Contemporary Authors

EDITORS' NOTE

Contemporary Authors, Volume 101, introduced two changes in the physical appearance of *Contemporary Authors* original volumes: a new cover design and a new numbering system.

Contemporary Authors, Volume 97-100, published in 1980, is the last volume with a four-unit number.

Contemporary Authors, Volume 101, Volume 102, and Volume 103, carry single volume numbers, as will all subsequent original volumes.

The only changes that have been made in *Contemporary Authors* are the cover design and the numbering plan. No change has been made in the amount or type of material included.

Contemporary Authors

A Bio-Bibliographical Guide to
Current Writers in Fiction, General Nonfiction,
Poetry, Journalism, Drama, Motion Pictures,
Television, and Other Fields

FRANCES C. LOCHER
Editor

volume 103

GALE RESEARCH COMPANY • THE BOOK TOWER • DETROIT, MICHIGAN 48226

EDITORIAL STAFF

Christine Nasso, *General Editor, Contemporary Authors*

Frances C. Locher, *Editor, Original Volumes*

Marie Evans, David Versical,
and Martha G. Winkel, *Associate Editors*
Tim Connor, Charity Anne Dorgan, Diane L. Dupuis, Nancy S. Gearhart,
Anne M. Guerrini, Michael L. LaBlanc, B. Hal May, Lillian S. Sims,
Les Stone, Mary K. Sullivan, and Susan M. Trosky, *Assistant Editors*
Denise M. Cloutier, Shirley Kuenz, Victoria M. Kurtz,
Norma Sawaya, and Shirley Seip, *Editorial Assistants*

Kathleen Ceton Newman and Adele Sarkissian, *Contributing Editors*
Peter Benjaminson, Trisha Gorman, Al Purdy,
Jean W. Ross, and Judith Spiegelman, *Interviewers*
Andrea Geffner, Arlene True, and Benjamin True, *Sketchwriters*
Eunice Bergin, *Copy Editor*

Special recognition is given to the staff of
Young People's Literature Department, Gale Research Company

Frederick G. Ruffner, *Publisher*   James M. Ethridge, *Editorial Director*

Copyright © 1982 by
GALE RESEARCH COMPANY

Library of Congress Catalog Card Number 62-52046
ISBN 0-8103-1903-9
ISSN 0010-7468

Authors Featured in This Volume

Among the 1,600 listings in *Contemporary Authors*, Volume 103,
are full-length sketches on these authors and media people.

Milton Acorn—Award-winning Canadian poet; author of several volumes of poetry, including *More Poems for People* and *Jackpine Sonnets.* (Sketch includes interview.)

Alan Alda—Award-winning American actor, writer, and director; well-known star of "M*A*S*H" television serial; recently turned to screenwriting and directing.

Jean Auel—American first novelist; wrote the highly praised 1980 novel, *The Clan of the Cave Bear.*

Rona Barrett—American entertainment industry columnist, television interviewer and correspondent; author of 1974 autobiography, *Miss Rona.* (Sketch includes interview.)

Mike Baxter—Award-winning American journalist for the *Miami Herald;* involved in investigative series on the Federal Housing Administration. (Sketch includes interview.)

William Maxwell Aitken Beaverbrook—Hailed as the "Hearst of Britain"; late publisher of *London Daily Express, London Sunday Express,* and *London Evening Standard.*

David Bowie—British rock music songwriter and performer; songs include "Panic in Detroit," "Young Americans," and "Changes"; actor in films and on stage.

Susan Brownmiller—Feminist and writer; author of bestselling *Against Our Will: Men, Women, and Rape.*

Susan Cheever—American writer; author of highly-acclaimed novels *Looking for Work* and *A Handsome Man;* daughter of Pulitzer Prize-winning author John Cheever. (Sketch includes interview.)

Kenneth C. Crowe—American journalist; awarded 1970 Pulitzer Prize for investigative reporting; author of *America for Sale,* 1978.

Bobby Fischer—American chess champion; international grand master of chess since 1958; author of books on chess.

Harvey Frommer—American educator, sports writer, and lecturer; wrote official centennial history of the National Baseball League; other books include *New York City Baseball* and *Rickey and Robinson: A Dual Biography.*

St. Clare Grondona—Australian economist and writer who formulated commodity price theory; author of books in his field.

Julie Harris—Noted American stage and screen actress, best known for portrayals of historical figures such as Mary Todd Lincoln in "The Last of Mrs. Lincoln"; wrote *Julie Harris Talks to Young Actors.*

Ursula Hicks—One of the world's leading experts in economic and governmental theory; among her works are *Federalism: Failure and Success* and *Federalism and Economic Growth in Underdeveloped Countries.*

Hugh Honour—British art historian and author of books on art and architecture, including *Neo-Classicism, Romanticism,* and *The New Golden Land: European Images of America From Discovery to the Present Time.*

Burl Ives—Popular American actor and ballad singer dedicated to ensuring the survival of America's folk heritage; author of song collections and autobiographical works, including *Wayfaring Stranger.*

Anne Jackson—American stage actress and winner of two Obie Awards; author of 1979 autobiography, *Early Stages.*

Stefan Kanfer—American writer; senior editor of *Time* magazine; author of *A Journal of the Plague Years* and two novels, *The Eighth Sin* and *Fear Itself.* (Sketch includes interview.)

Doris Kearns—American educator and biographer; assisted President Lyndon B. Johnson in compiling his official memoirs; later wrote biography, *Lyndon Johnson and the American Dream.*

Ted Koppel—American journalist; ABC-TV "Nightline" anchor; co-authored a 1977 novel, *In the National Interest,* with CBS-TV diplomatic correspondent Marvin Kalb.

Haldor Laxness—Prolific Icelandic author; winner of 1953 Stalin Prize and 1955 Nobel Prize.

Shirley MacLaine—Award-winning American stage and screen actress; author of two autobiographies, *Don't Fall Off the Mountain* and *You Can Get There From Here.*

Marty Mann—Late American lecturer and writer on alcoholism; founder of the National Council on Alcoholism; author of *Marty Mann Answers Your Questions About Drinking and Alcoholism.*

Wendell Mayes—American television writer and motion picture screenwriter; works include "Anatomy of a Murder," "Advise and Consent," and "The Poseidon Adventure." (Sketch includes interview.)

Edward R. Murrow—Renowned American broadcast journalist who died in 1965; well known for reports from Europe during World War II; the quality of his reporting helped make CBS the foremost American news network and set a standard of excellence in the profession.

J. Robert Oppenheimer—Late physicist known as the "father of the atomic bomb"; principal in development of atom bomb; later became a victim of McCarthyism for recommending nuclear control; *Robert Oppenheimer: Letters and Recollections* is among his published works.

Marlin Perkins—American zoologist and zoo curator; originator and host of the award-winning television shows "Wild Kingdom" and "Zooparade"; author of books in his field.

Anne Redmon—British author of novels *Emily Stone* and *Music and Silence;* won 1974 *Yorkshire Post* prize for best first work.

Tim Rice—British writer; award-winning lyricist for "Jesus Christ Superstar" and "Joseph and the Amazing Technicolor Dreamcoat."

Dale Evans Rogers—American actress, singer, and lyricist; well known as television co-star, with husband, on "Roy Rogers Show" during 1950's; author of inspirational books and books on children. (Sketch includes interview.)

Philip Rosenberg—American author of police nonfiction thrillers, including *Badge of the Assassin* and *The Spivey Assignment,* and a novel in the same genre, *Contract on Cherry Street.* (Sketch includes interview.)

Alan Saperstein—American novelist; author of much-reviewed novel *Mom Kills Kids and Self.*

Neil Sedaka—Award-winning American composer of popular music.

Stephen Sondheim—Famous American composer and lyricist of songs for musicals; works include "West Side Story," "Gypsy," and "Sweeney Todd."

Susan Stamberg—Award-winning co-host of National Public Radio's daily feature news program, "All Things Considered." (Sketch includes interview.)

Jean Strouse—American editor and writer; author of a book on legal rights for young people, *Up Against the Law,* a biography, *Alice James,* and a book of essays.

Lloyd Turner—American television writer, currently writing for "House Calls." (Sketch includes interview.)

Lionel White—American journalist and mystery novelist; considered an expert in the field of "caper novels."

J. Patrick Wright—American author and publisher; co-authored, with former GM executive John Z. De Lorean, *On a Clear Day You Can See General Motors;* originally self-published, the book became an instant best-seller and was picked up by trade publishers both in the United States and abroad.

Preface

The 1,600 entries in *Contemporary Authors,* Volume 103, bring to nearly 66,000 the number of authors, either living or deceased since 1960, now represented in the *Contemporary Authors* series. *CA* includes nontechnical writers in all genres—fiction, nonfiction, poetry, drama, etc.—whose books are issued by commercial, risk publishers or by university presses. Authors of books published only by known vanity or author-subsidized firms are ordinarily not included. Since native language and nationality have no bearing on inclusion in *CA,* authors who write in languages other than English are included in *CA* if their works have been published in the United States or translated into English.

Although *CA* focuses primarily on authors of published books, the series also encompasses prominent persons in communications: newspaper and television reporters and correspondents, columnists, newspaper and magazine editors, photojournalists, syndicated cartoonists, screenwriters, television scriptwriters, and other media people.

No charge or obligation is attached to a *CA* listing. Authors are included in the series solely on the basis of the above criteria and their interest to *CA* users.

Compilation Methods

The editors make every effort to secure information directly from the authors through questionnaires and personal correspondence. If authors of special interest to *CA* users are deceased or fail to reply to requests for information, material is gathered from other reliable sources. Biographical dictionaries are checked (a task made easier through the use of Gale's *Biography and Genealogy Master Index* and other volumes in the "Gale Biographical Index Series"), as are bibliographical sources, such as *Cumulative Book Index* and *The National Union Catalog.* Published interviews, feature stories, and book reviews are examined, and often material is supplied by the authors' publishers. All sketches, whether prepared from questionnaires or through extensive research, are sent to the authors for review prior to publication.

Informative Sidelights

Numerous *CA* entries contain Sidelights—in some cases providing a personal dimension to the sketch, and in other cases supplying information about the critical reception the authors' works have received. Some authors work closely with *CA*'s editors to develop lengthy, incisive Sidelights, as in the case of John Clive, a British novelist. When he describes how he conceived the idea for his book *KG 200,* based on the Luftwaffe bomber group that used captured Allied aircraft to aid the German war effort, Clive enables the reader to see the creative process behind the writing of a specific book. And American novelist Edward Keyes, for example, tells *CA* that he postponed full-time writing for ten years while he raised a family. He finally abandoned conventional employment fifteen years ago to write full time, though, and remains enthusiastic about writing. Keyes declares, "I could never work for anyone else again."

Broadcast journalists have a zeal for excellence and an awareness of the level of literacy possible in their craft, and some of them, too, work with *CA*'s editors to provide revealing Sidelights. For instance, though also a book author, British broadcast journalist and BBC documentary producer Philip French tells *CA*, "I regard the best of my radio work as equal, and in most cases superior, to the essays I've published." Claiming that "a good radio program depends as much on nuance, inflection, and vocal orchestration as it does on the quality of the written and spoken word," French considers his contribution to the communications medium as having "a status comparable to books."

Equally incisive Sidelights are written by *CA*'s editors when authors and media people of particular interest to *CA* readers are unable to supply Sidelights material, or when the demand for information about the critical reception their works have received is especially high. The Sidelights on American author Philip Rosenberg, for example, point out that while his first book, *The Seventh Hero*, written while he was a doctoral candidate at Columbia University, was found to be a notable work of scholarship, he did not pursue an academic career. Instead, Rosenberg became a full-time author and wrote several nonfiction and fictional thrillers critics have found to be "good, jolting, professional," and "told with insight, indignation, . . . inspiration." And Susan Cheever's Sidelights note that her first novel, *Looking for Work,* should be read "not because John Cheever's daughter wrote it but because it is well worth reading." Several reviewers praised her writing skills but suggested that she had not penetrated "the deeper paradoxes of her characters' behavior." However, critics felt that with her second novel, *A Handsome Man,* Cheever had "come of age" and produced a book of "effortless grace that comes from discipline, strength, and committed professionalism."

Writers of Special Interest

CA's editors make every effort to include a substantial number of entries in each volume on active authors and media people of special interest to *CA*'s readers. Since *CA* also includes sketches on deceased writers of special interest, a significant amount of work goes into the compilation of full-length entries on important deceased authors. Some of the prominent writers whose sketches are contained in this volume are noted in the list headed "Authors Featured in This Volume" immediately preceding the preface.

Exclusive Interviews

CA provides additional primary information on certain authors in the form of exclusive interviews. Prepared specifically for *CA,* the never-before-published conversations presented in the section of the sketch headed *CA INTERVIEW* give *CA* users the opportunity to learn the authors' thoughts, in depth, about their craft. Subjects chosen for interviews are, the editors feel, authors who hold special interest for *CA*'s readers.

Authors and journalists in this volume whose sketches include interviews are Milton Acorn, Rona Barrett, Mike Baxter, Susan Cheever, Stefan Kanfer, Wendell Mayes, Dale Evans Rogers, Philip Rosenberg, Susan Stamberg, and Lloyd Turner.

Obituary Notices Make *CA* Timely and Comprehensive

To be as timely and comprehensive as possible, *CA* publishes brief, one-paragraph obituary notices on deceased authors within the scope of the series. These notices provide date and place of birth and death, highlight the author's career and writings, and list other sources where additional biographical information and obituaries may be found. To distinguish them from full-length sketches, obituaries are identified with the heading *OBITUARY NOTICE.*

CA includes obituary notices for authors who already have full-length sketches in earlier *CA* volumes, thus effectively completing their sketches. Seventy-two percent of the obituary notices in this volume are for authors with listings already in *CA*. *CA also* contains obituary notices for authors not yet included in the series. Deceased authors of special interest presently represented only by obituary notices are scheduled for full-length sketch treatment in forthcoming *CA* volumes.

Cumulative Index Should Always Be Consulted

The most recent *CA* cumulative index is the user's guide to the volume in which an author's listing appears. The entire *CA* series consists of original volumes, containing entries on authors new to the series, and revision volumes, containing completely updated entries on authors with earlier sketches in the series. The cumulative index, which lists all original and revision volume entries, should always be consulted to locate the specific volume containing an author's original or most recently revised sketch.

For the convenience of *CA* users, the *CA* cumulative index also includes references to all entries in three related Gale series—*Contemporary Literary Criticism* (CLC), which is devoted entirely to current criticism of today's novelists, poets, playwrights, short story writers, filmmakers, screenwriters, and other creative writers, *Something About the Author* (SATA), a series of heavily illustrated sketches on authors and illustrators of books for young people, and *Authors in the News* (AITN), a compilation of news stories and feature articles from American newspapers and magazines covering writers and other members of the communications media.

Retaining *CA* Volumes

As new volumes in the series are published, users often ask which *CA* volumes in their collections, if any, can be discarded. The chart on the following page is designed to assist users in keeping their collections as complete as possible.

As always, suggestions from users about any aspect of *CA* will be welcomed.

IF YOU HAVE:	YOU MAY DISCARD:
1-4 First Revision (1967)	1 (1962) 2 (1963) 3 (1963) 4 (1963)
5-8 First Revision (1969)	5-6 (1963) 7-8 (1963)
Both 9-12 First Revision (1974) AND *Contemporary Authors Permanent Series,* Volume 1 (1975)	9-10 (1964) 11-12 (1965)
Both 13-16 First Revision (1975) AND *Contemporary Authors Permanent Series,* Volumes 1 and 2 (1975, 1978)	13-14 (1965) 15-16 (1966)
Both 17-20 First Revision (1976) AND *Contemporary Authors Permanent Series,* Volumes 1 and 2 (1975, 1978)	17-18 (1967) 19-20 (1968)
Both 21-24 First Revision (1977) AND *Contemporary Authors Permanent Series,* Volumes 1 and 2 (1975, 1978)	21-22 (1969) 23-24 (1970)
Both 25-28 First Revision (1977) AND *Contemporary Authors Permanent Series,* Volume 2 (1978)	25-28 (1971)
Both 29-32 First Revision (1978) AND *Contemporary Authors Permanent Series,* Volume 2 (1978)	29-32 (1972)
Both 33-36 First Revision (1978) AND *Contemporary Authors Permanent Series,* Volume 2 (1978)	33-36 (1973)
37-40 First Revision (1979)	37-40 (1973)
41-44 First Revision (1979)	41-44 (1974)
45-48 (1974) 49-52 (1975) 53-56 (1975) 57-60 (1976) ↓ ↓ 103 (1982)	NONE: These volumes will not be super-seded by corresponding revised vol-umes. Individual entries from these and all other volumes appearing in the left column of this chart will be revised and included in the *New Revision Series.*
Volumes in the *Contemporary Authors New Revision Series*	NONE: The *New Revision Series* does not replace any single volume of *CA*. All volumes appearing in the left column of this chart must be retained to have in-formation on all authors in the series.

CONTEMPORARY AUTHORS

ABBEY, Margaret
See YORK, Margaret Elizabeth

* * *

ACKERMAN, Robert W(illiam) 1910-1980

PERSONAL: Born February 1, 1910, in Swanton, Ohio; died October 13, 1980; married, 1962; children: two. *Education:* University of Michigan, A.B., 1931, A.M., 1933, Ph.D., 1938.

CAREER: University of Michigan, Ann Arbor, instructor in English, 1938; Washington State College (now University), Pullman, instructor in English, 1938-41; Illinois Institute of Technology, Chicago, instructor in English, 1941-42; Stanford University, Stanford, Calif., began as assistant professor, became professor of English, 1946-73, professor emeritus, 1973-80. Visiting professor at University of Wisconsin—Madison, 1974-75.

WRITINGS: Index to the Arthurian Names in Middle English, Stanford University, 1952, reprinted, AMS Press; (contributor) *Arthurian Literature in the Middle Ages,* Oxford University Press, 1959; *Review Notes and Study Guide to Hardy's Tess of the d'Urbervilles,* Monarch, 1964; (with Ruth H. Blackburn and Unicio J. Violi) *Review Notes and Study Guide to the Old Testament,* Monarch, 1964; (contributor) *The Medieval Literature of Western Europe,* New York University, 1966; *Backgrounds to Medieval English Literature,* Random House, 1966; (translator with Frederick W. Locke and Carlton W. Carroll) Chrestien de Troyes, *Ywain: The Knight of the Lion,* Ungar, 1977.*

* * *

ACKROYD, Joyce Irene

PERSONAL: Born in Newcastle, Australia; daughter of Alfred Walter and Constance (Lloyd) Ackroyd; married Frank Warren Speed (a writer), May 12, 1962. *Education:* University of Sydney, B.A. (with honors) and diploma in education, both 1940; Cambridge University, M.A., 1948, Ph.D., 1951. *Home:* 50 Vanwall Rd., Moggill, Queensland 4070, Australia. *Office:* Department of Japanese, University of Queensland, St. Lucia, Queensland 4067, Australia.

CAREER: Australian National University, Canberra, research fellow in Tokugawa history, 1952-58, senior lecturer, 1958-61, associate professor of Japanese and head of department, 1961-65; University of Queensland, St. Lucia,

Australia, professor of Japanese language and literature and head of department of Japanese, 1965—. *Member:* International House of Japan, Australian Universities Language and Literature Association, Japan-Australia Society, Asia Society, Modern Language Teachers Association of Queensland, University of Queensland Club. *Awards, honors:* Cultural award from Japan Translators, 1980, for *Told Round a Brushwood Fire.*

WRITINGS: Women in Feudal Japan, Asiatic Society of Japan, 1959; *The Unknown Japanese,* University of Queensland Press, 1967; *Japan Today,* Angus & Robertson, 1970; (with Teriko Sayeg and Diana Beresford) *Discovering Japan,* Angus & Robertson, Book I, 1970, Book II, 1972; *Your Journey Into Japan,* Angus & Robertson, 1973; *A Reassessment of the Poetry of Shimazaki Toson: Studies in Japanese Culture,* International P.E.N. (Tokyo, Japan), 1975; *Situational Conversational Japanese,* University of Queensland Press, 1976; (translator) Arai Hakuseki, *Told Round a Brushwood Fire* (autobiography), Tokyo University Press, 1979; *Ningyo no Opera* (five-act play for children; first produced in Brisbane, Australia, at Kenmore High School, 1973), text in English and Japanese, Kaitakusha Co., 1979; (translator and author of commentary) Hakuseki, *Studies in History,* University of Queensland Press, 1982. Editor of "Asia Today," a series published by Angus & Robertson.

SIDELIGHTS: Joyce Ackroyd told *CA:* "I work to assist in the removal of internationally dangerous ignorance—specifically, ignorance of the Japanese mind and its achievements.

"I am, I know, a sparrow attempting to demolish a mountain by pecking at it. I derive deep enjoyment and satisfaction from translating—trying to express well in English what has been well said in Japanese. Only those engaged in such work can understand the drudgery of research in Japanese—the arcane nature of the language, the ambiguity of its sentence structure, the esoteric readings and meanings of its ideographs, the conflicting accounts and points of view, the customs and ways of thought alien to the West combine to produce a mystification that requires great effort to penetrate.

"I work from morning to night, often seven days a week. Yet the rewards are almost nil, apart from having done the job."

ACORN, Milton 1923-

PERSONAL: Born March 30, 1923, in Charlottetown, Prince Edward Island, Canada; son of Robert Fairclough (a customs officer) and Helen (a secretary; maiden name, Carbonelle) Acorn; divorced. *Education:* Educated in Charlottetown, Prince Edward Island, Canada. *Politics:* "For the working class." *Religion:* "My own religion." *Home:* Waverley Hotel, 484 Spadina Ave., Toronto, Ontario, Canada, M5S 2H1.

CAREER: Poet, writer, and playwright. Worked as fireman, shipper, freight handler, longshoreman, and carpenter. *Military service:* Canadian Armoured Corps, 1939-43; served in England; received service medal. *Member:* Canadian Poets. *Awards, honors:* Canadian Poets award, 1970; Governor General's award, 1975.

WRITINGS: In Love and Anger (poems), privately printed, 1957; *The Brain's the Target* (poems), Ryerson, 1960; *Against a League of Liars* (poems), Hawkshead Press, 1960; *Jawbreakers* (poems), Contact Press, 1963; *I've Tasted My Blood: Poems 1956 to 1968,* edited by Al Purdy, Ryerson, 1969; *I Shout Love and Shaving Off His Beard* (poems and prose), Village Book Store Press, 1971; *More Poems for People,* NC Press, 1972; *The Island Means Minago* (poems and prose), NC Press, 1975; (with Cedric Smith) "Road to Charlottetown" (two-act musical), first produced in Toronto, Ontario, 1976; *Jackpine Sonnets,* Steel Rail, 1977. Editor of *Moment* (magazine), 1960-62.

WORK IN PROGRESS: Poetry; newspaper and periodical articles.

SIDELIGHTS: Acorn was one of Canada's first "public poets." Dubbed by a *Toronto Quill and Quire* reporter as a "troubadour of the working class," Acorn sees himself as the spokesman of the laborer, whether he be a Nova Scotia seaman or an Ottawa farmer. He was a frequent poetry reader on the coffee house scene in the 1950's. The poet read in such well-known coffee houses of that period as The Place, El Cortijo, The Bohemian Embassy, and l'Echourie. Acorn has often called himself a "revolutionary poet." He is probably the only poet in Canada to have one of his readings disrupted by the police. Although once a member of the Communist party, the Trotskyites, and the Canadian Liberation Movement, Acorn disagreed with and resigned from all the leftist groups in which he participated. Acorn, however, is still strongly political and espouses a left-wing, nationalist stand. Al Purdy observed that Acorn is "a maverick" who "fits no aperture or easy definition."

CA INTERVIEW

Milton Acorn was interviewed in his Toronto apartment by Al Purdy on November 6, 1979.

CA: You grew up in Charlottetown, Prince Edward Island. Tell me something about your childhood.

ACORN: I learned to read at age three, but not well; I didn't learn to read well until I was ten. I was sick much of the time then and didn't get over it until I was in my teens. Just sickly, weak, without any particular reason. But it was strange: I got into a lot of fights anyway and always got beat up. But I learned to fight at fourteen and after that over the years, many of them, I came to avoid fights.

CA: When did you start writing?

ACORN: I was pretty young, maybe eight or ten years old. Me and another kid, name of "Silly"—his real name was Sylvanus—we both wrote poems and made drawings. I kept on writing.

CA: What were your mother and father like?

ACORN: My father was a working man. He'd been in the army in World War I, and got shell-shocked. He was a customs officer after the war. I guess you'd say we were middle class. My mother was boss of the household: when she said do something, you did it. No argument was possible. And I was writing so early; it was like playing games with words. Later, the urge to write was worse than needing a drink. I had to write. When I got to be a carpenter, I remember walking down the street swinging a lunch pail chanting to myself, "I've got to write. I've got to write."

CA: Did anybody encourage you?

ACORN: All my family were amateur writers. My grandfather was a correspondent for the *London Times*. My aunt was writing too. In fact there was no one who didn't write. My older brother taught me scansion in poems; they all taught me something.

CA: What books did you read?

ACORN: The first I can remember is *Dracula,* by Bram Stoker. Early science fiction. And H. G. Wells, Mark Twain, Rider Haggard. . . .

CA: That's some apprenticeship for a carpenter. When did you become one?

ACORN: I was always doing carpenter work, but my mother said, "Milt, you're no carpenter; you have no knack of the hands." So I went to carpenter school in 1946.

CA: You were in the army before that?

ACORN: The Black Watch regiment, but only briefly. I joined them when I was underage, sixteen. They discharged me. Then I went back to the Canadian Armoured Corps, still underage, but I got away with it that time. I was shipped to England in January, 1942, on the *Cameronian.* We were attacked by a submarine in the Atlantic, but there were no casualties except for me. My ears were blasted in by shellfire. After that my ears bled all the time; they called it *otitis media,* in the middle ear. I also remember being on pack drill in England, marching with a heavy pack on my shoulders. And an officer said, "He's enjoying it; take him out of there!" Of course you weren't supposed to enjoy pack drill. Then the doctors decided my ear injuries were serious, and I got sent back to Canada. The war was over where I was concerned.

CA: All this time you were writing poems and reading?

ACORN: Yes, I was reading Dorothy Livesay, Joe Wallace, and when it came out in the sixties, *The New American Poetry, 1945-1960,* the book Donald Allen edited. And I read the classics, Shelley, Wordsworth, Coleridge, and many, many others.

CA: What were your politics in those years after the war?

ACORN: I was always a Red Tory, a red conservative, not a straight Communist. Anything the media attacked I was for. I don't mean the Nazis, of course, or Mussolini's fascists. It's just that anything the newspapers and television attack has a lot to be said for it.

CA: Apart from love poems, and many of yours are love poems, your largest subject is social injustice as you see it and wherever you see it. You wrote poems about Norman Bethune among the Chinese, about Ho Chi Minh, and Che Guevara.

ACORN: Sure, but I had to retract what I said about Guevara. He was a fine man but his tactics were absurd, though I agree with his goals.

CA: Should more writers be concerned with this kind of subject matter?

ACORN: Noble subjects and noble sentiments do not make noble poetry, not without noble work. I mean you have to have good syntax, scansion, rhyme if necessary.

CA: Should writers write from their own direct experience?

ACORN: Yes, the people-experience. One must write about people, the working class. But don't get too obsessed with it because poetry is a large area. The history of mankind is the history of poetry. And it's mankind that is the subject of all poetry.

CA: As it was with you in Jawbreakers?

ACORN: Yes, it was—after I learned something from other writers.

CA: Who were they?

ACORN: Frank Scott, Wilson MacDonald, the Russians Vladimir Mayakovsky (he was great, but couldn't handle rhetoric) and Boris Pasternak. Also the Russian moderns, Andrei Voznesensky and Yevgeny Yevtushenko. The Americans, Robert Duncan and Charles Olson. I met Olson once and loved him. But I'm not like the Black Mountain people; my stress is in the syllable rather than metaphor. And Walt Whitman—he had some great lines, but too much rhetoric. And Robert Lowell, nice, nice—I admire him as a man, or did before his death, but then poets don't die, do they? And Pablo Neruda, but he should have had better translators. The Roy Campbell translations of Lorca, though, were excellent.

CA: You're not partial to the Black Mountain people, but you liked Charles Olson?

ACORN: Those rules of prosody Olson had in the *New American Poetry* were a put-on. Olson said as much in answer to a question by John Colombo in my presence about 1963. He cooked them up to refute people who criticized him, people who knew very little about writing anyway and couldn't tell whether he was talking horse—— or not. And those rules were horse——. His Black Mountain disciples give me the creeps.

CA: Do you see yourself as belonging to any tradition in poetry?

ACORN: I'm the start of one. But really, I'm the umpteenth revival of romanticism.

CA: Aren't you, therefore, in your own work, a guardian and protector of tradition?

ACORN: I don't protect, I threaten: if things don't change—and I mean social injustice and the few dominating the many—then I and others will make them change. You have to understand: my material is the world, the world as seen from Canada.

CA: What about Auden's line, "Poetry makes nothing happen"?

ACORN: Auden was wrong; things will change. To make it happen, I plan campaigns.

CA: What kind of campaigns?

ACORN: In the poems and prose I write, there is a concentration on particular subjects relating to social change. For instance, I wrote a column about abortion for the *Toronto Globe and Mail*, in their "Mermaid Inn" section on the editorial page. I'm against abortion: a poet must be pro-life. But Canadians are difficult to move about anything. They're a passive people. They have the ability to do anything, but they have to be told to do it. Just tell 'em to take Vimy Ridge in World War I, and they did. But try to get them excited about any worthwhile cause and they sit on their asses. You have to light a fire under them. They're the most passive people in the world.

CA: Maybe that's because most of our directions come from the outside, such as in the case of multi-national companies from the United States. But not from across the sea, since we're not British any more.

ACORN: We're the other North Americans, Canadians are, and quite distinct from Americans. But they don't realize this. Quite recently there was a stage play here; it was about Billy Bishop and had an American producer. Bishop was the great air hero of World War I, who shot down seventy-two German planes. It was a good play and did well at the box office. In fact, it did so well that the producer wanted to stage the play in the United States. And he wanted Billy Bishop to have guilt feelings about killing. He didn't realize that Canadian soldiers and airmen were mercenaries. Bishop did what he was paid to do, and any onus of guilt was on his employers.

CA: Do you see the United States, Canada, and Mexico as representing a break with European tradition?

ACORN: True enough. They weren't far out of feudalism when Europe settled North America, the days of barons and serfs not long past. We had a chance to be egalitarian with an equal chance for all. Of course it didn't work out that way.

CA: Didn't you break with European literary tradition when you wrote your Jackpine Sonnets *by making some of them thirteen lines long?*

ACORN: Others had been there first, as long ago as Shakespeare's time.

CA: Why thirteen lines and not eighteen or nineteen?

ACORN: Thirteen is a prime number. You can't make a regular poem of a prime number of lines.

CA: Why not?

ACORN: Nothing will divide a prime number equally—in formal form. Most of my sonnets are fourteen lines, the power of tradition being strong—although some are thirteen. But you can't make a formal traditional poem of thirteen lines, or one that you have started out to be possibly thirteen, because of that number. Shakespeare had one in his "Passionate Pilgrim" series of poems. But others wrote them too.

CA: I see what you mean about the formal poem, but then why not make it seventeen or nineteen lines? Nothing will divide into those numbers either. Anyway, from what you've said, you write poems in order to change the world socially?

ACORN: You pay your dues for being here. You owe the good people in the world, people of both past and present, for being alive, for helping you along the way.

CA: And you do it with poems. How do you feel about poetry in Canada now, generally speaking?

ACORN: It's a terrible mess. There are too many bad poets around. Since about ten years ago Canadian poetry has ignored questions of both form and content. And this aspect is even more noticeable now because there are thousands of poets writing now as compared to perhaps one hundred twenty years ago. Many of them just scribble anything that comes into their heads and don't bother at all about cadence. The majority of poetry published in Canada is not even good prose. There is no knowledge of the mode and method of writing poems. One reason for this is the importation of anarchistic ideas from the United States.

CA: Do you see any good younger poets writing now in Canada?

ACORN: Ted Plantos.

CA: Any others?

ACORN: Mary di Michele.

CA: And the known writers you think are good?

ACORN: Frank Scott, Margaret Atwood—Atwood is an awfully good novelist, but she writes cold poems, cold. Dorothy Livesay, too.

CA: Scott tried to change the country politically when he helped write the Regina Manifesto *for the Canadian Cooperative Federation in the 1930's, and also with his poems. You want to do that politically as well as socially?*

ACORN: You can't do one without doing the other. I've always been trying to change the world. The best poets have always been world-changers and prophets: Shelley, Blake, Whitman, Mayakovsky.

CA: Philosophy and politics: I remember George Bowering saying that you shouldn't mix politics into your poems, that they don't mix.

ACORN: I once saw a sign in an army officers' mess that said: "Conversation apropos sex, politics, and religion is unbecoming to an officer and gentleman." In other words, what do you talk about to replace them? Life is forbidden.

CA: There's a great deal of violence in some of your poems. Is that related to your general plan of changing the world?

ACORN: Well, it's a part of life. And some violence must be resisted with violence.

CA: Surely you're not advocating violence just because it exists in the world?

ACORN: Of course not. But violence is sometimes necessary, may even be a positive good.

CA: Your publisher is Steel Rail, which is a rather political organization despite being a publisher. What are its aims?

ACORN: Its politics are left of center and Canadian nationalistic. It's a strong force for Canadian independence.

CA: Apart from your brother and family who encouraged you years ago, who else has done that over the years?

ACORN: Everyone I meet encourages me. Even when I didn't want to be known as a poet, everyone said I was, even when I denied it. And I've learned from everyone, Mao Tsetung as a poet and leader, Norman Bethune as a man, and a great man. And Shelley, more for what he said than how.

CA: Do you have any kind of personal philosophy?

ACORN: I was born six billion years ago and I shall never die.

CA: Do you therefore live by your writing? I mean money.

ACORN: I live to write, I write to live. And money, it comes, it goes. I've rarely lacked, not lately anyhow.

CA: What are you writing now?

ACORN: Poems of course. Also newspaper and periodical writing, prose. I have a new prose book, *On Being Severe to Children.* My subject is Western arrogance, which thinks itself superior to all other societies. Eastern culture is much older, goes back milleniums, with dozens of different cultures, each with its own peculiar virtues. Western arrogance gives no credit to any other society but the one in which we live. And that is simply stupid.

CA: What other writing have you done lately?

ACORN: The "Road to Charlottetown." It's a play I wrote with Cedric Smith. It was pretty successful, a lot of people came to see it. In fact, some students here from China came down and asked to tape the play.

CA: What's it about?

ACORN: John Acorn and his struggles with authority. The odd thing is that I invented John Acorn for purposes of the play, made him up completely. But then my relatives searched the Prince Edward Island records in Charlottetown and found that he really did exist. Under the same name too. The play is a romp through island history.

CA: And the play will change the world?

ACORN: It'll help.

BIOGRAPHICAL/CRITICAL SOURCES: University of Toronto Quarterly, July, 1961; *Culture,* June, 1964; *Canadian Forum,* July, 1969, March, 1974; *Canadian Literature,* autumn, 1969; *Authors in the News,* Volume 2, Gale, 1976; *Contemporary Literary Criticism,* Volume 15, Gale, 1980.

—*Interview by Al Purdy*

*   *   *

ADAMS, Kenneth Menzies 1922-

PERSONAL: Born October 28, 1922, in Melbourne, Australia; son of Frederick Reginald (a teacher) and Gertrude (a teacher; maiden name, Wright) Adams; married Verna Gilsenan (a teacher), May 22, 1948; children: David, Christopher, Phillip. *Education:* Melbourne Teachers College, Trained Primary Teachers' Certificate, 1947; University of Melbourne, B.A., 1952, B.Ed., 1956. *Religion:* Church of England. *Home:* 20 Leoni Ave., Heathmont, Victoria 3155, Australia.

CAREER: Teacher at high schools in Box Hill, Australia, 1949-51, Wangaratta, Australia, 1952-61, Mitcham, Australia, 1962-67, and Nunawading, Australia, 1968-73; deputy principal of high school in Hallam, Australia, 1974-77; Doveton High School, Australia, principal, 1977—. *Military service:* Australian Imperial Forces, 1942-46; served in southwest Pacific. *Member:* Royal Victorian Historical Society, North East Historical Society (life member; founding president).

WRITINGS: Seeing History, Volume I: *The First Australians,* Lansdowne, 1968, Volume II: *Gaol to Colony,* Angus & Robertson, 1970, Volume III: *Colonies to Commonwealth,* Lansdowne, 1971. Also author of Volume IV, *Twentieth-Century Australia,* 1972.

* * *

ADDEO, Jovita A. 1939-

PERSONAL: Born May 18, 1939, in Fond du Lac, Wis.; daughter of George N. and Thelma (Tagliapietra) Reichling; married Edmond G. Addeo, Jr. (a writer), May 28, 1960; children: Denise, Nicole. *Education:* Attended Immaculate Heart College and Queen of Angels School of Nursing. *Religion:* Roman Catholic. *Home:* 123 Alta Vista, Mill Valley, Calif. 94941.

CAREER: Private duty registered nurse; nurse at Sunny Hills (psychiatric facility for teenagers). Member of board of directors of local Alcohol Information Committee and Catholic Social Services.

WRITINGS: Why Our Children Drink, Prentice-Hall, 1975.

* * *

ADDY, Ted
See WINTERBOTHAM, R(ussell) R(obert)

* * *

ADES, Dawn 1943-

PERSONAL: Surname is pronounced A-*des;* born in 1943, in Ripley, England; daughter of A. E. and Ruth (Morton) Tylden-Pattenson; married Timothy Ades (a writer), July, 1966; children: Thomas, Harry. *Education:* Attended St. Hilda's College, Oxford, 1962-65; Courtauld Institute of Art, London, M.A. (with distinction), 1968. *Office:* Department of Art, University of Essex, Wivenhoe Park, Colchester, Essex, England.

CAREER: University of Essex, Colchester, England, faculty member in department of art history, 1968—.

WRITINGS: Dada and Surrealism, Dolphin, 1974; *Photomontage,* Thames & Hudson, 1976; *Dada and Surrealism Reviewed,* Arts Council of Great Britain, 1978; *Experimental Photography,* Arts Council of Great Britain, 1980; (contributor) *Joseph Cornell,* Museum of Modern Art (New York), 1980; *Salvador Dali,* Thames & Hudson, 1982.

SIDELIGHTS: Ades told *CA:* "*Salvador Dali* is a concise critical account of Dali's paintings, films, and objects, with some emphasis on his own writings, his relationship with the surrealist movement, and critical attidudes toward him."

* * *

AFTERMAN, Allen 1941-

PERSONAL: Born in 1941, in Los Angeles, Calif.; son of Sam (a worker) and Manya (a singer; maiden name, Soltrov) Afterman; married Susan Whiting (a poet); children: Adam, Gedaliah. *Education:* University of California, Los Angeles, B.A. (with honors), 1962; Harvard University, LL.B., 1965; Monash University, LL.M., 1969. *Home:* Pardes, Rocky Hall, New South Wales 2550, Australia.

CAREER: Victoria University of Wellington, Wellington, New Zealand, junior lecturer in law, 1966-67; Monash University, Clayton, Australia, lecturer in law, 1967-68; University of Singapore, Singapore, lecturer in law, 1968-70; University of Melbourne, Melbourne, Australia, senior lecturer in law, 1970-73; rancher and orchardist in Rocky Hall, Australia, 1973—.

WRITINGS: (With Robert Baxt) *Cases and Materials on Corporations and Associations,* Butterworth, 1972, 3rd edition, 1980; *Company Directors and Controllers,* Law Book Co., 1973; *The Maze Rose* (poems), Macmillan, 1974; (with Baxt) *Casebook on Companies and Securities,* Butterworth, 1976; *Purple Adam* (poems), Angus & Robertson, 1980. Contributor of articles to law journals, including *Virginia Law Review* and *Australian Law Review,* and poems to literary magazines, including *Transatlantic Review, Poetry Review, Bananas, Texas Quarterly, New Letters,* and *Meanjin,* and newspapers.

WORK IN PROGRESS: Master of Return, poems, publication expected in 1982; a book on the writings of Rabbi Nachman of Bratzlav, founder of "Bratzlav Hasidism," with Gedaliah Fleer, publication expected in 1982.

SIDELIGHTS: Afterman commented to *CA:* "I am no longer involved in law. I left the universities in 1973 to devote myself full time to poetry. I have no theories on poetics; I keep changing (hopefully evolving), and my views express this in a personal way. Over the past few years I have moved from a fairly hard existentialism towards Judaism, especially Hasidism.

"My mother was a famous gypsy singer and my father a working man in the garment industry. I worked my way through college as an investigator for a labor law and civil rights law firm. I travel extensively and currently live on a cattle ranch-fruit orchard in the far south coast mountains of New South Wales."

* * *

AGER, Cecelia 1902-1981

OBITUARY NOTICE: Born January 23, 1902, in Grass Valley, Calif.; died after a stroke, April 3, 1981, in Los Angeles, Calif. Film critic. Ager was best known as a commentator on the foibles and personalities of the entertainment world. Her early writings in *Variety* concentrated on fashions in films, including who was wearing what, and who designed it. Later she wrote about the films themselves and her work won her the admiration of fans such as British journalist Alistair Cooke. In addition to *Variety,* Ager's work appeared in *PM, Harper's Bazaar, Vogue,* and the *New York Times.* Obituaries and other sources: *New York Times,* April 4, 1981.

* * *

AITKEN, William Maxwell
See BEAVERBROOK, William Maxwell Aitken

* * *

AITMATOV, Chingiz 1928-

PERSONAL: Born December 12, 1928, in Sheker Village, Kirghizia, U.S.S.R.; son of Torekul and Nahima Aitmatov; married wife, Keres (a physician); children: two sons. *Education:* Received degree in animal husbandry from Kirghiz Agricultural Institute; attended Moscow Literary Institute of the Union of Soviet Writers. *Home:* 43 Dzerzhinsky Flat 1, Frunze, Kirghiz Soviet Socialist Republic, U.S.S.R. *Of-*

fice: c/o Kirghiz Branch of the Union of Writers of the U.S.S.R., Ulitsa Pushkina 52, Frunze, U.S.S.R.

CAREER: Writer, 1952—. Communist Party of the Soviet Union, assistant to the secretary of Sheker Village Soviet, c. 1943, member, 1959—; People's Writer of Kirghiz Soviet Socialist Republic, 1968. Candidate member of Central Committee of Kirghiz Soviet Socialist Republic; vice-chairman of committee of Solidarity With Peoples of Asian and African Countries; deputy of U.S.S.R. Supreme Soviet. Cinema Union of Kirghiz Soviet Socialist Republic, first secretary, 1964-69, chairman, 1969—. *Awards, honors:* Lenin Prize for literature and the fine arts, 1963, for *Tales of the Mountains and Steppes;* Order of the Red Banner of Labor (twice); U.S.S.R. State Prize, 1968; Hero of Socialist Labor, 1978.

WRITINGS—In English translation: *Dzhamilia* (novel), Pravda, 1959, translation published as *Jamila,* Foreign Languages Publishing House (Moscow); *Povesti gor i stepei,* Sovetskii Pisatel, 1963, translation published as *Tales of the Mountains and Steppes,* Progress Publishers, 1969; *Proschai, Gul'sary!* (novella), Molodia Guardiia, 1967, translation by John French published as *Farewell, Gulsary!,* Hodder & Stoughton, 1970; *Posle skazki, Belyj parokhod* (novel), 1970, translation by Mirra Ginsburg published as *The White Ship,* Crown, 1972 (translation by Tatyana Feifer and George Feifer published in England as *The White Steamship,* Hodder & Stoughton, 1972); (with Kaltai Mukhamedzhanov) *Voskhozhdenie na Fudzhiamu* (play; first produced in Moscow, U.S.S.R., 1973; produced as "The Ascent of Mount Fuji" in Washington, D.C., at Kreeger Theatre, 1975), translation by Nicholas Bethell published as *The Ascent of Mount Fuji,* Farrar, Straus, 1975. Also author of *Tri povesti,* translation published as *Short Novels,* Progress Publishers.

Other writings: *Rasskazy* (title means "Stories"), Sovetskii Pisatel, 1958; *Verbliuzhii glaz* (short stories and novellas; title means "The Camel's Eye"), Sovetskii Pisatel, 1962; *Materinskoe Pole* (novel; title means "The Field of Mothers"), Pravda, 1963; *Samanchy zholu* (short stories and novellas), Basmasy, 1963; *Povesti* (title means "Novellas"), Izvestia, 1967; *Pervyi uchitel* (novel; title means "The First Master"), Detskaia Literatura, 1967; *Atadan kalgan tuiak,* Mektep, 1970; *Povesti i rasskazy* (title means "Novellas and Stories"), Molodaia Guardiia, 1970; *Pegil pes, begushchij kraem moria,* Sovetskii Pisatel, 1977; *V soavtostve s zemleiu i vodoiu* (essays and lectures), Kyrgyzstan, 1978.

SIDELIGHTS: Unlike such dissident Soviet writers as Solzhenitsyn and Tsabour, Chingiz Aitmatov has managed to remain in the U.S.S.R. and write of life in the republic of his birth, Kirghizia. A member of one of the Soviet Union's central Asian minorities, he is the first Kirghiz author to become known throughout the world. His books have been widely translated, with several appearing in French, German, Polish, English, and Arabic editions. His work has also been the focus of several Soviet films.

Aitmatov is an active and prominent member of the Communist party. Nevertheless, as *Newsweek*'s Jay Axelbank noted, he "tries to steer clear of political ideology and concentrate on psychological portraits" in his writing. He incorporates aspects of the Kirghiz oral tradition into the reality of Soviet society and culture.

One of the best examples of this quality of Aitmatov's work is to be found in *Farewell, Gulsary!* This novella recounts the story of an old draughthorse, once a magnificent steed, and his aged master, Tanabai. The tale is strongly reminiscent of the old oral epics that focus on the cultural importance of horses and horseback riding. As Gulsary and his master

contemplate their shared past, Aitmatov illustrates the interwoven destinies of man and animal, the concordance of man and nature so vital to the Kirghiz oral heritage. The horse suffers a long, agonizing death which prompts deep soul-searching in his master. In the end, Tanabai accepts the passing of his old companion and the passing of the old days.

Underlying Aitmatov's support of the Soviet system is a strong determination to uphold the freedom of artistic expression. "Clearly among the things he believes," said Frank Getlein of *Commonweal,* "is the efficacy of facing facts, however unpleasant." These two aspects of Aitmatov's character have led him, occasionally, to violate certain literary taboos of the Soviet state. In *The White Ship,* for example, Aitmatov depicts the suicide of a seven-year-old boy who becomes despondent after witnessing the brutal slaying and consumption of a rare deer.

Some Soviet readers were offended by the pessimism of the story, and the outcry against it prompted the author to defend his artistic integrity in the *Literaturnaya Gazeta.* Countering suggested changes in the tale, Aitmatov was quoted in the *New York Times:* "I had a choice, either to write or not to write the story. And if to write it, then only as I did." The author also asserted that evil is inexorable and, lacking the capacity to overcome the adult evil surrounding him, the boy had to sacrifice his life or his childhood ideals. As Rosemarie Keiffer explained in *Books Abroad,* Aitmatov intended to provoke thought by allowing the young protagonist to take his own life: "The boy's fate is aimed at elucidating certain human faults: Who has been faithful to the most positive of childhood dreams? Who has measured up to the moral aspirations of adolescence? Who has remained truthful in his relations with children? Aitmatov does not pretend here to teach men how to live up to their most cherished and human ideals, only to prick their consciences with the disparities between those ideals and the realities of most people's lives."

Another of Aitmatov's more daring works is "The Ascent of Mount Fuji," a play he co-authored with Kaltai Mikhamedzhanov, another native of Kirghizia. This drama caused a sensation when it premiered in Moscow in 1973 because it openly treats the delicate subject of Soviet suppression of dissidents. The drama does not recount the many horrors suffered by dissidents in the Soviet state; instead, it is a psychological study of betrayal and quiescence. Four old schoolmates meet on a mountaintop to renew their friendship but find they must first confront and reconcile the absence of a fifth friend, Sabur, a poet who questioned some Red Army tactics. Sabur had been betrayed by one of his four friends while the other three remained silent. Each must now acknowledge his own portion of guilt in the case.

Assessing Aitmatov's appeal for both Western and Eastern readers, Rosemarie Kieffer declared: "Like the classical poets and epic bards, he is a patriot and a historian of his nation. He is an ardent lover of life and nature, possesses a deep understanding of such varied human passions as love and despair, admires the Leninist society's ideals of order and progress, and is optimistic about that society's potential for bringing prosperity to his native region. And permeating all his writing is a serene harmony between past and present, between man and nature, between joy and sadness, a spirit which unequivocally condemns such aberrations of the human ideal as war or personal cruelty but which also holds to the hope that such ideals will at least endure and possibly one day even be attained."

BIOGRAPHICAL/CRITICAL SOURCES: New York Times, July 30, 1970; *UNESCO Courier,* October, 1972; *Newsweek,*

June 24, 1974, June 30, 1975; *Commonweal*, July 18, 1975; *Nation*, August 30, 1975; *Books Abroad*, summer, 1975.*

* * *

ALDA, Alan 1936-

PERSONAL: Birth-given name, Alphonso Joseph D'Abruzzo; name legally changed; born January 28, 1936, in New York, N.Y.; son of Alphonso Giovanni Giuseppe Roberto (an actor under stage name Robert Alda) and Joan (Browne) D'Abruzzo; married Arlene Weiss (a teacher, photographer, and musician), March 15, 1957; children: Eve, Elizabeth, Beatrice. *Education:* Fordham University, B.S., 1956; attended Paul Still's Improvisational Workshop, 1963. *Residence:* Leonia, N. J.; and Hollywood, Calif. *Agent:* c/o CBS Inc., 7800 Beverly Blvd., Los Angeles, Calif. 90036.

CAREER: Actor, writer, and director. Worked as teacher at Compass School of Improvization, New York, N.Y., c. 1963; member of Commission on the Observance of International Women's Year, 1975; co-chairman of presidential subcommittee on the Equal Rights Amendment (ERA), 1976. Actor in stage productions, including "Only in America," 1959, "L'il Abner," 1960, "Darwin's Theories," 1960, "The Woman With Red Hair,' 1961, "Golden Fleecing," 1961, "Anatol," 1961, "Purlie Victorious," 1961, "A Whisper in God's Ear," 1962, "Memo," 1963, "King of Hearts," 1963, "Fair Game for Lovers," 1963, "Cafe Crown," 1964, "The Owl and the Pussycat," 1966, and "The Apple Tree," 1966; in motion pictures, including "Gone Are the Days," Hammer, 1963, "Paper Lion," United Artists, 1968, "The Extraordinary Seaman," MGM, 1968, "Jennie," Cinerama, 1970, "The Moonshine War," MGM, 1970, "The Mephisto Waltz," Twentieth Century-Fox, 1971, "To Kill a Clown," Twentieth Century-Fox, 1972, "California Suite," Columbia, 1978, "Same Time, Next Year," Universal, 1978, "The Seduction of Joe Tynan," Universal, 1979, and "The Four Seasons," Universal, 1981; in television productions, including "The Glass House," 1972, "Playmates," 1972, "Six Rms Riv Vu," 1974, "Kill Me if You Can," 1977, and in television series "M*A*S*H," 1972—. *Military service:* U.S. Army Reserve; served as gunnery officer; became second lieutenant.

MEMBER: American Federation of Television and Radio Artists, Actors Equity Association, Screen Actors Guild, Men for ERA. *Awards, honors:* Ford Foundation grant; award from *Theatre World*, 1964, for performance in "Fair Game for Lovers"; Antoniette Perry ("Tony") Award nomination, 1967, for performance in "The Apple Tree"; Emmy Awards for best actor from National Academy of Television Arts and Sciences, 1973 and 1974, both for performance in "M*A*S*H"; Golden Apple Award from *Cue* magazine, 1980.

WRITINGS: (With Darwin Venneri) "Darwin's Theories" (musical revue), first produced on Broadway at Madison Avenue Playhouse, October 19, 1960; "The Seduction of Joe Tynan" (screenplay), Universal, 1979; *The Senator* (novelization of "The Seduction of Joe Tynan"), Dell, 1979; (and director) "The Four Seasons" (screenplay), Universal, 1981. Also co-author of dictionary *The Language of Show Biz*. Author of scripts for television series "M*A*S*H," 1972—, and for "We'll Get By," 1974. Contributor with Marlo Thomas and others to "Free to Be . . . You and Me" (sound recording), Bell Records, 1973. Contributor of articles to periodicals, including *Ms*.

SIDELIGHTS: Since 1972 Alan Alda has charmed millions of Americans as the inimitable Captain Benjamin Franklin

"Hawkeye" Pierce, wise-cracking chief surgeon on the popular television series "M*A*S*H." Whether he is playing up to a pretty nurse or racing against the clock in the operating room, he never fails to captivate his audience. As writer Edwin Miller expressed, "When Hawkeye's familiar features crinkle into a smile, you nestle under the warmth of Alda's gentle personality as if you were plugged into an electronic security blanket."

Alda began his acting career at an early age; his first appearance on stage came while he was still in diapers, cradled in the arms of his father, actor Robert Alda. His first professional appearance, however, came in 1951 playing Costello to his father's Abbott at the Hollywood Canteen. The young actor subsequently gained experience in summer stock and local productions before making his Broadway debut in 1959 as the Telephone Man in "Only in America." Consistently praised for his comic flair and enthusiastic and earnest performances, he continued on Broadway and landed substantial roles in such productions as "L'il Abner," "Anatol," "Purlie Victorious," and "Fair Game for Lovers."

In addition to his theatrical roles, Alda appeared in numerous television series during the 1960's, including "Route 66," "The Nurses," "Trials of O'Brien," and the popular "That Was the Week That Was." The actor distinguished himself in these early appearances and was approached by the Columbia Broadcasting System, Inc. (CBS-TV) to star in two proposed pilot series, "Where's Everett?" and "Higher and Higher." Although both floundered, CBS was impressed with the talented young actor and remembered him when the pilot for "M*A*S*H" came out in the early 1970's.

During the late 1960's Alda appeared in several films. In his first, "Gone Are the Days," an adaptation of the stage play "Purlie Victorious," he recreated the role of Charlie Cotchipee, which he had played in the Broadway production. This was followed in 1968 by his portrayal of George Plimpton, the journalist-turned-football player, in "Paper Lion." In 1970 he starred in "Jennie," a light-hearted comedy about a young couple who arrange a "marriage of convenience" and subsequently fall in love.

Alda's dedication to his profession was especially highlighted in the 1972 demonic thriller, "The Mephisto Waltz." In the film Alda's character, a failed concert pianist, was called upon to perform a five-minute selection from the Franz Liszt composition that gave the film its title. Instead of using a dubbed-in recording of the piece played by an actual concert pianist, Alda decided to perform the music himself. For nearly two months he practiced the piano several hours each day to achieve the desired authenticity.

Alda's next motion picture, "To Kill a Clown," tells the story of a deranged army veteran who manages a group of seaside cottages. When a young couple comes to his resort for a quiet vacation, Alda, as the manager, subjects the husband to such hard physical labor as hauling rocks back and forth for no reason other than "military discipline." He later imprisons the couple in their own cottage, guarded by two vicious attack dogs who will kill them should they attempt to escape. Although considered an undistinguished film, Alda's portrayal of the twisted resort manager was hailed by critics as intense and moving.

Alda read the pilot script for the proposed television series "M*A*S*H" in the early 1970's. "It was the best pilot I'd ever read," he recalled to interviewer Joseph P. Bell, "and when Larry [Gelbart, a writer and producer for the series] assured me it wasn't going to turn into one of those hijinks-at-the-battlefront routines, I decided to do it." Alda's intuition proved correct as the series moved quickly into the elite "Top Ten" of the most-watched shows on television. But with this overwhelming success came also a sense of loss for the actor: "I had anonymity for years, and I really relished it," he confided to Bell. "I was getting good parts, acting with good people, making good money; yet nobody recognized me because the films I was making weren't very successful. Then M*A*S*H came along, and all of a sudden about 30 million people seemed to be responding to me. It's fun at first, but then comes the sadness of no longer having the luxury of anonymity."

Many writers have attempted to isolate the reason behind the tremendous popularity of "M*A*S*H." George Vecsey of the Reader's Digest, for instance, held that "what makes these characters so appealing—and the show so popular—is that, unlike most TV characters, the ones on 'M*A*S*H' are quite capable of being cruel to one another, of taking advantage, even of making mistakes with their patients." "They are so bitingly human," he asserted, "that they stand above almost everything else on the tube." Others point out the interplay of the actors and actresses and the absense of a "big star" figure whose character dominates every episode. Actor David Ogden Stiers, who plays fellow surgeon Charles Emerson Winchester III on the show, explained that "Alan is the core, the central figure, rather than the star, because 'star' implies a certain kind of behavior, and with Alan, there is none of that." Similarly, executive producer Burt Metcalfe recalled: "From the start there were no barracudas on this show, so no one had to fight for his survival. If Alan Alda, the star, is not a prima donna, how can someone sixth down the line be one?" Loretta Swit, Major Margaret Hoolihan on the series, summarized, "The star of M*A*S*H is M*A*S*H."

In addition to his leading role in the series, Alda writes numerous scripts for "M*A*S*H" and has become one of the show's creative consultants. In this he has begun to realize a long-awaited dream. As wife Arlene revealed, "He wants to act, but he yearns to write." Alda has worked hard to become an established writer. "To me, work is love," he maintained. "Work is at the heart of health. I had to work very hard to develop the skills I have. Since I was a little boy, I've wanted to be accepted as a writer—and now it's happening. And I find I have more energy and take more pleasure in acting since that's not all I'm doing."

In 1979 Alda's first screenplay, which he both wrote and starred in, was released by Universal Pictures. "The Seduction of Joe Tynan" concerns a U.S. senator who must make difficult choices between his career and family; he wants to be a successful politician, yet he also seeks a fulfilling family life. "It's a comedy about an ambitious man's drive for success and the demands on him to be a family man," Alda explained to a Horizon interviewer. "But it's not all funny. There is this conflict in our culture. Family, love, faithfulness, and devotion are supposed to come first. Human values. Then there is the other dictate of our culture that success comes first."

Although several critics complained that the plot of the film was time-worn, others contended that Alda handled the various situations and characters in new and innovative ways. Gene Siskel of the Chicago Tribune, for example, mentioned a particular scene in which Tynan pays a rather off-beat compliment to a beautiful woman lawyer when he likens her to John F. Kennedy: "At first it's a very funny line—a guy comparing a woman to another man. But then Alda explains what he means. He talks about the Kennedy-like fire in her eyes, the similar passion he has seen in both of them. Now it's more than a cute pickup scene; it's a tender moment that in a quiet way strikes a blow for the equality of the sexes. Why not compare a woman to a man? Why should that seem silly?" "It's fine dialog," Siskel concluded, "and Alda wrote it."

One common criticism of "The Seduction of Joe Tynan" is that the characters seem too nice to be believed. A New York writer deemed the film "overly earnest and inhibited by good intentions" and contended that "all the major characters are so well-meaning." "In other words, the movie is paralyzed by too much respect for characters—a highly unusual defect, I admit." A writer for the National Review was stronger in his criticism: "Very little of the movie has been thought through and worked out with mature understanding let alone penetrating insight." Frank Rich of Time, however, asserted that "Alda has an instinct for intelligent comic dialogue, a willingness to engage hard issues and a sure touch for creating characters of all ages and genders."

Alda's dedication to the women's rights movement and his staunch support of the Equal Rights Amendment (ERA) is widely known. An active participant in the struggle for equality between the sexes, he became a member of the Commission on the Observance of International Women's Year in 1975 and in 1976 served as co-chairman of the presidential subcommittee on the ERA. Alda has made it very clear that he is sincere in his commitment to the movement. "I didn't become a feminist because it was 'this year's cause,'" he once declared. "I became one because of the incredible waste of half the talent in the world." When asked why he has devoted so much time and energy to the women's movement, he explained simply, "I own my life to women." He went on to relate that he is indebted both to his mother for recognizing early signs of polio in him when he was seven years old, and also to Sister Elizabeth Kenny, the Australian nurse who first developed an effective treatment for the disease.

The Equal Rights Amendment is an extremely important issue to Alda. "I get asked to do a lot of things," he once stated, "but [the ERA] is the only thing I'll drop everything for." He feels it is imperative that equality between the sexes be a constitutional guarantee. But despite the tremendous importance he attaches to passage of the amendment, Alda discourages those who would support it for the wrong reasons. "I'm not endorsing the ERA like soap," he insists. "I don't want people to vote for it because I'm cute."

Alda maintains that equality is a human issue, not a political one; it involves mutual respect and understanding between the sexes by which everyone would prosper. He told writer Edwin Miller: "Feminism concerns everybody. It is a constant process of learning. We men need to learn to raise our consciousness too—just as women have—to see ourselves in a way that's more relaxed and open and vulnerable."

BIOGRAPHICAL/CRITICAL SOURCES: Milwaukee Journal, June 23, 1974; Biography News, Volume I, Gale, 1974; Newsweek, September 9, 1974; Good Housekeeping, November, 1974, February, 1979, November, 1980; Christian Science Monitor, April 16, 1975; Ladies' Home Journal, August, 1975; Ms., October, 1975, July, 1976, September, 1979; McCall's, January, 1976; Redbook, July, 1976; TV Guide, January 4, 1977, June 4, 1977, January 5, 1980; U.S. News and World Report, June 26, 1978; Horizon, September, 1978; Vogue, January, 1979; Time, May 28, 1979, August 20, 1979; Working Woman, August, 1979; Reader's Digest, August, 1979; Chicago Tribune, August 12, 1979, August 31, 1979, May 22, 1981; New York Times, August 17, 1979, May 22, 1981; New Yorker, August 20, 1979; Washington Post,

August 24, 1979; *New Republic,* August 25, 1979; *New York,* September 3, 1979; *Maclean's,* October 1, 1979; *New Leader,* October 8, 1979; *National Review,* October 26, 1979; *Seventeen,* November, 1979; *Christian Century,* November 7, 1979; *Saturday Review,* November 10, 1979.*

—*Sketch by Kathleen Ceton Newman*

* * *

ALESSANDRA, Anthony J(oseph) 1947-

PERSONAL: Born June 2, 1947, in New York, N.Y.; son of Victor E. (a printer) and Margaret (Imbriani) Alessandra; married Janice Van Dyel (a small business owner), August 30, 1970; children: Justin. *Education:* University of Notre Dame, B.B.A., 1969; University of Connecticut, M.B.A., 1970; Georgia State University, Ph.D., 1976. *Home:* 5443 Pacifica Dr., La Jolla, Calif. 92037. *Office:* Alessandra & Associates, 920 Kline St., No. 100, La Jolla, Calif. 92037.

CAREER: Susquehanna University, Selinsgrove, Pa., instructor in business and administration, 1970-73; Georgia State University, Atlanta, instructor in marketing, 1973-76; University of San Diego, San Diego, Calif., assistant professor of marketing, 1976-78; Alessandra & Associates (consultants), La Jolla, Calif., president, 1978—. Sales and management trainer; public speaker. *Member:* American Marketing Association, American Society for Training and Development.

WRITINGS: (With Phillip Wexler) *Non-Manipulative Selling,* Courseware, 1979; (with Phillip Hunsaker) *The Art of Managing People,* Spectrum, 1980; (with Jim Cathcart) *Selling by Objectives,* Reston, 1982.

WORK IN PROGRESS: Self-help articles on sales, management, and communication topics for national trade magazines.

SIDELIGHTS: Alessandra told *CA:* "After teaching for three years at Georgia State University, I started doing some marketing consulting for local businesses. The consulting engagements led to conducting training seminars. I enjoyed teaching the seminars so much that I designed an eighteen-hour program called 'Non-Manipulative Selling.' I put together some sketchy notes that served as a participant's workbook. I kept updating the workbook until, in June, 1978, it was nearly one hundred twenty-five single-spaced pages. At that time, I decided to actually make it a book. *Non-Manipulative Selling* has sold nearly eleven thousand copies in hard cover, and it has been released in paperback.

"In mid-1978, I decided to take many of the concepts in *Non-Manipulative Selling* and apply them from a management perspective. I asked a fellow faculty member at the University of San Diego, Phillip L. Hunsaker, to help write a new book, *The Art of Managing People.* Phil took the lead and became the senior author. This book sold more than ten thousand copies in its first three months.

"In April, 1981, Walt Disney Productions produced three films based on *Non-Manipulative Selling.* Disney will distribute the films worldwide. The company is planning up to twelve more films over the next four years using my sales material."

* * *

ALEXANDER, Ernest R(obert) 1933-

PERSONAL: Born December 11, 1933, in Dresden, Germany (now East Germany); came to the United States in 1969, naturalized citizen, 1978; son of Fritz Ludwig (an art critic)

and Malwina (Mund) Alexander; married Shulamith Stock (an interior designer), March 6, 1960; children: Michael, Dana. *Education:* University of Cape Town, B.Arch., 1954; University of California, Berkeley, M.C.P., 1971, Ph.D., 1974. *Home:* 2216 East Stratford Court, Shorewood, Wis. 53211. *Office:* Department of Urban Planning, University of Wisconsin, P.O. Box 413, Milwaukee, Wis. 53201.

CAREER: Rechter, Zarchi & Rechter, Tel-Aviv, Israel, architect, 1955-56; architect in London, England, 1956-57, in Accra, Ghana, 1957-59, and in Tel-Aviv, 1959-69; University of Wisconsin—Milwaukee, visiting associate professor, 1972-73, associate professor of urban planning, 1973—. Head of research team at Institute for Planning and Development, Tel-Aviv, 1966-69. Lady Davis Visiting Professor at Technion-Israel Institute of Technology, 1977-78, Neaman and Petrie Visiting Professor, 1979-80. Consultant to State of Wisconsin, Israel Ministry of the Interior, and other organizations. *Member:* American Planning Association, American Institute of Certified Planners.

WRITINGS: (With Robert M. Beckley) *Going It Alone?: A Case Study of Planning and Implementation at the Local Level,* U.S. Government Printing Office, 1975; (with Anthony J. Catanese and David S. Sawicki) *Urban Planning: A Guide to Information Sources,* Gale, 1979. Contributor to academic journals.

WORK IN PROGRESS: Coordination: Interorganizational Policymaking and Implementation in Urban and Regional Development and Renewal; Design for Policy and Planning: The Development of Alternatives in Organizational Contexts.

SIDELIGHTS: Ernest Alexander told *CA:* "The two problems that have engaged my attention since becoming a planner and undertaking planning research are: how do people and organizations actually make decisions—as opposed to how they ought to make them—and how do plans get implemented? These are questions to which there are, as yet, very few answers. Any addition to our knowledge in these areas may help to make planning, policy analysis, administration, and management more effective than they are today."

* * *

ALEXANDER, (Charles) K(halil) 1923-1980
(Basheer Qadar, Mario Quimber)

OBITUARY NOTICE: Born May 4, 1923, in Cairo, Egypt; died of cancer, September 2, 1980, in New York, N.Y. Playwright, actor, director, composer, and producer. During his lifelong involvement with the theatre, Alexander acted in numerous Broadway plays, including "Three Penny Opera" and "The Cherry Orchard." He also appeared on television programs, including "Studio One" and "The Dupont Show-of-the-Week." He composed music for such plays as "The Campbells of Boston" and "Francesca da Rimini." Alexander also produced, directed, and wrote a variety of Off-Broadway plays. He organized The Company of Twelve and Theater Explorations, Inc., both Off-Broadway production groups. Obituaries and other sources: *Notable Names in the American Theatre,* James T. White, 1976; *New York Times,* September 3, 1980.

* * *

ALGREN, Nelson 1909-1981

OBITUARY NOTICE—See index for *CA* sketch: Born March 28, 1909, in Detroit, Mich.; died of a heart attack, May 9, 1981, in Sag Harbor, N.Y. Salesman, migrant worker, editor, and author. One of the Chicago realists along with James T.

Farrell and Richard Wright, Algren wrote about life in Chicago's slums and tenements. His works about the underbelly of American society inspired Ernest Hemingway to name Algren the best contemporary American writer after Faulkner. Among the author's novels number *Somebody in Boots,* later reprinted as *A Walk on the Wild Side, Never Come Morning,* and *The Devil's Stocking.* Algren's most successful book, *The Man With the Golden Arm,* established his reputation and earned him the National Book Award in 1950. The writer also co-edited an experimental magazine entitled *New Anvil.* Obituaries and other sources: *New York Times,* May 10, 1981; *London Times,* May 11, 1981; *Newsweek,* May 18, 1981; *Publishers Weekly,* May 22, 1981; *Time,* May 25, 1981; *AB Bookman's Weekly,* July 13-20, 1981.

* * *

ALICE (MARY VICTORIA AUGUSTA PAULINE), Princess 1883-1981
(Countess of Athlone)

OBITUARY NOTICE: Born February 25, 1883, in Windsor Castle, Windsor, England; died January 3, 1981, in London, England. Member of the British royal family and author. A great-aunt to Queen Elizabeth II, Princess Alice was the last surviving grandchild of Queen Victoria. Noted for her vitality and her longevity, the princess lived in six reigns and was present at four coronations. From 1950 to 1971 she was chancellor of the University of the West Indies, and her fundraising efforts were credited with having expanded that facility from a few shacks into a full-scale university. She received several honorary degrees from universities, including University of London, McGill University, and St. Andrew's University. Her book of memoirs, *For My Grandchildren: Some Reminiscences,* was a best-seller. Obituaries and other sources: *Who's Who,* 126th edition, St. Martin's, 1974; *New York Times,* January 4, 1981.

* * *

ALLAUN, Frank (Julian) 1913-

PERSONAL: Born February 27, 1913, in Manchester, England; son of Harry (a salesman) and Hannah (Fine) Allaun; married Lilian Ball, September 9, 1941; children: David, Ruth. *Education:* University of London, B.Comm., 1934. *Home:* 1 South Dr., Manchester 21, England. *Office:* House of Commons, London S.W.1, England.

CAREER: Northern Voice (Labour party newspaper), Manchester, England, editor, 1945-67; *Manchester Evening News,* Manchester, northern industrial correspondent, 1947-51; northern industrial correspondent for *London Daily Herald* in London, England; Labour member of Parliament from East Salford, England, 1955—. *Member:* National Union of Journalists.

WRITINGS: Heartbreak Housing, Hodder & Stoughton, 1966; *No Place Like Home: Britain's Housing Tragedy,* Deutsch, 1972; *Nuclear Weapons: Questions and Answers,* Campaign for Nuclear Disarmament, 1981. Also author of *The Thirty Billion Pounds Wasted on False Security* and *Your Trade Union and You.* Contributor of articles to newspapers, including *London Daily Star, London Sunday Times,* and *Manchester Guardian.*

SIDELIGHTS: Allaun told *CA:* "I am a three-subject writer: on housing, on 'defense,' and on the media. I enjoy writing letters to the press on these subjects, because the correspondence column is the best-read part of most newspapers. As nearly all the capitalist press is against my ideas, it gives

me special pleasure to get printed by these papers, particularly as they reach a huge audience."

BIOGRAPHICAL/CRITICAL SOURCES: New Statesman, November 10, 1972; *Spectator,* December 9, 1972; *Times Literary Supplement,* April 6, 1973; *Books and Bookmen,* May, 1973.

* * *

ALLEN, David F(ranklyn) 1943-

PERSONAL: Born August 21, 1943, in Nassau, Bahamas; married wife, Victoria S. (a writer). *Education:* University of St. Andrews, MBChB, 1969; Harvard University, MPH, 1974. *Religion:* Christian. *Office:* Western Medical Centre, P.O. Box W7776, Nassau, Bahamas.

CAREER: Boston City Hospital, Boston, Mass., resident in psychiatry, 1970-73; inspector of mental health for Massachusetts Department of Mental Health, 1974-76; Yale Divinity School, New Haven, Conn., visiting professor in psychiatry and religion, beginning in 1976; currently psychiatrist with Western Medical Centre in Nassau, Bahamas. *Awards, honors:* Joseph P. Kennedy, Jr., Foundation fellow at Harvard School of Public Health, 1973-74.

WRITINGS: Trends in Mental Health Evaluation, Lexington Books, 1976; *Ethical Issues in Mental Retardation,* Abingdon, 1979. Contributor to journals, including *Yale Medical Journal* and *Christianity Today.*

* * *

ALLEN, Robert S(haron) 1900-1981

OBITUARY NOTICE—See index for *CA* sketch: Born July 14, 1900, in Latonia, Ky.; committed suicide, February 23, 1981, in Washington, D.C. Journalist, columnist, and author. Allen worked as a reporter and correspondent for several newspapers, including the *Capitol Times, Wisconsin State Journal, Milwaukee Journal,* and *Philadelphia Record.* In 1931, while chief of the Washington, D.C., bureau of the *Christian Science Monitor,* Allen, with reporter Drew Pearson, anonymously published a collection of reports on government operations that the *Monitor* would not print. The book, *Washington Merry-Go-Round,* caused a furor and when the authors' names were revealed, they lost their positions. The two journalists, however, soon syndicated a column under the same title and wrote a sequel called *More Merry-Go-Round.* Allen quit writing the column when he served in World War II. On his return, he started another syndicated column, "Inside Washington," and wrote many books. *Why Hoover Faces Defeat, Nine Old Men, Lucky Forward: The History of Patton's Third U.S. Army,* and *The Truman Merry-Go-Round* number among his works. Obituaries and other sources: *New York Times,* February 25, 1981.

* * *

AMBROSI, Hans Georg 1925-

PERSONAL: Born February 24, 1925, in Medias, Romania; son of Michael (a proprietor of a wine estate) and Julia (Mueller) Ambrosi; married wife, August, 1958; children: Nikolaus, Andreas, Denise, Birgit. *Education:* Attended University of Agriculture, Stuttgart-Hohenheim, 1952-53; Geisenheim Agricultural Institute, D.Ag., 1953. *Office:* Leiter der Verwaltung der Straatsweingueter, Schwalbacherstrasse 60, 6228 Eltville/Rheingau, West Germany.

CAREER: Institute for Vine Breeding and Grafting, Geisenheim, assistant, 1953-54; University of Stuttgart-Hohenheim, West Germany, assistant at institute for horticulture, 1954-55; University of Stellenbosch, Stellenbosch, South Africa, leader of the viticulture department, 1955-58; Paarl Wine and Brandy Ltd., South Africa, cellar manager, 1958-64; Stellenbosch Farmers Winery, Stellenbosch, leader of scientific section, 1964-66. Director of the government viticulture wine estate in Eltville, West Germany. Founder of and director of study at German Wine Academy, Kloster Eberbach-Rheingau. Chief judge of world wine competition at Club Oenologic's Bristol Wine Fair, England, 1979-81. *Awards, honors:* Gold medal from Frankfurt International Book Fair, 1979, for *Der Deutsch Wein.*

WRITINGS: Weinlagen-Atlas mit Wein-Lexikon Deutschland, Ceres Verlag, 1973, third edition, 1976, translation by Bill Gavin published as *Wine-Atlas Germany and Dictionary,* Ceres Verlag, 1976; *Where the Great German Wines Grow: A Guide to the Leading Vineyards,* translated by Gavin Hamilton and Thom Pringle, Hastings House, 1976; (editor with Helmut Becker, and contributor) *Der Deutsch Wein* (title means "The German Wine"), Graefe und Unzer Verlag, 1978; *Welt-Wein Atlas* (title means "World Wine Atlas"), Ceres Verlag, 1982.

"Vinothek der deutschen Weinberg-Lagen" series; published by Seewald Verlag: (With Bernhard Breuer) *Der Rheingau,* 1978; (with Breuer) *Die Ahr,* 1979; (editor) *Baden,* 1979; (with Breuer) *Der Mittelrhein,* 1980; (with Breuer) *Die Nahe,* 1980; (with Breuer) *Franken,* 1981; (with Breuer) *Hessische Bergstrasse,* 1981; (editor) *Rheinfalz,* 1981; (editor) *Mosel-Saar Ruwer,* 1981; (editor) *Wurttemburg,* 1981; (editor) *Rheinhessen,* 1981.

Also author of *Vom Weinfreund zum Weinkenner* (title means "From Wine Friend to Wine Connoisseur"), 1975, fourth edition, 1980; *Wine-Atlas Europa* (title means "Wine-Atlas Europe"), 1975, second edition, 1980; and *Das Grosse Lexicon vom Wein* (title means "The Great Lexicon of Wine"), 1979. Contributor of more than a hundred articles to international periodicals.

WORK IN PROGRESS: Guida ai Vini di Germania (title means "The Wines of Germany"), for Arnoldo Mondadore Editore.

SIDELIGHTS: Amborsi told *CA;* "I prefer to give direct, practical, and technical information to people who like wine. What I learn by teaching at wine seminars and at the German Wine Academy, I use in my writings. I am not a poet, but I like to teach about the subject that I have been handling since my childhood. I am using my practical experience to explain the technical background of viticulture and of wine making. I am the director of the biggest German wine estate. I also am forced to deal with wine culture as I have to take care of the oldest wine monastery in the Rheingau, Kloster Eberbach, which was founded in 1135."

*   *   *

AMIDON, Bill (Vincent)   1935-1979
  (Jesse Taylor)

OBITUARY NOTICE—See index for *CA* sketch: Born June 30, 1935, in Cleveland, Ohio; died of severe diabetes and chronic alcoholism, February 9, 1979. Writer whose works appeared under the pseudonym Jesse Taylor. Amidon had been a columnist with the *Village Voice* since 1973. He was the author of plays and books, including "The Temporary,"

The Pleasure Principle, and *Charge ...!* (Date of death provided by sister, Loretta Range.)

*   *   *

ANCKARSVARD, Karin Inez Maria   1915-1969

OBITUARY NOTICE—See index for *CA* sketch: Born August 10, 1915, in Stockholm, Sweden; died January 16, 1969. Author of children's books and mysteries. Anckarsvard's first book was a fantasy about a lizard, *Bonifacius the Green,* but she sometimes wrote for a specific audience, as with *Aunt Vinnie's Invasion* and *Aunt Vinnie's Victorious Six.* These latter two were books for girls. In 1964 *Doctor's Boy* received the Nils Holgersson Prize as one of the best children's books of the year in Sweden. Obituaries and other sources: *Third Book of Junior Authors,* Wilson, 1972; *Something About the Author,* Volume 6, Gale, 1974.

*   *   *

ANDERSON, Lester William   1918-1973

OBITUARY NOTICE—See index for *CA* sketch: Born August 14, 1918, in Freeborn County, Minn.; died in an automobile accident in March, 1973. Educator and author. Anderson worked as a teacher and administrator at junior and senior high schools before beginning his academic career at Arizona State University. From 1952 until his death he was a professor of education at the University of Michigan. He was the co-author of *Secondary School Administration,* published first in 1963 and again in a second edition in 1972. (Date of death provided by wife, Margaret L. Anderson.)

*   *   *

ANDERVONT, Howard Bancroft   1898-1981

OBITUARY NOTICE: Born March 8, 1898, in Canton, Ohio; died of a stroke, March 11, 1981, in Sarasota, Fla. Virologist, cancer researcher, and editor. Andervont was best known for his pioneer work in the study of viruses as cancer-causing agents. His research on the immunology of transplanted tumors in genetically-controlled mice developed methods of cancer research still valid today. In the early 1930's, while he was an instructor in epidemiology and preventive medicine at the Harvard School of Public Health and Medicine, Andervont helped to convince the U.S. Public Health Service that cancer was a public health problem, and he was instrumental in the formation of the National Cancer Institute. He served as the first chief of the biology laboratory with the institute from the 1940's until 1961 at which time he became editor of the institute's journal. Andervont was awarded a Distinguished Service Award from the Department of Health, Education, and Welfare in 1961, and the following year he received the National Civil Service League Award. He retired in 1968. A former president of the American Society of Cancer Research, Andervont was also the author of 165 scientific papers in his field. Obituaries and other sources: *American Men and Women of Science: The Physical and Biological Sciences,* 12th edition, Bowker, 1971-73; *Washington Post,* March 14, 1981.

*   *   *

ANGLADE, Jean   1915-

PERSONAL: Born March 18, 1915, in Thiers, France; son of Jean (a bricklayer) and Felistine (a servant; maiden name, Chaleron) Anglade; married Marie Ombret (a teacher), June 11, 1935; children: Michelle-Helene Anglade Vuillardot. *Education:* University of Clermont-Ferrand, agregation d'italien,

1947. *Religion:* Roman Catholic. *Home:* 32 avenue J. B. Marrou, Ceyrat, 63110 Beaumont, France.

CAREER: Teacher at primary schools in Thiers, France, 1934-35, and St.-Gervais-d'Auvergne, France, 1935-41; teacher of French at technical schools in Saint-Etienne, France, 1941-42, and Thiers, 1942-47; teacher of Italian at high schools in Tunis, Tunisia, 1947-48, and Gap, France, 1948-49; Commercial Institute, Clermont-Ferrand, France, teacher of Italian, 1949-75. *Military service:* French Air Force, 1936-38, 1939-40.

MEMBER: Societaire de la Societe des gens de lettres de France, Societe des Auteurs, Compositeurs et Editeurs de Musique, Societe des Auteurs et Compositeurs Dramatiques. *Awards, honors:* Prix populiste from Cerde Populiste, 1957, for *L'Immeuble Taub;* Prix de Libraires de France, 1962, for *La Foi et la montagne:* Prix Eugene Le Roy from French Agriculture Ministry, 1970, for *Une Pomme oubliee;* Prix de l'humour noir from Cerde de l'humour noir, 1970, for *Le Point de suspension;* Prix Scarron from Cerde Scarron, 1972, for *Riez pour nous;* Grand prix de la ville de Cannes from Cannes Council, 1974, for *Un Temps pour lancer des pierres.*

WRITINGS—In English translation: *Des Chiens vivants* (novel), Julliard, 1967, translation by Robert Bullen and Rosette Letellier published as *Better a Living Dog,* Prentice-Hall, 1971.

Other; novels: *Le Chien du Seigneur* (title means "The Lord's Dog"), Plon, 1952, reprinted, Julliard, 1973; *Les Mauvais Pauvres* (title means "The Bad Poor"), Plon, 1954; *Les Convoites* (title means "The Coveted Town"), Gallimard, 1955; *L'Immeuble Taub* (title means "Taub's House"), Gallimard, 1956; *Le Fils de Tiberio Pulci* (title means "The Son of Tiberio Pulci"), R. Laffont, 1959; *Le Peche d'ecarlate* (title means "The Scarlet Sin"), R. Laffont, 1960; *La Foi et la montagne* (title means "The Faith and the Mountain"), R. Laffont, 1961; *La Garance* (title means "The Madder"), R. Laffont, 1963; *Une Pomme oubliee* (title means "A Forgotten Apple"; adaptation for television first broadcast by Antenne 2 TV, 1973), Julliard, 1969; *Le Point de suspension* (title means "The Point of Suspension"), Gallimard, 1969; *Un Front de marbre* (title means "A Marble Brow"), Julliard, 1970; *Le Voleur de coloquintes* (title means "The Pumpkin Robber"), Julliard, 1972; *Un Temps pour lancer des pierres* (title means "A Time for Throwing Stones"), Julliard, 1974; *Le Tilleul du soir* (title means "The Evening Lime Tea"), Julliard, 1975; *Le Tour du doigt* (title means "The Finger Round"), Julliard, 1977; *Les Ventres jaunes* (title means "The Yellow Bellies"), Julliard, 1979.

Poetry: *Chants de guerre et de paix* (title means "War and Peace Songs"), Le Sol Clair, 1946.

Nonfiction: *Les Greffeurs d'orties: L'Eglise et le proletariat* (title means "To Graft Nettles: Church and Proletariat"), La Palatine, 1958; *Herve Bazin* (title means "Herve Bazin, Writer"), Gallimard, 1962; *Sidoine Apollinaire* (title means "Biography of Sidonius Apollinares"), Editions Volcans, 1963; (with R. Baron) *Cours de composition francaise* (title means "How to Write a French Essay"), 5th edition, Dunod, 1965; *Grands Mystiques,* P. Waleffe, 1967; *Celebration de la chevre,* R. Morel, 1971; *Le Vie quotidienne dans le Massif Central au dix-neuvieme siecle,* Hachette, 1971; *Riez pour nous* (title means "Laugh for Us"), R. Morel, 1971, 2nd edition, 1972; *Solarama Auvergne* (title means "Auvergne Prospects"), Solar, 1972; *La Vie quotidienne contemporaine en Italie* (title means "The Contemporary Living in Italy"), Hachette, 1973; *Histoire de l'Auvergne* (title means "History of Auvergne"), Hachette, 1974; *L'Auvergne que j'aime* (title

means "Auvergne I Like"), Sun, 1974; *Jean Anglade raconte* (title means "Jean Anglade Tells"), Editions Le Cercle d'Or, 1975; *Les Singes de l'Europe* (title means "The Monkeys of Europe"), Julliard, 1976; *La Vie quotidienne des immigres en France de 1919 a nos jours* (title means "The Daily Living of Immigrants in France From 1919 to Now"), Hachette, 1976; *Les Grandes Heures de l'Auvergne* (title means "Great Hours in Auvergne"), Librairie Academique Perrin, 1977; *Drailles et burons d'Aubrac* (title means "Wandering in Aubrac"), Le Chene, 1979; *Le bonne rosee,* Julliard, 1980.

Translator from Italian: Niccolo Machiavelli, *Le Prince* (title means "The Prince"), Le Livre de Poche, 1972; Giovanni Boccaccio, *Le Decameron* (title means "The Decameron"), Le Livre de Poche, 1974.

Contributor to journals.

SIDELIGHTS: Anglade commented to *CA:* "I have attempted all kinds of literary works—novels, poetry, essays, translations, biographies, history, plays, satires—but feel I am essentially a novelist because I can put in my novels all the range of literary attitudes. In France I am considered a specialist on the Auvergne area, the heart of the country, on which I have written more than a dozen books."

*   *   *

ANTHONY, Barbara 1932-
(Antonia Barber)

PERSONAL: Born December 10, 1932, in London, England; daughter of Derek (a box office manager) and Julie (a landscape gardener; maiden name, Jeal) Wilson; married Ken Anthony (a structural engineering consultant), August 6, 1956; children: Jonathan Charles, Nicholas James, Gemma Thi-Phi-Yen. *Education:* University College, London, B.A. (with honors), 1955. *Home:* Horne's Place Oast, Appledore, Kent, England. *Agent:* Murray Pollinger, 4 Garrick St., London, England.

CAREER: Writer. *Member:* National Book League.

WRITINGS—All under pseudonym Antonia Barber; all for children: *The Affair of the Rockerbye Baby,* J. Cape, 1966, Delacorte, 1970; *The Ghosts,* Farrar, Straus, 1969, published as *The Amazing Mr. Blunden,* Penguin, 1972.

WORK IN PROGRESS: The *Rough Stuff,* a children's book about the Thames sailing barges at the time of the first World War; *The Women,* a series of adult novels about the changing nature of women's lives over a period of five hundred years.

SIDELIGHTS: In Barber's first novel, *The Affair of the Rockerbye Baby,* three English children vacationing in New York City find adventure and mystery by joining a local gang in their search for the kidnapped son of a millionaire banker.

Barber's second novel, *The Ghosts,* combines suspense and the supernatural. A young brother and sister, James and Lucy Allen, are confronted by the ghosts of two children killed a hundred years earlier in a fire. The apparitions seek aid, and the Allen children are required to travel back in time in order to change the course of history. The story was made into a feature film, televised, and was a runner-up for the Carnegie Award.

Barber told *CA:* "I am an example of a contemporary phenomenon: the professional woman writer who takes a few years out for the fascinating experience of raising young children. After two successful children's books, both widely published and translated, I gave up writing for a while to bring up two adopted sons, intending to return to work when they reached school age. The chance to add a baby daughter, a Vietnamese war orphan, to our family delayed me again; but now that she has joined the boys in school, I have returned to writing full time. The marvelous years in between have been of inestimable value to me as a writer. Having seen childhood now from the outside as well as the inside, and knowing what it is to be a parent as well as to have parents, I have a much deeper understanding of human character and relationships.

"The question children ask me most often in their letters is: 'What made you write the book *The Ghosts*?' My answer is: J. W. Dunne's book *An Experiment with Time,* which I read when I was seventeen; T. S. Eliot's poem "Four Quartets," which I read when I was seventeen; a story about a real apparition, told to me by an elderly man when I was twenty-six; and an old house I visited for a furniture auction when I was thirty-two, which made all the other memories come together to make a story. The moral is: You never know what may be useful if you are a writer."

AVOCATIONAL INTERESTS: Reading, sailing, theatre, travel, gardening.

BIOGRAPHICAL/CRITICAL SOURCES: Times Literary Supplement, June 26, 1969.

*   *   *

ARCANA, Judith 1943-

PERSONAL: Surname is pronounced Ar-*cah*-nah; name legally changed c. 1978; born February 5, 1943, in Cleveland, Ohio; daughter of Norman (in real estate sales) and Ida (an artist; maiden name, Epstein) Rosenfield; married Michael Pildes, July 26, 1964 (divorced October 31, 1973); children: Daniel. *Education:* Northwestern University, B.A., 1964; Goddard College, M.A., c. 1978. *Home and office:* 564 West Roscoe St., Chicago, Ill. 60657. *Agent:* Jean V. Naggar, Jean V. Naggar Literary Agency, 336 East 73rd St., New York, N.Y. 10021.

CAREER: Teacher of English at high school in Skokie, Ill., 1964-70; Abortion Counseling Service Clinic, Chicago, Ill., medical worker, administrator, counselor, and driver, 1970-72; Columbia College, Chicago, teacher of women's studies, 1973-79; Parents Primary School, Chicago, teacher of human sexuality, 1979-80. Lecturer on women's issues throughout the United States, 1971—; co-convenor of women's writing workshops, 1978-79. *Member:* Chimera, Feminist Writers Guild.

WRITINGS: (Contributor) Ann Landers, editor, *The Ann Landers Encyclopedia,* Doubleday, 1978; *Our Mothers' Daughters,* Shameless Hussy Press, 1979. Contributor to *Journeywomyn, Chrysalis,* and *Frontiers.*

WORK IN PROGRESS: A book about mothers raising male children; *Rachel's Story,* a book for young adolescent girls; a collection of poetry from 1969 to the present; two performance pieces, one magic, one philosophical.

SIDELIGHTS: Arcana told *CA:* "My writing and all the rest of my life are informed and encouraged by the women's movement. That is, both the information and the courage I embody or put forth come largely from that source. I read the Tarot, I scan the sky, and I take criticism, loving, and support from a small circle of friends."

*   *   *

ARMSTRONG, Thomas 1899-1978

OBITUARY NOTICE—See index for *CA* sketch: Born September 3, 1899, in Airedale, Yorkshire, England; died August 2, 1978. Textile manufacturer and author. Armstrong had worked in his family's textile manufacturing trade since the end of World War I, but a large part of his time was spent writing what he called "massive novels." His *King Cotton* contains 440,000 words. He traveled widely, but avoided television and radio appearances, preferring his life and work in the countryside of Yorkshire. Among his other writings are *Adam Brunskill, The Face of a Madonna,* and *The Crowthers of Bankdam,* which was filmed as "The Master of Bankdam." Obituaries and other sources: *Who's Who,* 131st edition, St. Martin's, 1979.

*   *   *

ASHE, Penelope
See KARMAN, Mal

*   *   *

ASHMORE, Lewis
See RABORG, Frederick A(shton), Jr.

*   *   *

ATHLONE, Countess of
See ALICE (MARY VICTORIA AUGUSTA PAULINE), Princess

*   *   *

AUEL, Jean M(arie) 1936-

PERSONAL: Born February 18, 1936, in Chicago, Ill.; daughter of Neil S. (a painter and decorator) and Martha (Wirtanen) Untinen; married Ray B. Auel (a corporate operations planner), March 19, 1954; children: RaeAnn, Karen, Lenore, Kendall, Marshall. *Education:* Attended Portland State University; University of Portland, M.B.A., 1976. *Politics:* Independent. *Residence:* Portland, Ore. *Agent:* Jean V. Naggar Literary Agency, 336 East 73rd St., New York, N.Y. 10021. *Office:* c/o Crown Publishers, Inc., 1 Park Ave., New York, N.Y. 10016.

CAREER: Tektronix, Inc., Beaverton, Ore., clerk, 1965-66, circuit board designer, 1966-73, technical writer, 1973-74, credit manager, 1974-76; writer. *Member:* Mensa, P.E.N., Willamette Writers Club.

WRITINGS: The Clan of the Cave Bear (novel; first in "Earth's Children" series), Crown, 1980. Poetry anthologized in *From Oregon With Love,* edited by Anne Hinds, Heron's Quill.

WORK IN PROGRESS: The second book of the "Earth's Children" series.

SIDELIGHTS: Auel's first novel, *The Clan of the Cave Bear,* received praise as one of the most original and exciting works of 1980. The story takes place in prehistoric times during the overlapping of the Cro-Magnon and Neanderthal periods. The central figure is Ayla, a Cro-Magnon girl adopted by Neanderthals after her own family perishes in an earthquake. Though Ayla is considered an outsider by her more primitive adopters, she is also respected for her higher developed intelligence. Auel's novel deals primarily with the cooperative aspects of Ayla's relationship with the Neanderthals. "What distinguishes us from animals is caring and sharing," contends Auel. "Animals let their cripples die. We take care of our old, sick and lame. And hunting big mammals, which provided a principal source of fat and protein for prehistoric people, was a cooperative venture."

Many reviewers were impressed with Auel's knowledge of prehistoric man. "The credibility and immediacy of the novel are due in large part to the wealth of researched detail that has gone into it,'' wrote Dave Walsten in the *Chicago Tribune*. ''If Jean Auel had gone back in time and researched her material then and there, I have the conviction that her novel would have been much the same thing.'' In the *Baltimore Sun*, Jeanne Rose noted that Auel ''makes us see . . . that these primitive people were 'human and humane.' She describes their ceremonies, medicines, tools, and foods so realistically that she brings us right into their lives.''

Critics also praised Auel's abilities as a storyteller. ''She has written an exciting, imaginative and intuitively solid book,'' wrote John Pfeiffer in the *New York Times Book Review*. Similarly, Larry E. Neagle called the novel ''solid, enticing, and at times even exciting.'' And Roy E. Perry deemed it ''a stunning *tour de force*. Original, distinctive, and ingenious, it is a novel filled with tense excitement and adventure.''

Auel told *CA:* ''I had no background in paleontology, anthropology, or archeology, and no real background in writing—three poems published in a small anthology and one year as a technical writer. I never even had ambitions to write the 'Great American Novel' (whatever that is). But at age forty, after finally gaining a long desired master's degree, with children all but grown, and with no idea what I really wanted to do, I quit my job. I didn't know I was going to write a book, but late one evening I had this idea for a story of humans who lived long ago, prehistoric cave dwellers, and two different kinds of people. What began as research for a short story grew to enough material for a series, and *The Clan of the Cave Bear* is the first. For the first time in my life, I'm doing what I want to do more than anything else. With all the frustration, I love writing fiction and telling stories.''

BIOGRAPHICAL/CRITICAL SOURCES: Oregonian, September 6, 1979, September 14, 1980, December 6, 1980; *New York Times Book Review*, August 31, 1980, October 26, 1980; *Kansas City Star*, September 7, 1980; *Morganton News Herald*, September 12, 1980; *Buffalo News*, September 14, 1980; *Chicago Tribune*, September 14, 1980, September 21, 1980; *San Francisco Chronicle*, September 14, 1980, October 13, 1980; *Nashville Banner*, September 20, 1980; *Fort Worth Star-Telegram*, September 28, 1980; *Baltimore Sun*, October 19, 1980; *Valley News* (Los Angeles), November 9, 1980.

*   *   *

AWDRY, Wilbert Vere 1911-

PERSONAL: Born in June, 1911, at Ampfield, near Romsey, England; son of Vere (a vicar) and Lucy Louisa (a teacher; maiden name, Bury) Awdry; married Margaret Emily Wale, August, 1938; children: Christopher, Veronica, Hilary Margaret. *Education:* St. Peter's College, Oxford, B.A., 1932, M.A., 1936; Wycliffe Hall, Oxford, diploma in theology, 1933. *Home:* Sodor, 30 Rodborough Ave., Stroud, Gloucestershire GL5 3RS, England.

CAREER: Ordained priest of Church of England, 1937; schoolmaster at boys' school in Jerusalem, 1933-36; curate in Odiham, England, 1936-39, West Lavington, England, 1939-40, and Birmingham, England, 1940-46; rector in Elsworth and Knapwell, England, 1946-53; vicar in Emneth, England, 1953-65; Diocese of Gloucester, Gloucester, England, officiant, 1965—. Rural dean of Bourn, 1949-53.

WRITINGS—Children's books; all published by Kaye & Ward, except as indicated: *The Three Railway Engines*, 1945; *Thomas the Tank Engine*, 1946; *James the Red Engine*, 1948; *Tank-Engine Thomas Again*, 1949; *Troublesome Engines*,

1950; *Henry the Green Engine*, 1951; *Toby the Tram Engine*, 1952; *Gordon the Big Engine*, 1953; *Edward the Blue Engine*, 1954; *Four Little Engines*, 1955; *Percy the Small Engine*, 1956; *Eight Famous Engines*, 1957; *Duck and the Diesel Engine*, 1958; *Belinda the Beetle*, Brockhampton Press, 1958; *The Little Old Engine*, 1959; *The Twin Engines*, 1960; *Belinda Beats the Band*, Brockhampton Press, 1961; *Branch Line Engines*, 1961; *Gallant Old Engine*, 1962; *Stepney the Blueball Engine*, 1963; *Mountain Engines*, 1964; *Very Old Engines*, 1965; *Main Line Engines*, 1966; *The Small Railway Engines*, 1967; *Enterprising Engines*, 1968; *Oliver the Western Engine*, 1969; *Duke the Lost Engine*, 1970; *Map of the Island of Sodor*, 1971; *Thomas the Tank Engine's Surprise Packet*, 1972; *Tramway Engines*, 1972.

Editor: *The Industrial Archaeology of Gloucestershire*, Gloucester Community Council, 1973; (with Christopher Cook) *A Guide to the Steam Railways of Great Britain*, Pelham Books, 1979.

SIDELIGHTS: Awdry told *CA:* ''My earliest recollections date from about the age of four, when I used to go for walks with my father round his parish of Ampfield. Our favorite was to go to Baddesley Bridge, climb up the embankment, and walk along the railway tracks.

''No one ever turned us away. The track gang were all my father's parishioners, and knew him as a keen amateur expert on railways. Personally I do not remember ever asking him a question about railways which he could not answer or know where to find the answer.

''After we moved to Box, in Wiltshire, our house was within two hundred yards of the Great Western Railway's London-to-Bristol main line, at a place where it climbed at one in one hundred for just over two miles, and a banking or 'pusher' engine was stabled at Box Station.

''In bed at night I would hear heavy freights clawing up the grade, and it needed little imagination to hear, in the sounds they made, the engines talking to each other, or the bitter complaints of an engine climbing the grade unassisted. From that time there developed in my mind the idea that steam engines all have personality.

''Writing began in 1943 when my son, aged three then, had measles, and had to be kept amused. I told him stories about engines invented on the spur of the moment. These stories were liked and told over and over again until the wordage became fixed. Then I wrote them down on scraps of paper for future family use. I had no further idea than that.

''Mrs. Awdry had other ideas. With much prodding she induced me to offer them to an agent, and much to my surprise he liked them, too.

''Granted the fiction that steam engines have personality and can express it, great care is taken to ensure authenticity in other directions by following real practice. All stories are based on incidents which have happened to some engine somewhere, sometime. A great many are based on off-beat incidents recorded in the railway press.

''The first two illustrators of my books had little knowledge of railways, and there were often discrepancies between pictures of the same places or engines in different books. Children and their parents wrote to me about these. Such letters must be answered with great care. It is no use pointing out that it was the artist who made the mistake. That would not satisfy the child at all. The only thing to do was to think up a story to account for the discrepancy. After the third or fourth book there were so many letters that life began to get too short! In self-defence, and to ensure continuity, I was forced to find a geographical location for the railway, and I 'discovered' the island of Sodor lying between Barrow-in-Furness and the Isle of Man.

"The railway there serves towns, villages, and industries. Towns and villages have names, and these names are wrapped in history. The siting and nature of industries depends on geology; thus, before long I found myself developing a political and economic history of my imaginary island. This has led to extensive research in Irish, Manx, Scotch, Norwegian, Icelandic, and English history.

"The work is still incomplete, and I doubt if it will ever be finished, though a map of the island was published in 1971. I have from time to time tried to settle down to its history, only to find myself brought up short by gaps which can only be filled by further research.

"I have had great fun lecturing on 'Pages from Sodor History,' and treasure the memory of one such occasion. After my talk was finished, questions were invited. One member of the audience asked, 'You write about the people and railways of Sodor, don't you?' 'Yes,' I answered, 'that is so.' 'Well,' he went on, 'aren't you putting yourself in danger of being sued for libel?' "

*   *   *

AYRES, James Eyvind   1939-

PERSONAL: Born June 10, 1939, in London, England; son of Arthur James John (a sculptor) and Elsa (a painter; maiden name, Groenvold) Ayres; married Annabel Jane Crowther, November 20, 1971; children: Peter James, Alice Elsa. *Education:* Goldsmith's College, London, N.D.D., 1960, A.T.D., 1961; Royal Academy Schools, diploma, 1964; attended Museum School, Boston, Mass., 1964-65. *Religion:* None. *Home:* Tollhouse, Church Lane, Freshford, Bath BA3 6ED, England. *Agent:* David Higham Associates, 5-8 Lower John St., Golden Square, London W1R 4HA, England. *Office:* John Judkyn Memorial, Freshford Manor, Bath BA3 6EF, England.

CAREER: Museum of Fine Arts, Boston, Mass., guest lecturer, 1964-65; free-lance sculptor, London, England, 1965-66; John Judkyn Memorial, Bath, England, director, 1966—. Part-time director of animation for television series "Focus," British Broadcasting Corp. (BBC-TV), 1959-60; restorer of historic buildings, 1960—. *Member:* Museums Association. *Awards, honors:* Received several awards for sculpture, drawing, and craftsmanship from Royal Academy, 1961-64; first prize for sculpture from British Institute, 1962; Fulbright scholarship, 1964-65; Ford Foundation fellowship, 1964-65; arts program travel grant from Institute of International Education, 1965.

WRITINGS: American Antiques, Crescent, 1973; *British Folk Art,* Overlook Press, 1977; *English Naive Painting,* Thames & Hudson, 1980; *The Shell Book of the Home in Britain: Design, Decoration, and Construction of Vernacular Interiors, 1500-1850,* Faber, 1981.

WORK IN PROGRESS: Research on the relationship between the arts tradition and crafts; exhibitions on American art and history.

SIDELIGHTS: Ayres told *CA:* "My books are concerned with the work of carvers, joiners, plasterers, painters, and other craftsmen for whom designing and making were simultaneous activities."

BIOGRAPHICAL/CRITICAL SOURCES: Times Literary Supplement, October, 24, 1980.

B

BADEN-POWELL, Dorothy 1920-

PERSONAL: Born May 2, 1920, in Southampton, England; daughter of Alton Ewart (a scientist and lecturer) and Hilda (Salvesen) Clarence-Smith; married Peter Philip Baden-Powell (a barrister); children: Imogen Baden-Powell Ward, Roger, Victoria Baden-Powell Church, Harry. *Education:* Attended University of Grenoble, 1938-39. *Politics:* Conservative. *Religion:* Church of England. *Home:* Ballindoon House, Ballindoon, Boyle, County Roscommon, Ireland; and Clos des Pins, Village de Putron, St. Peter Port, Guernsey, Channel Islands. *Agent:* Hughes Massie, 31 Southampton Row, London W.C.1, England.

CAREER: Writer. Interpreter for Finnish Legation in political intelligence department of Foreign Office, 1940; affiliated with Special Operations Executive, 1940-45. *Member:* Sesame Club.

WRITINGS: Pimpernel Gold: How Norway Foiled the Nazis, St. Martin's, 1978; *H. VII* (sequel to *Pimpernel Gold*), R. Hale, 1981.

WORK IN PROGRESS: A series of short historical plays, including "Vercingetorix" and "Alaric the Great," for Australian Broadcasting Commission.

SIDELIGHTS: Dorothy Baden-Powell commented to *CA:* "In writing about heroes of any nationality, my motivation is that they shall not be forgotten. Too many brave men have been allowed to sink into obscurity. Heroes should never die. I have started with *Pimpernel Gold,* with heroes personally known to me—the fifteen men who, in 1940, brought eighty tons of gold bullion (Norway's national reserves) from Oslo to ships on the west coast of Norway, chased all the way by Germans. The sequel concerns the brave deeds of saboteurs and the Norwegian Home Front. As I worked during the war in Special Operations Executive—the secret department for the organization of sabotage in the occupied countries and the formation of secret armies therein—I am in a position to know details of many of these exploits, which, till recently, were not permitted to be published.

"All my life my chief interest has been people, whether alive now or from some other century. I have studied history in depth, and speak most European languages. I also speak Malay and a little Cantonese, from living for nine years in Malaya. My other concern is conservation. Mankind cannot flower if we destroy the natural beauty of the world in which we live."

BAEHR, Consuelo 1938-

PERSONAL: Born September 5, 1938, in San Salvador, El Salvador; came to the United States in 1944, naturalized citizen, 1962; daughter of Fred M. (a retailer) and Blanche (a keypunch operator; maiden name, Coto) Saah; married Richard Baehr (an artist), May 23, 1965; children: Andrew, Nicholas, Amanda. *Education:* George Washington University, A.A., 1959; attended New School for Social Research, 1959-60. *Home:* 34 Frost Creek Dr., Locust Valley, N.Y. 11560. *Agent:* Aaron M. Priest Literary Agency, Inc., 150 East 35th St., New York, N.Y. 10016.

CAREER: Macy Corp., Newark, N.J., copywriter, 1962-65; Grey Advertising, New York, N.Y., copywriter, 1965-67; free-lance copywriter, 1967-70; free-lance writer, 1974-76.

WRITINGS: Report From the Heart (nonfiction), Simon & Schuster, 1976; *Best Friends* (novel), Delacorte, 1980. Contributor to *Newsday* and newspapers.

WORK IN PROGRESS: Nothing to Lose, a novel, following the fortunes and transformations of a fat, pretty girl and an ambitious half-Puerto Rican boy, publication expected in 1981.

SIDELIGHTS: Consuelo Baehr told *CA:* "When I was ten years old I wrote a novel about the Gold Rush in which the liver of a horse was used to coax the poison of a snake bite from a young man. I lost that novel in one of my many moves from apartment to apartment and it breaks my heart not to be able to have it now. I can't remember any time when I did not want to write, although there were many years in my adult life when I did nothing about it.

"When I was thirty-six years old, however, it occurred to me that the future would be pretty dim without writing and I began again in earnest. My aim was to have a newspaper column, and I submitted some essays to the 'Op-Ed' page of the *New York Times.* The fifth one was accepted and ran under the headline, 'Maggie, Jiggs, Blondie, Dagwood, Us.' The following week several magazines and two publishers were clamoring (yes, clamoring) for my services. A book, *Report From the Heart,* resulted.

"*Best Friends,* my first novel, concerns itself with three different women and how they interact—willingly or unwillingly, they affect each other drastically. I love writing about women and their complex lives. There is so much texture and innuedo in the lives of the most ordinary women. Also, to me, the simple declarative sentence is king. I like to comfort the reader with the familiar—characters get headaches, get mail, brush their teeth, make tea.''

In a review of *Best Friends, Los Angeles Times* writer Marilyn Murray Willison compared the novel's exploration of the three women's lives to soap opera plots, adding, ''Like too many daytime TV shows, the flow of events in this novel continues to shock and surprise the reader and, like any good soap opera, it seems the action will never, ever end.'' Willison cited contrived or improbable plot elements and jarring diction as examples of the novel's weak points, but observed that ''Baehr has a solid talent for repartee.'' While speculating that Baehr may have tried to incorporate into her first novel some characteristics found in the fiction of currently popular female writers, Willison suggested that ''we'd have been better off with a book that gave us, instead, a sampling of pure Consuelo Baehr.''

BIOGRAPHICAL/CRITICAL SOURCES: Los Angeles Times, August 29, 1980.

*   *   *

BAEHR, Patricia Goehner 1952-

PERSONAL: Born May 14, 1952, in Long Island, N.Y.; daughter of Herman and Doris (Powers) Goehner; married Edward W. Baehr, October 14, 1972; children: Peter Edward. *Education:* Hofstra University, B.S., 1974, M.A., 1977. *Residence:* Bayville, N.Y. *Agent:* Jean V. Naggar Literary Agency, 420 East 72nd St., New York, N.Y. 10021.

CAREER: Archer Street and Leo F. Giblyn schools, Freeport, N.Y., teacher of instrumental music, 1974-80. *Member:* Society of Children's Book Writers. *Awards, honors:* Jane Tinkham Broughton fellow at Bread Loaf Writers' Conference, 1980.

WRITINGS—Juvenile novels: The Way to Windra, F. Warne, 1980; *The Dragon Prophecy,* F. Warne, 1980.

WORK IN PROGRESS: Knights of Windra, a juvenile novel, publication expected in 1982; a novel for adults

SIDELIGHTS: Baehr told *CA:* ''Making distinctions between writing for children and writing for adults tends to produce children's books that are limited in vocabulary, lacking in imagination, and of a tone that condescends to young readers. The qualities desirable in adult fiction—clear prose, good stories, true characterizations—are equally desirable in children's literature. The writer of children's tales who must try to remember what it was like to be a child is not as successful as the writer who still holds inside the child he was. I write stories for myself, never for some imagined audience.''

*   *   *

BAGNOLD, Enid 1889-1981
(A Lady of Quality)

OBITUARY NOTICE—See index for CA sketch: Born October 27, 1889, in Rochester, England; died March 31, 1981, in London, England. Poet, playwright, and author. Bagnold became well known after her novel *National Velvet* was made into a motion picture starring adolescent actress Elizabeth Taylor. Among her other successes are the novel *Serena Blandish; or, The Difficulty in Getting Married* and the plays ''The Chalk Garden'' and ''A Matter of Gravity.'' Bagnold also wrote *Sailing Ships,* a volume of poetry, and an autobiography. Obituaries and other sources: *London Times,* April 1, 1981; *New York Times,* April 1, 1981; *Chicago Tribune,* April 1, 1981; *Washington Post,* April 3, 1981; *Newsweek,* April 13, 1981; *Time,* April 13, 1981; *Publishers Weekly,* April 24, 1981.

*   *   *

BAKER, Rachel 1904-1978

OBITUARY NOTICE—See index for CA sketch: Born March 1, 1904, in Chernigov, Ukraine; died July 7, 1978. Educator and author. Baker was a free-lance writer who had taught creative writing classes since the early 1940's. She was the founder and first president of Fairfield County Organization for Mentally Ill Children, located in Connecticut, and a co-founder of Resources Unlimited, Inc., a creative fellowship for the physically handicapped. Her writings include *The First Woman Doctor* (1942), *Sigmund Freud* (1952), and *America's First Woman Astronomer: Maria Mitchell* (1958). (Date of death provided by daughter, Joanna Baker Merlen.)

*   *   *

BALASKAS, Arthur 1940-

PERSONAL: Born April 15, 1940, in Johannesburg, South Africa; son of Xenophon Constantine (a chemist) and Paraskivola (a restaurateur; maiden name, Poulos) Balaskas; married Mina Rywka Fisher, August, 1966 (divorced September, 1974); married Janet Marion Hanson (a teacher of pre-natal classes), August, 1976; children: Kira Ann, Kim Lisa, Jed Xenon. *Education:* Attended London Film School, 1968-71. *Home and office:* 32 Cholmeley Cres., Highgate, London N.6, England. *Agent:* Patrick Seale Books Ltd., 2 Motcombe St., Belgrave Sq., London SW1X 8JU, England; and A.P. Watt Ltd., 26/28 Bedford Row, London WC1R 4HL, England.

CAREER: Director of company in South Africa, 1961-67; owner of restaurants in Johannesburg and Cape Town, South Africa. *Member:* Physical Education Association of Great Britain and Northern Ireland, Philadelphia Club (associate member).

WRITINGS: Bodylife (physical education), Sidgwick & Jackson, 1977; (with wife, J. Balaskas) *Newlife* (physical education), Sidgwick & Jackson, 1978.

WORK IN PROGRESS: Back to Life, on self-treatment for back pain; *Variations,* ''a love book''; *The Complete Book of Stretching.*

SIDELIGHTS: Balaskas is currently studying to become a psychotherapist under the supervision of R. D. Laing.

*   *   *

BALDWIN, Dick
See RABORG, Frederick A(shton), Jr.

*   *   *

BALDWIN, Leland D(ewitt) 1897-1981

OBITUARY NOTICE—See index for CA sketch: Born November 23, 1897, in Fairchance, Pa.; died March 6, 1981, in Santa Barbara, Calif. Educator, librarian, editor, historian, and author. Baldwin worked as a professor and librarian at the University of Pittsburgh and as an editor at the University of Pittsburgh Press. He was also assistant director in charge of research with the Western Pennsylvania Historical Survey. Baldwin wrote several history books, including *Whiskey Rebels: The Story of a Frontier Uprising, The Stream of American History,* and *Reframing the Constitution: An Im-*

perative for Modern America. Obituaries and other sources: *New York Times,* March 7, 1981.

*   *   *

BALLEN, Roger 1950-

PERSONAL: Born April 11, 1950, in New York, N.Y.; son of Irving W. (an attorney) and Adrienne (Miller) Ballen; married Lynn Moross (an art teacher), October 5, 1980. *Education:* University of California, Berkeley, B.A., 1972; Colorado School of Mines, Ph.D., 1980. *Religion:* Jewish. *Home and office:* 100 East 42nd St., Floor 24, New York, N.Y. 10017.

CAREER: Union Corp., Johannesburg, South Africa, geologist, 1974-76; free-lance photographer, 1976-78; Inca, Golden, Colo., mineral economist, 1978-80. *Member:* Phi Beta Kappa.

WRITINGS: Boyhood, Chelsea House, 1979.

WORK IN PROGRESS: A book on the relationship between the African and the land on which he lives and which he shapes, expected in 1982.

SIDELIGHTS: Ballen commented: "Since graduating from the university I have spent my time working in the mineral business and traveling for the sake of my photography. My trips have taken me across Africa and Asia as well as to the Americas. *Boyhood* stressed the need to find my boyhood through understanding boys around the world."

*   *   *

BALZER, Robert Lawrence 1912-

PERSONAL: Born June 25, 1912, in Des Moines, Iowa; son of Albert Taylor and Selma Olivia (Peterson) Balzer; married Emily Abel, December 24, 1936 (divorced, 1945). *Education:* Stanford University, B.A. (cum laude), 1935; attended Royal Academy of Dramatic Art, 1936. *Religion:* Buddhist. *Home and office:* 10551 Hillsboro Rd., Santa Ana, Calif. 92705.

CAREER: Owner of Balzer's (wine and food retail store), Los Angeles, Calif., and The Tirol (restaurant), Idyllwild, Calif. Photographer for United Press International (UPI), *New York Mirror, Flighttime, Wine,* and *Travel/Holiday.* Instructor and lecturer on wine, food, and restaurant management at University of California, Irvine, 1967, University of California, Los Angeles, 1969-72; Lawry's California Center, 1972—, and Queen Mary, Long Beach, Calif., 1978—; consultant to Paul Masson Vineyards, 1967-70. Performer in "What Shall I Have for Dinner?," KMPC-Radio, 1940-41, and "Robert L. Balzer on Wine," KFI-Radio; guest on television programs; appeared in feature films "The Day of the Locust" and "Killer Bees." Member of Los Angeles-Bordeaux Sister City program; founder and president of Mulholland Property Owners Association, 1952. *Military service:* U.S. Army Air Forces, pilot and flight instructor, 1941-42.

MEMBER: Chaine de Rotisseurs, Society of Bacchus, Guild of Sommeliers, Southern California Wine Writers, Cordon Bleu Wine and Food Society, Pi Delta Phi. *Awards, honors:* First prize from Kaiser's Men's Cookout, 1960; distinctive dining award from *Holiday,* 1965, for The Tirol; decorated in Cambodia, France, and Italy.

WRITINGS: California's Best Wines, Anderson & Ritchie, 1948; *Beyond Conflict* (autobiography), Bobbs-Merrill, 1963; *The Pleasures of Wine,* Bobbs-Merrill, 1964; (and photographer) *Adventures in Wine: Legends, History, Recipes,* Ritchie, 1969; *This Uncommon Heritage: The Paul Masson Story,* Ritchie, 1969; *Robert Lawrence Balzer's Book of Wines and Spirits,* Ritchie, 1973; *Wines of California,* Abrams, 1978. Also author of *Chefs of the West Cook Book,*

1951, and *American Cooking: The Great West;* co-author, with Clifton Fadiman, Hugh Johnson, and Sam Aaron, of *The Joys of Wine,* 1976.

Author and publisher of *Robert Lawrence Balzer's Private Guide to Food and Wine,* 1971—. Author of "Wine Connoisseur," a weekly column syndicated by *Los Angeles Times,* and a column in *Sunset.* Contributor of articles and photographs to magazines, including *Flighttime* and *Wine,* and to newspapers. Food and beverage editor of *Travel/Holiday.*

WORK IN PROGRESS: The Winebook for Restaurateurs and Other Hosts; California Wine Country Cookbook; The Pleasures of Food.

SIDELIGHTS: The Pleasures of Food is drawn from Balzer's lifetime experience in the kitchen, at markets, in restaurants, and at the table. He travels to Europe, Mexico, Canada, and across the United States each year, conducting seminars, lecturing, and discovering and writing about restaurants for the annual "Travel/Holiday Guide to Fine Dining in North American Restaurants." He takes his wine students on tours through California wine country twice a year and to France and/or Italy once a year.

BIOGRAPHICAL/CRITICAL SOURCES: Robert Lawrence Balzer, *Beyond Conflict,* Bobbs-Merrill, 1963.

*   *   *

BARBER, Antonia
See ANTHONY, Barbara

*   *   *

BARBER, Philip W. 1903-1981

OBITUARY NOTICE: Born in 1903; died of cancer, May 8, 1981, in Pittsfield, Mass. Dramatist, public relations consultant, educator, and author. The president of Barber & Baar, a public-relations firm, and a graduate of Harvard University, Barber grew up in Mason City, Iowa, where he put on plays with his cousin Meredith Willson, author of "The Music Man." Early in his career Barber taught play writing at Yale University and served as assistant to the founder of the Yale Drama School. While at Yale he wrote *The Scene Technician's Handbook.* In the 1930's he directed the Works Progress Administration's Federal Theatre Project, and during World War II he worked for the War Relocation Authority and was chairman of the national committee planning the resettlement of Japanese-Americans on the West Coast. Co-founder of the Manhattan Theatre Club and founder of the Music Inn and Music Barn in the Berkshires, Barber also worked as a screenwriter for Metro-Goldwyn-Mayer and as a writer for radio shows such as "Gangbusters" and "Young Widow Brown." His dramatic works include "The Passionate Quest" and "I, Elizabeth Otis, Being of Sound Mind." Obituaries and other sources: *New York Times,* May 27, 1981.

*   *   *

BARBER, Samuel 1910-1981

OBITUARY NOTICE: Born March 9, 1910, in West Chester, Pa.; died of cancer, January 23, 1981, in New York, N.Y. Composer. One of America's most distinguished composers, Barber began studying piano at the age of six; at seven he wrote his first piano composition, and by twenty-one he was acclaimed for his first orchestral piece, "Overture to the School for Scandal." He won two Pulitzer Prizes, the first in 1958 for his opera "Vanessa" and the second in 1963 for his "First Piano Concerto." In addition, Barber was awarded a Pulitzer traveling scholarship, the Prix de Rome of the American Academy, a Guggenheim fellowship, and an honorary doctorate in music from Harvard University. Virtually all of Barber's works have been recorded. They include, "Adagio for Strings," "Second Essay," "Souvenir," "Capricorn Concerto," "Andromaches' Farewell," and "Despite and Still." Obituaries and other sources: *Current Biography,* Wilson, 1963; *International Who's Who,* Europa, 1980; *New York Times,* January 24, 1981; *Newsweek,* February 2, 1981; *Time,* February 2, 1981.

* * *

BARBETTE, Jay
See SPICER, Bart

* * *

BARBOUR, Nevill 1895-1972

OBITUARY NOTICE—See index for *CA* sketch: Born February 17, 1895, in Eastbourne, Sussex, England; died in 1972. Editor, author, and publicist who specialized in Middle Eastern and North African subjects. He was the editor of *Journal of Palestine Oriental Society* from 1935 to 1939 and worked as an Egyptian specialist in Britain's Ministry of Information. He was an assistant director with the British Broadcasting Company's Eastern Services from 1940 to 1956. Barbour's writings include *Palestine: Star or Crescent?* and *Morocco.* A third edition of his *Survey of North West Africa (the Maghrib)* was published by Oxford University Press in 1977. Obituaries and other sources: *The Writers Directory, 1976-78,* St. Martin's, 1976.

* * *

BARCIA, Jose Rubia
See RUBIA BARCIA, Jose

* * *

BARDWICK, Judith M(arcia) 1933-

PERSONAL: Born January 16, 1933, in New York, N.Y.; daughter of Abraham I. and Ethel Hardis; married John Bardwick III, December, 1954 (divorced July, 1977); children: Jennifer, Peter, Deborah. *Education:* Purdue University, B.S., 1954; Cornell University, M.S., 1955; University of Michigan, Ph.D., 1964. *Home:* 2132 Spruceway Lane, Ann Arbor, Mich. 48103. *Office:* Department of Psychology, University of Michigan, 580 Union Dr., Ann Arbor, Mich. 48109.

CAREER: University of Michigan, Ann Arbor, lecturer, 1964-66, assistant professor, 1966-69, associate professor, 1969-74, professor of psychology, 1974—, associate dean of College of Literature, Science, and Arts, 1977-80, senior fellow of Society of Fellows, 1975-80. Member of faculty at National Science Foundation-American Association for the Advancement of Science chautauqua course for college faculty, 1975-77; speaker at colleges, seminars, and meetings. Member of National Institute of Mental Health population study group, 1971-75. *Member:* American Psychological Association (fellow), American Psychosomatic Society, Midwest Psychological Association, New York Academy of Science, Phi Beta Kappa.

WRITINGS: (With Elizabeth Douvan, Martina Horner, and David Gutmann) *Feminine Personality and Conflict,* Brooks/Cole, 1970; *Psychology of Women,* Harper, 1971; (editor and contributor) *Readings in the Psychology of Women,* Harper, 1972; *In Transition,* Holt, 1979; *Essays on the Psychology of Women,* Harper, 1981.

Contributor: Barbara Gornick and Vivian Moran, editors, *Women in a Sexist Society,* Basic Books, 1971; J. T. Fawcett, editor, *Psychological Perspectives on Population,* Basic Books, 1973; William Uricchio and M. K. Williams, editors, *Natural Family Planning,* HLF, 1973; Ruth Unger and Florence Denmark, editors, *Women: Independent or Dependent Variables,* Psychological Dimensions, 1974; V. Burtle and V. Franks, editors, *Women in Therapy,* Brunner, 1974; Dorothy McGuigan, editor, *New Research on Women,* Continuing Education for Women, 1974; M. L. McBee and K. A. Blaise, editors, *The American Woman: Who Will She Be?,* Glencoe, 1974; Alice Sargent, editor, *Beyond Sex Roles,* West Publishing, 1976; McGuigan, editor, *New Research on Women,* University of Michigan Press, 1976; Rosalind Loring and Herbert Otto, editors, *New Life Options,* McGraw, 1976; F. McKinney and others, editors, *Developmental Psychology,* Dorsey, 1977; Gerda Lerner, editor, *The Female Experience: An American Documentary,* Bobbs-Merrill, 1977; B. L. Forisha and B. H. Goldman, editors, *Outsiders on the Inside: Women and Organizations,* Prentice-Hall, 1980; J. Leonard, editor, *The ABC of Psychology,* Life Cycle Publications, 1981.

Contributor to *Encyclopedia of Women.* Contributor of articles and reviews to psychology journals. Member of editorial board of *Women's Studies.*

WORK IN PROGRESS: He Said / She Said, with Eric Rapkin.

* * *

BARGATE, Verity 1941(?)-1981

OBITUARY NOTICE: Born c. 1941 in Exeter, England; died of cancer, May 18, 1981. Theatre artistic director and author. Bargate was the co-founder and artistic director of the Soho Poly Theatre, which introduced the work of such playwrights as James Leo Herlihy, Sam Shepard, Chris Wilkinson, and Barrie Keeffe. Her novels include *No Mama No, Children Crossing,* and *Tit for Tat.* Obituaries and other sources: *London Times,* May 20,, 1981.

* * *

BARKER, Ernest 1874-1960

PERSONAL: Born September 23, 1874, in Woodley, Cheshire, England; died February 17, 1960; son of George Barker; married Emily Isabel Salkeld, 1900 (died, 1924); married Olivia Stuart Horner, 1927; children: (first marriage) one son, two daughters; (second marriage) one son, one daughter. *Education:* Attended Balliol College, Oxford.

CAREER: Oxford University, Oxford, England, fellow and lecturer at Merton College, 1898-1905, lecturer in modern history at Waldham College, 1899-1909, fellow and lecturer at St. John's College, 1909-13, lecturer at New College, 1913-20; University of London, King's College, London, England, principal, 1920-27; Cambridge University, Cambridge, England, professor of political science, 1928-39, fellow of St. Peterhouse College. Visiting professor at Amherst College, 1920. *Member:* British Academy (fellow). *Awards, honors:* Knight of the Order of the British Empire, 1944; received numerous honorary degrees.

WRITINGS: The Political Thought of Plato and Aristotle, Methuen, 1906, revised and abridged edition published as *Greek Political Theory: Plato and His Predecessors,* 1918, 5th edition, Barnes & Noble, 1960, original edition reprinted, Dover, 1959; *All for Germany; or, The World's Respect Well Lost, Being a Dialogue, in the Satyrick Manner, Between*

Dr. Pangloss and M. Candide, Clarendon Press, 1914; *Nietzsche and Treitschke: The Worship of Power in Modern Germany*, Oxford University Press, 1914; *Political Thought in England From Herbert Spencer to the Present Day*, Holt, 1915; *Ireland in the Last Fifty Years, 1866-1916*, Burrup, Mathieson & Sprague, 1916, 2nd edition, Clarendon Press, 1919; *A Confederation of the Nations: Its Powers and Constitution*, Clarendon Press, 1918; *The Dominican Order and Convocation: A Study of the Growth of Representation in the Church During the Thirteenth Century*, Clarendon Press, 1918; *Linguistic Oppression in the German Empire*, Harper, 1918; *Mothers and Sons in War Time, and Other Pieces* (collection of newspaper articles), A. L. Humphries, 1918; (editor) *The Future Government of India and the Indian Civil Service*, Methuen, 1919.

The Crusades, Oxford University Press, 1923, reprinted, Books for Libraries Press, 1971; *Christianity and Nationality*, Clarendon Press, 1927; *The National Character and the Factors in Its Formation*, Methuen, 1927, 4th edition, 1948, reprinted, Hyperion Press, 1979; *Church, State, and Study* (essays), Methuen, 1930, published as *Church, State, and Education*, University of Michigan Press, 1957, original edition reprinted, Greenwood Press, 1974; *Burke and Bristol: A Study of the Relations Between Burke and His Constituency During the Years 1774-1780*, J. W. Arrowsmith, 1931; *Education for Citizenship*, Oxford University Press, 1936; *The Citizen's Choice*, Cambridge University Press, 1937, reprinted, Books for Libraries Press, 1972; *Oliver Cromwell and the English People*, Cambridge University Press, 1937, reprinted, Books for Libraries Press, 1971.

The Parliamentary System of Government, Oxford University Press, c.1940; *British Statesmen*, Collins, 1941; *The Ideas and Ideals of the British Empire*, Cambridge University Press, 1941, 2nd edition, Greenwood Press, 1969; *Britain and the British People*, Oxford University Press, 1942, 2nd edition, 1955; *Reflections on Government*, Oxford University Press (London, England), 1942, Oxford University Press (New York, N.Y.), 1958; *British Constitutional Monarchy*, Oxford University Press, 1944, revised edition, British Information Services, 1950; *The Development of Public Services in Western Europe, 1660-1930*, Oxford University Press, 1944, reprinted, Archon Books, 1966; *Essays on Government*, Clarendon Press, 1945, 2nd edition, 1951; *British Universities*, Longmans, Green, 1946; (translator) *The Politics of Aristotle*, Clarendon Press, 1946; (editor) *The Character of England*, Clarendon Press, 1947, reprinted, Greenwood Press, 1976; *Traditions of Civility: Eight Essays*, [England], 1948, reprinted, Archon Books, 1967; *Change and Continuity*, Gollancz, 1949; *Father of the Man: Memories of Cheshire, Lancashire, and Oxford, 1874-1898* (autobiography), National Council of Social Service, 1949.

Political Thought in England, 1848 to 1914, Oxford University Press, 1950, 2nd edition, 1959; (translator) Otto Friedrich von Gierke, *National Law and the Theory of Society, 1500-1800*, Cambridge University Press, 1950; *Principles of Social and Political Theory*, Clarendon Press, 1951; *Age and Youth: Memories of Three Universities; and, Father of the Man* (autobiography), Oxford University Press, 1953; (editor with George Clark and P. Vaucher) *The European Inheritance*, three volumes, Clarendon Press, 1954; (editor and translator) *From Alexander to Constantine: Passages and Documents Illustrating the History of Social and Political Ideas, 336 B.C.-A.D 337*, Clarendon Press, 1956; (editor and translator) *Social and Political Thought in Byzantium*, Oxford University Press, 1957; (editor) *Social Contract: Essays by Locke,*

Hume, and Rousseau, Oxford University Press, 1962. Also author of *Values of Life*, 1939.

SIDELIGHTS: Sir Ernest Barker was a respected political scientist and historian. His numerous books delve into political theory from the period of Plato and Aristotle to twentieth-century Europe. Rather than the historical or governmental approach adopted by many other scholars, Barker was concerned more with the philosophical aspects of politics: the ideologies behind the institutions as opposed to the evolution or development of the governments themselves.

OBITUARIES: New York Times, February 20, 1960; *Illustrated London News*, February 27, 1960; *Nature*, March 19, 1960; *Wilson Library Bulletin*, April, 1960; *Political Studies*, June, 1960; *American Historical Review*, July, 1960; *Americana Annual*, 1961; *Britannica Book of the Year*, 1961.*

*   *   *

BARKER, Joseph 1929-

PERSONAL: Born June 24, 1929, in Hounslow, England; son of Ronald Alfred and Isobella (Paris) Barker; married Nancy Petrie (a painter), November 17, 1960; children: Ian Stephen Petrie, Jason Jonathan Petrie. *Education:* Attended School of Oriental and African Studies, University of London, 1949-50. *Politics:* Conservative. *Religion:* Church of England. *Residence:* Hertfordshire, England. *Agent:* Hughes Massie Ltd., 31 Southampton Row, London WC1B 5HL, England.

CAREER: James Warren & Co. Ltd., London, England, manager in Malaya and Singapore, 1952-58; Lombard Banking Ltd., London, Far East director in Hong Kong and Singapore, 1959-61; worked for various companies in England, 1961-69; Philips & Pye Groups, Cambridge and London, England, chief executive, 1969-78; management consultant, 1978—. *Military service:* Royal Air Force, navigator, 1947-49. *Member:* Institute of Petroleum, Institute of Marketing, Naval and Military Club.

WRITINGS: Fourth at Junction (novel), R. Hale, 1979, St. Martin's, 1980. Contributor to magazines.

WORK IN PROGRESS: Mortal Shadow, a novel; *Pithinian Burial*, a suspense novel; *Executive Hunter*, a novel.

SIDELIGHTS: Barker told *CA:* "I found my writing as a young man insufficiently objective and recommenced writing in 1977 only when I was convinced I would not obtrude my personality into the characters.

"In the interim, I had acquired a knowledge of French, German, Persian, Malay, and Arabic while living in Rhodesia (now Zimbabwe), South Africa, Iran, Iraq, Bahrain, Singapore, Malaya, and Hong Kong and while visiting thirty or more other countries.

"My writing time is divided between thrillers and novels. Thrillers provide me with the opportunity to devise complex plots, which are set in locales with which I am familiar. My first two novels are based on business situations, and in the personal lives of the characters the pressures of modern commerce are reflected and played out. It is my conviction that there is a valid audience for business-based novels since they provide the backdrop of a familiar scene, contrasting with the relaxation and escapism provided by the thriller.

"On writing the first book of my maturity, *Fourth at Junction*, I plotted it carefully, although finding that my characters caused some diversions, which necessitated plot reorientation. Subsequently, I have plotted more loosely providing the opportunity for freer development of each book as it is written.

"I make use of experiences and scenes with which I am familiar, examining the motivations of those whom I meet. However, I never use as a character someone I know, feeling that this breaks the bonds of confidence and limits the development of the character.

"My living in, working in, and visiting many countries has provided an understanding of many peoples and their ways of life, giving me a wide variety of experience which I can never hope to utilize fully in my writing since I frequently prefer to use the colors which are fresh to my palette."

*   *   *

BARNES, Douglas 1927-

PERSONAL: Born July 1, 1927, in Twickenham, England; son of Arthur George (a teacher) and Margaret (Wing) Barnes; married Dorothy M. Raistrick (a researcher), December 30, 1954; children: Ursula, Richard Jeronym. *Education:* Received B.A., M.A., and certificate of education from Downing College, Cambridge. *Home:* 4 Harrowby Rd., Leeds LS16 5HN, England. *Office:* School of Education, University of Leeds, Leeds LS2 9JT, England.

CAREER: High school English teacher in Bradford, Yorkshire, England, 1950-53, Dartford, Kent, England, 1954-56, Raubon, Denbighshire, Wales, 1956-59, and London, England, 1959-66; University of Leeds, Leeds, England, lecturer, 1966-73, senior lecturer in education, 1973—. Project director for Social Science Research Council. *Member:* National Association for the Teaching of English (chairman, 1967-69).

WRITINGS: (With James Britten and Harold Rosen) *Language, the Learner, and the School,* Penguin, 1969, 2nd edition, 1971; *Language in the Classroom,* Open University Press, 1973; *From Communication to Curriculum,* Penguin, 1976; (with Frankie Todd) *Communication and Learning in Small Groups,* Routledge & Kegan Paul, 1977. Contributor to education and language journals.

WORK IN PROGRESS: Research on kinds of English language education offered to high school students and their relation to institutional contexts and students' attitudes.

SIDELIGHTS: Barnes told *CA:* "Two major influences on my thinking have been the critic F. R. Leavis—though I have never accepted his elitism—and the educationist J. N. Britton. Leavis first made me realize that each of us has to recreate literature for himself. Britton helped me to apply this to the whole of our knowledge of the world and therefore to all education. Emphasis upon the active participation of the learner in learning has thus informed all my writing about 'language' in the classroom—which is really about increasing the learner's control of learning.

"During most of my seventeen years as a school teacher I had no intentions of leaving the classroom, and now after many years in a university I still feel a conflict between the priorities implicit in each of these contexts. I have always wanted my work to be useful to teachers, but as time has passed my perspective has insensibly moved away from theirs, as I have become aware of assumptions that I no longer hold and beliefs about education that I now question.

"In the classroom and in the education system as a whole I see a conflict between forces making for custodialism and social reproduction on the one hand and those which seek to turn education into an instrument and a power in the

learner's hand. The latter has to colonize the crevices left by the massive inefficiency of the former."

*   *   *

BARNETSON, William Denholm 1917-1981

OBITUARY NOTICE: Born March 21, 1917, in Edinburgh, Scotland; died March 12, 1981, in London, England. Journalist and news executive. Barnetson was the chairman and managing director of United Newspapers, a major group of thirty regional morning, evening, and weekly publications, including the humor magazine *Punch.* Also chairman of *The Observer* of London and of Thames Television, Barnetson was the former chairman of Reuters, the international news agency, which he headed from 1968 to 1979. In addition to his journalistic activities Barnetson served as deputy chairman of British Electric Traction and as a board member of the English National Opera and the Bank of Scotland. In 1975 Queen Elizabeth II named him a life peer. Obituaries and other sources: *International Who's Who,* Europa, 1980; *Chicago Tribune,* March 13, 1981; *New York Times,* March 14, 1981.

*   *   *

BARNHOUSE, Donald

PERSONAL—Education: Harvard University, A.B.; Princeton Theological Seminary, Th.M., 1955. *Home:* 2203 Brandenburg Way, King of Prussia, Pa. 19406. *Office:* Department of Political Science, Eastern College, St. Davids, Pa. 19087.

CAREER: Personal research assistant for evangelist Billy Graham, 1955-59; WCAU-TV, Philadelphia, Pa., news analyst, 1960-72; Committee of Seventy, Philadelphia, executive director, 1973-76; Drexel University, Philadelphia, adjunct professor of political science and journalism, 1976-78; Eastern College, St. David's, Pa., associate professor of political science.

WRITINGS: Is Anybody Up There?, Seabury, 1977. Contributor to magazines, including *Realites.*

SIDELIGHTS: Barnhouse wrote: "One of my favorite activities is meeting groups of Americans face to face, in situations like workshops and lectures where there is opportunity for questions and dialogue. I have spoken to close to a million people on topics such as 'Middle East Prospects,' 'SALT and the Cold War,' 'Choosing Our President,' 'The Real Energy Story,' 'Ten Ways to End the World,' 'An Inside Look at Television News,' 'The Stealing of Elections,' 'Forces Shaping the Eighties,' 'A Practical Program for Crime Control,' and just about anything else that may turn up in the news.

"My travels have taken me to forty-five nations, giving me a working knowledge of five languages. More important, my seven years spent living and studying among people of other cultures have helped me to know how they feel and think."

*   *   *

BARNWELL, William Curtis 1943-

PERSONAL: Born February 11, 1943, in Macon, Ga.; married Jo Ann Weeks (an educational administrator), September 12, 1966; children: Anne, William Curtis, Jr. *Education:* Florence State College, B.A., 1966; University of Florida, Ph.D., 1972. *Home and office:* 6008 Yorkshire Dr., Columbia, S.C. 29209. *Agent:* Curtis Brown Ltd., 575 Madison Ave., New York, N.Y. 10022.

CAREER: University of South Carolina, Columbia, assistant professor of English, 1971-77; Columbia College, Columbia, writer-in-residence, 1977—. *Member:* Modern Language Association of America, American Committee for Irish Studies, Authors Guild, Authors League of America, South Atlantic Modern Language Association. *Awards, honors:* First prize in poetry from University of South Carolina writing conference, 1977, for "Krystal Burger."

WRITINGS: The Blessing Papers (novel), Pocket Books, 1980; *Imram* (novel), Pocket Books, 1981; *Curve of the Sigmoid* (novel), Pocket Books, in press. Contributor to language and literature journals.

WORK IN PROGRESS: Indefinite Reprieves, poems; *The Spearman Novel*, a novel; *Rounding Man*, a novel.

SIDELIGHTS: Barnwell commented: "Writing as a craft requires desire, will, and hard work. It is at times exciting, but then so are a lot of things. If fiction is a splinter pulled from autobiography, then each writer has his own reasons for pulling it out. It seems to me that one of the major tasks of the writers of our time will be the dramatization of the struggle between man's traditional humanistic values and his new tools; that is, technology. Will man be king, or will his tools?"

*   *   *

BARRETT, Judi
  See BARRETT, Judith

*   *   *

BARRETT, Judith   1941-
  (Judi Barrett)

PERSONAL: Married Ron Barrett (an artist). *Home:* 230 Garfield Place, Brooklyn, N.Y.

CAREER: Writer of books for children, art teacher, and freelance designer. *New York Times*, New York, N.Y., children's book reviewer, 1974—. *Awards, honors:* American Institute of Graphic Arts Book Show Awards, 1973-74, for *Benjamin's 365 Birthdays*, and 1979, for *Cloudy With a Chance of Meatballs;* Children's Book Showcase Award from Children's Book Council, 1974, for *Benjamin's 365 Birthdays*.

WRITINGS—All under name Judi Barrett, except as noted; all juvenile; all published by Atheneum, except as noted: (Under name Judith Barrett) *Old MacDonald Had an Apartment House* (illustrated by husband, Ron Barrett), 1969; *Animals Should Definitely Not Wear Clothing* (illustrated by R. Barrett), 1970; *An Apple a Day* (illustrated by Tim Lewis), 1973; *Benjamin's 365 Birthdays* (illustrated by R. Barrett), 1974; *Peter's Pocket* (illustrated by Julia Noonan), 1974; *I Hate to Take a Bath* (illustrated by Charles B. Slackman), Four Winds Press, 1975; *I Hate to Go to Bed* (illustrated by Ray Cruz), Four Winds Press, 1977; *The Wind Thief* (illustrated by Diane Dawson), 1977; *Cloudy With a Chance of Meatballs* (illustrated by R. Barrett), 1978; *Animals Should Definitely Not Act Like People*, 1980.

SIDELIGHTS: Judith Barrett's books have been praised for the quality of their texts, their bold, bright illustrations, and their whimsicality. "This is original humor," said Harriet B. Quimby when reviewing *Old MacDonald Had an Apartment House*. In this book, a New York apartment superintendent converts his building into a four-story farm complete with animals. Another character, Benjamin, in *Benjamin's 365 Birthdays*, loves opening presents so much that he wraps and unwraps every object in his house, and eventually he even wraps the house.

While Barrett's stories are entertaining, they inform young readers about the world. For example, *Animals Should Definitely Not Wear Clothing* emphasizes creatures's characteristics through humorous illustrations, such as a giraffe wearing seven neckties or an opossum sporting his clothes upside down. *I Hate to Go to Bed* and *I Hate to Take a Bath* teach a child to adjust to everyday routines.

BIOGRAPHICAL/CRITICAL SOURCES: Book World, November 9, 1969.*

*   *   *

BARRETT, Rona   1936-

PERSONAL: Given name, Rona Burstein; born October 8, 1936, in New York, N.Y.; daughter of Harry J. (a food market entrepreneur) and Ida (Lefkowitz) Burstein; married William Allan Trowbridge (a businessman), September 22, 1973. *Education:* Attended New York University, 1953-55. *Home address:* P.O. Box 1410, Beverly Hills, Calif. 90213. *Office:* National Broadcasting Company, Inc., 3000 West Alameda Ave., Burbank, Calif. 91523.

CAREER: Creator of column, "Rona Barrett's Young Hollywood," 1957; *Motion Picture* (magazine), columnist, 1960; syndicated columnist with North American Newspaper Alliance, 1961-64; American Broadcasting Co. (ABC-TV), Los Angeles, Calif., host of shows, "Dateline: Hollywood," 1967, and "Rona Barrett's Hollywood," 1969, featured journalist and interviewer on "Good Morning America," 1975-80, and host of special programs, including "Rona Looks at the Oscars," 1972, "Rona Looks at Raquel, Liza, Cher, and Ann Margaret," 1975, and "Rona Looks at James Caan, Michael Caine, Elliot Gould, and Burt Reynolds," 1976; journalist syndicated by Metromedia, 1969-74; publisher of fan magazines, *Rona Barrett's Hollywood*, 1969—, and *Rona Barrett's Gossip;* National Broadcasting Co. (NBC-TV), Los Angeles, interviewer and news correspondent with shows, "Today" and "Tomorrow," 1980—.

WRITINGS: The Lovo-Maniacs (novel), Nash Publishing, 1972; *Miss Rona* (autobiography), Nash Publishing, 1974.

WORK IN PROGRESS: A novel.

SIDELIGHTS: "I am a truth-teller, not a gossip mongerer," insists Rona Barrett. Covering the glamorous Hollywood scene, Barrett's big news breaks include the divorce of Dyan Cannon and Cary Grant, the separation of Elizabeth Taylor and Richard Burton, and the marriage of Elvis Presley. "When you become a public person, you no longer are a private person," she explains. "You can't use the press one day, then ask them to leave you alone the next." Some of the persons involved in Barrett's news items do not agree. Mia Farrow once dumped a bucket of champagne over the columnist's head, and Ryan O'Neal mailed her a tarantula. Despite such incidents, Barrett's juicy, informative columns and television spots have proved extremely popular. Her magazines, *Rona Barrett's Hollywood* and *Rona Barrett's Gossip,* sold more than one million copies combined in 1974, with circulation on the increase. In 1980 NBC lured Barrett away from rival network ABC in an effort to boost its falling viewer ratings. Barrett moved, though, because NBC offered her work as a straight news commentator. The trim, attractive reporter, who overcame muscular dystrophy as a child, once admitted, "I am still someone who, no matter how high I climb, always sees a higher pinnacle."

AVOCATIONAL INTERESTS: Redecorating houses.

CA INTERVIEW

Rona Barrett was interviewed on June 25, 1980, in her office, which is situated almost directly above the on-camera newsroom at the ABC news department in Los Angeles, Calif.

CA: A lot of people criticize what you do as gossip rather than journalism. Is it?

BARRETT: I think you would have to define for me what you mean by gossip, because I don't call it gossip, certainly not what I've been doing in the last five years on "Good Morning America." I don't think you could look at any one broadcast I'm doing right now and say that is gossip. You don't come on the air and discuss big business industry information and call that gossip. It is totally reliable information. It is not hearsay. It is not, "Someone told me that this might be happening." It is certainly not personal news on the level of who's sleeping with whom, which is what I consider and call gossip. I report about an industry that happens to be the second or third largest industry in the world, leisure time activity. It is not gossip.

CA: What you're doing really is like what Jack Anderson does, except that it's directed toward the entertainment industry.

BARRETT: There are moments when I am like Jack Anderson, when I have uncovered major stories that turn into major scandals. There are also times that I think I am much more a cross between the *New York Times, Daily Variety,* and a consumer paper, any consumer paper.

I really feel that the reason people sometimes call me a gossip has much to do with the fact that I am a woman and that the two women journalists [Hedda Hopper and Louella Parsons] who gained a reputation in the Hollywood community were gossips and did a different kind of reporting. They did what was right for their time. I feel that I am doing what is right for our time. We're just not living in the same times, and I think one has to progress. I've often said that if my name were Ronald Barrett, I don't think anybody would say, "Oh, he's a gossip." They would say, "He's a Hollywood journalist; he's a Hollywood commentator." They would never attach the word gossip. Gossip seems to be a very convenient word to attach to any woman who is in the business of talking about people. But I just don't talk about people. I talk about issues and an industry.

CA: How has the industry changed since you've been on the scene?

BARRETT: Well, when I first came here some twenty years ago, it was into its final phase, as I call it, where there were still the very well-known studio moguls, there were people who were under contract, actresses, producers, and directors, and there was what we call the old studio system. In the last twenty-two years we have seen the breakdown of that system. We have seen it go through all kinds of changes and transitions, and as we speak right now, I am convinced we are still in a transitional stage, about to make an assault into a scene that will be reminiscent of how this town was structured forty, fifty years ago, because it is the only way that the community is eventually going to survive.

For the last fifteen years I have always spoken of pay television, and I believe that that is what we're now into. The facts are that there is an attendance fall-off at the theatres, that commercial television as we know it has had a decline in its audience, and at the same time, that cable has had an increased hookup. The American middle class, which has gone to movies in the past, is now taking its money and putting it towards a monthly fee, towards a pay-TV system that permits them to watch major motion pictures several months after they're released into the theatres. They wait that time because it is much cheaper for them to do so and much more convenient for them, because most of their homes are a lot prettier than some of the theatres, which are terribly dirty and filthy, inefficiently run, and unsafe in many instances.

I think there's enough evidence at this time to say that we're changing, and why I say we're going to go back to some form of what once was in the thirties or forties is because there's going to be such an overwhelming need for product. There is right now. In order to ensure that various pay TV and cable systems, as well as commercial television and the few theatres that survive will have their kind of product, people are going to have to guarantee the ability to make that product. And the most efficient way to make that product is to always have your specific writers, your directors, your actors, and an ensemble company all prepared to work for you literally around the clock or twelve months out of the year. And I see various cottage industries or cottage companies, as we call them now, joining forces not unlike the way they did fifty years ago, sixty years ago, when Metro and Goldwyn and Mayer got together and you had Metro-Goldwyn-Mayer. Or when Fox got together with Twentieth Century and became Twentieth Century-Fox. They altered because that was the only way they could all survive. So what happened is you emerged with seven or eight major motion picture companies. I think there might be a few more than that when it all settles down, but I think we will see that kind of structuring again.

CA: Why did you write your autobiography at such an early age?

BARRETT: I didn't intend to. I started to write a novel, and as I was halfway into my novel, which was called "The Pinnacle," my friend Barbara Howar came out with an autobiography called *Laughing All the Way.* I stopped to read it, and I said, "Whoa. If Barbara can get away with saying the things she has said, maybe the time has come not to disguise stories but to be very upfront about them and let it all hang out." I think another one of the reasons was that I often felt people were not writing about me; they were taking their pot shots at me. I've always said everybody's entitled to do what they want to do, but I felt people were asking me things that were very trivial, and I really felt that I've never been a trivial person. I've never been able to make small talk, ever. Basically I was a very quiet, shy person who would sit in a corner and observe people because I was fascinated by them. I felt I had a very interesting story. I had rarely told anybody about my own personal handicaps, and I knew that those personal handicaps, my surviving them, enabled me to live. I knew by observation that the minute people come across an obstacle, the very first obstacle, most quit. Most people say, "Well, I can't go on." I felt that if I wrote my story maybe it would encourage others to have the faith to believe in themselves, that despite whatever obstacle comes in your path, you can be whomever you want to be, providing you believe. That's why I wrote the book.

CA: In the book you also focused on an era that nobody had written about yet, the time of your arrival in Hollywood, the fifties and sixties. So your book becomes sort of a history of that time, too.

BARRETT: I guess looking back you might say so. I mean if I had to rewrite it all over again, I think I would not leave out anything but would have embellished even more. There were so many things I left out, crucial observations about the time, but I had choices to make. The publisher only wanted a manuscript that was so many words long. I think in the last seven years since I wrote that book I have changed so dramatically. My perspective has again changed, and I probably would view things differently, not the details, not the facts, but the observations I make now; I think they would have clarified even a few more things.

The book is a social document to some degree. It's a human document, number one, but I think it's a social document, number two. It does tell us something about the period, the late fifties into the sixties in Hollywood, and the people who were there, what they thought, what they did, and things of that nature, and my own relationship with those people. How dreams were born in those days. I don't think the dreams could be the same today, I just don't. I think you can dream. I think part of the problem today is that most people have lost the dream. They have nothing to hold on to, or they don't know how to hold on, or they're afraid of holding on for fear that every time they do, something collapses. The idols are taken away; the idols have clay feet; the dreams never materialize. It's very difficult, it's a very difficult time we're living through.

CA: There do seem to be more people with a death wish, more self-destructive actors, singers, entertainers. Or are we just finding out more about it?

BARRETT: I think we're finding out more about it. Since the mid-seventies, and I would have to say after the real success of *Miss Rona*—I can't say it was really due to myself because that would be unfair, but I think I just hit it at the right time—people found it very necessary to reveal all. They wanted to be seen properly as real people and that was what I was concerned about in my interviewing of all these famous people. I realized that oftentimes the public image just never matches the private person. And in some instances it *did* match the private person; in other words the image up on the screen was very similar to the image in real life. But they were the exceptions to the rule. I found that most people underneath it all, even as famous as they were, laughed and cried and really cried a lot. Many of these very famous individuals were really very insecure, very shy. Sometimes very limited people, too, who, given the script and given the words of others, were able to capture those feelings on the screen but found it very difficult to articulate them as individuals, which is why they are actors and actresses.

CA: That's their liberation of emotion. And that, in turn, affects their personal lives, makes them tumultuous?

BARRETT: Yes. I think the fact that actors and actresses were willing to expose those things and that suddenly the personal kind of interview came into play (because nobody did that kind of personal interview until 1975, when I did the first of those big, major specials) created the atmosphere for the look at the four famous ladies who were the hottest names in Hollywood at that time: Raquel Welch, Liza Minelli, Ann Margaret, and Cher. When they revealed all, down to the most intimate parts of their lives, I think that was the beginning, I really do. No one in the sixties did their interviews like that. I was never given the opportunity in the sixties to do that kind of an interview, ever. I was always condemned, or people would say to me after I did an interview like that, "Oh my God, that was so personal. How did you get to ask those kinds of questions?" I didn't even think of them as

being out of the ordinary. They were just questions of purposeful curiosity.

CA: How do you feel about an interview? Do you feel it's more like a conversation and making friends with someone, or do you feel it's a formal, structured situation?

BARRETT: I think it really should be more of making friends with somebody, of being concerned about somebody. The most difficult aspect of doing interviews for "Good Morning America" is that basically they're anywhere between six and a half and eight minutes in length because that's the maximum. So I personally do maybe a ten- or twelve-minute interview with somebody, and then I edit to the best eight. So I'm taking out very little, but it doesn't really give me an opportunity, as opposed to when I do a special, to sit with somebody for an hour and a half, or two hours on tape. You get to break down the defenses, and there's just no other way to do it. It's like being in analysis: you don't automatically start blurting out everything to a doctor until you learn that the doctor really cares about you. And that's basically the kind of interview I do.

CA: How much preparation do you do? Is it a life-long preparation? For example, you had watched Cher's career from the very beginning.

BARRETT: That's really what happens, unlike some people who go in to interview a subject who has never met them before. These interviewers have to do a different kind of preparation. I might prep myself on some background information. As far as sitting down, most of these are people I have observed, so I know a great deal about them. But there's also something else. I don't think there's any difference between interviewing Robert Redford and interviewing President Carter. I really don't. I think the art is in the interviewing. I don't think there's any difference sitting down with one or the other.

There is a difference, however, in doing a news interview as opposed to a feature interview. In a news interview you're really dealing with specific information and basically, on television anyway, you're almost looking for somebody to answer one question that will enlighten someone as to what the whole purpose of this story is.

CA: And in a feature?

BARRETT: In a feature you're looking for lots of insights. You're looking for how somebody expresses themselves; you're looking for body language. I think you're looking for all kinds of things. How they respond, how they think. It tells you a lot about an individual. There are some people who talk incessantly and say nothing. And there are others—like one person—I don't know why she stands out in my mind right now. I did an interview with Nancy Walker, and we were talking about mothers and death. I asked her if she could recall what her feelings were like when she lost her mother at the age of eight. And there was this silent pause, and I could see Nancy's eyes going to the corner of her head and looking up, and she just shook her head and she said, "The lights went out." And she had nothing more to say, and yet that said it all. Sometimes you don't need twenty paragraphs in order to say what you're feeling, and that's the thing I love about television.

CA: Are you gossiped about?

BARRETT: It seems out of the New York and Chicago papers, lately anyway, that they mainly gossip about whether

I'm going to stay at ABC, or whether I'm going to go some-place else, or whether I'm going to retire, or whether I'm just going to quit. [Barrett moved to NBC in late 1980.] Professional gossip. Personal gossip I haven't had for a long, long time. When I first got married the *National Enquirer* just attacked me every two minutes.

CA: But otherwise, is there an unwritten code that journalists don't write about journalists?

BARRETT: I don't know if it's an unwritten code. Maybe it's just that my personal life isn't very exciting. I don't seek personal publicity. If one doesn't seek it, one doesn't have to deal with it. You put yourself on the firing line for that kind of thing and you'll get it.

CA: If you entertained you certainly wouldn't come out and say, "I had a lovely dinner party the other night."

BARRETT: Can you just see that as being part of the news. It's funny, because when President Carter gives, or anybody in the White House gives a party, it is news. It's interesting, and the funny thing that's always amazed me is why the people who run the news division feel that Hollywood news is gossip while Washington news is not. Yet you will hear more "sources at the White House said," more "sources at the Pentagon," more "sources at the CIA," more "sources here," and more "sources there," which are never revealed, while ninety-nine percent of my broadcasts are filled with "the president of Twentieth Century-Fox confirms," "the vice-president says this," "top executive named so and so says that," always people who *exist*. And who anyone could check with.

CA: Now, you do your interviews, your television program in the mornings. What other areas do you plan to pursue? Do you think you'll have a cable show?

BARRETT: No, not right now. First of all, I've been exclusive to the network, so I have not had the opportunity to go into cable. I also don't have the time. I really don't have the time. This job keeps me busy fourteen, sixteen hours a day. And when I'm into my specials we literally run around the clock with few of us getting more than three or four hours sleep a night.

CA: How many hours actually are put into preparing the small segment that you do?

BARRETT: Well, first of all, there are two news segments every day plus a minimum of two interviews a week. The segments run seven to eight minutes long, five days a week, so that's forty minutes of news, and two interviews of a minimum of eight minutes apiece is sixteen more minutes. You're talking about over an hour's worth of actual pro-gramming a week. That's like asking, "Well, what goes into it?" I get offended by even the words, "Well, how much time do you spend going into those little segments?" What you don't realize, I've got twelve people who work for me. I've just been out doing an interview this morning. I come back now, and I will begin culling all this information, check-ing, rechecking, then pulling all the information together.

CA: So when you talk about an hour of broadcast time a week, it's like putting on a "Movie of the Week" every week.

BARRETT: Absolutely. Totally.

CA: With a staff of twelve, which is kind of small for that type of indepth coverage.

BARRETT: Yes, we could use two or three more bodies here. If you think about it, just think about it, in each of my seg-ments there can be anywhere between three and six stories. Now, those are culled from a much larger number of potential stories. Most people get on the air and do one story. For every one that they do, I do twenty, because during the day I may start working on as many as twenty different pieces of information. Verifying, researching, writing, rewriting—hoping to get a comment from somebody perhaps that I can use on the air.

CA: And out of the twenty stories, fourteen may die?

BARRETT: Fourteen may die, for that day, and may get resurrected if somebody else doesn't break them or whatever. Actually, what I consider to be the most important goes on that day.

CA: I guess it's your exclusive responsibility?

BARRETT: Absolutely. Well, I really don't have that many PR people who call in and say, "Hi, here's a free story." I just don't have that happen.

CA: So you've got people out with feelers all the time?

BARRETT: We're on the phones all day long.

CA: What stories do you feel proudest of having done?

BARRETT: I don't know if the word is proud. I don't know how to answer that question. I really don't, because I'm not proud of a specific story. I am proud of my integrity. I am proud that I feel I do the best job possible at always ascer-taining the accuracy of a story. I am very concerned and very aware that many of the things I say affect a lot of people. They affect the marketplace, also meaning Wall Street, they affect this community, they affect the creative people. So I am always concerned and aware of attempting to put the facts into proper perspective. I am also proud of the fact that I cannot be bought, and I think that's why many Hollywood journalists have always caused this community to have a bad name. It is very easy to accept a free trip to Vegas, a free junket to anywhere in the world. When you do that, in my opinion, you are no longer a free person. You really have some form of an obligation to be sort of courteous to the individual who's picked up your tab.

If traveling is part of my job, then it is for ABC to pick up those expenses because that's what they're paying me for. Nobody forces me to do anything. The point is that it's part of my job. If my job is to cover a major opening of a brand new personality or a major star in Vegas for the very first time, I shouldn't go as a courtesy of the hotel. What if I hate that person? But that's part of my job. Those are legitimate expenses my job should pay for.

I can remember a couple of years ago, four or five years ago, somebody was doing the promotion that dealt with bicycles, and one day I came home and there was a bicycle at my door. So I returned the bicycle. Then they did a promotion on phonograph records or just phonographs and somebody sent me over a portable phonograph and I sent it back. The company finally got the message that just because they were doing this promotion didn't mean I would accept the gift. I remember George Barrie from Faberge when he came in to the world of entertainment. He insisted on sending God knows how many boxes of various kinds of Faberge goodies. I told him I couldn't accept them. He said, "Well, if you can't accept them, then give them to everybody else," which is exactly what I did.

CA: That is important.

BARRETT: To me that is very important. There are several producers still in this community who feel that if they buy me a dinner that will insure them of a good review of a film. It's just not the case.

CA: Because your responsibility really isn't to them at all.

BARRETT: No, never. The truth of the matter is this town was the very last place in the whole damn bloody world that ever gave me a break. This town tests your patience until you want to die and then one day you wake up and they say, "Guess who's on the new list of survivors? Add the name Rona Barrett. Forget her. We don't have to bother with her any more." You think about that. Those are the observations that I sort of missed in *Miss Rona*. But I don't think they really became as clear to me as they have in the last few years, anyway.

CA: But you can write more books.

BARRETT: I have every intention of writing more books. I'm in the midst of writing a novel right now. I've had to put it away for a while because I haven't been able to lick it. There's something wrong with my story. I've got the people down, but I don't have my story right yet.

CA: Have you ever been awed by anybody you've had to interview?

BARRETT: There've been a couple of people who have concerned me. Like the first time I ever interviewed Gregory Peck. I wasn't quite sure whether his public image was going to match his private person. But he was extremely responsive and it was probably one of my best two-part interviews. I don't know if I could use the word awed. I don't know if the word excitement is even applicable. I think concerned and nervous would probably be better.

BIOGRAPHICAL/CRITICAL SOURCES: Biography News, Volume I, Gale, 1974; *Philadelphia Bulletin,* July 12, 1974; *Detroit Free Press,* July 26, 1974; *Houston Post,* July 29, 1974; *Authors in the News,* Volume I, Gale, 1976.

—*Interview by Judith Spiegelman*

* * *

BARROW, Joseph Louis 1914-1981
(Joe Louis)

OBITUARY NOTICE: Born May 13, 1914, in Lexington, Ala.; died of a heart attack, April 12, 1981, in Las Vegas, Nev. Professional boxer and author. Known to millions of fans as the "Brown Bomber of Detroit," Joe Louis was the heavyweight boxing champion of the world for twelve years. He first captured the heavyweight crown in 1937, when he scored an eighth-round knockout of the titleholder, James J. Braddock. The next year he faced off for a second time with Nazi Germany's symbol of racial superiority, Max Schmeling. In their first meeting, in 1936, Schmeling won the battle with a twelfth-round knockout. But in the famous re-match, laden with overtones of racism and nationalism, Louis demolished Schmeling in the first round, winning by a knock-out that stunned the world and broke the myth of Nazi invincibility. During his reign as champion Louis defended his title twenty-five times (more than any other heavyweight champion), retiring undefeated in 1949. As a boxer Louis performed with a slow, flat-footed motion that was offset with the quickest, most powerful fists in the game, and many experts consider him the greatest fighter of all time. In the

bitter aftermath of his fight career, beset with marital problems, squabbles with the Internal Revenue Service, bouts with gambling and cocaine, and a nervous breakdown in 1970, Louis remained a man of dignity and grace, the model of sportsmanship, and a beloved American folk hero who advanced the cause of black people everywhere. In the words of the Reverend Jesse Jackson: "Joe Louis was to America what David was to Israel. . . . Heroes usually have to stand on the people's shoulders. When Joe Louis was our hero in the midst of a depression and World War, the nation stood on his shoulders. He literally lifted the morale of the nation." Louis was the author of *My Life Story* and *The Joe Louis Story.* Obituaries and other sources: *Current Biography,* Wilson, 1940, June, 1981; *The Ebony Success Library,* Volume I: *One Thousand Successful Blacks,* Southwestern Co., 1973; *Who's Who in Boxing,* Arlington House, 1974; *New York Times,* May 13, 1979, April 13, 1981; *Time,* April 27, 1981.

* * *

BARROW, William
See FULLER, Hoyt (William)

* * *

BARRY, John Vincent William 1903-1969

OBITUARY NOTICE—See index for *CA* sketch: Born June 13, 1903, in Albury, New South Wales, Australia; died November 8, 1969. Lawyer, judge, and author of books in his field. Barry served as a king's counsel in Australia for many years before becoming a justice of the Supreme Court of Victoria in 1947. He also served as chairman of the department of criminology at the University of Melbourne. His writings include *Introduction to Criminal Law in Australia* and *Studies in Criminal Law.* His most recent book, *The Courts and Criminal Punishments: Three Lectures by Sir John Vincent William Barry,* was published by the Wellington Government Printing Office in 1969. (Date of death provided by James H. Edwards, the author's associate.)

* * *

BARTH, Gunther 1925-

PERSONAL: Born January 10, 1925, in Duesseldorf, Germany (now West Germany); came to the United States in 1951, naturalized citizen, 1960; son of Clemens and Hedwig Barth; married Ellen Wood, September 10, 1960; children: Christine, Dominic, Gilbert, Giselle. *Education:* University of Oregon, B.A., 1955, M.A., 1957; Harvard University, Ph.D., 1962. *Home:* 642 Santa Rosa Ave., Berkeley, Calif. 94707. *Office:* Department of History, University of California, Berkeley, Calif. 94720.

CAREER: University of California, Berkeley, instructor, 1962-63, assistant professor, 1963-66, associate professor, 1967-71, professor of history, 1971—. Fulbright professor at University of Cologne, 1970-71. *Member:* American Historical Association, Organization of American Historians. *Awards, honors:* American Historical Association Pacific Coast Branch award, 1965; Guggenheim fellowship, 1968-69.

WRITINGS: All Quiet on the Yamhill, University of Oregon Press, 1959; *Bitter Strength,* Harvard University Press, 1964; (contributor) Frederic C. Jaher, editor, *The Age of Industrialization in America,* Free Press, 1968; *Instant Cities,* Oxford University Press, 1975; *City People,* Oxford University Press, 1980.

WORK IN PROGRESS: Landscape and Land Use, for Oxford University Press.

SIDELIGHTS: Anatole Broyard of the *New York Times* said that Barth's *City People* "is rather like an old Cecil B. De Mille 'spectacular,' only much better. Mr. Barth has an immense fund of knowledge, which he uses with wit and a fine sense of proportion. If you read this book, it may even make your heart feel 'gallant' again about the city."

BIOGRAPHICAL/CRITICAL SOURCES: New York Times, January 3, 1981.

* * *

BARTON, Del 1925-1971

OBITUARY NOTICE: Born in 1925 on an Indian Reservation near Painted Post, N.Y.; died in 1971. Author. Barton is best known for her book *A Good Day to Die,* based on the life story of her great-grandfather, Gray Wolf, the last Dakota chieftain. (Date of death provided by Doubleday.)

* * *

BASKIN, Barbara H(olland) 1929-

PERSONAL: Born August 27, 1929, in Detroit, Mich.; daughter of C. F. (an engineer) and Ruth (in sales; maiden name, Herman) Harriman; married Alex Baskin (a professor), August 15, 1952; children: Julie Susan, Amy Shael. *Education:* Wayne State University, B.A., 1951, Ed.D., 1968; University of Michigan, M.A., 1957. *Religion:* Jewish. *Home:* 32 Seville Lane, Stony Brook, N.Y. 11790. *Office:* Office of Special Education and Developmental Disabilities, State University of New York at Stony Brook, Stony Brook, N.Y. 11794.

CAREER: Special education teacher at public schools in Detroit, Mich., 1951-54, 1955-59; Fort Knox, Fort Knox, Ky., teacher in transitional training unit and elementary school, 1954-55; Wayne State University, Detroit, staff member until 1968; State University of New York at Stony Brook, Stony Brook, faculty member, 1971—, director of Office of Special Education and Developmental Disabilities, 1977—. Educational director of psychiatric center for children; director of institute for the gifted; president of Suffolk County Council for Exceptional Children, 1978; founding member of executive board of Awareness Coalition for the Exceptional, 1980. Developer of computer software. *Member:* American Association on Mental Deficiency, National Association for Gifted Children, National Organization for Women, Council for Exceptional Children. *Awards, honors: Notes From a Different Drummer* was named among fifty outstanding reference books of the year by American Library Association, 1978; citation from President's Committee for the Employment of the Handicapped, 1980, for *Notes From a Different Drummer.*

WRITINGS: (Editor with Karen Harris) *The Special Child in the Library,* American Library Association, 1976; (with Harris) *Notes From a Different Drummer: A Guide to Juvenile Fiction Portraying the Handicapped,* Bowker, 1977; (with Harris) *Books for the Gifted Child,* Bowker, 1980; (editor with Harris) *The Mainstreamed Library,* American Library Association, 1981. Contributor to education and library journals.

WORK IN PROGRESS: Notes From a Different Drummer, Volume II, with Karen Harris, publication by Bowker expected in 1983.

SIDELIGHTS: Barbara Baskin wrote: "Karen Harris and I have long been concerned about stereotyping attitudes toward those in our population who have disabilities. I discovered many of the same problems in writing about characters who were disabled as earlier researchers had uncovered in works on women and minorities, namely that distortions, exaggeration, and other forms of stereotyping were pandemic in juvenile literature.

"Moreover, many of these books appeared to have been written 'with the best of intentions,' but were innocent of the gritty realities of impairment. Although many titles were excellent, others presented characters and context with simplistic solutions, improbable plots, and roseate solutions widely at variance with actuality. Critics seemed reluctant to evaluate these titles using criteria similar to that employed with comparable novels, perhaps feeling that serious criticism about these juvenile books was tantamount to behaving callously towards the disabled. The consequence was that selectors who wished to acquire books that were accurate, non-stereotyped, realistic, and of commendable literary quality were in difficulty.

"*Notes From a Different Drummer,* the first hardcover book devoted to this single topic, tried to address that issue some years ago and is being updated. It not only provided for critical, detailed annotations of juvenile foreign and domestic novels on impairment, but examined their relationship with adult fiction on this topic, commented on portrayals of disability in popular media, and discussed the literary uses of disability.

"*The Special Child in the Library* was also a pioneering effort, being the first collection of articles (to our knowledge) on the role of the library in adapting to disabled patrons. This title subsequently generated other professional interest and a small but growing list of titles has emerged since 1976 directed toward improving access to books and media for this population.

"Although much attention has been given to book selection for youngsters whose functional reading level was low in relation to their age, little thought was directed to youngsters who read as preschoolers and those who read well above the level of their contemporaries. Harris and I addressed the issue of selecting juvenile books, both fiction and nonfiction, which contained attributes that matched characteristics most frequently ascribed to gifted children; that is, matter containing abstractions and ambiguities, humorous word play, et cetera. The first of its kind, *Books for the Gifted Child* provides guidance to the searcher of contemporary books, fiction and nonfiction, for this particular audience."

AVOCATIONAL INTERESTS: Reading, theatre, museums, bridge, puzzles, cryptography, travel (North Africa, the Middle East, Mexico, Europe).

* * *

BASLER, Thomas G(ordon) 1940-

PERSONAL: Born March 8, 1940, in Cleveland, Ohio; son of Gordon F. (an attorney and pharmacist) and Bertha E. (Gerspacher) Basler; children: William Thomas, Elizabeth E., Charles Gordon. *Education:* University of Miami, Coral Gables, Fla., B.Ed., 1962; Florida State University, M.S., 1964; Laurence University, Ph.D., 1977. *Home:* 2715 Walton Way, Augusta, Ga. 30909. *Office:* Library, Medical College of Georgia, Augusta, Ga. 30912.

CAREER: Teacher at public schools in Miami, Fla., 1962-63; Emory University, Atlanta, Ga., medical librarian intern, 1964-65; Miami-Dade Junior College, Miami, librarian and instructor in library science, 1965-66; Institute of Marine

Sciences, Miami, librarian and assistant professor of library science, 1966-68; American Museum of Natural History, New York City, librarian, 1968-70; New York Academy of Medicine, New York City, librarian, 1970-72; Medical College of Georgia, Augusta, director of libraries and professor of library science, 1972—. Member of Augusta Area Committee for Health Information Resources; consultant to Abbott Pharmaceutical Co., Archival Restoration Associates, and Ferrell & Hoyt Business Appraisals. *Member:* Medical Library Association (chairman of Southern Regional Group, 1975-76), Special Libraries Association (chairman of Biological Sciences Division, 1974-75), Georgia Health Sciences Library Association, Central Savannah River Library Association.

WRITINGS: (Editor with Beatrice K. Basler) *Health Sciences Librarianship: A Guide to Information Sources,* Gale, 1977. Contributor of more than a dozen articles to library journals and *Pet Life.*

* * *

BATES, Caroline (Philbrick) 1932-

PERSONAL: Born November 15, 1932, in Cleveland, Ohio; daughter of William Edwin and Irene (Goffeney) Philbrick; married Kenneth Bates (a photographer), August 21, 1954; children: Eliot. *Education:* Elmira College, B.A., 1953. *Home address:* P.O. Box 30821, Santa Barbara, Calif. 93105.

CAREER: Newsweek, New York City, researcher, 1953-55; *Gourmet,* New York City, contributing editor, 1958—. Staff consultant on cookery for *The Random House Dictionary of the English Language,* 1966.

WRITINGS: (With husband, Kenneth Bates) *Baja California,* Sunset Books, 1971. Author of "Specialites de la Maison, California," a monthly column in *Gourmet.**

* * *

BATTISTA, Miriam 1912(?)-1980

OBITUARY NOTICE: Born c. 1912; died of emphysema, December 22, 1980, in New York. Actress and author. A child star on stage and in the silent films of the 1920's, Battista was noted for her ability to cry on directorial command. During the 1930's she appeared in several Broadway productions, including Florenz Ziegfeld's "Hot Cha" and "Our Wife," with Humphrey Bogart. Battista and her second husband, Russell Malone, wrote the book and the lyrics for "Sleepy Hollow," a musical produced on Broadway in 1948. Obituaries and other sources: *New York Times,* December 27, 1980.

* * *

BAUER, Peter Thomas 1915-

PERSONAL: Born November 6, 1915, in Budapest, Hungary; *Education:* Gonville and Caius College, Cambridge, M.A., 1942. *Office:* London School of Economics and Political Science, University of London, Houghton St., Aldwych, London WC2A 2AE, England.

CAREER: University of London, London, England, reader in agricultural economics, 1947-48; Cambridge University, Cambridge, England, lecturer in economics, 1948-56, Smuts Reader in Commonwealth Studies, 1956-60, fellow of Gonville and Caius College, 1946-60 and 1968—; University of London, London School of Economics and Political Science, professor of economics, 1960—. Woodward Lecturer at Yale University, 1965; Roush Distinguished Visiting Scholar at

Hoover Institution on War, Revolution, and Peace, 1967; Sir William Meyer Lecturer at Madras University, 1969-70. *Member:* British Academy (fellow).

WRITINGS: Report on a Visit to the Rubber Growing Smallholdings of Malaya, July-September, 1946, Colonial Research Publications, 1946; *The Rubber Industry: A Study in Competition and Monopoly,,* Longmans, Green, 1948; *West African Trade: A Study of Competition, Oligopoly, and Monopoly in a Changing Economy,* Augustus M. Kelley, 1954; *Economic Analysis and Policy in Underdeveloped Countries,* Duke University Press, 1957; (with Basil Selig Yamey) *The Economics of Under-Developed Countries,* Nisbet, 1957; *United States Aid and Indian Economic Development,* American Enterprise Association, 1959.

Indian Economic Policy and Development, Allen & Unwin, 1961; *The Study of Underdeveloped Economies,* G. Bell, 1964; (with Yamey) *Markets, Market Control, and Marketing Reform: Selected Papers,* Weidenfeld & Nicolson, 1968; *Two Views on Aid to Developing Countries,* Institute of Economic Affairs, 1966; *Dissent on Development: Studies and Debates in Development Economics,* Harvard University Press, 1972; *Nigerian Development Experience: Aspects and Implications,* University of Ife Press, 1974; (with Irving Kristol) *Two Essays on Income Distribution and the Open Society,* Green Hill, 1977; *Class on the Brain: The Cost of a British Obsession,* Centre for Policy Studies, 1978. Contributor to economic journals.

* * *

BAUGH, Albert C(roll) 1891-1981

OBITUARY NOTICE: Born in 1891 in Philadelphia, Pa.; died March 21, 1981, in Philadelphia, Pa. Educator, philologist, and author. Baugh was best known for his writing on the English language and medieval literature and culture. Educated at the University of Pennsylvania, Baugh began his career there in 1912 as an instructor in English. He advanced to chairman of the department in 1942, and from 1946 until his retirement in 1961 he served as the Felix E. Schelling Memorial Professor of English. Baugh served as president of several organizations, including the Modern Humanities Research Association of Cambridge, England, the International Federation for Modern Languages and Literature, and the Fellows of Medieval Academy at Harvard University. He edited and was a contributing author to *A Literary History of England,* and he wrote *A History of the English Language.* Obituaries and other sources: *Lincoln Library of Language Arts,* 3rd edition, Frontier Press (Columbus, Ohio), 1978; *Who Was Who Among English and European Authors, 1931-1949,* Gale, 1978; *New York Times,* March 27, 1981; *AB Bookman's Weekly,* May 4, 1981.

* * *

BAUM, Paull F(ranklin) 1886-1964

OBITUARY NOTICE—See index for *CA* sketch: Born May 13, 1886, in Dover, Del.; died July 15, 1964. Educator and author. Baum was a professor at Duke University, where he taught English. His numerous critical studies of literature include *Principles of English Versification, Tennyson Sixty Years After,* and *Chaucer: A Critical Appreciation.* Obituaries and other sources: *Who Was Who in America,* 4th edition, Marquis, 1968.

BAUMGARDT, David 1890-1963

OBITUARY NOTICE—See index for *CA* sketch: Born April 20, 1890, in Erfurt, Germany; died in 1963. Educator and author. Baumgardt was a professor of philosophy at the University of Berlin until 1935, when he immigrated to England. Four years later he settled permanently in the United States, where he lectured and worked at Pendle Hill College in Pennsylvania, the Library of Congress, and Columbia University. Among his works are *The Goethe Centuries, Bentham and the Ethics of Today,* and *Great Western Mystics.* Baumgardt's most recent book, *Mystik und Wissenschaft: Ihr Ort im abendlaendischen Denken,* was published by Luther Verlag in 1963. Obituaries and other sources: Joseph Frank, Helmut Minkowski, and Ernest J. Sternglass, editors, *Horizons of a Philosopher: Essays in Honor of David Baumgardt,* E. J. Brill, 1963; *New York Times,* July 22, 1963; *Who Was Who,* Volume VI: *1961-1970,* A. & C. Black, 1972.

*   *   *

BAXTER, Michael John 1944-
(Mike Baxter)

PERSONAL: Born July 5, 1944, in Terre Haute, Ind.; son of Victor and Wilda Ione (Davis) Baxter; married Joanne Kay Stohlman, July 5, 1966; children: Bradley Scott, Jeffrey John, Michael Victor Martin, Matthew John. *Education:* University of Nebraska, B.A., 1967. *Home:* 13631 Southwest 103rd Ave., Miami, Fla. 33176. *Office:* Miami Herald, 1 Herald Plaza, Miami, Fla. 33101.

CAREER/WRITINGS: Journalist under name Mike Baxter. *Lincoln Evening Journal,* Lincoln, Neb., reporter, 1962-67; *Miami Herald,* Miami, Fla., reporter, 1967-76, city editor, 1976-79, executive city editor, 1980—. *Military service:* U.S. Army Reserve, 1967. *Member:* Kappa Tau Alpha. *Awards, honors:* Association Award from *Florida,* 1970, for series on phosphate strip-mining; George Polk Memorial Award from Long Island University, 1973, APME Public Service Award and Public Service Award from Florida Society of Newspaper Editors, both 1974, and Distinguished Achievement Award from Florida Society of Newspaper Editors, 1975, all for investigative series on corruption in the Federal Housing Administration; University of Nebraska Distinguished Journalist Award, 1975.

CA INTERVIEW

Mike Baxter was interviewed by *CA* on September 24, 1979.

CA: I read Leonard Downie, Jr.'s, account of the Gurney investigation in The New Muckrakers. *Would you give a synopsis of that very complex situation?*

BAXTER: Sure. We had a source who approached one of the editors at the *Miami Herald* and said there was some curious activity at the Federal Housing Administration in Miami. Another reporter and I had each written stories previously about an unusually generous mortgage given to the assistant director of the FHA and to the director, who had raised the profile of the agency quite a bit, so the tip and the tipster got quite a bit of attention. I had done the most recent story, and I was available. So Steve Rogers, who was then metropolitan editor, had Jim Savage, our investigative reporter, and myself sit down and talk to the source. One of his major allegations was that builder John Priestes, who had no track record and whom nobody knew, was purportedly getting the lion's share of allocations under a particular subsidized sin-

gle-family housing program. . . . So we checked the allegation, we got the records, after quite a bit of legal work, from the Department of Housing and Urban Development, and they indicated that Priestes was getting very very few allocations. Then we began taking the list apart and piercing corporate shields, and we found that a number of corporations getting those allocations were also very new and they had some tenuous connection with Priestes. We continued to develop that and finally demonstrate that Priestes was getting the majority of the allocations through about a dozen different corporate identities.

For some time we continued to look at that program and a host of other FHA programs in southern Florida and, eventually, throughout the state; we saw a lot of political influence. We had a tip that a man named Larry Williams, who was identified as an aid to Senator Gurney, had tried to shake down one builder, Phil Emmer of Gainesville, for a contribution to Gurney, in return for which Emmer would get substantial FHA approval of various mortgages. Emmer would not go on the record with that, and we could not independently confirm it for more than a year. At the time, Jim and I had no idea that Larry Williams had any involvement with Priestes. We thought we were investigating two different stories.

CA: That must have been frustrating, trying to get Emmer to get on the record with that.

BAXTER: It was. We tried it repeatedly, and finally Savage agreed to make the last phone call to Emmer. He and I both agreed that it was a matter of futility, but we were going into the paper with some routine folo [follow-up story], and we felt we ought to make one more stab at it. At that time, Gurney was on television with the Watergate hearings [as a member of the Senate investigation committee], and that may have influenced Emmer's attitude; he said it did. When we called, he agreed to talk to us on the record. We were pretty excited about that.

CA: What arguments had you been using previously to try to get Emmer to talk?

BAXTER: We had talked to him quite a bit by telephone and had gone up to Gainesville and talked to him once or twice. We simply argued that if the allegations were true, they were very serious and required investigation; that the FBI, as he said, had already interviewed him and nothing had happened, so he couldn't rely on a federal investigation; that if there were such activity, he was in the best position to put a stop to it and had a moral obligation to do so.

CA: That's a very straight way to talk to him. Was there any way you could have offered him anonymity?

BAXTER: We already had the information on a non-attribution basis, but we just couldn't use it.

CA: Because it was so serious?

BAXTER: It was a very serious allegation, and we felt we needed to have corroboration or at least to put Emmer on the record. Meanwhile, we'd gotten Priestes in trouble. We'd demonstrated that he had committed some relatively minor infraction of federal law; the FBI immediately jumped on that the same day of publication, which was a Sunday, talked to our named sources, and got sworn statements. As a matter of fact, from that point on, Priestes was pretty much in the chute for conviction. Eventually, under that kind of pressure, Priestes agreed to talk. The FBI was building a case, and we were putting our case in print. One of the first major revelations that Priestes had to make was that he had indeed paid bribes to the Miami FHA director and that he had made substantial amounts of cash payments to Larry Williams, who said he represented Ed Gurney.

CA: And that linked the two stories?

BAXTER Yep. Actually, we had first gotten Emmer on the record and were already pursuing Larry Williams very openly; we talked to Williams and had done some of those stories before Priestes produced that link. We'd pretty much forgotten about Priestes and were concentrating now on Williams when the link became apparent.

CA: How did you link the two?

BAXTER: We had a great many little things we began with. We had a tip that Gurney and his administrative assistant Jim Groot, who was later convicted, and Larry Williams had been on vacation in the British Honduras and had bought some real estate together down there. I went to the British Honduras and checked the real estate records and could not find them in real estate. But I did confirm that they had indeed vactioned together, which showed their closeness. We learned that Larry Williams's baby-sitter had taken phone calls at his home from Ed Gurney. We had a number of minor things like that that demonstrated to us a fairly close relationship between the two men.

CA: Did you eventually prove that Williams had actually collected the money on Gurney's behalf?

BAXTER: There was no question according to the evidence presented that Williams was collecting money, much of it on Gurney's behalf, some of which was utilized by Ed Gurney. What a jury did not accept was that Ed Gurney was aware of the shakedown tactics being used by Williams.

CA: Were there any other turning points in that investigation?

BAXTER: There were a number: when we were able to pierce the corporate veil to establish the linkage to Priestes and when we were able to get various women who bought Priestes projects to confirm that he had, first off, sold the houses to them illegally by waiving a federally-required downpayment, and, subsequently, offered them money to refute the stories they had given us. That led to an FBI charge on which he was convicted. It was a relatively minor charge, considering what Priestes was involved in, but it gave federal investigators leverage.

CA: In regard to the Gurney investigation, or any other investigation, do you ever feel some kind of guilt at having removed people from office, ruined their careers, or whatever?

BAXTER: We did our job. And whether Gurney remained in office or left office was independent of our objective, which was to report as completely as possible that situation. I don't think we feel any pride that he left office; we certainly don't feel any guilt either.

CA: I didn't mean to imply you should.

BAXTER: I think there is a phenomenon in investigative reporting—I've noticed this in some reporters—in which reporters are exposing a certain individual for a corrupt act, and while they do so with energy and integrity, they realize the man they're writing about is a human being and that there are personal consequences for the man they're writing about.

And there's occasionally a post-partum depression after publishing an investigative story about an individual. It doesn't mean that you're not going to publish it or that you're going to change anything. You realize there are consequences on the personal level.

CA: Were you thinking things as a reporter that you now see were perhaps erroneous, since you're looking at reporting from a different perspective? Or is it that much of a different perspective?

BAXTER: My perspective has changed a lot, but I don't think the accuracy of my original perspectives has. As an investigative reporter and as a reporter I was pretty much concerned with my job and what I did. And now my view in that respect is pretty much on the community outside the newsroom.

CA: You mean the effect that your stories might have on the community outside the newsroom?

BAXTER: No, I was looking for stories, and I was looking at stories, and I paid a great deal less attention to the newspapers as a whole. Clearly, now, I'm involved with much more of the newspaper, as an editor.

CA: Some papers have a theory that a reporter doing investigative work shouldn't be on a beat so that he can take time to get into the story and not be beholden to sources who have given him stories previously. And others have the opposite theory, that the beat reporter knows what's going on in the area and can see what's happening more clearly. Do you subscribe to either one of those theories?

BAXTER: We believe that the beat reporter more than any other reporter, once he identifies an investigative story, might need the help of an investigative reporter simply because the investigative reporter can be permitted more time. The beat reporter has other responsibilities. Our philosophy and our practice have been that the beat reporter who identifies an investigative story should be able to participate in the investigation, do it himself, be freed up from his beat, or at least work with another reporter on doing it. We think that all of our reporters should be independent and represent the *Miami Herald,* not the beat, and should have no fear of conducting investigative stories on their beat.

CA: Is journalism too negative today, just going after public officials? Do you think there's anything to the criticism that journalism should be more positive, should try to build up people rather than come down on our hardworking public officials?

BAXTER: I think that we do an awful lot of that so-called "positive" journalism. If you look carefully at a newspaper, I think you'll frequently find that it does not actually fit harmoniously with that conception. I think that one of the major definers of news is an aberration from the norm. It could be argued that public servants are of such a low character that that is the norm and that when we find somebody to be corrupt, it is really not an aberration. I think the fact that we do find it to be an aberration demonstrates our idealism, our belief that there is a norm of moral, qualified public servants, and that we are dealing with the aberrations. I think we have a constitutional responsibility and a moral responsibility.

BIOGRAPHICAL/CRITICAL SOURCES: James H. Dygert, *The Investigative Journalist: Folk Heroes of a New Era,*

Prentice-Hall, 1976; Leonard Downie, Jr., *The New Muck-rakers,* New Republic Books, 1976.

—Interview by Peter Benjaminson

*   *   *

BAXTER, Mike
See BAXTER, Michael John

*   *   *

BAYER, Oliver Weld
See PERRY, Eleanor

*   *   *

BEALS, Frank Lee   1881-1972

OBITUARY NOTICE—See index for *CA* sketch: Born September 2, 1881, in Morganton, Tenn.; died August 31, 1972. Soldier, educator, school administrator, and author. A veteran of the Spanish American War and World War I, Beals became a professor of military science and tactics at Chicago's Board of Education. He later became superintendant of schools and compulsory education in Chicago. He wrote several books about well-known heroes of the Old West, such as *Kit Carson, Davy Crockett, Chief Black Hawk,* and *Buffalo Bill,* as well as books based on famous adventure tales. Among these are *The Story of Robinson Crusoe, The Story of Lemuel Gulliver in Lilliput Land,* and *The Story of Treasure Island.* (Date of death provided by daughter, Bettina Byrd Iwersen.)

*   *   *

BEARDSWORTH, Millicent Monica   1915-

PERSONAL: Born March 10, 1915, in Liverpool, England; daughter of William Henry and Annie Newcombe (Hall) Beardsworth. *Education:* Penrhos College, L.G.S.M., 1931, L.R.A.M., 1933. *Religion:* Church of England. *Home:* 14 St. George's Rd., Rhos-on-Sea, Clwyd LL28 4HF, North Wales.

CAREER: Penrhos College, Clwyd, Wales, assistant teacher of speech and drama, 1934-37, head of department, 1947-68, deputy headmistress, 1968-76; writer, 1976—. *Member:* Royal Stuart Society (vice-president), Society of Teachers of Speech and Drama, National Book League.

WRITINGS—Historical novels; published by R. Hale: *King's Servant,* 1966; *King's Friend,* 1968; *King's Endeavour,* 1969; *King's Adversary,* 1972; *King's Contest,* 1974; *King's Victory,* 1978.

WORK IN PROGRESS: Research on the life of James II, "but I have no particular book in view at present."

SIDELIGHTS: Millicent Beardsworth commented: "My interest in history, particularly Stuart history, has been virtually lifelong, and I have been especially influenced by the writings of King Charles I."

*   *   *

BEATTY, Hetty Burlingame   1907-1971

OBITUARY NOTICE—See index for *CA* sketch: Born October 8, 1907, in New Canaan, Conn.; died August 20, 1971. Sculptor, illustrator, and author. Beatty was a trained sculptor whose works were exhibited nationally. She later became so interested in writing that she devoted most of her time to it. She also illustrated her own works, which include *Topsy, Little Owl Indian,* and *Voyage of the Sea Wind,* all children's books. Her last book, published by Houghton in 1968, was *Rebel, the Reluctant Racehorse.* Obituaries and other sources:

New York Times, August 25, 1971; *Something About the Author,* Volume 5, Gale, 1973.

*   *   *

BEATY, Shirley MacLean   1934-
(Shirley MacLaine)

PERSONAL: Professionally known as Shirley MacLaine; born April 24, 1934, in Richmond, Va.; daughter of Ira O. (a realtor) and Kathlyn (MacLean) Beaty; married Steve Parker (in business), September 17, 1954; children: Stephanie Sachiko. *Education:* Attended high school in Washington, D.C. *Politics:* Democrat.

CAREER: Chorus girl and dancer, 1950-53; stage actress, with performances in Broadway plays and revues including "Me and Juliet," 1953, "Pajama Game," 1954, and "A Gypsy in My Soul," 1976; screen actress, with performances in films including "The Trouble With Harry," 1954, "Around the World in 80 Days," 1956, "Some Came Running," 1958, "Ask Any Girl," 1959, "Can-Can," 1959, "The Apartment," 1959, "Irma la douce," 1963, "Two Mules for Sister Sara," 1969, "Sweet Charity," 1969, "Desperate Characters," 1971, "The Turning Point," 1977, "Being There," 1979, "Loving Couples," 1980, and "Change of Seasons," 1980; actress in television programs, including "Shirley's World" (series), 1971, (and producer) "Amelia," 1975, "If They Could See Me Now," 1974, and "Gypsy in My Soul" 1976. Delegate to the Democratic National Convention, 1968, 1972; member of platform committee, 1972; co-chairperson of McGovern-Shriver National Advisory Committee, 1972.

AWARDS, HONORS: International Stardom Award from Hollywood Foreign Press Association, 1954; Academy Award nomination for best actress from Academy of Motion Pictures Arts and Sciences, 1958, for "Some Came Running," 1960, for "The Apartment," 1963, for "Irma la douce," and 1977, for "The Turning Point"; Foreign Press award for best actress, 1958, 1961, 1963; Silver Bear Award for best actress from International Berlin Film Festival, 1959, for "Ask Any Girl"; best actress award from Venice Film Festival and British Film Academy Award for best actress, both 1960, both for "The Apartment"; Golden Globe Award from Foreign Press Association, 1964, for "Irma la douce"; best actress award from Italian Film Festival, 1964; Star of the Year Award from Theater Owners of America, 1967; best actress award from Berlin Film Festival, 1971, for "Desperate Characters"; two Emmy Awards from Academy of Television Arts and Sciences, including one in 1974 for "If They Could See Me Now"; female musical star of the year award from Las Vegas Entertainment Awards, 1976.

WRITINGS: Don't Fall Off the Mountain (autobiography), Norton, 1970; (editor) *McGovern: The Man and His Beliefs,* Norton, 1972; (editor and author of introduction) *The New Celebrity Cookbook,* Price, Stern, 1973; *You Can Get There from Here* (memoirs), Norton, 1975; (author of narration and producer) "The Other Half of the Sky: A China Memoir" (film documentary), broadcast by Public Broadcasting Service, 1975.

WORK IN PROGRESS: A novel.

SIDELIGHTS: Shirley MacLaine began taking dancing lessons before she was three years old; by age sixteen she was in New York dancing in the chorus of a City Center revival of "Oklahoma!" Four years later, she was dancing in the chorus of "Pajama Game" and acting as understudy to Carol Haney, the show's leading dancer. Several days after the show's opening, Haney injured her ankle and MacLaine replaced her in the lead. Her performance met with enthusiastic reviews; one member of her appreciative audience was Hollywood producer Hal B. Wallis, who shortly thereafter signed her to a long-term film contract.

Alfred Hitchcock directed MacLaine in her film debut as the screwball lead in "The Trouble With Harry." She has since appeared in over twenty-five motion pictures, where her elfin looks and her offbeat humor frequently gained her the role of the kook. In several films she played the "hooker with the heart of gold"; her portrayal of the Parisian madam in "Irma la douce" earned her the Golden Globe Award and her third of four Academy Award nominations.

MacLaine's on-screen personality belies her more serious side. She is a political activist and an international traveler whose sojourns have made her a humanitarian activist as well. In addition to having campaigned for several democratic presidential candidates, she has spoken out on such issues as civil rights, women's rights, and environmental protection. Chagrined by continued American involvement in the Vietnam war, she became a vocal supporter of George McGovern during his 1972 presidential campaign. That same year, as the first woman speaker in the history of the National Democratic Club, she spoke out on the dangers of overpopulation. MacLaine's extensive travels have taken her to such remote parts of the world as East Africa, where she lived among the Masai tribe, and the Himalayan kingdom of Bhutan, where she was detained by border guards during a political crisis. While traveling in India, she became sympathetic to the plight of the "gutter babies" and helped to establish an orphanage for them in Calcutta.

MacLaine details accounts of her childhood, her political activities, and her travels in her best-selling autobiography *Don't Fall Off the Mountain*. To the surprise of many reviewers, she wrote the book herself; they found it a far cry from the typically glossy, ghost-written Hollywood autobiography. "Her memoir has the feel of an individual," said *Newsweek*'s Alex Keneas. "It possesses a vigor that seems consistent with her convictions. It is also compassionate, witty and partly for what it avoids, amiable." John Leonard, a critic for *New York Times*, said that "what really distinguishes 'Don't Fall Off the Mountain' is Miss MacLaine's capacity and willingness to feel her way into 'other' realities—those of a Masai warrior, for instance, or a middle-aged Japanese male."

In 1973 MacLaine was invited to lead a delegation of twelve American women, including filmmaker Claudia Weill, on a six-week tour of the People's Republic of China. With Weill acting as her co-director, MacLaine produced and wrote the narration for the film "The Other Half of the Sky: A China Memoir" to document the trip. *Saturday Review*'s Hollis Alpert called the film "revelatory" because it "concentrates on the roles of women in China, and the reactions of the American delegation." He felt that what made the film valuable was "Shirley's continual probing into roles and relationships, and her constant desire to understand."

MacLaine discusses her China trip as well as her short-lived television series and her involvement with George McGovern's presidential campaign in her second autobiographical work, *You Can Get There From Here*. Critics found her discussion of China most interesting. The book, wrote Alpert, provides "an illuminating view of the new China, as seen through relatively unbiased American eyes." He called MacLaine a "skilled writer" who is "able to convey her intimate feelings and now and then an acerbic wit." Jean Zorn, a writer for *New York Times Book Review*, noted that

"hardly an author until MacLaine has reported China's effect on the American traveler." R. Z. Sheppard, in a review for *Time*, wrote, "she skips winningly over the quicksands of human nature and power politics, and still lands on her feet."

When she returned from China, MacLaine decided to put together an act for the stage. She attributed her renewed interest in singing and dancing to her experiences in China, where she realized the value of her ability to entertain. In 1976, after a twenty-two year hiatus, she returned to the theatrical stage and to rave reviews for her show "A Gypsy in My Soul." Her spirited performance in the show caused a writer for *Time* to remark, "Shirley MacLaine is still racing through life like a one-woman track team."

BIOGRAPHICAL/CRITICAL SOURCES: Time, June 22, 1959, March 3, 1975, March 7, 1977; *Look*, September 15, 1959; *Life*, February 17, 1961; *Redbook*, May, 1966; Shirley MacLaine, *Don't Fall Off the Mountain*, Norton, 1970; *New York Times*, October 29, 1970, August 8, 1971, April 18, 1976; *Newsweek*, January 11, 1971; *Saturday Review*, February 27, 1971, April 5, 1975; *Show*, May, 1971; MacLaine, *You Can Get There From Here*, Norton, 1975; *Ladies' Home Journal*, March, 1975, July, 1979; *New York Times Book Review*, March 16, 1975; *Esquire*, June, 1975, September, 1975.*

—*Sketch by Mary Sullivan*

*   *   *

BEAUMONT, Charles   1929-1967

OBITUARY NOTICE—See index for *CA* sketch: Born January 2, 1929, in Chicago, Ill.; died February 21, 1967, in Los Angeles, Calif. Author. Beaumont was a free-lance writer whose work included short stories, television and film plays, and several books. He was the author of *Run From the Hunter*, *The Intruder*, *The Fiend in You*, and *The Magic Man, and Other Science Fantasy Stories*. His last book was *Remember? Remember?* for Macmillan. Two books, *A Touch of the Creature* and *Where No Man Walks*, were never completed. Obituaries and other sources: *Science Fiction and Fantasy Literature*, Volume 2: *Contemporary Science Fiction Authors II*, Gale, 1979.

*   *   *

BEAVERBROOK, William Maxwell Aitken   1879-1964
(William Maxwell Aitken)

PERSONAL: Surname legally changed to Beaverbrook, 1917; born May 25, 1879, in Maple, Ontario, Canada; died June 9, 1964; son of William (a minister) and Jean (Noble) Aitken; married Gladys Drury, 1906 (died, 1927); married Marcia Christoforides, 1963; children: (first marriage) John William Max Aitken, Peter Aitken (died, 1947), Janet Aitken (Mrs. Drago Montagu). *Education:* Educated in Newcastle, New Brunswick, Canada. *Politics:* Conservative. *Residence:* London, England.

CAREER: Worked as bank clerk and insurance salesman; secretary in Halifax, Nova Scotia, Canada; managing director of Royal Securities Corp. in Canada; stockbroker and promoter in Montreal, Canada; British House of Commons, London, England, member of parliament for Ashton-under-Lyne, 1910-16; *London Daily Express* and *London Sunday Express*, London, publisher, 1917-64, editor, 1917-c. 1940; *Evening Standard*, publisher and editor, beginning in 1922. Member of cabinet as chancellor of Duchy of Lancaster and minister of information, 1918-19; minister of aircraft production, 1940-41; minister of state, 1941; minister of supply,

1941-42; lord privy seal, 1943-45. Chancellor of University of New Brunswick, 1947-53. *Military service:* Served as Canadian Government observer of the British Expeditionary Force, 1914, representative at front, 1916, and officer in charge of Canadian war records, 1917. *Awards, honors:* Knight of the Order of the British Empire, 1911; made a baronet, 1916; made first baron of Beaverbrook, 1917; LL.D. from University of New Brunswick, 1921, and named honorary chancellor, 1954; LL.D. from Toronto University, 1947; D.Litt. from Mount Allison University, 1948; D.C.L. from Bishops University, 1950; LL.D. from St. Thomas University, 1953.

WRITINGS—All nonfiction: (Under name William Maxwell Aitken) *Canada in Flanders: The Official Story of the Canadian Expeditionary Force,* two volumes, Hodder & Stoughton, 1916-17; *Success,* Small, Maynard, 1922, revised edition published as *Don't Trust to Luck,* London Express Newspapers, 1954, published as *The Three Keys to Success,* introduction by Joseph P. Kennedy, Duell, Sloan & Pearce, 1956; *Politicians and the Press,* Hutchinson, 1925; *Politicians and the War, 1914-1916,* Volume I, Doubleday, 1928, Volume II, T. Butterworth, 1932, both volumes published together in one volume, Shoe String, 1968; *My Case for Empire Free Trade* (speeches), Empire Crusade, 1930; *The Resources of the British Empire,* Lane, 1934; *Men and Power, 1917-1918,* Hutchinson, 1956, Duell, Sloan & Pearce, 1957; *Friends: Sixty Years of Intimate Personal Relations With Richard Bedford Bennett* (memoir), Heinemann, 1959; *Courage: The Story of Sir James Dunn Fredericton,* Brunswick, 1961; *The Divine Propagandist,* Duell, Sloan & Pearce, 1962; *The Decline and Fall of Lloyd George,* Duell, Sloan & Pearce, 1963, new edition published as *The Decline and Fall of Lloyd George; And Great Was the Fall Thereof,* Collins, 1966; *My Early Life,* Brunswick, 1965; *The Abdication of King Edward VIII,* edited by A.J.P. Taylor, Atheneum, 1966.

SIDELIGHTS: Hailed as the "Hearst of Britain," Beaverbrook helped change the complexion of British journalism. Ever interested in politics, he originally acquired the *London Daily Express, London Sunday Express,* and *Evening Standard* newspapers to further his political aims. When he bought the *Daily Express* in 1917, the paper was selling poorly and constantly losing ground to its rival, the *London Daily Mail.* In the first two years after the purchase, Beaverbrook's *Daily Express* lost $1.3 million. By the next year the paper broke even, and it soon became immensely profitable and influential.

Some of Beaverbrook's colleagues on Fleet Street felt the entrepreneur was not a journalist at all, but merely a rich politician. Sir William Haley, editor of the *London Times,* was quoted as saying: "He came into journalism with a fortune made elsewhere. He entered British politics and bought the *Daily Express* for political purposes. He was always a politician." Having become a millionaire in Canada, Beaverbrook arrived in Britain at the age of thirty-one intent on breaking into politics. He once remarked that if it was the prime occupation of an American to earn money, then the chief function of a European was to participate in politics. Thus he moved to England to pursue his interest.

Less than a year after his arrival, Beaverbrook was elected to the House of Commons. He established a strong association with Bonar Law, the leader of the Conservative party, and became his private secretary. After leaving Parliament in 1916, Beaverbrook bought the *Daily Express* to finance Law's bid for the office of prime minister. The two friends' goal was achieved in 1922 when Law defeated opponent Lloyd George. Law developed cancer, however, and was forced to resign as prime minister after less than one year.

Following this disappointment, Beaverbrook devoted his attention to increasing his newspapers' circulation. He fashioned an apartment for himself on an upper floor of his business place and involved himself in all facets of publication. Beaverbrook soon became known for his flamboyance. Linton Andrews and H. A. Taylor described him as "a man of histrionic temperament" with "many changes of mood." Andrews and Taylor added that Beaverbrook could shift "breathlessly from sneers to flattery; bubbling with joy, and then shaking with rage; using three telephones at once; sending down to the staff below his office flat an unending stream of ideas, reprimands, praise, and instructions." But Beaverbrook's methods brought rewards. The *Daily Express* became increasingly popular, sporting the American invention of news on the front page and making news more accessible to the everyday worker. He gave England an imported dose of William Randolph Hearst's brand of journalism.

Meanwhile, Beaverbrook furthered his political causes in newsprint. His main objective was to obtain "Empire Free Trade," which essentially was a policy of isolationism. The politician wanted the British Empire to trade with no other countries, only with its own colonies and holdings. He also vehemently opposed the League of Nations. In his papers he attacked those public figures who were not favorable to his ideas and praised those who were. His opinionated editorials prompted criticism from many quarters, including his own newspaper staffs.

In the 1930's Beaverbrook became embroiled in a fierce newspaper war. To increase their circulation, papers commonly offered free insurance to new subscribers. When the *Daily Herald* began giving away silk stockings, cameras, ink pens, and books, its rivals began to make available similar gifts to patrons. Competition heightened as customers received such commodities as shoes, boots, coats, underwear, and tea sets for subscribing to a newspaper for ten weeks. Such rivalry forced less profitable papers to scrimp on news coverage in order to supply free bonuses to their readers. Beaverbrook's wealth enabled him to offset the expenses, however, and he spent more money to provide even better news coverage. The *Daily Express* began to regularly treat its readers with important newsbreaks. By 1940 the *London Daily Express* was the largest-selling newspaper in the world.

With the outbreak of World War II, Beaverbrook returned to government service. Although he held several other positions, he distinguished himself particularly as the minister of aircraft production. He pursued the job of acquiring airplanes for the Battle of Britain with the same energy he used to acquire subscribers to his newspapers. After the war, though, Beaverbrook gradually lost his effectiveness in politics but continued until his death to oversee his newspapers and trumpet his political views on their editorial pages.

During his career Beaverbrook wrote several books about history and politics. Because of his close associations with many important governmental figures, the author was able to supply firsthand information and new insights on how the British government actually worked. *Politicians and the War, 1914-1916* was widely and favorably reviewed. Although many critics found the volume to be a blatant eulogy for his friend Bonar Law, they were also impressed. B. Munro of the *Living Age* declared: "The book is full of dramatic passages, for Lord Beaverbrook writes with insight as well as knowledge and has a keen eye for the picturesque. He is easy to read and worth reading." A *New Statesman* writer commented that the book is "full of good stories, new lights and acute observations," while a *Springfield Republican* reviewer added that it "is informative and will give to those who have never studied the British cabinet system a clear picture of what goes on behind the scenes."

A later effort, *Men and Power, 1917-1918,* made use of many private historical documents in Beaverbrook's possession. In compiling this history, he used the private papers and correspondence of Lloyd George, Lady Lloyd George, and Bonar Law. "A real contribution to history, organized in an unusual and compelling way," applauded the *New York Herald Tribune Book Review*'s H. W. Baehr. John Raymond of *New Statesman and Nation* called it "a remarkable achievement," but Malcolm Muggeridge was not so complimentary in the *Saturday Review*. He reflected: "As a source book for all the minor and mostly squalid intrigues out of which Lloyd George emerged triumphant during the last phase of the 1914-1918 war and its immediate aftermath, 'Men and Power' is invaluable. Yet somehow it is unsatisfying. Is this really government, one asks oneself—this grimy, tawdry scramble for office, for peerages, for privy councilorships? Are these men—Lloyd George himself, Curzon, Churchill, F. E. Smith, Carson, Austen Chamberlain, and many lesser hangers-on—as presented by Lord Beaverbrook, the heroes of their time?"

The Decline and Fall of Lloyd George generally fared well with critics. "He writes as well as any of the journalists whom he employs," commended Lindsay Rogers in the *New York Times Book Review*. The book "recaptures, authentically and vividly," wrote *Nation*'s David Thomson, "the atmosphere of the transient postwar phase . . . [and] the colorful figures who were to go on being of importance in British life and world politics a generation later."

Beaverbrook's last book, published after his death, was *The Abdication of King Edward VIII.* As a personal friend of King Edward, who dubbed Beaverbrook "Tornado" in acknowledgement of his zest and energy, the author revealed much new information about the abdication. According to Harold Hobson of the *Christian Science Monitor,* Beaverbrook viewed the incident "from a strictly legalistic and constitutional position. He thought that the King should place himself firmly and immovably on the letter of the law. The law says that a King of England can marry absolutely anyone he pleases provided that she is not Roman Catholic." An *Economist* reviewer refuted Beaverbrook's contention as being "sheer political naivety," which was strongly influenced by "a genuine compassion and sentimental high hope for the young and anti-Establishment Edward." A *Times Literary Supplement* reviewer, meanwhile, called *The Abdication of King Edward VIII* "a valuable contribution to the writing of history."

BIOGRAPHICAL/CRITICAL SOURCES: Times Literary Supplement, March 8, 1917, November 10, 1921, May 17, 1928, November 2, 1956, May 18, 1962, March 8, 1963, May 5, 1966; *Spectator,* December 10, 1921, May 11, 1962; *New York Times,* July 16, 1922, June 17, 1928, October 28, 1956, May 5, 1957; *Nation and Athenaeum,* May 26, 1928; *New Statesman,* June 2, 1928, May 11, 1962, March 8, 1963, April 22, 1966; *Collier's,* July 2, 1928; *Living Age,* October, 1928, September, 1930, March, 1932; *Saturday Review of Literature,* October 13, 1928, May 25, 1957; *Springfield Republican,* October 22, 1928; *New York Herald Tribune Books,* November 25, 1928; *Fortnightly Review,* December, 1929; *New Statesman and Nation,* May 16, 1931, November 3, 1956; *Time,* July 27, 1936, November 28, 1938, May 27, 1940, September 16, 1940, May 31, 1963, July 22, 1966; *American Mercury,* August, 1936; *Life,* August 5, 1940; *Readers' Digest,* November, 1940.

New York Herald Tribune Book Review, May 5, 1957; *Chicago Sunday Tribune,* May 5, 1957; *Christian Science Monitor,* May 9, 1957, May 23, 1963, July 19, 1966; *Nation,* June 29, 1957, May 25, 1963; *Guardian,* May 11, 1962; *New York Times Book Review,* May 19, 1963, September 11, 1966; *Newsweek,* May 20, 1963, August 1, 1966; *National Review,* June 4, 1963; *Saturday Review,* June 8, 1963; *Canadian Forum,* July, 1963; *Economist,* April 30, 1966; *Book Week,* July 31, 1966; *New York Review of Books,* September 8, 1966; C. M. Vines, *Little Nut-Brown Man: My Three Years With Lord Beaverbrook,* Frewin, 1968; David Farrer, *G for God Almighty: A Personal Memoir of Lord Beaverbrook,* Stein, 1969; Linton Andrews and H. A. Taylor, *Lords and Laborers of the Press: Men Who Fashioned the Modern British Newspaper,* Southern Illinois University Press, 1970; A.J.P. Taylor, *Beaverbrook,* Simon & Schuster, 1972; *Historian,* November, 1974; *Harper's,* September, 1975.*

—*Sketch by Anne M. Guerrini*

*   *   *

BEILENSON, Edna   1909-1981
(Elisabeth Deane)

OBITUARY NOTICE—See index for *CA* sketch: Born June 16, 1909, in New York, N.Y.; died after a long illness, February 28, 1981, in New York, N.Y. Publisher, editor, art director, and author. As president of Peter Pauper Press, Inc., Beilenson published decorative books noted for their quality. In addition to numerous single works, she edited the series of books "Simple Cookery" and the inspirational "Gifts of Gold." Beilenson also wrote many books, including *Holiday Cookbook, Abalone to Zabaglione: Unusual and Exotic Recipes,* and *The Christmas Stocking Book.* The publisher founded the Goudy Society for members of the graphic arts profession and was the first president of the American Institute of Graphic Arts. Obituaries and other sources: *New York Times,* March 4, 1981; *Publishers Weekly,* March 13, 1981.

*   *   *

BELL, John C.   1902 (?)-1981

OBITUARY NOTICE: Born c. 1902; died of cardiac arrest, march 12, 1981, in Washington, D.C. Architect, sportsman, and journalist. A government architect for more than thirty years, Bell began his career with the Federal Works Agency in 1930. In 1943 he joined the Rubber Development Corporation and spent the next five years exploring and charting jungles along the Amazon River in order to obtain rubber for the war effort. From 1948 until his retirement in 1961 Bell was a supervisory architectural engineer with the State Department. His assignments on U.S.-assisted construction programs took him to Ceylon, Pakistan, Afghanistan, and the Far East. Bell, also a noted hunter and angler, was a charter member of the Angler's Club of Washington, and in 1940 he won a prize for brook trout fishing in Canada. Throughout the 1940's Bell was wildlife editor and outdoors columnist with the *Washington Post.* He also contributed articles to magazines and books. Obituaries and other sources: *Washington Post,* March 20, 1981.

BENNETT, Alan 1934-

PERSONAL: Born May 9, 1934, in Leeds, England; son of Walter (a butcher) and Lilian Mary (Peel) Bennett. *Education:* Exeter College, Oxford, B.A. (with honors), 1957. *Religion:* Church of England. *Agent:* Michael Linnit Ltd., Globe Theatre, Shaftesbury Ave., London W.1, England.

CAREER: Playwright and actor on stage and television. President of North Craven Heritage Trust. *Military service:* Intelligence Corps, 1952-54. *Awards, honors:* Awards from *London Evening Standard,* 1961, for "Beyond the Fringe," 1968, for "Forty Years On," and 1971, for "Getting On"; Antoinette Perry (Tony) Award, 1963, for "Beyond the Fringe"; award from Guild of Television Producers, 1967, for "On the Margin."

WRITINGS—Plays: (With Peter Cook, Jonathan Miller, and Dudley Moore) *Beyond the Fringe* (comedy revue; first produced in Edinburgh, Scotland, at Royal Lyceum Theatre, August 25, 1960; produced on the West End at Fortune Theatre, May 8, 1961; produced in New York, N.Y., at John Golden Theatre, October, 1962), Souvenir Press, 1962, Random House, 1963; *Forty Years On* (two-act; first produced in Manchester, England, at Palace Theatre, September 30, 1968; produced on the West End at Apollo Theatre, October 31, 1968), Faber, 1969; (with Carol Brahms and Ned Sherrin) "Sing a Rude Song" (two-act), first produced in London at Greenwich Theatre, 1969; *Getting On* (two-act; first produced in Brighton, England, at Theatre Royal, September 28, 1971; produced on the West End at Queen's Theatre, October 14, 1971), Faber, 1972; *Habeas Corpus* (two-act; first produced in Oxford, England, at Playhouse Theatre, May 1, 1973; produced on the West End at Lyric Theatre, May 10, 1973; produced on Broadway at Martin Beck Theatre, November, 1975), Faber, 1973; *The Old Country* (first produced in Oxford at Playhouse Theatre, August 21, 1977; produced on the West End at Queen's Theatre, September 7, 1977), Faber, 1978; *Enjoy* (first produced at Richmond Theatre, September 29, 1980; produced on the West End at Vaudeville Theatre, October 15, 1980), Faber, 1980; *Office Suite* (adaptation of television plays "A Visit From Miss Prothero" and "Doris and Doreen"), Faber, 1981.

Television plays: "A Day Out," broadcast by British Broadcasting Corp. (BBC-TV), December 26, 1972; "Sunset Across the Bay," broadcast by BBC-TV, March, 1975; "A Little Outing," broadcast by BBC-TV, 1978; "A Visit From Miss Prothero," broadcast by BBC-TV, 1978. Also author of "Me, I'm Afraid of Virginia Woolf," "The Old Crowd," "Doris and Doreen," "Afternoon Off," "One Fine Day," and "All Day on the Sands." Author of television series, "On the Margin," broadcast by BBC-TV, 1966.

*   *   *

BENNETT, Jack Arthur Walter 1911-1981

OBITUARY NOTICE—See index for *CA* sketch: Born February 28, 1911, in Auckland, New Zealand; died January 29, 1981, in Los Angeles, Calif. Educator, editor, and author. An authority on medieval literature, Bennett taught at Oxford and Cambridge universities. He edited several books, including *The Knight's Tale, Essays on Malory,* and *Selections From John Gower,* and the "Clarendon Medieval and Tudor Series." He also wrote scholarly works, among which number *The Parlement of Foules: An Interpretation, The Humane Medievalist,* and *Chaucer's Book of Fame: An Exposition*

of "The House of Fame." Obituaries and other sources: *London Times,* February 5, 1981.

*   *   *

BENNETT, Josephine Waters 1899-1975

OBITUARY NOTICE—See index for *CA* sketch: Born January 15, 1899, in Lakeside, Ohio; died December 31, 1975, in Washington, D.C. Educator and author. Bennett joined the English faculty of Hunter College in 1942 and was a professor there from 1955 until 1970. She was the author of *The Evolution of "The Faerie Queene," The Rediscovery of Sir John Mandeville,* and *"Measure for Measure" as Royal Entertainment.* Obituaries and other sources: *AB Bookman's Weekly,* April 19, 1976.

*   *   *

BENSON, Rachel
See JOWITT, Deborah

*   *   *

BERGER, Morroe 1917-1981

OBITUARY NOTICE—See index for *CA* sketch: Born June 25, 1917, in New York, N.Y.; died of a heart attack, April 7, 1981, in Princeton, N.J. Educator, sociologist, editor, translator, and author. Berger was a professor of sociology at Princeton University for over twenty-five years. An expert on the Near East, he wrote numerous books on the subject, including *Bureaucracy and Society in Modern Egypt, The Arab World Today,* and *The New Metropolis in the Arab World.* Berger also edited and translated the volume *Madame de Stael on Politics, Literature, and National Character.* Obituaries and other sources: *New York Times,* April 8, 1981; *AB Bookman's Weekly,* May 4, 1981.

*   *   *

BERGHAHN, Volker R(olf) 1938-

PERSONAL: Born February 15, 1938, in Berlin, Germany; son of Alfred (an engineer) and Gisela (Henke) Berghahn; married Marion Koop (a publisher), December 29, 1969; children: Sascha, Vivian. *Education:* University of North Carolina, M.A., 1961; University of London, Ph.D., 1964; University of Mannheim, Habil., 1971. *Home:* 24 Binswood Ave., Leamington Spa CV32 5SQ, England. *Office:* Department of History, University of Warwick, Coventry CV4 7AL, England.

CAREER: University of East Anglia, Norwich, England, lecturer, 1969-71, reader in European history, 1971-75; University of Warwick, Conventry, England, professor of history, 1975—. *Awards, honors:* Fellow of Deutsche Friedengesellschaft, 1966-69; Leverhulme fellow, 1973.

WRITINGS: Germany and the Approach of War in 1914, Macmillan, 1973; *A History of Modern Germany,* Cambridge University Press, 1981.

In German: *Der Stahlhelm, B.D.F., 1918-1935,* Droste, 1966; *Der Tirpitz-Plan,* Droste, 1971; *Ruestung and Machtpolitik* (title means "Armaments Power Politics"), Droste, 1973.

Contributor to German and British history journals.

WORK IN PROGRESS: Entrepreneurial Political Attitudes in Germany and Britain, 1945-75, publication expected in 1982 or 1983.

SIDELIGHTS: Berghahn commented to *CA:* "My main interests are the influence of military and industrial elites on socioeconomic developments and policy-making in modern

Germany, comparative study of political and industrial cultures in Western Europe, and the relationship between economic costs of armaments and of social reform. This has been stated—in historical perspective—in my books and articles and—in a 1970's context—in my Warwick inaugural lecture, 'Armaments, Taxes and Status Quo.'

"Life and education in three different countries—Germany, the United States, and Britain—have, not surprisingly perhaps, acted as a major stimulus to making comparisons between divergent societies. Behind this there is a fascination but also a certain impatience with the weight of tradition and cultural conditioning in a period of rapid economic and technological change."

He added: "I am also interested in globalization of 'social question' in the context of the north-south conflict."

AVOCATIONAL INTERESTS: Astronomy, tennis.

*   *   *

BERGIN, Kenneth Glenny   1911-1981

OBITUARY NOTICE: Born June 10, 1911, in Clifton, Bristol, England; died March 26, 1981. Physician and author. Best known for his work in aviation medicine, Bergin began his specialization when he was commissioned into the medical branch of the Royal Air Force at the outbreak of World War II. After the war he joined the British Overseas Airways Corporation (BOAC) as assistant to the director of medical services, and from 1959 to 1963 he was director of personnel and medical services. He has been credited with helping to produce one of the finest airline medical services yet developed, and his textbook *Aviation Medicine* has become a standard in the field. Bergin was president of the Air League and the Airline Medical Directors' Association as well as Master of the Guild of Air Pilots and Air Navigators. At the time of his death he was director of the Cavendish Medical Centre and president of the International Academy of Aviation and Space Medicine. In addition to *Aviation Medicine*, Bergin's writings include *Medicine in Transport: Civil Air Transport Medical Services, Weight and Health*, and *The Transport of Invalids by Air*. Obituaries and other sources: *The Author's and Writer's Who's Who*, 6th edition, Burke's Peerage, 1971; *Who's Who*, 126th edition, St. Martin's, 1974; *The Writers Directory, 1976-78*, St. Martin's, 1976; *London Times*, April 2, 1981.

*   *   *

BERKEBILE, Fred D(onovan)   1900-1978
(William Donovan, William Ernest, Don Stauffer)

OBITUARY NOTICE—See index for *CA* sketch: Born October 7, 1900, in Kanter, Pa.; died in 1978. Educator, school administrator, and author. Berkebile began his career in education as a school teacher and principal in Pennsylvania. He later worked for federal and state educational programs in recreation and public instruction before joining the faculty of Pennsylvania State University. He was a professor of education at the university and a lecturer in children's literature. Berkebile wrote numerous short stories, and his books include *The Magic City* and *Moroccan Adventure*. A book that he had called *Idols in Buckskin* as a work in progress was published as *Captured* by David Cook in 1975. (Date of death provided by wife, Mary Z. Berkebile.)

*   *   *

BERNARD, Jay
See SAWKINS, Raymond H(arold)

BERNHARDT, Frances Simonsen   1932-

PERSONAL: Born May 4, 1932, in Kennecott, Alaska; daughter of Sigurd J. (a railway agent) and Amanda (a teacher; maiden name, Dettbarn) Simonsen; married Preston A. Bernhardt (a General Accounting Office auditor), June 24, 1968. *Education:* Attended St. Cloud State College (now University), 1949-50; University of Minnesota, B.S., 1955, M.A., 1958; further graduate study at Catholic University of America, 1979—. *Religion:* Methodist. *Home:* 5647 Mount Burnside Way, Burke, Va. 22015. *Office:* Library, Northern Virginia Community College, Annandale, Va. 22003.

CAREER: University of Minnesota, Minneapolis, acquisitions bibliographer at library, 1958-61, cataloger at library, 1961-64; University of Minnesota, St. Paul, acquisitions librarian, 1964-66; U.S. Army, Tongduchon, Korea, civilian special services librarian, 1966-67; University of Minnesota, Minneapolis, cataloger, 1967-68; Fort Sill Indian High School, Lawton, Okla., high school librarian, 1968-70; Clayton Junior College, Morrow, Ga., technical services librarian, 1971-78; Northern Virginia Community College, Annandale, acquisitions librarian, 1978—. *Member:* American Library Association, Church and Synagogue Library Association, Southeastern Library Association, Potomac Technical Processing Librarians.

WRITINGS: Introduction to Library Technical Services, H. W. Wilson, 1979.

SIDELIGHTS: Frances Bernhardt wrote: "*Introduction to Library Technical Services* was an outgrowth of teaching a technical class for three years and of my experience in technical services in various types of libraries. I tried to make the book relevant to libraries of all types, and to staff members with various levels of responsibility."

*   *   *

BEST, Charles H(erbert)   1899-1978

OBITUARY NOTICE—See index for *CA* sketch: Born February 27, 1899, in Pembroke, Me.; died March 31, 1978. Educator, scientist, and author. While still a graduate student at the University of Toronto, Best helped conduct the experiments that led to the discovery of insulin. Together with co-discoverer Frederick G. Banting, he established the Banting and Best Department of Medical Research at the university, where he also became a professor of physiology and an associate director of the school's Connaught Laboratories. He was honored throughout the world for the insulin discovery, and his birthplace in Pembroke was designated a historical landmark in 1968. He was the author of a number of books, including *The Internal Secretions of the Pancreas, The Human Body and Its Function*, and *The Physiological Basis of Medical Practice*. Obituaries and other sources: *Who's Who*, 126th edition, St. Martin's, 1974; *The Writers Directory, 1976-78*, St. Martin's, 1976. (Date of death provided by secretary, Linda Mahon.)

*   *   *

BEYTAGH, Gonville (Aubie) ffrench
See ffRENCH-BEYTAGH, Gonville (Aubie)

*   *   *

BIDDLE, Francis (Beverley)   1886-1968

OBITUARY NOTICE—See index for *CA* sketch: Born May 9, 1886, in Paris, France; died October 4, 1968. Lawyer, judge, and author. From 1912 to 1939 Biddle was a partner in Philadelphia law firms. He then became a U.S. attorney and a U.S. Circuit Court of Appeals judge for the third circuit. From 1941 to 1945 he was the U.S. attorney general in the Roosevelt administration, after which he served as a judge at the Nuremburg trials. His books include *The Llanfear Pattern, The World's Best Hope, The Fear of Freedom,* and *In Brief Authority.* Obituaries and other sources: *Current Biography,* Wilson, 1941, December, 1968; *New York Times,* October 5, 1968.

* * *

BIELER, Ludwig 1906-1981

OBITUARY NOTICE—See index for *CA* sketch: Born October 20, 1906, in Vienna, Austria; died May 2, 1981, in Dublin, Ireland. Educator, paleographer, editor, and author. Bieler taught at the University of Vienna and worked as a keeper of manuscripts at the National Library in Vienna before fleeing the Nazi occupation of his native country. He moved to Ireland where he lectured at the National University and later became a professor at the University College in Dublin. A scholar of ancient writings and inscriptions, Bieler wrote several books in this field. His works include *Theios Aner, Codices Patriciani Latini,* and *Boethius: Philosophiae Consolatio.* He also edited *Scriptores Latini Hibernaiae.* Obituaries and other sources: *London Times,* May 18, 1981.

* * *

BIGNELL, Alan 1928-

PERSONAL: Born June 15, 1928, in Tonbridge, England; son of Frank Richard (a mechanic) and Elizabeth Lucy (Colegate) Bignell; married Audrey Moreen Gray (a nurse), June 16, 1951; children: Brian, Eric, Judith Bignell Page. *Home:* 13 Southwood, Barming, Maidstone, Kent ME16 9EB, England.

CAREER: Office worker, 1949-57; Kent Messenger Group, Maidstone, England, journalist, 1957—, Kent local government special feature writer, 1969—. *Military service:* British Army, Royal Service Corps, 1946-48. *Member:* Institute of Journalists (chairman of Kent district, 1975—).

WRITINGS: Kent Villages, R. Hale, 1975; *Hopping Down in Kent,* R. Hale, 1977.

Children's plays: "The Wonderful Clock" (three-act musical), first produced in Faversham, England, at Faversham Children's Operetta Theatre, 1968; "Welcome to Obenderberg" (three-act musical), first produced in Faversham, at Faversham Children's Operetta Theatre, 1972.

Author of "Look at It This Way," a weekly column in *Kent Evening Post,* 1970—. Contributor of articles and stories to periodicals.

WORK IN PROGRESS: High Weald Run, a novel about smuggling in eighteenth-century Kent; *The Hoppers,* a novel about hop picking in Kent in the 1850's.

SIDELIGHTS: Bignell commented: "With comparatively brief exceptions, I have lived and worked in Kent all my life, and most of my writing is about the county. I am very concerned for the future of Kent and very apprehensive about some trends threatening to reduce the traditionally large farming acreage. Indeed, I extend that concern to the whole of England. I take a deep interest in Kentish history, particularly as it illuminates the lives of ordinary people through the ages."

BILLINGS, Richard N. 1930-

PERSONAL: Born August 29, 1930, in New York, N.Y.; son of Chester (in business) and Caryle (Pressinger) Billings; married Aileen C. Jackson, April 15, 1955 (divorced); children: Deborah, Sarah. *Education:* Princeton University, B.A. *Politics:* Democrat. *Religion:* Protestant. *Home and office:* 3416 Porter St. N.W., Washington, D.C. 20016.

CAREER: Life, New York, N.Y., 1956-68, began as correspondent, became bureau chief and associate editor; *Congressional Quarterly,* Washington, D.C., executive editor, 1969-72; Fact Research, Inc., Washington, D.C., president, 1973-76; *U.S. News Washington Newsletter,* Washington, D.C., executive editor, 1975-77; free-lance writer, 1977—. Managing director of National Tourism Resources Review Commission; editorial chief of U.S. House of Representatives Select Committee on Assassinations. *Military service:* U.S. Army, 1952-54. *Member:* National Press Club, Americans for Democratic Action.

WRITINGS: (With John Greenya) *Power to the Public Worker,* Luce, 1974; (with G. Robert Blakey) *The Plot to Kill the President* (nonfiction), Times Books, 1980.

* * *

BILLINGTON, Ray Allen 1903-1981

OBITUARY NOTICE—See index for *CA* sketch: Born September 28, 1903, in Bay City, Mich.; died of a heart attack, March 7, 1981, in San Marino, Calif. Educator, historian, editor, and author. Billington taught at several schools, including Clark University, Smith College, Northwestern University, and Oxford University. He also worked as a senior research associate at the Henry E. Huntington Library for more than fifteen years. Billington specialized in the history of the American West and espoused the theory of historian Frederick Jackson Turner that proposed the frontier played a major role in the development of the United States both economically and ideologically. Billington wrote several books, among which number *The Far Western Frontier, 1830-1860, The Westward Movement in the United States,* and *Land of Savagery, Land of Promise. Frederick Jackson Turner: Historian, Scholar, Teacher,* the author's biography of his mentor, won the 1974 Bancroft Prize for American History. In addition, Billington edited books such as *Massachusetts: A Guide to Its Places and People* and *The Making of American Democracy.* Obituaries and other sources: *Washington Post,* March 14, 1981; *Publishers Weekly,* March 20, 1981; *Time,* March 23, 1981.

* * *

BISHOP, Bonnie 1943-

PERSONAL: Born August 24, 1943, in Meriden, Conn.; daughter of Welles L. (a birdhouse manufacturer) and Julia (a registered nurse; maiden name, Nettleton) Bishop; married James H. Wells (a laboratory technician), May 21, 1975. *Education:* Skidmore College, B.S., 1965; attended New School for Social Research, 1969-76, and Parsons School of Design, 1970-76. *Residence:* Athens, Maine.

CAREER: Scholastic Magazines, Inc., New York, N.Y., artist, 1966-68, art editor, 1968-72, art director of language arts projects, 1972-76; Sterns, Waterville, Me. display director and advertising assistant, 1977-78; J.C. Penney & Co., Inc., Skowhegan, Me. merchandise presentation supervisor, 1978—. Instructor at Thomas College, autumns, 1978—. Participant in group and solo shows in New York and Maine. *Awards, honors:* Awards from Poster U.S.A. for "Get High on Life" poster; Creativity '73, 1973, for "Garbage Can Poster"; American Institute of Graphic Arts, 1973, for "Getting Together" and "Double Action" learning kits; Creativity '74, 1974, for poster, "You Are the American Dream."

WRITINGS—For children: *No One Noticed Ralph* (Xerox Book Club selection), Doubleday, 1979; *Ralph Rides Away,* Doubleday, 1979.

WORK IN PROGRESS: Short stories; poems.

SIDELIGHTS: Bonnie Bishop wrote: "I have always considered myself primarily an artist, and I hope to write more children's books and illustrate them myself. I am also involved in printmaking, and am beginning to show my work locally."

*   *   *

BISHOP of TRURO
See LEONARD, Graham Douglas

*   *   *

BISSET, Ronald 1950-

PERSONAL: Born August 10, 1950, in Aberdeen, Scotland; son of Hugh Ewen (a forester) and Ross Mary Dundas (Macleod) Bisset; married Lindsey Mary Urquhart (a lecturer in mathematics), December 16, 1972. *Education:* University of Edinburgh, M.A. (with honors), 1972; University of Salford, M.Sc., 1974. *Home:* 4 Holland St., Aberdeen AB2 3UU, Scotland. *Office:* Project Appraisal for Development Control, Department of Geography, University of Aberdeen, High St., Old Aberdeen, Aberdeen AB9 2UF, Scotland.

CAREER: University of Aberdeen, Aberdeen, Scotland, research assistant, 1974-77, research fellow, 1977—. Consultant to United Nations Environment Program, Latin America Office. *Member:* Royal Anthropological Institute of Great Britain and Ireland (fellow), Impact Assessment Association. *Awards, honors:* Grants from Natural Environment Research Council, Carnegie Trust for the Universities of Scotland (for the United States), and North Atlantic Treaty Organization (for the United States), all 1980.

WRITINGS: The Assessment of Major Industrial Applications: A Manual, Department of the Environment (London, England), 1976; *U.S. Environmental Impact Assessment: A Critical Review,* Department of the Environment and Transport (London, England), 1979; (contributor) Derek Lovejoy, editor, *Land Use and Landscape Planning,* Leonard Hill, 1979; *Environmental Impact Assessment: A Bibliography With Abstracts,* Bowker, 1980; (contributor) Timothy O'Riordan and R. K. Turner, editors, *An Annotated Reader in Environmental Planning and Management,* Pergamon, 1981; (contributor) O'Riordan and W.R.D. Sewell, editors, *Project Appraisal and Policy Review,* Wiley, 1981; *The Assessment of Major Developments: A Manual,* H.M.S.O., 1981. Contributor to professional journals.

WORK IN PROGRESS: Research on the role of post-development audits in environmental impact assessment.

SIDELIGHTS: Bisset commented: "Although interested in all aspects of environmental impact assessment (apart from the economic), I am concerned mainly in methods for impact assessment, social impact assessment, auditing of projects, and the role of impact assessment in less industrialized countries.

"From 1974 to 1975 I was engaged in preparing a structured method whereby local planning authorities could carry out a balanced assessment of the environmental, social, and economic effects of major developments. I examined U.S. procedures and methods to ascertain whether these could be used by United Kingdom planning authorities within the existing development control system.

"In 1978 I was involved with two colleagues in organizing a course on environmental impact assessment and development in conjunction with the Monitoring and Assessment Research Centre of Chelsea College, London, for senior administrators and academics from developing countries. An outcome of the training course was a request from the United Nations Environment Program (Regional Seas Activity Center) to develop a training package aimed at administrators dealing with development in coastal and marine environments.

"In 1980 I spent five weeks visiting the United States on a study tour. I visited Massachusetts Institute of Technology and various federal agencies such as the Department of Agriculture and Transportation, the Environmental Protection Agency, and the council on Environmental Quality. I also spent considerable time at the U.S. Army Construction Engineering Research Laboratory, the Oak Ridge National Laboratory, and the Argonne National Laboratory."

AVOCATIONAL INTERESTS: Natural history, walking, Russian literature, photography.

*   *   *

BLACKFORD, Staige D(avis) 1931-

PERSONAL: Born January 3, 1931, in Charlottesville, Va.; son of Staige Davis and Lydia (Fishburne) Blackford; married Bettina Balding, November 1, 1958; children: Linda Balding, Sheila Mason. *Education:* University of Virginia, B.A. (with honors), 1952; Oxford University, B.A., 1954. *Politics:* Independent. *Religion:* Episcopalian. *Home:* 1857 Westview Rd., Charlottesville, Va. 22903. *Office:* Virginia Quarterly Review, One West Range, Charlottesville, Va. 22903.

CAREER/WRITINGS: Southern Regional Council, Atlanta, Ga., research director, 1962-64; *Norfolk Virginian-Pilot,* Norfolk, Va., political reporter, 1964-69; press secretary to governor of Virginia, 1970-74; University of Virginia, Charlottesville, Va., special assistant to president, 1974—; *Virginia Quarterly Review,* Charlottesville, editor, 1975—. Member of board of directors of Council on Religion and International Affairs. *Military service:* U.S. Air Force, 1955-57; became first lieutenant. *Member:* Association of American Rhodes Scholars, P.E.N., Phi Beta Kappa, Boar's Head Sports Club. *Awards, honors:* Rhodes Scholar at Oxford University.

*   *   *

BLACKIE, Pamela 1917-

PERSONAL: Born June 20, 1917, in East Sheen, Surrey, England; daughter of Alfred James (an engineering professor and inspector of schools) and Joyce (Newman) Margetson; married John Blackie (a chief inspector of schools and writer), May 22, 1942; children: Carolyn Blackie de Grey, David, Sebastian, Catherine Blackie Shepherd. *Education:* Attended Royal Academy of Dramatic Art, 1937-39; graduated from University of London. *Home:* The Bell House, Alconbury, Huntingdon, Cambridge PE17 5DT, England. *Agent:* Curtis Brown Ltd., 1 Craven Hill, London W2 3EP, England.

CAREER: Drama adviser for Yorkshire Rural Community Council, Council for Encouragement of Music and the Arts, and Community Council of Lancashire, 1939-42; taught drama part-time in Borstal, Cambshire, England; writer. *Member:* Hinchingbrooke Geriatric Hospital (honorary librarian).

WRITINGS: A Drama Teacher's Handbook, Basil Blackwell, 1956; (with husband, John Blackie) *Family Holidays Abroad,* Hodder & Stoughton, 1962; (with Bess Bullough and Doris Nash) *Drama,* Citation Press, 1972. Author of "The Years of Parting and the Years of Return," broadcast by BBC; also author of several unpublished plays for amateurs, including "Christmas at Home," "The Frozen Road," "This Was His Life," "Standards," and "The Prayer That Is Made in This Place," first produced in Ely, England, at Ely Cathedral, as part of the thirteenth centenary celebration.

WORK IN PROGRESS: The Losing Side, a novel; *The Gamekeeper's Dog,* a fictionalized autobiographical tale; *The Children of Hamelin,* a tale.

SIDELIGHTS: Blackie told *CA:* "My chief interests which my writing reflects are: family life; children; reading; the significance of belief, legend, and history in what makes humans 'tick'; the love and care of the underprivileged and the contribution these people make to our society; the charismatic movement in the churches; and natural history and growing things.

"In the past I have traveled quite a bit and taken a lovely interest in the theatre, art, and music, but I am a bit too homebound now to be able to indulge these in an up-to-date fashion."

*   *   *

BLACKMAN, Victor   1922-

PERSONAL: Born September 20, 1922, in London, England; son of Walter Henry (a police officer) and Miriam (Humphries) Blackman. *Education:* Attended Gaddesden College, 1948-50. *Politics:* "Distrust them all." *Religion:* "Lapsed Roman Catholic." *Home:* 9 Barry Close, Orpington, Kent BR6 9TD, England. *Office: Daily Express,* Fleet St., London, England.

CAREER: Teacher of mathematics, 1950-55; free-lance photojournalist, 1955-56; *Daily Express,* London, England, staff photographer, 1956—. Air raid warden, 1940-41. Guest on television programs; lecturer. *Military service:* Royal Air Force, 1941-46; became sergeant; received Burma Star. *Awards, honors:* Photography awards include color picture of the year award, 1968.

WRITINGS: My Way With a Camera (autobiography), Focal Press, 1937. Author of "Blackman," a column in *Amateur Photographer,* 1961—.

SIDELIGHTS: Blackman commented: "I was much influenced by the late Lancelot Vining, who pioneered the use of 35mm film in press photography before World War II. I specialize in action photography, especially motor racing and aerobatic flying, and have been a qualified pilot since 1963."

*   *   *

BLACKWOOD, Andrew W(atterson)   1882-1966

OBITUARY NOTICE—See index for *CA* sketch: Born August 5, 1882, in Clay Center, Kan.; died March 28, 1966. Minister, educator, and author. Blackwood was a minister in the Presbyterian church before beginning his academic career at the Louisville Theological Seminary in 1925. He later taught as a professor of preaching at Princeton and Temple universities. His writings include *The Fine Art of Preaching, Preaching From the Bible,* and *Prayers for All Occasions.* Obituaries and other sources: *Who Was Who in America,* 4th edition, Marquis, 1968.

*   *   *

BLAKE, Patrick
See EGLETON, Clive (Frederick)

*   *   *

BLEIBERG, Robert Marvin   1924-

PERSONAL: Born June 21, 1924, in Brooklyn, N.Y.; son of Edward and Frances (DuBroff) Bleiberg; married Harriet Evans, May, 1948 (divorced March, 1953;) married Sally Diane Beverly, October 25, 1956; children: (first marriage) Ellen; (second marriage) Richard Beverly. *Education:* Columbia University, B.A., 1943; New York University, M.B.A., 1950; Hillsdale College, D.C.Sc., 1977. *Home:* 25 Central Park W., New York, N.Y. 10023. *Office:* 22 Cortland St., New York, N.Y. 10007.

CAREER: Prudden's Digest of Investment and Banking Options, New York City, associate editor, 1946; *Barron's National Business and Financial Weekly,* New York City, staff member, 1946-54, editor, 1955—. *Military service:* U.S. Army, 1943-45; served in Pacific Theatre; received Purple Heart. *Member:* New York Society of Security Analysts, New York Finance Writers Association, Economic Club of New York, Mont Pelerin Society, Phi Beta Kappa, Phi Beta Kappa Associates.

WRITINGS: Tax Reform: Real or Spurious?, Committee for Monetary Research and Education, Inc., 1977.

*   *   *

BLISS, (John) Michael   1941-

PERSONAL: Born January 18, 1941, in Canada; son of Quartus (a physician) and Anne (Crow) Bliss; married Elizabeth Haslam (a teacher), June 29, 1963; children: James, Laura, Sara. *Education:* University of Toronto, B.A., 1962, M.A., 1966, Ph.D., 1972. *Home:* 314 Bessborough Dr., Toronto, Ontario, Canada M4G 3L1. *Office:* Department of History, University of Toronto, Toronto, Ontario, Canada M5S 1A1.

CAREER: University of Toronto, Toronto, Ontario, lecturer, 1968-72, assistant professor, 1972-74, associate professor, 1974-78, professor of history, 1978—, member of governing council, 1976-78. *Member:* Canadian Historical Association, Business History Conference. *Awards, honors:* Sir John A. Macdonald Prize from Canadian Historical Association, 1978, medal for Canadian biography from University of British Columbia, 1978, book prize from city of Toronto, 1978, and award of merit from Toronto Historical Board, 1979, all for *A Canadian Millionaire.*

WRITINGS: Canadian History in Documents, 1763-1966, McGraw, 1966; *A Living Profit: Studies in the Social History of Canadian Business, 1883-1911,* McClelland & Stewart, 1974; *Confederation, 1867,* F. Watts, 1975; *A Canadian Millionaire: The Life and Business Times of Sir Joseph Flavelle, Bart., 1858-1939,* Macmillan, 1978. General editor of "Social History of Canada," a series, University of Toronto Press, 1971-76. Contributor of articles and reviews to Canadian magazines and newspapers. Member of editorial board of *Ontario History,* 1976—.

WORK IN PROGRESS: A History of the Discovery of Insulin; Banting: A Troubled Life.

*   *   *

BLUM, Harold P.   1929-

PERSONAL: Born July 8, 1929, in New York, N.Y.; son of Paul and Anna (Brown) Blum; married Elsa J. Fienberg (a psychologist), July 6, 1952; children: Lawrence, Linda, Daniel. *Education:* Cornell University, B.A., 1949; Boston University, M.D., 1953. *Home and office:* 23 The Hemlocks, Roslyn Estates, N.Y. 11576.

CAREER: New York University, New York, N.Y., clinical professor of psychiatry, 1979—. Chairman of Research on Reconstruction, Psychoanalytic Research and Development Fund. *Military service:* U.S. Navy, 1954-56; served with Medical Corps. *Awards, honors:* Mosby Prize for outstanding medical student, 1953; Margaret Mahler Prize, 1976, for "The Prototype of Preoedipal Reconstruction."

WRITINGS: (Editor) *Female Psychology,* International Universities Press, 1977; (editor) *Explorations in Psychoanalytic Technique: Discourse on Psychoanalytic Psychotherapy,* International Universities Press, 1980. Editor of *Journal of the American Psychoanalytic Association,* 1973-80.

SIDELIGHTS: Blum told *CA:* "My emphasis in work and lectures is on technique based on the foundation in the theory of technique, and the increasingly refined psychoanalytic understanding of the analytic process. Rational psychotherapy is derived from psychoanalytic principles."

*   *   *

BLUMENTHAL, Monica David   1930-1981

OBITUARY NOTICE—See index for *CA* sketch: Born September 1, 1930, in Tuebingen, Germany (now West Germany); died after a long illness, March 16, 1981, in Pittsburgh, Pa. Educator, psychiatrist, and author. Blumenthal taught at the University of Michigan for more than fifteen years before moving to the University of Pittsburgh where she was a professor and the program director of geriatric psychiatry at the Western Psychiatric Institute and Clinic. Blumenthal became nationally known as a specialist in geriatric psychiatry and the study of violence and aggression. She was nominated for an Emmy Award in 1980 for her work on the television program "What Shall We Do About Mother?" Blumenthal was the co-author of *Justifying Violence: Attitudes of American Men* and *More About Justifying Violence: A Methodological Study of Attitudes and Behavior.* She also contributed to numerous books. Obituaries and other sources: *New York Times,* March 17, 1981.

*   *   *

BLYTH, John
See HIBBS, John

*   *   *

BOARDWELL, Robert Lee   1926-

PERSONAL: Born December 30, 1926, in Portland, Ore.; son of Perry Leon (in theater) and Mary Amelia Boardwell; married Virginia Carol Miller (an artist and writer), May 17, 1948; children: Barbara Susan Boardwell Yeomans, Carol Kathleen Boardwell Jensen. *Education:* Lewis and Clark College, B.S., 1951; Reed College, M.A.L.S. *Home:* 16358 South Wilson Rd., Oregon City, Ore. 97045. *Office:* 13801 South Webster Rd., Milwaukie, Ore. 97222.

CAREER: Teacher of art and photography in Milwaukie, Ore., 1956—, became chairman of art and photography departments. Free-lance artist and photographer. Chairman of Ford Foundation research on the gifted child. Director of satellite tracking station, Oregon Moonwatch Team; state representative (from Clackamas County) to REACT. Charting chairman of Portland Power Squadron. *Military service:* Served in U.S. Navy during World War II; became Navy pilot.

MEMBER: Society of Calligraphic Handwriting (member of western American branch board of directors), National Education Association, Society for Italic Handwriting, Willamette Writers (member of board of directors). *Awards, honors:* Second place national chart correction award from Power Squadron; two awards from National Academy of Sciences and Smithsonian Institution, both for satellite tracking; named citizen of the year by *Oregon Journal.*

WRITINGS: Beginning Calligraphy, Touchstone, 1974. Contributor of articles, poems, and photographs to national magazines and newspapers.

WORK IN PROGRESS: Poetry and Photography: Zen Teaching Stories; a calligraphy book.

SIDELIGHTS: Boardwell wrote: "My book on calligraphy helps fulfill a need for those who must teach themselves. I have a background in science, and this explains my work and awards in satellite tracking. I am interested in boating and all forms of art. At present I am working on an extensive collection of color slides of Hawaii. I am also interested in extra-sensory perception as it relates to education and have conducted some interesting research in this area."

*   *   *

BOATENG, Yaw Maurice
See BRUNNER, Maurice Yaw

*   *   *

BODIAN, Nat G.   1921-

PERSONAL: Born February 12, 1921, in Newark, N.J.; son of Louis and Fannie (Gabot) Bodian; married Ruth Naiman, June 28, 1947; children: Mark, Lester. *Education:* Attended Essex Junior College, 1939-40; New School for Social Research, Certificate in Public Relations, 1947; attended City College (now of City University of New York), 1948. *Residence:* Cranford, N.J. *Office:* John Wiley & Sons, Inc., 605 Third Ave., New York, N.Y. 10158.

CAREER: Baker & Taylor Co. (wholesale booksellers), Hillside, N.J., sales and promotion manager, 1959-60; John F. Rider Publisher/Hayden Book Co., Inc., New York City, advertising and promotion manager, 1961-62; American Elsevier Publishing Co., New York City, marketing manager, 1963-71; Transaction Books, New Brunswick, N.J., marketing manager, 1971-72; Crane, Russak & Co., Inc., marketing manager, 1972-76; John Wiley & Sons, Inc., New York City, marketing manager of Interscience Division, 1976—. Past project coordinator in the Middle East for Elsevier Publishing Co., Amsterdam, Netherlands. Guest lecturer at Boston University. *Military service:* U.S. Army Air Forces, South Atlantic correspondent for *Yank* and editor of base publications, 1942-45. *Member:* New Jersey Writers Association.

WRITINGS: Book Marketing Handbook: Tips and Techniques for the Sale and Promotion of Scientific, Technical, Professional, and Scholarly Books and Journals, Bowker, 1980.

Work represented in anthologies, including *Yank: The Army Weekly,* Arno, 1968. Contributor to magazines and newspapers, including *Editor and Publisher, Tide,* and *Advertising Requirements.*

WORK IN PROGRESS: Revising *Book Marketing Handbook,* publication by Bowker expected in 1984.

SIDELIGHTS: Bodian told *CA:* "The marketing of scientific, technical, professional, and scholarly books is a profession learned largely on the job. As a consequence, while practiced successfully by many, it is also practiced in many different ways, based on the skills, experience, intelligence, and initiative of each individual practitioner.

"For some, the set of skills acquired in marketing books have been acquired with great difficulty and only after long experience. As a consequence, their learning experiences have long been viewed as their 'secrets,' something to be carefully guarded and utilized as circumstances warranted.

"It has long been my conviction that there are no 'secrets' in book marketing—only 'techniques,' and that these techniques are tools which can be applied by many different individuals in many different ways. *Book Marketing Handbook* is essentially a collection of these techniques assembled over twenty years in book marketing and promotion and carefully catalogued and sorted out so that they may be readily referred to and used by anyone in publishing. For many successful marketers, these techniques will undoubtedly represent a second or third opinion, or possibly confirm what they have known and practiced all along. On the other hand, for a newcomer to the work of professional and scholarly book marketing, the forty-four-chapter work, with its five thousand-entry index, represents a detailed catalog of steps, approaches, procedures, rules, laws, case histories, and guidelines to carry him or her through unfamiliar areas in conjunction with the marketing of books.

"The original idea for the book came from a top-ranking publishing executive drawn from another industry. In a conversation with me some years ago, he mentioned he had checked various reference sources and could find no reliable guide to the marketing of books. He also mentioned that it would have been an embarrassment to ask these questions of the more experienced publishing people serving under him. This led to an investigation in the Library of Congress catalog which confirmed that, indeed, there was no comprehensive hands-on manual published that offered guidance on the marketing and promotion of professional and scholarly books.

"Having been through two companies from inception to ultimate expansion and success in all areas of professional and scholarly publishing, and worn *all* the 'hats' involved in the marketing process, I felt uniquely qualified to first outline all the steps involved in the book marketing process and then to expand each step into an extensive discourse replete with techniques, case histories, and guidelines for success.

"The result was *Book Marketing Handbook.* The fact that the first year's sales projection was exceeded in less than six months attests to the fact that *Book Marketing Handbook* has been widely accepted as a working tool of the American book publishing industry and meets the objectives I set when I started writing it."

*   *   *

BOFF, Vic 1915-

PERSONAL: Born October 22, 1915, in Brooklyn, N.Y.; married Ann Johnson; children: George, Ken. *Education:* New York Institute of Massage, graduated; Macfadden Institute of Physical Culture, graduated, 1935; American School of Naturopathy and Chiropractic, N.D., D.C., 1938; Pennsylvania College of Chiropractic, graduated, 1943.

CAREER: Camp Hygiology, Verplank, N.Y., director of therapy, 1936; Yunborn Sanitarium, Butler, N.J., intern, 1939; Healthful Living Publications, editor, 1953-55; owner and director of Health and Fitness Enterprises; president of Iceberg Athletic Club. Licensed medical masseur in State of New York; registered physical therapist; consultant to Jowett Institute of Physical Culture and Bonomo Culture Institute. *Awards, honors:* Named Ray of Sun the Healer by United Association of American Indians, 1959; athletic awards include "world's greatest winter bather award," 1975.

WRITINGS: You Can Be Physically Perfect, Powerfully Strong, Arco, 1975; *What Herbs Will Do for You,* Bonomo Publishing, 1977; *Exercises for Busy People,* Bonomo Publishing, 1977; *Reducing Guide,* Bonomo Publishing, 1977; *Carbohydrate Counter: Diet Guide,* Bonomo Publishing, 1978; *Beautify Your Figure,* Bonomo Publishing, 1979. Contributor to magazines.

*   *   *

BOGAN, James 1945-

PERSONAL: Born September 9, 1945, in Chicago, Ill.; son of James J. (a sailor) and Virginia (a social worker; maiden name, Ruse) Bogan. *Education:* Loyola University, Chicago, Ill., B.S. (with honors), 1967; University of Kansas, M.A. (with honors), 1968, M.Phil. (with honors), 1972, Ph.D. (with honors), 1979. *Home address:* Route 3, Box 5, Rolla, Mo. 65401. *Office:* Department of Fine Arts, University of Missouri, Rolla, Mo. 65401.

CAREER: Factory worker in Argo-Summit, Ill., 1964-65; teacher in Head Start program in Chicago, Ill., 1966; cab driver in Chicago, 1967; University of Kansas, Lawrence, assistant instructor in English, 1968; University of Missouri, Rolla, instructor, 1969-79, assistant professor of fine arts, 1979—. Gives poetry readings and lectures; guest on radio programs; consultant. *Awards, honors:* Grants from Missouri Arts Council, 1976-77, 1977-78, 1979, 1979-80, 1980, and Missouri Committee for the Humanities, 1978; Indiana University National Endowment for the Humanities fellowship, summer, 1979.

WRITINGS: Trees in the Same Forest (poems), Cauldron, 1976; (editor) *A Directory of Missouri Film-Radio Artists, Lecturers, and Programmers,* Missouri Arts Council, 1980; (co-editor) *Sparks of Fire: A William Blake Anthology,* North Atlantic Books, 1982.

Work represented in anthologies, including *Ozark, Ozark: A Hillside Reader,* edited by Miller Williams, University of Missouri Press, 1980; *An Anthology of Missouri Poets,* edited by Robert Stewart, University of Missouri Press. Contributor of nearly fifty articles and poems to scholarly journals, literary magazines, and newspapers, including *Review of the Arts, Dance, Southwinds, Focus Midwest, River Styx,* and *Interface.*

WORK IN PROGRESS: Ozark Meanderings, poems and prose, publication expected in 1982; *Trance Arrows,* meditation poems, publication expected in 1982.

SIDELIGHTS: Bogan wrote: "I was born at dawn on September 9, 1945, by the shores of Lake Michigan, and grew up in a willow tree. I learned how to play third base instead of the violin. I was educated in Catholic schools in Chicagoland, Rome, Kansas, and the Ozarks. I received my Ph.D.

after years of studying William Blake, a fire source. I teach writing, film, books, and art for a living.

"I love boats without motors, music with saxophones, hard work, and no work at all. I was surprised into being a writer at age twenty-eight. I keep a clean desk, but near to hand are pictures of children and angels, a star chart, three dictionaries, a cream pitcher full of pens and screwdrivers, a couple of chert arrowheads, a two-foot cedar in a coffee can, sun-and-moon painted by daughters and sons, and out the window: oaks, a creek, hills, and the Ozark sky floating by."

BIOGRAPHICAL/CRITICAL SOURCES: Focus Midwest, summer, 1980.

* * *

BOHANA, Aileen Stein 1951-

PERSONAL: Born September 25, 1951, in New York, N.Y.; daughter of Philip (a businessman) and Doris (an administrative assistant; maiden name, Kramer) Stein; married Ira Bohana (a tax accountant), June 24, 1979. *Education:* Attended State University of New York at Stony Brook, 1968-70; New York University, B.A., 1972. *Home and office:* 370 East 76th St., New York, N.Y. 10021.

CAREER/WRITINGS: Gentlemen's Quarterly, New York, N.Y., copy editor, 1972-76, associate editor, 1976-79, grooming editor, 1977—, author of columns "Imagery," and "Groomers."

WORK IN PROGRESS: A book on hair, completion expected in 1981.

SIDELIGHTS: Bohana told *CA:* "I have specialized to date in the areas of grooming, beauty, and new products." *Avocational interests:* Theatre, film, music, travel, literature, dance, exercise.

* * *

BOLITHO, Harold 1939-

PERSONAL: Born January 3, 1939, in Mordialloc, Australia; son of Harold and Kathleen Sheila Bolitho; married Margaret Anne Bevan (a teacher), February 7, 1962; children: Harold Ennis, Elizabeth Emily. *Education:* University of Melbourne, B.A. (with honors), 1960; Yale University, Ph.D., 1969. *Religion:* Anglican. *Home:* 13 View St., Mont Albert, Victoria 3127, Australia.

CAREER: University of Melbourne, Parkville, Australia, senior lecturer, 1969-72; Monash University, Clayton, Australia, associate professor, 1973—. *Member:* Asian Studies Association of Australia (member of council, 1978-80), Japanese Studies Association of Australia (president, 1978-80).

WRITINGS: Treasures Among Men, Yale University Press, 1974; *Meiji Japan,* Cambridge University Press, 1977.

WORK IN PROGRESS: Research on nineteenth-century Japan.

* * *

BOLTON, James 1917(?)-1981

OBITUARY NOTICE: Born c. 1917; died February 24, 1981, in Sussex, England. Educator and author. Bolton, a tutor and praelector in Classics at Oxford University, was elected to the Fellowship at Queen's College in 1949. His writings include *Aristeas of Proconesus* and *Glory, Jest and Riddle.* Obituaries and other sources: *London Times,* March 3, 1981.

BOND, J. Harvey
See WINTERBOTHAM, R(ussell) R(obert)

* * *

BONNER, Paul Hyde 1893-1968

OBITUARY NOTICE—See index for *CA* sketch: Born February 14, 1893, in New York, N.Y.; died December 14, 1968, in Charleston, S.C. Industrialist and author. Bonner was the vice-president of Stehli Silks Corporation and a diplomat with the U.S. State Department. He wrote novels of international political intrigue, including *Hotel Talleyrand* and *Ambassador Extraordinary.* Obituaries and other sources: *Current Biography,* Wilson, 1955, March, 1969; *New York Times,* December 15, 1968; *Detroit Free Press,* December 16, 1968; *Publishers Weekly,* January 13, 1969; *Who Was Who in America,* 5th edition, Marquis, 1973. (Exact date of death provided by wife, Elizabeth M. Bonner.)

* * *

BONNEY, H(anning) Orrin 1903-1979

OBITUARY NOTICE—See index for *CA* sketch: Born May 14, 1903, in Idaho Springs, Colo.; died in 1979. Lawyer and author. Bonney was a partner in the law firm of Mathes, Bonney & Clawson from 1933 to 1951. After 1951 he practiced law privately in Houston, Texas. He wrote a number of books with his wife, Lorraine G. Bonney, including *Guide to Wyoming Mountains and Wilderness Areas, The Teton Range and Gros Ventre Range,* and *Battle Drums and Geysers.* Obituaries and other sources: *Who's Who in the South and Southwest,* 13th edition, Marquis, 1973. (Date of death provided by wife, Lorraine G. Bonney.)

* * *

BOOHER, Dianna Daniels 1948-

PERSONAL: Born January 13, 1948, in Hillsboro, Tex.; daughter of Alton B. (a postal supervisor) and Opal (Schronk) Daniels; married Daniel T. Booher (a minister of music and youth), June 23, 1967; children: Jeffrey Thomas, Lisa Christine. *Education:* North Texas State University, B.A. (cum laude), 1970; University of Houston, M.A., 1979. *Residence:* Houston, Tex. *Agent:* Carol Mann Literary Agency, 168 Pacific Ave., New York, N.Y. 11201. *Office:* Booher Writing Consultants, 11611 Barwood Bend, Houston, Tex. 77065.

CAREER: Fort Bruckner, Okinawa, secretary in Military Education Division, 1967-68; teacher of Spanish at public schools in Pampa, Tex., 1975-77; North Harris County College, Houston, Tex., instructor in creative writing, 1977-78; senior English teacher at public schools in Houston, 1979-80; Booher Writing Consultants, Houston, president, 1980—. *Member:* Houston Writers Workshop.

WRITINGS: Help, We're Moving (juvenile nonfiction), Broadman, 1978; *Coping When Your Family Falls Apart* (juvenile nonfiction), Messner, 1979; *The Faces of Death* (nonfiction), Broadman, 1980; *Not Yet Free* (novel), Broadman, 1981; *Rape: What Would You Do If . . . ?* (juvenile nonfiction), Messner, 1981; *The Last Caress* (novel), Zebra Books, 1981; *How to Write Right—in Business Reports, Letters, Memos* (textbook), Facts-on-File, 1982. Contributor to magazines. Book reviewer for *Houston Chronicle.*

WORK IN PROGRESS: Teacher, a novel on the teaching profession, completion expected in 1981; a self-help book on mother-daughter relationships, for young adults.

SIDELIGHTS: Dianna Booher told *CA:* "To have someone say, 'You've helped—your book got me through a rough time,' makes writing nonfiction worthwhile for me. Both my teaching and writing are branches of the same inner drive to achieve immortality through the values I foster in others. Far too few have realized that 'to give is to receive.' In my books I strive to motivate people to cope with problems as learning and giving experiences which can enrich their lives.

"In fiction, to make a reader 'feel' is of utmost importance. No matter how much I intend to paint a character despicable, in the end I find that I like him because I understand him. This is equally true to my personal experience. Understanding another's motives, circumstances, and background forces me to weigh his strengths more heavily than his weaknesses.

"I lived my first year of married life in Okinawa while my husband was in the Navy. That year was my first attempt to get outside my cocoon and view the American scene more objectively with a foreign culture as a background. My writing continues to reflect that view—of a nineteen-year-old away from home for the first time.

"Although timidly at first, my religious beliefs color everything I write. I'm often asked if my religious convictions don't inhibit my attempt to express reality for the majority. On the contrary, my Christianity serves as a catalyst to my understanding, to my finding meaning or lack of it in the mundane. Characters without a purpose in life move me to deeper expression of eternal truth.

"I began my writing in 1976 at the age of twenty-eight, with no more motivation than to find a career which would let me stay home with my children and a memory that I enjoyed writing English themes in school. I sold both the first magazine article and book manuscripts I submitted. Although later rejections were to come, the first sale hooked me. Four years and seven books later, I still read each acceptance with awe.

"My present interest is teaching business executives the principles of good writing—that business reports and letters should not be in a foreign language.

"*Help, We're Moving* is about both the physical and emotional adjustments necessary in our mobile society. Since teens primarily learn 'who they are' from peers' views of them, separation from friends can be a major crisis in their search for identity. The book attempts to help them widen their horizons in that search.

"*The Faces of Death* deals with understanding death and the grief process. The major thesis is that only when one faces death can he really learn to live.

"*Coping When Your Family Falls Apart* attempts to help teens through one of the most serious crises in their lives—divorce of their parents. Although a 'broken home' is the excuse behind many teens' emotional and behavioral problems, divorce often makes teens more mature, secure individuals. The book tries to point grieving teens to the choices they have in their reaction to the crisis of divorce.

"*Not Yet Free* is the story of a daughter searching for her illusive dream of 'freedom.' Only when she comes to understand that freedom is 'in her head' is she free to form mature relationships with significant others—her husband and mother.

"*Rape: What Would You Do If . . .?* confronts the preventive, medical, and legal aspects of rape and the teen victim. Great strides have been made in recent legislation against the violence of rape. To create the desire to take the movement further is the purpose of the book.

"*The Last Caress* concerns questions surrounding the governmental decision to suppress studies done in the 1960's about the links between leukemia and radiation leaks from nuclear testing sites. The protagonist of this novel, a research firm executive, finds herself facing the decision about whether to release such information to the public when her own teenage daughter is diagnosed as having leukemia. The woman's already tension-filled marriage to an insecure chaplain who uses their daughter as an ego-booster and weapon in their marital relationship adds to the difficulty of her decision. The novel, then, becomes a depiction of the couple's journey through the conflict-ridden grief process. The protagonist's dilemma and the ways in which it alters her family's relationships is one which will doubtlessly be repeated as American citizens come to grips with other environmental issues."

BIOGRAPHICAL/CRITICAL SOURCES: Houston Chronicle, February 18, 1981.

*   *   *

BOORSTIN, Paul (Terry) 1944-

PERSONAL: Born January 29, 1944, in Philadelphia, Pa.; son of Daniel Joseph and Ruth (Frankel) Boorstin; married Sharon Silver (a writer), December 23, 1967; children: Julia Frances. *Education:* Princeton University, B.A. (magna cum laude); attended London School of Film Technique and University of California, Los Angeles. *Home and office:* 9915 Westwanda Dr., Beverly Hills, Calif. 90210. *Agent:* William Morris Agency, 1350 Avenue of the Americas, New York, N.Y. 10019.

CAREER: Writer, producer, and director of documentary television films, 1968-76; writer, 1976—. Instructor at Sherwood Oaks Experimental College, summer, 1980. *Member:* Writers Guild of America West, Phi Beta Kappa. *Awards, honors:* Golden Eagle from Council on International Nontheatrical Events for film "People Who Make Things"; Emmy Award from Academy of Television Arts and Sciences and nomination for Academy Award from Motion Picture Academy of Arts and Sciences, both for documentary film "Journey to the Outer Limits."

WRITINGS: The Accursed, New American Library, 1977; *Savage,* Richard Marek Publishers, 1980; (with wife, Sharon Boorstin) *The Glory Hand* (suspense novel), Richard Marek Publishers, 1981.

Co-author of films, including "Journey to the Outer Limits." Contributor to magazines, including *New Times, New West, Smithsonian,* and *Travel and Leisure.*

WORK IN PROGRESS: "The Glory Hand," a feature film for Metro-Goldwyn-Mayer.

SIDELIGHTS: Boorstin wrote: "World travels for National Geographic television documentaries included visits to the Upper Amazon, India's Gujarat Peninsula, and the Dogon of Mali."

BIOGRAPHICAL/CRITICAL SOURCES: Time, March 24, 1980.

*   *   *

BOOTH, Geoffrey
See TANN, Jennifer

BORDES, Francois   1919-1981
(Francis Carsac)

OBITUARY NOTICE: Born in 1919; died April 30, 1981, in Tucson, Ariz. Archeologist, educator, and author. An internationally known archeologist, Bordes was considered an authority on Neanderthal culture and a pioneer in the study of how ancient man made and used stone tools. The director of the Laboratory of Quaternary Geology and History at the University of Bordeaux, Bordes made more than one hundred thousand replicas of early tools and spent many summers in Australia discussing toolmaking with aborigines. His book *The Stone Age* is an introduction to Old World archeology. Bordes also wrote several science-fiction books under the psuedonym Francis Carsac, including *Les Robinsons du cosmos, Terre en fuite,* and *La Vermine du lion.* Obituaries and other sources: *The Encyclopedia of Science Fiction: An Illustrated A to Z,* Grenada, 1979; *New York Times,* May 7, 1981; *Newsweek,* May 18, 1981.

*   *   *

BORRIE, John   1915-

PERSONAL: Born January 22, 1915, in Port Chalmers, New Zealand; son of William Henry (a physician) and Helen Borrie; married Mavis Helen Merrifield (an artist), March 4, 1950; children: Michael, Philip, Louise. *Education:* University of Otago, Dunedin, 1938. *Religion:* Church of England. *Home:* 37 Newington Ave., Dunedin, New Zealand. *Agent:* Kimber & Co., Queen Anne's Gate, London, England. *Office:* Southern Thoracic Surgical Unit, University of Otago, Dunedin, New Zealand.

CAREER: Dunedin Hospital, Dunedin, New Zealand, member of house staff, 1938-40; Middlesex Hospital, London, England, thoracic surgeon, 1945-46; Southend-on-Sea General Infirmary, Leeds, England, thoracic surgeon, 1946-47; General Infirmary, Leeds, England, thoracic surgeon, 1948; assistant thoracic Surgeon in Newcastle upon Tyne, England, 1949-51; Green Lane Hospital, Auckland, New Zealand, thoracic surgeon, 1951-52; University of Otago, Dunedin, surgeon in charge of Southern Thoracic Surgical Unit, 1952-79, honorary keeper of historic artifacts at Medical School. Member of council of Dunedin Public Art Gallery, 1957—(past president); member of management committee of Olveston Gallery, 1966—. *Military service:* New Zealand Army, Medical Corps, 1940-45, prisoner of war, 1941-45; became captain.

MEMBER: Cardiac Society of Australia and New Zealand (senior member), Surgical Research Society of Australia and New Zealand (senior member), Royal Australasian College of Surgeons (fellow), Royal College of Surgeons (fellow), Alumnus Association of Otago Medical School (president). *Awards, honors:* Member of Order of the British Empire, 1946; M. L. Nuffield surgical award, 1947; named Hunter Professor by Royal College of Surgeons, 1950; Jacksonian Prize, 1953; Jacksonian Medal, 1971; Rockefeller Foundation fellowship, 1960; distinguished service medal from Royal Australasian College of Surgeons, 1977.

WRITINGS: Thoracic Emergencies, Appleton-Century-Crofts, 1958, 3rd edition, 1979; *Lung Cancer: Surgery and Survival,* Appleton-Century-Crofts, 1965; *Olveston Gallery, Dunedin,* Allied Press (Dunedin, New Zealand), 1968, 12th edition, 1976; *Despite Captivity: A Doctor's Life as a German Prisoner of War,* Kimber, 1974; *Art and Observables,* Med-

ical School, University of Otago, 1975. Contributor of about one hundred fifty articles to medical, art, and history journals.

WORK IN PROGRESS: A biography of John H. O. Brown, a British prisoner-of-war secret agent in Germany from 1940 to 1945, publication by R. Hale expected in 1981.

AVOCATIONAL INTERESTS: Travel (Europe, Iran, Iraq, the United States, Japan), administering a coastal scenic reserve at Doctors' Point (Waitati, Otago), oil painting.

*   *   *

BOSS, Richard W(oodruff)   1937-

PERSONAL: Born October 31, 1937, in Arnhem, Netherlands; came to the United States in 1948, naturalized citizen, 1955; son of P. Johannes and Albertje (Lagro) Boss. *Education:* University of Utah, B.A., 1960; University of Washington, Seattle, M.A., 1962, doctoral study. *Home:* 10620 Muirfield Dr., Potomac, Md. 20854. *Office:* Information Systems Consultants, Inc., P.O. Box 34504, Bethesda, Md. 20034.

CAREER: University of Utah, Salt Lake City, order librarian, 1962-63, assistant director of libraries, 1963-64, associate director, 1964-70, instructor in library science, 1962-70; University of Tennessee, Knoxville, director of libraries, 1970-75, associate professor of library and information science, 1972-75; Princeton University, Princeton, N.J., university librarian, 1975-78; Information Systems Consultants, Inc., Bethesda, Md., senior consultant, 1978—. Consultant to National Commission on Libraries and Information Science, National Science Foundation, and Arthur D. Little Co. *Member:* American Library Association (member of council, 1977-80), American Society for Information Science, National Micrographics Association, Phi Beta Kappa. *Awards, honors:* Fellow of Council on Library Resources, 1970.

WRITINGS: (Contributor) *Advances in Understanding Approval and Gathering Plans in Academic Libraries,* Western Michigan University, 1970; *The Library Manager's Guide to Automation,* Knowledge Industry Publications, 1979; *Grant Money and How to Get It,* Bowker, 1980; *Fee-Based Information Services: The Commercial Sector,* Bowker, 1980. Contributor to library journals.

WORK IN PROGRESS: Developing Microform Facilities, with Deborah Raikes, for Microform Review Press.

SIDELIGHTS: Boss commented: "I specialize in the technology of information storage, transfer, and use, including automation, micrographics, and video disk technology. I believe the new technologies will augment rather than displace the book. We must become 'multi-literate,' or proficient in all of them."

BIOGRAPHICAL/CRITICAL SOURCES: Wilson Library Bulletin, June, 1980.

*   *   *

BOWDEN, Jim
See SPENCE, William John Duncan

*   *   *

BOWEN, John   1916-

PERSONAL: Born August 12, 1916, in London, England; son of Caswell (a dental surgeon) and Margaret (McMillan) Bowen; married Anne Elizabeth Muir Hopkin, October 27, 1944. *Education:* Attended University of Glasgow and Royal Technical College, Glasgow, Scotland. *Home:* 27 Springfield Gardens, Upminster, Essex RM14 3EH, England.

CAREER: Fairfield Shipping & Engineering Co., Glasgow, Scotland, ship draftsman, 1934-47; Vokins & Co. (tugboat and barge owners), London, England, repair yard manager, 1947-73; Thames & General Lighterage Ltd. (tugboat and barge owners), London, technical executive in fleet repairs, 1973-79; writer, 1979—. *Member:* Royal Institution of Naval Architects.

WRITINGS: Waterline Ship Models, Conway Maritime Press, 1972; (editor) *Scale Model Sailing Ships,* Conway Maritime Press, 1977; (editor) *Scale Model Warships,* Conway Maritime Press, 1978. Editor of *Model Shipwright.*

AVOCATIONAL INTERESTS: Building ship models, ship construction and design, photography, travel.

*   *   *

BOWIE, David
    See JONES, David Robert

*   *   *

BOWLEY, Rex Lyon   1925-

PERSONAL: Born July 27, 1925, in Exeter, England; son of Ernest Lyon (a civil servant) and Janet Elma (Hooper) Bowley; married Joan Miles (a teacher), April 20, 1950; children: Susan Lyon Bowley Dibley, Carol Lyon. *Education:* Trinity College, Dublin, M.A., 1954. *Home:* 16 Linden Cres., Woodford Green, Essex, England.

CAREER: Assistant master at headmaster's school in Exeter, England, 1952-53, grammar school in Weymouth, England, 1953-55, and school in Reading, England, 1955-60; boarding housemaster at boarding school in Reading, 1960-70; Bancroft's School, Essex, England, senior history master and housemaster, 1970—. Chairman of board of directors of Bowley Publications Ltd. *Military service:* Royal Air Force, 1944-47. *Member:* Society of Authors, Historical Association, Assistant Masters and Mistresses Association, Rural Preservation Association.

WRITINGS: The Isles of Scilly Standard Guidebook, Bowley Publications, 1936, 41st edition, 1981; *Teaching Without Tears: A Guide to Teaching Techniques,* Centaur Press, 1960, 4th edition, 1973; *The Fortunate Islands: The Story of the Isles of Scilly,* Bowley Publications, 1968, 7th edition, 1980; *Tresco Guidebook: The Standard Guidebook to Tresco, Isles of Scilly,* Bowley Publications, 1970; *Scillonian Quiz-Book: An Educational Handbook to the Isles of Scilly,* Bowley Publications, 1974; *Readings for Assembly,* Centaur Press, 1976.

*   *   *

BOYCE, David George   1942-

PERSONAL: Born November 7, 1942, in Lurgan, Northern Ireland. *Education:* Queen's University, Belfast, B.A. (with honors), 1965, Ph.D., 1968. *Office:* Department of Politics, University College of Swansea, University of Wales, Swansea SA2 8PP, Wales.

CAREER: Oxford University, Bodleian Library, Oxford, England, assistant in department of western manuscripts; University of Wales, University College of Swansea, Swansea, senior lecturer in politics, 1971—. *Member:* Royal Historical Society (fellow).

WRITINGS: Englishmen and Irish Troubles, M.I.T. Press, 1972; (co-editor), *Newspaper History,* Constable, 1978. Contributor to learned journals.

BOYER, John (William)   1946-

PERSONAL: Born October 17, 1946, in Chicago, Ill.; son of William Dana and Mary Frances Boyer; married Barbara A. Juskevich (a teacher), August 23, 1968; children: Dominic, Alexandra, Victoria. *Education:* Loyola University, Chicago, Ill., B.A., 1968; University of Chicago, M.A., 1969, Ph.D., 1975. *Religion:* Roman Catholic. *Home:* 5705 South Blackstone, Chicago, Ill. 60637. *Office:* Journal of Modern History, 1126 East 59th St., Chicago, Ill. 60637.

CAREER: University of Chicago, Chicago, Ill., assistant professor, 1974-80, associate professor of central European history, 1980—. *Military service:* U.S. Army Reserve, Signal Corps, 1968-80; became captain. *Awards, honors:* Theodor Koerner Prize, 1977; Koerner Stiftung from city of Vienna and Austrian Socialist party; Alexander von Humboldt fellow in West Germany, 1980-81.

WRITINGS: Political Radicalism in Late Imperial Vienna: Origins of the Christian Social Movement, 1848-1897, University of Chicago Press, 1980. Contributor to history journals. Editor of *Journal of Modern History,* 1979—.

WORK IN PROGRESS: The Crisis of Mass Politics: Bureaucracy and Machine Rule in Vienna, 1897-1920; a history of religion and politics in modern European history.

*   *   *

BOYLEN, Margaret Currier   1921-1967

OBITUARY NOTICE—See index for *CA* sketch: Born January 12, 1921, in Bozeman, Mont.; died in 1967. Author. Boylen wrote *Crow Field, The Marble Orchard,* and *A Moveable Feast.* Obituaries and other sources: *New York Times,* May 23, 1967.

*   *   *

BRADDOCK, Richard R(eed)   1920-1974

OBITUARY NOTICE—See index for *CA* sketch: Born June 14, 1920, in Glenridge, N.J.; died in September, 1974. Educator and author. Braddock joined the English faculty at the University of Iowa in 1955, becoming a professor of English and rhetoric in 1965. He was the editor of *Introductory Readings of the English Language* and the author of *A Little Casebook in the Rhetoric of Writing,* published by Prentice-Hall in 1971. Obituaries and other sources: *Who's Who in the Midwest,* 14th edition, Marquis, 1974; *Directory of American Scholars,* Volume II: *English, Speech, and Drama,* 6th edition, Bowker, 1974. (Date of death provided by English Department of University of Iowa.)

*   *   *

BRADLEY, Ian Campbell   1950-

PERSONAL: Born May 28, 1950, in Berkhamstead, England; son of William Ewart (a civil servant) and Mary Campbell (Tyre) Bradley. *Education:* New College, Oxford, B.A. (with first class honors), 1971, M.A., 1974, D.Phil., 1974. *Politics:* Liberal party. *Religion:* Church of England. *Agent:* Giles Gordon, Morwell St., London W.C.1, England. *Office: London Times,* Gray's Inn Rd., London WC1X 8EZ, England.

CAREER: Oxford University, Oxford, England, research fellow at New College, 1971-74; British Broadcasting Corp., London, England, member of staff, 1974-76; *London Times,* London, staff writer, 1977—.

WRITINGS: *The Call to Seriousness: The Evangelical Impact on the Victorians*, J. Cape, 1975; *William Morris and His World*, Thames & Hudson, 1977; *The Optimists: Themes and Personalities in Victorian Liberalism*, Faber, 1980. Writer for British Broadcasting Corp. Contributor to *History Today*. Member of editorial board of *New Universities Quarterly*.

WORK IN PROGRESS: A book on the English middle classes, publication by Collins expected in 1982.

SIDELIGHTS: Bradley commented: "I am interested in reporting on both the traditional and contemporary English political, social, and cultural scene." *Avocational interests:* Gilbert & Sullivan, nonconformist hymns, liberalism, tea shops in spa towns, provincial museums.

* * *

BRADLEY, Omar Nelson 1893-1981

OBITUARY NOTICE: Born February 12, 1893, in Clark, Mo.; died of cardiac arrest, April 4, 1981, in New York, N.Y.; buried in Arlington National Cemetary, Arlington, Va. Military officer, business executive, and author. The last of the nation's five-star generals, Bradley was best known as the leader of the historic Normandy invasion and as the first chairman of the Joint Chiefs of Staff. Bradley graduated from West Point in 1915, and although he was a career soldier he never saw action on the battlefield until he was fifty years old. Then, from 1943 to 1945, he led some of the bloodiest combat of the Second World War, including the defeat of the Germans' Afrika Korps, the invasion of Sicily, and, as commander of the U.S. First Army, the invasion of Normandy. Known as "the G.I.'s general," Bradley held twenty-eight different posts before he became a five-star general. By the end of World War II he had earned four stars and was commander of the Twelfth Army, the largest American force ever united under one man's command. After the war Bradley headed the Veterans Administration and was appointed the first chairman of the Joint Chiefs of Staff. It was at this time that he was awarded his fifth star. After two terms as head of the Joint Chiefs, Bradley joined the Bulova Watch Company where he was chairman from 1958 to 1973. Since, by act of Congress, five-star generals cannot retire, Bradley remained in the military until his death, thus having served sixty-nine years on active duty, longer than any other American soldier in history. He wrote *A Soldier's Story*. Obituaries and other sources: *International Who's Who*, Europa, 1980; *New York Times*, April 9, 1981; *Newsweek*, April 20, 1981; *Time*, April 20, 1981.

* * *

BRADSHAW, Gillian (Marucha) 1956-

PERSONAL: Born May 14, 1956, in Virginia; daughter of James Stanford (a professor) and Joan (a secretary; maiden name, Rouquette) Bradshaw; married Robin Christopher Ball (a research physicist), June 27, 1981. *Education:* University of Michigan, B.A. (with honors), 1977; Newnham College, Cambridge, M.A., 1979. *Politics:* "Liberal non-partisan." *Religion:* Anglican. *Home address:* c/o 324 Hiawatha Dr., Mount Pleasant, Mich. 48858. *Agent:* Lois Wallace, Wallace & Sheil Agency, Inc., 177 East 70th St., New York, N.Y. 10021.

CAREER: Writer, 1980—. *Awards, honors:* Jule and Avery Hopwood Award from University of Michigan, 1977, for *Hawk of May*.

WRITINGS: *Hawk of May*, Simon & Schuster, 1980; *Kingdom of Summer*, Simon & Schuster, 1981; *In Winter's Shadow*, Simon & Schuster, in press.

WORK IN PROGRESS: Another novel.

SIDELIGHTS: Gillian Bradshaw commented: "I write for pleasure, and never expected to be published so soon. However, far be it from me to look a gift horse in the mouth.

"I'm still very interested in the Greek and Latin classics. I love traveling, and spend some time every year touring cheaply. I am about to study French in Paris."

BIOGRAPHICAL/CRITICAL SOURCES: *New York Times Book Review*, May 31, 1981.

* * *

BRADY, Sally Ryder 1939-

PERSONAL: Born May 26, 1939, in Boston, Mass.; daughter of Francis C. (an administrator) and Dorothy (Childs) Ryder; married Upton R. Brady (director of Atlantic Monthly Press), November 17, 1962; children: Sarah, Andrew, Nathaniel, Alexander. *Education:* Attended Barnard College, 1956-57, 1960-61. *Politics:* Independent. *Religion:* Roman Catholic. *Residence:* Bedford, Mass.

CAREER: Writer.

WRITINGS: *Instar* (novel), Doubleday, 1976. Contributor to *Boston Review of the Arts* and newspapers.

WORK IN PROGRESS: *Ferly Stick* a novel; *Bolt*, a novel.

SIDELIGHTS: Sally Brady wrote: "Following a brief theatrical career, I had four children in five years, thereby limiting extra activities. While writing my first novel, I recognized the similarity between acting and writing, both arts demanding the same energetic and economical projection into other characters. This likeness intrigues me and makes me eager to attempt a screenplay at some point.

"I am also interested in psychic and electromagnetic energy and their effects on people. Thus far, my novels have been about fear and power. For lack of a better label, I call them psychological thrillers."

* * *

BRAINERD, Charles Jon 1944-

PERSONAL: Born July 30, 1944, in Lansing, Mich.; son of Charles Donald and Geraldine Elaine Brainerd; married Susan Haske (an audiologist), January 18, 1964; children: Tereasa Gail. *Education:* Michigan State University, B.S., 1966, M.A., 1968, Ph.D., 1970. *Home:* 431 Huron St., London, Ontario, Canada. *Office:* Department of Psychology, University of Western Ontario, London, Ontario, Canada.

CAREER: University of Windsor, Windsor, Ontario, assistant professor of psychology, 1970-71; University of Alberta, Edmonton, assistant professor, 1971-73, associate professor, 1973-76, professor of psychology, 1976; University of Western Ontario, London, professor of psychology, 1976—. *Member:* Canadian Psychological Association (fellow), American Psychological Association (fellow), American Association for the Advancement of Science, Society for Research in Child Development.

WRITINGS: (With L. S. Siegel) *Alternatives to Piaget*, Academic Press, 1978; *Piaget's Theory of Intelligence*, Prentice-Hall, 1978; *Structural/Process Models of Complex Human Behavior*, Sijthoff & Noordhoff, 1979; *Origins of the Number Concept*, Praeger, 1979; *Children's Logical and Mathematical Cognition*, Springer-Verlag, 1981. Editor of "Series in

Cognitive Development,'' Springer-Verlag. Contributor to education and psychology journals. Editor of *Progress in Cognitive Development Research;* associate editor of *Behavioral and Brain Sciences* and *Child Development.*

WORK IN PROGRESS: Piaget's Theory of Intelligence, 2nd edition; research on mathematical models of development and working-memory theories of cognitive development.

*   *   *

BRANDELL, (Erik) Gunnar 1916-

PERSONAL: Born October 1, 1916, in Soedertaelje, Sweden; son of Georg Albert and Frida Olavia (Franck) Brandell; married Kerstin K. V. Joenson (a teacher), 1937; children: Lars, Gerd (Mrs. Peter Becker), Inga (Mrs. Fausto Guidice), Eva (Mrs. Lars-Aake Brus). *Education:* University of Uppsala, Fil.mag., 1936; University of Stockholm, Fil.dr., 1950. *Home:* Murklevaegen 1, Uppsala, Sweden 752 46. *Office:* Litrraturvetenskapliga institutionen, Box 513, Uppsala, Sweden 751 20.

CAREER: High school teacher of Swedish language and literature in Storvik, Sweden, 1936-46; *Goeteborgs handelstidning,* Goeteborg, Sweden, Paris correspondent, 1946-48; *Svenska dagbladet,* Stockholm, Sweden, cultural editor, 1951-62; University of Uppsala, Uppsala, Sweden, professor of literary history, 1963—, dean of faculty, 1977-80. Lecturer at about thirty universities in the United States and Europe. Organizer of international Strindberg symposia, 1973—. *Military service:* Swedish Army, 1938-40. Swedish Navy, 1941-43; became lieutenant. *Member:* International P.E.N., Swedish Psychoanalytical Society (honorary member), Academie septentrionale Paris, Strindberg Society (chairman, 1965-75), Royal Academy of Letters and History, Royal Scientific Society. *Awards, honors:* Several prizes from Swedish Academy.

WRITINGS: Strindbergs Infernekris, [Sweden], 1950, translation by Barry Jacobs published as *Strindberg in Inferno,* Harvard University Press, 1974; *Freud och sekelslutet,* [Sweden], 1970, translation by Iain White published as *Freud: A Man of His Century,* Humanities, 1979.

In Swedish; all published in Sweden: *Bekaennare och uppfostrare* (title means ''Confessors and Educators''), 1937; *Den europeiska nihilismen* (title means ''The European Nihilism''), 1943; *Paa Strindbergs vaegar genom Frankrike* (title means ''On Strindberg's Roads Through France''), 1949; *Aattital och nittital* (title means ''The Eighties and the Nineties''), 1957; *Svensk litteratur, 1900-1950* (title means ''Swedish Literature, 1900-1950''), 1958, 2nd edition, 1967; *Vid seklets kaellor* (title means ''At the Sources of the Century''), 1961; *Konsten att citera* (title means ''The Art of Quoting''), 1968; *Skolreform och universitetskris* (title means ''School Reform and University Crisis''), 1969; *Drama i tre avsnitt* (title means ''Drama in Three Parts''), 1971; *Revolt i dikt* (title means ''Revolt in Literature''), 1977.

WORK IN PROGRESS: Research on Strindberg.

SIDELIGHTS: Brandell told *CA:* ''My main interest has been the new problematic view of man which emerged in the late years of the nineteenth century (with Strindberg and Freud) and connected with it the question, 'What kind of a humanism is possible in the light of these and other experiences?' That is why I took great interest in French existential literature in the forties. I have also devoted myself to literary and other cooperation on an international scale, thereby following a tradition in Swedish literary history.''

BRATT, Elmer Clark 1901-1970

OBITUARY NOTICE—See index for *CA* sketch: Born November 12, 1901, in Arapahoe, Neb.; died November 9, 1970. Educator and author. Bratt began his career as a teacher in 1918, becoming a principal and then superintendant of schools in Nebraska. He worked briefly at the National Bureau of Economics before joining the economics faculty at Lehigh University in 1929. There he became a professor of economics in 1941, serving as chairman of the department from 1958 to 1965 and as director of the Business Economic Center from 1966 to 1970. His writings include *Business Cycles and Forecasting, This Unbalanced World,* and *Business Forecasting.* His most recent book, *Availability and Reliability of Inventory Data Needed to Study Economic Change,* was published by the U.S. Bureau of the Budget in 1961. Obituaries and other sources: *Who Was Who in America,* 6th edition, Marquis, 1976.

*   *   *

BREDVOLD, Louis I(gnatius) 1888-1977

OBITUARY NOTICE—See index for *CA* sketch: Born July 20, 1888, in Springfield, Minn.; died February 9, 1977, in Tucson, Ariz. Educator and author. Bredvold was a professor of English at the University of Michigan until 1958. Among his writings are *The Brave New World of the Enlightenment, The Natural History of Sensibility,* and *The Relevance of Edmund Burke.* In 1973 Ronald Press Co. published a third edition of *Eighteenth Century Poetry and Prose,* a book Bredvold edited with others. (Date of death provided by wife, Emilie Bredvold.)

*   *   *

BREUGELMANS, Rene 1925-

PERSONAL: Born August 16, 1925, in Antwerp, Belgium; son of Frans (a school principal) and Josephine Maria (a teacher; maiden name, Hubrecht) Breugelmans; married Margaret Prud'homme, February 26, 1949; children: Nelly Breugelmans de Roeck. *Education:* University of Ghent, Lic. en Philosophie et Lettres (summa cum laude), 1948, Agrege de l'Enseignement Moyen du Degre Superieur (cum laude), 1948, Dr. en Philosophie et Lettres (maxima cum laude), 1953. *Home:* 330 15th Ave., Apt. 305, Calgary, Alberta, Canada T2R 0P8. *Office:* Department of Germanic Studies, University of Calgary, Calgary, Alberta, Canada T2N 1N4.

CAREER: Institut Royal Colonial Belge (now Academie Royale des Sciences), Tervuren, Belgium, scientific collaborator at Bureau de Documentation, 1948-49; Athenee Royal d'Elisabethville, Elisabethville, Congo (now Zaire), professor of Germanic languages, 1949-56; Athenee Royal d'Usumbura, Usumbura, Ruanda-Urundi (now Bujumbura, Burundi), professor of Germanic languages, 1955-56; Universite Officielle du Congo Belge et du Ruanda-Urundi, Elisabethville, docent, 1956-60, professor of German, English, and African ethnology, 1960-61; University of Calgary, Calgary, Alberta, assistant professor, 1961-65, associate professor, 1965-71, professor of modern languages, 1971—. Professor at Institut Preuniversitaire d'Usumbura, 1955-56, and Institut Preuniversitaire d'Elisabethville, 1956-57; visiting assistant professor at University of Alberta, summer, 1962; visiting associate professor at University of Texas, summer, 1966; public speaker; guest on radio and television programs. Research assistant at Museum of Central Africa, 1948-49.

MEMBER: International Comparative Literature Association, Internationaler Verein fuer Germanistic, Internationale Vereniging voor Neerlandistiek, Internationale Hofmannsthal-Gesellschaft, Canadian Association of Teachers of German, Canadian Association of University Teachers, Canadian Association for the Advancement of Netherlandic Studies (founding member), Overseas Institute of Canada, American Comparative Literature Association, American Association of Teachers of German, Modern Language Association of America, Association of Germanists (Belgium), Philological Association of the Pacific Coast, Pacific Northwest Conference on Foreign Languages. *Awards, honors:* Grant from Belgium's National Fund for Scientific Research, 1960-61; Canada Council grants, 1965, 1973, 1976, fellowship, 1968-69; research grant from University of Calgary, 1980.

WRITINGS: Jacques Perk, Twayne, 1974. Contributor of about fifty articles to scholarly journals. Co-editor of *Canadian Ethnic Studies,* 1971-75.

WORK IN PROGRESS: Research on comparative literature; research on literature and depth-psychology.

SIDELIGHTS: Breugelmans told *CA:* "My earlier articles deal mainly with thematic studies in comparative literature and studies of influence and reception. I have done studies comparing Oscar Wilde with such writers as Baudelaire, Renan, Sainte-Beuve, Hugo von Hofmannsthal, and Stefan George. I have also studied the critical reception of Wilde in Holland and Flanders, the Dutch-Flemish ethnic group in Canada, and 'alienation' in literature.

"The book on Jacques Perk and more recent articles deal with a method of literary criticism combining the viewpoints of traditional literary analysis, ethnology (social anthropology), and depth-psychological theories, mainly those of Freud and Jung. From this point of view, Novalis, Jacques Perk, and Hofmannsthal are interpreted in various articles. A study, 'Herman Hesse and Depth Psychology,' in the *Canadian Review of Comparative Literature* is in press."

*   *   *

BRIGHTBILL, Charles K(estner) 1910-1966

OBITUARY NOTICE—See index for *CA* sketch: Born February 15, 1910, in Reading, Pa.; died August 22, 1966. Recreation specialist, educator, and author. From 1934 to 1951 Brightbill worked for governmental departments of recreation, where he served in administrative capacities. He joined the University of Illinois at Urbana-Champaign as a professor of recreation in 1951 and became head of the department of recreation and municipal park administration in 1956. His writings include *Community Recreation: A Guide to Its Organization and Administration,* fifth edition published as *Leisure Services: The Organized Recreation and Park System* by Prentice-Hall in 1975; *Man and Leisure: A Philosophy of Recreation,* revised and condensed edition published by Prentice-Hall as *The Challenge of Leisure* in 1963; and *Educating for Leisure-Centered Living,* second edition published by Wiley in 1977. (Date of death provided by D. James Brademas of the University of Illinois.)

*   *   *

BRITT, Albert 1874-1969

OBITUARY NOTICE—See index for *CA* sketch: Born November 26, 1874, in Utah, Ill.; died February 18, 1969, in Worcester, Mass. Educator, historian, editor, and author. Britt began his career in 1900 as an editor of magazines. In 1925 he became the president of Knox College in Galesbury,

Illinois, a post he held until 1936 when he joined the Associated Colleges of Claremont as a professor of history. He was the author of *Wind's Will, Boys' Own Book of Frontiersmen, The Great Biographers, Great Indian Chiefs,* and *An America That Was,* among others. Obituaries and other sources: *National Cyclopedia of American Biography,* Volume 57, James T. White, 1977.

*   *   *

BROADHEAD, Helen Cross 1913-
(Helen Reeder Cross)

PERSONAL: Born August 26, 1913, in Wilmington, N.C.: daughter of Arthur Maurice and Helen (Newbold) Cross; married Edward Hall Broadhead, June 5, 1936 (divorced, 1961); children: David Edward, Cynthia Newbold (Mrs. Phillip M. Joseph). *Education:* Duke University, A.B., 1935; Trinity College, Hartford, Conn., M.A., 1958. *Politics:* Independent. *Religion:* Presbyterian. *Home:* Larchmont Palmer House, 1299 Palmer Ave., Larchmont, N.Y. *Agent:* Dorothy Markinko, McIntosh & Otis, 475 5th Ave., New York, N.Y. 10017.

CAREER: University of Hartford, Hartford, Conn., instructor in English, 1958-61; St. Margaret's School, Waterbury, Conn., English department head, 1961-67; Master's School, Dobbs Ferry, N.Y., English teacher, 1967-78; Westchester Community College, Valhalla, N.Y., adjunct professor, 1968—.

WRITINGS—All under name Helen Reeder Cross; all for children: *Life in Lincoln's America,* Random House, 1964; *A Curiosity for the Curious,* illustrated by Margot Tomes, Coward, 1978; *The Real Tom Thumb,* illustrated by Stephen Gammell, Four Winds Press, 1980. Contributor of stories and articles to newspapers and periodicals, including the *New York Times, Gourmet, History Today, English Journal,* and *New England Galaxy.*

WORK IN PROGRESS: Isabella, "a semi-autobiographical book about an eleven-year-old girl's life in the Tennessee mountains in the late 1920's."

*   *   *

BROCK, Emma L(illian) 1886-1974

OBITUARY NOTICE—See index for *CA* sketch: Born June 11, 1886, in Fort Shaw, Mont.; died August 17, 1974. Librarian, illustrator, and author. Brock was a librarian at the Minneapolis and New York Public Libraries between 1914 and 1932. She was the author and illustrator of thirty-five children's books, including *Runaway Sardine, To Market, to Market, One Little Indian Boy, Topsy Turvy Family, Ballet for Mary,* and *Sudden Mary on Roller Skates.* Obituaries and other sources: *Something About the Author,* Volume 8, Gale, 1976.

*   *   *

BRODIE, H(arlowe) Keith H(ammond) 1939-

PERSONAL: Born August 24, 1939, in Stamford, Conn.; son of Lawrence Sheldon and Elizabeth (Hammond) Brodie; married Brenda Ann Barrowclough (a nurse), January, 1967; children: Melissa Verdiun, Cameron Keith, Tyler Hammond, Bryson Barrowclough. *Education:* Princeton University, A.B., 1961; Columbia University, M.D., 1965. *Religion:* Presbyterian. *Home:* 63 Beverly Dr., Durham, N.C. 27707. *Office:* Department of Psychiatry, Medical Center, Duke University, Durham, N.C. 27710.

CAREER: Ochsner Foundation Hospital, New Orleans, La., intern, 1965-66; Columbia-Presbyterian Medical Center, New York, N.Y., assistant resident in psychiatry, 1966-68; National Institute of Mental Health, Laboratory of Clinical Science, Bethesda, Md., clinical associate in psychiatry section, 1968-70; Stanford University, Stanford, Calif., assistant professor of psychiatry, 1970-74, program director at General Clinical Research Center, 1973-74, chairman of medical school faculty senate and member of executive committee of School of Medicine, 1972-73; Duke University, Durham, N.C., professor of psychiatry and chairman of department, 1974—, adjunct professor of psychology, 1978—, senior lecturer in law, 1979—, member of executive committee of academic council, 1976-78, chief of Psychiatry Service at Duke Hospital, 1979—.

Certified ship's surgeon by U.S. Merchant Marine, 1966; certified by American Board of Psychiatry and Neurology, 1971, examiner, 1974—; postdoctoral fellow in community and social psychiatry at School of Public Health and Administrative Medicine, Columbia University, 1966-68; member of staff at Durham County General Hospital, 1978—. Member of President's biomedical research panel interdisciplinary cluster on pharmacology, substance abuse, and environmental toxicology, 1975, and National Advisory Council on Alcoholism and Alcohol Abuse, 1974-78; member of National Academy of Sciences Institute of Medicine, 1980—. Member of Area Mental Health Board, 1975—, chairman, 1980-81, now vice-president; member of North Carolina Alcoholism Research Authority, 1976—; vice-president of board of trustees of Durham Academy. *Military service:* U.S. Public Health Service, assistant surgeon, 1968-70.

MEMBER: American Association for the Advancement of Science, American Psychiatric Association (fellow; secretary and member of board of trustees and member of executive committee of board of trustees, all 1977-81), American Medical Association, American Psychosomatic Society, American College of Psychiatrists (fellow; chairman of publications committee, 1980—), American Association of Medical Colleges (member of council of academic societies, 1978—), Society of Biological Psychiatry, Society for Neuroscience, Group for Advancement of Psychiatry, Royal College of Psychiatrists, Southern Psychiatric Association, Southern Medical Association, North Carolina Neuropsychiatric Society, North Carolina Medical Society, Durham-Orange County Medical Society, Sigma Xi, Alpha Omega Alpha. *Awards, honors:* Dean Echols Award from Ochsner Foundation Hospital, 1965, for medical writing; Sol Ginsburg fellow of Group for the Advancement of Psychiatry, 1967-68; A. E. Bennett Clinical Research Award from Society of Biological Psychiatry, 1970, for original research in biological psychiatry; Psychopharmacology Award from American Psychological Association, 1971, for original research in psychopharmacology; Edward A. Strecker, M.D. Award from Institute of Pennsylvania Hospital, 1980, for outstanding contribution to the treatment of mental illness.

WRITINGS: (Editor and contributor) *American Handbook of Psychiatry,* Basic Books, Volume VI (with D. A. Hamburg; Brodie was not associated with earlier volumes), 1975, Volume VII (with Silvano Arieti), 1981; (editor with J. P. Brady) *Controversy in Psychiatry,* Saunders, 1977; (with J. L. Houpt, C. S. Orleans, and L. K. George) *The Importance of Mental Health Services to General Health Care,* Ballinger, 1979; (editor with Brady) *Psychiatry at the Crossroads,* Saunders, 1981; (editor with Jesse Cavenar) *Critical Problems in Psychiatry,* Lippincott, 1981.

Contributor: A. R. Foley, editor, *The Institute for Training in Community and Social Psychiatry,* Behavioral Publications, 1972; Seymour Levine, editor, *Hormones and Behavior,* Academic Press, 1972; Jules Masserman, editor, *Science and Psychoanalysis,* Grune, 1972; J. D. Barchas and Eugene Usdin, editors, *Serotonin and Behavior,* Academic Press, 1973; Carl Eisdorfer and W. E. Fann, editors, *Psychopharmacology and Aging,* Plenum, 1973; E. A. Spegel, editor, *Progress in Neurology and Psychiatry,* Volume XXVIII, Grune, 1974; R. C. Friedman, R. M. Richart, and R. L. Vande Wiele, editors, *Sex Differences in Behavior,* Wiley, 1974; A. H. Leighton, editor, *Further Explorations in Social Psychiatry,* Basic Books, 1975; E. W. Busse and Daniel G. Balzer, editors, *Handbook of Geriatric Psychiatry,* Van Nostrand, 1978; Barchas, Hamburg, and P. A. Berger, editors, *Psychiatry and Behavioral Sciences,* Oxford University Press, 1981.

Also contributor to *Drug Use in America: Problems in Perspective,* Volume I: *Patterns and Consequences of Drug Abuse,* National Commission on Marijuana and Drug Abuse, 1973; *The Impact of Science on Society,* United Nations Educational, Scientific, and Cultural Organization, 1973; *Research in the Service of Mental Health,* U.S. Government Printing Office, 1975; and *Comprehensive Textbook of Psychiatry,* Volume III, 1980.

Editor of "Psychiatry Sub-Series" in "Primary Care Series," for Addison-Wesley. Contributor to *Encyclopedia Americana* and *Encyclopaedia Britannica.* Contributor of more than fifty articles to medical and scientific journals. Member of editorial board of *Psychiatry Digest,* 1971—, and *Excerpta Medica-Psychiatry,* 1976—; associate editor of *American Journal of Psychiatry,* 1973-81.

WORK IN PROGRESS: Editing 10th edition of *Modern Clinical Psychiatry,* with Lawrence Kolb, for publication by Saunders.

*   *   *

BROGAN, Elise
   See URCH, Elizabeth

*   *   *

BRONSON, Wolfe
   See RABORG, Frederick A(shton), Jr.

*   *   *

BROOK, Victor John Knight   1887-1974

OBITUARY NOTICE—See index for *CA* sketch: Born June 22, 1887, in Bradford, Yorkshire, England; died in July, 1974. Chaplain and author. Brook was a curate at Wakefield Cathedral from 1912 to 1915 and at James Church in London from 1915 to 1916. Afterwards he was an assistant master at Charterhouse in Godalming before becoming a fellow and chaplain at Oxford University in 1921. Among his books are *The Claims of Duty, Divine Justice,* and *A Life of Archbishop Parker.* Obituaries and other sources: *Who's Who,* 125th edition, St. Martin's, 1973; *London Times,* July 3, 1974. (Date of death provided by second wife, Janet R. Brook.)

*   *   *

BROOMFIELD, Gerald W(ebb)   1895-1976

OBITUARY NOTICE—See index for *CA* sketch: Born May 26, 1895, in London, England; died in September, 1976. Anglican priest and author. Broomfield was a church administrator for education in East Africa and the canon chancellor of Zanzibar Cathedral. In 1936 he became general secretary of Universities' Mission to Central Africa, where he also served as vice-president after 1962. Broomfield was the author of *John, Peter, and the Fourth Gospel, Revelation and Reunion, The Chosen People; or, The Bible, Christianity, and Race,* and *Towards Freedom.* He also wrote a number of educational books in Swahili, including *Saruti ya Kiswahili.* (Date of death provided by wife, Charlotte Helen Broomfield.)

*   *   *

BROTHERS, (M.) Jay 1931-

PERSONAL: Born June 4, 1931, in Bronx, N.Y.; son of Henry Albert and Gladys (Rappaport) Hudson-Brothers; married Ferne Hoffman (a designer), April 9, 1954; children: Harlan Jay, Eric Mitchell, Meredith Ann. *Education:* Cornell University, B.S., 1954. *Politics:* Liberal Democrat. *Religion:* Jewish. *Home:* 300 Central Park W., New York, N.Y. 10024.

CAREER: McCann Erickson Advertising, group head, 1958-64; Benton & Bowles (advertising agency), New York City, group head, 1964-65; Grey Advertising, New York City, vice-president and associate creative director, 1965-68; Norman, Craig, Kummel (advertising agency), senior vice-president and creative director, 1968-70; free-lance writer. *Military service:* U.S. Air Force, pilot, 1954-57; became first lieutenant.

WRITINGS: Julie, Bobbs-Merrill, 1974; *Ox,* Bobbs-Merrill, 1975.

Author of "Power Play," a film, and short stories.

WORK IN PROGRESS: A sequel to "Power Play."

SIDELIGHTS: Brothers commented: "It was my love of the language, combined with the stifling atmosphere of advertising, that drove me to the typewriter at the age of forty. My wife and I have always put a premium on travel and have taken the family to Spain, North and West Africa, the Caribbean, and the Far East."

*   *   *

BROWN, Archibald Haworth 1938-

PERSONAL: Born in 1938 in Annan, Scotland; son of Alexander Douglas (a minister of Church of Scotland) and Mary (Yates) Brown; married Patricia Susan Cornwell, March 23, 1963; children: Susan Woolford, Alexander Douglas. *Education:* Attended City of Westminster College, 1958-59; London School of Economics and Political Science, London, B.Sc. (with first class honors), 1962; Oxford University, M.A., 1972. *Home:* 407 Banbury Rd., Oxford OX2 6JF, England. *Office:* St. Antony's College, Oxford University, Oxford OX2 6JF, England.

CAREER: University of Glasgow, Glasgow, Scotland, lecturer in politics, 1964-71; Oxford University, Oxford, England, lecturer in Soviet institutions and fellow of St. Antony's College, 1971—. British Council exchange scholar at Moscow University, 1967-68; visiting professor and Stimson Lecturer at Yale University and visiting professor at University of Connecticut, both 1980. *Member:* Political Studies Association of the United Kingdom (Communist Politics Group), British National Association for Soviet and East European Studies.

WRITINGS: Soviet Politics and Political Science, Macmillan, 1974, St. Martin's 1976; (editor with Michael Kaser) *The Soviet Union Since the Fall of Khrushchev,* Macmillan, 1975, 2nd edition, 1978, Free Press, 1976; (editor with Jack Gray)

Political Culture and Political Change in Communist States, Holmes & Meier, 1977, 2nd edition, 1979; (editor with T. H. Rigby and Peter Reddaway) *Authority, Power, and Policy in the U.S.S.R.,* St. Martin's, 1980; (editor with John Fennell, Kaser, and H.T. Willetts) *Encyclopedia of Russia and the Soviet Union,* Cambridge University Press, 1981. General editor of St. Anthony's College, Oxford, and Macmillan book series, 1977—. Member of editorial board of *British Journal of Political Science* and *Studies in Comparative Communism.*

WORK IN PROGRESS: Political Change Within Communist Systems; Political Culture and Communist Studies.

*   *   *

BROWN, Derek Ernest Denny
See DENNY-BROWN, Derek Ernest

*   *   *

BROWNMILLER, Susan 1935-

PERSONAL: Born February 15, 1935, in Brooklyn, N.Y. *Education:* Attended Cornell University, 1952-55, and Jefferson School of Social Sciences. *Home:* 61 Jane St., New York, N.Y. 10014.

CAREER: Actress in New York City, 1955-59; *Coronet,* New York City, assistant to managing editor, 1959-60; *Albany Report,* Albany, N.Y., editor, 1961-62; *Newsweek,* New York City, national affairs researcher, 1963-64; *Village Voice,* New York City, staff writer, 1965; American Broadcasting Co. (ABC-TV), New York City, network newswriter, 1966-68; free-lance journalist, 1968-70; writer. Lecturer; organizer of Women Against Pornography. *Member:* New York Radical Feminists (co-founder). *Awards, honors:* Grants from Alicia Patterson Foundation and Louis M. Rabinowitz Foundation; *Against Our Will: Men, Women, and Rape* was listed among the outstanding books of the year by *New York Times Book Review,* 1975; named one of *Time*'s twelve Women of the Year, 1975.

WRITINGS: Shirley Chisholm: A Biography (juvenile), Doubleday, 1971; *Against Our Will: Men, Women, and Rape* (Book-of-the-Month Club selection), Simon & Schuster, 1975. Contributor of articles to magazines, including *Newsweek, Esquire,* and *New York Times Magazine.*

WORK IN PROGRESS: A study of femininity, for Simon & Schuster.

SIDELIGHTS: Brownmiller was among the first of the politically active feminists in New York City during the 1960's. In 1968 she helped to found the New York Radical Feminists, and as a member of that group she took part in a number of protest demonstrations, including a sit-in at the offices of the *Ladies' Home Journal* opposing the magazine's "demeaning" attitude toward women. Her interest in women's liberation surfaced in much of her work as a free-lance journalist, and one article she wrote, about Shirley Chisholm, the first black U.S. congresswoman, developed into a biography for young readers. In 1971 Brownmiller helped to organize a "Speak-Out on Rape," and in the process she realized that once again she had the material for a book. She submitted an outline of her idea to Simon & Schuster, they contracted for the book, and Brownmiller began researching the subject of rape. After four years of research and writing, she published *Against Our Will: Men, Women, and Rape.*

Against Our Will explores the history of rape, exploding the myths that, the author says, influence our modern perspective. She traces the political use of rape in war from biblical times through Vietnam, explains the origins of American rape laws, and examines the subjects of interracial rape, homosexual rape, and child molestation. Brownmiller asserts that rape "is nothing more or less than a conscious process of intimidation by which *all men* keep *all women* in a state of fear." Supporting her thesis with facts taken from her extensive research in history, literature, sociology, law, psychoanalysis, mythology, and criminology, Brownmiller argues that rape is not a sexual act but an act of power based on an "anatomical fiat"; it is the result of early man's realization that women could be subjected to "a thoroughly detestable physical conquest from which there could be no retaliation in kind."

A best seller and a Book-of-the-Month Club selection, *Against Our Will* was serialized in four magazines; and its nationwide tour made Brownmiller a celebrity. Her appearance on the cover of *Time* as one of the twelve Women of the Year and on television talk shows as a frequent guest confirmed the timeliness of her book. Brownmiller herself remarked, "I saw it as a once-in-a-lifetime subject that had somehow crossed my path," and she expressed gratitude to the women's movement for having given her "a constructive way" to use her rage.

Since Brownmiller's analysis of rape presented a new and controversial viewpoint to an already provocative subject, *Against Our Will* was received with mixed and at times passionate reviews. Women lauded the book. Editor Carol Eisen Rinzler expressed her regret that Simon & Schuster, and not she, had published *Against Our Will*. "It is one of the two books I lay awake nights lusting after," she said. Mary Ellen Gale, reviewing for the *New York Times Book Review*, said Brownmiller's book "deserves a place on the shelf next to those rare books about social problems which force us to make connections we have too long evaded, and change the way we feel about what we know." And reviewer Helen E. Schwartz, writing in the *Nation*, indicated the significance *Against Our Will* held for women by relating, "One friend told me that the book was 'so politically important that any criticism you might have of it is secondary.'" Schwartz was also told that if she said anything bad about the book she would be regarded "as an Aunt Thomasina, or whatever the women's movement equivalent is of Uncle Tom."

Described in *Time* as "a kind of *Whole Earth Catalog* of man's inhumanity to women," *Against Our Will* at the same time won the applause of male critics. *Village Voice* critic Eliot Fremont-Smith praised it as "a landmark work in the literature of awareness. . . . Whatever its distorted premises and internal contradictions . . . [it] is a most important, eye-and-mind-opening book." Michael F. McCauley concurred when he said in *Commonweal*: "*Against Our Will* is a poignant, candid, and long overdue analysis of a subject that concerns all. As long as present legal outlooks and cultural mythologies prevail, we are, each one of us, victims of this unspeakable attack on our humanity."

In a review for *Village Voice*, Rinzler said, "It seems evident that 'Against Our Will' will stand up as a major work of history, a classic, if you will," but she also noted that "Brownmiller expects criticism." Indeed, because as Diane Johnson of the *New York Review of Books* observed, "no other subject, it seems, is experienced so differently by men and women as rape. . . . There are really two audiences for it [*Against Our Will*], one which will know much of what she [Brownmiller] has to say already, and another which is ill-equipped by training or sympathy to understand it at all."

The *National Review*'s M. J. Sobran, Jr., criticized Brownmiller, her book, and her supporters. He excoriated favorable *Village Voice* reviews by Fremont-Smith and Rinzler, labeling Rinzler as "some dizzy feminist," and ridiculed Brownmiller's scholarship and work as intellectually and stylistically sloppy. "The whole point of her book is the tendentiousness of her research," Sobran declared. "What she is engaged in, really, is not scholarship but henpecking—that conscious process of intimidation by which all women keep all men in terror."

Other critics shared Sobran's contention that Brownmiller's research was tendentious. *New Leader* critic Ellen Chesler maintained: "While helping to organize a feminist speak-out on rape, Susan Brownmiller made a discovery: Rape could be seen as an extraordinary historical metaphor, a fundamental 'way of looking at male-female relations, at sex, at strength, and at power. Now . . . she has given us a book that jams the facts—against their will—into the Procrustean bed of her original 'moment of revelation.'" In a review for *Commentary*, Michael Novak also complained that Brownmiller's assertions "are surrounded with much rhetoric, a great smokescreen of 'research,' evidence so selective and reasoning so tendentious that to contend against them is to involve oneself in intellectual corruption." Agreeing that "sometimes the book is strident in its tone and one-sided in its presentation," Helene E. Schwartz nevertheless argued that "we should recognize that anger and extremism may be necessary before we can reach the mean of re-education that this book advocates."

In researching and writing *Against Our Will*, Brownmiller was motivated by "a dual sense of purpose," theorized Carol Eisen Rinzler," a political desire that the book be of value to feminism, and a personal desire to make a lasting contribution to the body of thought." Brownmiller mentions yet another goal in her conclusion to *Against Our Will*, stating: "Fighting back. On a multiplicity of levels, that is the activity we must engage in, together, if we—women—are to redress the imbalance and rid ourselves and men of the ideology of rape. . . . My purpose in this book has been to give rape its history. Now we must deny it a future."

AVOCATIONAL INTERESTS: Travel.

BIOGRAPHICAL/CRITICAL SOURCES: Susan Brownmiller, *Against Our Will: Men, Women, and Rape*, Simon & Schuster, 1975; *Village Voice*, October 6, 1975; *New York Times Book Review*, October, 1975, December 28, 1975; *Time*, October 13, 1975, January 5, 1976; *Nation*, November 29, 1975; *Commonweal*, December 5, 1975; *New York Review of Books*, December 11, 1975; *New Statesman*, December 12, 1975; *New Leader*, January 5, 1976; *Commentary*, February, 1976; *National Review*, March 5, 1976.

—*Sketch by Lillian S. Sims*

*   *   *

BRUMMEL, Mark Joseph 1933-

PERSONAL: Born October 28, 1933, in Chicago, Ill.; son of Anthony William and Mary (Helmreich) Brummel. *Education:* Attended Loyola University of Los Angeles, 1952-55, Catholic University of America, A.B., 1956, S.T.L., 1961, M.S., 1964. *Religion:* Roman Catholic. *Home:* 400 North Euclid, Oak Park, Ill. 60302. *Office:* U.S. Catholic, 221 West Madison St., Chicago, Ill. 60606.

CAREER/WRITINGS: Entered Order of Claretians, 1952, ordained Roman Catholic priest, 1960; St. Jude Seminary, Momence, Ill., librarian and teacher, 1961-70; *U.S. Catholic*, Chicago, Ill., associate editor, 1971-72, editor, 1972—; Claretian Publications, Chicago, editor 1972—. Associated with Fides/Claretian Publications, Notre Dame, Ind., 1970—; editor of *Today,* 1970-71, and *Report,* 1972—. Member of board of directors of Eastern Province Claretians. 1973—; delegate to National Federation of Priests Councils, 1974-78; associated with Claretian Medical Center, 1976. *Member:* National Catholic Library Association, Associated Church Press, Catholic Press Association, Association of Chicago Priests.

* * *

BRUN, Ellen 1933-

PERSONAL: Born March 23, 1933, in Copenhagen, Denmark; daughter of Oscar Constantine and Julie (a translator; maiden name, Schepelern) Brun; married Jacques Hersh (a writer), October 13, 1964. *Education:* Attended Sorbonne, University of Paris, and University of Vienna; University of Copenhagen, D.Sc. *Residence:* Copenhagen, Denmark.

CAREER: Writer.

WRITINGS: (With husband, Jacques Hersh) *Socialist Korea,* Monthly Review Press, 1976; (with Hersh) *Kapitalismens udviklings system,* Gyldendal, 1972. Contributor to European and American journals.

WORK IN PROGRESS: An East-West project, with Hersh.

SIDELIGHTS: Ellen Brun wrote: "After working as a three-language secretary (Danish-German-French) I studied in France and Austria, where I met my husband. We have developed a close working relationship. We are very active in political debates in Denmark and are known as specialists in the field of international politics and the problems of underdevelopment. In order to survive as free-lance writers, we keep a rather modest standard of living and the highest respect for resources (both human and material)."

* * *

BRUNNER, Maurice Yaw 1950-
(Yaw Maurice Boateng)

PERSONAL: Born April 13, 1950, in Kumasi, Ghana; son of Charles Albert and Agnes Abenaa (Boateng) Brunner. *Education:* Swiss Federal Institute of Technology, Dipl. Bauing—E.T.H., 1976. *Religion:* Roman Catholic. *Home:* Solibodenstr 21, 8180 Buelach, Switzerland. *Office:* Institut Fuer H.T.B., ETH—Hoenggerberg, 8093 Zurich, Switzerland.

CAREER: Basler & Hofman, Zurich, Switzerland, civil engineer, 1977; Krarue Mercer & Partners, Accra, Ghana, civil engineer, 1978-79; Swiss Federal Institute of Technology, Zurich, assistant to professor, 1979—. *Member:* African Students Association (president, 1975-76), Ghana Institute of Engineers.

WRITINGS—Juvenile; under pseudonym Yaw Maurice Boateng: *The Return,* Heinemann, 1977.

Also author of five-act television play "Katier," first broadcast by Ghana Television, 1972.

WORK IN PROGRESS: To Kill a Lion and Other Stories.

SIDELIGHTS: Brunner told *CA:* "*The Return* is a novel of the slave trade in Ghana. Friendly questions by my Swiss hosts made me realize how ignorant I was of my country's pre-colonial history. I therefore made some research at the central library in Zurich and decided to write a novel as a modest contribution to lighting up Africa's 'unknown' past." *Avocational interests:* Athletics, boxing, soccer.

BRYAN, M(erwyn) Leonard 1937-

PERSONAL: Born September 25, 1937, in Decatur, Ind.; son of Lloyd (a teacher) and Nona Belle (Gunder) Bryan; children: Megan Wiley, Marc Leonard. *Education:* Indiana University, A.B., 1963; McGill University, M.Sc., 1965; University of Michigan, Ph.D., 1971. *Office:* Jet Propulsion Laboratory, 4800 Oak Grove Dr., Pasadena, Calif. 91106.

CAREER: Frostburg State College, Frostburg, Md., lecturer in geography, 1965-68; Environmental Research Institute of Michigan, Ann Arbor, research geographer, 1971-75; Jet Propulsion Laboratory, Pasadena, Calif., member of technical staff, 1975—; Glendale Community College, Glendale, Calif., instructor, 1976—. *Military service:* U.S. Navy, 1959-60. *Member:* International Glaciological Society, American Society of Photogrammetry, Association of American Geographers, Photogrammetric Society.

WRITINGS: (Editor) *Remote Sensing of Earth Resources: A Guide to Information Sources,* Gale, 1979. Contributor of about twenty articles to scientific journals. Review editor of *Remote Sensing Quarterly.*

WORK IN PROGRESS: A radar remote sensing slide set for use in public schools; research on applications of imaging radars to earth resources and on nonrenewable resources applications, including urban morphology, hydrology, and vegetation.

SIDELIGHTS: Bryan commented: "Due to the complex nature of the environment, it is doubtful if a single instrument or a set of instruments detecting and measuring a restricted portion of the electromagnetic spectrum will be suitable for obtaining a comprehensive view of a given scene. Consequently, work in the active microwave portion of the spectrum is continuing apace and will become increasingly important as we develop more accurate models of the radiative characteristics of the earth. Radars, such as Seasat and the SIR-A (Shuttle Imaging Radar) systems which operate from space, are sensitive to scene (physical) roughness and moisture characteristics as well as to angular variations between the components of the scene and the instrument. Thus, such instruments provide data about the observed scene that are not available from systems that operate in other (e.g., visible) portions of the spectrum. Consequently, the combination of such data will enhance our understanding of the interactive mechanisms and allow an expansion of our understanding of the earth's environment."

* * *

BRYANT, Willis Rooks 1892-1965

OBITUARY NOTICE—See index for *CA* sketch: Born August 22, 1892, in Portland, Ore.; died in 1965. Banker, real estate expert, and author of works in his fields. Bryant was vice-president of the Wells Fargo Bank when he accepted a position as president of Bryant-Johnson-Chamberlain Co. He was also vice-chairman of the Mortgage Bankers Association School of Mortgage Banking at Stanford University. He wrote *Mortgage Lending* and co-wrote *Home Mortgage Lending, California Real Estate and Land Development,* and *Profitable Farm Management.* (Date of death provided by wife, Fredda Bryant.)

BRYCHTA, Alex 1956-

PERSONAL: Surname is pronounced Bricktah; born January 13, 1956, in Prague, Czechoslovakia; son of Jan (a graphic designer) and Lida (a graphic designer; maiden name, Ambroz) Brychta. *Education:* London College of Printing, B.A., 1977; attended National Film School, Buckinghamshire, England, 1977-80. *Politics:* Conservative. *Home:* 9 Links View, Dollis Rd., London N-3, England.

CAREER: Writer, illustrator, and artist. Paintings shown in exhibitions at Gallery Mensch, Hamburg, Germany, 1967 and 1970, and at London and Preston, c. 1970. *Member:* British Film Institute.

WRITINGS: (Self-illustrated) *Numbers One to Ten and Back Again* (juvenile), Frank Book, 1977.

Illustrator: Perrott Philips, *When in Spain,* Dent, 1974; Helen Hoke, editor, *Ghostly, Grim, and Gruesome,* Dent, 1976; Hoke, editor, *Eerie, Weird, and Wicked,* Dent, 1977; Hoke, *The Little Riddle Book,* R. Enslow, 1977; David English, *Bee Gees Legend,* Entertainers Merchandise Management, 1979.

SIDELIGHTS: Brychta told *CA:* "I don't consider my experience as an illustrator wide enough to be able to comment on motivation or my modus operandi, except that up till now, my motivation has always been that of financial reward. The media I favor are virtually all, except oil. I prefer to draw in India ink and color the drawings with watercolors, inks, crayons, or markers.

"I was born in Czechoslovakia where I lived until the age of twelve and where my enthusiasm for art was constantly supressed by the educational authorities. I attended two schools in Prague and was almost daily punished in one form or another for attempting to draw in exercise books, on blotters, or just on scraps of paper under the desk. Ironically, my personal 'liberation' came with the Soviet occupation of Czechoslovakia in the fall of 1968. My parents decided to leave the country and we settled down in London. "In England things began to look up. The teachers at the William Ellis School in Highgate soon realized that art was my strong subject, and I was gradually allowed to drop most of the subjects in which I had no interest (math, chemistry, etc.) and substitute them with extra hours of drawing and painting."

AVOCATIONAL INTERESTS: Photography, automobile body designing, reading, music, sailing, swimming, squash, badminton, travel (especially to the United States).

*   *   *

BUCK, Robert N. 1914-

PERSONAL: Born January 29, 1914, in Elizabeth, N.J.; son of Abijan O. and Emilie F. (Bellingrath) Buck; married Jean Pearsall, February 21, 1938; children: Ferris Buck Urbanowski, Robert O. *Education:* Attended New York University and University of Maryland. *Politics:* Independent. *Home address:* P.O. Box 462, Moretown, Vt. 05660.

CAREER: Writer. Former captain, chief pilot, and adviser to president of Trans World Airlines. Member of Fayston Planning Commission. *Member:* Air Line Pilots Association, Soaring Society of America, Quiet Birdmen, Aero Club de France.

WRITINGS: Burning Up the Sky, Putnam, 1931; *Battling the Elements,* Putnam, 1933; *Weather Flying,* Macmillan, 1970; *Flying Know How,* Delacorte, 1974. Contributor to maga-

zines, including *Reader's Digest, Air Facts, Flying,* and *Flight Crew.*

WORK IN PROGRESS: Atmospheric research with a glider on thermals and standing waves.

*   *   *

BUCKINGHAM, Walter S(amuel), Jr. 1924-1967

OBITUARY NOTICE—See index for *CA* sketch: Born December 2, 1924, in Vero Beach, Fla.; died May, 1967. Economist, educator, and author of works in his field. Buckingham taught at the Georgia Institute of Technology and Drexel University, and served as a member of the U.S. House of Representatives Unemployment-Automation Subcommittee in 1961. His writings include *Theoretical Economic Systems* and *Automation: Its Impact on Business and People.* Obituaries and other sources: *Who Was Who in America,* 4th edition, Marquis, 1968.

*   *   *

BUCKLEY, Doris Heather
See BUCKLEY NEVILLE, Heather

*   *   *

BUCKLEY NEVILLE, Heather 1910-
(Doris Heather Buckley)

PERSONAL: Born July 16, 1910, in Lind, Wash.; daughter of William (a farmer) and Emza (a teacher; maiden name, Hiday) Godsey; married Daniel J. Buckley, January 1, 1933 (divorced, 1959); married Elmer J. Neville, December 12, 1970; children: (first marriage) Michael John, Patrick Stanton, Susan Buckley Harris. *Education:* Attended Willamette University and Oregon Educational Institution. *Religion:* "Universal." *Home and office:* 4018 Rincon Ave., Campbell, Calif. 95008.

CAREER: Teacher at rural schools in Oregon, 1930-32; *Eugene Register Guard,* Eugene, Ore., writer, 1958-60; State of California, Department of Motor Vehicles, motor vehicle assistant in Pomon, San Jose, and Los Gatos, 1969-77; writer and operator of book shop in Campbell, Calif., 1977—. *Member:* National League of American Pen Women.

WRITINGS—Under name Doris Heather Buckley: *Spirit Communication for the Millions,* Sherbourne, 1967; *Science of Mind for the Millions,* Sherbourne, 1970; *Conversations With the Beyond,* Sherbourne, 1971.

WORK IN PROGRESS: When a Child Dies, publication expected in 1982.

SIDELIGHTS: Heather Buckley Neville commented: "In 1956, as a result of a study group in esoteric matters, my first husband, Dan Buckley, discovered he had mediumistic capabilities. A year of instruction from people from the 'other side' and our experiences with other invisible entities were the basis of my books on spirit communication. Our sessions were taped, and the material in the books was taken from the tapes. Many situations from real life were extended to the invisible realm and were communicated to us, so the books give the beginner a glimpse into expanded awareness.

"The book on science of mind contains a background, history, and many examples of ways my friends used it in their daily lives. It is not a textbook, but a book the average person can relate to.

"Classes for further information from books and the spirit world met in my home. Additional books were needed, so I opened a small book store in my home. This has since grown and become a very specialized, personal store. Each person who comes here is special, an advancing, growing person seeking new horizons in expanded awareness, self-help, health, metaphysics of all kinds, ancient wisdom, and the like.

"I have other writing projects in the works, using channeled material that pertains to the world situation today. Except for small articles here and there that I haven't kept track of, the book store takes most of my time. This is my way of life. My husband and I are in our seventies and enjoying every minute of it."

*   *   *

BUDDEE, Paul Edgar 1913-

PERSONAL: Surname is pronounced Bude-*day;* born March 12, 1913, in Perth, Australia; son of Thomas Richards (a civil servant) and Florence Ida (Nenke) Buddee; married Elizabeth Vere Bremner, January 12, 1944; children: Jill Leslie Buddee Parish, Kim Ronald. *Education:* Attended State University and Teacher's College, Claremont, Australia. *Home:* 11 The Parapet, Burrendah Estate, Willetton, Western Australia 6155, Australia. *Agent:* Winant, Towers Ltd., 14 Cliffords Inn, London EC4A 1DA, England.

CAREER: Worked as principal and lecturer for Education Department of Western Australia, 1933-76; writer, 1976—. Concert performer (on flute) and composer; conducted boys' choir, 1935-40, and "Schools Singing Broadcasts," for Australian Broadcasting Commission, 1946-51. Branch president of Western Australia State School Teachers Union, 1947-49, founder of local branches, executive member of state union, 1947-57, vice-president, 1955-57. Member of South Perth City Council, 1963-71; trustee of Tom Collins House. *Military service:* Australian Imperial Forces, 1940-46; served in North Africa; became lieutenant.

MEMBER: Australian College of Education, Fellowship of Writers of Western Australia (president, 1947-49), Rotary Club of Thornlie (charter president, 1973-74). *Awards, honors:* Named Western Australia citizen of the year by Western Australian Week Council, 1977; grants from Literature Board of Australia Council, 1977, 1978, and Fellowship of Writers of Western Australia, 1978; Paul Harris fellow of Rotary International, 1980; one-hundred-fiftieth anniversary medal from City of South Perth, Australia, 1980.

WRITINGS: Stand to and Other War Poems, Elmsdale Press, 1944.

Children's books: *Osca and Olga,* three volumes, Currawong Press, 1935-43; *Rupert and Rita,* Currawong Press, 1944; *Rattigan Rat,* Imperial Press, 1947; *The Unwilling Adventurers,* Hodder & Stoughton, 1967; *The Mystery of Moma Island,* Hodder & Stoughton, 1967; *The Escape of the Fenians,* Longman, 1972; *The Escape of John O'Reilly,* Longman, 1973; *Air Patrol and the Hijackers,* Rigby, 1973; *Air Patrol and the Underwater Spies,* Rigby, 1973; *Air Patrol and the Saboteurs,* Rigby, 1973; *Air Patrol and the Secret Intruders,* Rigby, 1973; *Ann Rankin and the Boy Who Painted Horses,* Rigby, 1973; *Ann Rankin and the House on Coolabah Hill,* Rigby, 1973; *Ann Rankin and the Lost Valley,* Rigby, 1973; *Ann Rankin and the Great Flood,* Rigby, 1973; *Peter Devlin Fights for Survival,* Rigby, 1973; *Peter Devlin Range Rider,* Rigby, 1973; *Peter Devlin Buffalo Hunter,* Rigby, 1973; *Peter Devlin and the Road Bandits,* Rigby, 1973; *The Call of the Sky,* Lothian Publishing, 1978.

Country correspondent for West Australian and Australian Broadcasting Commission, 1952-58. Contributor to *Perth Daily News* and *Western Australia Sunday Times.* Author of column in *Western Mail.*

WORK IN PROGRESS: Jud Mudbury, Parkhurst Boy, for children; *The Parkhurst Boys in Western Australia* and *What Happened to the Artful Dodger?,* both for adults.

SIDELIGHTS: Buddee told *CA:* "Although it is four years since I left my active role as an educationalist, I still attend schools to talk to the children and encourage them to write. I visit hundreds of classes every year and take an active part in the Children's Book Week at the state level. I have also taken a very active role in the establishment of young writers groups sponsored by local writers, judging literary competitions, and recently traveled over two thousand miles to the eastern goldfields to organize a safari for young writers there.

"The first consideration of being a literate person is the ability to communicate by either written or oral means. My activities in encouraging children to write are not intended to turn out potential authors, but normal literate persons who enjoy writing even if it is only a letter home or the minutes of a corporation meeting. I consider many people are much better off once they no longer fear writing things down, for whatever purpose—to satisfy an examiner, to convey regards through the mail, or even in a few cases to produce worthwhile literary work of some sort. When dealing with children, I use a technique wherein the children help fill in the sessions by asking me questions about my writing and experiences, and in turn giving some of their own opinions and reading some of their own efforts.

"Once, when asked to provide the blurb for a cover for one of my books, I took the commission to my twelve-year-old students, who provided some biographical material which has become a classic of its kind. They began: 'Mr. Buddee used to be a school teacher but now he's a headmaster. He likes wild flowers animals and children. He is about five feet nine inches tall and getting a little round. He is very intelligent interesting and friendly. He speaks well and says all his words clearly. He dresses well with a small black moustache which he wears all the time.' With this I rest, feeling I have been well described."

*   *   *

BULMAN, Joan (Carroll Boone) 1904-

PERSONAL: Born December 23, 1904, in London, England; daughter of Henry Herbert (an artist) and Beatrice (a musician; maiden name, Boone) Bulman. *Education:* Newnham College, Cambridge, M.A. (with first class honors), 1927; attended University of Munich, 1926, and University of Stockholm, 1928-31. *Politics:* Conservative. *Religion:* Church of England. *Home:* 5 King St., Bishop's Stortford, Hertfordshire CM23 2NB, England.

CAREER: Translator for Air Ministry in England, 1938-47; free-lance writer and translator, 1947—. *Member:* Society of Authors, Translators Association.

WRITINGS: Strindberg and Shakespeare: Shakespeare's Influence on Strindberg's Historical Drama, J. Cape, 1933; *Jenny Lind: A Biography,* J. Barrie, 1956.

Translator: Ragnar Svanstroem and B.C.F. Palmstierna, *A Short History of Sweden,* Clarendon Press, 1934; Herbert Tingsten, *The Debate on the Foreign Policy of Sweden, 1918-1939,* Oxford University Press, 1949; Liv Balstad, *North of the Desolate Sea,* Souvenir Press, 1958; Henning G. Lundstroem, *The Kingdom of God in the Teaching of Jesus: A History of Interpretation From the Last Decades of the Nineteenth Century to the President Day,* Oliver & Boyd, 1963;

Gunnar Mattsson, *The Princess*, Heinemann, 1966; Hans Krister Roenblom, *Wennerstroem the Spy*, Hodder & Stoughton, 1966; Lars Wilsson, *My Beaver Colony*, Souvenir Press, 1969; Astrid Bergnam Sucksdorff, *Tiger in Sight*, Deutsch, 1970; Peter V. Glob, *Danish Prehistoric Monuments*, Faber, 1971; Lisa Melen, *Drawn Threadwork*, Van Nostrand Reinhold, 1972; Melen, *Knotting and Netting: The Art of Filet Work*, Van Nostrand Reinhold, 1973; Glob, *The Mound People: Danish Bronze Age Man Preserved*, Faber, 1974.

Contributor to *Britannica Year Book* and *Purcell's New English Encyclopaedia*. Editor of local parish magazine.

WORK IN PROGRESS: Short stories; translations.

*   *   *

BUNIM, Irving M.   1901(?)-1980

OBITUARY NOTICE: Born c. 1901 in Volozhin, Russia (now U.S.S.R.); died December 10, 1980, in Manhattan, N.Y. Businessman, lecturer, and author, best known for his work in Orthodox Jewish organizations. Bunim founded the Eden Textiles and Garden Fabrics companies in New York. As a leader of Orthodoxy, he began the Young Israel movement and was a primary spokesman for the National Council of Young Israel. His books, *Ethics From Sinai* and *Ever Since Sinai*, address the topic of Jewish ethics. Shortly before his death, Bunim was presented with the Jabotinsky Award for distinguished service to Israel by Prime Minister Menachem Begin. Obituaries and other sources: *New York Times*, December 16, 1980.

*   *   *

BURCH, Monte G.   1943-
(Mark Gregory)

PERSONAL: Born April 4, 1943, in Clinton, Mo.; son of George Marvin (a cabinetmaker) and Willa (Brown) Burch; married Joan Hinshaw, September 1, 1963; children: Mark, Jodi, Michael. *Education:* Attended Central Missouri State College. *Home and office address:* Route 1, Box 454, Humansville, Mo. 65674.

CAREER: Writer and editor.

WRITINGS: Outdoorsman's Fixit Book, Harper, 1971; (with Jay W. Hedden) *Making Mediterranean Furniture,* Arco, 1973; *Basic House Wiring,* Harper, 1975; (with wife, Joan Burch) *Home Canning and Preserving,* Reston, 1977; *Windows, Doors, Security, and Insulation,* Peterson Publishing, 1977; *The Outdoorsman's Workshop,* Winchester Press, 1977; *Gun Care and Repair,* Winchester Press, 1978; *Waterfowling,* Harper, 1978.

Under pseudonym Mark Gregory: *Good Earth Almanac,* Grosset, 1973; *The Good Earth Almanac: Survival Handbook,* Sheed, 1973; *The Good Earth Almanac Natural Gardening Handbook,* Sheed, 1974; *The Good Earth Almanac Old-Time Recipes,* Sheed, 1974.

Also author of *The Shotgunner's Guide,* Winchester Press; *Small Farm Outbuildings,* Garden Way Publishing; *Small Farm Workshop,* Garden Way Publishing; *Exteriors,* Peterson Publishing; *Furniture Restorations,* Peterson Publishing; and *How to Be Your Own Home Electrician,* Popular Science.

WORK IN PROGRESS: Tile, for Creative Homeowner Press; *The Home Cabinetmaker,* for Popular Science.

BURCHETT, Randall E.   (?)-1971

OBITUARY NOTICE—See index for *CA* sketch: Born in Clarksville, Tenn.; died May 1, 1971. Banker, religious worker, and author. Burchett began his career as a cashier at the First Trust & Savings Bank. He was associated with Youth for Christ and was a member of Camp of Gideons and the Christian Business Men's Committee. He wrote *Chart and Compass* and *When the Mountains Fall.* (Date of death provided by daughter, Mrs. Floyd Brown.)

*   *   *

BURCKEL, Nicholas C(lare)   1943-

PERSONAL: Born August 15, 1943, in Evansville, Ind.; son of Arthur J. (in sales) and Irene (a secretary; maiden name, Dorsey) Burckel; married Lenore M. Herriges (a teacher), June 21, 1969. *Education:* Georgetown University, B.A., 1965; University of Wisconsin—Madison, M.A., 1967, Ph.D., 1971. *Home:* 2422 West Lawn Ave., Racine, Wis. 53405. *Office:* University Archives and Area Research Center, University of Wisconsin—Parkside, Kenosha, Wis. 53141.

CAREER: University of Wisconsin—Madison, assistant archivist, 1971-72; University of Wisconsin—Parkside, Kenosha, director of Archives and Area Research Center, 1972—, executive assistant to chancellor, 1975—. Member of Tri-County Library Council, 1974—; member of board of directors of Racine County Planning Council, 1978—.

MEMBER: American Historical Association, American Association for State and Local History, American Library Association, National Trust for Historic Preservation, Society of American Archivists (chairman of College and University Archives Committee and of Committee on Committees, both 1977-79), Organization of American Historians, Midwest Archives Conference (vice-president, 1976-78; president, 1979-81), Society for History of Education, Association of College and Research Libraries, State Historical Society of Wisconsin. *Awards, honors:* Scholarly book award from Council for Wisconsin Writers, 1977, and award of merit from State Historical Society of Wisconsin, 1978, both for *Racine: Growth and Change in a Wisconsin County;* certificate of commendation from American Association for State and Local History, 1978, for work in local history.

WRITINGS: Racine: Growth and Change in a Wisconsin County, Racine County Board of Supervisors, 1977; *Guide to Archives and Manuscripts in the University of Wisconsin—Parkside Area Research Center,* State Historical Society of Wisconsin, 1977; (with John D. Buenker) *Immigration and Ethnicity,* Gale, 1977; (with Buenker) *Progressive Reform,* Gale, 1980; (with John Neuenschwander) *Kenosha Retrospective: A Biographical Approach,* Kenosha County Board of Supervisors, 1981; (with J. Frank Cook) *College and University Archives: An Introduction,* Society of American Archivists, 1982. Contributor to *Encyclopedia of Southern History.* Contributor of articles and reviews to history, library, and archival journals. Book review editor of *Midwestern Archivist,* 1973-79.

SIDELIGHTS: Burckel told *CA:* "After decades of neglect by professional historians, local history has at last begun to receive the attention it deserves. Long considered the special preserve of amateurs, antiquarians, and genealogists, local history has been discovered by the academic historian. One possible explanation for this new interest is the lack of mobility among professional historians. Historians formerly focused on national topics because they expected to move several times in their career and did not want to spend time on a local issue that might have little relation to their next position. Now, however, since historians remain at a specific institution for longer periods, they have turned to local history and found it a nearly unexploited resource for teaching and research. Another possible reason for their increased interest is that local history provides a manageable framework for testing theories and theses about larger regional and national questions. The growth of state and local historical societies and the increasing importance of the American Association for State and Local History are testimony to the vitality of local history and its importance to historical scholarship.''

*   *   *

BURFIELD, Eva
See EBBETT, (Frances) Eva

*   *   *

BURKE, Joseph (Terence Anthony) 1913-

PERSONAL: Born July 14, 1913, in London, England; son of R.M.J. (a bank manager) and Dora (a music teacher; maiden name, Teasdale) Burke; married Agnes Middleton (a registered nurse), November 20, 1940; children: Rickard Middleton. *Education:* Attended King's College, London, 1930-33, Courtauld Institute of Art, 1933-35, and Yale University, 1936-37. *Home:* Dormers, Falls Road, Mount Dandenong, Victoria 3767, Australia. *Office:* Department of Fine Arts, University of Melbourne, Parkville, Victoria, Australia.

CAREER: Associated with Victoria and Albert Museum, London, England, 1938-39; associated with Home Office and Minister of Home Security, London, 1939-41; private secretary to successive lord presidents of the Council, London, 1942-45; private secretary to Prime Minister Clement R. Attlee, London, 1945-46; University of Melbourne, Melbourne, Australia, professor of fine arts, 1946-78; fellow at Trinity College, 1973—. Trustee of Felton Bequest. *Member:* Australian Academy of the Humanities (fellow; president, 1971-73), Athenaeum Club (London), Melbourne Club. *Awards, honors:* Member of the Order of the British Empire, 1946, Commander, 1973, Knight Commander, 1980; D. Litt. from Monash University, Clayton, Australia, 1977.

WRITINGS: (Editor) William Hogarth, *Analysis of Beauty,* Clarendon Press, 1955; (author of text with Colin Caldwell) *Hogarth: The Complete Engravings,* Thames & Hudson, 1968; (author of foreword) Frank T. Morris, *Birds of Prey of Australia,* Lansdowne, 1973; *English Art, 1714-1800,* Clarendon Press, 1976.

Contributor of articles to magazines and journals, including *Burlington Magazine* and *Warburg Journal.*

WORK IN PROGRESS: Benjamin West and the Anglo-American Revival of History Painting.

SIDELIGHTS: In English Art, 1714-1800, Burke traces the interaction between the classic and romantic traditions in art during the eighteenth century. He reveals how the artists of the time laid the foundation for a reversal in English taste by combining familiar imagery with the prevailing concept of high art and by integrating realism and rococo.

Burke's ''aesthetic argument,'' according to Dennis Thomas, ''is that the 18th century's reputation for elegance and civilised recreation should yield to a higher claim: 'artistic excellence in the sphere of wit, inspired by humanitarian sympathy.''' In the *Times Literary Supplement,* Hugh Honour

called the commentary of *English Art* ''original and perceptive.'' He noted: ''Professor Burke gives great prominence to the landscape garden. His account of its origins is admirably judicious and he writes with sensitivity of the finest surviving examples.''

AVOCATIONAL INTERESTS: Golf, swimming.

BIOGRAPHICAL/CRITICAL SOURCES: Listener, May 20, 1976; *Times Literary Supplement,* January 31, 1977.

*   *   *

BURKE, Leda
See GARNETT, David

*   *   *

BURKERT, Walter 1931-

PERSONAL: Born February 2, 1931, in Neuendettelsau, Germany; son of Adolf (a minister) and Luise (Grossmann) Burkert; married Maria Bosch, August 1, 1957; children: Reinhard, Andrea, Cornelius. *Education:* University of Erlangen, Ph.D., 1955; attended University of Munich, 1952-53. *Home:* Wildsbergstrasse 8, Uster 8610, Switzerland. *Office:* Klassisch-Philologisches Seminar, University of Zurich, Florhofgasse 11, Zurich 8001, Switzerland.

CAREER: University of Erlangen, Erlangen, West Germany, assistant, 1957-61, privatdozent in classics, 1961-66; Technical University of Berlin, Berlin, West Germany, professor of classics, 1966-69; University of Zurich, Zurich, Switzerland, professor of classics, 1969—. Senior fellow of Center for Hellenic Studies, Washington, D.C., 1971—; Sather Professor of Classical Literature at University of California, Berkeley, 1977. *Member:* British Academy (corresponding fellow), Schweizerische Vereinigung fuer Altertumswissenschaft (president, 1978—), Schweizerische Gesellschaft fuer Religionswissenschaft (president, 1979—), Heidelberger Akademie der Wissenschaften (corresponding member).

WRITINGS: Weisheit und Wissenschaft, Carl Verlag, 1962, revised translation by Edwin L. Minar, Jr. published as *Lore and Science in Ancient Pythagoreanism,* Harvard University Press, 1972; *Structure and History in Greek Mythology and Ritual,* University of California Press, 1979.

In German: *Homo Necans: Interpretationen altgriechischer Opferriten und Mythen* (title means ''Man the Killer: Interpretations of Ancient Greek Sacrificial Ritual and Myths''), De Gruyter, 1972; *Griechische Religion der archaischen und klassischen Epoche* (title means ''Greek Religion of the Archaic and Classic Epochs''), Kohlhammer, 1977.

WORK IN PROGRESS: Research in the impact of the ancient Near East on the formative period of archaic Greek civilization.

SIDELIGHTS: Burkert wrote: ''A traditional education in humanities and philosophy was broadened by an interest in the more profound background of rational culture. This led to an analysis of the Pythagorean tradition; that is, the emergence of science from obscure antecedents, and to continuing research on mythology and religius ritual. Ancient Greek tradition is seen in connection with similar phenomena in both historical and functional perspectives, while philological-historical methods are supplemented by models taken from anthropology and ethology. The aim would be a more comprehensive understanding of human civilization and its alternatives.''

BIOGRAPHICAL/CRITICAL SOURCES: Religious Studies Review, June, 1980.

BURNS, Chester R(ay) 1937-

PERSONAL: Born December 5, 1937, in Nashville, Tenn.; son of Leslie A. and Margaret (Drake) Burns; married Ann Christine Griffey (a nurse), 1962; children: Margaret Christine, Michael Derek. *Education:* Vanderbilt University, B.A. (cum laude), 1959, M.D., 1963; Johns Hopkins University, Ph.D., 1969. *Home:* 2708 Beluche Dr., Galveston, Tex. 77551. *Office:* Institute for the Medical Humanities, University of Texas Medical Branch, Galveston, Tex. 77550.

CAREER: Licensed to practice medicine in Tennessee, 1963, and Texas, 1970; diplomate, National Board of Medical Examiners, 1964; University of Oklahoma Hospitals, Oklahoma City, intern, 1963-64; University of Texas Medical Branch at Galveston, Galveston, assistant professor, 1969-71, James Wade Rockwell assistant professor, 1971-74, assistant professor, 1974-75, associate professor and James Wade Rockwell associate professor, 1975-79, professor of preventive medicine and community health and James Wade Rockwell Professor of the History of Medicine, 1979—, director of history of medicine division, 1967-74, associate director of Institute for the Medical Humanities, 1975-80, acting director, 1980-81. Member of special studies section of National Institutes of Health, 1974-75 and 1980-81; member of national board of consultants of National Endowment for the Humanities, 1978—; member of advisory board of *The Journal of Medicine and Philosophy,* 1974—, and *Transactions and Studies of the College of Physicians of Philadelphia,* 1979—; consultant to *Texas Medicine,* 1978.

MEMBER: Societe Internationale d'Histoire de la Medicine, Cheiron: The International Society for the History of Behavioral and Social Sciences, American Medical Association, American Association of University Professors, American Historical Association, American Association for the Advancement of Science, American Osler Society, Organization of American Historians, Association of American Medical Colleges, Texas Medical Association, Osler Club of London, History of Science Society, Society for Health and Human Values (member of executive council, 1974-77; president, 1975-76), Sigma Xi, Rotary Club of Galveston (president, 1980-81). *Awards, honors:* Physician's Recognition Award from American Medical Association, 1969; grant from the University of Texas System, 1972; National Endowment for the Humanities grants, 1974-79 and 1978; grant from Hogg Foundation for Mental Health, 1975-78; grant from American Philosophical Society, 1975.

WRITINGS: (Editor with John P. McGovern) *Humanism in Medicine,* C. C. Thomas, 1973; (editor) *Legacies in Ethics and Medicine,* Science History Publications, 1977; (editor and contributor) *Legacies in Law and Medicine,* Science History Publications, 1977; (author of introduction) Thomas Percival, *Medical Ethics,* Robert E. Krieger, 1975.

Contributor: *Human Values Teaching Programs for Health Professionals,* Society for Health and Human Values, 1974, 3rd edition, 1976; H. T. Engelhardt, Jr., and S. Spicker, editors, *Evaluation and Explanation in the Biomedical Sciences,* Reidel, 1975; *Dictionary of American History,* Scribner, 1976; Engelhardt and Spicker, editors, *Mental Health: Philosophical Perspectives,* Reidel, 1977; Ronald L. Numbers, editor, *The Education of American Physicians: Historical Essays,* University of California Press, 1980. Contributor to periodicals, including *Journal of the American Medical Association, Yale Medicine, Bulletin of the History of Medicine,* and *Journal of Medicine and Philosophy.*

WORK IN PROGRESS: Ethics in Medical Practice: Essays Written by Physicians in the United States, 1769-1969; Professional Ethics in American Medicine: A History.

SIDELIGHTS: Burns told *CA:* "As an educator, I want to help move the humanities into a more central position in the training of health care professionals. As a scholar, I use historical and philosophical approaches in my journeys through the terrains of values in the health care sciences and professions."

*   *   *

BURNS, Edward McNall 1897-1972

OBITUARY NOTICE—See index for *CA* sketch: Born February 18, 1897, in Burgettstown, Pa.; died July 14, 1972. Educator and author. An expert in both history and political science, Burns taught at Rutgers University, the Free University of Berlin, and the University of California. Among his writings are *Ideas in Conflict, World Civilizations,* and biographies of James Madison and David Star Jordan. Burns also edited *Gertrude Stein on Picasso.* Obituaries and other sources: *Current Biography,* Wilson, 1954; *Who Was Who in America,* 5th edition, Marquis, 1973.

*   *   *

BURNS, Jean (Ellen) 1934-

PERSONAL: Born February 15, 1934, in Oakland, Calif.; daughter of Frank Robert (an electrical engineer) and Janet Elizabeth (Sommers) Burns. *Education:* University of California, Berkeley, B.A., 1955; University of Hawaii, M.A., 1966, Ph.D., 1970. *Home address:* P.O. Box 11066, Honolulu, Hawaii 96828. *Agent:* Peter L. Skolnik, Sanford J. Greenburger Associates, Inc., 825 Third Ave., New York, N.Y. 10022.

CAREER: University of Hawaii, Honolulu, researcher in solar physics, 1971-72; free-lance writer, researcher, and teacher of consciousness and psychic techniques, 1972-78; writer, 1978—. *Member:* Phi Beta Kappa.

WRITINGS: Burns Telepathy Course, privately printed, 1972; *Your Innate Psychic Powers,* Sphere Books, 1981. Contributor to *Solar Physics.*

WORK IN PROGRESS: "A book on consciousness—spontaneous activities and consciously directed ones, the merged state and the witness state, the principle of identification, the properties of consciousness."

SIDELIGHTS: Jean Burns writes: "My book *Your Innate Psychic Powers* details practical methods for pyschic work—telepathy, divination, etc.—which I have tested for myself and taught in classes to others. I have also compared techniques with many people who do psychic work, so as to have a range of ideas on how this work is done. I have seen the methods work, for myself and from teaching them, and I want to bring this knowledge out to others.

"My book also discusses the properties of consciousness (which I will discuss more fully in another forthcoming book). I hold that the physical world and consciousness are different things, with different properties. The physical world has such properties as mass, electric charge, and the like. Through these properties you can explain basically everything that happens in the physical world. The brain, for example, is part of the physical world and can be explained in these terms.

"Consciousness deals with such things as thoughts and emotions, the merged state and the witness state, and the like. These are completely different things than what is in the physical world. A major point in my book is that psychic phenomena are part of the realm of consciousness, not the physical world, and should be described in terms of the properties of consciousness. I list the properties of consciousness and compare them to those of the physical world, and in fact, you can gain insight into psychic happenings by looking at them in this way.

"This approach is not unique to me—it is an idea which circulates informally among many people in the physical sciences who take an interest in psychic phenomena. However, I am perhaps the first to set this forth in a definitive way in a published work.

"I hope to promote discussion by doing this and to encourage others to look at this viewpoint. It is a very simple idea—consciousness is different from the physical world and should be described in terms of its own basic properties. Consciousness does have properties—why not look for them?"

*   *   *

BURR, Lonnie 1943-

PERSONAL: Born May 31, 1943, in Dayton, Ky.; son of Howard A. and Dorothy (Burr) Babin. *Education:* California State University, Northridge, A.B., 1962, doctoral study, 1968-69; University of California, Los Angeles, M.A., 1964. *Home:* 5252 Corteen Pl., Suite 15, North Hollywood, Calif. 91607. *Agent:* Larry Grossman, 211 South Beverly Dr., Suite 206, Beverly Hills, Calif. 90212.

CAREER: Actor, singer, dancer, director, and choreographer, 1948—. Actor in television series, including "The Ruggles," and "The Mickey Mouse Club." Gave poetry readings in New York City and at Chicago Art Institute. *Awards, honors:* Poetry Award from *Nevadan,* 1969; poetry award from *DeKalb Literary Arts Journal,* 1971; awards from Kentucky State Poetry Society and South Carolina State Poetry Society, both 1972; two awards from Alabama State Poetry Society, 1973; Katherine Lyons Clark Award from Pennsylvania Poetry Society, and August Derleth Memorial Award, both 1974; Lubbe Award and Modern Award, both from National Federation of State Poetry Societies, both 1976; Artact Award from Kentucky Arts Council, 1977, for "Occam's Razor"; First American Radio Theater Award from American Radio Theatre, 1980, for "Cat's Out of the Closet".

WRITINGS: Two for the Show: Great Comedy Teams, Messner, 1979.

Plays: "Over the Hill" (two-act), first produced in Hollywood, Calif., at MET Theater, 1977; "Children Are Strangers" (two-act), first produced in Los Angeles, Calif., c. 1981. Also author of "Icons Are in Vogue," produced at University of California, Los Angeles.

Writer for radio programs, including "Heartbeat Theater." Past editor of *Quiddity.* Contributing editor of *Footnotes, Big Valley, Scriptwriter,* and *Valley Express.*

WORK IN PROGRESS: Funny Ladies and *Monsieur Dupin Returns,* novels; "Rumors of War" and "Spiders," screenplays; "Interval," a two-act drama.

SIDELIGHTS: Burr told *CA:* "I have found that in a world of compromise a solitary writer makes fewer compromises than an actor. I would rather place the majority of my creative instincts into relying on my own juices and convolutions rather than the convoluted juices of others; this holds true in writing but does not in an acting situation."

BURROWES, Michael Anthony Bernard 1937-
(Mike Burrowes)

PERSONAL: Born May 7, 1937, in Kitty, Guyana; son of Edward Rupert (an artist) and Maude Alice (Rogers) Burrowes; married Anna Mary Kennedy, December 15, 1972; children: David Anthony, Linda, Marianne Elizabeth. *Education:* Attended secondary school in Georgetown, Guyana. *Politics:* "Liberal, but I have no love for politicians." *Religion:* Agnostic. *Home:* 102 Moyne Close, Hove, Sussex BN3 7JX, England. *Office:* Government Post Office, Hove St., Hove, Sussex, England.

CAREER: Royal Free Medical School, London, England, laboratory technician, 1957-59; St. James' Hospital, London, laboratory technician, 1959-60; photographic technician for AGFA, 1960-62, and for ANCOR, 1962; professional singer of popular music, 1963; Government Post Office, Hove, England, postman in Hove and Brighton, 1964—.

WRITINGS—Western novels under name Mike Burrowes: *North of Paola,* Ward, Lock, 1965; *Chinook,* Ward, Lock, 1965; *Action at Las Animas,* Ward, Lock, 1966; *Blood Trail,* Ward, Lock, 1966; *Deadly Justice,* Ward, Lock, 1967; *Requiem for a Gunfighter,* Ward, Lock, 1967; *Wolf Creek Pass,* Ward, Lock, 1968; *Echoes of Shiloh,* Ward, Lock, 1968; *Hell in San Pedro,* R. Hale, 1971.

WORK IN PROGRESS: A suspense novel set in England and Brazil.

SIDELIGHTS: Borrowes told *CA:* "My nine published novels are westerns, though I have not yet managed to visit the land in which they are set. Inside my head at least another fifty westerns and thrillers are swimming about. I want to be able to write all the time, but to feed my family I need to work, hence my 4:00 A.M. alarm six days a week.

"By tradition painters are poor during their lifetimes. Indeed, my own father was made a member of the Order of the British Empire for his services to art, but died almost penniless. I often wonder if many of my fellow writers live so close to the breadline, or is it only in this country that they are paid so little and taxed so heavily for their creations?"

BIOGRAPHICAL/CRITICAL SOURCES: Daily Mirror, August 2, 1972.

*   *   *

BURROWES, Mike
See BURROWES, Michael Anthony Bernard

*   *   *

BURSTON, W. H. 1915-1981

OBITUARY NOTICE: Born July 26, 1915; died April 3, 1981, in London, England. Educator, historian, and author. Beginning as a lecturer and becoming a professor, Burston was with the University of London Institute of Education for thirty-three years. His writings include *Principles of History Teaching* and *Studies in the Nature of the Teaching of History,* and he edited several other volumes on education. At his death, Burston was editing *Chrestomathia,* a volume of writings by utilitarian Jeremy Bentham. Obituaries and other sources: *London Times,* April 16, 1981.

BURTON, John Wear 1915-

PERSONAL—Education: University of Sydney, B.A.; University of London, Ph.D. and D.Sc. Int. Rel. *Home:* 75-A Bedford Court Mansions, Bedford Ave., London W.C.1, England. *Office:* Rutherford College, University of Kent at Canterbury, Canterbury CT2 7NX, England.

CAREER: Permanent head of Australian Department of External Affairs, 1945-50; Australian high commissioner in Ceylon, 1951; Australian National University, Canberra, visiting research fellow, 1960-63; University of London, London, England, reader in international relations, 1963-78, director of Centre for the Analysis of Conflict, 1965-78; University of Kent at Canterbury, Canterbury, England, reader in international relations, 1978—.

WRITINGS: International Relations: A General Theory, Cambridge University Press, 1965; (editor and contributor) *Nonalignment,* Deutsch, 1966; *Systems, States, Diplomacy, and Rules,* Cambridge University Press, 1968; *Conflict and Comunication: The Use of Controlled Communication in International Relations,* Macmillan, 1969; *World Society,* Cambridge University Press, 1972; *Deviance, Terrorism, and War: The Process of Solving Unsolved Social and Political Problems,* Martin Robertson, 1980. Also author of *Peace Theory,* 1962.

*   *   *

BUTLER, George Tyssen 1943-

PERSONAL: Born October 12, 1943, in Chester, England; son of Tyssen Desmond (a major in the military) and Dorothy (West) Butler; married Victoria Leiter (marriage ended); children: Desmond, Tyssen. *Education:* University of North Carolina, B.A. (with honors); Hollins College, M.A. *Religion:* Episcopal. *Home address:* True Farm, Holderness, N.H. 03245. *Agent:* Lynn Nesbitt, International Creative Management, 40 West 57th St., New York, N.Y. 10019; and Sue Mengers, International Creative Management, 8899 Beverly, Los Angeles, Calif. *Office:* White Mountain Films, 165 East 80th St., New York, N.Y. 10021.

CAREER: White Mountain Films, New York, N.Y., president, 1975—. Producer of "Pumping Iron," a film released by Cinema Five.

WRITINGS: (Co-editor) *The New Soldier,* Macmillan, 1971; (co-author) *Pumping Iron,* Simon & Schuster, 1975. Contributor of photographs to popular magazines.

*   *   *

BUTLER, Grace Kipp Pratt
See PRATT-BUTLER, Grace Kipp

*   *   *

BUTLER, Stefan Congrat
See CONGRAT-BUTLER, Stefan

*   *   *

BUTRYM, Zofia Teresa 1927-

PERSONAL: Born April 27, 1927, in Polesie, Poland (now part of U.S.S.R.). *Education:* London School of Economics and Political Science, London, certificate in social science, 1949; Institute of Medical Science, London, professional certificate, 1950; further graduate study at Tavistock Clinic and Institute, 1954-55. *Religion:* Roman Catholic. *Office:*

London School of Economics and Political Science, University of London, Houghton St., London WC2A 2AE, England.

CAREER: Hammersmith Hospital, London, England, medical social worker, 1950-54, senior medical social worker, 1955-58; University of London, London School of Economics and Political Science, London, lecturer, 1958-70, senior lecturer in social work, 1970—. Committee chairman at Institute of Medical Social Work, London, 1966-70. *Member:* British Association of Social Workers (member of council, 1970-71), Association of Teachers in Social Work Education (vice-chairman, 1979—).

WRITINGS: Social Work in Medical Care, Routledge & Kegan Paul, 1967; *Medical Social Work in Action,* G. Bell, 1968; *The Nature of Social Work,* Macmillan, 1976; *Social Work: A Theory and Practice Text,* McDonald & Evans, 1981.

WORK IN PROGRESS: A book on health, doctors, and social workers, with J.F.M. Herder, publication by Routledge & Kegan Paul expected in 1981; "The Functions of Social Work," to be included in a social work textbook, edited by P. M. Brown.

SIDELIGHTS: Zofia Butrym commented to *CA:* "My professional concerns are predominantly with promoting social work as a caring and individualistic act within a society which has so many callous and dehumanizing facets. I am therefore particularly concerned with the ethical aspects of social work practice as well as with its links with health care. I believe the two to be interdependent."

*   *   *

BUTTERFIELD, Roger (Place) 1907-1981

OBITUARY NOTICE—See index for *CA* sketch: Born July 29, 1907, in Lyndonville, N.Y.; died of a heart attack, January 31, 1981, in Hartwick, N.Y. Journalist, editor, historian, consultant, and author. Butterfield worked as a reporter and editor with *Time* and *Life* magazines for more than fifteen years before becoming a consultant to Time, Inc. He wrote several books about American history, including *The American Past: A History of the United States From Concord to the Great Society* and *Henry Ford, the Wayside Inn, and the Problem of "History Is Bunk."* Obituaries and other sources: *Publishers Weekly,* February 20, 1981.

*   *   *

BUTTON, Kenneth John 1948-

PERSONAL: Born November 14, 1948, in Shoreham, England; son of Frank Alfred Arthur (in business) and Joyce (Tapson) Button; married Elizabeth Ruth Hallas (a teacher of modern languages), August 4, 1974. *Education:* University of East Anglia, B.A. (with honors), 1970; University of Leeds, M.A. (with distinction), 1971. *Home:* Merrion House, 133 Ashby Rd., Loughborough, Leicestershire, England. *Office:* Department of Economics, Loughborough University, Loughborough, Leicestershire, England.

CAREER: University of Leeds, Leeds, England, researcher, 1971-73; Loughborough University, Loughborough, England, lecturer in economics, 1973—. *Member:* Royal Economic Society, Chartered Institute of Transport, Regional Science Association.

WRITINGS: (With P. J. Barker) *Case Studies in Cost Benefit Analysis,* Heinemann, 1975; *Urban Economics: Theory and Policy,* Macmillan, 1976; (with David Gillingwater) *Case Studies in Regional Economics,* Heinemann, 1976; *The Eco-*

nomics of Urban Transport, Saxon House, 1977; (with A. D. Pearman) *The Economics of Urban Freight Transport*, Macmillan, 1981; (with Pearman) *Case Studies in Transport Economics*, Heinemann, 1981; (with Pearman and A. S. Fowkes) *Car Ownership Modelling and Forecasting*, Saxon House, 1981; *Transport Economics*, Heinemann, 1982.

Contributor: M.J.H. Magridge, editor, *Urban Traffic Models*, Planning and Transport Research and Compilation (PTRC), 1975; E. J. Visser, editor, *Transport Decisions in an Age of Uncertainty*, Nijhoff, 1977; M. J. Richards, editor, *Transportation Models*, PTRC, 1977; D. G. Abraham, editor, *Proceedings of Universities Transport Study Group Conference*, Universities Transport Studies Group, 1978; J. A. Fletcher, editor, *Proceedings of the Ninth National Conference of the Institute of Road Transport Engineers*, Institute of Road Transport Engineers, 1978; Richards, editor, *Transportation Models*, PTRC, 1978; A. S. Hakkert, editor, *Integration of Traffic and Transportation Engineering in Urban Planning*, Conference Associates Ltd., 1980; J. S. Yerrell, editor, *Transport Research for Social and Economic Progress*, Saxon House, 1980; W.P.J. Maunder, editor, *The British Economy in the 1970's*, Heinemann, 1980. Contributor of more than fifty articles and reviews to economic, management, and transportation journals.

WORK IN PROGRESS: Collected papers on transport investment appraisal, publication by Saxon House expected in 1982; an introductory textbook on economics, publication by Heinemann expected in 1984; researching freight transport policy and urban traffic congestion theory.

SIDELIGHTS: Button told *CA:* "My main concern about the future of transportation is that its study and operation increasingly seem to be moving away from considering the most efficient method of transporting people and goods and towards the support of specific modes of transport—i.e., the road lobby, the railway enthusiasts, etc. When studying the economics of the footwear industry one is not confronted by groups supporting boots and other groups supporting shoes, but in transportation parallel groupings of this type do exist and, what is worse, often influence and control decision making. Throughout my career I have tried to be objective, and I hope pragmatic, in my various writings, steering away from the emotive subjectivity which seems to form any moving part of transport studies.

"It is also important to recognize that people in virtually all circumstances wish to minimize transportation and not recognize it. Improved transportation often reduces miles traveled, stops made or time taken, but this is not always recognized by agencies supporting transportation services. Consequently, I feel that, although there is an increasing integration of transportation economics into the wide fields of urban economics and location theory, this integration needs to be entailed much further. Additionally, the rather complex mathematic theorizing in this area might give way to a more realistic approach which breaks away from the conventional idea of a circularity served by a simple radial transport system."

C

CABOT, John Moors 1901-1981

OBITUARY NOTICE: Born December 11, 1901, in Cambridge, Mass.; died after a stroke, February 23, 1981, in Washington, D.C. Ambassador and author. Cabot was a United States Ambassador to five nations between 1954 and 1965, spending much time in Latin America. During his forty-one year career in the Foreign Service, Cabot served as Assistant Secretary of State for Latin American Affairs during the Eisenhower Administration, Consul General in Shanghai, China until its communist takeover, and as charge d'affaires in Belgrade, Yugoslavia. There it is believed that Cabot's work was responsible for the division between Yugoslavia and the Soviet Union, thus preventing Yugoslavia's communization. After retiring in 1966, Cabot served as a lecturer and consultant on law, diplomacy, and foreign service at Tufts University in Massachusetts and at Georgetown University in Washington, D.C. His books include two volumes describing his experiences in the foreign service, *Toward Our Common American Destiny* and *The First Line of Defense.* He also wrote *The Racial Conflict in Transylvania.* Obituaries and other sources: *Who's Who in America,* 39th edition, Marquis, 1976; *Political Profiles: The Eisenhower Years,* Facts on File, 1977; *International Yearbook and Statesmen's Who's Who,* Kelly's Directories, 1980; *New York Times,* February 25, 1981; *Newsweek,* March 9, 1981; *Time,* March 9, 1981.

*   *   *

CADIEUX, (Joseph Arthur) Lorenzo 1903-1976

OBITUARY NOTICE—See index for *CA* sketch: Born November 10, 1903, in Granby, Quebec, Canada; died in 1976. Clergyman, educator, historian, and author. Cadieux taught at Laurentian University in Ontario, Canada, for many years. His works include *Afloat and Aloft: Joseph-Marie Couture.* Obituaries and other sources: *International Authors and Writers Who's Who,* 8th edition, Melrose Press, 1977.

*   *   *

CAILLOU, Alan
See LYLE-SMYTHE, Alan

CALASIBETTA, Charlotte M(ankey) 1917-

PERSONAL: Born June 2, 1917, in Williamsport, Pa.; daughter of Fred W. (a church organist and railroad clerk) and Katharine (a secretary; maiden name, Laux) Mankey; married Charles J. Calasibetta (a physician), June 26, 1954. *Education:* Carnegie Institute of Technology (now Carnegie-Mellon University), B.S., 1939; New York University, M.S., 1944, Ed.D., 1953; also attended University of Pittsburgh, 1939, and Columbia University, 1941; studied fine arts at Fairleigh Dickinson University, Montclair Museum, and Newark Museum. *Home:* 925 Campbell St., Williamsport, Pa. 17701.

CAREER: Edgewood Park Junior College, Briarcliff Manor, N.Y., head of merchandising course, 1940-43; Ohrbach's (specialty store), New York City, training director, 1944; Georgia State College for Women (now Georgia College), Milledgeville, associate professor of distributive education, 1944-52; Russell Sage College, Troy, N.Y., associate professor of business administration, 1952-54; New York University School of Retailing (now Institute for Retailing Management), New York City, lecturer in retailing, 1955-56; College of St. Elizabeth, Convent Station, N.J., lecturer in retailing, 1956-57; Bernard M. Baruch School of Business and Public Administration of the City College (now Bernard M. Baruch College of the City University of New York), New York City, part-time lecturer in fashion and textiles, 1964-70. Costume designer for community theatres; director of fashion shows; judge of fashion shows in Albany, N.Y., 1953-54. *Member:* American Association of University Women, Etat Mu Pi, Delta Pi Epsilon, Pi Gamma Nu. *Awards, honors:* Prize from School of Retailing, New York University, 1944.

WRITINGS: Fairchild's Dictionary of Fashion, self-illustrated, Fairchild Books & Visuals, 1975.

SIDELIGHTS: During her years as a teacher, Calasibetta recognized the need for a teaching aid that would serve the needs of her students while retaining its usefulness in a rapidly changing fashion world. She wrote *Fairchild's Dictionary of Fashion,* a compilation of approximately eighteen thousand fashion terms, plus six hundred illustrations, for use as a reference source by students of fashion. The book took seven years to complete, and in the process Calasibetta searched through some fifteen thousand periodicals and filled fourteen file drawers with her material and pen and ink drawings. Fifty of the drawings present a pictorial history of fashion from ancient Egypt to the 1970's.

Calasibetta relied on her personal fashion collection to provide her with much of the material for the dictionary. Her collection of periodicals, dating back to 1823, and her book collection were invaluable sources of historical fashion information and terminology. In addition to books and periodicals about fashion history, Calasibetta's collection contains costumes, accessories dating from 1848, and fashion plates from 1802.

AVOCATIONAL INTERESTS: Travel, reading, swimming, sewing, sketching, painting.

BIOGRAPHICAL/CRITICAL SOURCES: GRIT, August 19, 1973, June 22, 1975; *Williamsport Citizen's Press,* September 28, 1974.

* * *

CALDER, Daniel Gillmore 1939-

PERSONAL: Born February 10, 1939, in Lubec, Maine; son of Gillmore D. and Margaret (Burr) Calder. *Education:* Bowdoin College, A.B., 1960; University of Iowa, M.A., 1962; Indiana University, M.A., 1967, Ph.D., 1969. *Home:* 14447 Dunbar Pl., Sherman Oaks, Calif. 91423. *Office:* Department of English, University of California, 405 Hilgard Ave., Los Angeles, Calif. 90024.

CAREER: Bowdoin College, Brunswick, Maine, instructor in English and drama, 1962-64; University of Washington, Seattle, assistant professor of English, 1969-71; University of California, Los Angeles, assistant professor, 1971-75, associate professor, 1975-80, professor of English, 1980—. *Member:* Modern Language Association of America, Mediaeval Academy of America, Medieval Association of the Pacific.

WRITINGS: (Contributor) Lewis Nicholson and Dolores Frese, editors, *Anglo-Saxon Poetry: Essays in Appreciation,* University of Notre Dame Press, 1975; (with Michael J. B. Allen) *Sources and Analogues of Old English Poetry: The Major Latin Texts in Translation,* D. S. Brewer, 1976; (editor) *Old English Poetry: Essays on Style,* University of California Press, 1979; *Cynewulf,* Twayne, 1981. Contributor to language and philology journals.

WORK IN PROGRESS: Sources and Analogues of Old English Poetry: The Major Germanic and Celtic Texts, publication by D. S. Brewer expected in 1983; *The Development of Old English Prose Style,* completion expected in 1983.

* * *

CALDWELL, Irene Catherine (Smith) 1908-1979

OBITUARY NOTICE—See index for *CA* sketch: Born August 29, 1908, in Santa Fe, Kan.; died January, 1979. Clergywoman, educator, and author. Caldwell taught at Warner Pacific College and Anderson College School of Theology. At the time of her death, she was the head of the Christian education department at the Warner Southern College in Florida. Among Caldwell's writings are *Solving Church School Problems, Our Concern Is Children,* and *The Teacher as Evangelist.* Obituaries and other sources: *Who's Who in America,* 40th edition, Marquis, 1978. (Date of death provided by Jane Wiebe, instructor at Warner Southern College.)

CALIBAN
See REID, J(ohn) C(owie)

* * *

CAMERINI, Mario 1895-1981

OBITUARY NOTICE: Born February 6, 1895, in Rome, Italy; died February 6, 1981. Director and author of screenplays. Camerini is hailed as the creator of a genre of films, called white telephone films, characterized by humorous romantic intrigues and emotional upsets in upper middle class settings. (The white telephone was considered a bourgeois status symbol.) Camerini made two or three of these films per year during the 1930's and early forties, but later turned to more serious endeavors such as the screen versions of *I Promessi Sposi, Ulysses,* and *War and Peace.* Among the screenplays he wrote are "Jolly—Clown da Circo," "Gli Uomini Che Mascalzoni" ("Men Are Such Rascals"), and "Il Signor Max." Obituaries and other sources: *Dictionary of Film Makers,* University of California Press, 1972; *The World Encyclopedia of Film,* A. & W. Visual Library, 1972; *The Oxford Companion to Film,* Oxford University Press, 1976; *London Times,* February 26, 1981.

* * *

CAMERON, D. Y.
See COOK, Dorothy Mary

* * *

CAMERON, Kenneth 1922-

PERSONAL: Born May 21, 1922, in Burnley, England; son of Angus Whittaker (a tape-sizer) and Elizabeth Alice (Hargreaves) Cameron; married Kathleen Heap, August 12, 1947 (died July 1, 1977); children: Susan (Mrs. William Cole), Iain Stewart. *Education:* University of Leeds, B.A., 1947; University of Sheffield, Ph.D., 1951. *Politics:* Liberal. *Religion:* Methodist. *Home:* 292 Queens Rd., Beeston, Nottingham NG9 1JA, England. *Office:* Department of English Studies, University of Nottingham, Nottingham NG7 2RD, England.

CAREER: University of Sheffield, Sheffield, England, assistant lecturer, 1947-50; University of Nottingham, Nottingham, England, lecturer, 1950-59, senior lecturer, 1959-62, reader, 1962-63, professor of English language, 1963—. *Member:* Royal Historical Society (fellow), Viking Society (president, 1972-74), English Place-Name Society (honorary member of board of directors). *Awards, honors:* Sir Israel Gollancz Memorial Prize from British Academy, 1969.

WRITINGS: The Place-Names of Derbyshire, Volume I: *Introduction, River Names, High Peak Hundred,* Volume II: *Scarsdale Hundred, Wirksworth Hundred, Morleyston and Litchurch Hundred,* Volume III: *Appletree Hundred, Repton and Gresley Hundred, Analyses, Indexes,* Cambridge University Press, 1959; *English Place Names,* Batsford, 1961, 3rd edition, 1978; *Scandinavian Settlement in the Territory of the Five Boroughs,* University of Nottingham, Part I: *The Place-Names Evidence,* 1965, Part II: *In Medieval Scandinavia,* 1970, Part III: *In England Before the Conquest,* 1971; *Place-Name Evidence for the Anglo-Saxon Invasion and Scandinavian Settlements: Eight Studies,* English Place-Name Society, 1976; *The Significance of English Place-Names,* British Academy, 1976.

Contributor: M. W. Barley and R.P.C. Hanson, editors, *Christianity in Britain, 300-700,* [Leicester, England], 1968; Folke Sandregren, editors, *Otium et Negotium* (title means

"Work and Leisure"), 1973; Thorsten Andersson and Karl Inge Sandred, editors, *The Vikings*, [Uppsala, Sweden], 1978; *Ortnamnssaellskapets i Uppsala Arsskrift* (title means "Handbook of the Place-Name Society in Uppsala"), [Uppsala], 1978. Contributor to medieval and Scandinavian studies journals, and to *Journal of the English Place-Name Society*.

WORK IN PROGRESS: The Place-Names of Lincolnshire, publication by English Place-Name Society expected in mid-1980's.

SIDELIGHTS: Kenneth Cameron told *CA:* "The study of English place-names is basically to determine the etymology and meaning of individual place-names, and the technique involved is essentially philological. It involves the collection of the spellings of the place-name from the present day back to its earliest recorded form and the analysis of such a collection in the light of the known dialectal history of English sounds. The volumes of the English Place-Name Society contain, county by county, all the names recorded on the modern six-inch Ordnance Survey map, together with the names of fields from the nineteenth century to the Middle Ages. Such a collection takes fifteen years or more to assemble and years more to edit.

"During the past sixteen years or so, a good deal of work has been done using the evidence of place-names to throw light on settlement history in the Romano-British and Anglo-Saxon periods and in the effects of the Viking settlements in various parts of England. Much exciting work has been done, and a 'new look' in English place-name studies has as a result been seen. My own work in particular involves an assessment of Viking settlement, but also recently an attempt to trace Welsh or British survival in Anglo-Saxon England. All this may be summed up under the general heading 'The Significance of English Place-Names,' and in the next couple of decades we can anticipate tremendous advances in many different areas of study, where the evidence of place-names can be used to throw light on settlement history."

*   *   *

CAMPBELL, Ian 1899-1978

OBITUARY NOTICE—See index for *CA* sketch: Born October 17, 1899, in Bismarck, N.D.; died February 11, 1978. Educator, geologist and co-author of *The Earth and Human Affairs* and *Minerals: Nature's Fabulous Jewels.* Cambell was associated with the California Institute of Technology for more than forty years. (Date of death provided by wife, Catherine Chase Campbell.)

*   *   *

CAMPBELL, Patricia J(ean) 1930-
(Patty Campbell)

PERSONAL: Born November 20, 1930, in Hollywood, Calif.; daughter of Fred Duane and Frances (Griffith) Cowan; married Billy Wilmon Campbell, April 20, 1951 (divorced, September, 1970); children: Fred Campbell-Craven, Broos, Aisha, Cameron. *Education:* University of California, Los Angeles, B.A., 1952; University of California, Berkeley, M.L.S., 1953. *Politics:* Democrat. *Religion:* "Liberal Christian." *Home:* 2611 Fourth St., Santa Monica, Calif. 90405.

CAREER: Library of Hawaii, Honolulu, librarian, 1954-55; Office of Economic Opportunity, Los Angeles, Calif., housing organizer, 1967-69; Los Angeles Public Library, Los Angeles, young adult librarian, 1969-72, assistant coordinator of young adult services, 1972-78; writer, consultant, and belly

dancer, 1978—. *Member:* American Library Association (member of board of directors of Young Adult Services Division, 1979—), Women Library Workers, Young Adult Reviewers of Southern California (president, 1975), Phi Beta Kappa.

WRITINGS: Sex Education Books for Young Adults, 1892-1979, Bowker, 1979; *Passing the Hat: Street Performers in America,* Delacorte, 1981. Author of "Se Habla YA Aqui," a column in *Booklegger,* and "The YA Perplex," a column in *Wilson Library Bulletin.* Contributor to library magazines, under name Patty Campbell.

WORK IN PROGRESS: Passing the Hat Abroad: American Street Performers in Europe, with photographer D. Lincoln Shore; a revision of *An Ample Field,* for American Library Association; *Successful Divorce,* with Ruth Brice and D. Lincoln Shore.

SIDELIGHTS: Patricia Campbell wrote: "My strength and my weakness as a writer is that I care passionately about the people and books that are my subjects. This sometimes leads me to an outspokenness that has made me (I hope) a controversial figure in the library press. With the publication of *Passing the Hat* I have moved into the writing of books for the general public, and hope to continue as the Boswell of the cultural underworld."

*   *   *

CAMPBELL, Patty
See CAMPBELL, Patricia J(ean)

*   *   *

CAMUTI, Louis J(oseph) 1893-1981

OBITUARY NOTICE—See index for *CA* sketch: Born August 30, 1893, in Parma, Italy; died of a heart attack, February 24, 1981, near Mount Vernon, N.Y. Veterinarian and author. Camuti worked as a veterinarian for cats for more than sixty years. He was also an inspector of the New York City Department of Health, the president of a poultry firm, and the founding president of a company of food and drug regulations consultants. Camuti wrote two autobiographies, *Park Avenue Vet* and *All My Patients Are Under the Bed: Memoirs of a Cat Doctor.* Obituaries and other sources: Louis Camuti and Lloyd Alexander, *Park Avenue Vet,* Holt, 1962; Camuti and Haskell Frankel, *All My Patients Are Under the Bed: Memoirs of a Cat Doctor,* Simon & Schuster, 1980; *New York Times,* February 27, 1981.

*   *   *

CANNON, Ravenna
See MAYHAR, Ardath

*   *   *

CAPON, (Harry) Paul 1912-1969

OBITUARY NOTICE—See index for *CA* sketch: Born December 18, 1912, at Kenton Hall, Suffolk, England; died in November, 1969. Screenwriter, translator, editor of motion pictures, and author of science fiction and mysteries. Capon worked as a screenwriter and editor for London Films, Gaumont British, and Warner Brothers during the 1930's. He also worked for British International and Walt Disney before becoming head of the film division for Independent Television News. Capon translated books from the French for Walker & Co. Publishers. He wrote more than thirty novels, including *Battered Caravanserai, Image of a Murder, The Other Half of the Planet, Warrior's Moon,* and *Lord of the*

Chariots. Obituaries and other sources: *Science Fiction and Fantasy Literature*, Volume 2: *Contemporary Science Fiction Authors II*, Gale, 1979.

*   *   *

CAPPER, Douglas Parode   1898(?)-1979

OBITUARY NOTICE—See index for *CA* sketch: Born c. 1898 in Sydney, Australia; died July 24, 1979. Military officer and author. Capper served as commander of the British Naval Representative in Japan after World War II. His writings include *On the Pilgrims Way, The Vikings of Britain,* and *Famous Battleships of the World.* Obituaries and other sources: *London Daily Telegraph*, July 26, 1979. (Exact date of death provided by wife, Yolanda Capper.)

*   *   *

CARALEY, Demetrios   1932-

PERSONAL: Born June 22, 1932, in New York, N.Y.; son of Chris and Stella Caraley; married Jeanne Benner (a teacher of the handicapped), September 7, 1957; children: James Christopher (deceased), David Andrew, Anne Leslie. *Education:* Columbia University, B.A. (summa cum laude), 1954, Ph.D., 1962. *Politics:* Democrat. *Home:* 24 Hemlock Dr., North Tarrytown, N.Y. 10591.

CAREER: Barnard College and Columbia University, New York, N.Y., assistant professor, 1962-65, associate professor, 1965-68, professor of political science, 1968—, Janet H. Robb Professor of Social Sciences, 1980—, director of graduate program in public affairs, 1977—. Member of board of trustees and deputy mayor of North Tarrytown, N.Y., 1971-73. *Military service:* U.S. Navy, 1954-56; became lieutenant junior grade. *Member:* American Political Science Association, Academy of Political Science, Association for Public Policy Analysis and Management, Phi Beta Kappa.

WRITINGS: The Politics of Military Unification, Columbia University Press, 1966; *Party Politics and National Elections,* Little, Brown, 1966; *New York City's Deputy Mayor,* Citizens Budget Committee, 1966; (with R. H. Connery) *Governing the City,* Praeger, 1969; *American Political Institutions in the 1970's,* Columbia University Press, 1976; *City Governments and Urban Problems,* Prentice-Hall, 1977; (with M. A. Epstein) *The Making of American Foreign and Military Policy,* Dabor Science, 1978; *Congress and the Cities,* MIT Press, 1981. Editor of *Political Science Quarterly,* 1973—.

*   *   *

CARDOZO, Nancy

PERSONAL: Born in New York, N.Y.; daughter of Danforth and Constance (Mordecai) Cardozo; married James Egleson (divorced, 1953); married Russell Cowles (an artist), March 19, 1954 (deceased); children: (first marriage) Nicholas, Jan. *Education:* Attended Swarthmore College. *Home:* 179 East 70th St., Apt. 11-A, New York, N.Y. 10021; and R.D. 1, New Milford, Conn. 06776.

CAREER: Writer. Gives poetry readings. *Member:* International P.E.N.

WRITINGS: Helmet of the Wind (poems), Bobbs-Merrill, 1972; *Lucky Eyes and a High Heart: The Life of Maud Gonne* (Book-of-the-Month Club selection), Bobbs-Merrill, 1978 (published in England as *Maud Gonne: Lucky Eyes and a High Heart,* Gollancz, 1979).

Work represented in anthologies, including *Best Short Stories,* 1955; *A Time for Growing,* Random House, 1968; *Men*

and Women: The Poetry of Love, edited by Louis Untermeyer, American Heritage Publishing Co., 1970. Contributor of poems, stories, and articles to magazines, including *Redbook, Seventeen, Harper's Bazaar, New Yorker, Mademoiselle,* and *Hudson Review,* and newspapers.

WORK IN PROGRESS: A novel; a collection of poems.

SIDELIGHTS: Nancy Cardozo told *CA:* "I was born in New York City and grew up there and in New England. I live and work in an old stone house in New Milford. I have been writing poems since I was a child. When I was thirteen some of them were published in *Poetry* and *Scribner's.*"

*   *   *

CAREW, Dudley Charles   1903-1981

OBITUARY NOTICE: Born in 1903; died March 22, 1981. Journalist, critic, and author. A member of the *London Times* editorial staff for more than thirty years, Carew also reviewed films and books and contributed articles about cricket to the newspaper. Among his writings are two memoirs, *The House Is Gone* and *A Fragment of Friendship,* books about cricket, and several novels. Obituaries and other sources: *London Times,* March 27, 1981.

*   *   *

CARLISLE, D. M.
See COOK, Dorothy Mary

*   *   *

CARLTON, David   1938-

PERSONAL: Born July 16, 1938, in Bradford, England. *Education:* London School of Economics and Political Science, London, B.A. (with honors), 1960, Ph.D., 1966. *Residence:* Kent, England. *Agent:* A. P. Watt Ltd., 26/28 Bedford Row, London WC1R 4HL, England. *Office:* Polytechnic of North London, Prince of Wales Rd., London N.W.5, England.

CAREER: Polytechnic of North London, London, England, assistant lecturer, 1967-68, lecturer, 1968-70, senior lecturer in diplomatic history, 1970—. Labour candidate for Parliament, 1966, 1974. *Member:* International Institute for Strategic Studies, Royal Institute of International Affairs, Reform Club.

WRITINGS: MacDonald Versus Henderson: The Foreign Policy of the Second Labour Government, Humanities, 1970; (editor with Carlo Schaerf) *The Dynamics of the Arms Race,* Wiley, 1975; (editor with Schaerf) *International Terrorism and World Security,* Wiley, 1975; (editor with Schaerf) *Arms Control and Technological Innovation,* Wiley, 1977; (editor with Yonah Alexander and Paul Wilkinson) *Terrorism: Theory and Practice,* Westview Press, 1979; *Anthony Eden: A Biography,* Indiana University Press, 1981; (editor with Schaerf) *Contemporary Terror: Essays in Sub-State Violence,* Macmillan, 1981; (editor with Schaerf) *The Hazards of the International Energy Crisis,* Macmillan, 1981; (editor with Schaerf) *The Arms Race in the 1980's,* St. Martin's, in press; (editor with Schaerf) *South-Eastern Europe: A Powder Keg for the 1980's?,* St. Martin's, in press. Contributor of articles and reviews to political science and history journals. Associate editor of *Terrorism: An International Journal.*

*   *   *

CARMEL, Hesi   1937-

PERSONAL: Born March 24, 1937, in Vienna, Austria; son of Baruch and Gerda (Hellman) Carmel; married Reni Cherkinsky (a journalist), June 25, 1968; children: Dean, Elya. *Education:* Institut d'Etudes Politiques, Diplome d'Etudes Politiques, 1957. *Religion:* Jewish. *Home:* 128 Haeshel, Herzelya, Pituakh, Israel. *Agent:* Harold Lipton, 450 North Roxbury Dr., Beverly Hills, Calif. 90210.

CAREER: Tiberias, Jerusalem, Israel, member of Israeli delegation to Syra, Lebanon, and Jordan, 1957-60; Israel Foreign Service, attache in Paris, France, 1960-62, second secretary in the Congo, 1962-63, first secretary in Abidjan, Ivory Coast, 1963-64, Bangkok, Thailand, 1964-65, Singapore, 1965-66, and Tokyo, Japan, 1966-67; *Maariv,* Tel Aviv, Israel, member of editorial board, 1968-70; Israel Foreign Service, consul general in Los Angeles, Calif., 1970-72; *Maariv,* member of editorial board, 1972-74; *L'Express,* Paris, France, foreign correspondent, 1974—; author, 1974—. Chairman of Reca Press, 1974—. *Military service:* Israel Defense Forces, military correspondent, 1957-60. Israel Defense Forces Reserve, 1960—; present rank, captain.

WRITINGS: Kippour, [Israel], 1973, Hachette Litterature, 1974; *The Kissinger Connection,* Yedioth Publishing, 1975; (with Jacques Derogy) *Histoire secrete d'Israel,* Orban, 1978, translation published as *The Untold History of Israel,* Grove, 1979; *Embassy* (political fiction), translated from the original Hebrew by Michael Greenspun, Reca Press, 1980; *Foreign Correspondent* (novel), Reca Press, 1981.

WORK IN PROGRESS: Floreal, a novel about Napoleon in Palestine.

SIDELIGHTS: Carmel told *CA:* "As a journalist and a former senior diplomat, I believe in the special combination of facts and fiction; in the importance of an authentic background for a political drama in which the fiction completes and complements the event. The 'faction' (facts and fiction) gives us a new dimension for the understanding (and enjoyment) of the complexities of modern politics and enables us to tell history in a fascinating way."

*   *   *

CARMINES, Al(vin Allison, Jr.) 1936-

PERSONAL: Born July 25, 1936, in Hampton, Va.; son of Alvin Allison (a boat captain) and Katherine (a teacher; maiden name, Graham) Carmines. *Education:* Swarthmore College, B.A., 1958; Union Theological Seminary, New York, N.Y., B.D., 1961, S.T.M., 1963. *Politics:* Democrat. *Home:* 237 Thompson St., New York, N.Y. 10012. *Agent:* Arthur Zinberg, 11 East 44th St., New York, N.Y. *Office:* Judson Memorial Church, 55 Washington Sq. St., New York, N.Y. 10012.

CAREER: Ordained American Baptist minister; Judson Memorial Church, New York, N.Y., 1961, began as associate minister, became minister. Founder of Judson Poets' Theater, 1961; member of board of directors of Arts, Religion, Culture. Composer; actor, director, and producer; teacher. Guest on television programs, including "Tonight Show," "Today Show," and "Mike Douglas." *Awards, honors:* Obie Awards from *Village Voice,* 1964, for "What Happened" and "Home Movies," 1968, for "In Circles," and 1979, for sustained achievement; Vernon Rice Awards from Drama Desk, 1968, for score of "In Circles," 1969, for score of "Peace," named outstanding composer, 1974, for "The Faggot"; cultural award from city of New York, 1979.

WRITINGS—Plays; produced in New York City at Judson Poets' Theatre, except as noted: "The Sayings of Mao Tsetung" (opera), January 26, 1968; "The Urban Crisis," October 9, 1969; "Christmas Rappings" (oratorio), December

14, 1969; (co-author) "About Time," April 12, 1970; "The Playful Tyrant," October 18, 1970; "The Journey of Snow White" (oratorio), February 26, 1971; "Joan," November 19, 1971, produced Off-Broadway at Circle in the Square, June 19, 1972; "A Look at the Fifties," April 14, 1972; "Religion," October 28, 1973; "The Future," March 25, 1974; "The Duel," first produced in New York City at Brooklyn Academy of Music, April 24, 1974; "Sacred and Profane Love," February, 1975. Also author of play, "The Agony of Paul."

Composer of music and/or author of lyrics; produced in New York City at Judson Poets' Theatre, except as noted: "Vaudeville Skit," August 24, 1962; "The Wax Engine," June 13, 1963; "What Happened," September 19, 1963; "An Old Tune," December 19, 1963; "Home Movies," March 19, 1964; "Patter for a Soft Shoe Dance," July 9, 1964; "Sing Ho for a Bear," December 17, 1964; "Promenade," April 8, 1965; "A Beautiful Day," December 16, 1965; "Pomegranada," January 1, 1967; "Song of Songs," February, 1967; "Gorilla Queen," March 10, 1967; "Successful Life of Three," May 18, 1967; "Celebrations," June 15, 1967; "In Circles," October 6, 1967; "Untitled Play," 1967; "The Line of Least Existence," March 15, 1968; "Songs by Carmines" (solo show), first produced in New York City at Gramercy Arts Theatre, June 25, 1968; "Peace," November 1, 1968; "The Poor Little Match Girl," December 22, 1968; "Wanted," September 17, 1971; "The Life of a Man," September 29, 1972; "The Making of Americans," November 10, 1972; "The Faggot," April 13, 1973; "Listen to Me," October 18, 1974; "Christmas '74," December, 1974; "Why I Love New York," October, 1975. Also composer of music for "Dr. Faustus Lights the Lights."

Contributor to *Motive.*

SIDELIGHTS: Carmines's sound recordings include "In Circles," released by Avant-Garde; "Promenade," released by RCA Victor; "Peace," released by Metromedia; and "Joan," released by Judson.

Carmines commented: "Paul Tillich's *Systematic Theology* got me into the ministry. Reinhold Niebuhr, in *Nature and Deity of Man,* taught me about the single implication of good intention. Martin Heidegger's *Time and Being* is the most profound philosophy of our time. Becket's 'Waiting for Godot' is the first play of our time. Mozart and Bessie Smith are the two greatest geniuses of all time. 'Cosi fan tutte' is my favorite opera."

*   *   *

CAROLL, Nonie 1926-
(Nonie Carol Murphy)

PERSONAL: Married name, Nonie Carol Murphy, name legally changed in 1981; born October 31, 1926, in New York, N.Y.; daughter of Irving S. and Miriam Gambert; married Red Weiss (a marketing executive), November 9, 1945 (divorced, 1966); married Lee Murphy (a newscaster and producer), May 11, 1967 (divorced, 1980); children: Jane Margot Schreiber. *Education:* Attended Brooklyn College (now of the City University of New York), 1944. *Home:* 12 West 72nd St., New York, N.Y. 10023. *Agent:* Elaine Markson Literary Agency, Inc., 44 Greenwich Ave., New York, N.Y. 10011.

CAREER: Television actress, 1959-67; Douglas Elliman, New York, N.Y., realtor, 1973-74; writer, 1974—.

WRITINGS—All under name Nonie Carol Murphy: *Mutual Arrangements* (novel), Simon & Schuster, 1976. Contributor to *Vogue* and *Viva.*

WORK IN PROGRESS: Dream Vacations; or, How Not to Be a Tourist, "a book which is a philosophy of vacationing—so the readers may come home with more than a tan. During my research I have floated in a hot-air balloon over the Loire Valley, cruised up the Nile in a yacht, gone to a sex-therapy clinic in a chateau outside Paris, vacationed with thirty nuns in a cloister, etc."

SIDELIGHTS: Caroll told *CA:* "I was totally unqualified to author my first book. I had never taken a course in literature during my brief year in college, had never taken a course in writing at any time, and had hardly read (my reading block didn't clear until after I began writing myself). But then I was equally unqualified to begin an acting career at the age of thirty-three with no experience or credits. How do I (no genius, no extraordinary talent) attain these seemingly impossible goals? Well, to write, for instance, I arm myself with pencil and paper (two prime requisites) and turn a deaf ear on society's "belief systems." If I pay attention to them, I come up with too many reasons why it is absolutely *impossible* to do whatever it is I want to do—and make failure a self-fulfilling prophecy. Instead, I find it more fun to dig up equally valid reasons as to why I *can* do whatever it is I want to do. Get it? The secret is simple: write mental scripts with happy endings. . . ."

*   *   *

CARROLL, Thomas J. 1909-1971

OBITUARY NOTICE—See index for *CA* sketch: Born August 6, 1909, in Gloucester, Mass.; died April 24, 1971. Clergyman and director of Catholic Guild for All the Blind. Carroll was associated with various institutions for aid to the blind throughout his life. After his death, the Catholic Guild was renamed the Carroll Center for the Blind. He wrote *Blindness: What It Is, What It Does, and How to Live With It.* Obituaries and other sources: *New York Times,* April 25, 1971. (Date of death provided by Carol Dyer, secretary to the director of the Carroll Center for the Blind.)

*   *   *

CARR-SAUNDERS, Alexander 1886-1966

OBITUARY NOTICE—See index for *CA* sketch: Born January 14, 1886, in Reigate, England; died October 6, 1966. Educator and author. Carr-Saunders was director of the London School of Economics for nearly twenty years. He also worked during the 1920's and 1930's as a professor at the University of Liverpool. He wrote *Population Problem, Eugenics, Social Structure, Population, The Professions, World Population,* and *New Universities Overseas.* Obituaries and other sources: *Who Was Who:* Volume VI: *1961-1970,* A. & C. Black, 1972.

*   *   *

CARSAC, Francis
See BORDES, Francois

*   *   *

CARTER, John Mack 1928-

PERSONAL: Born February 28, 1928, in Murray, Ky.; son of William Z. and Martha (Stevenson) Carter; married Sharlyn Emily Reaves (an author), August 30, 1948; children: Jonna Lyn, John Mack II. *Education:* University of Missouri, B.J., 1948, M.A., 1949. *Politics:* Democrat. *Religion:* Disciples of Christ. *Home:* 144 East Wharf Rd., Madison, Conn. 06443. *Agent:* Scott Meredith, 845 Third Ave., New York,

N.Y. 10022. *Office:* 641 Lexington Ave., New York, N.Y. 10022.

CAREER: Assistant editor for *Better Homes and Gardens,* 1949-51; *Household,* Topeka, Kan., managing editor, 1953-57, editor, 1957-58; executive editor of *Together,* 1958-59; editor of *American Home,* 1959-61; *McCall's,* New York City, executive editor, 1961, editor, 1962-65; McCall corp., New York City, vice-president and director, 1962-65; *Ladies Home Journal,* editor in chief, 1965-74, publisher, 1967-70; Downe Communications Inc., president and chief operating officer, 1972-73, chairman of board and editor in chief, 1973-77; president of American Home Publishing Co., 1974-75; *Good Housekeeping,* New York City, editor in chief, 1975—. *Military service:* U.S. Naval Reserve, 1951-53; became lieutenant junior grade. *Member:* Sigma Delta Chi. *Awards, honors:* Walter Williams Award for writing, 1949.

WRITINGS: All the Lovely Ladies, Coward, 1981.

*   *   *

CARTWRIGHT, N.
See SCOFIELD, Norma Margaret Cartwright

*   *   *

CARVIC, Heron ?-1980

OBITUARY NOTICE—See index for *CA* sketch: Born in London, England; died February, 1980. Dancer, actor, designer, builder, decorator, market gardener, and author. Carvic wrote crime novels, including *Picture Miss Seeton, Miss Seeton Sings,* and *Odds on Miss Seeton.* (Date of death provided by Julie Laird, an associate of the Victoria and Albert Museum.)

*   *   *

CASE, Justin
See GLEADOW, Rupert Seeley

*   *   *

CASSEL, Mana-Zucca 1891-1981
(Mana-Zucca)

OBITUARY NOTICE: Born December 25, 1891, in New York; died March 8, 1981 in Miami, Fla. Composer best known for her songs "I Love Life," "Honey Lamb," and "Time and Time Again." The creator of hundreds of popular songs, two operas, a ballet, chamber music, and orchestral works, Mana-Zucca made her piano debut with the New York Symphony Orchestra at the age of eight and gave concerts throughout Europe as a child. Her husband, Irwin M. Cassel, supplied the lyrics for some of Mana-Zucca's compositions. Obituaries and other sources: *New York Times,* March 11, 1981.

*   *   *

CASSIDY, William L(awrence Robert)
(William Schwabe)

PERSONAL: Born in Indiana; son of Lawrence D. (an executive in the entertainment industry) and Mary (Fitzpatrick) Cassidy; married Virginia Sudymont, 1969 (divorced, 1971); married Shari Berne, 1971 (divorced, 1979); children: Christine. *Education:* Attended California Institute of Asian Studies, University of California, Berkeley, and Yale University. *Politics:* Conservative. *Religion:* Buddhist. *Office address:* P.O. Box 4596, Sather Gate Station, Berkeley, Calif. 94704.

CAREER: Company for Security Research, Berkeley, Calif., director, 1975—. Partner of Castle Knife Co., 1977—; vice-president of Black Manufacturing Co., Inc., 1979—; president of Intelligence Studies Foundation, Inc.; political adviser in Central America, 1978-79. Founding secretary of Tibetan Nyingmapa Meditation Center, 1969-70; chairman of board of chancellors of Vajrayana Buddhist Churches of America; chief of security for part of U.S. tour of the Dalai Lama of Tibet, 1979. Consultant to U.S. Departments of State, Justice, and the Treasury and U.S. Army.

MEMBER: Association of Former Intelligence Officers (life member), National Intelligence Study Center (life member), Security and Intelligence Fund (sponsoring member), Special Operations Association (associate member), Camp X Military Museum Society (life member), Knifemakers Guild (associate member), Heaven and Earth Society (honorary member), White Tiger Family Association (honorary member).

WRITINGS: The Complete Book of Knife Fighting, Paladin Press, 1975; *Planned Political Assassination,* International Association of Chiefs of Police, 1977; *Quick or Dead* (nonfiction), Paladin Press, 1978; *Political Kidnapping,* Sycamore Island Books, 1978; *Basic Manual of Knife Fighting,* Paladin Press, 1978.

Author of "The Diary of Mr. Grey," a feature film for Paramount Pictures, 1974. Contributor to magazines (sometimes under pseudonym William Schwabe), including *Guns, CoEvolution Quarterly,* and *Police Journal.* Executive editor of *Knife Digest,* 1974-76, and *American Blade,* 1976; contributing editor of *Soldier of Fortune,* 1978-79.

WORK IN PROGRESS: A book on the history of Anglo-American special intelligence training schools, publication expected in 1982; a biography of William Ewart Fairbairn.

SIDELIGHTS: Cassidy's assistant, Walter Singleton, told *CA:* "Mr. Cassidy is an internationally respected student of intelligence history and has been afforded unprecedented opportunities to record this history working in association with pioneer intelligence trainers, officers, and executives in the United States and abroad. A unique facet of his background is the esteem in which he is regarded by Tibetan Buddhists: he is regarded as a *tulku* or especially gifted being, and as such is held in great respect by Buddhist leaders the world over."

*   *   *

CASSON, Hugh Maxwell 1910-

PERSONAL: Born May 23, 1910, in London, England; son of Randal (in Indian Civil Service) and Mary Caroline (Man) Casson; married Margaret Macdonald Troup (an architect), 1938; children: Caroline Casson Ritchie, Nicola Casson Hessenberg, Dinah Casson Wood. *Education:* St. John's College, Cambridge, M.A., 1931; attended British School at Athens, 1933. *Religion:* Church of England. *Home:* 60 Elgin Crescent, London W.11, England. *Office:* Casson, Conder & Partners, 35 Thurloe Place, London S.W.7, England.

CAREER: Private practice of architecture in London, England, 1937-39; Air Ministry, London, camouflage officer, 1940-44; Ministry of Town and Country Planning, London, technical officer, 1944-46; Casson, Conder & Partners, London, senior partner, 1946—. Professor at Royal College of Art, 1953-75. Member of Royal Fine Art Commission, 1960—, and Royal Mint Advisory Committee, 1972—; director of architecture for Festival of Britain, 1948-51. Member of board of trustees of British Museum (Natural History)

and National Portrait Gallery, 1976—, and board of directors of British Council, 1977—.

MEMBER: Royal Institute of British Architects, Society of Industrial Artists (fellow), Royal Academy (president, 1976—), American Institute of Architects (honorary associate). *Awards, honors:* Royal Designer for Industry, 1951; Knight of the Order of the British Empire, 1952; Royal Artist, 1970; honorary doctorates from Royal College of Art, 1975, and University of Southampton, 1977; LL.D. from University of Birmingham, 1977; Knight Commander of Royal Victorian Order, 1978.

WRITINGS: New Sights of London, London Transport, 1937; *Bombed Churches,* Architectural Press, 1946; *Homes by the Million,* Penguin, 1947; (with Anthony Chitty) *Houses: Permanence and Prefabrication,* [London], 1947; *An Introduction to Victorian Architecture,* [London], 1948; (editor) *Inscape: The Design of Interiors,* Architectural Press, 1968; (with Joyce Grenfell) *Nanny Says,* Dobson, 1972; *Sketchbook,* Lion and Unicorn Press, 1975. Television and radio writer. Contributor to professional journals and popular magazines.

*   *   *

CATLIN, Warren Benjamin 1881-1968

OBITUARY NOTICE—See index for *CA* sketch: Born November 3, 1881, in Nemaha, Neb.; died July 10, 1968; Educator and author. Catlin was a Daniel B. Fayerweather Professor of economics and sociology at Bowdoin College from 1912 to 1952. He wrote *The Labor Problem in the United States and Great Britain* and *The Progress of Economics: A History.* Obituaries and other sources: *Who Was Who in America,* 5th edition, Marquis, 1973.

*   *   *

CERRUTI, James Smith 1918-

PERSONAL: Born July 12, 1918, in New York, N.Y.; son of James Joseph and Mary Agnes (Smith) Cerruti; married Hannah Brown (an attorney), March 8, 1941; children: Diana (Mrs. Ahmed Amin Ghanem), James Lawrence, Vera (Mrs. John Magruder). *Education:* City College (now of the City University of New York), B.A. (magna cum laude), 1939; Syracuse University, M.A., 1941. *Politics:* Independent. *Home:* 7800 Elba Rd., Alexandria, Va. 22306. *Office:* National Geographic, 17 and M Sts. N.W., Washington, D.C. 20036.

CAREER/WRITINGS: Syracuse University, Syracuse, N.Y., instructor, 1939-41; University of Illinois, Urbana, instructor, 1941-42; free-lance writer, 1946-47; *Holiday,* Philadelphia, Pa., senior editor, 1947-62; *National Geographic,* Washington, D.C., senior assistant editor, 1962—. Has contributed numerous articles to magazines, including *National Geographic, Holiday, Esquire,* and *Writer's Digest. Wartime service:* U.S. Signal Corps, 1942-46; served as civilian instructor. *Member:* International Confederation of Book Actors, Lach und Schiessgesellschaft, Phi Beta Kappa.

*   *   *

CHALIDZE, Valery Nikolaevich 1938-

PERSONAL: Born November 25, 1938, in Moscow, Soviet Union; came to the United States in 1972, naturalized citizen, 1979; son of Nikolai M. and Francesca I. (Janson) Chalidze; children: Maria Theresa. *Education:* Moscow University, B.A., 1958; Tbilisi University, M.A., 1965. *Home:* 145 East

92nd St., New York, N.Y. 10028. *Office:* Khronika Press, 505 Eighth Ave., New York, N.Y. 10018.

CAREER: Khronika Press (publisher), New York, N.Y., editor-in-chief, 1973—. President of Institute of Socialist Law, 1974—; director of International League for Human Rights.

WRITINGS: To Defend These Rights, Random House, 1974; *Criminal Russia,* Random House, 1977; (editor with Leon Lipsom) *Papers on Soviet Law,* Institute of Socialist Law, Volume I, 1977, Volume II, 1979; *Rabochee dvizhenee V SSSR* (in Russian; title means "The Workers' Movement in the U.S.S.R."), Khronika Press, 1979; *A Legal Aid for Travelers to the Soviet Union,* Helsinki Watch Group, 1981. Co-editor of *Chronical of Human Rights in the U.S.S.R.,* 1973—.

WORK IN PROGRESS: The U.S.S.R. and Covenant of Civil and Political Rights.

SIDELIGHTS: Chalidze commented to *CA:* "In 1970 in Moscow I founded, with Andrei Sakharov and Andrei Tverdokhlebov, the Moscow Human Rights Committee (the documents of which were published by the International League for Human Rights in 1972). I arrived in the United States in 1972 at the invitation of Georgetown University, at which time the Soviet government revoked my citizenship."

BIOGRAPHICAL/CRITICAL SOURCES: New York Times, December 14, 1972, December 15, 1972; *Time,* December 18, 1972; *Washington Post,* December 19, 1972; *Washington Star,* December 25, 1972; George Kline, *Dissent in the USSR: Politics, Ideology, and People,* Johns Hopkins Press, 1975.

* * *

CHAMBERLAIN, Wilt(on Norman)   1936-

PERSONAL: Born August 21, 1936, in Philadelphia, Pa.; son of William (a porter) and Olivia (a domestic) Chamberlain. *Education:* Attended University of Kansas, 1956-58. *Residence:* Bel Air, Calif. *Office:* c/o Big Wilt's Smalls Paradise Nightclub, 2294 Seventh Ave., New York, N.Y. 10030.

CAREER: Harlem Globetrotters basketball team, New York, N.Y., center, 1958-59; Philadelphia Warriors basketball team, Philadelphia, Pa., center, 1959-67; Philadelphia Seventy-Sixers basketball team, Philadelphia, center, 1967-72; Los Angeles Lakers basketball team, Inglewood, Calif., center, 1972-73. Owner of Big Wilt's Smalls Paradise Nightclub and Basin Street West (nightclub); actor in television commercials for products, including Brut aftershave lotion, Miller's Lite beer, and Volkswagen; executive producer of "Go for It" (movie documentary), 1976. Active in professional volleyball. *Awards, honors:* Named All-American center, University of Kansas, 1957-58; National Basketball Association (NBA) top scorer, 1959-65; NBA Rookie of the Year, 1960; NBA all-time single-season scorer, 1960; Hy Turkin Award for rookie of the year and Sam Davis Award for most valuable player, both from New York Basketball Writers, 1960; most valuable player of the NBA playoffs from *Sport,* 1972; elected to Basketball Hall of Fame.

WRITINGS: (With David Shaw) *Wilt: Just Like Any Other Seven-Foot Black Millionaire Who Lives Next Door,* Macmillan, 1973, published as *Wilt,* Warner Books, 1975.

SIDELIGHTS: Chamberlain's autobiography, *Wilt: Just Like Any Other Seven-Foot Black Millionaire Who Lives Next Door,* is about the man who has been called "the greatest offensive player in the history of basketball." The book candidly describes both Chamberlain's personal life and his basketball career, covering such topics as his unpopularity as

a player, his influence on the game of basketball, and the abilities of his former teammates. *Avocational interests:* Pet dogs, race horses, real estate and stock investments, jazz music, expensive automobiles, coaching and playing volleyball.

BIOGRAPHICAL/CRITICAL SOURCES: Newsweek, December 17, 1956, October 8, 1973; *New York Times Magazine,* April 29, 1972, June 3, 1973, September 13, 1975; Wilt Chamberlain and David Shaw, *Wilt: Just Like Any Other Seven-Foot Black Millionaire Who Lives Next Door,* Macmillan, 1973, published as *Wilt,* Warner Books, 1975; Dave Klein, *Pro Basketball's Big Men,* Random House, 1973; *Best Sellers,* October 1, 1973; *Village Voice,* November 1, 1973; *New York Times Book Review,* December 2, 1973; Bill Libby, *Goliath: The Wilt Chamberlain Story,* Dodd, 1977.*

* * *

CHAMBERS, Robin Bernard   1942-

PERSONAL: Born July 25, 1942; son of Bernard (a maintenance engineer) and Isabel Evelyn (a telephonist; maiden name, Stobbs) Chambers; married Elizabeth Ann Evertt (an information officer), November 12, 1965; children: Toby James. *Education:* Queen Mary College, London, B.A. (with honors), 1964, doctoral study, 1964-67. *Politics:* "Committed socialist." *Religion:* None. *Home:* 36 Colvestone Cres., London E8 2LH, England. *Office:* Clissold Park School, Clissold Rd., London N.16, England.

CAREER: English teacher and department head at schools in London, England, 1967-79; Clissold Park School, London, head teacher, 1979—.

WRITINGS: (With Tony Burgess and others) *Understanding Children Writing,* Penguin, 1973; *The Ice Warrior and Other Stories,* Kestrel, 1976; *The Fight of Neither Century and Other Stories,* Granada, 1980; *Shadows in the Pit,* Granada, 1980.

SIDELIGHTS: Chambers commented: "My motivation to write came and comes from the children I work with. They taught me how to write, and I have tried to learn with them. A lot of consumer research goes into the writing I do, which is little enough, because I am head teacher of an Inner London comprehensive school, with one thousand children, and that is more than a full-time job."

* * *

CHANDLER, Ruth Forbes   1894-1978

OBITUARY NOTICE—See index for *CA* sketch: Born July 17, 1894, in New Bedford, Mass.; died December 29, 1978. Educator and author. Chandler taught in New Bedford, Mass., for twenty-seven years before retiring in 1947. Her childrens' books include *Too Many Promises, The Happy Answer,* and *Middle Island Mystery.* (Date of death provided by Winona Strachan.)

* * *

CHAPIN, Louis Le Bourgeois, Jr.   1918-1981

PERSONAL: Born February 6, 1918, in New York, N.Y.; died April 1, 1981; son of Louis Le Bourgeois and Julia Appleton (Tuckerman) Chapin; married Mary Lee Smith (an administrative assistant), December 15, 1956; children: Julia Wyche. *Education:* Principia College, B.A., 1939; Boston University, A.M., 1948. *Religion:* Christian Scientist. *Home:* 7 Dandy Dr., Cos Cob, Conn. 06807.

CAREER: Held positions as radio announcer and director; Columbia Broadcasting System, staff director, 1944-45; Principia College, Elsah, Ill., instructor in fine arts and music, 1946-60; *Christian Science Monitor,* Boston, Mass., staff critic of music, theatre, film, and arts, 1960-63, drama critic, 1963-66; Earl Rowland Foundation, director, 1968-74; State University of New York Empire State College, State Springs, tutor in writing, 1973—. Church organist, 1980—. President of St. Botolph Citizens' Committee, 1961-62. *Member:* New Drama Forum Association.

WRITINGS: Favorite Paintings by Charles H. Russell, Crown, 1978; *Fifty Masterpieces by Frederick Remington,* Crown, 1979; (Contributor of pictures and captions) Owen Rachleff, editor, *Exploring the Bible With Your Children,* Abbeville Press, 1980. Author of a column in *Stamford Advocate,* 1980—. Connecticut critic for *Opera News;* drama critic for *Christianity and Crisis,* 1970—. Contributor of several hundred articles and reviews to magazines, including *Musical Heritage Review, Musical America, Art News, National Observer,* and *High Fidelity,* and newspapers.

WORK IN PROGRESS: Developing a seminar on sacred music; research on music as an accessible language.

SIDELIGHTS: Chapin told *CA:* "In my teaching I was involved mainly in a required introduction to all the arts. Since one person can't possibly *require* anyone else to enjoy or give any primal importance to the arts, my strong desire, first as a teacher and now mainly as a journalist, has been to show the arts as an escalating requirement of us all: not only for our full self-realization (and of course, enjoyment) but sooner or later—in league with our spiritual sense—for full human survival.

"So, as a writer and communicator-at-large, I have taken my own encounters with music, theatre, dance, visual, and other performing arts (like teaching) into dialogues among themselves and with any other accessible disciplines, not mostly academic dialogues, but rather more collaborative ones. In the *Christian Science Monitor* alone, aside from reviews in all the art fields and essays which may on occasion brush with etymology or ecology, I have appeared on feature pages devoted to business, living style, books, travel, children, and even sports—when I went unexpectedly to Sardinia and reviewed a new international golf course as a kind of earth sculpture.

"This diversification makes it hard to pigeonhole either an artist or writer—or for that matter just a human being, and since we are professionally programmed for pigeonholes it is not the easiest way to have a recognizable career (even as pigeons), but the arts are our languages for excellence, our keys to understanding who we *all* are and what is magnificently survivable out of all time (including the present), and this life of learning how to engineer and articulate the communicative bridges that we so vehemently need, is the career for me. Even if it means detonating pigeonholes.

"Speaking of which, I'm not even sure I'm an author. I feel more, as I. A. Richards once said about being a poet, like somebody to whom a message of some sort is handed, and he or she undertakes to transmit the thing with no pretense of having originated it.

"I guess one of my mottoes is the country's motto, *E pluribus unum.* Out of the whole marvelous, measureless *pluribus* of our world, we come to some degree to recognize the distinct *unum* that each of us is."

CHARDIET, Bernice (Kroll) 1927(?)-

PERSONAL: Married Oscar Chardiet (a doctor); children: two. *Education:* Queens College, B.A., 1949; later studied music composition with Hall Overton; graduate study at Juilliard School of Music, Yale Drama School, 1950-51, Hunter College, 1954, and Columbia University, 1956. *Office:* See-Saw Book Program, Scholastic Book Services, 50 West 44th St., New York, N.Y. 10036.

CAREER: Teacher of high school English and speech, 1954-59; Directory of Elementary Promotion, promotion copywriter, 1963-67; Scholastic Book Services, New York, N.Y., editor of See-Saw Book Program, 1967—. Has been vice-president and a member of the board of directors, Children's Film Associates; jazz pianist and recording artist.

WRITINGS: C Is for Circus (juvenile), illustrated by Brinton Turkle, Walker, 1971; (reteller) *Juan Bobo and the Pig: A Puerto Rican Folktale* (juvenile), illustrated by Hope Meryman, Walker, 1973. Lyricist and composer of "Puss in Boots: A Musical Production" (juvenile), Scholastic Records, 1969; also lyricist and composer of two Broadway revues, author of the script for a jazz series broadcast by Radio Free Europe, and contributor of articles to periodicals.*

*　　*　　*

CHARNIN, Martin (Jay) 1934-

PERSONAL: Born November 24, 1934, in New York, N.Y.; son of William (an opera singer) and Birdie (Blakeman) Charnin; married Lynn Ross (a dancer), March 2, 1958 (divorced, 1961); married Genii Prior (a dancer), January 8, 1962; children: (first marriage) Randy; (second marriage) Sasha. *Education:* Cooper Union, B.A., 1955. *Home:* 48 Jane St., New York, N.Y. 10014. *Office:* c/o Beam One Ltd., 850 Seventh Ave., New York, N.Y. 10019.

CAREER: Lyricist for plays, revues, and television programs, 1957—. Creator and producer of television programs, including "Annie: The Women in the Life of a Man," Columbia Broadcasting System (CBS-TV), 1970, (and director) "George M!," National Broadcasting Co. (NBC-TV), 1970, (and writer) "'S Wonderful, 'S Marvelous, 'S Gershwin," NBC-TV, 1972, "Dames at Sea," NBC-TV, 1972, "Get Happy: The Music of Harold Arlen," NBC-TV, 1973, "Cole Porter in Paris," NBC-TV, 1973, "Annie and the Hoods," 1974, "The Annie Christmas Show," 1977, and "'C'mon Saturday," 1977; producer of pilot program for Children's Television Workshop, summer, 1973. Director of plays, including "Ballad for a Firing Squad," 1968, (and creator) "Nash at Nine," 1973, "Music! Music!," 1974, "Annie," 1976, and "Bar Mitzvah Boy," 1978. Director and writer of night club acts for performers, including Shirley Jones, Abbe Lane, Dionne Warwick, and Nancy Wilson. Actor in plays and revues, including "West Side Story," 1957 and 1960, and "The Boys Against the Girls," 1959.

MEMBER: American Society of Composers, Authors, and Publishers, American Guild of Authors and Composers, Directors Guild of America, Writers Guild of America, New York Theatre Actors Society, Dramatists Guild. *Awards, honors:* Two Emmy awards from National Academy of Television Arts and Sciences for "Annie: The Women in the Life of a Man," 1970; two Emmy awards and George Foster Peabody Radio and Television award from the University of Georgia, all 1972, all for "'S Wonderful, 'S Marvelous, 'S Gershwin"; Antoinette Perry Award for best lyrics from

League of New York Theatres and Producers and Drama Desk awards for best lyrics and best director, all for "Annie"; Gold Record Award from Recording Industry Association of America for "The Best Thing You've Ever Done."

WRITINGS: The Giraffe Who Sounded Like Ol' Blue Eyes (for children), illustrations by Kate Draper, Dutton, 1976; *Annie: A Theatre Memoir,* Dutton, 1977. Author of television musical, "'S Wonderful, 'S Marvelous, 'S Gershwin," 1972.

Lyricist for plays and revues: "Kaleidoscope," 1957, (and sketchwriter) "Fallout Revue," 1959, "Upstairs at the Downstairs," 1959, "Pieces of Eight," 1959, "Little Revue," 1960, "Hot Spot," 1963, "Zenda," 1963, "Wet Paint," 1965, "Mata Hari," 1967, "Ballad for a Firing Squad," 1968, ":Two by Two," 1970, "Annie," 1976, and "I Remember Mama," 1979. Lyricist for television programs, including "Feathertop," American Broadcasting Co. (ABC-TV), 1961, and "Jackie Gleason Show," Columbia Broadcasting System (CBS-TV), 1961. Lyricist of songs, including "The Best Thing You've Ever Done," 1972, and "Maman."

SIDELIGHTS: Charnin's second book, *Annie: A Theatre Memoir,* chronicles the making of the award-winning musical "Annie." As creator, lyricist, and director of "Annie," Charnin was in a unique position to tell the story of the musical from its conception to its triumph on Broadway.

The show is based on Harold Gray's comic strip, "Little Orphan Annie." It is the story of a poor orphan who is rescued from the evil director of her orphanage by billionaire Oliver (Daddy) Warbucks. *Time* critic T. E. Kalem described the music as "wholesome family fare," and Clive Barnes of the *New York Times* said it was "lovable." "Annie" won a total of seven Tony awards, two Drama Desk awards, and the New York Drama Critics Circle award, following its Broadway opening on April 21, 1977.

AVOCATIONAL INTERESTS: Painting, travel.

BIOGRAPHICAL/CRITICAL SOURCES: New York Times, November 11, 1970, April 22, 1977, June 10, 1979; *New York Post,* April 22, 1977; *Time,* May 2, 1977.*

* * *

CHAVEZ, Patricia 1934-

PERSONAL: Born March 28, 1934, in Grants, N.M.; daughter of Joseph E. (an Army lieutenant colonel) and Mildred (a writer; maiden name, Stull) Chavez; married T. C. Newman (divorced, 1964); children: Robin Newman Langeliers, Laura Newman Smulktis. *Politics:* Independent. *Religion:* Christian. *Home:* Brahegaten 62, 114 37 Stockholm, Sweden. *Agent:* Cliff Cartland, 1519 Western Ave., Glendale, Calif. 91201. *Office:* Svenska World Vision, Vastmannangatan 41, 113 25 Stockholm, Sweden.

CAREER: Washington State University, Pullman, computer programmer, 1958-62; Information Systems Design, Oakland, Calif., systems analyst, 1963-66; I. Magnin & Carter Hawley Hale, San Francisco and Los Angeles, Calif., project manager, 1967-75; director of volunteer programs for World Vision International, Inc., 1975-79; Svenska World Vision for Scandinavia, Stockholm, Sweden, director, 1980—. *Member:* Data Processing Management Association.

WRITINGS: (With Cliff Cartland) *Picking Up the Pieces,* Thomas Nelson, 1980; *We Don't Have Wives* (guide for executive women), Thomas Nelson, in press. Also author of a screenplay, "Sky Storm."

SIDELIGHTS: Chavez remarked: "Mostly, the writing I have done, the book and several magazine articles, has been

a result of someone asking me to write about my experience. I think it's vital to share experiences and victories as well as failures."

* * *

CHEEVER, Susan 1943-

PERSONAL: Born July 31, 1943, in New York, N.Y.; daughter of John (an author) and Mary (a poet and teacher; maiden name, Winternitz) Cheever; married Robert Cowley (an editor), 1967 (divorced). *Education:* Brown University, B.A., 1965. *Residence:* New York, N.Y. *Agent:* Literistic, 32 West 40th St., New York, N.Y. 10018.

CAREER: Tarrytown Daily News, Tarrytown, N.Y., reporter, 1971-72; *Newsweek,* New York, N.Y., swing writer, 1974-75, religion editor, 1975-77, life-style editor, 1977-78; writer. Instructor in two creative writing classes at Hoffstra University, beginning in 1980. *Member:* Authors Guild.

WRITINGS: Looking for Work (novel), Simon & Schuster, 1980; *A Handsome Man* (novel), Simon & Schuster, 1981.

WORK IN PROGRESS: A novel, set in New York and New Hampshire, about female possessiveness and male passivity in an intense and violent marriage; a book about life in New York City.

SIDELIGHTS: Salley Potter Gardens, the daughter of a famous Columbia University literature professor, is the narrator-heroine of Susan Cheever's first novel, *Looking for Work.* Leaving a promising journalism career to marry a gifted editor, Salley "lives a pleasantly well-buttered life surrounded by ideas and celebrities," commented *Chicago Tribune Book World* critic Cyra McFadden; she also "gives little dinner parties, wears designer clothes, jogs and suffers from growing panic." Instead of happiness, she finds boredom and discontent. *Looking for Work* is, according to an *Atlantic* reviewer, the story of "the demise of a marriage, told by a young woman who mistakenly assumed that she should and could find meaning in her life by helping her husband to live his."

The similarities between the protagonist of *Looking for Work* and its author are obvious. Cheever, the daughter of Pulitzer Prize-winning author John Cheever, was a professional journalist before she began writing novels, and like Salley she married and divorced an editor. Admitting, "I borrowed from my life like a bandit," Cheever nevertheless maintains, "Salley is not me. She is a spinoff—calm, less complicated." Supporting his daughter's assertions, John Cheever remarked: "We have both agreed that fiction is not crypto-autobiography. This is an aesthetic mandate as well as a guarantee of the fact that I will not find in her novels any description of an old man who is too drunk to dance the Charleston." Although John Cheever does make a cameo appearance in *Looking for Work* as an honored guest at Salley's wedding, an *Atlantic* critic pointed out that "readers looking for a *roman a clef* about the senior novelist will be disappointed." McFadden suggested, "Read it not because John Cheever's daughter wrote it but because it is well worth reading."

Noting that "Miss Cheever shows considerable promise" and that "she produces occasional sentences that only a born writer achieves," *New York Times* critic Christopher Lehmann-Haupt also commented that "'Looking for Work' is not really much of a story.... [Cheever] has a voice, all right. But it will not be clearly heard until she finds something more to sing about." Several other critics shared Lehmann-Haupt's opinion, praising Cheever's writing skill while remarking that her first novel lacked depth. Susan Kennedy of the *Times Literary Supplement* acclaimed Cheever's "good descriptive writing," "her unobtrusive technical assurance," and "her respect for the just use of words"; but at the same time Kennedy argued that Cheever had not used her skills to "penetrate the deeper paradoxes of her characters' behavior." "It is clear she can write," agreed a *Newsweek* critic, but "by merely *telling* us how Salley feels instead of giving those feelings dramatic life, Cheever has created something less than a novel."

It seems that Cheever expected some criticism. In an interview with *Chicago Tribune Book World* critic Helen Dudar, Cheever commented that *Looking for Work* is "a beginner's book. It's a book in which I learned how to do a lot of things. I plan to get a lot better. But it's my first book and I love it. I just love it." Answering the critics, Cheever told *New York Times* reporter Judy Klemesrud, "one way my father has helped me is to show me that a writer can improve over the years. He certainly has gotten a lot better, and I hope that the same practice and hard work . . . will make me a better writer, too."

Cheever's second novel, *A Handsome Man,* is the story of thirty-two-year-old Hannah Bart, a book publicist, and her romantic involvement with Sam Noble, a glamorous and successful fifty-year-old publisher. Sam, who is divorced, is the "handsome man," and Hannah, though young and effervescent, is, Sam thinks, "a bit dowdy and definitely overweight." Hannah is flattered by Sam's interest in her, for she is aware of the frequency with which his affairs with women more beautiful and alluring than she were described in newspaper society columns and gossip magazines.

Despite the doubts that Sam and Hannah have about each other, things go fairly smoothly between them until they decide to meet in Ireland for a two-week vacation. Hannah suggests that Sam invite his estranged son Travis to join them, and with her encouragement, Sam attempts to reestablish his ties with the young man. Hannah's good intentions backfire when she finds herself relegated to a secondary position as Sam devotes himself more to his son than to her. The book's tension reaches its peak when the three decide to visit the troubled areas of Northern Ireland. "The mayhem in Ulster becomes a perfect paradigm for the mayhem—albeit the quiet mayhem—committed by three people," observed Joanne Kaufman in the *Detroit News.*

Kaufman noted that "*A Handsome Man* was written almost immediately after Cheever's first novel . . . but as surely as Hannah Bart comes of age, so Cheever has come of age as a writer." Elaine Kendall of the *Los Angeles Times* also praised the book, saying: "*A Handsome Man* is a literary ballet; Cheever demonstrates the illusion of effortless grace that comes from discipline, strength, and committed professionalism. . . . The author's second novel . . . fulfills every promise made by the first. In a couple of years Cheever and her endearing heroine should both be magnificent."

AVOCATIONAL INTERESTS: "My avocations are food (this causes me to eat more than I should), and sports (this causes me to work it off on the tennis court, the ski slope, exercise class, and jogging in the park). I also love to read fiction—it's magic for me."

CA INTERVIEW

CA interviewed Susan Cheever by phone on August 8, 1980, while she was vacationing in Vermont.

CA: You said that your novel Looking for Work *represents your transition from journalist to novelist. Were there great difficulties in making that transition?*

CHEEVER: There were great difficulties in that I wasn't sure I could do it. I was very restless at *Newsweek*, but everybody is. I knew that I wanted to write something more personal, but I didn't really know what. I thought my restlessness was just the restlessness that everyone feels at a news magazine. So I didn't have any confidence that this transformation could take place, and I wrestled with it for a long time before I even had the confidence to give myself a chance to try it, so in that way it was very difficult.

CA: You also said in connection with the novel that you were depressed at first and then you slowly became happy. Was the depression tied up with wondering if you could do it or was that later, after you had finished writing?

CHEEVER: The depression was when I had sent it off. When I sent it off I felt a sense of loss. At first I was exhilarated, and then I felt a sense of loss. When it was sold for a sum which exceeded my wildest expectations, to a publisher who exceeded my wildest expectations, I was very depressed, which isn't what I expected to feel; but then I got happy. Basically, the fact that I had been able to make the transformation from journalist to novelist has been a source of constant pleasure and satisfaction.

CA: Was your writing, as your father said, "a career chosen through emulation"?

CHEEVER: No, the opposite. I was determined not to be a writer until I was about thirty-five. Sometime in my adolescence I decided that that was the last thing I wanted to be. I became a teacher, and then I got married. When I was about thirty I was living with my husband in the suburbs, and we needed money. I had to get a job, and I didn't know what to do. I tried all kinds of things—I tried making macrame belts, I tried to get a job in public relations, and I tried to get a job at *Reader's Digest*, and I tried to get a job as a researcher, and I tried to get a job as a teacher, and I couldn't. The job I finally got was on a local newspaper, the *Tarrytown Daily News*, and I loved that immediately, but I still wouldn't admit that I was a writer. I would still say, "No, I'm a journalist." Years went by and I went to *Newsweek*, but I was still very adamant about not being a writer. And then, as I said, I got more and more restless at *Newsweek*, and I knew that I wanted to write something more personal, but I wouldn't admit that it was a novel until it was practically written. So it wasn't emulation—I fought the emulation right down to the wire.

CA: You told a writer for People *magazine that as a child you were unimpressed by your father's literary fame. When did that begin to change?*

CHEEVER: He wasn't really famous until quite recently. I'm thirty-seven, and back when I was sixteen and seventeen I was proud of him in the way one is proud of one's father, not for what he does. He wasn't really famous at all until the mid-1960's. And he never had any money. He has become much more famous in the last two to three years, so I didn't have much chance to be impressed.

CA: The Newsweek *interview you did with your father after the publication of* Falconer *seemed to mark a real turning point in his attitude toward his reading public. Did you sense that he was ready to talk more openly to his readers at that time?*

CHEEVER: The interview with *Newsweek* was another one of those things that we all backed into. I didn't want to do that either. A lot of people had asked me if I would interview my father and I said no, no, no. Harvey Shapiro, whom I like a lot, at the *New York Times Book Review* asked me and I said no. He said, well, it would just be Q and A—all I'd have to do was turn on the tape recorder—and I said no. He said, "Well, come on, I'll give you a list of questions and all you have to do is ask these questions and turn on the tape recorder." I asked my father and he said, "Okay with me," which surprised me. So then Harvey said, "Why don't you just think it over?" So what I very stupidly did was this: at *Newsweek* we had to ask permission if we did any outside writing, so I sent a memo to the editor, Ed Kosner, saying, "Would it be okay with you if I interviewed my father for the *New York Times Book Review*," assuming that he'd say no and I'd be off the hook. But he said, "No, you'll do it for *us*." At that point I couldn't explain that I was reluctant about doing it for Harvey anyway. I really trapped myself. None of that was planned at all.

I think that when he stopped drinking, my father became a much more open and reasonable man. I think a lot of his defenses fell away, and I certainly recognized that as a member of his family; and I recognized that *Falconer* in a way was a different kind of book than he had ever written and that he was more open about it than he had ever been. The interview really didn't have anything to do with that. It was just another accident. I was terrified; I thought that the whole thing was a horrible idea. We were both very, very nervous about it. It was as awkward as anything can be.

CA: Did he really not read your novel until you had found a publisher for it?

CHEEVER: I didn't give it to him, so he couldn't have read it. He didn't read it until it was almost in bound galleys.

CA: Your mother is also a writer. Any influence there?

CHEEVER: She wasn't writing when I was a kid, but I think that she's very literate and very intelligent. She has a different kind of mind than my father does. They both influenced me very much in terms of what I was given to read and who I could talk to about it. I was given a lot of things to read when I was very young, and my mother was as much a part of that as my father. So I wouldn't say I was influenced by her writing, but I was certainly influenced by her intellect.

CA: Has being from a writing family made the work more difficult in any specific way?

CHEEVER: Being from a writing family, I think, has made it easier. I grew up in a house where fiction was being written, and I saw all that. I saw how you did it. I saw that it was doable by a human being. There wasn't any violin music when my father went to work, he just went to work. It demystified fiction for me. I had a very clear sense that if you just sat down and wrote a novel, you would have written a novel. You didn't have to wait for some great calling. And I had a very clear sense that you used what you knew about, and that it was something that a person could do, as opposed to something that a person couldn't do. People say to me, "Well, I'd really like to write fiction but I don't have *the gift*." I never have sensed that there was any *the gift*, any more than there is with anything, so that was very helpful to me. It wasn't intimidating.

CA: Salley Gardens, the heroine of Looking for Work, *is a certain kind of feminist—not radical, but perhaps just want-*

ing the best of both worlds. Do her concerns as a woman reflect your own?

CHEEVER: Well, they *reflect* them. I think I'm much more political and tougher than she is. She's kind of confused. The answer to the question "Are you a feminist?" is "What do you mean by feminist?" It's amazing what people think a feminist is. I very emphatically feel that women should get equal pay for equal work and equal respect for equal work, and that everyone should have the same kind of domestic and professional opportunities, whether they be men or women. I don't think this has happened, and I think it ought to.

CA: Work figures strongly in the book. It seems to be equated, for Salley, with independence. You seem to feel very strongly about your work also.

CHEEVER: Yes. I feel much more strongly about it now in the sense that for me writing fiction is like finally plugging into the right current. I really feel that I'm able to put all my energies into my work now.

CA: You started at Newsweek *as an apprentice writer. Does that mean that seasoned writers are helping you with your work or that you just sit in a corner and do a lot of writing?*

CHEEVER: "Apprentice writer" is kind of a misleading term. I had what's called a tryout that lasts from two to six weeks, and then after that I was a writer. The system at *Newsweek* is that you write something and then it's edited by your senior editor, and then that in turn is edited—it's top-edited—and then that in turn is, not edited exactly, but sort of vetted by the editor of the magazine. Everything at *Newsweek* is vertical, nothing's lateral. It can be very frustrating. I think it was very good for me in that I learned to write under pressure to certain kinds of formulas, and I learned not to be overly in love with my own prose, and I learned all kinds of discipline that I honestly wouldn't have learned if I'd just started out writing fiction.

CA: What happened after the trial period?

CHEEVER: I started as religion editor after my tryout. In fact, my tryout was *in* religion. I got that job, so I was religion editor for about two years. During that time, the man who wrote "Newsmakers," the gossip section, took a leave of absence, and I filled in for him. Then I went back to being religion editor and then I was life-style editor.

CA: Was religion an interest, or did you just get that position because it was open?

CHEEVER: Both—mostly the latter. I had some education in religion, and I had some passing acquaintance with religion, but it certainly isn't a field that I have much expertise in.

CA: Was it difficult to act as an editor in a field you didn't have great knowledge in?

CHEEVER: Yes. But on the other hand, writing at *Newsweek* really does not require expertise in the subject. For one thing, there are other people doing the reporting, so that what you're often doing is taking the facts other people have found out and blending them into a story that makes sense and imparts the information. That doesn't require that you really know much about the facts.

CA: Do you miss working with other people, or are you delighted to be working on your own?

CHEEVER: I'm delighted to be writing fiction, just plain delighted. I miss the security and protection of that kind of job, however; writing fiction you never know if you're going to have any money or not. At *Newsweek*, if your editor was mean to you, you could go down the hall and drop in on someone's office and say, "That bastard," and they would say, "Boy, do you know what he did to me last week?" If you write a novel and someone creams it in a very personal, vindictive way, it hurts a lot more than anything ever hurt at *Newsweek*. I guess if you knew a lot of other writers, it would help, but I don't. I think writers are pretty isolated.

CA: How did you feel generally about the reviews of the novel?

CHEEVER: Well, I liked the good ones and I didn't like the bad ones. In some cases people were vindictive and in some cases they were generous; in some cases they were fair and intelligent. I got a lot of reviews, and I got every kind. I felt that for a first novel, the book got really a disproportionate amount of attention. I'm not sure why—I think it's timing and a lot of different things. As a result, I got many more reviews than I expected, much more attention than I expected. Some of them were nasty and some of them were lovely.

CA: A couple of reviewers seemed to be carping at the autobiographical aspects of the novel. Do you feel that anything an author writes must be to some extent autobiographical?

CHEEVER: Yes. That was one of the things I knew from growing up in my father's household. It's okay to use what you know, which is your own life, and it's very deceptive when somebody who writes fiction says to somebody who doesn't, "Yes, it's autobiographical." The person tends to think that means that these things actually happened, which of course they didn't. *Looking for Work* is a tremendous distortion of my life. I would never want anybody to read it and think that was what I was like because, although some of the facts are the same, it's not me at all. My family, when they had all read it, said, "Thank God it's not autobiographical." I think the closer you are to me, the more you realize it's not autobiographical. But if somebody didn't know me very well—yes, I was married to the son of a friend of my father's; yes, we were married for seven years; yes, we got divorced; yes, I got a job at *Newsweek*. So it's an interesting question. To say that it's autobiographical, I think, is true, but it's deceptive.

CA: The novel has been optioned by Warner Brothers. If it becomes a movie, will you have a hand in it?

CHEEVER: No, not at all. I love movies, but I have no expertise. I believe quite strongly that most things you do, you have to learn how to do, and I don't think that just because I can write novels means that I could write a screenplay. I wouldn't even know how to begin. I've just finished a second novel, which is a very different kind of novel, and with that I guess I might be more tempted to try the screenplay. No movie company has seen it yet or shown an interest in it. But on the other hand, I'm getting ready to write a third book. It's a question of time, too.

CA: You seem to be very happy being a novelist. Is there anything else you would like to say about that?

CHEEVER: I don't think it gets said enough that I feel fiction is a very, very serious enterprise, and I have the highest ambitions for it. I think that as much as I love doing it, it's hard. In some way it has to transcend your own experience.

The reason I do it is because I very much want to find a way in which I can make some kind of useful contribution to society and civilization, and this seems to me to be the way that I can best do it. That always sounds very corny, but I think it really is important to say.

BIOGRAPHICAL/CRITICAL SOURCES: New York Times, December 17, 1979; January 15, 1980; *Time*, December 24, 1979; *Atlantic*, January, 1980; *New York Times Book Review*, January 6, 1980; *Chicago Tribune Book World*, January 13, 1980, February 10, 1980, April 12, 1981; *Newsweek*, January 14, 1980; *Times Literary Supplement*, February 22, 1980, *People*, February 4, 1980; *New York*, April 7, 1980; *Contemporary Literary Criticism*, Volume 18, Gale, 1981; *Los Angeles Times*, May 28, 1981; *Detroit News*, July 21, 1981.

—*Sketch by Lillian S. Sims*
—*Interview by Jean W. Ross*

*   *   *

CHENERY, Janet (Dai) 1923-

PERSONAL: Born April 10, 1923, in New Rochelle, N.Y.; daughter of William Ludlow and Margaret Elizabeth (Miller) Chenery; married French H. Conway, January 30, 1943 (marriage ended, 1954). *Education:* Attended Sweet Briar College, University of Chicago, and University of North Carolina. *Home:* Winston Dr., Washington Depot, Conn. 06794.

CAREER: Western Publishing Co., New York City, editor, 1957-63; Harper & Row Publishers, Inc., New York City, senior editor, 1963-67; Simon & Schuster, Inc., New York City, editor-in-chief, 1967-73; Doubleday & Co., New York City, editorial director, 1973-79. *Member:* Women's National Book Association, Children's Book Council (treasurer). *WRITINGS*—For young people: *The Golden Book of Lost Worlds: Great Civilizations of the Past* (adapted for young readers from Leonard Cottrell's *The Horizon Book of Lost Worlds*), Golden Press, 1963; *The Toad Hunt*, illustrated by Ben Schecter, Harper, 1967; *Wolfie*, illustrated by Marc Simont, Harper, 1969; *Pickles and Jake*, illustrated by Lillian Obligado, Viking, 1975.

WORK IN PROGRESS: Length, Time, and Mass: A Guide to Usual and Unusual Measurements (adult reference); various free-lance articles; a novel for children.

*   *   *

CHEVALLIER, Raymond 1929-

PERSONAL: Born June 21, 1929, in Bourg, France; married Elizabeth Henrion (a professor of comparative literature), June 18, 1952. *Education:* Ecole Normale Superieure, licence es lettres, 1951, maitrise, 1952, agregation des lettres, 1953; Ecole Pratique des Hautes Etudes, Docteur es lettres. Attended Ecole Francaise de Rome (Scuola Francese di Roma), 1956-58. *Home:* 3 Square Debussy, 92160 Antony, France. *Office:* Universite de Tours, 3 rue des Tanneurs, 37000 Tours, France.

CAREER: University of Paris, Sorbonne, Paris, France, assistant professor, 1958-61; Ecole Pratique des Hautes Etudes, Paris, associate professor and lecturer, 1961-77; Universite de Tours, Tours, France, director of Institut d'Etudes Latines, 1964—. Director of archeological digs in France, Italy, and Morocco; member of Scientific Council of the University of Tours; president of A. Piganiol Center for Research. Professor-counselor at Sorbonne University Residence. President of International Commission of Photo-Interpretation, 1964-68; member of editing committee of *Revue de Photo-*

Interpretation and *Revue Francaise;* coordinator of three international aerial photography expositions. Member of Deputazioni di Storia Patria of Emilie-Romagne and of Veneties; member of Regional Inventory Commission. Emissary abroad for the French Foreign Affairs department. *Military service:* French Air Force; specialist in military photo-interpretation; became superior officer.

MEMBER: International Association of Classical Archeology, French Society of Photogrammetry and Teledetection, National Society of French Antiquarians, Pontifical Academy of Archeology, Tabula Imperii Romani (central committee), Geographical Society of Paris, Naturalists and Archeologists Society of Ain, Society of Latin Studies, Society of Emulation, Society of Commercial Geography. *Awards, honors:* Academie Francaise laureat, Geographical Society laureat, Officer of Public instruction, Gold Medal from Society for Encouragement of Progress, Medal of Archeology from Academy of Architecture.

WRITINGS—In English translation: *La France,* introduction by Pierre Gascar, Arthaud, 1971, translation by Roger Greaves published as *France From the Air,* Norton, 1972; *Les Voies romaines,* A. Colin, 1972, translation by N. H. Field published as *Roman Roads,* University of California Press, 1976.

In French, except as noted: *Bibliographie des applications archeologiques de la photographie aerienne,* Casablanca, 1959; *Les Etudes superieures de Latin: Initiation a la recherche,* preface by Marcel Durry, Societe d'Edition d'Enseignement Superieur, 1960; (with wife, E. Chevallier) *Emilie et Romagne: Ravenne, Bologne, Modene, Parme, Rimini, l'Adriatique,* Arthaud, 1963; *L'Avion a la decouverte du passe,* Fayard, 1964; *Rome,* three volumes, Editions Rencontre, 1964; *Dictionnaire de la litterature latine,* Larousse, 1968; (with M. Carbonnell and M. Guy) *Panorama des applications de la photographie aerienne,* S.E.V.P.E.N., 1968; *La Photographie aerienne,* A. Colin, 1971; *Epigraphie et litterature a Rome,* Fratelli Lega, 1972; *Aion: Le Temps chez les romains,* A. & J. Picard, 1976; *Romische Provence: Die Provinz Gallia Narbonensis* (in German), Atlantis-Verlag, 1979.

Editor: *Photographie aerienne: Panorama intertechnique,* Gauthier-Villars, 1965; *Melanges d'archeologie et d'histoire offerts a Andre Piganiol,* S.E.V.P.E.N., 1966; *Colloque international sur la cartographie archeologique et historique, Paris, Institut Pedagogique National, 24-26 janvier 1970,* Centre de Recherches A. Piganiol, 1972; *Litterature greco-romaine et geographie historique,* A. & J. Picard, 1974; (with R. Agache) *Tabula Imperii Romani: Lutetia, Atuatuca, Ulpia Noviomagus,* A. & J. Picard, 1975; *Influence de la Grece et de Rome sur l'Occident moderne,* Les Belles Lettres, 1977; *Presence de Virgile,* Les Belles Lettres, 1978.

Translator of works from German and Italian into French. Photographer for *Mezzogiorno,* by Elisabeth Chevallier, 1959.

WORK IN PROGRESS: La Romanisation de la celtique du Po; Villes et monuments; Les Mosaiques romaines du Maroc; La Province romaine de Lyonnaise.

BIOGRAPHICAL/CRITICAL SOURCES: Times Literary Supplement, April 20, 1973, August 13, 1976; *Classical Journal,* April, 1977; *Classical World,* April, 1977; *Scientific American,* September, 1977.

CHIDSEY, Donald Barr   1902-1981

OBITUARY NOTICE—See index for *CA* sketch: Born May 14, 1902, in Elizabeth, N.J.; died in 1981 in New London, Conn. Journalist, historian, novelist, and author. Chidsey worked as a newspaperman before becoming a full-time writer in 1928. He wrote several novels such as *Rod Rides High, Buccaneer's Blade,* and *The Flaming Island,* but is best-known for his historical and biographical works. Concentrating on English and American history and notable figures, the author's nonfictional books include *The Gentleman From New York: A Life of Roscoe Conkling, Elizabeth I, The Great Conspiracy: Aaron Burr and His Strange Doings in the West, Bonnie Prince Charlie,* and *The World of Samuel Adams.* Obituaries and other sources: *Something About the Author,* Volume 3, Gale, 1972; *AB Bookman's Weekly,* May 4, 1981.

*   *   *

CHILTON, Irma   1930-

PERSONAL: Born November 12, 1930, in Loughor, Wales; daughter of Iorwerth S. (in furnace work) and Esther (Muxworthy) Evans; married Henry T. J. Chilton (an industrial chemist), July 30, 1955; children: Dafydd Henry, Rhiannon Irma. *Education:* University College of Swansean University of Wales, B.A. (with honors), 1952. *Residence:* Llangollen, Wales.

CAREER: School teacher in charge of Welsh teaching in Dolgellau, Wales, 1952-55; teacher of history at secondary schools in Luton, Wales, 1955-56, and in Sheffield, England, 1956-59; teacher of Welsh at school in Wrexham, Wales, 1972-73; Boys' Modern Secondary School, Oswestry, England, teacher of history, 1973-74; writer, 1974—. Clerk for parish of Llangadwaladr, 1970-77. *Member:* Union of Welsh Authors (member of executive committee). *Awards, honors:* Tir-na-n Og Prize from Consortium of Children's Librarians in Wales and Welsh Joint Education Committee, 1980, for *Y Llong.*

WRITINGS—For young people: *Take Away the Flowers,* Heinemann, 1967; *Nightmare,* Scholastic Book Services, 1968 (published in England as *String of Time,* Macmillan, 1968); *Goldie,* Hamish Hamilton, 1969; *The Time Button,* Hamish Hamilton, 1970; *Strangers up the Lane,* Hamish Hamilton, 1970; *The Lamb,* Macmillan, 1973; *The Hundred,* Macmillan, 1974; *Club Books Four,* Cassell, 1975; *The Magic Cauldron,* Christopher Davies, 1976; *A Spray of Leaves,* Macmillan, 1977; *The Witch,* Macmillan, 1979; *Soul Ship,* Cassell, 1980; *Killer,* Cassell, 1980; *Flash,* Cassell, 1981.

In Welsh; for adults: *Cusanau* (title means "Kisses"), Christopher Davies, 1968; *Byd Fuller* (title means "Fuller's World"), Christopher Davies, 1970; *Rhwng Cwsg ac Effro* (title means "Between Sleeping and Waking"), Christopher Davies, 1975; *Storiau* (title means "Stories"), Christopher Davies, 1978.

Juvenile: *Met i Bompo* (title means "A Mate for Bompo"), Christopher Davies, 1975; *Breichled Modlen* (title means "Modlen's Bangle"), Christopher Davies, 1977; *Y Llong* (title means "The Ship"), Gomer, 1979; *Y Syrcas* (science fiction stories; title means "The Circus"), Gomer, 1980.

SIDELIGHTS: "Having been a school teacher for some years," Irma Chilton told *CA,* "I learned that one of the main hindrances to learning was a disinterest in reading. This motivated me to write short, snappy novels, the main purpose of which is to get young people interested in finding out what happens between the covers of a book. I write in both English and Welsh because I live in a bilingual community and need both languages to express what I have to say."

*   *   *

CHINERY, Michael 1938-

PERSONAL: Born June 5, 1938, in London, England; son of Oliver John (a grocer) and Dorothy (a seamstress; maiden name, Loveday) Chinery; married Jillian Ann Gray (a secretary), September 21, 1963; children: Roger, Tessa and Selena (twins). *Education:* Jesus College, Cambridge, B.A., 1960. *Home:* Mousehole, Mill Rd., Hundon, Sudbury, Suffolk CO10 8EG, England.

CAREER: Free-lance writer, 1965—. *Member:* Linnean Society of London. *Awards, honors:* Award from Austrian Minister of Education and Culture, 1973, for *Animal Communities;* Prix Dollfus from Society Entomologique de France, for *Field Guide to Insects.*

WRITINGS—All nonfiction: *Breeding and Growing: Foundations of Genetics, Anthropology, and Agriculture,* Low, 1966; (with David Larkin), *Patterns of Living: Foundations of Ecology,* Low, 1966; *A Pictorial Dictionary of the Animal World: An Illustrated Demonstration of Terms Used in Animal Biology,* Low, 1966; published as *A Science Dictionary of the Animal World,* F. Watts, 1969; (with Michael Gabb) *Human Kind: Foundations of Human Biology,* Low, 1966; (with Gabb) *The Life of Animals With Backbones: Foundations of Vertebrate Zoology,* Low, 1966; (with Gabb) *The Life of Animals Without Backbones: Foundations of Invertebrate Zoology,* Low, 1966; (with Gabb) *The World of Plants: Foundations of Botany,* Low, 1966.

Animal Communities (juvenile), F. Watts, 1972; *Concise Color Encyclopedia of Nature,* Crowell, 1972; *A Field Guide to the Insects of Britain and Northern Europe,* Collins, 1973, Houghton, 1974; *Animals in the Zoo* (juvenile), Collins, 1973, Taplinger, 1974; *Life in the Zoo* (juvenile), Taplinger, 1976; *Discovering Nature* (juvenile), Raintree, 1977; *Enjoying Nature With Your Family: Look, Learn, Collect, Conserve, Explore the Wildlife of Town and Country in Fascinating Projects and Experiments,* Crown, 1977; *The Natural History of the Garden,* Collins, 1977; *Discovering Animals,* Collins, 1978; *The Family Naturalist,* McDonald & Jane's, 1978; *Pictorial Atlas of Animals,* Ward, Lock, 1978; *Purnell's Find Out About Natural Wonders of the World,* Purnell, 1978; *Purnell's Nature All Around,* Purnell, 1978; *Guide to Wild Flowers,* Pan Books, 1979; *Killers of the Wild,* Salamander, 1979. Also author of *Pouched Mammals,* 1979.

Contributor to BBC radio wildlife programs.*

*   *   *

CHINN, Laurene Chambers 1902-1978

OBITUARY NOTICE—See index for *CA* sketch: Born in 1902 in Alburnet, Iowa; died March 17, 1978. Educator, researcher, and author. Chinn taught at schools in Kansas, and Texas. She wrote *The Unanointed, Voice of the Lord, Believe My Love, Marcus,* and *The Soothsayer.* (Date of death provided by husband, Harry Wing Chinn.)

*   *   *

CHINWEIZU 1943-

PERSONAL: Born March 26, 1943, in Eluama-Isuikwuato, Nigeria; son of Obediah Dimgba (in business) and Oluchi Akuji (Ejinwa) Ibekwe. *Education:* Massachusetts Institute of Technology, S.B., 1967; State University of New York at Buffalo, M.A., 1975; Ph.D., 1976. *Office address:* Okike, P.O. Box 53, Nsukka, Nigeria.

CAREER: Biafra Review, Cambridge, Mass., founder and editor, 1969-70; *Okike,* Nsukka, Nigeria, associate editor, 1973—. Associate professor at San Jose State University, 1978-79. *Awards, honors:* Rockefeller Foundation fellow in the United States, 1976.

WRITINGS: The West and the Rest of Us (history), Random House, 1975; *Energy Crisis and Other Poems,* NOK Publishers, 1978; (with Onwuchekwa Jemie and Ihechukwu Madubuike) *Toward the Decolonization of African Literature* (literary history and criticism), Fourth Dimension Publishers, Volume I, 1980, Volume II, 1981; *The Footrace and Other Satires,* Fourth Dimension Publishers, 1981. Contributor to journals, including *Africa, Black Scholar, First World, East African Journal,* and *New Age.* Contributing editor of *American Rag,* 1978—.

WORK IN PROGRESS: Poems; research on ecology and culture and on African development.

SIDELIGHTS: "Chinweizu demands of literature," wrote G. G. Darah of *Punch,* "the mental preparation of the people for the task of nation-building."

Since literature, as Chinweizu believes, has a fundamental role in shaping a people's consciousness, it is a central concern in African cultural autonomy. "For centuries," the author told Darah, "Africa has been under attack by colonialists. It needs to free itself in autonomous ways. Our writers have to do serious rethinking of their themes, styles, and centrally in our view, the audience for which they write. They should write about issues fundamental to Africa today and bear in mind the literary traditions of pre-colonial era."

Chinweizu suggests that African authors write for their countrymen using the official language, English, and that they explore contemporary issues the average individual can appreciate. Darah explained: "The writer should grasp the essence of political events and their impact on, say, the farmer, taxi driver and factory worker."

Chinweizu told *CA:* "I write because it is the way of contributing to my society that I find most appropriate to my talents and temperament.

"My primary audience is the Pan-African world—i.e., Africans of both the continental homeland and the diaspora. Most of my writing comes out of a consciousness shaped by the anti-colonial movement in Africa. Political, economic, and cultural nationalism saturated the very air in which I grew up in Nigeria. The great unfinished business of African decolonization and development is my theme, and my writing is devoted to raising consciousness about the sources of, the nature of, and the possible remedies for our condition. I am particularly concerned with helping to clean up the colonial cataracts and the hangover that still prevents us from seeing what our condition calls for.

"In the last few years, my interest has enlarged to include ecology. My focus is on the quest for ecological values, a quest guided by the question: What values, if any, are appropriate for both the survival of the human species and the health of the biosphere? If and when we discover ecologically valid values, we must work very hard to create a culture consistent with them, seeing as values and habits are extremely difficult to alter. Whether we can do all that before catastrophe overtakes us is in much doubt. However, I do see cause for some hope. If we do discover ecological values, we ought not have too much difficulty adopting them, for, after all, any species that could sell itself the virgin birth could sell itself anything.

"All that grave and serious stuff aside, I write satires for fun."

BIOGRAPHICAL/CRITICAL SOURCES: Daily Times, May 17, 1980; *Punch*, March 21, 1981.

*   *   *

CHITHAM, Edward (Harry Gordon) 1932-

PERSONAL: Born May 16, 1932, in Birmingham, England; son of Norman E. (an export official in steel tubing) and Elaine (Newman) Chitham; married Mary Tilley (in adult education), December 29, 1962; children: Eleanor M. E., John W. H., Rachel J. W. *Education:* Jesus College, Cambridge, B.A., 1955, M.A., 1959; University of Birmingham, Certificate in Education, 1956; University of Warwick, M.A., 1978. *Politics:* Liberal. *Religion:* Church of England. *Home:* 11 Victoria Rd., Harborne, Birmingham B17 0AG, England.

CAREER: Master in charge of Latin at grammar school in Old Hill, England, 1956-61, head of library department, 1961-67; Dudley College of Education, Dudley, England, lecturer, 1967-73, senior lecturer in English, 1973-77; Polytechnic, Wolverhampton, England, senior lecturer in education, 1977—. Tutor and counselor at Open University.

WRITINGS: The Black Country (local history), Longman, 1972; *Ghost in the Water* (children's novel), Longman, 1973; *The Poems of Anne Bronte*, Macmillan, 1979. Contributor to *Black Countryman*.

WORK IN PROGRESS: Poems of Emily Jane Bronte, with Derek Roper, publication by Oxford University Press expected in 1983 or 1984; *Bronte: Facts and Problems*, with Tom Winnifrith, Macmillan, c. 1983; a book on children's literature, concentrating on the work of Arthur Ransome.

SIDELIGHTS: Chitham told *CA:* "I often find myself passionately defending 'lost' causes. To take two: Latin is a most fascinating language, and if you can be patient, it rewards you by giving an accurate and painstaking turn of mind, as well as access to wild and extraordinary mythology; Liberalism in Great Britain *must* be renewed. It may have an over-optimistic strand, but it is only by ending 'confrontation' politics that Britain can survive as a positive force into the twenty-first century.

"Although I work in education, I think teaching is an art where you need to throw away the textbooks and use your own God-given common sense."

*   *   *

CHOMETTE, Rene Lucien 1898-1981
(Rene Clair)

OBITUARY NOTICE: Born November 11, 1898, in Paris, France; died March 15, 1981, in Neuilly, France. Journalist, film director, and author. Clair was a journalist in France when he took a bit part in a movie, and discovered his fascination for the cinema. Finding himself more comfortable behind the camera than in front of it, Clair directed twenty-eight films between 1928 and 1965. His works, produced primarily in France, are touched by surrealism. They include "Sous les toits de Paris" ("Under the Roofs of Paris"), "Un Chapeau de paille d'Italie" ("The Italian Straw Hat"), "I Married a Witch," and "It Happened Tomorrow." He also wrote three novels: *Adams, De fil en Aiguille,* and *La Princesse de Chine.* Obituaries and other sources: *Who's Who in the World*, 2nd edition, Marquis, 1973; *A Biographical*

Dictionary of Film, Morrow, 1976; *The International Who's Who*, Europa, 1977; *Chicago Tribune*, March 16, 1981; *New York Times*, March 16, 1981; *Newsweek*, March 30, 1981; *Time*, March 30, 1981.

*   *   *

CHRISTGAU, John (Frederick) 1934-

PERSONAL: Born February 11, 1934, in Crookston, Minn.; son of Rufus J. and Alice (Erickson) Christgau; married Peggy Barrett (an artist), August 20, 1960; children: Erick, Sally, Jennifer. *Education:* San Francisco State University, B.A., 1960, M.A., 1961. *Home:* 2704 Comstock, Belmont, Calif. 94002. *Agent:* Russell & Volkening, Inc., 551 Fifth Ave., New York, N.Y. 10017.

CAREER: Writer. Currently works as English teacher at Capuchino High School in San Bruno, Calif. *Military service:* U.S. Army, 1954-57. *Awards, honors: Spoon* was named best novel of the year by Society of Midland Authors, 1978.

WRITINGS: Spoon (novel), Viking, 1978.

WORK IN PROGRESS: Enemies, a dramatic history of the World War II Alien Enemy Interment Program in the United States.

SIDELIGHTS: According to the *Atlantic Monthly,* "*Spoon* is a sort of *Candide* of the Wild West, a whimsical satire that interprets history as melancholy comedy." An itinerant sketch artist, Alexander Featherstone, and his mystical Indian companion, Spoon, are "pursued by Indians as well as by the U.S. Army, escaping from one antic adventure only to fall into another. . . . John Christgau has created a deft and clever miniature epic, a novel that manages to be both provocative and delightfully entertaining."

BIOGRAPHICAL/CRITICAL SOURCES: Atlantic Monthly, September, 1978.

*   *   *

CHRISTIAN, Jill
See DILCOCK, Noreen

*   *   *

CHRISTIAN, Portia 1908-

PERSONAL: Born January 12, 1908, in Indiana; daughter of Paul Durbin (a farmer) and Julia Frances (Booth) Christian. *Education:* Attended Oxford College for Women, 1926-28, and Indiana University, 1939-40; Butler University, B.A., 1958; Columbia University, M.S., 1961. *Politics:* Independent. *Religion:* Roman Catholic. *Home:* 49 East Madison St., Franklin, Ind. 46131.

CAREER: Caldwell, Van Riper (advertising agency), Indianapolis, Ind., research director, 1935-55; Indiana University, Bloomington, registrar in department of library science, 1961-63, business assistant in School of Business, 1963-68; St. Joseph's College, Philadelphia, Pa., director of library of Academy of Food Marketing, 1968-74; writer, 1974—. *Military service:* U.S. Army, Signal Corps, 1944-46; became sergeant/technician; received Legion of Merit with citation. *Member:* American Association of University Women, American Association of Retired Persons, Indiana Historical Society, Society of Indiana Pioneers, Georgia Genealogical Society, Pennsylvania Horticultural Society, American Legion.

WRITINGS: (Editor) *Ethics in Business Conduct: Selected References From the Record,* Gale, 1970; (editor) *Agricultural Enterprises Management in an Urban-Industrial So-*

ciety: A Guide to Information Sources, Gale, 1978. Contributor to Delaware Valley food trade newspapers.

WORK IN PROGRESS: Editing *Tales Told by Daniel Deupree; Amos Durbin in Indiana; The Georgia Connection: Daniel Ragsdale Christian.*

SIDELIGHTS: Portia Christian wrote: "I cannot remember when I wasn't writing stories or articles, but the sheer effort of making a living through the years of the Depression, plus simply not getting at it, nipped many ideas before they were written." *Avocational interests:* Travel, reading, gardening and gardens, cooking.

* * *

CHRISTMAN, Henry 1906-1980

OBITUARY NOTICE: Born in 1906; died from injuries received in a fire, c. December, 1980. Journalist, editor, and author best known for his book *Tin Horns and Calico.* Christman was a reporter in New York for the *Evening News* and the *Knickerbocker Press* from 1928 to 1937. He also edited *The American Indian,* a journal on Native American affairs, and served as news editor for the American Cancer Society. *Tin Horns and Calico,* a study of the 1840's anti-rent war in the Hudson River Valley of New York, is widely used as a high school and college textbook. Obituaries and other sources: *New York Times,* December 4, 1980.

* * *

CILFFRIW, Gwynfor
See GRIFFITH, Thomas Gwynfor

* * *

CLAIR, Rene
See CHOMETTE, Rene Lucien

* * *

CLARE, Elizabeth
See COOK, Dorothy Mary

* * *

CLARFIELD, Gerard Howard 1936-

PERSONAL: Born January 9, 1936, in San Francisco, Calif.; son of Joseph Louis and Shirley Clarfield; married Julie Tick (a librarian), June 27, 1959; children: Leslie Elizabeth. *Education:* University of California, Berkeley, B.A., 1958, M.A., 1959, Ph.D., 1965. *Home:* 2401 Lynnwood Dr., Columbia, Mo. 65201. *Office:* Department of History, University of Missouri, 123 Arts and Science Building, Columbia, Mo. 65201.

CAREER: Sacramento State College, Sacramento, Calif., assistant professor of history, 1964-68; University of Missouri, Columbia, 1969—, began as associate professor, became professor of history. *Member:* Organization of American Historians.

WRITINGS: Timothy Pickering and American Diplomacy, University of Missouri Press, 1969; *U.S. Diplomatic History,* Volume I, Houghton, 1973; *Timothy Pickering and the American Republic,* University of Pittsburgh Press, 1980. Contributor to history journals.

WORK IN PROGRESS: The United States and Korea: 1945 to the Present; Nuclear America, a study of nuclear issues from 1940 to the present.

CLARK, Robert L(loyd), Jr. 1945-

PERSONAL: Born September 12, 1945, in McAlester, Okla.; son of Robert L. (a school administrator) and Ruth (a teacher; maiden name, Nelson) Clark; married first wife, Anetta Jean (divorced October 30, 1979); married Andrea Cantrell Hawkins, May 23, 1980. children: Roberta Jean, Jonathan Thomas. *Education:* University of Oklahoma, B.A., 1968, M.L.S., 1969. *Politics:* Democrat. *Home:* 2001 Cedar Ridge Rd., Edmond, Okla. 73034. *Office:* Oklahoma Department of Libraries, 200 Northeast 18th, Oklahoma City, Okla. 73105.

CAREER: Oklahoma Department of Libraries, Oklahoma City, head of Archives and Records Division, 1968-72; Jackson Metropolitan Library System, Jackson, Miss., assistant director, 1972-74; Mid-Mississippi Regional Library System, Kosciusko, director, 1974-76; Oklahoma Department of Libraries, director, 1976—. Member of White House Conference on Libraries and Information Services task force, Oklahoma Archives and Records Commission, and Oklahoma Historical Records Advisory Board. *Member:* American Library Association (committee chairman), Amigos Bibliographic Council (member of board of directors, 1978-80), Southwestern Library Association (president, 1980-82), Oklahoma Library Association (member of board of directors, 1977-78), Oklahoma Heritage Association.

WRITINGS: (Editor and contributor) *Archive-Library Relations,* Bowker, 1976; (contributor) Beth Hamilton, editor, *Multitype Library Cooperation,* Bowker, 1977; (contributor) E. J. Josey, editor, *Libraries in the Political Process,* Ornyx Press, 1980. Contributor to library and history journals and to *Oklahoma Observer.*

WORK IN PROGRESS: Research on legislative information management, state library agency responsibilities, national library legislation, and national information policy.

SIDELIGHTS: Clark wrote: "The right of public access to government information while protecting essential personal privacy rights and the mobilization of informational needs of our people requires constant attention. The vast influence of state government over these areas was of utmost interest to me. This led my attention into the arena of state politics which, because I am the head of an agency within the state government that reflects my career interest, has given challenges, job satisfaction, and oversight of the growth of projects, appropriations, and laws that I deem valuable for the public's access and preservation of information.

"Travels have afforded the opportunity to observe and study the great diversity of the methods and the range of depth to which state governments provide these services. This then has cleared the way to examine and contribute to national legislation and policies that support the public's right to know."

* * *

CLARKE, Captain Jafar
See NESMITH, Robert I.

* * *

CLARKE, Derrick Harry 1919-

PERSONAL: Born June 7, 1919, in London, England; son of Henry (a printer) and Emma (Callens) Clarke; married Molly Jessica Smith, February 16, 1942; children: Kester John. *Education:* Attended London School of Printing, 1936-37. *Politics:* "Ardent individualist." *Religion:* "Self-discipline.'' *Home:* Gables, Woolverstone, Ipswich, Suffolk IP9 1BA, England. *Agent:* Dominick Abel Literary Agency, 498 West End Ave., No. 12-C, New York, N.Y. 10024.

CAREER: Cox Marine Ltd., Ipswich, England, sales director, 1960-66; writer, 1967—. Supplier of small boat blue water records to Guinness Superlatives Ltd., 1969—; trimaran and small boat records consultant. *Military service:* Royal Air Force, pilot, 1937-46; received Air Force Cross and Distinguished Flying Cross; mentioned in dispatches. *Awards, honors:* J. B. Charcot Award from American Slocum Society, 1957.

WRITINGS: What Were They Like to Fly?, Ian Allen, 1965; *Trimarans: An Introduction,* Adlard Coles, 1969, revised edition, 1975; *The Lure of the Sea,* Adlard Coles, 1970; *East Coast Passage* (autobiography), Longman, 1971; *Trimaran Development,* Adlard Coles, 1972; *The Multihull Primer,* Adlard Coles, 1976; *An Evolution of Singlehanders,* McKay, 1976; *The Blue Water Dream,* McKay, 1981. Author of unpublished novels, including *Some Sharp Trial* and *The Night of the Pill,* and unpublished books on the occult, including *A Magick of Life and Death* and *Close to Death.* Contributor of more than three hundred articles to yachting and flying magazines and newspapers.

WORK IN PROGRESS: The Compleat Joat, an autobiography; *The Art and Practice of Survival Against All Odds; The History of the Blue Water Game;* continuing research on small boat blue water records.

SIDELIGHTS: Clarke told *CA:* "I claim to be a master jack-of-all-trades, having worked at (at least) one hundred twenty-seven different paid jobs. I joined the Royal Air Force in 1937 with the intention of saving enough money to buy a yacht and sail her single-handedly round the world. This was planned for 1942, but of course World War II spoiled my plans. If I had done so, I would have been the seventh single-handed circumnavigator (currently just under seventy have achieved this feat). Consequently my main interest has always been in small boat blue water records, and I am now considered the foremost authority on this subject in the world. During the past decade I have done my best to neutralize the extravagant claims made by sponsors on behalf of their sailing representatives, who have been suggesting 'firsts' and 'fastests' as though nobody else had ever put to sea in a small yacht. I have had some success, but there is a great deal that still needs doing.

"Of my own accomplishments, I can claim a few rare performances. I flew on three suicide jobs during World War II, including 'Operation Flash' at Dunkirk and 'Merchant Ship Fighter Unit' (better known as the 'Catafighters') for a year during the Battle of the Atlantic. I also carried the sole match that ignited the anti-invasion fuel pumped out into the English Channel in 1940. I was one of the few fighter pilots during the war who succeeded in picking up a fellow pilot who had been shot down and flying home with him some two hundred miles.

"After the war, I bought a 115-ton Thames sailing barge (no engine) which I converted and lived aboard with my wife and son for eleven years. We made the last east coast passage (Humber to Thames) ever to be completed by an engineless barge with only a husband/wife crew. For this we received the J. B. Charcot Award.

"In 1961 I introduced the first commercially successful trimarans into Britain, and later into Europe and Africa. During the years until 1966 I sold more trimarans than any other company in the world. In 1966 we moved ashore for the first

time in twenty years. This is not a record, but it is a rare accomplishment (particularly with the same wife).

"I have traveled through twenty-seven countries, but prefer now to stay at home. My last visit abroad was in 1976 when I acted as moderator at the First World Trimaran Symposium, held in Toronto. The symposium was all right, but the air travel was miserable—I'd rather do it in an open cockpit aircraft, or go by sea. I abhor the sardine mentality!

"I am interested in everything, including the occult (my father was a member of the Inner Magic Circle). I have even written two books on this subject (*A Magick of Life and Death* and *Close to Death*), but, alas, I was not able to sell them. It would seem that I am equally useless at writing fiction, since two attempts (*Some Sharp Trial* and *The Night of the Pill*) failed to find a publisher. I am now out of date with regard to multihulls, and I have no intention of writing any more books on this subject, so it would seem that small boat records are all that is left.

"There is, however, survival—which everyone thinks about, but few know what to do about. If this, my latest project, finds a publisher, I believe a new route will be opened up—certainly it is a subject that is sadly neglected by all authors (survival, *not* safety). Having survived over a dozen close-to-death encounters, when quite obviously I should have died but didn't, I consider that I know quite a bit about the subject. We shall have to wait and see if a publisher is interested enough to want to avoid Doomsday!''

*   *   *

CLARKE, Dwight Lancelot   1885-1971

OBITUARY NOTICE—See index for *CA* sketch: Born in 1885 in Berkeley, Calif.; died February 7, 1971. Banker, businessman, and author. Clarke worked in California throughout his banking career. He then moved to the Occidental Life Insurance Co., where he stayed nearly fifteen years. From 1951 to 1953 he was president of the American Cancer Society's Los Angeles County branch. He wrote *Stephen Watts Kearny: Soldier of the West* and edited *The Original Journals of Henry Smith Turner, 1846-47.* (Date of death provided by wife, Edna Marie Clarke.)

*   *   *

CLARKE, Thomas Ernest Bennett   1907-

PERSONAL: Born June 7, 1907, in Watford, England; son of Sir Ernest Michael Clarke; married Joyce Caroline Steele, 1932; children: one daughter, one son (deceased). *Education:* Attended Clare College, Cambridge. *Home:* Tanners Mead, Oxted, Surrey, England.

CAREER: Staff writer for *Answers,* 1927-35; member of editorial staff of *Daily Sketch,* 1936; free-lance writer, 1936—. *Awards, honors:* Member of Order of the British Empire, 1952; Academy Award from Academy of Motion Picture Arts and Sciences, 1952, for "The Lavender Hill Mob"; Venice Award for "The Lavender Hill Mob"; Academy Award nomination from Academy of Motion Picture Arts and Sciences, 1960, for "Sons and Lovers."

WRITINGS: Go South, Go West, John Long, 1932; *Jeremy's England,* John Long, 1934; *Second Impression,* John Long, 1937; *Two and Two Make Five,* John Long, 1938; *What's Yours?: The Student's Guide to Publand,* P. Davies, 1938; *Mr. Spirket Reforms,* John Long, 1940; (with Arthur Macrae and Eric Ambler) *Encore,* Heinemann, 1951; *The World Was Mine,* Bodley Head, 1964; *The Wide Open Door,* M. Joseph, 1966; *A Little Temptation* (three-act play), Evans Brothers,

1966; *The Trail of the Serpent*, M. Joseph, 1968; *The Wrong Turning*, R. Hale, 1971; *Intimate Relations; or, Sixty Years a Bastard*, M. Joseph, 1971; *This Is Where I Came In* (autobiography), M. Joseph, 1974; *The Man Who Seduced a Bank*, M. Joseph, 1977. Also author of *Cartwright Was a Cad*, 1936, and a play, "This Undesirable Residence."

Films: "Johnny Frenchman," released by Universal in 1948; "Against the Wind," released by Eagle Lion, 1949; "Passport to Pimlico," released by Eagle Lion, 1949; "Train of Events," released by J. Arthur Rank, 1951; "Hue and Cry," 1951; "The Blue Lamp," released by Eagle Lion, 1951; "The Magnet," released by Universal, 1951; "The Lavender Hill Mob," released by Universal, 1952; "Encore," released by Paramount, 1952; "The Titfield Thunderbolt," released by Universal, 1954; "Barnacle Bill," 1957; "A Tale of Two Cities," released by J. Arthur Rank, 1958; "All at Sea," released by Metro-Goldwyn-Mayer, 1958; "Gideon's Day," 1958; "Gideon of Scotland Yard," released by Columbia Pictures, 1959; "Sons and Lovers," released by Twentieth Century-Fox, 1960; "The Horse Without a Head," 1963; "A Man Could Get Killed," released by Universal, 1966. Also author of "The Rainbow Jacket," and "Who Done It?"

AVOCATIONAL INTERESTS: Racing, gardening.*

*   *   *

CLARKSON, Tom 1913-

PERSONAL: Born February 16, 1913, in Birmingham, England; son of Samuel and Editha (Shatz) Clarkson. *Education:* Attended grammar school in Hull, England. *Politics:* Labour. *Home:* Elim, 121 Westfield Rd., Mayford, Woking, Surrey, England. *Agent:* Rosemary Bromley, Colden Common, Winchester, Hampshire, England.

CAREER: Professional actor, painter, and writer. *Awards, honors:* Scholarship from Old Vic Drama School, 1933; *Daily Graphic* book find, 1952, for *The Pavement and the Sky*.

WRITINGS: The Pavement and the Sky: A Poet's Story, Farrar, Straus, 1952; *Love Is My Vocation* (biography), Farrar, Straus, 1953; *The Wounded*, Farrar, Straus, 1956; *A Certain Summer*, Farrar, Straus, 1963; *The Dirty Workers*, Farrar, Straus, 1973. Also author of *The Angel of My Bed* (poems), Farrar, Straus. Author of radio plays. Contributor of stories and poems to periodicals.

WORK IN PROGRESS: A philosophical and religious approach to the tarot; *Eve*, a biography; *My Friend the Minotaur*, an autobiography.

*   *   *

CLAYTON, Sylvia

PERSONAL: Born in Cheltenham, England; daughter of Arthur George (a headmaster and mayor) and Miria Ruth (Vincent) Dye; married Tom Clayton (a journalist); children: Nicholas Vincent, Richard Harvey. *Education:* Lady Margaret Hall, Oxford, M.A. *Home:* 54 Taylor Ave., Kew, Richmond, Surrey, England.

CAREER: British Broadcasting Corp., London, England, television script writer, 1952-54; free-lance writer, 1954-67; *Daily Telegraph*, London, television critic, 1967—. *Member:* Broadcasting Press Guild, Society of Authors, Critics Circle. *Awards, honors:* Fiction prize from *Guardian*, 1975, for *Friends and Romans*.

WRITINGS—Novels: The Crystal Gazers, Faber, 1961; *The Peninsula*, Faber, 1964; *Top Co.*, Faber, 1968; *Sabbatical*, Faber, 1972; *Friends and Romans*, Faber, 1975.

Translator: Sven Lindkvist, *China in Crisis*, Faber, 1965; Sven Holm, *Termush*, Faber, 1969.

Author of television play, "Preview," first broadcast by British Broadcasting Corp., 1980.

WORK IN PROGRESS: A novel covering fifty years of a woman's life, "with a strong satirical element."

SIDELIGHTS: Sylvia Clayton wrote: "I start writing novels or plays with the sound of people arguing, fighting, crying, mocking in my head. The characters define themselves as I work, and the stronger characters take over, shaping the plot in a way I tend to follow. I hate padding, love the right word."

AVOCATIONAL INTERESTS: Travel, "the company of children and animals."

*   *   *

CLELLAND, Catherine
See TOWNSEND, Doris McFerran

*   *   *

CLISSMANN, Anne
See CLUNE, Anne

*   *   *

CLIVE, John 1933-

PERSONAL: Born January 6, 1933, in London, England; son of Jess (a stevedore) and Irene Gardner; married Carole Anne White (a television production assistant), April 1, 1968; children: Alexander, Hannah. *Education:* Attended school in London and Liverpool, England, and Wales. *Religion:* Church of England. *Residence:* County Wicklow, Ireland. *Agent:* Arthur Pine Associates, Inc., 1780 Broadway, New York, N.Y. 10019.

CAREER: Professional actor, 1949—. *Military service:* Royal Air Force, 1951-53.

WRITINGS: (With J. D. Gilman) *KG 200* (novel), Simon & Schuster, 1977; *The Last Liberator* (novel), Delacorte, 1980; *Barossa* (novel), Delacorte, 1981. Also writer of lyrics and musical score for Thames Television Christmas show, 1974.

WORK IN PROGRESS: "Broken Wings," a screenplay and book, publication expected in 1982.

SIDELIGHTS: Clive told *CA:* "The compulsion to write is probably as different as the people who do so. For me it was frustration, frustration with my work as an actor. I wasn't getting the part that I wanted; I was working steadily, but doing the same thing again and again. There was no fear, nothing to stretch me. I know that 'typecasting' is a cliche, the heart cry of every actor, but it doesn't make it any easier to bear, any less of a truth. There were the exceptions of course—Sydney in 'Absurd Person Singular,' Lardface in Stanley Kubrick's 'A Clockwork Orange,' and perhaps my favorite, Rosko in 'Perils of Pendragon,' a television series for BBC—but they were few and far between.

"So, I needed to break out, find something else. The only thing I knew anything about was drama, words, scripts, motivation, etc. The choice was limited and simple. The one thing I didn't want to do was write some amusing show business autobiography. What I really wanted to do was write about something dramatic, adventurous, and exciting. I wanted to put myself, in my mind's eye at least, in an unfamiliar locale, where the elements as well as the people were in conflict, away from cities, studios, and theatres. I wanted to do in a story what I had yearned to do years ago when I sat entranced in the cinema, dreaming of wild adventure. Sounds a bit corny, I know, but what the hell! It's the truth.

"One Friday I opened up the magazine section of the *Daily Telegraph* and found an article on the draining of the Zuyder Zee in Holland and how a recovery unit was, as the waters receded, dragging out of the mud some World War II aircraft that had been missing for more than thirty years. There was a sentence in the article that went something like this: 'And one aircraft, a British Mosquito recovered in 1963, had German ammunition in the weapons system.' I read it again . . . *German* ammunition? What was German ammunition doing in a Second World War *British* aircraft?

"Well, to make a long story short, I was interested in World War II planes (I'd been brought up with them as a kid in London during the Blitz), so off I went to Holland to find out about the aircraft. I tracked down the Dutch major in charge of the recovery unit. He asked me back to his house and told me about KG 200, a Luftwaffe bomber group set up by Hermann Goering to make use of captured Allied aircraft. Later research disclosed that the group used Flying Fortresses, Liberators, Hurricanes, Spitfires, and Russian and French planes. They used them to drop spies behind the Allied lines and to infiltrate incoming and outgoing bomber formations, revealing the positions and numbers of the formations. In short, they used them for anything that would aid the German war effort. In the last year of the war, they flew over five hundred missions, though we knew very little about it at the time.

"The Germans destroyed all records of KG 200 at the end of the war. They broke the Geneva Convention and had many war crimes on their plate. The Allies? Well, it's my belief that in 1945 when they discovered how widespread this operation had been, they were in no mood to say, 'Hey, look how clever the Germans were.' Instead, the Allies sat on it.

"After researching KG 200, I knew I had what I needed to write a book. But instinct told me that without conflict, there was no drama; KG 200 did exist and carried out most of its missions without detection, but I had to invent an Allied response. The fiction lies in the plot, not the facts.

"I was a co-author on *KG-200* but wrote *The Last Liberator* on my own. I like my second book, and the critical reaction has been better than for the first, better than I dared hope. *Barossa,* my third book, is set in Australia in 1970. It is about to be published. My fingers are crossed; it's a bit like an opening night, but without the applause. I haven't given up acting; it's a marvelously social profession and complements the writing perfectly. If the right part came along I'd snap at it. I'm presently working on a screenplay and book called 'Broken Wings.' If there's a part in it that I'm right for, at least I won't have to audition.''

BIOGRAPHICAL/CRITICAL SOURCES: New York Times Book Review, January 27, 1980.

*   *   *

CLODFELTER, (William) Frank(lin) 1911-

PERSONAL: Born June 20, 1911, in Asheville, N.C.; son of James F. (a railway official) and Beulah Mae (Franklin) Clodfelter; married Anne Davis Jones (a teacher), July 8, 1940; children: Nelda Olivia (Mrs. John E. Coligan), Rebecca Anne (Mrs. Thomas Gordon Wilf III). *Education:* Attended Asheville-Biltmore College (now University of North Carolina at Asheville), 1931-32; attended Jones Business College,

Orlando, Fla., 1955-56. *Home:* 36 Westchester Dr., Asheville, N.C. 28803.

CAREER: Southern Railway, Asheville, N.C., coach cleaner, 1931-35; Crane Co., Asheville, receiving clerk, 1935-38; *Asheville Citizen-Times,* Asheville, chief photographer, 1938-42; Southern Railway, Washington, D.C., and Alexandria, Va., patrolman and photographer, 1942, locomotive fireman and engineer, 1943-49; Florida East Coast Railway, St. Augustine, Fla., clerk, 1949; traveled through United States, Canada, and Alaska, 1949-1952; Citrus Industry, Plymouth, Fla., personnel director, 1953-57; Southern Railway, locomotive engineer, 1957—. Director of North Carolina Transportation History Corp., Spencer, 1979—. Free-lance photographer and writer, 1933—. *Member:* National Audubon Society, National Geographical Society, National Wildlife Federation, Sierra Club. *Awards, honors:* Recipient of twenty-two local, state, and national awards for photography, including awards from *American Nature* and *Photography,* both 1943, both for photograph of a hibernating bear; "My Favorite Photo" first prize award from *Saturday Evening Post,* 1948; and awards from *Outdoors,* 1948, *Travel,* 1956, and *Saga,* 1957.

WRITINGS: Fogg and Steam, illustrated by Howard Fogg, Pruett, 1978. Contributor of articles and photographs to numerous magazines, including *American Nature, Saturday Evening Post, Trains,* and *Camera.*

WORK IN PROGRESS: Carolina Division, the story of railroading on Southern Railway's Asheville territory, completion expected in 1985; *My Affairs With Cameras and Locomotives,* a book of photographs dealing with a "search for beauty in landscape, wildlife, the power and thunder of trains, and the quiet kindness of character in the aging face," completion expected in 1987.

SIDELIGHTS: Railroading is a tradition in Clodfelter's family and has been the subject of much of his photography. In *Fogg and Steam,* his photographs and prose accompany twenty-six original oil paintings of steam locomotives by noted railroad artist Howard Fogg. Clodfelter is also known as a nature photographer; his photographs of a hibernating bear has been published in several popular magazines.

Clodfelter told *CA:* "I have never professed to be a writer. Photography has been my principal obsession, but I soon learned that few editors will publish photographs without accompanying captions or articles. This meant that I was forced to write in order to have my pictures published.

"Working on the railroad, my other passion, has provided me with experiences—and money—that have enabled me to capture some of the drama and beauty of man and his machines. This experience culminated in the publication of *Fogg and Steam.*

"People who create or work with their hands and souls are my preferred subjects: artists, writers, farmers, mountaineers, house builders, blacksmiths—everyday unsung people. I prefer anyone who creates things or makes them operate—people who wear work clothes, sweat, and use physical energy to accomplish their purpose."

BIOGRAPHICAL/CRITICAL SOURCES: Ties, July-August, 1971; *Locomotive Engineer,* July 28, 1972; *Asheville Times,* July 30, 1973; *Trains,* October, 1973; *Railroad Magazine,* August, 1976; *Modern Railroads,* March, 1979; *Winston-Salem Sentinel,* October 1, 1979.

CLOTFELTER, Mary (Eunice) L(ong)

PERSONAL: Born in Noble, Okla.; daughter of George Elmer (a farmer) and Emma Mae (Bradley) Long; married Cecil F. Clotfelter, September 20, 1957; children: two daughters. Education: University of Oklahoma, B.A., 1946, B.A.L.S., 1948; graduate study at Eastern New Mexico University, 1974—. Politics: Democrat. Religion: Baptist. Home address: Route 2, Box 43A, Portales, N.M. 88130. Office: Portales Public Library, 218 South Ave. B, Portales, N.M. 88130.

CAREER: Oklahoma Baptist University, Shawnee, assistant librarian and instructor in library science, 1947-59; worked part time as a church librarian and as a duplicating manager, 1959-62; Carnegie Public Library, Las Vegas, N.M., director, 1962-67; Bryan Public Schools, Library Processing Center, Bryan, Tex., library assistant, 1968-69; Eastern New Mexico University, Portales, part-time instructor in library science, 1969—, part-time reference librarian, 1975-79. Assistant librarian at Portales Public Library, 1979—.

MEMBER: American Library Association, American Association of University Women, League of Women Voters, Southwestern Library Association (executive secretary, 1973), New Mexico Library Association, Portales Garden Club (president, 1973-74, 1976), Portales Gem and Mineral Society, La Escalera Art Guild (president, 1974-75), Phi Delta Kappa, Faculty Dames of Eastern New Mexico University, Newcomers of Eastern New Mexico University (president, 1970-71).

WRITINGS: (Editor with husband, Cecil F. Clotfelter) Camping and Backpacking: A Guide to Information Sources, Gale, 1978.

WORK IN PROGRESS: Research on the history of libraries in New Mexico.

SIDELIGHTS: Mary Clotfelter commented: "I have been an avid gardener of both flowers and vegetables for years and am recognized for my floral arrangements, which are in demand for campus, civic, and public engagements. I believe that nature is the best instructor for all art, be it in a floral arrangement or on canvas. I have studied painting and have had oil, gouache, and pastel paintings exhibited locally.

"With my varied experience as a librarian and as a teacher of library science, my interest has been to help others enjoy life to the fullest—to share the flowers, the vegetables, the rocks, the trips, and the scenes. My philosophy is that life is too short to wait for tomorrow. Now is the time to appreciate the aesthetic beauty of our world.

"Since I was a small child, the out-of-doors has had a special appeal. From the cloud formations, to various types and colors of trees, flowers, wild vegetables and fruits—whatever is in God's world—I am thrilled to explore and examine. The lull of the wind in the mountain trees, the ice frozen on the fishing line, the different rock formations and colors—all intensify my yearning to know more of what is just beyond the next horizon. I believe that everyone, regardless of age, should have the privilege to camp or backpack anywhere in America, be it among the crowded campgrounds in a national park or forest or in some secluded nook away from all people."

*   *   *

CLOUD, Yvonne
See KAPP, Yvonne (Mayer)

CLUNE, Anne 1945-
(Anne Clissmann)

PERSONAL: Married name, Anne Clissmann; name legally changed to Clune; born January 6, 1945, in Dublin, Ireland; daughter of Patrick J. (a musician) and Mary (Clune) Connolly; married Frank Clissmann, May 31, 1969 (divorced July, 1978). Education: University of Sussex, B.A., 1967; Trinity College, Dublin, M.Litt., 1971. Politics: Irish Labour party. Religion: None. Home: 132 Richmond Court, Dartry, Dublin 6, Ireland. Office: Department of English, Trinity College, University of Dublin, Dublin, Ireland.

CAREER: University of Dublin, Trinity College, Dublin, Ireland, lecturer in English, 1968—. Member of board of directors of Academy Press and Irish Microforms Ltd. Member: Amnesty International, International Association for the Study of Anglo-Irish Literature (member of executive committee, 1980), Irish Federation of Teachers, Irish Council for Civil Liberties.

WRITINGS: (Under name Anne Clissmann) Flann O'Brien: A Critical Introduction to His Writings, Macmillan, 1975. Contributor to The Irish Short Story. Past editor of Journal of Irish Literature.

WORK IN PROGRESS: Editing The Poetry and Prose of Ireland; editing A Critical Guide to Anglo-Irish Literature, three volumes.

SIDELIGHTS: Anne Clune told CA: "It is my aim to help develop academic publishing in Ireland by my writing and editing and by my involvement in a publishing company and a microfilming company. This is the most exciting and exacting work I can do."

*   *   *

CLYDE COOL
See FRAZIER, Walt(er)

*   *   *

COAD, F(rederick) Roy 1925-

PERSONAL: Born February 5, 1925, in Kalene Hill, Zambia; son of Stanley Robert (a missionary and clerk) and Mildred (a missionary; maiden name, Woodbridge) Coad; married Joyce Kathleen Lomax, April 1, 1950; children: Malcolm, Rachel Coad D'Orazio, Stephen. Education: Attended secondary school in Winchester, England. Politics: Liberal. Religion: Christian Brethren. Home: 18 King's Ave., Carshalton, Surrey SM5 4NX, England. Office: 14 Welbeck St., London W1M 5AP, England.

CAREER: Griffin Stone Moscrop & Co. (chartered accountants), London, England, partner, 1949—. Member of council of Evangelical Alliance, 1971-77. Director of Charlton Sand & Ballast Co. Ltd.; member of board of trustees of Mueller Homes for Children; member of board of directors of In Contact and Care for Refugees and Immigrants. Member: Institute of Chartered Accountants in England and Wales (fellow), Arts Centre Group. Awards, honors: Institute Award from Institute of Chartered Accountants in England and Wales, Frederick Whinney Award, and Stephens Award, all 1943; Plender Award, 1948.

WRITINGS: Prophetic Developments With Particular Reference to the Brethren Movement, Christian Brethren Research Fellowship, 1966; A History of the Brethren Movement, Paternoster Press, 1968, 2nd edition, 1974; Biography of *Sir John Laing, C.B.E.,* Hodder & Stoughton, 1979; (contributor) G.C.D. Howley, F. F. Brace, and M. L. Ellison, editors, *A Bible Commentary for Today,* Pickering & Inglis, 1979. Contributor of poems to magazines. Honorary editor of publications of Christian Brethren Research Fellowship, 1963-73; honorary editor of *Harvester,* 1973—.

SIDELIGHTS: Coad told *CA:* "My writing has been strongly motivated by the influence of (and my loyalty to) the minority Christian religious tradition in which I was reared. It has probably arisen from the tension between the narrow horizons of a world-denying religious tradition and my wider natural sympathies with humanity in general. In recent years, close personal contacts with Italy and things Italian have had their effect. My business experience is of comparatively little influence on my literary interests. Recently I have turned to poetry as a more intense and versatile outlet for these tensions.

"A busy professional life as a practicing accountant leaves me with much less time for mental exploration than I would like. However, it presents me with ample raw study material in the shape of human character as distorted by financial pressures!"

                              *   *   *

COALSON, Glo   1946-

PERSONAL: Born March 19, 1946, in Abilene, Tex.; daughter of Bill L. (a teacher) and LaVerne (an elementary school teacher; maiden name, Bowles) Coalson. *Education:* Abilene Christian University, B.A., 1968; also attended University of Colorado, University of Texas, and Columbia University. *Home address:* Route 5, Box 860, Abilene, Tex. 79605.

CAREER: Ed Triggs/Al Boyd—Graphic Designers, Austin, Tex., graphic designer, 1969; artist in Kotzebue, Alaska, 1969-70; free-lance illustrator in New York, N.Y., 1971-78, and in Dallas, Tex., 1978—.

WRITINGS: The Stone Woman (juvenile folktale; self-illustrated), Atheneum, 1971.

Illustrator: Ann Herbert Scott, *On Mother's Lap* (juvenile), McGraw, 1972; E. C. Foster and Slim Williams, *The Long Hungry Night,* Atheneum, 1973; Arnold Griese, *At the Mouth of the Luckiest River* (juvenile), Crowell, 1973; Clyde Robert Bulla, *Dexter,* Crowell, 1973; Jonathan Gathorne-Hardy, *Operation Peeg,* Lippincott, 1974; Phyllis LaFarge, *Abby Takes Over,* Lippincott, 1974; Helen S. Rogers, *Morris and His Brave Lion* (juvenile), McGraw, 1975; Tom Robinson, *An Eskimo Birthday* (juvenile), Dodd, 1975; Hila Coleman, *That's the Way It Is, Amigo,* Crowell, 1975; Gloria Skurzynski, *In a Bottle With a Cork on Top* (juvenile), Dodd, 1976; Gathorne-Hardy, *The Airship Lady Ship Adventure,* Lippincott, 1977; Valentina P. Wasson, *The Chosen Baby* (juvenile), Lippincott, 1977; Griese, *The Wind Is Not a River,* Crowell, 1978; P. C. Hass, *Windsong Summer,* Dodd, 1978; Jay Leech and Zane Spencer, *Bright Fawn and Me* (juvenile), Crowell, 1979; Lee Bennett Hopkins, *By Myself* (juvenile), Crowell, 1980; Arnold Adoff, *Today We Are Brother and Sister* (juvenile), Crowell, 1981.

SIDELIGHTS: Coalson told *CA:* "All my life I've been making things—sculpture and pottery—and drawing things. I never thought about making books, though, until college. In 1968 I was sitting in a college figure drawing class, about to graduate that spring with a B.A. in art, which to me was the equivalent of stepping off the edge of the earth! I hadn't the foggiest idea what to do next. A classmate of mine, a little older and wiser about the ways of the world, came over to

me and said, 'You should illustrate books!' She was very sure. I probably looked at her in a peculiar way and asked, 'Do what?' The idea stuck. About two years later, while visiting Alaska, I collected some Eskimo folktales. I made up a couple of book presentations and took them to New York. I was fortunate enough to sell one of the books to Atheneum.

"I love Alaska, but I lived in New York City for seven years, and that left a profound impression. I try to spend a few weeks there each year—it's a revitalization process.

"In my book art, I try always to do things that people can identify with, the typical human experience. I like to pack energy into my drawings, as much as is appropriate for each manuscript. In my personal art I keep exploring, playing off ever-accumulating life experiences, hoping for the satisfaction that comes with learning how to express more about myself in a visual way. In my life experiences I hope to keep growing.

"I am in the process of learning sign language for the deaf. The graphic aspects of this language fascinate me."

AVOCATIONAL INTERESTS: Camping, sailing, snorkeling, "all watery things done on top of the water," her schnauzer, Meatloaf.

                              *   *   *

COCHRANE, Hugh (Ferrier)   1923-

PERSONAL: Born October 19, 1923, in Toronto, Ontario, Canada; son of Hugh (a miner) and Agnes (a nurse; maiden name, Robertson) Cochrane. *Education:* Attended Radio College Canada, Toronto, Ontario, Canada, 1949, 1953. *Religion:* Christian. *Home and office:* 100 Walpole Ave., Toronto 8, Ontario, Canada M4L 2J1.

CAREER: Worked in Ontario, Canada, on docks and in warehouses, 1941-45, in lumber mills and foundries, 1945-47; worked as a boat builder, 1948-50, and as a steelworker and construction worker, 1950-53; began work in electronics as a hi-fi technician, 1956; became television serviceman, 1963; free-lance writer, 1964—.

WRITINGS: Gateway to Oblivion, Doubleday, 1980. Contributor of articles to magazines, including *Rockhound, Gems and Minerals, Treasure, Outdoor Canada, Probe the Unknown,* and *Beyond Reality.*

WORK IN PROGRESS: A book tentatively titled *Third Millennium Threshold,* comparing historic and contemporary Fortean, UFO, psychic, and miraculous events and suggest undiscovered dimensions of reality.

SIDELIGHTS: Cochrane told *CA:* "My writing has stemmed from a desire to share information, anecdotes, and speculations gleaned from my own experiences and those of others."

AVOCATIONAL INTERESTS: Exploring historic sites, treasure hunting, mineral collecting, rockhounding, hunting, fishing, UFO's, psychic phenomena.

BIOGRAPHICAL/CRITICAL SOURCES: Toronto Quill & Quire, May, 1980; *In Review,* August, 1980.

                              *   *   *

COFFIN, William Sloane, Jr.   1924-

PERSONAL: Born June 1, 1924, in New York, N.Y.; son of William (a furniture store executive) and Catherine (Butterfield) Coffin; married Eva Anna Rubinstein (a ballet dancer and actress), December 12, 1956 (divorced, 1968); married Harriet Gibney, 1969; children: Amy Elizabeth, Alexander

Sloane, David Andrew. *Education:* Yale University, B.A., 1949, B.D., 1956; attended Union Theological Seminary, New York, N.Y., 1949-50. *Office:* Riverside Church, Riverside Dr. and 122nd St., New York, N.Y. 10027.

CAREER: Ordained minister of Presbyterian church, 1956; Phillips Academy, Andover, Mass., acting chaplain, 1956-57; Williams College, Williamstown, Mass., chaplain, 1957-58; Yale University, New Haven, Conn., chaplain, 1958-75; Riverside Church, New York, N.Y., senior minister, 1977—. Worked abroad on Russian affairs for Central Intelligence Agency (CIA), 1950-53; member of board of directors of President's Advisory Council for the Peace Corps. *Military service:* U.S. Army, 1943-47; became captain. *Member:* American Freedom of Residence Fund (director), National Association for the Advancement of Colored People (director of legal defense fund), Operation Crossroads Africa. *Awards, honors:* Connecticut Valley B'nai B'rith award for Americanism; D.D. from Wesleyan College.

WRITINGS: (Contributor) Franklin H. Littell, editor, *Sermons to Intellectuals From Three Continents*, Macmillan, 1963; (with Charles E. Whittaker) *Law, Order, and Civil Disobedience*, American Enterprise Institute for Public Policy Research, 1967; (with Morris L. Leibman) *Civil Disobedience: Aid or Hindrance to Justice?*, American Enterprise Institute for Public Policy Research, 1972; *Once to Every Man: A Memoir*, Atheneum, 1977. Author of pamphlets and published sermons.

SIDELIGHTS: In his book *Once to Every Man* Coffin discusses both his personal life and his role as a civil rights and anti-war activist. Daniel Yergin of the *New York Times Book Review* observed that Coffin's book can be read on two levels. "On one level," he said, "it is about success in America—about a rich boy whose father died when he was nine, who as a teen-ager practiced for hours a day in Paris to be a concert pianist, instead became a Central Intelligence Agency agent, a member of Skull and Bones, a minister, a national figure—and finally confronted failure, not once but twice, and not in politics but in the private realm, in the collapse of his two marriages. On another level, *Once to Every Man* is a perceptive and revelatory political history of America since World War II."

Richard John Neuhaus of *Christian Century* called Coffin's autobiography a "fight book." Neuhaus noted that "the end chapter is titled 'What Next?'; in it Coffin restlessly casts about for the next crusade in which the ambiguities of self can be submerged in a good clean fight."

Coffin's activism began with the civil rights movement of the early 1960's. He was arrested and convicted for disorderly conduct in 1961 as one of the eleven Freedom Riders who went to Montgomery, Alabama, to protest local laws that provided for racial segregation on buses and in restaurants. Seven years later Coffin and Dr. Benjamin Spock were the two most prominent defendants in a conspiracy trial in which they were charged with advocating resistance to the draft. Both were found guilty, but execution of their sentences—two years in federal prison and a $5,000 fine—was waived pending appeal.

Neuhaus observed that *Once to Every Man* offers an "essentially accurate view of 'the movement' as it was experienced by those at the center of it, or at least at one center of it."

BIOGRAPHICAL/CRITICAL SOURCES: Time, August 29, 1977; *Saturday Review*, October 29, 1977; *New York Times Book Review*, October 30, 1977; *Christian Century*, November

30, 1977; *Commonweal*, January 20, 1978; *America*, January 21, 1978; *National Review*, February 3, 1978.*

*   *   *

COHEN, Bernard 1937-

PERSONAL: Born November 16, 1937, in Suffern, N.Y.; son of Jacob and Edith Cohen; married Barbara Hecht (in real estate), March 8, 1960; children: Stuart, Michael, Ahuva, Jeffrey. *Education:* Yeshiva University, B.A., 1959, M.H.L., 1961; University of Pennsylvania, A.M., 1964, Ph.D., 1968. *Home:* 585 Green Pl., Woodmere, N.Y. 11598. *Office:* Department of Sociology, Queens College of the City University of New York, Flushing, N.Y. 11367.

CAREER: Queens College of the City University of New York, Flushing, N.Y., assistant professor, 1968-70, associate professor, 1970-81, professor of sociology, 1981—. Director of police research for Rand Corp., 1968-76. *Member:* American Sociological Association, American Society of Criminology. *Awards, honors:* J. Francis Finnegan Award in criminology from University of Pennsylvania, 1964; Bobbs-Merrill Award in sociology, 1965.

WRITINGS: The Police Internal Administration of Justice in New York City, New York City-Rand Institute, 1970; (with Marvin E. Wolfgang) *Crime and Race*, Institute of Human Relations Press, 1970; (with Isaac C. Hunt) *Minority Recruiting in the New York City Police Department: The Attraction of Candidates*, Rand Corp., 1971; (with Jan M. Chaiken) *Police Background Characteristics and Performance*, Lexington Books, 1973; (with Chaiken) *Police Civil Service Selection Procedures in New York City*, New York City-Rand Institute, 1973; (with Stephen H. Leinen) *Research on Criminal Justice Organizations: The Sentencing Process*, Rand Corp., 1974; *Deviant Street Networks: Prostitution in New York City*, Lexington Books, 1980. Book review editor of *Journal of Criminal Law and Criminology*, 1968-74.

WORK IN PROGRESS: Research on social deviance and on the police.

*   *   *

COHEN, Richard Murry 1938-

PERSONAL: Born May 4, 1938, in Ridgefield, Conn.; son of Leo and Betty Ruth Cohen; married Nancy Jean Naphols (a teacher and secretary), October, 1965; children: Brian E., Allison L. *Education:* Northeastern University, B.A., 1961. *Home:* 58 Mamanasco Rd., Ridgefield, Conn. 06877. *Office:* Sports Products, Inc., P.O. Box 392, Ridgefield, Conn. 06877.

CAREER: Sports Products, Inc., Ridgefield, Conn., president, 1973—. *Military service:* U.S. Army, 1961-63; became first lieutenant. *Member:* Publishers Alliance, Society for American Baseball Research, Professional Football Research Association.

WRITINGS: (With Jordan A. Deutsch, Roland T. Johnson, and David S. Neft) *The Sports Encyclopedia: Baseball*, Grosset, 1974, 4th edition, 1981; (with Deutsch, Johnson, and Neft) *The Sports Encyclopedia: Pro Football*, Grosset, 1974, 3rd edition published as *The Sports Encyclopedia: Pro Football, the Modern Era, 1960 to the Present*, 1978; (with Deutsch, Johnson, and Neft) *The Sports Encyclopedia: Pro Basketball*, Grosset, 1975; (with Deutsch, Johnson, and Neft) *The World Series*, Dial, 1976, revised edition, 1979; (with Deutsch and Neft) *The Scrapbook History of Pro Football, 1893-1979*, Bobbs-Merrill, 1976, revised edition, 1979; (with Deutsch and Neft) *The Complete All-Time Pro Baseball Reg-*

ister, Grosset, 1976, revised edition 1979; (with Deutsch and Neft) *The Notre Dame Football Scrapbook*, Bobbs-Merrill, 1977; (with Deutsch and Neft) *The Ohio State Football Scrapbook*, Bobbs-Merrill, 1977; (with Deutsch and Neft) *Pro Football: The Early Years, an Encyclopedic History, 1895-1959*, Sports Products, Inc., 1978.

*   *   *

COHEN, William A(lan) 1937-

PERSONAL: Born June 25, 1937, in Baltimore, Md.; son of Sidney Oliver (a U.S. Air Force officer) and Theresa (a teacher; maiden name, Bachman) Cohen; married Janice Stults, January 8, 1963 (divorced January 19, 1966); married Nurit Kovnator (a professor), May 28, 1967; children: William Alan II, Barak, Nimrod. *Education:* U.S. Military Academy, B.S., 1959; University of Chicago, M.B.A., 1967; Claremont Graduate School, M.A., 1978, Ph.D., 1979. *Politics:* Republican. *Religion:* Jewish. *Home:* 1556 North Sierra Madre Villa, Pasadena, Calif. 91107. *Office:* Department of Marketing, California State University, 5151 State University Dr., Los Angeles, Calif. 90032.

CAREER: U.S. Air Force, pilot, navigator, and program manager, 1959-70, leaving service as major; Israel Aircraft Industries, Lod, deputy manager of human engineering department and project manager, 1970-73; Sierra Engineering Co., Sierra Madre, Calif., manager of research and development, 1973-76; McDonnell-Douglas Astronautics Co., Huntington Beach, Calif., advanced technology marketing manager, 1976-78; California State University, Los Angeles, associate professor of marketing, director of Bureau of Business and Economic Research, and director of Small Business Institute, 1978—. President of Global Associates (management consultants), 1973—; member of U.S. Senatorial Business Advisory Board. *Military service:* Israeli Air Force, pilot, 1972-73; major. U.S. Air Force Reserve, Space Division, 1970—.

MEMBER: American Marketing Association, Society of American Military Engineers, Direct Mail Marketing Association (fellow, 1980), Combat Pilots Association, Reserve Officers Association, Association of Graduates of the U.S. Military Academy, Direct Marketing Club of Southern California (president; member of board of governors), West Point Society of Los Angeles (member of board of governors). *Awards, honors*—Military: Pierce Currier Foster Memorial Award from U.S. Military Academy, 1959; Distinguished Flying Cross with three oak leaf clusters; Air Medal with eleven oak leaf clusters; Meritorious Service Medal; Commendation Medal with oak leaf cluster; Vietnamese Cross of Gallantry with palm and star. Other: Gold medal from Daughters of the Confederacy, 1953; gold medal from *Chicago Tribune*, 1955, for academic achievement; outstanding service award from National Management Association, 1980; nominated for award from Freedoms Foundation, 1980.

WRITINGS: Writer's Guide to Publication and Profit, Global Associates, 1975; *Writer's Guide to Professional Writers' Secrets*, Global Associates, 1975; *Writer's Guide to Punctuation*, Global Associates, 1975; *The Executive's Guide to Finding a Superior Job*, American Management Association, 1978; *Principles of Technical Management*, American Management Association, 1980; *Selling to the U.S. Government*, Wiley, 1981; *Successful Marketing for Small Business*, American Management Association, 1981; *Mail Order Marketing*, Wiley, 1982. Contributor of about thirty articles to technical journals in the United States and abroad.

WORK IN PROGRESS: A book, *The Entrepreneur and Small Businessman's Problem Solver.*

SIDELIGHTS: Cohen wrote: "I am interested in writing books that show an individual how to become successful in some field of business. To write these books, I not only do conventional research, but rely on my own experience about the subject. For example, *The Executive's Guide to Finding a Superior Job* was based mainly on my own experiences as an executive recruiter. Similarly, I've been a technical manager, a small businessman, and so forth. These have all been topics of my books. I believe my contribution is to combine theory, research, and my experience and thinking about the subject.

"I have traveled in Europe, Asia, and the Middle East, including one year in Thailand and three years in Israel; I flew in the Yom Kippur War in 1973."

AVOCATIONAL INTERESTS: Physical conditioning, applied psychology, karate.

*   *   *

COIGNEY, Virginia 1917-
(Virginia Travers)

PERSONAL: Born October 2, 1917, in St. Louis, Mo.; married Robert Travers (marriage ended); married H. E. Cooper (marriage ended); married Rudy Coigney, October 25, 1945 (divorced December, 1969); children: (first marriage) Mary. *Education:* Attended high school. *Religion:* None. *Home:* 33 Limekiln Rd., West Redding, Conn. 06896. *Agent:* Phyllis Bellows Wender, Wender & Associates, 30 East 60th St., Room 903, New York, N.Y. 10022. *Office:* Community Health Center, Danbury Hospital, Danbury, Conn. 06810.

CAREER: Associated with *Albany Knickerbocker Press*, Albany, N.Y., *Louisville Courier-Journal*, Louisville, Ky., and *Schenectady Gazette*, Schenectady, N.Y.; member of staff of American Museum of Natural History; director of public relations for Compton Advertising, Inc.; Danbury Hospital, Danbury, Conn., director of patient and community relations, 1960—. Director of Interlude. Member of board of directors of Wooster School. *Member:* Writers Guild, Authors League of America, National Association for the Advancement of Colored People.

WRITINGS: Who Did It?: Biographies of Leaders in History, Science, Invention, Exploration, and Entertainment, Doubleday, 1963; *Rebel With a Cause: Biography of Margaret Sanger*, Doubleday, 1969; *Children Are People Too: How We Fail Our Children and How We Can Love Them*, Morrow, 1975. Also author of *The No Beef Cookbook*, Bantam; *Handbook for Foreign Medical Graduates;* several one-act plays; and several documentary series for the Anti-Defamation League.

Writer for radio and television programs (sometimes under name Virginia Travers), including "Edge of Night," "Armstrong Circle Theatre," "Love of Life," "Ever Since Eve," and "Young Doctor Malone." Contributor to *Science Encyclopedia*. Contributor to magazines and newspapers, including *Cosmopolitan, Ingenue, World Health, Nature and Science, New York Times, Women's Home Companion*, and *This Week.*

*   *   *

COLANERI, John Nunzio 1930-

PERSONAL: Born January 8, 1930, in New York, N.Y.; son of Donato (a bricklayer) and Chiarina (Ruta) Colaneri; married Ann Rose Raia (a college professor), July 1, 1967; children: John. *Education:* City College (now of the City University of New York), B.A., 1952; Columbia University, M.A., 1954, Ph.D., 1968. *Politics:* Conservative. *Religion:* Roman Catholic. *Office:* Department of Modern Languages, Iona College, 715 North Ave., New Rochelle, N.Y. 10801.

CAREER: Iona College, New Rochelle, N.Y., professor of Italian and chairman of department of modern languages, 1959—. Adjunct professor at College of New Rochelle, 1961—, Bronx Community College of the City University of New York, spring, 1962, and State University of New York College at Purchase, 1971-72. *Member:* American Association of Teachers of Spanish and Portuguese, American Association of Teachers of Italian (president, 1969-71).

WRITINGS: (Editor) Francesco De Vieri, *Lezzioni D'Amore,* Wilhelm Fink Verlag, 1973; *Italian Bilingual Dictionary: A Beginner's Guide in Words and Pictures,* Barron's, 1980. Contributor to academic journals.

WORK IN PROGRESS: Research on the place of the city in the nineteenth-century Romantic novel in Italy.

*   *   *

COLE, John Y(oung), Jr. 1940-

PERSONAL: Born July 30, 1940, in Ellensburg, Wash.; son of John Y. (a banker) and Alice (Van Leuven) Cole; married Nancy E. Gwinn (a librarian), April 28, 1973. *Education:* University of Washington, Seattle, B.A., 1962, M.L.S., 1963; Johns Hopkins University, M.L.A., 1966; George Washington University, Ph.D., 1971. *Home:* 6309 33rd St. N.W., Washington, D.C. 20015. *Office:* Center for the Book, Library of Congress, Washington, D.C. 20540.

CAREER: Library of Congress, Washington, D.C., librarian and library administrator, 1966-75, chairman of Librarian's Task Force on Goals, Organization, and Planning, 1976, executive director of Center for the Book, 1977—. Associate professorial lecturer at George Washington University, 1977—. *Military service:* U.S. Army, 1963-66; became first lieutenant. *Member:* American Library Association, Organization of American Historians, Society of American Archivists.

WRITINGS: (Editor) *Ainsworth Rand Spofford: Bookman and Librarian,* Libraries Unlimited, 1975; (editor) *Television, the Book, and the Classroom,* Library of Congress, 1978; (editor) *The Library of Congress in Perspective,* Bowker, 1978; *For Congress and the Nation: A Chronological History of the Library of Congress,* Library of Congress, 1979; (editor) *Responsibilities of the American Book Community,* Library of Congress, 1981.

WORK IN PROGRESS: Research on history of books and libraries in American society, with emphasis on the Library of Congress.

*   *   *

COLE, Leonard Leslie 1909-1980
(Cole Lesley)

PERSONAL: Born March 6, 1909, in Farningham, England; died January 4, 1980, in Les Avants, Switzerland; son of William James and Ellen Jane Cole. *Education:* Attended Church of England grammar school in Farningham, England. *Politics:* Conservative. *Religion:* Church of England. *Agent:* Irving Paul Lazar Agency, 211 South Beverly Dr., Beverly Hills, Calif. 90212; and Curtis Brown Ltd., 1 Craven Hill, London W2 3EP, England.

CAREER: Secretary to Noel Coward, 1936-73; writer, 1973-80. *Military service:* Royal Air Force, aircraftsman, 1940; served in Ireland and Scotland.

WRITINGS—Under pseudonym Cole Lesley: *Remembered Laughter: The Life of Noel Coward,* J. Cape, 1976; (with Graham Payn and Sheridan Morley) *Noel Coward and His Friends,* Weidenfeld & Nicolson, 1979.

SIDELIGHTS: In 1936, the eminent playwright Noel Coward hired Cole Lesley to be his cook and valet. Thirty-seven years later, until Coward's death, Lesley was still with the dramatist as his personal secretary, constant companion, and biographer.

Lesley's *Remembered Laughter: The Life of Noel Coward* is, according to Mel Gussow of the *New York Times Book Review,* "a treasure trove of anecdotes and memorabilia, a richly illustrated, affectionate love letter to a treasured friend." Included in the biography are Lesley's memories of life with Coward and stories of Coward's associations with other personalities of the stage. The book also features carefully culled excerpts from Sir Noel's personal diary and letters, to which Lesley was given access before his employer's death.

Remembered Laughter was warmly received by critics. In a *Times Literary Supplement* review, Alastair Forbes remarked, "If not a masterpiece, it is a masterly and surely definitive piecing-together of Coward's life and career, full of splendidly funny anecdotes." Arthur Marshall of the *New Statesman* proclaimed, "If there has been a better or more fascinating theatrical biography in the last fifty years, it has not come my way."

A second book, *Noel Coward and His Friends,* followed *Remembered Laughter.* Written by Lesley and two other companions of Coward, the volume is a melange of photos, sheet music and lyrics, programs, and other remembrances of Coward's career.

An heir to the writer's estate, Lesley died in his sleep at Chalet Coward, Sir Noel Coward's home in Switzerland.

BIOGRAPHICAL/CRITICAL SOURCES: New Statesman, October 22, 1976; *Times Literary Supplement,* October 22, 1976; *New York Times Book Review,* November 28, 1976; *New York Review of Books,* January 20, 1977; *New Yorker,* January 24, 1977; *Encounter,* May, 1977.

OBITUARIES: New York Times, January 9, 1980; *Newsweek,* January 21, 1980.

[Sketch verified by co-author Graham Payn]

*   *   *

COLLIER, Herbert L(eon) 1933-

PERSONAL: Born October 19, 1933, in Seattle, Wash.; son of Herbert L., Jr. (in oil business) and Lucina M. (Babin) Collier; married Sharon Lee Williams (a clinical assistant), September 2, 1956; children: Tracie L. and Scott J. (twins), Lisa J. *Education:* Whitman College, B.A., 1956; graduate study at University of London, 1956-57; University of Portland, M.S., 1958, Ph.D., 1962. *Agent:* Don Woodside, 2218 East Magnolia, Phoenix, Ariz. 85034. *Office:* Southwest Psychological Services, 4227 North 32nd St., Phoenix, Ariz. 85018.

CAREER: Began private practice in clinical psychology at Southwest Psychological Services, Phoenix, Ariz.; Portland Children's Center, Inc. (for the mentally retarded), Portland, Ore., supervisor, 1958-59; University of Portland, Portland, extern in child psychology with Psychological Services, 1959-

60; University of Oregon, Eugene, intern in psychology, 1960-61, fellow of Division of Child Psychiatry, 1961-62; Child Evaluation Center, Phoenix, chief clinical psychologist and administrative assistant, 1962-65; Maricopa County Health Department, Phoenix, director of mental health services, 1965-66; St. Joseph's Mental Health Center, Phoenix, staff psychologist, 1966-73; Greater Phoenix Psychiatric Center, Inc., Phoenix, president, 1973—. Extern in psychology at Oregon Fairview Home, 1958-59; lecturer at Arizona State University, 1964-67; member of board of directors of Crisis Nursery and San Pablo Home for Youth; consultant to National Organization of Mothers of Twins Clubs. *Member:* American Psychological Association, Arizona State Psychological Association (chairman of ethics committee, 1968-70), Maricopa County Society of Clinical Psychologists.

WRITINGS: The Psychology of Twins: A Practical Handbook for Parents, Doctors, Nurses, Counselors, and Teachers, C.O.L. Publishing, 1972, revised edition, 1974; (contributor) Walter Klopfer and Max Reed, editors, *Problems in Psychotherapy: An Eclectic Approach,* Wiley, 1974; *Homework: How to Study and Remember,* O'Sullivan, Woodside, 1976. Contributor to psychology and medical journals.

WORK IN PROGRESS: A book on the learning process; *What Is Psychotherapy and Who Needs It?*.

AVOCATIONAL INTERESTS: Tennis, travel.

*   *   *

COLLINS, Judy (Marjorie) 1939-

PERSONAL: Born May 1, 1939, in Seattle, Wash.; daughter of Charles T. (a musician and broadcaster) and Marjorie (Byrd) Collins; married Peter A. Taylor, April, 1958 (divorced, 1962); children: Clark Collins. *Office:* c/o Rocky Mountain Productions, Inc., 1775 Broadway, New York, N.Y., 10019.

CAREER: Musical performer and producer and director of motion pictures, including "Antonia: A Portrait of the Woman," 1974. Actress in stage production "Peer Gynt," 1969. *Awards, honors:* Silver Medal from Atlanta International Film Festival, Blue Ribbon from American Film Festival, and nomination for Academy Award for best documentary from Academy of Motion Picture Arts and Sciences, all 1974, all for "Antonia: A Portrait of the Woman"; Christopher Award.

WRITINGS: The Judy Collins Songbook: With Comments, Instructions, and Personal Reminiscences, Grosset, 1969.

Recordings; all for Elektra: "Maid of Constant Sorrow," 1961; "Golden Apples of the Sun," 1962; "Judy Collins No. 3," 1964; "The Judy Collins Concert," 1964; "Judy Collins' Fifth Album," 1965; "In My Life," 1966; "Wildflowers," 1967; "Who Knows Where the Time Goes?," 1968; "Recollections," 1969; "Whales and Nightingales," 1970; "Living," 1971; "True Stories and Other Dreams," 1972; "Colors of the Day: The Best of Judy Collins," 1972; "Judith," 1975; "Bread and Roses," 1976; "So Early in the Spring: The First Fifteen Years," 1977; "Hard Times for Lovers," 1979.

WORK IN PROGRESS: An autobiography; a book on Antonia Brico.

SIDELIGHTS: In 1964 *Time* described Collins as "a major contender for the feminine folk-music crown, second only to [Joan] Baez among today's flock of urban folk stylists and perhaps first to have lived the songs before learning to sing them." Since that article appeared, Collins has broadened her musical scope and added blues and even show tunes to

her repertoire. In the 1970's she began to receive recognition as one of the most durable and versatile vocalists of her generation.

The earliest musical influence on Collins was her father, a blind musician who hosted his own radio program in Denver. "Daddy was loud and definite about who he was," Collins recalled in *The Judy Collins Songbook,* "snarling at the world when it tumbled him, raving at it when it cheated him, embracing it in those rare moments when he was not having a fight with it. I think he believed I would avenge the fight somehow, being the firstborn and being like him, a musician and a stranger to a part of the everyday, common world that was his enemy."

Collins's formal musical training began when she was seven. She studied classical piano under Antonia Brico, a conductor for the Businessmen's Orchestra in Denver. Brico "studied conducting with Sibelius when she was a young woman," Collins acknowledged. "She visited Schweitzer every summer in Lambarene, Africa, and while the nurses tended the African patients and the big tarantulas crawled slowly through the makeshift hospital compound in the tropical heat, Dr. Brico and Schweitzer played Bach. . . . I was totally in awe of her."

Collins abandoned her classical studies in her teens when she discovered folk music. "I wanted to find some kind of music which would be an outlet for drama and storytelling," she said, "and it wasn't opera. I needed something which gave me more of a scope to explore through words, and that was folk music." Collins listened to Woody Guthrie and Pete Seeger, and performed their songs in bars in Colorado. Eventually she appeared at the Gate of Horn in Chicago. Her success there led to bookings in Greenwich Village, the hub of folk-music activity during the early 1960's.

After signing with Elektra Records in 1961, Collins released albums of songs written by folk songwriters such as Bob Dylan, Phil Ochs, Richard Farina, and Guthrie. The records were immensely successful with folk audiences and sparked a booking at the prestigious Carnegie Hall. By 1966, however, Collins was also recording material written by lesser known composers, including Randy Newman. "Wildflowers," her 1967 recording, included songs by Collins and then-budding singer/songwriter Joni Mitchell. Collins's music continued to evolve during the 1970's, as she included blues and jazz tunes in her concerts and recordings. Her rendition of Stephen Sondheim's "Send in the Clowns," from the stage musical "A Little Night Music," was a popular success and helped establish her as a commanding interpreter of a wide variety of songs. "These are very exciting times musically," she told the *New York Times* in 1976. "There are so many new forms. And we've finally gotten to the point where people don't stand up and shout, 'You can't sing that, Ella Fitzgerald should be singing that,' if a performer branches out."

By 1980 Collins seemed equally pleased with her development as a vocalist. "I've been studying for years, and now I'm becoming the kind of singer I want to be," she revealed in *Harper's Bazaar.* "This has really flowered for me just in the past year. I'm beginning to learn what I want to sound like and to get the kind of flexibility that comes only with training. My singing is stronger. I'm adding more humor and making more daring choices in the kind of material I sing."

In 1974, Collins departed from performing to collaborate with filmmaker Jill Godmilow on "Antonia: A Portrait of the Woman," a film about her former instructor Antonia Brico. Collins told *Mademoiselle* that "working in another field gives energy to your original field—all creativity is similar."

The documentary was highly regarded in the film industry, and won several festival awards and a nomination for best documentary from the motion picture academy.

Collins called 1980 "a very introspective period for me." She noted, "I'm very busy now—doing concerts, and looking for parts in movies. . . . I'm doing a lot of mulling over where I'd like to be in the next 10 years—and when I'm 60 or 70. I've had a lot of success in my music, but what I want to do is write, and that's only begun to happen in the last few years. I'm writing songs . . . , and I hope to do an autobiography."

BIOGRAPHICAL/CRITICAL SOURCES: Time, August 7, 1964; *Los Angeles Times,* February 4, 1967; *Newsweek,* January 6, 1969; *Life,* May 2, 1969; *Redbook,* October, 1969; *McCall's,* April, 1970; *Mademoiselle,* February, 1975; *New York Times,* December 1, 1976; *High Fidelity,* April, 1977; Vivian Claire, *Judy Collins,* Flash Books, 1977; *Rolling Stone,* May 3, 1979; *Harper's Bazaar,* October 1980.*

* * *

COLLINS, Max (Allan), Jr. 1948-

PERSONAL: Born March 3, 1948, in Muscatine, Iowa; son of Max Allan, Sr. (an executive) and Patricia Ann Collins; married Barbara Jane Mull (a secretary), June 1, 1968. *Education:* Muscatine Community College, A.A., 1968; University of Iowa, B.A., 1970, M.F.A., 1972. *Politics:* Independent. *Home and office:* 117 Lord Ave., Muscatine, Iowa 52761. *Agent:* Knox Burger Associates Ltd., 39½ Washington Sq. S., New York, N.Y. 10012.

CAREER: Professional musician, 1966-72; Muscatine Community College, Muscatine, Iowa, instructor in English, journalism, and creative writing, 1971-77; professional musician, 1977-79; writer, 1972—. Instructor at Mississippi Valley Writers Conference. *Member:* Mystery Writers of America, American Federation of Musicians.

WRITINGS—"Nolan" series; suspense novels; all published by Pinnacle Books, except as noted: *Nolan I: Bait Money,* Curtis Books, 1973, revised edition, Pinnacle Books, 1981; . . . *II: Blood Money,* Curtis Books, 1973, revised edition, 1981; . . . *III: Fly Paper,* 1981; . . . *IV: Hush Money,* 1981; . . . *V: Hard Cash,* 1982; . . . *VI: Scratch Fever,* 1982.

"Quarry" series; all published by Berkley Publishing: *Quarry I: The Broker,* 1976; . . . *II: The Broker's Wife,* 1976; . . . *III: The Dealer,* 1976; . . . *IV: The Slasher,* 1977.

Comic strip collections: *Dick Tracy Meets Angeltop,* Ace Books, 1980; *Dick Tracy Meets the Punks,* Ace Books, 1980; *The Mike Mist Minute Mist-eries,* Eclipse Enterprises, 1981.

Writer of comic strip "Dick Tracy," distributed by Chicago Tribune/New York News Syndicate, 1977—; writer of "The Comics Page," 1979-80. Contributor to magazines, including *Armchair Detective, Mystery Magazine,* and *Video Action.*

WORK IN PROGRESS: The Waste, a suspense novel dealing with dumping of hazardous wastes; research for a historical detective novel set in Chicago in the 1930's; comic strips.

SIDELIGHTS: Collins wrote: "My works to date have been in the mystery/suspense genre. I am proudest of my novels about the hired killer Quarry, but the series seems to be complete at four books. Despite the fact that I tend to make the 'heroes' of my novels criminals, I am probably most widely read as the writer of the syndicated comic strip 'Dick Tracy,' which appears in five hundred newspapers and which represents 'law and order' in its best and most traditional sense.

"My interest in comics had previously been reflected by the character Jon, a young aspiring cartoonist who is a sidekick of sorts to the fifty-ish, semi-retired thief Nolan. Cartooning had been my childhood ambition, and 'Dick Tracy' was my favorite comic strip. As I grew older my fondness for Tracy led me quite naturally into the works of Dashiell Hammett, Mickey Spillane, and other 'tough guy' crime writers, and I put drawing aside and concentrated on writing.

"I am a former rock musician (I recorded with the Daybreakers in Nashville, Tennessee, and in 1968 signed a songwriting contract with Tree Publishing of Nashville), and I am still interested in music in general and rock 'n' roll in particular (probably always will be). I collect original comic art and have assembled one of the major collections in the United States (or anywhere), with an excess of one hundred originals hanging in my home. I am an avid movie buff and have a growing library of old movies on video tape.

"My literary heroes include Hammett, James M. Cain, Donald E. Westlake, and Jim Thompson. I am in particular a supporter of Mickey Spillane, about whom I have written a number of articles, and I hope eventually, when time allows, to do a book-length study of this important, influential American writer.

"I plan to stay in the mystery/suspense area, but I am expanding beyond the notion of category fiction with my novel *The Waste* and with the work on Chicago in the 1930's."

* * *

COLLINSON, Laurence (Henry) 1925-

PERSONAL: Born September 7, 1925, in Leeds, England. *Education:* Attended University of Queensland and Julian Ashton Art School; received diploma from Mercer House, 1955. *Home:* 97 Edgwarebury Lane, Edgware, Middlesex HA8 8NA, England. *Agent:* Margery Vosper Ltd., 26 Charing Cross Rd., Suite 8, London WC2H 0DG, England.

CAREER: Free-lance writer, until 1954; high school teacher of mathematics and English in Australia, 1956-61; Victoria Education Department, Australia, editor of *Educational,* 1961-64; International Publishing Corp., London, England, magazine sub-editor, 1965-73. Transactional analysis therapist. *Member:* British Academy of Film and Television Arts, Society of Authors, Writers Guild of Great Britain, National Union of Journalists. *Awards, honors:* Prize from Society of Australian Authors, 1969; Australian Council of Arts fellowship, 1973, grant, 1974-75.

WRITINGS: Poet's Dozen (poems), privately printed, 1952; *The Moods of Love* (poems), Overland, 1957; *Who Is Wheeling Grandma?* (poems), Overland, 1967; *Cupid's Crescent* (novel), Grandma Press, 1973; *Hovering Narcissus,* Grandma Press, 1977. Also author of *Thinking Straight,* 1975, and *One Penny for Israel,* 1978.

Children's books: *The Lion and the Mouse,* Hamlyn, 1969; *My Book of Fables,* Odhams, 1969; *Swan Lake,* Hamlyn, 1969; *The Lion Who Ran Away,* Hamlyn, 1970; *Snow White and the Seven Dwarfs,* Hamlyn, 1971.

Plays represented in anthologies, including: "Friday Night at the Schrammers'" (first produced in Brisbane, Australia, 1949), published in *Australian One-Act Plays,* edited by Greg Branson, Rigby, 1962; "A Slice of Birthday Cake" (radio play; first broadcast in 1963), published in *Eight Short Plays,* Thomas Nelson, 1965; "The Wangaratta Bunyip," published in *Plays for Young Players,* edited by Branson and Colin Thiele, Rigby, 1970.

Unpublished stage plays: "No Sugar for George," first produced in Brisbane, Australia, 1949; "The Zelda Trio" (two-act), first produced in Melbourne, Australia, 1961. Also author of "Syllabus of Love: How Far Is a Little Bit?" (two-act comedy).

Television plays: "Uneasy Paradise," first broadcast in 1963; "Nude With Violin," first broadcast in 1964; "The Audition," first broadcast in 1964; "The Moods of Love," first broadcast in 1964; "Number Thirty Approximately," first broadcast in 1968; "Loving Israel," first broadcast in 1968; "The Girl From Upstairs," first broadcast in 1971.

Radio plays: "The Slob on Friday," first broadcast in 1969.

Writer for documentary film series "Export Action," 1964. Author of a column in *Quorum*, 1973—. Contributor to magazines and newspapers, including *Overland, Meanjin, Australian,* and *Age.*

SIDELIGHTS: As a poet, Collinson discounts the freedom of technique advocated by many of his contemporaries. The restrictions imposed by traditional forms, he suggests, allow a poet to shape a more valuable object.

Collinson's plays have been termed "unconventional" because they espouse the individual's rejection of social conventions in favor of personal freedom. Though Collinson advocates freedom of the spirit, he tempers his belief with warnings against the dangers of living in a fantasy world.*

*   *   *

COLM, Gerhard 1897-1968

OBITUARY NOTICE—See index for *CA* sketch: Born June 30, 1897, in Hanover, Germany; died December 25, 1968. Economist, educator, and author of works in his field. Colm taught at German universities during the 1920's. He arrived in the United States in 1933 and became a professor at New School for Social Research. During World War II he worked for the Bureau of the Budget. His many writings include *General Economic Feasibility of National Security Programs* and *The Economy of the American People: Progress, Problems, and Prospects.* Obituaries and other sources: *Who Was Who in America,* 5th edition, Marquis, 1973.

*   *   *

COMAY, Joan

PERSONAL: Born in Johannesburg, South Africa; daughter of Charles (in business) and Bertha (a lawyer and member of South African Parliament; maiden name, Schwartz) Solomon; married Michael Comay (Israel's former ambassador to England and the United Nations); children: Yochanan (deceased), Jill Comay Stern. *Education:* Attended University of the Witwatersrand, 1933-35, and University of Cape Town, 1940-45. *Religion:* Jewish. *Home:* 47 Harav Berlin St., Jerusalem 92505, Israel. *Agent:* International Creative Management, 40 West 57th St., New York, N.Y. 10019; and Elaine Greene Ltd., 31 Newington Green, Islington, London N16 9PU, England.

CAREER: Israel Speaks, New York, N.Y., Jerusalem correspondent and Israel bureau chief, 1948-52; lecturer, broadcaster, and feature writer in Canada and the United States, 1952-67; staff editor for *Encyclopaedia Judaica,* 1967-70; lecturer, broadcaster, and feature writer in England, 1970-74; author of column for *WIZO Review,* 1974-80. *Member:* Jerusalem Animal Protection Society (honorary president). *Awards, honors:* Nonfiction book of the year award from *Yorkshire Post,* 1971, for *Who's Who in the Old Testament.*

WRITINGS: The Sinai Campaign, Israel Book Publishing Co., 1957; *Everyone's Guide to Israel,* Doubleday, 1962, revised edition, 1966; *Introducing Israel,* Methuen, 1963, revised edition, 1969; (with Moshe Pearlman) *Israel,* Macmillan, 1964; *The United Nations in Action,* Macmillan, 1965; *Ben Gurion and the Birth of Israel,* Random House, 1967; *Israel: An Uncommon Guide,* Random House, 1969.

Who's Who in the Old Testament (Literary Guild selection), Holt, 1971; *Who's Who in Jewish History,* McKay, 1974; *The Temple of Jerusalem,* Holt, 1975; *The Hebrew Kings,* Morrow, 1976; *The Jerusalem I Love,* Leon Amiel, 1976; *The World's Greatest Story,* Holt, 1978; *The Diaspora Story,* Random House, 1981; *The Turbulent Inn,* Weidenfeld & Nicholson, 1981.

SIDELIGHTS: Joan Comay's books have been published in French, Italian, and Swedish. She told *CA:* "My intense interest and involvement with Israel, Jewish history, and the Diaspora was deepened by my settling in Israel in 1947, my contacts with the Jewish communities in countries of my husband's diplomatic service (in Canada, the United States, and England), and my three years of work on the staff of the *Encyclopaedia Judaica.*"

*   *   *

CONDRY, William Moreton 1918-

PERSONAL: Born March 1, 1918, in Birmingham, England; son of William Joseph (a gem-setter) and Elizabeth Agnes (Moreton) Condry; married Penny Bailey, April 17, 1946. *Education:* University of Birmingham, B.A., 1939, Dip.Ed., 1940; University of London, B.A. (with honors), 1945; University of Wales, M.A., 1952. *Home:* Ynys Edwin, Eglwysfach, Machynlleth, Powys, Wales. *Agent:* Curtis Brown Ltd., 1 Craven Hill, London W2 3EP, England.

CAREER: Lapley Grange Prep School, Furnace, Machynlleth, Wales, teacher, 1949-57; University of Wales, Aberystwyth, lecturer in natural history, 1958-68; Royal Society for the Protection of Birds, Ynys-hir Reserve, nature reserve warden, 1969-79, teacher and naturalist, 1979—. Free-lance broadcaster for British Broadcasting Corp. (BBC), 1948—; free-lance writer, 1954—. *Member:* British Trust for Ornithology, Botanical Society of the British Isles, West Wales Naturalists' Trust, North Wales Naturalists' Trust. *Awards, honors:* Silver Medal from Royal Society for the Protection of Birds, 1965; M.Sc., University of Wales, 1980.

WRITINGS: Thoreau (biography), Witherby, 1954; *The Snowdonia National Park,* Collins, 1966; *Birds and Wild Africa,* Collins, 1967; *Exploring Wales,* Faber, 1970; *Woodlands,* Collins, 1974; *Pathway to the Wild,* Faber, 1975; *World of a Mountain,* Faber, 1977; *The Natural History of Wales,* Collins, 1981. Author of column, "A Country Diary," in *London Guardian,* 1957—.

WORK IN PROGRESS: A handbook to nature reserves administered in Great Britain and Northern Ireland by the Royal Society for the Protection of Birds.

SIDELIGHTS: Condry told *CA:* "I have long studied the life and ideas of the American philosopher and naturalist Henry David Thoreau. This study accompanies my lifelong interest in natural history and nature conservation. I'm especially concerned with the conservation and natural history of the British Isles, the European Continent, and Africa; this last concern reinforced by my several visits to the national parks and wilderness areas of Tanzania, Zambia, and Kenya."

In his 1975 book, *Pathway to the Wild,* Condry, according to Harry Coombes, reflects on his travels in Wales, Ireland,

France, Spain, Switzerland, Africa, and Scotland while revealing his convictions about nature and ecology. The reviewer wrote in *Books and Bookmen:* "Condry is not specifically an ecologist, though he knows much about ecology. He is a naturalist without pedantry, enthusiastic but notably level-headed. That is, he is an intelligent man who loves flowers, trees, rocks and soils, animals and birds." As a conservationist, Condry is neither unrealistically optimistic nor resignedly dismal. Coombes continued, "He sees a lot that is dangerously wrong in the world; he sees signs of hope, and he does not cease from working for what he believes in."

BIOGRAPHICAL/CRITICAL SOURCES: London Observer, June 15, 1969; *Times Literary Supplement,* January 10, 1975, April 17, 1981; *Guardian Weekly,* January 25, 1976; *Books and Bookmen,* January, 1977; *Times Educational Supplement,* June 2, 1978; *Country Life,* April 9, 1981.

*   *   *

CONGRAT-BUTLER, Stefan   1914(?)-1979

PERSONAL: Born c. 1914 in Chicago, Ill.; died of leukemia, October 27, 1979, in New York, N.Y.; married wife, Caterina. *Education:* Columbia University, B.S.; graduate study at Aarhus University. *Residence:* New York, N.Y.

CAREER: Linguist, editor, and scholar of Russian culture. Reporter for *Chicago Daily News* prior to World War II; author of foreign language radio commercials; consultant on the preparation and production of multilingual texts, manuals, and reference books; photographer. *Military service:* U.S. Navy, served in World War II. *Member:* P.E.N.

WRITINGS: (Editor with Ad Stender Petersen) *Anthology of Old Russian Literature,* Columbia University Press, 1962; (compiler and annotator) *Posters of the Russian Revolution, 1917-1929,* Grove, 1967; (editor) *Russian Vest Pocket Dictionary,* Random House, 1974; (editor) *Translations and Translators: An International Directory and Guide,* Bowker, 1979. Contributor of photographs to Paul Goodman's *The Open Look,* Funk, 1969.

OBITUARIES: New York Times, October 30, 1979; *Publishers Weekly,* November 5, 1979.

*   *   *

CONLEY, Ellen Alexander   1938-

PERSONAL: Born November 5, 1938, in Carbondale, Pa.; daughter of Alexander (a dentist) and Sylvia (Eisner) Howard; married Steve Conley (an artist), August 13, 1967; children: Dalton, Alexandra. *Education:* Pennsylvania State University, B.A., 1960; Jefferson Medical School, M.T., 1961; Wagner College, M.S., 1975; also attended New School for Social Research and Columbia University. *Home:* 85 Columbia St., No. 21-F, New York, N.Y. 10002. *Agent:* Frances Goldin, 305 East 11th St., New York, N.Y. 10003.

CAREER: Jefferson Medical School, Philadelphia, Pa., research assistant in pediatrics, 1961-62; Hahnemann Medical School, Philadelphia, research assistant in pharmacology, 1962-63; Hospital for Special Surgery, New York City, rotating laboratory technologist, 1963-65; Schweitzer Hospital, St. Marc, Haiti, volunteer worker on classification and coding of diseases project, 1965; New York Infirmary, New York City, bacteriology technologist, 1965-67; Beth Israel Hospital, New York City, instructor in microbiology, 1967-68; Boro Medical Center, New York City, supervisor for general laboratory in Manhattan and Brooklyn subdivision, 1968-70; Hostos Community College of the City University of New

York, Bronx, N.Y., lecturer in medical technology and hospital laboratory training coordinator for six hospitals, 1970-72, summer, 1973; Wagner College, Staten Island, N.Y., internship instructor, 1974-75; State University of New York Empire State College, State Springs, lecturer on the Medusa Crisis/health system and expert credit evaluator in health science and English, 1975-78; New York School for Laboratory Technologists, New York City, laboratory internship coordinator, 1979—. Part-time bacteriologist at Long Island College Hospital, 1970-72; member of English department faculty at Pratt Institute, 1977—. *Member:* American Society of Clinical Pathologists. *Awards, honors:* New York fiction award from Creative Artists Public Service, 1979, for fiction.

WRITINGS: Soho Madonna (novel), Avon, 1980.

WORK IN PROGRESS: Soon to Be Immortal, a novel, publication expected in 1981.

SIDELIGHTS: Ellen Conley wrote: "I am not a hot-house writer. I must go out in the world in various occupations to earn my living. Though this does not increase the gracefulness of my sentences, it gives me richer contents. I have always devoted equal time to the study and performance of medicine and writing."

BIOGRAPHICAL/CRITICAL SOURCES: New York Times, June 11, 1980.

*   *   *

CONNALLY, Eugenia (Maye) Horstman   1931-

PERSONAL: Born March 11, 1931, in Washington, D.C.; daughter of Emanuel Eugene and Maye Mary (Hemphill) Horstman; married John Ronald Connally, January 1, 1962 (marriage ended, 1969); children: Lara Kay. *Education:* University of Maryland, B.A., 1961. *Home:* 3111 First St. N., Arlington, Va. 22201. *Office:* National Parks and Conservation Association, 1701 18th St. N.W., Washington, D.C. 20009.

CAREER: Technipress, Inc., Washington, D.C., editor and manager, 1963-69; National Parks and Conservation Association, Washington, D.C., executive editor of *National Parks* (formerly *National Parks and Conservation Magazine*), 1969—. Instructor in "Publication Specialist" program at George Washington University.

WRITINGS: (Editor) *Wilderness Parklands in Alaska,* National Parks and Conservation Association, 1978; *Welcome to Washington,* Interpretive Publications, 1980.

SIDELIGHTS: Eugenia Connally commented; "My love of nature and wildlife and my concern for the environment and our quality of life led me, quite by chance after six years in technical editing, to the field I love best—the outdoors and conservation."

*   *   *

CONNOLLY, Peter   1935-

PERSONAL: Born May 8, 1935, in Surrey, England; son of Harold (an artist) and Mollie (Naw) Connolly; married Maureen Jennings, July 4, 1959 (divorced, 1969); married Barbara Carpenter (a company secretary), August 2, 1973; children: Sarah, Anna, Matthew. *Education:* Attended Brighton College of Arts and Crafts, 1951-53. *Politics:* "Pragmatist; believe in democracy but opposed to party politics." *Religion:* "Agnostic (brought up Roman Catholic)." *Home and office:* Westhaven, Gosberton-Westhorpe, Lincolnshire PE11 4ER, England.

CAREER: Worked in various advertising studios, 1956-61; free-lance artist, 1959-60 and 1961-69; illustrator of children's books, 1969-74; writer and illustrator, 1974—. Painter for museums. *Military service:* Royal Air·Force, 1953-56. *Member:* Society for the Promotion of Roman Studies, Society for the Promotion of Hellenic Studies.

WRITINGS—All self-illustrated: (With R. Tomlin and B. Dobson) *Greece and Rome at War,* Macdonald & Co., 1981.

Children's books: *The Roman Army,* Macdonald & Co., 1975; *The Greek Armies,* Macdonald & Co., 1977; *Hannibal and the Enemies of Rome,* Macdonald & Co., 1978; *Pompeii,* Macdonald & Co., 1979. Contributor to *Cambridge Ancient History.*

WORK IN PROGRESS: A book on Caesar, publication by Macdonald & Co. expected in 1982; an educational book on the historical background of Jesus, publication by Oxford University Press expected in 1984.

SIDELIGHTS: Connolly told *CA:* "I became interested in Greek and Roman history while in the Royal Air Force. The subject became my consuming interest, particularly military history and architecture.

"My special field is ancient armor. In 1970 I met Russell Robinson, curator of the new armories at the Tower of London, and the leading authority on Roman armor. His motto was, 'If you want to understand how anything works, make a copy of it and try it out.' He had a profound effect on me and we became the closest of friends until his death in 1978. His motto has become my own and I have made copies of shields and cuirasses. During my researches I have visited most of the museums of Europe and North Africa, and also innumerable battlefields.

"I believe it is wrong to write about things one has not seen. This is, of course, not always possible. For my book on Caesar I would like to visit the battlefield of Dyrrhachium in Albania, but so far the Albanian government has not granted permission. It would be impossible to write the sort of books that I do if my motivation were profit. They require an enormous amount of research and travel; I have just returned from an eight thousand-mile trip around the Caesarian battlefields of western Europe.

"My great hero in ancient history is Hannibal. Over the past fifteen years I have visited the sites of all his battles and crossed every possible route that he could have taken over the Alps—several of them on foot as there is no road. A book on Hannibal will be published, possibly in 1987. My aim is to produce a complete library of deeply researched books of Greek and Roman history for children.

"I feel I must enlarge upon the subjects of religion and politics. I was brought up as a Roman Catholic and was educated by the Jesuits for nine years. As I became involved in historical research during my twenties, I found it impossible not to apply the same standards of criticism to religious writings that I would to any other ancient document. This resulted in constant revisions of my standpoint and final agnosticism in my late twenties. My political position went through a similar metamorphosis. Brought up in an ultra-conservative background, I flirted with socialism and communism in my twenties. I finally became convinced that there was no universal 'cure-all.' I am not opposed to any system as long as it allows for individuality and it works. I hold no other conviction than personal integrity. I am a pacifist, but admit that under certain circumstances I would fight."

AVOCATIONAL INTERESTS: Model making, photography, building topographical models of battlefields.

*   *   *

CONRAN, Shirley Ida   1932-

PERSONAL: Born in 1932 in London, England; daughter of W. Thirlby (a pilot) and Ida (Wakelin) Pearce; married Terence Conran (a company president; marriage ended); children: Sebastian Orby, Jasper Alexander Thirlby. *Education:* Attended girls' school in London, England. *Agent:* Morton Janklow, 598 Madison Ave., New York, N.Y. 10022.

CAREER: Conran Fabrics Ltd., London, England, founder and co-owner, 1957—. Solo exhibition of paintings at Architectural Association; judge for British Council of Industrial Design, 1961-69; judge for Duke of Edinburgh's design-of-the-year award; adviser to British jewelry industry.

WRITINGS: Superwoman: Everywoman's Book of Household Management, Sidgwick & Jackson, Volume I, 1975, Volume II, 1977, published in the United States in one volume as *Superwoman,* Crown, 1978; *Superwoman Yearbook,* Sidgwick & Jackson, 1976; *Superwoman in Action,* Penguin, 1977; *Futures: How to Survive Life After Thirty,* Sidgwick & Jackson, 1979. Also author of *Printed Textile Design for Studio Publication,* 1975, and *Forever Superwoman,* Penguin. Past member of editorial staff of *Observer* and *Daily Mail.*

SIDELIGHTS: Shirley Conran told *CA* that she hopes her books improve life for women. Offering advice to other writers, Conran said, "Be truthful to yourself, always plan what you intend to do before you do it, and pick a good editor." *Avocational interests:* Long-distance swimming, collecting houses and antique glass.

*   *   *

CONWAY, Theresa (Ann)   1951-

PERSONAL: Born June 8, 1951, in St. Louis, Mo.; daughter of Harold S. and Agnes M. Whitcomb; married Ronald Conway (an executive), April 23, 1971; children: Amy, Katherine. *Education:* Attended St. Louis Community College, 1969-71. *Religion:* Roman Catholic. *Home and office:* 15988 Meadow Oak Dr., Chesterfield, Mo. 63017. *Agent:* Helen Barrett, William Morris Agency, 1350 Avenue of the Americas, New York, N.Y. 10019.

CAREER: Dundee Cement Co., St. Louis, Mo., secretary, 1971-77; writer, 1977—. *Member:* Authors Guild.

WRITINGS: Gabrielle (historical romance), Fawcett, 1977; *Crimson Glory* (historical romance), Fawcett, 1979; *Honor Bound* (historical romance), Fawcett, 1980; *Paloma* (romance), Ballantine, 1981.

WORK IN PROGRESS: A saga set in St. Louis, Mo., publication by Fawcett expected in 1982.

SIDELIGHTS: Theresa Conway told *CA:* "My husband is my most important motivator. I usually write in my own office, after my two children are asleep, until midnight or so. I truly believe the greatest attribute a writer or potential writer must have is self-discipline, followed by imagination and a dash of introvertedness.

"My first three books were 'formula' historical romances. In *Paloma* I tried to 'stretch' and placed less emphasis on the sexual and more on the character and motivation of my Irish heroine. In my fifth work I tried to stretch even more, making the plot more complicated with two sisters getting equal time in the book. No title has been given to this book yet. Someday I'd like to deviate into a different genre entirely—perhaps science fiction or the occult!''

AVOCATIONAL INTERESTS: Travel.

*   *   *

COOK, David   1940-

PERSONAL: Born September 21, 1940, in Preston, Lancastershire, England; son of George T. and Beatrice (Jackson) Cook. *Education:* Attended Royal Academy of Dramatic Art, 1959-61. *Home:* 7 Sydney Pl., London S.W.7, England. *Agent:* Elaine Green Ltd., 31 Newington Green, Islington, London N16 9PU, England.

CAREER: Professional actor, 1961—. *Member:* Writers Guild of Great Britain, Society of Authors. *Awards, honors:* Award from Writers Guild of Great Britain, 1977, for ''A Place Like Home''; E. M. Forster Prize from American Academy of Arts and Letters, 1977, for *Happy Endings;* Hawthornden Prize for Literature from Society of Authors, 1978, for *Walter;* fiction award from Arts Council, 1979, for *Winter Doves.*

WRITINGS—Novels: *Albert's Memorial,* Secker & Warburg, 1972; *Happy Endings* Secker & Warburg, 1974; *Walter,* Secker & Warburg, 1978; *Winter Doves,* Secker & Warburg, 1979.

Television plays: ''Willy,'' first broadcast by Associated Television, June 3, 1973; ''Jenny Can't Work Any Faster,'' first broadcast by Associated Television, December 8, 1975; ''Why Here?,'' first broadcast by Associated Television, August 7, 1976; ''Repent at Leisure,'' first broadcast by Associated Television, January 11, 1978; ''Mary's Wife,'' first broadcast by British Broadcasting Corp. (BBC-TV), May 2, 1980. Writer for television series, ''A Place Like Home.''

WORK IN PROGRESS: A historical novel on life in an English village in the Cotswolds in the nineteenth century, publication by Secker & Warburg expected in 1982; a television drama series about the Salvation Army.

SIDELIGHTS: Cook told *CA:* ''When I am writing a book, I don't think about 'themes.' Getting inside my characters and telling a story are what concern me at the time of writing. Training and working as an actor with directors such as Vivian Matalon have helped me with the first, and with the latter I've had invaluable help from the playwright and novelist John Bowen.

''The reasons *why* one decides to write about such a situation or character are for me almost always accidental. Seeing a lady tramp at South Kensington Underground Station and wondering what had led up to her being there was the starting point of my first novel, *Albert's Memorial.* Meeting a mentally handicapped man who ran errands for the actors when I was playing in 'Othello' at the Ludlow Festival and who reminded me of a young man with whom I'd worked twenty years earlier sparked off an obsessive wanting to know how a mentally handicapped man perceives what goes on around him, and led to *Walter* and its sequel, *Winter Doves.*

''Most of my plays for television have been concerned with the 'walking wounded'—brain damage, autism, transvestism, children in care. In fact, as I look back at both the novels and the television plays, I see that there *is* a theme—innocence and the corruption of innocence—and since this was not intentional, it may be all the more valid as an insight into my work.

''What most of all fascinates me are relationships or the lack of them. We arrive in this world screaming and we go on screaming—for love, sex, emotional security—and we leave it whimpering at how little of any of these we've found. Although for the future I plan to write a historical novel and maybe a thriller, I don't think this primary concern will change. I should like to write a best-seller, however. Having won a share of the Glittering Prizes, I would now exchange good reviews for higher sales figures. I write to be read.''

*   *   *

COOK, Dorothy Mary   1907-
(D. Y. Cameron, D. M. Carlisle, Elizabeth Clare)

PERSONAL: Born February 13, 1907, in Gravesend, England; daughter of Percy Richard and Clara Elizabeth (Thornhill) Cook. *Education:* Attended grammar school in Rochester, England. *Politics:* ''Christian Socialist; if no candidate, Liberal.'' *Religion:* Society of Friends (Quakers). *Home:* Two Penn Cottage, West End, Herstmonceux, Hailsham, Sussex BN27 4NR, England. *Agent:* Laurence Pollinger Ltd., 18 Maddox St., London W1R 0EU, England.

CAREER: Writer, 1962—. *Member:* Romantic Novelists Association, Friends Historical Society, Fellowship of Reconciliation.

WRITINGS—Novels under pseudonym D. Y. Cameron; all published by R. Hale: *Chasing Shadows,* 1962; *Out of the Storm,* 1962; *Strange Byways,* 1963; *The Searching Heart,* 1964; *The Loving Cup,* 1965; *Love Unfolding,* 1966; *The Happy Awakening,* 1967; *A Puzzled Heart,* 1967; *Magic in the Air,* 1968; *Conflicting Tides,* 1969; *Enchanting Adventure,* 1969; *Moonlight and March Roses,* 1970; *Night-Scented Air,* 1974; *Scent of Jasmin,* 1975; *Music in the Wind,* 1978; *Jenny's Searching Heart,* 1979; *A Touch of Spring,* 1981.

Novels under pseudonym D. M. Carlisle: *Althea's Falcon,* Arthur Baker, 1974; *The Secret of the Chateau,* R. Hale, 1980.

Novels under pseudonym Elizabeth Clare; all published by R. Hale: *A Land of Stars,* 1966; *The Heart Is Hidden,* 1967; *Sunlight Through the Mist,* 1967; *The Enchanted Way,* 1968; *In Spring Time,* 1968; *A Royal Occasion,* 1970; *Magic of Springtime,* 1971; *Sunlit Waterways,* 1972; *Glade in the Woods,* 1974; *Down by the Willows,* 1977; *The Delightful Valley,* 1980.

Contributor of articles and stories to magazines.

WORK IN PROGRESS: Historical novels; light romantic mysteries.

SIDELIGHTS: Dorothy Cook told *CA:* ''Now, at my age, my personal life is private and simple, rooted in Quaker interests and activities, especially peace work. I am also interested in conservation and touring the country for historical research. I am devoted to cats. I give talks to women's clubs and show slides of my visits to Europe and the Near East. I am interested in archaeology and art galleries. It is not exciting, but interesting, and very useful for my writing.''

*   *   *

COOK, James Graham   1925-1966

OBITUARY NOTICE—See index for *CA* sketch: Born February 23, 1925, in Fayette, Ala.; died March 25, 1966. Journalist, educator, and author of *Remedies and Rackets* and *The Segregationists.* Cook worked as a reporter for United Press International (UPI), *Commercial Appeal,* the *New York Post,* and the *San Francisco Examiner.* In 1961 he began teaching at San Francisco State College. In 1962 he became an instructor at the Santa Barbara City College. (Date of death provided by Santa Barbara City College.)

*   *   *

COON, Gene L(ee)   1924-1973

OBITUARY NOTICE—See index for *CA* sketch: Born June 7, 1924, in Beatrice, Neb.; died July 8, 1973. Journalist, screenwriter, and author. Coon worked in the late 1940's and early 1950's as a radio and television news reporter. In the late 1950's he began writing screenplays. Some of his best known film scripts are "No Name on the Bullet" and the 1964 production of "The Killers." He also wrote two novels, *Meanwhile Back at the Front* and *The Short End of the Stick.* (Date of death provided by Reece Halsey Agency.)

*   *   *

COOPER, Martin Du Pre   1910-

PERSONAL: Born January 17, 1910, in Winchester, England; son of Cecil Henry Hamilton and Cecil Hatherley (Stephens) Cooper; married Mary Stewart, June 29, 1940; children: Felicity Cooper Cave, Dominic, Josephine Cooper Carrington, Imogen. *Education:* Attended Winchester College, 1922-28; Oxford University, B.A., 1931; studied music under Egon Wellesz in Vienna, Austria, 1931-34. *Religion:* Roman Catholic. *Home:* 34 Halford Rd., Richmond, Surrey, England.

CAREER: London Mercury, London, England, music critic, 1934-39; *Spectator,* London, music critic, 1939-45; *Daily Herald,* London, music critic, 1945-50; *Daily Telegraph,* London, music critic, 1950-76. Fellow of Trinity College School of Music, London, and Royal Academy of Music. *Member:* Critics Circle (president, 1959-60). *Awards, honors:* Commander of Order of the British Empire, 1972.

WRITINGS: Gluck, Chatto & Windus, 1935; *Bizet,* Oxford University Press, 1938; *Opera Comique,* Chanticleer, 1949; *Russian Opera,* Parrish, 1951; *French Music, 1870-1925,* Oxford University Press, 1951; *Ideas and Music,* Barrie & Rockliff, 1966; *Beethoven: The Last Decade,* Oxford University Press, 1970; (editor) *Oxford History of Music,* Volume X, Oxford University Press, 1974. Editor of *Musical Times,* 1953-56; member of editorial board of *New Oxford History of Music.*

WORK IN PROGRESS: Translations from German and Russian.

SIDELIGHTS: Cooper's languages are French, German, Italian, Russian, Spanish, Portuguese, Latin, and Greek.

*   *   *

COPE, Jackson I(rving)   1925-

PERSONAL: Born September 1, 1925, in Muncie, Ind.; son of Raymond M. and Helen (Jackson) Cope; married Jamie Heise, 1948 (marriage ended); married Susan Waller, 1969 (marriage ended); married Paula Doss, September 26, 1979; children: (first marriage) Dryden, Tami (Mrs. William Smith). *Education:* University of Illinois, B.A., 1950; Johns Hopkins University, Ph.D., 1952. *Office:* Department of English, University of Southern California, Los Angeles, Calif. 90007.

CAREER: Ohio State University, Columbus, instructor in English, 1952-54; Washington University, St. Louis, Mo., assistant professor of English, 1954-58; Rice University, Houston, Tex., associate professor, 1958-60, professor of English, 1960-62; Johns Hopkins University, Baltimore, Md., associate professor, 1962-63, professor of English, 1963-72;

University of Southern California, Los Angeles, Leo S. Bing Professor of English, 1972—. Member of James Joyce Foundation. *Military service:* U.S. Army Air Forces, 1943-45; became second lieutenant.

MEMBER: Modern Language Association of America, Renaissance Society of America, Malone Society, Phi Beta Kappa, Phi Kappa Phi. *Awards, honors:* Bissing fellowship from Johns Hopkins University, 1954-55; Folger Library fellowships, 1954, 1960; Guggenheim fellowship, 1958-59; American Council of Learned Societies fellowship, 1963-64.

WRITINGS: Joseph Glanvill, Anglican Apologist, Washington University Press, 1956; (editor) Glanvill, *Plus Ultra,* Scholar's Facsimiles, 1958; (editor with Harold Jones) Thomas Sprat, *History of the Royal Society,* Washington University Press, 1958; *The Metaphoric Structure of "Paradise Lost",* Johns Hopkins Press, 1962; *The Theater and the Dream: From Metaphor to Form in Renaissance Drama,* Johns Hopkins Press, 1973; *Joyce's Cities: Archaeologies of the Soul,* Johns Hopkins Press, 1981; *Genesis of Anti-Genres in the Theatre,* Johns Hopkins Press, 1982. Contributor of about a hundred articles and reviews to academic journals.

WORK IN PROGRESS: A book on the fiction and drama of Robert Coover.

SIDELIGHTS: Jackson Cope told *CA:* "Scholarly criticism is ephemeral, written on the wind. Its job is to reseed the future with the past."

*   *   *

CORFE, Thomas Howell   1928-
(Tom Corfe)

PERSONAL: Born November 1, 1928, in London, England; son of Arthur Charles (a dealer) and Dorothy (a teacher; maiden name, Howell) Corfe; married Sheila Dobson, December 22, 1964; children: Frances, Helen. *Education:* Pembroke College, Cambridge, B.A., 1948, M.A., 1952; further study at Institute of Education, London. *Home:* 8 Nilverton Ave., Sunderland SR2 7TS, England.

CAREER: Teacher of history at grammar school in Melton Mowbray, England, 1953-62; Sunderland College of Education, Sunderland, England, senior lecturer in history, 1962-75; Sunderland Polytechnic, Sunderland, senior lecturer in history, 1975—. *Member:* Historical Association (director of tours).

WRITINGS: The School on the Hill: An Informal History of King Edward VII Grammar School, Melton Mowbray, 1910-1960, King Edward VII Grammar School, 1960; (editor with others) *History Field Studies in the Durham Area: A Handbook for Teachers,* Durham University, 1966; (under name Tom Corfe) *The Phoenix Park Murders: Conflict, Compromise, and Tragedy in Ireland, 1879-1882,* Hodder & Stoughton, 1968; (editor under name Tom Corfe) *History in the Field,* Blond Educational, 1970; (under name Tom Corfe) *Sunderland: A Short History,* Frank Graham, 1973; *Wearside Heritage,* Civic Society, 1975; *Whitehall Palace,* Cambridge University Press, 1977.

For young readers; all under name Tom Corfe: *St. Patrick and Irish Christianity,* Cambridge University Press, 1973, Lerner, 1978; *Archbishop Thomas and King Henry II,* Cambridge University Press, 1975, published as *The Murder of Archbishop Thomas,* Lerner, 1977; *Samuel Pepys* (illustrated by Valerie Bell), Cambridge University Press, 1976; *The Great Fire of London* (illustrated by Bell), Cambridge University Press, 1978; *Queen Victoria* (illustrated by Edward

Ripley), Cambridge University Press, 1979; *Windsor Castle* (illustrated by Ripley), Cambridge University Press, 1979.

Editor, "History First" series, and deputy editor, "Cambridge Introduction to the History of Mankind" series, both Cambridge University Press. Author of television scripts on local history. Contributor of articles to periodicals, including *History Today, History of the English Speaking Peoples, Irish Times, Times Educational Supplement,* and *Teaching History.*

BIOGRAPHICAL/CRITICAL SOURCES: Observer Review, February 18, 1968; *Punch,* March 13, 1968.

*   *   *

CORFE, Tom
  See CORFE, Thomas Howell

*   *   *

CORLETT, William 1938-

PERSONAL: Born October 8, 1938, in Darlington, Durham, England; son of Harold and Ida (Allen) Corlett. *Education:* Attended Royal Academy of Dramatic Art, London, 1956-58. *Home:* Cottesbrook, Great Bardfield, Essex, England.

CAREER: Writer of fiction and drama; stage and television actor. *Member:* Screenwriters Guild, Society of Authors. *Awards, honors:* Pye television award, 1978, for children's drama; New York film and television international award, 1980, for "Barriers."

WRITINGS—Fiction; all for young people: *The Gate of Eden,* Hamilton, 1974, Bradbury, 1975; *The I Deal Tale,* Compton Russell, 1975; *The Land Beyond,* Hamilton, 1975, Bradbury, 1976; *Return to the Gate,* Hamilton, 1975, Bradbury, 1977; *The Dark Side of the Moon,* Hamilton, 1976, Bradbury, 1977; (with John H. Moore) *The Once and Forever Christmas,* Compton Russell, 1976.

Nonfiction series; all with Moore; all published by Hamilton: *The Question of Religion,* 1978, *The Christ Story,* 1978, *The Hindu Sound,* 1978, *The Judaic Law,* 1979, *The Buddha Way,* 1979, *The Islamic Space,* 1979, published under same titles as a six-volume series, "Questions of Human Existence As Answered by Major World Religions," Bradbury, 1980.

Published plays: *Another Round* (first produced in Farnham, England, 1962), Samuel French, 1963; *The Gentle Avalanche* (first produced in Farnham, 1962), Samuel French, 1964; *Return Ticket: A Comedy* (first produced in Farnham, 1962), English Theatre Guild, 1966; *Tinker's Curse* (first produced in Nottingham, England, 1968), Ungar, 1969.

Unpublished plays: "Flight of a Lone Sparrow," first produced in Farnham, 1965; "The Scallop Shell," first produced in Farnham, 1965; "The Scourging of Mathew Barrow," first produced in Leicester, England, 1966; "The Illusionist," first produced in Perth, Scotland, 1969; "We Never Went to Cheddar Gorge," first produced in Perth, 1969; "National Trust," first produced in Perth, 1970; "The Deliverance of Fanny Blaydon," first produced in Perth, 1971; "Orlando the Marmalade Cat Buys a Cottage" (juvenile; adapted from a story by Kathleen Hale), first produced in London, 1975; "Orlando's Camping Holiday," (juvenile; adapted from a story by Hale), first produced in London, 1976.

Also author of television plays, including: "Dead Set at Dream Boy," 1965; "The Story Teller," 1969; "A Memory of Two Loves," 1972; "Conversations in the Dark," 1972; "Mr. Oddy" (adapted from a story by Hugh Walpole), 1975; "The Orsini Emeralds" (adapted from a story by G. B.

Stern), 1975; "Emerdale Farm" series, 1975-77; "The Gate of Eden" (adapted from Corlett's own novel), 1979; "Barriers" series, 1980.

WORK IN PROGRESS: "The Christie Hour"; adaptation of Corlett's own novel "Return to the Gate."

*   *   *

COSTELLO, William Aloysious 1904-1969

OBITUARY NOTICE—See index for *CA* sketch: Born March 5, 1904, in St. Paul, Minn.; died of a heart attack, June 20, 1969, in Port-of-Spain, Trinidad; buried at sea. Journalist, diplomat, and author. Costello worked as a correspondent for the Columbia Broadcasting System (CBS) for ten years following the end of World War II. He had previously reported for several newspapers, including the *Minneapolis Journal* and *Omaha World Herald.* In 1967 he became American ambassador to Trinidad and Tobago. Costello wrote *Democracy vs. Feudalism in Post-War Japan* and *The Facts About Nixon.* Obituaries and other sources: *New York Times,* June 21, 1969; *Variety,* June 25, 1969; *Who Was Who in America,* 5th edition, Marquis, 1973.

*   *   *

COTTON, Norris 1900-

PERSONAL: Born May 11, 1900, in Warren, N.H.; son of Henry Lang and Elizabeth (Moses) Cotton; married Ruth Isaacs, May 11, 1927 (died, 1978); married Eleanor Coolidge, May 24, 1980. *Education:* Attended Wesleyan University, Middletown, Conn., 1920-22, and George Washington University, 1928. *Religion:* Methodist. *Home and office:* 15 Kimball St., Lebanon, N.H. 03766.

CAREER: High school teacher, member of New Hampshire House of Representatives, and editor of *Granite Monthly* (state magazine), all 1923; secretary to Republican State Committee and to U.S. Senator George H. Moses, 1924-28; admitted to the Bar of New Hampshire, 1928; Demond, Woodworth, Sulloway & Rogers, Concord, N.H., attorney, 1928-33; private practice of law in Lebanon, N.H., 1933; member of New Hampshire House of Representatives, 1943, serving as majority leader and chairman of Judiciary Committee; Cotton, Tesreau & Stebbins (law firm), Lebanon, partner, 1945-55; member of New Hampshire House of Representatives, 1945, serving as Speaker of the House; U.S. House of Representatives, congressman from 2nd New Hampshire district, 1946-54, serving on Appropriations Committee and Agricultural Committee; U.S. senator from New Hampshire, 1954-75. Served as clerk of New Hampshire Senate, 1928-33, district attorney for Grafton County (N.H.), 1933-39, and justice in municipal court of Lebanon, 1939-44. Member of board of directors of banks.

MEMBER: American Bar Association, Masons, University Club. *Awards, honors:* Briggs Prize from Wesleyan University, Middletown, Conn., 1922, for oratory; D.C.L. from New England College, 1954; LL.D. from University of Vermont, 1964, University of New Hampshire, 1965, Daniel Webster College, 1970, Franklin Pierce College, 1971, and New Hampshire College, 1980; named southern New Hampshire man of the year by city of Lebanon, 1966, and city of Nashua, 1970; Pettee Prize from University of New Hampshire, 1967, for distinguished public service; D.Hum. from Belknap College, 1968.

WRITINGS: In the Senate (nonfiction), Dodd, 1978. Author of column "Report from Congress," in numerous New Hampshire newspapers, 1949-75. Contributor to magazines and newspapers.

WORK IN PROGRESS: Research on legislative and elective processes, including presidential primary elections.

*   *   *

COVERT, Paul 1941-

PERSONAL: Born March 2, 1941, in Jersey City, N.J.; son of Byron (an engineer) and Evelyn (Snyder) Covert; married Elizabeth Hartman, June 21, 1961 (divorced June, 1971); children: Robert Carl. *Education:* Attended University of Wisconsin—Milwaukee, 1964-66. *Politics:* "Seeking workable." *Religion:* Christian. *Home and office:* 1007 North Marshall St., Milwaukee, Wis. 53202. *Agent:* Paul R. Reynolds, Inc., 12 East 41st St., New York, N.Y. 10017.

CAREER: Freeman, Huenink, Zilbert, Inc., Milwaukee, Wis., and Dallas, Tex., account executive, 1962-80; Pyramid World Entertainment Ltd., Hollywood, Calif., creative consultant, 1980—. *Military service:* U.S. Air Force, 1960-61. *Awards, honors:* ADDY award from American Advertising Foundation, 1968; best fiction award from Wisconsin Council of Writers, 1971, for *Cages;* special award from Milwaukee Ballet Co., 1979.

WRITINGS: Cages (novel), Liveright, 1971; *Escape to Nowhere* (novel), Major, 1974; "The Body and the Blood" (screenplay), Pyramid World Entertainment, 1982. Also author of unproduced screenplays, including "Twelfth Site" and "Brothers to the Dolphin."

WORK IN PROGRESS—Novels: *Brothers to the Dolphin; The Kerioth Chronicles; The Body and the Blood.*

SIDELIGHTS: Covert told *CA:* "The greatest influences upon my career have been the writings of Hemingway, Faulkner, Thomas Wolfe, Herman Wouk, and William Goldman; other influences include Salinger and Tennessee Williams. I strive to portray human beings in struggle with life in all its aspects, preferring to concentrate on humanity rather than exploitive action; there is enough refuse on television. I shy away from interviews and the like, having found them largely shallow and less than objective in the end result."

AVOCATIONAL INTERESTS: Religion, psychology, sports fishing.

*   *   *

COWAN, Edward James 1944-

PERSONAL: Born February 15, 1944, in Edinburgh, Scotland; son of William Edward (a civil servant) and Margaret (Macbryde) Cowan; married Alison Dawson (a preschool educator), December 14, 1963; children: Karen Jane, Morna Helen, David Edward. *Education:* University of Edinburgh, M.A., 1967. *Politics:* Socialist. *Religion:* None. *Home:* 34 Moore Ave., Guelph, Ontario, Canada N1G 1R4. *Office:* Department of History, University of Guelph, Guelph, Ontario, Canada.

CAREER: University of Edinburgh, Edinburgh, Scotland, lecturer in Scottish history, 1967-79; University of Guelph, Guelph, Ontario, associate professor of history, 1979—. *Member:* Scottish Society for Northern Studies (president, 1972-75), Scottish History Society (member of council, 1974-79). *Awards, honors:* Award from Scottish Arts Council, 1977, for *Montrose: For Covenant and King.*

WRITINGS: Montrose: For Covenant and King, Weidenfeld & Nicolson, 1977; *The Historical Highlands: A Guide to Reading,* Edinburgh University Press, 1977; *The People's Past: Scottish Folk in Scottish History,* Polygon Books, 1980.

Editor of *East Lothian Transactions,* 1970-78; co-editor of *Scottish Tradition.*

WORK IN PROGRESS: King Campbell: Archibald Marcus of Argyll, 1607-1661; Viking Scotland; The Highlands in Scottish History.

SIDELIGHTS: Cowan wrote: "I am dedicated to Scotland and Scottish history. I am now carrying the banner in the New World. My special interests are folk song and culture, oral and traditional history, also the North American vision of 'plastic Scotland.' I am interested in popularizing history in the best sense, accommodating the search for roots, taking history to the people and people to history. History must be alive or we must bury the corpse."

*   *   *

COWELL, (John) Adrian 1934-

PERSONAL: Born February 2, 1934; in Tongshan, China; son of Edmund C. (in business) and Phyllis (Newson) Cowell; married Pauline Chamberlayne (a potter), May 13, 1961; children: Lucinda, Xingu. *Education:* St. Catharine's College, Cambridge, degree in history (with honors), 1955. *Agent:* John Cushman Associates, Inc., 25 West 43rd St., Room 1520, New York, N.Y. 10036. *Office:* Nomad Films Ltd., 46 Anson Rd., London N.7, England.

CAREER: Associated Television Ltd., London, England, producer of documentary films, 1964-80; associated with Nomad Films Ltd., London, 1980—. Fellow of Institute for the Study of Human Issues, Philadelphia, Pa., 1974-80, and Instituto Goiano de Prehistoria e Antropologia, Universidad Catolico de Goias, 1979-80. *Awards, honors:* Awards from British Academy, 1970 and 1978, for documentary films; award from Scriptwriters Guild of Great Britain, 1970; Italia Award, 1970; Golden Gate Award, 1970; blue ribbon from American Film Festival, 1975; Golden Hugo from Chicago Film Festival, 1978.

WRITINGS: The Heart of the Forest, Knopf, 1962; *The Tribe That Hides From Man,* Stein & Day, 1973.

WORK IN PROGRESS: A documentary series on Rondonia, Brazil.

SIDELIGHTS: Cowell spent five years in the Brazilian Amazon country, studying Indian and ecological problems. He stayed two years in the Shan State of Burma with guerrilla opium armies, and another two years studying narcotics problems in other parts of Southeast Asia.

*   *   *

COX, (Christopher) Barry 1931-

PERSONAL: Born July 29, 1931, in London, England; son of Herbert Ernest (a civil servant) and May (Bell) Cox; married Sheila Morgan, April 6, 1961; children: Timothy David, Sally Ann, Justin Daniel. *Education:* Balliol College, Oxford, B.A. (with first class honors), 1953; St. John's College, Cambridge, Ph.D., 1956. *Home:* 9 Woodcote Close, Epsom, Surrey, England. *Office:* Department of Zoology, King's College, University of London, Strand, London WC2R 2LS, England.

CAREER: University of London, King's College, London, England, lecturer, 1956-66, senior lecturer, 1966-69, reader, 1969-76, professor of zoology, 1976—. Chairman of Epsom-Ewell Consultative Committee. Vice-chairman of governors of Epsom High School. *Member:* Paleontological Association (vice-president, 1980—), Epsom Protection Society (chairman). *Awards, honors:* Harkness fellow of Commonwealth Fund, Harvard University, 1959-60.

WRITINGS: Prehistoric Animals, Hamlyn, 1969; (with I. N. Healey and P. D. Moore) *Biogeography: An Ecological and Evolutionary Approach,* Blackwell Scientific Publications, 1973, 3rd edition (with Moore), 1980; *The Prehistoric World,* Samson Lowe, 1975.

WORK IN PROGRESS: Research on historical biogeography and its relationship to continental drift.

SIDELIGHTS: Cox wrote: ''My biogeographic research arose from my teaching the subject at undergraduate level. I am interested in, and enjoy, teaching as well as research, and I especially enjoy trying to make students think for themselves. I have been on fossil collecting expeditions to central Africa, the Andes of Argentina, Brazil, and Australia.

''It has been especially interesting to see the varying ways in which, over the last twenty years, different research workers have changed their views on the interpretation of biogeographic patterns from those based on the old stabilist-earth concept to the new tectonic-earth picture. Not surprisingly, the senior workers, already firmly committed to the older assumptions, often found the most difficulty in this. There's a moral here for us all!''

*   *   *

COX, Geoffrey Sandford 1910-

PERSONAL: Born April 7, 1910, in Palmerston North, New Zealand; son of Sandford (a banker) and Mary (MacGregor) Cox; married Cecily Turner, May 25, 1935; children: Peter S., Patrick T.S., Evelyn Cox Meaes, Rosemond Gallant. *Education:* Attended University of Otago, 1928-31, and Oxford University, 1932-35. *Religion:* Anglican. *Home:* Amadines, Coln St. Dennis, Gloucestershire, England. *Agent:* A. D. Peters & Co. Ltd., 10 Buckingham St., London WC2N 6BU, England. *Office:* London Broadcasting Co., London, England.

CAREER: Worked for *News Chronicle* and *Daily Express,* 1931-56; Independent Television News, editor and chief executive, 1956-68; Yorkshire Television, Yorkshire, England, deputy chairman, 1968-71; Tyne & Tees Television, England, chairman, 1971-74; London Broadcasting Co., London, England, chairman, 1977—. *Military service:* New Zealand Army, 1940-45; mentioned in dispatches. *Awards, honors:* Member of Order of the British Empire, 1946, commander of order, 1959; knighted, 1966.

WRITINGS: Defence of Madrid, Gollancz, 1937; *Red Army Moves,* Gollancz, 1941; *Road to Trieste,* Heinemann, 1946; *Race for Trieste,* Kimber, 1977.

*   *   *

COX, Oliver Cromwell 1901-1974

OBITUARY NOTICE—See index for *CA* sketch: Born August 25, 1901, in Trinidad, British West Indies; died in 1974. Educator, sociologist, and author of works in his field. Cox taught at Lincoln University for twenty-five years beginning in 1949. He wrote *Caste, Class, and Race: A Study in Social Dynamics, Foundations of Capitalism, Capitalism and American Leadership, Capitalism as a System,* and *Race Relations.* Obituaries and other sources: *National Union Catalog, 1973-1977,* Rowman & Littlefield, 1978.

COXE, Antony D(acres) Hippisley
See HIPPISLEY COXE, Antony D(acres)

*   *   *

COX-JOHNSON, Ann
See SAUNDERS, Ann Loreille

*   *   *

COYLE, David Cushman 1887-1969

OBITUARY NOTICE—See index for *CA* sketch: Born May 24, 1887, in North Adams, Mass.; died July 15, 1969, in Washington, D.C. Government worker, consultant, and author. Coyle began his career as a consulting engineer with the Gunvald Aus Co. He then worked for the Public Works Administration (WPA) during the Depression before becoming a consultant to the Natural Resources Committee on Unemployment and Relief. His numerous writings include *Roads to a New America, The American Way, National Development and How It Works,* and *Breakthrough to the Great Society.* Obituaries and other sources: *Washington Post,* July 17, 1969; *Who Was Who in America,* 5th edition, Marquis, 1973.

*   *   *

CRACKNELL, Basil Edward 1925-

PERSONAL: Born February 5, 1925, in Wickford, England; son of Frederick James (a commercial traveler) and Annie (Wilson) Cracknell; married Sylvia Gladys Rickerby, 1952; children: Joan, Peter, Paul, David. *Education:* London School of Economics and Political Science, London, B.Sc., 1949, Ph.D., 1953. *Religion:* Church of England. *Home:* 6 Raglan Close, Reigate, Surrey, England.

CAREER: Ministry of Agriculture, London, England, economist, 1952-64; Ministry of Land and Natural Resources, London, economist, 1964-66; University of Nottingham, Nottingham, England, senior research fellow, 1966-69; Overseas Development Administration, London, senior economic adviser, 1969—. Member of national council of Evangelical Urban Training Project. *Military service:* Royal Navy, Fleet Air Arm, 1943-46. *Member:* Agricultural Economics Society, Society for International Development. *Awards, honors:* Traveling fellowship from Kellogg Foundation, 1964; John Nicholls Prize for local history from University of Leicester, 1958, for article ''Canvey Island: The History of a Marshland Community.''

WRITINGS: Portrait of London River: The Tidal Thames From Teddington to the Sea, International Publications Service, 1968, 2nd edition, R. Hale, 1980; (with D. K. Britton) *Cereals of the United Kingdom: Production, Marketing, and Utilisation,* Pergamon, 1969; *Portrait of Surrey,* R. Hale, 1970, 2nd edition, International Publications Service, 1974; *Dominica,* David & Charles, 1973; *The West Indians: How They Live and Work,* David & Charles, 1974.

Contributor to *Readings in Recreation Research and Planning,* Allen & Unwin, 1972, and *Peoples of the Earth,* Volume V: *Islands of the Atlantic Including the Caribbean,* Danbury Press, 1973. Contributor of more than a hundred articles to magazines, including *Town and Country, Surrey, Geographical Magazine, Country Life,* and *Geography.*

WORK IN PROGRESS: Articles on topography; a book on the strange origins of everyday words and phrases.

SIDELIGHTS: Cracknell wrote: "I regard local histories that are tedious lists of musty facts as anathema. I am concerned with the 'personality of place' and try to paint a living portrait of the places I write about.

"I was trained as a geographer, and it is the inter-relationship between man and the land that interests me and which is the main theme in my books and articles, whether they be about local places near my family home, or the far-away places I visit in my work. I was fortunate enough to visit America for six months in 1964. I have traveled all over the world and have been able to write books and articles about the places I have visited.

"I am more interested in the 'feel' of a place than in the naked facts. Why is it that some places immediately attract me, and others repel? Do other people have similar reactions? Is it because every place has a personality—just as every person does? Of course you have to get to know that personality—but that, to me is the thrill of travel and the fascination of writing topographical books."

*   *   *

CRAIG, E(velyn) Quita 1917-
(Eve Langdale)

PERSONAL: Born January 5, 1917, in Bridgetown, Barbados; came to the United States in 1942, naturalized citizen, 1946; daughter of Hugo Hoffman (a planter) and Mable Vera (Cox) Gibbon; married William H. Craig (a U.S. Army officer), March, 1942 (died, 1944); children: John H., William H., Jr. *Education:* George Mason University, B.A. (with highest distinction), 1973, M.A., 1976. *Home:* 6020 North 27th St., Arlington, Va. 22207.

CAREER: Walsh-Driscol Construction Co., Fort Read, Trinidad, executive secretary, 1940-42; Miller & Chevalier (attorneys), Washington, D.C., legal secretary, 1946-47; U.S. Civil Service, Department of the Army, Washington, D.C., administrative secretary for Logistics Division and Office of the Chief of Information, 1948-65; student, traveler, and writer, 1965—. *Member:* American Theatre Association, American Association of Retired Persons, Retired Officers Association Auxiliary, Smithsonian Associates. *Awards, honors:* Eight outstanding and sustained superior service awards from Department of the Army.

WRITINGS: Black Drama of the Federal Theatre Era: Beyond the Formal Horizons, University of Massachusetts Press, 1980. Contributor to *A Dictionary of Black Theatre.* Contributor to *Trinidad Guardian,* under pseudonym Eve Langdale, and *Black American Literature Forum.*

SIDELIGHTS: Quita Craig wrote: "After educating my sons I returned to school myself, to join their world and return to writing. I felt it was important to keep up with a changing world if I was to be an active part of it. I have traveled extensively in England, Europe, Russia, the Far East, the Middle East, and Africa, and found a macrocosm of the West Indies, where I was raised. Take colonialism, for example. In whatever variation it has been practiced in the past, or is currently being practiced, it has the same aim: to corral and maintain, for the least possible cost, a labor force for the benefit of a dominant minority, with much the same effects on the captive populations—deprivation, degradation, and mounting hostility.

"In the broad context it is not exclusively a racial problem, although that aspect was particularly important in *Black Drama of the Federal Theatre Era: Beyond the Formal Horizons* and still is today in Southern Africa. It is basically a problem of distorted human values and priorities which become entrenched in the political philosophy, the educational and communication systems of a people. It encompasses a broad spectrum and often does not even turn out to be beneficial to the dominant faction. Take equal rights for women. After my husband was killed in World War II, the disparity in male and female salaries, for example, did not affect me only. It also had a detrimental effect on the quality of life of the two male children I had to raise and educate—by no means an isolated case of males, too, suffering from female inequality. I suppose at heart I am a crusader for human rights and dignity.

"I have just returned from South Africa and, as usual, have been jotting down poetry and notes on what I have observed. I have not had time yet to sort out exactly what I will work on next, but I would most like to incorporate in fiction the distorted human values I've found in many places; fiction reaches so many more people and is so much more alive and memorable than a preachment. I think most of us humans want to do the fair and honest thing by our fellow humans when we understand the effects of our actions on them, and I would like to continue trying to contribute to this sort of constructive change in our changing world."

AVOCATIONAL INTERESTS: Orchid horticulture, oil painting, poetry.

*   *   *

CRANE, William Earl 1899-

PERSONAL: Born September 14, 1899, in Yazoo City, Miss.; son of Edgar Shields (a hardware jobber) and Letitia (Gebhart) Crane; married Katharine Rowland, June 6, 1922; children: Effie Crane Rule, Paul Edgar, Katharine Crane Ross. *Education:* Davidson College, A.B., 1922; Union Theological Seminary in Virginia, B.D., 1925, Th.D., 1945; Xenia Theological Seminary, Th.M., 1930. *Religion:* Presbyterian. *Home and office:* Willowynde, Beech Haven, Athens, Ga. 30606.

CAREER: Ordained to Presbyterian ministry, 1925; pastor in Guntersville, Ala., 1925-27, Porterdale, Ga., 1927-30, Atlanta, Ga., 1930-40, and Charleston, W.Va., 1940-54; counseling pastor in Knoxville, Tenn., 1954-64; Pastoral Counseling Institute, Athens, Ga., founder and director, 1964-70; First Presbyterian Church, Athens, pastoral assistant, 1975-79. President of Knox area board of directors of the Mental Health Center in Knoxville, Tenn., 1958-59; president of Southeastern Council on Family Relations, 1963-64; president and member of executive board of Athens-Clarke County Association for Mental Health, 1973-74. *Member:* American Association of Marriage and Family Therapy (fellow emeritus), Academy of Religion and Mental Health. *Awards, honors:* Honorary D.D. from Davis and Elkins College, 1950; leadership award from Southeastern Council on Family Relations, 1977.

WRITINGS: Where God Comes In: The Divine Plus in Counseling, Word Books, 1970. Author of several religious counseling workshop manuals; contributor of religious counseling articles to magazines, including *Torch, Witness,* and *Osteopathic Physician.*

SIDELIGHTS: Crane told *CA:* "From early adolescense there was a nearly compulsive drive to help people, so as the years passed I felt the need for more special training to equip me better for this service. This is one reason the ministry made such a demand upon me. As a result, I majored in psychology in college and seminary, along with my theological education. My early pastorates made increasing demands upon my time in counseling individuals in youth work and conferences. Finally, I applied to be admitted as a candidate for the doctor's degree in pastoral counseling from Union Theological Seminary and received this degree (the first ever awarded by that seminary in this special field) in 1945. The years that followed brought the greatest tests and satisfaction of my life. In those years I was really a pioneer in this field of the ministry and was at first criticized by some of my peers for 'leaving the ministry.' On the contrary, I assured them that I felt this was the most needed and demanding phase of the Christian ministry, and so I had to struggle on with little encouragement from my fellow ministers. Now this is recognized as a very important part of the training of ministers in the seminaries.

"The Historical Foundation of the Presbyterian and Reformed churches, located at Montreat, North Carolina, has requested me to deposit with them my writings, records, sermons, correspondence and autobiography because of the fact that the director there insists that I am a 'pioneer in this field' [pastoral counseling]. I am in the process of committing these and all related materials to the foundation to be made available there for those interested in further research in this area of the ministry. I believe the life and influence of my Christian parents were, along with that of my minister brothers, vital factors of influence.

"I do not consider myself primarily a writer, though I always feel a strong desire to share with others, through print, some of the things I consider vital and, I hope, interesting to others. Because of my deep conviction that much of the success I enjoyed in my counseling ministry was the direct guidance of the Holy Spirit (the Wonderful Counselor), I was compelled to attempt to record this fact and give due credit to this invaluable 'Aide' in my counseling ministry. This led to my writing the volume *Where God Comes In: The Divine Plus in Counseling.* Many of my other articles and publications were directly or indirectly related to this desire to help others in the field of pastoral counseling."

AVOCATIONAL INTERESTS: Cabinetmaking, making reproductions of antique furniture, family history, photography, Boy Scouting.

*   *   *

CRAVEN, Margaret   1901-1980

PERSONAL: Born March 13, 1901, in Helena, Mont.; died July 19, 1980, in Sacramento, Calif.; daughter of Arthur John (a judge) and Clara Emily (Kerr) Craven. *Education:* Stanford University, A.B. (with great distinction), 1924.

CAREER: San Jose Mercury, San Jose, Calif., editorial writer and columnist, 1924-28; free-lance writer, 1928-80.

WRITINGS: I Heard the Owl Call My Name (novel), Clark, Irwin Co., of Canada, 1967, Doubleday, 1973; *Walk Gently This Good Earth* (novel), Putnam, 1977; *Again Calls the Owl* (autobiography), Putnam, 1980; *The Home Front* (short stories), Putnam, 1981.

Contributor of short stories to magazines, including *Ladies' Home Journal* and *Collier's,* 1928-41, and *Saturday Evening Post,* 1941-62.

SIDELIGHTS: Craven's first novel, *I Heard the Owl Call My Name,* explores the relationship between a dying Anglican priest and his parishioners, a tribe of British Columbian Indians. Set in a small fishing village in the Canadian wilderness, the novel depicts the Kwakiutl Indians of British Columbia struggling against assimilation into a modern civilization. Jennifer Farley Smith of the *Christian Science*

Monitor called the novel a "shining parable about the reconciliation of two cultures and two faiths." The story demonstrates that "the Red Indian philosophy, firmly rooted in nature, is both a challenge to modern man and an undeniable comfort," noted *Times Literary Supplement* critic Elaine Moss. A best-selling novel, *I Heard the Owl Call My Name* was made into a movie for television in 1973.

Walk Gently This Good Earth, Craven's second novel, also shows people responding to a changing world as it follows the Wescott family through the social upheavals of the Great Depression and World War II. Elizabeth Schmidt, writing in the *Christian Science Monitor,* found the book "comfortable and honest," saying also that "the characters are like old pieces of pewter, showing a faint stubborn luster." On the other hand, a *Kirkus Reviews* critic observed, "this brood . . . is noble and pure hearted beyond belief. Also cloying and a bit unreal."

Craven's autobiography, *Again Calls the Owl,* is largely devoted to the research and travel that provided the foundation for much of her writing. Craven once spent several weeks with the Kwakiutl Indians, and she recalled those experiences in writing *I Heard the Owl Call My Name.*

BIOGRAPHICAL/CRITICAL SOURCES: Christian Science Monitor, January 30, 1974, December 28, 1977; *New York Times Book Review,* February 3, 1974; *New Statesman,* August 2, 1974; *Junior Bookshelf,* December, 1974; *Times Literary Supplement,* December 6, 1974; *Kirkus Reviews,* October 1, 1977; *Wilson Library Bulletin,* February, 1978; *Atlantic Monthly,* April, 1980; *Booklist,* May 1, 1980; *Los Angeles Times,* May 25, 1981; *Contemporary Literary Criticism,* Volume 17, Gale, 1981.

OBITUARIES: Los Angeles Times, August 4, 1980.

[Sketch verified by niece, Elizabeth Craven]

*   *   *

CRAVEN, Wesley Frank (Jr.)   1905-1981

OBITUARY NOTICE—See index for *CA* sketch: Born May 19, 1905, in Conway, N.C.; died of cancer, February 10, 1981, in Princeton, N.J. Educator, historian, and author. Craven taught at New York University before moving to Princeton University where he was a professor of history for more than twenty years. His numerous historical works include *Dissolution of the Virginia Company: The Failure of a Colonial Experiment, New Jersey and the English Colonization of North America,* and *White, Red, and Black: The Seventeenth-Century Virginian.* Obituaries and other sources: *New York Times,* February 13, 1981; *AB Bookman's Weekly,* March 9, 1981.

*   *   *

CRAVENS, Hamilton   1938-

PERSONAL: Born August 12, 1938, in Evanston, Ill.; son of Charles Turner (a business owner) and Flora (Hamilton) Cravens; married Joan Pemberton (an editor), June 17, 1961; children: Heather Lee, Christopher Hamilton. *Education:* University of Washington, Seattle, B.A., 1960, M.A., 1962; University of Iowa, Ph.D., 1969. *Home:* 2722 Northwood Dr., Ames, Iowa 50010. *Office:* Department of History, Iowa State University, Ames, Iowa 50011.

CAREER: Ohio State University, Columbus, instructor in history, 1965-68; Iowa State University, Ames, instructor, 1968-69, assistant professor, 1969-73, associate professor, 1973-80, professor of history, 1980—. Visiting assistant professor at University of Maryland, 1971-72. *Member:* American Historical Association, American Studies Association, History of Science Society, Society for Research in Child Development, Society for the History of Technology, Intellectual History Group, Southern Historical Association. *Awards, honors:* Award from Washington State Historical Association, 1966, for magazine article "The Emergence of the Farmer-Labor Party in Washington Politics, 1919-1920"; award from National Science Teachers Association, 1976, for an essay, part of which was later published as "The Role of Universities in the Rise of Experimental Biology, 1880-1910"; grants from National Endowment for the Humanities, 1974, National Science Foundation, 1978-79, and Rockefeller Archive Center, 1978, 1981.

WRITINGS: The Triumph of Evolution: American Scientists and the Heredity-Environment Controversy, 1900-1941, University of Pennsylvania Press, 1978; (editor) *Ideas in America's Cultures: From Republic to Mass Society,* Iowa State University Press, 1982. Contributor to American studies and education journals. Chairman of editorial board of *American Studies,* 1976—.

WORK IN PROGRESS: Pioneer: The Iowa Child Welfare Research Station and the Science of the Child, completion expected in 1983; *The Child-Savers: The Rockefeller Foundation and Child Development,* completion expected in 1986.

SIDELIGHTS: Cravens commented: "As a scholar, I am interested in the cultural history of technology and science in modern America. That is, I am interested in more than the 'technical' history of technology and science; I am interested in how and why technology and science are used within culture and society."

* * *

CRAWFORD, Patricia

PERSONAL—Education: University of Pennsylvania, B.A., 1957. *Home address:* P.O. Box 195, McAllen, Tex. 78501. *Agent:* Helen Merrill, 337 West 22nd St., New York, N.Y. 10011.

CAREER: Writer.

WRITINGS: Homesteading, Macmillan, 1975; *Homesteading Recipe Book,* Macmillan, 1976.

WORK IN PROGRESS: A book on the Mexican-American border.

AVOCATIONAL INTERESTS: Gardening, cooking, Mexican and U.S. history, antiques of the southwest, medieval history.

* * *

CRITTENDEN, Mabel (Buss) 1917-

PERSONAL: Born February 23, 1917, in Provo, Utah; daughter of Fred Earle and Edith (Rumsey) Buss; married Max D. Crittenden, Jr. (a geologist), December 26, 1942; children: Elisabeth (Mrs. Gary Schwarzman), Joan M., Susan (Mrs. Fred Zoller), Laurel (Mrs. Richard Penniman). *Education:* San Jose State University, A.B., 1939, M.A., 1968; Stanford University, high school teaching certificate, 1940. *Religion:* Congregationalist. *Home:* 50 Alhambra Court, Portola Valley, Calif. 94025.

CAREER: High school biology teacher in Lodi, Calif., 1940-43; San Jose State University, San Jose, Calif., zoology teacher, 1947-49; Portola Valley Schools, Portola Valley, Calif., district librarian, 1960-75. Docent of Jasper Ridge Biological Preserve; volunteer ecology worker in Palo Alto, Calif. *Member:* Native Plant Society, Pacific Horticultural Society.

WRITINGS: (With Dorothy Telfer) *Wildflowers of the West,* Celestial Arts, 1975; (with Telfer) *Wildflowers of the East,* Celestial Arts, 1977; *Trees of the West,* Celestial Arts, 1977; *Ferns,* Celestial Arts, 1978. Co-author of "Science Corner," a column in *Early Years.*

WORK IN PROGRESS: Desert Wildflowers, publication by Celestial Arts expected in 1982 or 1983.

SIDELIGHTS: Mabel Crittenden told *CA:* "My books are for people who are not trained botanists, but who would like to be able to identify plants by characteristics they can observe. My writing teaches scientific identification without the scientific jargon."

* * *

CROSS, Helen Reeder
See BROADHEAD, Helen Cross

* * *

CROW, Elizabeth Smith 1946-

PERSONAL: Born July 29, 1946; daughter of Harrison Venture and Marlis (deGreve) Smith; married Charles Patrick Crow (an editor), March 2, 1974; children: Samuel Harrison, Rachel Venture. *Education:* Mills College, Oakland, Calif., B.A., 1968. *Home:* 211 East 35th St., New York, N.Y. 10016. *Office: Parents' Magazine,* 685 Third Ave., New York, N.Y. 10017; and 52 Vanderbilt Ave., New York, N.Y. 10017.

CAREER/WRITINGS: Parents' Magazine, New York, N.Y., editor-in-chief, 1978—. *Member:* Cosmopolitan Club.

* * *

CROWDER, Christopher M. D. 1922-

PERSONAL: Born September 26, 1922, in Weybridge, England; married, 1951; children: three. *Education:* Received B.A. from Oxford University, M.A., 1948, D.Phil., 1953. *Office:* Department of History, Queen's University, Kingston, Ontario, Canada K7L 3N6.

CAREER: Queen's University, Belfast, Northern Ireland, lecturer in history, 1953-66; Queen's University, Kingston, Ontario, associate professor, 1966-69, professor of history, 1969—, associate dean of graduate studies, 1976—. *Military service:* British Army, 1942-45; became lieutenant. *Member:* Royal Historical Society (fellow).

WRITINGS: Two Thousand Years of Handwriting (exhibition catalog), H.M.S.O., 1956; (contributor) *Das Konzie von Konstanz,* Herder, 1964; (editor and author of introduction) *English Society and Government in the Fifteenth Century,* Dufour, 1967 (published in England as *English Society and Government in the Fifteenth Century: A Selection of Articles From "History Today",* Oliver & Boyd, 1967); (editor) *Selections From History Today,* two volumes, Oliver & Boyd, 1968; *Politics and the Councils of the Fifteenth Century,* Canadian Catholic Historical Association, 1970; *Unity, Heresy, and Reform, 1378-1460: The Conciliar Response to the Great Schism,* St. Martin's, 1977 (published in England as *Unity, Heresy, and Reform, 1378-1459,* Edward Arnold, 1977). Contributor to scholarly journals.

BIOGRAPHICAL/CRITICAL SOURCES: Encounter, November, 1977; *American Historical Review,* June, 1978.*

CROWE, Charles Monroe 1902-1978

OBITUARY NOTICE—See index for *CA* sketch: Born February 6, 1902, in San Antonio, Tex.; died May 31, 1978. Clergyman, lecturer, and author. A Methodist pastor, Crowe served in several churches in Texas, Louisiana, Missouri, and Illinois. He lectured on television and radio programs and wrote prayers that were syndicated by National Council Religious Features. Among Crowe's books number *Sermons for Special Days, The Years of Our Lord,* and *In This Free Land.* Obituaries and other sources: *Who's Who in America,* 38th edition, Marquis, 1974. (Date of death provided by wife, Lucy-Avis Crowe.)

* * *

CROWE, Kenneth C(harles) 1934-

PERSONAL: Born August 19, 1934, in New York, N.Y.; son of William F. (a policeman) and Loretta (an industrial worker and union officer; maiden name, Connolly) Crowe; married Rae Lord (a nursing consultant and educator), September 8, 1956; children: Kenneth C. II, Roy, Daniel, Carol. *Education:* Fordham University, B.S., 1956. *Politics:* Democrat. *Religion:* Roman Catholic. *Home:* 37 East Lyons St., Melville, N.Y. 11747. *Agent:* Roslyn Targ, 250 West 57th St., Suite 1932, New York, N.Y. 10019. *Office:* Newsday, Long Island, N.Y. 11747.

CAREER: Associated with *Endicott Daily Bulletin,* Endicott, N.Y., 1958-59; and *Syracuse Herald-Journal,* Syracuse, N.Y., 1959-63; *Newsday,* Long Island, N.Y., journalist, 1963—, member of investigative team, 1967-71. Notable assignments include investigation of Bebe Rebozo and other associates of Richard Nixon, 1971, and Watergate, 1973. *Military service:* U.S. Army, 1956-58; became sergeant. *Awards, honors:* Pulitzer Prize for investigative reporting and special award from Society of Silvrians, both 1970, both for investigation of political and land scandals; Alicia Patterson fellowship, 1974.

WRITINGS: America for Sale, Doubleday, 1978.

WORK IN PROGRESS: A historical novel set in the 1870's in Europe and Asia, centering on the experiences of an American in the Paris Commune of 1871.

SIDELIGHTS: Crowe's book, *America for Sale,* is an inquiry into the enormous amount of money being funneled into U.S. businesses by foreign investors. Citing available government information on the identity of these investors and the amount of money involved, Crowe concludes that the sheer volume of the invested funds poses a threat to America's security and its economy.

Crowe fails to point out, noted John Helmer in the *Washington Post,* that American businessmen are investing abroad even more heavily than foreign capitalists are investing in the United States. Helmer declared that omissions such as this are "an incitement to greater stupidity than even [Crowe] alleges we have been guilty of so far."

Several critics complained that Crowe neglects to consider the potential benefits of foreign investment in U.S. businesses. *National Review* critic M. Stanton Evans said, "It is estimated that more than one million jobs were provided to U.S. workers by such investment in 1974." Robert Lekachman of *Saturday Review* claimed that "the communities in which foreign companies have opened new plants usually perceive their presence as a great blessing."

Crowe's book treats foreign investment as a recent development, but Lekachman pointed out that "foreign money has always been attracted to opportunities in the New World. . . . America has always been for sale. So, for that matter, has the rest of the world." Lekachman described *America for Sale* as "a useful volume," because it provides much-needed information about foreign funding of U.S. industry, but thought "it would be considerably more useful if its organization were less casual, its prose more attractive, its comparisons more frequent, and its analysis less primitive."

Crowe told *CA:* "*American for Sale* dealt fully with the positive aspects of foreign investment in the United States, including the jobs created and the history of foreign investment going back to Alexander Hamilton. The book was not a polemic, but it discussed the potential dangers of an economy dominated by foreign investors, particularly foreign government investors."

BIOGRAPHICAL/CRITICAL SOURCES: Saturday Review, September 16, 1978; *Washington Post,* October 2, 1978; *Christian Science Monitor,* October 25, 1978; *National Review,* October 27, 1978; *Harvard Business Review,* March-April, 1979.

* * *

CROWTHER, (Francis) Bosley 1905-1981

OBITUARY NOTICE—See index for *CA* sketch: Born July 13, 1905, in Lutherville, Md.; died of heart failure, March 7, 1981, in Mt. Kisco, N.Y. Journalist, editor, critic, consultant, playwright, and author. Employed by the *New York Times* for forty years, Crowther held a variety of positions, including rewrite man, assistant drama editor, assistant screen editor, screen editor, and film critic. As the film critic for the *Times,* he was well-known and respected for his scholarly, fair reviews. He wrote prodigiously, often supplying three or four reviews weekly in addition to articles for the *Times*'s Sunday drama section. Crowther served three times as president of the New York Film Critics and in 1954 became the first critic honored by the Screen Directors Guild. After retiring from the newspaper, he began working as a creative consultant at Columbia Pictures and later became an independent consultant. Crowther's works include the play "East of the Sun" and several books. Among his books number *The Lion's Share: The Story of an Entertainment Empire, Hollywood Rajah: The Life and Times of Louis B. Mayer,* and *Vintage Films.* Obituaries and other sources: New York Times, March 8, 1981; *Washington Post,* March 9, 1981; *Chicago Tribune,* March 9, 1981; *Newsweek,* March 16, 1981; *Time,* March 23, 1981.

* * *

CULLEN, Lee Stowell 1922-

PERSONAL: Born July 31, 1922, in Hull, Mass.; daughter of E. Fred (a biscuit manufacturer) and Mary (Stowell) Cullen. *Education:* Attended private secondary schools in Massachusetts and Connecticut. *Politics:* Republican. *Religion:* Episcopalian. *Home:* Apt. 629-W, 1204 South Washington St., Alexandria, Va. 22314. *Office:* National Wildlife Federation, 1204 16th St. NW, Washington, D.C. 20036.

CAREER/WRITINGS: Ladies' Home Journal, Philadelphia, Pa., assistant editor, 1948-62; *Woman's Journal,* London, England, senior editor, 1962-63; *Jack & Jill,* Philadelphia, Pa., associate editor, 1963-70; *Ranger Rick's Nature Magazine,* Washington, D.C., senior editor, 1970—. Contributor of numerous articles on wildlife and conservation to *Jack & Jill* and *Ranger Rick's Nature Magazine*.

SIDELIGHTS: Ranger Rick's Nature Magazine is a conservation and wildlife publication geared for children ages five to twelve. Affiliated with the National Wildlife Federation, *Ranger Rick* combines information about nature with leisure-time activities and projects for its young readers.

Cullen told *CA:* "Probably the fact that I love writing is what makes it sometimes seem easy, other times hard, but always gratifying (though I'm never *really* satisfied). There is something special about writing for children, but I do not write especially for them. I never think, 'Remember, you're writing for five to twelve year olds.' In other writers I admire the whimsy of A. A. Milne, the careful research and fine honing of Anya Seaton, and the wizardry of DuMaurier.

"Writing about conservation issues for children is a rewarding experience, particularly when a problem we have discussed in the magazine brings in responses from our young readers. In one instance we did an article on saving the Platte River in Nebraska for migrating birds, including the endangered whopping crane. At the end of the article we suggested that the children could contribute to 'Pennies for the Platte' to help purchase more land near the river. They came through in unbelievable numbers with pennies, dimes, and dollars. One little boy sent in fifty-three cents, but it cost his parents about eighty-seven cents to mail it! Another wrote, 'I'd like to send you more, but I have to feed my pet hamster.' That's what makes it all worthwhile, and then some!"

*   *   *

CULVER, Kenneth Leon   1903-

PERSONAL: Born November 21, 1903, in Stowe, Vt.; son of Leo (an engineer) and Adele (Swift) Culver; married Lillian Hogan, December 21, 1939; children: Kenneth L., Jr. *Education:* University of California, Berkeley, A.B., 1929, M.A., 1930, Ph.D., 1935. *Home:* 2500 H. Johnson Ave., Riverdale, N.Y. 10463. *Office:* Holt, Rinehart & Winston, 383 Madison Ave., New York, N.Y. 10017.

CAREER: Owl Drug Co., San Francisco, Calif., pharmacist, 1923-29; University of Hawaii, Honolulu, instructor in European history, 1930-31; Chico State College (now California State University), Chico, Calif., associate professor of history, 1933-34; University of Hawaii, instructor in European history, 1935-36; D. C. Heath & Co., Lexington, Mass., college field traveler, 1939-57, associate head of college department, 1958-60; Holt, Rinehart & Winston, Inc., New York City, history editor, 1961-68; Thomas Y. Crowell Co., New York City, editor of history and political science books, 1969-71, history consultant, 1972-73; Holt, Rinehart & Winston, Inc., special consultant, 1974—. *Member:* American Historical Association, Organization of American Historians, Society for French Historical Studies, Western History Association.

WRITINGS: (Editor) *Social Problems in America,* Holt, 1974.

WORK IN PROGRESS: Extended research on Edmund Burke, 1729-1797, with possible plans for some analyses of his *Reflections on the French Revolution.*

AVOCATIONAL INTERESTS: Travel.

*   *   *

CUNNINGHAM, Captain Frank
See GLICK, Carl (Cannon)

CUNNINGHAM, Donald H(ayward)   1935-

PERSONAL: Born May 21, 1935, in Columbia, Mo.; son of H. H. and E. F. (Crane) Cunningham; married Patsy A. Dickson, December 21, 1957; children: Mark. *Education:* University of Missouri, B.A., 1961, M.A., 1962, Ph.D., 1972. *Home:* 412 North Wilson St., Morehead, Ky. 40531. *Office:* Department of English, Morehead State University, Morehead, Ky. 40531.

CAREER: University of Missouri, Columbia, instructor in English, 1962-66; Southern Illinois University, Carbondale, assistant professor of English, 1966-72; Morehead State University, Morehead, Ky., associate professor, 1972-76, professor of English, 1976—. Consultant to government agencies, publishers, and other businesses. *Military service:* U.S. Navy, 1953-57. *Member:* National Council of Teachers of English, Society for Technical Communications, Association of Teachers of Technical Writing. *Awards, honors:* Award of Excellence from Society for Technical Communications, Piedmont/Carolina chapters, 1979, for *The Practical Craft: Readings for Business and Technical Writers.*

WRITINGS: (Editor) *A Reading Approach to Professional Police Writing,* C. C. Thomas, 1972; (editor with Herman A. Estrin) *The Teaching of Technical Writing,* National Council of Teachers of English, 1975; (with Thomas E. Pearsall) *How to Write for the World of Work,* Holt, 1978; (editor with W. Keats Sparrow) *The Practical Craft: Readings for Business and Technical Writers,* Houghton, 1978. Contributor of articles and book reviews to scholarly and professional journals, including *College Composition and Communcation, Journal of Technical Writing and Communication,* and *Technical Writing Teacher.* Editor of *Technical Writing Teacher,* 1973—.

WORK IN PROGRESS: A book, tentatively titled *Composition;* various instructional materials and manuals.

*   *   *

CUNNINGHAM, R(onnie) Walter   1932-

PERSONAL: Born March 16, 1932, in Creston, Iowa; son of Walter Wilfred and Gladys (Backen) Cunningham; married to Lo Ella Irby, July 12, 1956; children: Brian Keith, Kimberly Anne. *Education:* University of California, Los Angeles, B.A., 1960, M.A., 1961, doctoral study; attended Harvard University, 1974. *Home:* 701 West Friar Tuck, Houston, Tex. 77024. *Office:* Capital Group, 505 Stuart, Houston, Tex. 77006.

CAREER: Rand Corp., Santa Monica, Calif., physicist, 1960-63; National Aeronautics and Space Administration, Washington, D.C., astronaut (pilot of Apollo 7 Mission), 1963-68, chief of Skylab Branch of Astronaut Office, 1968-71; Century Development Corp., Houston, Tex., senior vice-president, 1971-74; HydroTech Development Co., Houston, president, 1974-76; 3D International, Houston, senior vice-president and director of Engineering Division, 1976-79; Capital Group (investment and merchant bankers), Houston, partner, 1979—. Residential and commercial real estate investor, 1972—. Founding director of Earth Awareness Foundation; member of board of directors of University Savings Association and Nitron, Inc. Lecturer on the environment and the space program. *Military service:* U.S. Marine Corps, fighter pilot, 1951-56. U.S. Marine Corps Reserve, 1956-76; became colonel.

MEMBER: American Institute of Aeronautics and Astronautics (associate fellow), Society of Experimental Test Pilots, American Geophysical Union, Explorers Club, Houston Chamber of Commerce, Sigma Xi, Sigma Pi Sigma. *Awards, honors:* Exceptional service medal from National Aeronautics and Space Administration, 1968; Astronaut Wings from U.S. Navy, 1969; Haley Astronautics Award from American Institute of Aeronautics and Astronautics, 1969; special trustee award from National Academy of Television Arts and Sciences, 1969; Medal of Valor from American Legion, 1974; Outstanding American Award from American Conservative Union, 1975.

WRITINGS: The All American Boys, Macmillan, 1977. Contributor to technical journals and popular magazines.

AVOCATIONAL INTERESTS: Hunting, tennis, sports cars.

*   *   *

CUOMO, Mario Matthew   1932-

PERSONAL: Born June 15, 1932, in Queens County, N.Y.; son of Andrea and Immaculata (Giordano) Cuomo; married Matilda N. Raffia, 1954; children: Margaret I., Andrew M., Maria C., Madeline C., Christopher C. *Education:* St. John's College, B.A. (summa cum laude), 1953; St. John's University, Jamaica, N.Y., LL.B. (cum laude), 1956. *Religion:* Roman Catholic. *Home:* 32 Court St., Brooklyn, N.Y. 11201. *Office:* Office of the Lieutenant Governor, State Capitol, Albany, N.Y. 12224.

CAREER: Admitted to New York Bar, 1956, and U.S. Supreme Court Bar, 1960; confidential legal assistant for New York State Court of Appeals, 1956-58; Corner, Weisbrod, Froeb & Charles, Brooklyn, N.Y., associate, 1958-63, partner, 1963-75; State of New York, Albany, secretary of state, 1975-79, lieutenant governor, 1979—. Member of faculty at St. John's University, Jamaica, N.Y., 1963-75. Counsel to Corona Homeowners, 1966-72. Charter member of First Ecumenical Commission of Christians and Jews for Brooklyn and Queens.

MEMBER: American Bar Association, American Judicature Society, Federation of Italian-American Democratic Organizations, New York State Bar Association, Nassau County Bar Association, Queens County Bar Association, Catholic Lawyers Guild of Queens County (president, 1966-67), Association of the Bar of the City of New York, Brooklyn Bar Association, Columbian Lawyers Association, St. John's University Alumni Federation (chairman of board of directors, 1970-72), Big Brothers of America (member of regional board of directors), Skull and Circle, Pi Alpha Sigma, Delta Theta Pi. *Awards, honors:* Pietas Medal from St. John's University, Jamaica, N.Y., 1972; named man of the year by Glendal chapter of Universal Cooperatives, 1974; humanitarian award from Long Beach lodge of B'nai B'rith, 1975; Rapallo Award from Columbia Lawyers Association, 1976; Dante Medal in Government from American Association of Teachers of Italian, 1976; silver medallion from Columbia Coalition, 1976; outstanding public administration award from C. W. Post College of Long Island University, 1977.

WRITINGS: The New York City Secondary School System, Thomas More Institute, 1966; *Forest Hills Diary: The Crisis of Low-Income Housing,* Random House, 1974. Contributor to law journals.*

CURRAN, Joseph M(aroney)   1932-

PERSONAL: Born August 9, 1932, in Rock Island, Ill.; son of John William (an engineer) and Margaret (Maroney) Curran. *Education:* College of St. Thomas, B.A., 1954; University of Chicago, M.A., 1955, Ph.D., 1959; attended Queen's University, Belfast, Northern Ireland, 1958-59. *Politics:* Democrat. *Religion:* Roman Catholic. *Home:* 753 James St., Syracuse, N.Y. 13203. *Office:* Department of History, Le Moyne College, Syracuse, N.Y. 13214.

CAREER: Fordham University, Bronx, N.Y., instructor in history, 1959-61; Le Moyne College, Syracuse, N.Y., assistant professor, 1963-67, associate professor, 1967-73, professor of history, 1973—. *Member:* American Historical Association, American Committee for Irish Studies, Conference on British Studies. *Awards, honors:* Fulbright scholar, 1958-59.

WRITINGS: The Birth of the Irish Free State, 1921-1923, University of Alabama Press, 1980. Contributor to history journals.

WORK IN PROGRESS: Research on the relationship between history and film, as recorded by fiction and nonfiction film.

*   *   *

CURRAN, Peter Malcolm   1922-

PERSONAL: Born September 18, 1922, in Salisbury, England. *Education:* Educated privately. *Home:* 29 Drive, Hove, Sussex BN3 3JE, England.

CAREER: Davies's School of English, Hove, England, senior tutor in English, 1957-75; lecturer and writer, 1975—. *Member:* Royal Overseas League (life member).

WRITINGS: Do You Speak English?, Harrap, 1967; *Beware of Idioms,* Tutor Tape, 1970; *Proverbs in Action,* Editypa, 1972; *English Structure Stories,* Stanley Thomas, 1975; (coauthor) *Hushed October* (play), Playwrights Network, 1976; *English Idiom Stories,* Stanley Thomas, 1977. Television and radio writer for British Broadcasting Corp. Contributor to *English Language Teaching Journal.*

WORK IN PROGRESS: English Proverb Stories, publication expected in 1981 or 1982; *A New Coursebook for Proficiency English,* publication expected in 1983.

SIDELIGHTS: Curran wrote: "I am a strong believer in voluntary euthanasia. I believe everyone has the right to a dignified death. I am a lifelong lover of Siamese cats, who are my constant companions. My philosophy of life is very simple: there's nothing worth the wear of winning but laughter and the love of friends. I have lectured extensively on euthanasia, oratory, cats, letter writing, and medieval architecture, but I am a very private person who would rather be a Pere Joseph than a Cardinal Richilieu any day."

*   *   *

CURTEIS, Ian Bayley   1935-

PERSONAL: Born May 1, 1935, in London, England; married Dorothy Joan Armstrong, 1964; children: Tobit, Mikol. *Agent:* Jenne Casarotto, Douglas Rae Management Ltd., 28 Charing Cross Rd., London WC2H 0DB, England.

CAREER: Actor and director at theatres in England, 1956-63; worked as drama director in England for British Broadcasting Corp. (BBC) and for Associated Television, 1963-67.

WRITINGS—Television plays: "The Folly," first broadcast by ITV, 1968; "The Haunting," ITV, 1969; "Beethoven," British Broadcasting Corp. (BBC-TV), 1970; "Sir Alexander Fleming," BBC-TV, 1970; *Long Voyage Out of War* (trilogy; BBC-TV, 1971), J. Calder, 1971; "A Distant Chill," BBC-TV, 1971; "Second Time Around," ITV, 1971; "Mr. Rolls and Mr. Royce," BBC-TV, 1972; "The Portland Millions," ITV, 1976; "Philby, Burgess, and Maclean," ITV, 1977; "Hess," ITV, 1978; "The Atom Spies," ITV, 1979; "Churchill and the Generals," BBC-TV, 1979; "Suez 1956," BBC-TV, 1979; "Miss Moberly's Ghosts," ITV, 1981; "The Mitford Girls," ITV, 1981.

Author of play "A Personal Affair," first produced on the West End, March, 1981. Originator and writer of numerous drama series for television.

WORK IN PROGRESS: A television trilogy of plays about Bernard Berenson and Lord Duveen for the British Broadcasting Corp.

* * *

CURTIS, Donald 1915-

PERSONAL: Born February 27, 1915, in Eugene, Ore.; son of Carl William (a farmer) and Josephine (Lacey) Rudolf; married Dorothy Mae Gessel (a teacher and minister), March 29, 1974; children: Chris, Daniel Curtis. *Education:* Northwestern University, B.A., 1936, M.A., 1937. *Office:* Unity Church of Dallas, 6525 Forest Lane, Dallas, Tex. 75230.

CAREER: Ordained minister of Unity School of Practical Christianity, 1954; Allegheny College, Meadville, Pa., instructor in speech, 1936-37; Duquesne University, Pittsburgh, Pa., associate professor of drama, 1937-38; Pasadena Community Playhouse, Pasadena, Calif., associate director, 1938-40; actor in films, on television, and on the Broadway stage, 1940-50; pastor of metaphysical churches, 1950-70; Unity Church of Dallas, Dallas, Tex., senior minister, 1970—. Actor, 1938-40, 1950-60; presents radio and television programs and seminars; public speaker in the United States, England, Switzerland, Germany, Ghana, South Africa, Greece, India, Japan, and the Caribbean. President of Texas district of International New Thought Alliance, 1969-80. *Member:* Association of Unity Churches.

WRITINGS: Love and Marriage, CSA Press, 1960; *The Twenty-Third Psalm,* CSA Press, 1961; *Your Thoughts Can Change Your Life,* Wilshire, 1961; *Human Problems and How to Solve Them,* Wilshire, 1962; *Daily Power for Joyful Living,* Wilshire, 1963.

How to Be Happy and Successful, CSA Press, 1970; *Ten Steps to Personal Power,* CSA Press, 1970; *New Age Understanding,* Unity, 1973; *The Way of the Christ,* Unity, 1974; *Science of Mind in Daily Living,* Wilshire, 1975; *The Christ-Based Teachings,* Unity, 1976; *Live It Up!,* CSA Press, 1976; *Master Meditations,* CSA Press, 1976; *Finding the Christ,* CSA Press, 1977; *How to Be Great,* CSA Press, 1978; *Songs of the Soul* (poems), CSA Press, 1979. Author of inspirational booklets. Contributor of more than a hundred articles to magazines, including *Science of Mind* and *New Thought Quarterly.*

SIDELIGHTS: Curtis's books are used as textbooks for healing, meditation, and spiritual education at churches and religious centers. His sales and executive leadership training seminars are in the business and professional fields, and he is in demand as a speaker at conventions. His favorite theme is "The Unlimited Potential Within You," and he presents techniques for developing this potential, "releasing the free,

full-flow of life through the individual as his consciousness expands and he experiences richer, fuller living." Through the Spiritual Unity of Nations and other organizations, he works for human understanding, international cooperation, and world peace, and carries on a large correspondence with readers, teachers, and students all over the world.

Curtis has studied with the holy men of India, spending time in their *ashrams,* and seeking out the counsel of Buddhist monks and Tibetan lamas. In Japan he studied Oriental techniques of healing, studied Zen, researched the traditional older religions, and spoke at religious centers. His broad background and approach to spiritual matters make him welcome by many religious denominations, and his sermons and tape recordings are distributed internationally.

* * *

CURTIS, Edith Roelker 1893-1977

OBITUARY NOTICE—See index for *CA* sketch: Born July 29, 1893, in East Greenwich, R.I.; died February 1, 1977. Author. Curtis wrote several books, including *Anne Hutchinson: A Biography, Lady Sarah Lennox: An Irrepressible Stuart, A Season In Utopia: The Story of Brook Farm,* and *Mexican Romance.* She also contributed stories, poems, and articles to magazines such as *Literary Review* and *American Heritage.* Obituaries and other sources: *Who's Who in the East,* 16th edition, Marquis, 1977. (Date of death provided by Smith College.)

* * *

CURTIS, Jack 1922-

PERSONAL: Born January 4, 1922, in Lincoln, Kan.; son of Ross E. (in sales) and Gladys (Knabe) Curtis; married Lavon Renaas (a bookstore owner), September 7, 1947; children: Micah, Lincoln, Melissa Jane, Ross. *Education:* Fresno State College (now California State University, Fresno), A.B., 1941. *Home:* Apple Pie Ranch, Big Sur, Calif. 93920. *Agent:* Bart Fles, 501 Fifth Ave., New York, N.Y. 10017.

CAREER: Writer, 1954—. *Military service:* U.S. Navy, 1942-45; became lieutenant junior grade; received four battle stars. *Member:* American Civil Liberties Union, Writers Guild of America, West.

WRITINGS: Green Again (novel), La Prensa d'Eduardo, 1951; *Pigeon Wing* (poems), Peregrine Press, 1955; *Cool of Kansas* (poems), Peregrine Press, 1955; *Artic Circle* (poems), The Guild, 1959; *The Kloochman* (novel), Simon & Schuster, 1966; *Banjo* (novel), Macmillan, 1972; (contributor) Russell Chatham, editor, *Silent Seasons* (anthology), Dutton, 1978; *Eagles Over Big Sur* (novel), Capra, 1980; *Watermoon of a Woman* (poems), NWS Press, 1980; *Occupations* (poems), NWS Press, 1980. Author of more than fifty plays for television. Contributor of short stories to *Reader's Digest.*

WORK IN PROGRESS: Two novels based on Big Sur.

SIDELIGHTS: Curtis commented: "The river finds death without life unacceptable." *Avocational interests:* Farming, travel.

* * *

CURTIS, Jackie [a pseudonym] 1947-

PERSONAL: Born February 19, 1947, in Stony Creek, Tenn.; son of John B. (a Veteran's Administration worker) and Jean (a certified public accountant; maiden name, Uglialoro) Holder; married Eric Emerson, July 21, 1969 (divorced June 6, 1970); married Artchie Dukeshire, October

28, 1970 (divorced April 17, 1971); married Hunter Robert Cayce, November 27, 1971 (divorced January 5, 1972); married Hiram Keller, February 14, 1972 (divorced March 1, 1973); married Lance Loud, June 9, 1973 (divorced August 7, 1975); married Peter Rufus Groby, December 24, 1976 (divorced May 14, 1978); married Kevin McPhee (a publicity manager), July 23, 1980. *Education:* Hunter College of the City University of New York, B.A., 1975; studied at Lee Strassberg Actors' Studio, 1975-76. *Politics:* "Ever since I said I do, I don't." *Religion:* Roman Catholic/Free Will Baptist. *Address:* Jackie Curtis Productions Unltd., c/o Joseph Preston, 114 East 11th St., New York, N.Y. 10003.

CAREER: Typist in New York City, 1964; cloak room attendant and elevator operator in Broadway theatres, 1965; Jackie Curtis Productions Unltd., New York City, president, 1979—. Performer in stage plays, including "Scrooge," 1965, "This Was Burlesque," 1966, "The Life of Lady Godiva," 1968-69, "Les Precieuses Ridicules," 1972, and "A Modern Hamlet," 1972; performer in all of own plays and films; co-director of "Lucky Wonderful," with Roz Kelly, 1968, and director of "Vain Victory," 1971. *Awards, honors:* Three playwright honorarium awards from La Mama Experimental Theatre Club and other companies, 1971; Soho Arts Award nomination, 1980.

WRITINGS—Plays: "Glamour, Glory, and Gold: The Life and Legend of Nola Noonan, Goddess and Star," first produced in New York City at Bastianos Theatre, 1967; "Lucky Wonderful: Thirteen Musicals About Tommy Manville," first produced in New York City at Bastianos Theatre, 1968; "Heaven Grand in Amber Orbit," first produced in New York City at Gotham Art Theatre, 1969; "Femme Fatale: The Three Faces of Gloria," first produced Off-Broadway at La Mama Experimental Theatre Club, 1970; "Vain Victory: The Vicissitudes of the Damned" (first produced in New York City), published in *The Great American Family,* WNET-TV, 1972.

Screenplays: "Flesh," Andy Warhol Enterprises, 1967; "Big Badge: The Brigid Polk Detective Story," Andy Warhol Enterprises, 1970; "WR—Mysteries of the Organism," Cinema Five, 1971; "Tits," Larry Rivers Productions, 1971; "Women in Revolt," Andy Warhol Enterprises, 1971.

WORK IN PROGRESS: "Champagne—The Bottle Beautiful," a tragi-comedy; *Selfish Lullaby, My Memoirs,* with David Dalton, publication by Dutton expected in 1985.

SIDELIGHTS: Jackie Curtis's plays deal largely with sex, social values, and life in general, in bizarre, outrageous manners. His first play, "Heaven Grand in Amber Orbit," is a melange of lines from comic books, Shakespeare, television scripts and commercials, old movies, and various other media. Rosalyn Regelson of the *New York Times* said of "Heaven Grand," "There is a script, and the players' loud declamations and frenetic staging give the disorienting impression that there must be plot and dialogue that you could follow if you knew how."

Throughout "Heaven Grand," Curtis floods the stage with simultaneous activity. While Heaven Grand, the leading female character, is dying at center stage, a set of Siamese triplets cavorts lewdly about while other cast members lecture from a toilet seat.

Because of their deviance from theatrical norms, Curtis's plays have received mixed reviews. Regelson, commenting on Curtis's knack for mocking social values, wrote: "For those in the audience who consider the old social values unfunctional, the actors are performing a satisfying rite of destruction. On the other hand, the buoyant nihilism of this

theater, which communicates itself so directly to the audience, causes those viewers who resent the attack on the basic constructs of their existence to find the performances ugly, sordid, stupid and infantile."

Mel Gussow of the *New York Times* said of "Vain Victory": "The jokes are abysmal, but the delivery is so ingenuous as to make almost the worst line excusable. A groan of recognition from the audience! For all the cornucopian theatricality, there is a lack of ostentation. One does not leave 'Vain Victory' humming the old nostalgia, but smiling at the energetic cavortings of this single-minded troupe."

Curtis often stars in his productions, frequently appearing as a woman. Consequently, his gender is the subject of much discussion. "[I'm] not a boy, not a girl, not a faggot, not a drag queen, not a transsexual—just me, Jackie," Curtis says. "I have to laugh at those people who say they feel like a woman trapped in a man's body. What is a man? What is a woman? . . . Those sex change operations—so 1950's. I am what I feel I am."

Curtis told *CA:* "Love is an astonishing thing, even in art. It can do what no amount of culture, criticism, or intellect can do, namely, connect the most widely divergent poles, bring together what is oldest and what is newest. It transcends time by relating everything to itself as a center. It alone gives certainty, it alone is right, because it has no interest in being right. Everything in the world can be imitated or forged, everything but love. Love can be neither stolen nor imitated; it lives only in the hearts that are able to give themselves wholly. It is the source of all art. To be loved is not happiness. Every man loves himself. To love: That is happiness."

BIOGRAPHICAL/CRITICAL SOURCES: New York Times, November 2, 1969, August 25, 1971; *New York Herald,* June 6, 1971; *New York Record,* September, 1971.

*   *   *

CURTIS, Michael Raymond   1923-

PERSONAL: Born September 11, 1923, in London, England; came to the United States in 1954; son of Philip and Mildred Curtis; married Laura Ann Goldsmith (a university teacher), August 26, 1956; children: Mike, Anthony. *Education:* London School of Economics and Political Science, London, B.Sc., 1951; Cornell University, Ph.D., 1958. *Home:* 294 Western Way, Princeton, N.J. 08540. *Office:* Department of Political Science, Rutgers University, New Brunswick, N.J. 08903.

CAREER: Polytechnic Institute of New York, New York, lecturer, 1951-54; Cornell University, Ithaca, N.Y., assistant professor, 1954-56; Yale University, New Haven, Conn., assistant professor, 1956-58; Connecticut College, New London, visiting professor, 1958-59; Oberlin College, Oberlin, Ohio, visiting professor, 1959-60; University of Massachusetts, Amherst, associate professor, 1960-61; Rutgers University, New Brunswick, N.J., associate professor, 1961-64, professor of political science, 1964—, chairman of department, 1971-74, chairman of West European Studies Group. Lecturer at Johns Hopkins University, University of California, Los Angeles, Princeton University, Naval War College, American University, Northwestern University, State University of New York at Albany, Korea University, Tokyo University, George Washington University, University of Colorado, University of Texas, Towson State University, Pembroke State University, and University of Illinois. Guest on television programs. Member of Conference on British Politics, 1976; member of National Science Foundation behavioral and social sciences panel. Testified before U.S.

Senate Foreign Relations Committee. *Member:* American Political Science Association, American Society for Eighteenth Century Studies. *Awards, honors:* Fulbright grant, 1954.

WRITINGS: Central Government: An Introduction to the British System, Pitman, 1956, 3rd edition, 1970; *Three Against the Third Republic,* Princeton University Press, 1959; (editor) *The Great Political Theories,* Avon, Volume I: *From Plato and Aristotle to Locke and Montesquieu,* 1961, Volume II: *From Burke, Rousseau, and Kant to Modern Times,* 1962; (editor) *The Nature of Politics,* Avon, 1963; *Western European Integration,* Harper, 1965; *Comparative Government and Politics,* Harper, 1968, 2nd edition, 1978; (editor) *The Middle East in the Contemporary World,* American Professors for Peace in the Middle East, 1968.

(With Carl Friedrich and Benjamin Barber) *Totalitarianism in Perspective: Three Views,* Praeger, 1970; (editor) *Marxism,* Atherton, 1970; (editor and contributor) *People and Politics in the Middle East,* Transaction Books, 1971; *Elementi di scienza politica* (title means "Elements of Political Science"), Il Mulino, 1972; (editor) *Israel: Social Structure and Change,* Transaction Books, 1973; *The British Constitution,* Oceana, 1974; *The Palestinians,* Transaction Books, 1975; (editor with Joseph Neyer) *Israel in the Third World,* Transaction Books, 1976; *Supplement to the United Kingdom Constitution,* Oceana, 1978; *Totalitarianism,* Transaction Books, 1979; (contributor) Irving L. Horowitz, editor, *Constructing Policy,* Praeger, 1979; (contributor) Ernest A. Menze, editor, *Totalitarianism Reconsidered,* Kennikat, 1981.

Editor of "Comparative Government and Politics," a series, Harper. Contributor to *Encyclopedia Americana* and *American Oxford Encyclopedia.* Contributor to scholarly journals and newspapers. Member of editorial board of *Society, Polity, Middle East Review,* and *Jerusalem Quarterly.*

WORK IN PROGRESS: A revision of both volumes of *The Great Political Theories;* a book, *Religion and Politics in the Middle East.*

*   *   *

CUTLER, Carl C(uster)   1878-1966

OBITUARY NOTICE—See index for *CA* sketch: Born August 12, 1878, in Kingston, Mich.; died February 20, 1966. Attorney, museum curator, and author. Cutler worked as a law clerk and lawyer in New York City and Seattle, Wash. In 1929 he founded the Marine Historical Association Inc., and was its secretary and marine museum curator for nearly twenty-five years. Cutler helped establish the association's "Mystic Seaport," a replica of a mid-nineteenth-century coastal village. He also studied how the effects of sea trade influenced early America. Cutler's works include *Greyhounds of the Sea: The Story of the American Clipper Ship, Five Hundred Sailing Records of American-Built Ships,* and *Queens of the Western Ocean: The Story of America's Mail and Passenger Lines.* (Date of death provided by the Mystic Marine Museum.)

*   *   *

CUTLER, Carol   1926-

PERSONAL: Born April 25, 1926, in Pittsburgh, Pa.; daughter of John Michael (a plant foreman) and Stella Rataic; married B. J. Cutler (a journalist), March 6, 1948. *Education:* Attended University of Pittsburgh, 1944-48; Carnegie Institute of Technology (now Carnegie-Mellon University), 1946-

47; Hunter College (now of the City University of New York), 1952-53; Sorbonne, University of Paris, 1959-61; Cordon Bleu, 1960-69; Ecole du Louvre, 1965-1966; and Ecole des Trois Gourmande, beginning 1968. *Home:* 2735 P St. N.W., Washington, D.C. 20007.

CAREER: Joseph Horne Co., Pittsburgh, Pa., advertising copywriter, 1948-51; free-lance writer in New York, N.Y., 1951-55; *New York Herald Tribune,* Paris edition, Paris, France, art critic, 1959-69; National Gallery of Art, Washington, D.C., coordinator of summer exhibition, 1970; *Washington Post,* Washington, D.C., author of food column, 1971-73; National Portrait Gallery, Washington, D.C., public affairs officer, 1974-78; writer, 1978—. Worked at restaurant near Geneva, Switzerland. Cultural affairs reporter for WTOP-Radio, 1972-73. Member of Beard-Glaser-Wolf Good Cooking School, 1974—. Member of Paris board of directors of United Service Organization, 1963-69; member of White House task force for study of U.S. representation in foreign art shows, 1970; consultant for International Exhibitions Foundation, 1972; consultant to U.S. Embassy in Paris and Metropolitan Museum. *Member:* Cercle des Gourmettes, Les Dames d'Escoffier (Washington chapter). *Awards, honors:* Tastemaker Award from R. T. French Co., 1976, for *The Six-Minute Souffle and Other Culinary Delights.*

WRITINGS: Haute Cuisine for Your Heart's Delight: A Low Cholesterol Cookbook for Gourmets, C. N. Potter, 1973; *The Six-Minute Souffle and Other Culinary Delights,* C. N. Potter, 1976; *The Woman's Day Low-Calorie Dessert Cookbook,* Houghton, 1980.

European correspondent for *Art in America,* 1961-71. Author of "The Arts," a column in *Kennedy Center,* 1972. Contributor to magazines in the United States, Australia, and Europe, including *Smithsonian, Harper's Bazaar, House and Garden, Washingtonian, Family Circle,* and *American Home,* and newspapers. Contributing editor of *Working Woman,* 1977-79, and *International Review of Food and Wine,* 1978-81.

SIDELIGHTS: Carol Cutler became interested in cooking after she was married. Suddenly, she told Ginger Mudd Galvez of *Food and Fine Living,* she "had an audience." When she and her husband moved to Moscow in 1955, "cooking became important in almost a negative way, because I had so little to work with—a small supply of canned goods and very few fresh ingredients."

From Moscow, Cutler moved to Paris, where she began studying the art of food preparation. She also had the opportunity to eat in restaurants all over France, an experience that she considers a vital part of her education. Her knack for identifying ingredients in the foods she tasted, along with her serious attitude toward the culinary arts, have made her a respected cook and food writer.

She told *CA:* "Generally I am concerned with maintaining high culinary standards by adapting them to today's lifestyle. If good cooking is made manageable, I believe people will eat fewer fast foods and convenience foods."

BIOGRAPHICAL/CRITICAL SOURCES: Food and Fine Living, June, 1978.

*   *   *

CUTLER, William Worcester III   1941-

PERSONAL: Born May 28, 1941, in Boston, Mass.; son of William Worcester, Jr., and Mary (Johnston) Cutler; married Penelope Cope (a teacher), December 28, 1965; children: Julia, Rachel, Rosemary. *Education:* Harvard University, B.A., 1963; Cornell University, Ph.D., 1968. *Office:* The

Graduate School, Temple University, Philadelphia, Pa. 19122.

CAREER: Temple University, Philadelphia, Pa., assistant professor, 1968-77, associate professor of history and education, 1977—, assistant dean of graduate school, 1979-80, associate dean, 1980—. Guest of radio programs. *Member:* American Studies Association (mid-Atlantic chapter vice-president, 1973-75, president, 1975-77), Organization of American Historians, Fellows in American Studies (vice-president, 1977-78), History of Education Society, Oral History Association. *Awards, honors:* Award from *American Quarterly,* 1972, for article "Status, Values, and the Education of the Poor: The Trustees of the New York Public School Society, 1805-1853."

WRITINGS: (Editor with Howard Gillette, Jr., and contributor) *The Divided Metropolis: Social and Spatial Dimensions of Philadelphia, 1800-1975,* Greenwood Press, 1980. Contributor of articles and reviews to history and education journals.

WORK IN PROGRESS: The Environment of American Education, "which will examine the way Americans have designed and used school environments," publication expected in 1984.

SIDELIGHTS: William Cutler told *CA:* "In America today most people believe that better schoolhouses mean better schools. Educators support this view no less than laymen do. In fact, the educational establishment is in part responsible for the assumptions that we make about the efficacy of the physical environment in the educational process. From the time of Horace Mann, teachers and school administrators have sought suitable facilities in the name of better teaching and learning.

"But the underlying assumption—that better schoolhouses mean better education—remains unproven. It is not clear at all what, if any, relationship exists between the where and the how of education. If this relationship is to be understood, what must be established first is how we came to regard the environment of education as so important. Beginning with the work of the common school reformers and extending to the present, I intend to do that."

*   *   *

CUTUL, Ann-Marie 1945-

PERSONAL: Born November 12, 1945, in Eskilstuna, Sweden; came to the United States in 1966; daughter of Ragnar (a civil engineer) and Ingegerd (Deurell) Bergholtz; married Anton Cutul (a contractor), May 6, 1978; children: Christian Carl. *Education:* Attended University of Stockholm, 1965-66; Pace University, B.A. (cum laude), 1971; Pratt Institute, M.L.S., 1973. *Religion:* Protestant. *Home:* 261 East 239th St., Bronx, N.Y. 10470.

CAREER: Pratt Institute Library, Brooklyn, N.Y., instructor, 1973-78, assistant professor, 1978. *Member:* Art Libraries Society of North America, Beta Phi Mu.

WRITINGS: (Editor) *Twentieth-Century European Painting: A Guide to Information Sources,* Gale, 1980.

SIDELIGHTS: Ann-Marie Cutul commented: "I am fluent in Swedish, French, and German. I grew up in Sweden, specializing in languages.

"My book is an annotated bibliographic guide to well-known artists and movements associated with the twentieth century. It emphasizes material in the English language and includes books, exhibition catalogs, special issues of periodicals, and

theses and dissertations, but it contains no periodical articles. It is selective in that it focuses upon up-to-date and reliable writings. The cut-off date for inclusion of material was July, 1977.

"I encountered several problems while working on this project. The most immediate one was the publisher's request that English-language material be emphasized. Many artists, including major ones such as Umberto Boccioni, Carlo Carra, and August Macke, have been poorly documented in English, as have been many Italian and French abstract artists, minor French Fauves and naive painters.

"Also, the abundance of material and artists to be considered for inclusion in the bibliography made it particularly difficult to accommodate the publisher's request that the manuscript not exceed 300 pages. A compromise was reached, and the final page number turned out to be 520.

"There were also many technical problems. There were variations of artists' names to deal with. Some artists, such as Mondrian, have had their names anglicized, while others, such as Kadinsky and Jawlensky, have had theirs transliterated. Still others, such as Hundertwasser, use pseudonyms. One version of an artist's name had to be established in the bibliography. Also, some artists' birthdates are surrounded by uncertainty or disagreement. The British vorticist Wyndham Lewis has been given three different birthdates by recognized authorities.

"As for all bibliographers, the most frustrating problem was the feeling of racing against time. New material on modern painting was constantly being published, and after a cut-off date was set, the editor struggled to publish a bibliography that was as up-to-date as possible but also correct and accurate. An effort was made to include all foreign accents and diacritical marks throughout the text, and these had to be applied by hand for the camera-ready copy at the publisher's."

*   *   *

CYR, Don(ald Joseph) 1935-

PERSONAL: Born February 17, 1935, in Cohoes, N.Y.; son of Donald Joseph, Sr., and Rita Cyr; married Joan Aili Helf, November 16, 1957; children: Cathy Ann, Bobby. *Education:* State University of New York College at New Paltz, B.S., 1957; Columbia University, M.A., 1959, Ed.D., 1965. *Home:* 80 Pound Ridge Rd., Cheshire, Conn. 06410. *Office:* Department of Art and Art History, Southern Connecticut State College, 501 Crescent St., New Haven, Conn. 06515.

CAREER: High school teacher of art and mechanical drawing in Levittown, N.Y., 1957-58; woodworking teacher at public schools in Edgewater, N.J., 1959-60; New Jersey State College, Jersey City, assistant professor of art, 1960-67; Southern Connecticut State College, New Haven, assistant professor of art, 1967—. Artist and photographer, with international exhibitions and solo shows in New York, New Jersey, Pennsylvania, and Italy; visiting artist for Connecticut Commission on the Arts, 1975 and 1976. *Member:* National Art Education Association, Society for Photographic Education (member of board of directors, 1972-76). *Awards, honors:* Visiting artist grant from Ziff-Davis Publications, 1975.

WRITINGS: Complete Photo-Course Handbook, Omega Arts, 1974; *Teaching Your Children Photography,* Amphoto, 1977; *Basic Darkroom Guide,* SanSem Publications, 1980. Author of "Turn Your Kid on to Photography" and "Kids and Kameras," series in *Popular Photography,* 1975-78. Contributor of more than one hundred fifty articles and photographs (including magazine covers) to periodicals, including *Petersen's Photographic, Popular Photography, Invitation to Photography, Design, Everyday Art, Ceramics Monthly,* and *Art Education.* Editor of *Spectrum* (newsletter of the Society for Photographic Education, New York City Region), 1973-76; contributing editor of *Popular Photography,* 1976-79; member of editorial advisory board of *Arts and Activities,* 1977-79.

WORK IN PROGRESS: Advanced Darkroom Guide, for SanSem Publications; a series of articles on photography.

SIDELIGHTS: Don Cyr commented: "Writing, for me, has always been a chore. As a visually oriented person (that kind of human animal now considered to be a 'right brain' creature), any required verbalization, especially in the form of writing, produced nothing short of a crisis. My limited attitude got me through most of my schooling, until that fatal day when I came face to face with a graduate dissertation. In no way could that verbal ordeal be turned into a visual project. Submitting to the system was a must.

"The strain and exertion of that ordeal eventually helped to break down my inhibitions to the point where the painfulness of my writing labors turned into pleasure. Making the inevitable journey from the right brain to the left, and having become comfortable with the terrain, traveling back and forth over that biological chasm has become more natural.

"It was because of this experience that I decided to make every effort to help demystify the visual (right side of the brain) activities that the vast majority of 'left brain' people find so difficult to deal with. In a practical way, I have tried to encourage the verbal majority to venture into unknown visual territories. We were meant to use both sides of the brain with equal facility. Unfortunately, our educational system tends to separate rather than consolidate functions."

*   *   *

CYR, John Edwin 1915-

PERSONAL: Born October 6, 1915, in Missoula, Mont.; son of John E. (a banker) and Alma (Krest) Cyr; married Joan Tuttle (a real estate executive), October 17, 1964; children: Gay Denise Cyr Jacobs, Suzanne Cyr Peluso, Joan Cyr Armstrong. *Education:* University of California, Berkeley, Real Estate Certificate, 1959. *Politics:* Libertarian. *Home:* 4466 Denby Lane, Stockton, Calif. 95207. *Office:* John Cyr, Realtors, Inc., 840 North El Dorado St., Stockton, Calif. 95201.

CAREER: City of Stockton, Calif., deputy assessor, 1940-42; Bank of Stockton, Stockton, assistant trust officer, 1942-44; Sims & Grupe (realtors), Stockton, sales manager, 1946-59; John Cyr, Realtors, Inc., Stockton, president, 1959—. President of Stockton Board of Realtors, 1964; member of board of governors of Farm and Land Institute, 1972—; member of University of California Presidents Real Estate Research and Education Advisory Committee, 1973—; vice-chairman of City of Stockton Community Development Committee, 1978-79. *Military service:* U.S. Navy, storekeeper, 1944-46. *Member:* National Association of Realtors (member of board of directors, 1976-78), California Association of Realtors (honorary lifetime director, 1969—, master instructor emeritus, 1978—, education chairman), Stockton Commercial-Exchange Club (president, 1979). *Awards, honors:* Named realtor of the year, 1964, by Stockton, California Board of Realtors; award from *Farm and Land Realtor,* 1974, for article "Soils + Management = Success"; named Farm and Land Broker for California by the California chapter of Farm and Land Institute, 1977.

WRITINGS: Training and Supervising Real Estate Salesmen, Prentice-Hall, 1973; *Psychology of Motivation and Persuasion in Real Estate Selling,* Prentice-Hall, 1975. Contributor to *Real Estate Review.* Contributing chairman of editorial board of *Farm and Land Journal.*

WORK IN PROGRESS: A book with Joan M. Sobeck, tentatively titled *Opening a Successful Real Estate Brokerage,* publication by Real Estate Education expected in 1981; research on real estate brokerage ownership sharing plans.

SIDELIGHTS: Cyr commented: "Graduating from high school in 1933 and coming from a rather poor family prevented me from going to college; hence, education has always been a consuming desire of mine. After entering the real estate business in 1946, I decided to devote my extra efforts (outside of earning a living) to the advancement and study of real estate education. Eventually I acquired a State of California Community College Teaching Credential in real estate, and then went into writing on real estate subjects."

D

DALY, Robert Welter 1916-1975

OBITUARY NOTICE—See index for *CA* sketch: Born March 13, 1916, in Chicago, Ill.; died September, 1975. Educator, historian, editor, and author. Daly taught at the U.S. Coast Guard Academy and at the U.S. Naval Academy. As a professor of history, he wrote several books on naval history, including *How the Merrimac Won: The Strategic Story of the C.S.S. Virginia, Age of Responsibility,* and *Raphael Semmes, Confederate Admiral.* Daly also edited *Aboard the U.S.S. Florida: The Letters of Paymaster William Frederick Keeler, U.S. Navy, to His Wife, Anne,* and *William Frederick Keeler: Aboard the U.S.S. Monitor, 1862, Letters to His Wife, Anne.* Among the author's fictional works are *Broadsides, To the Vigilant,* and *Guns of Roman Nose.* Obituaries and other sources: *Directory of American Scholars,* Volume I: *History,* 6th edition, Bowker, 1974. (Date of death provided by wife, Mary Kennedy Daly.)

* * *

DANIEL, Price, Jr. 1941-1981

OBITUARY NOTICE: Born June 8, 1941, in Austin, Tex.; died from gunshot wounds, January 19, 1981, in Liberty, Tex. Lawyer, state representative, book collector, and author. The son of Supreme Court Judge Price Daniel, Sr., Daniel at thirty-one was among the youngest men ever elected Speaker of the House of Representatives of Texas. In addition, he was an avid collector and seller of rare books and published numerous catalogues as reference tools to which other collectors and buyers could look for information concerning antique books. Daniel's wife admitted to shooting him. Obituaries and other sources: *Who's Who in Government,* Marquis, 1975; *AB Bookman's Weekly,* March 2, 1981.

* * *

DAVIDSON, Alan Eaton 1924-

PERSONAL: Born March 30, 1924, in Londonderry, Northern Ireland; son of William John (a civil servant) and Constance (Eaton) Davidson; married Jane Macatee, June 28, 1951; children: Caroline, Pamela, Jennifer. *Education:* Queen's College, Oxford, M.A. (with first class honors), 1948. *Home:* 45 Lamont Rd., World's End, London SW10 0HU, England. *Agent:* A. P. Watt Ltd., 26/28 Bedford Row, London WC1R 4HL, England.

CAREER: British Diplomatic Service, 1948-75, served in Foreign Office, London, then as private secretary to British ambassador in Washington, D.C., 1950-53, in The Hague, Netherlands, 1953-55, in Cairo, Egypt, 1959-60, and in Tunis, Tunisia, 1961-64; head of Central Department of Foreign Office, 1967-68; political counselor in United Kingdom delegation to NATO, 1968-71; head of Defense Department of Foreign and Commonwealth Office, 1972-73; British ambassador in Vientiane, Laos, 1973-75; Oxford University, Oxford, England, senior associate member of St. Antony's College, 1978—, Alastair Horne Research Fellow, 1978-79. Partner of Prospect Books. *Military service:* Royal Naval Volunteer Reserve, 1942-46; became lieutenant. *Member:* Society of Authors. *Awards, honors:* Commander of Order of St. Michael and St. George, 1974.

WRITINGS: Mediterranean Seafood, Penguin, 1972, 2nd edition, Louisiana State University Press, 1981; *Fish and Fish Dishes of Laos,* Tuttle, 1975; *Seafood of South-East Asia,* Federal Publications (Singapore), 1977; (editor of abridgement and translator, with wife, Jane Davidson) Alexandre Dumas, *Dumas on Food,* Folio Society, 1978; *North Atlantic Seafood,* Macmillan, 1979, Viking Penguin, 1980; *Science in the Kitchen,* Penguin, 1982. Contributor to magazines, including *Virginia Quarterly Review* and *American Scholar.*

WORK IN PROGRESS: The Oxford Companion to Food, publication by Oxford University Press expected in 1984; *Something Bigger Still,* a novel.

SIDELIGHTS: Davidson told *CA:* "I have written a novel, *Something Quite Big,* about the North Atlantic Treaty Organization and environmental problems. I was in the Birtish Diplomatic Service when I wrote it, and had to seek permission for publication. This was withheld, but anonymous copies have been in private circulation.

"I started to take a serious interest in seafood in Tunis in 1961, since the fish there were so good but difficult to identify. There being no book on the subject, I wrote a primitive little handbook on it myself and sold it for charity. It made several hundred dollars for the Tunisian Red Crescent, and I've kept up the tradition ever since by having the first edition or first impression of my fish books devoted to a charitable cause. What would quite possibly have been only a passing interest developed into a real hobby when Penguin Books asked me to expand my booklet on Tunisian fish into *Mediterranean Seafood.* I then developed the pattern I have followed in these books: the first half is natural history, the second half recipes. I think that many cookbook readers like to have more than just recipes; they enjoy background material about the foodstuffs and welcome being told whence recipes come.

"I'm a strong believer in giving credit to people who help with recipes and to other books that have aided my research. I think that the bibliography of *North Atlantic Seafood* may be the longest ever in a cookbook (seventeen pages of fine print, covering works in fourteen languages). I also like to put in quirkish recipes and anecdotes which appeal to me. My (American) wife Jane takes care that the proportion of practical recipes remains high enough to satisfy most people.

"Work in the Diplomatic Service was hard but enjoyable. At one time in London I worked seven days a week for fourteen straight weeks, sometimes with only a few hours sleep. This kind of pace ruled out much writing. Laos was different. Plenty to do, but not too much. Marvellous people, perhaps the most beautiful in the world, and certainly among the most amiable. I wrote two books there, and I could see that I'd never have it so good again if I stayed in the Service. So I left ten years early to become a full-time writer.

"I want to do more seafood books, but also to branch out into other aspects of writing about food. Hence the *Oxford Companion to Food,* which will cover them all on a global basis, not just concentrating on western Europe and North America. I'm also trying to promote the academic study of the history of foods and of cookery books. With Elizabeth David, my main source of inspiration, and others I set up a pigmy publishing concern called Prospect Books. We publish a journal (in English, although called *Petits Propos Culinaires*) which has a fair number of subscribers on both sides of the Atlantic. We've also started publishing books and have quite a few coming up, including what will become the definitive bibliographies of English-language cookery books. I love dealing with that sort of thing.

"Publishing has really taken the place of the Diplomatic Service as 'the other half' of my life. I reckon that a writer needs to have some other demanding activity. I don't get much written unless I have to struggle to find the time for it. Since Prospect Books has no staff, no premises, no telephone, no nothing (except for superb authors and a very distinguished U.S. distributor, the University Press of Virginia), the struggle is just about guaranteed for the foreseeable future.

"I'm strongly interested in environmental problems. My clandestine novel about them and NATO has a serious purpose, although it's handled lightly. Most of my colleagues in the Diplomatic Service loved it, but not those close up at the top, who deemed it irreverent. I suppose it was, but they'd really missed the point. I have another novel ready for birth, *Something Bigger Still,* but it's not as funny."

BIOGRAPHICAL/CRITICAL SOURCES: International Herald Tribune, November 26, 1974, November 4-5, 1978; *New York Times,* May 9, 1979, July 2, 1980; *Quest,* February, 1980.

*   *   *

DAVIES, D(avid) Jacob   1916-1974

OBITUARY NOTICE—See index for *CA* sketch: Born September 5, 1916; died February 11, 1974. Clergyman, educator, actor, broadcaster, translator, poet, editor, columnist, and author. Davies served as a minister for several years in addition to teaching at the University of Wales. The author of thousands of radio scripts, he also acted in and hosted many radio and television shows. He translated English works into

Welsh and wrote books in both languages. His works include *Cerddi'r Ddau Frawd* (title means "Songs of Two Brothers"), *Plwm Pwdin, A City Set on a Hill, The New Beginning,* and a volume of poetry, *Y mynydd teimladwy.* He edited the book, *History of the Old Meeting House* in addition to the magazines *Yr Ymofynnydd* (title means "The Inquirer") and *Pensioner of Wales.* Davies was also a columnist for *Welshman.* (Date of death provided by wife, Ann Lee Davies.)

*   *   *

DAVIES, Piers (Anthony David)   1941-

PERSONAL: Born June 15, 1941, in Sydney, Australia; son of Ernest Richard Lasham (an army officer) and Mary (a secretary; maiden name, McDougall) Davies; married Margaret Elaine Haswell (a teacher), August 24, 1973; children: Gretchen. *Education:* University of Auckland, LL.B., 1964; City of London College, diploma in English and comparative law, 1967. *Home:* 16 Crocus Pl., Remuera, Auckland 5, New Zealand.

CAREER: Admitted as a barrister in New Zealand, 1965, solicitor, 1968. Russell McVeagh & Co., Auckland, New Zealand, law clerk, 1959-65; intern at Lord Ilford's chambers, Inner Temple, London, England, 1966-67; associate solicitor with William Jordon, Auckland, 1968-69; Jordan, Smith & Davies (barristers and solicitors), Auckland, partner, 1970—. Poet, playwright, and author of film scripts; director of Phase Three Film Productions Ltd. Member of National Council of Churches' Church and Society Commission. Member of supervising committee of Grey Lynn Neighbourhood Law Office, 1977-80, chairman, 1979-80.

MEMBER: International Law Association (member of executive council of Australian branch, 1976—), International Poetry Society (fellow), Workshop New Poetry (New Zealand representative, 1967—), Auckland Law Society (coordinator of Citizens Advice Bureaux Legal Services, 1979—). *Awards, honors:* Best film award from Australian Film Institute, 1971, for "Homesdale"; silver plaque from Chicago Film Festival, 1974, for "The Cars That Ate Paris"; Bruce Elliot Memorial Award from Auckland Law Society and Bruce Elliot Trust, 1978, for Citizens Advice Bureaux Legal Services.

WRITINGS: Day Trip From Mount Meru (poetry), Ophir Press, 1969; *Deus Vult* (poetry), Ophir Press, 1971; (editor) *Central Almanac,* Central Press, 1974; "Diaspora" (one-act play; first produced in Auckland, New Zealand, at Central Theatre, 1974; "Bourgeois Homage to Dada" (cabaret), first produced in Auckland at Central Theatre, 1974.

Films: (Co-author) "Homesdale," Richard Brennan, 1971; (co-author) "The Cars That Ate Paris," Salt Pan Films, 1974; (co-author) "Skin Deep," Phase Three Films, 1978; "R. V. Huckleberry Finn," Alternative Cinema, 1979.

WORK IN PROGRESS: "Driving Force," a feature film; a video documentary on alternatives to prison; "The Lamb of God," a short film (black comedy).

SIDELIGHTS: Davies commented: "Although I have written films and poetry over the last fifteen years, the recent emphasis has been more heavily on film and video because of the great filmmaking boom in Australia in the early 1970's and New Zealand in the late 1970's."

*   *   *

DAVIS, Joe Lee   1906-1974

OBITUARY NOTICE—See index for *CA* sketch: Born February 22, 1906, in Lexington, Ky.; died of a heart attack,

February 19, 1974; buried in Lexington, Ky. Educator, editor, poet, and author. Davis taught at the University of Kentucky before moving to the University of Michigan, where he stayed for more than twenty-five years. He was also a consulting editor to Charles Scribner's Sons Publishers. His works include a volume of poetry, *Boyhood Dreams,* and the books *James Branch Cabell* and *The Sons of Ben: Jonsonian Comedy in Caroline England.* Obituaries and other sources: *Who Was Who in America,* 6th edition, Marquis, 1976. (Cause of death provided by wife, Lorene B. Davis.)

* * *

DAVIS, Louise Littleton

PERSONAL: Born in Paris, Tenn.; daughter of Grover C. (an army officer) and LaRue L. (a music teacher; maiden name, Littleton) Davis. *Education:* Attended Washington University, St. Louis, Mo.; received A.B. from Murray State University; received M.A. from Vanderbilt University; further study at University of North Carolina. *Religion:* Episcopal. *Home:* 2118 Ashwood Ave., Nashville, Tenn. 37212. *Office:* 1100 Broadway, Nashville, Tenn. 37202.

CAREER: Tennessean (newspaper), Nashville, Tenn., feature writer, 1950—. *Member:* Association for the Preservation of Virginia Antiquities, Tennessee Press Association, Tennessee Historical Society (vice-president), Tennessee Botanical Gardens and Fine Arts Center, Ladies Hermitage Association, Nashville Symphony Association, Blount Mansion Association. *Awards, honors:* Named woman of the year, Nashville, Tenn., 1953; historical achievement award from Metropolitan Nashville and Davidson County Historical Commission, 1974.

WRITINGS: Snowball Fight in the White House, Westminster Press, 1974; *Frontier Tales of Tennessee,* Pelican, 1976; *More Tales of Tennessee,* Pelican, 1978; (with John Egerton) *Nashville: The Faces of Two Centuries, 1780-1980,* Plus Media, 1979. Also author of the short histories *Children's Museum of Nashville,* 1973, and *The First Seventy-Five,* 1978. Member of board of editorial advisers, *Tennessee Historical Quarterly,* 1975—.

WORK IN PROGRESS: Stories of Nashville history.

SIDELIGHTS: Louise Davis told *CA* that newspaper assignments concerning international relations and business have taken her to the Caribbean and to most parts of Europe. Areas of personal interest, she said, are Tennessee business and the state's influence abroad.

Language is another of Davis's interests. She is "enthusiastic about Latin and its influence on the French and English languages." However, her "greatest fascination" is with the English language and with European and American history.

* * *

DAVIS, Monte 1949-

PERSONAL: Born November 6, 1949, in Dallas, Tex.; son of Robert Thomas and Dorothy (Crane) Davis; married Selby Lane Beebe, May 7, 1977 (divorced, 1980). *Education:* Attended Princeton University, 1966-67, 1968-69; Sarah Lawrence College, B.A., 1971. *Home:* 31 Washington St., Brooklyn, N.Y. 11201. *Office: Discover,* Time and Life Building, Rockefeller Center, New York, N.Y. 10020.

CAREER: Dalton School, New York City, teacher of literature and math, 1968-71; American School of Florence, Florence, Italy, teacher of history and science, 1971-72; freelance science writer, 1972-78; *Omni,* New York City, contributing editor, 1978-80; *Discover,* New York City, staff

writer, 1980—. Chairman of Brooklyn Loft Tenants, 1979—; science consultant to television and film industries. *Member:* National Association of Science Writers.

WRITINGS: (Contributor) R. A. Marshall, editor, *Great Events of the Twentieth Century,* Reader's Digest Press, 1977; (with Alexander Woodcock) *Catastrophe Theory,* Dutton, 1978.

WORK IN PROGRESS: A biography of mathematician John von Neumann, publication by Holt expected in 1982; a children's fantasy; continuing research on applied mathematics and history of mathematics and physics.

SIDELIGHTS: Davis commented: "Study with Joseph Campbell led me, when I later turned to science writing, to apply methods from comparative literature and mythology to the way science works. It's a truism to point out that scientists are human; what is not so obvious is that their choices of experiments and explanatory theories are shaped by many things besides logic and the desire for simplicity. Ideas of how the stars work and how our minds work have a life of their own, just like religious traditions or literary conventions.

"At first, I pursued science writing rather than science itself simply because I was interested in *all* the sciences, and I preferred the risks of dilettantism to the narrowing of interest that usually accompanies specialization. Now I think what I do matters because science matters, and because if the nonscientific public doesn't understand what it can and can't do, we won't survive this century. We can't afford to regard scientists as villains or saviors, and we can't afford to attack or defend their work from ignorance."

* * *

DEANE, Elisabeth
See BEILENSON, Edna

* * *

deFONTAINE, Wade Hampton 1893-1969

*OBITUARY NOTICE—*See index for *CA* sketch: Born September 22, 1893; died August 24, 1969, in Stamford, Conn. Stockbroker, editor, and author. A stockbroker for twenty-five years, Wade deFontaine also served as associate editor of *Yachting.* "Gadgets and Gilhickies," a column deFontaine wrote for the magazine, was also the title of one of his books. Among his other books on boating are *Boatowner's Handibook* and *Young Sportsman's Guide to Sailing.* Obituaries and other sources: *New York Times,* August 26, 1969.

* * *

de GUNZBURG, Nicholas
See GUNZBURG, Nicholas de

* * *

de HAMEL, Joan Littledale 1924-

PERSONAL: Born March 31, 1924, in London, England; daughter of Humphrey Rivers (a medical practitioner) and Eleanor (Littledale) Pollock; married Francis de Hamel (a professor of medicine), April 24, 1948; children: Michael, Christopher, William, Richard, Quentin. *Education:* Lady Margaret Hall, Oxford, B.A. (with honors), 1944, M.A., 1949. *Religion:* Church of England. *Home:* 26 Howard St., Macandrew Bay, Dunedin, New Zealand. *Agent:* A. P. Watt Ltd., 26/28 Bedford Row, London WC1R 4HL, England; and Dorothy Butler, Takapuna, Auckland, New Zealand.

CAREER: Teacher of languages at girls' preparatory school in Hemel Hempstead, England, 1944-45; senior teacher of modern languages at a school in London, England, 1945-48; part-time writer, 1948-67; Dunedin Teachers College, Dunedin, New Zealand, lecturer in French, 1967-78; writer, 1978—. *Member:* International P.E.N., New Zealand Association of Language Teachers. *Awards, honors:* Esther Glen Medal from New Zealand Library Association, 1979, for *Take the Long Path.*

WRITINGS—Juveniles: *"X" Marks the Spot,* Lutterworth, 1973; *Take the Long Path,* Lutterworth, 1978.

Also author of scripts, including "To Chartes in Three Hours," produced by British Broadcasting Corp. (BBC), "Mr. Timms and Mr. Mott," BBC, and "The Chaubord Omelette," produced by New Zealand Broadcasting Corp. Contributor to magazines. Editor of *Polyglot.*

WORK IN PROGRESS: *Te Marama,* a children's novel; *Hemi's Pet,* a children's story book; writing for children's television programs, including a serial.

SIDELIGHTS: Joan de Hamel commented: "I wrote for myself from early childhood, for money after marriage, and sold most of it. I emigrated to New Zealand in 1955 and turned mostly to radio writing. When my fifth son was at kindergarten, I began my first full-length novel, and in 1978, at last, became a full-time writer.

"Life has been full of action, interest, and travel. My particular interest is natural history, which has inspired the majority of my work. *"X" Marks the Spot* was based on personal experiences, lost in the bush. *Take the Long Path* is about penguins on Otago Peninsula."

AVOCATIONAL INTERESTS: Art, especially French art, history, literature, education.

* * *

DELL, Edmund 1921-

PERSONAL: Born August 15, 1921, in London, England; son of Reuben and Frances Dell; married Susanne Gottschalk, 1963. *Education:* Queen's College, Oxford, B.A. and M.A. (with first class honors), both 1947. *Home:* 4 Reynolds Close, London NW11 7EA, England.

CAREER: Oxford University, Queen's College, Oxford, England, lecturer in modern history, 1947-49; Imperial Chemical Industries Ltd., Manchester, England, executive, 1949-63; Victoria University of Manchester, Manchester, Simon research fellow, 1963-64; government of England, London, Labour member of Parliament for Birkenhead, 1964-79, parliamentary secretary to Ministry of Technology, 1966-67, joint parliamentary under-secretary of state in Department of Economic Affairs, 1967-68, minister of state at Board of Trade, 1968-69, and Department of Employment and Productivity, 1969-70, paymaster general, 1974-76, secretary of state for trade, 1976-78; Guinness Peat Group, London, England, chairman and chief executive, 1979—. Chairman of Channel Four Television Co. Ltd., 1980—. Member of Manchester City Council, 1953-60; president of Manchester and Salford Trades Council, 1958-61. Chairman of Public Accounts Committee, 1973-74; member of Committee of Three appointed by European Council to review procedures of the European Economic Community, 1978-79. *Military service:* British Army, Royal Artillery (Anti-Tank), 1941-45; became lieutenant. *Awards, honors:* Named boys' chess champion of London, 1936; Privy Council, 1970.

WRITINGS: (Editor with Christopher Hill) *The Good Old Cause: The English Revolution of 1640-60,* Lawrence, 1949;

Political Responsibility and Industry, Allen & Unwin, 1973. Contributor to scholarly journals.

* * *

DELORME, Andre
See JULIEN, Charles-Andre

* * *

DELUPIS, Ingrid 1939-
(Ingrid Detter, Ingrid Doimi di Delupis)

PERSONAL: Born November 24, 1939, in Stockholm, Sweden; daughter of Nils (a barrister and judge) and Thyra (a writer; maiden name, Hellberg) Detter; married Louis Delupis (a banker and barrister), April, 1968; children: Paola, Peter, Christina, Nicholas, Lawrence. *Education:* University of Stockholm, LL.B., 1958, LL.M., 1965, J.D., 1965; University of Turin, diploma in European law, 1960; University of Paris, Lic. en Droit, 1960; Oxford University, D. Phil., 1962. *Religion:* Roman Catholic. *Home:* 10 Wellington Court, Knightsbridge, London SW1X 7PL, England. *Office:* 1 Hare Court, Temple, London, E.C.4, England.

CAREER: University of Stockholm, Stockholm, Sweden, associate professor of international law, 1965-68; professor of the law of economic integration for Swedish State Council for Research, 1968-74; University of Uppsala, Uppsala, Sweden, professor of international law, 1974-76; called to the English Bar (Middle Temple), 1977; barrister in London, England, 1977—. Visiting professor at University of Melbourne, 1966; lecturer at London School of Economics and Political Science, London, 1974-75. *Member:* Royal Institute of International Affairs. *Awards, honors:* Fellow of St. Antony's College, Oxford, 1963-64; fellow of Lady Margaret Hall, 1964-68.

WRITINGS—Under name Ingrid Detter: *Law Making by International Organizations,* Norstedt, 1965; *Essays on the Law of Treaties,* Sweet & Maxwell, 1967.

Under name Ingrid Doimi di Delupis: *The East African Community,* Longmans, Green, 1970.

Under name Ingrid Delupis: *Finance and Protection of Investments in Developing Countries,* Gower Press, 1973; *International Law and the Independent State,* Gower Press, 1974; *Bibliography of International Law,* Gower Press, 1974, Bowker, 1975; *International Adoptions and the Conflict of Laws,* Almqvist & Wiksell, 1976; *Ekonomisk Integration* (title means "Economic Integration"), Almqvist & Wiksell, 1976. Contributor to law journals.

WORK IN PROGRESS: A general treatise on the law of the sea.

SIDELIGHTS: Delupis told *CA:* "I have specialized in such fields as the theory of international organizations (their structure and powers), economic integration, the law of treaties (their formation and legal effect), and the law of nationalization. I also specialize in the field of conflict of laws, especially in questions regarding recognition and legal effect of foreign adoptions and the status of the adopted child. I am now active as barrister in international cases bearing on public international law and conflict of laws."

* * *

de MANDIARGUES, Andre Pieyre
See PIEYRE de MANDIARGUES, Andre

DENKSTEIN, Vladimir 1906-

PERSONAL: Born February 3, 1906, in Dobrany, Czechoslovakia; son of Zdislav and Bozena (Vojtechovska) Denkstein; married Zdenka Vondraskova (an official), September 16, 1940; children: Tomas, Ondr ej. *Education:* Attended University of Warsaw and University of Krakow, both 1928-29; Charles University, Ph.D., 1932. *Home:* 9 Kyjevska, Prague 6, Czechoslovakia.

CAREER: Institute of Art History, Prague, Czechoslovakia, assistant instructor in art history, 1930-32; Regional Museum, Ceske Budejovice, Czechoslovakia, assistant curator, 1932-40; National Museum, Prague, assistant curator in department of historical archaeology, 1940-45, curator, 1945-56, director of museum, 1956-70, director emeritus, 1970—. Professor at Charles University, 1938-39, 1945-54. Chairman of Czechoslovak national committee of International Museums Council, 1960-69; member of Czechoslovak Central Museums Council, 1959-69. *Member:* International Association for the History of Glass. *Awards, honors:* D.Sc. from the Czechoslovak Academy of Sciences, 1966; distinguished prize for construction from government of Czechoslovakia, 1966.

WRITINGS: South Bohemian Gothic Art, Artia (Prague), 1953; *Pavises of the Bohemian Type,* Acta Musei Nationalis (Prague), Volume I, 1962, Volume II, 1964, Volume III, 1965; *Kresby Va'clava Hollara,* Odeon, 1977, translation by E. Ortovska published as *Hollar Drawings,* Orbis Publishing, 1980; *Great Centers of Art: Prague,* Allanheld & Schram, 1979. Also author of *Great Centers of Art: Prague,* Volume I, 1962, Volume II, 1964, Volume III, 1965. Contributor to scholarly journals.

WORK IN PROGRESS: "Iconographic analysis of attributes in the Romanesque sculptural motif of 'Madonna Enthroned'; a treatise on a caballa solar talisman from the time of Emperor Rudolph II; a treatise on a rare, small, silver figure of a crusader from the thirteenth century."

SIDELIGHTS: Denkstein told *CA:* "The masterworks of artists from fourteenth- and early fifteenth-century Bohemia rank among the greatest in the development of European art. An important collection of South Bohemian Gothic art was placed in the Castle of Hluboka in 1956 by the Ales South Bohemian Gallery. An outstanding and extensive collection of Czech Gothic art, which embraces all the best artifacts, was installed by the National Gallery in 1976 in the former nunnery of the beautiful Premyslide Romanesque basilica of St. George at Prague Castle.

"My former orientation toward Gothic architecture evolved later to Bohemian Gothic sculpture. My latest contribution to this field is an extensive treatise on a group of outstanding sculptures from 1300 to 1450, which are in the collection of the National Museum in Prague.

"I am also deeply attached to the drawings by Vaclav Wenceslas Hollar, a famous European painter and graphic artist of Czech origin. My interest in him resulted in the book *Hollar Drawings,* which contains some new important facts concerning his life and work. The London issue, with a foreword by Professor Michael Kitson, was favorably received by the London press.

"In 1980 I found a gouache miniature of high quality—'The Allegory of Fortuna'—from 1620. I specified it, on the basis of detailed critical analysis of style and contemporary accounts in historical sources, as one of the earliest works of Vaclav Hollar, who even at thirteen was an extraordinarily gifted book miniaturist.''

*   *   *

DENNY-BROWN, Derek Ernest 1901-1981

OBITUARY NOTICE: Born June 1, 1901, in Christchurch, New Zealand; died of cancer, April 20, 1981, in Cambridge, Mass. Neurologist, educator, and author, best known for his research on strokes, cerebral palsy, and Parkinson's disease. A professor of neurology at Harvard for more than twenty-five years and chief neurologist at Boston City Hospital, Denny-Brown introduced the theory that strokes can result from an insufficient supply of blood to the brain and first described the degeneration of nerves in cancer cases. Among his writings are *A Handbook of Neurological Examination and Case Recording, The Basal Ganglia in Relation to Disorders of Movement,* and *Reflex Activity of the Spinal Cord.* Obituaries and other sources: *International Who's Who,* Europa, 1978; *American Men and Women of Science,* 14th edition, Bowker, 1979; *New York Times,* April 23, 1981; *Newsweek,* May 4, 1981; *Time,* May 4, 1981.

*   *   *

de ROO, Anne Louise 1931-

PERSONAL: Born in 1931, in Gore, New Zealand; daughter of William Frederick (a health inspector) and Amy Louisa de Roo. *Education:* University of Canterbury, Christchurch, New Zealand, B.A., 1952. *Home:* 7C Rolleston St., Palmerston North, New Zealand. *Agent:* A. P. Watt & Son, 26-28 Bedford Row, London WC1R 4HL, England.

CAREER: Dunedin Public Library, Dunedin, New Zealand, library assistant, 1956; Dunedin Teachers' College, Dunedin, librarian, 1957-59; governess and part-time gardener in Church Preen, Shropshire, England, 1962-68; secretary in Barkway, Hertfordshire, England, 1969-73; medical typist in Palmerston North, New Zealand, 1974-78; full-time writer, 1978—.

WRITINGS—Juvenile fiction: *The Gold Dog,* Hart-Davis, 1969; *Moa Valley,* Hart-Davis, 1969; *Boy and the Sea Beast,* Hart-Davis, 1971, Scholastic Book Services, 1974; *Cinnamon and Nutmeg,* Nelson, 1974; *Mick's Country Cousins,* Macmillan (London), 1974; *Scrub Fire,* Heinemann, 1977; *Traveller,* Heinemann, 1979; *Because of Rosie,* Heinemann, 1980.

Plays: (With John Schwabe) *The Dragon Master* (children's musical), first produced in Palmerston North, New Zealand, 1978.

WORK IN PROGRESS: The second of two children's books dealing with the rebellion of the Maori chief Hone Heke in 1844-45; a second children's musical in collaboration with John Schwabe.

SIDELIGHTS: Realizing that the fiction of Europe and North America presents settings unnatural to a New Zealand child, Anne de Roo's goal is to create good stories with settings familiar to the children of her native land. De Roo characterizes herself as "a New Zealand writer, principally concerned with the building up in a young country of a children's literature through which children can identify themselves and their roots, whether European or Maori." An added purpose of de Roo's writing is to expose children of other parts of the world to New Zealand culture. "I do delight in having this additional usefulness as well," she writes, "although I will always feel that my chief responsibility is to young New Zealanders."

De Roo spent twelve years in England, where her first five books were written. She regards those years as a period of growth "which enabled me to return with a new perspective and a new and deeper appreciation of the natural beauty of New Zealand's forests, mountains, and sea. It has also given me the opportunity to concentrate in the last few years on historical stories, for which I now have the material available for research."

De Roo feels the need to "branch out from time to time into the realms of fantasy and fairy tale" as an escape from what she terms her "basically European reading and education." She has done this primarily through musical theatre for children. "The theatre is a lifelong love," she says, "and much of my spare time is devoted to amateur theatre, which is particularly strong in a small country with little scope for professional theatre. The spoken word, its sounds and possibilities, has always fascinated me, from youthful poetry writing onwards. Even in books, the dialogue is the part in which I always feel most at home."

*   *   *

DERRICK, Graham
   See RABY, Derek Graham

*   *   *

DETTER, Ingrid
   See DELUPIS, Ingrid

*   *   *

DEWDNEY, John Christopher   1928-

PERSONAL: Born June 8, 1928, in Woodford, England; son of William Alfred (a civil servant) and Irene (Hitchman) Dewdney; married Euphemia Jean Sinclair (a teacher), April 21, 1956; children: Peter John, Nicholas, Alexander. *Education:* University of Edinburgh, M.A. (with first class honors), 1952. *Politics:* Social Democrat. *Religion:* Church of England. *Home:* 48 South St., Durham DH1 4QP, England. *Office:* Department of Geography, Science Laboratories, University of Durham, South Rd., Durham DH1 3LE, England.

CAREER: University of Durham, Durham, England, lecturer, 1953-68, senior lecturer, 1968-71, reader in geography, 1971—. Professor at University of Sierra Leone, 1965-67; governor of Sunderland Polytechnic. *Military service:* Royal Air Force, 1946-48. *Member:* Institute of British Geographers, Geographical Association, British Society for Middle Eastern Studies, Commonwealth Human Ecology Council, Royal Scottish Geographical Society (fellow).

WRITINGS: A Geography of the Soviet Union, Pergamon, 1965, 3rd edition, 1979; (editor) *Durham County and City With Teesside,* British Association, 1970; *Turkey,* Chatto & Windus, 1971; *The U.S.S.R.: Studies in Industrial Geography,* Dawson, Hutchinson, 1976; (editor with D. W. Rhind) *People in Durham: A Census Atlas,* University of Durham, 1976; (with J. I. Clarke, Rhind, and others) *People in Britain: A Census Atlas,* H.M.S.O., 1980; *The U.S.S.R. in Maps,* Hodder & Stoughton, 1981. Contributor to geography and planning journals.

SIDELIGHTS: Dewdney has conducted field work in Malta, Turkey, and the Soviet Union and has traveled widely in Europe and Africa.

DIBBLE, Nancy Ann   1942-
   (Ansen Dibell)

PERSONAL: Born September 8, 1942, in New York, N.Y.; daughter of Ralph M. (a radio engineer) and Barbara (a social worker; maiden name, Waterman) Dibble. *Education:* Keuka College, B.A., 1964; University of Iowa, M.F.A., 1967, M.A., 1973, Ph.D., 1975. *Home and office:* 379 Amazon Ave., Cincinnati, Ohio 45220.

CAREER: High school English teacher in Perth Amboy, N.J., 1964-65; Wesley College, Dover, Del., instructor in English, 1970-71; Keuka College, Keuka Park, N.Y., instructor in English, 1971-74; State University of New York College at Fredonia, assistant professor of English, 1974-75; Northern Kentucky University, Highland Heights, assistant professor of English, 1976-80; free-lance editor and writer, 1980—. *Member:* Mensa, American Association of University Professors, Science Fiction Writers of America.

WRITINGS—Under pseudonym Ansen Dibell: *Pursuit of the Screamer* (science fiction), Daw Books, 1978; *Circle, Crescent, Star* (science fiction), Daw Books, 1981; *Summerfair,* Daw Books, 1981. Contributor of stories (sometimes under pseudonym Ansen Dibell) and poems to magazines, including *Iowa Review, Middle Earth, Louisville Review, Collage, Red Jacket,* and *Midwest Quarterly.*

WORK IN PROGRESS: Deucetown, a western novel.

SIDELIGHTS: Nancy Dibble wrote: "My books are 'alien anthropology'—exploring the nature and interaction of human and nonhuman cultures, with special emphasis on the relationship between emotion and intellect. I have taught popular fiction, especially science fiction and fantasy, on the college level for ten years. This set of courses grew out of my interest in reading and writing in popular genres rather than the reverse.

"All popular fiction is related, as is all human experience, by its understructures of myth, whether intended or unintended by the author. And the subjective experience of anyone else, whether separated from you by time, distance, culture, or merely the fact of inhabiting another body and seeing through another pair of eyes than your own, is finally alien experience. To the degree that popular fiction both reveals the extent of that gap and enables the reader, through imagination, to bridge it, it is of lasting value whatever genre it happens to fall into. However, science fiction and fantasy are the only genres which attempt to deal with this problem of the dual universality and uniqueness of individual experience as one of their primary concerns."

*   *   *

DIBELL, Ansen
   See DIBBLE, Nancy Ann

*   *   *

DICKERSON, Roy Ernest   1886-1965

OBITUARY NOTICE—See index for *CA* sketch: Born April 3, 1886, in Versailles, Ind.; died November 8, 1965. Lawyer, social worker, educator, and author. In addition to lecturing in education at the University of Cincinnati for many years, Roy Dickerson was involved in the field of social health. He held various posts in government agencies and served on both national and local committees on youth, sex education, and family relations. Dickerson contributed articles to magazines, including *Saturday Evening Post* and *Good House-*

keeping, and he wrote such books as *So Youth May Know, Home Study Course in Social Hygiene,* and *How Character Develops.* Obituaries and other sources: *Who Was Who in America,* 4th edition, Marquis, 1968.

*   *   *

DICKINSON, Margaret
   See MUGGESON, Margaret Elizabeth

*   *   *

DICKSON, Helen
   See REYNOLDS, Helen Mary Greenwood Campbell

*   *   *

di DONATO, Georgia   1932-

PERSONAL: Born July 24, 1932, in Seattle, Wash.; daughter of George J. (in business) and Helen C. (an artist; maiden name, Sutherland) Townsend; married Bill di Donato (a film-maker), April 28, 1957; children: Concetta. *Education:* University of Washington, Seattle, B.A., 1954. *Home:* 10603 Bradbury Rd., Los Angeles, Calif. 90064. *Agent:* Harvey Klinger, Inc., 301 West 53rd St., New York, N.Y. 10019.

CAREER: National Broadcasting Co., New York, N.Y., production assistant for "The Today Show," 1956-58; free-lance writer in California, 1958-61; University of California, Los Angeles, production assistant in motion picture and television department, 1961-63; American Broadcasting Co., Hollywood, Calif., researcher and writer for "The Rebus Game," 1963-64, production assistant for "Never Too Young," 1965-66, associate producer of "Dr. Loriene Chase," 1967-68; United Nations Food and Agriculture Organization, Rome, Italy, writer of documentary films, 1968-70; free-lance writer of feature film scripts, 1968-70; Columbia Broadcasting System, Hollywood, advertising manager of film division, BFA Educational Media, 1970-79; free-lance writer, 1979—. Co-owner with husband, Bill di Donato, of Forum Productions.

WRITINGS: Woman of Justice (historical novel), Doubleday, 1980; *Firebrand* (novel), Doubleday, 1982.

Author of "Le Hat" (feature film), released by Forum Productions in 1981.

WORK IN PROGRESS: A contemporary novel.

SIDELIGHTS: Georgia di Donato wrote: "*Woman of Justice* is my first novel. It received good reviews and has been optioned by CBS-TV for a movie-of-the-week. It also appeared in condensation in the British magazine *Fiction for Leisure.*

"The one notable feature of this rather modest debut is that I was a late starter—forty-seven years old when it was published. Writing had been at best a spare-time occupation over the years, while I earned a living at a succession of jobs which were only slightly less hazardous than writing. But a strong show-biz background combined with disciplined hard work and tenacity turned out to be the winning formula. When acceptance (luck) came, I was ready. I feel that when one reaches a certain point in life, the term 'overnight success' doesn't really apply—our whole lives are preparation for that moment when it all comes together. With some of us it just takes a little longer.

"The idea for *Woman of Justice* began to germinate in the mid-sixties, as a premise for a television series. But the timing was wrong. The day of the western was over, said the net-

works. Years passed and eventually the idea emerged as a novel. Now, with the prospect of a television movie, *Woman of Justice* will have come full circle."

*   *   *

DIEL, Paul   1893-

PERSONAL: Born July 8, 1893, in Vienna, Austria; son of Marguerite Diel; married Jane Blum, August 23, 1923. *Education:* Attended secondary school in Vienna, Austria. *Politics:* None. *Religion:* None. *Home:* 31 rue Maurice Ripoche, Paris 14, France.

CAREER: Algemein Hospital, Vienna, Austria, psychotherapist, 1930-37; Laboratoire de Psychobiologie de l'Enfant, Paris, France, psychotherapist, 1945-60; writer, 1947—. Attache to Centre National de la Recherche Scientifique, 1945-63. *Military service:* Volunteer French Army, 1939-41. *Member:* Societe des Gens de Lettres. *Awards, honors:* Prix de l'Academie Francaise, 1956, for *La Peur et l'angoisse.*

WRITINGS—In English translation: *Le Symbolisme dans la mythologie grecque,* Payot, 1952, translation by Vincent Stuart, Micheline Stuart, and Rebecca Folkman published as *Symbolism in Greek Mythology,* Shambhala, 1980.

Other writings: *Psychologie de la motivation* (title means "The Psychology of Motivation"), Presses Universitaires de France, 1947, 3rd edition, Payot, 1978; *La Divinite* (title means "God: Symbol and Meaning"), Presses Universitaires de France, 1950, reprinted, Payot, 1971; *La Peur et l'angoisse* (title means "Fear and Anguish"), Payot, 1956, 3rd edition, 1978; *Les Principes de l'education et de la reeducation* (title means "The Principles of Education and Reeducation"), Delachaux & Niestle, 1961, reprinted, Payot, 1976; *Le Journal d'une psychanalyse* (title means "The Diary of an Analysand"), Plon, 1964; *Psychologie curative et medecine* (title means "Psychotherapy and Medicine"), Delachaux & Niestle, 1968; *Le Symbolisme dans la Bible* (title means "Symbolism in the Bible"), Payot, 1975; (with Jeanine Solotareff) *Le Symbolisme dans l'Evangile de Jean* (title means "Symbolism in the Gospel of John"), Payot, 1981. Writer for French radio programs. Contributor to scholarly journals.

SIDELIGHTS: Diel's books have been translated into Spanish, Portuguese, Greek, English, and Yugoslavian. He wrote that he undertook "intensive philosophical studies as well as a study of Freud with the aim of getting to know myself and to find the meaning of life and how to adapt to it." He also carried on a long correspondence with Albert Einstein, who helped him to enter the Centre National du Recherche Scientifique after World War II. He prefaced his remarks to *CA* by noting that the central theme of all his books is "introspection."

Diel commented: "Intuitive introspection has always been the basis of all psychological thought. Thanks to it, Freud discovered the extra-conscious (at least, part of it). But the problem of all sciences is to establish a method. The problem of psychology is therefore to develop intuitive introspection into a scientific method capable of (a) self-analysis and (b) the analysis of symbolic language in all its forms (dream, psychopathic symptoms, and myth).

"This is of vital importance because if we do not understand mythical symbolism, we either believe that God is a real person, or else dismiss him as an illusion and believe that matter is a sort of God. This would only be of theoretical importance if these false epistomological bases did not lead to false ethical ideas: the meaning of life is to please God (moralism), or the meaning of life is to satisfy all desires indiscriminately (amoralism). Hence the books on symbolism.

"The understanding of dream symbolism leads to self-understanding and thus to self-control. The understanding of psychopathic symptoms leads to the possibility of therapy, of healing both the nervous disorders of the psyche and the up to now undiagnosed, 'banalized' disorders (unscrupulous unleashing of desires, mediocrity, loss of values). Only by establishing the scale of values on a scientific basis can one put life and all vital problems into perspective. This means establishing introspectively the laws of the human psyche and grounding them on their biological foundations. Hence the books on the human psyche, its biological evolution, and on education, the most important function in life, along with self-education.

"*Psychologie de la motivation* exposes the basis of the introspective method of studying our inner motivations and their symbolic expressions (dreams, myths, and psychopathological symptoms). Intuitive, semi-conscious auto-observation is at the bottom of all our knowledge about the human psyche, but it is often morbid. Hence the necessity of its development into a scientific method. Einstein wrote to me: 'I cannot but agree with all you develop relative to your method. I am convinced that it is an illness a la mode to camouflage introspection as the principal source of our psychological knowledge.'

"How else can we apprehend our inner motives, the fundamental cause of our activity? These motives are too often repressed and removed from conscious control, and yet they remain our reasons for acting. They combine in a very precise but hidden calculation of satisfaction, which can be true or false. Its understanding is essential if we want to improve individual and social life.

"Using symbolic language, mythology expresses the deepest working of the human mind in a precise though veiled manner. To understand the psychological significance of this symbolism, one must use a method of analysis that can unlock the true meaning of myths and their symbols: the introspective method is such a system. In *Le Symbolisme dans la mythologie grecque* several famous myths are thus 'translated,' such as Heracles, Dionysius, Oedipus, Jason, and the Theogony. The themes investigated include the appearance of social and sexual perversion in myths, the origin of a psychosomatic understanding of illness, and the significance of the Greek creation myths. The most common symbols that are used to represent the subconscious, the conscious, and the superconscious (or spiritual) processes of the mind are translated according to their psychological significance. Throughout the goal is to elevate psychology to a science by deciphering, accurately and intimately, the symbolic language of myth and thus of the mind.

"The methodology is based on the premise that the central phenomenon of life is desire. Suffering comes from the contrast between desire (what we want) and reality (what is possible and true). Unsatisfied desire, unsatisfied because it is unrealistic, constitutes suffering (anguish). Joy, on the other hand, comes from the harmonizing of multiple desires. This can only happen through the evolution of desire, the transformation of its energies. The hero or heroine represents the spiritualizing impulse and the struggle of the psyche to overcome unrealistic or banalized forms of thought and desire. Within this scheme, divinities symbolize the evolutionary ideal of the human species, the sublime ideal which is sought by the hero.

"*La Peur et l'angoisse* shows that anguish is the central phenomenon in life. It is by no means only a psychopathological phenomenon as is usually thought. All living beings are characterized by a fundamental disquiet (which is the seed of anguish) caused by their dependency (which is the seed of desire) on the outer world, which can be an obstacle to the satisfaction of their vital needs. The biological necessity of overcoming this vital disquiet is the motor of evolution both of the soma and of the psyche. This means a unifying conception of evolution and therefore of life and its meaning.

"On the human level there is a decisive transformation: the obstacle to satisfaction is no longer the outer world but the inner world, the imaginative play on desire. The effort to elucidate and master psychic life becomes the responsibility of man and indicates the direction of human evolution. But on the human level anguish, instead of being a factor of evolution, can become involutive and pathological, creating all the psychic disorders from which men suffer. This pathological anguish, however, can be overcome and dynamically reconverted into joy.

"*La Divinite* holds that the facade of all myths tells the story of how the hero-man, helped by the gods, fights against monsters and demons. The facade is symbolic and has a precise psychological meaning. It is quite impossible to admit that the divinities were a product of vain fabulation as it is historically proved that myths have founded every culture and that the image of the divinities has exerted a profound motivating influence on men. Myths are in fact a pre-scientific vision of man's inner conflict between antagonistic motives. God and the devil are thus seen to be motivating forces in man. This is the basis for a real understanding of the problem of values, imposed neither by God nor by society, but biogenetically immanent in the human psyche.

"*Le Journal d'une psychanalyse* was not written with an eye to being published. It was undertaken to keep a record of the contents of each analytic session so as to profit more fully from the explanations given. We can follow the cure step by step, the struggle against resistance, the successive victories, the gradual behavioral change due to better inner balance. In short, an example of the motivational method of therapy, based not on retrospection but on introspection, on the discovery of our hidden inner motivations.

"Like the Freudian approach, this method explores the subconscious, but with the difference that the predominating factor is shown to be not sexuality but the three drives which make up our psychic life: the material or social drive, the sexual drive, and the evolutionary drive. These drives are often deformed by vain egocentricity which will admit no fault. The analyst must uncover these hidden 'false motivations' and dismantle their false justifications in order to render to the psyche its original spontaneity.

"*Les Principes de l'education et de la reeducation* applies to education and reeducation the science of motives. Education is the most important event in everyone's life. It is the central problem which confronts the individual, the couple, and society. The solution—radically new—is to found education on a biological definition of the origin of values (love and sociability). The foreword was written in 1960 and analyzes the violent defiance which youth opposes to the adult world. Only by becoming able to distinguish, by methodological self-analysis, their false and true needs can adult educators and reeducators respond to the real needs of children and adolescents. They must not be passively adapted to a society itself deformed, but guided towards the meaning of life. The crisis of education has repercussions over life as a whole and expresses a general confusion of the mind. The science of motives detects the precise cause of this confusion and, going beyond ideological prejudices, gives its evolutionary solution.

"Depth psychology has shown that we have an extraconscious psychic functioning, but up to now there was no method capable of fully sounding the intrapsychic depths. Hence the quarrels between the different schools of psychology and the diversity of therapies proposed. The problem dealt with in *Psychologie curative et medecine* is to overcome the diversity of the doctrines which divide psychologists and psychiatrists concerning the method appropriate for healing psychically-ill people.

"The deepest cause of the confusion of our times is our centuries-old misunderstanding of those products of the psyche that have always founded each new culture: myths. This universal language of myths must be understood in conceptual language, the instrument of conscious thought. Without this understanding, man's mind is blocked in false metaphysical problems and their erroneous solutions. *Le Symbolisme dans la Bible* is not a translation of the whole of biblical symbolism, but of Genesis, the Prologue of John, and the Epistles of Paul."

AVOCATIONAL INTERESTS: Football, singing (opera and lieder), chess, mountaineering.

BIOGRAPHICAL/CRITICAL SOURCES: Jeanine Solotareff, *Le Symbolisme dans les reves: Methode de traduction de Paul Diel,* Payot, 1979.

* * *

DILCOCK, Noreen 1907-
(Norrey Ford; Jill Christian, Christian Walford, pseudonyms)

PERSONAL: Born March 28, 1907, in Hull, England; daughter of Robert (a captain in British Merchant Navy) and Esther Ford; married James Louis Christian Dilcock (a district registrar of High Court of Justice), July, 1945. *Education:* Attended convent school in Hull, England. *Politics:* Conservative. *Religion:* Anglican. *Home:* 10 Leigh Close, Leigh Rd., Walsall WS4 2DU, England. *Agent:* Peter Lewin, River House, The Croft, Sudbury, Suffolk, England.

CAREER: Writer, 1946—. Past chairman of Walsall Young Women's Christian Association; press secretary for Walsall Photographic Society. *Member:* Romantic Novelists Association (national chairman, 1963-64; vice-president, 1965—),Walsall Writers Circle (founding president, 1965—; life president, 1978—).

WRITINGS—Novels; under name Norrey Ford; all published by Mills & Boon: *Where Love Is,* 1952; *My Gentle Enemy,* 1952; *The Romantic Heart,* 1953; *Dragon Castle,* 1954; *Mistress of High Trees,* 1955; *The Rainbow in the Spray,* 1956; *Nurse With a Dream,* 1957; *Let Love Abide,* 1957; *Wild Waters,* 1958; *The House of My Enemy,* 1959; *The Far Sweet Thing,* 1960; *Wild Rowan,* 1961; *Doctor in the Dale,* 1966; *Rich Man, Poor Man,* 1968; *The Marriage Tree,* 1969; *Someone Different,* 1970; *The Trouble at Gilmores,* 1972; *Walk Tall Country,* 1973; *Life Most Dear,* 1974; *Call to the Castle,* 1974; *One Hot Summer,* 1974; *The Road of the Eagles,* 1975; *The Love Goddess,* 1976; *Fount of Love,* 1977.

Novels; under pseudonym Jill Christian: *Bid Me to Live,* Jenkins, 1952; *Heart in Waiting,* Jenkins, 1953; *Love in the Morning,* Jenkins, 1954; *Darling Girl,* Jenkins, 1954; *Harvest of the Heart,* Mills & Boon, 1955; *Beyond the Frost the*

Flower, Mills & Boon, 1955; *The Chosen One,* Mills & Boon, 1956; *Summer Shadow,* Mills & Boon, 1958; *This Day and for Ever,* Mills & Boon, 1959; *Lad's Love,* Mills & Boon, 1960; *The Tender Bond,* Mills & Boon, 1961; *The Long Summer Night,* Mills & Boon, 1962; *Castle of the Ravens,* Mills & Boon, 1967; *Snow on the Grass,* Mills & Boon, 1968; *Master of This House,* Mills & Boon, 1970; *Scent of Lemons,* Mills & Boon, 1972.

(Under pseudonym Christian Walford) *The Little Masters* (novel), Hurst & Blackett, 1969. Contributor of about two hundred stories to magazines in England and Europe.

SIDELIGHTS: Noreen Dilcock's novels have been translated into French, German, Italian, Norwegian, Danish, and Finnish, and have been published in Belgium. She wrote: "My interests are in the countryside, wildlife, farming and growing, the sea and small islands. Settings are important in my novels, and I like to share my best personal experiences with my readers. The settings range from north of the Arctic Circle (in *The Long Summer Night*) to Colorado (in *Walk Tall Country*), and include castles on the Rhine and in Wales, wine-growing country along the Moselle in Germany, and marine archaeology in the Mediterranean (in *The Love Goddess*).

"My characters fall truly into real love to create a permanent marriage relationship. I never use pre-marital or extra-marital sex. I write about one-man/one-woman relationships 'till death do us part.'"

AVOCATIONAL INTERESTS: Old houses, old furniture, industrial archaeology, photography.

* * *

DINES, Michael 1916-

PERSONAL: Original surname, Dinerstein; born February 1, 1916, in Manchester, England; son of Gabriel (a butcher) and Miriam (Silverstone) Dinerstein; married Rosemarie Freedman (a company director), March 27, 1951; children: Steve, Gail, Ruth, Jonathon. *Education:* Educated in England. *Politics:* Moderate Conservative. *Religion:* Jewish. *Residence:* Manchester, England.

CAREER: Writer. Designer of gowns in Manchester, England, 1938-39 and 1946-52; owner and director of bookmaker business in Manchester, 1952-76. Consultant on property and business; teacher in adult education. *Military service:* Royal Air Force, 1939-46; became sergeant; received Long Service Medal, Africa Star, and Defence Medal. *Member:* Writers Guild of Great Britain, Screen Writers Guild, Crime Writers Association. *Awards, honors:* Hirshman Esun Zionist Award, 1961.

WRITINGS: Operation: Deadline, R. Hale, 1967; *Operation: To Kill a Man,* R. Hale, 1968; *Operation: To Kill or Be Killed,* R. Hale, 1969; *Abrams and Jones: Homicide,* R. Hale, 1977.

Plays: *The Stranger of Vallenska* (one-act), Evans, 1959; *The Lullaby: A Play in One Act for Four Women,* Samuel French, 1960; *Viva Juarez!* (one-act), Samuel French, 1961; "*Absalom, My Son!*" (one-act), Samuel French, 1961; *The General Reviews the Troops* (one-act), Samuel French, 1963; *The Trial of Harry Man* (one-act comedy), H.R.W. Dean, 1964.

Also author of short stories, filmscripts, and numerous radio and television documentaries. Editor of *Jewish Life,* 1965-70. Author of column in *Jewish Gazette,* 1961-71.

WORK IN PROGRESS: A thriller, tentatively titled *Killing Around;* a sex-comedy thriller.

DIRKSEN, Louella Carver 1899-1979

PERSONAL: Born in 1899, in Pekin, Ill.; died of cancer, July 18, 1979, in Washington, D.C.; daughter of a wholesale tobacco dealer and a dressmaker; married Everett Dirksen (a U.S. senator), December 24, 1927; children: Joy (Mrs. Howard Baker). *Education:* Attended Illinois State Normal College.

CAREER: Worked as bookkeeper in Pekin, Ill., and at department store in Peoria, Ill.; Dirksen Brothers Bakery, Pekin, treasurer, beginning in 1927. Spokesperson for National Federation of Republican Women's "GOP Election Express," 1954; head of camp and hospital service of District of Columbia Red Cross during World War II; member of President Nixon's Committee on Aging; fundraiser for Everett McKinley Dirksen Memorial Library; organizer of charity tours.

WRITINGS: (With Norma Lee Browning) *The Honorable Mr. Marigold: My Life With Everett Dirksen*, Doubleday, 1972.

OBITUARIES: Washington Post, July 19, 1979.*

*   *   *

DIVINE, Arthur Durham 1904-
(David Divine, David Rame)

PERSONAL: Born July 27, 1904, in Cape Town, South Africa; son of Arthur and Mabel Divine; married Elizabeth Ann Macalister (a publisher), December 9, 1931; children: Janet May (Mrs. James Campbell), Sally Antoinette (Mrs. Alan Keir). *Education:* Attended secondary school in Grahamstown, South Africa. *Religion:* Church of England. *Home address:* Keats Grove, London, England. *Agent:* David Higham Associates Ltd., 5-8 Lower John St., Golden Sq., London W1R 4HA, England.

CAREER: Writer. *Sunday Times*, London, England, war correspondent, 1940-45. *Awards, honors:* Distinguished Service Medal; commander of Order of the British Empire.

WRITINGS: Sea Loot, Methuen, 1930; *Graveyard Watch*, Methuen, 1931; *Pelican Island*, Methuen, 1932; *Dark Moon*, Methuen, 1933; *They Blocked the Suez Canal*, Methuen, 1935; *Wings Over the Atlantic*, John Lane, 1936; *Seventy Fathom Treasure*, George Newnes, 1936; *Admiral's Million*, Methuen, 1936; *Diamond Coast*, Methuen, 1936; *Escape From Spain*, Methuen, 1936; *Fire in the Ice*, Basil Blackwell, 1937; *Lawless Voyage*, Hodder & Stoughton, 1937; *Pub on the Pool*, Collins, 1938; *Terror in the Thames*, Collins, 1938; *Slack Water*, Collins, 1939; *Deeds That Held the Empire: At Sea*, J. Murray, 1939.

The Wake of the Raiders: The Exploits and Failure of the Pocket Battleships and a Consecutive Account of Events at Sea, J. Murray, 1940; *U-Boat in the Hebrides*, Collins, 1940; (editor) *My Best Secret Service Story: A Collection of Stories Chosen by Their Own Authors*, Faber, 1940; *The Merchant Navy Fights: Tramps Against U-Boats*, J. Murray, 1940; *The Fighting Tramp and Other True Tales of the Sea*, J. Murray, 1940; *Behind the Fleets: A First-Hand Account of the Duties and Exploits of the Convoys, the Dover Patrol, the Mine-Sweepers, and the Other Subsidiary Fleets*, J. Murray, 1940; *Destroyer's War: A Million Miles by the Eighth Flotilla*, J. Murray, 1942; *Navies in Exile*, J. Murray, 1944; *Dunkirk: An Account of the Evacuation of the British Army From Dunkirk in May, 1940*, Faber, 1945; *Diamond Coast* (juvenile), Children's Books, 1949.

Under pseudonym David Divine: *The King of Fassarai*, J. Murray, 1951; *Atom at Spithead*, R. Hale, 1953; *The Golden Fool*, J. Murray, 1954; *Six Great Explorers: Frobisher, Cook, Mungo Park, Burton, Livingstone, Scott*, Hamish Hamilton, 1954; *Six Great Sailors: Howard of Effingham, Blake, Morgan, Bligh, Keyes, Ramsay*, Hamish Hamilton, 1955; *Boy on a Dolphin*, J. Murray, 1955; *The Story of Sea Warfare*, Hamish Hamilton, 1957; *These Splendid Ships: The Story of the Peninsular and Oriental Line*, Muller, 1960; *The Iron Ladies*, Hutchinson, 1961; *The Daughter of the Pangaran*, Hutchinson, 1963; *The Blunted Sword*, Hutchinson, 1964; *The Nine Days of Dunkirk*, Pan Books, 1964; *The Broken Wing: A Study in the British Exercise of Air Power*, Hutchinson, 1966; *The Key of England*, Macdonald & Co., 1968; *The North-West Frontier of Rome: A Military Study of Hadrian's Wall*, Macdonald & Co., 1969; *Mutiny at Invergordon*, Macdonald & Co., 1970; *The Three Red Flares*, Macdonald & Co., 1970; *Certain Islands: A Personal Selection*, Macdonald & Co., 1972; *The Opening of the World*, Collins, 1973.

Under pseudonym David Rame: *The Sun Shall Greet Them*, Macmillan, 1941; *Tunnel From Calais*, Macmillan, 1943; *Road to Tunis*, Macmillan, 1944.

*   *   *

DIVINE, David
See DIVINE, Arthur Durham

*   *   *

DOAN, Daniel 1914-

PERSONAL: Born February 23, 1914, in Summit, N.J.; son of Frank C. (a professor and Unitarian minister) and Isabel (Wilson) Doan; married Ernestine Elizabeth Crone, (a legal secretary), March 30, 1935; children: Ruth Doan MacDougal, Penelope Doan Nason. *Education:* Dartmouth College, B.A., 1936. *Home address:* R.F.D.1, No. 159, Laconia, N.H. 03246.

CAREER: Chicken farmer, 1936-39; free-lance writer, 1939-40; Scott & Williams, Inc. (manufacturer of circular knitting machines), Laconia, N.H., 1940-65, began as drill press operator, became time study and industrial heat treating foreman; worked at odd jobs, cost estimating, teaching, and in real estate, beginning 1964. Writer.

WRITINGS: The Crystal Years (novel), Abelard, 1952; *Amos Jackman* (novel), Beacon Press, 1957; *Fifty Hikes in the White Mountains of New Hampshire*, New Hampshire Publishing, 1973, 2nd edition, 1977; *Fifty More Hikes in New Hampshire*, New Hampshire Publishing, 1978, revised edition, in press; *Dan Doan's Fitness Book for Hikers and Cross-Country Skiers*, New Hampshire Publishing, 1978. Also author of *Indian Stream Republic* (a history of New Hampshire). Contributor of articles and stories to magazines, including *Cosmopolitan, Collier's, Country Gentleman, New Hampshire Profiles*, and *Field and Stream*.

WORK IN PROGRESS: A novel.

SIDELIGHTS: When asked about his motivation for writing, Doan replied: "I needed the money. In the 1930's magazines sometimes paid two thousand dollars a story, which was enough to live on luxuriously (for a writer) for a year."

Doan added: "The dream of not wealth, but moderate income to supplement a farm income and a simple life, turned out to be impractical. Even so, I wouldn't have missed it for anything.

"I had an early inclination to write about nature and a boy's adventures in the woods, and I did so in a diary and in little stories. My home life encouraged this, particularly my father, and his important influence continued following his premature death when I was thirteen. Two of my three older sisters were interested in writing and literature, and being near my age they were sympathetic towards my attempts at writing. I suppose we were a bookish family. My mother brought my attention to the writing of Henry Thoreau. This, and my love for New Hampshire, acquired through long summers there, undoubtedly influenced me to seek a livelihood by writing and farming.

"I raised chickens for three years and tried writing full time for a year, with the only success an article in *Field and Stream*. The obvious financial desert (fifty dollars from the article) and two daughters and a wife to support sent me job hunting, and I went to work on a drill press. My low income and dislike of the work (most of the time) were great incentives to continue writing in the hopes of more money and perhaps independence. My two novels and various short stories came from writing in evenings and on weekends. My daughter, Ruth Doan MacDougall, the novelist, says she used to go to sleep to the sound of my typewriter.

"The Breadloaf Writer's Conference in 1964 was a revelation to me as a would-be professional writer long trapped in industry. The next year I quit my job, realizing at age fifty that I'd had enough of the values of industry as compared to literature, although more through my wife's urging, and for health reasons as well. My wife kept on as a legal secretary, and we had accumulated a nest egg that would enable me to write for three years.

"I wrote another novel that didn't sell, and I began climbing mountains in New Hampshire once more. The hiking guidebooks I wrote did nicely, and I kept on writing for longer than the planned three years. We went to Europe in 1965. From that experience, and thinking about my parents' trips abroad, I began, between work on the guidebooks and the fitness book, to put together a novel.

"I'm quick to point out to aspiring young writers that writing is a tough racket, even tougher than when I began trying, now that short stories are no longer in demand. I point out that I never made a living at it, but I am very glad I kept on, although at times it seemed like an addiction (maybe it is). I think young writers should learn a good trade, one that they can always use—brick mason, for instance, or secretarial skills—any skill that brings in the needed money. And, don't mistake early talent for the ability to go the distance and win. Most teenagers are talented and creative. They must build up the habit of the daily stint.

"Probably most advice formulated from my experience isn't of much use. Those who want to write badly enough will write one way or another, just as I did and am doing."

*　　　*　　　*

DOBBIN, John E.   1914-1979

OBITUARY NOTICE—See index for *CA* sketch: Born July 8, 1914, in Eau Claire, Wis.; died of a heart attack in 1979, in Dallas, Tex. Educator and author. John Dobbin was involved in educational research and testing. He contributed to several books and journals in his field and co-wrote *Testing: Its Place in Education Today*. (Date of death provided by wife, Elizabeth Dobbin.)

DODD, James Harvey   1892-1969

OBITUARY NOTICE—See index for *CA* sketch: Born January 30, 1892; died June 10, 1969. Educator and author. For more than thirty years, James Dodd was a professor of economics at Mary Washington College of the University of Virginia (now Mary Washington College). He was the author of *Introductory Economics* and the co-author of *Economics: Principles and Applications*, both of which were published under new titles in later editions. (Date of death provided by wife, Eileen Dodd.)

*　　　*　　　*

DOENITZ, Karl   1891-1980

OBITUARY NOTICE: Born September 16, 1891, in Berlin, Germany; died December 24, 1980, in Hamburg, West Germany. Naval officer and author. Grand Admiral Doenitz succeeded Adolph Hitler as the leader of Nazi Germany and ordered the U-boat campaign against Allied ships during World War II. Arrested by the British in 1945, Doenitz was convicted of war crimes at the Nuremberg trials and was imprisoned for ten years. His book, *Memoirs: Ten Years and Twenty Days*, maintains that the admiral knew nothing of the atrocities committed by Hitler and that by participating in Nazi activities Doenitz was merely following military orders. Released from Berlin's Spandau Prison in 1956, Doenitz lived the remainder of his life as a recluse near Hamburg. Obituaries and other sources: *Current Biography*, Wilson, 1942, February, 1981; *Encyclopedia of the Third Reich*, McGraw, 1976; *Who Was Who in World War II*, Arms & Armour Press, 1978; *New York Times*, December 26, 1980.

*　　　*　　　*

DOIMI di DELUPIS, Ingrid
See DELUPIS, Ingrid

*　　　*　　　*

DOLLOFF, Eugene Dinsmore   1890-1972

OBITUARY NOTICE—See index for *CA* sketch: Born May 10, 1890, in Meredith, N.H.; died July 9, 1972. Minister and author. A Baptist minister for more than thirty years, Eugene Dolloff was the author of such books as *Maturing in the Ministry, It Can Happen Between Sundays,* and *The Pastor's Public Relations*. (Date of death provided by son, Lawrence S. Dolloff.)

*　　　*　　　*

DONALDSON, Betty   1923-

PERSONAL: Born May 24, 1923, in Longtown, England; came to the United States in 1957, naturalized citizen, 1963; daughter of Adam and Jane (Thomson) Burgess; married Norman Donaldson (a technical editor), March 19, 1947; children: Rosemary, Hilary, Andrew, Heather. *Education:* Attended girls' school in Edinburgh, Scotland. *Politics:* Democrat. *Home and office:* 1358 Inglis Ave., Columbus, Ohio 43212.

CAREER: Writer, 1974—.

WRITINGS: (Contributor) Arthur W. Upfield, *The New Shoe*, University of California, San Diego, 1976; (with husband, Norman Donaldson) *How Did They Die?*, St. Martin's, 1980; (contributor) John M. Reilly, editor, *Twentieth Century Crime and Mystery Writers*, St. Martin's, 1980. Contributor of articles and reviews to *Armchair Detective* and newspapers.

WORK IN PROGRESS: A sequel to *How Did They Die?*, with husband, N. Donaldson, publication by St. Martin's expected in 1982.

SIDELIGHTS: Betty Donaldson commented: "I have wanted to write since childhood, but until a few years ago I was content to bring up our family and help my husband with his writing. Now I enjoy working with him, particularly doing the research essential to nonfiction writing." *Avocational interests:* Books, music, "exploring this vast, wonderful continent of America."

*   *   *

DONALDSON, Elvin F. 1903-1972

OBITUARY NOTICE—See index for *CA* sketch: Born April 21, 1903, in Athens, Ohio; died October 29, 1972. Educator and author. A professor at Ohio State University for more than forty years, Elvin Donaldson wrote several books on finance, including *Business Organization and Procedure* and *Financial Handbook.* Another book, *Corporate Finance,* was published as *Corporate Finance, Policy, and Management* in a later edition. (Date of death provided by Ohio State University.)

*   *   *

DONALDSON, Margaret 1926-
(Margaret Lennox Salter)

PERSONAL: Born June 16, 1926, in Paisley, Scotland; daughter of James (in business) and Agnes (a teacher; maiden name, Lennox) Donaldson; married Stephen Salter (an engineer), April 24, 1973. *Education:* University of Edinburgh, M.A., 1947, B.Ed., 1953, Ph.D., 1956. *Residence:* Edinburgh, Scotland. *Agent:* A.P. Watt Ltd., 26/28 Bedford Row, London WC1R 4HL, England. *Office:* Department of Psychology, University of Edinburgh, One Roxburgh St., Edinburgh EH8 9TA, Scotland.

CAREER: University of Edinburgh, Edinburgh, Scotland, assistant lecturer, 1953-57, lecturer, 1958-69, reader, 1969-80, professor of developmental psychology, 1980—. Lecturer at American universities, including Harvard University, Stanford University, Carnegie-Mellon University, and New School for Social Research. *Member:* British Psychological Society, Association for Child Psychology and Psychiatry, British Educational Research Association. *Awards, honors:* John Hay Whitney fellowship from John Hay Whitney Foundation, 1962-63.

WRITINGS: A Study of Children's Thinking, Tavistock Publications, 1963; *Children's Minds,* Fontana, 1978, Norton, 1979; *Journey Into War* (juvenile novel), Deutsch, 1979; *Mindar* (juvenile novel), Methuen, 1979; *The Moon's on Fire* (juvenile; sequel to *Journey Into War*), Deutsch, 1980.

Under name Margaret Lennox Salter: *The Adventures of Magnus* (juvenile stories), three volumes, Holmes McDougall, 1976; *Mindar of Brannin* (juvenile stories), three volumes, Holmes McDougall, 1976; *Living on the Earth: Man* (juvenile nonfiction), three volumes, Holmes McDougall, 1976. Contributor to *Human Nature.*

WORK IN PROGRESS: Continuing research on children's thinking and language.

SIDELIGHTS: Donaldson told *CA:* "I believe that my writings as psychologist and as author of children's fiction complement one another in important ways. The two kinds of

activity are very different—which is good for me personally—and yet they are not unrelated. I do not apply psychological knowledge in a direct and conscious way when I write for children but do genuinely and seriously try to write *for* them. I hope that my knowledge of their thinking and language skills helps me to do this well. It is a common belief that writing for children is easier than writing for adults. I do not think this is true."

*   *   *

DONKIN, Nance (Clare) 1915-

PERSONAL: Born in 1915 in West Maitland, New South Wales, Australia; daughter of Archie T. Pender and Clara Russell; married Victor Donkin, January 14, 1939; children: Nicola Williams, Richard Donkin. *Home:* 8/8 Mooltan Ave., Balaclava, Victoria 3183, Australia.

CAREER: Maitland Daily Mercury, Maitland, New South Wales, journalist, 1932-35; *Newcastle Morning Herald,* Newcastle, New South Wales, journalist, 1935-39; writer, 1946—. Broadcaster for Australian Broadcasting Commission (ABC) program, "Women's Session"; children's book reviewer for *Melbourne Herald,* 1970—; tutor for Council of Adult Education, c. 1975—. *Member:* Children's Book Council (Victoria, Australia; president, 1968-75; vice-president, 1975-79), Australian Society of Authors, Fellowship of Australian Writers, Women's Writers Society, National Trust of Australia, Gallery Society of Victoria. *Awards, honors:* Australian Arts Council travel grant, 1972, senior fellowship, 1980.

WRITINGS—All for children; fiction: *Araluen Adventures* (illustrated by Edith B. Bowden), Cheshire, 1946; *No Medals for Meg,* Cheshire, 1947; *Julie Stands By* (illustrated by Joan Turner), Cheshire, 1948; *Blue Ribbon Beth,* Oxford University Press (Melbourne), 1948; *House by the Water* (illustrated by Astra Lacis Dick), Angus & Robertson, 1969; *Johnny Neptune,* Angus & Robertson, 1973; *A Friend for Petros,* Hamish Hamilton, 1974; *Patchwork Grandmother,* Hamish Hamilton, 1975, published as *Patchwork Mystery,* Beaver Books, 1978; *Green Christmas,* Hamish Hamilton, 1976; *Yellowgum Gil,* Hamish Hamilton, 1976; *The Maidens of Pefka,* Methuen, 1979; *Nini,* Rigby Reading, 1979.

Other; all published by Oxford University Press, except as noted: *Sheep* (illustrated by Jocelyn Jones), 1967; *Sugar* (illustrated by J. Jones), 1967; *An Emancipist* (illustrated by Jane Robinson), 1968; *A Currency Lass* (illustrated by Jane Walker), 1969; *An Orphan* (illustrated by Ann Culvenor), 1970; *Margaret Catchpole* (illustrated by Edwina Bell), Collins (Sydney), 1974; *Best of the Bunch,* Collins, 1978.

Work represented in anthologies, including *The Cool Man,* Angus & Robertson, 1973, and *A Handful of Ghosts,* Hodder & Stoughton, 1976.

WORK IN PROGRESS: A book on migrant lifestyles in Australia and Greece.

SIDELIGHTS: Nance Donkin began her literary career as an adolescent when she contributed stories to her local newspaper. Her efforts led to jobs as women's editor for the *Maitland Daily Mercury* and, later, for the *Newcastle Morning Herald.*

After residing briefly in England, Donkin settled in Melbourne and contributed verses to the Australian Broadcasting Commission's "Children's Session," and worked as a freelance broadcaster in other ABC programs.

Donkin's aim is to write uniquely Australian literature for children. *Green Christmas,* for example, is the story of a

European girl who is distraught over having to spend Christmas in a hot Australian climate until she discovers Australia's unique Christmas customs. *Margaret Catchpole,* the true story of an Australian convict, is Donkin's response to what she sees as a need for children's books on Australian history. *A Friend for Petros* and *Nini* are both concerned with Greek children in contemporary Australia, while *Maidens of Pefka* deals with an Australian family on a Greek island.

In addition to her books, Donkin writes stories for Australian magazines and was for many years involved in television programming for women and children. Out of concern for the plight of migrants in Australia, she has served as a volunteer teacher and home visitor of migrant families.

BIOGRAPHICAL/CRITICAL SOURCES: Times Literary Supplement, April 16, 1970.

* * *

DONOVAN, William
See BERKEBILE, Fred D(onovan)

* * *

DONSKOI, Mark Semyonovich 1901-1981

OBITUARY NOTICE: Born March 6, 1901, in Odessa, Russia (now U.S.S.R.); died c. March, 1981, in Moscow, U.S.S.R. Film director and author, best known for his biographical film trilogy on writer Maxim Gorki. Praised by Soviet leaders for his contributions to the cinema, Donskoi made patriotic films, including "The Rainbow," an adaptation of Wanda Wassilewska's novel about a Nazi-occupied village during World War II, and "The Tara Family," a story that he co-authored about the plight of Russian Jews following the Nazi invasion. Donskoi also wrote *How I Became a Director.* He was twice awarded the highest Soviet civilian prize, the Order of Lenin. Obituaries and other sources: *A Biographical Dictionary of Film,* Morrow, 1976; *The International Who's Who,* Europa, 1980; *New York Times,* March 26, 1981.

* * *

DOUGLAS-HOME, Henry 1907-1980

PERSONAL: Born November 21, 1907; died July 19, 1980; son of Charles Cospatrick Archibald (an earl) and Lilian (Lambton) Douglas-Home; married Margaret Spencer, 1931 (divorced, 1947); married Vera Johansen, 1947 (died, 1963); married Felicity Wills, 1966; children: (first marriage) Fiona Margaret (Mrs. Gregory Martin), Charles Cospatrick, another son; (second marriage) George Erik Montagu; (third marriage) Peregrine Montagu. *Education:* Attended Christ Church, Oxford.

CAREER: Broadcaster for British Broadcasting Corp. (BBC-Radio and -TV), beginning in 1930's. British Army, 1940-56; deputy assistant director of public relations, Scottish Command, beginning 1943; retired as honorary major. Ornithologist. *Member:* Puffins (Edinburgh). *Awards, honors:* Member of the Order of the British Empire.

WRITINGS: The Birdman: Memories of Birds (memoirs), Collins, 1977.

SIDELIGHTS: Douglas-Home was the brother of Alec, the former British prime minister, and William, the prominent playwright. As "The Birdman," he began broadcasting a popular program of birdsongs during the 1930's and continued throughout World War II.

He was a respected ornithologist, particularly noted for his research into the life and habits of the swift, a small bird which may fly as many as three million miles in its lifetime. He wrote and lectured on ornithology and was also well known for his paintings of birds.

OBITUARIES: London Times, July 21, 1980.*

* * *

DOUGLASS, Donald McNutt 1899-1975

OBITUARY NOTICE—See index for *CA* sketch: Born December 7, 1899, in Houston, Tex.; died in 1975. Draftsman and author. Donald Douglass was the owner of an architectural firm. He wrote several books, including *Rebecca's Pride* and *Mary Brave Hearts,* and he contributed to such magazines as *Yachting* and *Cosmopolitan.* Obituaries and other sources: *The Author's and Writer's Who's Who,* 6th edition, Burke's Peerage, 1971. (Date of death provided by agent, Shirley Collier.)

* * *

DOUMATO, Lamia 1947-

PERSONAL: Born August 26, 1947, in Homs, Syria; came to the United States, 1952, naturalized citizen, 1959; daughter of A. G. and Victoria (Peters) Doumato. *Education:* Rhode Island College, B.A., 1969; Pennsylvania State University, M.A., 1971; Simmons College, M.S., 1974; also attended Columbia University, 1977-78. *Office:* Reference Divison, National Gallery of Art, Washington, D.C. 20565.

CAREER: Museum of Modern Art, New York, N.Y., reference librarian, 1974-78; University of Colorado, Boulder, assistant professor of art bibliography, 1978-81; National Gallery of Art, Washington, D.C., head of Reference Division, 1981—. *Member:* College Art Association, Art Librarian Association. *Awards, honors:* Grant from Council on Research and Creative Work, 1979-80.

WRITINGS: American Drawings, Gale, 1979; (with Jeanne Weiffenbach) *Six Painters of the Figure,* Art Gallery, University of Colorado, 1979; *Museum Design, 1965-1979,* Council of Planning Librarians, 1980; (contributor), Elizabeth Sussman, editor, *Florine Stettheimer,* Institute of Contemporary Art (Boston, Mass.), 1980; *Dictionary of Women Artists,* Garland Publishing, 1982. Contributor to journals. Editor of *Muse.*

WORK IN PROGRESS: Research on women's art; architectural studies.

SIDELIGHTS: Lamia Doumato commented: "My interest in women's art was stimulated by a recent visit to Third World countries where I was able to meet with these women and discuss their views on art and life. These travels included countries such as Communist China, Japan, Taiwan, Indonesia, Sri Lanka, the Phillippines, and Egypt. A basic motivation for my work is to provide accessibility to information in areas which were previously neglected."

* * *

DOWNS, Cal W. 1936-

PERSONAL: Born September 21, 1936, in El Dorado, Ark.; son of Charles R. (a merchant) and Alma (a merchant; maiden name, Wright) Downs; married Alice O'Daniel (a university professor), February 23, 1963; children: Allyson, Kevin. *Education:* Harding College, B.A., 1958; Michigan State University, M.A., 1959, Ph.D., 1963. *Office:* Department of Communication Studies, University of Kansas, Lawrence, Kan. 66045; and Communication Management, Inc., P.O. Box 3242, Lawrence, Kan. 66044.

CAREER: Michigan State University, East Lansing, resident coordinator of Agency for International Development seminars, 1961-62; University of Maryland, College Park, assistant professor of speech, 1962-64; Northwestern University, Evanston, Ill., assistant professor of speech and business, 1964-67; University of Kansas, Lawrence, began as assistant professor, 1967, became professor of organization communication, 1976—. President of Communication Management, Inc. *Member:* International Communication Association (chairperson of Organizational Communication Division), Academy of Management (chairperson of Organizational Communication Division), Speech Communication Association of America, American Business Communication Association.

WRITINGS: The Organizational Communicator, Harper, 1977; *Professional Interviewing,* Harper, 1980. Contributor to speech and business journals.

* * *

DUANE, Jim
  See HURLEY, Vic

* * *

DUCKHAM, Baron Frederick 1933-

PERSONAL: Born May 20, 1933, in Leeds, England; son of Kenneth Luzon (a postal official) and Edith Faith (Baron) Duckham; married Helen Gertrud Ebbe Wegener (a secretary), March 30, 1959; children: Christopher Michael John, Katrin Sarah, Jonathan Stephen Andrew. *Education:* Victoria University of Manchester, B.A., 1954, M.A., 1956; University of Leeds, certificate in education, 1955. *Religion:* Anglican. *Home:* Bronllan, Betws Bledrws, Lampeter, Wales. *Office:* Department of History, St. David's University College, University of Wales, Lampeter, Dyfed, Wales.

CAREER: Cleveland Technical College, Cleveland, England, lecturer in history, 1958-60; Reading Technical College, Reading, England, lecturer in history, 1960-62; Doncaster College of Education, Doncaster, England, lecturer in history, 1962-66; University of Sheffield, Sheffield, England, part-time lecturer in history, 1964-66; University of Strathclyde, Glasgow, Scotland, lecturer, 1966-71, senior lecturer in economic history, 1971-78; University of Wales, St. David's University College, Lampeter, professor of history, 1978—. *Military service:* British Army, Royal Education Corps, 1956-58. *Member:* Royal Historical Society (fellow), Historical Association, Economic History Society.

WRITINGS: Navigable Rivers of Yorkshire, Dalesman, 1964; *The Yorkshire Ouse: History of a River Navigation,* David & Charles, 1967; *The Transport Revolution, 1750-1830,* Historical Association, 1967; *Yorkshire Ports and Harbours,* Dalesman, 1967; *History of the Scottish Coal Industry, 1700-1815,* David & Charles, 1970; (with wife, Helen Duckham) *Great Pit Disasters: Great Britain, 1700 to the Present Day,* David & Charles, 1973; *The Inland Waterways of East Yorkshire,* East Yorkshire Local History Society, 1973; (with John R. Hume) *Steam Entertainment,* David & Charles, 1974.

Editor; all published by David & Charles: R. L. Galloway, *History of Coal Mining in Great Britain,* 1969; H. S. Jevons, *The British Coal Trade,* 1969; Galloway, *Annals of Coal Mining and the Coal Trade,* 1971.

Contributor to history journals. Editor of *Transport History,* 1968-73.

WORK IN PROGRESS: Research on transportation during the British industrial revolution; research on road administration in Wales.

SIDELIGHTS: Duckham told *CA:* "I am basically a local or regional historian and believe that the preservation of the local approach is particularly important in an age of mass societies. Naturally, regional history is only one small element of historical studies, but it possesses its own rationale and has an intrinsic value quite apart from providing footnotes to general history. It is the duty of the historian to record and analyze man's struggle to earn his bread and live in his community. Local history provides a fruitful framework of study provided one resists the pitfalls of antiquarianism."

* * *

DUDLEY-SMITH, Timothy 1926-

PERSONAL: Born in 1926, in Manchester, England; son of Arthur (a headmaster) and Phyllis (Richards) Dudley-Smith; married June Arlette MacDonald, November 7, 1959; children: Caroline, Sarah, James. *Education:* Pembroke College, Cambridge, B.A., 1947; Ridley Hall, Cambridge, M.A., 1951. *Home:* Rectory Meadow, Bramerton, Norwich, England.

CAREER: Ordained minister of Church of England, 1950; assistant curate in Northumberland, Heath, England, 1950-53; head of Cambridge University mission in Bermondsey, 1953-55; Evangelical Alliance, London, England, editorial secretary, 1955-59; Church Pastoral-Aid Society, London, assistant secretary, 1959-65, secretary, 1965-73; archdeacon of Norwich in Bramerton, England, 1973-81; bishop of Thetford, England, 1981—. Member of General Synod of Church of England, 1975-80; commissary to archbishop of Sydney, Australia, 1971—. *Member:* Hymn Society of the United Kingdom, Hymn Society of America.

WRITINGS: Christian Literature and the Church Bookstall, Falcon, 1963; *What Makes a Man a Christian?,* Hodder & Stoughton, 1965; *A Man Named Jesus,* Falcon, 1971; *Someone Who Beckons,* Inter-Varsity Press, 1978. Contributor to hymnals. Editor of *Crusade,* 1955-59.

WORK IN PROGRESS: Hymn texts.

* * *

du JARDIN, Rosamond Neal 1902-1963

OBITUARY NOTICE—See index for *CA* sketch: Born July 22, 1902, in Fairland, Ill.; died March, 1963; buried in Glen Ellyn, Ill. Author. Although Rosamond du Jardin wrote several novels for adults, she was best known for her novels for teenagers, all of which have gone through numerous printings. Critics consistently praised her ability to write of the teenage years with humor and understanding. Most of her books have been published in other countries, including Japan, Italy, Holland, and Sweden. *Class Ring* and *Wait for Marcy* were adapted into three-act plays by Anne Martens. Included among du Jardin's many novels are *Double Date, A Man for Marcy, Senior Prom,* and *Young and Fair.* She also contributed more than one hundred short stories to such magazines as *Cosmopolitan, Good Housekeeping,* and *McCall's.* Obituaries and other sources: *Who Was Who in America,* 4th edition, Marquis, 1968; *Something About the Author,* Volume 2, Gale, 1971.

* * *

DUN, Mao
  See YEN-PING, Shen

DUNBAR, Maxwell John 1914-

PERSONAL: Born September 19, 1914, in Edinburgh, Scotland; son of William (a lawyer) and Elizabeth Mary (Robertson) Dunbar; married Joan Suzanne Jackson, August 1, 1945, (died August 22, 1959;) married Nancy Jane Wosstroff (a museum curator), December 14, 1960; children: (firt marriage) Douglas, William; (second marriage) Elisabeth, Andrew, Christine, Robyn. *Education:* Trinity College, Oxford, B.A, 1937, M.A., 1939; attended Yale University, 1937-38; McGill University, Ph.D., 1941. *Politics:* Liberal. *Religion:* Protestant. *Home:* 488 Strathcona Ave., Montreal, Quebec, Canada H3Y 2X1. *Office:* Marine Sciences Centre, McGill University, 3620 University, Montreal, Quebec, Canada H3A 2B2.

CAREER: Canadian Department of External Affairs, Consul in Greenland, 1941-46; McGill University, Montreal, Quebec, assistant professor, 1946-48, associate professor, 1948-59, professor of zoology, 1959—, chairman of Marine Sciences Centre, 1963-67. Arctic explorer, 1935-58. *Member:* American Association for the Advancement of Science (fellow), American Geographical Society (honorary fellow), Arctic Institute of North America (chairman, 1958-59; past member of board of directors), Royal Society of Canada (fellow). *Awards, honors:* Bruce Medal from Royal Society of Edinburgh, 1950, for polar exploration; Guggenheim fellow in Denmark, 1952-53; Fry Medal from Canadian Society of Zoologists, 1979; D.Sc. from Memorial University of Newfoundland, 1979.

WRITINGS: (Editor and contributor) *Marine Distributions,* University of Toronto Press, 1963; *Ecological Development in Polar Regions: A Study in Evolution,* Prentice-Hall, 1968; *Environment and Good Sense: An Introduction to Environmental Damage and Control in Canada,* McGill-Queen's University Press, 1971; (editor) *Polar Oceans,* Arctic Institute of North America, 1977; (editor and contributor) *Marine Production Mechanisms,* Cambridge University Press, 1979. Contributor of about one hundred articles and reviews to scientific journals.

SIDELIGHTS: Dunbar wrote: "I have two abiding interests and passions: ecosystem mechanisms and evolution, and history. I have lectured, and still do lecture, on comparative anatomy, general ecology, biological oceanography, and the history of biology, which is the subject I love most. History is not easy to teach at the school level, but wise children learn it well and continue to learn it throughout their lives."

*   *   *

DUNCAN, Julia Coley
See SATHER, Julia Coley Duncan

*   *   *

DUSSERE, Carol
See DUSSERE, Carolyn T(homas)

*   *   *

DUSSERE, Carolyn T(homas) 1942-
(Carol Dussere)

PERSONAL: Born January 11, 1942, in Rochester, N.Y.; daughter of John Wesley (a professor) and Lina Miriam Thomas; married David Dussere, 1963 (marriage ended, 1974). *Education:* Attended University of Tuebingen, 1960-61, 1965-66, and University of Arkansas, 1961-63, M.A.,

1968; Wisconsin State University—Superior (now University of Wisconsin, Superior), B.A., 1965; attended University of Wisconsin—La Crosse (formerly Wisconsin State University—La Crosse), 1969-72; University of Kentucky, Ph.D., 1978. *Politics:* "Feminist." *Home:* 1326½ West Cleveland, Fayetteville, Ark. 72701; and 116 Vanderbilt, Lexington, Ky. 40503. *Office:* Department of Foreign Languages, University of Arkansas, 425 Communications, Fayetteville, Ark. 72701.

CAREER: Arkansas State University, Jonesboro, instructor in German and English, 1968-69; Dussere Studio, La Crescent, Minn., and Holmen, Wis., potter, 1969-72; Louisiana Tech University, Ruston, assistant professor of German, 1978-79; University of Kentucky, Lexington, instructor in German, 1980; University of Arkansas, Fayetteville, lector in German, 1980—. Instructor at Wisconsin State University—La Crosse (now University of Wisconsin—La Crosse), 1970. Art work (etchings, woodcuts, silkscreen, sculpture, pottery, and political art) has been exhibited in professional shows.

MEMBER: National Organization for Women, Modern Language Association, New American Movement, Alpha Psi Omega, Delta Phi Alpha.

WRITINGS: The Image of the Primitive Giant in the Works of Gerhart Hauptmann, Hans-Dieter Heinz, 1979; (editor, translator, and author of introduction, with J. W. Thomas) *The Legend of Duke Ernst,* University of Nebraska Press, 1980. Contributor of about thirty-five articles and reviews to scholarly journals and newspapers, sometimes under name Carol Dussere.

WORK IN PROGRESS: An article on humor in Gerhart Hauptmann's *Ulrich von Lichtenstein;* an article on Hauptmann's "Lohengrin"; translations of Hauptmann's "Parsival" and "Lohengrin"; research on works of women writers, "particularly those reflecting the condition of women in the Middle Ages and the second half of the nineteenth century."

SIDELIGHTS: Carolyn Dussere wrote: "Fairly early in my assorted activities in the theatre, visual arts, literary criticism, and politics I became convinced that creative activity always transcends the boundaries of arbitrarily assigned categories. When I was doing primarily visual art I wanted to stretch the medium beyond its limits and tear down any fence I came to. Much of that was simply exuberance. In recent years I've contemplated the boundary between the humanities and political activism more soberly and concluded that those of us with some insight into the creative process have a responsibility to work for social change. In a society with as many contradictions and inequities as ours the question of what a work says about society is not a matter of marginal importance. The interaction of art and politics can indeed produce good art in the service of humanity and politics with a human face."

*   *   *

DYE, Frank Charles 1930-

PERSONAL: Born April 24, 1930, in Norfolk, England; son of Frank and Ada Dye; married Margaret Ann Bidwell (a teacher and writer), December 21, 1965. *Education:* Loughborough Engineering College, D.L.C., 1951. *Politics:* Conservative. *Religion:* Church of England. *Home and office:* Dyecraft Ltd., Kent Green, Stoke-on-Trent, England.

CAREER: Perkin's Diesel Engines, Peterborough, England, graduate apprentice, 1951-54; Ford Main Dealers, Central Norfolk, England, tractor sales and service manager, 1954-58, general manager and director of vehicle sales and service,

1958-68, managing director, 1968-74; Dyecraft Ltd., Stoke-on-Trent, England, director, 1974—. Owner of a marina.

WRITINGS: (With wife, Margaret Dye) *Dinghy Cruising,* Spurbooks, 1977; (with M. Dye) *Ocean Crossing Wayfarer: To Iceland and Norway in an Open Boat,* David & Charles, 1978; *Practical Dinghy Cruising,* David & Charles, 1981. Contributor to British yachting magazines.

SIDELIGHTS: Dye's wife, Margaret, wrote: "Frank is capable of long periods of hard work. He is a typical executive and a perfectionist. He is a complete loner and needs to do something nobody else has tried. His trips by open boat to Iceland and Norway prove this. He gets impatient if expected to conform. He and I are afraid of the sea, but fascinated by it. We need to explore by dinghy for we are much closer to the sea in all its moods in an open sailing boat without power than in any other type of craft. Our sixteen-foot dinghy, 'Wanderer,' is now in the British Maritime Museum in Greenwich, England, after some twenty years of cruising."

*   *   *

DYER, John Percy   1902-1975

OBITUARY NOTICE—See index for *CA* sketch: Born June 24, 1902, in New Albany, Miss.; died October 5, 1975. Educator and author. A professor of history for more than thirty years, John Dyer wrote several books, including *"Fightin' Joe" Wheeler, From Shiloh to San Juan,* and *Tulane: The Biography of a University.* (Date of death provided by Tulane University.)

E

EAGLESFIELD, Francis
See GUIRDHAM, Arthur

*   *   *

EASSON, James   1895-1979

OBITUARY NOTICE—See index for *CA* sketch: Born August 22, 1895, in Perthshire, Scotland; died May 13, 1979. Musician, educator, and author. Included among James Easson's books on music are *Classical Sight Reader, The Good Musician, Philharmonic Reader,* and *Opera Airs for Schools.* (Date of death provided by Easson's executor, A. A. Soutar.)

*   *   *

EAST, P. D.   1921-1971

OBITUARY NOTICE—See index for *CA* sketch: Born November 26, 1921, in Columbia, Miss.; died December 31, 1971. Editor and author. East was the author of a column, "Easy Chair," for *Harper's.* He also wrote *The Magnolia Jungle: The Life, Times, and Education of a Southern Editor.* (Date of death provided by wife, Mary Cameron East.)

*   *   *

EATON, Faith (Sybil)   1927-

PERSONAL: Born January 9, 1927, in London, England; daughter of Godfrey Lewis (a university tutor) and Sybil Annie Irene (Rees) Eaton. *Education:* Attended boarding school in Richmond, England; studied privately under governesses. *Residence:* London, England.

CAREER: Occupational therapist, 1948-53; doll designer commissioned by collectors and museums in England, India, the United States, and Europe, 1953—; writer and antique restorer, 1953—. *Member:* Doll Club of Great Britain, Doll Makers Circle (president), Dollshouse Society, Fan Circle, United Federation of Doll Clubs, National Trust.

WRITINGS: Making "Far and Near" Dolls, Hulton, 1959, revised and enlarged edition, 1966; *Dolls in Colour,* Blandford, 1975. Contributor to magazines in England, Germany, and the United States, including *Doll Reader, International Toy and Doll Collector, International Dolls' House News,* and *International Dollmaking and Collecting.*

WORK IN PROGRESS: A history of nineteenth-century dollhouse dolls and costumes, with patterns, for G. Bell; a book on conservation and restoration of dolls, for Batsford.

SIDELIGHTS: Eaton's doll designs include a set of wooden dolls under one inch tall dressed in Victorian costumes; a large unbreakable doll with a carved head and soft body costumed as a London "Pearlie Queen"; play dolls modeled after characters from history and nursery rhymes; a set of dolls representing characters from Lewis Carroll's "Alice" books which was made for the British Government as a gift for the museum in New Delphi, India; a scale model of the poets' room on Wimpole Street with Robert and Elizabeth Browning and her spaniel; a jointed wooden replica of a Tudor doll; and a model of Mary, Queen of Scots.

Faith Eaton told *CA:* "My main collection is of dolls and dolls' houses, toys, etc., antique and modern as I am particularly interested in researching the continuity and changes in their design: The 'streets' of dolls' houses, for example, will be a miniature record of households in England, decade by decade.

"Books, costumes, and fans have also accumulated over the years and are invaluable aids to the three branches of my work—designing original dolls and models, restoring antique ones, and advising film, television, and advertising companies, sometimes lending certain items for programs and projects."

BIOGRAPHICAL/CRITICAL SOURCES: Homes and Gardens, July, 1970; *Rostrum,* December, 1970, *Rappen und Speilzeug,* 1977.

*   *   *

EBBETT, (Frances) Eva   1925-
(Eva Burfield, Eve Ebbett)

PERSONAL: Born June 6, 1925, in Wellingborough, England; daughter of Francis Albert (a shoe repairer) and Winifred Bessie (Major) Burfield; married Trevor George Ebbett (a clerk), October 22, 1949; children: Susan Bronwen Ebbett Hopkins. *Education:* Attended high school in Waipukurau, New Zealand. *Religion:* Unaffiliated. *Home:* 17 Rose St., Waipawa, Hawkes Bay, New Zealand. *Agent:* Kay Routledge Associates, 176 Wardour St., London W1V 3AA, England.

CAREER: Free-lance writer, 1946—. Also worked as bank clerk. *Member:* International P.E.N., New Zealand Women Writers Society.

WRITINGS—Under name Eva Burfield; novels; published by Wright & Brown: *Yellow Kowhai*, 1957; *A Chair to Sit On*, 1958; *The Long Winter*, 1964; *After Midnight*, 1965; *Out of Yesterday*, 1965; *The White Prison*, 1966; *The New Mrs. Rainier*, 1967; *The Last Day of Summer*, 1968.

Under name Eve Ebbett: *Give Them Swing Bands* (novel), Witcombe & Tombs, 1969; *To the Garden Alone* (novel), Witcombe & Tombs, 1970; *In True Colonial Fashion* (nonfiction), A.H. & A.W. Reed, 1977; *Victoria's Daughters* (nonfiction), A. H. & A. W. Reed, 1981. Contributor of articles, stories, and reviews to magazines in New Zealand, England, Australia, and Scandinavia.

SIDELIGHTS: Eve Ebbett wrote: "I have had an earnest desire to write all my life, at least as far back as I can remember, and I was first rejected by editors and publishers when I was fifteen. In 1946 I sold my first short story, but the novel has always been my greatest interest. The market in New Zealand is very small, and I had to find an English publisher. *To the Garden Alone* is the book I like best—it is the type of novel I always wanted to write. At present I am writing nonfiction, commissioned by a New Zealand publisher.

"My family came to New Zealand when I was two, and only in 1980 have I left the country, when I went to England to see the land of my birth.

"I believe in meticulous research in nonfiction and in 'truth' in fiction, even if the type of novel is light."

*   *   *

EBBETT, Eve
See EBBETT, (Frances) Eva

*   *   *

EBENSTEIN, Ronnie Sue   1946-

PERSONAL: Born October 6, 1946, in Brooklyn, N.Y.; daughter of Murray (an office manager) and Pearl (a secretary; maiden name, Brussel) Willensky; married Alan H. Ebenstein (a president of an insurance brokerage), July 19, 1970; children: Amy Beth. *Education:* Pennsylvania State University, B.A. (cum laude), 1968. *Residence:* Ridgewood, N.J. *Office:* 410 West 24th St., New York, N.Y. 10011.

CAREER: Cosmopolitan, New York City, assistant beauty editor, 1970-72; Planned Communication Services, New York City, chief copywriter, 1972-76; free-lance writer, 1976—.

WRITINGS: (With Adrien Arpel) *Adrien Arpel's Three-Week Crash Makeover/Shapeover Beauty Program*, Rawson, Wade, 1977; (with Arpel) *How to Look Ten Years Younger*, Rawson, Wade, 1980. Contributor to magazines, including *Cosmopolitan*, *Family Circle*, and *Good Housekeeping Beauty Book*.

SIDELIGHTS: Ebenstein told *CA:* "Because women today are spending more time outside the home, knowledge of how to look their best is not just a matter of personal vanity (though there's nothing wrong with a little healthy self-interest!). Looking good can be as important a career 'skill' as good typing, etc. Women (as well as men) who don't look vital and well put-together rarely reach the top rungs of the corporate ladder. Our books teach the beauty and fashion tricks that can be quickly adopted by the busy woman—whether she's at home raising a child, out in the marketplace raising her standard of living, or (as I am) trying to do both."

BIOGRAPHICAL/CRITICAL SOURCES: New York Times Book Review, May 7, 1978.

*   *   *

EBSEN, Buddy
See EBSEN, Christian

*   *   *

EBSEN, Christian   1908-
(Buddy Ebsen)

PERSONAL: Born April 2, 1908, in Belleville, Ill.; son of Christian Ludolf (a dancing master) and Franciska (Wendt) Ebsen; married Ruth McCambridge, 1933 (divorced); married Nancy Wolcott (a theatre director), September 6, 1945; children: (first marriage) Alexandra Ebsen Able, Libby; (second marriage) Susannah, Catharine, Bonnie, Nancy Kiersten, Dustin Wolcott. *Education:* Attended Rollins College, 1926-27, and University of Florida, 1927-28. *Politics:* Republican. *Religion:* Protestant. *Home address:* P.O. Box 157, Balboa Island, Calif. 92662. *Office:* 1040 Las Palmas, Hollywood, Calif. 90038.

CAREER: Dancer, actor, and playwright. Dancer with his sister, Vilma Ebsen, in night clubs and on road tours, 1928-35; dancer in Broadway shows: "Whoopee," New Amsterdam Theatre, 1928-29; "Flying Colors," Imperial Theatre, 1932-33; "Ziegfeld Follies," Winter Garden Theatre, 1934. Actor in plays, including: "Yokel Boy," produced on Broadway at Majestic Theatre, 1939; "The Male Animal," on tour, 1941, 1947, and on Broadway at Music Box Theatre, 1952-53; "Good Night, Ladies," on tour, 1941-42; "Show Boat," produced on Broadway at Ziegfeld Theatre, 1946-47; and numerous others, including "Take Her, She's Mine," "Our Town," and "Apple of His Eye." Actor in motion pictures, including: "Broadway Melody of 1936," 1935; "Captain January," 1936; "Born to Dance," 1936; "Banjo on My Knee," 1936; "Broadway Melody of 1938," 1937; "The Girl of the Golden West," 1938; "My Lucky Star," 1938; "Four Girls in White," 1939; "Yellow Jack," 1939; "Kid From Texas," 1939; "They Met in Argentina," 1941; "Parachute Battalion," 1941; "Sing Your Worries Away," 1942; "Under Mexicali Skies," 1950; "Thunder in God's Country," 1951; "Silver City Bonanza," 1951; "The Rodeo King and the Senorita," 1951; "Utah Wagon Train," 1951; "Red Garters," 1954; "Night People," 1954; "Davy Crockett, King of the Wild Frontier," 1955; "Davy Crockett and the River Pirates," 1956; "Attack," 1956; "Between Heaven and Hell," 1956; "Breakfast at Tiffany's," 1961; "The Interns," 1962; "Mail Order Bride," 1964; "The One and Only Genuine, Original Family Band," 1967; "The Daughters of Joshua Cabe" (television movie), 1972; "Terror at 37,000 Feet" (television movie), 1972; "Stones" (television movie). Appeared in television programs, including: "Davy Crockett," 1954; "Walt Disney Presents," c.1955; "The Mickey Mouse Club," c.1955; "Northwest Passage," 1958; "Westinghouse Presents," 1962; "The Andersonville Trial," 1970; "Tom Sawyer," 1973. Starred in television series: "The Beverly Hillbillies," 1962-70; "Barnaby Jones," 1972-80. Owner of Polynesian Concept (catamaran manufacturer). Lecturer on history. *Military service:* U.S. Coast Guard, 1942-46; became lieutenant.

WRITINGS—Under name Buddy Ebsen: "The Champagne General" (play), first produced in Altadena, Calif., 1964; (with George A. Gunston) *Polynesian Concept* (nonfiction), Prentice-Hall, 1972; (with daughter, Bonnie Ebsen) "Lahaina" (television script), 1979. Also author of "Honest John" (play), first produced in Southampton, N.Y.

Author of television scripts for "Barnaby Jones" series. Composer of songs, including: (With Fess Parker) "Be Sure You're Right, Then Go Ahead," "Baby Blues," "Squeezin' Polka," "Handsome Stranger," "I'll See You," (with Paul Mason Howard) "Whispering Pines."

WORK IN PROGRESS: A book of memoirs tentatively titled *My First Fifty Years in Show Business.*

SIDELIGHTS: Although Buddy Ebsen is probably best known as star of the popular television series "The Beverly Hillbillies" and "Barnaby Jones," he actually began his entertainment career as a dancer in 1928. In a partnership with his sister Vilma, Ebsen danced in Broadway revues and on vaudeville for seven years before venturing to Hollywood. The team split up after dancing together in one motion picture, "Broadway Melody of 1936," but Ebsen went on to appear on his own in a variety of movies during the late 1930's.

When Ebsen declined a seven-year contract with Metro-Goldwyn-Mayer in 1938 he found himself effectively banished from the motion picture business for the next fifteen years. Nevertheless, he continued to perform in plays and eventually gained nationwide popularity for his role as Fess Parker's sidekick in the Walt Disney television series "Davy Crockett."

In 1962 Ebsen took on the role of Jed Clampett in "The Beverly Hillbillies." The comedy series featured the wacky adventures of a nouveau riche Ozark family who move to Beverly Hills, California, after striking oil on their homestead. Although the show was panned by critics, it was immensely popular with television audiences for its entire nine-season run. Ebsen then starred in the series "Barnaby Jones," in which he played a private detective.

One of Ebsen's hobbies is sailing his thirty-five-foot catamaran, "Polynesian Concept." His book of the same name is an account of his 1968 sailing trip to Hawaii from Long Beach, California. He won the trans-Pacific race in his catamaran, the smallest boat entered in the contest, in a corrected time of eleven days, sixteen hours, and twenty minutes.

AVOCATIONAL INTERESTS: Sailing, playing guitar, literature, music, art, American history, numismatics, solar energy.

BIOGRAPHICAL/CRITICAL SOURCES: Yacht, September, 1972; *TV Guide,* August 9, 1975.

*   *   *

ECCLES, Frank 1923-

PERSONAL: Born January 16, 1923, in Manchester, England; son of Ben (a steam locomotive driver) and Eliza (a factory worker; maiden name, Wren) Eccles; married Gladys Joy Marriott (a teacher), April 15, 1946; children: Barbara, John, Christine, Peter. *Education:* Attended Lancaster Teachers' Training College, 1947-49. *Politics:* "Middle of the road—Liberal/Labour." *Religion:* Church of England. *Home:* 14 St. Luke's Rd., Haverigg, Millom, Cumbria, England. *Office:* Black Combe Junior School, Millom, Cumbria, England.

CAREER: Teacher in Wakefield, England, 1949-52, and in Malton, England, 1952-54; headmaster at schools in Amotherby, England, 1954-56, Oldenburg, West Germany, 1956-61, Duesseldorf, West Germany, 1961-63, and Muenster, West Germany, 1963-69; Black Combe School, Millom, England, headmaster, 1969—. *Military service:* British Army, Manchester Regiment, 1939-40; Royal Artillery, 1940-42; Para-

chute Regiment, 1942-46, prisoner of war in Germany, 1944-45. *Member:* National Association of Headteachers, Rugby Union Club.

WRITINGS: The Barbary Run, Longman, 1971; *Fifty Thousand Overcoats* (juvenile), Dent, 1973.

WORK IN PROGRESS: And There Went Youth, a war novel.

SIDELIGHTS: Eccles told *CA* he began writing because "I just wanted to prove myself. I married a graduate of University of London, and I suppose I had an inferiority complex. There was always an interest in the sea, but I couldn't afford a boat, so I read everything going and eventually thought I had enough technical material for a book about the sea. This was *The Barbary Run.* I bought a sailing cruiser (modest) out of the royalties, and I've been sailing ever since. *Fifty Thousand Overcoats* followed, but by this time I had a fair practical knowledge of sailing, and probably the story had too much technical detail for the average boy.

"At the present time I am writing for television. And every year since 1960 I have written a musical play for the children of my schools. I find a musician to help but I have written several scores. I have never offered a play for publication. Maybe I shall one day, but the market in England for children's musicals is tough. This year I wrote 'St. Benedict,' which we performed in the local church, to commemorate his 1500th anniversary.

"I play the trumpet and violin badly. I also took part in the local operatic society's last two productions, 'Oklahoma' and 'Camelot,' playing Merlin in the latter. I enjoy a bit of drama and would love to play Hamlet."

AVOCATIONAL INTERESTS: "I have been involved in Rugby football all my life. Just after the war I tried my luck with the professional Rugby League when I played for Wakefield Trinity. I did not make the grade. Officially that was me finished for life, but I removed to a remote part of Yorkshire, where I was unknown, and returned to the amateur game of Rugby Union. In Germany I played for a German club and eventually became a referee on the German net. I officiated at several international competitions in the 1960's. Now I am involved with the local Rugby Union club.

"I have traveled on camping holidays through the Balkans and into Turkey, Rumania, and Hungary—everywhere, except Poland and Russia."

*   *   *

EGLETON, Clive (Frederick) 1927-
(Patrick Blake, John Tarrant)

PERSONAL: Born November 25, 1927, in Harrow, England; son of Frederick and Rose (Wildman) Egleton; married Joan Evelyn Lane (an editor), April 9, 1949; children: Charles, Richard. *Education:* Attended private school in Hampstead, England. *Politics:* Conservative. *Religion:* Church of England. *Home and office:* Dolphin House, Beach House Lane, Bembridge, Isle of Wight PO35 5TA, England. *Agent:* John Farquharson Ltd., Bell House, Bell Yard, London WC2A 2JU, England.

CAREER: British Army, trooper in Royal Armoured Corps, 1945-46, lieutenant and rifle platoon commander in Staffordshire Regiment in India, 1946-48, lieutenant and transportation officer in Japan, 1949-51, lieutenant and anti-tank platoon commander in Ireland and Germany, 1952, captain in Germany, Egypt, Libya, Cyprus, and England, 1953-59, major in England, Kenya, Uganda, and Germany, 1960-70, lieutenant colonel in Nottingham, England, 1970-75, retiring as lieutenant colonel; writer, 1975—. *Member:* Crime Writers Association.

WRITINGS—Novels, except as indicated: *A Piece of Resistance,* Coward, 1970; *Last Post for a Partisan,* Coward, 1971; *The Judas Mandate,* Coward, 1972; *Seven Days to a Killing,* Coward, 1973; *The Bormann Brief,* Coward, 1974 (published in England as *The October Plot,* Hodder & Stoughton, 1974); *Skirmish,* Coward, 1975; *State Visit,* Hodder & Stoughton, 1976; *The Mills Bomb,* Atheneum, 1978; *The Stealing of Muriel McKay* (nonfiction), Reader's Digest Association, 1978; *Backfire,* Atheneum, 1979; *The Eisenhower Deception,* Atheneum, 1981 (published in England as *The Winter Touch,* Hodder & Stoughton, 1981); *The Baldau Touch* (nonfiction), Reader's Digest Association, 1981.

Novels under pseudonym Patrick Blake: *Escape to Athena,* Berkley Publishing, 1979; *Double Griffin,* Jove, 1981.

Novels under pseudonym John Tarrant: *The Rommel Plot,* Lippincott, 1977; *The Claubert Trigger,* Macdonald & Jane's, 1978, Atheneum, 1979.

WORK IN PROGRESS: *A Falcon for the Hawks* (tentative title).

SIDELIGHTS: Egleton told *CA:* "With the exception of *State Visit,* all novels written under my own name have appeared in paperback in the United States. They have also been published in France, Germany, Italy, Sweden, Finland, Spain, Brazil, Japan, and Holland."

*   *   *

EHRLICH, Cyril   1925-

PERSONAL: Born September 13, 1925, in London, England; son of Henry (a tailor) and Dinah (a dressmaker; maiden name, Jay) Ehrlich; married Felicity Bell-Bonnett (a librarian), May 1, 1954; children: Ruth, Paul, Robert. *Education:* London School of Economics and Political Science, London, B.Sc., 1950, Ph.D., 1958. *Home:* 36 Cranmore Gardens, Belfast BT9 6JC, Northern Ireland. *Office:* Department of Social and Economic History, Queen's University, Belfast, Northern Ireland.

CAREER: Makerere University, Kampala, Uganda, lecturer, 1952-58, senior lecturer in economic history, 1958-61; Queen's University, Belfast, Northern Ireland, lecturer, 1961-65, senior lecturer, 1965-69, reader, 1969-74, professor of social and economic history, 1974—, dean of faculty of economics, 1978-81. Member of board of Arts Council of Northern Ireland, 1966-79. *Military service:* British Army, 1944-47; served in India; became sergeant. *Member:* Economic History Society, Royal Musical Association.

WRITINGS: The Piano: A History, Dent, 1976. Contributor to *Oxford History of East Africa* and *New Grove Dictionary of Music.* Contributor to economic and music journals.

WORK IN PROGRESS: Research for a book on the history of the music profession in England, publication by Oxford University Press expected in 1982.

SIDELIGHTS: Ehrlich wrote: "I have always been interested in economic and social history, and music. In recent years these interests have coalesced, leading to the piano book. I play piano, harpsichord, and clavichord. I think there's great scope for serious work on the social history of music. I hate jargon and admire clear English."

ELLIS, Mark Karl   1945-

PERSONAL: Born August 1, 1945, in Musoorie, India; son of Charles William (a lecturer) and Jean Mary (Erle) Ellis; married wife, Printha Jane, August 30, 1969; children: Nathaniel Bjorn, Carson Joel. *Education:* Christ's College, Cambridge, M.A., 1967; University of Leeds, Postgraduate Diploma in English as a Second Language, 1970. *Home:* 9 Alexandra Rd., Leyton, London E.10, England. *Agent:* Deborah Rogers Ltd., 5-11 Mortimer St., London W1N 7RH, England. *Office:* Language Training Services, 10 Essex St., London W.C.2, England.

CAREER: Regional Institute of English, Chandigarh, India, lecturer in English, 1967-69; University of Tripoli, Tripoli, Libya, assistant lecturer in English, 1970-73; Asian Institute of Technology, Bangkok, Thailand, assistant professor of English, 1973-78; Professional Language Services, course coordinator, 1978-80; Language Training Services, London, England, senior partner, 1980—.

WRITINGS—Novels: *Bannerman,* Secker & Warburg, 1973; *A Fatal Charade,* Secker & Warburg, 1974; *The Adoration of the Hanged Man,* Secker & Warburg, 1975; *Survivors Beyond Babel,* Secker & Warburg, 1979.

Contributor to *Language Training.*

WORK IN PROGRESS Death by Water, a novel; a series of textbooks on reading skills, for Thomas Nelson.

SIDELIGHTS: Ellis commented: "I see my writing in cycles. The first cycle, from the age of seventeen to age twenty-five, was a period of juvenile trivia, very productive, approximately six or seven finished unpublished novels. The second cycle was from 1972-78, when I wrote my four published novels, all written with ease and published with ease. None of these four books is very similar to another; all attracted reviews and criticism of a consistent range—from praise to damnation. I consider myself outside the ordinary horizon of English fiction, though I believe I could only be an English writer.

"My concerns are with the destruction of present British society, and a lack of apparent destiny. My characters are often very lonely people, and there is always a great sense of loss. I am probably too young to deal with these themes, and may never be old enough. Experience has shown me that I am inadequate much of the time to project what I see, and there is always a fear, a very real fear, that it is in fact the camera itself which is faulty—that time will not change anything for the better.

"I see myself now in my third cycle—reflective, having novels rejected, constantly experimenting, having certain moments of great confidence, and others when I wonder if I will ever be able to handle my subjects with the respect and care they deserve. Meanwhile, the deterioration in British society—which I first began to write about in detail ten years ago—gets worse."

*   *   *

ELY, John Hart   1938-

PERSONAL: Born December 3, 1938, in New York, N.Y.; son of John and Martha (Coyle) Ely; children: John, Robert. *Education:* Princeton University, A.B., 1960; Yale University, LL.B., 1963; attended London School of Economics and Political Science, London, 1965-66. *Home:* 63 Atlantic Ave., Boston, Mass. 02110. *Office:* School of Law, Harvard University, Cambridge, Mass. 02138.

CAREER: Staff attorney on Warren Commission, 1964, and law clerk to Chief Justice Earl Warren of U.S. Supreme Court, 1964-65; Defenders, Inc., San Diego, Calif., lawyer, 1966-68; Yale University, New Haven, Conn., associate professor, 1968-70, professor of law, 1970-73; Harvard University, Cambridge, Mass., professor of law, 1973—. General counsel for U.S. Department of Transportation, 1975-76. *Military service:* U.S. Army, 1963-69; became first lieutenant. *Awards, honors:* Fulbright scholarship, 1965-66; M.A. from Yale University, 1971, and Harvard University, 1973.

WRITINGS: Democracy and Distrust: A Theory of Judicial Review, Harvard University Press, 1980. Contributor to law reviews and popular magazines.

* * *

ENDE, Richard Chaffey von
   See von ENDE, Richard Chaffey

* * *

ENGLE, Jeff(rey) 1947-

PERSONAL: Born October 20, 1947, in Brooklyn, N.Y.; son of William (a realtor) and Faye (Appelbaum) Engle. *Education:* Attended Queens College of the City University of New York, 1965-67; Bernard M. Baruch College of the City University of New York, B.B.A., 1969; attended St. John's University, Jamaica, N.Y., 1969. *Residence:* San Francisco, Calif. *Office:* Destiny Business Consultants, Suite 1500, 2 Penn Plaza, New York, N.Y. 10001.

CAREER: Teacher of mathematics and science at public school in Flushing, N.Y., 1969-70; worked as assistant sales manager in Suffolk, N.Y., 1970-73; Bahama Realty Corp., New York City, owner and administrator, 1974-76; Dykeman Medical Center, New York City, in sales and promotions, 1977-78; Destiny Business Consultants, New York City, president, in promotion, consulting, and printing in New York City and San Francisco, Calif., 1978—. Member of New York Hospital Planning Board, 1975; lecturer on metaphysics.

WRITINGS: The Power of Prediction, Destiny Business Consultants, 1981; *The Art of Creative Foolishness: A Book on Making Your Everyday Life a Fantasy,* Destiny Business Consultants, 1981.

WORK IN PROGRESS: A book on reincarnation "and its applications to freeing individuals from current problems and discovering hidden talents through regression and dream therapy," publication by Destiny Business Consultants expected in 1982; *The Key to Personal Prosperity: Following Your True Destiny Path.*

SIDELIGHTS: Engle told *CA:* "Awakened by a psychic experience in 1975, I started to have many reincarnational experiences and became adept with the Tarot. I spent literally hundreds of hours using the Tarot to study reincarnation and my own personal reality as well as asking it questions about itself and its multitudinous records. As I began to trust my own intuition more, I developed clairvoyance and the ability to regress people through psychic channeling. This technique allows most people to see their past lives as if they were motion pictures.

"I presently do a Personal Destiny Workshop that closes the gap between dreams and their realization, by aligning an individual's desires to his beliefs and destiny.

"*The Power of Prediction* got its start at a baccarat table in Atlantic City, when against all odds the bank won twelve straight times, with me bucking the odds all the way. Later, while licking my financial wounds, I realized that had I bet on the bank after the third or fourth time, I could only have lost once and, as it turned out, would have won nine in a row. I began to see that all life is just ebbs and flows of probable happenings. The book started as part of my daily journal and unfolded more and more each day. Basically, it reiterates 'when you are hot, you're hot, and when you're not, you're not,' and explains in detail how to determine the flows in your own life in order to lead a simpler and more prosperous existence."

* * *

ENGLISH, E. Schuyler 1899-1981

OBITUARY NOTICE: Born October 12, 1899, in New York, N.Y.; died March 16, 1981, in Philadelphia, Pa. Editor and author, best known as editor of the Pilgrim edition of the King James Bible. A former purchasing agent with Curtis Publishing Company in Philadelphia, English abandoned his business career to pursue religious projects. For ten years he worked on his Pilgrim edition of the Bible, which was intended for children and for those desiring a simplified text. English later headed a committee that labored for eleven years revising the *Scofield Reference Bible.* In addition, English wrote *Studies in the Gospel According to Matthew, Studies in the Gospel of Mark,* and *Robert G. Lee: A Chosen Vessel.* Obituaries and other sources: *American Authors and Books, 1640 to the Present Day,* 3rd revised edition, Crown, 1972; *Who's Who in Religion,* Marquis, 1977; *New York Times,* March 18, 1981; *Publishers Weekly,* April 3, 1981; *AB Bookman's Weekly,* May 4, 1981.

* * *

ERNEST, William
   See BERKEBILE, Fred D(onovan)

* * *

ETHRIDGE, Mark Foster 1896-1981

OBITUARY NOTICE: Born April 22, 1896, in Meridian, Miss.; died of a stroke, April 5, 1981, in Moncure, N.C. Editor and journalist, best known for his editorials in which he cursed racism and poverty. Ethridge was with the *Louisville Courier-Journal* and *Louisville Times* for twenty-seven years and is credited with helping make both publications nationally known and respected. Prior to his stint in Louisville, Ethridge was city and managing editor for the *Macon Telegraph* and general manager and publisher of the *Richmond Times-Dispatch* and held other positions with the *Washington Consolidated Press, New York Sun,* and *Columbus Enquirer-Sun.* In 1961 he was named chairman of the board of the Louisville newspapers and remained on it until 1980. Retiring from his position in Louisville in 1963, Ethridge was vice-president and editor of *Newsday* until 1965 and taught journalism at the University of North Carolina until 1968. Ethridge's ardent opposition to widespread racism and poverty led to his appointment as chairman of the Fair Employment Practices Committee by President Roosevelt. This committee investigated racial discrimination in employment. Later, President Truman appointed Ethridge to study whether diplomatic recognition should be granted to Bulgaria and Romania. Obituaries and other sources: *Current Biography,* Wilson, 1946; *The International Who's Who,* Europa, 1980; *New York Times,* April 7, 1981; *Newsweek,* April 20, 1981; *Time,* April 20, 1981.

EVANS, Dale
    See ROGERS, Dale Evans

*   *   *

EVANS, Hubert Reginald   1892-

PERSONAL: Born May 9, 1892, in Vankleek Hill, Ontario, Canada; married Anna Winter, 1920 (died, 1960); children: three. *Home:* Roberts Creek, Strait of Georgia, British Columbia, Canada.

CAREER: Novelist, poet, and writer of children's fiction. Newspaper reporter in Toronto, Ontario, and British Columbia for four years; worked for commercial fisheries and as a fisheries officer in salmon conservation in British Columbia. *Military service:* Rocky Mountain Rangers, 1915-19; served in France and Flanders.

WRITINGS—All juvenile fiction, except as noted: *Forest Friends: Stories of Animals, Fish, and Birds West of the Rockies,* Judson Press, 1926; *The New Front Line* (for adults), Macmillan, 1927; *Derry, Airedale of the Frontier* (illustrated by F. C. Yohn), Dodd, 1928; *Derry's Partner* (illustrated by Frank E. Schoonover), Dodd, 1929, reprinted, Grosset, 1953; *Derry of Totem Creek* (illustrated by H.E.M. Sellen), Dodd, 1930; *The Silent Call* (illustrated by Sellen), Dodd, 1930; *North to the Unknown: The Achievements and Adventures of David Thompson* (illustrated by Ruth Collins), Dodd, 1949; *Mist on the River* (for adults), Copp, 1954, reprinted, McClelland & Stewart, 1973; *Mountain Dog,* Westminster Press, 1956; *Whittlings* (poems; illustrated by Robert Jack), Harbour Publishing, 1976.

Contributor to periodicals, including *Canadian Magazine* and *St. Nicholas.*

SIDELIGHTS: Hubert Evans has spent most of his adult years living in and writing about the Skeena River area of British Columbia. Many of his writings are directed toward readers in their early teens, although Evans has published novels for adults and also a collection of verse.

Evans's stories focus on life in the wilderness of the province while touching on such issues as conservation and discrimination against Indians. Several of his stories, including his "Derry" books *North to the Unknown* and *Mountain Dog,* have a dog as a primary character. Evans's Newfoundlands and Airedales are depicted as the most loyal of friends, accompanying and supporting their masters on numerous adventures.*

EVANS, Richard L(ouis)   1906-1971

OBITUARY NOTICE—See index for *CA* sketch: Born March 23, 1906, in Salt Lake City, Utah; died November 1, 1971; buried in Salt Lake City. Radio announcer, editor, and author. For more than forty years, Richard Evans was a writer, producer, and commentator for the Mormon Tabernacle Choir's weekly network radio program, "Music and the Spoken Word." He contributed articles to such magazines and newspapers as the *Christian Science Monitor* and *Look,* and he wrote many books, including *Unto the Hills, Thoughts for One Hundred Days as Heard on Radio,* and *These Are the Mormons.* Obituaries and other sources: *New York Times,* November 2, 1971; *Who Was Who in America,* 5th edition, Marquis, 1973.

*   *   *

EVERETT, Arthur (W., Jr.)   1914-

PERSONAL: Born October 1, 1914, in Battle Creek, Mich; son of Arthur W. (a railroad electrician) and Blanche (Stanley) Everett; married Marie Lago, July 5, 1941; children: Arthur W. III. *Education:* Attended University of Notre Dame, 1931-33; University of Missouri, B.J., 1935. *Religion:* Roman Catholic. *Home:* 144-07 Sanford Ave., Flushing, N.Y. 11355. *Office:* Associated Press, 50 Rockefeller Plaza, New York, N.Y. 10020.

CAREER: Battle Creek Enquirer and News, Battle Creek, Mich., reporter, 1936-37; *Bay City Times,* Bay City, Mich., reporter, 1937-41; reporter for Associated Press, New York, N.Y. *Military service:* U.S. Army Air Forces, 1941-45; served in Europe, Africa, and the Middle East; became staff sergeant; received Silver Star and Bronze Star.

WRITINGS: (With Kathryn Johnson and Harry F. Rosenthal) *Calley,* Dell, 1971.

BIOGRAPHICAL/CRITICAL SOURCES: New York Times Book Review, July 11, 1971.

*   *   *

EZELL, Harry E(ugene)   1918-1974

OBITUARY NOTICE—See index for *CA* sketch: Born June 12, 1918, in Leavenworth County, Kan.; died February 13, 1974. Methodist minister, educator, and author. Harry Ezell wrote *The Hall Family of Maple Hill* and contributed articles, fiction, and poetry to magazines and newspapers. (Date of death provided by wife, Mary Ellen Ezell.)

F

FABBRI, Nancy Rash 1940-
   (Mary Harrison)

PERSONAL: Born November 19, 1940, in Louisville, Ky.; daughter of Dillman A. (a financial adviser) and Nancy (Batson) Rash; married Remo Fabbri, Jr. (a physician), June 27, 1962; children: Gian-Dillman Rash. *Education:* Radcliffe College, B.A., 1962; Bryn Mawr College, M.A., 1965, Ph.D., 1971. *Residence:* Cornwall Hollow, Conn. *Agent:* Mary Yost Associates, Inc., 75 East 55th St., New York, N.Y. 10022. *Office:* Department of Art History, Connecticut College, New London, Conn. 06320.

CAREER: Connecticut College, New London, assistant professor, 1972-76, associate professor of art history, 1976—. Visiting lecturer at Yale University, summer, 1975. *Member:* International Center of Medieval Art, College Art Association, Renaissance Society, Phi Beta Kappa.

WRITINGS: Infertility, Houghton, 1977. Contributor to magazines, including *Good Housekeeping* (under pseudonym Mary Harrison), *Journal of the Warburg and Courtauld Institutes, Numismatic Chronicle,* and *Gesta.*

WORK IN PROGRESS: Life Begins at What?, with Art Milner; *Undiscovered Italy; Romanesque Mosaic Floors in South Italy,* with Clara Bargellini.

SIDELIGHTS: Nancy Fabbri commented: "Personal experiences and the lack of such a book led me to write *Infertility,* and the letters I have received demonstrate how many people needed help and sympathy. The medical community has also voiced an interest in using this book for patients. My other two areas of interest are history and the history of art, professionally motivated but personally satisfying. *Life Begins at What?* is the result of attempted humor over the mid-life crisis which is upon me."

*   *   *

FABISCH, Judith Patricia 1938-

PERSONAL: Born August 30, 1938, in Milwaukee, Wis.; daughter of Joseph (a building contractor) and Gertrude I. (Wollman) Theriault; married Edward J. Fabisch, June 28, 1958 (died, 1973); children: Scott Edward. *Education:* Grand Rapids Baptist College, B.A., 1977. *Home address:* Box 456, Goroka E.H.P., Papua New Guinea.

CAREER: Association of Baptists for World Evangelism, Cherry Hill, N.J., missionary in Goroka, Papua New Guinea, 1978—.

WRITINGS: Not Ready to Walk Alone, Zondervan, 1978.

WORK IN PROGRESS: A simplified church history; a Christian life text; assisting unwed mothers.

*   *   *

FAIRBAIRNS, Zoe Ann 1948-

PERSONAL: Born December 20, 1948, in England; daughter of John Joshua (an estate agent) and Isabel (a geologist; maiden name, Dippie) Fairbairns. *Education:* Attended College of William and Mary, 1969-70; University of St. Andrews, M.A. (with honors), 1972. *Politics:* "Feminist." *Religion:* "Feminist." *Agent:* A.M. Heath & Co., 40-42 William IV St., London WC2N 4DD., England.

CAREER: Writer.

WRITINGS: Live as Family, Macmillan, 1968; *Down: An Explanation,* Macmillan, 1969; *Study War No More,* CND, 1974; (with Jim Wintour) *No Place to Grow Up,* Shelter, 1977; (co-author) *Tales I Tell My Mother,* Journeyman, 1978; *Benefits,* Virago, 1979.

*   *   *

FAIRHALL, David Keir 1934-

PERSONAL: Born November 10, 1934, in Clacton-on-Sea, England; son of Henry William and Millicent Rebecca Fairhall; married Katherine Pamela Cole (an art teacher), February, 1960; children: Jim, David, Catherine. *Education:* London School of Economics and Political Science, London, B.Sc., 1956. *Home:* 10 Wellington Rd., Maldon, Essex, England. *Office: Guardian,* 119 Farringdon Rd., London E.C.1, England.

CAREER: Guardian, London, England, currently associate editor. *Military service:* Royal Navy, Russian interpreter, 1956-58. *Member:* International Institute of Strategic Studies, Royal United Services Institute for Defence Studies.

WRITINGS: Russia Looks to the Sea, Deutsch, 1970; *Black Tide Rising,* Deutsch, 1980. Author and presenter of documentary television programs.

WORK IN PROGRESS: A yachting textbook.

SIDELIGHTS: Fairhall commented: "I have a great interest in the sea, and much of my work has been connected with it. My naval service, for instance, included the first Icelandic 'cod war,' and I covered the last one as a journalist. My specialty in military affairs is the Soviet Union, especially Soviet maritime strategy. I live on the eastern coast of England so as to be near the water and my boat."

AVOCATIONAL INTERESTS: Music.

* * *

FALLON, Padraic 1905-1974

PERSONAL: Born January 3, 1905, in Athenry, Ireland; died October 9, 1974; married Dorothea Maher, 1930; children: six sons. *Education:* Educated at Mt. St. Joseph's College, Roscrea, County Tipperary, Ireland. *Home:* Hill Cottage, Scilly, Kinsale, County Cork, Ireland.

CAREER: Poet and playwright. Worked as a customs official in Wexford, Ireland, for forty years. *Member:* Irish Academy of Letters.

WRITINGS: Lighting Up Time (short stories), Orwell Press, 1938; "The Seventh Step" (play), produced in Dublin, Ireland, 1954; (editor) *The Poems of Emily Lawless,* Dufour, 1964; "Sweet Love Till Morn" (play), produced in Dublin, 1971; *Collected Poems,* Dolmen Press, 1974.

Radio plays: "Diarmuid and Grainne"; "The Vision of Maconglinne"; "The Wooing of Etain"; "Deirdre's King"; "The Poplar"; "Steeple Jerkin"; "Outpost; or, Out on a Limb"; "Last and Final Appearance"; "The Third Bachelor"; "The Five Stations"; "At the Bridge Inn"; "Two Men With a Face"; "The Hags of Clough". Also author of television play, "The Shield of Steel," 1966.*

* * *

FARBER, Leslie Hillel 1912-1981

OBITUARY NOTICE: Born July 12, 1912, in Carlsbad, N.M.; died of a heart attack, March 24, 1981, in New York, N.Y. Psychoanalyst and author, known as a leading proponent of the existential movement in psychiatry. A former chairman of the Association of Existential Psychology and Psychiatry and faculty chairman of the Washington School of Psychiatry, Farber wrote many essays and papers addressing various human problems and conditions. Among his writings are *Lying, Despair, Jealousy, Envy, Sex, Suicide, Drugs and the Good Life,* a collection of essays, and *The Ways of the Will,* which explains Farber's theory of the disordered will. Obituaries and other sources: *American Men and Women of Science: The Physical and Biological Sciences,* 12th edition, Bowker, 1973; *New York Times,* March 27, 1981; *Washington Post,* March 27, 1981.

* * *

FARBER, Stephen E. 1943-

PERSONAL: Born July 13, 1943, in Cleveland, Heights, Ohio; son of Lester J. and Zelda (Hantman) Farber. *Education:* Amherst College, B.A., 1965; University of California, Berkeley, M.A. (English), 1967; University of California, Los Angeles, M.A. (theatre arts), 1969. *Home:* 10611 Wilkins Ave., No. 6, Los Angeles, Calif. 90024.

CAREER: New West, Beverly Hills, Calif., film critic, 1976—. Extension instructor at University of California, Los Angeles, 1979—. *Member:* National Society of Film Critics, Writers Guild of America.

WRITINGS: The Movie Rating Game, Public Affairs Press, 1972. Contributor to magazines, including *Esquire, Partisan Review, Hudson Review, American Scholar, Film Quarterly,* and *Film Comment,* and newspapers.

* * *

FARBER, Thomas (David) 1944-

PERSONAL: Born April 26, 1944, in Boston, Mass.; son of Sidney and Norma (Holzman) Farber. *Education:* Harvard University, B.A., 1965. *Home:* 1827 Virginia St., Berkeley, Calif. 94703. *Agent:* Ellen Levine, 370 Lexington Ave., Suite 906, New York, N.Y. 10017.

CAREER: Writer. *Awards, honors:* Guggenheim fellow; National Endowment for the Arts fellow.

WRITINGS: Tales for the Son of My Unborn Child, Dutton, 1971; *Who Wrote the Book of Love?,* Norton, 1977; *Whatever the Cost,* Creative Arts, 1979; *Hazards to the Human Heart,* Dutton, 1980; *The Material Plane,* Dutton, 1980.

* * *

FARELY, Alison
See POLAND, Dorothy (Elizabeth Hayward)

* * *

FAULKNER, Harold Underwood 1890-1968

OBITUARY NOTICE—See index for *CA* sketch: Born February 25, 1890, in Taylor, Pa.; died June 17, 1968. Educator, historian, and author. A professor of history for more than thirty-five years, Harold Faulkner was a contributor of articles to encyclopedias, magazines, and professional journals. Among his books are *From Versailles to the New Deal, The Decline of Laissez Faire, 1897-1917,* and *Politics, Reform, and Expansion, 1890-1900.* Obituaries and other sources: *New York Times,* June 20, 1968; *Who Was Who in America,* 5th edition, Marquis, 1973.

* * *

FAVILLE, David Ernest 1899-1970

OBITUARY NOTICE—See index for *CA* sketch: Born December 8, 1899, in Doylestown, Pa.; died October 12, 1970, in Palo Alto, Calif.; buried in Alta Mesa Cemetery, Palo Alto, Calif. Educator and author. A professor of marketing at Stanford University for thirty-eight years, David Faville also served as a marketing consultant to major corporations and government agencies. He was the author of books, including *Selected Case Problems in Retailing* and *Selected Cases in Marketing Management.* Obituaries and other sources: *Who Was Who in America,* 5th edition, Marquis, 1973; *National Cyclopedia of American Biography,* Volume 57, 1977.

* * *

FAWKES, Richard (Brian) 1944-

PERSONAL: Born July 31, 1944, in Camberley, England; son of Stanley Victor and Dorothy Lawrance (Cooper) Fawkes; married Cherry Elizabeth Cole (a television producer), April 17, 1971. *Education:* St. David's University College, University of Wales, B.A. (with honors), 1967. *Politics:* Liberal. *Religion:* Agnostic. *Home:* 66 Castlebar Park, London W5 1BU, England. *Agent:* David Higham Associates Ltd., 5-8 Lower John St., Golden Sq., London W1R 4HA, England.

CAREER: British Broadcasting Corp. (BBC-TV), London, England, general trainee, 1967-68, director, 1969-71; free-lance assistant film director for commercials, documentaries, and feature films, 1971—. *Member:* Society of Authors, Society for Theatre Research, Association of Cinematograph, Television, and Allied Technicians.

WRITINGS: (With Michael Darlow) *The Last Corner of Arabia (nonfiction),* Quartet, *1976; Fighting for a Laugh* (nonfiction), Macdonald & Jane's, 1978; *Dion Boucicault: A Biography,* Quartet, 1979.

Television and radio plays: "Magic Boucicault" (first broadcast by BBC-Radio, April, 1976); "Don't Forget the Umbrella" (first broadcast by BBC-Radio, September, 1980); "The Shaughraun" (adapted from work of same title by Dion Boucicault; first broadcast by BBC-Radio, December, 1980); "Language at Work" (first broadcast by BBC-TV, January, 1980); "Something Different" (first broadcast by BBC-TV, October, 1980).

Documentary films: Three parts in series, "Risk Control for Profit," RM-EMI, 1975; "The Last Corner of Arabia," Stella Richman Productions 1976; "The Monarchy—A Family for Today," Central Office of Information, 1979; "Why Industry Matters," Video Arts, 1980.

Contributor to *Music and Musicians* and *Classical Music.*

WORK IN PROGRESS: With Michael Langdon, an autobiography of opera singer Michael Langdon, publication by Julia Macrae Books expected in 1982; a novel; the book and lyrics for a musical; stage plays; radio plays.

SIDELIGHTS: Fawkes told *CA:* "Most of my writing so far has been for money; very little has been the sort of work I would do if I didn't have to pay my mortgage regularly. I would, however, exclude my biography of Dion Boucicault from that. He became a fascination and will stay with me for the rest of my life, and if I have managed one worthwhile thing so far, it has been that I have helped in a small way to make him and his work better known."

AVOCATIONAL INTERESTS: Music (especially opera), theatre (especially musicals and nineteenth-century theatre), travel.

*   *   *

FEAVER, William Andrew 1942-

PERSONAL: Born December 26, 1942, in Salisbury, England; son of Douglas Russell (a minister) and Katharine (Stubbs) Feaver; married wife, Vicki (a poet); children: Jane, Emily, Jessica, Silas. *Education:* Keble College, Oxford, B.A., 1963, M.A., 1965. *Home:* 23 Somers Rd., London S.W.2, England. *Agent:* Deborah Rogers Ltd., 5-11 Mortimer St., London W1N 7RH, England.

CAREER: University of Newcastle-upon-Tyne, Newcastle-upon-Tyne, England, James Knott research fellow, 1971-73; *Observer,* London, England, art critic, 1975—. Member of Arts Council art panel, 1973-79.

WRITINGS: The Art of John Martin, Oxford University Press, 1975; *When We Were Very Young,* Thames & Hudson, 1977; *The Art of Caricature,* Weidenfeld & Nicolson, 1981. Writer for television, film, and radio. Contributor to magazines, including *London* and *Art News.* Art critic for *Listener,* 1970-74, and *Financial Times,* 1973-74. Art adviser for *Sunday Times,* 1973-75

*   *   *

FENG, Chin
See LIU, Sydney (Chieh)

FERGUSON, J(ohn) Halcro 1920-1968

OBITUARY NOTICE—See index for *CA* sketch: Born April 10, 1920, in Teddington, Middlesex, England; died July 5, 1968. Journalist and author. While serving as the Latin American correspondent for the *London Observer,* J. Halcro Ferguson wrote several books, including *Latin America: The Balance of Race Redressed* and *The Revolutions of Latin America.* He was co-author of *The River Plate Republics: Argentina, Paraguay, Uruguay* and translator of Enrique Meneses's book, *Fidel Castro.* (Date of death provided by wife, Valerie Ferguson.)

*   *   *

FEUCHT, Oscar E(mil) 1895-

PERSONAL: Surname is pronounced Foist; born December 25, 1895, in Cuyahoga Falls, Ohio; son of Christian (a woodworker) and Amalie (Heyer) Feucht; married Erna Christine Schultz (an executive secretary), June 5, 1930; children: Frederic Nathan, Henry Jerome, Eleanor Louise (Mrs. James Sudbrock), Richard Heyer. *Education:* Attended Concordia College, Fort Wayne, Ind., and Concordia Seminary, St. Louis, Mo. *Home:* 11823 Parklind Dr., St. Louis, Mo. 63127.

CAREER: Ordained Lutheran minister; pastor of Lutheran churches in Wartburg, Tenn., 1920-25, and Kansas City, Mo., 1925-45; Lutheran Church, Missouri Synod, St. Louis, secretary of adult education for Board of Parish Education, 1945-69; writer, 1969—. Past dean of St. Louis Lutheran Bible Institute. Director of training projects, "Bible Study Advance" and "Train Two." Created family life workshops and worked for annual observance of Christian Family Week. Past executive officer of Coordinating Committee for Parish Services. *Member:* American Bible Society (honorary life member), Lutheran Education Association, Lutheran Forum, Missouri Botanical Garden, St. Louis Bach Society, St. Louis Horticultural Society, Concordia Historical Society. *Awards, honors:* D.D. from Concordia Seminary, 1955.

WRITINGS: Manual of Practical Church Work, Lutheran Press, 1940; *Take the Sword of the Spirit,* Concordia, 1952; *The Practice of Prayer,* Concordia, 1956; *Ministry to Families,* Concordia, 1963; *Learning to Use Your Bible,* Concordia, 1969; *Christian's Worship,* Concordia, 1971; *Everyone a Minister,* Concordia, 1974.

Editor: *Studying His Word,* Concordia, 1948; *Christ and His Church,* Concordia, 1951; (also contributor) *Helping Families Through the Church,* Concordia, 1957, revised edition, 1971; (with others) *Engagement and Marriage,* Concordia, 1959; *Small Bible Study Groups,* Concordia, 1961; (with Harry G. Coiner, Alfred von Rohr Sauer, and Paul G. Hansen) *Sex and the Church,* Concordia, 1961; John W. Constable, *The Church Since Pentecost,* Concordia, 1969; Edward C. May, *Christian Family Living,* Concordia, 1970; Richard J. Schultz, *The Christian's Mission,* Concordia, 1970; (also contributor) *Family Relationships and the Church,* Concordia, 1970.

Contributor: Roy B. Zuck and Gene A. Getz, editors, *Adult Education in the Church,* Moody, 1970; Zuck and Getz, editors, *Ventures in Family Living,* Moody, 1971; Zuck and Robert E. Clark, editors, *Childhood Education in the Church,* Moody, 1975. Author of religious pamphlets and tracts. Editor of "Marriage and Family Research Series," Concordia, and "Adult Bible Class Series One Hundred," Concordia. Contributor to theology journals.

WORK IN PROGRESS: Guidelines for Women's Groups in the Church, for Concordia.

AVOCATIONAL INTERESTS: Reading.

*   *   *

ffRENCH-BEYTAGH, Gonville (Aubie) 1912-

PERSONAL: Surname is pronounced French-*Bee*-ta; born January 26, 1912, in Shanghai, China; son of Leo Michael and Edith (Watson) ffrench-Beytagh. *Education:* St. Paul's Theological College, Grahamstown, South Africa, L.Th., 1938. *Home and office:* St. Vedast's Rectory, Foster Lane, London EC2V 6HH, England.

CAREER: Sheepshearer and lumberjack in New Zealand, Australia, and South Africa, 1929-33; ordained Anglican priest, 1939; parish priest in Springs, Germiston, and Johannesburg, South Africa, 1938-55; dean of Salisbury, Rhodesia, 1955-65, and Johannesburg, South Africa, 1965-72; rector of St. Vedast's Church, London, England. Canon of Johannesburg and Canterbury.

WRITINGS: Prescription Sixty-Nine, Church of Province of South Africa, 1969; *Encountering Darkness*, Collins, 1973; *Encountering Light*, Collins, 1975; *Facing Depression*, Sisters of the Love of God Press, 1978.

SIDELIGHTS: ffrench-Beytagh moved to New Zealand in 1929. His decision to become a priest came after a beating he received in a Johannesburg subway. As a priest, he argued against apartheid in South Africa and welcomed all races to worship at his church. The white government of South Africa tried him in 1971 under the Terrorism Act, charging him with plotting the violent overthrow of the government. He was convicted by the Supreme Court of Transvaal and sentenced to five years in prison. The next year his conviction was overturned by the South Africa Supreme Court, and, suffering from heart problems and hypertension, ffrench-Beytagh left South Africa for England. He has toured Canada and the United States, lecturing on South Africa.

BIOGRAPHICAL/CRITICAL SOURCES: Esylt Newbury, *Parson's Daughter*, R. Hale, 1958; *New York Times*, August 14, 1971.

*   *   *

FIELD, Frank McCoy 1887-1978

OBITUARY NOTICE—See index for *CA* sketch: Born May 4, 1887, in Mason, Mich.; died May 20, 1978. Minister, editor, and author. A Methodist minister for more than thirty years, Frank Field was the author of *Where Jesus Walked: Through the Holy Land With the Master*. He was also associate editor of *Holy Land Pictorial News*. Obituaries and other sources: *Who's Who in America*, 39th edition, Marquis, 1976. (Date of death provided by daughter, Marjorie Field Hall.)

*   *   *

FILICCHIA, Ralph 1935-
(Ralph Michaels)

PERSONAL: Born November 5, 1935, in Boston, Mass.; son of Anthony (a taxicab owner) and Lydia (Prioli) Filicchia; married Carol Livingstone (a nurse), October 21, 1966; children: Juliane, Andrea Rose, Terri-Lynn. *Education:* Attended public schools in Watertown, Mass. *Politics:* Republican (conservative). *Religion:* Evangelical Baptist. *Home:* 121 Bellevue Rd., Watertown, Mass. 02172.

CAREER: Myerson Tooth, Cambridge, Mass., moldcutter, 1954-70; Spider Staging, Waltham, Mass., rigger, 1970-76;

Wise Potato Chips, Cambridge, route salesman, 1976—. Author. *Military service:* Massachusetts National Guard, 1958-64.

WRITINGS—Under pseudonym Ralph Michaels: *Share the New Life With a Catholic* (nonfiction), Moody, 1975; *Maybe I Sound Like a Nut* (novel), Herald Press, 1976; *A Broken Melody* (novel), Fleming Revell, 1977; *The Girl on First Base* (novel), Leisure Books, 1981. Also author of several unpublished novels, including *Bloody Sunday, One Angry Man, The Night of the Preacher, The Potato Chip Man*, and *The Ballplayers*.

Contributor of numerous articles and short stories to newspapers and periodicals, including *Christian Science Monitor, Denver Post, Applied Christianity, Southern Libertarian Review*, and *Weight Watcher's Magazine*.

SIDELIGHTS: Filicchia told *CA:* "I have two writing goals: to be a best-selling novelist and to someday have my own newspaper column in which I can tear apart the foolishness that passes for social and political intelligence. I consider political and religious liberalism dangers that should be exposed. I find that I do my best nonfiction writing when I am ripping mad about something.

"I would like to concentrate on evangelical Christian writing, but find this almost impossible because of the attitudes of Christian publishers. They live in a world of their own making that is totally divorced from reality and have set themselves up as guardians of the faith (which they are not). They refuse to recognize the place and power of the novel and concentrate instead on shallow and semi-psychological trivia that seems aimed at emotionally crippled housewives. Someday someone is going to get an honest and realistic Christian novel published by a secular publishing house—and it will sell big because the huge untapped audience is there just waiting for it. I'd like to be the one who writes it.

"I never took a writing course, but I read everything I can get my hands on. I have been influenced very much by the style of Stephen Crane and the forcefulness of Ayn Rand."

*   *   *

FISCHER, Bobby
See FISCHER, Robert James

*   *   *

FISCHER, Robert James 1943-
(Bobby Fischer)

PERSONAL: Born March 9, 1943, in Chicago, Ill.; son of Gerald (a biophysicist) and Regina (a schoolteacher and registered nurse; maiden name, Wender) Fischer. *Education:* Educated in Brooklyn, N.Y. *Agent:* Management III Ltd., 1345 Avenue of the Americas, New York, N.Y. 10019.

CAREER: International grand master of chess, 1958—. Won first United States Chess Championship, 1958; became world champion, 1972.

WRITINGS—All under name Bobby Fischer: *Games of Chess*, Simon & Schuster, 1959; (with Stuart Margulies and Donn Mosenfelder) *Bobby Fischer Teaches Chess*, Basic Systems, 1966; *My Sixty Memorable Games: Selected and Fully Annotated*, Simon & Schuster, 1969.

SIDELIGHTS: Fischer's name is synonymous with chess in the United States. In 1958, at the age of fifteen, Fischer became the youngest winner in the history of the U.S. chess championship. By that time, Fischer had been playing chess for nine years and had proven himself at the highly regarded

Manhattan Chess Club. Early tutelage from Carmine Nigro, president of the Brooklyn Chess Club, helped Fischer immensely while still a youngster, though he was not outstanding in early tournaments. In 1956, however, he became the United States' youngest junior champion, and the following year he bested a field of 175 players and earned the right to play U.S. champion Arthur B. Bisguier. Fischer defeated Bisguier in 1958 and won the Lessing J. Rosenwald and Frank J. Marshall trophies.

Fischer's career stalled in the mid-1960's when he began avoiding tournaments to protest meager prize money. He also refused to play in tournaments sanctioned by the Federation Internationale des Echecs (FIDE) and charged that the eminent chess organization was allowing Soviet players to monopolize the matches.

In 1970, after abandoning chess for one year, Fischer reentered the chess world, complaining that he was tired of being the "unofficial" champion of the world. In play unequaled in chess history, Fischer defeated ex-champion Tigran Petrosian, then shut out Mark Taimanov and Bent Larson, before defeating Petrosian again to determine the challenger in the match against Soviet player Boris Spassky. Although the match was marred by the press's emphasis on Fischer's eccentric behavior, Fischer persuaded chess enthusiasts to acknowledge his superiority by easily defeating Spassky. Fischer soon disappeared from tournament-level chess, though, and his title was eventually forfeited to another Soviet player, Anatoly Karpov.

BIOGRAPHICAL/CRITICAL SOURCES: New York Times Magazine, February 23, 1958, November 14, 1971, September 3, 1972; *Harper's,* January, 1962; *Saturday Review,* April 27, 1963; Frank Robert Brady, *Profile of a Prodigy: The Life and Games of Bobby Fischer,* McKay, 1965; *Time,* August 2, 1971, July 10, 1972, July 31, 1972, October 28, 1974; Brad Darrach, *Bobby Fisher vs. The Rest of the World,* Stein & Day, 1975; *Newsweek,* November 15, 1976, September 4, 1978.*

*   *   *

FISH, Robert L. 1912-1981
(Robert L. Pike)

OBITUARY NOTICE—See index for *CA* sketch: Born August 21, 1912, in Cleveland, Ohio; died of a heart attack, February 24, 1981, in Trumbull, Conn. Consulting engineer, novelist, and author. A consulting engineer to the plastic industry, Fish wrote his first novel, *The Fugitive,* at the age of forty-eight. He wrote many other books, including *The Diamond Bubble, Whirligig,* and *The Wager.* The Mystery Writers of America honored the author's work with three Edgar Allen Poe awards. Fish was also co-author of *My Life and the Beautiful Game,* the autobiography of soccer star Pele. Obituaries and other sources: *New York Times,* February 25, 1981; *Publishers Weekly,* March 13, 1981.

*   *   *

FISHEL, Elizabeth 1950-

PERSONAL: Born May 6, 1950, in New York, N.Y.; daughter of James Wilson (an advertising executive) and Edith (a potter; maiden name, Rubin) Fishel; married Robert Houghteling (a teacher), October 13, 1978. *Education:* Radcliffe College, B.A., (cum laude), 1972; Stanford University, M.A., 1974. *Religion:* Jewish. *Residence:* Oakland, Calif. *Agent:* Patricia Berens, Sterling Lord Agency, Inc., 660 Madison Ave., New York, N.Y. 10021.

CAREER: Free-lance writer, 1970—. Instructor in creative writing at University of California, Berkeley, 1976-79; gives workshops and lectures at San Francisco State College. *Member:* San Francisco Media Alliance, San Francisco Feminist Writers Guild.

WRITINGS: Sisters: Love and Rivalry Inside the Family and Beyond, Morrow, 1979. Contributor of nearly fifty articles and reviews to magazines, including *Ms., Human Behavior, Viva, New York,* and *Ramparts,* and newspapers.

WORK IN PROGRESS: The Men in Our lives.

SIDELIGHTS: Elizabeth Fishel commented: "My work always begins with the personal and grows from there through research into other people's lives and stories. *Sisters* began with my curiosity about my relationship with my younger sister, and our periods of closeness, distance and change. Where *Sisters* looked at the ways women learn about their lives from other women, *The Men in Our Lives* explores what we can learn about ourselves from crucial men, including fathers, lovers, and husbands."

BIOGRAPHICAL/CRITICAL SOURCES: Human Behavior, December, 1977.

*   *   *

FISHER, (Donald) Gary 1938-

PERSONAL: Born October 20, 1938, in Los Angeles, Calif.; son of Fred and Louise (Miller) Fisher; married Nanelle Marie (died September 10, 1979); married Barbara Anne Duncan, December 16, 1979; children: Shane Daniel. *Home:* 14846 Brentstone, Sunnymead, Calif. 92388.

CAREER: Non-denominational Christian minister and evangelist. *Military service:* U.S. Army, 1964. *Member:* Full Gospel Businessmen's Fellowship Association.

WRITINGS: (With Robert L. McGrath) *Satan's Been Cross Since Calvary,* Hawthorne, 1974; (with McGrath) *Abusers,* Mott Media, 1975.

WORK IN PROGRESS: Set Free.

SIDELIGHTS: Fisher's wife, Barbara, told *CA:* "Gary was dishonorably discharged from the army for drug abuse. He wants to share his life experiences in order to enlighten other people about drug abuse and what long-term using may do. For him and many others like him Jesus Christ is the only answer to a complete and normal life."

*   *   *

FISHER, Joe 1947-

PERSONAL: Born June 18, 1947, in Bristol, England; son of Graham (a Baptist minister) and Monica (a guest house proprietress; maiden name, Hilton) Fisher. *Education:* Wolverhampton College of Technology, certificate in journalism, 1969. *Residence:* Toronto, Ontario, Canada. *Office: Toronto Sun,* 333 King St. E., Toronto, Ontario, Canada M5A 3X5.

CAREER: Staffordshire Advertiser, Staffordshire, England, reporter, 1969-71, news editor, 1972; *Toronto Sun,* Toronto, Ontario, reporter, 1973-74; free-lance writer, 1974-77; *Toronto Sun,* assistant city editor, 1977-79; feature writer on Sunday edition, 1979—; free-lance writer.

WRITINGS: Skin Dive (novel), General Publishing, 1977; *Predictions* (nonfiction), Van Nostrand, 1980. Feature writer for *Showcase.*

WORK IN PROGRESS: The Graveyard Shift, a novel, publication expected in 1981; a collection of poetry; editing a travel journal he wrote while living in Ecuador.

SIDELIGHTS: Fisher wrote: "*Predictions* was written in four months, four months of full-time writing, seven days a week. It made me appreciate how important self-discipline is to a writer. I have traveled to Europe, Malaysia, South and Central America, and North Africa. I always keep a journal when traveling, because for me journals are a never-ending resource. *Skin Dive* was written in a ladies' washroom in a disused bowling club in Harrow, England, and on the Greek isle of Siphnos. Travel stimulates this writer's pen like nothing else."

*   *   *

FITZ-RANDOLPH, Jane (Currens)   1915-

PERSONAL: Name legally changed in 1951; born June 23, 1915, in Boulder, Colo; daughter of Jesse Wilson (a Presbyterian minister) and Gertrude (a teacher; maiden name, Fitz-Randolph) Currens; married Frederick Charles Porter (an engineer), June 19, 1935 (divorced, 1950); children: Frederick Charles, Jr., Philip Edward, Priscilla Jane. *Education:* University of Colorado, B.A., 1937; graduate study at Tulane University of Louisiana, George Washington University, and University of California, Los Angeles. *Politics:* Independent. *Religion:* Christian Science. *Home:* 1845 Bluebell Ave., Boulder, Colo. 80302.

CAREER: National Writers Club, Denver, Colo., critic and teacher, 1950-62, member of board of directors, 1972—, vice president, 1979—; University of Colorado, Denver and Boulder, instructor in writing, 1950-79. *Member:* Society of Children's Book Writers, Colorado Authors League. *Awards, honors:* Golden Eagle Award from Council on International Nontheatrical Events (CINE), 1978, for "What's So Great About Books?"; award of excellence from Society for Technical Communication, 1979, for *From Sundials to Atomic Clocks;* honorable mention from New York Academy of Sciences, 1980, for *Time and Clocks for the Space Age;*

WRITINGS: Writing for the Juvenile and Teenage Market, Funk, 1969, revised edition published as *How to Write for Children and Young Adults,* Barnes & Noble, 1980; (with James Jespersen) *From Sundials to Atomic Clocks,* U.S. Government Printing Office, 1978; (with Jespersen) *Time and Clocks for the Space Age,* Atheneum, 1980; (with Jespersen) *Mercury's Web,* Atheneum, 1981. Author of scripts for more than forty educational films and filmstrips, including "If You're for Colorado," 1966, "Pacific Neighbor States," 1968, "The Search for the Hidden Sugar," 1973, "Sharing Literature With Children," 1976, "What's So Great About Books?" 1978, and "America's Railroads: How the Iron Horse Shaped Our Nation," 1980.

WORK IN PROGRESS: A book on computers; a textbook on writing for audiovisual media.

SIDELIGHTS: Fitz-Randolph told *CA:* "I began writing part time for magazines in my college days, but I was first and foremost a career mother. When supporting my family became necessary, I began writing scripts for nontheatrical films and filmstrips. At one time I wrote for the national radio program of the Christian Science church. My church and religion are my central interest and activity; whatever I've done in writing or as a person would have been impossible without a foundation in spiritual values. My greatest joys are the achievements of my children and grandchildren, and, also, the achievements of my students and former students. I love to teach—it is the most exciting and rewarding profession in the world.

"I am admittedly a perfectionist and have no patience with 'good enough' or 'it will get by.' If I'm going to do something

at all, I expect to do it to the very best of my ability, and I want to work with others whose aims are the same."

AVOCATIONAL INTERESTS: The outdoors, gardening, hiking, swimming, birds, horses, reading, classical music.

*   *   *

FLETCHER, Geoffrey Scowcroft   1923-

PERSONAL: Born April 3, 1923; son of Herbert and Annie (Talence) Fletcher; married Mary Jean Timothy, 1953. *Education:* Received diploma in fine arts from University College, London; studied at British School in Rome, 1948. *Office:* Daily Telegraph, Fleet St., London E.C.4, England.

CAREER: Artist and writer. Drawings and painting in collections in England and abroad, including London's Selfridge Hotel.

WRITINGS—Self-illustrated: *Town's Eye View* (juvenile), Hutchinson, 1960; *The London Nobody Knows,* Hutchinson, 1962, Arco, 1964; *Popular Art in England,* Harrap, 1962; *City Sights: A City of London Portfolio,* Hutchinson, 1963; *London Overlooked,* Hutchinson, 1964; *Pearly Kingdom,* Hutchinson, 1965; (with G. Matchett) *En Vacances,* Harrap, 1966; (with Matchett) *Au Marche,* Harrap, 1966; *Offbeat in London,* Daily Telegraph, 1966; *London's River,* Hutchinson, 1966; *Elements of Sketching,* Allen & Unwin, 1966, A. S. Barnes, 1968; *Down Among the Meths Men,* Hutchinson, 1966; *London's Pavement Pounders,* Hutchinson, 1967; *Geoffrey Fletcher's London,* Hutchinson, 1968; *Sketching in Colour,* Allen & Unwin, 1968, A. S. Barnes, 1969; *Changing London: Drawings From the Peterborough Collection of "The Daily Telegraph,"* Collins, 1969; *London After Dark,* Arco, 1969.

The London Dickens Knew, Hutchinson, 1970; *London Souvenirs,* Allen & Unwin, 1973; *Paint It Yourself in Oils,* Daily Telegraph, 1973; *Italian Impressions,* Allen & Unwin, 1974; *Paint It in Water Colour,* Daily Telegraph, 1974; *Portraits of London,* Kingsmead Press, 1978.

Illustrator: John Bunyan, *Every Child's Pilgrim's Progress,* John Knox, 1957; Jennie Hawthorne, *David and the Penny Red,* White Lion Publishers, 1975. Also illustrator of Elisabeth De Stroumillo, *Guide to Paris.*

Writer for television and contributor of articles and drawings to newspapers, including *Daily Telegraph.*

SIDELIGHTS: "The London Nobody Knows" was released as a film by British Lion Films, Ltd., in 1969.*

*   *   *

FLETCHER, Harris Francis   1892-1979

OBITUARY NOTICE—See index for *CA* sketch: Born October 23, 1892, in Ypsilanti, Mich.; died July 16, 1979. Educator and author. During a long career as a professor of English, Harris Fletcher specialized in the study of poet John Milton. Among his works are *Milton's Semitic Studies and Some Manifestations of Them in His Poetry, Milton's Rabbinical Readings,* and *Contributions to a Milton Bibliography, 1800-1930: Being a List of Addenda to Stevens's Reference Guide to Milton. Milton Studies: In Honor of Harris Francis Fletcher,* a collection of essays edited by G. Blakemore Evans and others, was published in 1961. Obituaries and other sources: *Who's Who in America,* 39th edition, Marquis, 1976. (Date of death provided by board of trustees office, University of Illinois at Urbana-Champaign.)

FLORES, Angel 1900-

PERSONAL: Born October 2, 1900, in Barceloneta, P.R.; son of Nepomuceno (in business) and Paula (a teacher; maiden name, Rodriguez) Flores; married Kate Mann (a writer), 1936; children: Ralph, Juan, Barbara Flores Dederick. *Education:* New York University, A.B., 1923; Lafayette College, A.M., 1925; Cornell University, Ph.D., 1947. *Home:* 163 Malden Ave., Palenville, N.Y. 12463.

CAREER: Union College, Schenectady, N.Y. instructor in Spanish, 1924-25; Rutgers University, New Brunswick, N.J., instructor in Spanish language and literature, 1925-29; editor of *Alhambra,* 1929-30; Cornell University, Ithaca, N.Y., instructor in Spanish, 1930-33; editor of *Literary World,* 1934-45; Queens College of the City University of New York, Flushing, N.Y., assistant professor, 1945-47, associate professor, 1948-52, professor of romance languages and comparative literature, 1952-70, professor emeritus, 1970—. Visiting professor at University of Wisconsin (now University of Wisconsin—Madison), 1953-54; professor at Graduate Center of the City University of New York, 1968-70. Editor of Dragon Press, 1931-33. Member of Pan American Union's Division of Intellectual Cooperation, 1941-45. *Member:* Instituto Internacional de Literatura Iberoamericana.

WRITINGS—In English: *Spanish Literature in English Translation,* H. W. Wilson, 1926; *Lope de Vega: Monster of Nature,* Brentano's, 1930; (with M. J. Benardete) *Cervantes Across the Centuries,* Dryden, 1947; *Masterpieces of the Spanish Golden Age,* Rinehart, 1957; *The Medieval Age,* Dell, 1963; *The Literature of Spanish America,* five volumes, Las Americas, 1966-69; (with Helene M. Anderson) *Masterpieces of Spanish American Literature,* two volumes, Macmillan, 1972; *A Kafka Bibliography,* Gordian, 1976; *The Problem of "The Judgment,"* Gordian, 1977.

Editor: (With Benardete) *The Anatomy of Don Quixote,* Dragon Press, 1932; (with Dudley Poore) *Fiesta in November: Stories From Latin America,* Houghton, 1942; *The Kafka Problem,* New Directions, 1946, reprinted, Gordian, 1975; *Spanish Writers in Exile,* Bern Porter, 1947, reprinted, 1977; *Great Spanish Stories,* Modern Library, 1956; *An Anthology of Spanish Poetry From Nerval to Valery,* Doubleday, 1958; (with Homer Swander) *Franz Kafka Today,* University of Wisconsin Press, 1958; *Nineteenth Century German Tales,* Doubleday, 1959; *Spanish Stories* (in Spanish and English), Bantam, 1960, 8th edition, 1979; *An Anthology of German Poetry From Hoelderlin to Rilke,* Doubleday, 1960; *An Anthology of Spanish Poetry From Garcilaso to Garcia Lorca,* Doubleday, 1961; *Great Spanish Short Stories,* Dell, 1962; *Spanish Drama,* Bantam, 1962; *An Anthology of Medieval Lyrics,* Modern Library, 1962; *Leopardi: Poems and Prose,* Indiana University Press, 1966; *The Kafka Debate,* Gordian, 1977.

Translator: Jose E. Rodo, *The Motives of Proteus,* Brentano's, 1928; Ramon Gomez de la Serna, *Movieland,* Macaulay, 1930; T. S. Eliot, *Tierra baldia* (title means "The Waste Land"), Editorial Cervantes, 1930, reprinted, Ocnos, 1973; Miguel de Unamuno, *Three Exemplary Novels,* Boni, 1930, reprinted, Grove Press, 1956; Miguel A. Menendez, *Nayar,* Farrar & Rinehart, 1942; German Arciniegas, *Germans in the Conquest of America,* Macmillan, 1943; Benjamin Subercaseaux, *Chile: A Geographic Extravaganza,* Macmillan, 1943, reprinted, Haffner, 1971; Pablo Neruda, *Residence on Earth,* New Directions, 1946; Neruda, *Three Material Songs,* East River Editions, 1948; Jaime Sabartes, *Picasso: An In-*

timate Portrait, Prentice-Hall, 1948; Humberto Diaz Casanueva, *Requiem,* Grupo Fuego, 1958; (with Esther S. Dillon) Baldomero Lillo, *The Devil's Pit,* UNESCO Collection of Representative Works, 1959; Esteban Echeverria, *The Slaughter House,* Las Americas, 1959.

Other writings: (With Alberto Vasquez) *Paisaje y hombres de America,* Dryden, 1947; *Historia y antologia del cuento y la novela en Hispanoamerica,* Las Americas, 1959; *First Spanish Reader,* Bantam, 1964; *La literatura de Espana,* Las Americas, 1970; *Aproximaciones a Cesar Vallejo* (title means "Approaches to Cesar Vallejo"), two volumes, Las Americas, 1971; *Aproximaciones a Octavio Paz* (title means "Approaches to Octavio Paz"), Mortiz, 1974; *Aproximaciones a Pablo Neruda* (title means "Approaches to Pablo Neruda"), Ocnos, 1974; *Bibliografia de escritores hispanoamericanos, 1609-1974* (title means "Bibliography of Spanish-American Writers, 1609-1974"), Gordian, 1975; *Origenes del cuento hispanoamericana* (title means "Origins of the Spanish-American Short Story"), Premia, 1979; *Selecciones espanolas* (title means "Spanish Selections"), Macmillan, 1979; *Realismo magico* (title means "Magical Realism"), Premia, 1981; *Cesar Vallejo* (biography), Premia, 1981; *Narrativa hispanoamericana: Historia y antologia* (title means "Spanish-American Fiction: History and Anthology"), Siglo Veinte Uno, 1981.

*   *   *

FLOWER, Elizabeth Farquhar 1914-

PERSONAL: Born October 31, 1914, in Atlantic City, N.J. *Education:* University of Pennsylvania, Ph.D., 1939. *Office:* Department of Philosophy, University of Pennsylvania, Philadelphia, Pa. 19104.

CAREER: University of Pennsylvania, Philadelphia, 1945-76, began as assistant professor, became professor of philosophy, 1976—. *Member:* American Philosophical Association, Society of Ethical and Legal Philosophies, Society of Religious Higher Education. *Awards, honors:* Jusser fellowship, 1947; American Association of University Women fellowship, 1947.

WRITINGS: (Contributor) F.C. Gruber, editor, *Aspects of Value,* University of Pennsylvania Press, 1959; (contributor) R. Houde and J.P. Mullally, editors, *Philosophy of Knowledge,* Lippincott, 1960; (contributor) *Liberty,* Volume IV, Atherton, 1962; (with Murray G. Murphy) *A History of Philosophy in America,* two volumes, Putnam, 1977. Contributor to scholarly journals.

BIOGRAPHICAL/CRITICAL SOURCES: New England Quarterly, September, 1978.*

*   *   *

FLOWERDEW, Phyllis

PERSONAL: Born in Yorkshire, England; daughter of Charles (a stationer's representative) and Ethel (Scott) Flowerdew; married Arthur Kingbury; children: Noel Jonathan. *Education:* Educated in Wimbledon, England. *Home:* Fallows, Chartway, Sevenoaks, Kent, England.

CAREER: Adviser to primary schools in Oxfordshire, England; teacher in Surrey, England and in South Africa; writer, 1948—. *Member:* Society of Authors.

WRITINGS—Educational books; published by Oliver & Boyd, except as indicated: (With F. J. Schonell) *Wide Range Readers,* twelve volumes, 1948-53; (with Ronald Ridout) *Reading to Some Purpose,* six volumes, 1952-57; (with Schonell) *Happy Venture Playbooks,* Books III-IV, 1954; (with

Sam Stewart) *Reading On*, four volumes, 1958-63; (with Schonell) *Happy Venture Library Books*, twenty-seven volumes, 1963; *Flamingo Books*, 20 volumes, 1965-66; *Stories for Telling*, Johnston & Bacon, 1966; (with Schonell and A. Elliott-Cannon) *Widerange Interest*, four volumes, 1966-67; *Poetry Is All Around*, 1967; *More Stories for Telling*, Johnston & Bacon, 1968; *New Interest Books*, four volumes, 1972; *New Interest Activity Books*, four volumes, 1974; *True Books*, twelve volumes, 1974; *Pedro Books*, eight volumes, 1974; *Goodbye Candlelight*, 1974; *More Interest Books*, four volumes, 1977; *More Interest Quiz Books*, four volumes, 1977; *Wide Range Red Books*, Volumes I-VI, 1979-80, Volume VII, 1981, Volume VIII, in press; *Wide Range Quiz Books*, six volumes, 1980.

SIDELIGHTS: Flowerdew has provided individual help for children with reading difficulties. She has also taken Tibetan children into her home. She told *CA:* "I decided to be an author when I was six years old, and I never wavered. I did not intend to write for children, but when I began teaching I found it difficult to procure enough good stories to tell. I therefore wrote my own for whatever age I was teaching. I then became involved in writing reading books with controlled vocabulary-sentence structure. I am fascinated by words of language rather than by plots or characters. I would not reform English spelling entirely but I should like to make at least some changes to make life easier for the many clever but frustrated dyslexic children—e.g. we could use 'k' in every case where the sound is 'k.' This would eliminate many examples of 'c,' 'ch,' 'ck,' etc.

"It gives me great pleasure to know that my stories are enjoyed by so many children in Great Britain and other English-speaking countries; to know that I am able to help reading progress from a reading age of six to thirteen."

*   *   *

FONG, Wen Chih   1930-

PERSONAL: Born December 9, 1930, in Shanghai, China; came to the United States in 1948, naturalized citizen, 1961; son of Tse-tsing and Jen-yen (Sha) Fong; married Constance Chih-ming Tang, August 29, 1953; children: Laurence T., Peter C., Serena M. *Education:* Princeton University, A.B., 1951, M.F.A., 1954, Ph.D., 1957. *Home:* 83 Allison Rd., Princeton, N.J. 08540. *Office:* Department of Art and Archaeology, Princeton University, Princeton, N.J. 08540.

CAREER: Cleveland Museum of Art, Cleveland, Ohio, research assistant, 1953; Princeton University, Princeton, N.J., began as instructor, 1955, became chairman of doctoral program in Chinese and Japanese art and archaeology, 1964—, professor of art and archaeology and curator of Oriental art, 1967—, chairman of department of art and archaeology, 1970-73, chairman of executive committee of Art Museum, 1970—, Sanford Professor of Art and Archaeology, 1971—. Visiting curator of Oriental art at Art Gallery, Yale University, 1958-59; member of art committee of China Institute of America, 1971—, and gallery committee of Asia Society Art Gallery; consultant to Metropolitan Museum of Art.

MEMBER: College Art Association of America (member of board of directors, 1971—), Chinese Art Society. *Awards, honors:* Honorary fellow of Institute of Oriental Studies, University of Hong Kong, 1961-62, and Institute for Advanced Chinese Studies, Taiwan, 1966—; Guggenheim fellowship, 1961-62; American Council of Learned Societies fellowships, 1965-66 and 1969-70.

WRITINGS: (With Sherman E. Lee) *Streams and Mountains Without End*, Artibus Asiae, 1955, 2nd edition, 1967; *The*

Lohans and a Bridge to Heaven, Smithsonian Institution, 1958; (contributor) Boderick Whitfield, *In Pursuit of Antiquity: Chinese Paintings of the Ming and Ch'ing Dynasties From the Collection of Mr. and Mrs. Earl Morse*, Art Museum, Princeton University, 1969; (editor) Marilyn Fu, *Sung and Yuan Paintings*, Metropolitan Museum of Art, 1973; (with Fu) *The Wilderness Colors of Tao-chi*, Metropolitan Museum of Art, 1974; (translator with Robert R. Rorex) *Eighteen Songs of a Nomad Flute: The Story of Lady Wen-Chi*, Metropolitan Museum of Art, 1974; *Summer Mountains: The Timeless Landscape*, Metropolitan Museum of Art, 1975; (translator and author of introduction) *Returning Home: Tao-Chi's Album of Landscapes and Flowers*, Braziller, 1976. Also author of *Fu Ch'ing-chuhsien sheng*, 1970, and *The Bronze Age of China*. Contributor to journals.*

*   *   *

FORBES, Colin
See SAWKINS, Raymond H(arold)

*   *   *

FORD, Kirk
See SPENCE, William John Duncan

*   *   *

FORD, Lewis
See PATTEN, Lewis B(yford)

*   *   *

FORD, Norrey
See DILCOCK, Noreen

*   *   *

FOREST, Antonia

PERSONAL: Born in London, England. *Office:* c/o Faber & Faber Ltd., Three Queen Sq., London WC1N 3AU, England.

CAREER: Author of books for young people. *Awards, honors:* Commendation from British Library Association, 1961, for *Peter's Room.*

WRITINGS—Juvenile; published by Faber, except as noted: *Autumn Term*, illustrated by Marjorie Owens, 1948, reprinted, Puffin, 1977; *The Marlows and the Traitor*, illustrated by Doritie Kettlewell, 1953; *Falconer's Lure: The Story of a Summer Holiday*, illustrated by Tasha Kallin, 1957; *End of Term*, 1959, Puffin, 1978; *Peter's Room*, 1961; *The Thursday Kidnapping*, 1963, Coward, 1965; *The Thuggery Affair*, 1965; *The Ready-Made Family*, 1967; *The Player's Boy*, 1970; *The Players and the Rebels*, 1971; *The Cricket Term*, 1974; *The Attic Term*, 1976.*

*   *   *

FORNELL, Earl Wesley   1915-1969

OBITUARY NOTICE—See index for *CA* sketch: Born November 12, 1915, in Laketown, Wis.; died March 2, 1969. Educator and author. Included among Earl Fornell's books are *The Galveston Era: The Texas Crescent on the Eve of Secession* and *The Unhappy Medium: Spiritualism and the Life of Margaret Fox.* (Date of death provided by wife, Martha Fornell.)

FORREST, Alfred Clinton 1916-1978

OBITUARY NOTICE—See index for *CA* sketch: Born May 24, 1916, in Mariposa, Ontario, Canada; died December 27, 1978. Minister, editor, and author. A minister of the United Church of Canada for many years, Alfred Forrest also served as editor of the *United Church Observer.* He wrote a weekly syndicated newspaper column, "A Cleric Comments," and he was the author of books, including *Religion in Canada* and *The Unholy Land.* Obituaries and other sources: *Who's Who in Religion,* 2nd edition, Marquis, 1977; *The Canadian Who's Who,* Volume 14, University of Toronto Press, 1979. (Date of death provided by the general manager of *United Church Observer.*)

*   *   *

FORREST, Earle Robert 1883-1969

OBITUARY NOTICE—See index for *CA* sketch: Born June 29, 1883, in Washington, Pa.; died August 25, 1969. Journalist and author. Earle Forrest specialized in courthouse reporting and historical feature writing during his forty-six years as a journalist. *Missions and Pueblos of the Old Southwest, The Snake Dance of the Hopi Indians,* and *With a Camera in Old Navaholand* are among his many works. (Date of death provided by daughter, Margaret Forrest Brown.)

*   *   *

FORRESTER, Rex Desmond 1928-

PERSONAL: Born November 8, 1928, in Whangerei, New Zealand; son of Donald George (an electrician) and Henrietta (Mee) Forrester; married Isabella Phillips, June 2, 1950; children: Roger, Lorraine, Donna, Gary. *Education* Attended high school in Putaruru, New Zealand. *Politics:* National party. *Religion* Church of England. *Home:* 81 Grand Vue Rd., Kawaha, Rotorua, New Zealand. *Office:* New Zealand Government Tourist and Publicity Department, Fenton St., Rotorua, New Zealand.

CAREER: Trapper, bounty hunter, and ranger, 1945-56; New Zealand Safaris, owner, 1956-65; New Zealand Government Tourist and Publicity Department, Rotorua, hunting and fishing officer, 1965—. *Member:* Outdoor Writers Association, Professional Fishing Guides Association, Deercullers, Inc. *Awards, honors:* Nicest Listening Award from Radio Australia, 1966, for radio interviews.

WRITINGS: Hunter for Hire, A. H. & A. W. Reed, 1964; *Hunting in New Zealand,* A. H. & A. W. Reed, 1965; *Trout Fishing in New Zealand,* Whitcoulls, 1979; *True Hunting Adventures,* Whitcoulls, 1979.

Contributor to magazines, including *Kaleidoscope, Woman's Weekly, Alive, Man, Guns, Sporting Shooter,* and *Australia Outdoors.*

WORK IN PROGRESS: A book on the capture of live game by using helicopters, publication by Whitcoulls expected in 1982 or 1983.

SIDELIGHTS: Forrester told *CA:* "I left school to become a self-employed deer hunter. I became a government bounty hunter (for deer), then a field officer employing and training hunters. In the government eradication program of all imported animals, I killed ten thousand deer before I was twenty-one. I became a wildlife ranger (game warden), then a self-employed fur trapper. I owned and operated the first New Zealand safari company, guiding the world's sportsmen on safaris. Now I am employed by the New Zealand Government to inspect and promote hunting and fishing guides.

"All my books are factual, and although I have ambitions to write a novel, I have not yet delved into fiction. I enjoy writing, like to be busy, and have tremendous admiration for the professionals I write about. I find it easier to write about others. I carry two cameras and take all my own photographs. I have made three tours of the United States to promote New Zealand's sporting attractions."

AVOCATIONAL INTERESTS: Restoring a vintage 1927 Ford roadster, boat building, fishing, water skiing, collecting paintings by Charles Russell and Remington, vacationing in Arizona and Montana.

*   *   *

FORWARD, Robert L(ull) 1932-

PERSONAL: Born August 15, 1932, in Geneva, N.Y.; son of Robert T. and Mildred (a teacher; maiden name, Lull) Forward; married Martha Neil Dodson, August 29, 1954; children: Robert D., Mary Lois, Julie E., Eve Laurel. *Education:* University of Maryland, B.S., 1954, Ph.D., 1965; University of California, Los Angeles, M.S., 1958. *Religion:* Congregational. *Home:* 34 Carriage Sq., Oxnard, Calif. 93030. *Agent:* Ashley Darlington Grayson, 1342 18th St., San Pedro, Calif. 90732. *Office:* Hughes Research Laboratories, 3011 Malibu Canyon Rd., Malibu, Calif. 90265.

CAREER: Hughes Research Laboratories, Malibu, Calif., senior scientist, 1956—. *Military service:* U.S. Air Force, 1954-56; became captain. *Member:* American Institute of Aeronautics and Astronautics (associate fellow), American Astronautical Society, Institute of Electrical and Electronic Engineers, American Physical Society, American Geophysical Union, British Interplanetary Society (fellow), Sigma Xi, Sigma Pi Sigma. *Awards, honors:* Award for outstanding achievement in the field of gravity from Gravity Research Foundation, 1965; research award from Ventura Branch of the Scientific Research Society of America, 1969.

WRITINGS: Dragon's Egg (science-fiction), Del Rey/Ballantine/Random House, 1980; *Rocheworld,* Del Rey/Ballantine/Random House, in press. Contributor of seventeen articles and stories to magazines, including *Omni, Science 80, Analog, Galaxy,* and *Galileo.*

SIDELIGHTS: Forward told *CA:* "I write science articles and science fiction stories as accurately as I can so that the reader will learn some science while enjoying a story. However, I follow the rule: *'Don't let the facts stand in the way of a good story.'* But in both *Dragon's Egg* and *Rocheworld* I spent a year with my calculator designing the world and both the human and alien cultures and technologies *before* I wrote the story (which took another year)."

*   *   *

FOSCUE, Edwin Jay 1899-1972

OBITUARY NOTICE—See index for *CA* sketch: Born August 26, 1899, in Camden, Ark.; died in 1972. Educator and author. A professor of geography at Southern Methodist University for more than forty years, Edwin Foscue was the author of *Taxco: Mexico's Silver City* and the co-author of *Regional Geography of Anglo-America* and *Estes Park: Resort in the Rockies.* (Date of death provided by wife, Fannie Foscue.)

FOSSE, Alfred
See JELLY, George Oliver

*   *   *

FOWLER, John M(ajor) 1926-

PERSONAL: Born February 4, 1926, in Eufaula, Ala.; son of Earl D. and Ada E. Fowler; married Margaret Fogg, August 7, 1948 (marriage ended December 5, 1975); married Kathryn E. Mervine, December 27, 1975; children: Lee, Lynn, Kathryn, John Kurt, Leslie, Ada, Marian, John Mervine. *Education:* Earlham College, B.A., 1949; University of Oklahoma, M.A., 1950; Johns Hopkins University, Ph.D., 1954. *Home:* 1700 Priscilla Dr., Silver Spring, Md. 20904. *Office:* National Science Teachers Association, 1742 Connecticut Ave. N.W., Washington, D.C. 20009.

CAREER: Washington University, St. Louis, Mo., research associate, 1954-56, assistant professor, 1956-61, associate professor of physics, 1961-65; University of Maryland, College Park, director of Commission on College Physics, 1965-72, visiting professor of physics, 1967-74; National Science Teachers Association, Washington, D.C., director of special projects, 1975—. Member of executive board and secretary of Scientists Institute for Public Information; member of board of trustees of Earlham College; consultant to League of Women Voters, 1970-76. *Military service:* U.S. Army, 1944-46. *Member:* American Association for the Advancement of Science, National Science Teachers Association, American Physical Society. *Awards, honors:* Millikan Award from American Association of Physics Teachers, 1969.

WRITINGS: Fallout: A Study of Superbombs, Strontium 90, and Survival, Basic Books, 1960; *Energy and the Environment,* McGraw, 1975; *Energy-Environment Source Book,* National Science Teachers Association, 1975. Executive editor of *Environment.*

WORK IN PROGRESS: Fact sheets on biofuels, burning coal, wind power, electricity from the sun (both photovoltaic and solar thermal), oil shale and tar sands, solar heating and cooling, geothermal energy, energy conservation in home and buildings, industry, and transportation, conventional reactors, nuclear fusion, new fuels from coal, energy storage, global and long-range effects of energy conversion, fuel cells, a bibliography of energy technologies, and centralized versus decentralized energy production.

SIDELIGHTS: Fowler commented: "I consider myself a scientist concerned with interpreting the scientific content of socio-political issues. It is my strong belief that the scientist's responsibility is to provide objective information on such issues. There are crucial energy/environment/economic issues facing the nation now: the nuclear debate, the choice between centralized and decentralized energy production, and the relative emphasis on energy conservation and energy production. We are in a period of transition from an era in which energy was abundant and inexpensive to one in which the only certainty is that it will cost more. The scientist does not have a map to the best path, but his guidance can be helpful in pointing out the dangers along the various paths and in helping to weigh the technological, economic, environmental, and social advantages and disadvantages of the choices.

"This motivation places several responsibilities on the scientist as author. In my own case I have to understand and keep up with a broad field which crosses many disciplines.

I also have to write in a way that can be understood by the layman but does not oversimplify complex and difficult subjects. I find that my extensive public speaking—which now replaces teaching as a way of directly interacting with the public—enables me to keep my descriptions and explanations short and complete."

*   *   *

FOX, Frederic Ewing 1917-1981

OBITUARY NOTICE—See index for *CA* sketch: Born August 19, 1917, in Stamford, Conn.; died February 20, 1981, in Princeton, N.J. Clergyman, educator, journalist, and author. Following service with the U.S. Army during World War II, Fox became a Congregationalist minister and a contributor of articles on American life to the *New York Times Magazine.* In 1956 Fox joined the Eisenhower White House as a presidential assistant and speech writer, serving there until 1961 when he traveled to what was then Northern Rhodesia to instruct African clergymen in the basics of journalism. Fox detailed his African experiences in the book *Fourteen Africans vs. One American.* In 1963 he returned to the United States and was made recording secretary of Princeton University, later becoming a special assistant for public affairs and unofficial historian of the school. Obituaries and other sources: *New York Times,* February 21, 1981.

*   *   *

FOX, Gail 1942-

PERSONAL: Born February 5, 1942, in Williamantic, Conn.; daughter of Harry Wilbur (a professor of microbiology) and Margaret (Johnson) Seeley; married Michael Allen Fox, June 11, 1963 (divorced, 1978); children: Jason Daniel, Timothy Peter. *Education:* Cornell University, B.A., 1964; graduate study at Pontifical Institute of Medieval Studies, 1964-65. *Home:* 205 Vaughan Rd., Apt. 13N, Toronto, Ontario, Canada M6C 2M5.

CAREER: Epoch, assistant editor, 1962-63; University of Tuebingen, Tuebingen, West Germany, lecturer, 1972-73; *Quarry,* Kingston, Ontario, editor, 1975-78. Teacher at college preparatory school in Kingston, 1975, and at prison for women in Kingston, 1977. *Member:* League of Canadian Poets. *Awards, honors:* Award from *Quarry,* 1975; Canada Council grants, 1975-76, 1978-79, and 1980-81; Ontario Arts Council grants.

WRITINGS—Poems: *Dangerous Season,* Quarry Press, 1969; *The Royal Collector of Dreams,* Fiddlehead, 1970; *Flight of the Pterodactyl,* Oberon Press, 1973; *The Ringmaster's Circus,* Fiddlehead, 1973; *God's Odd Look,* Oberon, 1976; *In Search of Living Things,* Oberon Press, 1980.

Work represented in anthologies, including *Canadian Short Stories,* 1972. Contributor to magazines, including *Tamarack Review, Fiddlehead, Queen's Quarterly,* and *Alive.*

WORK IN PROGRESS: Grandfather and Gail, poems, with her grandfather; another book of poems.

*   *   *

FOX, Michael A(llen) 1940-

PERSONAL: Born May 7, 1940, in Cleveland, Ohio; son of Milton S. (an editor and publisher) and Ruby (an artist; maiden name, Canfield) Fox; married Gail Talmadge Seeley, June 11, 1963 (divorced September, 1978); children: Jason Daniel, Timothy Peter. *Education:* Cornell University, B.A., 1962; University of Toronto, M.A., 1964, Ph.D., 1970.

Politics: Independent. *Religion:* None. *Home:* 52 Oakridge Ave., Kingston, Ontario, Canada K7L 4S9. *Office:* Queen's *Quarterly,* Queen's University, Kingston, Ontario, Canada K7L 3N6.

CAREER: University of Toronto, Toronto, Ontario, instructor in philosophy, 1965-66; Queen's University, Kingston, Ontario, lecturer, 1966-70, assistant professor, 1970-76, associate professor of philosophy, 1976—, editor of Queen's *Quarterly. Member:* Canadian Philosophical Association, Canadian Association of University Teachers, Hegel Society of America, American Philosophical Association, Schopenhauer Society, Society for the Study of Ethics and Animals. *Awards, honors:* German academic exchange fellow of German Academic Exchange Service, 1973.

WRITINGS: (Editor) *Schopenhauer: His Philosophical Achievement,* Barnes & Noble, 1980. Contributor to philosophy and literary journals, including *Ethics, Metaphilosophy, Philosophy and Phenomenological Research, Dialogue, Dalhousie Review,* and *Owl of Minerva.*

WORK IN PROGRESS: The Ethics of Man's Treatment of Animals.

SIDELIGHTS: Fox commented: "I am a dedicated generalist, swimming against the tide in an age of specialization. Originally I came to philosophy to find the answers to 'large' questions. But now I see it mainly as a frustrating, though occasionally intensely rewarding, discipline, useful chiefly for its application to other subjects—for getting to the heart of the matter and separating bran from chaff.

"My generalism (which is not dilettantism) led me to seek the editorship of Queen's *Quarterly,* Canada's oldest, most respected, and most consistently polymathic review. I believe that only a generalist's all-sided perspective can produce a quarterly that can be (and has been) classed with more frequent and enormously wealthier, more influential periodicals like the New York *Review of Books, Encounter,* and *Times Literary Supplement.*

"I would describe myself as a pessimistic optimist—one who is gloomy about the short-term future of man, but hopeful about the long-term. I guess my streak of pessimism made Schopenhauer an attractive figure to me, one on whom I wanted to do a book. He's not a very compelling pessimist either, as his friends (if he had any) would have known. (Mine know this about me, too.)

"My major areas of vocational interest are nineteenth-century philosophy and existentialism, which I regard as more substantive philosophical movements than most—also more psychologically deep. Hegel and Kierkegaard are favorites—the former for his vastly encompassing generalism, the latter for his passion, humor, and psychological acumen. Philosophy and psychoanalysis and environmental ethics are other special interests."

AVOCATIONAL INTERESTS: Travel, new environments, carpentry, cooking, photography, camping, tennis, skiing, shopping.

BIOGRAPHICAL/CRITICAL SOURCES: Queen's Alumni Review, July-August, 1977.

*   *   *

FRANC, Helen M.   1908-

PERSONAL: Born May 17, 1908, in New York, N.Y.; daughter of James J. (a lawyer)) and Nellie (Steinberg) Franc. *Education:* Wellesley College, B.A., 1929; New York University, M.A., 1931; attended Institut d'Art et d'Archeologie,

summers, 1931-32. *Politics:* Democrat. *Religion:* Jewish. *Residence:* New York, N.Y.

CAREER: Pierpont Morgan Library, New York City, assistant to director, 1934-42; associated with Air Force Intelligence, Foreign Broadcast Intelligence Service, United Nations Relief and Rehabilitation Administration, and International Bank, all in Washington, D.C., 1942-48; Philadelphia Museum of Art, Philadelphia, Pa., associate in education, 1948-49; *Magazine of Art,* New York City, managing editor, 1949-53; Harry N. Abrams, Inc., New York City, associate editor, 1953-54; Museum of Modern Art, New York City, became editor-in-chief of publications, 1954-72; freelance writer and editor, 1972—. *Member:* National Trust for Historic Preservation, College Art Association of America, Society of Architectural Historians, Municipal Art Society, Wellesley College Friends of Art.

WRITINGS: The Animal Kingdom, Pierpont Morgan Library, 1941; *An Invitation to See: 125 Paintings From the Museum of Modern Art,* Museum of Modern Art, 1973; (with Jean Lipman) *Bright Stars: American Painting and Sculpture Since 1776,* Dutton, 1976. Also editor of volumes published by Museum of Modern Art, including *The Machine at the End of the Mechanical Age;* Barbara Rose, *Claes Oldenburg;* Albert Elsen, *Rodin,* 1963; *The New Italian Landscape;* and *Philip Johnson: Writings.* Assistant editor of *Art Bulletin,* 1938-42.

WORK IN PROGRESS: Editing a catalog of the David Rockefeller collection.

SIDELIGHTS: Helen Franc wrote: "My motivation in turning to art history as a profession was sparked by auditing a pioneering seminar on modern art taught by Alfred H. Barr, Jr., later the first director of the Museum of Modern Art. My editing work was an outgrowth of my early interest in writing. I believe an editor has the dual function of enabling the author to express his ideas as clearly and cogently as possible, and, as 'first reader,' clarifying any points that might be difficult for the public. Ensuring accuracy of all facts is, of course, elementary! The best preparation is to be a generalist as well as a specialist in one's field.

"I have traveled or resided in England, France, Italy, Germany, Austria, Belgium, Switzerland, Portugal, Spain, the Netherlands, Sweden, Greece, Yugoslavia, Turkey, the Soviet Union, including Soviet Central Asia, Morocco, Tunisia, Mexico, Guatemala, Ecuador, Peru, Puerto Rico, the Virgin Islands, the Leeward and Windward Islands of the Caribbean, and the People's Republic of China. I try to take one major trip a year and plan for it many months ahead.

"Since retiring in 1972, I have continued editing and writing as a 'cottage industry' and plan to keep on until I lose my marbles and/or nobody is interested in employing or commissioning me! Though my profession is not the most lucrative one in the world, I have never regretted it for a moment, as it has so many non-monetary rewards, not the least being that one is constantly learning."

*   *   *

FRANCE, Anna Kay   1940-

PERSONAL: Born May 4, 1940, in Baltimore, Md.; daughter of Walter Raleigh and Mae Beth Moses; married Denis H. France, August 17, 1980. *Education:* Radcliffe College, B.A., 1961; Yale University, Ph.D., 1966. *Home:* 1310 Delaware Ave., Buffalo, N.Y. 14209. *Office:* Department of English, State University of New York at Buffalo, Buffalo, N.Y. 14209.

CAREER: State University of New York at Buffalo, associate professor of English and theatre, 1965—. *Member:* American Association for the Advancement of Slavic Studies, American Association of Teachers of Slavic and East European Languages.

WRITINGS: Boris Pasternak's Translations of Shakespeare, University of California Press, 1978. Contributor to literature and Slavic studies journals.

SIDELIGHTS: Anna France commented: "I combine interests in scholarship and theatre. My Ph.D. is in comparative literature, with major emphasis on English and Russian, and French as a third field. My scholarly work has been and continues to be focused on drama. I have been interested in both theatrical production and translation as means of interpretation. At present my energies are devoted not simply to scholarship and writing, but also to acting and the teaching of acting."

* * *

FRANCHI, Eda
    See VICKERS, Antoinette L.

* * *

FRANCIS, Charles
    See HOLME, Bryan

* * *

FRANK, Harry Thomas   1933-1980

OBITUARY NOTICE—See index for *CA* sketch: Born June 7, 1933, in Williamston, N.C.; died in 1980. Minister, educator, and author. Harry Frank, a Baptist minister and professor of religion, was involved in a number of archaeological expeditions. Included among his books are *Bible, Archaeology, and Faith; An Archaeological Companion to the Bible;* and *Discovering the Biblical World.* Obituaries and other sources: *Directory of American Scholars,* Volume IV, *Philosophy, Religion, and Law,* 7th edition, Bowker, 1978. (Date of death provided by wife, Elizabeth Frank.)

* * *

FRANK, Lawrence K(elso)   1890-1968

OBITUARY NOTICE—See index for *CA* sketch: Born December 6, 1890, in Cincinnati, Ohio; died September 23, 1968. Authority in the field of family relations, educator, and author. During his career, Lawrence Frank held a variety of positions in the fields of education and human development. Together with his wife, child-guidance expert Mary Hughes Frank, he wrote such books as *How to Help Your Child in School* and *Your Adolescent at Home and in School.* Frank also wrote *Feelings and Emotions, Individual Development,* and *On the Importance of Infancy.* His numerous articles appeared in *Saturday Review, Look,* and other magazines. Obituaries and other sources: *New York Times,* September 24, 1968; *Publishers Weekly,* December 2, 1968; *Who Was Who in America,* 5th edition, Marquis, 1973.

* * *

FRASER, W(illiam) Hamish   1941-

PERSONAL: Born June 30, 1941, in Scotland; son of Hugh R.R. (a textile worker) and Charlotte (a shopkeeper; maiden name, Milne) Fraser; married Helen Tuach (a college lecturer), September 4, 1965; children: Louisa. *Education:* University of Aberdeen, M.A., 1963; University of Sussex,

D.Phil., 1966. *Office:* Department of History, University of Strathclyde, Glasgow G1 1XQ, Scotland.

CAREER: University of Strathclyde, Glasgow, Scotland, lecturer, 1966-75, senior lecturer in history, 1975—.

WRITINGS: Trade Union and Society: The Struggle for Acceptance, 1850-1880, Allen & Unwin, 1974; (editor with J. T. Ward) *Workers and Employers: Documents on Trade Unions and Industrial Relations Since the Eighteenth Century,* Macmillan, 1980. Editor of *Journal* of Scottish Labour History Society, 1968-74.

WORK IN PROGRESS: The Growth of the Mass Market, 1850-1914, for Macmillan; research on municipal socialism.

* * *

FRAZIER, Walt(er)   1945-
    (Clyde Cool)

PERSONAL: Born March 29, 1945, in Atlanta, Georgia; son of Walter (an automobile production line worker) and Eula Frazier; divorced; children: Walt III. *Education:* Attended Southern Illinois University, 1963-65, 1966-67. *Office:* Coliseum, 2923 Streetsboro Rd., Richfield, Ohio 44286.

CAREER Professional basketball player for New York Knickerbockers, New York City, 1967-77, and Cleveland Cavaliers, Cleveland, Ohio, 1977-79. President of Walt Frazier Enterprises; co-owner of hairstyling salon in New York City; operator of a basketball camp for boys in Pawling, N.Y. *Awards, honors:* National Invitation Tournament Most Valuable Player, 1967; voted best defensive player, National Basketball Association, 1968-69, 1969-70; All Star Game Most Valuable Player, 1975; National Basketball Association All-Defensive Squad, four consecutive years; National Basketball Association All Star Game, 1970-76.

WRITINGS: (With Joe Jares) *Clyde: The Walt Frazier Story,* Rutledge Books, 1970; (with Ira Berkow) *Rockin' Steady: A Guide to Basketball and Cool,* introduction by Bill Russell, Prentice-Hall, 1974.

SIDELIGHTS: Walt Frazier, better known as "Clyde Cool" to his fans, retired from a colorful basketball career after the 1978-79 season. The nickname "Clyde" was bestowed upon him because his 1930's-style attire reminded a teammate of Clyde Barrow's dress and because Walt "stole" basketballs the way Clyde robbed banks. "Cool" was added because of his demeanor both on and off the court. During the ten years he spent in New York City playing with the Knickerbockers, Frazier became known for his flashy style. His wardrobe included dozens of suits, shirts, shoes, and hats, as well as a full-length mink coat. His image earned him the *Esquire* America's Best-Dressed Jock award, and *Pageant* named him one of America's ten sexiest athletes.

The oldest of nine children, Frazier grew up in Atlanta, Georgia. He developed his athletic abilities in high school there, catching for the baseball team, quarterbacking for the football team, and playing guard on the basketball team. Two universities offered him scholarships to play football, but Frazier opted to accept a basketball scholarship at the University of Southern Illinois. After three years of college, Frazier dropped out to accept a $100,000 contract with the Knicks, who picked him in the first round of the 1967 draft.

Frazier was the leading scorer for the Knicks from 1970 through 1974, held their all-time assists record at the end of the 1973-74 season, and was the first Knick guard to lead the team in scoring with a 21.7 average in 1972. In the 1968-69 and 1969-70 seasons Frazier was voted the best defensive player in the National Basketball Association, and he made the NBA All-Defensive squad four consecutive years. Frazier was a leading ball stealer and rebounder. He was also known as one of the best fourth-quarter players in professional basketball.

After a foot ailment disabled Frazier during much of the 1978-79 season, he retired from the game, but he left the basketball court with a good feeling. As Frazier told a writer for the *New York Times*, "If this is a tragedy, I wish it to everyone. . . . I had a very successful career. I have my health, my wealth, my peace of mind. . . . What I did is in the books."

BIOGRAPHICAL/CRITICAL SOURCES—Books: Robert Liston, *The Pros*, Platt, 1968; Walt Frazier and Joe Jares, *Clyde: The Walt Frazier Story*, Rutledge Books, 1970; Louis Sabin and Dave Sendler, *Stars of Pro Basketball*, Random House, 1970; Frazier and Ira Berkow, *Rockin' Steady: A Guide to Basketball and Cool*, introduction by Bill Russell, Prentice-Hall, 1974; Larry Batson, *Walt Frazier*, Creative Education, Inc., 1974; Jim Benagh, *Walt Frazier: Superguard of Pro Basketball*, Scholastic Book Services, 1974; Bill Gutman, *Modern Basketball Superstars*, Dodd, 1975; S. H. Burchard, *Sports Star: Walt Frazier*, Harcourt, 1975; Howard Liss, *The Picture Story of Walt Frazier*, Messner, 1976; Louis Sabin, *Pro Basketball's Greatest*, Putnam, 1976; Sabin, *Walt Frazier: No. 1 Guard of the NBA*, Putnam, 1976.

Periodicals: *New York Times*, April 22,1973, April 21, 1974, February 16, 1975, January 29, 1976, October 9, 1977, December 11, 1978; *New York Times Book Review*, March 24, 1974; *Sports Illustrated*, February 10, 1975.*

*   *   *

FRENCH, Philip (Neville) 1933-

PERSONAL: Born August 28, 1933, in Liverpool, England; son of John (in insurance sales) and Bessie (a teacher; maiden name, Funston) French; married Kersti Elisabet Molin (a teacher and translator), December 31, 1957; children: Sean, Patrick, Karl. *Education:* Exeter College, Oxford, B.A., 1957; attended Indiana University, 1957-58. *Home:* 62 Dartmouth Park Rd., London N.W.5, England. *Office:* British Broadcasting Corp., Broadcasting House, London W1A 1AA, England.

CAREER: Bristol Evening Post, Bristol, England, journalist, 1958-59; British Broadcasting Corp. (BBC), London, producer of North American service, 1959-61, producer in talks and documentaries department, 1961—, senior producer, 1972—. Visiting professor at University of Texas, 1972. Member of British Film Institute production board, 1968-73, British Film Institute publications advisory board, 1974—, and National Film Archives advisory committee, 1979—. *Military service:* British Army, Duke of Cornwall's Light Infantry and Parachute Regiment, 1952-54; became lieutenant. *Member:* British Film Institute.

WRITINGS: (Editor with Michael Sissons) *The Age of Austerity*, Hodder & Stoughton, 1963; *The Movie Moguls*, Weidenfeld & Nicolson, 1969, revised edition, 1970; *Westerns*, Viking, 1974, revised edition, Oxford University Press, 1977; *Three Honest Men: Edmund Wilson, Lionel Trilling, F. R. Leavis*, Carcanet New Press, 1980.

Work represented in anthologies, including: *The Films of Jean-Luc Godard*, edited by Ian Cameron, Studio Vista, 1967; *Sight, Sound, and Society*, edited by David Manning White and Richard Averson, Beacon Press, 1968; *The Emergence of Film Art*, edited by Lewis Jacobs, Hopkinson & Blake, 1968; *Violence and the Mass Media*, edited by Otto Larsen, Harper, 1969; *Film and the Liberal Arts*, edited by T. J. Ross, Holt, 1970; *The Oxford Reader*, edited by Frank

Kermode and Richard Poirier, Oxford University Press, 1971; *The World of Rudyard Kipling*, edited by John Gross, Weidenfeld & Nicolson, 1972; *Next Year in Jerusalem: Portraits of the Jew in the Twentieth Century*, edited by Douglas Villiers, Viking, 1976; *The World of Raymond Chandler*, edited by Miriam Gross, Weidenfeld & Nicolson, 1977.

Author of an arts column in *New Statesman*, 1967-72; theatre critic for *New Statesman*, 1967-68; film critic for *Observer*, 1978—.

SIDELIGHTS: French told *CA:* "In 1959 I was diverted, temporarily I thought, from a career of journalism and authorship into broadcasting. I have been a radio producer ever since, specializing in programs on the arts and American affairs. My writing, therefore, has been done in the margins and interstices of a full-time job.

"The broadcasting side of my life involves not merely the producing of other people's work, but a great deal of programs in which I act as interviewer and writer. Although discussion, talk, and feature programs are usually intended for the ear alone, a good many are reprinted in the *Listener* and elsewhere. As a result, numerous books contain material that I have produced on the air. For instance, *The Novelist as Innovator*, published by BBC in 1966, and the series of Reith Lectures delivered for Richard Hoggart in 1971 and by Daniel Boorstein in 1975, are entirely composed of the texts of programs that I superintended. My book on Wilson, Leavis, and Trilling also contains the texts, which I compiled and presented, of multi-voice radio portraits of these three critics. Similar programs on S. J. Perelman and Graham Greene have been published (in part) in the *Listener* and given a certain permanent currency by being included in the BBC Transcription Service's catalogue of programs available on tape and disc for use by foreign broadcasting stations.

"Since the advent of the cassette, radio programs have a status comparable to books, and I regard the best of my radio work as equal, and in most cases superior, to the essays I've published. A good radio program depends as much on nuance, inflection, and vocal orchestration as it does on the quality of the written and spoken word. I have written articles on Perelman and Greene, but nothing comparable to my radio portraits of them, each of which includes comments from the subject together with contributions from friends and critics, readings by actors, and movie soundtrack. Print cannot match this. The radio portrait is a unique form of critical biography that does not attempt to replace written criticism or biographical writing, but that can be a useful adjunct to these traditional activities. In similar ways, the radio interview and discussion have unique qualities and involve as much skill, preparation, concentration, and editorial shaping as a literary composition does.

"One consolation of producing radio programs, to set against the nagging sense one always has about their ephemerality, is that they don't involve the destruction of forests. In addition, you can't wrap fish and chips or garbage in them, they don't pollute the air (or not permanently), and those who record them can wipe their tapes clean and substitute something fresh."

*   *   *

FRIEDENTHAL, Richard 1896-1979

PERSONAL: Born June 9, 1896, in Munich, Germany (now West Germany); died of a pulmonary embolism October 19, 1979, in Kiel, West Germany; son of Hans (a professor) and Martha (Elster) Friedenthal; married Elisabeth C. Bach-Guettermann, 1950. *Education:* Attended Humboldt University and Friedrich-Schiller University; received Ph.D. from University of Munich.

CAREER: Knaur Verlag, Berlin, Germany, reader and editor of *Konversationslexikon*, 1931-32; writer and editor, 1938—. Worked for British Broadcasting Corp. (BBC) during World War II. *Member:* P.E.N. (honorary chairman of West German center). *Awards, honors:* Grosses Bundesverdienstkreuz of West Germany.

WRITINGS—In English: *Der eroberer: Ein Cortes-roman*, Insel-Verlag, 1929, translation by Charles Hope Lumley published as *The White Gods*, Harper, 1931; (editor) *Facts*, four volumes, 1934; (editor) *Goethe Chronicle*, Acorn Press, 1949; *Leonardo: Eine Bibliographie*, Kindler, 1959, translation by Margaret Shenfield published as *Leonardo da Vinci: A Pictorial Biography*, Viking, 1959; *Goethe: Sein Leben und seine Zeit*, R. Piper, 1963, translation published as *Goethe: His Life and Times*, World Publishing, 1963; (editor) *Letters of the Great Artists*, two volumes, Random House, 1963; *Luther: Sein Leben und seine Zeit*, R. Piper, 1967, translation by John Nowell published as *Luther: His Life and Times*, Harcourt, 1970 (published in England as *Luther*, Weidenfeld & Nicolson, 1970).

In German: *Tanz und Tod* (poems), 1918; *Demeter* (poems), 1924; *Der Faecher mit der goldenen Schnur*, 1924; *Der Heuschober*, 1925; *Marie Rebschneider*, 1927; (editor) *Knaurs Lexikon*, Knaur Verlag, 1931; *Brot und Salz* (poems), 1943; (editor) Stefan Zweig, *Balzac*, S. Fischer, 1946, 2nd edition, Cassell, 1970.

Das Erbe des Kolumbus: Fuenf Novellen, Bechtle, 1950; *Die Welt in der Nusschale: Roman*, R. Piper, 1956; (editor) S. Zweig, *Balzac: Dichter und Abenteurer des Lebens*, Beuchergilde Gutenberg, 1957; (editor) Johann Wolfgang von Goethe, *Goethes Werke in zwei Baenden*, two volumes, Knaur Verlag, 1957; *Die Party bei Herrn Tokaido: Begegnungen im heutigen Japan*, R. Piper, 1958; *Georg Friedrich Handel in Selbstzeugnissen und Bilddokumenten*, Rowohlt, 1959; *London: Zwischen gestern und morgen*, W. Andermann, 1960; (editor) von Goethe, *Englische Werke*, Westerham Press, 1961; (editor) Rudolf Steiner, *Weltsilvester und Neujahrsgedanken: Fuenf Vortraege*, R. Steiner-Nachlessverwaltung, 1962; (editor) Zweig, *Die Dramen*, S. Fischer, 1964; (editor with Johann Waeger) *Kosmische und menschliche Geschichte*, Verlag de Rudolf Steiner-Nachlassverwaltung, seven volumes, 1964-74; *Gedichte fuer meine Freunde*, R. Piper, 1966; *Entdecker des Ich: Montaigne, Pascal, Diderot*, R. Piper, 1969.

Ketzer und Rebell: Jan Hus und das Jahrhundert der Revolutionskriege, R. Piper, 1972; (editor) *Soziales Verstaendis aus geisteswissenchaftlicher Erkenntnis*, Dornach/Schweiz, 1972; *Goethe-Weisheiten im ernsten und heiteren Ton: Goethe-Almanach fuer die Freunde und Mitglieder des Deutschen Buecherbundes*, Deutscher Buecherbund, 1974; *Grosse Erzaehlungen*, Herbig, 1976; *Und unversehens ist es Abend: Von und ueber Richard Friedenthal: Essays, Gedichte, Fragm., Wuerdigung, Autobiograph*, edited by Klaus Piper, R. Piper, 1976; (editor) S. Zweig, *Briefe an Freunde*, S. Fischer, 1978.

BIOGRAPHICAL/CRITICAL SOURCES: Washington Post, October 22, 1979; *AB Bookman's Weekly*, November 5, 1979; *New York Times*, November 5, 1979.*

*   *   *

FRIEDRICH, Dick
See FRIEDRICH, Richard

FRIEDRICH, Richard 1936-
(Dick Friedrich)

PERSONAL: Born May 11, 1936, in Chicago, Ill.; son of Harold E. (a factory worker) and Dorothea (a clerk; maiden name, Schwartz) Friedrich; married first wife, Alice Ann (divorced, 1968); married second wife, Linda (divorced, 1975); children: Larry, Lisa, Julie, Ursula. *Education:* St. Procopius College, A.B., 1959; University of Wisconsin (now Univeristy of Wisconsin—Madison), M.S., 1966. *Politics:* "Anarchist, Leftist, Radical." *Religion:* Atheist. *Residence:* St. Louis, Mo.

CAREER: Stout State College (now University of Wisconsin—Stout), Menominie, associate professor, 1961-68; Forest Park Community College, St. Louis, Mo., professor, 1968—. Member of local East-West Cultural Committee. *Awards, honors:* Teaching award from Lindbach Foundation, 1964; Danforth associate, 1966.

WRITINGS—Under name Dick Friedrich: (With David Kuester) *It's Mine and I'll Write It That Way*, Random House, 1970; (with Angela Harris) *Writing for Your Reader*, Kendall/Hunt, 1980.

Author of play, "J. C." Contributor of articles and poems to literature and language journals. Member of editorial board of *Teaching English in the Two-Year College*.

WORK IN PROGRESS: A biography of a World War II sailor; poems.

*   *   *

FRIENDLY, Henry Jacob 1903-

PERSONAL: Born July 3, 1903, in Elmira, N.Y.; son of Myer H. and Leah (Hallo) Friendly; married Sophie M. Stern, September 4, 1930; children: David Stern, Joan Pfaeizer (Mrs. Frank Goodman), Ellen (Mrs. Stephen Simon). *Education:* Harvard University, A.B., 1923, LL.B., 1927. *Home:* 1088 Park Ave., New York, N.Y. 10028. *Office:* U.S. Court House, New York, N.Y. 10007.

CAREER: Admitted to the Bar of New York State, 1928, and the Bar of District of Columbia, 1947; law clerk to U.S. Supreme Court Justice Brandeis in Washington, D.C., 1927-28; Root, Clark, Buckner & Ballantine, New York City, associate, 1928-36, partner, 1937-45; partner in law firm of Cleary, Gottlieb, Friendly & Hamilton, 1946-59; U.S. Court of Appeals, Second Circuit, New York City, judge, 1959—, chief judge, 1971-73, presiding judge of special court under Rail Reorganization Act, 1974—. Oliver Wendell Holmes Lecturer at Harvard University, 1962, and Dartmouth College, 1968; Carpentier Lecturer at Columbia University, 1972; overseer of Harvard University, 1964-69. Member of board of directors, vice-president, and general counsel of Pan American World Airways System, 1946-50; trustee-at-large of Federation of Jewish Philanthropies of New York.

MEMBER: American Bar Association, American Law Institute (member of council and executive committee), New York State Bar Association, Association of the Bar of the City of New York (honorary member), Harvard Alumni Association (president, 1960-61), Harvard Club, Harmonie Club, Century Association. *Awards, honors:* D.H.L. from Hebrew Union College, 1960; LL.D. from Syracuse University, 1962, Brooklyn Law School, 1964, Jewish Theological Seminary, 1965, Case Western Reserve University, 1967, Brandeis University and University of Cincinnati, 1968, University of Chicago, 1969, Harvard University, 1971, Columbia University, Northwestern University, and New York University; Presidential Medal of Freedom, 1977; Thomas Jefferson Memorial Award in Law, 1978; Louis Stern Award from Fordham University.

WRITINGS: The Federal Administrative Agencies: The Need for Better Definition of Standards, Harvard University Press, 1962; *In Praise of Erie, and of the New Federal Common Law*, Association of the Bar of the City of New York, 1964; *Benchmarks*, University of Chicago Press, 1967; *Federal Jurisdiction: A General View*, Columbia University Press, 1973. Contributor to law journals.*

*   *   *

FRIGGENS, Arthur (Henry) 1920-

PERSONAL: Born March 2, 1920, in Penzance, England; son of James Ede (a gas company manager) and Mary (Strick) Friggens; married Elsa Duthie, March 31, 1955; children: Christine Simpson (stepdaughter). *Education:* Oxford University, certificate, 1937. *Agent:* Elspeth Gordon, Manor House, Pope's Ave., Twickenham, Middlesex, England.

CAREER: Officer of customs and excise in England, 1948—. *Military service:* British Army, Royal Artillery, 1940-47; became captain. *Member:* Royal Overseas League, Folio Society.

WRITINGS—Science fiction novels; with Eric Burgess: *Anti-Zota*, R. Hale, 1973; *Mortorio*, R. Hale, 1973; *Mortorio Two*, R. Hale, 1975; *The Mants of Myrmedon*, R. Hale, 1977; *Hounds of Heaven*, R. Hale, 1979.

AVOCATIONAL INTERESTS: Reading modern languages, travel, cooking.*

*   *   *

FRIMBO, E. M.
See WHITAKER, Rogers E(rnest) M(alcolm)

*   *   *

FRINGS, Ketti 1915-1981

OBITUARY NOTICE—See index for *CA* sketch: Born in 1915 in Columbus, Ohio; died of cancer, February 11, 1981, in Los Angeles, Calif. Screenwriter, playwright, and author best known for her Pulitzer Prize-winning stage adaptation of Thomas Wolfe's *Look Homeward, Angel*, for which she also was awarded the New York Drama Critics Circle Award in 1958. Frings wrote the screen adaptation of William Inge's "Come Back, Little Sheba" in 1952 and the scenario for "The Shrike," the screen adaptation of Joseph Kramm's play, in 1955. Frings also wrote the novels *Hold Back the Dawn* and *God's Front Porch*. Obituaries and other sources: *New York Times*, February 13, 1981; *Time*, February 23, 1981.

*   *   *

FRITZE, Julius Arnold 1918-

PERSONAL: Born December 30, 1918, in Albuquerque, N.M.; son of Martin Herman and Mary (Staerkel) Fritze; married Marion Caroline Becker, June 4, 1944 (marriage ended); married Anita Carol Dozier, May 18, 1973; children: (first marriage) Christine, Timothy. *Education:* Attended St. Paul's Junior College, 1937-39; Concordia Seminary, St. Louis, Mo., diploma, 1944; University of New Mexico, B.A., 1943; Central Missouri State College, M.S., 1969. *Home:* 3240 Lancelot St., Dallas, Tex. 75229. *Office:* 2919 Welborn, Dallas, Tex. 75219.

CAREER: Ordained Lutheran minister, 1944; pastor of Lutheran churches in Corpus Christi, Tex., 1944-48, and Higginsville, Mo., 1948-57; Marriage and Parenthood Center, Dallas, Tex., executive director, 1957-59; private practice in marriage counseling in Dallas, Tex., 1959—. Industrial psychologist at North American Marketing, 1975-76; lecturer at Dallas County Junior College; lecturer to public and professional groups. *Member:* International Platform Association, American Association of Marriage Counselors, American Personnel and Guidance Association, National Vocational Guidance Association, National Council on Family Relations, American Psychological Association, American Lung Association (member of Dallas board of directors, 1976—), Southwestern Psychological Association, Texas Psychological Association.

WRITINGS: The Essence of Marriage, Zondervan, 1969. Contributor to national magazines.*

*   *   *

FROMMER, Harvey 1937-

PERSONAL: Born October 10, 1937, in Brooklyn, N.Y.; son of Max and Fannie (Wechsler) Frommer; married Myrna Katz (a writer, teacher, and free-lance editor), January 23, 1960; children: Jennifer, Freddy, Jan. *Education:* New York University, B.S., 1957, M.A., 1961, Ph.D., 1974. *Religion:* Jewish. *Residence:* North Woodmere, N.Y.

CAREER: United Press International (UPI), Chicago, Ill., sportswriter, 1957-58; New York public schools, New York City, high school English teacher, 1960-70; City University of New York, New York City, associate professor, 1970—. As a sports nostalgia and trivia expert, has appeared on television and radio talk shows. *Military service:* U.S. Army, 1958-59. *Member:* Association of American University Professors, Society for American Baseball Research.

WRITINGS: A Baseball Century: The First 100 Years of the National League, Macmillan, 1976; *A Sailing Primer*, Atheneum, 1977; *The Martial Arts: Judo and Karate*, Atheneum, 1978; *Sports Lingo*, Atheneum, 1979; *Sports Roots: How Nicknames, Namesakes, Trophies, Competitions, and Expressions Came to Be in the World of Sports*, Atheneum, 1979; *The Great American Soccer Book*, Atheneum, 1980; *New York City Baseball: The Last Golden Age, 1947-1957*, Macmillan, 1980; *The Sports Dates Book*, Grosset, 1981; *Rickey and Robinson: A Dual Biography*, Macmillan, 1982. Contributor of numerous articles to professional journals.

WORK IN PROGRESS: A book on basketball with Nancy Leiberman, publication by Scribner expected in 1981.

SIDELIGHTS: In 1974 Frommer wrote his doctoral dissertation in English on the influence of sports on television and of television on sports. His efforts to have the work published resulted in the opportunity to write *A Baseball Century*, the official centennial history of the National League.

Frommer told *CA:* "Sports and work and writing fascinate me, and gardening acts as a release. I am involved all the time with one of these or another. I have written ten books on sports in five years and look forward to doing many more. An auto accident—for a few frightening moments—made me wonder if I would ever do anything again. However, after a long healing process, I am starting to engage in all my projects again at full speed.

"I enjoy my dual careers—as professor of writing and speech and as sports author and lecturer. One acts as a change of pace for the other. Also, there is my wonderful family, my wife, Myrna—my editor, adviser, organizer, and inspirer—

and my lovely children. My two boys are totally involved in the world of sports, and we are able to share anecdotes and happy times playing games—especially baseball. I still find myself anchored in my own childhood world of games and fanhood. Perhaps that is what inspired *New York City Baseball* and *Rickey and Robinson*—both books deal with the golden heroes of my growing up years, when the world we all knew was very different.

"I am very pleased when reviewers say nice things about my writings. I try to give my work every ounce of effort and intelligence that I possess. I am especially pleased when I receive a fan letter or when I meet someone or hear of someone who has read one of my books and has expressed his or her appreciation. I look back over these things and am happy at how far a poor kid from a seedy neighborhood in Brooklyn came in the United States of America. I dream now of other journeys, other accomplishments, other big and significant books for the future."

BIOGRAPHICAL/CRITICAL SOURCES: New York Times, April 13, 1980; *New York Times Book Review,* June 15, 1980.

*   *   *

FUERMANN, George Melvin   1918-

PERSONAL: Born August 25, 1918, in Buffalo, N.Y.; son of Walter John and Viola Irene (Bishop) Fuermann; married Ruth Wagner Owens, July 9, 1970; children: Julie Ann, Walter. *Education:* Attended Texas A & M University, 1937-41. *Religion:* Episcopalian. *Home:* 4747 Southwest Freeway, Houston, Tex. 77001.

CAREER: Houston Post, Houston, Tex., columnist, 1950-70, editor of editorial page, 1971—. Chairman of Houston Municipal Art Commission, 1965-67, and Houston Municipal Art Foundation, 1966-67; member of Houston Commission on Foreign Relations, chairman, 1977. *Military service:* U.S. Army; became captain; received Bronze Star.

WRITINGS: (With F. Edward Cranz) *Ninety-Fifth Infantry Division History, 1918-1946,* A. Love Enterprises, 1947; *Houston: Land of the Big Rich,* Doubleday, 1951; *Reluctant Empire; The Mind of Texas,* Doubleday, 1957; *The Face of Houston,* Press of Premier, 1963; *Houston Recalled: Six Miniatures,* Baxter & Korge, 1968; *Houston: The Once and Future City,* Doubleday, 1971. Also author of *Houston: The Feast Years,* 1962.*

*   *   *

FUKUDA, Tsutomu   1905-

PERSONAL: Born September 24, 1905, in Tokyo, Japan; son of Teikichi and Masako (Bessho) Fukuda; married wife Momoyo (deceased); married wife Toshie, 1945; children: Toshiko Fukuda Matsuda, Shizuko Fukuda Kakiya, Katsuaki, Kimiko Fukuda Yanai, Miyoko Fukuda Yokoyama. *Education:* Fifth Teachers' Institute, teacher's license, 1925; attended Indiana University, Columbia University, and Harvard University, 1942, and Oxford University and Cambridge University, 1943. *Politics:* Social Democrat. *Religion:* Nichiren Buddhist. *Home:* 3-17 2-chome, Yakushidori, Nada, Kobe, Japan. *Office:* Department of English Language and

Literature, Kyoto University of Foreign Studies, Kyoto, Japan.

CAREER: Hirosaki University, Hirosaki City, Japan, professor of English, 1951-59; Kobe University, Kobe, Japan, professor of English, 1959-69; Tezukayama Women's Junior College, Osaka, Japan, professor of English, 1969-70; Kyoto University of Foreign Studies, Kyoto, Japan, professor of English, 1970—. *Awards, honors:* Fulbright fellow, 1942; prize from Stanford University, 1954, for translating *Spring Birds;* D.Litt. from Kanseigakuin University, 1968.

WRITINGS: Literary and Linguistic Travels in the United States and Europe, Daigakukyoikusha, 1936; *A Study of Charles Lamb's "Essays of Elia,"* Hokuseido Press, 1964; (translator and editor) *Sansho-Dayu and Other Short Stories,* Hokuseido Press, 1970; *The Hanging Bridge* (poems), Hokuseido Press, 1971; *A Study of Charles Lamb's Works,* Daigakukyoikusha Press, 1975; *Playing the Harp* (poems), Japan Society for the Promotion of Science, 1976; (translator and editor) *One Hundred Peonies* (poems), Sun-Lotus Haiku, 1977; *Literal and Liberal Translations,* Kenkyusha Press, 1978; *Allusions in Thomas Hardy's Works,* Thomas Hardy Society of Japan, 1978; (translator with James Kirkup) Yasunari Kawabata, *The Ring* [and]*Death Mask,* Pan Books, 1980.

Work represented in anthologies, including *Songs and Dreams,* edited by Kirkup, Blackie & Sons, 1970; *Listening to Japan,* Praeger, 1973; *Moving Along,* edited by John Glover, Evans Brothers, 1977. Contributor to literary journals, including *Orbis, Little Word Machine, Poet, Ocarina, Commonwealth Quarterly,* and *Poetry Nippon, Michi.* President of *Poetry Nippon;* Far East editor of *Poet.*

SIDELIGHTS: Fukuda commented: "For many years I taught English composition at high schools, which led me to take an interest in translation. I translated many literary works by famous Japanese authors into English, both stories and poems. Later on I began writing English poems and sending them to foreign magazines. My poems are influenced by *haiku* and *waka,* our traditional poems, which are heavily influenced by Buddhism. Naturally, my poems are short in imitation of them. Happily they are welcomed all over the world, perhaps because only a few Japanese write poems in English."

*   *   *

FULLER, Hoyt (William)   1927-1981
(William Barrow)

OBITUARY NOTICE—See index for *CA* sketch: Born September 10, 1927, in Atlanta, Ga.; died of a heart attack, May 11, 1981, in Atlanta, Ga. Editor, literary critic, and author. Under Fuller's editorship, *Negro Digest* (renamed *Black World* in 1970) became the springboard for the black aesthetic literary movement in the 1960's and 1970's. Fuller and other black intellectuals formed the First World Foundation to publish *First World* in Atlanta after *Black World* ceased publication in 1976. Fuller taught Afro-American literature at Wayne State, Indiana, and Northwestern universities. He was the author of *Journey to Africa.* Obituaries and other sources: *New York Times,* May 13, 1981; *Newsweek,* May 25, 1981; *Time,* May 25, 1981.

G

GALLOWAY, George Barnes 1898-1967

OBITUARY NOTICE—See index for CA sketch: Born January 9, 1898, in Brooklyn, N.Y.; died July 29, 1967, in Washington, D.C. Authority on American government and author. George Galloway, a senior specialist in American government with the Legislative Reference Service of the Library of Congress, wrote a number of books, including *Planning for America* and *The Legislative Process in Congress*. He also wrote *History of the United States House of Representatives*, which was published as *History of the House of Representatives* in a revised edition. Galloway was the author of public affairs bulletins for the Library of Congress, and his articles on congressional activities appeared in numerous political science and history journals. Obituaries and other sources: *New York Times*, July 30, 1967.

* * *

GAMMON, Roland I. 1920-1981

OBITUARY NOTICE—See index for CA sketch: Born November 18, 1920, in Caribou, Me.; died April 8, 1981, in New York, N.Y. Editor, executive, lecturer, and author. After working as a writer and editor for *Life*, Gammon founded and was president of Editorial Communications, Inc. and World Authors Ltd. He was also past president and dean of the all-faith chapel of the Universalist Church. Gammon was the author of five books on the subject of religion: *Truth Is One, Faith Is a Star, A God for Modern Man, All Believers Are Brothers*, and *Nirvana Now*. Obituaries and other sources: *New York Times*, April 12, 1981.

* * *

GARDINER, Charles Wrey 1901-1981

OBITUARY NOTICE: Born in 1901; died March 13, 1981. Editor, publisher, poet, and author. The editor of *Poetry Quarterly* and founder of the Grey Walls Press, Gardiner wrote several autobiographies depicting his life in England during the 1940's and 1950's, as well as his years spent on his yacht in the Mediterranean. Among his books are *The Colonies of Heaven, The Once-Loved God*, and *The Answer to Life Is No*. Obituaries and other sources: *London Times*, March 18, 1981.

GARDNER, John Edmund 1926-

PERSONAL: Born November 20, 1926, in Seaton Delaval, England; son of Cyril John (a priest of Church of England) and Lena (Henderson) Gardner; married Margaret Mercer, September 15, 1952; children: Alexis Mary, Simon Richard John. *Education:* St. John's College, Cambridge, B.A., 1950, M.A., 1951; attended St. Stephen's House, Oxford, 1951-52. *Residence:* Ashford, Ireland. *Agent:* Desmond Elliott, 3 Clifford St., Mayfair, London W1X 1RA, England.

CAREER: Writer. Ordained priest of Church of England, 1953, legally released from obligations of the priesthood, 1958; magician with American Red Cross, Entertainments Department, 1943-44; curator in Evesham, England, 1952-58; *Herald*, Stratford-upon-Avon, England, theatre critic and arts editor, 1959-65. Lecturer in the United States and Soviet Union. *Military service:* Royal Navy, Fleet Air Arm, 1944-46. Royal Marines, Commandos, 1946; served in Hong Kong and Malta; became chaplain. *Member:* Crime Writers Association.

WRITINGS—Novels, except as indicated: *Spin the Bottle* (autobiography), Muller, 1963; *The Liquidator*, Viking, 1964; *Understrike*, Viking, 1965; *Amber Nine*, Viking, 1966; *Madrigal*, Viking, 1968; *Hideaway* (stories), Corgi, 1968; *Founder Member*, Muller, 1969; *A Complete State of Death*, Viking, 1969.

Traitor's Exit, Muller, 1970; *Air Apparent*, Putnam, 1970 (published in England as *The Airline Pirates*, Hodder & Stoughton, 1970); *The Censor*, New English Library, 1970; *Every Night's a Festival*, Morrow, 1971 (published in England as *Every Night's a Bullfight*, M. Joseph, 1971); *The Assassination File* (stories), Corgi, 1972; *The Corner Men*, Doubleday, 1974; *The Return of Moriarty*, Putnam, 1974; *The Revenge of Moriarty*, Putnam, 1975; *A Killer for a Song*, Hodder & Stoughton, 1975; *To Run a Little Faster*, M. Joseph, 1976; *The Werewolf Trace*, Doubleday, 1977; *The Dancing Dodo*, Doubleday, 1978; *The Last Trump*, McGraw, 1980 (published in England as *Golgotha*, W. H. Allen, 1980); *The Garden of Weapons*, Hodder & Stoughton, 1980, McGraw, 1981; *License Renewed* (James Bond novel), Hodder & Stoughton/J. Cape, 1981.

The "Kruger Trilogy" *The Nostradamus Traitor*, Doubleday, 1979; *The Garden of Weapons*, Hodder & Stoughton,

1980, McGraw, 1981; *The Quiet Dogs,* Hodder & Stoughton, 1981, McGraw, in press.

WORK IN PROGRESS: Flamingo, a novel, publication by Doubleday expected in 1983; two James Bond suspense novels for Hodder & Stoughton/J. Cape, respective publications expected in 1981 and 1982.

SIDELIGHTS: Gardner wrote: "At the age of nine I announced that I would be a writer, and my father presented me with a notebook. On the title page I wrote, 'The Complete Works of John Gardner.' The book remained empty for a long while, but I knew that I should really be an actor or a writer. For a while, I took the wrong turning and entered the Church of England, even though the spark had been lighted at school by the English translator and editor J. M. Cohen. My trade was first learned at the *Stratford-upon-Avon Herald,* where I realized I would not be happy forever acting as a critic of other people's work. The job also gave me an even greater sense of the dramatic, and, I suppose, my work pattern is still based on that—I work rather like an actor, taking on a theme or role so that it, eventually, envelops me. After that, I need to work with a good editor, who I use as an actor uses a director. I have always been a loner (which does not mean I am lonely). Work is life and life is work, though I have no pretensions about being 'literary'—I greatly mistrust any so-called 'Literary Establishment,' I am a story-teller, a professional wordsmith—it is a job, like that of a carpenter or any other craftsman. Sometimes the piece works, sometimes not. I am drawn toward all secret worlds, those of espionage, crime, and the police."

"The Liquidator" was released as a feature film by Metro-Goldwyn-Mayer in 1965. *A Complete State of Death* was released as "The Stone Killer" by Columbia, 1973.

AVOCATIONAL INTERESTS: Reading, music.

*   *   *

GARIOCH, Robert Sutherland   1909-1981

PERSONAL: Born May 9, 1909, in Edinburgh, Scotland; died April 26, 1981; married Margaret Sutherland, 1941; children: two. *Education:* University of Edinburgh, M.A. (with honors). *Home:* 4 Nelson St., Edinburgh 3, Scotland. *Office:* School of Scottish Studies, University of Edinburgh, Edinburgh, Scotland.

CAREER: Schoolmaster in Kent, England, London, England, and Edinburgh, Scotland; University of Edinburgh, Edinburgh, transcriber at School of Scottish Studies, 1965—, writer-in-residence, 1971-73. Lexicographer for Dictionary of the Older Scottish Tongue, 1965—. *Military service:* British Army, Royal Signal Corps, 1941-46, prisoner of war, 1942-45. *Awards, honors:* Sloan Prize, 1930; Scottish Arts Council award, 1968.

WRITINGS: (With Somhairle MacGhill-Eathain) *Seventeen Poems for Sixpence: In Gaelic, Lowland Scots, and English,* Chalmers Press, 1940; *Chuckies on the Cairn: Poems in Scots and English,* Chalmers Press, 1949; *The Masque of Edinburgh* (play), M. Macdonald, 1954; (translator) George Buchanan, *Jephthah and the Baptist: Translatit Frae Latin in Scots,* Oliver & Boyd, 1959; *Selected Poems,* M. Macdonald, 1966; *The Big Music and Other Poems,* Caithness Books, 1971; *Doktor Faust in Rose Street* (poems), M. Macdonald, 1973; *Two Men and a Blanket: Memoirs of Captivity* (memoirs of World War II), Southside Publishers, 1974; (editor) *Made in Scotland: An Anthology of Fourteen Scottish Poets,* Dufour, 1974; (editor) Robert Fergusson, *Fergusson: A Bi-Centenary Handsel—Seventeen Poems* (bound with *A Vision*

of Angels by Anne Smith), Reprographia, 1974; *Collected Poems,* M. Macdonald, 1977.*

OBITUARIES: London Times, May 2, 1981.*

*   *   *

GARNETT, David   1892-1981
(Leda Burke)

OBITUARY NOTICE—See index for *CA* sketch: Born March 9, 1892, in Brighton, England; died February 17, 1981, in Montucq, France. Publisher, bookseller, and author. The last surviving member of the Bloomsbury group, Garnett became a bookseller following service as a conscientious objector during World War I. *Lady Into Fox,* the first novel Garnett wrote under his own name, received instant literary acclaim, winning the Hawthornden and the James Tait Black Memorial prizes. During the 1920's Garnett entered the publishing field and developed an interest in aviation. He became a pilot and during World War II served with the British Air Ministry as an intelligence officer, writing a graphic account of the British-German air war during the Battle of Britain. Although best known as a writer of short fantasies, Garnett worked in several genres. His work has been consistently praised. Among Garnett's books are *A Man in the Zoo, The Sailor's Return, The Letters of T. E. Lawrence, A Shot in the Dark,* and *Ulterior Motives.* Several books remained unpublished at the time of Garnett's death. Obituaries and other sources: *London Times,* February 19, 1981; *Publishers Weekly,* March 13, 1981.

*   *   *

GARRITY, Devin Adair   1906-1981

OBITUARY NOTICE: Born November 26, 1906, in Staten Island, N.Y.; died January 6, 1981, in Rye, N.Y. Publisher and editor of anthologies, including *New Irish Poets, The Irish Genius,* and *Mentor Book of Irish Poetry.* Garrity was president of the Devin-Adair Publishing Company for more than forty years. Obituaries and other sources: *American Authors and Books, 1640 to the Present Day,* 3rd revised edition, Crown, 1972; *Who's Who in America,* 40th edition, Marquis, 1978; *Publishers Weekly,* January 30, 1981.

*   *   *

GART, Murray Joseph   1924-

PERSONAL: Born November 9, 1924, in Boston, Mass.; son of John and Frieda (Fisher) Gart; married Jeanne Brooks, February 26, 1950; children: Mitchell Brooks, Marcia Anne. *Education:* Northeastern University, B.A., 1949. *Home:* 2126 Connecticut Ave. N.W., Washington, D.C. 20008. *Office: Washington Star,* 225 Virginia Ave. S.E., Washington, D.C. 20061.

CAREER/WRITINGS: Honolulu Star-Bulletin, Honolulu, Hawaii, reporter, 1949-50; *Weekly Independent Record,* Cape May County, N.J., editor, 1950-51; *Wichita Beacon,* Wichita, Kan., reporter and city editor, 1951-53; *Wichita Eagle,* Wichita, reporter and news editor, 1953-55; Time-Life News Service, bureau chief in Toronto, Canada, 1955-57, and Boston, Mass., 1957-59, chief midwest correspondent for *Time,* 1959-61, and bureau chief in Chicago, Ill., 1961-64, and London, England, 1964-66; *Fortune,* New York City, assistant managing editor, 1966-69; Time-Life News Service, New York City, chief, 1969-78, assistant managing editor of *Time,* 1972-78; *Washington Star,* Washington, D.C., editor, 1978—. Director of Universal Press Syndicate. *Military service:* U.S. Army, 1943-46. *Member:* Council on Foreign Relations, Century Association (New York City), Cosmos (Washington, D.C.), The Garrick (London).

*   *   *

GARTON, Malinda D(ean)   (?)-1976

OBITUARY NOTICE—See index for *CA* sketch: Born in Gallatin, Mo.; died May 8, 1976. Educator and author. An educator for more than thirty years, Malinda Garton specialized in teaching slow learners. She was the author of *Teaching the Educable Mentally Retarded: Practical Methods* and *Making Friends,* a basic reading series. (Date of death provided by publisher, Charles C Thomas.)

*   *   *

GARVEY, Terence Willcocks   1915-

PERSONAL: Born December 7, 1915, in Dublin, Ireland; son of Francis Willcocks and Ethel Margaret (Ray) Garvey; married Rosemary O'Neill; children: three. *Education:* Oxford University, B.A., 1938, M.A., 1976. *Home:* 11A Stonefield St., London N1 OHW, England.

CAREER: Foreign Service, London, England, posted in U.S., Chile, Germany, and Egypt, 1938-62, charge d'affaires in China, 1962-65, ambassador to Mongolia, 1963-65, assistant under-secretary of state in London, 1965-68, ambassador to Yugoslavia, 1968-71, high commissioner to India, 1971-73, ambassador to the Soviet Union, 1973-75; Oxford University, Oxford, England, senior associate member of St. Antony's College, 1976—. *Awards, honors:* Knight commander of St. Michael and St. George.

WRITINGS: Bones of Contention: An Enquiry Into East-West Relations, St. Martin's, 1978.

*   *   *

GAWRON, Jean Mark   1953-

PERSONAL: Surname is pronounced Gav-ron; born October 2, 1953, in Paris, France; son of Walter (a physician) and Henryan (Niewiadomska) Gawron. *Education:* New York Univeristy, B.A., 1974; University of California, Berkeley, M.A., 1980. *Residence:* Chicago, Ill.

CAREER: Taxicab driver in New York City, 1974-75; John Jay College of Criminal Justice of the City University of New York, New York City, tutor, 1977; writer, 1977—.

WRITINGS: An Apology for Rain (novel), Doubleday, 1974; *Algorithm* (novel), Putnam, 1977.

WORK IN PROGRESS: The Last Science Fiction Novel.

*   *   *

GAY, Francis
See GEE, H(erbert) L(eslie)

*   *   *

GAZI, Stephen   1914-1978

OBITUARY NOTICE—See index for *CA* sketch: Born August 9, 1914, in Peteranec, Croatia (now Yugoslavia); died September 15, 1978. Diplomat, educator, and author. Stephen Gazi wrote such books as *The Croatian Immigration to Alleghany County* and *A History of Croatia.* (Date of death provided by wife, Elizabeth Gazi.)

GEACH, Peter Thomas   1916-

PERSONAL: Born March 29, 1916; son of George Hender (a professor) and Eleonora Frederyka Adolfina (Sgonina) Geach; married Gertrude Elizabeth Margaret Anscombe (a professor), December 26, 1941; children: three sons, four daughters. *Education:* Balliol College, Oxford, B.A., 1938, M.A., 1951; Cambridge University, M.A., 1971. *Religion:* Roman Catholic. *Home:* 3 Richmond Rd., Cambridge CB4 3PP, England. *Office:* Department of Philosophy, University of Leeds, 3 Richmond Rd., Leeds, Yorkshire LS2 9JT, England.

CAREER: Cambridge University, Cambridge, England, researcher in philosophy, 1945-51; University of Birmingham, Birmingham, England, assistant lecturer, 1951-52, lecturer, 1952-59, senior lecturer in philosophy, 1959-61, reader in logic, 1961-66; University of Leeds, Leeds, England, professor of logic, 1966—. Adjunct professor of philosophy at University of Pennsylvania, 1968—; Stanton lecturer in philosophy of religion at Cambridge University, 1971-74; Haegerstroem lecturer at University of Uppsala, 1975. *Member:* British Academy (fellow), Union Society (Oxford, England). *Awards, honors:* Fellow of Balliol College, Oxford, 1979.

WRITINGS: Mental Acts: Their Content and Their Objects, Routledge & Kegan Paul, 1956, Humanities, 1957, revised edition, 1971; (with wife, Gertrude Elizabeth Margaret Anscombe) *Three Philosophers,* Cornell University Press, 1961; *Reference and Generality: An Examination of Some Medieval and Modern Theories,* Cornell University Press, 1962, 3rd edition, 1980; *God and the Soul* (essays), Shocken, 1969; *Logic Matters,* University of California Press, 1972; *Reason and Argument,* University of California Press, 1976; *Providence and Evil,* Cambridge University Press, 1977; *The Virtues,* Cambridge University Press, 1977; *Truth, Love, and Immortality: An Introduction to McTaggart's Philosophy,* University of California Press, 1979.

Editor: (With Max Black) Gottlob Frege, *Translations From the Philosophical Writings of Gottlob Frege,* Philosophical Library, 1952; (with A.J.P. Kenny) Arthur N. Prior, *Objects of Thought,* Clarendon, 1971; (and translator from the French, both with G.E.M. Anscombe) *Philosophical Writings,* introduction by Alexandre Koyre, Thomas Nelson (Melbourne), 1964, Bobbs-Merrill, 1971; (with Kenny) Prior, *Papers in Logic and Ethics,* University of Massachusetts Press, 1976; (with Kenny) Prior, *The Doctrine of Propositions and Terms,* University of Massachusetts Press, 1976; (also translator from the German with R. H. Stoothoff, and author of preface) Frege, *Logical Investigations,* Yale University Press, 1977.

BIOGRAPHICAL/CRITICAL SOURCES: Times Literary Supplement, October 16, 1969, February 2, 1973; *Encounter,* March, 1978; *Commonweal,* August 4, 1978; *Philosophical Review,* October, 1978; *Review of Metaphysics,* December, 1979.

*   *   *

GEARING, Catherine   1916-

PERSONAL: Born October 7, 1916, in Lemoore, Calif.: daughter of Ross Elliot (an auto mechanic) and Ida Pearl (Brown) Gearing. *Education:* Walla Walla College, B.S., 1961. *Politics:* Republican. *Religion:* Seventh-Day Adventist. *Residence:* Placerville, Calif.

CAREER: Registered nurse. Feather River Hospital, Paradise, Calif., floor supervisor, 1953-57, director of nurses, 1957-59, 1961-67, director of education, 1955-69; office nurse of physician in Placerville, Calif., 1970-79. Lecturer on processing of plant foods. *Member:* Association of Seventh-Day Adventist Nurses.

WRITINGS: Fieldguide to Wilderness Living, Southern Publishing Association, 1973.

WORK IN PROGRESS: Research for a book on wild edible plants.

SIDELIGHTS: Gearing told *CA:* "I took a course in wilderness survival at Walla Walla College. This caused me to have a keen interest in wild edible plants. I began to collect books and any literature available on the subject. I talked to Indians, Mexicans, woodsmen, backpackers, hunters—anyone who knew anything on the subject. Many took me out in the field and showed me various plants. "I began to give lectures with demonstrations on how to process certain plant foods. My display table is now fifty feet long. On this table are between fifty and sixty fresh plant samples: dry samples such as acorns (many varieties), pine nuts (several varieties), sumac cones (fruit), bamboo shoots, roots of various plants, cattail root stalk, shoots, sprouts, and green spikes, plus may other samples placed on trays. There are scores of frozen samples of wild foods out of season, and foods cooked or baked such as acorn bread, cattail yellow pollen muffins, buckeye casserole, cream of buckeye soup, thistle casserole, thistle stalks boiled as a vegetable, and much more."

*   *   *

GEE, H(erbert) L(eslie)   1901-1977
(Francis Gay)

OBITUARY NOTICE—See index for *CA* sketch: Born June 16, 1901, in Bridlington, Yorkshire, England; died of a heart attack, March 19, 1977. Journalist and author. H. L. Gee wrote newspaper features and an annual publication under a pseudonym, Francis Gay, from 1935 to 1964. Under his own name, Gee wrote more than seventy books, many of which are for children. Among his books are *A Pocketful of Humour, Comprising Hundreds of Twice-Told Tales Worth Telling Again; The Twins on Holiday;* and *Through the Year With H. L. Gee.* (Date of death provided by wife, Mary Gee.)

*   *   *

GELB, Leslie H(oward)   1937-

PERSONAL: Born March 4, 1937, in New Rochelle, N.Y.; son of Max R. and Dorothy (Klein) Gelb; married Judith Cohen, August 2, 1959; children: Adam, Caroline, Alison. *Education:* Tufts University, A.B. (magna cum laude), 1959; Harvard University, M.A. 1961, Ph.D., 1964. *Home:* 2405 Elba Court, Alexandria, Va. 22306.

CAREER: Wesleyan University, Middletown, Conn., assistant professor of government, 1964-65; executive assistant to U.S. Senator Jacob K. Javits in Washington, D.C., 1966-67; Office of the Secretary of Defense, Washington, D.C., deputy director of policy planning staff in international security affairs, 1967-68; director of Secretary of Defense Vietnam Task Force, 1967-68; director of policy planning staff, 1968, acting deputy assistant secretary of defense (policy planning and arms control staff), 1968-69; Brookings Institution, Washington, D.C., senior fellow, 1969-73; *New York Times,* New York, N.Y., diplomatic correspondent, 1973-76; Department of State, Bureau of Politico-Military Affairs, Washington, D.C., director, 1977-79, also chairman and chief

U.S. negotiator in conventional arms transfer restraint negotiations with the Soviet Union and chairman of North Atlantic Treaty Organization's special group on "Salt III"; Carnegie Endowment for International Peace, Washington, D.C., senior associate, 1979—. Visiting professor at Georgetown University, 1971-76; consultant to German Marshall Fund of the United States. *Member:* International Institute of Strategic Studies, Council on Foreign Relations. *Awards, honors:* Woodrow Wilson Award from American Political Science Association, 1980, for *The Irony of Vietnam.*

WRITINGS: (With Richard Betts) *The Irony of Vietnam: The System Worked,* Brookings Institution, 1979. Contributor to magazines and newspapers, including *Foreign Policy, Foreign Affairs, New Republic, Forbes,* and *Harper's.*

WORKS IN PROGRESS: A book on the future of arms control.

BIOGRAPHICAL/CRITICAL SOURCES: Time, April 24, 1978.

*   *   *

GELMAN, David Graham   1926-

PERSONAL: Born November 1, 1926, in New York, N.Y.; son of George and Rose Leah (Shulman) Gelman; married Elaine Edith Rodkinson (a pediatric nurse), April 6, 1952; children: Eric Adam, Andrew Seth, Amy Miriam. *Education:* Attended Brooklyn College (now of the City University of New York), 1947-55. *Home:* 229 West 78th St., New York, N.Y. 10024. *Office: Newsweek,* 444 Madison Ave., New York, N.Y. 10022.

CAREER/WRITINGS: New York Post, New York City, reporter, 1943-62; U.S. Peace Corps, Washington, D.C., evaluation officer and director of special projects, 1962-66; *Newsweek,* New York City, associate editor for national affairs and special projects, 1966-68; U.S. Research and Development, New York City, vice-president for education, 1968-69; *Newsday,* Garden City, N.Y., chief correspondent and national editor, 1969-75; *Newsweek,* New York City, general editor, 1975-78, senior writer, 1978—. *Military service:* U.S. Navy, 1944-46. *Awards, honors:* National Magazine Award, 1968, for *Newsweek* story "Negro in America"; citation for excellence from Overseas Press Club, 1973, for reporting from Vietnam; Page One Award from Newspaper Guild, 1978.

*   *   *

GEORGE, E(dgar) Madison   1907-1975

OBITUARY NOTICE—See index for *CA* sketch: Born November 10, 1907, in Bennetts Switch, Ind.; died April 6, 1975. Educator and author. George taught physical education and Spanish in high schools in Arizona and Virginia for more than thirty years. He wrote a book about communism, *Which Way, Young Americans,* for high school students. (Date of death provided by wife, Frances L. George.)

*   *   *

GERBER, John   1907(?)-1981

OBITUARY NOTICE: Born c. 1907 in Portland, Me.; died of a heart attack, January 28, 1981, in Houston, Tex. Contract bridge champion and author of *The Four Club Bid.* Gerber is known for inventing a bridge convention whereby a bid of four clubs is used to determine the number of aces the bidder's partner holds. Gerber won numerous bridge championships and was once considered one of the nation's best bridge players. Obituaries and other sources: *New York Times*, January 29, 1981; *Chicago Tribune*, January 31, 1981; *Time*, February 9, 1981.

* * *

GEROW, Josh(ua R.) 1941-

PERSONAL: Born April 29, 1941, in Liberty, N.Y.; married, 1967; children: one. *Education:* State University of New York at Buffalo, B.A., 1963; University of Tennessee, Ph.D., 1967. *Office:* Department of Psychology, Purdue University, 2101 East Coliseum Blvd., Fort Wayne, Ind. 46815.

CAREER: University of Colorado, Boulder, assistant professor of psychology, 1967-69; Purdue University, Fort Wayne, Ind., associate professor of psychology, 1969—.

WRITINGS: (With R. Douglas Lyng) *How to Succeed in College*, Scribner, 1975.*

* * *

GERSTAD, John (Leif) 1924-

PERSONAL: Original surname Gjerstad, name legally changed, 1925; born September 3, 1924, in Boston, Mass.; son of Leif Augustus (a journalist; in insurance sales) and Adelaide (an executive secretary of Norwegian consulate; maiden name, Johannessen) Gjerstad; married Annabel Lee Nugent, June 4, 1945; children: three. *Education:* Harvard University, B.A. *Home:* 345 East 57th St., New York, N.Y. 10022.

CAREER: Playwright, 1940—; actor in Broadway stage productions, 1943—, including "Othello," "Joy to the World," "The Male Animal," "The Trial of Lee Harvey Oswald," "Come Summer," "Oklahoma," and "All Over"; actor in motion pictures, including "Star," "The Swimmer," "Up the Down Staircase," and "What's So Bad About Feeling Good?"; actor in television programs and series, including "Certain Honorable Men," "A Case of Libel," "The Dillinger Story," "Galileo," "Give Us Barrabas," "Edge of Night," and more than twenty Hallmark Hall of Fame productions; director of stage productions, 1952—, including "The Seven Year Itch," "Howie," "The Wayward Saint," and "The Male Animal"; producer of stage productions and television programs, 1959—; producer, writer, and director of industrial films. Co-founder, officer, and director of Theatrical Interests Plan, Inc. Speech writer for Business Committee for the Arts, Inc. Dean of drama department of New England Conservatory and head of drama department of Hunter Lenox Day Center.

MEMBER: American Federation of Television and Radio Artists, American Institute of Science and Engineering, Dramatists Guild of America, Screen Actors Guild, Actors Equity Association (life member), League of New York Theatres, Society of Stage Directors and Choreographers (co-founder), Stage Managers' Club, Players Club.

WRITINGS—Plays: "Sun at Midnight" (three-act), first produced in Boston, Mass., at Peabody Playhouse, November, 1940; "The Wild Duck" (three-act; adapted and translated from the play by Henrik Ibsen), first produced in New York City at George Bruce Theatre, January, 1944; "Ghosts" (three-act; adapted from the play by Ibsen), first produced in New York City at Mendelsohn Theatre, 1945; (with James Lee) "The Monday Man" (three-act), first produced in Falmouth, Mass., at Falmouth Playhouse, July, 1947; (with Lee) "The French Have a Word for It" (three-act), first produced in Ridgefield, Conn., at Ridgefield Theatre, 1948.

(With Robert Scott) "When the Bough Breaks" (three-act), first produced in New York City at Master Arts Theatre, January, 1950; (with Norman Brooks) "O, Didn't He Ramble?" (one-act musical), first broadcast by CBS-TV, 1951; (with Brooks) "The Fig Leaf" (three-act), first produced in Chicago, Ill., at Erlanger Theatre, 1952; (with George Schaefer) "One Touch of Venus" (five-act), first broadcast by NBC-TV, 1953.

(With Oscar Brand) "Thunder Rock" (two-act musical), first produced in New York City at Lyric Theatre, January, 1979; "Jam" (two-act musical), first produced in New York City at Amas Theatre, April, 1980; "The High Bouncing Lover" (three-act), first produced in 1981.

Co-author with Charles A. McDaniel of musical book "A Joyful Noise." Writer for series "Lights Out," on NBC-TV, 1950-51, and "The Clock," on NBC-TV, 1950-51.

WORK IN PROGRESS: "Harz and Flowers," a three-act play; "Lost in the Stars," a musical book for Hallmark Hall of Fame television production.

SIDELIGHTS: John Gerstad commented: "As a playwright, my work has just begun when I write 'Curtain.' At this point the real job begins—to get a production. A play sitting on a shelf is not really a play: only when it fulfills its complete function—to be played by actors—for an audience. The actual writing comes fairly easily. I just sit with a large pad of legal paper and wait until drops of blood run from my brow."

* * *

GETHERS, Peter 1953-

PERSONAL: Born April 10, 1953, in New York, N.Y.; son of Steven and Judith Gethers. *Education:* Attended University of California, Berkeley, 1970-72, University of London, 1972-73, and University of California, Los Angeles, 1973-74. *Home:* 815 Greenwich St., New York, N.Y. 10014. *Agent:* International Creative Management, 40 West 57th St., New York, N.Y. 10019. *Office:* Random House, Inc., 201 East 50th St., New York, N.Y. 10022.

CAREER: Bantam Books, Inc., New York City, executive editor, 1975-80; Random House, Inc., New York City, editor, 1980—. *Member:* Writers Guild of America (East), National Academy of Television Arts and Sciences.

WRITINGS: The Dandy (novel), Dutton, 1978. Also author of television film "How to Pick Up Girls," broadcast by American Broadcasting Co.

WORK IN PROGRESS: Getting Blue, a novel.

* * *

GEYL, Pieter (Catharinus Arie) 1887-1966
(A. v.d. Merwe)

PERSONAL: Born December 15, 1887, in Dordrecht, Netherlands; died December 31, 1966, in Utrecht, Netherlands; son of Arie and Ada (van Erp Jaalman Kip) Geyl; married Maria Cornelia van Slooten, December, 1911 (died, 1933); married Garberlina Kremer, 1934; children: (first marriage) two. *Education:* University of Leyden, Litt.D., 1913.

CAREER: History master at high school in Schiedam, Netherlands, 1912; *Nieuwe Rotterdamsche Courant,* Rotterdam, Netherlands, correspondent from London, England, 1913-19; University of London, London, professor of Dutch studies, 1919-24, professor of Dutch history and institutions, 1924-35; University of Utrecht, Utrecht, Netherlands, professor of history, beginning in 1936. Terry Lecturer at Yale University. Press attache to Dutch legation in London. *Awards, honors:* Commander of Order of the British Empire; knight of Netherlands Lion; commander of Belgian Crown Order.

WRITINGS: *Holland and Belgium: Their Common History and Their Relations,* 1920; (contributor) *Problems of Peace and War,* Volume XII, Grotius Society, 1927; *Geschiedenis van de Nederlandsche stam,* Wereld Bibliotheek, Volume I, 1931, Volume II, 1934, reprinted in six volumes, Volume I: *Tot 1581,* Volume II: *1581-1648,* Volume III: *1648-1701,* Volume IV: *1701-1751,* Volume V: *1751-1792,* Volume VI: *1792-1798,* 1961-62, translation by Geyl and S. T. Bindoff published as *The Netherlands Divided, 1609-1648,* Williams & Norgate, 1930, Volume I published as *The Revolt of the Netherlands, 1555-1609,* 1932, 2nd edition, Barnes & Noble, 1958; *The Netherlands Divided,* 1936, revised edition published as *The Netherlands in the Seventeenth Century,* Volume I, *1609-1648,* Volume II: *1648-1715,* Barnes & Noble, 1961; *Oranje en Stuart, 1641-1672,* N.v.A. Oosthoek, 1939, 2nd edition, De Haan, 1963, translation by Arnold Pomerans published as *Orange and Stuart, 1641-72,* Weidenfeld & Nicolson, 1969, Scribner, 1970.

Napoleon: For and Against (translated into English by Olive Renier), Yale University Press, 1949; (with Arnold J. Toynbee and Pitirim A. Sorokin) *The Pattern of the Past: Can We Determine It?,* Beacon Press, 1949; *From Ranke to Toynbee: Five Lectures on Historians and Historiographical Problems,* Department of History, Smith College, 1952; *Debates With Historians,* J. B. Wolters, 1955, Philosophical Library, 1956; *Use and Abuse of History,* Yale University Press, 1955.

Encounters in History, Meridian, 1962; *History of the Low Countries, Episodes and Problems: The Trevelyan Lectures 1963 With Four Additional Essays,* St. Martin's, 1964; (editor with F.W.N. Hugenholtz) John Huizinga, *Dutch Civilisation in the Seventeenth Century and Other Essays* (translated by A. Pomerans), Collins, 1968, Harper, 1969; (editor) Francisco Pelsaert, *The Remonstrantie of Francisco Pelsaert: Jahangur's India* (translated from Dutch by Geyl and W. H. Moreland), Idarah-I Adabiyat-I, 1972.

Other writings: *Willem IV en Engeland,* 1924; *De Groot-Nederlandsche Gedachte: Historische en Politieke Benchonwingen* (title means "The Greater Netherlands Idea"), two volumes, H. D. Tjeenk Willink & Son, 1925. *Revolutiedagen te Amsterdam (augustus-september 1748): Prins Willem IV en de Doelistenbeweging,* Nijhoff, 1936.

(Under pseudonym A. v.d. Merwe) *Het wachtwoord* (sonnets), De Bezige Bij, 1944; *O vrijheid!* (sonnets), L.J.C. Boucher, 1945; *Eenheid en tweeheid in de Nederlanden,* De Tijdstroom, 1946; *Patriotten en N.S.B. ers: Een historische parallel,* J. van Campen, 1946; *Moord op de plas,* W. de Haan, 1946, 2nd edition, 1956; *Napoleon: Voor en tegen in de franse geschiedschrijving,* A. Oosthoek, 1946, reprinted, De Haan, 1965; *De patriottenbeweging, 1780-1787,* P. N. van Kampen, 1947.

Democratische tendenties in 1672, North-Holland Publishing, 1950; *Tochten en toernooien,* A. Oosthoek, 1950; *De Witten-oorlog: Een pennestrijd in 1757,* North-Holland Publishing, 1953; *Historicus un te tijd,* De Haan, 1954; *Gebruik en misbruik der geschiedenis,* J. B. Wolters, 1956; *Geschiedenis als medespeler,* Het Spectrum, 1958; *Studies en strijdschriften,* J. B. Wolters, 1958; *Die Diskussion ohne Ende: Auseinandersetzungen mit Historikern,* H. Gentner, 1958; *Franse figuren,* Wereld-Bibliotheek, 1959; *Vier maal Europa: Acht colleges in het kader van het Studium generale,* N. Samsom, 1959.

Nederlandse figuren, Wereld-Bibliotheek, 1960; *Noord en Zuid: Eenheid en tweeheid in de Lage Landen,* Het Spectrum,

1960; *Amerikaanse figuren,* Wereld-Bibliotheek, 1961; *Duitse en Italiaanse figuren,* Wereld-Bibliotheek, 1961; *Engelse figuren,* two volumes, Wereld-Bibliotheek, 1961; *van Bilderdijk tot Huizinga: Historische toetsingen,* Aula-Boeken, 1963; *Figuren en problemen,* Wereld Bibliotheek, 1964.

Pennestrijd over staat en historie: Opstellen over de vaderlandse geschiedenis aangevult met Geyl's levensverhaal (tot 1945), Wolters-Noordhoff, 1971; *La revolution batave, 1783-1798* (translated into French by J. Godard), Societe des Etudes Robespierristes, 1971; *Geyl en Vlaanderen: Uit het archief van P. Geyl, brieven en notities* (edited by P. van Hees and A. W. Willemsen), De Nederlandsche Boekhandel, 1973.

Translator into English: "Lancelot of Denmark" (play), 1924; *The Tale of Beatrice* (poem), 1927.

Contributor to *Encyclopaedia Britannica.* Contributor to history and political science journals in the Netherlands, England, the United States, and Germany. Co-founder and co-editor of *Leiding,* 1930-31, and *Nederlandsche Historiebladen,* 1938.

SIDELIGHTS: Geyl's strong views favoring Flemish nationalism were not popular before and during World War II, and he was arrested on several occasions. In 1940 he was imprisoned by the Germans in Buchenwald; he remained there and in prison camps in the Netherlands until 1944. During that time he wrote poetry, some of which was later published, and a novel. After his release he began writing for an illegal underground movement.

BIOGRAPHICAL/CRITICAL SOURCES: *Journal of the History of Ideas,* January, 1948, April, 1955; *Illustrated London News,* January 29, 1949; *Spectator,* February 25, 1949, March 9, 1956; *New Statesman,* February 26, 1949; *American Historical Review,* October, 1949, July, 1959, January, 1965; *Virginia Quarterly Review,* October, 1950; *New England Quarterly,* June, 1951; *Atlantic,* April, 1954; *Saturday Review,* November 19, 1955; *Nation,* February 23, 1957, April 13, 1957, April 14, 1966; *History Today,* December, 1957, March, 1967; *English Historical Review,* July, 1960; *New Yorker,* December 8, 1962; *Times Literary Supplement,* January 9, 1964, May 28, 1964; *Journal of Modern History,* March, 1965; *New York Review of Books,* April 8, 1965; *Encounter,* May, 1965, May, 1967.*

*   *   *

GIBBON, Vivian 1917-

PERSONAL: Born June 26, 1917, in Newcastle-upon-Tyne, England; daughter of Ernest (a dental surgeon) and Lily (Sheldon) Gibbon. *Education:* University of Durham, B.A., 1939, Diploma in Education, 1941; National Froebel Foundation, Certificate. *Religion:* Church of England. *Home:* 45 The Riding, Kenton, Newcastle-upon-Tyne, England.

CAREER: High school teacher in Stamford, England, 1941-44, and Sunderland, England (also head of preparatory department), 1944-46; St. Hild's College, Durham, England, began as lecturer, became senior lecturer and vice-principal, 1947-57; adviser for infant schools in Leicester, England, 1957-64; Newcastle College of Education, Newcastle-upon-Tyne, England, began as deputy principal, became acting principal, 1964-74; Newcastle Polytechnic, Newcastle-upon-Tyne, England, dean of education students, 1974-78; writer, 1978—.

WRITINGS: (With Leonard George William Sealey) *Communication and Learning in the Primary School,* Basil Blackwell, 1962, revised edition, Humanities, 1963; (editor with Ronald Philip Albert Edwards) *Words Your Children Use:*

A Survey of the Words Used by Children in Infants' Schools With the Resultant Graded Vocabulary, Burke Publishing, 1964, 2nd edition, 1973.

Children's books; all with Edwards; all published by Burke Publishing: *Our World*, 1965; *Eating and Drinking*, 1966, 2nd edition, 1973; *At Home With the Family*, 1966; *People We Meet*, 1966, 2nd edition, 1973; *Toys and Games: Indoors*, 1966; *Travelling by Land*, 1966; *Travelling by Sea and Air*, 1966; *Wild Animals*, 1967; *Tame Animals*, 1967, 2nd edition, 1973; *Seaside and Country*, 1967; *Playing Outdoors*, 1967; *Opposites*, 1967; *Myself and My Clothes*, 1967; *Listening*, 1968; *School*, 1968; *When*, 1968; *Buildings*, 1969; *Gardens and Flowers*, 1969; *Machines and Gadgets*, 1969; *Places*, 1969; *Things People Often Say*, 1969; *Weather*, 1969; *What Things Are Made Of*, 1969; *Where and Which Way*, 1969; *The Branch Line*, 1970; *The Bypass*, 1970; *Adventure*, 1970; *Counting and Measuring*, 1970.

Children's books in Welsh; all with Edwards; all published by Burke Publishing: *Bwyta ac yfed*, 1970; *Dywediadau a glywn ni yn aml*, 1970; *Gartre gyda'r teulu*, 1970; *Gerdii a blodau*, 1970; *I ble? pa ffordd?*, 1970; *Pobl ddoddorol*, 1970.

SIDELIGHTS: Vivian Gibbon commented: "There is still much work to be done in improving the teaching of mathematics to the youngest school children. Too many older pupils show lack of understanding of even basic arithmetic."

* * *

GIBSON, Margaret 1948-

PERSONAL: Born June 4, 1948, in Toronto, Ontario, Canada; daughter of H. Dane (a telephone company employee) and Audrey Elizabeth Gibson; married S. Gilboord (separated); children: Aaron Dane. *Education:* Attended high school in Toronto, Ontario. *Home and office:* 17 Monarch Park, Toronto, Ontario, Canada.

CAREER: Writer. *Member:* Writers Union of Canada. *Awards, honors:* Literary award from city of Toronto, Ontario, 1976.

WRITINGS: The Butterfly Ward, Oberon, 1977; *Considering Her Condition*, Gage, 1978; *Poem Aaron*, Aurora, 1978.

Author of scripts for television, including "Aida" and "Dark Angel, Pale Fire," and a film script, "Outrageous," based on her story, "Making It."

WORK IN PROGRESS: Sweet Poison and Other Songs, stories.

SIDELIGHTS: Margaret Gibson wrote: "I have wanted to be a writer all my life, and now, due to health problems, I must write to support my son and myself."

* * *

GIBSON, Shirley 1927-

PERSONAL: Born December 28, 1927, in Toronto, Ontario, Canada; daughter of Charles Stuart and Ivy Grace (Mann) White; married Graeme Cameron Gibson, 1959 (divorced, 1976); children: Thomas Matthew Mann, Graeme Charles Alexander. *Education:* Attended high school in Toronto, Ontario, Canada. *Religion:* Protestant. *Home:* 120 South Dr., Toronto, Ontario, Canada M4W 1R8.

CAREER: Associated with CHUM-Radio, Toronto, Ontario, 1944-45; London Art Museum, London, Ontario, assistant to curator, 1946-52; founder and manager of retail business, 1953-59; *Arts/Canada*, assistant to editor, 1969; House of Anansi Press, Toronto, managing editor, 1970-74, president and member of board of directors, 1972-74; Playwrights Co-

Operative, Toronto, executive director, 1977. Member of board of governors of Canadian Conference of the Arts. *Member:* Empire Club, Bookman's Club.

WRITINGS: I Am Watching (poems), House of Anansi Press, 1973.*

* * *

GIDAL, Peter 1946-

PERSONAL: Born December 21, 1946; son of Tim and Sonia Gidal; married Sarah Harding (a needlework designer, consultant, and technician). *Education:* Brandeis University, B.A., 1968; attended University of Munich, 1966-67; Royal College of Art, M.A., 1971. *Religion:* None. *Home and office:* 102 Holland Rd., London W.14, England.

CAREER: Filmmaker, writer, and lecturer. Associated with London College of Printing, 1971-72, and Royal College of Art, 1972—. Member of executive committee of London Filmmakers Cooperative, 1967-75, and British Film Institute Production Board, 1978-80; member of senate of Royal College of Art, 1980-81. Co-founder of Independent Filmmakers Association (member of executive committee). *Awards, honors:* Prix de la Recherche from Toulon Film Festival, 1974, for "Room Film 1973."

WRITINGS: Andy Warhol: Films and Paintings, Dutton, 1971; (editor) *Structural Film Anthology*, British Film Institute, 1976; (contributor) Stephen Heath and T. Lauretis, editors, *The Cinematic Apparatus*, St. Martin's, 1980; *Understanding Beckett*, Macmillan, 1982.

Films—All released by London Filmmakers Cooperative: "Hall," 1968; "Key," 1968; "Room Film 1973," 1973; "Film Print," 1974; "Condition of Illusion," 1975; "Silent Partner," 1977; "Fourth Wall," 1978; "Action at a Distance," 1980. Contributor to magazines, including *Studio International*, *Artforum*, *Screen*, *After-Image*, *Millenium Film Journal*, and *Ark*.

WORK IN PROGRESS: "Close Up," a sixty-minute color film with optical sound.

SIDELIGHTS: Gidal commented: "My work is in the framework of a structural-materialist aesthetic, and is theorized as such in certain of my writings and in the films; the major influences are Warhol, Beckett, Althusser, Delphy, and earlier on, Julia Margaret Cameron, Marx, Lenin, Lou Andreas Salome, Klee, and Goddard."

BIOGRAPHICAL/CRITICAL SOURCES: Screen, summer, 1977, summer, 1979; Malcolm LeGrice, *Abstract Film and Beyond*, M.I.T. Press, 1977; *Millenium Film Journal*, summer, 1978; Stephen Heath, *Questions of Cinema*, Macmillan, 1980; *Soho News* (New York City), January 14, 1981; *Wide Angle* (Ohio), September, 1981.

* * *

GILBERT, Christine B(ell) 1909-

PERSONAL: Born June 30, 1909, in Brooklyn, N.Y.; daughter of Frank C. (an insurance broker) and Madeline (Bell) Gilbert. *Education:* Mount Holyoke College, B.A., 1932; Columbia University, B.L.S., 1934, M.A., 1945. *Home and office address:* Star Route 70, Box 79L, Great Barrington, Mass. 01230.

CAREER: Columbia University, Teachers College, New York, N.Y., assistant librarian at Lincoln School, 1934-39, supervisor of School Library Laboratory, 1939-47; librarian at public schools in Manhasset, N.Y., and coordinator of school community relations, 1947-68; Long Island University, Long Island, N.Y., associate professor of library science, 1968-76; writer, 1976—. Member of faculty at Columbia University, Queens College of the City University of New York, State University of New York at Albany, and State University of New York College at Cortland. Past member of Newbery-Caldecott Awards Committees. *Member:* American Library Association, National Education Association, National Council of Teachers of English, New York State Library Association.

WRITINGS: (With Ruth Strang and Margaret Scoggin) *Gateway to Readable Books: A Booklist for Reluctant Readers,* H. W. Wilson, 1951; (with John Gillespie) *Best Books for Children,* Bowker, 1978, revised edition, 1981. Contributor to newspapers and magazines, including *New York Times, Instructor, Parents' Magazine,* and *School Library Journal.*

WORK IN PROGRESS: A third edition of *Best Books for Children,* publication by Bowker expected in 1983.

SIDELIGHTS: Christine Gilbert wrote: "I've always felt strongly that school librarianship is one of the most interesting and rewarding professions, giving one the opportunity of guiding young people into an appreciation of books and reading. I've tried in my teaching to convey my enthusiasm for children's books and to help future librarians and teachers realize the importance of children's literature." *Avocational interests:* Travel (Europe, Guatemala, the Caribbean, Alaska, Canada, Great Britain), reading.

* * *

GILBERT, Gordon Allan 1942-

PERSONAL: Born March 15, 1942, in Glasgow, Scotland; came to the United States in 1945, naturalized citizen, 1957; son of Arnold Bernard and Leila Esther (Bloom) Gilbert; married Judy Goldzader (a teacher), July 1, 1969; children: Ronete Ann, David Ari. *Education:* San Fernando Valley State College, B.A., 1965; California State University, Northridge, M.A., 1973. *Politics:* Democrat. *Religion:* Jewish. *Home:* 41 Mendes Rd., Danbury, Conn. 06810. *Office:* Business and Commercial Aviation, Hangar C-1, Westchester County Airport, White Plains, N.Y. 10604.

CAREER: Aero Products Research, Los Angeles, Calif., 1963-65; aviation writer, 1969-72; Pan American Navigation Service, Van Nuys, Calif., 1972-73; *Business and Commercial Aviation,* White Plains, N.Y., chief news editor, 1973—. *Military service:* U.S. Army, 1965-69; became captain; received Distinguished Service Medal. *Member:* Aviation/Space Writers Association, Sigma Delta Chi. *Awards, honors:* Osborne Award from Aviation/Space Writers Association, 1974, for "The Energy Crisis"; Northeast region award, 1979, for "Improving Cabin Safety."

WRITINGS: Flight Instruction Written Examination Guide, Pan American Navigation Service, 1971; *Staying Current,* Ziff-Davis, 1980.

AVOCATIONAL INTERESTS: Flying, motorcycling.

* * *

GILISON, Jerome Martin 1935-

PERSONAL: Born September 27, 1935, in New York, N.Y.; married, 1962; children: two. *Education:* Massachusetts Institute of Technology, B.S., 1956; Columbia University, Ph.D., 1965. *Office:* Department of Political Science, Johns Hopkins University, Baltimore, Md. 21218.

CAREER: Johns Hopkins University, Baltimore, Md., assistant professor, 1965-71, associate professor of political

science, 1971—. *Member:* American Political Science Association, American Association for the Advancement of Slavic Studies.

WRITINGS: British and Soviet Politics: A Study of Legitimacy and Convergence, Johns Hopkins Press, 1972; *The Soviet Image of Utopia,* Johns Hopkins Press, 1975; (editor) *The Soviet Jewish Emigre: Proceedings of the National Symposium on the Integration of Soviet Jews Into the American Jewish Community,* Baltimore Hebrew College, 1977. Contributor to scholarly journals.*

* * *

GILL, Peter 1939-

PERSONAL: Born September 7, 1939, in Cardiff, Wales; son of George John and Margaret Mary (Browne) Gill. *Education:* Attended secondary school in Cardiff, Wales. *Home:* 9 Lower Mall, London W.6, England. *Agent:* Margaret Ramsay Ltd., 14a Goodwin's Court, London WC2N 4LL, England. *Office:* London International, Park House, Park St., London W.1, England.

CAREER: Professional actor on stage and television, and in films, 1957-65; playwright and director, 1965—. Director of Riverside Studios; associate artistic director at Royal Court Theatre, 1970-72. *Awards, honors:* Prize from Belgrade International Theater Festival, 1968, for directing "The Daughter-in-Law"; George Devine Award, 1968.

WRITINGS: The Sleepers' Den and Over Gardens Out (contains "The Sleepers' Den," a play, first produced in London, England, at Royal Court Theatre, 1965; and "Over Gardens Out," a play, first produced in London, at Royal Court Theatre, 1969), Calder & Boyars, 1970; (contributor of notes) William Shakespeare, *Macbeth* (edited by Gordon Coggins), Festival Editions of Canada, 1972; *Small Change* (play; first produced in London, 1976), Samuel French, 1979.

Unpublished plays: "A Provincial Life" (adaptation of *My Life,* by Anton Chekhov), first produced in London, 1966; "The Merry-Go-Round" (adaptation of play by D. H. Lawrence), first produced in London, 1976.

Contributor to *Plays and Players.*

* * *

GILLES, Daniel 1917-

PERSONAL: Born May 7, 1917, in Bruges, Belgium; married Simone Lambinon, 1948; children: one daughter. *Home:* Park Kennedy, Avenue Churchill 161, Brussels 1180, Belgium.

CAREER: Caisse Privee, Brussels, Belgium, banker, 1950-60; Credit Lyonnais, Brussels, banker, 1960-78. *Awards, honors:* Prix Rossel from *Le Soir,* 1952; Grand Prix de la Critique Litteraire, 1967, for *Tchekhov;* Prix Triennal du Roman from Belgian government, 1977.

WRITINGS—In English: La Termitiere (novel), Gallimard, 1960, translation by Marigold Johnson published as *The Anthill,* Vanguard, 1962; *Tchekhov; ou, Le Spectateur desenchante,* Julliard, 1967, translation by Charles Lam Markman published as *Chekhov: Observer Without Illusion,* Funk, 1968.

In French: *Mort la douce* (novel; title means "Death Is Tender"), Editions des Artistes, 1952; *Jetons de presence* (novel), Julliard, 1954; *Le Coupon 44* (novel; title means "Dividends"), Julliard, 1956; *L'Etat de grace* (novel; title means "Love Is Grace"), Gallimard, 1958; *Tolstoi,* Julliard, 1959; *Les Brouillards de Bruges* (novel), Julliard, 1962; *D. H. Lawrence; ou, Le Puritain scandaleux,* Julliard, 1964; *La Rouille* (novel), Julliard, 1971; *Le festival de Salzbourg* (novel), A. Michel, 1974; *Nes pour mourir* (novel), A. Michel, 1976; *Le Tache de sang* (novel), A. Michel, 1977; *Le Spectateur brandebourgeois* (novel), A. Michel, 1979.

WORK IN PROGRESS: Laurence, publication expected in 1980; *God gegen uns,* publication expected in 1981.

SIDELIGHTS: Gilles wrote: "I was brought to literature as a child, by Stefan Zweig, but until 1940, I vacillated between painting and writing. My captivity in Germany decided the matter for me—I returned as a writer."

* * *

GILROY, Thomas Laurence   1951-
(Tom Gilroy)

PERSONAL: Born July 29, 1951, in Hot Springs, Ark.; son of Francis J. and Mary (Shay) Gilroy; married Barbara J. Smith (a banker), June 4, 1977. *Education:* University of Virginia, B.A., 1973; Columbia University, M.S., 1977. *Politics:* Independent. *Religion:* Roman Catholic. *Home and office address:* B.P. 1132, Douala, Cameroon, West Africa.

CAREER: McGraw-Hill World News, New York City, reporter, 1977-80; United Press International (UPI), New York City, reporter, 1980—. Free-lance reporter. U.S. Peace Corps volunteer in Senegal, West Africa, 1973-75. *Awards, honors: In Bikole* was named a "Wiggly Worm" outstanding children's book.

WRITINGS: (Under name Tom Gilroy) *In Bikole: Modern Stories of Life in a West African Village* (juvenile), Knopf, 1978. Contributor of articles to *Washington Monthly* and *Mother Jones.*

SIDELIGHTS: In Bikole is an anthology of eight short stories about real people and places. Evolving from Gilroy's experiences as a Peace Corps volunteer, the stories illustrate life in a Senegalese village. Contemporary mores and the tension between modern innovations and traditional ways are explored in the works.

* * *

GILROY, Tom
See GILROY, Thomas Laurence

* * *

GLASSGOLD, Peter   1939-

PERSONAL: Born May 13, 1939, in New York, N.Y.; son of George Millard (a lawyer) and Marjorie (a writer under name Damsey Wilson; maiden name, Wilson) Glassgold; married Suzanne Thibodeau (an editor), September 6, 1968. *Education:* Columbia University, A.B., 1960. *Residence:* Brooklyn, N.Y. *Office:* New Directions Publishing Corp., 80 Eighth Ave., New York, N.Y. 10011.

CAREER: Columbia University Press, New York City, staff writer and researcher for *The Columbia Encyclopedia,* 1961; New York Historical Society, New York City, editor of quarterly journal, 1965-66; *New Leader,* New York City, associate editor, 1968-70; New Directions Publishing Corp., New York City, managing editor and co-editor of series, "New Directions in Prose and Poetry," 1970—. Guest lecturer at Colgate University, 1976. *Member:* International P.E.N.

WRITINGS: Living Space: Poems of the Dutch "Fiftiers," New Directions, 1979. Contributor of stories, poems, articles, and reviews to magazines, including *Contact II, Modern Poetry in Translation, Nation, Mentemoca, New Leader,* and *New Directions in Prose and Poetry.*

WORK IN PROGRESS: Translating a novel from the West Flemish, *The Flaxfield,* by Stijn Streuvels, with Andre Lefevere.

* * *

GLEADOW, Rupert Seeley   1909-1974
(Justin Case)

OBITUARY NOTICE—See index for *CA* sketch: Born January 22, 1909, in Leicester, England; died October 30, 1974. Translator and author. Gleadow wrote several books on mysticism, magic, and astrology, including *Magic and Divination, The Unclouded Eye: An Exploration Among the Roots of Religion,* and *The Origin of the Zodiac.* His translations include *The Opening of the Way* by Isha Schwaller deLubicz, published by Inner Traditions in 1980. (Date of death provided by wife, Helen Gleadow.)

* * *

GLICK, Carl (Cannon)   1890-1971
(Captain Frank Cunningham, Peter Holbrook)

OBITUARY NOTICE—See index for *CA* sketch: Born September 11, 1890, in Marshalltown, Iowa; died March 7, 1971. Educator, theatrical director, and author, best known for his books about the Chinese in America. A prolific writer, Glick wrote adult and juvenile fiction and nonfiction, plays, and motion pictures. During the early 1920's he was the author of columns on theatre under the pseudonym Peter Holbrook and book reviews under the pseudonym Captain Frank Cunningham. Among his books are several that describe his lifelong associations with members of the Chinese community in New York. Obituaries and other sources: *Something About the Author,* Volume 14, Gale, 1978.

* * *

GLUCK, Felix   1923-1981

OBITUARY NOTICE: Born in 1923 in Bavaria, Germany (now West Germany); died after a long illness, February 22, 1981, in London, England. Publisher, artist, designer, and editor of the "Modern Publicity" series. Gluck also designed and produced facsimile editions of previously published books, including Godden's *Gulbadan.* Gluck, a survivor of a Nazi concentration camp, lived for several years in Hungary before immigrating to England where he became known for his excellent taste and artistic skill. Obituaries and other sources: *London Times,* March 3, 1981; *Publishers Weekly,* April 10, 1981.

* * *

GMELCH, George   1944-

PERSONAL: Born December 28, 1944, in Queens, N.Y.; son of George John (in business) and Edna (a photographer; maiden name, Bierlein) Gmelch; married Sharon Bohn (an anthropologist, writer, and editor), September 22, 1968. *Education:* Stanford University, B.A., 1968; University of California, Santa Barbara, M.A., 1970, Ph.D., 1975. *Home:* 127 Font Grove Rd., Slingerlands, N.Y. 12159. *Office:* Department of Sociology and Anthropology, Union College, Schenectady, N.Y. 12308.

CAREER: Memorial University of Newfoundland, St. John's, research fellow at Institute of Social and Economic Research, 1971-73; McGill University, Montreal, Quebec, assistant professor of anthropology, 1973-75; State University of New York at Albany, assistant professor of anthropology, 1975-

81; Union College, Schenectady, N.Y., visiting associate professor, 1981—. Visiting senior research fellow at National University of Ireland, University College, Dublin, 1978; visiting research fellow at Leicester Polytechnic, 1980-81.

WRITINGS: Irish Tinkers: The Urbanization of an Itinerant People, Cummings, 1976; (with Ben Kroup) *To Shorten the Road: Traveller Folktales From Ireland,* Macmillan, 1978; (with Walter P. Zenner) *Urban Life: Readings in Urban Anthropology,* St. Martin's, 1980; (editor) J. M. Synge, *In Wicklow, West Kerry, and Connemara,* Rowman & Littlefield, 1980. Contributor to anthropology and natural history journals.

WORK IN PROGRESS: Research on return migration and migration readjustment in Ireland and Newfoundland and on traveler migration and settlement in England and Wales, for Department of Environment, England.

*   *   *

GMELCH, Sharon Bohn 1947-

PERSONAL: Born June 2, 1947, in Panama Canal Zone; daughter of Harold Owen (a U.S. Air Force officer) and Patricia (in business; maiden name, Enright) Bohn; married George Gmelch (an anthropologist), September 22, 1968. *Education:* University of California, Santa Barbara, B.A., 1969, M.A., 1971, Ph.D., 1975. *Home:* 127 Font Grove Rd., Slingerlands, N.Y. 12159. *Office:* Department of Sociology, Union College, Schenectady, N.Y. 12308.

CAREER: State University of New York at Albany, Albany, adjunct assistant professor of anthropology, 1975—; Union College, Schenectady, N.Y., visiting assistant and associate professor, 1976—. Visiting research fellow at Leicester Polytechnic, 1980-81. Nonfiction editor for O'Brien Press, 1980—. *Member:* American Anthropological Association, Royal Society of Antiquaries of Ireland. *Awards, honors:* First prize nonfiction award from Books Ireland, 1976, for *Tinkers and Travellers.*

WRITINGS: Tinkers and Travellers, O'Brien Press, 1975; (editor) *Irish Life,* O'Brien Press, 1979; *Fairs and Pilgrimages* (juvenile), Folens Publishing, 1979. Contributor to natural history and anthropology journals.

WORK IN PROGRESS: A biography and social history of an Irish traveling woman, Nan Donoghue, publication expected in 1982; research on Irish traveler migration and settlement in England and Wales, for Department of Environment, England.

*   *   *

GNAGY, Jon
See GNAGY, Michael Jacques

*   *   *

GNAGY, Michael Jacques 1907(?)-1981
(Jon Gnagy)

OBITUARY NOTICE: Born c. 1907; died of a cardiac arrest, March 7, 1981, in Idyllwild, Calif. Artist, television performer, and author of books on art, including *The Doodler's Handbook, Learn to Draw With Jon Gnagy,* and *Learn to Draw Human Figures.* Gnagy made television history in 1946 when he appeared as the first performer on the first commercial television program. He became a well-known personality during the 1940's and 1950's when he hosted the popular television programs "You Are an Artist" and "Learn to Draw." Gnagy was also a student of aerodynamics and was involved in designing the first low-wing monoplane built

in America. Obituaries and other sources: *Chicago Tribune,* March 11, 1981; *Washington Post,* March 11, 1981.

*   *   *

GODOWN, Marian Bailey

PERSONAL: Born in Paterson, N.J.; daughter of James (a banker) and Anna Johanna (a realtor; maiden name, Pederson) Bailey; married Albert Wallingford Godown, 1947 (died April 30, 1976); children: Joanna, Jan. *Education:* Attended Paterson State Teachers College. *Home:* 1915 Hill Ave., Fort Myers, Fla. 33901.

CAREER: Paterson Evening News, Paterson, N.J., reporter, feature writer, and copy editor, 1942-46; *Hunterdon County Democrat,* Flemington, N.J., feature writer, 1946-66; freelance writer, 1966—. Publicist with Fred Maaloe Associates, American Red Cross, and Raritan Productions; member of Fort Lee County Historic and Scenic Preservation Task Force; lecturer on Florida history. *Member:* League of Women Voters, Florida Historical Society (member of board of directors), Southwest Florida Historical Society (librarian), Hunterdon County Historical Society, Friends of the Fort Myers Library.

WRITINGS: (With Alberta Rawchuck) *Yesterday's Fort Myers,* E. A. Seemann, 1976. Author of "Here's Florida," "Fort Myers Yesterday," and "The Passing Scene," columns in *Fort Myers News-Press.* Correspondent for *Philadelphia Bulletin.* Contributor to newspapers. Past editor of *Hunterdon County Republican* and *Hunterdon Historical Newsletter.*

WORK IN PROGRESS: Research for a book on the history of Lee County, Florida.

*   *   *

GOGGIN, Terrence P(atrick) 1941-

PERSONAL: Born November 8, 1941, in Los Angeles, Calif.; son of George Thomas and Mary Adelaide (Hare) Goggin; married Jill Anne Tronvic, November 28, 1963; children: Brian, Patrick, Colin. *Education:* Georgetown University, A.B., 1963; University of Southern California, J.D., 1966. *Religion:* Roman Catholic. *Home:* 855 Edgemont, San Bernardino, Calif. 92405. *Office:* State Capitol, Sacramento, Calif. 95814.

CAREER: Inland Empire Committee to Re-Elect Governor Pat Brown, California, campaign coordinator, 1966; U.S. Military Academy, West Point, N.Y., assistant professor, 1967-70; U.S. House of Representatives, Washington, D.C., administrative assistant to Representative George E. Brown, Jr., 1973-74; California State Assembly, Sacramento, Democratic member of assembly, 1975—. Partner of Goggin, Goggin & Commons (law firm), 1971—; consultant to White House Urban Affairs Council. *Military service:* U.S. Army, 1966-70; became captain. *Member:* California Bar Association, Native Sons of the Golden West, San Bernardino Bar Association. *Awards, honors:* Named legislator of the year by American Society of Professional Engineers, 1976; Kennedy fellowship for Harvard University, 1977.

WRITINGS: (Editor with John M. Seidl) *Politics American Style: Race, Environment, and Central Cities,* Prentice-Hall, 1972. Contributor to law journals.*

GOLDBERG, Arnold I(rving) 1929-

PERSONAL: Born May 21, 1929, in Chicago, Ill.; son of Morris H. (a laundry proprietor) and Rose (Auerbach) Goldberg; married Phylis Magida, August 8, 1963 (divorced, June, 1970); married Constance O. Obenhaus (a psychiatric social worker), April 22, 1971; children: (first marriage) Andrew; (second marriage) Sarah. *Education:* University of Illinois at Chicago Circle, B.S., 1949, M.D., 1953. *Religion:* None. *Home:* 844 Chalmers St., Chicago, Ill. 60614. *Office:* 180 North Michigan Ave., Suite 2407, Chicago, Ill. 60601.

CAREER: Cincinnati General Hospital, Cincinnati, Ohio, intern, 1953-54; Illinois Neuropsychiatric Institute, Chicago, resident in psychiatry, 1954-55; Michael Reese Medical Center, Chicago, Ill., resident in psychiatry at Psychosomatic and Psychiatric Institute for Research and Training, 1957-59; private practice of psychiatry in Chicago, 1959—. Member of faculty at Chicago Institute for Psychoanalysis, 1966—, training and supervising analyst, 1973—, member of council, 1974-78; research associate at Northwestern University, Chicago, 1966-71; member of Center for Advanced Psychoanalytic Studies, Princeton, N.J., 1970—; clinical professor at University of Chicago, 1972—; visiting professor at Rush-Presbyterian-St. Luke's School of Medicine, 1976—; attending psychiatrist at Michael Reese Medical Center, 1959—, director of psychiatric resident supervision at Psychosomatic and Psychiatric Institute for Research and Training, 1970—. *Military service:* U.S. Army, 1955-57; became captain.

MEMBER: American Psychiatric Association (fellow), American Psychoanalytic Association, American Society for Adolescent Psychiatry (fellow), Illinois Psychiatric Society, Chicago Psychoanalytic Society, Chicago Society for Adolescent Psychiatry (president), Phi Beta Kappa, Alpha Omega Alpha, Phi Kappa Phi. *Awards, honors:* Joan Fleming Award from Chicago Institute for Psychoanalysis, 1973, for teaching excellence.

WRITINGS: (With John Gedo) *Models of the Mind: A Psychoanalytic Theory* (monograph), University of Chicago Press, 1973; (contributor) Therese Benedek and James Anthony, editors, *The Human Condition,* Little, Brown, 1975; (editor) *Psychology of the Self: A Casebook,* International Universities Press, 1978; (contributor) Judith Mishne, editor, *Clinical Social Book,* Gardner Press, 1979; (editor) *Advances in Self Psychology,* International Universities Press, 1980. Contributor to *Academic American Encyclopedia.* Contributor of more than twenty articles and numerous reviews to medical journals.

WORK IN PROGRESS: Editing a book on the future of psychoanalysis.

SIDELIGHTS: Arnold Goldberg commented: "I have an interest in the changes in psychoanalytic theory and practice brought about by the new ideas of self psychology. This interest lies in both the formal structure of psychoanalysis as well as the social and political implications of a change in a science. Especially as new psychoanalytic theories allow for exchanges with other discipline such as linguistics and history, my book in progress will highlight the possible directions that psychoanalysis might pursue."

*   *   *

GOLDBERG, Dorothy K(urgans)

PERSONAL: Born in St. Louis, Mo.; married Arthur Joseph Goldberg; children: Robert, Barbara (Mrs. David A. Cra-

mer). *Education:* University of Chicago, B.A.; attended Art Institute, Chicago, Ill.; studied art privately. *Home:* 2801 New Mexico Ave., Washington, D.C. 20007.

CAREER: Artist. Program director at Associated Artists Gallery. *Member:* United Nations Association (member of board of directors), National School Volunteer Program.

WRITINGS: The Creative Woman, Luce, 1963; *A Private View of a Public Life,* Charterhouse, 1975. Contributor to magazines.*

*   *   *

GOLDBERG, Maxwell Henry 1907-

PERSONAL: Born October 22, 1907, in Malden, Mass. *Education:* University of Massachusetts, B.S., 1928; Yale University, A.M., 1932, Ph.D., 1933. *Home:* 1865 Fernwood Glendale Rd., Spartanburg, S.C. 29302.

CAREER: University of Massachusetts, Amherst, instructor in English, 1928-30, 1933-34, assistant professor, 1934-47, associate professor, 1947-48, professor, 1948-62, Commonwealth Professor of Humanities, 1960-62, professor emeritus, 1962—, head of department, 1955-60; Pennsylvania State University, State College, professor of humanities and English, 1962-72, professor emeritus, 1972—, associate director of Center for Continuing Liberal Education, 1962-72; Converse College, Spartanburg, S.C., Andrew J. R. Helmus Distinguished Professor of Humanities and Literature and director of continuing liberal studies at Center for Humanities, 1972-76, professor emeritus, 1976—. President of Humanities Center for Liberal Education, Inc., 1962-71. Lecturer at Oak Ridge Associated Universities, 1965; Danforth visiting lecturer, 1968-72. Member of National Council of Churches advisory committee on technological change and society, 1965-67; education director of Wildacres Retreat, 1978—; consultant to Public Broadcasting Corp., National Endowment for the Humanities, and U.S. Department of Health, Education and Welfare.

MEMBER: Society for the Advancement of Education (member of board of trustees, 1966—), Modern Language Association of America, College English Association (executive director, 1950-59; president-elect, 1967), American Association for Higher Education (member of executive committee, 1960-62), Adult Education Association of the United States of America, Society for the History of Technology. *Awards, honors:* Fund for Adult Education fellowship, 1956-57.

WRITINGS: Amherst as Poetry, Newell Press, 1941; (with Patricia Kochanek) *Technological Change and Human Dignity: A Study in Human Values,* Center for Continuing Liberal Education, Pennsylvania State University, 1966; (editor with John R. Swinton) *Blindness Research: The Expanding Frontiers—A Liberal Studies Perspective,* Pennsylvania State University Press, 1969; (editor) *Needles, Burrs, and Bibliographies: Study Resources in Technological Change, Human Values, and the Humanities,* Center for Continuing Liberal Education, Pennsylvania State University, 1969; *Design in Liberal Learning,* Jossey-Bass, 1971; *Cybernation, Systems, and the Teaching of English: The Dilemma of Control,* National Council of Teachers of English, 1972; (editor with Frederick F. Ritsch, Jr.) *Probes and Projections: Papers From the CCH-SCCH Humanities Project on Greater Spartanburg in Transition,* Center for Humanities, Converse College, 1974; (editor) *Community Self-Renewal and Telec Imaging: Humanistic Perspectives,* Center for Humanities, Converse College, 1976. Contributor to *Yearbook of Comparative Criticism.* Contributor to education journals. Editor for College English Association, 1950-59; member of editorial board of *Educational Forum*, 1972-75; associate literary editor of *Intellect*, 1974—.*

*   *   *

GOLDING, Peter 1947-

PERSONAL: Born September 3, 1947, in London, England; son of Tony (a bookkeeper) and Kitty (a school secretary; maiden name, Koss) Golding; married Jennifer Bostock, 1975; children: Ben. *Education:* University of London, B.Sc., 1969; University of Essex, M.A., 1970. *Office:* Centre for Mass Communication Research, University of Leicester, 104 Regent Rd., Leicester, England.

CAREER: University of Leicester, Leicester, England, research officer at Centre for Mass Communication Research, 1970—.

WRITINGS: The Mass Media, Longman, 1974; *Making the News*, Longman, 1979; *Images of Welfare*, Martin Robertson, 1981; (editor) *Mass Media and Social Policy*, Martin Robertson, 1982.

WORK IN PROGRESS: A study of the political economy of the mass media, with Graham Murdock.

*   *   *

GOLDSTEIN, Michael J(oseph) 1930-

PERSONAL: Born June 28, 1930, in Brooklyn, N.Y.; married, 1953; children: one. *Education:* University of Iowa, B.A., 1952; Washington State University, M.S., 1953; University of Washington, Seattle, Ph.D., 1957. *Office:* Department of Psychology, University of California, Los Angeles, Calif. 90024.

CAREER: Veterans Administration, Washington, D.C., trainee, 1953-57; University of California, Los Angeles, instructor, 1957, assistant professor, 1958-65, associate professor, 1965-71, professor of psychology, 1971—. Staff psychologist at Kings County Hospital, summer, 1957; fellow at Institute of Gerontology, University of Connecticut, summer, 1958. *Member:* American Psychological Association. *Awards, honors:* Fulbright scholar at Psychology Laboratory, University of Copenhagen, 1960-61.

WRITINGS: (Editor with James O. Palmer) *The Experience of Anxiety: A Casebook*, Oxford University Press, 1963, 2nd edition, 1975; (editor with Palmer) *Perspectives in Psychopathology: Readings in Abnormal Psychology*, Oxford University Press, 1966; (with Harold Sanford Kent and John J. Hartman) *Pornography and Sexual Deviance: A Report of the Legal and Behavioral Institute, Beverly Hills, California*, University of California Press, 1973; (with others) *Abnormal Psychology: Experiences, Origins, and Interventions*, Little, Brown, 1980. Contributor to psychology journals.*

*   *   *

GOLDSTEIN, Stanley 1922-

PERSONAL: Born December 7, 1922, in New York, N.Y.; married, 1947; children: two. *Education:* Brooklyn College (now of City University of New York), B.A., 1947; University of Michigan, M.A., 1949, Ph.D., 1952. *Home:* 3432 Woodstock Lane, Mountain View, Calif. 94040.

CAREER: Veterans Administration Mental Hygiene Clinic, St. Louis, Mo., clinical psychologist, 1951-58; Veterans Administration Hospital, Salt Lake City, Utah, clinical psychologist, 1958-60; Veterans Administration Hospital, Palo Alto, Calif., chief counseling psychologist, 1960—. *Military*

service: U.S. Army Air Forces, 1942-45. *Member:* American Psychological Association.

WRITINGS: Troubled Parents—Troubled Children: The Way Out, Atheneum, 1979.*

*   *   *

GOLOMB, Claire 1928-

PERSONAL: Born January 30, 1928, in Germany; daughter of Chaskel and Fanny (Monderer) Schimmel; married Dan Golomb (a physical scientist), 1954; children: Mayana, Anath. *Education:* Hebrew University of Jerusalem, B.A., 1954; New School for Social Research, M.A., 1959; Brandeis University, Ph.D., 1968. *Office:* Department of Psychology, University of Massachusetts, Boston, Mass. 02125.

CAREER: Worked as clinical psychologist in Israel, 1954-58; Wellesley College, Wellesley, Mass., instructor in psychology, 1969-70; Brandeis University, Waltham, Mass., assistant professor of psychology, 1971-74; University of Massachusetts, Boston, associate professor of psychology, 1974—.

WRITINGS: Young Children's Sculpture and Drawing: A Study of Representational Development, Harvard University Press, 1974. Contributor to journals in the behavioral sciences.

WORK IN PROGRESS: Continuing research on child art and child play.

*   *   *

GOLOMBEK, Harry 1911-

PERSONAL: Born March 1, 1911, in London, England; son of Barnet and Emma Golombek. *Education:* Attended University of London. *Home:* Albury, 35 Albion Cres., Chalfont St. Giles, Buckinghamshire HP8 4ET, England.

CAREER: British Chess, England, editor, 1938-40; associated with Foreign Office, London, England, 1942-45; *British Chess*, co-editor, 1949—. Represented England in nine Chess Olympiads; captain of British chess team in Finland, 1952, the Netherlands, 1954, West Germany, 1958, East Germany, 1960, and Bulgaria, 1962; president of zone one of World Chess Federation, 1974—. *Military service:* British Army, Royal Artillery, 1940-42. *Member:* Athenaeum Club, Surrey County Cricket Club. *Awards, honors:* First prize in four international chess tournaments; British chess champion, 1947, 1949, 1955; named international master by Federation Internationale des Echecs, 1948; officer of Order of the British Empire, 1966.

WRITINGS: (Author of foreword to reprint) Richard Reti, *Modern Ideas in Chess* (edited by John Hart), G. Bell, 1943; *The World Chess Championship, 1948*, G. Bell, 1948, McKay, 1949; *The Maroczy Memorial Tournament, Budapest, 1952*, British Chess, 1952; *The Game of Chess*, Penguin, 1954, 3rd edition, 1980; *The World Chess Championship, 1954*, MacGibbon & Kee, 1954; *The World Chess Championship, 1957*, MacGibbon & Kee, 1957; *Instructions to Young Chess-Players*, Pitman, 1958, revised edition published as *Improve Your Chess*, 1976; *The Twenty-Second U.S.S.R. Chess Championship*, British Chess, 1959; (with Hubert Phillips) *Chess*, H. F.& G. Witherby, 1959, Crowell, 1963; *Prague, 1946*, Sutton Coldfield, 1959; *The 1959 Candidates Tournament, Bled, Zagreb, Belgrade, September-October, 1959*, British Chess, 1959; *Modern Opening Chess Strategy*, Pitman, 1959; (contributor) Harold J.R. Murray, editor, *A Short History of Chess*, Clarendon Press, 1963.

(Translator) Paul Keres, *Grandmaster of Chess: The Complete Games of Paul Keres,* Arc Books, 1972; *Fischer versus Spassky: The World Chess Championship, 1972,* Barrie & Jenkins, 1973; *Chess: A History,* Putnam, 1976 (published in England as *A History of Chess,* Routledge & Kegan Paul, 1976); *The Laws of Chess and Their Interpretations,* Pitman, 1976, 4th edition published as *The Law of Chess: Being the Translation Authorized by the Federation Internationale des Echecs at Gothenburg,* 1976.

Editor and translator: Savely Grigor'evich Tartakover, *My Best Games of Chess, 1905-1930,* G. Bell, 1953, Van Nostrand, 1957; Gideon Stahlberg, *Chess and Chessmasters,* G. Bell, 1955; Tartakover, *My Best Games of Chess, 1931-1954,* Van Nostrand, 1956; Hans Bouwmeester, *Modern End-Game Studies for the Chess-Player,* G. Bell, 1959; Paul Keres and A. A. Kotov, *The Art of the Middle Game,* Penguin, 1964; Keres, *Grandmaster of Chess: The Early Games of Paul Keres,* Herbert Jenkins, 1964; Keres, *Grandmaster of Chess: The Later Years of Paul Keres,* Herbert Jenkins, 1969; (with E. Strauss) Aleksei P. Sokolskii, *The Modern Openings in Theory and Practice: Their Influence on the Middle Game,* Pitman, 1972.

Editor: Aleksandr Aleksandrovich Alekhin, *The World's Chess Championship, 1937: Official Account of the Game,* Pitman, 1938, Dover, 1973; *Fifty Great Games of Modern Chess,* McKay, 1942; Jose Raul Capablanca y Graupera, *Hundred Best Games of Chess,* Harcourt, 1947, reprinted, McKay, 1978 (published in England as *Capablanca's Hundred Best Games of Chess,* G. Bell, 1947, reprinted, 1972); (with Richard Clewin Griffith) Griffith and J. H. White, *The Pocket Guide to the Chess Openings,* revised edition (Golombek was not associated with 1st edition), G. Bell, 1949, revised edition, 1952, Transatlantic, 1974; (also author of introduction) Richard Reti, *Reti's Best Games of Chess,* G. Bell, 1954, Dover, 1974; (with William Hartston) Hugh O'Donel Alexander, *The Best Games of C. H. O'D. Alexander,* Oxford University Press, 1976; *Golombek's Encyclopedia of Chess,* Crown, 1977 (published in England as *The Encyclopedia of Chess,* Batsford, 1978).

Chess correspondent for *Times,* 1945—, and *Observer,* 1955—.

BIOGRAPHICAL/CRITICAL SOURCES: Economist, November 6, 1976; *Times Literary Supplement,* December 24, 1976; *Choice,* July-August, 1977; *Booklist,* May 15, 1979.*

*   *   *

GONZALEZ, Jaime Jose   1925-

PERSONAL: Born February 11, 1925, in Matanzas, Cuba; married, 1955; children: one. *Education:* Matanzas Preuniversity Institute of Cuba, B.S., 1944; University of Havana, Ed.D., 1962; University of Tennessee, M.A., 1965; Vanderbilt University, Ph.D., 1969. *Office:* Department of Foreign Languages, Georgia College, Milledgeville, Ga. 21061.

CAREER: Vedado Preuniversity Institute, Havana, Cuba, instructor in Spanish, 1946-54; Matanzas School of Business Administration, Matanzas, Cuba, professor and head of department, 1956-62; Tusculum College, Greenville, Tenn., instructor, 1963-65, assistant professor, 1965-66, associate professor of Spanish, chairman of department, and director of language laboratories, 1966-69; Georgia College, Milledgeville, associate professor, 1969-74, professor of Spanish, 1974—. *Member:* Modern Language Association of America, American Association of Teachers of Spanish and Portuguese, National Association for Foreign Student Affairs,

American Association of University Professors, South Atlantic Modern Language Association.

WRITINGS: Elementos absurdos en el teatro de Enrique Jardiel Poncela, privately printed, 1974; *A Gull Against the Wind,* Doubleday, 1977. Contributor to Spanish studies journals.*

*   *   *

GONZALEZ, Nancie L(oudon)   1929-

PERSONAL: Born December 9, 1929, in Chicago, Ill.; daughter of Archibald Niven (a chemist) and Dorothy Helen (a nutritionist; maiden name, Ayers) Loudon; children: Ian, Kevin, Tania. *Education:* University of North Dakota, B.S. (with honors), 1951; University of Michigan, M.A., 1955, Ph.D., 1959. *Home:* 228 12th St. S.E., Washington, D.C. 20003. *Office:* Office of the Vice-Chancellor for Academic Affairs, University of Maryland, College Park, Md. 20742.

CAREER: Jamestown College, Jamestown, N.D., instructor in nutrition, 1952-53; University of California, Berkeley, visiting lecturer in anthropology, 1959-60; Institute of Nutrition of Central America and Panama, Guatemala City, Guatemala, research anthropologist, 1961-64; University of New Mexico, Albuquerque, visiting assistant professor, 1965, associate professor of anthropology and sociology, 1965-69; University of Iowa, Iowa City, professor of anthropology, 1969-72, chairperson of department, 1970-72; Boston University, Boston, Mass., professor of anthropology and chairperson of department, 1972-75; National Science Foundation, Washington, D.C., program director for anthropology, 1975-77; University of Maryland, College Park, professor of anthropology, 1977—, vice-chancellor for academic affairs, 1977-81. Professor at University of San Carlos, summers, 1957, 1961-63; visiting distinguished professor at Southern Methodist University, summer, 1977; lecturer at colleges and universities all over the United States and in the Dominican Republic. Conducted field studies in Guatemala, Belize, the Dominican Republic, and the United States. Member of executive board of Council on Anthropology and Education, 1969-72; member of joint committee on agricultural development of Board for International Food and Agricultural Development; consultant to National Science Foundation, National Institute of General Medical Sciences, and Agency for International Development.

MEMBER: American Anthropological Association, American Association for the Advancement of Science, American Ethnological Society (member of executive board, 1970-73), Society for Applied Anthropology (member of executive board, 1970-76; president, 1974-75), Current Anthropology (associate), Latin American Studies Association (coordinator of women's committee, 1973-75), Society for Medical Anthropology, National Association of State Universities and Land Grant Colleges (member of executive board of council of academic affairs, 1978—), Philosophical Society of Washington, Phi Beta Kappa, Sigma Xi, Phi Kappa Phi, Mortar Board. *Awards, honors:* Research grants from Henry L. and Grace Doherty Foundation, 1955 and 1956, for Guatemala; Wenner-Gren Foundation travel grants, 1964, for the Soviet Union and Spain, 1970, for Peru; grant from Mexican-American Study Project (Ford Foundation), 1965-66; National Science Foundation grants, 1966, for travel to Argentina, 1967-68, for research in the Dominican Republic, 1968-69, 1976, for Guatemala; research grants from U.S. Office of Education, 1970, 1971; Ford Foundation grant, 1977-78; Smithsonian Institution travel grant, 1978, for India.

WRITINGS: A Heritage of Pride: The Spanish Americans of New Mexico, University of New Mexico Press, 1969; *Black Carib Household Structure: A Study of Migration and Modernization,* University of Washington Press, 1969; (editor with Eleanor Leacock and Gilbert Kushner) *Training Programs for New Opportunities in Applied Anthropology,* Society for Applied Anthropology and American Anthropological Association, 1974; (editor) *Social and Technological Management in Dry Lands,* Westview Press, 1978; *Saga of Santiago: Development and Dependency in the Dominican Republic,* Institute for the Study of Human Issues, 1981; *Collected Articles on the Garifuna,* Westview Press, 1982.

Contributor: Morris Freilich, editor, *Marginal Natives: Anthropologists in Cross-Cultural Research,* Harper, 1970; Norman Whitten, editor, *Afro-American Anthropology: Problems in Theory and Method,* Free Press, 1970; Deward D. Walker, Jr., editor, *Systems of North American Witchcraft and Sorcery* (monograph), University of Idaho, 1970; Michael Horowitz, editor, *Peoples and Cultures of the Caribbean,* Doubleday, 1971; William M. Moore, M. M. Silverberg, and M. S. Read, editors, *Nutrition, Growth, and Development of North American Indian Children,* U.S. Government Printing Office, 1972; Arnold Strickon and Sidney Greenfield, editors, *Structure and Process in Latin America,* University of New Mexico Press, 1972; John Bennett, editor, *The New Ethnicity,* American Ethnological Society, 1973; *A Sampler of Women's Studies,* Center for Continuing Education for Women, University of Michigan, 1973; Roberta M. Delson, editor, *Readings in Caribbean History,* Gordon & Breach, 1974; George Foster and R. V. Kemper, editors, *Anthropologists in Cities,* Little, Brown, 1974; Brian du Toit and Helen Safa, editors, *Migration and Urbanization,* Mouton, 1976; Nevin S. Scrimshaw and Moises Behar, editors, *Nutrition and Agricultural and Economic Development in the Tropics,* XIV International Biological Symposium in Latin America, 1976; Ronald K. Wetherington, editor, *Colloquia in Anthropology,* Volume II, Fort Burgwin Research Center, 1978; M. H. Brenner, Anne Mooney, and T. J. Nagy, editors, *Assessing the Contributions of the Social Sciences to Health,* American Association for the Advancement of Science, 1979.

Contributor to *Encyclopaedia Britannica.* Contributor of about seventy articles and reviews to anthropology journals and popular magazines. Member of editorial board of *Third World Studies,* 1973—, *Reviews in Anthropology,* 1975-78, *Medical Anthropology,* 1976—, and *Human Organization,* 1977—; advisory editor of *Reviews in Anthropology,* 1978—.

SIDELIGHTS: Nancie Gonzalez wrote: "All my books are the result of anthropological field work, which is part and parcel of my life. I have done quite a lot of it and in many different places. At present I am still attempting to continue my work with the Garifuna or Black Caribs, many of whom have migrated to the South Bronx in New York City.

"For me, travel is both a professional and a recreational interest. I have visited nearly every country in South and Central America and the Carribean. In addition, I have traveled extensively in eastern and western Europe, and more recently, in Asia. For the anthropologist, travel is like a preview or an abstract, whetting the appetite for a longer, more contemplative and rigorous study.

"I will certainly continue writing. At present I have at least three or four books in my head, and all I need is the time to be able to sit down and write them! One of these will be a social anthropological and analysis of higher education ad-

ministration. Another will be a biography/autobiography based on family records going back to the 1830's. The focus will be on my great grandmother, her daughter, her daughter's daughter, and finally myself. I will deal with how educated and professional women's roles have changed over these generations in response to a more permissive environment and different demands. The women in my family have had no brothers for four generations. I think this has made a difference in my view of myself and the world. Certainly I have never thought there was anything I couldn't do because of being female."

BIOGRAPHICAL/CRITICAL SOURCES: Anthropology Newsletter, February, 1980.

* * *

GOOD, H(arry) G(ehman) 1880-1971

OBITUARY NOTICE—See index for *CA* sketch: Born July 14, 1880, in Lancaster County, Pa.; died April 11, 1971. Educator and author, best known for his books on the history of American education. Among Good's writings are *A History of Western Education, A History of American Education,* and *They Made Our Schools.* (Date of death provided by Macmillan Publishing Co.)

* * *

GOODE, John 1927-

PERSONAL: Born in 1927 in London, England; married Clare McDonald; children: three sons. *Education:* Attended technical high school in Brighton, England. *Home:* 12 Roberts St., Frankston, Victoria 3199, Australia.

CAREER: Australian Motor News, southern editor and manager, 1957-59; Consolidated Public Relations, Australia, manager, 1959-61; Australian Department of Trade and Industry, journalist, 1962-67; free-lance writer, editor, and photographer, 1967—. *Member:* Australian Society of Authors, Fellowhsip of Australian Writers.

WRITINGS: Freshwater Tortoises of Australia and New Guinea (in the Family Chelidae), Lansdowne, 1967; *Wood, Wire, and Fabric: A Saga of Australian Flying,* Lansdowne, 1968; *Smoke, Smell, and Clatter: The Revolutionary Story of Motoring in Australia,* Lansdowne, 1969; *Turtles, Tortoises, and Terrapins* (juvenile), Scribner, 1971; *The Australian Fish Cook Book,* Sun Books, 1971; *Tortoises, Terrapins, and Turtles,* Angus & Robertson, 1972; *The Air of Reality: New Essays on Henry James,* Methuen, 1972; *The World Guide to Cooking With Fruits and Vegetables,* Macmillan (Australia), 1973, Dutton, 1974; (editor) *George Gissing: The Nether World,* Fairleigh Dickinson University Press, 1974; *Practical Nature Study: Reptiles and Freshwater Animals,* Sun Books, 1974; *Rape of the Fly* (nonfiction), Thomas Nelson, 1977; *George Gissing,* Barnes & Nobles, 1978; *The Original Australian and New Zealand Fish Cookbook: An Alphabetical Guide to the Fishes of the Region, Their Preparation and Cookery,* A. H. & A. W. Reed, 1979. Contributor to magazines, including *Age, Australian, New Idea, Walkabout, Victoria Naturalist,* and *Autocar,* and to newspapers. Editor of *Australian Motor Sports Review,* 1959.*

* * *

GOODMAN, A(lvin) Harold 1924-

PERSONAL: Born July 14, 1924, in Solomon, Ariz.; son of Ralph N. and Marie O. Goodman; married Naomi Foster (a teacher), August 25, 1945; children: Steven H., Gordon D., Karen (Mrs. Brian Reeder). *Education:* University of

Arizona, B.A., 1947; University of Southern California, M.M., 1951, Ed.D., 1960. *Religion:* Church of Jesus Christ of Latter-day Saints (Mormons). *Home:* 725 East Stadium Ave., Provo, Utah 84601. *Office:* Department of Music, Brigham Young University, Provo, Utah 84601.

CAREER: Music supervisor at public schools in Snowflake, Ariz., 1947-50; orchestra conductor at public schools in Tucson, Ariz., 1950-52; Northern Arizona University, Flagstaff, assistant professor, 1952-55, associate professor, 1955-60, conductor of symphony 1952-60, chairman of department of music, 1956-57; Brigham Young University, Provo, Utah, professor of music and conductor of symphony, 1960—, chairman of department, 1964-80. Guest conductor and lecturer in the United States, Canada, Central America, Mexico, and Europe. Conductor and musical director of Tucson Symphony Orchestra, 1950-52, Northern Arizona Symphony Orchestra, 1952-80, Utah Valley Youth Symphony Orchestra and Utah Valley Symphony Orchestra, 1960-66. Chairman of executive committee of international music department of Church of Jesus Christ of Latter-day Saints, 1970-78.

MEMBER: Music Educators National Conference (president of Western Division; member of national executive board; member of research council), National Association of Schools of Music (regional chairman), American Federation of Musicians (member of board of directors), National Council of Accreditation of Teacher Education, Young Audiences of America (member of board of directors), North Central Accrediting Association, Utah Music Educators Association.

WRITINGS: Music Administration in Higher Learning, Utah Press Publishing, 1975; *We Can Become Perfect,* Utah Press Publishing, 1976; *Instrumental Music Guide,* Brigham Young University Press, 1977. Contributor to music journals.

WORKS IN PROGRESS: Exemplars in Music Education in the United States of America, publication expected in 1982; *Expressive Musical Performance,* publication expected in 1985.

SIDELIGHTS: Goodman told *CA:* "Music can do the following to improve educational objectives. Music can produce within the individual an awareness of patterns of sound as an aesthetic component in his world of experience. No other form of art has this potential. Music can increase each person's ability to control the availability of this aesthetic component, through singing, listening, performing instruments, rythmics, and creative activities. Music can present a wealth of culture into a recognized part of each person's environment, especially through a literature approach. Every performance organization, general music class, and classroom music program should excell with superb literature that demonstrates performance styles and practices of each of the major historical periods.

"Music can provide a means of communication that is near universal, a manner of expressing feelings, stimulating each individual's imagination, creating responsiveness within the lives of individuals. The affective and intellectual responses to music cannot be denied. Music can assist in finding the 'good life' through a deliberate guidance of behavior, helping each individual's whole affective nature and assisting each person to live on a higher plane. The spirit of man needs to be fed, and music can assist in this spiritual realization. Music can discover and give special opportunities for continual individual enrichment, relaxation, appreciation, and aesthetic experience throughout life.

"The above purposes have been stated from the intrinsic values that may accrue from music. Even though music, through a secondary nature, can assist the 'Seven Cardinal

Principles of Education,' this is not the prime purpose of music in the school. The 'instrumentalism' of John Dewey has influenced music educators to the degree that the full essence of music in the public schools' programs may not be realized. Whenever the values of music are stated on a basis other than aesthetic experience, music educators will not bring to fruition the potentialities of this great profession."

*   *   *

GOODMAN, Leonard H(enry)   1941-

PERSONAL: Born December 6, 1941, in New York, N.Y.; son of Joseph A. (a clerk) and Lillian (a garment worker; maiden name, Zelnick) Goodman; married Claire L. Sadle (a registered nurse), August 28, 1966; children: Stephen, Scott. *Education:* Ricker College, A.B., 1964; University of Virginia, M.Ed., 1967, D.Ed., 1973. *Religion:* Jewish. *Home:* 6804 Rambling Rose Dr., Charlotte, N.C. 28212. *Office:* Fox-Morris, 1742 Southern National Center, Charlotte, N.C. 28202.

CAREER: University of Virginia, Charlottesville, assistant director of placement, 1970-73; Kennesaw College, Marietta, Ga., director of counseling, 1973-76; University of North Carolina, Charlotte, career development coordinator, 1976-81; Fox-Morris, Charlotte, N.C., health care specialist, 1981—. Lecturer; presents workshops; consultant. *Military service:* U.S. Army, 1964-66. *Member:* American Personnel and Guidance Association, National Vocational Guidance Association, American Society for Training and Development.

WRITINGS: Sharter File of Free Occupational Literature, B'nai B'rith, 1970; *What Shall I Order for Our Career Placement Library?,* College Placement Council, 1975, 2nd edition, 1981; *Current Career and Occupational Literature, 1973-77,* H. W. Wilson, 1978; *Current Career and Occupational Literature, 1977-79,* H. W. Wilson, 1980; *Alternative Careers,* Garnett Park Press, 1982. Contributor to counseling and education journals. Book editor of *Journal of College Placement,* 1971—.

WORK IN PROGRESS: Finding a Career You Feel Good About, publication expected in 1982.

SIDELIGHTS: Goodman commented: "My past work has been oriented toward the career library and resource center. Now that I'm consulting and conducting workshops I'm putting emphasis on personal endeavor and life-change planning. I have been successful in regional workshops dealing with career planning, goal setting, and career changes. I'm an executive search consultant for health care professionals."

*   *   *

GOODMAN, Saul   1919-

PERSONAL: Born April 20, 1919, in New York, N.Y.; son of Morris (a merchant) and Bertha (Mantell) Goodman. *Education:* Attended City College (now of the City University of New York). *Home:* 157 East 18th St., New York, N.Y. 10003. *Office:* 745 Fifth Ave., New York, N.Y. 10151.

CAREER: Jade Hosiery, New York, N.Y., sales manager for ladies' hosiery wholesaler, 1940—; writer, 1954—; lecturer on dance, 1975—.

WRITINGS: Dancers You Should Know, Dance Magazine, 1964; *Baryshnikov: A Most Spectacular Dancer,* Harvey House, 1979. Author of "Brief Biographies," a monthly series in *Dance,* 1954-74. Contributor to *Dance, Ballet Today,* and *American Scandinavian Review.*

WORK IN PROGRESS: Two dance books; theatre memoirs; an album of candid snapshots of film stars.

SIDELIGHTS: Goodman wrote: "I am primarily interested in writing about performing arts subjects with which I have had personal contact, either as an interviewer or as a critical member of the audience, so that my own personal experience can enhance the historical value of the material."

BIOGRAPHICAL/CRITICAL SOURCES: Dance, September, 1964.

*   *   *

GORDON, Anne Wolrige
See WOLRIGE GORDON, Anne

*   *   *

GORDON, Caroline   1895-1981

OBITUARY NOTICE—See index for *CA* sketch: Born October 6, 1895, in Trenton, Ky.; died after surgery, April 11, 1981, in San Cristobal de las Casas, Chiapas, Mexico. Educator, literary critic, novelist, and author. After working as a newspaper reporter for several years, Gordon turned to teaching English at the University of North Carolina, and later became a lecturer in creative writing at Columbia University. Gordon's fiction examined life in the American South and has been compared to the work of other Southern women writers such as Eudora Welty and Katherine Anne Porter. Gordon's novels, short stories, and books of literary criticism include *Penhally, Aleck Maury: Sportsman, The Garden of Adonis, None Shall Look Back, The Malefactors,* and *A Good Soldier: A Key to the Novels of Ford Madox Ford.* Obituaries and other sources: *New York Times,* April 14, 1981; *Newsweek,* April 27, 1981; *Time,* April 27, 1981; *Publishers Weekly,* May 1, 1981; *AB Bookman's Weekly,* May 4, 1981.

*   *   *

GORDON, John William   1925-

PERSONAL: Born November, 1925, in Jarrow, England; son of Norman (a teacher) and Margaret (Revely) Gordon; married Sylvia Ellen Young, January 9, 1954; children: Sally, Robert. *Education:* Attended secondary school in Wisbech, England. *Home:* 99 George Borrow Rd., Norwich, Norfolk NR4 7HU, England.

CAREER: Isle of Ely and Wisbech Advertiser, Wisbech, England, reporter, 1947-49, sub-editor, 1949-51; *Bury Free Press,* Bury St. Edmunds, England, sub-editor, 1951-58; *Western Evening Herald,* Plymouth, England, sub-editor, 1958-62; *Eastern Evening News,* Norwich, England, sub-editor, 1962-73; *Eastern Daily Press,* Norwich, sub-editor, 1973—. *Military service:* Royal Navy, 1943-47.

WRITINGS—Children's books: *The Giant Under the Snow,* Hutchinson, 1968, Harper, 1970; *The House on the Brink,* Hutchinson, 1970, Harper, 1971, Peacock, 1972; *The Ghost on the Hill,* Kestrell, 1976, Viking, 1976, Peacock, 1977; *The Waterfall Box,* Kestrell, 1978; *The Spitfire Grave and Other Stories,* Kestrell, 1979.

Work represented in anthologies. Contributor of articles and stories to journals.

WORK IN PROGRESS: A novel, publication expected in 1982.

SIDELIGHTS: Gordon told *CA:* "Writing is always an attempt to get to the edge of things, to reach that strangest of all places where one thing ends and another begins. Within a story there must be a reality that is all but touchable, a place in which things can happen. The starting point must be a place that already exists. But from there a story must go toward the edge of the next real thing. The young know this. They inhabit border country, and so do story-tellers. The boundary between imagination and reality and the boundary between being a child and being an adult are on the same frontier. It is a passionate place in which to work."

BIOGRAPHICAL/CRITICAL SOURCES: Signal, May, 1972; Edward Blishen, *The Writer's Approach to the Novel,* Harrap, 1976; Naomi Lewis, *Fantasy Books for Children,* National Book League, 1977.

*   *   *

GORYAN, Sirak
See SAROYAN, William

*   *   *

GOULD, Carol C.   1946-

PERSONAL: Born January 24, 1946, in New York, N.Y. *Education:* University of Chicago, B.A., 1966; Yale University, M.Phil., 1969, Ph.D., 1971. *Home:* 333 Central Park W., New York, N.Y. 10025. *Office:* Department of Philosophy, Stevens Institute of Technology, Hoboken, N.J. 07030.

CAREER: State University of New York College at New Paltz, assistant professor of philosophy, 1970-72; Herbert H. Lehman College of the City University of New York, Bronx, N.Y., assistant professor of philosophy, 1972-75; Swarthmore College, Swarthmore, Pa., assistant professor of philosophy, 1975-79; University of Pittsburgh, Pittsburgh, Pa., visiting associate professor of philosophy, 1979-80; Stevens Institute of Technology, Hoboken, N.J., associate professor of philosophy, 1980—. *Member:* Committee on International Cooperation, American Philosophical Association, Metaphysical Society of America, Committee on Defense of Professional Rights, Society for Philosophy and Public Affairs, Society for Women in Philosophy.

WRITINGS: (Editor with Marx Wartofsky) *Women and Philosophy: Toward a Theory of Liberation,* Putnam, 1976; *Marx's Social Ontology: Individuality and Community in Marx's Theory of Social Reality,* MIT Press, 1978. Contributor of scholarly articles to *Philosophical Forum, Journal of Philosophy, Boston Studies in the Philosophy of Science,* and *Dialectics and Humanism.* Member of editorial board of *Praxis International.*

WORK IN PROGRESS: A book manuscript tentatively titled *The New Democracy: From Politics to Participation,* completion expected in January, 1982.

SIDELIGHTS: Through her books, Gould adds a philosophical dimension to scholarly questions and contemporary issues. For example, the intention of *Women in Philosophy,* noted Patricia Lyden of the *New Leader,* is "to lay the groundwork for a theory of liberation." In this book Gould asks if philosophy is capable of addressing "the woman question," so she analyzes a woman's position in philosophy as well as her place in society. "Those unfamiliar with philosophy will have difficulty appreciating the novelty of this book's subject," said Nancy Holmstrom in *Sex Roles: A Journal of Research.* "It is novel in philosophy both because it deals with a concrete social problem, whereas philosophy traditionally deals with universalistic and consequently abstract questions, and because it does so from an explicit and critical social-political viewpoint." The twenty-one essays included in *Women in Philosophy* cover topics such as the theoretical and political conceptions of women, abortion, and preferential hiring.

In her second book, *Marx's Social Ontology,* Gould approaches Marx as a philosopher who formulated an original theory of a social system. Her purpose, said A. Belden Fields of the *Journal of Politics,* is to prove that Marx "did indeed possess conceptions of human freedom and human justice." Using the philosopher's *Grundisse* as a text, Gould establishes, in the words of critic Tony Flood, that "Marx, presupposing as absolute the value of human freedom, interpreted history in terms of the realization and frustration of man's fundamental desire to control his destiny." In this book Gould concludes that, because of his social ontology, Marx "is a great systematic philosopher in the tradition of Aristotle, Kant and Hegel."

BIOGRAPHICAL/CRITICAL SOURCES: New Leader, July 19, 1976; *Review of Metaphysics,* June, 1979; *American Political Science Review,* September, 1979; *Journal of Politics,* Volume XLI, 1979; *Sex Roles: A Journal of Research,* January 25, 1980; *New International Review,* winter-spring, 1980; *Philosophiche Rundschau,* 1980; *Teaching Philosophy,* 1980.

* * *

GOULDING, Brian 1933-

PERSONAL: Born November 6, 1933, in Leicester, England; son of Fred Baden and Florence Ada (Mason) Goulding; married Frances Mary Perkins, July 6, 1956; children: Guy, Anthony. *Education:* Attended school in Nottingham, England. *Religion:* Church of England. *Office:* Lloyds Bank Ltd., N. & E. Midlands Regional Office, Market Square House, St. James's Street, Nottingham, England.

CAREER: Lloyds Bank Ltd., England, office junior and teller, 1950-67, assistant manager in Boston, Lincolnshire, England, 1963-67, personal assistant to general manager in London, England, 1967-68, instructor in staff college in Kingswood, Surrey, England, 1969, manager in Blackpool, Lancashire, England, 1970-74, manager in Burton on Trent, Staffordshire, England, 1974-77, general manager of Lewis's Bank, Liverpool, England, 1977-78, group representative to Lloyd's Bank in Los Angeles, Calif., 1978-80, deputy regional general manager, Nottingham, England, 1980—. *Military service:* Royal Air Force Reserve, 1965-70. *Member:* Institute of Bankers (London).

WRITINGS—All with Mike Garbett: *The Lancaster I,* Profile, 1966; *The Avro Lancaster in Unit Service,* Osprey, 1970; *Story of a Lanc,* Lincolnshire Chronicle and Royal Air Force Scampton, 1975; *Lancaster at War,* Ian Allan, Volume I, 1971, Volume II, 1979; *Lincoln at War: 1944-66,* Ian Allan, 1979. Contributor of numerous articles on World War II aviation to magazines, including *Air Pictorial, Control Column,* and *Aircraft Illustrated.*

WORK IN PROGRESS: Continued research with Mike Garbett on the Lancaster bomber.

SIDELIGHTS: The first volume of the *Lancaster at War* series is a collection of anecdotes about the World War II bomber, the Lancaster. The second volume, according to a writer for *Aircraft Illustrated,* grew out of the mass of material supplied to the authors by readers of the first book. A critic for *Aviation News* admitted an initial bias against yet another book on the Lancaster, but conceded that the book makes it "possible to gain intimate knowledge of the aircraft (such as the acrobatics required to prime the engines) in an ef-

fortless way whilst reading an absorbing account related to the authors by former crew members."

Goulding recalled for *CA:* "My interest in the Lancaster bomber began during World War II when I lived near the operational stations from which raids on Germany were launched. I began serious research in the early 1950's and joined with co-author, Mike Garbett, several years later."

BIOGRAPHICAL/CRITICAL SOURCES: Aircraft Illustrated, January, 1980; *Aviation News,* January 18-31, 1980.

* * *

GOURI, Haim 1923-

PERSONAL: Born October 9, 1923, in Tel-Aviv, Israel; son of Israel and Gila Gouri; married Aliza Becker (a teacher), September 16, 1952; children: Yael, Noa, Hamutal. *Education:* Hebrew University of Jerusalem, B.A., 1952. *Religion:* Jewish. *Home:* 5 Pinsker St., Jerusalem, Israel. *Agent:* Bertha Klausner, International Literary Agency, Inc., 71 Park Ave., New York, N.Y. 10016.

CAREER: Associated with newspaper *Lemerhav,* 1954-70; author of column in *Davar,* Israel, 1970—. *Military service:* Palmach, 1941-49. Israel Army, 1949—. *Member:* Hebrew Writers Association, Israeli Association of Writers and Composers. *Awards, honors:* Ussishkin Prize for literature, 1961, for *Prihei-Esh;* Sokolov Prize for journalism, 1962, for *Mul Ta Ha'zchuchit;* Bialik Prize for literature, 1975, for *Mariot Greizhazi;* Akum Prize from Israeli Association of Writers and Composers, 1979, for achievement in poetry; Walenrode Prize for *Ha-Chakira, Sipur Reuel.*

WRITINGS—In English translation: *Iskat Ha-Shokolad* (novel), Ha Kibbutz Hamehuda, 1964, translation by Seymour Simkes published as *The Chocolate Deal,* Holt, 1965.

Poetry; all published by Ha-Kibbutz Ha-Meuhad, except as noted: *Prihei-Esh* (title means "Flowers of Fire"), Sifriat Poalim, 1949; *Shirei Hotam* (title means "Seal Poems"), 1954; *Shoshanat Ruhot* (title means "Rose of Winds"), 1960; *Tnauh Lemaga* (title means "movement to Contact"), 1968; *Moreot Geihazi* (title means "The Vision of Gehazi"), 1974; *Ad Kav Nesher* (title means "To the Eagle Line"), 1975; *Ayuma* (title means "Terrible"), 1979.

Other; all published by Ha-Kibbutz Ha-Meuhad, except as noted: *Ad Alot Hashachar* (title means "Till Dawn"), 1950; *Mul Ta Ha'zchuchit* (title means "The Glass Cage"), 1962; *Dapim Yerushalmiim* (commentary; title means "Jerusalem Years"), 1968; *Hasefer Hameshuga* (novel; title means "The Crazy Book"), Am Oved, 1971; *Mi Maker et Yosef G.?* (adventure; title means "Who Knows Joseph G.?"), 1980; *Ha-Chakira, Sipur Reuel* (novel; title means "The Interrogative Reuel's Story"), Am Oved, 1981.

SIDELIGHTS: Gouri's book *Mul Ta Ha'zchuchit* is the diary of the Eichman trial. *Ayuma*'s title, the author reported, comes from a passage from the "Song of Songs": "Thou art beautiful, O my love, as Tirzah, comely as Jerusalem, *terrible* as an army with banners."

Gouri told *CA:* "Aside from the impulses and passions which characterize any writer anywhere in the world and at any time, my writing is largely influenced by my place of birth, the days of my growing up, and my later life as a conscious adult in Israel.

"Coming from a pacifist family and having to take part in the violence and the painful struggle in a torn country created a conflict in me. As a young man, it was almost a heartbreaking experience to confront the first survivors of the

Holocaust. I suddenly became acutely aware of the historical and national burden, of the age-old heritage which will follow me as a constant reminder throughout my life. I never had any religious education and have little knowledge of Judaica. All of a sudden, a voice from the past, a voice in me, recalled me slowly to the sources.

"The dualistic, ever dynamic, attraction-repulsion relationship with the Arabs created yet another important conflict. I feel a natural attraction to the smells and tastes of Arab scenery, to Arab customs and language, to their colorful, noisy, ever-changing markets. And I have the fear, the bitterness, and the anguish of living on the other side in a country besieged by neighbors who refuse to recognize our sovereignty.

"These conflicts, together with personal passions and feelings, are all interwoven in my writing."

* * *

GRAHAM, Andrew Guillemard 1913-1981

OBITUARY NOTICE: Born February 1, 1913, in Uppingham, England; died April 30, 1981. Soldier, journalist, and author. Graham's first book, *Interval in Indo-China*, describes his experiences as a military attache in Saigon. He later wrote novels and short stories, including *The Club, A Foreign Affair*, and *The Regiment*. Obituaries and other sources: *The Author's and Writer's Who's Who*, 6th edition, Burke's Peerage, 1971; *Who's Who*, 131st edition, St. Martin's, 1979; *London Times*, May 4, 1981.

* * *

GRAHAM, Brenda Knight 1942-

PERSONAL: Born September 17, 1942, in Clarkesville, Ga.; daughter of Floyd S. (an artist) and Eula (Gibbs) Knight; married Charles Graham (a veterinarian), December 20, 1965; children: William Stacey, Julie Victoria. *Education:* Young Harris College, A.A., 1963; University of Georgia, A.B.J., 1965. *Religion:* Baptist. *Home:* 1280 South Broad St., Cairo, Ga. 31728.

CAREER: Elementary school teacher in Habersham County, Ga., 1965; University of Georgia, Athens, secretary in department of housing, 1966-68; writer for children and adults, 1970—. Volunteer worker, teacher in adult literacy program, and speaker in children's classrooms. *Member:* American Veterinary Medical Association Auxiliary. *Awards, honors:* Scholar of Dixie Writers Conference, 1963; first prize from *Baptist Student* poetry contest, 1964, for "Sympathy."

WRITINGS: Stone Gables (nonfiction), Broadman, 1978; *The Pattersons at Turkey Hill House* (juvenile fiction), Broadman, 1979; *The Pattersons and the Mysterious Airplane* (juvenile fiction), Broadman, 1980; *The Pattersons and the Goat Man* (juvenile fiction), Broadman, 1981.

Work represented in anthologies, including *Yearbook of Modern Poetry*, 1971. Contributor to magazines, including *Home Life, Grit*, and *Baptist Student*, and newspapers.

WORK IN PROGRESS: Eulalie of Clover Hill, a fictionalized story of a girl growing up in the early 1900's in northern Georgia, publication expected in 1982 or 1983.

SIDELIGHTS: Brenda Graham commented: "I have wanted to write almost as long as I've been able to hold a pencil. My motivation is basically that of a songbird's: he sings because he *must* sing, I write because I *must* write. God has given me this talent as He gave the bird his song, and it is my joy to exercise it.

"My desire is to put wholesome, family-oriented literature into the hands of young and old alike. I believe that stable loving homes are one of America's biggest strengths. I also believe it is important for the education of our children that they *enjoy* reading; therefore, one of my biggest aims is to give them a good time!

"My father, a retired artist, began at the age of forty-two to teach his children at home rather than send them to public school. There ended up being ten of us, and none of us, except the oldest two, had any schoolteachers through the elementary grades other than Mom and Dad. Most of us had no other teachers until we went to college. Our life on a northern Georgia tree farm was unusual and most wonderful. Many of our episodes of growing up are included in *Stone Gables*.

"People tell me they like my descriptions most. I dearly love to make my readers aware of the beauty around them, whether it be shifting sun circles on a sandy brook bottom, or a bare tree silhouetted against an evening sky."

* * *

GRAHAM, Henry 1930-

PERSONAL: Born December 1, 1930. *Education:* Attended Liverpool College of Art.

CAREER: Liverpool Polytechnic, Liverpool, England, lecturer in art history, 1969—. Artist, with exhibitions of paintings in London and northern England. Also worked as jazz musician. *Awards, honors:* Award from *Ambit*, 1968; Arts Council Award, 1969; Arts Council Award, 1971, for *Passport to Earth*.

WRITINGS: (With Jim Mangnall) *Soup City Zoo: Poems*, Anima Press, 1968; *Good Luck to You, Kafka/You'll Need It Boss* (poems), Rapp & Whiting, 1969; *Passport to Earth* (poems), Rapp & Whiting, 1971.

Work represented in numerous anthologies, including *Come on Everybody; New Poems, 1971-72; The House That Jack Built*. Poetry editor of *Ambit*.*

* * *

GRASSI, Joseph A(ugustus) 1922-

PERSONAL: Born November 4, 1922, in New Rochelle, N.Y.; son of Joseph (a plastering contractor) and Marie G. (DiNunzio) Grassi; married Carolyn M. Cook (a teacher of philosophy at a community college), September 20, 1968; children: Edwin, Peter. *Education:* Attended Manhattan College, 1939-41; Maryknoll College, B.A., 1943; Maryknoll Seminary, B.D., 1948; Angelicum, S.T.D., 1949; Pontifical Biblical Institute, S.S.L., 1951. *Home:* 1746 Emory St., San Jose, Calif. 95126. *Office:* Department of Religious Studies, University of Santa Clara, Santa Clara, Calif. 95053.

CAREER: Maryknoll Seminary, Ossining, N.Y., assistant professor of Old Testament, 1951-57; served as missionary in Guatemala, 1957-60; Maryknoll Seminary, associate professor of New Testament, 1960-67; Drew University, Madison, N.J., associate professor of New Testament, 1968-70; University of Santa Clara, Santa Clara, Calif., associate professor, 1971-74, professor of religious studies, 1975—, chairman of department, 1972-79. Presented summer workshops in Chile, Colombia, Peru, Bolivia, Mexico, and Guatemala, 1966; visiting scholar at Union Theological Seminary, New York, N.Y., summer, 1968, and Columbia University, 1968-69; conducts classes in New Testament and in Christian origins. *Member:* Catholic Biblical Association.

WRITINGS: A World to Win: The Missionary Methods of Paul the Apostle, Maryknoll Publications, 1965; (contributor) W. Richardson, editor, *The Church as Sign,* Maryknoll Press, 1968; (contributor) R. E. Brown, J. Fitzmyer, and R. E. Murphy, editors, *Jerome Biblical Commentary: Ephesians, Colossians,* Prentice-Hall, 1968; (contributor) M. Zeik and M. Siegel, editors, *The Root and the Branch,* Roth, 1973; *The Teacher in the Primitive Church and the Teacher Today,* University of Santa Clara Press, 1973; (contributor) T. M. McFallen, editor, *Does Jesus Make a Difference?,* Seabury, 1974; *Underground Christians in the Earliest Church,* Diakonia Press, 1975; *The Secret of Paul the Apostle,* Orbis, 1978; *Jesus as Teacher,* St. Mary's College Press, 1978. Contributor to *New Catholic Encyclopedia.* Contributor of articles and reviews to religious journals.

WORK IN PROGRESS: A book, *Toward a Whole Earth Spirituality.*

SIDELIGHTS: Grassi has written a cassette series for Alba Communications, "The Spiritual Message of the Four Gospels," and he has edited and contributed to a record and cassette series, "The New Testament for Today," for the same company.

He told *CA:* "Teaching, studying, and writing in my special field of the New Testament and Christian origins are my main interests. In addition, my wife and I enjoy conducting groups and classes in meditation and personal growth. This has proved to be a rewarding personal experience for us. We also donate our services to coordinate 'Skip-a-Meal,' a non-profit organization whose members skip a meal each week and send the savings directly to purchase food for starving and hungry people throughout the world."

AVOCATIONAL INTERESTS: The ocean, hiking, camping.

*　　*　　*

GRAUBARD, Paul S. 1932-

PERSONAL: Born March 20, 1932, in Elizabeth, N.J.; married, 1954; children: four. *Education:* University of Michigan, B.A., 1952; Columbia University, M.A., 1954; Yeshiva University, Ed.D., 1965. *Office:* Department of Special Education, Yeshiva University, 55 Fifth Ave., New York, N.Y. 10003.

CAREER: Teacher at school in Brooklyn, N.Y., 1957-59; teacher at private school, 1959-62; supervisor of remedial education at boys' school, 1962-65; Yeshiva University, New York, N.Y., assistant professor, 1965-68, associate professor of special education and director of programs for education of the behavior-disordered, 1968—. Lecturer at Bank Street College of Education, 1965—. *Member:* American Orthopsychiatric Association (fellow; chairman of school committee, 1966-69), American Psychological Association, Council on Children's Behavior Disorders, Council on Exceptional Children.

WRITINGS: (Editor) *Children Against Schools: Education of the Delinquent, Disturbed, Disruptive,* Follett, 1969; (with Abraham Givner) *A Handbook of Behavior Modification for the Classroom,* Holt, 1974; (with Harry Rosenberg) *Classrooms That Work: Prescription for Change,* Dutton, 1974; *Positive Parenthood: Solving Parent-Child Conflicts Through Behavior Modification,* Bobbs-Merrill, 1977. Contributor to education journals. Associate editor of *Exceptional Children,* 1965—.

BIOGRAPHICAL/CRITICAL SOURCES: New York Times Book Review, July 24, 1977.*

GRAY, Jack 1927-

PERSONAL: Born December 7, 1927, in Detroit, Mich.; son of John Russell and Jessie Parsons (Patterson) Gray; married Araby Lockhart, December 4, 1952; children: John, Nicholas, Rebecca, Susannah, Felix. *Education:* Attended Queen's University, Kingston, Ontario; received B.A. and M.A. from University of Toronto. *Home:* 32 Binscarth Rd., Toronto, Ontario, Canada M4W 1Y1. *Agent:* Blanche Marvin, Elspeth Cochrane Agency, 1 The Pavement, London SW4 0HY, England.

CAREER: Maclean's, Toronto, Ontario, assistant editor, 1953-57; free-lance writer, 1957—. President of John Gray Productions Ltd. Executive director and resident playwright at Neptune Theatre, Halifax, Nova Scotia, 1963; secretary-general of Canadian Theatre Centre, 1971-73. Professor at University of Waterloo, 1969-71. *Member:* International Writers Guild (president), Association of Canadian Television and Radio Artists (president; member of executive board and chairman of Writers Council, 1970—), Writers Guild of Great Britain, League of Dramatists.

WRITINGS—Plays: Chevalier Johnstone (first produced as "Louisbourg" in Halifax, Nova Scotia, at Neptune Theatre, 1964), Playwrights Cooperative (Toronto), 1972; *Susannah, Agnes, and Ruth* (first broadcast in 1969), Playwrights Cooperative, 1972; *Striker Schneiderman* (first produced in Toronto at St. Lawrence Theatre, 1970), University of Toronto Press, 1973.

Unpublished plays: "Bright Sun at Midnight," first produced in Toronto at Crest Theatre, 1957; (co-author) "Ride a Pink Horse" (musical), first produced in Toronto at Crest Theatre, 1958; "The Teacher," first produced in Stratford, Ontario, 1960; "Emmanuel Xoc," first produced in Toronto at Crest Theatre, 1965; "Godiva," first produced in Coventry, England, at Belgrade Theatre, 1967.

Radio plays: "To Whom It May Concern," first broadcast in 1958; "The Lost Boy," first broadcast in 1959; "The Cracker Man," first broadcast in 1970; "And I Mayakovsky," first broadcast in 1976.

Television plays: "The Ledge," first broadcast in 1959; "The Glove," first broadcast in 1961; "Man in Town," first broadcast in 1962; "The Enemy," first broadcast in 1962; "The Guard," first broadcast in 1963; "Miss Hanago," first broadcast in 1964.

Editor of "Canadian Play Series," University of Toronto Press.*

*　　*　　*

GRAY, John Morgan 1907-

PERSONAL: Born June 12, 1907, in Toronto, Ontario, Canada; son of Samuel Morgan and Helen Harris (Putnam) Gray; married Frances Antoinette Lalonde, July 30, 1932; children: John Anthony Morgan. *Education:* Attended University of Toronto, 1925-27. *Office:* 70 Bond St., Toronto, Ontario, Canada.

CAREER: Chairman of board of directors of Macmillan Co. of Canada Ltd., Toronto, Ontario. Member of board of governors of York University; governor of Lakefield College School. *Military service:* Canadian Army, Scotland Regiment, Intelligence, 1941-42; served in European theater; became general staff officer, second class; mentioned in dispatches. *Member:* York Club, Canadian Club (president,

1970-71). *Awards, honors:* Member of Order of the British Empire; LL.D. from Mount Allison University, 1969.

WRITINGS: (Editor with Frank A. Upjohn and J. J. Knights) *Prose of Our Day,* Macmillan, 1940; *Lord Selkirk of Red River,* Macmillan of Canada, 1963, Michigan State University Press, 1964; *History of Gambia,* Biblio Distribution, 1966; *Fun Tomorrow: Learning to Be a Publisher and Much Else,* Macmillan of Canada, 1978, published as *Fun Tomorrow: Memoirs of a Canadian Publisher, 1907-1946,* St. Martin's, 1979. Also author of *History of Zanzibar: From the Middle Ages to 1856,* 1962; *James and William Tassie: Gem Cutters,* Saifer; *A History of Jerusalem.**

*   *   *

GRAY, Michael H(aslam)   1946-

PERSONAL: Born August 11, 1946, in Newcastle, Australia; came to the United States in 1946, naturalized citizen, 1946; son of John Duncan (an engineer) and Enid (Haslam) Gray; married Dorothy Allman Pollet (a librarian), August 11, 1980. *Education:* University of North Carolina, B.A., 1968, M.S.L.S., 1972. *Home:* 3656 Gunston Rd., Alexandria, Va. 22302. *Office:* Voice of America, 330 Independence Ave. S.W., Washington, D.C. 20547.

CAREER: Library of Congress, Washington, D.C., librarian, 1972-76; Voice of America, Washington, D.C., librarian, 1976—. Discography editor of Greenwood Press, 1979—. *Military service:* U.S. Army, 1969-71. *Member:* International Association of Sound Archives, Association for Recorded Sound Collections (chairman of publications committee, 1977—), Music Library Association.

WRITINGS: (Editor with Gerald D. Gibson) *Bibliography of Discographies,* Volume I: *Classical Music,* Bowker, 1977; (compiler) *Beecham: A Centenary Discography,* Holmes & Meier, 1979. Editor of *Journal* (of Association for Recorded Sound Collections), 1977—.

WORK IN PROGRESS: Bibliography of Discographies, Volume II: *Popular and Folk Music,* with co-editor Gerald D. Gibson, publication by Bowker expected in 1983.

SIDELIGHTS: Michael Gray told *CA:* "My works have aimed for accuracy in a field where too much work has not. I seek to encourage the discographic work of others through my editorships at the Association for Recorded Sound Collections and Greenwood Press. I hope to establish, through myself and through the work of others I can assist, discography as a discipline on an equal footing with bibliography. I also seek to have discographic works used in conjunction with formal music research and teaching."

*   *   *

GRAY, Nicholas Stuart   1922-1981

OBITUARY NOTICE—See index for *CA* sketch: Born October 23, 1922, in Scotland; died March 17, 1981, in London, England. Actor, playwright, and author best known for writing plays for children. After having his first play produced professionally when he was seventeen, Gray wrote and acted in an adaptation of "Beauty and the Beast." Other plays written by Gray include "The Princess and the Swineherd," "The Tinder-Box," "The Marvellous Story of Puss in Boots," and "New Clothes for the Emperor." Gray was also the author of novels, including *Down in the Cellar, The Stone Cage, The Apple Stone,* and *Killer's Cookbook.* Obituaries and other sources: *London Times,* March 20, 1981.

GRAY, Nicolete (Mary)   1911-

PERSONAL: Born July 20, 1911, in Stevenage, England; daughter of Laurence (a poet and art historian) and Cicely (Powell) Binyon; married Basil Gray (a museum keeper), July 20, 1933; children: Marius, Camilla (Mrs. Oleg Prokofiev; deceased), Edmund, Cecilia (Mrs. Tassilo Wolff-Metternich), Sophia. *Education:* Lady Margaret Hall, Oxford, M.A., 1932. *Religion:* Roman Catholic. *Home:* Dawbers House, Long Wittenham, Abingdon, Oxfordshire OX14 4QQ, England.

CAREER: Free-lance writer and researcher, 1932-66; Central School of Art and Design, London, England, lecturer in lettering, 1966—. Part-time teacher, 1940-43. Organizer of international exhibitions. *Member:* Association Typographique Internationale, International Society of Christian Artists, Society for English Liturgy, Printing Historical Society.

WRITINGS: Nineteenth-Century Ornamented Types and Title Pages, Faber, 1938, revised edition published as *Nineteenth-Century Ornamented Typefaces,* 1976; *Rossetti, Dante, and Ourselves,* Faber, 1947; *The Paleography of Latin Inscriptions in the Eighth, Ninth, and Tenth Centuries in Italy,* Papers of the British School at Rome, 1948; *Jacob's Ladder: A Bible Picture Book From Anglo-Saxon and Twelfth-Century English Manuscripts,* Faber, 1949; *Lettering on Buildings,* Architectural Press, 1960; (editor) Richard Egenter, *The Desecration of Christ,* Burns & Oates, 1967; *Lettering as Drawing,* Volume I: *Contour and Silhouette,* Volume II: *The Moving Line,* Oxford University Press, 1971; *The Helen Sutherland Collection: A Pioneer Collection of the 1930's—Catalogue of an Exhibition,* Arts Council of Great Britain, 1971; *The Painted Inscriptions of David Jones,* Gordon Fraser, 1981.

WORK IN PROGRESS: The Running Script, a new method and model for teaching handwriting, based on the ball-point pen; *The Central Lettering Record,* a photographic collection of lettering (from all periods) at Central School of Art and Design.

SIDELIGHTS: Nicolete Gray wrote: "My chief interests have been modern art, the Catholic faith, and lettering. As it has worked out, most of the writing I have produced has been on lettering; I have been fortunate in having been asked to teach at the Central School, and so combine my activity in scholarship with the creative arts. I also enjoy designing and carving lettering myself. During the years that I have taught, we have worked out a new attitude and a new method to bring the art of lettering back into contact with contemporary art and technology."

*   *   *

GRAY, Wellington Burbank   1919-1977

OBITUARY NOTICE—See index for *CA* sketch: Born April 25, 1919, in Albany, N.Y.; died November 29, 1977. Painter, designer, educator, and author. Gray served as an instructor of art and design at public schools and colleges before becoming dean of the School of Art at East Carolina College in Greenville, N.C. A contributor of articles to numerous art and education journals, Gray also wrote *Student Teaching in Art.* (Date of death provided by wife, Norma W. Gray.)

GREATOREX, Wilfred 1921-

PERSONAL: Born May 27, 1921, in Blackburn, England; married Beryl Thornley. *Education:* Attended grammar school in Blackburn, England. *Home:* Foxwell, Berry Hill, Taplow, Buckinghamshire, England.

CAREER: Assistant editor of *John Bull,* 1956-59. Writer. *Member:* Writers Guild of Great Britain, Society of Film and Television Arts, Press Club, Arts Theatre Club. *Awards, honors:* Awards from Writers Guild of Great Britain, 1965, for drama series script "The Plane Makers," and 1967, for drama series script "The Power Game."

WRITINGS: Diamond Fever (travel book), Cassell, 1957; (editor) Robert Elliott Urquhart, *Arnhem,* Cassell, 1958; (with John Burke) *The Power Game,* Pan Books, 1966; *The Freelancers,* Weidenfeld & Nicolson, 1975; *Crossover,* Weidenfeld & Nicolson, 1976, published as *Three Potato, Four,* Coward, 1977; *Quicksand,* Weidenfeld & Nicolson, 1979.

Television plays: "The Curtis Affair," first broadcast in 1968; "The Eleventh Commandment," first broadcast in 1970; "Dying Gets You Nowhere," first broadcast in 1970; "Night of the Tanks," first broadcast in 1972; "The Inheritors," first broadcast in 1974; "Did Machiavelli Have Welch Blood?," first broadcast in 1974. Also author of screenplays "Nobody Runs Forever: The High Commissioner" and "Battle of Britain." Writer for television series "The Power Game," 1965, "The Plane Makers," 1967, "Hine," 1971, and "Man From Haven," 1972.

SIDELIGHTS: A two-volume novel, *1990,* by Maureen Gregson, is based on one of Wilfred Greatorex's television series.

BIOGRAPHICAL/CRITICAL SOURCES: New York Times Book Review, February 20, 1977.*

* * *

GREAVES, (Brian) John 1898-

PERSONAL: Born July 25, 1898, in London, England; son of Leonard William and Annie Eliza (Wright) Greaves; married Beatrice Mabel Siddon, June 12, 1926 (died, 1961); children: Derek William, Brian John, Jr. *Office:* 48 Doughty St., London W.C.1, England.

CAREER: Clerk with T. J. Harries Co. (drapers), London, England; shipping clerk with E. J. Winser & Co. (hide merchants), London, and M. Blackett & Colombie (merchants), London; Abbey National Buildings Society, London, began as clerk and cashier, became manager of West End branch and chief personnel officer. Honorary secretary and member of board of trustees of Dickens House Museum and Library, 1947—. Lecturer for Dickens Fellowship and British Council on England, Scandinavia, Europe, Canada, and the United States. *Military service:* Royal Navy, Air Service. Royal Air Force. *Member:* Chartered Institute of Secretaries, Dickens Fellowship.

WRITINGS: (Editor) *Who's Who in Dickens,* Elm Tree Books, 1972, Taplinger, 1973; *Dickens at Doughty St.,* Elm Tree Books, 1975.*

* * *

GREEN, Elmer Ellsworth 1917-

PERSONAL: Born October 10, 1917, in La Grande, Ore.; son of Mable F. and Marie L. (Bolton) Green; married Alyce M. Mattson, February 25, 1941; children: Patricia, Douglas, Sandra, Judith. *Education:* University of Minnesota, B.S.,

1942; attended University of California, Los Angeles, 1946; University of Chicago, Ph.D., 1962. *Home:* 279 Lakewood Hills, Ozawkie, Kan. 66070. *Office:* Menninger Foundation, P.O. Box 829, Topeka, Kan. 66601.

CAREER: Honeywell Corp., Minneapolis, Minn., fire control assembly methods engineer, 1942-43, technical representative to U.S. Army Air Forces, 1934-35; U.S. Naval Ordnance Test Station, China Lake, Calif., physicist, 1947-51, head of data reduction branch, 1951-53, and photophysics branch, 1953-55, head of assessments division for evaluation of research on rockets and guided missiles, 1955-58; University of Chicago, Chicago, Ill., research associate in medical psychology, 1962-64; Menninger Foundation, Topeka, Kan., head of biomedical electronics laboratory, 1964-66, director of psychophysiology laboratory and voluntary controls program in research department, 1966—. Member of advisory board of Canadian Institute for Psychosynthesis, 1971—, and American Institute for Psychosynthesis, 1973—; director of Institute for Transpersonal Psychology, 1972—; adviser to Gladman Medical Foundation, 1976—. Member of field faculty of Union Graduate School, 1973—. Member of working groups of U.S. Department of Defense, 1952-57.

MEMBER: Scientific Research Society of America, American Association for the Advancement of Science, American Society for Psychical Research, Biofeedback Society of America (president, 1978), Society for Psychophysiological Research, Association for Humanistic Psychology, Association for Transpersonal Psychology, Kansas Psychological Association, Sigma Xi. *Awards, honors:* National Institute of Mental Health grants, 1968-69, 1972-73; grants from Millicent Foundation, van Ameringen Foundation, Stranahan Foundation, Weyerhaeuser Foundation, Murdock Charitable Trust, and Joseph and Sadie Danciger Fund.

WRITINGS: (With wife, Alyce Green) *Beyond Biofeedback,* Delacorte, 1977.

SIDELIGHTS: Green and his wife have made sound recordings for Big Sur Recordings, including "Biofeedback for Mind-Body Self-Regulation," 1969, "Eastern and Western Science," 1970, and "Biofeedback and Psychophysiological Training," 1972.

BIOGRAPHICAL/CRITICAL SOURCES: Best Sellers, October, 1977.*

* * *

GREEN, Hollis Lynn 1933-

PERSONAL: Born January 6, 1933, in Rhea County, Tenn.; son of Herbert Barton (a manager) and Grace Irene (a teacher; maiden name, Curton) Green; married Peggy Jean Lane, December 8, 1951 (marriage ended, 1972); married Gloria Gale Parks (an insurance underwriter), 1974; children: (first marriage) Barton Lynn, Brian Lane. *Education:* Attended Beckley College, 1952-54, and University of Cincinnati, 1957-58; Southwestern College, B.A., 1962; Luther Rice Seminary, B.D., 1968, M.Ed., 1974, Th.D., 1968; Walden University, Ph.D., 1978. *Politics:* Republican. *Home:* 6236 Pinelock Dr., Jacksonville, Fla. 32211. *Office:* 1820 Monument Rd., Jacksonville, Fla. 32225.

CAREER: Ordained Southern Baptist minister, 1959; West Virginia state director of Christian education, 1952-58; pastor of churches in Milford, Ohio, 1958-59, Greenville, S.C., 1959-61, Columbus, Ind., 1961-62, and Hialeah, Fla., 1963-64; Church of God, Executive Offices, director of public relations, 1964-72; Provident Investment Corp., Atlanta, Ga., director, 1972-74; Luther Rice Seminary, Jacksonville, Fla., vice-president and professor of evangelism and church growth, 1974-79; Greenleaf Foundation, Inc., Jacksonville, president, 1979—. President of Aid Ltd., 1966—; vice-president of P.A.C.E. Inc., 1980; executive director of Greenleaf Retreat and Resource Center, 1980—; vice-president of Transition Dynamics, 1980—. Member of Inter-Racial Study Commission of the South, 1962-64, U.S. Postal Forums, 1968-69, and board of trustees of Luther Rice Seminary, 1968-73; Protestant Armed Forces field representative, 1969. *Military service:* U.S. Air Force Auxiliary, chaplain, 1964-74; became major.

MEMBER: International Platform Association (fellow), International Public Relations Association, Public Relations Society of America, Religious Public Relations Council, Evangelical Press Association, Society of Pentecostal Scholars, National Sunday School Association (member of board of directors, 1958-62), Kiwanis. *Awards, honors:* Public service awards from U.S. Postal Service, 1968, and U.S. Senatorial Business Advisory Board, 1980.

WRITINGS: Hitching Your Star to a Wagon, Pathway Press, 1958; *Dynamics of Christian Discipleship,* Pathway Press, 1962; *Christian Education Cyclopedia,* Pathway Press, 1965; *Marchings as to War,* Pathway Press, 1969; *Understanding Pentecostalism,* Pathway Press, 1970; *Where in the World Are You Going?,* Pathway Press, 1971; *Why Churches Die,* Bethany Fellowship, 1972; *Why Wait Till Sunday,* Bethany Fellowship, 1975; *Why Disciple-Making Fails,* Bethany Fellowship, 1981; *Life-Cycle Leadership,* P.A.C.E., 1982.

SIDELIGHTS: Green told *CA:* "I am presently developing the Greenleaf Retreat and Resource Center near Dayton, Tenn. This facility will include a retirement village, a seminar and retreat center, and a counseling service for professionals in transition. I am also pioneering a new counseling model for mid-life, mid-career understanding called Transition Dynamics."

* * *

GREEN, Paul (Eliot) 1894-1981

OBITUARY NOTICE—See index for *CA* sketch: Born March 17, 1894, near Lillington, N.C.; died of congestive heart failure, May 4, 1981, in Chapel Hill, N.C. Playwright, educator, and author. Green taught philosophy and the dramatic arts at the University of North Carolina from 1923 until 1944. He was awarded the Pulitzer Prize in drama in 1927 for his Broadway play "In Abraham's Bosom," the story of black life in the South during the early part of the twentieth century. Green also wrote screenplays, including the 1933 version of "State Fair" and "Black Like Me," the story of a white man who changes his skin color in order to examine racial prejudice. Green pioneered the symphonic outdoor drama in 1937 with his production of "The Lost Colony." An outspoken supporter of civil rights for blacks, Green aroused the anger of some people when he collaborated with black novelist Richard Wright on the stage adaptation of Wright's book *Native Son.* He was the author of short stories and novels, including *The Laughing Pioneer* and *This Body the Earth.* Obituaries and other sources: *New York Times,* May 6, 1981; *Washington Post,* May 6, 1981; *Newsweek,* May 18, 1981; *Time,* May 18, 1981.

* * *

GREENBERG, Uri Zvi 1898-1981

OBITUARY NOTICE: Born October 17, 1898, in Bialykamien, Eastern Galicia (now Ukrainian S.S.R.); died May 8,

1981, in Israel. Author of books of poetry, including *Jerusalem.* His poems were also published in *The Door Standing Open, Modern Hebrew Poetry,* and *Poetry.* A leading Hebrew poet, Greenberg used his art to promote Jewish nationalism. During the 1940's he fought as a member of various guerrilla groups that sought to establish an independant Jewish nation in Palestine. After the formation of the state of Israel, Greenberg served as a member of the Israeli parliament for one term. Obituaries and other sources: *Who's Who in World Jewry: A Biographical Dictionary of Outstanding Jews,* Pitman, 1972; *World Authors, 1970-75,* H. W. Wilson, 1980; *Chicago Tribune,* May 10, 1981; *New York Times,* May 10, 1981.

* * *

GREENLEE, Douglas 1935-1979

OBITUARY NOTICE—See index for *CA* sketch: Born November 20, 1935, in El Paso, Tex.; died of cancer, January 10, 1979. Educator and author. A professor of philosophy at Temple University in Philadelphia, Pa., Greenlee was an expert on the writings of philosopher Charles Sander Peirce. He wrote *Peirce's Concept of Sign,* edited a book on Peirce, and contributed articles to anthologies and periodicals. In 1977 he served as president of the Charles S. Peirce Society. (Date of death supplied by wife, Ruth Nelson Greenlee.)

* * *

GREENSPAN, Bud 1927-

PERSONAL: Born September 18, 1927, in New York, N.Y.; son of Benjamin E. (a judge) and Paychel P. (a lawyer; maiden name, Perry) Greenspan; married Constance Anne Petrash (an executive producer and associate director), February 28, 1965. *Education:* New York University, B.A., 1947. *Politics:* Democrat. *Religion:* Jewish. *Home:* 252 East 61st St., New York, N.Y. 10021. *Agent:* Jay Acton, Edward J. Acton, Inc., 17 Grove St., New York, N.Y. 10014. *Office:* Cappy Productions, Inc., 33 East 68th St., New York, N.Y. 10021.

CAREER: WHN-Radio, New York City, sports director and broadcaster, 1947-51; Gumbinner Agency, New York City, television producer, 1959-61; Dancer-Fitzgerald-Sample, New York City, television producer, 1961-66; Sullivan, Stauffer, Colwell & Bayles, New York City, creative television supervisor, 1966-68; Cappy Productions, New York City, president, 1968—; writer. Instructor in film at New York University; lecturer. *Military service:* U.S. Army, in military intelligence; became captain. *Member:* American Federation of Television and Radio Artists, Writers Guild of America, Directors Guild of America. *Awards, honors:* Emmy Award from Academy of Television Arts and Sciences, 1977, for "The Olympiad."

WRITINGS—Sports: *Play It Again, Bud,* Wyden Books, 1973; *We Wuz Robbed,* Grosset, 1976; (with Wilma Rudolph) *Wilma: The Story of Wilma Rudolph,* New American Library, 1977. Also author of *Numero Uno* and *The Olympiad,* as yet unpublished.

Teleplays on sports, and director: "Jesse Owens Returns to Berlin," 1968; "The Charlie Boswell Story"; "The Glory of Their Times" (adapted from the book by Lawrence Ritter), 1977; "Wilma," 1977. Also author and director of sports shorts for television.

Contributor of more than one hundred articles to periodicals, including *Reader's Digest, Sports Illustrated, New York Times,* and *Washington Post.*

WORK IN PROGRESS: "The Al Oerter Story," a documentary film about the American Olympic discus champion who won four successive Olympic gold medals from 1956 to 1968.

SIDELIGHTS: Greenspan's projects have always received critical acclaim, but the commercial television networks have been reluctant to schedule them. "Jesse Owens Returns to Berlin," although filmed in 1964, was not aired by a major network until 1972, when it was nominated for three Emmy awards. "The Glory of Their Times," a look at baseball's beginnings through rare photographs and film clips, was considered "too low-key" by the major networks. Rather than submit to pressure to change the program, Greenspan bought the film back and waited eight years before the Public Broadcasting System ran it uncut in 1977.

Greenspan and his wife, Cappy Petrash, began filming a documentary in 1971 about the Ethiopian runners who had dominated the marathon competition at the 1960, 1964, and 1968 Olympic games. Greenspan soon decided that the best way to get a sports documentary on the air was to compile a series and sell the episodes as a package. The resulting series, "The Olympiad," was so successful that it was expanded from ten to eighteen segments in 1980 and was aired in more than eighty countries.

Greenspan has also been successful in making spoken-word recordings. His first record album, "Great Moments in Sport," earned him a Gold Record Award. It was followed by eighteen more albums, including "Witness," on the Army-McCarthy hearings, "Voices of the Twentieth Century," "The Nuremburg War Crime Trials," "The Day F.D.R. Died," "Madison Square Garden," and "December 7, 1941."

BIOGRAPHICAL/CRITICAL SOURCES: Best Sellers, October 15, 1973.

* * *

GREER, Rebecca Ellen 1935-

PERSONAL: Born October 15, 1935, in Washington, D.C.; daughter of Frank Upton and May (Mann) Greer. *Education:* University of Florida, B.S., 1957. *Home:* 50 King St., New York, N.Y. 10014. *Agent:* Anita Diamant, Writer's Workshop, Inc., 51 East 42nd St., New York, N.Y. 10017. *Office:* Woman's Day, 1515 Broadway, New York, N.Y. 10036.

CAREER: Worked as assistant editor for *Parents' Magazine,* 1959, and *Ladies' Home Journal,* 1960-61; editor-in-chief of *Teen Age,* 1962; features editor of *Bride's,* 1965-68; New School for Social Research, New York, N.Y., teacher of nonfiction writing, 1973—. *Member:* Authors Guild, Authors League of America, Women in Communications, Society of Professional Journalists (member of executive council).

WRITINGS: The Book for Brides, Fawcett, 1963; *The Bride's Book of Etiquette,* Grosset, 1967; *Why Isn't a Nice Girl Like You Married?,* Macmillan, 1969; *How to Live Rich When You're Not,* Grosset, 1975. Contributor to magazines and newspapers, including *McCall's, House Beautiful, Mademoiselle,* and *Parents' Magazine.* Articles editor of *Woman's Day,* 1968—.

* * *

GREGORY, Mark
See BURCH, Monte G.

GREISMAN, Joan Ruth 1937-

PERSONAL: Born May 4, 1937, in New York, N.Y.; daughter of Jack and Pearl Greisman. *Education:* Hunter College of the City University of New York, B.A., M.S. *Religion:* Jewish. *Home and office:* 185 East 85th St., New York, N.Y. 10028. *Agent:* Curtis Brown Ltd., 575 Madison Ave., New York, N.Y. 10028.

CAREER: Associated with Board of Education of New York City, 1958—; teacher and reading specialist at elementary schools in New York City, until 1966; assistant principal at elementary school in East Harlem, N.Y.; instructor at Long Island University, 1966-75; writer.

WRITINGS: (With Harriet Joan Wittels) *The Clear and Simple Thesaurus-Dictionary,* Grosset, 1971; (with Wittels) *The Perfect Speller,* Grosset, 1973; (with Wittels) *Things I Hate,* Behavioral Publications, 1973.

WORK IN PROGRESS: Jeff Fights for Justice, a teenage novel, with Wittels; *The Budding Business Bureau,* a teenage novel, with Wittels; *Preparing Your Child for Success With Reading,* a reference book for parents, with Wittels.

* * *

GREW, James Hooper 1906-

PERSONAL: Born December 16, 1906, in Boston, Mass.; married, 1938; children: three. *Education:* Harvard University, A.B., 1929; University of Paris, Dr. es Lettres, 1932. *Home:* 128 Johnson St., North Andover, Mass. 01845.

CAREER: Teacher of French at private schools, 1933-72; teacher of French at Belmont Hill School, 1972—. *Member:* Modern Language Association of America, American Association of Teachers of French, American Council of Teachers of Foreign Languages, National Education Association, New England Modern Language Association. *Awards, honors:* Palmes Academiques, 1949; chevalier of Legion d'Honneur, 1954.

WRITINGS: (Contributor) William F. Bottiglia, editor, *The Language Classroom,* New England Conference of Teachers of Foreign Languages, 1957; (with Daniel D. Olivier) *One Thousand One Pitfalls in French,* Barron's, 1974.*

* * *

GRIDLEY, Marion E(leanor) 1906-1974

OBITUARY NOTICE—See index for *CA* sketch: Born November 16, 1906, in White Plains, N.Y.; died October 31, 1974. Publisher, editor, and author, best known for her books on American Indians. Adopted by the Omaha and Winnebago Indian tribes, Gridley wrote numerous volumes on Indian legends, leaders, and lore. In 1923 she founded the Indian Council Fire, serving as its executive secretary for more than forty years. She also published and edited *The Amerindian.* Gridley's writings include *The Story of Pocahontas, Contemporary American Indian Leaders, Maria Tallchief,* and *American Indian Women.* Obituaries and other sources: *Who Was Who in America,* 6th edition, Marquis, 1976.

* * *

GRIFFIN, Emilie Russell Dietrich 1936-

PERSONAL: Born July 22, 1936, in New Orleans, La.; daughter of Norman Edward and Helen (Russell) Dietrich; married Henry William Griffin, August 31, 1963; children: Lucy Adelaide, Henry Francis, Sarah Jeannette. *Education:*

Tulane University, B.A., 1957. *Office:* Helen R. Dietrich, Inc., 333 St. Charles Ave., New Orleans, La. 70130.

CAREER: Fuller & Smith & Ross, Inc., New York City, advertising copywriter, 1959-62; Norman, Craig & Kummel, New York City, advertising copywriter, 1962-64; Compton Advertising, Inc., New York City, copywriter and copy group head, 1964-70, vice-president, 1968-70; creative marketing consultant and free-lance writer, 1970-74; Council of Better Business Bureaus, National Advertising Division, New York City, director of Children's Advertising Review Unit, 1974-77; Compton Advertising, Inc., vice-president and creative supervisor, 1977-80; Helen R. Dietrich, Inc., New Orleans, La., executive vice-president and director of marketing, 1980—. Film reviewer for National Catholic Office for Motion Pictures (now Division of Film and Broadcasting, U.S. Catholic Conference), 1963-69; panel co-chairman at Airlie House Conference on Telecommunications Policy, 1978; member of Forest Hills Roman Catholic pastoral care program and eucharistic ministry, 1978-80; consultant for Office of Pastoral Communications, Diocese of Brooklyn, 1980; testified before Federal Communications Commission and U.S. House of Representatives.

MEMBER: Daughters of the American Revolution, Louisiana Historical Society, New York C. S. Lewis Society, Phi Beta Kappa. *Awards, honors:* Seven awards from American Television Commercials Festival and one from Venice Film Festival, 1962, for Alcoa advertisements; American Television Commercials Festival named her "Ivory Bar" advertisement among the one hundred best-read advertisements of 1968; first prize from Louisiana Council for Music and the Performing Arts, 1971, for playscript, "The Only Begotten Son."

WRITINGS: (Contributor) Herbert S. Dordick, editor, *Proceedings of the Sixth Annual Telecommunications Policy Research Conference,* Lexington Books, 1978; (contributor) Edward Palmer and Aimee Dorr, editors, *Children and the Faces of Television,* Academic Press, 1980; *Turning: Reflections on the Experience of Conversion* (Catholic Book Club selection; Book-of-the-Month Club alternate selection), Doubleday, 1980. Contributor to *American Catholic Catalog.* Contributor to journals and magazines, including *Cross Currents, Journal of Advertising, Publishers Weekly,* and *CSL: The Bulletin of the New York C. S. Lewis Society.*

WORK IN PROGRESS: A volume on prayer.

* * *

GRIFFITH, Thomas Gwynfor 1926-
(Gwynfor Cilffriw)

PERSONAL: Born March 29, 1926, in Cilffriw, Wales; son of William Rhys and Mary Ann (Thomas) Griffith; married Rhiannon Howell (a medical practitioner), July 11, 1953 (died December 21, 1980); children: Nia Rhiannon, Sian Mererid, Megan Eleri. *Education:* Attended Queen's College, Oxford, B.Litt., 1944, M.A., 1948. *Religion:* Congregationalist. *Office:* Department of Italian Studies, Victoria University of Manchester, Manchester M13 9PL, England.

CAREER: University of Leeds, Leeds, England, lecturer in Italian, 1948-52; University of Dublin, Dublin, Ireland, lecturer, 1952-55, reader in Italian, 1955-58, fellow of Trinity College, 1955-58; Oxford University, Oxford, England, lecturer in Italian, 1958-65; fellow of St. Cross College, 1965; University of Hull, Hull, England, professor of Italian, 1966-71; Victoria University of Manchester, Manchester, England, professor of Italian language and literature, 1971—. Adju-

dicator for National Eisteddfod of Wales. *Member:* Society for Italian Studies of Great Britain (vice-chairman, 1971-74; chairman, 1974-79), Manchester Dante Society (chairman, 1971—), Gorsedd of Bards (honorary member). *Awards, honors:* Named Cavaliere Ufficiale, Ordine al Merito della Repubblica Italiana, 1974.

WRITINGS: Bandello's Fiction: An Examination of the Novelle, Basil Blackwell, 1955; *Avventure Linguistiche del Cinquecento* (title means "Linguistic Adventures of the Sixteenth Century"), Le Monnier, 1961; (editor and translator) Bruno Migliorini, *The Italian Language,* Faber, 1966; *Italian Writers and the Italian Language,* University of Hull, 1967; (editor with P.R.J. Hainsworth) *Petrarch: Selected Poems,* Manchester University Press, 1971.

In Welsh: (Editor and translator) *Boccaccio: Detholion o'r Decameron* (title means "Boccaccio: Selections from the Decameron"), University of Wales Press, 1951. Contributor to British, Italian, and Welsh periodicals (Welsh writing sometimes under pseudonym Gwynfor Cilffriw). Co-editor of *Italian Studies,* 1971—, senior editor, 1974—.

WORK IN PROGRESS: A study of the works of Giangiorgio Trissino.

SIDELIGHTS: Griffith wrote: "I am a native speaker of Welsh, educated through the medium of English; hence, my interest in minority languages and cultures. My special interests are Romance languages, Italian dialects, regional cultures of Italy, Welsh literature, and the literature of the Italian Renaissance."

* * *

GRIFFITHS, Percival Joseph 1899-

PERSONAL: Born January 15, 1899; son of J. T. Griffiths; married Kathleen Mary Wilkes; children: three sons. *Education:* Received B.Sc. and M.A. from Peterhouse, Cambridge. *Home:* St. Christopher, Abbots Dr., Wentworth, Virginia Water, Surrey, England.

CAREER: Associated with Indian Civil Service, 1922-37; member of Indian Legislative Assembly, 1937-47, leader of European group, 1946. Central organizer of National War Front in India; adviser to Indian Tea Association, 1937-47; publicity adviser to government of India. Company director. *Member:* India, Pakistan, and Burma Association (past president), Oriental Club, City of London Club, Bengal Club. *Awards, honors:* Companion of Order of the Indian Empire, 1943; knighted, 1947; knight commander of Order of the British Empire, 1963; fellow of London School of Oriental and African Studies, London, 1971.

WRITINGS: Better Towns: A Study of Urban Reconstruction in India, Kitabistan, 1945; *The British in India,* R. Hale, 1946; *The British Impact on India,* Macdonald & Co., 1952, Archon Books, 1965; *Modern India,* Praeger, 1957, 4th edition, 1965; *The Changing Face of Communism,* Bodley Head, 1961; *The Road to Freedom,* Ampersand, 1965; *The History of the Indian Tea Industry,* Humanities, 1967; *Empire Into Commonwealth,* International Publications Service, 1969; *To Guard My People: The History of the Indian Police,* Benn, 1971; *A Licence to Trade: The History of English Chartered Companies,* Benn, 1974; *A History of the Inchcape Group,* Inchcape, 1977. Contributor to magazines and newspapers.*

* * *

GRIMES, Johnnie Marie

PERSONAL: Born in Bellville, Tex.; married, 1947; children: one. *Education:* Southwestern University, A.B., 1927; Union

Theological Seminary, New York, N.Y., M.A., 1948; received M.A. from Columbia University. *Home:* 3314 Drexel Dr., Dallas, Tex. 75205.

CAREER: Southern Methodist University, Dallas, Tex., assistant to the president in research and planning, 1953-72; member of Texas State Board of Education, 1973—.

WRITINGS: (Editor) Willis M. Tate, *View and Interviews,* Southern Methodist University Press, 1978.*

*   *   *

GROMBACH, John V(alentin)   1901-

PERSONAL: Born January 2, 1901, in New Orleans, La.; son of Andre (a diplomat) and Marcelle (Valentin) Grombach; married Olga Alice Lohinecz, July 17, 1959. *Education:* U.S. Military Academy, B.S., 1923; State University of New York, C.E., 1929. *Politics:* Conservative Republican. *Religion:* Protestant. *Home:* 40 Park Ave., Newton, N.J. 07860. *Office:* 111 West 57th St., New York, N.Y. 10019.

CAREER: U.S. Army, police and prison officer at Governor's Island, N.Y., 1923-25, head coach of Second Corps football team, 1923-26, acting junior military attache in Paris, France, 1924, assistant provost marshal in Panama Canal Zone, 1926-28, liaison officer between War Department and film producers and technical advisers to theatre producers, leaving service as second lieutenant; president of Jean V. Grombach, Inc., 1929-41; U.S. Army, member of general staff of War Department, State Department, liaison to Federal Bureau of Investigation and Federal Communications Commission, 1942-46, leaving service as brigadier general; president of Universal Service Corp., 1947-75.

Radio sports commentator. Consultant to State Department, 1947-55. Adviser to Recreation Service, 1930-41. President of Industrial Reports, Inc., 1942-76; international business consultant. Secretary of International Amateur Boxing Federation, 1924-28; member of U.S. Olympic boxing team in Paris, France, 1924; member of U.S. international fencing teams in London, England, 1926, and Paris, 1937; member of U.S. Olympic Games Committee, 1956-68; secretary-general of International Fencing Federation, 1960-64. *Military service:* New York National Guard Reserve, 1956; became brigadier general.

MEMBER: New York Athletic Club, New York Fencers Club, Union Club (Panama), Army-Navy Club. *Awards, honors*—Military: Legion of Merit; New York State Conspicuous Service Cross. Other: Intercollegiate heavyweight boxing champion, 1922, army champion, 1924; won national and international fencing championships, 1924-40; National Open (Masters) Epee Champion, 1950.

WRITINGS: (With F. Laurent) *Touch Football,* Ronald Press, 1945; *The Saga of the Fist,* A. S. Barnes, 1947, 4th edition, 1979; *Olympic Cavalcade of Sports,* Ronald Press, 1952. Also author of *How to Box: The Olympic Guide,* 1956, 25th edition, 1980; and *The Saga of Sock.* Author of military intelligence manuals. Radio and film writer and producer. Contributor to magazines, including *Adventure, Argosy,* and *American Mercury.*

WORK IN PROGRESS: Ran Runnels, Panama Sheriff, completion expected in 1982.

SIDELIGHTS: Grombach told *CA:* "I am very much against planned socialization of amateur and Olympic sports and financial support by government taxpayers with personal economics."

GRONDONA, L(eo) St. Clare   1890-

PERSONAL: Born August 12, 1890, in Melbourne, Australia; son of Charles Henry (a merchant) and Margaret (Dineen) Grondona; married Peggy Adair Hyland, May 11, 1929 (died March 17, 1967); children: John (deceased), Peter. *Education:* Attended Xavier University, Melbourne. *Politics:* "Sometimes conservative, lately—no." *Religion:* Agnostic. *Home:* 6 Knightsbridge Court, Sloane St., London S.W.1, England.

CAREER: Worked as jackaroo, turns drover, stockrider, and junior overseer on a sheep and cattle station in Queensland, Australia, 1909-11; *The Age,* Melbourne, Australia, reporter, c. 1911-14; Federal Department of Repatriation, chief executive officer of New South Wales branch, c. 1919-1923; Imperial Economic Conference, London, England, staff member of Australian delegation, 1923; British Empire Exhibition, director of the Australian section, Wembley, 1924-25; Australian High Commissioner, London, consultant, beginning in 1925; Special Depressed Areas, England and Wales, district commissioner, 1934; Intercement (S.A.), Paris, France, economic consultant, 1937-39; economist, 1940—; writer, 1948—.

Reporter for newspapers and periodicals, including *Morning Post, Daily Telegraph, Financial Times, Manchester Guardian;* London representative for *Sydney Bulletin;* correspondent for Australian journals. Founder of Tudor Rose League of British Employment Providers, 1931. *Military service:* Australian Imperial Force, 1914; became lieutenant. British Army, 1940-48; served as commandant of No. 2 Combined Services Detailed Interrogation Centre and as commandant of Political Re-Education Centre for German War Prisoners; became lieutenant colonel. *Member:* Army and Navy Club, Naval and Military Club (Melbourne).

WRITINGS: The Romantic Story of Australia, introduction by Viscount Bruce, J. Marlow, Savage & Co., 1924; *The Kangaroo Keeps on Talking,* introduction by Stanley Baldwin, Victoria Publishing House, 1924; *Empire Stock-Taking,* Simpkin Marshall, 1930, abridged version published as *Empire Stock-Taking, 1932,* Haycock Press, 1932; *Britons in Partnership,* Lovat Dickson, 1932; *National Reserves for Safety and Stabilization,* Allen & Unwin, 1939; *Commonwealth Stocktaking,* preface by Bruce, Butterworths Publications, 1953; *Utilizing World Abundance,* Allen & Unwin, 1958.

Australia in the 1960's, preface by Robert Menzies, Anthony Blond, 1962, revised edition, 1964; *A Firm Foundation for Economy,* Anthony Blond, 1962; *A Built-In Basic-Economy Stabilizer,* Economic Research Council, 1972; *Economic Stability Is Attainable,* Hutchinson, 1975. Also author of *The Adventures of a Jackaroo,* 1910, and *Agricultural Reconstruction,* 1933.

SIDELIGHTS: The major economic problems of industrialized nations in the 1970's and 1980's, suggested Patrick Collins, an economist and writer for the *London Times,* are "inflation and recession arising from prolonged government deficit financing." According to Collins, these are the result of Keynesian economic theory, which has served as the foundation of this generation's economic policy.

Around 1940, before Keynesian economic policy was accepted, St. Clare Grondona proposed a theory for stabilizing the trade cycle and preventing deflation by reducing cyclical fluctuations of commodity prices. Grondona's theory, which is explained in *Economic Stability Is Attainable,* calls for the establishment of reserves, which means excess supplies, and for fixed "floor" prices. The government, Grondona decided, should establish a Price Stabilizing Corporation which, wrote Peter Jay, economics editor of the *London Times*, "declares for each durable essential basic commodity an initial index value related to the average price of that commodity over the past few years." This corporation controls commodity price and currency value fluctuations while breaking long-term trends in commodity prices. Under this system, the market forces dictate values, and there are no artificial controls on the free market or on output.

Initially, fixed "floor" prices were considered economically unfeasible because they were thought to distort the market and to require a financial commitment beyond most countries, and excess stocks were frightening. But Grondona's system overcame these problems. His "most important innovation," said Collins, "was an automatic price-adjustment process which would limit sharp fluctuations in commodity prices but would allow market forces to control the price range of each commodity. This innovation eliminates the danger of excessive accumulations of stocks (the bane of attempts to stabilize commodity prices within a *fixed* range.)" Collective bargaining, the other apparent red herring in Grondona's system, was not really detrimental to his proposal either, since, according to Jay, "collective bargaining can only inflate costs and prices if governments inject the necessary inflationary purchasing power into their economies. If they do this, then under the Grondona system commodity prices will steadily rise under the influence of rising world monetary demand, but with less fluctuations."

Grondona's policies received support as early as the 1940's. The British Government was urged to use the economist's theories to prevent a postwar depression. On October 15, 1940, the *London Times* expressed a preference for Grondona's theories over Keynes's and declared: "There could be no more effective reply to the Nazi gibes about pluto-democracy than to show by practical action of this kind that democracy is capable of reconciling the claims of individual and national liberty with those of economic security." It was not until the 1950's, when the postwar depression was forgotten, that the British Government decided to consider Grondona's policies, but by then they were no longer needed. In the fifties and sixties, Jay noted, industrial countries "were not yet really worried about the inflation and currency disorders which the combination of Keynesian fiscal policies and free collective bargaining were progressively injecting into the world economy." But, he submitted, "the 1970s have changed all that."

The seventies mark a bleak era in the world's economic history. As Collins observed, inflation runs rampant in industrial nations while recession grows. The search for a stable international monetary system has all but been foresaken, and confusion and panic loom. "Now that the Keynesian bubble has burst," Collins lamented, "and the trade cycle has returned with a vengeance, Grondona's ideas merit re-examination." He went on to suggest that "Grondona's policies would help to stimulate recovery by becoming a source of non-inflationary export demand on the economy." Jay applauded the economist's proposals, saying that they "could one and at the same time restore the initiative to Britain and set our own and the world's economy back on the path to stability and openness." Yet another, David Barran, a bank chairman and the former chairman of Shell Petroleum, concurred by commenting: "Having studied this book [*Economic Stability Is Attainable*] myself, I believe the implementation

of the system it describes would have an unprecedented stabilizing effect on international currency."

Grondona began formulating his commodity price theory in 1904 when his father died. Copper was worth £17 per ton when the family was settling the estate; eighteen months later it was worth £70 per ton, and that, explained Grondona, "started the suspicion; the analysis came later."

BIOGRAPHICAL/CRITICAL SOURCES: London Times, October 15, 1940, April 3, 1975, July 29, 1975, August 12, 1975, December 15, 1980, December 16, 1980; *Financial Times*, January 11, 1954.

*   *   *

GROSSINGER, Richard (Selig) 1944-

PERSONAL: Born November 3, 1944, in New York, N.Y.; son of Paul Leonard and Martha Washington (Rothkrug) Grossinger; married Lindy Downer Hough, June 21, 1966; children: Robin, Miranda. *Education:* Amherst College, B.A., 1966; University of Michigan, M.A., 1968, Ph.D., 1975. *Office:* North Atlantic Books, 635 Amador St., Richmond, Calif. 94805.

CAREER: University of Maine, Portland-Gorham, lecturer in anthropology and geography, 1970-72; North Atlantic Books, Richmond, Calif., founder and editor, 1973—. Member of faculty at Goddard College, 1972-77, and visiting member of faculty at Kent State University, 1973; research associate at University of California, Berkeley, 1978-79; gives prose readings. *Member:* Society for the Study of Native Arts and Sciences, Coordinating Council of Literary Magazines. *Awards, honors:* Grant from Vermont Council on the Arts, 1975; fellow of National Endowment for the Arts, 1976.

WRITINGS: Solar Journal: Oecological Sections, Black Sparrow Press, 1970; *Spaces Wild and Tame*, Mudra Books, 1971; *Book of the Earth and Sky*, Black Sparrow Press, 1971; *Mars: A Science-Fiction Vision*, North Atlantic Books, 1971; *The Continents*, Black Sparrow Press, 1973; *Early Field Notes From the All-American Revival Church*, North Atlantic Books, 1973; *Book of the Cranberry Islands*, Harper, 1974; *The Long Body of the Dream*, North Atlantic Books, 1974; *The Windy Passage From Nostalgia*, North Atlantic Books, 1974; *The Book of Being Born Again Into the World*, North Atlantic Books, 1974; *The Slag of Creation*, North Atlantic Books, 1974; *Martian Homecoming at the All-American Revival Church*, North Atlantic Books, 1974; *The Provinces*, North Atlantic Books, 1975; *The Unfinished Business of Dr. Hermes*, North Atlantic Books, 1976; (editor with Kevin Kerrane) *Baseball, I Gave You All the Best Years of My Life*, North Atlantic Books, 1977, 3rd edition, 1979; (editor) *Ecology and Consciousness*, North Atlantic Books, 1978; (editor) *Alchemy: Pre-Egyptian Legacy, Millenial Promise*, North Atlantic Books, 1979; *Planet Medicine: From Stone Age Shamanism to Post-Industrial Healing*, Doubleday, 1980; (with Kerrane) *Baseball Diamonds*, Doubleday, 1980; *The Night Sky*, Sierra Club Books, 1981. Founder and editor of *Io*, 1965—.

WORK IN PROGRESS: The Dream Work, publication expected in 1982.

SIDELIGHTS: Grossinger told *CA*: "I began writing autobiographical prose in high school. By the time I was a freshman in college, I was attempting fictional novels, much influenced by Faulkner and Lawrence. A faculty member there put me in touch with an editor at a New York publisher, and I worked with her for a year on an attempted novel called *The Moon* and another called *The Cloud*. About the middle of the time I was in college, I met the poet Robert Kelly, and he interested me in whole other genres of writing. I realized that the things I wanted to say were more apparent in the poetry tradition, so I wrote poetry for a year, but then ultimately went back to prose, and began writing it in my own style and genre.

"Over the years, I produced some fourteen experimental prose books (basically from 1966 through 1974), published initially by Black Sparrow Press, Mudra Books, and Harper & Row, and then later by myself after starting North Atlantic Books, to maintain the integrity of the text. After completing this intense process, which involved work virtually every day and a continuous attention to subjective data, I stopped writing for a couple of years, doing only occasional fragments and reviews. When I began again, in 1977, I decided to deal with the objective elements, and I have since been at work on a series of books, beginning with *Planet Medicine,* that deal with the origin and meaning of critical forms in our society and culture. The second, *The Night Sky,* is about the formation of an image of the creation in time and space. The third is about dreams, and the fourth will be about plants, animals, genetics, and life. These are prose narrative books, meant as literature (the same as novels in that sense), but without characters and without the standard fictional, or even nonfictional, sense of what constitutes a literary topic.

"Like many poets, I am primarily concerned with language, the source of meaning, and the complex interrelation of objective and subjective shapes. Like most prose writers, I am interested in narrative, exposition, and conventional use of sentences and paragraphs."

* * *

GRUBER, Helmut 1928-

PERSONAL: Born July 20, 1928, in Austria; married, 1957. *Education:* City College (now of City University of New York), B.S.S., 1950; Columbia University, M.A., 1951, Ph.D., 1962. *Office:* Department of Social Sciences, Polytechnic Institute of New York, 333 Jay St., Brooklyn, N.Y. 11201.

CAREER: Polytechnic Institute of New York, Brooklyn, began as instructor, 1957, became assistant professor, then associate professor, until 1965, professor of history, 1965—, head of department of social sciences, 1965-76. *Member:* American Historical Association.

WRITINGS: (Editor) *International Communism in the Era of Lenin: A Documentary History,* Cornell University Press, 1967; (editor) *Social Science Theory and Method: An Integrated Historical Introduction,* Volume I (with Eleanor Leacock, Louis Menashe, and I. L. Leeb): *Understanding, Perception, and Reality: A Book of Readings,* Volume II (with Leacock, Menashe, and Leeb): *What Are Laws?: Concepts and Reality,* Volume III (with Leacock, Menashe, and Leeb): *Unity, Diversity, and Levels of Integration,* Volume IV (with Leacock, Menashe, and Leeb): *Language, Understanding, and Misunderstanding,* Volume V (with Leacock, Menashe, and Leeb): *The Emergence of Social Science: Antiquity Through the Enlightenment,* Volume VI (with Leacock, Menashe, and Leeb): *Modern Social Science: The Analysis of Class in Relation to Political Power and Social Change,* Volume VII (with Leacock, Menashe, and Leeb): *Modern Social Science: Biology and Society—Society and Ideology as Levels of Integration,* Volume X (with Leacock, S. Millman, and M. Gettleman): *Theory, Data, and Analysis,* Department of Social Sciences, Polytechnic Institute of New York, 1967; *Soviet Russia Masters the Comintern: Inter-*

national Communism in the Era of Stalin's Ascendancy, Anchor Press, 1974; *The Temptation of Adam,* Everest House, 1979. Contributor to history journals.*

* * *

GRUNDBERG, Andy
See GRUNDBERG, John Andrew

* * *

GRUNDBERG, John Andrew 1947-
(Andy Grundberg)

PERSONAL: Born June 25, 1947, in Bryn Mawr, Pa.; son of Curtis A. and Jean (Billings) Grundberg; married wife, Jeanne, 1969 (marriage ended, 1980). *Education:* Cornell University, B.A., 1969; University of North Carolina, Greensboro, M.F.A., 1971. *Home:* 205 West End Ave., New York, N.Y. 10023. *Office:* ABC Leisure Magazines, 825 Seventh Ave., New York, N.Y. 10019.

CAREER: Hackensack Record, Hackensack, N.J., copy editor, 1972-74; ABC Leisure Magazines, New York, N.Y., picture editor of *Modern Photography,* 1974—. *Member:* Society for Photographic Education.

WRITINGS—Under name Andy Grundberg: *Sympathetic Explorations,* Plains Art Museum, 1978; (contributor) *The Camera Viewed,* two volumes, Dutton, 1979. Contributor of articles and photographs to magazines, including *Art in America* and *Afterimage.* Photography critic for *Soho News,* 1979—.

WORK IN PROGRESS: A critical history of photography since World War II.

SIDELIGHTS: Grundberg wrote: "I came to New York as a poet with an interest in photography, found work as a journalist, and through no fault of my own became a photography critic. I continue to write and to photograph in my own time.

* * *

GUARDO, Carol Joan 1939-

PERSONAL: Born April 12, 1939, in Hartford, Conn. *Education:* St. Joseph College, West Hartford, Conn., B.A., 1961; University of Detroit, M.A., 1963; University of Denver, Ph.D., 1966. *Office:* Office of the Dean, Utica College, Burrstone Rd., Utica, N.Y. 13502.

CAREER: Eastern Michigan University, Ypsilanti, assistant professor of psychology, 1966-68; University of Denver, Denver, Colo., assistant professor, 1968-71, became associate professor of psychology, 1971, counselor, 1968-72, and staff psychologist; associated with Drake University, Des Moines, Iowa; currently associated with Utica College, Utica, N.Y. *Member:* American Psychological Association, Society for Research in Child Development.

WRITINGS: (Editor) *The Adolescent as Individual: Issues and Insights,* Harper, 1975. Contributor to education and psychology journals.*

* * *

GUDJONSSON, Halldor Kiljan 1902-
(Halldor Laxness)

PERSONAL: Born April 23, 1902, in Reykjavik, Iceland; son of Gudjon Helgason (a road builder) and Sigridur Halldorsdottir; married Ingibjorg Einarsdottir, 1930 (marriage ended); married Audur Sveinsdottir, 1945; children: one son, two daughters. *Education:* Educated in Iceland. *Address:* P.O. Box 664, Reykjavik, Iceland.

CAREER: Writer. *Awards, honors:* Literature prize from International Peace Movement, 1953; Stalin Prize for literature, 1953; Nobel Prize for literature, 1955; Sonning Prize, 1969.

WRITINGS—All under pseudonym Halldor Laxness; in English translation: *Thu vinvidur hreini,* [Iceland], 1931, translation by F. H. Lyon published with *Fuglinn i fjorunni* (see below) as *Salka Valka: A Novel of Iceland,* Houghton, 1936, reprinted, Allen & Unwin, 1963; *Fuglinn i fjorunni,* [Iceland], 1932, translation by Lyon published with *Thu vinvidur hreini* as *Salka Valka: A Novel of Iceland* (see above); *Sjalfstaett folk I,* [Iceland], 1934, reprinted, Helgafell, 1961, translation by J. A. Thompson published with *Sjalfstaett folk II* (see below) as *Independent People: An Epic,* Allen & Unwin, 1945, Knopf, 1946, reprinted, Greenwood Press, 1974; *Sjalfstaett folk II,* [Iceland], 1935, reprinted, Helgafell, 1961, translation by Thompson published with *Sjalfstaett folk I* as *Independent People: An Epic* (see above); *Ljos heimsins,* [Iceland], 1937, translation by Magnus Magnusson published with *Holl sumarlandsins, Hus skaldsins,* and *Fegurd himinsins* (see below) as *World Light,* University of Wisconsin Press, 1969; *Holl sumarlandsins,* [Iceland], 1938, translation by Magnusson published in *World Light* (see above); *Hus skaldsins,* [Iceland], 1939, translation by Magnusson published in *World Light* (see above); *Fegurd himinsins,* [Iceland], 1940, translation by Magnusson published in *World Light* (see above).

Atomstodin, [Iceland], 1948, reprinted, Helgafell, 1961, translation by Magnusson published as *The Atom Station,* Methuen, 1961; *Gerpla,* [Iceland], 1952, translation by Katherine John published as *The Happy Warriors,* Methuen, 1958; *Brekkukotsannall,* Helgafell, 1957, translation by Magnusson published as *The Fish Can Sing,* Methuen, 1966, Crowell, 1967; *The Honor of the House,* translated from the original *Jomfruin goda og husid,* Helgafell, 1959; *Paradisarheimt,* Helgafell, 1960, translation by Magnusson published as *Paradise Reclaimed,* Crowell, 1962; *Kristnihald undir Jokli,* Helgafell, 1968, translation published as *Christianity at the Glacier,* Helgafell, 1972; *A Quire of Seven,* translated by Alan Boucher from the original Icelandic, Iceland Review, 1974.

Other writings; all published in Iceland: *Barn natturunnar* (title means "Child of Nature"), 1919, reprinted, Helgafell, 1964; *Nokkrar sogur* (title means "Several Stories"), 1923; *Undir Helgahnuk* (title means "Under Helgahnukur"), 1924, reprinted, Helgafell, 1967; *Katholsk vidhorf* (title means "A Catholic View"), 1925; *Vefarinn mikli fra Kasmir* (title means "The Great Weaver From Kashmir"), 1927, reprinted, Helgafell, 1957; *Althydubokin* (title means "The People's Book"), 1929; *Kvaedakver,* 1930, reprinted, Helgafell, 1956; *I Austurvegi* (title means "On the Eastern Road"), 1933; *Fotatak manna* (title means "Footsteps of Men"), 1933; *Straumrof* (title means "Short Circuit"), 1934; *Thordur gamli halti* (title means "Old Thordur the Lame"), 1935; *Dagleid a fjollum,* Helgafell, 1937; *Gerska aefintyrid* (title means "The Russian Adventure"), 1938.

Sjo toframenn (title means "Seven Magicians"), 1942; *Vettvangur dagsins,* 1942, reprinted, Helgafell, 1962; *Islandsklukkan* (first novel in trilogy; title means "The Bell of Iceland"), 1943; *Hid ljosa man* (second novel in trilogy; title means "The Fair Maiden"), 1944; *Sjalfsagdir hlutir* (title means "Things Taken for Granted"), 1946; *Eldur i Kaupinhafn* (third novel in trilogy; title means "Fire in Copen-

hagen"), 1946; *Reisubokarkorn* (title means "A Little Travel Book"), 1950; *Snaefridur Islandssol* (title means "Snaefridur, Iceland's Sun"), 1950; *Heiman eg for* (title means "I Went From Home"), 1952; *Silfurtunglid* (title means "The Silver Moon"), 1954; *Dagur i senn* (title means "A Day at a Time"), 1955; *Gjorningabok* (title means "Miscellany"), Helgafell, 1959.

Strompleikurinn (title means "The Chimney Game"), Helgafell, 1961; *Prjonastofan Solin,* Helgafell and Mal og menning, 1962; *Skaldatimi* (essays; title means "Poets' Time"), Helgafell, 1963; *Sjostafakverid,* Helgafell, 1964; *Upphaf mannudarstefnu* (title means "The Origins of Humanism"), Helgafell, 1965, *Dufnaveislan* (title means "The Dove Feast"), Helgafell, 1966; *Islendingaspjall,* Helgafell, 1967; *Vinlandspunktar,* Helgafell, 1969.

Innansveitarkronika (title means "A Local Chronicle"), Helgafell, 1970; *Ua,* Helgafell, 1970; *Yfirskygdir staoir* (title means "Overshadowed Places"), Helgafell, 1971; *Gudsgjafathula* (title means "A Narration of God's Gifts"), Helgafell, 1972; *Nordanstulkan,* Helgafell, 1972; *Pjodhatidarrolla* (title means "The Girl From the North"), Helgafell, 1974; *I tuninu heima* (autobiographical; title means "My Childhood Home"), Helgafell, 1975; *Ungur eg var* (autobiographical), Helgafell, 1976; *Seiseiju, mikil oskop,* Helgafell, 1977; *Sjomeistarasaga* (autobiographical; title means "The Story of the Seven Masters"), Helgafell, 1978; *Grikklandsarid* (autobiographical; title means "The Year in Greece"), Helgafell, 1980.

Translator of numerous works into Icelandic, including Ernest Hemingway's *Farewell to Arms* and Voltaire's *Candide.*

SIDELIGHTS: Although his writings are popular in his native Iceland as well as throughout Europe and the Soviet Union, Halldor Laxness remains relatively unknown in the United States. According to the author himself, this partial obscurity of his work is due to the Americans' lack of understanding of his wit and humor. To the Scandinavians, he is quick to point out, he is known as "The Humorist of the North," and in France he is affectionately referred to as "The Nordic Voltaire." He is at a loss to explain the "apparent lack of interest" in his writings exhibited by the American public. Of his more than fifty books, less than fifteen have been translated into English. And the novel *Vefarinn mikli fra Kasmir* ("The Great Weaver From Kashmir"), held by some to be his masterwork, is conspicuously absent from this list. Laxness reports, however, that he "constantly [gets] letters from English readers who say how much they have enjoyed the book. The reason, I think, is that the novel is listed in my bibliography by its English title. I find it all very weird."

Laxness has led an almost nomadic life. He journeyed to Denmark and worked as a journalist, lived in a monastery in the Duchy of Luxembourg where he was converted to Catholicism, studied with the Jesuits in London, and embraced socialism while visiting North America. His writings, however, are firmly grounded in the people and traditions of Iceland. *Independent People,* for example, one of his best-loved works, is the story of a peasant who struggles for twenty years to gain enough funds to purchase a farm of his own, only to find he must struggle just as hard in order to keep it. "Bitter and somber as the story is," noted reviewer Bruce Lancaster, "there is a rare beauty in its telling, a beauty as surprising as the authentic strain of poetry that lies in the shoving, battering Icelander." Ernestine Evans of the *Weekly Book Review* also praised the work: "The book is bold and forward-looking, melodramatic yet pensive, full of wry statements and sneers, and the harmony is dependent upon discordance." Roger Butterfield, moreover, summarized that *Independent People* is "a hard but truly great novel, which goes far to explain an entire nation."

BIOGRAPHICAL/CRITICAL SOURCES: Saturday Review of Literature, July 27, 1946; *New York Times,* July 28, 1946, February 23, 1971; *Weekly Book Review,* July 28, 1946; *New Yorker,* August 17, 1946; *Atlantic Monthly,* September, 1946; *New Republic,* September 23, 1946; *Books,* January, 1970; *Books Abroad,* spring, 1970, winter, 1971; Peter Hallberg, *Halldor Laxness,* Twayne, 1971; *Scandinavica,* Volume 2, No. 1, 1972.

* * *

GUIRDHAM, Arthur 1905-
(Francis Eaglesfield)

PERSONAL: Born March 9, 1905, in Workington, England; son of Arthur (a steel technologist) and Emma (Scoon) Guirdham; married Mary Lacy Addison, September 29, 1934; children: Ingrid Guirdham Marsden, Tessa Guirdham Gowan, John Quentin. *Education:* Attended Keble College, Oxford, 1927, and Charing Cross Hospital, 1929. *Politics:* "Anti-socialist/anti-communist." *Religion:* Anglican. *Home:* 146 High St., Bathford, Bath, England.

CAREER: Assistant medical officer at Royal Earlswood Institution, 1929-30; assistant medical officer at Brentwood Mental Hospital, 1931-35; private practice of psychiatry in Bath, England, 1935-73; writer, 1968—. Medical superintendent at Bailbrook House (psychiatric hospital), 1935-69; Child Guidance Clinic, Bath, consultant psychiatrist, 1938-73; National Health Service, Bath Clinical Area, Bath, senior consulting psychiatrist, 1948-68. *Military service:* British Army, Royal Army Medical Corps, 1930-31; became lieutenant. *Member:* Society of Authors. *Awards, honors:* Llewellyn Prize and Clerical Gold Medal from Charing Cross Hospital, 1929; Saville Prize from West End Hospital for Nervous Diseases, 1936, for monograph on epilepsy; Bronze Medal from Royal Medico-Psychological Association for research on Rorschach Test.

WRITINGS: Disease and the Social System, Allen & Unwin, 1942; *A Theory of Disease,* Allen & Unwin, 1957; *Christ and Freud,* Allen & Unwin, 1959; *Man: Divine or Social,* Vincent Stuart, 1960; *Cosmic Factors in Disease,* Duckworth, 1963; *The Nature of Healing,* Allen & Unwin, 1964; *The Cathars and Reincarnation,* Neville Spearman, 1970, Quest Books, 1978; *Obsession,* Neville Spearman, 1972; *A Foot in Both Worlds,* Neville Spearman, 1973; *We Are One Another,* Neville Spearman, 1974; *The Lake and the Castle,* Neville Spearman, 1976; *The Great Heresy,* Neville Spearman, 1977; *The Psyche in Medicine,* Neville Spearman, 1978; *The Island,* Neville Spearman, 1980; *Paradise Found,* Turnstone Press, 1980; *The Psychic Basis of Psychiatry,* Turnstone Press, 1981.

Novels: *The Lights Were Going Out,* Quality Press, 1944; *These Paid,* Quality Press, 1946; *I a Stranger,* Quality Press, 1949; *The Gibbet and the Cross,* Neville Spearman, 1971.

Under pseudonym Francis Eaglesfield: *Silent Union,* Stuart & Watkins, 1966.

Contributor to magazines.

WORK IN PROGRESS: A novel that introduces a new concept of medicine.

SIDELIGHTS: Guirdham's books have been translated into Spanish, Italian, French, Swedish, and Japanese.

He wrote: "My main interest is the influence of parapsychology, not only on psychiatry, but on life as a whole. I write books on reincarnation and books involving my special attitude to medicine, such as *A Theory of Disease* and *The Psyche in Medicine.* I am now engaged in writing novels because I think that some of my views on current life and the permissive society are best expressed in art form rather than written as directly informative books."

BIOGRAPHICAL/CRITICAL SOURCES: Colin Wilson, *Strange Powers,* Random House, 1973.

* * *

GUISINGER, Stephen Edward 1941-

PERSONAL: Born January 14, 1941, in Kansas City, Kan.; married, 1965; children: two. *Education:* Yale University, B.A., 1963; Harvard University, M.P.A., 1965, Ph.D., 1970. *Office:* Department of Economics, Southern Methodist University, Dallas, Tex. 75222.

CAREER: Southern Methodist University, Dallas, Tex., assistant professor, 1970-73, associate professor of economics, 1973—. Consultant to International Finance Corp. and International Bank for Reconstruction and Development. *Member:* American Economic Association, Society for International Development.

WRITINGS: (Co-author) *Evaluation of MDTA Training in Correctional Institutions,* Volume II, Abt Associates, 1969; (with Daniel M. Schydlowsky) *The Empirical Relationship Between Nominal and Effective Rates of Protection,* [Cambridge, Mass.], 1971; *Protection in Twelve IFC Projects,* International Finance Corp., 1971; (contributor) *The Structure of Protection in Developing Countries,* Johns Hopkins Press, 1971; (contributor) *Effective Tariff Protection,* Unipub, 1971; (editor) *Trade and Investment Policies in the Americas,* Southern Methodist University Press, 1973; *Private Enterprise and the New Global Economic Challenge,* Bobbs-Merrill, 1979. Contributor to economic journals.*

* * *

GUNNELL, Bryn 1933-

PERSONAL: Born in October, 1933, in England; son of Bernard (an architect) and Dora (Fathers) Gunnell; married Louise Orsini (a teacher); children: Yanni B. *Education:* Attended University of Southampton, 1953; University of London, B.A., 1961, M.A., 1969; Ecole Superieure d'Interpretes et de Traducteurs, Diploma, 1963. *Home:* 66 rue de la Fontaine, 92 Bagneux, France.

CAREER: Worked at a private language school in Madrid, Spain, 1955-57; teacher at schools in France, 1958-61; Karnatak University, Dharwar, India, lecturer in English, 1964-66; British Institute, Paris, France, lecturer in English language and literature, 1966—. Lecturer at University of London.

WRITINGS: Calabrian Summer (travel book), Hart-Davis, 1965, Rand McNally, 1966; *The Cashew-Nut Girl and Other Stories of India,* Elek, 1974. Contributor to magazines, including *London, Cornhill, Stand, Good Housekeeping, Malahat Review, Vole,* and *Contemporary Review.* Translator of English edition of *Le Monde,* 1966-68.

WORK IN PROGRESS: A Shadow Round the Day; T. F. Powys: The Maker, a critical study; a collection of short stories; "Autumn Revels," a play; "An Overflowing Emptiness," a prose poem.

SIDELIGHTS: Bryn Gunnell told *CA:* "I married a French girl of Italian origin and have settled down here in France. I am very fond of the French countryside, particularly Sologne and the Cevennes, but in any case the countryside is really my prevailing passion. I frequently return to Britain and could be called a nostalgic exile. Every year we go hiking, always in out-of-the-way places (Iceland, Lapland, Yugoslavia, Algeria), just with a rucksack and sleeping rough, and wherever we go I try to learn a little of the language to be able to make contact with people. I have hitchhiked from India to Europe.

"India was perhaps the greatest experience of my life, but I cannot say much about so vast a subject in a few lines: what I felt about the country at the time is to be found in my short story collection, *The Cashew-Nut Girl*.

"T. F. Powys has always fascinated me. I began to make notes on his work a few years ago, and these notes have now become a critical study. Powys needs to be pondered deeply—that's why so little has been written about him—and does not lend himself to the usual kind of dismal scholarship.

"To me writing is a way of recreating the world I see in the hope that other people will begin to use their eyes. It is an exhausting occupation but one that frees you completely from the naggings of society. Writing is its own reward, and I know it is virtually impossible to make a living out of it. In the last resort, of course, I think one writes the kind of book one would like to read. There is great satisfaction in looking at a page one has written that reads passably well: it's like looking at a patch of well-dug earth."

AVOCATIONAL INTERESTS: The countryside, walking, birdwatching, solitude, oil painting, Indian music.

*   *   *

GUNTHER, Richard (Paul) 1946-

PERSONAL: Born September 8, 1946, in Los Angeles, Calif.; son of Paul O. (an electricity company supervisor) and Agnes M. (a nurse; maiden name, Johnson) Gunther; married Linda Kahn (a physical therapist), December 20, 1980; children: Elizabeth Kahn. *Education:* University of California, Berkeley, B.A., 1968, M.A., 1971, Ph.D., 1977. *Home:* 148 Fallis Rd., Columbus, Ohio 43214. *Office:* Department of Political Science, Ohio State University, Columbus, Ohio 43210.

CAREER: Ohio State University, Columbus, assistant professor of political science, 1976—.

WRITINGS: Public Policy in a No-Party State: Spanish Planning and Budgeting in the Twilight of the Franquist Era, University of California Press, 1980; (contributor) J. Oltra, S. Proctor, and T. McCoy, editors, *Spain and the United States: A Panorama of Relations,* University Presses of Florida, 1981; (contributor) J. Crispin, E. Pupo Walker, and J. Cagiagao, editors, *Spain 1975-1980: The Conflicts and Achievements of Democracy,* Vanderbilt University Press, 1981. Contributor to political science journals.

WORK IN PROGRESS: A study of the re-emergence of a democratic party system in Spanish politics, publication expected in 1981; a study of negotiation processes in drafting a new Spanish constitution and autonomy statutes, 1981 or 1982; a study of regional nationalist movements in Spain, especially in the Catalan and Basque provinces, 1981.

SIDELIGHTS: Richard Gunther commented: "*Public Policy in a No-Party State* is a study of the consequences of Franco's authoritarian regime relevant to taxation and public expenditures in Spain. It was based upon nearly one hundred interviews with Spanish government officials involved in economic decision making under that regime.

"The forthcoming book on the new Spanish party system will be based upon survey data collected through over five thousand, four hundred interviews with Spanish citizens and 125 interviews with the highest-ranking leaders of Spain's six largest political parties. It will describe and analyze the process by which party organizations were founded or reestablished after the death of Franco, the parties' strategies for long-term institutional growth, and the short-term strategies and tactics employed in the 1979 parliamentary election campaign. It will also explore the response to these campaign strategies by the Spanish electorate as well as the differences between the party systems of the Basque region and Catalunya and that of the rest of Spain."

*   *   *

GUNZBURG, Nicholas de 1904-1981

OBITUARY NOTICE: Born in 1904 in Paris, France; died after a stroke, February 20, 1981, in New York, N.Y. Editor of style and fashion magazines, including *Town and Country, Harper's Bazaar,* and *Vogue.* Gunzburg was known as an expert on matters of fashion and etiquette. Obituaries and other sources: *World of Fashion: People, Places, Resources,* Bowker, 1976; *New York Times,* February 21, 1981.

*   *   *

GUSTAFSON, Alrik 1903-1970

OBITUARY NOTICE—See index for *CA* sketch: Born April 23, 1903, in Sioux City, Iowa; died March 24, 1970; buried in Minneapolis, Minn. Educator and author. An instructor in Scandinavian, English, and comparative literature, Gustafson wrote numerous books on European authors and writings. He also translated several works into Swedish from the original English. Among his writings are *Six Scandinavian Novelists, A History of Swedish Literature, A Bibliographical Guide to Swedish Literature,* and *A History of Modern Drama.* At the time of his death, Gustafson was working on books about Swedish authors August Strindberg and Paar Lagerkvist. Obituaries and other sources: *Publishers Weekly,* May 25, 1970; *Who Was Who in America,* 5th edition, Marquis, 1973.

*   *   *

GUTHRIE, William Keith Chambers 1906-1981

OBITUARY NOTICE—See index for *CA* sketch: Born August 1, 1906, in London, England; died May 17, 1981. Historian, scholar, educator, and author. Guthrie was a historian of Greek philosophy, holding positions at Cambridge University from 1932 until his retirement in 1973, except for four years of service with the British Intelligence Corps during World War II. He was a fellow and director of studies at Peterhouse College, Cambridge, until 1957, when he was elected master of Downing College. Guthrie was also Laurence Professor of Ancient Philosophy and remained in that post until his retirement. Guthrie's books on ancient Greek philosophy include *Orpheus and Greek Religion, The Greeks and Their Gods, Myth and Reason, Protagoras and Meno, Socrates and Plato,* and *A History of Greek Philosophy.* Obituaries and other sources: *London Times,* May 18, 1981.

*   *   *

GUTTING, Gary (Michael) 1942-

PERSONAL: Born April 11, 1942, in St. Louis, Mo.; married, 1965; children: two. *Education:* St. Louis University, B.A.,

1964, Ph.D., 1968. *Office:* Department of Philosophy, University of Notre Dame, Notre Dame, Ind. 46556.

CAREER: St. Louis University, St. Louis, Mo., instructor in philosophy, 1967-68; University of Notre Dame, Notre Dame, Ind., assistant professor, 1969-74, associate professor of philosophy, 1974—. *Member:* American Philosophical Association, Philosophy of Science Association. *Awards, honors:* Fulbright fellow at Catholic University of Louvain, 1968-69.

WRITINGS: (With Michael Loux) *The Synoptic Vision: The Philosophy of Wilfrid Sellars,* University of Notre Dame Press, 1977; (contributor) *The Philosophy of Wilfrid Sellars,* Reidl, 1978; (contributor) *Current Research in Philosophy of Science,* Philosophy of Science Association, 1978. Contributor to philosophy journals.*

H

HABERLER, Gottfried 1900-

PERSONAL: Born July 20, 1900, in Purkersdort, Austria; came to the United States in 1936, naturalized citizen, 1943; son of Franz and Francisca (Mosing) Haberler; married Friederike Kaan, 1931. Education: University of Vienna, Dr.Rer.Pol., 1923, LL.D., 1925. Home: 4108 48th St. N.W., Washington, D.C. 20016. Office: American Enterprise Institute for Public Policy Research, 1150 17th St. N.W., Washington, D.C. 20036.

CAREER: University of Vienna, Vienna, Austria, lecturer, 1928-34, professor of economics and statistics, 1934-36; Harvard University, Cambridge, Mass., professor of economics, 1936-57, Galen L. Stone Professor of International Trade, 1957-71, professor emeritus, 1971—; American Enterprise Institute for Public Policy Research, Washington, D.C., resident scholar, 1971—. Visiting lecturer at Harvard University, 1931-32; expert attached to financial section of League of Nations, 1934-36; member of staff of board of governors of Federal Reserve System, 1943-44; president of National Bureau of Economics, 1955; consultant to U.S. Department of the Treasury, 1961-79.

MEMBER: International Economic Association (president, 1950-51; honorary president, 1953—), American Economic Association (president, 1963), Royal Economic Society. Awards, honors: Rockefeller Foundation fellowship for University of London and universities in the United States, 1927-29; honorary degrees from University of St. Gallen, 1949, University of Saarland, 1967, and University of Innsbruck, 1970.

WRITINGS: Der Internationale Handel: Theorie der Weltwirtschaftlichen Zusanmenhaenge Sowie Darstellung und Analyse ober Aussenhandelspolitik, Verlag von Julius Springer, 1933, translation by Frederic Benham published as The Theory of International Trade With Its Applications to Commercial Policy, Macmillan, 1935; Prosperity and Depression (in English and French), League of Nations, 1937, 4th edition, Harvard University Press, 1958; Consumer Instalment Credit and Economic Fluctuations, National Bureau of Economic Research, 1942; Inflation: Its Causes and Cures, revised edition published as Inflation: Its Causes and Cures, With a New Look at Inflation in 1966, American Enterprise Institute for Public Policy Research, 1966; (with Thomas D. Willett) U.S. Balance-of-Payments Policies and International Monetary Reform: A Critical Analysis, American En-

terprise Institute for Public Policy Research, 1971; (with Willett) A Strategy for U.S. Balance of Payments Policy, American Enterprise Institute for Public Policy Research, 1971; Incomes Policy and Inflation: An Analysis of Basic Principles, American Enterprise Institute for Public Policy Research, 1971; (with Michael Parkin and Henry Smith) Inflation and the Unions, Institute of Economic Affairs, London, 1972; Economic Growth and Stability: An Analysis of Economic Change and Policies, Nash Publishing, 1974. Also author of A Survey of International Trade Theory, 1955.

Other writings: Derr Sinn der Indexxahlen: Eine Untersuchung ueber den pegriff des Presisnivoaus und die Methoden seiner Messung (title means "The Meaning of Price Index Numbers: The Concept of the Price Level and the Methods of Its Measurement"), Verlag von J.C.B. Mohr, 1927; (with Stephen Verosta) Liberale und Planwirtschaftliche Handelspolitik (title means "Liberal and Plausible Commercial Policy"), Junker und Dunnhaupt Verlag, 1934; Problemas de Conjuntura e de Politica Economica (title means "The Problem of the Business Cycle and Political Economy"), Fundacao Getulio Vargas, 1948.

SIDELIGHTS: Haberler's books have been translated into French, Japanese, Swedish, Spanish, and Greek.

*   *   *

HABERLY, Loyd 1896-1981

OBITUARY NOTICE: Born December 9, 1896, in Ellsworth, Iowa; died March 27, 1981, in Vero Beach, Fla. Educator, poet, and author of more than forty books. Although most of Haberly's books are volumes of poetry, he also wrote a biographical work, Pursuit of the Horizon: A Life of George Catlin, and a memoir, An American Bookbuilder in England and Wales: Reminiscences of the Seven Acres and Gregynog Presses. Obituaries and other sources: Directory of American Scholars, Volume I: History, 6th edition, Bowker, 1974; Who's Who in America, 38th edition, Marquis, 1974; New York Times, March 28, 1971.

*   *   *

HABERMAN, Shelby J(oel) 1947-

PERSONAL: Born May 4, 1947, in Cincinnati, Ohio; son of Jack Leon and Miriam Leah Haberman; married Elinor Penny Levine (a pediatrician), February 18, 1979; children: Shoshanah Zahavah. Education: Princeton University, A.B.,

1968; University of Chicago, Ph.D., 1970. *Home:* 2938 West Arthur, Chicago, Ill. 60645. *Office:* Department of Statistics, University of Chicago, 5734 South University, Chicago, Ill. 60637.

CAREER: University of Chicago, Chicago, Ill., assistant professor, 1970-75, associate professor of statistics, 1975—. *Member:* American Statistical Association (vice-president for workshops, 1974-75), Institute of Mathematical Statistics (fellow), Sigma Xi. *Awards, honors:* Guggenheim fellowship, 1977-78.

WRITINGS: The Analysis of Frequency Data, University of Chicago Press, 1974; *Analysis of Qualitative Data,* Academic Press, Volume I, 1978, Volume II, 1979. Associate editor of *Journal of the American Statistical Association.*

WORK IN PROGRESS: A book on maximum likelihood, publication expected in 1983.

*   *   *

HADLEY, Franklin
See WINTERBOTHAM, R(ussell) R(obert)

*   *   *

HAENTZSCHEL, Adolph T(heodore) 1881-1971

OBITUARY NOTICE—See index for *CA* sketch: Born December 24, 1881, in Addison, Ill.; died June 5, 1971. Educator, minister, and author. Haentzschel was a professor of classics before becoming the pastor of Calvary Lutheran University Church in Madison, Wisconsin. He became a professor emeritus at Valparaiso University, Valparaiso, Indiana, in 1957. His writings include *Learning to Know the Child, The Great Quest,* and *How About Christianity?* (Date of death provided by Valparaiso University.)

*   *   *

HAGER, Alice Rogers 1894-1969

OBITUARY NOTICE—See index for *CA* sketch: Born August 3, 1894, in Peoria, Ill.; died December 5, 1969, in Manassas, Va. Journalist, editor, and author, best known for her coverage of aviation news and her books on the growth of Brazil. Hager was an aviation writer for the *Washington Star* and *New York Times* before becoming a war correspondent and Washington editor for *Skyways.* She later served as public information and affairs officer for the U.S. government. Among her numerous books are *Wings Over the Americas, Frontier by Air: Brazil Takes the Skyroad, Brazil: Giant to the South, Washington Secretary,* and *Cathy Whitney: President's Daughter.* Obituaries and other sources: *Washington Post,* December 6, 1969.

*   *   *

HAGERTY, James C(ampbell) 1909-1981

OBITUARY NOTICE: Born May 9, 1909, in Plattsburg, N.Y.; died of a heart attack, April 11, 1981, in Bronxville, N.Y. Broadcasting executive and journalist. Hagerty became widely known following his appointment to the post of press secretary to President Dwight Eisenhower. Hagerty's reputation for efficiency and honesty earned him the respect of White House newsmen, who credited Hagerty with influencing Eisenhower to establish good relations with the press corps. Hagerty was responsible for inaugurating the practice of holding regular presidential press conferences before live television cameras. After leaving the White House in 1961, Hagerty was employed by the American Broadcasting Com-

pany as vice-president of news. He retired in 1975 following a stroke. Obituaries and other sources: *Current Biography,* Wilson, 1953; Patrick Anderson, *Presidents' Men,* Doubleday, 1968; *Who's Who in Public Relations (International),* 4th edition, PR Publishing, 1972; *Who's Who in America,* 40th edition, Marquis, 1978; *New York Times,* April 13, 1981; *Newsweek,* April 20, 1981; *Time,* April 27, 1981.

*   *   *

HAILPERIN, Herman 1899-1973

OBITUARY NOTICE—See index for *CA* sketch: Born April 6, 1899, in Newark, N.J.; died January 9, 1973. Rabbi, educator, and author. A lecturer on Jewish thought and history, Hailperin wrote several books, including *A Rabbi Teaches, Gentile Reactions to Jewish Ideals,* and *Rashi and the Christian Scholars.* Obituaries and other sources: *Who Was Who in America,* 5th edition, Marquis, 1973.

*   *   *

HAISLIP, Harvey (Shadle) 1889-1978

OBITUARY NOTICE—See index for *CA* sketch: Born July 12, 1889, in Fredericksburg, Va.; died September 3, 1978. Military officer and author, best known for his Academy Award-winning documentary film, "The Secret Land." After retiring as a captain from the U.S. Navy, Haislip tried his hand at writing screenplays, including "Navy Blue and Gold," "Flight Command," and "Guided Missile." "The Secret Land," about Richard Byrd's Deep Freeze expedition, won the 1941 Oscar for best full-length documentary of the year. Haislip also wrote several books, among which are *Sailor Named Jones, Sea Road to Yorktown,* and *Escape From Java.* (Date of death provided by Haislip's executor.)

*   *   *

HALAS, Celia (Mary) 1922-

PERSONAL: Born October 6, 1922, in Lenox, Iowa; daughter of Frank (a well driller) and Mary (a seamstress; maiden name, Fabritz) Schaub; married W. H. Mike Halas (a business owner and manager), August 17, 1946; children: Mary, Anthony, Therese. *Education:* Marquette University, Ph.B., 1948; Arizona State University, M.C., 1970, Ph.D., 1974. *Politics:* Democrat. *Religion:* Roman Catholic. *Home:* 5123 East McDonald Dr., Paradise Valley, Ariz. 85253. *Agent:* Sterling Lord Agency, Inc., 660 Madison Ave., New York, N.Y. 10021. *Office:* 4541 North Seventh St., Phoenix, Ariz. 85014.

CAREER: Studio Quilting Service, Chicago, Ill., designer, 1941-46; Quilting by Halas, Phoenix, Ariz., owner and designer, 1956-67; Arizona State University, Tempe, faculty associate of Department of Counseling Psychology, 1970-74; private practice of psychology in Phoenix, 1974—. *Member:* American Psychological Association, Arizona State Psychological Association, Charter One Hundred.

WRITINGS—All published by Macmillan: (With Roberta Matteson) *I've Done So Well, Why Do I Feel So Bad?,* 1978; *Why Can't a Woman Be More Like a Man?,* 1981; *For Women: The Garbage We Carry Around,* 1982. Contributor to journals in the behavioral sciences.

SIDELIGHTS: Celia Halas told *CA:* "I write books in order to interpret professional concepts for the general public. My concerns with women's psychological issues date from my school days. My doctoral dissertation dealt with the effect of early socialization experiences on the lives of mature women. Most of my professional work has grown out of this basic concern.''

* * *

HALE, Agnes Burke 1890-1981

OBITUARY NOTICE: Born November 23, 1890, in Morristown, N.J.; died May 23, 1981, in Portland, Me. Journalist and author of the novel *So Wise, So Young.* Hale also contributed short stories to popular magazines, including *New Yorker, Collier's Weekly,* and *Saturday Evening Post.* Before Hale turned to writing fiction, she had been employed as a social worker, a reporter for the *New York Evening Sun,* and an assistant editor for *McCalls.* Obituaries and other sources: *Who's Who of American Women,* Marquis, 1958; *Washington Post,* May 27, 1981.

* * *

HALL, Challis A(lva), Jr. 1917-1968

OBITUARY NOTICE—See index for *CA* sketch: Born September 1, 1917, in Kansas City, Kan.; died September 15, 1968. Educator and author. A professor of economics, Hall served as a consultant to the U.S. War Department and U.S. Treasury Department. He wrote *Effects of Taxation: Executive Compensation and Retirement Plans,* and *Fiscal Policy for Stable Growth.* (Date of death provided by Hall's business manager, Mary Y. Doody.)

* * *

HALL, Daniel George Edward 1891-1979

PERSONAL: Born November 17, 1891, in Offley, England; died; son of Daniel and Elinor Ann (Field) Hall; married Helen Eugenie Banks, 1919 (died, 1962); children: three sons (one deceased), two daughters. *Education:* University of London, B.A. (with first class honors), 1916, M.A., 1918, D.Litt., 1930. *Religion:* Congregationalist. *Home:* 4 Chiltern Rd., Hitchin, Hertfordshire SG4 9PL, England.

CAREER: University of London, King's College, London, England, assistant lecturer in history, 1916-17; associated with Officers' Training Corps in Berkhampstead, England, 1917-19; senior history master at private boys' grammar school in Worcester, England, 1919, and at school in Hampshire, England, 1919-21; University of Rangoon, Rangoon, Burma, professor of history, 1921-34; headmaster of private boys' school in Surrey, England, 1934-49; University of London, London School of Oriental and African Studies, London, England, professor of history of southeast Asia, 1949-59, professor emeritus, 1959—, fellow, 1959. Worked with Lena Ashwell Concert Parties, 1916-17. Temporary member of Legislative Council of Burma, 1923-24; corresponding member of Indian Historical Records Commission, 1925. Visiting lecturer at Johns Hopkins University at School of Advanced International Studies, 1955; visiting professor at Cornell University, 1959-60, 1963, 1966, 1967-69, 1970-71, and 1972, Syracuse University, summer, 1963, University of British Columbia, 1964-65, 1965-66, and 1967, Monash University, 1965, and University of Michigan, 1966. *Member:* Royal Historical Society (fellow), Royal Asiatic Society (fellow), Society of Authors. *Awards, honors:* Silver medal from Royal Society of Arts, 1944.

WRITINGS: Imperialism in Modern History, Six Lectures, Government Printer (Rangoon, Burma), 1923; *English Constitutional History,* Harrap, 1925; *Early English Intercourse With Burma, 1587-1743,* Longmans, Green, 1928, 2nd edition (bound with *The Tragedy of Negrais*), Frank Cass, 1968;

(editor and author of introduction and notes) *The Dalhousie-Phayre Correspondence, 1852-1856: The Correspondence of the Marquis of Dalhousie and Sir Arthur P. Phayre on the Relations Between Great Britain and Burma, With the Letters of Thomas Spears to Sir A. P. Phayre,* Oxford University Press, 1932; (with A. M. Druitt) *A High School British History, 1714-1930, for Burma, India, and the East,* Oxford University Press, 1935, revised edition, 1946; *A Brief Survey of English Constitutional History,* new revised edition, Harrap, 1939.

Europe and Burma: A Study of European Relations With Burma to the Annexation of Thibaw's Kingdom, 1866, Oxford University Press, 1945; *Burma,* Hutchinson, 1950, 3rd edition, 1960, reprinted, AMS Press, 1974; *A Handbook of Oriental History,* edited by C. H. Philips, Royal Historical Society, 1951; (editor and author of introduction and notes) Michael Symes, *Journal of His Second Embassy to the Court of Ava in 1802 and Other Related Documents,* Allen & Unwin, 1955; *A History of South-East Asia,* St. Martin's, 1955; (editor and contributor) *Historians of South East Asia,* Oxford University Press, Volume I, 1961, Volume II, 1962; *Henry Burney: A Political Biography,* Oxford University Press, 1974. Also author of *A Handbook to the League of Nations for India, Burma, and Ceylon,* with J. M. Sen, 1926, *Studies in Dutch Relations,* with Arakan, 1936, and *Dutch Trade With Burma in the Seventeenth Century,* 1939. Contributor to history journals and newspapers.

AVOCATIONAL INTERESTS: Music.

BIOGRAPHICAL/CRITICAL SOURCES: New England Quarterly, October, 1975; C. D. Cowan and O. W. Wolters, editors, *Southeast Asian History and Historiography: Essays Presented to D.G.E. Hall,* Cornell University Press, 1976.*

* * *

HALL, Luella J(emima) 1890-1973

OBITUARY NOTICE—See index for *CA* sketch: Born October 18, 1890, in Duluth, Minn.; died June 21, 1973; buried in Palo Alto, Calif. Educator and author. Hall was a social science instructor for more than forty years, holding teaching positions at junior and senior high schools and colleges. Her writings include *A History of the Formation of Counties in North Dakota* and *The United States and Morocco: 1776-1956.* Obituaries and other sources: *Who Was Who in America,* 6th edition, Marquis, 1976.

* * *

HALLER, Ellis M(etcalf) 1915-1981

OBITUARY NOTICE: Born March 20, 1915, in Carthage, N.Y.; died of a heart attack, April 7, 1981, in Orlando, Fla. Journalist. During Haller's forty-two years as a journalist he worked as a reporter, editor, bureau chief, and columnist. At the time of his death he was an assistant managing editor of *U.S. News and World Report.* Obituaries and other sources: *Who's Who in America,* 40th edition, Marquis, 1978; *Washington Post,* April 10, 1981.

* * *

HALLETT, Robin 1926-

PERSONAL: Born December 13, 1926, in Gaya, India; son of Sir Maurice (a civil servant) and Gladys (Veasey) Hallett; married Ingeborg Friedl, August 19, 1950; children: Elisabeth, Susan, Stephen. *Education:* New College, Oxford, M.A., 1950. *Home:* Tyte Brook House, Sandford St. Martin, Oxfordshire OX5 4AH, England.

CAREER: Norfolk Workers' Educational Association, Norfolk, England, extra-mural tutor in history, 1950-55; University of Ibadan, Ibadan, Nigeria, extra-mural tutor in history, 1956-59; British Council, London, England, assistant representative in Zanzibar and Tanganyika, 1959-61; free-lance writer, 1961-65; Oxford University, Oxford, England, research officer at Institute of Commonwealth Studies, 1965-71; University of Cape Town, Cape Town, South Africa, senior lecturer in history, 1972-78; lecturer and free-lance writer, 1978—. *Military service:* British Army, 1945-48.

WRITINGS: Records of the African Association, 1788-1831, Thomas Nelson, 1964; *The Penetration of Africa,* Routledge & Kegan Paul, 1965; *The Niger Journal of Richard and John Lander,* Routledge & Kegan Paul, 1965; *People and Progress in West Africa,* Pergamon, 1966; *Africa to 1875,* University of Michigan Press, 1971; *Africa Since 1875,* University of Michigan Press, 1974.

SIDELIGHTS: Robin Hallett told *CA:* "Scholarly historical works can be written only by those who enjoy either a substantial private income or a comfortable academic sinecure. For a brief period of my life I enjoyed such a sinecure and was able to write some lengthy historical works. Now I possess a modest private income that I supplement by writing articles on international affairs for small local newspapers in remote parts of the world. I find it a good discipline to have to write in order to make ends meet. Once one acquires the habit of writing regularly for several hours each day, everything that comes one's way—everything one sees, hears, reads, or thinks—becomes grist to one's mill.

"I appreciate the populist nature of writing for newspapers; what I write is likely to be read by several hundred people. When I wrote scholarly articles for academic journals, I knew that only a few dozen people, at the most, would ever bother to look at them. I have not got a proper pension, and the real value of my private income is steadily being eroded by inflation. I have no alternative but to go on writing till I drop; I find this an immensely cheering prospect."

*   *   *

HALLS, Geraldine (Mary) 1919-
(Charlotte Jay; G. S. Jay)

PERSONAL: Born December 17, 1919, in Adelaide, Australia; daughter of Hubert Melville (an eye, ear, nose, and throat physician) and Dorathea (van Doussa) Jay; married Albert James Halls (a specialist in Oriental art). *Education:* Attended University of Adelaide. *Politics:* "My own." *Religion:* "My own." *Home and office:* 21 Commercial Rd., Hyde Park, Adelaide, South Australia. *Agent:* Richard Simon, 32 College Cross, London N.1, England.

CAREER: Writer, 1951—. Worked as shorthand typist in Australia and England; Supreme Court, Port Moresby, Papua New Guinea, stenographer, 1942-50; Oriental antiques dealer in Somerset, England, and Adelaide, Australia. *Awards, honors:* Edgar Allan Poe Award from Mystery Writers of America, 1952, for *Beat Not the Bones.*

WRITINGS—All novels: The Silk Project, Heinemann, 1964; *The Cats of Benares,* Harper, 1967; *The Cobra Kite,* Constable, 1971; *The Last Summer of the Men Shortage,* Constable, 1976; *The Felling of Thawle,* Constable, 1979, published in the United States as *The Last Inheritor,* St. Martin's, 1980.

Under pseudonym Charlotte Jay, except as noted: *The Knife Is Feminine,* Collins, 1951; *Beat Not the Bones,* Harper, 1953; *The Yellow Turban,* Harper, 1955; *The Brink of Silence,* Harper, 1956 (published in England as *The Feast of the Dead,*

under name G. S. Jay, R. Hale, 1956); *The Stepfather,* Harper, 1958 (published in England as *The Man Who Walked Away,* Collins, 1958); *Arms for Adonis,* Collins, 1960, Harper, 1961; *A Hank of Hair,* Harper, 1964; *The Voice of the Crab,* Harper, 1974.

SIDELIGHTS: Geraldine Halls wrote: "In my books I have always aimed at economy: the most possible said in the fewest possible words. The books I have most admired have spaces in them where the reader's imagination can wander. The writer should not do all the work. The reader should be given the opportunity to cooperate. The best books make demands on the reader and extend the reader's understanding of life. I believe that a good novel should be built around a structure which, although strong and shapely, does not show, and that the writer should keep out of sight. The most tempting danger, for a writer, is self-indulgence."

*   *   *

HALSEY, George Dawson 1889-1970

OBITUARY NOTICE—See index for CA sketch: Born January 3, 1889, in Volusia, Fla.; died October, 1970. Businessman, educator, and author. Halsey was an employment and personnel manager for several department stores and a credit association in Ohio, Washington, D.C., New York, and South Carolina. In addition, he lectured in management at the University of South Carolina. Motivated by a desire to help others achieve success, Halsey wrote numerous books on business and management, including *How to Be a Leader, Selecting and Developing First-Line Supervisors,* and *How to Achieve Success and Happiness in Business.* (Date of death provided by wife, Mary Halsey.)

*   *   *

HAMILTON, Alex John 1939-

PERSONAL: Born November 5, 1939, in Bristol, England; married Stephanie Nettell; children: two sons. *Education:* Received B.A. from Oxford University. *Home:* 24 Weymouth St., London W1N 3FA, England. *Agent:* Rainer Heumann, Mohrbooks, Klosbachstrasse, 8030 Zurich, Switzerland.

CAREER: Writer, 1962—. Presenter of program, "The World of Books."

WRITINGS: As If She Were Mine (novel), New Authors, 1962; *Wild Track* (short stories), Hutchinson, 1963; *Town Parole* (novel), Hutchinson, 1964; *Beam of Malice: Fifteen Short, Dark Stories,* Hutchinson, 1966, McKay, 1967; *The Dead Needle* (novel), Hutchinson, 1969; *Flies on the Wall* (short stories), Hutchinson, 1972. Also author of children's books *Bad Boys* and *Pick of Puffin Post* and of nonfiction books *Along the Trans-Siberian Railway, Critical Introduction to Jorrocks,* and *The Autobiography of a Film Star.*

Editor: *If You Don't Watch Out,* McKay, 1965; *The Cold Embrace and Other Stories,* Transworld, 1966; *Splinters: A New Anthology of Modern Macabre Fiction,* Hutchinson, 1968, Walker & Co., 1969; *A Long Look at the Short Story: A List of Books,* National Book League, 1972; *Triangles: Original Stories,* Hutchinson, 1973; *Best Horror Stories Three,* Faber, 1972; (with Giles Gordon) *Factions,* M. Joseph, 1974; (with James Kelman and Tom Leonard) *Three Glasgow Writers: A Collection of Writing,* Molendinar Press, 1976. Also editor of *My Blood Ran Cold.*

Work represented in anthologies, including *The Midnight Ghost Book, The Bedside Book of Horror,* and *The Best Science Fiction of the Year 1973.*

Author of radio play, "The Searchlight." Writer of programs for British Broadcasting Corp. (BBC), including "Outlook," "Twenty-Four Hours," "Bookshelf," "The Paperback Programme," "The Book Programme," and "Infants' Nativity." Feature writer for *Guardian*, 1970—; radio critic for *Listener*, 1974—. Author of a column in *London Times*, 1967-70. Contributor to magazines, including *Folio, Scotsman, Harper's, Cosmopolitan, Puffin Post*, and *Penthouse*, and to newspapers. Editor of *Books and Bookmen*, 1966-67.

WORK IN PROGRESS: Do You Speak Hellish?, a novel for Hutchinson; *English People*, for Penguin; *Fattitudes*, for Transworld.

* * *

HAMILTON, James Robertson 1921-

PERSONAL: Born May 23, 1921, in Glasgow, Scotland; son of James Phillips (a dentist) and Millicent Wilhelmina (Gow) Hamilton; married Elaine Margaret Maddigan, December 23, 1953; children: Claire Margaret (Mrs. Ian Johnston), John Keith, Neil James. *Education:* University of Edinburgh, M.A. (with first class honors), 1948; Peterhouse, Cambridge, degree in classics (with first class honors), 1950. *Politics:* Conservative. *Religion:* Presbyterian. *Home:* 8 Glenveagh Dr., Waikowhai, Auckland 4, New Zealand.

CAREER: University of Hull, Hull, England, assistant lecturer in classics, 1950-51; University of Otago, Dunedin, New Zealand, lecturer, 1951-56, senior lecturer, 1956-63, reader in classics, 1963-70; University of Auckland, Auckland, New Zealand, associate professor of classics and ancient history, 1970—. *Military service:* British Army, Royal Artillery and Intelligence Corps, 1941-46; became sergeant. *Member:* Association of University Teachers (president, 1958), Classical Association of New Zealand (president, 1958, 1968, and 1976-78). *Awards, honors:* Commonwealth fellow, 1966.

WRITINGS: Plutarch Alexander: A Commentary, Oxford University Press, 1969, (editor) *The Campaigns of Alexander (Arrian),* Penguin, 1971; *Alexander the Great,* Hutchinson, 1973. Contributor to classical studies and history journals. Co-editor of *Prudentia.*

WORK IN PROGRESS: Alexander and the Romans; Plutarch's Political Writings.

SIDELIGHTS: Hamilton commented: "My writings have generally arisen from my teaching, and partly in reaction against Sir William Tarn's *Alexander the Great.* My main interests are historical and biographical."

* * *

HAMM, Charles Edward 1925-

PERSONAL: Born April 21, 1925, in Charlottesville, Va.; married, 1949; children: three. *Education:* University of Virginia, B.A., 1947; Princeton University, M.F.A., 1950, Ph.D., 1960. *Office:* Department of Music, Dartmouth College, Hanover, N.H. 03755.

CAREER: Cincinnati Conservatory of Music, Cincinnati, Ohio, instructor in music theory and music history, 1950-57; Tulane University, New Orleans, La., associate professor of composition and musicology at Newcomb College, 1959-63; University of Illinois, Urbana, professor of musicology, 1963-76; Dartmouth College, Hanover, N.H., professor of musicology and head of department, 1976—. Director of musicological archive for Renaissance manuscript studies, University of Illinois, 1963-74. *Member:* International Musicological Society, American Musicological Society (president), Italian Society Musical. *Awards, honors:* American

Council of Learned Societies grant-in-aid, 1961; Center for International Composition Studies research grant, Poland, 1966; Guggenheim fellowship, 1967-68; Fulbright research grant, Italy, 1967-68.

WRITINGS: A Chronology of the Works of Guillaume Dufay, Princeton University Press, 1964; *Opera,* Allyn & Bacon, 1966; (editor) Igor Fedorovich Stravinskii, *Petrushka,* Norton, 1967; (with Bruno Nettl and Ronald Byrnside) *Contemporary Music and Music Cultures,* Prentice-Hall, 1975; *Yesterdays: Popular Song in America,* Norton, 1979. Contributor of articles to music journals.

Composer of musical compositions, including "Sinfonia," 1954, "Canto," 1963, "Mobile for Piano and Tape," "Portrait of John Cage," "Round," and "Anyone Lived in a Pretty How Town;" also composer of six operas and several chamber, piano, and vocal works.

SIDELIGHTS: Hamm's book, *Yesterdays: Popular Song in America,* is a history of American song from its origins to the present. Robert Palmer of the *New York Times Book Review* conceded that Hamm "has amassed impressive documentation, and he spins an engaging, readable yarn," but contended that Hamm's definition of popular song is too narrow. Palmer also pointed out that Hamm neglects to consider the influence that African-American music and popular instrumental music such as ragtime have had on American song. He concluded that "while *Yesterdays* is an interesting and worthwhile book, it isn't a holistic history of American pop and shouldn't be taken as such."

BIOGRAPHICAL/CRITICAL SOURCES: Music Educators Journal, April, 1975; *Notes,* March, 1976; *New York Times Book Review,* November 11, 1979; *West Coast Review of Books,* January, 1980; *Best Sellers,* March, 1980.*

* * *

HAMMOND, Albert L(anphier) 1892-1970

OBITUARY NOTICE—See index for *CA* sketch: Born September 25, 1892, in Baltimore, Md.; died June 6, 1970. Educator and author. A professor emeritus of philosophy at Johns Hopkins University, Hammond wrote *Properties and Vagaries* and *Ideas About Substance.* (Date of death provided by associate, Stephen Barker.)

* * *

HAMMOND, Jane
See POLAND, Dorothy (Elizabeth Hayward)

* * *

HANCOCK, Carol Helen Brooks
See HANCOCK, Morgan

* * *

HANCOCK, Morgan 1941-
(Carol Helen Brooks Hancock)

PERSONAL: Born July 10, 1941, in Los Angeles, Calif.; daughter of John Howard and Carol G. (Henley) Brooks; married Roger Lester Edwards, August 22, 1959 (divorced December, 1964); married Taylor Hancock (a lawyer), March 29, 1969 (divorced April 17, 1980); children: (first marriage) Laura Anne; (second marriage) April. *Education:* Attended Los Angeles City College, 1959, and University of Florida, 1959-61; California State College, Dominguez Hills, M.B.A., 1977. *Politics:* Libertarian. *Religion:* Episcopalian/Scientologist. *Home and office:* 135 South Harper Ave., Los Angeles, Calif. 90048.

CAREER: Latta & Co. (public relations firm), Glendale, Calif., secretary, 1956-59; University of Florida, Gainesville, head secretary in field services, department of educational administration, 1959-60; Jim Hope Electric, Inc., Gainesville, assistant office manager and bookkeeper, 1960-64; University of Florida, executive secretary to supervisor of pathology department at Health Center, 1963; Lincoln Estates, Inc., Gainesville, office manager, 1963-65; Gallerie La Colline, Paris, France, director, 1965; Bolo Corp., Los Angeles, Calif., vice-president, 1966-69; vice-president of Bolo International Ltd., Nassau, Bahamas, 1968-69; Orangefair Mall, Fullerton, Calif., executive director, 1969-71; Greentree Distributors, Los Angeles, general partner, 1971; Feminist Book Club, Los Angeles, general partner, 1971-73; Greenberg, Bernhard, Weiss & Karma, Inc. (law firm), Los Angeles, manager, 1973-74; Charles Burke Associates, Los Angeles, business manager, 1974-75; U.S. Life Savings and Loan Association, Los Angeles, assistant corporate secretary, 1975-76; Snyder Heathcote, Inc./Shorthand Reporting Corp., Los Angeles, operations manager, 1976-77; affirmative action consultant and business methods analyst in Los Angeles, 1977—. Owner and managing director of Morgan Marketing, Computer Reference Guide, and Star-Rated Satellite Services, 1981—. Member of board of directors of Bo-Lomb South, Inc. and Bo-Lomb West, Inc., 1968-72.

MEMBER: National Women's Political Caucus (co-founder of southern California section), National Organization for Women, American Economic Council, Safe Environment Fund, Silence Speaks, Inc.

WRITINGS: (Under name Carol Helen Brooks Hancock; with husband, Taylor Hancock) *Only a Damn Fool: The Pacific Voyage of the Dagny Taggert*, McKay, 1977.

WORK IN PROGRESS: Fools in Paradise: The Continuing Pacific Voyage of the Dagny Taggert, with T. Hancock, publication expected in 1981.

*   *   *

HANDL, Irene 1902-

PERSONAL: Born December 26, 1902, in London, England; daughter of Frederick (a banker) and Marie (Schuepp) Handl. *Education:* Attended girls' high school in London, England. *Home:* 31 Viscount Court, 1 Pembridge Villas, London W2 4XA, England. *Agent:* Curtis Brown Group Ltd., 1 Craven Hill, London W2 3EP, England.

CAREER: Actress on stage, radio, and television and in films, 1928—. *Member:* British Actors' Equity Association. *Awards, honors:* Pye Female Comedy Award, 1980, for portrayal of Mrs. Perry in "Maggie and Her."

WRITINGS: The Sioux (novel), New American Library, 1965, reprinted as *The Green and Purple Dream*, Mayflower Books, 1973; *The Gold Tip Pfitzer* (novel), Allen Lane, 1973. Writer for radio.

SIDELIGHTS: Irene Handl commented: "I write, when I have time, because I love it. Acting takes precedence. Novels are my real talent, I think. I never research. The process goes on all the time subconsciously and suddenly bursts out. I do very little revision. Of my two books *The Sioux* is probably more exciting, but *The Gold Tip Pfitzer* is better written. My comment for both: they may be good, bad, or indifferent as literary works, but they are unique."

HANKEY, Cyril Patrick 1886-1973

OBITUARY NOTICE—See index for *CA* sketch: Born March 17, 1886, in Folkestone, England; died December, 1973, in Dorchester, England. Clergyman and author. A vicar at several parishes in England, Hankey wrote *Lives of the Serbian Saints, A Confession of My Faith,* and *Signposts on the Christian Way.* (Date of death provided by M. S. Carey, dean of Ely Cathedral.)

*   *   *

HANSON, Howard (Harold) 1896-1981

OBITUARY NOTICE: Born October 28, 1896, in Wahoo, Neb.; died February 26, 1981, in Rochester, N.Y. Educator, conductor, and composer of more than forty-five musical compositions. Hanson's major works include the opera "Merry Mount" and his "Symphony No. 4," winner of a Pulitzer Prize in 1944. Hanson inaugurated a variety of innovative programs at the Eastman School of Music of the University of Rochester during the forty years that he served as its director. Most notable is the Festival of American Music, featuring the Eastman-Rochester Symphony Orchestra performing the compositions of young American composers. As a result of these festivals, Hanson became the most influential man in American music. A *New York Times* reporter observed that "nearly every American composer after World War I was in Hanson's debt to some degree." Hanson was also well known as a conductor and made guest appearances with numerous orchestras throughout the United States and abroad, including the New York Philharmonic-Symphony, the Boston Symphony, and the Rome Symphony Orchestra. Obituaries and other sources: *Current Biography,* Wilson, 1966; *Music Journal,* July, 1972; *Baker's Biographical Dictionary of Musicians,* 6th edition, Schirmer Books, 1978; *Who's Who in America,* 41st edition, Marquis, 1980; *New York Times,* February 28, 1981; *Newsweek,* March 9, 1981.

*   *   *

HANSON, Philip 1936-

PERSONAL: Born December 16, 1936, in London, England; son of Eric Hugh (a bank executive) and Doris (a hairdresser; maiden name, Ward) Hanson; married Evelyn Rogers (a medical administrator), October 22, 1960; children: Paul Edward, Nicholas James. *Education:* Cambridge University, B.A., 1960; University of Birmingham, Ph.D., 1971. *Politics:* "Undecided." *Religion:* "Undecided." *Office:* Centre for Russian and East European Studies, University of Birmingham, Birmingham 15, England.

CAREER: British Treasury, London, England, economic assistant, 1960-61; University of Exeter, Exeter, England, lecturer in economics, 1961-67; University of Michigan, Ann Arbor, visiting lecturer in economics, 1967-68; University of Birmingham, Birmingham, England, lecturer, 1968-73, senior lecturer, 1973-80, reader in Soviet economics, 1980—. Visiting professor at University of Michigan, 1977. First secretary of British embassy in Moscow, Soviet Union, 1971; senior research officer at Foreign and Commonwealth Office, 1971-72; consultant to Economist Intelligence Unit. *Military service:* British Army, 1955-57; became sergeant. *Member:* British National Association for Soviet and East European Studies, Birmingham Jazz Society.

WRITINGS: The Wage-Packet: How the Economy Works, Anthony Blond, 1967; *The Consumer in the Soviet Economy,* Macmillan, 1968; *Advertising and Socialism,* Macmillan, 1974; *U.S.S.R.: The Foreign Trade Implications of the 1976-80 Plan,* Economist Intelligence Unit, 1976; *Trade and Technology in Soviet-Western Relations,* Macmillan, 1981; (editor with Karen Dawisha) *Soviet and East European Dilemmas,* Heinemann, 1981. Member of editorial board of "Soviet and East European Studies" (a monograph series), Cambridge University Press, 1973-77. Contributor to journals, including *Political Quarterly, Soviet Studies, International Affairs, Quarterly Economic Review of the U.S.S.R., Jazz Monthly,* and *Jazz Journal.*

WORK IN PROGRESS: Analysis of current Soviet economic developments.

SIDELIGHTS: Hanson commented: "I have a long-standing interest in socialist ideas and economics, but my interest in jazz is more passionate." *Avocational interests:* Playing and watching cricket.

*   *   *

HARBURG, E(dgar) Y(ipsel) 1896-1981
(Yip Harburg)

OBITUARY NOTICE—See index for *CA* sketch: Born April 8, 1896, in New York, N.Y.; died in an automobile accident, March 5, 1981, in Los Angeles, Calif. Lyricist and author best known for his Academy Award-winning song "Over the Rainbow." Harburg began songwriting after his electric appliance business failed at the start of the Great Depression. His first hit song was "Brother, Can You Spare a Dime," written with composer Jay Gorney in 1932. Harburg continued to write lyrics for Hollywood musicals, producing such popular songs as "It's Only a Paper Moon," "April in Paris," and "Suddenly." He was teamed with composer Harold Arlen for the 1939 MGM classic "The Wizard of Oz" and wrote lyrics for its well-known songs, including "We're Off to See the Wizard," "Ding, Dong, the Witch is Dead," "If I Only Had a Brain," and "Over the Rainbow." Blacklisted in Hollywood following World War II because of his political views, Harburg turned to Broadway in 1947. Here he co-wrote the libretto and was lyricist for "Finian's Rainbow" and also worked on the Broadway show "Flahooley." Over the years Harburg worked with such musical legends as Jerome Kern, John Green, Vernon Duke, Burton Lane, Arthur Schwartz, and former college classmate Ira Gershwin. Harburg was co-author of the librettos for "Jamaica" and "The Happiest Girl in the World." He also wrote two books of poetry entitled *Rhymes for the Irreverent* and *At This Point in Rhyme: E. Y. Harburg's Poems.* Obituaries and other sources: *Chicago Tribune,* March 7, 1981; *New York Times,* March 7, 1981; *Washington Post,* March 7, 1981; *Newsweek,* March 16, 1981; *Time,* March 16, 1981.

*   *   *

HARBURG, Yip
See HARBURG, E(dgar) Y(ipsel)

*   *   *

HARMSEN, Dorothy B. Bahneman

PERSONAL: Born in Minneapolis, Minn.; daughter of Otto Paul and Celia (Holmblade) Bahneman; married William D. Harmsen, May 6, 1939; children: William Dorrington, Robert John, Michael Whittaker. *Education:* Attended University of Minnesota, 1932-33. *Home address:* Polo Club, 3131 East

Alameda St., Denver, Colo. 80209. *Office:* Jolly Rancher Candy Co., 5060 Ward Rd., Wheatridge, Colo. 80033.

CAREER: Dayton Co., Minneapolis, Minn., fashion model, 1934; Sell Elertson Photographers, Minneapolis, fashion model, 1940; Jolly Rancher Candy Co., Wheatridge, Colo., executive vice-president, 1949—. Vice-president of Sweetners, Inc., 1963—. Member of Western Heritage Center, Foothills Art Center, Phoenix Art Museum, Denver Art Museum, El Paso Art Museum, and St. Anthony Hospital Women's Auxiliary. *Member:* Gilpin County Art Association, Denver University Library Association. *Awards, honors:* Member of National Cowboy Hall of Fame; Wrangler Award from Western Heritage Center, 1972; award from Rounce and Coffin Club, 1970, for *Harmsen's Western Americana.*

WRITINGS: Harmsen's Western Americana: A Collection of One Hundred Western Paintings With Biographical Profiles of the Artists, Northland Press, 1971, 2nd edition, Harmsen Publishing, 1978; *American Western Art: A Collection of One Hundred Twenty-Five Western Paintings and Sculpture With Biographies of the Artists,* Harmsen Publishing, 1977. Author of *Sugar 'n' Spice,* 1961-69.*

*   *   *

HARPER, John C(arsten) 1924-

PERSONAL: Born July 17, 1924, in Winthrop, Mass.; son of Ralph M. Harper (a minister); married Barbara Quarles, 1953; children: Deborah Moore, Jeffrey Rhodes, Elizabeth Warren. *Education:* Harvard University, A.B., 1946; Episcopal Theological School, B.D., 1953; also attended Aspen Institute for Humanistic Studies, 1971, St. George's College, Jerusalem, Israel, 1973, and Episcopal Seminary of the Southwest, 1979. *Home:* 2303 Bancroft Pl. N.W., Washington, D.C. 20008. *Office:* St. John's Church, 1525 H St. N.W., Lafayette Sq., Washington, D.C. 20005.

CAREER: English teacher at private school in Watertown, Conn., 1946-50; ordained Episcopal minister, 1953; curate of Episcopal church in Providence, R.I., 1953-57; rector of Episcopal church in Bedford, N.Y., 1957-63; St. John's Church, Washington, D.C., rector, 1963—. Rector of Episcopal church in Foxboro, Mass., 1954-57; visiting preacher at Westminster Abbey, St. Martin-in-the-Fields, St. Paul's Cathedral, and American Cathedral in Paris. Member of board of directors or trustees of Woodrow Wilson House Council, International Student House, Protestant Episcopal Cathedral Foundation of the District of Columbia, St. John's Child Development Center, Traveler's Aid Society, St. Francis Burial and Counseling Society, Madeira School, St. George's College, Jerusalem, Israel, and North American Regional Committee for St. George's College. *Military service:* U.S. Navy, 1942-45. *Member:* Metropolitan Club, Century Association. *Awards, honors:* D.D. from George Washington University, 1966.

WRITINGS: Sunday: A Minister's Story, Little, Brown, 1974; *Fifty-Two Windows on Lafayette Square,* privately printed, 1978.

*   *   *

HARPER, John Dickson 1910-

PERSONAL: Born April 6, 1910, in Louisville, Tenn.; son of Lafayette Rodgers and Mary Alice (Collier) Harper; married Samma Lucille McCrary, October 21, 1937 (died November 13, 1979); children: Rodgers McCrary, John Dickson, Jr., Thomas William. *Education:* University of Tennessee, B.S.E.E., 1933. *Politics:* Republican. *Religion:*

Presbyterian. *Home:* 880 Old Hickory Rd., Pittsburgh, Pa. 15243. *Office:* 1501 Alcoa Building, Pittsburgh, Pa. 15219.

CAREER: Aluminum Company of America, assistant district power manager, 1943-51, works manager in Rockdale, Tex., 1951-55, assistant general manager of smelting division in Pittsburgh, Pa., 1955-56, general manager, 1956-60, vice-president of smelting and fabrication, 1960-62, vice-president of production, 1962, executive vice-president, 1962-63, president, 1963-70, member of board of directors, 1962, chief executive officer, 1965-75, chairman of executive committee, 1966—, chairman of board of directors, 1970-75. Member of board of directors of U.S.-Korea Council, Communications Satellite Corp. (chairman), Mellon National Corp., Metropolitan Life Insurance Co., Goodyear Tire and Rubber Co., Proctor & Gamble Co. (chairman), National Alliance of Businessmen, AEA Investors, Crutcher Resources Corp., and Paribas North America. Member of public oversight board of American Institute of Certified Public Accountants; past chairman of International Primary Aluminum Institute (member of committee for economic development). Member of Business Advisory Council of Stanford University Graduate School, University of Tennessee Development Board, and President's Labor-Management Committee. Founding member of Rockefeller University Council. Member of national council of Boy Scouts of America (past president of Northeast Region). Trustee of Carnegie-Mellon University and Council for Latin America.

MEMBER: National Academy of Engineering, American Society of Mechanical Engineers (fellow), American Society for Metals (distinguished life member), Institute of Electrical and Electronics Engineers (fellow; life member), Aluminum Association (past president), Engineers' Society of Western Pennsylvania, Business Council (past vice-chairman), Tau Beta Pi, Eta Kappa Nu, Beta Gamma Sigma, Duquesne Club, Fox Chapel Club, St. Clair Club, Rolling Rock Club, Links Club, Sky Club, Metropolitan Club, International Club. *Awards, honors:* Knight's cross of Order of St. Olav; William Metcalf Award; Nathan W. Dougherty Award from University of Tennessee; Professional Engineers' Distinguished Service award from Pennsylvania Society of Professional Engineers, 1966; Engineers' Gold Medal from Pennsylvania Society, 1970; Gantt Memorial Medal; D.Eng. from Lehigh University, Maryville College, and Rensselaer Polytechnic Institute; LL.D. from University of Evansville; D.Sc. from Clarkson College; D. Commercial Science from Widener College.

WRITINGS: A View of the Corporate Role in Society, Carnegie-Melon University Press, 1977.

AVOCATIONAL INTERESTS: Hunting, golf.

* * *

HARPER, Kate
   See HARPER, Katherine E(rna)

* * *

HARPER, Katherine E(rna)   1946-
   (Kate Harper)

PERSONAL: Born December 7, 1946, in Oak Ridge, Tenn.; daughter of Stirling Hart (an architect) and Gertrude Hannah (Zdunek) Harper; divorced. *Education:* Hastings College, B.A., 1968. *Home address:* RD 2, Waterbury, Vt. 05676.

CAREER: Child care worker in Lincoln, Neb., 1969-70; homebound teacher in Scottsbluff, Neb., 1973; secretary, 1974-76; welfare case worker, 1976-77; librarian, 1977-80;

State of Vermont, Montpelier, training specialist, 1980—. Member of board of directors of Planned Parenthood of Vermont, 1975-78. *Member:* League of Vermont Writers.

WRITINGS: (Under name Kate Harper) *The Childfree Alternative,* Stephen Greene, 1980; *A Field Guide to ANFC,* Vermont Department of Social Welfare, 1980.

WORK IN PROGRESS: "A novel about a family, using material from 1890 to the present. Not strictly historical fiction, this book is about a father who died when his children were small and the children's attempt to come to terms with that death after they are grown up."

SIDELIGHTS: Harper commented: "Writing has always been my way of finding out what I'm thinking. Most of my writing has been for myself; my journals were my constant listeners during many years when I felt alone in the world. Being alone a great deal has probably shaped me, and my writing, more than any other single thing. I can enjoy the solitude of writing, but the best part of it for me is the sense of discovery, finding out what is happening by seeing it appear on the page in front of me.

"My concerns about the world are many. To me, the question of how we decide to use limited resources today and in the near future is the most pressing one. I am vitally interested in helping spread the word about the richness of simplicity. It is clear to me that some kinds of abundance can be a curse and that we need to be much more rational in our uses of technology than we have been in the past."

AVOCATIONAL INTERESTS: Taking long walks, the natural world, talking with good friends, gardening, writing letters, reading, baking bread.

* * *

HARR, Wilber C.   1908-1971

OBITUARY NOTICE—See index for *CA* sketch: Born in 1908 in Easton, Mo.; died November 29, 1971. Minister, educator, and author. Harr pastored at Evangelical United Brethren churches before becoming a professor at the Evangelical Theological Seminary in Naperville, Ill. He edited *Frontiers of the Christian Mission Since 1938: Essays in Honour of Kenneth Scott Latourette.* (Date of death provided by wife, Juanita Harr.)

* * *

HARRINGTON, Curtis   1928-

PERSONAL: Born September 17, 1928, in Los Angeles, Calif.; son of Raymond Stephen and Isabel (Dorum) Harrington. *Education:* University of Southern California, B.A., 1947; graduate study at University of California, Los Angeles, 1948-49. *Politics:* Democrat. *Religion:* Episcopalian. *Agent:* Eisenbach-Greene-Duchow, Inc., 760 North La Cienega Blvd., Los Angeles, Calif. 90069.

CAREER: Writer. Executive assistant with Jerry Wald Productions; associate producer with Twentieth Century-Fox, 1958-62. Producer of films, including "Hound Dog Man," American International, 1959, "Return to Peyton Place," American International, 1962, "The Stripper," Universal, 1963, and "What's the Matter With Helen?," United Artists, 1971; director of films, including "Queen of Blood," American International, 1966, "The Killing Kind," Universal, 1967, and "Who Slew Auntie Roo?," American International, 1971, and of television movies, "How Awful About Allan," 1970, "The Cat Creature," 1973, "The Dead Don't Die," 1974, and "Killer Bees," 1974. *Member:* Academy of

Motion Picture Arts and Sciences, Directors Guild of America, Count Dracula Society (member of board of directors).

WRITINGS: Josef Von Sternberg, Gordon Press, 1979.

Screenplays: "Fragment of Seeking," 1946; "Picnic," 1948; "On the Edge," 1949; "The Assignation," 1953; "The Wormwood Star," 1957; "Mardi Gras," Twentieth Century-Fox, 1958; "Night Tide," American International, 1963; "Voyage to a Prehistoric Planet," 1964; "The Four Elements" (documentary), U.S. Information Agency, 1965; (with George Edwards) "Games," Universal, 1968; "Ruby," Dimension, 1977; "Dog of Darkness," 1978.

BIOGRAPHICAL/CRITICAL SOURCES: Curtis Harrington: An American Film Institute Seminar on His Work, Microfilming Corp. of America, 1977.*

*   *   *

HARRIS, Julie 1925-

PERSONAL: Birth-given name Julia Ann Harris; born December 2, 1925, in Grosse Pointe Park, Mich.; daughter of William Picket (an investment banker) and Elsie (a nurse; maiden name, Smith) Harris; married Jay I. Julien (a lawyer and producer of motion pictures), August 16, 1946 (divorced July, 1954); married Manning Gurian (a stage manager), October 21, 1954 (divorced, 1967); married William Erwin Carroll (a writer), April 27, 1977; children: (second marriage) Peter Alston. *Education:* Attended Yale University, 1944-45, and New York Actors Studio, 1946-48. *Agent:* Ed Bondy, 151 El Camino Dr., Beverly Hills, Calif. 90210.

CAREER: Actress in stage productions, including "It's a Gift," 1945, "I Am a Camera," 1951, "Romeo and Juliet," 1960, "A Streetcar Named Desire," 1967, and "The Belle of Amherst," 1977; motion pictures, including "The Member of the Wedding," 1952, "East of Eden," 1955, "Reflections in a Golden Eye," 1967, and "The Hiding Place," 1974; and television productions, including "Wind From the South," 1955, "Pygmalion," 1962, and "Anastasia," 1967, and series, including "Tarzan," 1967, and "The Big Valley," 1968. Narrator of recordings of stories, including "Curious George," "The Diary of a Young Girl," and "Little House in the Big Woods." *Member:* Actors' Equity Association, American Guild of Variety Artists, Screen Actors Guild, Actor's Studio.

AWARDS, HONORS: Donaldson Award for best supporting actress, 1950, for "The Member of the Wedding"; Antoinette Perry Award from League of New York Theatres and Producers, award from New York Drama Critics Circle, and Donaldson Award, all for best actress, all 1951, all for "I Am a Camera"; nomination for Academy Award for best actress from Academy of Motion Picture Arts and Sciences, 1952, for "The Member of the Wedding"; Sylvania Award, 1955, for "Wind From the South"; Antoinette Perry Award for best actress, 1956, for "The Lark"; Emmy Award for best actress from Academy of Television Arts and Sciences, 1958, for "Little Moon of Alban," and 1961, for "Victoria Regina"; nomination for Antoinette Perry Award for best actress, 1966, for "Skyscraper"; Antoinette Perry Award for best actress, 1969, for "Forty Carats"; Drama Desk Award, Outer Circle Award, and Antoinette Perry Award for best actress, all 1973, all for "The Last of Mrs. Lincoln"; nomination for Antoinette Perry Award for best actress, 1974, for "The Au Pair Man"; honorary doctorate from Mount Holyoke College, 1976; Antoinette Perry Award for best actress, 1978, for "The Belle of Amherst"; and other awards and honors.

WRITINGS: (With Barry Tarshis) *Julie Harris Talks to Young Actors,* Lothrop, 1971.

SIDELIGHTS: With five Antoinette Perry (Tony) Awards to her credit, Harris is one of the most successful actresses of the American stage. She is best known for her portrayals of historical characters, including Joan of Arc, Mrs. Abraham Lincoln, and Emily Dickenson. "I've played glamorous roles, all kinds of different people," she told an interviewer. "That's the fun of acting anyway. You walk into a room, find this dress and you can be somebody else, anyone—beautiful, plain."

Among the most satisfying roles of her stage career was that of Mary Lincoln in "The Last of Mrs. Lincoln." Harris commented: "The part of Mrs. Lincoln was a rare experience because the audience was always so moved by the play. You know Mary Todd Lincoln wrote that when she met Abe Lincoln, 'He came toward me and I saw the look of God in his eyes.' To have that kind of greatness talked about on stage is important. There is humanity in it that is very intense."

Roles like that of Mrs. Lincoln are part of the greater value Harris finds in the theatre itself. "The theatre gives me a sense of identity with life, with the past and the future," she told Barbara Hoover of the *Detroit News.* "A playwright tells us what life can mean or does mean and the actor is part of this. A play doesn't have life until it's performed and when it is it becomes an experience that is lived out and that we share with the audience. It is capable of changing us."

AVOCATIONAL INTERESTS: Reading, tennis, cooking, gardening, knitting.

BIOGRAPHICAL/CRITICAL SOURCES—Books: Cecil Walter Hardy and Kenneth Tynan, *Persona Grata,* Putnam, 1954; Yousuf Karsh, *Portraits of Greatness,* Nelson, 1959; C. Isherwood, *Double Exposure,* Delacorte, 1966; Roy Newquist, *Showcase,* Morrow, 1966; *Biography News,* Volume I, number 8, 1974; David Shipman, *Great Movie Stars,* A & W Visual Library, 1976.

Periodicals: *Life,* January 23, 1950, December 24, 1951, April 7, 1952, February 15, 1954, April 14, 1958, January 19, 1959; *Coronet,* December, 1950; *Saturday Review,* December 22, 1951, December 3, 1955; *Theatre Arts,* July, 1952, March, 1953; *Collier's,* January 17, 1953; *Good Housekeeping,* April, 1953, May, 1973; *Vogue,* April 1, 1954, February 1, 1962; *New York Post Magazine,* August 7, 1955; *New York Times Magazine,* November 6, 1955, November 5, 1961; *Time,* November 28, 1955, December 3, 1965, May 9, 1977; *Newsweek,* November 28, 1955, October 30, 1961; *Scholastic,* March 15, 1956; *McCall's,* December, 1956; *Seventeen,* October, 1963; *Saturday Evening Post,* December 5, 1964; *New York Post,* October 21, 1972; *Detroit News,* June 30, 1974; *Cue,* February 17, 1975.*

*   *   *

HARRIS, Karen H(arriman) 1934-

PERSONAL: Born January 25, 1934, in Detroit, Mich.; daughter of Carl F. (in business) and Ruth (Herman) Harriman; married William Baird, June 5, 1954 (divorced June, 1964); married Louis Harris (an engineer), July 16, 1966; children: (first marriage) David, Bruce; (second marriage) Myra, Seth. *Education:* Wayne State University, B.A., 1957, M.Ed., 1964. *Home:* 5332 Magazine, New Orleans, La. 70115. *Office:* Department of Curriculum and Instruction, College of Education, University of New Orleans, Lakefront, New Orleans, La. 70122.

CAREER: Wayne State University, Detroit, Mich., administrative librarian, 1964-66; media librarian at public schools in New Orleans, La., 1967-70; University of New Orleans, New Orleans, assistant professor, 1970-76, associate professor of library science, 1976—. *Member:* American Library Association, American Association of School Librarians. *Awards, honors:* Named Harriet Dickson Reynolds Endowment Speaker by Houston Public Library, 1980.

WRITINGS—All with sister, Barbara Baskin: *The Special Child in the Library*, American Library Association, 1976; *Notes From a Different Drummer: The Handicapped Character in Juvenile Fiction*, Bowker, 1977; *Books for the Gifted Child*, Bowker, 1980; *The Mainstreamed Library*, American Library Association, 1981. Contributor to education, special education, and language journals.

WORK IN PROGRESS: A successor to *Notes From a Different Drummer*, with Baskin, publication by Bowker expected in 1982; a child's book on language play, with Baskin.

SIDELIGHTS: Karen Harris told *CA:* "I have loved books for as long as I can remember, so a career as a librarian seemed a natural, almost inevitable, choice. My sister and co-author, Barbara Baskin, a teacher of both handicapped and gifted children, has made me aware of the special needs of these youngsters. We discovered that our respective fields were almost mutually exclusive: special education teachers neither expected nor demanded library service and librarians rarely sought out or welcomed disabled youngsters. Working together we investigated what services were appropriate for these children and what adaptations libraries would need to make to supply them. The result was *The Special Child in the Library*. Our timing was fortuitous since the publication immediately preceded implementation of the national law requiring 'mainstreaming'—the integration of disabled children into regular classrooms whenever feasible. What we were proposing as proper policy had just been mandated by Congress.

"Between the legal necessity and actual implementation of the spirit as well as the letter of the law lay tremendous problems. One immediate result was that many handicapped children enjoyed greater academic opportunities. A tragic corollary was that social rejection, even ostracism, was common. Other youngsters too frequently regarded their new classmates as unacceptable companions. Barbara and I looked at the origins of attitudes toward disability and their manifestation in children's literature. Our research led to *Notes From a Different Drummer*, which assesses contemporary juvenile fiction in terms of its depiction of handicapped characters and recommends using books to reshape perceptions and foster sensitivity.

"The gift of a children's book addressed to young readers who need expertise in history, lexicography, mythology, geography, and classical literature in order to understand its contents focused our attention on gifted youth. We had recently finished some minor projects which necessitated the use of materials written for children with poor language skills and were aware that the market was flooded with such titles. We found far fewer contemporary books addressed to very intelligent, knowledgeable, and highly competent readers. The search for such books and the identification of qualities that make them suitable for gifted youngsters ended in the publication of *Books for the Gifted Child*.

"We are committed to revisions of our first two books, but after that several possibilities tempt us. Whatever we choose will keep us writing about books, children with special needs, and the means to bring them together."

HARRIS, Richard H. 1942-

PERSONAL: Born March 30, 1942, in New York, N.Y.; son of Richard H. (a foreman) and Helen (Walsh) Harris; married wife, Linda L., June 6, 1970 (separated). *Education:* Iona College, B.A., 1964; Columbia University, M.A., 1965, Ph.D., 1972. *Politics:* "Left." *Home:* 501 West 110th St., New York, N.Y. 10025. *Office:* WBAI-FM Radio, 505 Eighth Ave., New York, N.Y. 10018.

CAREER: WBAI-FM Radio, New York, N.Y., drama and literature director, 1977—. Adjunct assistant professor at York College of the City University of New York. *Awards, honors:* Woodrow Wilson fellowship, 1964-65; grant from New York State Council on the Arts, 1977-78.

WRITINGS: (Editor) *Gale Research Guide to Contemporary Drama in America and England, 1950-1970*, Gale, 1981.

SIDELIGHTS: Harris wrote: "My major activity is directing and producing radio dramas. I am director and producer for the 99.5% Perfect Players, a group which has done productions of Sartre's 'No Exit,' Brecht's 'Galileo,' and a comedy revue."

*   *   *

HARRIS, Ricky 1922-

PERSONAL: Born March 8, 1922, in Los Angeles, Calif.; daughter of Abraham (in sales) and Rose (Marder) Polim; married Robert E. Harris, June 6, 1952 (divorced, 1972); married Paul A. Piazzese (an interior designer), March 1, 1973; children: (first marriage) Hillary Ann, John Patrick. *Education:* University of California, Irvine, B.A. (cum laude), 1969, M.F.A., 1971. *Home and office address:* P.O. Box 2112, Newport Beach, Calif. 92663.

CAREER: Skater in Ice Follies, 1946-48, and in Sonja Henie Ice Show, 1949; ice skating teacher in Los Angeles, Calif., 1949-52; Los Angeles Dance Theater, Los Angeles, public relations director, 1960-61; Chapman College, Orange, Calif., professor of dance, 1972-74, professor with World Campus Afloat, 1972; Olympic Training Center, Squaw Valley, Calif., member of support staff, 1978-79; international stylist and choreographer at ice skating rinks and ballet studios, 1979—. Co-director of Children's Theatre Guild in Newport Beach, Calif., 1952-70; presenter of "Dancethnics Show" on cablevision, Newport Beach, 1970. *Military service:* Women's Army Corps, 1943-45; became staff sergeant. *Member:* International Professional Skating Union, Professional Skaters Guild of America, U.S. Figure Skating Association, Los Angeles Skating Club. *Awards, honors:* Grant from University of California, 1972.

WRITINGS: Choreography and Style for Ice Skaters, St. Martin's, 1980. Contributor to *Skating, Canadian Skater*, and *PSGA Newsletter*.

WORK IN PROGRESS: Busybody Exercises for Bodies Too Busy to Exercise, with daughter, Hillary Ann Harris, publication expected in 1982.

SIDELIGHTS: Ricky Harris wrote: "My primary motivation has always been the original approach. After years of experimentation, this resulted in new teaching concepts for competitive and professional skaters that helped to develop their artistic and athletic skills simultaneously.

"Besides teaching academic dance classes to skaters in ballet studios inside skating rinks, I indoctrinated into their schedules classes in drama techniques. This culminated in workshops for skaters that I conduct all over the world. I feel that skating is becoming more and more an artistic endeavor and that skaters must be trained as dancers and actors. I am the artistic coach of Scott Hamilton, the men's world figure skating champion.

"It is important to me that skaters become more knowledgeable about the choreographic process in order to help themselves develop original and individual styles. In the past, the skating professionals, who sometimes had ten to sixty students, were expected to do this, and overlapping in style occurred.

"I was inspired to conceive an academic approach to teaching skaters how they can develop movement styles that suited their individual bodies and needs. This resulted in *Choreography and Style for Ice Skaters*, so I could reach skaters throughout the world with these techniques. I am happy to note that just as many competitive roller skaters as ice skaters are using my book.

"I have an affinity for the fine arts and feel it is important to indoctrinate regular doses of it, not only in my life, but in the life of anyone studying to be a performing artist. I encourage skaters to visit museums and galleries and to attend concerts and the theatre.

"Recently I became interested in developing original approaches to exercise for people who feel they are too busy for it, and I also wanted to make exercise fun.

"Travel is important to me. It makes me realize how much there is to learn and see, and how exciting life is. I recently returned from the 1981 world's figure skating competition in Hartford, Connecticut. One of the most wonderful times in my life was the four months I spent on a ship with World Campus Afloat going through Africa, Asia, and the Orient. A safari, originating in East Africa, was one of the highlights of that trip. I love Paris and speak a smattering of French, but I intend to speak it fluently one day."

*   *   *

HARRISON, Mary
See FABBRI, Nancy Rash

*   *   *

HARROD, Roy Forbes   1900-1978

OBITUARY NOTICE—See index for *CA* sketch: Born February 13, 1900, in London, England; died March 8, 1978. Educator and author best known for his books on economics. A past president of the Royal Economic Society, Harrod wrote numerous books, including *Are These Hardships Necessary?*, *The Life of John Maynard Keynes*, *The International Monetary Fund*, *Economic Dynamics*, and *Sociology, Morals, and Mystery*. (Date of death provided by wife, Wilhelmine Harrod.)

*   *   *

HARROWE, Fiona
See HURD, Florence

*   *   *

HARSCH, Hilya
See JELLY, George Oliver

*   *   *

HART, Basil Henry Liddell
See LIDDELL HART, Basil Henry

HART, Kate
See KRAMER, Roberta

*   *   *

HARTLEY, Peter (Roy)   1933-

PERSONAL: Born June 17, 1933, in London, England; son of Laurence Walter Erle (an engineer) and Evelyn Hartley; married Josephine Swindells, February 25, 1972; children: Charlotte Polly, Annabelle Josephine, Rosemary Frances Elaine. *Education:* Attended Chelsea Polytechnic, 1957. *Religion:* "Monotheistic non-aligned." *Home:* 7 Kennard Close, Borstal, Rochester, Kent ME7 3LH, England. *Office:* Design Council, *Engineering*, 28 Haymarket, London SW1Y 4SU, England.

CAREER: Borax Consolidated Ltd., London, England, assistant chemist in chemical engineering development, 1954; North Thames Gas Board, London, technical assistant in chemical engineering development, 1955-57; Associated Lead Manufacturers, London, research assistant in development of nuclear and electronic materials of high purity, 1958-60; Mullard Valve Co., Croydon, England, senior assistant in development of materials in electronics manufacture, 1960-64; Iliffe Books Ltd., London, assistant editor, 1964-67; full-time writer, 1968—. *Military service:* British Army, radar technician in Royal Electrical and Mechanical Engineers, 1952-54. *Member:* National Union of Journalists, Institution of Mechanical and General Technician Engineers, Vintage Motor Cycle Club, Brooklands Society.

WRITINGS: Bikes at Brooklands in the Pioneer Years, Goose & Son, 1973; *Brooklands Bikes in the Twenties*, Argus, 1980; *The Ariel Story*, Argus, 1980; *Matchless Motorcycles*, Osprey, 1981; *A History of Royal Enfield Motorcycles*, Patrick Stephens, 1981. Assistant editor of *Design and Components in Engineering*, 1968-72; associate editor of *Design and Engineering*, 1972-77; editor of *Maintenance Engineering*, 1977-78, *OEM Design*, 1978-80, and *Materials*; assistant editor of *Engineering*.

SIDELIGHTS: Hartley commented: "My father was a well-known motor racing engineer and this gave me the right environment for acquiring an interest in both engineering design and motor vehicle development. A serious illness in my early twenties caused me to rethink my career along the lines of technical journalism. My books have been researched and written essentially on my own time."

*   *   *

HARTUNG, Albert Edward   1923-

PERSONAL: Born October 8, 1923, in Woodcrest, N.J.; married, 1946; children: two. *Education:* Lehigh University, B.A., 1947, M.A., 1949, Ph.D., 1957. *Office:* Department of English, Lehigh University, Bethlehem, Pa. 18015.

CAREER: Lehigh University, Bethlehem, Pa., instructor, 1949-57, assistant professor, 1957-61, associate professor, 1961-68, professor of English, 1968—. *Member:* Modern Language Association of America, Mediaeval Academy of America.

WRITINGS: (Editor) *A Manual of the Writings in Middle English, 1050-1500*, Volume III (Hartung was not associated with earlier volumes), Connecticut Academy of Arts and Sciences, 1972, Volume IV, Connecticut Academy of Arts and Sciences, 1973, Volume V, Connecticut Academy of Arts and Sciences, 1975, Volume VI, Shoe String, 1980. Contributor to language and medieval studies journals.*

* * *

HARTWELL, Dickson Jay 1906-1981

OBITUARY NOTICE—See index for *CA* sketch: Born May 1, 1906, in Portland, Ore.; died March 21, 1981, in Honolulu, Hawaii. Journalist, public relations executive, editor, and author. An expert in public relations, Hartwell was a public information officer for the United Nations Children's Fund and a vice-president of the Hill & Knowlton public relations firm. In 1962 he became a contributing editor to the weekly newspaper *Arizonian.* With Andrew Rooney he edited *Off the Record,* a collection of reports by foreign correspondents. Hartwell contributed more than one hundred fifty articles to national magazines and wrote *Dogs Against Darkness: The Story of the Seeing Eye.* Obituaries and other sources: *New York Times,* March 21, 1981; *Chicago Tribune,* March 24, 1981.

* * *

HARWOOD, Jonathan 1943-

PERSONAL: Born February 27, 1943, in Lockport, N.Y.; son of W. W. (a manager) and Virginia (a teacher; maiden name, Oakes) Tyler; married Heide Ingenohl (a teacher), 1968; children: Rebecca Renate, Roland Jock. *Education:* Wesleyan University, Middletown, Conn., B.A., 1965; Harvard University, Ph.D., 1970; University of Bristol, Diploma in Sociology, 1971. *Politics:* Socialist. *Office:* Department of Liberal Studies in Science, Victoria University of Manchester, Manchester M13 9PL, England.

CAREER: Bath College of Education, Bath, England, lecturer in sociology, 1971-72; University of Edinburgh, Edinburgh, Scotland, research fellow in science studies, 1973-74; Victoria University of Manchester, Manchester, England, lecturer in sociology of science and knowledge, 1974—. *Member:* Phi Beta Kappa, Sigma Xi. *Awards, honors:* Fulbright grant, 1965-66.

WRITINGS: (With Michael Banton) *The Race Concept,* Praeger, 1975; (contributor) Barry Barnes and Steven Shapin, editors, *Natural Order: Historical Studies in Scientific Culture,* Sage Publications, 1979; (contributor) J. V. Smith and David Hamilton, editors, *The Meritocratic Intellect: Studies in the History of Educational Research,* Aberdeen University Press, 1980. Contributor to *Social Studies of Science.*

WORK IN PROGRESS: A study of styles of thought in the field of genetics in Germany, 1915-33.

SIDELIGHTS: Harwood commented: "My published work so far has dealt with the social underpinnings of the controversy, since 1969, over racial differences in intelligence. I am prompted, no doubt, by my training as both a biologist and sociologist as well as by my experiences as a spectator of racial conflict in the United States in the late sixties. My most recent work is sustained by a powerful fascination with the society and culture of the Weimar Republic and by the belief that science was an integral part of that culture."

* * *

HASKIN, Gretchen 1936-

PERSONAL: Born November 18, 1936, in Bound Brook, N.J.; daughter of Harry Wolfe and Marguerite (Granieri) Swartz; married David Haskin (a physician), January 24, 1971; children: Claudia Leslie Baker. *Education:* Attended Radcliffe College and Bucknell University; University of Hawaii, B.A. (with honors), 1959; graduate study at University of Pennsylvania, 1962. *Home and office:* 1264 Laurel Hill Dr., San Mateo, Calif. 94402. *Agent:* Ellen Levine, Ellen Levine Literary Agency, 370 Lexington Ave., New York, N.Y. 10017.

CAREER: General Electric Missile and Space Vehicle Center, Philadelphia, Pa., technical writer, 1959; Smith Kline & French Pharmaceutical, Philadelphia, medical writer, 1960-63; Bancroft-Whitney (legal publisher), San Francisco, Calif., legal editor, 1963-64; Century Schoolbook Press, San Francisco, writer and editor, 1964-72; free-lance writer, 1972—.

WRITINGS: An Imperial Affair (novel), Dial, 1980. Contributor to magazines, including *Classic, Horse Play, Horse Lovers, American Horseman,* and *Horse of Course.*

WORK IN PROGRESS: Thunder of Captains, a novel dealing with intrigue in the world of horse shows "and with the people who inhabit this bizarre world."

SIDELIGHTS: Gretchen Haskin wrote: "After an exhaustive love affair with things Russian, I tried to get it out of my system with a novel set in post-revolutionary Russia. That book was *An Imperial Affair.* Russian history continues to fascinate me, however, and after my second (strictly non-Russian) book, I plan to return to the 1918 period in eastern Russia. I have been writing since I was six and will probably continue till I'm sixty-six."

BIOGRAPHICAL/CRITICAL SOURCES: San Francisco Chronicle, January 27, 1970, June 27, 1980; *San Mateo Times,* April 10, 1980; *Kansas City Star,* May 5, 1980; *San Diego Union,* June 25, 1980.

* * *

HASKINS, Sam(uel Joseph) 1926-

PERSONAL: Born November 11, 1926, in Kroonstad, South Africa; son of Benjamin G. and Anne A. (Oelofse) Haskins; married Alida Elzabe van Heerden, 1952; children: Ludwig, Konrad. *Education:* Attended Witwatersrand Technical College, 1947, and Bolt Court School of Photography, 1950. *Home and office:* 9A Calonne Rd., London SW19 5HH, England.

CAREER: Free-lance photographer and designer, 1950—, with solo shows in Johannesburg, Tokyo, London, Paris, and Amsterdam. Lecturer at international seminars. *Member:* Royal Photographic Society (fellow), Society of Industrial Artists and Designers (fellow), Association of Fashion Advertising & Editorial Photographers. *Awards, honors:* Prix Nadar from Government of France, 1964, for *Cowboy Kate and Other Stories;* three awards for *Haskins Posters,* including gold award from New York Art Directors, all 1974.

WRITINGS: Five Girls, Bodley Head, 1962; *Cowboy Kate and Other Stories* (photography), Bodley Head, 1964; *African Image* (photography), Bodley Head, 1966; (with Desmond Skinner) *November Girl* (photography), Bodley Head, 1967; *Haskins Posters,* Haskins Press, 1972. Contributor to international photographic magazines.

WORK IN PROGRESS: Haskins Photo Graphics, publication expected in 1981.

AVOCATIONAL INTERESTS: Vintage automobiles.

HATHAWAY, Sibyl Collings 1884-1974

OBITUARY NOTICE—See index for *CA* sketch: Born January 13, 1884; died July 14, 1974 on Sark, Channel Islands, United Kingdom. Seigneur of Sark and author. Hathaway succeeded her father in 1927 as seigneur of Sark, one of the Channel Islands in the English Channel near France. She remained the island's feudal ruler until her death. During her rule no divorces or serious crimes occurred among Sark's six hundred inhabitants, nor were taxes imposed on income, liquor, or cigarettes. Hathaway was bestowed with the title of Dame in 1965 by Queen Elizabeth II. A contributor to English and French journals, Hathaway wrote *Maid of Sark* and *Dame of Sark*. Obituaries and other sources: *New York Times*, July 15, 1974.

* * *

HATTERSLEY, Ralph (Marshall, Jr.) 1921-

PERSONAL: Born March 13, 1921, in Conrad, Mont.; son of Ralph Marshall and Ruth Claire Hattersley; married Mitzi Myers, 1946 (divorced, 1957); married Allisa Loeb, August 2, 1962; children: (first marriage) Cleve Marshall, Craig Robert, Lissa Ann. *Education:* Attended University of Washington, Seattle, 1939-40, Montana State College (now University), 1940-42, and Rochester Institute of Technology, 1946-48. *Home:* 542 Collicello St., Harrisonburg, Va. 22801. *Office:* Popular Photography, 1 Park Ave., New York, N.Y. 10016.

CAREER: Rochester Institute of Technology, Rochester, N.Y., associate professor, 1948-61; Birmingham College of Arts and Crafts, Birmingham, England, instructor, 1959-60; Columbia University, New York City, instructor, 1961-66; Pratt Institute, Brooklyn, N.Y., instructor, 1963-64; Germain School of Photography, New York City, instructor, 1965-72; School of Visual Arts, New York City, instructor, 1966-74; Smithsonian Institution, Washington, D.C., instructor, 1971-73; Maryland Institute College of Art, Baltimore, 1971-74. *Popular Photography*, New York City, contributing editor, 1957—. *Military service:* U.S. Naval Reserve, active duty as photographer's mate, 1942-46. *Member:* Society for Photographic Education.

WRITINGS: Beginner's Guide to Photography, Doubleday, 1974; *Discover Your Self Through Photography*, Morgan & Morgan, 1976; *Beginner's Guide to Darkroom Techniques*, Doubleday, 1976; *Photographic Printing*, Prentice-Hall, 1977; *Beginner's Guide to Photographing People*, Doubleday, 1978; *Photographic Lighting*, Prentice-Hall, 1979; *Beginner's Guide to Color Photography*, Doubleday, 1980. Contributor to magazines. Editor of *Infinity*.

WORK IN PROGRESS: Elsewhere, a novel about after-death activity; *Beginner's Guide to Photographic Lighting*, for Doubleday.

SIDELIGHTS: Hattersley wrote: "My ambition is to make photography accessible to everyone by writing clearly about difficult subjects. I want people to see that photography is a language, a form of therapy, a special psychology, and an effective means of self-expression as an art form. I also want to use language well in talking about things."

* * *

HATTERSLEY, Roy (Sydney George) 1932-

PERSONAL: Born December 28, 1932, in Sheffield, England; son of Frederick Roy and Enid (Brackenbury) Hattersley; married Edith Mary Loughran, 1956. *Education:* Received B.Sc. from University of Hull. *Office:* House of Commons, Westminster, London S.W.1, England.

CAREER: Sheffield City Council, Sheffield, England, member of council and chairman of housing and public works committees, 1957-65; Parliament, London, England, Labour member of House of Commons for Sparkbrook Division of Birmingham, 1964—, Parliamentary private secretary to minister of pensions and national insurance, 1964-67, joint Parliamentary secretary to ministry of labor, 1967-68, and department of employment and productivity, 1968-69, minister of defense for administration, 1969-70, Labour party spokesman on defense, 1972, on education and science, 1972-74, and on the environment, 1979, minister of state at Foreign and Commonwealth Office, 1974-76, secretary of state for prices and consumer protection, 1976—. Visiting fellow at Institute of Politics, Harvard University, 1971 and 1972. Director of Campaign for a European Political Community, 1966-67. Consultant to International Business Machines Corp. (IBM). *Member:* Reform Club. *Awards, honors:* Member of Privy Council, 1975.

WRITINGS: The Overload Performance of Powder Couplings: The Prevention of the Fire Hazard, Safety in Mines Research Establishment, 1957; *Nelson*, Saturday Review Press, 1974; *Goodbye to Yorkshire*, Gollancz, 1976. Contributor to journals.

BIOGRAPHICAL/CRITICAL SOURCES: New Statesman, October 6, 1972.*

* * *

HAWKINSON, Lucy (Ozone) 1924-1971

PERSONAL: Born in 1924 in California; died December 6, 1971; married John Samuel Hawkinson (an author and illustrator), September 20, 1954; children: Anne Miyo, Julia Eiko. *Education:* Attended Chicago Academy of Art. *Residence:* Chicago, Ill.

CAREER: Author and illustrator of children's books. Associated with a publishing firm.

WRITINGS—All juveniles; all self-illustrated, except as noted: *All in One Day*, Albert Whitman, 1955; *Pockets*, Albert Whitman, 1955; *Surprise!*, Rand McNally, 1956; *Dance, Dance, Amy-Chan!*, Albert Whitman, 1964; *Days I Like*, Albert Whitman, 1965; *That New River Train*, Albert Whitman, 1970; *Picture Book Farm*, illustrated by Robert Pippenger, Childrens Press, 1971.

With husband, John Hawkinson: *Winter Tree Birds*, Albert Whitman, 1956; *City Birds*, Albert Whitman, 1957; *Robins and Rabbits*, Albert Whitman, 1960; *Birds in the Sky*, Childrens Press, 1965; *Little Boy Who Lives Up High*, Albert Whitman, 1967.

Illustrator: Jene Barr, *Good Morning, Teacher*, Albert Whitman, 1957; Carla Greene, *I Want to Be a Fisherman*, Childrens Press, 1957; Barr, *Miss Terry at the Library*, Albert Whitman, 1962; (with J. Hawkinson) Mabel Gee and Mary Bongiorno, *How Can I Find Out*, Childrens Press, 1963; Margaret Friskey, *Mystery of the Farmer's Three Fives*, Childrens Press, 1963; Jane Hefflefinger and Elaine Hoffman, *At the Pet Hospital*, Melmont, 1964; Dorothy Koch, *Up the Big Mountain*, Holiday House, 1964; Florence Schulz, *I Am Andrew*, CLC Press, 1965; Natalie Miller, *Story of the Statue of Liberty*, Childrens Press, 1965; Miriam Schlein, *Billy the Littlest One*, Albert Whitman, 1966; Friskey, *Indian Two Feet and His Eagle Feather*, Childrens Press, 1967; Patricia Miles Martin, *One Special Dog*, Rand McNally, 1968; Muriel

Novella Stanek, *Left, Right, Left, Right!*, Albert Whitman, 1969; Fran Harvey, *Why Does It Rain?*, Harvey House, 1969; Patrick Mayers, *Just One More Block*, Albert Whitman, 1970; Stanek, *Tall Tina*, Albert Whitman, 1970; Helen Ross Russell, *The True Book of Buds: Surprise Packages*, Childrens Press, 1970.

Author of filmstrip "Birds in the Sky," adapted from Hawkinson's own book, released by Westport Communication Group, 1969.*

* * *

HAYDEN, Torey L(ynn) 1951-

PERSONAL: Born May 21, 1951, in Livingston, Mont.; daughter of Joyce (a secretary) Jansen. *Education:* Whitman College, B.A., 1972; Eastern Montana College, M.S., 1973; doctoral study at University of Minnesota, 1975-79. *Residence:* Anglesey, Wales. *Agent:* Peter L. Ginsberg, James Brown Associates, Inc., 25 West 43rd St., New York, N.Y. 10036.

CAREER: Special education teacher for the emotionally disturbed; university teacher; psychiatric researcher; children's unit teacher in a state mental institution; Coleg Prifysgol Gogledd Cymru, Bangor, Wales, writer, 1979—.

WRITINGS: One Child (nonfiction), Putnam, 1980; *Somebody Else's Kids* (nonfiction), Putnam, 1981. Contributor to professional journals.

WORK IN PROGRESS: Murphy's Boy, the third book in her nonfiction trilogy, publication by Putnam expected in late 1982; a children's novel set in the West in the nineteenth century; a book on sexual abuse.

SIDELIGHTS: Torey Hayden wrote: "Because most of my writing involves real-life people recovering from mental illness, I prefer not to have locations and dates of my previous employment published.

"I started my writing career twenty-some-odd years ago when I was just over seven. At that time, when I first discovered that I was able to capture a moment—especially the emotions of a moment—on paper, I was hooked. The real love affair began when I was twelve. Too old to live out my elaborate fantasies of another world I had created, I began to write about it, starting a cycle of stories which was to extend over twelve years and more than two-and-a-half million words.

"Writing continues to be an affair of the heart for me. Never having been much of a reader, never being especially interested in the outcome of the material once it is completed, I have always written solely for the joy of writing. I tend to work only when in the mood, and this has resulted in an erratic schedule of several months off, then intense periods of work when I am at the typewriter ten or twelve hours a day. My average output when I am working is about ten thousand words a day. I wrote *One Child* in eight days. I still find it incredibly difficult to believe anyone would actually pay me to enjoy myself, but I don't complain!

"I am a completely unredeemed workaholic and fill the time not spent writing with continuations of other work, primarily research on childhood emotional disturbances. I continue to teach, both children and adults, and lecture at regular intervals. In addition, I moved to North Wales early in 1980 after a long-standing love affair with the country and its people. I am bilingual and devote time to helping the programs for prevention of the deterioration of the Welsh culture and language, which is the oldest living Western language."

BIOGRAPHICAL/CRITICAL SOURCES: Washington Post, May 8, 1981; *New York Times Book Review*, April 26, 1981.

* * *

HAYS, Samuel Pfrimmer 1921-

PERSONAL: Born April 5, 1921, in Corydon, Ind.; son of Clay Blaine and Clara Ridley (Pfrimmer) Hays; married Barbara Darrow, June 11, 1948; children: Peter Darrow, Mary Elizabeth, Michael Pfrimmer, Rebecca deSchweinitz. *Education:* Swarthmore College, B.A., 1948; Harvard University, M.A., 1949, Ph.D., 1953. *Religion:* Society of Friends (Quakers). *Home:* 1421 Wightman St., Pittsburgh, Pa. 15217. *Office:* Department of History, University of Pittsburgh, Pittsburgh, Pa. 15260.

CAREER: University of Illinois, Champaign-Urbana, instructor in history, 1952-53; University of Iowa, Iowa City, 1953-60, began as assistant professor, became associate professor of history; University of Pittsburgh, Pittsburgh, Pa., professor of history and head of department, 1960—, distinguished service professor, 1973—. Member of board of directors of Harry S Truman Library Institute, 1958-70; member of Social Science Research Council, 1967-72. *Member:* American Historical Association, Organization of American Historians, American Association of University Professors.

WRITINGS: Response to Industrialization, 1885-1914, University of Chicago Press, 1957; *Conservation and the Gospel of Efficiency: The Progressive Conservation Movement, 1890-1920*, Harvard University Press, 1959; (contributor) W. N. Chambers and W. D. Burnham, editors, *The American Party Systems*, Oxford University Press, 1967; *American Political History as Social Analysis: Essays by Samuel P. Hays*, University of Tennessee Press, 1980. Contributor to history and political science journals.

BIOGRAPHICAL/CRITICAL SOURCES: Living Wilderness, June, 1980.*

* * *

HAYTHORNTHWAITE, Philip John 1951-

PERSONAL: Born April 22, 1951, in Colne, England; son of John (a company director) and Joyce (a company director; maiden name, Duckworth) Haythornthwaite. *Education:* Attended University of Lancaster. *Religion:* Christian. *Home:* Park Hill, Parrock Rd., Barrowford, Nelson, Lancashire BB9 6QF, England.

CAREER: H. Gerrard Ltd. (booksellers), Nelson, England, company director, 1970—.

WRITINGS: Uniforms of the Napoleonic Wars, Hippocrene, 1973, 2nd edition, Blandford, 1977; *Uniforms of Waterloo*, Hippocrene, 1975; *Regiment of the Line: A History of the Duke of Wellington's Regiment*, Halifax Antiquarian Society, 1975; *Uniforms of the Civil War*, Macmillan, 1975 (published in England as *Uniforms of the American Civil War*, Blandford, 1975, 2nd edition, 1980); *World Uniforms and Battles, 1815-50*, Hippocrene, 1976; *Uniforms of the Retreat From Moscow*, Hippocrene, 1976; *Uniforms of the Peninsular War*, Sterling, 1978; *Weapons and Equipment of the Napoleonic Wars*, Sterling, 1979; *Uniforms of the French Revolutionary Wars, 1789-1802*, Blandford, 1981. Contributor to history and antiquarian journals and to popular magazines, including *Art and Antiques Weekly*, *Lancashire Life*, and *Cumbria*.

WORK IN PROGRESS: Research on the social and military history of the British Volunteer Force of 1794-1814, the home guard formed to combat the threatened invasion by Napoleonic France.

AVOCATIONAL INTERESTS: History, archaeology, antiques and antiquities, natural history and conservation, history and modern practice of the game of cricket.

* * *

HAZLEHURST, Cameron 1941-

PERSONAL: Born October 12, 1941, in Harrogate, England; son of George Henry (an advertising and marketing consultant) and Eileen Leonie (Carmody) Hazlehurst; married Janette Doughty, January 18, 1964 (separated, 1980); children: David, Peter, Jane. *Education:* University of Melbourne, B.A. (with first class honors), 1963; attended Balliol College, Oxford, 1966, and Nuffield College, Oxford, 1966-68; Oxford University, D. Phil., 1969. *Residence:* Australia. *Agent:* Georges Borchardt, Inc., 136 East 57th St., New York, N.Y. 10022; and A. P. Watt Ltd., 26-28 Bedford Row, London WC1R 4HL, England. *Office:* Department of History, Research School of Social Sciences, Institute of Advanced Studies, Australian National University, P.O. Box 4, Canberra, Australian Capital Territory 2600, Australia.

CAREER: Monash University, Melbourne, Australia, teaching fellow in history, 1964-65; Oxford University, Oxford, England, lecturer in politics at Nuffield College and research fellow at Queen's College, 1970-72; Australian National University, Canberra, fellow in history, 1972—, fellow at Burgmann College, 1978—, academic assistant to vice-chancellor, 1979. Guest lecturer at Colgate University (London program), 1970-71; lecturer and seminar leader for Commonwealth Public Service Board, 1976-77; visiting fellow at Griffith University, 1978-80. Acting director of Beaverbrook Library, summer, 1967. Assistant secretary and head of Information Service, Australian Department of Urban and Regional Development, 1973-75; member of Department of Home Affairs Museums and national historical collections advisory committee, 1980. Co-producer of "Peach's Australia," on Australian Broadcasting Commission-Television, 1974-75; consultant to Australian Broadcasting Commission-Television and BBC-TV.

MEMBER: Australian Historical Association, Australian Society of Archivists, National Press Club (Australia), Royal Society of Literature (fellow), Royal Historical Society (fellow), Royal Society of Arts (fellow), Historical Association (England), National Liberal Club (England). *Awards, honors:* Grants from England's Social Science Research Council, 1968-70, Leverhulme Foundation, 1970-72, Twenty-Seven Foundation, 1971, Australian War Memorial, 1976-78, and Utah Foundation, 1978-80.

WRITINGS: Politicians at War, July 1914 to May 1915, Knopf, 1971; (with Christine Woodland) *A Guide to the Papers of British Cabinet Ministers, 1900-1951,* Royal Historical Society, 1974; (editor) *The History of the Ministry of Munitions,* Harvester, 1974; (editor with J. R. Nethercote, and contributor) *Reforming Australian Government: The Coombs Report and Beyond,* Australian National University Press, 1977; (editor) *The Mastermind Book,* Australian Broadcasting Commission, 1979; (editor and contributor) *Australian Conservatism: Essays in Twentieth-Century Political History,* Australian National University Press, 1979; *Menzies Observed,* Allen & Unwin, 1979; *Chalk: An Australian Political Portrait,* Allen & Unwin, 1981.

Contributor: (Author of introduction) Winston S. Churchill, *The People's Rights,* J. Cape, 1970, Taplinger, 1971; (author of introduction) *The Lloyd George Liberal Magazine, 1920-23,* six volumes, Harvester, 1973; John P. Mackintosh, editor, *British Prime Ministers in the Twentieth Century,* Volume I: *Balfour to Chamberlain,* Weidenfeld & Nicolson, 1977. Historical correspondent for *Observer,* 1969. Contributor to *Encyclopedia Americana.* Contributor to scholarly journals and newspapers, including *Age* and *New Statesman.* Contributing editor of *Times Higher Education Supplement,* 1971-72.

WORK IN PROGRESS: Editing, with Woodland, *A Liberal Chronicle: The Political Journals of J. A. Pease, First Lord Gainford, 1908-15,* publication by J. Cape expected in 1983; *The Triumph of Lloyd George: A Study of the Political Crisis of 1916,* for J. Cape, completion expected in 1983.

SIDELIGHTS: Hazlehurst wrote: "British political history in 1916 is probably better documented than any period before or since. Letter-writing and diary-keeping were still commonplace, and the creation and preservation of official reocrds had rapidly reached a level of comprehensiveness that has not been surpassed since. Accordingly, the student of politics has a uniquely rich field in which to explore not only one of the major events in modern British history (the advent of Lloyd George as Prime Minister), but also more general problems of political behavior which transcend the particular time and place. My trilogy on politics in the First World War will take a total of about twenty-five years to write. Other projects continue to intervene, including service in government—an extraordinarily enriching experience for a writer on politics."

AVOCATIONAL INTERESTS: Soccer, cricket.

* * *

HECHT, Warren Jay 1946-

PERSONAL: Born December 31, 1946, in Brooklyn, N.Y.; son of Abraham (in sales) and Evelyn (a teacher; maiden name, Birnhaum) Hecht; married Christine Holowicki, July 28, 1973. *Education:* City College of the City University of New York, B.A., 1969. *Home:* 906 Gott St., Ann Arbor, Mich. 48103. *Office:* Residential College, East Quad, University of Michigan, Ann Arbor, Mich. 48013.

CAREER: University of Michigan, Ann Arbor, head of creative writing program at Residential College, 1970—; Street Fiction Press, Ann Arbor, editor, 1973—; Crowfoot Press, Ann Arbor, editor, 1978—. *Awards, honors:* Grant from Theodore Goodman Foundation, 1969; good teaching award from Amoco, 1980.

WRITINGS: Babyburgers, Street Fiction, 1975. Editor of "Periodical Lunch Collection" series and anthologies for Street Fiction, 1973; editor of poetry series for Crowfoot Press.

* * *

HECKART, Beverly Anne 1938-

PERSONAL: Born May 17, 1938, in Harrisburg, Pa. *Education:* Hood College, B.A., 1959; Washington University, St. Louis, Mo., M.A., 1964, Ph.D., 1968. *Office:* Department of History, Central Washington State College, Ellensburg, Wash. 98926.

CAREER: Central Washington State College, Ellensburg, 1967—, began as assistant professor, became associate professor of history. *Member:* American Historical Association, Organization of American Historians. *Awards, honors:* Fulbright fellow at Max Planck Institute of History, 1964-66.

WRITINGS: From Bassermann to Bebel: The Grand Bloc's Quest for Reform in the Kaiserreich, 1900-1914, Yale University Press, 1974.

BIOGRAPHICAL/CRITICAL SOURCES: American Historical Review, April, 1976.*

* * *

HEDIN, Mary

PERSONAL: Surname is pronounced He-*deen;* born in Minneapolis, Minn.; daughter of Carl William and Augusta Emilia Hawkinson; married Roger W. Hedin (a physician); children: four. *Education:* University of Minnesota, B.S.; California State University, San Francisco, M.A. *Residence:* San Anselmo, Calif. *Agent:* Julie Fallowfield, McIntosh & Otis, Inc., 475 Fifth Ave., New York, N.Y. 10017. *Office:* Department of Humanities, College of Marin, Kentfield, Calif. 94904.

CAREER: College of Marin, Kentfield, Calif., instructor in humanities, 1965—, chairman of department, 1975-77. Past member of San Anselmo Parks and Recreation Commission, Human Rights Commission, and San Anselmo School District board of trustees. *Member:* Poetry Society of America, Authors Guild. *Awards, honors:* Yaddo fellow; short fiction award from Iowa School of Letters, 1979, for *Fly Away Home;* John H. McGinnis Award for short fiction from Southern Methodist University, 1980, for "The Middle Place."

WRITINGS: Fly Away Home (stories), University of Iowa Press, 1980.

Other stories: "Places We Lost," published in *Best American Short Stories, 1966,* Houghton, 1966, and in *McCall's,* October, 1975; "Mountain Man, Mountain Man," published in *Brushfire,* 1969; "Everyone Should Laugh," published in *Mariner,* 1969; "The Followers," published in *South Dakota Review,* summer, 1970; "Sixty Seven," published in *Southwest Review,* winter, 1971; "Oatmeal," published in *Descant,* spring, 1971; "Pookie," published in *Southwest Review,* winter, 1972; "Ladybug, Fly Away Home," published in *Southwest Review,* October, 1975, and in *O. Henry Prize Stories, 1977,* Doubleday, 1977; "The Loon," published in *Great River Review,* spring, 1978; "The Middle Place," published in *Southwest Review,* summer, 1978, and in *Best American Short Stories, 1979,* Houghton, 1979; "The Peculiar Vision of Mrs. Winkler," published in *Redbook,* May, 1979.

Poetry represented in anthologies *The Literature of South Dakota, The Poetry of Horses, Contemporary Women Poets,* and *Peace and Pieces;* contributor of poems to journals and magazines, including *Shenandoah, Perspective, Epos, Descant, South,* and *Southern Poetry Review.* Contributor of personal essays to *McCall's* and *California Living.*

WORK IN PROGRESS: Finding Happiness, a novel, "a tale of three families struggling for balance in their lives, for commitment, meaning, and happiness, that elusive reward."

SIDELIGHTS: Hedin told *CA:* "Some children know from their earliest exposure to music that they will become musicians, and some children know from the time they first listen to stories or hear poems that they will be writers. I made up my mind very early that I would be a writer.

"For me, the drive to write is rooted in an innate love of language itself. I am sensitive to the sounds and rhythms of language, and that involves me in the form we call poetry. However, my fictions—the stories and the novel—though in prose form, are written with a keen awareness of the tone, nuance, rhythm, and sound of language.

"Of course, good writing is not composed of language alone, and poems and tales also have to contain experience, thought, and meaning. Through my writing, then, I record and interpret the human events about me and my experience of them.

I write more often of the dark aspects of that human experience than the light. That may be true because I am fascinated by the mysteries of human love, human courage, human greed and lust, human dreams and sacrifices. I need to understand why men and women and children do what they do, and how they deal with the consequences of their own choices. The people I write about are most often decent, dignified, earnest folk who are brought into a testing that forces insight and results in change. Most often the people in my tales are good, and when they are not, they are evil in the ordinary ways of ignorance, selfishness, and greed.

"Storytelling is old as man's social structures, and it seems obvious that the tales people attend have greater significance than the simple events therein. The best stories touch upon myth, and my best stories and my novel reach beyond the level of plot and specific character to the lodestone of mythic significance.

"I write in all forms—articles, essays, poems, fictional tales. My poems are the most directly personal, and therefore of largest importance to me. My stories are for others: In them I am the professional writer, offering the works of her imagination to the world. I've had most success in the short story, which many people feel is a difficult form. For me, it is delightful and natural. I enjoy the brevity and tension of the short story.

"I am currently finishing a novel, *Finding Happiness.* It has a large cast of characters and a plot that draws these people into relationships in which each is altered. Then, after problems and sufferings, the characters are set free to spin out of the novel into the onward march of time, enlightened a little, happier for a while."

* * *

HEIDE, Robert 1939-

PERSONAL: Born May 9, 1939, in Irvington, N.J.; son of Ludwig and Olga (Straefle) Heitke. *Education:* Northwestern University, B.A., 1962. *Home:* 84 Christopher St., New York, N.Y. 10014.

CAREER: Writer. Worked as dialogue writer for Metro-Goldwyn-Mayer (MGM); teacher at East Harlem Youth Employment Service, New York, N.Y.; production assistant for Living Theatre. *Awards, honors:* National Catholic Theater Award, 1969, for "Why Tuesday Never Has a Blue Monday."

WRITINGS: (With John Gilman) *Dime Store Dream Parade: Popular Culture, 1925-1955,* Dutton, 1979; (with Gilman) *Popular Culture on Parade, 1925-1955,* Dutton, 1979.

Published plays: *Moon* (first produced in New Brunswick, N.J., at Brecht West, 1970), Breakthrough Press, 1971; *Why Tuesday Never Has a Blue Monday,* Breakthrough Press, 1971.

Unpublished plays: "West of the Moon," 1964; "The Bed," 1965; "At War With the Mongols," 1970; "Split Levels," 1972. Also author of "Hector."

BIOGRAPHICAL/CRITICAL SOURCES: Show Business, March 14, 1970.*

* * *

HEIDINGSFIELD, Myron S. 1914-1969

OBITUARY NOTICE—See index for *CA* sketch: Born February 3, 1914, in New York, N.Y.; died May 29, 1969, in Gainesville, Fla.; buried in Gainesville, Fla. Educator, marketing executive, and author. Heidingsfield had been a professor of marketing at several universities and was named National Marketing Educator of the Year in 1966 by Salesmen Marketing Executive International. At the time of his death, he was a marketing consultant for various companies. Heidingsfeld wrote several books, including *Market and Marketing Analysis, Marketing and Business Research,* and *Changing Patterns in Marketing: A Study in Strategy.* Obituaries and other sources: *New York Times,* June 3, 1969; *Who Was Who in America,* 5th edition, Marquis, 1973.

* * *

HEISERMAN, Arthur Ray   1929-1975

OBITUARY NOTICE—See index for *CA* sketch: Born January 10, 1929, in Evansville, Ind.; died December 9, 1975. Educator and author. A professor of English at the Universities of Nebraska, Illinois, and Chicago, Heiserman wrote *Skelton and Satire* and *The Novel Before the Novel: Essays and Discussions About the Beginnings of Prose Fiction in the West.* Obituaries and other sources: *Who Was Who in America,* 6th edition, Marquis, 1976.

* * *

HELD, Julius Samuel   1905-

PERSONAL: Born April 15, 1905, in Mosbach, Germany; came to the United States in 1934, naturalized citizen, 1940; son of Adolf and Nannette (Seligmann) Held; married Ingrid-Maerta Nordin-Pettersson, October 31, 1936; children: Anna-Brita (Mrs. Louis G. Audette II), James Michael. *Education:* Attended University of Heidelberg, 1923, University of Berlin, 1923-24, 1927-28, and University of Vienna, 1925-26, 1929; University of Freiburg, Ph.D., 1930. *Home:* 81 Monument Ave., Old Bennington, Vt. 05201.

CAREER: Staatliche Museen, Berlin, Germany, assistant, 1931-33; New York University, New York City, lecturer in art, 1935-41; Columbia University, Barnard College, New York City, lecturer, 1937-44, assistant professor, 1944-50, associate professor, 1950-54, professor of art, 1954-70, professor emeritus, 1970—, chairman of department of art history, 1967-70. Carnegie Lecturer at National Gallery, Ottawa, Ontario, 1936-37; visiting lecturer at Bryn Mawr College, 1943-44; visiting professor at New School for Social Research, 1946-47, and Yale University, 1954 and 1958; lecturer with American College Council for Summer Study Abroad, 1957; Robert Sterling Clark Professor at Williams College, 1969, 1973-74, and 1975-76; Andrew W. Mellon Visiting Professor at University of Pittsburgh, 1972-73. Academic adviser at Marlboro College, 1965—; member of Institute for Advanced Study, Princeton, N.J., 1967; consultant to Museum of Art, Ponce, P.R.

MEMBER: College Art Association of America (member of board of directors, 1959-64; honorary member of board of directors, 1975—), Mediaeval Academy of America, Renaissance Society of America, American Friends of Musee Plantin Moretus (president, 1969-72), Societe de l'Histoire de l'Art Francais, Deutscher Verein fuer Kunstwissenschaft. *Awards, honors:* Carnegie fellow, 1935; advanced fellow of Belgian American Educational Foundation, 1947; Guggenheim fellow, 1952-53 and 1966-67; Fulbright fellow, 1952-53; L.H.D. from Williams College, 1972; officer of Ordre de la Couronne (Belgium), 1974; Litt.D. from Columbia University, 1977.

WRITINGS: (Contributor) Jan Albert Goris, editor, *Rubens in America,* Standaard Boekhandel, 1947; *Rubens: Selected Drawings,* two volumes, Phaidon, 1959; (contributor) *Essays*

in Honor of Erwin Panofsky, New York University Press, 1961; (contributor) *Studies in Western Art: Acts of the Twentieth International Congress of the History of Art,* Princeton University Press, 1963; *Paintings of the European and American Schools,* Museo de Arte de Ponce, 1965; *Rembrandt's Aristotle and Other Rembrandt Studies,* Princeton University Press, 1969; (with Donald Posner) *Seventeenth and Eighteenth Century Art: Baroque and Rococo,* Abrams, 1971; (with Posner) *Seventeenth and Eighteenth Century Art: Baroque Painting, Sculpture, and Architecture,* edited by H. Janson, Abrams, 1971; (editor) *Rubens and the Book: Title Pages by Peter Paul Rubens,* Williams College, 1977; *The Oil Sketches of Peter Paul Rubens: A Critical Catalogue,* Princeton University Press, 1978.

Other: (Editor) *Handzeichnungen: Eine Auswahl,* Phaidon, 1960. Also author of *Duerer's Wirkung auf die Niederlaendische Kunst,* 1931. Contributor to art journals. Member of editorial board of *Art Bulletin,* 1942-68, and *Art Quarterly,* 1959-74.

BIOGRAPHICAL/CRITICAL SOURCES: Times Literary Supplement, January 30, 1981.*

* * *

HELTERMAN, Jeffrey A.   1942-

PERSONAL: Born July 31, 1942, in Brooklyn, N.Y.; son of Myron (an owner of a school supplies store) and Rae (an owner of a school supplies store; maiden name, Hausner) Helterman; married wife, Josephine M., October 12, 1968 (divorced, 1979); children: JoJo, Trudy, Sara, Miranda, Jamie. *Education:* University of Rochester, B.A., 1963, Ph.D., 1967; Northwestern University, M.A., 1964. *Religion:* Jewish. *Home:* 364 Ranch Rd., Apt. 21-3, Columbia, S.C. 29206. *Office:* Department of English, University of South Carolina, Columbia, S.C. 29208.

CAREER: Vanderbilt University, Nashville, Tenn., assistant professor of English, 1967-71; University of South Carolina, Columbia, assistant professor, 1971-75, associate professor of English, 1975—. *Awards, honors:* Grant from South Atlantic Modern Language Association, 1977.

WRITINGS: (Editor with Rick Layman) *Dictionary of Literary Biography,* Volume II: *American Novelists Since World War II,* Gale, 1978; *The Blue Frogs* (novel), Manor, 1980; *Symbolic Action in the Plays of the Wakefield Master,* University of Georgia Press, 1981.

WORK IN PROGRESS: Guinevere, a novel; a historical romance set in Restoration England.

* * *

HENDERSON, Lawrence W.   1921-

PERSONAL: Born February 6, 1921, in Yankton, S.D.; son of Lewis W. (an attorney) and Lucile (a teacher; maiden name, Johnson) Henderson; married Muriel Woods (a social worker), July 4, 1943; children: Kathleen M. Henderson Ashley, Nancy Henderson-James, David N., Mark W. *Education:* University of Puget Sound, B.A., 1942; Yale University, M.Div., 1945; Hartford Seminary Foundation, M.A., 1958. *Home:* 29800 Southwest 153rd Ct., Leisure City, Fla. 33033.

CAREER: Ordained minister of United Church of Christ; United Church Board for World Ministries, New York, N.Y., missionary in Angola, 1947-69, executive, 1969-77; United Church of Leisure City, Leisure City, Fla., minister, 1977—. *Member:* African Studies Association.

WRITINGS: (Contributor) Robert T. Parsons, editor, *Windows in Africa: A Symposium,* E. J. Brill, 1971; *Africa: Five Centuries of Conflict,* Cornell University Press, 1979. Contributor to Portuguese journals.

WORK IN PROGRESS: A book on the roles of the church in Angola since 1880.

SIDELIGHTS: Henderson wrote: "Living twenty-two years in Angola convinced me that Africa is not the Dark Continent. One goal of my writing is to reveal the values and rich heritage of African culture to Americans and Europeans. African authors are now doing this job more effectively for most areas, but there are still very few Angolans who are writing their own story."

*   *   *

HENDRICKS, Walter   1892-1979

OBITUARY NOTICE: Born July 24, 1892, in Chicago, Ill.; died September 29, 1979, in Brattleboro, Vt. Educator, publisher, and author of volumes of poetry, including *Double Dealer: Early Poems,* and nonfiction books, including *My Quarrel With Robert Frost.* Hendricks maintained a long-term friendship with the poet Robert Frost that began when Hendricks was a student of Frost's at Amherst College. Between 1946 and 1964 Hendricks established Marlboro College and two other liberal-arts colleges in Vermont. He also founded Hendricks House, Inc., a New York publishing firm. Obituaries and other sources: *Leaders in Education,* 5th edition, Bowker, 1974; *Directory of American Scholars,* Volume II, *English, Speech, and Drama,* 7th edition, Bowker, 1978; *Who's Who in America,* 40th edition, Marquis, 1978; *New York Times,* October 3, 1979.

*   *   *

HENIGE, David   1938-

PERSONAL: Born March 26, 1938, in Toledo, Ohio; son of Bernard James (a bookkeeper) and Rhoda (a cashier; maiden name, Tierney) Henige; married Suzanne Freiheit (an auditor), July 11, 1959; children: Cynthia, Christopher, Brian. *Education:* University of Toledo, B.A., 1959, M.A., 1967; University of Wisconsin—Madison, Ph.D., 1973. *Politics:* "None or less." *Religion:* Roman Catholic. *Home:* 722 Chapman St., Madison, Wis. 53711. *Office:* Memorial Library, University of Wisconsin, 728 State St., Madison, Wis. 53706.

CAREER: University of Wisconsin—Madison, bibliographer of African studies, 1971-72; University of Birmingham, Birmingham, England, lecturer in history, 1973-74; University of Wisconsin—Madison, bibliographer of African studies, 1974—. *Military service:* U.S. Army, 1959. *Member:* African Studies Association, African Studies Association of the United Kingdom.

WRITINGS: Colonial Governors From the Fifteenth Century to the Present, University of Wisconsin Press, 1970; *The Chronology of Oral Tradition,* Clarendon Press, 1974; *Reviews in African History, 1960-1974,* African Studies Association, 1975; *Reviews in African History, 1974-1978,* Crossroads Press, 1979; *Catholic Missionary Journals Relating to Africa: A Provisional Checklist and Union List for North America,* Crossroads Press, 1980.

WORK IN PROGRESS: A monograph on oral historiography, especially as it relates to Africa, publication expected in 1982.

SIDELIGHTS: Henige wrote: "The major intent of my work in progress is to demonstrate that it is necessary to view contemporary oral historiography in a perspective of historical method, both oral and written, from other places and other times."

*   *   *

HENRIES, A. Doris Banks   1913(?)-1981

OBITUARY NOTICE: Born c. 1913 in Live Oak, Fla.; died of cancer, February 16, 1981, in Middleton, Conn. Educator and author of more than twenty-five books on education in Liberia. Henries lived in Liberia for forty-one years. There, in addition to her teaching and writing activities, she served as assistant minister of education. Henries left Liberia when her husband Richard A. Henries, speaker of the Liberian House of Representatives, was executed following the overthrow of the government of William R. Talbot, Jr., by the revolutionary forces of Samuel K. Doe. Obituaries and other sources: *New York Times,* February 18, 1981.

*   *   *

HENRY, Robert Selph   1889-1970

OBITUARY NOTICE—See index for *CA* sketch: Born October 20, 1889, in Clifton, Tenn.; died August 18, 1970, in Alexandria, Va.; buried in Mount Olivet Cemetery, Nashville, Tenn. Railroad executive, historian, and author. Henry was best known for his books on railroad history, the Civil War, and the Mexican War. Among his many books are *The Story of the Confederacy, Portraits of the Iron Horse: The American Locomotive in Pictures and Story, The Fascinating Railroad Business,* and *The Story of the Mexican War.* Obituaries and other sources: *Who Was Who in America,* 5th edition, Marquis, 1973.

*   *   *

HENSHAW, Tom   1924-

PERSONAL: Born October 18, 1924, in Hubbardston, Mass.; son of Tom (a telegrapher) and Ellen (a shoe worker; maiden name, Anderson) Henshaw; married Marilyn J. Coffey, April 15, 1961 (divorced, 1964); children: Ian M. *Education:* Boston University, A.A., 1950, B.S., 1952. *Politics:* Social Democrat. *Home:* 387 Commercial St., Braintree, Mass. 02184.

CAREER: Associated Press, Boston, Mass., writer, 1952-56; Associated Press Newsfeatures, New York, N.Y., writer, 1956-66; *Boston Herald-Traveler,* Boston, writer, 1966-72. *Military service:* U.S. Marine Corps, 1943-46. *Member:* Professional Hockey Writers Association.

WRITINGS: (With Saul Pett, Sid Moody, and Hugh Mulligan) *The Torch Is Passed,* Associated Press, 1964; *The Boston Celtics,* Prentice-Hall, 1974. Editor of *Yankee Hockey.*

WORK IN PROGRESS: A novel about small-city politics; research for a history of hockey in the United States.

*   *   *

HEPPENSTALL, (John) Rayner   1911-1981

OBITUARY NOTICE—See index for *CA* sketch: Born July 27, 1911, in Huddersfield, Yorkshire, England; died May 23, 1981. Crime historian, translator, critic, and author. Following a stint as a schoolmaster and a free-lance writer, Heppenstall served with the British Army during World War II. From the end of the war until 1967 he was a producer for BBC-Radio, writing and translating radio plays. Heppenstall was also the author of novels and nonfiction, including *The Blaze of Noon, Saturine, The Connecting Door, The Woodshed, The Shearers, French Crime in the Romantic*

Age, The Sex Wars and Others, and *Two Moons.* Obituaries and other sources: *London Times,* May 25, 1981.

* * *

HERBERT, Martin 1933-

PERSONAL: Born in 1933 in Durban, South Africa; married Margaret Batten. *Education:* Attended University of Natal and University of London. *Agent:* International Authors Agency, Wadhurst, Sussex, England.

CAREER: Writer. Assistant director of Child Guidance Clinic, Durban, South Africa; associated with University of Natal, Durban, and University of London, London, England; clinical psychologist at Institute of Psychiatry. *Member:* British Sociological Association.

WRITINGS: (Editor with Sidney Gillmore McKenzie) *Freud and Psychology: Selected Readings,* Penguin, 1970; *Emotional Problems of Development in Children,* Academic Press, 1974; *Problems of Childhood: A Complete Guide for All Concerned,* Pan Books, 1975. Also author of *The Emotional Problems of the School-Going Child,* Penguin, and *Introducing Psychology,* with J. T. Reason, Kahn & Averill. Contributor to *Book of Life.* Contributor to psychology journals and popular magazines, including *Your Child, New Society, Good Housekeeping,* and *Woman.*

AVOCATIONAL INTERESTS: Reading, music.*

* * *

HERMAN, Masako

PERSONAL: Born in New York, N.Y.; married Elliot Herman (deceased); children: Hunter Ken, Ellyn Akemi, Amy Mariko. *Education:* Adelphi College (now University), B.A., 1951; Massachusetts General Hospital, certificate in medical illustration, 1954. *Home and office:* 49 Hudson St., Hastings-on-Hudson, N.Y. 10706.

CAREER: Free-lance medical illustrator, 1968—.

WRITINGS: (Editor) *The Japanese in America, 1843-1973,* Oceana, 1974.

* * *

HERNES, Helga Maria 1938-

PERSONAL: Born January 16, 1938, in Germany; daughter of Heinz Wolfgang and Lucy Mary (a physician; maiden name, Goedicke) Jahncke; divorced; children: Stein. *Education:* Mount Holyoke College, B.A., 1961; Johns Hopkins University, M.A., 1967, Ph.D., 1970. *Home:* Oeyjordsveien 71, 5000 Bergen, Norway. *Office:* Institute of Comparative Politics, University of Bergen, Bergen, Norway.

CAREER: University of Bergen, Bergen, Norway, senior lecturer in comparative politics, 1973—. Member of Norwegian Social Science Research Council, 1976-79, and government advisory board of disarmament and arms control; chairperson of board of directors of Oslo Office of Women's Studies. *Member:* International Political Science Association, Norwegian Political Science Association, American Political Science Association.

WRITINGS: The Multinational Corporation, Gale, 1977. Also author of *Concepts of Community in Modern Theories of International Law,* 1970. Contributor to political science journals.

WORK IN PROGRESS: A book on Norwegian women's access to the state, in Norwegian.

HERRMANN, Luke John 1932-

PERSONAL: Born March 9, 1932, in Berlin, Germany; son of F. H. Herrmann; married wife, Georgina; children: Mark, Jeremy. *Education:* New College, Oxford, M.A. *Home:* Old Manse, Clipston, near Market Harborough, Leicestershire, England. *Office:* Department of Art History, University of Leicester, Leicester, England.

CAREER: Illustrated London News, London, England, assistant editor, 1955-58; Oxford University, Ashmolean Museum, Oxford, England, began as assistant keeper, became senior assistant keeper in department of western art, 1958-67; University of Leicester, Leicester, England, Paul Mellon Foundation lecturer, 1967-70, senior lecturer and head of department, 1970-73, professor of art history, 1973—. *Member:* Society of Antiquaries (fellow).

WRITINGS: (Translator) Ludwig Muenz, *Bruegel's Drawings,* Phaidon, 1961; *J.M.W. Turner,* Methuen, 1963; *Il Paesaggio nella pittura inglese dell'Ottocento,* Fratelli Fabbri, 1967; *Ruskin and Turner,* Faber, 1968; *British Landscape Painting of the Eighteenth Century,* Faber, 1973; *Turner,* Phaidon, 1975. Author of exhibition catalogs for British Council. Contributor of articles and reviews to magazines and newspapers, including *Apollo, Burlington, Connoisseur,* and *Country Life.*

* * *

HERSH, Jacques 1935-

PERSONAL: Born March 27, 1935, in Paris, France; son of Mordecai (a tailor) and Helen (Najman) Herzkowicz; married Ellen Brun (a writer), October 13, 1964. *Education:* City College (now of the City University of New York), B.A.; University of Copenhagen, D.Sc. *Residence:* Copenhagen, Denmark.

CAREER: Free-lance writer. *Military service:* U.S. Army.

WRITINGS: (With wife, Ellen Brun) *Kapitalismens udviklings system,* Gyldendal, 1972; (with Brun) *Socialist Korea,* Monthly Review Press, 1976. Contributor to journals in Europe and the United States.

WORK IN PROGRESS: A project on the consequences of East-West relations in the field of economics and politics, with wife, Ellen Brun.

SIDELIGHTS: Hersh commented: "Although French-American, I have been living in Denmark and working together with my wife. We met as students in Vienna in the beginning of the 1960's and became interested in international politics and economics. We followed courses in Vienna, but have done much work on our own and are rather self-taught. I have traveled in Asia, including China, Vietnam, North Korea, Japan, and Hong Kong."

* * *

HERTZLER, Joyce O(ramel) 1895-1975

OBITUARY NOTICE—See index for *CA* sketch: Born January 20, 1895, in Jordan, Minn.; died September 25, 1975. Educator, sociologist, and author. Among Hertzler's books are *History of Utopian Thought, Social Thought of the Ancient Civilizations, Crisis in World Population,* and *Laughter: A Socio-Scientific Analysis.* At the time of his death Hertzler was professor emeritus at the University of Nebraska. (Date of death provided by University of Nebraska.)

HERZOG, Chaim   1918-

PERSONAL: Born September 17, 1918, in Belfast, Northern Ireland; son of Isaac (a rabbi) and Sarah (Hillman) Herzog; married Aura Ambache (an environmentalist), May 8, 1947; children: Joel, Michael, Isaac, Runit. *Education:* Attended Royal Military College; University of London, LL.B., 1941. *Religion:* Jewish. *Residence:* Israel. *Office:* Herzog Fox & Co., 5 Bn. Guirol St., 25 Tel-Aviv, Israel.

CAREER: G.U.S. Industries, Tel-Aviv, Israel, managing director, 1962-72; Herzog Fox & Co. (law firm), Tel-Aviv, senior partner, 1972—. Israel's ambassador to the United Nations, 1975-78; president of World Organization for Rehabilitation Through Training Union and Organization for Rehabilitation Through Training of Israel. Member of board of governors of Hebrew University of Jerusalem, Bar-Ilan University, and Weilmann Institute of Science; member of board of directors of Israel Discount Bank, Industrial Development Bank of Israel, Israel Aircraft Industries, and Paz Oil Corp. Member of Leadership Bureau of Labour party. Political and military commentator for Israel Broadcasting Authority; television and radio commentator in Israel and abroad. *Military service:* British Army, 1939-45; served in Europe; became lieutenant colonel. Israel Defense Forces, 1948-62, defense attache at Israel's embassy in Washington, D.C., director of military intelligence, 1948-50, 1959-62, military governor of the West Bank, 1967; became major-general. *Member:* Harmonie Club. *Awards, honors:* Knight commander of Order of the British Empire, 1970; honorary doctorates from Yeshiva University, 1976, Jewish Theological Seminary, 1976, and Bar-Ilan University, 1977.

WRITINGS: Israel's Finest Hour, Maariv Book Guild, 1967; *Days of Awe,* Weidenfeld & Nicolson, 1973; (editor) *Judaism, Law, and Ethics,* Soncino, 1974; *The War of Atonement,* Little, Brown, 1975; *Who Stands Accused?,* Random House, 1978; (co-author) *Battles of the Bible,* Random House, 1978. Author of columns in *Jerusalem Post* and *Maariv.* Contributor to newspapers in Israel and abroad.

WORK IN PROGRESS: A book on the United Nations; a book on Israel's wars.

*   *   *

HEVENER, John W(atts)   1933-

PERSONAL: Born March 21, 1933, in Dunmore, W.Va.; son of John U. and Mabel M. Hevener; married Mary Sisson (a teacher), May 6, 1961; children: John Mark, Anne Elizabeth. *Education:* Marshall University, B.A., 1956, M.A., 1960; Ohio State University, Ph.D., 1971. *Politics:* Democrat. *Religion:* United Church of Christ. *Home:* 3261 Allentown Rd., Lima, Ohio 45805. *Office:* Lima Campus, Ohio State University, Lima, Ohio 45804.

CAREER: High school history teacher in McArthur, Ohio, 1956-61, and Columbus, Ohio, 1961-62; Wisconsin State University (now University of Wisconsin), Whitewater, historian, 1966-70; Mankato State University, Mankato, Minn., historian, 1970-74; Ohio State University, Lima Campus, Lima, historian, 1974—. *Member:* American Historical Association, Coal Miners Research Association (member of executive committee, 1979-81), Southern Historical Association. *Awards, honors:* W. D. Weatherford Award from Berea College, 1978, for *Which Side Are You On?*

WRITINGS: Which Side Are You On?: The Harlan County Coal Miners, 1931-1939, University of Illinois Press, 1978.

WORK IN PROGRESS: Bradley's Kingdom: The Elk River Coal and Lumber Company, Widen, West Virginia, 1904-63.

*   *   *

HEXNER, Ervin Paul   1893-1968

OBITUARY NOTICE—See index for *CA* sketch: Born August 13, 1893, in Czechoslovakia; died May 15, 1968. Lawyer, educator, and author. Hexner was an executive at companies in Czechoslovakia until 1939 when he immigrated to the United States. He became a professor of political science and economics at the University of North Carolina, Chapel Hill, and at Pennsylvania State University. A frequent adviser at monetary, trade, and labor conferences, Hexner served as assistant general counsel for the International Monetary Fund in Washington, D.C. His writings include *Studies in Legal Terminology, The International Steel Cartel,* and *The Constitutional Structure of the International Monetary Fund.* Obituaries and other sources: *Who Was Who in America,* 5th edition, Marquis, 1973.

*   *   *

HIBBERD, Jack   1940-

PERSONAL: Born April 12, 1940, in Warracknabeal, Australia; son of James George (a plumber) and Moira (a singer; maiden name, Richardson) Hibberd; married first wife, Jocelyn, February 8, 1969 (divorced, 1976); married Evelyn Krape (an actress), January 3, 1978; children: Lillian Margaret, James Benjamin, Samuel Spike Mendel. *Education:* University of Melbourne, M.B.B.S., 1964. *Home:* 87 Turner St., Abbotsford, Victoria 3067, Australia. *Agent:* Harvey Unna & Beaumont Mews, Marylebone High St., London W1N 4HE, England.

CAREER: Writer. Physician in general practice in Australia, 1965-66 and 1970-73; St. Vincent's Hospital, Department of Social Medicine, Melbourne, Australia, registrar, 1967. Member of Australian Performing Group.

WRITINGS: Dimboola: A Wedding Reception Play (first produced in Carlton, Australia; bound with "The Last of the Knucklemen"), Penguin, 1974; *A Stretch of the Imagination* (first produced in Carlton, 1972), Currency Press, 1973; *Three Popular Plays* (contains "One of Nature's Gentlemen"; "A Toast to Melba," first produced in Adelaide, Australia, 1976; and "The Les Darcy Show," first produced in Adelaide, 1973), Outback Press, 1976; (translator) Charles Baudelaire, *Le Vin des amants: Poems From Baudelaire,* Gryphon Books, 1977.

Work represented in anthologies, including *Buzo, Hibberd, Romeril: Four Australian Plays* (includes "White With Wire Wheels," first produced in Melbourne, Australia, 1970, and "Who"), Penguin, 1970.

Unpublished plays: "Brain Rot," first produced in Carlton, 1967; "The Last Days of Epic J. Remorse," 1969; "Customs and Excise," first produced in Carlton, 1970 (produced as "Proud Flesh" in Carlton, 1972); "Klag," first produced in Melbourne, 1970; (co-author) "Marvelous Melbourne," first produced in Melbourne, 1970; "Aorta," first produced in Melbourne, 1971; "Women!" (adaptation of play by Aristophanes), first produced in Carlton, 1972; "Captain Midnight VC," first produced in Carlton, 1973; "The Architect and the Emperor of Assyria" (adaptation of play by Fernando Arrabel), first produced in Carlton, 1974; "Peggy Sue," first produced in Carlton, 1974; "The Overcoat" (adaptation of story by Nikolai Gogol), first produced in Carlton, 1976;

"Sin," 1978; "A Man of Many Parts," 1980; "Smash Hit!," 1980.

WORK IN PROGRESS: Three plays, "Silver Threads Among the Gold," "Odyssey of a Prostitute," and "Is Tonight the Night?"; a six-part television comedy, "Tall Tales."

SIDELIGHTS: Hibberd told *CA:* "My plays are non-autobiographical and generally anti-naturalistic. My ambition is to write bizarre comedies that depict the sad, mad paradoxes of contemporary existence within and without Australia. Major influences on my work are vaudeville and popular demotic comedy, the theatre of the absurd, Bertolt Brecht, German expressionism, Baudelaire, and the French symbolists."

BIOGRAPHICAL/CRITICAL SOURCES: Peter Fitzpatrick, *After the Doll,* Edward Arnold, 1979; *Quadrant,* March, 1979.

*   *   *

HIBBS, John 1925-
(John Blyth)

PERSONAL: Born May 5, 1925, in Birmingham, England; son of Alfred Leonard (a minister) and Sylvia (Blyth) Hibbs; married Constance Tillyard, July 8, 1950 (divorced September, 1975); children: Michael, Robin, Alison. *Education:* University of Birmingham, B.Com. Social Study, 1950; London School of Economics and Political Science, London, M.Sc., 1954; doctoral study at University of Birmingham. *Religion:* United Reformed. *Home:* Copper Beeches, 134 Wood End Rd., Erdington, Birmingham B24 8BN, England. *Agent:* Rupert Crew Ltd., King's Mews, Gray's Inn Rd., London W1N 2JA, England. *Office:* Birmingham Polytechnic, Perry Barr, Birmingham B42 2SU, England.

CAREER: Premier Travel Ltd., Cambridge, England, personal assistant to managing director, 1950-52; technical journalist and transport consultant, 1954-56; Corona Coaches Ltd., Sudbury, England, managing director, 1956-60; British Railways, Eastern Region, London, England, traffic survey officer and market research officer, 1961-67; City of London Polytechnic, London, senior lecturer, 1967-69, principal lecturer in transport, 1969-73; Birmingham Polytechnic, Birmingham, England, principal lecturer in transport and business studies, 1973—. Member of Liberal party advisory panel on transport, 1969—, chairman of panel, 1971-75; member of Liberal Industrial Partnership Committee, 1968-70; member of transport board of Council for National Academic Awards, 1978—.

MEMBER: Chartered Institute of Transport (fellow; member of council), Institute of Transport Administration, British Institute of Management, Organization of Teachers of Transport Studies (past chairman), Transport Economists Group, Transport History Group, Charles Williams Society, Saffron Walden Constituency Liberal and Radical Association (chairman, 1964-67; president, 1967-68; honorary organizer, 1968-72; honorary election agent for general election, 1970).

WRITINGS: Transport for Passengers, Institute of Economic Affairs, 1962, 2nd edition, 1971; *The History of British Bus Services,* David & Charles, 1968; *Transport Studies: An Introduction,* John Baker, 1970, revised edition, Grove, 1981; (editor) *The Omnibus,* David & Charles, 1971; *How to Run the Buses,* John Baker, 1972; *People and Transport,* Unservile State Group, 1973; *The Bus and Coach Industry: Its Economics and Organization,* Dent, 1975.

Books of poems; under pseudonym John Blyth: *New Found Land,* Outposts, 1963; *Being a Patient,* Breakthru, 1965. Contributor to transport, history, and banking journals.

WORK IN PROGRESS: A comparative study of the licensing and control of public road passenger transport in selected countries outside England.

SIDELIGHTS: Hibbs commented: "It is proper to pay tribute to those who have influenced me, notably Charles Williams. Two quotations underlie what I would want my work to be remembered by. Dante said, 'We are created for our function, not our function for us.' And Jakob Boehme said, 'If a man did only cast stones into the sea (if his brother be pleased with it, and that he get his living by it) then he is as acceptable to God as a preacher in a pulpit.' As I see it, neither in economics, nor in politics, nor in art, dare we tell other people what is good for them."

*   *   *

HICKMAN, C(harles) Addison 1916-

PERSONAL: Born June 11, 1916, in Sioux City, Iowa; married wife in 1940; children: three. *Education:* University of Iowa, B.A., 1937, M.A., 1938, Ph.D., 1942. *Office:* Department of Economics, Southern Illinois University, Carbondale, Ill. 62901.

CAREER: Stetson University, De Land, Fla., instructor in economics, 1938-40; University of Iowa, Iowa City, 1940-50, began as instructor, became professor of economics; University of Illinois, Urbana-Champaign, research professor of economics, 1950-53; North Carolina State University, Raleigh, professor of economics, 1953-60, chairman of department, 1953-55, dean of School of Liberal Arts, 1955-60; Southern Illinois University, Carbondale, Vandeveer Professor of Economics, 1960—, dean of graduate school, 1963-64. Member of boards of directors and commissions of American Council on Education, Social Science Research Council, and National Academy of Sciences. *Member:* American Economic Association, Association for Comparative Economics (vice-president, 1967-68), American Association for Higher Education (member of board of directors; past president).

WRITINGS: (With P. R. Olson) *Pan American Economics,* Wiley, 1943; (with others) *World Economic Problems: Nationalism, Technology, and Cultural Lag,* Pitman, 1947; *Our Farm Program and Foreign Trade: A Conflict of National Policies,* Council on Foreign Relations, 1949, reprinted, 1971; (with Manford H. Kuhn) *Individuals, Groups, and Economic Behavior,* Dryden, 1956; (contributor) M. L. Greenhut and W. T. Whitman, editors, *Essays in Southern Economic Development,* University of North Carolina Press, 1964; (co-author) *Faculty Participation in Academic Governance,* American Association for Higher Education, 1967; *J. M. Clark,* Columbia University Press, 1975. Editor of "Series in Economics," Dryden, 1950-60.*

*   *   *

HICKS, Tyler Gregory 1921-
(Louis J. Murphy)

PERSONAL: Born June 21, 1921, in New York, N.Y.; son of Ernest Tyler and Mary B. (O'Brien) Hicks; married Saretta M. Gratke, February 23, 1946 (died March, 1974); married Mary T. Shanley, August, 1975; children: (first marriage) Gregory T., Barbara L., Steven D. *Education:* Cooper Union, B.M.E., 1948. *Home:* 24 Canterbury Rd., Rockville Centre, N.Y. 11570. *Office:* McGraw-Hill Book Co., 1221 Avenue of the Americas, New York, N.Y. 10036.

CAREER: Engineer with Merport Realty Co., 1942-46; Lockwood-Greene Engineers, Inc., design engineer, 1946-49; McGraw-Hill Book Co., New York, N.Y., editor-in-chief of P & RB Division, 1962—. Owner of International Engineering Associates, 1950—; president of International Wealth Success, Inc. Instructor at Cooper Union, 1951—; lecturer. *Member:* International Oceanographic Foundation, Institute of Electrical and Electronics Engineers, American Society of Mechanical Engineers, U.S. Naval Institute.

WRITINGS: (Under pseudonym Louis J. Murphy) *The Plant Engineer's Easy Problem Solver*, Conover-Mast Publications, 1954; *Pump Selection and Application*, McGraw, 1957; *Pump Operation and Maintenance*, McGraw, 1958; *Successful Technical Writing: Technical Articles, Papers, Reports, Instruction and Training Manuals, and Books*, McGraw, 1959; *Writing for Engineering and Science*, McGraw, 1961; (with John J. Pippenger) *Industrial Hydraulics: Fluids, Pumps, Motors, Controls, Circuits, Servo Systems, Electrical Devices*, McGraw, 1962, 3rd edition, 1979; *Professional Achievement for Engineers and Scientists: How to Earn More Money and Greater Success in Engineering and Science*, McGraw, 1963; *How to Build a Second-Income Fortune in Your Spare Time*, Parker Publishing, 1965; *Smart Money Shortcuts to Becoming Rich*, Parker Publishing, 1966; *Successful Engineering Management: Modern Techniques for Effective and Profitable Direction of the Engineering Function*, McGraw, 1966; *Estimating and Controlling Engineering and Manufacturing Costs*, Industrial and Commercial Techniques, 1966; *How to Start Your Own Business on a Shoestring and Make up to One Hundred Thousand Dollars a Year*, Parker Publishing, 1968.

How to Borrow Your Way to a Great Fortune, Parker Publishing, 1970; *Pump Application Engineering*, McGraw, 1970; *Magic Mind Secrets for Building Great Riches Fast*, Parker Publishing, 1971; (editor) *Standard Handbook of Engineering Calculations*, McGraw, 1972; *How to Make a Quick Fortune: New Ways to Build Wealth Fast*, Parker Publishing, 1973; *How to Make One Million Dollars in Real Estate in Three Years Starting With No Cash*, Prentice-Hall, 1976; *How to Make a Quick Fortune*, Prentice-Hall, 1977; (editor) *How to Borrow Your Way to Real Estate Riches*, International Wealth Success, 1978; (with Sean C. Beach) *Tyler Hicks' Encyclopedia of Wealth-Building Secrets*, Parker Publishing, 1980. Also author of *Controlling and Reducing Maintenance Costs*, 1968, *Business Capital Sources*, 1969, and *Budgeting and Controlling Research and Development and Design Costs*, 1969.*

*   *   *

HICKS, Ursula Kathleen (Webb) 1896-

PERSONAL: Born February 17, 1896, in Dublin, Ireland; daughter of William Fisher (a lawyer) and Isabella Mary (a botanist; maiden name, Hayward) Webb; married John Hicks (a professor), December 17, 1935. *Education:* Somerville College, Oxford, M.A., 1918; London School of Economics and Political Science, London, B.Sc., 1932, graduate study, 1932-35. *Politics:* "Middle of the road." *Religion:* Society of Friends (Quakers). *Home:* Porch House, Blockley, Gloucestershire GL56 9BW, England. *Office:* Linacre College, Oxford University, St. Cross St., Oxford OX1 3JA, England.

CAREER: University of London, London School of Economics and Political Science, London, England, assistant lecturer, 1935; University of Liverpool, Liverpool, England, lecturer in economics and head of department, 1941-46; Oxford University, Oxford, England, university lecturer in pub-

lic finance, 1947-65, fellow of Linacre College, 1965-67, fellow emeritus, 1967—. Fiscal commissioner of Uganda, 1962, and Eastern Caribbean, 1962-63; consultant to governments, including those of Jamaica, 1955, British colonies, 1955-62, and Cyprus, 1980-81. *Wartime service:* Women's Land Army, local organizer, 1940-45. *Awards, honors:* D.Sc., University of Belfast, 1966; fellow of Institute of Social Studies (The Hague, Netherlands), 1967; honorary president of International Institute of Public Finance, 1979; honorary fellow of London School of Economics, 1981.

WRITINGS: Finance of British Government, 1920-1936, Oxford University Press, 1938, reprinted with new introduction, Clarendon Press, 1970; (with husband, John R. Hicks, and Laszlo Rostas) *Taxation of War Wealth*, Clarendon Press, 1941; (with J. R. Hicks) *Standards of Local Expenditure*, Cambridge University Press, 1943; (with J. R. Hicks and C.E.V. Leser) *The Problem of Valuation for Rating*, Cambridge University Press, 1944; (with J. R. Hicks) *The Incidence of Local Rates in Great Britain*, Cambridge University Press, 1945; *Public Finance*, introduction by C. W. Guillebaud, Nisbet, 1947, 3rd edition, Cambridge University Press, 1968; *Indian Public Finance*, United Nations Publishing Division, 1952; *British Public Finances: Their Structure and Development, 1880-1952*, Oxford University Press, 1954, revised edition, 1958; (with J. R. Hicks) *Report on Finance and Taxation in Jamaica*, Government of Jamaica, 1955.

Development From Below: Local Government and Finance in Developing Countries of the Commonwealth, Oxford University Press, 1961; (with F. G. Cavnell, W. T. Newly, and J. R. Hicks) *Federalism and Economic Growth in Underdeveloped Countries*, Oxford University Press, 1961; *Federation of East Caribbean Territories: Report of the Fiscal Commissioner*, H.M.S.O., 1963; *Development Finance: Planning and Control*, Oxford University Press, 1965; *The Large City: A World Problem*, Wiley, 1974; *Federalism: Failure and Success*, Macmillan, 1978; (contributor) *Handbuch der Finanzwissenschaft*, [Frankfort], 1981. Founder and managing editor of *Review of Economic Studies*, 1933—. Contributor of articles and reviews to journals including *Economic Journal*, *Economica*, and *Public Administration*.

WORK IN PROGRESS: Research on taxation of women; a study of the fiscal aspects of world regionalism.

SIDELIGHTS: Hicks is recognized as one of the world's leading experts in economic and governmental theory. Richard H. Leach of the *American Political Science Review* asserted that "among living scholars, Ursula K. Hicks is certainly one of the most knowledgeable and experienced students of government and finance in a variety of institutional and cultural settings."

The author's book *Federalism* examines the successes and failures of ten federal systems of government. Much of the research for the book is based on information collected during the author's visits to those countries featured. Leach observed that "however extensive her own background, she pays little or no attention to the vast (and some of it very good) literature on federalism in those countries." A *Choice* reviewer remarked that although *Federalism* was "not of the same calibre" as her *Federalism and Economic Growth in Underdeveloped Countries*, Hicks's "general reflections are those of one of the world's senior authorities on federalism, and worthy of consideration."

Hicks told *CA:* "Although always interested in travel, I took a professional interest in travel dating from my first visit to India in 1950. Since then, I have visited most parts of the world and have been to India seven times. I have never lost interest in my native Ireland, and both my husband and I are particularly devoted to Italy, which is almost a second home for us. It is also a particular joy to visit former students working in foreign countries all over the world.''

Hicks's books have been translated into Japanese, Spanish, and French.

AVOCATIONAL INTERESTS: Painting, horticulture.

BIOGRAPHICAL/CRITICAL SOURCES: Public Finance, Planning, and Economic Development: Essays in Honour of Ursula Hicks, edited by Wilfred David, Macmillan, 1973; *Annals of the American Academy of Political and Social Sciences,* July, 1979; *Choice,* September, 1979; *American Political Science Review,* March, 1980; *Journal of Economic History,* March, 1980.

*   *   *

HIGHTOWER, Florence Cole   1916-1981

OBITUARY NOTICE—See index for *CA* sketch: Born June 9, 1916, in Boston, Mass.; died March 6, 1981, in Boston, Mass. Author. Hightower and her sinologist husband, James Hightower, traveled to China from 1940 to 1941 and again for two years after the end of World War II. She was the author of six books for children: *Mrs. Wappinger's Secret, The Ghost of Follonsbee's Folly, Dark Horse of Woodfield, Fayerweather Forecast, Dreamwold Castle,* and *The Secret of the Crazy Quilt.* Obituaries and other sources: *Publishers Weekly,* May 15, 1981.

*   *   *

HILLER, Flora
See HURD, Florence

*   *   *

HILLS, Patricia Gorton Schulze   1936-

PERSONAL: Born January 31, 1936, in Baraboo, Wis.; daughter of Hartwin A. and Glennie Gorton (Baker) Schulze; married Frederic W. Hills, January 17, 1958 (divorced February, 1974); married Guy Kevin Whitfield, January 3, 1976; children: (first marriage) Christina, Bradford. *Education:* Stanford University, B.A., 1957; Hunter College of the City University of New York, M.A., 1968; New York University, Ph.D., 1973. *Home:* 36 Harrison St., Brookline, Mass. 02146. *Office:* 945 Madison Ave., New York, N.Y. 10021.

CAREER: Museum of Modern Art, New York City, curatorial assistant, 1960-62; Whitney Museum of American Art, New York City, guest curator, 1971-72, associate curator of eighteenth- and nineteenth-century art, 1972-74; York College of the City University of New York, Jamaica, N.Y., associate professor of fine arts and performing arts, 1974-78; Boston University, Boston, Mass., associate professor of art history, 1978—. Visiting assistant professor at Hunter College of the City University of New York, 1973; adjunct associate professor at New York University, 1973-74, and Columbia University, 1974-75; adjunct curator of Whitney Museum of American Art, 1974—. *Member:* College Art Association of America. *Awards, honors:* Fellow of Danforth Foundation, 1968-72.

WRITINGS: Eastman Johnson: Retrospective Exhibition, C. N. Potter, 1972; *The American Frontier: Images in Myths,* Whitney Museum of American Art, 1973; *The Painters' America: Rural and Urban Life, 1810-1910,* Praeger, 1974; *The Genre Painting of Eastman Johnson: The Sources and*

Development of His Style and Themes, Garland Publishing, 1977; *Turn-of-the-Century America: Paintings, Graphics, Photographs, 1890-1910,* Whitney Museum of American Art, 1977.

BIOGRAPHICAL/CRITICAL SOURCES: Choice, February, 1975; *Journal of American History,* September, 1975.*

*   *   *

HILTEBEITAL, Alf   1942-

PERSONAL: Born April 10, 1942, in New York, N.Y.; son of George W. (an artist) and Lucille (a real estate broker; maiden name, Barnett) Hiltebeital; married Wendy Randenbush, December 30, 1963 (divorced February, 1968); married Helen Nelson (a counselor), February 26, 1968; children: Adam, Simon. *Education:* Haverford College, B.A., 1963; University of Chicago, M.A., 1966, Ph.D., 1973. *Residence:* Washington, D.C. *Office:* Department of Religion, George Washington University, Washington, D.C. 20052.

CAREER: Seabury Press, New York, N.Y., editorial assistant, 1963-64; editorial assistant for *History of Religions,* 1967-68; George Washington University, Washington, D.C., assistant professor, 1968-74, associate professor of religion, 1974—. *Member:* American Society for the Study of Religion, American Academy of Religion, American Oriental Society, Association on Asian Studies, Conference on Religion in South India. *Awards, honors:* American Institute of Indian Studies fellow in Pune, India, 1974-75, 1978; National Endowment for the Humanities grant for England and India, 1977.

WRITINGS: (Translator) Georges Dumezil, *The Destiny of the Warrior,* University of Chicago Press, 1969; (translator) Dumezil, *The Destiny of a King,* University of Chicago Press, 1973; *The Ritual of Battle: Krishna in the Mahabharata,* Cornell University Press, 1976; (contributor) Bardwell L. Smith, editor, *Hinduism: New Essays in the History of Religions,* E. J. Brill, 1976; (contributor) Fred Clothey, editor, *Change and Continuity in South Asian Religion,* Manohar, 1981. Contributor to *Abingdon Dictionary of World Religions.* Contributor of more than twenty-five articles and reviews to scholarly journals.

WORK IN PROGRESS: The Indian Epics, the Goddess, and the Continuity of Hinduism, a book on Draupadi as epic heroine and goddess of a South Indian fire-walking cult; ''Krsna at Mathura,'' to be included in *Conference on Ancient Mathura: Seminar Papers,* edited by Doris Srinivasan; research on the relationship between the *Mahabharata* and the *Ramayana.*

AVOCATIONAL INTERESTS: ''Climbing medium-sized mountains.''

*   *   *

HINDE, Wendy   1919-

PERSONAL—Home: 5 The Keep, Blackheath, London SE3 0AG, England.

CAREER: Economist, London, England, member of editorial staff, 1950-71; Royal Institute of International Affairs, London, editor of *International Affairs,* 1971—.

WRITINGS: George Canning, Collins, 1973, St. Martin's, 1974.*

HIPPISLEY COXE, Antony D(acres)   1912-
(Charles Lacy)

PERSONAL: Born March 21, 1912, in London, England; son of Robert (a writer) and Helen de Lacy (Lacy) Hippisley Coxe; married Araminta Peel (a writer), January 29, 1942; children: Nicolas Charles, Helen Penelope Hippisley Coxe Bugge, Araminta Sophie. *Education:* Attended Royal Naval College, Dartmouth, 1925-28, and Architectural Association School of Architecture, 1929-32. *Politics:* "Liberalish Conservative." *Religion:* Church of England. *Home:* Ackworthy, Hartland, Devonshire EX39 6DZ, England.

CAREER: Gainsborough Pictures Film Production, London, England, assistant art director, 1932-35; *Harper's Bazaar,* London edition, London, assistant art editor, 1935-39, subeditor, 1936-39, author of "Let's Eat Out," a food and wine column, 1937-39; British Broadcasting Corp., Overseas Monitoring Service, London, copytaster in London and Evesham, England, 1939-40; *News Chronicle,* London, features editor, 1945-48; Festival of Britain, London, representative of Council of Industrial Design, 1948-51; National Farmers Union, London, head of publicity, 1952-55; Granada Television Co., London, director of press and publicity, 1955-56; Shell International Petroleum Co., London, head of media and Middle East adviser on trade relations, 1956-70; British Plastics Federation, London, head of press and publicity, 1970-72; writer, 1972—. Member of advisory council of Theatre Museum; past member of board of governors of Overseas Visual Aid Centre; guest on television and radio programs; lecturer. *Military service:* Royal Naval Volunteer Reserve, Naval Intelligence, 1941-45; served in destroyers; became lieutenant commander. *Member:* Society of Authors, Circus Fans Association of Great Britain (president, 1951), Le Club du Cirque (member d'honneur), West Country Writers Association (vice-chairman, 1980), Devonshire Association (vice-chairman of arts and literature section).

WRITINGS: (With sister, Tacina Coxe) *Galley-Wise: A Guide to "Boat Cooking",* Hamish Hamilton, 1938; *A Seat at the Circus,* Evans Brothers, 1951, revised edition, Archon, 1980; (with H. J. Lijsen) *Training Horses at Liberty,* J. A. Allen, 1956; (with Lijsen) *Trick-Riding and Voltige,* J. A. Allen, 1956; (with Lijsen) *Classic and Circus High School Riding,* J. A. Allen, 1957; (with Lijsen) *Mounted Quadrilles, Carrousels, and Other Equestrian Manoeuvres,* J. A. Allen, 1957; *Haunted Britain,* McGraw, 1973; (with wife, Araminta Hippisley Coxe) *The Book of the Sausage,* Pan Books, 1978; *Concerning Clovely,* Clovely Estate Co., 1980.

Contributor: Leonard Russell, editor, *The Saturday Book,* Volume 8, Hutchinson, 1948; T. H. Tracy, editor, *The Book of the Poodle,* Harville Press, 1951; W. E. Lyon, editor, *The Horseman's Year,* Collins, 1952; John Hadfield, editor, *The Saturday Book,* Volume 34, Hutchinson, 1975; M. Renevey, editor, *Le Grand Livre du Cirque* (title means "The Big Book of the Circus"), Edito-Service, 1977; D. Bradby, L. James, and B. Sharralt, editors, *Performance and Politics in Popular Drama,* Cambridge University Press, 1980.

Author of introduction to *The Circus and Allied Arts,* Volume 3, edited by R. Toole Scott, Harper, 1962, and *Just Cats,* by Ylla, Harville Press. Author of pamphlets, including one under pseudonym Charles Lacy. Writer for television. Contributor to *Encyclopaedia Britannica* and to periodicals, including *Country Life, Tatler, Geographical, Listener, Spectator,* and *Journal of the Gypsy Lore Society.* Co-editor of *I-Spy Annual* (juvenile).

WORK IN PROGRESS: An autobiography; a book on the conversion of country cottages; research on smuggling, 1700-1850, for a thematic exhibition.

SIDELIGHTS: "Most of my writing," Hippisley Coxe told *CA,* "has been about the circus. My first article in 1936 led to criticism from the anti-performing animal fanatics. I decided to see for myself and trained a troupe of domestic cats, entirely by kindness, to work in a circus, in cabarets, and in variety shows. This led to my collection of books, then of photographs, programs, prints, posters, contracts, and route books. The Hippisley Coxe Circus Collection is now in the Theatre Musuem, London, and I write their information cards on the circus. I have seen circuses in eighteen different countries and in cities from Tashkent to New York, including a Brazilian circus in Hong Kong.

"My second interest seems to be food. The common factors in circuses and sausage is that both are international. I am also interested in Romany. I spent two years in Iran, and wrote a monograph on Persian words in the Gypsy language.

"I have had a good many different jobs, but if one is a journalist one is inquisitive. I have also been lucky that people have asked me to write. If I thought the subject might be interesting and lead to better financial return I would probably take it. For the Festival of Britain, I made a free balloon ascent, and as a publicity stunt, produced the first man to cross the Thames on a tightrope. But I also showed how seaside rock was made."

BIOGRAPHICAL/CRITICAL SOURCES: Times Literary Supplement, December 21, 1951.

*   *   *

HIRSCH, Morris Isaac   1915-

PERSONAL: Born October 30, 1915, in Johannesburg, South Africa; son of Louis Philip (an advertising agent) and Rebecca (Rubin) Hirsch; married Joan E. Sullivan, March 3, 1943; children: Brian John, Diana, I. David. *Education:* University of the Witwatersrand, M.B., B.Ch., 1938. *Home:* 305 Russell Sq., 26 Hillbrow St., Berea, Johannesburg, South Africa 2198. *Office:* Electricity Supply Commission, P.O. Box 1091, Johannesburg, South Africa 2000.

CAREER: Private practice of medicine, 1946-76; Electricity Supply Commission, Johannesburg, South Africa, corporate medical officer, 1979—. Member of Rhodesian Parliament, 1958-62; mayor of Que Que, Rhodesia, 1953-56, member of municipal council, 1948-75; past member of Rhodesian Drug Council. *Military service:* South African Army, Medical Corps, 1940-46; became captain. *Member:* South African Medical Association, South African Society of Occupational Medicine, South African Institute of Race Relations, American Academy of Family Physicians, Rhodesian College of General Practice.

WRITINGS: Focus on Southern Rhodesia, Stuart Manning, 1964; *For Whom the Land,* A. & W. Bardwell & Co., 1967; *A Decade of Crisis,* Peter Dearlove, 1973. Also contributor to *South Africa: Dilemmas of Evolutionary Change,* edited by Van Zyl Slabbert and Jeff Opland, 1980. Author of columns in *Rhodesian Herald* and *Midlands Observer,* both before 1975. Contributor to journals, including *Rhodesia Medical Journal.*

WORK IN PROGRESS: Research on people from medieval history and on political philosophy and trends.

SIDELIGHTS: Hirsch commented: "I love challenge, especially the challenge of seeking answers to interpersonal and intergroup conflicts to contribute to community development to face the truth. I am interested in all aspects of medicine and surgery, and in constitutional answers for multiracial communities. I participated in and contributed to the 1961 Rhodesian Constitutional Settlement.''

AVOCATIONAL INTERESTS: Squash, swimming.

*   *   *

HITCHING, (John) Francis 1933-

PERSONAL: Born December 3, 1933, in Wolverhampton, England; son of Leonard Levesley and Luise Hitching; married Judith Wellstood, February 6, 1958; children: Emma, Suzie, Polly. *Education:* Attended private boys' school in Warwick, England. *Home:* 20 St. George's Rd., Twickenham TW1 1QR, England. *Agent:* Michael Sissons, A. D. Peters & Co. Ltd., 10 Buckingham St., London WC2N 6BU, England.

CAREER: Alan Landsburg Productions, Los Angeles, Calif., executive producer in Europe; currently full-time writer. *Member:* Royal Archaeological Institute, Prehistoric Society, Society for Psychical Research, British Society of Dowsers, American Society of Dowsers.

WRITINGS: Earth Magic, Morrow, 1977; *Dowsing: The Psi Connection,* Doubleday, 1978; *Mysterious World: An Atlas of the Unexplained,* Holt, 1979.

WORK IN PROGRESS: Fraud, Mischief, and the Supernatural; Instead of Darwin.

SIDELIGHTS: Hitching wrote: "I write about and film phenomena. I am more interested in what science hasn't explained than what it has, and more interested in what the mind can do than what it can't.''

*   *   *

HOARE, Merval Hannah 1914-

PERSONAL: Born June 17, 1914, in Wellington, New Zealand; daughter of Michael and Agnes (Aynsley) Connelly; married Percy Raymond Hoare, 1949; children: Ann Merval Burke. *Education:* Attended St. Dominics College, Dunedin, New Zealand. *Home address:* New Cascade Rd., Norfolk Island, South Pacific.

CAREER: Writer, 1943—. *Member:* Australian Society of Authors, Norfolk Island Conservation Society, Norfolk Island Historical Society, Norfolk Island Museum Trust.

WRITINGS: Twelve Poems, Harry H. Tombs, 1943; *Twenty-Eight Poems,* Caxton Press, 1951; *Norfolk Island Poems,* Pegasus Press, 1951; *Rambler's Guide to Norfolk Island,* Pacific Publications, 1965, 6th edition, 1977; *Norfolk Island: An Outline of Its History, 1774-1977,* St. Lucia, 1969, 2nd edition, University of Queensland Press, 1978; *The Discovery of Norfolk Island,* Australian Government Publishing Service, 1974; *Norfolk Island: A History Through Illustration, 1774-1974,* Australian Government Publishing Service, 1979.

WORK IN PROGRESS: A survey of fundamental changes on Norfolk Island since 1950.

SIDELIGHTS: Merval Hoare wrote: "I have lived on Norfolk Island (an Australian territory) for thirty-one years, but even before arriving I had begun research on its history, social life, economy, and environment. Although it is closely woven into Australian history, Norfolk's story is also linked with that of Pitcairn Island and many other islands in the South Pacific region. I consider myself one of the little people in the literary world, working in comparative isolation.''

HOBSON, William 1911-

PERSONAL: Born September 5, 1911, in Leeds, England; son of William and Lilian (May) Hobson; married Lucy Muriel Wilson, 1937 (marriage ended December 23, 1953); married Heather McMahon Greer (a registered nurse), 1953 (divorced June, 1973); children: (first marriage) one daughter, one son; (second marriage) one daughter. *Education:* University of Leeds, B.Sc. (with first class honors), 1933, D.P.H. (with distinction), 1938, M.D. (with distinction), L.R.C.P. *Home:* Strand Cottage, Myrtleville, County Cork, Ireland.

CAREER: University of Leeds, Leeds, England, lecturer in physiology and hygiene, 1936-38; City of Leeds, assistant school medical officer, 1938-39; Hampshire County Council, England, assistant county medical officer, 1939-40; Borough of Lymington, England, medical officer of health, 1940-42; University of Bristol, Bristol, England, senior lecturer in preventive medicine, 1946-48; University of Sheffield, Sheffield, England, professor of social and industrial medicine, 1949-58; World Health Organization, Geneva, Switzerland, visiting professor in India, 1957-58, chief of education and training at European office in Denmark, 1958-68, chief of staff training in Geneva, 1968-71, consultant to Regional Office for the East Mediterranean in Alexandria, Egypt, 1971-72, consultant in medical education, 1971—. Honorary patron of Western Foundation of Vertebrate Zoology, Los Angeles, Calif., 1968. *Military service:* British Army, Royal Army Medical Corps, specialist in epidemiology and hygiene, 1942-46; became major; mentioned in dispatches. *Awards, honors:* Prize from CIBA Foundation, 1955, for *The Health of the Elderly at Home;* commander of Conferie des Chevaliers de Tastevin de Bourgogne, 1963.

WRITINGS: (With John Pemberton) *The Health of the Elderly at Home: A Medical, Social, and Dietary Study of Elderly People Living at Home in Sheffield,* Butterworth, 1955; (editor) *Modern Trends in Geriatrics,* Butterworth, 1956, Harper, 1957; (editor) *Theory and Practice of Public Health,* Oxford University Press, 1961, 5th edition, 1979; *World Health and History,* Williams & Wilkins, 1963. Contributor of about fifty articles to medical journals.

AVOCATIONAL INTERESTS: Ornithology in Greenland, Scandinavia, all European countries, North America, and Mongolia.

*   *   *

HOCHBAUM, H(ans) Albert 1911-

PERSONAL: Born February 9, 1911, in Greeley, Colo.; came to Canada, 1938; naturalized Canadian citizen; son of Hans Weller (an agriculturist) and Gertrude Stone (Schenck) Hochbaum; married Eleanor Joan Ward, May 26, 1939; children: Albert Ward, Peter Weller, George Sutton, Trudi Ann. *Education:* Cornell University, B.Sc., 1933; University of Wisconsin (now University of Wisconsin—Madison), M.Sc., 1941. *Politics:* Conservative. *Religion:* Protestant. *Home and office address:* R.R.1, Box 4, Portage la Prairie, Manitoba, Canada R1N 3A1.

CAREER: U.S. National Park Service, Washington, D.C., wildlife technician, 1934-37; Delta Waterfowl Research Station, Delta, Manitoba, director, 1938-70; free-lance artist and writer, 1970—. *Member:* Canadian Society of Zoologists, American Ornithologists Union (fellow), American Association for the Advancement of Science, Manitoba Naturalists Society, Wildlife Society, Beta Theta Pi, Sigma Xi. *Awards, honors:* Brewster Medal from American Ornithologists Union, 1945, for *The Canvasback on a Prairie Marsh;* literary award from Wildlife Society, 1945, for *The Canvasback on a Prairie Marsh,* and 1957, for *Travels and Traditions of Waterfowl;* Guggenheim fellowship, 1961; Manitoba LL.D. from University of Manitoba, 1962; Centennial Medal of Honour, 1970; Wilderness Award from Canadian Broadcasting Corp., 1970; Canadian Council explorations grant, 1975-76; member of Order of Canada, 1979; Leopold Medal, 1980.

WRITINGS: The Canvasback on a Prairie Marsh, American Wildlife Institute, 1944; *Travels and Traditions of Waterfowl,* University of Minnesota Press, 1955; *To Ride the Wind,* Harlequin Press, 1973. Contributor to scientific journals and popular magazines.

WORK IN PROGRESS: Tundra Wolves and Caribou (tentative title), based on annual travels in the Canadian arctic since 1961.

SIDELIGHTS: Hochbaum commented: "I am motivated by my interest in wildlife and the wild environment. Currently my art and writing deal with the Canadian arctic and arctic wildlife. I have made twenty-two arctic field trips since 1961. I am deeply concerned with the role of private citizens in the conservation of wildlife and wild places."

*   *   *

HOCHMAN, Stanley Richard 1928-

PERSONAL: Born October 15, 1928, in New York, N.Y.; son of Isador and Rose (Merman) Hochman; married Gloria S. Honickman, October 30, 1961; children: Anndee Elyn. *Education:* New York University, B.A., 1948, M.A., 1950. *Home:* 44 Trent Rd., Philadelphia, Pa. 19151. *Office: Philadelphia Daily News,* 400 North Broad St., Philadelphia, Pa. 19101.

CAREER: Member of staff of *Brownsville Herald,* Brownsville, Tex., 1953-54, *Corpus Christi Caller-Times,* Corpus Christi, Tex., 1954-56, *Waco News-Tribune,* Waco, Tex., 1956-58, and *San Bernardino Sun,* San Bernardino, Calif., 1958-59; *Philadelphia Daily News,* Philadelphia, Pa., member of staff, 1959—, sports editor, 1971-74. *Military service:* U.S. Army, 1951-53.

WRITINGS: A Library of Film Criticism: American Film Directors; With Filmographies and Index of Critics and Films, Ungar, 1974; *Yesterday and Today: A Dictionary of Recent American History,* McGraw, 1979; (with Louis DeVries) *French-English Science Dictionary,* McGraw, 1976.

Translator: Jules Renard, *Poil De Carotte and Other Plays,* Ungar, 1977; Vitaliano Brancati, *Bell'Antonio,* Ungar, 1978; Eric Rohmer and Claude Chabrol, *Hitchcock: The First Forty-Four Films,* Ungar, 1979.

BIOGRAPHICAL/CRITICAL SOURCES: Booklist, April 1, 1975.*

*   *   *

HOCHSCHILD, Harold K. 1892-1981

OBITUARY NOTICE: Born May 20, 1892, in New York, N.Y.; died after a long illness, January 23, 1981, in New York, N.Y. Industrialist, historian, conservationist, and author of books about the history of the Adirondacks, including *Lumberjacks and Rivermen in the Central Adirondacks, 1850-1950* and *Township Thirty-Four.* Hochschild's efforts on behalf of the Adirondack State Park contributed to the establishment of a state agency to insure conservation within the park. Obituaries and other sources: *Who's Who in Amer-*

ica, 39th edition, Marquis, 1976; *New York Times,* January 25, 1981.

*   *   *

HODGES, John C(unyus) 1892-1967

OBITUARY NOTICE—See index for *CA* sketch: Born March 15, 1892, in Cotton Valley, La.; died in 1967. Educator and author. A professor English for more than fifty years, Hodges wrote prolifically on William Gongreve and composed several English textbooks. Included among his writings are *William Congreve, the Man; Harbrace Handbook of English; Harbrace College Handbook;* and *The Library of William Congreve.* Obituaries and other sources: *Who Was Who in America,* 5th edition, Marquis, 1973.

*   *   *

HOGAN, Thom(as Eugene, Jr.) 1952-

PERSONAL: Born July 22, 1952, in Redwood City, Calif.; son of Thomas Eugene (in business) and Yvonne Shirley (a teacher; maiden name, Lange) Hogan; married Eva Katherine Langfeldt (an editor), January 5, 1973. *Education:* Washington State University, B.A., 1974; Indiana University, M.A., 1978, A.B.D., 1980. *Residence:* Palo Alto, Calif. *Office: Infoworld,* 530 Lytton Ave., Palo Alto, Calif. 94301.

CAREER: Squaw Valley U.S.A. (ski resort), Squaw Valley, Calif., public relations representative, 1974-75; Indiana University, Bloomington, associate instructor in telecommunications, 1976-80; Data Domain (retail computer store), Bloomington, manager, 1976-80; *Infoworld* (bi-weekly computer newspaper), Palo Alto, Calif., editor, 1980—. Second trumpet in Spokane Symphony, 1971-72. Managing editor of *Media Montage,* 1976-77. *Member:* Association of Masters of Business Administration Executives, University Film Association.

WRITINGS: The Osborne CP/M Users Guide, Osborne & Associates, 1981; (editor) *Software Buyers' Guide,* Infoworld, 1981. Author of television drama, "Labor Day," WTIU-TV, 1979. Author of computer equipment manuals. Contributor of articles to *Media Montage, Kilobaud Microcomputing,* and *Infoworld.*

WORK IN PROGRESS: Debuzzing Computers, an explanation of computers to lay persons using fiction narrative technique; *Wait State,* a novel; a bookette project involving translation of books to computer media.

SIDELIGHTS: Hogan told *CA:* "The information explosion is about to put all persons in the middle of computing data processing and telecommunications technology. I intend to be one of those people who make others' transitions easier. I write using two computers, both at work and at home."

*   *   *

HOLBROOK, Peter
See GLICK, Carl (Cannon)

*   *   *

HOLLANDER, Hans 1899-

PERSONAL: Born October 6, 1899, in Breclav, Austria (now Czechoslovakia). *Education:* Received Ph.D. from University of Vienna. *Home:* Gidleigh Lodge, Changford, Devonshire, England.

CAREER: In charge of music in the German department of a radio station in Brno, Czechoslovakia, 1929-39; University of Exeter, Exeter, England, tutor in music, 1940-78, honorary research fellow. Broadcaster.

WRITINGS—In English: *Leos Janacek: Leben und Werk,* Atlantis, 1964, translation by Paul Hamburger published as *Leos Janacek: His Life and Work,* St. Martin's, 1963; *Early Medieval Art,* Weidenfeld & Nicolson, 1974.

Other writings: *Die Musik in der Kulturgeschichte des 19 und 20 Jahrhunderts,* Kloen, 1967; *Musik und Jugendstil,* Atlantis, 1974. Also author of *Janacek,* 1963. Contributor to music journals.

* * *

HOLLEB, Arthur Irving 1921-

PERSONAL: Born April 1, 1921, in New York, N.Y.; son of Simon and Kate (Liss) Holleb; married Carolyn R. Oglesby, June 16, 1951; children: Susan Jane and David Gene (twins). *Education:* Brown University, A.B., 1941; New York University, M.D., 1944. *Home:* 3 Highridge Rd., Larchmont, N.Y. 10538. *Office:* 777 Third Ave., New York, N.Y. 10017.

CAREER: Queens General Hospital, Jamaica, N.Y., intern, 1944-45; Meadowbrook Hospital, Hempstead, N.Y., resident in surgery and pathology, 1945-46, chief resident in general surgery, 1948-50; Memorial Hospital, New York, N.Y., member of staff, 1950—, associate chief of medical service, 1966-67. Diplomate of American Board of Surgery. Assistant director of tumor service at Meadowbrook Hospital, 1954-56; associate clinician at Sloan-Kettering Institute, 1961-67; associate visiting surgeon at James Ewing Hospital, 1966-67; member of staff, associate professor, member of research staff, and associate director of education at M.D. Anderson Hospital and Tumor Institute, 1967-68. Instructor and clinical associate professor at Cornell University, 1965-67; associate professor at University of Texas, 1967-68. Member of evaluation panel of cancer control branch of U.S. Public Health Service, 1965-69; member of cancer control advisory committee, diagnostic research advisory group, and therapy committee of National Cancer Institute, 1972—. *Military service:* U.S. Naval Reserve, active duty, 1946-48.

MEMBER: American Cancer Society (senior vice-president for medical affairs and research, 1968—; chief medical officer, 1968—; member of board of directors, 1964-67), American Association for Cancer Education, American Association for Cancer Research, American Medical Association, American College of Surgeons, American Radium Society (vice-president, 1969-70), Association of American Medical Colleges, American Society of Clinical Oncology, Association of Hospital Directors of Medical Education (chairman of surgical education committee, 1965-67), James Ewing Society (president, 1972-73), New York Academy of Medicine, New York Academy of Sciences, New York Cancer Society (president, 1971), New York Surgical Society, Harris County Medical Society, New York County Medical Society, Brown Club, Marco Polo Club.

WRITINGS: (With Jane E. Brody) *You Can Fight Cancer and Win,* Quadrangle, 1977. Editor-in-chief of *Journal CA;* member of editorial advisory board of *Journal of Cancer* and *American Journal of Preventive Medicine.*

BIOGRAPHICAL/CRITICAL SOURCES: *New York Review of Books,* June 9, 1977.*

HOLLINDALE, Peter 1936-

PERSONAL: Born April 5, 1936, in Chesterfield, England; son of Wilfred Arthur (a wheelwright) and Dorothy (Fennell) Hollindale; married Anne Rosemary Botham, July 29, 1967; children: Philip Edward, Nicholas Daniel. *Education:* Jesus College, Cambridge, B.A. (with first class honors), 1957, M.A., 1962; University of Bristol, Certificate in Education (with distinction), 1959. *Home:* 17 Chalfonts, York YO2 2EX, England. *Office:* Department of English and Related Literature, University of York, York YO1 5DD, England.

CAREER: Assistant English master at cathedral choir school in Gloucester, England, 1959-62, and at college in Bristol, England, 1962-65; University of York, York, England, lecturer, 1965-75, senior lecturer in English and education, 1975—. *Member:* National Association for the Teaching of English.

WRITINGS: *A Critical Commentary on Shakespeare's King Henry IV, Part Two,* Macmillan, 1971; (editor) William Shakespeare, *As You Like It,* Macmillan, 1974; *Choosing Books for Children,* Elek, 1974; (editor) Shakespeare, *King Henry IV, Part One,* Macmillan, 1975; (contributor) Dennis Butts, editor, *Good Writers for Young Readers,* Hart-Davis, 1977; (editor) Joseph Conrad, *Lord Jim,* Macmillian, in press; *William Shakespeare,* Ward, Lock, in press. General editor of "Macmillan Shakespeare," a series, Macmillan, 1972—. Contributor to literature and education journals. Guest editor of *Use of English,* autumn, 1979.

WORK IN PROGRESS: *To Seek a Newer World,* on the importance of fantasy in contemporary literature.

SIDELIGHTS: Hollindale told *CA:* "I am two things: a literary critic and a practical drama teacher, where my program includes workshops in experimental drama, movement, and improvisation. I believe that work in my field habitually tends to complicate language and simplify experience. I try to do the opposite.

"As a literary critic I see my job as helping to open up understanding of literature by expressing difficult ideas simply, so that I can illuminate rather than terrorize. As a drama teacher I base my work on the supposition that we rarely know ourselves or each other very well, and that, under the conditions of controlled risk that drama can offer, we are able to achieve new insights into our own and others' ideas and emotions, which will prevent us from settling for easy social generalizations and cliches.

"I believe that most people (including most children) are far more creative and daring than ordinary life allows for, and that that creativity is nurtured and given expression by many activities. Storytelling, drama, and dance are three of the most important. I concentrate in my work on the first two of these, but dance is my essential point of reference and my personal ideal of artistic achievment.

"Although I teach and write for adults, everything in my program derives special purpose and delight from its direct concern with children. One day, when I've time at last, I want to write a novel for children—one that some children enjoy and that pleases me. Without that, everything else that I've written and taught will be incomplete."

AVOCATIONAL INTERESTS: Birdwatching, steam locomotives.

HOLLOWOOD, Albert Bernard   1910-1981

OBITUARY NOTICE—See index for *CA* sketch: Born June 3, 1910, in Burslem, Staffordshire, England; died of a brain hemorrhage, March 28, 1981, in Guildford, England. Journalist, cartoonist, economist, educator, and author. Hollowood lectured in economics at Stoke and Loughborough College in London, England, for eleven years before joining the staff of the *Economist* in 1944. He also became the editor of *Pottery and Glass* in 1944, remaining in that position until 1950. As the editor of *Punch* from 1958 to 1968, Hollowood added political and social commentaries to the British humor magazine, beginning with a 1965 editorial criticizing United States involvement in Vietnam. Other editorials called for famine relief for Africa and India and reported on the state of British labor. An accomplished cartoonist, Hollowood drew for the *London Times* and the *Sunday Telegraph* and illustrated several of his books, including *Direct Economics* and *Money Is No Expense.* Among Hollowood's other works are *The Story of Morro Velho, These Fuelish Things, Cricket on the Brain,* and *Tales of Tammy Barr.* Obituaries and other sources: *New York Times,* March 29, 1981; *Time,* April 13, 1981.

*   *   *

HOLME, Bryan   1913-
(Charles Francis)

PERSONAL: Born June 25, 1913, in Church Crookham, England; came to the United States, 1932, naturalized citizen, 1946; son of Charles Geoffrey (a publisher) and Margaret Nina (Bolton) Holme; married Edith Elfrida Mary Bell, March 7, 1936; children: Christopher Bryan, Charles Francis. *Education:* Attended Columbia University. *Home:* 157 East 75th St., New York, N.Y. 10021.

CAREER: Editor and publisher. *Studio,* London, England, staff member, 1930-32; Studio Publications, New York City, co-founder, 1932, editor, 1932—; Viking Press, New York City, director of Studio Books, 1959—. *Member:* Coffee House Club. *Awards, honors:* Certificate from Eastern Arts Associates, 1955, for contributing to art education in public schools.

WRITINGS—Published by Studio Publications, except as noted: *A Book of Animals,* 1943; (editor) *The Classical Figure,* 1943; *Master Drawings,* 1943; (with Marcel Vertes) *Art and Fashion,* 1944; (editor) *Masterpieces in Color at the Metropolitan Museum of Art, New York,* American Studio Books, 1945; (editor with Thomas Forman) *Poet's Camera,* American Studio Books, 1946; (editor) *Master Drawings in Line,* 1948; (editor) *Cats and Kittens,* 1950; (editor) *Horses,* 1951; (with Anne Freemantle) *Europe: A Journey With Pictures,* 1954; (under pseudonym Charles Francis) *Make Your Own Greeting Cards,* 1955; (picture editor) Emily Davie, *Profile of America,* P. Owen, 1959.

Published by Viking, except as noted: *Pictures to Live With* (juvenile; Junior Literary Guild selection), 1959; (co-editor) *The World in Vogue,* 1963; *Drawings to Live With* (juvenile), 1966; (editor) *The Churchill Years: 1874-1965,* 1965; (co-editor) *The Journal of the Century,* 1976; (editor) *The Kate Greenaway Book: A Collection of Illustration, Verse, and Text,* 1976; (editor) *Tales From Times Past* (juvenile), 1977; (editor) Thomas Bulfinch, *Bulfinch's Mythology: The Greek and Roman Fables Illustrated,* 1979; *Enchanted World: Pictures to Grow Up With* (juvenile), Oxford University Press, 1979 (published in England as *Enchanted World: The Magic*

of Pictures, Thames & Hudson, 1979); *Creatures of Paradise: Pictures to Grow Up With* (juvenile), Oxford University Press, 1979; *Hiroshige: A Shoal of Fishes,* 1979; *Nursery Songs,* Thames & Hudson, 1980.

Contributor to periodicals, including *Christian Science Monitor, American Artist, Design, Popular Photography, Art World,* and *House and Garden.*

WORK IN PROGRESS: Gardens of Delight; Visual History of Advertising; The Drawings of Grandville.

SIDELIGHTS: Bryan Holme represents "the complete publisher in a classic tradition," according to Paul D. Doebler. "He is at once a skilled entrepreneur, editor, art director, buyer of graphic reproductions, [and] manipulator of complex schedules and relationships." Using all of these skills, Holme and his staff publish approximately forty-five new books each year. "One of Mr. Holme's publishing principles," wrote Doebler, "is that every art or photography book he produces must have a clear editorial theme."

Holme explained to Doebler that "most really successful art books must sell in more than one country, and the economics involved requires international cooperation among publishers and book manufacturers." Such was the case with *Minerals and Crystals,* a co-publishing venture which resulted in American, English, French, and German editions. "The market estimate for 'Minerals and Crystals,'" Holme told Doebler, "substantiated what is the case for most co-published volumes—that the U.S. market alone was not large enough to generate all the sales needed. Foreign editions were required." Like most co-publishing contracts, the agreement for the international publication of *Minerals and Crystals* was secured at the Frankfurt Book Fair where "the exhibit floor is something like a stock exchange on one of its business days."

As a successful art publisher, Holme perpetuates a family tradition that began in the late nineteenth century. His paternal grandfather, Charles, was the founder of *Studio* magazine (*International Studio* in the United States). Though the magazine has been sold and though the family has moved into the book publishing industry, Holme shows "no regrets, for the challenges of publishing art books now surpass those involved in publishing an art magazine."

BIOGRAPHICAL/CRITICAL SOURCES: Publishers Weekly, May 8, 1972, September 24, 1973; *New Republic,* January 1-8, 1977; *New York Times Book Review,* May 13, 1979; *Christian Science Monitor,* May 14, 1979.

*   *   *

HOME, Henry Douglas
See DOUGLAS-HOME, Henry

*   *   *

HONOUR, Hugh   1927-

PERSONAL: Born September 26, 1927, in Eastbourne, Sussex, England; son of Herbert Percy and Dorothy Margaret (Withers) Honour. *Education:* Received B.A. from St. Catherine's College, Cambridge. *Address:* Villa Marchio, Tofori, Lucca, Italy; and c/o Traveller's Club, Pall Mall, London S.W.1, England.

CAREER: Assistant director of Leeds City Art Gallery and Temple Newsan House, 1953-54; Italian correspondent for *Connoisseur,* 1956-61; guest curator for exhibition The European Vision of America, appeared at Gallery of Art (Washington, D.C.), Cleveland Museum of Art (Cleveland), and Grand Palais (Paris), 1976. *Member:* Traveller's Club.

WRITINGS: Horace Walpole, Longmans, Green, 1957, reprinted with amendments and additions, 1970; *Chinoiserie: The Vision of Cathay*, J. Murray, 1961, Dutton, 1962; *The Companion Guide to Venice*, Collins, 1965, Harper, 1966, published as *Fodor's Venice: A Companion Guide*, practical information section edited by Eugene Fodor, McKay, 1971; (with Nelly Schargo Hoyt) *An Exhibition of Chinoiserie*, organized by the Smith College Museum of Art, 1965; (with John Fleming and Nikolas Pevsner) *The Penguin Dictionary of Architecture*, drawings by David Etherton, Penguin, 1966, enlarged and revised edition published as *A Dictionary of Architecture*, Allen Lane, 1975, Overlook Press, 1976; *Neo-Classicism*, Penguin, 1968; *Cabinet Makers and Furniture Designers*, Putnam, 1969; *Canova's Theseus and the Minotaur*, Phaidon, 1969.

(With Fleming) *A Heritage of Images: A Selection of Lectures*, introduction by E. H. Gombrich, Penguin, 1970; *Goldsmiths and Silversmiths*, Putnam, 1971; *The European Vision of America: A Special Exhibition to Honor the Bicentennial of the United States*, Kent State University Press, 1975; *The New Golden Land: European Images of America From Discovery to the Present Time*, Pantheon, 1975; (with Fleming) *Dictionary of the Decorative Arts*, Harper, 1977 (published in England as *The Penguin Dictionary of the Arts*, Allen Lane, 1977); *Romanticism*, Harper, 1979. Contributor of numerous articles to periodicals.

SIDELIGHTS: Through his books, Hugh Honour, a British art historian, provides a short cut by which his readers may arrive at a comprehension of major artistic movements, styles, and concepts. For example, Honour's book *The New Golden Land* is the first general reference survey of the Europeans' visual images of America, which, as Alan Trachtenburg of the *New York Times Book Review* pointed out, "are often fantastic." The European artists' impressions of America are misrepresentations which have resulted, said Ruth Berenson in the *National Review,* in "stereotypes that have determined the way Europeans looked at us ever since."

In *The New Golden Land,* Honour states that Europeans visualized America through "bifocal vision." They either saw an earthly paradise full of curious creatures and strange vegetation or a combination of jungles, deserts, and sky-scraper forests inhabited by cannibals and savages. Some artists pictured America as the new Promised Land, "an unspoiled Eden," wrote Berenson, "peopled with noble savages, naked or at most sporting a few feathers, whose idyllic existence before the white man came was one of pure innocence." Trachtenburg added that Europeans saw in America the "ripe image of the wealth they dreamed of possessing." But other artists, Berenson noted, "depicted Indians as brutal, cruel, devil-worshippers." In fact, the standard image of America in the sixteenth and seventeenth centuries was a severed limb, a representation of cannibalism. Softened by the passage of time, although just as fantastic, the European image of America evolved into the allegorical figure of "an almost naked classical goddess wearing the regulation feathers on her head, and somewhat uncomfortably perched on the regulation American animal, an armor-plated armadillo," reported J. H. Elliot of the *New York Review of Books.*

Berenson explained the reason for the artists' misconceptions about America when she revealed that "relatively few had a first-hand acquaintance with their subject; they based their images, especially during the early centuries, on written descriptions." Europe, then, shaped America in its own image and likeness. The cultural, political, and psychological needs of the Europeans found a symbol in America, and "European

societies," suggested Trachtenburg, "assimilated and used the images of America to serve their own internal purposes." Many artists dealt only with the curiosity, not the reality, of America while others, however few, were able to transcend their preconceived images.

In another work, *Neo-Classicism,* Honour presents the reflections of an insecure and unstable age in western history (1760-1815) in which artists, spurred by a Greco-Roman influence, concentrated on ideal form and content. Honour "fuses fact with idea" in the scholarly, yet broadly interpretive book. Robert Rosenblum of the *New York Review of Books* judged: "What distinguishes Mr. Honour's book . . . is that it is written by someone who is not a dilettante but a professional art historian, thoroughly attuned to the high degree of specialization demanded today, yet willing to apply refined art-historical data to problems of a broad, interpretive nature." The art historian is conscious of cultural influences and of technical innovations and qualities when exploring the artistic principles that illustrate the break between the modern and Old worlds.

Nevertheless, David Watkins of the *Observer Review* cited that Honour addresses only one style, neglecting several other important styles. Rosenblum found a problem with the art historian's time sequence. "Mr. Honour," he complained, "ends his book with the art of the Napoleonic Empire, and suggests that this is the last and decadent phase of Neoclassicism, where high-minded goals and pure, virile forms become trivial, pretty, and diminutive, and that this feeble coda is to be followed by something new and vital called Romanticism. Yet this rupture appears to terminate Neoclassicism far too early and to start Romanticism much too late." Both critics agree that neither flaw is significant enough to detract from Honour's book as a whole. When commenting on another reviewer's notion that "neoclassicism is 'so hydra-headed that the historian who attacks it from a single approach is sure to be defeated,'" Watkins insisted that "'defeat' is the last word to evoke to the justifiable triumph with which he [Honour] lays at our feet the single startling head he chose with admirable skill to make his own."

A counterpart of *Neo-Classicism* is Honour's *Romanticism,* a book which investigates the visual themes of that era of art history. Romanticism, unlike any other artistic movement, synthesized past and present art forms. It was a movement, concludes Honour, through time that is constantly changing and varied. Envisioning the historical time's instability, he argues that painters unconsciously strove to be non-representational in order to soothe their insecurity. Common themes of romantic artists include nature as a manifestation of God and landscapes as a vehicle for expressing profound sentiments and religious ideas.

Again, a major criticism of *Romanticism* is that it addresses subjects only by themes. In another issue of *National Review,* Berenson criticized Honour for ignoring the premature realists. "The author," she argued, "has a tendency to neglect those artists of the period who do not fit into his subject categories because of their perverse refusal to be concerned with anything but the here and now." Charles Rosen and Henri Zerner of the *New York Review of Books* agree that Honour's scheme of organization limited his book. These critics, like Berenson, claim that eccentric works do not fit under Honour's subject titles.

Though they agree that "Hugh Honour has written the best book yet available (and perhaps ever written) on romanticism in the visual arts," Rosen and Zerner felt that the art historian "fails, except intermittently, to convey a feeling of the historical development of Romanticism in the visual arts because his decision to attack the subject exclusively by themes leaves him no place for the two aspects of the arts of the time which would allow us to understand the nature and direction of most of the changes: the division of genres in the romantic period, and the marginal arts—book illustration, caricature, decoration, prints, works by amateurs, and so forth." The critics also asked why Honour did not divulge what the artistic developments were to which romanticism was leading. They wanted to know why the art historian did not deal with the "absurd magnitude of ambition" which permeated the artists' minds. Berenson, however, defended Honour. She stated: "Still, one can hardly fault him for sticking to his subject, especially since he does so with such knowledge and insight."

BIOGRAPHICAL/CRITICAL SOURCES: New Statesman, December 27, 1968, April 9, 1976, April 13, 1979; *Economist,* October 9, 1965; *Times Literary Supplement,* November 18, 1965, December 10, 1971, July 22, 1977; *Observer Review,* December 15, 1968, August 30, 1970; *New York Review of Books,* April 9, 1970, January 22, 1976, November 22, 1979; *National Review,* March 5, 1976, November 23, 1979; *New York Times Book Review,* March 21, 1976; *Best Sellers,* April, 1976; *New Republic,* May 8, 1976; *Yale Review,* autumn, 1976.*

—*Sketch by Charity Anne Dorgan*

*   *   *

HONRI, Peter 1929-

PERSONAL: In surname, the "h" is not silent; born October 11, 1929, in London, England; son of Baynham (a film technician) and Dorothy (an actress; maiden name, Wilkins) Honri; married June Bernice Ansell (an actress and skater), October 29, 1955; children: Sarah Anne Jane Honri Gray, Caroline Emma, Paul Simon. *Education:* Attended London Academy of Music and Dramatic Art, 1947. *Religion:* Church of England. *Home:* 32 Complins, Holybourne, Alton, Hampshire, England. *Agent:* Laurence Pollinger Ltd., 18 Maddox St., London W1R 0EU, England.

CAREER: Actor and variety artist, 1948—. Joint managing director of Music Hall Investigations; honorary artistic director of Wilton's Grand Music Hall; member of council of management of British Theatre Institute, 1977—. *Member:* British Actors Equity Association (member of council, 1965—), Society of Authors, Mechanical Copyright Protection Society, Authors Lending Rights Society, Society for Theatre Research, British Music Hall Society, London Music Hall Protection Society (member of board of directors, 1978).

WRITINGS: Working the Halls (nonfiction), Atheneum, 1973. Contributor to magazines, including *Theatre Quarterly, Stage, Music Hall, Call Boy,* and *Wilton's Newsletter.*

WORK IN PROGRESS: The Handsomest Room in Town!, the history of Wilton's Grand Music Hall, for Lennard; *Behind the Laughter,* a history of the Variety Artistes Federation, 1906-1967; "The Lion Comique," the tragedy of George Leybourne; "Very Awkward Fellow," a dramatized television documentary of the 1907 music hall strike.

SIDELIGHTS: Honri told *CA:* "An important aspect of Wilton's Grand Music Hall project will be the provision of research facilities for the study of popular entertainments history. The strength of the variety tradition in entertainment demands accurate assessment of the impact made by the

performers of previous eras. I am a performer, and see my writing activities as an extension of my *persona.*

"To succeed, the vaudeville performer has to identify with the aspirations of an audience. It is the ultimate individualist's performing art. A multiplicity of skills may be honed for the act—above all here is an art concealing art; it is a very crafty craft. Max Wall has been my greatest influence, though he does not play the concertina. Music hall/vaudeville/cabaret is a theatre of personalities; it is larger than life because today life seems to revolve around the micro-chip. It is a radical-reactionary theatre art that never stands still; the umbilical cord with the audience remains uncut."

*   *   *

HOOPER, Byrd
See St. CLAIR, Byrd Hooper

*   *   *

HORN, Peter (Rudolf Gisela) 1934-
(Roger Skelton)

PERSONAL: Born December 7, 1934, in Teplitz-Schoenau, Czechoslovakia; son of Alfred (a woodcarver) and Paula (a teacher; maiden name, Gloeckner) Horn; married Magdalena Siem (a nurse), November 27, 1958; children: Ulysses, Roland, Hauke, Immo. *Education:* University of the Witwatersrand, B.A., 1958, B.A. (with honors), 1959, Ph.D., 1971. *Home:* 51 Cleveland Rd., Claremont, South Africa. *Office:* Department of German, University of Cape Town, Private Bag, Rondebosch 7700, South Africa.

CAREER: Teacher of German at a private school in Johannesburg, South Africa, 1959-64; University of the Witwatersrand, Johannesburg, junior lecturer in German, 1964; University of South Africa, Pretoria, lecturer in German, 1965; University of Zululand, Kwa-Dlangezwa, Empangeni, senior lecturer in German, 1966-73; University of Cape Town, Cape Town, South Africa, professor of German, 1974—. Co-editor of Ophir Press, 1967-74. *Member:* Internationaler Germanistenverband, Suedafrikaanischer Germanistenverband. *Awards, honors:* Pringle Award from English Academy of South Africa, 1974, for critical essay on concrete poetry.

WRITINGS—Poetry: Voices From the Gallows Tree, Ophir Press, 1969; *Walking Through Our Sleep,* Ravan Press, 1974; (editor with Walter Saunders) *It's Gettin' Late,* Ravan Press, 1974; *Silence in Jail,* Scribe Press, 1979.

Other: (Editor with Jan Kruger) *Deutsche Gedichte* (title means "German Poems"), McGraw, 1973; (editor) *Heinrich von Kleists Erzaehlungen* (title means "Heinrich von Kleist's Stories"), Scriptor Verlag, 1978; *Kleist-Chronik* (title means "A Chronicle of Kleist's Life"), Athenaeum Verlag, 1979; (editor and translator) *Kap der Guten Hoffnung: Lyrik aus dem suedafrikanischen Widerstand* (title means "Cape of Good Hope: Poetry From the South African Resistance"), Athenaeum Verlag, 1980. Contributor of poems, sometimes under pseudonym Roger Skelton, to *Ophir.*

WORK IN PROGRESS: A book on the third world in German literature since 1945; a biography of nineteenth-century writer Georg Buechner; a series of poems on the history of South African resistance from 1652 to the present.

SIDELIGHTS: Horn commented: "I write poems in a situation where most of the masses live in dire poverty and under inhuman conditions of injustice and exploitation. Unless my poetry had some relevance to this situation, I would feel a parasite of a state and a social system which I abhor. My poetry is thus squarely located in the struggle of the masses against Apartheid and capitalist exploitation in South Africa and elsewhere in the world.''

*   *   *

HORNBY, Leslie 1949-
(Twiggy)

PERSONAL: Born September 19, 1949, in London, England; daughter of William Norman (a scenery builder) and Helen (Reeman) Hornby; married Michael Whitney (an actor), 1977; children: Carly. *Residence:* Hollywood Hills, Calif.

CAREER: Photographic model, actress, and singer. Manager and director of Twiggy Enterprises Ltd., beginning in 1966. Actress appearing in motion pictures, including "The Boy Friend," 1971, "W," 1974, and "There Goes the Bride"; and in television productions, including "Queen Victoria's Scandals." Recordings as professional singer include "Get the Name Right," "Twiggy," and "Here I Go Again."

WRITINGS—Under pseudonym Twiggy: *Twiggy: How I Probably Just Came Along on a White Rabbit at the Right Time, and Met the Smile on the Face of the Tiger,* Hawthorne, 1968; *Twiggy: An Autobiography,* Hart-Davis, 1975.

SIDELIGHTS: In 1965 Leslie Hornby was a skinny sixteen-year-old London schoolgirl; in 1966 she was an international celebrity whose waif-like countenance graced the covers of many high-fashion magazines in Europe. Twiggy, as she was dubbed by her boyfriend/manager Justin de Villeneuve, was the new face of the sixties. Her larger-than-life eyes (due to three pairs of false eyelashes worn simultaneously) and slight build were so much in demand that her modeling fees doubled from $120 an hour to $240 within a few short weeks after her New York debut in 1967. She modeled everything from the creations of the top designers to dresses made from newly-developed synthetic fibers for the Monsanto Chemical Company. Twiggy also endorsed such diverse products as cosmetics, sweatshirts, lunch boxes, and ball-point pens.

By 1968 Twiggy grew weary of the rigorous and demanding life of a model and temporarily retired from the profession. On the advice of her manager she tried acting. "The Boy Friend," in which she both sang and danced, was her first venture. Her success in this film led to two additional motion pictures and numerous television appearances. In recent years she has also become a recording artist, with three albums to her credit, and an author. Published in 1975, Twiggy's autobiography chronicles her rise from Cockney origins to international celebrity status in one year.

BIOGRAPHICAL/CRITICAL SOURCES: Newsweek, April 10, 1967, August 18, 1980; *New York Times,* December 1, 1971, January 2, 1972; Twiggy, *Twiggy: An Autobiography,* Hart-Davis, 1975; *Observer,* November 30, 1975; *Times Literary Supplement,* December 19, 1975.*

*   *   *

HORNE, Donald Richmond 1921-

PERSONAL: Born December 26, 1921, in Sydney, Australia; son of David (a teacher) and Florence (Carpenter) Horne; married Myfanwy Jane Anna Gollan (a writer), March 22, 1960; children: Julia Jane, Nicholas Ross. *Education:* Attended University of Sydney, 1939-41, and Canberra University College (now Australian National University), 1944-45. *Home:* 53 Grosvenor St., Woollahra, New South Wales 2025, Australia. *Agent:* Curtis Brown Ltd., 86 William St., Paddington, New South Wales, Australia.

CAREER: Daily Telegraph, Sydney, Australia, political correspondent, general reporter, and feature writer, 1946-49; free-lance writer, 1950-52; Associated Newspapers, London, England, foreign correspondent, 1952-53; Australian Consolidated Press, Sydney, foreign correspondent in London, 1953-54, managing editor of subsidiary publications in Sydney, 1954-62; Jackson Wain (advertising agency), Sydney, creative director, 1963-66; *Bulletin,* Sydney, editor, 1967-72; University of New South Wales, Kensington, research fellow at School of Political Science, 1973-75, senior lecturer, 1975-80, associate professor, 1980—. Chairman of International Seminar on Literary Journals and Journals of Opinion, 1962; member of organizing committee of Quadrant Seminar on Development in South East Asia, Kuala Lumpur, 1966; member of New South Wales Cultural Grants Advisory Council, 1976-79, and chairman of history, literature, broadcasting, and film committee; convener of National Conference for a Democratic Constitution, 1977, and National "Change the Rules" Conference, 1980. *Military service:* Australian Imperial Forces, 1942-44. *Member:* Australasian Political Studies Association, Australian Institute of International Affairs.

WRITINGS: The Lucky Country, Penguin, 1964, 4th edition, 1971; *The Permit* (novel), Sun Books, 1965; *The Education of Young Donald* (autobiography), Angus & Robertson, 1967; (with David Beal) *Southern Exposure,* Collins, 1967; *God Is an Englishman,* Penguin, 1969; *The Next Australia,* Angus & Robertson, 1970; *But What If There Are No Pelicans?* (novel), Angus & Robertson, 1971; *The Australian People,* Angus & Robertson, 1972; *Death of the Lucky Country,* Penguin, 1976; *Money Made Us,* Penguin, 1976; *His Excellency's Pleasure,* Thomas Nelson, 1977; *Right Way, Don't Go Back,* Sun Books, 1978; *In Search of Billy Hughes,* Macmillan, 1979; *Time of Hope: Australia, 1966-1972,* Angus & Robertson, 1980; *Winner Take All,* Penguin, 1981.

Contributor: Peter Coleman, editor, *Australian Civilization,* F. W. Cheshire, 1962; Geoffrey Dutton, editor, *Australia and the Monarchy,* Sun Books, 1966; Sibnarayan Ray, editor, *Vietnam, Seen From East and West,* Thomas Nelson, 1966; (author of foreword) Frank Hardy, *The Unlucky Australians,* Thomas Nelson, 1968; Hammond Innes, editor, *Introducing Australia,* Deutsch, 1971; Michael Boddy and Robert Ellis, *The Legend of King O'Malley,* Angus & Robertson, 1974; Richard Lucy, editor, *The Pieces of Australian Politics,* Macmillan, 1975; Mari Davis and George Sedden, editors, *Man and Landscape in Australia,* UNESCO and Australian Government Publishing Service, 1976; Edward P. Wolfers, editor, *Australia's Northern Neighbors,* Australian Institute of International Affairs, Thomas Nelson, 1976; *The Queen,* Allen Lane, 1977; Geoffrey Dutton and Max Harris, editors, *Republican Australia?,* Sun Books, 1977; Sol Encel, Donald Thompson, and Elaine Thompson, editors, *Change the Rules!,* Penguin, 1977. Also contributor to *World Book Encyclopedia* and *Australian Encyclopedia.*

Contributor to magazines and newspapers. Editor of Sydney newspapers, *Observer,* 1958-61, and *Bulletin,* 1961-62; co-editor of *Quadrant,* 1963-66; contributing editor of *Newsweek International,* 1972-76; advisory editor of *Australian Encyclopedia,* 1972—.

WORK IN PROGRESS: A book on the European imagination as it is expressed in monuments; a sequel to *The Education of Young Donald;* a book on power and democracy in Australia.

SIDELIGHTS: Horne told *CA:* "One of the results of my writing books has been the way it has changed me. I sit there and think, 'What could I possibly believe?' Later, when it is done, I think, 'Could I possibly believe that?' Too late.

"Although I do big sweeps of new reading, giving myself the chance for new perspectives, a lot of my developing has been inner-driven, not reactive, although done, of course, in a social context. For example, a big year of change for me— a definite program of change, observed and recorded in a diary—was 1972. That was the year of the eye operation that resulted in two-and-a-half months of recovery, mishaps, and the like that gave me a definite point of departure."

*   *   *

HORNER, J. C.
See HORNER, John Curwen

*   *   *

HORNER, John Curwen   1922-
(J. C. Horner)

PERSONAL: Born May 15, 1922, in Sandringham, Australia; son of Arthur (a postal official) and May (Templeman) Horner; married Jean Cowtan (an artist and weaver), August 23, 1947. *Education:* Attended East Sydney Technical College, 1940-42, 1946-48; Wolsey Hall, Oxford, Diploma in Bookselling, 1957. *Politics:* Christian Socialist. *Religion:* Anglican. *Home and office address:* Irwins Rd., East Kurrajong, New South Wales 2758, Australia.

CAREER: Scenic designer for theatres in Sydney, Australia, 1947-50, and London, England, 1950-53; book shop assistant in Sydney, 1953-66; researcher and writer, 1967—. Honorary secretary of Aboriginal Australian Fellowship, 1958-66; secretary to general secretary of Cooperative for Aborigines Ltd., 1964-65; secretary of ad hoc committee and of referendum campaign of NSW Aboriginal Rights Vote Yes Committee, 1967; coordinator, 1967, general secretary, 1969-70, and secretary to the general secretary, 1972-73, of Federal Council for Advancement of Aborigines and Torres Strait Islanders. *Military service:* Australian Army, Engineers, 1943-45; served in Papua New Guinea and in Merauke, Dutch New Guinea (now Irian Jaya). *Member:* Australian Institute of Aboriginal Studies (associate member), Australian Society of Authors.

WRITINGS: (Under name J. C. Horner; with Arthur Reginald Barnes) *A Dictionary of Australian History,* Cassell Australia, 1970; (contributor) F. S. Stevens, editor, *Racism: The Australian Experience,* Volume II, Australia and New Zealand Book Co., 1971; *Vote Ferguson for Aboriginal Freedom,* Australia and New Zealand Book Co., 1974; (editor) Monica Clare, *Karobran* (autobiographical), Alternative Publishing Cooperative, 1978. Australian correspondent for *Race Today,* 1970-74. Contributor to journals, including *Aboriginal Identity, Aboriginal History, Mankind, Politics, St. Mark's Review,* and *Australia 1938, a Bicentennial History Bulletin.*

WORK IN PROGRESS: A People of Courage, "an autobiographical book on my work as a white man among the blacks"; contributor to *The Aboriginal Fellowship,* edited by Faith Bardles.

SIDELIGHTS: Horner commented: "In London, in 1953, I met racial tensions for the first time and returned to Australia that year vividly recalling the incidents. From 1957 to 1973 I was active in removing restrictive laws, breaking down white ignorance and indifference. I traveled to many parts of eastern Australia to acquaint myself with the conditions of blacks.

"The vast gap between blacks and whites in Australia has historical, academic, and political, even fictional, origins, for people are unaware of the history. Irony should be a strong factor in writing about the willful mistakes and misunderstandings. Working in the book trade has given me knowledge of British law and Australian literature, giving broader reason to social commitment. Creative motivation stems from the human difficulties on both sides.

"*A People of Courage* is about South Sea Islands indentured laborers in Australia in the nineteenth century."

BIOGRAPHICAL/CRITICAL SOURCES: Sunday Mirror, May 3, 1963; *Australian,* November, 1972; *Historical Studies,* October, 1976; *Politics,* May, 1977.

*   *   *

HORWITZ, Simi L(ouise)   1949-

PERSONAL: Born June 2, 1949, in New York, N.Y.; daughter of Nathan (a news editor) and Mildred (a teacher; maiden name, Brodsky) Horwitz. *Education:* Hunter College of the City University of New York, B.A., 1973, M.A., 1978. *Home:* 317 West 93rd St., New York, N.Y. 10025. *Agent:* Collier Associates, 280 Madison Ave., New York, N.Y. 10016. *Office:* Department of English, Hunter College of the City University of New York, 695 Park Ave., New York, N.Y. 10021.

CAREER: Bernard M. Baruch College of the City University of New York, New York City, tutor in English, 1974-75; Hunter College of the City University of New York, New York city, master tutor, 1979-80, adjunct lecturer in English, 1980—.

WRITINGS: South of the Navel (memoir), Crowell, 1973. Contributor to magazines, including *Seventeen, Ladies' Home Journal, New Dawn, National Health, Family Weekly, Pilots Only,* and *Travel Agent.*

WORK IN PROGRESS: A novel.

SIDELIGHTS: Horowitz told *CA:* "I never intended to be a writer. However, after having had a very bad experience in a theatre arts school in the late 1960's, I had a need to sort out, describe, and understand what had happened. And that's when I started to write my book, *South of the Navel,* a memoir-critique of theatre training in the late 1960's. It received excellent reviews all over the country. As a result, I felt encouraged to continue writing—I also enjoyed it very much—and I have been doing so ever since."

*   *   *

HOUEDARD, Pierre-Sylvester   1924-

PERSONAL: Born February 16, 1924, in Guernsey, Channel Islands. *Education:* Attended Jesus College, Oxford; received Ph.L. from Collegio Santanselmo. *Home and office:* Prinknash Abbey, Gloucester GL4 8EX, England.

CAREER: Writer. Became Benedictine monk, 1949; librarian at Farnborough Abbey, 1959-61; associated with Prinknash Abbey in Gloucester, England. Visual poetry has been exhibited throughout the world. *Military service:* Served in the Far East. *Member:* Association of Little Presses (founding member; vice-president), Poetry Society (vice-president, 1974).

WRITINGS—Poetry: Yes-No, Daneway Press, 1963; *Thalamus-Sol,* St. Albert's Press, 1964; *Rock Sand Tide,* Daneway Press, 1964; *Frog-Pond Plop,* Openings Press, 1965; *Atom,* Openings Press, 1965; *Kinkon,* Writers Forum, 1965, revised edition published as *Op and Kinkon Poems and Some Non-Kinkon,* 1965; *Plakat I,* Openings Press, 1965; (contributor) Bob Cobbing, editor, *Eyearun*, Coptic Press, 1966; *A Book of Chakras (Eight Yantrics): Studies Towards Mechanical Fingers by dsh for Inner Moon Pointing*, Watford School of Art, 1966; *To Catch a Whiteman by His Manifesto*, Openings Press, 1967; *Tantric Poems, Perhaps*, Writers, Forum, 1967; *Book of Twelve Mudras*, Openings Press, 1967; *Book of Mazes and Troytowns*, Openings Press, 1967; *Easter Frog Toy for Pesach-Skipover*, Openings Press, 1967; *Eros A-Gape*, Lisson Delta Publications, 1967; *Semaine Euclidienne*, South Street Publications, 1968; *The Sun-Cheese-Wheel-Ode: A Double-Rolling-Gloster Memorial for Ken Cop*, South Street Publications, 1968; *Poster for the Breakdown of Nations Fourth-World Conference*, Resurgence Publications, 1968; *Deus-Snap*, Openings Press, 1968; *Miniposters*, South Street Publications, 1968; *A Snow Mouse*, Axis Multiple, 1969; *En Trance*, Axis Multiple, 1969; *Twelve Nahuatl Dancepoems From the Cosmic Typewriter*, South Street Publications, 1969; *Texts* (edited by John Sharkey), Lorrimer Books, 1969; *Streets Go Both Crazy Ways at Once*, South Street Publications, 1969; *Book of Battledores*, South Street Publications, 1969; *Book of Onomastikons*, South Street Publications, 1969; *Splendid Weeping*, Openings Press, 1969.

Successful Cube Tranceplant in Honor of Chairman Mao, Openings Press, 1970; *Grove Sings: Reflecting Poem for ihf*, Ceolfrith Bookshop & Gallery, 1970; *The Sign*, Stanbrook Abbey Press, 1971; (contributor) *Dorothy's Umbrellas*, Openings Press, 1971; *Auto-de-Chakra-Struction*, Bear Lane Gallery, 1971; *Five Tripestacks*, Covent Garden Press, 1972; *Main Calm Line*, National Poetry Centre, 1972; *Like Contemplation*, Writers Forum, 1972; *Begin Again: A Book of Reflections and Reversals*, LYC Publications, 1975.

Translator: (With Michael Hanbury) *Office of Our Lady: The Encalat Office*, Darton Longman Todd, 1962. Contributor to journals, including *Typographica*.

BIOGRAPHICAL/CRITICAL SOURCES: Charles Verey, editor, *Dom Sylvester Houedard*, Ceolfrith Arts Centre, 1972.*

* * *

HOUFE, Simon (Richard) 1942-

PERSONAL: Born September 13, 1942, in Bedford, England; son of Eric Alfred (an architect) and Kathleen (Richardson) Houfe. *Education:* Attended secondary school in Stowe, England. *Religion:* Anglican. *Agent:* c/o White Crescent Press, Ltd., Crescent Rd., Luton LU2 0AG, England.

CAREER: Associated with Victoria and Albert Museum, London, England, 1963-65; free-lance researcher in Italy, 1965; *Antique Collector*, editor, 1970-74; *Homes and Gardens*, antiques correspondent, 1976—. Member of National Art Collections Fund, 1970-79. *Member:* Historic Houses Association, Georgian Group.

WRITINGS: *Old Bedfordshire*, White Crescent Press, 1975; *The Dictionary of British Book Illustrators and Caricaturists, 1800-1914*, Antique Collectors Club, 1978; *Sir Albert Richardson: The Professor*, White Cresent Press, 1980. Contributor to magazines, including *Apollo, Antique Collector*, and *Antique Collecting*.

WORK IN PROGRESS: A biography of nineteenth-century illustrator John Leech, 1817-1864.

SIDELIGHTS: Houfe wrote: "I am interested in all aspects of book production and run a small private press, Bunyan Press, at Ampthill in Bedfordshire. I am also interested in

Christian poetry and drama, and am involved in conservation and preservation work."

Houfe's book *Sir Albert Richardson: The Professor* is a memoir of his grandfather. Gavin Stamp of the *Times Literary Supplement* described the volume as "a collection of anecdotes and funny stories" about a man who was "ebullient, eccentric and entertaining and. . . [who] became a legend in his own long lifetime." He added also that it "is an evocative and very entertaining tribute to Richardson the man—and the eccentric."

BIOGRAPHICAL/CRITICAL SOURCES: Times Literary Supplement, January 30, 1981.

* * *

HOUSTON, Jeanne Wakatsuki 1934-

PERSONAL: Born September 26, 1934, in California; daughter of Ko (a fisherman) and Riku (Sugai) Wakatsuki; married James D. Houston (a writer), March 27, 1957; children: Corinne, Joshua, Gabrielle. *Education:* University of San Jose, B.A., 1956; also attended Sorbonne, University of Paris. *Residence:* Santa Cruz, Calif. *Agent:* Elaine Berman, 12680 Viscaino Rd., Los Altos Hills, Calif. 94022; (films) George Diskant, Zigler, Diskant, Inc., 9255 Sunset Blvd., No. 1122, Los Angeles, Calif. 90069.

CAREER: Writer. Group worker and juvenile probation officer in San Mateo, Calif., 1955-57. *Member:* Writers Guild, Screen Writers Guild. *Awards, honors:* Humanitas Prize and Christopher Award, both for screenplay "Farewell to Manzanar"; award from National Women's Political Caucus.

WRITINGS: (With husband, J. D. Houston) *Farewell to Manzanar: A True Story of Japanese American Experience During and After the World War II Internment* (nonfiction), Houghton, 1973. Also author of teleplays, "Farewell to Manzanar," broadcast by MCA-TV, 1976, and "Barrio," broadcast by National Broadcasting Co. (NBC). Contributor to magazines.

WORK IN PROGRESS: Picture Bride, a novel about first generation Japanese.

* * *

HOWARD, Kenneth Samuel 1882-1972

OBITUARY NOTICE—See index for *CA* sketch: Born April 12, 1882, in Le Roy, N.Y.; died June 22, 1972. Advertising and promotion specialist, salesman, editor, and author. Howard was a chess expert, and his many books on the subject include *How to Solve Chess Problems, Classic Chess Problems*, and *The Enjoyment of Chess Problems*. (Date of death provided by associate, Frank L. Paeltler.)

* * *

HOWARD, Ted
See HOWARD, Theodore Korner

* * *

HOWARD, Theodore Korner 1915-
(Ted Howard)

PERSONAL: Born August 20, 1915, in Norfolk, Va.; son of Willard Mallilau and Eva Dora (Korner) Howard; married Marie White, May 28, 1935; children Norma Jean Howard Warren, Donald Willard. *Education:* Gramling New Era University, D.Lit., 1944; Fundamental Christian College, D.D., 1957. *Home:* 1167 George St., Norfolk, Va. 23502. *Office:* 1173 George St., P.O. Box 12226, Norfolk, Va. 23502.

CAREER: Ordained minister of Pentecostal Free-Will Baptist church, 1946; co-founder of Pentecostal Church of Christ in Virginia Beach, Va., 1950; founder and pastor of Pentecostal church in Chesapeake, Va., 1951-54; Faith Temple, Norfolk, Va., founder and pastor, 1963—. Chartered King James Bible School, Norfolk, 1965; president of local Community Counseling Center. *Member:* Association of Fundamental Ministers and Churches (member of state board of directors, 1955-69).

WRITINGS—Under name Ted Howard: *The P.B.C., a History, 1971-1976: The Peoples Bicentennial Commission, 1976-1984, the Peoples Business Commission,* People's Bicentennial Commission, 1976; (with Jeremy Rifkin) *Who Should Play God?: The Artificial Creation of Life and What It Means for the Future of the Human Race,* Delacorte, 1977; (with Rifking) *The Emerging Order: God in the Age of Scarcity,* Putnam, 1979; (with Rifkin) *Entropy: A New World View,* Viking, 1980.

BIOGRAPHICAL/CRITICAL SOURCES: Horn Book, August, 1978; *Progressive,* September, 1979; *Discussion,* January, 1980.*

* * *

HOXIE, R(alph) Gordon   1919-

PERSONAL: Born March 18, 1919, in Waterloo, Iowa; son of Charles Ray and Ada May (Little) Hoxie; married Louise Lobtiz, December 23, 1953. *Education:* Iowa State Teachers College (now University of Northern Iowa), B.A., 1940; University of Wisconsin (now University of Wisconsin—Madison), M.A., 1941; Columbia University, Ph.D., 1950. *Politics:* Independent. *Religion:* Episcopalian. *Home:* 224 Laurel Cove Rd., Oyster Bay Cove, N.Y. 11771. *Office:* Center for the Study of the Presidency, 926 Fifth Ave., New York, N.Y. 10021.

CAREER: Columbia University, New York City, Roberts fellow, 1946-47, Roberts traveling fellow, 1947-48, assistant to provost, 1948-49; University of Denver, Denver, Colorado, assistant professor of history, general editor of Social Science Foundation, and assistant to chancellor, 1950-53; Long Island University, Greenvale, N.Y., dean of College of Liberal Arts, 1954-55, acting dean of Merriweather Campus (now C. W. Post Center), 1954-55, dean, 1955-60, provost, 1960-62, president, 1962-68, chancellor of university, 1964-68, consultant, 1968-69; Center for the Study of the Presidency, New York City, president, 1969—. Visiting lecturer at universities throughout the United States, including Columbia University, Northwestern University, Colorado State University, and University of Texas at El Paso. Project associate, Columbia University bicentennial history, 1953-54; member of board of directors of Council of Higher Educational Institutions; director of Greater New York Council on Foreign Studies; chairman and president of board of directors of American Friends of Chung-ang University, Seoul, Korea.

Member of advisory council of Robert A. Taft Institute of Government; secretary of Nassau County Commission on Government Revision; member of advisory board of the American Association of the United Nations; director of Greater New York Safety Council, vice-president of education and home division; member of board of governors of Human Resources Center; member of Long Island Council on Alcoholism (Brooklyn chapter) and Long Island United Fund; co-chairman of Nassau-Suffolk Conference of Christians and Jews. President of Mitchel chapter of U.S. Reserve Officers Association; member of advisory board of Long

Island Air Reserve Center; public member of Foreign Service Officer Selection board, U.S. Department of State, 1969. Consultant to Franklin National Bank, 1968-69; trustee of Long Island Theatre Society (honorary member), Kosciuszko Foundation, and Tibetan Foundation. *Military service:* U.S. Army Air Forces, 1942-46, served in North Pacific; became captain; received Meritorious Service Award and Legion of Merit. Served with U.S. Air Force Reserve; became brigadier general.

MEMBER: International Association of University Presidents, American Historical Association, American Political Science Association, Academy of Political Science, American Red Cross, American Polar Society, American Legion, Veterans of Foreign Wars, Air Force Association, Navy League, Brooklyn Institute of Arts and Sciences, Downtown Brooklyn Association, Friends of New York Library, Delta Sigma Pi, Kappa Delta Pi, Alpha Sigma Lambda, Pi Gamma Mu, Gamma Theta Upsilon, Metropolitan Club (Washington, D.C.), Columbia University Faculty House, Century Association, Adventurers, Old Westbury Golf and Country Club (honorary), Mill River Club (honorary). *Awards, honors:* American Bill of Rights Award, 1964; LL.D. from Chung-ang University, New York City distinguished service medal, University of Northern Iowa alumni achievement award, and Korean cultural medal, all 1965; Litt.D. from D'Youville College and Paderewski Foundation man of the year award, both 1966; American Studies Association fellow; Eloy Alfaro International Foundation award; named honorable citizen of Seoul, Korea.

WRITINGS: Command Decision and the Presidency: A Study in National Security Policy and Organization, Reader's Digest Press, 1977; (editor) *Frontiers for Freedom,* University of Denver Press, 1952; (contributor) *Freedom and Authority in Our Time* (conference proceedings), Harper, 1953; (with Sally Falk Moore and others) *A History of the Faculty of Political Science, Columbia University,* Columbia University Press, 1955; (editor) *The White House: Organizations and Operations* (symposium proceedings), Center for the Study of the Presidency, 1970; (editor) *The Presidency of the 1970's* (symposium proceedings), Center for the Study of the Presidency, 1973; (contributor) *The Coattailless Landslide* (symposium on presidential elections), Texas Western Press, 1974; (contributor) Philip C. Dolce and George H. Skall, editors, *Power and the Presidency,* Scribner, 1976. Contributor to *Encyclopaedia Britannica* and *World Book Encyclopedia;* contributor to professional journals, including *Presidential Studies Quarterly.*

SIDELIGHTS: In *Command Decision and the Presidency* Hoxie provides an in-depth study of presidential authority and leadership, particularly in the formulation of national-security policy. Jeff Greenfield of the *New York Times Book Review* wrote, "Dr. R. Gordon Hoxie (whose own battles included stormy tenures at C. W. Post College and Long Island University) is determined to demonstrate that strong Presidential leadership is an absolute necessity despite what he delicately labels the 'excesses' of the Nixon Administration." Greenfield also noted that "what makes this book work . . . is a thorough review of important national security questions of the Truman and Eisenhower years."

BIOGRAPHICAL/CRITICAL SOURCES: New York Times Book Review, March 12, 1978.*

* * *

HSIANG, Yeh
See LIU, Sydney (Chieh)

HUBBARD, Barbara Marx   1929-

PERSONAL: Born December 22, 1929, in Washington, D.C.; daughter of Louis (a toy manufacturer) and Rene (Saltzman) Marx; married Earl Wade Hubbard (an artist; divorced); children: Suzanne Fletcher, Woodleigh, Alexandra Bryant, Earl Wade, Lloyd Frost. *Education:* Bryn Mawr College, B.A. (cum laude), 1951; also studied at Sorbonne, University of Paris, 1949-50. *Politics:* "Up Winger." *Religion:* Universal. *Home and office:* 2325 Porter St. N.W., Washington, D.C. 20008. *Agent:* Chris Tomasino, 7 West 51st St., New York, N.Y. 10019.

CAREER: International Committee for the Future, Washington, D.C., co-founder, 1970—; Futures Network (communications products), Washington, D.C., co-founder and president, 1978—. Administrator of The New Worlds Center (educational center), Washington, D.C. Member of National Advisory Board of the Institute of Noetic Sciences; lecturer. *Member:* World Future Society (member of board of directors, 1968—), L-5 Society (member of board of directors, 1976—).

WRITINGS: (Editor with husband, Earl Hubbard) *The Search Is On*, R. D. Pace, 1969; *The Hunger of Eve: A Woman's Odyssey Toward the Future* (autobiography), Stackpole, 1976; *Evolutionary Journal*, privately printed, 1978; *Theatre for the Future*, Celestial Arts, 1981. Also author of audio tape series. Frequent contributor to *Futurist* and other publications; editor of *The Center Letter*, 1967.

WORK IN PROGRESS: An "evolutionary interpretation" of the New Testament.

SIDELIGHTS: "When I first read Genesis in my youth," Barbara Marx Hubbard wrote, "I was on Eve's side." Perhaps this is the reason why Marx compares herself to Eve in her autobiography, *The Hunger of Eve*. As Delphine Kolker of *Best Sellers* noted, "the analogy between herself and Eve is appropriate." "This modern Eve," Kolker went on to say, "recounts her search for a cause that would give meaning to her life." Like Eve, Hubbard searches for something to which she can be totally dedicated. And she is willing to accept some of the responsibility for mankind's future, just as Eve was.

Discontent with earthbound existence, Hubbard began searching for a higher purpose in life. Her quest ended when, while she was strolling near her home in Connecticut, she received a "call" to make the world aware of cosmic consciousness. Hubbard's mission was to become midwife of mankind's birth into the future. And she accepted her role, which is to affirm that mankind is capable of rising above a resource-depleted earth.

To prepare for mankind's tomorrow, Hubbard organized the Committee for the Future. The Committee conducts worldwide workshops and seminars that attempt to make people realize that they must control their future evolution. One special project that the Committee for the Future considered was launching a citizen-sponsored lunar expedition. Such an expedition would be important since, as Hubbard and the Committee contend, mankind will be united in the conquest of space.

Hubbard commented: "My interest is in communicating the reality of our potentials to create a choiceful future for humanity. I am enlarging my activity to create an expanded Futures Network to produce television products and other media on a positive future."

Hubbard is the daughter of toy magnate Louis Marx.

BIOGRAPHICAL/CRITICAL SOURCES: Barbara Marx Hubbard, *The Hunger of Eve: A Woman's Odyssey Toward the Future*, Stackpole, 1976; *Best Sellers*, January, 1977; *West Coast Review of Books*, January, 1977; *New Yorker*, March 28, 1977; *Communication Notes*, December, 1978; *World Future Society Bulletin*, March-April, 1979; *Alternatives*, fall, 1979; *Indianapolis Star*, December 6, 1979; *Parade*, December 13, 1979; *Movement*, May, 1980.

*   *   *

HUBBARD, (Andrew) Ray   1924-

PERSONAL: Born December 7, 1924, in Los Angeles, Calif.; son of Lloyd E. (in insurance) and Gertrud (employed by an airline; maiden name, Bartmus) Hubbard; married Marion Cohen (a dog breeder), June 10, 1950; children: Bruce, Gregory, Stephen. *Education:* California College of Arts and Crafts, B.A.Ed., 1946; Stanford University, M.A., 1951. *Agent:* Edward J. Acton, Inc., 17 Grove St., New York, N.Y. 10014. *Office:* Ray Hubbard Associates, Inc., Beall Mountain Rd., Potomac, Md. 20854.

CAREER: Writer. KPIX, San Francisco, Calif., art director, 1951-56, program director, 1957-65; Westinghouse Broadcasting Co., New York, N.Y., national program director, 1965-69; Post-Newsweek Stations, Inc., Washington, D.C., vice-president of programs, 1969-76; Ray Hubbard Associates, Inc., Potomac, Md., president, 1976—. Chairman of Dramacourt Ltd., 1974-76; vice-president of Unicorn Projects, Inc., 1978—. *Awards, honors:* Robert E. Sherwood Award from the Fund of the Republic, 1956, for "Let Freedom Ring"; Peabody Broadcasting Award from Academy of Television Arts and Sciences, 1963, for "San Francisco Pageant"; Dupont Award, 1964, for news excellence at KPIX; gold medal from Atlanta Film Festival, 1974, for "The Age of Ballyhoo," and 1975, for "We All Came to America"; Golden Gate Award from San Francisco Film Festival, 1976, for "Black Shadows on a Silver Screen"; two Emmy Awards from Academy of Television Arts and Sciences, one in 1976, for "How We Got the Vote."

WRITINGS: Majestic: A Hollywood Novel, Bantam, 1981; *The Water War* (novel), Delacorte, in press. Also author of television films "San Francisco Pageant," 1962-64, "The American Documents," 1974-76, and "Lewis Mumford: Toward Human Architecture," Public Broadcasting System, 1978.

WORK IN PROGRESS: "Castle," an hour-long film based on David Macaulay's book, for Public Broadcasting System.

*   *   *

HUDSPETH, Robert N.   1936-

PERSONAL: Born November 21, 1936, in Sweetwater, Tex.; married, 1959; children: three. *Education:* University of Texas, A.B., 1961; Syracuse University, A.M., 1963, Ph.D., 1967. *Office:* Department of English, Pennsylvania State University, University Park, Pa. 16802.

CAREER: University of Washington, Seattle, assistant professor, 1967-71, associate professor of English, 1971-72; Pennsylvania State University, University Park, associate professor of English, 1972—. *Member:* Modern Language Association of America, American Studies Association.

WRITINGS: (Editor with Donald F. Sturtevant) *The World of Language: A Reader in Linguistics*, American Book Co., 1967; *Ellery Channing*, Twayne, 1973. Contributor to literature journals.*

HUGHES, Everett Cherrington 1897-

PERSONAL: Born November 30, 1897, in Beaver, Ohio; son of Charles Anderson and Jessamine Blanche (Roberts) Hughes; married Helen Gregory MacGill, August 18, 1927; children: Helen MacGill Cherrington Brock, Elizabeth Gregory Cherrington Schneewind. *Education:* Ohio Wesleyan University, A.B., 1918; University of Chicago, Ph.D., 1928. *Politics:* Democrat. *Religion:* Episcopalian. *Home:* 27 Shepard St., Cambridge, Mass. 02138.

CAREER: McGill University, Montreal, Quebec, assistant professor of sociology, 1927-38; University of Chicago, Chicago, Ill., assistant professor, 1938-43, associate professor, 1943-49, professor of sociology, 1949-61, chairman of department, 1952-56; Brandeis University, Waltham, Mass., professor of sociology, 1961-68, professor emeritus, 1968—; Boston College, Chestnut Hill, Mass., professor of sociology, 1968-76, professor emeritus, 1976—. Visiting professor at Laval University, 1942-43, University of Frankfurt, 1948, 1953, and 1958, Columbia University, summer, 1951, Radcliffe College, 1957-58, Stanford University, summer, 1963, University of Vienna, 1964, McGill University and University of Montreal, 1965; Rose Morgan Professor at University of Kansas, 1959 and 1961. Member of research and advisory committees of American Nurses' Foundation, 1953-60; member of public health and nursing study section of National Institutes of Health and cooperative research branch of U.S. Office of Education; member of United Nations Educational, Scientific & Cultural Organization's (UNESCO) mission to Switzerland, the Soviet Union, and Czechoslovakia.

MEMBER: American Association for the Advancement of Science (fellow), American Sociological Association (fellow; president, 1962-63), American Anthropological Association (fellow), American Academy of Arts and Sciences (fellow), Canadian Sociology and Anthropology Association (honorary life president), Society for Applied Anthropology (president, 1950-51), Society for the Study of Social Problems, Eastern Sociological Society (president, 1968-69), Alpha Sigma Phi. *Awards, honors:* Social Science Research Council fellow in Germany, 1931-32; LL.D. from Sir George Williams University, 1966, Boston College, 1967, Queen's University, Kingston, Ontario, 1969, and McGill University, 1970; L.H.D. from Michigan State University, 1967, and Ohio Wesleyan University, 1969; merit award from Eastern Sociological Society, 1972; Malinowski Award from Society for Applied Anthropology, 1974; D.S.S. from Laval University, 1977; Litt.D. from University of Montreal, 1978.

WRITINGS: The Chicago Real Estate Board: The Growth of an Institution, Society for Social Research, 1931, reprinted (edited by Lewis A. Coser and Walter W. Powell), Arno, 1979; *French Canada in Transition,* University of Chicago Press, 1943, reprinted, 1963; (with wife, Helen MacGill Hughes) *Where Peoples Meet: Racial and Ethnic Frontiers,* Free Press, 1952; (editor with Edgar Tristram Thompson) *Race: Individual and Collective Behavior,* Free Press, 1958; (with H. M. Hughes and Irwin Deutsche *Twenty Thousand Nurses Tell Their Story: A Report on Studies of Nursing Functions Sponsored by the American Nurses' Association,* Lippincott, 1958; *Men and Their Work,* Free Press, 1958.

Students' Culture and Perspectives: Lectures on Medical and General Education, School of Law, University of Kansas, 1961; (with Howard Saul Becker and Blanche Geer) *Making the Grade: The Academic Side of College Life,* Wiley, 1968; *The Sociological Eye: Selected Papers,* two

volumes, Aldine-Atherton, 1971; (co-author) *Education for the Professions of Medicine, Law, Theology, and Social Welfare,* McGraw, 1973; (co-editor) *The Collected Papers of Robert Park,* Volume I: *Race and Culture,* Volume II: *Human Communities: The City and Human Ecology,* Volume III: *Society: Collective Behavior, News and Opinion, Sociology and Modern Society,* Arno, 1974. Contributor to sociology journals. Associate editor of *American Journal of Sociology,* 1941-52, editor, 1952-60.

BIOGRAPHICAL/CRITICAL SOURCES: Howard Saul Becker and other editors, *Institutions and the Person: Essays Presented to Everett C. Hughes,* Aldine, 1968.*

*   *   *

HUGHES, Irene Finger

PERSONAL: Born in Saulsbury, Tenn.; daughter of Joseph and Easter Bell (Carter) Finger; married William John Hughes, December 23, 1945; children: William John III, Karen Frances, Patricia Ilene, Kathleen Laurie. *Education:* Attended high school. *Agent:* c/o Rudolph Steiner Publications, 100 South Western Hwy., Blauvelt, N.Y. 10913.

CAREER: Secretary in New Orleans, La., 1941-45; *Calumet Index,* Chicago, Ill., reporter, 1949-55; associated with Domestic Engineering Co., Chicago, 1956-61; Golden Path (teachers of extrasensory perception, prayer, meditation, and astrology), Chicago, founder and manager, 1963—. Managing editor of *International Journal of Neuropsychiatry,* 1963-66. *Member:* National Federation of Press Women, Spiritual Frontiers Fellowship, Illinois Women's Press Association, Chicago Press Club. *Awards, honors:* Award from Mate Palmer Fund; award from Illinois Women's Press Association.

WRITINGS: ESPecially Irene: A Guide to Psychic Awareness, Rudolf Steiner, 1972. Author of column "ESPecially . . . Irene."*

*   *   *

HUGHES, James Monroe 1890-1971

OBITUARY NOTICE—See index for *CA* sketch: Born October 17, 1890, in Sharpsville, Ind.; died October 26, 1971. Educator and author. Hughes began his teaching career in rural schools in Indiana. He later became an education instructor in Minnesota, and in 1924 he joined the faculty of Northwestern University. From 1941 to 1951 he served as dean of the School of Education at Northwestern. Hughes wrote several books on education, including *Education in America,* which has been brought out in several editions. Obituaries and other sources: *Who Was Who in America,* 5th edition, Marquis, 1973.

*   *   *

HUGHES, Riley 1915(?)-1981

OBITUARY NOTICE: Born c. 1915 in New Haven, Conn.; died of a heart attack, March 8, 1981, in Washington, D.C. Educator, critic, and author of novels, short stories, poems, and books on writing. Hughes is best known for his science-fiction novel *The Hills Were Liars.* Obituaries and other sources: *The Encyclopedia of Science Fiction: An Illustrated A to Z,* Grenada, 1979; *Washington Post,* March 11, 1981.

*   *   *

HUMPHRIES, Sydney Vernon 1907-
(Michael Vane)

PERSONAL: Born January 24, 1907, in Middleburg, South Africa; son of Sydney William (a bank manager) and Violet

(Ersell) Humphries; married Mareuil Elizabeth Albertyn Coetzee (a physiotherapist), June 17, 1936. *Education:* Received LRCP, 1932; Pembroke College, Cambridge, M.A., 1935. *Politics:* Socialist. *Religion:* Atheist. *Home:* Calle Nueva 1, 136 Estepona, Malaga, Spain.

CAREER: Associated with St. Thomas's Hospital, London, England, 1929-31; held positions at various hospitals in England, 1932-35; Van Dyk Mine, Transvaal, South Africa, mine medical officer, 1936-40 and 1943-49; physician in mine, government, and mission hospitals in Africa, the Bahamas, Australia, and Naura Island; Lilongwe Hospitals, Malawi, surgeon, 1959-62; worked at Mission Hospital in Liaganj, India, 1965. Writer. *Military service:* South African Medical Corps, Field Ambulance, 1940-43. *Member:* British Medical Association. *Awards, honors:* Hippocrates prize, 1951; Royal College of Surgeons fellow.

WRITINGS: The Life of Hamilton Bailey, British Book Center, 1974.

Under pseudonym Michael Vane: *The Hun in Africa: The Aims and Methods of German Imperialism,* Libertas, 1942; *The South African Indians* (pamphlet), Society of the Friends of Africa, 1948; *Black Magic and White Medicine: A Mine Medical Officer's Experiences in South Africa, the Belgian Congo, Sierra Leone, and the Gold Coast,* W. & R. Chambers, 1957. Also author of *Apathy Supercharged,* 1943, and *Snobbery Under Arms,* 1944. Contributor to *Central African Journal of Medicine.*

SIDELIGHTS: Humphries commented: "My main objects in life have been to be free, to be useful, to lead a life of travel and adventure, and to write."

*   *   *

HUNT, June 1944-

PERSONAL: Born December 31, 1944, in Dallas, Tex.; daughter of H. L. (an oil producer) and Ruth (Ray) Hunt. *Education:* Southern Methodist University, B.Mus., 1966. *Religion:* Baptist. *Office:* c/o Hunt Oil Co., 1401 Elm St., Dallas, Tex. 75202.

CAREER: Free-lance entertainer and speaker, 1973—. Performed for United Services Organizations in Vietnam, 1972; guest soloist with Billy Graham's evangelistic crusades; guest on national television programs, including "The Today Show."

WRITINGS: Above All Else, Revell, 1975. Contributor to *Church Revelation.*

WORK IN PROGRESS: A book on unconditional love, publication by Revell expected in 1982.

SIDELIGHTS: June Hunt told *CA:* "As a singer and speaker, I do not view myself as a 'performer,' but as a 'communicator.' I use many methods to communicate the message, but it is the method that is most important—the living principles, based on God's word, which will enhance the quality of our lives and increase understanding of spiritual growth and God himself. The writings and talks are practical, often containing projects which can 'walk out on feet.'"

BIOGRAPHICAL/CRITICAL SOURCES: Time, January 13, 1975; *Shophar,* April, 1979; *Journal of Christian Camping,* September 10, 1979; *World Wide Challenge,* October, 1979.

*   *   *

HUNT, Nancy (Ridgely) 1927-

PERSONAL: Born February 1, 1927; son of Ridgely (a publisher and librarian) and Julia (Cheney) Hunt; married Con-

stance Farley (divorced); married Sue Allman (a nurse and nursing instructor; divorced); children: Ridgely, Constance, Alice. *Education:* Yale University, B.A., 1950. *Politics:* Republican. *Religion:* Episcopalian. *Residence:* Chicago, Ill. *Agent:* Dominick Abel Literary Agency, 498 West End Ave., 12C, New York, N.Y. 10024. *Office: Chicago Tribune,* 435 North Michigan Ave., Chicago, Ill. 60611.

CAREER: New Haven Register, New Haven, Conn., copy editor, 1953-57; *Chicago Daily News,* Chicago, Ill., copy editor, 1958-63; *Chicago Tribune,* Chicago, associate magazine editor, 1963, became copy editor, national-foreign desk; writer. *Military service:* U.S. Army, 1945-46; became sergeant. U.S. Air Force, 1950-51; became sergeant.

WRITINGS: Mirror Image: The Odyssey of a Male-to-Female Transsexual (autobiography), Holt, 1978. Contributor of numerous articles to the *Chicago Tribune Magazine.*

SIDELIGHTS: For many years, Hunt was a successful reporter for the *Chicago Tribune,* serving as the paper's Vietnam war correspondent. In 1976 Hunt underwent sex change surgery; her transformation from a man to a woman is the subject of her autobiography, *Mirror Image.*

In *Mirror Image* Hunt told of an unhappy childhood, a "supermasculine" life as a soldier, police reporter, and war correspondent, and a growing awareness of feminine feelings. When those feelings could be repressed no longer, Hunt's wife assisted the metamorphosis, sharing clothes, giving hormone injections, and finally accompanying him to the hospital for the operation. In an interview in *People,* Hunt said: "All the years as a man I would look in the mirror and hate myself. Now I'm an avowed sexual freak. Yet I look in that mirror, and after a lifetime of self-loathing I can say, "Hey, I like me."

Hunt commented to *CA:* "I am appalled by the low estate into which the English language has fallen since World War II and from which flow many of the evils of the day—political and commercial as well as journalistic. On quite a different tack, I have lately become manic about flying small airplanes, which I find a joyous expression of life."

BIOGRAPHICAL/CRITICAL SOURCES: Nancy Hunt, *Mirror Image,* Holt, 1978; *Best Sellers,* February, 1979; *People,* February 12, 1979.

*   *   *

HUNT, Noreen 1931-

PERSONAL: Born September 15, 1931, in Oldham, England. *Education:* Royal Holloway College, London, B.A., 1955; Institute of Historical Research, London, Ph.D., 1958; Cavendish Square Teacher Training College, certificate, 1959. *Office:* Neville's Cross College, Durham DH1 4SY, England.

CAREER: Writer. Associated with Neville's Cross College in Durham, England. *Member:* Society of Authors, Ecclesiastical History Society, Institute of Religion and Theology.

WRITINGS: Cluny Under Saint Hugh, 1049-1109, Edward Arnold, 1967, University of Notre Dame Press, 1968; (editor) *Cluniac Monasticism in the Central Middle Ages,* Archon, 1971. Contributor to journals, including *Ampleforth Journal, Tablet,* and *Cistercian Studies.**

*   *   *

HUNT, Patricia Joan

PERSONAL: Born in Sefton Park, England; daughter of Harold and Ida (Campion) Hunt. *Education:* Attended girls' high school in Altringham, England. *Religion:* Anglican.

Home: 7 St. John's Rd., Knutsford, Cheshire WA16 0DL, England. *Agent:* Juvenilia, Colden Common, near Winchester, Hampshire SO21 1TB, England.

CAREER: Cheshire County Council, England, town and country planning assistant, 1948-73; Macclesfield Borough Council, Macclesfield, England, town and country planning assistant, 1974-79; writer, 1979—.

WRITINGS—Juveniles: *The King and the Traffic Lights: A Play for Children in Four Acts*, N.S.S.U., 1963; *Puffin the Vicarage Cat*, Mowbray, 1966; *Sunday School Single Handed*, Denholm House Press, 1967; *The History of Our Bible*, Ladybird, 1971; *What to Look for Inside a Church*, Ladybird, 1972; *What to Look for Outside a Church*, Ladybird, 1972; *A First Look at Churches and Chapels*, F. Watts, 1974; *A First Look at Temples and Other Places of Worship*, F. Watts, 1975; *A First Look at Water*, F. Watts, 1977; *St. Michael Book of Bible Stories*, Sundial Publications, 1978; *Book of Bible Stories*, Ward, Lock, 1981. Also author of *First Steps in Teaching* (for adults), 1966, and *In and Around the Church*, 1969. Contributor to religious journals and *Home Life*.

WORK IN PROGRESS: Architecture, for young people.

* * *

HUNTINGTON, Henry S., Jr.   1892-1981

OBITUARY NOTICE: Born in 1892 in Gorham, Me.; died February 13, 1981, in Philadelphia, Pa. Former clergyman, editor, and author of *Defense of Nudism.* Huntington was a pioneer of the nudist movement in the United States. He helped to establish one of the country's first nudist camps and was the first editor of *Nudist* (now *Sunshine and Health*). Obituaries and other sources: *New York Times*, February 17, 1981; *Newsweek*, March 2, 1981; *Time*, March 2, 1981.

* * *

HURD, Florence   1918-
(Fiona Harrowe, Flora Hiller)

PERSONAL: Born November 4, 1918, in Chicago, Ill.; divorced. *Education:* University of Chicago, B.A. *Religion:* Unitarian-Universalist. *Home and office:* 1732 Old Mill Rd., Encinitas, Calif. 92024. *Agent:* Donald MacCampbell, Inc., 12 East 41st St., New York, N.Y. 10017.

CAREER: Worked as welfare worker in San Diego, Calif., 1946-50; writer, 1965—.

WRITINGS—Novels: *Secret of Canfield House*, Fawcett, 1966; *Wade House*, New American Library, 1966; *The Possessed*, Belmont-Tower, 1969; *The Gorgon's Head*, Macfadden, 1971; *The House on Trevor Street*, Manor, 1972; *Witches Pond*, Manor, 1972; *Seance for the Dead*, Macfadden, 1972; *Moorsend Manor*, Manor, 1973; *Storm House*, Manor, 1973; *Nightmare at Mountain Aerie*, Manor, 1973; *House of Shadows*, Fawcett, 1973; *Curse of the Moors*, Manor, 1975; *Terror at Seacliff Pines*, Manor, 1976; *Secret of Awen Castle*, Avon, 1975; *Secret of Hayworth Hall*, Avon, 1975; *Voyage of the Secret Duchess*, Avon, 1976; *Rommany*, Avon, 1976; *The House on Russian Hill*, New American Library, 1976; *Legacy*, Avon, 1977; *Nightwind at Northriding*, New American Library, 1977; *Shadows of the Heart*, Avon, 1980; *Passion's Child*, Fawcett, 1982; *Dark Palms of Paradise*, Harlequin, 1982.

Under pseudonym Fiona Harrowe: *Love's Scarlet Banner*, Fawcett, 1977; *Fountains of Glory*, Fawcett, 1979; *Forbidden Wine*, Fawcett, 1981.

Under pseudonym Flora Hiller: *Love's Fiery Dagger*, Popular Library, 1978.

WORK IN PROGRESS: Past All Dishonor (tentative title), a post-Civil War novel, for Fawcett.

SIDELIGHTS: Florence Hurd commented: "I did not start writing seriously until I was forty-five, at which time I decided to quit piddling around with creative writing courses and the amateur short stories. I sat down and penned my first book, a gothic novel, which sold to Fawcett. I have been at the typewriter, and selling, ever since. History fascinates me. One can find dozens of readymade plots, characters, and crises in the records of the past. If I had my choice I'd spend my days at research, so much more fun than filling up all those blank pages—that's hard work."

* * *

HURLEY, Vic   1898-1978
(Jim Duane, Duane Richards)

OBITUARY NOTICE—See index for *CA* sketch: Born October 6, 1898, in Springfield, Mo.; died June, 1978, in Lacey, Wash. Naval officer and author. A contributor of articles and short stories to many magazines, Hurley also wrote several books, including *Southeast of Zamboanga*, *The Parthian*, and *Arrows Against Steel: The History of the Bow.* (Date of death provided by brother, James Hurley.)

* * *

HURT, Freda M(ary) E(lizabeth)   1911-

PERSONAL: Born June 14, 1911, in London, England; daughter of Harry F. J. (an artist) and Martha (Armer) Hurt. *Education:* Attended school in London, England. *Politics:* "Non-party." *Religion:* "Non-denominational." *Home:* 298 Pickhurst Rise, West Wickham, Kent BR4 0AY, England. *Agent:* Strathmore, Park Rd., St. John's Wood, London, England.

CAREER: Writer. Worked in art shop in Forest Hill, England, 1929; nurse in day nursery, 1941; deputy matron in day nursery, 1945. *Member:* Society of Authors, Conservation Society, Kent Trust for Nature Conservation.

WRITINGS—Novels; published by R. Hale, except as noted: *The Body at Busman's Hollow*, Macdonald & Co., 1959; *Death by Bequest*, Macdonald & Co., 1960; *Sweet Death*, Macdonald & Co., 1961; *Acquainted With Murder*, 1962; *Death and the Bridegroom*, 1963; *Cold and Unhonoured*, 1964; *A Cause for Malice*, 1966; *Death and the Dark Daughter*, 1966; *So Dark a Shadow*, 1967; *Seven Year Secret*, 1968; *Death in the Mist*, 1969; *A Witch at the Funeral*, 1970; *Dangerous Visit*, 1971; *Dark Design*, 1972; *Return to Terror*, 1974; *Fatal Fortune*, 1975.

Juveniles: *The Wonderful Birthday*, Thomas Nelson, 1953; *Two to Make Friends*, Thomas Nelson, 1955; *Norgy in Little Land*, Epworth, 1955; *The Exciting Summer*, Thomas Nelson, 1956; *Intruders at Pinetops*, Thomas Nelson, 1958; *Thirteen for Luck*, Thomas Nelson, 1958; *The Caravan Cat*, Roy, 1963; *Crab Island*, Epworth, 1965, Roy, 1966; *Benny and the Dolphin*, Roy, 1968; *Benny and the Space Boy*, Epworth, 1970. Also author of *And in Trouble.*

"Mr. Twink" series; published by Epworth, except as noted: *Clever Mr. Twink*, 1953; *. . . Takes Charge*, 1954; *. . . Finds Out*, 1956; *. . . , Detective*, 1957; *. . . and the Kitten Mystery*, 1958; *. . . and the Pirates*, Roy, 1959; *. . . and the Jungle Garden*, Roy, 1960; *. . . Finds a Family*, 1961; *. . . and the Cat Thief*, 1962.

"Andy" series; published by Thomas Nelson: *Andy in Trouble*, 1953; . . . *Keeps a Secret*, 1954; . . . *Takes the Lead*, 1955; . . . *Gets the Blame*, 1956; . . . *in Danger*, 1957; . . . *Finds a Way*, 1959; . . . *Goes Abroad*, 1960; . . . *Wins the Prize*, 1961; . . . *and Her Twin*, 1963; . . . *Meets a Hero*, 1964; . . . *Looks for Gold*, 1965.

Plays: *Morning in Bethlehem: A Play of the Nativity for Child Players*, Epworth, 1953; "*The Weather Imp*" and "*The King of Nowhere*", Macmillan, 1955. Also author of *The Fortune Teller*, Macdonald & Co.

Contributor of poems to magazines and newspapers.

WORK IN PROGRESS: Girl With a Secret, a novel; poems.

SIDELIGHTS: Freda Hurt told *CA:* "I believe that to do anything creative is good for the soul and for the health of the body, too. I write because it gives me satisfaction to do so and I hope will give pleasure and entertainment to others. My favorite author has always been Charles Dickens.

"When I was very young I was torn between the desire to be a poet and an equal ambition to be a painter. Later I developed a singing voice and an interest in music. It was hard to decide which of the arts to choose as a career. Writing won, but I realize now that all the arts are allied and each can contribute to the other.

"The author's world is a private one. He produces something that is received by individuals, usually in the seclusion of their own homes, for reading is private, too. I think he has a peculiar responsibility not to abuse this privilege. Sadism, blatant sex, and violence for its own sake I regard as such abuse."

*   *   *

HURWITZ, Stephan   1901-1981

OBITUARY NOTICE: Born June 20, 1901, in Copenhagen, Denmark; died after a long illness, January 22, 1981, in Copenhagen, Denmark. Educator, jurist, and author. His books include *Criminology, Human Responsibility*, and *Respect for the Human Individual*. Hurwitz served on the United Nations War Crimes Commission in 1945 and later was appointed Denmark's first parliamentary commissioner for public affairs. Obituaries and other sources: *The International Who's Who*, Europa, 1976; *Who's Who in World Jewry: A Biographical Dictionary of Outstanding Jews*, Pitman, 1978; *New York Times*, January 25, 1981.

*   *   *

HUTCHINSON, (William Patrick Henry) Pearse   1927-

PERSONAL: Born February 16, 1927, in Glasgow, Scotland. *Education:* Attended University College, Dublin. *Office:* School of English, University of Leeds, Leeds LS2 9JT, England.

CAREER: International Labor Organization, Geneva Switzerland, translator, 1951-53; drama critic for Radio Eireann in Ireland, 1957-61; drama critic for Telefis Eireann in Ireland, 1968; associated with University of Leeds, Leeds, England. Attended Salzburg Seminar in American Studies, 1952. *Awards, honors:* Butler Award, 1969; Gregory fellowship from University of Leeds, 1971-73.

WRITINGS—Poetry: *Tongue Without Hands*, Dolmen Press, 1963; *Faoistin Bhacach* (title means "Imperfect Confession"), Clochomhar, 1968; *Expansions*, Dolmen Press, 1969; *Watching the Morning Grow*, Gallery Press, 1973; *Frost Is All Over*, Gallery Press, 1975.

Translator: Josep Carner, *Poems*, Dolphin Book Co., 1962; *Friend Songs: Medieval Love-Songs From Galaico-Portuguese*, New Writers Press, 1970.*

*   *   *

HUTCHISON, (William) Bruce   1901-

PERSONAL: Born June 5, 1901, in Prescott, Ontario, Canada; son of John and Constance Mary (Leslie) Hutchison; married Dorothy Kidd MacDiarmid, 1925; children: Joan Edith, Robert Bruce. *Education:* Attended high school in Victoria, British Columbia, Canada. *Home:* 810 Rogers Ave., Victoria, British Columbia, Canada V8X 3P9.

CAREER: Victoria Times, Victoria, British Columbia, journalist and political writer, 1918-36; Imperial Conference, London, England, correspondent, 1937; *Vancouver Sun*, Vancouver, British Columbia, editorial writer and author of column, 1938-43; *Free Press*, Winnipeg, Manitoba, associate editor, 1944-50; *Daily Times*, Victoria, editor, 1950-63; *Vancouver Sun*, editorial director, 1963-74; free-lance writer, 1974—. Director of Sun Publishing Co. Political reporter from Ottawa, Ontario, for *Vancouver Province*, 1925; correspondent for *Vancouver World* and *Vancouver Star*. Guest on radio programs.

MEMBER: Victoria Union Club. *Awards, honors:* Canadian Governor-General's literary award, 1943, for *The Unknown Country*, 1952, for *The Incredible Canadian*, and 1957, for *Canada: Tomorrow's Giant;* LL.D. from University of British Columbia, 1951; president's medal from University of Western Ontario, 1952, for *The Incredible Canadian;* national newspaper awards, 1952, 1958, and 1959; Lorne Pierce Medal, 1955; award for distinguished journalism in the Commonwealth from Royal Society of Arts, 1961; D.D.U. from University of Calgary, 1967; medal of service from Order of Canada, 1967; made a member of Canadian News Hall of Fame, 1968; L.H.D. from Yale University, 1968; C.C.A. Award, 1977, for *The Far Side of the Street*.

WRITINGS: The Unknown Country: Canada and Her People, Coward, 1942, reprinted, Greenwood Press, 1977 (published in England as *The Unknown Dominion: Canada and Her People*, Jenkins, 1946); *The Hollow Men* (novel), Coward, 1944; *The Fraser*, Rinehart, 1950; *Winds of Chance*, Northern Electric Co., 1951; *The Incredible Canadian: A Candid Portrait of Mackenzie King, His Works, His Times, and His Nation*, Longmans, Green, 1952; *Canada's Lonely Neighbour*, Longmans, Green, 1954; *The Struggle for the Border*, Longmans, Green, 1955; *Canada: Tomorrow's Giant* (travel), Knopf, 1957, 4th edition, Academic Press, 1957; *Mr. Prime Minister, 1867-1964*, Longmans Canada, 1964, Harcourt, 1965, abridged edition published as *Macdonald to Pearson: The Prime Ministers of Canada*, Longmans Canada, 1967; *Western Windows*, Longmans Canada, 1967; *Canada: A Year of the Land*, Queen's Printer, 1967; *The Far Side of the Street: A Personal Record*, Macmillan of Canada, 1976. Also author of *Manners, Morals, Myths: Analysis of Canadian-U.S. Relations*, 1954.

Work represented in anthologies, including *Canadian Anthology*, edited by C. F. Klinck and R. E. Watters, Gage, 1955; *British Columbia: A Centennial Anthology*, edited by Watters, McClelland & Stewart, 1958; *Maclean's Canada*, edited by L. F. Hannon, McClelland & Stewart, 1960.

Author of "The Unknown Country Revisited," first broadcast by Canadian Broadcasting Corp. (CBC), March 26, 1961. Contributor of stories to magazines and newspapers, including *Saturday Evening Post, Collier's, Cosmopolitan, Fortune, National Geographic*, and *Saturday Night*.

SIDELIGHTS: Hutchison's many books on Canada have fared well with reviewers. His first effort, *The Unknown Country,* was described by *Atlantic*'s W. H. Chamberlin as an "informal, chatty, colorful, descriptive book." Joan Dangelzer elaborated that in Hutchison's survey of Canada, its people, its history, and its probable future, the author "diagnoses Canada like a doctor, feels it like a poet and writes of it like a competent journalist." *The Incredible Canadian* is a biography of Mackenzie King, a major figure in Canadian politics for more than twenty-five years. Impressed with the volume, A. L. Burt of the *American Historical Review* claimed that Hutchison "is incapable of turning out a dull paragraph, for he wields the magic pen of a fine literary artist." Agreeing in the *Canadian Forum,* F. H. Underhill noted that the book "is written in high spirits, with wit and imagination." "This is certainly the best biography of Mackenzie King that has yet appeared," commented the *Times Literary Supplement.* "It reveals much that has hitherto been unknown, and it is an able analysis of a man of moods and mystery, difficult to understand, and remote from his fellows."

Canada: Tomorrow's Giant chronicles a cross-Canada trip Hutchison took with his family. R. C. Nelson of the *Christian Science Monitor* observed that in the author's descriptions of the land and its people "is the craftsmanship of a reporter— almost a poet—who knows how to use the English language at full strength to capture sights and sounds and smells." The *New York Times*'s Mason Wade contended that "it is an exciting and lively book, which should do much to dispel the ignorance of which its author justly complains."

AVOCATIONAL INTERESTS: Fishing, gardening.

BIOGRAPHICAL/CRITICAL SOURCES: New York Times, February 15, 1942, February 22, 1953, October 20, 1957; *New York Herald Tribune,* February 15, 1942; *Canadian Forum,* April, 1942, December, 1952; *Canadian Historical Review,* June, 1942, June, 1953; *Atlantic,* July, 1942; *Weekly Book Review,* October 1, 1944; *New York Herald Tribune Book Review,* November 19, 1950, March 1, 1953, November 27, 1955; *American Historical Review,* July, 1953; *Times Literary Supplement,* December 4, 1953; *Saturday Review,* December 10, 1955; *Christian Science Monitor,* November 1, 1957; *New York Times Book Review,* February 14, 1965.*

*   *   *

HUTH, Mary Jo(sephine) 1929-

PERSONAL: Born April 2, 1929, in South Bend, Ind.; daughter of Edward A. and Margaret (Emonds) Huth. *Education:* University of Dayton, B.S., 1950; Indiana University, M.A., 1951; St. Louis University, Ph.D., 1955. *Religion:* Roman Catholic. *Office:* Department of Social Science, University of Dayton, Dayton, Ohio 45409.

CAREER: St. Mary's Dominican College, New Orleans, La., head of department of sociology, 1954-55; St. Mary's College, Notre Dame, Ind., associate professor of social sciences, 1955-62; University of Dayton, Dayton, Ohio, associate professor, 1962, head of department, 1965-70, currently professor of sociology. Research sociologist with National Bureau of Standards, 1972-74; member of workshop staff at Mexico City college, summer, 1958, and University of Detroit, summers, 1959-63. Chairperson of program committee of South Bend Council on Community Services, 1960-61; vice-president of St. Joseph County International Relations Council, 1961-62; member of educational advisory committee of Ohio Civil Rights commission, 1969—; member of board of directors of Mishawaka Family and Children's Center, 1956-61,

South Bend Civic Music Association, 1960-62, Dayton Catholic Charities, 1963-69, Dayton Urban League, 1965-68, Travelers Aid Society, 1967-72, and local chapter of National Council of Christians and Jews, 1974—.

MEMBER: American Sociological Association, American Catholic Sociological Association (member of executive council, 1957-59 and 1969-71; vice-president, 1961-62), American Association of University Women (chairperson of committee on the status of women in Indiana, 1958-60; vice-president, 1960-62), Gamma Pi Epsilon, Alpha Kappa Delta, Alpha Sigma Tau.

WRITINGS: The Urban Habitat: Past, Present, and Future, Nelson-Hall, 1978. Contributor to sociology journals. *

*   *   *

HYDEN, (Sten Gustav Vilhelm) Goeran 1938-

PERSONAL: Born July 23, 1938, in Nykoeping, Sweden; son of Sten G. E. and Ida-Marie (a nurse; maiden name, Larsson) Hyden; married Melania Kobulungo (a nursing officer), January 29, 1966; children: Michael, Jane, Erik. *Education:* University of Lund, B.A., 1961, M.A., 1964, Ph.D., 1968; attended Oxford University, 1962, and University of California, Los Angeles, 1962-63. *Religion:* Lutheran. *Home:* Trollebogatan 6, S-552 58 Joenkoeping, Sweden. *Office:* Ford Foundation, P.O. Box 41081, Nairobi, Kenya.

CAREER: University of Lund, Lund, Sweden, lecturer in political science, 1963-64 and 1966-68; Makerere University, Kampala, Uganda, lecturer in political science, 1965-67; University of Nairobi, Nairobi, Kenya, senior lecturer in government, 1968-71; University of Dar es Salaam, Dar es Salaam, Tanzania, professor of political science, 1971-77; University of California, Berkeley, visiting lecturer in political science, 1977-78; Ford Foundation, Nairobi, program adviser, 1978-80, representative, 1980—. Consultant to World Bank, Food and Agriculture Organization of the United Nations, and Swedish International Development Agency. *Military service:* Swedish Army, Infantry, 1957-58. *Member:* Swedish Writers Society, African Association for Public Administration and Management, Society for International Development.

WRITINGS: Politik och samhaelle i Afrika (title means "Politics and Society in Africa"), Cavefors, 1967, 2nd edition, 1969; *Political Development in Rural Tanzania,* East African Publishing House, 1969; *Efficiency Versus Distribution in East African Cooperatives,* East African Literature Bureau, 1973; (editor with Anthony Rweyemamu) *A Decade of Public Administration in Africa,* East African Literature Bureau, 1975; *Beyond Ujamaa in Tanzania,* University of California Press, 1980. Reporter for *Svenska Dagbladet.*

WORK IN PROGRESS: A book on problems of development facing the countries of sub-Saharan Africa, publication expected in 1982.

SIDELIGHTS: Hyden commented: "My vocational interests are rural development, public administration, management, and politics. I am currently involved in administering the Ford Foundation program for eastern and southern Africa, in which support of new initiatives aimed at strengthening progressive development measures, particularly at the community level, forms a significant ingredient. In applying my own judgment to this work I stand guided by my conviction that conventional modes of analyzing development are of limited value and must be substituted by fresh looks at the African situation."

AVOCATIONAL INTERESTS: Playing squash.

I

IBINGIRA, G(race) S(tuart) K(atebarirwe) 1932-

PERSONAL: Born May 23, 1932, in Uganda; son of Alfred and Eva (Kera) Katebarirwe; married Monica Ntarumbana, January 31, 1965; children: Jacqueline, Sandra. *Education:* University of Wales, LL.B. (with honors), 1958; attended King's College, Budo, and King's College, London. *Office:* 801 Second Ave., New York, N.Y. 10017.

CAREER: Called to the Bar at Middle Temple, 1959; High Court, Uganda, advocate, 1959-62; Uganda Government, Kampala, Uganda, minister of justice, 1962-64, minister of state, 1964-66; United Nations, New York, N.Y., permanent representative of Uganda, 1971-74. Member of Uganda Parliament, 1960-66; secretary-general of Uganda People's Congress, 1964-66; consultant to Carnegie Endowment for International Peace. *Member:* Uganda Law Society, Society of the Middle Temple. *Awards, honors:* Award from government of Sudan, 1963; award from government of Ethiopia, 1964.

WRITINGS: The Forging of an African Nation: The Political and Constitutional Evolution of Uganda From Colonial Rule to Independence, 1894-1962, Viking, 1973; *African Upheavals Since Independence,* Westview Press, 1980.*

*　　*　　*

ILLES, Robert E(noch) 1914-

PERSONAL: Surname is pronounced *Ill*-ess; born July 11, 1914, in St. Louis, Mo.; son of Arpad E. (in business and founder of Illes Co.) and Sylvina (Martin) Illes; married Billie McLeod, October 17, 1942; children: Stephanie Illes Ladewig, Nick. *Education:* Rice University, B.A., 1937. *Politics:* Conservative. *Religion:* "Hardshell agnostic." *Residence:* Dallas, Tex. *Office:* Illes Co., P.O. Box 35412, Dallas, Tex. 75235.

CAREER: Illes Co., (flavoring and food manufacturing company), Dallas, Tex., 1927—, currently president. *Military service:* U.S. Army Air Forces, 1942-46; became captain. *Member:* Institute of Food Technologists.

WRITINGS: Men in Stitches (nonfiction), Van Nostrand, 1975.

WORK IN PROGRESS: Wayrider; or, The Sixth Book, a science fiction novel, publication expected in 1981.

SIDELIGHTS: Illes commented: "I have psychic powers, *Wayrider,* a novel set in 1955 with transfer to Henry III's court, Windsor Castle, and Oxford (1255 A.D.), has to do with 'distance influence' or telepathic hypnotism, plus intrigue and historical data. All data is authentic as to history, characters, and dates, with the exception of my people and the fantastic happenings."

Men in Stitches, continued Illes, "is a 'how-to-do' book" which explains "the method of painting pictures in thread using hypodermic needles to embroider."

AVOCATIONAL INTEREST: Travel (South America, Africa, Europe, Asia).

*　　*　　*

IMMERMAN, Leon Andrew 1952-

PERSONAL: Born December 9, 1952, in New York, N.Y.; son of Adolph A. (a lawyer) and Rita (a political scientist; maiden name, Silverman) Immerman. *Education:* Carleton College, B.A., 1973; University of Minnesota, M.A. (philosophy), 1976; Princeton University, M.A. (religion), 1976, Ph.D., 1978; postdoctoral study at Yale University, 1979—. *Home:* 160 Nevins St., Brooklyn, N.Y. 11217.

CAREER: Fund for Open Information and Accountability, New York, N.Y., researcher, 1978-79; writer, 1979—.

WRITINGS: (With Ann Mari Buitrago) *Are You Now or Have You Ever Been in the F.B.I. Files?: How to Secure and Interpret Your F.B.I. Files,* Grove, 1980. Contributor to *Academic American Encyclopedia;* contributor to *Religious Studies.*

*　　*　　*

INFIELD, Glenn (Berton) 1920-1981
(George Powers, Frank Rodgers, Arthur Tolby)

OBITUARY NOTICE—See index for *CA* sketch: Born September 12, 1920, in New Castle, Pa.; died April 15, 1981, in Beaver County, Pa. Screenwriter and author. A combat bomber pilot and flight instructor during World War II, Infield rose to the rank of major before leaving active duty to join the U.S. Air Force Reserve in 1953. Specializing in military subjects, Infield contributed more than two hundred articles to national magazines, wrote television and film scripts, and was the author of books, including *Fighting Eagles, The Kennedy War Heroes, Disaster at Bari, The Poltava Affair,* and *Secrets of the S.S.* Obituaries and other sources: *New York Times,* April 18, 1981; *Publishers Weekly,* May 22, 1981.

INGRAM, Collingwood 1880-1981

OBITUARY NOTICE—See index for CA sketch: Born October 30, 1880, in London, England; died May 19, 1981. Horticulturist and author. Ingram traveled the world in search of plants and had one of the world's finest collections of ornamental cherry trees. He was awarded the Victoria Medal of Honour in 1952. In addition to articles for botanical journals, Ingram wrote books on ornithology and botany, including In Search of Birds, Migration of the Swallow, Ornamental Cherries, and A Garden of Memories. Obituaries and other sources: London Times, May 22, 1981.

*   *   *

INGRAMS, Richard (Reid) 1937-
(Philip Reid)

PERSONAL: Born August 19, 1937; son of Leonard St. Clair and Victoria (Reid) Ingrams; married Mary Morgan, 1962; children: two sons, one daughter. Education: Attended University College, Oxford. Agent: Anthony Sheil Associates Ltd., 2-3 Morwell St., London WC1B 3AR, England. Office: c/o Private Eye, 34 Greek St., London W.1, England.

CAREER: Private Eye, London, England, editor, 1963—.

WRITINGS: (With Christopher Booker and William Rushton) Private Eye on London, Weidenfeld & Nicolson, 1962; (with Booker and Rushton) Private Eye's Romantic England, Weidenfeld & Nicolson, 1962; (with John Wells) Mrs. Wilson's Diary, Anthony Blond, 1966 (also see below); (with Wells) Mrs. Wilson's Second Diary, Anthony Blond, 1966, published with Mrs. Wilson's Diary as Mrs. Wilson's Diaries, illustrated by Rushton, Sphere Books, 1968; (with Ralph Steadman) Tale of Driver Grope, Dobson, 1970; (with Barry Fantoni) The Bible Motorist, Hobbs, 1971; (under pseudonym Philip Reid; with Andrew Osmond) Harris in Wonderland, J. Cape, 1973, published as The Fun House, Houghton, 1974; (with Michael Heath) Book of Bores, Deutsch, 1976; God's Apology: A Chronicle of Three Friends, Deutsch, 1977. Also author of Goldballs, 1979.

Editor: What the Press Never Meant to Say: Private Eye's Second Book of Boobs, illustrated by Bill Tidy, MacDonald & Co., 1968; The Life and Times of Private Eye, 1961-1971, Penguin, 1971; "Private Eye" Book of Pseuds, Deutsch, 1973; "Private Eye's" Bumper Book of Boobs, Deutsch, 1973; Beachcomber: The Words of J. B. Morton, Muller, 1974; Cobbett's Country Book: An Anthology of William Cobbett's Writings on Country Matters, David & Charles, 1975; Lord Gnome of the Rings, Private Eye, 1976; Psecond Book of Pseuds, Private Eye, 1977; "Private Eye" Book Covers, Deutsch, 1978. Also editor, with Wells, of Dear Bill: The Collected Letters of Denis Thatcher, Deutsch, c. 1980.

"Best of Private Eye" series: Anatomy of Neasden, Deutsch, 1972; A Load of Rubbish, Quartet Books, 1974; Wholly Libel, Deutsch, 1978.

BIOGRAPHICAL/CRITICAL SOURCES: Times Literary Supplement, October 17, 1980.

*   *   *

INMERITO
See JAVITCH, Daniel Gilbert

IONESCU, Ghita G. 1913-

PERSONAL: Born in 1913 in Bucharest, Rumania; married Valence de Bois MacLaren. Education: Attended Bucharest University. Agent: Curtis Brown Ltd., 1 Craven Hill, London W2 3EP, England. Office: Department of Government, University of Manchester, Manchester M13 9PL, England.

CAREER: Victoria University of Manchester, Manchester, England, professor of government, 1969—; University of Strasbourg, Strasbourg, France, professor of government, 1974—. Member: International Political Science Association (chairman of research committee on European unification, 1975—), Athenaeum Club.

WRITINGS: Communism in Rumania, 1944-1962, Oxford University Press, 1964, Greenwood Press, 1976; The Reluctant Ally: A Study of Communist Neo-Colonialism, Ampersand, 1965; The Break-up of the Soviet Empire in Eastern Europe, Penguin, 1965; The Politics of the European Communist States, Weidenfeld & Nicolson, 1967; L'Avenir politique de l'Europe orientale, Futuribles, 1967. (with Isabel de Madariaga) Opposition: Past and Present of a Political Institution, C. A. Watts, 1968; (editor with Ernest Gellner) Populism: Its Meanings and National Characteristics, Macmillan, 1969; The New Politics of European Integration, St. Martin's, 1972; Comparative Communist Politics, Macmillan, 1972; (editor) Between Sovereignty and Integration, Halsted, 1973; The Political Thought of Saint-Simon, Oxford University Press, 1976; Centripetal Politics: Government and the New Centres of Power, Hart-Davis, 1979. Also author of The European Alternatives, 1979. Editor of Government and Opposition.

WORK IN PROGRESS: The Concept of Jacobism.

*   *   *

IRVIN, Bob
See IRVIN, Robert W.

*   *   *

IRVIN, Robert W. 1933-1980
(Bob Irvin)

OBITUARY NOTICE: Born March 3, 1933, in Highland Park, Mich.; died of a heart attack, December 1, 1980, in Chicago, Ill. Journalist. Robert Irvin, a highly-regarded automotive writer for nearly thirty years, contributed articles to numerous publications, including the New York Times, the Washington Star, AAA Motor News, and Motor Trend. At the time of his death, he was editor-at-large of Automotive News and publisher of Auto Week. Previously he had served as automotive writer for the Detroit News. Obituaries and other sources: Newsweek, December 27, 1971; 1977 Ward's Who's Who Among U.S. Motor Vehicle Manufacturers, Wards Communications, 1977; New York Times, December 4, 1980.

*   *   *

ISH-KISHOR, Judith 1892-1972

OBITUARY NOTICE—See index for CA sketch: Born March 26, 1892, in Boston, Mass.; died in 1972. Editor and author. Ish-Kishor edited a children's weekly and wrote for a food magazine before becoming a free-lance writer. Her books include Adventure in Palestine, The World Over Story Book, and Tales From the Wise Men of Israel. Obituaries and other sources: Something About the Author, Volume 11, Gale, 1977.

ISRAEL, Marion Louise 1882-1973

OBITUARY NOTICE—See index for *CA* sketch: Born in 1882 in Peabody, Mass.; died January 7, 1973. Secretary, visual education administrator, editor, and author. Israel worked in the public school system of Los Angeles County, Calif., for thirty-four years before beginning a new career as a free-lance writer in 1947. She also researched local history as a community service. Her books for children include several on native Americans, among them *Apaches, Dakotas, Cherokees,* and *Ojibway.* (Date of death provided by Butte County Library, Butte County, Calif.)

* * *

IVES, Burl (Icle Ivanhoe) 1909-

PERSONAL: Born June 14, 1909, in Hunt City Township, Ill.; son of Frank (a contractor) and Cordella (White) Ives; married Helen Peck Ehrlich, December 6, 1945 (divorced, 1971); married Dorothy Koster, April 19, 1971; children: (first marriage) Alexander Frank. *Education:* Attended Eastern Illinois State Teachers College (now Eastern Illinois University), 1927-30, Indiana State Teachers College (now Indiana State University), beginning 1933, New York University, c. 1937-38, and Julliard School, late 1930's; also private study in voice and acting. *Politics:* Independent. *Religion:* Protestant. *Home:* 1880 East Valley Rd., Santa Barbara, Calif. 93106. *Office:* Fitelson & Meyers, 1212 Avenue of the Americas, New York, N.Y. 10036.

CAREER: Actor and singer. Worked as a banjo player, professional football player, bus boy, singer with the Reverend Frank J. Norris's traveling evangelical company, waiter, and singer in bars and cafes, 1913-38. Actor in plays, including "Ah, Wilderness," 1938, "Pocahontas Preferred," 1938, "Flight," 1938, "Knickerbocker Holiday," 1938, "I Married an Angel," 1938, "The Boys From Syracuse," 1938, "Heavenly Express," 1940, "This Is the Army," 1942, "Sing Out, Sweet Land," 1944, "She Stoops to Conquer," 1949, "Paint Your Wagon," 1952, "Show Boat," 1954, "Cat on a Hot Tin Roof," 1955, "Joshua Beene and God," 1961, and "Dr. Cook's Garden," 1967. Also appeared in cabaret in Reno, Nevada, 1974. Actor in own theatrical company's summer productions.

Performer on radio shows, including folksinging engagements for National Broadcasting Co. (NBC-Radio), 1940, "Back Where I Come From," 1940, "Wayfaring Stranger," 1940, "G.I. Jive," 1942, "Radio Reader's Digest," 1945, and weekly song series with Mutual Broadcasting System, 1946.

Actor in motion pictures, including "Earthbound," 1940, "The Man Who Wouldn't Die," 1942, "Smokey," 1946, "Green Grass of Wyoming," 1948, "Station West," 1948, "So Dear to My Heart," 1948, "Sierra," 1950, "East of Eden," 1955, "The Power and the Prize," 1956, "Cat on a Hot Tin Roof," 1958, "The Big Country," 1958, "Wind Across the Everglades," 1958, "Robin and the Seven Hoods," 1958, "Day of the Outlaw," 1959, "Our Man in Havana," 1960, "Let No Man Write My Epitaph," 1960, "The Spiral Road," 1962, "Summer Magic," 1963, "The Brass Bottle," 1964, "Ensign Pulver," 1964, "Mediterranean Holiday," 1964, "The Daydreamer," 1966, "Blast-Off," 1967, "Rocket to the Moon," 1967, "Those Fantastic Flying Fools," 1967, "The McMasters," 1969, "The Only Way Out Is Dead," 1971, "Baker's Hawk," 1976, and "Just You and Me, Kid," 1979. Also appeared in "The Adversaries," "The

Carrier Weather Office," "New Adventures of Heidi," and "Bermuda Depths."

Actor in television programs, including "OK Crackerby" series, 1965, "The Bold Ones" series, 1969-72, and "Roots" mini-series, 1977. Also appeared in "Rudolph," "The Great Easter Bunny," "Celebration," "Sing America," "On Eagle's Wings," and "Oddessy."

Consultant for Academy Insurance; spokesman for United Nations, Salvation Army, and Johnny Horizon Program. *Military service:* U.S. Air Force, 1942-43, stationed with shows "This Is the Army" and "G.I. Jive"; became sergeant.

MEMBER: American Federation of Television and Radio Artists, American Federation of Musicians, Screen Actors Guild, Writers Guild. *Awards, honors:* Donaldson Award for "Sing Out, Sweet Land," 1945; Academy Award for best supporting actor from Academy of Motion Picture Arts and Sciences, 1958, for "The Big Country"; Grammy Award from National Academy of Recording Arts and Sciences, 1962, for "Funny Way of Laughing"; Lincoln Lauriette Award from state of Illinois, 1975; LL.D., Farleigh Dickinson University; D.F.A., Western Illinois University; Mus.D., Carl Sandburg College; Phi Mu Alpha Award from Boston University; Others Award from Salvation Army; National Award from President Gerald Ford; Minnesota Heritage Award; Carl Sandburg Award; National Boy Scouts Award; Crystal Humanitarian Award from Crystal Cathedral; "E" Award from U.S. Navy.

WRITINGS: The Wayfaring Stranger (music), edited by Herbert Haufrecht, Leeds Music, 1945; *Wayfaring Stranger* (autobiography), Whittelsey House, 1948; *Burl Ives Song Book,* Ballantine, 1953; *Tales of America,* World, 1954; *Sailing on a Very Fine Day* (verse), Rand McNally, 1954; (author of introduction) Paul Kapp, *A Cat Came Fiddling and Other Rhymes of Childhood,* Harcourt, 1956; *Burl Ives Book of Irish Songs,* Duell, 1958; *Song in America: Our Musical Heritage,* Duell, 1962; *A Wayfaring Stranger's Notebook,* Bobbs-Merrill, 1962; *The Burl Ives Sing-Along Song Book,* F. Watts, 1963; *Albad, the Oaf,* Abelard, 1965; *More Burl Ives Songs,* Ballantine, 1966; *Guitar for Beginners,* Lorenz Press, 1976. Also author of *Burl Ives Book of Sea Songs,* 1961, and *Sing a Fun Song,* Peer-Southern.

Recordings: "The Wayfaring Stranger," 1949, "Ballads and Folk Songs," volumes 1-3, 1949, "The Return of the Wayfaring Stranger," 1949, "Riders in the Sky," 1949, "Captain Burl Ives' Ark," 1952, "Christmas Day in the Morning," 1952, "Australian Folk Songs," 1952, "Marianne," 1957; "Coronation Concert," 1958, "Down to the Sea in Ships," 1958, "Folk Songs Dramatic and Humorous," 1958, "Songs of Ireland," 1958, "Songs for and About Men," 1958, "Women—Folk Songs about the Fair Sex," 1958, "Old Time Varieties," 1958, "Christmas Eve With Burl Ives," 1958, "Cheers With the Charles Singers," 1959, "Versatile Burl Ives," 1961, "Best of Burl Ives," 1961, "A Little Bitty Tear," 1962, "Call Me Mr. In-Between," 1962, "Funny Way of Laughing," 1962, "Sunshine in My Soul," 1962, "Songs of the West," 1962, "Mary Ann Regrets," 1962, "This Is All I Ask," 1963, "Burl," 1963, "Singin' Easy," 1963, "Brave Man," 1963, "The Same Old Hurt," 1963, "True Love Goes On and On," 1963, "Pearly Shells," 1964, "My Gal Sal," 1965, "The Return of Frank James," 1974.

"The Wild Side of Life," "In the Quiet of the Night," "Rudolph, the Red-Nosed Reindeer," "Burl Ives Sings for Fun," "The Lonesome Trail," "So Dear to My Heart," "The Best of Burl for Boys and Girls," "Burl's Broadway," "Johnny Horizon," "Something Special," "Sing Out, Sweet

Land,'' ''On the Beach at Waikiki,'' ''Burl's Choice,'' ''Holly Jolly Christmas,'' ''Burl Ives Big Country Hits,'' ''Sweet, Sad, and Salty,'' ''Paying My Dues Again,'' ''A First Easter Record for Children,'' ''The Lollipop Tree,'' ''The Times They Are A-Changin','' ''Peace on Earth,'' ''Songs for All Ages,'' ''Little White Duck and Other Favorites,'' ''Animal Fair,'' ''All-Star Children's Album,'' ''Mother Goose Songs,'' ''More Folk Songs,'' ''Singtime with Burl Ives,'' ''Burl Ives Animal Folk.''

''Chim Chim Cheree and Other Children's Choices,'' ''Burl Ives Folk Lullabies,'' ''Summer Magic,'' ''America Sings,'' ''Burl Ives Live in Europe,'' ''Songs I Sang in Sunday School,'' ''How Great Thou Art,'' ''Burl Ives and the Korean Orphan Choir Sing Songs of Faith and Joy,'' ''Shall We Gather at the River,'' ''Two Hundred Years Experience,'' ''A Day at the Zoo,'' ''Big Rock Candy Mountain,'' ''She's a Very Fine Lady,'' ''Salute to America,'' ''Twelve Days of Christmas,'' ''Bicentennial America,'' ''Christmas at the White House,'' ''The Children at Christmas,'' ''We Americans,'' ''Great American Poems,'' ''Burl Ives Presents America's Musical Heritage,'' ''Burl Ives Sings Irving Berlin,'' ''Manhattan Troubador,'' ''Roving Gambler,'' ''Bonnie Wee Lassie,'' ''Mule Train.''

''Grier County Bacheler,'' ''River of Smoke,'' ''The Bachelor's Life,'' ''Blessed Assurance,'' ''When the Roll Is Called Up Yonder,'' ''Got the World by the Tail,'' ''My Mamma Told Me,'' ''Ballanderie,'' ''Robin, He Married,'' ''I've Got No Use for Women,'' ''Foggy, Foggy Dew,'' ''Rodger Young,'' ''Blue Tail Fly,'' ''I'm Goin' Down the Road,'' ''Down in the Valley,'' ''Cowboy's Lament,'' ''It Makes No Difference Now,'' ''I'm Thinking Tonight of My Blue Eyes,'' ''Diesel, Smoke, Dangerous Curves,'' ''The Little Green Valley,'' ''Burl Ives Sings Songs for All Ages,'' ''Children's Favorites,'' ''More Folksongs,'' ''Historical America in Song'' (six records for series of Encyclopaedia Britannica Films).

WORK IN PROGRESS: After Sixty—, an autobiography written with Jesse Stern.

SIDELIGHTS: Carl Sandburg once described Burl Ives as ''the mightiest ballad singer of any century,'' but to his audiences and friends Ives is a unique cross between a favorite uncle and Santa Claus. *Variety*'s Henry Pleasants wrote that Ives ''has become genial Uncle Burl, inviting family, friends and neighbors to gather round the fireside and listen to the often melancholy tales and legends of long ago.''

While bringing pleasure to those who share his stories and songs, Ives has dedicated himself to ensuring that America's folk heritage survives for future generations. Not an academic folklorist, Ives is a grass roots folksinger and anthologist of folk literature. His first exposure to folk music came nearly seventy years ago when he was formally introduced to the folksongs of the Irish, the Scotch, and the English by his Scottish grandmother, Kate White. Ives told Harry Bowman of the *Dallas Morning News* about the folksinging lessons at his grandmother's knee: ''She taught my sister and me some verses with 4-letter words in them. In that way, we were introduced to 4-letter words in a humorous way so when

we got to school we didn't think anything about them. I think that was a rather ingenious educational method.''

At the age of four, Ives began his folksinging career at an old soldiers' picnic when he received a quarter for singing the ballad ''Barbara Allen.'' From the picnic engagement, Ives moved on to appearances as a child entertainer and as an evangelistic singer for small-town gatherings.

During the 1930's, Ives succumbed to wanderlust and took to the road. As a musical hobo, he traveled extensively through the United States, Mexico, and Canada, adding to his repertoire of folksongs, collecting stories, and adventuring. Once, while wandering through Mona, Utah, Ives was arrested for singing ''Foggy, Foggy Dew,'' a favorite song long associated with the folksinger, because the police considered the song ribald.

Ives captured these vagabond days in his autobiography, *Wayfaring Stranger*. A *New York Times* reviewer described the book as ''an account of the struggle of the folk spirit to speak its piece, to make its voice heard above the crash and clatter of the modern world.'' Relating reminiscences and correspondences with a mixture of humor and sincerity, *Wayfaring Stranger* tells the story of Ives, the balladeer.

Though he never totally abandoned his vagabond way of life, Ives lighted in New York in the late 1930's. Here he continued doing odd jobs while he studied classical music. But he still dedicated his musical talent to ballads. Even after beginning his professional acting career in 1938 at the Rockridge Theatre in Carmel, New York, Ives remained chiefly a ballad singer.

His chance for a big break into radio arrived in June, 1940, with a job as a balladeer for NBC-Radio. Sadly, his debut performance was interrupted by a news bulletin reporting the fall of France. Nobody heard Ives sing. It was not until later, during his performance in ''Sing Out, Sweet Land,'' that Burl Ives experienced fame as a folksinger.

In addition to folksinging, Ives has found much success in the theatre, films, and television. His popularity earned him the nickname ''Big Daddy,'' a sobriquet that evolved from the folksinger's role in both the stage and screen versions of Tennessee Williams's ''Cat on a Hot Tin Roof.'' Ives is also well recognized as the narrator of the Christmas television classic ''Rudolph.''

In 1979, the International Year of the Child, seventy-year-old Burl Ives gave some advice to a concert audience. Keith Blogg of *Variety* recorded his words: ''Don't forget to care for the child in yourself.''

AVOCATIONAL INTERESTS: Dogs, camping, sailing, cooking, traveling, raising Nubian goats.

BIOGRAPHICAL/CRITICAL SOURCES: Burl Ives, *Wayfaring Stranger*, Whittlesey House, 1948; *Chicago Sun*, November 7, 1948; *New York Herald Tribune Book Review*, November 7, 1948, November 22, 1953, December 2, 1954; *New York Times*, November 7, 1948, November 22, 1953, November 14, 1954; *San Francisco Chronicle*, December 8, 1948, November 11, 1953, November 18, 1954; *Saturday Review of Literature*, January 8, 1949; *Canadian Forum*, May, 1949; *Music Library Association*, March, 1949; *Chicago Sunday Tribune*, June 8, 1958; *Variety*, June 6, 1979; *Dallas Morning News*, September 18, 1980.

J

JACKSON, Anna J. 1926-
(Anne Jackson)

PERSONAL: Born September 3, 1926, in Allegheny, Pa.; daughter of John Ivan (a barber) and Stella Germaine (Murray) Jackson; married Eli Wallach (an actor), March, 1948; children: Peter Douglas, Roberta Katherine, another daughter. *Education:* Attended New School for Social Research, 1943, Neighborhood Playhouse School of the Theatre, New York, N.Y., 1943-44, and Actors' Studio, 1948. *Home:* 90 Riverside Dr., New York, N.Y. 10024.

CAREER: Actress in stage plays, including "The Cherry Orchard," 1944, "Henry VIII," 1946, "John Gabriel Borkman," 1946, "Arms and the Man," 1950, and "The Glass Menagerie," 1959; performances in Broadway plays include "Summer and Smoke," 1948, "The Last Dance," 1948, "Love Me Long," 1949, "Never Say Never," 1951, "Oh Men! Oh Women!," 1953, "Middle of the Night," 1956, "Major Barbara," 1956, "Rhinoceros," 1961, "Luv," 1964, "The Front Page," 1969, and "Inquest," 1970. Actress in motion pictures, including "So Young So Bad," 1950, "The Journey," 1959, "How to Save a Marriage and Ruin Your Life," 1968, and "Lovers and Other Strangers," 1970; actress in television programs, including "Johnny Pickup," 1951, "Lullaby," 1960, "The Typists," 1971, and "Blinded by the Light," 1980. *Member:* American Federation of Television and Radio Artists, Screen Actors Guild, Actor's Equity Association. *Awards, honors:* Off-Broadway (Obie) Award from *Village Voice*, 1962, for "The Typists" and "The Tiger"; Tinker Award from *Brighton Argus*, 1964.

WRITINGS: (Under name Anne Jackson) *Early Stages* (autobiography), Little, Brown, 1979.

SIDELIGHTS: Although Anne Jackson's stage and film career could no doubt have provided her with ample material with which to write her memoirs, she chose instead to write about her growing-up years. *Early Stages* covers only Jackson's first twenty-five years and contains just a fleeting glimpse of her marriage to Eli Wallach and her experiences as an actress. This choice of material surprised some critics, who expected, as Thomas Lask of *New York Times Book Review* put it, "a reprise of Miss Jackson's theatrical career [or] a gossipy peek behind the theatrical curtain."

The focus of *Early Stages* was not the only aspect of the book to surprise its reviewers. The fact that Jackson wrote it herself instead of enlisting the services of a ghostwriter earned the praise of several critics, including John F. Baker of the *Chicago Tribune,* who called the book "astonishingly vivid and well-written."

Jackson and her two older sisters were the products of a particularly turbulent marriage between two very different personalities. Jackson's father, an expansive, somewhat reckless Croatian barber, had advertised for a companion; her mother, a prim, austere Irishwoman, had answered the ad. The resulting union was a stormy one, punctuated by frequent moves around rural Pennsylvania and later to various tenement houses in New York. The mother's difficulty in adjusting to the stress of the constant moves led eventually to her mental breakdown and permanent institutionalization. Though Jackson reacted to her mother's breakdown with guilt and remorse, the effect of the domestic discord in her childhood was outweighed by what Baker called her "irrepressible determination to enjoy life." He wrote that "the enjoyment in 'Early Stages' lies in watching the creation of an optimistic and plucky personality against almost insuperable odds."

The family's move to New York provided Jackson with her first real exposure to movies; she saw as many as her meager budget and disapproving mother would allow. She had shown an interest in acting by the age of seven, staging her first public performance in the yard of a neighbor's home in Pennsylvania. Already there was the glimmer of the "star" to come, and in the last pages of her autobiography she writes of the beginnings of her acting career. She went on to become, according to Seymour Peck of *New York Times Book Review,* "one of the foremost actresses of the American theater."

In an interview with Jackson for *Publishers Weekly,* Robert Dahlin learned that while writing *Early Stages* she had "tapped into" the memories of her sisters and other relatives instead of relying solely on her own recollections. "The web of memories are knit together in a group portrait," wrote Dahlin. Jackson "does not dwell on herself." The result, according to Baker, is a "composite portrait of an extraordinary family." In *Early Stages,* remarked Peck, Jackson has written "a rare and loving memoir of her family . . . that culminates, most poignantly, in the deaths of her mother and father. . . . For all the family's travail, [she] remembers it without bitterness. She writes of it vividly, sensitively, modestly."

AVOCATIONAL INTERESTS: Ice skating, bicycling, water colors.

BIOGRAPHICAL/CRITICAL SOURCES: Anne Jackson, *Early Stages,* Little, Brown, 1979; *New York Times Book Review,* February 18, 1979, July 8, 1979; *Publishers Weekly,* April 16, 1979; *Chicago Tribune,* August 12, 1979.*

*   *   *

JACKSON, Anne
    See JACKSON, Anna J.

*   *   *

JACKSON, Barbara (Ward)   1914-1981
    (Barbara Ward)

*OBITUARY NOTICE—*See index for *CA* sketch: Born May 23, 1914, in Yorkshire, England; died of cancer, May 31, 1981, in Lodsworth, England. Economist, broadcaster, and author best known as an evangelist for developing Third World countries. Jackson began her career as an assistant editor of *The Economist* in 1939, and she went on to become that publication's foreign editor. She served as the president of the International Institute for Environment and Development for seven years and helped to found the Sword of the Spirit, an organization bent on preserving the values and traditions of the West, which were threatened by World War II. Jackson was a member of the governing council of the Institute of International Affairs as well as one of the first female members of the Pontifical Commission for Justice and Peace. A governor of the British Broadcasting Corporation (BBC), Jackson appeared on BBC's "Brain Trust" and on American television programs such as "The Great Challenge" and "Meet the Press." In addition to teaching at Radcliffe and at Harvard, from which she received an honorary doctorate in 1957, the economist was also a Schweitzer Professor of International Economic Development at Columbia University. Throughout her career she contributed to periodicals, among them *Foreign Affairs* and *New York Times Sunday Magazine.* Her works include *India and the West, Rich Nations and Poor Nations, Only the Earth: The Care and Maintenance of a Small Planet,* and a work on global environment and social justice left incomplete at the time of her death. Obituaries and other sources: *London Times,* June 1, 1981; *New York Times,* June 1, 1981; *Newsweek,* June 15, 1981; *Time,* June 15, 1981.

*   *   *

JACKSON, Everatt
    See MUGGESON, Margaret Elizabeth

*   *   *

JACOB, Paul   1940-

PERSONAL: Born April 27, 1940, in Kerala, India. *Education:* Attended Madras Christian College and St. Stephen's College, Delhi, India. *Office: Enact,* Paul's Press, B-258 Naraina, Industrial Area Phase, New Delhi 110028, India.

CAREER: Century, New Delhi, India, member of editorial staff, 1963-65; *Enact,* Delhi, India, member of editorial staff, 1966—. Gives readings of his works on television programs. *Member:* Writer's Workshop (Calcutta, India).

*WRITINGS—*Books of poems: *Sonnets,* Writer's Workshop (Caluctta, India), 1968; *Alter Sonnets,* Writer's Workshop (Calcutta, India), 1969; *Swedish Exercises,* Writer's Workshop (Caluctta, India), 1973, InterCulture, 1975. Also author of *Inlands in Selestina,* 1971. Work represented in anthologies, including *Modern Indian Poetry in English,* 1969, and

English Poetry in India, 1973. Contributor to magazines, including *Miscellany* and *Junior Statesman.**

*   *   *

JACOBS, Melville   1902-1971

*OBITUARY NOTICE—*See index for *CA* sketch: Born July 3, 1902, in New York, N.Y.; died July 31, 1971; buried in Seattle, Wash. Educator, anthropologist, folklorist, and author. Jacobs became a faculty member in the department of anthropology at the University of Washington in 1928 and taught there for over four decades. A field researcher among native Americans in the northwestern United States, he wrote widely on the folklore and myths gathered during his research. Jacobs wrote anthropology texts, including *Outlines of Anthropology* and *Pattern in Cultural Anthropology.* He also compiled and wrote the foreword of *The Anthropologist Looks at Myth.* Obituaries and other sources: *Who Was Who in America,* 5th edition, Marquis, 1973.

*   *   *

JACOBS, Susan
    See QUINN, Susan

*   *   *

JACOBS, Vivian   1916(?)-1981

OBITUARY NOTICE: Born c. 1916; died after a long illness, April 4, 1981, in Livingston, N.J. Poet and writer. Vivian Jacobs collaborated with her brother, Isaac Rosensohn Jacobs, on articles for the *Harvard Theological Review.* She was co-author with her sister, Wilhelmina Jacobs, of articles on language for *American Speech.* She also contributed poetry to the *New York Times* and the *New York Herald Tribune.* Obituaries and other sources: *New York Times,* April 6, 1981.

*   *   *

JAFFE, Sherril   1945-

PERSONAL: Born September 12, 1945, in Walla Walla, Wash.; daughter of Sam (a publisher) and Vera (a secretary; maiden name, Berger) Jaffe; married David Bromige, September 5, 1970 (divorced December 17, 1979); married Alan Lew (a writer), December 23, 1979; children: (second marriage) Hannah Jaffe. *Education:* University of California, Berkeley, B.A., 1967; San Francisco State College, M.A., 1970. *Religion:* Jewish. *Home:* 880 First St., Sebastopol, Calif. 95472.

CAREER: Santa Rosa Junior College, Santa Rosa, Calif., instructor in creative writing, 1973—. Assistant professor at California State College, Rohnert Park, 1975—, and University of California, Berkeley, 1979.

WRITINGS: Scars Make Your Body More Interesting (stories), Black Sparrow Press, 1975; *This Flower Only Blooms Every Hundred Years* (novel), Black Sparrow Press, 1979.

WORK IN PROGRESS: The Unexamined Wife, a novel; *From the Window,* poems; *The Lost Key,* stories.

SIDELIGHTS: Sherril Jaffe commented: "My first book is a collection of condensed short stories which probe contemporary manners and mores with irony and satire. My novel examines the process of the development of consciousness and value systems. It is a comedy. *The Unexamined Wife* is also a comedy, though a very dark one. It looks at the mechanism of unexamination in a marriage. My collection of poems is titled *From the Window,* as most are inspired by the view from a particular window. Many are love poems for my husband.

"My aim with fiction is to provoke self-discovery and to entertain. I do not believe there should be any wasted words in fiction any more than there should be extra words in poetry. I am very grateful to Jane Austen and Emily Dickinson for all they have given me; I am trying to return something worthy of them."

*   *   *

JAGGER, Peter (John)   1938-

PERSONAL: Born January 31, 1938, in Yorkshire, England; son of Willie (a provision merchant) and Annie (Pullen) Jagger; married Margaret Thompson (a manager of St. Deiniol's Library), March 12, 1960; children: John Mark, Catherine Sarah. *Education:* Attended Wesley College, Leeds, 1962-66, and College of the Resurrection, 1967-68; Lambeth, M.A., 1971; Leeds University, M.Phil., 1976. *Office:* St. Deiniol's Library, Hawarden, Deeside, Clwyd CH5 3DF, Wales.

CAREER: Manager of family business, 1958-62; ordained minister of Church of England, 1969; curate of Church of England in Leeds, England, 1968-71; vicar of Bolton cum Redmire, England, 1971-76; St. Deiniol's Library, Hawarden, Wales, warden, chief librarian, and director of Self Supporting Ministry, 1976—. Member of Archbishop of Canterbury's Lambeth Diploma Committee; regional representative for Lambeth Diploma of Theology; member of Theological Colleges Principals Conference; lecturer. *Member:* Royal Historical Society (fellow), Alcuin club.

WRITINGS: Christian Initiation, 1552-1969: Rites of Baptism and Confirmation Since the Reformation Period, S.P.C.K., 1970; *The Alcuin Club and Its Publications, 1897-1972,* Alcuin Club, 1972; (editor) *Being the Church Today: A Collection of Sermons and Addresses by Bishop Henry de Candole,* Faith Press, 1974; *Bishop Henry de Candole: His Life and Times, 1895-1971,* Faith Press, 1975; *The Alcuin Club and Its Publications: An Annotated Bibliography, 1897-1974,* Alcuin Club, 1976; *A History of the Parish and People Movement,* Faith Press, 1978; (contributor) *A Social History of the Diocese of Newcastle,* Oriel Press, 1981. Contributor to theology journals and to newspapers.

WORK IN PROGRESS: Initiation in the Church of England: The Mid-Victorian Period, 1850-1875; research on the Bishopric Bill of 1878, the formulation of the Four Northern Sees of Newcastle, Wakefield, Liverpool, and Southwell; *Christian Initiation 1969 to 1980: Rites of Baptism and Confirmation;* an annotated bibliography of the W. E. Gladstone Tract Collection; a history of St. Deiniol's Library.

AVOCATIONAL INTERESTS: Sailing, canoeing, shooting, walking, gardening, classical music and opera.

*   *   *

JAINI, Padmanabh S.   1923-

PERSONAL: Born October 23, 1923, in Mangalore, India; came to the United States in 1967; married, 1956; children: two. *Education:* Received B.A., 1947, M.A., 1949; Vidyodaya Pirivena, Tripitakacarya, 1951; University of London, Ph.D., 1959. *Office:* Department of South and Southeast Asian Language and Literature, University of California, 246 Dwinelle, Berkeley, Calif. 94720

CAREER: Banaras Hindu University, Varanasi, India, lecturer in Sanskrit and Pali, 1952-56; University of London, London, England, lecturer, 1956-64, reader in Pali and Buddhist Sanskrit, 1965-67; University of Michigan, Ann

Arbor, professor of Indic languages, 1967-72; University of California, Berkeley, professor of Buddhism, 1972—. Visiting lecturer at University of Michigan, 1964-65.

WRITINGS: The Jaina Path of Purification, University of California Press, 1979.

In Sanskrit: (Editor and author of notes and English introduction) *Abhidharmadipa With Vibhashaprabhavritti Dipakara,* Kashi Prasad Jayaswal Research Institute, 1959, 2nd edition, 1977; (editor) *Milinda-Tika,* Pali Text Society, 1961; (editor) *Aryastasahasrikayah Prajnaparamitayah Saratamakhya panjika: Ratnakara-santivitacita* (introduction in English), Kasi Prasada-Jayasavala-Anusilana Samstha, 1979. Contributor to scholarly journals.*

*   *   *

JAMES, Coy Hilton   1915-

PERSONAL: Born December 21, 1915, in Clarkston, Mo.; married, 1939; children: three. *Education:* Missouri State College, B.S., 1937; University of Iowa, M.A., 1938; Michigan State University, Ph.D., 1956. *Home:* 422 Linden Ave., Albion, Mich. 49224. *Office:* Department of History, Albion College, Albion, Mich. 49224.

CAREER: High school history teacher in Missouri, 1938-45; Albion College, Albion, Mich., instructor, 1946-56, assistant professor, 1956-58, associate professor, 1958-63, professor of history, 1963—, chairman of department and director of European study-travel program, 1961—. High school teacher in Munich, West Germany, 1950-52. *Military service:* U.S. Army, 1944-45. *Member:* American Historical Association, Organization of American Historians.

WRITINGS: Silas Dean: Patriot or Traitor?, Michigan State University Press, 1975.

BIOGRAPHICAL/CRITICAL SOURCES: Annals of the American Academy of Political and Social Science, March, 1976; *Journal of American History,* September, 1976.*

*   *   *

JAMESON, Judith
See NEYLAND, James (Elwyn)

*   *   *

JAQUES, Faith   1923-

PERSONAL: Born December 13, 1923, in Leicester, England; daughter of Maurice Thompson (a businessman) and Gladys Jaques. *Education:* Attended Central School of Art, London, England, 1946-48. *Home and office:* 16 Hillcrest, 51 Ladbroke Grove, London W11 3AX, England.

CAREER: Artist and illustrator. Guildford School of Art, England, visiting lecturer, 1950-54; Hornsey College of Art, London, England, visiting lecturer, 1958-64. Work shown in exhibitions at The Workshop Gallery, London, 1972 and 1976, Nicholas Hill Gallery, London, 1975, Chichester Gallery, Sussex, England, 1976, and Piccadilly Gallery, London, 1977. *Military service:* Women's Royal Naval Service, 1941-45; became petty officer. *Member:* Association of Illustrators, Society of Authors.

WRITINGS—Self-illustrated: Drawing in Pen and Ink, Studio Vista, 1964; *Tilly's House,* Atheneum, 1979; *Tilly's Rescue,* Atheneum, 1981.

Illustrator: Dorothy Wellesley, *Rhymes for Middle Years,* James Barrie, 1954; Jo Manton, *A Portrait of Bach,* Abelard, 1957; Rene Guillot, *The White Shadow,* Oxford University Press, 1959; Gaskell, *Lois the Witch,* Methuen, 1960; *The*

Hugh Evelyn History of Costume, Sixth Century B.C.—1900 A.D., four volumes, Hugh Evelyn, 1960-70; *A Peck of Pepper,* Chatto & Windus, 1961; Josephine Kamm, *Mrs. Pankhurst,* Methuen, 1961; Eric Mathieson, *Jumbo the Elephant,* Hamish Hamilton, 1963, published as *The True Story of Jumbo the Elephant,* Coward, 1964; Henry Treece, *The Windswept City,* Meredith, 1967; Kamm, *Joseph Paxton,* Methuen, 1967; Roald Dahl, *Charlie and the Chocolate Factory,* Allen & Unwin, 1967; Ivan Turgenev, *The Torrents of Spring,* Folio, 1967; Samuel Butler, *The Way of All Flesh,* Heron Books, 1967; Henry James, *The Turn of the Screw,* abridged edition, Longman Books, 1967; R.D. Blackmore, *Lorna Doone,* Heron Books, 1968; Robert Louis Stevenson, *Treasure Island,* Heron Books, 1968; Mary Treadgold, *The Humbugs,* Methuen, 1968; Charles Dickens, *The Magic Fish-Bone* (picture book), Chatto & Windus, 1969, Harvey House, 1970.

Ursula Moray Williams, *Johnny Golightly and His Crocodile* (picture book), Chatto & Windus, 1970, Harvey House, 1971; Eric Houghton, *The Mouse and the Magician* (picture book), Lippincott, 1970; Monica Dickens, *The Great Fire,* Kaye & Ward, 1970; Edith Nesbit, *The Island of the Nine Whirlpools,* Kaye & Ward, 1970; John Cunliffe, *The Giant Who Stole the World* (picture book), Deutsch, 1971; Arthur Ransome, *Old Peter's Russian Tales,* Thomas Nelson, 1971; C. Dickens, *David Copperfield,* American Educational Publications, 1971; Gillian Avery, *A Likely Lad,* Collins, 1971; Philippa Pearce, *What the Neighbours Did and Other Stories,* Longman Young Books, 1972, Crowell, 1973; Jane Austen, *Persuasion,* abridged version, Longman Books, 1972; Margaret Crush, *A First Look at Costume,* C. A. Watts, 1972; Williams, *A Picnic With the Aunts* (picture book), Chatto & Windus, 1972; Cunliffe, *The Giant Who Swallowed the Wind* (picture book), Deutsch, 1972.

Nina Bawden, *Carrie's War,* Lippincott, 1973; Margery Fisher, editor, *Journeys,* Brockhampton Press, 1973; Robert Newton Peck, *A Day No Pigs Would Die,* Knopf, 1973; Cunliffe, *The King's Birthday Cake* (picture book), Deutsch, 1973; Kathleen Lines, editor, *The Faber Book of Greek Legends,* Faber, 1973; Dahl, *Charlie and the Great Glass Elevator,* Allen & Unwin, 1973; Hilary Seton, *Beyond the Blue Hills,* Heinemann, 1973; Seton, *A Lion in the Garden,* Heinemann, 1974; Elizabeth Yandell, *Henry,* Bodley Head, 1974; Maurice Duggan, *Falter Tom and the Water Boy,* Kestrel, 1974; John Rae, *The Golden Crucifix,* Brockhampton Press, 1974; George Eliot, *The Mill on the Floss,* Collins, 1974; Margery Sharp, *The Magical Cockatoo,* Heinemann, 1974; Williams, *Grandpapa's Folly and the Woodworm-Bookworm,* Chatto & Windus, 1974; Helen Cresswell, *Lizzie Dripping Again,* BBC Publications, 1974; Rae, *The Treasure of Westminster Abbey,* Brockhampton Press, 1975; Nesbit, *The Old Nursery Stories,* Hodder & Stoughton, 1975; Barbara Willard, editor, *Field and Forest,* Kestrel, 1975; Houghton, *A Giant Can Do Anything* (picture book), Deutsch, 1975; Rae, *Christmas Is Coming,* Brockhampton Press, 1976; Sharp, *Bernard the Brave,* Heinemann, 1976; Andrew Lang, *The Red Fairy Book,* Viking, 1976; Alison Uttley, *A Traveller in Time,* Puffin, 1977; Avery, *Mouldy's Orphan,* Collins, 1978; Uttley, *The Little Grey Rabbit Book,* Heinemann, 1980.

All by Leon Garfield; all published by Heinemann: *Moss and Blister,* 1976; *The Cloak,* 1976; *The Valentine,* 1977; *Labour in Vain,* 1977; *The Fool,* 1977; *Rosy Starling,* 1977; *The Dumb Cake,* 1977; *Tom Titmarch's Devil,* 1977; *The Filthy Beast,* 1978; *The Enemy,* 1978.

Contributor of articles to magazines, including *Cricket.*

SIDELIGHTS: Jaques told *CA:* "I care as much for the word as the picture when I select the books I illustrate. The quality of the writing matters very much and I like to feel the book will stand the test of time. Fortunately the standard of writing in children's books is so high now that a degree of choice is possible. But I regret that the publishers are tending to neglect black and white illustration in favor of so many full-color picture books. The latter are great fun to do, and a proportion of them are really worthwhile, but to me the problems are not so interesting as those of trying to complement a full-length text, strong in mood and characterization and with the author's particular 'flavor.' This requires *illustration* not *decoration,* which means abilities of draftsmanship and technique are necessary, as well as a wide background knowledge. I'm always thankful that I was trained at a time when life drawing was predominant, in addition to studies of architecture and perspective, and furniture and costume styles. I wouldn't consider myself a 'documentary' illustrator, but I'm grateful for the work I had to put in years ago on these subjects and for the lifelong interest in social history that has resulted. I can't create in a void—I need practical knowledge as a jumping-off point for the imagination.

"The major influences on my work have stemmed from my childhood reading. I read Dickens, Thackeray, the Brontes, and other Victorian writers when I was quite young and became fond of the steel and wood-engraved pictures by Cruikshank, 'Phiz,' and so on, which accompanied the texts. I still love this sort of illustration because it accomplished so much in the way of mood and scene-setting. It is capable of great subtlety and never dominates the text.

"I started at the Central School of Art in January, 1946, on a tiny grant lasting for four terms only. So my entire art school training was very short, but I made up for it by working about eighteen hours a day. I had to get any commissions I could while still a student, so I worked in every sort of illustration then and for the next fifteen years: newspapers, books, magazines, advertising, postage stamps, filmstrips, wallpapers, pottery, textiles, etc. Only in the last fifteen years have I been able to concentrate on book illustration, which is what I wanted to do ever since I was a child. I have also sold several illustrations to the British Museum, have work in various private collections, and did the four 1978 Christmas stamps on the theme of caroling."

BIOGRAPHICAL/CRITICAL SOURCES: Guardian, February 10, 1975; *Mother,* September, 1975.

*   *   *

JAQUES, Florence Page 1890-

PERSONAL: Born March 7, 1890, in Decatur, Ill.; daughter of Henry Putnam and Anna (Farrell) Page; married Francis Lee Jacques (an artist), May 12, 1927. *Education:* Millikin University, A.B., 1911; graduate study at Columbia University. *Home:* 610 West 116th St., New York, N.Y. 10027.

CAREER: Writer. *Member:* Society of Women Geographers, Pi Beta Phi. *Awards, honors:* John Burroughs Medal, 1946, for *Snowshoe Country;* alumni award from Millikin University, 1959.

WRITINGS—Nonfiction: Canoe Country, University of Minnesota Press, 1938, reprinted, 1967; *The Geese Fly High,* University of Minnesota Press, 1939, reprinted, 1964; *Birds Across the Sky,* Harper, 1942; *Snowshoe Country,* University of Minnesota Press, 1944, reprinted, 1979; *Canadian Spring,* Harper, 1947; *As Far as the Yukon,* Harper, 1951; *There Was Once a Puffin and Other Nonsense Verse,* Wake-Brook, 1956; *Francis Lee Jaques: Artist of the Wilderness World,*

Doubleday, 1973. Contributor of stories and poems to adult and children's magazines, including *Natural History, American Girl, Child Life, Audubon, Naturalist,* and *Beaver.*

BIOGRAPHICAL/CRITICAL SOURCES: Audubon, January, 1950.*

*   *   *

JARVIS, Rupert Charles   1899-

PERSONAL: Born December 10, 1899, in Sudbury, England; married Marjorie Wilson Hare; children: two sons, one daughter. *Education:* Attended University of Berlin. *Home:* Shelley, Station Rd., Hockley, Essex, England.

CAREER: City Literary Institute, London, England, lecturer in history and archaeology, 1958-69; librarian and archivist for British Customs and Exise, until 1964; lecturer in manuscript studies and archive administration at University of London. *Member:* Society of Antiquaries (fellow), Royal Archaeological Institute (fellow), Royal Historical Society (fellow). *Awards, honors:* Haldane Medal; companion of Imperial Service Order.

WRITINGS: (Editor) *The Jacobite Risings of 1715 and 1745,* Cumberland County Council, 1954; *The Administration of the Anti-Papist Laws With Particular Reference to the North of England,* John Rylands Library, 1964; (editor and author of introduction) *Customs Letter-Books of the Port of Liverpool, 1711-1813,* Chetham Society, 1964; (with Robert Craig) *Liverpool Registry of Merchant Ships,* Manchester University Press, 1967; (author of introduction to reprint) Elizabeth Evelynola Hoon, *The Organization of the English Customs System, 1696-1786,* David & Charles, 1968; (contributor) *Studies in London History,* Hodder & Stoughton, 1969; *Collected Papers on the Jacobite Risings,* Barnes & Noble, Volume I, 1971, Volume II, 1972; (co-author) *Prisca Munimenta: Studies in Archival and Administrative History,* University of London Press, 1973. Also author of *The Customs in the Ports,* 1974. Contributor to learned journals.*

*   *   *

JASPAN, Norman

PERSONAL—Office: Norman Jaspan Associates, Inc., 60 East 42nd St., Suite 1620, New York, N.Y. 10017.

CAREER: Norman Jaspan Associates, Inc. (management engineers), New York, N.Y., currently president. President of Investigations, Inc. Member of National Committee on Technical Distribution Research and domestic distribution committee of Chamber of Commerce of the United States; consultant to U.S. General Accounting Office.

WRITINGS: (With Hillel Black) *The Thief in the White Collar,* Lippincott, 1960; *Mind Your Own Business,* Prentice-Hall, 1974; (editor with Walter Nagel) *Theft in the Health Care Industry,* Aspen Systems Corp., 1978. Contributor to magazines, including *Newsweek, Business Week,* and *Fortune,* and newspapers.

SIDELIGHTS: Jaspan's firms operate as international management consultants, combining fact-finding procedures with management engineering functions and specializing in safeguarding company assets, developing shortage controls, evaluating methods and systems, and designing educational training programs. His more than two hundred clients include companies that deal in heavy industry, soft goods manufacturing, and airlines, hotels, and hospitals.

JAVITCH, Daniel Gilbert   1941-
(Inmerito)

PERSONAL: Born June 13, 1941, in Cannes, France; married, 1968. *Education:* Princeton University, A.B., 1963; Cambridge University, B.A., 1965, M.A., 1970; Harvard University, M.A., 1966, Ph.D., 1970. *Office:* Department of English, Columbia University, 416 Hamilton Hall, New York, N.Y. 10027.

CAREER: Columbia University, New York, N.Y., assistant professor of comparative literature, 1970—. Director of New Directions Publishing Corp., 1972—. Fellow at Harvard University's Center for Italian Renaissance Studies, Florence, Italy, 1976-77. *Member:* Modern Language Association of America, Renaissance Society of America. *Awards, honors:* American Council of Learned Societies fellowship, 1977.

WRITINGS: (Under pseudonym Inmerito) *The Use of Italian Sources in Spenser's Ideal of Courtesy,* privately printed, 1967; *Poetry and Courtliness in Renaissance England,* Princeton University Press, 1978. Contributor to language and literature journals.

BIOGRAPHICAL/CRITICAL SOURCES: Times Literary Supplement, October 6, 1978.*

*   *   *

JAY, Charlotte
See HALLS, Geraldine (Mary)

*   *   *

JAY, G. S.
See HALLS, Geraldine (Mary)

*   *   *

JEFFREY, Richard Carl   1926-

PERSONAL: Born August 5, 1926, in Boston, Mass.; son of Mark M. and Jane (Markovitz) Jeffrey; married Edith Kelman, January 2, 1955; children: Daniel, Pamela. *Education:* Attended Boston University, 1943-44; University of Chicago, M.A., 1951; Princeton University, Ph.D., 1957. *Home:* 55 Patton Ave., Princeton, N.J. 08540. *Office:* Department of Philosophy, Princeton University, Princeton, N.J. 08540.

CAREER: Massachusetts Institute of Technology, Cambridge, designer of computers at Digital Computer Laboratory and Lincoln Laboratory, 1952-55, assistant professor of electrical engineering, 1958-59; Stanford University, Stanford, Calif., assistant professor of philosophy, 1959-63; City College of the City University of New York, New York, N.Y., associate professor of philosophy, 1964-67; University of Pennsylvania, Philadelphia, professor, 1967-73, Adam Seybert Professor of Philosophy, 1973-74; Princeton University, Princeton, N.J., professor of philosophy, 1974—. Visiting member of Institute for Advanced Study, Princeton, 1963; visiting associate professor at Princeton University, 1964; member of National Science Foundation panel on history and philosophy of science, 1967-69. *Military service:* U.S. Naval Reserve, active duty, 1944-46. *Member:* American Philosophical Association, Association for Symbolic Logic, Philosophy of Science Association (member of governing board, 1969-71). *Awards, honors:* National Science Foundation grants, 1965-69.

WRITINGS: The Logic of Decision, McGraw, 1965; *Formal Logic: Its Scope and Limits,* with instructor's manual, McGraw, 1967; (contributor) Wesley C. Salmon, editor, *Statistical Explanation and Statistical Relevance,* University of Pittsburgh Press, 1971; (editor with Rudolf Carnap) *Studies in Inductive Logic and Probability,* University of California Press, Volume I, 1971, Volume II, 1980; (with George Boolos) *Computability and Logic,* Cambridge University Press, 1974.*

*   *   *

JEFFRIES, John Worthington 1942-

PERSONAL: Born April 6, 1942, in Oxford, Miss.; married, 1964; children: two. *Education:* Harvard University, B.A., 1963; Yale University, M.Phil., 1971, Ph.D., 1973. *Office:* Department of History, University of Maryland, Baltimore County, 5401 Wilkens Ave., Baltimore, Md. 21228.

CAREER: Princeton University, Princeton, N.J., instructor in history, 1972-73; University of Maryland, Baltimore, assistant professor, 1973-78, associate professor of history, 1978—. *Member:* Organization of American Historians.

WRITINGS: Testing the Roosevelt Coalition: Connecticut Society and Politics in the Era of World War II, University of Tennessee Press, 1979. Contributor to scholarly journals.

BIOGRAPHICAL/CRITICAL SOURCES: Choice, December, 1979.*

*   *   *

JEFFRIES, Lewis I(ngles) 1942-

PERSONAL: Born January 28, 1942, in Roanoke, Va.; son of Melville Lewis (a journalist) and Mary Lewis (Ingles) Jeffries; married Mary Ann Veirs (a teacher), June 7, 1969; children: Mary Jennifer, John. *Education:* Virginia Polytechnic Institute and State University, B.S., 1964; attended Armed Forces Staff College, 1975-76. *Home:* 7713 Hayfield Rd., Alexandria, Va. 22310. *Office:* Headquarters, Department of the Army, Pentagon, Washington, D.C. 20310.

CAREER: U.S. Army, 1964—; battery officer in Augsburg, West Germany, 1965-66; ranger instructor in Fort Benning, Ga., 1966-67; battalion officer in Vietnam, 1967-68; stationed in Fort Sill, Okla., 1968-69; battalion officer in Schwienfurt, West Germany, 1969-72; Reserve Officers Training Corps (ROTC) instructor at Virginia Military Institute in Lexington, Va., 1972-75; North Atlantic Treaty Organization (NATO) detachment commander in Corlu, Turkey, 1976-77; staff officer at Fort Hood, Tex., 1977-80; Department of Army staff officer in Washington, D.C., 1980—; present rank, lieutenant colonel. *Member:* Association of the U.S. Army, U.S. Naval Institute, Railway and Locomotive Historical Society, Omicron Delta Kappa. *Awards, honors*—Military: Silver Star, Meritorious Service Medal, Bronze Star.

WRITINGS: Norfolk and Western: Giant of Steam, Pruett, 1980.

SIDELIGHTS: Jeffries wrote: "I was reared in southwestern Virginia on the Allegheny plateau. My boyhood was spent on the family farm, which did much to influence my formative years toward outdoor activities, our American heritage, and individual resourcefulness.

"My fascination with Norfolk & Western did not just come about. It was a growing romance from early boyhood, when I watched the steam giants on the main line through nearby towns and on a branch line through the farm. I literally grew up with Norfolk & Western steam around me. In my younger years, the biggest thrill was going to Roanoke to see the 'hub' of steam operations in action. My book is the culmination of a lifelong association with and a special interest in a railway that epitomizes the free enterprise system in America.

"The full story about the Norfolk and Western Railway and its home-designed and home-built steam locomotives had never been written. This prompted me to begin the project while I had access to those who had the information and while I was near to the railway itself. I felt the documentary must be told, and the whole endeavor became a hobby with a crusading torch. Helpful advice from scores of former and present officials of the railway made the project possible.

"Although the book is oriented toward the Norfolk & Western steam operations, it also outlines the whole story of the industry between 1896 and 1964. Specifically, it is not just about mighty steam locomotives, but also about how operating conditions and events dictated the great coal hauler's motive power policy. Norfolk & Western locomotives of the late steam era did not come about suddenly, they evolved after many years of using various types of older power— some successfully, some unsuccessfully. My intent is to show how various types of locomotives evolved and why, and I want to perpetuate the free enterprise system of this great country and the private ownership of the U.S. railroad industry."

AVOCATIONAL INTERESTS: Horseback riding, farming, shooting sports, camping.

*   *   *

JELLY, George Oliver 1909-
(Alfred Fosse, Hilya Harsch)

PERSONAL: Born April 20, 1909, in Bury, England; son of George Aubrey (an ophthalmologist) and Kitty Olive Jelly; married Phyllis Hilda Russell, July 25, 1934; children: Elisabeth Jelly Taylor, Georgina, John Oliver. *Education:* Magdalen College, Oxford, M.A., 1927, M.Ch., 1930. *Religion:* Church of England. *Home:* Rocket Carthouse, Angle, Pembroke, Dyfed, Wales.

CAREER: Associated with Guy's Hospital in London, England, 1930-37; Manchester Royal Infirmary, Manchester, England, chief surgical assistant, 1939-41; Manchester Regional Hospital Board, Manchester, consultant surgeon, 1948-74; writer, 1974—. *Military service:* British Army, Royal Medical Corps, 1942-46.

WRITINGS: (Under pseudonym Alfred Fosse) *Minor Malady Malignant,* Johnson Publications, 1958; *An Essay on Eyesight,* Hodder, 1963; *Ditchcraft: Essays Around Medicine,* Johnson Publications, 1965; *We Three* (novel), Johnson Publications, 1965; *The Two, the Three, and the Four* (poems), Johnson Publications, 1973; (under pseudonym Hilya Harsch) *Fives Court* (novel in verse), Exposition Press, 1979.

WORK IN PROGRESS: My Thesis on Failure, a novel, expected in 1982; short stories.

SIDELIGHTS: Jelly commented: "I am an authentic amateur, motivated by years of reading other authors' books and by professional fatigue. I am also an amateur painter and draftsman. I find I start writing when I am tired and paint (or engrave) when I am revived. I am clearly a hopeless case and certainly not in literature for the money. I should stick to golf!"

JENKINS, Ray(mond Leonard) 1935-

PERSONAL: Born September 1, 1935, in Oxford, England; son of Richard Owen Glyndwr and Catherine (Leonard) Jenkins; married Annie Daniele Lecomte, December 30, 1961; children: Pascale Sian, Ceri Daniel. *Education:* Trinity College, Cambridge, B.A. (with honors), 1959. *Politics:* "Left." *Home:* 187 Pitshanger Lane, London W5 1RQ, England. *Agent:* Margaret Ramsay Ltd., 14A Goodwin's Court, St. Martin's Lane, London WC2N 4LL, England.

CAREER: Head of drama department at comprehensive school in London, England, 1960-63; City of Leicester College of Education, Leicester, England, lecturer in English, 1963-65; free-lance television writer, 1965—. Extramural lecturer at University of London, 1967-68. *Military service:* British Army, Royal Artillery, bombardier, 1953-56. *Member:* Writers Guild of Great Britain (chairman, 1976-77).

WRITINGS: The Lawbreakers (nonfiction), Penguin, 1969; *The World of Colonel Kelly* (juvenile novel), Macmillan, 1977.

Plays: "Clair de lune" (one-act), first produced in London at Arts Theatre, August 5, 1959; "The Reliever" (one-act), first produced in London at Hovenden Theatre Club, February 2, 1962; "Alas, Good Friday" (one-act), first produced in England at Piccadilly One Studio, December 12, 1966; *Julian* (juvenile), Cassell, 1968; *Five Green Bottles* (juvenile), Cassell, 1968; "Boy Dudgeon" (one-act), first produced at Leeds Playhouse, February 2, 1977; *Incident* (juvenile), Macmillan, 1979. Author of about one hundred fifty television and radio scripts.

Work represented in anthologies, including *Playbill Three*, 1969.

SIDELIGHTS: Jenkins wrote: "When you've worked with the inarticulate, as I have with kids, you realize *somebody* has to speak up for them. That is why I like writing for and about kids. This leads naturally to my preoccupation with police, education, and law; now my best friend is a cop!"

* * *

JENNINGS, Patrick
See MAYER, S(ydney) L(ouis)

* * *

JENNY, Hans H(einrich) 1922-

PERSONAL: Surname is pronounced *Yen*-ny; born April 11, 1922, in Ennenda, Switzerland; came to the United States in 1947, naturalized citizen, 1957. *Education:* Attended Ecole Superieur de Commerce, 1938-42, and University of Lausanne, 1942-43; University of Bern, Lic. Rer. Pol., 1947, Dr. Rer. Pol., 1950; attended George Washington University, 1947, and Yale University, 1949. *Home address:* U.S. Route 250 E, Box 157, Polk, Ohio 44866. *Office:* Department of Economics, College of Wooster, Wooster, Ohio 44691.

CAREER: Lucerne Recruit School, Lucerne, Switzerland, instructor, 1944; College of Wooster, Wooster, Ohio, instructor, 1949-51, assistant professor, 1951-54, associate professor, 1954-59, professor of economics, 1959—, director of institutional research, 1962—, vice-president for budgetary affairs, 1966—, vice-president of Wooster Student Aid Fund, 1954—. Associated with John Minter Associates (consultants), 1978. Lecturer at colleges and universities in the United States and Europe. Member of technical and advisory councils of Western Interstate Commission for Higher Education—Management Information Systems, 1970—; member of National Commission on the Financing of Postsecondary Education, 1973, and Twentieth Century Fund task force on college and university endowment policy, 1975; member of board of directors of National Center for Higher Education Management Systems, 1975—; committee member of American Council on Education, 1977; consultant to General Electric Co. and Cummins Mid-America Manufacturing. *Member:* National Association of College and University Business Officers, Association of American Colleges (member of advisory council, 1975). *Awards, honors:* Grants from Ford Foundation, 1973, Lilly Foundation, 1975, Cleveland Foundation, 1978, and Exxon Corp., 1978.

WRITINGS: (Contributor) K. E. Boulding and W. A. Spivey, editors, *Linear Programming and the Theory of the Firm*, Macmillan, 1960; *The Golden Years: A Study of Income and Expenditure Growth and Distribution of Forty-Eight Private Four-Year Liberal Arts Colleges, 1960-1968*, College of Wooster, 1970, revised edition published as *The Turning Point: A Study of Income and Expenditure Growth and Distribution of Forty-Eight Private Four-Year Liberal Arts Colleges, 1960-1970*, 1972; *The Consolidated Net Worth of Private Colleges: Recommendation of a Model*, College of Wooster, 1973; *The Bottom Line*, College of Wooster, 1978; *Financial Viability in Postsecondary Education: Data Requirements for Sound Policy Formulation and Control During the 1980's and 1990's*, College of Wooster, 1978; *Institutional Financial Assessment: Methodology and Meaning; Research in Higher Education*, APS Publications, 1977; (with others) *Another Challenge: Age Seventy Retirement in Higher Education*, Teachers Insurance and Annuity Association/College Retirement Equities Fund, 1979. Contributor to economic and education journals.

* * *

JENSEN, Laura (Linnea) 1948-

PERSONAL: Born November 16, 1948, in Tacoma, Wash.; daughter of Theodore Jonas and Linnea Serena Jensen. *Education:* University of Washington, Seattle, B.A., 1972; University of Iowa, M.F.A., 1974. *Religion:* Lutheran. *Residence:* Tacoma, Wash.

CAREER: Writer. *Awards, honors:* Honors award from Washington State Arts Commission, 1978, for *Bad Boats*; fellow of National Endowment for the Arts, 1980.

WRITINGS—Poetry, except as noted: *After I Have Voted*, Gemini Press, 1972; *Anxiety and Ashes*, Penumbra Press, 1976; *Bad Boats*, Ecco Press, 1977; *Tapwater*, Graywolf, 1978; *The Story Makes Them Whole* (pamphlet), Porch, 1979; *Memory*, Dragon Gate, 1981.

* * *

JESPERSEN, James 1934-

PERSONAL: Born November 17, 1934, in Weldona, Colo.; son of Andrew James and Margaret (Irene) Jespersen; children: Ann, Christine, Andrew. *Education:* University of Colorado, B.A., 1956, M.S., 1961. *Home:* 1110 Poplar Ave., Boulder, Colo. 80302.

CAREER: Central Radio Propagation Laboratories, Boulder, Colo., physicist, 1958-63; Radio Research Laboratories, Slough, England, exchange scientist, 1963-64; National Bureau of Standards, Boulder, physicist, 1965-72; Department of Commerce, Washington, D.C., science fellow, 1973-74; National Bureau of Standards, Boulder, physicist, 1975—. Consultant to United Nations. *Member:* Institute of Electronic and Electrical Engineers, Consultative Committee on

International Radio, Colorado Authors League, Sigma Pi Sigma, Sigma Psi. *Awards, honors:* Emmy Award from Academy of Television Arts and Sciences, 1980, for developing closed-captioning for the hearing impaired.

WRITINGS—All with Jane Fitz-Randolph: *From Sundials to Atomic Clocks,* U.S. Government Printing Office, 1977; *Time and Clocks for the Space Age,* Atheneum, 1979; *Mercury's Web,* Atheneum, 1981.

WORK IN PROGRESS: A book on computers for the layman, publication by Atheneum expected in 1983.

SIDELIGHTS: Jespersen commented: "I have traveled extensively in Asia as a consultant on telecommunications for the United Nations."

*   *   *

JESSEL, George (Albert) 1898-1981

OBITUARY NOTICE—See index for *CA* sketch: Born April 3, 1898, in New York, N.Y.; died of a heart attack, May 24, 1981, in Los Angeles, Calif. Comedian, singer, actor, public speaker, and author. Jessel began his career in vaudeville when he was nine years old. He went on to become a successful actor, starring in the Broadway production of "The Jazz Singer," though he lost the movie role to Al Jolson. Later, he was a producer, actor, and screenwriter in Hollywood and also performed on radio and television. Deeply patriotic, he often entertained U.S. troops abroad and liked to appear in what he called his "U.S.O. uniform." He was very active as a speaker at fund-raising dinners of all sorts, for which President Harry Truman dubbed him "toastmaster general of the United States." Jessel was the author of books on public speaking as well as collections of his jokes and comedy routines. He wrote an autobiography, *So Help Me,* and a book of memoirs, *This Way Miss.* Obituaries and other sources: *Chicago Tribune,* May 26, 1981; *New York Times,* May 26, 1981; *Washington Post,* May 26, 1981; *Newsweek,* June 8, 1981; *Time,* June 8, 1981.

*   *   *

JEZEWSKI, Bohdan O(lgierd) 1900-1980

OBITUARY NOTICE—See index for *CA* sketch: Born February 16, 1900, in Warsaw, Poland; died August 9, 1980, in London, England. Tourism director, journalist, editor, and author. After a decade with the Polish Army, Jezewski spent the thirties as a director of tourism in Warsaw. During World War II he worked at the Polish Ministry of Information in London and remained in Britain after the war, publishing books of particular interest to Polish expatriates. Among these are *Poles Abroad, Year Book and Directory, Directory of Polish Newspapers and Periodicals in the Free World,* and *Polish Guide to London.* (Date of death provided by associate, H. G. Graham.)

*   *   *

JOESTING, Edward Henry 1925-

PERSONAL: Born June 28, 1925, in St. Paul, Minn. *Education:* Pomona College, B.A. *Office:* C. Brewer & Co. Ltd., P.O. Box 3200, Honolulu, Hawaii 96801.

CAREER: Pasadena Star News, Pasadena, Calif., assistant advertising manager, 1949-51; Lund-Heitman, manager, 1951-53; N.Y. Ayer & Son, account representative, 1953-56; First National Bank of Hawaii, assistant vice-president, 1956-69; C. Brewer & Co. Ltd., Honolulu, Hawaii, vice-president of corporate communications, 1971—. Member of East-West

Center. *Member:* Public Relations Society of America, Hawaiian Historical Society (president, 1964-65), Honolulu Press Club (member of board of directors).

WRITINGS: The Islands of Hawaii (photographs by Ansel Adams), privately printed, 1958; *An Introduction to Hawaii* (photographs by Adams), Five Associates, 1964; (with O. A. Bushnell) *Hawaii: A Pictorial History* (edited by Joseph Feher), Bishop Museum Press, 1969; *Hawaii: An Uncommon History,* Norton, 1972; *Eternal Hawaii,* C. H. Belding, 1976.*

*   *   *

JOHNSON, Ann Cox
See SAUNDERS, Ann Loreille

*   *   *

JOHNSON, Charles Ellicott 1920-1969

OBITUARY NOTICE—See index for *CA* sketch: Born September 7, 1920, in Worland, Wyo.; died June 17, 1969, in a traffic accident. Accountant, educator, and author. Johnson was a practicing accountant while studying for his advanced degrees, then began teaching at the University of Minnesota in 1948. After a year at Berkeley as a lecturer, Johnson became associate professor at the University of Oregon in 1952. He remained at the University of Oregon for seventeen years, becoming head of the department of accounting and statistics, dean of College of Liberal Arts, and, from 1968 to his death in 1969, acting president of the University. Johnson also co-authored several accounting textbooks. Obituaries and other sources: *New York Times,* June 18, 1969; Ken Metzler, *Confrontation: The Destruction of a College President,* Nash Publishing, 1973; *Who Was Who in America,* 5th edition, Marquis, 1973.

*   *   *

JOHNSON, Fridolf (Lester) 1905-

PERSONAL: Born February 24, 1905, in Chicago, Ill.; son of Herman Oscar and Sophia Maria (Hanson) Johnson; married Madeline Chiville, November 17, 1933 (divorced, 1958); married Heidi Ruth Lenssen (a painter), July 19, 1958. *Education:* Attended School of Art Institute of Chicago, 1923-25. *Home and office:* 34 Whitney Dr., Woodstock, N.Y. 12498.

CAREER: Frankel-Rose Advertising Agency, Chicago, Ill., art director, 1925-34; free-lance artist in Chicago, 1934-42, and Los Angeles, Calif., 1942-43; publicity designer for Universal-International, 1943-47; free-lance designer and calligrapher in San Francisco, Calif., 1947-48, and New York City, 1950-52; Contempo Art Service, Hollywood, Calif., owner, 1948-50; Norcoss Co., New York City, planning director, 1952-62; Mermaid Press, New York City, owner and operator, 1958—; *American Artist,* New York City, executive editor, 1962-70; free-lance writer and designer, 1970—. Lecturer on graphic art; calligrapher, with group exhibitions and work in collections, including Victoria and Albert Museum, London, England; co-founder of Society of Graphic Arts, San Francisco, Society of Calligraphers, Los Angeles, The New York Chappell of Private Presses, New York City, and "The Junketeers."

WRITINGS: Ornamentation and Illustrations for the Kelmscott Chaucer, Dover, 1973; *The Illustrations of Rockwell Kent,* Dover, 1976; *Mythical Beasts Coloring Book* (self-illustrated), Dover, 1976; (with Clarence P. Hornung) *Two Hundred Years of American Graphic Art,* Braziller, 1976; *A Treasury of Bookplates From the Renaissance to the Present,* Dover, 1977; *American Illustrators in Line,* Dover, 1981;

Rockwell Kent, Knopf, 1981; *The Worlds of Rockwell Kent,* Knopf, 1981.

Illustrator: Frederika Shumway Smith, *The Magic Stairway,* Alliance Book Corp., 1942; Ben Aronin, *The New Mother Goose Rhymes,* Remington-Morse, 1943.

Contributor to *Encyclopedia of Collectibles.* Contributor of articles and reviews to magazines and newspapers, including *New York Historical Society Quarterly.* Executive editor of *American Artist,* 1962-70.

WORK IN PROGRESS: A book about mermaids; a book on handwriting.

SIDELIGHTS: Johnson wrote: "I have always been an avid bibliophile, with a library of about seven thousand volumes on fine printing, typography, design, art, social history, folklore, illustration, illuminated manuscripts, publishing, costume and decoration, natural history, and good literature. I learned to write by reading good books. Though for many years I was active in calligraphic and private press circles, and have written articles on these subjects and exhibited my calligraphy and printing in numerous shows, I now find my time taken up mostly by writing. I have not printed anything of consequence since my miniature book, *Nasty Nancy and Her Cat: A Horrid ABC Book,* 1962, but I keep my press oiled up just in case."

He added: "During its existence of several years, I was secretary and co-founder of the Junketeers, a group of designers, printers, and librarians organized for the purpose of making pilgrimages to such graphic art and bibliographic centers as Boston, Washington, D.C., Providence, and Chicago."

BIOGRAPHICAL/CRITICAL SOURCES: John Ryder, *Miniature Folio of Private Presses,* Miniature Press, 1960; Roderick Cave, *The Private Press,* Watson-Guptill, 1971; *American Artist,* October, 1976; *Ulster County Townsman,* October 7, 1976.

*   *   *

JOHNSTON, Alan (William)   1942-

PERSONAL: Born March 4, 1942, in Blackpool, England. *Education:* Merton College, Oxford, B.A., 1965, Diploma of Classical Archaeology, 1967, D.Phil., 1971. *Politics:* "No." *Religion:* "No." *Office:* Department of Classical Archaeology, University College, University of London, Gower St., London WC1E 6BT, England.

CAREER: National University of Ireland, University College, Dublin, assistant lecturer in classics, 1969-72; University of London, University College, London, England, lecturer in classical archaeology, 1972—. Representative of Ireland on the Comite Scientifique of the *Lexicon Iconographicum Mythologiae Classicae.* *Member:* Society for the Promotion of Hellenic Studies (member of council, 1976-79).

WRITINGS: Greek Vases in Public Collections in Ireland, Royal Irish Academy, 1973; *The Emergence of Greece,* Phaidon, 1976; *Trademarks on Greek Vases,* Aris & Phillips, 1980. Contributor to European and American periodicals.

WORK IN PROGRESS: Research on Greek pottery (especially undecorated) and Greek epigraphy, and on Greek and Etruscan archaeology—"the whole bracketed approximately by the geographical range Larnaca to Tarquinia, the chronological 800-300 B.C."

SIDELIGHTS: Johnston wrote: "I am concerned that 'popular' books on the ancient world should be written by competent and literate experts; that the ancient world should not

be seen as a series of exquisite masterpieces; that the true status of any masterpiece preserved should be seen in perspective; that the negative arguments implicit in the last statement should not go unrecognized, especially by the 'media'; and that all archaeology should be properly funded and protected from the rapacity of many private collectors."

*   *   *

JOLLIFFE, H(arold) R(ichard)   1904-1978

OBITUARY NOTICE—See index for *CA* sketch: Born February 26, 1904, in Winnipeg, Manitoba, Canada; died January 6, 1978. Educator, journalist, and author. A specialist in the classics, Jolliffe was a reporter and feature writer for the *Toronto Daily Star* in the early thirties. He taught classics and journalism at various universities before joining the Michigan State University faculty in 1949 as a professor of journalism. Here he became professor emeritus in 1969. In 1960 Jolliffe was chosen Smith-Mundt grant professor, teaching for one year at the University of Kabul in Afghanistan, where he wrote, in Persian, *The Basics of Journalism.* His other books include *Tales From the Greek Drama* and a translation of Agricola's *Bermannus.* (Date of death provided by wife, Margaret M. Jolliffe.)

*   *   *

JONES, Alan Griffith   1943-

PERSONAL: Born August 16, 1943, in Llanellis Wales; son of W. Trefor (a teacher) and Beryl (a teacher; maiden name, Griffiths) Jones; married Jennifer Payne (a lecturer), July 19, 1975. *Education:* Balliol College, Oxford, B.A. (with first class honors), 1966, M.A., 1968; University of York, Postgraduate Certificate in Education, 1967; Ealing Technical College, Postgraduate Diploma in German, 1976. *Politics:* "Floating Liberal/Labour." *Religion:* Society of Friends (Quakers). *Home:* 51 Roe Green Close, Hatfield , Hertfordshire AL10 9PF, England. *Office:* Hatfield Polytechnic, Hatfield, Hertfordshire AL10 9AB, England.

CAREER: Hatfield Polytechnic, Hatfield, England, lecturer, 1968-72, senior lecturer in German, 1973—. Organizer of Hatfield District Young Volunteers, 1971-73. *Member:* Institute of Linguists (fellow), Modern Language Association (member of executive council).

WRITINGS: (Editor) *Anglo-German Songbook,* Pond Press, 1968; *The Germans: An Englishman's Notebook,* Pond Press, 1968; (editor with Martin Deutschkron) *Deutsche Schueler in England* (title means "German Students in England"), University of London Press, 1972; (editor with Deutschkron) *British Teenagers on the Rhine,* Staedtisches Schulamt, 1975; (editor with Sheila Rowell and David Bennett) *A Handbook of Information for Teachers of German,* Association of Teachers of German, 1979; *This Is Germany,* European Schoolbooks, 1980. Editor of *treffpunkt.*

WORK IN PROGRESS: Research on use of actuality recordings as a basis for teaching employment-related lexis in German, with publication expected to result.

SIDELIGHTS: Jones told *CA:* "Writing about Germany and editing my journal are the points where work and hobby overlap. A major headache is how to treat East Germany. On the one hand, I detest the place, on the other I feel it gets much too little attention in the teaching of German in the West. I write for fun, not for profit.

"My first two books were for a small publisher who had neither catalogs nor reps, and they sold few copies. But I can never repay Bob Pond for what he taught me by involving me at every stage of book production. I am frequently told that *treffpunkt* is a nicely produced journal; if this is so then it is largely due to what I learned from Bob Pond.

"As a journal editor, I am in the happy position of having more material coming in than I can use. But I still firmly believe that a journal must solicit a major part of its contents; letting the make-up depend entirely on what happens to come in is a disservice to the reader. Even academic journals should put the reader before the contributors."

*   *   *

JONES, Alexander 1906-1970

OBITUARY NOTICE—See index for *CA* sketch: Born in 1906 in Liverpool, England; died November 1, 1970, in Liverpool, England. Biblical scholar, educator, editor, and author. Beginning in 1966 Jones undertook the general editorship of *The Jerusalem Bible*, which has been hailed as a major achievement in biblical scholarship. *The Jerusalem Bible* is a contemporary, ecumenical translation made up of separate studies of the biblical books and is based directly on the original language texts. In addition to commentaries on the gospels of Sts. Mark and Matthew, Jones also wrote *The Kingdom of Promise, Unless Some Man Show Me,* and *God's Living Word*. Obituaries and other sources: *London Times*, November 4, 1970; *AB Bookman's Weekly*, January 4, 1971.

*   *   *

JONES, Aubrey 1911-

PERSONAL: Born November 20, 1911, in Merthyr Tydfil, Wales; son of Evan (a miner) and Margaret (a teacher; maiden name, Aubrey) Jones; married Joan Marie Godfrey-Isaacs (a civil servant), September 7, 1948; children: David Andrew, Simon Rodney. *Education:* London School of Economics and Political Science, London, B.Sc. (with first class honors), 1933. *Politics:* Liberal. *Religion:* Anglican. *Home:* 4 Plane Tree House, Duchess of Bedford's Walk, London W8 7QT, England. *Agent:* A. P. Watt Ltd., 26/28 Bedford Row, London WC1R 4HL, England.

CAREER: London Times, London, England, member of foreign and editorial staff, 1937-39; British Iron and Steel Federation, England, member of staff, 1949-55, economic director, 1954, general director, 1955; British Parliament, London, Conservative member of Parliament for Birmingham Hall Green, 1950-65, minister of fuel and power, 1955-57, minister of supply, 1957-59; Staveley Industries Ltd., England, director, 1962-65, chairman, 1964-65; National Board for Prices and Incomes, London, chairman, 1965-70; Laporte Industries Ltd., England, chairman, 1970-72; Cornhill Insurance Co. Ltd., England, director, 1971—, chairman, 1972-74. Member of foreign and editorial staff of *London Times,* 1947-48. Member of board of directors of Courtalds Ltd., 1960-63, Guest Keen & Nettlefolds Steel Co. Ltd., 1960-65, Thomas Tilling, 1971—, and Black & Decker, 1976-81. Leading adviser to Nigerian Public Service Review Commission, 1973-74, and Government of Iran, 1974-78. *Military service:* British Army, Intelligence, 1940-46; served in Mediterranean theater.

MEMBER: Oxford Energy Policy Club (president, 1976—). *Awards, honors:* D.Sc. from University of Bath, 1968; industrial fellow commoner of Churchill College, Cambridge, 1972; visiting fellow of New College, Oxford, 1979; senior research associate of St. Antony's College, Oxford, 1979—.

WRITINGS: The Pendulum of Politics, Faber, 1946; *Industrial Order,* Falcon Press, 1950; *The New Inflation: The Pol-*

itics of Prices and Incomes, Deutsch, 1973; (editor) *Economics and Equality,* P. Allan, 1976; *Oil: The Missed Opportunity,* Deutsch, 1981. Contributor to magazines and newspapers, including *Observer, Encounter,* and *Spectator.*

AVOCATIONAL INTERESTS: Skiing.

*   *   *

JONES, David Robert 1947-
(David Bowie)

PERSONAL: Born January 8, 1947 (listed in some sources as 1948), in London, England; son of Haywood Stenton (in public relations) and Margaret Mary (Burns) Jones; married Mary Angela Barnett (a model), March 20, 1970 (divorced c. 1978); children: Zowie. *Education:* Educated in England; studied mime under Lindsay Kemp. *Residence:* New York, N.Y.; and Kyoto, Japan.

CAREER: Songwriter and performer. Member of numerous musical groups, including "The Lower Third" and "David Jones and the King Bees," c. 1966-68; actor in motion pictures, including "The Man Who Fell to Earth," 1976, and "Just a Gigolo," 1979, and stage productions, including "The Elephant Man," 1980. Producer of recordings; narrator of "Peter and the Wolf" by Sergei Prokofiev, RCA, 1978.

WRITINGS—All under name David Bowie; recordings as composer and lyricist, unless otherwise noted: "David Bowie: Man of Words, Man of Music" (contains "Space Oddity," "Cygnet Committee," "An Occasional Dream," "The Wild Eyed Boy From Freecloud," "Janine," "God Knows I'm Good," "Memory of a Free Festival," "Letter to Hermoine," and "Unwashed and Somewhat Slightly Dazed"), Mercury, 1969, re-released as "Space Oddity," RCA, 1972; "The Man Who Sold the World" (contains "The Man Who Sold the World," "Width of a Circle," "Savior Machine," "Black Country Rock," "She Shook Me Cold," "After All," "The Supermen," "All the Madmen," and "Running Gun Blues"), Mercury, 1970, re-released by RCA, 1972.

"Hunky Dory" (contains "Changes," "Life on Mars?," "Kooks," "Bewlay Brothers," "Quicksand," "Fill Your Heart," "Andy Warhol," "Queen Bitch," "Song for Bob Dylan," "Oh! You Pretty Thing," and "Eight Line Poem"), RCA, 1971; "The Rise and Fall of Ziggy Stardust and the Spiders From Mars" (contains "Five Years," "Soul Love," "Lady Stardust," "Moonage Daydream," "Rock and Roll Suicide," "Starman," "Star," "Hang on to Yourself," "Suffragette City," "Ziggy Stardust"), RCA, 1972.

"Aladdin Sane" (contains "Watch That Man," "The Jean Genie," "Panic in Detroit," "Drive-in Saturday," "Cracked Actor," "Time," "Aladdin Sane," "Prettiest Star," and "Lady Grinning Soul"), RCA, 1973; "Diamond Dogs" (contains "Future Legend," "Diamond Dogs," "Sweet Thing," "Candidate," "Sweet Thing [Reprise]," "Big Brother," "1984," "Rock and Roll With Me," "We Are the Dead," "Rebel, Rebel," and "Chant of the Evercircling Skeletal Family"), RCA, 1974.

"Young Americans" (contains "Young Americans," "Win," "Fascination," "Right," "Somebody Up There Likes Me," "Can You Hear Me," and [with Carlos Alomar and John Lennon] "Fame"), RCA, 1975; "Station to Station" (contains "Station to Station," "Word on a Wing," "Stay," "TVC15," and "Golden Years"), RCA, 1975; "Low" (contains "Be My Wife," "Breaking Glass," "What in the World," "Always Crashing in the Same Car," "Sound and Vision," and instrumental compositions "Speed of Life,"

"Art Decade," "Weeping Wall," "Subterraneans," and [with Brian Eno] "Warszawa"), RCA, 1977.

"'Heroes'" (contains [with Eno] "'Heroes,'" "Sons of the Silent Age," "Beauty and the Beast," "Blackout," "Joe the Lion," [with Alomar] "The Secret Life of Arabia," and instrumental compositions "V-2 Schneider," "Sense of Doubt," and [with Eno] "Moss Garden/Neukoln"), RCA, 1978; "Lodger" (contains [with Eno] "Fantastic Voyage," "Move On," [with Eno] "African Night Life," "Move On," [with Eno] "Yassassin," [with Eno] "Red Sails," [with Alomar] "Red Money," [with Alomar] "D. J.," [with Eno] "Look Back in Anger," [with Eno] "Boys Keep Swinging," and "Repetition"), RCA, 1979; "Scary Monsters (and Super Creeps)" (contains "It's No Game [Part 1]," "Up the Hill Backwards," "Scary Monsters [and Super Creeps]," "Ashes to Ashes," "Fashion," "Teenage Wildlife," "Scream Like a Baby," "Because You're Young," and "It's No Game [Part 2]"), RCA, 1980.

Music only; lyrics by Iggy Pop: "The Idiot" (contains "Nightclubbing," [with Alomar] "Sister Midnight," "Funtime," "Baby," "China Girl," "Dum Dum Boys," "Tiny Girls," and "Mass Production"), RCA, 1977; "Lust for Life" (contains "Lust for Life," "Some Weird Sin," "Tonight," "Success," "Turn Blue," "Neighborhood Threat," and "Fall in Love With Me"), RCA, 1978.

Also author of songs contained on "David Bowie: Images, 1966-67," and of songs recorded by other performers, including "All the Young Dudes," "Hey Ma, Get Papa," and "John, I'm Only Dancing."

Author of unpublished autobiography, *The Return of the Thin White Duke,* and an unproduced screenplay, "Dogs."

WORK IN PROGRESS: Organizing an exhibition of paintings.

SIDELIGHTS: Many followers of rock music consider Bowie one of the most talented and innovative creators in that medium. He was a forerunner of both glitter-rock and disco, and his collaborations with Brian Eno placed him squarely in the rock avant-garde. Throughout his career, Bowie has abandoned musical styles and images when verging on mass acceptance, thereby avoiding the kind of typecasting that usually spells a performer's demise. In 1978 he acknowledged that his iconoclasm possessed certain limitations. "It's not very profitable nor very rewarding in terms of thanks, to be ahead of your time," he contended. But more than fifteen years in rock—a medium that is as much business as creative expression—convinced Bowie that his method was most suitable for his needs. "I think my albums make an impression," he considered, "and it's a position that I'm quite happy with. I once wanted to be a big commercial success . . . , but that was never to be. I lost that desire when I realized how exciting it was to do things musically that other people don't do."

Bowie obtained little exposure to the arts as a youth. He spent his childhood in a working-class district in south London. It was a disorderly life, for his parents' children from previous marriages were seen infrequently by Bowie, and many of his other relatives shuttled in and out of mental institutions. At sixteen, Bowie left school and began reading books recommended by his step-brother Terry, a veteran of the Royal Air Force whose discharge precipitated his own mental breakdown. Two books, Franz Kafka's *The Metamorphosis* and Jack Kerouac's *On the Road,* powerfully influenced Bowie. Kafka's book in particular, with its insect imagery and persecution portrayal, left a marked psychological impression on him. "I saw myself become something unrecognizable," Bowie recalled. "And if you are imagi-

native, it does strike home very hard and leaves lots of very definite impressions. . . , enigmatic little corners, nooks and crannies with shadows in them that will haunt you for a lifetime."

On the Road exerted a more positive influence on Bowie. Kerouac's ode to revelry inspired Bowie to pursue the Bohemian life. He began painting, meditating, and playing the saxophone. Briefly, he even considered entering a monastery. "I got to the point where I wanted to be a novice monk," he told William Burroughs, "and about two weeks before I was actually going to take those steps, I broke up and went out on the streets and got drunk and never looked back."

Bowie also began studying mime and listening to recordings by Little Richard. Enthralled by Richard's sound, Bowie formed his own musical groups, including David Jones and the Buzz, David Jones and the King Bees, and the blues-oriented Lower Third. As he developed a following, he was forced to change his name, for one of the members of the Monkees had already popularized it. He decided on Bowie—after Jim Bowie, creator of the twin-edged Bowie knife—because "I wanted a truism about cutting through the lies."

In 1969, while performing in a small club, Bowie met Angela Barrett and her escort, a representative from Mercury Records. Though the fellow was unimpressed with Bowie, Barrett insisted that he offer Bowie a contract if the fellow wished to continue dating her. He relented and offered Bowie a recording contract. Soon afterward, Bowie and Angela married.

Bowie's first recording for Mercury, "David Bowie: Man of Words, Man of Music," sold reasonably well due to a hit single, "Space Oddity." Impressed with Stanley Kubrick's film "2001: A Space Odyssey," Bowie penned his song about an astronaut, Major Tom, who breaks contact with earth and continues journeying through the universe instead of returning home to his wife. For Major Tom, the unknown was infinitely more interesting than the expected.

Seemingly cast from the same type as Donavon—a British folksinger whose popularity peaked in the mid-1960's with a flurry of psychedelic flower-power songs—Bowie developed a reputation as a soft-spoken, self-conscious performer. His second album, however, rebuked the "shy folkie" image. In "The Man Who Sold the World," Bowie replaced the starry-eyed innocence of "Man of Words, Man of Music," with violence and lust. Songs like "Running Gun Blues" and "She Shook Me Cold" portrayed cynical characters for whom brutality was pleasurable and sex was parasitic. Other tunes seemed inspired by the writings of Friedrich Nietzsche, the philosopher who conceptualized a race of "supermen" and contended that "God is dead" before succumbing to insanity in 1889. And in "All the Madmen," Bowie reiterated the notion already voiced by Major Tom in "Space Oddity," that uncertainty is preferable to society.

The cover photography for "The Man Who Sold the World" probably had as great an effect on Bowie's career as did any of the music from that album. Bowie was shown heavily made-up, wearing an evening dress and jewelry and reclining on a sofa. He called the pose "a parody of Gabriel Rossetti." The idea for the cover occured to him after he discovered that he had developed a small audience from the gay community. He recounted: "I said, 'Fine, don't try to explain it; nobody is going to bother to try to understand it.' I'll play along, absolutely *anything* to break me through. . . . All the papers wrote *volumes* about how sick I was, how I was helping to kill off true art. In the meantime, they used up all the space they could have given over to true artists.''

Bowie's behavior drew further criticism in 1971 when he confessed to an interviewer that he was bisexual. He was condemned by the rock establishment as both decadent and morally corrupt, much to his publicity-seeking pleasure. Unfortunately, his revelations had no effect on record sales, and he was dropped from Mercury's roster. RCA quickly signed him, however, and in 1971 they released Bowie's third album, ''Hunky Dory.'' The record vaguely resembled the musical style of his first album, with catchy melodies and tongue-in-cheek vocals. Lyrically, though, ''Hunky Dory'' seemed more poetic than its predecessors; William Burroughs even compared one song to T. S. Eliot's ''The Waste Land.'' Thematically, songs such as ''Quicksand'' and ''Bewlay Brothers'' were stark, introspective laments about surviving in a society where nonconformity was either ridiculed or condemned.

Boosted by a successful single, ''Changes,'' and a cover photograph that recalled the controversial ''The Man Who Sold the World,'' ''Hunky Dory'' proved to be Bowie's most popular album. He wanted more than just a reliable public, however; he sought adulation and wealth. ''I began to wonder what it would be like to be a rock and roll star,'' he said, ''so I wrote a script.'' The script was derived from an actual incident involving Vince Taylor, an American rock performer whom Bowie had befriended during the mid-1960's. ''He was slowly going crazy,'' Bowie noted. ''Finally, he fired his band and went onstage one night in a white sheet. He told the audience to rejoice, that he was Jesus. They put him away.''

Bowie turned his script into a song cycle entitled ''The Rise and Fall of Ziggy Stardust and the Spiders From Mars.'' The plot, set in the future, concerns a rock musician, Ziggy Stardust, who begins singing the news instead of fictional songs. Though the news is extremely pessimistic—with prophesies of pollution and genocide—people flock to Ziggy's concerts, for his shows are the only entertainment left on earth. As his popularity increases, Ziggy believes that he is being visited in his sleep by aliens called Infinites. He begins singing about Starman, an Infinite whom Ziggy is convinced will save the earth. Ziggy eventually believes that he is the Infinite and begins informing the public that he is the savior. At the height of his notoriety, however, Ziggy is destroyed by the actual Infinites, who attend his performance in the guise of black holes.

Bowie's Ziggy Stardust saga quickly rose up the British record charts on the strength of the single, ''Starman.'' He then commenced performing as Ziggy, replete with makeup, orange-dyed hair, and bizarre, effeminate, space-age clothes. The concept was an enormous success: Bowie's concerts sold to capacity and his records became best-sellers. And his unique appearance and manner attracted publicity wherever he traveled. Before 1972 ended, he was among the most popular performers in Europe and America. And his futuristic vision spawned a new kind of music—glitter rock—that emphasized visuals, particularly theatrics, as well as music.

The Ziggy Stardust phenomenon held a threatening aspect for Bowie, though. He submerged his personality into the Ziggy persona so thoroughly that his public was convinced that Bowie *was* Ziggy. Listeners eager for a new approach to rock music hailed Bowie/Ziggy as the savior of their music and took him as their role model. ''What I did with my Ziggy Stardust was package a totally credible, plastic rock-'n'-roll singer,'' Bowie claimed. ''*My* plastic rock-'n'-roller was

much more plastic than anybody's. . . . Most people still want their idols and gods to be shallow, like cheap toys. Why do you think teenagers are the way they are? They run around like ants, chewing gum and flitting onto a certain style of dressing for a day; that's as deep as they go. It's no surprise that Ziggy was a huge success.''

Bowie's next recording, ''Aladdin Sane,'' was a series of songs commemorating incidents, both real and imagined, that occured in specific cities during his tours of America and Britain in 1972 and 1973. The title is probably Bowie's pun on his mental state while touring with the Spiders, for he later acknowledged that he was unable to function outside the Ziggy persona during those years. The album, however, was another success, and it yielded several hits, including ''The Jean Genie,'' ''Drive-in Saturday,'' and ''Panic in Detroit.'' In the latter, Bowie summed up America's obsession with celebrities: a fellow fails to prevent a murder but has the foresight to obtain an autograph from the killer.

In late 1973, Bowie unveiled plans to present theatrical presentations of both ''Ziggy Stardust'' and an adaptation of George Orwell's *1984*. He released ''Pinups,'' his final recording with the Spiders, which contained his interpretations of songs popularized by other groups during his early years as a musician. After an appearance on American television and another tour with the Spiders, Bowie announced his retirement from performing.

The retirement was simply a publicity hoax, however, for Bowie was soon recording another album, ''Diamond Dogs.'' His plans for staging ''Ziggy Stardust'' and *1984* failed to materialize, so Bowie decided to build a review around his new recording. The album was panned by reviewers annoyed by its solemn, apocalyptic tone. But the concerts, which employed props from Bowie's unrealized projects, were hailed as revolutionary; he called the new shows ''Thea-Tour.'' The entire stage supported paper skyscrapers inspired by Fritz Lang's film ''Metropolis,'' and included a footbridge and streetlight. Near the end of each concert, Bowie enacted a mime skit that concluded with the destruction of the buildings, and followed it with Ziggy's finale, ''Rock and Roll Suicide.''

Unfortunately, as the press and rock followers heaped adulation on Bowie, he deceived himself into believing that he was the salvation of rock music. ''At first I assumed the character on stage,'' he told *Playboy*. ''Then everybody started to treat me as they treated Ziggy; as though I were the Next Big Thing, as though I moved masses of people. I became convinced I was the messiah.'' To thwart continued suppression of his own identity by Ziggy, Bowie systematically destroyed his alter ego. ''I stripped myself down and took myself apart, layer by layer,'' he related. ''I used to sit in bed and pick on one thing a week that I either didn't like or couldn't understand. And during the course of the week, I'd try to kill it off.''

By 1974, the Ziggy persona had vanished. Bowie changed physically as well as mentally: he cut his hair, reduced his use of makeup, and began wearing fashionable men's clothing. But the changes only resulted in another character that Bowie couldn't control. He couldn't bear to face either the press or the public without a persona to hide behind. ''I didn't have the nerve to sing my songs onstage,'' Bowie explained. ''I decided to do them in disguise so that I didn't have to actually go through the humiliation of going onstage and being myself. And that became obsessive with me. I continued designing characters with their own complete personalities and environments.''

The Aladdin Sane guise proved quite profitable for Bowie. He released another recording, "Young Americans," that contained two of his most popular songs, the title track and "Fame," co-written with John Lennon. A new career for Bowie as a soul singer seemed likely, for most of the new album was either soul music or disco. Within one year, however, Bowie dismissed "Young Americans" as "thoroughly plastic" and told *Playboy* that if anyone had told him during his years as Ziggy that he would someday record a soul album, "I would have laughed. Hysterically." He summed it up as "the squashed remains of ethnic music as it survives in the age of Muzak rock, written and sung by a Limey."

After the release of "Young Americans," Bowie abandoned music to work as an actor in Nicholas Roeg's film, "The Man Who Fell to Earth." The plot centered around an alien arriving on earth to evaluate the planet's water supply for possible consumption by his own people. Armed with valuable blueprints for unpatented inventions, the alien (played by Bowie), quickly becomes wealthy enough to finance his return voyage by constructing a spaceship. During his time in America, however, the alien becomes an alcoholic and, during a series of scientific tests, is permanently fixed to his disguise. For Bowie, the film opened new creative avenues, and he announced plans to form his own film company and direct a film entitled "Dogs." When plans were delayed by litigation involving his former manager, Bowie decided to record another album and follow it with a tour that would "make an obscene amount of money" for financing his film ventures.

Released in 1976, "Station to Station" was viewed by the rock world as an unlikely fusion of disco, soul music, and rock. It contained only six songs, including his next popular single, "Golden Years," and two others designed to showcase Bowie's newest persona, a Frank Sinatra-like singer called the Thin White Duke. As the Duke, Bowie appeared on a number of television programs, including "The Dinah Shore Show," "Soul Train," and Bing Crosby's Christmas special, in which Bowie and Crosby sang "The Little Drummer Boy."

Though Bowie's expanding popularity in yet another guise seemed assured, his newest persona resulted in his most severe psychological setback. The court battle with ex-manager Tony DeFries, together with the frantic pace of filming, recording, and touring, exhausted Bowie. He moved into the exclusive Bel Air section of Beverly Hills, California, and became semi-reclusive. Former advisor Michael Lippman recalled: "He would not come out of his house . . . He was overworked and under a lot of pressure . . . and unable to accept the realities of certain facts." Bowie began using amphetamines and dividing his time between painting unintelligible works and writing an encyclopedic autobiography.

When Bowie relented to interviewers for *Rolling Stone* and *Playboy*, he spouted fascist comments and condemned rock music. "We've had the high with rock," he claimed. "It's got to go the other way now . . . , the dark era. . . . I feel that we're only heralding something even darker than ourselves." He told *Rolling Stone* that rock music was evil "because it supplements people's sensitivity." In *Playboy*, Bowie contended, "Adolf Hitler was one of the first rock stars. Look at some of his films and see how he moved. . . . The world will never see his like. He staged a country." Perhaps his most outrageous comments involved politics. "I'd adore to be Prime Minister," he said. "And yes, I believe very strongly in fascism. The only way we can speed up the sort of liberalism that's hanging foul in the air at the moment is to speed up the progress of a right-wing, totally dictatorial tyranny and get it over as fast as possible."

Early in 1976, Bowie sensed that the Thin White Duke was beyond control. "I was totally out of hand and spouting for hours at two people who were either terrified or bored with what I was saying," he admitted. Two years later, he told *Crawdaddy* that his comments as the Duke were "incredibly insane mutterings of a very hurt, broken mentality." He called the Duke "a fractured person, brought on by . . . confounding myself with images and characters that I found I was living with—and actually *seeing* them in my apartment." Bowie was also hallucinating. While being interviewed by *Rolling Stone,* he thought he saw a human body hurtle past a window. At home, he felt his various characters were plotting the destruction of his own identity. "I was being threatened by my own characters," he explained, "feeling them coming in on me and grinning at me saying *'We're gonna take you over completely!'*"

Bowie realized that his sanity depended on more than systematic elimination of his flaws as the Duke. He decided to leave Los Angeles and quit music temporarily. He moved to Berlin and rented a two-room apartment over a gas station. There, Bowie swore off drugs and revived his interest in painting. Vowing not to relinquish his identity to anymore "characters," Bowie immersed himself in his studies of German expressionist films and the paintings of Egon Schiele, an expressionist whose work profoundly influenced Bowie.

Within the year, Bowie was prepared to return to music by directing his talents towards experimentation. Enlisting Brian Eno, whose work ranged from rock to classical to avant-garde, Bowie made "Low," the recording he ranks as his best effort. The two sides of the album reflect Bowie's twin interests as an experimentalist: short, drum-emphasized pieces with improvised lyrics fill the first side; and long instrumental compositions that evolve into Gregorian chants complete the recording.

"Low" was hailed in most rock quarters as a stunning surprise from Bowie. But he refused to promote the album with concerts and continued painting in Berlin. In mid-1977, he produced and composed the music for Iggy Pop's comeback effort, "The Idiot," which was the singer's first recording since his own crisis in Los Angeles with alcoholism. Bowie further assisted Pop by supporting the performer as pianist during a tour of America. The concerts were an enormous success for Pop, as Bowie helped draw a larger audience than Pop would have attracted by himself. For Bowie, the tour was his first trip to America since his traumatic experiences in Bel Air, and he found himself relaxing much more than he had on his tour performing "Station to Station." After recording "'Heroes,'" his second collaboration with Eno, Bowie decided to tour the States once again. His popularity seemed revived with the tour, in which he devoted portions of his concerts to his avant-garde compositions and audience favorites from "Ziggy Stardust."

Bowie also spent part of 1978 appearing in his second film, "Just a Gigolo." He played an escort/prostitute whose decadent behavior flourished in Nazi Germany. Despite the presence of Bowie and actresses Marlene Dietrich and Kim Novak, the film failed to impress viewers at the European film festivals and was never commercially distributed.

A near-fatal tragedy additionally marred Bowie's success that year. Angela, realizing that her husband would receive custody of their son Zowie following their divorce, attempted suicide. Soon after her return to health, Bowie and Zowie moved to Japan.

In 1979 Bowie completed "Lodger," his third recording with Eno. The album retained the experimental sound of its two predecessors but confined it within traditionally structured songs. Most of the music revealed Bowie's renewed interest in foreign—particularly African—music styles. Tunes such as "Move On" and "African Night Flight" featured chants and supplementary percussion, while other pieces, including "Yassassin" and "Red Sails," displayed Turkish and German elements respectively.

Bowie moved back to New York City the following year and recorded "Scary Monsters." The album differs substantially from "Lodger," and its melodic tunes recall his earlier work on "Hunky Dory" and "Ziggy Stardust." But some of Bowie's vocals seem derived from his collaborations with Eno. He called the album "psychotic rock and roll" and dubbed his singing "radical and alarming." Among the more bizarre nuances are relentless Japanese intonations on "It's No Game (Part 1)," and barking sounds and screams on both "Scary Monsters" and the hit single "Ashes to Ashes."

Bowie also made his Broadway debut in 1980 as "The Elephant Man." The play was based on the life of John Merrick, a horribly deformed side-show freak who became a favorite of Victorian social circles before his premature death. Unlike the film version of Merrick's life, the play required the lead actor to reproduce Merrick without benefit of makeup. Bowie used extreme face and body contortions to resemble the grotesque character. Each performance left him exhausted. "After a show, you can't just suddenly leap out of . . . position," Bowie explained. "I spend ten or fifteen minutes just straightening up."

The play was a huge commercial success, despite pre-performance apprehensions from cynical reviewers. Many critics questioned director Jack Hofsiss's decision to cast Bowie. Hofsiss, however, insisted that it was Bowie's acting, not his popularity as a rock singer, that inspired him to offer Bowie the role. "I was familiar with his music, and I had seen him in concert," Hofsiss recounted. "But the piece of work he did that was most helpful in making the decision was *The Man Who Fell to Earth,* in which I thought he was wonderful, and in which the character he played had an isolation similar to the Elephant Man's."

Bowie's performances in "The Elephant Man" drew nearly unanimous critical raves and his reputation as a rock star *did* help fill theatres to capacity. And his fellow actors matched reviewers and audiences with their appreciation of his talent. "Bowie has the technique of magnetizing people," acknowledged co-star Concetta Tomei. "He's not a rock performer going into acting—he's an actor."

Working as both an actor and experimental recording artist, Bowie has broadened his perspective outside the rock domain. He seems firmly convinced that diversity and a disregard for commercial taste has brought him both personal and artistic stability. "I've been getting happier and happier," he proclaimed. "Not with myself and my situation, but happier in my realization that I can face up to things a lot better than I could when I was living a *heavily* rock & roll life in America. I feel happy that I can travel about in some kind of anonymity and circulate within cities I've always dreamed of going to see. More and more, I'm prepared to relinquish sales, so far as records go, by sticking to my guns about the kind of music I really wish to make."

AVOCATIONAL INTERESTS: Travel, classical music, painting.

BIOGRAPHICAL/CRITICAL SOURCES: Rolling Stone, February 18, 1971, January 6, 1972, July 20, 1972, July 19, 1973, February 28, 1974, August 1, 1974, February 12, 1976, April 21, 1977, November 13, 1980; *Melody Maker,* February 18, 1972, October 6, 1973, January 24, 1976, March 12, 1977, October 1, 1977; *Crawdaddy,* February 20, 1972, August, 1974, June, 1975, February, 1978; *Philadelphia Bulletin,* July 5, 1974; *Biography News,* Volume I, Gale, 1974; George Tremlett, *The David Bowie Story,* Warner Books, 1975; *Playboy,* September, 1976; Jim Miller, editor, *The Rolling Stone Illustrated History of Rock and Roll,* Random House, 1976; *Creem,* September, 1978; *Stereo Review,* October, 1979; *Trouser Press,* October, 1979; *Chicago Tribune,* August 3, 1980; *Contemporary Literary Criticism,* Volume 17, Gale, 1981.*

—*Sketch by Les Stone*

*   *   *

JONES, Henry Albert 1889-1981

OBITUARY NOTICE: Born May 6, 1889, in Deer Park, Ill.; died of cancer, February 24, 1981, in Cave Creek, Ariz. Horticulturist, geneticist, and author. Henry Jones's 1925 discovery of a form of male sterility in onions led him to develop a commercially practical method of producing hybrid onions. Subsequent research led to the development of approximately two thousand types of hybrid onions as well as to the development of hybridization techniques for such other crops as spinach, corn, and sugar beets. The first hybrid onion based on Jones's research was made available in 1944, while Jones was serving as principal horticulturist for the Department of Agriculture's Bureau of Plant Industry. He later became director of the Dessert Seed Company in El Centro, California, one of the largest onion-seed growers in the United States. Co-author of *Onions and Their Allies,* Jones also wrote and co-wrote several other books and numerous articles on horticulture. Obituaries and other sources: *Science,* May 31, 1957; *American Men and Women of Science,* 14th edition, Bowker, 1979; *Washington Post,* March 6, 1981; *New York Times,* March 6, 1981.

*   *   *

JONES, Lyndon Hamer 1927-

PERSONAL: Born April 15, 1927, in Bolton, England; son of John and Lilian (Hamer) Jones; married Phillis Manzoni, November 6, 1947; children: Gail Megan. *Education:* Victoria University of Manchester, B.A., 1950; Manchester College of Science and Technology, Diploma in Industrail Administration, 1951; Bolton College of Education, Teachers' Certificate, 1954. *Religion:* Methodist. *Home:* 20 Wolsey Close, Kingston-upon-Thames, Surrey, England. *Office:* Association of Business Executives, 3 Station Parade, Balham High Rd., London SW12 9AZ, England.

CAREER: Fothergill & Harvey Ltd., Littleborough, England, works manager, 1951-53; Bolton Technical College, Bolton, England, assistant lecturer, 1954-57; Southwest Essex Technical College, Dagenham, England, lecturer, 1957-59; Thurrock Technical College, Grays, England, head of management and business studies, 1959-65; South West London College, London, England, principal, 1965—. Director of Editype Publications, 1963—, editorial director, 1974—; director of Answerbank Ltd. and Harmala Ltd. President of Kingston-upon-Thames Liberal Party; vice-president of Havering Liberal party. Vice-chairman of National Examination Board in Supervisory Studies; member of Business Education Council, Council for the Accreditation of Correspondence Colleges, British Rail Joint Industrial Training Board, British Broadcasting Corp. Further Education Advisory

Committee, National Computer Centre committee for training of systems analysts, and Overseas Students Advisory Committee; industrial, social, and educational consultant. *Military service:* British Army, 1946-48. *Member:* Association of Business Executives (chairman). *Awards, honors:* Leverhulme fellow, 1944.

WRITINGS: (With Geoffrey Dart) *Forms of Business Organisation and Their Finance,* Editype, 1965; (with Dart) *National Income,* Editype, 1965; (with Dart) *Wage Determination,* Editype, 1966; (with Dart) *Manpower,* Editype, 1966; (contributor) John Robinson, editor, *New Media and Methods in Instructional Training,* BBC Publications, 1968; *One Hundred One Questions and Answers on Economics,* Pitman, 1972; *Bogus Degrees,* Harmala, 1977; (contributor) John Coffey, editor, *Opening Learning Systems for Mature Students,* Council for Educational Technology, 1980. Contributor of more than two hundred articles to professional journals. Editorial director of *Education and Training.*

WORK IN PROGRESS: Behavior Modification: Principles and Practice, publication by Harmala.

SIDELIGHTS: Jones wrote: "We live in a world where change is the only permanent thing. We are all engaged in a race between mental obsolescence and retirement. Accordingly, I believe that both academics and graduates should cease to put the name of their university after their degree (as in M.B.A., Harvard). Instead, they should list the year they graduated (as in M.B.A., 1947)."

*   *   *

JONES, Malcolm V(ince) 1940-

PERSONAL: Born January 7, 1940, in Stoke-sub-Hamdon, England; son of Reginald Cross (in life insurance) and Winifred Ethel (Vince) Jones; married Jennifer Rosemary Durrant, July, 1963. *Education:* University of Nottingham, B.A. (with first class honors), 1962, Ph.D., 1966. *Residence:* Nottingham, England. *Agent:* Frances Kelly, 9 King Edward Mansions, 629 Fulham Rd., London S.W.6, England. *Office:* Department of Slavonic Studies, University of Nottingham, Nottingham NG7 2RD, England.

CAREER: University of Sussex, Brighton, England, assistant lecturer in Russian, 1965-67; University of Nottingham, Nottingham, England, lecturer, 1967-73, senior lecturer, 1973-80, professor of Slavonic studies and head of department, 1980—, vice-dean of faculty of arts, 1976-79. *Member:* International Dostoevsky Society (member of executive committee), British Universities Association of Slavists, Association of Teachers of Russian (honorary vice-president).

WRITINGS: Dostoyevsky: The Novel of Discord, Barnes & Noble, 1976; (editor) *New Essays on Tolstoy,* Cambridge University Press, 1981. Member of editorial board of "Birmingham Slavonic Monographs." Contributor to Slavic studies and history journals.

WORK IN PROGRESS: A two-volume book on Dostoevsky, publication by Cambridge University Press expected in 1982.

SIDELIGHTS: Jones wrote: "I first took up the study of Russian, not only because of its intrinsic interest and its cultural, economic, and political importance, but also because I am convinced that an almost exclusive concentration on French and German in the British educational system was a totally inadequate response to the complexity of international and intercultural relations in the modern world. I remain convinced of this, and also of the fact that it is impossible to understand a foreign culture in depth without a good knowledge of the native language. If more people in positions

of responsibility understood this, many errors of judgment might be avoided which threaten catastrophic results for our world."

*   *   *

JONES, Peter 1920-

PERSONAL: Born June 12, 1920, in Wem, England; son of William and Sarah Lillian (Francis) Jones; married Jeri Sauvinet (an actress); children: Selena Carey, Charles D., William D. *Education:* Attended Ellesmere College. *Home:* 32 Acacia Rd., London NW8 6AS, England.

CAREER: Actor, 1936—. Actor in plays, including "The Composite Man," 1936; "The Doctor's Dilemma," 1942; "The Imaginary Invalid," "The Rivals," "The Constant Couple," "Misalliance," "The Watched Pot," and "The Magistrate," all 1943; "The Rest Is Silence" and "How Are They at Home?," both 1944; "The Simpleton of the Unexpected Isles" and "An Italian Straw Hat" both 1945; "Crime and Punishment," 1946; "Love in Albania," 1949; "The Vortex" and "Sweet Madness," both 1952; "The Confidential Clerk" and "The Heart of the Matter," both 1953; "Morning's at Seven," 1955; "Late Interlude," 1956; "Touch It Light," 1958; "In the Red" and "The Darling Buds of May," both 1959; "Doctor at Sea," 1961; "The Rag Trade," 1962; "Boeing-Boeing," 1964; "Angie and Ernie," 1966; "It's Underneath That Counts," 1970; "The Night of the Blue Demands," 1971; "Small Craft Warnings," 1973; "Hamlet," 1976; "Cinderella," 1979.

Actor in films, including "Fanny by Gaslight," 1943; "Dead of Night," 1945; "Private Angelo," 1949; "Twenty-Four Hours of a Woman's Life," 1952; "A Day to Remember," 1953; "Private's Progress," 1956; "Romanoff and Juliet," 1961; "Return of the Pink Panther," 1975; "Seven Nights in Japan," 1976.

Star of television series, including "The Rag Trade," British Broadcasting Corp. (BBC-TV); "Mr. Digby Darling," YTV; "Oneupmanship," BBC-2; "Beggar My Neighbour," BBC-1; "Mr. Big," BBC-1; "My Lords, Ladies and Gentlemen," Granada TV; "From a Bird's Eye View," Associated Television Ltd. (ATV); "Mild and Bitter," BBC-2; "Night Train to Surbitron," BBC-2; "The Hitchhiker's Guide to the Galaxy," BBC-1.

Guest on television programs, including "The Sheila Hancock Show," "The Goodies," "Father, Dear Father," and "Zodiac." Star in radio shows, including "In All Directions" and "The Hitchhiker's Guide to the Galaxy." Panelist on radio shows, including "Just a Minute" and "Quote-Unquote." Performer in cabarets; lecturer and after-dinner speaker.

WRITINGS—Plays: "Sweet Madness" (three-act), first produced on the West End at Vaudeville Theatre, 1952; "Marion," first produced by BBC-TV, 1953; (with John Jowett) "The Party Spirit" (three-act), first produced on the West End at Piccadilly Theatre, 1954; "The New Man," first produced by ARTV, 1960; (with Kevin Laffan) "Angie and Ernie" (three-act), first produced in Guildford, England, at Yvonne Arnaud Theatre, 1966; *The Rescue* (first produced by BBC-TV, 1973), Samuel French, 1973. Also author of "Mr. Big," with Christopher Bond, of scripts for "Comedy Playhouse," and of scripts, with Peter Ustinov, for radio program "In All Directions," beginning in 1950.

WORK IN PROGRESS: "Mummy and Daddy," a series for BBC-TV; a pilot, with Laffan, for ATV.

SIDELIGHTS: Jones told CA: "The show I wrote with Christopher Bond, 'Mr. Big,' is under option to a U.S. company, and I am hoping to work on it there in a writing capacity, if they do a pilot. My wife is American, and this year we spent three months in California—I would like to go back there to work. I have several ideas I feel sure Americans would like."

*   *   *

JONES, Reginald Victor   1911-

PERSONAL: Born September 29, 1911, in London, England; son of Harold Victor and Alice Margaret (May) Jones; married Vera Margaret Cain, March 21, 1940; children: Susan (Mrs. Archibald Addison), Robert, Rosemary. Education: Wadham College, Oxford, M.A., D. Phil., 1934; attended Balliol College, Oxford, 1934-36. Home: 8 Queen's Ter., Aberdeen AB1 1XL, Scotland. Agent: John Farquharson Ltd., Bell House, 8 Bell Yard, London, WC2A 2JU, England. Office: Department of Natural Philosophy, University of Aberdeen, Aberdeen AB9 2WE, Scotland.

CAREER: Air Ministry, London, England, director of intelligence, 1939-46; University of Aberdeen, Aberdeen, Scotland, professor of natural philosophy, 1946—. Physicist. Director of scientific information for Ministry of Defence, 1952-54. Member: Royal Society (fellow), Royal Society of Edinburgh (fellow), Royal Society of Arts (fellow), Royal Astronomical Society (fellow), College of Preceptors (fellow), Institute of Physics and Physical Society (fellow), Institute of Measurement and Control. Awards, honors: U.S. Medal of Freedom with silver palm, 1946; U.S. Medal for Merit, 1947; Duddell Medal, 1960, Parsons Medal, 1967, and Hartley Medal from Institute of Measurement and Control, 1972, all for scientific instrument design; D. Sc. from University of Strathclyde, 1969, and University of Cantebury; D. Univ. from University of York, 1976, Open University, 1978, and University of Surrey; Rutherford Medal from USSR Academy of Sciences, 1977; Companion of Order of the Bath; Commander of Order of the British Empire; Telecommunications Medal from Mexico; LL. D. from University of Bristol.

WRITINGS: The Wizard War: British Scientific Intelligence, 1939-1945, Coward, 1978 (published in England as Most Secret War, Hamilton, 1978). Contributor to science and history journals. Editor of Notes and Records of the Royal Society of London.

WORK IN PROGRESS: Research on the impact of technology on conflict.

*   *   *

JONES, Richard Allan   1943-

PERSONAL: Born July 7, 1943, in Kearny, N.J.; son of Richard Ditzel (a minister) and Evelyn Antoinette (Allen) Jones; married Lilianne Plamondon (a teacher), June 8, 1974; children: Marie-Noelle, Stephanie Nancy, Serge-Andre, Claude-Denis. Education: Princeton University, B.A., 1965; Universite Laval, M.A., 1966, Ph.D., 1972. Religion: Presbyterian. Residence: St. Cyrille-de-L'Islet, Quebec, Canada G0R 2W0. Office: Department of History, Universite Laval, Quebec, Quebec, Canada G1K 7P4.

CAREER: College Ste-Anne-de-la-Pocatiere, La Pocatiere, Quebec, professor of history, 1966-68; Universite Laval, Quebec, Quebec, assistant professor, 1970-75, associate professor of history, 1975—.

WRITINGS: Community in Crisis: French-Canadian Nationalism in Perspective, McClelland & Stewart, 1967, revised edition, 1972; L'Ideologie de "L'Action catholique," Presses de l'Universite Laval, 1974; (with Jean Hamelin) Histoire du Quebec, Maison Ed. Privat, 1976; Vers une hegemonie liberale: Apercu de la politique canadienne de Laurier a King (title means "Toward a Liberal Hegemony: Canadian Politics From Laurier to King"), Presses de l'Universite Laval, 1980.

WORK IN PROGRESS: Research on contemporary Quebec and on Canadian politics and society.

*   *   *

JORDAN, John   1930-

PERSONAL: Born April 8, 1930, in Dublin, Ireland. Education: University College, Dublin, National University of Ireland, B.A., 1951, M.A., 1954; Pembroke College, Oxford, B.Litt., 1961. Religion: Roman Catholic. Home: 18 Parkvew Ave., Harold's Cross, Dublin 6, Ireland.

CAREER: National University of Ireland, University College, Dublin, assistant lecturer, 1955-65, lecturer in English, 1965-69; free-lance writer, 1969—.

WRITINGS: Patrician Stations (poems), New Writers' Press, 1971; A Raft From Flotsam (poems), Gallery Press, 1975; Blood and Stations (poems and prose), Gallery Press, 1976; Yarns (stories), Poolbeg Press, 1977; (editor) The Pleasures of Gaelic Literature, Mercier Press, 1977.

Contributor: Ronald Ayling, editor, S'oc: Modern Judgments, Macmillan, 1969; John Ryan, editor, A Bash in the Tunnel, Clifton Books, 1970; Thomas Kilroy, editor, Sean O'Casey, Prentice-Hall, 1975.

Work represented in anthologies, including Best Irish Short Stories, edited by David Marcus, Elek; Soft Day, edited by Peter Fallon and Sean Golden, University of Notre Dame Press, 1980; The Penguin Book of Irish Short Stories, edited by Benedict Kiely, Penguin. Contributor to literary journals, including Hibernia. Editor of Poetry Ireland Two, 1962-66.

WORK IN PROGRESS: With Whom Did I Share the Crystal, poems; All That Is Lent to Loving (tentative title), a novel.

SIDELIGHTS: Jordan commented: "The disruption of my academic career in 1969 was the spur to more courageous publication. The serious creative writer is often sidetracked at an early age by considerations of financial security, as in my case, the comparative affluence attaching to academic competence. In every teacher of English there is a writer, good or bad, howling for expression."

AVOCATIONAL INTERESTS: Travel (including France and Spain.)

*   *   *

JORGENSEN, James (Aleck)   1931-

PERSONAL: Born April 11, 1931, in Omaha, Neb.; son of Niels N. (an accountant) and Vivetta (a nurse; maiden name, Aleck) Jorgensen; married Patricia S. Smith, October 23, 1954; children: Richard, Nancy. Education: University of California, Berkeley, B.S., 1954; American College, Bryn Mawr, Pa., C.L.U., 1975. Agent: Mel Berger, William Morris Agency, 1350 Avenue of the Americas, New York, N.Y. 10019. Office: Jorgensen, Moo & Wentz, P.O. Box 610, Santa Clara, Calif. 95052.

CAREER: Jorgensen, Moo & Wentz (pension and employee benefits firm), Santa Clara, Calif., senior partner, 1975—. Military service: U.S. Marine Corps, Air Wing, 1954-57; became first lieutenant. *Member:* California Alumni Club, Rotary Club (past president).

WRITINGS: The Graying of America, Dial, 1980.

WORK IN PROGRESS: How to Retire Without Inflation.

SIDELIGHTS: In *The Graying of America,* James Jorgensen demonstrates how the Social Security system, established at a time when the average married woman in America did not work outside the home, has become archaic. "The facts, as he outlines them, are grim," wrote Susan Jacoby of the *New York Times Book Review.*

Jorgensen told *CA:* "I am currently designing and installing retirement plans, and arranging investments for the plans. My new book is a result of what I see as the problems confronting most Americans as they try to save for retirement in the face of continuing double-digit inflation. *The Graying of America* outlined the nation's problem with our private pension system and with Social Security. The new book will allow the American worker to 'save with inflation,' so that by the end of the decade their assets will be preserved."

BIOGRAPHICAL/CRITICAL SOURCES: New York Times Book Review, October 26, 1980.

*   *   *

JOSEPH, Stephen   1921-1967

OBITUARY NOTICE—See index for *CA* sketch: Born June 13, 1921, in London, England; died in 1967. Actor, stage director, lecturer, and author. Joseph obtained drama degrees from both the University of Iowa and Cambridge University before becoming the director of several theatrical companies in England, many of which he himself formed in accordance with his innovative ideas for the theatre. Joseph was one of England's main proponents of theatre-in-the-round, a subject of one of his books. Among his other works are *Adaptable Theatres, Planning for New Forms of Theatre,* and *New Theatre Forms.* Obituaries and other sources: *London Times,* October 6, 1967.

*   *   *

JOWITT, Deborah   1934-
(Rachel Benson)

PERSONAL: Born February 8, 1934, in Los Angeles, Calif.; daughter of Anthony Jowitt and Doris Anderson; married Murray H. Ralph (a musicologist), September 6, 1962; children: Tobias Ralph. *Education:* Attended University of California, Los Angeles, 1951-52, New School for Social Research, 1959-60, and Hunter College of the City University of New York, 1960-62. *Home:* 78 Christopher St., New York, N.Y. 10014. *Office: Village Voice,* 842 Broadway, New York, N.Y. 10003.

CAREER: Professional dancer, 1953—; toured with numerous companies, including Julliard Dance Theatre, 1957-59, Dance Theatre Workshop, John Begg's "Ballet Carnival," Mara's "Legends of Cambodia," and troupes led by Mary Anthony, Valerie Bettis, Pauline Koner, Pearl Land, Sophie Maslow, and Charles Weidman; appeared in several television programs, including "Lamp Unto My Feet," and in several plays. Choreographer, 1962—; worked with Valerie Bettis's Dancer's Studio, Dance Uptown, Choreoconcerts, Dance Theatre Workshop, and American Theatre Laboratory; choreographed several business and industrial films. Member of faculty at New York University, 1975, and Brooklyn College of the City University of New York, spring, 1976; teacher of drama and dance at elementary and high schools

in Jersey City, N.J. and Englewood, N.J., and at Camp Beaupre in Stockbridge, Mass; lecturer at colleges and universities, including Pratt Institute, Kingsborough Community College of the City University of New York, London School of Contemporary Dance, George Washington University, American University, Ohio State University, Ohio University, Harvard University, University of Waterloo, York University (Toronto), and Swarthmore College. Member of advisory dance panel of National Endowment for the Arts, 1969-72, co-chairman of panel, 1971-72; director of dance critics conference at American Dance Festival, 1973-78; critic for WBAI-FM Radio. *Member:* Actors Equity Association, Dance Critics Association. *Awards, honors:* Camus Prize from New School for Social Research, 1960, for an essay on Paris in 1900.

WRITINGS: (Translator, under pseudonym Rachel Benson) *Nine Latin American Poets,* Las Americas, 1968; *Dance Beat* (collected reviews), Dekker, 1977; *Contemporary Dance* (essay), Abbeville Press, 1978.

Work represented in anthologies, including *New Poetry of Mexico.* Author of "Dance," a weekly column in *Village Voice,* 1967—. Contributor of articles, translations, and reviews to magazines and newspapers, including *New York Times, Mademoiselle, Art in America, Artscanada, Horizon, Dance Scope,* and *Dance.*

WORK IN PROGRESS: Research for a book on the history of dance as a profession.

SIDELIGHTS: Jowitt told *CA:* "Although now I choreograph less frequently than I used to, I find that my critical eye stays acute and my sympathies high when I am involved in the creative process."

*   *   *

JOY, David Anthony Welton   1942-

PERSONAL: Born June 14, 1942, in Ilkley, England; son of Richard Clapham (a journalist) and Annie Doreen (Welton) Joy; married Judith Margaret Agar, March 28, 1967; children: Fiona Rachel, Richard Gabriel, Thomas Christian Appleton. *Education:* Attended Leeds College of Commerce, 1961-62. *Politics:* "Apolitical." *Religion:* Church of England. *Home:* Hole Bottom, Hebden, Skipton, North Yorkshire, England. *Office:* Dalesman Publishing Co. Ltd., Clapham, Lancaster, England.

CAREER: Yorkshire Post, Leeds, England, general reporter, 1962-65; Dalesman Publishing Co. Ltd., Lancaster, England, editorial assistant, 1965-70, books editor, 1970—. Member of national executive and planning committees of Council for the Protection of Rural England; member of Yorkshire Dales National Park Committee, 1973—. *Member:* Country Landowners Association, Railway and Canal Historical Society, Cumbrian Railways Association.

WRITINGS—All published by Dalesman Publishing, except as indicated: (With W. R. Mitchell) *Settle-Carlisle Railway,* 1966; *Main Line Over Shap,* 1967; *Cumbrian Coast Railways,* 1968; *Whitby-Pickering Railway,* 1969; *Railways in the North,* 1970; *Traction Engines in the North,* 1970; (with A. J. Peacock) *George Hudson of York,* 1971; *Steamtown,* 1972; *Railways of the Lake Counties,* 1973; *Regional History of the Railways of Great Britain: South and West Yorkshire,* David & Charles, 1975; *Railways in Lancashire,* 1975; (with W. R. Mitchell) *Settle-Carlisle Centenary,* 1975; *Railways of Yorkshire: The West Riding,* 1976; (with Peter Williams) *North Yorkshire Moors Railway,* 1977; *Steam on the North York Moors,* 1978; (with Alan Haigh) *Yorkshire Railways,*

1979; *Regional History of the Railways of Great Britain: Cumbria,* David & Charles, 1982. Contributor to *Shell Book of Railways.* Editor of Cumbrian Railways Association, 1975—.

SIDELIGHTS: "My interest in railways dates back to my teens," Joy told *CA,* "when I was at boarding school in York, close to the East Coast main line. I spent as much leisure time as possible at York station, instead of on school playing fields.

"I am also keenly interested in the conservation of the countryside, as a result of inheriting a seventeenth-century farmhouse in a beautiful part of the Yorkshire Dales; hence, my involvement with conservation bodies. My future plans are to write something on this theme, rather than just about railways."

*   *   *

JUDAH, Aaron 1923-

PERSONAL: Born October 19, 1923, in Bombay, India; son of Joseph (a fund secretary) and Kate Judah; married October 19, 1978; children: Daniel. *Education:* Attended Lawrence College, India, 1942-43. *Politics:* "All party sympathy." *Religion:* Jewish agnostic." *Home:* 35 Drayton Grove, London W13 OLD, England.

CAREER: Worked as bridge-boy on Cunard ship, 1943-44; draftsman in munitions factory in London, England, 1945-46; trainee physiotherapist, 1946-49; physiotherapist in London, Norway, Israel, India, Australia, France, and Spain, 1949-72; part-time physiotherapist and writer, 1972—. *Member:* Chartered Society of Physiotherapists (London).

WRITINGS—Juvenile: *Tommy With the Hole in His Shoe,* Faber, 1957; *The Adventures of Henrietta Hen,* Faber, 1958; *Tales of Teddy Bear,* Faber, 1958; *Basil Chimpy Isn't Bright,* Faber, 1959; *Miss Hare and Mr. Tortoise,* Faber, 1959; *The Pot of Gold, and Two Other Tales,* Faber, 1959, Barnes, 1960; *Anna Anaconda: The Swallowing Wonder,* Faber, 1960; *Basil Chimpy's Comic Light,* Faber, 1960; *God and Mr. Sourpuss,* Barnes, 1960; *Henrietta in the Snow,* Faber, 1960; *Henrietta in Love,* Faber, 1961; (self-illustrated) *The Proud Duck,* Faber, 1961; *The Elf's New House,* Faber, 1962; *The Careless Cuckoos,* Faber, 1963; (self-illustrated) *Ex-King Max Forever!,* Faber, 1963; (self-illustrated) *The Fabulous Haircut,* Faber, 1964; *On the Feast of Stephen,* Faber, 1965.

Novels: *Clown of Bombay,* Faber, 1963, Dial, 1968; *Clown on Fire,* Macdonald, 1965, Dial, 1967; *Cobweb Pennant,* Dent, 1968; *Lillian's Dam,* Dent, 1970.

WORK IN PROGRESS: A novel, *Revenge in Florence.*

SIDELIGHTS: In his writings for children, Aaron Judah employs a range of experience and emotion. The people and animals in his tales are balanced between wonder and reality, fear and joy, harshness and tenderness, humor and sadness. According to numerous critics, Judah illustrates in a simple and direct manner a variety of morals in his children's stories.

Sensitivity and humor are Judah's keys to success in his adult novels *Clown on Fire* and *Clown of Bombay.* The main character in these works, a rebellious teenager by the name of Joe Hosea, is the grandson of a clown. In the *New York Times Book Review,* Joseph Hitrec wrote of *Clown on Fire:* "Hosea . . . did his pubescent best to pick clean the adult world as it confronted him in India during the last war. Joe's verve and glee in his galloping disengagement from society had a purity so close to moral it joined him to the elite of fictional teen-age rebels from Huck Finn to Kim and Holden Caulfield. Joe's frontal assault on the mysteries of existence

at a preposterous prep-school in the Himalayas was a tonic of zaniness and truth: It proved Aaron Judah to be a comic writer of considerable gifts."

Judah commented to *CA:* "A few decades ago the complaint of the serious novelist was that the majority of the reading public read 'trash.' But readers they were, and there was always the hope of catching their interest with some inspired phrase and eventually uplifting their literary tastes. The flight from 'trash' was then no more rare than spiritual enlightenment. Now that challenge no longer exists. The novelist doesn't try to write a second novel better than his first; he must write better than television.

"In my own home the television—even this impoverished black and white affair—is singing, laughing, weeping, whispering, yelling, shooting, killing, raping, and looting its way into the house for over fifty hours a week. The horrendous end results of television on the young mind has been the storm center of national scandals, yet not for one precious minute has its mouth been stopped up. For the 1970's, at least, the battle is lost, and many excellent writers have given up trying to write better than television. Instead, they write *for* it.

"Another and more insidious evil particular to 'the box' is its readaptation of the classics to the myopic demands of the viewers. A much-voiced argument of the television buffs is that sales of a great novel (unabridged!) always increases after its depiction on television. One wonders what the 'imbecilified' hordes of buyers get out of the real thing. The process of enlightenment here is like that of a youth introduced to the joys of sex by a poxy whore, being next inspired to try marriage."

BIOGRAPHICAL/CRITICAL SOURCES: Time, May 19, 1967; *Saturday Review,* June 3, 1967; *New York Times Book Review,* June 11, 1967, May 12, 1968; *Christian Science Monitor,* June 29, 1967, June 25, 1968.

*   *   *

JUKIC, Ilija 1901-1977

OBITUARY NOTICE—See index for *CA* sketch: Born April 19, 1901, in Svilaj, Yugoslavia; died February 18, 1977, in London, England. Attorney, politician, editor, and author. Jukic held various positions with the Yugoslavian government and devoted his study to the problems of his native land. His writings include *Tito Between East and West* and *The Fall of Yugoslavia.* (Date of death provided by associate, N. Grisogono.)

*   *   *

JULIEN, Charles-Andre 1891-
(Andre Delorme)

PERSONAL: Born September 2, 1891, in Caen, France; son of Etienne (a professor) and Elise (Jugier) Julien; married Lucie Momy, October 29, 1921; children: Nicole (Mrs. Jean Daniel Reynaud). *Education:* Sorbonne, University of Paris, D.es Lettres, 1947. *Politics:* Socialist. *Religion:* "Protestant agnostic." *Home:* 1 Sq. de Port Royal, 75013 Paris, France.

CAREER: Teacher in Algeria and France, 1912-36; secretary general of Haut Comite Mediterraneen et de l'Afrique du Nord, 1936-39; lecturer at university in Paris, 1939-47; University of Paris, Sorbonne, Paris, France, professor of history, 1947-61, professor emeritus, 1961—. Member of council of l'Assemblee de l'Union Francaise, 1947-58, and delegate to National Commission for United Nations Educational, Scientific and Cultural Organization. Dean of faculty of letters of University of Rabat, 1957-61, dean emeritus, 1961—. *Military service:* French army, 1914-15. *Member:* Ruvue historique (past secretary general). *Awards, honors:* Grand cordon of Ouissam Alaouite (Morocco), 1957; grand cordon of Ordre de l'Independance (Tunisia), 1977.

WRITINGS—In English translation: *Histoire de l'Afrique du Nord (Tunisie-Algerie-Maroc),* Payot, 1931, 2nd edition in two volumes, Volume I: *Des Origines a la conquete arabe* (edited by Christian Courtois), 1951, Volume II: *De la conquete arabe a 1830* (edited by Roger Le Tourneau), 1953, reprinted, 1978, translation by John Petrie published as *History of North Africa,* Routledge & Kegan Paul, 1970.

Other writings: *Un Medecin romantique* (title means "A Romantic Doctor"), Carbonel, 1925; *La Question italienne en Tunisie, 1868-1938* (title means "The Italian Problem in Tunisia, 1868-1938"), Cahiers d'Information Francaise, 1939; *Histoire de l'Afrique,* Presses Universitaires de France, 1941, reprinted as *Histoire de l'Afrique blanche* (title means "A History of White Africa"), 1966; *Histoire de l'Oceanie,* Presses Universitaires de France, 1942, 4th edition (edited by Jean Guiart), 1971; (with Robert Delavignette) *Les Constructeurs de la France d'outre-mer* (title means "The Builders of French-Colonial Expansion"), Correa, 1946; *Les Debuts de l'expansion et de la colonisation francaises: Quinzieme-siezieme siecles* (title means "The Beginnings of French-Colonial Expansion: Fifteenth and Sixteenth Centuries"), Presses Universitaires de France, 1948, 2nd edition (edited by Gerard Montfort), 1979; *L'Afrique du Nord en marche: Nationalismes musulmans et souverainete francaise*

(title means "North Africa's Forward March: Muslim Nationalities and French Sovereignty"), Rene Julliard, 1952, 3rd edition, 1972; *Histoire de l'Algerie contemporaine,* Volume I: *La Conquete et les debuts de la colonisation* (title means "A History of Contemporary Algeria: Conquest and the Beginnings of Colonization"), Presses Universitaires de France, 1964, 2nd edition, 1979; *Le Maroc face aux imperialismes, 1415-1956* (title means "Morocco Confronted With Imperialism"), Jeune Afrique, 1978; (with Magali Morsy) *Une Pensee anticoloniale: Positions 1914-1979* (title means "Anti-Colonial Attitudes, 1914-1979"), Sindbad, 1979; *La Crise franco-tunisienne, 1951-1957* (title means "The Franco-Tunisian Crisis, 1951-1957"), Jeune Afrique, 1981; *Memoires d'un nonagenaire* (title means "Memoirs of a Ninety-Year-Old Man"), Grasset, 1982.

Also author of numerous articles under pseudonym Andre Delorme. Member of editorial board of "Pays d'Outre-Mer," a series, Presses Universitaires de France.

WORK IN PROGRESS: Revising *L'Afrique du Nord en marche,* publication by Sindbad expected in 1982.

SIDELIGHTS: Julien is considered a pioneer of anti-colonialism in France. He told *CA:* "I have been intimately involved in political action. Since 1917 I have played an important role in the struggle for feminist causes. From then on, I was president of the League of Human Rights for French North Africa. I have pursued journalistic activities since 1914, and I have always thought that intellectual production and political action are intimately connected."

K

KAHN, Lawrence E(dwin) 1937-

PERSONAL: Born December 8, 1937, in Troy, N.Y.; son of Moe and Ann Kahn; married Michele Kagan, September 15, 1968; children: Tamara, Alyssa, Daniel. *Education:* Union College, Schenectady, N.Y., A.B., 1959; Harvard University, J.D., 1962; graduate study at Oxford University. *Agent:* Edward J. Acton, Inc., 17 Grove St., New York, N.Y. 10014. *Office:* Albany County Courthouse, Albany, N.Y. 12207.

CAREER: City of Albany, Albany, N.Y., assistant corporation counsel, 1963-69; County of Albany, Albany, surrogate judge, 1973-79; New York State Supreme Court, Albany, justice, 1979—. *Military service:* New York State National Guard, 1955-65. *Awards, honors:* Named among five outstanding young men of New York State by New York State Jaycees, 1967.

WRITINGS: (With brother, Robert W. Kahn) *Divorce Lawyers' Casebook,* St. Martin's, 1972; *When Couples Part,* F. Watts, 1981.

*   *   *

KALMAN, Harold David 1943-

PERSONAL: Born June 22, 1943, in Montreal, Quebec, Canada; son of Maxwell M. (an architect) and Frances (Glasberg) Kalman; married Jacqueline Ritchie, June 25, 1964 (divorced, 1975); children: Diane Rebecca, Hilary Lynn. *Education:* Princeton University, B.A., 1964, M.F.A., 1966, Ph.D., 1971. *Home:* 530 Laurier Ave. W., Apt. 1706, Ottawa, Ontario, Canada K1R 7T1. *Office:* 46 Elgin St., Suite 19, Ottawa, Ontario, Canada K1P 5K6.

CAREER: University of British Columbia, Vancouver, assistant professor, 1968-73, associate professor of fine arts, 1973-75; free-lance writer and consultant, 1975—. Managing editor of *RACAR: Revue d'Art Canadienne/Canadian Art Review,* 1977-81. Member of Vancouver Heritage Advisory Committee, 1971-75, and Ottawa Local Architectural Conservation Advisory Committee, 1980—. *Member:* Heritage Canada, Society of Architectural Historians (vice-chairman for Canada of Committee on Architectural Preservation, 1975-79), Universities Art Association of Canada (member of executive council, 1970-74), Association for Preservation Technology.

WRITINGS: The Railway Hotels, Maltwood Museum, 1968; *Exploring Vancouver,* University of British Columbia Press, 1974, 2nd edition, 1978; *Pioneer Churches,* Norton, 1976; *The Evaluation of Historic Buildings,* Parks Canada, 1979; *The Sensible Rehabilitation of Older Buildings,* Canada Mortgage and Housing Corp., 1979; (with Robert Bailey and Keith Wagland) *Encore: Recycling Public Buildings for the Arts,* Corpus, 1979; *Exploring Ottawa,* University of Toronto Press, in press. Author of "Viewpoint," a column in *Canadian Heritage,* 1980—. Contributor to professional journals.

WORK IN PROGRESS: A book tentatively titled *The Face of Main Street,* publication by Heritage Canada expected in 1982.

SIDELIGHTS: Kalman wrote: "I have always been interested in older buildings and their conservation, formerly as a teacher, now as a consultant, and always as a writer. Society is finally recognizing that the preservation of the best of the past is essential to the health of our future. By writing about historical architecture and preparing guidebooks to cities, I can help to raise the popular appreciation of buildings and thereby play a part in their conservation. My consulting work faces this issue even more squarely by advising those property owners and officials whose actions have a direct effect on our environment."

*   *   *

KAMIN, Leon J. 1927-

PERSONAL: Born December 29, 1927, in Taunton, Mass.; son of Jonas and Jean (Rybak) Kamin; married Marie-Claire Fay, April 21, 1970; children: John, Katherine. *Education:* Harvard University, B.A., 1949, Ph.D., 1954. *Home:* 307 Hartley Ave., Princeton, N.J. 08540. *Office:* Department of Psychology, Princeton University, Princeton, N.J. 08540.

CAREER: McGill University, Montreal, Quebec, professor of psychology, 1954-55; Queen's University, Kingston, Ontario, professor of psychology, 1955-57; McMaster University, Hamilton, Ontario, professor of psychology, 1957-68; Princeton University, Princeton, N.J., Dorman T. Warren Professor of Psychology and chairman of department, 1968—. *Military service:* U.S. Army, 1946-47. *Member:* American Psychological Association, Psychonomic Society, Society for Experimental Psychology.

WRITINGS: The Science and Politics of I.Q., L. Erlbaum Associates, 1974.

BIOGRAPHICAL/CRITICAL SOURCES: Scientific American, July, 1975; *Science,* September 26, 1975.*

*   *   *

KAMMERER, Gladys M.   1909-1970

OBITUARY NOTICE—See index for *CA* sketch: Born May 13, 1909, in St. Louis, Mo.; died July 17, 1970. Educator and author. A political scientist, Kammerer devoted some study to child welfare and social work. She wrote numerous monographs and civic information pamphlets, including *Requirements for State Social Work Positions in the South, The Changing Urban County,* and *Against Long Odds: The Theory and Practice of Successful Governmental Consolidation.* Her books include *Impact of War on Federal Personnel Administration, 1939-1945* and *British and American Child Welfare Services.* Obituaries and other sources: *American Men and Women of Science: The Social and Behavioral Sciences,* 12th edition, Bowker, 1973. (Date of death provided by University of Florida Political Science Department.)

*   *   *

KANE, George   1916-

PERSONAL: Born July 4, 1916; son of George Michael and Clara Kane; married Katherine Bridget Montgomery; children: one son, one daughter. *Education:* University of British Columbia, B.A., 1936; University of Toronto, M.A., 1937; attended Northwestern University, 1937-38; University of London, Ph.D., 1946. *Office:* Department of English, University of North Carolina, Greenlaw Hall, Chapel Hill, N.C. 27514.

CAREER: University of London, London, England, assistant lecturer, 1946-48, lecturer, 1948-53, reader, 1953-55, professor of English language and literature and head of department of English at Royal Holloway College, 1955-65, Chambers Memorial Lecturer, 1965, professor of English language and medieval literature at King's College, 1965-76, professor emeritus, 1976—, head of department of English, 1968-76, fellow of University College, 1971, and King's College, 1976, public orator, 1962-66, member of governing body of London School of Oriental and African Studies, 1970-76; University of North Carolina, Chapel Hill, William Rand Kenan, Jr. Professor of English, 1976—. British Academy lecturer at Accademia Nazionale dei Lincei, 1976. *Military service:* British Army, Artist's Rifles and Rifle Brigade, 1939-46; mentioned in dispatches.

MEMBER: Mediaeval Academy of America (fellow), American Academy of Arts and Sciences (fellow), British Academy (fellow; member of council, 1974-76), Early English Text Society (member of council, 1969), Athenaeum Club. *Awards, honors:* Sir Israel Gollancz Memorial Prize from British Academy, 1963; Haskins Medal from Mediaeval Academy of America, 1978.

WRITINGS: Middle English Literature: A Critical Study of the Romances, the Religious Lyrics, Piers Plowman, Methuen, 1951, Folcroft, 1969; (editor) William Langland, *Will's Visions of Piers Plowman and Do-Well,* Athlone Press, 1960; *Piers Plowman: The A Version,* Athlone Press, 1960; *Piers Plowman: The Evidence for Authorship,* Humanities, 1965; (editor with E. Talbot Donaldson) *Piers Plowman: The B Version,* Humanities, 1965; *What's the Next Move?,* Scribner, 1974. General editor of "Piers Plowman," a series, Ath-

lone Press, 1960—. Contributor of articles and reviews to scholarly journals.*

*   *   *

KANFER, Stefan   1933-

PERSONAL: Born May 17, 1933; son of Allen (a teacher) and Violet (a scriptwriter; maiden name, Leonard) Kanfer; married May Markey (a teacher), 1956; children: Lillian, Ethan. *Education:* New York University, B.A., 1953, graduate study, 1955-57. *Agent:* Lynn Nesbit, International Creative Management, 40 West 57th St., New York, N.Y. 10019. *Office: Time,* 1271 Avenue of the Americas, New York, N.Y. 10019.

CAREER: New York Herald Tribune, New York City, copy boy, 1951-53; television writer for the "Patty Duke Show" in the early 1960's and for Victor Borge and Allen Funt, 1964-65; *Time,* New York City, show business writer, cinema critic, essay anchor man, and book review editor, 1967-75, senior editor, 1975—. *Military service:* U.S. Army, 1953-55. *Member:* Writers Guild of America, Dramatists Guild. *Awards, honors:* J. C. Penney-University of Missouri Journalism Award, 1975.

WRITINGS: A Journal of the Plague Years (nonfiction), Atheneum, 1973; *The Eighth Sin* (novel), Random House, 1978; *Fear Itself* (novel), Putnam, 1981.

Plays: "I Want You" (two-act musical), first produced Off-Broadway at Maidman Playhouse, 1958; "The Coffee Lover" (two-act comedy), first produced in eastern United States at summer stock theatres, 1964.

Author of short stories. Contributor of articles and reviews to publications, including *Atlantic, Harper's,* and *New Republic.*

SIDELIGHTS: Kanfer's first two books reminded readers of two dark periods of the twentieth century. His 1973 work, *Journal of the Plague Years,* is an account of the "blacklisting and persecution" in the entertainment industry during the McCarthy era. Convinced that such a plague could again afflict the United States, Kanfer warned that complacency in such matters "is extremely ill-advised." The author offered another admonition in his second book, *The Eighth Sin,* where the sin of the title is to forget about the Nazi Holocaust.

The Eighth Sin tells the story of Benoit, a gypsy survivor of the Auschwitz prison camp where the rest of his family has died. He is adopted by an American and his wife in England and then moves with his new family to New York City. His talent for painting is obscured by a penchant for shoplifting, a term in prison, and later a troubled marriage and alcoholism. In addition to his personal problems, Bensit carries with himself the haunting memory of prison camp life. As Richard Freedman pointed out, "Benoit cannot and will not forget; the memory of the horror blights his life.... Ultimately Benoit must seek revenge on Elezar Jassy, a gypsy who collaborated with the Nazis while protecting the boy when he was in Auschwitz."

Critics saw *The Eighth Sin* as a flawed but powerful work. It is an "alert but wobbly first novel," said Ross Feld. Freedman, meanwhile, objected to the "factual 'Items,'" that "obstruct the fictional flow, suggesting cool authorial research rather than genuine remembrance of nightmares past. This only slightly mars an absorbing narrative otherwise compounded of hot rage and ribald humor." And Curt Leviant viewed the gypsy motif as "bookish and contrived" while regarding some scenes as a betrayal "to the impassioned honesty of the rest of the book.'' That honesty is ''Kanfer's eloquent cry. . . : Do not forget! The Germans, he says, not only destroyed the dead, they destroyed—marked forever—those who survived; among them is the lonely, anguished Benoit.''

CA INTERVIEW

CA interviewed Kanfer at his New York City office on May 14, 1980.

Stefan Kanfer is nothing if not prolific. He has written novels and short stories, television comedy, plays (with music and lyrics), a nonfiction book, essays, newspaper and magazine articles, television and film reviews, book criticism, and even cartoon captions for *New Yorker*. The only medium it seems he hasn't written for is radio, but then his mother, scriptwriter Violet Leonard Kanfer, covered that for him.

Writing is something of a family tradition. Grandfather Oscar Leonard wrote for the Yiddish theatre, while his grandmother Leah is the author of the perennial bestseller *Jewish Cookery*. Stefan's father, Allen Kanfer, wrote his first poem in his early forties and has published hundreds since.

''We're late bloomers in my family,'' observes the son, who published his first novel at forty-four and feels he didn't hit his literary stride until his fourth decade. He had joined *Time* magazine in the mid-1960's as a show business writer. ''I never thought I would stay for long, since I had never been formally trained as a journalist,'' says Kanfer, who went on to become cinema critic, essay anchor man, and in 1976, an editor in the book section. Author of numerous cover stories, he writes an annual piece for the magazine on the state of the American language. Many of his essays—which range from discussions of Watergate and Vietnam veterans to Sherlock Holmes—have been reprinted in textbook anthologies.

''My father was a very profound influence on my life. He once told me something that I have since passed on to my children, that once you know how to read, you're on your own. The rest is up to you; you'll find all your own answers there.'' He cites Chekhov, Proust, and ''early Cheever'' as personal favorites.

One of his books contains this passage: ''Max knew, as all teachers knew, that once a student is truly hooked on reading he is hooked for life. Thereafter, the victim will read candy-bar wrappers if they are all that is available, and will stock his bathroom with everything from Kafka to Raymond Chandler.''

Kanfer's first book was published in 1973. *A Journal of the Plague Years* was called an ''eloquent chronicle'' and ''the best researched and most evocative study we have of black-listing during the McCarthy era''; yet other critics scolded him for resorting to language they labeled ''Time-ese.'' ''I think critics who accused me of that hadn't read me, but were remembering the old *Time* of the late 1940's and 1950's,'' argues Kanfer.

Perhaps the most meaningful project for Kanfer has been his first novel, *The Eighth Sin*, which traces the fate of a gypsy boy who escapes Hitler's concentration camps but is obsessed by memories of the past. Notes the author: ''This is the serious Kanfer. I had always wanted to write about the Holocaust, but felt it had already been done by Elie Wiesel and others. One day I picked up a book, *The Destiny of Europe's Gypsies*, and found my story. Though I felt some might think me impertinent for writing without direct experience, I had it in my blood, so to speak. My grandfather

had been involved with the rehabilitation of Holocaust victims, so I'd heard about it all of my life.''

Wiesel, head of the President's Commission on the Holocaust, was so moved by the book that he permitted Kanfer to join the group as the only journalist on a trip to the camps. In the conclusion to the article he wrote for *Time* about the experience, Kanfer rhetorically asks why we continue to recall the horrors of history: ''Why not let the unbearable past recede into the anaesthesia of history books?'' He quotes Wiesel as saying that the resurrection of the past is ''not to remember, but to warn.'' Kanfer's ''eighth sin,'' the sin of forgetting, ''was a theme,'' he says, ''that had a mystical power for me.''

Kanfer's second novel, the thriller *Fear Itself,* is not a Holocaust novel, he says, though the character is a survivor and one scene takes place in a concentration camp. The book concerns itself with the attitude of the Franklin Roosevelt administration to the refugees and the killing of the Jews.

The person who emerges from these writings is a man with a strong sense of injustice, but one who also wears a mask of comedy along with the mask of sorrow. He tempers his anguished vision with humor. ''I don't know what I'd do without it,'' says Kanfer.

BIOGRAPHICAL/CRITICAL SOURCES: Washington Post Book World, June 3, 1973, May 21, 1978; *Time*, June 11, 1973, May 15, 1978, August 20, 1979; *New York Times*, June 11, 1973, May 11, 1978; *World*, June 19, 1973; *New York Times Book Review, July 8, 1973, April 30, 1978; Saturday Review*, May 13, 1978; *Nation*, June 17, 1978.

—*Interview by Trisha Gorman*

* * *

KANNER, Leo 1894-1981

OBITUARY NOTICE—See index for *CA* sketch: Born June 13, 1894, in Klekotow, Austria; died of heart failure, April 3, 1981, in Sykesville, Md. Psychiatrist and author. Kanner was known as ''the father of child psychiatry.'' He was the first to identify early infantile autism, also known as Kanner Syndrome, an affliction characterized by the victim's total withdrawal from the world. He was the founder of the Johns Hopkins Children's Psychiatric Clinic and the author of numerous books, including the classic textbook *Child Psychiatry* and popular books on child rearing. Obituaries and other sources: *Chicago Tribune*, April 7, 1981; *Washington Post*, April 7, 1981; *New York Times*, April 7, 1981; *Time*, April 20, 1981.

* * *

KAPP, Yvonne (Mayer) 1903-
(Yvonne Cloud)

PERSONAL: Born in London, England. *Education:* Attended King's College, London. *Address:* c/o Lloyd's Bank Ltd., Highgate Village, London N6, England.

CAREER: Author and translator. *Member:* Writers' Guild of Great Britain, Society of Authors.

WRITINGS—Under name Yvonne Cloud: *Pastiche: A Music-Room Book*, drawings by Edmond X. Kapp, Faber & Gwyer, 1926; *Short Lease*, D. Harmsworth, 1932; *Nobody Asked You*, Willy-Nilly Press, 1932; *Mediterranean Blues*, J. Lane, 1933, Vanguard Press, 1934; (editor) *Beside the Seaside: Six Variations* (essays), Stanley Nott, 1934; (with Richard Ellis) *The Basque Children in England: An Account of Their Life at North Stoucham Camp*, Gollancz, 1937; *The*

Houses in Between: A Domestic Comedy in Several Districts, J. Lane, 1938.

Under Yvonne Kapp: (Editor) *The Ninth Wave,* Lawrence & Wishart, 1955; (editor) *Short Stories of Russia Today,* Houghton, 1959; *Eleanor Marx,* Beekman, Volume I: *Family Life,* 1972, Volume II: *The Crowded Years,* 1976.

Translator: (With Mollie Guiart) Andre Stil, *The First Clash* (novel), Lawrence & Wishart, Volume I, 1953, Volume II, 1954; (with Anna Bostok) Ilya Ehrenburg, *Julio Jurenito,* MacGibbon & Kee, 1958; Paul Lechat, *Italy,* Viking Press, 1959; *Correspondence Between Friedrich Engels and Paul and Laura Lafargue,* Lawrence & Wishart, Volume I, 1959, Volume II, 1960; (with Michael Hamburger) Bertolt Brecht, *Tales From the Calendar,* Methuen, 1961; Ehrenburg, *People and Life* (autobiography), six volumes, MacGibbon & Kee, 1961-66, Volumes I and II translated with Bostock, Volumes III-VI translated with Tatiana Shebunina; (with Bostock and Shebunina) Ehrenburg, *Chekhov, Stendhal, and Other Essays,* Knopf, 1963.

General editor of *Library of Contemporary Soviet Novels,* Lawrence & Wishart, 1955—. Contributor to magazines and periodicals, including *Vogue* and *Times Literary Supplement.*

SIDELIGHTS: Eleanor Marx, youngest daughter of German political philosopher Karl Marx, was "a great tragic heroine of the international socialist movement," wrote James Joll of the *New York Times Book Review.* Several critics have noted that Yvonne Kapp's tone is largely sympathetic in her two-volume biography of this writer, translator, union organizer, and actress. Kapp's discussion of the various aspects of Marx's life, including her political beliefs, her relationship with her famous father (whom she idolized), and the events that led to her suicide, "dispels some of the atmosphere of melodrama but rouses even greater interest in Eleanor's historical importance," commented *Nation*'s James Sloan Allen.

In his review of Kapp's book, Joll called Marx a "tempestuous, passionate, warm-hearted woman whose sympathy for the oppressed started with her dedication from the age of 12 to the cause of 'the Poor Neglected Nation,' Ireland." This dedication continued throughout her life; much of her time was devoted to speaking, organizing, and writing pamphlets for the socialist cause. She was the first person to propose a union for secretaries, and she was the founder of the first women's branch of the National Union of Gasworkers and General Labourers of Great Britain and Ireland. In Eleanor Marx, declared Allen, "Marxism passed from socialist theory to working-class organization."

Kapp explains that much of the mystique that continues to surround Eleanor Marx is due to her tumultuous relationship with Edward Aveling, her common-law husband of fourteen years. Aveling was, wrote Joll, "an actor both on and off the stage who was capable of inspiring devotion in women in spite of what seemed to many an unattractive and even repulsive appearance." Marx remained devoted to Aveling throughout her life, despite his frequent infidelity. Together they translated the first volume of Karl Marx's *Das Kapital,* worked actively on behalf of working class organizations, and promoted the teachings of playwright Henrik Ibsen. E. J. Hobsbawm, in a review for *New Statesman,* observed of Aveling that "with all his unremitting lechery and sponging he never ceased to be an able and devoted socialist militant."

In 1898 (when she was forty-four years old), Eleanor Marx swallowed a dram of cyanide and was dead within an hour. There is some difficulty, as several critics noted, in determining the causes leading to a suicide which occurred so long

ago. In the last months of her life, Kapp maintains, Marx had become disillusioned with her socialist activities and had despaired of ever seeing her political dreams—and those of her father—realized. She saw that Marxism was becoming "a game played at universities without the smallest application to the life of the people." Some believe that Eleanor Marx poisoned herself after learning that Aveling had secretly married a young actress; others doubt that she ever knew of the marriage. It is generally believed, though, that the relationship between Marx and Aveling had soured, and that this disappointment, coupled with Eleanor's political frustrations, were the primary factors that led to her suicide. Eleanor "could not, apparently, appreciate her own substantial achievements, nor could she recognize that, whatever she did, she managed to illumine the life of nearly everyone she touched," wrote Naomi Bliven of the *New Yorker.*

Critics have applauded Yvonne Kapp's biography of Marx, calling it magnificent, well-written, and definitive. Kapp "possesses the three major qualifications of a biographer: exact, unmystifiable scholarship, a clever and loving eye, and a knowledge of the world," wrote Hobsbawm. "Moreover, she writes with enormous, unrhetorical, skill, style and wit." Joll suggested that the biography was too long, but conceded that because Marx "was involved in so many aspects of late Victorian life as well as in the international socialist movement . . . [a biography about her] needs a mass of detail to do justice to the many aspects of her career."

BIOGRAPHICAL/CRITICAL SOURCES: *Spectator,* November 17, 1933; *New York Times,* July 29, 1934; *Times Literary Supplement,* July 7, 1977; *New Statesman,* January 7, 1977; *Nation,* December 31, 1977; *New York Times Book Review,* January 8, 1978; *New Yorker,* April 17, 1978; *Commentary,* September, 1978.*

*   *   *

KARMAN, Mal 1944-
(Penelope Ashe)

PERSONAL: Born July 12, 1944, in New York, N.Y.; son of Sam (a sales manager) and Jane Karman. *Education:* Attended State University of New York Agricultural and Technical College at Farmingdale, 1962; Hofstra University, B.A., 1966; University of Stockholm, M.A., 1968; also attended San Francisco State University, 1970-71. *Residence:* San Francisco, Calif., and Marina del Rey, Calif. *Agent:* Barbara Lowenstein, 250 West 57th St., New York, N.Y. 10019.

CAREER: Iversen Associates, New York City, designer and production assistant, 1962-63; *Newsday,* New York City, reporter, 1965-68, correspondent from Stockholm, Sweden, 1968, editor, 1968-69; copy editor, 1969, free-lance writer, 1969-81. Writer and film producer for KGO-TV, U.S. Department of Health, Education and Welfare, Urban and Rural Systems Associates, and KPIX-TV, 1976-78. *Member:* Writers Guild of America. *Awards, honors:* National awards from Newspaper Guild of America, 1964, for outstanding news story, 1965, for outstanding feature story, and 1966, for outstanding sports story; named one of ten outstanding young men of America by U.S. Jaycees, 1981.

WRITINGS: *The Foxbat Spiral* (political novel), Dell, 1980; "Terminal Circle" (screenplay), PMS Productions, 1982.

Under pseudonym Penelope Ashe: (With twenty-one others) *Naked Came the Stranger,* Lyle Stuart, 1969.

Author of "Film Notes," a column in *City,* 1975-76. Contributor of articles and photographs to magazines and newspapers, including *Mother Jones, Rolling Stone, Ladies Home*

Journal, Oui, Millimeter, and *Filmmakers Newsletter.* Contributing film editor of *Pacific Sun,* 1974-77.

WORK IN PROGRESS: Wind From the Sun, a novel, publication expected in 1982; "Lord of the Rings, Part II," a screenplay, release by United Artists expected in 1982 or 1983; "China Basin," a screenplay.

SIDELIGHTS: While working as a film reviewer, Karman interviewed such actors as Woody Allen, Liv Ullman, Michael Crichton, Robert Mitchum, Burt Lancaster, Jane Fonda, and Lillian Gish. As a journalist and filmmaker, he covered Robert Kennedy's assassination, race riots, the attempted assassination of Nassau County executive Eugene Nickerson, military deserters in Sweden during the war in Vietnam, and such issues as child abuse and neglect.

Karman wrote: "I have traveled widely in Europe, and in 1968 I journeyed to northern Sweden and Lake Stoersjon in search of the Swedish 'Loch Ness monster' for a lighthearted magazine article. Realizing I would not be happy as a career journalist unless I could do something as creative as running my own paper, I moved to California in 1969 in search of my first love—fiction writing. I struggled several years before breaking through with my creative work.

"I believe that personal growth parallels creative growth, so I continue to seek ways in which I can learn about myself and those around me via psychology, holistic medicine, spiritual exploration, and physical well-being. I can't write without being physically active.

"Cultivating new contacts isn't all that important for new writers and I would encourage them to put their energies into creating something, rather than trying to cultivate 'the big break' through personal acquaintances. If what you do is good enough, people will want it, whether they know you or not, and in the end you will feel better about yourself.

"As for my own work, I try to spring into totally different areas each time I start a project. This allows fresh ideas to germinate, like rotating crops in the soil. Hence, if I'm working on a totally bizarre fantasy like 'Terminal Circle,' it would follow that I would next begin something as unrelated as 'China Basin,' a period-piece love story set against the Chinese tong wars."

BIOGRAPHICAL/CRITICAL SOURCES: San Francisco Examiner, September 11, 1980.

*　　*　　*

KARSH, Bernard 1921-

PERSONAL: Born August 25, 1921, in Chicago, Ill.; son of David and Harriet (Pugach) Karsh; married Annette Eleanor Shier, June 9, 1946; children: Paul I., Aaron N. *Education:* Attended Roosevelt University, 1946; University of Chicago, M.A., 1948, Ph.D., 1953. *Home:* 1412 West William St., Champaign, Ill. 61820. *Office:* Department of Sociology, University of Illinois, Urbana, Ill. 61801.

CAREER: University of Chicago, Chicago, Ill., instructor, 1952-53, assistant professor of industrial relations, 1953-54; University of Illinois, Urbana, assistant professor, 1954-58, associate professor, 1958-63, professor of sociology and industrial relations, 1963—, head of department of sociology, 1973—, associate director of Institute of Aviation, 1976—. Visiting lecturer at University of Kansas, 1951, and Indiana University, 1952; visiting professor at Keio University, 1966, and Florida Atlantic University, 1972; consultant to Ford Foundation and Asia Foundation. *Military service:* U.S. Army Air Forces, 1939-43; became master sergeant.

MEMBER: American Sociological Association (fellow), Industrial Relations Research Association, Association for Asian Studies, American Association of University Professors, Midwest Conference on Asian Studies (vice-president, 1970-71; president, 1971-72). *Awards, honors:* Fulbright scholarship, 1960.

WRITINGS: Diary of a Strike, University of Illinois Press, 1958; (with others) *The Worker Views His Union,* University of Chicago Press, 1958; (contributor) *Labor and the New Deal,* University of Wisconsin Press, 1959; (contributor) *Society Today,* CRM Books, 1971; (editor with Kazuo Okochi and Solomon B. Levine) *Workers and Employers in Japan: The Japanese Employment Relations System,* University of Tokyo Press, 1973, Princeton University Press, 1974. Contributor to sociology journals.*

*　　*　　*

KARVE, Dinakar Dhondo 1899-1980

OBITUARY NOTICE—See index for *CA* sketch: Born July 13, 1899, in Poona, India; died July 6, 1980. Educator and author. Karve's career as an educator began at Fergusson College in Poona, India, in 1925. In 1962 he became executive officer of the American Institute of Indian Studies in Poona, a position he held until his retirement in 1972. Among his writings are *Comparative Educational Administration* and *The New Brahmans: Five Maharashtrian Families.* (Date of death provided by daughter, Gauri Karve Deshpande.)

*　　*　　*

KASARDA, John Dale 1945-

PERSONAL: Born June 16, 1945, in Wilkes-Barre, Pa.; son of Edward and Stella (Scott) Kasarda; married Mary Ann Dudascik (a conference coordinator), August 24, 1968; children: Jason, Kimberly. *Education:* Cornell University, B.S., 1967, M.B.A., 1968; University of North Carolina, Ph.D., 1971. *Home:* 707 Gimghoul Rd., Chapel Hill, N.C. 27514. *Office:* Department of Sociology, University of North Carolina, Chapel Hill, N.C. 27514.

CAREER: University of Chicago, Chicago, Ill., assistant professor of sociology, 1971-74; Florida Atlantic University, Boca Raton, associate professor of sociology, 1974-76; University of North Carolina, Chapel Hill, professor of sociology and chairman of department, 1976—. *Member:* International Sociological Association, American Sociological Association, Population Association of America, Sociological Research Association.

WRITINGS: Contemporary Urban Ecology, Macmillan, 1977; *Ecological Models of Organizational Structuring,* University of Chicago Press, in press; *Female Status and Fertility,* Academic Press, in press. Contributor of more than thirty articles to sociology journals. Member of editorial board of *American Journal of Sociology, Social Forces, Western Sociological Review, Urban Affairs Quarterly,* and *Sociological Symposium;* book review editor of *American Journal of Sociology.*

WORK IN PROGRESS: Population Redistribution and National Urban Policy.

*　　*　　*

KATCHADOURIAN, Herant A(ram) 1933-

PERSONAL: Born January 23, 1933, in Alexandretta, Syria; came to the United States in 1958, naturalized citizen, 1973; son of Aram A. (in business) and Efronia (Nazarian) Katchadourian; married Stina Lindfors (a writer), August 30, 1964; children: Nina, Kai. *Education:* American University of Beirut, B.A. (cum laude), 1954, M.D. (cum laude), 1958. *Home:* 956 Mears Court, Stanford, Calif. 94305. *Office:* Office of the Dean of Undergraduate Studies, Stanford University, Stanford, Calif. 94305.

CAREER: American University of Beirut, Beirut, Lebanon, intern, 1957-58; University of Rochester, Rochester, N.Y., resident in psychiatry, 1958-61; National Institute of mental Health, Bethesda, Md., visiting associate of U.S. Public Health Service, 1961-62; American University of Beirut, assistant professor of psychiatry, 1962-66; Stanford University, Stanford, Calif., assistant professor, 1966-70, associate professor, 1970-76, professor of psychiatry and behavioral sciences, vice-provost, and dean of undergraduate studies, 1977—. Member of board of trustees of Haigazian College and corporation visiting committee of Massachusetts Institute of Technology, both 1978—. *Member:* Alpha Omega Alpha.

WRITINGS: (With D. T. Lunde) *Fundamentals of Human Sexuality,* with instructor's manual, Holt, 1972, abridged edition, 1979, 3rd edition, 1980; *Human Sexuality: Sense and Nonsense,* Stanford Alumni Association, 1972; (with Lunde) *Biological Aspects of Human Sexuality,* Holt, 1975; *The Biology of Adolescence,* W. H. Freeman, 1977; (contributor) L. Carl Brown and Norman Itzkowitz, editors, *Psychological Dimensions of Near Eastern Studies,* Darwin Press, 1977; (editor) *Human Sexuality: A Comparative and Developmental Perspective,* University of California Press, 1979. Contributor of more than twenty articles to medical and psychiatry journals.

*   *   *

KATZ, Herbert Melvin 1930-

PERSONAL: Born November 13, 1930, in New York, N.Y.; son of Charles and May (Tonkin) Katz; married Marjorie Phillis Pearle, January 5, 1958 (divorced, May, 1974); married Nancy Beth Jacobs, August 15, 1974; children: (first marriage) Daniel Seth, Nina Judith. *Education:* New York University, B.A., 1951; Columbia University, M.A., 1952. *Office:* M. Evans & Co., Inc., 216 East 49th St., New York, N.Y. 10017.

CAREER: Viking Press, Inc., New York City, publicity writer, 1952-53; Pyramid Publications, Inc., Moonachie, N.J., editor-in-chief, 1953-55; Funk & Wagnalls Co., Scranton, Pa., editorial director, 1955-61; G. P. Putnam's Sons, New York City, editor, 1961-63; M. Evans & Co., Inc., New York City, vice-president and editor-in-chief, 1964—. Editorial director of Wilfred Funk, Inc., 1955-61.

WRITINGS: (With Marjorie Katz) *Museums, U.S.A.: A History and Guide,* Doubleday, 1965; (with M. Katz) *Museum Adventures: An Introduction to Discovery* (juvenile), Coward, 1969; *Love and Marriage* (novel), Arbor House, 1975; *Nicolette* (novel), Arbor House, 1976.*

*   *   *

KATZ, Marjorie P.
See WEISER, Marjorie P(hillis) K(atz)

*   *   *

KAYE, H. R.
See KNOX, Hugh (Randolph)

KEAN, Benjamin Harrison 1912-

PERSONAL: Born December 2, 1912, in Chicago, Ill.; son of Harrison and Tillie (Rhodes) Kean; married, 1948. *Education:* University of California, A.B., 1933; Columbia University, M.D., 1937. *Home:* 435 East 70th St., New York, N.Y. 10021. *Office:* College of Medicine, Cornell University, 1300 York Ave., New York, N.Y. 10021.

CAREER: Gorgas Hospital, Canal Zone, intern and resident, 1937-39, senior pathologist, 1940-45; New York University, New York City, assistant professor of pathology, 1946-52; Cornell University, New York City, 1952-65, began as assistant professor, became associate professor, professor of tropical medicine, 1965—, professor of public health, 1972—. Diplomate of American Board of Pathology and American Board of Microbiology; private practice of medicine in New York City, 1946—. Attending pathologist at New York University-Bellevue Medical Center, 1946-52; attending physician and parasitologist at New York Hospital and director of parasitology laboratory, 1952—; attending physician at Doctors Hospital, 1952—. Member of World Health Organization scientific advisory committee on tropical diseases; consultant to General Motors Corp., Travelers Health Institute, and Development and Resources Corp. *Military service:* U.S. Army, Medical Corps, 1942-46; became lieutenant colonel.

MEMBER: American College of Physicians (fellow), College of American Pathologists (fellow), American Medical Association (fellow), American Society of Clinical Pathology, American Society of Tropical Medicine, American Association of Pathology and Bacteriology, Royal Society of Tropical Medicine and Hygiene, New York Society of Tropical Medicine. *Awards, honors:* Presidential award of the Golden Heart from Philippine Government, 1968.

WRITINGS: (With Roger C. Breslau) *Parasites of the Human Heart,* Grune, 1964; (with Harold Atherton Tucker) *The Traveler's Health Guide,* C. C Thomas, 1965; (with Tucker) *The Traveler's Medical Guide for Physicians,* C. C Thomas, 1966; (editor with Kenneth E. Mott and Adair J. Russell) *Tropical Medicine and Parasitology: Classic Investigations,* two volumes, Cornell University Press, 1978. Contributor to medical journals.*

*   *   *

KEANEY, Marian 1944-

PERSONAL: Born March 26, 1944, in Sligo, Ireland; daughter of Patrick (a farmer) and Mary Ellen (a sales representative; maiden name, Reynolds) Keaney. *Education:* Attended convent school in Longford, Ireland. *Home:* 24 Newlands, Mullingar, Westmeath, Ireland. *Office:* Longford/Westmeath Joint Library Committee, Mullingar, Westmeath, Ireland.

CAREER: Longford/Westmeath Joint Library Committee, Mullingar, Ireland, library assistant, 1962-68, assistant librarian, 1968-73; Regional Technical College, Athlone, Ireland, librarian, 1973-74; Longford/Westmeath Joint Library Committee, county librarian and secretary, 1974—. *Member:* Library Association of Ireland (member of executive board, 1975-77), Irish Red Cross Society, Gorta, Mullingar Historical and Archaeological Society, Mullingar Art Guild. *Awards, honors:* Library Association of Ireland fellowship, 1968.

WRITINGS: Westmeath Authors: A Biographical and Bibliographical Study, Longford/Westmeath Joint Library Committee, 1969; *They Brought the Good News,* Veritas, 1980.

Contributor to magazines, including *Deirdre, Midland Topic, Books Ireland, Era,* and *Teathbha.*

WORK IN PROGRESS: Only the Rock Remained, a historical novel for children; research on the life and works of poet Padraic Colum, on artist Robert Gregory, and on the literary and local history of Westmeath.

SIDELIGHTS: Marian Keaney wrote: "*Westmeath Authors* was the first work of its kind to be published in Ireland. It was originally presented as a thesis in support of application for a fellowship from the Library Association of Ireland. *Irish Times* described it as 'a serious valuable work of bibliography and biography.'

"In recent years I have done research on various aspects of Irish biography, particularly the life and work of Padraic Colum. *They Brought the Good News* deals with the lives of eight twentieth-century Irish missionaries who I consider have made major contributions in the fields of education, medicine, and sociology. My children's novel is set in nineteenth-century Ireland and Scotland, during the time of the Great Famine."

BIOGRAPHICAL/CRITICAL SOURCES: Helen Maher, *Roscommon Authors,* Roscommon County Library, 1978.

* * *

KEARNS, Doris Helen 1943-

PERSONAL: Born January 4, 1943, in Rockville Centre, N.Y.; daughter of Michael Alouisius (a bank examiner) and Helen Witt (Miller) Kearns; married Richard Goodwin (a writer). *Education:* Colby College, B.A. (magna cum laude), 1964; Harvard University, Ph.D., 1968. *Religion:* Roman Catholic. *Office:* 78 Mt. Auburn St., Cambridge, Mass. 02139.

CAREER: U.S. Government, Washington, D.C., State Department intern, 1963, House of Representatives intern, 1965, Department of Health, Education, and Welfare, research associate, 1966, special assistant to Willard Wirtz, Department of Labor, 1967, special assistant to President Lyndon Johnson, 1968; Harvard University, Cambridge, Mass., assistant professor, 1969-71, associate professor of government, 1972—, assistant director of Institute of Politics, 1971—, member of faculty council. Special consultant to President Johnson, 1969-73. Hostess of television show, "What's the Big Idea," WGBH-TV, Boston, Mass., 1972; political analyst for news desk, WBZ-TV, Boston. Member of Democratic party platform committee, 1972; member of Women's Political Caucus in Massachusetts (member of steering committee, 1972—). Trustee of Wesleyan University and Robert F. Kennedy Foundation.

MEMBER: American Political Science Association, Council on Foreign Relations (member of nominating and reform committees, 1972), Women Involved (chairman and member of board of advisers), Group for Applied Psychoanalysis, Phi Beta Kappa, Phi Sigma Iota, Signet Society. *Awards, honors:* Fulbright fellow, 1966; Outstanding Young Woman of the Year award from Phi Beta Kappa, 1966; White House fellow, 1967.

WRITINGS: Lyndon Johnson and the American Dream, Harper, 1976; (contributor) Marc Pachter, editor, *Telling Lives: The Biographer's Art,* New Republic Books, 1979. Contributor of articles to *New Republic.*

SIDELIGHTS: Doris Kearns first met Lyndon Johnson at a White House dance in 1967. At the time, she was a White House fellow working as special assistant to Willard Wirtz. She had recently co-authored an article for *New Republic*

entitled "How to Remove LBJ in 1968," in which she was sharply critical of Johnson's foreign policy. Johnson was aware of her criticism when he met her, but instead of arguing with her, he danced with her. At the end of the evening, he suggested that she be assigned to work with him in the White House. In befriending Kearns, Johnson had apparently heeded the advice of John Roche, one of his aides, who told him that having a White House fellow who was critical of the administration would cause him to appear open-minded and unthreatened by the growing anti-war sentiment in America. When Johnson eventually asked Kearns to help him write his memoirs, she agreed; after his retirement, she traveled to the Johnson ranch in Austin, Texas, on weekends, holidays, and vacations to help Johnson write the "official" version of his presidency.

Johnson's choice of Kearns as his biographer was one many critics found noteworthy. In addition to begin critical of his administration, she was, as a Harvard graduate student, a member of a group Johnson had long felt inferior to. Johnson was certain that many of the elite Eastern intellectuals despised him, but with Kearns (as one of their own) telling his story, he believed that the group he felt excluded from would finally, if not accept him, at least listen to his story. He had, as a writer for *New Yorker* put it, become "preoccupied with the verdict of history." He wanted to be remembered as a successful president; he sought out writers who would be friendly in their judgment of him. Johnson is reported to have told Kearns that she reminded him of his mother, and as he spent more and more time with her, he apparently came to believe that she felt sympathetic towards him and that she would write a flattering portrayal of him.

In an article in *New York Review of Books,* Garry Wills recounted Johnson's history of manipulating reporters in order to elicit favorable stories from them. Johnson was most persistent in his efforts to overcome whatever objections a writer might have had to complying with his wishes. According to Wills, when Kearns objected to working with Johnson because "she had to study, do social work, [and] meet different people," Johnson "promised her hot-and-cold running scholars, poor people, and millionaire bachelors at the turn of a spigot." His promises were, said Wills, very much in character. "It was the old routine; but Ms. Kearns presents it as something peculiar to her and her situation." Was she not aware, he asked, that "this was the standard Johnson pitch?" *Nation's* Ronnie Dugger, however, believed that Kearns was aware of Johnson's tactic. He agreed that Johnson probably tried to hoodwink her, but "she saw the dangers, and she is no fool."

In helping Johnson compose his memoirs, Kearns was hindered by Johnson's desire to sound "presidential." She wanted him to include, for example, a particularly astute quote about Wilbur Mills. Johnson had observed that Mills, who was reluctant to allow any bill to come out of his Ways and Means Committee unless he was certain of its passage in the House, was "always so concerned about saving his own face that someday that man will fall on his ass." Johnson was enraged Kearns found the quote suitable. It was not included, Johnson had his way, and his book, *The Vantage Point: Perspectives of the Presidency, 1963-1969,* was criticized for being, as Paul D. Zimmerman of *Newsweek* put it, "dry stuff, conforming to Johnson's notion of Presidentiality—formal, remote, like his speeches on television." Kearns agreed with Zimmerman, calling the Johnson memoirs stilted, bureaucratic, and tedious. He felt, she wrote in *New Republic,* that he "had to drain the color from his life in order to give it the appropriate dignity."

Kearns had the opportunity, three years after Johnson's death, to include some of Johnson's more colorful quotes in her own book, *Lyndon Johnson and the American Dream.* According to Larry McMurtry of *Saturday Review,* however, Kearns failed to capture the flavor of Johnson's speech. Although he called her analysis of Johnson tactful and intelligent, he wrote that since Johnson "knew he was . . . speaking to history, he made the characteristic mistake of toning himself down—either that or Miss Kearns herself toned him down, out of tact. But a toned-down Johnson is not the real Johnson: his vulgarity was an element of his greatness, and profanity the true accent of his passion."

As Kearns sees it, Johnson's political ambitions, his quest for power, and his plan for the "Great Society" all stemmed from an effort to free himself from the conflict he felt torn by from birth. His mother was shy, genteel, and dignified; his father was easy-going, flamboyant, and frequently illmannered. "Without appearing to labor the point," wrote McMurtry, "Miss Kearns demonstrates again and again how Johnson's youthful need to keep the peace between his parents affected his style as a politician, a style dependent upon endless and often very subtle personal negotiation." Paul Zimmerman praised Kearns for "producing a sensible, scrupulous, compassionate study of the connections between Lyndon Johnson's psychological drives and his political fortunes. . . . She identifies those repeated patterns of mind and behavior that served Johnson splendidly as Senate Majority Leader in the 1950s but conspired to undo him a decade later in an institutional setting with wholly different demands."

Kearns commented on the difficulty Johnson had in making the transition from president to civilian. "Having been so obsessive about the pursuit of power for so many years, he had no other purpose," she wrote in her *New Republic* article, "so he had to invent an imitation power. He was so used to staff meetings each morning with men from Capitol Hill, or with cabinet officials and White House aides, that he had to imitate those sessions back on the ranch. He would call conferences to decide which fields should be plowed at what time, which cows should be given what medicine, and which tractors would be fixed when. He would force his field hands to write out assignments so that he could check up on them in the afternoon."

One of the more controversial aspects of the book was Kearns's analysis of Johnson's dreams; several critics wondered about the validity of her interpretations. "She seems," wrote Wills, "insufficiently aware of the fact that dreams told in a persuasive context cannot have the evidentiary value of those discussed in analysis." McMurtry, however, wrote that Kearns "makes a tentative, fair, never very dogmatic use of the tools of psychoanalysis," and that no other biography of Johnson is "likely to offer a sharper, more intimate portrait of Lyndon Johnson in full psychological undress." James M. Perry of *National Observer* found that although Kearns presents "some pretty heavy character analysis amounting to psychohistory" in her book, "she is honest enough to admit that there are vast empty spaces in what we know about the human mind and human behavior."

In the *New Republic* article, Kearns wrote that she would rather have waited a number of years before writing *Lyndon Johnson and the American Dream,* so that she could "really understand and convey its human value." But she was a young Harvard professor, and as she said, "I had to publish." The book is at its best, wrote David Halberstam of the *New York Times Book Review,* when Kearns is "personal," when she draws upon the "special relationship and special access" to Johnson. "When she is not personal, when she is doing

the requisite work for her tenure, it slogs along, often dull, not very original, shedding relatively little new light." *Spectator*'s Peter Jenkins said, however, "This is no mere I-was-confidante-of-the-President memoir but a thoroughly serious piece of research." McMurtry called the book "a triumph—partly Miss Kearns's and partly Lyndon Johnson's." Johnson's choice of Kearns as his biographer was both shrewd and wise, McMurtry wrote, for "the effort she has made to untangle the psychic knots of his character and relate them to his actions is . . . extremely loyal, requiring much empathy and a long application of effort and intelligence."

BIOGRAPHICAL/CRITICAL SOURCES: Newsweek, May 31, 1976; *New York Times Book Review,* June 6, 1976; *New Yorker,* June 7, 1976; *Saturday Review,* June 12, 1976; *National Observer,* June 19, 1976; *New York Review of Books,* June 24, 1976; *Commentary,* August, 1976; *New Republic,* August 7 & 14, 1976, March 3, 1979; *Nation,* September 4, 1976; *New Statesman,* October 8, 1976; *Spectator,* October 16, 1976; *Times Literary Supplement,* December 10, 1976.*

—Sketch by Mary Sullivan

*   *   *

KELEN, Emery 1896-1978

OBITUARY NOTICE—See index for *CA* sketch: Born December 22, 1896, in Gyor, Hungary; died October 9, 1978, in Vienna, Austria. Artist, caricaturist, journalist, and author. Having left Hungary in 1919, Kelen was a newspaper correspondant in Europe before immigrating to the United States in 1938. A naturalized U.S. citizen, Kelen wrote a syndicated newspaper column before becoming television director for the United Nations. He later served as a United Nations radio newscaster. His television coverage of historic speeches before the United Nations General Assembly won him an Emmy and a Peabody Award. Among his writings are *Peace in Their Time: Men Who Led Us In and Out of War, 1914-1945, Hammarskjold: The Dangerous Man, The Political Platypus,* and *Hammarskjold: The Political Man.* Kelen's books for children include *Yussuf the Ostrich, Food for the Valley, Stamps Tell the Story of John F. Kennedy,* and *Mr. Nonsense: A Life of Edward Lear.* (Date of death provided by daughter, Julia Kelen.)

*   *   *

KELLETT, Arnold 1926-

PERSONAL: Born May 13, 1926, in Wibsey, Bradford, West Yorkshire, England; son of Horace and Gladys (Denton) Kellett; married Patricia Horsfall (a library assistant), July 25, 1953; children: Ruth, Rachel, Ann, Timothy. *Education:* University of Liverpool, B.A. (with first class honors), 1952; also attended Sorbonne, University of Paris. *Politics:* Independent. *Home:* 22 Aspin Oval, Knaresborough, North Yorkshire, England.

CAREER: Teacher of chemistry and modern languages at Methodist school in Harrogate, England, 1952-56; King James's School, Knaresborough, North Yorkshire, England, teacher of French, German, and religion, 1956-64, head of modern languages department, 1964—. Methodist lay preacher, 1953—. Town of Knaresborough, member of town council, 1976—, mayor, 1979-80. *Military service:* British Army, Intelligence Corps, 1944-48. *Member:* Yorkshire Dialect Society.

WRITINGS: (Editor) *Prayers for Patients,* Arthur James, 1964, *Isms and Ologies,* Epworth, 1965; (editor) *Maupassant: Contes du surnaturel* (title means "Maupassant: Tales of the

Supernatural''), Pergamon, 1969; *The Knaresborough Story,* Advertiser Press, 1972; *Heros de France* (title means ''Heroes of France''), Dent, 1973; (editor and translator) *Tales of Supernatural Terror,* Pan Books, 1973; *Le Prisonnier en pyjama* (title means ''Prisoner in Pajamas''), Dent, 1974; (translator) *A Night of Terror* (Maupassant stories in simplified English), Oxford University Press, 1976; (editor and translator) *Diary of a Madman and Other Tales of Horror,* Pan Books, 1976; *French for Science Students,* Macdonald & Evans, 1976; *Basic French,* Macdonald & Evans, 1977, 2nd edition, 1978; *Harrogate,* Dalesman Press, 1978; *The Queen's Church,* Friends of Knaresborough Parish Church, 1978; *Know Your Yorkshire,* Dalesman Press, 1980. Writer for local radio programs. Contributor of articles and poems to magazines, including *Dalesman* and *Methodist Recorder.*

WORK IN PROGRESS: Research on local history.

SIDELIGHTS: Kellett told *CA:* ''Writing is an escape from the world of full-time teaching. My principal interests are local history and religion, but I am fascinated by a great variety of subjects. My heroes are universal and wide-ranging men, especially Blaise Pascal and John Wesley.

''This is the age of the narrow specialist and the type-cast writer. I would like to try all kinds of writing—fiction as well as nonfiction. But time is a problem, as is the present economic restraint on publishing in Britain.

''I am currently organizing literary weekends based on Harrogate to introduce visitors to the places and landscapes that have inspired Yorkshire writers from the Brontes to James Herriot.''

*   *   *

KELLOGG, James C. III   1915-1980

OBITUARY NOTICE: Born in 1915 in New York, N.Y.; died of a stroke, December 29, 1980, in Point Pleasant, N.J. Stockbroker and author. A member of the New York Stock Exchange since 1936, James Kellogg served as governor and later as chairman of the board of governors of the exchange. At the time of his death, he was the senior board member of the Port Authority of New York and New Jersey. He was also a senior partner of Spear, Leeds & Kellogg, a New York stockbroker firm. With William E. Downie, Kellogg wrote *The Stock Market Crash of 1929.* Obituaries and other sources: *New York Times,* December 30, 1980.

*   *   *

KELLY, John Rivard   1939-

PERSONAL: Born December 7, 1939, in Chicago, Ill.; married, 1965. *Education:* Mexico City College, A.B., 1961; University of Southern California, M.A., 1964, Ph.D., 1967. *Office:* Department of Spanish and Portuguese, University of California, Santa Barbara, Calif. 93106.

CAREER: University of California, Santa Barbara, assistant professor of Spanish and Portuguese, 1965—. *Member:* Modern Language Association of America, Philological Association of the Pacific Coast, Pacific Coast Council on Latin American Studies.

WRITINGS: Pedro Prado, Twayne, 1974; (with Clement L. McGowan) *Top-Down Structured Programming Techniques,* Van Nostrand, 1975. Contributor to language and Latin American studies journals.*

KELLY, (Alison) Linda   1936-

PERSONAL: Born October 1, 1936, in Kent, England; daughter of Ronald Guthrie (a writer) and Mary Cecilia McNair Scott; married Laurence Kelly (in business; a writer), April 20, 1963; children: Rosanna, Rachel, Nicholas. *Education:* Attended Byam Shaw School of Art, 1954-56. *Religion:* Roman Catholic. *Home:* 44 Ladbroke Grove, London W.11, England. *Agent:* Richard Scott Simon, 32 College Cross, London N.1, England.

CAREER: Vogue, London, England, copy writer, 1957-60, travel editor, 1960-63; writer, 1963—.

WRITINGS: The Marvellous Boy: The Life and Myth of Thomas Chatterton, Weidenfeld & Nicolson, 1971; *The Young Romantics: Paris, 1827-37,* Random House, 1976; *The Kemble Era: John Philip Kemble, Sarah Siddons, and the London Stage,* Random House, 1980. Contributor to magazines and newspapers, including *Reader's Digest, Washington Post,* and *Times Literary Supplement.*

WORK IN PROGRESS: Women of the Revolution, a book on the role of women in the French Revolution, 1789.

SIDELIGHTS: Kelly told *CA:* ''French is my second language, and my early interest in French history and literature has been stimulated by my marriage—my husband is French on his mother's side. Both of my husband's parents were writers—his father, Sir David Kelly, was the author of *The Ruling Few.* My father was a novelist and reviewer, and two of my sisters write, so writing is in the family. My husband is the author of a recent biography of the Russian poet Lermontov.''

*   *   *

KELSEY, Robert J(ohn)   1927-

PERSONAL: Born February 24, 1927, in Los Angeles, Calif.; son of Roland (an attorney) and Mary (a writer; maiden name, Tudor) Gray; married Theodosia Thompson (an occupational therapist), June 15, 1950; children: Robert J., Jr., Patricia T., Charles R., Christopher E. *Education:* University of Massachusetts, B.S., 1949. *Home and office:* 271 Orchard Pl., Ridgewood, N.J. 07450.

CAREER: U.S. Department of Agriculture, Processed Products Inspection Division, Winter Haven, Fla., inspector, 1949-51; Curtice Brothers Co., Rochester, N.Y., quality control manager and assistant plant manager, 1951-55; *Food Engineering,* New York City, engineering editor, 1955-59; *Modern Packaging,* engineering editor, 1959-66, editor-in-chief, 1966-71, executive editor, 1971-73; *Food and Drug Packaging,* New York City, technical editor, 1973—. Packaging consultant, 1973—; director of Packaging Education Foundation; adjunct professor at Rutgers University, 1973—. *Military service:* U.S. Navy, 1944-46. *Member:* American Society of Mechanical Engineers, American Society for Testing Materials, Packaging Institute (fellow), Society of Packaging and Handling Engineers, Sierra Club, Adirondack Mountain Club.

WRITINGS: Walking in the Wild, Crowell, 1973; *Packaging in Today's Society,* St. Regis Paper Co., 1978; *The World of Packaging Technology: A Handbook,* Magazines for Industry, 1982.

SIDELIGHTS: Kelsey commented: ''I have spent more than thirty years applying principles of structural design, mechanical engineering, and microbiology to the solution of problems in packaging development, packaging line operations, and materials handling.

"In seven years as an independent packaging consultant, I have been responsible for project management, packaging coordination, machine specification and redesign, and the design and specification of inner and outer containers for products ranging from small consumer items to large industrial unit loads. "Areas in which I have worked include foods, medical devices, soft goods, household and industrial chemicals, and industrial hardware and OEM components.

"My training and initial experience has provided a solid background for my consulting work. The U.S. Navy contributed a practical foundation in mechanical engineering. A degree in food engineering added a knowledge of processing and packaging methods, chemistry, and microbiology. The U.S. Department of Agriculture's Processed Products Inspection Service provided two years in quality control, testing methods, and product development. Six more years as an assistant plant superintendent in the canning and freezing of perishable foods developed an extensive knowledge of package development, the design and specification of materials handling and packaging equipment and machinery maintenance. I continue my development with regular courses in the technology and mechanics of packaging.

"In seventeen years as engineering and chief editor, I have had an unparalleled opportunity to study the design and action of over six hundred packaging operations and technical packaging developments in the United States, Europe, and the Far East."

AVOCATIONAL INTERESTS: Backpacking, canoeing, pre-Columbian Indian culture, ski touring.

*   *   *

KENNAWAY, James (Pebles Ewing)   1928-1968

PERSONAL: Born June 5, 1928, in Perthshire, Scotland; died in an automobile accident, December 21, 1968, near London, England; son of Charles Gray and Marjory Helen Kennaway; married wife, Susan, 1951; children: Emma, Jane, Guy, David. *Education:* Attended Trinity College, Oxford.

CAREER: Longmans, Green (publisher), London, England, editor, 1951-57; writer, 1957-68. *Military service:* British Army, Cameron Highlanders, 1946-48. *Member:* Royal Institution, Chelsea Arts Club, Raffles Club.

WRITINGS—Novels: *Tunes of Glory,* Harper, 1956; *Household Ghosts,* Atheneum, 1961; *The Bells of Shoreditch,* Longmans, Green, 1963, Atheneum, 1964; *The Mind Benders: A Novel of Suspense,* Atheneum, 1963; *Some Gorgeous Accident,* Atheneum, 1967; *The Cost of Living Like This,* Atheneum, 1969; *Silence,* edited by Lynn Hughes, J. Cape, 1972.

Screenplays, excepted as noted: "Tunes of Glory" (adapted from own novel), United Artists, 1960; "The Mind Benders" (adapted from own novel), Anglo-Amalgamated, 1963; "Country Dance" (play; adapted from own novel *Household Ghosts*) first produced in Hampstead, England, at Hampstead Theatre Club, 1967; "Brotherly Love" (adapted from own play "Country Dance"), Metro-Goldwyn-Mayer, 1970.

SIDELIGHTS: Frank Littler of the *New York Times Book Review* found James Kennaway's *The Cost of Living Like This* a "hard novel to understand." The principal characters in the book, which was published posthumously, are Julian, an economist who is dying of cancer, his wife, Christabel, and his lover, Sally. The story involves the interrelationship of the three and focuses on the women's jealousy and their

reactions to Julian as he wrestles with and eventually succumbs to his disease. Paul Bailey, writing for *London Magazine,* proclaimed *The Cost of Living Like This* a brilliant book, saying that "for once the word 'brilliant' really is appropriate—the writing sparkles, even in the book's darkest moments." In *Punch,* David Pryce-Jones criticized Kennaway's melodramatic tone and his "gimmicky narrative method." Bailey was also bothered by this, noting that "once or twice the heightened language rings false. . . . But these are mere quibbles when set beside the many sad truths about human nature it [the book] manages to convey. Had he lived," declared Bailey, "Kennaway might well have gone on to produce a masterpiece."

Kennaway adapted his novel *Household Ghosts* for the stage, under the title "Country Dance," and later adapted it for the screen, under the title "Brotherly Love." The movie version, starring Peter O'Toole and Susannah York, was directed by J. Lee Thompson. The film explores the incestous relationship between a brother (O'Toole) and his sister (York). "The theme is ancient," observed Stanley Kauffmann in the *New Republic.* "But, to supply a double and symbolic doom, it is intertwined here and there with a theme of declining aristocracy, which makes it somewhat remote for us." In his review for the *New York Times,* Vincent Canby complained that the movie "is so tasteful . . . that it seems downright platonic, which, under the circumstances, is a bit of a bore."

BIOGRAPHICAL/CRITICAL SOURCES: Twentieth Century, April, 1957; *Observer,* July 2, 1967; *New York Times,* December 25, 1968; April 23, 1970; *Publishers Weekly,* January 20, 1969; *Life,* September 5, 1969; *New York Times Book Review,* September 14, 1969; *Punch,* October 1, 1969; *London Magazine,* December, 1969; *New Republic,* May 9, 1970; *Times Literary Supplement,* September 15, 1972; *Listener,* March 1, 1973.*

*   *   *

KENNEDY, Adrienne (Lita)   1931-

PERSONAL: Born September 13, 1931, in Pittsburgh, Pa.; daughter of Cornell Wallace and Etta (Haugabook) Hawkins; married Joseph C. Kennedy, May 15, 1953; children: Joseph C., Adam. *Education:* Ohio State University, B.A., 1952; graduate study at Columbia University, 1954-56; also studied at New School for Social Research, American Theatre Wing, Circle in the Square Theatre School, and Edward Albee's workshop. *Home:* 172 West 79th St., New York, N.Y. 10024. *Agent:* Bridget Aschenberg, 40 West 57th St., New York, N.Y. 10019.

CAREER: Playwright. Lecturer in writing at Yale University, 1972-74. *Member:* Actors' Studio. *Awards, honors:* Obie distinguished play award from *Village Voice,* 1964, for "Funnyhouse of a Negro"; John Simon Guggenheim memorial fellowship, 1967; Rockefeller grants, 1967-69, 1970; National Endowment for the Arts grant, 1973; Stanley award for writing plays; New England Theatre Conference grant.

WRITINGS—Plays: *Funnyhouse of a Negro* (one-act; first produced Off-Broadway at Circle in the Square Theatre, 1962), Samuel French, 1969; "The Owl Answers" (one-act; first produced in Westport, Conn., at White Barn Theatre, 1963; produced Off-Broadway at Public Theatre, January 12, 1969), published in *Cities in Bezique,* Samuel French, 1969; "A Lesson in a Dead Language" (first produced in 1964), published in *Collision Course,* edited by Edward Parone, Random House, 1968; "A Rat's Mass" (first produced in Boston, Mass., by the Theatre Company, April, 1966; produced Off-Broadway at La Mama Experimental Theatre

Club, November, 1969), published in *New Black Playwrights,* edited by William Couch, Jr., Louisiana State University Press, 1968; "A Beast's Story" (one-act; first produced in 1966; produced Off-Broadway at Public Theatre, January 12, 1969), published in *Cities in Bezique* (see above); (with John Lennon and Victor Spinetti) *The Lennon Play: In His Own Write* (adapted from Lennon's *In His Own Write* and *A Spaniard in the Works;* first produced in London by National Theatre, 1967; produced in Albany, N.Y., at Arena Summer Theatre, August, 1969), Simon & Schuster, 1972; "Sun: A Poem for Malcolm X Inspired by His Murder" (first produced on the West End at Royal Court Theatre, 1968), published in *Scripts 1,* November, 1971; "Boats," first produced in Los Angeles, 1969; "An Evening With Dead Essex," first produced in New York, 1973; "A Lancashire Lad" (for children), first produced in Albany, N.Y., at Governor Nelson A. Rockefeller Empire State Plaza Performing Arts Center, May, 1980.

Contributor of plays to anthologies, including: *Kuntu Drama,* edited by Paul C. Harrison, Grove Press; *New American Plays,* edited by William M. Hoffman, Hill & Wang, 1968.

SIDELIGHTS: "While almost every black playwright in the country is fundamentally concerned with realism . . . Miss Kennedy is weaving some kind of dramatic fabric of poetry," Clive Barnes commented in the *New York Times.* "What she writes is a mosaic of feeling, with each tiny stone stained with the blood of the gray experience. Of all our black writers, Miss Kennedy is most concerned with white, with white relationship, with white blood. She thinks black, but she remembers white. It gives her work an eddying ambiguity."

In her complex and introspective plays, Martin Duberman remarked in *Partisan Review,* Kennedy is "absorbed by her private fantasies, her interior world. She disdains narrative, 'everyday' language and human interaction; the dream, the myth, the poem are her domain." James Hatch and Ted Shine also noted that "in a tradition in which the major style has long been realism, Adrienne Kennedy has done what few black playwrights have attempted: used form to project an interior reality and thereby created a rich and demanding theatrical style."

Kennedy's first play, "Funnyhouse of a Negro," examines the psychological problems of Sarah, a young mulatto woman who lives with a Jewish poet in a boarding house run by a white landlady. Dealing with the last moments before Sarah's suicide, the play consists of what Doris Abramson called "a series of mad fantasies." Tortured by an identity crisis, Sarah is "lost in a nightmare world where black is evil and white is good, where various personages, including Queen Victoria, Patrice Lumumba, and Jesus Himself, materialize to mock her," said *New Yorker*'s Edith Oliver. "Funnyhouse of a Negro" earned Kennedy an Obie award and, noted *Variety,* a reputation as "a gifted writer with a distinctive dramatic imagination."

"The Owl Answers" was described by Oliver as another fantasy of "a forbidden and glorious white world, viewed with a passion and frustration that shred the spirit and nerves and mind of the dispossessed heroine." This time the illegitimate child of a black cook and the wealthiest white man in Georgia, the heroine is riding on a New York subway. The subway doors become the doors to the chapel of the Tower of London through which appear masked historical characters, including Chaucer, Shakespeare, Anne Boleyn, and the Virgin Mary, who at times unmask to become other characters, such as the heroine's mother and father.

"A Beast's Story," produced with "The Owl Answers" under the title "Cities in Bezique," was described as more elaborate, hallucinatory and obscure than the first play. It draws analogies, said Steve Tennen in *Show Business,* "between inhuman beings and man's bestial tendencies." Kennedy's later play, "A Rat's Mass," staged as a parody mass, was also abstract, centering around the relationship between a black brother and sister and their childhood involvement with the white girl next door.

In all of these plays, Kennedy's writing is poetic and symbolic; plot and dialogue are secondary to effect. Her works have been defined as nightmarish rituals and as poetic dances. Marilyn Stasio explained in *Cue* : "Kennedy is a poet, working with disjointed time sequences, evocative images, internalized half-thoughts, and incantatory language to create a netherworld of submerged emotions surfacing only in fragments. Events are crucial only for the articulated feelings they evoke."

Kennedy's reliance on such devices as masks, characters who become other characters, characters played by more than one actor, and Christian symbolism makes her work difficult, and several reviewers have commented that they do not understand her plays. But even those who concluded, as did Walter Kerr, that the plays "don't work," were engaged by the intensity of the theatrical experience. As Kerr said of the playwright, "There is a spare, unsentimental intensity about her that promises to drive a dagger home some day."

During 1971, Kennedy joined five other women playwrights to found the Women's Theatre Council, a theatre cooperative devoted to producing the works of women playwrights and providing opportunities for women in other aspects of the theatre, such as directing and acting. Mel Gussow of the *New York Times* noted that the council's "founding sisters all come from Off Off Broadway, are exceeding prolific, have had their plays staged throughout the United States and in many foreign countries and feel neglected by the New York commercial theater. Each has a distinctive voice, but their work is related in being largely non-realistic and experimental. The women feel unified as innovators and by their artistic consciousness."

Kennedy branched out into juvenile theatre in 1980 after being commissioned by the Empire State Youth Theatre Institute. "A Lancashire Lad," which Frank Rich described as "a beautiful play of great poetry and feeling," is a fictionalized version of Charles Chaplin's childhood. Narrated by the hero, the play traces his life growing up in Dickensian England and beginning his career in the British music halls. Although an entertaining musical, the show confronts the poverty and pain of Chaplin's youth. Praising Kennedy's language for achieving "powerful emotional effects with the sparest of means," Rich concluded: "The difference between 'The Lancashire Lad' and an adult play is, perhaps, the intellectual simplicity of its ambitions. Yet that simplicity can also be theater magic in its purest and most eloquent form."

BIOGRAPHICAL/CRITICAL SOURCES: New York Times, January 15, 1964, June 20, 1968, July 9, 1968, January 13, 1969, January 19, 1969, November 1, 1969, February 22, 1972, May 21, 1980, February 15, 1981; *New Yorker,* January 25, 1964, January 25, 1969; *Observer Review,* June 23, 1968; *International Times,* September 22, 1968; Doris E. Abramson, *Negro Playwrights in the American Theater, 1925-1959,* Columbia University Press, 1969; *Cue,* January 18, 1969, October 4, 1969; *Show Business,* January 25, 1969, October

4, 1969; *Variety,* January 29, 1969; *Village Voice,* August 14, 1969, September 25, 1969; *Partisan Review,* Number 3, 1969; James V. Hatch and Ted Shine, editors, *Black Theater U.S.A.,* Free Press, 1974.*

* * *

KENNY, Ellsworth Newcomb   1909-1971
(Ellsworth Newcomb)

OBITUARY NOTICE—See index for *CA* sketch: Born December 16, 1909, in Washington, D.C.; died November 15, 1971. Author of several novels and nonfiction works and contributor to various magazines and newspapers. Among Kenny's books are *Anchor for Her Heart, Window on the Sea,* and *Three Came Riding.* In addition, she collaborated with her husband, Hugh Kenny, on books such as *Miracle Fabrics, Alchemy to Atoms, African Adventures,* and *Miracle Metals.* (Date of death provided by sister, Holly N. Leichert.)

* * *

KENT, Deborah Ann   1948-

PERSONAL: Born October 11, 1948, in Little Falls, N.J.; daughter of Gordon L. and Doris M. (Vandermay) Kent; married Richard Conrad Stein (a writer), December 15, 1979. *Education:* Oberlin College, B.A., 1969; Smith College, M.S.W., 1971; Instituto Allende, M.F.A., 1976. *Home:* 1 Morningside Circle, Little Falls, N.J. 07424. *Agent:* Amy Berkower, 21 West 26th St., New York, N.Y.

CAREER: Associated with University Settlement, New York, N.Y., 1971-75, and Centro de Crecimiento, San Miguel de Allende, Mexico, 1977-80; writer.

WRITINGS: Belonging, Dial, 1978. Contributor to *Disabled U.S.A.* and *Journal of Visual Impairment and Blindness.*

WORK IN PROGRESS: Cindy, for teenagers.

* * *

KENWARD, Michael   1945-

PERSONAL: Born July 12, 1945, in Brighton, England. *Education:* University of Sussex, B.Sc. *Home:* Grange Cottage, Staplefield, West Sussex, England. *Agent:* Murray Pollinger, 4 Garrick St., London WC2 9BH, England. *Office:* Commonwealth House, New Oxford St., London, England.

CAREER: Writer. *Member:* Association of British Science Writers. *Awards, honors:* Glaxo British Science Writers Award.

WRITINGS: Potential Energy, Cambridge University Press, 1976. Contributor to scientific journals.

* * *

KENWORTHY, Brian J(ohn)   1920-

PERSONAL: Born December 7, 1920, in Stroud, England; son of John Frederick (a farmer) and Constance I. (Foster) Kenworthy; married C. Winifred Rotter, September 2, 1946 (died February 24, 1974); married Mary A. Forsyth Brown (an assistant head of a primary school, October 21, 1974; children: James Brian, David Clive, Ruth Helen Kenworthy Easton. *Education:* University of Bristol, B.A. (with first class honors), 1942, diploma in education, 1943; University of Aberdeen, Ph.D., 1952. *Home:* 91 Duthie Ter., Aberdeen, Scotland. *Office:* Department of German, King's College, University of Aberdeen, Old Aberdeen AB9 2UB, Scotland.

CAREER: Teacher of modern languages at grammar school in Bristol, England, 1943-46; Control Commission for Ger-

many, interpreter and translator, 1946-47; University of Aberdeen, Aberdeen, Scotland, assistant lecturer, 1947-52, lecturer, 1952-68, senior lecturer in German, 1968—.

WRITINGS: Georg Kaiser, Basil Blackwell, 1957; (translator with W. A. Coupe) W. Braunbek, *The Drama of the Atom,* Oliver & Boyd, 1958; (with F. M. Fowler and Margarete Wuerzel) *A Manual of German Prose Composition for Advanced Students,* Harrap, 1966; (contributor) Edwin Rhodes, editor, *First Steps in German Literature,* Magee University College, 1968; (contributor of translations) Kaiser, *Five Plays,* J. Calder, 1971; (contributor) H. A. Pausch and E. Reinhold, editors, *Georg Kaiser Symposium,* Agora Verlag, 1980; (contributor of translations and author of introduction) Kaiser, *Plays,* Volume II, J. Calder, 1981.

In German: (Editor, and author of introduction and notes) G. Kaiser, *Die Koralle, Gas I, Gas II* (title means "The Coral, Gas I and Gas II"), Harrap, 1968; (editor and author of introduction and notes) Hermann Sudermann, *Litauische Geschichten* (title means "Lithuanian Tales"), Harrap, 1971; (contributor) A. Arnold, editor, Interpretationen zu Georg Kaiser, Klett, 1980. Contributor to journals.

WORK IN PROGRESS: Research on nineteenth-century Austrian realist writers.

SIDELIGHTS: Kenworthy told *CA:* "My writing has been primarily concerned with the illumination of aspects of German literature and, in particular, with making them more accessible to students of German. In my research on Austrian nineteenth-century realism, I hope to make a contribution towards a definition of the term by a study of the non-creative writings of Marie von Ebner-Eschenbach, L. Anzengruber, P. Rosegger, and Ferndinand von Saar (e.g., their letters, reviews, essays, aphorisms, etc.).''

* * *

KERN, Canyon
See RABORG, Frederick A(shton), Jr.

* * *

KERR, Howard Hastings   1931-

PERSONAL: Born November 23, 1931, in Los Angeles, Calif.; married, 1963; children: three. *Education:* University of California, Berkeley, B.A., 1953; University of California, Los Angeles, M.A., 1963, Ph.D., 1968. *Office:* Department of English, University of Illinois at Chicago Circle, Box 4348, Chicago, Ill. 60680.

CAREER: University of Illinois at Chicago Circle, Chicago, instructor, 1966-68, assistant professor, 1968-72, associate professor of English, 1972—. *Member:* Modern Language Association of America, American Studies Association.

WRITINGS: Mediums, and Spirit-Rappers, and Roaring Radicals: Spiritualism in American Literature, 1850-1900, University of Illinois Press, 1972; (contributor) *Literature and the Occult: Essays in Comparative Literature,* University of Texas, Arlington, 1977.*

* * *

KERR, Hugh Thomson   1909-

PERSONAL: Born July 1, 1909, in Chicago, Ill.; son of Hugh Thomson and Olive May (Boggs) Kerr; married Dorothy DePree, December 28, 1938; children: Stephen T. *Education:* Princeton University, A.B., 1931; Western Theological Seminary, Pittsburgh, Pa., B.D., 1934; University of Pittsburgh, M.A., 1934; University of Edinburgh, Ph.D., 1936; University of Tuebingen, Ph.D., 1936. *Home:* 707 Rosedale Rd.,

Princeton, N.J. 08540. *Office:* P.O. Box 29, Princeton, N.J. 08540.

CAREER: Ordained Presbyterian minister, 1934; Louisville Presbyterian Theological Seminary, Louisville, Ky., began as instructor, became associate professor of doctrinal theology, 1936-40; Princeton Theological Seminary, Princeton, N.J., associate professor, 1940-55, professor of systematic theology, 1955-74, Benjamin B. Warfield Professor of Theology Emeritus, 1974—, chairman of department of theology, 1949-56. Director of Westminster Foundation, 1954-65, and Gallahue Conference Quo Vadis, 1968; chairman of curriculum committee of Council on Theological Education, 1949-53; member of national council of Committee on Church Architecture; member of commission on women of World Council of Churches, 1950-54; North American delegate to World Alliance of Reformed Churches, 1945-60. *Member:* American Theological Society, Society of Biblical Literature, National Association of Bible Instructors, American Society of Church History, American Academy of Religion, American Association of University Professors, Duodecim. *Awards, honors:* Guggenheim fellow, 1960.

WRITINGS: A Compend of Luther's Theology, 1943, Westminster, 1966; *Positive Protestantism: An Interpretation of the Gospel,* Westminster, 1950; *Mystery and Meaning in the Christian Faith,* Ryerson, 1958; *What Divides Protestants Today,* Association Press, 1958; *Origen of Alexandria,* Princeton Theological Seminary, 1958; (editor) *Sons of the Prophets: Leaders in Protestantism From Princeton Seminary,* Princeton University Press, 1963; *Positive Protestantism: A Return to First Principles,* Prentice-Hall, 1963; (editor) John Calvin, *A Compend of the Institutes of the Christian Religion,* Westminster, 1964; (editor) *Readings in Christian Thought,* Abingdon, 1966; *Our Life in God's Light: Essays* (edited by John M. Mulder), Westminster, 1979; (editor) *Protestantism: A Concise Survey of Protestantism and Its Influence on American Religious and Social Traditions,* Barron's, 1979.

Contributor to *Interpreter's Bible, Encyclopedia Americana, Collier's Encyclopedia,* and *Book of Knowledge.* Contributor to theology journals. Associte editor of *Theology Today,* 1945-50, editor, 1950—.

BIOGRAPHICAL/CRITICAL SOURCES: Commonweal, February 1, 1980.*

*   *   *

KEW, Stephen 1947-

PERSONAL: Born March 7, 1947, in Reading, England; married wife, Katinka (an artist and illustrator). *Education:* Attended University of Sussex, 1966-70.

CAREER: Invalid Children's Aid Association, London, England, research officer, 1970-74; Institute of Family and Environmental Research, London, research associate, 1974—.

WRITINGS: Handicap and Family Crisis, Pitman, 1975; (with R. Rapoport, R. M. Rapoport, and Z. Strelitz) *Fathers, Mothers, and Others,* Routledge & Kegan Paul, 1977; *Fathers, Mothers, and Society,* Basic Books, 1977; *Crisis and Community Support,* Institute of Family and Environmental Research, 1980; (with R. Rapoport, M. Dower, and Strelitz) *Leisure Provision and People's Needs,* H.M.S.O., 1980.

WORK IN PROGRESS: Research on ethnic minorities.

KEYES, Edward 1927-

PERSONAL: Born July 20, 1927, in New York, N.Y.; son of Edward A. (a banker) and Jane M. Keyes; married Eileen Walsh (a teacher), April 14, 1952; children: seven. *Education:* Fordham University, B.A., 1949. *Residence:* New Rochelle, N.Y. *Agent:* Owen Laster, William Morris Agency, 1350 Avenue of the Americas, New York, N.Y. 10019.

CAREER: New Rochelle Standard-Star, New Rochelle, N.Y., reporter, 1949-50; *Yonkers Herald-Statesman,* Yonkers, N.Y., sports writer and editor, 1950-52; *Look* magazine, New York City, writer, 1952-54; *Quick* magazine, New York City, writer, 1952-54; free-lance writer for periodicals, newspapers, and radio programs, 1954-56; Sheraton Corporation of America, New York City, in public relations, 1956-62; B. Relin & Associates, New York City, in public relations, 1963-65; writer. *Military service:* U.S. Army Air Corps, 1945-46. *Awards, honors:* Special award for suspense nonfiction from Mystery Writers of America, 1976, for *The Michigan Murders.*

WRITINGS: (With Al Schacht) *My Own Particular Screwball,* Doubleday, 1955; (with Robin Moore) *The French Connection,* Little, Brown, 1969; *The Michigan Murders,* Reader's Digest Press, 1976; *Double Dare,* McGraw, 1981; *Interpol Anthology (Reader's Digest* Condensed Book), Reader's Digest Press, 1982. Contributor of articles to magazines, including *Look, Sports Illustrated,* and *Cosmopolitan.*

SIDELIGHTS: Keyes told *CA:* "I started out as a writer after college at twenty-two, but got sidetracked by economic realities when my budding family grew faster than my career. I was ten years in the commercial world before I could get back to it; and now, after some fifteen years as a full-time author, I can only wonder how it might have turned out had I risked all while still in my twenties. I know this: I could never work for anyone else again.

"Successful collaboration with Robin Moore on *The French Connection* enabled me to try my own in writing books. My first completed solo work was *The Michigan Murders,* which took me three years and, in the raw, consisted of some 1,300 pages of typescript, or perhaps 250,000 words. To my shock, the publisher who had contracted for this book rejected my manuscript as unmanageable. It took my agent eight months to find another publisher who would chance it. Judicious editing pared the manuscript by more than one half. The finished product subsequently was a major book club selection and winner of a special Mystery Writers Award.

"I say my first 'completed' solo work was *The Michigan Murders* because earlier, in 1969, I'd contracted with a publisher for a novel I was then calling "The Informer"—about an ordinary guy who gets himself involved with some illegal types, then is coerced by the law to betray them. I never could finish it and ultimately had to repay the publisher's advance. However, years later I happened upon a similar real-life situation in New York, the circumstances of which helped fill in the blanks I'd drawn in my own aborted effort. Fleshed out and embellished, this became the novel *Double Dare.*

"Writing is everything to me now. I love it, and hate it. I can't imagine doing anything else, yet it's often agony in the doing. I hate to start, but I'm disoriented and out of sorts when I neglect it. I feel guilty any day I haven't sat at the typewriter. There are days when nothing comes, and I torture myself with doubt. And there are days—or an hour, or just moments—when I know I've written something just the way I'd wanted, and the exhilaration and satisfaction are cosmic.

"My advice to writers is a cliche, perhaps, but the only eternal truth: write, write, write. Listen, observe, absorb; and write. Nobody can teach you to write, even if there are fundamental do's, don'ts, and techniques that *can* be learned. Either you have it in you or you don't. But the only way to find that out is to try it.

"Every writer has his own modus operandi. I'm a morning man, at my best—or at least my most ambitious, if not creative—from eight or nine in the morning to lunch about one or two in the afternoon. Occasionally, if I feel I'm on a 'hot roll,' I'll go back for another hour or two in the afternoon; but not often. Rarely, perhaps under deadline pressure or impelled by sudden inspiration, I can get a couple of hours in at night after dinner. I use typewriter only, a manual; if I had to write in longhand, or on an electric typewriter, I would not write. I do not write a rough draft, then go back and do revision after revision: I stumble, creep, crawl painstakingly through a single manuscript—each page, each paragraph, frequently each word—as though it will be the final version. And generally, except for inevitable editing, cutting, transposing, filling in, my 'rough draft' *is* essentially the finished product. For better or worse."

AVOCATIONAL INTERESTS: Golfing, swimming, bicycling, watching baseball and football.

*   *   *

KEYNES, Geoffrey Langdon   1887-

PERSONAL: Born March 25, 1887, in Cambridge, England; son of John Neville and Ada Florence (Brown) Keynes; married Margaret Elizabeth Darwin, May 12, 1917 (died, 1974); children: Richard Darwin, Quentin George, William Milo, Stephen John. *Education:* Attended Pembroke College, Oxford, 1906-10; Cambridge University, M.D. *Home:* Lammas House, Brinkley, Newmarket, Suffolk CB8 0SB, England.

CAREER: St. Bartholomew's Hospital, London, England, intern, 1910-13, Brackenbury Surgery Scholar and Willett Medal Operative Surgery Scholar, 1913, chief assistant, 1920, surgeon, 1929-56, consulting surgeon, 1956, surgeon emeritus. Consulting surgeon at New End Endocrine Clinic and City of London Truss Society. Hunterian Professor of Royal College of Surgeons, 1923, 1929, and 1945; Harveian Orator of Royal College of Physicians, 1958; Fitzpatrick Lecturer of Royal College of Physicians, 1966; Wilkins Lecturer of Royal Society, 1967; Osler Orator of Royal College of Physicians, 1968; Sir Arthur Sims Commonwealth Traveling Professor, 1956. Trustee of National Portrait Gallery, 1942-66, chairman, 1958-66; founder and chairman of William Blake Trust, 1949; Hunterian Trustee, 1958. Honorary fellow at Pembroke College, Oxford, and at Darwin College, Cambridge. *Military service:* Royal Army Medical Corps, 1914-18; served as surgical specialist with British Expeditionary Forces; became major; mentioned in dispatches. Royal Air Force, 1939-45; served as acting air vice-marshal and senior consulting surgeon.

MEMBER: Royal College of Surgeons (fellow; honorary librarian; member of council, 1944-52), Royal College of Physicians (fellow), Royal Society of Medicine (honorary fellow), Royal College of Obstetricians and Gynaecologists (fellow), Royal College of Surgeons of Canada (fellow), American Association of Surgeons (honorary fellow), Modern Language Association of America (honorary member), Society of Apothecaries (honorary freeman), Bibliographical Society

of London (former president), Grolier Club (honorary foreign corresponding member). *Awards, honors:* Cecil Joll Prize from Royal College of Surgeons, 1953; James Tate Black Memorial Prize, 1966, for *The Bibliography of John Harvey;* Osler Gold Medal from Royal College of Physicians, 1968; gold medal from Royal College of Surgeons, 1969; decorated Knight Bachelor of Order of the British Empire; LL.D. from University of Edinburgh; D.Litt. from Oxford University, Cambridge University, University of Birmingham, University of Reading, and University of Sheffield.

WRITINGS: A Bibliography of the Works of Dr. John Donne, Dean of Saint Paul's, Cambridge University Press, 1914, 4th edition published as *A Bibliography of Dr. John Donne, Dean of Saint Paul's,* Oxford University Press, 1973; *The Commonplace Book of Elizabeth Lyttleton, Daughter of Sir Thomas Browne,* Cambridge University Press, 1919; *A Bibliography of William Blake,* Grolier Club (New York), 1921, reprinted, Kraus Reprint, 1969; *Blood Transfusion,* Hodder & Stoughton, 1922; *A Bibliography of Sir Thomas Browne, kt., M.D.,* Cambridge University Press, 1924, 2nd edition, Clarendon Press, 1968; *William Pickering, Publisher: A Memoir and a Hand-List of His Editions,* Fleuron, 1924, revised edition published as *William Pickering, Publisher: A Memoir and a Check-List of His Editions,* B. Franklin, 1969; *A Bibliography of the Writings of William Harvey, M.D., Discoverer of the Circulation of the Blood,* Cambridge University Press, 1928, 2nd edition published as *A Bibliography of the Writings of Dr. William Harvey, 1578-1657,* 1953; *Jane Austen: A Bibliography,* Nonesuch, 1929, reprinted, B. Franklin, 1968.

A Bibliography of William Hazlitt, Nonesuch, 1931, reprinted, Folcroft, 1970; *The Early Diagnosis of Malignant Disease* (monograph), J. Bale, 1935; (author of introduction) *A Bibliography of the Works of Thomas Fuller, D.D.,* edited by Strickland Gibson, Oxford University Press, 1936; *The Illustrations of William Blake for Thornton's Virgil* Nonesuch, 1937; *John Evelyn: A Study in Bibliophily and a Bibliography of His Writings,* Grolier Club (New York), 1937, 2nd edition, Clarendon Press, 1968; *Blake Studies: Notes on His Life and Works,* Hart-Davis, 1949, 2nd edition published as *Blake Studies: Essays on His Life and Work,* Clarendon Press, 1971; *The Personality of William Harvey,* Cambridge University Press, 1949; *The Portraiture of William Harvey,* Royal College of Surgeons, 1949.

John Ray: A Bibliography, Faber, 1951, published as *The Bibliography of John Ray,* Milford House, 1973; (author of foreword) William Blake, *Jerusalem,* Trianon Press, 1952; *A Bibliography of Rupert Brooke,* Hart-Davis, 1954, 3rd edition, 1964; *Engravings by William Blake, the Separate Plates: A Catalogue Raisonnee,* Emery Walker, 1956; (author of notes and select bibliography) Blake, *Poems and Prophesies,* edited by Max Plowman, Dutton, 1959; *A Bibliography of Dr. Robert Hooke,* Clarendon Press, 1960; *A Bibliography of Siegfried Sassoon,* Hart-Davis, 1962; *Dr. Timothie Bright, 1550-1615: A Survey of His Life With a Bibliography of His Writings,* Wellcome Historical Medical Library, 1962; *Bibliotheca Bibliographici: A Catalogue of the Library Formed by Geoffrey Keynes,* Trianon Press, 1964; *A Study of the Illuminated Books of William Blake, Poet, Printer, Prophet,* Orion Press, 1964; *The Life of William Harvey,* Clarendon Press, 1966.

Drawings of William Blake: Ninety-Two Pencil Studies, Dover, 1970; (author of introduction and commentary) Blake, *Songs of Innocence and of Experience,* Oxford University Press, 1970, published as *Songs of Innocence and of Experience: Showing the Two Contrary States of the Human Soul,*

1789-1794, 1977; *A Bibliography of Sir William Petty and of "Observations on the Bills of Mortality" by John Graunt*, Clarendon Press, 1971; *The Life of William Blake*, 3rd edition, Oxford University Press, 1971; (author of introduction and commentary) *Water-Colours Illustrating the Poems of Thomas Gray*, J. P. O'Hara, 1972; *William Blake's Water-Colour Designs for the Poems of Thomas Gray*, Eyre, Methuen, 1972; *The Marriage of Heaven and Hell*, Oxford University Press, 1975; *A Bibliography of George Berkeley, Bishop of Cloyne: His Work and His Critics in the Eighteenth Century*, Pittsburgh Press, 1976; *William Blake's "Auguries of Innocence,"* Cygnet Press, 1976; (author of essay) *The Complete Portraiture of William and Catherine Blake*, Trianon Press, 1977; *A Bibliography of Henry King, Bishop of Chichester*, Douglas Cleverdon, 1979.

Editor: *Ten Sermons Preached by the Late Learned and Reverend Divine John Donne, Doctor in Divinity*, Nonesuch, 1923; John Donne, *Paradoxes and Problems: With Two Characters and an Essay of Valour*, Nonesuch, 1923; (and author of introduction) *Letters From William Blake to Thomas Butts, 1800-1803*, Clarendon Press, 1926, reprinted, Folcroft, 1969; John Evelyn, *Memoirs for My Grandson*, Nonesuch, 1926; *The Anatomical Exercises of Dr. William Harvey*, Nonesuch, 1928; *The Works of Sir Thomas Browne*, six volumes, Faber & Gwyer, 1928-31, Volume VI also published separately as *The Letters of Sir Thomas Browne*, Faber, 1946, revised four-volume edition, University of Chicago Press, 1964; Izaak Walton, *The Compleat Angler: The Lives of Donne, Wotton, Hooker, Herbert, and Sanderson; With Love and Truth and Miscellaneous Writings*, Nonesuch, 1929.

Selected Essays of William Hazlitt, Nonesuch, 1930, reprinted as *Hazlitt: Selected Essays*, Merrimack Book Service, 1978; Anthony Alfred Bowlby, *Surgical Anatomy and Morbid Anatomy*, 8th edition (Keynes was not associated with earlier editions), J. & A. Churchill, 1930; Evelyn, *Directions for the Gardiner at Saya-Court, but Which May Be of Use for Other Gardens*, Nonesuch, 1932; (with Brian Hill) *Letters Between Samuel Butler and Miss E.M.A. Savage, 1871-1885*, J. Cape, 1935; *The Note-Book of William Blake, Called the Rossetti Manuscript*, Nonesuch, 1935, reprinted, Cooper Square, 1970.

Thomas Browne, *Religio Medici and Christian Morals*, Thomas Nelson, 1940; *The Complete Poetry and Selected Prose of John Donne*, Random House, 1941; *The Poetical Works of Rupert Brooke*, Faber, 1946, 2nd edition, 1970; H. F. Brewer and others, *Blood Transfusion*, John Wright, 1949; *William Blake's Engravings*, Faber, 1950; John Maynard Keynes, *Essays in Biography*, Hart-Davis, 1951; (with Hill) *Samuel Butler's Note-Books*, J. Cape, 1951; (and author of introduction) *The Apologie and Treatise of Ambroise Pore: Containing the Voyages Made Into Divers Places With Many of His Writings Upon Surgery*, Falcon Educational Books, 1952; *Poems of Rupert Brooke*, Thomas Nelson, 1952; (with Edwin Wolf) *William Blake's Illuminated Books: A Census*, Grolier Club (New York), 1953; Blake, *Pencil Drawings: Second Series*, Nonesuch, 1956; Blake, *Illustrations to the Bible*, Trianon Press, 1957.

Poetry and Prose of William Blake, Nonesuch, 1961; *The Complete Writings of William Blake*, Oxford Univeristy Press, 1966; Blake, *The Gates of Paradise: For Children, For the Sexes*, three volumes, Trianon Press, 1968; *The Letters of Rupert Brooke*, Harcourt, 1968; *The Letters of William Blake*, Harvard University Press, 1968, 3rd edition, Oxford University Press, 1980; *Selected Writings of Sir Thomas Browne*, University of Chicago Press, 1968; Donne, *Death's Duell*, David R. Godine, 1973; *"On the Morning of Christ's*

Nativity": Milton's Hymn With Illustrations by William Blake, reprint of original 1923 edition, Folcroft, 1977; *Edward Gibbon's Library: A Catalogue*, University Press of Virginia, 1980.

Contributor of articles to medical and scholarly journals.

SIDELIGHTS: A highly respected surgeon in England before his retirement in 1956, Geoffrey Langdon Keynes is also an admired writer. His biographies and bibliographies of such well-known figures as William Harvey, Sir Thomas Browne, Rupert Brooke, William Blake, and Dr. Robert Hooke have been consistently lauded by reviewers and the general public alike. *The Life of William Harvey*, for instance, Keynes's 1967 biography of the physician who first discovered the circulation of blood through the body, was praised by *New Statesman* writer Christopher Hill as the "undoubtedly . . . definitive biography" of the man. A reviewer for the *Times Literary Supplement* likewise commended the work: "[Keynes] has created not only a vivid picture of the medical, court and social world of the seventeenth century but has also shown us how the man of science fitted into this world."

A William Blake scholar, Keynes has written numerous works on the English poet and artist. In a review of *A Study of the Illuminated Books of William Blake*, Anthony Blunt of the *New York Review of Books* declared that the author "has written an admirably clear and concise account" of the various methods Blake used in his illuminated books. *Nation*'s J. E. Grant held, "In this volume [Keynes] has written a very readable and informative summary of many matters relating to Blake's art and life." In writing of Keynes's *Blake Studies*, a *Times Literary Supplement* reviewer assessed, "These studies, as meticulously detailed as all Sir Geoffrey's editorial and bibliographical work, lay the solid foundation of knowledge on which the further work of interpretation must build."

BIOGRAPHICAL/CRITICAL SOURCES: Nation, January 25, 1965; *New York Review of Books*, October 28, 1965; *Times Literary Supplement*, August 18, 1966, December 10, 1971; *New Statesman*, September 2, 1966; *New York Times Book Review*, January 8, 1967; *Science*, August 18, 1967.*

*　　　*　　　*

KEYS, Ivor Christopher Banfield 1919-

PERSONAL: Born March 8, 1919, in Littlehampton, England; son of Christopher Richard Keys; married Margaret Anne Layzell, 1944; children: two sons, two daughters. *Education:* Christ Church, Oxford, M.A. and D.Mus.; attended Royal College of Music. *Home:* 6 Eastern Rd., Selly Park, Birmingham 29, England. *Office:* Department of Music, Barber Institute of Fine Arts, University of Birmingham, Birmingham B15 2TS, England.

CAREER: Christ Church Cathedral, Oxford, England, assistant organist, 1938-40, 1946-47; Queen's University, Belfast, Northern Ireland, lecturer, 1947-50, reader, 1950-51, Sir Hamilton Harty Professor of Music, 1951-54; University of Nottingham, Nottingham, England, professor of music, 1954-68; University of Birmingham, Birmingham, England, professor of music, 1968—. Director of music at school in Oxford, 1946-47. *Military service:* Royal Pioneer Corps, 1940-46. *Member:* Royal Academy of Music (honorary member), Royal College of Organists (fellow; president, 1968-70). *Awards, honors:* D.Mus. from Queen's University, Belfast, 1972.

WRITINGS: The Texture of Music: From Purcell to Brahms, Dufour, 1961; (contributor) August Closs, editor, *Twentieth*

Century German Literature, Cresset, 1963, Barnes & Noble, 1969; *Ten Composers,* British Broadcasting Corp., 1964; *Brahms Chamber Music,* British Broadcasting Corp., 1973; *Mozart: His Music in His Life,* Elek, 1980.

Musical compositions include "The Wheel of the Year," "Prayer for Pentecostal Fire," "Anthem for Advent," "A Garland of Carols," and "The Road to the Stable." Contributor to music journals.

BIOGRAPHICAL/CRITICAL SOURCES: Times Literary Supplement, January 16, 1981.*

*   *   *

KHARASCH, Robert Nelson 1926-

PERSONAL: Born December 13, 1926, in Washington, D.C.; son of Morris S. and Ethel (Nelson) Kharasch; married Shari Barton, December 26, 1966; children: Mark Robert, Frank William. *Education:* University of Chicago, Ph.B., 1946, B.S., 1948, J.D., 1951. *Home:* 2914 Fessenden St. N.W., Washington, D.C. 20008. *Office:* Galland, Kharasch, Calkins & Short, 1054 31st St. N.W., Washington, D.C. 20007.

CAREER: Private practice of law in Washington, D.C., 1952-54; Galland, Kharasch, Calkins & Short, Washington, D.C., partner, 1955—. Director of Computer Operations, Inc., 1974—. Member of National Academy of Sciences study group on legal impediments to intermodal transportation; member of Maritime Transportation Research Board, 1974-75; consultant to U.S. Department of Transportation. *Member:* American Bar Association, Maritime Administrative Bar Association, Maritime Law Association, District of Columbia Bar Association, Phi Beta Kappa, Coif.

WRITINGS: The Institutional Imperative, Longman, 1973.*

*   *   *

KIEFER, Christie Weber 1937-

PERSONAL: Born July 11, 1937, in Bremerton, Wash.; married, 1960; children: three. *Education:* University of California, Berkeley, A.B., 1960, Ph.D., 1968. *Home:* 30 San Mateo Rd., Berkeley, Calif. 94707.

CAREER: Langley Porter Neuropsychiatric Institute, San Francisco, Calif., research assistant in anthropology and psychology, 1967-68, research specialist in anthropology, 1968-70; University of California, Berkeley, assistant professor of anthropology, 1970—, associate director of human development program, 1975—. Lecturer at University of California, San Francisco, 1969—; consultant to National Council on Aging. *Member:* American Anthropological Association, Gerontological Society, Society for Medical Anthropology, Society of Applied Anthropology, Japanese Sociological Society.

WRITINGS: (Contributor) *Perspectives in Urban Anthropology,* Free Press, 1971; *Changing Cultures, Changing Lives: An Ethnographic Study of Three Generations of Japanese Americans,* Jossey-Bass, 1974. Contributor to anthropology journals.*

*   *   *

KILSON, Martin Luther, Jr. 1931-

PERSONAL: Born February 14, 1931, in East Rutherford, N.J.; son of Martin Luther and Louisa (Laws) Kilson; married Marion Dusser de Barenne, August 8, 1959; children: Jenny Greene, Peter Dusser de Barenne, Hannah Laws. *Education:* Lincoln University, B.A. (magna cum laude), 1953; Harvard University, M.A., 1958, Ph.D., 1959; post-

doctoral study at Oxford University, 1959. *Religion:* African United Methodist. *Home:* 4 Eliot Rd., Lexington, Mass. 02173. *Office:* Department of Government, Harvard University, Littauer Center, 16 Holyoke St., Cambridge, Mass. 02138.

CAREER: Harvard University, Cambridge, Mass., tutor, 1961-62, lecturer in government, 1962-63, fellow at Center of International Affairs, 1961-63; University of Ghana, Legon, visiting professor of government, 1964-65; Harvard University, lecturer, 1965-67, assistant professor, 1967-69, professor of government, 1969—, fellow at Center of International Affairs, 1965—. Consultant to Ford Foundation. *Member:* American Academy of Arts and Sciences (fellow), Black Academy of Arts and Letters (founding fellow), American African Studies Association (member of board of directors, 1967-68), National Association for the Advancement of Colored People. *Awards, honors:* Ford Foundation fellowship for West Africa, 1959-61; Phi Beta Kappa scholarship, 1974-75; Guggenheim fellowship, 1975-76.

WRITINGS: (Editor with Rupert Emerson) *The Political Awakening of Africa,* Prentice-Hall, 1965; *Political Change in a West African State: A Study of the Modernization Process in Sierra Leone,* Harvard University Press, 1966; (editor with Adelaide Cromwell Hill) *Apropos of Africa: Sentiments of Negro Leaders From the 1800's to the 1850's,* Cass, 1969, published in the United States as *Apropos of Africa: Afro-American Leaders and the Romance of Africa,* Anchor Books, 1971; (editor and author of introduction, with Wilfred Cartey) *The Africa Reader,* Volume I: *Colonial Africa,* Volume II: *Independent Africa,* Random House, 1970; (editor with Nathan I. Huggins and Daniel M. Fox) *Key Issues in the Afro-American Experience,* two volumes, Harcourt, 1971; (editor) *New States in the Modern World,* Harvard University Press, 1975; (editor with Robert I. Rotberg) *The African Diaspora: Interpretive Essays,* Harvard University Press, 1976. Contributor to academic journals.

BIOGRAPHICAL/CRITICAL SOURCES: Esquire January, 1973.*

*   *   *

KIMCHE, David

PERSONAL—Education: Attended Hebrew University of Jerusalem. *Office: Jewish Observer,* 36 Whitefriars St., London E.C.4, England.

CAREER: Writer. Worked as correspondent for *Jerusalem Post* in Jerusalem, Israel, and for *Jewish Observer* in London, England.

WRITINGS: (With Jon Kimche) *The Secret Roads: The "Illegal" Migration of a People, 1938-1948,* Secker & Warburg, 1954, Farrar, Straus, 1955, reprinted, Hyperion Press (Westport, Conn.), 1976; (with J. Kimche) *Both Sides of the Hill: Britain and the Palestine War,* Secker & Warburg, 1960; (with J. Kimche) *A Clash of Destinies: The Arab-Jewish War and the Founding of the State of Israel,* Praeger, 1960; (with Dan Bawly) *The Sandstorm: The Arab-Israeli War of June, 1967, Prelude and Aftermath,* Stein & Day, 1968, reprinted as *The Six-Day War: Prologue and Aftermath,* 1971; *The Afro-Asian Movement: Ideology and Foreign Policy of the Third World,* Halsted, 1973.*

*   *   *

KING, Betty (Alice) 1919-

PERSONAL: Born June 17, 1919, in Enfield, England; daughter of Oswald Nelson (a company director) and Winifred Martin; married Douglas King (a chartered surveyor), June 14, 1941; children: Caroline King Yannaghas, Malcolm, Jeffrey. *Education:* Attended secondary school in Hatfield, England. *Religion:* Christian. *Home:* Monkswood Cottage, Camlet Way, Hadley Wood, Hertfordshire, England. *Agent:* A. M. Heath & Co. Ltd., 40-42 William IV St., London WC2N 4DD, England.

CAREER: Writer, 1960—. *Member:* Society of Authors, Society of Women Writers and Journalists, Old Queenswoodian Society (governor, 1955-58).

WRITINGS—Novels: The Lady Margaret, Jenkins, 1965; *The Captive James,* Jenkins, 1967; *The Lord Jasper,* Jenkins, 1969; *The King's Mother,* R. Hale, 1969; *The Beaufort Secretary,* R. Hale, 1970; *The Rose Both Red and White,* Pinnacle Books, 1970; *The Flight of the Merlin,* R. Hale, 1972; *The Beaufort Bastard,* R. Hale, 1973; *Margaret of Anjou,* R. Hale, 1974; *Bright Is the Ring,* R. Hale, 1974; *Boadicea,* R. Hale, 1975; *Emma Hamilton,* R. Hale, 1976; *Mountains Divide Us,* R. Hale, 1977; *Owen Tudor,* R. Hale, 1977; *Nell Gwyn,* R. Hale, 1979; *Claybourn,* R. Hale, 1980; *Historical Enfield,* Percy Press, 1981.

WORK IN PROGRESS: In Sad or Singing Weather, a novel; research for a biography of Margaret Beaufort, mother of Henry VIII.

SIDELIGHTS: Betty King told *CA:* "Writing is a necessary part of my life and, although I realize my limitations, it is a method of communication with immense interest attached. It is most important that research for a historical novel be thorough, as the reader must have faith in the author." *Avocational interests:* Genealogy, painting, old porcelain, travel ("with an obvious bias to antiquity").

*   *   *

KING, Jerome Babcock 1927-

PERSONAL: Born May 1, 1927, in New York, N.Y.; married wife, 1953; children: four. *Education:* Dartmouth College, B.S., 1949; Stanford University, M.A., 1954, Ph.D., 1958. *Office:* Department of Government, University of Massachusetts, Amherst, Mass. 01002.

CAREER: University of Arkansas, Fayetteville, instructor in government, 1958-59; Middlebury College, Middlebury, Vt., instructor in contemporary civilization, 1959-61; Williams College, Williamstown, Mass., lecturer, 1961-63, assistant professor of political science, 1963-67; University of Massachusetts, Amherst, association professor of government, 1967—. Visiting lecturer at University of Vermont, 1961. *Military service:* U.S. Navy, 1945-46. *Awards, honors:* Fulbright fellowship.

WRITINGS: (Co-author) *Politics and Civil Liberties in Europe,* Van Nostrand, 1967; *Law Versus Order: Legal Process and Free Speech in Contemporary France,* Archon Books, 1975. Contributor to political science journals.*

*   *   *

KING, Philip 1904-

PERSONAL: Born October 30, 1904, in Beverley, England. *Home:* 3 Woodland Way, Withdean, Brighton BN1 8BA, England.

CAREER: Playwright, actor, and director, 1939—. *Member:* Constitutional Club, Savage Club, Dramatists' Club.

WRITINGS—Plays: Without the Prince: A Country Comedy (three-act), Samuel French, 1939; (with Thomas Falkland Litton Cary) *Holiday Eve* (one-act comedy), Charles H. Fox,

1946; (with Cary) *The Telephone Never Rings* (one-act comedy), Charles H. Fox, 1946; (with Cary) *Crystal Clear* (comedy), W. Thornley & Son, 1946; (with Cary) *Beyond the West* (one-act comedy), Charles H. Fox, 1947; *See How They Run* (three-act farce), Samuel French, 1947, revised edition, 1949; (with Cary) *Holiday Home* (one-act comedy), Charles H. Fox, 1948.

On Monday Next (three-act comedy), Samuel French, 1950; (with George Antony Armstrong Willis) *Here We Come Gathering* (comedy), Samuel French, 1952; *Serious Charge* (three-act), Samuel French, 1956; (with Cary) *Sailor, Beware!* (three-act comedy), Samuel French, 1958; (with Cary) *An Air for Murder: A Crime Play* (three-act), Samuel French, 1958; (with Cary) *The Dream House* (three-act comedy), Samuel French, 1959.

(With Robin Maugham) *The Lonesome Road* (three-act), Samuel French, 1960; (with T.F.L. Cary) *Watch It, Sailor!* (three-act comedy), Samuel French, 1961; *Pools Paradise* (three-act farce), Samuel French, 1961; *As Black as She's Painted* (farce), Walter H. Baker, 1962; *"How Are You, Johnnie?": A Murder Play* (three-act), Samuel French, 1963; (with Cary) *Rock-a-Bye, Sailor* (three-act comedy), Samuel French, 1963; *Milk and Honey* (comedy), Samuel French, 1968; *I'll Get My Man* (farce), Samuel French, 1968; (with Cary) *Big—Bad—Mouse!* (two-act farce; first produced on the West End at Prince of Wales' Theatre, September 14, 1971), Samuel French, 1969.

Go Bang Your Tambourine (comedy; first produced in Bexhill, England, at De La Warr Pavilion, July 6, 1970), Samuel French, 1970; (with P. Bradbury) *Dark Lucy,* Samuel French, 1971; *So Far—No Further* (first produced at Little Theatre, September 17, 1970), Samuel French, 1971; *Housekeeper Wanted* (farce), Samuel French, 1972; (with John Boland) *Murder in Company,* Samuel French, 1973; *The Hairless Mexican; and The Traitor,* Heinemann, 1974; (with Boland) *Elementary, My Dear,* Samuel French, 1975; (editor) Michael Hardcastle, *Don't Tell Me What to Do,* Heinemann, 1975; (with Boland) *Who Says Murder?,* Samuel French, 1975.

Also author of "Come to the Fair," "Distant Shore," "Wife Required," "The Gypsy Warned Me," "My Blessed Aunt," and "There Is a Green Hill."*

*   *   *

KING, Willard L. 1893-1981

OBITUARY NOTICE—See index for *CA* sketch: Born December 9, 1893, in Batavia, Ill.; died March 5, 1981, in Barbados. Attorney and author. King was a senior partner in a Chicago law firm, but he was best known as an Abraham Lincoln scholar. He wrote numerous articles about President Lincoln and was working on a biography, *Lincoln the Lawyer,* when he died. He also wrote biographies of Supreme Court Chief Justice Melville Weston Fuller and Associate Justice David Davis. Obituaries and other sources: *New York Times,* March 11, 1981; *AB Bookman's Weekly,* May 25, 1981.

*   *   *

KING, Woodie, Jr. 1937-

PERSONAL: Born July 27, 1937, in Mobile, Ala.; son of Woodie and Ruby (Johnson) King; married Willie Mae Washington; children: Michelle, Woodie Geoffrey, Michael. *Education:* Attended Will-o-Way School of Theatre, 1958-62, Wayne State University, 1961, and Detroit School of Arts and Crafts. *Office:* Woodie King Associates, Inc., 417 Convent Ave., New York, N.Y. 10031.

CAREER: Professional model, 1955-68; Mobilization for Youth, New York City, cultural arts director, 1965-70; New Federal Theatre, New York City, founder and co-director, 1970—. Co-founder and manager of Concept East Theatre, Detroit, Mich., 1960-63; president of Woodie King Associates; associate producer at Lincoln Center. Consultant to Rockefeller Foundation. *Awards, honors:* John Hay Whitney fellow, 1965-66; award from Venice Festival, 1968, for "The Game"; Oberhausen Award, 1968, for "The Game"; International Film Critics Award, 1970, for "Right On!"; A. Phillip Randolph Award from New York Film Festival, 1971, for "Epitaph."

WRITINGS: (Editor with Ron Milner) *Black Drama Anthology,* Columbia University Press, 1971; (editor) *A Black Quartet: Four One-Act Plays,* New American Library, 1971; (editor) *Black Spirits: A Festival of New Black Poets in America,* Random House, 1972; (editor with Earl Anthony, and contributor) *Black Poets and Prophets: The Theory, Practice, and Esthetics of the Pan-Africanist Revolution,* New American Library, 1972; (editor and contributor) *Black Short Story Anthology,* Columbia University Press, 1972; (editor) *The Forerunners: Black Poets in America,* Howard University Press, 1975.

Scripts: "The Weary Blues" (two-act play; adaptation of work by Langston Hughes), first produced in New York City at Lincoln Center Library, 1966; "Simple Blues" (one-act play; adaptation of work by Hughes), first produced in New York City at Clark Center of Performing Arts, 1967; (co-author) "The Long Night," a film released by Mahler Films of New York, 1976.

Work represented in anthologies, including *Best Short Stories by Negro Writers,* edited by Hughes; *Black Theatre Anthology; City Street.* Writer for television series, including "Sanford and Son" and "Hot 1 Baltimore." Drama critic for *Detroit Tribune,* 1959-62. Contributor of stories and reviews to magazines, including *Liberator, Negro Digest,* and *Negro History Bulletin,* and newspapers.

SIDELIGHTS: King has worked as director and producer of plays and films, including "Right On!," "Ghetto," and "Where We Live." His acting credits include "Serpico" and "Together for Days." He produced two record albums for the Motown label, "New Black Poets in America" and "Nation time," both in 1972.

BIOGRAPHICAL/CRITICAL SOURCES: Negro Digest, January, 1968.

*   *   *

KINGERY, Robert E(rnest)   1913-1978

OBITUARY NOTICE—See index for *CA* sketch: Born August 5, 1913, in Dayton, Ohio; died June 23, 1978. Librarian, educator, and author. Kingery was affiliated for over thirty years with the New York City Public Library while instructing library service at Pratt Institute in Brooklyn and serving as consultant to libraries and library systems throughout the United States. He was chief bibliographer of the 1950 *Collier's Encyclopedia.* His other writings include *Opportunities in Library Careers* and *Book Catalogs.* (Date of death provided by executor of estate, Russell A. Needham.)

KINGSTON, Jeremy Henry Spencer   1931-

PERSONAL: Born in 1931 in London, England; married Meg Ritchie; children: two sons. *Education:* Attended secondary school in London, England. *Home:* 4 Short Rd., Chiswick, London W.4, England.

CAREER: Punch, London, England, theatre critic, 1964—.

WRITINGS: No Concern of Mine (three-act play), Samuel French, 1959; *Love Among the Unicorns* (novel), Constable, 1968; *The Dustbin Who Wanted to Be a General* (juvenile), Faber, 1971; *The Bird Who Saved the Jungle,* Faber, 1973; *Signs of the Times* (play), Samuel French, 1974. Contributor to magazines, including *New Yorker* and *Atlantic Monthly.**

*   *   *

KINLOCH, A. Murray   1923-

PERSONAL: Born April 18, 1923, in Greenock, Scotland; son of Alexander and Helen Maclachlan (Stewart) Kinloch; married wife, Jean Elizabeth (an office manager), December 28, 1950. *Education:* University of St. Andrews, M.A., 1944, M.A. (with honors), 1950, D.Phil., 1956. *Religion:* Anglican. *Home:* New Maryland, R.R. 5, Fredericton, New Brunswick, Canada E3B 4X6. *Office:* Department of English, University of New Brunswick, Bag Service 45555, Fredericton, New Brunswick, Canada E3B 6E5.

CAREER: University College of Wales, lecturer, 1955-59, associate professor of English, 1959-72; University of New Brunswick, Fredericton, professor of English, 1972—. *Military service:* British Army. Canadian Army; became captain. *Member:* American Dialect Society (member of executive committee, 1977—).

WRITINGS: (With Walter S. Avis) *Writings on Canadian English, 1792-1975: An Annotated Bibliography,* Fitzhenry & Whiteside, 1978. Associate editor of *American Speech.*

WORK IN PROGRESS: Research in phonetics, phonemics, and dialectology, especially Canadian dialects.

*   *   *

KINTNER, Robert Edmonds   1909-1980

OBITUARY NOTICE: Born September 12, 1909, in Stroudsburg, Pa.; died December 20, 1980, in Washington, D.C. Journalist, broadcasting executive, and author. Robert Kintner began his journalistic career as the White House correspondent for the *New York Herald Tribune.* In collaboration with journalist Joseph W. Alsop, Jr., Kintner wrote the syndicated newspaper column "Capitol Parade." The two also co-wrote the best-selling books *Men Around the President* and *American White Paper.* In 1944 Kintner joined the public relations staff of the American Broadcasting Co. (ABC), and in 1949 became that company's president. He left ABC in 1956, and in 1958 he assumed the presidency of the National Broadcasting Co. (NBC). Kintner's special interest was the news department, and his decision to televise the McCarthy hearings of the 1950's helped precipitate the political demise of Senator Joseph R. McCarthy. Throughout his career as a broadcasting executive, Kintner was criticized for what some saw as irresponsible and excessive programming of westerns and other violence-oriented television shows. Under his leadership, however, both ABC and NBC were financially successful. After leaving NBC in 1966, Kintner joined the Johnson administration, serving as cabinet secretary and as special assistant to the president. Obituaries and other sources: *Current Biography,* Wilson, 1950, February, 1981; *Time*, November 16, 1959, January 27, 1967; *Newsweek*, December 20, 1965; Milton Viorst, *Hustlers and Heroes*, Simon & Schuster, 1971; *New York Times*, December 23, 1980.

* * *

KIPNIS, Claude 1938-1981

OBITUARY NOTICE: Born April 22, 1938, in Paris, France; died of cancer, February 8, 1981, in New York, N.Y. Pantomimist, educator, and author. Claude Kipnis, who studied under French mime artist Marcel Marceau, was the founder of the Israeli Mime Theatre. It was that company's 1965 performance at the Festival of the Theatre of Nations in Paris that earned Kipnis his international reputation. In 1966 he moved to the United States, founding the Claude Kipnis Mime Theatre and later the Claude Kipnis School of New York. The author of *The Mime Book,* Kipnis created mime acts using the classical compositions of such musical artists as Stravinsky, Schoenberg, and Mozart. He also served as director-in-residence of the Boston Opera Company and as artist-in-residence for the University of Illinois. Obituaries and other sources: *Who's Who in America,* 40th edition, Marquis, 1978; *New York Times,* February 9, 1981.

* * *

KIRBY, Gilbert W(alter) 1914-

PERSONAL: Born September 7, 1914, in London, England; son of Alfred William (in business) and Eleanor Lottie (a teacher) Kirby; married Constance Heddle, August 2, 1944; children: Gillian J. Kirby Hylson-Smith, Gilbert David, Ruth Elizabeth Kirby Calver, Peter John. *Education:* Fitzwilliam College, Cambridge, B.A., 1936, M.A., 1938. *Home:* 39 Eastcote Lane, South Harrow, Middlesex HA2 2DE, England.

CAREER: Ordained Congregational minister, 1938; pastor of Congregational churches in Halstead, England, 1938-45, and Middlesex, England, 1945-56; Evangelical Alliance, London, England, general secretary, 1956-66; London Bible College, Northwood, England, principal, 1966-80; Evangelical Alliance, president, 1979—.

WRITINGS: The Protestant Churches of Britain, Hodder & Stoughton, 1963; (editor) *Remember, I Am Coming Soon,* Victory Press, 1964; (editor) *The Question of Healing,* Victory Press, 1967; *Pastor and Principal: E. F. Kevan,* Victory Press, 1968; (editor) *Evangelism Alert,* World Wide Publications, 1972; *The Way We Care,* Scripture Union, 1977, reprinted as *Understanding Christian Ethics,* Scripture Union, 1978; *Too Hot to Handle,* Marshall, Morgan & Scott, 1978; *I Want to Know What the Bible Says About Christian Living,* Kingsway Publications, 1979. Editor of "I Want to Know What the Bible Says About . . . ," a series, Kingsway Publications, 1979-80.

WORK IN PROGRESS: Evangelism in Britain Since World War II.

SIDELIGHTS: Kirby commented: "My interests are essentially inter-church and inter-denominational. I have a particular concern for evangelism and for Christian ethics. I am essentially interested in the practical application of biblical teaching. I am also interested in church history, particularly that of the present century. I have recently been asked to write something on prophecy as it is understood in the church today."

KIRK, Robert Warner ?-1980

OBITUARY NOTICE—See index for *CA* sketch: Born in Amory, Miss.; died of cancer, June 19, 1980. Musician, educator, and author. Prior to World War II, Kirk was a professional trombonist in the southwestern United States. He later became a professor of English at El Camino College in California. A contributor of essays to *Georgia Review*, Kirk also wrote *Faulkner's People: A Complete Guide and Index to Characters in the Fiction of William Faulkner.* (Date of death provided by wife, Rose Marie Kirk.)

* * *

KIRSCH, Anthony Thomas 1930-

PERSONAL: Born May 29, 1930, in Syracuse, N.Y.; married, 1968. *Education:* Syracuse University, B.A., 1952, M.A., 1959; Harvard University, Ph.D., 1967. *Office:* Department of Anthropology, Cornell University, Ithaca, N.Y. 14850.

CAREER: Princeton University, Princeton, N.J., lecturer, 1966-67, assistant professor of anthropology, 1967-69; Cornell University, Ithaca, N.Y., associate professor of anthropology and Asian studies, and chairman of department of anthropology, 1969—. Research associate at Peabody Museum, Harvard University, 1974-75. *Military service:* U.S. Army, Medical Corps, 1953-55. *Member:* American Anthropological Association (fellow), Association for Asian Studies, Society for the Scientific Study of Religion. *Awards, honors:* Senior fellow of National Endowment for the Humanities, 1974-75.

WRITINGS: (With James L. Peacock) *The Human Direction: An Evolutionary Approach to Social and Cultural Anthropology,* Appleton, 1970, 3rd edition, Prentice-Hall, 1980; (contributor) *Southeast Asia: The Politics of National Integration,* Knopf, 1972; *Feasting and Social Oscillation: A Working Paper on Religion and Society in Upland Southeast Asia,* Southeast Asia Program, Cornell University, 1975; *Change and Persistence in Thai Society: Essays in Honor of Lauriston Sharp* (edited by G. William Skinner), Cornell University Press, 1975. Contributor to scholarly journals.*

* * *

KIVY, Peter Nathan 1934-

PERSONAL: Born October 22, 1934, in New York, N.Y. *Education:* University of Michigan, A.B., 1956, M.A., 1958; Yale University, M.A., 1960; Columbia University, Ph.D., 1966. *Office:* Department of Philosophy, Rutgers University, New Brunswick, N.J. 08903.

CAREER: Rutgers University, New Brunswick, N.J., assistant professor, 1967-70, associate professor, 1970-76, professor of philosophy, 1976—. *Member:* American Society of Aesthetics, American Musicological Society, American Philosophical Association.

WRITINGS: Speaking of Art, Nijhoff, 1973; (editor and author of introduction and notes) *Thomas Reid's Lectures on the Fine Arts,* Nijhoff, 1973; *The Seventh Sense: A Study of Francis Hutchinson's Aesthetics and Its Influence in Eighteenth-Century Britain,* B. Franklin, 1976; *The Corded Shell: Reflections on Musical Expression,* Princeton University Press, 1980. Contributor to philosophy journals.

BIOGRAPHICAL/CRITICAL SOURCES: Journal of Aesthetics, winter, 1977.*

KLARE, Hugh J(ohn) 1916-

PERSONAL: Born June 22, 1916, in Berndorf, Austria; son of Fritz Alfred and Ella Helen (Baumgarten) Klare; married Eveline Rankin, September 18, 1946. *Education:* Attended University of Geneva, 1935-39. *Home:* 28 Pittville Court, Albert Rd., Cheltenham, Gloucestershire, England.

CAREER: Control Commission for Germany, British Section, Minden, Germany, deputy director of economic organization branch, 1946-47, deputy economic adviser to joint Anglo-American Control Commission in Frankfurt, Germany, 1947-50; Howard League for Penal Reform, London, England, executive secretary, 1950-71; Council of Europe, Strasbourg, France, head of Division of Crime Problems, 1971-73; writer, 1973—. Member of Parole Board of England and Wales, 1972—; member of Gloucestershire Probation Committee and Community Service Committee. Founder of Cheltenham and North Cotswolds Eye Therapy Trust, 1974; consultant to United Nations and British television networks. *Military service:* British Army, 1939-46; became major. *Member:* International Society of Criminology (member of council, 1960-66), British Institute of Human Rights (member of board of governors, 1974-79), Authors Club. *Awards, honors:* Commander of Order of the British Empire, 1967.

WRITINGS: Anatomy of Prison, Hutchinson, 1960; (editor and contributor) *Changing Concepts of Crime and Its Treatment,* Pergamon, 1966; (editor with David Haxby) *Frontiers of Criminology,* Pergamon, 1967; *People in Prison,* Pitman, 1973. Author of column "As I See It," in *Justice of the Peace,* 1972—. Contributor to *Encyclopaedia Britannica.* Contributor to journals, including *Spectator, New Statesman, New Society,* and *Justice of the Peace,* and newspapers. Editor of *Howard Journal of Penology,* 1971.

WORK IN PROGRESS: A study of crime victims; an autobiography.

SIDELIGHTS: Klare told *CA:* "Probably a sublimated criminal myself, I consider crime (which is *very* widespread) a significant aspect of human behavior which is worth trying to understand. With the world population growing so fast, and basic resources still so limited, there's going to be a lot of crime around.

"I greatly enjoy writing, but anything else faintly resembling work is now anathema to me. I am a pessimist who enjoys life, the mountains of Austria, and peaceful Gloucestershire."

* * *

KLEINFELD, Gerald R. 1936-

PERSONAL: Born November 8, 1936, in New York, N.Y. *Education:* New York University, B.A., 1956, Ph.D., 1961; University of Michigan, M.A., 1957. *Office:* Department of History, Arizona State University, Tempe, Ariz. 85281.

CAREER: Bates College, Lewiston, Maine, instructor in history, 1961-62; Arizona State University, Tempe, began as assistant professor, 1962, professor of history, 1977—. Visiting assistant professor at State University of New York College at Fredonia, 1967-68. *Member:* American Historical Association, Conference Group on Central European History, American Committee on the History of the Second World War, Western Association for German Studies.

WRITINGS: (With Lewis A. Tambs) *Hitler's Spanish Legion: The Blue Division in Russia,* Southern Illinois University Press, 1979. Editor of *German Studies Review,* 1977—.*

KLINCK, George Alfred 1903-1973

OBITUARY NOTICE—See index for *CA* sketch: Born July 23, 1903, in Elmira, Ontario, Canada; died in 1973. Educator, editor, and author. Klinck was editor of Canadian *Modern Language Review* and compiler of several widely-used anthologies, including *Allons Gai!: A Topical Anthology of French Canadian Prose and Verse, En Avant,* and *Entre Nous.* Among Klinck's other works are *Parlons Francais!,* a three-part French language text, and *Down to the Sea.* He edited Louis Frechette's *Memoires Intimes,* reprinted in 1977. (Date of death provided by wife, Gladys Jean Klinck.)

* * *

KNAPP, Ron 1952-

PERSONAL: Born February 11, 1952, in Battle Creek, Mich.; son of Donald Loyd (a blacksmith) and Cecelia (an account clerk; maiden name, Maurer) Knapp. *Education:* University of Detroit, B.A., 1974; graduate study at Western Michigan University, 1975-78. *Politics:* "Democrat-Citizens Party." *Religion:* Roman Catholic. *Home:* 314 Charlotte St., Union City, Mich. 49094. *Office:* Union City Elementary School, Walnut Lane, Union City, Mich. 49094.

CAREER: Battle Creek Enquirer and News, Battle Creek, Mich., reporter and sportswriter, 1968-79; Union City Elementary School, Union City, Mich., teacher, 1974—, teacher of gifted children, 1975-78. Co-founder of jogging club, Local Yokels.

WRITINGS: (Contributor) Nicholas Colangelo and Ronald T. Zaffrann, editors, *New Voices in Counseling the Gifted,* Kendall-Hunt, 1979; *Tutankhamun and the Mysteries of Ancient Egypt* (juvenile), Messner, 1979; *From Prison to the Major Leagues: The Picture Story of Ron LeFlore* (juvenile), Messner, 1980. Author of "Rapping With Ron," a sports column in *Battle Creek Enquirer and News,* 1974, 1978.

WORK IN PROGRESS—Children's books: *Sojourner,* a biography of anti-slavery black feminist, Sojourner Truth; *Being a Kid in America,* a history of children in the United States; *The War We Didn't Win,* on U.S. involvement in Vietnam; *My Sister Kissed Pumpkin Blossoms,* a short novel on love and death.

SIDELIGHTS: Knapp commented: "When I was sixteen I won the grand prize in an area youth talent exhibit for a play, 'Lyndon Johnson,' a re-working of 'Julius Caesar.' From that time my goal was to write books.

"After college, I became an elementary school teacher, and it seemed natural for me to write for young people. My students gave me ideas and inspiration. Listening to kids all day helped me know how I should say what I was writing for them at night.

"I still use my classes as guinea pigs to sample my work. Unlike most adults, kids are very honest. Just the direction of their heads while I read is an excellent indicator of the quality of my work.

"My goal is to present interesting slices of information in clear paragraphs. In nonfiction, I'd like to concentrate on important topics that are usually ignored—like Vietnam, Watergate, or Islam. I'd also like to use short novels to address topics like loneliness and death."

BIOGRAPHICAL/CRITICAL SOURCES: Battle Creek Enquirer and News, October 28, 1980; *Coldwater Daily Reporter,* November 11, 1980.

KNIGHT, Bertram 1904-

PERSONAL: Born March 21, 1904, in Northampton, England; son of Charles Henry and Maria Knight; married Enid Maude Scott (died, 1966); married Elizabeth Lilian Smith, April 16, 1969; children: Philip Beverley, Judith Knight Roumani. *Education:* Attended Borough Road College, London, England, 1922-24. *Home:* Byways, Ecton, Northampton NN6 0QA, England.

CAREER: Assistant master at school in Northampton, England, 1924-34; headmaster of Rothersthorpe Road Evening Institute, Northampton, and St. George's Evening Institute, Northampton, 1934-53; Bective Junior School, Northampton, England, deputy headmaster, 1946-66; writer, 1966—. Warden of Northampton Teachers Training Centre, 1972. *Member:* National Union of Teachers (president, 1957-58).

WRITINGS: Sending Messages (juvenile), Basil Blackwell, 1970; *Time to Look Around Ecton* (juvenile), Stanton, 1971. Contributor to education journals and newspapers.

WORK IN PROGRESS: Research on the British roots and family origins of Benjamin Franklin.

SIDELIGHTS: Knight commented: "After a long career as a schoolmaster, it is a joy to sit back and assume the same basic role of a storyteller to one's grandchildren and young friends. Sometimes these stories find their way into print, but that is not essential. On the research side, I feel that there is much light to be shed on the pre-emergent fire of Benjamin Franklin's genius that was smothered on this side by the bigotry and hatred that was aroused at the time of the American Revolution."

*   *   *

KNIGHT, Gareth
See WILBY, Basil Leslie

*   *   *

KNIGHT, John Shively 1894-1981

OBITUARY NOTICE—See index for *CA* sketch: Born October 26, 1894, in Bluefield, W.Va.; died of a heart attack, June 16, 1981, in Akron, Ohio. Journalist, editor, and publisher. Knight was one of the most respected newspapermen in the United States. In 1933 he inherited the Akron Beacon-Journal from his father and from that base built Knight-Ridder Newspapers, a chain of thirty-three daily papers with a combined circulation of more than nine million. He believed strongly in an independent press and never interfered with his editors' decisions, even when they contradicted positions he took in his own Pulitzer Prize-winning column, "The Editor's Notebook." The "Knight formula" for a successful newspaper was simple: "Get the truth and print it." Knight continued to report for his papers throughout his career, getting several important stories, including the selection of vice-presidential candidates Richard Nixon in 1952 and Lyndon Johnson in 1960. Under his management, Knight-Ridder Newspapers won twenty-six Pulitzer Prizes, becoming in 1968 the first newspaper group ever to win three Pulitzers in one year. Obituaries and other sources: *Detroit Free Press,* June 17, 1981; *New York Times,* June 18, 1981; *Newsweek,* June 29, 1981; *Time,* June 29, 1981.

KNOPP, Josephine Zadovsky 1941-

PERSONAL: Born in 1941, in Chicago, Ill. *Education:* University of Illinois, B.A., 1961, M.A., 1965; University of Wisconsin—Madison, Ph.D., 1971. *Office:* Department of Religion, Temple University, Philadelphia, Pa. 19122.

CAREER: University of Illinois at Chicago Circle, Chicago, assistant professor of English, literature, and the humanities, 1971-76; Temple University, Philadelphia, Pa., adjunct professor of religion, 1976—. Research director at National Institute on the Holocaust, 1976. *Member:* American Association of University Professors, American Academy of Religion, Modern Language Association, Association for Jewish Studies, Northeast Modern Language Association.

WRITINGS: The Trial of Judaism in Contemporary Jewish Writing, University of Illinois Press, 1974. Contributor to academic journals.

BIOGRAPHICAL/CRITICAL SOURCES: American Literature, November, 1975.*

*   *   *

KNOWLTON, Robert A(lmy) 1914-1968

OBITUARY NOTICE—See index for *CA* sketch: Born July 17, 1914, in Scituate, Mass.; died of a heart attack, May 24, 1968, in Washington, D.C. Journalist and author. Knowlton was a correspondent for United Press in Washington, D.C., prior to his first service with the U.S. Naval Intelligence Office during World War II. Following the war, Knowlton rejoined United Press as managing editor of the foreign department. In 1950 he began a second period of service with the Naval Intelligence Office, which ended in 1958 when the author was injured in a plane crash in India. Most of Knowlton's short stories were written in the last decade of his life, appearing in numerous magazines, including *Good Housekeeping, Cosmopolitan, New Yorker, Esquire,* and *Saturday Evening Post.* His novel, *Court of Crows,* was published in 1961. Obituaries and other sources: *New York Times,* May 28, 1968; *Publishers Weekly,* July 1, 1968.

*   *   *

KNOX, Hugh (Randolph) 1942-
(H. R. Kaye)

PERSONAL: Born August 12, 1942, in Artesia, N.M.; son of Hugh (in automobile body repair) and Bethel (Swisher) Knox; married Elena Segal; children: Nicole. *Agent:* Alex Jackinson, 55 West 42nd St., New York, N.Y. 10036.

CAREER: Free-lance writer.

WRITINGS: The Satyr (novel), Holloway, 1970; *The Queen of Snakes: A Poem,* Abattoir, 1978. Also author of *Cult of Flesh.*

Under pseudonym H. R. Kaye: *A Place in Hell: The Autobiography of Wild Bill Henderson as Told to H. R. Kaye* (about the motorcycle gang Hell's Angels), Holloway, 1968; *Eros 2000 A.D.* (novel), Brandon House, 1970.*

*   *   *

KNOX, (Thomas) Malcolm 1900-1980

PERSONAL: Born November 28, 1900, in Birkenhead, England; died April 6, 1980, in Crieff, Scotland; son of James (a Congregationalist minister) and Isabella Russell (Marshall) Knox; married Margaret Normana McLeod Smith (died, 1930); married Dorothy Ellen Jolly; children: (first marriage)

Tarbert, Harris. *Education:* Pembroke College, Oxford, degree (with honors), 1923.

CAREER: Lever Brothers Ltd., 1923-31, began as secretary to Lord Leverhulme, became executive in charge of West African interests; Oxford University, Oxford, England, lecturer in philosophy at Jesus College, 1931-33, fellow and tutor, 1933-36, lecturer in Greek philosophy at Queen's College, 1934-36; University of St. Andrews, St. Andrews, Scotland, professor of moral philosophy, 1936-53, deputy principal of university, 1951-52, acting principal, 1952-53, principal, 1953-66. Gifford Lecturer at University of Aberdeen, 1965-66, 1967-68; fellow of Pembroke College, Oxford. Member of Catering Wages Commission, 1943-46, and National Reference Tribunal for the Coal Industry of Great Britain, 1943-56; chairman of Advisory Council on Education in Scotland, 1957-61; member of review body on doctors' and dentists' remuneration, 1962-65. Chairman of board of governors of Morrison's Academy, 1946-62, and Scottish Universities Entrance Board. *Awards, honors:* Knighted, 1961; LL.D. from University of Edinburgh, University of Pennsylvania, and University of Dundee; D.Litt. from University of Glasgow.

WRITINGS: Plato's Republic, Murby, 1957; *Action,* Humanities, 1968; *A Layman's Quest,* Humanities, 1969; (editor) Robin George Collingwood, *The Idea of History,* Oxford University Press, 1970; *A Heretic's Religion,* University of Dundee, 1976; (editor) *Hegel's Introduction to Aesthetics: Being the Introduction to the Berlin Aesthetics Lectures of the 1820's* (translated by Charles Karelis), Oxford University Press, 1979.

Translator: (Also author of notes) Georg Wilhelm Freidrich Hegel, *The Philosophy of Right,* Oxford University Press, 1942, reprinted as *Hegel's Philosophy of Right,* Clarendon Press, 1965; Hegel, *Early Theological Writings,* University of Chicago Press, 1948; (also author of notes) Hegel, *The Philosophy of Right* (bound with *The Philosophy of History,* translated by John Sibree), Encyclopaedia Britannica, 1955; *Hegel's Political Writings,* 1964; Hegel, *Aesthetics: Lectures on Fine Art,* two volumes, Oxford University Press, 1975; Hegel, *Natural Law,* University of Pennsylvania Press, 1975.

Contributor of articles and reviews to scholarly journals. Past editor of *Philosophical Quarterly.*

BIOGRAPHICAL/CRITICAL SOURCES: London Times, April 16, 1980.*

*   *   *

KOCH, Michael   1916(?)-1981

OBITUARY NOTICE: Born c. 1916; died in 1981 in Scarsdale, N.Y. Author. Michael Koch, collector of railroad memorabilia and author of books on steam locomotives, wrote *The Shay Locomotive* and *Steam and Thunder in Timber.* Obituaries and other sources: *AB Bookman's Weekly,* April 27, 1981.

*   *   *

KOCHAN, Miriam (Louise)   1929-

PERSONAL: Born October 5, 1929, in London, England; daughter of Martin (a guide lecturer) and Bessie (Bradlaw) Buchler; married Lionel Kochan (a university history teacher), December 23, 1951; children: Nicholas, Anna, Benjamin. *Education:* University College of the South-West of England, B.Sc., 1950. *Religion:* Jewish. *Home:* 237 Woodstock Rd., Oxford, England.

CAREER: Reuters Economic Services, London, England, sub-editor, 1950-54; free-lance writer, 1954-77; *Past and Present* (a journal of historical studies), Oxford, England, assistant sub-editor, 1977-80.

WRITINGS: Life in Russia Under Catherine the Great, Batsford, 1969; (editor with husband, Lionel Kochan) *The Jewish Family Album,* Routledge & Kegan Paul, 1975; *Catherine the Great,* Wayland Publishers, 1976; *The Last Days of Imperial Russia,* Weidenfeld & Nicholson, 1976; *Prisoners of England,* Macmillan, 1980.

Translator: Jeanne Roux and Georges Roux, *Greece,* Nicholas Vane, 1958; Marcel Aubert, *Gothic Cathedrals of France,* Nicholas Vane, 1959; Paul Rivet, *Maya Cities,* Elek, 1960; Marcel Brion, *The World of Archaeology,* Elek, 1961; Gilbert Picard, *Carthage,* Elek, 1964; Pierre Leveque, *The Greek Adventure,* Weidenfeld & Nicholson, 1968; Paul Akamatsu, *Mekji,* Harper, 1968; Fernand Braudel, *Capitalism and Material Life,* Weidenfeld & Nicolson, 1973; Leon Poliakov, *History of Anti-Semitism,* Volume III, Routledge & Kegan Paul, 1975; Poliakov, *The Jewish Bankers and the Holy See,* Routledge & Kegan Paul, 1977.

WORK IN PROGRESS: The Internees, on interment in England in 1940, for Macmillan.

SIDELIGHTS: Miriam Kochan wrote: "I am currently very interested in contemporary history, specifically living history based on oral evidence from personal interviews with the people who actually experienced it."

*   *   *

KOERTE, Mary Norbert   1934-

PERSONAL—Home: 7034 Mesa Dr., Aptos, Calif. 95003.

CAREER: Roman Catholic nun (Dominican Order), legally released from obligations of the order, 1968; teacher of English, Latin, music, and religion, and director of poetry workshop at St. Rose Academy (private girls' college preparatory school). *Awards, honors:* National Endowment for the Arts grant, 1969.

WRITINGS—Poems: Hymn to the Gentle Sun, Oyez, 1967; *The Beginning Is the Life, Is the Word,* Oyez, 1967; *Beginning of Lines: Response to "Albion Moonlight",* Oyez, 1968; *The Generation of Love* (edited by Clayton C. Barbeau), M. M. Bruce, 1969; *"My Day Was Beautiful, How Was Yours?"* and *"The Going",* Oyez, 1969; *A Breviary in Time of War,* Cranium Press, 1970; *The Midnight Bridge,* Oyez, 1970; *Mammals of Delight: Poems, 1972-1977,* Oyez, 1978.*

*   *   *

KOHN, George C(hilds)   1940-

PERSONAL: Born May 27, 1940, in Hartford, Conn.; son of P. Corbin (a lawyer) and Elizabeth (Childs) Kohn; married Jutta Knechtsberger, August 27, 1966; children: Christina, Peter. *Education:* University of Pennsylvania, B.A., 1963; University of Hartford, M.Ed., 1968. *Home:* 104 Liberty St., Madison, Conn. 06443. *Office:* 724 Boston Post Rd., Madison, Conn. 06443.

CAREER: West Hartford News, West Hartford, Conn., advertising manager, 1964-67; high school English teacher in Deep River, Conn., 1969-73; Laurence Urdang, Inc. (editorial service for reference books), Essex, Conn., vice-president and editor, 1976-80; operated own editorial service, 1980—.

WRITINGS: Wentworth, Vantage, 1975; (senior editor) *Young Students Encyclopedia,* Xerox Education Publications, revised edition, 1977; (compiler with Walter C. Kidney)

Twentieth-Century American Nicknames, H. W. Wilson, 1979; (managing editor) *Raintree Illustrated Science Encyclopedia,* Macdonald-Raintree, 1979; (editor of revision) Laurence Urdang, *Timetables of History,* Simon & Schuster, revised edition, 1979; (managing editor) *Nelson's Encyclopedia for Young Readers,* Thomas Nelson, 1980; (assistant editor) *Dictionary of Allusions,* Gale, 1981; (managing editor) *Timetables of American History,* Simon & Schuster, 1981.

Contributor to *Random House Encyclopedia,* 1977. Contributor to magazines and newspapers, including *Human Events, New Guard, Adolescence, Law and Order, National Educator,* and *Christian Science Monitor.*

WORK IN PROGRESS: Revising a children's encyclopedia and compiling part of a historical reference book.

SIDELIGHTS: Kohn told *CA:* "I have always liked information and reference books, and have had a natural skepticism about 'facts'—their accuracy and presentation. My years in teaching made me even more convinced of the need for accurate and objective reference works, since young people take dictionaries, encyclopedias, and almanacs as 'bibles'—that is, as the last word on anything. Almost! I enjoy compiling, rewriting, editing, or updating—making a book a little bit (or a lot) better, if I can, with the help of others."

*   *   *

KOHN, Jacob 1881-1968

OBITUARY NOTICE—See index for *CA* sketch: Born September 13, 1881, in Newark, N.J.; died September 9, 1968. Rabbi, educator, and author. Kohn was rabbi of several congregations in New York and California before joining the faculty of University of Judaism in Los Angeles in 1948, where he also became dean of the graduate school. In addition to his contributions to professional journals, Kohn's writings include *The Moral Life of Man: Its Philosophical Foundations* and *Evolution as Revelation.* Obituaries and other sources: *Who Was Who in America,* 5th edition, Marquis, 1973.

*   *   *

KOLNAI, Aurel (Thomas) 1900-1973

PERSONAL: Born December 5, 1900, in Budapest, Hungary; died June 28, 1973; son of Armin and Valeria (Glueck) Stein; married Elisabeth Gemes, February 19, 1940. *Education:* University of Vienna, certificate, 1922, Ph.D. (with distinction), 1926.

CAREER: Writer. Laval University, Quebec, Quebec, professor of modern philosophy, 1945-51, professor of political philosophy, 1951-55; University of London, Bedford College, London, England, visiting lecturer in ethics, 1959-73. Guest lecturer at Ateneo de Madrid, 1952-73; member of faculty at King's College, London, 1960-61; research fellow at University of Birmingham, 1961-62; guest professor at Marquette University, 1968.

WRITINGS—In English: *Psychoanalyse und Soziologie,* Internationaler Psychoanalytischer Verlag, 1920, translation published as *Psycho-Analysis and Society,* Allen & Unwin, 1921; *The War Against the West,* Viking, 1938; (contributor) Balduin V. Schwarz, editor, *The Human Person and the World of Values,* Fordham University Press, 1960; (contributor) *The Human Agent,* St. Martin's, 1968; (contributor) R. L. Cunningham, editor, *Situationism and the New Morality,* Appleton, 1970; *Ethics, Values, and Reality: Selected*

Papers of Aurel Kolnai (edited by David Wiggins and Bernard Williams), Athlone Press, 1977.

Other writings: *Der ethische Wert und die Wirklichkeit* (title means "Ethical Value and Reality"), Herder, 1927; *Sexualethik,* Shoeningh, 1930; *Errores del anticomunismo* (translated by Salvador Pons; title means "Errors of Anti-Communism"), Rialp, 1952; *La Divinizacion y la suma esclavatud del hombre* (title means "The Divinization and Supreme Enslavement of Man"), Ateneo, 1952; *Critica de las utopias politicas* (title means "Critique of the Utopian Political Ideals"), Ateneo, 1959.

Contributor of nearly two hundred articles and reviews to scholarly journals and popular magazines, including *World Tomorrow, Nation, American Teacher, Free Europe, Liberation,* and *Voice of Austria.*

*   *   *

KOPPEL, Ted 1940(?)-

PERSONAL: Born c. 1940, in England; naturalized United States citizen in 1963; married wife, Grace Anne (an attorney); children: four. *Education:* Attended Syracuse University and Stanford University. *Office:* American Broadcasting Co., 1124 Connecticut Ave. N.W., Washington, D.C. 20036.

CAREER: American Broadcasting Co., (ABC News), radio correspondent, 1963-67, 1967-71, began as head of Miami bureau, became head of Hong Kong bureau, diplomatic correspondent, 1971-76 and 1977-79, anchorman of Saturday television news, 1976-77, host of television news show, "Nightline," Washington, D.C., 1980—. Free-lance writer, 1976-77. *Awards, honors:* Overseas Press Club award; DuPont-Columbia award, 1979, for "World News Tonight" series, "Second to None?"

WRITINGS: (Compiler) *The Wit and Wisdom of Adlai Stevenson,* Hawthorn, 1965; (with Marvin L. Kalb) *In the National Interest* (novel), Simon & Schuster, 1977.

SIDELIGHTS: In November, 1979, the Iranian siege on the American embassy in Tehran commanded national attention, prompting ABC to feature a series of late-night television updates, "America Held Hostage," often hosted by Ted Koppel. These live, nightly specials soon brought Koppel recognition from millions of viewers who appreciated his informed, direct interviewing style. By March, 1980, the television specials had evolved into "Nightline," a half-hour, late-night, live news show featuring Koppel's special brand of television journalism. *Newsweek* called the show "global in perspective, intimate in presentation and always rivetingly spontaneous."

Koppel had been with ABC for sixteen years before he became widely known for his coverage of the hostage crisis. He joined ABC News as a radio correspondent in 1963, covering controversial topics such as the Viet Nam War and civil rights. After heading the network's Miami and Hong Kong bureaus, he became diplomatic correspondent in 1971, and traveled to China for President Nixon's 1972 visit. It was as diplomatic correspondent that Koppel began covering, from the State Department, the Iranian crisis. Howard Rosenberg declared that "as occasional anchor of *America Held Hostage,* Koppel showed a new dimension as a facile, pugnacious interviewer." The same article in *Washington Journalism Review* called Koppel "sure-footed, feisty, and phraseworthy," and cited television critic Tom Shales: "What makes *Nightline* click is Koppel's bulls-eye interviewing style . . . a succession of jabs, rejoinders, and judicious-to-delicious interruptions: Koppel *a cappella.*" *Newsweek* praised

Koppel as an "outspoken commentator . . . equipped with a quick and eclectic memory" and admired "his unflappable temperament and on-camera presence."

Koppel took a leave of absence from his position as diplomatic correspondent in 1976 while his wife attended law school. He assumed household duties, cared for their four children, and anchored ABC-TV's Saturday night news. During this time he also collaborated with Marvin Kalb, a diplomatic correspondent for rival network CBS-TV News, on the novel *In the National Interest*. Both Koppel and Kalb had previously accompanied former U.S. Secretary of State Henry Kissinger on his diplomatic negotiations in the Middle East, and their novel portrays a similar Mideast shuttle diplomacy junket.

The novel's protagonist, Darius Kane, is, like Kalb and Koppel, a foreign correspondent for a major television network. The character covers diplomatic negotiations in the Middle East that are threatened when the secretary of state's wife is kidnapped and then mysteriously released. The book "flavorfully moves through assassinations, chase scenes, White House backbiting, secret agentry—all standard meat in the Washington fiction stewpot, but in this case sauced with three-and-a-half-star pungency by two veteran cooks," wrote Les Whitten in the *Washington Post*. As correspondent Kane searches out the story, continued Whitten, "he rounds out to a hard-working, more than a little self-important, loyal, funny, brave newsman who devotedly cares about chasing down the truth. . . . We see the squalor and the splendor of reporting, and exactly why America can neither be comfortable with it, nor safe without it." Darius Kane's final dilemma reflects a major theme of the book, as Richard R. Lingeman explained in the *New York Times Book Review*: "Ultimately, when he gets his story, he faces the classic conflict between the imperatives of freedom of the press and the national interest."

One of the novel's main characters, Secretary of State Vandenberg, is in part patterned after Henry Kissinger. In the *New York Times Book Review* Kissinger offered some remarks about *In the National Interest* and its fictional secretary of state: "It is fascinating to me, and great fun, to see how these two particularly able journalists visualize high-stakes diplomacy on the inside. . . . But overall, I am afraid that in seeking balance Kalb and Koppel have let their literary imagination run wild in the interests of an (admittedly) exciting plot and characterization." Kissinger noted that the unfavorable portrayal of Vandenberg's professional ethics, "raises profound issues of the way public officials are treated in our democracy," but then good-humoredly qualified the statement, adding, "any two authors who have spent 33 days cooped up in an airplane shuttling through the Middle East must be excused for any minor shortcomings, such as the incredible description of a Secretary of State who is fallible."

BIOGRAPHICAL/CRITICAL SOURCES: New York Times Book Review, November 13, 1977; *Washington Post*, November 15, 1977; *Newsweek*, February 16, 1981; *Washington Journalism Review*, March, 1981; *TV Guide*, April 18, 1981.*

* * *

KORTE, Mary Norbert
    See KOERTE, Mary Norbert

KOSTIS, Nicholas

PERSONAL: Born in Sanford, Maine. *Education:* Bowdoin College, B.A., attended University of Nancy, 1961, and University of Aix-Marseille, 1962; Columbia University, M.A., 1963, Ph.D., 1965. *Home:* 718 Commonwealth Ave., Boston, Mass. 02215. *Office:* Department of French, Boston University, Boston, Mass. 02215.

CAREER: Brown University, Providence, R.I., instructor in French, 1963-65; Boston University, Boston, Mass., associate professor of French, 1965—. *Member:* Modern Language Association of America. *Awards, honors:* Fulbright grants, 1961-62.

WRITINGS: The Exorcism of Sex and Death in Julien Green's Novels, Mouton, 1973. Contributor to language journals.*

* * *

KOUTS, Hertha Pretorius   1922-1973
    (Hertha Pretorius)

OBITUARY NOTICE—See index for *CA* sketch: Born September 7, 1922, in New Orleans, La.; died June 1, 1973. Kouts's book, *Tallien's Children*, was published in 1961 under the name Hertha Pretorius. (Date of death provided by husband, Herbert Kouts.)

* * *

KOZAR, Andrew Joseph   1930-

PERSONAL: Born May 11, 1930, in St. Michael, Pa.; married, 1954; children: three. *Education:* University of Tennessee, B.S., 1953; University of Michigan, M.A., 1957, Ph.D., 1961. *Office:* Department of Health, Physical Education, and Recreation, University of Tennessee, Knoxville, Tenn. 37916.

CAREER: University of Michigan, Ann Arbor, 1958-65, began as instructor, became assistant professor of physical education; University of Tennessee, Knoxville, professor of physical education and chairman of department of health, physical education, and recreation, 1966—. Coordinator of physical education for public schools in Ann Arbor, 1961-65. *Military service:* U.S. Army, physical education instructor, 1953-55. *Member:* American College of Sports Medicine (fellow), American Alliance for Health, Physical Education, Recreation, and Dance, College Physical Education Association, Tennessee Association for Health, Physical Education, and Recreation, Tennessee College Physical Education Association (president, 1973-74).

WRITINGS: (Co-author) *Physical Fitness*, W. C. Brown, 1967; (with Rodney J. Grambeau and Earl N. Riskey) *Beginning Paddleball*, Wadsworth, 1967; (with Ben A. Plotnicki) *Handball*, Kendall/Hunt, 1970; *R. Tait McKenzie: The Sculptor of Athletes*, University of Tennessee Press, 1975. Contributor to scholarly journals. Art editor of newsletter of American Alliance for Health, Physical Education, Recreation, and Dance, 1965-66.*

* * *

KOZICKI, Henry   1924-

PERSONAL: Born March 20, 1924, in Detroit, Mich.; married, 1950; children: two. *Education:* Wayne State University, B.A., 1962, M.A., 1963, Ph.D., 1969. *Office:* Department of English and Linguistics, Indiana University-Purdue University at Fort Wayne, Fort Wayne, Ind. 46805.

CAREER: Wayne State University, Detroit, Mich., 1965-70, began as instructor, became assistant professor of English; University of Wisconsin—Parkside, assistant professor of English, 1970-76; Indiana University-Purdue University at Fort Wayne, Fort Wayne, professor of English and chairman of department of English and linguistics, 1976—. *Member:* Modern Language Association of America, Midwest Modern Language Association.

WRITINGS: (Editor with Robert H. Canary) *The Writing of History: Literary Form and Historical Understanding,* University of Wisconsin Press, 1978; *Tennyson and Clio: History in the Major Poems,* Johns Hopkins Press, 1979. Contributor to language and literature journals. Co-editor of *Clio: An Interdisciplinary Journal of Literature, History, and Philosophy,* 1971—.*

*   *   *

KRAFSUR, Richard Paul 1940-

PERSONAL: Born December 16, 1940, in New York, N.Y.; son of Samuel S. and Dixie (Scoville) Krafsur. *Education:* George Washington University, B.A., 1965, M.Phil., 1972. *Home:* 3457 Adina Dr., Los Angeles, Calif. 90068.

CAREER: American Film Institute, Washington, D.C., executive editor of *American Film Institute Catalog,* 1973-77; Academy of Television Arts and Sciences, Los Angeles, Calif., administrator of Emmy Awards, 1977-80, editor of *Emmy* magazine, 1981—. *Military service:* Air National Guard, 1962-67. U.S. Air Force, 1968.

WRITINGS: (Executive editor) *The American Film Institute Catalog: Feature Films, 1961-1970,* Bowker, 1976; (editor) *Emmy Awards Director,* Academy of Television Arts and Sciences, 1979.

WORK IN PROGRESS: A novel tentatively titled *Sinking Slowly in the West,* "in the form of an autobiography, with strong thematic emphasis upon murder, food, sex, and the clash of values between the East and West Coast."

*   *   *

KRAFT, Charlotte 1922-

PERSONAL: Born July 8, 1922, in Palmerton, Pa.; daughter of Charles B. (an engineer) and Ruth (a music teacher; maiden name, Fitch) Conover; married Reynold R. Kraft, February 26, 1944 (divorced, 1969); children: Reynold, Douglas, Charles, Stephanie, Roger. *Education:* Colby Junior College, A.A., 1941; University of Michigan, B.A., 1943. *Politics:* Democrat. *Religion:* Unitarian-Universalist. *Home address:* Box 775, Groton, Mass. 01450. *Office:* 103 Reade St., New York, N.Y. 10013.

CAREER: Consolidated Vultee Aircraft, Allentown, Pa., editor of employee's weekly newspaper, 1943-44; *Charleston Evening Post,* Charleston, S.C., reporter, 1944-45; high school English teacher in Morristown, N.J., 1969-75; Human Resources Institute, Morristown, editor, writing consultant, and staff assistant for systems development, 1975—. *Member:* Dramatists Guild, Authors League of America.

WRITINGS: (With Robert F. Allen) *Beat the System: A Way to Create More Human Environments,* McGraw, 1980; (with Allen) *A Cultural Approach to Organization Development,* Human Resources Institute Press, 1980; (with Allen) *The Handbook for Cultural Analysis and Change,* Human Resources Institute Press, 1980.

Plays: "Snooks Goes to Colby" (revue), first produced in New London, N.H., at Colby Junior College, May, 1941; "Kuber's Secret" (two-act), first produced in Chester, N.J., at Black River Theatre, July, 1968; "Geneva Crossroads" (one-act), first produced in Morristown, N.J., at Morristown Unitarian Fellowship, October, 1968; "Binary" (three-act), first produced in Morristown at Morristown Unitarian Fellowship, 1969; "Jump!" (one-act comedy), first produced in Hartford, Conn., on WEDH-TV, 1969; "A Day in the Life of . . ." (one-act), first produced in Chester at Black River Theatre, 1972; "Sky-Jack" (one-act), first produced in Chester at Black River Theatre, 1972; "Children's Magical Theatre" (one-act), produced in San Francisco, Calif., in several public schools, 1972-73.

"God and the New Math" (one-act), first produced in Morristown at Wit's End Theatre Experience, May, 1975; "Trappings" (three-act), first produced in Morristown at Wit's End Theatre Experience, May, 1975; (co-author) "Feel Free" (three-act comedy), first produced in New York City at Gene Frankel Theatre, November, 1976; "Red Riding Hood and the Nuclear Power Wolf" (one-act), first produced in New York City at Tompkin's Square Park, May 9, 1980; (co-author) "Snow White and the Seven Solutions" (one-act), first produced in New York City at Artists-for-Survival Street Festival, May 10, 1980.

Unproduced plays: "The Wise Bird Sings Twice"; "The Floaters"; "Mahatma" (three-act); "Now I Lay Me" (three-act); "Keys to the Cadillac" (one-act); "Harter Collins" (one-act); "Double Take" (one-act); "Four Eggs on the Half Shell, Please" (one-act); "The Enemy, the Enemy" (one-act); "The Spaceman's Hallowe'en" (a play framework for children), published in *Instructor* magazine, October, 1965.

Author of pamphlets and training materials. Author of "Undercover Angles," a book review column on children's books, in *Ypsilanti Daily News* and Citizens Newspapers of Denville, N.J., 1946-48. Contributor of stories and articles to magazines, including *Instructor, Parents' Magazine, Customer Courtesy, Organizational Dynamics,* and *Personnel,* and newspapers.

WORK IN PROGRESS: A book on development of supportive environments, with Robert F. Allen, publication expected in 1982; political theatre pieces for street theatre and festivals; a three-act play about John Calvin and Michael Servetus.

SIDELIGHTS: Charlotte Kraft told *CA:* "A very recent performing arts tour which I escorted to China sparked an interest in Chinese theatre and the Chinese way of life. I plan to explore more in this direction. I have been corresponding with a Chinese theatre director and will escort another tour in fall, 1981, during which we will see more of the marvelous Chinese opera spectacles, new, original comedy, and serious drama. We also hope to see indigenous theatre. Last year we discovered theatre groups were active in communes, ironworks factories, housing developments, etc. Many of these are new plays, rooted in people's experience and political beliefs. The Chinese love theatre and support it by filling the theatres night after night. They talk aloud in the theatre during the performance, but three mikes on stage overcome this, and the chatter makes it easy for interpreters to speak loud enough for American visitors to understand the play without disturbing the audience.

"Chinese play directors are familiar with Stanislowski methods through their contact with Russia, but have not yet absorbed later European and American experimental-theatre techniques. Their sense of humor is akin to our American sense, so their wit is readily understandable. There are no sexual references, and the most torrid love scene we saw was a boy and girl sitting close together on a bench—not even holding hands. Even this brought titters from the audience.

"I am interested in finding more ways in which the theatre can contribute to people's consciousness of environmental and political problems. I also want to discover ways in which theatre can influence involvement and community activism."

* * *

KRAMER, Judith Rita 1933-1970

OBITUARY NOTICE—See index for *CA* sketch: Born January 5, 1933, in New York, N.Y.; died, 1970. Sociologist, educator, and author. Kramer's sociological research focused upon analysis of the minority situation. Her books include *Children of the Gilded Ghetto: Conflict Resolutions of Three Generations of American Jews* and *The American Minority Community*. Obituaries and other sources: *American Men and Women of Science: The Social and Behavioral Sciences,* 12th edition, Bowker, 1973.

* * *

KRAMER, Roberta 1935-
(Kate Hart)

PERSONAL: Born May 20, 1935, in Paterson, N.J.; daughter of John Orville (a mechanic) and Frances (Moore) McLean; married Jerome Kramer; children: Fran Kramer Young, Julie Kramer Davis, Laura and Karen (twins). *Education:* Queens College of the City University of New York, B.A. (summa cum laude), 1972, M.A., 1975; doctoral study at Graduate Center of the City University of New York, 1975—. *Home:* 3 Terrace Dr., Great Neck, N.Y. 11021. *Office:* Department of English, Nassau Community College, Garden City, N.Y. 11530.

CAREER: Queens College of the City University of New York, Flushing, N.Y., instructor in English, 1972-77; Nassau Community College, Garden City, N.Y., instructor in English, 1977—. Instructor at New York Institute of Technology, 1975-78. *Member:* Phi Beta Kappa. *Awards, honors:* Providenza Weiss Prize in Poetry for "Paterson Childhood," Durling-Tobin Prize for best group of poems, Emory Holloway Prize in Literary Criticism for essay "The Search for Identity and the Kierkegaardian Choice in Max Frisch's Novel, 'I'm Not Stiller,'" and Peter Pauper Press Award, all from Queen's College, Oxford, all 1971.

WRITINGS: A Book of Curiosities, Jonathan David, 1975. Contributor to *Whereas.* Also author of poems and essays under pseudonym Kate Hart.

WORK IN PROGRESS: Poems; research on the "Confessional Poets," Lowell, Plath, Sexton, Snodgrass, Roethke, and Wakoski.

SIDELIGHTS: Roberta Kramer commented: "In 1968, as my twins entered second grade, I returned to college because I'd been talking about doing so since 1953. I was scared stiff and figured I'd disgrace myself by not being able to learn any more.

"In my senior year I began writing poems, under the pseudonym Kate Hart, and entered them in the English department's annual competition, and won four of the nine prizes awarded that year. I also wrote a booklet, 'Twins Are Two People,' for the Queens Mothers of Twins Club, to keep busy

when my twins were infants, and my 1975 book, to keep me out of mischief one summer.

"I've been too busy studying, raising my family, and trying to get a permanent teaching position to have done much else. Now I have the position and have begun to write again.

"A major interest right now is sign language. After working with several deaf students, I began to study it—it's interesting and very beautiful. I don't know why it calls to me, but it does. Sometimes now I dream in sign language."

* * *

KRASNOW, Erwin G(ilbert) 1936-

PERSONAL: Born January 8, 1936, in Brooklyn, N.Y.; son of Charles (an owner of a clothing store) and Etta (Simowitz) Krasnow; married E. Judith Levine (a social worker), September 5, 1960; children: Michael Andrew, Catherine Beth. *Education:* Boston University, A.B. (summa cum laude), 1958; Harvard University, J.D., 1961; Georgetown University, LL.M., 1965. *Religion:* Jewish. *Home:* 5604 Surrey St., Chevy Chase, Md. 20015. *Office:* National Association of Broadcasters, 1771 N St. N.W., Washington, D.C. 20036.

CAREER: Massachusetts Government Internship Program, Boston, assistant to commissioner of administration and finance, summer, 1960; U.S. House of Representatives, Washington, D.C., administrative assistant to Representative Torbert H. Macdonald, 1962-64; Kirkland, Ellis & Rowe, Washington, D.C., law partner and communications specialist, 1964-76; National Association of Broadcasters, Washington, D.C., senior vice-president and general counsel, 1976—. Visiting professor at Ohio State University, 1974; professional lecturer at American University, 1974, adjunct professor, 1975; distinguished visiting lecturer at Temple University, 1976. Admitted to practice before Massachusetts Supreme Judicial Court, U.S. District Court, U.S. Court of Appeals for the District of Columbia, and U.S. Supreme Court. Co-chairman of Lawbooks U.S.A., 1971-73. Member of board of directors of Minority Broadcast Investment Fund, 1978—.

MEMBER: American Bar Association (chairman of communications law committee, administrative law section, 1980—), Federal Bar Association (chapter president, 1963-64; co-chairman of communications law committee, 1970-71), Federal Communications Bar Association (chairman of committee on legislation, 1969-76, committee on continuing legal education, 1974-76, and committee on minority legal internship program, 1978-80; member of executive committee, 1976-79), Boston University National Alumni Association (member of board of directors, 1966-68; regional vice-president, 1971, 1973), Phi Beta Kappa, Boston University Alumni Club of Washington, D.C. (president, 1967-70), B'nai B'rith (vice-president of Argo lodge, 1966-68).

WRITINGS: (With Lawrence Longley) *The Politics of Broadcast Regulation,* St. Martin's, 1974, 3rd edition, 1982; (editor) *National Association of Broadcasters Legal Guide to FCC Broadcast Rules, Regulations, and Policies,* National Association of Broadcasters, 1977; (with John C. Quale) *A Candidate's Guide to the Law of Political Broadcasting,* National Association of Broadcasters, 1977, 2nd edition, 1980; *When Citizens Complain: UCC Versus FCC, a Decade Later,* Association of American Law Schools, 1978; *Acquiring a Broadcast Station: A Buyer's Guide,* National Association of Broadcasters, 1979.

Contributor: Don R. Le Duc, editor, *Issues in Broadcast Regulation* (monograph), Broadcast Education Association,

1974; *CATV Today: A Discussion of Current Issues,* School for Summer and Continuing Education, Georgetown University, 1975; Carol Weinhaus, editor, *Bibliographic Tools,* Harvard University Press, 1975, 2nd edition, 1976; Michael Botein, editor, *Legal Restrictions on Ownership of the Mass Media,* Advanced Media Publishing Associates, 1977.

Contributor of about thirty articles to law and communications journals and popular magazines, including *Variety* and *Television Quarterly.* Member of editorial advisory board of *Journal of Broadcasting,* 1972—; member of board of editors of *Federal Communications Bar Journal,* 1973-75.

AVOCATIONAL INTERESTS: Painting.

BIOGRAPHICAL/CRITICAL SOURCES: Choice, October, 1973, February, 1979; *Broadcasting,* November 15, 1976.

*   *   *

KRAUSE, Herbert 1905-1976

OBITUARY NOTICE—See index for *CA* sketch: Born May 25, 1905, in Fergus Falls, Minn.; died September 22, 1976, in Sioux Falls, S.D. Educator and author. As a Fulbright lecturer and Rockefeller visiting professor, Krause spent several years in Africa and the Philippines, but his novels and poems mainly reflect his native-American, middle-western background. He taught for one year at the University of Iowa before beginning a tenure of over three decades with Augustana College in Sioux Falls, South Dakota, where he was professor of English, writer-in-residence, and, beginning in 1970, director of the Center for Western Studies. In addition to a volume of poetry, *Neighbor Boy,* Krause also wrote several novels, including *Wind Without Rain, The Thresher,* and *The Oxcart Trail.* His nonfiction works include historical and ornithological studies. (Date of death provided by associate, R. L. Johnson.)

*   *   *

KRAUTHEIMER, Richard 1897-

PERSONAL: Born July 6, 1897, in Fuerth, Germany (now West Germany); came to the United States in 1935, naturalized citizen, 1942; son of Nathan and Martha (Landmann) Krautheimer; married Trude Hess, March 18, 1924. *Education:* Attended University of Munich, University of Berlin, and University of Marburg; Halle-Wittenberg University, Ph.D., 1923. *Home:* 28 Via Gregoriana, Rome, Italy. *Office:* Institute of Fine Arts, New York University, 1 East 78th St., New York, N.Y. 10021.

CAREER: University of Marburg, Marburg, Germany, privatdozent, 1928-35; University of Louisville, Louisville, Ky., assistant professor of art history, 1935-37; Vassar College, Poughkeepsie, N.Y., professor of history of art, 1937-52; New York University, New York, N.Y., professor of history of art, 1952-65, Jayne Wrightsman Professor, 1965-71, Samuel F. B. Morse Professor of Art, 1971—. Senior research analyst with Office of Strategic Services, 1942-44. Guest professor at Hertziana Library, Rome, Italy, 1929-30, 1931-32; guest lecturer at Courtauld Institute of Art, London, 1934, and Pontifical Institute for Christian Archaeology and New York University, both 1938-49; art historian in residence at American Academy in Rome, 1956, 1967.

MEMBER: American Academy of Arts and Sciences (fellow), Mediaeval Academy of America (fellow), College Art Association of America, American Philosophical Society (fellow), Jewish Academy of Arts and Sciences (fellow), British Academy (corresponding fellow), Pontifical Academy of Archaeology (fellow), German Archaeological Institute,

Max Planck Society. *Awards, honors:* Guggenheim fellowships, 1950-51, 1963-64; honorary degrees include D.H.L. from University of Louisville, 1957, and honorary doctorates from University of Frankfurt, 1964, University of Marburg, 1967, Pontifical Institute for Christian Archaeology, 1968, and University di Studi, Siena, 1976; Alice David Hitchcock Book Award from Society of Architectural Historians, 1965, for *Early Christian and Byzantine Architecture;* fellow of Accademia Nazionale dei Lincei, 1977.

WRITINGS: Die Kirchen der Bettelorden in Deutschland, F. J. Marcan, 1925; *Corpus basilicarum christianarum Romae: The Early Christian Basilicas of Rome (Fourth to Ninth Centuries),* Pontificio Istituto di Archeologia Cristiana, 1937; (with wife, Trude Krautheimer-Hess) *Lorenzo Ghiberti,* two volumes, Princeton University Press, 1956; *Early Christian and Byzantine Architecture,* Penguin, 1965; *Studies in Early Christian, Medieval, and Renaissance Art,* New York University Press, 1969; *Ghiberti's Bronze Doors,* Princeton University Press, 1971; *Rome: Profile of a City,* Princeton University Press, 1979. Also author of *Collected Essays,* 1969.

BIOGRAPHICAL/CRITICAL SOURCES: American Institute of Architecture Journal, April, 1967.*

*   *   *

KREMER, Laura Evelyn 1921-

PERSONAL: Born January 4, 1921, in Munson, Pa.; daughter of William David and Augusta Anna (Sinfelt) Hill; married William Frederick Kremer, September 27, 1947; children: Corinne Virginia, Valerie Hill. *Education:* Attended Pennsylvania State University, 1938-41; Hahnemann Medical College, M.D., 1944; postdoctoral study at University of Pennsylvania, 1945-46. *Politics:* Republican. *Home address:* Route 1, Box 42A, Dickerson, Md. 20753.

CAREER: Chesapeake and Ohio Hospital, Clifton Forge, Va., intern, 1944-45, resident in general surgery, 1946-48; New England Hospital, Boston, Mass., resident in general surgery, 1948-49; U.S. Army Hospital, Aberdeen, Md., head of department of obstetrics and gynecology, 1949-51; private practice of obstetrics and gynecology in Clearfield, Pa., 1951-53, Pittsburgh, Pa., 1953-57, and Hartsdale, N.Y., 1957-68; *Medical World News,* New York, N.Y., medical director, 1968-71; Hood College, Frederick, Md., staff gynecologist, 1973—. Vice-president of Pharmaceutical Research and Products Corp., Inc., 1967—; consultant to Maryland Department of Public Health. *Member:* American Medical Association, Maryland Medical Association, Planned Parenthood of Maryland (member of board of directors), Frederick County Medical Society, Planned Parenthood of Frederick County (member of board of directors).

WRITINGS: (With husband, William Frederick Kremer) *The Doctors' Metabolic Diet,* Avon, 1976.*

*   *   *

KRULEWITCH, Melvin Levin 1895-1978

PERSONAL: Born November 11, 1895, in New York, N.Y.; died in 1978; son of Harry and Ann (Levin) Krulewitch; married Helen Rothstein, 1937 (deceased); married Hellen Sulzbacher, February 2, 1968; children: (first marriage) Ann, Elihu. *Education:* Columbia University, B.A., 1916, LL.B., 1920.

CAREER: Goldstein, Gurfein, Shames & Hyde, New York City, attorney. Special counsel to New York State Public Service Commission and Public Utilities Commission; chairman of New York State Athletic Commission, 1959-67; official referee for Superior Court. Honorary member of board of directors of Young Men's-Young Women's Hebrew Association; member of board of trustees of National Jewish Welfare Board; member of board of trustees of Federation of Jewish Philanthropies of New York; honorary member of board of trustees of Park Avenue Syndicate; vice-chairman of board of directors and vice-president of United Service Organizations in New York City; sponsor of General Krulewitch Fund at Columbia University. *Military service:* U.S. Marine Corps, beginning in 1918; served in Korea; became major general; received two Bronze Stars with Gold Star, Purple Heart, Individual Fourragere, French Croix de Guerre, and Medaille d'Or de Verdun. *Member:* Military Order of the World Wars (commander).

WRITINGS: Now That You Mention It, Quadrangle, 1973.

BIOGRAPHICAL/CRITICAL SOURCES: New York Times, May 26, 1978.*

*　　*　　*

KUPER, Adam (Jonathan) 1941-

PERSONAL: Born December 29, 1941, in Johannesburg, South Africa; son of Simon Meyer (a judge) and Gertrude (a teacher; maiden name, Hesselson) Kuper; married Jessica Cohen (a writer and publisher), December 15, 1966; children: Simon, Jeremy, Hannah. *Education:* University of the Witwatersrand, B.A., 1961; Cambridge University, Ph.D., 1966. *Religion:* Jewish. *Home:* Rijnsburgerweg 104, Leiden, Netherlands. *Office:* Institute of Cultural Anthropology, University of Leiden, Stationsplein 10, Leiden, Netherlands.

CAREER: Makerere University, Kampala, Uganda, lecturer in social anthropology, 1967-70; University of London, London, England, lecturer in anthropology, 1970-76; University of Leiden, Leiden, Netherlands, professor of African cultural anthropology, 1976—. Fellow at Center for Advanced Study in the Behavioral Sciences, Palo Alto, Calif., 1980-81. *Member:* Association of Social Anthropologists, Royal Anthropological Institute. *Awards, honors:* Honorary doctorate from University of Gothenburg, 1978.

WRITINGS: Kalahari Village Politics: An African Democracy, Cambridge University Press, 1970; (editor with A. I. Richards) *Councils in Action,* Cambridge University Press, 1971; *Anthropologists and Anthropology: The British School, 1922-1972,* Universe Books, 1973; *Changing Jamaica,* Routledge & Kegan Paul, 1976; (editor) *The Social Anthropology* of *Radcliffe-Brown,* Routledge & Kegan Paul, 1977; *Wives for Cattle,* Routledge & Kegan Paul, 1982.

WORK IN PROGRESS: Work on the cognitive structure of dreams; continuing work in African anthropology.

SIDELIGHTS: Kuper's 1981 book concerns marriage and bride-wealth in pre-industrial southern Bantu society. He told *CA:* "I work hard at writing, and think of myself as a writer, not simply as an anthropologist who is obliged to 'write up' his stuff. I enjoy journalism (nowadays mainly for *New Society*) and have seriously considered writing on other topics. At the same time I have a special admiration for formal analysis in the social sciences, and would like to develop more formal models in my own discipline. Probably this divided ambition helps to account for my rather ordinary level of achievement in either field, but there are, of course, inspiring examples—John Maynard Keynes, for instance—of what can be done.''

*　　*　　*

KYME, Ernest Hector 1906-

PERSONAL: Born April 2, 1906, in Sheffield, England; son of Herbert (a master builder) and Sarah A. (a maid; maiden name, Outram) Kyme; married Dora Silcock, January 7, 1933 (died, 1980); children: Andrew John, Sheila. *Education:* Attended London City Guilds for Handicraft Teaching in Woodwork and Metalwork; also studied building construction. *Politics:* Liberal. *Home and office:* 29 Cecil Rd., Dronfield, Sheffield S18 6GW, England.

CAREER: Worked as joiner for Sheffield Corp., 1927; teacher of handicrafts, 1930-40; foreman, 1940-46; teacher of photography, 1950—; free-lance photographer. Lecturer. *Awards, honors:* Award from *Sheffield Telegraph;* and other awards.

WRITINGS: A Million and More Strides (illustrated with photographs by Kyme), R. Hale, 1975. Contributor of photographs to magazines.

WORK IN PROGRESS: A book of photographs.

SIDELIGHTS: Kyme wrote: "Having seen a little of Europe, including Switzerland, I felt the earth is very large. In a lifetime I could not hope to see more than a little, so I took a good walk at leisure. I wanted to excite others who saw the glories of my own country and to give an account of the folk one misses in city, town, or village. I wanted to send my book abroad, especially to America, to induce travelers to come see Britain, whose skies, woods and fields, coastlines, rivers, and lakes are the best in the world."

L

LACHMANN, Frank M(ichael) 1929-

PERSONAL: Born December 9, 1929, in Breslau, Germany; came to the United States in 1938, naturalized citizen, 1944; son of Hans (a certified public accountant) and Kate (Landsberg) Lachmann; married Annette Schamroth (a learning disabilities specialist), July 15, 1962; children: Suzanne, Peter. *Education:* New York University, B.A., 1951; Northwestern University, M.A., 1953, Ph.D., 1955. *Religion:* Jewish. *Home:* 221 West 82nd St., New York, N.Y. 10024. *Office:* 333 West End Ave., New York, N.Y. 10023.

CAREER: Dyslexia Memorial Institute, Chicago, Ill., staff psychologist, 1951-52; Northwestern University, Evanston, Ill., extern in psychology at School of Medicine, 1952-53; Bellevue Psychiatric Hospital, New York City, intern in psychology, 1953-54; Dyslexia Memorial Institute, staff psychologist, 1954-55; F. D. Roosevelt Veterans Administration Hospital, Montrose, N.Y., research fellow, 1955-56; Veterans Administration, Regional Office, New York City, clinical psychologist, 1956-60; private practice of psychotherapy, psychoanalysis, and diagnostic testing in New York City, 1960—. Diplomate of American Board of Examiners in Professional Psychology; associate psychologist at Postgraduate Center for Mental Health, 1960—, lecturer, 1964—, supervisor of department of community services and education, 1964-66, senior supervisor, 1971—, and training analyst; member of Klein-Rapaport Study Group, 1975—. Adjunct supervisor at Teachers College of Columbia University, 1969-70; lecturer at Pace College, 1956-57, and Hunter college (now of the City University of New york), 1957-60; visiting lecturer at New York University, 1970-71; Theodor Reik Lecturer of National Psychological Association for Psychoanalysis, 1979, and control analyst; consultant to Psychiatric Treatment Center for Adolescents and Parents Without Partners. *Member:* American Psychological Association, American Orthopsychiatric Association, New York State Psychological Association, Postgraduate Psychoanalytic Society.

WRITINGS: (With Robert D. Stolorow) *The Psychoanalysis of Developmental Arrests*, International Universitites Press, 1980; (contributor) Dale Mendell, editor, *Early Female Development: Current Psychoanalytic Views*, spectrum, 1981; (contributor) Stanley Cath, Alan Gurwitt, and John M. Ross, editors, *Fatherhood*, Little, Brown, 1981; (with Lloyd Silverman and Robert Milich) *The Search for Oneness*, International Universitites Press, 1981. Contributor to *Annual of Psychoanalysis*. Contributor of about a dozen articles to psychoanalysis and psychology journals.

*   *   *

LACKEY, Douglas Paul 1945-

PERSONAL: Born August 27, 1945, in New York, N.Y. *Education:* Michigan State University, B.A., 1966; Yale University, Ph.D., 1970. *Home:* 50 Juniper Rd., Wayne, N.J. 07470. *Office:* Bernard M. Baruch College of the City University of New York, New York, N.Y. 10010.

CAREER: New York University, New York City, assistant professor of philosophy, 1970; Bernard M. Baruch College of the City University of New York, New York City, assistant professor of philosophy, 1972—. *Awards, honors:* Woodrow Wilson fellowship, 1967.

WRITINGS: (Editor) Bertrand Russell, *Essays in Analysis*, Braziller, 1973. Contributor to philosophy journals.*

*   *   *

LACY, Charles
See HIPPISLEY COXE, Antony D(acres)

*   *   *

LADYMAN, Phyllis

PERSONAL: Born in Bromley, England; married James Lucas; children: two daughters. *Education:* Attended Thanet School of Art, Royal College of Art, and Margate School of Art. *Agent:* c/o Hodder & Stoughton Children's Books, Arlen House, Salisbury Rd., Leicester LE1 7QS, England.

CAREER: Free-lance artist and writer. *Member:* Society of Industrial Artists.

WRITINGS—For children: *About a Motor Car*, Penguin, 1946, revised edition, 1956; *About Television*, Brockhampton Press, 1960; *Things About the House*, Brockhampton Press, 1962; *Grasshopper, Dragonfly, and Daddy-Long-Legs*, Methuen, 1964; *Ladybird, Butterfly, and Earwig*, Methuen, 1964; *Frog, Stickleback, and Pond Snail*, Methuen, 1966; *Water Boatman, Caddis Fly, and Water Spider*, Methuen, 1966; *About Flowering Plants*, Brockhampton Press, 1966, published in the United States as *Learning About Flowering Plants: Observing, Identifying, Experimenting*, illustrated by Grambs Miller, Scott Publishing, 1970; *Starfish, Shore Crab, and Mussel*, Methuen, 1968; *Blenny, Prawn, and Sea Ane-*

mone, Methuen, 1968; *About Farm Machines,* Brockhampton Press, 1968, revised edition, Hodder & Stoughton, 1980; *Inside the Earth,* Scott Publishing, 1969; *Honeybee and Garden Ant,* Methuen, 1971; *Mosquito, Housefly, and Common Clothes Moth,* Methuen, 1971; (with Arthur Leslie Frost) *Billy the Buck Jumper,* Goose & Son, 1972; *About Natural Gas,* Goose & Son, 1973; *Things From the Earth: The Basic Resources of Our World and How They Are Used,* Brockhampton Press, 1975; *How Machines Work,* Hodder & Stoughton, 1977; *Electronics,* self-illustrated, Hodder & Stoughton, 1980.

Contributor to *Child Education.**

* * *

LADY OF QUALITY, A
See BAGNOLD, Enid

* * *

LAITHWAITE, Eric Roberts 1921-

PERSONAL: Born June 14, 1921, in Atherton, England; son of Herbert (a farmer) and Florence Laithwaite; married Sheila Margaret Gooddie, September 8, 1951; children: Martin John Herbert, Helen Fiona, Vanda Louise, Dennis William. *Education:* Victoria University of Manchester, B.Sc., 1949, M.Sc., 1950, Ph.D., 1957, D.Sc., 1964. *Religion:* "Changes from week to week." *Residence:* Surrey, England. *Office:* Department of Electrical Engineering, Imperial College of Science and Technology, University of London, London SW7 2BT, England.

CAREER: Victoria University of Manchester, Manchester, England, assistant lecturer, 1950-53, lecturer, 1953-67, senior lecturer in electrical engineering, 1957-64; University of London, Imperial College of Science and Technology, London, England, professor of heavy electrical engineering, 1964—. Professor at Royal Institution of Great Britain, 1967-76. Member of board of directors of Linear Motors Ltd., Landspeed Ltd., and Cotswold Research Ltd.; consultant to industry. *Military service:* Royal Air Force, 1941-46; became flying officer. *Member:* Association for Science Education (president, 1970), Institute of Electrical and Electronics Engineers (fellow), Institution of Electrical Engineers (fellow; chairman of Power Board, 1971-72), Royal Society of Arts (fellow), Athenaeum Club. *Awards, honors:* S. G. Brown Award and medal from Royal Society, 1966, for work on linear induction motors.

WRITINGS: Induction Machines for Special Purposes, George Newnes, 1966; *Propulsion Without Wheels,* English Universities Press, 1966, 2nd edition, 1970; *The Engineer in Wonderland,* English Universities Press, 1967; *Linear Electric Motors,* Mills & Boon, 1971; *Exciting Electrical Machines,* Pergamon, 1974, 2nd edition, 1979; (with Allan Watson and Paul E. S. Whalley) *The Dictionary of Butterflies and Moths in Colour,* M. Joseph, 1975; *All Things Are Possible: An Engineer Looks at Research and Development,* IPC Electrical-Electronic Press, 1976; (with M. W. Thring) *How to Invent,* Macmillan, 1977; *Why Does a Glow-Worm Glow?,* Beaver Books, 1977; (editor) *Transport Without Wheels,* Elek, 1977; *Engineer Through the Looking-Glass,* BBC Publications, 1980; (with L. L. Freris) *Electric Energy: Its Generation, Transmission, and Use,* McGraw, 1980; *History of Linear Electric Motors,* Peter Peregrinus, in press; *Engineering and Biology,* W. Foulsham, in press. Contributor of more than two hundred fifty articles to technical journals.

SIDELIGHTS: Laithwaite commented: "I do 80 percent of my writing on public transport where there are no telephones. I like to have several books in progress at the same time, so that I can work on the one which appears most exciting on any particular day."

BIOGRAPHICAL/CRITICAL SOURCES: Vogue, March, 1977.

* * *

LAKOFF, Robin Tolmach 1942-

PERSONAL: Born November 27, 1942, in Brooklyn, N.Y.; married, 1963; children: one. *Education:* Radcliffe College, B.A., 1964; Indiana University, M.A., 1965; Harvard University, Ph.D., 1967. *Office:* Department of Linguistics, University of California, Berkeley, Calif. 94720.

CAREER: Language Research Foundation, Cambridge, Mass., textbook editor, 1968-69; University of Michigan, Ann Arbor, assistant professor of linguistics, 1969-71; Stanford University, Stanford, Calif., fellow of Center for Advanced Study of Behavioral Sciences, 1971-72; University of California, Berkeley, associate professor of linguistics, 1972—. Lecturer in classics and linguistics at University of Illinois, Urbana, 1968; visiting associate professor at University of Michigan Linguistics Institute, 1973. *Member:* Linguistics Society of America.

WRITINGS: Abstract Syntax and Latin Complementation, M.I.T. Press, 1968; *Language and Woman's Place,* Harper, 1975.

SIDELIGHTS: Lakoff is a leader in the field of generative semantics, a linguistic theory whose followers recognize language as a psychological phenomenon, with word order, choice, and meaning functioning as integral and inseparable grammatical components. She also has worked extensively in sociolinguistics, examining the socio-cultural impact on language as well as the functioning of language in society.

Lakoff's book *Language and Woman's Place* discusses language's part in indicating and reinforcing society's attitude about women. Reviewer Ann Scott of the *English Journal* commented: "*Language and Woman's Place* goes a long way toward elucidating for the open-minded reader the reasons for the feminist attack upon language use, separating the sense from the nonsense. . . . Less controversial, but probably more socially revealing, are Lakoff's observations about the language spoken by women themselves." Lakoff identifies certain speech patterns and word choices found almost exclusively in the linguistic behavior of women. Lakoff observes, for example, that women more frequently than men add a tag question at the end of a declarative assertion, such as, "He's with the Philharmonic, isn't he?" The tag question diminishes the force of the sentence and may be indicative of a sense of subordination. Lakoff notes many other areas in which women's language is both characteristic and socially revealing. Her analysis is based upon personal observation and interpretation rather than scientifically collected data. "In the absence of experimental proof," said Scott, "[Lakoff] invites the reader to make his (?!) own observations and draw his own conclusions."

BIOGRAPHICAL/CRITICAL SOURCES: English Journal, May, 1976; *Reviews in Anthropology,* May, 1976.*

* * *

LAMBERTI, Marjorie 1937-

PERSONAL: Born September 30, 1937, in New Haven, Conn.; daughter of James and Anna Lamberti. *Education:*

Smith College, B.A., 1959; Yale University, M.A., 1960, Ph.D., 1965. *Home:* 3 Benedict Lane, Middlebury, Vt. 05753. *Office:* Department of History, Middlebury College, Middlebury, Vt. 05753.

CAREER: Middlebury College, Middlebury, Vt., instructor, 1964-66, assistant professor, 1966-69, associate professor, 1969-75, professor of history, 1975—. *Member:* American Historical Association, Phi Beta Kappa. *Awards, honors:* Fellow of National Endowment for the Humanities, 1968 and 1981.

WRITINGS: Jewish Activism in Imperial Germany: The Struggle for Civil Equality, Yale University Press, 1978. Contributor to history journals.

WORK IN PROGRESS: Research on the state, society, and primary education in Prussia, 1870-1914.

* * *

LAMBERTON, Donald McLean 1927-

PERSONAL: Born July 29, 1927, in Casino, Australia; son of Leslie Thomas (a farmer) and Isabel Mary (Montgomery) Lamberton; married Clare Margaret McSullea, November 20, 1965; children: Hugh McLean, Anna. *Education:* University of Sydney, B.Ec., 1949; Oxford University, D.Phil., 1963. *Office:* Department of Economics, University of Queensland, St. Lucia, Brisbane, Queensland 4067, Australia.

CAREER: Member of branch staff at Rank of New South Wales in various locations in Australia, 1942-45; *Sydney Morning Herald,* Sydney, Australia, member of financial staff, 1949; Sydney Stock Exchange, Sydney, junior executive, 1949-50, editor of publications, 1950-53; University of New England, Armidale, Australia, lecturer in economics, 1953-58; University of New South Wales, Kensington, Australia, senior lecturer, 1960-65, associate professor of economics, 1966-69; Case Western Reserve University, Cleveland, Ohio, professor of economics, 1969-72; University of Queensland, Brisbane, Australia, professor of economics, 1973—, head of department, 1974-77. Visiting Fulbright associate professor at Stanford University and University of Pittsburgh, 1966. Visiting Professor at Stanford University and visiting fellow at Oxford Centre for Management Studies, 1978. Member of Australian Government Committee of Inquiry Into Public Libraries, 1975-76; member of Organization for Economic Cooperation and Development's group of experts on economic analysis of information activities and the role of electronics and telecommunications technologies, 1977-79; consultant to United Nations Educational, Scientific and Cultural Organization.

MEMBER: Australia and New Zealand Association for the Advancement of Science, Australian Academy of Science, Pacific Science Committee, Pacific Science Association (chairman of scientific committee for social sciences and humanities). *Awards, honors:* Scholarship from Services Canteens Trust Fund of Australia, 1957-60; studentship from Nuffield College, Oxford, 1958-60; grant from Australian-American Educational Foundation, 1966.

WRITINGS: Share Price Indices in Australia, Law Book Co. of Australasia, 1958; *The Australian Economy,* Tudor Press, 1969; *The Theory of Profit,* Basil Blackwell, 1965; *Science, Technology, and the Australian Economy,* Tudor Press, 1970; (editor) *Economics of Information and Knowledge,* Penguin, 1971; (editor) *Industrial Economics,* Penguin, 1972; (with N. D. Karunaratne, P. Murnane, and R. A. Stayner) *Cost Analysis of Public Libraries,* University of Queensland Press,

1976; (editor with Meheroo Jussawalla, and contributor) *Communication and Development,* Pergamon, 1981.

Contributor: G. W. Ford, editor, *Automation: Threat or Promise?,* Law Book Co. of Australasia, 1969; C. F. Carter and J. L. Ford, editors, *Uncertainty and Expectations in Economics,* Basil Blackwell, 1972; *Productivity Through Technology,* Productivity Promotion Council of Australia, 1973; Gordon McCarthy, editor, *Industrial Australia, 1975-2000,* Australia and New Zealand Book Co., 1974; K. A. Tucker, editor, *Economics of the Australian Service Sector,* Croom Helm, 1977; (S. A. Rahim, Dan Wedemeyer, John Holstrom, and others, editors) *Planning Methods, Models, and Organization: A Review Study for Communication Policy Making and Planning,* East-West Center, 1978; *Technological Change in Australia,* Australian Government Publishing Service, 1980; B.R.B. Crough and Shankariah Chamala, editors, *Extension Education and Rural Development: International Experience in Communication and Innovation,* Wiley, 1980; Mangalam Srinivasan, editor, *Technology Assessment and Development,* Praeger, 1981.

Contributor to *International Encyclopedia of Higher Education.* Contributor of about fifty articles and reviews to professional journals. Editor of *Annals of the American Academy of Political and Social Science,* March, 1974; associate editor of *Journal of Industrial Economics;* member of editorial board of *Telecommunications Policy.*

WORK IN PROGRESS: New Dimensions of Information Policy; Economics of Information, a revised and enlarged edition of 1971 publication; *The Trouble With Technology,* with S. Macdonald and T. Mandeville; numerous papers and projects on the economics of information and technical change.

SIDELIGHTS: Lamberton told *CA:* "Technological change does not provide 'free lunches.' There are so many costs (and benefits) that are not and cannot be perceived in advance that it is foolish to define technological change as productivity gains. Australia and other countries need to probe, imagine, and invent their futures. If the conflicts involved in what is euphemistically called modernization are not faced, social costs can continue to escalate.

"It is widely believed that the income gap between rich and poor countries can be closed by transferring information. However, the more information flow created, the less appropriate the information may be to the needs of the recipient. There is an important aspect of irreversibility involved: the information flows cannot be switched on and off, and they cannot be reversed. The result is that information is as often the chains by which peoples are bound as the instrument of their progress and freedom. My writing attempts to address such problems, report research, develop new ideas, and influence the thoughts of decision makers."

* * *

LAMBRIGHT, William Henry 1939-

PERSONAL: Born July 7, 1939, in Baltimore, Md.; married, 1963. *Education:* Johns Hopkins University, A.B., 1961; Columbia University, M.A., 1962, Ph.D., 1966. *Home:* 555 Cumberland Ave., Syracuse, N.Y. 13210. *Office:* Syracuse University, Syracuse, N.Y. 13210.

CAREER: Inter-University Case Program, Inc., Syracuse, N.Y., case writer in political science, 1965-66, assistant director of program, 1966—. Associate professor at Syracuse University, 1966—; consultant to Educational Resources and Research, Inc. *Military service:* U.S. Army Reserve, 1957-

65. *Member:* American Association for the Advancement of Science, American Political Science Association, American Society for Public Administration.

WRITINGS: (With Edwin A. Bock) *Launching NASA's Sustaining University Program,* Inter-University Case Program, 1969; (with Byron Thomas Hipple) *Delay in Washington: A State View of Grant-in-Aid Administration,* [Syracuse, N.Y.], 1969; *Governing Science and Technology,* Oxford University Press, 1976; (with Paul J. Flynn) *Technology Transfer to Cities: Processes of Choice of the Local Level,* Westview Press, 1979.*

*   *   *

LAMPMAN, Robert James 1920-

PERSONAL: Born September 25, 1920, in Plover, Wis.; son of Harry Gordon and Bernice (Pierce) Lampman; married JoAnn Cockrell, June 27, 1943; children: Jonathan William, James Henry, Rebecca Jo, Thomas Robert. *Education:* University of Wisconsin (now University of Wisconsin—Madison), B.A., 1942, Ph.D., 1950; attended University of California, Berkeley, 1947-48. *Home:* 729 Oneida Pl., Madison, Wis. 53711. *Office:* Department of Economics, University of Wisconsin—Madison, Madison, Wis. 53706.

CAREER: University of Washington, Seattle, assistant professor, 1948-53, associate professor of economics, 1953-58; University of Wisconsin (now University of Wisconsin—Madison), professor of economics, 1958—, chairman of department, 1961-62, 1964-65. Visiting associate professor at American University of Beirut, 1951-52; visiting professor at University of Wisconsin, 1955-56, University of the Philippines, 1966-67, and Cornell University, 1973-74. Research associate at National Bureau of Economic Research, 1957-58; staff member of President's Council of Economic Advisers, 1962-63. *Military service:* U.S. Naval Reserve, 1942-53, active duty, 1942-46; became lieutenant senior grade. *Member:* American Economic Association, American Association of University Professors, Industrial Relations Research Association, Phi Beta Kappa, Phi Kappa Phi. *Awards, honors:* Ford Foundation fellowship, 1960-61.

WRITINGS: (With Joseph L. Fisher and Edward Boorstin) *The Low Income Population and Economic Growth* [and] *The Adequacy of Resources for Economic Growth in the United States* (the former by Lampman, the latter by Fisher and Boorstin), U.S. Government Printing Office, 1959; *The Share of Top Wealth-Holders in National Wealth, 1922-56,* Princeton University Press, 1962; (contributor) Leonard H. Goodman, editor, *Economic Progress and Social Welfare,* Columbia University Press, 1966; (editor with Sar A. Levitan and Wilbur J. Cohen) *Towards Freedom From Want,* Industrial Relations Research Association, 1968; *Ends and Means of Reducing Income Poverty,* Markham, 1971. Also author of *Administration of Washington Medical Service Corporations,* 1962. Contributor to economic journals.*

*   *   *

LANCASTER, Otis Ewing 1909-

PERSONAL: Born January 28, 1909, in Pleasant Hill, Mo.; son of Hayden Guard and Ida May (Seaton) Lancaster; married Hildreth Adele Herald, December 5, 1942; children: Elaine Adele, Hayden Ewing, Patricia, Dale Burkham, Matthew. *Education:* Central Missouri State Teachers College, B.A., 1929; University of Missouri, M.A., 1934; Harvard University, Ph.D., 1938; California Institute of Technology,

Aero.Engr., 1945. *Home:* 268 Ellen Ave., State College, Pa. 16801.

CAREER: High school teacher of science and mathematics; junior high school teacher of science and mathematics in Independence, Mo., 1929-33; Harvard University, Cambridge, Mass., instructor in mathematics, 1936-37; University of Maryland, College Park, 1937-42, began as instructor, became assistant professor of mathematics; U.S. Department of the Navy, Washington, D.C., head of applied mathematics branch in Research Division of Bureau of Aeronautics, 1946-54, assistant director of Research Division, 1954; Internal Revenue Service, Washington, D.C., member of planning staff, 1954-55; U.S. Post Office Department, Washington, D.C., director of Statistics and Economics Division of Bureau of Finance, 1955-57; Pennsylvania State University, University Park, George Westinghouse Professor of Engineering Education, 1957-75, associate dean of College of Engineering, 1967-74, director of Summer Institute on Effective Teaching for Young Engineers; chairman of mathematics and statistics for Interstate Commerce Commission, 1976—. Director of National Science Foundation Academic Year Institute, 1964-71, and Summer Institute on Engineering Concepts for High School Teachers; consultant to National Aeronautics and Space Administration, Federal Aviation Authority, and United Nations Educational, Scientific, and Cultural Organization. *Military service:* U.S. Naval Reserve, active duty, 1942-46; became lieutenant senior grade.

MEMBER: American Society for Engineering Education (chairman of Allegheny section, 1961-62; chairman of Educational Methods Division, 1963-64; chairman of Aerospace Division, 1964-65; vice-president of eastern section, 1965-67; president, 1977-78), American Society of Mechanical Engineers (chairman of aircraft gas turbine committee, 1962-67), Mathematical Association of America, Institute of Mathematical Statistics, American Institute of Aeronautics and Astronautics (associate fellow), Institute of Aeronautical Sciences (fellow), Sigma Xi, Sigma Chi.

WRITINGS: (With Ivan H. Driggs) *Gas Turbines for Aircraft,* Ronald, 1955; (editor) *Jet Propulsion Engines,* Princeton University Press, 1959; (editor and contributor) *Effective Teaching and Learning,* Gordon & Breach, 1974. Contributor to *Sawyer's Gas Turbine Engineering Handbook.* Contributor to scientific journals. Contributing editor of *Gas Turbines Aviation.**

*   *   *

LANDAUER, Jerry Gerd 1932-1981

OBITUARY NOTICE: Born January 16, 1932, in Rexinger, Germany; died of a heart attack, February 27, 1981, in Washington, D.C. Journalist. Jerry Landauer, a correspondent for the Washington bureau of the *Wall Street Journal,* was the recipient of several awards for investigative reporting. Among them were the Drew Pearson Prize and the Worth Bingham Memorial Prize, both of which he received in 1974 after reporting that Vice-President Spiro Agnew was under investigation by the Justice Department for suspected tax fraud. Landauer, known for his untiring efforts to expose government and corporate wrongdoings, began his career in journalism at the *New York Times.* Before joining the *Wall Street Journal,* he worked for the *Washington Post* and United Press International. Obituaries and other sources: *Who's Who in America,* 40th edition, Marquis, 1978; *New York Times,* March 1, 1981; *Washington Post,* March 1, 1981.

LANDES, David Saul 1924-

PERSONAL: Born April 29, 1924, in New York, N.Y.; son of Harry and Sylvia (Silberman) Landes; married Sonia Tarnopol, March 19, 1944; children: Jane, Richard Allen, Alison. *Education:* City College (now of the City University of New York), A.B., 1942; Harvard University, A.M., 1943, Ph.D., 1953. *Home:* 24 Highland St., Cambridge, Mass. 02138. *Office:* Department of History and Political Science, Harvard University, Cambridge, Mass. 02138.

CAREER: Columbia University, New York, N.Y., assistant professor, 1952-55, associate professor of economics, 1955-58; University of California, Berkeley, professor of history and economics, 1958-64; Harvard University, Cambridge, Mass., professor of history, 1964-72, Leroy B. Williams Professor of History and Political Science, 1972-75, Robert Walton Goelet Professor of French History, 1975—, director of Center for Middle Eastern Studies, 1966-68. Fellow at Center for Advanced Study in the Behavioral Sciences, 1957-58; fellow at Churchill College, Cambridge, 1966-69. Ellen McArthur Lecturer at Cambridge University, 1964; associate professor at Sorbonne, University of Paris, 1972-73. Chairman of National Academy of Sciences-Social Science Research Council history panel, 1966-70, and Council for Research on Economic History, 1963-66. *Military service:* U.S. Army, Signal Corps, 1943-46; became first lieutenant.

MEMBER: American Academy of Arts and Sciences (fellow), American Historical Association, Economic History Association (president, 1976-77; member of board of trustees), Society for French Historical Studies, British Academy (fellow), Royal Historical Society, Economic History Society (England), Societe d'Histoire Moderne, Gesellschaft fuer Sozial-und Wirtschaftgeschichte. *Awards, honors:* D.H.C. from University of Lille; Social Science Research Council grant for France, 1960-61; Rockefeller Foundation fellow, 1960-61.

WRITINGS: Bankers and Pashas: International Finance and Economic Imperialism in Egypt, Harvard University Press, 1958; (editor) *The Rise of Capitalism,* Macmillan, 1966; *The Unbound Prometheus: Technological Change and Industrial Development in Western Europe From 1750 to the Present,* Cambridge University Press, 1969; (editor with Charles Tilly) *History as Social Science,* Prentice-Hall, 1971; (co-author) *Estudios sobre al naciemiento y desarrollo del capitalismo* (translated into Spanish by Jorge Fabra Utray), Ayuso, 2nd edition, 1972; (editor) *Western Europe: The Trials of Partnership,* Lexington Books, 1977. Contributor to history journals. Associate editor of *Journal of Economic History,* 1954-60.

SIDELIGHTS: Theodore Roszak, writing for the *Nation,* called David Landes's *The Unbound Prometheus: Technological Change and Industrial Development in Western Europe From 1750 to the Present* "an indispensable reference guide." "With impressive authority," Roszak added, "it covers a wide range of most important interpretive emphases on and insights into modern economic thought and scholarship. . . . Further, the more technical features of industrialization are treated by Landes with admirable breadth; the context of social and political history is never lost from sight in the often detailed discussion of machines, techniques and organizational forms."

Although Roszak found "a naivete at the heart of this highly sophisticated work," he felt that Landes had "produced a history of such authority and critical substance, that it fully

deserves the place it is bound to hold for the next generation or more as a standard comparative study of industrial development in England, Germany, France and . . . America."

BIOGRAPHICAL/CRITICAL SOURCES: Nation, November 24, 1969.*

*   *   *

LANDRITH, Harold Fochone 1919-

PERSONAL: Born December 23, 1919, in Seneca, S.C.; son of Walter Louis and Ethel (Powell) Landrith. *Education:* Clemson University, B.S., 1948; Vanderbilt University, M.A., 1949; University of Houston, Ed.D., 1960. *Home address:* Fair Play Rd., Seneca, S.C. 29678. *Office:* College of Education, Clemson University, Clemson, S.C. 29631.

CAREER: Keesler Air Force Base, Miss., civilian educational specialist and teacher, 1951-55; South Texas College, Houston, head of department of social science, 1955-61; Clemson University, Clemson, S.C., associate professor of history and education, 1961—, dean of College of Education, 1965—. Instructor at University of Mississippi, Biloxi Center, 1952-55; president of department of higher education of South Carolina State Supported Colleges; consultant to International Telephone & Telegraph and Modern Optics, Inc. *Military service:* U.S. Army Air Forces, 1939-45. *Member:* South Carolina Education Association (president of department of higher education, 1969-70; vice-president). *Awards, honors:* Distinguished service award from South Carolina Recreation and Park Society.

WRITINGS: Introduction to the Community Junior College, Interstate, 1971. Contributor to education journals.*

*   *   *

LANDSBURG, Alan William 1933-

PERSONAL: Born May 10, 1933, in White Plains, N.Y.; son of Harry and Fanny (Koslovsky) Landsburg; married Sally Breit (divorced, 1975); married Linda Otto (a film producer), March 7, 1976; children: Valerie, Michael. *Education:* New York University, B.A., 1953. *Home:* 2204 North Beverly Dr., Beverly Hills, Calif. 90210. *Agent:* Julian Bach Literary Agency, Inc., 747 Third Ave., New York, N.Y. 10017. *Office:* Alan Landsburg Productions, 1554 South Sepulveda Blvd., Los Angeles, Calif. 90025.

CAREER: National Broadcasting Co., New York City, producer in news department, 1951-59; Columbia Broadcasting System, New York City, producer and writer, 1959-60; Metromedia Productions, Los Angeles, Calif., executive vice-president, 1961-70; Alan Landsburg Productions, Los Angeles, chairman of board of directors, 1970—. Instructor at University of California, Los Angeles, 1968-70. Executive producer of television series, including "The Undersea World of Jacques Cousteau," "March of Time," "In Search of . . . ," "Those Amazing Animals" (ABC-TV, 1980), "That's Incredible" (ABC-TV, 1980), and "National Geographic Specials." Executive producer of television films, including "Fear on Trial," "Storm in Summer," "Savage Bees," "Triangle Factory Fire," "The Chisolms," and "And Baby Makes Six." *Military service:* U.S. Army, 1953-55. *Awards, honors:* Peabody Broadcasting Awards from Academy of Television Arts and Sciences, 1964, for "Biography" series, and 1966, for "National Geographic Specials"; Emmy Award from Academy of Television Arts and Sciences, 1970, for producing.

WRITINGS: (With Sally Landsburg) *In Search of Ancient Mysteries,* Bantam, 1974; (with S. Landsburg) *Outer Space*

Connection, Bantam, 1975; *The Insects Are Coming*, Warner Books, 1978; *Secrets of the Bermuda Triangle*, Warner Books, 1978; *In Search of . . .*, Everest House, 1978.

*   *   *

LANDVATER, Dorothy 1927-

PERSONAL: Born August 23, 1927, in Lancaster, Pa.; daughter of Cleon and Miriam S. (Hess) Kahler; married John Howard Landvater (a consultant), June 11, 1948; children: Darryl Vincent, Gregory Lee, Lance Eric, David Ashley. *Religion:* Methodist. *Home:* 77 Holly Glen Lane S., Berkeley Heights, N.J. 07922. *Office:* Sharing, 1788 Springfield Ave., New Providence, N.J. 07974.

CAREER: Book reviewer with Alice Black Agency in South Orange, N.J., beginning 1966; Sharing (nonprofit organization for the handicapped), New Providence, N.J., president, 1978—. Creative writing teacher in North Plainfield adult education program, 1976—. Co-chairman of Union County Advisory Board for the Handicapped. *Member:* Berkeley Heights Woman's Club. *Awards, honors:* First prize for book review from New Jersey State Federation of Woman's Clubs, 1955.

WRITINGS: David (nonfiction), Prentice-Hall, 1976. Editor of *Sharing*, 1978—.

SIDELIGHTS: Dorothy Landvater wrote: "After our fourth son's accident, which resulted in his being multiply handicapped, I turned to help those who are disabled. At Sharing, we are all volunteers. In addition to publishing a newsletter for the handicapped, we are helping to create a barrier-free society, mainstream handicapped people into the employment world, and educate society that the handicapped are real people and that disabilities should not interfere with personal relations."

*   *   *

LANEY, James Thomas 1927-

PERSONAL: Born December 24, 1927, in Wilson, Ark.; son of Thomas Mann and Mary (Hughey) Laney; married Berta Joan Radford, December 20, 1949; children: Berta Joan (Mrs. Mark Anderson), James T., Arthur Radford, Mary Ruth, Susan Elizabeth. *Education:* Yale University, B.A., 1950, B.D., 1954, Ph.D., 1966. *Home:* 1463 Clifton Rd., Atlanta, Ga. 30329. *Office:* Office of the President, Emory University, Atlanta, Ga. 30322.

CAREER: Ordained Methodist minister, 1955; chaplain at private school in Wallingford, Conn., 1953-55; pastor of Methodist church in Cincinnati, Ohio, 1955-58; Board of Missions of the Methodist Church, Seoul, Korea, secretary of Korean Students Church Council, 1959-62; Yonsei University, Seoul, associate professor of ethics, 1962-64; Vanderbilt University, Nashville, Tenn., assistant professor of Christian ethics, 1966-69; Emory University, Atlanta, Ga., dean of Candler School of Theology, 1969-77, president of university, 1977—. Assistant lecturer at Yale University, 1954-55; Lilly Lecturer at DePauw University, 1967; visiting professor at Harvard University, 1974. President of Nashville Community Relations Coucil, 1968-69; member of board of directors of Trust Company of Georgia, Fund for Theological Education, and Christian Education in Asia; chairman of board of directors of United Service Organizations in Korea, 1962-64. *Military service:* U.S. Army, 1946-48.

MEMBER: American Association of Theological Schools (chairman of Resources Planning Commission), American Society of Christian Ethics, Society for the Scientific Study

of Religion, Society for Religion in Higher Education (fellow), Atlanta Theological Association (chairman of board of governors), Phi Beta Kappa, Omicron Delta Kappa. *Awards, honors:* Leadership award, 1970-71; D.D. from Florida Southern College, 1977; L.H.D. from Southwestern College at Memphis, 1979.

WRITINGS: (Editor with James M. Gustafson) *On Being Responsible: Issues in Personal Ethics*, Harper, 1968; (contributor) Liston O. Mills, editor, *Perspectives on Death*, Abingdon, 1969; (editor) *Evangelism: Mandates for Action*, Hawthorn, 1975. Contributor to theology journals and *Annals of the American Academy of Politcal and Social Science.**

*   *   *

LANG, Paul Henry 1901-

PERSONAL: Born August 28, 1901, in Budapest, Hungary; came to the United States in 1928, naturalized citizen, 1934; married Anne Pecheux; children: two sons, two daughters. *Education:* Attended Budapest Royal Academy of Music, University of Heidelberg, University of Paris, and Cornell University. *Office:* Department of Music, Columbia University, New York, N.Y. 10027.

CAREER: Vassar College, Poughkeepsie, N.Y., assistant professor of music, 1930-31; Wells College, Aurora, N.Y., associate professor of music, 1931-33; Columbia University, New York, N.Y., began as assistant professor, became associate professor, 1933-39, professor of musicology, 1939-70. *Member:* International Musicological Society (president), American Academy of Arts and Sciences (fellow), French Musicological Society, Dutch Musicological Society, Belgian Musicological Society. *Awards, honors:* L.H.D.

WRITINGS: Music in Western Civilization, Norton, 1941, reprinted, 1969; (with Otto Bettmann) *A Pictorial History of Music*, Norton, 1960; (editor) *One Hundred Years of Music in America*, Schirmer Books, 1961; (editor) *The Creative World of Mozart*, Norton, 1963; (editor) *Stravinsky: A New Appraisal of His Work*, Norton, 1963; *Ceremony and Celebration*, Concordia, 1965; (editor with Nathan Broder) *Contemporary Music in Europe: A Comprehensive Survey*, Schirmer Books, 1966; *George Frederic Handel*, Norton, 1966; (editor) *The Concerto, 1800-1900*, Norton, 1969; (editor) *The Symphony, 1800-1900*, Norton, 1969; (editor) *The Creative World of Beethoven*, Norton, 1970; *Critic at the Opera*, Norton, 1971, reprinted as *The Experience of Opera*, 1973. Also author of *Problems of Modern Music: The Princeton Seminar in Advanced Musical Studies*, 1960.

Music critic for *New York Herald Tribune*, 1954-66, chief music critic, 1957-63. Contributor to music journals. Editor of *Musical Quarterly*, 1945—.

SIDELIGHTS: George Frederic Handel, Paul Henry Lang's biography of the German-born composer of operas, oratorios, and church and chamber music, "is the product of many years of research," noted Winthrop Sargeant in the *New Yorker*. It "is delightfully readable as well as thoroughly documented; and it will probably stand for many years as the definitive book about Handel and his work."

The *Messiah*, generally the best known of Handel's oratorios, is not typical of the composer's work, Lang asserts. "Lang is at pains at the outset to show that Handel's reputation for holiness and monumentality rests mainly on a nineteenth-century Victorian misunderstanding of his musical intentions as well as of his character," Sargeant explained. In reality, Handel "was neither particularly religious nor at all pompous."

A *Times Literary Supplement* critic agreed that Lang's book would "command attention," calling it a "labour of love spread over years of investigation in depth." He complained, however, that Lang's thesis (that, with the exception of *Messiah,* Handel's work did not generally have religious themes) was not an original discovery, but had been set forth sixty years earlier by Ernest Walker. Lang discussed Walker in his book but dismisses him, observed the *Times Literary Supplement* critic, "because he does not agree with some of his [Walker's] value judgments."

Denis Arnold of the *Listener* thought that although Lang had provided a great deal of much-needed biographical information about Handel, he had at times supplied background material that was irrelevant. Still, Arnold commented, the book "offers a wryly witty account of Handel's career. It is only as a final word on the subject that it is inadequate."

BIOGRAPHICAL/CRITICAL SOURCES: New Yorker, June 10, 1967; *Times Literary Supplement,* July 13, 1967; *Listener,* April 4, 1968; *New York Times,* October 22, 1971.*

* * *

LANG, Ronald William 1933-

PERSONAL: Born April 26, 1933, in St. Mary's, Ontario, Canada; son of Harold DeFoe (a judge) and Marion Christine (Grieve) Lang; married Birthe Anna Simonsen, June 5, 1954; children: Harold DeFoe, Heather Anne, Stephen Ronald, John Douglas, Christopher Simon, Sheldon. *Education:* Attended Ontario Agricultural College, 1950-52, and Labour College of Canada, 1964; University of Waterloo, B.A., 1968, M.A., 1969; London School of Economics and Political Science, London, Ph.D., 1974. *Politics:* New Democrat. *Religion:* United Church of Canada. *Home:* 293 John St. N., Arnprior, Ontario, Canada K7S 2P5. *Office:* Canadian Labour Congress, 2841 Riverside Dr., Ottawa, Ontario, Canada K1V 8N4.

CAREER: Farm worker, 1952-53; farmer in St. Mary's, Ontario, 1953-63; York University, Downsview, Ontario, assistant professor of Canadian government and politics, 1971-72; Canadian Labour Congress, Ottawa, Ontario, director of research and legislation. Honorary life member of Woodstock and Ingersoll District Labour Council (president, 1963); member of Canadian Economic Policy Committee and Canadian-American Committee. *Member:* United Cement, Lime, and Gypsum Workers International Union (shop steward, 1959; president, 1961-64), Masons. *Awards, honors:* Canada Council fellow, 1969.

WRITINGS: The Politics of Drugs: A Comparative Pressure-Group Study of the Canadian Pharmaceutical Manufacturers Association and Association of the British Pharmaceutical Industry, 1930-1970, Lexington Books, 1974, revised edition published as *The Politics of Drugs: A Comparative Study of the British and Canadian Pharmaceutical Industries, 1930-1973,* 1975.

AVOCATIONAL INTERESTS: Ice hockey, gardening.*

* * *

LANG, William Rawson 1909-

PERSONAL: Born February 16, 1909, in Kanowna, Western Australia, Australia; son of William Rawson (a clergyman) and May (a hospital matron; maiden name, Griggs) Lang; married Helen Lindley Wansbrough, December 28, 1938; children: John David Rawson, Ross James Alan. *Education:* University of Western Australia, B.Sc., 1931, B.A., 1934, M.Sc., 1939, D.Sc., 1961. *Religion:* Christian. *Home:* 13

Humble St., Geelong East, Victoria 3219, Australia. *Office:* The Geelong Hospital, Box 281, Geelong, Victoria 3220, Australia.

CAREER: Wesley College, Perth, Western Australia, Australia, science master, 1931-34; Perth Technical College, Perth, science lecturer, 1934-36; University of Western Australia, Nedlands, research physicist at Institute of Agriculture, 1937-38; Gordon Institute of Technology, Geelong, Victoria, Australia, scientific investigations officer, 1938-45, head of Textile College, 1945-70, head of School of Applied Sciences and deputy principal, 1970-74. Victoria Institute of Colleges, member of board of studies, 1970-73, member of higher degrees committee, 1970-78. President of Geelong branch of Young Men's Christian Association (YMCA), 1954-58; president of Geelong Rotary Club, 1966. Geelong Hospital, honorary archivist, 1975-80, member of board of management, 1975—; member of board of directors of Geelong Medical and Hospital Benefits Association, 1978—. Historic research officer for Mosaic Mural for state of Victoria, 1977-80. *Member:* Australian College of Education (fellow; chairman of Victoria chapter, 1969-71), Australian Institute of Physics (fellow), Institute of Physics (United Kingdom; fellow), Textile Institute (United Kingdom; fellow). *Awards, honors:* Service medal, 1960, and Warner Memorial Medal, 1966, both from Textile Institute; Paul Harris fellowship from Rotary Foundation, 1979.

WRITINGS: (With Arthur James Farnsworth) *Textile Education in the Union of Burma,* UNESCO, 1957; (with Edmund Barrington Thomas) *The Televiewing Habits of Secondary School Children in Geelong,* Australian College of Education, 1965; *Sheep and Wool: Industry in Australia,* Longman Cheshire, 1967, 2nd edition, 1972; *Visions and Realities: A History of the Geelong Infirmary and Benevolent Asylum,* Neptune Press, 1980; *James Harrison: Pioneering Genius,* Neptune Press, 1981.

WORK IN PROGRESS: A sequel to *Visions and Realities,* covering the history of the Geelong Hospital from 1925 to 1980.

SIDELIGHTS: Lang told *CA:* "My interest in local, Victorian, and Australian history led to my collaboration with Harold Freedman, state artist for the State of Victoria, on a mosaic mural. I supplied some six hundred items for a pageant, or cavalcade, of the history of Geelong and the surrounding district, with dossiers on the people and their symbols. From these, Freedman chose 185 for use on the thirty-one-by-three-meter mural. It was unveiled on November 6, 1980, and is unique in that it covers a city's entire 144-year history rather than a single incident in that history. The mural will provide a basis for student projects and attract tourists to the Geelong area."

* * *

LANGDALE, Eve
See CRAIG, E(velyn) Quita

* * *

LANGE, Oliver [a pseudonym] 1927-

PERSONAL: Born December 14, 1927, in New York, N.Y.; married Nancy Henderson (a writer), July 20, 1979; children: Johanna, Jennifer, Jason, Thaddeus, Cassandra, Joshua. *Education:* Columbia University, B.S., 1956. *Politics:* None. *Religion:* None. *Home and office:* 530 Eagle Cove Dr., Friday Harbor, Wash. 98250. *Agent:* JET Literary Associates, Inc., 124 East 84th St., Suite 4A, New York, N.Y. 10028.

CAREER: Associated with *New Yorker* in New York City, beginning 1956; writer, 1956—; worked as a carpenter, handyman, night watchman, and psychiatric social worker. *Military service:* U.S. Army, 1945-51.

WRITINGS—Novels: *Vandenberg,* Stein & Day, 1971; *Incident at La Junta,* Stein & Day, 1973; *Red Snow,* Seaview, 1978; *Next of Kin,* Seaview, 1980; *The Land of the Long Shadow,* Seaview, 1981; *Defiance: An American Novel,* Stein & Day, 1981.

WORK IN PROGRESS: A novel, *Pas de deux,* publication expected in 1982.

SIDELIGHTS: Distinguishing himself from historic, journalistic, and pedantic writers, Oliver Lange wishes to be known as a storyteller. Characterization is the heart of his stories; he develops a cast of characters and then, as he words it, "steps aside and watches what kind of mischief they'll get into."

Lange's knack for storytelling has been praised by numerous critics. His first novel, *Vandenberg,* is a story about a man's escape from a detention center in a Russian-controlled United States and the escapee's subsequent fight to destroy the center. Peter Sourian of the *New York Times Book Review* wrote of *Vandenberg:* "The author draws his characters with a melodramatic flair, yet he does not generally sacrifice psychological verisimilitudes. [When he] stops to dabble in ideas themselves, he maintains an enviably hard-nosed sense of just how long he can afford to do so, never missing the train of his narrative." William Decker of *Saturday Review* postulated: "In his narrative writing, Mr. Lange is in the class of Hemingway of *For Whom the Bell Tolls.* His style is admirably taut."

Perseverance is a key characteristic of Oliver Lange. He wrote his novel *The Land of the Long Shadow* and then continuously revised it for nineteen years before it was finally accepted for publication. Lange also exhibits determination in his writing habits. When involved in the composition process, he writes as long as eighteen hours per day, breaking only occasionally for food or a nap. He maintains such a pace for weeks, but explains, "This is how books get written."

BIOGRAPHICAL/CRITICAL SOURCES: New York Times Book Review, February 28, 1971, August 12, 1973; *Best Sellers,* March 1, 1971, August 15, 1973; *New Republic,* March 13, 1973; *Saturday Review,* March 13, 1971; *Washington Post Book World,* March 2, 1980; *Detroit News,* March 9, 1980.

* * *

LANGFORD, Gary R(aymond) 1947-

PERSONAL: Born in 1947 in Christchurch, New Zealand; son of Maurice and May (Philpott) Langford; children: Kim. *Education:* University of Canterbury, B.A., 1969, M.A. (with honors; history), 1970, M.A. (with honors; English), 1972; Christchurch Secondary Teachers College, Diploma in Teaching, 1973. *Politics:* Socialist. *Home:* 36 Dean St., West Pennant Hills, Sydney, New South Wales, Australia. *Agent:* Curtis Brown Proprietary Ltd., P.O. Box 19, Paddington, Sydney, New South Wales 2119, Australia.

CAREER: Co-editor of *Edge,* 1970-72, and editor of *Superbox,* 1971, and *Shard,* 1972, all in New Zealand; teacher at secondary school in Sydney, Australia, 1974-76; Milperra College of Advanced Education, Sydney, lecturer in drama, 1977—. *Awards, honors:* Vera Bladen Poetry Award from *Expression,* 1970, for "Epilogue"; Patricia Hackett Prize from *Westerly,* 1974, for creative writing; grants from New

Zealand Literary Fund, 1974, and Australia Council, 1975; Australia Council fellow, 1977.

WRITINGS: The Family (poetry), Fragments Press, 1973; *Death of the Early Morning Hero* (novel), Angus & Robertson, 1976; *Getting On* (sketches), Milperra College of Advanced Education Press, 1978; *Reversals* (sketches), Milperra College of Advanced Education Press, 1978; *The Death of James Dean* (short stories), Randolph Press, 1978; *Players in the Ballgame* (novel), Macmillan, 1979; *The Adventures of Dreaded Ned* (novel), Randolph Press, 1980; *Four Ships* (poems), Randolph Press, 1981; *The Last Giants* (novel), Randolph Press, 1982.

Plays: "Lovers" (one-act), first produced in Sydney, Australia, at Milperra Theatre, November 20, 1977; "I Didn't Ask to Grow Old" (one-act), first produced in Sydney at Milperra Theatre, November 22, 1978; "Going Back" (two-act), first produced in Sydney at Nimrod Theatre, February 19, 1979; "The True Story of Superman" (two-act), first produced in Sydney at Hotel Manly, November 4, 1979.

Television and radio plays: "Quartet," first broadcast by New Zealand Broadcasting Commission, November 19, 1972; "Golden Handshake," first broadcast by New Zealand Broadcasting Commission, October 10, 1974; "The Bush Ranger," first broadcast by TCN Television, April 15, 1976.

SIDELIGHTS: Langford commented: "I write in all forms and like the idea of the artist as a court jester who reflects life's contradictions and absurdities. A comic, often bizarre, dark style is present in most of my writing, as I believe that laughter is one way of meeting the world without getting completely wiped out. I frequently perform my own poetry, stories, and sketches, and get out in the marketplace where the dust rarely settles.

"People are more important than place in my work. Many of the characters who have interested me have done so because they are individuals in an increasingly mass-produced world. Like me, they join few movements, yet remain aware that social change only happens through such movements. Irony and paradox abound.

"As soon as we take on a label we are classified and, therefore, dehumanized. Complexity is removed, for it is so much easier to join a group pecking at a form resembling ourselves in the town square. Yet it may be worse to be the solitary figure on the edge of the crowd, for one day, he may turn. . . .

"It is that feeling of individual, often helpless, courage that interests me. It may dangle people above the dark spaces, yet many survive with humanity and style. To hold that humanity is never easy. For me writing is as natural as breathing and eating (even if I sometimes feel like I'm in a queue at a fast-food outlet), and as paradoxical as life itself."

BIOGRAPHICAL/CRITICAL SOURCES: Canta, April 30, 1971; *Affairs,* October, 1971; *Review,* November 15, 1974; *Landfall No. 116,* 1975; *Bulletin,* November 26, 1977; *Campaign,* October, 1979.

* * *

LANSDALE, Robert Tucker 1900-1980

OBITUARY NOTICE: Born January 22, 1900, in Elmira, N.Y.; died November 29, 1980, in St. Petersburg, Fla. Social worker, educator, and author. In his lengthy career in the field of social welfare, Robert Lansdale held such various positions as assistant to the commissioner of the U.S. Office of Indian Affairs, commissioner of New York State's Department of Social Welfare, and consultant to the Maryland Commission on the Aging. A professor of social work at

Florida State University and the University of Maryland, Lansdale was the author of several books, including *Inadequacies of Statewide Programs of Public Assistance in Urban Areas, Supplemental Security Income: The First Six Months,* and *Supplemental Security Income: State Variations.* Obituaries and other sources: *Who's Who in America,* 40th edition, Marquis, 1978; *New York Times,* December 2, 1980.

*   *   *

La PLACE, John 1922-

PERSONAL: Born April 26, 1922, in New York, N.Y.; married Olang Klokkhammer, December 22, 1962; children: Ellen. *Education:* Columbia University, B.S., 1948, M.A., 1949, Ph.D., 1952. *Home:* 128 Howard Ter., Leonia, N.J. 07605.

CAREER: City College of the City University of New York (formerly City College), New York, N.Y., tutor, 1948-53, lecturer and instructor, 1953, assistant professor, 1953-59, associate professor, 1959-71, professor of health and physical education, 1971-77, professor emeritus, 1977—; Queensborough Community College of the City University of New York, Bayside, N.Y., professor of health, 1977-78; William Paterson College, Wayne, N.J., professor of health science, 1978-80. Charter member of New Jersey Trails Council. *Military service:* U.S. Army Air Forces, 1943-46. *Member:* American Association of Sex Educators, Counselors, and Therapists, New Jersey League for Conservation Legislation (member of board of directors).

WRITINGS: Health, Appleton-Century-Crofts, 1972, 3rd edition, Prentice-Hall, 1980.

SIDELIGHTS: La Place wrote: "My interests and concerns in the field of health reflect my firm belief in the importance of health to the individual and to society. A society that is replete with health problems is as handicapped in its ability to function as is the individual who is in poor health. The magnitude of the problems that confront us is enormous and there is a question as to whether we will ever address them appropriately. Such problems as the impact of man and technology upon the environment, the exploitation of the health consumer by fraudulent practitioners, and the inability of our present system of medical services to reach all parts of our society adequately demand greater attention than they have received so far.

"I am a physically active person. Over the years I have cycled in most of Europe, from Norway to Spain. I am a hiker and have been a tour leader with the Appalachian Mountain Club. At one point in my life I was rather extensively involved in mountaineering and have been a member of both the American Alpine Club and the Alpine Club of Canada. In 1967 I participated in the Yukon Alpine Centennial Expedition Sponsored by the Alpine Club of Canada. I have been in the forefront of the ski-touring movement and have led ski tours sponsored jointly by the Appalachian Mountain Club and the Eastern Ski-Touring Council. I participated in the 'Ski for Light' program in 1977 and 1980. I have also been running for over forty years but have never felt inclined to participate in a competitive event.

"I have traveled in the U.S. Virgin Islands, Mexico, Bermuda, all fifty U.S. states, and all of the Canadian provinces. I have been throughout central and northern Europe, and Iceland as well—and the health services in many of these areas are far superior to what we provide in the United States."

"I am involved in the political life of my community and my state; I'm also very committed to the educational process. I am presently serving in my fourth year as a school board trustee in the borough of Leonia, with two years remaining to my present terms of office."

*   *   *

LARN, Richard (James Vincent) 1930-

PERSONAL: Born September 1, 1930, in Norwich, England; son of Cyril (a market gardener) and Margaret (Vincent) Larn; married second wife, Bridget; children: (first marriage) Victoria Larn Newman, Tracy. *Education:* Attended a naval academy in England. *Religion:* Church of England. *Home:* 50 Sea Rd., Carlyon Bay, St. Austell, Cornwall, England. *Office:* Prodive Ltd., Falmouth Docks, Falmouth, Cornwall, England.

CAREER: British Merchant Navy, deck officer's apprentice with South American Saint Line, 1946-49; Royal Navy, diver, 1949-71, served in Korea, leaving service as chief petty officer; Partech Electronics Ltd., Charlestown, England, works manager, 1971-74, works director, 1974—. Managing director of Prodive Ltd., a professional diving training school, 1974—. *Member:* British Sub-Aqua Club, Society for Nautical Research, Society for Nautical Archaeology, Royal Cornwall Institute.

WRITINGS: Land's End Shipwrecks, Taplinger, 1968; (with Clive Carter) *Cornish Shipwrecks: The South Coast,* Taplinger, 1969; *Cornish Shipwrecks: The Isles of Scilly,* Taplinger, 1971; *Devon Shipwrecks,* Taplinger, 1973; *Goodwin Sands Shipwrecks,* Taplinger, 1977; *Shipwrecks of the British Isles,* David & Charles, 1980; (with Zelide Cowan) *Dictionary of Historic Divers, 1961-1825,* two volumes, Duckworth, 1982. Contributor to *The Second Underwater Book* and *The Wreck Hunters.* Contributor to magazines, including *Underwater World, Watersport, Triton, Diver,* and *Skin Diver.* Consulting editor of *Underwater World.*

WORK IN PROGRESS: A history of Charlestown, Cornwell, publication by Charlestown Estate Ltd., expected in 1981.

SIDELIGHTS: Larn wrote: "I have spent a lifetime connected with the sea, ships, and diving, and have dived on shipwrecks around the world. I have established a shipwreck computer center for the United Kingdom, which will eventually hold a record of over 250,000 shipping incidents, ranging from 1100 to 1981. It will probably be the most sophisticated and comprehensive wreck index, for any one country, in the world. In addition, my partner Roy Davis and I provide the contents and exhibits for a very active shipwreck museum center, which is based at Charlestown near St. Austell, Cornwall; this too is a unique activity in this country.

"I suppose that I have had more than my share of diving experiences, including treasure wrecks and modern salvage, but I still like to participate in new projects and adventures."

*   *   *

LaSALLE, Peter 1947-

PERSONAL: Born May 27, 1947, in Providence, R.I.; son of A. Norman (a lawyer) and Hope (a school librarian; maiden name, Conroy) LaSalle. *Education:* Harvard University, B.A., 1969; University of Chicago, M.A., 1972. *Politics:* Liberal Democrat. *Religion:* Roman Catholic. *Office:* Department of English, University of Texas, Austin, Tex. 78712.

CAREER: Johnson State College, Johnson, Vt., lecturer in creative writing and literature, 1974-76; University of Texas at the Permian Basin, Odessa, visiting assistant professor of creative writing, 1976-77; Iowa State University, Ames, assistant professor of English, 1977-80; University of Texas at Austin, assistant professor of English, 1980—. Fiction writer-in-residence at Green Mountain Writers Workshop, summer, 1980. *Awards, honors:* Grant from Iowa State University to interview writers in Cameroon, 1979; short story award from *Kansas Quarterly,* 1981.

WRITINGS: The Graves of Famous Writers and Other Stories, University of Missouri Press, 1980. Work represented in anthologies, including *The Best American Short Stories, 1979,* edited by Joyce Carol Oates, Houghton, 1979. Contributor of stories, poems, articles, and reviews to magazines, including *Esquire, Fiction International, Epoch, New Republic, Nation,* and *Progressive,* and newspapers. Associate editor of *Poet and Critic,* 1977—.

WORK IN PROGRESS: Short stories.

SIDELIGHTS: LaSalle commented: "I write, simply enough, about life in contemporary America. If any note recurs in my stories about 'everyday people' (such as nightclub owners, priests, beauty queens, FBI agents, and real estate agents), it is that life here today sometimes must seem so strange to them that it takes on the texture of a dream."

BIOGRAPHICAL/CRITICAL SOURCES: Georgia Review, summer, 1980; *Sewanee Review,* summer, 1980.

*   *   *

LASKER, Edward 1885-1981

OBITUARY NOTICE—See index for *CA* sketch: Born December 3, 1885, in Kempen, Germany; died March 23, 1981, in New York, N.Y. Engineer and author. Lasker won the United States Open chess championship five times, in 1916, 1917, 1919, 1920, and 1921, and competed in several other major tournaments. He was the author of books on chess and other games, including the classic *Chess Strategy,* which became a standard work soon after it was published in 1911. The 1945 revision was retitled *Modern Chess Strategy.* Obituaries and other sources: *New York Times,* March 26, 1981.

*   *   *

LATHAM, Earl Ganson 1907-

PERSONAL: Born October 28, 1907, in New Bedford, Mass.; son of Artemas Leroy and Irene Florence (Ganson) Latham; married Margaret Victoria Perrier, August 21, 1935; children: Peter Samuel, Susan Gail. *Education:* Harvard University, A.B., 1930, Ph.D., 1939. *Office:* Department of Political Science, Amherst College, Amherst, Mass. 01002.

CAREER: Harvard University, Amherst, Mass., instructor in government, 1936-40; University of Minnesota, Minneapolis, assistant professor, 1940-44, associate professor of government, 1944-48; Amherst College, Amherst, Mass., Joseph B. Eastman Professor of Political Science, 1948—, distinguished lecturer, 1973—, chairman of department, 1949-73. Instructor at Radcliffe College, 1938-40; visiting professor at Mount Holyoke College, 1951-52; visiting professor at Harvard University, 1959-60, and summers, 1947, 1949, 1953-56, 1958; Sperry-Hutchinson Foundation Lecturer at University of Florida, 1962. Senior administrative analyst for U.S. Bureau of the Budget, 1942-43, assistant chief of field service, 1943-46, chief budget examiner and chief economist, 1946, member of advisory committee, 1952—; member of executive council of Administrative Office of the United States, 1961-63. Delegate to international congresses; member of board of directors of Social Science Research Council, 1954-60, chairman of committee of social science personnel,

1959-60. Political science editor for St. Martin's Press, Inc., 1962-66; past political science editor for Harcourt Brace Jovanovich, Inc. Consultant to United Nations and federal government agencies.

MEMBER: American Academy of Arts and Sciences (fellow), American Political Science Association (member of executive committee, 1953-55; program chairman, 1955-56; vice-president, 1957-58), American Society for Public Administration, American Association of University Professors, New England Political Science Association (president, 1953-54), Psi Upsilon, Pi Sigma Alpha, Cosmos Club. *Awards, honors:* Social Science Research Council fellowship, 1935-36, grant, 1961-62; A.M. from Amherst College, 1949; citation from Woodrow Wilson Foundation, 1957; David Demaret Lloyd Prize from Harry S. Truman Library Institute, 1966, for *The Communist Controversy in Washington.*

WRITINGS: (Co-author) *Federal Field Service,* [Chicago], 1947; (editor) *John D. Rockefeller: Robber Baron or Industrial Statesman?,* Heath, 1949, revised edition, 1956; *The Group Basis of Politics: A Study in Basing-Point Legislation,* Cornell University Press, 1952; (editor and author of introduction) *The Declaration of Independence and the Constitution,* Heath, 1956, 3rd edition, 1976; (with George Goodwin) *Massachusetts Politics,* Citizenship Clearing House, 1956, revised edition, Tufts Civic Education Center, 1960; (co-author) Ivan Hinderaker, editor, *American Government Annual, 1958-59,* Holt, 1958; (co-author) *American Government Annual, 1959-60,* Holt, 1959; *The Politics of Railroad Coordination, 1933-1936,* Harvard University Press, 1959.

(Editor) *The Meaning of McCarthyism,* Heath, 1965, 2nd edition, 1973; *The Communist Controversy in Washington: From the New Deal to McCarthy,* Harvard University Press, 1966; (editor and author of introduction) *J. F. Kennedy and Presidential Power,* Heath, 1972.

Also author of *Ideas and Issues in Public Administration,* 1953, *Political Behavior,* 1956, *The Corporation and Modern Society,* 1959, *American Politics and Government,* 1965, and *Teaching Political Science,* 1965. Co-author of *Public Policy,* 1942. Special correspondent for the *Washington Post,* 1937-39. Contributor of articles and reviews to political science journals.

BIOGRAPHICAL/CRITICAL SOURCES: Esquire, April, 1967.*

*   *   *

LAUF, Detlef I. Charles 1936-

PERSONAL: Born March 24, 1936, in Wurzburg, Germany (now West Germany); came to the United States in 1971; son of Alfred (a physician) and Theresa (Sierp-Koenig) Lauf; married Gudrun Klempnauer, September 27, 1963; children: Sigrun (daughter). *Education:* University of Munich, Ph.D., 1965; Indiana University, Ps.D., 1971; University of Zurich, diploma of psychology, 1972. *Home:* 625 Post St., No. 246, San Francisco, Calif. 94109; and P.O. Box 44, Schaffhausen 8202, Switzerland. *Office:* C. G. Jung Institute Zurich, 28 Hornweg, Kusnacht 8700, Switzerland.

CAREER: C. G. Jung Institute, Zurich, Switzerland, professor of comparative religion, 1968—. Visiting professor at University of Ghent, 1971-73, Royal Academy of Arts, Antwerp, Belgium, 1971-74, California Institute of Asian Studies, San Francisco, 1976—, University of California, Berkeley, 1977, and John F. Kennedy University, Martinez, Calif., 1979; member of Jean Gebser Center at Ohio University. *Member:* International Society for the History of Religions,

International Platform Association, International Biographical Association (fellow), American Association of University Professors, American Oriental Society, Smithsonian Associates, Association of Swiss Psychologists, Eranos Institute of Classical Studies, Societe des Etudes Asiatiques, Suisse.

WRITINGS: Tibetan Sacred Art, Shambhala, 1976; *Secret Revelation of Tibetan Thangkas,* Aurum, 1976; (contributor) Mircea Eliade, Joseph Campbell, and Alexander Eliot, editors, *Myths of the World,* McGraw, 1976; *Secret Doctrines of the Tibetan Book of the Dead,* Shambhala, 1977; *Terrifying Deities of Vajrayana Buddhism,* Marco Polo, 1978; *Mandalas: Blockprints From Ladakh,* Kossodo (Geneva), 1978.

In German: *Das Bild als Symbol in Tantrismus* (title means "The Image as Symbol in Tantrism"), H. Moos, 1973; *Symbole: Verschiedenheit und Einheit in westlicher und oestlicher Kultur* (title means "Symbols: Variety and Unity of Western and Eastern Culture"), Insel, 1976; *Eine Ikonographie des tibetischen Buddhismus* (title means "An Iconography of Tibetan Buddhism"), [Graz, Austria], 1979.

Author of art catalogs. Contributor of more than fifty articles to religious and Asian studies journals.

WORK IN PROGRESS: Fundamente der mythischen Welt (title means "Foundations of the Mythic World"), publication by Insel expected in 1981 or 1982; *Phaenomenologie des Numinosen* (title means "Phenomenology of the Numinous in World Religions), publication by Insel expected in 1984; research on fundamentals of mythic thought, cultural philosophy, and religion.

SIDELIGHTS: Lauf told *CA:* "After intensive studies and research in eastern philosophy and religions, with field work in India, Nepal, Ladakh, Sikkim, and Bhutan, I realized that the heritage and values of eastern ways of thinking should be compared to western thought and finally be integrated to enhance a broader and integral consciousness. Cross-cultural studies of eastern and western thought, religions, myths, and culture are particularly in demand for our time; they will serve essentially for the understanding of human culture and the psychological and socio-political background in fast-growing worldwide relations.

"My special interest is focused on comparative mythology and phenomenology of religions, because these are open fields in the dynamics of the human mind, and they have an important influence on the future development of integration and culture. Therefore, my studies and coming publications will be concentrated on basic structures, origins and archetypal powers or patterns of human consciousness and their functioning in contemporaneous thought. Knowing the roots and origins of thought helps us to formulate a phenomenology that can serve to develop integral studies and cross-cultural understanding, as well as the mutual appreciation of cultures."

In addition to German and English, Lauf speaks Pali, Sanskrit, Hindi, Tibetan, Chinese, Mongolian, Russian, Italian, and French.

*   *   *

LAUNITZ-SCHURER, Leopold (Sidney), Jr.   1942-

PERSONAL: Born April 19, 1942, in Montreal, Quebec, Canada; son of Leopold Sidney (an investment banker) and Rose Marjory (Springett) Launitz-Schurer; married Caroline Turner (an art gallery officer), February 9, 1974. *Education:* Sir George Williams University, B.A., 1963; McGill University, M.A., 1966, Ph.D., 1970. *Religion:* Episcopalian. *Home:* 53 Moolanda St., Brisbane, Queensland 4074, Aus-

tralia. *Office:* Division of External Studies, University of Queensland, Brisbane, Queensland 4067, Australia.

CAREER: Sir George Williams University, Montreal, Quebec, part-time lecturer in European history, 1963-65; Dawson College, Montreal, Quebec, lecturer in Canadian history, 1971-74; University of Queensland, Brisbane, Australia, lecturer, 1974-79, senior lecturer in American history, 1980—. *Member:* Australian Historical Association, Australian and New Zealand American Studies Association, American Historical Association, Organization of American Historians, Southern Historical Association, New York State Historical Association, New York Historical Society.

WRITINGS: Loyal Whigs and Revolutionaries: The Making of the Revolution in New York, 1765-1776, New York University Press, 1980.

Contributor: Neville Meaney, editor, *Studies on the American Revolution,* Macmillan, 1976; Norman Harper, editor, *Pacific Circle Three: American Studies From Down Under,* University of Queensland Press, 1976; John A. Moses, editor, *Historical Disciplines and Culture in Australasia: An Assessment,* University of Queensland Press, 1979. Contributor to history journals.

WORK IN PROGRESS: A biography of New York loyalist William Smith, Jr.

SIDELIGHTS: Launitz-Schurer wrote: "I have had a lifelong interest in American history and view the Revolutionary period as the key to understanding the importance of the United States and American national character."

*   *   *

LAURE, Ettagale   1940-

PERSONAL: Born June 8, 1940, in New York, N.Y.; daughter of Samuel and Minnie Blauer. *Education:* Hunter College (now Herbert H. Lehman College of the City University of New York), B.A., 1961. *Home:* 8 West 13th St., New York, N.Y. 10011.

CAREER: Chemstrand Co., New York City, writer, 1961-66; Chilton Co., New York City, writer, 1971—. *Awards, honors:* National Book Award nomination, 1975, for *Joi Bangla;* Jesse Neal Editorial Achievement Award from American Business Press, 1977, for stories on women and discrimination, and 1979, for a series on gold; American Library Association notable book citation for *South Africa: Coming of Age Under Apartheid.*

WRITINGS: (With Jason Laure) *Joi Bangla: The Children of Bangladesh* (young adult), Farrar, Straus, 1974; (with J. Laure) *Jovem Portugal: After the Revolution* (young adult), Farrar, Straus, 1977; (with J. Laure) *South Africa: Coming of Age Under Apartheid* (young adult), Farrar, Straus, 1980. Contributor to magazines, including *Signature, Junior Scholastic,* and *Savvy.*

SIDELIGHTS: Ettagale Laure told *CA:* "As a writer of nonfiction, I consider it both my task and my pleasure to learn about foreign subjects and people and bring that information to my readers who cannot make those same journeys except through my writings."

BIOGRAPHICAL/CRITICAL SOURCES: Los Angeles Times Book Review, August 3, 1980; *Chicago Times Book World,* November 9, 1980.

LAURIA, Frank (Jonathan)   1935-

PERSONAL: Born October 26, 1935, in Brooklyn, N.Y.; son of Melchiorre (a structural engineer) and Vittoria (a teacher; maiden name, Agneta) Lauria; married E. Margareta Prins (a fashion designer), June 3, 1965. *Education:* Manhattan College, B.S., 1958.

CAREER: Worked as professional actor, model, photographer, and social worker; Bantam Books, Inc., New York, N.Y., assistant copy chief, 1967-68; Pyramid Publications, Moonachie, N.J., special projects editor, 1968; senior editor of Paperback Library, 1969-70; account executive for Wunderman Ricattasklien, 1972; free-lance writer, 1972—. *Member:* International P.E.N., Actors' Equity Association, Screen Actors Guild, National Organization for Reform of Marijuana Laws. *Awards, honors:* First prize for poetry from Valley Writers Conference, 1963.

WRITINGS: Doctor Orient (novel), Bantam, 1970; *Raga Six* (novel), Bantam, 1972; *Lady Sativa* (novel), Curtis Books, 1973; *Baron Orgaz* (novel), Bantam, 1974; *Communion,* Bantam, 1977; *The Seth Papers,* Ballantine, 1979. Also author of *The Priestess.* Contributor to *Arkangel.**

*   *   *

LAVENSON, James H.   1919-
(Jim Lavenson)

PERSONAL: Born June 8, 1919, in Philadelphia, Pa.; son of Jay and Caroline (Wolf) Lavenson; married Susan Barker (an art director), April 22, 1973; children: Joel, Michael, Gary, Peter, Ellen. *Education:* Williams College, B.A., 1941; Harvard University, M.B.A., 1955. *Politics:* Democrat. *Religion:* None. *Home:* 1831 East Mountain Dr., Montecito, Calif. 93108. *Office:* San Ysidro Ranch, Montecito, Calif. 93108.

CAREER: President of Lavenson Bureau of Advertising, Inc., 1950-64; Plaza Hotel, New York City, president, 1972-75; Lavenson Management Enterprises, Inc., New York City, president, 1976—. Director of Young Presidents Organization, 1955-69; member of Chief Executives Forum, 1969—; volunteer consultant to International Executive Service Corp., 1970—; president and chief executive officer of San Ysidro Ranch Corp.; president of Sunwear Inc.; chairman of Doxee Food Co.; senior partner of McCaffrey Associates; director of Sonesta Hotels. Member of American Cancer Society and Albert Schweitzer Foundation. *Military service:* U.S. Army, 1942-46; became captain. *Awards, honors:* Gold medals from Direct Mail Association, for employee motivation, and Hotel Association, for advertising for the Plaza Hotel, both 1974.

WRITINGS—Under name Jim Lavenson: *Sensuous Animal* (fiction), Dell, 1973. Author of "Jaundiced Eye," a column in *Sales Management and Marketing,* 1971—. Contributor to *Saturday Evening Post* and *Sales and Marketing Management.*

*   *   *

LAVENSON, Jim
See LAVENSON, James H.

LAWLER, Raymond Evenor   1922-

PERSONAL: Born in 1922 (birthdate listed in some sources as 1921) in Footscray, Australia; married Jacklyn Kelleher; children: three. *Education:* Attended grammar school in Australia.

CAREER: Worked in factories in Australia; stage manager of Variety Theatre, Brisbane, Australia; actor, director, and producer with National Theatre Co., Melbourne, Australia; director of Melbourne University Repertory Co., Melbourne. Playwright. *Member:* Dramatists League. *Awards, honors:* First prize from Australian National Theatre Commonwealth Jubilee Play Competition, 1952, for "Cradle of Thunder"; award from *Evening Standard,* 1958.

WRITINGS—Plays: *Summer of the Seventeenth Doll* (first produced in Melbourne, Australia, at Union Theatre, 1955; produced on the West End at New Theatre, April 30, 1957; produced in New York at Coronet Theatre, January 22, 1958; produced Off-Broadway at Players Theatre, October 13, 1959), Random House, 1957; *The Picadilly Bushman* (first produced in Melbourne, 1959; produced in Watford, England, at Palace Theatre, September 28, 1965), Angus & Robertson, 1961.

Unpublished plays: "Cradle of Thunder," first produced in Edinburgh, Scotland, at Lyceum Theatre, 1963, produced in London, c. 1963; "A Breach in the Wall," first produced in Canterbury, England, at Marlowe Theatre, 1970 (also see below); "The Man Who Shot the Albatross" (three-act), first produced in Melbourne at Princess Theatre, 1971; "Kid Stakes," first produced in Melbourne, 1975.

Television plays: "A Breach in the Wall," 1967; "Cousin Bette" (series; adapted from the novel by Balzac), 1971; "The Visitors" (series; adapted from the novel by Mary McMinnies), 1972; "Two Women" (series; adapted from the novel by Alberto Moravia), 1972; "Mrs. Palfrey at Claremont" (adapted from the novel by Elizabeth Taylor), 1973; "Seeking the Bubbles," 1975; "True Patriots All," 1975; "Husband to Mrs. Fitzherbert," 1975.

Also author of children's shows, 1950. Ghost writer for Will Mahoney.

SIDELIGHTS: With the production of "Summer of the Seventeenth Doll," Ray Lawler became one of Australia's few internationally known playwrights. The principal characters are two aging sugarcane cutters who come to realize that their friendship, with its roots in earlier times, was appropriate in their youth but is no longer meaningful. "Summer of the Seventeenth Doll," which Jack Kroll of *Newsweek* called a "solid, well-crafted realist work," challenges several popular Australian myths that have outlived their validity. Lawler's work provided a new range of material for Australian playwrights and prompted them to tackle other existing myths.

One aspect of Australian theatre that had outlived its validity was the traditional portrayal of the working class as speakers of a coarse, hackneyed version of English. In "Summer of the Seventeenth Doll," Lawler created dialogue that was colorful, unstilted, and authentic. In his attempt to capture the native vernacular for the stage, Lawler destroyed the outdated and inaccurate image of the language of the Australian laborer.

The notorious Captain William Bligh is the subject of another Lawler play, "The Man Who Shot the Albatross." The play explores the enigmatic personality of Bligh who, seventeen years after the *Bounty* mutiny of 1789, is still haunted by memories of that historic event. As governor of New South Wales, he is once again faced with dissension and insurrection. This time it is the military who revolt, in what came to be known as the Rum Rebellion. Lawler draws parallels between the current uprising and the earlier *Bounty* mutiny and examines Bligh's reaction to both. The play, which a writer for *Stage* called "the year's theatrical event in Australia," initially met with mixed reviews and later underwent extensive revision. A critic for *Variety* called Lawler's dialogue and scene plotting "skillful" and praised him for writing a historically accurate play.

BIOGRAPHICAL/CRITICAL SOURCES: Newsweek, March 4, 1968; *Stage,* October 28, 1971; *Variety,* December 15, 1971.*

*　*　*

LAWSON, Joan 1906-

PERSONAL: Born January 30, 1906, in London, England; daughter of Robb and Edith Marion (Usherwood) Lawson. *Education:* Attended Choreographic School in Moscow, Leningrad Choreographic School, and Seraphina Astafieva School of Dance. *Home:* 11 Hallswelle Rd., London NW11 0DH, England.

CAREER: Critic for *Dancing Times,* 1940-60; Royal Ballet School, London, England, teacher of classical and national dance and history of ballet, 1963—. Lecturer to military forces for Advisory Council for Education, 1940-47. *Member:* International Folk Music Society, Critics' Circle, Imperial Society of Teachers of Dancing (national vice-chairman, 1952—), Society for Theatre Research. *Awards, honors:* Imperial Award for special services to national dance.

WRITINGS: (Translator, with Stephen Garry) Valerian Mikhailovich Bogdanov-Berezovsky, *Ulanova and the Development of the Soviet Ballet,* MacGibbon & Kee, 1952; *European Folk Dance: Its National and Musical Characteristics,* Pitman, 1953, reprinted, Imperial Society of Teachers of Dancing, 1976, Arno, 1980; *Mime: The Theory and Practice of Expressive Gesture, With a Description of Its Historical Development,* Pitman, 1957, Dance Horizons, 1973; (with Peter Revitt) *Dressing for the Ballet,* A. & C. Black, 1958.

Classical Ballet: Its Style and Technique, A. & C. Black, 1960; *A History of Ballet and Its Makers,* Pitman, 1964, Dance Horizons, 1972; (editor and translator) Tamara Stepanovna Tkachenko, *Soviet Dances,* Imperial Society of Teachers of Dancing, 1964; (editor and translator) Tkachenko, *More Soviet Dances,* Imperial Society of Teachers of Dancing, 1967; (editor) Tkachenko, *A Third Set of Soviet Dances,* Imperial Society of Teachers of Dancing, 1968.

The Teaching of Classical Ballet: Common Faults in Young Dancers and Their Training, Theatre Arts, 1973; *Teaching Young Dancers: Muscular Coordination in Classical Ballet,* Theatre Arts, 1975; *The Story of Ballet,* Taplinger, 1976; *Beginning Ballet: A Concentrated Primer for Ballet Students of All Ages,* A. & C. Black, 1977; *Ballet Stories,* Mayflower, 1978; *The Principles of Classical Dance,* A. & C. Black, 1979; *The Kay Ambrose Ballet Companion,* A. & C. Black, 1979. Also author of *Pas de deuce,* 1978. Contributor to *Oxford Junior Encyclopedia, Enciclopedia Della Spectaccolo,* and *Encyclopaedia Britannica.* Contributor to dance journals.

SIDELIGHTS: Joan Lawson told *CA:* "I started dancing at the age of six, after recovering from a serious illness. I have traveled widely in professional dance companies throughout

England and Europe. I am currently working with an orthopedic surgeon on the rehabilitation of dancers after serious injuries."

*　*　*

LAXNESS, Halldor
See GUDJONSSON, Halldor Kiljan

*　*　*

LEACH, Eleanor Winsor 1937-

PERSONAL: Born August 16, 1937, in Providence, R.I.; married, 1962. *Education:* Bryn Mawr College, A.B., 1959; Yale University, M.A., 1960, Ph.D., 1963. *Office:* Department of Classical Studies, Indiana University, 547 Ballantine Hall, Bloomington, Ind. 47401.

CAREER: Villanova University, Villanova, Pa., assistant professor of classical languages, 1965-71; University of Texas, Austin, visiting associate professor of classical studies, 1972-74; Wesleyan University, Middletown, Conn., visiting associate professor of classical studies, 1974-76, fellow of Humanities Center, 1974; Indiana University, Bloomington, associate professor of classical studies, 1976—. *Member:* American Philological Association, Archaeological Institute of America, Classical Association of the Midwest and South. *Awards, honors:* Grants from American Philosophical Society, 1971, and American Council of Learned Societies, 1972; Guggenheim fellow, 1976-77.

WRITINGS: Vergil's Eclogues: Landscapes of Experience, Cornell University Press, 1974. Contributor to scholarly journals.*

*　*　*

LEAGANS, John Paul 1911-

PERSONAL: Born September 11, 1911, in Mocksville, N.C.; married, 1934; children: three. *Education:* North Carolina State University, B.S., 1934; University of Chicago, Ph.D., 1949. *Office:* Department of Education, Cornell University, 109 Stone Hall, Ithaca, N.Y. 14850.

CAREER: High school teacher of agriculture in North Carolina, 1934-36; North Carolina Cooperative Extension Service, assistant county agent, 1936-38, county agent, 1938-39; North Carolina State University, Raleigh, assistant professor of extension education, 1939-49; Cornell University, Ithaca, N.Y., professor for extension and continuing education programs, 1949—, chairman of graduate program, 1949—. Visiting professor at Flordia A & M University, 1972-73. Member of research committee of National Commission on Professional Adult Education; member of steering committee of National Extension Education Curriculum Development Seminar; member of national advisory board of Educational Resources Information Center/Clearinghouse for Adult Education; consultant to U.S. Agency for International Development. *Member:* American Academy of Political and Social Science, Adult Education Association of the United States, Phi Delta Kappa, Alpha Zeta, Epsilon Sigma Phi.

WRITINGS: Training in Extension Education for Community Development in India, Ford Foundation, 1960; (co-editor and contributor) *Workers in Agribusiness,* Agricultural Experiment Station, Cornell University, 1970; (with Harlan G. Copeland and Gertrude E. Kaiser) *Selected Concepts From Educational Psychology and Adult Education for Extension and continuing Educators,* Syracuse University Publications in Continuing Education, 1971; (editor with Charles P. Loomis) *Behavioral Change in Agriculture: Concepts and*

Strategies for Influencing Tradition, Cornell University Press, 1971. Contributor to *Encyclopedia Americana.* Contributor to journals.*

* * *

LEAP, Harry P(atrick) 1908-1976

OBITUARY NOTICE—See index for *CA* sketch: Born February 23, 1908, in Philadelphia, Pa.; died in 1976. Mechanic and author. Leap worked at more than forty jobs before becoming a mechanic in 1938 at Bayuk Cigars, Inc., where he remained until his retirement in 1973. Leap's book, *The Spice of Life,* was published in 1961. (Date of death provided by wife, Julia Leap.)

* * *

LEBERGOTT, Stanley 1918-

PERSONAL: Born July 22, 1918, in Detroit, Mich.; son of Isaac and Lillian (Weiss) Lebergott; married Ruth Wellington, January 1, 1941; children: Steven, Karen. *Education:* University of Michigan, B.A., 1938, M.A., 1939. *Home:* 146 Mount Vernon St., Middletown, Conn. 06457. *Office:* Department of Economics, Wesleyan University, Middletown, Conn. 06457.

CAREER: U.S. Government, Washington, D.C., associated with Department of Labor, 1940-45, International Labor Office, 1946-47, and Bureau of the Budget, 1948-61; Stanford University, Stanford, Calif., visiting professor of economics, 1961-62; Wesleyan University, Middletown, Conn., professor of economics, 1962—, Chester D. Hubbard Professor, 1963-71, university professor, 1971—. Member of Presidential Commission on Federal Statistics, 1970—; member of board of directors of Social Science Research Council, 1962-66, and executive committee, 1964—. *Member:* American Economic Association, American Statistical Association (fellow). *Awards, honors:* Public service award from Rockefeller Foundation, 1958.

WRITINGS: Manpower in Economic Growth: The American Record Since 1800, McGraw, 1964; (editor) *Men Without Work: The Economics of Unemployment,* Prentice-Hall, 1964; *Wealth and Want,* Princeton University Press, 1975; *The American Economy: Income, Wealth, and Want,* Princeton University Press, 1976. Contributor to economic and statistics journals.

BIOGRAPHICAL/CRITICAL SOURCES: Annals of the American Academy of Political and Social Science, September, 1976.*

* * *

LEDWIDGE, William (Bernard) John 1915-

PERSONAL: Born November 9, 1915, in London, England; son of Charles Bernard (an architect) and Eileen (O'Sullivan) Ledwidge; married Anne Kingsley, June 1, 1948 (divorced, 1970); married Flora Groult (a novelist), October 3, 1970; children: Francis John Kingsley, Natacha. *Education:* King's College, Cambridge, M.A., 1937; Princeton University, A.M., 1939. *Residence:* Paris, France. *Office:* Foreign Office, Downing St., London S.W.1, England.

CAREER: Foreign Office, London, England, first secretary, 1948-49; associated with British Consul, St. Louis, Mo., 1949-52; first secretary at British Embassy in Afghanistan, 1952-56; political adviser to British military governor in Berlin, 1956-61; Foreign Office, London, counselor, 1961-65; minister to France, 1965-69, ambassador to Finland, 1969-72,

and ambassador to Israel, 1972-75. Chairman of United Kingdom Committee for UNICEF, 1976—; member of United Kingdom Police Complaints Board, 1977—. *Military service:* British Army, 1940-41. Indian Army, 1941-46; became major. *Member:* Travellers Club. *Awards, honors:* Knight commander of St. Michael and St. George, 1974.

WRITINGS: Frontiers (novel), Weidenfeld & Nicolson, 1979; (with Groult, Guimard, and De Caunes) *Nouvelles de la famille,* Mazarine, 1980. Contributor to *Jane Austen Society Journal.*

WORK IN PROGRESS: A biography of Charles De Gaulle.

SIDELIGHTS: Ledwidge wrote: "By temperament I am a nomad, nowhere at home, everywhere at ease. That is why I chose diplomacy as a career. Now, as a writer, I shall go on being a nomad.

"I think freedom of the press is vital. It contains all freedoms."

* * *

LEDWITH, Frank 1907-

PERSONAL: Born February 6, 1907, in London, England; son of Richard James (a printer) and Minnie Eliza (Glover) Ledwith; married Constance Barnard, December 10, 1932; children: Brian, Veronica Ledwith Lawson. *Education:* Studied at boarding school in Horsham, England. *Politics:* Conservative. *Religion:* Church of England. *Home:* 168 Bickenhall Mansions, London W1H 3DF, England.

CAREER: Thos. R. Miller & Son (managers of mutual insurance associations for shipowners), London, England, held a number of positions, including management training officer and container risks underwriter, 1924-52, partner, 1952-72; industrial consultant in London, 1972—. Member of Baltic Mercantile and Shipping Exchange. *Member:* Chartered Insurance Institute (life member), Charles Lamb Society (vice-chairman), Christ's Hospital Club.

WRITINGS—Memoirs: *Ships That Go Bump in the Night,* R. Hale, 1974; *Ships Afloat in the City,* R. Hale, 1977.

Contributor to magazines, including *New World News,* and newspapers.

WORK IN PROGRESS: A novel set in the business world, tentatively titled *Fire and Water,* publication expected in 1982.

SIDELIGHTS: Ledwith commented: "Most of my writing has not been published in the usual sense. It includes about two hundred thousand business letters, two insurance policies (and to compose such documents is equivalent to a symphony in the world of music), technical handbooks, a centenary booklet for my firm, and a management training course.

"I suppose that all my writing owes much to two influences. One is a basic conviction that the world can become a saner and more progressive place, a belief fostered by a long association with Moral Re-Armament. The other is half a century of satisfying and exciting business experience, based in London, but in daily touch with many countries, about thirty of which I have visited, particulary North America, Europe, and Asia. I have lectured in London, Cambridge, Bombay, and New York."

BIOGRAPHICAL/CRITICAL SOURCES: Seatrade, November, 1972.

LEE, Betty 1921-

PERSONAL: Born December 18, 1921, in Sydney, Australia; daughter of Albert George and Violet (Haffenden) Lee. *Education:* Attended University of Sydney and Columbia University. *Residence:* Scarborough, Ontario, Canada. *Office: Chatelaine,* Maclean-Hunter Ltd., 481 University Ave., Toronto, Ontario, Canada.

CAREER: Radio-2UE, Sydney, Australia, scriptwriter, 1944-46; feature writer and editor for K. G. Murray Publishing Co., Sydney; associated with *Argus,* Melbourne, Australia, 1949-51; *Daily Mirror,* London, England, reporter, 1951-52; Wembley Stadium, England, press officer, 1952-53; *Globe and Mail,* Toronto, Ontario, senior reporter and editor, 1953-54; free-lance writer in the United States, 1954-57; *Globe and Mail,* reporter and feature writer, 1957-78; *Chatelaine,* Toronto, senior editor, 1978—. *Member:* American Newspaper Guild. *Awards, honors:* National award for spot news reporting from Canadian Women's Press Club, 1965; national newspaper award for feature writing, 1966; Southam fellow at University of Toronto, 1972-73.

WRITINGS: Insurance: The Magic of Averages, Globe and Mail, 1966; *Love and Whisky: The Story of the Dominion Drama Festival,* McClelland & Stewart, 1973; *Lutiapik: The Little One Who Cares,* McClelland & Stewart, 1975. Also author of *The Borrowers,* 1964, and *The Stock Market Story.* Contributor to Canadian magazines.*

*   *   *

LEECH, Kenneth 1939-

PERSONAL: Born June 15, 1939, in Ashton-under-Lyne, England. *Education:* King's College, London, B.A., 1961; Trinity College, Oxford, B.A., 1963, M.A., 1968. *Home:* St. Matthew's Rectory, Hereford St., Bethnal Green, London E2 6EX, England.

CAREER: Ordained priest; Holy Trinity Church, Hoxton, England, assistant curate, 1964-67; St. Anne's Church, London, England, assistant curate, 1967-71; chaplain at secondary school in Canterbury, England, 1971-74; St. Matthew's, London, rector, 1974—. Associate of King's College, London.

WRITINGS: (With Brenda Jordan) *Drugs for Young People: Their Use and Misuse,* Pergamon, 1967, 2nd edition, Religious Education Press, 1974; (contributor) Maurice B. Reckitt, editor, *For Christ and the People,* [London], 1968; *The Drug Subculture: A Christian Analysis,* Church Information Office, 1969; *Pastoral Care and the Drug Scene,* Allenson, 1970, revised edition published as *A Practical Guide to the Drug Scene,* Sheldon Press, 1974, British Book Centre, 1978; *The Real Jesus Revolution,* Church Literature Association, 1972; *Keep the Faith, Baby: A Close-Up of London's Drop-Outs,* S.P.C.K., 1973; *Youthquake: The Growth of a Counter-Culture Through Two Decades,* Sheldon Press, 1973, Littlefield, Adams, 1977; *Action for Revival,* Church Literature Association, 1974; *The Resurrection of the Catholic Social Voice,* Church Literature Association, 1976; *Believing in the Incarnation and Its Consequences,* Church Literature Association, 1977; *The Charismatic Movement and the Demons,* Church Literature Association, 1977; *Soul Friend: A Study of Spirituality,* British Book Centre, 1977; *Contemplation and Resistance: As Seen in the Spirituality of Thomas Merton,* Church Literature Association, 1978; *Catholic Theology and Social Change,* Church Literature Association,

1978; (editor) Ramon Lull, *Blanquerna: Libre d'amic et amat* (title means "The Book of the Lover and the Beloved"), Sheldon Press, revised edition, 1978. Contributor to theology journals and newspapers.

SIDELIGHTS: Christian Century's J. R. Mathers called Kenneth Leech's *Pastoral Care and the Drug Scene* informative and lucid. He described the book as a "first-rate manual for pastors and Christian laymen who find themselves concerned with young people using drugs." *Avocational interests:* Mimicry, practical jokes, drawing cartoons.

BIOGRAPHICAL/CRITICAL SOURCES: Christian Century, December 16, 1970, April 19, 1978; *Times Literary Supplement,* October 6, 1978.*

*   *   *

LEES, Carlton Brown 1924-

PERSONAL: Born February 16, 1924, in Windsor, Conn.; son of Carlton Brown and Dorothy (St. John) Lees; married Marian Louise Wicks, April 13, 1946; children: Peter St. John, Stephen Wicks, Barbara Ellen, James Carlton. *Education:* University of Connecticut, B.S., 1950; Cornell University, M.S., 1952. *Home address:* Enoch Crosby Rd., R.D.1, Brewster, N.Y. 10509. *Office:* New York Botanical Garden, Bronx, N.Y. 10458.

CAREER: Brooklyn Botanical Garden, Brooklyn, N.Y., assistant horticulturist, 1950-51; West Virginia University, Morgantown, instructor, 1952-54; Kingswood Center, Mansfield, Ohio, horticulturist, 1954-59; Pennsylvania Horticultural Society, Philadelphia, director, 1959-63; Massachusetts Horticultural Society, Boston, executive director, 1963-73; New York Botanical Garden, Bronx, vice-president, 1973-77, senior vice-president, 1977—. Publisher and member of board of directors of *Horticulture,* 1963-73. *Military service:* U.S. Naval Reserve, active duty, 1943-46. *Member:* American Horticultural Society, Garden Writers of America (president, 1971-75), Phi Alpha Xi, Alpha Zeta. *Awards, honors:* Helen Hull Certificate of Merit for Horticultural Literature from National Council of State Garden Clubs, 1972.

WRITINGS: Budget Landscaping, Holt, 1960; *Gardens, Plants, and Man,* Prentice-Hall, 1970; *New Budget Landscaping,* Holt, 1979.*

*   *   *

LEFKOWITZ, Mary Rosenthal 1935-

PERSONAL: Born April 30, 1935, in New York, N.Y.; daughter of Harold L. and Mena G. (Weil) Rosenthal; married Alan L. Lefkowitz, July 1, 1956 (divorced, 1981); children: Rachel G., Hannah W. *Education:* Wellesley College, B.A. (with honors), 1957; Radcliffe College, A.M., 1959, Ph.D., 1961. *Home:* 7 Norfolk Ter., Wellesley, Mass. 02181. *Office:* Departments of Greek and Latin, Wellesley College, Wellesley, Mass. 02181.

CAREER: Wellesley College, Wellesley, Mass., 1959—, began as instructor, became professor of Greek and Latin, 1965, chairman of department, 1970-72, 1975—, Andrew W. Mellon Professor of Humanities. Visiting professor at University of California, Berkeley, 1978; visiting fellow at Radcliffe Institute, 1966-67, 1972, 1973, and St. Hilda's College, Oxford, 1979-80; consultant to National Endowment for the Humanities. *Member:* American Philological Association (member of national board of directors, 1974-77), Phi Beta Kappa. *Awards, honors:* Woodrow Wilson fellow, 1957-58; American Council of Learned Societies fellow, 1972-73; National Endowment for the Humanities fellow, 1979-80.

WRITINGS: The Victory Ode: An Introduction, Noyes Press, 1976; (editor with Maureen B. Fant) *Women in Greece and Rome,* Samuel Stevens, 1977, revised edition published as *Women's Life in Greece and Rome,* Duckworth, 1981; *Heroines and Hysterics,* Duckworth, 1981. Contributor of articles and reviews to scholarly journals. New England editor of *Classical Journal.*

WORK IN PROGRESS: The Lives of the Greek Poets, for Duckworth.

*   *   *

LEIBENSTEIN, Harvey 1922-

PERSONAL: Born August 7, 1922, in U.S.S.R.; came to the United States in 1942, naturalized citizen, 1949; son of Joseph and Gusta (Bendick) Leibenstein; married Margaret Libnic, 1954. *Education:* Northwestern University, B.S., 1945, M.A., 1946; Princeton University, Ph.D., 1951. *Home:* 47 Larchwood Dr., Cambridge, Mass. 02138. *Office:* Department of Economics, Harvard University, 204 Littauer Center, Cambridge, Mass. 02138.

CAREER: Illinois Institute of Technology, Chicago, instructor in economics, 1946-47; Princeton University, Princeton, N.J., instructor in economics, 1947-48; University of California, Berkeley, assistant professor, 1951-60, professor of economics, 1960-67; Harvard University, Cambridge, Mass., visiting professor, 1966-67, Andelot Professor of Economics and Population, 1967—. Member of Institute for Advanced Study, Princeton, 1978-79; consultant to RAND Corp. *Member:* International Union for the Scientific Study of Population, American Economic Association, Population Association of America. *Awards, honors:* Social Science Research Council fellow, 1957-60; Guggenheim fellow, 1963.

WRITINGS: A Theory of Economic-Demographic Development, Princeton University Press, 1954, reprinted, Greenwood Press; *Economic Backwardness and Economic Growth: Studies in the Theory of Economic Development,* Wiley, 1957; *Economic Theory and Organizational Analysis,* Harper, 1960; *Beyond Economic Man,* Harvard University Press, 1976; *General X-Efficiency Theory and Economic Development,* Oxford University Press, 1978; *Inflation, Income Distribution, and X-Efficieny Theory: A Study Prepared for the International Labour Office Within the Framework of the World Employment Programme,* Barnes & Noble, 1980. Contributor to economic journals.

BIOGRAPHICAL/CRITICAL SOURCES: Science, November 12, 1976.*

*   *   *

LENTIN, Antony 1941-

PERSONAL: Born May 30, 1941, in Leicester, England; married, 1967; children: one. *Education:* Cambridge University, B.A., 1963, M.A., 1967, Ph.D., 1969. *Office:* Department of History, University of Waterloo, Waterloo, Ontario, Canada N2L 3G1.

CAREER: University of Keele, Keele, England, lecturer in Russian studies, 1967-69; University of Waterloo, Waterloo, Ontario, assistant professor, 1969-72, associate professor of history, 1972—. Member of Inter-University Center for European Studies, 1973—. *Awards, honors:* Canada Council grants, 1970, 1971, and 1972.

WRITINGS: (Editor) Mikhail Mikhailovich Shcherbatov, *On the Corruption of Morals in Russia,* Cambridge University Press, 1969; *Russia in the Eighteenth Century: From Peter the Great to Catherine the Great, 1696-1796,* Barnes & Noble,

1973; (editor) Francois Marie Arouet de Voltaire, *Voltaire and Catherine the Great: Selected Correspondence,* Oriental Research Partners, 1974.*

*   *   *

LENTON, Henry Trevor 1924-

PERSONAL: Born in 1924, in Rangoon, Burma; married Daphne Edwina Dear; children: two sons, two daughters. *Education:* Attended Royal Naval College, Greenwich. *Home:* 5 Chaucers Court, Ewelme, Oxford, England.

CAREER: Mercantile Marine, 1939-41 and 1948-58; naval correspondent for *Shipbuilding and Shipping Record,* 1960-68; editor of *Naval Record,* 1968—. Director of Monitor Ltd. (naval publishers), 1969—. *Military service:* Royal Navy, 1941-48. *Member:* World Ship Society, U.S. Naval Institute.

WRITINGS: (With James Joseph Colledge) *Warships of World War II,* Ian Allan, Volume I: *Capital Ships, Cruisers, and Aircraft Carriers of the Royal and Dominion Navies,* 1962, Volume II: *Destroyers and Submarines of the Royal and Dominion Navies,* 1962, Volume III: *Sloops of the Royal and Dominion Navies,* 1963, Volume IV: *Miscellaneous and Auxiliary Vessels Engaged in Trade Protection,* 1963, Volume V: *Miscellaneous Vessels Engaged in Harbour, Towing, and Salvage Vessel Duties,* 1963, Volume VI: *Trawlers, Drifters, and Whalers,* 1963, Volume VII: *Coastal Forces, Motor Minesweepers, and Motor Fishing Vessels,* 1963, Volume VIII: *Landing Craft, Landing Ships, and Landing Barges,* 1964, revised edition in one volume, 1973, published in the United States as *British and Dominion Warships of World War II,* Doubleday, 1968; *ABC of British Warships,* Ian Allan, 1962 edition (Lenton was not associated with earlier editions), 1962, 1964 edition, 1964; *British Warships,* Ian Allan, 7th edition, 1964; *Navies of the Second World War,* Volume I: *German Submarines,* Parts 1 and 2, Macdonald & Co., 1965, 2nd edition, 1968, Doubleday, 1966, Volume II: *German Surface Vessels,* Parts 1 and 2, Macdonald & Co., 1966, Doubleday, 1967; (with Colledge) *Warship Losses of World War II: British and Dominion Fleets,* Ian Allan, 1965; *German Warships: Navies of the Second World War,* Volume I, Macdonald & Co., 1966; *Warships of the British and Commonwealth Navies,* Ian Allan, 1967, 3rd edition, 1972; *American Battleships, Carriers, and Cruisers,* Doubleday, 1968, 2nd edition, 1970; *Royal Netherlands Navy,* Doubleday, 1968.

Warships: From 1860 to the Present Day, Hamlyn, 1970, Grosset (edited by Jacques Simmons), 1971; *British Fleet and Escort Destroyers: Navies of the Second World War,* two volumes, Macdonald & Co., 1970, Doubleday, 1971; *American Fleet and Escort Destroyers: Navies of the Second World War,* two volumes, Doubleday, 1971; *British Battleships and Aircraft Carriers,* Doubleday, 1972; *British Submarines: Navies of the Second World War,* Doubleday, 1972; *American Submarines: Navies of the Second World War,* Doubleday, 1973; (with Alan Raven) *Dido Class Cruisers,* Bivouac Books, 1973; *British Cruisers,* Doubleday, 1973; *American Gunboats and Minesweepers: World War II Fact Files,* two volumes, Arco, 1974; *British Escort Ships: World War II Fact Files,* Macdonald & Jane's, 1974, Arco, 1975; *German Warships of the Second World War* (edited by Antony Preston), Macdonald & Jane's, 1975, Arco, 1976. Contributor to shipping and marine periodicals.*

LEONARD, Graham Douglas 1921-

PERSONAL: Born May 8, 1921, in London, England; son of Douglas Leonard (a minister); married Vivien Priscilla Swann, 1943; children: two sons. *Education:* Balliol College, Oxford, B.A., 1943, M.A., 1947. *Home:* Lis Escop, Truro, Cornwall, England.

CAREER: Ordained priest of Church of England, 1948; vicar of Ardleigh, England, 1952-55; Diocese of St. Albans, England, director of religious education, 1955-58, canon residentiary, 1957-58, canon emeritus, 1958; secretary of Church of England Schools Council and general secretary of national society, 1958-62; archdeacon of Hampstead, examining chaplain to bishop of London, and rector of St. Andrew Undershaft with St. Mary Axe in London, England, all 1962-64; bishop suffragen of Willesden, England, 1964-73; bishop of Truro, England, 1973—. Honorary canon of St. Albans, 1955-57; chairman of Church of England committee for social work and social services, 1967-76, and Church of England Board for Social Responsibility, 1976—; member of Churches Unity Commission, 1977—, and Commission for Anglican Orthodox Joint Doctrinal Discussions; foreign affairs counselor to Archbishop of Canterbury, 1974. Member of House of Lords, 1977—. Select preacher at Oxford University, 1968; fellow of Gonville and Caius College, Cambridge. Member of governing board and publishing committee of Society for Promoting Christian Knowledge. *Military service:* British Army, Oxfordshire and Buckinghamshire Light Infantry and Army Operational Group, 1941-45; became captain. *Member:* Middlesex Association (president, 1970-73), Army and Navy Club. *Awards, honors:* D.D. from Episcopal Seminary, Ky., 1974.

WRITINGS: (With John Bissell Carroll) *The Effectiveness of Programmed "Grafdrils" in Teaching the Arabic Writing System,* Harvard University Press, 1963; *The Gospel Is for Everyone,* Morehouse, 1971, 2nd edition, Church Literature Association, 1977; *New Dimensions: The Report of the Bishop of Willesden's Commission on the Objects and Policy of the Mother's Union,* S.P.C.K., 1972. Co-author of *Growing Into Union,* 1970.

Contributor to *The Christian Religion Explained,* 1960; *Retreats Today,* 1962; *Communicating the Faith,* 1969; *A Critique of Eucharistic Agreement,* 1975. Contributor to journals.

AVOCATIONAL INTERESTS: Reading (especially biography), music.*

*   *   *

LESHER, Stephan 1935-

PERSONAL: Born July 26, 1935, in Brooklyn, N.Y.; son of Murray and Lila Lesher; married Nancy Ball; children: Michael, Robert, Jeffrey, Joseph, Julia. *Education:* Attended University of Missouri, 1952-54; Salem College, Winston-Salem, N.C., A.B., 1952; also attended Wake Forest University, 1960. *Agent:* Gerard McCauley Agency, Inc., Box AE, Katonah, N.Y. 10536. *Office:* Stephan Lesher Associates, Federal Bar Building W., Suite 950, 1819 H St. N.W., Washington, D.C. 20006.

CAREER: Reporter for *Montgomery Advertiser,* Montgomery, Ala., *Columbus Ledger,* Columbus, Ga., and *Winston-Salem Journal,* Winston-Salem, N.C., 1955-63; press secretary to U.S. Senator Birch Bayh, 1963-69; *Newsweek,* New York, N.Y., national correspondent in Atlanta, Ga., 1960-

72, deputy bureau chief in Los Angeles, Calif., 1972-73, national correspondent in Washington, D.C., 1973-77; Stephan Lesher Associates (public affairs consultants), Washington, D.C., president, 1977—. *Awards, honors:* Congressional fellow of American Political Science Association, 1963-64.

WRITINGS: A Coronary Event (nonfiction), Lippincott, 1976; *Vested Interest* (nonfiction), Doubleday, 1977.

Co-author of revues "Son of Spread Eagle," 1969, "A Fifth of Spread Eagle," 1970, both produced at the Washington Theatre Club. Creative collaborator for "The Lazarus Syndrome," first broadcast by ABC-TV, 1979. Contributor of articles to magazines and newspapers, including *New York Times Magazine* and *New York Times.*

WORK IN PROGRESS: A book on the impact of modern reporting on the nation's perceptions of events, publication by Houghton expected in 1982.

SIDELIGHTS: Lesher commented: "The speed, ubiquity, and repetition of modern news media have overwhelmed thoughtful, measured, and dispassionate evaluation of significant events. Journalism always has been a hit-or-miss, seat-of-the-pants exercise; now, however, its built-in affinity for error has been magnified by its omnipresence—not only through television, but through major print-media outlets as well. The result is that 'big' journalism's mistakes, when they occur, are more difficult to overcome by subsequent inquiry. Meanwhile, the likelihood of making mistakes has been compounded by the growth of a legal shield surrounding journalism; the more difficult it is for people to sue and collect for libel, the more likely it is that media will include more value judgments in their reportage. The more a reporter makes judgments, the more he will make mistakes. Although doctors are accused of burying their mistakes, and industries of lobbying theirs away, journalism either ignores its errors or suffuses them in First Amendment arguments. A critic may be told, for example, 'Sure, we make mistakes, but that's the price we must pay for freedom.' Obviously, that begs the question of the nature of journalism's errors, both their extent and their influence on major decisions made by government and in the private sector."

*   *   *

LESLEY, Cole
See COLE, Leonard Leslie

*   *   *

LEVINE, Isaac Don 1892-1981

OBITUARY NOTICE—See index for *CA* sketch: Born February 1, 1892, in Mozyr, Russia (now U.S.S.R.); died of a heart attack, February 15, 1981, in Venice, Fla. Journalist and author. As a foreign correspondent and columnist, Levine was considered an expert on the Soviet Union. He covered the Russian Revolution in 1917 and the civil war during the early 1920's, and he visited the U.S.S.R. again in the early 1960's. He was opposed to communism and the Soviet regime but did not consider himself a conservative; he once described himself as "an inveterate libertarian." He wrote several books on Russian history and society as well as biographies of Joseph Stalin and Nikolai Lenin. His autobiography is entitled *Eyewitness to History: Memoirs and Reflections of a Foreign Correspondent for Half a Century.* Obituaries and other sources: *New York Times,* February 17, 1981; *Chicago Tribune,* February 17, 1981; *Washington Post,* February 17, 1981.

LEVINE, Laurence William 1931-

PERSONAL: Born April 9, 1931, in New York, N.Y.; son of Robert L. and Molly (Brunner) Levine. *Education:* Union College, B.A., 1952; Harvard University, LL.B., 1955. *Home:* 1435 Redford St., Apt. 12-B, Stamford, Conn. 06905. *Office:* Walsh & Levine, 60 Wall Tower, 70 Pine St., New York, N.Y. 10005.

CAREER: Walsh & Levine, New York, N.Y., law partner, 1958—. Counsel to Northeast Airlines, 1958-67, British Eagle Airlines, 1963-69, Aerolineas Argentinas, 1960—, Banco de la Nacion Argentina and Banco de Intercambio Regional Argentina, 1977—; secretary-treasurer of Kabuki Japanese Restaurant, 1958—; partner of San Francisco Merchandise Mart, Westbury Hotel, and Kaanapoli Hotel; member of board of directors of New York Venture Fund, Foothill Group, Erickson Educational Foundation, and Pan Australian Fund; public member of Blue Cross/Blue Shield; chairman of creditors committees of Imperial 400 motel chain. Aide to Adlai Stevenson and office manager of New York committee for Stevenson, Kefauver, and Wagner, 1956; member of New York Committee for Democratic Votes, 1962-63. *Member:* New York County Lawyers Association, Association of the Bar of the City of New York, Argentine-American Chamber of Commerce (member of board of directors), Downtown Athletic Club, Georgetown Club, Harvard Club, World Trade Center Club, Sands Point Club.

WRITINGS: U.S.-China Relations, Robert Speller, 1972. Also author of *Gullibles Travels Through Harvard*, 1955. North American correspondent for *Cambio*, 1974—. Contributor to magazines and newspapers in the United States and Argentina, including *East-Europe.**

*   *   *

LEVINSON, Olga May

PERSONAL: Born in Transvaal, South Africa; daughter of Edward (a stockbroker) and Cecily (an artist and pianist; maiden name, Steinberg) Cohen; married Jack Louis Levinson (a company director), July 18, 1943; children: Clive, Gil, Orde. *Education:* University of the Witwatersrand, B.A.; Trinity College of London, licentiate. *Religion:* Jewish. *Home:* Heynitz Castle, P.O. Box 458, Windhoek, South-West Africa.

CAREER: Writer. Broadcaster for South African Broadcasting Commission; member of South-West Africa Broadcasting Board, 1978—. *Member:* South African Association of Arts (president, 1958-76), South-West African Performing Arts Council (chairman of opera and ballet), Le Cercle Francais (honorary life president).

WRITINGS: Call Me Master, C.N.A., 1958; *The Ageless Land*, Tafelberg, 1961; *Adolph Jentsch*, Human & Rousseau, 1973; *South West Africa*, Tafelberg, 1976; *The Story of Namibia*, Tafelberg, 1978. Chief scenario writer of short advertising films for Empire Films. Contributor to periodicals.

WORK IN PROGRESS: A novel, publication expected in 1982; a book about August Stauch, the man who discovered the first diamonds in South Africa, publication expected in 1983.

SIDELIGHTS: Olga Levinson commented: "I am madly interested in all matters pertaining to Africa and its indigenous inhabitants; also the arts."

LEVY, Harry L(ouis) 1906-1981

OBITUARY NOTICE—See index for *CA* sketch: Born December 5, 1906, in New York, N.Y.; died January 11, 1981, in Durham, N.C. Educator, administrator, and author. Levy was a professor of classics at Hunter College of the City University of New York and later served as a dean and a vice-chancellor of the university. He also taught at Fordham University and was a visiting professor at Duke University at the time of his death. He was the author of major works on the Latin poets Claudian and Ovid, and he edited the dialogues of the Greek satirist Lucian. He also wrote articles on ancient and modern Mediterranean cultures. His books include *A Latin Reader for Colleges* and *Claudian's "In Rufinum": An Exegetical Commentary*. Obituaries and other sources: *New York Times*, January 12, 1981.

*   *   *

LEVY, Julien 1906-1981

OBITUARY NOTICE: Born January 22, 1906, in New York, N.Y.; died February 10, 1981, in New Haven, Conn. Art dealer, educator, and author. Julien Levy introduced the New York art world to the work of such artists as Max Ernst, Joseph Cornell, and Arshile Gorky. During the 1930's and 1940's, Levy's gallery served as a center for surrealist and neoromantic artists. He recalled those years in his book *Memoir of an Art Gallery*. A lecturer in art history, Levy also wrote several other books, including *Surrealism*. At the time of his death, he was preparing for publication his correspondence with poet Mina Loy, who was the mother of his first wife. Obituaries and other sources: *Who's Who in American Art*, Bowker, 1978; *New Yorker*, July 4, 1977; *New York Times*, February 11, 1981; *Time*, February 23, 1981.

*   *   *

LEWIS, Stephen 1947(?)-1981
(Jennifer Sills)

OBITUARY NOTICE: Born c. 1947; died January 23, 1981, in Los Angeles, Calif. Fashion writer, columnist, and author of paperback books. Stephen Lewis, prolific writer of books with titles such as *Sex Among the Singles*, *The Love Merchants*, and *The Watergate Girls*, was the author of gossip columns for *Movie World* and *Screen Stars*. Under the pseudonym Jennifer Sills he wrote *Massage Parlor*. At the time of his death, Lewis had completed two more novels, *Olivia's Children* and *Expensive Pleasures*. For his book *The Best Sellers* he received a Gold Medal Award from the *West Coast Review of Books*. Obituaries and other sources: *Authors in the News*, Volume 1, Gale, 1976; *Publisher's Weekly*, February 20, 1981.

*   *   *

LIDDELL HART, Basil Henry 1895-1970

PERSONAL: First part of last name is pronounced *lid*-el; born October 31, 1895; died January 29, 1970, in Marlow, England; son of H. Bramley (a minister) and Clara (Liddell) Hart; married Jessie Stone, 1918 (divorced); married Kathleen Sullivan Nelson, 1942; children: (first marriage) Adrian John. *Education:* Attended Corpus Christi College, Cambridge. *Home:* States House, Medmenham, Marlow, Buckinghamshire, England.

CAREER: Military tactician, historian, and writer. *Daily Telegraph*, London, England, military correspondent, 1925-

35; *London Times*, London, military correspondent, 1935-39. Lees-Knowles Lecturer on military history at Trinity College, Cambridge, 1932-33; Leverhulme research fellow, 1934; member of British delegation to International Studies Conference, 1935; adviser to British minister of state for war, 1937-38; member of County of London Territorial Association; advisory member of Executive Committee of League of Nations Union. Visiting professor at University of California, Cambridge University, Naval War College, and others. *Military service:* King's Own Yorkshire Light Infantry, 1914-18; became captain. *Member:* Society for Army Historical Research, P.E.N. Club (former vice-president), Association of Writers for Intellectual Liberty, Athenaeum Club. *Awards, honors:* Chesney Gold Medal from Royal United States Institution; D.Litt from Oxford University, 1964; honorary fellow of Corpus Christi College, Cambridge, 1965; knighted by Queen Elizabeth II, 1966.

WRITINGS: Paris; or, The Future of War, Dutton, 1925, revised edition, Garland, 1972; *A Greater Than Napoleon, Scipio Africanus*, W. Blackwood, 1926, reprinted, Biblo & Tannen, 1971; *Great Captains Unveiled*, W. Blackwood, 1927, reprinted, Books for Libraries, 1967; *The Remaking of Modern Armies*, J. Murray, 1927, reprinted, Greenwood Press, 1980; *Reputations, Ten Years After*, Little, Brown, 1928, reprinted, Books for Libraries, 1968; *The Decisive Wars of History: A Study in Strategy*, Little, Brown, 1929; *Sherman: Soldier, Realist, American*, Dodd, Mead, 1929, reprinted, Greenwood Press, 1978 (published in England as *Sherman: The Genius of the Civil War*, Benn, 1930, reprinted, Praeger, 1958).

The Real War, 1914-1918, Little, Brown, 1930, enlarged edition published as *History of the World War, 1914-1918*, 1934, also published as *History of the First World War*, 1964, enlarged edition, Pan Books, 1972; *Foch, the Man of Orleans*, Eyre & Spottiswoode, 1931, Little, Brown, 1932, reprinted, Greenwood Press, 1980; *The British Way in Warfare*, Faber, 1932, published as *When Britain Goes to War*, Faber, 1935, revised edition published under original title, Penguin, 1942; *The Future of Infantry*, Faber, 1933, Military Service Publishing Co., 1936; *The Ghost of Napoleon*, Faber, 1933; *Colonel Lawrence, the Man Behind the Legend*, Dodd, Mead, 1934, reprinted, Greenwood Press, 1979 (published in England as *T. E. Lawrence in Arabia and After*, J. Cape, 1934), enlarged edition published as *The Man Behind the Legend, Colonel Lawrence*, Halcyon House, 1937.

T. E. Lawrence to His Biographer, Robert Graves [and] *T. E. Lawrence to His Biographer, Liddell Hart*, Doubleday, 1938, published as *T. E. Lawrence to His Biographers, Robert Graves and Liddell Hart*, 1963; *The War in Outline, 1914-18*, Random House, 1936, reprinted, Award Books, 1965; *Europe in Arms*, Random House, 1937; *Through the Fog of War*, Random House, 1938; *The Defence of Britain*, Random House, 1939.

Dynamic Defence, Faber, 1940; *The Current of War*, Hutchinson, 1941; *The Way to Win Wars: Strategy of Indirect Approach*, Faber, 1942, published as *Strategy*, Praeger, 1954, 2nd revised edition, 1967; *This Expanding War*, Faber, 1942; *Thoughts on War*, Faber, 1944; *Why Don't We Learn From History?*, Allen & Unwin, 1944, reprinted, Hawthorn Books, 1972; *The Revolution in Warfare*, Faber, 1946, Yale University Press, 1947, reprinted, Greenwood Press, 1980; *The German Generals Talk*, Morrow, 1948 (published in England as *The Other Side of the Hill: Germany's Generals, Their Rise and Fall*, Cassell, 1948, revised and enlarged edition, Pan Books, 1978).

Defence of the West, Morrow, 1950; *The Tanks: The History of the Royal Tank Regiment and Its Predecessors, Heavy Branch, Machine-Gun Corps, Tank Corps, and Royal Tank Corps, 1914-1945*, Praeger, 1959; *Deterrent or Defense: A Fresh Look at the West's Military Position* (essays), Praeger, 1960; *The Liddell Hart Memoirs*, Putnam, Volume I: *1895-1938*, 1965, Volume II: *The Later Years*, 1966; *History of the Second World War*, Cassell, 1970, Putnam, 1971. Also author of *Lawn Tennis Masters Unveiled*, 1926.

Other: (Editor and author of foreword) William Wheeler, *The Letters of Private Wheeler, 1809-1828*, M. Joseph, 1951; (editor) Erwin Rommel, *The Rommel Papers* (translated by Paul Findlay), Harcourt, 1953; (editor) *The Red Army* (essays), Harcourt, 1956 (published in England as *The Soviet Army*, Weidenfeld & Nicolson, 1956); (editor with Barrie Pitt) *History of the Second World War*, Purnell, 1966, revised edition published as *World War II: An Illustrated History*, 1977; (compiler) *The Sword and the Pen: Selections From World's Greatest Military Writings* (essays; edited by son, Adrian Liddell Hart), Crowell, 1976.

Contributor of articles to periodicals, including *Encounter, Fortune, Yale Review, American Heritage, New Republic, Life, Reporter, National Review, Harper's, Atlantic Monthly*. Military editor of the 14th edition of *Encyclopaedia Britannica* and editor of *Small Arms Training*, an official manual of the British War Office.

SIDELIGHTS: Known as one of the world's foremost military tacticians, Liddell Hart was also a renowned military historian, publishing over thirty books on the tactics, history, and personages of warfare.

At the outbreak of World War I, Liddell Hart joined the British forces, serving as a captain in the infantry for four years. He was wounded twice, once severely. After the war Liddell Hart gained attention as a military tactician, and at age twenty-five he was commissioned by the British government to write the official post-war manual on infantry training. He was also appointed by the War Office to edit the official manual *Small Arms Training*.

In 1926 Liddell Hart wrote his first military biography, *A Greater Than Napoleon: Scipio Africanus*. Marryat Dobie, reviewing for *Saturday Review of Literature*, hailed the book: "In straightforward language, unaided by the tricks which are supposed to give vividness, the author gives a clear and lively picture of men, times, and events."

Hart's next three biographies were *Great Captains Unveiled, Sherman: Soldier, Realist, American*, and *Reputations, Ten Years After*. In reviewing *Sherman* for *Saturday Review of Literature*, A. H. Meneely praised Liddell Hart for the qualities that became the trademarks of his work. "There is no attempt to jazz up the narrative, no withholding of criticism, no effusive laudation," noted Meneely. "Frankness is as characteristic of the author's presentation as it was of Sherman himself." Later biographies on Ferdinand Foch and T. E. Lawrence further enhanced Liddell Hart's reputation.

Prior to World War II, Liddell Hart worked closely with Leslie Hore-Belisha, then British minister of war. Advising the minister on the reorganization and mechanization of national forces, Liddell Hart expounded the defense principle and favored air power and armored forces. His theories on the policy of a waiting war were presented in his book *The Defence of Britain*. The reputation of both author and book suffered in 1940 with the fall of France, but Liddell Hart and others claimed that his theories would have proved valid had they been adhered to with greater consistency.

Following World War II, Liddell Hart's writing continued to provide new insights and perspectives on the history and stratagem of war. In 1946 he published *Revolution in Warfare,* describing the development of modern weaponry and its probable effect on future wars. He theorized that the atomic bomb would be ruled out of future use by agreement. In *Defence of the West,* 1950, Liddell Hart offered an analysis of the western world's chances for survival in a conflict with the Soviet Union. A *New Yorker* reviewer called the book "provocative and sobering," noting that Liddell Hart "comes to the inarguable conclusion that there had just better not be another war." Ten years later, in 1960, Liddell Hart published *Deterent or Defense: A Fresh Look at the West's Military Position,* once again presenting a discomforting look at military policy, tactics, and world politics. The book prompted a *Spectator* reviewer to remark, "At a time when a new wave of ostrichism in regard to defence is sweeping the country it is as well to be reminded . . . that the best way of safeguarding peace is to think about war."

In the last five years of his life, Liddell Hart wrote *The Liddell Hart Memoirs* and *The History of the Second World War.* He also compiled a collection of essays that was edited by his son, Adrian Liddell Hart, and published posthumously. In a review of *Memoirs,* Alastair Buchan praised the work while lamenting that Liddell Hart had not presented a more personal picture of himself. "There is a great deal of fun, of illumination, of tears, in these memoirs, much fine detail," Buchan said. "What is missing is the portrait of the author himself."

AVOCATIONAL INTERESTS: Lawn tennis, discussion, croquet, chess, history of fashion and habit.

BIOGRAPHICAL/CRITICAL SOURCES: New York Times Book Review, June 5, 1927, December 2, 1928, January 12, 1930, March 9, 1930, September 14, 1930, August 22, 1937, January 8, 1939, October 22, 1939, October 17, 1948, December 2, 1956, August 25, 1963, May 30, 1971; *New York Herald Tribune Books,* August 21, 1927, March 20, 1932, November 28, 1938, January 8, 1938, August 18, 1963; *Saturday Review of Literature,* October 22, 1927, November 23, 1929, March 5, 1932, February 2, 1935, September 4, 1937, October 14, 1939; *Current History Magazine of the New York Times,* April, 1930; *New Statesman and Nation,* November 5, 1938, July 22, 1939, June 17, 1950; *Time,* March 18, 1940, August 27, 1945, October 25, 1948, May 17, 1971; *Times Literary Supplement,* May 22, 1948, June 23, 1950, May 17, 1965, November 6, 1970; *New Yorker,* November 18, 1950; *Saturday Review,* October 28, 1954, September 3, 1960; *Spectator,* July 15, 1960; *New Statesman,* June 4, 1965, October 30, 1970; *Reporter,* February 24, 1966; *Book Week,* August 28, 1966, May 2, 1971; *Observer Review,* October 25, 1970; *Nation,* June 7, 1971.

OBITUARIES: New York Times, January 30, 1970; *Washington Post,* January 30, 1970; *Newsweek,* February 9, 1970.*

* * *

LINDSAY, Martin Alexander 1905-1981

OBITUARY NOTICE: Born August 22, 1905, in London, England; died May 5, 1981. Explorer, member of British Parliament, and author. Martin Lindsay, known for his numerous expeditions to such remote areas of the world as the Inturi Forest in Africa's Belgian Congo, was chosen in 1934 to lead an expedition to Greenland. With two others, he traveled over more than seven hundred miles of previously unexplored territory in northern Greenland. His book *Those Greenland Days* contains an account of that journey. Num-

bered among Sir Lindsay's later works are *The Epic of Captain Scott, Three Got Through,* and *The House of Commons.* He also contributed articles to magazines and periodicals, including the *Observer,* the *Listener,* and *Spectator.* Obituaries and other sources: *Who Was Who Among English and European Authors,* Gale, 1978; *London Times,* May 7, 1981.

* * *

LINDSTROM, Carl E(inar) 1896-1969

OBITUARY NOTICE—See index for *CA* sketch: Born March 1, 1896, in Wallace, Mich.; died April 2, 1969, in Ormond Beach, Fla., of a cerebral hemorrhage. Journalist, editor, educator, and author. Lindstrom began as copy editor and music critic for the *Hartford Times* in 1917, became managing editor in 1946, and executive editor in 1953. In 1959 Lindstrom accepted a post as journalism professor at University of Michigan. He served as a member of the Pulitzer Prize screening jury and the Nieman Fellowships selection committee. Lindstrom's 1960 book, *The Fading American Newspaper,* contains the author's criticisms of the newspaper business but also reveals his fondness for his profession. The book was considered a notable but controversial discussion of the press. Obituaries and other sources: *New York Times,* April 4, 1969; *Who Was Who in America,* 5th edition, Marquis, 1973.

* * *

LING, Roger (John) 1942-

PERSONAL: Born November 13, 1942, in Watford, England; son of Leslie James (a laboratory technician) and Kathleen Clara (Child) Ling; married Lesley Ann Steer (a lecturer), December 30, 1967. *Education:* St. John's College, Cambridge, B.A., 1964, M.A., 1968, Ph.D., 1969. *Politics:* "Indeterminate." *Religion:* "Non-existent." *Office:* Department of History of Art, Victoria University of Manchester, Manchester M13 9PL, England.

CAREER: University of Wales, University College, Swansea, lecturer in classics, 1967-71; Victoria University of Manchester, Manchester, England, senior lecturer in classical art and archaeology, 1971—. Member of faculty of archaeology, history, and letters at British School at Rome, 1974-78. *Member:* Society for the Promotion of Roman Studies (member of council, 1978—), Royal Archaeological institute, Society of Antiquaries (fellow), British Pompeii Research Committee, Cambrian Archaeological Association, Derbyshire Archaeological Society, North Derbyshire Archaeological Trust. *Awards, honors:* Rome scholar at British School at Rome, 1965-67.

WRITINGS: The Greek World, Phaidon, 1976; (editor of revision with T.C.B. Rasmussen) Axel Boethius, *Etruscan and Early Roman Architecture,* Penguin, 1978; (contributor) H. M. Blake, T. W. Potter, and D. B. Whitehouse, editors, *Papers in Italian Archaeology,* British Archaeological Reports, 1978; (contributor) Fausto Zevi, editor, *Pompei 79: Raccolta di studi per il decimonono centenario dell' eruzione Vesuviana* (title means "Pompeii 79: Collection of Studies for the 1900th Anniversary of the Eruption of Vesuvius"), Macchiavoli (Naples), 1979. Contributor of articles and reviews to archaeology and classical studies journals.

WORK IN PROGRESS: Romano-British Painted Wall Plaster, with Norman Davey, publication expected in 1982; *The Hellenistic World,* 2nd edition of *Cambridge Ancient History,* publication by Cambridge University Press expected in 1984.

SIDELIGHTS: Roger Ling told *CA:* "Though brought up in the traditional school of classical archaeology, which concentrates on classical art to the exclusion of the other material remains of antiquity, I find this an unduly blinkered and restrictive approach. I am interested in all the material evidence of life in the past, in the various techniques by which that evidence is collected, and in the social and economic conclusions that can be drawn from it. Art is only one aspect of the evidence, and to focus solely on the aesthetic and stylistic development of art is a sterile exercise. Yet for too long excavations of classical sites have been entrusted to people trained in art history rather than in archaeological techniques, and for too long publications have concentrated on spectacular and artistic discoveries rather than on the anonymous bric-a-brac of everyday life. Only in recent years has there come a greater awareness of the value of, say, statistical studies of animal and human bones or distribution patterns of coarse pottery fabrics. But this, in my opinion, is the stuff from which history can be reconstructed.''

AVOCATIONAL INTERESTS: Sports, popular music, cinema, Watford Football Club.

*   *   *

LIPSKY, David Bruce   1939-

PERSONAL: Born April 27, 1939, in Bethlehem, Pa.; son of William Ray and Gertrude May Lipsky; married Alexandra Anne Chapko, June 9, 1962; children: Anne Alexandra. *Education:* Attended Lehigh University, 1957-58; Cornell University, B.S., 1961; Massachusetts Institute of Technology, Ph.D., 1967. *Home:* 241 Valley Rd., Ithaca, N.Y. 14850. *Office:* New York School of Industrial and Labor Relations, Cornell University, 293 Ives, Ithaca, N.Y. 14853.

CAREER: State University of New York College at Buffalo, assistant professor of industrial relations, 1965-69, Cornell University, Ithaca, N.Y., assistant professor, 1969-73, associate professor, 1973-79, professor of industrial and labor relations, 1979—. Member of faculty at Harvard University, summers, 1972—, co-director of Institute in Employment and Training Administration, 1979—; visiting associate professor at Massachusetts Institute of Technology and Boston University, 1976-77; adjunct lecturer at Brandeis University, summers, 1978—. Member of New York Public Employment Relations Board panel of mediators and factfinders, 1970—; consultant to Abt Associates and National Science Foundation. *Member:* American Economic Association, Industrial Relations Research Association, Society for Professionals in Dispute Resolution (charter member), Phi Kappa Phi. *Awards, honors:* Grants from Ford Foundation, 1973, 1974-75, 1975-76, and W. E. Upjohn Institute, 1980—.

WRITINGS: (Contributor) Donald Gerwin, editor, *The Employment of Teachers,* McCutchan, 1974; (contributor) Anthony M. Cresswell and Michael J. Murphy, editors, *Education and Collective Bargaining: Readings in Policy and Research,* McCutchan, 1976; (editor) *Union Power and Public Policy,* New York School of Industrial and Labor Relations, Cornell University, 1975; (with Thomas A. Kochan and Lee Dyer) *The Effectiveness of Union-Management Safety and Health Committees,* Upjohn, 1977; (editor with Abraham J. Siegel) *Unfinished Business: An Agenda,* M.I.T. Press, 1978; *The Labor Market Experience of Workers Displaced and Relocated by Plant Shutdowns,* Garland Publishing, 1979; *Essentials of Collective Bargaining,* Prentice-Hall, 1981. Contributor of more than a dozen articles to business and industrial relations journals. Associate editor and member of editorial board of *Industrial and Labor Relations Review,* 1971-75, 1977—, editor, 1975-76.

WORK IN PROGRESS: Research on government transfer payments and strike activity.

SIDELIGHTS: Lipsky told *CA:* "My current research project, funded by the Upjohn Institute, deals with the effect of welfare payments—such as Aid to Families with Dependent Children (AFDC) and General Assistance, unemployment compensation, and food stamps—on strike activity. In New York and Rhode Island, strikers routinely receive unemployment compensation after a waiting period of seven or eight weeks. In other states strikers may receive unemployment compensation under more restricted circumstances. In twenty-two states strikers who meet the eligibility requirements may receive payments under the AFDC-Unemployed Parents program. Eligible strikers may receive food stamps in all states. Using the data for all states during the years from 1960 to 1976, I am investigating whether the availability of these various forms of state assistance affects the number of strikes or the duration of strikes in the United States.

"Needless to say, this topic has been an extremely controversial one. Several cases have been heard by the Supreme Court (and more by the lower courts) on the legality and constitutionality of paying state benefits to strikers. Several judges have lamented the lack of systematic empirical research on the topic. My research is an attempt to fill the gap by evaluating, in an impartial, nonpartisan fashion, the true effect of transfer payments on strike activity."

*   *   *

LITTLE, Lester Knox   1935-

PERSONAL: Born October 21, 1935, in Providence, R.I. *Education:* Dartmouth College, B.A., 1957; attended University of Chicago, 1957-58; Princeton University, M.A., 1960, Ph.D., 1962. *Office:* Department of History, Smith College, Northampton, Mass. 01060.

CAREER: Princeton University, Princeton, N.J., instructor in history, 1961-63; University of Chicago, Chicago, Ill., assistant professor, 1963-69, associate professor of history, 1969-71; Smith College, Northampton, Mass., associate professor, 1971-76, professor of history, 1976—. Member of Institute for Advanced Studies, Princeton, 1969-70. *Member:* International Society for Franciscan Studies, American Historical Association, Mediaeval Academy of America. *Awards, honors:* Woodrow Wilson fellowship, 1957-58; American Council of Learned Societies fellowship, 1970-71.

WRITINGS: (Co-editor) *Nature, Man, and Society in the Twelfth Century,* University of Chicago Press, 1968; (editor) *Becket,* Armon Books, 1971; (contributor) *Order and Innovation in the Middle Ages: Essays in Honor of J. R. Strayer,* Princeton University Press, 1976; *Religious Poverty and the Profit Economy in Medieval Europe,* Cornell University Press, 1978. Contributor to history journals.*

*   *   *

LIU, Sydney (Chieh)   1920-
(Chin Feng, Yeh Hsiang)

PERSONAL: Born February 13, 1920, in Shanghai, China; son of Yuan-chang and Fu-ju (Chao) Liu; married Annie Young, October 6, 1956; children: Michael King-sun, Josephine Wen-ting, Victor Kin-tung. *Education:* National Chiao Tung University, B.S., 1942. *Home:* Silver Fair Mansion, Apt. F-2, Shiu Fai Ter., Stubbs Rd., Hong Kong. *Office:* *Newsweek,* 20 Kennedy Ter., Flat 6-B, Hong Kong.

CAREER: Reporter, feature writer, and foreign affairs editor of *Hsin Min Pao* in Chengtu and Chungking, China, 1943-

45, and in Nanking China, 1945-47, managing editor of Nanking bureau, 1947-49, and of Chungking bureau, 1949-50; reporter for Reuters News Agency, 1946-47; free-lance writer, translator, and columnist in Hong Kong, 1951-53; *New Life Evening Post*, Hong Kong bureau, managing editor, 1954-62; *Hindustan Times*, New Delhi, India, special correspondent and columnist, 1960-65; *Newsweek*, Hong Kong bureau, China specialist and staff correspondent, 1963-79; independent consultant on Asian affairs, 1979—. Research associate at Harvard University East Asian Research Center, Cambridge, Mass., 1965-66. Member of standing committee of Hong Kong Human Rights Council. *Member:* International P.E.N., Royal Asiatic Society, Foreign Correspondents Club (Hong Kong; honorary member).

WRITINGS: (Under pseudonym Chin Feng) *Liu Long Tse* (novel; title means "The Wanderer"), Asia Publication House, 1955; (with Lai Ying and Edward Behr) *Thirty-Sixth Way* (nonfiction), Doubleday, 1969; (contributor) Ruprecht Kurzrock, editor, *Asien Im 20. Jahrhundert* (title means "Asia in the Twentieth Century"), Collogium Verlag (Berlin), 1972. Also author, under pseudonym Yeh Hsiang, of screenplay "Su Man Zu: Poet Monk," 1948. Contributor to magazines, including *China Quarterly, Reporter's, National Review,* and *Formosa Today.* Member of editorial board of *Italiano-China Quarterly.*

WORK IN PROGRESS: A book on Chinese military history from 1921 to 1949.

SIDELIGHTS: Sydney Liu told *CA:* "I have always felt that reading is a pleasure, but writing is not. Everytime, when writing, I feel like a coolie carrying a heavy load up a mountain slope; when I finish an article or a book, I suddenly feel totally relieved and the pleasure is beyond description. As a trained engineer, I had no intention in the beginning to be a writer. I was sucked accidently into duty as a journalist on a daily paper and began to know many writers. I tried, or rather, was impressed into trying all sorts of writing, ranging from editorials, essays, and features to novels and movie scripts, upon the urging of friends or editors. These proved interesting exercises in expressing concepts or telling stories with brevity and conciseness. After decades of such forced discipline, I still want to move on like an opium smoker. To outline a theme is hard, but to put the idea into words is harder. I am now working on an academic work on modern Chinese military history, retracing much of the same ground I did as a journalist, but searching for greater insights and complexities of the labyrinths of often contradictory and conflicting sources. I am finding this a much taller mountain."

*   *   *

LIVERSIDGE, Joan (Eileen Annie)

PERSONAL: Born in London, England; daughter of Harold and Louise (Appleyard) Liversidge. *Education:* Newnham College, Cambridge, diploma in prehistoric archaeology, 1943, M.Litt., 1949. *Home:* 10 Richmond Rd., Cambridge, England. *Office:* Department of Archaeology, Cambridge University, Cambridge, England.

CAREER: Cambridge University, Cambridge, England, honorary keeper of Roman collections at Museum of Archaeology and Anthropology, 1951, researcher on Roman Britain, 1951-55, 1958-60, research fellow at Newnham College, 1955-58, fellow of Lucy Cavendish College, 1960—, lecturer in archaeology, 1973—. *Member:* Society of Antiquaries (fellow), Cambridge Antiquarian Society.

WRITINGS: Furniture in Roman Britain, Tiranti, 1955; *Roman Britain,* Longmans, Green, 1958; *Britain in the Roman*

Empire, Praeger, 1968; *Roman Gaul,* Longman, 1975; *Everyday Life in the Roman Empire,* Putnam, 1977. Contributor to *Encyclopaedia Britannica.* Contributor to scholarly journals.

WORK IN PROGRESS: Research on the interior decoration of Roman buildings in the Western Empire, with special reference to furniture and wall-painting; a book on religion in Roman Britain, for Hutchinson.

SIDELIGHTS: Liversidge told *CA:* "My major project is the production of a corpus of Roman wall-painting in Britain. This has been a neglected subject outside of Italy, but now, with modern methods of excavation and conservation, it is becoming important. A Cambridge seminar in 1980 attracted major papers from several countries, including Holland, France, and Germany, on Roman provincial wall-painting which I am editing for publication by British Archaeological Reports International. I have also contributed reports on the painted walls surviving from Verulamium (St. Albans) and the Lullingstone villa house-church for books edited by S. Frere and G. W. Meates."

*   *   *

LLOYD, Howell Arnold   1937-

PERSONAL: Born November 15, 1937, in Carmarthen, Wales; son of John Lewis (a secondary school principal) and Elizabeth Mary (a teacher; maiden name, Arnold) Lloyd; married Gaynor Ilid Jones, September 15, 1962; children: Susanna, Becky, Jonathan, Tim, Christian. *Education:* University of Wales, University College of Wales, Aberystwyth, B.A. (with first class honors), 1958; Jesus College, Oxford, D.Phil., 1964. *Home:* 23 Strathmore Ave., Hull HU6 7HJ, England. *Office:* Department of History, University of Hull, Cottingham Rd., Hull HU6 7RX, England.

CAREER: University of Hull, Hull, England, lecturer, 1962-73, senior lecturer in history, 1973—.

WRITINGS: The Gentry of South-West Wales, 1540-1640, University of Wales Press, 1968; (with Gordon Connell-Smith) *The Relevance of History,* Heinemann, 1972; *The Rouen Campaign, 1590-1592: Politics, Warfare, and the Early-Modern State,* Oxford University Press, 1973; *The State, France, and the Sixteenth Century,* Allen & Unwin, in press. Contributor to history journals.

WORK IN PROGRESS: A study of Robert Devereux, second Earl of Essex; a political history of sixteenth-century France, publication by Longman expected in 1986.

*   *   *

LOEW, Sebastian   1939-

PERSONAL: Born June 6, 1939, in Paris, France; son of George M. (in business) and Elisabet (Cohen) Loew. *Education:* University of Buenos Aires, Architect, 1965; Architectural Association, London, England, diploma in town planning, 1970. *Home:* 17/17 Broad Court, London W.C.2, England. *Office:* Department of Planning, Polytechnic of the South Bank, Borough Rd., London, England.

CAREER: Mario R. Alvarez & Partners, Buenos Aires, Argentina, assistant architect, 1965; Greater London Council, Architects Department, London, England, assistant architect, 1967-68; Islington Borough Council, London, planning officer in planning department, 1969-72, principal planning officer in directorate of development, 1972-73; Polytechnic of the South Bank, London, lecturer, 1973-76, senior lecturer in planning, 1976—. Member of Covent Garden Conservation Area Advisory Committee.

WRITINGS: Local Planning, Shoe String, 1979. Contributor to British planning journals and newspapers.

WORK IN PROGRESS: Research on tourism, town planning, urban design, and design control.

AVOCATIONAL INTERESTS: Music (singing), yoga.

* * *

LONG, E(verette) B(each) 1919-1981

OBITUARY NOTICE—See index for *CA* sketch: Born October 24, 1919, in Whitehall, Wis.; died March 31, 1981, in Chicago, Ill. Journalist, historian, and author. E. B. Long was one of America's foremost experts on the Civil War. He worked as a reporter in Chicago for ten years before deciding to devote himself to historical research and teaching. "I got interested in the Civil War as a hobby," he explained. "Then it became an avocation, then a way of life." Long was the chief researcher for Bruce Catton's *Centennial History of the Civil War* and worked on Allan Nevins's *Ordeal of the Union.* He also wrote and edited several works on the Civil War, including *The Civil War: A Picture Chronicle* and *The Civil War Day by Day.* Long's last book, *The Saints and the Union: The Utah Territory in the Civil War,* was published the day before his death. Obituaries and other sources: *Chicago Tribune,* April 2, 1981; *New York Times,* April 13, 1981; *AB Bookman's Weekly,* May 4, 1981.

* * *

LOPEZ, Adalberto 1943-

PERSONAL: Born March 12, 1943, in Cidra, P.R.; son of Miguel and Juanita (Hernandez) Lopez; married Miriam Habib, 1965; children: Karim, Hassan. *Education:* Harvard University, B.A., 1966, M.A., 1968, Ph.D., 1972. *Office:* Department of History, State University of New York at Binghamton, Binghamton, N.Y. 13901.

CAREER: Brandeis University, Waltham, Mass., visiting lecturer in history, 1969-70; State University of New York at Binghamton, assistant professor, 1970-75, associate professor of history, 1975—, director of Latin American and Caribbean area studies program and coordinator of overseas academic programs, 1975—.

WRITINGS: (Editor with James Petras) *Puerto Rico and Puerto Ricans: Studies in History and Society,* Schenkman, 1974; *The Revolt of the Comuneros, 1721-1735: A Study in the Colonial History of Paraguay,* Schenkman, 1976; *The Puerto Ricans: Their History, Culture, and Society,* Schenkman, 1980. Contributor to academic journals.

* * *

LORD, Albert Bates 1912-

PERSONAL: Born September 15, 1912, in Boston, Mass.; son of Robert Whiting and Corinne Adeline (Bates) Lord; married Mary Louise Carlson, August 24, 1950; children: Nathan Eliot, Mark Edwards. *Education:* Harvard University, A.B., 1934, A.M., 1936, Ph.D., 1949. *Home:* 23 Francis Ave., Cambridge, Mass. 02138.

CAREER: Harvard University, Cambridge, Mass., lecturer, 1950-52, associate professor, 1952-58, professor of Slavic studies and contemporary literature, 1958—, Arthur Kingsley Porter Professor, 1972—, honorary curator of Milman Parry Collection at library, 1959—. Conducted research in Yugoslavia, 1934-35, 1937, 1950-51, 1961-64, 1966-67, Albania, 1937, and Bulgaria, 1958, 1959.

MEMBER: International Comparative Literature Association, American Academy of Arts and Sciences (fellow), American Folklore Society (fellow), American Association for the Advancement of Slavic Studies, American Philological Association, Archaeological Institute of America, American Comparative Literature Association, Mediaeval Academy of America, Modern Language Association of America, Modern Greek Studies Association, Phi Beta Kappa. *Awards, honors:* Guggenheim fellow, 1949-50; Yugoslavian Order of St. Sava.

WRITINGS: (Editor and translator) Bela Bartok, *Serbo-Croatian Folk Songs,* Columbia University Press, 1951; (editor and translator) *Serbo-Croatian Heroic Songs,* Harvard University Press, Volume I, 1953, Volume II, 1954, Volume III (with David E. Bynum), 1975, Volume IV (with Bynum), 1975; (editor) *Slavic Folklore: A Symposium,* American Folklore Society, 1956; *Beginning Serbocroatian,* 's-Gravenhage, 1958; *The Singer of Tales,* Harvard University Press, 1960; *Beginning Bulgarian,* 's-Gravenhage, 1962; (editor with Bynum) *A Bulgarian Literary Reader,* Mouton, 1968; (editor) *Russian Folk Tales,* Limited Editions Club, 1970; (editor) *The Multinational Literature of Yugoslavia,* St. John's University (Jamaica, N.Y.), 1974; (translator and author of introduction and notes, with Bynum) Avdo Mededovic, *The Wedding of Smailagic Meho,* Harvard University Press, 1974. Contributor to academic journals.*

* * *

LORIE, James Hirsch 1922-

PERSONAL: Born February 23, 1922, in Kansas City, Mo.; son of Alvin J. and Adele (Hirsch) Lorie; married Sally Rosen, June 16, 1948 (divorced, 1953); married Nancy A. Wexler, June 19, 1958 (died, 1966); married Vanna Metzenberg Lautman, August 27, 1967; children: (first marriage) Susan; (second marriage) Katherine, Jeffrey (stepchildren); (third marriage) Erika, Victoria, Karl (stepchildren). *Education:* Cornell University, A.B., 1942, A.M., 1945; University of Chicago, Ph.D., 1947. *Home:* 5825 Blackstone Ave., Chicago, Ill. 60637. *Office:* Graduate School of Business, University of Chicago, Chicago, Ill. 60637.

CAREER: Seminar on American Civilization, Salzburg, Austria, member of staff, 1947; University of Chicago, Chicago, Ill., assistant professor, 1947-50, associate professor, 1950-56, professor of business administration, 1956—, associate dean of Graduate School of Business, 1956-61, director of research, 1961-65, director of Center for Research in Security Prices, 1960-75. Member of National Market Advisory Board, 1975-77. Chairman of board of directors of Woodlawn Hospital; member of board of directors of Square D Co., Acorn Fund, Standard Shares, Inc., Fundamerica of Japan, Chicago Board Options Exchange, Sealy, Inc., Lionel D. Edie Capital Fund, Vulcan Materials Co., Inc., Elsinore Corp., Merrill Lynch Capital Fund, Wallace Business Forms, and International Clearing Corp.; consultant to Federal Reserve System and U.S. Department of the Treasury. *Military service:* U.S. Coast Guard Reserve, 1942-44. *Member:* American Economic Association, National Association of Securities Dealers (member of board of governors, 1972-75), Mont Pelerin Society, Phi Beta Kappa, Economic Club, Quadrangle Club.

WRITINGS: Causes of Annual Fluctuations in the Production of Livestock and Livestock Products, University of Chicago Press, 1947; (with Harry V. Roberts) *Basic Methods of Marketing Research,* McGraw, 1951; (with Lawrence Fisher) *Rates of Return on Investments in Common Stocks,*

1926-1965, Center for Research in Security Prices, University of Chicago, 1963; (editor with Richard Brealey) *Modern Developments in Investment Management: A Book of Readings*, Praeger, 1972, 2nd edition, Dryden, 1978; (with Mary T. Hamilton) *The Stock Market: Theories and Evidence*, Irwin, 1973; (with Fisher) *A Half-Century of Returns on Stocks and Bonds*, Graduate School of Business, University of Chicago, 1977. Contributor to journals.*

*   *   *

LORRAH, Jean

PERSONAL: Born in Canton, Ohio; daughter of Walter and Marie (Unger) Lorrah. *Education:* Western Reserve University (now Case Western Reserve University), B.A., 1962, M.A., 1963; Florida State University, Ph.D., 1968. *Home:* 301 South 15th St., Murray, Ky. 42071. *Office:* Department of English, Murray State University, Murray, Ky. 42071.

CAREER: English teacher at private school in Montverde, Fla., 1963-66, department head, 1964-66; Murray State University, Murray, Ky., assistant professor, 1968-72, associate professor, 1972-80, professor of English, 1980—. *Member:* National Writers Club, Modern Language Association of America, Science Fiction Writers of America, American Name Society, Popular Culture Association of the South, South Atlantic Modern Language Association.

WRITINGS: (With Jacqueline Lichtenberg) *First Channel* (novel), Doubleday, 1980; (contributor) Marion Zimmer Bradley, editor, *The Keeper's Price*, DAW Books, 1980; (contributor) Collins and Pearce, editors, *The Scope of the Fantastic*, Greenwood Press, 1981; *Savage Empire* (novel), Playboy Press, 1981; (contributor) Susan Shwartz, editor, *Hecate's Cauldron*, DAW, 1981; *Channel's Destiny* (novel), Doubleday, 1982; *Dragon Lord of the Savage Empire* (novel), Playboy Press, 1982. Also contributor to *Feminist Criticism of Science Fiction*, edited by Jessica Amanda Salmonson. Associate editor of *Pandora*, 1981—.

WORK IN PROGRESS: Two novels, *Captives of the Savage Empire* and *Ambrov Keon*, completion of both expected in 1983; *Outplacement: The Teacher's Guide to a Non-Teaching Career*.

SIDELIGHTS: Jean Lorrah commented: "I have had the incredible good fortune to have the field of literature that I love, science fiction, open to me both creatively and academically in the past five years. I have been reading and writing science fiction since my teens; in the 1970's, pioneering women authors broke through the subject/theme barrier against the *kind* of science fiction I write, and opened the field to me. Meanwhile, via popular culture, the world of academe was becoming responsive to research in a field now called 'the fantastic.' Suddenly I can write what I want and be published, and research what I want and be published. Could anyone be more fortunate? I particularly owe a debt to Jacqueline Lichtenberg, whose allowing me to collaborate with her in a universe she created helped me to my first creative publication."

*   *   *

LOUIS, Joe
See BARROW, Joseph Louis

*   *   *

LOUX, Michael Joseph   1942-

PERSONAL: Born August 17, 1942, in St. Paul, Minn.; married, 1966; children: three. *Education:* College of St. Thomas,

B.A., 1964; University of Chicago, A.M., 1965, Ph.D., 1968. *Office:* Department of Philosophy, University of Notre Dame, Notre Dame, Ind. 46556.

CAREER: University of Notre Dame, Notre Dame, Ind., associate professor of philosophy, 1968—. *Member:* American Philosophical Association, American Association of University Professors.

WRITINGS: (Editor) *Universals and Particulars: Readings in Ontology*, Anchor Books, 1970; (translator) William Ockham, *Ockham's Theory of Terms*, University of Notre Dame Press, 1975; *Substance and Attribute: A Study in Ontology*, D. Reidel, 1978; (editor and author of introduction) *The Possible and the Actual: Readings in the Metaphysics of Modality*, Cornell University Press, 1979. Contributor to philosophy journals.*

*   *   *

LOVEJOY, David Sherman   1919-

PERSONAL: Born November 30, 1919, in Pawtucket, R.I.; son of Edmund Matteson and Ida Elizabeth (Louks) Lovejoy; married Elizabeth Richards Bowers, September 13, 1941; children: Elizabeth Grant (Mrs. Nicholas W. Fisher). *Education:* Bowdoin College, B.S., 1941; Brown University, A.M., 1947, Ph.D., 1954. *Home:* 110 Vaughn Court, Madison, Wis. 53705. *Office:* Department of History, University of Wisconsin, Madison, Wis. 53706.

CAREER: Affiliated with Marlboro College, 1950-53; Michigan State University, East Lansing, assistant professor of history, 1954-55; Brown University, Providence, R.I., assistant professor of history, 1955-59; Northwestern University, Evanston, Ill., visiting assistant professor of history, 1959-60; University of Wisconsin (now University of Wisconsin—Madison), 1965—, began as assistant professor, became professor of American colonial history, 1960—. Fulbright lecturer at University of Aberdeen, 1964-65; member of council of Institute of Early American History and Culture, 1975-78. *Military service:* U.S. Army, infantry, 1942-45; served in Europe; became captain; received Bronze Star. *Member:* American Historical Association, Organization of American Historians, American Civil Liberties Union, Audubon Society. *Awards, honors:* Guggenheim fellow, 1967-68; John Carter Brown Library fellow, 1970; Folger Library fellow, 1974-75; Rockefeller Foundation fellow, 1978-79.

WRITINGS: Rhode Island Politics and the American Revolution, 1760-1776, Brown University Press, 1958; (editor) *Religious Enthusiasm and the Great Awakening*, Prentice-Hall, 1969; *The Glorious Revolution in America*, Harper, 1972. Contributor to history journals.*

*   *   *

LOVELL, Ernest J(ames), Jr.   1918-1975

OBITUARY NOTICE—See index for *CA* sketch: Born August 28, 1918, in Roanoke, Va.; died June 22, 1975. Educator and author. An expert on Lord Byron, Lovell was a professor of English for almost thirty years at the University of Texas at Austin and served as editor of *Texas Studies in Literature and Language*. Among his books are *Byron: The Record of a Quest* and *Captain Medwin: Friend of Byron and Shelley*. Obituaries and other sources: *Who Was Who in America*, 6th edition, Marquis, 1976.

LUCE, Gay Gaer 1930-

PERSONAL: Born October 2, 1930, in Berkeley, Calif.; daughter of Joseph and Fay (Ratner) Gaer. *Education:* Radcliffe College, B.A., 1951; Stanford University, M.A., 1957.

CAREER: Boston Museum of Science, Boston, Mass., in public relations, 1952-53; City of Palo Alto, Palo Alto, Calif., consultant, 1954-55; Jewish Theological Seminary, New York City, in public information, 1956-57; Concord Control, Inc., Boston, writing consultant, 1958-59; associated with public affairs programs at Columbia Broadcasting System (CBS-TV), New York City, 1959-61; President's Scientific Advisory Committee, Washington, D.C., editor, 1962-63; National Institute of Mental Health, Washington, D.C., writer, 1963-67. *Member:* International Loners Club, Association of Psychophysiological Study of Sleep, Psychophysiological Research Society. *Awards, honors:* American Psychology Foundation scientific writing award, 1962; American Psychology Foundation scientific writing award, 1966, for *Sleep.*

WRITINGS: Current Research On Sleep and Dreams, U.S. Government Printing Office, 1965; (with Julius Segal) *Sleep,* Coward, 1966 (published in England as *Sleep and Dreams,* Panther, 1969); (with Segal) *Insomnia: The Guide for Troubled Sleepers,* Doubleday, 1969; *Biological Rhythms in Psychiatry and Medicine,* U.S. Government Printing Office, 1970, published as *Biological Rhythms in Human and Animal Physiology,* Dover, 1971; *Body Time: Physiological Rhythms and Social Stress,* Pantheon, 1971; *Your Second Life: Vitality in Middle and Later Age,* Delacorte, 1979.

SIDELIGHTS: Luce has devoted herself to researching and writing about biological and physiological occurrences in humans and animals, particularly the phenomenon of sleep. Her book, *Sleep,* co-authored with Julius Segal, was hailed as the best popular science book of 1966. Norman MacKenzie of the *New York Times Book Review* said of their effort, "Gay Gaer Luce and Julius Segal, whose commission seems to have been to provide a complete popular introduction to the subject of sleep, have done remarkably well, not least in providing a much better bibliography than is customary in books of this sort."

In their second book, *Insomnia,* Luce and Segal study problems associated with sleep. While defining and citing differences between various forms of insomnia, the authors explore the many reasons why millions of Americans suffer from poor sleep, among them being deficient diet and nocturnal rituals that promote habitual sleeplessness. They also emphasize that "one of the strongest and most dangerous sleep myths of our day is that a person can simply swallow a pill to cure insomnia." Hypnosis, meditation, and electrosleep (a Russian technique of electrically stimulating the brain to reestablish sleeping patterns) are suggested by Luce and Segal as alternatives to sleep-inducing chemicals.

Critics have praised *Insomnia.* David Rorvik of *New York* wrote that "*Insomnia* is a provocative mix of authoritative research findings, engaging anecdotes and personal, but always informed, opinions." J. H. Plumb of *Saturday Review* agreed: "A magnificent book, lucid and sane, it combines scientific wisdom with a warm human approach to a problem that haunts maybe thirty million Americans." Rorvik predicted that, ironically, *Insomnia* may actually cause some to lose sleep. He quipped, "*Insomnia* is full of surprising information bound to keep even sound sleepers up beyond their bedtimes."

In *Your Second Life,* Luce traces the growth of the SAGE (Senior Actualization and Growth Explorations) program and discusses its goal of improving the lives of the elderly through such methods as mind control, stress therapy, self-healing, meditation, and nutritive counseling. In addition to being a history of SAGE, *Your Second Life* is "a guide for people who want to join or expand the movement," said Helen Kelley of the *Washington Post Book World.* "And in very significant part it can serve as a handbook for younger people who want to enjoy their youth and middle age as well as to control or prevent some of the stress and depression which characterize the lives of many older people."

BIOGRAPHICAL/CRITICAL SOURCES: New York Times Book Review, June 12, 1966; *Saturday Review,* July 26, 1969; *New York,* September 8, 1969; *Washington Post Book World,* August 26, 1979.*

*   *   *

LUKAS, Mary

PERSONAL: Daughter of Alex J. and Margaret (McGuire) Lukas. *Education:* Attended College of New Rochelle and Fordham University; graduate study at Catholic University of America. *Religion:* Roman Catholic. *Agent:* Paul R. Reynolds, Inc., 12 East 41st St., New York, N.Y. 10017.

CAREER: Writer and lecturer. *U.S.A.-1* (magazine), general editor, 1963; *Show* (magazine), theatre editor, 1963-64; *Look,* New York, N.Y., entertainment editor, 1964; free-lance writer, 1966—. *Member:* International P.E.N., Authors Guild, New York Teilhard Association (member of advisory board of directors), Kappa Gamma Pi. *Awards, honors:* History-biography prize from Religious Media, Inc., 1977, for *Teilhard.*

WRITINGS: (With sister, Ellen Lukas) *Teilhard: A Biography,* Doubleday, 1977, annotated edition, McGraw-Hill, 1981; (editor and translator) *Teilhard's Letters to Pierre Leroy,* Paulist, 1980. Contributor to magazines, including *America, Quest,* and *Jubilee.*

WORK IN PROGRESS: A historical novel.

SIDELIGHTS: Lucas spent seven years researching her biography of Pierre Teilhard de Chardin. "The result," said *New York Times Book Review* critic Frank Gibney, "is a highly illuminating book" about the French Jesuit who attempted "to construct a new theology and virtually a new Christian metaphysics out of the discoveries of modern science."

BIOGRAPHICAL/CRITICAL SOURCES: New York Times Book Review, February 20, 1977; *Saturday Review,* April 2, 1977; *Best Sellers,* July, 1977.

*   *   *

LUKENBILL, Willis B(ernard) 1939-

PERSONAL: Born March 27, 1939, in Mount Sylvan, Tex.; son of Lee Roy and Tommie Lee (McCorkle) Lukenbill; married Shirley Ann Hebert (an educator), June 1, 1968; children: James Frederick. *Education:* Tyler Junior College, A.A., 1957; North Texas State University, B.S., 1961; University of Oklahoma, M.L.S., 1964; Indiana University, Ph.D., 1973. *Politics:* Democrat. *Home:* 4906 Canyonwood Dr., Austin, Tex. 78735. *Office:* Graduate School of Library and Information Science, University of Texas at Austin, Austin, Tex. 78712.

CAREER: High school librarian in Seguin, Tex., 1961-63; Austin College, Sherman, Tex., reference librarian, 1964;

Louisiana Tech University, Ruston, instructor in library science, 1964-69; University of Maryland, College Park, assistant professor of library science, 1972-74; University of Texas at Austin, assistant professor of library science, 1975-80, associate professor of library and information science, 1980—. *Member:* American Library Association, Popular Culture Association, Assembly on Adolescent Literature, Texas Library Association.

WRITINGS: (Contributor) Zena Sutherland and May Hill Arbuthnot, *Children and Books,* 4th edition, Scott, Foresman, 1972, 5th edition, 1977; (editor) *Media and the Young Adult, 1950-1972,* American Library Association, 1977; (contributor) JoAnn Rogers, editor, *Libraries and Young Adults: Media, Services, and Librarianship,* Libraries Unlimited, 1979; (contributor) Millicent A. Lenz and Ramona Mahood, editors, *Young Adult Literature: Background and Criticism,* American Library Association, 1980; (co-editor) *Media and the Young Adult, 1973-77,* American Library Association, 1981. Contributor of about twenty articles to library journals.

SIDELIGHTS: Lukenbill wrote: "During my career, I have been concerned with both practical and theoretical ways of understanding how people's social, personal, and workplace needs relate to information. With this focus in mind, I consider my writing and teaching to be client-directed in terms of understanding the social and psychological phenomena that influence and direct one's need for information. This premise has been the focus of my work in documenting the information-seeking behavior of adolescents. Most of my writings reflect this concern."

*   *   *

LUNDGREN, Paul Arthur   1925-1981
(James McCutcheon)

OBITUARY NOTICE: Born January 4, 1925, in Kansas City, Mo.; died in 1981 in Topeka, Kan. Rare book dealer and author. In addition to his lengthy career as a dealer in the rare book trade, Paul Lundgren wrote numerous short stories and articles. Under the pseudonym James McCutcheon he was a contributor to magazines and periodicals, including *Kansas Quarterly, New Pacific,* and *Boys' Life.* Obituaries and other sources: *AB Bookman's Weekly,* May 4, 1981.

*   *   *

LUST, Peter   1911-

PERSONAL: Born January 15, 1911, in Nuremberg, Germany (now West Germany); son of Arthur (a hop dealer) and Luise (a writer and theatre critic; maiden name, Bloch) Lust; married Evelyn Heymannsohn (an operatic singer), June 23, 1953; children: Patricia, Arthur, Peter, Jr. *Education:* University of Geneva, M.A., 1931. *Politics:* "Completely neutral." *Religion:* Roman Catholic. *Home:* 13 Thompson Point, Beaconsfield, Quebec, Canada H9W 5Y8. *Office:* Box 2, Dorval Airport, Dorval, Quebec, Canada H4Y 1A2.

CAREER: Hop dealer, 1933-46; *Montreal Herald,* Montreal, Quebec, writer, 1946-52; free-lance journalist, 1952-70; *Suburban* (newspaper), Cote St. Luc, Quebec, author of column "Commentary," 1970—. Canadian correspondent for *Der Spiegel,* 1967-70, and *Der Stern,* 1971—. *Military service:* U.S. Army, 1941-45. *Awards, honors:* Nonfiction prize from government of Quebec, 1967, for *The Last Seal Pup.*

WRITINGS: Two Germanies: Mirror of an Age, Harvest House, 1966; *The Last Seal Pup: The Story of Canada's Last Seal Hunt,* Harvest House, 1967; *Cuba: Time Bomb at Our Door,* Chateau Books, 1973.

WORK IN PROGRESS: Research for a book on the explosive situation in Quebec; a novel.

SIDELIGHTS: "I used to live in the United States," Lust told *CA.* "I had to sell hops for my father's firm and hated every moment of it. I am by nature a writer, perhaps a dreamer. Business is not my thing. It actually frightens me to think of myself as a businessman. I had the chance after I left the army to go to Canada, where I started as a journalist at the old *Montreal Herald.* My life started in that year, by that I mean my *real* life. For the first time I did what I liked to do.

"My main effort has been to travel to as many internationally important areas as possible and research facts. Often I learned that generally held opinions were wrong. For instance, in 1965 I received invitations from both the West German and East German governments to visit their respective countries and report my findings. At that time the German Democratic Republic was still internationally isolated and few reporters from western countries visited there. After my visit I had to conclude that the country was stable and would endure. I reported my findings through the Canadian Broadcasting Corporation and other media. Naturally, I was immediately called 'soft on communism.'

"In 1971 the U.S. Information Service gave me a chance to visit Vietnam to observe 'the cooperation between the U.S. Army and the Thieu government.' To make certain that I would see both sides of the war, several months after my return from Vietnam I applied to North Vietnam for permission to visit Hanoi. I got it, and I researched and reported. This time I found that public opinion again did not conform to my findings. It was the time of American anti-war protests. According to many young Americans, everything that happened in Vietnam was wrong. Sorry—my findings showed that the North Vietnamese were as cruel, if not more so, than some of the U.S. Army units. I visited the 'tiger cages' where Thieu's soldiers held and tortured captured North Vietnamese. But I also investigated the Hue massacre where North Vietnamese and Viet Kong troops had massacred more than six thousand innocent civilians, including small children and old men and women. On the average, the North's crimes exceeded those of the South and the U.S. Army. After my report came in I was called—you might have guessed it—pro-Fascist.

"In West Germany (my native country) I interviewed some of the captured Baader-Meinhof terrorists (in fact, I knew Ulrike Meinhof reasonably well before she became a terrorist), and I had to report that, while their methods were to be roundly condemned, their idealism was based on humanitarian thoughts.

"I would say that my main purpose in life is to deflate false images and correct my readers' information about existing facts. I have tried to achieve this with my three books. Presently I am researching the political situation here at home in Quebec—Rene Levesque might have lost the last referendum, but his movement is by no means dead.

"I am writing a novel, which I hope will merit the term 'thriller,' about a future war involving a Quebec revolution and the breakup of Canada. I have enough background knowledge of such a possible situation to write what I hope may be a reasonably exciting novel."

LYLE-SMYTHE, Alan 1914-
(Alan Caillou)

PERSONAL: Born November 9, 1914, in Redhill, Surrey, England; naturalized U.S. citizen in 1978; son of Walter and Edith (Lyle) Smythe; married Aliza Sverdlova, May 6, 1939; children: Nadia. *Education:* Studied acting at Oscar Lewis Academy. *Religion:* None. *Residence:* Tarzana, Calif. *Agent:* Dorris Halsey, Reece Halsey Agency, 8733 Sunset Blvd., Los Angeles, Calif. 90069; and Scott Meredith Literary Agency, Inc., 845 Third Ave., New York, N.Y. 10022.

CAREER: Palestine Police, Jerusalem and Haifa, Palestine, police officer, 1936-39; Reserved Areas of Ethiopia, Dire Dawa, chief of police, 1946-48; British Government Foreign Office, Garoe, Somalia, district officer, 1948-50; actor, touring in Africa, and writer, 1950-52; television actor and writer in Toronto, Ontario and Vancouver, British Columbia, 1952-57; film and television actor and writer in Tarzana, Calif., 1957—. *Military service:* British Army, Intelligence Corps, 1939-45; served in Africa; became major; received Medal of Order of the British Empire, Military Cross, and seven campaign medals. *Member:* Institute of Canine Psychology. *Awards, honors:* Edgar Allan Poe Award from Mystery Writers of America, 1970, for *Assault on Ming.*

WRITINGS—All under pseudonym Alan Caillou; nonfiction: *The World Is Six Feet Square,* P. Davies, 1954, Norton, 1955; *Sheba Slept Here,* Abelard, 1974; *South From Khartoum,* Hawthorne, 1974.

Novels: *Rogue's Gambit,* P. Davies, 1955; *Alien Virus,* P. Davies, 1957, published in the United States as *Cairo Cabal,* Pinnacle Books, 1974; *The Mindanao Pearl,* P. Davies, 1959, Pinnacle Books, 1973.

The Plotters, Harper, 1960; *The Walls of Jolo* (Dollar Book Club selection), Appleton, 1960; *Rampage* (Dollar Book Club selection), Appleton, 1961; *Field of Women,* Appleton, 1963; *Marseilles,* Pocket Books, 1964; *The Hot Sun of Africa,* Signet Books, 1964; *A Journey to Orassia,* Doubleday, 1965; *Khartoum* (novelization of screenplay), Signet Books, 1966; *Who'll Buy My Evil?,* Pocket Books, 1966; *Charge of the Light Brigade,* Pyramid Publications, 1968; *Assault on Kolchak,* Avon, 1969; *Bichu the Jaguar* (Reader's Digest Condensed Book selection), World Press, 1969.

Assault on Loveless, Avon, 1970; *Assault on Ming,* Avon, 1970; *The Cheetahs* (Reader's Digest Condensed Book selection), World Press, 1971; *The Dead Sea Submarine,* Pinnacle Books, 1971; *Terror in Rio,* Pinnacle Books, 1971; *Congo War-Cry,* Pinnacle Books, 1971; *Afghan Onslaught,* Pinnacle Books, 1971; *Assault on Fellawi,* Avon, 1972; *Assault on Agathon,* Avon, 1972; *Swamp War,* Pinnacle Books, 1973; *Death Charge,* Pinnacle Books, 1973; *The Garonsky Missile,* Pinnacle Books, 1973; *Assault on Aimata,* Avon, 1975; *Diamonds Wild,* Avon, 1979.

Work represented in anthologies, including *The Writers' Guild Anthology.*

Films: "The Plotters," released by Ida Lupino in 1962; "Clarence, the Cross-Eyed Lion," released by Metro-Goldwyn-Mayer in 1964; "The Losers," released by Fanfare Productions in 1970; "The 'Star of India'," a documentary released by Copley Productions in 1970; "Evel Knievel," released by Fanfare Productions in 1971; "The Good Life," a documentary released by Copley Productions in 1973; "Assault on Agathon," released by Agathon Productions in 1974; "Thermoliath," released by John Brand Productions

in 1975; "Kingdom of the Spiders," released by Arachnid Productions in 1977; "Tennessee Work Farm," released by Dimension Pictures in 1978; (co-author) "Devilfish," released by First Artists in 1978; "The Mindanao Pearl," an independent production.

Author of television and radio plays and documentary film scripts for Canadian Broadcasting Corp. and Canada's National Film Board. Writer for television series, including "The Six Million Dollar Man," "The Man From U.N.C.L.E.," "The Rogues," "Voyage to the Bottom of the Sea," "Thriller," "Behind Closed Doors," "Man From Atlantis," "U.S. Steel Hour," "The Fugitive," "Flipper," "Daktari," "Bus Stop," "77 Sunset Strip," "The Bob Cummings Show," "The Outlaws," "Bulldog Drummond," and "Cannonball." Contributor of articles to *Geographical* and novellas to *Coven Thirteen.*

WORK IN PROGRESS: The Entwhistle Saga, the story of four generations of an Anglo-Indian army family who immigrate to America, for Morrow.

SIDELIGHTS: Caillou told *CA:* "I went to Palestine in 1934, served three years in the Palestine police, and spent the next two years traveling between Palestine and Egypt, the Sudan, Lebanon, Syria, and Trans-Jordan.

"At the outbreak of the War, in 1939, I joined the British Army; being able to speak Arabic, I was sent at once to the Western Desert. I then joined the Intelligence Corps, and spent 1941 and 1942 operating behind enemy lines in the Libyan Desert and Tunisia. I was captured by the Italians in Tunisia in January, 1943, court-martialed on charges of espionage, sentenced to be shot, and escaped in March; I headed across the Libyan Desert and was picked up by the Germans five days and a hundred-twenty miles later, largely on account of water difficulties. I was sent to a civilian prison in Italy, escaped again in September, and reached the British lines at Salerno two months later. I spent the remainder of the war with the guerrillas in Yugoslavia and Italy, as intelligence officer to the Partisan Ninth Corps.

"At the end of hostilities in Europe I was sent to Ethiopia to take over the administration of the Reserved Areas Police, with headquarters in Dire Dawa. I was chief of police there for the next two years, and then went to Somalia as a district officer—to the Mijertein, which is practically unexplored territory. I had a 'one-man' station for the next twelve months at a place called Garoe—a water-hole which served three mutually hostile Somali tribes—and I had many duties rolled into one: magistrate, prosecuting officer, defending officer, mineralogist, doctor, veterinarian, midwife, and general factotum.

"I was constantly on safari over an area of roughly ten thousand square miles, inhabited by a dozen mutually warring tribes and by almost every known African species of game. Communication with headquarters (in Mogadiscio) was by once-monthly truck which brought up the rations and mail, and by a radio which was operated by a Somali policeman. In case of real trouble, a small fort was provided, and there was a landing strip which was, however, out of commission (because of a sand storm) on the only occasion it was required—a police mutiny.

"After I became a civilian again in October, 1947, I took up my old professions, writing and acting. I toured extensively in Kenya, Tanganyika, Uganda, Eritrea, and Zanzibar. I had an interest in a safari organization as well, and worked as a hunter and trapper, as gun to camera-safaris, and as guide and interpreter to tourists and hunters. I spent the next four years in these territories, sometimes living in the bush for months at a time. I have hunted lion, leopard, elephant, rhino, buffalo, crocodile, wild boar, and almost all the smaller animals, and have kept as pets lion, ostrich, gazelles of various kinds, and six cheetahs.

"I once drove a Model-A Ford across the Sahara Desert (alone); I have driven from Addis Ababa to Nairobi (parts of this trip are considered impossible), and was a member of the second party in history to cross the Great Sand Sea of the Sahara Desert in a truck; I also made my home, for three months, in a dried-up Roman well in the middle of the Fezzan Desert.

"My first book, *The World Is Six Feet Square,* is about my life in prison. *Sheba Slept Here* is also autobiographical, covering my years as chief of police in Ethiopia. *Rampage* was made into a movie by Warner Brothers, with Robert Mitchum and Jack Hawkins. *The Walls of Jolo* is a story of the Spanish-American War in the Philippines. Novels of the late 1970's, in series form, concern the adventures of one Cabot Cain, and one has been made into a motion picture. Many of my books have been translated into French, German, Spanish, Dutch, Norwegian, Swedish, Finnish, Italian, Portuguese, and Japanese.

"I left Africa in 1952 and went to Canada. After five years of writing and acting for television in Toronto and Vancouver, I came to the United States and my permanent home in California. In the years I have been here I have written some sixty television plays and acted in about eighty. I have also appeared in twenty-one motion pictures.

"I work very long hours, usually on two projects at a time, probably averaging ten or twelve hours a day seven days a week. When I can, I put in spare time in my garden, which is large: some four hundred rose bushes, many of which I imported from England, fifty-odd fruit trees, a certain amount of vegetables, and a lot of weeds.

"I speak French and Italian fluently and have a working knowledge of English. My Hebrew is fair to middling (I once lived in a kibbutz near Haifa), my Arabic quite forgotten, my German very limited, and my Spanish almost non-existent though I could once manage fairly well. I once studied Amharic for a year, but gave up, it's an impossible language. I am studying Portuguese. I believe that a civilized man should speak at least six languages, fluently. I once managed very well in eight, but I have been living in a mono-lingual country for years and not traveling nearly enough; who can afford, these days, to spend any time at all in Paris, Rome, or Athens, where a decent meal now costs fifty dollars and you can't buy a cheap shirt for less than thirty?

"I keep Doberman Pinschers, used to breed and train them for police work (in Palestine, as it was then). I am still (I think) a member of the Institute of Canine Psychology which has its headquarters in Vienna and wonders why dogs behave

as they do. I used to be an expert on this breed; no longer. *Sic transit gloria Doberman.*

"I have one wife and one daughter, and believe very strongly in an old-fashioned concept—the value of family above all else.

"I'd be a vintage car buff if I could afford it, which I can't. But I do drive a 1934 Bentley, the only two-seater roadster in America, and one of five left world-wide.

"I have a philosophy about writing that may possibly be of interest: if you wait for 'inspiration' you're just not going to make a living. On those (frequent) days when I feel I'm writing badly, I write anyway, because I discovered long ago that it's far easier tomorrow to correct today's lousy work than it is to sit down tomorrow and stare at that same blank page of yellow paper and wonder what to do next."

AVOCATIONAL INTERESTS: Gardening, gourmet cooking, playing chess, classical music (particularly Italian, French, and Russian opera, but not German).

*　　*　　*

LYNN, Ruth Nadelman 1948-

PERSONAL: Born September 26, 1948, in Kalamazoo, Mich.; daughter of Alfred H. (a paper technology consultant) and Hilde (Wolfe) Nadelman; married Bruce A. Lynn (a computer company planner), August 19, 1973; children: Joshua Benjamin. *Education:* University of Michigan, B.A., 1970; Rosary College M.L.S., 1974. *Politics:* Independent. *Home:* 33 Maple St., Lexington, Mass. 02173.

CAREER: Elementary school teacher at public schools in Hingham, Mass., 1970-72; Skokie Public Library, Skokie, Ill., children's librarian, 1974-77; Waltham Public Library, Waltham, Mass., head of children's department, 1977-80. *Member:* American Library Association, New England Library Association, Massachusetts Library Association, Roundtable of Children's Librarians, Beta Phi Mu.

WRITINGS: Fantasy for Children: An Annotated Checklist, Bowker, 1979.

WORK IN PROGRESS: A revision of *Fantasy for Children,* publication by Bowker expected in 1984.

SIDELIGHTS: Ruth Lynn wrote: "I would love to write for children, eventually. As a child, my favorite books were fantasies and I kept a mental list of the best of these. In library school I started a written list, and six years later it became a book." *Avocational interests:* Music, art, dance, film architecture, birdwatching, travel (once lived in France).

*　　*　　*

LYTE, Richard
See WHELPTON, (George) Eric

M

MABERLY, Allan   1922-1977

PERSONAL: Born May 2, 1922, in Sydney, Australia; died July 26, 1977; son of Egbert Henry (a master builder) and Mabel (a seamstress; maiden name, Gisby) Maberly; married Ivy Bertha Findley (a diet aide), April 28, 1948; children: Dawn Ivy Giblett, Carol Ellen McKean, Ruth Iris Jackson. *Education:* Avondale College, B.A., 1945. *Religion:* Seventh Day Adventist. *Home:* 84 Redgrave St., Normanhurst NSW 2076, Australia.

CAREER: Ordained to Seventh Day Adventist ministry, 1950; church pastor in Queensland and Victoria, Australia, 1947-53; missionary in northern India, 1954-61; Signs Publishing Co., Warburton, Victoria, sales manager, 1965-72; associate of Institute of Sales and Marketing Executives, 1972-77.

WRITINGS: God Spoke Tibetan, Pacific Press Publishing Association, 1971.

[Sketch verified by wife, Ivy Bertha Maberly]

*   *   *

MACAINSH, Noel Leslie   1926-

PERSONAL: Born June 15, 1926, in Horsham, Victoria, Australia; son of Leslie John (a journalist) and Elsie May (Morrison) Macainish; married Beryl Hilda Ferguson; children: Gregory John, Andrew James, Helen Rilka. *Education:* University of Melbourne, Diploma in Public Administration, 1958, B.A., 1961; University of Munich, M.A., 1964, Ph.D., 1967. *Office:* Department of English, James Cook University of North Queensland, Townsville, Queensland 4810, Australia.

CAREER: Australia Post, Melbourne, communications engineer, 1948-60; James Cook University of North Queensland, Townsville, Australia, lecturer, 1969-75, senior lecturer in English, 1975—. Member of literature board of Australia Council for the Arts, 1974-76. *Member:* Goethe Society of Townsville (president, 1972—).

WRITINGS: Clifton Pugh, Georgian House, 1961; *Eight by Eight* (poetry), Jacaranda Press, 1963; *Nietzsche in Australia,* Verlag Dokumentation and Werbung, 1975; *Voss: His Character, Communications, and Irony,* James Cook University of North Queensland, 1981.

Work represented in anthologies, including *Verse in Australia,* 1960; *The Penguin Book of Australian Verse,* Penguin,

1976; *World Anthology,* 1980. Contributor of articles, stories, poems, and translations to magazines, including *Poetry Australia, Age, Meanjin, Quadrant, Overland,* and *Australian Letters,* and newspapers.

WORK IN PROGRESS: Research on the writing of Rosa Campbell Praed, the aesthetic movement in Australian poetry, and problems of Australian literary history.

SIDELIGHTS: Macainsh commented: "While writers often claim to pursue beauty, truth, and a vision of a better world, it is modern discoveries about the nature of language that interest me as sources of literary criticism. Just as artists and philosophers have been close to each other in the past, it seems that new developments such as semiotics now offer the possibility of overcoming old dichotomies of high-brow and popular forms, helping us to produce new types of work more appropriate to our age.

"I admire writers such as Friedrich Durrenmatt, Leonardo Sciasca, and George Batailles, as examples of this. They are not just intuitives, flying by the seat of their pants, but imaginative intellectuals in touch with the 'deep structures' of everyday life.

"In my work I am interested in transcending the now obsolete boundaries between verse, prose-fiction, and the essay. But as always with me, this is ever a renewed beginning."

*   *   *

MACDONALD, Ronald St. John   1928-

PERSONAL: Born August 20, 1928, in Montreal, Quebec, Canada; son of Ronald St. John (a military officer) and Elizabeth Marie (Smith) Macdonald. *Education:* St. Francis Xavier University, B.A., 1949; Dalhousie University, LL.B., 1952; International Law Commission Seminar, diploma, 1952; University of London, LL.M., 1954; Harvard University, LL.M., 1955. *Politics:* Liberal. *Religion:* Roman Catholic. *Home:* 1173 Beaufort Ave., Halifax, Nova Scotia, Canada B3H 3Y3. *Office:* Faculty of Law, Dalhousie University, Halifax, Nova Scotia, Canada.

CAREER: Called to the Bar of Nova Scotia, 1955, and the Bar of Ontario, 1956, created Queen's Counsel for Ontario, 1968; associated with McInnes, Cooper & Robertson, 1952, and McInnes, MacQuarrie & Cooper, Halifax, Nova Scotia; Osgoode Hall, Toronto, Ontario, lecturer, 1955-57, professor of law, 1957-59; University of Western Ontario, London, professor of law, 1959-61; University of Toronto, Toronto, professor of law, 1961-72, dean of School of Law, 1967-72; Dalhousie University, Halifax, Weldon Professor of Law and dean of faculty of law, 1972—. Visiting professor at Colegio de Mexico, 1965; senior fellow of Massey College. Canadian representative to General Assembly of United Nations, 1965, 1966, 1968, and 1977; member of National UNICEF Committee, 1966—; member of United Nations committee on elimination of racial discrimination, 1972—. Member of advisory board of Alcoholism and Narcotic Drug Foundation, Toronto, 1961-72; chairman of Canadian Pension Plan Advisory Committee, 1967-72; president of Canadian Council on International Law, 1972-77; consultant to Canadian Department of External Affairs. *Military service:* Royal Canadian Naval (Volunteer) Reserve, 1945-46; became sub-lieutenant. *Member:* International Law Association (member of national executive committee, 1957—), Canadian Bar Association, Canadian Institute of International Affairs (member of national executive committee), Law Society of Upper Canada, London Institute of World Affairs, St. Andrew's Society, Zeta Psi.

WRITINGS: (Editor) *Changing Legal Objectives,* University of Toronto Press, 1963; (editor) *The Arctic Frontier,* University of Toronto Press, 1966; (editor with Gerald L. Morris and Douglas M. Johnston) *Canadian Perspectives on International Law and Organization,* University of Toronto Press, 1974; (editor with John P. Humphrey) *The Practice of Freedom: Canadian Essays on Human Rights and Fundamental Freedoms,* Butterworth, 1979. Contributor to law journals. Editor of *University of Toronto Law Journal,* 1961-72; assistant editor of *Ontario Reports* and *Ontario Weekly Notes,* 1956-57; founding editor of *Current Law and Social Problems,* 1959-62.

AVOCATIONAL INTERESTS: Reading, walking, sailing, travel.*

* * *

MacDONALD, Sandy 1949-

PERSONAL: Born February 13, 1949, in New York, N.Y.; child of William G. and Margaret S. MacDonald. *Education:* Attended Sorbonne, University of Paris, 1965-66, and Barnard College, 1966-68. *Home:* 23 Ware St., Cambridge, Mass. 02138. *Office: New Age,* 32 Station St., Brookline, Mass. 02146.

CAREER: Drama Review, New York City, assistant editor, 1968-70; *Performance,* New York City, assistant editor, 1970-71; *Aphra,* New York City, editor, 1970-77; *New Age,* Brookline, Mass., associate editor, 1975—. *Member:* American Literary Translators Association, National Book Critics Circle, Word Guild.

WRITINGS: (Translator) Andre Pochan, *The Mystery of the Great Pyramid,* Avon, 1977; (translator) Simone Waisbard, *Machu Picchu,* Avon, 1979. Contributor to magazines.

SIDELIGHTS: Sandy MacDonald wrote: "I translate from French, Spanish, and Italian, and am particularly interested in fiction and poetry. I have also written profiles of women active in the fields of energy, ecology, consciousness, and music."

* * *

MACK, Mary Peter 1927-1973

OBITUARY NOTICE—See index for *CA* sketch: Born May 26, 1927, in Englewood, N.J.; died May 22, 1973. Historian, educator, and author. Mack was a recipient of Rockefeller Foundation and Guggenheim fellowships. She contributed

to *International Encyclopedia of Social Sciences,* wrote *Jeremy Bentham: An Odyssey of Ideas,* and edited *A Bentham Reader.* (Date of death provided by Connecticut College.)

* * *

MACKARNESS, Richard 1916-

PERSONAL: Born August 17, 1916, in Murree, Punjab, India; son of Cuthbert (Conservator of Forests of Assam, India) Eileen (Godfrey) Mackarness; married Margaret Perry-Walker, May, 1947; children: Patrick. *Education:* Attended Westminster School of Art, 1936-39; Westminster School of Medicine, M.B., B.S., 1944; Wessex Regional School of Psychiatry, D.P.M., 1967. *Politics:* Radical Conservative. *Home:* Broadacre, Longparish Near Andover, Hampshire SP11 6QQ, England. *Agent:* Curtis Brown Ltd., 1 Craven Hill, London W2 3EP, England. *Office:* Basingstoke District Hospital, Basingstoke, Hampshire RG24 9NA, England.

CAREER: General practice of medicine in Kew Gardens, Surrey, England, 1952-64; Basingstoke District Hospital, Basingstoke, Hampshire, England, psychiatrist, 1965—. Medical correspondent for *London News Chronicle,* 1957-61, *London Daily Mail,* 1961-62, and *Today,* 1962-63. Chairman of Chemical Victims Club, 1975—. *Military service:* Royal Army Medical Corps, 1944-46; became captain. *Member:* British Medical Association, Royal Society of Medicine, Medical Journalists Association, London Press Club.

WRITINGS: Eat Fat and Grow Slim, Collins, 1958, revised edition, Fontana Books, 1975; *Not All in the Mind,* Pan Books, 1976; *Chemical Victims,* Pan Books, 1980; *Living Safely in a Polluted World: How to Protect Yourself and Your Children From Chemicals in Your Food and Environment,* Stein & Day, in press. Contributor of articles to magazines, including *Practitioner, International Journal of Social Psychiatry, John Bull, Today, Homes and Gardens,* and *Nursing Times.*

WORK IN PROGRESS: Research on clinical ecology; a textbook for medical practitioners and students on clinical ecology.

SIDELIGHTS: Mackarness told *CA* that his interests include "holistic medicine, anthropology, man in relation to his environment, psychology, and psychiatry.

"My books and articles are all on aspects of clinical ecology, a new branch of medicine aimed at helping people made sick by a failure to adapt to facets of our modern, polluted environment. Adverse reactions to processed foods and their chemical contaminants, and to indoor and outdoor air pollution with petrochemicals, are becoming more and more widespread and so far these reactions are being misdiagnosed by mainstream medical practitioners and so are not treated effectively.

"In America there is a growing medical group, called the Society For Clinical Ecology, which has three to four hundred members. In Britian and Europe the subject is just beginning to interest doctors. My writings are aimed at stimulating this interest by appealing both to doctors and their patients. Clinical ecology is the medicine of the future."

AVOCATIONAL INTERESTS: Gardening, country walks, driving and looking after his automobile, attending horse races, fishing, lecturing, designing visual teaching aids.

MacKENZIE, Jean 1928-

PERSONAL: Born March 22, 1928, in Traynor, Saskatchewan, Canada; daughter of F. J. (a writer) and Jean B. (Irving) Whiting; married Edward D. MacKenzie (a systems consultant), July 5, 1952; children: Bruce, Ross. *Education:* Educated in Vancouver, Canada. *Home:* 3815 Merriman Dr., Victoria, British Columbia V8P 2S8, Canada.

CAREER: Worked as assistant cook and children's nurse for R. W. Large Memorial Hospital, 1947-48; display assistant for Birk's Jewellers, 1948-52, and display manager, 1952-54; display manager for Firbank's, 1954-55; writer, c. 1968—.

WRITINGS: Storm Island, Macmillan (Toronto), 1968; *River of Stars,* McClelland & Stewart, 1971. Contributor to periodicals, including *Western Living, Pacific Yachting,* and *United Church Observer.*

SIDELIGHTS: MacKenzie worked for "almost two years" in a hospital in a remote Indian village along the coastline of British Columbia. Her two books for children evolved from her experiences there. Both books deal with the struggle to survive and adapt to modern life in the rugged country. Her first book, *Storm Island,* relates the experience of a young boy sent to a British Columbia lighthouse to live with relatives while his mother recovers from an accident. The story deals with the family's survival during a winter storm. MacKenzie presents vivid descriptions of the Pacific coast setting. In *River of Stars* MacKenzie again devotes ample space to scenery description. The story concerns a young Indian boy's transformation to manhood amidst the racial and economic tensions of the west coast salmon fisheries.

MacKenzie told *CA:* "I have been doing a lot of writing for magazines over the past ten years, as well as travel articles for British Columbia tourism. I hope now to get back into children's books."

BIOGRAPHICAL/CRITICAL SOURCES: Canadian Books for Children, autumn, 1976.

*   *   *

MACKIE, Philip 1918-

PERSONAL: Born November 26, 1918, in Broughton, England; son of Leslie Alan (an engineer) and Matilda (Summersfield) Mackie; married Cynthia Louise Curtis Clarke (an art historian), January 24, 1949; children: Susan Caroline, Charlotte Ann, Alexandria Harriet, Barbara Jane. *Education:* University of London, B.A. (with honors), 1939. *Politics:* "Not much, but a persistent Labour voter." *Religion:* "Church of England, but not much." *Home:* Lower House, Kelmscott, Lechlade, Gloucestershire GL7 3HG, England. *Agent:* Emanuel Wax, ACTAC Ltd., 16 Cadogan Lane, London S.W.1, England. *Office:* Flat 1, 18 Buckingham St., London WC2N 6DU, England.

CAREER: Central Office of Information, London, England, film production supervisor, 1946-49; European Cooperation Administration, Films Division, Paris, France, film production supervisor in Paris and Rome, 1949-51; Cinetone Studios, Amsterdam, Netherlands, film producer, 1952; Madeleine Films, Paris, film producer, 1952-53; British Broadcasting Corp. (BBC-TV), London, drama staff scriptwriter, 1954-55; free-lance writer, 1955-58; Granada Television, London, head of drama in London and Manchester, England, 1958-59, producer, 1960-67; Granada Films, London, managing director, 1967-70; writer, 1970—. *Military service:* British Army, 1939-46; became captain.

MEMBER: International P.E.N., Writers Guild of Great Britain (past member of executive council), Society of Authors, Dramatists Guild, American Dramatists Guild. *Awards, honors:* Award from Guild of Television Producers and Directors, 1963, for producing "The Victorians" and "Maupassant," and 1965, for producing "Paris 1900"; awards from Writers Guild of Great Britain, 1968, for television play, "The Caesars," and 1972, for *The Organisation;* first prize for drama from Adelaide International Film Festival, 1969, for producing "The Caesars"; Prix Italia from Concorso Internazionale per Opere Radiofoniche e Televisive, award from Academy of Television Arts and Sciences, and award from Broadcasting Press Guild, all 1976, all for "The Naked Civil Servant."

WRITINGS: Hurrah! The Flag (novel), Deutsch, 1957; *All the Way Up* (novel), Mayflower, 1968; *Napoleon and Love* (novel), Quartet, 1974; *The Organisation* (novel), Quartet, 1974.

Plays: *The Right Person* (one-act; first produced on BBC-TV, 1954), Samuel French, 1955; *The Whole Truth* (three-act; first produced in London at Aldwych Theatre, 1955), Evans Brothers, 1956; *Open House* (three-act; first produced in folkstone, England, at Leas Pavilion Theatre, 1957), Evans Brothers, 1958; *The Key of the Door* (three-act; first produced in Conventry, England, at Belgrade Theatre, 1957), Evans Brothers, 1959; *The Big Killing* (three-act; first produced in London at Princes Theatre, 1962), Evans Brothers, 1962; *The Chairman* (three-act; first produced in London at Globe Theatre, 1976), Samuel French, 1976; "A Marriage" (three-act), first produced in Leatherhead, England, at Thorndike Theatre, 1977.

Writer for television series.

WORK IN PROGRESS: "Cover," a television spy series, for Thames TV; a film biography of 1930's dance band singer, Al bowlly, for Euston Films; a television series on Cleopatras of ancient Egypt, for BBC-TV.

SIDELIGHTS: Mackie commented: "I always wanted to be a writer, and I've found it the way of earning a living most compatible with my temperament. My spells as a producer were really a way of making sure that I did any writing there was and making sure that the writing got to the screen (or whatever) with the minimum of alteration from the producer. Now I'm fairly old and important, and producers don't dare to muck about with my work, so I've gone back to just being a writer. And now I don't have to go to offices in the morning."

*   *   *

MacKINNON, John Ramsay 1947-

PERSONAL—Office: c/o Holt, Rinehart & Winston, Inc., 383 Madison Ave., New York, N.Y. 10017.

CAREER: Writer. Free-lance zoologist.

WRITINGS: In Search of the Red Ape, Holt, 1974; (with Kathleen MacKinnon) *Animals of Asia: The Ecology of the Oriental Region,* Holt, 1974; (with others) *Borneo,* Time-Life, 1975; *The Ape Within Us,* Holt, 1978.*

*   *   *

MACKINTOSH, John (Pitcairn) 1929-1978

PERSONAL: Born in 1929, in England; died July 30, 1978; son of Colin and Mary (Pitcairn) Mackintosh; married Una Maclean (a physician); children: Charlotte, Malcolm, Stuart, Deirdre. *Education:* Attended Edinburgh University, 1946-

50, Balliol College, Oxford, 1950-52, and Princeton University, 1952-53. *Residence:* Edinburgh, Scotland.

CAREER: University of Glasgow, Glasgow, Scotland, assistant lecturer in history, 1953-54; University of Edinburgh, Edinburgh, Scotland, lecturer in history, 1954-61; University of Ibadan, Ibadan, Nigeria, senior lecturer in government, 1961-63; University of Glasgow, senior lecturer in politics, 1963-65; University of Strathclyde, Glasgow, professor of politics, 1965-66; Parliament, London, England, Labour member of Parliament for Berwick and East Lothian, 1966-78, Parliamentary member of select committees on procedure, 1966-70, agriculture, 1967-69, and Scottish affairs, 1968-70, Visiting professor at Birkbeck College, London, 1973; professor at University of Edinburgh, 1977-78. Chariman of Scottish Labour Committee for Europe, 1975.

WRITINGS: History of Europe, 1815-1939, Blackie & Son, 1946; *The British Cabinet,* Stevens, 1962, 3rd edition, 1977; *Nigerian Government and Politics: Prelude to the Revolution,* Northwestern University Press, 1966; *The Devolution of Power: Local Democracy, Regionalism, and Nationalism,* Penguin, 1968; *The Government and Politics of Britain,* Hutchinson, 1970, 4th edition, 1977; *Specialist Committees in the House of Commons: Have They Failed?,* Department of Politics, University of Edinburgh, 1971; (editor) *British Prime Ministers in the Twentieth Century,* St. Martin's, 1977 (published in England in two volumes, Weidenfeld & Nicolson, Volume I: *Balfour to Chamberlain,* 1977, Volume II: *Churchill to Callaghan,* 1978); (editor) *People and Parliament,* Praeger, 1978. Co-editor of *Political Quarterly,* 1975—.

SIDELIGHTS: Mackintosh made two sound recordings for Holt Information Systems in 1972, "Decision Makers," with P. G. Richards, and "Who Rules Britain?," with Anthony Stephen King.

[Sketch verified by wife, Una Maclean Mackintosh]

*   *   *

MacLAINE, Shirley
See BEATY, Shirley MacLean

*   *   *

MACNAMARA, Ellen   1924-

PERSONAL: Born September 14, 1924, in London, England; daughter of Patrick (an admiral in the Royal Navy) and Ellen (Nickerson) Macnamara. *Education:* University of London, B.A., 1954, Diploma in Italian Archaeology, 1957, Ph.D., 1968. *Home:* 1 Thistle Grove, London S.W.10, England.

CAREER: Free-lance writer. *Member:* Society of Antiquaries (London; fellow), Society of Antiquaries (Scotland; fellow).

WRITINGS: The Everyday Life of the Etruscans, Putnam, 1973.

WORK IN PROGRESS: A book on Etruscan bronzes.

SIDELIGHTS: Ellen Macnamara is the founder and administrator of the Ellaina Macnamara Memorial Scholarship, given annually to a student of any nationality who will undertake research on the Italian late Bronze Age, early Iron Age, and Etruscan archaeology.

*   *   *

MADER, (Stanley) Chris(topher, Jr.)   1943(?)-1980

OBITUARY NOTICE: Born c. 1943; died in a hotel fire, December 4, 1980, in Westchester County, N.Y. Business-

man, educator, and author. As founder and president of Mader Group, Inc. of Narberth, Pennsylvania, Mader pioneered the use of computer programs as training exercises for managers in such fields as health care, real estate, manufacturing, and insurance. Using his own computer games as tools for instruction, Mader led more than three hundred managerial training seminars. For fifteen years he lectured in management training at the University of Pennsylvania's School of Business and Finance. Under the name Chris Mader, he was the author of several books, including *The Dow Jones-Irwin Guide to Real Estate Investing.* With Robert Hagin, Mader also wrote *The Dow Jones-Irwin Guide to Common Stocks and Information Systems: Technology, Economics, Applications.* Obituaries and other sources: *New York Times,* December 7, 1980.

*   *   *

MADSEN, Brigham Dwaine   1914-

PERSONAL: Born October 21, 1914, in Magna, Utah; son of Brigham and Lydia (Cushing) Madsen; married Betty McAllister, August 11, 1939; children: Karen Madsen Loos, David B., Linda Madsen Dunning, Steven M. *Education:* University of Utah, B.A., 1938; University of California, Berkeley, M.A., 1940, Ph.D., 1948. *Politics:* Republican. *Religion:* Church of Jesus Christ of Latter-day Saints (Mormons). *Home:* 2181 Lincoln Lane, Salt Lake City, Utah 84117. *Office:* Department of History, University of Utah, Salt Lake City, Utah 84112.

CAREER: Principal of elementary and junior high schools in Pingree, Idaho, 1938-39; Brigham Young University, Provo, Utah, associate professor of history, 1948-54; Madsen Brothers Construction Co., Salt Lake City, Utah, president and manager, 1954-61; Utah State University, Logan, professor of history, 1961-64; U.S. Peace Corps, Washington, D.C., assistant director of training, 1964-65; Volunteers in Service to America (VISTA), Washington, D.C., director of training, 1965; University of Utah, Salt Lake City, dean of Division of Continuing Education, 1965-66, deputy academic vice-president, 1966-67, administrative vice-president, 1967-71, director of libraries, 1971-73, professor of history, 1973—, chairman of department, 1974-75; Director of state National Endowment for the Humanities program in Utah, 1974-75. *Military service:* U.S. Army, infantry, 1943-46; served in European theater; became first lieutenant. *Member:* Phi Kappa Phi, Phi Alpha Theta.

WRITINGS: The Bannock of Idaho, Caxton, 1958; (editor) *The Now Generation,* University of Utah Press, 1971; *The Lemhi: Sacajawea's People,* Caxton, 1979; *The Northern Shoshoni,* Caxton, 1979; (with wife, Betty M. Madsen) *North to Montana!: Jehu, Bullwhackers, and Mule Skinners on the Montana Trail,* University of Utah Press, 1980; *Corinne: The Gentile Capital of Utah,* Utah State Historical Society, 1980. Also editor of *The Violent Year: 1970,* 1972, and *Letters of Long Ago,* 1973.

*   *   *

MAHLER, Margaret S(choenberger)   1897-

PERSONAL: Born May 10, 1897, in Sopron-Oedenburg, Hungary; married Paul Mahler (deceased). *Education:* University of Vienna, M.D., 1923. *Home and office:* 10 West 66th St., No. 26-K, New York, N.Y. 10023.

CAREER: University Children's Clinic, Jena, East Germany, intern, 1922-23; Children's Hospital, resident child psychiatrist, 1923-27; Steinhof Psychiatric Hospital, resident psychiatrist, 1928-29; Child Guidance Centers, Vienna, Austria, resident psychiatrist, 1928-33, head of outpatient department, 1933-38; University Psychiatric Hospital and Clinic, Vienna, resident psychiatrist, 1936-37; New York State Psychiatric Institute, New York City, assistant chief clinician, 1941-42 and 1944-45, consultant to children's services, 1941-53; Columbia University, New York City, instructional psychiatrist, 1942-43, associate psychiatrist, 1943-56; Albert Einstein College of Medicine, New York City, associate clinical professor, 1956-59, clinical professor of psychiatry, 1959-72, professor emeritus, 1972—. Diplomate of American Board of Child Psychiatry; member of faculty at New York Psychoanalytic Institute, 1946—, and Philadelphia Psychoanalytic Institute, 1950— (chairman of child analysis curriculum, 1950-62); visiting professor at Medical College of Pennsylvania, 1971; lecturer in Austria, Denmark, France, Germany, the Netherlands, Italy, Mexico, Norway, and Portugal; chief consultant to Children's Service at New York State Psychiatric Institute, Columbia University, and Roosevelt Hospital.

MEMBER: International Psychoanalytic Association, American Academy of Child Psychiatry (charter member), American Psychiatric Association (life fellow), American Association for Child Psychoanalysis (charter member), American Psychoanalytic Association, American Orthopsychiatric Association, Philadelphia Psychoanalytic Society (honorary member), New York Psychoanalytic Society (president, 1971-73). *Awards, honors:* Brill Memorial Plaque, 1962, Freud Anniversary Lecturer Scroll, 1970, and Heinz Hartmann Award, 1975, all from New York Psychoanalytic Society; Agnes Purcell McGavin Award from American Psychiatric Association, 1969; "Margaret S. Mahler Symposium" was named in her honor by Medical College of Pennsylvania and Philadelphia Psychoanalytic Society and Institute, 1969; Frieda-Fromm-Reichman Award from American Academy of Psychoanalysis, 1970; Sc.D. from Medical College of Pennsylvania, 1971; Wilfred C. Hulse Memorial Award from New York Council on Child Psychiatry, 1979; Barnard Medal of Distinction from Barnard College, 1980.

WRITINGS: (With Manuel Furer) *On Human Symbiosis and the Vicissitudes of Individuation,* International Universities Press, 1969; (with Fred Pine and Anni Bergman) *The Psychological Birth of the Human Infant: Symbiosis and Individuation,* Basic Books, 1975; *The Selected Papers of Margaret S. Mahler,* Volume I: *Infantile Psychosis and Early Contributions,* Volume II: *Separation-Individuation,* Jason Aronson, 1979.

Contributor: Ruth S. Eissler and others, editors, *Psychoanalytic Study of the Child,* International Universities Press, 1963; *Psychoanalysis: A General Psychology,* International Universities Press, 1966. Contributor of about one hundred twenty articles to scientific journals, including *International Journal of Psychoanalysis* and *Psychoanalytic Quarterly.*

SIDELIGHTS: Margaret Mahler's books have been translated into French, German, Italian, Spanish, Portuguese, and Japanese.

*   *   *

MAHOOD, Kenneth   1930-

PERSONAL: Born February 4, 1930, in Belfast, Northern Ireland. *Education:* Attended school in Belfast. *Residence:* London, England.

CAREER: Cartoonist, illustrator, author of books for children. Free-lance illustrator for magazines, 1950—; *Punch,* London, England, assistant art editor, 1960-65; *London Times,* London, political cartoonist, 1966-69; topical cartoonist for *Punch* and the *Financial Times,* London.

WRITINGS—All for children; self-illustrated: *Not a Word to a Soul* (cartoons), Hammond, 1958; *Fore!* (drawings), Hammond, 1959; *The Laughing Dragon,* Scribner, 1970; *Clanky, the Mechanical Boy,* Collins, 1971; *Why Are There More Questions Than Answers, Grandad?,* Bradbury, 1974; *Losing Willy,* Prentice-Hall, 1978; *The Crack-a-Joke Book,* Puffin, 1978.

Illustrator: Albert Bernard Hollowood, *Tory Story,* Hammond, 1964; Sandie Oram, *Italy,* Macdonald & Co., 1972; Jennifer Vaughan, *Japan,* Macdonald & Co., 1973; Roger Benedictus, *Fifty Million Sausages,* Deutsch, 1975; *The Wizard of Gauze,* compiled by Charles Keller, Prentice-Hall, 1979.

SIDELIGHTS: Although he has had no formal art training, Kenneth Mahood has been successful as an illustrator and cartoonist. He sold his first cartoon to *Punch* magazine in London at eighteen and has been free-lancing since he was twenty. In addition, he writes nonsensical children's stories and illustrates them with drawings in brilliant and bold colors.

Among Mahood's zany storybook characters is Hojo in *The Laughing Dragon.* A beloved pancake-making, chess-playing dragon who lives in the Emperor of Japan's palace, Hojo is plagued with a mouth that shoots flames when he laughs. After setting the palace afire, Hojo faces eviction unless he can learn to control his flames.

Another Mahood character, Sandy, asks silly questions in *Why Are There More Questions Than Answers, Grandad?* A young, orphaned boy, Sandy puzzles his grandfather with such questions as "Does a young prune have wrinkles?" and "Does dirty water need a bath?" Frustrated by his grandson's foolishness, Grandad sends Sandy to the attic, telling him to clean it before dinner. With the help of a magic book whose contents come to life, Sandy transforms the disheveled attic into a beautiful drawing room. The result? A further baffled Grandad with many questions of his own.

BIOGRAPHICAL/CRITICAL SOURCES: Times Literary Supplement, December 11, 1971, December 6, 1974.*

*   *   *

MAKEPEACE, Joanna
See YORK, Margaret Elizabeth

*   *   *

MALAND, David   1929-

PERSONAL: Surname is pronounced *May*-land; born October 6, 1929, in Leeds, England; son of Gordon Albert (a Methodist minister) and Florence Maud (Bosence) Maland; married Edna Foulsham, March 25, 1953; children: Oliver, Nicholas. *Education:* Wadham College, Oxford, B.A. (with honors), 1951, M.A., 1957. *Religion:* Anglican. *Office:* Manchester Grammar School, Manchester, England.

CAREER: Assistant master at grammar school in Brighton, England, 1953-56; senior history master at private boys' school in Stamford, England, 1956-66; headmaster of boys' high school in Cardiff, Wales, 1966-68; headmaster of independent boarding school of Denstone College in Uttoxeter, England, 1969-78; Manchester Grammar School, Manchester, England, high master, 1978—. Member of board of governors of Stoneyhurst College, 1971-79, and Abingdon School, 1979—. *Military service:* Royal Air Force, Education Branch, 1951-53; became flying officer. *Member:* East India Club, Sports and Public Schools Club. *Awards, honors:* Robert Herbert Memorial Essay Prize from Oxford University, 1959, for essay on Duke of Wellington.

WRITINGS: Europe in the Seventeenth Century, Macmillan, 1966; (translator with John Hooper) Georges Pages, *La Guerre de trente ans* (title means "The Thirty Year War"), A. & C. Black, 1970; *Culture and Society in Seventeenth-Century France*, Batsford, 1971; *Europe in the Sixteenth Century*, Macmillan, 1973; *Europe at War, 1600-1660*, Macmillan, 1980.

* * *

MALANOS, George J(ohn) 1919-1962

OBITUARY NOTICE—See index for *CA* sketch: Born August, 1919, in Athens, Greece; died January 28, 1962. Educator, economist, and author. Malanos wrote *Intermediate Economic Theory*. (Date of death provided by wife, Alexandria Malanos.)

* * *

MALCOLMSON, Robert W(illiam) 1943-

PERSONAL: Born February 8, 1943, in Toronto, Ontario, Canada; married, 1967; children: one. *Education:* University of Toronto, B.A., 1965; University of Sussex, M.A., 1966; University of Warwick, Ph.D., 1970. *Office:* Department of History, Queen's University, Kingston, Ontario, Canada K7L 3N6.

CAREER: Queen's University, Kingston, Ontario, lecturer, 1969-70, assistant professor, 1970-74, associate professor of history, 1974—.

WRITINGS: Popular Recreations in English Society, 1700-1850, Cambridge University Press, 1973; (contributor) J. S. Cockburn, editor, *Crime in England, 1550-1800*, Methuen, 1977.*

* * *

MALINS, Edward (Greenway) 1910-

PERSONAL: Born October 1, 1910, in Warwick, England; married Meta Leo, 1937; children: three daughters. *Education:* Worcester College, Oxford, M.A., 1930. *Home:* Tuckingmill House, Compton Dando, near Bristol, England.

CAREER: English teacher and department head at private boys' school in Horsham, Sussex, England, 1933-40, 1945-58; College of St. Matthias, Bristol, England, lecturer in English, 1967-70; associated with Bath Academy of Art and St. Peter's College, Oxford, 1970-72. *Military service:* Indian Army, 47th Cavalry, 1941-43; became captain. *Member:* Kildare Street, University Club (Dublin, Ireland).

WRITINGS: Recorded Time, Christ's Hospital (Horsham, England), 1954; *Yeats and Music*, Dolmen Press, 1964; *English Landscaping and Literature, 1660-1840*, Oxford University Press, 1966; *Samuel Palmer's Italian Honeymoon*, Oxford University Press, 1968; (with Morchard Bishop) *James Smetham and Francis Danby: Two Nineteenth-Century Romantic Painters*, Eric & Joan Stevens, 1974; *A Preface to Yeats*, Scribner, 1974; *The Red Books of Humphry Repton*, Volume IV (Malins was not associated with earlier volumes), Basilisk Press, 1976; (editor with James P. McGarry) *Place Names in the Writings of William Butler Yeats*, Smythe, 1976; *Lost Demesnes: Irish Landscape Gardening*, Barrie & Jenkins, 1977; (with Desmond Fitz-Gerald) *Irish Gardens and Demesnes From 1830*, Barrie & Jenkins, 1977; *Irish Gardens*, Jarrolds, 1977. Contributor to periodicals, including *Quarterly Bulletin* of the Irish Georgian Society.

BIOGRAPHICAL/CRITICAL SOURCES: New Statesman, December 13, 1968.

* * *

MALTESE, Michael 1909(?)-1981

OBITUARY NOTICE: Born c. 1909; died of cancer in 1981 in Los Angeles, Calif. Cartoon animator and writer. Michael Maltese, co-creator of well-loved animated cartoon characters, including Sylvester Cat and Road Runner, concocted innumerable comic situations for them and for such others as Porky Pig, Daffy Duck, and Elmer Fudd. Obituaries and other sources: *Time*, March 9, 1981.

* * *

MANA-ZUCCA
See CASSEL, Mana-Zucca

* * *

MANDINO, Og 1923-

PERSONAL: Born December 12, 1923, in Boston, Mass.; son of Silvio and Margaret T. (Lee) Mandino; married Bette L. Lang, December 9, 1957; children: Dana, Matthew. *Education:* Attended Bucknell Junior College, 1941. *Home:* 6130 East Via Estrella Ave., Scottsdale, Ariz. 85253.

CAREER: Metropolitan Life Insurance Co., Boston, Mass., sales representative, 1948-60; Combined Insurance Co., Chicago, Ill., sales manager, 1960-65; *Success Unlimited*, Chicago, Ill., executive editor, 1965-72; Success Unlimited, Inc., Chicago, president, 1972-76; Matt-Dana Ltd., president and member of board of directors, 1974—. *Military service:* U.S. Army Air Forces, 1942-45; became first lieutenant; received Distinguished Flying Cross and Air Medal with five oak leaf clusters. *Member:* Authors Guild, National Speakers Association.

WRITINGS: A Treasury of Success Unlimited, Hawthorn, 1966; *The Greatest Salesman in the World*, Fell, 1968; *The U.S. in a Nutshell*, Hawthorn, 1971; (with Edward R. Dewey) *Cycles: The Mysterious Forces That Trigger Events*, Hawthorn, 1971; *The Greatest Secret in the World: Featuring Your Own Success Recorder Diary With the Ten Great Scrolls for Success From "The Greatest Salesman in the World,"* Fell, 1972; *The Greatest Miracle in the World*, Fell, 1975; (with Buddy Kaye) *The Gift of Acabar*, Lippincott, 1978; *The Christ Commission*, Crowell, 1980; *The God Memorandum*, Fell, 1980.

BIOGRAPHICAL/CRITICAL SOURCES: Sales Management, August 5, 1974.*

* * *

MANHIRE, Bill 1946-

PERSONAL: Born December 27, 1946, in Invercargill, New Zealand; son of Jack (a publican) and Madeline Mary (a teacher; maiden name, Aitken) Manhire; married Barbara Marion McLeod (a teacher), July 31, 1970; children: Vanessa, Tobias Joseph. *Education:* University of Otago, New Zealand, B.A., 1967, M.A. (with honors), 1968, M.Litt., 1970; University College, London, M.Phil., 1973. *Agent:* Toby Eady Associates, 313 Fulham Rd., London, England. *Office:* Department of English, Victoria University of Wellington, Private Bag, Wellington, New Zealand.

CAREER: Victoria University of Wellington, Wellington, New Zealand, lecturer, 1973-78, senior lecturer in English, 1978—. Editor of Amphedesma Press. *Awards, honors:* New Zealand Book Award for poetry, 1977, for *How to Take Off*

Your Clothes at the Picnic; Nuffield traveling fellowship, 1980-81.

WRITINGS: Malady (poems), Amphedesma Press, 1970; *The Elaboration* (poems), Square & Circle, 1972; *How to Take Off Your Clothes at the Picnic* (poems), Wai-te-ata Press, 1977; (editor) *New Zealand Listener Short Stories,* Methuen, 1977, Volume II, 1978; *Dawn/Water,* Hawk Press, 1979; *Good Looks* (poems), Auckland University Press, in press. General editor of "New Zealand Stories" series, published jointly by Price Milburn and Victoria University of Wellington Press.

WORK IN PROGRESS: A critical book on novelist Maurice Gee for "New Zealand Writers and Their Work" series for Oxford University Press; research on Icelandic sagas; research on W. H. Auden.

SIDELIGHTS: Manhire's poetry, which has been influenced by Ezra Pound and John Crowe Ransom, reflects both humor and sadness and is often tinged with surrealism. The books he has edited concern the arts and stories native to New Zealand.

*   *   *

MANN, Edward Andrew 1932-

PERSONAL: Born January 23, 1932, in Los Angeles, Calif.; married Lorna Mundy (a travel consultant and proprietor of nursery schools), November 20, 1968. *Education:* Received B.A., J.D., and LL.B. from University of California, Los Angeles. *Politics:* Independent. *Religion:* "My own." *Residence:* Beverly Hills, Calif. *Agent:* Harold Ober Associates, Inc., 40 East 49th St., New York, N.Y. 10017; and David Higham Associates Ltd., 5-8 Lower John St., Golden Sq., London W1R 4HA, England.

CAREER: Writer. Associated with U.S. Attorney's Office in Los Angeles, Calif., and Shearer & Fields (attorneys) in Beverly Hills, Calif. *Military service:* U.S. Army; became lieutenant. *Member:* Writers Guild of America (West).

WRITINGS: (With M. Schofield) *Goering's Diary,* New English Library, 1968; *The Portals* (novel), Simon & Schuster, 1970. Writer for television, including adaptation of "Crash of '79."

WORK IN PROGRESS: Novels, writing for films and television.

SIDELIGHTS: "I write because I enjoy it," Mann commented, "or it is a compulsion. I also like to tell a story, to entertain. My philosophy is reality; my stories are not necessarily. My interests are catholic; my knowledge is more limited. It is necessary to dream but folly to believe in dreams. To expect too much of the world or oneself is foolish; to expect nothing is not to live."

*   *   *

MANN, Marty 1904-1980

PERSONAL: Born October 15, 1904, in Chicago, Ill.; died of a stroke, July 22, 1980, in Bridgeport, Conn.; daughter of William Henry (a business executive) and Lillian (Christy) Mann; married John Blakemore, 1927 (divorced, 1928). *Education:* Attended schools in New York and Florida, 1922-24, and in Florence, Italy, 1924-25. *Office:* 733 Third Ave., New York, N.Y. 10017.

CAREER: International Studio, assistant editor, 1928-30; partner in photography business, London, England, 1930-36; Covent Garden Opera, London, publicity work, 1935; R. H. Macy & Co., New York, N.Y., fashion publicity director,

1940-42; American Society of Composers, Authors and Publishers (ASCAP), research director and radio script writer, 1942-44; National Council on Alcoholism, founder, 1944, executive director, 1944-68, founder-consultant, 1968-80. Addressed joint sessions of state legislatures of South Carolina, 1946, Michigan, 1952, and Tennessee, 1965; served as official delegate to the International Congress on Alcoholism, Luzerne, Switzerland, 1948; adviser on government action on alcoholism to Union of South Africa, 1951; lecturer and adviser to alcoholism to Union of South Africa, 1951; lecturer and adviser to alcoholism groups in New Zealand and Australia, 1961, and in London, Belfast, Northern Ireland, and Dublin, Ireland, 1964; lecturer at the School of Alcohol Studies, Yale University, and at University of Washington, University of Utah, University of Texas, University of Colorado, University of Georgia, Millsaps College, and Menninger Foundation; research associate at Columbia Teachers College; lecturer in pharmaceutical science at University of Arizona; consultant on alcoholism to National Institute on Alcoholic Abuse and Alcoholism, Silver Hill Foundation, New Canaan, Conn., and numerous professional and lay organizations and church and civic groups. *Member:* American Psychiatric Association (honorary fellow), American Public Health Association (fellow), Society of Public Health Educators (fellow), Royal Society of Health (London; fellow). *Awards, honors:* Elizabeth Blackwell Award from Hobart and William Smith Colleges, 1963; D.Hum. from Adelphi University, 1975.

WRITINGS: Primer on Alcoholism, Rinehart, 1950; *New Primer on Alcoholism,* Rinehart, 1958; *Marty Mann Answers Your Questions About Drinking and Alcoholism,* Holt, 1970. Contributor of articles to popular and professional journals.

SIDELIGHTS: "I am an alcoholic," Mann once wrote. "I no longer mind that appellation, for I have a disease like several million other Americans who are victims of alcoholism. I am no more ashamed of it than if I had diabetes. I know I cannot safely touch alcohol in any form." After her own recovery, Mann devoted most of her life to aiding other alcoholics in need. "Helping alcoholics who wanted help became my avocation," Mann wrote in 1946, "and it has remained so. In my case it so happens that educating the general public about alcoholism is my vocation just as well."

Mann had been a successful businesswoman in London during the early 1930's until her problems with alcoholism forced her to return to the United States for treatment. Medical doctors she consulted became apathetic toward her when they discovered that her problems were alcohol-related. She finally admitted herself to Blythewood Sanitarium for psychiatric treatment in January, 1938, and after her release fifteen months later joined a group of recovered alcoholics who aided in her rehabilitation. It was during this period that Mann became convinced that alcoholism was a disease; she described it as "an obsession of the mind, coupled with an allergy of the body."

Aware of the need for public education on alcoholism, Mann founded the National Council on Alcoholism in 1944. Dr. Elvin Jellinek of the Yale School of Alcohol Studies was enlisted for his scientific expertise and under his sponsorship the group adopted three tenets: alcoholism is a disease; the alcoholic can and should be helped; alcoholism is a public health problem and a public responsibility. Within a year of its founding, the National Council on Alcoholism had established twelve local committees around the United States and by 1949 that number had grown to 52 groups in the United States, Canada, and Mexico. In 1980 there were 200 local groups.

Mann soon became known as a prominent promoter of alcoholism education. The U.S. Department of State chose her to serve as one of three delegates to the International Congress on Alcoholism held in Luzerne, Switzerland, in 1948 and again in 1972. Until shortly before her death, Mann addressed an average of 200 groups annually, including alcoholism groups and governmental agencies around the world, university alcoholism study groups, groups of health care professionals, and civic organizations. Her *New Primer on Alcoholism* came to be regarded as a classic by alcoholism professionals and has been translated into several languages.

BIOGRAPHICAL/CRITICAL SOURCES: Modern Hospital, January, 1946; *New York Times,* July 24, 1980.*

* * *

MANNING, David John 1938-

PERSONAL: Born April 8, 1938, in Newcastle, England; son of Louis Henry (a technical representative) and Marjory (Richards) Manning; married Michele Casamayou, May 27, 1967 (divorced March 1, 1976); married Jean Marie di Meo, July 2, 1976; children: (first marriage) Harold Pierre, Helen. *Education:* London School of Economics and Political Science, London, B.Sc., 1960, Ph.D., 1964. *Politics:* "Uncommitted." *Religion:* "None." *Home:* Flass Hall, Esh Winning, County Durham DH7 90D, England. *Office:* Department of Politics, University of Durham, 23-26 Old Elvet St., Durham DH1 3HY, England.

CAREER: Regent Street Polytechnic, London, England, lecturer in politics, 1964-65; University of Durham, Durham, England, senior lecturer in politics, 1965—. Visiting professor at University of Texas, 1973; guest professor at University of Tuebingen, 1976, 1980; lecturer at Durham County Police Headquarters. *Member:* United Kingdom Political Studies Association, Oxford Political Theory Group.

WRITINGS: The Mind of Jeremy Bentham, Longmans, Green, 1968; *Liberalism,* Dent, 1976; (editor and contributor) *The Form of Ideology,* Allen & Unwin, 1980; *The Philosophical Understanding of Politics,* Routledge & Kegan Paul, 1982. Contributor of poems to literary journals.

SIDELIGHTS: Manning commented: "Writing is the investigation of experience and it is not least revealing when it serves as a mirror in which we glimpse the self. However, no matter on what it constitutes a reflection to prove, revealing it demands the perfection of images whether they be of persons, societies or things. It is only in the perfect representation of reality that an author can command communication and without it writing could be what it is often said to be, a lonely business.

"My main area of vocational interest is the philosophy of action, particularly in an account of ideologically motivated action. Traditionally ideology has been represented as epiphenomenal, parasitic or irrational thought that misguides the unfortunate, ignorant or confused in the pursuit of what must prove unobtainable. I have argued that these conceptions are confused. Properly understood ideology is an expression of emotional commitment yielding information about human aspirations rather than solutions to human problems. An ideology is not a theory to be put into practice it is an imaginative portrayal of the value of a way of life that legitimizes the relationships that constitute our political institutions."

AVOCATIONAL INTERESTS: "Although I find the achievement of craftsmanship and the exercise of skill in the fabrication of artifacts very impressive, the variety in human character and the intricacy of human relationships is for me the most fascinating aspect of everyday life."

* * *

MANO, M(oshe) Morris 1927-

PERSONAL: Born April 3, 1927, in Salonika, Greece; came to the United States in 1947, naturalized citizen, 1961; son of David and Esther (Errera) Mano; married Sandra D. Fried, March 29, 1958; children: Susan, Robin. *Education:* New York University, B.E.E., 1952; Northwestern University, M.S., 1958; Worcester Polytechnic Institute, Ph.D., 1968. *Home:* 434 La Terraza St., South Pasadena, Calif. 91030. *Office:* Department of Electrical and Computer Engineering, California State University, 5151 State University Dr., Los Angeles, Calif. 90032.

CAREER: Beckman Instruments, Richmond, Calif., electrical engineer, 1957-58; Ampex Computer Products, Culver City, Calif., electrical engineer, 1959-60; California State University, Los Angeles, professor of engineering, 1960—. Electrical engineer in electronics development department of Israel Air Force, 1953-56; computer engineer in Space and Information Systems Division at North American Aviation, 1962-66; consultant to Burroughs Corp. City Industry, 1969-72. *Member:* Institute of Electrical and Electronics Engineers (senior member), Sigma Xi, Eta Kappa Nu.

WRITINGS: Computer Logic Design, Prentice-Hall, 1972; *Computer System Architecture,* Prentice-Hall, 1976; *Digital Logic and Computer Design,* Prentice-Hall, 1979.

WORK IN PROGRESS: Computer System Architecture, 2nd edition, publication expected in 1982.

* * *

MANSFIELD, Bruce Edgar 1926-

PERSONAL: Born March 30, 1926, in Brisbane, Australia; son of Edgar James (a warehouse employee) and Ethel (Greenberg) Mansfield; married Joan Isobel Wood, May 19, 1950; children: Martin Bruce, Paul Leon, Nicholas James. *Education:* University of Sydney, B.A. (with first class honors), 1948, M.A. (with first class honors), 1951. *Religion:* Uniting Church in Australia. *Home:* 60 Darnley St., Gordon, New South Wales 2072, Australia. *Office:* Office of the Deputy Vice-Chancellor, Macquarie University, North Ryde, New South Wales 2113, Australia.

CAREER: University of Sydney, Sydney, Australia, temporary lecturer, 1949-51, lecturer, 1951-58, senior lecturer, 1958-64, associate professor of history, 1964-65; Macquarie University, North Ryde, Australia, professor of history, 1965-75, deputy vice-chancellor, 1976—. *Member:* Australian Historical Association (president, 1977-78), Royal Australian Historical Society, Renaissance Society of America. *Awards, honors:* Nuffield Dominions fellow, 1953.

WRITINGS: Australian Democrat: The Career of Edward William O'Sullivan, 1846-1910, Sydney University Press, 1965; *Knox: A History of Knox Grammar School, 1924-1974,* Knox Grammar School, 1974; *Phoenix of His Age: Interpretations of Erasmus, c. 1550-1750,* University of Toronto Press, 1979. Editor of *Journal of Religious History,* 1959—.

WORK IN PROGRESS: A sequel to *Phoenix of His Age,* covering interpretations of Erasmus from the eighteenth to the twentieth centuries, for the "Erasmus Studies" series of University of Toronto Press.

SIDELIGHTS: Mansfield commented: "My first research was in Australian history. I was interested in the formation of political parties in Australia. Teaching Reformation history, I became interested in Erasmus, especially the conflicting views about him over the generations. An enigmatic personality with distinctive views as church reformer and social critic, Erasmus was bound to attract comment from the warring parties of early modern Europe. This kind of work is partly history of ideas, partly historiography. But I would wish to emphasize my role in the *Journal of Religious History,* which has been a meeting ground for scholars over a wide range of historical interests.''

* * *

MARENCO, Ethne (Elsie) K(aplan)   1925-

PERSONAL: Born December 8, 1925, in New York, N.Y.; daughter of Robert and Mary (Banks) Kaplan; married Enzo Carlo Marenco (an engineer), September 4, 1953. *Education:* Attended Brooklyn College (now of the City University of New York), 1942-45; Hunter College (now of the City University of New York), B.A. (magna cum laude), 1946; attended Musee de l'Homme, 1952; Columbia University, Ph.D., 1963.

CAREER: United Nations, New York City, guide, 1952-54; Babies' Hospital, New York City, medical research assistant on premature infant mortality study, 1956-59, research assistant in obstetrics and gynecology, 1959-60; Fairleigh Dickinson University, Teaneck, N.Y., assistant professor of sociology and anthropology, 1964-66; Long Island University, Brooklyn Center, Brooklyn, N.Y., visiting associate professor of anthropology, 1967-69; Queensborough Community College of the City University of New York, Bayside, N.Y., assistant professor of anthropology, 1970-73; Marymount Manhattan College, New York City, visiting assistant professor of anthropology, 1973-74; Rutgers University, New Brunswick, N.J., assistant professor of anthropology, 1975; free-lance editor. Visiting assistant professor at Hunter College (now Herbert H. Lehman College of the City University of New York), 1956, 1967, and City College (now of the City University of New York), 1959-60. *Member:* American Anthropological Association (fellow), Society for Applied Anthropology, Society for Medical Anthropology, Authors Guild, Authors League of America, New York Academy of Sciences (honorary member), Eta Sigma Phi. *Awards, honors:* Fellowship from French government, 1952.

WRITINGS: (With E. N. Papert) *The Invader* (historical novel), Pyramid Publications, 1973; *The Transformation of Sikh Society,* Heritage Publishers, 1976.

Illustrator: William D. Strong, *The Cultural Stratigraphy of the Viru Valley,* Columbia University Press, 1949. Also illustrator of *Amazon Town* by Charles Wagley, 1949. Contributor to *McGraw-Hill Dictionary of Art, Columbia Encyclopedia,* and *Encyclopedia of Sikhism.* Contributor to anthropology and archaeology journals and *Journal of Ultimate Reality.* Member of advisory editorial board of *Journal of Comparative Sociology and Religion.*

WORK IN PROGRESS: A book on Sikhs outside India, publication by Heritage Publishers expected in 1983.

SIDELIGHTS: Ethne Marenco wrote: "I have maintained a constant interest in archaeology, history, and languages. French, Italian, Latin, classical Greek, Danish, Hebrew, and Arabic are among the languages I've studied."

BIOGRAPHICAL/CRITICAL SOURCES: Journal of Asian Studies, October-December, 1978.

MARLAND, Michael   1934-

PERSONAL: Born December 28, 1934, in London, England. *Education:* Sidney Sussex College, Cambridge, M.A., 1957. *Home:* 22 Compton Ter., London N1 2UN, England; and Green Farmhouse, Cranmer Green, Walsham-le-Willows, Bury St. Edmunds, Suffolk, England. *Office:* North Westminster Community School, Penfold St., London N.W.1, England.

CAREER: Teacher at school in Hamburg, West Germany, 1957-58, and grammar school in Canterbury, England, 1958-61; head of English studies at school in London, England, 1964-68, director of studies, 1968-71; headmaster of school in London, 1971-79; North Westminster Community School, London, headmaster, 1980—. Chairman of Schools Council English committee, past chairman of drama committee; vice-chairman of Committee of Enquiry Into the Supply of Books to Schools; past member of schools committee of Independent Television Authority and Bullock Committee on the Teaching of Reading and the Uses of English. Honorary professor at University of Warwick, 1980; lecturer to teachers and administrators in England and the United States; founder of Organisation in Schools Courses, 1977. Broadcaster, including appearances on "Today," "A Word in Edgeways," and "Man of Action"; gives touring book exhibitions for National Book League. *Member:* National Book League (member of executive committee). *Awards, honors:* Commander of Order of the British Empire, 1977; Senior Page Scholar of English-Speaking Union in the United States, 1978.

WRITINGS: Towards the New Fifth, Longmans, Green, 1969; (with Graham Owens) *The Practice of English Teaching,* Blackie & Son, 1970; *Head of Department,* Heinemann, 1971; *Pastoral Care,* Heinemann, 1974; *The Craft of the Classroom,* Heinemann, 1975; *Language Across the Curriculum,* Heinemann, 1977; *English in the 1980's: A Programme of Support for Teachers,* Methuen, 1979; *Education for the Inner City,* Heinemann, 1980; (with Syd Hill) *Departmental Management,* Heinemann, 1981; *Comprehensive School Management,* Heinemann, in press; *Sex Differentiation and Schooling,* Heinemann, in press.

For children: (Editor) *Spotlight,* Blackie & Son, 1966; *Following the News,* Chatto & Windus, 1967; *Looking at Advertising,* Chatto & Windus, 1967; (editor) *Pictures for Writing,* Blackie & Son, 1967; (with Denys Thompson) *English for the Individual,* Heinemann, 1967; (editor) *More Pictures for Writing,* Blackie & Son, 1968; *Conflicting Generations,* Longmans, Green, 1968; (editor) D. H. Lawrence, *"The Widowing of Mrs. Holroyd" and "The Daughter-in-Law,"* Heinemann, 1968; *The Experience of Colour,* Longmans, Green, 1969; *First Choice,* Longmans, Green, 1970; *Discovering Poetry,* four volumes, Longmans, Green, 1970; *Peter Grimes* (dramatization of the poem by George Crabbe), Heinemann, 1971; *Theatre Choice,* Blackie & Son, 1972; *Scene Scripts,* Longman, 1972; *Friends and Families,* Longman, 1973; *The Experience of Work,* Longman, 1973; (with Marilyn Davies) *Breaking Away,* Longman, 1974; *The Question of Advertising,* Chatto & Windus, 1974; *Loves, Hopes, and Fears,* Longman, 1975; *Scene Scripts Two,* Longman, 1978; (with Sarah Ray) *The Minority Experience,* Longman, 1978; *Could It Be?,* Longman, 1978; (editor) *Caribbean Stories,* Longman, 1978; *The Pressures of Life,* Longman, 1979; *The Experience of Love,* Longman, 1980; *Growing Up,* Longman, in press.

Contributor: Thompson, editor, *Directions in the Teaching of English,* Cambridge University Press, 1969; Kenyon Calthrop and Graham Owens, editors, *Teachers for Tomorrow,* Heinemann, 1971; Jennifer Rogers, editor, *Young Adults in School,* BBC Publications, 1972; Nicholas Bagnall, editor, *New Movements in the Study and Teaching of English,* Maurice Temple Smith, 1973; Elizabeth Hunter-Grundin and Hans U. Grundin, editors, *Reading: Implementing the Bullock Report,* Ward, Lock, 1978; L. John Chapman and Pam Czerniewska, editors, *Reading: From Process to Practice,* Routledge & Kegan Paul, 1978; Ron Best, editor, *Perspectives on Pastoral Care,* Heinemann, 1979.

General editor of "Organisation in Schools" series, Heinemann, "Student Drama" series, Blackie & Son; "The Times' Authors," London Times; "Imprint Books," Longman. Contributor to education journals.

SIDELIGHTS: Marland commented: "My work all relates to my actual activities in education, and I try to fill needs as far as I can see them. I find anthologizing a fascinating occupation, and am particularly proud of some of my collections. These try to give balanced selections in which minority groups are well featured, and the position of women properly portrayed. I am very pleased at how many teachers tell me that my books on aspects of teaching and school organization have been helpful to them."

*   *   *

MARLEY, Bob
See MARLEY, Robert Nesta

*   *   *

MARLEY, Robert Nesta   1945-1981
(Bob Marley)

OBITUARY NOTICE: Born February 6, 1945, in Rhoden Hall, Jamaica; died of cancers of the brain and lungs, May 11, 1981, in Miami, Fla. Performer and lyricist. Third World superstar Bob Marley was a dynamic performer who was credited with bringing reggae music to international attention. The music, with its message of protest, was described by the *New York Times* as having "syncopated rhythms, Caribbean lilt, American black soul, [and] biblical chantings." Bob Marley and his group, the Wailers, recorded their first song in 1963, but it was not until 1976, when Eric Clapton recorded Marley's "I Shot the Sheriff," that the group received notoriety and reggae came into vogue. Numbered among his other songs that speak to the "downpressed" of Jamaica and other Third World countries are "Concrete Jungle," "Rebel Music," and "Burnin' and Lootin'." Marley was an outspoken member of the Rastafarians, a religious cult whose adherents believe that they are the true Israelites, that Ethiopia is Zion, that the Western world is Babylon, and that Armageddon is at hand. They also advocate reggae music and the use of marijuana, and they believe in the divinity of the late Emperor Haile Selassie of Ethiopia. As is characteristic of Rastafarians, Marley wore his long, uncombed hair in braids called "dreadlocks." Obituaries and other sources: *New York Times,* August 14, 1977, May 12, 1981, May 21, 1981; *Newsweek,* May 25, 1981; *Time,* May 25, 1981.

*   *   *

MARSH, David Charles   1917-

PERSONAL: Born January 9, 1917, in Aberdare, Wales; son of F. C. Marsh; married Maisie Done, 1941; children: one son. *Education:* Attended University of Birmingham. *Home:* 239 Chilwell Lane, Bramcote, Nottinghamshire, England.

CAREER: University of Birmingham, Birmingham, England, research scholar, 1938-39; University of Wales, University College of Swansea, lecturer, 1947-49; Victoria University of Wellington, Wellington, New Zealand, professor of political science, 1949-54; University of Nottingham, Nottingham, England, professor of applied social science, 1954—. *Military service:* British Army, Royal Artillery, 1940-45.

WRITINGS: National Insurance and Assistance in Great Britain, Pitman, 1950; *Social Research and the Welfare State,* University of Nottingham, 1955; *The Changing Social Structure of England and Wales, 1871-1951,* Humanities, 1958, revised edition, 1965; *The Future of the Welfare State,* Penguin, 1964; (with Arthur John Willcocks) *Focus on Nurse Recruitment: A Snapshot From the Provinces,* Oxford University Press, 1965; (editor) *The Social Sciences: An Outline for the Intending Student,* Routledge & Kegan Paul, 1965; (editor) *An Introduction to the Study of Social Administration,* Routledge & Kegan Paul, 1965; *The Welfare State,* Longman, 1970, 2nd edition, 1980; (with Wyn Grant) *The Confederation of British Industry,* Hodder & Stoughton, 1977; *Introducing Social Policy,* Routledge & Kegan Paul, 1979.*

*   *   *

MARSHALL, Helen Lowrie   1904-1975

PERSONAL: Born August 21, 1904, in Atlanta, Neb.; died September 30, 1975, in Denver, Colo.; daughter of Charles Stuart (a grain elevator operator) and Louella Evelyn (Barr) Coffey; married Patrick Houston Lowrie, December 9, 1929 (marriage ended); married John S. Marshall (a printer), July 23, 1950; children: Patrick Houston Lowrie, Jr., Harold Watkins Lowrie III. *Education:* Attended Kearney State Teachers College, 1921-22, and University of Colorado, 1925-26; graduate of Parks Business College, 1926. *Religion:* Methodist. *Residence:* Denver, Colo.

CAREER: Writer. Teacher at school in Axtell, Neb., 1922-25; Lowrie & Co. (brokers), Denver, Colo., secretary, 1926-28; secretary to Senator Charles Thomas in Denver, 1929; Chevrolet Motor Division, Denver, secretary, 1939-50; associated with Helvern Press, beginning in 1954. Writer for Hallmark Cards Inc. Producer of plays for local theatre groups; lecturer. *Member:* National League of American Pen Women (Colorado state president, 1968-69), National Federation of Press Women, Colorado Authors League, Poetry Society of Colorado, Colorado Press Women, Delta Kappa Gamma (honorary member), Executives Club, Women's Press Club. *Awards, honors:* First prize from National Press Women for *Aim for a Star;* award from National League of American Pen Women, 1966.

WRITINGS—Books of poems; published by Doubleday, except as noted: *Bright Horizons,* privately printed, 1954; *Close to the Heart,* Helvern Press, 1966; *Dare to Be Happy,* Helvern Press, 1966; *Aim for a Star,* Helvern Press, 1966; *Hold to Your Dream,* Helvern Press, 1966; *The Gift of Wonder,* 1967; *Moments of Awareness,* 1968; *Walk the World Proudly,* 1969; *A Gift So Rare,* 1969; *Quiet Power,* 1970; *A Treasury of Inspiration,* 1970; *Happy Anniversary, Darling,* 1971; *Let Me Love the Little Things,* 1971; *A World That Sings,* 1971; *Starlight and Candleglow,* 1971; *Success Is a Journey,* 1972; *Aren't You Glad!,* 1973; *Leave a Touch of Glory,* 1976.

SIDELIGHTS: Helen Marshall's husband, John, wrote: "Helen lived in the rural areas of Nebraska and at an early age was attracted to the beauties of poetry. Her folks moved around frequently due to her father's occupation, and she attended several schools.

"In 1925 Helen moved with her brother to Denver, where she continued her schooling. She studied the writing of short stories and plays. She wrote a few short stories and wrote and directed plays for her church and civic groups; she reveled in expressing her thoughts in poetry.

"Helen was urged repeatedly to publish her poetry in book form. Her brother owned a modest printing plant which was an invitation to get busy. In 1954 they organized Helvern Press, and brought me into the project to print the first book. Knowing nothing about book publishing, we started to learn the hard way by trial and error—mostly error. Helen learned to set type, one letter at a time; I gradually became adept at running the letter press. When the sheets were finally printed, there remained nothing to be done but the bookbinding. Not knowing where to tread, we tore books apart to discover how they went together. As the need arose, I created jigs, folding machines, book presses, and other gadgets from vegetable crates, jar lids, or anything that was the right shape to do the job. Helen collated and sewed by hand the more than three thousand sections required for the job.

"From then on we decided to have the books printed and bound commercially. The marketing became a team project. Helen concentrated on her writing, autograph parties, and poetry programs. Her programs were unique in that she gave from memory practically all of the poems she offered. Together we traveled all over the country.

"Helen's books provide a storehouse of inspiration, comfort, and cheerfulness that the world always needs. They serve to radiate a joyful outlook on life. Her poetry is known for its simplicity and clarity. If it is profound, it is because it is easily understood, warm, and cheerful, expressing a devotion, faith, and philosophy that many can associate with. She felt that dreams are important and that a reality begins with a dream. She wrote many poems to emphasize this, including the title poem for her book, *Hold to Your Dream*.

"Many approaches to wholesome and worthwhile living were reflected in Helen's life. Many times, filled with awe by what she had written, she would say, 'I can't believe those lines are mine. No—some Force guided my hand, and I am merely an instrument to help someone to a happier life.' Helen died in Denver, Colorado, in 1975. However, she still lives in her heritage of inspiration, humor, comfort, cheer, and truth."

[Sketch verified by husband, John S. Marshall]

* * *

MARSLAND, Amy 1924-

PERSONAL: Born March 23, 1924, in Saskatoon, Saskatchewan, Canada; daughter of Richard A. (a principal) and Alberta G. (a teacher; maiden name, Amy) Downey; married William D. Marsland (a publisher), September 8, 1951; children: Alicia Marsland Geromel, Stephen, David, Adam. *Education:* University of Saskatchewan, B.A. (with honors), 1944; University of Michigan, Ph.D. (summa cum laude), 1950. *Agent:* McIntosh & Otis, Inc., 475 Fifth Ave., New York, N.Y. 10017. *Office address:* P.O. Box 248, Greene, N.Y. 13778.

CAREER: Writer. Twin Valley Publishers, Inc., Greene, N.Y., treasurer, 1958—. Teacher at State University of New York at Binghamton, 1963-67, Carleton College, and Broome Community College. Chairman of Greene Bicentennial Committee. *Member:* Authors Guild, National Organization for Women, Greene Art Group, Greene Performing Arts Forum, Historic Preservation. *Awards, honors:* Hopwood Drama Award from University of Michigan, 1945.

WRITINGS: (With husband, William D. Marsland) *Venezuela Through Its History,* Crowell, 1954; *Cache-Cache,* Doubleday, 1980. Also author, with George Klin, of Cliff's Notes editions on *Andromache* and *Les Miserables.*

WORK IN PROGRESS: Seguidilla, a suspense novel; *The Mischief in Monaghan,* a suspense novel; *Snow White, the Wolf, and the Unicorn,* nonfiction.

SIDELIGHTS: Amy Marsland wrote: "My first love is scholarship, which circumstances prevented me from pursuing consistently, but one can be satisfactorily curious about the tax laws and whodunit as well as the origins of western culture." *Avocational interests:* Travel, aerobic walking, painting in oils, moral philosophy.

* * *

MARTIN, Betty
See MARTIN, Elizabeth DuVernet

* * *

MARTIN, David 1915-
(Spinifex)

PERSONAL: Born December 22, 1915, in Budapest, Hungary; came to Australia, 1949; son of Leo and Hedirig (Rosner) Detsinyi; married Elizabeth Richenda Powell, 1941; children: one son. *Education:* Educated in Germany. *Home:* 3 Finch St., Beechworth, Victoria 3747, Australia. *Agent:* c/o Curtis Brown Pty. Ltd., 24 Renny St., Sydney, New South Wales 2021, Australia.

CAREER: Worked in European service for British Broadcasting Corp. (BBC), as foreign correspondent for *London Daily Express,* and literary editor for *Reynolds News,* all in London, England, 1938-47; foreign correspondent in India, 1948-49; writer, 1949—. *Military service:* International Brigade, 1937-38; served in Spain. *Member:* Australian Society of Authors and Reporters (council member, 1973—), Australian Literature Board. *Awards, honors:* Australia Council senior fellowship, 1973-76.

WRITINGS—Novels: Tiger Bay, Martin & Reid, 1946; *The Stones of Bombay,* Wingate, 1950; *The Young Wife,* Macmillan (London), 1962; *The Hero of the Town,* Morrow, 1965 (published in England as *The Hero of Too,* Cassell, 1965); *The Littlest Neutral,* Crown, 1966 (published in England as *The King Between,* Cassell, 1966); *Where a Man Belongs,* Cassell, 1969.

Juvenile fiction: *Hughie,* St. Martin's 1971; *Gary,* Cassell, 1972; *Frank and Francesca,* Thomas Nelson, 1972; *The Chinese Boy,* Hodder & Stoughton, 1973; *The Cabby's Daughter,* Hodder & Stoughton, 1974; (with wife, Elizabeth Richenda Martin) *Katie,* Hodder & Stoughton, 1974; *Mister P and His Remarkable Flight,* Hodder & Stoughton, 1975; *The Devilfish Mystery of the Flying Mum,* Thomas Nelson, 1977; *The Mermaid Attack,* Outback Press, 1978; *The Man in the Red Turban,* Hutchinson, 1978; *Peppino Says Goodbye,* Rigby, 1980.

Poetry: *Battlefields and Girls,* Maclellan, 1942; (with Hubert Nicholson and John Manifold) *Trident,* Fore, 1944; (editor) *Rhyme and Reason: Thirty-four Poems,* Fore, 1944; *From Life: Selected Poems,* Current, 1953; (under pseudonym, Spinifex) *Rob the Robber: His Life and Vindication,* J. Waters, 1954; *Poems, 1938-1958,* Edwards & Shaw, 1958; *Spiegel the Cat: A Story-Poem Based on a Tale By Gottfried Keller,* F. W. Cheshire, 1961, C. N. Potter, 1971; *The Gift: Poems, 1959-1965,* Jacaranda, 1966; *The Idealist,* Jacaranda, 1968; *I Rhyme My Time* (juvenile), Jacaranda, 1980.

Other: *The Shepherd and the Hunter* (three-act play; first produced in London, 1945), Wingate, 1946; *The Shoes Men Walk In* (short stories), Pilot Press, 1946; (with F. E. Emery) *Psychological Effects of the "Western" Film: A Study in Television Viewing* (nonfiction), University of Melbourne, 1957; *Television Tension Programmes: A Study Based on a Content Analysis of Western, Crime, and Adventure Programmes Televised by Melbourne Stations, 1960-61* (nonfiction), Australian Broadcasting Control Board, 1963; "The Young Wife" (play; adaptation of Martin's own novel), first produced in Melbourne, 1966; *On the Road to Sydney* (travel), Thomas Nelson, 1970; *Foreigners*, Rigby, 1981. Also author of *I'll Take Australia*.

WORK IN PROGRESS: A satirical novel on life in an Australian country town.

SIDELIGHTS: Martin told *CA:* "I was described by the *Times Literary Supplement* as 'Australia's outstanding literary acquisition from post-war immigration.' I am one of my adopted country's most prolific writers. Having first won a reputation as a poet (though my mother language is German), I later became well-known as a novelist. My most widely read work of fiction is *The Young Wife,* which tells of a Greek migrant woman in Melbourne. I have also written 'young' novels. They, too, deal mainly with the insider-outsider theme, often using Australia's colorful background. I am sometimes criticized for my partisanship, but I never moralize. I must be counted among the half-dozen or so most successful writers for young people in Australia.

"The chief motivation of my work is the rage for expressing the various, and sometimes conflicting, parts of my personality. I call myself, though, an 'international nationalist.'"

*　　*　　*

MARTIN, Elizabeth DuVernet 1910-
(Betty Martin)

PERSONAL: Born January 12, 1910, in Greenville, S.C.; daughter of Robert Parker (in agriculture) and Ella (Pratt) DuVernet; married William Bertrand Martin, July 21, 1934 (died, 1957); children: William Bertrand, Jr., Walter Hugh. *Education:* Furman University, M.A., 1962; also attended University of North Carolina, University of Michigan, University of Denver, and Rutgers University. *Religion:* Episcopalian. *Agent:* c/o Shoe String Press Inc., Box 4327, 995 Sherman Ave., Hamden, Conn. 06514. *Residence:* Greenville, S.C. 29609.

CAREER: Associated with Fisk University, Nashville, Tenn., University of South Carolina, Columbia, and Furman University, Greenville, S.C.; high school librarian and director of District Materials Center; School District of Greenville County, Greenville, S.C., director of library services, beginning in 1957; writer. Member of board of directors of Friends of the Greenville County Library, 1969-73. *Member:* American Association of School Librarians (member of executive board of directors, 1963-66; chairman of supervisors' section, 1968-69), Southeastern Library Association (president, 1974-76), South Carolina Library Association (president, 1964), South Carolina Association of School Librarians (president, 1970-71), Alpha Delta Kappa (president of Zeta chapter, 1973-74), Soroptimist International.

WRITINGS—Under name Betty Martin: (With Ben Carson) *The Principal's Handbook on the School Library Media Center,* Gaylord, 1978; (with Linda Sargent) *The Teacher's Handbook on the School Library Media Center,* Shoe String, 1980; (with Frances Hatfield) *The School District Media*

Director: A Handbook for the Novice, Shoe String, 1981. Contributor to library journals.

WORK IN PROGRESS: A book on student use of library media resources; research on the school library media program.

SIDELIGHTS: Betty Martin told *CA:* "I'm afraid I've always been a 'workaholic,' very much achievement oriented. In our family we've always referred to this as 'the DuVernet drive.' There must be something in my genes. Both my parents had the courage, ambition, and determination to achieve, which caused them to come to America, my mother from England and my father from Canada.

"My motivation has been to promote the school library media facilities program and the use of a professional staff to help all students develop lifetime skills for using these resources effectively.

"I believe that librarians in all types of libraries should strive to give excellent service to all segments of the population they serve, should seek out the 'unserved,' and offer programs for them that meet their needs and interests. In these times of inflation and tax-revolt, when there is a danger of cutbacks in library staff, collections, and programs, all librarians should increase their efforts to demonstrate the effectiveness of their services and their contributions to the education and quality of life of children and adults. All librarians should be receptive to the products of communications technology as they are developed and should evaluate them for their unique roles in achieving the goals of excellent library services. I believe that librarians, whether in public schools, colleges, public libraries, or other libraries, should involve themselves actively in the planning, implementation, and evaluation of the curricula and/or programs of the institutions or community they serve. Cooperative ventures between all types of libraries should be instituted and librarians should seek diligently to identify ways of sharing resources and programs effectively. All librarians should pursue a program of professional growth and, as one aspect of this, should be active in professional organizations.

"Above all, I believe that librarians' concern for the efficient administration of their libraries should never cause them to neglect the human facet of their interaction with their patrons."

AVOCATIONAL INTERESTS: Exercise and health, reading, travel (England, Europe, the Soviet Union).

*　　*　　*

MARTIN, Hubert M., Jr. 1932-

PERSONAL: Born May 7, 1932, in Chattanooga, Tenn.; son of Hubert M. Martin; married, 1952; children: two. *Education:* University of Chattanooga, A.B., 1954; Johns Hopkins University, M.A., 1955, Ph.D., 1958. *Office:* Department of Classical Languages, University of Kentucky, Lexington, Ky. 40506.

CAREER: Randolph-Macon College, Ashland, Va., associate professor, 1958-59, professor of Greek, 1959-60; University of North Carolina, Chapel Hill, 1960-69, began as assistant professor, became associate professor of classics; University of Kentucky, Lexington, associate professor, 1969-74, professor of classics, 1974—, chairman of department of classical languages, 1976—. Fellow at Center for Hellenic Studies, 1962-63; member of managing committee of American School of Classical Studies, Athens, Greece, 1970—. *Member:* American Philological Association, Archaeological Institute of America, American Classical League, American Association of University Professors,

Vergilian Society, Classical Association of the Midwest and South. *Awards, honors:* Grant from Southern Fellowships Fund, 1960; American Council of Learned Societies grant, 1973.

WRITINGS: Alcaeus, Twayne, 1972. Contributor to philology and classical studies journals.*

* * *

MARTIN, John Sayre   1921-

PERSONAL: Born November 24, 1921, in England; married, 1956; children: three. *Education:* University of California, Berkeley, A.B., 1943, M.A., 1948, Ph.D., 1958. *Office:* Department of English, University of Calgary, Calgary, Alberta, Canada T2N 1N4.

CAREER: University of California, Berkeley, lecturer in English, 1955-56; University of Illinois, Urbana, instructor in English, 1957-62; Hiram College, Hiram, Ohio, assistant professor of English, 1962-65; University of Calgary, Calgary, Alberta, associate professor of English, 1965—. *Military service:* U.S. Navy, 1943-45 and 1950-52; became lieutenant. *Member:* Modern Language Association of America, Association of Canadian University Teachers of English, Philological Association of the Pacific Coast.

WRITINGS: E. M. Forster: The Endless Journey, Cambridge University Press, 1976. Contributor to literature journals.*

* * *

MARTIN, Robert (Lee)   1908-1976
(Lee Roberts)

OBITUARY NOTICE—See index for *CA* sketch: Born October 16, 1908, in Chula, Va.; died February 1, 1976, in Tiffin, Ohio. Personnel manager and author. Martin wrote mystery novels as an avocation. Several of his novels were adapted for television, including *The Widow and the Web* and *Sleep My Love.* Among Martin's other books are *Just a Corpse at Twilight, She, Me and Murder,* and *Bargain for Death.* He also wrote several novels under the pseudonym Lee Roberts, including *Death of a Ladies' Man* and *Suspicion.* (Date of death provided by daughter, Mrs. Charles Dryfuse.)

* * *

MARTINSEN, Ella Barbara Lung   1901-1977

PERSONAL: Born January 6, 1901, in Dominion Creek, Yukon Territory, Canada; died in 1977; daughter of Edward Burchall and Velma Deborah (Clement) Lung; married Perry J. Martinsen, August 25, 1921; children: Rowena Barbara (Mrs. Charles McQueen Taylor). *Education:* Attended Santa Barbara State Teachers College, 1931. *Home:* 3033 Lomita Rd., Santa Barbara, Calif. 93105. *Office:* 30 East Victoria St., Santa Barbara, Calif. 93101.

CAREER: Concert singer, beginning 1917; writer and lecturer. Co-founder of Cross Town Freeway Committee (treasurer, 1961-65). *Member:* National League of American Pen Women (president, 1966-67, 1970-71, 1974-75), Santa Barbara Historical Society, International Alaska-Yukon Club, Alaska Club (vice-president, 1968-69), Strollers Club (president, 1942-43), Women's Montecito Country Club. *Awards, honors:* Gold plaques from National League of American Pen Women.

WRITINGS: (Editor) Edward B. Lung, *Black Sand and Gold: True Alaska-Yukon Gold-Rush Story,* Metropolitan Press, 1967; (editor) Velma D. Lung, *Trail to North Star Gold: A Sequel to Black Sand and Gold, True Story of the Alaska-*

Klondike Gold Rush, Binford & Mort, 1969. Contributor to *New Voices in American Poetry,* 1973, and *The Alaska Book.* Contributor to magazines, including *Alaska* and *Alaska Sportsman.**

* * *

MARX, Samuel   1902-

PERSONAL: Born January 26, 1902, in New York, N.Y.; son of Max and Edna Marx; widower; children: Richard, Kenneth. *Education:* Attended Columbia University, 1918-19. *Politics:* Democrat. *Religion:* Jewish. *Home and office:* 10341 Rossbury Pl., Los Angeles, Calif. 90064.

CAREER: Worked as editor of *New York Amusements;* Metro-Goldwyn-Mayer, Hollywood, Calif., story editor, 1930, producer, 1940-50, story consultant, 1981—. Producer of motion pictures for Universal, Columbia, and Desilu. Lecturer at Columbia University, California State University, and University of Oklahoma. *Member:* Academy of Motion Picture Arts and Sciences, Writers Guild of America (West), Authors League of America.

WRITINGS: Mayer and Thalberg: "The Make-Believe Saints," Random House, 1975; (with Jan Clayton) *Rodgers and Hart: "Bewitched, Bothered, and Bedeviled,"* Putnam, 1977; *Queen of the Ritz,* Bobbs-Merrill, 1978. Contributor to *New Yorker,* 1923-29.

WORK IN PROGRESS: Always New Year's Eve, a novel of New York City in the 1920's.

SIDELIGHTS: Marx wrote: "My desire to write books has been constantly sidelined by job offers (too good to reject) in the motion picture field. I am very interested in student preoccupation with films."

BIOGRAPHICAL/CRITICAL SOURCES: Los Angeles Times, February 13, 1981.

* * *

MASON, Edmund (John)   1911-

PERSONAL: Born April 25, 1911, in London, England; son of Edmund Montgomery Foster (an engineer) and Ellen Ethel (Jago) Mason; married Dorrien Annie Mary Ryan (a lecturer), 1939; children: Edmund Jeffery, Vivien Mary Mason Allen. *Education:* Attended high school in London, England. *Politics:* "None particularly." *Home:* 33 Broadleys Ave., Henleaze Park, Henleaze, Bristol BS9 4LY, England.

CAREER: Worked as rating surveyor in London, England, 1933-34; Workers Educational Association, Bristol, England, adult education lecturer, 1948—, vice-chairman of western district, 1965-68, 1973-76, chairman of district, 1969-72. Broadcaster for British Broadcasting Corporation (BBC). District estate supervisor for Department of the Environment, 1934-76; archaeological consultant to Dan Yr and Ogof Caves Ltd., 1939—, and Wookey Holes Caves Ltd., 1947-72; chairman and member of board of trustees of Steepholm Trust, 1968-74; member of board of trustees of South Brecons Field Study Centre, 1969—.

MEMBER: Society of Authors, Royal Institution of Chartered Surveyors (fellow), Cave Diving Group of Great Britain (founding member), Mendip Nature Research Committee (chairman), Wells Natural History Society (life member), Bristol Exploration Society (life member), Bristol Folkhouse Archaeological Society, South Wales Caving Club (founding member). *Awards, honors:* Second prize from Civil Service Council for Further Education, 1975.

WRITINGS: (With A. W. Coysh and Vincent Waite) *The Mendips,* R. Hale, 1954, 4th edition, 1977; (translator) Guy de Lavaur, *Caves and Cave Diving,* R. Hale, 1956; *The Story of Wookey Hole,* Wookey Hole Caves, 1963, 3rd edition, 1970; *Portrait of the Brecon Beacons,* R. Hale, 1975; *Caves and Caving in Britain,* R. Hale, 1977; *Avon Villages,* R. Hale, 1981. Also author of screenplay "Wookey Hole Divers," Rayant Pictures Ltd., 1951, and television script "The Mendips," BBC-TV, 1976.

SIDELIGHTS: Mason wrote: "As an archaeologist and former cave explorer, my literary works were first in connection with caves and archaeology. This also applied to my early radio talks, television programs, and a couple films. On the publication of *Portrait of the Brecon Beacons,* British Broadcasting Corp. in Wales asked for an anecdote in the work to be put into radio script form and read by me. That was followed by a demand for other short stories for a series, not necessarily on caves. I traveled extensively for the Department of the Environment, so publishers' demands also included topographical works and my bias at present is this kind of literature."

*　　　*　　　*

MASON, Francis K(enneth)　1928-

PERSONAL: Born September 4, 1928, in London, England; son of Kenneth (a professor of geography) and Dorothy Helen Mason; married Jane Ann Cawston, March 26. 1955; children: Andrea Louise, Charles Kenneth Knowles, Christopher Alexander. *Education:* Royal Air Force College, Cranwell, graduated, 1951. *Home and office:* Beechwood, Watton, Thetford, Norfolk IP25 6AB, England.

CAREER: Hawker Aircraft Ltd., senior project engineer, 1956-63; *Flying Review International,* editor, 1963-64; Profile Publications Ltd., Windsor, England, managing director, 1964-67; Guinness Superlatives Ltd., Enfield, England, managing editor, 1968-71; Alban Book Services Ltd., Watton, England, managing director and member of Institute of Directors, 1971—. Freeman of City of London, 1955—. Guest on television programs; lecturer. *Military service:* Royal Air Force, flying officer, 1948-56; became flight lieutenant. *Member:* Royal Historical Society (fellow), Royal Aeronautical Society (associate member), Royal Air Forces Association, Worshipful Company of Drapers (liveryman, 1955—). *Awards, honors:* International literary diploma, 1973.

WRITINGS: Hawker Aircraft Since 1920, Putnam, 1961, 2nd edition, 1971; *The Hawker Hurricane,* Macdonald & Co., 1962; *The Gloster Gladiator,* Macdonald & Co., 1964; *Battle Over Britain: A History of the German Air Assaults on Great Britain, 1917-18, and July-December 1940, and of the Development of Britain's Air Defences Between the World Wars,* McWhirter Twins, 1969; *British Fighters of World War II,* Hylton Lacy Publishers, 1970; (editor with Martin C. Windrow) *The Guinness Book of Air Facts and Feats,* Guinness Superlatives, 1970, 2nd edition, 1974; *The Hawker F. 1/T. 66 in Royal Air Force and Foreign Service,* Osprey, 1971; *The De Havilland Mosquito in the Royal Air Force, Fleet Air Arm, Royal Australian Air Force, South Africa Air Force, Royal New Zealand Air Force, Royal Canadian Air Force, and U.S. Army Air Forces,* Osprey, Volume I, 1972; *Know Aviation* G. Philip, 1973; *Know Britain: The Heritage and Institutions of and Offshore Island,* G. Philip, 1973, 2nd edition, 1975; *Ribbons and Medals: The Worlds Military and Civil Awards,* G. Philip, new edition, 1974; *A Concise Dictionary of Military Biography: Two Hundred of the Most Significant Names in Land Warfare, Tenth to Twentieth*

Century, Osprey, 1975. Also author of *Aviation Profiles,* 1965, and *Dictionary of Aviation, 1970.* Contributor to about one dozen magazines, including *Flying Review* and *Flight.*

WORK IN PROGRESS: Research for an "aviation who's who of all time," from 1896 to the present and including all nationalities.

SIDELIGHTS: Mason wrote: "I am basically a historian with interests in Anglo-Saxon and military history, but am obliged to concentrate on aviation as it is lucrative. I travel extensively and write fulltime, preferring country to city life. I seem to have become 'officially' recognized as the authority on the Battle of Britian as *Battle Over Britain* has been accepted as the definitive work. Continuing research on this brings me into contact with many British and German veterans.

"I am an artist in my own right and have illustrated a number of publications. My favorite holiday location is the Seychelles, in the Indian Ocean. I infinitely prefer them to the United States (I have visited thirteen states). It is nothing personal, but I am an island animal.

"I became editor of *Flying Review International* in 1963, but only lasted a year as I thoroughly disliked the job of interviewing our particularly nasty brand of socialist politician, and I'm afraid my columns tended to reflect this dislike. In any case I had become bitten by the publishing bug and started my own publishing company. In three years I decided to sell the company and start up again. I then wrote *Battle Over Britain,* which has really become something of an institution both financially and academically. Incidentally, I published this book myself, doing all design, editing, print purchase, marketing, and distribution—so I reckon I am able to say I found out about publishing the hard way. The book has gone to four editions and is now accepted as the standard textbook on this aspect of history in universities, schools, military establishments, and government departments. It has brought in its wake an extraordinary social expansion for me, not to mention considerable travel throughout the world.

"Although I grew up in Oxford, I have always preferred the low-key honesty of country folk. I now live in a small country village with all the necessary amenities within spitting distance, and I get more work done in a nine-hour day than I ever did when I lived close to London. I don't have a phone at my office so that if anyone wants to contact me they have to write; if I want to contact anyone, I walk a dozen yards and pick up someone else's phone. It's very cheap that way. It's rather like giving up smoking your own cigarettes.

"Please don't be offended by my stated dislike of the United States. As a matter of fact I have a very great admiration for Americans, especially having to live where they do. Being used to an island, I find that if I go anywhere I get somewhere; in a place like the U.S.A. you seem to go and get nowhere. Having said that, my favorite state is Texas, where the horizons seem to be as wide as the Texans' outlook; they are nice genuine people with a big sense of humor. I least like New York and California where horizons seem confined.

"I am a traditionalist and hate change for the sake of change. I am also an imperialist and a capitalist. I have very simple (possibly naive) political views. My attitude can perhaps best be summed up as: If a way of life has taken the human race several thousand years to evolve, why change it? Let it change itself. Certainly I am a conservationist. I am also a supporter of capital punishment. As such, I believe in punishment fitting the crime. I support fox hunting but abhor whale hunting (mainly because fox hunting is strictly controlled, and the other is not, and because in fox hunting someone usually falls off his horse and breaks his leg or neck). I support 'the bomb' because the worse it gets the less likely it is to be used. One day a small country will use it on its neighbor and the world will see how dangerous it really is; but if it wasn't the bomb it would be something else.

"I object to objectors; more often than not they are like children, crying because they can't get what they want. They would be better employed in useful work.

"I resent the world telling Britain that it had no right to possess an empire. Since we got rid of ours, the rest of the world has been busy trying to get its hands on it—and in a much more subversive and unethical way. Britain did a far more humane and useful job in civilizing the world during the one hundred fifty years of its great empire than either Russia or America will ever do. I know, for I lived in India, saw the vast amount of good we did for the people in trade, administration, and defense, and the moment we got out, most of those countries got back to the business of fratricide and civil war.

"These are my outlooks. I consider the fellow human being as the most arrogant, selfish, and deceitful of all animals. I prefer the cat family. My favorite human trait is a sense of humor; humans are almost human when they are laughing. My gardener is a graduate in sociology, but a boring young man he is except when he is talking about something he *really* likes in my garden. He is almost deaf now, having subjected himself to years of pop festivals. A pity, because he was just beginning to get to like some of the great music masters."

AVOCATIONAL INTERESTS: Listening to music (classical), motoring, fishing.

* * *

MASON, Miriam E(vangeline)   1900-1973

OBITUARY NOTICE—See index for *CA* sketch: Born January 23, 1900, in Goshen, Ind.; died February 20, 1973. Freelance writer and author of children's books. Reared on an Indiana farm, Mason drew upon her own childhood experiences as material for her books. Among her many writings are *The Little Story House, Matilda and Her Family, A Pony Called Lightning, The Grey Nosed Kitten, Becky and Her Brave Cat, Bluegrass,* and *Mary Mapes Dodge, Jolly Girl.* Also a prolific contributor to periodicals, Mason wrote more than four hundred articles, short stories, and plays. Obituaries and other sources: *Who Was Who in America,* 6th edition, Marquis, 1976.

* * *

MATANZO, Jane Brady   1940-

PERSONAL: Born May 9, 1940, in LaPorte, Ind.; daughter of John Leonard (a machinist) and Helen (Schmitz) Brady; married Francisco Matanzo (an engineer), September 18, 1965; children: Megan Elise. *Education:* Ball State University, B.S., 1962; Ohio State University, M.A., 1965; University of Maryland, Ph.D., 1974. *Residence:* Damascus, Md. *Office:* The Reading Place, 10916 Middleboro Dr., Damascus, Md. 20750.

CAREER: Teacher at public schools in Columbus, Ohio, 1962-66; media specialist at public schools in Bel Air, Md., 1966-67; teacher at public schools in Upper Marlboro, Md., 1970-71; Hood College, Frederick, Md., assistant professor of education and coordinator and supervisor of early childhood student teachers, 1973-77, coordinator of Children's Literature Conference, 1977, director of Reading Center and graduate reading program, 1977-79; The Reading Place, Da-

mascus, Md., president and educational consultant, 1979—. Instructor at University of Maryland, 1973-74, Western Maryland College, 1976, and Johns Hopkins University, 1979; adjunct professor at Antioch College, 1975-77; speaker at workshops and conferences; consultant to Maryland School for the Deaf.

MEMBER: International Reading Association, College Reading Association (member of board of directors), National Council of Teachers of English, Children's Literature Assembly, Assembly on Literature for Adolescents, National Association for Gifted Children, Association for Supervision and Curriculum Development, Maryland Higher Education Reading Association, Phi Kappa Phi (founding member of local chapter; president, 1977-79), Phi Delta Kappa, Delta Kappa Gamma.

WRITINGS: (With James R. Geyer) *Programmed Reading Diagnosis for Teachers With Prescriptive References,* with cassette tapes, C. E. Merrill, 1977; (with Linda Lamme, Vivian Cox, and Miken Olson) *Raising Readers: Sharing Literature With Young Children,* Walker & Co., 1980. Author of "Traveling Around the Reading World," a column in *Reading News,* 1977-80. Contributor to education journals. Associate editor of *Reading News,* 1977-80, editor, 1980—.

WORK IN PROGRESS: Children's literature resource materials; parenting materials; research on multi-ethnic literacy, gifted readers, and the deaf learner.

SIDELIGHTS: Jane Matanzo commented: "I was a participant, in summer, 1979, in the International Children's Literature Study Tour to mainland China, Hong Kong, Macao, Thailand, Singapore, the Philippines, and Japan. The tour included the perusal of published materials for children, seminars with authors, illustrators, professors, librarians, publishers, teachers, literary translators, and education ministers, and visits to related institutions.

"As an independent consultant, I specialize in a number of inservice facets of the curriculum and work primarily in the areas of staff development, curriculum development, program planning, and program implementation with administrators, teachers, specialists, aides, students, parents, and any other relative personnel."

* * *

MATHEWS, J(oseph) Howard   1881-1970

OBITUARY NOTICE—See index for *CA* sketch: Born October 15, 1881, in Auroraville, Wis.; died April 15, 1970; buried in Madison, Wis. Educator and author. Mathews was best known for his work in the identification of firearms for criminal investigations. He established a research laboratory for the purpose of identifying firearms, and he wrote *Firearms Identification.* Obituaries and other sources: *Who Was Who in America,* 5th edition, Marquis, 1973.

* * *

MATISOFF, James A(lan)   1937-

PERSONAL: Born July 14, 1937, in Boston, Mass.; married, 1962; children: two. *Education:* Harvard University, A.B., 1958, A.M., 1959; University of California, Berkeley, Ph.D., 1967. *Office:* Department of Linguistics, University of California, Berkeley, Calif. 94720.

CAREER: Columbia University, New York, N.Y., 1966-70, began as instructor, became assistant professor of linguistics; University of California, Berkeley, associate professor of linguistics, 1970—. Visiting scholar at Summer Institute of Linguistic Society of America, 1973. *Member:* Linguistic

Society of America, Northern Thai Society. *Awards, honors:* American Council of Learned Societies grant for Asia, 1970.

WRITINGS: The Loloish Tonal Split Revisited (monograph), Cellar Book Shop, 1972; *The Grammar of Lahu,* University of California Press, 1973; *Variational Semantics in Tibeto-Burman: The "Organic" Approach to Linguistic Comparison,* Institute for the Study of Human Issues, 1978; *Blessings, Curses, Hopes, and Fears: Psycho-Ostensive Expressions in Yiddish,* Institute for the Study of Human Issues, 1979. Contributor to linguistic and Oriental studies journals.*

* * *

MATTHEWS, Clyde   1917-

PERSONAL: Born July 8, 1917, in New York, N.Y.; son of Albert and Caroline (Brandel) Matthews; married Florence Eisner, March 3, 1940; children: Roberta (Mrs. Lawrence M. Monat), Mark. *Education:* New York University, B.S., 1938; graduate study at Columbia University, 1938. *Home and office:* 2863 Harbor Rd., Merrick, N.Y. 11566.

CAREER: Woodside Herald, reporter and author of column, 1937-38; WWRL-Radio, news commentator, 1938; *Brooklyn Eagle,* Brooklyn, N.Y., reporter, 1938-39; director of public relations at Barbizon School of Modeling, 1939-47; president of Clyde Matthews Associates, 1948-51; director of public relations and advertising at MacLevy Affiliated Companies, 1952-53; director of public relations at Barton's Candy Co., 1954-56; Max Rogel, Inc., executive vice-president and president of Rogel International, 1956-60; Matthews International, New York City, president, 1960-62; Etkes, Matthews, Inc., New York City, executive vice-president, 1962-64; Public Relations Board, Inc., New York City, president, 1964-73; president of Matthews Communications, 1973—. Guest lecturer at New School for Social Research, 1963; instructor at Adelphi University, 1968—. Founding chairman of arts advisory council of New York Board of Trade, 1965-68; member of board of directors of National Businessman's Council. *Member:* Public Relations Society of America, American Management Association, National Press Club. *Awards, honors:* Silver Anvil Award from Public Relations Society of America, 1967.

WRITINGS: The Ides of March Conspiracy: The Year the IRS Got What It Deserves, Arbor House, 1979.*

* * *

MATTHEWS, Denis (James)   1919-

PERSONAL: Born February 27, 1919, in Coventry, England; son of Arthur and Elsie Randall (Culver) Matthews; married Mira Pauline Howe, November 3, 1941 (divorced November, 1960); married Brenda McDermott, August 23, 1963; children: (first marriage) Rachel, Miranda, Sophie, James; (second marriage) one son, one daughter. *Education:* Attended Royal Academy of Music, 1935-40; received M.A. from Trinity College, London. *Office:* Department of Music, University of Newcastle upon Tyne, Newcastle upon Tyne NE1 7RU, England.

CAREER: Concert pianist, 1939—. Professor at University of Newcastle upon Tyne, 1971—; lecturer at Royal Academy of Music and Royal College of Music. Member of Arts Council of Great Britain, 1972-73. Guest on media programs; broadcaster; recording artist; soloist for Royal Philharmonic Society, 1945; performed in the United States, Canada, Europe, Africa, Latin America, and the Far East. *Military service:* Royal Air Force Orchestra, 1940-46. *Awards, honors:* Medal, 1938, and Cobbett Medal, 1973, both from Worshipful

Company of Musicians; M.A. from University of Newcastle upon Tyne, 1971; fellow of Trinity College, London, 1972, and of Royal Academy of Music; commander of Order of the British Empire, 1975; D.Mus. from University of St. Andrews, 1973, and University of Hull, 1978.

WRITINGS: In Pursuit of Music (autobiography), Gollancz, 1966; *Beethoven Piano Sonatas,* BBC Publications, 1967, University of Washington Press, 1969; *Keyboard Music,* Praeger, 1972; *Brahms Piano Music,* BBC Publications, 1978. Compositions include *Serenade for 'Cello and Piano,* Oxford University Press, 1943.

SIDELIGHTS: Matthews's sound recordings include Beethoven's "Sketchbooks," released by Discourses, 1971-74. *Avocational interests:* Astronomy, filing systems, reading aloud, eighteenth-century English furniture.

BIOGRAPHICAL/CRITICAL SOURCES: Music Library Association Notes, December, 1979.*

* * *

MAUDE, H(enry) E(vans)   1906-

PERSONAL: Born October 1, 1906, in Patna, India; son of Walter (in Indian civil service) and Carrie Maude; married Honor Courtney King (a writer and publisher), September 6, 1929; children: Alaric Mervyn. *Education:* Jesus College, Cambridge, B.A. (with honors), 1929, M.A., 1933. *Politics:* "No political affiliations, views, or interests." *Religion:* Unitarian-Universalist. *Home:* 77 Arthur Circle, Forrest, Canberra, Australian Capital Territory 2603, Australia.

CAREER: British Colonial Service, London, England, administrative cadet at Gilbert and Ellice Islands Colony, 1929-32, administrative officer, 1932-33, secretary to government, 1933-34, chief lands commissioner, 1934-38, officer in charge of Phoenix Islands settlement scheme, 1938-40, administrator of Pitcairn Island, 1940-41, British agent and consul of Tonga, 1941-42, first assistant secretary of Western Pacific High Commission, 1942-46, resident commissioner of Gilbert and Ellice Islands Colony, 1946-49, deputy secretary-general and executive officer for social development of South Pacific Commission, 1949-57; Australian National University, Canberra, senior research fellow at Research School of Pacific Studies, Institute of Advanced Studies, 1957-59, senior fellow, 1959-63, professorial fellow, 1963-70; writer, 1970—. Visiting fellow at Australian National University, 1971, 1978; honorary professor at University of Adelaide, 1973. Founder of South Pacific Literature Bureau, 1949, and Pacific Manuscripts Bureau, 1969.

MEMBER: Polynesian Society, Societe des Oceanistes, Societe d'Etudes Oceaniennes, Centre de Recherches Historiques pour le Pacifique (member of comite d'honneur, 1974—), Association for Social Anthropology in Oceania (fellow), Pacific History Association. *Awards, honors:* Member of Order of the British Empire, 1939, officer of order, 1949; Australian literary grant from Literature Board of the Australian Council for the Arts, 1974; Independence Medal from Republic of Kiribati, 1979.

WRITINGS: (With wife, Honor Courtney Maude) *String Figures From the Gilbert Islands,* University Press of Hawaii, 1958; *The Evolution of Gilbertese Boti: An Ethnohistorical Interpretation,* Polynesian Society, 1963, revised edition, Institute of Pacific Studies, University of the South Pacific, 1977; *Of Islands and Men: Studies in Pacific History,* Oxford University Press, 1968; *The Gilbertese Maneaba,* Institute of Pacific Studies, University of the South Pacific, 1980; *Slavers in Paradise: The Peruvian Labour Trade in*

Polynesia, 1862-64, Stanford University Press, 1981. Founder and general editor of "Pacific History" series, Australian National University Press, 1968, and "Pacific Monograph" series, Australian National University Press, 1970. Contributor of about one hundred articles to journals. Co-founder and editor of *Journal of Pacific History,* 1966.

WORK IN PROGRESS: Editing *The Grimble Book,* previously unpublished anthropological notes and papers of Sir Arthur Grimble, publication by Australian National University Press, expected in 1984; an autobiography.

SIDELIGHTS: Maude wrote: "My study and working library is in the garden, behind the pear and apple trees, but my main Pacific Islands Library (of ten thousand items) has outgrown our capacity to house it and is now located as a separate section of the Barr Smith Library at the University of Adelaide. I keep only what I require for current work. I never accept work on commission and never sign a contract, because I only research and write on what intrigues me personally at the time and I find that to work for others inhibits spontaneity. When I finish a paper, monograph, or book I send it unsolicited to whatever publisher I think might like it and I have never had a knock-back yet, touch wood.

"I've been described as an 'island monomaniac' and certainly ever since I was a teenager I have had only one aim in life: to read about, live in, study, and write about the South Sea islands, which fascinate me as much now as they did over half a century ago. The gods proved kind and enabled me to live on over eighty islands in every corner of the island world, and now that my field work days are over, except for occasional return visits, I am content to select unsolved problems relating to the history of the island peoples of Polynesia and Micronesia, and research them for publication, using primary documentary sources blended with oral tradition. No one else can ever duplicate my experiences in Oceania, for my life straddles two eras: the old days when the islands were a colonial backwater, and the new in which the islanders, many of them the grandchildren of old friends, have taken over the management of their own mini-states."

BIOGRAPHICAL/CRITICAL SOURCES: Niel Gunson, editor, *The Changing Pacific: Essays in Honour of H. E. Maude,* Oxford University Press, 1978.

*   *   *

MAUGHAM, Robert Cecil Romer   1916-1981
(Robin Maugham)

OBITUARY NOTICE—See index for *CA* sketch: Born May 17, 1916, in London, England; died after a long illness, March 13, 1981, in Brighton, England. Attorney and author. Trained in the law, Maugham gave up his career as a barrister after he was wounded in World War II. While recovering from his wounds, he wrote his first book, *Come to Dust,* and decided to become a writer. He was the author of novels, plays, film scripts, and nonfiction books, including two books of reminiscences about his uncle, Somerset Maugham. Robin Maugham traveled widely and his research was reflected in such books as *Nomad, North African Notebook,* and *The Slaves of Timbuktu.* A new novel, *The Deserters,* was in press at the time of his death. Obituaries and other sources: *Chicago Tribune,* March 14, 1981; *New York Times,* March 14, 1981; *Time,* March 23, 1981; *Publishers Weekly,* April 3, 1981; *AB Bookman's Weekly,* May 25, 1981.

MAUGHAM, Robin
See MAUGHAM, Robert Cecil Romer

*   *   *

MAURY, Reuben   1899-1981

OBITUARY NOTICE: Born September 2, 1899, in Butte, Mont.; died of pneumonia, April 23, 1981, in Norwalk, Conn. Journalist. Maury, an editorial writer for the *New York Daily News* for forty-six years, once called the United Nations "a glass cigar box . . . jam-packed with pompous do-gooders, nervy deadbeats, moochers, saboteurs, spies and traitors." From 1926 to 1972 he was an influential spokesman for the conservative viewpoint of the *Daily News,* campaigning against communism, bad grammar, and public figures, yet he was also the anonymous author of liberal, pro-Roosevelt commentaries published in *Collier's* magazine in the 1940's. "An editorial writer," he explained, "is like a lawyer or a public relations man: his job is to make the best possible case for his client." Obituaries and other sources: *The International Year Book and Statesmen's Who's Who,* Kelly's Directories, 1978; *Who's Who in America,* 40th edition, Marquis, 1978; *New York Times,* April 25, 1981; *Time,* May 4, 1981; *Newsweek,* May 4, 1981.

*   *   *

MAYER, S(ydney) L(ouis)   1937-
(Patrick Jennings)

PERSONAL: Born August 2, 1937, in Chicago, Ill.; son of Sidney Louis (in business) and Elizabeth (a teacher; maiden name, Sandorf) Mayer; married Charlotte W. M. Bouter (a writer and translator), July 10, 1970; children: Patrick Michael (deceased). *Education:* University of Michigan, B.A., 1962, A.M., 1963; doctoral study at Yale University, 1963-65. *Politics:* Republican. *Home:* 23 Bryanston Sq., London W.1, England. *Office:* 4 Cromwell Pl., London S.W.7, England.

CAREER: University of Maryland, lecturer in history, 1966-78; British Printing Corp., England, executive editor, 1967-69, consulting editor, 1969-72; Ballantine books, consulting editor, 1969-73; Bison Books Ltd., London, England, chairman, 1975—. Visiting assistant professor at University of Southern California, 1969-80. *Member:* Royal Geographical Society (fellow), Yale Club (London), Savage Club (London), Yale Club (New York City), Presidents Club (Ann Arbor, Mich.).

WRITINGS: (With Harry J. Benda and John Larkin) *The World of southeast Asia,* Harper, 1967; *MacArthur,* Ballantine, 1970; *MacArthur in Japan,* Ballantine, 1973; *Signal: Hitler's Wartime Picture Magazine,* Prentice-Hall, 1976; (with William J. Koenig) *European Manuscript Sources of the American Revolution,* Bowker, 1976; *Signal: Years of Triumph,* Prentice-Hall, 1977; (with Koenig) *The Two World Wars,* Bowker, 1978; *Signal: Years of Retreat,* Prentice-Hall, 1979.

Editor: *World War I,* Octopus, 1973; *World War II,* Octopus, 1973; *Russian War Machine,* Chartwell, 1976; *The Japanese War Machine,* Chartwell, 1977; *Encyclopedia of World War II,* Rand McNally, 1977; *Wars of the Twentieth Century,* Octopus, 1977; (with Masami Tokoi) *Der Adler: The Luftwaffe Magazine,* Crowell, 1977; *Der Fuehrer: The Life and Times of Adolf Hitler,* Chartwell, 1978; *Who Was Who in World War II,* Crowell, 1978. Executive editor of *History of Second World War,* British Printing Corp., consulting editor of *History of the First World War*, British Printing Corp., and consulting editor of *History of the Violent Century*, Ballantine Books.

Contributor of articles to magazines under pseudonym Patrick Jennings.

WORK IN PROGRESS: The Netherlands Indies in World War II, publication expected in 1983.

SIDELIGHTS: Mayer commented: "I have traveled in every state and some fifty countries, and lived in England, France, and the Netherlands for fifteen years. I have probably written and edited more works on World War II and related subjects than any living person and am Britain's leading publisher in the genre. Reading, writing, teaching, and editing history has been my life's ambition and my life's work. I have founded and directed Bison Books Ltd. on this basis. I suppose I am one of the lucky few who have been able to make his living out of a pastime and abiding interest."

*   *   *

MAYES, Wendell 1919-

PERSONAL: Born in 1919 in Hayti, Mo.; son of Von (a lawyer) and Irene (a teacher; maiden name, Haynes) Mayes. *Education:* Attended Columbia University, 1939-40, and Johns Hopkins University, 1941-42. *Residence:* Los Angeles, Calif. *Agent:* Zeigler-Diskant, 9255 Sunset Blvd., Los Angeles, Calif. 90069.

CAREER: Actor, 1946-53; writer for television, 1953-60; screenwriter, 1956—. *Military service:* U.S. Navy, 1942-45. *Member:* Academy of Motion Picture Arts and Sciences, Writers Guild of America. *Awards, honors:* Nomination for Academy Award for best screenplay adapted from another source by Academy of Motion Picture Arts and Sciences, and nomination for award from Writers Guild of America, both 1959, both for "Anatomy of a Murder"; nomination for award from Writers Guild of America, 1978, for "Go Tell the Spartans."

WRITINGS—Screenplays: (With Billy Wilder) "The Spirit of St. Louis" (adapted from the autobiography by Charles A. Lindbergh), Warner Bros., 1957; "The Enemy Below" (adapted from the novel by Commander D. A. Rayner), Twentieth Century-Fox, 1957; (with Robert H. Buckner) "From Hell to Texas" (adapted from the novel by Charles O. Locke, *The Hell-Bent Kid*), Twentieth Century-Fox, 1958; "The Hunters" (adapted from the novel by James Salter), Twentieth Century-Fox, 1958; (with Halsted Welles) "The Hanging Tree" (adapted from the novel by Dorothy M. Johnson), Warner Bros., 1959; "Anatomy of a Murder" (adapted from the novel by Robert Traver), Columbia, 1959.

"Advise and Consent" (adapted from the novel by Allen Drury), Columbia, 1962; (with Joseph Landon) "Von Ryan's Express" (adapted from the novel by David Westheimer), Twentieth Century-Fox, 1965; "In Harm's Way" (adapted from the novel by James Bassett), Paramount, 1965; "Hotel" (adapted from the novel by Arthur Hailey), Warner Bros., 1967; "The Stalking Moon" (adapted from the novel by Theodore V. Olsen), National General Pictures, 1968.

"The Revengers," National General Pictures, 1972; (with Stirling Silliphant) "The Poseidon Adventure" (adapted from the novel by Paul Gallico), Twentieth Century-Fox, 1972; "Death Wish" (adapted from the novel by Brian Garfield), Paramount, 1974; "Bank Shot" (adapted from the novel by Donald E. Westlake), United Artists, 1974; "Go Tell the Spartans" (adapted from the novel by Daniel Ford), Amer-

ican Cinema, 1978; "Love and Bullets," International Television Corp. (ITC), 1979.

Contributor of teleplays to numerous television shows, including "Studio One" and "Kraft Theatre."

WORK IN PROGRESS: A screenplay, "The Princess With the Golden Hair," adapted from the story by Edmund Wilson, for Springfield Productions.

CA INTERVIEW

CA interviewed Wendell Mayes on May 12, 1980, at his home in Los Angeles.

CA: You started your career as an actor. Was it your ambition to become a writer?

MAYES: Actually, no. I think what I wanted to do was get into show business, and in the course of getting into show business, I did a bit of everything. Finally with the advent of television in the early 1950s, I began to write plays, and that became the main source of income, so it became the profession.

CA: Could you talk about your work in television?

MAYES: Until about 1957 or 1958, all television was live. There was no such thing as taped television. Shows were done for not a great deal of money, and the stars in those days were in fact the writers; it was the writer's name that was featured. While I wasn't as well known as some of the others—say, Paddy Chayefsky or Reginald Rose—I was in that group. We wrote for "Pond Theatre" and "Kraft Theatre" and "Studio One" and any number of programs. They were one-hour plays, and a lot of them were exceptional—mainly because the writer had a free hand. It was a new medium, and it was wide open for anything. There were no Nielsen ratings; shows were not assessed by ratings and thereby reduced to the banal. Some of the plays I did were repeated a couple of times, several of them that were quite famous in their time. Among the best known were "No Riders," "Death Is a Spanish Dancer," "Hang Up My Guns," and "Most Blessed Woman."

CA: Then you went from television to motion pictures?

MAYES: Billy Wilder brought me to the motion picture industry on the strength of one of my plays that he saw on television. I worked with Billy on "The Spirit of St. Louis," which was made in 1956 with Jimmy Stewart. I was with Billy for a year, and he was my instructor in the business of writing screenplays.

CA: Did you have reservations about leaving your successful work in television?

MAYES: For a time I went back and forth. As a matter of fact, my residence was in New York until about 1963. So I did continue to do some work for television. Finally, however, it became obvious that if you're going to be a writer of plays to be put on film or tape, Hollywood is the place to be. I haven't done anything for television for many years now.

CA: When you were doing both, was there any difficulty involved in switching from one form to the other?

MAYES: No. I was quite familiar with the needs of TV and also rapidly became familiar with the needs of motion pictures. It presented no difficulty.

CA: Can you pinpoint any early influences on your work?

MAYES: Billy Wilder had a great influence on my work. Wilder had certain rules he had developed across the years in his work. I had his instruction in those rules, and that had a great deal to do with what I have written and have not written. I can't point to any of his pictures and say that those pictures influenced me; it's rather things he told me about screenwriting. I can give you one cardinal rule that is perhaps the single most effective thing I learned from Wilder: that cold gray logic is death to entertainment; that you must be free to be illogical, not be bound by logic in creating a screenplay.

CA: You wrote and produced the movie "Hotel." Is that the only movie you've both written and produced?

MAYES: Yes. I intended at that time to be a writer-producer. But that first experience sort of cooled me, because I found the nuts and bolts of making a picture to be very boring. At least it is to me. And that was the end of my producing career, mainly because I just wasn't interested in doing it.

CA: Did you study "Grand Hotel" in any way when you were working on the screenplay for "Hotel"?

MAYES: No. As a matter of fact, I don't think I've ever seen "Grand Hotel." A lot of those old movies that we're supposed to be influenced by I've simply never seen. I do think some of the younger writers, cinema-school graduates, have been caught in the sticky web of old movies. My generation is always striving for something new.

CA: What is most difficult in adapting a novel for film?

MAYES: The main difficulty is that most novels are internal. Much of a novel is concerned with what its characters are thinking. When you write a screenplay, you can only show what they do and what they say. The problem is how to tell the story with only action and dialogue.

CA: Have you ever had any response from an author of a novel you've adapted for the screen?

MAYES: Most novelists resent the screenwriter. However, I had one novelist, Robert Traver, who liked my screenplay. That was *Anatomy of a Murder.* Traver was very kind to write me a note and say that he thought in fact I had improved on his story. It astounded me.

CA: Have you pretty much decided on your own what to write, or have things largely been assigned to you?

MAYES: The word *assigned* is a holdover from the days when writers were contracted by studios and were permanent employees of one studio. They were *assigned* to certain *properties,* another buzzword. But assignments don't exist anymore. All screenwriters now are free-lance. If they have a following, as many do, they have some choice in what they write. They can pick and choose among things that are sent to them. Happily, I have been in that situation for some years now.

CA: You did the screenplay for "The Poseidon Adventure," a so-called disaster movie. Is there a lot of research involved in writing such screenplays?

MAYES: No. "The Poseidon Adventure" is a simpleminded movie. All I really had to do was imagine what it would be like in a ship that's turned upside down. As I wrote it, I thought of people walking on ceilings instead of floors, climbing upside-down staircases, that sort of thing.

CA: You don't have to know how the ship is normally navigated, for instance?

MAYES: A minimal amount of knowledge is required because the audience isn't interested in it. You don't bother them with details like that.

CA: Aside from "Hotel," have you been closely involved with the production of any of your screenplays?

MAYES: Yes, I've been closely involved with many of them, but not involved with what kind of trousers the actor wears or how an actress does her hair. This is what a producer has to do, you know. I've only been involved with the script, scenes, dialogue, locations.

CA: How sensitive are you to criticism?

MAYES: Insensitive. In the beginning I was thin-skinned, but now it means almost nothing to me, good or bad.

CA: Are there critics you consider fairly decent?

MAYES: I believe most critics are fairly decent, not deliberately malicious, but I consider all motion picture criticism to be a rather foolish endeavor. It's like trying to sort out a can of worms. You really can't make much critical sense about a motion picture because whatever it is it's an accident. If it's bad it's an accident, if it's good it's an accident.

CA: What exactly do you mean when you say a good or a bad motion picture is an accident?

MAYES: It just happens. You can't, as with a stage play, try it out, polish it, improve it. You shoot it one time and put it on the screen; and if it doesn't work, it doesn't work. That's one reason motion picture is not a true art. It's like a roll of the dice instead of being an art. It really needs another definition.

CA: Do you have a favorite among your screenplays?

MAYES: Yes. I'm still very fond of "Anatomy of a Murder." I still have an affection for a screenplay called "The Enemy Below," and I have a fondness for a picture called "The Hanging Tree," that was Gary Cooper's last Western. He was one of my favorite people in Hollywood; maybe that's the reason I have affection for the picture. I like a recent screenplay called "Go Tell the Spartans." It made up into a damn good picture. Its subject matter, the Vietnam War, kept it from being popular.

CA: What changes stand out in your mind of those that have taken place in Hollywood in the years you've been there?

MAYES: The most obvious change is the material that you can put on the screen now. I'm not altogether sure that it's for the best. Maybe it is in some ways; it's been abused, obviously. The language you can use, the sexual scenes that you can show, those are the greatest changes. Apart from that, I don't know that there's much difference in most of the basic stories being done then and those being done now.

CA: How do you feel about the changes that have taken place in television since the beginning of your career?

MAYES: I would simply have to say that with commercial television it's been downhill all the way. After I look at the news, unless there's an old movie I want to see, I turn on the PBS channel and leave it there.

CA: Is there any hope for improvement with commercial television?

MAYES: No, I don't think with commercial television there is. Pay television is going to provide possibly better material, if it doesn't slip over into exploitation, which it may very well do.

CA: Are you working on something now that you'd like to talk about?

MAYES: I have something now of my own. There's a collection of stories called *Memoirs of Hecate County* by Edmund Wilson. In it there's a novella called "The Princess with Golden Hair," and I have turned that into a screenplay. It's making the rounds now, and I hope to get it made. That's on my own front. On a second front I have a couple of screenplays that I was employed to write that are waiting for production.

CA: Is there any chance that you might go back to television work?

MAYES: Maybe. In show business you can't rule anything out.

CA: Is there any kind of writing you haven't done that you'd like to try?

MAYES: Somerset Maugham said we don't write what we wish but what we can. I'd like to write novels, stage plays, essays; but my metier, I'm afraid, is the screenplay.

CA: Do you foresee any trends in movies?

MAYES: It's a very trendy business. I think we are trending away from overblown sci-fi at the moment. We may be trending down to what we used to call kitchen drama, the most recent example being "Kramer vs. Kramer": a very small story, the kind of thing that could have been done on television back in 1955.

CA: Is there any aspect of your work we've left out that you'd like to talk about?

MAYES: Well, there's the aspect of how important the work is. Although I earn my living as a screenwriter, enjoy it, and feel I've accomplished something, I don't think a motion picture has any lasting importance—not in the way a novel or a stage play or a concerto can have a lively value across a couple of centuries or more. A movie is very quickly fossilized. Its actors get old and die and finally it's nothing more than a curiosity like snapshots of long-dead relatives in a family album. I suppose to film-school graduates and motion picture critics who're inclined to be solemn about movies, that's a wicked heresy, but I think it's very likely the truth.

—*Interview by Jean W. Ross*

*   *   *

MAYFAIR, Bertha
   See RABORG, Frederick A(shton), Jr.

*   *   *

MAYHAR, Ardath   1930-
   (Ravenna Cannon)

PERSONAL: Born February 20, 1930, in Timpson, Tex.; daughter of Bert Aaron (a farmer) and Ardath (a farmer; maiden name, Ellington) Hurst; married Joe Mayhar (an expressman), June 7, 1958; children: Frank Edward, James Anthony; (stepsons) Robert William, William Earl. *Politics:*

Independent. *Religion:* Independent. *Home address:* Route 1, Box 140, Chireno, Tex. 75937. *Agent:* Valerie Smith, Virginia Kidd, Literary Agent, 528 East Harford St., Milford, Pa. 18337.

CAREER: Partner in dairy farm in Nacogdoches County, Tex., 1942-57; owner and manager of book store in Nacogdoches, Tex., 1957-62; proofreader in Salem, Ore., 1968-75, and Nacogdoches, 1979-80; writer, 1980—. Raised chickens in Nacogdoches County, 1976-78. *Member:* Science Fiction Writers of America, Small Press Writers and Artists Organization.

WRITINGS: Journey to an Ending (poetry chapbook), South and West, 1965; *How the Gods Wove in Kyrannon* (fantasy), Doubleday, 1979; *The Seekers of Shar-Nuhn* (fantasy), Doubleday, 1980; *Soul-Singer of Tyrnos* (young adult fantasy), Atheneum, 1981; *Warlock's Gift* (fantasy), Doubleday, 1982.

Work represented in anthologies, including *Stories to Be Read With the Lights On* and *Swords Against Darkness, Number Four.* Author of "View From Orbit," a column, 1980. Contributor of stories and poems to magazines, including *Fiction, Gothic, Weirdbook, Dark Fantasy,* and *Mummy!*

WORK IN PROGRESS: Feud at Sweetwater Creek, a western novel under pseudonym Ravenna Cannon; *The Tulpa,* an occult suspense novel; *The Saga of Grittel Sundotha,* a fantasy novel.

SIDELIGHTS: Ardath Mayhar told *CA:* "I have spent most of my adult life shoveling manure, writing poetry, and looking up at the stars. At the age of forty-three, I 'reformed' and stopped writing poetry, took up yoga and writing fantasy novels, and haven't looked back in the almost eight years since. I have been influenced, to a greater or lesser extent, by Dickens, Shakespeare, Ayn Rand, Andre Norton, William Faulkner, and all the 'old heads' in the science fiction field.

"I earnestly believe that being upside down (yoga) directly stimulated my bursting forth into fantasy novels, short stories, and even a regular newspaper column.

"From the ages seventeen to twenty-seven, I ran my father's dairy. Not as some sort of lordly supervisor, but hand-to-hand (sometimes face-to-hoof) with the cows, the cruddy milking machines, the manure, the hay, the weather. In that time, I also studied Latin, Greek, German, French, Spanish, and Italian. At one time I read most of them with some ease, but I haven't kept my hand in. As I get older, time seems to telescope inward. In that time, I also mastered several forms of poetry. I was a very good poet, having work in many magazines (such as *Mark Twain Quarterly*). However, I finally realized that English teachers have destroyed any love of poetry that might remain in the English-speaking race.

"I escaped from the dairy into a bookstore. There I met my husband, for he worked just around the corner, and snared him infallibly with books. In the next few years we achieved two sons (he already had two), moved to Houston (which I will insist be deducted from any time in Hell, when and if) and Oregon. There I met mountains, yoga, and proofreading, all of which were seminal influences. We moved back to Texas in 1975, glad to have gone but gladder still to get back home to individualist country.

"Now we live in the mutilated edge of the Big Thicket, near Sam Rayburn Lake. We are so poor that church mice look affluent beside us, but we grow fine gardens and hear the wolves howl at night. Occasionally we see a bobcat. There are bear and deer and cougar in the woods around us. It is ideal for writing the sort of fantasy I do best, and I've written more than twelve books in the years since we moved here. I don't even count short stories any more. If I ever quit writing, the U.S. Postal Service will go broke, for I buy enough stamps to keep them in business.

"I believe that hard work and early lack of success probably fitted me, more than anything else, to achieve what I wanted to: a control of my material which, whether it seems so or not, is deliberate. I have written some of my best poetry—stuff that won prizes—while shoveling manure. Many writers, I note, would be far better craftsmen for a closer acquaintance with actual, rather than metaphysical, manure. The combination of physical labor and wild imagination works extremely well for me.

"I am by nature a hermit. I do squeeze myself out of my burrow to go to science fiction conventions, at times. I also, being a study in contradictions, love to speak to groups of intelligent people, so I do a bit of that. I am becoming pretty adept at pushing my own books, as big publishers don't give new authors any visible help at all. I am a hard-core independent. Worse yet, I am objective and logical. Sacred cows, I find, make excellent steak."

BIOGRAPHICAL/CRITICAL SOURCES: Nacogdoches Daily Sentinel, October 10, 1979, July 10, 1980; Beaumont Enterprise-Journal, October 5, 1980.

*   *   *

MAYNARD, Harold Bright   1902-1975

OBITUARY NOTICE—See index for CA sketch: Born October 18, 1902, in Northampton, Mass.; died March 10, 1975. Management engineer and author. Maynard was best known for developing Methods-Time Measurement (MTM), a system that sets work standards by analyzing the time and motion required to accomplish a task. He was co-author of Methods-Time Measurement. Written in 1948, the book is still considered a classic in its field. Among Maynard's other works are New Developments in Management and Practical Control of Office Costs. He also edited several handbooks, including Top Management Handbook, Handbook of Business Administration, and Handbook of Modern Manufacturing Management. Obituaries and other sources: New York Times, March 11, 1975.

*   *   *

MAYO, Nick   1922-

PERSONAL: Birth-given name, Nickoli Martoff; born October 31, 1922, in Philadelphia, Pa.; son of Louis (a restaurateur) Martoff; married wife, Lee (marriage ended); married Janet Blair (an actress and singer), October 5, 1952; children: (first marriage) one daughter; (second marriage) one son, one daughter. Education: Los Angeles City College, B.A., 1941. Home: 2901 Antelo View Dr., Los Angeles, Calif. 90024. Office: 20600 Ventura Blvd., Woodland Hills, Calif. 91364.

CAREER: KIDO-Radio, Boise, Idaho, chief newscaster, 1940-41; radio performer in New York, N.Y., 1941-45; professional actor, stage and production manager, producer, and director, 1945—. Member of faculty at American Group Theater, 1945. Co-founder of Valley Music Theater, 1963; past president of Music Theatres, Inc. Producer and director of "The Witness," a series on CBS-TV. Member: Directors Guild of America.

WRITINGS: The Benefit, Stein & Day, 1979.*

MAYO, Patricia Elton   1915-

PERSONAL: Born September 7, 1915, in Brisbane, Australia; daughter of George Elton (a professor) and Dorothea (McConnel) Mayo; married Walter Goetz, 1940 (divorced, 1949); married Dunstan Curtis (a lawyer and international civil servant), June 24, 1950. Education: Cambridge University, diplomas in history and economics (with honors), 1936. Home: Penybryn Hall, Montgomery, Powys SY15 6TY, Wales.

CAREER: Associated with Industrial Welfare Society, London, England, 1938; personnel manager in aircraft industry, 1940-45; Royal Commission for the Cutlery Industry, Sheffield, England, independent member of commission, 1945-46; British Institute of Management, London, head of field research group, 1946-48; University of Strasbourg, Strasbourg, France, lecturer in industrial sociology, 1950-52; Organization for European Economic Cooperation (now Organization for Economic Cooperation and Development), Paris, France, manager of trade union projects, 1952-54; French Ministry of Justice, France, conducted experimental work in probation for adult offenders, 1954-58; European Commission on Crime Problems, Strasbourg, consulting sociologist, 1958-62; writer, 1963—. Member of Cadmos Group at University of Geneva, 1977-78. Member: University Women's Club (London). Awards, honors: Chevalier of Les Palmes Academiques.

WRITINGS: Probation and After-Care in Europe, European Commission on Crime Problems, 1963; The Making of a Criminal: A Comparative Case Study of Two Delinquency Areas, Weidenfeld & Nicolson, 1969; The Roots of Identity: Three National Movements in Contemporary European Politics, Allen Lane, 1974. Contributor to magazines and newspapers.

WORK IN PROGRESS: Continuing sociological research.

SIDELIGHTS: Patricia Mayo commented: "My career was upset when I followed my husband to France in 1950. I chose the marriage over the work, hence, the rather sporadic types of activity since then. Recently my fields have been the structure of government as it is related to the solution of regional problems, particularly the regional movement in Europe and elsewhere, and the growth of separatist movements."

*   *   *

MAYTHAM, Thomas N(orthrup)   1931-

PERSONAL: Born July 30, 1931, in Buffalo, N.Y.; son of Thomas Edward and Lorana Margaret (Northrup) Maytham; children: Gifford. Education: Williams College, B.A., 1954; Yale University, M.A., 1956. Home: 211 Ivanhoe St., Denver, Colo. 80220. Office: Denver Art Museum, 100 West 14th Avenue Parkway, Denver, Colo. 80204.

CAREER: Wadsworth Atheneum, Hartford, Conn., museum assistant, summer, 1955; Museum of Fine Arts, Boston, Mass., assistant in department of painting, 1956-57, head of department, 1957-67, assistant curator of paintings, 1967; Seattle Art Museum, Seattle, Wash., 1967-74, began as associate director, became acting director; Denver Art Museum, Denver, Colo., director, 1974—. Lecturer; juror of national and regional art exhibits. Member of National Endowment for the Arts museum advisory council; member of board of directors of Colorado Celebration for the Arts; member of agency council of United Arts Council; past member of airport art advisory committee of Port of Seattle. Member: International Council of Museums, American Federation of Arts (member of board of trustees, 1977), Association of Art Museum Directors, American Association of Museums.

WRITINGS: *Henri Labrouste, Architect: A Bibliography,* American Association of Architectural Bibliographers, 1955; *Great American Paintings From the Boston and Metropolitan Museums,* Seattle Art Museum, 1970; (author of foreword) *Vance Kirkland: Fifty Years,* Denver Art Museum, 1978. Also editor of *American Painting in the Boston Museum,* two volumes, 1968. Writer for National Educational Television. Contributor to magazines, including *Boston Museum Bulletin, Antiques,* and *Canadian Art.**

*   *   *

MAZOW, Julia Wolf 1937-

PERSONAL: Born May 21, 1937, in Houston, Tex.; daughter of Harry Arthur (a certified public accountant) and Joyce (Dannenbaum) Wolf; married Jack Bernard Mazow (a physician), March 12, 1961; children: Claire, Leo, Joshua. *Education:* Brandeis University, B.A., 1959; University of Houston, M.A., 1969, Ph.D., 1974. *Politics:* Liberal Democrat. *Religion:* Jewish. *Residence:* Houston, Tex. *Office:* The Word Department, P.O. Box 6762, Houston, Tex. 77005.

CAREER: University of Houston, Houston, Tex., instructor in English, 1974-77; The Word Department, Houston, co-owner, 1978—. Houston Community College, Houston, instructor in English, 1976. Member of board of directors of American Jewish Committee and Neighborhood Centers-Day Care Association; community adviser for Women's Caucus for Art. *Member:* International Association of Business Communicators, South Central Women's Studies Association. *Awards, honors:* Award of merit for interpretive writing from International Association of Business Communicators, 1980, for "Where's the Cat; or the Trials of Being Transferred."

WRITINGS: (Editor) *The Woman Who Lost Her Names: Selected Writings of American Jewish Women,* Harper, 1980. Contributor to corporate publications.

WORK IN PROGRESS: A study of women and failure.

SIDELIGHTS: Mazow told *CA:* "I hope that the selections in *The Woman Who Lost Her Names* will put to rest—once and for all—the negative stereotypes of Jewish women that have been perpetrated primarily by American Jewish male writers. We need to look at the picture that emerges when Jewish women write about themselves, other women, and their relationships. In both my research and personal experience I have found that there are no stereotypes and there is no single vision.

"Although I suppose that role models have a function, I have learned more from women who have not achieved what they wanted; I have been drawn to their stories of how they lived their lives *after* they 'failed' at a certain task. My current work on women and the ways they think about failure is leading me, I think, to conclude that failure is a great motivator."

BIOGRAPHICAL/CRITICAL SOURCES: *Houston Chronicle,* March 23, 1980; *Houston Post,* April 29, 1980; *Jewish Exponent,* June 13, 1980; *New Mexican,* July 17, 1980; *Philadelphia Inquirer,* August 17, 1980; *Arlington Daily News,* October 15, 1980.

McBEE, Mary Louise 1924-

PERSONAL: Born June 15, 1924, in Strawberry Plains, Tenn. *Education:* East Tennessee State University, B.S., 1946; Columbia University, M.A., 1951; Ohio State University, Ph.D., 1961. *Office:* Department of Psychology, University of Georgia, Athens, Ga. 30601.

CAREER: Worked as high school geography teacher, 1946-47; East Tennessee State University, Johnson City, instructor in physical education, 1947-50, assistant dean of women, 1951-56 and 1957-59, dean of women, 1961-63; University of Georgia, Athens, associate professor of psychology, 1963—, dean of women, 1963-69, associate dean of students, 1970-74, dean of student affairs, 1974—. English teacher at girls' school in Rotterdam, Netherlands, 1956-57; professor and dean of women for Chapman College's World Campus Afloat, 1967. Chairman of education committee of Georgia governor's Commission on the Status of Women, 1963—. *Member:* American Psychological Association, National Association of Women Deans and Counselors, Georgia Association of Women Deans and Counselors (president, 1969-71), Phi Kappa Phi. *Awards, honors:* Fulbright grant for the Netherlands, 1956-57.

WRITINGS: (Editor with Kathryn A. Blake) *The American Woman: Who Will She Be?,* Glencoe, 1974; (editor with Blake) *Essays,* Glencoe, 1978. Contributor to education journals.*

*   *   *

McCANN, Kevin 1904-1981

OBITUARY NOTICE: Born October 12, 1904, in County Tyrone, Ireland; died February 21, 1981, in Phoenix, Ariz. Administrator, speech writer, and author. McCann was President Eisenhower's chief speech writer and the author of *Man From Abilene,* a biography of Eisenhower published in 1952. His long association with the general began in 1946, when Eisenhower was named Army chief of staff at the Pentagon, and continued until Eisenhower's death in 1969. McCann also served as president of Defiance College from 1951 to 1964. Obituaries and other sources: *Who's Who in American Law,* 2nd edition, Marquis, 1979; *New York Times,* February 24, 1981.

*   *   *

McCARRICK, Earlean M. 1930-

PERSONAL: Born September 25, 1930, in New Orleans, La.; daughter of James William (a railroad worker and farmer) and Earlean Alice (Cure) McCarrick. *Education:* Louisiana State University, B.A., 1954, M.A., 1955; Vanderbilt University, Ph.D., 1964. *Home:* 1507 Crest Rd., Silver Spring, Md. 20902. *Office:* Department of Government and Politics, University of Maryland, College Park, Md. 20942.

CAREER: Texas Technological Institute, Lubbock, instructor in government, 1958-59; Louisiana State University, Baton Rouge, instructor in government, 1959-60; University of New Orleans—Lakefront, New Orleans, La., assistant professor of government, 1960-66; University of Maryland, College Park, assistant professor of government and politics, 1966—.

WRITINGS: (Editor) *United States Constitution: A Guide to Information Sources,* Gale, 1980. Contributor to *Polity* and *Journal of Public Law.*

WORK IN PROGRESS: The Constitutional Status of Federalism in the 1980's; The Constitutional Power of Congress to Resolve Competing Rights.

*   *   *

McCARRY, Charles   1930-

PERSONAL: Born June 14, 1930, in Pittsfield, Mass. Agent: Owen Laster, William Morris Agency, 1350 Avenue of the Americas, New York, N.Y. 10019.

CAREER: Lisbon Evening Journal, Lisbon, Ohio, editor and reporter, 1952-55; Youngstown Vindicator, Youngstown, Ohio, reporter and columnist, 1955-56; assistant to Secretary of Labor in Washington, D.C., 1956-57; worked for Central Intelligence Agency, Washington, D.C., 1958-67; free-lance writer, 1967—.

WRITINGS—Nonfiction: Citizen Nader (biography), Saturday Review Press, 1972; (with Ben Abruzzo, Maxie Anderson, and Larry Newman) Double Eagle, Little, Brown, 1979; (co-author) Isles of the Caribbean, National Geographic Society, 1979; The Great Southwest, National Geographic Society, 1980.

Novels: The Miernik Dossier, Saturday Review Press, 1973; The Tears of Autumn, Saturday Review Press, 1974; The Secret Lovers, Dutton, 1977; The Better Angels, Dutton, 1979.

Contributor of about one hundred stories and articles to magazines, including Saturday Evening Post, Life, National Geographic, Esquire, Saturday Review, and True.

WORK IN PROGRESS: A novel; a screenplay; magazine writing.

*   *   *

McCARTHY, Paul Eugene   1921-

PERSONAL: Born April 18, 1921, in Des Moines, Iowa; married, 1948; children: five. Education: University of Iowa, B.A., 1948, M.F.A., 1951; University of Texas, Ph.D., 1962. Home: 1621 Browning Ave., Manhattan, Kan. 66502. Office: Department of English, Kansas State University, Manhattan, Kan. 66506.

CAREER: Iowa State University, Ames, instructor in English, 1951-53; University of Texas, Austin, instructor in English, 1956-58; University of Idaho, Moscow, instructor in English, 1958-60; University of North Dakota, Grand Forks, instructor in English, 1960-62; University of Alabama, 1962-67, began as assistant professor, became associate professor of English; Kansas State University, Manhattan, associate professor, 1967-75, professor of English, 1975—. Member: Modern Language Association of America, Melville Society of America, John Steinbeck Society.

WRITINGS: (Editor) Long Fiction of the American Renaissance: A Symposium on Genre, Transcendental, 1974; John Steinbeck, Ungar, 1979. Contributor to literature journals.*

*   *   *

McCLELLAND, Vincent Alan   1933-

PERSONAL: Born March 3, 1933, in Clitheroe, England; son of Robert and Elizabeth (Walsh) McClelland; married Maria Goretti O'Callaghan (a teacher), July 8, 1972; children: Alkelda Marianne Elizabeth. Education: University of Sheffield, B.A., 1954, M.A., 1955, Diploma in Education, 1956, Ph.D., 1968; University of Birmingham, M.A., 1958. Religion: Roman Catholic. Office: Institute of Education, University of Hull, Hull, England.

CAREER: Teacher at public schools in Spinkhill, England, 1958-59, and Oldham, England, 1959-62; Mount Pleasant College of Education, Liverpool, England, lecturer in English and history, 1962-64; University of Liverpool, Liverpool, lecturer in education, 1964-69; National University of Ireland, Cork, professor of education, 1969-77; University of Hull, Hull, England, professor of educational studies and director of Institute of Education, 1978—. Governor of Hull College of Higher Education, Hull College of Further Education, and Scarborough College; member of Humberside Regional Consortium for Further Education.

MEMBER: Royal Society of Arts (fellow), National Foundation for Educational Research, Universities Council for the Education of Teachers, History of Education Society, Catholic Record Society, Latin Mass Society, North West Catholic History Society, Challoner Club.

WRITINGS: Cardinal Manning: His Public Life and Influence, 1865-92, Oxford University Press, 1962; English Roman Catholics and Higher Education, 1830-1903, Oxford University Press, 1973; (contributor) John Cumming and Paul Burns, editors, The Church Now, Gill & Macmillan, 1980. Contributor to New Catholic Encyclopedia. Contributor of articles and reviews to history and education journals and newspapers.

WORK IN PROGRESS: An Anglican Life of Cardinal Manning, with Alphonse Chapeau, publication expected in 1982 or 1983.

SIDELIGHTS: McClelland told CA: "Cardinal Manning's reputation in the Roman Catholic church has been overshadowed by that of John Henry Newman. This is unfortunate because, as is becoming increasingly recognized, Manning's work is social and educational reform was of major and permanent importance. A good deal of my work has been concerned with illustrating this importance within the context of nineteenth-century religious policy."

*   *   *

McCLENNEN, Sandra Elaine   1942-

PERSONAL: Born October 28, 1942, in Huntington, W.Va.; daughter of Sol S. and Doris R. (Weintraub) Swiss; married Douglas McClennen (a psychotherapist), August 20, 1966; children: Michael Joshua, Marjorie Ann. Education: University of Michigan, B.S., 1963, M.A. (education), 1965, M.A. (psychology), 1970, Ph.D., 1973. Religion: "Humanistic Judaism." Home: 619 North Sheldon Rd., Plymouth, Mich. 48170. Office: Department of Special Education, Eastern Michigan University, 236 Rackham, Ypsilanti, Mich. 48197.

CAREER: Plymouth Center for Human Development, Northville, Mich., teacher, 1963-66, mental retardation program director, 1966-70; psychologist at elementary schools in Dearborn, Mich., summer, 1970; Eastern Michigan University, Ypsilanti, lecturer, 1970-71, instructor, 1971-73, assistant professor, 1973-80, associate professor of special education, 1980—. Licensed psychologist; court-appointed monitor at Plymouth Center for Human Development, 1978-79. Presenter of workshops. Member of board of directors of Community Opportunity Center Non-Profit Housing, Inc., 1973—.

MEMBER: American Association on Mental Deficiency (state vice-president for psychology, 1976-79; regional vice-president for psychology, 1980-83), American Educational Research Association, American Psychological Association, Association for Behavior Analysis, Association for the Severely Handicapped, Association for Supervision and Curriculum Development, American Civil Liberties Union, League of Women Voters, Association for Retarded Citizens/ Michigan (member of board of directors, 1975—; member of executive board, 1978—; chairperson of education committee, 1979—), Phi Kappa Phi. *Awards, honors:* Named educator of the year by Northwest Communities Association for Retarded Citizens and Association for Retarded Citizens/ Michigan, 1976.

WRITINGS: (With Ronald Hockstra and James Bryan) *Social Skills for Severely Retarded Adults,* Research Press, 1980. Contributor to special education journals.

WORK IN PROGRESS: Developing a functional curriculum in basic arithmetic skills for severely retarded adolescents and adults; research on developmental drama with developmentally disabled adults.

SIDELIGHTS: Sandra McClennen commented: "For as long as I can remember, a major concern of mine has been that persons with handicaps, both physical and mental, not be treated as second-class citizens.

"In 1978 I was one of five monitors appointed by U.S. District Judge Charles Joiner to the Plymouth Center for Human Development. It was our responsibility to spend up to twenty hours per week each, working in pairs, on the living units at Plymouth Center, and to present monthly reports to him of our observations. Having worked in this institution for seven years, but many years prior to the legal action taken against the center, I began to look at institutionalization in a different way, as often happens when one is an onlooker rather than a part of the system. I now recognize that professionals created institutions for handicapped people, and that these institutions have been accepted by both professionals and society for decades. Today, both humane and legal concerns about the rights of people, including those who are handicapped, are making us question institutions as appropriate living situations. People who are handicapped have the same right as the rest of us to live in a home in a community and to be a part of the mainstream of life.

"I became involved in developmental drama because I believe in the value of play—for the quality of pleasure it brings and for the learning it fosters. I also believe that people who are retarded should have the same opportunities for quality of life, for development, which we all cherish. Developmental drama takes place in a playful, no-audience, noncompetitive, no-right-or-wrong atmosphere in which the leaders are also participants in the play community. Sense awareness, sense memory, observation, free association, hypothetical suggestions, and dramatic involvement all provide opportunities for development. The heart of the creative process, transformation, which allows the individual to combine ideas in an unusual or fresh way for her/himself, is encouraged by emphasizing aspects of play which stimulate spontaneous and intuitive responses."

                    *   *   *

McCLOY, James F(loyd)   1941-

PERSONAL: Born February 13, 1941, in Collingswood, N.J.; son of Charles Dunham (a credit manager) and Evelyn (Floyd) McCloy; married Virginia Stap (a teacher and vice-principal), August 21, 1965; children: Karen, David. *Education:* Glassboro State College, B.A., 1964, M.A., 1967. *Home:* 402 Rosewood Dr., Newark, Del. 19713.

CAREER: Teacher at public schools in Magnolia, N.J., 1964-65, and Edgewater Park, N.J., 1966-68; Wilmington College, New Castle, Del., assistant professor of history, 1968-74;

Delaware Department of Labor, Newark, interviewer, 1975—. Part-time assistant professor at Wilmington College, 1976—; member of New Jersey folklife advisory council of New Jersey Historical Commission. *Member:* New Jersey Folklore Society.

WRITINGS: (With Ray Miller, Jr.) *The Jersey Devil,* Middle Atlantic Press, 1976; *Dogs at Work* (juvenile), Crown, 1979; *Delaware Periodical Library,* Wilmington College Library, 1981. Contributor of more than a hundred articles to history and education journals.

WORK IN PROGRESS: A sequel to *The Jersey Devil,* publication by Middle Atlantic Press expected in 1982.

SIDELIGHTS: McCloy wrote: "*The Jersey Devil* is about a legendary creature that dates back at least to 1735. The story of the legend, once confined mostly to New Jersey, is now becoming nationally known as interest in monsters and the supernatural is increasing.

"*Dogs at Work* is an illustrated children's book that describes eleven breeds of dogs that have worked for people in the past and that continue to work for people in different but equally important ways today. I find research as challenging and stimulating as writing."

                    *   *   *

McCLURE, Gillian Mary   1948-

PERSONAL: Born October 29, 1948, in Bradford, England; daughter of Paul Curtis (a poet) and Jean Mary (a music teacher; maiden name, Parker) Coltman; married Ian Patrick McClure (a picture restorer), September 26, 1970; children: Calum Hugh, Brendan Paul. *Education:* Received degree with honors from University of Bristol, 1970. *Home and office:* 40 Buchanan St., Balfron, Glasgow G63 0TR, Scotland. *Agent:* Curtis Brown Ltd., 1 Craven Hill, London W2 3EP, England.

CAREER: Writer and illustrator of children's books, 1970—. Infant and nursery teacher at schools in Midlothian, Scotland and Glasgow, Scotland, 1971-74.

WRITINGS—Self-illustrated children's books: *The Emperor's Singing Bird,* Deutsch, 1974; *Prickly Pig,* Deutsch, 1976, Dutton, 1980; *Fly Home McDoo,* Dutton, 1979; *What's the Time Rory Wolf?,* Deutsch, 1982.

WORK IN PROGRESS: *Teddy Bear's Picnic* and *Norrie the Knee-Creeper, the Deep Freezer Thief,* both for children.

SIDELIGHTS: Gillian McClure wrote: "I find many children's picture books on the market today too sophisticated; they are books for adults posing as children's books. When I am writing and illustrating a book I like to try it out on children, either my own or groups of children in libraries and schools. Very often they contribute ideas. I have also made puppets and masks of all the characters in my books for the children to use.

"Being a writer and illustrator, it is hard to distinguish whether my books start from a visual or a literary idea, for the text and illustrations tend to be closely integrated. Although I am not short of new ideas for books, I take a long time to execute them and do a lot of reworking. I have been working on my current book on and off for two years."

BIOGRAPHICAL/CRITICAL SOURCES: Scottish Field, September, 1974; *Stirling Observer,* October 12, 1979; *Glasgow Evening Times,* Scotland, October 26, 1979.

McCORMICK, E(ric) H(all) 1906-

PERSONAL: Born June 17, 1906, in Taihape, New Zealand; son of William J. (a shopkeeper) and Ellen (a dressmaker; maiden name, Powrie) McCormick. *Education:* Victoria University of Wellington, M.A., 1928; Clare College, Cambridge, M.Litt., 1935; University of New Zealand, D.Litt., 1962. *Politics:* "Radical." *Religion:* None. *Home:* 30 Harrybrook Rd., Green Bay, Auckland 7, New Zealand. *Office:* Department of History, University of Auckland, Auckland, New Zealand.

CAREER: Country school teacher in Nelson, New Zealand, 1926-29; Hocken Library, Dunedin, New Zealand, librarian, 1935-36; National Historic Committee, Wellington, New Zealand, secretary and assistant dominion archivist, 1936-38, editor of centennial publications, 1939-40; University of Auckland, Auckland, New Zealand, senior lecturer in arts, 1947-51; free-lance writer, editor, and researcher, 1951-73; University of Auckland, research fellow in arts, 1973—. *Military service:* New Zealand Army, Expeditionary Force, 1941-45; served in the Middle East and Italy; became captain. *Member:* International P.E.N. (president of honor of New Zealand Centre, 1976-77). *Awards, honors:* Hubert Church Award from New Zealand Literary Fund, 1955, for *The Expatriate*.

WRITINGS: Letters and Art in New Zealand, Department of Internal Affairs, 1940; *The Expatriate* (nonfiction), New Zealand University Press, 1954; *Work of Frances Hodgkins,* Auckland City Art Gallery, 1954; *Eric Lee-Johnson,* Paul's Book Arcade, 1956; *New Zealand Literature,* Oxford University Press, 1959; *Tasman and New Zealand,* Government Printer, 1959; *The Inland Eye,* Auckland Gallery Associates, 1959.

The Fascinating Folly, University of Otago Press, 1961; *Alexander Turnbull,* Alexander Turnbull Library, 1974; *Omai, Pacific Envoy,* Auckland University Press, 1978; *Portrait of Frances Hodkins,* Auckland University Press, 1981; *Charles and Carlino,* Auckland University Press, 1982.

Editor: *Making New Zealand,* Department of Internal Affairs, 1941; Edward Markham, *New Zealand; or, Recollections of It,* Government Printer, 1963; Augustus Earle, *Narrative of a Residence in New Zealand,* Clarendon Press, 1966.

Contributor to magazines, including *Islands, Landfall, Art New Zealand,* and *Southerly.*

SIDELIGHTS: McCormick wrote: "As I look back on a long and erratic career, I recognize that my ambition was always to be a writer. After several false starts I discovered a vocation as critic of literature and art, but have since found myself more at home in the disciplines of history and biography. If my work has one general theme, it is the study, in all its implications, of what it means to be a New Zealander. The subject is by no means exhausted, and in recent years has been enlarged to embrace the South Pacific and its Polynesian people."

BIOGRAPHICAL/CRITICAL SOURCES: Colin MacInnes, *Australia and New Zealand,* Time Inc., 1964; *Islands,* May, 1978.

*   *   *

McCOURT, Edward (Alexander) 1907-1972

OBITUARY NOTICE—See index for *CA* sketch: Born October 10, 1907, in Mullingar, Ireland; died January 6, 1972, in Saskatoon, Saskatchewan. Educator and author. McCourt was best known for his novels, which demonstrate the influence of the Canadian prairie environment on character. In 1947 McCourt was the recipient of the Ryerson Award and won the All Canada Fiction Award for his novel *Music at the Close.* Among his other books are *The Flaming Hour, Home Is the Stranger, Walk Through the Valley,* and *The Yukon and Northwest Territories.* At the time of his death, McCourt was professor of English at the University of Saskatchewan. Obituaries and other sources: *The Macmillan Dictionary of Canadian Biography,* 4th edition, Macmillan, 1978.

*   *   *

McCRAW, Louise Harrison 1893-1975

OBITUARY NOTICE—See index for *CA* sketch: Born in 1893; died January 26, 1975. Secretary, free-lance writer, and author. Among McCraw's books are *Hearts That Understood, On Wings of Morning, My Heart's at Liberty,* and *It Shall Be Forever.* (Date of death provided by Gladys W. Billings, corresponding secretary of Braille Circulating Library, Richmond, Va.)

*   *   *

McCULLY, Ethel Walbridge 1896-1980

OBITUARY NOTICE: Born May 13, 1896, in New York, N.Y.; died December 21, 1980, on St. John, Virgin Islands. Author. In 1947, when the captain of her Caribbean cruise ship refused to dock at St. John Island, McCully went over the side with a basketful of belongings and swam ashore. She bought four acres on the island, designed her dream house, and spent eleven years building her home, "Island Fancy," despite her difficulties with workmen, suppliers, and boat captains. When Congress authorized expansion of the Virgin Islands National Park in 1962, the National Park Service threatened to condemn and confiscate McCully's property and that of other islanders. McCully, however, went to Washington to "raise a little hell," won national attention for her cause, and successfully lobbied against the Park Service plan. Although she eventually sold her home to the Park Service, she was given life tenancy in "Island Fancy." She was the author of *Grandma Raised the Roof,* describing her struggle to build "Island Fancy," and mystery novels, including *Death Rides Tandem, Doctors, Beware!,* and *Blood on Nassau's Moon.* Obituaries and other sources: *Who's Who of American Women,* 2nd edition, Marquis, 1961; *New York Times,* January 4, 1981.

*   *   *

McCUTCHEON, James
See LUNDGREN, Paul Arthur

*   *   *

McDOWELL, John (Henry) 1942-

PERSONAL: Born in 1942, in England; son of Henry McLorian (a civil servant) and Norah (a teacher; maiden name, Douthwaite) McDowell; married Andrea Lee Lehrke, June 16, 1977. *Education:* University College of Rhodesia and Nyasaland (now University of Zimbabwe), B.A., 1962; New College, Oxford, B.A., 1965, M.A., 1969. *Home:* 17 Merton St., Oxford, England. *Office:* University College, Oxford University, Oxford, England.

CAREER: Oxford University, Oxford, England, fellow and praelector at University College, 1966—, lecturer in philosophy, 1967—. James C. Loeb fellow at Harvard University, 1969; visiting professor at University of Michigan, 1975.

WRITINGS: (Translator) Plato, *Theaetetus,* Clarendon Press, 1973; (editor with Gareth Evans) *Truth and Meaning,* Clarendon Press, 1976. Contributor to philosophy journals.

WORK IN PROGRESS: "Research on Greek philosophy (especially ethics), philosophy of language (especially its boundaries with philosophy of mind and metaphysics), and ethics (especially the related issues in philosophy of mind and metaphysics)."

* * *

McDOWELL, Robert Emmett   1914-1975

OBITUARY NOTICE—See index for *CA* sketch: Born April 5, 1914, in Sentinal, Okla.; died March 29, 1975. McDowell's works include *Switcheroo, City of Conflict, The Hound's Tooth,* and *Rediscovering Kentucky: A Guide for Modern-Day Explorers.* (Date of death provided by agent, Paul R. Reynolds, Inc.)

* * *

McELDOWNEY, (Richard) Dennis   1926-

PERSONAL: Born January 29, 1926, in Wanganui, New Zealand; son of Arthur Joseph (a social worker) and Margery (Chambers) McEldowney; married Zoe Greenhough, December 2, 1967. *Education:* Attended primary schools in Christchurch, New Zealand. *Home:* 54a Challenger St., St. Heliers, Auckland, New Zealand. *Office:* Auckland University Press, University of Auckland, Private Bag, Auckland, New Zealand.

CAREER: Free-lance writer, 1945-63; School of Physical Education, Dunedin, New Zealand, assistant typist, 1963-66; Auckland University Press, Auckland, New Zealand, editor, 1966-72, managing editor, 1972—. Librarian at Knox College; member of Church and Society Commission of New Zealand National Council of Churches, 1969-79. *Member:* International P.E.N. *Awards, honors:* Hubert Church Memorial Prize from New Zealand Centre of International P.E.N., 1957, for *The World Regained.*

WRITINGS: The World Regained, Beacon Press, 1957, 2nd edition, John McIndoe, 1976; *Donald Anderson: A Memoir,* Blackwood & Janet Paul, 1966; (editor) Sygurd Wisniowski, *Tikera,* Auckland University Press, 1972; *Arguing With My Grandmother* (nonfiction), John McIndoe, 1973; *Frank Sargeson in His Time,* John McIndoe, 1976.

Work represented in anthologies, including *New Zealand Short Stories,* edited by Dan Davin, Oxford University Press, 1953; *Critical Essays on the New Zealand Novel,* edited by Cherry Hankin, Heinemann Educational, 1976; *The Seventies Connection,* edited by David Hill and Elizabeth Smither, John McIndoe, 1980. Author of "To My Way of Thinking," a column in *Outlook.* Contributor of stories and articles to journals, including *Islands, Landfall,* and *New Zealand Listener.*

SIDELIGHTS: McEldowney commented: "I was born with a heart condition that progressively restricted activity until it was relieved by surgery at the age of twenty-four. This experience and the world as it appeared to one who emerged into it as an adult was the subject of my first book. A sense of celebration plus a delight in the manipulation of words (in prose form only) has, I think, informed most of my writing since; my special interest has come to be biography. Since further surgery in 1961 pitched me more fully into everyday life and the need to earn a living, my own writing has come

second-best to midwifery for other writers, which I enjoy and do not complain about."

BIOGRAPHICAL/CRITICAL SOURCES: Maurice Shadbolt, *Love and Legend,* Hodder & Stoughton, 1976.

* * *

McFATE, Patricia Ann   1932-

PERSONAL: Born in 1932, in Detroit, Mich. *Education:* Michigan State University, B.A., 1954; Northwestern University, M.A., 1958, Ph.D., 1965. *Office:* Office of the Vice-Provost, University of Pennsylvania, 106 College Hall, Philadelphia, Pa. 19104.

CAREER: Columbia University, New York City, staff psychologist at School of Engineering and Applied Science, 1960-62; City College of the City University of New York, New York City, lecturer in English, 1962; University of Illinois at Chicago Circle, Chicago, instructor in humanities, 1962-64; Columbia University, member of staff at physiology research laboratory, 1964; University of Illinois at Chicago Circle, assistant professor and associate professor of English, 1965-75, assistant dean of liberal arts and science, 1967-73, associate vice-chancellor for academic affairs and executive assistant to chancellor, 1974-75; University of Pennsylvania, Philadelphia, associate professor of folklore and English, 1975—, professor of technology and sociology, 1975—, vice-provost, 1975—. Member of board of directors of Bishop Anderson House Foundation, 1971; member of attending scientific staff in hematology at Rush-Presbyterian-St. Luke's Medical Center, 1973—. Visiting associate professor at Rush University, 1974—. Member of board of directors of Philadelphia National Bank, 1976—, Pennsylvania Ballet, 1977—, and Associated Dry Goods Corp., 1978—; member of humanities committee of WHYY-TV, 1976—; member of board of trustees of Institute for Cancer Research, Fox Chase Cancer Center, 1977—, and United Way of Southeastern Pennsylvania, 1977-80. *Member:* International Association for Anglo-Irish Studies, Modern Language Association of America, American Association for the Advancement of Science, American Committee for Irish Studies, New York Academy of Sciences.

WRITINGS: The Writings of James Stephens: Variations on a Theme of Love, St. Martin's, 1979. Contributor to *Toward the Modern: Portents of the Movement, 1880-1920,* Southern Illinois Press, 1972. Contributor to literature and Irish studies journals.

BIOGRAPHICAL/CRITICAL SOURCES: Economist, February 24, 1979.*

* * *

McFEAT, Tom Farrar Scott   1919-

PERSONAL: Born February 5, 1919, in Montreal, Quebec, Canada; married, 1947; children: two. *Education:* McGill University, B.A., 1950; Harvard University, A.M., 1954, Ph.D., 1957. *Office:* Department of Anthropology, University of Toronto, 1000 St. George St., Toronto, Ontario, Canada M5S 1A3.

CAREER: University of New Brunswick, Fredericton, associate professor of anthropology, 1954-59; National Museum of Canada, Ottawa, Ontario, senior ethnologist, 1959-63; Carleton University, Ottawa, senior ethnologist, 1963-64; University of Toronto, Toronto, Ontario, professor of anthropology, 1964—, chairman of department, 1964-74. *Military service:* Canadian Army, 1940-45. *Member:* Canadian

Political Science Association, American Anthropological Association (fellow).

WRITINGS: Museum Ethnology and the Algonkian Project, Department of Northern Affairs and National Resources (Ottawa, Ontario), 1962; (editor and author of introduction) *Indians of the North Pacific Coast: Studies in Selected Topics,* McClelland & Stewart, 1966, University of Washington Press, 1967; *Small-Group Cultures,* Pergamon, 1974. Contributor to anthropology journals.*

*   *   *

McFERRAN, Ann
   See TOWNSEND, Doris McFerran

*   *   *

McFERRAN, Doris
   See TOWNSEND, Doris McFerran

*   *   *

McGLYNN, James V(incent)   1919-1973

OBITUARY NOTICE—See index for *CA* sketch: Born July 20, 1919, in Cleveland, Ohio; died August 3, 1973. Clergyman, educator, translator, and author. A Jesuit priest, McGlynn was a teacher and administrator at the University of Detroit for fifteen years, serving as vice-president and dean of faculties from 1970 to 1971. He wrote *A Metaphysics of Being and God* and was co-author of *Modern Ethical Theories.* McGlynn also translated Thomas Aquinas's *Truth.* (Date of death provided by Marioara Maneca, administrative supervisor of the graduate school of University of Detroit.)

*   *   *

McGRADY, Patrick Michael, Sr.   1908-1980

PERSONAL: Born January 15, 1908, in Anaconda, Mont.; died of cancer March 2, 1980, in Lansing, Mich.; married, 1931; children: three sons (including Patrick Michael, Jr.). *Education:* Attended University of Washington, Seattle, 1924-26, 1929-30, and New York University, 1927-28.

CAREER: North China Daily News, Shanghai, staff writer and editor, 1930-31; *China Press,* staff writer and editor, 1931-32; foreign correspondent for U.S. newspapers and a Jewish agency in Europe, 1933-34; Associated Press, New York City, staff writer and editor, 1934-42; Farm Security Administration, Pennsylvania, regional information director, 1942-47; American Cancer Society, New York City, science editor, 1947-68; free-lance writer and consultant, 1968-80. Chairman of Associated Press unit of American Newspaper Guild, 1938-39; member of awards committee of American Institute of Physics, 1968, 1970, 1971, and board of directors of Biological Research Institute, Inc., 1972-80; founder of Scientist Writers Seminar, 1960; consultant to Research to Prevent Blindness, Inc. *Military service:* U.S. Marine Corps Reserve, active duty in air combat intelligence, 1944-46; served in the South Pacific; became first lieutenant. *Awards, honors:* Fulbright fellowship for France and western Europe, 1950-51; D.Sc. from University of Portland, 1967; *The Savage Cell* was named outstanding book by American Library Association.

WRITINGS: The Savage Cell: A Report on Cancer and Cancer Research, Basic Books, 1964; *The Persecuted Drug: The Story of DMSO,* Doubleday, 1973, revised edition published as *DMSO: The Persecuted Drug,* Charter Books, 1979; (with Nathan Pritikin) *The Pritikin Program for Diet and Exercise,* Grosset, 1979. Author of consumer information pamphlets

for New York Public Affairs Committee, including "Cigarettes and Health," "Cigarettes Equal Lung Cancer?," "Science Against Cancer," and "Leukemia: Key to the Cancer Puzzle?" Editor of quarterly newsletter of National Association of Science Writers, 1958-64.

SIDELIGHTS: Since the 1940's McGrady was critical of the Federal Drug Administration for its interference with public access to such controversial drugs as DMSO. He was a founder and director of the American Tentative Society, established as a force against scientific orthodoxy. When he contracted cancer himself, McGrady and his son Pat (also a writer) left the United States to try alternative treatments not available at home; he succumbed to the disease at the age of seventy-two.

BIOGRAPHICAL/CRITICAL SOURCES: New York Times, March 3, 1980; *Chicago Tribune,* March 4, 1980; *Washington Post,* March 4, 1980.*

*   *   *

McGRATH, William Thomas   1917-

PERSONAL: Born October 12, 1917, in Pointe du Chene, New Brunswick, Canada; son of William Thomas (a laborer) and Maude (Tucker) McGrath; married Flora MacDonald Wilkie (a watercolor artist), June 14, 1946; children: Patricia McGrath Feasey, Maude McGrath Barlow, Christine McGrath Jefferson. *Education:* Mount Allison University, B.A., 1941; University of Toronto, M.S.W., 1948. *Politics:* "No." *Religion:* "No." *Office:* Canadian Association for the Prevention of Crime, 55 Parkdale Ave., Ottawa, Ontario, Canada K1Y 1E5.

CAREER: Regional supervisor of Department of Public Welfare in Nova Scotia, 1948-51; secretary of Delinquency and Crime Division, and associate secretary of Public Welfare Division for Canadian Welfare Council, 1951-52; Canadian Association for the Prevention of Crime, Ottawa, Ontario, executive director, 1952—. Chairman of board of consultants at University of Ottawa's Centre of Criminology, 1968—. Member of Canadian Committee on Corrections, 1965-69; member of research advisory board of Ministry of Health and Welfare's welfare grants program, 1966-71, and advisory board of advisory committee on delinquent and socially maladjusted children and young people, International Union for Child Welfare; member of Working Group on Maximum Security Penitentiaries, of Ministry of the Solicitor General, 1971, member of assistance group on minimum security accomodation and strategic planning committee, both 1979; member of Task Force on the Role of Communications in the Canadian Corrections Service, 1978; consultant to Royal Commission on the Status of Women. *Military service:* Canadian Army, Infantry, 1941-45; served in England and Europe; became captain.

MEMBER: International Society of Criminology (national representative for Canada, 1965—), American Correctional Association (member of board of directors). *Awards, honors:* Named John Howard Man of the Year by John Howard Society of Ontario, 1971; J. Alex Edmison Award from Canadian Association of Professional Criminologists, 1979.

WRITINGS: Should Canada Abolish the Gallows and Lash?, Stovel-Advocate Press, 1956; *Youth and the Law,* Gage, 1963, 2nd edition, 1973; (contributor) Richard Laskin, editor, *Canadian Social Problems: A Sourcebook of Information and Opinion,* McGraw, 1964; (editor) *Crime and Its Treatment in Canada,* Macmillan, 1965, 2nd edition, 1975; (contributor) C.H.S. Jayewardene, editor, *The Criminal Justice System in Canada,* Department of Criminology, University of Ottawa, 1975; (with A. M. Kirkpatrick) *Crime and You,* Macmillan, 1976; (with M. P. Mitchell) *The Police Function in Canada,* Methuen, 1980. Contributor to *Encyclopedia Canadiana* and *Encyclopaedia Britannica*. Contributor of about forty articles to law and criminology journals, magazines, and newspapers, including *Canadian Forum*.

WORK IN PROGRESS: Revising *Crime and Its Treatment in Canada*.

SIDELIGHTS: McGrath wrote: "I have played down the search for causes of crime as useless. My position is that crime is a normal activity, as normal as breathing. We human beings are by nature aggressive and acquisitive creatures, and it is perfectly natural for us to take what we want without regard to the effect on other people. The interesting question is why some people do *not* commit crime, or at least avoid many kinds of crime."

* * *

McHALE, Philip John 1928-

PERSONAL: Born July 20, 1928, in Birmingham, England; son of Thomas P. (in business) and Lilian (Duggins) McHale; married Joyce Middleton (an opera singer), November 14, 1953; children: Patrick Michael, John Philip, Kerri Marion. *Education:* Teachers Training College, Auckland, New Zealand, Trained Teachers Certificate, 1963; Massey University, diploma in teaching, 1980. *Home:* 8 Buller Grove, Naenae, Lower Hutt, New Zealand. *Office:* New Zealand Technical Correspondence Institute, Wyndrum Ave., Lower Hutt, New Zealand.

CAREER: Parks Department and City Treasurers Department, Birmingham, England, clerk, 1944-46; Empire Box Co. Ltd., Lower Hutt, New Zealand, clerk, 1955-56; National Film Unit, Wellington, New Zealand, assistant producer and scriptwriter, 1956-59, director of motion picture "We Lead the World," 1958; New Zealand Broadcasting System, program organizer of television service in Auckland and Wellington and senior television producer, 1959-61; free-lance writer, 1962; teacher at primary schools in Auckland, New Zealand, 1963-66; special education teacher at secondary school in Auckland, New Zealand, 1966-77; New Zealand Technical Correspondence Institute, Lower Hutt, instructional videotape producer and director, 1978—. Lecturer on writing and filmmaking. Part time staff member at Crescent Theatre, Birmingham. *Military service:* Royal Air Force, photographer with Junior Air Photographic Interpretation Corps, 1946-48. *Member:* Society of Motion Picture and Television Engineers, New Zealand Producers, Writers, and Directors Guild. *Awards, honors:* Top award in documentary film section from Chicago Film Festival, 1959, awards of merit from Brussels Film Festival, 1960, and award of merit from Antwerp Film Festival, 1960, all for directing film, "We Lead the World."

WRITINGS—Published by Playset International, except as noted: *Inside Broadcasting,* School Publications of New Zealand, 1968; *Communications in the Post Office,* School Publications of New Zealand, 1969; *Plays of Total Theatre* (contains "Music on the Waters," "The Vibrating Man," and "Time Off"), 1971 (also see below); *Saint on a Pig's Back* (three-act play; first produced in Auckland, New Zealand, at Northcote College Theatre, 1969), 1971; *The Vibrating Man* (three-act play; first produced in Auckland, at Westbridge Theatre Club, 1971), 1971; *Limbo* (three-act play; first produced in Wellington, New Zealand, at Unity Theatre, 1958), 1971; *Island of Mulabeeka* (three-act play; first produced in Auckland, at Auckland Training College Theatre,

1963), 1971; *No Flowers for the Fool* (three-act play; first produced in Birmingham, England, at Crescent Theatre, 1955), 1972; *Short Stories for Reading Aloud, 1972; More Short Stories for Reading Aloud,* 1976.

Unpublished scripts: "The Ideal Realist" (three-act radio play), first broadcast by BBC-Radio, 1953; "Ballyhoo Castle" (three-act play), first produced in Birmingham, England, at Crescent Theatre, 1957; "The Art of Maori Legend," first broadcast by New Zealand Broadcasting System Television, WNTVI, 1960; "Legend of Birds," a film released by National Film Unit, 1961; "Danger—Men at Work" (three-act play), first broadcast by New Zealand Broadcasting Service Radio, 1961; "The Visitor" (one-act play), first broadcast by New Zealand Broadcasting Service Television, AKTV2, 1961; "No More Limbo" (three-act play), first broadcast by CBC, 1963; "I Miss the 'Orses," first broadcast by New Zealand Broadcasting Service Television, 1963; "Firm Foundation," 1967; "Plough of Peace," a film released by Atlantic Oil Co., 1967; "Time Off" (one-act play), first produced in Auckland, at Northcote College Theatre, 1968; "Prometheus" (one-act play), first produced in Auckland at Grafton Theatre, 1969; "Music on the Waters" (three-act play), first produced in Auckland, at Northcote College Theatre, 1969; "Watch It Daddio" (one-act play), first produced in Auckland at Northcote Theatre Club, 1971.

Short stories have been broadcast in England, Ireland, New Zealand, and Australia. Contributor of about one hundred poems, stories, and articles to education journals, magazines, and newspapers, including *Joy, Short Story International, Catholic Fireside,* and *Public Service Journal*.

WORK IN PROGRESS: Don't Close the Curtain, a novel, completion expected in 1982.

SIDELIGHTS: In 1977 McHale was named New Zealand's chief film censor, a position he did not accept.

He told *CA:* "New Zealand television service appointed me as the first staff member to help launch television in New Zealand. After developing AKTV2 in Auckland in to a full weekly broadcast, I moved to Wellington to plan the first transmission from the Wellington Station. I saw television as an educational and cultural force and when the commercial elements moved in, I realized I had lost the battle. I returned to writing and to education.

"When people regard me as a pioneer of New Zealand television, I think today they should blame me. I believe passionately in what television can be and shudder at what it is.

"Being a writer in New Zealand is very difficult. Even a national success cannot pay for the hours of writing. We become amateurs in order to preserve our professionalism and integrity.

"I believe in the fundamental importance of reason and science in the world of morals, ethics, politics, and human behavior, the obligation of all people to extend the limits of eccentricity to preserve democracy, and the integration of all art with science to achieve precision of observation and accuracy of description."

BIOGRAPHICAL/CRITICAL SOURCES: New Zealand Women's Weekly, October 5, 1970; *New Zealand Herald,* June 11, 1977.

McHUGH, John (Francis)   1927-

PERSONAL: Born August 3, 1927, in Stalybridge, England; son of Joseph (a clerk) and Margaret (Buck) McHugh. *Education:* Gregorian University, Ph.L., 1949, S.T.L., 1953, S.T.D., 1957. *Politics:* "Strictly independent on all issues." *Home address:* Ushaw College, Durham DH7 9RH, England. *Office:* Department of Theology, University of Durham, Abbey House, Palace Green, Durham DH1 3RS, England.

CAREER: Ordained Roman Catholic priest, 1953; Ushaw College, Durham, England, lecturer in biblical studies, 1957-76, director of studies, 1967-72; University of Durham, Durham, lecturer, 1976-78, senior lecturer in theology, 1978—. Honorary canon of Diocese of Shrewsbury, 1981. *Member:* Society for Old Testament Studies, Studiorum Novi Testamenti Societas. *Awards, honors:* Award, 1962, for translation of *Ancient Israel.*

WRITINGS: (Translator) Roland de Vaux, *Ancient Israel: Its Life and Institutions,* Darton, Longman & Todd, 1961; (editor and translator) Xavier Leon-Dufour, *The Gospels and the Jesus of History,* Collins, 1968; (editor) de Vaux, *The Bible and the Ancient Near East,* Darton, Longman & Todd, 1971; *The Mother of Jesus in the New Testament,* Doubleday, 1975; (contributor) John Emerton, Andrew Mackintosh, and David Frost, editors, *The Psalms: A New Translation for Worship,* Collins, 1977.

WORK IN PROGRESS: New edition of *International Critical Commentary on the Gospel According to St. John.*

AVOCATIONAL INTERESTS: Ancient classics, Dante, annual holidays in Germany, Italy, France, or Scandinavia.

*   *   *

McHUGH, Thomas Cannell   1926-
(Tom McHugh)

PERSONAL: Born April 17, 1926, in Cleveland, Ohio; son of Thomas Cartier (a paint manufacturer) and Zella (a teacher; maiden name, Cannell) McHugh. *Education:* Attended Oberlin College, 1944-45, and Miami University, Oxford, Ohio, 1945; University of Wisconsin—Madison, B.A., 1948, M.A., 1950, Ph.D., 1952. *Home:* 8560 Franklin Ave., Los Angeles, Calif. 90069. *Agent:* J. W. Schults, 60 East 56th St., New York, N.Y. 10022. *Office:* Cally Curtis Co., 1111 North Las Palmas, Los Angeles, Calif. 90038.

CAREER: W. Colston Leigh, Inc., New York City, platform lecturer, 1950-52; Walt Disney Productions, Burbank, Calif., field cameraman in Wyoming, Alberta, and western United States and director for "True-Life Adventure Series," 1952-56; Jack Douglas Organizations, Los Angeles, Calif., cameraman, director, and producer, 1957-66; Photo Researchers, Inc., New York City, photographer, 1965—; Cally Curtis Co., Los Angeles, director of photography, 1966—. Cameraman for feature films, including "The Sea Gypsies," Warner Bros., 1977, and "When the North Wind Blows," NBC, 1976. *Military service:* U.S. Navy, 1944-45. *Member:* American Society of Mammalogists, National Buffalo Association. *Awards, honors:* Spur Award from Western Writers of America and Wrangler award from National Cowboy Hall of Fame and Western Heritage Center, both 1972, both for *The Time of the Buffalo.*

WRITINGS—Under name Tom McHugh: *The Time of the Buffalo,* Knopf, 1972; (contributor) Martin W. Schein, editor, *Benchmark Papers in Animal Behavior,* Volume III, Dowden, 1975. Contributor to *Encyclopaedia Britannica.* Con-

tributor of articles and photographs to magazines, including *Zoologica, Natural History, Audubon, Sports Afield, National Geographic, Time,* and *Life.*

WORK IN PROGRESS: Research and photographs for a book on the American bison.

SIDELIGHTS: McHugh told *CA:* "Some reviewers have called my book, *The Time of the Buffalo,* the definitive work on the subject. The book actually had its beginnings in my doctoral thesis, a study of social behavior in buffalo that was later published in the journal *Zoologica.* For the book I expanded my thesis to include not only all aspects of behavior but also the effect of the buffalo on the life of ancient hunters, the Plains Indians, and the American frontier. Photographs of buffalo behavior that I originally made for the thesis eventually led to my being chosen as director of photography for Walt Disney's Academy Award-winning feature, "The Vanishing Prairie." The making of the movie required some unusual filming techniques."

One technique involved McHugh disguising himself as a buffalo. He hid under a buffalo hide in the middle of the herd in order to get close enough to film the animals. McHugh added: "This incident was featured on one program of 'Disney's Wonderful World' and has been re-broadcast several times since. Because of this repeated television exposure, it seems that almost everyone remembers 'the guy who crawled into a buffalo herd under a buffalo hide.' It worked, but I also might add that I am not about to try it again."

BIOGRAPHICAL/CRITICAL SOURCES: Turner Browne and Elaine Partnow, editors, *The Complete Book of Photographers,* Macmillan, 1982.

*   *   *

McHUGH, Tom
See McHUGH, Thomas Cannell

*   *   *

McKINLAY, Brian John   1933-

PERSONAL: Born May 3, 1933, in Geelong, Australia; son of Alan John and Eve (Skene) McKinlay; married Moira Trenery (a secretary), March 1, 1959; children: David, Mark, John. *Education:* Toorak Teachers College, teaching diploma, 1955; LaTrobe University, B.A., 1973, B.Ed., 1980. *Politics:* Socialist—Australian Labour party. *Home:* 2 De Blonay Cres., Greensborough, Victoria 3008, Australia. *Office:* Education Department of Victoria, 234 Queensberry St., Melbourne, Victoria, Australia.

CAREER: Teacher at primary school in Victoria, Australia, 1955-65; technical school teacher of history in Australia, 1965-70; Melbourne Teachers College, Melbourne, Australia, tutor in librarianship, 1970-75; Education Department of Victoria, Melbourne, regional history editor for Corangamite region, 1973—. Broadcaster and current affairs commentator. *Member:* Library Association of Australia, Labor History Society.

WRITINGS: *Primary Mathematics,* Methuen, 1965; *The First Royal Tour,* Rigby, 1970; *Western District Sketchbook,* Rigby, 1971; *Diamond Valley Sketchbook,* Rigby, 1973; *Carlton Sketchbook,* Rigby, 1974; *Collingwood and Fitzroy Sketchbook,* Rigby, 1978; *A Documentary History of the Australian Labour Movement, 1850-1975,* Drummond, 1978. Also author of *A.L.P.: A Short History,* 1980. Contributor to academic journals and popular magazines, including *Nation Review* and *Labour History.*

WORK IN PROGRESS: A picture study of ethnic communities in Australia.

SIDELIGHTS: McKinlay told *CA:* "My interest in the history of the Australian labour movement is linked to my belief in the need for socialist change in Australian society, and that socialists must understand the past in order to better cope with the future." *Avocational interests:* Travel (Europe, the Middle East, Southeast Asia).

* * *

McKISACK, May 1900-1981

OBITUARY NOTICE: Born March 30, 1900, in Belfast, Northern Ireland; died March 14, 1981. Educator and author. McKisack was a professor of history at Westfield College in the University of London. She began her teaching career as a lecturer in medieval history at Liverpool University in 1927 and published her first work of scholarship, *Parliamentary Representation of the English Boroughs,* in 1932. Her next study, *The Fourteenth Century,* appeared in 1959 as Volume V in the Oxford History of England. Long attracted to the work of Tudor historians, she undertook a description of the writings, collections, and topographies of Tudor antiquaries in *Mediaeval History in the Tudor Age* (1971). According to the *London Times,* McKisack's work was "marked by wide-ranging though in the main conservative scholarship, by a preference for the study of men in action over that of the institutions within which this action took place . . . , by a belief in the value of narrative in the writing of history, by strong good sense, an imaginative feeling for period, and by a clear, pleasant and flexible prose style which reflected the qualities of her mind." Obituaries and other sources: *Who's Who,* 126th edition, St. Martin's, 1974; *London Times,* March 17, 1981.

* * *

McLAREN, Ian A. 1928-

PERSONAL: Born April 17, 1928, in Naseby, New Zealand; son of David Lillie (a butcher) and Agnes Hay (a dressmaker; maiden name, Gunton) McLaren; married Margaret Cameron Lewis (a lecturer in business communication), August 31, 1957; children: David Lionel, Kirsten Aroha. *Education:* University of Otago, B.A., 1948, M.A., 1949; attended Institute of Education, London, 1953-54; University of Chicago, A.M., 1958; Victoria University of Wellington, Ph.D., 1966. *Home:* 216 Hillcrest Rd., Hamilton, New Zealand. *Office:* School of Education, University of Waikato, Private Bag, Hamilton, New Zealand.

CAREER: Palmerston North Teachers College, Palmerston North, New Zealand, lecturer in history, 1956-57 and 1959; Victoria University of Wellington, Wellington, New Zealand, 1960-71, began as lecturer, became reader in education; University of Waikato, Hamilton, New Zealand, professor of education, 1972—, dean of School of Education, 1975—. *Member:* Comparative Education Society, Australia and New Zealand History of Education Society, New Zealand Educational Administration Society, History of Education Society (England).

WRITINGS: (With Michael Turnbull) *The Land of New Zealand,* Longmans, Green, 1964; *British Education, 1870-1970,* Heinemann, 1969; *Education in a Small Democracy: New Zealand,* Routledge & Kegan Paul, 1974. Co-editor of *New Zealand Journal of Educational Studies.*

WORK IN PROGRESS: A collection of essays on New Zealand educational history; a documentary history of New Zealand education.

SIDELIGHTS: McLaren commented: "I am particularly interested in education in developing countries, especially South Pacific states."

* * *

McLAREN, Moray (David Shaw) 1901-1971 (Michael Murray)

PERSONAL: Born in March, 1901, in Edinburgh, Scotland; died in 1971, in Edinburgh; son of John Shaw and Eva Helen (Inglis) McLaren; married Lennox Milne (an actress), 1946. *Education:* Corpus Christi College, Cambridge, B.A. *Religion:* Roman Catholic.

CAREER: London Mercury, London, England, assistant editor; *Listener,* editor, 1929; British Broadcasting Corp., second in command of Scottish region, 1930, program director in Scotland, 1933, chief assistant editor; Foreign Office, London, head of Polish Political Institute, 1940-45; free-lance writer, 1945-71. *Awards, honors:* Officer of Order of the British Empire.

WRITINGS: Return to Scotland: An Egoist's Journey, Duckworth, 1930; *A Wayfarer in Poland,* Methuen, 1934; *Lord Lovat of the '45: The End of an Old Song,* Jarrolds, 1957; *A Dinner With the Dead* (stories), Serif Books, 1947; *Stern and Wild: A New Scottish Journey,* Chapman & Hall, 1948; *"By Me. . .": A Report Upon the Apparent Discovery of Some Working Notes of William Shakespeare in a Sixteenth-Century Book* (edited by Raymond Postgate), J. Redington, 1949; (with Osborne Henry Mavor) *A Small Stir: Letters on the English,* Hollis & Carter, 1949; *The Capital of Scotland,* Douglas & Foulis, 1950; (editor) *The House of Neill, 1749-1949,* Neill & Co., 1950; *The Capital of Scotland: A Twentieth-Century Contemplation on Edinburgh,* Douglas & Foulis, 1950; *Stevenson and Edinburgh: A Centenary Study,* Folcroft, 1950, reprinted, Richard West, 1973; *The Scots,* Penguin, 1951; (editor of revision) Desmond Campbell Miller, *Questions and Answers on Evidence,* Sweet & Maxwell, 1951; *A Singing Reel,* Hollis & Carter, 1953; *The Highland Jaunt: A Study of James Boswell and Samuel Johnson Upon Their Highland and Hebridean Tour of 1773,* Jarrolds, 1954, W. Sloane, 1955; *Scotland in Colour,* Batsford, 1954; *Understanding the Scots: A Guide for South Britons and Other Foreigners,* Muller, 1956, 2nd edition, International Publications Service, 1974; *The Pursuit,* Jarrolds, 1959.

(With Robert Neil Stewart) *Fishing as We Find It* (letters), Stanley Paul, 1960; *The Wisdom of the Scots: A Choice and a Comment,* M. Joseph, 1961, St. Martin's, 1962; *If Freedom Fail: Bannockburn, Flodden, the Union,* Secker & Warburg, 1964; *The Shell Guide to Scotland* (edited by Yorke Crompton), Ebury Press, 1965, 3rd edition (edited by Donald Lamond Macnie) published as *The New Shell Guide to Scotland,* 1977; *Poland's Thousand Years: The Vanguard of Christendom,* Catholic Institute for International Relations, 1965; *Pure Wine; or, In Vino Sanitas: A Centenary Celebration of, Quotation From, and Comment on Dr. Robert Druitt's Remarkable Book, "A Report on Cheap Wines, 1865,"* A. Campbell, 1965; *Corsica Boswell: Paoli, Johnson, and Freedom,* Secker & Warburg, 1966; *Sir Walter Scott: The Man and the Patriot,* Heinemann, 1970; *Bonnie Prince Charlie,* Saturday Review Press, 1972; (with William B. Currie) *The Fishing Waters of Scotland,* J. Murray, 1972; *Scotland,* Ebury Press, 1977.

Also author of *Escape and Return, Scottish Delight: A Contribution to Scotland in Quest of Her Youth,* and, under pseudonym Michael Murray, *The Noblest Prospect.*

Plays: "One Traveller Returns"; "Heather on Fire"; "The Non-Resident." Contributor to magazines and newspapers, including *Week End Review* and *Saturday Review*.

BIOGRAPHICAL/CRITICAL SOURCES: Books, October, 1970.*

* * *

McLEAN, Robert 1891-1980

OBITUARY NOTICE: Born October 1, 1891, in Philadelphia, Pa.; died December 5, 1980, in Montecito, Calif. Newspaper publisher. McLean was publisher of the family-owned *Philadelphia Bulletin* and a director and president of the Associated Press (AP). When his father died in 1931, McLean inherited a newspaper that had grown from seven thousand readers in 1895 to more than two hundred thousand. Under the younger McLean's direction, the *Bulletin* continued to prosper, swelling in circulation to 725,000 customers in the 1960's, until stronger competition from rival newspapers and television captured much of the *Bulletin*'s audience. McLean also served as director of the Associated Press from 1924 to 1968, an unequaled forty-four-year tenure as head of the nation's largest wire service during the period of greatest growth for the news organization. McLean remained active as a publisher even after his departure from the AP and the *Bulletin:* upon moving to California in 1964, he purchased the *Santa Barbara News-Press* for $8 million. Obituaries and other sources: *Current Biography,* Wilson, 1951, February, 1981; *The International Who's Who,* Europa, 1974; *Who's Who in the East,* 15th edition, Marquis, 1975; *New York Times,* December 7, 1980.

* * *

McLELLAN, David S(tanley) 1924-

PERSONAL: Born December 24, 1924, in New York, N.Y.; son of Charles (a bricklayer) and Jessie (Stevenson) McLellan; married Ann Handforth, May 18, 1945; children: Hilary, Michele, Marjorie McLellan Greenberg, Eric. *Education:* Yale University, B.A., 1948, M.A., 1951, Ph.D., 1954; University of Geneva, Lic. es Science Politique, 1949. *Home:* 611 South Main, Oxford, Ohio 45056. *Office:* Department of Political Science, Miami University, Oxford, Ohio 45056.

CAREER: University of California, Riverside, assistant professor, 1955-61, associate professor, 1961-67, professor of political science, 1967-71, director of Study Center and junior-year-abroad program in Bordeaux, France, 1966-68; Miami University, Oxford, Ohio, professor of political science, 1971—. Editor of Miami University Press, 1975-78; chairman of editorial board of "Miami University Imprint." *Military service:* U.S. Army Air Forces, navigator, 1943-46; served in Pacific theater; became first lieutenant. *Member:* International Studies Association (Midwest president, 1980-81), Phi Beta Kappa. *Awards, honors:* Rotary International fellow in Switzerland, 1948-49; Ford Foundation fellow, 1959-60; fellow at Washington Center of Foreign Policy Research, Johns Hopkins University, 1962-63; visiting fellow, Clare Hall, Cambridge University, 1981.

WRITINGS: (With William C. Olson and Fred Sondermann) *The Theory and Practice of International Relations,* Prentice-Hall, 1960, 5th edition, 1979; *The Cold War in Transition,* Macmillan, 1966; *Dean Acheson: The State Department Years,* Dodd, 1976; (editor with Acheson) *Among Friends: The Personal Letters of Dean Acheson,* Dodd, 1980. Contributor to political science and international studies journals.

WORK IN PROGRESS: The Vietnam War: Where Did the System Go Wrong?, completion expected in 1983; an analysis of post-Vietnam writing on foreign policy with reference to the return of "Cold War realism" in *Commentary* and other journals and organizations, 1981.

SIDELIGHTS: McLellan told *CA:* "Fifty hours a week, year in and year out, I teach courses on U.S. foreign and national security, international political theory, comparative foreign policy (Soviet, Chinese, Third World, and European), weapons, war, and strategic doctrines, and the moral and ethical aspects of U.S. foreign policy. I also give seminars on specialized topics.

"I began publishing to get promoted, but became interested in Dean Acheson as exemplary of U.S. Cold War leadership and in the development of U.S. foreign policy based on internationalism. I think we became carried away and involved ourselves in a form of globalism and intervention that has led to excesses and has been excessive in itself."

* * *

McLEMORE, Richard Aubrey 1903-1976

OBITUARY NOTICE—See index for *CA* sketch: Born June 6, 1903, in Perry County, Miss.; died August 31, 1976. Educator, historian, and author. McLemore specialized in the history of Mississippi. Among his books are *An Outline of Mississippi, The Mississippi Story, A High School History of Modern America,* and *A History of Mississippi Baptists: 1780-1970.* (Date of death provided by son, Harry Kimbrell McLemore.)

* * *

McMICHAEL, George 1927-

PERSONAL: Born August 20, 1927, in Tulsa, Okla.; married, 1953; children: one. *Education:* Northwestern University, B.S., 1950, M.A. and Ph.D., 1959. *Office:* School of Arts, Letters, and Social Science, California State University, Hayward, Calif. 94542.

CAREER: Roosevelt University, Chicago, Ill., instructor in English, 1957-59; Chico State College (now California State University), Chico, Calif., assistant professor of English, 1959-62; California State University, San Bernardino, professor of American literature, 1962-70, dean of faculty, 1962-67; California State University, Hayward, professor of English and dean of School of Arts, Letters, and Social Science, 1972—. Fulbright visiting professor at University of Thessalonika, 1968-69. *Member:* Modern Language Association of America, American Studies Association. *Awards, honors:* American Philosophical Society grant, 1967.

WRITINGS: (Editor with Edgar M. Glenn) *Shakespeare and His Rivals: A Casebook on the Authorship Controversy,* Odyssey, 1962; *Journey to Obscurity: The Life of Octave Thanet,* University of Nebraska Press, 1965; (editor) *Anthology of American Literature,* Volume I: *Colonial Through Romantic,* Volume II: *Realism to the Present,* Macmillan, 1974, 2nd edition, 1980, abridged edition published as *Concise Anthology of American Literature,* 1974.*

* * *

McMULLEN, Jeremy (John) 1948-

PERSONAL: Born in 1948 in Lancashire, England; married; children: two. *Education:* Attended Oxford University, London School of Economics and Political Science, and Inns of

Court Law School. *Home:* 9 Clifton Ave., London W12 9DR, England.

CAREER: Barrister, Middle Temple, 1971; Kelley Drye & Warren, New York, N.Y., attorney, 1972-73; General and Municipal Workers' Union, legal officer in Esher, England, 1973-77, district officer in London, England, 1977-79, regional officer in London, 1979—. Member of Trade Union Congress Working Party on Law Reform, 1976-78. *Member:* Industrial Law Society (member of executive committee, 1976—).

WRITINGS: Rights at Work: A Worker's Guide to Employment Law, Pluto Press, 1978; *Employment Law Under the Tories,* Pluto Press, 1981. Contributor to magazines and newspapers, including *Tribune, New Statesman, Labour Weekly,* and *Labour Research.*

*   *   *

McMURRAY, George R(ay) 1925-

PERSONAL: Born October 14, 1925, in Grinnell, Iowa; married, 1950. *Education:* Mexico City College, B.A., 1949; University of Nebraska, M.A., 1951, Ph.D., 1955. *Office:* Department of Foreign Languages, Colorado State University, Fort Collins, Colo. 80521.

CAREER: Washington State University, Pullman, instructor in Spanish, 1955-56; University of Nevada, Reno, instructor, 1956-57, assistant professor of romance languages, 1957-60; Colorado State University, Fort Collins, associate professor, 1960-66, professor of romance languages, 1966—. *Military service:* U.S. Army, 1943-46; became staff sergeant. *Member:* Modern Language Association of America, American Association of Teachers of Spanish and Portuguese. *Awards, honors:* Fulbright fellowship for France, summer, 1959.

WRITINGS: (Contributor) *El cuento hispanoamericano ante la critica,* Castalia, 1973; *Gabriel Garcia Marquez,* Ungar, 1977; *Jose Donoso,* Twayne, 1979; *Jose Luis Borges,* Ungar, 1980. Contributor to scholarly journals.*

*   *   *

McNALLY, Dennis 1949-

PERSONAL: Born December 1, 1949, in Fort Meade, Md.; son of John F.J., Jr. and Adeline (a legal secretary; maiden name, Jacobson) McNally. *Education:* St. Lawrence University, B.A., 1971; University of Massachusetts, M.A., 1972, Ph.D., 1977. *Politics:* "Philosophical Anarchist." *Religion:* "Pagan." *Home and office:* 1492 Pacific Ave., No. 4, San Francisco, Calif. 94109. *Agent:* Robert Lescher, 155 East 71st St., New York, N.Y. 10022.

CAREER: Writer. Weizmann Institute of Science, Rehovot, Israel, fund raiser and administrative assistant in San Francisco, Calif., 1977-79. Worked as film grip and copy editor, and in public relations.

WRITINGS: Desolate Angel, A Biography: Jack Kerouac, the Beat Generation, and America, Random House, 1979. Contributor to magazines, including *Western American Literature, Newsday,* and *California Living.*

WORK IN PROGRESS: A novel about contemporary sexuality in San Francisco.

SIDELIGHTS: McNally wrote that he considers it vital to resist censorship of any sort.

McNULTY, James Edmund, Jr. 1924-1965

OBITUARY NOTICE—See index for *CA* sketch: Born August 16, 1924, in Oak Park, Ill.; died April 29, 1965. Educator, economist, and author. At the time of his death, McNulty was professor of industry at the Wharton School of Finance and Commerce of the University of Pennsylvania. He wrote *Decision and Influence Processes in Private Pension Plans* and *Some Economic Aspects of Business Organization.* (Date of death provided by wife, Ramona R. McNulty.)

*   *   *

McQUADE, Walter 1922-

PERSONAL: Born May 1, 1922, in Port Washington, N.Y.; son of Walter P. and Theresa (Dwyer) McQuade; married Ann Aikman, November 25, 1950; children: Molly Elizabeth, Benjamin Barr, Kate Maud. *Education:* Cornell University, B.Arch., 1947. *Home:* 3 Grosvenor Pl., Great Neck, N.Y. 11021. *Office: Fortune,* Time and Life Building, Rockefeller Center, New York, N.Y. 10020.

CAREER: Architectural Forum, New York City, staff writer, 1947-64; *Fortune,* New York City, member of board of editors, 1964—. Visiting critic at Yale University, 1962. Member of New York City Planning Commission, 1967-72. *Military service:* U.S. Army, 1942-46. *Member:* American Institute of Architects (fellow).

WRITINGS: (Editor) *Schoolhouse: A Primer About the Building of the American Public School Plant, Produced in the Public Service by the Joint School Research Project,* Simon & Schuster, 1958; (editor) *Cities Fit to Live In,* Macmillan, 1971; (with wife, Ann Aikman) *Stress: What It Is, What It Can do to Your Health, How to Handle It,* Dutton. 1974; (with Aikman) *The Longevity Factor,* Simon & Schuster, 1979. Contributor to magazines, including *Life.* Architecture and design critic for *Nation, 1959-65.*

BIOGRAPHICAL/CRITICAL SOURCES: American Institute of Architects Journal, March, 1974; *American Journal of Public Health,* December, 1974.

*   *   *

McWILLIAMS, Wilson Carey 1933-

PERSONAL: Born September 2, 1933, in Santa Monica, Calif.; son of Carey and Dorothy Janet (Hedrick) McWilliams; married Carol Golder, June, 1955 (marriage ended, 1961); married Nancy Riley (a psychoanalyst), September 16, 1966; children: Susan Jane, Helen Elizabeth. *Education:* University of California, Berkeley, A.B., 1955, M.A., 1960, Ph.D., 1966. *Politics:* Democrat. *Religion:* Presbyterian. *Home:* 9 Mine St., Flemington, N.J. 08822. *Office:* Department of Political Science, Livingston College, Rutgers University, New Brunswick, N.J. 08903.

CAREER: Oberlin College, Oberlin, Ohio, instructor, 1961-67; Brooklyn College of the City University of New York, Brooklyn, N.Y., instructor, 1967-70; Rutgers University, New Brunswick, N.J., instructor in political science, 1970—. Vice-president of Institute for the Study of Civic Values. *Military service:* U.S. Army, 1955-57; became first lieutenant. *Member:* American Political Science Association. *Awards, honors:* Prize from National Historical Society for *The Idea of Fraternity In America.*

WRITINGS: (With George Lanyi) *Crisis and Continuity in World Politics,* Random House, 1965; (editor) *Garrisons and*

Government, Chandler, 1967; *The Idea of Fraternity In America*, University of California Press, 1973. Contributor to magazines, including *Commonweal*. Member of editorial board of *Worldview*.

*   *   *

MEAD, Stella   ?-1981

OBITUARY NOTICE: Died March 30, 1981. Journalist and author best known for her books of children's tales, including *The Land of Happy Hours*, *The Land Where Dreams Come True*, *Princes and Fairies*, and *Magic Journeys*. Obituaries and other sources: *Who's Who*, 126th edition, St. Martin's, 1974; *London Times*, April 14, 1981.

*   *   *

MEAD, William Richard   1915-

PERSONAL: Born July 29, 1915, in Aylesbury, Buckinghamshire, England; son of William and Catharine Sarah (Stevens) Mead. *Education:* London School of Economics and Political Science, London, B.Sc., 1937, M.Sc., 1939, Ph.D., 1946, D.Sc., 1968. *Home:* Flat 2, 1 Hornton St., London W.8, England. *Office:* Department of Geography, University of London, London, England.

CAREER: University of Liverpool, Liverpool, England, assistant lecturer, 1947-49; University of London, London, England, lecturer, 1950-53, reader, 1953-66, professor of geography and head of department 1966—. *Military service:* Royal Air Force, 1940-46. *Member:* Institute of British Geographers (president, 1971), Royal Geographical Society (honorary secretary, 1968-77, vice-president, 1977—), Anglo-Finnish Society (chairman, 1966—), Geographical Association (president, 1981-82), Finnish Geographical Society (honorary member), Fenno-Ugrian Society (honorary member), Det norske Videnskaps Akademi (honorary member). *Awards, honors:* Rockefeller Foundation fellowship for Finland, 1949-50; Gill Memorial Award from Royal Geographical Society, 1951; chevalier of Finnish Order of the Lion, 1953, commander, 1963; chevalier of Swedish Order of Vasa, 1962; D.H.C. from University of Uppsala, 1966; D.Phil. from University of Helsinki, 1969, commander of Finnish Order of the White Rose, 1976; commander of Swedish Order of the Polar Star, 1977; fellow of London School of Economics and Political Science, 1979; Founder's Medal, 1980.

WRITINGS: Farming in Finland, Athlone Press, 1953; *An Economic Geography of the Scandinavian States and Finland*, University of London Press, 1958; *How People Live in Norway*, Educational Supply Association, 1959.

Norway, Educational Supply Association, 1960; (with David C. Large) *How People Live in the United States of America*, Educational Supply Association, 1961; *The United States and Canada: A Regional Geography*, Hutchinson, 1962; (with Eric Herbert Brown) *Saltvik: Studies From an Aland Parish*, Geographical Field Group, University of Nottingham, 1964; *Finland*, Ward, Lock, 1965, Praeger, 1968; *How People Live in Finland*, Ward, Lock, 1965; (with Helmer Smeds) *Winter in Finland*, Hugh Evelyn, 1967; (with R. J. Harrison Church, Peter Hall, and others) *An Advanced Geography of Northern and Western Europe*, Hulton Educational Publications, 1967.

(With Wendy Hall) *Scandinavia*, Thames & Hudson, 1972; *The Scandinavian Northlands*, Oxford University Press, 1974; (editor) *The American Environment*, Athlone Press, 1974; (with Stig Tyrgil Hjalmason Jaatinen) *The Aland Is-*

lands, David & Charles, 1974; *An Historical Geography of Scandinavia*, Academic Press, 1981.

WORK IN PROGRESS: A book on early nineteenth-century Finnish agricultural census material.

AVOCATIONAL INTERESTS: Music, riding, gardening.

BIOGRAPHICAL/CRITICAL SOURCES: Times Literary Supplement, April 27, 1967.

*   *   *

MEANS, Florence Crannell   1891-1980

OBITUARY NOTICE—See index for *CA* sketch: Born May 15, 1891, in Baldwinsville, N.Y.; died November 19, 1980, in Boulder, Colo. Author. Means was one of the first writers to deal with racial problems in children's literature. In *The Moved-Outers* she wrote about the evacuation of Japanese-American children during World War II, and in other books she explored the lives of blacks, native Americans, and Hispanics. She won a number of awards for her writing, including a Childhood Education Association Award for *The Moved-Outers* and a Nancy Bloch Annual Award for *Knock at the Door, Emmy*. Obituaries and other sources: *Publishers Weekly*, February 6, 1981.

*   *   *

MEEK, S(terner St.) P(aul)   1894-1972

OBITUARY NOTICE—See index for *CA* sketch: Born April 8, 1894, in Chicago, Ill.; died June 10, 1972. Military officer and author. Meek served in the U.S. Army for thirty years before retiring, with the rank of colonel, in 1947. He is best known as the author of juvenile animal stories, including *Jerry: The Adventures of an Army Dog, Franz: A Dog of the Police, Gustav: A Son of Franz, Bell Farm Star: The Story of Pacer*, and *Pierre of the Big Top: The Story of a Circus Poodle*. Meek also wrote adult fiction and science fiction. Obituaries and other sources: *Who Was Who in Ameica*, 5th edition, Marquis, 1973.

*   *   *

MEIGGS, Russell   1902-

PERSONAL: Born October 20, 1902, in London, England; son of William Herrick and Mary Gertrude (May) Meiggs; married Pauline Gregg, 1941; children: Sylvia, Rosalind. *Education:* Keble College, Oxford, M.A., 1928. *Home:* The Malt House, Garsington, Oxford, England.

CAREER: Oxford University, Oxford, England, fellow of Keble College, 1930-39, fellow and tutor in ancient history at Balliol College, 1939-70, honorary fellow, 1970, lecturer in ancient history, 1939-70, praefectus of Holywell Manor, 1945-69. Chief labour officer of Ministry of Supply, 1941-45; visiting professor at Swarthmore College, 1960, 1970-71, 1974, 1977; Kipling Fellow at Marlborough College, 1967. *Member:* British Academy (fellow). *Awards, honors:* D.H.L. from Swarthmore College, 1971.

WRITINGS: Home Timber Production, 1939-1945, Crosby Lockwood, 1949; (editor with Antony Andrewes) *Sources for Greek History Between the Persian and Peloponnesian Wars*, Oxford University Press, c.1950, new edition, Clarendon Press, 1951; (author of revision) John Bagnell Bury, *A History of Greece to the Death of Alexander the Great*, 3rd edition (Meiggs was not associated with earlier editions), Macmillan, 1951, St. Martin's, 1959, 4th edition, 1975; *Roman Ostia*, Oxford University Press, 1960, 2nd edition, 1974; (editor with David Malcolm Lewis) *A Selection of Greek Historical Inscriptions*, Volume I: *To the End of the Fifth*

Century, B.C., Clarendon Press, 1969; *The Athenian Empire*, Clarendon Press, 1972, Oxford University Press, 1979; *Trees and Timber in the Ancient World*, Oxford University Press, 1982.

SIDELIGHTS: Meiggs told *CA:* "I deplore the tendency to regard teaching as a necessary evil to provide financial basis for research. Teaching, for me, is a valuable stimulant for writing, and I have particularly enjoyed the contrasting problems of teaching in America and England. My main preoccupation has been the combination of literary and archaeological evidence, but I am frightened of pollen analysis and carbon dating, and I feel that the use of models, though occasionally fruitful, has done more harm than good to the study of ancient history."

*   *   *

MEIRING, Jane (Muriel) 1920-

PERSONAL: Surname is pronounced *May*-ring; born February 24, 1920, in Johannesburg, South Africa; daughter of Arthur Francis (an engineer) and Beatrice (Dale) Rose; married Pieter Meiring, April 30, 1943 (deceased); children: Andre, Mary Meiring Laver, Paula Meiring Velthuysen. *Education:* Rhodes University, B.A., 1940. *Home:* 32 Kariega Rd., Kenton-on-Sea 6191, Cape Province, South Africa. *Agent:* Glenn Cowley, 60 West 10th St., New York, N.Y. 10011.

CAREER: Secretary to consulting geologist, 1941-43; South African Broadcasting Corp., Johannesburg, South Africa, secretary, 1943-44; writer, 1966—. *Member:* International P.E.N.

WRITINGS: Candle in the Wind (novel), Muller, 1959; *Sundays River Valley* (nonfiction), Balkema, 1960; *Thomas Pringle: His Life and Times*, Balkema, 1968; *The Magic Calabash* (juvenile fiction), Mambo Press, 1970; *The Truth in Masquerade* (biography), Juta & Coy, 1974; *The Art of Edmund Caldwell*, Frank Read, 1978. Also author of radio play "Departure of the Bridge." Contributor of articles and stories to magazines.

WORK IN PROGRESS: A collection of Shona and Ndebele folktales from Zimbabwe; *The Gorah*, a novel about Addo province elephants; research on old Rhodesia and Zimbabwe, 1880-1980, with a book expected to result.

SIDELIGHTS: Jane Meiring wrote: "I am intensely interested in the history and indigenous peoples of southern Africa."

*   *   *

MERRILL, John Nigel 1943-

PERSONAL: Born August 19, 1943, in London, England; son of Ian Nuttal (a chemical engineer) and Ivy Mabel (a teacher; maiden name, Phillips) Merrill; married Sheila Margaret Munro (a company director), September 15, 1979. *Education:* Attended Chesterfield College of Education, 1963-67. *Politics:* Conservative. *Religion:* Church of England. *Home:* Flat 16, Rutland Court, Rutland St., Matlock, Derbyshire, England. *Office:* Yew Cottage, West Bank, Winster, Matlock, Derbyshire DE4 2DQ, England.

CAREER: Merrill Pumps Ltd., Sheffield, England, commercial manager, 1965-72; free-lance writer and lecturer, 1972—. Founder and managing director of Walking Boots Ltd., 1979—, and Trail Blazer (a hiking and camping supplies store), 1980. Guest on radio and television programs; gives illustrated lectures; consultant to Blacks of Greenock Ltd. and Berghaus of Newcastle. *Member:* Society of Authors,

Sierra Club, Appalachia Mountain Club, Appalachian Trail Conference, Pacific Crest Club, Derbyshire Archaeological Society, Rotary Club of Matlock, Rotary Club of Dronfield (founding member; honorary member).

WRITINGS: Walking in Derbyshire, Dalesman, 1970; *Motoring in Derbyshire*, Dalesman, 1971; *Famous Derbyshire Homes*, Dalesman, 1973; *Peak District Walks*, Dalesman, Volume I: *Short Walks for the Motorist*, Volume II: *Long Walks for the Rambler*, 1974; *Legends and Folklore of the Midlands*, Wayland, 1974; *Legends and Folklore of the North West*, Wayland, 1974.

Derbyshire Facts and Records, Dalesman, 1975; *Discovering South Yorkshire*, Shire Publications, 1975; (contributor) Michael Davidson, editor, *No Through Road*, AA Publications, 1975; *Bakewell*, Dalesman, 1976; *The Peak District A to Z*, Dalesman, 1976; *The Peakland Way*, Dalesman, 1976; *Exploring Derbyshire by Car*, Dalesman, 1976; *Walking in South Derbyshire*, Dalesman, 1977; *Explore the Peak District*, Dalesman, 1977; *Derbyshire Trails*, Dalesman, 1977; *Matlock*, Dalesman, 1977; *Ashbourne*, Dalesman, 1977; *A Look at Winster*, privately printed, 1977; *Lockwood and Carlisle Ltd.: A Hundred Years of History*, Crosby & Lockwood, 1977; *The Limey Way*, Dalesman, 1979; *Turn Right at Lands End*, Oxford Illustrated Press, 1979.

From Arran to Orkney, Spurbooks, 1981; *Derbyshire Inns*, Dalesman, 1981; *Derbyshire Myths*, Dalesman, 1981; *The John Merrill Walk Book*, Chatto & Windus, 1981; *Walks in the White Peak*, Dalesman, 1981; *Walks in the Dark Peak*, Dalesman, 1982; *My Favourite Walks in Britain*, Dalesman, 1982; *Don't Feed the Skunks*, Walking Boots Ltd., 1982; *My British Walks*, Walking Boots Ltd., 1982; *Do's and Don'ts of Walking*, Walking Boots Ltd., 1982; *Himalayan Trekking*, Walking Boots Ltd., 1982.

Contributor of more than two hundred articles to magazines, including *Lady, Camping, Climber and Rambler, Do It Yourself, Countryman*, and *This England*.

WORK IN PROGRESS: My World Walks, publication by Walking Books Ltd. expected in 1983.

SIDELIGHTS: A marathon walker, both in England and abroad, Merrill averages about four thousand miles a year. His travels include a thousand-mile walk in the Hebrides in 1970, walks through Ireland and virtually all over England, including a coastal walk of nearly seven thousand miles in 1978, and a two thousand-mile walk along the Appalachian Trail in the United States.

Describing his most recent activities, Merrill wrote: "During April, 1980, I successfully led a trek to Everest Basecamp. The route taken was not the usual approach, but an 'Alpine style' route up three valleys and crossing an eighteen thousand-foot pass to Everest. My illustrated lecture on it includes stunning views of many world-renowned Himalayan giants and insight into Sherpa life and trekking at high altitudes.

"During the summer of 1980 I became the first person to walk the Pacific Crest Trail that year, from Mexico to Canada, twenty-seven hundred miles. The walk took 118 days, the fastest time so far! The trail lies up the western side of America through California, Oregon, and Washington. Much of the trail is above six thousand feet as it weaves its way through the High Sierras and the Oregon and Washington cascades. It is a walk of stunning beauty through the remotest country in North America. The walk had to be extended because of the volcanic eruptions of Mount St. Helens. Before leaving America I climbed Mount Whitney, and my lecture on it covers this absorbing mountaineering trail.

"My 1981 walks include a trek round the Annapurna area of the Himalayas and a twenty-three hundred-mile walk across the whole of the European Alps and the Pyrenees. Apart from planning to walk the Continental Divide Trail in America I plan to do a fifty-five hundred-mile walk from the west coast to the east coast of America during the summer of 1983.

"Why I walk is rather complex. I walk because it is the only way to see and appreciate the countryside, to get the material for writing books and to take numerous photographs for illustrating lectures—but I also like the physical challenge of doing a very long walk because you have to walk at least fifteen hundred miles per year to really get into what you are doing. On all my walks I have carried all my own equipment, somewhere in the order of fifty pounds, and camp out wherever possible. In the last eight years I have walked thirty-eight thousand miles and taken thirty-five thousand color slides."

AVOCATIONAL INTERESTS: Natural history, folklore and customs, historical buildings, industrial archaeology.

*   *   *

MERWE, A. v.d.
See GEYL, Pieter (Catharinus Arie)

*   *   *

MESSEGUE, Maurice   1921-

PERSONAL: Born December 14, 1921, in Colayrac, St. Cirq, France; children: Didier, Franck, Marc. *Home:* Domaine de Bazillac, 32000 Auch, France. *Agent:* Opera Mundi, 100 Avenue Raymond Poincare, 75284 Paris, France.

CAREER: Writer and naturalist. Worked as technical consultant to "Fleurance chez soi"; administrator of Ecole Universelle; mayor and councellor general of Fleurance, Gers, France, 1971—.

WRITINGS—In English translation: *Des hommes et des plantes*, R. Laffont, 1970, translation by Pamela Swinglehurst published as *Of Men and Plants: The Autobiography of the World's Most Famous Plant Healer*, Weidenfeld & Nicolson, 1972, Macmillan, 1973; *C'est la nature qui a raison*, R. Laffont, 1972, translation by Clara Winston published as *Maurice Messegue's Way to Natural Health and Beauty*, Macmillan, 1974; *Mon Herbier de sante*, Laffont/Tchou, 1975, translation published as *Health Secrets of Plants and Herbs*, Morrow, 1979.

Other writings: *Cherche et tu trouveras: La Vie d'un guerisseur*, foreword by Marcel Jouhandeau, La Passerelle, 1953; *Et Pourtant je gueris: Memoires d'un guerisseur*, Calmann-Levy, 1960; *Votre Poison quotidien*, Lanore, 1961; *Sommes-nous des assassins?*, Plon, 1965; *Pour les guerisseurs et la medecine libre*, Berger-Levrault, 1967; (with Andre Gayot) *Ce Soir, le diable viendra ta prendre, la sorcellerie aux Antilles*, R. Laffont, 1968; *Reapprenons a aimer*, R. Laffont, 1974; *Tout une vie a se battre*, R. Laffont, 1977. Also author of *Mon Herbier de beaute*.

*   *   *

MESSEL, Harry   1922-

PERSONAL: Born March 3, 1922, in Levine Siding, Manitoba, Canada; son of James Nikola and Katrina Messel; married Patricia Iona Pegram, November 1, 1949; children: Naomi Wendy Messel Woo, Iona Messel Jeffrey. *Education:* Royal Military College, Kingston, Ontario, graduated, 1942;

Queen's University, Kingston, B.A. (with honors) and B.Sc. (with honors), both 1948; attended University of St. Andrews, 1948-49; Dublin Institute for Advanced Studies, Ph.D., 1951. *Residence:* Darling Point, New South Wales, Australia. *Office:* School of Physics, University of Sydney, Sydney, New South Wales 2006, Australia.

CAREER: University of Adelaide, Adelaide, Australia, senior lecturer in theoretical physics, 1951-52; University of Sydney, Sydney, Australia, professor of physics, head of School of Physics, and founding director of Science Foundation for Physics, all 1952—. Scientific adviser to Australian attorney-general and minister for customs and excise, 1973-75, and to minister for minerals and energy, 1975; member of Australian Atomic Energy Commission, 1974—. *Military service:* Canadian Army, 1942-46; became lieutenant.

MEMBER: International Union for the Conservation of Nature (Australian vice-chairman of Survival Service Commission, 1979—), Institute of Physics, Australian Institute of Physics, American Association for the Advancement of Science, Mathematics Society, Royal Institution, Elizabethan Trust. *Awards, honors:* Commander of Order of the British Empire, 1979.

WRITINGS: (Contributor) *Progress in Cosmic Ray Physics*, Volume II, North-Holland Publishing, 1953; (editor and contributor) *Selected Lectures in Modern Physics for School Science Teachers*, Nuclear Research Foundation, University of Sydney, 1958, reprinted as *Selected Lectures in Modern Physics*, Macmillan, 1960; *Lecture Notes on an Introductory Course in Modern Physics*, Shakespeare Head Press, 1958.

(Editor with S. T. Butler) *From Nucleus to Universe*, Shakespeare Head Press, 1960, reprinted (bound with *Space and the Atom*) as *The Universe and Its Origin*, Macmillan, 1964, *An Introduction to Modern Physics*, Macmillan, 1964, and *Space Physics and Radio Astronomy*, Macmillan, 1964; (editor with Butler, and contributor) *Space and the Atom*, Shakespeare Head Press, 1961, reprinted (bound with *From Nucleus to Universe*) as *The Universe and Its Origin*, Macmillan, 1964, *An Introduction to Modern Physics*, Macmillan, 1964, and *Space Physics and Radio Astronomy*, Macmillan, 1964; (editor and contributor with Butler,) *A Modern Introduction to Physics*, Volume III: *Atomic Physics, Light*, Horwitz-Grahame, 1961, reprinted in two volumes as *A Modern Introduction to Physics*, Volume V: *Atomic Physics*, 1965, Volume VI: *Light and Optics*, 1965; (editor with Butler, and contributor) *A Journey Through Space and the Atom*, Shakespeare Head Press, 1962; (editor with Butler, and contributor) *The Universe of Time and Space*, Shakespeare Head Press, 1963; (editor with Butler, and contributor) *Light and Life in the Universe*, Shakespeare Head Press, 1964; (editor and contributor) *Science for High School Students*, with teacher's manual, Science Foundation for Physics, University of Sydney, 1964, revised edition, 1970.

(Editor with Butler, and contributor) *Time*, Shakespeare Head Press, 1965; (editor and contributor) *Abridged Science for High School Students*, with teacher's manual, Volume I: *Physics*, Volume II: *Chemistry*, Volume III: *Biology*, Science Foundation for Physics, University of Sydney, 1965; (editor with Butler) *Atoms to Andromeda*, Shakespeare Head Press, 1966; (editor with Butler) *Apollo and the Universe*, Shakespeare Head Press, 1967; (editor with Butler) *Man in Inner and Outer Space*, Shakespeare Head Press, 1968; (editor with Butler) *Nuclear Energy Today and Tomorrow*, Shakespeare Head Press, 1969.

(With D. F. Crawford) *Electron-Photon Shower Distribution Function*, Pergamon, 1970; (editor with Butler) *Pioneering in Outer Space*, Shakespeare Head Press, 1970; (editor with Butler) *Molecules to Man*, Shakespeare Head Press, 1971; (editor with Butler) *Brain Mechanisms and the Control of Behaviour*, Shakespeare Head Press, 1972; (editor with Butler) *Focus on the Stars*, Shakespeare Head Press, 1973; (editor with Butler) *Solar Energy*, Shakespeare Head Press, 1974.

(Editor and contributor) *Multistrand Senior Science for High School Students*, with teacher's manual and student's manual, Science Foundation for Physics, University of Sydney, 1975; (editor with Butler) *Our earth*, Shakespeare Head Press, 1975; (editor with Butler, and contributor) *Australian Animals and Their Environment*, Shakespeare Head Press, 1977; (with L.R.B. Elton) *Time and Man*, Pergamon, 1978; (editor) *Energy for Survival*, Pergamon, 1979. Contributor of about seventy articles to scientific journals.

WORK IN PROGRESS: Surveys of Tidal River Systems in the Northern Territory of Australia and Their Crocodile Populations, a seventeen-volume monograph series, with A. G. Wells, W. J. Green, and others, for Pergamon.

SIDELIGHTS: Messel has built up the School of Physics at University of Sydney from a single-professor school to one of the largest undergraduate and post-graduate schools of physics in the British commonwealth countries. It has seven research departments, specializing in theoretical physics, high-energy nuclear physics, electronic computing, astronomy, astrophysics, plasma physics, and environmental physics, including a solar energy section.

When he was appointed to University of Sydney, he realized that government funds for research were insufficient, and through his efforts the Science Foundation for Physics was established in 1954. The foundation has contributed toward the development of secondary education in Australia, with annual international science schools for high school students, and with the publication of a textbook series, which has had an impact in several countries outside Australia.

A specialist in theoretical nuclear physics, Messel has undertaken more than eighty international tours associated with his scientific work. His own research interests have turned toward interdisciplinary fields, including a field research program on saltwater crocodiles in northern Australia, a program which is also being used to explore systematically, for the first time, most of the rivers of Australia's remote north.

AVOCATIONAL INTERESTS: Conservation, hunting, fishing, water skiing, photography.

*   *   *

MEZVINSKY, Edward M.   1937-

PERSONAL: Born January 17, 1937, in Ames, Iowa; son of Abe and Fannie (Grundman) Mezvinsky; married second wife, Marjorie Margolies, October 5, 1975; children: Margot, Vera, Elsa, Eve, Lee Heh, Holly, Marc. *Education:* University of Iowa, B.A., 1960; University of California, M.A., 1963, J.D., 1965. *Politics:* Democrat. *Residence:* Penn Valley, Pa. 19072. *Office:* 4 Penn Center Plaza, Philadelphia, Pa. 19103.

CAREER: Admitted to the Bar of Iowa State, 1965; legislative assistant to Congressman Neal Smith of Iowa, Washington, D.C., 1965-67; private practice of law, Iowa City, Iowa, 1967-68; Iowa House of Representatives, Des Moines, representative from Johnson County, 1969-70; private practice of law, 1970-72; U.S. House of Representatives from first Iowa district, 1972-77; United Nations Commission on Human Rights, New York, N.Y., Geneva, Switzerland, U.S. representative,

1977-79; admitted to the Supreme Court of Pennsylvania, 1980; private practice of law, Philadelphia, Penn., 1980—. *Awards, honors:* Presidential commendation, 1967, for work to protect the public in areas of traffic and highway safety and meat inspection.

WRITINGS: (With John Greenya and Kevin McCormally) *A Term to Remember*, Coward, 1977.

SIDELIGHTS: As a freshman congressman Mezvinsky was appointed to the House Judiciary Committee and took part in its deliberations on whether or not to impeach President Richard M. Nixon for his part in the Watergate scandal. Mezvinsky's book, *A Term to Remember*, describes his experiences during that period. A *New York Times Book Review* critic pointed out that the book was "a thoughtful, balanced look at one branch of government working in the midst of a constitutional crisis."

Mezvinsky told *CA:* "President Nixon had no choice but to resign due to the inevitability of his impeachment. However, justice would have been better served by President Gerald Ford not granting a pardon to President Nixon prior to the completion of the judicial process."

BIOGRAPHICAL/CRITICAL SOURCES: New Yorker, November 21, 1977; *New York Times Book Review*, December 18, 1977.

*   *   *

MICALLEF, Benjamin A(nthony)   1925-1980

OBITUARY NOTICE—See index for *CA* sketch: Born March 21, 1925, in Detroit, Mich.; died May 8, 1980. Educator and author. Micallef wrote *Electric Accounting Machine Fundamentals, An Introduction to Data Processing*, and *Keypunching: A Basic Office Skill*. (Date of death provided by wife, Mrs. Benjamin A. Micallef.)

*   *   *

MICHAELS, Ralph
See FILICCHIA, Ralph

*   *   *

MICHAELY, Michael   1928-

PERSONAL: Born October 3, 1928, in Kinneret, Israel; son of Aharon (a clerk) and Yona (Skolnik) Michaely; married Ora Avni-Steiner (a librarian), March 25, 1952; children: Ailon, Yoav, Boaz Aharon. *Education:* Hebrew University of Jerusalem, M.A., 1952; Johns Hopkins University, Ph.D., 1955. *Politics:* "Non-affiliated." *Religion:* Jewish. *Home:* 24 Havatzelet St., Mevasseret, Jerusalem, Israel. *Office:* Department of Economics, Hebrew University of Jerusalem, Jerusalem, Israel.

CAREER: Hebrew University of Jerusalem, Jerusalem, Israel, lecturer, 1955-61, senior lecturer, 1961-65, associate professor, 1965-69, professor of economics, 1969—, Aron and Michael Chilewich Professor of International Trade, 1970—, chairman of department of economics, 1961-65, dean of faculty of social sciences, 1968-71. Adviser to research department of Bank of Israel, 1955-59 and 1968-71; member of research staff of Falk Institute for Economic Research in Israel, 1960-65; visiting member of research staff at National Bureau of Economic Research, New York, N.Y., 1965-67, senior research associate, 1969-73; visiting senior economist at International Bank for Reconstruction and Development, 1974-75. Visiting professor at Graduate Center of the City University of New York, 1966-67, University of Stockholm, 1972 and 1973, and Monash University, 1979. *Military ser-*

vice: Palmach, 1945-48. Israel Defense Force, Infantry, 1948-49. Israel Defense Force Reserve, 1950—; became major.

WRITINGS: Concentration in International Trade, North-Holland Publishing, 1962; *Balance-of-Payment Adjustment Policies: Japan, Germany, and the Netherlands,* National Bureau of Economic Research, 1968; *Ma'arecht sha'arei hahalafin be'Israel,* Falk Institute for Economic Research in Israel, 1968, translation published as *Israel's Foreign Exchange Rate System,* 1971, volume of tables (in Hebrew), 1969, volume of appendixes (in Hebrew), 1970; *The Responsiveness of Demand Policies to Balance of Payments: Postwar Patterns,* Columbia University Press, 1971; *Foreign-Trade Regimes and Economic Development: Israel,* Columbia University Press, 1975; *Theory of Commercial Policy: Trade and Protection,* University of Chicago Press, 1977.

In Hebrew only: *Sahar hahautz vivoo hahon be'Israel,* (title means "Foreign Trade and Capital Imports in Israel"), Am-Oved, 1963.

Contributor: E. F. Jackson, editor, *Economic Development in Africa,* Basil Blackwell, 1966; Erik Lundberg and Sven Grassman, editors, *The Past and Prospects of the International Economic Order,* Macmillan, 1980; David Bigman and Teizo Taya, editors, *The Functioning of Floating Exchange Rates: Theory, Evidence, and Policy Implications,* Ballinger, 1980; Peter Oppenheimer, editor, *Issues in International Economics,* Oriel, 1980. Contributor to *International Encyclopedia of the Social Sciences.* Contributor of about twenty articles to professional journals in the United States, Israel, Canada, and Europe.

WORK IN PROGRESS: Trade Structure, Income Levels, and Economic Dependence.

SIDELIGHTS: Michaely told *CA:* "As reflected in my writings, I have attempted in conducting economic research to pay equal attention to general issues in international economics and to specific problems of the Israeli economy. Since Israel's economic performance has sometimes proven to anticipate developments and phenomena which later assumed worldwide scope, these two areas of interest have often merged."

*   *   *

MICKLEM, Nathaniel   1888-1976

PERSONAL: Born April 10, 1888, in London, England; died in 1976; son of Nathaniel (a lawyer) and Ellen Ruth (Curwen) Micklem; married Agatha Frances Silcock, 1916 (died, 1961); children: three sons. *Education:* New College, Oxford, M.A.

CAREER: Ordained minister of United Reformed church; pastor of United Reformed churches; Selly Oaks Colleges, Birmingham, England, professor of Old Testament literature and theology, 1921-27; Queen's University, Kingston, Ontario, professor of New Testament literature and criticism, 1927-31; Oxford University, Oxford, England, professor of dogmatic theology and principal of Mansfield College, 1932-53, principal emeritus, 1953-76, Wilde Lecturer in Natural and Comparative Religion, 1948-51. President of Liberal party, 1957-58, and Liberal International party, 1959-71. Select preacher at Oxford University, 1960. Patron of World Liberal Union, 1973. Visiting professor and Cole Lecturer at Vanderbilt University, 1954. *Awards, honors:* Fellow of Mansfield College, Oxford, 1972; Companion of Honor, 1974; LL.D. and D.D. from Queen's University, Kingston, Ontario; D.D. from University of Glasgow.

WRITINGS: The Open Light: A Enquiry Into Faith and Reality, Royal Institute of International Affairs, 1919.

The Galilean: The Permanent Element in Religion, J. Clarke & Co., 1920, 2nd edition, 1921; *A First Century Letter: Being an Exposition of Paul's First Epistle to the Corinthians,* S.C.M. Press, 1920; (with Herbert Morgan) *Christ and Caesar: On the Nature of Social Obligation,* Swarthmore Press, 1921; *God's Freemen: A Tract for the Times,* J. Clarke & Co., 1923; (contributor) *Arnold Thomas of Bristol: Collected Papers and Addresses,* Allen & Unwin, 1925; *Prophecy and Eschatology,* Allen & Unwin, 1926; (translator with Kenneth A. Saunders) Wilhelm Herrmann, *Systematic Theology,* Allen & Unwin, 1927.

The Church Catholic, S.C.M. Press, 1935; (editor) *Christian Worship: Studies in History and Meaning,* Clarendon Press, 1936; *What Is the Faith?,* Hodder & Stoughton, 1936; (author of foreword) A. Rosenberg, *Protestant Pilgrims to Rome: The Betrayal of Luther—An English summary of "Protestantische Rompilger,"* Friends of Europe, 1938; (editor) *A Book of Personal Religion,* Independent Press, 1938, new edition, 1953; *The Crisis and the Christian,* S.C.M. Press, 1938; *May God Defend the Right!: On the Moral and Religious Issues in the War Between England and Germany,* Hodder & Stoughton, 1939; *National Socialism and Christianity,* Farrar & Rinehart, 1939; *National Socialism and the Roman Catholic Church: Being an Account of the Conflict Between the National Socialist Government of Germany and the Roman Catholic Church, 1933-1938,* Oxford University Press, 1939, reprinted, AMS Press, 1979.

The Creed of a Christian: Being Monologues Upon Great Themes of the Christian Faith, S.C.M. Press, 1940, 2nd edition, 1940; *The Theology of Politics,* Oxford University Press, 1941; (editor and author of introduction) *Prayers and Praises,* Hodder & Stoughton, 1941, 2nd edition, Independent Press, 1954, reprinted, University of St. Andrews Press, 1975; *The Doctrines of Our Redemption,* Eyre & Spottiswoode, 1943; 2nd edition, 1960, Cokesbury Press, 1948; *Congregationalism and the Church Catholic,* Independent Press, 1943; *Europe's Own Book,* B. & F.B.S., 1944; *The Labyrinth* (poem), Oxford University Press, 1945; *Religion,* Oxford University Press, 1948, reprinted, Greenwood Press, 1973.

(Editor of abridgement, with G. W. Briggs and G. B. Caird) *The Shorter Oxford Bible,* Oxford University Press, 1951; *The Tree of Life and Other Verses,* Oxford University Press, 1952; *Reason and Revelation: A Question From Duns Scotus: An Interpretation of the First Question in the Prologue to the "Quaestiones super libro primo sententiarum" of Duns Scotus,* Thomas Nelson, 1953; *Law and the Laws: Being the Marginal Comments of a Theologian,* W. Green & Son, 1952; *A Gallimaufry* (poems), Parthenon Press, 1954; *Ultimate Questions,* Abingdon, 1955; *The Abyss of Truth,* Bles, 1956; *The Idea of Liberal Democracy,* Christopher Johnson, 1957; *The Box and the Puppets, 1888-1953* (reminiscences), Bles, 1957.

The Labyrinth Revisited: A Philosophical Poem, Oxford University Press, 1960; *Faith and Reason,* Allenson, 1963; *The Places of Understanding and Other Poems,* Bles, 1963; *A Religion for Agnostics,* S.C.M. Press, 1965; *My Cherry-Tree* (essays), Bles, 1966; *Christian Thinking Today,* Allenson, 1967; (contributor) Elaine Kaye, editor, *The History of the King's Weigh House Church,* 1968; *Behold the Man: A Study of the Fourth Gospel,* Bles, 1969; (with wife, Agatha Frances Micklem) *Walking Together: Poems,* Abbey Press, 1969.

The Art of Thought, Epworth, 1970; *The Religion of a Sceptic,* Acton Society Trust, 1976. General editor of "The Christian Revolution Series," Headley Brothers, 1919.

SIDELIGHTS: Micklem's books have been translated into German, Italian, French, and Dutch.*

*   *   *

MILLER, David E(ugene)   1909-1978

OBITUARY NOTICE—See index for *CA* sketch: Born June 5, 1909, in Syracuse, Utah; died August 21, 1978, in Salt Lake City, Utah. Educator, historian, and author. At the time of his death, Miller was professor emeritus at the University of Utah. His works include *Great Salt Lake: Past and Present, Hole-in-the-Rock: An Epic in the Colonization of the Great American West,* and *Westward Migration of the Mormons.* He also edited several books, including *Utah History Atlas* and *The Golden Spike.* (Date of death provided by second wife, Mabel P. Miller.)

*   *   *

MILLER, Libuse (Lukas)   1915-1973

OBITUARY NOTICE—See index for *CA* sketch: Born February 28, 1915, in San Francisco, Calif.; died March 6, 1973. Artist and author. Miller wrote *The Christian and the World of Unbelief, In Search of Self: The Individual in the Thought of Kierkegaard,* and *Knowing, Doing and Surviving: Cognition in Evolution.* (Date of death provided by husband, Franklin Miller, Jr.)

*   *   *

MILLER, Madelaine Hemingway   1904-

PERSONAL: Born November 28, 1904, in Oak Park, Ill.; daughter of Clarence Edmonds (a doctor) and Grace (a musician and artist; maiden name, Hall) Hemingway; married Kenneth Sinclair Mainland, January 28, 1938 (died); married Ernest John Miller, August 8, 1951 (died); children: (first marriage) Ernest Hemingway. *Religion:* Protestant. *Home:* 6502 Lake Grove Rd., Petoskey, Mich. 49770; and 1450 South East 14th Dr., Deerfield Beach, Fla. 33441.

CAREER: Musician. Worked as medical secretary in Chicago, Ill., and as legal secretary in Petoskey, Mich.

WRITINGS: Ernie Hemingway's Sister "Sunny" Remembers (nonfiction), Crown, 1975.

SIDELIGHTS: Miller told *CA* that she reluctantly wrote her book about Ernest Hemingway because she had read so much "froth" by supposedly responsible authors. "At least my stuff did not come from someone who hardly knew him," she said. Miller also hoped people would realize Hemingway's worth as a writer, rather than seek out "juicy bits" for satisfaction or jealousy.

*   *   *

MILLETT, John (Antill)   1922-

PERSONAL: Born February 3, 1922, in Niangla, New South Wales, Australia; son of John (a farmer) and Doris (Antill) Millett; married Marion Moss (a secretary), July 28, 1960; children: Scott, Shelley. *Education:* University of Sydney, L.L.B., 1952. *Home and office:* 'Alcheringa,' Lytton Rd., Moss Vale 2577, New South Wales, Australia.

CAREER: Called to the Bar in Australia, 1952; solicitor in New South Wales, Victoria, and Queensland, Australia, 1952—. Partner in own law firm, J. Antill Millett & Partners, Sydney, Australia. Managing editor of *Poetry Australia,* New South Wales, 1970—. Guest editor of *Issue,* 1974-75. *Member:* Australian Society of Accountants, Australian Institute of Valuers, Chartered Institute of Secretaries. *Awards, hon-*

ors: Annual award for best book of poetry from Australian Poetry Society, 1974, for *The Silences;* Australia Council Literary Board awards, 1975 and 1980.

WRITINGS—Poetry; all published by South Head Press: *Calendar Adam,* 1971; *The Silences,* 1973; *Love Tree of the Coomera,* 1975; *West of the Cunderang,* 1977.

Also author of "One Man's War" (radio play), first broadcast by Australian Broadcasting Corp., 1981. Translator of work of Swiss poet Pierre Etienne. Contributor to numerous poetry journals, magazines, and newspapers, including *New York Quarterly, Hiram Poetry Review, Fiddlehead, Contemporary Review, Sydney Morning Herald, Canberra Times,* and *Quadrant.*

WORK IN PROGRESS: A book of poetry, publication by South Head Press expected in 1981 or 1982; two plays, "Dr. Longsleep" and "Silver Corner"; *The Conscript,* short stories.

SIDELIGHTS: John Millett told *CA:* "I have been interested in the interplay of long and short lines, close-ups and panoramas, local speech and technical terms, and the articulation of imaginative vision as distinct from 'received' views of reality. By opening my little eye, I could unlock them from their timeless suspension and put something else against the model that tradition had made normal. The poem created because it knew what was possible for it. I would sacrifice logic in favor of a dramatic pattern of shards and nonsequiturs to convey a process in action, like a mobile, rather than represent a complete and static configuration.

"Now, however, I am developing towards a more static posture, more integrated by use of a single threat of comparable images or ideas frozen together in the poem.

"I enjoy racehorses and an occasional small wager. I live on a small farm and breed thoroughbred racehorses. I now have a two-year-old filly in training for the spring racing carnival."

AVOCATIONAL INTERESTS: Water skiing.

*   *   *

MILLS, Carley   1897-1962

OBITUARY NOTICE—See index for *CA* sketch: Born September 9, 1897, in Deal, N.J.; died October 20, 1962, in New York, N.Y. Composer and author. Mills was the co-author of "The World's My Oyster," an Off-Broadway musical comedy. He also wrote several popular songs, including "Time and Time Again," "On the Outside Lookin' In," and "The Things You Said Last Night," and a book, *A Nearness of Evil.* Obituaries and other sources: *New York Times,* October 22, 1962; *The ASCAP Biographical Dictionary of Composers, Authors, and Publishers,* American Society of Composers, Authors and Publishers, 1966.

*   *   *

MILLS, John FitzMaurice   1917-

PERSONAL: Born in 1917, in Cheam, England; married Lucilla Margaret; children: one son. *Education:* Attended Architectural Association School. *Home:* Poulstone Court, King's Caple, Herefordshire, England.

CAREER: Writer. *Member:* Society of Antiquaries (fellow), Royal Society of Arts (fellow).

WRITINGS: The Practice and History of Painting: A Book for Schools, Edward Arnold, 1959; *The Painter and His Materials,* Artist Publishing Co., 1960; *Art for Fun: A Quiz Book,* Hutchinson, 1960; *Instructions to Young Artists,* Museum Press, 1960, 2nd edition, 1964, published in the United

States as *Painting Made Easy*, Sterling, 1961, 2nd edition published as *The Young Artist*, 1968; *Careers Through Art*, Museum Press, 1961; *Flower Painting*, Pitman, 1961; *Oil Painting*, Pitman, 1961; *Tackle Print-Making This Way*, Stanley Paul, 1961; *Look at Pictures*, Hamish Hamilton, 1962; (editor) *The Uffa Fox Book of Sailing*, Longacre Press, 1963; *The Care of Antiques*, Arlington Books, 1964, Hastings House, 1965; *Peacock Festival: Selected Color Woodcuts*, J. Domjan, 1964; *Sketching*, Collins, 1964; *Studio and Art-Room Techniques*, Pitman, 1965; *The Pergamon Dictionary of Art*, Pergamon, 1965; *Acrylic Painting*, Pitman, 1965; (with Reginald Robert Tomlinson) *The Growth of Child Art* University of London Press, 1966.

How to Detect Fake Antiques, Arlington Books, 1972; *Collecting and Looking After Antiques*, Hamlyn, 1972; *Treasure Keepers*, Doubleday, 1973; *Carpets in Pictures*, National Gallery, 1975; *The Technique of Sculptures*, Watson-Guptill, 1976; *Painting for Pleasure*, Hamlyn, 1977; *The Guinness Book of Art Facts and Feats*, Guinness Superlatives, 1978; *The Guinness Book of Antiques*, Guinness Superlatives, 1979; *The Genuine Article*, BBC Publications, 1979. Also author of *Oil Painting Step by Step* and *Audio Visual History of Art*, fourteen volumes. Fine arts correspondent for *Irish Times*.*

*   *   *

MILUNSKY, Aubrey 1936-

PERSONAL: Born November 3, 1936, in Johannesburg, South Africa; son of Harry L. Milunsky; married wife, Babette (a finance and insurance adviser and agent); children: Jeffrey. *Education:* University of the Witwatersrand, M.B.B.Ch., 1960, M.R.C.P. and D.C.H., both 1965; postdoctoral study at Great Ormond Street Hospital, 1965. *Residence:* Wayland, Mass. *Office:* Eunice Kennedy Shriver Center, 200 Trapelo Rd., Waltham, Mass. 02254.

CAREER: Johannesburg General Hospital, Johannesburg, South Africa, surgical intern, 1961; Baragwanath Hospital, Johannesburg, medical intern, 1961, resident in medicine and pediatrics, 1961-64; Queen Mary's Hospital for Children, Surrey, England, pediatric registrar, 1965-66; Tufts New England Medical Center, Boston, Mass., assistant pediatrician, 1966-70; Eunice Kennedy Shriver Center, Waltham, Mass., director of Genetics Division, 1971—. Diplomate of American Board of Pediatrics. Research fellow and research associate in neurology at Massachusetts General Hospital and Harvard University, 1969-70; instructor at Tufts University, 1966-70, assistant professor, 1970; assistant professor at Harvard University, 1971—. Director of Birth Defects and Genetics Clinic at Massachusetts General Hospital, 1971-73, assistant pediatrician, 1971—, associate director of Cystic Fibrosis Clinic, 1975—. *Member:* Society for Pediatric Research, American Society of Human Genetics, American Society of Law and Medicine, American Association of Medical Writers, Royal Society of Medicine (fellow), New England Pediatric Society, Massachusetts Medical Society.

WRITINGS: The Prenatal Diagnosis of Hereditary Disorders, C. C. Thomas, 1973; (editor) *Clinics in Perinatology*, Volume II, Saunders, 1974; (editor) *The Prevention of Genetic Disease and Mental Retardation*, Saunders, 1975; (editor with G. J. Annas) *Genetics and the Law*, Plenum, Volume I, 1976, Volume II, 1980; *Know Your Genes*, Houghton, 1977; (editor) *Genetic Disorders and the Fetus: Diagnosis, Prevention, and Treatment*, Plenum, 1979; (editor with E. A. Friedman and L. Gluck) *Advances in Perinatal Medicine*, Volume I, Plenum, 1980; (editor) *Coping With Crisis and Handicap*, Plenum, 1981.

Contributor: B. Nilton, D. Callahan, and other editors, *Ethical Issues in Human Genetics: Genetic Counseling and the Use of Genetic Knowledge*, Plenum, 1973; *Clinics in Perinatology*, Volume I, Saunders, 1974; M. M. Kaback and C. Valenti, editors, *Intrauterine Fetal Visualization: A Multidisciplinary Approach*, American Elsevier, 1976; B. W. Volk and L. Schneck, editors, *Symposium on Current Trends in Sphingolipidoses and Allied Disorders*, Plenum, 1976; H. Lubs and F. DeLaCruz, editors, *Genetic Counseling*, Raven Press, 1977; A. J. Schaffer and M. E. Avery, editors, *Diseases of the Newborn*, 4th edition (Milunsky was not included in earlier editions), Saunders, 1977; E. B. Hook and I. H. Porter, editors, *Population Cytogenetics*, Academic Press, 1977; B. F. Crandall and M.A.B. Brazier, editors, *Proceedings of a Workshop on Alpha-Fetoprotein*, Academic Press, 1978; K. Berg, editor, *Genetic Damage in Man Caused by Environmental Agents*, Academic Press, 1979; Kaback, editor, *Genetics Issues in Pediatrics, Perinatology, and Obstetrical Practice*, Year Book Medical Publishers.

Contributor to *Encyclopedia of Bioethics* and *Encyclopedia Americana*. Contributor of nearly two hundred articles to medical journals. Member of board of editors of *American Journal of Law and Medicine*, 1974—, *American Journal of Medical Genetics*, 1977—, and *Prenatal Diagnosis*, 1980—; member of editorial advisory board of *Bioethics Digest*, 1977-78.

*   *   *

MINOR, Audax
See RYALL, George (Francis Trafford)

*   *   *

MINOR, Marz 1928-

PERSONAL: Born February 27, 1928, in Nebraska; daughter of Don (a cattle rancher and writer) and Nell Minor. *Home:* 4815 Fairmount Ave., Kansas City, Mo. 64112.

CAREER: Co-owner and operator of Discos Mexicanos (record store), beginning 1949; Nelson Gallery-Atkins Museum, Kansas City, Mo., co-founder and manager of Sacred Circles Bookstore, 1977; free-lance writer and photographer; co-owner of advertising agency. Guest on radio programs, including "Authors in the News" and "Analogue." *Member:* Mystery Writers of American, Authors Guild, Society of Professional Journalists, Missouri Press Women, Kansas City Press Club, Sigma Delta Chi.

WRITINGS: (With sister, Nono Minor) *The American Indian Craft Book*, Popular Library, 1972. Writer for television program "Garden Party." Contributor to newspapers. Past editor of *Inter-American News*.

WORK IN PROGRESS: Novels set in the prairie, with sister, Nono Minor.

SIDELIGHTS: Marz Minor and her sister have been writing about the American Indian for more than ten years, and their writings have spread as far as China, where they rest in the National Library of Peking. Their research is aided by the fact that they own one of the few sets of "Annual Reports of the Bureau of American Ethnology," beginning in 1879. They also have an extensive library on Tibetan and Chinese history, culture, and art, ranging from ancient to modern.

MINOR, Nono 1932-

PERSONAL: Born March 2, 1932, in Nebraska; daughter of Don (a cattle rancher and writer) and Nell Minor. *Home:* 4815 Fairmount Ave., Kansas City, Mo. 64112.

CAREER: Worked as co-owner and operator of Discos Mexicanos (record store); Kansas City Museum of History and Science, Kansas City, Mo., began as associate curator of Plains Indians, became curator; Nelson Gallery-Atkins Museum, Kansas City, co-founder and manager of Sacred Circles Bookstore, 1977. Co-owner of advertising agency. Guest on radio and television programs, including "Authors in the News" and "Analogue." *Member:* Authors Guild, Authors League of America, Mystery Writers of America, Society of Professional Journalists, Missouri Press Women, Kansas City Press Club, Sigma Delta Chi.

WRITINGS: (With sister, Marz Minor) *The American Indian Craft Book,* University of Nebraska Press, 1978. Writer for television program, "Garden Party." Author of a column in *Real West.* Contributor to magazines and newspapers, including *American History Illustrated, Frontiers,* and *Heritage.*

WORK IN PROGRESS: Novels with a prairie background, with sister, Marz Minor.

SIDELIGHTS: Nono Minor's main writing interests are the American Indian and Tibetan and Chinese history, culture, and art, both ancient and modern. She has been writing about North Amerian Indians for more than ten years, aided in her research by her copy of one of the few sets of "Annual Reports of the Bureau of American Ethnology," dating from 1879. In 1972 she visited the mosques and villages of eastern Turkey, studying rugs to correlate the Oriental rug with American Indian designs.

*   *   *

MITCHELL, Donald (Charles Peter) 1925-

PERSONAL: Born February 6, 1925, in London, England; married Kathleen Burbidge. *Education:* Attended private boys' school in London, England. *Home:* 83 Ridgmount Gardens, Tarrington Pl., London W.C.1, England; and Lawn Cottage, Barcombe Mills, near Lewes, Sussex, England.

CAREER: Music Survey, London, England, founder and co-editor, 1947-52; *Musical Times,* London, London music critic, 1953-57; Faber & Faber Ltd., London, head of music department, 1958, music editor, 1958; *Tempo,* London, editor, 1958-62. *Daily Telegraph,* London, member of music staff, 1959-64; *Listener,* London, music critic, 1964; Faber Music Ltd., London, managing director, 1965-77, chairman, 1977—; Faber & Faber Ltd., director, 1973—. Visiting fellow at University of Sussex, 1970, professor of music, 1971-76. Music adviser for Boosey & Hawkes, 1963-64. Member of British Broadcasting Corp. central music advisory committee, 1967. Lecturer in England, the United States, and Australia. Director of academic studies at Britten-Pears School for Advanced Musical Studies. *Member:* Performing Right Society (member of general council, 1971), Reform Club. *Awards, honors:* Mahler Medal from Bruckner Society of America, 1961; M.A. from University of Sussex, 1973.

WRITINGS: (Editor with Hans Keller) *Benjamin Britten: A Commentary on His Works From a Group of Specialists,* Barrie & Rockliff, 1952, Philosophical Library, 1953; (editor with Howard Chandler Robbins Landon) *The Mozart Companion,* Oxford University Press, 1956, new edition, Norton,

1969; *Wolfgang Amadeus Mozart, 1756-1956: A Short Biography,* Decca Record Co., 1956; (editor with Keller) Milein Cosman, *Musical Sketchbook,* Bruno Cassirer, 1957; *Gustav Mahler: The Early Years,* Barrie & Rockliff, 1958, revised edition, University of California Press, 1980.

The Language of Modern Music, St. Martin's, 1963, 2nd edition, 1966; (author of introduction) Alma Mahler Werfel, *Gustav Mahler: Erinnerungen und Briefe,* Ullstein, 1968, 2nd edition, 1971, translation by Basil Creighton published as *Gustav Mahler: Memories and Letters,* 2nd edition (Mitchell was not associated with 1st edition), University of Washington Press, 1968, 3rd edition, J. Murray, 1974, University of Washington Press, 1975; *Every Child's Book of Nursery Songs,* Crown, 1968, reprinted as *The Gambit Book of Children's Songs,* Gambit, 1970 (published in England as *The Faber Book of Nursery Songs,* Faber, 1968).

The Faber Book of Children's Songs, Faber, 1970; (with Jean Reti) *Notes on Playing the Piano: Illustrated With Scenes From the Childhood of Schumann,* Special Collections, Main Library, University of Georgia, 1974; *Gustav Mahler: The Wunderhorn Years—Chronicles and Commentaries,* Faber, 1975, Westview Press, 1976; *Benjamin Britten, 1913-1976; Pictures From a Life—A Pictorial Biography,* Faber, 1978; *Britten and Auden in the Thirties: The Year 1936,* Faber, 1981. Contributor to *Encyclopaedia Britannica* and *Chambers's Encyclopaedia.*

Contributor to journals, including *Music Review, Music and Letters,* and *Opera,* and newspapers.

WORK IN PROGRESS: Two more books about Gustav Mahler.

SIDELIGHTS: Donald Mitchell is Benjamin Britten's authorized biographer, and he plans to write a major account of the composer's life and works.

BIOGRAPHICAL/CRITICAL SOURCES: Economist, January, 1976; *New Statesman,* January 9, 1976; *Times Literary Supplement,* April 30, 1976; *Choice,* July-August, 1976; *Encounter,* August, 1976; *Music Library Association Notes,* December, 1976; *Music Quarterly,* January, 1977; *Opera News,* March 31, 1979.

*   *   *

MITCHELL, Thomas N(oel) 1939-

PERSONAL: Born December 7, 1939, in Castlebar, Ireland; children: three. *Education:* National University of Ireland, B.A., 1961, M.A., 1962; Cornell University, Ph.D., 1966. *Office:* Department of Classics, Swarthmore College, Swarthmore, Pa. 19081.

CAREER: Cornell University, Ithaca, N.Y., instructor in classics, 1965-66; Swarthmore College, Swarthmore, Pa., assistant professor of classics, 1966-67; National University of Ireland, Dublin, lecturer in classics, 1967-68; Swarthmore College, assistant professor, 1968-73, associate professor of classics, 1973—. *Member:* American Philological Association. *Awards, honors:* American Council of Learned Societies fellow, 1971-72.

WRITINGS: Cicero: The Ascending Years, Yale University Press, 1979. Contributor to philology and history journals.*

*   *   *

MOFFAT, John Lawrence 1916-

PERSONAL: Born December 4, 1916, in Brookside, New Zealand; son of Albert Edward Henry (a builder) and Ethel Maude Moffat; married Edmee Liliane Griesser, June 19,

1948; children: John Claude, Francis Mark. *Education:* Christchurch Teachers' College, teachers' "B" certificate, 1938; University of Canterbury, M.A., 1939; University of Bristol, Ph.D., 1948. *Politics:* Conservative. *Religion:* "Universal." *Home and office:* Soul's Repose, 51 London St., Christchurch 1, New Zealand.

CAREER: Language master at boys' high school in Christchurch, New Zealand, 1939-53; Christchurch Teachers' College, Christchurch, principal lecturer in post-primary language, Secondary Division, 1954-79; teacher of Greek, writer, composer, and lecturer, 1979—. *Military service:* New Zealand Army, Medical Corps, 1942-45; served in Fiji; became staff sergeant. *Member:* New Zealand Language Teachers Association, New Zealand Classical Teachers Association, New Zealand Homosexual Law Reform Society, Christchurch Classical Association, Christchurch Savage Club, Canterbury Sun Club (patron).

WRITINGS: The Structure of English, Pegasus Press, 1968; *A Guide to Study,* Government Printer (Wellington, New Zealand), 1971. Author of "Learn and Live," a column in *Christchurch Star,* 1965—, "Teach In," in *Auckland Star,* 1969-75, and "Learnabout," in *Napier Daily Telegraph,* 1971-76.

WORK IN PROGRESS: Bios Hellados, a history of the human race, publication expected in 1990; books on various aspects of human civilization growing out of Greek thought; a collection of Greek Byzantine historians; research on chronology.

SIDELIGHTS: Moffat commented: "I work every day, reading and writing, in English, French, German, Latin, and classical Greek, but since I retired my center of gravity is in Greek history, philosophy, science, and literature (from the seventh century, B.C., up to and including the sixteenth century, A.D.).

"Research work gives me spontaneous joy. For me, writing books is fun. I don't want the money, or even to have them published. The two books that have been published were asked for by the publishers. They had already appeared as a series of articles in the *Christchurch Star.*

"When I sit down to write an article for the *Star* I do not decide the topic or treatment until I have the paper lined up in the typewriter. For me it is a point of honor to have the article ready for posting an hour later. It would not be onerous for me to type a new book in a fortnight. All the fruits of my research are carefully filed away in two thousand manila folders in six filing cabinets, and when I am typing an article straight off I have one of these folders of notes alongside me.

"My advice to aspiring writers would be twofold: (1) Do your homework, and (2) be yourself. Having another source of income helps too. I taught for forty-five years."

AVOCATIONAL INTERESTS: "I ride a motor-bike, play piano in my own chamber music group, read naked in my geodesic solar dome for two hours every day, even in midwinter, and type all my articles and letters there. I have composed 9 violin sonatas, 6 cello sonatas, 5 trios, 214 organ pieces, set 40 Psalms to music, and composed innumerable works for piano. I have done a score of watercolor paintings and have made hundreds of enlargements of photographs in my own darkroom. I eat fish and onions six nights a week."

*   *   *

MOISE, Lotte E(lla) 1917-

PERSONAL: Surname is pronounced Mo-eese; born December 17, 1917, in Duesseldorf, Germany (now West Ger-

many); came to the United States in 1937, naturalized citizen, 1944; daughter of Kurt (a physician) and Minnie (Freundlich) Bardach; married Alfred H. Moise (a printer), August 22, 1947; children: Karen, David, Barbara. *Education:* Columbia University, B.S., 1940, M.A., 1943. *Home and office:* 30401 Sherwood Rd., Fort Bragg, Calif. 95437.

CAREER: Long Island University, Brooklyn, N.Y., assistant to dean of women, 1940-43; Hunter College of the City University of New York, New York City, student placement administrator, 1943-44; Rockefeller Center, Inc., New York City, in personnel department, 1946-47; Naval Petroleum Reserve, Fairbanks, Alaska, secretary, 1947-49; co-founder and teacher at Paul Bunyan School in Fort Bragg, Calif., 1960-66; Paul Bunyan Activity Center, Fort Bragg, director and adult education teacher, 1966-69; Potential Unlimited, Fort Bragg, retardation consultant, 1969-71; writer, lecturer, and consultant on community living for persons with special needs, 1971—. Faculty member of Naomi Gray Associates, 1975; presents workshops. Founding member and past member of board of trustees of North Coast Regional Center; charter member of Area I Developmental Disabilities Board and policy board of Sonoma County Citizen Advocacy; member of California Protection and Advocacy Panel; chairperson of Northcoast Continuum. *Military service:* U.S. Coast Guard, 1944-46; became ensign. *Member:* American Association on Mental Deficiency. *Awards, honors:* Special Education grant from Crown Zellerbach Foundation, 1959; Rosemary F. Dybwad International Award from National Association for Retarded Citizens, 1971, for study in Denmark.

WRITINGS: (Contributor) Gunnar Dybwad and Carolyn Cherington, editors, *New Neighbors: The Retarded Citizen in Quest of a Home,* President's Committee on Mental Retardation, 1974; (with daughters, Karen Moise and Barbara Moise) *The Skinny Book,* Gull Press, 1976; *We Are the Lucky Ones,* Gull Press, 1977; *As Up We Grew With Barbara,* Dillon, 1980. Author of "Never Say Can't," a column in *Fort Bragg Advocate News.* Contributor to magazines, including *Child Welfare, CAR Challenger,* and *Mendocino Medicine.*

SIDELIGHTS: Lotte Moise told *CA:* "I like to write but do not consider myself a writer. When our third child, Barbara, turned out to have a diagnosis of 'mental retardation,' I found myself writing about her more and more often. I wanted to tell others about our discoveries and new perceptions. Parents can and should be the first line of defense for other parents. We can be the dreamers of dreams of ideally appropriate programs for our sons and daughters, and at the same time their severest critics. 'Irritants make pearls' is my motto. As long as I have the energy I plan to live up to it!

"Much remains to be done to raise the consciousness of the American public about our retarded sons and daughters. I plan, sometime, to move into our daughter's group home to take photographs, make tape recordings, listen, and put together a book that might be called *My House: A Group Home.* In my spare time I'll continue to hit tennis balls and make believe that they are bureaucratic adversaries, and will hide in the photography darkroom from telephone bells."

AVOCATIONAL INTERESTS: Baking bread, playing tennis, photography.

*   *   *

MOLLOY, M(ichael) J(oseph) 1917-

PERSONAL: Born March 3, 1917, in Milltown, Ireland; son of William (a salesman) and Maria (a teacher; maiden name,

Tucker) Molloy. *Politics:* None. *Religion:* Catholic. *Residence:* Milltown, County Galway, Ireland.

CAREER: Playwright. Worked as farmer in Milltown, Ireland, 1950-72. *Member:* Society of Irish Playwrights, Authors Guild of Ireland. *Awards, honors:* Received award for "The Bitter Pill," 1965; Irish Arts Council award, 1977.

WRITINGS—Plays: *Old Road* (three-act; first produced in Dublin at Abbey Theatre, 1943), Progress House, 1961; "The Visiting House" (three-act; first produced in Dublin at Abbey Theatre, 1946), published in *Seven Irish Plays, 1946-1964,* edited by Robert G. Hogan, University of Minnesota Press, 1967; *The King of Friday's Men* (three-act; first produced in Dublin at Abbey Theatre, 1948; first produced in New York City at Playhouse Theatre, 1951), James Duffy, 1953; *The Paddy Pedlar* (one-act; fist produced in Dublin at Abbey Theatre, 1953), James Duffy, 1954; *The Wood of the Whispering* (three-act; first produced in Dublin at Abbey Theatre, 1953; first produced Off-Broadway, 1975), Progress House, 1961; *The Will and the Way* (three-act; first produced in Dublin at Abbey Theatre, 1955; produced in New York at Theatre East, 1956) P. J. Bourke, 1957; "A Right Rose Tree" (three-act), first produced in Dublin at Abbey Theatre, 1958; *Daughter From Over the Water* (three-act; first produced in Dublin at Gaiety Theatre, 1964), Progress House, 1963; *The Bitter Pill* (one-act; first produced in Dublin at Gate Theatre, 1965), Progress House, 1965; *Petticoat Loose* (three-act; first produced in Dublin at Abbey Theatre, 1979), Proscenium, in press.

Work anthologized in *Prizewinning Plays of 1964,* Progress House, 1964. Contributor of reviews and articles to periodicals.

WORK IN PROGRESS: A three-act play on terrorism c. 1880-1885, tentatively entitled "The Earl of Hell."

SIDELIGHTS: Molloy told *CA:* "I was influenced by Synge and Yeats far more than by Joyce. Lady Gregory also influenced me. My main objective as a writer is to be a storytelling dramatist in the tradition of Shakespeare and Synge. I also hold before my eyes the axiom that style is a main preservative of literature."

*   *   *

MONAGHAN, (James) Jay (IV)   1891-1981

OBITUARY NOTICE—See index for *CA* sketch: Born March 19, 1891, in West Chester, Pa.; died in 1981 in Santa Barbara, Calif. Historian and author. Monaghan worked as a cowboy in his youth and owned and operated cattle and sheep ranches until 1934. In 1911 he became involved in the Madero revolution in Mexico and was arrested as a spy. From the 1930's, he pursued his historical interests and became known as a leading authority on Abraham Lincoln and as one of the most distinguished historians of the American West. His books include *Lincoln Bibliography, Last of the Bad Men: The Legend of Tom Horn, Custer,* and an autobiography, *Schoolboy, Cowboy, Mexican Spy.* Obituaries and other sources: *AB Bookman's Weekly,* May 4, 1981.

*   *   *

MONTAG, Thomas   1947-
(Tom Montag)

PERSONAL: Born August 31, 1947, in Fort Dodge, Iowa; son of Philip John (a farmer) and Oma Marie (Allen) Montag; married Mary Kathryn Whitford (a registered nurse), 1969; children: Jenifer, Jessica. *Education:* Dominican College of Racine, B.A., 1972. *Home and office address:* P.O. Box A,

Fairwater, Wis. 53931. *Agent:* Hintz Literary Agency, 2879 North Grant Blvd., Milwaukee, Wis. 53210.

CAREER: Country Beautiful Publications, Waukesha, Wis., researcher, 1968; St. Mary's Burn Center, Milwaukee, Wis., orderly, 1969-72; Karl Bostrom/Center for Venture Management, Milwaukee, researcher and writer, 1970-72; *Margins: A Review of Little Magazines and Small Press Books,* Milwaukee, editor and publisher, 1972-76; *Fox River Patriot,* Princeton, Wis., associate editor, 1976-79; Ripon Community Printers, Ripon, Wis., shift supervisor and sheet-fed press operator, 1980—. Editor and publisher of Monday Morning Press and Margins Books, 1972—, Midwestern Writer's Publishing House, and *Midwestern Letters,* 1980; member of board of directors of Boox, Inc., 1974-76; member of literature panel of Wisconsin Arts Board, 1977-80.

WRITINGS—All under name Tom Montag; poems: *Wooden Nickel,* Albatross Press, 1972; *Twelve Poems,* Monday Morning Press, 1972; *Measures,* Harpoon Press, 1972; *To Leave/ This Place,* Monday Morning Press, 1972; *Making Hay,* Fault Publications, 1973; *Making Hay and Other Poems,* Pentagram Press, 1975; *Ninety Notes: Toward Partial Images and Lover Prints,* Pentagram Press, 1976; *Naming the Creeks,* Morgan Press, 1976; *Instructions for the Would-Be Assassin,* Grand River Publications, 1978; *The Farmer's Manifesto,* Grand River Publications, 1978; *Things I Could Tell You,* Grand River Publications, 1979; "Silence: Light", Pentagram Press, 1979; *Letters Home,* Sparrow Press, 1979; *This Gathering Season,* Juniper Books, 1980; *Middle Ground: Selected Poems, 1970-1980,* Midwestern Writers' Publishing House, 1981; *Between Zen and Midwestern,* Salt-works Press, 1981.

Nonfiction: (Editor with Forest Stearns) *The Urban Ecosystem: A Holistic Approach,* Dowden, 1974; *Learning to Read/Again,* Cat's Pajamas Press, 1976; *Concerns: Essays and Reviews, 1972-76,* Pentagram Press, 1977. Founder and contributing editor of *Pushcart Prize,* 1976.

WORK IN PROGRESS: Dear Esther, poems, adapted from the Civil War letters of George H. Cadman; *When the Sun Goes Down, the Sky Turns Dark: A Farmer's Notebook and Manifesto,* poems; *Married to Prairie,* a poem series of a pioneer widow struggling to make a life for herself and her children on the prairie; a collection of essays, publication by Juniper Books expected in 1982; essays exploring the relationship between place/region and literature and life.

SIDELIGHTS: Montag told *CA:* "It's not write-ups that are important to me, but my writing. Those who want a true and thoughtful explanation will have to wait till my autobiography is published; but don't hold your breath, because I have no plans for one. I am about as unfamous as a writer can be without disappearing from the face of the earth."

BIOGRAPHICAL/CRITICAL SOURCES: Wisconsin Academy Review, June, 1980.

*   *   *

MONTAG, Tom
See MONTAG, Thomas

*   *   *

MOONMAN, Eric   1929-

PERSONAL: Born April 29, 1929, in Liverpool, England; son of Bonach (a milkman) and Leah (Bernstein) Moonman; married wife, Jane (a writer and magistrate), September 9, 1962; children: Daniel, Natasha, Joshua. *Education:* University of Liverpool, Diploma in Social Science, 1953; Victoria University of Manchester, M.Sc., 1968. *Religion:* Jewish. *Home:* 1 Beacon Hill, London N.7, England. *Office:* Centre for Contemporary Studies, Heron House, 163-175 Shoreditch High St., London E.1, England.

CAREER: Daily Mirror, London, England, journalist, 1954-56; British Institute of Management, London, human relations adviser, 1956-62; Victoria University of Manchester, Manchester, England, senior research fellow in management sciences, 1962-66; British Parliament, London, Labour member of Parliament for Billericay, Essex, 1966-70, Parliamentary Private Secretary, 1968-70; British Parliament, Labour member of Parliament for Basildon, 1974-79. Founder and chairman of Parliamentary Committee on Mental Health, 1967; leader of council of London Borough of Shepney, 1959-61; member of Tower Hamlet's Council, 1962-66. Director of Radio Essex. Vice-chairman of Britain/Israel Public Affairs Committee. *Military service:* British Army, King's Regiment, 1951-53. *Member:* Royal Society of Arts (fellow), British Institute of Management (fellow), Institute of Personnel Management (member). *Awards, honors:* Japanese Management Award from Japanese Management Association, 1969.

WRITINGS: The Manager and the Organization, Tavistock Publications, 1960; (editor) *European Science and Technology,* Penguin, 1968; *Communication in an Expanding Organization,* Tavistock Publications, 1969; *Reluctant Partnership,* Gollancz, 1970; (editor) *The British Computer Industry and Industrial Innovation,* Allen & Unwin, 1972. Contributor to *London Times* and other newspapers.

SIDELIGHTS: Eric Moonman commented: "I have tried to introduce humor into my politics. I have often failed to make 'em laugh, and that's why I lose the occasional election." *Avocational interests:* Travel.

*   *   *

MOORE, Harry T(hornton)   1908-1981

OBITUARY NOTICE—See index for *CA* sketch: Born August 2, 1908, in Oakland, Calif.; died April 11, 1981, in Carbondale, Ill. Educator, critic, and author. Moore is best remembered for his studies of the life and works of D. H. Lawrence, though he also wrote and edited books on Steinbeck, Forster, Durrell, Rilke, and other authors. He wrote a biography of Lawrence, *The Intelligent Heart* (later revised and retitled *The Priest of Love*), that became the basis for a motion picture in 1981. Other works include *Poste Restante: A Lawrence Travel Calendar, Twentieth Century German Literature,* and *The World of Lawrence Durrell.* Moore taught at several universities in the United States and Great Britain and served in the U.S. Army Air Forces during World War II. Obituaries and other sources: *London Times,* May 15, 1981; *AB Bookman's Weekly,* May 25, 1981.

*   *   *

MOORE, Lilian

PERSONAL: Born in New York, N.Y.; married second husband, Sam Reavin (a farmer), 1969; children: (first marriage) Jonathan. *Education:* Hunter College, B.A.; graduate study at Columbia University.

CAREER: Teacher in New York City; staff member of New York City Bureau of Educational Research; Scholastic Book Services, New York City, editor of Arrow Book Club, beginning 1957; editor of easy reader series in Wonder Books Division of Grosset & Dunlap, New York City; series editor for Thomas Y. Crowell, New York City. Reading specialist and contributor to *Humpty Dumpty's Magazine.* Founding

member of the Council on Interracial Books for Children. *Awards, honors: Old Rosie, the Horse Nobody Understood* was on the *New York Times* list of best 100 books, 1960; *Sam's Place: Poems From the Country* was chosen for the American Institute of Graphic Arts Children's Books Show, 1973.

WRITINGS—All for children: *A Child's First Picture Dictionary,* Wonder Books, 1948; (with Leone Adelson) *Old Rosie, the Horse Nobody Understood,* Random House, 1952; (with Adelson) *The Terrible Mr. Twitmeyer,* Random House, 1952; *The Golden Picture Dictionary,* Simon & Schuster, 1954; *The Important Pockets of Paul,* McKay, 1954; *The Golden Picture Book of Stories to Hear and to Read,* Simon & Schuster, 1955; *Daniel Boone* (biography), Random House, 1956; *My First Counting Book,* Simon & Schuster, 1956, published as *My Big Golden Counting Book,* 1957; *Wobbly Wheels,* Abingdon, 1956; *The Snake That Went to School,* Random House, 1957; *Once Upon a Holiday,* Abingdon, 1959; *Tony the Pony,* Whittlesey House, 1959.

Bear Trouble, Whittlesey House, 1960; *Everything Happens to Stuey,* Random House, 1960; *Too Many Bozos,* Golden Press, 1960; *A Pickle for a Nickel,* Golden Press, 1961; *Once Upon a Season,* Abingdon, 1962; *Little Raccoon and the Thing in the Pool,* Whittlesey House, 1963; (with Adelson) *Mr. Twitmeyer and the Poodle,* Random House, 1963; *Papa Albert,* Atheneum, 1964; *Little Raccoon and the Outside World,* Whittlesey House, 1965; *The Magic Spectacles, and Other Easy-to-Read Stories,* Parents' Magazine Press, 1966; *I Feel the Same Way* (poems), Atheneum, 1967; *Just Right,* Parents' Magazine Press, 1968; *I Thought I Heard the City* (poems), Atheneum, 1969; *Junk Day on Juniper Street, and Other Easy-to-Read Stories,* Parents' Magazine Press, 1969.

(With others) A. Bennett, compiler, *Picture Dictionary, ABC's and Telling Time, Counting Rhymes, Riddles, and Finger Play* (previously published as *A Child's First Picture Dictionary, My ABC Book, What Time Is It?, The Wonder Book of Counting Rhymes, The Wonder Book of Finger Plays and Action Rhymes, Ten Little Fingers,* and *My First Book of Riddles*), Grosset, 1970; *The Riddle Walk,* Garrard, 1971; *Little Raccoon and No Trouble at All,* McGraw, 1972; (retold by Moore) *The Ugly Duckling by Hans Christian Andersen,* Scholastic Book Services, 1972; (compiler with Lawrence Webster) *Catch Your Breath: A Book of Shivery Poems,* Garrard, 1973; *Sam's Place: Poems From the Country,* Atheneum, 1973; *Spooky Rhymes and Riddles,* Scholastic Book Services, 1973; (editor) Hans Christian Andersen, *The Ugly Duckling and Two Other Stories,* Scholastic Book Services, 1973; (compiler with Judith Thurman) *To See the World Afresh* (poems), Atheneum, 1974; (with Remy Charlip) *Hooray for Me!,* Parents' Magazine Press, 1975; *Little Raccoon and Poems From the Woods,* McGraw, 1975; *See My Lovely Poison Ivy, and Other Verses About Witches, Ghosts, and Things,* Atheneum, 1975; (compiler) *Go With the Poem,* McGraw, 1979.

Also author of *The Girl in the White Hat, The House That Jack Built, The Kid, Miss Esta Maude's Secret, Old Mother Hubbard and Her Dog, The Old Woman and Her Pig, Sophocles the Hyena, Tony's Good Luck,* and *Count to Ten.* Editorial consultant for two books by Paul Newman, *The Birthday Party,* Grosset, 1964, and *No Place to Play,* Grosset, 1969.

SIDELIGHTS: In hopes of teaching Elizabethan literature to college students, Lilian Moore majored in English. Instead, she found herself teaching truant children how to read. Although she enjoyed the challenge of working with those children, she was frustrated by the lack of easy-to-read books with which to teach them and decided to write her own. She wanted to write books that were both exciting and not too difficult, so that a child with a reading problem could know the pleasure of being able to read independently.

The more than forty children's books that Moore has since written have been consistently well received. Critics have praised her ability to write simple sentences using an easy vocabulary. "Lilian Moore is very clever at handling the kind of simple stories that do not discourage those who are still fumbling with the newly acquired ability to read," wrote M. S. Libby of the *New York Herald Tribune Book Review*.

While working as an editor at Scholastic's Arrow Book Club, Moore became involved in a program that made quality paperback books available to children. Children and teachers alike were enthusiastic about this program that, for the first time, enabled children to buy many of their favorite books.

A number of Lilian Moore's popular stories have been adapted into short films, including *Bear Trouble, Too Many Bozos, A Pickle for a Nickel, Tony's Good Luck,* and *The Girl in the White Hat*.

AVOCATIONAL INTERESTS: Chamber music, bicycling, ice skating, gardening, and traveling.

BIOGRAPHICAL/CRITICAL SOURCES: New York Times, November 23, 1952; *New York Herald Tribune Book Review,* April 26, 1959; *New York Times Book Review,* November 9, 1969, April 29, 1979.*

*   *   *

MOORE, Paul L.   1917-1976

OBITUARY NOTICE—See index for *CA* sketch: Born November 5, 1917, in North Baltimore, Ohio; died April 14, 1976. Clergyman and author. Moore wrote *Seven Words of Men Around the Cross.* (Date of death provided by *Sidney Daily News,* Sidney, Ohio.)

*   *   *

MOREAU, Jules Laurence   1917-1971

OBITUARY NOTICE—See index for *CA* sketch: Born December 9, 1917, in Irvington, N.J.; died June 12, 1971. Educator, translator, and author. Moreau wrote *Language and Religious Language* and *Faith and Fact: A Traditio-Historical Inquiry Into the Primitive Strata of Christian History.* He also translated Thorlief Borman's book *Hebrew Thought Compared With Greek.* (Date of death provided by Seabury-Western Theological Seminary.)

*   *   *

MORGAN, Robert   1921-

PERSONAL: Born April 17, 1921, in Wales; son of William Henry and Else Jane Morgan; married Jean Elizabeth Florence; children: Allison Mary, Marion Lesley. *Education:* Attended Fircroft College, 1949-51; Bognor Regis College of Education, 1951-53; Southampton University, 1969-71. *Home:* 72 Anmore Rd., Denmead, Hampshire P07 6NT, England. *Office:* Teachers' Centre, Gosport, Hampshire, England.

CAREER: Coal miner, 1936-47; teacher in primary schools, 1951-64, and head of remedial department at secondary school in Cowplain, England, 1964-74; Gosport Education Authority, Gosport, England, advisory teacher for special education, 1974—. *Member:* Welsh Academy, Guild of Anglo-Welsh Writers.

WRITINGS: The Night's Prison (poems and verse play), Hart-Davis, 1967; *Poems and Extracts,* Exeter University, 1968; *The Storm* (poems and drawings), Christopher Davies, 1974; *On the Banks of the Cynon* (poems and drawings), A.R.C. Publications, 1976; *Voices in the Dark* (verse play), A.R.C. Publications, 1976; *My Lamp Still Burns* (autobiography), Gomer Press, 1981; *Impressions* (poems), Davis-Poynter, 1981.

Verse plays: "Rainbow Valley," first broadcast by BBC-Radio, August 4, 1967; "The Master Miners," first broadcast by BBC-Radio, June 16, 1974.

WORK IN PROGRESS: Another volume of his autobiography, publication by Gomer Press expected in 1982; poems; verse plays; *One Place, One Time,* a novel.

SIDELIGHTS: Morgan commented: "Almost all my work is devoted to coal miners and the mining landscape of South Wales. A small amount is connected with the pupils I taught between 1957 and 1964."

BIOGRAPHICAL/CRITICAL SOURCES: Writers on Tour, Welsh Arts Council, 1979.

*   *   *

MORGELLO, Clemente Frank   1923-

PERSONAL: Born December 3, 1923, in New York, N.Y.; son of Joseph and Maria Sophia (Romano) Morgello; married Kilda Laufer, June 11, 1949 (marriage ended); children: Susan, Peter. *Education:* City College of New York (now of the City University of New York), B.S., 1947; University of Wisconsin, M.A., 1948. *Home:* 136 Waverly Place, New York, N.Y. 10014. *Office:* 666 Fifth Ave., New York, N.Y. 10019.

CAREER/WRITINGS: Canandaigua Daily Messenger, Canandaigua, N.Y., staff member, 1948-49; *Wall Street Journal,* New York City, staff member, 1949-50; *Newsweek,* New York City, staff member, 1950-70, senior editor, 1959-75; *Dun's Review,* New York City, editor, 1976—. *Military service:* U.S. Army, 1943-45; received Purple Heart. *Member:* Financial Writers' Association. *Awards, honors:* Award for distinguished performance, 1966; award for business writing from Deadline Club, 1968; Gerald Loeb Award from University of Connecticut, 1972.

*   *   *

MORITA, James R.   1931-

PERSONAL: Born June 13, 1931, in Salem, Ore.; married; children: two. *Education:* University of Michigan, M.A., 1959, M.A., 1960; University of Chicago, Ph.D., 1968. *Office:* Department of East Asian Language and Literature, Ohio State University, Columbus, Ohio 43210.

CAREER: University of Chicago, Chicago, Ill., Japanese librarian at Far Eastern Library, 1961-69, instructor, 1966-68, assistant professor of Japanese literature, 1968-69; University of Oregon, Eugene, assistant professor of Japanese literature, 1969-72; Ohio State University, Columbus, associate professor of East Asian language and literature, 1972—. *Member:* Modern Language Association of America, Association of Teachers of Japanese, Association for Asian Studies. *Awards, honors:* Fellowships from American Council of Learned Societies and Social Science Research Council, 1970, and Japan Foundation, 1977-78.

WRITINGS: Keneko Mitsuharu, Twayne, 1980. Contributor to literature journals.

MORRILL, Claire 1900(?)-1981

OBITUARY NOTICE: Born c. 1900; died in 1981 in Taos, N.M. Bookseller and author. Morrill was a co-owner of the Taos Book Shop and a collector of Southwestern Americana. She wrote *A Taos Mosaic.* Obituaries and other sources: *AB Bookman's Weekly,* April 27, 1981.

* * *

MORRIS, Stephen 1935-

PERSONAL: Born August 14, 1935, in Smethwick, England; son of Rex (a television and radio retailer) and Muriel (a clerk; maiden name, Griffin) Morris; married Michele Madaleine Warren (a lecturer), August 31, 1963; children: Claudia, Daniel, Caroline. *Education:* Attended Fircroft College, 1958-59, and Marieborgs Folk High School (Sweden), 1959-60; University of Wales, University College, Cardiff, D.Soc.Sci., 1963; University of Leicester, Diploma in Sociology and Psychology, 1966. *Politics:* "Left." *Religion:* "Nominal Roman Catholic." *Home:* 12 Zulla Rd., Mapperley Park, Nottingham NG3 5DB, England. *Agent:* J. Sweet, 23 Bell Lane, Ludlow, Shropshire, England. *Office:* Department of Related Studies, Faculty of Art and Design, Polytechnic, Wolverhampton, England.

CAREER: Whitchurch Hospital, Cardiff, Wales, research worker, 1963-65; Mansfield Art College, Mansfield, England, assistant lecturer in art, 1966-67; Polytechnic, Wolverhampton, England, assistant lecturer, 1967-69, lecturer, 1969-72, senior lecturer in art, 1972—. Visiting tutor at Portsmouth College of Art. Gives poetry readings and solo exhibitions of experimental visual poetry and paintings in the United States, Denmark, The Netherlands, Sweden, the Far East, and England. *Military service:* Royal Air Force, 1953-56; became senior aircraftsman. *Awards, honors:* Scholar of Swedish Institute, 1959-60; British Council grant for India, 1980.

WRITINGS: Alien Poets (poetry), Claudia Publications, 1965; (with Peter Finch) *Wanted for Writing Poetry,* Avon Publications, 1968; *Penny Farthing Madness* (poetry), Summerstar, 1969; *Born Under Leo* (poetry), Aquila, 1972; *The Revolutionary* (poetry), Aquila, 1972; *The Kingfisher Catcher* (poetry), Aquila, 1974; *Death of a Clown* (poetry), Aquila, 1976; *The Moment of Truth* (poetry), Aquila, 1977; *Too Long at the Circus* (poetry), Aquila, 1980; *Czech Mate* (novel), Aquila, 1982; *In Search of Christie* (novel), Aquila, 1982.

Work represented in anthologies, including *Widening Circles,* 1977. Contributor to magazines, including *Observer,* and newspapers.

WORK IN PROGRESS: Children's Short Stories.

SIDELIGHTS: Morris told *CA:* "I only write when I think I've got something worthwhile to say. If it were the late 1960's, I could write ten thousand words a day. Now, in 1980, I fear for the future of the world, and I'm not sure that its worth writing ten words a day. I feel that mankind has reached a watershed. However, I don't know any answers at all. I don't think I even know the questions any more. Since visiting the Far East on three occasions from 1977 to 1980, my values have been turned upside down, culturally, politically, socially, and emotionally. Generally I think living is fantastic and I enjoy it. Inspiration comes from many things and I like many writers, not all that a particular individual writes, but odd things here and there."

AVOCATIONAL INTERESTS: Sport, French food, loving, sunshine, drinking wine and whisky, films.

BIOGRAPHICAL/CRITICAL SOURCES: Wolverhampton Express and Star, January 19, 1968, June 19, 1968; Caroline Hillier, *The Western Midlands,* Gollancz, 1976; *Penang Star,* July, 1977; *Waste Paper,* March, 1978; *Delphi Recorder,* January, 1980; *Moseley Arts,* March, 1980.

* * *

MORRIS, Taylor 1923-

PERSONAL: Born March 7, 1923, in Rayville, La.; son of Edgar Taylor (a lawyer and agent) and Aphra (Vairin) Morris; married Gale Tomlinson, September, 1958 (divorced, 1972); married Janice Dolan (a painter), September 12, 1978; children: (first marriage) Charlotte, Taylor, Jr., Jack, Lucy, Beverly. *Education:* Attended Texas A & M University, 1942; Tulane University, B.A., 1948; Columbia University, M.A., 1972. *Home:* 46 Union St., Peterborough, N.H. 03458. *Agent:* Heide Lange, Sanford J. Greenburger Associates, Inc., 825 Third Ave., New York, N.Y. 10022.

CAREER: Teacher and librarian at private school in New York City, 1960-61; teacher of mathematics and Spanish at private school in New York City, 1962-64; Hunter College of the City University of New York, New York City, instructor in English literature, 1964-66; Franklin Pierce College, Rindge, N.H., assistant professor, 1967-72, associate professor of English, 1972—. Founder and director of Bi-Lingual School, Jaltipan, Mexico. *Military service:* U.S. Marine Corps, pilot, 1943-46, 1949-51; became first lieutenant.

MEMBER: New Hampshire Poets and Writers, Arts Exchange. *Awards, honors:* Fellow of MacDowell Colony, 1966, 1975, 1977, 1978; grants from National Institute for Arts and Letters, MacDowell Foundation, and Foundation Six, 1967, Ford Foundation, 1969, Virginia Center for Creative Arts, 1971, and Carnegie Fund for Writers, 1974.

WRITINGS: The Walk of the Conscious Ants, Knopf, 1972; *Sam* (novel), Volume I, McGraw, in press. Contributor to magazines, including *New Yorker* and *Windfall,* and newspapers.

WORK IN PROGRESS: Goat Song, a novel, 1982; *The World at Our Feet,* nonfiction, 1982.

SIDELIGHTS: "I write," Morris told *CA,* "because it makes more sense to me than any other thing I can do. As well, I write because no one can possibly reproduce (in prose or any other form) my own vision of the world, precisely because it is my own. If I don't do it it will not be done. The artist's ego makes this tremendously important.

"I am a teacher and have supported myself and children by teaching; writing has had to wait on those priorities. Doing for the children is a different art form and there are no apparent honors or publications involved. I wouldn't have it different, but will simply have to live to 120 years old, which I intend to do.

"Mark Van Doren, under whom I studied at Columbia, once said that the difference between comedy and tragedy was whether the writer felt that God, from his perch, would look down on the human scene and laugh at it or cry over it. If the writer's attitude is that God would cry then the writer is doomed to write (or try to write) tragedy. My viewpoint is that God, presuming he (or she) is on duty and still cares, would shake his head and smile, while tears ran down his cheeks.

"I think that the novel allows the maximum opportunity to write songs, poems, talk, essays, meanderings, and is the greatest vehicle for the widest range of verbal expression. My longest unpublished novel, *Goat Song* (begun long before Frank Yerby used the same title), is like a seven hundred-page sentence. While doing it, I had the feeling that I must get the words out of the way of the experience. That apprenticeship has cost me thirteen years, and, since then, I have become much more interested in humor—humor with a hook in it.

"*Sam* is a novel in three parts. Sam, hero and novel's namesake, is convinced that the earth is doomed—consequently he sees his task as twofold: to kill hope for the world and to go out and kiss it goodbye. Of course, he discovers that with each breath we hope, and he intends to keep breathing.

"My own growing up in New Orleans seems vital and a novel about that is in the wings, along with another about an ideological revolution which, of course, changes the direction of life on earth.

"I am also the author of a pamphlet, 'Soldiers for Peace.' Soldiers for Peace would involve a massive exchange of Russian and American students on a yearly basis as voluntary hostages, in order for them to learn about each other's countries and form links between the two countries, eventually making war unthinkable.

"In trying to get my students and myself out of school to 'really' teach them what needs to be taught, I have organized long 'walks.' The first was from school to Canada, a forty-day walk in which we all slept in an old army squad tent. The second was a seven-hundred-mile walk across Spain under the same conditions. The third was a four hundred-mile walk up the southwest coast of Mexico, and the fourth another walk across Spain, in a different area, followed by a walk across England, or rather from London to Edinburgh. In 1979, with my wife and twenty-two students (including our five children), we walked from Spain inland to France, across to Italy, down to Pisa, into Florence, and up to Trieste, into and down the coast of Yugoslavia to Dubrovnik. The walk took about four months and covered sixteen hundred miles. *The World at Our Feet* is about that walk. I have also lived in Mexico, for about six years, and have traveled in the Caribbean islands and northern South America."

* * *

MORRISON, John Gordon 1904-

PERSONAL: Born January 29, 1904, in Sunderland, England; son of John (a telegraph construction foreman) and Mary (Turnbull) Morrison; married Rosina Jones, September 1, 1928 (died January 9, 1967); married Rachel Gordon, March 24, 1969; children: (first marriage) John, Marie Morrison Finlay. *Education:* Attended primary school in Sunderland, England. *Politics:* "Anywhere left of the Australian Liberal party." *Religion:* None. *Home:* 127 Brighton Rd., Flat 5, Elwood, Victoria 3184, Australia.

CAREER: Sunderland Museum, Sunderland, England, assistant to curator, 1918-20; gardener in England, 1920-23, and Australia, 1923—. *Member:* Fellowship of Australian Writers, Australian Society of Authors (member of council, 1968—). *Awards, honors:* Commonwealth Literary Fund fellow, 1947, 1949; gold medal from Australian Literature Society, 1962, for *Twenty-Three;* emeritus fellowship from Literary Board of Australia Council, 1980.

WRITINGS: Sailors Belong Ships (short stories), Dolphin Publications, 1947; *The Creeping City* (novel), Cassell, 1949; *Port of Call* (novel), Cassell, 1950; *Black Cargo* (short sto-

ries), Australasian Book Society, 1955; *Twenty-Three* (short stories), Australasian Book Society, 1962; *Selected Stories,* Rigby, 1972; *Australian by Choice* (short stories), Rigby, 1973.

Work represented in anthologies, including *Australian Short Stories,* Oxford University Press, Series I, 1951, Series II, 1963; *Eine Rose oder Zwei,* Paul Neff Verlag, 1963; *Classic Australian Short Stories,* Wren Publishing (Melbourne), 1974. Stories broadcast by Australian Broadcasting Commission. Contributor of stories to magazines, including *Meanjin* and *Overland.* Past reviewer for *Age,* Melbourne, Australia.

WORK IN PROGRESS: A collection of short stories, publication by Penguin (Australia) expected in 1982.

SIDELIGHTS: Morrison commented: "On leaving school at fourteen I took a job as boy assistant to the curator of Sunderland Museum. There I developed what was to be a lifelong interest in natural history, which as the years passed became a deep concern with the environment conservation problem. I also laid the foundations of a taste for good reading and an ambition to be a writer myself one day. Without higher education, however, I outgrew the job, and after a stint of two years as a learner gardener I came to Australia in 1923. In this country, except for a short visit to Europe in the early sixties, I have remained happily ever since, working on farms, sheep stations, and the Melbourne waterfront.

"I am, and have been for many years, concerned with the urgent social problems of the day. It doesn't seem to me an oversimplification to suggest that these problems all trace back to the age-old struggle of man to curb his animal instincts and to work out a social system in which he can get along peacefully with his fellow creatures. This concern inevitably colors much of my work, but I've tried never to lose sight of the prime importance of telling a readable story, of presenting men and women as I've really found them to be, and of preserving a sense of the ludicrous in human nature. I take the view that we're nothing if not fallible, and that the writer who is without a sense of humor is in danger of becoming a bore. My pet aversion is the fanatic, no matter of what persuasion. And my favorite among the pearls of wisdom which have come down to us from the wise is, 'The only men worthy of governing other men are those who don't want to.'"

BIOGRAPHICAL/CRITICAL SOURCES: John Hetherington, *Forty Faces,* F. W. Cheshire, 1962; *Meanjin,* Volume XVIII, number 4, 1962; *Overland,* Volume VIII, number 58, 1974; Graeme Kinross Simth, *Australia's Writers,* Thomas Nelson, 1980.

* * *

MORTON, H(enry Canova) V(ollam) 1892-1979

PERSONAL: Born July 25, 1892, in Birmingham, England; died in 1979, near Cape Town, South Africa; son of Joseph Vollam and Margaret Constance MacLean (Ewart) Morton. *Education:* Attended school in Birmingham, England.

CAREER: Birmingham Gazette, Birmingham, England, began as journalist, became assistant editor, 1910-12; *Empire,* London, England, editor, 1913; *Daily Mail,* London, subeditor, 1913-14; *Evening Standard,* London, member of editorial staff, 1919-21; *Daily Express,* London, member of editorial staff, 1921-31; *Daily Herald,* London, special writer, 1931-42; free-lance writer, 1942-79. *Military service:* British Army, Warwickshire Yeomanry, during World War I; served in France. *Awards, honors:* Knight commander of Greece's

Order of the Phoenix, 1937; cavaliere ufficiale of Italy's Order of Merit, 1965.

WRITINGS: The Heart of London, Methuen, 1925; *The London Year: A Book of Many Moods, Decorated From a London Sketch Book by A. E. Horne*, Methuen, 1926; *The Spell of London*, Methuen, 1926; *When You Go to London*, Harper, 1927; *In Search of England*, Methuen, 1927, 3rd edition, 1928, R. M. McBride & Co., 1928, revised edition, Dodd, 1935, reprinted, 1960; *London*, R. M. McBride & Co., 1928; *The Land of the Vikings: From Thames to Humber*, Richard Clay & Sons, 1928; *The Call of England*, R. M. McBride & Co., 1928; *In Search of Scotland*, Methuen, 1929, Dodd, 1930, reprinted, 1966.

In Search of Ireland, Methuen, 1930, 3rd edition, 1931, Dodd, 1931, reprinted, 1966, abridged edition (edited by Patricia Haward) published as *The Magic of Ireland*, 1978; *In Search of Wales*, Dodd, 1932; *Blue Days at Sea and Other Essays*, Dodd, 1933; *In Scotland Again*, Dodd, 1933, 15th edition, 1949; *In the Steps of the Master*, Dodd, 1934, reprinted, 1959, 24th edition, Methuen, 1971; *The London Scene*, R. M. McBride & Co., 1935; *Our Fellow Men*, Methuen. 1936; *In the Steps of Saint Paul*, Dodd, 1936; *London: A Guide*, Methuen, 1937; *Through Lands of the Bible*, Dodd, 1938, reprinted, 1959; *Ghosts of London*, Methuen, 1939, Dodd, 1940.

Women of the Bible, Methuen, 1940, Dodd, 1941; *The Middle East: A Record of Travel in the Countries of Egypt, Palestine, Iraq, Turkey, and Greece*, Dodd, 1941; *H. V. Morton's London: Being "The Heart of London," "The Spell of London," and "The Nights of London"; With an Introduction, "The Battle of London"*, Dodd, 1941, 18th edition published as *London: Being "The Heart of London," "The Spell of London," and "The Nights of London"; With an Introduction, "The Battle of London"*, Methuen, 1957; *I Saw Two Englands: The Record of a Journey Before the War, and After the Outbreak of War, in the Year 1939*, Methuen, 1942, 2nd edition, 1943, Dodd, 1943; *I, James Blunt* (fictitious autobiography), Dodd, 1942; *Atlantic Meeting: An Account of Mr. Churchill's Voyage in H.M.S. Prince of Wales, in August, 1941, and the Conference With President Roosevelt Which Resulted in the Atlantic Charter*, Dodd, 1943; *In Search of South Africa*, Dodd, 1948.

In Search of London, Dodd, 1951; *In the Steps of Jesus*, Dodd, 1953; *A Stranger in Spain*, Dodd, 1955; *A Traveller in Rome*, Dodd, 1957.

This Is Rome: A Pilgrimage in Words and Pictures, Conducted by Fulton J. Sheen (introduction by Sheen; photographs by Yousuf Karsh), Hawthorn, 1960; *This Is the Holy Land: A Pilgrimage in Words and Pictures, Conducted by Fulton J. Sheen* (introduction by Sheen; photographs by Karsh), Hawthorn, 1961; *A Traveller in Italy*, Dodd, 1964; *The Fountains of Rome*, Macmillan, 1966 (published in England as *The Waters of Rome*, M. Joseph, 1966); *H. V. Morton's Britain* (edited by Gilbert Carter), Dodd, 1969; *A Traveller in Southern Italy*, Dodd, 1969.

The Splendour of Scotland, Eyre Methuen, 1976; *In Search of the Holy Land* (edited by Christopher Derrick), Dodd, 1979.

OBITUARIES: AB Bookman's Weekly, August 20, 1979.*

* * *

MOSS, Stephen Joseph 1935-

PERSONAL: Born April 1, 1935, in New York, N.Y.: son of Hyman H. and Beatrice (Nadelstein) Moss; married Lydia Irene Wallack, December 16, 1962; children: Jonathan H., David L. *Education:* Queens College (now of the City University of New York), B.S., 1955; New York University, D.D.S., 1959, M.S., 1963, further graduate study, 1964-67. *Home:* 1 Washington Square Village, New York, N.Y. 10012. *Office:* Dental Center, New York University, 421 First Ave., New York, N.Y. 10016.

CAREER: Private practice of dentistry in New York, N.Y., 1959—. Diplomate of American Board of Pedodontics; instructor at New York University, 1964-67, assistant professor, 1967-70, associate professor, 1970-76, professor, 1976—, chairman of department of dentistry for children, 1971—, attending oral surgeon at university hospital Medical Center, 1965—, director of dental services at Irvington House, 1964-71. Director of Children's Comprehensive Dental Care Program at Beth Israel Medical Center, 1968-72; director of children's dentistry at Brookdale Hospital Center, 1966—, and Jewish Hospital and Medical Center, 1964—; member of advisory committee of Salvation Army Day Nursery. Film producer and editor.

MEMBER: American Academy of Pedodontics (member of board of directors, 1974-76; research chairman, 1971), American College of Dentists (fellow), Scientific Research Society of America, Association of Pedodontic Diplomates (member of board of directors; president, 1976—), American Society of Dentistry for Children (scientific program chairman, 1970), New York State Society of Dentistry for Children (member of executive council).

WRITINGS: Preventive Dentistry, Medicom, 1972; *Your Child's Teeth: A Parent's Guide to Making and Keeping Them Perfect*, Houghton, 1977. Also author of *Esthetics*, 1973; *Persuasive Prevention* (monograph), 1975; and *Fluoride: An Update for Dental Practice* (monograph), 1976.*

* * *

MOTT, Paul E.

PERSONAL—Education: Purdue University, B.S., 1952; University of Michigan, M.A., 1955, Ph.D., 1960. *Office:* Mott-McDonald Associates, Inc., 2011 I St. N.W., Suite 501, Washington, D.C. 20006.

CAREER: Associated with University of Michigan, Ann Arbor, 1960-64, member of Institute for Social Research, 1960-68; University of Pennsylvania, Philadelphia, associate professor of sociology, 1964-71; U.S. Department of Health, Education and Welfare, Washington, D.C., special assistant to administrator of Social and Rehabilitation Service, 1970-73; Mott-McDonald Associates, Inc., Washington, D.C., chairman of board of directors, 1975—. Consultant to U.S. Congress, Child Welfare League of America, and U.S. Bureau of the Budget.

WRITINGS: (With Mann, McLoughlin, and Warwick) *Shift Work: Social, Psychological, and Physical Consequences*, University of Michigan Press, 1965; (contributor) C. Dankert and other editors, *Hours of Work*, Harper, 1965; (editor with Michael Aiken, and contributor) *The Structure of Community Power*, Random House, 1970; *The Characteristics of Effective Organizations*, Harper, 1972; (with Elsa A. Porter) *A Case Report on a Comprehensive Planning and Management System*, Byrd Associates, 1973; *Foster Care and Adoptions: Key Policy Issues*, U.S. Government Printing Office, 1975; *Expanding Management Technology and Professional Accountability in Social Service Programs*, National Conference on Social Welfare, 1976; *Meeting Human Needs: The Political and Social History of Title XX*, National Conference on Social Welfare, 1976; (with L. Rivkin and C. Wheeler)

The American Family in Transition, National Conference on Social Work, 1977; *Home-Based Family-Centered Services for Children and Their Families,* Children's Bureau, U.S. Department of Health, Education and Welfare, 1980. Contributor to journals, including *Nursing Outlook* and *Sociological Inquiry.*

WORK IN PROGRESS: A book about what occurs in the executive branch of the U.S. government when administrations change.

SIDELIGHTS: Mott wrote: "After a decade of academic teaching and research, concentrated primarily in the areas of public and industrial organization and social change, I devoted the next decade to direct efforts at social policy formulation and social change. During this period, I helped to shape governmental policy in the human service area, draft legislation, and implement numerous projects intended to solve or ameliorate a variety of social problems. These experiences have given me considerable knowledge and skill in a unique and useful combination of areas: teaching, research, policy formulation and implementation, knowledge of the workings of government, an understanding of the potential contributions of the private sector to the solution of social problems, and a practical, as well as theoretical, knowledge of the effective techniques of social change.

"Mott-McDonald Associates was founded in order to implement several initiatives in the human service area, including the application of management technologies to the human service area, development of programs to move children from foster care to adoptive homes, development of rural human service programs, and the encouragement of private corporate involvement in the solution of such problems as special needs adoption, rural services, and domestic violence.

"During the next several years I want to use my combination of skills and knowledge to train interested students in the techniques of policy formulation, legislation, and organizational change; conduct change efforts in the human service area which involve partnerships among private corporations, foundations, universities, and public agencies; and write and publish articles and books on social and organizational change."

*   *   *

MOYNIHAN, John Dominic   1932-

PERSONAL: Born July 31, 1932, in London, England; son of Rodrigo M. (an artist) and Elinor (an artist; maiden name, Bellingham Smith) Moynihan; married Diana Ashe (divorced); married Judy Innes (divorced); married Clare Morice (a hospital researcher); children: Candida, Rose, Leo. *Education:* Attended Chelsea School of Art. *Home:* 4 Kildare Ter., London W.2, England. *Agent:* Irene Josephy, 35 Craven St., Strand, London WC2N 5NG, England. *Office:* Sunday Telegraph, Fleet St., London, England.

CAREER: Bromley Mercury, Bromley, England, junior reporter, 1953-54; *Evening Standard,* London, England, reporter, 1954-59, author of column "In London Last Night," 1959-61, diarist, 1961-63, feature writer, 1962-63; *Daily Express,* London, feature writer, 1963-64; *Sun,* London, diarist, 1964-65; *Sunday Telegraph,* London, feature writer and book reviewer, 1966-72, assistant literary editor, 1968-72, sportswriter, 1972—. *Military service:* British Army, editor of military newspaper, 1950-52; served in Europe. *Member:* International Sportswriters Club, Sports Writers Association, Football Writers Association, Chelsea Arts Club, Scribes,

Fleet Street Club, Battersea Park Football Club, Sportsmans Club, Lawn Tennis Writers Association.

WRITINGS: The Soccer Syndrome, MacGibbon & Kee, 1966; *Not All a Ball* (autobiography), Granada Publishing, 1970; *Park Football,* Pelham Books, 1970; *Football Fever,* Quartet Books, 1974; *Soccer,* Macmillan (London), 1975; *The Chelsea Story,* Arthur Barker, 1981. Contributor to magazines and newspapers, including *New Statesman, Spectator, Harper's, Queen,* and *Observer.*

WORK IN PROGRESS: A history of World Cup soccer, publication by Macdonald & Jane's expected in 1982.

SIDELIGHTS: Moynihan wrote: "Working as a columnist for Lord Beaverbrook's *Evening Standard* in the 1950's and early 1960's was an ideal platform for observing the famous at play—even though crusty performers like Evelyn Waugh, Frank Sinatra, and Ava Gardner were not always the easiest to interview. In later years, I found that the many adventures I had were valuable inspiration for a budding author. Now sportswriting dominates my life—hard work, but marvelous for global traveling—and traveling and discovering new places and meeting new people are essential for a writer."

*   *   *

MUELLER, Merrill   1916-1980
(Red Mueller)

OBITUARY NOTICE: Born January 27, 1916, in New York, N.Y.; died November 30, 1980, in Santa Monica, Calif. Journalist. After several years as a print journalist with *Newsweek* magazine, Mueller became a correspondent for NBC-Radio during World War II. His work took him to Allied headquarters all over the world, including Europe, Africa, and Asia, and brought him wide recognition. He returned to Asia during the Korean War and then joined NBC-TV to report on New York City politics. In the 1960's Mueller covered the manned space program from Cape Canaveral. Obituaries and other sources: *Who's Who in America,* 40th edition, Marquis, 1978; *New York Times,* December 2, 1980.

*   *   *

MUELLER, Red
See MUELLER, Merrill

*   *   *

MUGGESON, Margaret Elizabeth   1942-
(Margaret Dickinson; Everatt Jackson, pseudonym)

PERSONAL: Born April 30, 1942, in Gainsborough, England; daughter of John Everatt and Edna Mary (Copley) Dickinson; married Dennis Muggeson (a branch manager of a retail store), September 19, 1964; children: Amanda, Zoe Marie. *Education:* Attended Lincoln College of Technology, 1960-61. *Home:* Laurels, 3 Norwood Rd., Skegness, Lincolnshire PE25 3AD, England. *Agent:* Anthony Sheil Associates Ltd., 2-3 Morwell St., London WC1B 3AR, England.

CAREER: Skegness District Education Office, Skegness, England, local government officer, 1963-70; writer, 1970—. *Member:* Society of Authors.

*WRITINGS—*Historical romances; under name Margaret Dickinson: *Pride of the Courtneys,* R. Hale, 1968; *Brackenbeck,* R. Hale, 1969; *Portrait of Jonathan,* R. Hale, 1970; *Sarah,* R. Hale, 1981; *Adelina,* R. Hale, 1981; *Carrie,* R. Hale, 1981.

Under pseudonym Everatt Jackson: *The Road to Hell* (suspense novel), R. Hale, 1975.

WORK IN PROGRESS: A historical romance set during the Crimean war, under name Margaret Dickinson; an adventure-suspense novel set in the coastal area of Skegness, tentatively under pseudonym Everatt Jackson.

SIDELIGHTS: Margaret Muggeson told *CA:* "I have written since the age of fourteen and always with the ambition of being published. My main interest is the novel, and I am now attempting to move away from the light historical romance towards a more substantial type of novel with a greater depth of historical background. The Abbeyford trilogy—*Sarah, Adelina,* and *Carrie*—covers three generations of the same families, the first novel set in 1795, the second from 1815 to 1819, and the third from 1841 to the end of the Crimean War in 1856. Much as I enjoy writing the historical novel, occasionally I feel the need to tackle a completely different type. Hence the adventure/suspense novel set in a coastal town in the present day."

*   *   *

MULLARKY, Taylor   1922-

PERSONAL: Born October 29, 1922, in Detroit, Mich.; daughter of Harris Tweed and Pearl Mullarky; married I. Lett, June 20, 1959; children: Polly, Esther. *Education:* Attended girls' vocational school in Detroit, Mich. *Politics:* "Look for the union label." *Home and office:* 221 Lewiston Rd., Grosse Pointe Farms, Mich. 48236.

CAREER: Seagull's (clothing store), Detroit, Mich., seamstress in alterations department, 1940-42; American Costumes, Detroit, seamstress, 1945-46, designer, 1946-49; Detroit Theatre Group, Detroit, 1949-55, began as costume designer, became wardrobe supervisor; Querida's Bridal Salon, Detroit, owner, designer, and seamstress, 1955-59; free-lance designer, 1959—; writer, 1974—. *Wartime service:* Sewed uniforms for U.S. Armed Forces and sewed bandages for Red Cross, 1942-45. *Member:* International Sisterhood of Seamsters.

WRITINGS: One Thousand and One Halloween Costumes for Children, For Tomorrow Books, 1975; *Don't Needle Me!* (autobiography), Boben, 1977; *Machine Embroidery to Keep You in Stitches,* Zigzag Productions, 1978; *Thread Bear and Other Stories* (juvenile), Tapestry Books, 1978; *The Seamy Side of Life* (novel), Boben, 1980.

WORK IN PROGRESS: Zipper Foot, "the story of an agile Sioux who is preparing to run the Boston Marathon"; *Knitwit,* a novel for young adults.

SIDELIGHTS: Mullarky told *CA:* "I have always enjoyed fabricating stories, and in *Thread Bear* I proved my ability to spin a good yarn. Simple yet engaging, the stories that I wrote for this volume do not emphasize material goods. Rather, they present children with a moral, an answer to some of the 'so whats?' that spring into kids' minds. Similar to Aesop's fables, each story in *Thread Bear* includes an adage like 'a stitch in time saves nine' so that the moral will be recognizable and, hopefully, reinforced.

"My first novel, *The Seamy Side of Life,* was extremely difficult to write. A novel, to me, was an insurmountable task, so I hesitated to begin—perhaps longer than I should have. I thought it would be easier for the proverbial camel to pass through the eye of a needle than for me to piece together a lengthy work. Nevertheless, once I finally started *Seamy Side,* I needed only six months to complete the book and to finalize the publishing contracts. Like my earlier stories, *Seamy Side* is strongly didactic in that it teaches the

reader to look for a silver lining. The main character, Monsieur Applique, a hobo in New Orleans, lives in gutters and doorways, scrounging through garbage cans for food and scavenging through Salvation Army 'drop boxes' for his clothes. One day he discovers a pair of magical socks that becomes both a curse and a blessing. Through half of the novel he grumbles, 'Darn these socks!,' but in the end they are Monsieur Applique's salvation."

*   *   *

MULLER, John P(aul)   1940-

PERSONAL: Born December 31, 1940, in New York, N.Y. *Education:* Fordham University, A.B., 1964, M.A., 1966; Harvard University, Ph.D., 1971. *Office:* Austen Riggs Center, Stockbridge, Mass. 01262.

CAREER: Bridge Over Troubled Waters, Boston, Mass., director, 1970-71; Sinte Gleska College, Rosebud, S.D., chairman of department of human services, 1971-74; University of Cincinnati, Cincinnati, Ohio, assistant professor of psychology in pediatrics, 1974-75; Austen Riggs Center, Stockbridge, Mass., research associate and member of therapy staff, 1975—. Chairman of Rosebud Sioux Tribe Mental Health Advisory Committee, 1973-74; consultant to U.S. Office of Child Development, 1973-75. *Member:* American Psychological Association, American Association for the Advancement of Science, Council for Exceptional Children, New York Academy of Sciences.

WRITINGS: (With William J. Richardson) *Lacan and Language: Reader's Guide to the Ecrits,* International Universities Press, 1981. Contributor to psychology and literary journals.

WORK IN PROGRESS: Research on Lacan's views on aggression, the ego, cognitive defensiveness, language, and spirits in M. H. Kingston's *The Woman Warrior.*

SIDELIGHTS: Muller commented: "My first language is Hungarian, and I still speak it well enough to communicate with my many relatives in Romania. My current interests include the role of language in psychoanalysis, the cultural imperialism shown by psychology and psychoanalysis in the face of non-western cultures, and the evaluation of mental health treatment outcomes."

*   *   *

MULLER, Robert George   1923-

PERSONAL: Born March 11, 1923, in Waimes, Belgium; son of Robert and Leonie (Schneider) Muller: married Margarita Gallo (a professor of international relations), June 11, 1952; children: Gisele, Solange, Francois, Philippe. *Education:* University of Strasbourg, Doctorate of Law and Economics, 1948. *Religion:* Roman Catholic. *Home:* 144 Langdon Ave., Dobbs Ferry, N.Y. 10522. *Agent:* Ron Bernstein Agency, 200 West 58th St., New York, N.Y. 10019. *Office:* United Nations, Room 2977A, New York, N.Y. 10017.

CAREER: United Nations, New York, N.Y., intern, summer, 1948, economist in financial branch of department of economic affairs, 1948-58, secretary of capital development fund committee, 1958-59, special assistant to under-secretary-general for economic and social affairs, 1959-62, chief of steel and engineering section of Economic Commission for Europe, 1962-64, political adviser to United Nations Forces in Cyprus, 1964-65, counselor to secretary-general of United Nations Trade Conference, 1966-68, associate director of Natural Resources Division, 1968-69, director of budget, 1969-70, director of office of secretary-general, 1970-

73, deputy to under-secretary-general for inter-agency affairs and coordination, 1974-79, secretary of Economic and Social Council, 1979—. *Wartime service:* Member of French underground movement. *Member:* Pacem in Terris Society of the United Nations (president). *Awards, honors:* D.H.C. from University of Bridgeport, 1974; citations from New Jersey and Pennsylvania Senates and Houses of Representatives, 1980, for distinguished international service and book, *Most of All, They Taught Me Happiness;* officer of French order La Pleiade.

WRITINGS: Le Rattachement economique de la Sarre a la France, Riber, 1950; *Most of All, They Taught Me Happiness,* Doubleday, 1978; *Global Spirituality; or, The Planet of God,* Doubleday, in press; *A World of Humour,* World Happiness and Cooperation, in press; *Sima mon amor* (novel; title means "Sima, My Love"), Editions Pierron, in press. Contributor to magazines, including *Saturday Review, Success, New Age,* and *New Realities.*

SIDELIGHTS: Muller wrote: "After many years of observing the world at the United Nations, I believe I have a message about life and a positive, hopeful vision of the future of humankind. Most of my writing is devoted to world affairs, to a new world view, and to the art of living. I give an average of 150 speeches, and television and radio interviews a year. Thirty-three years of service in the U.N. have made me a rather unique being, and it is my duty to give back what I have received. From 1983 on, I intend, God willing, to devote the rest of my life to writing and to drawing the conclusions from my life. I plan to write several works: a diary of my work at the U.N.; memories from war and peace; a book entitled *There Will Be No World War III;* a philosophy for our time; a book on global education; a major novel; analects on happiness and the art of living; and collections of my essays on world affairs, philosophy, religion, and world government."

Muller's interests include political affairs, the environment and natural disasters, space communication, water problems, the handicapped, hijacking, solar energy, and biology.

AVOCATIONAL INTERESTS: Art, folklore, gardening, painting.

BIOGRAPHICAL/CRITICAL SOURCES: Sign (of the U.N.'s Prophet of Hope), September, 1979; Margaret McGurn, *Global Spirituality: Planetary Consciousness in the Thought of Teilhard de Chardin and Robert Muller,* World Happiness and Cooperation, 1981.

* * *

MULLIN, Michael 1944-

PERSONAL: Born November 30, 1944, in Chicago, Ill.; married wife, M. Catherine (a nurse), 1966; children: Catherine Mariah, Bridget Drusilla, Margaret Anne, Elizabeth Ellen. *Education:* College of the Holy Cross, A.B., 1966; Yale University, M.Phil., 1970, Ph.D., 1972. *Office:* Department of English, University of Illinois, Urbana, Ill. 61801.

CAREER: University of Illinois, Urbana, instructor, 1970-72, assistant professor, 1972-76, associate professor of English, 1976—. Director of Shakespeare Film Cooperative, 1973—; consultant to Public Broadcasting Service and British Broadcasting Corp. *Member:* American Theatre Association, American Society for Theatre Research, Shakespeare Association of America, Modern Language Association of America, Society for Theatre Research (England).

WRITINGS: (Contributor) Ronald Gottesman, editor, *Focus on Orson Welles,* Prentice-Hall, 1975; *"Macbeth" Onstage:*

An Annotated Facsimile of Glen Byam Shaw's 1955 Promptbook, University of Missouri Press, 1976; *Theatre at Stratford-upon-Avon: A Catalogue-Index to Productions of the Shakespeare Memorial/Royal Shakespeare Theatre, 1879-1978,* two volumes, Greenwood Press, 1980. Contributor to theatre journals.

* * *

MUMFORD, Bob 1930-

PERSONAL: Born December 29, 1930, in Steubenville, Ohio; son of Bernard C., Sr. and Margaret (Foster) Mumford; married Judith Lee Huxoll, May 12, 1954; children: Keren A., Beth Mumford Hensley, Bob, Jr., Eric. *Education:* Attended Northeast Bible College, 1955-58, Missionary Medical School, Toronto, Ontario, 1958-59, and University of Delaware, 1967-68; Reformed Episcopal Seminary, Philadelphia, Pa., B.D., 1967. *Office:* Life Changers, 6301 Pembroke Rd., Hollywood, Fla. 33023.

CAREER: Ordained Assemblies of God minister, 1960; professor of Bible and missions, and dean at Elim Bible Institute, 1961-64; pastor of churches in Pennsylvania and Delaware, 1964-67; Life Changers, Hollywood, Fla., Bible teacher, 1970—. *Military service:* U.S. Navy, Medical Department, 1950-54.

WRITINGS: Fifteen Steps Out, Logos International, 1969; *Take Another Look at Guidance,* Logos International, 1971; *The Problem of Doing Your Own Thing,* CGM Publishing, 1972; *Christ in Session,* CGM Publishing, 1973; *Living Happily Ever After,* Revell, 1973; *The Purpose of Temptation,* Revell, 1973; *The King and You,* Revell, 1974; *Entering and Enjoying Worship,* Manna Christian Outreach, 1976; *Handling God's Glory,* CGM Publishing, 1976; *Prison of Resentment,* CGM Publishing, 1977.

WORK IN PROGRESS: In the Arena of Truth, publication expected in 1982.

SIDELIGHTS: Mumford has worked as evangelist and seminar teacher in the United States and abroad.

* * *

MUNONYE, John 1929-

PERSONAL: Born April 28, 1929, in Akokwa, Nigeria; son of Reuben (a farmer) and Agnes (Obi) Munonye; married Regina Nwokeji, December 27, 1957; children: Beatrice, Clement. *Education:* University of Ibadan, B.A., 1952; Institute of Education, London, Post-Graduate Certificate in Education, 1953. *Religion:* Roman Catholic. *Home and office address:* P.O. Box 23, Akokwa, Orlu, Imo State, Nigeria. *Agent:* David Higham Associates Ltd., 5-8 Lower John St., Golden Sq., London W1R 4HA, England.

CAREER: Ministry of Education in Western and Eastern Nigeria, teacher, 1954-57, administrator and inspector, 1958-70; Ministry of Education in Eastern Nigeria, principal of Advanced Teachers College, 1970-73, chief inspector of education, 1973-76; writer, 1976—. Past assistant secretary of Education Review Committee of Eastern Nigeria; past member of board of directors of East Central State Broadcasting Services; past member of National Education Research Council, national committee of West African Examinations Council, and Imo State Curriculum Committee; member of Akokwa Development Committee. *Awards, honors:* Member of Order of the Niger, 1980.

WRITINGS: (With John Cairns) *Drills and Practice in English Language,* African Universities Press, 1966; *The Only Son* (novel), Heinemann, 1966; *Obi* (novel), Heinemann,

1969; *Oil Man of Obange* (novel), Heinemann, 1971; *A Wreath for the Maidens* (novel), Heinemann, 1973; *A Dancer of Fortune* (novel), Heinemann, 1974; *Bridge to a Wedding* (novel), Heinemann, 1978. Contributor to *Catholic Life*.

WORK IN PROGRESS: A novel for Heinemann.

SIDELIGHTS: Munonye commented: "All my novels are 'children of the soil,' set in the Igbo area of Nigeria to which I belong and in which I am deeply rooted. Happily, after twenty-three years in public service, I am now back to the roots, in retirement. Here I have my home, and am quietly plumbing for new dimensions of self. There is a problem. We move straight from school, to university, to public service, then to old age and retirement, without a substantial break somewhere to adjust the bearings.

"The mental span of my writings is fifty years. It is a privilege to be able to write about men in these parts during that period, but nothing nostalgic. *Bridge to a Wedding* attempts a dialogue between the old and the new, traditional and modern. We do need the bridge. There are, right now, pressing contemporary issues which ought to feature in my next novels. The great thing is that the field is so vast and green, the characters sparkling, and the events quite commonplace—you don't strain for the melody."

BIOGRAPHICAL/CRITICAL SOURCES: Dem-Say, African and Afro-American Studies Research Center, University of Texas, Austin, 1974.

* * *

MUNROW, David John 1942-

PERSONAL: Born August 12, 1942, in Birmingham, England; died in May, 1976; son of Albert Davis and Hilda Ivy Munrow; married Gillian Veronica Reid, 1966. *Education:* Pembroke College, Cambridge, M.A.; also attended University of Birmingham.

CAREER: Associated with Markham College, 1960-61; associated with Cambridge University, Cambridge, England, 1961-64; University of Birmingham, Birmingham, England, researcher, 1964-65; member of Wind Band in Royal Shakespeare Theatre, 1966-68; Early Music Consort of London, London, England, founder and director, 1967—. Professor at Royal Academy of Music, 1969-73; lecturer at University of Leicester, 1967—. Performer on recorder; specialist on early musical instruments; composer, including music for television series, "The Six Wives of Henry VIII," "Elizabeth R," 1970-71, and "The Devils," 1971, and films, "The Pied Piper of Hamlyn," 1968, "Chaucer's Tale," 1969, "Henry VIII and His Six Wives," 1972, "Zardoz," 1974, and "La Course en Tete," 1974; created BBC-Radio series, "Pied Piper," 1971. *Member:* Royal Academy of Music (associate), ISM, RMA.

WRITINGS: Instruments of the Middle Ages and Renaissance (foreword by Andre Previn), Oxford University Press, 1976.

SIDELIGHTS: Munrow's sound recordings include "Instruments of the Middle Ages and Renaissance," released by Angel in 1976. *Avocational interests:* Collecting musical instruments, sailing, travel.*

* * *

MURPHY, Dervla (Mary) 1931-

PERSONAL: Born November 28, 1931, in County Waterford, Ireland; daughter of Fergus Joseph (a librarian) and Kathleen Rochfort (Dowling) Murphy; children: Rachel

Dervla. *Education:* Attended convent school in County Waterford, Ireland. *Politics:* "Supporter of community politics for all countries." *Religion:* "None and all." *Home:* Clairvaux, Lismore, County Waterford, Ireland.

CAREER: Writer, 1952—. *Member:* Royal Geographical Society (fellow), Royal Asiatic Society, Tibet Society. *Awards, honors:* Literary award from American-Irish Foundation, 1975; Ewart-Biggs Memorial Prize, 1978, for *A Place Apart*.

WRITINGS—All on travel, except as noted; all published by J. Murray: *Full Tilt*, 1965; *Tibetan Foothold*, 1966; *The Waiting Land*, 1967; *In Ethiopia With a Mule*, 1968; *On a Shoestring to Coorg*, 1976; *Where the Indus Is Young*, 1977; *A Place Apart*, 1978; *Wheels Within Wheels* (autobiography), 1979; *Race to the Finish* (on politics), 1981. Contributor to magazines, including *Blackwood's*, and newspapers.

WORK IN PROGRESS: A book on Peru, publication by J. Murray expected in 1982.

SIDELIGHTS: Dervla Murphy commented: "Unless young writers set themselves high standards of precision, our language will soon become a blunt instrument. To me slang is good if it's strong and colorful, like 'get your act together!' But mindless phrases like 'at this moment in time' are unforgivable. There is an urgent need for the academic young to rebel against jargon. Technical terms are necessary but it is not necessary to turn the language inside out because you happen to be an anthropologist or a nuclear physicist or a political scientist. If 'experts' took the trouble to write plainly, many more people could benefit from their research and thought. If, on the other hand, their research and thought sound unimpressive in simple language, then surely it would be best to refrain from writing about them."

* * *

MURPHY, Louis J.
See HICKS, Tyler Gregory

* * *

MURPHY, Nonie Carol
See CAROLL, Nonie

* * *

MURRAY, Bruce C(hurchill) 1931-

PERSONAL: Born November 30, 1931, in New York, N.Y.; son of Churchill and Esther Murray; married Suzanne Moss, 1954; children: five. *Education:* Massachusetts Institute of Technology, S.B., 1953, S.M., 1954, Ph.D., 1955. *Office:* Jet Propulsion Laboratory, California Institute of Technology, 4800 Oak Grove Dr., Pasadena, Calif. 91103.

CAREER: Worked as exploration and exploitation geologist in Louisiana for Standard Oil Co., 1955-58; Air Force Cambridge Research Laboratories, Cambridge, Mass., geodesist, 1958-60; California Institute of Technology, Pasadena, research fellow, 1960-63, associate professor, 1963-68, professor of planetary science, 1968—, director of Jet Propulsion Laboratory, 1976—.

Geophysicist at Geophysical Research Directorate, L.G. Hanscom Field, Mass., 1958-60; guest observer at Mount Wilson and Palomar Observatories, 1960-65, staff associate, 1965-69; experimenter for Mariner 4, 6, 7, and 9 projects, leader of imaging team for Mariner 10 Mission, 1973-75; consultant to RAND Corp. *Military service:* U.S. Air Force, 1958-60.

MEMBER: American Geophysical Union (president of planetology section, 1974-75), American Astronomical Society, American Association for the Advancement of Science (fellow). *Awards, honors:* Exceptional scientific achievement medal, 1971, and distinguished public service medal, 1974, both from National Aeronautics and Space Administration; Guggenheim fellow, 1975-76; American Academy of Arts and Sciences fellow, 1980.

WRITINGS: (With Merton E. Davies and P. K. Eckman) *Planetary Contamination,* RAND Corp., 1967; (with Davies) *The View From Space: Photographic Exploration of the Planets,* Columbia University Press, 1971; *Navigating the Future,* Harper, 1975; (with Eric Burgess) *Flight to Mercury,* Columbia University Press, 1977; (with Michael Malin and Ronald Greeley) *Earthlike Planets: Surfaces of Mercury, Venus, Earth, Moon, Mars,* W. H. Freeman, 1981. Contributor to scientific journals.

Associate editor of *Journal of Geophysical Research,* 1965-68; member of board of editors of *Science,* 1970-72.

BIOGRAPHICAL/CRITICAL SOURCES: New York Times, April 1, 1979.

* * *

MURRAY, Michael
See McLAREN, Moray (David Shaw)

* * *

MURRAY, Ruth Lovell   1900-

PERSONAL: Born October 20, 1900, in Detroit, Mich.; daughter of Neil William (a printer) and Clara (Southwick) Murray. *Education:* Detroit Normal School, certificate, 1919; Columbia University, B.S., 1925, M.A., 1933; studied dance privately. *Politics:* Independent Democrat. *Religion:* Unitarian-Universalist. *Home:* 8900 East Jefferson Ave., Apt. 1215, Detroit, Mich. 48214.

CAREER: Worked as physical education teacher at elementary school, 1919-21; teacher at Marr Training School, 1921-23; Detroit Teachers College, Detroit, Mich., 1925-30, began as instructor, became assistant professor; Wayne State University, Detroit, assistant professor, 1930-43, associate professor, 1943-54, professor of physical education, 1954-71, professor emeritus, 1971—, director of dance workshop, 1927-54, chairperson of women's staff of Division of Health and Physical Education, 1943-61, coordinator of dance, 1961-71. Visiting professor at University of Michigan, autumn, 1928, summer, 1950, University of Iowa, summers, 1936-38, 1953, Mills College, summer, 1940, West Virginia University, summer, 1954, Connecticut College, summers, 1953, 1956, and University of Oregon, summer, 1959. Member of Federal Security Agency's National Council on Physical Fitness, 1945. Member of board of directors of Michigan Cultural Commission and chairperson of its committee on dance, 1960-66; member of board of directors and executive committee of Michigan State Council for the Arts and chairperson of its committee on dance, 1966-70, member of advisory dance panel, 1971—; chairperson of Detroit Adventure Conversations in Dance, 1962-63. Director and choreographer of dance group, 1928-53; choreographer for Detroit Friends of Opera and Detroit International Institute.

MEMBER: International Association of Physical Education and Sports for Girls and Women, American Alliance for Health, Physical Education, Recreation and Dance (chairperson of national dance section, 1935-37), National Dance Association, American Academy of Physical Education (fellow), American Association of University Professors, American Dance Guild (member of board of directors, 1965-66),

Midwest Association for Physical Education of College Women (life member), Midwest Association of College Teachers of Physical Education for Women (member of governing board, 1945-47, 1955-57; chairperson of teacher education committee, 1945-47, and educational policies committee, 1955-57), Michigan Physical Education Association (president, 1931-32), Michigan Dance Association (life member), Arizona Dance Arts Alliance (life member), Detroit Health and Physical Education Club (life member; president, 1933-34), Detroit Metropolitan Dance Project (life member), Saginaw Valley Dance Council (life member), Wayne State University Dance Alumni Association (life member), Wayne State University Association of Faculty Women (charter member; vice-president, 1957-58), Wayne State University Faculty Women's Club (vice-president, 1957-58; president, 1958-59), Delta Kappa Gamma (life member).

AWARDS, HONORS: Ruth Lovell Murray Scholarship was named in her honor by Wayne State University Dance Alumni Association, 1954; honor award from American Alliance for Health, Physical Education and Recreation, 1955, annual heritage award from Dance Division, 1969, Luther Halsey Gulick Medal, 1979; honor award from Michigan Association for Health, Physical Education and Recreation, 1958; service award from Michigan Council for the Arts, 1971; honorary fine arts medal from Michigan Academy of Science, Arts, and Letters, 1973; annual award from American Dance Guild, 1973; fine arts achievement award for dance from Wayne State University, 1976; named scholar of the year by National Dance Association, 1979-80.

WRITINGS: Dance in Elementary Education, Harper, 1953, 3rd edition, 1975; *And So to Teach: A Guidebook for Student Teachers of Physical Education,* Bookstore, Wayne State University, 1940, 3rd edition (with Delia Hussey) published as *From Student to Teacher in Physical Education: A Guidebook for Students and New Teachers,* Prentice-Hall, 1959; (editor) *Designs for Dance,* American Alliance for Health, Physical Education and Recreation, 1968.

Contributor: *Dancing in the Elementary Schools,* A. S. Barnes, 1933; Vaughn S. Blanchard and Laurentine B. Collins, editors, *A Modern Physical Education Program,* A. S. Barnes, 1940; *Children in Focus,* American Alliance for Health, Physical Education and Recreation, 1954; Martin Haberman and Tobie Garth Meisel, editors, *Dance: An Art in Academe,* Teachers College Press, 1970. Also contributor to *Children's Dance.* Contributor to physical education and dance journals.

SIDELIGHTS: Though she retired from university teaching in 1971, Ruth Murray has remained active in Michigan's dance community, through counseling and in-service education. *Avocational interests:* Travel (Europe, Japan, Australia, New Zealand), theatre, concerts, reading (including poetry), swimming.

BIOGRAPHICAL/CRITICAL SOURCES: Kate O'Neill, editor, *Dance Education in Michigan: Recollections of Three Pioneers,* Michigan Dance Association, 1974.

* * *

MURRAY-SMITH, Stephen   1922-

PERSONAL: Born September 9, 1922, in Melbourne, Australia; son of William David (a merchant) and Alice Margrett Murray-Smith; married Nita Bluthal (a teacher), February 6, 1948; children: Cleeve, David, Joanna. *Education:* University of Melbourne, B.A. (with honors), B.Ed., Ph.D. *Politics:* Social democrat. *Religion:* None. *Home address:* Ti-Tree Lane, Mount Eliza, Victoria 3930, Australia.

CAREER: Australian Peace Council, Melbourne, national organizing secretary, 1952-58; Victorian Teachers' Union, Melbourne, Australia, editor and research officer, 1958-61; University of Melbourne, Parkville, Australia, Nuffield research fellow, 1961-65, lecturer, 1966-74, reader in education, 1975—. Chairman of governing council of National Book Council of Australia, 1981—. Military service: Australian Imperial Force, 1941-45. Member: Order of Australia.

WRITINGS: (Editor) The Tracks We Travel, Australasian Book Society, 1953; Henry Lawson, Lansdowne Press, 1963; (editor) An Overland Muster, Jacaranda Press, 1965; (editor) Marcus Clarke, His Natural Life, Penguin, 1970; (editor with Judah Waten) Classic Australian Short Stories, Wren Publishing, 1974. Also author of Mission to the Islands, 1979, and Happy in the Circus? (literary autobiography), 1981. Editor of Overland, 1954—, and Melbourne Studies in Education, 1973-77.

WORK IN PROGRESS: Histories of technical education in Australia, and of the Bass Strait region.

*   *   *

MURROW, Edward R(oscoe) 1908-1965

PERSONAL: Original name Egbert Roscoe Murrow; name legally changed; born April 25, 1908, in Greensboro, N.C.; died April 27, 1965; son of Roscoe C. (a railroad engineer for a logging company) and Ethel (Lamb) Murrow; married Janet Huntington Brewster, 1932; children: Charles Casey. Education: Attended Leland Stanford University and University of Washington, Seattle; Washington State College (now University), B.A., 1930.

CAREER: Compassman and topographer for timber cruisers in northwestern Washington, British Columbia, and Alaska; National Student Federation of America, president, 1929-32; Institute of International Education, New York City, assistant director in charge of foreign offices, 1932-35; Columbia Broadcasting System, New York City, director of talks and education, 1935-37, director of European Bureau, 1937-46, war correspondent, 1939-45, vice-president and director of public affairs, 1945-47, news broadcaster, 1947-61, director, 1949-61; U.S. Information Agency, Washington, D.C., director, 1961-64. Host of radio programs "Hear It Now" and "This I Believe" and television programs "Person to Person," "See It Now," "Small World," and "CBS Reports"; lecturer on international relations in the United States and abroad. Secretary of Emergency Commission for the Aid of Displaced German Scholars, 1933-35. Member of board of trustees of Institute of International Education and Carnegie Endowment for International Peace, and of board of directors of National Institute of Foreign Affairs. Military service: U.S. Army Reserve; became first lieutenant.

AWARDS, HONORS: Honorary degrees include D.Journalism from Temple University, LL.D. from Washington State University, University of North Carolina, Muhlenberg College, Mount Holyoke College, Grinnell College, Oberlin College, Brandeis University, University of Rochester, University of Michigan, Johns Hopkins University, and Colby College, L.H.D. from Hamilton College, and H.H.D. from Rollins College; Freedom House Award, 1954; Emmy Award from Academy of Television Arts and Sciences, 1956, for "See It Now"; U.S. President's Medal of Freedom, 1964; knight commander of Order of the British Empire, 1965; two George Foster Peabody Awards from School of Journalism at University of Georgia; awards from Overseas Press Club of America; two George Polk Memorial Awards from Long Island University; Dupont Annual Award; National Head-

liners Award; One World Award; L. S. Weiss Memorial Award; arts and letters award from Air Force Association; awards from Southwest Journalism Forum, School of Journalism at Syracuse University, Ohio State University, and Poor Richard Club.

WRITINGS: (Editor) American Field Service Fellowships for French Universities, Institute of International Education, 1933; This Is London (edited by Elmer Davis), Simon & Schuster, 1941; (author of preface) Ernestine Carter, editor, Bloody But Unbowed: Pictures of Britain Under Fire, Scribner, 1941 (published in England as Grim Glory: Pictures of Britain Under Fire, Lund, 1941); (editor) This I Believe, Simon & Schuster, Volume I, 1952, Volume II, 1954; (editor with Fred W. Friendly) See It Now, Simon & Schuster, 1955; (with others) Watch: The Television Guide to the 1956 Conventions, the Campaign, and the Election; the Personalities, Events, Issues, the Whole Story in Words and Pictures by CBS News Correspondents, Maco Magazine Corp., 1956; In Search of Light: The Broadcasts of Edward R. Murrow, 1938-1961 (edited by Edward Bliss, Jr.), Knopf, 1967, abridged edition (foreword by Harold Macmillan), Macmillan, 1968. Contributor to education journals and popular magazines, including Saturday Review of Literature.

SIDELIGHTS: One of the most eminent of American journalists, Murrow brought to radio a level of intelligence and professionalism that helped make it, for the first time, a major news medium. The pace of events during World War II gave broadcast journalism much of its importance, but the high quality of Murrow's reporting gave it much of its character. He was "a rare figure, as good as his legend," wrote David Halberstam in the Atlantic Monthly. "In many ways, because he was what he was, CBS News is today what it is. . . . He helped make radio respectable as a serious journalistic profession, and more than a decade later, simply by going over to television, had a good deal to do with making that journalistically legitimate too."

Murrow, unlike many broadcasters, was not trained as a reporter and never worked on a newspaper. His job as CBS's European representative was non-journalistic until the Nazi invasion of Austria in 1938, when he chartered a plane to Vienna to cover the entry of German troops into the city. He covered the events leading to war and became famous for his broadcasts from London during the Battle of Britain, being "transformed in the public mind, as by magic, from being one of the many reporters covering the Battle of Britain to the reporter covering that battle," as Edward Bliss observed in Saturday Review. Murrow assembled a staff of highly talented correspondents, including William Shirer and Eric Sevareid, and made CBS the foremost American news network.

Murrow soon became one of the most respected war correspondents in Europe, pioneering a new style of journalism grounded in the immediacy of eyewitness accounts. He was devoted to accuracy and objectivity, but he was equally concerned with the qualities of human experience, with what the war felt like to those whose lives it touched. He had an "almost poetic insight into the feelings of the war-stricken English," and he resorted to innovative techniques to convey those feelings to Americans, interviewing citizens as well as officials and telling of the courage of civilians as well as soldiers. He insisted on experiencing as much as he could, and was known for his willingness to take risks to get a story. The Christian Science Monitor noted Murrow's "unorthodox manner of news-getting. . . . When an air raid is on he has the habit of going up on the roof to see what is happening, or of driving around town in an open car to see what has been hit.'' Such ''eyewitness'' reporting, then considered dramatically unconventional, is now standard in radio and television.

In pursuit of colorful stories, Murrow flew on a bombing run over Berlin and, in defiance of orders from CBS, took a cruise on a North Sea minesweeper. He faced an unusual challenge when he decided to do a live broadcast from a rooftop during an air raid. British censors feared that such a broadcast might provide information that would help the bombers find their targets, so Murrow had to choose his words carefully and describe the raid without revealing where the bombs fell. These and other broadcasts from 1939 and 1940 were collected in the book *This Is London*.

Murrow's reports were an important influence on American public opinion, helping to overcome isolationist sentiment; Archibald Macleish praised Murrow for destroying ''in the minds of many men and women in this country the superstition that what is done beyond 3,000 miles of water is not really done at all.'' Murrow's London broadcasts were also commended as exemplary journalism. ''Mr. Murrow clearly is a reporter of very considerable merit. . . . He has a clear eye for important detail, but he has equally the rarer gifts of sympathy and a sense of communion,'' concluded the *Times Literary Supplement*'s review of *This Is London*. The style as well as the substance of his reporting won praise. ''Mr. Murrow's broadcasts read well,'' remarked R. G. Swing of *Books*, ''because the language of good spoken speech is good language, and so good prose.'' Murrow was a powerful and articulate speaker who, Halberstam noted, ''had just the right touch: enough drama in his voice to make what he was saying unusually effective, but not so much as to sound like a phony or a ham. . . . The very manner of his reporting, as well as his words, seemed to embody what was at stake in the war, the values being fought for.''

After the war, Murrow undertook a brief stint as CBS vice-president in charge of news, but he found his talents and temperament unsuited to administration and returned to reporting. Along with his daily news broadcasts, he did two popular radio programs, ''Hear It Now'' and ''This I Believe.'' In the latter, people discussed their philosophies of life. Herbert Hoover, Thomas Mann, and dozens of others, not all of them prominent, were featured on the five-minute show.

Murrow was at first suspicious of television. He considered it too unsubtle to be a good medium for ideas, and he preferred radio's flexibility. Nevertheless, he turned to the new medium in 1951 with ''See It Now,'' which followed the format established by its radio predecessor: a weekly documentary interpreting current events and probing social and political problems. The program was often controversial, never more so than in 1954 when Murrow took on the anti-Communist Senator Joseph McCarthy, examining McCarthy's career and criticizing him strongly for his chilling effect on civil liberties. ''We are not descended from fearful men,'' Murrow concluded on that program, ''not from men who feared to write, to speak, to associate with, and to defend causes which were for the moment unpopular.'' The McCarthy program is considered the most dramatic moment in Murrow's lifelong defense of freedom of speech and of the press.

On another television show, ''Person to Person,'' Murrow interviewed celebrities in their homes. Some critics felt that ''Person to Person'' was superficial, lowbrow, and unworthy of Murrow's talent and stature. Murrow himself once called the show ''demeaning,'' but it brought him widespread popularity that enabled him to withstand the attacks that followed

the McCarthy show and other controversial ''See It Now'' documentaries.

Nonetheless, CBS executives were upset by the controversy and attempted to restrict Murrow's autonomy. Murrow found himself embroiled in conflicts that led eventually to the cancellation of ''See It Now.'' He became increasingly frustrated by the political and commercial constraints on television news, and in 1958 he made a speech accusing television of ''decadence, escapism, and insulation from the realities of the world.'' Finally he left CBS for government service under the John F. Kennedy administration. His last broadcast was his report on Kennedy's inauguration on January 20, 1961.

Many of Murrow's broadcasts have been transcribed and published in books, including *This I Believe* and *See It Now*. A posthumous anthology, *In Search of Light*, covers the whole of Murrow's career, from the earliest radio newscasts to his departure from broadcasting. Described by Stuart W. Little of *Saturday Review* as ''a unique historical record from the Second World War to the Kennedy inaugural,'' *In Search of Light* was praised as ''illustrative of the discipline of the best in broadcast journalism'' by Jack Gould of the *New York Times Book Review*. ''Beneath the printed word,'' Little wrote, ''one finds oneself listening to . . . the Murrow temperateness and fairness, his judiciousness as a reporter even where he had strong feelings, his compassion and conscience. . . . The underlying theme of reports and comments that are widely scattered in time and place, is his declaration for free expression as the first line of defense of a free society.''

Murrow remains a model for newscasters, ''one who set standards for his profession,'' wrote Edward Bliss. ''He was forever asking himself, 'Is this good enough?' That is what troubled him—not who would be upset by what he said, but whether it was right. And if it was right, was he communicating? Could the language be improved? How could the issues, so complicated, be made plain? He had standards—unexcelled today—that he was trying to meet.'' And Edward Weeks of *Atlantic* recalled, ''I have never known anyone who was so affectionately regarded by other journalists: we loved him for his courage, which he disguised; for his candor, which could be hot; and for his honor, which he wore lightly but which was always there.''

BIOGRAPHICAL/CRITICAL SOURCES—Books: Alexander Kendrick, *Prime Time: The Life of Edward R. Murrow*, Little, Brown, 1969; Irving E. Fang, *Those Radio Commentators*, Iowa State University Press, 1977; Robert Franklin Smith, *Edward R. Murrow: The War Years*, New Issues Press, 1978.

Periodicals: *Scribner's*, December, 1938; *Living Age*, November, 1939; *Time*, June 17, 1940, December 15, 1941; *Christian Science Monitor*, April 25, 1941, December 11, 1948; *Publishers Weekly*, July 12, 1941; *PM*, July 16, 1941; *Times Literary Supplement*, November 15, 1941; *Cue*, December 27, 1941, February 21, 1953; *Newsweek*, March 9, 1953; *New York Times*, April 28, 1965; *Saturday Review*, June 10, 1967, May 31, 1975; *Atlantic*, August, 1967, January, 1976; *New York Times Book Review*, September 10, 1967.*

—*Sketch by Tim Connor*

* * *

MUUS, Bent J(oergen) 1926-

PERSONAL: Born July 15, 1926, in Bragenaes, Denmark; son of Elias Bruun (a manufacturer) and Wilhelmine (Hoffmeyer) Muus; married Kirsten von Buelow (a university teacher), November 11, 1954. *Education:* University of Copenhagen, M.Sc., 1954, Ph.D., 1968. *Home:* Dronninggaards Alle 87, 2840 Holte, Denmark. *Agent:* c/o Gads Forlag, Vimmelskaftet 32, 1611 Copenhagen, Denmark.

CAREER: Worked as scientific assistant and leader of estuarine research for Danish Institute for Fishery and Marine Research, 1954-67; member of scientific expeditions, 1966; Zoological Museum, Copenhagen, Denmark, director, 1968-73; University of Copenhagen, Copenhagen, Denmark, professor of zoology, 1969—. Chairman of board of directors of Copenhagen Zoo; chairman of Council on Conservation, Ministry of the Environment; vice-chairman of World Wildlife Fund [Denmark]; consultant to United Nations Educational, Scientific and Cultural Organization and Danish Foreign Aid Office. *Member:* Baltic Marine Biologists, Royal Danish Geographic Society, Danish Natural History Society, Thai-Danish Society, Ornithological Society Denmark, Societas pro Fauna et Flora Fennica. *Awards, honors:* Officer of Crown of Thailand, 1966; knight of Order of Dannebrog, 1979.

WRITINGS: The Fauna of Danish Estuaries and Lagoons, Hoest, 1967; *The Freshwater Fishes of Britain and Europe,* Collins, 1971; *Sea Fishes of Britain and North-Western Europe,* Collins, 1974.

In Danish: *Blaeksprutter: Denmark's Fauna,* Volume 65, Gads Forlag, 1959; *Harvfisk,* Gads Forlag, 1964; *Europas Ferskvandsfisk,* Gads Forlag, 1967; (with Finn Salomonsen and Christian Vibe) *Groenlands Fauna,* Gyldendals Forlag, 1981. Contributor to scientific journals.

WORK IN PROGRESS: An English translation of *Groenlands Fauna,* to be titled *The Fauna of Greenland: Fishes, Birds, and Mammals,* publication expected in 1982.

SIDELIGHTS: Muus commented: "As a marine biologist I have joined expeditions in the North Atlantic, the South China Sea, and the Andaman Sea. I have traveled widely in the Far East. My travels have opened my eyes to the grave problems of over-exploitation of the earth and conservation, and I try to apply my knowledge to the benefit of World Wildlife Fund projects.

"I wish to stimulate a more focused approach to living resource conservation and to stress the need for action before the planet's capacity to support people is irreversibly reduced. I share the belief that 'we have not inherited the earth from our parents, we have borrowed it from our children.'"

*   *   *

MYHILL, Henry (James)   1925-1977

PERSONAL: Born October 26, 1925, in Leicester, England; died in 1977. *Education:* Attended Jesus College, Cambridge; St. Catherine's College, Oxford, M.A.; also attended University of Grenoble and Sorbonne, University of Paris; studied in Austria.

CAREER: Coal miner, 1944-47; travel agency representative in France and Spain, 1954-62; writer, 1962-77.

WRITINGS: Introducing the Channel Islands, Faber, 1964; *The Spanish Pyrenees,* Faber, 1966, Transatlantic, 1967; *The Canary Islands,* Faber, 1968; *Brittany,* Faber, 1969; *Portugal,* Transatlantic, 1972; *North of the Pyrenees,* Faber, 1973, Transatlantic, 1974; *Motor Caravanning: A Complete Guide,* Transatlantic, 1976; *The Loire Valley: Plantagenet and Valois,* Faber, 1978. Contributor to magazines and newspapers, including *Financial Times, Motor Caravan and Camping, Stock Exchange Gazette,* and *Caravaning.**

N

NAESLUND, Erik 1948-

PERSONAL: Born November 20, 1948, in Stockholm, Sweden; son of Hugo and Margot Naeslund. *Education:* University of Stockholm, B.A., 1972. *Home and office:* Bondegatan 55, 11633 Stockholm, Sweden.

CAREER: Dance critic and journalist, 1972—; *Dans/Dance,* Stockholm, Sweden, editor, 1973—. Script editor and literary adviser to Swedish Television drama department, 1976—; assistant director; translator. *Military service:* Swedish Army, 1971-72. *Member:* Swedish Journalists Association, Swedish Theater Critics Association, Friends of Stockholm Dance Museum (member of board of directors).

WRITINGS: Birgit Cullberg: A Biography, Norstedts, 1978; *Carina Ari: A Biography,* Bonniers, 1981. Contributor to dance and music journals in Sweden and abroad, including *Dance News* and *Opera Canada.*

SIDELIGHTS: Naeslund told *CA:* "My theatre interest was nurtured from early childhood. While still a teenager, I attended a theatre school, and later studied the history of theatre and participated in the Stockholm Student Theatre as an actor. I was inclined to become a director when chance directed me into dance criticism and dance writing. To develop myself in this particular field I have traveled extensively throughout Europe and the United States to study ballet and theatre. I have returned to the latter field in recent years, since I feel it is important not to isolate yourself in one art, as ballet, but to take interest in several theatrical arts. All of them relate to one another, and besides I feel it important to combine theoretical and practical work."

*   *   *

NAGLER, Alois Maria 1907-

PERSONAL: Born September 14, 1907, in Graz, Austria; came to the United States in 1938, naturalized citizen, 1944; son of Alois and Auguste (Schupp) Nagler; married Erna Scheinberger, August 19, 1933. *Education:* University of Graz, D.Phil., 1930; attended University of Vienna. *Home:* 174 Linden St., New Haven, Conn. 06511.

CAREER: Drama and music critic in Berlin, Germany, 1930-32; literary editor and theatre critic for daily paper in Vienna, Austria, 1932-38; visiting lecturer, 1938-40; U.S. Department of the Navy, Office of Intelligence, Washington, D.C., civilian supervisor of cross-cultural survey, 1941-45; Yale University, New Haven, Conn., 1946-65, began as assistant professor, became professor, Henry McCormick Professor of Dramatic History, 1965-76, professor emeritus, 1976—. Visiting professor at Columbia University, 1960-61, and City University of New York, 1968-69.

MEMBER: International Federation for Theater Research (president, 1959-63), American Society for Theater Research (chairman, 1960-63), Society for History of the Theater, Austrian Academy of Arts and Sciences. *Awards, honors:* Rockefeller Foundation fellowship, 1940-41, grant, 1949; M.A. from Yale University, 1960; Cross of Honor, first class, from Republic of Austria, 1967, for sciences and art; special award from New England Theater Conference, 1976.

WRITINGS: Hebbel und die musik (title means "Hebbel and Music"), J. P. Bachem, 1928; (editor) *Sources of Theatrical History,* Theatre Annual, 1952, reprinted as *A Source Book in Theatrical History,* Dover, 1959; *Shakespeare's Stage* (translated by Ralph Manheim), Yale University Press, 1958; *Theatre Festivals of the Medici, 1529-1637* (translated by George Hickenlooper), Yale University Press, 1964; *The Medieval Religious Stage: Shapes and Phantoms* (translated by George C. Schoolfield), Yale University Press, 1976. Also author of *Ferdinand von Saar as a Short Story Writer,* 1930. Contributor to theatre journals.

BIOGRAPHICAL/CRITICAL SOURCES: Times Literary Supplement, March 11, 1977.*

*   *   *

NARAYAN, Ongkar 1926-

PERSONAL: Born February 20, 1926, in Essequibo, Guyana; naturalized Canadian citizen; son of Sase (a merchant) and Taijhertie (Sawh) Narayan; married Manorama Narine, March 24, 1957; children: Narendra, Alita, Surendra, Keeran. *Education:* Susquehanna University, B.A., 1947; Bucknell University, M.A. (English), 1948; Northeast Missouri State University, M.A. (educational administration), 1956; Pennsylvania State University, D.Ed., 1972. *Home:* 30 Menlo Cres., Sherwood Park, Alberta, Canada T8A 0R9.

CAREER: Worked as school principal, secretary-treasurer, and head of English and physical education departments in Guyana, 1944-62; instructor in physics in Aruba, 1953-54; Teachers' College, Guyana, tutor in English methods, 1961-62; Edmonton Public School Board, Edmonton, Alberta, English teacher, 1963—.

WRITINGS: Bye Bye Mista (novel), Philosophical Library, 1973.

WORK IN PROGRESS: Shadow of a Woman, a novelette; *Toward Relevance in English.*

SIDELIGHTS: Narayan commented: "People suffer themselves unduly because of careless oral communication. Scholars can be taught to write most effectively. What the world of abundance needs is within the power of individuals to give—love and more love. Every living thing can become better if nourished with love."

*   *   *

NASLUND, Erik
See NAESLUND, Erik

*   *   *

NATUSCH, Sheila (Ellen)   1926-

PERSONAL: Surname is pronounced Na-*toosh;* born February 14, 1926, in Invercargill, New Zealand; daughter of Robert Henry (a ranger) and Dorothea Ellen (a painter in watercolors) Traill; married Gilbert Gardner Natusch (a civil engineer), November 28, 1950. *Education:* University of Otago, M.A., 1948. *Home:* 46 Ohiro Bay Parade, Wellington 2, New Zealand.

CAREER: Full-time writer. Has worked as teacher and laboratory assistant; worked briefly at National Library of New Zealand, 1949, and Dominion Museum (now National Museum), Wellington, New Zealand. *Member:* New Zealand Ship and Marine Society, Royal Society of New Zealand, Royal Astronomical Society, Wellington Botanical Society. *Awards, honors:* Hubert Church Award from International P.E.N., 1969, for *Brother Wohlers: A Biography.*

WRITINGS: Native Plants, Pegasus, 1956, revised edition, 1976; (with N. S. Seaward) *Stewart Island,* Pegasus, 1951, 5th edition, 1973; *Native Rock,* A. H. & A. W. Reed, 1959; *Animals of New Zealand,* Whitcombe & Tombs, 1967; *A Bunch of Wild Orchids,* Pegasus, 1968, 2nd edition, 1981; *New Zealand Mosses,* Pegasus, 1969; *Brother Wohlers: A Biography,* Pegasus Press, 1969; *On the Edge of the Bush: Women in Early Southland,* Craig Printing, 1976; *Hell and High Water: A German Occupation of the Chatham Islands, 1843-1910,* Pegasus Press, 1977; *The Cruise of the Acheron: Her Majesty's Steam Vessel on Survey in New Zealand Waters, 1848-51,* Whitcoulls, 1978; *Roaring Forties,* privately printed, 1978; *Wild Food for Wilderness Foragers,* Collins, 1979; *Wellington With Sheila Natusch,* Millwood Press, 1981.

WORK IN PROGRESS: A book about the search for land in New Zealand in 1844.

SIDELIGHTS: Sheila Natusch commented: "I have always been a poker about on the edge of the tide, up mountainsides, among fossils and minerals, and like to be in view of a clear night sky. Born a Stewart Islander, I also grew up boat-minded. Though not exactly gregarious, or not all the time, I like to share my interests. I am fond of the outdoors and interested in bird life, but not fond of television, automobiles, and the like. I sail a cockleshell-class boat. Politics and religion are more of a spectator sport with me: live and let live is the nearest I have to a policy."

*   *   *

NEALON, Eleanor

PERSONAL: Born in Washington, D.C.; daughter of Stephen William (a physician) and Eleanor (O'Donoghue) Nea-

lon. *Education:* Attended Rosemont College, 1958-61. *Religion:* Roman Catholic. *Home and office:* 4000 Tunlaw Rd. N.W., Washington, D.C. 20007. *Agent:* Edward J. Acton, Inc., 17 Grove St., New York, N.Y. 10014.

CAREER: Washingtonian, Washington, D.C., member of editorial staff, 1967-70; Georgetown University, Washington, D.C., science writer, 1971-77, assistant director of Medical Center public relations, 1971-75, director, 1975-77; free-lance writer, 1977-78; Robert Wood Johnson Foundation, Princeton, N.J., communications officer dealing with national health programs, 1978-79; free-lance writer and communications consultant, 1979—. *Member:* National Press Club, American Newspaper Women's Club, National Association of Science Writers, Washington Independent Writers. *Awards, honors:* MacEachern Citation from Academy of Hospital Public Relations, 1974, for public relations community program; award of distinction from Mid-Atlantic Division of American Medical Writers Association, 1976, for "Quick Help for Troubled Patients"; award for outstanding medical writing, 1980, for *Living With Surgery: Before and After.*

WRITINGS: (With Paul Melluzzo) *Living With Surgery: Before and After,* Lorenz, 1979, revised edition, Saunders, 1981. Contributor of more than forty articles to magazines, including *Smithsonian,* and newspapers.

SIDELIGHTS: Eleanor Nealon commented: "*Living With Surgery* was written with the hope of helping people meet the difficult challenges of major surgery—both physical and psychological. To do this we offered information, practical tips on daily living, and true stories that would bring better understanding of ourselves and of each other's feelings and needs. We presented not only facts and the wisdom of experts, but also the shared experiences of those who had been through the surgery themselves."

*   *   *

NEFF, William Lee   1906-1973

OBITUARY NOTICE—See index for *CA* sketch: Born December 7, 1906, in Sangamon County, Ill.; died August, 1973. Educator and author. Neff was the co-author of *World History for a Better World* and *Freedom Under Law: A History of the United States.* (Date of death provided by wife, Virginia Neff.)

*   *   *

NEIMAN, LeRoy   1926-

PERSONAL: Born June 8, 1926, in St. Paul, Minn.; son of Charles and Lydia (Serline) Runquist; married Janet Byrne, June 22, 1957. *Education:* Attended School of Art Institute of Chicago, 1946-50, University of Illinois, 1951, and DePaul University, 1951. *Home:* 1 West 67th St., New York, N.Y. 10023.

CAREER: Professional artist. Work represented in one-man exhibitions, including Hammer Galleries and Hermitage Museum, Leningrad, U.S.S.R., and in group shows all over the world, including Art Institute of Chicago, Corcoran Gallery, Smithsonian Institution, and Royal College of Art; represented in permanent collections, including Madison Square Garden Center. Instructor at School of Art Institute of Chicago, 1950-60, Saugatuck Summer School of Painting, 1957-58 and 1963, School of Arts and Crafts, Winston-Salem, N.C., 1963, and Atlanta Youth Council, 1968-69; visiting professor at University of Kentucky. Illustrator for *Playboy,* beginning in 1954. Resident artist for New York Jets, 1968—; artist reporter for ABC-TV's "Wide World of Sports," 1969—;

official artist for Major League Baseball Promotions, 1971—, and Olympic Games, 1972—; computer artist for CBS-TV presentation of "The Superbowl," 1978. Guest on numerous television talk shows. *Military service:* U.S. Army, 1942-46; served in European theater; received five battle stars. *Awards, honors:* First prize from Twin City Show, 1953; Clark Memorial Prize from Chicago Show of Art Institute of Chicago, 1957, municipal prize, 1958; Hamilton-Graham Prize from Ball State College (now University), 1958; purchase prize from Mississippi Valley Show, 1959; gold medal from Salon d'Art Modern, 1961; award of merit from Amateur Athletic Union of the United States, 1976; Litt.D. from Franklin Pierce College, 1976; Gold Plate Award from American Academy of Achievement, 1977; named artist of the year by Beaux Arts Gallery, 1981; named sportsman of the year by B'nai B'rith, 1981.

WRITINGS: (With Dave Anderson) *Countdown to Superbowl*, Random House, 1969; *This Great Game*, Prentice-Hall, 1971; *LeRoy Neiman: Art and Life Style*, Felicie, 1974; (illustrator) Herman Melville, *Moby Dick; or, The Whale* (preface by Yves-Jacques Cousteau), Artist's Limited Editions, 1975; *Horses*, Abrams, 1979; *Posters*, Abrams, 1980; *Catalogue Raisonne*, Knoedler, 1980. Contributor of art work to magazines, including covers for *Time*.

WORK IN PROGRESS: A book of drawings for Knoedler.

SIDELIGHTS: LeRoy Neiman's paintings and drawings of sports figures can be seen anywhere from the cover of *Playboy* magazine to the inside of Burger King restaurants to the television show "Wide World of Sports." One of the wealthiest artists in the world, Neiman receives a large amount of publicity. His dealer Maury Leibovitz assessed that "no other artist in the world has LeRoy Neiman's exposure." Neiman once described his life as a well-known artist : "I can't pay for a suit of clothes. I can't pay for a drink in a restaurant. People want to buy for me." "I don't want to sound like a braggart," he concluded, "but there's never been anything like me."

Despite his popularity and monetary rewards, though, Neiman is not accepted in serious art circles. Most critics consider him an illustrator rather than an artist. His style has been called a "stylistic mishmash, a kind of warmed-over impressionism" by *Village Voice* critic David Bourdon, and many others accuse his paintings of being decorative and shallow. Neiman, however, disagrees. "I can draw," he contended. "There's no one in the world like me." He further explained: "I came out of America as a world power. The fun and games America, where sports and recreation are an industry. I paint the bright, glossy exterior of things and I myself identify with the world I paint. It wasn't like I lived in a hut and just went and visited Vegas. I was into it. . . . I mean, what I do is valid."

BIOGRAPHICAL/CRITICAL SOURCES: American Artist, April, 1961; *Saturday Evening Post*, May 9, 1976; *New Times*, February 6, 1978; *New Yorker*, February 5, 1979.

*   *   *

NELLES, Henry Vivian   1942-

PERSONAL: Born November 9, 1942, in Galt, Ontario, Canada; son of Henry and Dorothy Nelles; married Diane Dilworth, 1967; children: one daughter. *Education:* University of Toronto, B.A., 1964, M.A., 1965, Ph.D., 1970. *Office:* Department of History, York University, 4700 Keele St., Downsview, Ontario, Canada M3J 1P3.

CAREER: University of Toronto, Toronto, Ontario, lecturer in history, 1967-68; University of British Columbia, Van-

couver, assistant professor of history, 1968-70; York University, Downsview, Ontario, assistant professor, 1970-73, associate professor of history, 1973—. Visiting professor at University of Tsukuba, Keio University, International Christian University, 1976-77, and Harvard University, 1981-82. *Member:* Canadian Historical Association, American Historical Association. *Awards, honors:* Newcomen Award from Business History Association, 1973; City of Toronto book award, 1977; Japan Society for the Promotion of Science traveling fellowship, 1979.

WRITINGS: (Editor) Thomas Coltrin Keefer, *Philosophy of Railroads and Other Essays*, University of Toronto Press, 1972; (contributor) *Olivar Mowat's Ontario*, Macmillan, 1972; *The Politics of Development: Forests, Mines, and Hydro-Electric Power in Ontario, 1849-1941*, Archon, 1974; (with Christopher Armstrong) *The Revenge of the Methodist Bicycle Company*, P. Martin, 1977; (contributor) P. Ward and K. Carty, editors, *Entering the Eighties*, Oxford University Press, 1981. Contributor to history journals.

SIDELIGHTS: D. C. MacDonald of the *Canadian Forum* called Nelles's work, *The Politics of Development* perhaps "the most important book of the seventies in the field of Ontario politics and economic development."

BIOGRAPHICAL/CRITICAL SOURCES: Canadian Forum, May-June, 1974; *Journal of American History*, June, 1975.

*   *   *

NELSON, Bryan   1932-

PERSONAL: Born March 14, 1932, in Shipley, England; son of Thomas William and Ida Nelson; married June Davison, December 31, 1960; children: Simon Philip and Rebecca Sarah (twins). *Education:* University of St. Andrews, B.Sc. (with honors), 1959; Oxford University, D.Phil., 1963. *Politics:* Liberal. *Home:* Quilquox Croft, Ythanbank, Aberdeen, Scotland. *Office:* Department of Zoology, University of Aberdeen, Tillydrone Ave., Aberdeen, Scotland.

CAREER: City of Bradford Corp., Bradford, England, analytic chemist at Esholt Sewage Works, 1953-56; Azraq International Biological Station, Jordan, director, 1968-69; University of Aberdeen, Aberdeen, Scotland, senior lecturer, 1973-80, reader in zoology, 1980—. *Member:* British Ornithologists Union, British Trust for Ornithology, Association for the Study of Animal Behavior.

WRITINGS: Galapagos: Islands of Birds, Longmans, Green, 1968; *Azraq: Desert Oasis*, Penguin, 1974; *Sulidae: Gannets and Boobies*, Oxford University Press, 1978; *The Gannet*, Poyser, 1978; *Seabirds: Their Biology and Ecology*, Hamlyn, 1980. Contributor to scientific journals and popular magazines, including *Natural History*.

WORK IN PROGRESS: An anthology on island living, publication expected in 1983; an introductory text on animal behavior, publication expected in 1984; a major comparative review of seabird behavior, publication by Cambridge University Press expected in 1987.

SIDELIGHTS: Nelson commented: "I have worked in the Galapagos, Christmas Island in the Indian Ocean, Aldabra, the Peruvian guano islands, and British seabird islands, including Ban Rock and Ailse Craig. I am a loner and not, I hope, materialistic. I am keen on alternative lifestyles, though not of the lunatic fringe.

"I write partly because I hate waste. Twenty years of field work, often in remote and beautiful places, produces a mass of information, and the challenge is to do something useful with it. Scientists usually write badly. They use jargon and are forced by journals to adopt a style devoid of all grace and personality. Books enable one to do more justice to one's material. This need not mean wordy rambling, but it can allow digression. The reviews of my own works which please me most are those which praise the quality of the writing.

"Also, I want to convert others to an appreciation of wildlife and man's obligation to this beautiful world. I loathe and detest the despoilation that one sees everywhere, and I am totally convinced that the world we ought to be striving towards is almost the opposite of the kind of world we are in fact rapidly, suicidally, creating.

"It would be immensely satisfying if I could write something that was conceptually important, but this is a very tall order. Darwin said that he became a machine for grinding out generalizations from a vast number of facts, and, although I do not have his capacity, I know just what he meant. Facts are fairly useless until they are synthesized and interpreted.

"I have been extremely lucky in that I have studied seabirds. Not only are seabirds ideal material for ecological and behavioral studies, but they and their breeding haunts are highly evocative. One can write vividly about them. If I studied fossil echinoderms I could interest only a handful of specialists.

"Most of all, I would like to write, with insight, about human behavior, but the task is so daunting that I may never try."

*   *   *

NELSON, Lawrence E(rnest)   1928-1977

OBITUARY NOTICE—See index for *CA* sketch: Born October 4, 1928, in Des Moines, Iowa; died December 17, 1977. Clergyman, editor, and author. A Lutheran pastor, Nelson was best known for his work in the field of youth guidance. His writings include *Working With Young People, Ways to Teach Teens, Move It,* and *Creative Ways to Use Youth Forum Books.* He was also former editor of *Viewpoint,* a newspaper for youths. (Date of death provided by wife, Mary Jane Nelson.)

*   *   *

NELSON, William   1908-1978

OBITUARY NOTICE—See index for *CA* sketch: Born January 18, 1908, in New York, N.Y.; died October 26, 1978. Educator and author. Nelson's works include *John Skelton: Laureate, The Poetry of Edmund Spenser,* and *Fact or Fiction.* Among the books he edited are *Out of the Crocodile's Mouth* and *A Fifteenth Century School Book.* (Date of death provided by wife, Elsa R. Nelson.)

*   *   *

NESMITH, Robert I.   1891-1972
(Captain Jafar Clarke)

OBITUARY NOTICE—See index for *CA* sketch: Born September 16, 1891, in Lynn, Mass.; died July 28, 1972. Photographer, numismatist, and author. Nesmith was the founder and owner of the Foul Anchor Archives, a treasure research center. Considered an authority on pirates, sunken galleons, and early Spanish coinage, Nesmith was a consultant to treasure hunters. He wrote *The Coinage of the First Mint of the Americas at Mexico City, 1536-1572,* and *Dig for Pirate Treasure.* He was also the co-author of *Treasure Hunters,* which was published in a revised edition as *Treasure Hunter's Guide: How and Where to Find It.* (Date of death provided by American Numismatic Society.)

NEUHAUS, Ruby (Hart)   1932-

PERSONAL: Born December 23, 1932, in New York, N.Y.; daughter of Coy Elkin and Pauline (Thorn) Hart; married Robert Neuhaus (a professor of health administration), 1955; children: Leah, Paul, Rachel. *Education:* Brooklyn College (now of the City University of New York), B.A., 1955; Fordham University, M.S.W., 1957; New York University, Ph.D., 1974. *Religion:* Lutheran. *Home:* 128 Burtis Ave., Oyster Bay, N.Y. 11771. *Office:* Department of Health Services, Herbert H. Lehman College of the City University of New York, Bedford Park Blvd., Bronx, N.Y. 10468.

CAREER: Associated with Adelphi University, Garden City, N.Y., 1973-74; State University of New York at Old Westbury, 1974-76; Nassau County Mental Health Center, regional director, 1975-77; Herbert H. Lehman College of the City University of New York, Bronx, N.Y., chairman of department of health services and director of health services administration program, 1977—. *Member:* Association of University Programs in Health Administration, Academy of Health Administrators, American Public Health Association, American Society for Public Administration, Orthopsychiatric Conference, National Association of Social Workers. *Awards, honors:* Fellowship from Wheatridge Foundation, 1955-57; Beta Mu Award from Brookly College, 1955.

WRITINGS: (With husband, Robert Neuhaus) *Family Crises,* C. E. Merrill, 1974; (with R. Neuhaus) *Successful Aging,* Wiley, 1981.

SIDELIGHTS: Ruby Neuhaus told *CA:* "*Successful Aging* deals with a holistic concept of aging from social, psychological, and physiological perspectives. This is a useful approach for health professional students in health administration, medicine, social work, nursing, and other fields."

*   *   *

NEUMAN, William Frederick   1919-1981

OBITUARY NOTICE: Born June 2, 1919, in Petoskey, Mich.; died January 4, 1981, in Rochester, N.Y. Biochemist and author. Neuman was an authority on the biochemistry of bone tissue. Before joining the faculty of the University of Rochester in 1944, he headed the biochemistry section of the Atomic Energy Commission at the university and helped develop the field of health physics. In 1965 he was a member of the scientific team that studied the effects of space flight on astronauts Frank Borman and James A. Lovell after their fourteen-day flight on Gemini 7. Neuman was the author or co-author of more than two hundred scholarly publications. Obituaries and other sources: *Who's Who in America,* 40th edition, Marquis, 1978; *American Men and Women of Science,* 14th edition, Bowker, 1979; *New York Times,* January 6, 1981.

*   *   *

NEUMANN, Robert   1897-1975

PERSONAL: Born May 22, 1897, in Vienna, Austria; died January 3, 1975, in Munich, West Germany; son of Samuel and Josephine (Pilpel) Neumann; married Stephanie Grunwald, 1920 (divorced, 1941); married Lore Fraziska Becker, 1941 (divorced, 1952); married Evelyn Hengerer, 1953 (died, 1958); married Helga Heller, September 9, 1960; children: (first marriage) Henry (deceased); (third marriage) Robert Michael Henry. *Education:* Attended University of Vienna. *Residence:* Locarno-Monti, Switzerland.

CAREER: Writer. Associated with Film Group, Inc., 1930-75. *Member:* P.E.N., Deutsche Akademie fur Sprache und Dichtung, Freie Deutsche Akademie der Kunste, Schweizerischer Schriftstellerverein. *Awards, honors:* Austrian Cross of Honor, first class in arts and sciences, 1965; Vienna Gold Medal of Honor.

WRITINGS: The Scene in Passing, Dent, 1942, published as *Mr. Tibbs Passes Through,* Dutton, 1943; *The Inquest* (novel), Hutchinson, 1944, Dutton, 1945; *Children of Vienna* (novel), Gollancz, 1946, Dutton, 1947; *Blind Man's Buff,* Hutchinson, 1949; *Insurrection in Poshansk,* Hutchinson, 1952; *Shooting Star* (novels; contains "Shooting Star" and "Circe's Island"), Hutchinson, 1954; *The Plague House Papers* (autobiography), Hutchinson, 1959; *The Dark Side of the Moon,* Hutchinson, 1961.

In English translation: *Sintflut* (novel), J. Engelhorns, 1929, translation by William A. Drake published as *Flood,* Covici, Friede, 1930; *Passion: Sechs dichter-ehen,* Phaidon, 1930, translation by Brian W. Downs published as *Passion: Six Literary Marriages,* Harcourt, 1932; *Das Schiff "Esperance,"* P. Zsolnay, 1931, translation by G. C. Grant published as *Ship in the Night,* P. Davies, 1932; *Karriere,* J. Engelhorns, 1931, translation by Laurence Vail published as *On the Make,* P. Davies, 1932; *Die Macht,* P. Zsolnay, 1932, reprinted, K. Desch, 1963, translation by Dorothy M. Richardson published as *Mammon,* P. Davies, 1933; *Sir Basil Zaharoff: Der Koenig der waffen,* Bibliothek Zeitgenoessischer Werke, 1934, translation by R. T. Clark published as *Zaharoff,* Knopf, 1935.

Struensee: Doktor, Diktator, Favorit, und Armer Suender (novel), Querido, 1935, translation by Edwin Muir and Willa Muir published as *The Queen's Doctor, Being the Strange Story of the Rise and Fall of Struensee, Dictator, Lover, and Doctor of Medicine,* Knopf, 1936; *Eine Frau hat geschrien* (novel), Humanitas, 1938, translation by E. Muir and W. Muir published as *A Woman Screamed,* Dail, 1938; *By the Waters of Babylon,* translated by Anthony Dent, Dent, 1936, Simon & Schuster, 1940; *Twenty-three Women: The Story of an International Traffic,* translated by Heinz Norden and Ruth Norden, Dial, 1940; (with Helga Koppel) *Hitler: Aufstieg und Untergang des Dritten Reiches,* K. Desch, 1961, translation published as *The Pictorial History of the Third Reich,* Bantam, 1962; *Festival* (novel), K. Desch, 1962, translated by Michael Bullock, Barrie & Rockliff, 1963.

In German: *Mit fremden Federn, Parodien von Robert Neumann,* T. Engelhorns, 1927, reprinted in two volumes, K. Desch, 1955; *Die Pest von Lianora,* J. Engelhorns, 1927; *Jagd auf Menschen und Gespenster* (reminiscences), J. Engelhorns, 1928; *Die Blinden von Kagoll,* P. Reclam, 1929; *Panaptikum, Bericht ueber fuenf ehen aus der Zeit,* Phaidon, 1930; *Hochstaplernovelle,* J. Engelhorns, 1930; *Unter falscher Flagge: Ein Lesebuch der deutschen Sprache fuer Fortgeschrittene,* P. Zsolnay, 1932; *Die blinden Passagiere* (novella), Bibliothek Zeitgenoessischer Werke, 1935; *Mein altes Haus in Kent: Erinnerungen an Menschen und Gespenster* (reminiscences), K. Desch, 1957; *Die Freiheit und der General* (novel), K. Desch, 1958; *Ausfluechte unseres Gewissens: Dokumente zu Hitlers "Endloesung der Judenfrage" mit Kommentar and Bilanz der politischen Situation,* Verlag fuer Literatur und Zeitgeschechen, 1960; *Der Favorit der Koenigin* (novel), Verlag Ullstein, 1962; (with Oswald Meichsner) *Die Staatsaffaere,* K. Desch, 1964.

(Contributor) Leonard Freed, *Deutsche Juden heute,* Hans Hermann Koeper, 1965; (editor) *Vierunddreissig mal erste Liebe: Schriftsteller aus zwei Generation unseres Jahrhun-*

derts beschreiben erste erotische Erlebnisse, Barmeier & Nikel, 1966; (with Lindi) *Hotel Sexos: Eine erotische Revolte* (caricatures and cartoons), Tabu Verlag, 1968; (with Lindi) *Palace Hotel de la Plage und der finstere Hintergrund: Eine politische Entlarvung* (caricatures and cartoons), Gala-Verlag, 1968; (with Lindi) *Komma sutram oder Die altindische Liebeskunst* (caricatures and cartoons), Scherz, 1969; (with Lindi) *Deutschland deine Oesterreicher; Oesterreich deine Deutschen,* Hoffmann & Campe, 1970; (contributor) *Erstes Internationales Festival des Erotischen Films, 1971,* Olympia, 1972; *Zwei mal zwei ist fuenf: Eine Anleitung zu Rechtbehalten,* Claassen, 1974.

Omnibus volumes; all published by K. Desch: *Vielleicht das Heitere; Tagebuch aus einem andern Jahr,* 1968; *Daemon Weib; oder, Die Selbstverzauberung durch Literatur, samt techischen Hinweisen, wie man dorthin gelangt,* 1969; *Nie wieder Politik oder von der Idiotie der Schriftsteller; Eine Krankengeschichte mit vielen grausigen Beispielen samt einem unpolit,* 1969; *Vorsicht Buecher: Parodien samt einem Lese-Leitfaden fuer Fortgeschrittene,* 1969; *Oktoberreise mit einer Geliebten,* 1970; *Ein unmoeglicher Sohn,* 1972.

Gesammelte Werke in Einzelaugaben, Volume I: *Die dunkle Seite des Mondes* (novel), 1959, Volume II: *An den Wassern von Babylon; Treibgut,* 1960, Volume III: *Olympia* (novel), 1961, Volume IV: *Die Parodien,* 1962, Volume V: *Festival,* 1962, Volume VI: *Ein leichtes Leben; Bericht ueber mich selbst und Zeitgenossen,* 1963, Volume VII: *Macht,* 1964, Volume VIII: *Der Tatbestand; oder, der gute Glaube der Deutschen,* 1965; *Karrieren: Hochstaplernovelle, Karriere, Blinde Passagiere, Luise,* 1966.

Author of screenplays, including "Abdui the Damned," 1934, "Dynamite Nobel," 1937, "Those Are the Men," 1941, "Herrscher ohne Krone," 1956, "The Life of Adolph Hitler," 1962, "Die Begnadigung," 1969, "Emigration," 1970, "Geschichte einer Geschichte," and "Schiosspension Furstenhorst."*

* * *

NEVILLE, Heather Buckley
 See BUCKLEY NEVILLE, Heather

* * *

NEWCOMB, Ellsworth
 See KENNY, Ellsworth Newcomb

* * *

NEWELL, William H(are)   1922-

PERSONAL: Born December 21, 1922, in Vanarasi, India; son of Herbert William (an Anglican priest) and Mary Irene Newell; married Pauline Marsh (a university lecturer), July 8, 1958; children: Elizabeth, Gertrude, William, Susan. *Education:* Victoria University of Wellington, M.A., 1945; Mansfield College, Oxford, Diploma in Anthropology, 1947; West China Union University, Diploma in Chinese, 1949; Victoria University of Manchester, Ph.D., 1958. *Politics:* Labour. *Religion:* Anglican. *Home:* 14 Olive St., Ryde, New South Wales 2112, Australia. *Office:* Department of Anthropology, University of Sydney, Sydney, New South Wales 2006, Australia.

CAREER: Victoria University of Manchester, Manchester, England, lecturer in social anthropology, 1950-53; University of Malaya, Singapore, fellow in social research unit, 1953-57; Victoria University of Manchester, lecturer in social anthropology, 1957-60; International Christian University, Tokyo, Japan, professor of sociology and head of department,

1960-69; University of Sydney, Sydney, Australia, associate professor of anthropology, 1969—. Chairman of Keston College, New South Wales. *Military service:* Royal New Zealand Air Force, Meteorological Service, 1942-45. *Member:* South Seas Society, Australian Anthropological Society (chairman), American Anthropological Association, Royal Anthropological Institute, British Association of Social Anthropologists, Nippon Minzoku Gakkai, Industrial Relations Society of New South Wales. *Awards, honors:* Fellow of Churchill College, Cambridge, 1969-70.

WRITINGS: Scheduled Castes and Tribes of Himachel Pradesh, Government of India Press, 1961; *Treacherous River,* University of Singapore Press, 1962; (editor with Kiyomi Morioka) *Sociology of Japanese Religion,* E. J. Brill, 1968; (editor) *Ancestors,* Mouton, 1974; (editor) *Japan in Asia, 1942-1945,* University of Singapore Press, 1981. Correspondent for *Economic and Political Weekly,* 1959-68.

WORK IN PROGRESS: Research on status in Indian factories, religious organization in Okinawa, and mainland Chinese social organization.

SIDELIGHTS: Newell commented: "I have spent most of my life in Asia. I have been lucky enough actually to have been involved in the Chinese Liberation, the Kashmir independence movement, the emergency in Malaysia and elsewhere. There are few Asian countries that I dislike living in and I have developed many loyal friends, both colleagues and students, partly through my strong interest in religions. During the last five years my interest in Communist countries has increased. I am especially fascinated with China and the U.S.S.R."

BIOGRAPHICAL/CRITICAL SOURCES: Okubo Akinori, *Gai koku jin no mita Tenri kyo* (title means "Foreigners Look at Tenri"), Tenri Kyodo Yosha, 1968.

* * *

NEWTON, Virgil Miller, Jr. 1904-1977

OBITUARY NOTICE—See index for *CA* sketch: Born April 12, 1904, in Atlanta, Ga.; died December 13, 1977, in Tampa, Fla. Journalist and editor. Newton was best known for his efforts to prevent secrecy in government. He was considered the catalyst for Florida's "sunshine" law which opened all government meetings to the public. A newspaperman for forty-two years, Newton was a former president of Sigma Delta Chi, the largest journalism fraternity in the United States. He was also a past president of the Associated Press Managing Editors Association, serving on its board of directors for eleven years. He wrote *Crusade for Democracy.* Obituaries and other sources: *New York Times,* December 14, 1977.

* * *

NEYLAND, James (Elwyn) 1939-
(Judith Jameson, Gerry Romero)

PERSONAL: Surname is pronounced *Nee*-land; born December 4, 1939, in Leon County, Tex.; son of James Rarden (a pulpwood contractor) and Velma Olene (a department store catalog manager; maiden name, Hodges) Neyland; married Ellen Jane Raphael, July 19, 1964 (divorced, 1975); children: Douglas Brian, Laura Meredith. *Education:* Attended University of Texas, 1958-63. *Politics:* Democrat. *Religion:* Episcopalian. *Home and office:* 1308 Brakenridge, Palestine, Tex. 75801. *Agent:* Dorris Halsey, Reece Halsey Agency, 8733 Sunset Blvd., Los Angeles, Calif. 90069.

CAREER: Wunderman, Ricotta & Kline (advertising agency), New York City, assistant art director, 1963-64; Prentice-Hall, Inc., Englewood Cliffs, N.J., production editor of college texts, 1964-65; Thomas Y. Crowell Co., New York City, senior editor of college texts, 1965-69; Macmillan Publishing Co., Inc., New York City, editor, 1969-72; Hawthorn Books, Inc., New York City, senior editor, 1972-75; free-lance writer, 1975—. Editor-at-large operating on the West Coast, Grosset & Dunlap, Inc., 1977-79. Artist and photographer. Delegate to Texas Democratic Convention, 1979. Member of Texas Historical Commission, 1977—. *Member:* Leon County Genealogical Society (vice-president, 1980—).

WRITINGS: (Under pseudonym Gerry Romero) *Sinatra's Women,* Manor, 1976; *The Carter Family Scrapbook,* Grosset, 1977; *The Official Battlestar Galactica Scrapbook,* Grosset, 1978; *Write a Better Resume and Get a Better Job,* Grosset, 1981.

Plays: "A Memory of People" (one-act), first produced Off-Off Broadway at Judson Poets' Theatre, August 4, 1961 (also see below); "Serpentine" (one-acts; includes "A Memory of People" and "Simon Sez"), first produced Off-Off Broadway at Playbox Studio, June 4, 1969; "The Assassin Guiteau and the Lord God Himself" (three-act), first produced in Brooklyn, N.Y., at Heights Playhouse, July 19, 1972; "How Does Your Garden Grow?" (three-act), first produced in New York, 1973.

WORK IN PROGRESS: A novel under pseudonym Judith Jameson, *The Runaway Heiress;* three other novels, *Breakdown, Strangler Fever,* and *The Town That Came and Went.*

SIDELIGHTS: Neyland told *CA:* "I have been, for the last five years, what is generally known as a 'hack writer.' I have written six books of my own, two under pseudonyms, and ten more as a ghost writer. I don't reveal the titles or authors of those books. Good skeletons stay in closets. But four were novels, four were celebrity books, one was a diet book, and one would have to be described as investigative journalism. I have also taken on numerous book-doctoring jobs for various publishers.

"My motivation for all of this work has been survival. During my years as an editor in New York, I managed to maintain a degree of integrity and self-respect. Even during the first year-and-a-half of my attempt to survive by writing, I managed to keep a certain pride in what I was doing.

"I am now in Texas, attempting to restore my soul, gathering the remnants of my integrity and self-respect, in hopes that there is enough left to produce something of value. This is not an easy process and is not easy to describe.

"Among the arts, writing is special. It is the only one in which conviction must be absolute and unwavering, with no room for ambiguity. Yet it is the one most easily pandered, especially in recent years, since the absorption of publishers by business conglomerates. Publishing decisions are no longer made by editors, but by marketing analysts. Books live briefly and die swiftly.

"It is significant that none of my sixteen books were originated by me. In all cases, I was approached by a publisher or an agent to write a book on a specific subject. In a few cases—notably the Carter book and some of the novels—I was able to put genuine conviction into the assignments. But none stemmed from a deep spiritual need to comment upon the world I am passing through.

"This is particularly distressing to me because I am a part of a generation that believed the world could be changed by idealism and conviction. In college, I was one of the leaders of the civil rights movement, and I witnessed change and progress, as genuine as it was brief.

"This brings me to work in progress, and I hesitate to discuss it because I have no idea if any of the works I am planning will ever see publicaion. They are not contracted by publishers, nor are they aimed at well-defined markets. *Breakdown* is set in the sixties, centering on a group of civil rights activists. In it, societal breakdown parallels the emotional breakdown of the central character. Its theme is the fine line between creativity and destructiveness. It attempts to show that progress stems from genuine human need and that the institutionalization of change can only be destructive.

"The Little Town That Came and Went follows a similar theme. It covers the creation and destruction of a small Texas town caused by the building of a railroad. The period is the years between 1915 and 1945, and the principle characters are the members of a farming family whose simple values are changed irrevocably by the economic promises of industrialization. By the time the railroad goes, leaving the empty stores and factories to the rats and spiders, the family members are bitter enemies."

*   *   *

NICHOLS, Marie Hochmuth   1908-1978

PERSONAL: Born July 13, 1908, in Dunbar, Pa.; died in 1978; daughter of Alexander and Mary (Flydell) Hochmuth; married Alan Nichols, August 18, 1960. *Education:* University of Pittsburgh, A.B., 1931, A.M., 1936; University of Wisconsin (now University of Wisconsin—Madison), Ph.D., 1945.

CAREER: Mount Mercy College for Women, Pittsburgh, Pa., instructor in speech, 1935-38; University of Illinois, Urbana, began as instructor in 1938, became professor of speech in 1958. Visiting professor at University of Southern California, summers, 1957, 1967, 1969, and University of Hawaii, 1962; lecturer at Louisiana State University, summer, 1960. *Member:* Speech Communication Association (member of council, 1960—; president, 1969), National Education Association.

WRITINGS: (Editor) *American Speeches*, Longmans, Green, 1954; (editor) *History and Criticism of American Public Address*, 3rd volume, Longmans, Green, 1955; *Rhetoric and Criticism*, Louisiana State University Press, 1963. Associate editor of *Quarterly Journal of Speech*, 1942-45, editor, 1963-65.*

*   *   *

NICKELL, Lesley J(acqueline)   1944-

PERSONAL: Surname is pronounced Nick-*ell;* born March 18, 1944, in Harrow, England; daughter of Jack Edward (an accountant) and Lorna (an accountant; maiden name, Townley-Taylor) Nickell. *Education:* London College of Dance and Drama, Teachers' Diploma, 1965; attended Bognor College of Education, 1966-67; University of Southampton, Certificate of Education, 1967. *Politics:* "Democratic Labour." *Religion:* "Pantheist." *Home:* 17 Clopton Court, Clopton Rd., Stratford-upon-Avon, Warwickshire, England.

CAREER: High school teacher of drama, English, and dance in Kent, England, 1965-66; high school teacher of drama in Buckinghamshire, England, 1967-68; British Council, London, England, assistant in books department, 1969-70; British Council, Stratford-upon-Avon, England, assistant area officer, 1970—. Founder member of City of Birmingham Symphony Orchestra Chorus, 1974—. *Member:* Royal Society for the Protection of Birds.

WRITINGS: The White Queen (historical novel), Bodley Head, 1978, St. Martin's, 1979. Contributor to *Church of England Newspaper.*

WORK IN PROGRESS: Perkin, a novel on the life of Perkin Warbeck, fifteenth-century pretender to the throne of Henry VII, publication by Bodley Head expected in 1982; a novel about Margaret of Anjou, wife of Henry VI.

SIDELIGHTS: Lesley Nickell told *CA:* "I have had a compulsion to write since my school days. Publication has merely added external pressure to inner urge. Being quite unsympathetic to the twentieth century, my field must be historical, mainly the fifteenth century. I would like to build a bridge of understanding between then and now. Research is exhaustive and has taken me all over Europe (which is also a pleasure). Greece and France are my great loves.

"Place is very important to me, as important as people. I try to visit all the major locations of my novels, to extract their essence and to dig out whatever remains of their character in the times of which I write. We are fortunate in Europe: there is a surprising amount left. For this reason, too, I love living in Stratford-upon-Avon, which has been a market town for 1,000 years. I could not work happily in a city or a place with no visible past. Cities are unnatural and produce unnatural and aggressive people. The greatest tragedy of our century is that man is taking too much, destroying the environment which supports and delights him. I reach into the past for a sense of stability, when man knew where he was: on God's earth, with hell below and heaven above."

AVOCATIONAL INTERESTS: Music (including media appearances and recordings), walking, birdwatching, reading, attending theatre, talking.

BIOGRAPHICAL/CRITICAL SOURCES: Harrow Observer, April 11, 1978; *Coventry Evening Telegraph*, October 28, 1978; *Stratford-upon-Avon Herald*, November 3, 1978; *Warwickshire Focus*, December, 1978; *Birmingham Post*, April 3, 1979.

*   *   *

NICOLSON, Marjorie Hope   1894-1981

OBITUARY NOTICE—See index for *CA* sketch: Born February 18, 1894, in Yonkers, N.Y.; died March 9, 1981, in White Plains, N.Y. Educator and author. Marjorie Nicolson was the first woman to hold a full professorship on the graduate faculty of Columbia University and the first woman president of Phi Beta Kappa. She served as dean of Smith College for eleven years. Nicolson wrote prolifically on the influence of science and philosophy on English literature of the seventeenth century, winning the Rose Mary Crawshay Prize of the British Academy for her book *Newton Demands the Muse*. Other works include *A World in the Moon: A Study of the Changing Attitude Toward the Moon in the Seventeenth and Eighteenth Centuries* and *John Milton: A Reader's Guide to His Poetry.* Obituaries and other sources: *New York Times*, March 10, 1981.

*   *   *

NIEDERHOFFER, Arthur   1917-1981

OBITUARY NOTICE: Born October 26, 1917, in New York, N.Y.; died January 14, 1981, in New York, N.Y. Policeman, educator, and author. Niederhoffer was a former member of the New York City Police Department and a professor of sociology at John Jay College of Criminal Justice. He held teaching posts at several colleges and universities, among them Hofstra and New York universities, before joining the faculty of John Jay College in 1961. His books about police work include *Behind the Shield: The Police in Urban Society*, *The Ambivalent Force*, and *The Police Family*. He also was co-author of *The Gang: A Study in Adolescent Behavior*. Obituaries and other sources: *American Men and Women of Science: The Social and Behavioral Sciences*, 13th edition, Bowker, 1978; *New York Times*, January 16, 1981.

*   *   *

NIELSEN, Waldemar August   1917-

PERSONAL: Born March 27, 1917, in Greensburg, Pa.; son of Malta August and Mary Pauline (Shaffer) Nielsen; married Marcia Kaplan, April 22, 1943; children: Signe. *Education:* University of Missouri, A.B. and B.S., both 1939, M.A., 1940; attended Oxford University, 1939, and University of Wisconsin (now University of Wisconsin—Madison), 1940. *Home:* 15 East 91st St., New York, N.Y. 10028. *Office:* 717 Fifth Ave., New York, N.Y. 10022.

CAREER: U.S. Department of Agriculture, Washington, D.C., economic researcher and field director of Division of Program Surveys, Bureau of Agricultural Economics, 1941-44; U.S. Department of State, Washington, D.C., economic researcher and director of public opinion studies, 1946-47; U.S. Department of Commerce, Washington, D.C., special assistant to Secretary of Commerce, 1947-48; Headquarters of U.S. Special Representative in Europe, Paris, France, deputy director of Office of Information, 1948-51, director, 1951-52; Ford Foundation, New York City, deputy director of Behavioral Sciences Division, 1952-53, assistant to president, 1953-55, associate director of international affairs program, 1956-61; African-American Institute, New York City, president, 1961-70; philanthropic adviser to Empress of Iran, 1970-74; Waldemar A. Nielsen Inc. (consultants on corporate social policy), New York City, president, 1974—. Executive director of President's Committee on U.S. Information Activities Abroad, 1960; member of board of directors of Experiment in International Living; member of U.S. National Commission for United Nations Educational, Scientific and Cultural Organization (UNESCO). Senior fellow of Aspen Institute for Humanistic Studies. *Military service:* U.S. Naval Reserve, active duty, 1944-46, member of U.S. Strategic Bombing Survey in Japan, 1945-46; became lieutenant junior grade.

MEMBER: International Planned Parenthood Association, World Society of Ekistics, United Nations Association (director), Foreign Policy Association (member of board of directors), Council on Foreign Relations, American Association of Rhodes Scholars, American Economic Association, American Political Science Association, Phi Beta Kappa, Beta Gamma Sigma, Century Association. *Awards, honors:* Rhodes scholar, 1939; commander of Italy's Legion of Merit, 1961; senior fellow of Council on Foreign Relations, 1962-68; commander of Greece's Royal Order of the Phoenix, 1962; chevalier of France's Ordre de la Valeur Cameroanaise, 1963; commander of Ordre National du Senegal, 1966; LL.D. from University of Lagos, 1970.

WRITINGS: African Battleline: American Policy Choices in Southern Africa, Harper, 1965; *Africa*, Atheneum, 1966; *The Great Powers and Africa*, Praeger, 1969; *The Big Foundations*, Columbia University Press, 1972; *The Endangered Sector*, Columbia University Press, 1979. Contributor to *Encyclopaedia Britannica*. Contributor to popular magazines, including *Harper's* and *New Yorker*.

BIOGRAPHICAL/CRITICAL SOURCES: New York Times, November 11, 1972; *Change*, January, 1980; *Christian Cen-*

tury, March 5, 1980; *America*, March 22, 1980; *Choice*, June, 1980.

*   *   *

NIGHTINGALE, Anne Redmon   1943-
(Anne Redmon)

PERSONAL: Born December 13, 1943; daughter of Brian Collins (a chemist) and Elizabeth (a social worker; maiden name, Howe) Redmon; married Benedict Nightingale (a drama critic), August 8, 1964; children: Christopher, Magdalen, Piers. *Education:* Attended University of Pennsylvania, 1961-63. *Politics:* Democrat. *Religion:* Roman Catholic. *Residence:* London, England. *Agent:* A. D. Peters & Co. Ltd., 10 Buckingham St., London WC1, England; and Harold Matson Co., Inc., 22 East 40th St., New York, N.Y. 10016.

CAREER: Writer. *Member:* Royal Society for Asian Affairs, Royal Society of Literature (fellow). *Awards, honors:* Yorkshire Post prize for best first work, 1974, for *Emily Stone*.

WRITINGS—Novels; under name Anne Redmon: *Emily Stone*, Secker & Warberg, 1974, Praeger, 1975; *Music and Silence*, Holt, 1979.

WORK IN PROGRESS: A novel about Outer Mongolia; short stories.

SIDELIGHTS: Redmon's first novel, *Emily Stone*, is a first-person analysis of the upheavals that affect the title character's friends and family. A cold and solitary woman, Emily views her own emotional austerity as the source of her strength. Her remoteness provides a sharp contrast to the vulnerability of her husband and the exuberance of her friend Sasha. *Ms.* reviewer Leslie Garis said *Emily Stone* "is so complex I can only hope to suggest its depth. . . . The two characters [Emily and Sasha] oppose each other with a kind of moral intensity that D. H. Lawrence would have admired."

In her second novel, *Music and Silence*, Redmon once again brings together contrasting personalities: Beatrice, a quiet, meditative doctor, and Maud, an intense, talented cellist. The two women, neighbors in the same London flat, are drawn together when a religious fanatic intrudes upon their lives. Describing Beatrice and Maud's relationship, a *New York Times Book Review* critic commented, "Their solitudes, guilts and gifts intertwine in a counterpoint of haunting subtlety."

Redmon told *CA:* "I find it difficult to say what motivates me. My religious faith informs much of what I do. Since my early childhood, I have been fascinated by religion. Although I prefer not to sound solemn about it—or pretentious—my chief area of exploration is where God and the soul meet—or fail to.

"My husband encouraged me to write when I was bringing up small children. I have always felt that my writing should be of a piece with my commitment to my family. I feel that the time I take out from my writing often enhances it, as in this way I pick up a great deal of material. As my husband is a successful writer, who also works at home, I feel that my work gives us a great deal in common. I also like to think that the children benefit from my writing.

"I am very interested in travel and, in particular, central Asia. I speak a little Russian (very badly), and this I wanted to learn because of my great love of Russian literature. My husband and I recently made a journey from London to Moscow, Irkutz (in Siberia), Ulan Bator (capital of Mongolia), and Peking.

"My chief pleasure is classical music, particularly Bach. I have a great interest in Southern literature as my family came from Kentucky originally. Although I have lived abroad for many years, I feel very much a part of American culture. I recently gave a lecture in Budapest for the USIS (U.S. Information Service) on Flannery O'Conner, in which I attempted to explain something about Southern religious sensibilities. I particularly admire Faulkner and Henry James among other American writers."

BIOGRAPHICAL/CRITICAL SOURCES: Ms., June, 1975; *Listener,* March 1, 1979; *Kirkus Reviews,* April 15, 1979; *Christian Science Monitor,* June 25, 1979; *New York Times Book Review,* November 4, 1979, November 2, 1980; *Times Literary Supplement,* November 30, 1979.

*   *   *

NIVISON, David Shepherd   1923-

PERSONAL: Born January 17, 1923, in Farmingdale, Maine; son of William and Ruth (Robinson) Nivison; married Cornelia Green, September 11, 1944; children: Louise, Helen Thom, David Gregory, James Nicholas. *Education:* Harvard University, A.B. (summa cum laude), 1946, M.A., 1948, Ph.D., 1953. *Home:* 1169 Russell Ave., Los Altos, Calif. 94022. *Office:* Department of Philosophy, Stanford University, Stanford, Calif. 94305.

CAREER: Stanford University, Stanford, Calif., instructor, 1948-54, lecturer, 1955-58, assistant professor, 1958-59, associate professor, 1959-66, professor of Chinese and philosophy, 1966—, chairman of department of philosophy, 1969-72 and 1975-76, Walter Y. Evans-Wentz Lecturer, 1980. *Military service:* U.S. Army, 1943-46. *Member:* American Philosophical Association (vice-president of Pacific Division, 1978-79; president, 1979-80), American Oriental Society (vice-president of western branch, 1964-65; president, 1971-72), American Association of University Professors (president of northern California conference, 1964-66), Association for Asian Studies, Phi Beta Kappa. *Awards, honors:* Fulbright scholar in Japan, 1954-55; Prix Stanislas-Julien from Institut de France, 1967, for *The Life and Thought of Chang Hsueh-ch'eng, 1738-1801;* American Council of Learned Societies fellowship, 1973; Guggenheim fellowship, 1973-74.

WRITINGS: (Editor with Arthur F. Wright) *Confucianism in Action,* Stanford University Press, 1959; *The Life and Thought of Chang Hsueh-ch'eng, 1738-1801,* Stanford University Press, 1966; (editor with P. J. Ivanhoe and P. K. Urcic) *The Stanford Chinese Concordance Series,* four volumes, Chinese Materials Center, 1979. Contributor to scholarly journals.

WORK IN PROGRESS: A book on the history of the western Chou period, reconstructed from inscriptions on ritual bronze vessels and the resulting reevaluations of old texts.

*   *   *

NORD, Paul   1900(?)-1981

OBITUARY NOTICE: Born c. 1900 in Greece; died April 24, 1981, in Athens, Greece. Author. Nord was a poet who, in 1936, emigrated from Greece to the United States and became an American citizen. He wrote screenplays and worked in the theatre until the U.S. Government gave its support in 1967 to the military dictatorship in Greece. From 1967 to 1974 Nord lived in Sweden, then returned to his homeland after the restoration of Greek democracy in 1974. Obituaries and other sources: *The Reader's Encyclopedia of World Drama,* Crowell, 1969; *Chicago Tribune,* April 25, 1981.

NORGATE, Matthew   1901-

PERSONAL: Born May 10, 1901, in London, England; son of G. LeGuys (a historian and literary journalist) and Edith (a teacher; maiden name, Hickman) Norgate; married Phyllis May Berry, May 1, 1936. *Education:* Graduate of University College School, 1918. *Home:* 7 Lloyd Sq., London WC1X 9BA, England.

CAREER: Free-lance journalist, 1927—, and broadcaster, 1938—. Lecturer; film critic for British Broadcasting Corp., 1939-43, member of news staff, 1939-63; freeman of city of Norwich. *Member:* Critics' Circle (president, 1947-48; general secretary, 1952-64, 1975—), Savage Club (chairman, 1965-68).

WRITINGS: (Translator) Grigory Bessedovski, *Memoirs of a Soviet Diplomat,* Williams & Norgate, 1928; (with Alan Wykes) *Not So Savage* (history of Savage Club), Jupiter Books, 1976. Author of "London After Dark," a column in *Evening Standard,* 1934-39. Contributor to numerous newspapers and magazines, including *Drama Quarterly.* Editor of *Critics' Circular,* 1952-64; drama critic for *Daily Express,* 1937; and film critic for *Evening Standard,* 1938-39.

WORK IN PROGRESS: A series of London theatre programs, with a book expected to result.

SIDELIGHTS: Among the authors Matthew Norgate lists as personal influences are George Bernard Shaw, Richard Winnington, M. Willson Disher, James Agate, and J. M. Barrie. He credits the start of his writing career, in 1927, to one of his teachers, who recommended him to the editor of *Nation and Athenaeum.* "Madness about the theatre and a youthful ambition to be a drama critic," he says, became the chief motivating factors in the years that followed, allowing that "self-satisfaction and money" are what he hopes to achieve through his books.

*   *   *

NOVICK, Julius Lerner   1939-

PERSONAL: Born January 31, 1939, in New York, N.Y.; son of Solomon J. and Ethel (Lerner) Novick. *Education:* Harvard University, B.A., 1960; attended University of Bristol, 1960-61; Yale University, D.F.A., 1965. *Home:* 3 Washington Square Village, New York, N.Y. 10012.

CAREER: New York University, New York, N.Y., 1966-72, began as instructor, became assistant professor of English; State University of New York College at Purchase, associate professor, 1972-80, professor of literature, 1980—. *Member:* American Theatre Association, American Theatre Critics Association (member of executive committee), New York Drama Critics Circle. *Awards, honors:* Fulbright scholarship, 1960-61; Woodrow Wilson fellowship, 1961-62; Ford Foundation grant, 1965-66; special award from New England Theatre Conference, 1969; Guggenheim fellowship, 1977.

WRITINGS: Beyond Broadway: The Quest for Permanent Theatres, Hill & Wang, 1968. Author of a column in *Village Voice.* Contributor to magazines and newspapers, including *Nation.*

WORK IN PROGRESS: A book on George Bernard Shaw; a book on not-for-profit theatre in America; a history of the American theatre since World War II; research on late nineteenth-century English theatre and late twentieth-century American and English theatre.

SIDELIGHTS: Novick wrote: "I'm a theatre critic. What's most important to me is to set the immediate experience of a performance in the widest possible context, without losing the immediacy of the experience. It's the connection between the imaginary world onstage and the real world outside that I want to catch."

*   *   *

NUGENT, Elliott (John)   1899-1980

OBITUARY NOTICE—See index for *CA* sketch: Born September 20, 1899 (some sources list birth year as 1896 or 1900), in Dover, Ohio; died August 9, 1980, in New York, N.Y. Actor, director, producer, and author. Nugent was best known for "The Male Animal," a play that he wrote with James Thurber, starred in on Broadway, and directed as a motion picture. Nugent was also well known for having co-produced "The Seven Year Itch" on Broadway. He was co-author, with his father J. C. Nugent, of several plays, including *Kempy, The Poor Nut,* and *Money to Burn.* He also wrote two books, *Of Cheat and Charmer* and *Events Leading Up to the Comedy.* Obituaries and other sources: *New York Times,* August 11, 1980.

*   *   *

NYE, Wilbur S.   1898-1970

OBITUARY NOTICE—See index for *CA* sketch: Born October 12, 1898, in Canton, Ohio; died June, 1970. Military officer, historian, editor, and author. Nye served in the U.S. Army for thirty-four years before retiring as a colonel in 1954. Prior to retirement he was chief historian of the U.S. Army in Europe. At the time of his death he was managing editor of the *Civil War Times Illustrated* and *American History Illustrated.* Among his books are *Carbine and Lance: The Story of Old Fort Sill, Bad Medicine and Good: Tales of the Kiowas, Here Come the Rebels!,* and *Plains Indian Raiders: The Final Phases of Warfare From the Arkansas to the Red River.* He was also the co-author of *I Fought With Geronimo, The Battle of Gettysburg: A Guided Tour,* and *How to Lose Friends and Alienate People.* (Date of death provided by *Civil War Times Illustrated.*)

*   *   *

NYGARD, Roald   1935-

PERSONAL: Born September 25, 1935, in Skjerstad, Norway; son of Moeller and Magny (Marvoll) Nygard; married Kari Stensvold (a speech therapist), September 6, 1958; children: Bjoern Ivar, Liv Toril. *Education:* Teachers Training College, Oslo, Norway, teacher's certificate, 1958; University of Oslo, Cand.Paed., 1968, Dr.Philos., 1974. *Residence:* Skedsmokorset, Norway. *Office:* Institute for Educational Research, University of Oslo, Blindern, Oslo 3, Norway.

CAREER: Elementary school teacher in Oslo, Norway, 1958, and Bodoe, Norway, 1960-63; junior high school teacher of languages and social studies in Skedsmo, Norway, 1963-65; University of Oslo, Oslo, lecturer, 1968-69, research fellow, 1970-74, associate professor of educational psychology, 1975—.

WRITINGS: Personality, Situation, and Persistence: A Study With Emphasis on Achievement Motivation, Universitetsforlaget, 1977; (contributor) T. Nordin and B. Sjoevall, editors, *Individualism och Samhoerighet* (title means "Individualism and Solidarity"), Doxa, 1977. Contributor to psychology and education journals.

WORK IN PROGRESS: Research on interactional psychology and personality by situation interaction.

SIDELIGHTS: Roald Nygard told *CA:* "The work on the book *Personality, Situation, and Persistence* originated from an interest in motivational questions which developed from my own experience as a teacher. Briefly, the study of motivation can be said to cover problems of selection, intensity, and persistence of behavior. The book reports a study focusing on the latter of these aspects, that of persistence. This aspect was focused upon because persistence is assumed to be both a key factor in the level of performance at the particular tasks with which the individual is confronted, and, through its cumulative effects, a significant determinator of the individual's general course of development.

"The study shows that individuals who, according to the results on a motive test, were achievement-oriented were more attracted to a situation where the outcome was uncertain, and displayed more resistence towards routine, repetitive tasks than failure-oriented individuals. This serves as a good illustration of the general principle that the individual who adapts well under one condition does not necessarily do so under another. Through their cumulative effects, the two different modes of reactions described above are expected to affect the individual's development, the achievement-oriented individual maximizing his possibilities of developing greater problem-solving skills and freedom to use his abilities, and the avoidance-oriented individual minimizing his possibilities of developing skills, implying less utilization of talents and abilities. Since achievement-orientation as well as failure-orientation are considered to a considerable extent as resulting from early learning experiences, the importance of early learning environments that promote a positive motivational orientation is stressed.

"I am still absorbed by studies of how human behavior may be understood as a result of personality characteristics in interaction with situation characteristics. In my opinion, the research area which especially has caught my interest, that of achievement motivation research, has, through its theory and results, a capacity to enrich that branch of psychology which has been termed interactional psychology, and which hitherto has been somewhat humble with respect to theory on *how* personality and situation interact. On the other hand, I am also convinced that ideas from the more general interactional psychology can enrich achievement-motivation thinking. Work is in progress which pulls together strands in both recent interactional psychology and motivation research.

"The interactional consideration of behavior strongly calls to the mind that each of us, through our being part of each other's environment, may help bring about the actualization of the very best of human capacities. Herein lies an enormous challenge, not least for educators. Maybe little more than what is obvious, but the obvious is too often ignored!"

In his review of *Personality, Situation, and Persistence,* Charles P. Smith wrote: "Nygard's purpose is to present a motivational theory of persistence which stresses the interaction of personality and situation. The author cogently develops his viewpoint, beginning with a review of past research which is followed by the presentation of his own theory and the report of an empirical investigation. . . . What is important is that an informed theoretical and empirical study of persistence has been presented which exemplifies the merits of the personality-situation interaction approach, and which provides for the specialist new techniques, interpretations, and empirical results that must be taken seriously."

*BIOGRAPHICAL/CRITICAL SOURCES: Contemporary
Psychology,* Volume 23, number 3, 1978.

O

OAKLEY, Giles (Francis) 1946-

PERSONAL: Born March 15, 1946, in Beaconsfield, England; son of Kenneth Page and Edith Margaret Oakley; married Hilary Margaret Joseph (a television assistant floor manager), May 19, 1979. *Education:* University of Nottingham, B.A. (honors), 1968. *Politics:* "Libertarian left." *Religion:* Church of England. *Home:* 22 Coval Rd., London S.W.14, England. *Office:* British Broadcasting Corp., Villiers House, Haven Green, London W.5, England.

CAREER: British Broadcasting Corp. (BBC), London, England, television researcher in department of further education, 1969-77, television director in department of continuing education, 1976—. Member of Labour Party and National Council for Civil Liberties. *Member:* Amnesty International, Association of Broadcasting Staff, Association of Cinematograph Television and Allied Technicians, Anti-Nazi League, Campaign Against Racism in the Media.

WRITINGS: The Devil's Music: A History of the Blues, BBC Publications, 1976, Taplinger, 1977.

Author (and director) of "The Devil's Music: A History of the Blues," first broadcast by BBC-TV, November 14, 1976; "People's Echo," first broadcast by BBC-TV, April 10, 1977; (and director) "The 607080 Show," first broadcast by BBC-TV, March 5, 1978; (contributor and director) "Whistle Blowers," first broadcast by BBC-TV, July 9, 1979; (and director) "The Devil's Music: The Blues," first broadcast by BBC-TV, July 9, 1979. Contributor to *A Dictionary of World History.* Contributor to magazines, including *Gong* and *Listener.* Editor of *Gongster,* 1967-68; co-editor of *Groundswell,* 1978-80.

WORK IN PROGRESS: The Bromyard Volunteer, "a biography of an obscure British soldier and his even more obscure death in the Boer War"; producing a five-part BBC-TV series on the subject of television, tentatively entitled "Medium and Message."

SIDELIGHTS: Oakley wrote: "Most of my working life has been spent in television. I started as a free-lance researcher in 1969, eventually becoming an assistant producer and director, which has involved scriptwriting, interviewing, and film and video directing. In over ten years, I have contributed to well over a hundred television programs, mainly in series of five or ten parts, using a wide variety of film and video techniques. Some have been documentary film series, some dramatized historical reconstructions, some have mixed sev-

eral different techniques. A large proportion of these series have been accompanied by books to which I have contributed research material. My own book, *The Devil's Music,* originally accompanied a five-part documentary film series that I also worked on.

"The range of subjects I have covered reflects my own interests: English social history in the sixteenth, eighteenth, and nineteenth centuries, history and politics of Ireland, history, politics, and economics of the Middle East, painting and fine art, the role of television in society, investigative journalism, cinema, American history, blues and jazz, English folk music, old age and aging, politics, and community action. Working on these subjects has taken me to Ireland, America, and the Middle East, often going into socially or politically sensitive areas. I have also traveled in over a dozen other countries.

"The motive force behind my work has been a deep commitment to a concept of democratically accountable public service broadcasting, and especially the educational part of it that I consider to be an essential part of any just, harmoniously pluralistic society. This, in turn, is based on the belief that knowledge and understanding is a form of political power, and like all power it should be shared."

AVOCATIONAL INTERESTS: Art.

* * *

OATMAN, Eric F(urber) 1939-

PERSONAL: Born November 6, 1939, in New York, N.Y.; son of Frederic (in advertising) and Margery (in retailing; maiden name, Ward) Oatman; married Jane Langenbacher (a teacher), November 28, 1969; children: Alison. *Education:* Hamilton College, A.B., 1961; attended University of Paris, 1961-63; University of Iowa, M.F.A., 1972. *Home:* 318-B Greenwich St., New York, N.Y. 10013. *Office:* Scholastic, Inc., 50 West 44th St., New York, N.Y. 10036.

CAREER: Teacher at country day school in Lake Forest, Ill., 1963-64; free-lance writer, 1964-70; University of Iowa, Iowa City, instructor in rhetoric and English, 1970-72; Kirkwood Community College, Cedar Rapids, Iowa, instructor in reading, 1972; Scholastic, Inc., New York, N.Y., assistant editor of *Senior Scholastic,* 1973-74, associate editor, 1974-75, associate editor of *Junior Scholastic,* 1975-76, editor of *Scholastic Search,* 1976—. *Member:* Organization of American Historians. *Awards, honors:* Ed-Press Award from Educational Press Association, 1974, for "John Dean—Watergate's Favorite Witness."

WRITINGS: (Editor) *Medical Care in the United States,* H. W. Wilson, 1978; (editor) *Crime and Society,* H. W. Wilson, 1979; (editor) *Prospects for Energy in America,* H. W. Wilson, 1980. Contributor of stories and articles to magazines, including *Retirement Living,* and newspapers. Editor of *Manhattan Review,* 1965-68.

WORK IN PROGRESS: A suspense novel for young people, set "during the turmoil of the Vietnam era"; biographical sketches of American reformers.

SIDELIGHTS: Oatman commented: "My first goal was to write fiction for adults. I drifted into publishing, the 'accidental profession,' as an educational journalist. Now my life, as an editor and writer, is devoted to making young people aware of the complexities of their world. The esthetic kick I get out of this work sometimes surprises me. Best of all, I get paid (not handsomely, but enough) to learn—pretty nice work, and I've got it."

*   *   *

OATTS, Henry Augustus   1898-1980

OBITUARY NOTICE—See index for *CA* sketch: Born January 16, 1898, in Roslin, Midlothian, Scotland; died January 23, 1980. Military officer and author. Oatts served in the Indian Army for thirty-three years before retiring as a colonel in 1948. During his retirement he wrote *Loch Trout,* and *Brown Trout in Lakes: The Complete Fly-Fisher.* (Date of death provided by wife, Audrey M. Oatts.)

*   *   *

OBER, Stuart Alan   1946-

PERSONAL: Born October 2, 1946, in New York, N.Y.; son of Paul (a teacher) and Gertrude (Stollerman) Ober. *Education:* Wesleyan University, Middletown, Conn., B.A., 1968; Sorbonne, University of Paris, License, 1970; graduate study at City University of New York, 1972. *Home:* Mill Hill Rd., Woodstock, N.Y. 12498. *Agent:* Joanne Michaels, Route 212, Woodstock, N.Y. 12498. *Office:* Beekman Publishers, Inc., Route 1, Box 506, Woodstock, N.Y. 12498.

CAREER: Beekman Publishers, Inc., Woodstock, N.Y., president, 1972—. President and director of Resource Control Management Corp., 1980—; president of Ober Enterprises. Tax shelter specialist for Loeb, Rhoades & Co., 1976-77; division director in tax shelter department of Josephthal Co., 1977-78; founder and manager of tax shelter department of Bruns, Nordeman, Rea & Co., 1978-80. Investment and tax shelter consultant, 1972—. *Member:* National Association of Security Dealers, Charter Life Underwriters, New York Stock Exchange, Chicago Board of Trade. *Awards, honors:* Sheldon Merrill Award.

WRITINGS: Everybody's Guide to Tax Shelters, Playboy Press, 1980.

Author of "Blue Skies," a film released by Wesleyan University, 1968. Contributor to *New York Times, Barron's, Executive Wealth Advisory, Financial Review,* and *Tax Shelter Digest.*

WORK IN PROGRESS: A book on tax shelters and investments.

SIDELIGHTS: Ober told *CA:* "I have counseled clients about their best tax shelter opportunities for over ten years, formerly as founder and manager of the department of a leading Wall Street brokerage firm and now with my own

firm, Ober Enterprises. My first loyalties lie with the investors I represent. The most important aspect of a tax shelter is first that it makes economic sense and second that it makes tax shelter sense. Too many times this process gets reversed to the detriment of investors. I thoroughly investigate the programs and the sponsors to place investors in programs that comply both with the spirit and the letter of the tax code.

"Drawing from my years of daily experience dispensing advice on Wall Street to shelter-seeking taxpayers, I have tried to design the first easy-to-understand, authoritative book about tax shelters for all people, whether they are millionaires or of the middle class. *Everybody's Guide to Tax Shelters* provides concise, tax-smart advice one should use before making an investment decision. With the examples, checklists, and work sheets in this guide, an individual can quickly determine exactly what tax shelters would be wise for him or her.

"When one is finally ready to organize investments around the realities of an overtaxed life, there are chapters on the sheltering potential of real estate, equipment leasing, farming, horse racing syndications, timber growing, and even becoming an angel for a Broadway show (if you absolutely cannot resist the glamour of it). I have tried to show how to analyze a tax shelter program and what to be wary of. (As Samuel Goldwyn said, 'A verbal contract isn't worth the paper it's written on.') I hope this book will make the reader aware that successful investing *must* take tax considerations into account."

*   *   *

O'BRIAN, Jack   1921-

PERSONAL: Born August 16, 1921, in Buffalo, N.Y.; son of Charles Joseph and Josephine Loretto (Kelleher) O'Brian; married Yvonne Johnston, January 15, 1947; children: Bridget Mary, Kate Mary. *Politics:* "Independent—no affiliation." *Religion:* Roman Catholic. *Home:* 225 East 73rd St., New York, N.Y. 10021. *Office:* WOR-Radio, 1440 Broadway, New York, N.Y. 10018.

CAREER: Journalist with *Buffalo Times,* Buffalo, N.Y., 1939, *New York World Telegram,* New York City, 1939-40, *Buffalo News,* Buffalo, 1940, and *Buffalo Courier-Express,* Buffalo, 1940-43; Associated Press (AP), New York City, film and music critic and author of two columns, 1943-49; *New York Journal-American,* New York City, author of column, 1949-67; King Features Syndicate, New York City, author of syndicated column, "Voice of Broadway," 1967—. Past host of "Critics Circle," on WOR-Radio. Member of board of directors of Damon Runyan-Walter Winchell Fund for Cancer Research. *Member:* National Catholic Actors Guild (national president, 1978—). *Awards, honors:* Nominated for Pulitzer Prize, 1942, 1961, and 1962; Christophers Award, 1955; awards from United Jewish Appeal, 1955, American Legion, 1958, and National Catholic War Veterans, 1972; Morality in Media Award, 1971 and 1973; Deems Taylor Award from American Society of Composers, Authors, and Publishers, 1974, 1976, and 1979; D.Litt. from Niagara University, 1975, St. John's University, Jamaica, N.Y., 1978, Canisius College, 1979, and St. Joseph's College, Wyndham, Maine.

WRITINGS: The Great Godfrey, 1953. Contributor to popular magazines, including *Harper's Bazaar, Collier's,* and *Cosmopolitan.*

SIDELIGHTS: O'Brian wrote to *CA:* "Originally my motivation was ideological. I wanted to get away from the docks where I was proficient enough at any work not requiring brains to become a foreman, due to my superior intelligence, my exquisite capacity for executive perspiration—and the fact that I was the only white man in a gang of forty-five laborers. The gang had at least a dozen who were better equipped for the job than I. The alternative seemed to be starvation in the depth of the Depression. This happened in Buffalo, which reminds me of the lines from 'Chorus Line.' In the play, one of the chorus boys confessed that he had attempted suicide in Buffalo. The response to his revelation was the cruncher, 'suicide in Buffalo is a redundancy.'"

*   *   *

O'BRIEN, George Dennis   1931-

PERSONAL: Born February 21, 1931, in Chicago, Ill.; son of George Francis and Helen (Fehlandt) O'Brien; married Judith Alyce Johnson, June 21, 1958; children: Elizabeth Belle, Juliana Helen, Victoria Alyce. *Education:* Yale University, A.B., 1952; University of Chicago, Ph.D., 1961. *Home:* 103 University Ave., Lewisburg, Pa. 17837. *Office:* 219 Marts Hall, Bucknell University, Lewisburg, Pa. 17837.

CAREER: University of Chicago, Chicago, Ill., instructor in humanities, 1957-58; Princeton University, Princeton, N.J., instructor, 1958-61, assistant professor of philosophy, 1961-65; Middlebury College, Middlebury, Vt., associate professor, 1965-69, professor of philosophy, 1969-76, chairman of department, 1970-71, dean of men, 1965-67, dean of college, 1967-75, dean of faculty, 1975-76; Bucknell University, Lewisburg, Pa., professor of philosophy and president of university, 1976—. Lecturer at LaSalle College, 1963-65, member of board of trustees, 1968—; member of board of trustees of St. Michael's College, Winooski, Vt., 1975-76. *Member:* American Philosophical Association, Phi Beta Kappa. *Awards, honors:* American Council of Learned Societies fellow in England, 1971-72.

WRITINGS: (Contributor) Donald A. Giannella, editor, *Religion and the Public Order*, Cornell University Press, 1968; *Hegel on Reason and History: A Contemporary Interpretation*, University of Chicago Press, 1975. Contributor to history, philosophy, and theology journals, and *Commonweal*.

*   *   *

OERKENY, Istvan
See ORKENY, Istvan

*   *   *

O'FARRELL, Patrick (James)   1933-

PERSONAL: Born September 17, 1933, in Greymouth, New Zealand; son of Patrick Vincent (a tailor) and Mai Briget (a teacher; maiden name, O'Sullivan) O'Farrell; married Deirdre Genevieve MacShane, December 29, 1956; children: Clare, Gerard, Virginia, Richard, Justin. *Education:* University of Canterbury, B.A., 1954, M.A. (with honors) 1956; Australian National University, Ph.D., 1961. *Religion:* Roman Catholic. *Office:* School of History, University of New South Wales, P.O. Box 1, Kensington, New South Wales 2033, Australia.

CAREER: University of New South Wales, Kensington, Australia, lecturer, 1959-64, senior lecturer, 1964-68, associate professor, 1969-71, professor of history, 1972—. Visiting professor at National University of Ireland, University College, Dublin, 1965-66, and Trinity College, Dublin, 1972-73. *Member:* Australian Academy of the Humanities (fellow).

WRITINGS: Harry Holland, Militant Socialist, Australian National University Press, 1964; *The Catholic Church in*

Australia: A Short History, 1788-1967, Thomas Nelson, 1968; (editor) *Documents in Australian Catholic History*, Volume I: *1788-1884*, Volume II: *1884-1968*, Geoffrey Chapman, 1969; *Ireland's English Question*, Schocken, 1971; *England and Ireland Since 1800*, Oxford University Press,1975; *The Catholic Church and Community: A History*, Thomas Nelson, 1977.

WORK IN PROGRESS: The History of the Irish in Australia, publication by Thomas Nelson expected in 1983.

SIDELIGHTS: O'Farrell told *CA:* "I am not sure that explaining why I write does much good, being complex and readily open to misunderstanding—including intimations of pomposity. *What* I write is available for judgment, and people will judge it in different ways and for their different purposes; to impose on it some detailed declared personal aims (aside from the attempt to pursue scholarly criteria) would seem to me both pretentious and irrelevant. The fact that I write for a mixture of fun and serious purpose highlights this problem. Which is which, and when? I'm happy to leave the reader to decide.

"A lot of history is dull or trivial. I prefer the lively bits in which things that are humanly important can also be amusing or at least entertaining. Thus my interest in religion and the Irish. In my view, this combination allows for the ranges of mood and depth and drama and irony that make up the paradoxes, contradictions, and obscurities that constitute history."

*   *   *

O FIAICH, Tomas   1923-

PERSONAL: Born November 3, 1923, in Anamar, Ireland; son of Patrick and Annie (Caraher) Fee. *Education:* Attended St. Patrick's College, Maynooth, 1940-44, and St. Peter's College, Wexford, 1945-48; National University of Ireland, University College, Dublin, B.A. (with first class honors), 1943, M.A. (with first class honors), 1950; Catholic University of Louvain, Lic.Sc.Hist. (with great distinction), 1952. *Home address:* Ara Coeli, Armagh, Ireland.

CAREER: Ordained Roman Catholic priest of the Archdiocese of Armagh, 1948; curate of Roman Catholic church in Moy, Ireland, 1952-53; St. Patrick's College, Maynooth, Ireland, lecturer, 1953-59, professor of modern history, 1959-74, registrar, 1968-70, vice-president of college, 1970-74, president, 1974-77; named Archbishop of Armagh and Primate of All Ireland, 1977, created Cardinal, 1979. Chairman of Government Commission on Restoration of the Irish Language, 1959-63, and Government Advisory Council on Irish, 1965-68; member of senate of National University of Ireland, 1964-72 and 1974-77; member of Higher Education Authority, 1972-74. Chairman of Irish Episcopal Conference, 1977—. *Member:* Catholic Society of Ireland, Society of Irish-Speaking Priests (president, 1955-67).

WRITINGS: (Editor) *The Patrician Years, 1961-1962*, J. English, 1962; *Columbanus in His Own Words*, Veritas Publications, 1974; *Oliver Plunkett: Ireland's New Saint*, Veritas Publications, 1975; *Irish Cultural Influence in Europe: Sixth to Twelfth Century*, Mercier, 1971.

Other: *Gaelscrinte i gcein*, F.A.S., 1960; (with Padraig De Barra) *Imeacht na nIarlai*, Foilseachain Naisiunta Teoranta, 1972; *Ma Naud*, An Sagart, 1972; *Danta: Art Mac Cumhaigh*, Clochomhar a d'fhoilsigh do Choiste Eigse Oirlalla, 1973. Contributor to history and literary journals. Editor of *Seanchas Ard Mhacha*, 1953-77.

AVOCATIONAL INTERESTS: Reading, travel, sports.

OGILVIE, Elisabeth May 1917-

PERSONAL: Born May 20, 1917, in Boston, Mass.; daughter of Frank Everett (in insurance) and Maude (a teacher; maiden name, Coates) Ogilvie. *Education:* Attended public schools in Massachusetts. *Politics:* Republican. *Religion:* Baptist. *Home addresss:* Gay's Island, Pleasant Point, Me. 04563. *Agent:* A. Watkins, Inc., 77 Park Ave., New York, N.Y. 10016.

CAREER: Writer. *Member:* Authors Guild, Mystery Writers of America, Foster Parents' Plan, Nature Conservancy. *Awards, honors:* New England Press Association fiction award, 1945, for *Storm Tide*.

WRITINGS: High Tide at Noon, Crowell, 1944, reprinted, Avon, 1975; *Storm Tide*, Crowell, 1945, reprinted, Avon, 1975; *The Ebbing Tide*, Crowell, 1947, reprinted, Avon, 1976; *Honeymoon* (based on story by Vicki Baum), Bartholomew House, 1947; *Rowan Head*, Wittlesey House, 1949; *My World Is an Island* (personal account), Whittlesey House, 1950; *The Dawning of the Day*, McGraw, 1954; *Whistle for a Wind: Maine, 1820*, Scribner, 1954; *Blueberry Summer* (juvenile; Junior Literary Guild selection), Whittlesey House, 1956; *No Evil Angel*, McGraw, 1956; *The Fabulous Year* (juvenile), Whittlesey House, 1958; *How Wide the Heart* (juvenile), Whittlesey House, 1959; *The Witch Door*, McGraw, 1959.

Published by McGraw, except as noted: *The Young Islanders* (juvenile), Whittlesey House, 1960; *Becky's Island*, Whittlesey House, 1961; *Call Home the Heart*, 1962; *Turn Around Twice*, Whittlesey House, 1962; *Ceiling of Amber*, 1964; *There May Be Heaven*, 1964; *Masquerade at Sea House*, 1965; *The Seasons Hereafter*, 1966; *The Pigeon Pair*, 1967; *Waters on a Starry Night*, 1968; *Bellwood*, 1969; *Come Aboard and Bring Your Dory*, 1969; *The Face of Innocence*, 1970; *A Theme for Reason*, 1970; *Weep and Know Why*, 1972; *Strawberries in the Sea*, 1973; *Image of a Lover*, 1974; *Where the Lost Aprils Are*, 1975; *The Dreaming Swimmer*, 1976; *An Answer in the Tide*, 1978; *A Dancer in Yellow*, 1979; *A Steady Kind of Love*, Scholastic Book Service, 1979; *The Devil in Tartan*, 1980; *Beautiful Girl*, Scholastic Book Service, 1980; *The Silent Ones*, 1981.

Contributor of short stories to magazines, including *Woman's Day*.

WORK IN PROGRESS: A novel set in Scotland.

SIDELIGHTS: Ogilvie began writing books after taking a college extension course dealing with writing for publication. Her instructor, a literary agent, helped her with her first novel and was her agent for nineteen years afterward. Ogilvie's books are primarily concerned with life on the Maine coast and the islands situated just off of it. *High Tide at Noon*, the author's first novel, tells the story of the Bennetts, a family who dwells on a Maine island. Critics were impressed by Ogilvie's effort. Sterling North of *Book Week* declared that "there can be no doubt that Miss Ogilvie has a brilliant future," while the *New York Times*'s Margaret Wallace noted that she "has a warm and homespun quality which suits her story well." David Tilden wrote in the *Weekly Book Review*, "You feel and delight in the distinctive zestful life of a particular place and a particularly engaging family." He added: "Beyond these, the book has a vigor and substance which would do credit to an author with a long string of titles to her credit." Ogilvie continued the saga of the Bennett family and especially Jo Bennett in two later novels, *Storm Tide* and *Ebbing Tide*.

Ogilvie told *CA:* "I would rather write than do anything else. In fact, I can't imagine a day going by without my having put *something* down, if it's only notes or a paragraph of description. Along with being a compulsive writer who likes to type in the dark at four in the morning so as to have an extra-long morning, I'm an outdoor person, and life on the coast of Maine gives me plenty of opportunities for scraping and painting boats, fishing, beachcombing, digging clams, and just wandering around.

"I hope my writing has matured over the years. The Bennetts and Sorensens of my earliest books are still very much alive to me and I return to them at intervals. Many things have changed with the times on Bennett's Island, and the six young Bennetts of *High Tide at Noon* have gray in their hair and grown-up kids. But they're still islanders in their own kingdom.

"I've branched out into suspense stories and to some settings away from the Maine coast such as Nova Scotia and Scotland, which is where *The Silent Ones* takes place. I know I'm far from being a *great* writer, but I think I'm a good storyteller."

BIOGRAPHICAL/CRITICAL SOURCES: Book Week, April 9, 1944; *Weekly Book Review*, April 16, 1944; *New York Times*, April 16, 1944.

*   *   *

O'HARA, Frederic James 1917-

PERSONAL: Born June 22, 1917, in Watertown, Mass.; son of Walter A. and Helena (Nugent) O'Hara; married Rose M. Tiernan, 1958 (divorced); married Florence Kennedy, 1970; children: (first marriage) Susan K., Frederic James. *Education:* Boston College, A.B., 1940; Columbia University, B.S. in L.S., 1947, M.S., 1950, Ed.D., 1954. *Religion:* Unitarian Universalist. *Office:* Graduate Library School, Long Island University, Greenvale, N.Y. 11548.

CAREER: City College (now of the City University of New York), New York, N.Y., reference assistant at library of School of Business, 1947-49; State University of New York Maritime College, Bronx, assistant librarian in public services, 1949-53; Texas Women's University, Denton, assistant professor of library science, 1955-56; Western Michigan University, Kalamazoo, associate professor of library science, 1956-61; Pratt Institute, Brooklyn, N.Y., associate professor of library science, 1961-63; Long Island University, Greenvale, N.Y., professor of library science, 1963—. *Military service:* U.S. Army Air Forces, 1942-46; became first lieutenant. *Member:* American Library Association (life member; chairman of scholarship committee, 1965-68), Special Libraries Association.

WRITINGS: (Editor) *Over Two Thousand Free Publications: Yours for the Asking*, New American Library, 1968; (editor) *Reader in Government Documents*, NCR Microcard Editions, 1973; *Bibliographical Essays on Government Documents and Diverse Matters*, Palmer Graduate Library School, Long Island University, 1974; *Guidance for the Adult Learner: A Book of Readings and References*, Palmer Graduate Library School, Long Island University, 1977; *The Library in the Community: A Book of Readings and References*, Palmer Graduate Library School, Long Island University, 1978; *A Guide to Publications of the Executive Branch*, Pierian, 1979. Editor of "Selected Government Publications," a monthly feature in *Wilson Library Bulletin*, 1968-73, "Government Serials and Services," a quarterly feature in *RSR: Reference Services Review*, 1974-76, and "Views and Overviews of Government Publications," an irregular feature in

Government Publications Review. Contributor to professional journals.

WORK IN PROGRESS: The second revised edition of *Over Two Thousand Free Publications: Yours for the Asking,* entitled *A Librarian's Guide to Free and Inexpensive Government Publications.*

SIDELIGHTS: O'Hara told *CA:* "I believe a course in government documents should be required in all library schools. Further, I believe all school, college, and public libraries need to develop collections of federal, state, and local government publications where these do not now exist. The library should provide the opportunity for its patrons to become informed and intelligent citizens by learning about their government and how it is run. They need to find out about what the government has to say on a wide variety of topics that might interest them: from stained glass windows, to drugs, to babysitting, to jazz, to Robert Frost and Carl Sandburg. The patron needs to know where to turn to satisfy his informational needs. The library is one such place and the documents collection is one possible source there."

*   *   *

O'KELLY, Elizabeth   1915-

PERSONAL: Born May 19, 1915, in Manchester, England; daughter of Alfred (an agent) and N. M. (Stevens) O'Kelly. *Education:* Royal Manchester College of Music, A.R.M.C.M., 1941; attended Selly Oak Colleges, 1946-47. *Politics:* Liberal. *Religion:* Church of England. *Home:* 3 Cumberland Gardens, London WC1X 9AF, England.

CAREER: Overseas Civil Service, London, England, principal community development officer in the Cameroons, 1950-62, adviser on women's welfare to Government of Sarawak, 1962-65; World Council of Churches, Asian Christian Service, Vietnam, director, 1967-69; Associated Country Women of the World, London, general secretary, 1969-72; consultant in rural development and use of intermediate technology, 1972—. Volunteer worker for charity organizations in England. *Military service:* Women's Royal Naval Service, 1941-46; became second officer. *Member:* Associated Country Women of the World, Intermediate Technology Development Group, Institute of Rural Life, Transnational Network for Appropriate/Alternative Technologies (TRANET). *Awards, honors:* Member of Order of the British Empire, 1959; Order of the Star of Sarawak, 1964.

WRITINGS: Aid and Self Help, Benn, 1973; *Simple Technologies for Rural Women in Bangladesh,* UNICEF, 1977; *Rural Women: Their Integration in Development Programmes,* privately printed, 1978. Contributor to journals.

WORK IN PROGRESS: A book, tentatively titled *Letters of a Woman Colonial Officer in West Africa.*

SIDELIGHTS: Elizabeth O'Kelly wrote: "I went out to Vietnam in 1967 as acting director of an organization set up by the World Council of Churches to aid refugees, and I was there for eighteen months, during the time of the heaviest fighting.

"I organized a country-wide literacy campaign in the Cameroons as part of the rural development program and set up the women's Corn Mill Societies which have since attracted considerable interest in other developing countries.

"When in Sarawak, I founded the Federation of Women's Institutes, now the largest rural women's organization in Malaysia. I became general secretary of the Associated Country Women of the World in 1969. This is the coordinating body for rural women's movements throughout the world.

"I have traveled widely, visiting most countries in Asia and Africa and driving across Africa from east to west. I lived in Ceylon for eighteen months. I was made a Queen Mother of the Nsaw tribe with the title of 'Ya o Ngalim,' the queen who works.

"After living amongst them for so many years I am greatly concerned with the problems of the rural women in the developing countries and the need to raise their standard of living without destroying their existing customs and cultures."

*   *   *

OLDS, Helen Diehl   1895-1981

OBITUARY NOTICE—See index for *CA* sketch: Born April 19, 1895, in Springfield, Ohio; died January 1, 1981. Educator and author. Olds wrote books and magazine articles for children and teenagers. One of her most successful children's books was *Miss Hattie and the Monkey.* She also wrote biographies of Lyndon Johnson and Richard Nixon. Olds taught juvenile writing at Queens College in New York City for fifteen years. Obituaries and other sources: *School Library Journal,* February, 1981.

*   *   *

OLGYAY, Victor   1910-1970

OBITUARY NOTICE—See index for *CA* sketch: Born September 1, 1910, in Budapest, Hungary; died in 1970. Architect, educator, and author. Olgyay wrote *Design With Climate: Bioclimatic Approach to Architectural Regionalism.* He was also co-author of *Application of Climate Data to House Design* and *Solar Control and Shading Devices.* (Date of death provided by wife, Ilona Olgyay.)

*   *   *

OLIVER, Anthony   1923-

PERSONAL: Born July 4, 1923, in Abersychan, Monmouthshire, England; son of George (a car repairman and salesman) and Florence (Le Blond) Oliver. *Education:* Attended Monmouth School, 1932-38. *Agent:* A. P. Watt Ltd., 26/28 Bedford Row, London WC1R 4HL, England. *Office:* c/o Oliver-Sutton Antiques, 34c Kensington Church St., London W8, England.

CAREER: Actor in plays in England and the United States, including "Hay Fever," 1946, "Boys in Brown," 1947, "The Hidden Years," 1947-48, "The Browning Version" and "Harliquinade," both 1948, "French Without Tears," 1949, "Accolade," 1950, "The Gay Dog," 1952, "Red-Headed Blonde," 1953, "The Moon is Blue," 1954, "A Month of Sundays," 1957, "The Mousetrap," 1959 and 1963, "The Lizard on the Rock," 1962, "Too True to be Good," 1965, "After the Rain," 1966-67; actor in motion pictures, including "Once Jolly Swagman," 1948, "The Clouded Yellow," 1950, "Glory at Sea," 1953, "The Runaway Bus," 1954, "Tears for Simon," 1956, "The Fourth Square," 1961. Oliver-Sutton Antiques, London, England, co-proprietor, 1968—; freelance writer, 1968—. *Military service:* Royal Air Force, 1941-46; became leading aircraftman.

WRITINGS: The Victorian Staffordshire Figure, Heinemann, 1971, St. Martin's, 1972; *The Pew Group* (novel), Heinemann, 1980, Doubleday, 1981; *Staffordshire Pottery: The Tribal Art of England,* Heinemann, 1981. Author of several stories for television. Contributor of articles on antiques and collecting to numerous magazines, including *Art & An-*

tiques Weekly, Apollo Magazine, Country Life, and *Collector's Guide.*

WORK IN PROGRESS: A novel set in the world of antiques dealing.

SIDELIGHTS: Oliver told *CA:* "I find it difficult to think of myself as an author. Throughout the quarter-century that I earned my living as an actor, any writing I did was really only a way of indulging myself with the luxury of discussing a hobby in public without being interrupted.

"Ever since I was a child the naive primitive art of the English Staffordshire potters intrigued and fascinated me. The fact that almost nothing was known about it—the British know more about the folk art of ancient Egypt than they do of their own—was a spur to discovering and researching it for myself. There are not many parts of Britain I did not visit as an actor touring with a new play, and whenever I could, I added to my collection of primitive Staffordshire pottery figurines. Many were portraits whose identity or significance was unknown. If the play was a success, I spent my days in musuems and libraries trying to find out what these figurines were. I once missed a matinee performance doing that.

"I rather enjoyed acting and I suppose I must have been adequate or I wouldn't have worked as much as I did. But it's a tough life, and of course sometimes when I should have been diligently looking for work I was in the musuems working for nothing. More and more I hated to leave London to act in New York or Boston, or on tour, so when a publisher suggested that I write a book about Staffordshire pottery, I took a deep breath and quit cold to become an antiques dealer and sell these strange primitive figurines that no one else seemed to know anything about.

"My novel, *The Pew Group,* was written purely for my own pleasure. In my textbooks I longed to talk about auction sales and the collectors, both British and American, who visit my shop. But who wants to be sued? The way out was a novel. By inventing fictional collectors I could indulge myself; but should anyone be tempted to think my characters wildly improbable, they should see some of the real ones."

AVOCATIONAL INTERESTS: Pipe-smoking, cats.

BIOGRAPHICAL/CRITICAL SOURCES: Times Literary Supplement, January 7, 1972; *Antiques,* May, 1973, *Chicago Tribune Book World,* April 19, 1981.

*   *   *

OLIVER, Egbert S(amuel) 1902-

PERSONAL: Born December 27, 1902, in Yankton, Ore.; son of Harry Orville and Iris (Tarbell) Oliver; married Helen Albee, April 20, 1924 (died April 11, 1977); married Marguerite Sappington Reese (a psychiatric social worker), February 18, 1979; children: Lillian E. Oliver McLaughlin, Keats. *Education:* University of Washington, Seattle, B.A., 1927, M.A., 1929, Ph.D., 1939; attended University of Oregon, 1932, and University of California, Berkeley, 1934. *Religion:* Congregational. *Home:* 1220 Northeast 17th Ave., Portland, Ore. 97232.

CAREER: Williamette University, Salem, Ore., instructor, 1929-35, assistant professor, 1935-39, associate professor, 1939-42, professor of English, 1942-50; Oregon State System of Higher Education, general extension division, assistant professor, 1950-51, associate professor of English, 1951-55; Portland State College (now Portland State University), Portland, Ore., professor of English, 1955-73, professor emeritus, 1973—, head of department, 1961-67. Lecturer at Ahmednagar College, 1955; Fulbright lecturer in American literature

at Osmania University, 1956-57, and Kurukshetra University, 1964-65; participated in U.S. Information Service seminars in India. Director of A-T Industries, Inc., 1977—. Coorganizer of Portland Area Literature Conference; public speaker. Moderator of Oregon Conference of Congregational Churches, 1942-43; director of Board of Home Missions of Congregational Churches of America, 1942-54. *Member:* Thoreau Society, Melville Society, Japanese Garden Society, Oregon Historical Society.

WRITINGS: (Editor) *Readings for Ideas and Form,* Doubleday, 1935; (editor) *Giving Form to Ideas,* Odyssey, 1946; (editor) *Melville's Piazza Tales,* Farrar, Straus, 1948; *How Our Bible Grew* (pamphlet), Pilgrim Press (Boston, Mass.), 1952; (contributor) Robert T. Oliver, *Conversation: The Development and Expression of Personality,* Thomas Co., 1961; (contributor) John C. Broderick, editor, *Whitman, the Poet,* Wadsworth, 1962; *Studies in American Literature,* Eurasia Press, 1965; (editor) *American Literature, 1890-1965: An Anthology,* Eurasia Press, 1967; (editor) *The Tarbells of Yankton,* Hapi Press, 1978; (contributor) M. Thomas Inge, editor, *Bartleby the Inscrutable,* Archon, 1979; *The Shaping of a Family: A Memoir,* Hapi Press, 1979; *The Columbia County Tarbells,* Columbia County Historical Society, 1980. Contributor of several dozen articles, poems, and reviews to journals and newspapers, including *Nation, New Outlook, American Review,* and *Philadelphia Forum.*

WORK IN PROGRESS: A history of the Milton Creek basin in Columbia County, Oregon, from 1875-1915, publication by the Columbia County Historical Society expected in 1982.

SIDELIGHTS: Oliver wrote: "My early working experience was largely in the forest industry. I wrote a personal account, 'Sawmilling the Grays Harbor in the Twenties,' for *Pacific Northwest Quarterly.* My autobiography, *The Shaping of a Family,* emphasizes boyhood, education, and professional work as an educator. As a professor and Christian layman I have traveled widely in the United States and most parts of the world.

"The highlights of my professional life are my contributions to Melville scholarship and my introduction of the teaching of American literature in Indian universities. Aside from the Melville work, my most important, most personal work is my autobiography."

In *Quest,* a 1958 publication of Osmania University, Oliver remarked: "Literature is one of the great doors which a person can open for himself upon the world of people. Each of us lives in a geographical area—smaller or larger—and in a piece of time—longer or shorter. The great problem of education is to extend our own intellectual and emotional horizons beyond the little area in which we live. This does not necessarily mean traveling.

"Henry Thoreau made himself supremely at home in the world by becoming well acquainted with Concord . . . and by reading widely in the great literatures of Europe and Asia. The seeing of the life around him, nature and human activity, was very important. The reading of Homer, Plato, the Gita, Confucius, and all the other great treasures of literature was an indispensible part of his growing out of provincialism."

*   *   *

OLSEN, Alfa-Betty 1947-

PERSONAL: Born November 30, 1947; daughter of Alf Karl and Borghild (Seime) Olsen; married David Patch (a bartender), August 31, 1967 (divorced). *Politics:* "Slightly to the left of the Russian Tea Room." *Religion:* "Zen-Lutheran."

Agent: Harold Cohen, Associated Management, 9200 Sunset Blvd., Suite 808, Los Angeles, Calif. 90069.

CAREER: Writer. *Awards, honors:* Award from Action for Children's Television, 1976, and Emmy Award from Academy of Television Arts and Sciences, 1978, both for television program, "Marshall Efron's Illustrated, Simplified, Painless Sunday School."

WRITINGS: (With Mel Brooks) "The Producers" (screenplay), Avco Embassy, 1968; (with Marshall Efron) *Bible Stories You Can't Forget No Matter How Hard You Try*, Dutton, 1976; *Just for Fun* (anthology), Dutton, 1977; (with Efron) *Omnivores: They Said They Would Eat Anything and They Did*, Viking, 1979. Author with Efron of "Great Aspirations," a screenplay, and "Marshall Efron's Illustrated, Simplified, and Painless Sunday School," a television program.

WORK IN PROGRESS: A novel set in New York City in the middle of the nineteenth century; "Hospital City," a musical comedy, with Efron.

AVOCATIONAL INTERESTS: Disco roller skating, fine food, good wine.

*   *   *

OLTON, Roy   1922-

PERSONAL: Born August 4, 1922, in Richmond Hill, N.Y.; son of Bertrand Fitzroy and Miriam (Knies) Olton; married Priscilla June Smith, September 17, 1946; children: Bertrand Lee, Leslie Miriam. *Education:* Ohio Wesleyan University, B.A., 1947; Fletcher School of Law and Diplomacy, M.A., 1948, Ph.D., 1954. *Office:* Department of Political Science, Western Michigan University, Kalamazoo, Mich. 49008.

CAREER: Massachusetts Institute of Technology, Cambridge, instructor, 1949-54, assistant professor of political science, 1954-57; Western Michigan University, Kalamazoo, assistant professor, 1957-61, associate professor, 1961-65, professor of political science, 1965—, chairman of department, 1969-79. *Military service:* U.S. Army, Infantry, 1943-46. *Member:* International Studies Association, American Political Science Association, Midwest Political Science Association, Michigan Political Science Association.

WRITINGS: (With Jack C. Plano) *The International Relations Dictionary*, Holt, 1969, 3rd edition, ABC-CLIO Press, 1981; (with Plano, Milton Greenberg, and Robert Riggs) *Political Science Dictionary*, Dryden, 1973.

*   *   *

OMAN, Charles Chichele   1901-

PERSONAL: Born June 5, 1901, in Oxford, England; son of Sir Charles and Mary (Maclagan) Oman; married Joan Trevelyan, 1929 (died, 1973); children: one son, one daughter. *Education:* Attended New College, Oxford, 1920-23, and British School at Rome, 1923-24. *Home:* 13 Woodborough Rd., Putney, London S.W.15, England.

CAREER: Associated with Victoria and Albert Museum in London, England, 1924-39; worked with Ministry of War Transport, England, 1940-44; Victoria and Albert Museum, keeper of department of metalwork, 1945-66; writer, 1966—. *Member:* Royal Archaeological Institute (honorary vice-president), Society of Antiquaries (fellow), Company of Goldsmiths (liveryman), Hispanic Society of America (honorary member).

WRITINGS: Catalogue of Wallpapers in the Victoria and Albert Museum, South Kensington Museum, 1929; *Catalogue of Rings in the Victoria and Albert Museum*, South Kensington Museum, 1930; *English Domestic Silver*, A. & C. Black, 1934, 7th edition, 1968; (editor of revision and author of preface) Herbert W. Macklin, *Monumental Brasses*, 7th edition (Oman was not associated with earlier editions), Allen & Unwin, 1953; *English Church Plate, 597-1830*, Oxford University Press, 1957; *The English Silver in the Kremlin, 1557-1663*, Methuen, 1961; *A Catalogue of Plate Belonging to the Bank of England*, Bank of England, 1967; (editor) *The Golden Age of Hispanic Silver, 1400-1665*, H.M.S.O., 1968; *Caroline Silver, 1625-1688*, Faber, 1971; *British Rings, 800-1914*, Batsford, 1973, Rowman & Littlefield, 1974; *English Engraved Silver, 1150-1900*, Faber, 1978.

WORK IN PROGRESS: Editing the travel diary of his grandfather's visit to America and Canada in 1853, entitled *Robert in America*.

SIDELIGHTS: Oman told *CA:* "Although I have written much on silver and jewelry, I have never been tempted to become a collector."

*   *   *

OPPENHEIMER, J(ulius) Robert   1904-1967

PERSONAL: Born April 22, 1904, in New York, N.Y.; died of throat cancer, February 18, 1967, in Princeton, N.J.; son of Julius (a textile importer) and Ella (an artist; maiden name, Friedman) Oppenheimer; married Katherine Puening Harrison, November 1, 1940; children: Peter, Katherine (Toni). *Education:* Harvard University, B.A. (summa cum laude), 1925; attended Cambridge University, 1925-26; University of Goettingen, Ph.D., 1927; postdoctoral study at Harvard University and California Institute of Technology, 1927-28, and University of Leiden and Polytechnic Academy, Zurich, 1928-29.

CAREER: University of California, Berkeley, and California Institute of Technology, Pasadena, 1929-47, began as associate professor, became professor of physics; director of U.S. atomic energy laboratory, Los Alamos, N.M., 1942-45; chairman of general advisory committee of United Nations Atomic Energy Commission, 1946-52; Princeton University, Princeton, N.J., director of Institute for Advanced Study, 1947-66. *Member:* American Physical Society (president, 1948), National Academy of Arts and Sciences, American Philosophical Society, American Academy of Arts and Sciences (fellow), Royal Society (fellow), Royal Danish Academy, Brazilian Academy, Japanese Academy (honorary member), Phi Beta Kappa. *Awards, honors:* U.S. Medal for Merit, 1946; French Legion of Honor, 1958; Enrico Fermi Award from Atomic Energy Commission, 1963.

WRITINGS: Science and the Common Understanding, Simon & Schuster, 1954; *The Open Mind*, Simon & Schuster, 1955; *The Flying Trapeze: Three Crises for Physicists*, Harper, 1969; *Lectures on Electrodynamics*, Gordon & Breach, 1970; *Robert Oppenheimer: Letters and Recollections*, edited by Alice Kimball Smith and Charles Weiner, Harvard University Press, 1980.

SIDELIGHTS: Often referred to as the "father of the atomic bomb," J. Robert Oppenheimer was instrumental in changing the nature of international defense and warfare. Though praised by the U.S. Government for his pioneering work in atomic research and honored for creating the weapon that helped hasten the end of World War II, Oppenheimer was later accused of disloyalty and declared a security risk by the country.

Oppenheimer first demonstrated his intellectual prowess as a student at New York's Ethical Culture School. Although adept in all his studies, he had a particular interest in science. At age eleven he was the only non-adult member of the New York Mineralogical Club, and at twelve he wrote and presented his first professional paper to his fellow mineralogists. Continuing his education, Oppenheimer studied physics at Harvard, where he completed his undergraduate courses in three years, graduating summa cum laude.

From Harvard he ventured to Cambridge University in England to study atomic theory with leading physicists of the day such as Joseph Thomson and Ernest Rutherford. His year at Cambridge, however, was a restless one. Assigned by Thomson to make metallic films used in testing the penetrating power of electrons, Oppenheimer found he was unskilled at the task. He became discouraged with his dream of being one of the first Americans to make a mark in the field of atomic research, a field dominated by the Germans, French, Danish, and English. He regained his self-confidence later when he transferred to Germany to begin his doctoral work at Goettingen, the world's principal center for atomic research. He received his doctorate in 1927 after submitting a thesis on quantum theory.

Returning to the United States, Oppenheimer took concurrent teaching positions at the California Institute of Technology (Caltech) and the University of California, Berkeley, where he developed the first school of theoretical physics in the United States. As a teacher, Oppenheimer was both feared and revered by his students. Though they recognized his genius, many of his students could not keep up with Oppenheimer's rapid pace in the classroom. Some students took their complaints to Berkeley's physics department chief, Raymond Birge, who also heard a complaint from Oppenheimer. Oppenheimer lamented that the class was not progressing because he had been moving *too slowly*. In Peter Michelmore's *The Swift Years: The Robert Oppenheimer Story,* Birge is quoted as saying, "It was my first intimation not only of the speed with which Oppenheimer's mind worked, but also of his complete failure at the time to realize how slowly, comparatively speaking, the minds of most other people worked."

Facing similar conflicts at Caltech, Oppenheimer once discovered that among the twenty-six students in his classroom, only one had registered for the class; the others were onlookers. After the first lecture, the sole registered student approached Oppenheimer and told him he could not survive Oppenheimer's pace. Oppenheimer replied: "Nonsense. You'll get good grades whatever happens. You have to; you're my only student." Three years later the student, Carl Anderson, won the Nobel Prize for discovering the positron, a positively-charged particle that constitutes the antiparticle of the electron.

Though physics preoccupied him, Oppenheimer had a keen interest in languages, literature, and art. He cared little for world affairs, however, until the mid-1930's, when he heard of the Fascist movement in Italy and the abuse of Jews in Nazi Germany. Oppenheimer became interested in Communism, reading leftist newspapers, attending Communist rallies, and becoming friends with several party members. He later dismissed the party as ineffective, though he maintained the friendships he had formed for the rest of his life.

In 1943 Oppenheimer became part of a secret team of scientists and engineers who met in Los Alamos, New Mexico, to build the first atomic bomb. As the bomb neared completion, several of the men involved, especially Oppenheimer and Niels Bohr, began to contemplate the moral and political implications of creating a weapon powerful enough to level cities and kill tens of thousands of people. Hoping that the development and fear of such a destructive force would inspire world peace, Oppenheimer went to Washington and suggested that Russia, France, and China be informed of the bomb and help govern the weapon's use. He also expressed the concerted opinion of those at Los Alamos and elsewhere that the bomb should be detonated in order for its power and danger to be fully realized; they felt that only atrocities, not words, could demonstrate the bomb's potential.

On July 16, 1945, "Fat Man," one of two types of fission bombs manufactured at Los Alamos, was tested in the New Mexico desert. Oppenheimer said that as he watched the explosion, two lines from the Hindu *Bhagavad Gita* came to his mind. The first: "The radiance of a thousand suns." The second: "I am become death, The Shatterer of Worlds." The bomb, indeed, proved immensely destructive in actual use, destroying the Japanese cities of Hiroshima and Nagasaki in August, 1945. The world had never seen such a cataclysm, but those responsible for building the bomb were already planning a weapon of far greater power—the hydrogen bomb.

Oppenheimer and many of his colleagues were hesitant about making an H-bomb, arguing that further creation of nuclear weaponry would deter world peace. Their feelings were expressed by Oppenheimer, who upon accepting a presidential scroll for their work at Los Alamos predicted: "If atomic bombs are to be added as new weapons to the arsenals of a warring world, or to the arsenals of nations preparing for war, then the time will come when mankind will curse the name of Los Alamos and of Hiroshima." He later warned: "When we are blind to the evil in ourselves, we dehumanize ourselves, and we deprive ourselves not only of our destiny, but of any possibility of dealing with the evil in others."

In 1946 Oppenheimer wrote the Acheson-Lilienthal Report, calling for worldwide control of nuclear energy, and the Baruch Plan, which sought to control atomic power with supervision from the United Nations. The Soviet Union rejected both proposals. Oppenheimer continued his fight for atomic regulation, however, as chairman of the General Advisory Committee of the United Nation's Atomic Energy Commission (AEC) while concurrently serving as director of Princeton's Institute for Advanced Study.

When the Soviet Union tested its first atomic bomb in 1949, Oppenheimer and the AEC proposed development of smaller nuclear weapons rather than massive air-delivered nuclear bombs. Because of his hesitancy to recommend U.S. participation in a full-scale arms race, some began to question his loyalty to the United States. William Liscum Borden, an Air Force security officer, accused Oppenheimer of having been a Soviet espionage agent for the previous fourteen years, basing his accusation on Oppenheimer's doubts about the H-bomb and his relationships with Communists at Berkeley. Despite the fact that Oppenheimer's friendships with leftists were known of even before he was approved for the Los Alamos team, President Eisenhower, who had promised in his campaign to rid the government of subversives, revoked Oppenheimer's security clearance. Lewis Strauss of the AEC gave Oppenheimer the option of either resigning from the commission or requesting a hearing. Oppenheimer did the latter. The three-member hearing board decided that Oppenheimer's opposition to the building of the hydrogen bomb was not grounds for dismissal from the AEC, but ruled that he was a security risk. His continuous associations with people of questionable political affiliation, contended the board, demonstrated a "serious disregard for the requirement of the security system."

Some observers have felt that Oppenheimer was a victim of McCarthyism and the Cold War. "What the accusations that Oppenheimer was a Communist agent, a subversive opponent of the H-bomb, and a security risk really meant," proposed Christopher Lehmann-Haupt of the *New York Times,* "was that history had caught up with him. Conduct that was acceptable in the urgency of the hot war was not longer permissable in the stringency of the cold war. So in 1954 he was found 'guilty' of what he had been judged innocent when the A.E.C. gave him clearance in 1947." Geoffrey Woolf of *Newsweek* also noted the wave of McCarthyism that swept the United States at the time of Oppenheimer's hearing. Woolf then declared, "The security hearing was an act of consummate ingratitude toward a dedicated national servant, and it deprived the United States of a supremely valuable national resource."

Although his case was never reopened, Oppenheimer was somewhat vindicated in 1963 when he received the Enrico Fermi Award, the highest honor given by the AEC, to recognize scientific achievement and engineering in the development of atomic energy. Despite this acknowledgement, he was never again privy to secret, government information, and he returned to Princeton to resume his work.

Many of Oppenheimer's personal notes, letters, and thoughts are documented in *Robert Oppenheimer: Letters and Recollections.* One of his speeches in the book, "Secrecy and Science," explains his steadfast opinion that scientific achievements should be shared worldwide. It reads in part: "Secrecy strikes at the very root of what science is, and what it is for. It is not possible to be a scientist unless you believe that it is good to learn. It is not good to be a scientist, and it is not possible, unless you think that it is of the highest value to share your knowledge, to share it with anyone who is interested. It is not possible to be a scientist unless you believe that the knowledge of the world, and the power which this gives, is a thing of intrinsic value to humanity, and that you are using it to help in the spread of knowledge, and are willing to take the consequences."

In a *New York Times Book Review* critique of the collection of Oppenheimer's writings, Ronald Clark commented that "not even the Atomic Energy Commission doubted Oppenheimer's loyalty. Its members seem, rather, to have asked themselves whether he was the sort of man to wield the influence he did wield; or, perhaps more accurately, they asked whether he was, to use an English phrase, the sort of man to go tiger-shooting with. They decided 'no,' being helped in their decision by the weapons Oppenheimer too frequently left around for his enemies to pick up. These letters suggest that the answer should have been 'yes.'"

BIOGRAPHICAL/CRITICAL SOURCES—Books: Peter Michelmore, *The Swift Years: The Robert Oppenheimer Story,* Dodd, 1969; I. I. Rabi, Robert Serber, Victor F. Weisskopf, Abraham Pais, and Glenn T. Seaborg, *Oppenheimer,* Scribner, 1969; Philip M. Stern, *The Oppenheimer Case: Security on Trial,* Harper, 1969; Thomas W. Wilson, Jr., *The Great Weapons Heresy,* Houghton, 1970.

Periodicals: *New York Times,* November 3, 1969; *Newsweek,* November 10, 1969; *New Republic,* November 22, 1969; *New York Times Book Review,* January 4, 1970; *Washington Post,* April 17, 1970; *Nation,* April 27, 1970; *New York Review of Books,* July 2, 1970; *Observer,* June 13, 1971.

OBITUARIES: New York Times, February 19, 1967; *London Times,* February 20, 1967; *Time,* February 24, 1967.*

—Sketch by Nancy S. Gearhart

ORFIELD, Olivia 1922-

PERSONAL: Born April 5, 1922, in Charleston, S.C.; daughter of Rex George (an architect) and Olivia (an executive of Young Women's Christian Association; maiden name, Connor) Fuller; married H.M. Orfield (an oil company chemical engineer), August 5, 1950; children: John Erik, Daniel Gregory. *Education:* Rice University, B.A., 1943, graduate study, 1978. *Politics:* "Center veering to left." *Religion:* "Grew up Episcoplian." *Home and office:* prism press, 11706 Longleaf Lane, Bunker Hill Village, Houston, Tex. 77024.

CAREER: Associated Press, New York City, secretary to executive director, 1943-44; *Newsweek,* New York City, assistant to publisher's assistant, 1944-45; worked with Broadway producer Alfred de Linagre, Jr.; Bobbs-Merrill Co., Inc., New York City, manuscript reader for "Young People's Books," 1969-70; writer, 1970—. Editor for prism press. *Member:* Dramatists Guild, Authors League of America, Committee of Small Magazine Editors and Publishers, Authors Unlimited of Houston, Phi Beta Kappa, Pi Delta Pi (vice-president, 1943). *Awards, honors:* Russell Sharp Drama Award from Webster Groves Theatre Guild, 1977, for "Death Trap"; first prize and honorable mention from Current Literature Club of Houston, for two short stories.

WRITINGS: Death Trap (one-act play; first produced in Webster Groves, Mo., at Theatre Guild, August 12, 1977), Performance Publishing, 1979; *Vortex: A Personal Quest Into the Nature of What Is,* prism press, 1981.

Unpublished plays: "Somebody Let Me Be Queen" (three-act), 1977; "'T' Is a Gift" (juvenile), first produced in Houston, Tex., at Memorial Drive Elementary School, December 16, 1975, also produced as "Uncle Sam and Saint Nick."

WORK IN PROGRESS: A book of "psychological observations from the viewpoint of an ex-psychoanalysand"; a fictionalized autobiography; a three-act play; a one-act play.

SIDELIGHTS: Olivia Orfield wrote: "My favorite prescription for how to write comes from J.D. Salinger. In *Seymour: An Introduction* Seymour advises his brother to 'sit very still and ask yourself, as a reader, what piece of writing in all the world Buddy Glass would most want to read if he had his heart's choice. The next step is terrible, but so simple I can hardly believe as I write it. You just sit down shamelessly and write the thing yourself.'

"I didn't adopt this method, at least not consciously, in writing *Vortex.* Possibly I lacked the audacity to admit to myself any such intent. Yet if in fact I'd deliberately followed Salinger instruction, *Vortex* is the book I'd have produced. I don't mean to imply it perfectly expresses what I want to say, but I've revised it to a point at which I suspect I'd sacrifice freshness if I tried for further refinement of articulation.

"It actually began as writing I intended to include within a novel, the autobiography I'm working on now. Developing a larger work I became engrossed with what I originally planned as one small piece of it—a subjective journey from one point to another. Almost sheepishly I confess I'm glad I have *Vortex* to read. I believe its statements. It reminds me of those experiences it speaks of, and so helps to evoke them for me again. None I've had seem, to me more critical in almost every way.

"Any book I would want to wallow in most would neccessarily concern philosophy. I considered graduate work in the field, but vetoed the possibility on the hunch that I'd use further academic study to over-intellectualize, to remove my subject from my own experience, rather than to explore on my own. I always considered philosophizing a personal responsibility and privilege of mine—a project very incomplete, however, until I'd finished *Vortex*. And now? As a result of happenings which motivated my writing it, I'm no longer interested in primarily logical construct. *Vortex* is not mainly a reasoning book.

"When I was six years old I finished my first poem. Ever since then I've continued to write: to give form to my formlessness and so to learn about myself. Much of my past output I haven't tried to sell because it didn't satisfy me. Also, I underwent psychoanalysis, driven there by my laboring over a play which turned out to be lousy, and my inability to become pregnant, fortunately not permanent. In combination these difficulties caused me to fear I couldn't accomplish anything. While on the couch, and again when my children were young, I hardly wrote at all. I had faith that my time would come later. Now it's my opinion that before I began *Vortex* I wasn't the person who could have produced it."

BIOGRAPHICAL/CRITICAL SOURCES: Houston Chronicle, July 31, 1977, November 29, 1977; *Suburbia Reporter,* Spring Branch Edition, March 28, 1979.

*   *   *

ORGANSKI, A(bramo) F(imo) K(enneth)   1923-

PERSONAL: Born May 17, 1923, in Rome, Italy; came to the United States in 1939, naturalized citizen, 1944; son of Menasce and Anna (Feinstein) Organski; married Katherine Davis Fox, May 29, 1947; children: Eric Fox, Elizabeth Anna. *Education:* New York University, B.A., 1947, M.A., 1948, Ph.D., 1951. *Home:* 460 Hillspur Rd., Ann Arbor, Mich. 48105. *Office:* Center for Political Studies, Institute for Social Research, University of Michigan, Ann Arbor, Mich. 48106.

CAREER: Brooklyn College of the City University of New York, Brooklyn, N.Y., assistant professor, 1952-57, associate professor, 1958-60, professor of political science, 1960-64; University of Michigan, Ann Arbor, professor of political science, 1965—, program director at Center for Political Studies, 1970—. Visiting associate professor at Columbia University, 1961; visiting professor at Dartmouth College, summers, 1963-64, Fletcher School of Law and Diplomacy, 1963-69, and Harvard University, 1963-69; lecturer in the United States and abroad, 1960—; consultant to government institutions. *Military service:* U.S. Army, 1943-45. *Member:* International Political Science Association, American Political Science Association (member of council, 1972). *Awards, honors:* Cavaliere della Republica Italiana.

WRITINGS: World Politics, Knopf, 1958, 2nd edition, 1968; (with wife, Katherine Fox Organski) *Population and World Power,* Knopf, 1961; *The Stages of Political Development: Politics and Industrialization,* Knopf, 1965; (with Jacek Kugler) *The War Ledger,* University of Chicago Press, 1980. Contributor to political science journals. Member of board of editors of *Journal of Conflict Resolution, Comparative Political Studies,* and *Comparative Politics;* member of international editorial board of *Affari Sociali Internazionali.*

WORK IN PROGRESS: Birth, Death, and Taxes: Demographic and Political Transitions, with Kugler, Youssef Cohen, and J. Timothy Johnson; *National Development: An Inquiry Into the Code of Growth; Capacity to Govern,* with Kugler.

ORKENY, Istvan   1912-1979

PERSONAL: Born April 5, 1912, in Budapest, Hungary; died in June, 1979, in Budapest; son of Hugo and Margit (Peto) Orkeny; married Zsuzsa Radnoti, August 15, 1965; children: Angela, Antal. *Education:* Received degree in chemical engineering from Technical University of Budapest.

CAREER: Writer. *Military service:* Served with Hungarian forces during World War II; spent one year in a Soviet prison camp. *Awards, honors:* Jozsef Attila Award, 1952 and 1968; Kossuth Prize, 1973.

WRITINGS: Egyperces novellak (title means "One Minute Stories"), Magveto, 1977. Also author of novels *Hazastarsak* (title means "Consorts"), 1951, and *The Playing Cat,* 1967.

Plays: "Voronyezs," 1948; "Soetet galamb" (title means "The Dark Pigeon"), 1958; "Macskajatek" (title means "Catsplay"), 1969, produced in Washington, D.C.; "Totek" (title means "The Tot Family"), 1967, first produced in Budapest, Hungary, produced in Washington, D.C., at Arena Stage; "Pisti in the Holocaust," 1970; "Rekviem egy hadseregert" (title means "Requiem for an Army"), 1973; "Verrokonok" (title means "Kinsfolk"), 1974; *Kulcskeresot,* Magveto, 1977; "Steve in the Holocaust" (autobiography), produced in 1978. Also author of "Looking for the Key" and "The Silence of the Dead."

Author of short stories.

BIOGRAPHICAL/CRITICAL SOURCES: New York Times, July 29, 1979.*

*   *   *

ORNSTEIN, Jack H(ervey)   1938-

PERSONAL: Born March 1, 1938, in Flin Flon, Manitoba, Canada; son of Irving and Gertrude (Morganstern) Ornstein; married Toby Morantz (a researcher), May 28, 1964; children: Gillian Faye. *Education:* University of British Columbia, B.A., 1961, M.A., 1964; University of California, San Diego, La Jolla, Ph.D., 1970. *Home:* 1100 Greene Ave., Montreal, Quebec, Canada H3Z 1Z9. *Office:* Department of Philosophy, Concordia University, 1455 de Maisonneuve Blvd. W., Montreal, Quebec, Canada.

CAREER: Memorial University of Newfoundland, St. John's, lecturer in philosophy, 1969-70; University of Windsor, Windsor, Ontario, assistant professor of philosophy, 1970-72; Concordia University, Montreal, Quebec, associate professor of philosophy, 1972—. *Member:* Mind Association, Aristotelian Society, Canadian Philosophical Association, Canadian Professors for Peace in the Middle East (chapter chairman, 1978-79).

WRITINGS: The Mind and the Brain, Nijhoff, 1972.

WORK IN PROGRESS: Research on philosophy of mind and action, on theory of knowledge, and on ethics of belief.

SIDELIGHTS: Ornstein wrote: "I think that my 1972 book went a long way toward solving the ancient mind-body problem. It would be nice to hear that others agree with me . . . and why they do (or do not). In my book, I argued that the only promising approach to the mind-body problem is a multi-aspect approach. Irving Thalberg's recent presentation of his 'component' approach is basically the same thing. Both reductive materialism and Cartesian dualism are mistaken. Consciousness is neither a ghostly separable process nor reducible to brain activity. It is an emergent power which enables humans to become free, to become, for example, self-determined. Skinnerian determinism is mistaken as is every type of psychological determinism. If everything is reducible to its ultimate material constituents and/or is utterly determined, then determinists and their theories must be so reducible and/or determined . . . so why should we take them seriously? This reductio ad absurdum shows that these theories are self-refuting and cannot be correct. Now if we could only understand in some detail how it is that consciousness emerges from certain brain activity!''

*   *   *

OWEN, Edmund
  See TELLER, Neville

*   *   *

OZY
  See ROSSET, B(enjamin) C(harles)

P

PAAUW, Douglas Seymour 1921-

PERSONAL: Born December 13, 1921, in Hancock, Minn.; son of Jacob D. and Elsie (Algra) Paauw; married Helen K. Horan, September 10, 1948; children: Scott H., Douglas S. Education: Calvin College, B.A., 1943; attended University of Washington, Seattle, 1946-47; Harvard University, M.A., 1949, Ph.D., 1950. Home: 4430 Marquis Lane, Birmingham, Mich. 48010. Office: Department of Economics, Wayne State University, Detroit, Mich. 48202.

CAREER: Harvard University, Cambridge, Mass., instructor in economics, 1950-52; Massachusetts Institute of Technology, Cambridge, research associate, 1953-54; Harvard University, lecturer in economics, 1954-56; Lake Forest College, Lake Forest, Ill., professor of economics, 1956-59; Universitas H.K.B.P. Nomensen, Pematang Siantar, Indonesia, visiting professor of economics, 1959-61; Yale University, New Haven, Conn., associate professor of economics, 1961-63; National Planning Association, Washington, D.C., director of research and of Center for Development Planning, 1963-70; Wayne State University, Detroit, Mich., professor of economics, 1970—, chairman of department, 1970-75. Member of executive committee of South East Asia Development Advisory Group, 1968—; member of Inter-University Southeast Asia Committee, 1969-71; consultant to Agency for International Development and International Labour Organization. Military service: U.S. Army Air Forces, 1943-46. Member: American Economic Association, Association for Asian Studies. Awards, honors: Harvard-Yenching fellow at Harvard University, 1951-52.

WRITINGS: Financing Economic Development: The Indonesian Case, Free Press, 1960; (editor and contributor) Prospects for East Sumatran Plantation Industries: A Symposium, Cellar Book Shop, 1962; Development Planning in Asia, Center for Development Planning, National Planning Association, 1965; (with Forrest E. Cookson) Planning Capital Inflows for Southeast Asia, Center for Development Planning, National Planning Association, 1966; Development Strategies in Open Dualistic Economies, Center for Development Planning, National Planning Association, 1970; (with John C. H. Fei) The Transition in Open Dualistic Economies: Theory and Southeast Asian Experience, Yale University Press, 1973. Contributor to economic journals.

PADILLA, Victoria 1907-

PERSONAL: Born January 4, 1907, in San Francisco, Calif.; daughter of Julio L. (a photographer) and Agatha (an artist; maiden name, Nelson) Padilla. Education: University of California, Los Angeles, A.B., 1928; University of Southern California, M.A., 1937. Politics: Independent. Religion: Roman Catholic. Home: 647 South Saltree Ave., Los Angeles, Calif. 90049.

CAREER: Worked as secretary, 1929-35; teacher at high schools in Los Angeles, Calif., 1938-45; Los Angeles City College, Los Angeles, Calif., professor of English, 1946-69. Lecturer. Member: American Orchid Society, Southern California Horticultural Society, Rhododendron Society, Bromeliad Society, Friends of the Library. Awards, honors: Awards from Bromeliad Guild of Los Angeles, 1965, for achievement in horticulture, from Southern California Horticultural Society, 1970, for achievement in horticulture, and from Bromeliad Society for work with bromeliads and for editing Bromeliad Society Journal.

WRITINGS: Southern California Gardens, University of California Press, 1961; Bromeliads in Color, Bromeliad Society, 1966; Bromeliads, Crown, 1973; A Bromeliad Glossary, Bromeliad Society, 1978; The Colorful Bromeliads, Bromeliad Society, 1981. Contributor to magazines. Editor of Bromeliad Society Journal, 1960—.

SIDELIGHTS: Victoria Padilla has led horticultural expeditions to the Amazon, Central America, the West Indies, and Europe. She told CA: "I was probably the first amateur to rent a plane and take a group to study the bromeliads of the upper Amazon region of Peru. As one of the founders of the Bromeliad Society in 1950, I have always believed that this plant family has been sorely neglected. The various species of bromeliads make beautiful indoor plants and are easy to grow."

AVOCATIONAL INTERESTS: Gardening, collecting plants, library work.

*　　*　　*

PADOVER, Saul K(ussiel) 1905-1981

OBITUARY NOTICE—See index for CA sketch: Born April 13, 1905, in Vienna, Austria; died after a strike, February 22, 1981, in New York, N.Y. Political scientist and author. Padover was a distinguished political scientist and an authority on Thomas Jefferson and Karl Marx. He wrote biographies of both men and edited collections of their writings. He finished work on *A Pictorial Biography of Karl Marx* shortly before his death. Padover also wrote or edited books on other major figures in American and European political history, including Alexander Hamilton, James Madison, Louis XVI of France, and Joseph II of Austria. Other of his works deal with the nature of American democracy and problems of foreign policy. He served in the Office of Strategic Services during World War II and was decorated for his intelligence-gathering work. For more than thirty years he taught at the New School for Social Research in New York City. Padover's books include *Jefferson, Experiment in Germany: The Story of an American Intelligence Officer, U.S. Foreign Policy and Public Opinion,* and *Karl Marx: An Intimate Biography.* Obituaries and other sources: *New York Times,* February 24, 1981; *Washington Post,* February 26, 1981; *Publishers Weekly,* March 13, 1981; *Time,* March 16, 1981; *AB Bookman's Weekly,* May 25, 1981.

*   *   *

PAFFARD, Michael Kenneth   1928-

PERSONAL: Born May 21, 1928, in Loose, England; son of Hugo Kenneth (a farmer) and Katharine (Clark) Paffard; married Helen Taylor (a teacher), August 8, 1953; children: Mark Neil, Frances Katherine, Lewis Emil Charles. *Education:* University of Bristol, B.A., 1949, M.A., 1964. *Home:* Church Bank, Keele, Staffordshire ST5 5AT, England. *Office:* Department of Education, University of Keele, Keele, Staffordshire ST5 5BG, England.

CAREER: Teacher at grammar schools in Wiltshire and Gloucestershire, England, 1949-53; University of Keele, Keele, England, assistant lecturer, 1953-56, lecturer, 1956-65, senior lecturer in education and English, 1965—.

WRITINGS: Inglorious Wordsworths, Hodder & Stoughton, 1973; *The Unattended Moment,* S.C.M. Press, 1976; *Thinking About English,* Ward, Lock, 1978. Contributor to education journals and literary magazines.

WORK IN PROGRESS: A study of twentieth-century literary autobiography.

SIDELIGHTS: Paffard told *CA:* "Though professionally concerned with training teachers of English, my interests are as much psychological as literary or linguistic. In particular I am interested in the biographical circumstances that initiate and encourage creativity in the arts, in 'peak experiences,' and the religious and aesthetic 'overbeliefs' that get constructed around them."

*   *   *

PAGE, Robin   1943-

PERSONAL: Born May 3, 1943, in Barton, Cambridgeshire, England; son of Mervyn Charles Odams (a farmer) and Enid Mary (a teacher; maiden name, Crow) Page. *Education:* Attended boys' high school in Cambridge, England. *Home:* Bird's Farm, Barton, Cambridgeshire, England. *Agent:* John Farquharson Ltd., Bell House, Bell Yard, London WC2A 2JU, England.

CAREER: Associated with Department of Health and Social Security, Cambridge, England, 1964-69; Birds Farm Publications, Barton, England, partner, 1976—. Farmer. Member of South Cambridgeshire District Council.

WRITINGS: (Contributor) Rhodes Boyson, editor, *Down With the Poor,* Churchill Press Ltd., 1971; *The Benefits Racket,* Tom Stacey, 1972; *Down Among the Dossers,* Davis-

Poynter, 1973; *The Decline of an English Village,* Davis-Poynter, 1974; *The Hunter and the Hunted,* Davis-Poynter, 1977; *Weather Forecasting: The Country Way,* Davis-Poynter, 1977, Summit Books, 1978; *Cures and Remedies the Country Way,* Summit Books, 1978; *Weeds the Country Way,* Davis-Poynter, 1979; *Animal Cures the Country Way,* Davis-Poynter, 1979; *The Journal of a Country Parish,* Davis-Poynter, 1980. Also author of *Journeys Into Britain,* 1982. Contributor to magazines and newspapers.

WORK IN PROGRESS: Travels Into Africa, publication by Hodder & Stoughton expected in 1983 or 1984.

SIDELIGHTS: "My writing deals with countryside and conservation matters," Page told *CA,* "mainly because man is destroying his natural surroundings so quickly that I want to see and record details of what is left before it is too late. There is wildlife to appreciate, beautiful places to experience, and people to meet who have not yet been conditioned by suburban twentieth-century living. Consequently, I try to record the feeling of the countryside and the spirit of the people. This applies as well to Africa, which has become one of my obsessions: I have visited Namibia, Kenya, Zaire, Trinidad, and South Africa. Africa is a place where it is still possible to find true wilderness, but which is again threatened by development and the pressures for change."

*   *   *

PALLIDINI, Jodi
See ROBBIN, (Jodi) Luna

*   *   *

PALLISTER, John C(lare)   1891-1980

*OBITUARY NOTICE—*See index for *CA* sketch: Born June 12, 1891, in Cleveland, Ohio; died March 6, 1980; buried in family grounds in Ohio. Entomologist, educator, and author. Pallister took part in several entomological research expeditions, including explorations in the Amazon Valley, Mexico, Peru, and British Honduras. He wrote *The Insect World* and *In the Steps of the Great American Entomologist, Frank Eugene Lutz.* He was also the co-author of *Insects of Pacific World* and *The Animal Kingdom.* (Date of death provided by wife, Domenica Pallister.)

*   *   *

PALMER, (John) Carey (Bowden)   1943-

PERSONAL: Born January 26, 1943, in Torquay, England. *Education:* St. Catherine's College, Oxford, B.A., 1964, M.A., 1968. *Office:* Richmond Tutorial College, 37 Kew Rd., Richmond, Surrey, England.

CAREER: Tutor at tutorial colleges in London, England, 1966-74; Richmond Tutorial College, Richmond, England, founder and principal, 1975—. *Member:* Oxford Union Society (life member).

WRITINGS: Decline and Fail (novel), Wingate, 1970; *Crammers* (nonfiction), Duckworth, 1977. Contributor to education journals and newspapers, including *Observer.*

SIDELIGHTS: Palmer commented: "I worked in three tutorial colleges (crammers), during which time I wrote *Crammers* and a novel about life in private schools. I am best known as founder and principal of Richmond Tutorial College, an experimental alternative to state schooling. It prepares boys and girls in small groups for their school-leaving certificates, and the college has aroused broad interest as an experiment in education. I write particularly about my strong belief in the need for a more broadly based private educational system in England.''

* * *

PALMER, Madelyn 1910-
(Geoffrey Peters)

PERSONAL—Education: Attended collegiate girls' school in Adelaide, Australia. *Home:* 14 Park Lane, Fareham, Hampshire, England. *Agent:* David Higham Associates Ltd., 5-8 Lower John St., Golden Sq., London W1R 3PE, England.

CAREER: Employed as office worker in Australia and London, England; film actress in Australia; Office of Population Censuses and Surveys, Titchfield, England, clerical officer; currently writer. *Member:* Crime Writers Association, National Trust.

WRITINGS—Crime novels: Dead Fellah, J. Cape, 1961; *Fareham Creek,* Cedric Chivers, 1974; *The Scottish Barbarian,* Historical Romance Series, 1976, reprinted as *The Monk of Falconsway,* 1977, and as *Quite by Chance,* Woman's Weekly Library, 1978.

Crime novels under pseudonym Geoffrey Peters: *The Claw of a Cat,* Ward, Lock, 1964; *The Eye of a Serpent,* Ward, Lock, 1964; *The Whirl of a Bird,* Ward, Lock, 1965; *The Twist of a Stick,* Ward, Lock, 1966; *The Flick of a Fin,* Ward, Lock, 1967; *The Mark of a Buoy,* Ward, Lock, 1967; *The Chill of a Corpse,* Ward, Lock, 1968.

Author of documentary scripts. Contributor of stories and articles to periodicals.

WORK IN PROGRESS: A crime novel.

SIDELIGHTS: Madelyn Palmer commented: ''I have traveled widely in Australia, Europe, and the British Isles. I preferred freedom to marriage and don't regret it. I write just for the fun of it; I certainly don't make a fortune!'' *Avocational interests:* Reading, travel, painting.

* * *

PALMER, Peter John 1932-

PERSONAL: Born September 20, 1932, in Melbourne, Australia; son of Roy Tasman (a clerk) and Marjorie (a tailor; maiden name, Evans) Palmer; married Elizabeth Fischer, December 22, 1955 (divorced March, 1974); children: David, Ellen. *Education:* University of Melbourne, B.A., 1953, B.Ed., 1967. *Religion:* None. *Home:* 34 Ardgower Cres., Lower Templestowe, Victoria 3107, Australia. *Office:* Preston East High School, Tyler St., East Preston, Victoria 3072, Australia.

CAREER: High school teacher of history and geography in Ouyen, Australia, 1954-57, in Alexandra, Australia, 1958-60, in Luton, England, 1961, in Alexandra, 1962-63, in Burwood, Australia, 1964-68, in Ashwood, Australia, 1969, and in Waverley, Australia, 1970-76; Koonung High School, Box Hill North, Australia, deputy principal, 1977-80; Preston East High School, Victoria, Australia, principal, 1981—. Part-time tutor at University of Melbourne, 1965-67; part-time lecturer at Monash University, 1968.

WRITINGS—Textbooks; self-illustrated; published by F. W. Cheshire: The Past and Us, 1957; *The Twentieth Century,* 1964.

Editor, contributor, and illustrator; all published by Macmillan: *Confrontations,* 1971; *Interaction,* 1973; *Expansion,* 1974; *Survival,* 1975; *Three Worlds,* 1977; *Earth and Man,* 1980; *Man on the Land,* 1981.

WORK IN PROGRESS: Editing, illustrating, and contributing to two geography textbooks for secondary school children, publication by Macmillan expected in 1982 and 1983.

SIDELIGHTS: Palmer commented: ''In Australia, at least, I believe that during the past decade the methodologists have led school geography into a dreary wasteland of jargon and statistics; whereas the subject should be one of interest, enjoyment, and enlightenment. I have tried to produce books which will help ordinary kids, who will never be teachers or professional geographers, gain an understanding of the world around them and an awareness of the physical, economic, and political agents which have shaped and continue to change that world.''

AVOCATIONAL INTERESTS: Painting, war games.

* * *

PALUSZNY, Maria Janina 1939-

PERSONAL: Born April 16, 1939, in Warsaw, Poland; daughter of Joseph and Janina (Gallot) Domaszewski; married Antoni Paluszny, July 16, 1960; children: Mark, Tadeus and Kristina (twins). *Education:* Wayne State University, A.B., 1960; University of Michigan, M.D., 1962. *Home:* 939 Forest Rd., Ann Arbor, Mich. 48105. *Office:* 130 South First St., Ann Arbor, Mich. 48108.

CAREER: St. Joseph's Mercy Hospital, Ann Arbor, Mich., intern, 1962-63; Neuropsychiatric Institute, Ann Arbor, resident, 1963-65; Children's Psychiatric Hospital, Ann Arbor, resident, 1965-67, instructor, 1967-68; University of Michigan, Ann Arbor, instructor, 1968-71, assistant professor, 1971-75, associate professor, 1975-79, professor of psychiatry, 1979—, program director for child psychiatry at Institute for the Study of Mental Retardation and Related Disabilities, 1973-75, chief of clinical services, 1975—. Diplomate of American Board of Psychiatry and Neurology; assistant director of outpatient service at Children's Psychiatric Hospital, 1968-73; consultant to Dearborn Downriver Child Guidance Clinic and Wyandotte Vocational Rehabilitation Center. *Member:* American Academy of Child Psychiatry (fellow), American Psychiatric Association, Michigan Medical Society, Washtenaw County Medical Society.

WRITINGS: Autism: A Practical Guide for Parents and Professionals, Syracuse University Press, 1979. Contributor to medical journals.

WORK IN PROGRESS: Writing about twins.

* * *

PAO, Ping-Nie 1922-

PERSONAL: Born March 31, 1922, in Shanghai, China; came to the United States in 1948, naturalized citizen, 1956; son of Zung-Sheng (in business) and Yu-Chuang (Sih) Pao; married Pearl Shen (a psychiatrist); children: Maryland, William. *Education:* National Medical College of Shanghai, M.D., 1947. *Home:* 8209 Fenway Rd., Bethesda, Md. 20034. *Office:* Chestnut Lodge, 500 West Montgomery Ave., Rockville, Md. 20850.

CAREER: First Hospital of the Red Cross Society of China, Shanghai, intern, 1946-47, resident, 1947-48; Thomas D. Dee Hospital, Ogden, Utah, intern, 1948; Seton Institute, Baltimore, Md., resident, 1949-53; Sheppard & Enoch Pratt Hospital, Towson, Md., resident, 1953-54, staff psychiatrist, 1954-57; University of Maryland, Psychiatric Institute, Baltimore, psychiatrist at Children's Psychiatric Clinic, 1954-55; Johns Hopkins University, Baltimore, psychiatrist at Psychiatric Liaison Service, 1955-57; Chestnut Lodge, Rockville, Md., staff psychiatrist, 1957-67, director of psychotherapy, 1967—. Diplomate of American Board of Psychiatry; member of faculty at Washington Psychoanalytic Institute. *Member:* International Psychoanalytic Association, American Psychiatric Association (fellow), American Psychoanalytic Association, Washington Psychoanalytic Society, Washington Psychiatry Society, District of Columbia Medical Society.

WRITINGS: Schizophrenic Disorder: Theory and Treatment From a Psychodynamic Point of View, International Universities Press, 1979.

Contributor: C. W. Socarides, editor, *The World of Emotions,* International Universities Press, 1977; Colette Chiland and Paul Bequart, editors, *Long-Term Treatment of Psychotic States,* Human Sciences, 1977; Joseph M. Natterson, editor, *The Dream in Clinical Practice,* Jason Aronson, 1980; George Pollock and Stanley Greenspan, editors, *Psychoanalysis and Human Development,* Government Press, 1981. Contributor of about thirty articles and reviews to medical journals.

WORK IN PROGRESS: Research on psychotherapy of schizophrenia.

SIDELIGHTS: Ping-Nie Pao told *CA:* "As a member of the senior staff of a mental hospital, I supervise the work of the younger staff. After being stimulated by their way of thinking about their patients and after being asked the same type of questions by them, I concluded that it might make sense to put down in writing what I have experienced with hospitalized psychiatric patients in long-term, intensive psychotherapy. This conclusion brought forth the book *Schizophrenic Disorder.*

"What I had intended to write, in terms of my own experience, was how to help these patients become interested in living again. However, as soon as I launched the project, I realized that I must first delineate the rationale for my approach—to put it another way, the theoretical orientation for my approach. This realization steered the book into a direction which was not originally intended.

"To put one's thoughts into words is not as simple as one might imagine. Writing an essay is perhaps far simpler than writing about one's own experience. One's own experience is personal. The concern that I might not express myself adequately led me often to think of giving up the whole project. Fortunately, I was spurred on and encouraged not to give up by my family and friends."

*   *   *

PARHAM, William   1914-

PERSONAL: Born April 16, 1914, in Comanche, Tex.; son of Stith Rowland and Anne Minerva (Presley) Parham; married Lois Ruth Pierce (a broker), April 3, 1937; children: Michael Anthony. *Education:* Attended University of Hawaii, 1951-52. *Politics:* Republican. *Religion:* Protestant. *Home and office:* 3824 South 12th St., Arlington, Va. 22204.

CAREER: U.S. Marine Corps, career officer, 1932-62; served in North China, 1945-46, and in Korea, 1953-54, both with First Marine Division; served at Marine Corps Schools, Quantico, Va., and at U.S. Marine Corps Headquarters, 1955-62, retiring as lieutenant colonel. WADAPA Enterprises, Inc. (manufacturing and general contracting firm), Arkansas, president and chief executive officer, 1962-65; Planning Research Corp., McLean, Va., vice-president, staff criminologist, and instructor, 1965-73; writer and free-lance criminologist, 1973—. Co-chairman of Republican Central

Committee, Hot Springs, Ark., 1963-64. *Member:* Masons, Shriners. *Awards, honors:* Commendation Medal and Korean Chung-Mu Medal with Silver Star, both for service in Korea.

WRITINGS: The Book of Melvin (humorous verse), Veritas Publications, 1980; *Requiems and Other Celebrations* (verse), Veritas Publications, 1981; *A Habitation of Devils* (nonfiction), Veritas Publications, 1981. Contributor to magazines and newspapers.

SIDELIGHTS: Parham received his decorations from the Republic of Korea for his services during the repatriation of prisoners of war after the Korean War and for his work as G-1 adviser to the Korean Marine Corps.

He wrote: "Practical experience as a criminologist, both in the national and in the international arenas, provided the motivation to write *A Habitation of Devils.* Work with police, courts, correctional personnel and criminals of every persuasion, provided a wealth of factual information—and some prejudices! Prior to the revolution in Iran, I taught a number of courses to the late Shah's Imperial National Police."

*   *   *

PARHAM, William Thomas   1913-

PERSONAL: Born July 11, 1913, in London, England; son of Thomas William (a caterer) and Lily Jane (a draper; maiden name, Smith) Parham; married Helena Pilkington (a medical secretary), April 29, 1944; children: Anne Christine (Mrs. M. J. Burkinshaw). *Education:* Attended Kingston-upon-Thames Technical College. *Politics:* None. *Religion:* None. *Home:* 19 Lincoln Ave., Tawa, Wellington, New Zealand.

CAREER: Worked in the paper industry, 1934-78; writer, 1960—. Broadcaster. Worked in conservation and bird banding for Royal Forest and Bird Protection Society (Auckland chairman, 1965) and Department of Scientific and Industrial Research, Wellington. Co-founder of Whakatane Museum. *Military service:* Royal Navy, Fleet Air Arm, 1943-46. *Member:* Whakatane and District Historical Society. *Awards, honors:* Nicholson-London Trophy from Whakatane and District Historical Society, 1978.

WRITINGS—Nonfiction: *Von Tempsky, Adventurer,* Hodder & Stoughton, 1969; *Island Volcano,* Collins, 1973; *Man at Arms,* Whakatane and District Historical Society, 1977; *Away From It All,* Whakatane and District Historical Society, 1977. Contributor of articles and reviews to magazines and newspapers.

WORK IN PROGRESS: A book tentatively titled *South of the Rio Grande,* on the author's travels in Latin America; a biography of Lieutenant Colonel John M. Roberts, N.Z.C.; research for a biography of Major Charles Heaphy, V.C.

SIDELIGHTS: Parham wrote: "I hold dual citizenship of the United Kingdom and New Zealand. I have lived in four countries and traveled through nearly fifty, including the United States, on five world tours. My interest in history has taken me through Central and South America and is now my main writing activity. I intend to spend the rest of my life filling in gaps in the historical record of my present country of residence, New Zealand."

BIOGRAPHICAL/CRITICAL SOURCES: Historical Record, Wanganui, New Zealand, May, 1980.

*   *   *

PARKER, Adrian David   1947-

PERSONAL: Born May 7, 1947, in Ravensworth, Durham, England; son of George and Winifred (Reed) Parker; married

Ingrid Milveden (a psychologist), 1978. *Education:* University of Edinburgh, M.A., 1969, Ph.D., 1977; Tavistock Clinic, diploma, 1972. *Office:* Stora Nygatan 11, S-411 08 Goeteborg, Sweden.

CAREER: University of Edinburgh, Edinburgh, Scotland, researcher in clinical psychology, 1972-80; clinical psychologist at a family psychiatric clinic in Goeteborg, Sweden, 1980—. *Member:* Swedish Psychological Society, American Psychological Society, British Psychological Society, Society for Psychical Research, Parapsychology Association.

WRITINGS: States of Mind: ESP and Altered States of Consciousness, Taplinger, 1975. Contributor of articles to scientific journals.

SIDELIGHTS: Parker told *CA:* "As a psychologist I chose to research ESP and altered states of consciousness because they relate to fundamental philosophical problems." *Avocational interests:* Travel, music, reading.

BIOGRAPHICAL/CRITICAL SOURCES: Times Literary Supplement, October 10, 1975; *Economist,* October 18, 1975.

*   *   *

PARKER, Elliott S(evern) 1939-

PERSONAL: Born December 13, 1939, in Kansas City, Kan.; son of Richard S. (a florist) and Mary (Hassig) Parker; married Emelia Marcellino (a librarian), June 19, 1970. *Education:* Kansas State University, B.A., 1962; Ohio University, M.F.A. and M.A., both 1970, doctoral study. *Home:* 101 East Bellows, Mount Pleasant, Mich. 48858. *Office:* Department of Journalism, Central Michigan Univeristy, Mount Pleasant, Mich. 48859.

CAREER: United Press International (UPI), free-lance photographer in Kansas City, Kan., 1958-64; free-lance photographer, 1964-67; Associated Press (AP), free-lance photojournalist in Kansas City, Saigon, and Singapore, 1968-70; Mara Institute of Technology, Shah Alam, Malaysia, senior lecturer in photography and head of department, 1971-75; Temple University, Philadelphia, Pa., instructor in graphics and news editing, 1975-76; Central Michigan University, Mount Pleasant, assistant professor, 1976-80, associate professor of journalism, 1980—, research professor, 1980-81. Photographer for Dianying Ltd., 1979—. *Member:* National Press Photographers Association, Association for Education in Journalism, Association for Asian Studies, Society for Photographic Education. *Awards, honors:* Paul Schutzer fellowship from *Life* and Ohio University, 1970.

WRITINGS: (With wife, Emelia Parker) *Asian Journalism: A Selected Bibliography of Sources on Journalism in China and Southeast Asia,* Scarecrow, 1979. Contributor to *World Encyclopedia of the Press.* Contributor to scholarly journals.

WORK IN PROGRESS: Research on the development and evolution of documentary photography in nineteenth-century Southeast Asia, with a book expected to result; an audio filmstrip presentation on journalism in East and Southeast Asia; a statistical and comparative analysis of newspapers in Singapore and Malaysia across all languages for a constructed week during 1974-75; analyzing election coverage by newspapers in a plural society, particularly Malaysia.

SIDELIGHTS: Parker told *CA:* "Our idea in publishing *Asian Journalism* was to expose the contemporary journalism researcher to a body of historical and descriptive work on Asian journalism. Most scholars have little idea (or interest?) that there exists a significant and important body of work on journalism in this section of the world, preferring to believe

that this type of study is limited to American (North and South) and European communications.

"My current major interest is in the photography of colonial Southeast Asia. I would like to place this work in a social and cultural context and investigate the difference between the perceptions of local people and foreigners.

"In both of the above projects, my overall concern is to discover what, if any, ideas, concepts, or theories of communications, developed for an industrialized Western world, are applicable to other societies."

*   *   *

PARKER, Gordon 1940-

PERSONAL: Born February 28, 1940, in Newcastle, England; son of John Eden (an electrical engineer) and Mary Robson (Anderson) Parker; married Ann Jane Hopkins (a dental receptionist), March 3, 1962; children: Kim, Tracey. *Education:* Attended Newcastle Polytechnic, 1965-68. *Politics:* "Left-wing Tory." *Religion:* Christian. *Home and office:* 14 Thornhill Close, Seaton Delaval, Northumberland, England. *Agent:* David Higham Associates Ltd., 5/8 Lower John St., Golden Sq., London W1R 4HA, England.

CAREER: Clark Chapman Ltd., Gateshead, England, area sales representative, 1962-67, area sales manager, 1967-78, sales manager in Engineering Division, 1978-80; Essen Steels Ltd., Birmingham, England, sales manager, 1980—. Member of Northumberland County Council Amenities Committee, 1980—. Book reviewer for BBC-Radio; literary critic for Tyne-Tees-TV.

WRITINGS—All novels, except as noted: *The Darkness of the Morning,* Bachman & Turner, 1975; *Lightning in May,* Bachman & Turner, 1976; *The Pool,* Bachman & Turner, 1978; "The Seance" (radio play), first broadcast by BBC-Radio, March, 1978; *Action of the Tiger,* Macdonald Futura, 1981; *The House in Kostroma,* Macdonald Futura, 1982.

SIDELIGHTS: Parker told *CA:* "My first novel, *The Darkness of the Morning,* was based on events leading up to an actual mining disaster in 1862. The disaster occurred only a few miles from where my home is located. The memorial in the village churchyard has 204 names on it, and the ages of the victims ranged from ten to seventy. I tried to recreate these forgotten, faceless people, their lifestyles, their hopes, and their dreams. Former President Jimmy Carter sent me a handwritten letter saying how much he enjoyed the novel. Detente? A little, perhaps, but nevertheless flattering.

"My second novel was again parochial inasmuch as it involved the general strike of 1926 and the derailment of an express train, The Flying Scotsman, by a gang of striking miners. Though the book was based on fact, I created fictional characters and tried to examine their plight and what drove them to such a desperate act.

"*The Pool* brought about a change of style dictated by the subject—corruption in local government—and by the period—the present. Again I tried to explore the human being as a species, vulnerable and prone to temptations beyond the law. Then another change: *Action of the Tiger* was written purely as a thriller, commercially dressed for general international interest and possible film rights. *Tiger* involves the CIA, MI5, and World War II Nazis still at large.

"My latest novel is another thriller—a genre I enjoy immensely. *The House in Kostroma* involves the CIA and a Russian sect that dictates Russian foreign policy. Initial reactions are very favorable.

"What next? More thrillers or perhaps another experiment. I admire Salinger and Joseph Heller. They've sewn ideas in my head for style and for oblique observation. Basically I'm a storyteller. That is the object of my novels. If there's any art or philosophy between the lines . . . great."

Parker's *The Darkness of the Morning* has been published in the Soviet Union and has been translated into Dutch.

* * *

PARKER, Robert Stewart 1915-

PERSONAL: Born February 19, 1915, in Sydney, Australia; son of Robert H. J. (a manager) and Mary (Stewart) Parker; married Nancy Martyr Bolton, August 30, 1939 (divorced, 1965); married Cecily Margaret Nixon (a psychotherapist), July 25, 1966; children: (first marriage) Roderick Bolton, Katrina Mary, Quentin Stewart. *Education:* University of Sydney, B.Ec., 1937, M.Ec., 1941. *Politics:* Labor. *Religion:* None. *Home:* 54 Munro St., Curtin, Canberra, Australian Capital Territory 2605, Australia.

CAREER: Australian National University (formerly Canberra University College), Canberra, Australia, lecturer in public administration, 1938; Victoria University of Wellington, Wellington, New Zealand, lecturer in political science, 1939-45; Australian National University, lecturer in political science, 1946-47, social science research fellow, 1947-48; Victoria University of Wellington, professor of political science and public administration, 1949-53; Australian National University, reader, 1954-62, professor of political science, 1963-78, professor emeritus, 1978—. Member of council of Papua New Guinea Administrative College, 1962-69; member of Papua New Guinea Public Services Conciliation and Arbitration Tribunal, 1972. Member of Australian Prime Minister's Committee of Inquiry Into Commonwealth Public Service Recruitment, 1957-58. *Military service:* Royal New Zealand Air Force, 1943-44.

MEMBER: International Political Science Association, Academy of the Social Sciences in Australia (fellow), Australian Institute of Public Administration (chairman of Australian groups, 1970-72), Australian Political Studies Association (president, 1963-64), Australian National University Staff Association (president, 1955, 1970-72), Canberra Chamber Music Society (president, 1956-59). *Awards, honors:* Member of Order of the British Empire, 1959.

WRITINGS: Public Service Recruitment in Australia, Melbourne University Press, 1942; (editor) *Economic Stability in New Zealand,* New Zealand Institute of Public Administration, 1953; *Highlights of New South Wales Local Government Legislation Over the Last Fifty Years,* New South Wales Local Government Association, 1956; (contributor) S. R. Davis, editor, *The Government of the Australian States,* Longmans, Green, 1960; (editor with A. L. Epstein and Marie Reay) *The Politics of Dependence,* Australian National University Press, 1971; *Administrative Development in Papua New Guinea,* Asia Society, 1971; (with P. N. Troy) *Politics of Urban Growth,* Australian National University Press, 1972; (editor with Peter Loveday and A. W. Martin) *The Emergence of the Australian Party System,* Hale & Iremonger, 1977; *The Government of New South Wales,* University of Queensland Press, 1978. Contributor to history and political science journals.

WORK IN PROGRESS: A comparison of American and Australian colonial administration in the Pacific, with Norman Meller, publication expected in 1982.

SIDELIGHTS: Parker told *CA:* "My interest in politics and administration stems from my first four working years as a state public servant in New South Wales, and from the reordering of Australian politics in the post-Depression years. My work as consultant to the administration of Papua New Guinea aroused my interest in that emergent state and less developed countries generally. That led to travel through western and eastern Africa and to studies in the United States and Europe, as well as my current research project.

"My writing is a by-product of my academic profession, not an artistic enterprise in its own right. It aims at helping readers to understand particular political happenings and trends at specific places and times. And not only to understand events, but also to evaluate them as guides to future action. Thus some political values are at least implicit in much of what I write. My writings about Papua New Guinea were implied or overt criticisms of Australian rule.

"I have written mainly for specialized audiences: political scientists, civil servants, politicians. A number of them have said that they found it easier to understand my writings than some other academic writings in the field. This may have resulted partly from my empathy as a former official; partly also, I would hope, from a conviction that academic writers owe as much dedication to the craft of writing as do literary people. It is obvious that effective academic exposition must be logical and unambiguous, but direct, grammatical, rhythmic English also has the appeal of all good art. On the other hand, wordy, pretentious or slovenly writing alienates the reader; it indicates poor thinking, or laziness, or both. So I regard precise, concise expression as an integral part of the academic quality of written work, and try to inculcate it in students. It is not easy to achieve. It takes painful effort to produce painless prose. My advice to aspiring writers is: soak yourself in good literature, study a foreign language, imagine yourself in the reader's place as you revise your drafts, and take Strunk's *Elements of Style* as your bible.

"The literature of social science is nine-tenths mediocre. Although I labor with care at my writing, I do not publish it with confidence. I expect it to have few readers and little influence. Occasionally this expectation is pleasantly disappointed. My writing rarely blesses or damns, exhorts or preaches. I hope it sometimes amuses, teaches, and warns."

* * *

PARKER, Stanley R(obert) 1927-

PERSONAL: Born November 21, 1927, in London, England. *Education:* University of London, B.Sc., M.Sc., Ph.D. *Home:* 46 Hurstwood Rd., London NW11 0AT, England. *Office:* Office of Population Censuses and Surveys, 10 Kingsway, London W.C.2, England.

CAREER: Office of Population Censuses and Surveys, London, England, social survey officer, 1973—. Visiting associate professor at University of Waterloo, 1974; visiting fellow at Kuring-gai College of Advanced Education, 1980-81. *Member:* International Sociological Association, British Sociological Association, Leisure Studies Association.

WRITINGS: (With Louis Moss) *The Local Government Councillor,* [London], 1967; (with R. Brown, J. Child, and M. Smith) *The Sociology of Industry,* Praeger, 1967, 4th edition, 1981; (with C. Thomas, N. Ellis, and W.E.J. McCarthy) *Effects of the Redundancy Payments Act,* H.M.S.O., 1971; *The Future of Work and Leisure,* Praeger, 1971; (editor with Michael A. Smith and C. Smith) *Leisure and Society in Britain,* Allen Lane, 1973; (with Geoffrey

Godbey) *The Sociology of Leisure,* Saunders, 1976. Also author of *Workplace Industrial Relations.*

WORK IN PROGRESS: A book on work and retirement, publication expected in 1982.

SIDELIGHTS: Parker wrote: "Having started with the sociology of work and industry, my interests have now turned to the study of leisure and retirement, because opportunities for work seem to be diminishing in our society."

*   *   *

PARKER, Stewart 1941-

PERSONAL: Born October 20, 1941, in Belfast, Northern Ireland; son of George Herbert (a tailor's cutter) and Isobel (Lynas) Parker; married Kate Ireland, 1964. *Education:* Queen's University of Belfast, B.A., 1964, M.A., 1966. *Home and office:* 103 Harrison Rd., Edinburgh EH11 1LT, Scotland. *Agent:* London Management, 235/241 Regent St., London W1A 2JT, England.

CAREER: Hamilton College, Clinton, N.Y., instructor in English, 1964-67; Cornell University, Ithaca, N.Y., instructor in English, 1967-69; writer, 1969—. *Member:* Writers Guild of Great Britain, Dramatists Guild. *Awards, honors:* Most promising playwright award from *Evening Standard,* 1976, for "Spokesong"; prize from Christopher Ewart-Biggs Memorial Trust, 1979, for "I'm a Dreamer, Montreal"; special commendation from Italia Prize, 1980, and Giles Cooper Award from British Broadcasting Corp., 1981, both for "The Kamikaze Ground Staff Reunion Dinner."

WRITINGS: (Editor) Sam Thompson, *Over the Bridge,* Gill & Macmillan, 1971; *Spokesong* (two-act play; first produced in Dublin, Ireland, at Dublin Theatre Festival, 1975), Samuel French, 1979; *Catchpenny Twist* (two-act play; first produced in Dublin at Peacock Theatre, 1977), Samuel French, 1980; *Nightshade* (two-act play; first produced in Dublin at Peacock Theatre, 1980), Co-Op Books (Dublin), 1980; "The Kamikaze Ground Staff Reunion Dinner" (radio play; first broadcast on British Broadcasting Corp. [BBC-Radio], 1980), published in *Best Radio Plays of 1980,* Methuen, 1981.

Unpublished plays: "Speaking of Red Indians" (radio play), first broadcast on BBC-Radio, 1967; "Minnie and Maisie and Lily Freed" (radio play), first broadcast on BBC-Radio, 1970; "The Iceberg" (radio play), first broadcast on BBC-Radio, 1975; "The Actress and the Bishop" (one-act), first produced in London at King's Head Theatre, 1976; "Kingdom Come" (two-act musical), first produced in London at King's Head Theatre, 1978; "I'm a Dreamer, Montreal," first broadcast on Thames-Television, 1979.

WORK IN PROGRESS: "Iris in the Traffic, Ruby in the Rain," a film for BBC-TV; "Pratt's Fall," a stage play.

BIOGRAPHICAL/CRITICAL SOURCES: New York Times, March 11, 1979.

*   *   *

PARKS, Arva Moore 1939-

PERSONAL: Born January 19, 1939, in Miami, Fla.; daughter of Jack and Anne (Parker) Moore; married Robert L. Parks (an attorney), August 19, 1959; children: Jacqueline Carey, Robert Downing, Gregory Moore. *Education:* Attended Florida State University, 1956-58; University of Florida, B.A. (with high honors), 1960; University of Miami, Coral Gables, Fla., M.A., 1971. *Politics:* Democrat. *Religion:* Methodist. *Home and office:* 1006 South Greenway Dr., Coral Gables, Fla. 33134.

CAREER: Teacher of social studies at junior high school in Hyattsville, Md., 1960-63, and senior high school in Miami, Fla., 1963-64; Everglades School for Girls, Miami, teacher of social studies, 1965-66; consultant, 1966-70; free-lance research historian, 1970—. Chairperson of City of Coral Gables Historic Preservation Board, 1974-79, Florida Governor's Mansion Advisory Council, Dade County Historical Board, and board of directors of Florida Endowment for the Humanities; past member of Florida Historic Sites and Properties Commission.

MEMBER: American Association for State and Local History, National Trust for Historic Preservation, Florida Historical Society (member of board of directors), Historical Association of Southern Florida (second vice-president; president, 1973-74). *Awards, honors:* Certificate of commendation from American Association for State and Local History, 1978, for *The Forgotten Frontier;* Headliner Award from Women in Communications, Inc., 1980, for distinguished service to the community; Humanitarian Award from Urban League Guild, 1980, for outstanding contributions to multi-ethnic groups; Museum of Science award, 1981, for contributions to history and literature.

WRITINGS: The Forgotten Frontier, Banyan Books, 1978; *Miami: The Magic City,* Continental Heritage, 1981. Author of "Miami Past," a column in *Miami* magazine. Associate editor of *Tequesta.*

Films; all released by Junior League of Miami, Inc.: "Coconut Grove," 1971; (co-author) "Ours Is a Tropic Land," 1973; "Miami: The Magic City," 1980.

SIDELIGHTS: Arva Parks told *CA:* "As a native Miamian, I have enjoyed combining my love of history with my love for my hometown. Miamians have long believed they have no history. My greatest thrill is convincing them otherwise. I see Miami's history as the best vehicle for bringing our diverse multi-ethnic community together. Miami is what we all have in common."

*   *   *

PARLETT, David (Sidney) 1939-

PERSONAL: Born May 18, 1939, in London, England; son of Sidney Thomas (a mechanic) and May (Nunan) Parlett; married Barbara Hoare (a teacher), March 26, 1966; children: Elizabeth Jane, Edward Frank. *Education:* University College of Wales, Aberystwyth, B.A., 1961. *Politics:* Liberal. *Religion:* Society of Friends (Quakers). *Home and office:* 1 Churchmore Rd., Streatham, London SW16 5UY, England. *Agent:* John McLaughlin, Campbell, Thomson & McLaughlin, 31 Newington Green, London N16 9PU, England.

CAREER: Teacher of modern languages at state schools in London, England, 1963-67; House Information Services Ltd. (promotional publishers), London, editorial manager, 1967-73; Taylor-Alden Marketing Ltd. (public relations agency), London, technical writer, 1974; writer, games inventor, and consultant, 1975—. *Member:* International Playing-Card Society, Society of Authors, Institute of Journalists, Institute of Linguists.

WRITINGS: A Short Dictionary of Languages, Hodder & Stoughton, 1967; *Learning a Language Alone,* Pitman, 1968; *Know the Game Patience,* E. P. Publishing, 1976; *Card Games for Three,* Hodder & Stoughton, 1977; *Card Games for Four,* Hodder & Stoughton, 1977; *Original Card Games,* Batsford, 1977; *All the Best Card Games,* Batsford, 1978; *Card Games for Two,* Hodder & Stoughton, 1978; *The Pen-*

guin Book of Card Games, Viking, 1979; *Solitaire,* Pantheon, 1979 (published in England as *The Penguin Book of Patience,* Allen Lane, 1979); *Poker and Brag,* Hodder & Stoughton, 1980; *The Penguin Book of Word Games,* Penguin, 1981. Contributing editor of *Games and Puzzles,* 1975, and *House's Guide to the Construction Industry,* 1968-78.

WORK IN PROGRESS: A History of Card Games (tentative title); translation of *Carmina Burana.*

SIDELIGHTS: Parlett told *CA:* "After a short career as a modern language teacher I wrote a couple of books on linguistic subjects and discovered I was a writer, not a teacher. So, I landed a post as technical writer with a promotional publishing company and did quite well at it. Technical writing and journalism suit me: I never did enjoy the literary side of language studies, and retain a deep suspicion of most so-called creative writing. (True, I indulge myself by writing poetry now and then, but not while anyone is looking. I subscribe to the belief that the only good poet is a dead one.) Even now my voracious reading is largely confined to fact rather than fiction; history, ethnology, philosophy, and astronomy are among my favorite subjects.

"I have been a games player and inventor for as long as I can remember, though only recently in a professional capacity. This led from an invitation in 1975 to edit *Games and Puzzles* magazine, which (though I have since given up the editorship) enabled me to realize an ambition to go freelance. At present I am entirely self-supporting in the games line, by means of writing books and articles, especially on card games, royalties from the invention of board and table games, and consultancy to games manufacturers.

"Playing games should be regarded by any civilized society as a cultural pursuit of comparable value to music-making, dancing, poetry-reading, and so on. Unfortunately it is degraded by the fact that some people regard games as kids' stuff and others just see them as a means to the end of gambling. Equally, of course, game production is expensive and manufacturers cannot afford to promote themselves as purveyors of culture.

"It is no doubt through my studies and travels as a language-lover that I have come to feel a greater sense of patriotism towards Europe as a whole than just my native corner of it. This, coupled with a penchant for history, has led me to take greater pleasure in medieval literature than modern. Some years ago I started a translation into English verse of the *Carmina Burana* and between bread-and-butter books I periodically dust it off and extend and revise it. Some time, I hope, it may see the light of day."

*   *   *

PARR, Letitia (Evelyn)   1906-

PERSONAL: Born January 5, 1906, in Sydney, Australia; daughter of John Lile Lewis and Elizabeth Christina Forsyth; married Harold George Parr (an optometrist), 1927; children: Patricia Lovell, Geoffrey, Susan Woods. *Education:* Attended girls' high school in Sydney, Australia. *Politics:* "On the side of mankind, not machines." *Religion:* "Christian, I hope." *Home:* Greenway, Flat CO5, Milsons Point, New South Wales 2061, Australia.

CAREER: Worked as a stenographer until 1927; Christian Education Home Correspondence Sunday School, Sydney, Australia, organizing secretary, 1964-68; writer, 1968—. Helped to establish free library at local community center; worked in after-school care at local primary school. *Member:* Australian Society of Authors, Australian Women's Writers,

Fellowship of Australian Writers. *Awards, honors: Green Is for Growing* was included in "Best of the Best" by United Nations Educational, Scientific and Cultural Organization's International Youth Library, 1969; Design award from Australian Book Publishers Association, 1969, for *Green Is for Growing.*

WRITINGS—Children's books: *Green Is for Growing,* illustrations by John Watts, Angus & Robertson, 1968; *When Sea and Sky Are Blue,* illustrations by Watts, Angus & Robertson, 1970; *Seagull,* photographs by son, Geoffrey Parr, Angus & Robertson, 1970; *Dolphins Are Different,* Angus & Robertson, 1972; *Flowers for Samantha,* Methuen of Australia, 1975; *Getting Well in Hospital,* Methuen of Australia, 1977; *Grandpa Pearson,* Methuen of Australia, 1979.

Work represented in anthologies, including *Stuff and Nonsense,* Collins, 1974. Stories and poems have been broadcast on "Kindergarten of the Air," by Australian Broadcasting Commission. Contributor to *Australian Author.*

WORK IN PROGRESS: A children's book, *Mr. Moriarty's Mate;* research for a biography of John Cadman, a convict, for elementary school children.

SIDELIGHTS: Letitia Parr wrote: "I appreciate the importance of the early years to the whole of life and have a natural empathy with children. In the main, my stories are about perceptions. *Dolphins Are Different* was written when Sheila, a zoo dolphin, died. *Flowers for Samantha* was the outcome of an editorial request for a story dealing with death. *Grandpa Pearson* expresses my belief that the old and the young are accepting of each other."

*   *   *

PARRISH, Bernard P.   1936-
(Bernie Parrish)

PERSONAL: Born April 29, 1936, in Long Beach, Calif.; son of Charles A. and Margaret (Fitzpatrick) Parrish; married wife, Carol (marriage ended); children: Nina, Teresa, Bernard, Holly, Amy. *Education:* University of Florida, B.B.C. *Home:* 19 Cottonwood Trace, Edwardsville, Ill. 62025. *Agent:* Gerard McCauley Agency, Inc., Box AE, Katonah, N.Y. 10536.

CAREER: Cleveland Browns, Cleveland, Ohio, professional football player, 1959-66; International Brotherhood of Teamsters, St. Louis, Mo., administrator, 1968-73; R & M Construction, Inc., Edwardsville, Ill., general contractor, 1973—. *Awards, honors:* All America baseball award, 1958; named athlete of the year, 1958; All Pro Award from National Football League, 1964; award from *Coach and Athlete.*

WRITINGS: (Under name Bernie Parrish) *They Call It a Game,* Dial, 1971. Contributor to *Look.*

*   *   *

PARRISH, Bernie
See PARRISH, Bernard P.

*   *   *

PARROTT, Cecil (Cuthbert)   1909-

PERSONAL: Born January 29, 1909, in Plymouth, England; son of Jasper William Alfred (a captain in Royal Navy) and Grace Edith (West) Parrott; married Ellen Julie Matzow, June 12, 1935; children: Hans Christopher, Michael Erik, Jasper William. *Education:* Peterhouse, Cambridge, M.A., 1930. *Residence:* Lancaster, England. *Agent:* Andrew Hewson of John Johnson, Clerkenwell House, 45-47 Clerkenwell Green, London EC1R 0HT, England.

CAREER: Assistant master at Edinburgh Academy, Edinburgh, Scotland, 1931-34; tutor to King Peter of Yugoslavia, 1935-39; British Legation, assistant press attache in Oslo, Norway, 1939-40, and assistant press attache, second secretary, and head of Press Reading Bureau in Stockholm, Sweden, 1940-45; British Embassy, Prague, Czechoslovakia, first secretary and press attache, 1945-48; Foreign Office, London, England, first secretary in information research department, 1948-49; assistant in United Nations Political Department, 1949-50, counselor and head of department, 1950-52; British Embassy, counselor and charge d'affaires in Brussels, Belgium, 1952-54, minister and charge d'affaires in Moscow, U.S.S.R., 1954-57; Foreign Office, London, librarian, keeper of the papers, and director of research, 1957-60; British Embassy, Prague, ambassador, 1960-66; University of Lancaster, Lancaster, England, professor of Russian and Soviet studies, 1966-71, professor of Central and Southeastern European studies, 1971-76, professor emeritus, 1976—. Director of Comenius Centre, 1967-76, honorary president, 1976—. Vice-chairman of D'Oyly Carte Opera Trust, 1971-78.

MEMBER: Royal Literary Society (fellow), Institute of Linguists (vice-president, 1970-77). *Awards, honors:* Officer of Order of British Empire, 1947; companion of Order of St. Michael and St. George, 1953, knight commander, 1964.

WRITINGS: (Translator) Jaroslav Hasek, *The Good Soldier Svejk,* Crowell, 1973; *The Tightrope* (memoirs), Faber, 1975; *The Serpent and the Nightingale* (memoirs), Faber, 1977; *The Bad Bohemian Hasek* (biography), Bodley Head, 1977; *The Works of Jaroslav Hasek: A Literary and Historical Study,* Cambridge University Press, in press.

Broadcasts; all produced by British Broadcasting Corp. (BBC): "The Good Bohemian Hasek," first broadcast August 31, 1973; "The Moscow Merchants," first broadcast October, 1974; "The Pasternaks," first broadcast October 9, 1975; "The Twilight of Dynasty," first broadcast January 12, 1975; "Liberated Theatre," first broadcast September 22, 1980.

WORK IN PROGRESS: Research on eastern European history, literature, music, and art; a translation of the short stories of Jaroslav Hasek, for Heinemann.

SIDELIGHTS: Parrott told *CA:* "It was my experience as tutor to a Balkan monarch that whetted my appetite for a career in diplomacy. This was only made possible by the war, which found me in Stockholm. Although I was keen on Scandanavia because my wife was Norwegian, my closest interests were the Slav countries and the Balkans. I was finally established in the British Foreign Service in 1946, and from then on my interest lay more in *where* I might be posted than in the positions I might hold. I maneuvered myself to Brussels because my family had been ill and I wanted a post near England. I was greatly intrigued by political life in Belgium and was one of the first British diplomats, I believe, to master Flemish. I was invited to go to Moscow after two years and was sorry to leave Brussels. It was only later that the Foreign Office found out that I spoke Russian! 'That will be a help,' they commented.

"It was worth joining the Foreign Service just to get to Moscow, because, as a diplomat, I could see and experience things that even the most faithful foreign communist would not be shown. I could have stayed there another three years. Knowledge of Czech and previous experience was a great help to me when I returned to Prague as an ambassador. Although it was a dull time politically, I enjoyed the musical life and the beauties of the country, including its myriad castles. I made countless friends.

"My aim as an academic and a writer has been to try and tell the British something about eastern Europe, which is no easy task because they only want to know about the things they know about. Sometimes it is discouraging, but it is a worthy aim and one that I am more fitted to pursue than anything else.

"I have given numerable talks on Czech music and other subjects on the BBC and would have given further talks on Russian and Yugoslavian music if they had only let me. There are so many fresh and unexplored cultural gems in these eastern European countries, which, except for Russia, prefer to be called central European or southeastern European countries. Our own civilization is getting rather played out, and we would do well to freshen ourselves up with closer acquaintance with the music, art, national songs, poetry, and folk costumes of these remarkable countries, without being infected by the stultifying political systems that they unfortunately have had thrust upon them."

*   *   *

PARRY, John
  See WHELPTON, (George) Eric

*   *   *

PARSONS, C(hristopher) J(ames) 1941-

PERSONAL: Born August 8, 1941, in Epsom, England; son of Cecil James and Marjorie (Budgell) Parsons; married Janelle Cooper (a writer and consultant), September 7, 1979; children: Katharine Ellen. *Education:* University of Nottingham, B.A., 1963; University of London, Ph.D., 1968. *Home:* 12 Berber Rd., London SW11 6RZ, England. *Agent:* Hope Leresche & Sayle, 11 Jubilee Pl., Chelsea, London SW3 3TE, England.

CAREER: Kidderminster College of Further Education, Kidderminster, England, lecturer in English, 1963-64; Canterbury Technical College, Canterbury, England, lecturer in English, 1964-67; Merton Technical College, London, England, senior lecturer in English, 1967-74; Hammersmith and West London College, London, principal lecturer in communication, 1974—. *Member:* National Association of Teachers in Further and Higher Education, Association for Liberal Education, Society of Authors, British Institute of Management.

WRITINGS: (With S. J. Hughes) *Written Communication for Business Students,* Edward Arnold, 1970; *Theses and Project Work,* Allen & Unwin, 1973; *Library Use in Further Education,* Edward Arnold, 1973; *How to Study Effectively,* Arrow Books, 1976; *Problems in Business Communication,* Edward Arnold, 1977; *Communication for Business Students,* Edward Arnold, 1978; (with Angela Nevstatter) *Getting the Right Job,* Pan Books, 1979; (with Nevstatter) *Work for Yourself,* Pan Books, 1980; *Communication Skills Library,* Holdsworth Audio-Visual, 1980; (with Brendan Moore) *English for Business Studies,* Macmillan, 1981; *Assignments in Communications Skills,* Edward Arnold, 1981.

SIDELIGHTS: Parsons told *CA:* "I like writing books that explain complicated subjects in a simple and straightforward manner and which in the long run help people communicate more effectively. Some of my books are college texts; others are intended for general readership. However, in all the books my aim is to teach. Basically, I am a teacher who writes because he wants to teach a larger audience than he finds in the classroom. If, at the end of it all, a few more people can communicate better, then I will feel well satisfied.''

AVOCATIONAL INTERESTS: Historic buildings, travel, photography, walking.

*   *   *

PARTRIDGE, Astley Cooper   1901-

PERSONAL: Born February 11, 1901, in Cape Town, South Africa; son of Astley Cooper (a conveyancer) and Frances (a teacher; maiden name, Commaille) Partridge; married Isabelle Mary Wiggett, October 5, 1935; children: Timothy Cooper. *Education:* University of South Africa, B.A., 1925; University of Pretoria, M.A., 1933; attended Magdalene College, Cambridge, 1933-34; University of Cape Town, Ph.D., 1946. *Religion:* Congregational. *Home and office:* 12 Cluny Rd., Forest Town, Johannesburg 2193, South Africa.

CAREER: Cape Provincial Administration, Cape Town, South Africa, public servant, 1919-32; Treasury, Department of Agriculture, and Transvaal Education Department, Pretoria, South Africa, public servant, 1932-35; University of Pretoria, Pretoria, senior lecturer in English, 1935-54; University of the Witwatersrand, Johannesburg, South Africa, professor of English and head of department, 1954-66, professor emeritus, 1966—. Dominion fellow at St. John's College, Cambridge, 1950; senior research fellow at University of Witwatersrand, 1967-69, honorary research associate, 1971-75, professorial research fellow, 1976—. British Council visiting lecturer at University of Keele, 1963; distinguished visiting professor at University of Alberta, 1971. Member of drama committee of Performing Arts Council, 1961—; judge of Central News Agency literary award, 1961-76. Member of Friends of Shakespeare Birthplace Trust. *Member:* International P.E.N. (chairman of South Africa Center, 1969-70), International Shakespeare Association. *Awards, honors:* Senior grant from South Africa Council for Social Research, 1950; grants from Italian Government, 1960, and British Council, 1973; D.Litt. from University of Cape Town, 1970.

WRITINGS: Readings in South African English Prose, Van Schaik, 1941, 3rd edition, 1954; *The Problem of Henry VIII Re-Opened: Some Linguistic Criteria for the Two Styles Apparent in the Play,* Bowes & Bowes, 1949; (with F. P. Wilson) *Gentleness and Nobility,* Oxford University Press, 1950; *The Accidence of Ben Jonson's Plays, Masques, and Entertainments,* Bowes & Bowes, 1953; *Studies in the Syntax of Ben Jonson's Plays,* Bowes & Bowes, 1953.

Orthography in Shakespeare and Elizabethan Drama, Edward Arnold, 1964; *Modern Prose,* Edward Arnold, 1964; *The Tribe of Ben,* Edward Arnold, 1966; *The Story of Our South African Flag,* Purnell, 1966; *Scenes From South African Life,* Evans Brothers, 1969; *Tudor to Augustan English,* Deutsch, 1969; *Thus the Bowl Should Run,* Keartland, 1969. *Lives, Letters, and Diaries,* Purnell, 1971; *The Language of Renaissance Poetry: Spenser, Shakespeare, Donne, and Milton,* Deutsch, 1971; *The Foundations of English Criticism,* Nasou, 1972; *Landmarks in the History of English Scholarship,* Nasou, 1972; *Folklore of Southern Africa,* Purnell, 1973; *English Biblical Translation,* Deutsch, 1973; *The Language of Modern Poetry: Yeats, Eliot, Auden,* Deutsch, 1976; *A Substantive Grammar of Shakespeare's Non-Dramatic Texts,* University Press of Virginia, 1976; *John Donne: Language and Style,* Deutsch, 1978; *A Companion to Old and Middle English Studies,* Deutsch, 1981.

Contributor of nearly two hundred articles and reviews to scientific, literary, and popular journals, including *Shakespeare Quarterly, South African Opinion,* and *Scenaria.* Founder and editor of *English Studies in Africa,* 1958-64.

WORK IN PROGRESS: The Celtic Spirit and the English Tongue: A Study in Cultural History, publication expected in 1983.

SIDELIGHTS: Partridge wrote: ''I believe in education through individual research, because every writer is his own teacher. Like human gestation, writing is painful, but the most rewarding of all activities. It exercises all the faculties and disciplines the mind. Much academic training indoctrinates, regiments, and stultifies the spirit for creative tasks. The developing minds of children are more interesting to me than the rigid opinions of some adults. My admiration is for those who educate through entertaining and instructive stories for the young.

''English is a difficult subject to teach, and one defect of the academic system in the past has been the separation of language and literature studies. The *raison d'etre* of my contributions to Deutsch's 'Language Library' has been to show that the disciplines are complementary. I am unsure whether the dilemma has been solved to my satisfaction by demonstrating the relationships of syntax to style and certain principles of rhetoric to composition. The introduction of structural linguistics, as initiated by de Saussure, has not been altogether fruitful for literary interpretation. The tendency of rhetoric to categorize has led to some misrepresentation of its true function.

''There are two *lacunae* that I should like to have seen thoroughly investigated: the language of romantic poetry from Coleridge to Keats and the language of the Old and New Testaments from four standpoints—demography, iconography, historiography, and lexicography. More light seems needed on man's devious paths, through the written word, to find his cultural identity.

''No writer seeks retirement from his vocation as long as he has material on hand that demands completion or reformulation. Whatever his philosophy, a categorical imperative urges him to write in order to discover himself.''

BIOGRAPHICAL/CRITICAL SOURCES: Witwatersrand Student, April 17, 1964; *Star,* Johannesburg, South Africa, November 23, 1966; *South African Digest,* December 2, 1966.

*   *   *

PATERSON, George W(illiam)   1931-

PERSONAL: Born January 1, 1931, in Perry, Iowa; son of J. W. (a farmer) and Jennie (a bookkeeper; maiden name, Mendon) Paterson; married Ida Belle Clark (a secretary), June 2, 1952; children: Jennifer Paterson Rendall, William, Richard, Elisabeth. *Education:* Simpson College, B.A., 1952; Drew University, B.D., 1955; University of Iowa, Ph.D., 1969. *Residence:* Iowa City, Iowa. *Office:* Department of Pastoral Services, University Hospital, University of Iowa, Iowa City, Iowa 52242.

CAREER: Ordained United Methodist elder, 1957; pastor of United Methodist churches in Russell, Iowa, 1955-59, and Churdan, Iowa, 1959-61; Wesley Foundation, Iowa City, Iowa, minister, 1961-70; University of Iowa, Iowa City, assistant professor of religion and internal medicine, 1970-75, associate professor, 1975—, hospital chaplain, 1970—. *Member:* Society for Values in Higher Education (fellow).

WRITINGS: Helping Your Handicapped Child, Augsburg, 1975; *The Cardiac Patient,* Augsburg, 1978; (contributor) William E. Clements, editor, *Ministry With the Aging,* Harper, 1980.

WORK IN PROGRESS: Death and Dying: Pastoral and Theological Dimensions; Religious Dimensions of Pain and Suffering.

AVOCATIONAL INTERESTS: Camping, playing jazz trombone.

* * *

PATMORE, Derek Coventry 1908-1972

OBITUARY NOTICE—See index for *CA* sketch: Born January 15, 1908, in London, England; died in 1972. Interior decorator, journalist, translator, editor, playwright, and author. An authority on interior decoration, Patmore wrote several books on that subject, including *Colour Schemes for the Modern Home, Decorations for the Small Home,* and *A Decorator's Notebook.* He also worked as a war correspondent for the *London News-Chronicle* and the *Christian Science Monitor.* Patmore edited many volumes written by his great-grandfather, the noted poet Coventry Patmore, including *Selected Poems of Coventry Patmore* and *The Rod, the Root, and the Flower.* Among Patmore's plays number "Life of a Lady" and "French for Love." Obituaries and other sources: *London Magazine,* August, 1968; *Stage,* November 23, 1972.

* * *

PATTEN, Lewis B(yford) 1915-1981
(Lewis Ford)

OBITUARY NOTICE—See index for *CA* sketch: Born January 13, 1915, in Denver, Colo.; died May 22, 1981, in Denver, Colo. Author of western novels and short stories. Patten wrote more than one hundred books, including *Death of a Gunfighter,* which was filmed in 1969. In 1979 the Western Writers of America presented him with the Golden Saddleman's Award for his collected works. Obituaries and other sources: *Chicago Tribune,* May 26, 1981; *Washington Post,* May 27, 1981; *AB Bookman's Weekly,* July 13-20, 1981.

* * *

PATTERSON, A(lfred) Temple 1902-

PERSONAL: Born November 27, 1902, in Gosforth, England; son of Alfred (a commercial clerk) and Mary Ellen (Temple) Patterson; married Helen Axon (a university lecturer), July 28, 1934. *Education:* University of Durham, B.A., 1924, M.A., 1926. *Home:* 24 Regniem Court, North Walls, Chichester, Sussex, England. *Agent:* Curtis Brown Ltd., 1 Craven Hill, London W2 3EW, England.

CAREER: Senior history master at school in England, 1926-29; Municipal College, Portsmouth, England, lecturer in charge of history, 1929-40; University of Leicester, Leicester, England, lecturer in history and head of department, 1940-49; University of Southampton, Southampton, England, lecturer, 1949-57, senior lecturer, 1957-60, reader, 1960-66, professor of regional history, 1966-68, professor emeritus, 1968—. *Member:* Royal Historical Society (fellow), Navy Records Society (council member), Society for Nautical Research (southern branch). *Awards, honors:* Leverhulme fellowship, 1947-48.

WRITINGS: (Translator with H. T. Patterson) Rene Grousset, *The Sum of History,* Tower Bridge Publications, 1951; *Radical Leicester,* Pitman, 1954; *The Other Armada,* Manchester University Press, 1960; *The University of Southampton,* Camelot Press, 1962; (editor) *The Jellicoe Papers,* Navy Records Society, Volume I, 1966, Volume II, 1968; *History of Southampton, 1700-1914,* Camelot Press, Volume I, 1966,

Volume II, 1971, Volume III, 1974; *Jellicoe: A Biography,* Macmillan, 1969; *Southampton: A Biography,* Macmillan, 1970; *Tyrwhitt of the Harwich Force,* McDonald & Jane, 1973; *History of Portsmouth,* Moonraker Press, 1976; *Hampshire,* Batsford, 1977. General editor of "The Portsmouth Papers," a monograph series, Corporation of Portsmouth, 1967-77. Contributor to history and military journals.

WORK IN PROGRESS: A biography of Lord Chatfield, Admiral of the Fleet, with Eric J. Grove; *They Say the French Are Coming,* a study of nineteenth-century scares of French invasion.

SIDELIGHTS: Patterson told *CA* that he has "two fields of interest: local history and naval history and biography."

* * *

PATTERSON, Geoffrey 1943-

PERSONAL: Born October 6, 1943, in Wimbledon, London, England; son of Walter (a carnival hat designer) and Yvonne (Still) Patterson; married Rosumund Mary Inglis, 1970; children: Ruth, Oliver. *Education:* Attended private boys' school. *Home and office:* Beech Tree Farm, Wingfield, near Diss, Suffolk, England.

CAREER: John Siddeley (interior designer), London, England, designer, 1961-64; BBC-TV, London, set designer, 1964-77; writer, 1977—. Teacher of visual and three-dimensional arts. *Member:* Society of Industrial Artists.

WRITINGS—Self-illustrated children's books; all published by Deutsch: *The Oak,* 1978; *Chestnut Farm, 1860,* 1980; *The Story of Hay,* 1981; *A Pig's Tale,* 1982; *The Story of Dairying,* 1982.

SIDELIGHTS: Patterson told *CA:* "I live in the country where things have changed very little in many ways over the last fifty years. So I write about and illustrate English country life as it used to be and is now. The books are always for children, six to twelve years old.

"I am concerned about the changing landscape of the English countryside and with the disappearance of the hedgerows and trees in the name of progress and modern farming; quite often it is just greed. So in the children's books I illustrate and write I try to make the next generation aware of what they will and are losing. The books also show that the old ways of farming, although incredibly hard and not as romantic as you may imagine, gave the community a feeling of strength and closeness to the land.

"Everything about country life fascinates me. In my spare time I run my small holding and restore my sixteenth-century farmhouse to its former glory."

* * *

PATTERSON, Rebecca Elizabeth Coy 1911-1975

PERSONAL: Born August 6, 1911, in Ola, Ark.; died December 24, 1975; daughter of Patrick Henry and Katherine (Weaver) Coy; married Thomas McEvoy Patterson, September 14, 1936 (divorced July, 1953); children: Thomas McEvoy, Anne Elizabeth. *Education:* University of Texas, B.A. (summa cum laude), 1934, M.A., 1935, Ph.D., 1938.

CAREER: University of Texas, Main University (now University of Texas at Austin), instructor in English, 1938-40; Amarillo College, Amarillo, Tex., instructor in English, 1945-46; Stanford University, Stanford, Calif., instructor in English, 1947-49; University of North Carolina, Chapel Hill, instructor in English, 1950-51; Kansas State College, Pittsburg, assistant professor, 1954-56, associate professor, 1956-

58, professor of American literature, 1958-75. *Awards, honors:* American Association of University Women fellow, 1949.

WRITINGS: The Riddle of Emily Dickinson, Houghton, 1951, reprinted, Cooper Square, 1972; *Emily Dickinson's Imagery,* edited by Margaret H. Freeman, University of Massachusetts Press, 1979. Contributor to scholarly journals. Editor-in-chief of *Midwest Quarterly,* 1967-75.*

* * *

PATTERSON, Walter C(ram)   1936-

PERSONAL: Born November 4, 1936, in Winnipeg, Manitoba, Canada; son of Walter Thomas (a lawyer) and Helen (Cram) Patterson; married Cleone Davis (a dentist), July 15, 1966; children: Perdita, Tabitha. *Education:* University of Manitoba, B.Sc. (with honors), 1958, M.Sc., 1960. *Home and office:* 10 Chesham Rd., Amersham, Buckinghamshire HP6 5ES, England. *Agent:* Abner Stein, The Vicarage, Studley Villa, 54 Lyndhurst Grove, Camberwell, London SE15 5AH, England.

CAREER: Private tutor in mathematics, physics, and chemistry in London, England, 1960-65, and Hertfordshire, England, 1965-70; *Your Environment,* London, editor, 1970-73; Friends of the Earth Ltd., London, energy specialist, 1972-78; *Bulletin of the Atomic Scientists,* Chicago, Ill., international editor, 1979—. International speaker; expert witness on energy and the environment; broadcaster on radio and television in England and abroad; consultant to Foe Ltd. *Member:* International Solar Energy Society, Association of British Science Writers, British Nuclear Energy Society.

WRITINGS: Nuclear Power, Penguin, 1976; *The Fissile Society,* Earth Resources Research, 1977; (with Richard Griffiths) *Fluidized-Bed Energy Technology: Coming to a Boil,* Inform, 1978. Contributor to magazines, including *New Scientist, Energy Policy, Environment, Nature,* and *New Statesman,* and newspapers.

WORK IN PROGRESS: The second edition of *Nuclear Power,* publication by Penguin expected in 1983.

* * *

PAUL, I(rving) H.   1928-

PERSONAL: Born April 8, 1928, in Montreal, Quebec, Canada; married wife, Edith (a teacher); children: Sarah, Ezra. *Education:* McGill University, B.A., 1949, M.A., 1950; University of Pennsylvania, Ph.D., 1954. *Home:* 330 West 72nd St., New York, N.Y. 10023.

CAREER: Austen Riggs Center, Inc., associate psychologist, 1954-56; New York University, New York City, assistant professor, 1957-63; City College of the City University of New York, New York City, associate professor, 1963-67, professor of psychology, 1967—.

WRITINGS: Studies in Remembering: The Reproduction of Connected and Extended Verbal Material, International Universities Press, 1959; *Letters to Simon: On the Conduct of Psychotherapy,* International Universities Press, 1973; *The Form and Technique of Psychotherapy,* University of Chicago Press, 1979.

* * *

PAYNE, Charles   1909-

PERSONAL: Born March 11, 1909, in Brooklyn, N.Y.; son of Henry Edwin and Isabella (Walls) Payne. *Education:* Yale University, B.A. and LL.D. *Home:* 504 West 48th St., New

York, N.Y. 10036. *Agent:* International Creative Management, 40 West 57th St., New York, N.Y. 10019.

CAREER: American Ballet Theatre, New York, N.Y., director, 1941—. *Military service:* U.S. Naval Reserve, active duty, 1942-46; became lieutenant.

WRITINGS: American Ballet Theatre, Knopf, 1978. Designer and editor of American Ballet Theatre souvenir programs, 1946—.

WORK IN PROGRESS: Nijinsky and Daghilev, for Knopf.

* * *

PEACOCK, Basil   1898-

PERSONAL: Born April 2, 1898, in Newcastle upon Tyne, England; son of James (a merchant) and Jane (Briggs) Peacock; married Lilian Carr (a nurse), July 4, 1923 (deceased); children: Gerald Page. *Education:* Attended University of Durham, 1920-24. *Religion:* Presbyterian. *Home:* 11 Harcourt Field, Wallington, Surrey, England.

CAREER: British Army, Royal Northumberland Fusiliers and Royal Artillery, career officer, 1916-54, retiring as major; St. Helier Hospital, Carshalton, England, dental specialist, 1953-63, emeritus dental specialist, 1963—. Dental officer with Colonial Service in Borneo, 1953-56. *Member:* Civil Service Club. *Awards, honors—*Military: Military Cross.

WRITINGS: Peacock's Tales, privately printed, 1964; *Prisoner on the Kwai,* W. Blackwood, 1966; *History of the Royal Northumberland Fusiliers,* Leo Cooper, 1970; *Discursive Dentist,* Heineman, 1972; *Tinker's Mufti: Memoirs of a Part Time Soldier,* Seeley Service, 1974. Stories have been broadcast by British Broadcasting Corp. Contributor to magazines.

WORK IN PROGRESS: My Boyish Days, about his life in a Victorian family; research on military history.

SIDELIGHTS: Peacock commented: "Though a qualified dental surgeon, my main interest is soldiering. I have traveled widely in the Far East and the Antipodes. I have recently been granted armorial bearings by the Kings of Arms of the English College of Arms. My motto, shown with my coat of arms, is 'wherever my country calls.'"

* * *

PEACOCK, Molly   1947-

PERSONAL: Born June 30, 1947, in Buffalo, N.Y.; daughter of Edward Frank and Pauline (Wright) Peacock. *Education:* State University of New York at Binghamton, B.A. (magna cum laude), 1969; Johns Hopkins University, M.A. (with honors), 1977. *Residence:* Wilmington, Del. *Office:* Delaware State Arts Council, Ninth and French Sts., Wilmington, Del. 19801.

CAREER: State University of New York at Binghamton, director of academic advising, 1970-73, coordinator of innovational projects in office of the dean, 1973-76; Johns Hopkins University, Baltimore, Md., honorary fellow, 1977-78; Delaware State Arts Council, Wilmington, poet-in-residence, 1978—. Director of Wilmington Writing Workshops, 1979—. *Member:* Poetry Society of America. *Awards, honors:* Resident at MacDowell Colony and Yaddo Colony, 1975-80; awards from Creative Artists Public Service, 1977; award from Ingram Merrill Foundation, 1981.

WRITINGS: And Live Apart (poems), University of Missouri Press, 1980. Contributor to magazines, including *Shenandoah, Mississippi Review, New Letters, Southern Review, Massachusetts Review,* and *Ohio Review.*

WORK IN PROGRESS: A collection of poems tentatively titled *All at Once.*

*   *   *

PEAIRS, Lillian Gehrke   1925-

PERSONAL: Born December 2, 1925, in Coshocton, Ohio; daughter of Henry (a farmer) and Louise (Mader) Gehrke; married Richard Hope Peairs (an industrial psychologist), December 18, 1954; children: Mark Andrew Sinclair, John Michael David, Nina Anne Louise. *Education:* Attended Missouri Valley College, 1944-46; Muskingum College, B.S.Ed., 1949. *Religion:* Methodist. *Home:* 370 Loyola Dr., Millbrae, Calif. 94030.

CAREER: Teacher of business education at secondary schools in Fresno, Newcomerstown, and Columbus, Ohio, 1946-56; Battelle Memorial Institute, Columbus, part-time teacher and consultant for stenographic development program, 1951-53; free-lance writer and researcher, 1958-76; American Association of University Professors, San Francisco, Calif., private secretary in western regional office, 1972-74; Lone Mountain College, San Francisco, project coordinator, 1975-76; Wright & Co. (real estate firm), Burlingame, Calif., realtor, 1978—.

WRITINGS: (With husband, Richard Peairs) *What Every Child Needs,* Harper, 1974. Also author of *Manual of Punctuation for the Secretary,* 1956. Contributor of articles to *Balance Sheet* and *Typewriting News.*

SIDELIGHTS: Peairs told *CA:* "My purpose in writing is to educate parents, to help them understand that children learn aggression and intimidation from parents and playmates who are aggressive and intimidating. Basically, the three-year-old reacts to the world as he has come to perceive himself from the experiences parents supply and the behavior we model as we respond to him and the outside world. Each child deserves a chance to develop a positive self-image, but few parents have the time, patience, or positive early backgrounds of their own.

"It takes time to guide children with the respect we accord adult friends. The alternative to anger and authoritarian discipline takes longer to carry out, so it is slowly given up as a means of guiding behavior.

"My current reflection is that the world cannot be changed from reading a book. Education for parenthood must start in infancy. In order to create a more peaceful world, schools may need to supplement parents by providing behavioral psychology courses as a regular part of the curriculum. Then children whose parents do not provide appropriate models or experiences at home will have a chance to unlearn and reshape their own inaccurately learned attitudes and behavior. Then slowly, perhaps, a more peaceful world will evolve."

*   *   *

PEARCE, Brian Louis   1933-

PERSONAL: Born June 4, 1933, in Acton, England; son of Louis Alfred James (a carpenter) and Marjorie Alison (a civil servant; maiden name, Longhurst) Pearce; married Margaret Wood (a teacher), August 2, 1969; children: Ann Gillian. *Education:* Attended West London School of Librarianship, 1961; University of London, M.A., 1976. *Politics:* "Liberal/Moderate." *Religion:* Protestant. *Home:* 72 Heathfield S., Twickenham, Middlesex TW2 7SS, England. *Office:* Richmond-upon-Thames College, Egerton Rd., Twickenham, Middlesex TW2 7SJ, England.

CAREER: Chiswick Public Library, Chiswick, England, librarian, 1949; Acton Public Library, Acton, England, librarian, 1950-51; Buckinghamshire County Library, Buckinghamshire, England, librarian, 1954-57; Twickenham Public Library, Twickenham, England, reference librarian, 1958-61; Acton Technical College, Acton, England, librarian, 1962-66; Twickenham College of Technology, Twickenham, tutor and librarian, 1966-77; Richmond-upon-Thames College, Richmond, England, college librarian, 1977—. Library Association examiner in English literature from 1750 to present, 1964-70; tutor in creative writing, 1981—. Chairman of Twickenham United Christian Council, 1974-75, 1980-81. *Military service:* Royal Air Force, 1951-53. *Member:* International P.E.N., National Association of Teachers in Further and Higher Education, Royal Society of Arts (fellow), Poetry Society, Library Association (fellow), Richmond Poetry Group (founding member, 1961; chairman, 1970—), Greater London College Libraries Group (vice-chairman, 1976-79).

WRITINGS—Poems: *The Americas and Other Poems,* Outposts Publications, 1962; *A Sense of Wonder,* Scrip, 1963; *Saga,* Guild Press, 1963; *Paola and Francesca,* privately printed, 1965; *Thames Music: A Poem,* privately printed, 1968; *Coombe Hill: A Poem,* Ore Publications, 1969; *Holman,* Mitre Press, 1969; *The Argonauts and Other Poems,* Quarto Press, 1970; *Requiem for the Sixties: Verse Sequence,* privately printed, 1971; (editor) *Twickenham Eyot: An Anthology,* Quarto Press, 1973; (editor) *Versed XI,* Twickenham College of Technology, 1977; *Selected Poems, 1951-1973,* Outposts Publications, 1978; (editor) *Makers Dozen,* Richmond-upon-Thames College, 1980; *The Vision of Piers Librarian,* Woodruff Press, 1981.

Plays: *Conchubar: A Play in Verse* (one-act; first produced in Twickenham at Richmond Poetry Group, 1964), privately printed, 1963; *The Blind Man at the Gate of Lethe: A Lyric Play* (one-act; first produced in Twickenham at Richmond Poetry Group, 1965), privately printed, 1964; *The Frozen Forest: A Contemporary Play* (one-act; first produced in Twickenham at Richmond Poetry Group, 1966), privately printed, 1965; *The Eagle and the Swan* (three-act; first produced in Twickenham at Richmond Poetry Group, 1966), Mitre Press, 1966.

Nonfiction: *My Grandfather's Uncle: A Memoir of the Reverend Caleb Mark Longhurst (Baptist), 1840-1928,* privately printed, 1964; (editor) *Old Ascot: Diaries of George and G. A. Longhurst, 1833-1881,* privately printed, 1964; *The Ascot of Gilbert Longhurst: A Memoir,* privately printed, 1967; *The Art of Eric Ratcliffe: An Appreciation,* privately printed, 1970; *Twickenham College of Technology: A History, the First Thirty-Five Years, 1937-1972,* Twickenham College of Technology, 1974; (contributor) A. B. Cotterell and E. W. Haley, editors, *Tertiary: A Radical Approach to Post-Compulsory Education,* Stanley Thornes, 1980; *Libraries in English Further Education, 1926-76: A Bibliography With an Historical Introduction,* Library Association, in press.

Work represented in anthologies, including *New Poems, 1976-77; New Poems, 1977-78; New Poetry, Number 3,* 1977; and *New Poetry, Number 6,* 1980.

Editor of "Quarto Poets Series," Quarto Press, 1973-76, and "Richmond Poets," Richmond Poetry Group, 1975-77. Contributor to journals and newspapers, including *Enigma, Green River Review, Guardian, Manifold, Poetry Review,* and *Message.* Editor of *Expression,* 1965-67; past associate editor of *Envoi;* past advisory editor of *Ore.*

WORK IN PROGRESS: Two books of poems, *Winter Sketching* and *Gwen John Talking;* a novel, *Victoria Hammersmith.*

SIDELIGHTS: Pearce wrote: "I would summarize myself as poet, author, and librarian. Sometimes the three intermingle, sometimes they don't. My current interest is the novel, though poetry has been my abiding concern since the age of sixteen. I am grateful for my nonconformist background, initially at Acton as a Baptist. Among my literary heroes are Yeats, Eliot, Pound, Rilke, Ted Hughes, George Barker, and Arthur Waley, as well as Joyce, Woolf, Forster, Isherwood, Hesse, Proust, Cyril Connolly, and Mark Rutherford, but such lists change with the years.

"I see the poem as an emotionally or aesthetically charged, intellectually ordered, carefully made *thing,* with meaning and/or value integrated with and inherent in its shape, structure, and form, just like music or a landscaped garden, a conscientious piece of carpentry or a painting. It will have its roots in one's own time and place but may sometimes have historical or nostalgic, overt subject matter while keeping one's contemporary problems and anxieties at heart. I like it to have sound energy and a satisfying (ear-wise, heart-wise, and mind-wise) pattern of sounds. It should have 'bounce' and be on its own terms 'fun.' Lately, I have been exploring the poetry on the borders of prose and inherent in prose. This trend may take me over, may represent a parallel development on a wider canvas, or may be only a phase. One accepts the present, the past, and the need for developmental experiment."

AVOCATIONAL INTERESTS: Walking, chess, turn-of-the-century English and European painting.

*   *   *

PEARCE, Moira

PERSONAL: Born in New York; daughter of John C. and Mary (Travis) Brady; married John M. Pearce (died, 1960); married Silas M. R. Giddings (a lawyer), 1962. *Education:* Attended Smith College. *Religion:* Protestant. *Residence:* New York, N.Y. *Agent:* Marie Rodell-Frances Collin Literary Agency, 156 East 52nd St., Suite 605, New York, N.Y. 10022.

CAREER: Writer.

WRITINGS: *A Sunset Touch,* Scribner, 1960; *Upstairs at the Bull Run* (novel), Norton, 1971.

WORK IN PROGRESS: Novels.

*   *   *

PECK, Theodore P(arker)   1924-

PERSONAL: Born January 13, 1924, in Brooklyn, N.Y.; son of Charles Theodore (a broker) and Angeline Corning (Naugle) Peck; married Carol Nielsen (divorced November, 1976); children: Alison, Evan, Stephanie, Meryl. *Education:* Gettysburg College, B.A., 1950; Columbia University, M.S.L.S., 1952; St. Cloud State University, M.S., 1980. *Home address:* Route 5, Box 26, Princeton, Minn. 55371. *Office:* University of Minnesota, St. Paul Campus, St. Paul, Minn. 55108.

CAREER: Brooklyn Public Library, Brooklyn, N.Y., reference librarian, 1951-53; System Development Corp., Santa Monica, Calif., documents officer, 1952-59; General Dynamics Corp., San Diego, Calif., technical information specialist, 1959-64; Chattauqua-Chattaraugus Library System, Jamestown, N.Y., assistant director, 1964-67; associated with University of Minnesota, St. Paul Campus. Branch librarian at Enoch Pratt Free Library, Baltimore, Md., 1953-57; consultant to Addis Ababa University. *Member:* American Personnel and Guidance Association, American Library Association, Special Libraries Association, American Vocational Guidance Association, American Society for Engineering Education, Minnesota Library Association. *Awards, honors:* Fellow of Council on Library Sciences, 1972.

WRITINGS—Editor: *Occupational Safety and Health: A Guide to Information Sources,* Gale, 1974; *Chemical Industries Information Sources,* Gale, 1977; *Employee Counseling in Industry and Government: A Guide to Information Sources,* Gale, 1979; *The Troubled Family: A Guide to Information Sources,* McFarland Publications, 1981.

WORK IN PROGRESS: A parents' manual on career guidance; *Biochemical Sciences Resource Guide.*

SIDELIGHTS: Peck commented: "My motivation to compile an information guide comes from awareness of the need for such a tool. There is also a drive to do something creative. Working with information is a valuable learning experience that can be realized without formal educational programs. It is satisfying to know these materials are used and to hear from users."

*   *   *

PEGLER, (James) Westbrook   1894-1969

PERSONAL: Born August 2, 1894, in Minneapolis, Minn.; died June 24, 1969, in Tucson, Ariz.; son of Arthur James (a journalist) and Frances (Nicholson) Pegler; married Julia Harpman (a reporter), August 28, 1922 (died, 1955); married Pearl W. Doane, 1959 (divorced, 1961); married Maud Towart, 1962. *Education:* Attended school in Illinois. *Residence:* Tucson, Ariz.

CAREER: United Press (now United Press International), telephone reporter in Chicago, Ill., reporter and bureau manager in Texas, Des Moines, Iowa, and St. Louis, Mo., 1912-16, correspondent in London, England, 1916-17, war correspondent with American Expeditionary Force, 1917-18, sports editor in New York City, 1919-25; *Chicago Tribune,* Chicago, eastern sports correspondent, 1925-33; *New York World-Telegram and Sun,* New York City, syndicated columnist, 1933-44; King Features Syndicate, New York City, syndicated columnist, 1944-62; free-lance writer and journalist, Tucson, Ariz., 1962-69. *Military service:* U.S. Navy, 1918-19. *Member:* National Press Club (Washington, D.C.), Jonathan Club (Los Angeles). *Awards, honors:* Pulitzer Prize for reporting, 1941, for expose of labor union racketeering; LL.D. from Knox College, 1943; Gold Medal award from Nassau County Bar Association, 1944; American Legion Award; two National Headliners Club awards, both for achievement in journalism; and numerous other citations.

WRITINGS: *'T Aint Right,* Doubleday, 1936; *The Dissenting Opinions of Mister Westbrook Pegler,* Scribner, 1938; *George Spelvin, American, and Fireside Chats,* Scribner, 1942, reprinted, Arno, 1972. Contributor of articles to newspapers and journals, including *Jacksonville Chronicle* and *American Opinion.*

SIDELIGHTS: Pegler's controversial journalism career began at age sixteen when United Press hired him to telephone short news stories to small dailies. Later, Pegler gained national attention with his sports commentaries on the funny or unusual side of athletics. During this period he developed the outspoken, caustic style that he later used in "Fair Enough," his popular syndicated column on national affairs.

According to a *Washington Post* reporter, Pegler established his reputation as "one of the most controversial Americans of his time" by using his typewriter "like a meat ax" on a long list of well known personalities and institutions. His targets included Franklin and Eleanor Roosevelt, Huey Long, Upton Sinclair, Frank Sinatra, Drew Pearson, the Newspaper Guild, Communism, gambling, and income tax.

Pegler was especially virulent in his treatment of labor union officials, whom he regarded as either gangsters or Communists. His 1940 investigation into racqueteering involving George Scalise, head of the Building Service Employees International Union, resulted in a prison sentence for Scalise and a Pulitzer Prize for Pegler. Another of Pegler's targets, Hollywood union official William Bioff, was exposed by Pegler as an extortionist; Bioff also went to jail.

Even Pegler's employers were not immune from his assaults. In 1962 Pegler's contract with King Features was canceled when he wrote articles attacking the syndicate's owner, William Randolph Hearst, Jr., and other members of the Hearst organization. He then began working as a free-lance journalist and writing articles for the John Birch Society's publication *American Opinion*. A dispute with the society's founder, Robert Welch, over an article on Chief Justice Earl Warren prompted Pegler to quit, saying, "I had enough of that with Hearst. I don't have to take it any more."

Pegler was involved in two widely publicized law suits, both resulting from a 1949 column in which he attacked magazine writer Quentin Reynolds. Reynolds brought a libel suit against the journalist claiming that Pegler had falsely accused him of cowardice and of being a Communist sympathizer. Pegler lost the suit and Reynolds was awarded $175,000 in punative damages. The second suit came about when "A Case of Libel," a dramatization of the Reynolds litigation, was televised on "The Ed Sullivan Show." Pegler claimed that the program distorted the issues in the case and charged Sullivan and CBS-TV with invasion of privacy. The suit was still pending at the time of Pegler's death.

William F. Buckley, Jr., once proclaimed Pegler "the greatest satirist in American journalism . . . and sometimes the most amusing polemical journeyman in the country." Nevertheless, interest in Pegler's column began to decline significantly during the last of its thirty-year run because, said Richard Weiner in *Syndicated Columnists*, Pegler's continual "carping and criticism" began to be "boring and predictable."

BIOGRAPHICAL/CRITICAL SOURCES: Oliver Ramsay Pilat, *Pegler: Angry Man of the Press*, Greenwood Press, 1973; *Fair Enough: The Life of Westbrook Pegler*, Arlington House, 1975; Richard Weiner, *Syndicated Columnists*, 3rd edition, Richard Weiner, 1979.

OBITUARIES: Washington Post, June 25, 1969; *London Times*, June 25, 1969; *New York Times*, June 25, 1969; *Variety*, July 2, 1969.*

* * *

PELL, Olive Bigelow 1886-1980

OBITUARY NOTICE: Born c. 1886; died December 8, 1980, in Princeton, N.J. Painter and author. Pell was a painter of oil portraits and the stepmother of Senator Claiborne Pell of Rhode Island. During World Wars I and II she sold many of her paintings to raise money for the Red Cross. In postwar years her work was exhibited at numerous galleries, among them the Paris Salon, the Museum of the City of New York, and the Royal Academy in London. She was the author of the *Olive Pell Bible,* a condensed version of the King James

Bible. Obituaries and other sources: *New York Times,* December 10, 1980.

* * *

PELTON, Robert D(oane) 1935-

PERSONAL: Born October 1, 1935, in Cleveland, Ohio; son of Mark Doane (in sales) and Margaret (a librarian; maiden name, McKay) Pelton. *Education:* Yale University, B.A., 1957; St. Mary's University and Seminary, Baltimore, Md., S.T.B., 1961, S.T.L., 1963; attended McGill University, 1965-67; University of Chicago, M.A., 1970, Ph.D., 1974. *Home:* Madonna House, Combermere, Ontario, Canada K0J 1L0.

CAREER: Ordained Roman Catholic priest, 1963. Writer. Visiting lecturer at University of Chicago, 1976. Managing editor of *History of Religions Journal,* 1976.

WRITINGS: The Trickster in West Africa, University of California Press, 1980. Contributor to *Restoration.*

WORK IN PROGRESS: A book of his articles on spiritual and liturgical subjects.

SIDELIGHTS: Pelton wrote: "I am a member of a small community of lay men and women and priests. Our purpose is to create a community of Gospel faith and love, thus to serve the poor by sharing with them the life that we have received. Since 1975, I have been spending three days a week in *ponstinia* (a Russian word for 'desert'), where I pray, fast, garden, and write, trying simply to live in silence before God."

* * *

PENDLE, George 1906-1977

OBITUARY NOTICE—See index for *CA* sketch: Born February 20, 1906, in London, England; died July 13, 1977. Diplomat, businessman, and author. Pendle served as a representative in Paraguay for the British Council before becoming managing director of Pendle & Rivett Ltd., a firm of wool merchants. He wrote several books on Paraguay and other South American countries, including *Much Sky: Impressions of South America, Paraguay: A Riverside Nation, Argentina,* and *The Land and People of Chile.* Pendle also served as a regular contributor to the British Broadcasting Corp. (BBC) and *Encyclopaedia Britannica.* (Date of death provided by wife, Olwen Pendle.)

* * *

PENNINGROTH, Paul W(illiam) 1901-1974

OBITUARY NOTICE—See index for *CA* sketch: Born May 27, 1901, in Tipton, Iowa; died July 13, 1974, in Atlanta, Ga. Educator, administrator, psychologist, and author. Penningroth taught psychology at the American University of Beirut and St. Petersburg Junior College before becoming director of the Child Guidance Clinic in Florida. He later served as assistant director of training and research in mental health at the Southern Regional Education Board in Atlanta, Ga. His work includes the book *Programs for Emotionally Disturbed Children.* (Date of death provided by Kathy Penningroth.)

* * *

PEPIN, Jacques Georges 1935-

PERSONAL: Born December 18, 1935, in Bourg-en-Bresse, France; came to the United States in 1959, naturalized citizen, 1965; son of John Victor and Jeanne V. (Bourdeille)

Pepin; married Gloria Evelyn Augier (an administrative assistant), September 18, 1966; children: Claudine. *Education:* Columbia University, B.A., 1970, M.A., 1972. *Politics:* Democrat. *Religion:* Roman Catholic. *Home and office:* 214 Durham Rd., Madison, Conn. 06443.

CAREER: Personal chef to Felix Gaillard, Pierre Pfimlin, and Charles De Gaulle, 1956-58; Le Pavillon, New York City, chef, 1959-60; director of research and development for Howard Johnson Co., 1960-69; La Potagerie, New York City, co-owner and developer, 1970-74; World Trade Center, New York City, consultant to food operation, 1975-78; free-lance writer, chef, cooking teacher, and restaurant consultant, 1980—. Guest on numerous television programs, including "Dinah Shore Show," "Mike Douglas Show," "Tomorrow Show," "What's My Line?," and "To Tell the Truth." *Military service:* French Navy, 1956-58. *Member:* Vatel Club. *Awards, honors:* Tastemaker Award from R. T. French Co., 1980, for *La Methode.*

WRITINGS: (With Helen McCully) *The Other Half of the Egg: Or One Hundred Eighty Ways to Use up Extra Yolks, or Whites,* Barrows, 1967; *A French Chef Cooks at Home,* Simon & Schuster, 1975; *La Technique,* New York Times Co., 1976; *La Methode,* New York Times Co., 1979. Contributor to magazines and newspapers, including *House Beautiful, Travel and Leisure, Pleasures of Cooking, New York Times, Cuisine,* and *Family Circle.*

WORK IN PROGRESS: A combined and revised edition of *La Technique* and *La Methode.*

SIDELIGHTS: Pepin wrote: "I want to write articles wherein, as in my books, I explain the intricacies of cooking techniques. I am interested in teaching, whatever the medium. I give approximately thirty weeks of courses each year in the United States, as well as some in Canada and Europe." *Avocational interests:* Painting, sculpturing, carpentry.

BIOGRAPHICAL/CRITICAL SOURCES: New York Times Book Review, December 7, 1975, March 13, 1977.

*   *   *

PEPPER, Stephen Coburn   1891-1972

OBITUARY NOTICE—See index for *CA* sketch: Born April 29, 1891, in Newark, N.J.; died May 1, 1972, in Berkeley, Calif. Educator, aesthetician, philosopher, and author. Pepper taught aesthetics and the philosophy of art at the University of California, Berkeley, for nearly forty years. He wrote a number of books in his field, including *Aesthetic Quality, The Basis of Criticism in the Arts, The Sources of Value,* and *Concept and Quality.* Obituaries and other sources: Andrew J. Reck, *New American Philosophers,* Louisiana State University Press, 1968; *New York Times,* May 6, 1972; *Who Was Who in America,* 5th edition, Marquis, 1973.

*   *   *

PERELMAN, Chaim   1912-

PERSONAL: Born May 20, 1912, in Warsaw, Poland; son of Abraham and Lea (Garbownik) Perelman; married Felicie Liwer, January 13, 1935; children: Noemi Mattis. *Education:* Free University of Brussels, Dr. en droit, 1934, D.Phil., 1938. *Home:* 32 rue de la Pecherie, Brussels, Belgium.

CAREER: Free University of Brussels, Brussels, Belgium, professor of logic and metaphysics and dean of faculty of philosophy and letters, 1939-78; writer, 1978—. Past secretary-general of Federation Internationale Societes Philosophie; member of board of governors of Hebrew University;

past president of Menorah Centre des Jeunes. *Member:* International Institute of Philosophy (past president), International Institute of Political Philosophy (past president), Societe Belge de Philosophie (past president). *Awards, honors:* Honorary degrees from the universities of Florence, Jerusalem, and Montreal; officer of Order of Leopold, 1955, and Order of Merit (Italy), 1965; great officer of Order of the Crown, 1978.

WRITINGS—In English translation: *The Idea of Justice and the Problem of Argument,* translation by John Petrie, Humanities, 1963; *An Historical Introduction to Philosophical Thinking,* translated by Kenneth A. Brown, Random House, 1965; *Justice,* Random House, 1967; (with Lucie Olbrechts-Tyteca) *Traite de argumentation: La Nouvelle rhetorique,* 2nd edition, Editions de l'Institut de Sociologie de l'Universite Libre de Bruxelles, 1970, translation by John Wilkinson and Purcell Weaver published as *The New Rhetoric: A Treatise on Argumentation,* University of Notre Dame Press, 1969; *The Reminiscences of Chaim Perelman,* Microfilming Corp., 1975; *The New Rhetoric and the Humanities: Essays on Rhetoric and its Applications,* Reidel, 1979; *Justice, Law, and Argument,* Reidel, 1980.

In French: *De la justice,* Office de Publicite, 1945; (with Olbrechts-Tyteca) *Rhetorique et philosophie pour une theorie de l'argumentation en philosophie,* Presses Universitaires de France, 1952; *Cours de logique,* 5th edition, Volume I: *Introduction historique: Antiquite,* Volume II: *Introduction historique: Moyen age et temps modernes,* Volume III: *Logique formelle et theorie de l'argumentation,* Presses Universitaires de Bruxelles, 1961; *Justice et raison,* Presses Universitaires de Bruxelles, 1963, 2nd edition, 1972; *Raisonnement et demarches de l'historien,* Edition de l'Institut de Sociologie de l'Universite Libre de Bruxelles, 1963; (editor) *Les Antinomies en droit,* E. Bruylant, 1964.

Philosophie moral, two volumes, Presses Universitaires de Bruxelles, 1967; *Le Probleme des lacunes en droit,* E. Bruylant, 1968; *Logique et argumentation,* [Brussels], 1968, 3rd edition, Presses Universitaires de Bruxelles, 1974; *Elements d'une theorie de l'argumentation,* Presses Universitaires de Bruxelles, 1968; *Droit, morale et philosophie,* Librairie Generale de Droit et de Jurisprudence, 1968, 2nd revised and enlarged edition, 1976; (editor) *Les Categories en histoire,* Editions de l'Institut de Sociologie de l'Universite Libre de Bruxelles, 1969; *Logique et morale,* Presses Universitaires de Bruxelles, 1969; *Le Champ de l'argumentation,* Presses Universitaires de Bruxelles, 1970; *La Regle de droit,* E. Bruylant, 1971; *Logique juridique: Nouvelle Rhetorique,* Dalloz, 1976, 2nd edition, 1979; *L'Empire rhetorique: Rhetorique et argumentation,* J. Vrin, 1977.

*   *   *

PERKINS, (Richard) Marlin   1905-

PERSONAL: Born March 28, 1905, in Carthage, Mo.; son of Joseph Dudley (a judge) and Mynta Mae (Miller) Perkins; married Elise More, September 12, 1933 (divorced October, 1953); married Carol M. Cotsworth, August 13, 1960; children: (first marriage) Suzanne. *Education:* Attended University of Missouri, 1924-26. *Address:* 520 North Michigan Ave., Chicago, Ill. 60611.

CAREER: St. Louis Zoo, St. Louis, Mo., workman, 1926, curator of reptiles, 1926-38; Buffalo Zoo, Buffalo, N.Y., curator, 1938-44; Lincoln Park Zoo, Chicago, Ill., director, 1945-62; St. Louis Zoo, director, 1962-70, director emeritus, 1970—. Originator and host of television programs "Zooparade," 1949-57, and "Mutual of Omaha's Wild Kingdom," with Don Meier, 1962—. Member of Sir Edmund Hillary's Expedition on Yeti Investigation in the Himalayas, 1960. *Member:* International Union of Directors of Zoological Gardens, American Society of Ichthyologists and Herpetologists, American Association of Zoological Parks and Aquariums, World Wildlife Fund, East African Wildlife Society, Adventurers Club (Chicago), Explorers Club (New York City). *Awards, honors:* Peabody Award, 1950, Look Award, and Sylvania Award, all for "Zooparade"; four Emmy Awards from National Academy of Television Arts and Sciences, all for "Mutual of Omaha's Wild Kingdom"; honorary doctorate from University of Missouri, 1971, Rockhurst College, and Northland College.

WRITINGS: (And photographer) *Animal Faces*, Foster & Stewart, 1944; (with Peggy Tibma) *One Magic Night: A Story From the Zoo*, Regnery, 1952; *Zoo Parade*, Rand McNally, 1954; (with wife, Carol M. Perkins) *"I Saw You From Afar": A Visit to the Bushmen of the Kalahari Desert*, Atheneum, 1965; (author of introduction) Richard Cromer, *The Miracle of Flight*, Doubleday, 1968; (author of introduction) Allan W. Eckert, *Bayou Backwaters*, Doubleday, 1968; (author of introduction) Eckert, *In Search of a Whale*, Doubleday, 1970; (author of introduction) Robert Martin, *Yesterday's People*, Doubleday, 1970; (author of introduction) Lewis Wayne Walker, *Survival Under the Sun*, Doubleday, 1971. Contributor to magazines, including *Copeia* and *Parks and Recreation*.

SIDELIGHTS: Perkins began his zoological career at the age of twenty-one. He was hired as a workman at the St. Louis Zoo, but within two weeks became the curator in charge of reptiles. During his tenure at the zoo, the young man expanded the snake collection by going on numerous hunting expeditions to Illinois and the southern states. Perkins then moved to the Buffalo Zoo, where he organized the material for his first book, *Animal Faces*. In this publication Perkins studied and compared the various facial expressions of animals. A *New York Times* critic observed: "The photographs are beautifully done, and they go far toward proving the author's contention that the faces of animals are just as revealing as are those of human beings."

In 1962 Perkins and producer Don Meier developed the television series "Mutual of Omaha's Wild Kingdom." Acclaimed for its emphasis on animal conservation, the show has been honored by almost every wildlife organization in the United States. In an article for *Variety*, a reviewer noted that "superb photography and editing and the actual physical participation of the narrators keep the show at high tempo."

AVOCATIONAL INTERESTS: Photography, archeology, scuba diving, music.

BIOGRAPHICAL/CRITICAL SOURCES: Weekly Book Review, March 19, 1944; *New York Times*, April 16, 1944; *New York Times Book Review*, May 9, 1965; *Variety*, January 15, 1969.

*   *   *

PERRY, Eleanor 1915(?)-1981
(Oliver Weld Bayer)

OBITUARY NOTICE: Born c. 1915 in Cleveland, Ohio; died of cancer, March 14, 1981, in New York, N.Y. Screenwriter. Perry was an accomplished screenwriter whose first screenplay, "David and Lisa," won an Academy Award in 1963. Her other screen credits included "Diary of a Mad Housewife," "The Swimmer," "Trilogy," "Last Summer," and "The Man Who Loved Cat Dancing." In addition to screen-

plays, Perry wrote two Emmy Award-winning television films, "Christmas Memory" and "House Without a Christmas Tree," and a full-length Broadway play, "Third Best Sport." Perry was a staunch supporter of the women's movement and strongly criticized Hollywood's portrayal of women as victims and sex objects. "It seems women are always getting killed or raped," she charged, "and those are men's fantasies we're seeing, right?" Perry's first novel, *Blue Pages*, published in 1979, described a female screenwriter who is exploited by her filmmaker husband. With her first husband, Leo Bayer, she also wrote a series of thrillers under the pseudonym Oliver Weld Bayer. Obituaries and other sources: *Contemporary Dramatists*, 2nd edition, St. Martin's, 1977; *International Motion Picture Almanac*, Quigley, 1980; *Who's Who in America*, 41st edition, Marquis, 1980; *New York Times*, March 17, 1981; *Washington Post*, March 18, 1981; *Chicago Tribune*, March 18, 1981; *Time*, March 30, 1981; *Newsweek*, March 30, 1981.

*   *   *

PERRY, George 1935-

PERSONAL: Born January 7, 1935, in London, England; son of George Cox (a civil servant) and Irene (Sadler) Perry; married Susanne Puddefoot, March 25, 1959 (divorced, 1976); married Frances Nicola Murray-Scott (a magazine executive), July 1, 1976; children: Matthew Richard Scott. *Education:* Trinity College, Cambridge, B.A., 1957, M.A., 1961. *Home:* 4 Swan Pl., Barnes, London SW13 9LT, England. *Agent:* Deborah Rogers Ltd., 5 Mortimer St., London W1N 7RH, England. *Office:* Sunday Times, 200 Gray's Inn Rd., London WC1X 8EZ, England.

CAREER: Sphere, London, England, member of editorial staff, 1957-58; J. Walter Thompson Co., London, England, advertising copywriter, 1958-62; *Sunday Times*, London, projects editor, 1965-70, assistant editor, 1970-77, senior editor of *Sunday Times Magazine*, 1977—. Managing editor of *Crossbow*, 1966-70. Director of Cinema City, an exhibition and film festival, 1970. Organizer of exhibition at National Portrait Gallery, 1979. Member of advisory committee of Minnesota Symposium of Visual Communication, 1974-77. *Member:* British Film Institute, American Film Institute, Cambridge Society (external examiner). *Awards, honors:* B.A. from Harrow College of Higher Education, 1980.

WRITINGS: The Films of Alfred Hitchcock, Dutton, 1965; (with Terence Kelly and Graham Norton) *A Competitive Cinema*, Institute of Economic Affairs, 1966; (with Alan Aldridge) *The Penguin Book of Comics*, Penguin, 1967, 3rd edition, 1975; *The Great British Picture Show*, Hill & Wang, 1974, revised edition, 1975; *The Moviemakers: Hitchcock*, Doubleday, 1975; *Movies From the Mansion*, Elm Tree, 1976; *Forever Ealing*, Pavillion, 1981.

Editor: *The Book of the Great Western*, Times Books, 1970; *King Steam*, Times Books, 1971; *Wheels of London*, Times Books, 1972; (with Nicholas Mason) *The Victorians: A World Built to Last*, Viking, 1974 (published in England as *Rule Britannia: The Victorian World*, Times Books, 1974); *The Great British*, New York Graphic Society, 1979.

Contributor to *One Thousand Makers of the Twentieth Century*, David & Charles, 1971, *Eureka*, Thames & Hudson, 1973, and *John Lennon: The Life and Legend*, Times Newspapers, 1980. Writer for British Broadcasting Corp. (BBC) radio and television programs. Contributor to periodicals, including *Radio Times* and *Los Angeles Times*.

WORK IN PROGRESS: Editing a book on chief influences on the twentieth century, publication by Weidenfeld & Nicolson expected in 1981.

SIDELIGHTS: Perry told *CA:* "I seem to have a preoccupation with things that move, whether they be large railway locomotives, glossy automobiles, or motion pictures, and that is coupled with a keen awareness of the visual popular arts, which include photography, graphic design, and even comic strips. The book I care most about is *The Penguin Book of Comics* because before it was published nobody in the United Kingdom took comics seriously. Nowadays they are a popular subject for university theses. Obviously I want to write about the things that interest me; there is therefore only one criterion of success—can I interest other people? Can I get them to use their eyes and look at the things that have given me pleasure? I like the movies of Alfred Hitchcock, about which I have written two books, and the movies of the British film industry, which for all its faults still survives, struggling on, and badly in need of a chronicler. My new book is about Ealing, the most individual of studios to be found anywhere in the world, alas no more, but it represented during its brief heyday the nearest thing in Britain to a totally indigenous style of filmmaking.

"I like the idea of books being collectable objects to be cherished over the years. It was with this thought in mind that I produced *The Book of the Great Western, King Steam,* and others, which were sumptuous productions and for their day wildly expensive. After the passage of a few years they don't seem to have been so extravagant after all, especially as they now change hands at far more than their original cost.

"Thanks to many years on the *Sunday Times,* where design and the importance of photography have long been recognized, I have had the training and experience as well as the opportunity to do many of the things I wanted to do. But that doesn't mean to say the well is dry. On the contrary, I'm still a raw beginner."

AVOCATIONAL INTERESTS: Travel (United States and Canada, Europe, the Soviet Union, Poland, the Middle East, Thailand, Singapore, Malaysia, Hong Kong, Australia, and New Zealand), photography, video, film.

*   *   *

PERSON, Bernard   1895(?)-1981

OBITUARY NOTICE: Born c. 1895 in the Netherlands; died March 9, 1981, in Albuquerque, N.M. Journalist. Person was a Dutch newspaper reporter who immigrated to the United States in 1939, the year before the Nazi invasion and occupation of his homeland. Throughout the war years he delivered daily shortwave broadcasts over Radio Netherlands and was later decorated by the Dutch Government for his work. After the war he represented Dutch newspapers at the United Nations. Person is perhaps best known, however, as the founder of *Facts on File.* The news digest, launched in 1940 and now widely used by journalists and librarians, was the first reference source of its kind in the Western Hemisphere to have a cumulative index. Obituaries and other sources: *New York Times,* March 11, 1981.

*   *   *

PERSONS, Stow Spaulding   1913-

PERSONAL: Born June 15, 1913, in Mount Carmel, Conn.; son of Frederick Torrell and Florence Isabel (Cummings) Persons; married Dorothy Mae Reuss, September 4, 1943; children: Catherine. *Education:* Yale University, B.A., 1936, Ph.D., 1940. *Home:* 1433 Oaklawn Ave., Iowa City, Iowa

52240. *Office:* Department of History, University of Iowa, Iowa City, Iowa 52242.

CAREER: Princeton University, Princeton, N.J., instructor, 1940-45, assistant professor of history, 1945-50; University of Iowa, Iowa City, professor of history, 1950—, research professor, 1956-57, Carver Distinguished Professor, 1978—, acting dean of Graduate College, 1960-61. Visiting professor at Salzburg Seminar, 1955, 1961, Stetson University, 1957, San Francisco State College (now San Francisco State University), 1959, University of Wyoming, 1960, and University of Colorado, 1964. *Member:* American Historical Association, Organization of American Historians (member of executive committee, 1960-63), American Studies Association. *Awards, honors:* Fund for the Advancement of Education fellowship, 1954-55; National Endowment for the Humanities senior fellowship, 1967-68.

WRITINGS: Free Religion: An American Faith, Yale University Press, 1947; (editor) *Evolutionary Thought in America,* Yale University Press, 1950; (editor with Donald Drew Egbert) *Socialism and American Life,* two volumes, Princeton University Press, 1952; *American Minds: A History of Ideas,* Holt, 1958, revised edition, Robert E. Krieger, 1975; (editor) *Social Darwinism: Selected Essays of William Graham Sumner,* Prentice-Hall, 1963; (editor) Laurence Gronlund, *The Cooperative Commonwealth* (reprint of *The Cooperative Commonwealth in Its Outlines: An Exposition of Modern Socialism*), Belknap Press, 1965; *The Decline of American Gentility,* Columbia University Press, 1973. Member of editorial board of *Mississippi Valley Historical Review,* 1954-57, and *American Quarterly,* 1958-61.

*   *   *

PETACCO, Arrigo   1929-

PERSONAL: Born August 8, 1929, in La Spezia, Italy; married Lucetta De Martino, May 6, 1957; children: Monica, Carlotta. *Home:* via Bradano 38, Rome 00199, Italy. *Office:* RAI-TV, via Teulada 66, Rome 00100, Italy.

CAREER: Writer. Works for RAI-TV, Rome, Italy.

*WRITINGS—*In English: *Joe Petrosino,* Mondadori, 1972, translation by Charles Lam Markmann, Macmillan, 1974.

Other writings: *L'anarchico che venne dall'America,* Mondadori, 1969; (with Sergio Zavoli) *Dal gran consiglio al gran sasso: Una storia da rifare,* Rizzoli, 2nd edition, 1973; *Il prefetto di ferro,* Mondadori, 1975; *Le battaglie navali del Mediterraneo nella seconda guerra mondiale,* Mondadori, 1976; *Il Cristo dell'Amiata: Storia di David Lazzaretti,* Mondadori, 1978; *Reservato per il Duce: I segreti del regime conservati nell'archivio personale di Mussolini,* Mondadori, 1979.

*   *   *

PETERS, Geoffrey
See PALMER, Madelyn

*   *   *

PETERSON, Houston   1897-1981

OBITUARY NOTICE: Born December 11, 1897, in Fresno, Calif.; died of a heart attack, May 19, 1981, in Dennis, Mass. Educator and author. Peterson was a professor of philosophy at Rutgers University, but he was best known for conducting a series of free lectures at Cooper Union between 1938 and 1946. Among those who participated in the lecture program were Eleanor Roosevelt, Thomas Mann, and Margaret Mead.

Peterson was the author of thirteen books, including scholarly studies of Havelock Ellis and Thomas Huxley. Obituaries and other sources: *Twentieth Century Authors: A Biographical Dictionary of Modern Literature*, H. W. Wilson, 1942, 1st supplement, 1955; *The Reader's Encyclopedia of American Literature*, Crowell, 1962; *New York Times*, May 21, 1981.

* * *

PETERSON, Jeanne Whitehouse
See WHITEHOUSE, Jeanne

* * *

PETERSON, M(ildred) Jeanne   1937-

PERSONAL: Born November 26, 1937, in Hibbing, Minn.; daughter of Clifford Woodrow and Mildred Amelia Peterson; marriage ended, 1963. *Education:* University of California, Berkeley, A.B., 1966, Ph.D., 1972. *Home:* 3334 Eden Dr., Bloomington, Ind. 47401. *Office:* Department of History, Indiana University, Bloomington, Ind. 47405.

CAREER: Indiana University, Bloomington, assistant professor, 1972-78, associate professor of history, 1978—, director of undergraduate studies, 1979—. *Member:* American Historical Association, Society for the Social History of Medicine, Conference on British Studies, Midwest Victorian Studies Association. *Awards, honors:* Woodrow Wilson fellow, 1966-67; grant from National Endowment for the Humanities, 1973, fellow, 1975; American Council of Learned Societies grant, 1975.

WRITINGS: The Medical Profession in Mid-Victorian London, University of California Press, 1978; (editor with J. Williams and E. Smithburn) *Lizzie Borden: A Case Book of Family and Crime in the 1890's*, T.I.S. Publications, 1981. Contributor to *Encyclopedia of Bioethics*. Contributor to scholarly journals. Member of editorial board of *Victorian Studies*, 1972-75, member of advisory board, 1975—.

WORK IN PROGRESS: The Pagets: A Nineteenth-Century English Family in Science, Education, and the Church.

SIDELIGHTS: Jeanne Peterson commented: "My major interests are the social history of Victorian England, the history of the professions, and the history of Victorian women and the Victorian family."

* * *

PETERSON, Willard James   1938-

PERSONAL: Born August 1, 1938, in Oak Park, Ill.; son of Otto S. and Catherine (Esin) Peterson; married Toby Black (a historian), 1960. *Education:* University of Rochester, B.A., 1960; University of London, M.A., 1964; Harvard University, Ph.D., 1970. *Office:* Department of East Asian Studies, Princeton University, Jones Hall, Princeton, N.J. 08540.

CAREER: Dartmouth College, Hanover, N.H., assistant professor of history, 1970-71; Princeton University, Princeton, N.J., assistant professor, 1971-78, associate professor of East Asian studies, 1978—.

WRITINGS: (Contributor) W. T. de Bary, editor, *The Unfolding of Neo-Confucianism*, Columbia University Press, 1975; *Bitter Gourd: Fang I-chih and the Impetus for Intellectual Change*, Yale University Press, 1979. Contributor to philosophy and Asian studies journals.

BIOGRAPHICAL/CRITICAL SOURCES: Times Literary Supplement, December 7, 1979.

PFALTZ, Marilyn   1933-

PERSONAL: Born February 26, 1933, in Jamaica, N.Y.; daughter of George O. (in advertising) and Mildred (Wheaton) Muir; married Hugo M. Pfaltz (an attorney), September 29, 1956; children: Elizabeth, William, Robert. *Education:* Bryn Mawr College, B.A., 1954. *Home:* 118 Prospect St., Summit, N.J. 07901. *Office:* P & R Associates, 382 Springfield Ave., Summit, N.J. 07901.

CAREER: P & R Associates (public relations and publicity firm), Summit, N.J., partner. Member of advisory board of Summit Elizabeth Trust Co., board of directors of New Jersey Automobile Club and Public Service Electric and Gas of New Jersey, and board of trustees of local library. *Member:* Authors Guild, Authors League of America.

WRITINGS: (With Ann Reed) *Your Secret Servant*, Scribner, 1970; (with Reed) *Ladies Who Lunch*, Scribner, 1972; (with Reed) *Stop the World, We Want to Get On*, Scribner, 1974; (with Reed) *How to Move Your Family Successfully*, H. P. Books, 1979.

SIDELIGHTS: Marilyn Pfaltz commented: "My major interest is in the humanness of life: how to communicate insights and observations by word and by photograph."

* * *

PHELPS, Digger
See PHELPS, Richard

* * *

PHELPS, Richard
(Digger Phelps)

PERSONAL: Born in Beacon, N.Y.; married wife, Terry; children: Karen, Ricky, Jennifer. *Education:* Earned degree from Rider College, 1963. *Office:* Department of Physical Education, University of Notre Dame, Notre Dame, Ind. 46556.

CAREER: Teacher and basketball coach at junior high school in Hazleton, Pa.; University of Pennsylvania, Philadelphia, freshman basketball coach, 1966-70; associated with Fordham University, Bronx, N.Y., 1970-71; University of Notre Dame, Notre Dame, Ind., head basketball coach, 1971—. Committee member of Joseph Kennedy Foundation. *Awards, honors:* Named coach of the year by Metropolitan Basketball Writers Association, 1971 and 1974, and by United Press International (UPI), *Sporting News*, and *Basketball Weekly*, 1974.

WRITINGS: (Under name Digger Phelps, with Larry Keith) *A Coach's World*, Warner Books, 1975.

SIDELIGHTS: Phelps took over the unseasoned Notre Dame basketball team in 1971 and in only eight seasons has coached it to more than one hundred fifty victories, taken six teams to National Collegiate Athletic Association tournaments, and led five clubs to twenty-victory campaigns.

* * *

PHILBRICK, Helen L.   1910-

PERSONAL: Born February 23, 1910, in Fall River, Mass.; daughter of Franklin (a silversmith) and Ethel Louise Borden (Chase) Porter; married John Hatch Philbrick (an Episcopalian priest). *Education:* Wheaton College, Norton, Mass., B.A., 1932; Boston School of Occupational Therapy, O.T.Reg., 1936. *Religion:* Episcopalian. *Residence:* Duxbury, Mass. *Agent:* c/o Garden Way Publishing Co., Charlotte, Vt. 05445.

CAREER: Silversmith in Danvers, Mass., 1925-35; Massachusetts General Hospital, Boston, occupational therapist, 1935-39; writer.

WRITINGS: Gardening for Health and Nutrition, Rudolf Steiner, 1962; (with Richard B. Gregg) *Companion Plants and How to Use Them,* Devin-Adair, 1965, revised edition, 1966; (with husband, John Philbrick) *Gardening for Health: The Organic Way,* Multimedia Publishing, 1973; (with J. Philbrick) *The Bug Book: Harmless Insect Controls,* Garden Way Publishing, 1974; *Powder Point Priest Keeps Pigs,* privately printed, 1978. Also author of *Biography of Franklin Porter, Silversmith,* Essex Institute.

* * *

PHILIPS, Cyril Henry 1912-

PERSONAL: Born December 27, 1912, in Worcester, England; son of William H. and Mary E. Philips; married Dorcas Rose, 1939 (deceased); married Joan Rosemary Marshall, 1975; children: (first marriage) Margaret, one son (deceased). *Education:* University of Liverpool, M.A., 1938; University of London, Ph.D., 1938. *Office:* Department of History, London School of Oriental and African Studies, University of London, Malet St., London WC1E 7HP, England.

CAREER: University of London, London School of Oriental and African Studies, London, England, assistant lecturer, 1936-39, lecturer, 1939-45, senior lecturer, 1945-46, professor of Oriental history and head of department of history, 1946—, director of London School of Oriental and African Studies, 1957-76, Creighton Lecturer, 1972, vice-chancellor of university, 1972-76, member of court of university, 1970-77. Montague Burton Lecturer at University of Leeds, 1966. Member of Colonial Office community development mission in Africa, 1947, member of social development committee, 1947-55, and research council, 1955-57; member of Commonwealth Education Commission, 1961-70, postgraduate awards committee of Ministry of Education, 1962-64, and modern languages committee, 1964-67; chairman of Royal Commission on Criminal Procedure, 1978—. Member of governing council of Chinese University of Hong Kong, 1965—, and Inter-University Council for Higher Education Overseas, 1967—; chairman of University Grants Committee committee on Oriental, African, and Slavonic studies, 1965-70, and committee on Latin American studies, 1966-70; chairman of India committee of Inter-University Council and British Council, 1972—. *Military service:* British Army, Suffolk Infantry and Army Education Corps, 1940-46, commandant of Army School of Education, 1943.

AWARDS, HONORS: Bishop Chavasse Prize from University of Liverpool, 1934, for history; Gladstone Memorial fellowship from University of Liverpool, 1935, for historical research; Frewen Lord Prize from Royal Empire Society, 1938, for historical research; Alexander Prize from Royal Historical Society, 1938, for an essay; Sir Percy Sykes Memorial Medal from Royal Society for Asian Affairs, 1976, for Asian studies; D.Litt. from University of Warwick, 1967; LL.D. from Chinese University of Hong Kong, 1971; knighted, 1974; Tagore Medal from government of India, 1976, for services to India.

WRITINGS: The East India Company, 1784-1834, Manchester University Press, 1940, 2nd edition, 1961; *India,* Hutchinson, 1949; *The Correspondence of David Scott: Relating to Indian Affairs, 1787-1805,* two volumes, Royal His-

torical Society, 1951; (editor) *Handbook of Oriental History,* Royal Historical Society, 1951.

(Editor) *Historians of India, Pakistan, and Ceylon,* Oxford University Press, 1961; (editor with H. L. Singh and B. N. Pandey) *The Evolution of India and Pakistan,* Oxford University Press, 1962; (editor) *Politics and Society in India,* Praeger, 1962; *Fort William India House Correspondence,* Government of India, 1964; *Select Documents on the History of India and Pakistan,* Oxford University Press, 1965; *The School of Oriental and African Studies, University of London, 1917-1967: An Introduction,* London School of Oriental and African Studies, London, 1967; (editor with Mary Doreen Wainwright) *The Partition of India: Policies and Perspectives, 1935-1947,* M.I.T. Press, 1969; *Indian Society and the Beginnings of Modernisation, Circa 1830-1850,* London School of Oriental and African Studies, London, 1976; *The Correspondence of Lord William Cavendish Bentinck, Governor-General of India,* two volumes, Oxford University Press, 1977. Advisory editor of "Asia Historical Series," Asia Publishing House, 1963.

WORK IN PROGRESS: Strategies of Development: Bentinck and Dalhousie in India.

BIOGRAPHICAL/CRITICAL SOURCES: Times Literary Supplement, February 3, 1978.*

* * *

PHILLIPS, Mac
See PHILLIPS, Maurice J(ack)

* * *

PHILLIPS, Maurice J(ack) 1914-1976
(Mac Phillips)

OBITUARY NOTICE—See index for *CA* sketch: Born September 8, 1914, in Chelsea, Mass.; died July 29, 1976. Editor, businessman, and author. Phillips was an editor with several publishing firms, including A. A. Wyn Inc., Metcalf Associates, Ace Books, and H. S. Stuttman Co., Inc. He then worked in public relations with the Economic Development Administration of the Commonwealth of Puerto Rico. Phillips wrote two books, *Parents' Guide to College Planning* and *Lightning on Ice.* (Date of death provided by wife, Elisabeth Phillips.)

* * *

PHILLIPS, Patricia 1935-

PERSONAL: Born September 29, 1935, in Nottingham, England; daughter of William E. (an ophthalmic optician) and Evelyn B. (Purdy) Phillips; married Christopher W. Outhwaite (a university lecturer), April 21, 1977. *Education:* University of Nottingham, B.A. (with honors), 1956; University of California, Los Angeles, M.A., 1967; University of London Institute of Archaeology, London, Ph.D., 1970. *Residence:* Sheffield, England. *Agent:* Curtis Brown (Academic) Ltd., 1 Craven Hill, London W2 3EW, England. *Office:* Department of Prehistory and Archaeology, University of Sheffield, Sheffield, Yorkshire S10 2TN, England.

CAREER: Stanton Ironworks Co., Ilkeston, England, translator, 1957-59; Golden Eagle Refining Co., Inc., Los Angeles, Calif., executive secretary, 1959-66; University of California, Los Angeles, lecturer in archaeology and anthropology, 1966-67; University of Maryland, European Division, England, lecturer in archaeology and anthropology, 1969-70; University of Sheffield, Sheffield, England, research fellow, 1970-72, lecturer, 1972-79, senior lecturer in prehistory and archaeology, 1979—. *Member:* Society of Antiquaries (fellow), Prehistoric Society of Great Britain, Society for American Archaeology, Societe Prehistorique Francaise. *Awards, honors:* French Government scholarship, 1968-69; British Academy grants, 1977-78, 1979; Science Research Council grant, 1979.

WRITINGS: Early Farmers of West Mediterranean Europe, Hutchinson, 1975; *The Preshistory of Europe,* Allen Lane, 1980; *The Middle Neolithic of Southern France: Culture Process or Culture History,* British Archaeological Report, 1982. Contributor to anthropology and archaeology journals.

WORK IN PROGRESS: Research on central England, both Neolithic and Bronze Ages, especially regarding movement of raw materials and finished goods; research on Sardinia, "where I want to continue research into *nuraghic* (stone tower) building and settlement organization."

SIDELIGHTS: Patricia Phillips commented: "My languages are French, German, Italian, and Spanish. This linguistic background persuaded me to concentrate more on prehistory of Europe than, say, Africa or America. It has been invaluable in preparing *The Prehistory of Europe.*

"I feel that study of the past is an essential part of understanding man's present and future role in the world; it unravels the strands of influence from the natural and social environments of the past, and gives a warning that stable life-ways can change very rapidly if there is too much pressure on food procurement systems or social organizations. The fine art and architecture of the past, in contrast, symbolize the possible achievements of human societies, even with primitive tools."

*　*　*

PHILLIPS, Steven 1947-

PERSONAL: Born June 26, 1947, in New York, N.Y.; son of Raymond and Malvina Phillips; married Susan Hope Postow (an artist), May 20, 1973; children: Valerie Ann, Victoria Elizabeth. *Education:* Williams College, B.A., 1968; Columbia University, J.D., 1971. *Agent:* Wallace & Sheil Agency, Inc., 118 East 61st St., New York, N.Y. 10021. *Office:* Kreindler & Kreindler, 99 Park Ave., New York, N.Y. 10016.

CAREER: Kreindler & Kreindler (law firm), New York, N.Y., partner, 1975—. Assistant district attorney of Bronx County, N.Y.

WRITINGS: No Heroes No Villains, Doubleday, 1977; *Resisting Arrest,* Doubleday, 1980.

*　*　*

PICKEN, Mary Brooks 1886(?)-1981

OBITUARY NOTICE: Born c. 1886; died March 8, 1981, in Williamsport, Pa. Fashion expert and author. Pickens was an authority on dress, fabric, design, and sewing. She was the first woman to be named a trustee of the Fashion Institute of Technology. Her ninety-six books on sewing and decorating include *The Language of Fashion.* Obituaries and other sources: *New York Times,* March 11, 1981.

*　*　*

PICKERING, James Sayre 1897-1969

OBITUARY NOTICE—See index for *CA* sketch: Born October 28, 1897, in Newark, N.J.; died February 14, 1969, in Millburn, N.J. Salesman, astronomer, and author. Pickering worked in commercial and retail sales for more than twenty-five years before becoming an astronomer at the American

Museum-Hayden Planetarium. He wrote several books, including *The Stars Are Yours, Captives of the Sun,* and *Famous Astronomers.* Obituaries and other sources: *New York Times,* February 15, 1969; *Publishers Weekly,* March 10, 1969.

*　*　*

PIERCE, Arthur Dudley 1897-1967

OBITUARY NOTICE—See index for *CA* sketch: Born November 17, 1897, in Camden, N.J.; died December 18, 1967, in Bennington, Vt. Journalist, editor, critic, philatelist, and author. Pierce worked as an editor for the Courier-Post Newspapers, the *Philadelphia Record,* and the *Philadelphia Inquirer.* He was also music critic for *American Mercury* magazine. A collector of rare stamps, Pierce was American director of Robson, Lowe, Ltd., an English firm of stamp auctioneers. His books are historical works and include *Iron in the Pines: The Story of New Jersey's Ghost Towns and Bog Iron, Smugglers' Woods,* and *Family Empire in Jersey Iron.* Obituaries and other sources: *New York Times,* December 20, 1967.

*　*　*

PIERROT, George Francis 1898-1980

OBITUARY NOTICE—See index for *CA* sketch: Born January 11, 1898, in Chicago, Ill.; died February 16, 1980. Journalist, editor, television personality, lecturer, and author. Pierrot began his career as a reporter and editor of *Business* and *American Boy* magazines. He then started his successful "World Adventure Series" of travel lectures and television shows, which he hosted for more than forty-five years. The travel series was the oldest adventure show on television. Pierrot visited nearly eighty countries during his lifetime. His works include *Yea Sheriton* and *The Vagabond Trail.* Obituaries and other sources: *Authors in the News,* Volume II, Gale, 1976; *Detroit Free Press,* February 17, 1980.

*　*　*

PIEYRE de MANDIARGUES, Andre 1909-

PERSONAL: Born March 14, 1909, in Paris, France; son of David and Lucie (Berard) Pieyre de Mandiargues; married Bona Tibertelli (an artist), February 2, 1950; children: Sibylle. *Home and office:* 36 rue de Sevigne, 75003 Paris, France.

CAREER: Writer, 1943—.

WRITINGS—In English translation: *Le Lis de mer* (novel), Laffont, 1956, translation by Richard Howard published as *The Girl Beneath the Lion,* Grove, 1958; *Feu de braise* (short stories), Grasset, 1959, translation by April Fitzlyon published as *Blaze of Embers,* Calder & Boyars, 1971; *La Motocyclette* (novel), Gallimard, 1963, translation by Howard published as *The Motorcycle,* Grove, 1965, translation by Alexander Trocchi published as *The Girl on the Motorcycle,* Calder & Boyars, 1966; *Jacinthes* (poems), Olv, 1967, translation by Edward Lucie Smith published as *Hyacinths: Thirteen Poems,* 1967; *La Marge* (novel), Gallimard, 1967, translation by Howard published as *The Margin,* Grove, 1969; *Arcimboldo le merveilleux* (nonfiction), Laffont, 1977, translation by I. Mark Paris published as *Arcimboldo the Marvelous,* Abrams, 1978.

Other writings: *Le Musee noir* (short stories), Laffont, 1946; *Dans les annees sordides* (prose poems), Gallimard, 1948; *Les Incongruites monumentales* (poems), Laffont, 1948; *Soleil des loups* (short stories), Laffont, 1951, revised edition, 1966; *Les Masques de Leonor Fini* (essay), A. Bonne, 1951;

Marbre (novel), Laffont, 1953; *Le Cadran lunaire* (nonfiction), Laffont, 1958; *Le Belvedere* (nonfiction), Grasset, 1958.

L'Age de craie, suivi de Hedera (poems), Gallimard, 1961, reprinted with *Dans les annees sordides,* 1967; *La Maree* (short stories), Cercle du Livre Previeux, 1962; *Deuxieme Belvedere* (nonfiction), Grasset, 1962; *Le Point ou jen suis, suivi de Dalila exaltee et de La nuit l'amour* (poems), Gallimard, 1964; *Asyntax: Precede de les incongruites monumentales et suivi de Cartolines et Dedicaces* (poems and prose), Gallimard, 1964; *Porte devergondee* (short stories), Gallimard, 1965; (with Frederic Barzilay) *Les Corps illumines* (nonfiction), Mercure de France, 1965; *Larmes de generaux: Lithographies de Baj* (nonfiction), Herman Igell, 1965; *Critiquettes* (nonfiction), Editions Fata Morgana, 1967; *Le Marronnier,* Mercure de France, 1968; *Ruisseau des solitudes* (poems), Gallimard, 1968.

Bona, l'amour et la peinture (essay), Albert Skira, 1971; *Mascarets* (short stories), Gallimard, 1971; *Troiseme belvedere* (nonfiction), Gallimard, 1971; (author of text) *Ljuba* (nonfiction), Galerie de Seine, 1972; *Croiseur noir: Eauxfortes de Lam* (poem), Olv, 1972; *Isabella Morra: Piece en deux actes* (play), Gallimard, 1973; *Chagall* (nonfiction), Maeght, 1974; *Le Desordre de la memoire: Entretiens avec Francine Mallet* (nonfiction), Gallimard, 1975; *Sous la lame* (short stories), Gallimard, 1976; *Parapapillonneries: Lithographies de Meret Oppenheim* (nonfiction), Casse, 1976; *Le Tresor cruel de Hans Bellmer* (essay), Le Sphinx, 1979; *La Nuit seculaire* (play), Gallimard, 1979; *L'Ivre oeil* (poems), Gallimard, 1979; *L'Anglais decrit dans le chateau ferme* (novel), Gallimard, 1979. Also author of *Sugai* (nonfiction), 1960.

Translator: Tommaso Landolfi, *La Femme de Gogol et autres recits* (nonfiction), Gallimard, 1969; Octavio Paz, *La Fille de Rappacini,* Mercure de France, 1972; W. B. Yeats, *Le Vent parmi les roseaux,* Olv, 1972; Filippo de Pisis, *La Petite bassaride,* L'Herne, 1972; de Pisis, *Undici piu uno* (poems; title means "Eleven Plus One"), Carlo Bestetti, 1975; Yukio Mishima, *Madame de Sade,* Gallimard, 1976.

WORK IN PROGRESS: A play, *Arsene et Cleopatre,* publication expected in 1981.

SIDELIGHTS: Pieyre de Mandiargues told *CA:* "On my father's side I'm of Languedocien origin, and on my mother's side I'm Norman. Both families came out of a Calvinist tradition. My grandfather, Paul Berard, was a friend of Renoir and Monet and is linked to the history of impressionism.

"When I was about twenty I began to write poems for myself in secret in the hope of recapturing the fever I felt reading Agrippa d'Aubigne, the Elizabethans, the German romantics, Poe, Coleridge, Lautreamont, Mallarme, and the surrealists. These poems weren't published until, selected and corrected, they appeared in 1961 under the title *L'Age de craie.*

"I took refuge in Monte Carlo during the war, publishing my first book there in 1943. *Dans les annees sordides* is a collection of prose poems or strange little stories. Then, in 1945, I wrote a long poem of surrealist inspiration, *Hedera; ou, La Persistance de l'amour a travers une reverie.* Since then I have not ceased to write and publish. In 1947 I began to participate in the activities of Andre Breton's surrealist group. The three passions of my life are love, language, and liberty."

*   *   *

PIKE, Robert L.
   See FISH, Robert L.

PINKERTON, Kathrene Sutherland (Gedney)   1887-1967

OBITUARY NOTICE—See index for *CA* sketch: Born June 9, 1887, in Minneapolis, Minn.; died of cancer, September 6, 1967, in New York, N.Y. Secretary and author. Pinkerton worked for the Wisconsin Anti-Tuberculosis Association before becoming a writer. Many of her books are based on her life in the Canadian wilderness, where she lived with her husband for five years. Her books include *Wilderness Wife, The Silver Strain, Year of Enchantment,* and *Steer North.* Obituaries and other sources: *New York Times,* September 7, 1967; *Current Biography,* December, 1967; *Who Was Who in America,* 4th edition, Marquis, 1968.

*   *   *

PINTORO, John   1947-

PERSONAL: Born December 20, 1947, in Jacksonville, Fla.; son of John Peter (a typographer) and Wilma Inez (a nurse; maiden name, Parham) Pintoro; married Barbara Ann Harasimowicz (an executive legal secretary), August 9, 1970. *Education:* Suffolk Community College, A.A.S., 1970; State University of New York at Stony Brook, B.A., 1972. *Religion:* None. *Home and office:* 2589-A New Haven Dr., Atlanta, Ga. 30345. *Agent:* Hy Cohen Literary Agency Ltd., 111 West 57th St., New York, N.Y. 10019.

CAREER: Writer.

WRITINGS: The Summoning, Avon, 1979.

WORK IN PROGRESS: Three novels, tentatively entitled *Dark Soul, Resurrection,* and *The Killer.*

SIDELIGHTS: Pintoro wrote: "I view my writing the way most storytellers have in history, as an avenue by which the motivations of humankind can be explored. In the genre of the horror-thriller, love and hate and bravery and fear, the four elements of the human psyche, can be magnified and, in the extreme, can perhaps be more easily examined and understood."

*   *   *

PLA, Josep   1897-1981

OBITUARY NOTICE: Born in 1897 in Spain; died April 23, 1981, in Llofriu, Spain. Author. Pla was known as the grand old man of Catalan letters, an author whose writings describe and encompass more than fifty years of Catalan literature. He was one of Spain's most prolific writers, penning novels, short stories, biographies, travelogues, diaries, and essays, and his collected works number twenty-nine volumes. Obituaries and other sources: *Cassell's Encyclopaedia of World Literature,* revised edition, Morrow, 1973; *Chicago Tribune,* April 24, 1981.

*   *   *

PLESSET, Isabel R(osahoff)   1912-

PERSONAL: Born August 22, 1912, in N.Y.; daughter of Aaron J. (a psychiatrist) and Isabel (a teacher; maiden name, Ross) Rosanoff; married Milton S. Plesset (a physicist), March 28, 1934; children: Michael, Jean Plesset Grey, Marjorie Judith. *Education:* University of California, Los Angeles, B.A., 1933. *Politics:* Democrat. *Home:* 860 Orlando Rd., San Marino, Calif. 91108.

CAREER: Alhambra Neuropsychiatric Hospital, Alhambra, Calif., administrator, 1939-68; writer. *Member:* International P.E.N.

WRITINGS: Noguchi and His Patrons, Fairleigh Dickinson University Press, 1980.

SIDELIGHTS: Plesset told *CA:* "*Noguchi and His Patrons* is a psychological study of the Japanese microbiologist Hideyo Noguchi, a victim as well as a contributor to significant social developments of his time both in Japan and in the United States.

"Noguchi was born in 1876, when Japan was just emerging from nearly three centuries of feudal isolation from the rest of the world. His family were impoverished peasants, too burdened by their misfortunes to prevent his crawling into the household firepit in his infancy and suffering a burn that resulted in the permanent deformity of his left hand. In the still rigid class structure of Japan, he was denied the opportunity of an education because of his social, financial, and physical deficiencies, and he fled to America.

"With a combination of intense hard work, some good luck, natural ability, and charm, he attracted the attention of some influential scientists in America. His professional career (1904-28) was to be spent entirely as a member of the newly established Rockefeller Institute for Medical Research in New York, an institution that was to exert enormous influence on the policies that still govern the American medical profession today.

"In the highly competitive atmosphere of the beginnings of American medical research, some of Noguchi's work was prematurely published and highly publicized to gain prestige and draw public attention both to this new field and to the institution in which he worked. When some of these claims proved to be mistaken, he became a highly controversial figure, and his record of unique accomplishments was overwhelmed by the controversy over his errors.

"Now, some fifty years after his death, his work has been reevaluated and the substantial value of his lasting contributions has been recognized. Furthermore, the new material that has recently become available in the papers and memoirs of his contemporaries in various parts of the world has made it possible to make this study of Noguchi's colorful personality and to see his role in the events of his life and times."

*   *   *

POCOCK, Thomas Allcot Guy   1925-
(Tom Pocock)

PERSONAL: Born August 18, 1925, in London, England; son of Guy Noel (a writer) and Dorothy (Bowers) Pocock; married Penelope Casson, April 26, 1969; children: Laura Jane, Hannah Lucy. *Education:* Attended Cheltenham College, England, *Religion:* Church of England. *Home:* 22 Lawrence St., London S.W.3, England. *Office:* New Standard, London, England.

CAREER: Leader, London, England, war correspondent, 1945, feature writer, 1945-48; *Daily Mail,* London, naval and military correspondent and special writer, 1949-52; *Times,* London, naval correspondent, 1952-55; *Daily Express,* London, Middle East correspondent and feature writer, 1955-57; *Elizabethan,* London, co-editor, 1957-59; *Evening Standard,* London, defense and war correspondent, 1960-74, travel editor, 1974—. Member of board of governors of Foudroyant Trust, 1980—. *Military service:* Royal Navy, 1943-44. *Member:* Royal Geographical Society, Royal United Service In-

stitution, Chelsea Society (member of council, 1965-75), Garrick Club.

WRITINGS—Under name Tom Pocock: *Nelson and His World,* Thames & Hudson, 1968; *Chelsea Reach,* Hodder & Stoughton, 1970; *London Walks,* Thames & Hudson, 1973; *Fighting General,* Collins, 1973; *Remember Nelson,* Collins, 1977; *The Young Nelson in the Americas,* Collins, 1980; (editor) *Three British Revolutions,* Princeton University Press, 1981. Author of documentary film scripts for public service groups. Contributor to magazines.

WORK IN PROGRESS: The Summer of 1945, publication expected in 1982; a book on the Seven Years War, 1756-63.

SIDELIGHTS: Pocock commented: "I am a journalist rather than an academic historian, and have used my long experience as a newspaper correspondent (including covering wars in Algeria, Malaya, Arabia, Borneo, Cyprus, Aden, India, and Vietnam, as well as the end of World War II) to recreate the physical and emotional background to historical events. I have visited all the scenes of Lord Nelson's activities around the world, using the knowledge gained to give depth to material gathered through documentary research."

*   *   *

POCOCK, Tom
See POCOCK, Thomas Allcot Guy

*   *   *

POLAND, Dorothy (Elizabeth Hayward)   1937-
(Alison Farely, Jane Hammond)

PERSONAL: Born May 3, 1937, in Barry, Wales; daughter of Edwin Albert (a chief engineer in British Merchant Navy) and Doris Burrell (Nankervis) Hayward; married George Poland, September 20, 1969; children: Elizabeth Yvette Georgina. *Education:* Attended commercial high school in Barry, Wales. *Religion:* Church of England. *Home:* Horizons, 95 Dock View Rd., Barry, Glamorganshire CF6 6PA, Wales.

CAREER: General Post Office, Cardiff and Penarth, Wales, civil servant, 1954-67; full-time writer, 1967—. *Member:* Romantic Novelists Association.

WRITINGS—Novels under pseudonym Alison Farely; all published by R. Hale: *The Shadows of Evil,* 1963; *Plunder Island,* 1964; *High Treason,* 1966; *Throne of Wrath,* 1967; *Crown of Splendour,* 1968; *Devils Royal,* 1968; *The Lion and the Wolf,* 1969; *Last Roar of the Lion,* 1969; *Leopard From Anjou,* 1970; *King Wolf,* 1974; *Kingdom Under Tyranny,* 1975; *Last Howl of the Wolf,* 1975; *The Cardinal's Nieces,* 1976; *Tempestuous Countess,* 1976; *Archduchess Arrogance,* 1980.

Novels under pseudonym Jane Hammond; all published by R. Hale: *The Hell Raisers of Wycombe,* 1970; *Fire and the Sword,* 1971; *The Golden Courtesan,* 1975; *Shadow of the Headsman,* 1975; *The Doomtower,* 1975; *Witch of the White House,* 1976; *The Red Queen,* 1976; *Gunpowder Treason,* 1976; *The Silver Madonna,* 1977; *The Queen's Assassin,* 1977; *Woman of Vengeance,* 1978; *Conspirators Moonlight,* 1978; *The Admiral's Lady,* 1978.

WORK IN PROGRESS: The Black Knight, under pseudonym Jane Hammond, a novel set in medieval England; three historical novels, *Scheming Spanish Queen, Spain for Mariana,* and *Malevolent Queen Mother.*

SIDELIGHTS: "Whenever interviewers come to see a writer," Dorothy Poland told *CA,* "the first thing they seem to ask is, 'Why do you write at all?' Inevitably, a writer begins to ask himself the same question. I believe there have always been two reasons why I write. I certainly began because I suffered badly with asthma as a child and was debarred from a normal, active life. But *why* do I write? Surely I have used writing as an escape route from daily reality, much as other people sit down and read a book. It's a welcome trip to an oasis. But it must be confessed, as I have matured, I need it less and less for this purely selfish purpose. I have discovered that I like my own personality quite well as it is, and no longer have the need to lose myself in other characters in order to find a more interesting identity than the one I thought I owned.

"So what does this leave me with now? Obviously, it is honesty. I now feel that I can look my craft squarely in the face and acknowledge that I write because I *have* to do it. I still care very much about my 'people'—those who are fact and those who are fiction. I want these faceless ones of history to be understood better. They sound so very dull in history books, but they lived, loved, and were frightened just as we are. They are fascinating, these people of the past; just as we are, just as the people of the future will be.

"I want to make it very plain just what were the mental traumas of a Thomas Becket and an Anne Boleyn, the tortured and bewildered state of mind of a Philip of Spain, the paranoid excesses of a King John. It is a difficult task I give myself, but how worthwhile it becomes if someone out there suddenly, having read my efforts, sees these people as 'real.' How good it is if, even with the worst of them, we can end by at least gaining a measure of sympathy and empathy. Oh yes, and I want to make everyone love the sheer beauty and majestic sweep of history, just as I do!

"I have been writing for a long time now and have many books on my own shelves and upon the shelves of the world's libraries. It's still a good feeling to go and stand in front of them and think, 'I did all that.' It's not big-headed, just a lovely peaceful feeling of achievement that lingers.

"I don't work too well with other people. I'm at my best when I'm on my own with a subject. I prefer things done my way with my books because I honestly think I know best about them; but I do of course pay heed to criticism. Even so, I find that I am unable to make changes until I can really believe in them myself.

"I have brought back out into the light a rather extraordinary novel, which I wrote at some length and with some inefficiency at the age of seventeen. It is not my normal kind of work at all, being concerned with some very colorful South American bandits, gunfighters, and a heroine who is apparently a Latin American Scarlett O'Hara. I shall have some fun with this one, I think.

"I don't travel much. I lead a very ordinary life as a British housewife most of the time, caring for my husband and daughter. This gives me honest satisfaction, and I hate the way some people apologize for this way of life. I'm not a women's liberation addict, though I will not see my sex denigrated unjustly and say nothing; far from it. I read, but mostly for research. I am a firm believer in God and in dedicating my life to what He wants for me. I live from day to day and take the future as it comes; I never, never pine for the past. In general, I can describe myself as a productive and happy woman."

AVOCATIONAL INTERESTS: Driving, swimming, walking.

POLDERVAART, Arie 1909-1969

OBITUARY NOTICE—See index for *CA* sketch: Born October 21, 1909, in Vierpolders, Netherlands; died June 3, 1969; buried in Albuquerque, N.M. Librarian, lawyer, educator, and author. Poldervaart worked as the state librarian to the Supreme Court of New Mexico before he moved to the University of New Mexico to teach law and serve as a law librarian. Poldervaart wrote several books, including *Black-Robed Justice, New Mexico Justice of the Peace Manual,* and *New Mexico Probate System.* Obituaries and other sources: *Who Was Who in America,* 5th edition, Marquis, 1973.

* * *

POLHAMUS, Jean Burt 1928-

PERSONAL: Surname is pronounced Paul-*hay*-muss; born April 30, 1928, in Mississippi; daughter of John Owen (a farmer) and Ellen (Sanders) Burt; married John Polhamus (an engineer), May 10, 1952; children: Jean Ellen, John Burt. *Education:* University of Arizona, B.S., 1950. *Home:* 4056 Honeycutt St., San Diego, Calif. 92109.

CAREER: Writer. U.S. Naval Station, San Diego, Calif., technical librarian, 1950-52; copywriter for an advertising agency in Tucson, Ariz., 1952-53; U.S. Park Service, Dinosaur National Monument, Utah, summer fireguard, 1953; Hughes Aircraft, Tucson, technical librarian, 1953-55.

WRITINGS: Dinosaur Funny Bones (juvenile), Prentice-Hall, 1974; *Dinosaur Dos and Don'ts* (juvenile), Prentice-Hall, 1975. Contributor of articles to magazines, including *Good Housekeeping.*

WORK IN PROGRESS: Beulah Brontosaurus, a story-poem about a brontosaurus who tries to be skinny; *Dinosaur Holiday Book,* a collection of twelve poems, one for each month of the year; *A Houseful of Dinosaurs and Pten Pteranodons; Dinosaur Safety Bones.*

SIDELIGHTS: Polhamus told *CA:* "I write for fun, to inspire laughter and nudge people's funny bones, including my own. I don't write exclusively in rhyme, but I lean toward it because I enjoy the meter and precision, as well as the challenge of creating a story or an idea with comparatively few words. The idea of treating lightly such awesome, exciting creatures as the formidably named dinosaurs occurred to me when I was volunteer librarian in my children's elementary school. I discovered that dinosaurs fascinated almost every child and that humor delighted even more. Therefore, why not funny dinosaurs? I began creating some, and found it so much fun, I'm still at it!"

* * *

POLON, Linda Beth 1943-

PERSONAL: Born October 7, 1943, in Baltimore, Md.; daughter of Harold B. (a realtor) and Edith (a realtor) Wolff; married Martin Polon (an editor and educator), December 18, 1966. *Education:* University of California, Los Angeles, B.A., 1966, teaching credential, 1967. *Home:* 1515 Manning Ave., Apt. 3, Los Angeles, Calif. 90024.

CAREER: Elementary school teacher in Los Angeles, Calif., 1966—. *Member:* Society of Children's Book Writers.

WRITINGS—All for children: (With Wendy Pollitt) *Creative Teaching Games,* Denison, 1974; (with Pollitt) *Teaching Games for Fun,* Denison, 1976; (with Aileen Cantwell; self-illustrated) *Making Kids Click,* Goodyear Publishing, 1979; (with Cantwell; self-illustrated) *Write Up a Storm,* Goodyear

Publishing, 1979; (self-illustrated) *Using Words Correctly,* Frank Schaffer Publications, 1981; (self-illustrated) *Using Words Correctly,* Frank Schaffer Publications, 1981; *Paragraph Production,* Learning Works, 1981; *Stir Up a Story,* Learning Works, 1981; (with Cantwell; self-illustrated) *Real World of Math,* Goodyear Publishing, 1982; (with Cantwell; self-illustrated) *Real World of Money Math,* Goodyear Publishing, 1982; (with Cantwell; self-illustrated) *Fests, Frolics, and Fiestas,* Goodyear Publishing, 1982; (self-illustrated) *Cartoon/Writing Book,* Goodyear Publishing, 1982.

WORK IN PROGRESS: A sequel to *Making Kids Click,* with Barbara Sayble, publication by Goodyear Publishing expected in 1982; a creative nonfiction book for children.

SIDELIGHTS: Polon told *CA:* "Through teaching I became involved in the wonderful world of children and in writing things that they would enjoy. Many of my cartoons and ideas are drawn from the children I've worked with in my classrooms through the years."

*   *   *

POOLE, Herbert (Leslie)

PERSONAL: Born in Pittsboro, N.C.; son of Luther Herbert, Jr., and Sarah Thelma (Thrift) Poole; married Eva Joan Newlin, July 15, 1973; children: Luther, Wesley. *Education:* University of North Carolina, A.B. (with honors), 1962, M.S.L.S., 1964; Rutgers University, Ph.D., 1979. *Home address:* Route 3, Box 86A, Summerfield, N.C. 27358. *Office:* Library, Guilford College, Greensboro, N.C. 27410.

CAREER: North Carolina Memorial Hospital, Chapel Hill, scrub nurse trainee, 1961; University of North Carolina, Chapel Hill, descriptive cataloger at library, 1961-63, supervisor of Interlibrary Center, 1962-63, fellow at Wilson Library, 1963-64; University of Alabama, University, head of library's circulation department, 1964-66; Guilford College, Greensboro, N.C., library director, 1966—, special assistant to president for admissions and financial aid, 1976—. President of Consortium Shuttleservices, Inc., 1974—. Visiting lecturer at Emory University, 1967, 1971, and North Carolina Central University, 1972; library coordinator of Greensboro Regional Consortium, 1969-75; consultant to Redstone Scientific Information Center, Redstone Arsenal. *Military service:* U.S. Army, Russian interpreter, 1956-59.

MEMBER: American Association of University Professors (vice-president, 1968-69), American Library Association, Southeastern Library Association, North Carolina Friends Historical Society (vice-president, 1976—), North Carolina Library Association (past chairman of college and university section), Greensboro Library Club (vice-president, 1967-68; president, 1968-69), Sigma Xi, Alpha Phi Omega, Beta Phi Mu (president of Epsilon chapter, 1969-71), Delta Phi Alpha, Hancock Field Aero Society (president).

WRITINGS: (Editor with Nelsie P. Rothschild) *Monographic Materials Pertaining to Asia, South Asia, Southeast Asia, East Asia, Southwest Asia, Africa, and Latin America,* Library, Guilford College, 1973; (editor with Rothschild) *Man Will Never Fly: A Comprehensive Bibliography of Science Fiction Titles in the Guilford College Library,* Friends of Guilford College Library, 1975; (editor) Elizabeth H. Ragan, *The Lineage of the Amos Ragan Family,* privately printed, 1976; (editor) Henry G. Hood, Jr., *The Public Career of John Archdale, 1642-1717,* North Carolina Friends Historical Society, 1976; (editor and contributor) *Academic Libraries by the Year Two Thousand: Essays Honoring Jerrold Orne,* Bowker, 1977. Contributor of more than twenty articles to library journals and Quaker magazines. Editor of college and

university section of *North Carolina Libraries,* 1968-72, editor-in-chief, 1972-79; associate editor of *Southeastern Librarian,* 1973, 1976-79; founding co-editor of *Southern Friend: Journal of the North Carolina Friends Historical Society,* 1979—.

WORK IN PROGRESS: Theories of the Middle Range on Information Use: A New Research Paradigm in Information Science, tentative title; historical articles.

SIDELIGHTS: Poole has lived and traveled in Europe and the United Kingdom. He has taught bagpiping and operated a bagpipe school *Avocational interests:* Beekeeping, flying, antique aircraft.

*   *   *

POPE, Clifford Hillhouse   1899-1974

OBITUARY NOTICE—See index for *CA* sketch: Born April 11, 1899, in Washington, Ga.; died June 3, 1974. Herpetologist and author. Pope worked at the American Museum of Natural History as a member of the amphibian and reptile department and later as assistant curator of herpetology. He then served as the curator of amphibians and reptiles at the Field Museum of Natural History. He wrote several books in his field, including *The Reptiles of China, Turtles of the United States and Canada,* and *The Giant Snakes.* Obituaries and other sources: *Who Was Who in America,* 6th edition, Marquis, 1976.

*   *   *

PORADA, Edith   1912-

PERSONAL: Born August 22, 1912, in Vienna, Austria; came to the United States in 1938, naturalized citizen, 1943; daughter of Alfred and Catherine (Magnus) Porada. *Education:* University of Vienna, Ph.D., 1935. *Home:* 400 West 119th St., Butler Hall, Apt. 13-R, New York, N.Y. 10027. *Office:* Department of Art History and Archaeology, 815 Schermerhorn Hall, Columbia University, New York, N.Y. 10027.

CAREER: Affiliated with Metropolitan Museum of Art, New York City, 1945-46; Queens College (now of the City University of New York), Flushing, N.Y., assistant professor of art history, 1950-58; Columbia University, New York City, assistant professor, 1958-62, associate professor, 1962-64, professor, 1964-73, Arthur Lehman Professor of art history and archaeology, 1973—, chairman of seminar on archaeology of the eastern Mediterranean, eastern Europe, and the Near East, 1966—. Pierpont Morgan Library, New York City, honorary curator of seals and tablets, 1956—, fellow. Norton Lecturer of Archaeological Institute of America, 1967.

MEMBER: American Academy of Arts and Sciences (fellow), American Philosophical Society, Society for American Archaeology, American Oriental Society, Archaeological Institute of America, British Academy (corresponding fellow), Deutsche Orientgesellschaft, Austrian Academy of Sciences (corresponding member), New York Oriental Club. *Awards, honors:* American Philosophical Society fellowship, 1940-42, grants, 1946, 1956; fellow at American Schools of Oriental Research, 1943-44; Guggenheim fellowship, 1950-51; grants from Bollingen Foundation, 1947-49, 1954, 1958, and American Council of Learned Societies, 1960; Litt.D. from Smith College, 1967; distinguished achievement award from Archaeological Institute of America, 1978.

WRITINGS: Seal Impressions of Nuzi, American Schools of Oriental Research, 1947; *Mesopotamian Art in Cylinder Seals of the Pierpont Morgan Library,* Pierpont Morgan

Library, 1947; *Corpus of Ancient Near Eastern Seals in North American Collections*, Bollingen Foundation, 1948; (with R. H. Dyson and C. K. Wilkinson) *Alt-Iran: Die Kunst in vorislamischer Zeit*, Holle, 1962, translation published as *The Art of Ancient Iran: Pre-Islamic Cultures*, Crown, 1965, revised edition, Greystone, 1969 (published in England as *Ancient Iran: The Art of Pre-Islamic Times*, Methuen, 1965); (contributor) Mogens Weitemeyer, editor, *Some Aspects of the Hiring of Workers in the Sippar Region at the Time of Hammurabi*, Munksgaard, 1962.

(With Roman Ghirshman) *Tchoga Zanbil IV: La Glyptique* (title means "Glyptic Art"), P. Geuther, 1970; (contributor) Jack Leonard Benson, editor, *Bamboula at Kourion: The Necropolis and the Finds Excavated by J. F. Daniel*, University of Pennsylvania Press, 1972; (editor) *Ancient Mesopotamian Art and Selected Texts*, Pierpont Morgan Library, 1976; (editor) *Ancient Art in Seals: Essays by Pierre Amiet, Nimet Ozguc, and John Boardman*, Princeton University Press, 1980. Contributor to art history and archaeology journals.

WORK IN PROGRESS: An article, "The Cylinder Seals From Thebes in Boeotia."

BIOGRAPHICAL/CRITICAL SOURCES: Archaeology, March, 1978.

* * *

PORTER, Donald 1939-

PERSONAL: Born April 16, 1939, in New Orleans, La.; son of Don R. (in business) and Olga (in business; maiden name, Lyons) Porter. *Education:* University of the South, B.A. (cum laude), 1960; King's College, Cambridge, B.A., 1963, M.A., 1964. *Home and office:* 120 West 70th St., New York, N.Y. 10023.

CAREER: Pahlavi University, Shiraz, Iran, lecturer in English literature, 1965-66; *New Orleans States-Item*, New Orleans, La., reporter, 1967; Relco, Inc. (manufacturer's representative and distributor), Gallion, Ala., executive vice-president, 1967-75; Grand Street Holding Co., New York City, president, 1975-77; Manhattan Development Corp., New York City, founder and owner, 1977—. Director and founder of The Writing Workshop, New York City, 1977—. *Member:* Mystery Writers of America, Authors Guild.

WRITINGS: As If a Footnote, Assembling Press, 1974; (with Diane Taxson) *The EST Experience*, Universal Publishing and Distributing, 1976; *Inner Running*, Grosset, 1978; *Sight Unseen*, Warner Brooks, 1981; *The War Against the Apache*, Dell, 1981. Contributor of articles and reviews to magazines, including *Transatlantic Review*, *Beyond Baroque*, and *Forum*.

WORK IN PROGRESS: A novel for Warner Books; a novel about the Sioux and another about the Kiowa Indians, for Dell.

AVOCATIONAL INTERESTS: Chess, finance and business, running, swimming, bicycling, group and depth psychology, the psychology of creation, religions of the world, Iran, Persia, France, England, New York City, classic mysteries of the 1930's—particularly those by Cain and Chandler.

BIOGRAPHICAL/CRITICAL SOURCES: New York Times Book Review, December 24, 1978.

* * *

PORTER, J(ene) M(iles) 1937-

PERSONAL: Born August 21, 1937, in Wichita, Kan.; son of Gilbert and Vernice (Nash) Porter; married Susan Mar-

garet Speer; children: Edmund, Cliff, Tom, Julia, Jeannette. *Education:* Park College, B.A., 1959; University of Wyoming, M.A., 1960; Duke University, Ph.D., 1967. *Office:* Department of Economics and Political Science, University of Saskatchewan, Saskatoon, Saskatchewan, Canada S7N 0W0.

CAREER: Drury College, Springfield, Mo., assistant professor of American government and political philosophy, 1963-67; University of Saskatchewan, Saskatoon, assistant professor, 1967-70, associate professor, 1970-76, professor of economics and political science, 1976—, associate head of department, 1978-79. Visiting scholar at Tulane University, 1974-75. Program director of International Seminar for Philosophy and Political Theory, 1981. *Member:* Canadian Political Science Association (member of board of directors, 1980—), American Political Science Association, Conference for the Study of Political Thought, Phi Gamma Mu, Phi Kappa Phi. *Awards, honors:* Grants from National Humanities Faculty, 1974, Canada Council, 1976, Social Sciences and Humanities Research Council of Canada, 1980, Kemper Educational and Charitable Fund, 1981, and Earhart Foundation, 1981.

WRITINGS: (Editor) *United States Foreign Policy and South Vietnam*, Drury College, 1966; (editor) *Contemporary Developments in the Theory and Practice of Communism*, Drury College, 1967; (editor and author of introduction) *Martin Luther: Selected Political Writings*, Fortress, 1974; (contributor) William C. Harvard, Richard Bishirjian, and William Corrington, editors, *Gnosticism and Modernity*, Louisiana State University Press, in press. Contributor of articles and reviews to political science and history journals and *Queen's Quarterly*.

WORK IN PROGRESS: Research on the dimensions of the relationship between analytical philosophy and political science.

* * *

POST, Emily Price 1873-1960

PERSONAL: Born October 3, 1873, in Baltimore, Md.; died September 25, 1960; buried in St. Mary's in the Churchyard, Tuxedo Park, N.Y.; daughter of Bruce (an architect) and Josephine (Lee) Price; married Edwin Main Post (a banker), 1892 (divorced, c. 1901); children: Edwin Main, Jr., Bruce (died, 1927). *Education:* Educated in private schools. *Politics:* Republican. *Religion:* Episcopalian. *Address:* 39 East 79th St., New York, N.Y.

CAREER: Novelist, c. 1905-1925; writer of etiquette manuals, 1922-60. Commentator of radio program beginning in 1929; syndicated newspaper columnist, 1932-60. Founder of Emily Post Institute, 1946. *Member:* Colony Club, Tuxedo Club.

WRITINGS—Novels: The Flight of a Moth, Dodd, 1904; *Purple and Fine Linen*, D. Appleton, 1905; *Woven in Tapestry*, Moffat, Yard, 1908; *The Title Market*, Dodd, 1909; *The Eagle's Feather*, Dodd, 1910; *By Motor to the Golden Gate*, D. Appleton, 1916; *Parade: A Novel of New York Society*, Funk, 1925.

Etiquette manuals: *Etiquette in Society, in Business, in Politics and at Home*, Funk, 1922, 10th edition, 1964, published as *Etiquette: "The Blue Book of Social Usage,"* 1928, 11th edition, revised by Elizabeth L. Post, 1965, abridged edition published as *Emily Post's Pocket Book of Etiquette*, revised by E. L. Post, Pocket Books, 1967, published as *Etiquette*, revised by E. L. Post, Funk, 1969, published as

The New Emily Post's Etiquette, revised by E. L. Post, 1975; *How to Behave—Though a Debutante*, Doubleday, 1928; *The Letters We Write*, White & Wyckoff, 1935; *The Secret of Keeping Friends*, Rust Craft, 1938; *One Hundred and One Common Mistakes in Etiquette—And How to Avoid Them*, A. D. Steinbach & Sons, 1939; *Children are People, and Ideal Parents Are Comrades*, Funk, 1940, revised edition published as *Children Are People: How to Understand Your Children*, 1959.

Other: *Bridal Silver and Wedding Customs*, Towle Silversmiths, 1929; *The Personality of a House: The Blue Book of Home Design and Decoration*, Funk, 1930, revised edition, 1939, published as *The Personality of a House: The Blue Book of Home Charm*, 1948; *How to Give Buffet Suppers* (cookbook), Chase Brass & Copper, 1933; (with son, Edwin M. Post, Jr.) *The Emily Post Cookbook*, Funk, 1951. Also author of *Weddings*, Simon & Schuster. Daily columnist for Bell Syndicate newspapers, 1932-60. Contributor of articles to numerous publications.

SIDELIGHTS: The only child of Josephine Lee and renowned architect Bruce Price, Emily Post enjoyed wealth and social position as a child. Her affluent upbringing included a varied education: she was taught at home by a German governess, attended private schools, and traveled abroad.

In 1892, Post made a stunning debut into New York society. Her beauty and grace caused a flurry of excitement among male suitors, and it was rumored that four men were required to transport the many tokens of affection which the debutante received after an evening of dancing at society balls.

During her first season as a debutante, Post married society banker Edwin Main Post. Unfortunately, in the panic of 1901, her husband lost his fortune. Their subsequent divorce left Post to support herself and her two sons.

At the suggestion of her friends, Post turned to a career in writing. At first, she wrote fictional accounts of Americans living in European society. Later, in 1922, she began writing etiquette manuals at the prompting of publisher Richard Duffy. Originally, Post believed that she had no knowledge of etiquette, and she was opposed to etiquette books in general. Though Duffy attempted to convince the novelist that her books were overflowing with manners, she did not agree to write a book on manners until she read a contemporary etiquette manual and was appalled by its inaccuracies. "Mrs. Post," said Justin Kaplan of *Harper's*, "was determined to protect and perpetuate the decorums of her own upbringing."

With the publication of *Etiquette*, Post became the arbiter of American manners and social behavior. In its early edition, *Etiquette* advised its readers of behavior in "best society." For instance, a member of best society, instructed Post, does not pull his coat over the head of the individual seated ahead of him in the theatre. Also, one does not employ a maid who will deal plates around a dinner table "like a pack of cards."

The most recent edition of *Etiquette*, which was revised by Post's granddaughter-in-law, Elizabeth L. Post, concerns itself with ordinary society. Kaplan noticed that "the concept of the book . . . has shifted over the years from a guide to forms and etiquette to a general encyclopedia which now gives practical and for the most part sensible advice." Throughout Post's career, she believed that which fork an individual used was the least of his worries. Instead, she purported that the spirit of etiquette, which is derived from kindness, is the essence of good manners.

Newsweek critic Peter S. Prescott scoffed at the "practical counsel" given by Post in *Etiquette* and laughed at her warning "not to cut on my first wife's tombstone the words 'greatest love' for fear of offending her successor." He also complained that Emily Post was a "huckster of manners" who took advantage of the population's fear of using the wrong fork and thereby promulgated dullness throughout society. On the other hand, many reviewers agreed with the *Book List* critic who acclaimed *The New Emily Post's Etiquette* as "the incontestable first source" of the etiquette conscious.

BIOGRAPHICAL/CRITICAL SOURCES: New York Times, September 27, 1960; *Newsweek*, October 10, 1960, November 8, 1978; *Time*, October 10, 1960; *Harper's*, March, 1969; *Book List*, April 1, 1975.*

*   *   *

POST, Steve(n A.)   1944-

PERSONAL—Home: 155 West 71st St., New York, N.Y. 10023.

CAREER: WBAI-FM Radio Station, New York, N.Y., began as bookkeeper, 1965, became announcer, program host, producer, and general manager. Instructor at School of Visual Arts.

WRITINGS: Playing in the FM Band: A Personal Account of Free Radio, foreword by Julius Lester, illustrations by Ira Epstein, Viking, 1974.

BIOGRAPHICAL/CRITICAL SOURCES: Washington Post Book World, July 7, 1974; *New York Review of Books*, August 8, 1974.*

*   *   *

POSTAL, Bernard   1905-1981

OBITUARY NOTICE—See index for *CA* sketch: Born November 1, 1905, in New York, N.Y.; died of a heart attack, March 5, 1981, in Oceanside, Long Island, N.Y. Editor and author best known for his books on Jewish-American history. Postal began his career in the 1920's as a reporter in New York. He went on to become editor-in-chief of the *Jewish Daily Bulletin* as well as the editor of the *Jersey City Jewish Standard* and the *Jewish War Veteran*. At the time of his death, Postal was the associate editor of *Jewish Week*. His works include *Traveler's Guide to Jewish Landmarks of Europe*, *American Jewish Landmarks*, *Guess Who's Jewish in American History*, and *A Guide to Jewish Sites in Europe*. Obituaries and other sources: *New York Times*, March 7, 1981; *Publishers Weekly*, April 3, 1981.

*   *   *

POTTS, Eve   1929-

PERSONAL: Born August 27, 1929, in Hamden, Conn.; daughter of Italo and Eleanor (Tirone) Morra; married Robert Potts (a publisher), September 8, 1956; children: Mark, Matthew, Amy, Abby. *Education:* Attended New Haven College (now University of New Haven), 1948-51. *Residence:* Westport, Conn. *Office:* Avon Books, 959 Eighth Ave., New York, N.Y. 10021.

CAREER: Author of medical-oriented writings for various editorial and sales promotional departments, 1946-56; freelance medical writer, 1957—. Co-curator of Westport Art Collection; chairman of Historic District Commission; member of board of directors of Westport Historical Society. Guest on numerous radio and television programs.

WRITINGS: (With sister, Marion Morra) *Choices: Realistic Alternatives in Cancer Treatment,* Avon, 1980. Contributor to *Good Housekeeping.*

SIDELIGHTS: Choices, a guidebook for cancer patients and their families, explores different types of cancer, traditional cancer treatments such as chemotherapy and radiation, and experimental treatment such as immunotherapy and laetrile. Based on conversations Potts and Mora had with hundreds of cancer patients over a three-year period, *Choices* is intended to be a supplement to a doctor's care and a straight-forward reference on cancer.

Potts and Morra were inspired to write *Choices* when one of their friends, a lung-cancer patient, had a sore throat and feared her cancer was spreading. Not knowing that radiation treatments had been irritating her throat, the friend was afraid to talk with her doctor: she feared he would tell her that her cancer had spread. Realizing the widespread ignorance about cancer, Potts and Morra saw a need for a nontechnical, informative source to alleviate some of the fears that cancer patients have.

As well as answering general questions about cancer and its treatments, Potts and Morra stress that cancer is not always a death sentence. "It's true no miracle cures have been found," they wrote, "but advances in treatment have been made, and cancer no longer is considered an incurable disease. In fact, more people today are living with cancer than dying from it."

The authors also emphasize the importance of communication between cancer patients and their families, friends, and doctors. "So many cancer patients tell us how lonely they are, how their friends won't discuss the disease, how people are afraid to say the word 'cancer'," Potts and Morra revealed. "We think it's important for people to know how much the support of family and friends means to cancer patients." With reference to doctors, they urged, "ask, ask, ask, and ask again. Don't take anything for granted and don't be put off by medical jargon or a doctor who doesn't want to talk. Remember, you are a consumer and are entitled to answers to your questions."

Choices has been hailed by critics as a valuable aid to cancer victims, their families and friends, and anyone interested in the subject of cancer. In a *Chicago Sun-Times* column, Jory Graham called *Choices* "the best single source of a vast amount of information."

Potts told *CA:* "I'm a curious, plugging writer and was impelled to work on this book by the obvious need for it."

BIOGRAPHICAL/CRITICAL SOURCES: Chicago Sun-Times, November 10, 1980.

*   *   *

POTTS, Richard   1938-

PERSONAL: Born May 15, 1938; son of William and Marion Potts; married Alison McMorland (a singer); children: Anna, Kirsty, Katy. *Education:* University of Keele, B.Ed., 1972. *Home:* 3 Abbotsway, York, England. *Agent:* Sheila Watson, Bolt & Watson Ltd., 8-12 Old Queen St., Storey's Gate, London SW1H 9HP, England. *Office:* Great Ouseburn Primary School, York, England.

CAREER: Great Ouseburn Primary School, York, England, head teacher, 1977—.

WRITINGS—For children: *An Owl for His Birthday,* Lutterworth, 1966; *The Haunted Mine,* Lutterworth, 1968; *A*

Boy and His Bike, Dobson, 1976; *Tod's Owl,* Hodder & Stoughton, 1980.

SIDELIGHTS: Potts commented: "All my stories are motivated by childhood memories, elaborated and interwoven with observations from the present day."

The Haunted Mine was serialized on "Jackanory," on BBC-TV in 1970.

*   *   *

POWELL, Dorothy Baden
See BADEN-POWELL, Dorothy

*   *   *

POWELL, Larson Merrill   1932-

PERSONAL: Born March 8, 1932, in Pittsfield, Mass.; son of Harry LeRoy and Elsie Madeline (Larson) Powell; married Anne C. Millet, December 8, 1956; children: Larson Merrill, Anne Coleman, Miles Sloan. *Education:* Harvard University, A.B., 1954; attended Columbia University Law School, 1957-59. *Office:* Young Men's Christian Association of Greater New York, Westside Branch, 5 West 63rd St., New York, N.Y. 10023.

CAREER/WRITINGS: Boston Daily Globe, Boston, Mass., news editor and reporter, 1954 and 1956-57; Moody's Investors Service, New York City, security analyst, 1959-62, regional manager, 1964-67, vice-president, 1967-68; Anchor Corp., Elizabeth, N.J., president of institutional investment management division, 1968-70; Reserve Research Ltd., New York City, president, 1971—. Editor and publisher of *Powell Monetary Analyst,* 1971—, *The Powell Alert,* 1972—, *Powell Gold Industry Guide,* 1972—, and *Powell International Mining Analyst.* Member of Borough of Manhattan Community Planning Board Seven, 1966-69; chairman of men's committee of American Museum of Natural History, 1970-72; Young Men's Christian Association of Greater New York (YMCA), New York City, member of board of managers of Westside branch, 1970—, member-at-large of city-wide board, 1976—; member of board of directors of Episcopal Camp and Conference Center, 1978—. *Military service:* U.S. Army, 1954-56. *Member:* Financial Analysts Federation (fellow), New York Social Security Analysts, New York Newsletter Publishers Association, India House, Harvard Club (New York City), Cumberland (Portland, Me.).*

*   *   *

POWELL, Terry   1949-

PERSONAL: Born October 2, 1949, in Rutherford County, N.C.; son of George Hoyle and Irene Ruth (Conner) Powell; married Dolly Marie Wardell, June 5, 1971; children: John Mark, Stephen Floyd. *Education:* Wingate Junior College, A.A., 1969; Carson-Newman College, B.A., 1971; Wheaton College, Wheaton, Ill., M.A. (communications), 1973, M.A. (Christian education), 1975; further graduate study at Trinity Evangelical Divinity School, 1979—. *Home:* 306 North Court, Island Lake, Ill. 60042. *Office:* 2002 South Arlington Heights Rd., Arlington Heights, Ill. 60005.

CAREER: Radiant Tidings Evangelistic Association, Charlotte, N.C., Bible teacher, 1970-72; Southeastern Bible College, Birmingham, Ala., instructor in Christian education, 1975-76; presented classes on leadership training for Bible teachers in and around Indianapolis, Ind., 1977-79; Baptist General Conference, Evanston, Ill., writer and seminar leader, 1979—.

WRITINGS: Making Youth Programs Go, Victor Books, 1973; *Nobody's Perfect,* Victor Books, 1979; *You Want Me to Know What?,* Board of Christian Education of the Baptist General Conference, 1981. Author of church school curriculum material. Contributor to magazines, including *Reflections, Campus Life, Young Ambassador, Junior Pupil,* and *Family Life Today,* and newspapers. Editor of *Radiant Tidings,* 1970-73.

SIDELIGHTS: Powell commented: "My motivation, as an evangelical Christian, is to serve Jesus Christ through my gifts of writing and teaching. The messages I write must be prepared in my life and heart, not just in my mind."

* * *

POWELL, Violet Georgiana 1912-

PERSONAL: Surname is pronounced *Poe*-ell; born March 13, 1912, in London, England; daughter of Thomas (a soldier; Fifth Earl of Longford) and Mary Villiers (Countess of Longford); married Anthony Powell (a writer), December 1, 1934; children: Tristram, John. *Education:* Attended private girls' school in Bushey, England. *Politics:* Conservative. *Religion:* Church of England. *Home:* Chantry, near Frome, Somerset, England.

CAREER: Writer, 1935-39 and 1953—. Chairman of Whatley Parish Council, 1960—.

WRITINGS—All published by Heinemann: *Five Out of Six* (autobiography), 1960; *A Substantial Ghost: The Literary Adventures of Maude ffloulkes* (biography), 1967; *The Irish Cousins: The Books and Background of Somerville and Ross,* 1970; (editor) *A Compton-Burnett Compendium* (literary criticism), 1973; *Within the Family Circle* (autobiography), 1976; *Margaret, Countess of Jersey* (biography), 1978; *Flora Annie Steel: Novelist of India,* 1981. Contributor to magazines, including *Vogue* and *Harper's,* and newspapers.

WORK IN PROGRESS: A study of the life and work of British novelist Margaret Kennedy, publication by Heinemann expected in 1982.

SIDELIGHTS: Violet Powell commented: "Early study of painting has left me with the ability to illustrate my own travel diaries. I find this a relaxation and an aid to observation that is a help when writing. My book on Flora Annie Steel owes a great deal to two Indian tours. I am actively interested in the conservation of the countryside and of historical monuments. In this the habit of observation, gained by the practice of painting, has been a great help particularly in deciding what features of landscape or buildings are vital to a harmonious whole."

BIOGRAPHICAL/CRITICAL SOURCES: Times Literary Supplement, April 3, 1981.

* * *

POWERS, George
See INFIELD, Glenn (Berton)

* * *

PRATT, (Mildred) Claire 1921-

PERSONAL: Born March 18, 1921, in Toronto, Ontario, Canada; daughter of Edwin John (a professor and poet) and Viola (a writer and editor; maiden name, Whitney) Pratt. *Education:* University of Toronto, B.A., 1944; attended Columbia University, 1944-45. *Home:* 5 Elm Ave., Apt. 7, Toronto, Ontario, Canada M4W 1N1.

CAREER: University of Toronto Press, Toronto, Ontario, editor, 1948-52; Harvard University Press, Cambridge, Mass., editor, 1952-54; McClelland & Stewart Ltd., Toronto, editor, 1955-65; free-lance editor, 1965—. Woodcut artist, with solo shows in Canada and the United States and group shows in France, Italy, and Luxembourg. *Member:* Print and Drawing Council of Canada, Canadian Haiku Society, Centro Studi e Scampi Internazionale, World Federalists, Amnesty International, Planetary Citizens, World Goodwill.

WRITINGS: Haiku (poems), privately printed, 1965; *The Silent Ancestors,* McClelland & Stewart, 1971; *The Music of Oberon* (poems), Robert A. Massmann, 1975.

Work represented in anthologies, including *Touchstone 2,* Musion Book Co., 1972, and *Canadian Haiku Anthology,* 1979. Contributor to magazines, including *Canadian Forum, Fiddlehead, Cicada, Portals,* and *Haiku West.*

SIDELIGHTS: Pratt told *CA:* "My most natural outlet had, until 1965, been in the medium of art, chiefly woodcuts. Writing followed a debilitating illness during which I experienced strange psychological and out-of-body events. I had in mind to express these in woodcut at a time when I might be restored to health. During the extremely long convalescence I had not the strength to do much more than think about them, and when I was given a book on haiku I seized the opportunity of jotting down captions that might be used later visually. These developed into verses in their own right which were published in 1965, the first book of haiku to be published in Canada. Seventeen of these were set to music for soprano and flute in 1973.

"In both art and writing I seek to expand awareness of the world and our environment, both visible and invisible. My work tends to show circular or spiral motion, which gathers and completes and at the same time suggests growth and expansion. I believe in the unity of all living things, and that each of us is touched by all. My beliefs grow and expand as I express them, so that I am being taught by my own work.

"Other interests are human rights, both the exoteric and esoteric aspects, and genealogy, which has been responsible for many of my travels and has taken me to remote areas of England and to New Zealand. The result of that was *The Silent Ancestors,* in which I sought to 'enter the pit from which we are digged.' My feeling about genealogy is not to know 'who' our ancestors were in terms of names and status, but rather to reach back and join hands with the peoples of the earth separated from us by the illusion of time. It is a reaching back and a taking hold of the ages as they in their endless variety keep faith with the circling seasons, ringing the changes from birth to death, from death to birth again.

"While in Fiji, on the way home from New Zealand, I picked up some fantastic seashells that were washed ashore in a recent storm. These have been drawn and redrawn by me, and some of the drawings are in *The Music of Oberon.* They have been exhibited as woodcuts and made into cards, and are constantly on display. They also initiated an anthology of seashell poetry which it is my hope someday to publish."

* * *

PRATT-BUTLER, Grace Kipp 1916-

PERSONAL: Born April 25, 1916, in Yonkers, N.Y.; daughter of Arthur Pembroke and Grace Mildred (Clark) Pratt; married Alan Jay Butler, May 17, 1971. *Education:* Ethical Culture School, diploma, 1937; New York University, B.S., 1942, M.A., 1947, Ph.D., 1959. *Home:* 5166 Post Rd., Bronx, N.Y. 10471.

CAREER: Teacher in New York City at Froebel League School, 1937-38, Riverdale Country School, 1938-44, and Ethical Culture School, 1944-52, 1954-55; State University of New York at Buffalo, assistant professor of education, 1952-54; Long Island University, Brooklyn, N.Y., assistant professor, 1955-60, associate professor, 1961-63, professor of education, 1963-71, 1973-79, director of Institute for Human Religious Education, 1955-65, chairman of department of early childhood and elementary education, 1962-67, acting associate dean and division director of education, 1969-70, director of graduate studies in teacher education, 1970-71, director of education and special programs, 1979; Cleveland State University, Cleveland, Ohio, professor of education and chairman of early childhood and elementary education department, 1971-73. Visiting instructor at New York University, 1944-53, visiting assistant professor, 1957, visiting associate professor, 1963. National director of religious education of American Ethical Union, 1960-61; consultant in religious education, Long Island Ethical Culture Society, 1961-62; member of admissions committee of Encampment for Citizenship, 1967-68, and scholarship committees of National Conference of Christians and Jews, 1962-65, and Brooklyn Human Relations Council, 1963-65; consultant in ethics, Brooklyn Ethical Culture School, 1968-70; consultant on gifted kindergarten children, New York City Board of Education, District 15, 1981—. Co-founder and president of People for Animal Welfare, 1975-79; co-director of volunteers for Animal Rescue, 1979—.

MEMBER: American Philosophical Association, American Association of University Professors (member of Long Island University Chapter executive board, 1956-58, president, 1970), History of Education Society, Philosophy of Education Society (fellow), Society for Educational Reconstruction (past treasurer), Middle Atlantic States Philosophy of Education Society, New York Society for Ethical Culture, Riverdale-Yonkers Society for Ethical Culture. *Awards, honors:* New York University Founder's Day certificate for scholarship, 1960; humanitarian award from Save the Children Federation, 1968; Long Island University alumni award for twenty-five years of service, 1980.

WRITINGS: (Contributor and co-editor) *Proceedings,* Philosophy of Education Society, 1962; *How to Care for Living Things in the Classroom,* National Science Teachers Association, 1965, revised edition, 1978; *Helping Children Learn Science,* National Science Teachers Association, 1966; *Let Them Write Creatively,* C. E. Merrill, 1973; *The Three-, Four-, and Five-Year-Old in a School Setting,* C. E. Merrill, 1975. Contributor of numerous articles, reviews, columns, and poems to education journals.

WORK IN PROGRESS: Study in the areas of humane education and children's philosophy and literature.

SIDELIGHTS: Pratt-Butler told *CA:* "As a philosopher, professor, and author, I have been able to pursue my varied interests and only regret that there are but twenty-four hours in a day. To have more time to write has been a lifelong desire beginning with my first story, begun at about age eight. The story was supposed to be the life story of a horse. But I was told to 'put it away' and 'go to bed.' I learned at an early age to write in bed!"

*   *   *

PRAWER, S(iegbert) S(alomon) 1925-

PERSONAL: Surname is pronounced Prah-ver; born February 15, 1925, in Cologne, Germany (now West Germany); came to England, 1939; British citizen, 1945; son of Marcus

and Eleonora Prawer; married Helga Alice Schaefer, December 25, 1949; children: David Marcus (died, 1968), Daniela Sylvia, Deborah Joy, Jonathan Roy. *Education:* Attended Jesus College, Cambridge; Christ's College, Cambridge, B.A., 1947, M.A., 1950; University of Birmingham, Ph.D., 1953. *Office:* The Taylor Institution, Queen's College, Oxford University, Oxford, England.

CAREER: University of Birmingham, Birmingham, England, assistant lecturer, 1948-51, lecturer, 1951-58, senior lecturer in German, 1958-63; University of London, Westfield College, London, England, professor of German, 1964-69; Oxford University, Oxford, England, Taylor professor of German language and literature, 1969—. Visiting professor at City College (now of the City University of New York), 1957-58, University of Chicago, 1963-64, Harvard University, 1968, Hamburg University, 1969, University of California, Irvine, 1975, Otago University, 1976, Pittsburgh University, 1977, Australian National University, 1980, and Brandeis University, 1981. Fellow of Queen's College, Oxford, 1969—; resident fellow of Knox College, Dunedin, New Zealand, 1976. Honorary director of University of London Institute of Germanic Studies, 1966-68; member of board of Leo Baeck Institute. *Awards, honors:* Litt.D., Cambridge University, 1962; M.A. and D.Litt., Oxford University, 1969; Goethe Medal, 1973; Isaac Deutscher Memorial Prize, 1977, for *Karl Marx and World Literature.*

WRITINGS: German Lyric Poetry, Routledge & Kegan Paul, 1952; *Moerike und seine Leser* (title means "Moerike and His Readership"), 1960; *Heine's "Buch der Lieder": A Critical Study,* Edward Arnold, 1960; *Heine: The Tragic Satirist,* Cambridge University Press, 1961; *Comparative Literary Studies: An Introduction,* Duckworth, 1973, Barnes & Noble, 1974; *Karl Marx and World Literature,* Oxford University Press, 1976; *Caligari's Children: The Film as Tale of Terror,* Oxford University Press, 1978.

Editor: *The Penguin Book of Lieder,* Penguin, 1964; (with V. J. Riley) *Theses in Germanic Studies: 1962-67,* Institute of Germanic Studies, University of London, 1969; (with R. H. Thomas and Leonard W. Forster) *Essays in German Language, Culture, and Society,* Institute of Germanic Studies, University of London, 1969; *The Romantic Period in Germany,* Schocken, 1970; *Seventeen Modern German Poets,* Oxford University Press, 1971. Contributor of numerous articles on German, English, and comparative literature to scholarly journals, including *Cambridge Journal, German Review, Modern Language Review,* and *Modern Philology.*

WORK IN PROGRESS: Further research on Heine for a book tentatively titled *Heine's Jewish Comedy.*

AVOCATIONAL INTERESTS: Attending the cinema.

BIOGRAPHICAL/CRITICAL SOURCES: Times Literary Supplement, October 16, 1970, February 1, 1974, February 4, 1977; *Modern Language Review,* January, 1972, July, 1972, October, 1977; *Spectator,* October 16, 1976; *Journal of Aesthetics and Art Criticism,* winter, 1977; *Prairie Schooner,* summer, 1977; *American Political Science Review,* September, 1978.

*   *   *

PRESTIDGE, Pauline 1922-

PERSONAL: Born April 29, 1922, in Harrow, England; daughter of Frank Sydney (a civil servant) and Clara Jane (Batchelor) Cooper; married James Philip Prestidge, September 26, 1940; children: Janet, Margaret Prestidge Warren,

Mary. *Education:* Attended secondary school in Chingford, Essex, England. *Home:* Roselea, Ball Lane, Brownedge, Stoke-on-Trent, Staffordshire, England.

CAREER: Addressograph multilithe operator in London, England, 1936-39; Ladywell Gymnastics Club, London, England, director of gymnastic coaching, 1967-76; North Staffs Gymnastics Club, Burslem, England, director of gymnastic coaching, 1976—. Honorary national gymnastics coach, British Amateur Gymnastics Association, 1965-76; coach of British gymnastics team at Olympic Games in Mexico, 1968, West Germany, 1972, and Canada, 1976. *Member:* British Amateur Gymnastic Association (honorary life member).

WRITINGS: (With husband, Jim Prestidge) *Your Book of Gymnastics,* Faber, 1964, 3rd edition, 1979; *Women's Gymnastics for Performer and Coach,* Faber, 1972; *Better Gymnastics,* Kaye & Ward, 1977, Plays, 1979; *A Guide to Gymnastics Coaching,* British Amateur Gymnastic Association, 1975; *How to Start a Gym Club,* British Amateur Gymnastics Association, 1978.

SIDELIGHTS: Pauline Prestidge told *CA:* "I helped to pioneer modern gymnastics in Great Britain after World War II. I was a competitor from 1946 to 1950 and began writing to fill a need for gymnastic information. My children are gymnastic enthusiasts. My daughter Mary represented Great Britain in gymnastics at the Olympics in Mexico, and my daughter Margaret writes gymnastic coaching books and is an artist specializing in gymnastic figurines. Even my three grandsons are gymnasts. My husband recently edited *The Love of Gymnastics* for Octopus Books and photographs gymnasts as a hobby."

*　　　*　　　*

PRESTON, Florence (Margaret) 1905-

PERSONAL: Born May 1, 1905, in Invercargill, New Zealand; daughter of William James (a farmer) and Lilian (Robinson) Munro; married Eric Henry James Preston (a barrister and solicitor), November 2, 1928; children: Roger Neill, John Nicholas, Gillian Mary Hutcherson, James Christopher. *Education:* Attended University of Otago, New Zealand, 1923-26. *Home:* 17 Melbourne St., Queenstown, New Zealand.

CAREER: Writer, 1956—. *Member:* International P.E.N., New Zealand Women Writers Society.

WRITINGS: A Gallows Tree (novel), Cassell, 1956; *Harvest of Daring* (novel), Cassell, 1957; *Great Refusals* (novel), Cassell, 1958; *The Gay Pretensions* (novel), Cassell, 1959; *Out and About in Queenstown* (travelogue), A. H. & A. W. Reed, 1975; *Finding Fiordland* (travelogue), A. H. & A. W. Reed, 1977; *From Rocks to Roses* (nonfiction), Craigs, 1978; *Who Rides the Tiger* (novel), Craigs, 1980.

WORK IN PROGRESS: Some Women of Rome, from the Vestal Virgins to Clementine Sobieska.

SIDELIGHTS: Florence Preston told *CA:* "If my novels have been motivated by any one thing, it is the desire to be more articulate on paper than I am in conversation, about things that matter to me; and included with this is the urge to write not just clear prose in the manner of Hemingway and his imitators, but something more rich, even beautiful (*The Old Man and the Sea* always excepted). After all, writing *is* one of the arts.

"I would that I could write a powerful indictment against blatant materialism and its concomitant, war. Concerning the latter, more political involvement of women—their instincts being much less aggressive and destructive than men's—

would seem to be the world's best hope for ridding humankind of this monstrous evil which, if not speedily outlawed, will assuredly rid our long-suffering planet of all life—with the possible exception of the salamander, which, Mr. Attenborough assures us, can tolerate a very high level of nuclear fallout.

"My vocational interests? Since I am neither young enough nor sufficiently competent to practice my own advocacy of women in politics, I feel able to enjoy with a reasonably clear conscience the pursuits of an old age freed from the strains and stresses, especially the emotional stresses, of youth. Chief among these joys are writing, in spite of the hard work involved, reading, especially history and biography, gardening, especially landscaping, and walking, in our own native forests and in the medieval cities of Europe such as York and Chester, Lyon and Lisbon, Salzburg and Innsbruck, Venice and Vienna, and especially Rome.

"Freedom, did I say, from emotional stresses? Alas, I suspect that even the saints never quite conquered their particular demons. My own pet hates are mostly the offspring of television: the wailings and wigglings and screamings and grimacings of pop singers, female and male; claque audiences in the wings; and 'spectacular' shows during which for no apparent reason the artists keep changing their clothes. Backstage, of course; such entertainments are usually impeccably correct—and incredibly dull."

*　　　*　　　*

PRETORIUS, Hertha
See KOUTS, Hertha Pretorius

*　　　*　　　*

PRICE, Barbara Pradal

PERSONAL: Born in New York, N.Y.; daughter of Martin John and Amelie Marie Josephine (Pradal) Price. *Education:* Attended high school. *Religion:* "Catholic-Protestant." *Home:* 265 Burns St., Forest Hills, N.Y. 11375.

CAREER: Worked as account executive for Carson-Ruff Associates, 1948-51; Barbara Pradal Price Public Relations, New York, N.Y., owner and operator, 1952—.

WRITINGS: Ancient Egypt From A to Z, Bobbs-Merrill, 1971; *Miracle of the Golden Doors,* Prentice-Hall, 1971. Contributor to education journals.

WORK IN PROGRESS: A humorous story about a cat.

SIDELIGHTS: Barbara Price commented: "I became interested in ancient Egypt when I was very young, read widely, and spent many years compiling my research."

*　　　*　　　*

PRICE, George 1901-

PERSONAL: Born June 9, 1901, in Coytesville, N.J.; son of George and Camille (Vidal) Price; married Florence Schwank, December 3, 1927; children: George, Wilfrid, Charles, Susan. *Education:* Attended high school in Fort Lee, N.J. *Home:* 81 Westervelt Ave., Tenafly, N.J. 07670.

CAREER: Cartoonist, artist, and writer, 1920—. Held one-man shows in New York, N.Y., and exhibited in group shows in London, Paris, Munich, and Basel, Switzerland; cartoons collected in museums, libraries, and private collections.

WRITINGS:—Self-illustrated cartoon books: *George Price, Good Humor Man,* Farrar & Rinehart, 1940; *It's Smart to Be People,* foreword by S. J. Perelman, Farrar & Rinehart, 1942; *Who's in Charge Here?,* Farrar & Rinehart, 1943; *Is*

It Anyone We Know?, Murray-Hill News, 1944; *George Price's Ice Cold War*, H. Schuman, 1951; *We Buy Old Gold: An Album of Cartoons*, H. Schuman, 1951; *George Price's Characters: More Than Two Hundred of His Best Cartoons*, Simon & Schuster, 1955; *My Dear Five Hundred Friends: Embalmed and Treasured Up by George Price*, Simon & Schuster, 1963; *Browse at Your Own Risk*, Simon & Schuster, 1977.

Illustrator: Mary Lasswell, *Suds in Your Eye*, Houghton, 1942; Frank Sullivan, *A Moose in the Hoose*, Random House, 1959; Steven Allen, *Little Red Riding Hood*, Simon & Schuster, 1965; Bill Adler, editor, *Love Letters to the Mets*, Simon & Schuster, 1965; Stephen Josephs, *The People Zoo*, Windmill Books, 1971; Olive Wong, *Here Comes Pops*, Ginn, 1974.

Contributor of cartoons to magazines, including *New Yorker*.

BIOGRAPHICAL/CRITICAL SOURCES: Ernest W. Watson, *Forty Illustrators and How They Work*, Watson-Guptill, 1946.

* * *

PRICHARD, Caradog   1904-1980

PERSONAL: Born in 1904 in Bethesda, Wales; died February 25, 1980, in London, England; married Mattie Wyn; children: Mari.

CAREER: Welsh Herald, Caernarfon, journalist, beginning 1921; *Cambrian News*, Aberystwyth, Wales, journalist; *Western Mail*, Cardiff, Wales, journalist; *News Chronicle*, London, England, journalist, beginning 1927; *Daily Telegraph*, London, began as sub-editor, became chief parliamentary sub-editor, 1947-72, part-time reporter after 1972. Chaired Bard at Llanelli. *Military service:* British Army, served during World War II; served in India. *Awards, honors:* Crowned bard at National Eisteddfod, 1927, 1928, 1929; grant from Welsh Arts Council, 1972.

WRITINGS: Tantalus: Casgliad o gerddi (poems), Gwasg Gee, 1957; *Un Nos Ola Leuad* (novel), Gwasg Gee, 1961, translation by Menna Gallie published as *Full Moon*, Hodder & Stoughton, 1972; *Llef un yn llefain: Detholiad o weithiau*, Llyfrau'r Dryw, 1963; *Y genod yn ein bywyd*, Gwasg Gee, 1964; *Afal Drwg Adda: Hunangofiant methiant* (autobiography), Gwasg Gee, 1973.

OBITUARIES: London Times, February 27, 1980; *Chicago Tribune*, March 2, 1980; *AB Bookman's Weekly*, May 12, 1980.*

* * *

PRILL, Felician   1904-

PERSONAL: Born June 9, 1904, in Koniiz, Germany; son of Ferdinand (a solicitor) and Martha (Semrau) Prill; married Hildegard Nebelung, October 27, 1930; children: Meinrad, Renata Prill Betson, Norbert. *Education:* Attended University of Wuerzburg, 1923, and University of Cologne, 1923-24; University of Jena, LL.D., 1924. *Religion:* Roman Catholic. *Home:* Giersbergstrasse 9, 5300 Bonn-Holzlar, West Germany.

CAREER: Judge, 1926-31; worked as a county manager, 1931-33; administrator of finance in Germany and Danzig, Poland, 1933-46; Federal Ministry of Finance, Germany, counselor, 1946-54, member of German delegation to international conferences, 1951-54; Foreign Office, Bonn, diplomat sent on missions to several countries, 1954-56, ambassador to Ireland, 1956-60, permanent representative to Council of Europe in Strasbourg, 1960-67, ambassador to Ireland, 1967-69, ambassador extraordinary and plenipotentiary. *Military service:* German Air Force, 1941-46; prisoner of war. *Member:* Association for Foreign Affairs, German-Irish Society. *Awards, honors:* Knight commander's cross of German Order of Merit, 1960; grand cross of Sovereign Order of Malta, 1965.

WRITINGS: The Social Partners in West German Industry, Irish Industry, 1958; *Germany's Position in the Defense of the Free World*, Chrisus Rex, 1959; *Sean Lester: High Commissioner in Danzig, 1933-1937*, Hudics Autirnum, 1960; *Ireland, Britain, and Germany, 1871-1914: Problems of Nationalism and Religion in Nineteenth-Century Europe*, Barnes & Noble, 1975. Contributor to political science journals.

WORK IN PROGRESS: Research on the League of Nations, Danzig, and his homeland, West Prussia.

SIDELIGHTS: Prill commented: "I am a specialist in finance and a diplomat at an important center of the European movement."

* * *

PROCTOR, E(velyn) E(mma) S(tefanos)   1897-1980

PERSONAL: Born June 6, 1897; died in 1980. *Education:* Somerville College, Oxford, received degree in modern history (with first class honors).

CAREER: Employed at private girls' school in Southwold, England; Oxford University, Oxford, England, Mary Somerville Research Fellow, tutor, 1925-46, principal of St. Hugh's College, 1946-52, honorary fellow, 1962-80. Authority on medieval Spain. Maccoll Lecturer at Cambridge University, 1949. *Awards, honors:* Chevalier of French Legion of Honor, 1948.

WRITINGS: (Contributor) *Transactions of the Royal Historical Society*, Royal Historical Society, 1931; *Alfonso X of Castile: Patron of Literature and Learning*, 1951; *Curia and Cortes in Leon and Castile, 1072-1295*, Cambridge University Press, 1980.

OBITUARIES: London Times, March 26, 1980.*

* * *

PUGSLEY, John A.   1934-

PERSONAL: Born January 5, 1934, in Minneapolis, Minn.; son of Lawrence Eugene (an inventor) and Cleota Rae (Johnson) Pugsley; married Gloria J. Terry (a sculptor), January 11, 1958; children: Joseph, Hollis, Tamara. *Education:* University of California, Los Angeles, B.A., 1960. *Politics:* None. *Residence:* Santa Ana, Calif. *Office:* Common Sense Press, Inc., 711 West 17th St., No. G-6, Costa Mesa, Calif. 92627.

CAREER: Porta-Shop Tool Corp., Detroit, Mich., president, 1962-66; Club Caribbean, Inc., Newport Beach, Calif., president, 1967-68; investment adviser in Newport Beach, 1969—. Associated with Common Sense Press. *Military service:* U.S. Army, 1954-56.

WRITINGS: Common Sense Economics, Common Sense Press, 1954, 2nd edition, 1976; *The Alpha Strategy*, Common Sense Press, 1980. Also author of *Bio-Economics*, 1982, and *The Doomsday Factory*, 1982. Contributor to business and finance journals. Editor of *Metals Investor* and *Common Sense Viewpoint*.

SIDELIGHTS: Bio-Economics is a book on the biological foundations of economics and investment values. *The Doomsday Factor* is about the economic causes of war.

Pugsley wrote: "My economic views are heavily influenced by the Australian School of Economics and Education at the Free-Enterprise Institute of Los Angeles. My experience in the investment field, my education, and heavy reading in biology and sociobiology are also major influences."

*   *   *

PURSER, John Whitley   1942-

PERSONAL: Born in 1942, in Glasgow, Scotland; son of Sean (a poet) and Elizabeth (Jellett) Purser; married Wilma Paterson (a composer), July 6, 1965; children: Sean, Sarah. *Education:* Royal Scottish Academy of Music and Drama, D.R.S.A.M., 1963; University of Glasgow, M.A. (with honors), 1980, doctoral study, 1980—. *Home:* 27 Hamilton Dr., Glasgow G12 8DN, Scotland.

CAREER: University of Glasgow, Glasgow, Scotland, extramural lecturer in music, 1965—. Cello teacher for Lanarkshire County Council, 1964-67; composer and music critic. Member of board of directors of Scottish International, 1968-70, and Occasional Words Ltd., 1969. *Member:* Scottish Society of Composers (concert manager), Musicians Union. *Awards, honors:* Award from Royal Philharmonic Society, 1962, for a ballet score; Carolan Prize from Radio Eireann, 1963, for variations on an Irish theme; prize from government of Ireland, 1966, for "Epitaph 1916"; composers' award from Scottish Arts Council, 1969; award from Glasgow Educational Trust, 1974, for study in Italy; New Writers Award from Scottish Arts Council, 1976, for *The Counting Stick;* Buchan Award from Glasgow University, 1977, for poetry.

WRITINGS: The Counting Stick (poems), Aquila Publishing, 1976; *A Share of the Wind* (poems), Aquila Publishing, 1980.

Radio plays: "Papageno," first broadcast by BBC-Scotland-Radio 4, October 19, 1976; "Heartwood," first broadcast by BBC-Scotland-Radio 4, April 4, 1978.

Composer of operas, orchestral and chamber works, music for exhibitions, and incidental music for theatre and radio. Contributor to periodicals, including *Scotsman, Words, Aquarius, Prospice, Lines,* and *Times Educational Supplement.*

WORK IN PROGRESS: Research on the literary work of Jack B. Yeats; a string quartet.

SIDELIGHTS: Purser told *CA:* "I keep bees, but I leave them as much as possible to their own devices. They are not a peaceable breed of bee, but I love them all the same. In the early spring I watch them prize open the crocusses and disappear inside: Then all you can see is the flower shaking as the bee wrestles with the anthers for pollen."

*   *   *

PYNE, Mable Mandeville   1903-1969

OBITUARY NOTICE—See index for *CA* sketch: Born January 15, 1903, in Mount Vernon, N.Y.; died September 19, 1969. Fashion artist, illustrator, and author. Pyne worked as an illustrator for nearly thirty years. Her works include *The Little History of the United States, The Little Geography of the United States,* and *When We Were Little.* Pyne's books about the United States were distributed by the U.S. Information Agency in Turkey, Korea, and Malay. Obituaries and other sources: *Something About the Author,* Volume 9, Gale, 1976.

Q

QADAR, Basheer
   See ALEXANDER, C(harles) K(halil)

* * *

QUARRIE, Bruce (Roy Bryant) 1947-

PERSONAL: Born June 15, 1947, in London, England; son of Ian Andrew (in Royal Navy) and Yvonne (Roy) Quarrie; married Linda Berry (a teacher), October 27, 1973. *Education:* Peterhouse, Cambridge, B.A. (with honors), 1968. *Politics:* Conservative. *Religion:* Agnostic. *Home:* 5 Edward St., Cambridge, England. *Office:* Patrick Stephens Ltd., Bar Hill, Cambridge CB3 8EL, England.

CAREER: Medical News, reporter, beginning 1968, deputy news editor, until 1970; free-lance writer and designer, 1970-71; *Heating and Ventilating News,* editor, 1971-72; Patrick Stephens Ltd., Cambridge, England, editor of *Airfix,* 1972-78, senior editor, 1976-78, managing editor, 1978—. *Member:* Cambridge Professional Book Association, English Civil War Society.

WRITINGS: Napoleonic Wargaming, Patrick Stephens, 1974; *Afrika Korps,* Patrick Stephens, 1974; *Tank Battles in Miniature,* Patrick Stephens, Volume II (Quarrie was not associated with Volume I): *Wargamers Guide to the Russian Campaign, 1941-45,* 1975, Volume III: *Wargamers Guide to the North-West European Campaign, 1944-45,* 1976, Volume V (Quarrie was not associated with Volume IV): *Wargamers Guide to the Arab-Israeli Wars Since 1948,* 1978; (editor) *Modelling Miniature Figurines,* Patrick Stephens, 1975.

Napoleon's Campaigns in Miniature, Patrick Stephens, 1976; *World War II Wargaming,* Patrick Stephens, 1976; *Panzer-Grenadier Division "Grossdeutschland",* Osprey, 1977; *Fallschirmpanzerdivision "Hermann Goering",* Osprey, 1978; *Panzers in the Desert,* Patrick Stephens, 1978; *Waffen-SS in Russia,* Patrick Stephens, 1978; (editor) *Modelling Military Vehicles,* Patrick Stephens, 1978; *2nd SS Panzer Division "Das Reich",* Osprey, 1979; *Panzers in North-West Europe,* Patrick Stephens, 1979; *German Paratroops in the Med,* Patrick Stephens, 1979; *Panzers in Russia, 1941-1943,* Patrick Stephens, 1979; *Panzers in Russia, 1943-1945,* Patrick Stephens, 1980; *German Mountain Troops,* Patrick Stephens, 1980; *PSL Guide to Wargaming,* Patrick Stephens, 1980; *Fallschirmjager,* Osprey, 1981.

Editor of *Airfix Magazine Annual for Modellers,* 1974-77, *Airfix Magazine Annual for Aircraft Modellers,* 1978, and *Airfix Magazine Annual for Military Modellers,* 1978. Contributor to magazines and newspapers, including *Nature* and *Bookseller.*

SIDELIGHTS: Quarrie wrote: "Being born into a family with a strong naval tradition, I have always had an interest in military affairs. I began wargaming in my teens and my first book has become a standard text. Since then, I have written widely on wargaming and military topics, my main interests being the Napoleonic Wars and the German Army during World War II. My ambition is to write a novel, probably with a military background. I confess that I cannot write dialogue, but writing nonfiction is easy if the subject interests me, and most people could write good books on their hobbies, if they tried.

"I recently joined the English Civil War Society, an organization which re-enacts seventeenth-century battles for charity, and my current aim is to write a definitive book on the military forces of this period."

* * *

QUIGLEY, Harold Scott 1889-1968

OBITUARY NOTICE—See index for *CA* sketch: Born February 13, 1889, in Minneapolis, Minn.; died July 22, 1968, in Oakland, Calif. Educator and author. Quigley, a Rhodes scholar, taught political science at the University of Minnesota for more than thirty years. He was also a professor at Tsinghua University in Peking, China, for three years. His works include *The Immunity of Private Property From Capture at Sea in Time of War, Far Eastern War,* and *China's Politics in Perspective.* Obituaries and other sources: *New York Times,* July 22, 1968; *Publishers Weekly,* August 26, 1968.

* * *

QUIMBER, Mario
   See ALEXANDER, C(harles) K(halil)

* * *

QUINN, Susan 1940-
   (Susan Jacobs)

PERSONAL: Born March 6, 1940, in Chillicothe, Ohio;

daughter of Robert Emmet (a physician) and Esther (a teacher; maiden name, Taft) Quinn; married Daniel Howard Jacobs (a psychoanalyst), September 29, 1964; children: Thomas Quinn, Anna Taft. *Education:* Oberlin College, A.B., 1962. *Residence:* Brookline, Mass. *Agent:* Susan Ann Protter, 156 East 52nd St., New York, N.Y. 10022.

CAREER: Cleveland Playhouse, Cleveland, Ohio, apprentice and fellow, 1962-64; *Lake County News Herald,* Willoughby, Ohio, general assignment reporter, 1964-66; Mills College, Oakland, Calif., assistant to director of publications, 1966-67; free-lance writer, 1967-77; *Boston,* Boston, Mass., senior staff writer, 1977-79; Boston College, Chestnut Hill, Mass., instructor in journalism, 1979—. *Member:* Authors Guild. *Awards, honors:* Penney-Missouri Magazine Award from University of Missouri School of Journalism and J. C. Penney Foundation, 1979, for article "Dangerous Cargo"; Golden Hammer Award from National Association of Home Builders, 1979, for article "Inspecting the Home Inspectors."

WRITINGS: (Under name Susan Jacobs) *On Stage: The Making of a Broadway Play* (for young adults), Knopf, 1972. Contributor to magazines and newspapers, including *Glamour, Ms., New England,* and *New York Times Magazine.*

WORK IN PROGRESS: A nonfiction book for Dial, *Blood Is Thicker.*

QUINT, Barbara Gilder 1928-

PERSONAL: Born March 6, 1928, in New York; daughter of Saul H. and Ethel H. Gilder; married George Quint (an investor), June 1, 1952; children: Andrew, Douglas, Thomas. *Education:* Vassar College, A.B., 1947; attended Harvard University, 1950. *Home and office:* 14 Avondale Rd., White Plains, N.Y. 10605. *Agent:* Rhoda Weyr, William Morris Agency, 1350 Avenue of the Americas, New York, N.Y. 10019.

CAREER: Stockbroker at Dreyfus & Co., 1950-60; Iona College, New Rochelle, N.Y., instructor in finance department, 1960-63; New York University, New York City, instructor at Management Institute, 1963-65; *Glamour,* New York City, money management and financial editor, 1976—; *Family Circle,* New York City, money management editor, 1978—. Lecturer; guest on television programs, including "The Merv Griffin Show" and "AM America."

WRITINGS: Corporate Finance: College Level, Monarch, 1965; *Securities and Investment: College Level,* Monarch, 1965; *Accounting,* College Notes, 1968; *Bookkeeping Made Simple,* Simon & Schuster, 1981. Author of special projects, annual reports, and consumer booklets for numerous organizations, including Master Charge and American Council of Life Insurance. Contributor to magazines, including *Ladies' Home Journal* and *Money,* and to newspapers.

R

RABINOWITZ, Sandy 1954-

PERSONAL: Born October 22, 1954, in New Haven, Conn.; daughter of Harold W. (an artist) and Kiki (a designer; maiden name, Harris) Rabinowitz. *Education:* Parsons School of Design, Certificate of Illustration, 1975. *Residence:* Bethany, Conn. 06525.

CAREER: Illustrator, 1975—.

WRITINGS—Self-illustrated; juveniles: *The Red Horse and the Bluebird,* Harper, 1975; *What's Happening to Daisy?,* Harper, 1977; *A Colt Named Mischief,* Doubleday, 1979; *How I Trained My Colt,* Doubleday, 1981.

WORK IN PROGRESS: The Nature of Wild Horses, a self-illustrated children's book.

SIDELIGHTS: Sandy Rabinowitz commented: "I am a full-time horsewoman. I illustrate and write children's books in order to buy hay and grain. My experiences with my animals inspire my stories, and my horses are references for my illustrations. I am at ease writing for children because I am a perpetual child myself."

*   *   *

RABORG, Frederick A(shton), Jr. 1934-
(Lewis Ashmore, Dick Baldwin, Wolfe Bronson, Canyon Kern, Bertha Mayfair)

PERSONAL: Surname is pronounced *Ray*-borg; born April 10, 1934, in Richmond, Va.; son of Frederick Ashton (a boilermaker) and Marguerette (Smith) Ashton; married Eileen Mary Bradshaw (a layout artist), October 19, 1957; children: Frederick Ashton III, Donald Wayne, Marguerette Jeannette Raborg Cluck, Wayne Patrick, Jayne Alyson, Kevin Douglas. *Education:* Bakersfield College, A.A., 1970; California State College, Bakersfield, B.A., 1973, Secondary Teaching Credential, 1974, graduate study, 1974-75. *Politics:* Democrat. *Religion:* Roman Catholic. *Home:* 329 E St., Bakersfield, Calif. 93304. *Agent:* Anita Diamant, 51 East 42nd St., New York, N.Y. 10017; (for plays) Lawrence R. Harbison, Samuel French, Inc., 25 West 45th St., New York, N.Y. 10036.

CAREER: Huebsch Originators, Bakersfield, Calif., office manager, 1962-63; Southern Pacific Railroad, Bakersfield, editor, 1963-64; writer, 1964—. Instructor at Bakersfield College, 1970-74; judge of poetry contests and drama festivals; playwright and actor with Bakersfield Community Theatre and North of the River Recreation Department Theatre. *Military service:* U.S. Army, Infantry, 1952-55; served in Korea; became sergeant major. *Member:* Authors Guild, Dramatists Guild, Poetry Society of America. *Awards, honors:* First prize from *Class* International Intercollegiate Creative Writing Competition, 1969, for story, "The Clamming"; Eastside Herald Award from New York Poetry Forum, 1974, for "Heigh Ho, Heigh Ho"; award and grant from *Guideposts* Writers Workshop, 1973, for "God and Joe Dun"; second prize from International Thespian Association, 1975, for play "Ramon and the Artist."

WRITINGS—Novels published by Greenleaf Classics, except as noted: *Gin Street Rhythms,* 1971; *Why Should the Devil Have All the Good Tunes?* (poetry), Parvenu Press, 1972; *Checkers,* 1972; *Lovers Island,* 1972; *The Judas Match,* 1972; *The Gay Vigilantes,* 1972; *The Purple Feather,* 1972; *Jail Rape,* 1972; *Dude on Second Avenue,* 1972; *Houseboy,* 1973; *The Resurrectionist,* 1973; *Gang Rape!,* 1973.

Novels published by Hamilton House, except as noted: (Under pseudonym Wolfe Bronson) *Tall Timber,* 1974; (under pseudonym Dick Baldwin) *Hunk!,* 1974; (under Baldwin pseudonym) *Truck Stop,* 1974; (under Bronson pseudonym) *The Big Pipe,* 1974; (under Bronson pseudonym) *Mountain Stud,* 1974; (under Bronson pseudonym) *Brawny,* 1974; (under Baldwin pseudonym) *Chicken Hawk,* 1975; *The Modesto Messiah* (nonfiction), Universal Press, 1977.

Plays: "The Other Side of the Island" (two-act), first produced in Bakersfield, Calif., at Bakersfield Community Theatre, March, 1973; "Making It!" (one-act), first produced in Bakersfield at Bakersfield Community Theatre, April, 1974; "Ramon and the Artist" (one-act), first produced in Bakersfield at North High School, 1974; "Tribal Rites" (three-act), first produced in Bakersfield at Playwrights and Actors Conservatory Theatre, 1975.

Work represented in anthologies, including *Valley Light: Writers of the San Joaquin,* edited by Jane Watts; *Proud Harvest,* edited by Art Cuelho; *Ocarina,* edited by Sandra Fowler; *99 Vintage,* edited by Cuelho; and *Peopled Patterns,* New York Poetry Forum.

Author of "The Bowers Hill News," a column in *Portsmouth Star,* 1946-48, "A Straw to Chew," a column in *Bakersfield News-Bulletin,* 1968-70, and "The View From the Hill," a column in *Friendship House Journal,* 1970. Contributor of poems (some under pseudonym Canyon Kern), stories, and articles (sometimes under pseudonym Bertha Mayfair) to dozens of magazines, including *Chic, Statesman, Westways, Cavalier, Christian Living, Short Story International,* and *National Wildlife.* Editor of *Pantry,* 1963-65, and *Oildale News,* 1968-69; reviewer for *Bakersfield California,* 1972-78.

WORK IN PROGRESS: The Attic, a suspense novel, publication expected in 1982; *The Glass,* a suspense novel, publication expected in 1982; research on time warp in relation to black holes, for a science fiction novel; "Daisy at the Dance," a play.

SIDELIGHTS: Raborg wrote: "Perhaps my chief concern, both as a writer and as a secondary teacher who prefers to write instead, is the lack of abilities in the humanities today, not just among high school students but college graduates as well. When I was a high school student in the mid-forties, I was required to take four years of English (students now take two); I also took four years of Latin, a year of French, and a year of Spanish—not to overlook four years of history, mathematics through trigonometry, three sciences, mechanical drawing, et cetera. Using that as a yardstick, students today receive about one-fifth an education. I would carry placards for the return of Latin.

"Of course I would like to write *only* quality material, but two things limit that quest—the need to eat and the drive to reach as many of those readers as possible who might otherwise not read even the backs of cereal boxes. Therefore, I have written and continue to write even the sexual backwash of good writing. Get a man, woman, or child to read something—*anything*—often enough, and sooner or later the good book or story will be investigated. If they see *my* name often and everywhere, I may be the carrot that leads them to the stacks of literature.

"Now, with several hundred credits to my name, probably I can be resigned never to become a Hemingway or Steinbeck or Clavell, but every now and then a story—a *real* story—does break through and shines (stories like I've had in *Short Story International* and *Prairie Schooner*) just enough to justify all the painful moments of doubt."

* * *

RABY, Derek Graham 1927-
(Graham Derrick)

PERSONAL: Born May 18, 1927, in Bournemouth, England; son of Victor Harry (a civil servant) and Dorothy Alys (Buzzard) Raby; married Elsa Jean White, July 14, 1956; children: Charles Rupert Gordon. *Education:* Attended King's School, Bruton, England. *Religion:* Church of England. *Home:* "The Little House," Elm Grove Rd., Cobham, Surrey, England. *Agent:* Margery Vosper Ltd., Suite 8, 26 Charing Cross Rd., London WC2H 0DG, England. *Office:* People's Dispensary for Sick Animals, South St., Dorking, Surrey, England.

CAREER: National Coal Board, London, England, office administration staff, 1948-51; People's Dispensary for Sick Animals, Dorking, England, appeals director, 1952—. *Military service:* Royal Air Force, 1945-48. *Member:* Writers Guild of Great Britain.

WRITINGS—Radio plays; all first broadcast by BBC-Radio 4, except as noted: "The Office," 1973; "Tiger," 1974; "A Cat Called Willie," 1975; "Bandstand," first broadcast by BBC-Radio 3, 1975; "Put an Egg in Your Tank," 1977; "Passing Through," 1978; "Robinson," 1979; "Nightshift," 1979; "Letters to the Editor," 1979.

Stage plays: *We Need a Man* (one-act), Samuel French, 1975.

Also author (under name Graham Derrick) of "The Legend of the Siamese Cat" and "Catty Pieces." Contributor to periodicals.

WORK IN PROGRESS: "There's More to Christmas Than Soggy Sprouts," a radio play; "Pavementum," a radio play.

SIDELIGHTS: Raby commented: "I write for pleasure, relaxation, and to let off steam more than for profit, so I feel something of a fraud in the company of the dedicated, highly gifted, and wholly professional writer. I always expect my last play to be my last play. I am delighted that one title, 'Tiger,' has been taken up by the University of Wisconsin's 'Earplay.'

"I have an aversion to greed, aggressiveness, and people high on personal ambition, which is something of a disadvantage nowadays. Whenever possible, I prefer the old-fashioned values of gentleness, courtesy, service to others, and anything which will contribute to a mode of living that does not frighten people into preferring (and trusting) the company of pet animals over humans, or to behaving against their (hopefully) better natures 'just to survive.' (My apologies for sounding pompous.)

"I like writing for radio because there is an intimacy in using the pace and beauty of words to build an image and create a response in the mind of a total stranger. I am pleased at the success of my limited excursion into radio-dialogue style advertising.

"I hope to make people laugh and think and take themselves less seriously. I would dearly like to sit in a theatre and hear an audience enjoying the words I have written. There's always hope."

* * *

RAEBURN, Michael 1943-

PERSONAL: Born January 22, 1943, in Cairo, Egypt; son of W. W. (a headmaster) and Noemi (Bemaroio) Wilson; married wife, Anna (a writer and broadcaster; divorced, 1977); living with Karen Black (an actress). *Education:* Received degree (with honors) from University of London, 1966; graduate study at University of Aix en Provence and at Institut des Hautes Etudes Cinematographiques, 1966-68. *Home:* 108 Fremont Pl., Los Angeles, Calif. 90005; and 10 Spencer Park, London S.W.18, England.

CAREER: Writer and director of films, 1968—. Producer of films, including "Requiem for a Village." *Awards, honors:* Mannheim Peace Prize for "Rhodesia Countdown"; citation for outstanding film of the year from London Film Festival, 1975, for "Requiem for a Village"; citation for outstanding film of the year from London Film Festival, 1976, and prize from France's Centre National du Cinema, both for "Beyond the Plains Where Man Was Born."

WRITINGS: Black Fire! (novel), Julian Friedmann Publishers, 1978, Random House, 1979; *We/Are/Everywhere,* Random House, 1979. Author of screenplays and director of films, including "Rhodesia Countdown," "The Plastic Shamrock," "This Is Renee," "It's in My Blood," "This Game of Golf," "Beyond the Plains Where Man Was Born," and "The Grass Is Singing," Swedish Film Institute and Chibote Ltd., 1981.

Also author of scripts for television series "Sunday Sweet Sunday," first broadcast by Independent Television Network (ITV), 1978—.

WORK IN PROGRESS: Raven, a novel; "Giovanni's Room," a screenplay based on a book by James Baldwin.

SIDELIGHTS: Raeburn writes that he has a "special interest in Africa," a concern that his books and films confirm. The author calls his novel *Black Fire!* "a fictionalized documentary about Southern Africa." Set in East Africa, "Beyond the Plains Where Man Was Born" tells the story of a herdsman's son, and Zambia serves as the site of "The Grass Is Singing."

But the film writer does not deal exclusively with African themes. He considers the "memories" of a nineteenth-century village in "Requiem for a Village," and the effects of industrialization on Ireland, which is the subject of "The Plastic Shamrock," has also captured Raeburn's interest.

* * *

RAFFERTY, Kathleen Kelly 1915-1981

OBITUARY NOTICE: Born in 1915 in Chester, Iowa; died March 22, 1981, in New York, N.Y. Rafferty was editor in chief of puzzle publications at Dell Publishing Company. She also wrote the *Dell Crossword Puzzle Dictionary*. Obituaries and other sources: *Foremost Women in Communications*, Bowker, 1970; *Who's Who of American Women*, 7th edition, Marquis, 1972; *New York Times*, March 24, 1981.

* * *

RAINE, Richard
See SAWKINS, Raymond H(arold)

* * *

RAISZ, Erwin J(osephus) 1893-1968

OBITUARY NOTICE—See index for *CA* sketch: Born March 1, 1893, in Loecse, Hungary; died December 1, 1968, in Bangkok, Thailand. Educator, cartographer, and author. Raisz taught the art of map-making at several institutions, including Columbia University, the University of Florida, and Clark University. He was also a lecturer at Harvard University's Institute of Geographical Exploration for nearly twenty years. Among his works number *The Scenery of Mount Desert Island, Maine, Mapping the World*, and *Principles of Cartography*. Obituaries and other sources: *New York Times*, December 5, 1968; *Publishers Weekly*, December 30, 1968; *Association of American Geographers Annals*, March, 1970.

* * *

RAMBERT, Marie 1888-

PERSONAL: Born February 20, 1888, in Warsaw, Poland; daughter of Yakov (a bookseller) and Yevguenia Rambert; married Ashley Dukes (a playwright), 1918; children: Angela, Helena. *Education:* Studied with Jaques Dalcroze and Enrico Cecchetti. *Office:* Mercury Theatre Trust Ltd., 94 Chiswick High Rd., London W4 1SH, England.

CAREER: Diaghilev's Ballets Russes, professional dancer, 1912-25; Ballet Rambert, London, England, founder and director, 1926-66; Modern Dance Company, London, founder and director, 1966—. Founder of Rambert School of Ballet, 1920, and Mercury Theatre's Ballet Club, 1930; director of Mercury Theatre Trust Ltd.; guest on radio and television programs.

MEMBER: Imperial Society of Teachers (member of grand council), Royal Academy of Dancing (fellow; vice-president), Royal Society of Arts (fellow), Institute of Directors. *Awards, honors:* Commander of Order of the British Empire, 1953; Queen Elizabeth Coronation Award from Royal Academy

of Dancing, 1956; Legion d'Honneur, 1957; diploma from Manchester College of Art, 1960; dame of the British Empire, 1962; D.Litt. from University of Sussex, 1964; Jubilee Medal from Queen Elizabeth II, 1977; award from Composers Guild of Great Britain, 1978, for services to British ballet; gold medal of Polish Order of Merit, 1979.

WRITINGS: (With Mary Clarke) *Dancers of Mercury: The Story of Ballet Rambert*, A. & C. Black, 1960; (translator) M. I. Sizova, *Ulanova: Her Childhood and Schooldays*, A. & C. Black, 1962; *Quicksilver* (autobiography), Macmillan, 1972; (contributor) Anya Sainsbury, Clement Crisp, and Peter Williams, editors, *Fifty Years of Ballet Rambert*, Mercury Theatre Trust Ltd., 1976.

SIDELIGHTS: Dame Marie Rambert made a sound recording with Tamara Karsavina for Jupiter Records, "Marie Rambert on Ballet."

* * *

RAME, David
See DIVINE, Arthur Durham

* * *

RANDALL, Ruth (Elaine) Painter 1892-1971

OBITUARY NOTICE—See index for *CA* sketch: Born November 1, 1892, in Salem, Va.; died January 22, 1971. Author of several books about Abraham Lincoln and his family. Randall became interested in Lincoln studies through her husband, a scholar in that subject. Her books include *Mary Lincoln: Biography of a Marriage, The Courtship of Mr. Lincoln*, and *Colonel Elmer Elsworth*, and an autobiography, *I, Ruth*. Obituaries and other sources: *Current Biography*, Wilson, 1957; *I, Ruth*, Little, Brown, 1968; *The Author's and Writer's Who's Who*, 6th edition, Burke's Peerage, 1971; *Something About the Author*, Volume 3, Gale, 1972.

* * *

RANKIN, Herbert David 1931-

PERSONAL: Born June 21, 1931, in Belfast, Northern Ireland; son of Walter and Anna (Douglas) Rankin; married Anne Margaret Isobel Vannan (a teacher), January 11, 1957; children: Aidan. *Education:* Trinity College, Dublin, degree (with first class honors), 1954, graduate study, 1954-55. *Office:* Department of Classics, University of Southampton, Southampton SO9 5NH, England.

CAREER: Monash University, Clayton, Australia, Foundation Professor of Classics, 1965-73; University of Southampton, Southampton, England, professor of classics, 1973—. *Member:* Society for the Preservation of Hellenic Studies, Athenaeum Club. *Awards, honors:* Lefroy Stein Research Award, 1954-55.

WRITINGS: Plato and the Individual, Methuen, 1964; *Petronius the Artist*, Nijhoff, 1971; *Archilochus of Paros*, Noyes Press, 1977. Founder and editor of *Apeiron, Journal for Ancient Philosophy and Science*, 1966—. Contributor of articles, poems, and reviews to professional journals.

WORK IN PROGRESS: A monograph on the sophist Antisthenes.

* * *

RANSOHOFF, Paul M(artin) 1948-

PERSONAL: Born October 9, 1948, in Cincinnati, Ohio; son of William (a physician) and Regine (a school psychologist; maiden name, Weiss) Ransohoff. *Education:* Harvard University, B.A. (cum laude), 1970; University of Chicago, M.A., 1974; University of California, Berkeley, M.S., 1976; University of California, San Francisco, D.M.H., 1979. *Home:* 318 Maple St., San Francisco, Calif. 94118. *Office:* 422 Judah St., San Francisco, Calif. 94122.

CAREER: Private practice of psychotherapy and psychoanalysis in San Francisco, Calif., 1979—. Research fellow at University of California, San Francisco, 1979-81; clinical coordinator in psychiatry department at Mount Zion Hospital, 1980—. *Member:* Doctor of Mental Health Association (member of executive committee).

WRITINGS: (Editor with Donald Capps and Lewis Rambo) *Psychology of Religion: A Guide to Information Sources,* Gale, 1976. Contributor to psychiatry and sociology journals.

WORK IN PROGRESS: Research on the paintings of Rene Magritte, predictions of early termination of psychotherapy, and the restrictiveness of psychiatric care.

SIDELIGHTS: Ransohoff wrote: "My interests are in psychoanalysis, psychotherapy and clinical research, mental health education, and psychology of art. I am interested in empirical investigations of how psychotherapy and psychoanalysis work. In the psychology of art, I look at the psychological conflicts that artists struggle to master and the mechanisms by which responses are evoked in the audience or viewer."

* * *

RAUCH, Mabel Thompson   1888-1972

OBITUARY NOTICE—See index for *CA* sketch: Born November 30, 1888, in Carbondale, Ill.; died in 1972. Author. Rauch wrote many books, including *The American Scene, Vinnie and the Flag-Tree,* and *The Little Hellion.* She also contributed short stories and articles to magazines such as *Saturday Evening Post, Parents' Magazine,* and *Woman's Day.* (Date of death provided by son, Lawrence Lee Rauch.)

* * *

RAVEN, J(ohn) E(arle)   1914-1980

PERSONAL: Born December 13, 1914; died March 5, 1980; son of C. E. Raven (a minister); married Faith Hugh Smith, 1954; children: three daughters, two sons. *Education:* Trinity College, Cambridge, degree in classics (with first class honors).

CAREER: Social worker in London, England, and in Wales (as alternative service for a conscientious objector to military duty) during World War II; Cambridge University, Cambridge, England, fellow of Trinity College until 1948, and King's College, 1948-56, senior tutor in classics and fellow, 1956-58; writer, botanist, and consultant on gardening, 1958-80. J. H. Gray Memorial Lecturer at Cambridge University, 1976.

WRITINGS: Pythagoreans and Eleatics: An Account of the Interaction Between the Two Opposed Schools During the Fifth and Early Fourth Centuries B.C., Cambridge University Press, 1948; (with S. Max Walters) *Mountain Flowers,* Macmillan, 1956; (with Geoffrey Stephen Kirk) *The Presocratic Philosophers,* Cambridge University Press, 1957; *Plato's Thought in the Making: A Study of the Development of His Metaphysics,* Cambridge University Press, 1965; *A Botanist's Garden,* Collins, 1971.

BIOGRAPHICAL/CRITICAL SOURCES: London Times, March 7, 1980.*

RAVITZ, Shlomo   1885-1980

OBITUARY NOTICE: Born in 1885 in Novogrudok, Russia (now U.S.S.R.); died December 28, 1980, in Tel Aviv, Israel. Cantor and composer of numerous choral works. Ravitz led the Oneg Shabbat Choir for many years and later founded the Selah Seminary for Cantors. He also organized the Bilu Elementary School, where, according to Cantor Joseph Malovany, he "taught several generations of youngsters how to sing, pray and love music." In 1964 Ravitz edited *The Voice of Israel.* Obituaries and other sources: *New York Times,* December 29, 1980.

* * *

RAWLINGS, Hunter Ripley III   1944-

PERSONAL: Born December 14, 1944, in Norfolk, Va.; son of Hunter Ripley, Jr., and Tucker (Trapnell) Rawlings; married Irene Kukawka (a curator of art), January 7, 1967; children: Elizabeth, Hunter. *Education:* Haverford College, B.A., 1966; Princeton University, Ph.D., 1970. *Home:* 1510 Mariposa Ave., Boulder, Colo. 80302. *Office:* Department of Classics, University of Colorado, Boulder, Colo. 80309.

CAREER: University of Colorado, Boulder, assistant professor, 1970-75, associate professor, 1975-80, professor of classics, 1980—, associate vice-chancellor in Office of Academic Affairs, 1980—. Member of executive board of Denver Committee on Foreign Relations. *Member:* American Philological Association, Classical Association of the Middle West and South (member of executive board).

WRITINGS: The Structure of Thucydides' History, Princeton University Press, 1981. Contributor to periodicals. Editor of *Classical Journal.*

SIDELIGHTS: Rawlings wrote: "My major areas of research are Greek and Roman history and historiography. I read Greek, Latin, French, and German. I give frequent public lectures to universities and civic groups."

* * *

RAWSON, Wyatt Trevelyan Rawson   1894-1980

OBITUARY NOTICE—See index for *CA* sketch: Born January 2, 1894, in London, England; died February 11, 1980. Educator, editor, and author. Rawson taught at schools in Germany, England, and the United States, before founding and directing four independent schools in England. He also was an instructor in comparative religion with the Workers' Educational Association. His works include *The Werkplaats Adventure, The Way Within,* and *The Story of the New Education.* Rawson also edited the books *A New World in the Making* and *The Freedom We Seek.* (Date of death provided by daughter, Irmeli Gwendolen Rawson.)

* * *

RAYFIELD, (Patrick) Donald   1942-

PERSONAL: Born February 12, 1942, in Oxford, England; son of Harry Heron (an accountant) and Joan Rachel (a professor) Rayfield; married Rosalind Moore, July 27, 1963; children: Harriet, Gabriel, Barnaby. *Education:* Magdalene College, Cambridge, B.A., 1963, Ph.D., 1977. *Politics:* "Liberal with a small 'l.'" *Religion:* None. *Office:* Department of Russian, Queen Mary College, University of London, Mile End Rd., London E1 4NS, England.

CAREER: University of Queensland, Brisbane, Australia, lecturer in Russian, 1964-66; University of London, Queen Mary College, London, England, lecturer, 1967-78, senior lecturer in Russian, 1978—.

WRITINGS: (Translator and author of introduction) Nadezhda Mandel'shtam, *Ch.42*, Menard Press, 1973; (translator and author of introduction) Osip Mandel'shtam, *The Goldfinch*, Menard Press, 1973; *Chekhov: Evolution of His Art*, Barnes & Noble, 1975; (translator) Galaktion Tabidze, *Ati Leksi* (title means "Ten Poems"), Ganatleba, 1975; *The Dream of Lhasa*, Ohio State University Press, 1976.

Work represented in anthologies, including *The Elek Book of Oriental Verse; Cambridge Essays in Drama.* Contributor to literature and Slavic studies journals.

WORK IN PROGRESS: Research on folk poetry of the Khevsurs and on the Georgian language of the Soviet Union.

SIDELIGHTS: Rayfield commented: "Academics usually write books for the wrong reasons. They become obsessed with minutiae, polemics, and the search for authority. Readers and publishers should help them by insisting on the Pushkinian virtues of 'brevity, clarity, and simplicity,' and the Chekhovian standards of 'feeling, sense, and taking time.' Readers might also call for a return to multilingual standards, so that the art of translation might revive from its present insular inertia and make up for its deficient inspiration."

AVOCATIONAL INTERESTS: Breeding otters and wallabies, propagating shrubs, language study (especially languages of eastern Europe and the Near East).

* * *

RAYNER, John Desmond 1924-

PERSONAL: Original name Hans Sigismund Rahmer, name legally changed in 1944; born May 30, 1924, in Berlin, Germany; son of Ferdinand Josef and Charlotte (Landshut) Rahmer; married Jane Heilbronn (a secretary), June 19, 1955; children: Jeremy, Benjamin, Susan. *Education:* Emmanuel College, Cambridge, B.A., 1949, Diploma in Hebrew, Part I, 1951, Part II, 1952, M.A., 1954; attended Hebrew Union College-Jewish Institute of Religion, Cincinnati, Ohio, 1963-65. *Residence:* London, England. *Office:* Liberal Jewish Synagogue, 28 St. John's Wood Rd., London N.W.8, England.

CAREER: Ordained minister, 1953, and rabbi, 1965; Liberal Jewish Synagogue, London, England, associate minister, 1957-61, senior minister, 1961—. Lecturer at Leo Baeck College, 1966—; chairman of Council of Reform and Liberal Rabbis, 1969-71. *Military service:* British Army, 1943-47; became captain. *Awards, honors:* D.D. from Hebrew Union College-Jewish Institute of Religion, 1980.

WRITINGS—All published by Union of Liberal and Progressive Synagogues, except as noted: (Editor with Henry F. Skirball) *The Jewish Youth Group: A Handbook for Progressive Jewish Youth Groups*, Youth Section, World Union for Progressive Judaism, 1956; *The Practices of Liberal Judaism*, 1958; *Towards Mutual Understanding Between Jews and Christians*, Clarke, 1960; (editor with Chaim Stern) *Service of the Heart*, 1967; (editor with Stern) *Gate of Repentence*, 1973; *Guide to Jewish Marriage*, 1975; (with Bernard Hooker) *Judaism for Today*, 1978; (editor with Stern) *Passover Haggadah*, 1981.

WORK IN PROGRESS: A book on Judaism, with David J. Goldberg, publication by Penguin expected in 1982 or 1983.

SIDELIGHTS: Rayner commented: "My life and writing are primarily dedicated to the promotion of Liberal Judaism. By this I mean the preservation of all that is of permanent value in the religious and cultural heritage of the Jewish people (duly adapted in the light of contemporary knowledge and circumstances) for the sake of the enhancement of the quality of the life of the individual Jew. The preservation is also for the sake of the contribution which, I belive, Judaism can and should make in the life of humanity as a whole."

* * *

READ, Sylvia Joan

PERSONAL: Born on the ninth of April in London, England; daughter of John and Sylvia (a singer; maiden name Gothard) Read; married Alexander Francis William Fry, November 7, 1970; children: (previous marriage) Christobel Jane Albery, Jonathan Peter Albery. *Education:* Attended Froebel Educational Institute; received diploma and L.G.S.M. from Royal Academy of Dramatic Art. *Religion:* Anglican. *Home and office:* 859 Finchley Rd., London NW11 8LX, England.

CAREER: Writer. *Here and Now,* co-editor, 1940-49; Theatre Roundabout Ltd., London, England, leading actress, scriptwriter, and director of theatre, 1961—. Past lecturer for Poet's Theatre Guild; director of Radius, 1977-80. *Member:* British Actors Equity. *Awards, honors:* Gold Medal from Poetry Society.

WRITINGS: The Poetical Ark (poems), Acorn Press, 1946; *Harvest,* BBC Publications, 1951; *Burden of Blessing* (novel), Ward, Lock, 1952; *A Case of Arms* (novel) Heinemann, 1962; *Travelling Actors* (poems), Autolycus, 1973; *Poems,* BBC Publications, 1979. Also author of plays with husband William Fry, including "Lovely Day for the Race," "Living and Giving," "Pride and Prejudice" (adaptation of the novel by Jane Austen), "Vanity Fair" (adaptation of the novel by William Makepeace Thackeray), and "Elizabeth and Robert Browning." Contributor to magazines and newspapers, including *Outposts* and *Country Life.*

WORK IN PROGRESS: "Jane Eyre," play adapted from the novel by Charlotte Bronte, for Theatre Roundabout Ltd.

* * *

READING, Peter 1946-

PERSONAL: Born July 27, 1946, in Liverpool, England; son of Wilfred (an electrical engineer) and Mary (Catt) Reading; married Diana Gilbert, October 5, 1968; children: Angela. *Education:* Liverpool College of Art, B.A., 1967. *Home:* 1 Ragleth View, Little Stretton, Shropshire, England.

CAREER: School teacher in Liverpool, England, 1967-68; Liverpool College of Art, Liverpool, lecturer in art history, 1968-70; worked as a laborer and at an animal feed compounding mill, Shropshire, England, 1970-81; writer, 1970—. Sunderland Polytechnic, writer-in-residence, 1981-82. *Awards, honors:* Award from Arts Council of Great Britain, 1976; Cholmondeley Award for Poetry from the Society of Authors, 1978.

WRITINGS—Poetry collections; all published by Secker & Warburg, except as noted: *Water and Waste,* Outposts Publications, 1970; *For the Municipality's Elderly,* 1974; *The Prison Cell and Barrel Mystery,* 1976; *Nothing for Anyone,* 1977; *Fiction,* 1979; *Tom O'Bedlam's Beauties,* 1981.

* * *

REBBOT, Olivier 1951(?)-1981

OBITUARY NOTICE: Born c. 1951 in France; died of gunshot wounds sustained in El Salvador, February 10, 1981, in Hialeah, Fla. Journalist and photographer. Rebbot covered a Bolivian coup, the Guatemalan earthquake, and Lebanese and Nicaraguan civil wars. He was shot by a sniper while covering the civil war in El Salvador. Obituaries and other sources: *New York Times*, February 11, 1981; *Time*, February 23, 1981.

*   *   *

REDMON, Anne
See NIGHTINGALE, Anne Redmon

*   *   *

REED, Carroll E(dward) 1914-

PERSONAL: Born November 21, 1914, in Portland, Ore.; son of Edward R. and Cora (Schienle) Reed; married Elizabeth Eshom, December 26, 1938; children: John, Carolyn, Robin Reed Dale, Janet, Paul, Carl, Michelle. *Education:* University of Washington, Seattle, B.A., 1936, M.A., 1937; Brown University, Ph.D., 1941. *Home:* 190 Shays St., Amherst, Mass. 01002. *Office:* Department of Germanic Languages and Literatures, University of Massachusetts, Amherst, Mass. 01003.

CAREER: Brown University, Providence, R.I., instructor in German, 1941-42; War Department, Washington, D.C., cryptanalyst, 1942-46; University of Georgia, Athens, assistant professor of German, 1946; University of Washington, Seattle, instructor, 1946-48, assistant professor, 1948-52, associate professor, 1952-59, professor of German and linguistics, 1959-66; University of California, Riverside, professor of German and linguistics and chairman of department of German and Russian, 1966-69; University of Massachusetts, Amherst, professor of Germanic languages and literatures, 1969—, head of department, 1971-76. Lecturer at Columbia University, 1950, and University of Texas, 1958. *Member:* Modern Language Association of America, American Dialect Society, Linguistic Society of America, American Association of Teachers of German, Canadian Linguistic Association, Pennsylvania German Society, Phi Beta Kappa. *Awards, honors:* Fulbright scholar in Germany, 1953-54.

WRITINGS: The Pennsylvania German Dialect Spoken in the Counties of Lehigh and Berks, University of Washington Press, 1949; (editor) *Conference on Critical Languages in Liberal Arts Colleges,* Association of American Colleges, 1965; *Dialects of American English,* World Publishing, 1967, revised edition, University of Massachusetts Press, 1977; (editor) *The Learning of Language,* Appleton, 1971; (contributor) Glenn G. Gilbert, editor, *The German Language in America,* University of Texas Press, 1971; (contributor) Evelyn Firchow and others, editors, *Studies for Einar Haugen,* Mouton, 1972; (contributor) Ulrich Engel, editor, *Sprache der Gegenwart* (title means "Current Language"), Schwann, 1973; (contributor) Wolf von Schmidt, editor, *Streadbeck Festschrift,* Lang, 1981. Contributor to language, literature, and linguistic journals. Editor of *Modern Language Quarterly,* 1956-63.

WORK IN PROGRESS: The Dialect of Sachsenhausen in 1821.

*   *   *

REED, Donald A(nthony) 1935-

PERSONAL: Born November 22, 1935, in St. Bernard, La.; son of Roscoe and Mildred (Fauria) Reed. *Education:* Loyola University of Los Angeles (now Loyola Marymount University), B.S., 1957; University of Southern California, M.S.L.S., 1958, graduate study 1958-65, J.D., 1968. *Politics:* Democrat. *Religion:* Roman Catholic. *Home:* 334 West 54th St., Los Angeles, Calif. 90037.

CAREER: California Institute of the Arts, Los Angeles, instructor in history, 1963-64; Los Angeles Valley College, Van Nuys, Calif., lecturer in history, 1964, instructor in library services, 1964-66; Woodbury College, Los Angeles, librarian, 1972-79; Arthur T. Berggren (law firm), law librarian, 1979—; University of Beverly Hills, Beverly Hills, Calif., adjunct professor, 1980—. *Member:* American Association of Law Librarians, American Associaton of University Professors, Academy of Science Fiction, Fantasy, and Horror Films (president, 1972—), Science Fiction Writers Association, Mystery Writers of America, Count Dracula Society (president, 1962—), Beta Phi Mu, Phi Alpha Theta, Phi Kappa Alpha. *Awards, honors:* Mrs. Ann Radcliffe Award, 1964, Horace Walpole Gold Medal, 1968, and Rev. Dr. Montague Summers Memorial Award, 1969, all from Count Dracula Society; award from Academy of Science Fiction, Fantasy, and Horror Films, 1977; award of excellence from Film Advisory Board, 1980; award from Los Angeles Film Teachers Association, 1980.

WRITINGS: The Vampire on the Screen, Wagon & Star, 1964; *Admiral Leahy at Vichy France,* Adams Press, 1965; *Robert Redford,* foreword by Tom Kirk, Sherbourne, 1975; (with Patrick Pattison) *Science Fiction Film Awards,* ESE California, 1980.

WORK IN PROGRESS: An autobiography.

SIDELIGHTS: Reed told *CA:* "Most of my time is now taken up by activities of the Academy of Science Fiction, Fantasy, and Horror Films, a nonprofit, tax-exempt association of some three thousand members. As founder and national president, I supervise all its divisions: films, literature, television, art, and theatre. I also appear on its annual syndicated television awards program. This leaves very little time for writing, particularly as I now view some two hundred feature films a year and many, many television programs."

AVOCATIONAL INTERESTS: Films, television, books, history.

BIOGRAPHICAL/CRITICAL SOURCES: West Coast Review of Books, May, 1977.

*   *   *

REED, Douglas 1895-1976

PERSONAL: Born in 1895 in London, England; died in 1976; married, 1922; children: one son, one daughter.

CAREER: Office boy for publisher, 1908; bank clerk, 1914; clerk for wine merchant and canvasser for maps, 1918-21; Northcliffe Newspapers, began as stenographer, became private secretary to Lord Northcliffe, 1921-24; *Times,* London, England, sub-editor, 1924-26, reporter, 1926-29, assistant correspondent in Berlin, Germany, 1929-35, chief Central European correspondent, covering Austria, Rumania, Hungary, Czechoslovakia, Bulgaria, and Yugoslavia, 1935-38; *News Chronicle,* special correspondent, 1938-39; freelance writer, 1939-73. War correspondent in Normandy, 1944; foreign editor of Kemsley Newspapers, 1945; founder of newspaper, *Tidings,* 1946. *Military service:* British Army, Infantry and Air Service, 1914-18; mentioned in dispatches.

WRITINGS: The Burning of the Reichstag, Gollancz, 1934; *Insanity Fair: A European Cavalcade* (autobiography), Random House, 1938 (published in England as *Insanity Fair,* J. Cape, 1938); *Disgrace Abounding,* J. Cape, 1939; *Nemesis?: The Story of Otto Strasser,* Houghton, 1940 (published in England as *The Story of Otto Strasser and the Black Front,* J. Cape, 1940); *A Prophet at Home,* J. Cape, 1941; (translator) Strasser, *History in My Time,* J. Cape, 1941; *All Our To-*

morrows, J. Cape, 1942; *Lest We Regret,* J. Cape, 1943; *From Smoke to Smother, 1939-1948: A Sequel to Insanity Fair,* J. Cape, 1948; *Somewhere South of Suez,* J. Cape, 1950, published in the United States as *Somewhere South of Suez: A Further Survey of the Grand Design of the Twentieth Century,* Devin-Adair, 1951; *Far and Wide,* J. Cape, 1951, Omni Publications, Part 2 reprinted as *Behind the Scene,* Noontide, 1976; *The Prisoner of Ottawa: Otto Strasser,* J. Cape, 1953; *The Battle for Rhodesia,* Haum, 1966, Devin-Adair, 1967, reprinted as *Insanity Fair '67,* Gibbs, 1967; *The Siege of Southern Africa,* Macmillan South Africa, 1974.

Novels: *The Next Horizon; or, Yeoman's Progress,* J. Cape, 1945, published in the United States as *Yeoman's Progress,* Bobbs-merrill, 1946; *Galanty Show,* J. Cape, 1947; *Reasons of Health,* J. Cape, 1949; *Rule of Three,* J. Cape, 1950.

Author of *Downfall* (three-act play), J. Cape, 1942, Appleton, 1943.

SIDELIGHTS: The Burning of the Reichstag described the event, which Reed witnessed in 1933, and the ensuing trial. Reed also happened to be an eyewitness when Hitler's forces invaded Austria in 1938 and Prague in 1939, but he returned to England before World War II began in earnest. The Agreement of Munich, signed in 1938, convinced him that journalism was not an effective means of informing the public, and most of the rest of his career was devoted to writing books.

His autobiography, *Insanity Fair,* predicted World War I and World War II. *Disgrace Abounding* expressed his views on the dangers of communism and Zionism, which Reed predicted would grow more dominant after World War II began. *Somewhere South of Suez* described his visit to South Africa in 1948, and *Far and Wide* covered his travels in the United States and Canada in 1949.

*   *   *

REED, John Q(uincy)   1918-1978

OBITUARY NOTICE—See index for *CA* sketch: Born December 30, 1918, in Slippery Rock, Pa.; died May 20, 1978. Educator and author. Reed taught at Buena Vista College and Kansas State College (now Pittsburgh State University), where he became an English professor. His work includes *Benjamin Penhallow Shillaber.* Reed also contributed to the publications *American Literature* and *Midwest Quarterly.* Obituaries and other sources: *Directory of American Scholars,* Volume II: *English, Speech, and Drama,* 7th edition, Bowker, 1978. (Date of death provided by wife, Mary Reed.)

*   *   *

REED, Thomas (James)   1947-

PERSONAL: Born November 5, 1947, in New York, N.Y.; son of Charles Claude (a chemist) and Margo (Zellner) Reed. *Education:* Yale University, B.A. (magna cum laude), 1969; Princeton University, M.P.A., 1971; also attended New School for Social Research and Parsons School of Design. *Home:* 328 East 73rd St., New York, N.Y. 10021.

CAREER: Mobilization for Youth Legal Services, Inc., New York City, interne, caseworker, and researcher, summer, 1970; Princeton Survey Research Center, Princeton, N.J., interviewer for Gallup Poll, summer, 1971; substitute teacher at high school in Trenton, N.J., 1971; New York City Addiction Services Agency, New York City, program researcher and evaluator in department of research and evaluation, 1972-76; Yankelovich, Skelly & White, Inc., New York City, contract survey researcher, 1977-78; New York City Department of Health, New York City, manager and principal evaluator of district evaluation project, 1976—; freelance illustrator. Speaker at colleges. *Member:* Phi Beta Kappa.

WRITINGS: Melissa on Parade (self-illustrated juvenile), Bradbury, 1979. Contributor of articles to scholarly journals, and of illustrations and political cartoons to popular magazines and newspapers, including *Harper's, Good Housekeeping, American Bookseller,* and *Foreign Policy.*

WORK IN PROGRESS: Another self-illustrated children's book.

SIDELIGHTS: Reed told *CA:* "Basically, *Melissa* is a story about a child's efforts to overcome obstacles to get the world to take her seriously. The story's humor revolves largely around Melissa's sometimes imperfect, sometimes offbeat, but always persistent efforts to make sense of a world that is not so easily tamed or predictable. Melissa's grapplings with the meanings and limitations of her behavior reflect, I think, some common preoccupations of children, and the story introduced some themes which I would like to explore further.

"I became interested in trying to do a children's book during graduate school. While pursuing coursework, I had been doing some substitute teaching, which had introduced me to a cross-section of children's books. I was attracted by the children's book format as a vehicle for bringing writing and illustrating together.

"My illustrating and cartooning interests have always grown along, contended, and coexisted with other interests, studies, and work pursuits. While sometimes this arrangement has made for jostling and juggling, it has managed to endure and has had some important advantages. For one thing, it has meant that my various art activities could take direction from and be enriched by my studies and work experiences. It has also allowed creative pursuits to be buffered enough from the marketplace so that they could grow more naturally, following their own dictates."

*   *   *

REICH, Tova Rachel   1942-

PERSONAL: Born December 24, 1942, in Liberty, N.Y.; daughter of Moshe and Miriam Weiss; married Walter Reich (a psychiatrist), June 10, 1965; children: Daniel Salo, David Emile, Rebecca Zohar. *Education:* Brooklyn College of the City University of New York, B.A., 1964; New York University, M.A., 1965. *Home:* 200 Primrose St., Chevy Chase, Md. 20015. *Agent:* Georges Borchardt, Inc., 136 East 57th St., New York, N.Y. 10022.

CAREER: Southern Connecticut State College, New Haven, instructor in English, 1972-73; American University, Washington, D.C., instructor in English, 1974-77; writer, 1977—.

WRITINGS: Mara (novel), Farrar, Straus, 1978. Author of "Hers," a column in *New York Times,* 1978-81. Contributor of stories to magazines, including *Harper's* and *Commentary,* and articles and reviews to *New York Times* and *Washington Post.*

WORK IN PROGRESS: Two novels, one entitled *Birth Wish;* stories and articles.

*   *   *

REICHLER, Joseph Lawrence   1918-

PERSONAL: Surname is pronounced *Rike*-ler; born January

1, 1920, in New York; son of Daniel Reichler; married Ricky Cooper, December 3, 1946; children: Paul. *Education:* Received B.A. from St. John's University, Brooklyn, N.Y. (now Jamaica, N.Y.). *Home:* 39 Oakdale Rd., Roslyn Heights, N.Y. 11577. *Office:* Office of the Baseball Commissioner, 75 Rockefeller Plaza, New York, N.Y.

CAREER: Sportswriter for Associated Press (AP), 1942-65; Office of the Baseball Commissioner, New York, N.Y., director of public relations and special assistant to commissioner, 1965—.

WRITINGS: History of Baseball, Prentice-Hall, 1958; *It's Good to Be Alive* (biography of Roy Campanella), Little, Brown, 1959; *Unforgettable Games,* Ronald, 1960; *Mickey Walker: Toy Bulldog,* Random House, 1962; *Baseball's Greatest Moments,* Crown, 1970; *Encyclopedia of Baseball,* Macmillan, 1973, 3rd edition, 1978; *The Game and the Glory,* Prentice-Hall, 1976; *The World Series,* Simon & Schuster, 1977. Contributor to magazines in the United States and Japan, including *Saturday Evening Post, Look,* and *Sports Illustrated,* and newspapers.

WORK IN PROGRESS: Revisions of *History of Baseball* and *Encyclopedia of Baseball,* for Macmillan; *The All-Star Game; The Ultimate Baseball Record Book; Fabulous Baseball Facts, Figures, and Features,* for Macmillan; *Great Sports Oddities.*

*   *   *

REID, J(ohn) C(owie) 1916-1972
(Caliban)

OBITUARY NOTICE—See index for *CA* sketch: Born January 4, 1916, in Auckland, New Zealand; died May 31, 1972. Educator, broadcaster, editor, and author. Reid taught for more than twenty years at the University of Auckland. He also hosted the radio program "Critics" and the television show "Comment." Reid edited such works as *The Kiwi Laughs: An Anthology of New Zealand Prose Humour* and *Forty Short Short Stories,* and he wrote several books, including *The Mind and Art of Coventry Patmore; Francis Thompson, Man and Poet;* and *Gerard Manley Hopkins, Priest and Poet: A Centennial Tribute.* Obituaries and other sources: *The Author's and Writer's Who's Who,* 6th edition, Burke's Peerage, 1971. (Date of death provided by wife, Joyce Helena Reid.)

*   *   *

REID, Philip
See Ingrams, Richard (Reid)

*   *   *

REMMERS, H(ermann) H(enry) 1892-1969

OBITUARY NOTICE—See index for *CA* sketch: Born November 25, 1892, in Norden, Germany (now West Germany); died in 1969. Educator and author. Remmers taught psychology and education at Purdue University for forty years. He wrote several books in these fields, including *Educational Measurement and Evaluation, Introduction to Opinion and Attitude Measurement,* and *Anti-Democratic Attitudes in American Schools.* Obituaries and other sources: *American Men and Women of Science: The Social and Behavioral Sciences,* 12th edition, Bowker, 1973.

*   *   *

RENA, Sally
See RENA, Sarah Mary

RENA, Sarah Mary 1941-
(Sally Rena)

PERSONAL: Born March 26, 1941, in Glasgow, Scotland; daughter of Ian Hervey and Margaret Helen (Periera) Stuart Black; married Oliver Dollfus Rena (a banker), July 11, 1961; children: Nicholas, Julian, Francesca, Sophie. *Education:* Attended Sorbonne, University of Paris, and University of Florence. *Politics:* Conservative. *Religion:* Roman Catholic. *Home and office:* 12 Campden Hill Court, London, England. *Agent:* Michael Motley, Gloucester Ter., London, England.

CAREER: Writer. Justice of the peace and juvenile magistrate in London. *Member:* Magistrates Association.

WRITINGS—Under name Sally Rena: *The Sea Road West* (novel), Bobbs-Merrill, 1974; *The Night Flower* (novel), Weidenfeld & Nicolson, 1978.

WORK IN PROGRESS: Another novel; an anthology on food, flowers, and poetry.

SIDELIGHTS: Sarah Rena commented to *CA:* "I was lucky to be asked to become a juvenile magistrate in the city of London at a time when I thought I should find a lot of excellent material and ideas for fiction. Although I find the job exacting and absolutely fascinating, the tales of horror with which we are often faced would have to be greatly watered down to make them fiction."

The Sea Road West was adapted for radio and broadcast by BBC-Radio 3.

*   *   *

RENDEL, George William 1889-1979

OBITUARY NOTICE—See index for *CA* sketch: Born February 23, 1889, in Italy; died May, 1979. Diplomat, lecturer, and author. Rendel worked in the British Diplomatic and Foreign Office Service for more than fifty years. He held several positions, such as head of the Middle East Department, ambassador to Yugoslavia and Belgium, and chairman of the first Constitutional Commission in Singapore. Rendel was made Knight Commander of the Order of St. Michael and St. George for his service. He also lectured in many countries. Rendel's work includes *The Sword and the Olive.* Obituaries and other sources: *Who's Who,* 131st edition, St. Martin's, 1979. (Date of death provided by R. Rendel.)

*   *   *

REYNOLDS, Dickson
See REYNOLDS, Helen Mary Greenwood
Campbell

*   *   *

REYNOLDS, Helen Mary Greenwood Campbell 1884-1969
(Helen Dickson, Dickson Reynolds)

OBITUARY NOTICE—See index for *CA* sketch: Born in 1884 in Regina, Saskatchewan, Canada; died January 21, 1969. Illustrator and author. Reynolds wrote several books, including *Yoshio, Cherries Are Ripe, Carol of Long Chance Mine,* and *Summer of Surprise.* She also contributed numerous self-illustrated short-stories and articles to magazines. (Date of death provided by granddaughter, Helen Hughes.)

REYNOLDS, Pamela 1923-

PERSONAL: Born June 6, 1923, in New York, N.Y.; daughter of George Peter (an accountant) and Erma (a marine biologist; maiden name, Cary) Stemler; married John Cornelius Reynolds (an attorney); children: Nora Dare, Brian Drew, Diana Putman. *Education:* Wells College, B.A., 1945; Columbia University, M.A., 1948. *Agent:* Bertha Klausner, International Literary Agency, Inc., 71 Park Ave., New York, N.Y. 10016.

CAREER: Writer, 1965—. Substitute teacher of English at Fox Lane High School, 1967—. *Member:* U.S. Pony Club, Goldens Bridge Hounds Pony Club.

WRITINGS: Horseshoe Hill, Lothrop, 1965; *A Different Kind of Sister,* Lothrop, 1967; *Earth Times Two* (science fiction novel), Lothrop, 1970; *Will the Real Monday Please Stand Up?,* Archway, 1976.

WORK IN PROGRESS: The Stone Child, a historical mystery novel set in Sag Harbor, Long Island, New York.

SIDELIGHTS: "I was born with a caul," Pamela Reynolds commented. "One of my grandmothers was a Gypsy. I traveled to Clutchin Hye to see the temple where I was sacrificed in a former life. I share telepathy with one of my daughters."

*   *   *

REYNOLDS, Robert Leonard 1902-1966

OBITUARY NOTICE—See index for *CA* sketch: Born January 17, 1902, in Janesville, Wis.; died April 29, 1966. Educator, historian, editor, and author. Reynolds was a professor of history at the University of Wisconsin, Madison, for over thirty-five years. He co-edited an eight-volume work entitled *Notai Liguri del Secolo XII* and another book, *Twelfth-Century Europe.* He wrote *Europe Emerges: Transition Toward an Industrial Worldwide Society, 600-1750* and *Commodore Perry in Japan.* (Date of death provided by the University of Wisconsin.)

*   *   *

RHEA, Claude H(iram), Jr. 1927-

PERSONAL: Surname is pronounced Ray; born October 26, 1927, in Carrollton, Mo.; son of Claude H. (in sales) and Cecile Virginia (Walden) Rhea; married Carolyn Priscilla Turnage (a writer and teacher of English), August 26, 1951; children: Claude Hiram III, Charles Randall, Margaret Elizabeth. *Education:* William Jewell College, A.B., 1950; graduate study at University of Missouri, 1950-51; Florida State University, B.Mus.Ed., 1953, M.Mus.Ed., 1954, Ed.D., 1958; attended University of Rochester, summer, 1961. *Politics:* Republican. *Religion:* Baptist. *Home:* 3701 River Oaks Lane, Birmingham, Ala. 35223. *Office:* School of Music, Samford University, 800 Lakeshore Dr., Birmingham, Ala. 35209.

CAREER: New Orleans Baptist Theological Seminary, New Orleans, La., professor of music and dean of School of Music, 1954-63; Houston Baptist University, Houston, Tex., music professor and administrative vice-president, 1963-67; Southern Baptist Convention, Foreign Mission Board, Richmond, Va., music and mass media consultant, 1967-69; Samford University, Birmingham, Ala., dean of School of Music, 1969—. Member of board of directors of Learning Laboratories of Georgia. Chairman of youth activities for Birmingham Symphony; member of board of directors of Birmingham Civic Opera; member of Birmingham Children's Theater Board. *Military service:* U.S. Army, chaplain's assistant, 1945-47; served in Germany.

MEMBER: American Association of University Administrators, Music Educators National Conference, American Society of Composers, Authors, and Publishers (fellow), Newcomen Society of North America (fellow), Royal Society of Arts (fellow), Alabama Federation of Music Clubs (member of executive committee), Phi Eta Sigma, Beta Beta Beta, Phi Mu Alpha Sinfonia, Omicron Delta Kappa, Pi Kappa Lambda, Phi Kappa Phi, Kiwanis. *Awards, honors:* Certificate of achievement from William Jewell College, 1961; citation from city of Houston, Tex.; silver bowl from city of Birmingham, Ala., 1975; named honorary consul of Republic of Liberia, 1979.

WRITINGS: (With wife, Carolyn Rhea) *A Child's Life in Song,* Broadman, 1964; *The Lottie Moon Cook Book,* Word, Inc., 1969; (with Carolyn Rhea) *Sing While You Grow,* Lilleanas, 1975; *With My Song I Will Praise Him* (autobiography), Broadman, 1977.

WORK IN PROGRESS: Missionary Cookbook, eight hundred recipes from eighty nations.

SIDELIGHTS: Rhea wrote: "My autobiography catalogs my travels, my bout with cancer (successful so far), and the concerts I have given in more than fifty nations around the world. I have visited Central and South America, Europe, the Middle East, North and East Africa, Southeast Asia, the Orient, Australia and New Zealand, and the South Seas islands. My interests include composing music."

Rhea's record albums, all on the Word label, include "Claude Rhea Sings," "Sacred Masterpieces," 1957, "Majestic Themes," 1960, and "The Radiance of Christmas," 1962.

*   *   *

RHODES, John J(acob) 1916-

PERSONAL: Born September 18, 1916, in Council Grove, Kan.; son of John Jacob, Sr. (a retail lumber dealer and state treasurer) and Gladys Anne (Thomas) Rhodes; married Mary Elizabeth Harvey, May 24, 1942; children: John Jacob III, Thomas H., Elizabeth Campbell, James Scott. *Education:* Kansas State University, B.S., 1938; Harvard University, LL.B., 1941. *Religion:* Methodist. *Office:* U.S. House of Representatives, 2310 Rayburn Bldg., Washington, D.C. 20515.

CAREER: Rhodes, Killian & Legg (law firm), Mesa, Ariz., partner, 1946-52; U.S. Congress, Washington, D.C., Republican member of House of Representatives, 1953—, minority leader, 1973-81. Vice-president and member of board of directors of Farm and Home Life Insurance Co., 1951—. Vice-chairman of Arizona Board of Public Welfare, 1951-52. Delegate to Republican national convention, 1964-76, chairman of platform committee, 1972, chairman of convention, 1976 and 1980; member of executive committee of Republican National Committee, 1974; chairman of House Republican Policy Committee, 1965-73. *Military service:* U.S. Army Air Forces, 1941-46; became lieutenant colonel. U.S. Army Reserve, Judge Advocate General's Corps, 1948—; became colonel.

MEMBER: Kansas Bar Association, Arizona Bar Association, District of Columbia Bar Association, Mesa Chamber of Commerce (president, 1950), Sons of the American Revolution, American Legion (past senior vice-commander), Beta Theta Pi, Blue Key, Scabbard and Blade, Benevolent and Protective Order of Elks, Loyal Order of Moose, Free and Accepted Masons, Burning Tree Country Club, Congressional Country Club, Capitol Hill Club, Arizona Club, Mesa Golf and Country Club, Rotary. *Awards, honors:* Watchdog of the Treasury Award from U.S. Congress, 1970; honorary degrees from University of Arizona and Arizona State University.

WRITINGS: The Futile System: How to Unchain Congress and Make the System Work Again, EPM Publications, 1976.

SIDELIGHTS: Rhodes was the first Republican ever sent to the House of Representatives by Arizona voters. On the whole he has remained a conservative, supporting such issues as a strong military and voting against assistance programs. He supported Richard Nixon through the early part of the Watergate investigations, but eventually came to support the president's impeachment. His efforts have been dedicated consistently toward preserving and strengthening the viability of the Republican party.

BIOGRAPHICAL/CRITICAL SOURCES: Knoxville News-Sentinel, December 9, 1973; *New York Times,* December 29, 1973, August 16, 1976; *Best Sellers,* October, 1976; *Congressional Digest,* December, 1979.

*   *   *

RICE, Tim 1944-

PERSONAL: Born November 10, 1944, in Amersham, Buckinghamshire, England; son of Hugh Gordon and Joan Odette (Bawden) Rice; married Jane McIntosh (a farmer), August 19, 1974; children: Eva, Donald. *Education:* Attended Sorbonne, University of Paris, 1963; studied law in London, England, 1963-66. *Agent:* David Land, 118 Wardour St., London W.1, England. *Office:* Heartaches Ltd., Romeyns Court, Great Milton, Oxfordshire, England.

CAREER: Singer with music group, Aardvarks, 1958-62; EMI Records, London, England, management trainee, 1966-68; Norrie Paramor Organisation, London, assistant record producer, 1968-69; writer, 1969—. Broadcaster for radio and television networks, including British Broadcasting Corp. (BBC); host of "Friday Night Saturday Morning," on BBC-TV 2, "Musical Triangles," and "Disco"; singer. Operator of Heartaches Cricket Club. Member of Rick Nelson International and Bernard Levin Appreciation. *Awards, honors:* Numerous awards, including two Antoinette Perry ("Tony") Awards and seven Ivor Novello Awards, for "Jesus Christ Superstar" and "Evita."

WRITINGS: (With Paul Gambaccini, Mike Read, and Jo Rice) *The Guinness Book of British Hit Singles,* Guinness Superlatives, 1977, 4th edition, 1981; (editor) *The Lord's Taverners Sticky Wicket Book,* Queen Anne Press, 1980; (with J. Rice and others) *The Guinness Book of Hits of the Seventies,* Guinness Superlatives, 1980.

Musicals; lyricist, all with music by Andrew Lloyd Webber: "Joseph and the Amazing Technicolor Dreamcoat," first produced in 1968, revised version produced in 1972 (soundtrack released in 1972); "Jesus Christ Superstar," first produced in 1971 (soundtrack released by Decca, 1970; adapted for motion picture, Universal, 1973); "Evita," first produced in London, 1978 (soundtrack released by MCA, 1977).

Songs: "That's My Story," Mills Music, 1965; (with Marvin Hamlisch) "The Only Way to Go," 1975; "It's Easy for You," 1977; (co-author) "Hearts Not Diamonds," 1980; (co-author) "A Remarkable Woman," 1980. Author of lyrics for songs used in films, including "Gumshoe," and "The Odessa File," both with Webber, and "The Fan," with Hamlisch.

SIDELIGHTS: Rice gained notoriety in 1971 as lyricist of the immensely popular rock musical "Jesus Christ Superstar." The musical became a phenomenon of the entertainment industry by earning profits as a stage production, re-

cording, and motion picture. "It is several things," wrote Malcolm Boyd, "a Rockette operetta, a Barnumian put-on, a religioso-cum-showbiz pastiche, and a musicalized 'Sweet Sweetback's Baadassssss Judas Song.'" He added, "Even the controversy of Jesus . . . is made marketable in a plasticware production." James R. Huffman attributed the musical's success to its broad appeal. "Whatever can be all things to all people—or the most things to the most people—will be the most successful," he observed. "Works like *Jesus Christ Superstar,* which 'ask the right questions' but allow each individual to provide his own answers, will be appropriated by nearly all—the atheist, the agnostic, and the believer." Clifford Edwards agreed. "It has avoided cliches, sentimentality, and mere ficitonalizing," he observed, "presenting Jesus' real humanity forcefully while allowing the audience great latitude for personal interpretation."

Many critics noted Webber and Rice's portrayal of Jesus as a humanitarian. William Bender declared that "both libretto and music are provocatively ambiguous about Christ's divinity. What Webber and Rice seem certain of is that Christ was a profoundly humanitarian radical thinker, not unlike Martin Luther King and Robert F. Kennedy." Clifford Edwards wrote: "Where does the portrayal of Christ focus? On Jesus as a flesh-and-blood human being. . . . A common reaction to Superstar is 'It was the first time I ever thought of Jesus as a real person.' The phantom-like portrayals of an otherwordly Christ on decades of funeral-home calendars and Sunday School walls apparently makes the focus on Jesus as a real person a remarkable revelation to this generation." And Boyd charged that "Jesus Christ Superstar" "gives us a confused, tired but plucky Jesus who is going to the cross even if it kills him."

The music of "Jesus Christ Superstar" was generally praised as innovative and ambitious. Richard Williams called the music "a considerable achievement," and Douglas Watt deemed it "vibrant, richly varied, and always dramatically right." William Bender wrote: "Whatever the reaction to *Superstar* may be, Webber and Rice have fused words and music into such a convincing narrative style that rock may never be quite the same again. . . . Webber and Rice do not outdo the Beatles or the Rolling Stones or the Edwin Hawkins Singers, Prokofiev, Orff, Stravinsky, or any other musical influence found in their work. But they have welded these borrowings into a considerable work that is their own."

Buoyed by the success of "Jesus Christ Superstar," Webber and Rice revised their first musical, "Joseph and the Amazing Technicolor Dreamcoat," for production in 1972. Like "Superstar," "Joseph" draws its subject from the Bible. It is the Old Testament tale of Joseph, the son of a sheepherder who is abandoned by his eleven brothers after receiving a multi-colored coat from his father. Clive Barnes praised the musical as "fresher and brighter than 'Superstar'" and called it "totally unpretentious and . . . totally charming." *Variety* praised the musical's "charm, wit and inventive staging."

Webber and Rice enjoyed less success in the mid-1970's. "Jesus Christ Superstar" was released as a motion picture and was reviewed unfavorably by several critics. Directed by Norman Jewison, and written by Jewison and Melvyn Bragg, the film used Webber and Rice's music less successfully than the stage production. Loraine Alterman called the film "unmitigated boredom," and Jon Landau contended that "Jesus' character is so poorly drawn that we never understand either the appeal that he generates or the hostility he provokes."

In 1976 Clive Barnes dismissed a restaging of "Joseph and the Amazing Technicolor Dreamcoat." "The show looks good," he conceded, "but it just doesn't sound good. One musical number after another plonks lifeless on the deck. . . . The music is soft-rock, and nowadays seems a paraphrase of a pastiche. It has no originality—a few liturgical notes with a great deal of rock frenzy—and the lyrics are merely simplistic."

Webber and Rice's careers rebounded in 1978, though, with "Evita," their rock-opera about actress Eva Duarte's rise to political power as wife of Argentinian dictator Juan Peron. The musical begins with Eva's funeral, then retraces her life as a promiscuous actress who eventually marries the dictator. With the accompaniment of film footage, Eva is shown as the idol of the Argentinian working class that she abuses. The show concludes with her death of cancer at age thirty-three.

Although "Evita" proved enormously popular with the public, few critics were impressed. Edwin Wilson wrote, "'Evita' is hopelessly muddled." Eric Salzman complained, "In the end, we cannot untangle the dramatic, verbal, and musical skeins, and . . . the authors' ambitions do not permit us to do so." Similarly, Barnes charged, "The fault of the whole construction is that it is hollow." And Walter Kerr contended, "It is rather like reading endless footnotes from which the text has disappeared."

Most of the praise for "Evita" was for the grandeur of the production and the direction of Harold Prince. Barnes called it "a virtually faultless piece of Broadway fantasy that has shadow exultantly victorious over substance, and form virtually laughing at content. . . . The gloss of the surface is meant to be impenetrable—and it is." Jack Kroll applauded Prince's staging as "dazzling" and praised his ability to control the large production. Martin Gottfried declared that "there is no question of the entire production's strength and uniqueness," though he granted that "the intellectual content takes second place to theatricality." T. E. Kalem agreed. "*Evita* is a spectacular eye-catcher," the reviewer noted, "but it seldom gets a grip on the playgoer's feelings."

BIOGRAPHICAL/CRITICAL SOURCES: Melody Maker, March 3, 1970, October 10, 1970, June 16, 1973; *Time,* November 9, 1970, October 8, 1979; *Rolling Stone,* December 2, 1970, June 24, 1971, August 2, 1973, April 7, 1977; *New York Daily News,* October 13, 1971; *New York Times,* October 13, 1971, October 24, 1971, September 5, 1972, December 31, 1976, September 26, 1979; *Women's Wear Daily,* October 14, 1971, September 26, 1979; *Newsweek,* October 25, 1971, October 8, 1979; *Journal of Popular Culture,* fall, 1972; *Variety,* March 7, 1973; *Christian Century,* June 27, 1973; *Commentary,* September, 1973; *Esquire,* October, 1973; *Stereo Review,* April, 1977; *Catholic World,* August, 1977; *Saturday Review,* October 14, 1978; *New York Post,* September 26, 1979; *Wall Street Journal,* September 26, 1979; *Contemporary Literary Criticism,* Volume 21, Gale, 1982.

* * *

RICHARD, Olga 1914-

PERSONAL: Born November 15, 1914, in Altoona, Pa.; daughter of George (a farmer and factory worker) and Kathryn (Peilich) Mikelson; married Gene Richard (a design engineer), June 10, 1935; children: Toni Richard Marsnik, George, Susan Richard Fredlund. *Education:* Layton School of Art, diploma, 1935; University of California, Los Angeles, B.A., 1948, M.A., 1952. *Residence:* North Hollywood, Calif. *Office:* 11570 Victory Blvd., North Hollywood, Calif. 91606.

CAREER: Art teacher in Flint, Mich., Burbank, Calif., Northridge, Calif., and Los Angeles, Calif., 1935-52; University of California, Los Angeles, supervisor of art education at university elementary school, 1952-79. Art education consultant. *Awards, honors:* Dutton-Macrae Award.

WRITINGS: (With Donnarae MacCann) *The Child's First Books,* H. W. Wilson, 1973; (contributor) Zena Sutherland, editor, *Arbuthnot Anthology of Children's Literature,* 4th edition (Richard was not associated with earlier editions), Scott, Foresman, 1976. Author of "Children Arrange Shapes and Mix Colors.," a film strip released by Teacher Education Laboratory, University of California, Los Angeles, 1974. Author with Donnarae MacCann of column "Picture Books for Children," in *Wilson Library Bulletin.*

WORK IN PROGRESS: A book on sequential development in the use of visual language by children at the elementary school level, publication expected in 1984.

SIDELIGHTS: Olga Richard commented: "I have been absorbed with children's aesthetic predisposition throughout my long teaching career in art education. I find that children are responsive to, assimilate, and reflect the culture in which they live with honest, intense, and varied vividness. They do this in all expressive arts, but I have been particularly concerned with their diversity of expression in the visual arts. Sadly, though, the adult environment often restricts and impinges on children's creativity and reduces imagination to imitation. For example, those adults—teachers, librarians, parents—who make visual materials available to children often select these materials for reasons other than aesthetic standards of excellence. These choices reflect narrow, restrictive, and personal subjective judgments that are usually based on ignorance and/or tastes, styles, and modes of another generation. Prevailing literature in the field was of little help to adults since 'traditionalism' was stressed, rather than basic concepts from fields of art and literature. This dichotomy presented a challenging area for study and analysis. With the assistance of the Dutton-Macrae Award, Donnarae MacCann and I collaborated on a study of children's books. We examined hundreds of picture books and analyzed and evaluated both illustrations and stories. The collaboration led to *The Child's First Books* and continues to this day."

* * *

RICHARDS, Duane
See HURLEY, Vic

* * *

RICHARDSON, Frank McLean 1904-

PERSONAL: Born March 3, 1904, in St. Andrews, Scotland; son of Hugh and Elizabeth (MacLean) Richardson; married Sylvia Innes, 1944; children: Jennifer Jane, Hugh Alexander, Alastair Neil. *Education:* University of Edinburgh, M.B. Ch.B., 1926, M.D., 1938. *Politics:* Conservative. *Religion:* Scottish Episcopalian. *Home:* 4-B Barnton Ave. W., Edinburgh EH4 6DE, Scotland.

CAREER: British Army Medical Corps, career officer, 1927-61, director of Medical Services for British Army of the Rhine, 1957-61, retiring as major general; Civil Defence, Scotland, medical adviser, 1963-69; writer, 1969-. *Member:* Royal Medical Society of Edinburgh (fellow; past president), Piobaireachd Society (vice-president), Royal Scottish Pipers Society. *Awards, honors—*Military: Distinguished Service Order, 1941; officer of Order of the British Empire, 1945;

Companion of Order of the Bath, 1960. Honorary surgeon to the queen, 1957-61.

WRITINGS: Napoleon: Bisexual Emperor, William Kimber, 1972; *Napoleon's Death: An Inquest,* William Kimber, 1974; *Fighting Spirit: Psychological Factors in War,* Leo Cooper, 1978. Contributor to magazines, including *Blackwood's Magazine* and *Army Quarterly.*

WORK IN PROGRESS: Mars Without Venus, a study of homosexuality and sublimation; *Two Scottish Sergeants; Piobaireachd and Its Interpretation; The Public and the Bomb.*

SIDELIGHTS: Richardson wrote to *CA:* "Here in Scotland we've been unashamedly wallowing in emotional sentimentality over the chief thing we do better than most—wonderful parades for our beloved 'Royals'—including a musical tribute here in Edinburgh. At times I feel very sorry for my numerous American friends who had only Miz Lilian to compare with our adored Scottish great lady, the Queen Mum."

On the 1980 presidential campaign in the United States, Richardson reflected: "Your president matters almost as much— I might even say every bit as much—to us as he matters to you. The choices that were open to you struck most of my friends as too awful to contemplate: a peanut farmer or a clapped-out actor in second-rate films (second-rate even by American standards). I can't believe you could ever adopt the utterly discredited Kennedy, and we'd never forgive you if you did—he's an avowed enemy of our country and the son of another.

"From this side of the Atlantic, George Bush and that independent chap certainly looked human! But don't consider me anti-U.S.A. Apart from the horrible films that our television people will buy from you, I am a confirmed admirer as any of those who stay here with me would confirm."

AVOCATIONAL INTERESTS: Playing and judging classical music of the piobaireachd (Great Highland bagpipe).

*   *   *

RICHARDSON, Neil R(yan)   1944-

PERSONAL: Born February 12, 1944, in Hamilton, Ohio; son of John S. and Helen K. Richardson; married Jane Zimmerman (a director of a social agency), December 16, 1966; children: Sarah, Amy. *Education:* Miami University, Oxford, Ohio, A.B., 1965; Ohio State University, M.A., 1967; University of Michigan, Ph.D., 1974. *Home:* 1925 Regent St., Madison, Wis. 53705. *Office:* Department of Political Science, University of Wisconsin—Madison, Madison, Wis. 53706.

CAREER: University of Texas at Austin, instructor, 1971-74, assistant professor of government, 1974-79; University of Wisconsin—Madison, assistant professor of political science, 1979—. *Member:* International Studies Association, American Political Science Association.

WRITINGS: Foreign Policy and Economic Dependence, University of Texas Press, 1978; (contributor) Patrick J. McGowan and Charles W. Kegley, Jr., editors, *The Political Economy of Foreign Policy Behavior,* Sage Publications, 1981. Contributor of articles and reviews to political science and international studies journals.

WORK IN PROGRESS: Quantitative and longitudinal research on causes of detente in cold-war relations between the United States and the Soviet Union since 1950.

RICHELIEU, Peter
See ROBINSON, P. W.

*   *   *

RICKARDS, Maurice   1919-

PERSONAL: Surname adopted c. 1927; surname is accented on first syllable; born in 1919, in London, England; son of Eric and Rosa Mansbridge; married Yolanda Martelli, 1945 (divorced, 1978). *Education:* Attended Westminster School of Art. *Home:* 12 Fitzroy Sq., London W1P 5HQ, England.

CAREER: Carlton Studios, London, England, photographic apprentice, 1938-39; free-lance writer, editor, graphic designer, and photographer, 1945—. *Wartime service:* Social relief, London, 1940-45. *Member:* Society of Industrial Artists and Designers (fellow), Institute of Incorporated Photographers (fellow), Ephemera Society (founder; chairman), Society of Authors, Arts Club, Salmagundi Club.

WRITINGS: Offbeat Photography, Studio, 1959; *The Pye Book of Science,* Longacre, 1960; *Posters at the Turn of the Century,* Evelyn, Adams & Mackay, 1968; *Posters of the 1920's,* Evelyn, Adams & Mackay, 1968; *Posters of the First World War,* Evelyn, Adams & Mackay, 1968; *Brews and Potions,* Hugh Evelyn, 1968; (editor) *Engine Driving Life,* Hugh Evelyn, 1968; *Banned Posters,* Evelyn, Adams & Mackay 1969; (editor) *New Inventions,* Hugh Evelyn, 1969.

Posters of Protest and Revolution, Adams & Dart, 1970; *The World Saves Life* (juvenile), Longman, 1971; *The World Fights Fire* (juvenile), Longman, 1971; *The Rise and Fall of the Poster,* David & Charles, 1971; *The World Communicates* (juvenile), Longman, 1972; *The World Fights Crime* (juvenile), Longman, 1972; *Where They Lived in London,* David & Charles, 1972; *The Public Notice: An Illustrated History,* David & Charles, 1973; *The First World War: Ephemera, Mementoes, Documents,* Jupiter, 1975; *Railway Relics and Regalia,* Country Life, 1975; *This Is Ephemera: Collected Printed Throwaways,* David & Charles, 1978.

Ephemera of Travel and Transport, New Cavendish, 1981; *Dictionary of Printed Ephemera,* New Cavendish, 1982. Contributor to *Library of World Knowledge* and *Heritage of Britain.* Editor of *The Ephermerist.*

WORK IN PROGRESS: The Origins of Advertising, publication by New Cavendish expected in 1984.

SIDELIGHTS: Rickards told *CA:* "As writer, graphic designer, and minor social historian, I discern in my own published work a reflected fusion of these interests. I am concerned with the interplay of social history and the graphic image—especially the transient image expressed in posters, leaflets, tickets, and other throwaway material.

"As founder of the Ephemera Society, and after a lifelong preoccupation with the social role of printed trivia, I see my work in the *Dictionary of Printed Ephemera* as an attempt to express the whole thing in a single volume.

"My basic concern is with the phenomenon of human communication, truly a miraculous business. This also accounts for an incurable interest in speech and language. As an art student, I spent some time devising visual aids for the teaching of speech to deaf-mutes, and I have a passable working knowledge of a number of European languages. I am also greatly stirred by radio and television, for which I have done a fair amount of work—much of it, lately, in connection with the study and conservation of printed ephemera.

"In my earlier years I used my capacity to communicate in general free-lance advocacy. My most worthwhile client was the charity Christian Aid (whose title and logo I am proud to have devised), an organization which by now has raised millions for refugees, relief, and rehabilitation.

"In these latter years I find myself in advocacy not only of causes and services but of the study of advocacy."

* * *

RIDOUT, Ronald 1916-

PERSONAL: Born July 23, 1916, in Farnham, England; son of Gilbert Harry (a schoolmaster) and Ethel Mary (Phillips) Ridout; married Betty Elsie Dolley, February 10, 1940; children: Jessica Ridout Paget, Simon, Veronica. *Education:* Oxford University, B.A. (with honors), 1939. *Home and office address:* P.O. Box 224, Soufriere, St. Lucia, West Indies. *Agent:* A. P. Watt Ltd., 26/28 Bedford Row, London WC1R 4HL, England.

CAREER: National Provincial Bank, Alton, England, clerk, 1933-35; assistant teacher at schools in Bolton, Woking, Nuneaton, Shrewesbury, Luton, and Portsmouth, England, 1939-46; Ginn & Co. Ltd., London, England, publisher's representative, 1946-50; writer, 1950—. *Member:* Society of Authors (chairman of educational writers group, 1960), Society of Bookmen.

WRITINGS: English Today, five volumes, Ginn, 1948; *English Workbooks,* ten volumes, Ginn, 1950; *Self-Help English,* five volumes, Macmillan, 1952; (with Phyllis Flowerdew) *Reading to Some Purpose,* seven volumes, Oliver & Boyd, 1953; *Wide Horizon Readers,* five volumes, Heinemann, 1953; *English for Africans,* three volumes, Ginn, 1954; *Word Perfect,* ten volumes, Ginn, 1957; (with Kenneth McGregor) *English for Australian Schools,* five volumes, F. W. Cheshire, 1957; (with Ruth Ainsworth) *Look Ahead Readers,* thirty-two volumes, Heinemann, 1958; *Carnatic English Course,* seven volumes, Macmillan, 1959.

International English, six volumes, Macmillan, 1960; *Better English,* six volumes, Ginn, 1961; (with N. K. Vaniasingham) *English Today for South East Asia,* Federal Publications, 1962; *Transition English,* two volumes, Federal Publications, 1962; (with Paul Townsend) *This Is Life,* Edward Arnold, 1963; *The Facts of English,* Ginn, 1963; *New English Workbooks,* ten volumes, Federal Publications, 1963; (with Ruth Ainsworth) *Books for Me to Read,* twenty-four volumes, Heinemann, 1964; (with John Gunn) *Self-Help English for Australia,* five volumes, Macmillan, 1964; (with Philip Sherlock) *Self-Help English for the Caribbean,* Macmillan, 1964; *World-Wide English,* fifteen volumes, Macmillan, 1965; *English Now,* five volumes, Ginn, 1966; (with Eldred Jones) *Adjustments,* Edward Arnold, 1966; *English Workbooks for the Caribbean,* Ginn, 1966; (with Patricia Clements) *Ahmed and Rehan Workbooks,* seven volumes, Oxford University Press, 1966; *Structural English Workbooks,* eight volumes, Pilgrim Books, 1967; (with Clifford Witting) *English Proverbs Explained,* Pan Books, 1967; (with Stanley Mason) *Modern English Structures,* four volumes, Macmillan, 1968; *English for Schools and Colleges in West Africa,* eleven volumes, Macmillan, 1968; *Books for Me to Write In,* six volumes, Purnell, 1968.

(With Michael Vodden) *English for India,* ten volumes, Ginn, 1971; (with Waldo Clarke) *A Reference Book of English,* Macmillan, 1971; *Books for Me to Count In,* six volumes, Purnell, 1971; (with Michael Holt) *Now I Can Read,* four volumes, Purnell, 1971; (with Van Moll) *In English, Please,* seven volumes, Bosch, 1971; (with Terence Creed) *Guided Conversations,* two volumes, Macmillan, 1971; (with Holt) *The Big Book of Puzzles,* two volumes, Penguin, 1971; (with David Faulds) *Mastering English,* Macmillan, 1972; *Fun With Words,* three volumes, Piccolo, 1972; *Books for Me to Begin In,* six volumes, Purnell, 1972; *Facts of English,* Pan Books, 1972; (with Anthony Hern) *Word Puzzles,* Pan Books, 1973; *Dragon Puzzle Books,* six volumes, Granada, 1975; *All Round English,* nine volumes, Longman, 1975; *Write Now,* Ginn, 1975; *Puzzle It Out,* five volumes, Evans Brothers, 1975; *Evans Graded Readers,* two volumes, Evans Brothers, 1976; *Evans Graded Verse,* five volumes, Evans Brothers, 1977; *Just the Word,* six volumes, Hart-Davis, 1978; *My Learning to Write Books,* six volumes, Purnell, 1978; *Say It in English,* eleven volumes, Efstathiadis, 1978; *Nation-Wide English,* eighteen volumes, Evans Brothers, 1979; *ELT Pocket Dictionary,* Thomas Nelson, 1979.

Pan Spelling Dictionary, Pan Books, 1980; *My First Dictionary,* six volumes, Purnell, 1980.

WORK IN PROGRESS: An illustrated dictionary for children, publication by Granada Children's Books expected in 1982.

SIDELIGHTS: Ridout told *CA:* "I write books for teaching English, both as a native and as a foreign language. The total sales now exceed seventy million, and their success is largely due to the self-help method I have developed, whereby the student is able to do his own practice correctly by being given the means to come to the right answer, since he clearly cannot otherwise get it right if he doesn't already know it."

* * *

RIEU, E(mile) V(ictor) 1887-1972

OBITUARY NOTICE—See index for *CA* sketch: Born in 1887 in London, England; died May 11, 1972, in London, England. Publishing executive, editor, translator, and author. Rieu was editor of Penguin Classics. He translated some of the works he published, such as *The Odyssey, Virgil's Pastoral Poems,* and *The Four Gospels.* Before working at Penguin, Rieu established and managed the Oxford University Press in India. He also wrote books for children, including *Cuckoo Calling* and *The Flattered Flying Fish and Other Poems.* Obituaries and other sources: *New York Times,* May 13, 1972.

* * *

RIGGAN, William (Edward, Jr.) 1946-

PERSONAL: Born February 15, 1946, in Norfolk, Va.; son of William Edward and Dorothy (Farmer) Riggan; married Linda Kay Pursley (an editor and staff coordinator), August 30, 1975. *Education:* University of North Carolina, B.A. (summa cum laude), 1969; Indiana University, M.A., 1970, Ph.D., 1978; also attended University of Goettingen, 1966-67, and University of Hamburg, 1973-74. *Home:* 113 Brookwood Dr., Noble, Okla. 73068. *Office:* World Literature Today, University of Oklahoma, 110 Monnet Hall, Norman, Okla. 73019.

CAREER: University of Oklahoma, Norman, assistant editor of *World Literature Today,* 1974-76, associate editor, 1976—. *Awards, honors:* Goettingen exchange scholarship from University of North Carolina, 1966-67; fellowship from Indiana University, 1969-72; academic exchange service fellowship from University of Hamburg, 1973-74.

WRITINGS: (Translator) Ulrich Weisstein, *Comparative Literature and Literary Theory,* Indiana University Press, 1973; *Picaros, Madmen Naifs, and Clowns,* Oklahoma University Press, 1981.

WORK IN PROGRESS: Two plays set during and after the Vietnam War.

RIGGS, Sidney Noyes 1892-1975

OBITUARY NOTICE—See index for *CA* sketch: born April 14, 1892, in Newark, N.J.; died June, 1975. Educator, inventor, lecturer, and author. Riggs worked with Thomas A. Edison for two years before becoming a teacher and school principal in New Jersey. He also gave travel lectures. Rigg's work includes *Vineyard Poems and Prints, From Off Island,* and *Arrows and Snakeskin.* (Date of death provided by wife, Dionis Coffin Riggs.)

*   *   *

RING, Elizabeth 1912-
(Nerissa Scott)

PERSONAL: Born February 8, 1912, in London, England; daughter of Herbert (a clerk) and Susan (a domestic servant; maiden name, Yull) Scott; married William Ring (a technical librarian), July 31, 1937; children: Susan Ring Weatherly. *Education:* Trinity College of Music, received certificate; attended City Literary Institute. *Home:* 8 Honeymeade, Sawbridgeworth, Hertfordshire CM21 0AR, England.

CAREER: Associated with Ministry of Information in England, 1942-45; *Islington Gazette,* London, England, author of column, 1972-73.

WRITINGS: Up the Cockneys (nonfiction), Elek, 1974. Writer for British Broadcasting Corp. Contributor of about two hundred articles (many humorous) to popular magazines, including *She* and *Club International* (under pseudonym Nerissa Scott), *Punch,* and *Reveille.*

WORK IN PROGRESS: Cockney Into Bumpkin, a sequel to *Up the Cockneys,* with more details on marriage and motherhood; *The Daimler Road Lot,* a New Town novel.

SIDELIGHTS: Elizabeth Ring commented: "I wrote *Up the Cockneys* to try to change the customary beliefs about cockneys. We weren't all badly spoken and ignorant, quite the reverse. Children born in central London have the world on their doorstep, and it is up to them to take advantage of cultural opportunities.

"In middle age, I belive that Sex is Forever, and have had much publicity for my views. Sex keeps a woman beautiful and is the easiest way to retain her girlish figure."

AVOCATIONAL INTERESTS: Classical music, opera.

*   *   *

RIVIERE, Peter Gerard 1934-

PERSONAL: Born January 17, 1934, in London, England; son of Eugene Gonzague and Eleanor Eilleen Riviere; married Sarah Heyman, May 26, 1962 (marriage ended, 1977); married Sandra Jean Ott (a lecturer), October 7, 1978; children: Amelia, Arabella, Peregrine. *Education:* Magdalene College, Cambridge, B.A., 1957, M.A., 1960; Magdalen College, Oxford, B.Litt., 1963, D.Phil., 1965. *Home:* Quoin Barn, Beaulieu Court, Sunningwell, Abingdon OX13 6RB, England. *Office:* Institute of Social Anthropology, Oxford University, Oxford, England.

CAREER: University of London, London, England, research fellow, 1966-68; Harvard University, Cambridge, Mass., visiting professor of social anthropology, 1968-69; Cambridge University, Cambridge, England, lecturer in social anthropology, 1970-71; Oxford University, Oxford, England, lecturer in social anthropology, 1971—. Fellow of Linacre College, Oxford, 1971—. *Military service:* Royal Air Force, pilot

officer, 1951-53. *Member:* Royal Anthropological Institute, Association of Social Anthropologists.

WRITINGS: Marriage Among the Trio, Clarendon Press, 1969; *The Forgotten Frontier,* Holt, 1971. Contributor to scholarly journals. Editor of *Man,* 1973-77.

WORK IN PROGRESS: Variance and Invariance: The Case of Guianan Amerindians.

*   *   *

ROBBIN, (Jodi) Luna 1936-
(Jodi Pallidini)

PERSONAL: Born June 30, 1936, in New York, N.Y.; married Dan Robbin (marriage ended); children: Noah, Syam, Inca. *Education:* Bennington College, B.A., 1958; University of California, M.A., 1963. *Religion:* Unionista Espiritista de Filipinas. *Address:* c/o Emerald Press, Box 388, Santa Rosa, Calif. 95402.

CAREER: American Friends Service Committee, co-director of community development project in Mexico, 1958-60; DeYoung Museum Art School, San Francisco, Calif., instructor in art, 1969-70; University of California, Santa Cruz, instructor in art, 1970-75; photographer and artist, 1975—.

WRITINGS: (Under name Jodi Pallidini) *Roll Your Own,* P. Collier, 1974. Illustrator of books, including *Tweedles and Foodles, Little Boxes, The Muse of Parker Street,* and *Things That Sometimes Happen.*

WORK IN PROGRESS: A book on pyramids.

SIDELIGHTS: Luna Robbin wrote: "I am not actually a writer, but an artist, photographer, parent, and healer. I had become involved in healing circles in the Bay area in about 1975. Around 1978 a biopsy revealed that I had cancerous tumors but, as I am strongly opposed to chemotherapy, I embarked on an alternative healing program. The following year I was healed by Paz Navalta and other members of the Unionista Espiritista de Filipinas in Rosales, Pangasin, Philippines. Currently, although I am contributing to some books, my creative talents are focused on healing, the completion of a spiritual documentary on the Espiritista healers, and several multi-media presentations on themes of ecology and care of the planet Earth."

BIOGRAPHICAL/CRITICAL SOURCES: Mr./Ms., March 25, 1980.

*   *   *

ROBERTS, Lee
See MARTIN, Robert (Lee)

*   *   *

ROBERTS, Leslie 1896-1980

PERSONAL: Born June 3, 1896, in Newport, Wales; died May 16, 1980; son of John Henry and Martha (Kenyon) Roberts; married Gladys Isobel Cornell, April 20, 1921; children: Grant (deceased), William Leslie. *Education:* Attended McGill University. *Politics:* Independent Liberal. *Religion:* Anglican. *Home:* 28 Anwoth Rd., Westmount, Quebec, Canada H3Y 2E7.

CAREER: Free-lance writer, 1929-39; Ministry of National Defence, Ottawa, Ontario, special assistant to minister, 1939-40; free-lance writer, 1940-80. Editorial commentator for CJAD-Radio; foreign correspondent in Europe and the Soviet Union. *Military service:* Canadian Army, 1914-19, with Canadian Field Ambulance, also attached to Canadian Mounted Rifles, Royal Canadian Air Force, and Royal Air Force;

became lieutenant. *Member:* International P.E.N., Canadian Authors Association, Canadian War Correspondents Association, Aviation-Space Writers Association, Royal Society of Arts (fellow), Brome County Historical Society (life member), Windsor Club. *Awards, honors:* Centennial Medal, 1967.

WRITINGS: When the Gods Laughed (novel), Musson, 1930, Sears Publishing, 1931; (contributor) Tom A. Deacon and Wilfred Reeves, editors, *Open House*, Graphic, 1931; *So This Is Ottawa*, Macmillan of Canada, 1933; *We Must Be Free: Reflections of a Democrat*, Macmillan of Canada, 1939; *Canada's War in the Air*, A. M. Beatty, 1943; (with George F. Beurling) *Malta Spitfire*, Oxford University Press, 1943; *Home From the Cold Wars*, Beacon Press, 1948; *The Mackenzie*, Rinehart, 1949, reprinted, Greenwood Press, 1974.

Canada: The Golden Hinge, Rinehart, 1952; *From Three Men*, Dominion Rubber Co., 1954; *Noranda*, Clarke, Irwin, 1956; *C.D.: The Life and Times of Clarence Decatur Howe*, Clarke, Irwin, 1957; (with George Hunter) *Canada in Colour*, Clarke, Irwin, 1959; *There Shall be Wings: A History of the Royal Canadian Air Force*, Clarke, Irwin, 1959; *The Chief* (biography of Maurice LeNoblet Duplessis), Clarke, Irwin, 1963; *Montreal: From Mission Colony to World City*, Macmillan of Canada, 1969. Contributor to magazines in Canada and the United States, including *Saturday Evening Post*, *Harper's*, *Reader's Digest*, *Saturday Night*, *Canadian*, and *Maclean's*.

WORK IN PROGRESS: A book of memoirs, for Clarke, Irwin, uncompleted.

[Sketch verified by wife, Gladys C. Roberts]

*   *   *

ROBERTS, Paul McHenry   1917-1967

OBITUARY NOTICE—See index for *CA* sketch: Born October 6, 1917, in San Louis Obispo, Calif.; died after a fall, September 14, 1967, in Rome, Italy. Educator, linguist, and author. Roberts taught English and linguistics at San Jose State College (now San Jose State University) and Cornell University before ·becoming director of languages at the Rome Center of American Studies. He wrote several books about linguistics for high school and college students. Robert's works include *Understanding Grammar*, *Patterns of English*, *English Sentences*, and *Modern Grammar*. Obituaries and other sources: *New York Times*, September 15, 1967; *Publishers Weekly*, September 25, 1967.

*   *   *

ROBINSON, Charles Knox (Jr.)   1909-1980

PERSONAL: Born April 28, 1909, in New York, N.Y.; died June 4, 1980, in Pomona, N.Y.; married Geraldine O'Loughlin; children: Charles Knox III, Toni Robinson Thalenberg, Judith Robinson Nielsen.

CAREER: Lyceum Theater, New York, N.Y., assistant general stage manager; Metro-Goldwyn-Mayer, Hollywood, Calif., actor, beginning in 1931; actor, playwright, and television producer, 1931-80.

WRITINGS—Plays: (Co-author) "Sailor Beware," produced in New York, N.Y., 1932; (co-author) "Apple of His Eye," produced in 1946. Also author of "Swing Your Lady," "The Ride," and "Miss Otis Regrets."

Author of more than one hundred forty television plays, including work for "Theater Guild of the Air" and "Suspense."

SIDELIGHTS: Robinson wrote the play that became "Taxi," a film released in 1932 by Warner Brothers starring James Cagney.

BIOGRAPHICAL/CRITICAL SOURCES: New York Times, June 6, 1980.*

*   *   *

ROBINSON, P. W.   1893-
(Peter Richelieu)

PERSONAL: Born November 18, 1893, in Birmingham, England; son of William Frederick (a hospital registrar) and Annie Edith (Pitt) Robinson; married Katherine Ryan (a registered nurse), April 24, 1933. *Education:* St. John's College, Cambridge, B.A., 1914, LL.B., 1919. *Politics:* Liberal. *Religion:* "Occultist." *Residence:* Durban, South Africa.

CAREER: Company director in Ceylon, 1919-39; writer and lecturer in South Africa, 1945—. *Military service:* British Army, 1914-19, 1939-45; became major.

WRITINGS—Under pseudonym Peter Richelieu: *From the Turret* (nonfiction), Graphic Stationers & Publishers, 1953, revised edition published as *A Soul's Journey*, Turnstone Press, 1972, Doubleday, 1973.

WORK IN PROGRESS: A sequel to *A Soul's Journey*.

SIDELIGHTS: Robinson told *CA:* "I was born in Birmingham, Warwickshire, England, and my parents were well-to-do. I had no real contact with them at any time of my life, but I owe them a great debt of gratitude for giving me a first-class education which has enabled me to make sufficient money to retire at an early age, write a couple of books, and be the means of helping people with advice when they could not afford to go to a lawyer. I have also studied Eastern philosophy, commonly known as 'occultism' (the word occult means 'sacred wisdom'), and it includes Christianity, which also started in the Near East, although it was Ireland that first was known as the 'island of scholars' when England, France, Germany, and the Romans were interested mainly in conquering other countries and peoples from whom they acquired wealth and slaves.

"I was an only child. By the age of eight I had received some good education (including Latin) from a kindergarten school which I attended from the age of three-and-a-half. At fourteen I was supposed to go to a public school, but there was trouble there and I was not allowed to go. My father chose for me a Cambridge graduate, who taught me for four-and-a-half years much more than I would have learned at a public school. But personally I think the experience one gains at school is something one misses if one's education is contained within the parental home.

"I entered Cambridge toward the end of my eighteenth year, but two years later the First World War broke out and I volunteered for service the day after. I was badly wounded in 1916 when a German bomb burst within yards of me, killing seventeen of my companions and wounding twenty-three of us. I was not expected to live and heard the receiving surgeon tell the sister, 'Give this poor devil anything he asks for as he can't last long.' I asked for half a bottle of vintage champagne immediately. I was put to bed and repeated of the request three times daily for another two days, when I was abruptly refused further requests and had my first operation.

"I was called up for the Second World War, as I was on the officers' reserve list for non-combatant service, and was employed in welfare and intelligence work.

"I have not lived in England since 1919 when I was invalided out of the Army and given a pension. I went to Ceylon and spent two years in the open air learning about tea.

"After I gave a course of lectures on 'Life After Death' and 'How to Tread the Occult Path' at the capital of Natal, I was persuaded by one of the audience to write a book for the man in the street. That produced *From the Turret. A Soul's Journey* is the same book, with fewer pages. Both books are mainly factual, for the character Henry was a pupil of mine in Ceylon, and the episodes reported during my early teaching actually happened. I represented the only hypothetical figure in the book, named Acharya, a Hindustani word meaning teacher.

"I have the nucleus of another book which I am not allowed to publish. My Master, who is an Adept and lives mostly at the astral and mental levels, will not give permission. The information could be of value to the Black Forces, who at present are extremely dominant and the cause of wars, insurrections, and the many coups d'etat that have occured in recent years. The date of the coming of the person you know as Christ (referred to as the Lord Maitreya by occultists) is most likely to be 1982, if you accept the hieroglyphs explained in Davidson's *History of the Great Pyramid*."

*   *   *

ROBISON, Sophia Moses 1888-1969

OBITUARY NOTICE—See index for *CA* sketch: Born November 28, 1888, in New York, N.Y.; died August 3, 1969, in New Brunswick, N.J. Sociologist, educator, lecturer, research consultant, and author. An expert on juvenile delinquency, Robison taught sociology at several institutions, including Columbia University, Smith College, Yeshiva University, and Adelphi University. She researched and lectured on juvenile delinquency, crime, and population statistics. Numbering among Robison's many books are *Can Delinquency Be Measured?*, *Jewish Population Studies,* and *Juvenile Delinquency: Its Nature and Control.* Obituaries and other sources: *New York Times,* August 4, 1969; *Washington Post,* August 4, 1969.

*   *   *

ROBITSCHER, Jonas B(ondi, Jr.) 1920-1981

OBITUARY NOTICE—See index for *CA* sketch: Born October 28, 1920, in New York, N.Y.; died of cancer, March 25, 1981, in Atlanta, Ga. Attorney, psychiatrist, professor, and author, best known as a crusader against abuses in forensic psychiatry. At one time, Robitscher was the director of the Legal Psychiatry Program at the University of Pennsylvania School of Medicine and a lecturer at Villanova Law School. He was also the first to hold the Henry R. Luce Chair in Law and Behavioral Sciences at Emory University. In his controversial critique of the abuses in the psychiatric profession, *The Powers of Psychiatry,* Robitscher warned against psychiatrists' arbitrary definition of mental illness and the power of their opinions in the judicial system. For his work in legal and forensic psychiatry, Robitscher received the Isaac Ray Award from the American Psychiatric Association in 1976 and the Golden Apple Award from the American Academy of Psychiatry and the Law in 1980. In 1979 George Washington University presented the psychiatrist with an alumni achievement award. His other writings, all of which deal with the legal and social ramifications of science, include *Pursuit of Agreement: Psychiatry and the Law* and *Eugenic Sterilization.* Obituaries and other sources: *New*

York Times, March 26, 1981; *Washington Post,* March 27, 1981; *Time,* April 6, 1981.

*   *   *

ROBSON, William Alexander 1895-1980

PERSONAL: Born July 14, 1895, in London, England; died May 12, 1980; son of Jack Robson (a dealer in pearls); married Juliette Alvin (a music therapist); children: two sons, one daughter. *Education:* London School of Economics and Political Science, London, B.Sc. (with first class honors), 1922, LL.M., Ph.D., 1924.

CAREER: Called to the Bar, 1922; Graham White Aviation Co., began as clerk, 1910, became assistant manager; barrister at law, 1922-26; University of London, London School of Economics and Political Science, London, England, lecturer, 1926-47, professor of public administration, 1947-67, professor emeritus and honorary fellow, 1967-80. Founder and chairman of Greater London Group; vice-president of Institute of Public Administration; committee member of Greater London Planning Administration. Principal of Mines Department, 1940-42, and Ministry of Fuel and Power, 1942-43; assistant secretary of Air Ministry, 1943, and Civil Aviation, 1945; consultant to governments of Lebanon, Turkey, Nigeria, and Japan. *Military service:* Royal Flying Corps, fighter pilot during World War I. *Awards, honors:* D.H.C. from University of Paris, University of Lille, University of Grenoble, and University of Algiers; D.Litt. from University of Durham and Victoria University of Manchester; D.Soc.Sc. from University of Birmingham.

WRITINGS: Aircraft in War and Peace, Macmillan, 1916; *The Relation of Wealth to Welfare,* Allen & Unwin, 1924; (with Clement Richard Attlee) *The Town Councillor,* Labour Publishing Co., 1925; *Justice and Administrative Law: A Study of the British Constitution,* Macmillan, 1928, 3rd edition, Stevens, 1951, Greenwood Press, 1970.

The Law Relating to Local Government Audit: Being a Statement of the Law Relating to the Audit of the Accounts of Local Authorities by District Auditors and Borough Auditors, Sweet & Maxwell, 1930; *The Development of Local Government,* Allen & Unwin, 1931, 3rd edition, 1954, reprinted, Greenwood Press, 1978; *Civilisation and the Growth of Law: A Study of the Relations Between Men's Ideas About the Universe and the Institutions of Law and Government,* Macmillan, 1935, reprinted, Arno, 1975; (editor with Harold J. Laski and W. Ivor Jennings) *A Century of Municipal Progress, 1835-1935,* Allen & Unwin, 1935, reprinted, Greenwood Press, 1978, also published as *A Century of Municipal Progress: The Last Hundred Years,* AMS Press, 1976; (editor and contributor) *The British Civil Servant,* Allen & Unwin, 1937; (editor) *Public Enterprise: Developments in Social Ownership and Control in Great Britain,* Allen & Unwin, 1937; *The Government and Misgovernment of London,* Allen & Unwin, 1939, 2nd edition, 1948; (editor) *Social Security,* Allen & Unwin, 1943, 3rd edition, 1948.

(Editor) *Problems of Nationalized Industry,* Oxford University Press, 1952; *The University Teaching of Social Sciences: Political Science,* United Nations Educational, Scientific and Cultural Organization, 1954; (editor) *Great Cities of the World: Their Government, Politics, and Planning,* Allen & Unwin, 1954, Macmillan, 1955, 3rd edition (with D. E. Regan), two volumes, Sage Publications, 1972; (editor) *The Civil Service in Britain and France,* Macmillan, 1956; (author of preface) Gunnar Heckscher, *The Study of Comparative Government and Politics,* Allen & Unwin, 1957; *Nationalized Industry and Public Ownership,* Allen & Unwin, 1960, 2nd* edition, 1962; *Local Government in Crisis,* Allen & Unwin, 1962, 2nd edition, 1968; *The Governors and the Governed,* Louisiana State University Press, 1964; *Politics and Government at Home and Abroad,* Allen & Unwin, 1967; *Report on Tokyo Metropolitan Government,* Tokyo Institute for Municipal Research, 1968.

(Editor with Bernard Crick) *The Future of the Social Services,* Penguin, 1970; (editor with Crick) *Protest and Discontent,* Penguin, 1970; (editor) *"The Political Quarterly" in the Thirties,* Allen Lane, 1971; (editor) *Man and the Social Sciences,* Allen & Unwin, 1972, Sage Publications, 1974; (editor with Crick) *Taxation Policy,* Penguin, 1973; (editor with Crick) *China in Transition,* Sage Publications, 1975; *From Policy to Administration,* Allen & Unwin, 1976; *Welfare State and Welfare Society: Illusion and Reality,* Allen & Unwin, 1976. Also author of *Population and the People* and *British Government Since 1918.* Contributor to political science journals. Founder and co-editor of *Political Quarterly,* 1930-75.

SIDELIGHTS: Robson was considered to be a reformer and humanist, optimistic about the future despite some disappointments in the present; he was the last of the scholars of the Fabian Society, for whom he wrote several pamphlets. He also made a sound recording with Norman Hunt, "Government Tomorrow," released by Holt Information Systems in 1972.

BIOGRAPHICAL/CRITICAL SOURCES: London Times, May 15, 1980.*

* * *

ROCKWELL, F(rederick) F(rye) 1884-1976

OBITUARY NOTICE—See index for *CA* sketch: Born April 2, 1884, in Brooklyn, N.Y.; died April 18, 1976. Editor, illustrator, photographer, lecturer, gardener, and author. Rockwell worked for the *New York Time* as the editor of the Sunday garden section before joining *Home Garden* magazine (now *Flower Grower-Home Garden*) as an editor. He wrote numerous books on gardening with his own drawings and photographs. His works include *Roses; Peonies; Home Vegetables Gardening: A Complete and Practical Guide to the Planning and Care of All Vegetables, Fruits, and Berries Worth Growing for Home Use;* and *The Book of Bulbs: A Guide to the Selection, Planting and Cultivating of Bulbs for Spring, Summer, and Autumn Flowering—and to Winter-Long Beauty From Bulbs Indoors.* (Date of death provided by wife, Esther C. Grayson Rockwell.)

* * *

RODGERS, Frank
See INFIELD, Glenn (Berton)

* * *

ROEHRS, Walter R(obert) 1901-

PERSONAL: Born August 24, 1901, in Clinton, Wis.; son of Henry (a minister) and Lydia (Schaller) Roehrs; married Louise Winkelmann, January 1, 1933; children: Walter R. (deceased), Sara Louise (Mrs. David Robinson), Mary Louise (Mrs. Clifford Bischoff). *Education:* Attended Concordia College, Milwaukee, Wis., 1915-20, and Concordia Seminary, St. Louis, Mo., 1920-25; University of Chicago, M.A., 1926, Ph.D., 1934. *Office:* Office of Seminary Relations, Concordia Seminary, 801 DeMun Ave., St. Louis, Mo. 63105.

CAREER: Ordained Luteran minister, 1926; pastor of Lutheran church in Western Springs, Ill., 1926-31; St. Paul's College, Concordia, Mo., professor of Hebrew and German, 1931-41; Concordia Teachers College, River Forest, Ill., professor of religion, 1941-44; Concordia Seminary, St. Louis, Mo., professor of Old Testament, 1944-68, professor emeritus, 1969—. Participant in European conferences. *Awards, honors:* D.D. from Concordia Seminary, 1963.

WRITINGS: (Contributor) Carl F. H. Henry, editor, *The Bible Expositor,* A. J. Holman, 1960; (with Martin H. Franzmann) *Concordia Self-Study Commentary,* (contributor) Merrill F. Ungar and William White, Jr., editors, *Expository Dictionary of the Old Testament,* Thomas Nelson, 1980. Editor of *Concordia Theological Monthly,* 1954-64.

* * *

ROETHENMUND, Robert 1956-

PERSONAL: Born July 21, 1956, in San Francisco, Calif.; son of Otto and Ermina (Grassi) Roethenmund. *Education:* Dartmouth College, B.A., 1978; Harvard University, M.B.A., 1982. *Residence:* Badhus, Heimenschwand, Thun, Switzerland. *Address:* c/o Books in Focus, Inc., 160 East 38th St., Suite 31B, New York, N.Y. 10016.

CAREER: Associated with Bank Leu in Zurich, Switzerland, and Trammel Crow Co., in Dallas, Tex. *Member:* Explorers Club.

WRITINGS: The Swiss Banking Handbook, Books in Focus, 1980.

SIDELIGHTS: Roethenmund wrote: "*The Swiss Banking Handbook* describes the advantages and disadvantages of having a Swiss account. From a Swiss perspective the use of the banking industry through history is described and the implications of its history on future development are addressed. The book explains what types of accounts are available for the investor, and how he/she can take advantage of the Swiss banking system. The implications of U.S. law on foreign banking are discussed. This book is a guide for investors both large and small to the ins and outs of the Swiss account and the mechanism for opening accounts in Switzerland."

* * *

ROGERS, Dale Evans 1912-
(Dale Evans)

PERSONAL: Birth-given name, Frances Octavia Smith; born October 31, 1912, in Uvalde, Tex.; daughter of Walter Hillman (a farmer) and Bettie Sue (Wood) Smith; married Thomas Frederick Fox, January, 1927 (died, 1929); married Robert Dale Butts (a pianist; divorced, 1945); married Roy Rogers (an actor and singer), December 31, 1947; children: (first marriage) Thomas Frederick Fox, Jr.; (third marriage) Robin Elizabeth (deceased); stepchildren: (third marriage) Cheryl Rose, Linda Lou Johnson, Roy, Jr.; adopted children: (third marriage) John David (Sandy; deceased), Mary Little Doe Stanley, Marion Swift, Deborah Lee (deceased). *Education:* Attended business school in Memphis, Tenn. *Religion:* Christian. *Address:* Roy Rogers-Dale Evans Museum, 15650 Seneca Rd., Victorville, Calif. 92392. *Office:* c/o Fleming H. Revell Co., Old Tappan, N.J. 07675.

CAREER: Actress, singer, and lyricist. Worked as stenographer. Singer on radio station WHAS in Louisville, Ky., and on WFAA in Dallas, Tex.; vocalist with Anson Week's orchestra; staff singer for Columbia Broadcasting System (CBS) on WBBM radio station in Chicago, Ill., and star of show, "That Girl From Texas," 1940-41; featured vocalist on radio shows of Edgar Bergen and Charlie McCarthy, Jack Carson, Garry Moore, Jimmy Durante, and "The Chase and Sanborn Hour"; actress in Twentieth Century-Fox motion pictures "Orchestra Wives," and "Girl Trouble," both 1942; actress in more than thirty-five motion pictures for Republic, including "Swing Your Partner," 1943, "The West Side Kid," 1943, "Casanova in Burlesque," 1944, "Lights of Old Santa Fe," 1944, "The Big Show-Off," 1945, "Along the Navajo Trail," 1945, "Song of Arizona," 1946, "Helldorado," 1946, "My Pal Trigger," 1946, "Apache Rose," 1947, "The Trespasser," 1947, "Slippy McGee," 1948, "Susanna Pass," 1949, "Twilight in the Sierras," 1950, "Trigger, Jr.," 1950, "South of Caliente," 1951, and "Pals of the Golden West," 1951; star with husband Roy Rogers on National Broadcasting Co. (NBC-TV) program, "The Roy Rogers Show," 1951-56, and 1962; recorder of several record albums, including "The Bible Tells Me," "Faith, Hope, and Charity," "Jesus Loves Me," "Sweeter as the Years Go By," and "Peter Cottontail and Other Eastern Favorites"; entertainer at rodeos, state fairs, and television specials. Fund raiser for charities. *Wartime service:* Entertainer at training camps and performer in more than five hundred fifty United Service Organizations (U.S.O.) shows.

MEMBER: American Society of Composers, Authors, and Publishers, American Federation of Television and Radio Artists, Screen Actors Guild, American Pen Women, American Bible Society (honorary life member), Eastern Star, Hollywood Christian Group, Lambda Theta Chi. *Awards, honors:* Money-Making Western Star award from *Motion Picture Herald-Fame*, 1947, 1950, 1951, and 1952; George Spelvin Award from Masquers' Club, 1956, for humanitarian services; public interest award from National Safety Council; citations from National Association for Retarded Children, American Red Cross, Muscular Dystrophy Association, National Nephrosis Foundation, American Legion, Round Table International, and General William Westmoreland; woman of the year award from International Orphans, Inc.; church woman of the year award from Religious Heritage of America; Texan of the year award from Texas Press Association, 1966; mother of the year award, 1967.

WRITINGS—All published by Revell, except as noted; all nonfiction: *Angel Unaware*, 1953, revised edition, Pyramid Books, 1963; *My Spiritual Diary*, 1955; *Prayer Book for Children*, Simon & Schuster, 1956; *To My Son: Faith at Our House*, 1957; *Christmas Is Always*, 1958; *No Two Ways About It!*, 1963; *Dearest Debbie: In Ai Lee*, 1965; *Salute to Sandy*, 1967; *Time Out, Ladies!*, 1966; *God Has the Answers: Selections from "No Two Ways About It!" and "Time Out, Ladies!"*, 1969, revised edition published as *Finding the Way: Selections From the Writings of Dale Evans Rogers*, 1973; *The Woman at the Well*, 1970; *Dale: My Personal Picture Album*, 1971; *Cool It or Lose It!: Dale Evans Rogers Raps With Youth*, 1972; *Where He Leads*, 1974; (with Frank S. Mead) *Let Freedom Ring!*, 1975; *Trials, Tears, and Triumph*, 1977; (with Mead) *Hear the Children Crying*, 1978; (with Carole C. Carlson) *Woman, Be All You Can Be*, 1980.

Lyricist of songs: "Will You Marry Me, Mr. Laramie?," "Aha, San Antone," "Down the Trail to San Antone," "Lo Dee Lo Di," "T for Texas," "Happy Trails to You," "I'm Gonna Lock You Out-a My Heart," "Buckeye Cowboy," "The Bible Tells Me So," "Happy Birthday, Gentle Saviour," "No Bed of Roses," "I Wish I Had Never Met Sunshine."

SIDELIGHTS: "Queen of the Cowgirls" Dale Evans Rogers got her start in show business while working as a stenographer at an insurance company. One day while Rogers was singing over her secretarial labors, her boss overheard and suggested she sing on a local radio station. She did, and soon her voice could be heard over the wireless in Louisville, Dallas, and Chicago. It was while she was singing one of her own songs in Chicago at the Chez Paree supper club that Rogers got her break into motion pictures. After seeing her performance there, a Paramount agent asked her to audition for the lead opposite Bing Crosby in "Holiday Inn." She tried out for the part, but was not hired. Instead, Twentieth Century-Fox acquired Rogers's screen test and signed her to a one-year contract. At Twentieth Century-Fox, Rogers acted in her first two films. When her contract was not renewed, the singing star signed with Republic in 1943. She had made several films, including one with John Wayne, when she was cast opposite "King of the Cowboys" Roy Rogers for the first time in 1944. Their film, "The Cowboy and the Senorita," was followed by a string of successful collaborations. Their "horse operas" rivaled Gene Autry's westerns in popularity.

Meanwhile, Rogers's personal life was also in flux. Her first marriage to Frederick Fox ended in 1929, and Rogers was left to support her young son through her singing jobs. Rogers later married pianist Robert Dale Butts, but the couple divorced in 1945. In 1946, Roy Rogers's wife of ten years died after giving birth to their son Roy Rogers, Jr., leaving the star with three children. Dale and Roy continued to make their profitable films, though, and churned out eight in 1946 alone.

In 1947, while awaiting their entrance to a rodeo in Chicago, Dale and Roy decided to marry. They did so on December 31, 1947, at the home of the governor of Oklahoma. On August 26, 1950, the couple's daughter Robin Elizabeth was born afflicted with Down's syndrome and a weak heart. Instead of institutionalizing the child, Dale and Roy cared for her at home. She died a few days before her second birthday after a bout with the mumps. Robin's death left Rogers stricken with grief and she vented her sorrow in her first book, *Angel Unaware*. The inspirational volume sold well and Rogers donated all proceeds to the National Association for Retarded Children.

The couple went on with their lucrative careers and continued to expand their family by adopting four more children. They moved into television with "The Roy Rogers Show" in 1951. Singing their theme song, "Happy Trails to You," one of Dale's own compositions, Dale and Roy became known to Americans all over the country. In addition to their television work, the husband-and-wife team toured the British Isles and participated in a number of religious programs. They attended Billy Graham's Crusades in London and Washington, D.C. In 1953 Dale wrote her second book, *My Spiritual Diary*. The volume earned favorable reviews. T. A. Gill of *Christian Century* noted that "a sweet, sincere, earnest, indiscriminate Christianity is chronicled in this diary," while N. K. Burger remarked in the *New York Times* that the work "is certain to be one of the year's most popular books." All the earnings of *My Spiritual Diary* were donated to Children's Hospital of Los Angeles.

In 1964 the Rogers' Korean daughter Debbie was killed along with six other children in a bus accident. Returning from a church distribution of food and clothing in Mexico, the bus blew a tire and ran into a tree. Dale again exorcised her sorrow in a book called *Dearest Debbie: In Ai Lee*. As with her previous books, the proceeds of this volume also went to a charitable organization, World Vision, Inc. A year later, tragedy again visited Dale and Roy when their son Sandy died while in the army in Germany. In Sandy's memory, the singing couple entertained the servicemen in Vietnam in 1966, and Dale wrote a book, *Salute to Sandy,* in 1967.

Dale and her husband continue to raise money for a number of charities. In acknowledgement of their contributions, Round Table International bestowed them with a citation never before given to show business performers. The award commended the couple for "distinguished service to humanity and to their country in the fields of clean entertainment, of unselfish and effective leadership in service of homeless and orphaned children, and to the mentally retarded, and as volunteer entertainers to the armed forces."

CA INTERVIEW

Dale Evans Rogers was interviewed by telephone on May 20, 1980.

CA: In your autobiography, I noted that you tried to write short stories at one point.

ROGERS: Yes. When I was in high school, the best marks I made were in English and composition. I enjoyed doing little essays and short subjects and things like that because I've always been on the creative side. And then, when I was about fifteen, possibly, or sixteen, I tried writing lyrics to songs. I've always been better with lyrics than I have been with the music itself. And that's really the way I started. The first little song I ever did was a pop song and I think it was called "He's Mine, All Mine." I took it to a publisher in Memphis, Tenn., and I played and sang it and sang my heart out, and nothing ever came of it—I never heard from anybody. And then, oh, several months later, there used to be music stands way back in those years—like variety stores, you know, and I walked into one and there was a song with my title. The song was changed just slightly and there was somebody else's name on it. So, that was the end of the song writing at that point.

CA: It hasn't changed much nowadays, either, has it?

ROGERS: No, it hasn't. But that didn't discourage me too much. Later on, when I was in radio, nightclubs, and band work in Chicago, I wrote a little song during leap year called, "Will You Marry Me, Mr. Laramie?" I was at the Chez Paree in Chicago and Ray Bolger was the headliner with Ethel Chappey, who used to be married to George Olson. They were headlining and I was kind of a show opener. At that time I was under contract to CBS in Chicago as a staff singer. And so, some scouts came to me and said that they liked my voice, but said I needed some special material and asked if I didn't have something that was different. When you do clubs you usually have to have material written for you and I didn't; I was just a radio singer singing pop songs.

So, I sang the song for them. They liked it, and commented, "Well, you do a second chorus in the song that's sort of demure, but a little double entendre, you know just a little. . . ." They explained to me that "you'd never get away with a very risque lyric—you just don't look it." I said "well, I didn't want to do that, anyway." So, I wrote a little thing adding a misunderstanding between the girl and her father and Ray Bolger said he would stooge for me. With his Adam's apple, he pretended to be the suitor, and was very red-faced when I proposed to him. And that really—that song itself—landed me a contract. I came out to Hollywood with it to do a test at Paramount Studios. I did that song in the test, but I didn't get a contract at Paramount, I got a contract at Twentieth Century-Fox. So, you might say that sort of started me on the writing situation.

CA: And your writing sort of started your whole film career.

ROGERS: Yes, it did. From there I went to "The Chase and Sanborn Hour," "The Jimmy Durante Show," and "The Jack Carson Show"—both of them are gone now. And then I went to Republic Studios and wrote some little western things and I continued to write and I still do. Most of my writing now is Gospel music that I do for myself for tours, concerts, things like that. But the book writing started with our baby—the baby that Roy and I had that was retarded.

CA: Yes, now was it the burden on your heart to share that or was that a way to deal with your grief?

ROGERS: That had nothing to do with wanting to be a writer, actually, nothing at all. The fact is that when Robin was about six or seven months old, most of the press knew the extent of her handicap, but they were very kind not to divulge it to the public. Except for that she had a bad heart, which she did, they didn't mention Down's syndrome. It was a tremendous strain during the course of her lifetime because Roy was number one in westerns at the box office and there was a great deal of curiosity about our home and about our new baby. It really wasn't easy. One of the fan magazines wanted me to do a faith article. They knew I was a very committed Christian, and they wanted me to do an article on faith about this baby of ours, because we'd been told she wouldn't live very long. During the course of her lifetime, I said, "Well, I just don't know what's going to happen to her and I really can't, but some day I promise I will."

After she died, at age two, I was looking at this color etching of her over my desk, and these words from Paul's letter to the Hebrews in the Bible "be not forgetful to entertain strangers, but thereby some have entertained angels unawares," seemed to flash into my head. I thought, well, that's what this child was to us, because she accomplished so much in our family, teaching us lessons of gratitude for our normal children, humility, patience, dependence upon God, and faith in a power beyond ourselves and beyond the doctors. I couldn't stop writing. I started to write and it just flowed as if someone was pushing my hand.

CA: Now, you do *get that feeling, as though you are the instrument and it's being written through you?*

ROGERS: That's right—that's exactly the way it is. It just took wings, that little book. After *Angel Unaware,* I did a book called, *My Spiritual Diary,* because I had gotten so many letters from fans and other people who had this same problem. They wanted to know the basis of my faith and how I could accept this kind of handicap in that light. So, I wrote the second book to sort of explain the first one. All my writing has been of a very personal nature, explaining what I see in my world: what I have experienced, and what I've seen others experience. My writing is a quest for life itself. What is life? What is joy?

Then I did a book for our little girl who was killed on the bus, Debbie. Then our boy who died. He was an abused child who died in Germany. His name was John David. And for him I wrote *Salute to Sandy.* All of the proceeds of my books are donated to various organizations. I tithe right off the top to philanthropic works, Christian work, and where I see need.

CA: Your life, largely now, is sort of surrounding your Christian mission. Which part of that do you find the most satisfying?

ROGERS: I love writing. I enjoy writing, but, I think what I love most is testifying my faith, and how I found the answer in my life to joy, purpose, and the God-sustaining strength and understanding that has been given me in time of sorrow and great trial.

CA: Your writing does that, too. But you mean the person-to-person contact?

ROGERS: The person-to-person contact. Because, usually when I go out there, there is somebody in that audience who will inevitably come up and say, "I identify with you." And really, that is the reason why *Angel Unaware* was written—the prime reason was to help other people with the same problem.

CA: Today, in 1980, there is a real Christian awakening that is just all over the world. And it's particularly saturating the entertainment industry.

ROGERS: Yes, I think probably that is because most entertaining people are very giving by nature. I think that most of them are extroverts. They like to express their faith, probably more than the person who is not in the entertainment industry and hasn't had to face the public a whole lot. And that goes for people who have been in politics, too.

CA: But, you know, people used to be very quiet about it. But now, everyone is so vocal about it, they're just preaching.

ROGERS: Well, the thing is, we've already reached a terrific crisis in this country, and I think people are beginning to realize that. We have been blessed to live in this country, and to have the freedom to express ourselves. I think people are beginning to become quite aware of the fact that we might lose it. You know, the Bible says that under God we're free. We can be free under him, or live under the tyranny of man—there's no in-between. It's one or the other. I mean, we have to acknowledge him, understand that he is the creator, and that he holds the world in his hands. He really does. And if we get too obstreperous, all he has to do is just turn it upside down.

CA: Your latest book, Woman, *has stirred up quite a bit of controversy in the reviews I've been reading.*

ROGERS: Oh, yes. I'll tell you something: I don't expect to get any pats on the head for this book.

CA: What do you attribute the controversy to? You knew what you were doing when you went into it?

ROGERS: Yes, of course, because I've been watching this thing pretty closely for about five years. I mean the feminist movement. I understand those girls, because I used to feel the same way.

CA: I noticed that in the autobiography, and I thought when I saw the title, Woman, Be All You Can Be, *that now, Dale Evans has been through raising one child alone, raising another man's children, adopting children, and keeping a career going. She's really going to have some things to say. And this is going to be a real liberationist book coming from this Christian woman. And I was curious to see how you put this together.*

ROGERS: Well, I had to really speak from my heart, because I have been on both sides of the fence. I understand it, and

the other side never really made me happy. I mean to say, not ultimately happy. Always, there is in women a need to mother, most women, whether it be a child or a little pet, a mother or a father, a brother or a sister, or somebody's neighbor. But, it's there, that is in us. And, you know, until we get an opportunity to express it, we can be awfully shrill. I had never been really happy and I was really a *pushing* career woman. I mean, I was pushing and trying hard to make it. But the more I did, the less satisfied I was. Not the less satisfied, I should say, but the less secure I felt inside. I was always having to prove myself, over and over and over and over. And I thought, there must be something else in my life. Of course, when you've been independent, it's very, very difficult to change when you've had to go it by yourself for a long time. But, God did do a pretty good work on me, not that I haven't had to say, "Down girl," a lot of times, and a lot of times, "Down, Down." But I've found that, like Roy says, it's 90/10 on both sides—it should be; you both have to try. This book, *Woman,* is a pleading for the little people, the children. That's exactly what it is in a nutshell. They need their mothers to be women.

CA: I think the most interesting controversy about Woman *deals with your position on abortion.*

ROGERS: Abortion is a hard thing on a woman. A terrible thing on a woman. And because I know firsthand, I've seen, I've talked, and I know what the feeling is. The feeling of having done something terrible. The sin against your own body. You've sinned against God, against creation, and sometimes you get infections, and sometimes you have a child that is not quite normal later, and you think, that's punishment for what I did. I mean there's all kinds of ramifications from abortion. God does forgive, but I do believe in abortion in the case of incest, if you catch it early. I believe in that. I believe in abortion in the case of rape, wanton rape. In cases like that, I think it should be done, and I believe in abortion if the mother's life is at stake and there are other children to raise. If the doctor sees that it's the mother or the child, and when there are others to consider, little ones, I think it has to be. I mean, I'd hate to have to make the choice, but that's what I believe. But, there are so many other people who want little babies and then can't have them. The women won't even have the children and give them up for adoption. Women are using abortion as a contraceptive now. I knew I was going to get rapped on this book and I didn't mind because I think that we all have to say our say, and we've got to reason together about it.

CA: You don't speak too much in the autobiography of your religious beliefs before.

ROGERS: Oh, well, I was just a nominal Christian. I mean I went to Sunday school at the church. I took my little boy because I wanted him to be close to God.

CA: But, then, this wasn't a complete turnaround, was it?

ROGERS: Well, you see, I had joined the church when I was ten. I had accepted Christ as my savior, but in no way did I commit my life to the leading of the spirit in me. I wanted—I had been bitterly hurt by my son's father—to prove to myself, and prove to everybody else, but mostly to him that I could succeed. I had a real chip on my shoulder. I'd have been right in the middle of the feminist movement if there had been one. Really.

CA: So, you were in the middle of your own feminist movement.

ROGERS: That's right. That's right. Very antagonistic about women's lot.

CA: *Now, during all this time of the tragedies in your life, has your faith ever waivered?*

ROGERS: No. Well, not really. Sometimes, when a tragedy hits you, it's like somebody slapping you or knocking you on the head, and out of a reflex movement, you'll put yourself up to shield or try to ward it off. But, never, never, since I committed my life totally to God. Never. Even when our little girl was killed on the bus. That was the hardest thing I've ever had to handle. Harder than Robin. And because of the circumstances—she was such a delightful child—it was very difficult for me to handle. I did a little screaming for a few minutes, you know, "Why? why? why? It's not fair." And, then, of course, the Holy Spirit settled down on me and said, "Hey, wait a minute here." And our son, Dusty (Roy, Jr.) said, "Listen, Mom, you've been telling me ever since I can remember anything, that I'd better trust Jesus. You had better start right now. Don't you know that Debbie's with God? You know she is." And then I was settled. I'm not saying that I didn't grieve, because I did, terribly. When I wrote *Dearest Debbie*, it was in the midst of the hardest grief I had.

CA: *What is your next book going to be about?*

ROGERS: I don't know. I thought I'd do something about, "this, I really believe," but I'm not sure. I really don't know what I'm going to do next. I don't have any leading on it yet. I've been toying with several things, and I thought, well, maybe I should just do something like a devotional thing. Usually women like devotional books. But I'm not really sure yet, and I don't ever start until I am, you know? Until I feel the nudge.

CA: *What does Roy do while you're out gallivanting all over the country?*

ROGERS: Well, Roy runs a museum here at Victorville. He has a horse ranch and he bowls quite a bit. He's on leagues. Roy is on the board of His Life, which is out of Campus Crusade. And he has restaurants for the Marriott Corp.

CA: *He's got plenty to keep himself busy.*

ROGERS: Yes, he has. He sure does.

CA: *Is that what keeps you two so young?*

ROGERS: Well, I think it helps. That and faith in the Lord.

CA: *It keeps the worry lines away when you have faith.*

ROGERS: Well, they're there, but when you don't look so tense, they don't show so bad.

CA: *Well, when I see you two I never think of worry lines. They're laugh lines.*

ROGERS: They are. Yes, they really are. Well, we both have a sense of humor and we both can laugh about things. We can laugh at ourselves and at each other. And that helps.

BIOGRAPHICAL/CRITICAL SOURCES—Books: Dale Evans Rogers, *My Spiritual Diary*, Revell, 1955; Elise Miller Davis, *Answer Is God: The Inspiring Personal Story of Dale Evans and Roy Rogers*, McGraw, 1955; Dorothy Haskin, *Twice-Born Stars You Would Like to Know*, Zondervan, 1955; Maxine Garrison, *Angel Spreads Her Wings*, Revell, 1956; D. E. Rogers, *Woman at the Well*, Revell, 1970; D. E.

Rogers, *Dale: My Personal Picture Album*, Revell, 1971; Cyril Davey, *Fifty Lives for God*, Judson Press, 1973; Robert James Parish and Lennard DeCarl, *Hollywood Players: The Forties*, Arlington House, 1976.

Periodicals: *Time*, March 7, 1955; *Springfield Republican*, March 20, 1955; *Christian Century*, March 23, 1955; *New York Times*, March 27, 1955; *Biography News*, Volume I, Gale, 1974; *Columbia State*, January 20, 1974; *Louisville Courier Journal*, August 17, 1974; *West Coast Review of Books*, November, 1978.

—*Interview by Judith Spiegelman*

* * *

ROGERS, Floyd
See SPENCE, William John Duncan

* * *

ROGGE, Oetje John 1903-1981

OBITUARY NOTICE—See index for CA sketch: Born October 12, 1903, in Cass County, Ill.; died of cancer, March 22, 1981, in New York, N.Y. Attorney and author. As the assistant attorney general in the criminal division of the Justice Department, Rogge investigated and ended the Huey Long political machine in Louisiana. Four years later, in 1943, he conducted the sedition case against thirty-three pro-Nazi Americans; the case, however, ended in a mistrial when the presiding judge died. In 1946 Rogge was dismissed from the Justice Department after he revealed details of a report that cited twenty-four Congressmen as collaborators with a Nazi agent. A champion of civil rights, the attorney often defended those whose civil liberties he felt had been violated. Rogge's works include *Our Vanishing Civil Liberties*, *Why Men Confess*, *The First and the Fifth*, and *Obscenity Litigation in Ten American Jurisprudence Trials*. Obituaries and other sources: *New York Times*, March 23, 1981; *Newsweek*, April 6, 1981; *Time*, April 6, 1981.

* * *

ROHMER, Richard 1924-

PERSONAL: Born January 24, 1924, in Hamilton, Ontario, Canada; son of Ernest and Marion (Wright) Rohmer; married Mary Olivia Whiteside; children: Catherine, Ann. *Education:* University of Western Ontario, B.A., 1948; graduated from Osgoode Hall, 1951. *Office:* Joseph & Lyson, 2180 Yonge St., Toronto, Ontario, Canada M4S 2B9.

CAREER: Called to the Bar in Ontario, 1951, and the Bar of the Northwest Territories, 1970; appointed Queen's Counsel, 1961; in private law practice, 1951—. Counsel with Joseph & Lyson. Chairman of Royal Commission on Book Publishing, 1970-72; counsel to Royal Commission on Metropolitan Toronto, 1975-77. Founder and chairman of Mid-Canada Development Corridor Concept and Conference. Member of governing body of Canadian Corps of Commissionnaires; patron of Metro Toronto Branch of St. John Ambulance. Member of Council of Township North York, 1958-59, and chairman of works and personnel committees; member of board of directors of Mediacom Ltd. and Herbert A. Watts Contests Ltd.; past member of board of governors of North York General Hospital. Principal founder and chairman of Don Mills Foundation for Senior Citizens Inc. Chancellor of University of Windsor, 1978—. *Military service:* Royal Canadian Air Force, fighter pilot, 1942-45; served in Europe; received Distinguished Flying Cross. Royal Canadian Air Force Reserve, pilot, commander of Toronto and

York squadrons, 1945-53, retiring as wing commander. Appointed brigadier general and senior air reserve adviser to chief of defense staff and commander of Air Command, 1975, and commander of Air Reserve Group, 1976; appointed major general of reserves responsible to chief of defense staff for militia and naval, air, and communications reserves, 1978; appointed chief of reserves of the Canadian Armed Forces, 1979.

MEMBER: Canadian Bar Association, Community Planning Association of Canada, Northwest Territories Bar Association, County of York Law Association, Delta Chi, Lambda Alpha, Civitan International (judge advocate, 1962-63 and 1966-67; vice-president, 1963-64), Don Mills Civitan Club (president, 1961-62), Order of St. John (officer brother), Albany Club. *Awards, honors:* Honor key from Canadian district of Civitan International, 1965, international honor key, 1966; Centennial Medal, 1967, Jubilee Medal, 1977; Commissioner's Award for Public Service to the Northwest Territories, 1972; LL.D. from University of Windsor, 1975.

WRITINGS: The Green North: Mid-Canada (nonfiction), Maclean-Hunter, 1970; *The Arctic Imperative: An Overview of the Energy Crisis* (nonfiction), McClelland & Stewart, 1973; *Ultimatum* (novel), Clarke, Irwin, 1973, Pocket Books, 1975; *Exxoneration* (novel), McClelland & Stewart, 1974; *Exodus* (novel), McClelland & Stewart, 1975; *Separation* (novel), McClelland & Stewart, 1976; *E. P. Taylor: The Biography of Edward Plunket Taylor,* McClelland & Stewart, 1978; *Balls!* (novel), General Publishing, 1979; *Periscope Red,* Beaufort Book, 1980. Also author of *Separation II* (novel), 1981, *Triad* (novel), 1981, *Patton's Gap* (nonfiction), 1981, and *Images* (poems), 1981.

BIOGRAPHICAL/CRITICAL SOURCES: Windsor Star, November 1, 1980.

*   *   *

ROLAND, Betty   1903-

PERSONAL: Name legally changed in 1951; born July 22, 1903, in Kaniva, Australia; daughter of Roland (a physician) and Matilda (Blayney) Maclean; married Ellis H. Davies, April 23, 1923 (divorced, 1934); married Guido Baracchi (a journalist; died, 1975); children: (first marriage) Peter Ellis (deceased); (second marriage) Gilda. *Education:* Attended Church of England girls' grammar school in Melbourne, Australia. *Politics:* Liberal. *Religion:* None. *Home:* 59/4 Ward Ave., Potts Point, Sydney 2011, Australia. *Agent:* David Bolt, Bolt & Watson Ltd., 8-12 Old Queen St., Storey's Gate, London SW1H 9HP, England.

CAREER: Writer. *Member:* International P.E.N., Australian Society of Authors, Australian Writers Guild, Fellowship of Australian Writers, Society of Women Writers.

WRITINGS: Morning (one-act play), Angus & Robertson, 1937; *The Touch of Silk* (three-act play), Melbourne University Press, 1942, reprinted, Currency Press, 1974; *The Forbidden Bridge* (children's book), Bodley Head, 1961; *Jamie's Discovery* (children's book), Bodley Head, 1963; *Lesbos, the Pagan Island* (memoirs), F. W. Cheshire, 1963; *Jamie's Summer Visitor* (children's book), Bodley Head, 1964; *Sydney in Colour and Black and White* (travel book), Lansdowne Press, 1965; *The Bush Bandits* (children's book), Lansdowne Press, 1966; *Jamie's Other Grandmother* (children's book), Bodley Head, 1970; *The Other Side of Sunset* (novel), Mills & Boon, 1972; *No Ordinary Man* (novel), Collins, 1974; *Beyond Capricorn* (novel), Collins, 1976; *Caviar for Breakfast* (memoirs), Quartet Books, 1979.

Author of radio plays, including "The First Gentleman," "Daddy Was Asleep," "The White Cockade," "A Woman Scorned," "The Drums of Manalao," and "In His Steps," all written and broadcast c. 1942-49. Author of "Granite Peak" (television play), first broadcast by London Radio-Diffusion, August, 1957. Contributor to newspapers and magazines, including *Harper's Bazaar, Girl, Swift, Woman's Own, Women's Weekly, Sydney Morning Herald,* and *Overland.*

WORK IN PROGRESS: The Devious Being, an autobiographical novel, completion expected in 1995.

SIDELIGHTS: Betty Roland told *CA:* "My early formative years were spent in the Australian bush. I began to write while still at school and never wanted to do anything else. After the breakup of an early marriage I went abroad and spent many years traveling and living in different countries: Italy, the U.S.S.R., and the Greek islands, but staying principally in London, with brief returns to Australia. All the while, I wrote as I went. I decided that Australia was the place I most wanted to live in and returned in 1971. I have not regretted it. Writing is a tough game and getting worse, but I still keep on. It is as addictive as any drug, once you are 'hooked' you can't give it up, but I would not encourage anyone to start!"

*   *   *

ROMERO, Gerry
See NEYLAND, James (Elwyn)

*   *   *

ROMIG, Edna Davis   1889-1978

OBITUARY NOTICE—See index for *CA* sketch: Born January 16, 1889, in Rarden, Ohio; died June 26, 1978. Educator and poet. Romig was the author of several volumes of poetry, including *These Are the Fields, Flash of Wings,* and *The Heart Affirming.* She also contributed poems and articles to *Atlantic, Yale Review, Outlook,* and other literary journals. (Date of death provided by son, William Davis Romig.)

*   *   *

ROPE, Henry Edward George   1880-1978

OBITUARY NOTICE—See index for *CA* sketch: Born October 23, 1880, in Shrewsbury, England; died March 1, 1978. Roman Catholic priest, poet, and author of nonfiction books, including *Benedict XV* and *The Schola Saxonum, the Hospital and the English College in Rome.* Rope also wrote several volumes of poetry, including *The City of the Grail* and *The Hills of Home.* (Date of death provided by Pallotti Hall, Macclesfield, Cheshire, England.)

*   *   *

ROPER, Steve   1941-

PERSONAL: Born February 13, 1941, in Oklahoma; son of Edwin Ellis (a chemist) and Elberta (a librarian; maiden name, Henabery) Roper; married Katherine Gelus (a professor of history), October 21, 1977. *Education:* Attended Oregon State College (now University). *Home:* 63 Abbott Dr., Oakland, Calif. 94611. *Office:* 1452 Scenic Ave., Berkeley, Calif. 94708.

CAREER: Writer. *Military service:* U.S. Army, 1963-65; served in Vietnam.

WRITINGS: Climber's Guide to Pinnacles National Monument, Ski Hut, 1966; *Climber's Guide to Yosemite Valley,*

Sierra Books, 1971; *The Climber's Guide to the High Sierra,* Sierra Books, 1976; (with Allen Steck) *Fifty Classic Climbs of North America,* Sierra Books, 1979. Co-editor of *Ascent,* 1967—.

* * *

ROSCOE, Edwin Scott   1896-1978

OBITUARY NOTICE—See index for *CA* sketch: Born May 15, 1896, in Delaware, Ohio; died January 8, 1978. Engineer, educator, and author of books on industrial management, including *Organization for Production* and *Project Economy.* (Date of death provided by wife, Dorothea Palmer Roscoe.)

* * *

ROSE, Frank   1949-

PERSONAL: Born January 8, 1949, in Norfolk, Va.; son of Edmund and Ruth (Moseley) Rose. *Education:* Washington and Lee University, B.A., 1971. *Residence:* New York, N.Y. *Agent:* Virginia Barber, 353 West 21st St., New York, N.Y. 10011.

CAREER: Free-lance writer. *Member:* Writers Guild.

WRITINGS: (Contributor) Dave Marsh, editor, *The Rolling Stone Record Guide,* Random House, 1979; (contributor) Marianne Partridge, editor, *Rolling Stone Visits "Saturday Night Live,"* Dolphin, 1979; *Real Men: Sex and Style in an Uncertain Age,* photographs by George Bennett, Doubleday/ Dolphin, 1980. Contributor to periodicals, including *Esquire, Village Voice, New York, TV Guide, Washington Post, New Times, Quest,* and *Rolling Stone.*

WORK IN PROGRESS: Various articles.

SIDELIGHTS: Real Men: Sex and Style in an Uncertain Age received a favorable review from Dennis Drabelle in the *Washington Post Book World.* The book features interviews and photographs of several men from diverse backgrounds. Describing the volume as a "fascinating and seamless collaboration," Drabelle also observed: "Rose has drawn out . . . candid—sometimes even intemperate—self-revelations of seven men living in what he calls 'an uncertain age.' All seven have strength of character yet admit to being confused about themselves, unsure of what comes next." The reviewer concluded that "their willingness to share these doubts without fear of forfeiting their masculinity is what makes these men more real than their predecessors."

Rose told *CA:* "My concerns are the vagaries of pop culture. Several years ago I began writing about music and sexual politics for the *Village Voice* and *Rolling Stone;* then I wrote a book about the way men identify with their own masculinity; and most recently, in *Esquire,* I've been exploring various subcultures—the Pentagon and the new wave scene in New York—that have little in common except their ability to give some indication of where we're headed. My basic premise is that every new development is culturally interconnected, whether it takes place in Hollywood, in Washington, D.C., or in Soho. My job is to trace those connections."

BIOGRAPHICAL/CRITICAL SOURCES: Washington Post Book World, May 10, 1980.

* * *

ROSE, Gilbert J(acob)   1923-

PERSONAL: Born May 9, 1923, in Malden, Mass.; son of M. Edward (a lawyer and poet) and Sara (Freedman) Rose; married Anne Kaufman (a writer), March 10, 1946; children:

Renee Rose Shield, Daniel Asa, Cecily Rose-Itkoff, Aron Dana. *Education:* Harvard University, A.B., 1943; Boston University, M.D., 1947; State University of New York Downstate Medical Center, Certificate of Training in Psychoanalytic Medicine, 1959. *Office:* 25 Sammis St., Rowayton, Conn. 06853.

CAREER: Associate with Brooklyn Jewish Hospital, Brooklyn, N.Y., 1947-48; State University of New York Downstate Medical Center, Brooklyn, began in 1948, visiting psychiatrist and clinical instructor of psychiatry, 1950-53; private practice of psychoanalysis and psychiatry, 1955—; Yale University, New Haven, Conn., assistant professor, 1960-67, associate professor of psychiatry, 1967—. *Military service:* U.S. Air Force, Medical Corps, 1953-55; became captain. *Member:* American Psychiatric Association (fellow), American Psychoanalytic Association. *Awards, honors:* Sandor Lorand Essay Award from Psychoanalytic Association of New York, 1961, for article, "Screen Memories in Homicidal Acting-Out."

WRITINGS: The Power of Form: A Psychoanalytic Approach to Aesthetic Form, International Universities Press, 1980. Member of editorial board of *Psychoanalytic Study of Society.*

WORK IN PROGRESS: Book reviews and articles.

SIDELIGHTS: Rose commented: "You might ask, 'What's a psychoanalyst who's still in full-time private practice after twenty-five years doing trying to build a bridge between aesthetic form and psychoanalysis? Doesn't he have enough on his hands already?' My answer is in the first place the relationship between art and psychoanalysis, at least for me, has always been mutually informing, central and intimate. The condescension and naivete of 'explaining' art by reducing it to psychopathology always bugged me, as did exalting it as something ineffable and divine. In the second place, I did not know I was writing a book until I began to think about the many professional papers I had written over the years and asked myself, much as I would a patient in analysis, 'What's between the lines—what are they getting at?' In other words, I began to *listen* to my own papers *as a whole.* It then dawned on me that their sum total was pressing in a direction I had not suspected and, more than that, suggesting possibilities that surprised and excited me. What I began to see was that our perception of time, of place, and of person has a double aspect, corresponding to the two different cognitive styles in which the brain seems to process all information; that one can often find this doubleness reflected in aesthetic form; and that it is far more harmoniously accomodated in aesthetic form than the mind is able to do in its moment-by-moment workaday activity. Does aesthetic form, then, serve a *biological* function by serving as a model for the smooth orchestration of discordant data—the kind that the mind is always struggling to reconcile in order to keep itself oriented in the ever-lasting ambiguity between thought and feeling, past and present.

"I hope it is clear from these remarks that my aim is to suggest a direction for applied psychoanalysis, one more in line with current thinking in ego psychology as well as other fields. More specifically, I propose that we pay less attention to unconscious *motivations* which are, in any event, ubiquitous and therefore do not distinguish art from anything else; and pay more attention to the preconscious and unconscious ego task of continuing orientation in a reality which is always changing somewhat, never totally constant. An emphasis on form rather than content, the continuing need for adaptive orientation in a fluid, present reality in the light of the past rather than early motivations and regression to the past, accords to art an ongoing present biological significance—aspects heretofore overlooked.''

* * *

ROSE, Harold 1921-1967

OBITUARY NOTICE—See index for *CA* sketch: Born April 12, 1921; died in 1967. Scriptwriter, journalist, public relations consultant, broadcaster, editor, and author. Among Rose's writings are the ''Your Guide'' series of travel books, including *Your Guide to Malta, . . . to Bulgaria,* and *. . . to Ireland.* He also wrote *Available Light Photography.* (Date of death provided by wife, Beryl Brewer Rose.)

* * *

ROSE, Paul (Bernard) 1935-

PERSONAL: Born December 26, 1935, in Manchester, England; son of Arthur (an engineer) and Norah (a teacher; maiden name, Helman) Rose; married Eve Marie-Therese Lapu, September 13, 1957; children: Howard Imre, Michelle Alison, Daniel Sean. *Education:* Victoria University of Manchester, LL.B. (with honors), 1956. *Home:* 47 Lindsay Dr., Kenton, Harrow, Middlesex, England. *Office:* 10 King's Bench Walk, Temple, London E.C.4, England.

CAREER: Called to the Bar at Gray's Inn, 1958; barrister-at-law, 1958—. Legal adviser to Cooperative Union Ltd., 1957-60; deputy circuit judge, 1974—; member of Bar Council. Lecturer at University of Salford, 1960-62. Labour member of Parliament for Blackley Division of Manchester, 1964-79, Parliamentary private secretary to minister of transport, 1967-68, front bench spokesman on employment, 1971, member of Labour committee for Europe. Past member of Council of Europe; past chairman of Campaign for Democracy in Ulster and Family Action Information and Rescue. *Member:* Society for Electoral Reform, League for Democracy for Greece.

WRITINGS: Law Relating to Industrial and Provident Societies, Cooperative Union, 1962; *Weights and Measures Law,* Cooperative Union, 1964; *The Manchester Martyrs,* Lawrence & Wishart, 1970; *History of the Fenians in England,* J. Calder, 1980; *The Westminster Treadmill,* Muller, 1980. Contributor to journals and newspapers, including *Contemporary Review.*

WORK IN PROGRESS: Research on the extreme right, extreme pseudo-religious cults, South African involvement in Europe, and Northern Ireland.

SIDELIGHTS: Rose commented: ''I am particularly concerned about individual freedom, open government, and access to information. As a libertarian I feel that much political argument is irrelevant, as power does not lie in Parliament. I have a special interest in the Caribbean and have been deeply involved in Greece. I have also visited Mauritius, Kenya, Ethiopia, and the Middle East.''

* * *

ROSENBERG, Philip 1942-

PERSONAL: Born March 30, 1942, in Worcester, Mass.; son of Oscar (a manufacturer) and Eva (Weiner) Rosenberg; married Charlotte Schmidt, December 27, 1979; children: Mark Elijah, Matthew Isaiah. *Education:* Boston University, B.A., 1963; Columbia University, M.A., 1965, Ph.D., 1972. *Home:* 685 West End Ave., New York, N.Y. 10025. *Agent:* Robert Datilla, 150 East 74th St., New York, N.Y. 10017.

CAREER: Prentice-Hall, Inc., Englewood Cliffs, N.J., editor, 1965; free-lance editor, 1965-74; writer, 1974—.

WRITINGS—All nonfiction, except as noted: *The Seventh Hero: Thomas Carlyle and the Theory of Radical Activism,* Harvard University Press, 1974; *Contract on Cherry Street* (novel), Crowell, 1975 (also see below); (with Sonny Grosso) *Point Blank,* Grosset, 1978; (with Robert Tanenbaum) *Badge of the Assassin,* Dutton, 1979; *The Spivey Assignment: A Double Agent's Infiltration of the Drug Smuggling Conspiracy* (Literary Guild alternate selection), Holt, 1979. Also author of television screenplay ''Contract on Cherry Street'' (adapted from own novel), first broadcast in 1977. Contributor of articles to magazines, including *Esquire.*

WORK IN PROGRESS: Cartwheel (working title), a novel set in the Pacific during World War II.

SIDELIGHTS: In his first book, *The Seventh Hero,* Philip Rosenberg argued that the Victorian social critic Thomas Carlyle was a major precursor of modern activism. It was a notable work of scholarship, described by some critics as ''original,'' ''alive and readable,'' and ''brilliant, difficult, controversial.'' It might have marked the beginning of Rosenberg's academic career but for the serious reservations he had about working as both scholar and teacher [see *CA INTERVIEW,* below]. After leaving Columbia University with his Ph.D., Rosenberg hoped to make his living as a full-time writer. He has since written a novel and three nonfiction books, all joined to the theme of crime and punishment.

Contract on Cherry Street was Rosenberg's second book and his first attempt at fiction. The main character of the story, Frank Hovannes, is a detective in the New York City Police Department. When his partner is gunned down by the mob, to the apparent unconcern of the department, Hovannes sets out to avenge the killing. He forms his own undercover unit and launches a private ''war against crime,'' carrying out a series of executions that spreads panic throughout the underworld. Unable to identify its real enemies, the mob strikes out at false targets and turns violently against itself. Hovannes' strike force, however, in its effort to remain undiscovered, must commit another round of murders. Internal dissent and violence eventually overtake Hovannes's men as well.

Critics were impressed by this first novel. Gene Lyons of the *New York Times Book Review* commented: ''[Rosenberg] has written an admirably crafted entertainment that engages one's attention from beginning to end and gives one something to think about in between. To have done all that without violating one's sense of probability and proportion, while dealing with a subject and theme which do, is no small thing.'' Another reviewer, Michael Irwin of the *Times Literary Supplement,* observed that the author ''has done plenty of homework and written a good, jolting, professional thriller. His narrative is a little over-populated for anything much in the way of character definition, especially as cops and crooks alike converse in gangland Esperanto; but the action is fast and clever.''

Rosenberg followed up *Contract on Cherry Street* with another look at crime and police work. Although presented in the form of a novel, *Point Blank* is a work of nonfiction based on the story of police detective Joe Nunziata, named Joe Longo in the book. The source for the story is one that other authors, notably Peter Maas (*Serpico*) and William Phillips (*Rogue Cop*), have found especially rich for books, articles, and films: the revelation of widespread police corruption in New York City during the late sixties and early seventies. In collaboration with Sonny Grosso, the detective who broke the "French Connection" case, Rosenberg dramatizes the events that ended with Nunziata's suicide.

The authors portray Joe Longo as "a devoted father and dedicated cop who was driven to his death by callous manipulators." In the course of a drug investigation, Longo accepts a bribe from a drug dealer and informant working as a double agent of the Bureau of Narcotics and Dangerous Drugs (B.N.D.D.). "When Joe is finally trapped," explained Evan Hunter of the *New York Times Book Review,* "we are asked to believe he accepted a bribe from the bad guy only to tighten his grip on the man. Why he *really* took the money remains one of the book's mysteries." Officials of the B.N.D.D. confront Longo with three choices: "You can work with us, you can go to jail, or you can blow your brains out." Longo's suicide note makes it clear that he blamed agents of the B.N.D.D. for his death.

Point Blank "reads more like a complicated spy story than a straightforward police narrative, with more double agents and double-crosses than can be found this side of le Carre country," Hunter said. "Joe's eventual death is predicted throughout in flash-forwards, . . . creating a foregone-conclusion suspense that does not detract from the cat-and-mouse game Joe and the drug dealer-informant-double agent are playing. . . . [It is] a story told with insight, indignation and—yes—at times inspiration."

In his next book, *Badge of the Assassin,* Rosenberg teamed with prosecuting attorney Robert Tanenbaum for a detailed examination of the criminal justice system, starting with the murder of two New York City policemen in 1971. Officers Joseph Piagentini and Waverly Jones were among the first policemen killed by members of the self-proclaimed Black Liberation Army, which construed the slayings as political acts in the cause of racial war. *Badge of the Assassin* is about the difficult and often frustrating manhunt that went on for four years, the eventual capture of the murderers, and the two courtroom trials needed for a successful prosecution.

According to reviewers, *Badge of the Assassin* is a suspenseful, well-written book that provides some insight into the fragile traditions of American justice. Dan Greenburg of the *New York Times Book Review* remarked: "The accounts of the two murder trials in New York, at which co-author Robert Tanenbaum served as prosecutor, and an intervening chase down to a remote farm in Mississippi where one of the murder weapons (the 'badge of the assassin') is believed to be buried, are almost as suspenseful as the stalking and capture of the killers. . . . The book is nicely researched and documented. The story is complex but easy to follow. The characterizations are brief but ring true, and the scenes build well. The writing is generally as spare and clean as a news story."

Christopher Lehmann-Haupt, whose review appeared in the *New York Times,* responded with mixed feelings to the book. He wondered at first if the story reflected the "true legacy of black militancy" in the early seventies: "Does it all come down to this—a story of shots in the back in the dark of night, by vicious punks mouthing incoherent revolutionary slogans?" But the authors make a distinction between being militant and being evil, and "in the long run," he conceded, "Mr. Tanenbaum and Mr. Rosenberg win you over. . . . I was fully caught up in the building drama of the book and turning pages without any awareness of time at all. And if you had interrupted me here and asked me then about its larger meaning, I guess I would have snapped that it signified nothing but right and wrong and justice. And hurriedly gone back to finish an exciting story."

In *The Spivey Assignment,* another nonfiction thriller, Rosenberg delivers a portrait of "the narc as hero." The book purports to be a tribute to narcotics agents who, the author attests, "are roundly damned on the one hand for interfering with the rights of citizens to smoke, snort or ingest the chemicals of their choice, while on the other hand, they are mocked for their failure to win the war against drugs." The hero of *The Spivey Assignment* is Larry Spivey himself, a Georgian who had made and lost a small fortune in the construction business and, finding himself at loose ends, joins the Georgia Bureau of Investigation. During his six months as an undercover agent, Spivey infiltrates a number of drug-smuggling operations, travels to Mexico, Guatemala, and Jamaica, kills two men, and encounters eighteen other homicides.

Donald Goddard, writing in the *New York Times Book Review,* called *The Spivey Assignment* "a Central American macho trip, full of gun law and gun lore, high-speed chases by land, sea and air, virile adventurers, dashing entrepreneurs, treacherous Latins, [and] beautiful women. . . . The action is fast and frantic; the expertise crisp and convincing, the characters stock, but sufficient for an exercise in the New Romanticism, which sets as much store on jungle country and automatic weapons as it does on psychological insight." In the end, Goddard observed, "Spivey had to be as ruthless, as unprincipled and . . . as brutal as the dopers he tried to catch."

CA INTERVIEW

CA interviewed Philip Rosenberg by phone on July 14, 1980, at his home in New York City.

CA: Your first book, The Seventh Hero, *is a scholarly study on Thomas Carlyle. Did that grow out of your doctoral dissertation?*

ROSENBERG: Yes. Except for minor editing, it is my doctoral dissertation.

CA: At the point when you were getting that book ready, were you also working as an editor?

ROSENBERG: Yes, I was doing free-lance editing. I had worked as an editor in a textbook publishing house for a year, and I did free-lance editing while I was going through graduate school.

CA: Had you already decided when you were in graduate school that you wanted to be a writer?

ROSENBERG: No, not then. It was actually after I had finished the dissertation and got the degree that I thought about looking for a teaching job. I realized then that I was more interested in the writing than the teaching. I had some experience teaching and found it to be very rewarding but very much a full-time commitment. I didn't like the system of giving little time to the students and saving most of it for yourself and your research. I thought that if I were going to teach I would do it the way it should be done, which wouldn't leave me any time for writing. Either you're a teacher or you're not. Under the circumstances, the best thing seemed to be to see if I could make it just as a writer, without having a university support me while I was doing it.

CA: Was the editing experience a great help to you when you started your own writing?

ROSENBERG: Very much so. In fact, I found it more help than graduate study of literature. Somehow in graduate study of literature you're not looking at books the way a writer does. As an editor, you have to take a piece of prose—a textbook on accounting or geography or any of the other things I edited—and make each paragraph work to mean what it's supposed to mean. That's a lot of what writing is. I learned to edit myself in the process. I've found that since I've been writing, I've gone back and read a lot of the classic novels that I had read before as a graduate student, but I read them very differently. As a writer, you're interested in seeing how things are done, how other writers make their books do what they want them to. That's not a way in which literature is taught, with any eye toward the craft of putting it together and making things work, how things are structured. It's all done in a very rarified way that I don't feel very close to anymore.

CA: You went from Thomas Carlye to Contract on Cherry Street, *which was quite a change. The idea grew out of all the talk about what was going on at the time about war on crime?*

ROSENBERG: Yes, I think it was Lyndon Johnson who first used the phrase "war on crime," and then the Nixon administration picked up on it. I just asked myself what would happen if anyone actually took it not as a metaphor but as a code that declared war on crime—an open, shooting war. The book was more or less an experiment in following that logic out. That was the start of it anyway. The story as I originally conceived it is rather different from the book as it evolved.

CA: Did you do a lot of research before you started writing?

ROSENBERG: No, in fact I actually didn't. I thought of trying to get close to some police officers to see how they think, but then it dawned on me that it would probably be a mistake. To write a novel strictly from a police officer's point of view, to the extent that that's different from a civilian's point of view, would be a mistake, because the specialized concerns would get in the way and would make the hero someone the average person couldn't relate to, someone foreign and exotic. I just wanted a man I imagined to be a strong and forceful character. How would such a person relate to the situation I wanted to put him in? That was the question the book had to ask and answer.

CA: Did you have to do interviews of policemen and reporters?

ROSENBERG: No. A good friend of mine was a reporter at the time for the *New York Daily News,* and I would call her and check the plausibility of certain things—for example, do the police have target ranges within the city limits—and questions on the various precincts. Technical details—that was the extent of it.

CA: Had you had any previous interest in the police or police novels?

ROSENBERG: Not in the least. When I was at Columbia I wasn't politically active, but intellectually I was in sympathy with the students of the late '60's. My attitude at the time was strongly antipolice. Since *Contract on Cherry Street* I've met a lot of cops and I've developed a tremendous respect for them. Some of the most intelligent, most perceptive people I've met have been detectives in the New York City Police Department, and in a few police departments elsewhere around the country.

CA: Did you get a lot of letters in response to that book?

ROSENBERG: Not that one so much, but the two nonfiction books that followed: *Point Blank,* which I did with retired detective Sonny Grosso, and *Badge of the Assassin,* which was about the murder of two police officers by black militants. On those I did get a fairly heavy response from people who knew of the incidents. Mostly positive.

CA: In your third book, Point Blank, *Detective Grosso wrote a section at the back. Did the two of you collaborate on the entire book?*

ROSENBERG: The whole book was done in the same way. I did the writing, and then we had very intense meetings. He's an extremely bright guy, with a very good dramatic sense and excellent editorial instincts. We would get together every week with whatever I had produced—five pages, twelve pages, fifteen pages in a good week—and go over it—through the night, usually. The reason the third part is identified as being by him is because the narrative there concerns incidents that occurred after the death of the protagonist. We wanted a first-person narrator to replace the omniscient narrator we used in the first two parts of the book. By putting his name there, having him sign it in effect, we felt we would avoid confusion. But the whole thing was done in the same writing method. It was a completely collaborative effort.

CA: Did you find it difficult to work that closely with someone?

ROSENBERG: Just the opposite. I found it one of the most exciting writing experiences I've ever had. I like that kind of input. With most writing, you don't get that kind of feedback. You write a book, it appears in print a few months later, and then it gets very general reviews. With *Point Blank* there was an automatic, immediate, spontaneous feedback that was very stimulating. As I said, Sonny and I would spend eight, ten, or twelve hours going over every five or six pages. It was a very intense process—a lot of shouting—but the result is a book where I think I know exactly why every sentence is there. That's the way you want to feel about everything you write, but if you're honest with yourself you have to admit that most of the time you fall short of that ideal.

CA: Was the collaboration with Robert Tanenbaum similar in Badge of the Assassin?

ROSENBERG: Not in the least. That was a totally nominal collaboration. He supplied the information mainly in the form of transcripts of the trials. There were two trials—the first ended in a hung jury—so there were about eighteen thousand pages of trial transcripts. He delivered those to me and was available to answer questions. His name on the title page was totally a contractual arrangement.

CA: In addition to the trial transcriptions, you were dealing with a mass of information about the murders and manhunt, which covered a period of several years.

ROSENBERG: From the killings to the last trial to the verdict was about six years, and there was a huge amount of information. In a thing like that, it's just a question of steeping yourself in the material until you get a real sense of how the story is laid out and what's important to it, then going back and digging into the incidents you want to work with. And I had available most of the people who had worked on the case. I could call the detectives in San Francisco and New Orleans and all over the country and get their detailed recollections of particular incidents.

CA: Were people cooperative?

ROSENBERG: Oh, yes, very much so.

CA: In a review of that book in the New York Times, *Christopher Lehmann-Haupt said, ''The issue it explores is black revolutionaries versus the law-enforcement establishment.'' Did you approach the story from a political or racial point of view?*

ROSENBERG: No. Lehmann-Haupt wrote that review as though the book told a story of the police versus the black radical movement, which wasn't the way I saw it in the least. I think somewhere a line has to be clearly drawn between a very legitimate black-power movement and shooting people in the back. I didn't see it as a racial book. It was a book about two homicides. I think the reviewer unfortunately was hung up on the race issue, so that the book in his mind automatically turned into a reflection of his concerns. In fact, the major detective in the case and the major witnesses were all black people who saw the issue as simply a homicide, and Tanenbaum tried throughout the trials to keep them from turning political. I tried to do the same thing with the book.

CA: Have you ever gotten involved in any kind of research that you felt might present personal danger to you?

ROSENBERG: No, I honestly don't think there is much of that. The cases I've been dealing with, as a semi-novelist, have all been retrospective, after the fact. I'm not an investigative reporter, so I don't imagine I present much of a threat to the bad guys. In *Badge of the Assassin,* I imagine that if any of the murderers were out of jail and decided they didn't like the way they were portrayed, something like that might creep up on me, but I think it's a very remote possibility.

CA: Did you get a lot of response to Badge of the Assassin?

ROSENBERG: Yes, a lot of it from police officers. Most of them just wanted to write and thank me for telling their story. I'd say the bulk of it was that. There was nothing really negative. I don't think the book was seen by general readers as racial. It's hard to tell who reads a book—there's no rating system or anything like that—but I didn't get the idea that it was a racially sensitive book, except from certain reviews.

CA: How do you feel about reviewers?

ROSENBERG: I don't know. I've written reviews myself and I understand. I don't get upset as long as I get a feeling that a reviewer is being honest with himself. I've been lucky. Most of the reviews have been positive. There have been some negative ones, and I've been disappointed and wished that they had been more sympathetic. But the books on the whole have been well received, so I don't have any particularly bad experiences. In some cases I thought I could see where the reviewer was coming from and what made it inevitable that he would see it the way he did. If I get annoyed with anything, it's the assignment of certain books to particular reviewers. I think that's more of a problem.

CA: Do you write regular hours every day?

ROSENBERG: I try to. I reach points every once in a while when I'm not sure what comes next, and then it's best to back off. But I'm doing something now that involves a lot of research, so when the writing bogs down I can simply switch desks, as it were, and just do research. I find that if I try to press it and write when nothing seems to be coming, I only write things that I end up throwing out anyway.

CA: Do you read your work in progress to friends or family?

ROSENBERG: Yes, my wife Charlotte. She has very good instincts. Sometimes I tell her that she's not understanding what I'm saying when she doesn't like something I've done. But usually in a week or so, when I go back to it, I find out that I'd better do something about whatever it is that's giving her trouble. She was an editor, too, for a number of years. In fact, that's how we met. She's the only person I regularly try things out on. She's very helpful.

CA: Do you do a lot of revision?

ROSENBERG: Yes. I like to write as much of it as I can just to get through, whether I'm fully happy with it or not—a chapter or section—and then go back and fix it. Lots of times you can find out what you *should* be doing by coming to terms with why what you *are* doing doesn't work. Besides, with a lot of the small things you worry about, you find that when you get a longer view they weren't worth the trouble because they are coming out anyway or moving somewhere else in the book where they are going to be changed. So I try to put all the pieces in place and then find out how I'm going to handle it when I see how everything fits in. I would guess I usually end up with two or three pages of outtakes for every manuscript page I end up with.

CA: Did The Spivey Assignment *differ a lot in research and approach from the earlier books?*

ROSENBERG: I had one primary source for the research, and that was Mr. Spivey. The book concerned his career as an undercover investigator, and it's the sort of thing where there won't be any records and there aren't many people who can be talked to about it. He was working in narcotics in southeast Georgia as well as South America and Mexico and Jamaica, with very little contact with the law enforcement officials he was working for, dealing mainly with people he was working against. Naturally they're not accessible to interview. So it was based on his narration. It was a very different sort of research task, simply getting the story out of him.

CA: Did you enjoy doing it?

ROSENBERG: Well, he was a very fascinating character, so it was fun in that way; but I wouldn't care to do that sort of thing again, no.

CA: You wrote a 1973 Esquire *article on the business of selling research papers to students. Do you know whether the article had any effect on that practice?*

ROSENBERG: I know the individual I wrote about, who more or less invented the business—and this was six or seven years ago—retired under a large number of indictments and hasn't been heard from since. I don't know to what extent he has or doesn't have successors. I suppose that sort of stuff always went on in a clandestine way, where there were people who would hang around campuses to perform this service. He brought it out into the open and turned it into a business with franchised offices around a number of campuses. My guess is there's not much of that going on anymore, but I haven't followed up on it and can't really answer with any certainty.

CA: Are you doing any other free-lance articles?

ROSENBERG: No. Except for occasional reviews, I don't like writing articles. One of my major investments in time, with anything I write, is finding out how the thing is going to lay out and just getting started. It's as hard for me to get an article started as a book. The exciting part comes once it gets going. But with short-form stuff, it's over as soon as it's started. I feel like I'm cranking up a large furnace just to warm up a TV dinner. It just doesn't pay for me emotionally, financially, or in any other way to do articles. I'd rather spend the time getting a book started.

CA: Do you have time to do any reading?

ROSENBERG: Yes. I'm doing a book now involving the history of the early part of the Second World War, the war in the Pacific, so most of my reading has been in that area for the past year and a half or two years. I don't read much modern fiction because I don't have time, and I'm not particularly interested in it. I think of myself as a storyteller, a very old-fashioned sort of writer. I take a story and try and tell it from beginning to end. I guess that's also reflected in my reading tastes; I like the nineteenth-century novelists. I don't have much taste for the more experimental and modern approaches. I don't mean to sound arrogant about it, but there has got to be a simpler way to say what you have to say than *Gravity's Rainbow.* A book like that seems an imposition and a self-indulgence to me.

CA: Do you have any long-range goals?

ROSENBERG: I don't have any long-range goals except to find stories that I'm interested in. I'd like to do a novel—that is, an out-and-out novel, not based on factual material. I have one in mind that I want to do after the book I'm working on now. But in terms of how many volumes I want to complete, no. And I don't really have anything I'm conscious of as an overall design. I just want to find something that interests me, get to the bottom of it, and tell it. That's what I plan to keep doing. I don't think there's a shortage of material; I'm not concerned that the world's going to run out of stories to be told.

BIOGRAPHICAL/CRITICAL SOURCES: New York Review of Books, June 27, 1974; *New York Times Book Review,* July 21, 1974, May 11, 1975, July 2, 1978, July 8, 1979, December 2, 1979; *Commentary,* September, 1974; *Choice,* November, 1974; *Nation,* December 21, 1974; *Best Sellers,* June, 1974, July, 1979; *Times Literary Supplement,* February 27, 1976; *Washington Post Book World,* January 21, 1979; *New York Times,* July 12, 1979.

—*Sketch by B. Hal May*

—*Interview by Jean W. Ross*

*   *   *

ROSENGARTEN, Theodore 1944-

PERSONAL: Born December 17, 1944, in Brooklyn, N.Y.; son of Charles and Hannah (Sokal) Rosengarten; married Dale Rosen, May, 1979; children: Rafael. *Education:* Amherst College, A.B., 1966; Harvard University, Ph.D., 1975. *Religion:* Jewish. *Home address:* P.O. Box 8, McClellanville, S.C. 29458. *Agent:* Lois Wallace, Wallace & Sheil Agency, Inc., 177 East 70th St., New York, N.Y. 10021.

CAREER: Writer. Also works as carpenter and mechanic. *Awards, honors:* National Book Award, 1974, for *All God's Dangers.*

WRITINGS: All God's Dangers: The Life of Nate Shaw, Knopf, 1974; (contributor) *Telling Lives,* New Republic Books, 1979.

WORK IN PROGRESS: A Civil War novel; editing an antebellum plantation journal, publication by Harper expected in 1982.

*   *   *

ROSS, Martha 1951-

PERSONAL: Born June 7, 1951, in Reading, Pa.; daughter of Dean Preston (in business) and Barbara (an executive of the Young Women's Christian Association; maiden name, Stokes) Ross. *Education:* Mount Holyoke College, A.B., 1973; Boston University, A.M., 1974; Trinity College, Dublin, Diploma in Anglo-Irish Literature, 1975. *Home and office:* 45 Dollar St., Cirencester, Gloucestershire GL7 2AS, England.

CAREER: Free-lance writer and editor, 1975—.

WRITINGS: (Compiler) *Rulers and Governments of the World,* Volume I: *From Earliest Times to 1491,* Bowker, 1978. Contributor of poems to American magazines.

WORK IN PROGRESS: Poems.

*   *   *

ROSS, Terrence 1947-

PERSONAL: Born December 20, 1947, in Washington, D.C.; son of Merle James (a business consultant) and Helen (Carney) Ross. *Education:* Attended Providence College, 1965-67; New School College, B.A., 1969. *Home:* 8 Spring St., New York, N.Y. 10012.

CAREER: Masseur to dancers and teacher of massage techniques, 1975—.

WRITINGS: Bitter Graces, Avon, 1980.

WORK IN PROGRESS: A novel "about people passing through the 1960's."

*   *   *

ROSSET, B(enjamin) C(harles) 1910-1974 (Ozy)

OBITUARY NOTICE—See index for *CA* sketch: Born June 7, 1910, in Russia (now U.S.S.R.); died December 22, 1974. Author of *Shaw of Dublin: The Formative Years.* (Date of death provided by wife, Ida Stephenson.)

*   *   *

ROTH, Arlen 1952-

PERSONAL: Born October 30, 1952, in New York, N.Y.; son of Abraham J. (a cartoonist) and Sylvia (owner of a cartoon publishing firm; maiden name, Heller) Roth. *Education:* Attended Philadelphia College of Art, 1969-71. *Religion:* Jewish. *Home:* 46 Warren St., New York, N.Y. 10007.

CAREER: Touring musician in the United States, Canada, Japan, and Europe, 1970—, studio musician, 1973—. Guitarist for Art Garfunkel, 1978; guitarist and musical director for Phoebe Snow, 1979. Teacher at Guitar Study Center, New York, N.Y., 1975. Owner of HotLicks (a firm that sells tape-recorded guitar lessons by mail).

WRITINGS: Slide Guitar, Oak Publications, 1975; *How to Play Blues Guitar,* Acorn Publications, 1975; *Nashville Guitar,* Oak Publications, 1976; (with Happy Traum and Pete Seeger) *Great Guitar Lessons,* Oak Publications, 1978; *Arlen Roth's Advanced Lead Guitar,* Oak Publications, 1981; *Rhythm and Blues Guitar,* Oak Publications, 1981; *Arlen*

Roth's Electric Guitar, Doubleday, 1981. Contributor to *Sing Out!* and *Guitar Player*.

SIDELIGHTS: Roth has made two recordings for Rounder Records, "Arlen Roth—Guitarist" and "Hot Pickups."

He wrote: "In my books, I try as well as I can to recreate the self-learning process that occurred and is still prevalent in my own development as a guitarist. My first book was written, for the most part, on buses and in hotel rooms while I was on the road as a guitarist in 1975. I taught myself music in order to write it and that was a valuable experience in terms of helping me to understand what I did when I played the guitar. I look at my writing as part of an ongoing self-education and growth process that is the perfect supplement to my very busy performing and recording career."

AVOCATIONAL INTERESTS: Photography, wildlife, fishing, folk art, African art, vintage musical instruments, tennis, plants.

BIOGRAPHICAL/CRITICAL SOURCES: Guitar Player, September, 1979, July, 1980.

* * *

ROTHSCHILD, Norman 1913-

PERSONAL: Born June 8, 1913, in Hamburg, Germany (now West Germany) son of Alfred and Franziska Rothschild. *Education:* Attended high school in Brooklyn, N.Y. *Home:* 4 Park Ave., New York, N.Y. 10016. *Office: Popular Photography,* 1 Park Ave., New York, N.Y. 10016.

CAREER: Writer and free-lance photographer. Associated with *Popular Photography,* New York, N.Y., 1961—. Teacher at Ogunquit School of Photography and Camera Club of New York; speaker at Chilmark Workshop. *Military service:* U.S. Army, photographer in Signal Corps. *Member:* Photographic Society of America (associate), Society of Photographic Engineers. *Awards, honors:* Anny Award, 1971; D.H.L. from Philathea College.

WRITINGS: Making Slide Duplicates, Titles, and Filmstrips, Amphoto, 1962, 3rd edition, 1973; (with Cora Wright Kennedy) *Filter Guide: For Color and Black and White,* Amphoto, 1971. Also author with George Wright of *Mounting, Protecting, and Storing Your Slides.* Contributor to photography magazines.

WORK IN PROGRESS: A book on color photography; a book on close-up photography.

SIDELIGHTS: Rothschild wrote: "My writing begins with a practical photographic idea. I write only after I have made suitable images using conventional, or sometimes unconventional, techniques. This experience is then written of in straightforward language (although a bit of humor or biting personal opinion is not barred). I work mostly in color, but intend to expand my black and white photography."

* * *

ROTHWELL, Talbot (Nelson Conn) 1916-1981

OBITUARY NOTICE: Born November 12, 1916, in Bromley, Kent, England; died February 28, 1981, in Worthing, Sussex, England. Writer best known for his scripts for the "Carry On" series of motion pictures. Rothwell developed his humorous style during World War II when, as a prisoner of war, he diverted the attention of German guards away from escape attempts by telling them jokes. After the war Rothwell wrote plays for Arthur Askey and the Crazy Gang. In the late 1950's Rothwell began writing bawdy and semi-scatological screenplays for the British "Carry On" series. His scripts include "Carry On Nurse," "Carry On Regardless,"

and "Carry On Camping." He also wrote for television's "Up Pompeii," which featured his well-known joke, " 'What's a Grecian urn?' 'Five drachmas an hour.' " Obituaries and other sources: *The Author's and Writer's Who's Who,* 6th edition, Burke's Peerage, 1971; *Who's Who in the World,* 3rd edition, Marquis, 1976; *The Writer's Directory, 1980-82,* St. Martin's, 1979; *London Times,* March 2, 1981.

* * *

ROWE, Viola Carson 1903-1969

OBITUARY NOTICE—See index for *CA* sketch: Born January 28, 1903, in Melrose Park, Ill.; died December 4, 1969, in Elmhurst, Ill. Journalist, free-lance writer, and author of books for children, including *True to You* and *Freckled and Fourteen.* (Date of death provided by daughter, Joan V. Wren.)

* * *

ROWLEY, Charles (Dunford) 1906-

PERSONAL: Born in 1906 in Rylstone, Australia; son of George Charles (a police officer) and Mary (Dunford) Rowley; married Irene Janet Klingner (a stenographer and typist), December 22, 1934; children: Bryan Charles. *Education:* University of Sydney, B.A. (with first class honors), 1927, M.A. (with first class honors), 1939. *Home:* 19 Ambalindum St., Hawker, Canberra, Australian Capital Territory 2614, Australia.

CAREER: Universities Commission, Sydney, Australia, officer in charge of Sydney branch office and assistant secretary, 1946-49; Commonwealth Office of Education, Sydney, chief education officer in adult education publications, 1949-50; Australian School of Pacific Administration (now International Training Institute of Department of Foreign Affairs), Sydney, principal, 1950-64; Social Science Research Council (now Academy of the Social Sciences in Australia), Canberra, Australia, director of aborigines project, 1964-67; University of Papua New Guinea, Port Moresby, Foundation Professor of Political Studies, 1968-74; Academy of the Social Sciences in Australia, executive director, 1974-78; Australian National University, Canberra, visiting fellow at Research School of Social Sciences, 1978—. Chairman of Aboriginal Land Fund Commission, 1975-80. Distinguished visiting professor at Drake University, 1972; visiting professor at University of California, Santa Cruz, 1972. Participated in international conferences of United Nations Educational, Scientific, and Cultural Organization. *Military service:* Australian Imperial Forces, 1942-46; became lieutenant colonel; mentioned in dispatches. *Member:* Academy of the Social Sciences in Australia (fellow), National Press Club. *Awards, honors:* Research medal from Royal Society of Victoria, 1972, for *Aboriginal Policy and Practice;* D.Litt. from University of Sydney, 1974, for *Aboriginal Policy and Practice.*

WRITINGS: The Australians in German New Guinea, 1914-1921, Melbourne University Press, 1958; *The Lotus and the Dynamo,* Angus & Robertson, 1960; *The New Guinea Villager,* Praeger, 1965; *Aboriginal Policy and Practice,* Australian National University Press, Volume I: *The Destruction of Aboriginal Society,* 1970, Volume II: *Outcasts in White Australia,* 1971, Volume III: *The Remote Aborigines,* 1971; *The Politics of Educational Planning* (bilingual English-French edition), I.E.E.P., 1972; *A Matter of Justice,* Australian National University Press, 1978.

Contributor: I. G. Sharpe and C. M. Tatz, editors, *Aborigines in the Economy,* Jacaranda Press, 1966; Frances McReynolds

Smith, editor, *Micronesian Realities: Political and Economic,* Center for South Pacific Studies, University of California, Santa Cruz, 1967; *Anatomy of Australia,* Sun Books, 1968; W. J. Hudson, editor, *Australia and Papua New Guinea,* Sydney University Press, 1971; Peter Hastings, editor, *Papua New Guinea: Prospero's Other Island,* Angus & Robertson, 1971. Contributor to *Readings in Pacific and Australian Anthropology,* edited by Ian Hogbin and L. R. Hiatt, 1966. Contributor to *Australian Encyclopaedia* and *Encyclopaedia Britannica.* Contributor of about thirty articles and reviews to scholarly journals and popular magazines, including *Quadrant, South Pacific,* and *Australian Outlook.*

WORK IN PROGRESS: A survey of aboriginal living conditions and opportunities in New South Wales.

SIDELIGHTS: Rowley wrote: "My dominating interest has been the aftermath of western colonialism and its impact on former colonized societies and on such entrapped minorities as Amerindian, Maori, and aborigines. I have had many opportunities to study the politics of race relations."

* * *

RUBENSTEIN, Joshua 1949-

PERSONAL: Born July 18, 1949, in New Britain, Conn.; son of Bernard Alfred (a furrier) and Ruth (Ruden) Rubenstein. *Education:* Columbia University, B.A., 1971. *Home and office:* 12 Parker St., Cambridge, Mass. 02138. *Agent:* Ellen Levine Literary Agency, 370 Lexington Ave., No. 906, New York, N.Y. 10017.

CAREER: Worked as teacher of English in Jerusalem, Israel, 1971-72; teacher of Hebrew in Swampscott, Mass., 1972-74; Polaroid Corp., Cambridge, Mass., teacher of English, 1974-75; teacher of Hebrew in Chestnut Hill, Mass., 1974-79; writer. Part-time field organizer and New England coordinator for Amnesty International, 1975—.

WRITINGS: (Editor and author of introduction) Anatoly Marchenko, *From Tarusa to Siberia,* Strathcona Publishing, 1980; *Soviet Dissidents: Their Struggle for Human Rights,* Beacon Press, 1980. Author of educational filmstrips. Contributor to magazines, including *Art News, New York Times Book Review, Commentary, New Republic, Canto, Moment,* and *Columbia Journalism Review.*

WORK IN PROGRESS: A biography of Adolf Hitler, for F. Watts; research for a book on the third wave of Soviet immigrants in the United States, Israel, and Europe.

SIDELIGHTS: Rubenstein told *CA:* "I happened on the subject of Soviet dissent almost by accident. I spent my first year in Boston living in a small, run-down apartment in the North End, trying to write fiction. Having produced one-half of a worthless novel and several mediocre short stories, I was in such a profound rut that I longed for something new to do. During my year in Israel I had managed to produce an article on a young artist I had met in Leningrad (in the summer of 1970) who had since immigrated to Jerusalem and then Paris. His name was William Brui. With his help, I was able to write an article about him and his work that appeared in *Art News* in December 1971. Entitled 'Refreezing the Thaw,' it described William's efforts to revive the traditions of Constructivism and Suprematism, artistic movements that flourished in the early years of the Soviet regime only to be extinguished by Stalin.

"Armed with this article, I was able to show book review editors, first at the *Boston Phoenix,* then the *New Republic* and *Commentary,* that I could write about Russia. By 1975,

I managed to place reviews in *The New York Times Book Review* as well and wrote my first extended piece on the Soviet dissident movement and the Jewish emigration movement for *Moment.* This article later served as the basis for a chapter of my book.

"Meanwhile, after teaching Hebrew school Sunday mornings and four afternoons a week for two years, I was able to relinquish the afternoon commitment in favor of a position teaching at Polaroid Corporation. This job, unfortunately, lasted only about half a year when the effects of the recession limited the company's willingness to provide classes for their employees on company time. My classes were simply dissolved and I was left with regular work only on Sunday mornings. For a time, my writing was able adequately to supplement my income. I wrote my first set of filmstrips that year for Guidance Associates, at the time a subsidiary of Harcourt Brace Jovanovich.

"It was during this period that I joined Amnesty International. I clipped a membership form from *The New York Review of Books* and sent in a donation. By April, 1975, I formed a local chapter in Cambridge, and our efforts began on behalf of Prisoners of Conscience. In the fall, the woman who had been serving as New England coordinator resigned to join the Foreign Service. I immediately applied for the position and was hired in October, 1975.

"I work part time for Amnesty as New England coordinator and field organizer. Aside from my responsibilities in the Northeast, where I do a good deal of organizing and public speaking, I also help to organize Amnesty chapters in the Midwest and South. Between 1976 and 1978, I took numerous trips to areas of the country, like Indiana, Texas, Iowa, Ohio, Tennessee, and Georgia, where there was no organized Amnesty International activity but where a number of contributors to Amnesty International lived.

"I don't have the facility to describe how lucky I am to be able to work for Amnesty International and still have the time to pursue my interests as a writer."

BIOGRAPHICAL/CRITICAL SOURCES: Boston Ledger, October 10, 1980.

* * *

RUBIA BARCIA, Jose 1914-

PERSONAL: Born July 31, 1914, in Galicia, Spain; married, 1945; children: two. *Education:* University of Granada, Lic. en Filos. y Let., 1934. *Office:* Department of Spanish and Portuguese, University of California, 5303 Humanities Bldg., Los Angeles, Calif. 90024.

CAREER: University of Granada, Granada, Spain, lecturer in Spanish literature, 1935-36; Princeton University, Princeton, N.J., lecturer in Spanish literature, 1943-44; University of California, Los Angeles, 1947—, began as lecturer, became professor of Spanish literature, 1961. *Member:* Modern Language Association of America. *Awards, honors:* Guggenheim fellowship, 1961.

WRITINGS—In English: *A Biobibliography and Iconography of Valle Inclan, 1866-1936,* University of California Press, 1960; (editor with M. A. Zeitlin) *Unamuno: Creator and Creation,* University of California Press, 1967; (translator with Clayton Eshleman) *Vallejo's Spain: Take This Cup From Me,* Grove, 1974; (editor with Selma Margaretten) *Americo Castro and the Meaning of Spanish Civilization,* University of California Press, 1976.

In Spanish: (Author of epilogue) Juan Bartolome de Roxas (pseudonym), *Tres an Uno: Lo escribar encinco cuadros y tres journadas Juan Bartolome de Roxas,* La Veronica, 1940; (with Eugenio F. Granell and Armando del Moral) *Umbral de Suenos,* Obre Publications, 1961; *Lengua y Cultura,* Holt, 1967; *Prosas de Razon y Hiel,* Casuz, 1976. Contributor to language journals.

* * *

RUBINOW, Sol (Isaac)   1923-1981

OBITUARY NOTICE: Born November 6, 1923, in New York, N.Y.; died February 22, 1981, from complications following brain surgery. Biomathematician, educator, author, bridge player, and chess player. Rubinow taught at Cornell University and was the author of *Introduction to Mathematical Biology.* He achieved the rank of master in both chess and bridge. Obituaries and other sources: *Who's Who in World Jewry: A Biographical Dictionary of Outstanding Jews,* Pitman, 1972; *American Men and Women of Science,* 14th edition, Bowker, 1979; *New York Times,* February 24, 1981.

* * *

RUCKER, Frank Warren   1886-1975

OBITUARY NOTICE—See index for *CA* sketch: Born March 21, 1886, near Literberry, Ill.; died July 18, 1975. Journalist, publisher, and author of books on journalism. Rucker's books include *Tested Newspaper Promotion* and *Walter Williams: Pioneer in Journalism Education.* (Date of death provided by daughter, Barbara Jean Bunyar.)

* * *

RUOTOLO, Andrew K(eogh)   1926(?)-1979

PERSONAL: Born c. 1926; died of a heart attack August 8, 1979, in France; son of Alice Sweeney Ruotolo; married Claire E. Murphy (divorced, 1973); children: Andrew Keogh, Jr., Cynthia, Denise, Diane. *Education:* Yale University, graduated, 1945; Cornell University, M.D., 1948; postdoctoral study at American Institute for Psychoanalysis, Karen Horney Institute.

CAREER: Martland Hospital, Newark, N.J., intern; Worcester State Hospital, Worcester, Mass., resident in psychiatry until 1956; private practice of psychoanalysis in New Jersey until 1979. Member of board of trustees of Karen Horney Institute; consultant psychiatrist at counseling center of Seton Hall University. *Military service:* U.S. Navy, First Marine Division; served in Korea; became lieutenant senior grade.

WRITINGS: Once Upon a Murder (interviews with alleged murderers), Grosset, 1978; *Murder and Other Fairy Tales,* Grosset, 1978. Contributor to medical journals.

BIOGRAPHICAL/CRITICAL SOURCES: New York Times, August 16, 1979.*

* * *

RUSHER, William Allen   1923-

PERSONAL: Born July 19, 1923, in Chicago, Ill.; son of Evan Singleton and Verna Rae (Self) Rusher. *Education:* Princeton University, A.B., 1943; Harvard University, J.D., 1948. *Religion:* Anglican. *Home:* 30 East 37th St., New York, N.Y. 10016. *Office:* 150 East 35th St., New York, N.Y. 10016.

CAREER: Shearman & Sterling & Wright (law firm), New York City, associate, 1948-56; U.S. Senate, Washington, D.C., associate counsel to internal security subcommittee, 1956-57; *National Review,* New York City, publisher, direc-

tor, and vice-president, 1957—. Appeared on television program "The Advocates," 1970-73. Special counsel to finance committee of New York Senate, 1955; member of Advisory Task Force on Civil Disorders, 1972; member of National News Council; member of board of directors of Chinese Cultural Center, New York City; past vice-chairman of American Conservative Union. *Military service:* U.S. Army Air Forces, 1943-46; became captain. *Member:* American Bar Association, American African Affairs Association (cochairman, 1965-75; member of board of directors), University Club, Metropolitan Club. *Awards, honors:* D.Lit. from Nathaniel Hawthorne College, 1973; distinguised citizen award from School of Law, New York University, 1973.

WRITINGS: Special Counsel, Arlington House, 1968; (with Mark Hatfield and Arlie Schardt)*Amnesty?,* Sun River Press, 1973; *The Making of the New Majority Party,* Sheed, 1975; *How to Win Arguments (Most of the Time),* Doubleday, 1981. Author of "The Conservative Advocate," a column distributed by Universal Press Syndicate, 1973—.

* * *

RUSK, Howard A(rchibald)   1901-

PERSONAL: Born April 9, 1901, in Brookfield, Mo.; son of Michael Yost and Augusta Eastin (Shipp) Rusk; married Gladys Houx, October 20, 1926 (died October, 1980); children: Martha Eastin (Mrs. Preston Sutphen, Jr.), Howard Archibald, John Michael. *Education:* University of Missouri, A.B., 1923; University of Pennsylvania, M.D., 1925. *Religion:* Protestant. *Home:* 330 East 33rd St., New York, N.Y. 10016. *Office:* Institute of Rehabilitation Medicine, New York University Medical Center, 400 East 34th St., New York, N.Y. 10016.

CAREER: Internist in St. Louis, Mo., 1926-42; New York University, New York City, professor of physical medicine and rehabilitation and chairman of department, 1946—, director of Institute of Rehabilitation and Physical Medicine (now Institute of Rehabilitation Medicine), 1947—. Diplomate of American Board of Internal Medicine and American Board of Physical Medicine and Rehabilitation; instructor at Washington University, St. Louis, 1929-42. Associate chief of staff at St. Luke's Hospital, St. Louis, 1937-45. Member of President's Committee for Study of Government Medical Services, 1945; past chairman of advisory committee of New York Veterans Service Center; past member of advisory council of National Arthritis Research Foundation; chairman of health resources advisory committee of Office of Defense Mobilization, 1950-57; member of public health council of New York Department of Health; president of International Society for the Welfare of Cripples, 1954-57, and World Rehabilitation Fund, 1955—. Chairman of American-Korean Foundation, 1953-73, chairman emeritus, 1973—; chairman of public policy committee of Advertising Council; member of board of directors of Chemical Fund, Inc., Companion Life Insurance Co., Graphic Arts Mutual Insurance Co., IPCO Hospital Supply Corp., and New York Foundation; member of board of trustees of University of Pennsylvania, 1962-67; consultant to United Nations and Veterans Administration. *Military service:* U.S. Army Air Forces, Medical Corps, chief of Convalescent and Rehabilitation Branch of Professional Services Division and chief of Convalescent Services Division of Office of the Air Surgeon, 1942-45; became colonel; received Distinguished Service Medal. U.S. Air Force Reserve, 1942-45; became brigadier general.

MEMBER: International Society for Rehabilitation of the Disabled, American Medical Association, American College of Physicians (fellow), National Association of Science Writers, Royal College of Physicians (fellow), New York Academy of Medicine, New York State Medical Society, Westchester County Medical Society, Phi Beta Kappa, Alpha Omega Alpha, Phi Delta Theta, Nu Sigma Ni, Dutch Treat Club. *Awards, honors:* Honorary degrees include LL.D. from University of Missouri, 1947, Westminster College, 1950, Hahnemann Medical College, 1952, Chungang University, 1956, Long Island University, 1957, and Missouri Valley College, 1965; D.Sc. from Boston University, 1949, Lehigh University, 1956, Middlebury College, 1957, Trinity College, 1961, Woman's Medical College, 1962, University of Portland, 1969, and Hofstra University, 1972; L.H.D. from Adelphi College, 1957; Litt.D. from Ithaca College, 1961; M.D. from University of Rennes, 1965; D.M.Sc. from Brown University, 1969; chevalier of French Legion of Honor; design award from National Rehabilitation Association, 1944, meritorious service award, 1948; citation from American Academy of Physical Education, 1944; research award from American Pharmaceutical Manufacturers Association, 1951; Dr. C.C. Criss Award from National Multiple Sclerosis Society, 1952, modern medicine award, 1954; Lasker Award from American Public Health Association, 1952; medal of honor from National Association of Women Artists, 1953; gold medals from National Institute of Social Science, 1954, and International Benjamin Franklin Society, 1955; gold medal and national medal of Republic of Korea, 1955; Colombia's Order of Jose Fernandez Madrid, 1955; Lasker Award from International Society for Rehabilitation of the Disabled, 1957 and 1960; Robles Award, 1957; Gold Key Award from American Congress of Physical Medicine and Rehabilitation, 1958; bronze plaque from Association for Help to Retarded Children, 1958; grand master of Bolivia's Order of the Condor of the Andes, 1960; commander of Greece's Royal Order of the Phoenix, 1963.

WRITINGS: (With Eugene J. Taylor) *New Hope for the Handicapped: The Rehabilitation of the Disabled From Bed to Job* (foreword by Bernard M. Baruch), Harper, 1949; (with Taylor, Muriel Zimmerman, and Julia Judson) *Living With a Disability,* Blakiston Co., 1953; (with Mary E. Switzer) *Doing Something for the Disabled,* New York Public Affairs Committee, 1953; *A Manual for Training the Disabled Homemaker,* Institute of Rehabilitation and Physical Medicine, New York University-Bellevue Medical Center, 1955, 4th edition, 1970; (with Taylor and others) *Rehabilitation Medicine: A Textbook on Physical Medicine and Rehabilitation,* Mosby, 1958, 4th edition, 1977; *Specialized Placement of Quadriplegics and Other Severely Disabled,* Vocational Rehabilitation Association, U.S. Department of Health, Education, and Welfare, 1963; *A World to Care For: The Au-*

tobiography of Howard A. Rusk, M.D., Random House, 1972.

Author of a column in *New York Times.* Contributor to *Encyclopaedia Britannica.* Contributor to medical journals. Contributing editor of *New York Times,* 1946—, associate editor; contributing editor of *Medical World News.*

BIOGRAPHICAL/CRITICAL SOURCES: Collier's, August 19, 1950; *Weekly Underwriter,* December 20, 1952, May 2, 1953; Edward R. Murrow, *This I Believe,* Simon & Schuster, 1954; *Reader's Digest,* March, 1955; *Journal of Health, Physical Education, and Recreation,* October, 1960; Caroline A. Chandler, *Famous Modern Men of Medicine,* Dodd, 1965; David Hendon, *Life Givers,* Morrow, 1976.

*   *   *

RUSSELL, Edward (Frederick Langley)   1895-1981

OBITUARY NOTICE: Born April 10, 1895, in Liverpool, England; died April 8, 1981, in Hastings, England. Military jurist and author. Russell was prosecutor of war criminals in the British zone of Germany after World War II. He resigned from that post in 1954 after Lord Chancellor Simonds threatened to discharge him for writing *The Scourge of the Swastika,* an indictment of Nazism as a consequence of Aryan beliefs. Russell then wrote an account of Japanese war crimes entitled *The Knights of the Bushido.* His other books include *Deadman's Hill* and *Knight of the Sword,* a biography of Admiral Sidney Smith. Obituaries and other sources: *The Author's and Writer's Who's Who,* 6th edition, Burke's Peerage, 1971; *Who's Who in the World,* 2nd edition, Marquis, 1973; *The Writer's Directory, 1980-82,* St. Martin's, 1979; *New York Times,* April 10, 1981; *London Times,* April 10, 1981; *Time,* April 20, 1981.

*   *   *

RYALL, George (Francis Trafford)   1887(?)-1979 (Audax Minor)

PERSONAL: Born c. 1887 in Toronto, Ontario, Canada; died October 8, 1979, in Columbia, Md.; married Jacqueline Ryall (died, 1965); children: George Francis Trafford, Jr. *Education:* Attended private boys' secondary school in Haileybury, England.

CAREER: Exchange-Telegraph, London, England, began as general assignment reporter, became racing writer, 1907-20; *World,* New York City, reporter, beginning in 1920; *New Yorker,* New York City, feature writer and author of racing column (under pseudonym Audax Minor), 1926-78.

BIOGRAPHICAL/CRITICAL SOURCES: New York Times, October 10, 1979.*

S

SADD, Susan 1951-

PERSONAL: Born March 28, 1951, in Newark, N.J.; daughter of Hiram (a chemical engineer) and Janette (Bernfeld) Sadd. *Education:* Michigan State University, B.A. (with honors), 1971; New York University, M.A., 1974, Ph.D., 1977. *Office:* Vera Institute of Justice, 275 Madison Ave., New York, N.Y. 10016.

CAREER: American Express Co., New York City, trainee, 1975-76, consultant for Travel Division, 1976-77; Vera Institute of Justice, New York City, deputy director of evaluation of Court Employment Project and of Alternative Youth Employment Strategies Project, 1977—. Project director for Societal Data Corp., 1977—; adjunct assistant professor at New York University, 1979—. *Awards, honors:* James M. Cattell Award from New York Academy of Sciences, 1978, for dissertation.

WRITINGS: (With Carol Tavris) *The Redbook Report on Female Sexuality,* Delacorte, 1977. Contributor to journals in the behavioral sciences and popular magazines, including *Ms.*

WORK IN PROGRESS: "A book on pretrial diversion reporting results of Court Employment Project evaluation," with S. Hillsman, publication expected in 1981.

* * *

**St. CLAIR, Byrd Hooper 1905-1976
(Byrd Hooper)**

OBITUARY NOTICE—See index for *CA* sketch: Born September 29, 1905, in Cerro Gordo, Ark.; died January 25, 1976. Librarian and author. She wrote *Beef for Beauregard,* a book for children about the American Civil War. She also contributed articles to children's magazines. (Date of death provided by Maricopa County Library.)

* * *

SAKAMAKI, Shunzo 1906-1973

OBITUARY NOTICE—See index for *CA* sketch: Born July 15, 1906, in Olaa, Hawaii; died July 19, 1973. Educator, editor, and author of books about Japan. His writings include *Japan and the United States, 1790-1853, Ryukyuan Research Resources at the University of Hawaii,* and *Asia.* Sakamaki was awarded the Third Class of the Sacred Treasure by the Japanese Government in recognition of his distinguished service in education, goodwill, and cultural interchange between Japan and Hawaii. (Date of death provided by wife, Yoshiko Ikeda Sakamaki.)

* * *

SALTER, Elizabeth 1918-1981

OBITUARY NOTICE—See index for *CA* sketch: Born in 1918 in Anguston, Australia; died March 14, 1981. Author. Salter began her career as a mystery writer in 1957, the same year that she became Dame Edith Sitwell's secretary. Later Salter became a biographer who specialized in Australian subjects, such as Daisy Bates and John Peter Russell. Her works include *Death in a Mist, Once Upon a Tombstone, The Last Years of a Rebel,* and *Edith Sitwell.* Obituaries and other sources: *London Times,* March 20, 1981.

* * *

**SALTER, Margaret Lennox
See DONALDSON, Margaret**

* * *

SALTONSTALL, Richard, Jr. 1937-1981

OBITUARY NOTICE—See index for *CA* sketch: Born March 14, 1937, in Boston, Mass.; died of a heart attack, May 12, 1981, in Belfast, Me. Journalist, editor, and author. Owner and editor-in-chief of the *Republican Journal,* the *Bar Harbor Times,* and the *Camden Herald,* Saltonstall began his journalism career as a police reporter with the *Seattle Times.* He was associated with the Time-Life bureau in San Francisco, and he served as the White House correspondent for *Time* during the Johnson administration. In addition, Saltonstall was an environmentalist primarily concerned with energy problems. His works include *Maine Pilgrimage, Brownout and Slowdown,* and *Your Environment and What You Can Do About It.* Obituaries and other sources: *New York Times,* May 14, 1981; *Washington Post,* May 14, 1981.

* * *

**SAMUELS, E. A.
See TIFFANY, E. A.**

SANDERS, James Edward 1911-

PERSONAL: Born March 4, 1911, in Dargaville, New Zealand; son of Percy Vivian (a timber contractor) and Evelyn Margaret Sanders; married Dorothy Irene Piggott, November 6, 1943; children: Diana Faye, Michael James. *Education:* Attended technical high school in Auckland, New Zealand. *Religion:* Church of England. *Home and office:* Landfall, 42 Roberta Ave., Glendowie, Auckland, New Zealand. *Agent:* Gloria Safier, Inc., 667 Madison Ave., New York, N.Y. 10021; Ray Richards, P.O. Box 31240, Milford, Auckland 9, New Zealand; and Laurence Pollinger Ltd., 18 Maddox St., London W1R 0EU, England.

CAREER: Worked as farm worker and sheep station manager, 1928-36; *New Zealand Observer,* Auckland, New Zealand, journalist, 1936; *Northland Times,* Northland, New Zealand, journalist, 1937-39; worked in advertising and commercial art, 1948-54; James Sanders Advertising Ltd., Auckland, proprietor, 1954-69; free-lance writer, 1969-71; *New Zealand Herald,* Auckland, author of columns "Property" and "Around Auckland," feature and financial writer, and book reviewer, 1971—. *Military service:* Royal New Zealand Air Force, pilot, 1939-48, attached to Royal Air Force, 1939-45; served in England, the Middle East, and Malta. *Member:* Advertising Institute of New Zealand (life fellow), Advertising Institute of Australia (fellow), Officers Club.

WRITINGS: The Time of My Life (autobiography), Minerva, 1967; *The Green Paradise* (novel), R. Hale, 1971; *The Shores of Wrath* (novel), R. Hale, 1972; *Kindred of the Winds* (novel), R. Hale, 1973; *High Hills of Gold* (novel), R. Hale, 1973; *Our Explorers* (nonfiction), Wilson & Horton, 1974; *New Zealand Victoria Cross Winners,* Wilson & Horton, 1974; *Fire in the Forest* (novel), R. Hale, 1975; *The Lamps of Maine* (novel), R. Hale, 1975; *Where Lies the Land?* (novel), R. Hale, 1976; *Desert Patrols* (nonfiction), Wilson & Horton, 1976; *Chase the Dragon* (novel), R. Hale, 1978; *Dateline: N.Z.P.A.* (nonfiction), Wilson & Horton, 1979; *Frontiers of Fear* (novel), R. Hale, 1980.

WORK IN PROGRESS: Running Free, a novel set during the War of 1812; *The Shoreless Sea,* a novel set in Hong Kong; *Beggar on Horseback,* an autobiography.

SIDELIGHTS: Sanders told *CA:* "After some youthful years spent on New Zealand sheep stations—or ranches as you call them in the United States—I abandoned my free, open life as a shepherd, drover, horsebreaker, and later, sheep station manager to take up journalism on a small daily newspaper. I liked the life and feel that the discipline of concise writing to meet deadlines has been of considerable help to me in my later work as a novelist.

"Since my retirement from day-to-day journalism I have continued to earn my livelihood by writing. I got into authorship the comparatively easy way. Because I had moved around in strange places and had done many things to earn a living, I began at a mature age to write my autobiography, with what I hoped was a light touch. A New Zealand publisher saw the first seven chapters, liked what I had done, and gave me a contract to finish the book.

"It was well received, and after that I was hooked. I promptly sat down and produced my first novel. I sent the typescript to London and the first publisher who saw it took it. Since then I have continued to hammer out books at the rate of one or two a year.

"Fiction writers get scant encouragement from New Zealand publishers, who understandably argue that a total New Zealand population of only three million does not give sufficient reader absorbency for storytellers' flights of fancy. So we hardy individualists who scorn the aid of a state literary grant, and who are prepared to march unaided, get our novels published outside this country. This often means, of course, that not much of our work is seen by our own countryfolk as, in my case for example, publishers' agents in New Zealand don't indent many copies into this country.

"Whereas I began writing historical fiction, using early New Zealand as a setting, I have lately cast aside these themes in favor of broader canvases. My last two novels, for example, are set in Southeast Asia and Hong Kong. But I like historical novels with nautical settings. Maybe I will get back to writing another seafaring yarn before long. They don't seem to become dated."

*　　*　　*

SANFORD, Fillmore H(argrave) 1914-1967

OBITUARY NOTICE—See index for *CA* sketch: Born January 26, 1914, in Chatham, Va.; died August 5, 1967. Educator, consultant, and author of books on psychology, including *Psychology: A Scientific Study of Man* and *Advancing Psychological Science.* Sanford also edited books on psychology, including *Research in Developmental, Personality, and Social Psychology.* Obituaries and other sources: *Who Was Who in America,* 4th edition, Marquis, 1968.

*　　*　　*

SANTONI, Georges V. 1938-

PERSONAL: Born March 4, 1938, in Geneva, Switzerland. *Education:* Attended College of Geneva; University of Colorado, M.A., Ph.D., 1969. *Home:* Aspen Hills, Slingerlands, N.Y. 12159. *Office:* State University of New York at Albany, Albany, N.Y. 12222.

CAREER: University of Michigan, Ann Arbor, assistant professor, 1966-73; State University of New York at Albany, associate professor, 1973—. Director of National Endowment for the Humanities Institute on Contemporary French Culture and Society, summer, 1979. *Member:* American Association of Teachers of French, American Council on the Teaching of Foreign Languages.

WRITINGS: (With Jean Noel Rey) *Quand les Francais parlent,* Newbury, 1975; (with Rey) *Montbraye Village de France,* Hachette, 1976; *Contemporary French Culture and Society,* State University of New York Press, 1980. Contributor of numerous articles to *French Review, Foreign Language Annals,* and *Le Francais dans le Monde.*

*　　*　　*

SAPERSTEIN, Alan

PERSONAL—Address: c/o Macmillan, Inc., 866 Third Ave., New York, N.Y. 10022.

CAREER: Novelist. *Awards, honors:* P.E.N. Award; Ernest Hemingway Foundation Award.

WRITINGS: Mom Kills Kids and Self (novel), Macmillan, 1979.

SIDELIGHTS: With a title as sensational as the headline of a supermarket tabloid, Saperstein's first novel, *Mom Kills Kids and Self,* has commanded much attention. The book is about a nameless narrator who returns home from work only to discover that his wife has killed their two small sons and herself. Speaking of this narrator, Suzanne Fields of the *Washington Post Book World* said: "His is the story of a guilt-stricken husband whose narrative juxtaposes surreal situations with photo-album images of family life, pictures that will be broken into the thousands of tiny dots that make up the grainy photographs in the newspaper. He flogs himself with the details that deprive him of the anonymity of his existance, but do nothing to relieve him of the banality of his own evil." Through the narrator, Saperstein explores a husband's guilt and examines love, marriage, and family life in contemporary society.

After finding his family, the narrator swims, drinks, smashes things (including his toe) with golf clubs, mows the lawn, and reflects. His refections take the form of flashbacks, streams of consciousness, in which he attempts to sort out the reasons for his wife's tragic behavior. After three days of rumination, the narrator concludes that, by his neglect, he killed his family. This belief becomes so salient that he rearranges the bodies, telephones the police, and confesses to murder. The coroner's report indicates otherwise.

One critic, Christopher Lehmann-Haupt of the *New York Times,* found Saperstein's plot contrived. Lehmann-Haupt contended that the novel's plot is unbelievable: "Moms don't tend to kill kids and self," he said. "Mr. Saperstein's novel may be an interesting anatomy of a husband's guilt, but it finally has little to say about how women suffer."

Two other critics, Michael Blankfort of the *Los Angeles Times Book Review* and Ivan Gold of the *New York Times Book Review,* felt that Mr. Saperstein had taken "admirable risks" in producing his first novel. Both reviewers found the novel's theme uncomfortable; yet they agreed that the book is lively, bold, informative, and well done.

BIOGRAPHICAL/CRITICAL SOURCES: Kirkus Reviews, July 1, 1979; *New York Times Book Review,* August 12, 1979; *Washington Post Book World,* August 19, 1979; *Los Angeles Times Book Review,* August 26, 1979; *New York Times,* September 10, 1979; *Chicago Tribune Book World,* October 14, 1979.*

*   *   *

SAPOSS, David Joseph 1886-1968

OBITUARY NOTICE—See index for *CA* sketch: Born February 22, 1886, in Kiev, Ukraine (now U.S.S.R.); died November 13, 1968. Labor historian, economist, and author. Saposs wrote several books on the labor movement, including *Case Studies in Labor Ideology: Philosophic, Structural, and Procedural Adaptations Since World War I* and *The Labor Movement in Post-War France.* He edited *Readings in Trade Unionism* and was co-founder and editor of *American Labor Monthly.* Obituaries and other sources: *New York Times,* November 16, 1968; *Current Biography,* Wilson, January, 1969.

*   *   *

SARHAN, Samir 1941-

PERSONAL: Born December 8, 1941, in Cairo, Egypt; son of Gaber and Nefissa (Hassaneih) Sarhan; married Nihad Gad (a magazine editor), September 30, 1967; children: Hatem, Khaled. *Education:* University of Cairo, B.A., 1961; Indiana University, Ph.D., 1968. *Religion:* Moslem. *Home:* 7 Botros Ghali St., Heliopolis, Cairo, Egypt. *Office:* Department of English, University of Cairo, Giza, Cairo, Egypt.

CAREER: Theatre, Cairo, Egypt, managing editor, 1961-64; University of Cairo, Cairo, Egypt, lecturer, 1968-71, assistant professor, 1971-78, professor of English, 1978—, dean of Higher Institute of Dramatic Arts, 1980—.

WRITINGS: Ibsen: From Romanticism to Realism, Anglo-Egyptian Bookshop, 1974; (editor) *Who's Who in Saudi Arabia,* Europa, 1976-77, 2nd edition, 1977-79; *Realism-Naturalism in Modern Arabic Literature,* Anglo-Egyptian Bookshop, 1979; *The Concept of Influence in Comparative Literature,* University of Cairo, 1979; *Harold Pinter,* Anglo-Egyptian Bookshop, 1980; *Tajabib Jadidah fil fan al Masrahi* (title means "New Experiments in Theatrical Arts"), Gharib (Cairo), 1981; *Egyptian and Arab Drama in the Sixties,* Anglo-Egyptian Bookshop, 1982.

Plays: "Al-Kithb" (title means "To Mendacity"; three-act), first produced in Cairo, Egypt, at Al-Hakim State Theatre, 1965; *Malik Yabhath an Wadhijah* (title means "A King in Search of a Job"; three-act; first produced in Cairo at Al Hadith State Theatre, 1971), Al Najah (Lebanon), 1972; "Sittul Mulk" (two-act), first produced in 1978.

Drama critic. Contributor to Egyptian and Arabic magazines and newspapers. Editor of *Modern Drama.*

WORK IN PROGRESS: "Al-Hakim and O'Neill: A Comparative Study," an article for *Cairo University Journal;* *O'Neill in Egypt; Forms and Styles of Arabic Drama;* a play, *"Imra'atul Aziz"* (title means "The Wife of Al-Aziz").

SIDELIGHTS: Sarhan told *CA:* "Since boyhood, I have always wanted to become a professor of English literature and a playwright. I was always fascinated by the world of the theatre, the lighted stage with actors moving on it assuming identities not their own. It was a magical world that fired my imagination. I started my career, however, by writing and translating short stories at the age of fifteen. My translations were published in book form which enabled me to become a member of a literary clique who gathered together every evening at the famous Cairo Cafe. This discussions opened up for me wonderful vistas of art and literature.

"My preoccupation with the professional theatre started in the late 1950's and early 1960's when I translated some plays by Chekhov, Ionesco, Tennessee Williams, and others in collaboration with my friend and colleague Dr. M. Enany, himself a playwright and scholar. These were professionally produced and launched both of us into the professional theatre. The 1960's were for the Egyptian literary movement a period of great activity and achievement, and I tried hard to become part of the bustling literary theatrical scene.

"For me, art is a revelation of one's inner self, of other people and the world we live in. In drama, particularly, a writer projects himself in various characters and feels like a God toying with his diversified creation. It gives me immense pleasure.

"However, writing for me is an agonizing experience. The pain, worry, and fear of failure almost paralyzes my will before I take up pen and paper. I keep postponing it for as long as I can, then I write frantically until I finish. I always hate to take a second look at my writing and wish I could never see it again. But when my wife and friends tell me it is good, I consider sending it for performance or publication, hardly believing what they say. My works, however, were generally very successful on stage. Perhaps I should believe it one day!

"A writer should be the voice of his generation. He carries an enormous responsibility of correcting the world through showing his audience their truth. Some people tell me, 'Your plays should be rendered in foreign languages so that you can become an "international writer."' The Arabic audience are one hundred million who speak the language and I believe if I can capture the imagination of that much audience I'm 'international' enough by the standard of my own culture. One of my plays, 'Sittul Mulk,' however, is now being translated into English to be published and the thought thrills me.''

"We in the Arab world suffer from a scarcity of great playwrights, which is the case everywhere in the world now because of the onslaught of television and cinema. A playwright may be an anachronism in this day and age, but we playwrights carry more than ever the historical responsibility of preserving an age-old art which molded human consciousness throughout the ages. I also prefer stage drama because it is a writer's art, not that of the filmmaker's or contemporary technology where the writer is only one cog in a great big machine.

"I was influenced by Shakespeare, first and foremost, and the whole tradition of Western drama together with great dramatists of my nation. I hope that my work has added something of value of their achievement. As critic and scholar, I find the job facile enough and I do it with great ease. I am at my best, nevertheless, when I write about plays and the theories of drama.''

*   *   *

SAROYAN, William 1908-1981
(Sirak Goryan)

OBITUARY NOTICE—See index for *CA* sketch: Born August 31, 1908, in Fresno, Calif.; died of cancer, May 18, 1981, in Fresno, Calif. Novelist, playwright, composer, and author. One of the few proletarian writers of the 1930's who was never Marxist, Saroyan wrote romantic celebrations of American life. His first success came with the publication of "The Daring Young Man on the Flying Trapeze," a short story that received an O. Henry Award in 1934. From this work, the author went on to generate over four hundred short stories, of which "My Name is Aram" is held to be most notable. Saroyan once completed a novel in thirty-eight days because that was the amount of time he allotted to do so. He composed his Pulitzer Prize-winning play, "The Time of Your Life," in six days in a hotel room in New York and refused the award on the grounds that wealth and business are incapable of judging art. He also wrote what has been called "the first anti-war novel of World War II," *The Adventures of Wesley Jackson,* which the author called "anti-dishonesty and only incidentally anti-war." *The Human Comedy,* Saroyan's most famous novel, was made into a movie starring Mickey Rooney, and the song "Come On-A My House," which the novelist composed, became a hit for Rosemary Clooney in 1951. Before embarking on his career as a writer, Saroyan worked as a Western Union messenger and branch manager. He issued the following quote to the Associated Press five days before he died: "Everybody has got to die, but I have always believed an exception would be made in my case. Now what?" Saroyan's many writings include his autobiography *The Bicycle Rider in Beverly Hills,* two plays, *My Heart's in the Highlands* and *The Beautiful People,* and novels such as *Papa You're Crazy.* Obituaries and other sources: *Washington Post,* May 19, 1981; *New York Times,* May 19, 1981; *Detroit News,* May 24, 1981; *Newsweek,* June 1, 1981; *Time,* June 1, 1981; *Publishers Weekly,* June 5, 1981.

*   *   *

SATHER, Julia Coley Duncan 1940-
(Julia Coley Duncan)

PERSONAL: Born August 20, 1940, in Alexander City, Ala.; daughter of Thomas Edward and Julia (Coley) Duncan; mar-

ried R. Alan Sather, December, 1965 (marriage ended April, 1975); children: Julia, Kristin. *Education:* Agnes Scott College, B.A., 1962; University of Minnesota, M.A., 1964. *Religion:* Protestant. *Home:* 3813 Halbrook Lane, Birmingham, Ala. 35243. *Agent:* Freya Manston Literary Associates, Inc., 115 West 58th St., New York, N.Y. 10019.

CAREER: Worked as school psychologist and advertising copywriter; free-lance writer.

WRITINGS—Under name Julia Coley Duncan: *Halfway Home,* St. Martin's, 1979. Contributor to magazines.

WORK IN PROGRESS: A novel; a biography of Southern madam Louise Katherine Wooster.

SIDELIGHTS: Julia Sather told *CA:* "I write about characters, real and fictional, whose philosophy of life (as they live it) impresses me as being honest, compassionate, and otherwise admirable. Lou Wooster is a case in point. Though she was a wealthy, successful madam, she was also tenacious, loyal, shrewd, loving, and lived in a time when women in her position had little or no opportunity for growth or personal fulfillment. *Halfway Home* is also about Southern men and women who tried to cope compassionately in a system that was overwhelming.''

*   *   *

SAUNDERS, Alexander Carr
See CARR-SAUNDERS, Alexander

*   *   *

SAUNDERS, Ann Loreille 1930-
(Ann Cox-Johnson)

PERSONAL: Born in 1930 in London, England; daughter of George (a surveyor) and Joan Loreille (a headmistress; maiden name, Clowser) Cox-Johnson; married Bruce Kemp Saunders (an engineer), June 4, 1960; children: Matthew, Katherine. *Education:* University of London, B.A. (with honors), 1951; University of Leicester, Ph.D., 1965. *Religion:* Church of England. *Home and office:* 3 Corringway, London NW11 7ED, England.

CAREER: Lambeth Palace, London, England, deputy librarian, 1952-55; British Museum, London, assistant keeper, 1955-56; St. Marylebone Public Library, London, archivist, 1956-63; *British Journal of the Archaeology Association,* England, sub-editor, 1964-75; writer. Lecturer in history at Richardson College. *Member:* Society of Antiquaries (fellow).

WRITINGS: (Under name Ann Cox-Johnson) *Handlist to the Ashbridge Collection on the History and Topography of St. Marylebone,* Borough Council, 1959; *Handlist of Painters, Sculptors, and Architects,* Public Libraries Committee, Borough of St. Marylebone, 1963; *Regent's Park: A Study of the Development of the Area From 1086 to the Present Day,* Augustus M. Kelley, 1969; (editor of revision) Arthur Mee, *London North of the Thames, Except the City and Westminster,* Hodder & Stoughton, 1972; (editor) *The City and Westminster,* Hodder & Stoughton, 1975; *Art Historian's Guide to the Greater London Area,* Reclam of Stuttgart c. 1982. Editor of *Costume,* 1967—, and *London Topographical Record,* 1975—.

*   *   *

SAWKINS, Raymond H(arold) 1923-
(Jay Bernard, Colin Forbes, Richard Raine)

PERSONAL: Born in 1923, in Hampstead, England; married Jean Robertson; children: one daughter. *Education:* Attended grammar school in Harrow, England. *Home:* Prospect, Elm Rd., Horsell, Woking, Surrey, England. *Agent:* Elaine Greene Ltd., 31 Newington Green, Islington, London N16 9PU, England.

CAREER: Free-lance writer. *Military service:* British Army, 1942-46. *Member:* Society of Authors, Crime Writers' Association.

WRITINGS—All novels, except as noted: *Snow on High Ground,* Heinemann, 1966; *Snow in Paradise,* Heinemann, 1967; *Snow Along the Border,* Harcourt, 1968.

Under pseudonym Colin Forbes: (With Alan Fletcher and Bob Gill) *Graphic Design: Visual Comparisons* (nonfiction), Studio Books, 1964; *Tramp in Armour,* Collins, 1969, published as *Tramp in Armor,* Dutton, 1970; *The Heights of Zervos,* Collins, 1970, Dutton, 1971; *The Palermo Affair,* Dutton, 1972 (published in England as *The Palermo Ambush,* Collins, 1972); (editor) Robert Welch, *Robert Welch,* Lund, Humphries, 1973; *Target Five,* Dutton, 1973; *Year of the Golden Ape,* Dutton, 1974; *The Stone Leopard,* Collins, 1975, Dutton, 1976; *Avalanche Express,* Dutton, 1977.

Under pseudonym Richard Raine: *The Corder Index,* Harcourt, 1967 (published in England as *A Wreath for America,* Heinemann, 1967); *Night of the Hawk,* Harcourt, 1968; *Bombshell,* Harcourt, 1969.

Under pseudonym Jay Bernard: *The Burning Fuse,* Harcourt, 1970.

SIDELIGHTS: Sawkins's books are primarily thriller and mystery novels. His "Snow" series involves the detective John Snow and his various adventures. The youngest superintendent at Scotland Yard before opting for private investigation, Snow is adept at solving mysteries while uncovering murders and indulging in international chases. *Tramp in Armor* is a thriller about five British soldiers trapped in a tank behind enemy lines in World War II. In their effort to rejoin their division, they endure such trials as getting stuck in quicksand, nearly being buried alive in a tunnel cave-in, and almost burning to death when a match is thrown in the haystack under which they are hiding. *The Stone Leopard* details policeman Marc Grelle's search for a man called the "leopard." A World War II hero of the French Resistance, the Leopard is suspected of being a government official bent on orchestrating a coup d'etat in France.

AVOCATIONAL INTERESTS: Foreign travel.

BIOGRAPHICAL/CRITICAL SOURCES: Christian Science Monitor, May 5, 1976; *New York Times Book Review,* May 9, 1976, September 4, 1977; *Best Sellers,* June, 1976, November 1, 1977.*

* * *

SCHAFFER, Frank   1910-

PERSONAL: Born April 6, 1910, in London, England; son of Robert Joseph and Jane (Knight) Schaffer; married Gladys Barber (a bank official), October 9, 1937. *Education:* University of London, LL.B., 1931. *Home:* Langwood, Smallfield Rd., Horley, Surrey RH6 9LP, England.

CAREER: Inland Revenue Department, London, England, examiner in Estate Duty Office, 1929-41; Expert Committee on Compensation and Betterment, London, assistant secretary, 1941-42; Post-War Reconstruction Group, London, principal, 1942-43; Ministry of Town and Country Planning (now Department of the Environment), London, principal, 1943-45, assistant secretary, 1945-65; Commission of the New Towns, London, secretary, 1965-73; Location of Offices

Bureau, London, member of bureau, 1975-80. *Member:* Town and Country Planning Association (member of council, 1969-80), Land Use Society (chairman, 1977), Farmers' Club.

WRITINGS: (Editor) Robert Dymond, *Death Duties,* 8th edition (Schaffer was not associated with earlier editions), Solicitor's Law Stationery Society, 1937; *The New Town Story,* Macgibbon & Kee, 1970, revised edition, Paladin, 1972; (contributor) Hazel Evans, editor, *New Towns: The British Experience,* Charles Knight, 1972; (contributor) Gideon Gollany, editor, *International Urban Growth Policies,* John Wiley, 1978. Contributor to journals and newspapers.

SIDELIGHTS: Schaffer wrote: "My interest in planning dates from the early days of World War II when, having been bombed out of our London office and moved to North Wales, I was asked to return to London at the height of the bombing to join the secretariat of the Uthwatt Committee, which was appointed by Lord Reith to study and report on the subject of compensation and betterment, in preparation for the postwar reconstruction of Britain.

"I soon found the 'land problem' quite fascinating, and when the Uthwatt Report was completed (the far-reaching recommendations caused quite a stir at the time) I joined the Reconstruction Group, became a founding member of the new Ministry of Town and Country Planning when it was set up in 1943, played a leading part under the minister Lewis (later Lord) Silkin in the preparation of the Town and Planning Act of 1947, and for some years helped in the subsequent administration of the new planning system in Britain, including the building and management of the New Towns.

"My book, *The New Town Story,* was written rather by accident! The British New Towns soon became famous, and visitors from all over the world came to see them and find out 'how it was done.' One day I had a visitor from Japan. While I was talking to him I thought he was 'doodling,' which seemed rather rude, until I realized he was trying to take notes in Japanese script. Finally he threw down his pencil in despair and exclaimed, 'Why isn't this all written down in a Penguin book I can read?' So I decided to do just that."

* * *

SCHALM, Bernard   1928-1974

OBITUARY NOTICE—See index for *CA* sketch: Born December 12, 1928, in Poland; died February 2, 1974, in Edmonton, Alberta, Canada. Baptist minister and author of *The Church at Worship.* At the time of his death Schalm was academic dean at North American Baptist College. Obituaries and other sources: *The Writers Directory, 1976-78,* St. Martin's, 1976. (Exact date of death provided by wife, Verda Scheeler Schalm.)

* * *

SCHMIDT, Wilson Emerson   1927-

PERSONAL: Born March 22, 1927, in Madison, Wis.; son of Emerson Peter and Gertrude (Wilson) Schmidt; married Eleanor Butt Parker, December 26, 1950; children: Eric Emerson, Carl Wilson, Orrin Edward. *Education:* University of Maryland, B.S., 1947; University of Pittsburgh, M.A., 1948; University of Virginia, Ph.D., 1952. *Home:* 1514 Palmer Dr., Blacksburg, Va. 24060. *Office:* Department of Economics, Virginia Polytechnic Institute and State University, Blacksburg, Va. 24061.

CAREER: University of Virginia, Charlottesville, member of staff at Bureau of Population and Economic Research, 1948-49, instructor in economics, 1949-50; George Washington University, Washington, D.C., instructor, 1950-53, assistant professor, 1953-58, associate professor, 1958-60, professor of economics, 1960-66; Virginia Polytechnic Institute and State University, Blacksburg, professor of economics, 1966—, head of department, 1966-77. Visiting professor at Johns Hopkins School of Advanced International Studies, 1960, professor at Bologna Center, 1963. Member of President's Balance of Payments Task Force, 1968—; deputy assistant secretary of U.S. Treasury, 1970-72; consultant to American Enterprise Institute for Public Policy Research and U.S. Agency for International Development. *Member:* American Economic Association, National Association of Business Economists, Mont Pelerin Society, Beta Gamma Sigma, Cosmos Club.

WRITINGS: (With J. N. Behrman) *International Economics,* Holt, 1957; *The Rescue of the Dollar,* American Enterprise Institute for Public Policy Research, 1963; *The U.S. Balance of Payments and the Shrinking Dollar,* New York University Press, 1979. Contributor to economic journals.

WORK IN PROGRESS: International Economic Externalities and International Public Goods: The Economic Foundations for Intergovernmental Cooperation in Anarchial Circumstances.

SIDELIGHTS: Wilson Schmidt told *CA:* "Entering someone else's mind is the greatest privilege a person can obtain. It cannot be done without the greatest clarity of thinking and then exposition, oral and written. Too often it is the exposition and not the thinking that fails."

*   *   *

SCHMITT, Bernadotte Everly   1886-1969

OBITUARY NOTICE—See index for *CA* sketch: Born May 19, 1886, in Strasburg, Va.; died after a long illness, March 22, 1969, in Alexandria, Va. Educator, author, and internationally recognized authority on modern history. Schmitt was awarded the Pulitzer Prize for history in 1931 for his book *The Coming of the War, 1914.* Among his other books are *The Annexation of Bosnia, 1908-1909* and *The Origins of the First World War.* Schmitt edited several books on history and was also editor of the *Journal of Modern History.* He was a Rhodes scholar, a Guggenheim fellow, and a recipient of the George Louis Beer Prize for history from the American Historical Association. Obituaries and other sources: *Washington Post,* March 24, 1969; *New York Times,* March 24, 1969; *Publisher's Weekly,* April 14, 1969; *Current Biography,* Wilson, May, 1969.

*   *   *

SCHMITZ, James H(enry)   1911-

PERSONAL: Born October 15, 1911, in Hamburg, Germany (now West Germany); came to the United States, 1938; son of Joseph Henry (in business) and Catherine (Davis) Schmitz; married Betty Mae Chapman, January 11, 1957. *Education:* Attended high school in Berlin, Germany. *Agent:* Scott Meredith Literary Agency, Inc., 845 Third Ave., New York, N.Y. 10022.

CAREER: Worked for International Harvester Co. in various cities in Germany, 1932-38; writer, 1938-42; self-employed builder of automobile trailers, 1946-49; writer, 1949—. *Military service:* U.S. Army Air Forces, 1942-45; served in Pacific theater. *Member:* Science Fiction Writers of America, Authors Guild. *Awards, honors:* Invisible Little Man Award from Elves', Gnomes' and Little Men's Science Fiction, Chowder, and Marching Society, 1973.

WRITINGS—Science fiction novels, except as noted: *Agent of Vega,* Gnome Press, 1960; *A Tale of Two Clocks,* Dodd, 1962; *The Universe Against Her,* Ace Books, 1964; *A Nice Day for Screaming and Other Tales of the Hub* (stories), Chilton, 1965; *The Witches of Karres,* Chilton, 1966; *The Demon Breed,* Ace Books, 1968; *A Pride of Monsters* (stories), Macmillan, 1970; *The Eternal Frontiers,* Putnam, 1973; *The Lion Game,* DAW Books, 1973; *The Telzey Toy,* DAW Books, 1973. Contributor to science fiction magazines, including *Analog, Unknown Worlds,* and *Astounding.*

*   *   *

SCHNEIDER, Duane   1937-

PERSONAL: Born November 15, 1937, in South Bend, Ind.; son of William and Lillian (Pitchford) Schneider; married Jo Anne Bennett, February, 1959; children: four. *Education:* Miami University, Oxford, Ohio, B.A., 1958; Kent State University, M.A., 1960; University of Colorado, Ph.D., 1965. *Office:* Department of English, Ohio University, Athens, Ohio 45701.

CAREER: University of Colorado, Boulder, instructor in English, 1960-65; Ohio University, Athens, assistant professor, 1965-70, associate professor, 1970-75, professor of English, 1975—. Editor and publisher of Croissant & Co. *Member:* Modern Language Association of America, Charles Lamb Society, Thomas Wolfe Society (president, 1979-81), Society for the Study of Southern Literature.

WRITINGS: An Interview With Anais Nin, Village Press, 1973; *A Thomas Wolfe Collection: An Exhibition of Books,* Croissant, 1977; (contributor) Matthew J. Bruccoli, editor, *First Printings of American Authors,* Gale, 1977; (with Franklin V. Benjamin) *Anais Nin: An Introduction,* Ohio University Press, 1979. Contributor to journals. Associate editor of *Ohio Review;* contributing editor of *Thomas Wolfe Review,* 1979—.

WORK IN PROGRESS: Editing *New Essays on Thomas Wolfe.*

SIDELIGHTS: Schneider's company, Croissant & Co., is a publisher of small press poetry, along with books and pamphlets related to Thomas Wolfe.

*   *   *

SCHREIBER, Daniel   1909-1981

OBITUARY NOTICE—See index for *CA* sketch: Born April 18, 1909, in New York, N.Y.; died March 6, 1981, in Boca Raton, Fla. Educator and author best known as a specialist in the problems of disadvantaged children. Schreiber initiated the New York City Higher Horizons Program. A panelist at the White House Conference on Education in 1965, the educator was also associated with the Pentagon group that studied the Anti-Poverty Job Corps Program. He directed a project on dropouts from 1961 to 1965 for the National Education Association, and during the seventies he was Chancellor Irving Anker's assistant superintendent. His writings include *Profile of a School Dropout* and *Holding Power: Large City School Systems.* Obituaries and other sources: *New York Times,* March 9, 1981.

*   *   *

SCHULMAN, Arnold   1925-

PERSONAL: Born August 11, 1925, in Philadelphia, Pa.; son of H. (an innkeeper) and Eva (Blank) Schulman; married Jean Alexander, June 27, 1954; children: one daughter. *Ed-*

ucation: Attended University of North Carolina, 1942-43, 1945-46. *Home:* 411 East 53rd St., New York, N.Y. 10022.

CAREER: Actor and playwright. Associate producer of General Electric Theater, a series on CBS-TV, 1954-55. *Military service:* U.S. Navy, aerial photographer; became photographer's mate first class. *Member:* Writers Guild of America (West), Dramatists Guild. *Awards, honors:* Nominations for awards from Writers Guild, 1957, for "Wild Is the Wind," and 1959, for "A Hole in the Head"; nomination for Academy Award for best screenplay from Academy of Motion Picture Arts and Sciences, and award from Writers Guild, both 1963, both for "Love With the Proper Stranger"; award from Writers Guild and nomination for Academy Award for best screenplay, both 1969, both for "Goodbye, Columbus."

WRITINGS: Baba, Macmillian, 1972, Pocket Books, 1973.

Plays: "A Hole in the Head," first produced in New York City, at Plymouth Theater, February 28, 1957; "Jennie," first produced at Majestic Theater, October 17, 1963.

Screenplays: "Wild Is the Wind," released by Paramount in 1957; "A Hole in the Head," released by United Artists in 1959; "Love With the Proper Stranger," released by Paramount in 1963; (co-author) "The Night They Raided Minsky's," released by Tandem Productions in 1967; "Goodbye, Columbus" (adapted from the novella by Philip Roth), released by Paramount in 1969.

Author of nearly seventy television plays, including "Lost"; "The Heart's a Forgotten Hotel," first broadcast by NBC-TV; and works for "Philco Playhouse," "Studio One," "Omnibus," and "Kraft Television Theater."*

* * *

SCHULTZ, Harold John   1932-

PERSONAL: Born May 28, 1932, in Port Burwell, Ontario, Canada; came to the United States in 1954, naturalized citizen in 1966; son of Allan John and Alice Edith (Leach) Schultz; married Carolyn June Mast, August 27, 1955; children: Susan, Lori, Christopher. *Education:* Goshen College, B.A., 1953; University of Michigan, M.A., 1954; Duke University, Ph.D., 1959. *Religion:* Mennonite. *Home:* 200 East 24th St., North Newton, Kan. 67117. *Office:* Office of the President, Bethel College, North Newton, Kan. 67117.

CAREER: Goshen College, Goshen, Ind., instructor in history, 1954-56; Stetson University, DeLand, Fla., assistant professor, 1959-62, associate professor, 1962-64, professor of history, 1964-71, chairman of international studies, 1967-71, chairman of department of history, 1968-71; Bethel College, North Newton, Kan., president, 1971—. Visiting professor at Oxford University, 1969-70; president of Associated Independent Colleges of Kansas, 1972-73. Chairman of Council of Mennonite Colleges, 1980—; member of Commission on Overseas Missions of General Conference of the Mennonite Church, 1974—.

MEMBER: American Historical Association, African Studies Association (fellow), American Association for Higher Education, Christian Historians Association, Canadian Historical Association, Newton Chamber of Commerce, Omicron Delta Kappa, Rotary. *Awards, honors:* Carnegie fellowship, 1958-59; Fulbright-Hays grant for Africa, 1967.

WRITINGS: (With M. A. Ormsby, J. R. Wilbur, and B. J. Young) *Politics of Discontent,* University of Toronto Press, 1967; *History of England,* Barnes & Noble, 1968; *English Liberalism and the State: Individualism or Collectivism,* Heath, 1972. Contributor to history and religious journals.

Recordings: "Western Civilization: Origins and Directions," five volumes, Everett/Edwards, 1971.

WORK IN PROGRESS: Centennial goals study document for Bethel College, publication expected in 1981; seventy-fifth anniversary article on Alberta politics, publication expected in 1982.

SIDELIGHTS: Schultz told *CA:* "The third edition of *The History of England* highlights the current difficulties of the English economy and the power struggle between the trade unions and the government."

* * *

SCHURER, Leopold (Sidney) Launitz, Jr.
See LAUNITZ-SCHURER, Leopold (Sidney), Jr.

* * *

SCHUSCHNIGG, Kurt von
See von SCHUSCHNIGG, Kurt

* * *

SCHVANEVELDT, Jay D.   1937-

PERSONAL: Born January 15, 1937, in Preston, Idaho; son of Delbert George and Ruth (Schwartz) Schvaneveldt; married Karren Balls (a registered nurse), September 16, 1959; children: Cindy, Shane, Todd, Paul. *Education:* Utah State University, B.S., 1961; Florida State University, M.S., 1962, Ph.D., 1964; postdoctoral study at University of Minnesota. *Politics:* Democrat. *Religion:* Church of Jesus Christ of Latter-day Saints (Mormons). *Home:* 308 West Center, Logan, Utah 84321. *Office:* Department of Family and Human Development, Utah State University, Logan, Utah 84321.

CAREER: Florida State University, Tallahassee, assistant professor of home and family life, 1964-66; Utah State University, Logan, assistant professor of family and child development, 1967-72; University of Minnesota, Minneapolis, associate professor of family sociology and research associate, 1972-73; Utah State University, professor of family and human development and chairman of department, 1973-80. Visiting summer professor at Brigham Young University, 1968, Colorado State University, 1969-70, and University of Utah, 1971; visiting scholar at University of North Carolina, Greensboro, 1980-81. Chairman of Logan Historical Restoration, 1972-74. *Member:* National Council on Family Relations (chairman of research and theory section, 1977-79), American Sociological Association, American Home Economics Association, Utah Council on Family Relations (president, 1970-71).

WRITINGS: Understanding Research Methods, Wadsworth, 1981. Contributor to journals in the behavioral and social sciences. Associate editor of journal of the National Council on Family Relations, *Journal of Marriage and the Family, Family Relations, Family Perspective,* and *Western Sociological Quarterly.*

WORK IN PROGRESS: Research on pets as family members, the automobile and the family, family ritual, and siblings in the family.

SIDELIGHTS: Schvaneveldt told *CA:* "It has always been my belief and style to generate scientific data about family interaction and process and then help to improve the quality of family life as a result of the data. It is not enough to research and publish for professionals in one's discipline; one has an obligation to help enhance the community as well. As a family sociologist my work has focused on topics that have an impact on families in everyday life. My task is to help understand what the process is and then to facilitate education to enhance that process."

*   *   *

SCHWAB, Paul Josiah 1894-1966

OBITUARY NOTICE—See index for *CA* sketch: Born November 9, 1894, in Sutton, Neb.; died October 1, 1966; buried in Naperville, Ill. Minister, educator, and author of religious books and articles. His books include *The Attitude of Wolfgang Musculus Toward Religious Toleration* and *A Church-Related College Anticipates Its Centennial*. Obituaries and other sources: *Who Was Who in America*, 4th edition, Marquis, 1968.

*   *   *

SCHWABE, William
See CASSIDY, William L(awrence Robert)

*   *   *

SCHWARTZ, Lynne Sharon 1939-

PERSONAL: Born March 19, 1939, in Brooklyn, N.Y.; daughter of Jack M. (a lawyer and accountant) and Sarah (Slatus) Sharon; married Harry Schwartz (a city planner), December 22, 1957; children: Rachel Eve, Miranda Ruth. *Education:* Barnard College, B.A., 1959; Bryn Mawr College, M.A., 1961; further graduate study at New York University, 1967-72. *Residence:* New York, N.Y. *Agent:* Virginia Barber Literary Agency, Inc., 44 Greenwich Ave, New York, N.Y. 10011.

CAREER: Writer (magazine), Boston, Mass., associate editor, 1961-63; Operation Open City (civil rights-fair housing organization), New York City, writer, 1965-67; Hunter College of the City University of New York, New York City, lecturer in English, 1970-75; writer. Member of faculty at New York University, 1979. *Member:* International P.E.N., Authors Guild, Authors League of America, National Book Critics Circle. *Awards, honors:* James Henle Award from Vanguard Press, 1974, for "Lucca"; Lamport Award from Lamport Foundation, 1977, for short story "Rough Strife"; American Book Award nomination for first novel, 1981, for *Rough Strife*.

WRITINGS: Rough Strife (novel), Harper, 1980; *Balancing Acts* (novel), Harper, 1981.

Work represented in anthologies, including *Best American Short Stories, 1978; Best American Short Stories, 1979; Banquet,* Penmaen Press, 1979; *O. Henry Prize Stories, 1979*. Contributor of stories, articles, translations, and reviews to literary journals and popular magazines, including *Ontario Review, Transatlantic Review, New York Times Book Review, Washington Post Book World, Ploughshares, Redbook,* and *Chicago Review*.

WORK IN PROGRESS: Another novel, publication by Harper expected in 1983.

SIDELIGHTS: Schwartz's first novel, *Rough Strife,* deals with the twenty-year-old marriage of two middle-aged professionals. "Schwartz registers the fluctuations of marital feeling with the fidelity of a Geiger counter," noted Katha Pollitt in the *New York Times Book Review*. "She understands the permanent resentments that can be mixed with love . . . and the alternating currents of weakness and strength that pass between two people whose lives are joined together." The *New Republic*'s Dorothy Wickenden also complimented

Rough Strife and described it as "a wise novel, rewarding in its honesty and clarity of vision."

Balancing Acts, the author's next work, is about the growing friendship between a lonely teenager and an old man living in a nursing home. The unlikely companions find in each other the emotional support they lack.

BIOGRAPHICAL/CRITICAL SOURCES: Ms., June, 1980; *New Republic,* June 14, 1980; *Publishers Weekly,* June 15, 1980; *New York Times Book Review,* June 15, 1980; *Nation,* August 16-23, 1980.

*   *   *

SCHWARZ, Jack
See SCHWARZ, Jacob

*   *   *

SCHWARZ, Jacob 1924-
(Jack Schwarz)

PERSONAL: Born April 26, 1924, in Dordrecht, Netherlands. *Home and office:* Aletheia Foundation, 515 Northeast Eighth, Grants Pass, Ore. 97526. *Agent:* Robert Briggs, San Francisco, Calif.

CAREER: Writer.

WRITINGS—Under name Jack Schwarz: *The Path of Action,* Dutton, 1977; *Voluntary Controls,* Dutton, 1978; *Human Energy Systems,* Dutton, 1979.

SIDELIGHTS: Schwarz is currently involved in work at a health and research training center in Gold Hill, Oregon.

*   *   *

SCIFRES, Bill(y N.) 1925-

PERSONAL: Surname is pronounced *Sy*-fers; born February 16, 1925, in Crothersville, Ind.; son of Jacob W. (employed by American Can Co.) and Laura Belle (Dobbs) Scifres; married Helen Hacker, August 4, 1949 (divorced); married Nancy W. Wellington, September 4, 1954; children: Billie Jane Scifres Royalty, Donna, Joan, Patty. *Education:* Attended Hanover College and Indiana University. *Religion:* Presbyterian. *Home:* 1360 East 111th St., Indianapolis, Ind. 46280. *Office:* Sports Department, *Indianapolis Star,* P.O. Box 145, Indianapolis, Ind. 46206.

CAREER: Fort Wayne Journal-Gazette, Fort Wayne, Ind., reporter and copy editor; *Indianapolis Star,* Indianapolis, Ind., currently outdoor editor. Member of advisory council of Indiana Department of Lands, Forests, and Wildlife Resources; member of governor's committee on conservation education. *Military service:* U.S. Navy, 1943-46; served in European theater; received battle star.

MEMBER: Indiana Nature Conservancy (member of board of directors), Sigma Chi, Indianapolis Alumni Club. *Awards, honors:* Named Indiana conservation writer of the year by Sears Foundation, 1967, and National Wildlife Federation, 1973; Chase S. Osborn Award in Wildlife Conservation from Purdue University, 1969; named Indiana outdoor writer of the year by Indiana Department of Natural Resources, 1977.

WRITINGS: Indiana Outdoors, Indiana University Press, 1976. Contributor to national and regional magazines, including *Outdoor Life* and *Field and Stream*.

WORK IN PROGRESS: Indiana Streams and Rivers; a book on squirrel hunting.

SIDELIGHTS: Scifres wrote: "I am most interested in nature—all phases—and in conservation of natural resources.

Wildlife photography and nature photography are important activities for me, but I have at least one crusading book in mind right now and there could be others as I get more time to write. I would also like to write fiction with outdoor settings and themes and have written some verse and poetry (some published) with this theme in the past."

*   *   *

SCOFIELD, Norma Margaret Cartwright 1924-
(N. Cartwright)

PERSONAL: Born February 15, 1924, in Beamsville, Ontario, Canada; daughter of Harvey Elmer and Margaret Janet (Wilson) Cartwright; married Ray Daniel Scofield, August 19, 1957 (died December 5, 1962). *Education:* University of Saskatchewan, B.A., 1947; University of North Carolina, M.A., 1953. *Religion:* Roman Catholic. *Home address:* Route 1, Box 183, Moncure, N.C. 27559. *Agent:* George Scheer, Kings Mill Rd., Chapel Hill, N.C. 27514. *Office: Social Forces,* University of North Carolina, Chapel Hill, N.C. 27414.

CAREER: CKRM-Radio, Regina, Saskatchewan, in promotion and publicity services, 1947-50; Canadian Players, Montreal, Quebec, stage director, 1953; Grand Lodge of F & AM Masons, New York, N.Y., editor (under pseudonym N. Cartwright) and public relations representative of *Empire State Mason,* 1954-57; University of North Carolina, Chapel Hill, publications coordinator at Institute for Research in Social Science, social sciences managing editor of *Social Forces,* 1963—, editor of institute's *Research Previews,* 1965-74. *Awards, honors:* Best technical book award from Dog Writers Association of America, 1974, for *Your Dog: His Health and Happiness.*

WRITINGS: (Editor) Louis L. Vine, *Your Dog: His Health and Happiness,* Arco, 1973, revised edition, Winchester Press, 1975; (editor) Vine, *Behavior and Training of Dogs and Puppies,* Arco, 1977; (editor) Vine, *Breeding, Whelping, and Natal Care of Dogs,* Arco, 1977; (editor) Vine, *The Total Dog Book,* Popular Library, 1977; (editor) Vine, *Common Sense Book of Complete Cat Care,* Morrow, 1978; (editor) Vine, *Neurotic Dogs and Their Owners,* Dial, 1981.

Plays: "The End Is Not Yet" (one-act), first produced in Banff, Alberta, at School of Fine Arts, 1950; "The Glass Men" (three-act), first produced in 1952.

Contributor to *University of North Carolina Newsletter.*

SIDELIGHTS: Norma Scofield wrote: "My first love was writing plays—satirical comedies with 'social significance.' When the social significance of bread and roof became personal, I got a job. As editor of *Empire State Mason* my name appeared on the masthead as N. Cartwright, because the Masons were to assume I was male. The given name didn't matter a fig to me after hearing a tongue-in-cheek story that in the eighteenth century two London Temple charwomen were found floating in the Thames the morning after they were discovered watching a third-degree ceremony through a crack in the door.

"As a kid I desperately wanted to be a veterinarian. In those days in Saskatchewan it would have involved many miles traveling alone from an ailing horse to a sick cow to a lambing ewe, and my mother's veto held sway. But I have always had pets and my wishes have come together in my work with Dr. Vine on the dog and cat books.

"The first issue of *Social Forces* was published a little over a year before I was born, and several of its founders are still living in Chapel Hill. When I compiled the *SF Fifty Volume Index* in 1972 they were of inestimable help in adding substance to bare facts. The magazines of those fifty years turned out to be fascinatingly rich, including an article by Woodrow Wilson on Robert E. Lee, a review by Houdini of a book entitled *Haunted Houses,* and an article, 'Political Machine Strategy Against Investigation,' by V. O. Key, published in October, 1935, which spoke to the Watergate affair all that many years before."

*   *   *

SCOTFORD, John Ryland 1888-1976

OBITUARY NOTICE—See index for *CA* sketch: Born September 7, 1888, in Chicago, Ill.; died September 9, 1976, in Hamilton, N.Y. Congregational minister, expert on church architecture, and author. Scotford served as a building consultant for more than fourteen-hundred churches. In 1968 he received the Conover Award from the Church Architectural Guild of America for his contribution to church architecture. Scotford wrote several books on church design, including *When You Build Your Church* and *How to Decorate Your Church.* He was also editor of *The Advance,* the national organ of the Congregational Christian Church. Obituaries and other sources: *New York Times,* September 10, 1976.

*   *   *

SCOTT, Austin (Wakeman) 1885(?)-1981

OBITUARY NOTICE: Born c. 1885 in New Brunswick, N.J.; died April 9, 1981, in Boston, Mass. Educator and author. Scott taught at Harvard University's law school for more than fifty years and was renowned for his expertise in the field of trusts. He wrote *Scott on Trusts* and *The Law of Trusts.* In 1928 Scott was president of the Association of American Law Schools. Obituaries and other sources: *New York Times,* April 10, 1981; *Chicago Tribune,* April 11, 1981; *Newsweek,* April 20, 1981; *Time,* April 20, 1981.

*   *   *

SCOTT, Nerissa
See RING, Elizabeth

*   *   *

SCOTT, Rachel (Ann) 1947-

PERSONAL: Born April 20, 1947, in Shenandoah, Iowa; daughter of Duane Clarence and Elizabeth Ann (Clark) Scott. *Education:* Kansas State University, B.S., 1969; graduate study at University of Texas, Medical Branch at San Antonio, 1980—. *Residence:* San Antonio, Tex. *Agent:* Gail Hochman, Paul R. Reynolds, Inc., 12 East 41st St., New York, N.Y. 10017.

CAREER: Winston-Salem Journal, Winston-Salem, N.C., reporter, 1969; free-lance writer in Washington, D.C., 1970-71, and Brownsville, Md., 1972-74; *Baltimore Sun,* Baltimore, Md., reporter, 1974; Illinois Industrial Commission, director of health and safety, 1974-75; free-lance writer in Washington, D.C., 1975-76; *Environmental Action,* reporter and editor, 1977; free-lance writer, 1977—. Silversmith, 1977-78. Writer and editor for Occupational Safety and Health Administration of U.S. Department of Labor, 1978-79; public information specialist for Environmental Protection Agency, 1979—. Reporter on WRC-TV. *Awards, honors:* Grants from Fund for Investigative Journalism, 1970, 1972, 1975, Abelard Foundation, 1972, and Ford Foundation, 1972-73; award from *Mademoiselle,* 1974.

WRITINGS: Muscle and Blood, Dutton, 1974.

SCRIMSHER, Lila Gravatt 1897-1974

OBITUARY NOTICE—See index for *CA* sketch: Born December 26, 1897, in Talmage, Neb.; died September 12, 1974. Librarian and author of books on history for children. Among Scrimsher's writings are *General Pershing, Strong Man* and *The Pumpkin Flood of Harpers Ferry.* (Date of death provided by the Lincoln Main Library, Lincoln, Neb.)

*   *   *

SCULLY, Julia S(ilverman) 1929-

PERSONAL: Born February 9, 1929, in Seattle, Wash.; daughter of Julius and Rose (Hohenstein) Silverman; married Edward C. Scully, August 3, 1963 (marriage ended, 1980). *Education:* Stanford University, B.A., 1951; New York University, M.A., 1970. *Office: Modern Photography,* 825 Seventh Ave., New York, N.Y. 10019.

CAREER: Modern Photography, New York, N.Y., editor, 1967—.

WRITINGS: (With Peter Miller) *Disfarmer: The Heber Springs Portraits,* Addison House, 1976; (project editor) *Family of Women,* Ridge Press, 1979. Author of "Seeing Pictures" and co-author of "Currents in American Photography," columns in *Modern Photography.*

*   *   *

SEALEY, Leonard (George William) 1923-

PERSONAL: Born May 7, 1923, in London, England; came to the United States in 1967; son of George William (a civil servant) and Gertrude (Holmes) Sealey; married Joan Mary Hearn, March 11, 1944 (died, 1972); married Nancy Marie Verre (a teacher), August 29, 1972; children: Richard, Andrew, Nicholas, Edward, Christopher. *Education:* Loughborough College of Advanced Technology, Aeronautical Engineer's Certificate, 1944; Peterborough Teacher Training College, Teacher's Certificate, 1948; University of Leicester, Diploma in Education, 1959, M.Ed., 1964. *Religion:* Church of England. *Home and office:* 11 Chilton St., Plymouth, Mass. 02360.

CAREER: Elementary school teacher in Leicestershire, England, 1948-54; Thringstone Primary School and Community Centre, Leicestershire, principal and warden, 1954-55; adviser for primary schools in Leicestershire, 1956-65; North Buckinghamshire College of Education, Bletchley, England, principal, 1965-67; Education Development Center, Newton, Mass., director of Regional Educational Laboratory program, 1967-68; writer and consultant, 1968—. Consultant to Ford Foundation, British Council, and Weyerhaeuser Company Foundation. *Military service:* Royal Navy, air engineer officer, 1942-46. *Member:* Royal Society of Arts (fellow), Phi Delta Kappa.

WRITINGS—Children's textbooks: *The Creative Use of Mathematics,* six volumes, Basil Blackwell, 1961; (with Vivian Gibbon) *Beginning Mathematics,* four volumes, Basil Blackwell, 1963; *Introducing Mathematics,* four volumes, Basil Blackwell, 1968-70; *Exploring Language,* two volumes, Thomas Nelson, 1968; *Early Number Multi-Group Laboratory,* Responsive Environments Corp., 1969; *Basic Skills in Learning,* Thomas Nelson, 1970; *Let's Find Out About Mathematics,* two volumes, Thomas Nelson, 1971; *Let's Think About Mathematics,* four volumes, Thomas Nelson, 1971; *Metrikit Work Cards,* Metric-Aids, 1971; *Practice and Pro-*

cesses, four volumes, Basil Blackwell, 1972; *Lively Reading,* four volumes, Thomas Nelson, 1973.

Other children's books: *Finding Out About the World of Numbers,* Purnell, 1963; *About Numbers,* Basil Blackwell, 1964; *The Shapes of Things,* Basil Blackwell, 1965.

Other writings: (With Gibbon) *Communication and Learning in the Primary School,* Basil Blackwell, 1962, revised edition, Humanities, 1963; *Junior School Mathematics,* Basil Blackwell, 1964; *The Teaching of Elementary School Mathematics,* Encyclopaedia Brittannica, 1964; (contributor) Z. P. Dienes, editor, *Mathematics Reform in the Primary School,* United Nations Educational, Scientific, and Cultural Organization, 1967; (contributor) Brian Rose, editor, *Modern Trends in Education,* Macmillan, 1971; *The Post Office Books,* three volumes, Macmillan, 1971; *Introducing Computation,* Invicta, 1971; *The Lively Readers,* sixteen volumes, Thomas Nelson, 1973; *Open Education,* Hazen Foundation, 1977; (with wife, Nancy Sealy, and Marcia Millmore) *Children's Writing,* International Reading Association, 1978.

General editor of *Our World: A First Topic Encyclopedia,* Macmillan, 1974. Contributor to education journals.

WORK IN PROGRESS: A novel about industrial espionage; short stories for children of elementary school age; research on the development of language in children, ages two to four.

SIDELIGHTS: Leonard Sealy commented: "My career has changed direction several times, and I have seized every opportunity to travel widely and tackle problems rooted in a variety of cultures. Throughout, I have persisted with my interest in art. As a painter and sculptor, I have exhibited internationally and am now working toward one or more shows. A love of the sea is obvious in much that I do, and I am an avid sailor. Such an open and multi-faceted approach provides the detailed and well-rounded view of the world that is of immense help to any writer."

*   *   *

SEDAKA, Neil 1939-

PERSONAL: Born March 13, 1939, in Brooklyn, N.Y.; son of Mac (a taxi driver) and Eleanor (Appel) Sedaka; married Leba Margaret Strassberg, September 11, 1962; children: Dara Felice, Marc Charles. *Education:* Attended Julliard School of Music, New York City, 1948-52. *Office:* 1370 Avenue of the Americas, New York, N.Y. 10019.

CAREER: Composer and recording artist, 1958—. Appeared in concert tours, in night clubs, and on television programs, 1959—. *Member:* American Federation of Musicians, American Federation of Television and Radio Artists, American Guild of Variety Artists. *Awards, honors:* Numerous gold records; Grammy Award, 1976, for "Love Will Keep Us Together"; six Broadcast Music Incorporated awards.

WRITINGS: Composer and lyricist of more than one hundred songs, including "Stupid Cupid," 1958; "The Diary," 1958; and "Oh! Carol," "Stairway to Heaven," "Calendar Girl," "Happy Birthday, Sweet Sixteen," "Next Door to an Angel," "Breaking Up Is Hard to Do," "Working on a Groovy Thing," "That's When the Music Takes Me," "Laughter in the Rain," "New York City Blues," "You Gotta Make Your Own Sunshine," "Lonely Night (Angel Face)," "Love Will Keep Us Together," "Should've Never Let You Go."

SIDELIGHTS: Neil Sedaka's devotion to music began at age nine when he was accepted as a scholarship student in the preparatory division of the Julliard School of Music to study piano. After playing solely classical music for four years, Sedaka tried his hand at pop music when his neighbor Howard

Greenfield asked him to write music for a poem he had written. Thus, Sedaka wrote his first pop song, entitled "My Life's Devotion." Though he continued his studies in classical piano, Sedaka enjoyed the attention and popularity he gained by playing the music that his peers enjoyed. Therefore, he continued to collaborate with Greenfield, writing many soft ballads and rock and roll tunes during the following years.

After graduation from high school, Sedaka studied for two years under Adele Marcus at Julliard and planned to become a concert pianist. But when his song "Stupid Cupid" was successfully recorded by Connie Francis in 1958, Sedaka abandoned his previous career plans. He signed with Aldon Music, where he wrote songs with Greenfield for many pop singers, then eventually began recording his songs himself. On a contract with RCA records, Sedaka sold more than twenty-five million records with such hits as "Oh! Carol," "Calendar Girl," and "Breaking Up Is Hard to Do."

Sedaka experienced great success until 1964 when the Beatles and other British rock groups offered a new and different sound to pop music while his own sound lost its public appeal. Sedaka's record sales plunged, and he had only moderate success writing songs for other performers. Finally in 1970 he moved to London where his songs were well received once again. After three best-selling albums in England, Sedaka released "Laughter in the Rain" in the United States and found himself on his way to a comeback. "Laughter" sold more than one million copies in two months. "Love Will Keep Us Together," recorded by the Captain and Tennille, followed in 1975 and won a Grammy Award as Record of the Year in 1976. Since 1976, Sedaka has steadily enjoyed hit recordings, sold-out concerts, and numerous television appearances.

AVOCATIONAL INTERESTS: Tennis, skiing.

BIOGRAPHICAL/CRITICAL SOURCES: Newsweek, June 18, 1962, February 24, 1975; *Time,* September 15, 1975.*

* * *

SENIOR, Michael 1940-

PERSONAL: Born April 14, 1940, in Llandudno, Wales; son of Geoffrey (a company director) and Julia (Cotterell) Senior. *Education:* Open University, B.A., 1978 and 1980. *Home:* Bryn Eisteddfod, Glan Conwy, Colwyn Bay, North Wales. *Agent:* David Higham Associates Ltd., 508 Lower John St., Golden Sq., London W1R 4HA, England.

CAREER: Farmer.

WRITINGS: Portrait of North Wales, R. Hale, 1973; *Portrait of South Wales,* R. Hale, 1974; *Greece and Its Myths,* Gollancz, 1978; *Myths of Britain,* Orbis Publications, 1979; (contributor) Antonia Fraser, editor, *Heroes and Heroines,* Weidenfeld & Nicolson, 1979; (editor) *Sir Thomas Malory's Tales of King Arthur,* Collins, 1980; *Richard II,* Weidenfeld & Nicolson, 1981.

Author of "The Coffee Table," first broadcast by BBC-Radio, January, 1964. Work represented in anthologies, including *New Poetry 2,* edited by Patricia Beer and Kevin Crossley-Holland, Arts Council of Great Britain, 1976; *Green Horse,* edited by Meic Stephens and Peter Finch, Christopher Davies, 1978. Contributor of articles and poems to magazines, including *Anglo-Welsh Review, Ecologist, Folklore,* and *New Scientist,* and to newspapers.

SIDELIGHTS: Senior commented: "My main interests are mythology, history, and places. I have traveled widely in Europe, Africa, and the Americas. I believe that myth has a functional significance as a combined expression of universal human experiences and universal conceptual problems: as a necessary formalization of both psychological and proto-historical occurrences. My interest in history arises from a realization of the extent to which the past is manifested in the present. In writing of places it is particularly satisfactory to be able to combine a sense of history with a sense of place, and the most fruitful results occur when the three interests mentioned above combine, as in my book *Greece and Its Myths.* There is scope now for something of this sort extended to a wider sphere."

* * *

SEWEL, John 1946-

PERSONAL: Born January 15, 1946, in London, England; son of Leonard (a social worker) and Hilda (a social worker; maiden name, Brown) Sewel; married Rosemary Langeland (a social worker), July, 1968; children: Tom, Kate. *Education:* University of Durham, B.A., 1967; University College of Swansea, University of Wales, M.Sc., 1970; University of Aberdeen, Ph.D., 1977. *Politics:* Labour. *Religion:* None. *Residence:* Aberdeen, Scotland. *Office:* Institute for the Study of Sparsely Populated Areas, University of Aberdeen, Aberdeen, Scotland.

CAREER: University of Aberdeen, Aberdeen, Scotland, lecturer, 1975—. Member and past leader of Aberdeen City Council; member of Convention of Scottish Local Authorities.

WRITINGS: Colliery Closure and Social Change, University of Wales Press, 1975; *Education and Migration,* Highlands and Islands Development Board, 1976; (editor) *The Promise and the Reality,* Institute for the Study of Sparsely Populated Areas, University of Aberdeen, 1978; (contributor) G. F. Summers and A. Selvik, editors, *Nonmetropolitan Industrial Growth,* Heath, 1979; (with Frank Bealey) *Politics of Independence,* University of Aberdeen Press, 1981. Contributor to *Town Planning Review.*

WORK IN PROGRESS: Research on economic and social effects of employment fluctuations in oil-affected areas of northern Scotland, the role of rural primary schools, population change in northern Scotland, and relations between local and central governments in England and Scandinavia.

SIDELIGHTS: Sewel told *CA:* "The roles of academic and politician do not sit happily together. Although some skills are transferable, it is essential to make absolutely clear which role one is fulfilling at any given time. However, in both politics and social science it is necessary to resist the temptation of criticizing the present by reference to some past 'golden age' when concord and social jubilee prevailed. It never was like that."

* * *

SHALLCRASS, John James 1922-

PERSONAL: Born in 1922, in Auckland, New Zealand; son of Robert E. (in sales) and Mabel Margaret Shallcrass; married Aithna Susan Cato (a teacher), November, 1947; children: Jane, Simon. *Education:* Victoria University of Wellington, Diploma in Education, 1951, M.A., 1959, Advanced Diploma in Teaching, 1960. *Religion:* None. *Home:* 11 Pembroke Rd., Wellington 5, New Zealand. *Office:* Department of Education, Victoria University of Wellington, Private Bag, Wellington, New Zealand.

CAREER: Teacher at schools in Marlborough and Wellington, New Zealand, 1940-53; Wellington Teachers College, Wellington, began as lecturer in education, became senior lecturer in history and geography, 1953-63, vice-principal, 1963-67; Victoria University of Wellington, Wellington, reader in education, 1968—. Broadcaster and commentator, 1957—. Councillor of United Nations Educational, Scientific, and Cultural Organization; consultant to New Zealand Child Care Association and New Zealand Play Centre Federation. *Military service:* New Zealand Navy, 1941-45; served in Atlantic, Pacific, and Mediterranean theaters and on the Indian Ocean. *Member:* New Zealand Council for Civil Liberties (vice-president), Association for the Study of Childhood (past president), Association of University Teachers, Homosexual Reform Association, Community Volunteers (member of council), Defense and Aid Fund for Southern Africa (chairman).

WRITINGS: Educating New Zealanders, A. H. & A. W. Reed, 1967; (editor with J. L. Ewing) *An Introduction to Maori Education,* Price-Milburn, 1973; (editor and contributor) *Secondary Schools in Change,* Post Primary Teachers Association, 1973; (editor and contributor) *The Spirit of an Age,* A. H. & A. W. Reed, 1975; *Foreward to Basics,* New Zealand Educational Institute, 1978; (editor with R. Stothart and R. Larkin, and contributor) *Recreation Reconsidered,* New Zealand Council of Recreation and Sport, 1981. Also author of *Tales Out of School,* 1981.

Contributor: A. Haas, editor, *The Right to Dissent,* New Zealand University Students' Association, 1965; Beverley J. Morris, editor, *Women's Position in the World Today,* Victoria University of Wellington, 1968; R. J. Bates, editor, *Prospects in New Zealand Education,* Hodder & Stoughton, 1969; N. McLeod and B. Farland, editors, *Wellington Prospect,* Hicks, Smith & Son, 1970; D. Day, editor, *Education at the Crossroads,* Waikato, 1970; *New Horizons in Social Codes,* Auckland Principals' Association, 1971; *Recreation in New Zealand,* Volume II, Auckland Regional Authority, 1972; D. R. Cook and N. K. La Fleur, editors, *A Guide to Education Research,* Allen & Bacon, 1975; A. Codd and G. Hermansson, editors, *New Directions in Secondary Education,* Hodder & Stoughton, 1976; Jane Ritchie, *Chance to Be Equal,* Cape-Catley, 1978; *Environmental Education Handbook,* Canterbury Environment Centre, 1979; G. Robinson and B. O'Rourke, editors, *Schools in New Zealand Society,* Longman Paul, 1980; G. Melling, *Open School House,* Caveman Press, 1980; P. Macaskill, editor, *Ailo Pai,* Price-Milburn, 1980; G. Bryant, editor, *New Zealand 2000,* Cassells, 1981.

Contributor of about two hundred articles to magazines, journals, and newspapers. Editor of *Liberal Studies Briefs,* 1968-76; editor of fourteen-volume series for Price-Milburn.

WORK IN PROGRESS: A collection of oral archives on education in New Zealand.

SIDELIGHTS: Shallcrass wrote: "I am a teacher whose greatest pleasure is to be midwife to other people's views. I am competent and undistinguished, but saved from total insignificance by unsatisfied multiple interests. These include theater, literature, politics, sport, music, art, human adaptability, teaching, and family. I am constantly surprised at the ignorance and fallibility of the learned and powerful. I wonder if the species can adapt to a cooperative ethic before the individual ego brings general chaos."

*　　*　　*

SHAW, Helen 1913-

PERSONAL: Born February 20, 1913, in Timaru, New Zealand; daughter of Walter and Jessie Helen (Gow) Shaw; married Frank Hofmann (a photographer), December 24, 1941;

children: Mike, Stephen Rainer. *Education:* Teachers' Training College, Christchurch, New Zealand, Certified Teacher, 1933; University of Canterbury, B.A., 1937. *Home:* 42 Bassett Rd., Auckland 5, New Zealand.

CAREER: Poet, critic, and writer, 1937—. *Member:* International P.E.N., International Poetry Society. *Awards, honors:* Grant from New Zealand Literary Fund, 1965.

WRITINGS: (Editor) *The Puritan and the Waif: Essays on Frank Sargeson's Work,* Hofmann, 1954; *The Orange Tree and Other Stories,* Pelorus Press, 1957; *Out of Dark* (poems), Mitre, 1968; *Poetry Broadsheet,* Handcraft Press, 1970; (editor) *The Letters of D'Arcy Cresswell,* University of Canterbury, 1971; *The Girl of the Gods* (poems), Diparun, 1973; *The Word and Flower* (poems), ORE Publications, 1975; (editor) *D'Arcy Cresswell Sonnets,* Nag's Head Press, 1976; (editor with Robert Thompson) *Poems by Several Hands,* Pompallier Press, 1976; *The Gypsies and Other Stories,* Victoria University of Wellington, 1978.

Work represented in anthologies, including *Coast to Coast,* Angus & Robertson, 1955-56; *New Zealand Short Stories,* House of Belle Lettres, 1963; *Summer's Tales Two,* Macmillan, 1965.

Author of occasional columns in *New Zealand Observer,* 1942-45. Editor of "Cresswell Letters," University of Canterbury, 1965. Contributor of articles, poems, stories for children and adults, and reviews to magazines and newspapers, including *Image, Landfall, Islands,* and *Southern Review.* Poetry broadcast by Radio New Zealand.

WORK IN PROGRESS: A collection of stories; editing *Lady Ottoline Morrell and D'Arcy Cresswell: An Exchange of Letters.*

SIDELIGHTS: Helen Shaw wrote: "My interests lie in the direction of Spanish mystical poetry and the poetry of William Blake, W. B. Yeats and Kathleen Raine. I have written a sequence of poems on themes drawn from the life of Heloise, with reference to Heloise's love for Peter Abelard.

"I was brought up in the home of my grandfather, who influenced me in the direction of literature." In *Islands,* she wrote: "If, when a child, my grandfather had given me a key to the gardens of literature, by his death I had received a second key, one that, in the course of time, unlocked my own life I had not known. Liberated from the repressive Victorians by whom I was nurtured and haunted, and whom I loved, I could see beyond self. In that creative glass coloured by my psychological make-up, in the mirror of dream, I now saw a more catholic view of life. I began to see, in the darkened not totally dark creative mirror, a procession, beginnings, the characters of untold stories."

Shaw described her work further: "Characters in my stories may suggest the surreality of a Jungian underworld of dreams, if measured by their appearances and conversations. At the same time the stories are based on *terra firma.* A samovar significant to one story is a real Russian samovar. In another, the military coat of a long dead soldier, worn by a hippie artist and woven through her dream soliloquy of despair, is a substantial garment in spite of playing a part at dream-level.

"The past with its perils and marvels lives with us, but it must face the opposition we offer it by our conscious and collective attitudes. In today's world of technology and mass entertainment we are constantly pressured into conforming, persuaded to turn from the past in spite of its richness and illuminations and meanings. The world of the imagination needs to be maintained and on occasions strongly defended. I work for that objective and for that world in the midst of the present scene. I swing backwards, forwards, range from present to past to future to present.

"I tend to draw together a small group of characters and place them in the setting of a spacious, usually derelict house to work out their destinies. Once released or liberated from the creative source of my mind they are the controllers of the story. Perhaps the obsessive imaging of the spacious or threatened house is idiosyncratic as well as symbolic. Strange characters in derelict houses may act as voices to suggest the right to survival of the rich memory-depths which color and sustain thoughts and acts."

BIOGRAPHICAL/CRITICAL SOURCES: E. H. McCormick, *New Zealand Literature,* Oxford University Press, 1959; H. Winston Rhodes, *New Zealand Fiction Since 1945,* John McIndoe Ltd. (Dunedin), 1968; G. A. Wilkes and J. C. Reid, *The Literatures of the British Commonwealth: The Literatures of Australia and New Zealand,* University Park, Pennsylvania State University Press, 1970; *Islands,* Volume 7, number 1, 1978, Volume 7, number 3, 1979.

*   *   *

SHAW, Thurstan 1914-

PERSONAL: Born June 27, 1914, in Plymouth, England; son of John Herbert (a minister of the Church of England) and Irene (Woollatt) Shaw; married Ione Magor, January 21, 1939; children: Rosanne Shaw Gough, Gilian Shaw Green, Timothy, Jonathan, Joanna Shaw Newland. *Education:* Cambridge University, B.A., 1936, M.A., 1943, Ph.D., 1966; University of London, postgraduate teacher's diploma, 1937; attended Open University, 1981. *Politics:* Socialist Democrat. *Religion:* Society of Friends (Quakers). *Home:* 37 Hawthorne Rd., Stapleford, Cambridge, England. *Agent:* Curtis Brown Ltd., 1 Craven Hill, London W2 3EP, England. *Office:* Clare Hall, Cambridge University, Cambridge, England.

CAREER: Achimota College, Ghana, curator of Museum of Anthropology, 1937-45; associated with Cambridgeshire Education Committee, England, 1945-51; Cambridge Institute of Education, Cambridge, England, tutor, 1951-63; University of Ibadan, Ibadan, Nigeria, professor of archaeology and head of department, 1963-74; Cambridge University, Cambridge, lecturer in archaeology, 1975—, director of studies at Magdalene College, 1976—. Member of Cambridge Community Relations Council, 1980—. Visiting professor at Harvard University, 1975, Yale University, 1979, and University of Calgary, 1980.

MEMBER: International Union of Pre- and Proto-Historic Sciences (member of comite d'honneur, 1974—), Society of Antiquaries (fellow), Prehistoric Society, Royal Anthropological Institute (fellow), Panafrican Congress on Prehistory (vice-president, 1967-77), Athenaeum Club, Ramblers Association, Explorers Club. *Awards, honors:* Amaury Talbot Prize from Royal Anthropological Institute, 1970, for *Igbo-Ukwu,* and 1978, for *Nigeria;* commander of Order of the British Empire, 1972; Richard Corley Hunt Memorial Fellow of Wenner-Gren Foundation for Anthropological Research, 1975-77.

WRITINGS: Igbo-Ukwu: An Account of Archaeological Discoveries in Eastern Nigeria, two volumes, Faber, 1970; *Africa and the Origins of Man,* Ibadan University Press, 1973; *Why "Darkest" Africa?,* Ibadan University Press, 1975; (editor and contributor) *Discovering Nigeria's Past,* Oxford University Press, 1975; *Unearthing Igbo-Ukwu,* Oxford University Press, 1977; *Nigeria,* Thames & Hudson, 1978.

Contributor to *UNESCO History of Africa,* Volume 1 and Volume 3, and to *McDonald's Atlas of Archaeology.* Co-editor with Andrew Sherratt of *The Cambridge Encyclopaedia of Archaeology.* Contributor of more than a hundred articles to journals. Editor of *West African Archaeological Newsletter,* 1964-70, and *West African Journal of Archaeology,* 1971-75; member of advisory editorial board of *World Archaeology, West African Journal of Archaeology,* and *Interdisciplinary Science Reviews.*

WORK IN PROGRESS: A book on archaeology of West Africa, publication by Heinemann expected in 1984; research on the development of man's manipulation of energy from the earliest beginnings, the beginnings of sub-Saharan agriculture, and the analysis of West African bronzes.

SIDELIGHTS: Shaw wrote: "In connection with my work, studying archaeological sites and museum collections, I have traveled widely in the African continent, having at one time or another visited about two-thirds of its countries. In 1973, the Igbo-Ukwu community in eastern Nigeria conferred upon me the title of 'Onuna-Ekwulu Ora,' which means 'the mouth that speaks on behalf of Igbo-Ukwu.' In the same year I was made a second-class elder of Nembe in the Niger Delta.

"One of the principal motivations of my life has been the belief that white-skinned people have done awful things to darker-skinned people, and still do if they get the chance. I also believe in something called truth and that it is worth going after, even though it is a difficult concept philosophically."

AVOCATIONAL INTERESTS: "I like listening to music, play the piano very indifferently, enjoy poetry and scribbling some purely for my own satisfaction (and often dissatisfaction), and much enjoy walking. In 1979 I fulfilled a fifty-year-old ambition by walking two hundred fifty miles along the Icknield Way, from the Norfolk Coast to Wiltshire."

*   *   *

SHEBAR, Sharon Sigmond 1945-

PERSONAL: Born July 24, 1945, in Brooklyn, N.Y.; daughter of Joseph and Sara Libby (Stein) Sigmond; married Jonathan Shebar (a teacher), December 16, 1967; children: Tom Joseph Franklin, Susan Ethel. *Education:* Hofstra University, B.Sc., 1966; Fairleigh Dickinson University, Montessori Society Certificate, 1968; graduate study at Queens College of the City University of New York and at C. W. Post College of Long Island University. *Home:* 15 Connecticut Ave., Freeport, N.Y. 11520. *Agent:* Denise Marcil Literary Agency, 316 West 82nd St., New York, N.Y. 10024.

CAREER: Elementary school teacher in Amityville, N.Y., 1966-68; William Mount School, Rego Park, N.Y., teacher of Montessori education, 1969-74, director of Montessori education, 1972-74, special education teacher, 1980—.

WRITINGS—Children's books: The Montessori Enrichment Program, privately printed, 1970; *Groundhog Day,* Aro Publishing, 1977; *Whaling for Glory!,* Messner, 1978; *The Mysterious World of Honeybees,* Messner, 1979; *Milk,* Aro Publishing, 1979; *The Night Monsters,* Aro Publishing, 1979; (with husband, Jonathan Shebar) *Animal Dads Take Over,* Simon & Schuster, 1981; *Flight 25, New York to Los Angeles,* Messner, 1981; (with Judith Schoder) *Vampires* (nonfiction), Messner, 1981; *The Cardiff Giant,* Messner, 1981; *The Bell Witch,* Messner, in press. Author of "Our Kids," a column in *Freeport Leader.* Contributor to magazines, including *Weight Watchers, Animals, Catholic Digest, Young Judean,* and *Rainbow.*

WORK IN PROGRESS: Mysty Bayous, a historical romance, with Judith Schoder; *Mysty Death,* a ghost story, with Schoder; *Snowcap Love,* a contemporary romance, with Schoder and Celeste Wenzel.

SIDELIGHTS: Sharon Shebar wrote: "I write because I have to write; my nature will not allow me to do otherwise. For me, writing is an obsession and a passion. And when that passion is combined with talent and an interesting topic it brings both financial reward and a sense of accomplishment that is hard to equal in other areas of life."

*   *   *

SHENNAN, Joseph Hugh 1933-

PERSONAL: Born March 13, 1933, in Liverpool, England; son of Hugh (a school headmaster) and Mary (a teacher; maiden name, Jones) Shennan; married Margaret Price (a college lecturer), August 23, 1958; children: Andrew, Robert, Christopher. *Education:* University of Liverpool, B.A. (with first class honors), 1955; Cambridge University, Ph.D., 1960. *Home:* Bullbeck House, Four Acres, Brookhouse, Caton, Lancaster, England. *Agent:* Curtis Brown Academic Ltd., 1 Craven Hill, London W2 3EP, England. *Office:* Department of History, Furness College, University of Lancaster, Bailrigg, Lancaster LA1 4YG, England.

CAREER: University of Liverpool, Liverpool, England, assistant lecturer, 1960-63, lecturer in history, 1963-65; University of Lancaster, Bailrigg, England, 1965-71, began as lecturer, became senior lecturer, reader, 1971-74, professor of European studies, 1974—, head of department. *Member:* Royal Historical Society.

WRITINGS: The Parlement of Paris, Cornell University Press, 1968; *Government and Society in France, 1461-1661,* Barnes & Noble, 1969; *The Origins of the Modern European State, 1450-1725,* Hutchinson, 1974; *Philippe, Duke of Orleans: Regent of France, 1715-1723,* Thames & Hudson, 1979. Also editor of *Early Modern Europe Today,* Allen & Unwin, and *History of France,* Longman. Executive editor of *Dictionary of World History,* 1973. Founding editor of *European Studies Review,* 1971-79, advisory editor, 1979—.

WORK IN PROGRESS: A biography of Louis XV, 1710-74, and a history of France, 1715-1789, both for Allen & Unwin.

*   *   *

SHEPPARD, David Stuart 1929-

PERSONAL: Born in 1929 in Reigate, England; son of Stuart (a solicitor) and Barbara (Shepherd) Sheppard; married Grace Isaac (a teacher), June 19, 1957; children: Jenny. *Education:* Trinity Hall, Cambridge, B.A., 1953; Ridley Hall, Cambridge, M.A., 1955. *Politics:* "Christian socialist." *Home:* Bishop's Lodge, Woolton Park, Liverpool L25 6DT, England. *Office:* Church House, 1 Hanover St., Liverpool L1 3DW, England.

CAREER: Ordained minister of Church of England, 1955; curate of Church of England in Islington, 1955-57; Mayflower Family Centre, Canning Town, England, warden, 1957-69; bishop of Woolwich, England, 1969-75; bishop of Liverpool, England, 1975—. Chairman of Urban Ministry Project, 1969-75, Evangelical Urban Training Project, 1970-75, Martin Luther King Memorial Trust, 1972-75, Fair Cricket Campaign, 1971, and Special Programmes Board for Merseyside and Cheshire of Manpower Services Commission.

WRITINGS: Built as a City: God and the Urban World Today, Hodder & Stoughton, 1974. Also author of *Parson's Pitch,* 1964.

WORK IN PROGRESS: "A picture book on the urban mission of the church."

SIDELIGHTS: Sheppard's main interests are urban and industrial life and the church's task within it. Another interest is cricket, which he played from 1947 to 1963, first at Cambridge University and later in Sussex.

*   *   *

SHEPPARD, Eugenia

PERSONAL: Born in Columbus, Ohio; daughter of James Taylor and Jane (Benbow) Sheppard; married Walter Millis (died, 1968). *Education:* Received degree from Bryn Mawr College (cum laude). *Home:* 171 West 57th St., New York, N.Y. 10019.

CAREER: Women's Wear Daily, New York City, fashion writer, 1938-40; *New York Herald Tribune,* New York City, writer in women's features department, 1940-47, fashion editor, 1947-49; *World Journal Tribune,* New York City, head of women's staff, 1949-56; Publishers Hall Syndicate, New York City, author of syndicated column, "Inside Fashion," 1956—.

WRITINGS: (With Earl Blackwell) *Crystal Clear,* Doubleday, 1978; (with Blackwell) *Skyrocket,* Doubleday, 1980.

*   *   *

SHERATON, Neil
See SMITH, Norman Edward Mace

*   *   *

SHERMAN, Charles Bezalel 1896-1971

OBITUARY NOTICE—See index for *CA* sketch: Born January 14, 1896, in Kiev, Russia (now U.S.S.R.); died January 1, 1971, in New York, N.Y. Organization executive, educator, editor, and author. Sherman worked throughout his life with various Jewish organizations, including the Labor Zionist Movement and the Anti-Defamation League. He wrote *Jews and Other Ethnic Groups in the U.S., Labor Zionism in America,* and *The Jew Within American Society: A Study in Ethnic Individuality.* He also wrote pamphlets dealing with Jewish issues and contributed articles to Jewish journals. Obituaries and other sources: *New York Times,* January 3, 1971. (Exact date of death provided by daughter, Selma Sherman Stone.)

*   *   *

SHERMAN, Ingrid 1919-

PERSONAL: Born June 25, 1919, in Cologne, Germany (now West Germany); came to the United States in 1940, naturalized citizen, 1944; daughter of Abraham (a textile merchant) and Gertrude (Schloss) Kugelmann; married Morris Sherman (a high school teacher), May 22, 1943; children: Robert Arnold, Gordon Leroy (deceased). *Education:* Anglo-American Institute of Drugless Therapy, N.D., 1961, D.O., 1962; Science of Truth Institute, Pss.D., 1969, D.D., 1970. *Religion:* Jewish. *Home and office:* Peace of Mind Studio, 102 Courter Ave., Yonkers, N.Y. 10705.

CAREER: Reifenberg & Co., Cologne, Germany, secretary, 1936-38; Renson & Stafford, London, England, secretary, 1939-40; associated with General Stamp Co., New York, N.Y., 1941-45, and with Jan Kiepura and Martha Eggerth, 1958-63; Peace of Mind Studio, Yonkers, N.Y., founder, director, and counselor, 1958—, teacher of metaphysics and poetry therapy, 1963—. High school teacher of foreign languages, music, art, science, and commercial subjects in Yonkers, 1963-70. Lecturer and public speaker; guest on television and radio programs. Chancellor of University of Danzig, 1977.

MEMBER: International Clover Poetry Society (life member), United Poets Laureate International, Centro Studi e Scambi Internazionale, International Federation of Scientific Research Societies, International Platform Association, Educational Society of Parapsychology (honorary member), Association of Social Psychology (district director), Academy of American Poets (co-founder), American Poets Fellowship Society, American Poetry League, National Health Federation, Society of Naturopathic Physicians, ESP Research Association Foundation, Robert Louis Stevenson Society, Academy of Asia, Westchester Philo-Cultural Society (founder).

AWARDS, HONORS: Gold pin from International Academy of Poets and Artists, 1964; poetry awards from United Poets Laureate International, 1967; certificate from Accademia Internazionale Leonardo da Vinci, 1968, for "God's Giving Heart"; diploma from Centro Studi e Scambi Internazionale, 1968, for outstanding cultural activities, gold medal, 1968; N.D. from College of Natural Therapeutics (Ceylon), 1969; Ph.D. from International University of India, 1969, and Academy of Philosophy (Brazil), 1973; D.P.Th. from International University of India, 1970; D.Hum. from International Academy, 1970; D.Litt. from Sovereign Order of Alfred the Great, and from World Academy of Languages and Literature (Brazil), both 1970; Hereditary Paladine and Dame Grande Cross, both from Sovereign Order of Alfred the Great, both 1970; named Grand Naturopath by Alfredian Order of Mercy and Compassion and by Order of St. Veronica, both 1970; patron of honor of Sovereign Order of Alfred the Great, 1970; Right Reverend of Alfredian Order, 1970; Titular Lady Abbess of Alfredian Order, 1970; high honor and estate of knighthood from Sovereign and Royal Order of Piast (Poland), 1970; D.Lib.A. from Greater China Arts College, 1970; order of merit from Greater New York Citizens Society, 1971; distinguished service citation from World Poetry Society, 1972; named baroness by Chancery of Miensk and Byelorussia, 1973; Ps.D. from World University, 1974; D.W.Litt. from University Lincoln (Brazil), 1974; Ms.D. from College of Metaphysics, 1974; D.C.A. from Institute of Comparative Art, 1974; Sc.D. from University of Danzig, 1977; D.Ps.E. from Psycho-Embriologio College, 1978; D.Th. from Collegium and Seminarium Sancti Spirits (Brazil), 1978; D.C.R. from Christian Orthodox Church, 1978; Parapsicologia Emerita from University of Danzig, 1979.

WRITINGS: For Your Reading Pleasure, Spearman, 1964; *Thoughts for You,* Candor Press, 1965; *Gems From Above,* Candor Press, 1966; *Ripples of Wisdom,* Candor Press, 1966; *Poems That Speak of Love,* Candor Press, 1966; *Radiations for Self-Help,* Candor Press, 1967; *Prayer Poems That Heal,* Candor Press, 1967; *Philosophical Tidbits,* Candor Press, 1967; *Strange Patterns,* Candor Press, 1967; *Let Thy Heart Sing,* Academy Internat-Leonardo Da Vinci, 1967; *Face to Face With Nature,* Candor Press, 1969; *Natural Remedies for Better Health,* Naturegraph, 1970, revised edition, 1981; *The Simple Life,* Candor Press, 1977; *In Praise of God,* Candor Press, 1978; *On Healing,* Candor Press, 1978.

WORK IN PROGRESS: As I Recall It, an autobiography.

SIDELIGHTS: Ingrid Sherman wrote: "I help humanity through my spiritual gifts of counseling, healing, and writing. The purpose is brotherhood of man and lasting peace. I have discovered poetry therapy, a new creative healing art, which is today used in hospitals, mental institutions, rehabilitation centers, and by psychologists, psychiatrists, and psychotherapists. I have written a study course for self-help and psychotherapy on poetry therapy and a study course on metaphysics."

AVOCATIONAL INTERESTS: Painting with watercolors, composing (including ten songs that have been recorded).

BIOGRAPHICAL/CRITICAL SOURCES: Westchester County Herald Statesman, May 8, 1976.

* * *

SHERMAN, Patrick 1928-

PERSONAL: Born March 16, 1928, in Newport, England; son of Daniel James and Kathleen (Crowley) Sherman; married Kathleen Maureen Haggerty, September 29, 1951; children: Michael, Susan, Janet, Wendy. *Education:* Attended secondary school in Newport, England. *Home:* 556 Newdale Rd., West Vancouver, British Columbia, Canada. *Office: Vancouver Province,* 2250 Granville St., Vancouver, British Columbia, Canada.

CAREER: Worked for Yorkshire Conservative, Leeds, England, 1949-52; *Vancouver Province,* Vancouver, British Columbia, reporter and political columnist, 1952-65, editor, 1965—, publisher, 1972—. Director of Pacific Press Ltd.; vice-president of Southam, Inc., 1972. Member of board of directors of Westwater Research Centre at University of British Columbia; chairman of Canadian section of International Press Institute. Founding director of Mountain Rescue Group of British Columbia, 1956, and Outward Bound of British Columbia; leader of mountaineering expeditions in North America and South America. *Member:* Alpine Club of Canada, American Alpine Club, Explorers Club, University Club.

WRITINGS: Cloud Walkers, Macmillan, 1964; *Bennett,* McClelland & Stewart, 1965; *Expeditions to Nowhere* (nonfiction), McClelland & Stewart, 1981.

* * *

SHINNIE, Peter Lewis 1915-

PERSONAL: Son of Andrew James; married Margaret Blanche Elizabeth Cloake, 1940 (marriage ended); married Ama Nantwi; children: two sons, one daughter. *Education:* Christ Church, Oxford, B.A., 1938, M.A., 1942. *Politics:* Liberal. *Home:* 908 First Ave. N.W., Calgary, Alberta, Canada T2N 0A5. *Office:* Department of Archaeology, University of Calgary, Calgary, Alberta, Canada.

CAREER: Ashmolean Museum, Oxford, England, assistant keeper, 1945; assistant commissioner for government of Sudan, 1946-48, commissioner for archaeology, 1948-55; director of antiquities for government of Uganda, 1956; University of Ghana, Legon, professor of archaeology, 1958-66; University of Khartoum, Khartoum, Sudan, professor of archaeology, 1966-70; University of Calgary, Calgary, Alberta, professor of archaeology, 1970—. *Military service:* Royal Air Force, 1939-45; served in Africa and Italy; became squadron leader. *Member:* Society of Antiquaries (fellow).

WRITINGS: Medieval Nubia, J. Thornton, 1954; (with D. B. Harden) *Excavations at Soba,* J. Thornton, 1955; (with H. Neville Chittick) *Excavations at Ghazali,* J. Thornton, 1961; *The African Iron Age,* Oxford University Press, 1971; *Debeira West: A Mediaeval Nubian Town,* Aris & Phillips, 1979. Also author of *Ghazali: A Monastery in Northern Sudan,* 1960, and *Meroe: Civilization of the Sudan,* 1967. Contributor to archaeology journals.

WORK IN PROGRESS: A book on the history of Meroitic and medieval times in Sudan; a book on the origins of the Gonja state in Ghana.

SIDELIGHTS: Shinnie wrote: "My basic interest is in the study of Africa at all times in the past and to some extent in the future. I am interested not only in the archaeology of Africa (though that is my main interest) but also in the country's modern political and economic development. I am deeply committed to the idea of African independence. Other interests are the history, language, and literature of modern Greece. I speak Arabic, French, modern Greek, with some Italian, German, Twi, and Nubian."

*   *   *

SHIPLER, David Karr 1942-

PERSONAL: Born December 3, 1942, in Orange, N.J.; son of Guy Emery, Jr. (a journalist) and Eleanor (a teacher; maiden name, Karr) Shipler; married Deborah S. Isaacs (a teacher), September 17, 1966; children: Jonathan Robert, Laura Karr, Michael Edmund. *Education:* Dartmouth College, A.B., 1964; attended Columbia University, 1975. *Religion:* Protestant. *Home:* 21 Hovevei Zion, Jerusalem, Israel. *Office:* c/o *New York Times,* 229 West 43rd St., New York, N.Y. 10036.

CAREER: New York Times, New York, N.Y., news clerk, 1966-68, reporter, 1968-73, foreign correspondent in Saigon, 1973-75, foreign correspondent in Moscow, 1975-79, chief of Moscow bureau, 1977-79, chief of Jerusalem bureau, 1979—. Notable assignments include coverage of corruption in New York's construction industry, war in Indochina, and trials of Moscow dissidents. *Military service:* U.S. Naval Reserve, 1964-66; became lieutenant. *Member:* New York Newspaper Guild, Foreign Press Association of Israel. *Awards, honors:* Award from Society of Silurians, 1971, for distinguished reporting; award from American Political Scientists Association, 1971, for distinguished public affairs reporting; Page One Award from New York Newspaper Guild, 1973, for best local reporting, co-winner of Page One Award from New York Newspaper Guild, and award from New York Chapter of Sigma Delta Chi, all 1973. Contributor to periodicals, including *Atlantic, Harper's, New Republic, McCall's, Nation,* and *New York Times Magazine.*

WORK IN PROGRESS: A book on the Soviet Union.

*   *   *

SHIPLEY, Peter (Samuel) 1946-

PERSONAL: Born December 26, 1946, in Leicester, England; son of Clifford (an engineer) and Mildred (Tomlinson) Shipley; married Fiona Margaret Douglas, July 24, 1971; children: Alexandra, Catriona. *Education:* University of York, B.A. (with honors), 1969. *Home:* 17 Park Ave., Caterham, Surrey, England. *Office:* 32 Smith Sq., London S.W.1, England.

CAREER: Leicester Mercury, Leicester, England, journalist, 1965-66; Ministry of Defense, London, England, civil servant, 1970-76; Conservative Research Department, London, research officer in political affairs, 1977—. Broadcaster for British Broadcasting Corp. (BBC-Radio).

WRITINGS: Revolutionaries in Modern Britain, Bodley Head, 1976; (editor) *Guardian Directory of Pressure Groups,* Wilton House, 1976, 2nd edition, Bowker, 1979. Author of pamphlets for Institute for the Study of Conflict. Contributor to magazines, including *Spectator,* and newspapers.

WORK IN PROGRESS: A novel, publication expected in 1982.

SIDELIGHTS: Shipley told *CA:* "My interest in radical movements began in the late 1960's, when I was a student. It was stimulated by the events of the time, in the protests and demonstrations that were a constant feature of university life, and through my academic work, in studies of the great revolutions of history—English, French, and Russian.

"By about 1973 I felt there was a gap in public knowledge about some of the groups that were active in Britain, such as the Trotskyists, International Socialists, and Anarchists. So I set about studying their writings in as systematic a way as possible. For two years or so I spent much of my spare time attending meetings and tracking down collections of newspapers, pamphlets, etc., to build up a picture of the aims and activities of revolutionary groups in Britain and where they fitted into the world picture of revolutionary movements, Marxist or otherwise. The result was my first book published in 1976.

"Parallel to this, it was apparent that outside the mainstream of conventional parliamentary and party politics new styles of political activity were emerging as a reflection of society's tensions and rapid changes. My second work, *Guardian Directory of Pressure Groups,* focuses on single-issue campaigns and pressure groups, and tries to encompass the many facets of this development.

"Working in these areas holds many fascinations. The subject itself I find absorbing. The psychology of the revolutionary, the twilight world he (or she) so often inhabits and the subterranean stirrings of discontent he attempts to express are a mirror image of everything that passes for 'normality.' But who is to say what is real and what is unreal? In the radical and sometimes extreme movements I have studied many, sometimes contradictory, qualities existing side by side: there is an undoubted idealism, a striving to find new, better ways of conducting human affairs, but there is a dark side too, when ideals as well as ideology harden into an intolerant fanaticism or descend into violence and terror.

"To convey through writing a world many people would prefer to ignore presents its own challenge. The need is for clarity and directness. The research that precedes writing, that exposes the anarchist cell or the fascist clique to the light of day, contains other challenges. It involves much 'detective work,' some danger (when one is caught in the middle of a riot by stone-throwing mobs), and tedium (in plowing through obscure tracts that were conceived in an attic apartment but proclaim world revolution).

"But the bizarre incongruities of the subject, however absorbing, lead in directions other than historical description or political analysis. In the world of the revolutionary there is much drama, a suggestion of the sinister, an earth-moving heroism, and an irresistable urge to destroy as well as to create. There is in short no reality except that which exists in the minds of activists, who see themselves as latter-day Jesuses or Lenins. Perhaps this is why I have turned to fiction as a form in which my accumulated impressions of these complex human currents can be best expressed."

*   *   *

SHOCKLEY, Donald G(rady) 1937-

PERSONAL: Born August 12, 1937, in Birmingham, Ala.; son of Ira B. and Maggie (Davis) Shockley; married Mary Jim Lyons, November 22, 1958; children: Donald Scott, James Ira, Allison Lyons. *Education:* Birmingham-Southern

College, B.A., 1959; Emory University, B.D., 1962; San Francisco Theological Seminary, S.T.D., 1975. *Politics:* Democrat. *Home:* 1751 Vickers Circle, Decatur, Ga. 30030. *Office:* Office of the Chaplain, Emory University, Atlanta, Ga. 30322.

CAREER: Ordained Methodist minister, 1963; Birmingham-Southern College, Birmingham, Ala., chaplain, 1964-72; University of Redlands, Redlands, Calif., chaplain, 1972, associate provost, 1977-78, vice-president for academic affairs, 1978-79; Emory University, Atlanta, Ga., chaplain, 1979—. *Member:* National Association of College and University Chaplains, American Academy of Religion.

WRITINGS: Free, White, and Christian, Abingdon, 1975; *The Light Shines in Darkness,* Graded Press, 1976. Contributor of articles and reviews to magazines, including *Christian Century, Commonweal, Religion and Life,* and *Southern Living,* and newspapers.

WORK IN PROGRESS: Private Prayers in Public Places; Finding the Seeker: Meditations From Contemporary Literature.

SIDELIGHTS: Shockley commented: "*Free, White, and Christian* is an autobiographical and sympathetic response to black consciousness and black liberation theology. I am interested in social justice, and some of my articles have focused on prisons and equal rights. Lately I've struggled to express fresh perspectives on spirituality and the quest for personal meaning."

*   *   *

SHONE, Ronald   1946-

PERSONAL: Born July 15, 1946, in Liverpool, England; son of George Richard (a boatswain) and Ellen (McGuire) Shone. *Education:* University of Hull, B.Sc., 1968; University of Essex, M.A., 1969. *Home:* 41 Chisholm Ave., Causewayhead, Stirling FK9 5QU, Scotland. *Office:* Department of Economics, University of Stirling, Stirling FK9 4LA, Scotland.

CAREER: University of Sheffield, Sheffield, England, lecturer in economics, 1971-73, Esmee Fairbairn research fellow, 1974-76; University of Stirling, Stirling, Scotland, lecturer in economics, 1976—. Lecturer at London School of Economics and Political Science, University of Wales, University of York, University of Edinburgh, Haile Selassie I University, and University College, Cardiff.

WRITINGS: The Pure Theory of International Trade, Macmillan, 1972; *Microeconomics: A Modern Treatment,* Academic Press, 1975; (with Frank Neal) *Economic Model Building,* Macmillan, 1976; *Applications in Intermediate Microeconomics,* Martin Robertson, 1981. Contributor of articles and reviews to economic journals.

WORK IN PROGRESS: Self Hypnosis and Its Non-Medical Uses, publication by Thorsons Publishers Ltd. expected in 1982; *Applications in the Balance of Payments,* Martin Robertson, 1982.

SIDELIGHTS: Ronald Shone commented: "All my recent writings have a common approach, whether they are technical material in the areas of economics or on hypnosis. My aim is to apply theory to come to some understanding of the real world, including ourselves. *The Applications in Intermediate Microeconomics* takes this approach, as does my more recent work in the area of international monetary economics. In the same vein, the book on self hypnosis applies theories of right and left hemispheres of the brain to understand and, more particularly, to use in helping oneself. I hope

to extend this work by developing uses of reactive visualization along with hypnotic technique."

*   *   *

SHORE, Norman
See SMITH, Norman Edward Mace

*   *   *

SHORE, Sidney   1921-1981

OBITUARY NOTICE: Born September 13, 1921, in Philadelphia, Pa.; died of cancer, May 19, 1981, in Penn Valley, Pa. Civil engineer, artist, educator, and author of more than eighty articles and reports. Shore helped research electronic computers and solar energy. He taught at Princeton University and the University of Pennsylvania. Obituaries and other sources: *Who's Who in America,* 40th edition, Marquis, 1978; *American Men and Women of Science,* 14th edition, Bowker, 1979; *New York Times,* May 20, 1981.

*   *   *

SHORT, Clarice   1910-1977

OBITUARY NOTICE—See index for *CA* sketch: Born March 30, 1910, in Ellinwood, Kan.; died December 15, 1977. Educator and poet. Short wrote *The Old One and the Wind* and contributed to literary journals, including *Victorian Poetry, Modern Language Notes,* and *Western Humanities Review.* (Date of death provided by cousin, Dorothy Calvert.)

*   *   *

SHORT, James R.   1922(?)-1980

OBITUARY NOTICE: Born c. 1922 in Gastonia, N.C.; died of cancer, August 16, 1980, in Williamsburg, Va. Historian, educator, and author. Short served as general editor of publications for the Colonial Williamsburg Foundation of Virginia. He also taught at the University of Tennessee and worked as historian for the Virginia State Library. Short wrote many articles on Virginia's history and edited *Historic Preservation Today,* a collection of essays included in *The Journal of Major George Washington.* Obituaries and other sources: *Washington Post,* August 17, 1980.

*   *   *

SHRIMSLEY, Bernard   1931-

PERSONAL: Born January 13, 1931, in London, England; son of John and Alice (Rose) Shrimsley; married Norma Jesse Alexandra Porter, August 2, 1952; children: Amanda Alicia. *Education:* Educated in England. *Agent:* John Farquharson Ltd., Bell House, 8 Bell Yard, London WC2A 2JU, England. *Office:* Associated Newspapers, Carmelite House, London EC4Y 0JA, England.

CAREER: Sunday Express, Manchester, England, deputy editor, 1958-61; *Daily Mirror,* editor in Manchester, 1961-64, assistant editor in London, England, 1964-68; *Liverpool Daily Post,* Liverpool, England, editor, 1968-69; *Sun,* London, deputy editor, 1969-72, editor, 1972-75; *News of the World,* London, editor, 1975-80; Associated Newspapers, London, editor-designate of projected new Sunday newspaper, 1981—. *Military service:* Royal Air Force, 1949-51; became sergeant.

WRITINGS: The Candidates (novel), Secker & Warburg, 1968.

Co-author of "The Candidates," a play, first broadcast by BBC-Radio, February, 1977.

WORK IN PROGRESS: A historical novel set in the early seventeenth century.

BIOGRAPHICAL/CRITICAL SOURCES: Simon Regan, *Rupert Murdoch,* Routledge & Kegan Paul, 1975.

* * *

SHTEMENKO, Sergei Matveyevich 1907-1976

PERSONAL: Born in 1907, in Uriupinsk, Russia (now U.S.S.R.); died April 23, 1976. *Education:* Moscow Artillery College, graduated, 1926; Military Academy of Mechanization and Motorization, graduated, 1937; Military Academy of the General Staff, graduated, 1938.

CAREER: Soviet Army, career officer, 1926-76, platoon leader, division chief of staff, and regimental deputy chief of staff, 1926-37, commander of armored battalion, 1937-38, member of general staff of ground forces and military fleet, 1938-42, head of Operations Division, chief of staff, 1943-48, chief of general staff of ground forces and military fleet and deputy minister of Armed Forces, 1948-52, chief of staff of Soviet forces in Germany, 1953, chief of staff and first deputy chief of staff, 1953-62, head of main administration of army intelligence, 1957, supreme commander of Soviet forces in Hungary, 1958-60, deputy commander of Volga military district, first deputy commander of Transcaucasian military district, and head of Tbilisi garrison, 1960-65, chief of staff of land forces, 1962-64, deputy chief of general staff of ground forces and military fleet, 1965-68, first deputy chief of staff, 1968-76, chief of Warsaw Pact forces, 1968-76; became general. *Awards, honors:* Order of Lenin; Order of Red Banner; Order of Suvarov, first class; Order of Kutuzov, first class.

WRITINGS—In English translation: *General'nyi shtab v grody voiny,* Voyenizdat, 1968, reprinted in two volumes, translation by Robert Daglish published as *The Soviet General Staff at War, 1941-1945,* Progress Publisher, 1970, reprinted as *The General Staff in the War Years,* two volumes, U.S. Joint Publications Research Service, 1975, and as *The Soviet General Staff at War: Soviet Forces in the Anti-Hitler War,* Beekman, 1975; *The Last Six Months: Russia's Final Battles With Hitler's Armies in World War II* (translated from Russian by Guy Danicls), Doubleday, 1977.

Other writings: *Novyi zakon i voinskaia sluzhba,* Voyenizdat, 1968; *Sovetskie sukhoputnye voiska,* DOSAAF, 1968; *Marele Stat-Mazhor yn anii rezboiuiui,* Kartya Moldovenyaskeh, 1969.*

* * *

SHULMAN, Milton 1913-

PERSONAL: Born September 1, 1913, in Toronto, Ontario, Canada; son of Samuel (a merchant) and Ethel Shulman; married Drusilla Beyfus (a writer and editor), 1956; children: Jason, Alexandra, Nicola. *Education:* University of Toronto, B.A., 1934; studied at Osgoode Hall, 1934-37. *Home:* 51 Eaton Sq., Flat G, London S.W.1, England.

CAREER: Barrister in Toronto, Ontario, 1937-40; *Evening Standard,* London, England, film critic, 1948-58, theatre critic, 1953—, television critic, 1964-73, commentator on arts and current affairs, 1972—. Executive producer for Granada Television, 1958-62, including "Head On," "Animal Story," and "Who Goes Next?"; assistant controller of programs for Rediffusion Television, 1962-64, including "Decision"; broadcast "Stop the Week" on BBC-Radio, 1976-81. *Military service:* Canadian Army, Armoured Corps and Intelligence, 1940-46; served in France; became major; mentioned in dispatches. *Member:* Hurlingham Club, Savile Club. *Awards,*

honors: Hannen Swaffer Award from International Press Corporation, 1966, for "best critic of the year."

WRITINGS: Defeat in the West, Secker & Warburg, 1947, 2nd edition, 1949, reprinted, Coronet, 1973, Dutton, 1948, revised edition, Ballantine, 1968; *How to Be a Celebrity,* Reinhardt & Evans, 1950; *Carl Foreman's "The Victors"* (based on *The Human Kind* by Alexander Baron), Dell, 1963 (published in England as *The Victors,* Hamilton & Co., 1963); *Kill Three* (novel), Random House, 1967; (with Herbert Kretzmer) *Every Home Should Have One; or, The Goldilocks Conspiracy* (novel), Hodder & Stoughton, 1970; *The Least Worst Television in the World,* Barrie & Jenkins, 1973; *The Ravenous Eye: The Impact of the Fifth Factor,* Cassell, 1973, revised edition, Coronet, 1975.

Children's books: *Preep, the Little Pigeon of Trafalgar Square,* Random House, 1964; *Preep in Paris,* Collins, 1967; *Preep and the Queen,* Random House, 1970.

Author of a social and political affairs column in *Daily Express,* 1973-75; film critic for *Sunday Express,* 1948-58, book critic, 1957-58; film critic for *Vogue,* 1975—. Contributor to periodicals, including *New York Times, Saturday Evening Post, Vogue,* and *Encounter.*

WORK IN PROGRESS: The Coward Tapes, interviews with Noel Coward; collected film criticism.

SIDELIGHTS: Shulman told an *Evening Standard* interviewer: "The trouble is, I can do my work standing on my head. I find everything too easy. Perhaps if I aspired to something harder, I would be better, but one is so terrified of failure." *Avocational interests:* Tennis, modern art.

BIOGRAPHICAL/CRITICAL SOURCES: Evening Standard, March 13, 1967; *Books and Bookmen,* May, 1967.

* * *

SHULTZ, William J(ohn) 1902-1970

OBITUARY NOTICE—See index for *CA* sketch: Born April 25, 1902, in Brooklyn, N.Y.; died May 23, 1970, in New Harbor, Me. Educator, consultant, and author of books on business and finance. Shultz's book *Taxation of Inheritance* received the Hart Schaffner & Marx publication award. Also included among his works are *The Humane Movement in the United States, 1910-1922, Marketing in Action,* and *Problems in Credits and Collections.* Obituaries and other sources: *Who Was Who in America,* 5th edition, Marquis, 1973.

* * *

SHYRE, Paul 1929-

PERSONAL: Born March 8, 1929, in New York, N.Y.; son of Louis Philip and Mary (Lee) Shyre. *Education:* Attended University of Florida, 1945-46; graduated from American Academy of Dramatic Arts, 1947. *Home:* 162 West 56th St., New York, N.Y. 10019. *Agent:* Brigid Aschenberg, International Creative Management, 40 West 57th St., New York, N.Y. 10019.

CAREER: Professional theatrical director and producer, 1953—; actor, 1956—. Artistic director of Fred Miller Theater, Milwaukee, Wis., 1962-63. Professor at Cornell University, 1980. *Military service:* U.S. Army, 1944-45. *Member:* Actors Equity Association, Screen Actors Guild, American Federation of Television and Radio Artists, Society of Stage Directors and Choreographers, Dramatists Guild, Directors Guild of America, Writers Guild of America. *Awards, honors:* Obie Award from *Village Voice,* 1957, for "U.S.A."; Vernon Rice Award from New York Drama Desk, 1958, for "Pictures in the Hallway"; creative arts award from Brandeis University, 1958, for achievement in theatre; nomination for Antoinette Perry Award (Tony) from American Theatre Wing, 1958, for "I Knocked at the Door"; Boston University established a collection of papers in his name, 1965.

WRITINGS: Pictures in the Hallway (two-act; adaptation of work by Sean O'Casey; first produced on Broadway at The Playhouse, September, 1956), Samuel French, 1958; *U.S.A.* (two-act; adaptation of work by John Dos Passos; first produced Off-Broadway at Martinique Theatre, October, 1959), Samuel French, 1960; *I Knocked at the Door* (two-act; adaptation of work by O'Casey; first produced on Broadway at Belasco Theater, September, 1957), Dramatists Play Service, 1960; *Drums Under the Windows* (two-act; adaptation of work by O'Casey; first produced Off-Broadway at Cherry Lane Theater, December, 1960), Dramatists Play Service, 1960; *The Child Buyer* (two-act; adaptation of work by John Hersey; first produced Off-Broadway at Garrick Theater, October, 1964), Samuel French, 1966; *A Whitman Portrait* (two-act; adaptation of work by Walt Whitman; first produced Off-Broadway at Gramercy Arts Theater, December, 1966), Dramatists Play Service, 1967; "An Unpleasant Evening With H. L. Mencken" (two-act; adaptation of work by Mencken), first produced in Washington, D.C., at Ford's Theatre, November, 1972; "Will Rogers' U.S.A." (two-act; adaptation of work by Will Rogers), first produced on Broadway at Helen Hayes Theatre, September, 1973; "Blasts and Bravos: An Evening With H. L. Mencken" (two-act; adaptation of work by Mencken; solo performance), first produced Off-Broadway at Cherry Lane Theatre, October, 1975; "Paris Was Yesterday" (two-act; adaptation of work by Janet Flanner), first produced in New York City at Harold Clurman Theatre, January, 1980; "Ah, Men" (two-act), first produced in New York City at South Street Theatre, May, 1981.

Author of "Carl Sandburg," first broadcast by WNET-TV, December, 1981.

WORK IN PROGRESS: "An Evening With Art Buchwald," a revue with music.

* * *

SICKER, Philip 1951-

PERSONAL: Born August 16, 1951, in Covington, Ky.; son of Julius P. (an accountant) and Betty (Quinn) Sicker. *Education:* University of Cincinnati, B.A., 1973; University of Virginia, M.A., Ph.D. *Home:* 201 West 77th St., No. 17H, New York, N.Y. 10024.

CAREER: Fordham University, Bronx, N.Y., professor of English, 1978—. *Member:* Modern Language Association of America.

WRITINGS: Love and the Quest for Identity in the Fiction of Henry James, Princeton University Press, 1979.

* * *

SIDNEY, Kathleen M(arion) 1944-

PERSONAL: Born October 19, 1944, in Paterson, N.J.; daughter of Paul (a jeweler) and Kathleen (Mulgrue) Sidney. *Education:* Fairleigh Dickinson University, B.A., 1966; graduate study at Kean College of New Jersey. *Residence:* Nova Scotia.

CAREER: Teacher at schools in Paterson, N.J., 1971-78; writer, 1978—.

WRITINGS: Michael and the Magic Man, Berkley Publishing, 1980. Work represented in anthologies, including *Orbit 17,* edited by Damon Knight, Harper, 1975; *Orbit 18,* edited

by Knight, Harper, 1976; *Clarion,* edited by Kate Wilhelm, Berkley Publishing, 1977.

WORK IN PROGRESS: A novel.

SIDELIGHTS: Kathleen Sidney commented: "If mainstream fiction were a mansion with an infinite number of rooms, then science fiction would be what happens when we step outside. I like both environments but can most often be found in the vicinity of an open door, peering out or peering in."

* * *

SIEMON, Jeff 1950-

PERSONAL: Surname is pronounced *See*-man; born June 2, 1950, in Rochester, Minn.; son of Glenn (an ophthalmologist) and Isobel (Jones) Siemon; married Dawn Donnelly, January 21, 1973; children: Jeff, Maile, Kelley. *Education:* Stanford University, B.A., 1972. *Religion:* Christian. *Home:* 5401 Londonderry Rd., Edina, Minn. 55436. *Office:* Minnesota Vikings, 7110 France Ave. S., Edina, Minn. 55435.

CAREER: Minnesota Vikings, Edina, Minn., middle linebacker, 1972—. Chairman of executive committee of Pro Athletes Outreach. *Member:* Fellowship of Christian Athletes (chairman of state board of directors), Delta Tau Delta.

WRITINGS: (With Jim Klobucher) *Will the Vikings Ever Win the Super Bowl?,* Harper, 1976. Contributor to Christian magazines.

SIDELIGHTS: Siemon commented: "The motivation for writing my book came from sportswriter Jim Klobucher. My involvement in the Christian ministry is the primary focus of my life. My interest at Stanford was Reformation history, of which I continue to read voraciously." *Avocational interests:* Hawaii, fishing, hunting, golf, tennis.

* * *

SIEVERS, W(ieder) David 1919-1966

OBITUARY NOTICE—See index for *CA* sketch: Born September 23, 1919, in St. Louis, Mo.; died March, 1966. Actor, stage manager, radio writer and director, educator, and author. He wrote *Freud on Broadway: A History of Psychoanalysis and the American Drama* and *Directing for the Theatre.* Sievers also contributed articles to theatre journals. (Date of death provided by California State University.)

* * *

SILLS, Jennifer
See LEWIS, Stephen

* * *

SILVERMAN, Burt(on Philip) 1928-

PERSONAL: Born June 11, 1928, in Brooklyn, N.Y.; son of Morris Daniel (an accountant) and Anne (a bookkeeper; maiden name, Firstenberg) Silverman; married Helen Worthman, March 4, 1957 (divorced April, 1969); married Claire Guss (a psychologist), June 12, 1969; children: Robert Arthur, Karen Lila. *Education:* Attended Pratt Institute, 1937-39, and Art Students League, 1941-49; Columbia University, B.A., 1949. *Politics:* "Left independent." *Religion:* Jewish. *Home and office:* 324 West 71st St., New York, N.Y. 10023.

CAREER: Artist, 1949—, with solo and group shows all over the United States; illustrator, 1959—. Instructor at School of Visual Arts, New York, N.Y., 1962-64; gives private art classes. Commissions for Metropolitan Opera, Princeton University, Mobil Oil Corp., Exxon, Columbia Records, and

Columbia Broadcasting System; work exhibited at Davis Gallery, Kenmore Galleries, Genesis Gallery, Sindin Gallery, University of Utah, National Academy of Design, Wadsworth Athenaeum, and American Academy of Arts and Letters. *Military service:* U.S. Army, 1951-53.

MEMBER: National Academy of Design (member of governing council, 1980-83), American Watercolor Society, Artists Equity Association, Graphic Artists Guild. *Awards, honors:* Art prizes from National Academy of Design, 1961, 1966, and 1967; Henry W. Ranger Purchase Prize, 1965; Benjamin Altman Figure Prize, 1969; Dillard Collection purchase prize for "Art on Paper" from University of North Carolina, 1966; purchase prize from Portsmouth Museum, 1979; figure prize from Pastel Society of America, 1977; gold medal from American Watercolor Society, 1979; prizes from American Watercolor Society, 1980 and 1981.

WRITINGS: (With Louise Bernikow) *Abel,* Simon & Schuster, 1967; *Portfolio of Drawings,* Kenmore, 1968; *Painting People,* Watson-Guptill, 1977.

Illustrator: S. Carl Hirsch, *Globe for the Space Age,* Viking, 1963; Wilhelm Hauff, *The Caravan,* Crowell, 1964; Rudyard Kipling, *Phantoms and Fantasies* (short stories), Doubleday, 1965; Phyliss Bentley, *The Adventures of Tom Leigh* (Junior Literary Guild selection), Doubleday, 1966; P. Bentley, *Oath of Silence,* Doubleday, 1967. Contributor of illustrations to magazines, including *McCall's, Redbook, Psychology Today,* and *Sports Illustrated.* Contributor of articles to art journals and magazines, including *Art News, Book World, Life, Fortune, Esquire, Time, Newsweek,* and *New Yorker.*

WORK IN PROGRESS: On Watercolor (tentative title), "an art historical approach to watercolor and selective use of the medium, with conceptual and practical problems in six demonstrations from work in the studio and outdoors," publication by Watson-Guptill expected in 1982.

SIDELIGHTS: "Almost all of my writing has been about my art," Silverman told *CA,* "and occasionally the larger issue of aesthetics, especially those critical conventions surrounding the modernist period of history. Specifically it has involved an attempt to define, both for myself and hopefully others, a viable concept of realism. *Painting People* was conceived partly to present my particular views of realism and to provide a historical footnote to the 1950's and 1960's when the New York School (non-objective or abstract art) dominated the consciousness of the art world. I wanted to establish, or rather document, the existence of a realist underground, of which my group was a small, but I think influential, part. Since the early 1970's, all kinds of realisms have surfaced, creating an atmosphere of pluralism in a once serenely homogeneous international art community. This has dismayed many art historians and critics who thereby lost their hold on the nation's aesthetic perceptions. Tom Wolfe's essay 'The Painted Word,' while written off as lacking real scholarship by the New York critical establishment, was nevertheless a comprehensive and witty attack on the *fundamental* aesthetic contradictions of modernism and a harbinger of change in the art world.

"I am primarily a visual artist, but I enjoy writing and find it most satisfying as a format for my particular prejudices in regard to art.

"In 1967 I was commissioned by the French National Tourist Bureau to make drawings of historic sites in France for a series of travel ads. This took me to nine provinces in twenty-five days and produced over a hundred drawings, in what turned out to be a rather exhausting and bewildering junket. I went on a similar commission for *Esquire* in 1966, that time

to make paintings of eight countries in the South Pacific and the Far East for a travel piece.

"In 1967 I prepared for a trip to Moscow as part of my research for the book on the celebrated Russian agent, Colonel Rudolph Abel. I had known Abel in his cover *persona,* Emil Goldfuss. I was trying to re-establish contact with him after ten years, an attempt that ended in failure—largely because of Russian xenophobia, if not because of an exaggerated notion of security.

"Since 1972 I have been going to Italy every summer for work-vacations. I go to Pietrasanta, a small town on the Mediterranean which is part of a historically interesting art and artisan community around Carrara, and one which developed out of the nearby marble quarries that were first opened up by Michelangelo in the sixteenth century. Now sculptors from all over the world come to Pietrasanta, both for the stone and the numerous sculpture foundries which abound in the town. This town has become special to me as a kind of second home and as a source of much of my painting of the last few years."

AVOCATIONAL INTERESTS: "I have played folk guitar for many years, but largely gave that up in response to other small passions, at the moment making models of antique ships."

BIOGRAPHICAL/CRITICAL SOURCES: American Artist, October, 1964, June, 1971; Joseph Singer, *How to Paint Portraits in Pastel,* Watson-Guptill, 1972; *American Artist,* July, 1981.

* * *

SILVERMAN, Judith 1933-

PERSONAL: Born August 26, 1933, in Brooklyn, N.Y.; daughter of David and Shirley (Maltz) Marks; married Myron Silverman (a teacher), July 3, 1955; children: Brian Scott. *Education:* Brooklyn College (now of the City University of New York), B.A., 1960; Pratt Institute, M.L.S., 1963. *Residence:* Roslyn Heights, N.Y. *Office:* R. R. Bowker Co., 1180 Avenue of the Americas, New York, N.Y. 10036.

CAREER: Fairchild Publications, New York City, secretary, 1954-56; associated with New York City Board of Education, Brooklyn, N.Y., 1956-62; Brooklyn Public Library, Brooklyn, senior librarian, 1964-68; Queens Borough Public Library, Jamaica, N.Y., librarian, 1973-76; Baldwin Public Library, Baldwin, N.Y., assistant director, 1976-80; R. R. Bowker Co., New York City, writer and consultant, 1970—. *Member:* American Library Association, New York Library Association, Nassau County Library Association, Beta Phi Mu.

WRITINGS: Index to Young Readers' Collective Biographies, Bowker, 1970, 3rd edition published as *Index to Collective Biographies for Young Readers,* 1979.

WORK IN PROGRESS: Who Filed Frances?, a mystery.

* * *

SIMMONS, Anthony 1922-

PERSONAL: Born December 16, 1922, in London, England; son of Joseph (a shopkeeper) and Miriam (Corb) Simmons; children: Jonathan, Daniel, Mathew, Luke. *Education:* London School of Economics and Political Science, London, LL.B., 1947. *Religion:* Jewish. *Agent:* I.C.M., 22 Grafton St., London, W.1, England. *Office:* West One Film Producers Ltd., 2 Lower James St., London W.1, England.

CAREER: Called to the Bar at Lincoln's Inn, 1948; screenwriter, film producer, and director, 1950—. *Military service:*

British Army, Royal Signal Corps, 1945-46; became lieutenant. *Member:* Writers Guild of Great Britain, Association of Cine and Television Technicians. *Awards, honors:* Grand Prix from Venice Film Festival, 1953, for short film "Sunday by the Sea"; award from Society of Film and Television Arts, 1962, for screenplay "Dispute"; Grand Prix from Locarno Film Festival, 1965, for screenplay "Four in the Morning"; Prix Femina (Belgium), 1974, for screenplay "The Optimists of Nine Elms"; international Emmy Award from Academy of Television Arts & Sciences, 1979, for screenplay "On Giant's Shoulders."

WRITINGS: The Optimists of Nine Elms (novel), Methuen, 1973, Pantheon, 1975.

Screenplays: "The Passing Stranger," Interdependent Film Distributors, 1954; "Four in the Morning," West One Film Producers, 1965; "The Optimists of Nine Elms," Sagittarius Productions, 1973; "On Giant's Shoulders," BBC, 1979; "Green Ice," Universal, 1981; "Naughty Girls," Southern Pictures Ltd., 1981. Also author of "Dispute" (documentary), 1962, "Black Joy," 1977, and "Sunday by the Sea."

Radio plays: "Two Days in Love," first broadcast by British Broadcasting Corporation (BBC), 1975; "Oil Rig," first broadcast by BBC, 1976.

WORK IN PROGRESS: A screenplay for BBC, production expected in 1982.

SIDELIGHTS: Simmons told *CA:* "Because of the nature of the film industry, a lot of one's work is never published. 'The Optimists of Nine Elms' was a story I originally wrote for Buster Keaton, but it was shelved after two years of preproduction. Rather than see the story vanish, I rewrote it as a novella, which was then published and later became the name of a film I directed with Peter Sellers. Though in recent years I have written for the media, particularly radio, my main love is still being an 'auteur.' I am always preparing myself for making a movie."

*   *   *

SIMON, Robert A. 1897(?)-1981

OBITUARY NOTICE: Born c. 1897 in New York, N.Y.; died April 27, 1981, in New York, N.Y. Writer best known for his music reviews in *New Yorker* from 1925 to 1948. Simon wrote librettos for operas such as "Garrick" and "Rehearsal Call." According to the *New York Times,* Simon's writings include "a detective story, spoofs of the music world and a collection of 'Bronx Ballads.'" Obituaries and other sources: *The ASCAP Biographical Dictionary of Composers, Authors, and Publishers,* 3rd edition, American Society of Composers, Authors, and Publishers, 1966; *New York Times,* April 28, 1981.

*   *   *

SIMPSON, O(renthal) J(ames) 1947-

PERSONAL: Born July 9, 1947, in San Francisco, Calif.; son of Jimmie (a chef) and Eunice (a hospital administrator; maiden name, Durton) Simpson; married Marguerite Whitley (an artist), June 24, 1968 (divorced, 1980); children: Arnelle, Jason, Aaren (deceased). *Education:* Attended San Francisco City College, 1966-67; University of Southern California, B.A., 1969. *Residence:* Los Angeles, Calif. *Office:* 11661 San Vincente Blvd., Los Angeles, Calif. 90049.

CAREER: Buffalo Bills, Orchard Park, N.Y., running back, 1969-77; San Francisco 49'ers, San Francisco, Calif., running back, 1977-79. Actor in motion pictures, including "The Towering Inferno," 1974, "Killer Force," 1975, "Cassandra

Crossing," 1976, "Firepower," 1978, "Goldie and the Boxer" (TV), 1978, and "Goldie and the Boxer Go to Hollywood" (TV), 1980. Executive producer of Orenthal Productions, 1978—. Television sports commentator for Summer Olympics, Montreal, Quebec, 1976, and "Wide World of Sports" (ABC-TV); guest on television variety shows, specials, and dramatic series. *Awards, honors:* Named All-American collegiate football player, 1965-68; named outstanding player in Rose Bowl game, 1967; Walter Camp Memorial Trophy, Maxwell Memorial Trophy, and Heisman Trophy for collegiate football player of the year from New York Downtown Athletic Club, all 1968; named Man of the Year by *Sport* magazine, 1969; named College Player of the Decade by American Broadcasting Co. (ABC-Sports), 1970; named to American Football Conference All-Star team, 1970, and to Pro Bowl team, 1972-76; named Most Valuable Player in American Football Conference, 1972, 1973, 1975, and National Football League, 1973; Hickok Belt for professional athlete of the year, 1973.

WRITINGS: (With Pete Axthelm) *O. J.: The Education of a Rich Rookie,* Macmillan, 1970.

SIDELIGHTS: As a child, O. J. Simpson had to wear leg braces because he suffered from a calcium deficiency. The children in his neighborhood nicknamed him "pencil legs," never suspecting that he would one day be a star running back in both collegiate and professional football.

Simpson began his collegiate career at San Francisco City College, where he scored fifty-four touchdowns in two years, including six in a single game. He continued his record-setting pace at the University of Southern California, rushing for 3,295 yards and thirty-four touchdowns in twenty-two games. After the final game of the 1968 season, USC Coach John McKay praised Simpson by saying, "This is not only the greatest player I ever had, but the greatest anyone ever had." *Sport* magazine also called him the greatest running back in the history of college football, and in 1969 they chose Simpson as their Man of the Year. It was the first time the honor had ever been awarded to a college football player. In his last year as a collegiate player Simpson carried the ball an average of thirty-five times a game, gaining a record 1,709 yards and a Heisman Trophy.

Simpson's professional football career was as illustrious as his collegiate career. In 1969 he signed with the Buffalo Bills, and during the eight years he spent with the club he continued making football history. From 1972 through 1976 he rushed for over one thousand yards per season, and he was named annually to the Pro Bowl team. In 1975 he was both rushing and scoring leader in the American Football Conference. Six times between 1975 and 1976, he rushed two hundred yards or more in a single game; his game high was 273 yards. He retired in 1979, two years after he was traded to the San Francisco 49'ers.

People magazine credits Hertz Rent-a-Car advertisements with making Simpson one of the most recognizable faces in America, pointing out that more people have watched him sprint across crowded airports on television commercials than ever saw him make his famous runs down a football field. "The Hertz commercials gave me more national recognition in one year than I had received after playing football for fourteen years," Simpson commented. Whatever the source of his growing fame and fortune, by 1979 Simpson's estimated annual income was over two million dollars, and he had successfully made the transition from retired athlete to media celebrity.

BIOGRAPHICAL/CRITICAL SOURCES: Life, October 27, 1967; *Sports Illustrated,* November 20, 1967, December 25, 1967, July 14, 1969, August 25, 1969, November 26, 1979; *Look,* October 15, 1968; *Ebony,* December, 1968; John Durant and Les Elter, *Highlights of College Football,* Hastings House, 1970; Bill Libby, *Heroes of the Heisman Trophy,* Hawthorn, 1973; *People,* June 12, 1978, April 2, 1979; *New York Times Magazine,* July 30, 1978; *Sport,* November, 1978.

*   *   *

SIMPSON, Robert (Wilfred Levick) 1921-

PERSONAL: Born March 2, 1921, in Leamington, England; son of Robert Warren and Helena Hendrika (Govaars) Simpson; married Bessie Fraser, April 26, 1946. *Education:* Westminster City School, D.Mus., 1951. *Politics:* Socialist. *Religion:* None. *Home:* Cedar Cottage, Chearsley, Aylesbury, Buckinghamshire HP18 0DA, England.

CAREER: British Broadcasting Corp. (BBC), London, England, music producer, 1951-80; composer and writer, 1980—. *Member:* Incorporated Society of Musicians, Royal Astronomical Society (fellow). *Awards, honors:* Carl Nielsen Gold Medal, 1956; Medal of Honor from Bruckner Society of America, 1962, for contributions to studies on Anton Bruckner.

WRITINGS: Carl Nielsen, Symphonist, 1865-1931, Dent, 1952, revised edition, Kahn & Averill, 1979, Taplinger, 1979; (editor with Oliver Press) *Guide to Modern Music on Records, 1958,* Anthony Blond, 1958; (editor) *The Symphony,* Penguin, Volume I: *Haydn to Dvorak,* 1966, Volume II: *Elgar to the Present Day,* 1967, reprinted as *Mahler to the Present Day,* David & Charles, 1972; *The Essence of Bruckner: An Essay Towards the Understanding of His Music,* Gollancz, 1967, 2nd edition, 1977, Chilton, 1968; *Beethoven Symphonies,* BBC Publications, 1970, University of Washington Press, 1971; *The Proms and Natural Justice,* Kahn & Averill, 1981.

Compositions include seven symphonies, eight string quartets, one violin concerto, one piano concerto, and numerous other musical pieces.

WORK IN PROGRESS: Symphony No. 8.

SIDELIGHTS: Simpson wrote: "I resigned from my job in 1980 in protest at the degeneration of the British Broadcasting Corp. as a result of its decision to compete with commercial broadcasting on its own terms. Writing books is a sideline; my chief work is composition of music."

*   *   *

SINISGALLI, Leonardo 1908-1981

OBITUARY NOTICE: Born in 1908 in Potenza, Italy; died in 1981 in Rome, Italy. Physicist and poet. Sinisgalli co-published the magazine *Literary Italy* and founded the magazine *The Civilization of Machines.* His poetry was collected in several volumes, including *Geometric Notebook.* Sinisgalli also worked with renowned scientist Enrico Fermi. Obituaries and other sources: *Cassell's Encyclopaedia of World Literature,* revised edition, Morrow, 1973; *AB Bookman's Weekly,* April 27, 1981.

*   *   *

SIRC, Ljubo 1920-

PERSONAL: Born April 19, 1920, in Kranj, Slovenia, Yugoslavia; came to Great Britain in 1956, naturalized citizen, 1963; son of Franjo (an industrialist) and Zdenko (a pharmaceutical chemist; maiden name, Pirc) Sirc; married Susan

Powell (a lecturer in German literature), September 18, 1976; children: Nadia. *Education:* University of Ljubljana, Dip.Iur., 1943, graduate study, 1946-47; University of Fribourg, Dr.Rer.Pol., 1960. *Home:* 41A Westbourne Gardens, Glasgow G12, Scotland. *Office:* Department of Political Economy, University of Glasgow, Adam Smith Building, Glasgow G12 8RT, Scotland.

CAREER: Government of Slovenia, Yugoslavia, editor and translator in daily news section of Press Office, 1945; Yugoslav News Agency, Ljubljana, Yugoslavia, editor and translator, 1945; arrested and imprisoned in Yugoslavia, 1947-54; free-lance translator, 1954-55; British Broadcasting Corp., Monitoring Service, Reading, England, Serbo-Croat and Russian monitor, 1957-58; University of Dacca, Dacca, East Pakistan (now Bangladesh), visiting lecturer in economics, 1960-61; Institute of Economic Affairs, London, England, researcher, 1961-62; University of St. Andrews, Dundee, Scotland, lecturer in economics, 1962-65; University of Glasgow, Glasgow, Scotland, lecturer, 1965-68; senior lecturer in economics, 1968—. Translator and announcer (in Slovene and Serbo-Croat) for British Broadcasting Corporation's European Service, 1956—. *Military service:* Member of underground resistance movement in Yugoslavia, 1941-43; served in National Liberation Army of Yugoslavia, 1944-45. *Member:* Liberal International, National Association of Soviet and East European Studies, Association of University Teachers, Scottish Economic Society, Mont Pelerin Society.

WRITINGS: Kommunistische Agrarpolitik und Asien (title means "Communist Agricultural Policy and Asia"), Schweizerisches Ost-Institut, 1963; *Nesmisel in smisel* (autobiography; title means "Nonsense and Sense"), Pika Print, 1968; *Economic Devolution in Eastern Europe,* Praeger, 1969; *Outline of International Trade: Commodity Flows and Division of Production Between Countries,* Weidenfeld & Nicolson, 1973, Wiley, 1974; *Outline of International Finance: Exchange Rates and Payments Between Countries,* Wiley, 1974; *The Yugoslav Economy Under Self-Management,* St. Martin's, 1979.

Contributor: Arthur Selden, editor, *Advertising in a Free Society,* Institute of Economic Affairs (London, England), 1962; Seldon, editor, *Communist Economy Under Change,* Deutsch, 1963; Leszek Kolakowski and Stuart Hampshire, editors, *The Socialist Idea: A Reappraisal,* Weidenfeld & Nicolson, 1974; Seldon, editor, *Can Workers Manage?,* Institute of Economic Affairs, 1977; *Le Liberalism de Karl Marx a Milton Friedman,* Editions de la Revue Politique et Parlementaire, 1977; A. Clayre, editor, *The Political Economy of Cooperation and Participation: A Third Sector,* Oxford University Press, 1980; I. Jeffries, editor, *The Industrial Enterprise in Eastern Europe,* Praeger, 1981.

Contributor to *Collier's Encyclopedia.* Contributor of articles and reviews to scholarly journals and newspapers.

WORK IN PROGRESS: Industrial Democracy in Europe, for the Institutum Europaeum (Brussels); *Economic Malaise 1960-1980;* English translation of autobiography, *Nesmisel in smisel;* contributing chapter to *Human Rights in Yugoslavia,* edited by O. Gruenwald and K. Rosenblum-Cale.

SIDELIGHTS: Sirc told *CA:* "In 1941 my home town was occupied by Germans; my family had to escape to Italian-occupied Lujbljana to avoid deportation, and all their property was confiscated. In Ljubljana I joined an underground group that belonged to the Liberation Front together with the Communists. In 1942 the Communists were expelled, because they opposed a 'decree' that anybody fighting the Germans outside the Liberation Front was to be considered a traitor and be liquidated. In 1943 I escaped to Switzerland via Italy to report to the London exile government what was happening at home. When this government concluded an agreement with Marshal Titos' National Committee, I made my way back to Yugoslavia and enrolled in the National Liberation Army under Marshal Tito's command.

"In 1947 I was arrested by the Communist secret police and tried because of my connection with the leaders of democratic opposition and my friendly relations with Western representatives. I was tried with fourteen other defendants and sentenced to death, but the sentence was commuted to twenty years forced labor. After Stalin expelled Tito from the Cominform in 1948, the Yugoslav regime changed its tack and improved its relations with the West, so that I was finally released from prison six years later, but even then not without pressures that I should work for the Communist secret police. All I could do was to escape to Italy, where I made my way to Britain.

"I will not deny that I am very critical of East European economies (and dictatorships), but I maintain that I have painstakingly substantiated all my arguments and that I am not biased in my professional work in spite of my terrible experience. But while Communist economies both of the Soviet and of the Yugoslav type are disintegrating (the crisis there is incomparably worse that in the West), I would be foolish to say that they are functioning well.

"My teaching has so far not been concerned with Eastern Europe but has specialized in international trade and international finance. I became particularly interested in customs unions and monetary unions, both in conjunction with the European community. My sympathies are all with a confederated Europe, but I think that it should be primarily a political union, and that attempts at premature economic harmonization will do more harm than good.

"I would dearly love to have the English version of my memoirs published, but so far I have not had any success. It surprises me no end, since the deputy editor of the *Daily Telegraph* of London, for instance, wrote to me: 'In order to avoid hurting feelings I often say I have read what I have not had time to do. In this case, I started to read and could not stop—this material is absolutely fascinating, even if it does here and there need a little skilled editing, as what does now?' By now I have become sufficiently paranoid to think that the cult of the good Communist dictator, Tito, has reached such proportions in the West that nobody wants to know the truth about this Oriental despot."

Paul M. Johnson, writing in *Prospective,* commented that *The Yugoslav Economy Under Self-Management* "is intended both as an outline history of evolving Yugoslav economic institutions and policies and as an empirical contribution to the ongoing debate about the economic viability of workers' self-management. The book makes useful contributions in both respects, although the polemical style and occasionally one-sided presentation of complex issues will likely offend unnecessarily those readers most in need of an honest confrontation with the points he raises." In a review for the *Economic Journal,* D. A. Dyker observed: "In terms of the breadth and depth of source material used, and the range of topics covered, this is perhaps the most sustained research effort on the Yugoslav economy to have appeared for some time.... The book is full of real insights at the level of specific problem areas. The treatment of the complex of issues relating to investment, banking and money supply, and debts is particularly illuminating."

BIOGRAPHICAL/CRITICAL SOURCES: Economist, February 16, 1980; *Prospective,* May, 1980; *Economic Journal,* September, 1980; *Journal of Economic Literature,* March, 1981.

* * *

SKAER, Peter M(acKall) 1953-

PERSONAL: Born September 22, 1953, in San Rafael, Calif.; son of Peter Harry and Helena (MacKall) Skaer; married Hisae Yabe (an Asian import representative), April 2, 1978. *Education:* University of California, Davis, B.A. (linguistics), 1976, B.A. (English), 1976; graduate study at University of Washington, Seattle, 1979—. *Home:* 5502 15th N.E., No. 7, Seattle, Wash. 98105. *Office:* Department of Linguistics, University of Washington, GN-40, Seattle, Wash. 98195.

CAREER: Aoyama Gakuin, Shibuya, Tokyo, instructor in American culture, drama, and speech, 1976-79; University of Washington, Seattle, instructor in English as a second language and linguistics, 1979—. Also worked as English program coordinator at University of Tokyo Hospital and Taiyo Kobe Bank.

WRITINGS: Thinking and Thought in English, Eiyusha, 1981; *Knock Knock* (nonfiction), Eiyusha, 1981; *Creativity in English,* Eiyusha, 1982.

WORK IN PROGRESS: Research on language and cognition, "with emphasis on brain processing and respective cerebral dominances in the retention of phonological units compared to ideographic or serial units."

SIDELIGHTS: Skaer wrote: "I am interested in studying the activity of learning and acquiring meaning. Primarily, I am hopeful of using whatever insights I might gain from such a study in the aim of providing better learning situations for the acquisition of any type of information system. This study is done with language as the central focus, for I believe that the patterns developed to describe language closely resemble the imaginable patterns of the brain and its interworkings. Having lived in Japan for several years as an English teacher, I speak Japanese fluently, though reading is somewhat less proficient. Because of the scarcity of adequate educational resources, I found myself impelled to write most of my own educational materials for the Japanese students. *Thinking and Thought in English* and *Creativity in English* are condensations of my writings, and are published at this moment solely for Japanese readership in Japan. *Knock Knock* is a nonfictional work based loosely on my various impressions and thoughts from living in the huge expanses of Tokyo."

* * *

SKELTON, Roger
See HORN, Peter (Rudolf Gisela)

* * *

SKOLSKY, Sidney 1905-

PERSONAL: Born May 2, 1905, in New York, N.Y.; son of Louis and Mildred (Arbeit) Skolsky; married Estelle Lorenz, August 27, 1928; children: Nina Skolsky Marsh, Steffi Skolsky Grant. *Education:* Attended New York University, 1925. *Office:* New York Post, 75 West St., New York, N.Y.

CAREER: Press agent, 1925-29; *New York Daily News,* New York City, author of Broadway column, 1929-33; *New York Post,* New York City, author of Hollywood column, 1933—. Producer of "The Jolson Story," a film released by Columbia Pictures in 1946, and "The Eddie Cantor Story," a film released by Warner Bros., 1953; producer of "Hollywood, the

Golden Era," first televised in 1961, and "Hollywood and the Movies"; actor in film "Don't Make Waves."

WRITINGS: Times Square Tintypes: Being Typewriter Caricatures of Those Who Made Their Names Along the Not So Straight and Very Narrow Path of Broadway, Ives Washburn, 1930; *Don't Get Me Wrong—I Love Hollywood,* Putnam, 1975.

Co-author of film "The Daring Young Man," Twentieth Century-Fox, 1937; author of television program "Hollywood, the Golden Years," 1970. Author of a column distributed by United Features Syndicate; author of "From a Stool at Schwabs," a column in *Photoplay,* and "Tintypes," a weekly column in *New York Sun.*

BIOGRAPHICAL/CRITICAL SOURCES: Editor and Publisher, June 25, 1949; *Time,* June 4, 1954; *Best Sellers,* March, 1976.*

*   *   *

SLIVE, Seymour   1920-

PERSONAL: Born September 15, 1920, in Chicago, Ill.; son of Daniel and Sonia (Rapoport) Slive; married Zoya Gregorevna Sandomirsky, June 29, 1946; children: Katherine, Alexander, Sarah. *Education:* University of Chicago, A.B., 1943, Ph.D., 1952. *Home:* 1 Walker Street Pl., Cambridge, Mass. 02138. *Office:* Fogg Art Museum, Harvard University, Cambridge, Mass. 02138.

CAREER: Oberlin College, Oberlin, Ohio, instructor in fine arts, 1950-51; Pomona College, Claremont, Calif., assistant professor of art and chairman of department, 1952-54; Harvard University, Cambridge, Mass., assistant professor, 1954-57, associate professor, 1957-61, professor of fine arts, 1961—, Gleason Professor of Fine Arts, 1973—, chairman of department, 1968-71, director of Fogg Art Museum, 1975—. Exchange professor at University of Leningrad, 1961; Ryerson Lecturer at Yale University, 1962; Slade Professor of Fine Art at Oxford University, 1972-73. Member of board of trustees of Solomon R. Guggenheim Foundation, 1978—. *Military service:* U.S. Naval Reserve, active duty as commanding officer of small craft, 1942-46; served in Pacific theater; became lieutenant junior grade.

MEMBER: American Academy of Arts and Sciences (fellow), Renaissance Society of America, College Art Association of America (member of board of directors, 1958-62, 1965-69), Karel van Mander Society (honorary member), Dutch Society of Sciences (foreign member). *Awards, honors:* Fulbright fellow in the Netherlands, 1951-52, 1959-60; Guggenheim fellow, 1956-57, 1979-80; M.A. from Harvard University, 1958, and Oxford University, 1972; officer of Order of Orange Nassau, 1962.

WRITINGS: Rembrandt and His Critics, 1630-1730, Nijhoff, 1953; *Drawings of Rembrandt: With a Selection of Drawings by His Pupils and Followers,* two volumes, Dover, 1965; (with Jakob Rosenberg) *Dutch Art and Architecture, 1600-1800,* Penguin, 1966, revised edition (with Rosenberg and E. H. ter Kuile), 1972; *Frans Hals,* three volumes, Phaidon, 1970-74; *Jacob van Ruisdael* (catalog of exhibition), Abbeville Press, 1981. Contributor to journals.

*   *   *

SLOMA, Richard Stanley   1929-

PERSONAL: Born March 14, 1929, in Chicago, Ill.; married Dee Schennum, October 27, 1951; children: Lynn Catherine, Karen Gail. *Education:* Northwestern University, Sc.B., 1950; University of Chicago, M.B.A., 1962; DePaul University, J.D., 1979. *Home:* 325 Talcott Park, Park Ridge, Ill. 60068. *Office:* Qonaar Corp., 751 Pratt Blvd., Elk Grove Village, Ill. 60007.

CAREER: International Telephone & Telegraph, president of division; Bastian-Blessing, Inc., president and chief executive officer; Golconda Corp., president of division, executive vice-president and chief operating officer, and president and chief executive officer; Qonaar Corp., Elk Grove Village, Ill., executive vice-president and chief operating officer, 1977—. Guest lecturer at Northwestern University, Loyola University, Chicago, Ill., New York University, and Lake Forest College; conducts management seminars. *Military service:* U.S. Air Force, pilot; became first lieutenant.

WRITINGS: No-Nonsense Management (Fortune Book Club selection), Macmillan, 1977; *How to Measure Managerial Performance* (Fortune Book Club selection), Macmillan, 1979. Contributor to business and management journals.

WORK IN PROGRESS: No-Nonsense Government.

*   *   *

SMALLEY, Beryl   1905-

PERSONAL: Born June 3, 1905, in Cheadle, England. *Education:* St. Hilda's College, Oxford, M.A.; Victoria University of Manchester, Ph.D. *Home:* 5c Rawlinson Rd., Oxford, England.

CAREER: University of London, Royal Holloway College, London, England, assistant lecturer, 1931-35; Cambridge University, Girton College, Cambridge, England, research fellow, 1935-40; Oxford University, Oxford, England, temporary assistant in department of Western manuscripts at Bodleian Library, 1940-43, tutor in history, 1943-69, Ford's Lecturer, 1966-67, vice-principal of St. Hilda's College, 1957-69, emeritus fellow, 1969—. *Member:* British Academy (fellow), University Women's Club. *Awards, honors:* D.Litt. from University of Southampton, 1974.

WRITINGS: The Study of the Bible in the Middle Ages, Clarendon Press, 1941, 2nd edition, Philosophical Library, 1952; *English Friars and Antiquity in the Early Fourteenth Century,* Basil Blackwell, 1960, Barnes & Noble, 1961; (editor and author of introduction) *Trends in Medieval Political Thought,* Barnes & Noble, 1965; (editor with J. R. Hale and J.R.L. Highfield) *Europe in the Late Middle Ages,* Northwestern University Press, 1965; *The Becket Conflict and the Schools: A Study of Intellectuals in Politics,* Rowman & Littlefield, 1973; *Historians in the Middle Ages,* Thames & Hudson, 1974, Scribner, 1975.

Contributor to *Transactions of the Royal Historical Society,* Series IV, Volume XXX, 1948; *Mediaeval and Renaissance Studies,* Volume III, 1954; and *Archivum Fratrum Praedicatorum,* Volume XXVI, 1956. Also contributor to history journals.

BIOGRAPHICAL/CRITICAL SOURCES: Economist, November 23, 1974.*

*   *   *

SMALLEY, Stephen Stewart   1931-

PERSONAL: Born May 11, 1931, in London, England; son of Arthur Thomas (a civil servant) and May Elizabeth Selina (Kimm) Smalley; married Susan Jane Paterson (a lecturer), July 13, 1974; children: Jovian James Thomas. *Education:* Jesus College, Cambridge, B.A., 1955, M.A., 1958; attended Ridley Hall, Cambridge, 1955-56, 1957-58; Eden Theological

Seminary, B.D., 1957. *Home:* 35 Morningside, Coventry, West Midlands CV5 6PD, England. *Office:* Cathedral Offices, Pelham Lee House, Priory Row, Coventry CV1 5ES, England.

CAREER: Ordained minister of Church of England, 1958; assistant curate of St. Paul's Church of England in London, 1958-60; Cambridge University, Cambridge, England, dean and chaplain of Peterhouse, 1960-63; University of Ibadan, Ibadan, Nigeria, lecturer, 1963-67, senior lecturer in religious studies, 1967-69; Victoria University of Manchester, Manchester, England, lecturer, 1970-77, senior lecturer in New Testament studies, 1977; Coventry Cathedral, Coventry, England, canon residentiary and precentor, 1977—. Select preacher at Cambridge University, 1963-64; examining chaplain to bishop of Norwich, 1971—; member of Archbishop of Canterbury's Doctrine Commission. *Military service:* British Army, Royal Army Educational Corps, 1949-51; became captain. *Member:* Studiorum Novi Testamenti Societas, Tyndale Fellowship for Biblical Research. *Awards, honors:* Ph.D. from Cambridge University, 1979.

WRITINGS: Building for Worship: Biblical Principles in Church Design, Hodder & Stoughton, 1967; *Heaven and Hell: A Study of Last Things,* Daystar (Ibadan), 1968; (editor and contributor) *Work,* Africa Christian Press, 1968; *The Spirit's Power: The Teaching of the Bible About the Holy Spirit,* Africa Christian Press, 1972; (editor with Barnabas Lindars, and contributor) *Christ and Spirit in the New Testament: Essays in Honor of Professor C.F.D. Moule,* Cambridge University Press, 1973; *John: Evangelist and Interpreter,* Paternoster, 1978.

Contributor: H. D. Merchant, editor, *Encounter With Books: A Guide to Christian Reading,* Inter-Varsity Press, 1970; Rudolf Pesch and Rudolf Schnackenburg, editors, *Jesus und der Menschensohn: Fuer A. Voegtle* (title means "Jesus and the Son of Man"), Herder, 1975; I. H. Marshall, editor, *New Testament Interpretation,* Paternoster, 1977; D. H. Hagner and M. J. Harris, editors, *Pauline Studies in Honor of Professor F. F. Bruce,* Eerdmans, 1980.

Contributor to *The Illustrated Bible Dictionary* (formerly *New Bible Dictionary*), *Baker's Dictionary of Christian Ethics,* and *The New International Dictionary of the Christian Church.* Contributor to numerous theology journals.

WORK IN PROGRESS: A Commentary on the Greek Text of the Johannine Epistles, publication by Word Books expected in 1983; *A Commentary on the Greek Text of the Fourth Gospel,* completion expected in 1988.

SIDELIGHTS: Smalley told *CA:* "I have always loved words, both spoken and written. As a teenager, I spent hours reading great literature aloud: long passages of Chaucer, complete plays of Shakespeare, whole chapters of Jane Austen, and so on. Not surprisingly, I was also devoted to the stage: playing then and since multifarious roles, from the name-part in 'Hamlet' to the lead in 'Hadrian VII' and the mayor in Ibsen's 'Enemy of the People.' From my college days until recently, I have also directed amateur dramatic productions.

"Thus developed my great love of English literature: my first subject at university. When, after two years at Cambridge, I changed to theology, my literary sensibilities remained with me; and specializing in the New Testament gave me a welcome opportunity to bring my training in English to bear on the structure and interpretation of the biblical text.

"My Christian sympathies are evangelical, but over the years, and especially as a result of living in other countries than my own, I have learned to listen to those of other per-

suasions and indeed to those of other faiths and to those without faith. My concentration on biblical subjects, and in particular my exploration into the earliest forms of the Jesus tradition, so far as these can be recovered from the New Testament, is complemented by my wife's professional interest in historical and contemporary theology from a more 'catholic' standpoint.

"It has always been one of my concerns to encourage young people of university age (and others) to fulfill their own vocations in the world: both within the infrastructures of the church and beyond. (Thus my pastoral links with students in Africa, my responsibilities as the warden of a hall of residence in Manchester University, and my interest in the selection and training of men for the ministry of the church, especially as a selector and inspector for the Anglican Advisory Council for the Church's Ministry.)

"Since my conversion to Christianity as a university student, I have consistently combined the work of an Anglican priest with that of a teacher and writer. I am at my happiest when researching and writing, and write best when my wife is literally or metaphorically 'over my shoulder'!"

AVOCATIONAL INTERESTS: Literature, music, drama.

*   *   *

SMITH, Alson Jesse   1908-1965

OBITUARY NOTICE—See index for *CA* sketch: Born August 12, 1908, in Danbury, Conn.; died May 17, 1965. Methodist minister, lecturer, and author. His books include *Live All Your Life, A View of the Spree,* and *Men Against the Mountains: Jedediah Smith and the South West Expedition of 1826-1829.* Smith's biography of William Wesley Van Orsdel, *Brother Van,* was made into a motion picture by Republic Pictures. Obituaries and other sources: *Who Was Who in America,* 5th edition, Marquis, 1973.

*   *   *

SMITH, C. Busby
See SMITH, John (Charles)

*   *   *

SMITH, Desmond   1927-

PERSONAL: Born September 7, 1927, in Manchester, England; son of Arthur Phillip and Lilian (Pinegar) Smith; married Marjaleena Jappinen (a writer); children: Charly Elena, Nicholas Eino Desmond. *Education:* Victoria University of Manchester, B.Sc., 1952; attended Trinity College, Cambridge. *Religion:* Church of England. *Home:* 110 Pricefield Rd., Toronto, Ontario, Canada M4W 1Z9. *Agent:* Peter Shepherd, Harold Ober Associates, Inc., 40 East 49th St., New York, N.Y. 10017. *Office:* Canadian Broadcasting Corp., 354 Jarvis St., Toronto, Ontario, Canada M4W 1Z9.

CAREER: Television producer and writer for Canadian Broadcasting Corp., 1953-55, and National Broadcasting Co., 1955-57; American Broadcasting Co., New York City, news producer, 1961-67; Columbia Broadcasting System, New York City, senior news producer, 1968-73; Canadian Broadcasting Corp., television director in Montreal, Quebec, 1973-77, news producer in Toronto, Ontario, 1977—. Writer and producer for National Broadcasting Co. *Military service:* Royal Air Force, navigator, 1943-46. *Member:* Canadian Producers Association, Writers Guild. *Awards, honors:* Ohio State Award.

WRITINGS: Smith's Moscow, Knopf, 1974, 3rd edition, 1980 (published in England as *Smith's Guide to Moscow,* J. Cape, 1976); *Smith's Montreal,* Knopf, 1976; *The Rise of Mass Media in America,* MIT Press, in press. Contributor of more than one hundred articles to magazines and newspapers, including *Nation, TV Guide, Harper's, Reader's Digest,* and *Economist;* contributing editor of *Panorama.*

WORK IN PROGRESS: The Information Storm.

SIDELIGHTS: Smith wrote: "I came to Canada in 1953 as a journalist, joined Canadian television 'at the creation,' then left in the mid-1950's to work in New York. In the late 1950's I lived and worked as a journalist in Copenhagen, Denmark. I joined ABC-News as a documentary producer, covered the Indonesian revolution in the last days of Sukarno, went to Vietnam and covered the entire war, went to Moscow and produced two documentaries, 'Ivan Ivanovich' and 'Comrade Soldier,' the first extensive look at the Red Army.

"I joined CBS-News, where my major stories included the Berkeley riots, Black Panthers, civil rights, the Vietnam War, the Chicago Democratic Convention in 1968, and the counterculture.

"In recent years much of my writing has reflected my concern with the break-up of mass media and the emergence of micromedia, a profound and revolutionary change in the way Americans will get their news in the future. Also, the shift from a national economy based on the production of goods to an economy increasingly based on information—the so-called 'information society.' An optimist about the United States, I believe that the American Century will begin in the year 2000. No nation on earth is as well-equipped for the age of communications as this one. But how we all shall live in an age when we 'trade' information is a most extraordinary puzzle. Writing, thinking, and talking about the knowledge-based society seems to me the most useful task in the years ahead."

* * *

SMITH, Ernest A(llyn) 1911-1977

OBITUARY NOTICE—See index for *CA* sketch: Born July 6, 1911, in New York, N.Y.; died May 28, 1977. Educator and author of *American Youth Culture.* (Date of death provided by Hunter College.)

* * *

SMITH, George (Henry) 1922-

PERSONAL: Born October 27, 1922, in Vicksburg, Miss.; son of George Henry and Maria Eve (Poche) Smith; married M. Jane Deer (a writer), February 10, 1950. *Education:* University of Southern California, B.A., 1950. *Politics:* Social Democrat. *Religion:* Agnostic. *Home and office:* 4113 West 180th St., Torrance, Calif. 90504. *Agent:* John Boswell Associates, 45 East 51st St., New York, N.Y. 10022.

CAREER: Free-lance writer, 1950—. *Military service:* U.S. Navy, Quartermaster Corps, 1942-45. *Member:* Science Fiction Writers of America, Authors Guild, Authors League of America, U.S. Naval Institute.

WRITINGS—Novels, except as noted: *Satan's Daughter,* Epic Books, 1961; *Scourge of the Blood Cult,* Epic Books, 1961; *1976: Year of Terror,* Epic Books, 1961; *The Coming of the Rats,* Pike Books, 1961; *Doomsday Wing,* Monarch, 1963; *The Unending Night,* Monarch, 1964; *The Forgotten Planet,* Avalon, 1965; *The Four Day Weekend,* Belmont-Tower, 1966; *Druids' World,* Avalon, 1967; *Who Is Ronald Reagan?* (nonfiction), Pyramid Publications, 1968; *Witch*

Queen of Lochlann, New American Library, 1969; *Kar Kaballa: King of the Gogs,* Ace Books, 1969.

Martin Luther King, Jr. (nonfiction), Lancer Books, 1971; *The Second War of the Worlds,* DAW Books, 1976; *The Island Snatchers,* DAW Books, 1978; *The Devil's Breed,* Playboy Press, 1980. Also author of *The Rogues* and *The Firebrands.* Contributor to magazines.

WORK IN PROGRESS: Novels about World War II, for Pocket Books; novels for "American Freedom Series," Playboy Press.

SIDELIGHTS: Smith commented: "I sold my first science fiction story in 1951, my first science fiction novel in 1961. Since then I have written a great variety of fiction and nonfiction, most recently historical novels. I majored in history in college and over the years have accumulated an extensive library which has proven invaluable in research for various projects."

AVOCATIONAL INTERESTS: Collecting, casting, and painting toy soldiers.

* * *

SMITH, George O(liver) 1911-1981

OBITUARY NOTICE—See index for *CA* sketch: Born April 9, 1911, in Chicago, Ill.; died May 27, 1981, in Rumford, N.J. Engineer and author. Smith, an electronics engineer, worked for the International Telephone and Telegraph Corporation from 1959 to 1974. His experience working with radar and guided missiles in World War II made Smith the first technically qualified science-fiction writer in the areas of satellites and space communication. For his work Smith received the National Defense Council Certificate of Merit in 1945 and the Fandom Award at the 1980 World Science-Fiction Convention. His writings include *Highways in Hiding, Fire in the Heavens, Hellflower,* and *Mathematics: The Language of Science.* Obituaries and other sources: *New York Times,* June 4, 1981.

* * *

SMITH, Henry Peter 1910-1968

OBITUARY NOTICE—See index for *CA* sketch: Born March 22, 1910, in Willard, Kan.; died April 23, 1968, in Boston, Mass. Educator and author of books on psychology. Among his works are *Psychology in Teaching Reading* and *Psychology in Teaching.* Obituaries and other sources: *American Men and Women of Science: The Social and Behavioral Sciences,* 12th edition, Bowker, 1973. (Exact date of death provided by wife, Zona Wilson Smith.)

* * *

SMITH, James Morton 1919-

PERSONAL: Born May 28, 1919, in Bernie, Mo.; married Kathryn Hegler, 1945; children: Melissa Jane, James Morton, Jr. *Education:* Southern Illinois University, B.Ed., 1941; University of Oklahoma, M.A., 1946; Cornell University, Ph.D., 1951. *Office:* Winterthur Museum, Winterthur, Del. 19735.

CAREER: Butler University, Indianapolis, Ind., instructor in history, 1946-48; Cornell University, Ithaca, N.Y., research associate in industrial and labor relations, 1951-52; Ohio State University, Columbus, instructor in history, 1952-55; College of William and Mary, Williamsburg, Va., lecturer in history, 1955-66; Cornell University, professor of American history, 1966-70; University of Wisconsin—Madison, professor of American history, 1970-76; University of Delaware, Newark, professor of American history, 1976—. Visiting professor at Duke University, 1962-63, and University of Wisconsin, Madison, 1964-65; lecturer at colleges and universities. Publications editor of Institute of Early American History and Culture, 1955-66; director of Coe Foundation Institute in American Studies at Hampton Institute, summer, 1966; director of Winterthur Museum, 1976—. Member of International Commission for the History of Representative and Parliamentary Institutions; chairman of council of Institute of Early American History and Culture, 1970-76, and Wisconsin Humanities Committee, 1971-74; executive vice-president of Historic Sites Foundation, Circus World Museum, 1970-76; vice-president of Museum Council of Philadelphia, 1978; member of executive committee of National Conference of State Historic Preservation Officers, 1974-75, 1976-77; Wisconsin state preservation officer, 1970-76. Member of international center committee of Advisory Council on Historic Preservation, 1976—; member of national advisory council of Girl Scouts of the United States of America, 1978—; member of Wisconsin History Foundation; member of board of directors of Menominee Indian Historical Museum, 1971-76, and board of governors of Northeast Museums Conference, 1978—; consultant to National Endowment for the Humanities and New Jersey History Commission.

MEMBER: Association of Art Museum Directors, American Historical Association, Organization of American Historians, National Trust for Historic Preservation, American Association for State and Local History (member of council), American Association of Museums (member of council), American Antiquarian Society, Southern Historical Association, Historic Madison. *Awards, honors:* Grants from Institute of Early American History and Culture, 1952, Social Science Research Council, 1953, American Philosophical Society, 1954, and Fund for the Republic, 1955; grants from Thomas Jefferson Memorial Foundation, 1959, American Council of Learned Societies, 1960, and National Endowment for the Humanities, 1971, 1974; Guggenheim fellowship, 1960-61.

WRITINGS: Freedom's Fetters: The Alien and Sedition Laws and American Civil Liberties, Cornell University Press, 1956; (with Paul L. Murphy) *Liberty and Justice: A Historical Record of American Constitutional Development,* Knopf, 1958, reprinted in two volumes, Volume I, 1965, Volume II, 1968; (editor) *Seventeenth-Century America: Essays in Colonial History,* University of North Carolina Press, 1959; *George Washington: A Profile,* Hill & Wang, 1969; (editor) *The Constitution: The Origins of American Federalism,* Harper, 1971; *Politics and Society in American History,* two volumes, Prentice-Hall, 1973.

Member of board of editors of "The Documentary History of the Ratification of the Constitution," "The Papers of John Marshall," 1972-76, "The Papers of George Mason," "The Papers of James Madison," and "Black Abolitionist Editorial Project." Contributor of articles and reviews to scholarly journals. Past member of board of editors of *Journal of Southern History, William and Mary Quarterly,* and *Journal of Legal History.*

WORK IN PROGRESS: Reign of Witches: The Kentucky and Virginia Resolutions; The Jefferson-Madison Letters, 1778-1826.

SMITH, John (Charles)   1924-
(C. Busby Smith)

PERSONAL: Born April 5, 1924, in High Wycombe, England; son of John Albert and Mabel (Busby) Smith. *Education:* Attended school in Gerrard's Cross, England. *Home:* 3 Adelaide Ct., 15 Adelaide Crescent, Hove, Sussex, England.

CAREER: Christy & Moore Ltd. (literary agents), London, England, director, 1946-58, managing director, 1959-71, advisory director, 1972—. *Awards, honors:* Adam International Review Prize, 1952, for "Snow: A Meditation"; Second Borestone Mountain Prize, 1971, for "Thoughts From Torcello."

WRITINGS—Poems: (Under pseudonym C. Busby Smith) *Gates of Beauty and Death,* Fortune Press, 1948; *The Dark Side of Love,* Hogarth Press, 1952; *The Birth of Venus,* Hutchinson, 1954; *Excursus in Autumn* (Poetry Book Society choice), Hutchinson, 1958; *A Letter to Lao Tze,* Hart-Davis, 1961; *A Discreet Immorality* (Poetry Book Society recommendation), Hart-Davis, 1965; *Five Songs of Resurrection,* privately printed, 1967; *Four Ritual Dances,* privately printed, 1968; *Twentieth-Century Love Poems,* Studio Vista Ltd., 1969; *Entering Rooms* (Poetry Book Society choice), Chatto & Windus, 1973.

Nonfiction: *The Arts Betrayed,* Universe Books, 1978.

Children's books: (Editor) *My Kind of Verse,* Burke Publishing, 1965; *The Broken Fiddlestick,* Longman, 1971; (editor) *My Kind of Rhymes,* Burke Publishing, 1972; *The Early Bird and the Worm* (poems), Burke Publishing, 1972.

Editor: (With William Kean Seymour) *The Pattern of Poetry: The Poetry Society Verse-Speaking Anthology,* Burke Publishing, 1963, F. Watts, 1967; *Modern Love Poems,* Studio Vista, 1966; (with Seymour) *Happy Christmas,* Westminster, 1968; *Jan Le Witt,* Routledge & Kegan Paul, 1971, Library Press, 1972.

Plays: "The Mask of Glory" (three-act), first produced in Gerrards Cross, at Memorial Centre, 1956; "Mr. Smith's Apocalypse: A Jazz Cantata" (two parts), first produced in Farnham, Surrey, England, at Farnham Festival.

Work represented in anthologies, including *New Poems,* 1954, and *Mavericks,* 1957. Editor of *Poetry Review,* 1962-65.

WORK IN PROGRESS: The Stirring, a cantata, with music by Michael Garrick; *New Songs for Farinelli,* a book of poems; *Catherine Cookson: A Biographical Portrait.*

SIDELIGHTS: John Smith wrote: "I started writing poetry when I was in my late teens and have been writing ever since, though looking back I see that my output has been slowing down during the past ten years or so. My major interest has always been lyric poetry, though I realize that, along with most poets, I seem to grow less lyrical with age! Although poets should take no notice of fashion or critical denigration or acclaim, it is rare that one can swim entirely against the stream, and the whole development in art has been toward complexity on the one hand, so as to form a kind of exclusive elite, and on the other an attempt to be widely popular, which has resulted for the most part in an excessive vulgarity. Pop songs are not poetry; neither are Campbell soup cans art. Much of what I feel about the development in the arts during the century is expressed in my book *The Arts Betrayed.* And while there are many things in it which I would now like to change, by and large I am prepared to stand by those opinions.

"As regards my writing habits, I am pretty spasmodic and lazy; what talent I have is a minor one, and I am not goaded by the extreme urgency that drives great artists throughout their lives. In a world of such inhumanity and surrounded by so much violence it is often difficult to see what even the purest gem of poetry can do to help atone.

"I remember once talking to a remarkable man who had at that time published only one fine book; then silence for many years. 'When are you going to publish another book?' I asked. 'When I have something else to say that I think is worth saying,' he replied. I think that answer influenced me more than any other I have heard. I would like to write more, but poems cannot be manufactured. In my forthcoming collection, *New Songs for Farinelli*, there is a long poem which is more complex than anything I have attempted so far, and it is also in many ways more 'modern.' It suggests, at the end, that the important poem is the reader's individual life. That may explain why I have been moving away from the arts for some time. It seems to me that, as in the world at large, there is a great deal of shouting going on—'listen to me, listen to me'—but not all that much worth listening to. I recall Yeats's great poem, ''The Second Coming,'' perhaps the most important poetic statement of our time, with the prophetic words, 'The best lack all conviction, while the worst/ Are full of passionate intensity.'

"The above may indicate a nature of discontent or despair, but that would be very far from the truth, I am an exceedingly lucky man in this torn world, having food, drink, clothing, a warm and comfortable home, and above all many loves and friends. Who knows, with equal good fortune I may in the future have more poems."

*   *   *

SMITH, John Edwin   1921-

PERSONAL: Born May 27, 1921, in Brooklyn, N.Y.; son of Joseph Robert and Florence Grace (Dunn) Smith; married Marilyn Blanche Schulhof, August 25, 1951; children: Robin Dunn, Diana Edwards. *Education:* Columbia University, A.B., 1942, Ph.D., 1948; Union Theological Seminary, New York, N.Y., B.D., 1945. *Home:* 300 Ridgewood Ave., Hamden, Conn. 06517. *Office:* Department of Philosophy, Yale University, 1562 Yale Station, New Haven, Conn. 06520.

CAREER: Vassar College, Poughkeepsie, N.Y., instructor in religion and philosophy, 1945-46; Barnard College, New York City, assistant professor of philosophy and religion, 1946-52; Yale University, New Haven, Conn., assistant professor, 1952-56, associate professor, 1956-59, professor of philosophy, 1959—, Clark Professor of Philosophy, 1972—, chairman of department, 1961-64. Guest professor at University of Heidelberg, 1955-56; visiting professor at University of Michigan, 1958, and Union Theological seminary, New York City, 1959; Dudleian Lecturer at Harvard University, 1960; lecturer at University of Munich, 1961; Suarez Lecturer at Fordham University, 1963; public lecturer at King's College, London, 1965; Aquinas Lecturer at Marquette University, 1967; Warfield Lecturer at Princeton Theological Seminary, 1970; Fulbright Lecturer at Kyoto University, 1971; Sprunt Lecturer at Union Theological Seminary, Richmond, Va., 1973; Mead-Swing Lecturer at Oberlin College, 1975; H. Richard Niebuhr Lecturer at Elmhurst College, 1977; Merrick Lecturer at Ohio Wesleyan University, 1977; Roy Wood Sellars Lecturer at Bucknell College, 1978; Alain Locke Lecturer at Howard University, 1980. Member of board of directors of Pierre Lecomte du Nouy Foundation, 1967—; director of National Humanities Institute, 1977-78.

MEMBER: Culinary Institute of America (member of local board of directors), American Philosophical Association (Eastern Division, vice-president, 1980, president, 1981), American Theological Society (president, 1967-68), Metaphysical Society of America (president, 1970-71), Hegel Society of America (president, 1971), Pierce Society. *Awards, honors:* M.A. from Yale University, 1959; named honorary alumnus of Divinity School at Harvard University, 1960; LL.D. from University of Notre Dame, 1964; American Council of Learned Societies fellowship, 1964-65.

WRITINGS: Royce's Social Infinite: The Community of Interpretation, Liberal Arts Press, 1950; (translator) Richard Kroner, *Kant's Weltanschauung*, Chicago University Press, 1956; (editor) Jonathan Edwards, *Religious Affections*, Volume II, Yale University Press, 1959; *Reason and God: Encounters of Philosophy With Religion*, Yale University Press, 1961; *The Spirit of American Philosophy*, Oxford University Press, 1963; *Philosophy of Religion*, Macmillan, 1965; (contributor) Paul Ramsey, editor, *Religion*, Prentice-Hall, 1965; *Religion and Empiricism*, Marquette University Press, 1967; (author of introduction) Josiah Royce, *The Problem of Christianity*, University of Chicago Press, 1968; *Experience and God*, Oxford University Press, 1968.

Themes in American Philosophy: Purpose, Experience, and Community, Harper, 1970; (editor) *Contemporary American Philosophy*, second series, Humanities, 1970; *The Analogy of Experience: An Approach to Understanding Religious Truth*, Harper, 1973; *Purpose and Thought: The Meaning of Pragmatism*, Yale University Press, 1978. General editor of ''Works of Jonathan Edwards,'' Yale University Press, 1964—. Member of editorial board of *Monist*, 1962—, *Journal of Religious Studies*, 1965—, *Philosophy East and West*, 1968—, *International Journal for Philosophy of Religion*, and *Journal of Chinese Philosophy*.

BIOGRAPHICAL/CRITICAL SOURCES: Yale Review, winter, 1969; *Commonweal*, March 16, 1979.

*   *   *

SMITH, Kathleen J(oan)   1929-

PERSONAL: Born June 25, 1929, in Luton, Bedfordshire, England; daughter of Joseph (in business) and Kathleen (in business; maiden name, Bacon) Smith. *Education:* Attended University of North Wales, Bangor. *Home:* Felin Faesog, Clynnog, Gwynedd, Wales.

CAREER: Actress in traveling and resident repertory companies, 1950-57; Holloway Prison, London, England, assistant governor, 1957-60; farmer, writer, and lecturer, 1960-80; Felin Faesog Museum of Old Caernarvonshire, Felin Faesog, Wales, director, 1980—. Guest on television and radio programs; public speaker. *Member:* Work and Leisure Society (founder).

WRITINGS: Twelve Months, Mrs. Brown, Duckworth, 1965; *A Cure for Crime*, Duckworth, 1965; *The Young and the Pity*, Duckworth, 1966; *Devil's Delight*, Duckworth, 1968; *The Company of God*, Duckworth, 1975; *Considering the Victim*, C. C Thomas, 1975; (contributor) *Restitution in Criminal Justice*, Lexington Books, 1977; *Help for the Bereaved*, Duckworth, 1978.

Author of ''A Regular Friend,'' a play, first broadcast by Thames Television, 1974. Writer for ''Within These Walls,'' a series on London Weekend Television. Editor of *Time for Living*.

WORK IN PROGRESS: A book on the effects of new technology based on micro-electronics, publication expected in 1982.

SIDELIGHTS: Kathleen Smith holds the view that convicted criminals should be required to pay compensation to their victims. She proposes a system whereby the criminal, in addition to the rehabilitation provided by the act of compensation itself, would be eligible for the added reward of reduction in sentence. This system, which she calls "the self-determinate prison sentence," is described in detail in *A Cure for Crime*.

Smith wrote: "I want so much of life. I want success and from it the disappointment that it is not enough. I want failure and from it learning that it does not exist. I want illness and from it a new self. I want bereavement and from it the comfort of the dead. I want love and from it freedom. I want God and from God knowledge of the Devil. I want death and from death another birth."

*   *   *

SMITH, Michael Stephen   1944-

PERSONAL: Born February 19, 1944, in Kansas City, Mo.; son of Warren Watson (a civil servant) and Hope (Hollinger) Smith; married Carol Ann Reid (in university administration), August 19, 1967; children: Laura Jeannette. *Education:* University of Oklahoma, B.A., 1965; Cornell University, M.A., 1968, Ph.D., 1972; University of South Carolina, M.B.A., 1981. *Office:* Department of History, University of South Carolina, Columbia, S.C. 29208.

CAREER: St. Louis University, St. Louis, Mo., began as instructor, became assistant professor of history, 1970-73; University of South Carolina, Columbia, assistant professor of history, 1973—. *Member:* American Historical Association, Economic History Society, Society for French Historical Studies.

WRITINGS: (Contributor) Frank N. Magill, editor, *Great Events in History: European Series,* Salem Press, 1973; *Tariff Reform in France, 1860-1900: The Politics of Economic Interest,* Cornell University Press, 1980. Contributor to history journals.

*   *   *

SMITH, N(orman) J(ames)   1930-

PERSONAL: Born November 14, 1930, in St. Helens, England; son of James Garrett (a laborer) and Elsie (Frodsham) Smith; married Peggy Bunt, September 30, 1953 (divorced September 17, 1970); married Helen Miller Cameron (a social researcher); children: Nigel, Andrew, Robin. *Education:* University of Liverpool, certificate in social sciences, 1958; London School of Economics and Political Science, London, diploma in mental health, 1964; University of Bradford, M.A., 1971, Ph.D., 1977. *Politics:* Socialist. *Home:* 6 Chapman Blvd., Glen Waverley, Victoria 3150, Australia. *Office:* Department of Social Work, Monash University, Wellington Rd., Clayton, Victoria 3168, Australia.

CAREER: Railway worker in England, 1944-46, railway clerk, 1946-48; Whiston Hospital, Prescot, England, nurse, 1948-50; Lancashire Southwest Probation Area, Prescot, social worker (probation and psychiatric social work), 1956-65; Liverpool Education Committee, Liverpool, England, 1965-69; University of Bradford, Bradford, England, lecturer in social work, 1969-77; Monash University, Clayton, Australia, senior lecturer in social work, 1977—. *Member:* Australian

Association for Social Work Education, Australian Association of Social Workers.

WRITINGS: (Contributor) A. E. Forder, editor, *Penelope Hall's Social Service of England and Wales,* Routledge & Kegan Paul, 1968, 2nd edition, 1970; *A Brief Guide to Social Legislation,* Methuen, 1971, 2nd edition, 1975; (with A. E. Philip and J. W. McCulloch) *Social Work Research and the Analysis of Social Data,* Pergamon, 1975; *Disabled People in a Handicapped Society,* Macmillan, 1982; (co-author) *The Organisational Determinants of Social Work,* M. Arnold, 1982.

SIDELIGHTS: Smith told *CA:* "Ever since I can remember, I have always written either prose or poetry, but it was only after going to university later in life that I published. These have all been academic works, apart from one poem, primarily because it is an expected part of the 'scholarly way of life.' Writing has been both exhilarating and frightening, the latter because of my lack of basic writing skills. So far my academic writing has enabled me to learn the writer's craft. Now I have reached the point when my interests and ideas are taking me into much broader areas that are interdisciplinary and concerned with the nature of knowledge itself. I am interested in exploring the positive relationships between technology and social change, particularly computer applications in human interaction.

"More and more I am convinced that the poet and science-fiction writer are becoming the principal communicators in modern life. I intend to work more on poetry and plan a volume on the theme of 'man, minds, and machines.' The major influences on my thinking and writing have been the poets Ted Hughes and Sylvia Plath and the writers and thinkers Jacob Bronowski, Alistair Cooke, and C. G. Jung. The single work that captured me for a number of reasons was Robert Pirsig's *Zen and the Art of Motorcycle Maintenance*."

*   *   *

SMITH, Norman Edward Mace   1914-
(Neil Sheraton, Norman Shore)

PERSONAL: Born December 7, 1914, in London, England; son of Edward Albert (an accountant) and Edith Hamlyn (Byron) Smith; married Margaret Heather Mawson, 1941; children: Graham, Heather. *Education:* Attended high school in Bury St. Edmunds, England. *Home:* 67 St. Alban's Ave., Bournemouth BH8 9EG, England.

CAREER: British Overseas Airway Corp. (now British Airways), London, England, 1946-71, began as pilot, became captain; writer, 1971—. *Military service:* Royal Air Force, pilot, 1940-45; became flight lieutenant; received Distinguished Flying Cross and Bar.

WRITINGS—All novels; under pseudonym Neil Sheraton: *They Found a Way Back,* R. Hale, 1960; *The Princess and the Pilot,* R. Hale, 1961.

Under pseudonym Norman Shore: *The Lonely Russian,* R. Hale, 1972; *Hong Kong Nightstop,* R. Hale, 1973; *Russian Hi-Jack,* R. Hale, 1975.

SIDELIGHTS: Smith wrote: "I took up fiction writing as a hobby because it was creative, which airline flying is not, and because I had so much time in hotels overseas. I retired from flying in 1971, and had three novels published since then, but have now stopped writing—at least for awhile, and have taken up landscape painting. I am not a dedicated writer, and do not seek publicity. I am just an ordinary family man with home interests."

AVOCATIONAL INTERESTS: Gardening, physical fitness.

SMITH, S(idney) G(erald) Denis   1932-

PERSONAL: Born October 3, 1932, in Edmonton, Alberta, Canada; son of Sidney Bruce (a lawyer and judge) and Doris Gertrude (Charlesworth) Smith; married Dawn Louise Banks (a professor of Spanish literature), July 8, 1961; children: Alastair, Stephen, Andrea. *Education:* McGill University, B.A., 1953; Oxford University, B.A., 1955, M.A. and B.Litt., both 1959. *Religion:* Anglican. *Home address:* R.R.3, Lakefield, Ontario, Canada K0L 2H0. *Office:* Department of Political Studies, Trent University, Peterborough, Ontario, Canada K9J 7B8.

CAREER: University of Toronto, Toronto, Ontario, instructor, 1956-57, lecturer in political economy, 1957-58; York University, Downsview, Ontario, lecturer, 1960-61, assistant professor of political science, 1961-63, registrar, 1960-61; Trent University, Peterborough, Ontario, assistant professor, 1963-65, associate professor, 1965-68, professor of politics, 1968—, chairman of department, 1966-70, vice-president, 1964-67, master of Champlain College, 1969-71. *Member:* Canadian Political Science Association, Writers Union of Canada. *Awards, honors:* Medal from University of British Columbia, 1973, for *Gentle Patriot.*

WRITINGS: Bleeding Hearts, Bleeding Country, Hurtig, 1971; *Gentle Patriot,* Hurtig, 1973. Editor of *Journal of Canadian Studies,* 1966-75, and *Canadian Forum,* 1975-79.

WORK IN PROGRESS: Canada: The American Alliance and the Cold War, 1913-1949, publication expected in 1982.

*   *   *

SMITH, Stephen Murray
See MURRAY-SMITH, Stephen

*   *   *

SMITH, Timothy Dudley
See DUDLEY-SMITH, Timothy

*   *   *

SMITH, William Frank   1925-

PERSONAL: Born December 28, 1925, in California; son of Frank Porter (a custodian) and Evelyn LaVerne (Lemmon) Smith; married Dorothy Lagerstrom, December 15, 1951; children: Anne Elizabeth, Stephen Porter. *Education:* Stanford University, B.A. (with great distinction), 1949, M.A., 1950; California State University, Los Angeles, M.A., 1962. *Home:* 932 Boxwood Ave., Fullerton, Calif. 92635. *Office:* Division of Humanities, Fullerton College, 321 East Chapman Ave., Fullerton, Calif. 92634.

CAREER: Fullerton College, Fullerton, Calif., professor of English, 1958—, chairman of Division of Humanities, 1962-74. *Military service:* U.S. Army, 1944-46; became technical sergeant. *Member:* Faculty Association of California Community Colleges, Phi Beta Kappa. *Awards, honors:* Fulbright scholar in Belgium, 1964-65.

WRITINGS: From Thought to Theme, Harcourt, 1965, 6th edition, 1980; *Communicating Through Word and Image,* Winthrop Publishing, 1975.

SIDELIGHTS: Smith's interests include the English novel and American expatriate writers of the 1920's. *Avocational interests:* European travel.

SNEIDER, Vern(on) John   1916-1981

OBITUARY NOTICE—See index for *CA* sketch: Born October 6, 1916, in Monroe, Mich.; died May 1, 1981. Author best known for *Teahouse of the August Moon,* a novel that recounts the writer's experiences as an occupation officer on Okinawa during World War II. *Teahouse* was adapted into a Broadway play that ran for 1,032 performances and into a motion picture starring Marlon Brando. His other novels include *West of North Star, The King of Ashtabula,* and *A Long Way From Home.* Obituaries and other sources: *Washington Post,* May 3, 1981.

*   *   *

SOBY, James Thrall   1906-1979

PERSONAL: Born December 14, 1906, in Hartford, Conn.; died January 29, 1979, in Norwalk, Conn.; son of Charles (in tobacco business) and Anna (Hazlewood) Soby; married Melissa Wadley, April 10, 1952; children: Peter Allyn. *Education:* Attended Williams College, 1924-26.

CAREER: Art collector until 1942; Museum of Modern Art, New York, N.Y., director of painting and sculpture and member of board of trustees, 1942, assistant director, 1943-45, chairman of department of painting, 1946-68, vice-president of museum, beginning in 1968. Worked at Wadsworth Athenaeum, 1931; partner in bookshop in Hartford, Conn.; organized exhibitions. *Awards, honors:* L.H.D. from Williams College, 1962; Italy's Star of Solidarity.

WRITINGS: (Editor) *The Booklover's Diary,* Dodd, 1930; *After Picasso,* Dodd, 1935; *Eugene Berman: Catalogue of the Retrospective Exhibition of His Paintings, Illustrations, and Designs,* Institute of Modern Art (Boston, Mass.), 1941; *The Early Chirico,* Dodd, 1941, reprinted as *Giorgio Chirico,* Museum of Modern Art, 1955; *Paintings, Drawings, Prints: Salvador Dali,* Museum of Modern Art, 1941, revised edition published as *Salvador Dali,* 1946, reprinted, Arno, 1969; *Pavel Tchelitchew: Paintings, Drawings, 1942,* reprinted, Arno, 1972; (with Dorothy C. Miller) *Romantic Painting in America,* 1943, reprinted, Arno, 1969; *Georges Rouault: Paintings and Prints,* Museum of Modern Art, 3rd edition, 1947, reprinted, Arno, 1972; *Contemporary Painters,* Museum of Modern Art, 1948, 2nd edition, 1948; (with Alfred H. Barr, Jr.) *Twentieth-Century Italian Art,* Museum of Modern Art, 1949, reprinted, Arno, 1972; *Paintings, Drawings, and Prints by Paul Klee: From the Klee Foundation, Berne, Switzerland, With Additions From American Collections,* Museum of Modern Art, 1949.

Modigliani: Paintings, Drawings, Sculpture, Museum of Modern Art, 1951, 3rd edition, 1963; *Yves Tanguy,* Museum of Modern Art, 1955; *Modern Art and the New Past,* University of Oklahoma Press, 1957; *Ben Shahn: His Graphic Art,* Braziller, 1957; (editor) *Arp,* Museum of Modern Art, 1958; *Juan Gris,* Museum of Modern Art, 1958; *Joan Miro,* Museum of Modern Art, 1959.

The James Thrall Soby Collection of Works of Art Pledged or Given to the Museum of Modern Art, Museum of Modern Art, 1961; *Paintings* (of Ben Shahn), Braziller, 1963; (with James Elliott and Monroe Wheeler) *Bonnard and His Environment,* Museum of Modern Art, 1964; *The School of Paris: Paintings From the Florene May Schoenbrorn and Samuel A. Marx Collection,* Museum of Modern Art, 1965; *Rene Magritte,* Museum of Modern Art, 1965. Also author of *Recent Sculpture, U.S.A.,* 1959. Author of monthly column of art criticism in *Saturday Review of Literature,* 1946-57. Contributor to art journals. Editor of *Magazine of Art,* 1950-51, chairman of editorial board, 1951-52.

BIOGRAPHICAL/CRITICAL SOURCES: Carnegie, September, 1952; *New Yorker,* February 4, 1961; *Time,* February 10, 1961; *Vogue,* February 15, 1961; *Art in America,* February, 1964; *New York Times,* January 30, 1979.*

*   *   *

SODERBERG, Paul Stephen 1949-

PERSONAL: Born May 31, 1949, in Glendale, Calif.; son of Richard Reuben (a professor and diplomat) and Betty Lee (a teacher; maiden name, Van deMark) Soderberg; married Maureen Maeve (a teacher), May 19, 1974; children: Geoffrey Richmond. *Education:* Arizona State University, B.A., 1971. *Politics:* None. *Agent:* L. Geoffrey Young, 335 Willow Lane, Ellenton, Fla. 33532. *Office:* Pendragon Communications Corp., 1027 Ninth St. W., Bradenton, Fla. 33505.

CAREER: Centre for Thai National Reference Collections, Bangkok, Thailand, adviser and curator of herpetology, 1966; Government of Thailand, Bangkok, adviser to Royal Forestry Department, 1967; U.S. Peace Corps, Washington, D.C., volunteer worker in Afghanistan, 1971-73; warehouse worker and free-lance writer in Tempe, Ariz., 1973-75; Jaques Cattell Press, Tempe, text editor, 1976-78; developmental editor, 1977-78; *Pinellas Review* (legal and business newspaper), St. Petersburg, Fla., staff writer, 1978; Manatee County Department of Planning, Bradenton, Fla., document specialist, 1978-79; Sarasota County Office of Management Control, Sarasota, Fla., editorial consultant, publications and communications specialist, editor, and emergency assistant to director of civil defense, 1979-80; Pendragon Communications Corp., Bradenton, secretary, 1980—. Artist, with work in private collections. Nature guide for Boy Scouts of America in Tempe, 1976; model ship builder for Longman's Hobbycraft, Tempe, 1977-78; journalism judge for Golden Herald Awards program, 1981; consultant to U.S. Agency for International Development. Member of Sarasota County Chamber of Commerce and Manatee County Chamber of Commerce. *Member:* International Association of Business Communicators, Florida Magazine Association, Soderberg-Brasel-Young, Collecting Club, Siam Society, Alpha Mu Gamma, Phi Alpha Theta, Phi Kappa Phi.

WRITINGS: (Editor) Jaques Cattell Press, *The Big Book of Halls of Fame in the United States and Canada: Sports,* Bowker, 1977; *Chinese Food: Biography of a Family,* Pendragon, 1982. Contributor to magazines, including *Conservation News* and *Journal of the Bombay Natural History Society,* and newspapers. Editor of *Student Science Society Bulletin,* Bangkok, Thailand, 1965-66; editor of *Pendragon's Gulf Coast Review,* 1981—.

WORK IN PROGRESS: Toward the Sun-Rising Chamber, a novel set in Afghanistan, publication by Pendragon expected in 1984; *The Melon Man,* a historical novel, completion expected in 1985 ("the 500th anniversary of the birth of Babur Shah"); *Who's Who in the Kingdom,* ten volumes, 1990.

SIDELIGHTS: Soderberg commented: "In Delhi, India, there is a ruined place called Purana Qa'lah. When I was nine, mucking about the scree there, I discovered a human skull. Very old, it had been battleaxed at the end of its life Lord knows how many centuries before. I held it up in agitation and delight, gazed at a largish spider crouched in orbit (the left one), and paraded it home. My father made me put it back.

"In Afghanistan, when I was two years and some months old, a bird of no distinction and uncertain age had bungled into a bucket of water beneath the compound wall. I waddled up to find it floating. My mother informed, when I'd dragged it indoors, about death and the like, but (to humor me, I'm sure) placed the sodden thing where sunlight warmed a windowsill. I whispered things to its plum-colored tummy, in the garble babies use as speech, until, after ten minutes, the bird moved. In another five it was flapping. Perplexed and delighted, my mother later stood with me as I let it go.

"Gazing now at those two instances honestly and long enough, I find everything of importance I've subsequently learned. Life after age nine, in other words, has been predominantly reiteration.

"My preoccupation now is with questions of quality versus quantity, which leads to no end of excitingly unpopular positions. For example, where many are concerned at the number of people migrating to Florida, I'd have to insist that it's the quality of the immigrants which determines whether population growth is good or bad. The same must apply to life itself: what one does with it transcends the length of time one manages to retain it. And who would dispute the same thinking applied to creativity to state that one exquisite paragraph has greater merit than a ream of ramblings somebody paid to have bound in a book? This preoccupation, in short, is with excellence. Excellence in all its manifestations—though essentially opposed to the tenets of the Technological Society—is one of the traditional values to which I'd much like to see this nation return. Excellence, after all—quality over quantity—is much more permanent. It's all that really counts between the drowned bird that lives and the skull one returns to the earth.

"Thus my narrower preoccupation is with art language (which is one thing rather than two). To represent visually what I want to attain in writing, I invented an art form: eye art. Utterly realistic animal eyes in oil or watercolor can become abstracts when 'viewed' from several inches away. Eye art takes you that close to the subject—demands active confrontation rather than passive observation, since the animal is both close enough to bite you and looking straight back at you. It is highly instructive and can be unnerving. I seek essentially the same through words."

AVOCATIONAL INTERESTS: Model ship building, mountain climbing (Soderberg means "south mountain" in Swedish), languages (Persian, Russian, German, French, Thai, Greek, Hindi, and others), mythology.

BIOGRAPHICAL/CRITICAL SOURCES: Bangkok World, March 1, 1964; *Arizonian,* March 6, 1969; *Arizona,* December 15, 1974; *Sarasota Herald-Tribune,* May 28, 1980, August 25, 1980; *Bradenton Herald,* March 15, 1981.

*   *   *

SOHL, Robert (Allen) 1941-

PERSONAL: Born May 25, 1941, in Omaha, Neb.; son of Gerald Thomas (an insurance underwriter) and Roberta (a secretary; maiden name, Young) Sohl. *Education:* Occidental College, B.A., 1964; graduate study at University of Hawaii, 1964-66. *Politics:* Republican. *Religion:* Presbyterian. *Home:* 406 Oak St., Glendale, Calif. 91204.

CAREER: J. C. Penney & Co., Inc., Glendale, Calif., in sales, 1966-68; Security Pacific Bank, Los Angeles, Calif., service representative, 1971-75; Tricor America, Los Angeles, service representative, 1978—. *Member:* California Young Republicans, Phi Gamma Delta.

WRITINGS: (Editor with Audrey Carr) *The Gospel According to Zen: Beyond the Death of God,* New American Library, 1970; (editor with Carr) *Games Zen Masters Play: The Writings of R. H. Blyth,* New American Library, 1976.

WORK IN PROGRESS: The Buddha Game: Strategies of Meditation.

SIDELIGHTS: Sohl wrote: "Although I was born in Omaha, I have spent most of my life in southern California. During my sophomore year in college I had an experience that was quite liberating but one for which my Protestant background seemed to offer no explanation. It seemed as if I had awakened from a long dream, that all of life was a single consciousness rather than a collection of separate individuals.

"It was shortly thereafter that I became acquainted with the eastern religions of Zen Buddhism and Vedanta. It was obvious they were describing my own unitary experience better than any of the Christian theologies, Catholic or Protestant.

"In my books I have tried to share this so-called 'perennial philosophy.' From our dreams at night we realize that the appearance of multiplicity is a subtle illusion, that it is all created by our own minds.

"On a larger scale, life itself is on the very same principle. What appears to be a complex arrangement of many separate individuals and events is like a dream, a creation of one mind only."

*   *   *

SOLNIT, Albert J.   1919-

PERSONAL: Born August 26, 1919, in Los Angeles, Calif.; son of Benjamin and Bertha Solnit; married Martha Benedict, October 22, 1949; children: David, Ruth, Benjamin, Aaron. *Education:* University of California, Berkeley and San Francisco, B.A., 1940, M.A., 1942, M.D., 1943. *Religion:* Jewish. *Home:* 107 Cottage St., Apt. 4C, New Haven, Conn. 06511. *Office:* Child Study Center, Yale University, 333 Cedar St., New Haven, Conn. 06510.

CAREER: Long Island University, Brooklyn, N.Y., resident in rotating internship, 1944-45; University of California, San Francisco, resident in pediatrics and communicable diseases, 1947-48; Yale University, New Haven, Conn., resident in psychiatry, 1948-50, instructor, 1952-53, assistant professor, 1953-60, associate professor, 1960-64, professor of pediatrics and psychiatry, 1964—, Sterling Professor of Pediatrics and Psychiatry, 1970—, chief psychiatrist at Child Study Center, 1964—, director of center, 1966—. Training and supervising analyst for Western New England Institute for Psychoanalysis, 1962; member of New York Psychoanalytic Institute, 1962—, training and supervising analyst, 1966—; member of program monitoring team in department of children and youth, Connecticut Valley Hospital, 1976—.

Chairman of Connecticut Advisory Council on Children and Youth Services, 1976—; chairman of advisory council of Connecticut Department of Children and Youth Services, 1977—; member of Connecticut Justice Commission task force on Juvenile Justice and Delinquency Prevention Standards, 1979. Member of advisory board of Action for Children's Television, 1973—, board of directors of Human Services Institute for Children and Families, Inc., 1973—, national advisory council of HOSPICE, 1974-75, board on maternal, child, and family health research of Assembly of Life Science, 1976—, panel of Child Welfare Resource Information Exchange, of National Center for Child Advocacy (Children's Bureau of Administration for Children, Youth, and Families), 1978—, board of directors of National Center for Clinical Infant Programs, 1978—, and multidisciplinary

committee of health and behavior research agenda, Institute of Medicine, National Academy of Sciences, 1979.

Member of advisory council of Center for Advanced Psychoanalytic Studies, Princeton, N.J., 1963—, Erikson Institute for Early Childhood Education, 1966—, and Conference on Psychiatry and Medical Education, 1966—; scientific adviser to Center for Preventive Psychiatry, White Plains, N.Y., 1970—; member of national advisory committee of Center for the Study of Families and Children, at Vanderbilt University, 1978—. Member of American professional advisory committee of Jerusalem Mental Health Center, 1971—, professional advisory committee of Research Center for Human Sciences, at Hebrew University of Jerusalem, 1976—, and New England academic advisory committee of Ben-Gurion University of the Negev, 1977—.

Member of advisory medical committee of Foster School, 1964, and board of managers of Dixwell Community House, 1965—; member of professional advisory board of BenHaven School, 1976—; member of New Haven community health research advisory council of Community Progress, Inc. and South Central Connecticut Regional Mental Health Planning Council, 1965—; member of health subcommittee of White House Conference on Children and Youth, and planning committee of advisory council for children and mental health, Connecticut State Department of Mental Health, 1969—. *Military service:* U.S. Army Air Forces, psychiatrist, 1945-47; became captain.

MEMBER: International Psychoanalytical Association, International Association for Child and Adolescent Psychiatry and Allied Professions (secretary-general, 1970-74; president, 1974-78; vice-president, 1979—), International Society of Family Law, American Psychoanalytic Association (member of board on professional standards, 1967; chairman of committee on child analysis, 1964-68; member of executive committee, 1969—), Association for Child Psychoanalysis, American Psychiatric Association (fellow), American Academy of Pediatrics, American Academy of Child Psychology, American National Red Cross, American Orthopsychiatric Association, American Association for the Advancement of Science (fellow), Society of Professors of Child Psychiatry, Association for Mental Health Aid to Israel (member of advisory board), Israel Psychoanalytic Society (corresponding member), Western New England Psychoanalytic Society, Connecticut Child Welfare Association, Tourette Syndrome Association. *Awards, honors:* Mount Airy Gold Medal from Mount Airy Foundation, 1975; fellow of Institute of Medicine, National Academy of Sciences, 1979—; William C. Menninger Award from Menninger Foundation, 1979; Agnes Purcell McGavin Award from American Psychiatric Association, 1980; award from Washington Council of Child Psychiatry, 1980.

WRITINGS: (Editor with Sally A. Provence, and contributor) *Modern Perspectives in Child Development: In Honor of Milton J.E. Senn, M.D.,* International Universities Press, 1963; (editor with Rudolph M. Loewenstein, Lottie M. Newman, and Max Schur) *Psychoanalysis, a General Psychology: Essays in Honor of Heinz Hartmann,* International Universities Press, 1966; (with Milton J.E. Senn) *Problems in Child Behavior and Development,* Lea & Febiger, 1968; (with Anna Freud and Joseph Goldstein) *Beyond the Best Interests of the Child,* Free Press, 1973; (editor with Freud, Ruth S. Eissler, and Marianne Kris, and contributor) *An Anthology of the Psychological Study of the Child: Physical Illness and Handicap in Childhood,* Yale University Press, 1977; (with Freud and Goldstein) *Before the Best Interests of the Child,* Free Press, 1979.

Contributor: *Teaching Psychiatry in Medical School*, Garamond American Pridemark Press, 1967; Oliver Cope, editor, *Man, Mind, and Medicine: The Doctor's Education*, Lippincott, 1968; Grete L. Bibring, editor, *The Teaching of Dynamic Psychiatry*, International Universities Press, 1968; *Orthopsychiatry and the Law*, Wayne State University Press, 1968; P. L. Adams, H. H. Work, and J. B. Cramer, editors, *Academic Child Psychiatry*, Society of Professors of Child Psychiatry, 1969; C. C. Wilson and E. A. Wilson, editors, *Healthful School Environment*, National Education Association, 1969.

Laura L. Dittman, editor, *What We Can Learn From Infants*, National Association for the Education of Young Children, 1970; Rudolph Ekstein and Rocco L. Motto, editors, *From Learning for Love to Love of Learning*, Brunner, 1970; Ruth S. Eissler, Anna Freud, and other editors, *The Psychoanalytic Study of the Child*, International Universities Press, 1970; *Currents in Psychoanalysis*, International Universities Press, 1972; Evelyn K. Oremland and Jerome D. Oremland, editors, *The Effects of Hospitalization on Children*, C. C Thomas, 1973; E. James Anthony and Cyrille Koupernik, editors, *The Child in His Family*, Wiley, 1973; Peggy Charren and Evelyn Sarson, editors, *Who Is Talking to Our Children?*, Educational Resources Information Center/Clearinghouse on Media and Technology, 1973; *Psychological Bases of War*, Quadrangle, 1973; Daniel Bergsma, editor, *The Infant at Risk*, Symposia Specialists, 1974; Nicholas Hobbs, editor, *Issues in the Classification of Children*, Jossey-Bass, 1974.

Studies in Child Psychoanalysis: Pure and Applied, Yale University Press, 1975; E. James Anthony and Doris C. Gilpin, editors, *Three Clinical Faces of Childhood*, Spectrum, 1976; (author of introduction) Ann S. Kliman, *Crisis: Psychological First Aid for Recovery and Growth*, Holt, 1977; Morris Green and Robert Haggerty, editors, *Ambulatory Pediatrics*, Saunders, 1977; L. Eugene Arnold, editor, *Helping Parents Help Their Children*, Brunner, 1978; Anthony and Colette Chiland, editors, *The Child in His Family: Children and Their Parents in a Changing World*, International Association for Child and Adolescent Psychiatry and Allied Professions, 1978; *Adolescent Behavior and Health*, National Academy of Sciences, 1978; (author of introduction) Max Sugar, *Female Adolescent Development*, Brunner, 1979; Joseph Noshpitz, editor, *Basic Handbook of Child Psychiatry*, Volume I, Basic Books, 1979; Edward Zigler and Jeannette Valentine, editors, *Project Head Start: A Legacy of the War on Poverty*, Free Press, 1979; Joy D. Osofsky, editor, *The Handbook of Infant Development*, Wiley, 1979; C. K. Hofling and J. M. Lewis, editors, *The Family: Evaluation and Treatment*, Brunner, 1980.

Contributor to *American Handbook of Psychiatry*. Contributor of more than one hundred articles and reviews to professional journals. Member of editorial board of *Journal of the American Psychoanalytic Association*, 1972-74; associate editor of *American Journal of Psychiatry*, July, 1979; member of advisory board of *Children's Literature*, 1979—; editor of *Psychoanalytic Study of the Child*.

WORK IN PROGRESS: Role and Limitation of the Clinical Expert (tentative title), with Joseph Goldstein, Anna Freud, and Sonja Goldstein, for Free Press.

*   *   *

SOLOMON, (Neal) Brad(ley)   1945-

PERSONAL: Born January 10, 1945, in Syracuse, N.Y.; son of Irving and Bea Solomon. *Education:* Brandeis University,

B.A., 1966; University of California, Los Angeles, M.F.A., 1968. *Home:* 35-36 76th St., Jackson Heights, N.Y. 11372. *Agent:* Ned Leavitt, William Morris Agency, 1350 Avenue of the Americas, New York, N.Y. 10019.

CAREER: Writer.

WRITINGS—Suspense novels: *The Gone Man*, Random House, 1977; *The Open Shadow*, Summit Books, 1978; *Jake and Katie*, Dial, 1979.

*   *   *

SOLOMON, Richard H(arvey)   1937-

PERSONAL: Born June 19, 1937, in Philadelphia, Pa.; son of Bertram Harvey and Ellen (Harris) Solomon; married Carol Schwartz (a social worker), November 24, 1960; children: Lisa, Jonathan. *Education:* Massachusetts Institute of Technology, S.B., 1960, Ph.D., 1966. *Home:* 369 Las Casas Ave., Pacific Palisades, Calif. 90272. *Office:* RAND Corp., 1700 Main St., Santa Monica, Calif. 90406.

CAREER: University of Michigan, Ann Arbor, assistant professor, 1966-70, associate professor, 1970-75, professor of political science, 1976; National Security Council, Washington, D.C., senior staff member, 1971-76; RAND Corp., Santa Monica, Calif., head of social science department, 1976—, director of international security policy research, 1977—. Member of board of directors of Graphic Arts Research Foundation; member of Social Science Research Council joint committee on contemporary China, 1977-80; International Research and Exchanges Board. *Member:* National Committee on U.S.-China Relations, Committee on Scholarly Communication With the People's Republic of China, Asia Society (member of southern California advisory council), New York Council on Foreign Relations.

WRITINGS: Mao's Revolution and the Chinese Political Culture, University of California Press, 1971; *A Revolution Is Not a Dinner Party: A Feast of Images of the Maoist Transformation of China*, Doubleday, 1976; (editor) *Asian Security in the 1980's: Problems and Policies for a Time of Transition*, Oelgeschlager, Gunn & Hain, 1980; *The China Factor: Sino-American Relations and the Global Scene*, Prentice-Hall, 1981. Contributor to *Foreign Affairs, China Quarterly*, and *Yale Review*.

WORK IN PROGRESS: "Coalition-Building or Condominium," a chapter in a study of the Soviet Union in Asia to be published by Yale University Press in 1981.

SIDELIGHTS: Solomon told *CA:* "China and Asia remain esoteric subjects for most American readers, yet United States trade with Asia now surpasses commerce with Europe, and political trends in the region play an increasingly important role in American security. Our last three wars were fought in Asia (against Japan, in Korea, in Vietnam). My writings are intended to make Asia comprehensible to American readers and to contribute to the deliberations of policymakers as they open United States approaches to dealings with China and the region."

*   *   *

SONDHEIM, Stephen (Joshua)   1930-

PERSONAL: Born March 22, 1930, in New York, N.Y.; son of Herbert (a dress manufacturer) Sondheim, and Janet (a fashion designer and interior decorator; maiden name, Fox) Sondheim Leshin. *Education:* Williams College, B.A. (magna cum laude), 1950; graduate study in music composition and theory with Milton Babbitt; studied privately with Oscar

Hammerstein II. *Residence:* New York, N.Y. *Office:* c/o Flora Roberts, 65 East 55th St., New York, N.Y. 10022.

CAREER: Composer and lyricist, 1956—. *Member:* American Society of Composers, Authors, and Publishers, Writers Guild of America, Dramatists Guild (president, 1973-81). *Awards, honors:* Hutchinson Prize, 1950; best musical award from *Evening Standard,* 1959, for "Gypsy"; named outstanding composer by Drama Desk, 1970, named best composer by *Variety* New York Critics Poll, 1970, New York Drama Critics Award for best musical, 1970, Antoinette Perry (Tony) Awards for best musical, for best musical score, and for best lyricist, all 1971, all for "Company"; named best composer and best lyricist by *Variety* New York Critics Poll, 1971, Antoinette Perry Award for best musical score and lyrics, and Antoinette Perry Award nomination for best musical, 1972, all for "Follies."

Best musical award from *Evening Standard,* 1973, named outstanding composer and lyricist by Drama Desk, 1973, Antoinette Perry Awards for best musical and for best score and lyrics, both 1973, and Los Angeles Drama Critics Circle Award for best music and lyrics, 1974, all for "A Little Night Music"; New York Drama Critics Awards for best musical, 1976, for "Pacific Overtures"; Grammy Award from National Academy of Recording Arts and Sciences for best song of the year, 1976, for "Send in the Clowns"; best musical production award from Drama Desk, Antionette Perry Awards for best musical and for best score and lyrics, all 1979, all for "Sweeney Todd."

WRITINGS—Composer and lyricist of songs for plays: (With Leonard Bernstein) "Jet Song," "Something's Coming," "Maria," "Tonight," "America," "Cool," "One Hand, One Heart," "I Feel Pretty," "Somewhere," "Gee, Officer Krupke!," "A Boy Like That,"and "I Have a Love" from Arthur Laurents's *West Side Story* (first produced on Broadway at Winter Garden Theatre, September 26, 1957), Random House, 1958, published in *Romeo and Juliet and West Side Story,* Dell, 1965; (with Jule Styne) "Let Me Entertain You," "Some People," "Small World," "Mr. Goldstone," "Little Lamb," "You'll Never Get Away From Me," "Broadway," "If Momma Was Married," "All I Need Is the Girl," "Everything's Coming Up Roses," "Together Wherever We Go," "You Gotta Get a Gimmick," "Mamma's Talkin' Soft," and "Rose's Turn" from Laurents's *Gypsy* (first produced on Broadway at the Broadway Theatre, May 21, 1959), Random House, 1960.

"Comedy Tonight," "Love, I Hear," "Free," "The House of Marcus Lycus," "Lovely," "Pretty Little Picture," "Everybody Ought to Have a Maid," "I'm Calm" "Impossible," "Bring Me My Bride," "That Dirty Old Man," "That'll Show Him," "Funeral Sequence," "Love Is in the Air," and "The Echo Song" from Burt Shevelove and Larry Gelbart's *A Funny Thing Happened on the Way to the Forum* (first produced on Broadway at Alvin Theatre, May 8, 1962), Dodd, 1963; "I'm Like the Blue Bird," "Me and My Town," "Miracle Song," "Simple," "A-1 March," "Come Play Wiz Me," "Anyone Can Whistle," "A Parade in Town," "Everybody Says Don't," "I've Got You to Lean On," "See What It Gets You," and "With So Little to Be Sure Of" from Laurents's *Anyone Can Whistle* (first produced on Broadway at Majestic Theatre, April 4, 1964), Random House, 1965; (With Richard Rodgers) "Someone Woke Up," "This Week Americans," "What Do We Do? We Fly!," "Someone Like You," "Bargaining," "Here We Are Again," "Thinking," "No Understand," "Take the Moment," "Moon in My Window," "We're Gonna Be All Right," "Do I Hear a Waltz?" "Stay," "Perfectly Lovely Couple," and "Thank You So Much" from Laurents's *Do I Hear a Waltz?* (first produced on Broadway at Forty-Sixth Street Theatre, March 18, 1965), Random House, 1966.

"Company," "The Little Things You Do Together," "Sorry-Grateful," "You Could Drive a Person Crazy," "Have I Got a Girl For You," "Someone Is Waiting," "Another Hundred People," "Getting Married Today," "Side by Side by Side," "What Would We Do Without You." "Poor Bobby," "Barcelona," "The Ladies Who Lunch," and "Being Alive," from George Furth's *Company* (first produced on Broadway at Alvin Theatre, April 26, 1970), Random House, 1970; "Beautiful Girls," "Don't Look at Me," "Waiting for the Girls Upstairs," "Rain on the Roof," "Ah, Paris," "Broadway Baby," "The Road You Didn't Take," "Bolero d'Armour," "In Buddy's Eyes," "Who's That Woman?," "I'm Still Here," "Too Many Mornings," "The Right Girl," "One More Kiss," "Could I Leave You?," "Loveland," "Your Gonna Love Tomorrow," "Love Will See Us Through," "The God-Why-Don't-You-Love-Me Blues," "Losing My Mind," "The Story of Lucy and Jessie," "Can That Boy Foxtrot!," and "Live, Laugh, Love" from James Goldman's *Follies* (first produced on Broadway at Winter Garden Theatre, April 14, 1971), Random House, 1971.

"Send in the Clowns," "Night Waltz," "Now," "Later," "Soon," "Every Day a Little Death," "The Sun Won't Set," "Perpetual Anticipation," "The Glamorous Life," "Remember?," "You Must Meet My Wife," "Liaisons," "In Praise of Women," "A Weekend in the Country," "It Would Have Been Wonderful," and "The Miller's Son" from Hugh Wheeler's *A Little Night Music* (first produced on Broadway at Shubert Theatre, February 25, 1973), Dodd, 1974; "Invocation to the Gods and Instructions to the Audience," "The Frogs," "Evoe!," "It's Only a Play," "Fear No More," "The Sound of Poets," "Hymn to Dionysos," and "Travelling Music" from "The Frogs," first produced in New Haven, Conn., at Yale Repertory, 1974.

"The Advantages of Floating in the Middle of the Sea," "There Is No Other Way," "Four Black Dragons," "Chrysanthemum Tea," "Poems," "Welcome to Kanagawa," "Someone in a Tree," "Lion Dance," "Please Hello," "A Bowler Hat," "Pretty Lady," and "Next" from John Weidman's *Pacific Overtures* (first produced on Broadway at Winter Garden Theatre, January 11, 1976), Dodd, 1977; "Prelude," "The Ballad of Sweeney Todd," "No Place Like London," "The Barber and His Wife," "The Worst Pies in London," "Poor Thing," "My Friends," "Green Finch and Linnet Bird," "Ah, Miss," "Johanna," "Pirelli's Miracle Elixir," "The Contest," "Wait," "Kiss Me," "Ladies in Their Sensitivities," "Pretty Women," "Epiphany," "A Little Priest," "God, That's Good!," "By the Sea," "Wigmaker Sequence," "The Letter," "Not While I'm Around," "Parlor Songs," and "Final Sequence" from Christopher Bond and Wheeler's *Sweeney Todd, the Demon Barber of Fleet Street* (first produced on Broadway at Uris Theatre, March 1, 1979), Dodd, 1979.

"Two Fairy Tales," "Saturday Night," "Can That Boy Foxtrot!," All Things Bright and Beautiful," Bang!," "All Things Bright and Beautiful (Part II)," "The Girls of Summer," "Uptown, Downtown," "So Many People," "Your Eyes Are Blue," "A Moment With You," "Marry Me a Little," "Happily Ever After," "Pour Le Sport," "Silly People," "There Won't Be Trumpets," and "It Wasn't Meant to Happen" from Craig Lucas and Norman Rene's "Marry Me a Little," first produced in New York at Production Company, October 29, 1980.

Composer of incidental music for plays: (And song) "The Girls of Summer" from "The Girls of Summer," first produced on Broadway at Longacre Theater, November 19, 1956; "Invitation to a March," first produced on Broadway at Music Box Theatre, October 26, 1960; (and song) "Hollywood and Vine" from "Twigs," first produced in Detroit at Fisher Theatre, September 6, 1972; "The Enclave," first produced Off-Broadway at Theatre Four, November 15, 1973. Composed song, with Mary Rodgers, "The Boy From . . ." for Steven Vinaver's "The Mad Show," first produced Off-Broadway at New Theatre, January 10, 1966. Also collaborated with Rodgers and Martin Charnin on song "Don't Laugh" from show "Hot Spot," 1963.

Compositions represented in musical shows, including "By Bernstein," first produced Off-Broadway at Chelsea Theatre of Brooklyn Westside Theatre, November 23, 1975; "The Madwoman of Central Park West," first produced on Broadway at Twenty-Two Step Theatre, June 13, 1979. Also wrote additional lyrics for Leonard Bernstein's "Candide," first produced Off-Broadway at Chelsea Theatre of Brooklyn, December 11, 1973, produced on Broadway Theatre, March 10, 1974.

Work anthologized in Ned Sherrin's "Side by Side by Sondheim," first produced in London at Memorial Theatre, 1976, produced on Broadway at Music Box Theatre, April 18, 1977.

Composer and lyricist of music for television and for motion pictures: "Evening Primrose," American Broadcasting Co. (ABC-TV), 1966; "Stavisky," Cerito Films, 1974; "The Seven Percent Solution," Universal Pictures, 1977; "Reds," Paramount, 1981.

Recordings—All original cast albums, except as noted: "West Side Story," Columbia, 1957; "Gypsy," Columbia, 1959; "A Funny Thing Happened on the Way to the Forum," Capitol, 1962; "Anyone Can Whistle," Columbia, 1964; "Do I Hear a Waltz?," Columbia, 1965; "Company," Columbia, 1970; "Follies," Capitol, 1971; "A Little Night Music," Columbia, 1973; "Stavisky" (soundtrack), Polydor, 1973; "Sondheim/A Musical Tribute" (from a show of the same title; first produced on Broadway at Shubert Theatre, March 11, 1973), Warner Bros., 1973; "Pacific Overtures," RCA, 1976; "Side by Side by Sondheim," RCA, 1977; "Sweeney Todd," RCA, 1979.

Author of television scripts and screenplays: "Topper" (television series), National Broadcasting Co. (NBC-TV), 1953; "The Last Word" (televison series), Columbia Broadcasting System (CBS-TV), c. 1956; (with Anthony Perkins) "The Last of Sheila" (motion picture), Warner Bros., 1973.

Other: (Author of introduction) Richard Lewine and Alfred Simon, *Songs of the American Theatre,* Dodd, 1973; (contributor) Otis L. Guernsey, Jr., editor *Playwrights, Lyricists, Composers on Theatre,* Dodd, 1974; (author of introduction) Hugh Fordin, *Getting to Know Him* (biography of Oscar Hammerstein), Random House, 1977; *Stephen Sondheim's Crossword Puzzles,* Harper, 1980. Contributor of crossword puzzles to *New York* magazine, 1968-69.

WORK IN PROGRESS: Music and lyrics for George Furth's "Merrily we Roll Along," 1981.

SIDELIGHTS: Stephen Sondheim began playing the piano at the age of four. By the time he was fifteen, he was able to submit an original musical to an old family friend, Oscar Hammerstein II, for objective criticism. Hammerstein pronounced the work "terrible—although not without talent,"

and Sondheim's career as America's Noel Coward commenced.

Sondheim was introduced to the musical theatre while he was growing up in Pennsylvania. When he was eleven, just after his parents divorced, the composer found himself and his mother in the Keystone State while his father remained in New York. As a friend of the Hammerstein family, particularly as a buddy of the celebrated composer's son, Sondheim spent a considerable amount of the time at Hammerstein's farm. It was there that he learned the fine art of songwriting—in one afternoon. Sondheim recalled: "I wrote a musical called *By George,* a thinly disguised version of campus life with the teachers' names by changed by one vowel or consonant. I thought it was pretty terrific, so I asked Oscar to read it—and I was arrogant enough to say to him, 'Will you read it as if it were just a musical that crossed your desk as a producer? Pretend you don't know me.' He said, 'O.K.,' and I went home that night with visions of being the first 15-year-old to have a show on Broadway. I knew he was going to love it. Oscar called me in the next day and said, 'Now you really want me to treat this as if it were by somebody I don't know?' and I said, 'Yes, please,' and he said, 'Well, in that case it's the worst thing I ever read in my life.'

From that time on Hammerstein became, in Sondheim's own words, "my guide and mentor." Using "By George" as an example, Hammerstein taught his student to build songs, to write lyrics that tell a story, and to relate songs to characters. "I dare say, at the risk of hyperbole," Sondheim confessed in *Playwrights, Lyricists, Composers on Theatre,* "that I learned in that afternoon more than most people learn about songwriting in a lifetime."

At this time, Hammerstein became a father figure to the fledgling composer, someone to emulate. "I wanted to be exactly like him," Sondheim reflected in a *Newsweek* interview with Charles Michener. "In a way I still do."

With Hammerstein as a role model and instructor, Sondheim received a general exposure to musical theatre, but he started at the bottom: typing scripts and bringing coffee. Still the apprentice songwriter gained much knowledge. He told *Time:* "Oscar taught me that a song should be like a one-act play, with an exposition, a development and a conclusion; at the end of a song the character should be moved to a different position from where he was emotionally at the beginning. This was how Hammerstein and Dick Rodgers revolutionized the American theatre."

To Sondheim, the Broadway musical comedy is "one of the most popular and influential outcroppings of this century," and the composer has proved to be one of the most popular influences on the Broadway musical. Many of his peers hold Sondheim to be the foremost lyricist on Broadway. When Otis L. Guernsey, Jr., editor of *Playwrights, Lyricists, Composers on Theatre,* compiled the *Dramatists Guild Literary Quarterly*'s list of the best lyricists, he included Sheldon Harnick's response. "I suppose it's Stephen Sondheim," Harnick opined, "for the following reason: while there are a number of lyricists whose new work I look forward to, I invariably anticipate a new Sondheim score with special excitement because I know it will have a particularly high level of invention, wit, meticulous craftmanship, taste and comment."

Arthur Laurents said that "without question, the best Broadway lyricist past or present is Stephen Sondheim. Any lyric he has written can be quoted to illustrate this contention. I think Sondheim is the only lyricist who almost always writes a lyric which could *only* be sung by the character for which it was designed, who never pads with unnecessary fillers, who never sacrifices meaning or intention for a clever rhyme and who knows that a lyric is the shortest of one-act plays, with a beginning, a middle and an end. Moreover, he knows how the words must sit on a musical phrase. I am not his agent." And Burt Shevelove replied: "Far and away the best of the new lyric writers is Stephen Sondheim. Beside wit, ingenuity, and warmth, he brings a sense of the character to every word that is sung. He is the first and perhaps the only true *theatre* lyricist we have."

Sondheim's contributions to the musical theatre have been so significant that the *Dramatists Guild Literary Quarterly* has designated its first ten years as the "Sondheim decade." "There can hardly have been an issue since," the editors commented, "when a work by Stephen Sondheim . . . wasn't a major attraction on the Broadway scene, and often more than one. . . ."

In nearly thirty years in the theatre, Sondheim has been instrumental in revolutionizing the musical. The composer's ability to incorporate a variety of musical styles into his scores has caused T. E. Kalem of *Time* to claim after seeing a Sondheim production that the "entire score is an incredible display of musical virtuosity." Using music, Sondheim creates an attitude for the dramatic situation so that individual songs may push the drama along. Sometimes, unlike most of his predecessors, the composer strays from the traditional rhyming structure. Too, his lyrical cynicism and satire have moved the musical comedy from the lighter and simpler shows of Rodgers and Hammerstein to what is termed "conceptual musicals."

Instead of escapism, his musicals present serious concerns and dramatic subtexts. As conceptual musicals, each of the composer's works depends on one fundamental concept to act as a framework. Though every theatrical production should have a unifying theme, "every Sondheim-Prince [renowned director Harold Prince] show," argued Jeff Sweet, a critic, composer, and librettist, "begins with a prologue in which the plot isn't entered into, saying to the audience, 'These are what your expectations should be for this show. These are our priorities, these are the ideas we're going to be concentrating on.' They are conceptual musicals, they get the concept up there in the first number." One of the creators of the new, unromantic musical production, Sondheim has helped to place the musical on a more serious level than that of the traditional Broadway show. In fact, after assessing the contemporary musical, Ray Evans decided that "many musicals today tend to the opera form, and there are marvelous counterpoints, involvements and dramatics which, when done well—as in the case of Sondheim—are a new plateau in the art."

Sondheim, a puzzle enthusiast, compares lyric writing to solving brainteasers. He disclosed: "On one level, I suppose, lyric writing is an elegant form of a puzzle, and I am a great puzzle fan. There is a great deal of joy for me in the sweat involved in the working out of lyrics." Yet the lyricist calls himself an undisciplined writer who responds well to working under pressure. He writes "lying down so I can go to sleep easily." "I write about ten minutes and sleep for two, on the average," Sondheim quipped. "I write on legal pads in very small writing, partly for frugality—I used to write on both sides of the page, and Leonard Bernstein got annoyed because he would be constantly trying to find lyrics and turning the pages over and over, so I don't do that anymore." His routine includes "lots of recopying," and the composer recommends the use of very soft lead pencils. "Supposedly,"

he advised aspiring lyricists, "that makes the writing easier on your wrist, but what it really does is allow you to sharpen it every five minutes."

When Sondheim composes, it is a cooperative effort. "I go about starting a song first with the collaborators," he divulged, "sometimes just with the book writer, sometimes with the director. We have long discussions and I take notes, just general notes, and then we decide what the song should be about, and I try to make a title." The composer, according to Sondheim, must stage numbers or draw "blueprints" so that the director or the choreographer may see the uses of a song.

For Sondheim, collaboration usually begins with the book and the book writer from whom "you should steal." Since a good production sounds as though one writer is responsible for both the book and the score, the book writer and composer must work together if a play is to have texture. "Any book writer I work with knows what I'm going to do," explained Sondheim, "and I try to help him out wherever I can, that's the only way you make a piece, make a texture." "I keep hearing about people," he continued, "who write books and then give them to composers or composers who write scores and then get a book writer. I don't understand how that works."

Collaboration allows not only borrowing ideas but challenging each other's work as well, and, as the composer stated earlier, it extends beyond the writers to the choreographer and to the director—in Sondheim's case, director Harold Prince in particular. "Judging from what I see on the stage," maintained Sweet, "they understand each other so well now that you can consider them one consciousness. Incidentally, this is one of the few cases I can think of where the director has been so greatly credited for the content and attitude of musical productions."

Sondheim's first Broadway collaboration has an unusual history. At the age of twenty-five, the composer completed the music and lyrics for "Saturday Night," a musical that never saw the Broadway stage owing to the death of its producer Lemuel Ayers. But "Saturday Night" still served Sondheim well. "It was my portfolio," he vaunted, "and as a result of it I got *West Side Story.*" Remembering the circumstances of his collaboration with Leonard Bernstein, Sondheim related: "I was at an opening night party, and I saw one familiar face, Arthur Laurents, and I went over to make small talk with him. I asked him what he was doing, and he said, 'I'm about to begin a musical of *Romeo and Juliet* with Leonard Bernstein and Jerry Robbins.' I asked 'Who's doing the lyrics?—just idly, because I didn't think of myself as a lyric writer, I thought of myself as a songwriter, I was composing all the time. Arthur literally smote his forehead (I think it's the only time I have ever seen anybody literally smite his forehead). He said, 'I never thought of you and I liked your lyrics very much. I didn't like your music very much, but I did like your lyrics a lot.' (Arthur is nothing if not frank.)"

Originally titled "East Side Story," Laurents's play was to be a story of racial prejudice involving a Jewish girl and a Catholic boy on New York's east side. After much deliberation, however, the creators decided that the Jewish-Catholic theme was exhausted, so they shelved the project for a later date. The "later date" arrived in six years when an influx of Puerto Rican immigrants to New York's west side created racial tension. Thus, "East Side Story" became "West Side Story."

The story of the ugly life on a city street, with only glimpses of beauty and love, "West Side Story" is considered one of the masterpieces of the American theatre. Beginning its first run in New York in 1957, "West Side Story" ran for 734 performances on Broadway. After an extended tour of the United States, the play began a second Broadway run of 249 performances. In 1961, "West Side Story" was adapted into a motion picture that captured ten Academy Awards and that became one of the greatest screen musicals in terms of commercial success.

Many critics have attributed much of "West Side Story"'s popularity to its musical score. In *The Complete Book of the American Theatre,* David A. Ewen named the score as "one of the most powerful assets to this grim tragedy." Ewen cited "Maria," "I Feel Pretty," and "Somewhere" as "unforgettable lyrical episodes." Sondheim's comic songs, such as "America" and "Gee, Officer Krupke!," have also been applauded for their wittiness and their roles as satirical commentaries.

Besides its success in the United States, "West Side Story" achieved international recognition. It played throughout Europe to critical praise, and, in 1968, the play entered the repertory of the Volksper, Vienna's distinguished opera house. Ironically, American officials were not enthusiastic about the play's presentation abroad. Ewen recorded that, in spite of "West Side Story"'s success, "plans to produce it at the World's Fair in Brussels and in the Soviet Union collapsed because of opposition from some high American government quarters to present to foreign audiences so sordid and realistic a portrait of American life."

Looking back on his first endeavor, Sondheim finds some of its score distressing. "Maria" he called "a very fruity lyric," and "Somewhere," he felt, contains "one of the most embarrassing lyric lines ever written."

Sondheim's next production was "Gypsy," a musical based on the autobiography of burlesque star Gypsy Rose Lee. Initially, Sondheim was contracted to write both the music and the lyrics for this show, but actress Ethel Merman felt uneasy with a little known composer. So Jule Styne composed "Gypsy"'s music while Sondheim wrote the lyrics, a collaboration that produced, according to Harvey Schmidt, "the ideal Broadway show score." Although the play is entertaining in the tradition of Broadway musicals, its "real distinction," said Schmidt, "is in the fact that at its heart it is a 'serious' musical dealing with deep human drives and needs. And it manages to avoid pitfalls that work against most attempts at 'seriousness' in musicals: sentimentality and pretentiousness. Each song is strongly rooted in character and story, yet bounces off the stage with artful simplicity, never once violating its promise to 'Let Me Entertain You.'" One song from "Gypsy," "Some People," is considered, at least by Jerry Herman, to be the "best single lyric ever written." "It's perfectly metered and rhymed," he proclaimed. "It's a lyric in the Larry Hart sense of a *song* lyric, and at the same time it is a piece of dramatic literature, poetry that defines the character of Madame Rose [Gypsy's mother] as clearly as three scenes of dialogue. You know this woman after hearing it. It's harsh, it's bitter, its unrelenting, it's skillfull, it works on, like, three levels for me, and I admire it enormously." "In fact," he concluded, "I admire the *Gypsy* lyrics and score more than any other I can think of at this moment."

An old-fashioned burlesque, "A Funny Thing Happened on the Way to the Forum," followed "Gypsy." Sondheim and playwrights Burt Shevelove and Larry Gelbart adapted "Forum" from the comedies of Plautus, a classical Roman playwright. The play is bawdy, rough-and-tumble, and fun.

A low comedy of lechers and courtesans done in a combination of ancient Roman and American vaudeville techniques, "Forum" is packed with ambiguous meanings, risque connotations, and not-so-subtle innuendos. For instance, a slave carrying a piece of statuary is told by a matron: "Carry my bust with pride." Typically Sondheim, the score is saturated with humor. Some critics have cited "Everybody Ought to Have a Maid" as particularly amusing while "Lovely" has been suspected, at least by one critic, of being Sondheim's satire of Sondheim's "Tonight." For "Forum," unlike most of his previous plays, Sondheim wrote both the lyrics and the music. "With *Forum*," a *Time* reviewer noted, "Sondheim finally proved that he, like Noel Coward, could indeed go it alone." "Forum" received a Tony Award as the season's best musical, and, in 1966, it was released by United Artists as a motion picture starring Zero Mostel, Jack Gilford, Phil Silvers, and Buster Keaton.

Sondheim's next play, "Anyone Can Whistle," hit a sour note. Highly experimental in form and technique, it was a box-office failure that closed after only nine performances. Though disappointing in its reception, "Anyone Can Whistle" has been referred to as a "sacrificial lamb" in musical comedy; that is, a show that does not receive critical commendations, but that alters critical perceptions allowing similar productions, as Al Carmines said, to "make it because the first show changed the consciousness of the critic."

The following year, "Do I Hear a Waltz?" received a similar welcome. Ewen commented that, though the play was written with good intentions, it met with bad results from reviewers. And "the public apparently agreed," he continued, "for *Do I Hear a Waltz?* . . . promised much but, in the end, reneged on those promises." Among the criticisms of "Waltz," however, was praise for Sondheim's lyrics. Some songs, such as "What Do We Do? We Fly!," which illuminates the horror of air travel, or "This Week Americans," which is the vehicle through which an Italian manager of a boarding house comments on the eccentricities of her American guests, were singled out for their humor.

Sondheim followed "Waltz" with two hard-core conceptual musicals, "Company" and "Follies." The plays "were critical successes," noted Sweet, "but they weren't huge box-office successes" since many audiences were not prepared for serious musicals.

For instance, "Company," Walter Kerr announced in Ewen's book, "gets right down to brass tacks and brass knuckles without a moment's hestitating, staring contemporary society in the eye before spitting in it." Basically, the play is a sociological commentary on marriage. It tells the story of a thirty-five-year-old bachelor, Bobby, who lives in New York in the midst of his married, matchmaker friends. At the final curtain, Bobby remains a bachelor, but a bachelor with doubts about the single life.

Sweet charged audiences with "missing the point" of the show. "People would come out of *Company* debating whether the show was pro- or anti-marriage," he accused. "I mean, if nothing else, all you have to do is listen to the lyrics of 'Being Alive' and that question is laid to rest." Sondheim explained that "Company" is "the most pro-marriage show in the world." He told *Time:* "It says, very clearly, that to be emotionally committed to somebody is very difficult, but to be alone is impossible." Some critics, noticing the similarities between the character of Bobby and the life-long bachelor Sondheim, considered "Company" autobiographical.

In "Follies," Sondheim's use of dramatic lyrics and subtexts is exemplary. The song "The Road You Didn't Take" is a case in point. This song, Sondheim suggests, portrays a man who "on the surface is . . . saying, 'Oh, I never look back on the past, I mean, my goodness, it just wouldn't be worth it.' He's doing it to con himself as well as the lady he is with; in point of fact, he is ripped to shreds internally." "There's also a stabbing dissonance in the music," the composer explained, "a note that tells you, the audience, that something is not quite Kosher about what this guy is saying."

He goes on to discuss "In Buddy's Eyes," which is a woman's lie to the man who jilted her thirty years earlier. She tells him that she is married and happy, but the subtext reveals the woman's true feelings. "Nothing in the lyric," Sondheim pointed out, "nothing, not a single word tells you that maybe it isn't true. Nothing in the music tells you. . . . The actress has to tell you, and if you watch her deliver that song with intense anger because she feels she has been had . . . the whole song takes on a very peculiar quality. It isn't quite what it seems to be, and yet there's nothing in the lyrics or music that tells you this."

Produced during the nostalgia craze of the early seventies, "Follies" is reminiscent of Ziegfeld girls and feather boas. Utilizing theatrical modes of the twenties, thirties, and forties, it is a sentimental play that established Sondheim as *the* Broadway lyricist. A *Time* reviewer remarked: "For the musical, he has written some of the glossiest, wittiest lyrics in Broadway history. His melodies gracefully genuflect to Kern and Gershwin, Berlin and Arlen. His words bow to no one. With *Follies* he has established himself, beyond a doubt, as the theatre's supreme lyricist."

Nearly two years after "Follies," when Charles Michener worried that the Broadway musical had degenerated to an embarrassing state of high camp and rock music, Sondheim's "A Little Night Music" appeared on Broadway and restored some of the reviewer's faith in the musical theatre. "Sondheim," he wrote, "is virtually alone in trying to preserve the great tradition of dramatic songwriting that Jerome Kern and Oscar Hammerstein II began more than 40 years ago with 'Showboat.'" Critics recognized "Night Music" to be as spectacular as the great musicals that had gone before it, but, as Michener noted, the play was serious, too, "pertinent as well as diverting."

Sondheim composed all the songs for "Night Music" in three-quarter time or multiples of that meter; this served as the play's concept and tied it together. Three-quarter time was the foundation to which the composer added a Greek chorus, conons, and fuguetos. Subtexts were injected into almost every song—most notably in "Every Day a Little Death," which allows a countess to express her feelings of loneliness as a philanderer's wife. In addition, Sondheim devoted himself to the "inner monologue song," which is a song, a *Time* critic explained, "in which characters sing of their deepest thoughts, but almost never to each other."

Though "Night Music" addresses the standard musical-comedy subject—love, it "is a masquelike affair, tailor-made to fit Sondheim's flair for depicting confused people experiencing ambivalent thoughts and feelings," the *Time* reviewer assessed. Many of his songs illustrate ambivalence because Sondheim likes neurotic people. He revealed: "I like troubled people. Not that I don't like squared-away people, but I *prefer* neurotic people. I like to hear rumblings beneath the surface." The show's cast of confused characters includes the giddy child bride whose middle-aged husband takes up with his ex-mistress while his adolescent son has

a crush on his new stepmother. Of course, the above-mentioned countess laments the sadness of her marriage to a straying husband, and a lusty chambermaid salutes carnal love through the play.

Critically, "Night Music" was a triumph. "This is a jewelled music box of a show," asserted Kalem, "lovely to look at, delightful to listen to, perhaps too exquisite, fragile and muted to ever be quite humanly affecting." "It is a victory of technique over texture," the reviewer bubbled, "and one leaves it in the odd mental state of unbridled admiration and untouched feelings."

Many reviewers agreed that the strongest element in the play was Sondheim's score. "It is a beauty," Kalem gushed, "his best yet in an exceedingly distinguished career." "Night Music," another critic insisted, "is Sondheim's most brilliant accomplishment to date." "Literate, ironic, playful, enviably clever, altogether professional," praised Kalem, "Sondheim is a quicksilver wordsmith in the great tradition of Cole Porter, Noel Coward and Lorenz Hart."

Written next, "Pacific Overtures" employed stylistic techniques of the Orient, including Kabuki theatre techniques, haiku, dance, and masks. Throughout the play, which is the Japanese version of Commander Matthew Perry's visit to the islands in 1835, Sondheim illustrates the ramifications of the diplomatic and trade relations that Japan engaged in at this time. "Pacific Overtures," then, demonstrates the havoc that foreigners brought when they arrived in feudal Japan.

"The overall effect of Sondheim's next show," "Side by Side by Sondheim," said Jack Kroll of *Newsweek*, "is to turn Sondheim into a kind of American Noel Coward." An anthology of the composer's work, "Side by Side" is a British tribute to the composer, and most critics are quick to add their homage. Brendan Gill of the *New Yorker* wrote that "the apotheosis of Stephen Sondheim proceeds apace, and I am eager to do my bit. At forty-seven, Mr. Sondheim may feel that he is a trifle young to be hoisted up onto a plinth as the Good Gray Tunesmith of Turtle Bay, but the body of his work is already impressively large, and his admirers are as numerous as they are importunate; besides, it is an ineradicable defect of homage that it must be accepted when it is offered, and not when it is convenient." *New York*'s Alan Rich added: "These Britishers have journeyed to our midst to remind us of what we all should be aware of: That Sondheim is one of our treasures. . . ."

Sondheim once again made his presence known on Broadway with "Sweeney Todd, the Demon Barber of Fleet Street." Sondheim became interested in the play in 1973, related Mel Gussow of the *New York Times*, "when he saw a production of the melodrama at the Stratford East Theatre in England. He was captivated by it, although, as he said, 'I found it much more passionate and serious than the audience did.'"

Composed as if it were an opera, "Sweeney Todd" is the story of a murderous barber who sends his victims downstairs to a pie shop where they become the secret ingredients in Mrs. Lovett's meat pies. By Sondheim's own admission, the play "has a creepy atmosphere." The main character, Todd, is out for revenge. Judge Turpin, who desired Todd's wife and daughter, shipped the barber off to Australia as punishment for a crime that he did not commit. Todd escapes and returns seeking vengeance. His attempt to kill the judge fails, causing his revenge to snowball into mass murder. In the end, Todd kills Turpin, but by then the barber, too, is doomed.

"Sweeney Todd" is about revenge. Harold Prince's production, however, mirrors the industrial age, its influences, and its effects. "We are invited to see Sweeney Todd not as a man obsessed with an insane desire for revenge," Gill observed, "but as the sorry victim of the workings of a vicious society—that nineteenth century England which was reaping the rich fruit of the Industrial Revolution by dint of ignoring the cost in human suffering."

The real purpose of "Sweeney Todd" is, as Gill pointed out, "to give us all a good old-fashioned scare," which it does. For as Gill said after seeing the play, "I am steering clear these days of trapdoors, straight razors, and the more complexly bestrewn pizzas."

"Sweeney Todd" received numerous Drama Desk Awards and eight Tony Awards in 1979, including best score of a musical. In the opinion of director Harold Prince, the play's music is "the most melodic and romantic score that Steve has ever written. The music is soaring. . . ." Nearly 80 percent of the show is music, and musical motifs recur throughout the score to maintain the audience's emotional level. Sondheim even incorporated a musical clue, a theme associated with a character, into the score.

In March, 1981, "Marry Me a Little," a musical collage of Sondheim's songs, opened Off-Broadway at the Actors Playhouse after appearing at the Production Company. Conceived and developed by Craig Lucas and Norman Rene, "Marry Me a Little" incorporates the music from Sondheim's earlier shows, including three songs from "Saturday Night." The songs are worked into a dramatic background, but there is no dialogue and little stage business. "A young man and a young woman, an average, unglamorous pair, are each alone on a Saturday night," noted a reviewer in the *New York Times*. "As they go through their solitary rituals they daydream songs by Mr. Sondheim, and in their fantasies they eventually meet." The songs presented in "Marry Me a Little," the reviewer declared, "further consolidate Mr. Sondheim's position as our pre-eminent Broadway composer and lyricist." But that should not be surprising since, as Sondheim's mother revealed to *Time:* "Steve always wanted to be an American Noel Coward."

Sondheim told *CA:* "It was my mother who wanted me to be the American Noel Coward, not I. If I wanted to be like anybody (which I don't), it wouldn't be Noel Coward."

AVOCATIONAL INTERESTS: Puzzles, games, record collecting, talking.

BIOGRAPHICAL/CRITICAL SOURCES—Books: David A. Ewen, *The Complete Book of the American Musical Theatre*, Holt, 1970; Richard Lewine and Alfred Simon, *Songs of the American Theatre*, Dodd, 1973; Otis L. Guernsey, Jr., editor, *Playwrights, Lyricists, Composers on Theatre*, Dodd, 1974; Craig Zadan, *Sondheim and Company*, Avon, 1976; Catharine Hughes, editor, *New York Theatre Annual*, Gale, Volume I, 1978, Volume II, 1978; Catharine Hughes, editor, *American Theatre Annual 1978-1979*, Gale, 1980; Catharine Hughes, editor, *American Theatre Annual 1979-1980*, Gale, 1981.

Periodicals: *Time*, April 12, 1971, May 3, 1971, March 12, 1973, March 19, 1973, February 25, 1980; *Newsweek*, April 23, 1973, May 2, 1977, March 19, 1979; *New York Times*, April 19, 1977, February 1, 1979, February 25, 1979, March 2, 1979, June 2, 1979, February 14, 1980, March 14, 1981; *New York Post*, April 19, 1977, March 2, 1979, February 15, 1980; *Variety*, April 20, 1977, February 20, 1980; *New York*, May 2, 1977, March 3, 1979, March 19, 1979, March 3, 1980; *New Yorker*, May 2, 1977, March 12, 1979; *Daily News*, March 2, 1979, February 15, 1980; *Chicago Tribune*, June 5, 1979.

—*Sketch by Charity Anne Dorgan*

SONDRUP, Steven P(reece) 1944-

PERSONAL: Born May 27, 1944, in Salt Lake City, Utah; son of Walter E. and Louise P. Sondrup. *Education:* University of Utah, B.A. (with honors), 1968; Harvard University, A.M., 1969, Ph.D., 1974. *Politics:* Independent. *Religion:* Church of Jesus Christ of Latter-day Saints (Mormons). *Home:* 1346 South 18th E., Salt Lake City, Utah 84108. *Office:* Department of Comparative Literature, Brigham Young University, Provo, Utah 84602.

CAREER: Brigham Young University, Provo, Utah, assistant professor, 1973-77, associate professor of comparative literature, 1977—. *Member:* International Comparative Literature Association, Modern Language Association of America, Society for the Advancement of Scandinavian Studies, Hugo von Hofmannsthal-Gesellschaft, Phi Beta Kappa. *Awards, honors:* Woodrow Wilson fellow, 1968-69; award from Association for Mormon Letters, 1979, for "Literary Aspects of Mormon Autobiography."

WRITINGS: Hofmannsthal and the Symbolist Tradition, Lang, 1976; (editor with Craig Inglis) *Konkordanz zu den Gedichten Hugo von Hofmannsthals* (title means "Concordance to the Poetry of Hugo von Hoffmannsthals"), Brigham Young University Press, 1977; (editor) *Arts and Inspiration: Mormon Perspectives on the Arts*, Brigham Young University Press, 1980; (with David Chisolm) *Konkordanz zur Lyrik C. F. Meyers* (title means "Concordance to the Poetry of C. F. Meyer"), Atheneum, 1982; (translator with Dianna Wormuth), Artur Lundkvist, *Talk Trees and Other Poems*, Brigham Young University Press, 1982.

SIDELIGHTS: Sondrup told *CA:* "In my view, writing about writing is not a parasitic activity, but rather a means of securing the sense of continuity and tradition upon which literature in the best sense of the word is ultimately based. Literature today exists, at least in part, because it existed yesterday, last year, and millennia ago. The more that is understood about literary intertextuality, which is the foundation of literary meaning, the richer and deeper literary experience will be."

*   *   *

SOPER, Eileen Louise 1900-

PERSONAL: Born December 14, 1900, in Sydney, Australia; daughter of Edwin Curwen (an accountant) and Olga Louise (Varcoe) Service; married Frederick George Soper (a professor of chemistry and university administrator), February 14, 1938. *Education:* University of Otago, B.A., 1923. *Religion:* Church of England. *Home:* 6 Howard St., Macandrew Bay, Dunedin, New Zealand.

CAREER: Otago Witness, Otago, New Zealand, associate editor, 1924-32; *Otago Daily Times*, Otago, editor of "Notes for Women," 1932-38; writer and producer of plays and pageants for Otago Women's Club, 1938-41; Otago Girl Guides Association, Otago, provincial commissioner, 1941-54; University of Otago, Otago, hostess in University Lodge, 1954-64. Joint New Zealand representative at Girl Guides Commissioners Conference at Evian, 1946; president of Victoria League of Otago, 1964-66. *Member:* Dunedin Business and Professional Women's Club (first president, 1932-38), University of Otago Staff Wives' Association (first president, 1948).

WRITINGS: The Otago of Our Mothers (centennial history), Whitcombe & Tombs, 1948; *Young Jane* (juvenile), Whitcombe & Tombs, 1955; *The Green Years* (autobiography),

John McIndoe, 1969; *The Month of the Brittle Star* (juvenile), John McIndoe, 1971; *The Leaves Turn* (autobiography), John McIndoe, 1973.

WORK IN PROGRESS: A study of Henry James's *Virtuous Attachments;* a novel for children; an autobiography.

SIDELIGHTS: Eileen Soper told *CA:* "The desire to write persists, though one grows older. What seems to be lacking is time—or is it that one takes longer over everything one does? A greatest hope is that eyesight will not fail. I read more poetry, more literature, fewer novels, and wonder why anything more need be written, as it has already been so splendidly said by others. Yet does that deter one from again taking up the pen? No!"

*   *   *

SORUM, Paul Clay 1943-

PERSONAL: Born January 7, 1943, in Madison, Wis.; son of C. Harvey and Emma-Lou (Bachelder) Sorum; married Christina Elliott (a professor of Greek and Latin), June 15, 1968; children: Eve Christina. *Education:* Stanford University, A.B., 1965; Harvard University, M.A., 1966, Ph.D., 1972; University of North Carolina, M.D., 1980. *Home:* 601 Rock Creek Rd., Chapel Hill, N.C. 27514. *Office:* North Carolina Memorial Hospital, Chapel Hill, N.C. 27514.

CAREER: University of North Carolina, Chapel Hill, assistant professor of modern European history, 1971-76; North Carolina Memorial Hospital, Chapel Hill, resident in medicine and pediatrics, 1980—.

WRITINGS: Intellectuals and Decolonization in France, University of North Carolina Press, 1977.

SIDELIGHTS: Sorum told *CA:* "My switch from academic history to medicine was prompted by my failure to receive tenure, by the lack of enjoyment and satisfaction that I found in historical research, and by my discouragement with the pomposity, narrow-minded self-importance, and inhumanity of many historians in their dealings with graduate students, colleagues, and professional rivals."

*   *   *

SPARKS, Fred 1916(?)-1981

OBITUARY NOTICE: Born c. 1916; died February 18, 1981. Journalist best known as the recipient of the 1951 Pulitzer Prize for his reports from Berlin. Sparks wrote for the *Chicago Daily News,* the *New York World-Telegram,* and *The Sun.* He also contributed humorous pieces to periodicals, including *New Yorker, Saturday Evening Post,* and *Esquire.* Obituaries and other sources: *New York Times,* February 19, 1981.

*   *   *

SPARKS, John 1939-

PERSONAL: Born in April, 1939, in Colchester, England; son of Dennis John and Nancy Kate (Skeet) Sparks; married Anne Fowler; children: Nicola, Justin. *Education:* Queen Mary College, London, B.Sc., 1961; University of London, Ph.D., 1964. *Religion:* Atheist. *Office:* British Broadcasting Corp., Whiteladies Rd., Bristol, England.

CAREER: British Broadcasting Corp., Bristol, England, radio and television producer with natural history unit, 1965—. *Member:* Zoological Society (fellow), Association for the Study of Animal Behaviour.

WRITINGS: Penguins, David & Charles, 1967; *Bird Behavior,* Paul Hamlyn, 1969; *Owls: Their Natural and Unnatural*

History, David & Charles, 1970; *Animals in Danger,* Paul Hamlyn, 1972; *Animal Design,* BBC Publications, 1974; *The Air Around Us,* Aldus, 1976; *Island Life,* Aldus, 1976; *The Sexual Connection,* David & Charles, 1978. Contributor to scientific journals and popular magazines, including *Animals, New Scientist,* and *Birds Illustrated.*

WORK IN PROGRESS: A book on animal behavior, publication by BBC Publications expected in 1982.

SIDELIGHTS: Sparks commented: "I have produced one hundred natural history television programs, which have involved filming throughout the world. Recently, I was one of the producers of 'Life on Earth,' the prize-winning and highly acclaimed series presented by David Attenborough. Presently, I am working on a series of six prestigious programs, 'Discovering Animal Behavior,' which will, with the help of dramatic reconstruction, trace, from medieval times to the present day, the story of our understanding of why animals behave as they do."

*   *   *

SPARROW, John (Hanbury Angus) 1906-

PERSONAL: Born November 13, 1906, in New Oxley, near Wolverhampton, England; son of Isaac Saredon and Margaret (Macgregor) Sparrow. *Education:* New College, Oxford, M.A. (with first class honors), 1929. *Home:* Beechwood House, Iffley Turn, Oxford OX4 4HW, England.

CAREER: Called to the Bar at Middle Temple, England, 1931; High Court, Chancery Division, Middle Temple, lawyer, 1931-39, 1945-52, and honorary bencher, 1952; All Souls College, Oxford, England, warden, 1952-77. Fellow of All Souls College, Oxford, 1929-52; fellow of Winchester College, 1951. *Military service:* British Army, Oxfordshire and Buckinghamshire Light Infantry, Coldstream Guards, and War Office, 1940-45. *Member:* Garrick Club, Reform Club, Beefsteak Club. *Awards, honors:* Officer of Order of the British Empire, 1946; fellow of New College, Oxford, 1956; D.Litt. from University of Warwick, 1967.

WRITINGS: The Poems of Bishop Henry King, Nonesuch, 1925, reprinted, Folcroft, 1974; *Half Lines and Repetitions in Virgil,* Clarendon Press, 1931, reprinted (edited by Steele Commager), Garland Publishing, 1977; *Sense and Poetry: Essays on the Place of Meaning in Contemporary Verse,* Constable, 1934, Folcroft, 1973; *Robert Bridges,* British Book Center, 1962; *Independent Essays,* Faber, 1963, Greenwood Press, 1977; *Controversial Essays,* Faber, 1966; *Mark Pattison and the Idea of a University,* Cambridge University Press, 1967; *After the Assassination: A Positive Appraisal of the Warren Report,* Chilmark Press, 1967; *Visible Words: A Study of Inscriptions in Books as Works of Art,* Cambridge University Press, 1969; *Too Much of a Good Thing,* University of Chicago Press, 1977; (editor with Alessandro Perosa) *Renaissance Latin Verse: An Anthology,* Duckworth, 1979. Contributor of articles and reviews to magazines.

*   *   *

SPECHT, Robert 1928-

PERSONAL: Born April 30, 1928, in New York, N.Y.; son of Joseph (a waiter) and Hella (Frankl) Specht; married Judith Lee Adkins, September 16, 1961; children: Raphael Richard, Allegra Judith. *Education:* City College (now of the City University of New York), M.S., 1960. *Religion:* "Non-sectarian." *Agent:* Eisenbach-Green-Duchow, Inc., 760 North La Cienega Blvd., Los Angeles, Calif. 90069.

CAREER: Editor, 1961-65; free-lance television writer and story editor, 1965—.

WRITINGS: Tisha, St. Martin's, 1976.

WORK IN PROGRESS: Another Set of Beasts, a novel.

* * *

SPENCE, Bill
   See SPENCE, William John Duncan

* * *

SPENCE, Duncan
   See SPENCE, William John Duncan

* * *

SPENCE, William John Duncan   1923-
   (Bill Spence, Duncan Spence; Jim Bowden, Kirk Ford, Floyd Rogers, pseudonyms)

PERSONAL: Born April 20, 1923, in Middlesbrough, England; son of John Robert (a teacher) and Anne (Payne) Spence; married Joan Mary Rhoda Ludley, September 8, 1944; children: Anne Spence Hudson, Geraldine Spence Jones, Judith Spence Gilbert, Duncan. *Education:* Attended St. Mary's College, Strawberry Hill, England, 1940-42. *Religion:* Roman Catholic. *Home address:* Post Office, Ampleforth College, York YO6 4EZ, England. *Agent:* Laurence Pollinger Ltd., 18 Maddox St., London W1R 0EU, England.

CAREER: Teacher in primary school in Middlesbrough, England, 1942; Ampleforth College, York, England, store manager, 1946-77; writer, 1977—. Tutor at writing school. *Military service:* Royal Air Force, Bomber Command, 1942-46. *Member:* Society of Authors, Hakluyt Society, Whitby Literary and Philosophical Society.

WRITINGS—Under name Bill Spence: (With wife, Joan Spence) *Romantic Ryedale,* Ryedale Printing Works, 1977; *Harpooned* (nonfiction), Conway Maritime Press, 1980; (with J. Spence) *The Medieval Monasteries of Yorkshire,* Ryedale Printing Works, 1981; *Bomber's Moon* (war novel), R. Hale, 1981.

Under name Duncan Spence: *Dark Hell* (novel), Brown Watson, 1959.

Novels under pseudonym Jim Bowden; published by R. Hale: *The Return of the Sheriff,* 1960; *Wayman's Ford,* 1960; *Two Gun Justice,* 1961; *Roaring Valley,* 1962; *Revenge in Red Springs,* 1962; *Black Water Canyon,* 1963; *Arizona Gold,* 1963; *Trail of Revenge,* 1964; *Brazo Feud,* 1965; *Guns Along the Brazo,* 1967; *Gun Loose,* 1969; *Valley of Revenge,* 1971; *Trail to Texas,* 1973; *Thunder in Montana,* 1973; *Showdown in Salt Fork,* 1975; *Hired Gun,* 1976; *Incident in Bison Creek,* 1977; *CAP,* 1978; *Dollars of Death,* 1979; *Renegade Riders,* 1980; *Gunfight at Elm Creek,* 1980.

Novels under pseudonym Kirk Ford: *Trail to Sedalia,* R. Hale, 1967; *Feud Riders,* R. Hale, 1974.

Novels under pseudonym Floyd Rogers; published by R. Hale: *The Man From Cheyenne Wells,* 1964; *Revenge Rider,* 1964; *The Stage Riders,* 1967; *Montana Justice,* 1973; *Hangman's Gulch,* 1974; *Incident at Elk River,* 1979.

Contributor of articles and reviews to magazines, including *Country Life, Coast and Country, Yorkshire Life,* and *North,* and to newspapers.

WORK IN PROGRESS: Two historical novels about whaling; research on the history of whaling, polar regions, and medieval monasteries.

SIDELIGHTS: Spence commented: "As a peace-loving individual I think that all decisions can be achieved without violent argument, but rather by rational discussion. This tends to be reflected in my latest writing when characters become opposed. Though there may be extreme conflict this does not necessarily result in extreme violence. Maybe this has been worked out of my system in my Westerns!"

* * *

SPICER, Bart   1918-
   (Jay Barbette, a joint pseudonym)

PERSONAL: Born in 1918 in Richmond, Va.; married Betty Coe (a writer).

CAREER: Worked as journalist and radio writer; in public relations for Universal Military Training; free-lance writer. Formerly associated with Scripps-Howard Syndicate and World Affairs Council. *Military service:* U.S. Army; served in the South Pacific; became captain.

WRITINGS—Novels: *The Dark Light,* Dodd, 1949; *Blues for the Prince,* Dodd, 1950; *Black Sheep, Run,* Dodd, 1951; *The Golden Door,* Dodd, 1951; *The Long Green,* Dodd, 1952; *The Wild Ohio,* Dodd, 1953; *The Taming of Carney Wilde,* Dodd, 1954; *The Day of the Dead,* Dodd, 1955; *The Tall Captains,* Dodd, 1957; *Brother to the Enemy,* Dodd, 1958; *Exit Running,* Dodd, 1959; *The Day Before Thunder,* Dodd, 1960; *Act of Anger,* Atheneum, 1962; *The Burned Man,* Atheneum, 1966; *Kellogg Junction,* Atheneum, 1969; *Festival,* Atheneum, 1970. Also author of *The Adversary,* 1973.

Co-author of books with wife, Betty Coe, under joint pseudonym Jay Barbette. Work represented in anthologies, including *Not Me, Inspector,* edited by Helen Kieran Reilly, Black, 1959.

SIDELIGHTS: Spicer's books have been published in France, Germany, Spain, Sweden, Denmark, Norway, the Netherlands, Japan, Italy, Yugoslavia, and the Soviet Union. They have also been adapted for television.*

* * *

SPIEGEL, John P(aul)   1911-

PERSONAL: Born March 17, 1911, in Chicago, Ill.; son of Modie and Lena (Strauss) Spiegel; married Babette Schiller, August 1, 1935; children: Heli, Adam, Mary, Pauline. *Education:* Dartmouth College, B.A., 1934; Northwestern University, M.D., 1938; Chicago Institute of Psychoanalysis, Diploma, 1949. *Home:* 10 Channing Pl., Cambridge, Mass. 02138. *Office:* Florence Heller Graduate School for Advanced Studies in Social Welfare, Brandeis University, Waltham, Mass. 02254.

CAREER: Michael Reese Hospital, Chicago, Ill., intern, 1938-40, resident in neuropsychiatry, 1940-42, chief of psychiatric clinic, 1946-51, attending physician, 1950-54, associate director of Institute for Psychiatric and Psychosomatic Research and Training, 1951-54; Harvard University, Cambridge, Mass., lecturer, 1953-66, research associate at Laboratory of Social Relations, 1954-66, associate clinical professor of psychiatry, 1957-66; Brandeis University, Waltham, Mass., professor of social psychiatry at Florence Heller Graduate School for Advanced Studies in Social Welfare, 1966—, director of Lemberg Center for the Study of Violence, 1966-73, director of training in ethnicity and mental health, 1977—. Lecturer at University of Chicago, 1949-51, and Institute of Psychoanalysis, Chicago, 1953; Edward T. Gibson Lecturer at University of Kansas, 1956; lecturer at Tulane University, 1958. Associate attending physician at Cook

County Psychopathic Hospital, 1947-49; assistant psychiatrist at Children's Medical Center, Boston, Mass., 1954-66. Member of National Research Council committee on disaster studies, 1952-58; member of Josiah Macy, Jr. Foundation conference on group processes, 1954-58; member of National Institute of Mental Health behavioral science study section, 1958-61, and Mental Health Film Board. *Military service:* U.S. Army Air Forces, Medical Corps, 1942-46, chief of professional services at U.S. Air Force Hospital, St. Petersburg, Fla., 1944-46; became major.

MEMBER: American Sociological Association (fellow), American Psychiatric Association (fellow; president-elect, 1973), Group for the Advancement of Psychiatry (chairman of committee on the family, 1950—), American Public Health Association, American Psychosomatic Society, Society for Applied Anthropology, American Medical Association (fellow), National Council on Family Relations, American Academy of Psychoanalysis, American Association for the Advancement of Science, Australian and New Zealand College of Psychiatrists, Illinois Society of Mental Health (past vice-president), Chicago Psychoanalytic Society, Association of Psychiatric Facilities of Chicago.

WRITINGS: (With Roy Richard Grinker) *War Neuroses in North Africa: The Tunisian Campaign, January-May, 1943,* Josiah Macy, Jr. Foundation, 1943; (with Grinker) *Men Under Stress,* Blakiston, 1945, reprinted, Irvington, 1979; *The Dynamics of Dissent,* Grune, 1968; (contributor) Gertrude Einstein, editor, *Learning to Apply New Concepts to Casework Practice,* Family Service Association of America, 1968; (contributor) William Gray and others, editors, *General Systems Theory and Psychiatry,* Little, Brown, 1969.

Transactions: The Interplay Between Individual, Family, and Society (edited by John Papajohn), Science House, 1971; (with Pavel Machotka) *Messages of the Body,* Free Press, 1974; (with Papajohn) *Transactions in Families,* Jossey-Bass, 1975; (editor with Donald Light, Jr., and C. J. Lammer) *The Dynamics of University Protest,* Nelson-Hall, 1977; (with Machotka) *The Articulate Body,* Irvington, 1980; *Ethnicity and Family Therapy,* Guilford Press, 1982. Contributor to medical journals and journals in the behavioral sciences.

WORK IN PROGRESS: An article for *Models of Family Treatments.*

SIDELIGHTS: Spiegel told *CA:* "My research has included: (1) studies of combat neuroses and reaction to stress during World War II, which resulted in two books co-authored with Roy R. Grinker (*War Neuroses in North Africa* and *Men Under Stress*); (2) systems theory constructed so as to interrelate the social and behavioral sciences, described in the book *Transactions;* (3) studies of the dynamics of riots and civil disorders conducted when I was director of the Lemberg Center for the Study of Violence, resulting in a number of publications focusing on the dynamics of third-party intervention in general and mediation in particular; (4) studies of the relations between conflict in cultural value orientations among various minority and ethnic subcultural groups in the process of acculturation, family interaction processes, and mental illness in a family member. This last interest then led me to develop a mental health training program for mainstream professionals to enable them to provide culturally appropriate mental health services for the various immigrant and ethnic groups.

"Two themes have guided all my work: (1) How to relate environmental stress from whatever source to intrapsychic conflict and mental health problems, both in theory and in the empirical setting; and, (2) how to develop concepts that will make it easier for members of the various mental health disciplines to work together."

BIOGRAPHICAL/CRITICAL SOURCES: American Journal of Psychiatry, July 2, 1975.

*   *   *

SPIGELGASS, Leonard 1908-

PERSONAL: Born November 26, 1908, in Brooklyn, N.Y.; son of Abraham and Rebecca (Ratner) Spigelgass. *Education:* New York University, B.A., 1929. *Office:* Dramatists Guild, 234 West 44th St., New York, N.Y. 10036.

CAREER: Worked as reader and story editor in Hollywood, Calif., 1930; writer. *Military service:* Served during World War II; became lieutenant colonel. *Member:* Dramatists Guild, Writers Guild of America, Authors Guild.

WRITINGS: A Majority of One (play), Random House, 1959; *Scuttle Under the Bonnet,* Doubleday, 1962; *Dear Me, The Sky Is Falling* (three-act play), Samuel Franch, 1963; *Fed to the Teeth,* Doubleday, 1964; (with Edward G. Robinson) *All My Yesterdays,* Hawthorn, 1973.

Unpublished plays: "Princess O'Hara," first produced in 1935; "A Remedy for Winter," first produced in 1965; "The Wrong Way Light Bulb," first produced in 1969; "Look to the Lillies," (musical; adapted from the motion picture "The Lillies of the Field"), first produced in 1970.

Screenplays: (With Gertrude Purcell) "Service Deluxe," Universal, 1938; (with Gibney Sheridan) "Letter of Introduction," Universal, 1938; (with Charles Grayson) "Unexpected Father," Universal, 1939; (with Grayson and Paul Gerard Smith) "The Boys From Syracuse" (adapted from the play by George Abbott), RKO, 1940; (with Grayson and Peter Milne) "Private Affairs" (adapted from the short story by Walton Green, "He Was One of the Boston Bullertons"), Universal, 1940; (with Art Arthur) "Tight Shoes" (adapted from the short story by Damon Runyon), Universal, 1941; "Butch Minds the Baby" (adapted from the short story by Runyon), Universal, 1942; (with George Oppenheimer and Charles Lederer) "The Youngest Profession" (adapted from the novel by Lillian Day), Metro-Goldwyn-Mayer (MGM), 1942; "The Big Street" (adapted from the story by Runyon, "Little Pinks"), RKO, 1942; (with Edward Gilbert) "All Through the Night," Warner Brothers, 1942; "The Perfect Marriage" (adapted from the play by Samson Raphaelson), Paramount, 1946; (with Ronald Millar) "So Evil My Love" (adapted from the novel by Joseph Shearing), Paramount, 1948; (with Lederer and Hagar Wilde) "I Was a Male War Bride" (adapted from the nonfiction work by Henri Rochard), Twentieth Century-Fox, 1949.

(With Karl Tunberg) "The Law and the Lady" (adapted from the play by Frederick Lonsdale, "The Last of Mrs. Cheyney"), MGM, 1951; (with Tunberg) "Night Into Morning," MGM, 1951; (with Norman Corwin and Tunberg) "Scandal at Scourie" (adapted from the short story by Mary McSherry, "Good Boy"), MGM, 1953; (with William Ludwig) "Athena," MGM, 1954; "Deep in My Heart" (adapted from the biography of Sigmund Romberg by Elliott Arnold), MGM, 1954; (with Ludwig, Art Cohn, and Laslo Vadnay) "Ten Thousand Bedrooms," MGM, 1957; (with Leonard Gershe) "Silk Stockings" (adapted from the musical play by George Kaufman, Leueen McGrath, and Abe Burrows), MGM, 1957; "A Majority of One" (adapted from the play by Spigelgass), Warner Bros., 1962; "Gypsy" (adapted from the musical play by Arthur Laurents based on the memoirs of Gypsy Rose Lee), Warner Bros., 1962.

WORK IN PROGRESS: "Consenting Adults," a play co-written with Laura Z. Hobson; a musical adaptation of "A Majority of One," with Hobson.

*   *   *

SPINIFEX
See MARTIN, David

*   *   *

SPROTT, W(alter) John Herbert   1897-1971

OBITUARY NOTICE—See index for *CA* sketch: Born April 19, 1897, in Crowborough, Sussex, England; died September 2, 1971. Educator and author of books on social psychology. Among Sprott's books are *Miniatures: Orations Delivered by W.J.H. Sprott, Human Groups,* and *Sociology.* Also, Sprott translated from the German Ernst Kretschmer's *Physique and Character* and Sigmund Freud's *New Introductory Lectures.* Sprott's own books have been translated into seven languages, including Hebrew, Japanese, and Portuguese. Obituaries and other sources: *London Times,* September 6, 1971; *Who's Who,* 124th edition, St. Martin's, 1972.

*   *   *

STACKPOLE, Edward J(ames)   1894-1967

OBITUARY NOTICE—See index for *CA* sketch: Born June 21, 1894, in Harrisburg, Pa.; died October 1, 1967. Business executive, publisher, and author of books about the American Civil War. Among Stackpole's books are *They Met at Gettysburg, Chancellorsville: Lee's Greatest Battle,* and *Sheridan in the Shenandoah.* During the Second World War Stackpole became a brigadier general in the U.S. Army. He later joined the Pennsylvania National Guard and retired as a major general. Obituaries and other sources: *Who Was Who in America,* 4th edition, Marquis, 1968.

*   *   *

STAFFORD, David (Christopher)   1943-

PERSONAL: Born December 4, 1943, in Leamington Spa, England; son of Frederick and Barbara (Dew) Stafford; married Lesley Anne Hatfield, November 20, 1964; children: Fiona, Miles, Guy. *Education:* University of Exeter, B.A. (with honors), 1971. *Politics:* Conservative. *Home:* Old Vicarage, Topsham, Exeter, Devonshire, England. *Office:* Department of Economics, University of Exeter, Exeter, England.

CAREER: University of Exeter, Exeter, England, tutor, 1971-72, lecturer, 1972-80, senior lecturer in economics, 1980—. Member of Exeter City Council, 1976-79, deputy leader, 1979—, deputy chairman of housing committee, 1976-77, chairman of committee, 1977-79; chairman of Junior Chamber of Commerce, 1976. *Member:* Institute of Bankers (associate).

WRITINGS: (With D. C. Corner) *China Clay Sand: Liability or Asset?,* Devon County Council, 1972; *Open-Ended Funds: Bank Experience in France and Britain,* Societe Universitaire Europeene de Recherches Financieres, 1975; (with Corner) *Mutual Funds in the European Economic Community and Switzerland,* Macmillan, 1978; *Economics of Housing Policy,* Croom Helm, 1978; *Bank Advertising,* Advertising Association, 1981. Assistant editor of *Social Policy and Administration.*

WORK IN PROGRESS: Economics of Rent Control, publication expected in 1982.

SIDELIGHTS: Stafford wrote: "The double life that I lead as an academic and as a local politician permits me a degree of schizophrenia often denied to others of 'sound mind.' But this life of contrasting roles adds both balance and color. Academic research requires an objective and critical approach while politics is heavy on subjectivity and light on analysis. When I find myself confusing the roles I shall retire!"

*   *   *

STALLINGS, James O.   1938-

PERSONAL: Born January 11, 1938, in Memphis, Tenn. *Education:* Mississippi College, B.S., 1958; University of Pennsylvania, M.D., 1962; University of Iowa, M.S., 1968. *Home:* Park Fleur Apartments, 3131 Fleur Dr., Des Moines, Iowa 50321. *Office:* Plastic Surgery Institute, 1025 Ashworth Rd., 528 Univac Bldg., West Des Moines, Iowa 50265.

CAREER: University of Pennsylvania Hospital, Philadelphia, rotating intern, 1962-63; Veterans Administration Hospital, Iowa City, Iowa, resident in general surgery, 1963-64; Mercy Hospital, Mason City, Iowa, resident in general surgery, 1964-65; University of Iowa Hospital, Iowa City, resident in otolaryngology, 1965-68; New York University, Medical Center, New York, N.Y., resident in plastic surgery at Institute of Reconstructive Plastic Surgery, 1970-72; Plastic Surgery Institute, West Des Moines, Iowa, currently plastic surgeon. Diplomate of American Board of Otolaryngology and American Board of Plastic Surgery. *Military service:* U.S. Air Force, chief of otolaryngology at U.S. Air Force Hospital at Elmendorf Air Force Base, Alaska, 1968-70; became major. *Member:* American Medical Association, Iowa State Medical Society, Polk County Medical Society. *Awards, honors:* Neck fellowship, 1967-68.

WRITINGS: A New You: How Plastic Surgery Can Change Your Life, Mason/Charter, 1977. Contributor of about forty articles to medical journals.

SIDELIGHTS: Stallings has created more than one hundred (so far unpublished) operations, concepts, and modifications in the area of plastic surgery.

*   *   *

STAMBERG, Susan   1938-

PERSONAL: Born September 7, 1938, in Newark, N.J.; daughter of Robert I. (a manufacturer's representative) and Anne (a bookkeeper; maiden name, Rosenberg) Levitt; married Louis Collins Stamberg (a U.S. Department of State official), April 14, 1962; children: Joshua Collins. *Education:* Barnard College, A.B., 1959; graduate study at Brandeis University, 1959. *Agent:* Robert Lescher, 155 East 71st St., New York, N.Y. 20036. *Office:* National Public Radio, 2025 M St. N.W., Washington, D.C. 10021.

CAREER/WRITINGS: Daedalus (magazine), Cambridge, Mass., editorial assistant, 1960-62; *New Republic,* Washington, D.C., editorial assistant, 1962-63; WAMU-FM, Washington, D.C., program director, station manager, and producer and host of show "Kaleidoscope," 1963-70; National Public Radio, Washington, D.C., tape editor, 1971, co-host of show "All Things Considered," 1971—. Contributor to newspapers and periodicals. Host of interview segments "In Conversation With . . . ," 1980. Moderator of television specials and radio programs. *Member:* Maryland Council of the Arts. *Awards, honors:* Major Armstrong Award for educational broadcasting, 1968; honor award from Ohio University, 1977, for "pioneering humanistic selection of news and incisive interviewing techniques"; Clarion Award, 1978, for "Interviews With Susan Stamberg" (series of interviews with women artists); D.H.L. from Marlboro College, 1979; Edward R. Murrow Award from Corporation for Public Broadcasting, 1980, for "increasing the image, audience awareness, and listenership of public radio."

WORK IN PROGRESS: A book tentatively titled *Susan Stamberg's All Things Considered Book,* publication by Pantheon expected in 1982.

SIDELIGHTS: Susan Stamberg, co-host of National Public Radio's award-winning "All Things Considered," likes to think of the news and public affairs program as a radio-newspaper. In addition to news summaries, the ninety-minute program features commentaries, reviews, essays, and interviews. "My hope," Stamberg told Marjorie Harvey of the *Barnard Alumnae,* "is that if you haven't had time to read the newspaper that day, 'All Things Considered' makes sure you still know what's happened. . . . We answer the questions you're left with when you've *finished* the paper."

"ATC," as the show has come to be known, airs nightly on nearly two hundred fifty National Public Radio (NPR) stations and attracts an estimated weekly audience of five million. The reason for the show's popularity, Stamberg explained to *New York*'s Roger Piantadosi, is that "we respect people. We say, 'We are not the all-knowing voice from the top of the mountain, but we have a lively curiosity in the events around us. The world is confusing; let's get together and figure it out—we'll have some laughs, we'll be upset a little, things'll puzzle us, we're not going to understand it all, but let's make an effort.'"

Stamberg, who in 1971 became the first woman ever to anchor a network news program, is frequently praised for her conversational interviewing style, which has been called unique, direct, and effective. Her warm, comforting voice puts her guests at ease, and her ability to listen actively rarely allows a guest to mislead her. "Someone she may be interviewing will come up with an answer which is very obviously trying to fob something off on her," cartoonist Gahan Wilson, a confessed addict of "ATC," told Piantadosi. "The great thing about Susan is that she'll come back and say, 'Aren't you sort of fobbing something off on me?'" She is the key, declared a *Time* writer, "to the program's ingratiating charm. In interviews she is confiding and insouciant, first disarming her subjects, then enlisting them in a delicious conspiracy."

Direct confrontation can make her uncomfortable, Stamberg admits; she believes that an indirect line of questioning is frequently a more effective means of eliciting information from a guest, especially when the guest is defensive. She demonstrated her use of this method to Jean Lawrence, a writer for the *TWA Ambassador,* by recounting her interview of John Ehrlichman. She asked Ehrlichman, a former adviser to President Nixon who was convicted of Watergate-related crimes, "what kind of reaction he got when, say, a gas station attendant in California recognized him. He said he didn't get any kind of reaction, that the rest of the country was nothing like Washington. That in Washington there was only one king, and it was everyone else's job to knock him off the mountain. Now, if I had asked him why the Nixon administration was always so paranoid, I don't think I would have gotten a better description of their real feelings than the last remark."

Stamberg acknowledges that "the power . . . in the radio world lie[s] in producing." She declines, however, invitations to produce "All Things Considered" because, according to Harvey, she is committed to the daily challenge of anchoring

what a *Time* critic called "the most literate, trenchant, and entertaining news program on radio."

AVOCATIONAL INTERESTS: Reading, cooking, exercise, films, concerts, theatre, relaxation.

CA INTERVIEW

Susan Stamberg was interviewed by *CA* on May 23, 1980, at her office in Washington, D.C.

CA: "All Things Considered" has been very successful. Is there any one reason, you think, that it has been such a successful program?

STAMBERG: I think it's because it tries to do what other news organizations, especially electronic ones, don't: provide a kind of alternative service. That means to try to do more analytic reporting, to redefine news to a certain extent, to say that it's not simply what the makers of news on Capitol Hill and in New York and on the West Coast say it is, but that it's also what's happening in the middle of the country and in the small events of life. The fact that it's a national program, a network program, and a public radio program is extremely important. What we try to do is put the country in touch with itself and put ordinary people, just plain citizens, on the air as often as we do people who are in elected office or who hold extremely high positions in business or government.

CA: You mentioned analytic reporting. How do you define that in terms of a radio program?

STAMBERG: What we try to do regularly is to get through the "who," "what," "where," "when," and "how" of the story as quickly as possible, in order to focus on the "why." That's where our major emphasis is: Why has this event happened? What led up to it? What's the background? What's the context? What sorts of implications will the event have?

CA: ATC started out popular in the Midwest and remains popular there. Why?

STAMBERG: Public radio began in the middle of the country. The oldest public station in the system is WHA in Madison, Wisconsin. I think they've been on the air for about fifty-five years. There has been a long tradition of commitment to public radio in the Midwest, which accounts for some of our popularity there. We also put the Midwest on the air—we listen to that part of the country. What we're noticing now is that our listening patterns are changing. Metropolitan areas, like Chicago and New York, have had few listeners, but I understand that is changing; we have much larger audiences in New York, for instance, than we had suspected.

The reason for our popularity in small towns is that people see us as an alternative service, and we are most popular in places where thare is less competition for attention. A place like New York City, for instance, has excellent daily newspapers and the residents of New York City are very well served by their local media; but in a place like Murfreesboro, Tennessee, or in other small communities, ATC is an oasis of information. The local media just don't serve those people in the way that we can.

CA: You talk about "All Things Considered" as an alternative. Why haven't the commercial networks imitated the program?

STAMBERG: I don't know. I think ABC's "Nightline" comes closest to what we do. ABC's "20/20" and NBC's

"Prime Time" try. So there are imitations. But there's no way that television can do what we do on a daily basis, because it would be so expensive for them. They just couldn't afford it. As far as radio goes, I think commercial networks find they can sell more of their time through much simpler kinds of disc jockey and talk shows. We do rather elaborate production work here, and we're reinventing the medium as we go along. That involves a commitment of resources that I doubt the commercial stations would want to make. It's much less expensive for them to put on a record or to open their phone lines to listeners. It's much easier to do a show like that and sell commercial time on it.

CA: What do you mean by "reinventing the medium"?

STAMBERG: People like to say that ATC is like the golden age of radio—the 1930's and the 1940's when radio really was king. But if you go back and listen to any of those programs, you'll find them embarrassing. The announcers sound stentorian, too deep-throated, and too oratorical—not simply rhetorical, but oratorical. So I think it's wrong to say we have revived the golden days of radio. What we are doing is a kind of radio that I don't believe has ever existed. By speaking very simply and warmly to people, sounding like human beings rather than plastic wind-up dolls, we're using the medium in new and very creative ways: playing with it, stretching it, seeing how far we can push it.

I think a recent piece I did on Pablo Picasso was an example of how we can use this medium as a new kind of art form. By artfully mixing ambient sound (the sound that you'd find in a playground, for instance) with effectively used silences, tapes of people talking, and music from all sorts of discs, we can create our own musical interludes and sounds. A freelance producer named Larry Masset created that piece with me. It was an experiment in sound production that had never been done before.

CA: That really is an art form, the way you describe it. It must take a tremendous amount of brain work.

STAMBERG: It takes a tremendous amount of time, but that's really where the fun of it is—playing with the medium, exploring it, trying to create those mixes and sounds. It's very hard to do and it takes very good people, very good engineers. We hear these perfect radio programs in our heads all the time, and we so rarely get a chance to translate them out of our heads and get them into the ears of our listeners. Even with the best work that we do, the most carefully produced pieces, there's always something else that could have been just a little bit better if we'd only had the time.

CA: Have there been any big mistakes you've made, or mistreatments of subjects you now regret?

STAMBERG: Of course! One example is an interview with Charlotte Ford, who had written a book on contemporary manners [*Charlotte Ford's Book of Modern Manners*]. We spoke about the impact of new living arrangements, how you bring your "livewith" home to Momma for Thanksgiving, what you do about sleeping arrangements. She was wonderful in the interview, I thought. She said, "Well, you just talk with your mother, confront the situation, say 'Look, we've been living together for two years, it's absurd that we have to come home and sleep in separate rooms,' just face up to the reality of the situation." She's very modern, very contemporary about it. A production assistant, Dee Clarke Wells, intercut that interview with tape of people telling their life stories, what happened when they went home to Momma with their unmarried companions. It was a very funny piece—

very light. But I got quite a bit of critical mail, saying that it was so one-sided, that we really hadn't paid the proper respect to the morals of the house, that I should have pressed Ford to confront the fact that there are parents for whom this is simply unacceptable. For young people it may be acceptable, but not for the older generation. And I think the criticism was justified. It was an ommission. Mistakes are never deliberate. They happen through oversight, too many distractions, or too many other things cropping up to deflect attention. But it's inexcusable.

CA: It's always what you're not paying attention to that goes wrong.

STAMBERG: Certainly. And with this kind of pressure, and these daily demands, it's very hard.

CA: What are your criteria for selecting feature material for the program?

STAMBERG: It has to feel right to us. That's one of those infuriating answers that's no help to you, but there are some things it's just very clear the program does. They're just natural kinds of stories for us.

CA: Would it necessarily be something that someone else hasn't done?

STAMBERG: Yes. And if everybody else is doing it, like the Picasso piece (pegged to the opening of a retrospective exhibit at the Museum of Modern Art; it was on the cover of *Newsweek* and *Time* and all over the place), we see what we can do with it that no one else will do. What we did was to explore the idea of Picasso, rather than talk about the exhibit itself. We barely mentioned the exhibit. We used the fact of the exhibit as a peg for exploring the idea, for taking on the challenge of doing doing visual art on the radio.

CA: It's very unusual for a radio show to cover art exhibits.

STAMBERG: I do it all the time though. I love that because it's impossible to do. It's a favorite challenge.

CA: "All Things Considered" has been criticized in the past for being too Washington-oriented. [The show is produced in Washington, D.C.]

STAMBERG: I think that's been a valid criticism. But it's becoming less and less true. We have a separate unit now that deals with our member stations across the country, and gives them a lot of support and assistance in preparing their pieces and getting them ready for broadcast. Since this unit was created, it's tripled the amount of non-Washington material available to us.

CA: When you say non-Washington material you mean it's prepared by people at other stations?

STAMBERG: All over the country. But the program does have a Washington angle, because most of our reporters are based here, covering important stories at the White House and in Congress.

CA: You started off on the show by filling in for someone else. What was your first show like? Did you know what you were doing?

STAMBERG: Yes, I knew very well what I was doing. It was a job that I wanted very much, and I had come to it from having done a daily hour-long program. That local program was not nearly as well staffed or as sophisticated as "All Things Considered," but it gave me experience as a host.

I knew that certain things were needed on the program, such as writing continuity that would link one piece to another and make a program rather than a bunch of separate items.

CA: Did you get any immediate comment on your first show?

STAMBERG: They applauded in the control room, which really was amazing, and there were some telegrams. It was quite nice.

CA: Why do you think your audience identifies so strongly with you per se, especially when you're interviewing people?

STAMBERG: I think it's because I don't try to stand away from my subject. In fact, I don't think I do interviews so much as conversations. I mix up and scramble up with the people I'm talking to and get engaged in the ideas that they're discussing. I think that's appealing. The audience doesn't hear that elsewhere. Also, I don't mind laughing, and I do that a lot on the air. I have a good time and I think it shows. I enjoy doing the program, and I think that gets a good reaction. Also, I think I'm not very intimidating to people, because I'm not afraid to ask silly questions or naive ones as well as very well-informed and very well-prepared ones.

CA: What was your most successful interview?

STAMBERG: The interview I did with Joan Didion. It ran a full half hour on "All Things Considered." Both of us really forgot about the microphone, which is something you're always hoping for, but it rarely occurs. It didn't make any difference that we were sitting and recording, we just were very involved in what we were saying. The concentration level and the level of communication got very high, so that it just became two people talking to one another who happened to be in front of a microphone. But it was not a performance. It was a real interaction. She and I both revealed ourselves in ways that we wouldn't have been able to predict. I was very pleased with that.

CA: It's interesting you chose her, because she's extremely pessimistic in her writing, and you're very optimistic.

STAMBERG: Well, that gave us a good clashing point, so we could really explore that difference between us.

CA: What do you see in general as the advantage of public over private radio?

STAMBERG: We're not subject to any commercial pressures, which gives us such wonderful freedom, not just journalistic freedom, but also the chance to be the very best. Here the guideline is delivering information, not selling deodorant. Our goal is not to be the most popular with the most listeners; it's to be as good as we can all the time, on any subject. I think the best letter we ever received from a listener said, "Thanks for being so much better than you have to be, considering the competition." I'm not sure that's always true of us, since we have a lot of ups and downs, but it's certainly what we try to do all the time.

BIOGRAPHICAL/CRITICAL SOURCES: Ms., May, 1976, January, 1980; *Baltimore News American*, December 19, 1978; *Amherst Journal Inquirer*, March 7, 1979; *Rutland Daily Herald*, May 31, 1979; *People*, August 6, 1979; *Time*, August 27, 1979; *Barnard Alumnae*, fall, 1979; *Books & Arts*, October 12, 1979; *New York Times*, October 14, 1979; *Washington Post*, October 21, 1979; *New York*, October 22, 1979; *TWA Ambassador*, Volume XII, number 11, 1979.

—*Interview by Peter Benjaminson*

STAUDENRAUS, P(hilip) J(ohn)   1928-1971

OBITUARY NOTICE—See index for *CA* sketch: Born December 28, 1928, in Oshkosh, Wis.; died January 15, 1971. Educator and author of *The African Colonization Movement, 1816-1865.* Staudenraus also edited several volumes on American history. Perhaps the best known of these is *Mr. Lincoln's Washington: Selections From the Writings of Noah Brooks, Civil War Correspondent.* (Date of death provided by wife, Nancy MacWhorter Staudenraus.)

*   *   *

STAUFFER, Don
See BERKEBILE, Fred D(onovan)

*   *   *

STAUM, Martin Sheldon   1943-

PERSONAL: Born July 9, 1943, in Perth Amboy, N.J.; son of William (a manufacturer) and Sylvia (a secretary; maiden name, Eisenberg) Staum; married Sarah Shewin, December 8, 1974; children: Nina. *Education:* Princeton University, A.B., 1964; Cornell University, Ph.D., 1971. *Home:* 5935 Silver Ridge Dr. N.W., Calgary, Alberta, Canada T3B 3S2. *Office:* Department of History, University of Calgary, Calgary, Alberta, Canada T2N 1N4.

CAREER: University of British Columbia, Vancouver, visiting assistant professor of history, 1969-70; Simon Fraser University, Burnaby, British Columbia, visiting assistant professor of history, 1970-71; University of Calgary, Calgary, Alberta, assistant professor, 1971-77, associate professor of history, 1977—. *Member:* Canadian Society for the Study of the History and Philosophy of Science, American Historical Association, Society for French Historical Studies, American Society for Eighteenth Century Studies.

WRITINGS: (Contributor) William Coleman and Camille Limoges, editors, *History of Biology*, Volume II, Johns Hopkins Press, 1978; *Cabanis,* Princeton University Press, 1980. Contributor to history journals.

WORK IN PROGRESS: Research on the early history of social sciences in France at the end of the French Revolution.

BIOGRAPHICAL/CRITICAL SOURCES: Times Literary Supplement, January 9, 1981.

*   *   *

STEDMOND, John Mitchell   1916-

PERSONAL: Born May 14, 1916, in Leicester, England; son of John Butler and Margaret Hunter (Mitchell) Stedmond; married Nona Fay Horne, September 14, 1940 (died June, 1969). *Education:* University of Saskatchewan, B.A., 1950, M.A., 1951; University of Aberdeen, Ph.D., 1953. *Home:* 8 Barclay Rd., Kingston, Ontario, Canada K7M 2S4. *Office:* Department of English, Queen's University, Kingston, Ontario, Canada K7L 3N6.

CAREER: University of Aberdeen, Aberdeen, Scotland, assistant lecturer in English, 1951-52; University of Saskatchewan, Saskatoon, instructor, 1953-56, special lecturer, 1956-57, assistant professor of English, 1957-58; Queen's University, Kingston, Ontario, assistant professor, 1958-60, associate professor, 1960-63, professor of English, 1963—, R. Samuel McLaughlin Research Professor, 1964-65, chairman of department, 1968-77. Associate director of McGill-Queen's University Press, 1971-74. Chairman of Humanities Research

Council of Canada, 1972-74. *Military service:* Canadian Army, Royal Ordnance Corps, 1942-45; served in Europe.

MEMBER: Royal Society of Canada (fellow), Humanities Association of Canada (vice-president, 1958-60; president, 1972-73), Association of Canadian University Teachers of English, Canadian Association of University Teachers, Modern Language Association of America. *Awards, honors:* Overseas grant from Nuffield Foundation, 1960.

WRITINGS: The Comic Art of Laurence Sterne: Convention and Innovation in Tristram Shandy and A Sentimental Journey, University of Toronto Press, 1967; (editor with Arthur H. Cash) *The Winged Skull: Papers From the Laurence Sterne Bicentenary Conference,* Kent State University Press, 1971. Contributor to scholarly journals. Editor of *Queen's Quarterly,* 1959-63.

* * *

STEDWELL, Paki 1945-

PERSONAL: Born November 14, 1945, in New York, N.Y.; daughter of John Balfour (an artist) and Miriam Standeven (a laboratory technician; maiden name, Sheppard) Ker; married Chuck Stedwell, May 25, 1969 (divorced June, 1975); children: Kegan Erika. *Education:* City College of the City University of New York, B.A., 1966. *Politics:* "Slightly left of center." *Residence:* Point Reyes, Calif. *Agent:* Michael Larsen/Elizabeth Pomada, 1029 Jones St., San Francisco, Calif. 94109.

CAREER: Saul Krieg Associates, New York, N.Y., public relations account executive, 1967-70; free-lance writer, 1970-72; Lake County Flea Market, Lakeport, Calif., organizer, 1973-75; *Ukiah Daily Journal,* Ukiah, Calif., staff reporter, 1975; free-lance writer, 1975-76; *Point Reyes Light,* Point Reyes, Calif., reviewer-at-large, 1977-79. Public relations consultant.

WRITINGS: Vaulting: Gymnastics on Horseback, Simon & Schuster, 1980.

Author of "Falling in Love" (one-act play), first produced in Point Reyes, Calif., at Dance Palace, 1976. Contributor of articles and reviews to magazines, including *Equus, Horse of Course, California Living,* and *Viva,* and to newspapers.

WORK IN PROGRESS: "A Personal Affair," a romantic comedy for the screen; a contemporary psychic mystery novel.

SIDELIGHTS: Paki Stedwell commented: "Aside from being a relatively new but deliriously devoted horsefreak (genus dressage), which predisposes me to numerous equine book, article, and movie ideas, my main writing interest is in how strong-but-vulnerable, witty-but-not-always-wise women find their niches in our conspicuously cockeyed contemporary scene. I have written novels and screenplays on this theme, but have sold only nonfiction to date. I turn a blind eye to the implications of this fact.

"Another major interest is the exploration/postulation of the powerful psychic forces—for good and ill—within each of us, and I am a student of the high art of humor, believing that a good laugh is right up there with sex and food."

AVOCATIONAL INTERESTS: Reading, music, dressage, psychic healing.

* * *

STEIBLE, Daniel J(oseph) 1912-1976

OBITUARY NOTICE—See index for *CA* sketch: Born June 3, 1912, in Cincinnati, Ohio; died April 4, 1976. Educator and poet. A selection of Steible's poems was published in his volume, *Flight From Time;* other poems appeared in various journals. Steible also wrote *A Concise Handbook of Linguistics.* (Date of death provided by wife, Bertha Jaeger Steible.)

* * *

STEIN, Jack M(adison) 1914-1976

OBITUARY NOTICE—See index for *CA* sketch: Born April 25, 1914, in Newark, N.J.; died October 2, 1976. Educator and author. A professor of German at Harvard University from 1958 until his death, Stein chaired the Department of Germanic Languages and Literatures and served as the coordinator of Germanic languages courses. His scholarly interests involved the interrelations of music and literature. Distinguished in Wagner studies, Stein was the commentator of the Bayreuth Festival. He was a member of the executive committee of the American Council on Teaching of Foreign Languages and a member of the New England Goethe Society's board of directors. His works include *The German Heritage, Richard Wagner and the Synthesis of the Arts,* and *Poem and Music in the German Lied From Gluck to Hugo Wolf.* At the time of his death, Stein was preparing a study of the word-tone relationships in the operas of Richard Strauss and Alban Berg. Obituaries and other sources: *Harvard Gazette,* January 13, 1978.

* * *

STEINER, Gary A(lbert) 1931-1966

OBITUARY NOTICE—See index for *CA* sketch: Born August 3, 1931, in Vienna, Austria; died January 17, 1966, in Chicago, Ill. Authority on human behavior, educator, and author. Steiner was a professor of pychology at the University of Chicago and a consultant for television programs. His major works include *The People Look at Television* and a highly acclaimed study of behavioral science, *Human Behavior: An Inventory of Scientific Findings,* which he wrote with sociologist Bernard Berelson. Obituaries and other sources: *Chicago Herald Tribune,* January 20, 1966.

* * *

STEVENSON, (Arthur) Lionel 1902-1973

PERSONAL: Born July 16, 1902, in Edinburgh, Scotland; came to Canada, c. 1907; died December 21, 1973, in Vancouver, British Columbia, Canada; son of Henry and Mabel Rose (Cary) Stevenson; married Lillian Sprague Jones, April 19, 1954; children: one daughter. *Education:* University of British Columbia, B.A, 1922; University of Toronto, M.A., 1923; University of California, Ph.D., 1925, Oxford University, B.Litt., 1935. *Home:* 3106 Devon Rd., Hope Valley, Durham, N.C. 27707.

CAREER: University of California, Berkeley, instructor in English, 1925-30; Arizona State College at Tempe (now Arizona State University), professor of English and head of department, 1930-37; University of Southern California, Los Angeles, assistant professor, 1937-41, associate professor, 1941-44, professor of English, 1944-55, head of department, 1943-55; Duke University, Durham, N.C., professor of English, 1955-72, chairman of department, 1964-67; University of Houston, Houston, Tex., professor of English, 1972. Visiting lecturer or professor during summers at University of British Columbia, 1930, 1940, and 1954, New York University, 1948, 1962, and 1967-68, University of Colorado, 1950, University of Illinois, 1952-53, and Oxford University, 1960.

MEMBER: International P.E.N. (delegate to International Congresses, Vienna, 1929, Edinburgh, 1934, Paris, 1937, Lausanne, 1951; president of Los Angeles chapter, 1943-53), Royal Society of Literature of the United Kingdom (fellow), Canadian Authors Association, Western College Association (vice-president, 1946-47), Philological Association of the Pacific Coast (president, 1948-50), College English Association (vice-president, 1954), English-Speaking Union of the United States (president of the Raleigh-Durham branch, 1958-60), Southern Humanities Conference (chairman, 1959-60). *Awards, honors:* Guggenheim fellowship, 1960.

WRITINGS: Appraisals of Canadian Literature, Macmillan, 1926, reprinted, Norwood, 1978; *Darwin Among the Poets,* University of Chicago Press, 1932, revised edition, Russell, 1963; *The Wild Irish Girl: The Life of Sydney Owenson, Lady Morgan,* Chapman & Hall, 1936, reprinted, Russell, 1969; *Dr. Quicksilver: The Life of Charles Lever,* Chapman & Hall, 1939, reprinted, Russell, 1969; *The Showman of Vanity Fair: The Life of William Makepeace Thackeray,* Scribner, 1947; (with John D. Cooke) *English Literature of the Victorian Period,* Appleton-Century-Crofts, 1949, Russell, 1971.

The Ordeal of George Meredith: A Biography, Scribner, 1953; (editor and author of introduction) George Meredith, *Egoist: A Comedy in Narrative,* Houghton, 1958; *The English Novel, A Panorama,* Houghton, 1960; (editor) Robert Ashley and others, *Victorian Fiction: A Guide to Research,* Harvard University Press, 1964; *Yesterday and After* (volume 11 of *The History of the English Novel*), Barnes & Noble, 1967; *The Pre-Raphaelite Poets,* University of North Carolina Press, 1972. Editor of *Borestone Mountain Poetry Awards* (best poems of the year), volumes 11, 13, 16, 17, 19-26, Pacific Books, 1959-74.

Contributor of articles to periodicals, including *American Literature, South Atlantic Quarterly, Nineteenth Century Fiction, Western Humanities Review,* and *Modern Fiction Studies.*

SIDELIGHTS: Among Stevenson's works are five biographies, highly acclaimed for their scholarship and accuracy. *The Ordeal of George Meridith,* for example, was well received by literary critics. A reviewer for *New York Times* wrote: "It may be that Lionel Stevenson's critical biography prefigures a changing wind. Marked by clarity, conscientious scholarship and intellectual sympathy, it deserves our praise not least by illuminating the reasons behind the comparative and undeserved neglect of this pyrotechnical poet, wit and champion of civilized comedy." *New Yorker* also gave the book a favorable review: "Mr. Stevenson has drawn not only a moving likeness of a bedevilled artist, but a powerful study of fortitude as well."

BIOGRAPHICAL/CRITICAL SOURCES: Times Literary Supplement, June 2, 1927, December 20, 1947, April 15, 1965, June 22, 1973; *New York Herald Tribune Books,* August 28, 1927; *New York Herald Tribune Book Review,* January 12, 1947, September 27, 1953; *Saturday Review of Literature,* February 8, 1947; *New York Times,* February 16, 1947; *Christian Science Monitor,* March 1, 1947, October 1, 1953; *Canadian Forum,* June, 1947; *Yale Review,* summer, 1947; *Chicago Tribune,* September 13, 1953; *Saturday Review,* October 3, 1953; *Time,* October 12, 1953; *New Yorker,* October 17, 1953; *San Francisco Chronicle,* October 18, 1953; *New York Times,* October 25, 1953.

OBITUARIES: New York Times, December 15, 1973; *Nineteenth Century Fiction,* June, 1974.*

STEVENSON, Michael Ian 1953-

PERSONAL: Born June 12, 1953, in Fall River, Mass.; son of Alexander and Margaret (Evans) Stevenson. *Education:* Tufts University, B.A., 1975; Simmons College, M.L.S., 1978. *Politics:* Social Democrat. *Home:* 344 Godwin Ave., Midland Park, N.J. 07432. *Office:* Library, Ramapo College of New Jersey, 505 Ramapo Valley Rd., Mahwah, N.J. 07430.

CAREER: Ramapo College of New Jersey, Mahwah, media librarian, 1978—. *Member:* Association of College and Research Libraries, American Library Association.

WRITINGS: (With Joan Ash) *Health: A Multimedia Source Guide,* Bowker, 1976. Contributor to *Wares Where.*

WORK IN PROGRESS: Mountain Time, a novel set in Colorado in the 1970's.

SIDELIGHTS: Stevenson commented: "I am interested in the relationship between literature, visual arts, and popular culture. I feel Andy Warhol was generous in allotting each of us a full fifteen minutes as a celebrity. There will come a time when certain people float from politics to mass media to the space program to writing and back again (also into sports). I hope to capture this phenomenon in print before it happens.

"*Mountain Time,* my new book, focuses on college-age men and women who are leading rather self-indulgent lives in the Rockies. Some of them work for a roofing concern, run shakily by a medical school dropout who prefers spending his time racing dirt bikes, and the small business gets into big financial straits.

"Part of the action occurs at an alternative (actually, ex-alternative, now dyspeptic) college, such as sprung up in the sixties and seventies. This institution is making itself more attuned to the student market as its hired-gun recruiting experts perceive this pool. Fortunately, I have been a librarian at a New Jersey college that is providing an excellent model for such prevarication.

"I like the New West as a setting because of the mix of people gravitating there: space cowboys, ski bums, capitalists, wildcatters, and so on. Thomas McGuane and Edward Abbey in particular have been influences on me in the way they portray this peoplescape.

"Literature, I feel, is in for some good times, what with the increasing educational level of the populace. I hope shortly we will rediscover that recreational reading is one of the least energy-intensive activities available.

"The dark cloud on the horizon is the increasing reactionism of publishers as more of them are conglomerated into the information management companies. These concerns (such as CBS and Xerox) are purveying information of a very narrow sort via satellites, cablevision, and word-processing systems as well as printed products.

"There is a safe, celebrity-oriented pandering going on. Someone who made his/her entire reputation on the TV talk show circuit is ghostwritten up into an alleged autobiography which the celeb then flogs coast to coast. The information management companies can often publish the book, promote it through one of their TV subsidiaries, produce the film version through a studio they own, and narrowcast the final product on a cable controlled by still another subsidiary.

"Readers, bookstores, and libraries should help support small presses. Maybe enough support can counteract the effect of the conglomerates on literature and provide more variety in what is available to the reader. Doing a little research, one can often find fine reading is being produced outside the major concerns.''

*   *   *

STOB, Ralph   1894-1965

OBITUARY NOTICE—See index for *CA* sketch: Born April 1, 1894; died April 5, 1965. Educator and author. Associated with Calvin College and Seminary since 1917, Stob began as a professor of Greek and became president of the college in 1933. He resumed his professorial duties in 1939. In 1953, Stob became a professor of New Testament at Calvin Theological Seminary. His works include *Christianity and Classical Civilization* and *Thinking and Smiling*. (Date of death provided by wife, Evelyn Mokma Stob)

*   *   *

STOCKWIN, (James) Arthur (Ainscow)   1935-

PERSONAL: Born November 28, 1935, in Sutton Coldfield, England; son of Wilfred Arthur (a dental surgeon) and Edith Mary (a physician; maiden name, Ainscow) Stockwin; married Audrey Lucretia Hobson Wood (a potter), January 30, 1960; children: Katrina Mary, Jane Clare, Rupert Arthur, Timothy James. *Education:* Exeter College, Oxford, B.A., 1959; Australian National University, Ph.D., 1965. *Politics:* "Aware." *Religion:* None. *Home:* 16 Darambal St., Aranda, Canberra, Australian Capital Territory 2164, Australia. *Office:* Department of Political Science, Faculty of Arts, Australian National University, Box 4, Canberra, Australian Capital Territory 2600, Australia.

CAREER: Australian National University, Canberra, lecturer, 1964-66, senior lecturer, 1966-72, reader in political science, 1972—. Academic-in-residence of Australian Department of Foreign Affairs, 1975-76. *Military service:* British Army, 1954-56. *Member:* Australian Institute of International Affairs, Australian Political Studies Association, Japan Studies Association of Australia, Asian Studies Association of Australia.

WRITINGS: The Japanese Socialist Party and Neutralism: A Study of a Political Party and Its Foreign Policy, Melbourne University Press, 1968; (editor) *Japan and Australia in the Seventies,* Angus & Robertson, 1972; (editor) *Japan: Divided Politics in a Growth Economy,* Norton, 1975. Contributor to *Encyclopedia of Political Parties* and *Encyclopedia of Japan.* Contributor to Asian and Pacific studies journals.

WORK IN PROGRESS: A study of crises in Japanese politics; research on Japanese political parties and Australian-Japanese relations.

SIDELIGHTS: Stockwin wrote: "My work on Japanese politics is based on the general principle that the functioning of the Japanese political system contains a wealth of experience that is of relevance to the student of politics. I am hostile to the notion that is implicit in some 'orientalist' writing that Japan is in some way 'unique' and should only be studied for its own sake and in its own terms.

"Since Japan is Australia's largest trading partner and Japan is heavily dependent on Australia for supplies of some of her basic raw materials, the study of Australia-Japan relations is a study of how two countries with differing historical and cultural traditions have been learning to come to terms with each other in the context of the international relations of the Pacific Basin."

STOKES, Charles (Herbert)   1932-

PERSONAL: Born August 28, 1932, in Adelaide, Australia; son of Clement Sismey and Edith Stokes. *Education:* University of Adelaide, B.A., 1956. *Religion:* Anglican. *Home:* 6/22 Central St., Labrador, Queensland 4215, Australia. *Office:* Journalism Studies, Department of Government, University of Queensland, St. Lucia, Queensland 4067, Australia.

CAREER: Anglican, Sydney, Australia, correspondent from Adelaide diocese, 1954-58; Australian Consolidated Press Ltd., Sydney, Australia, journalist, 1958-59; John Fairfax & Sons Ltd., Sydney, journalist, 1959-60; Australian Broadcasting Commission, Sydney, radio and television producer and interviewer in federal talks/current affairs department, 1960-63; Mirror Newspapers Ltd., Sydney, reporter, feature editor, medical correspondent, leader writer, and letters editor for *Daily Mirror, Sunday Mirror,* and *Australian,* 1963-65; British Travel Association, London, England, assistant press officer, editor, and feature writer for *This Month in London,* 1965; British Broadcasting Corp., London, producer and interviewer for radio current affairs programs in Home Service and reporter, interviewer, and production assistant for "The World at One" and "The World This Weekend," 1966-69; *Guardian,* London, reporter, feature writer, and senior editor, 1969-73; University of Queensland, St. Lucia, Australia, lecturer in journalism, 1973—, coordinator of journalism studies, 1980—, fellow of St. John's College, 1979-80.

Reporter and feature writer for *News,* Adelaide, 1956-58; production editor and feature writer for *Observer;* reporter and feature writer for *Daily Telegraph,* Sydney; reporter, feature writer, and churches correspondent for *Sydney Morning Herald.* News journalist for Radio-5DN, 1956-58; freelance broadcaster from London for Australian Broadcasting Commission, 1965-70. Member of state executive committee of Liberal and Country League of South Australia, 1953-56; founder of Committee for Commonwealth Citizens in China, 1968-73; member of Council for the Advancement of Arab-British Understanding, 1968—; member of Queensland Council for Civil Liberties, 1978—, and Queensland branch committee of Musica Viva, 1978—. *Military service:* Royal Australian Air Force Active Reserve, 1956—; present rank, pilot officer. *Member:* Journalism Education Association (vice-president, 1979—), University of Queensland Journalism Alumni Association (founder).

WRITINGS: (Editor) *White Australia: Time for a Change?,* New South Wales Association for Immigration Reform, 1963; (editor with I. F. Nicolson) *Mass Media in the Seventies: The Impact on Public Administration,* Royal Institute of Public Administration, 1974; (contributor) John S. Western, editor, *Australian Mass Media: Controllers, Consumers, Producers,* Australian Institute of Political Science, 1975; (contributor) Richard Lucy, editor, *The Pieces of Politics,* Macmillan, 1975, revised edition, 1979; (contributor) *The Communication Revolution,* United Nations Educational, Scientific and Cultural Organization, 1975; (with Kenneth W. Wiltshire) *Government Regulation and the Commercial Electronic Media,* Committee for Economic Development of Australia, 1976; (with Wiltshire) *Government Controls and the Printed Media,* Committee for Economic Development of Australia, 1977.

Queensland correspondent for *Advertiser,* Adelaide, Australia, and *West Australian,* 1979—; correspondent for *Guardian,* 1981—. Contributor to Australian magazines, including *Nation.* Contributing editor of *Media Reporter,*

1977—; editor of annual, *Eating Out in Brisbane and the Gold Coast,* 1978—.

WORK IN PROGRESS: A comparative study of broadcasting and televising of parliamentary proceedings in Australia, the United Kingdom, and New Zealand, publication expected in 1982.

SIDELIGHTS: Stokes has traveled widely in Europe, the Middle East, Asia, and Africa. He studied in Hong Kong, Thailand, Canada, and the United States in 1978.

He wrote: "I am particularly interested in Australian-Asian relations and in Australian assistance in the training of young Asian journalists for English-language newspapers and other media in Southeast Asia."

*   *   *

STOKES, Eric (Thomas) 1924-1981

OBITUARY NOTICE: Born July 10, 1924, in London, England; died February 5, 1981. Educator, historian, and author of works in his field, including *The English Utilitarians and India* and *The Peasant and the Raj.* While Stokes's chief interest was the history of colonial India, he was also well known for his essays on Rudyard Kipling. He taught at the University of Malaya, the University of Bristol, University College of Rhodesia and Nyasaland, and St. Catherine's College, Cambridge. Obituaries and other sources: *Who's Who in the World,* 4th edition, Marquis, 1978; *The Writer's Directory, 1980-82,* St. Martin's, 1979; *London Times,* February 11, 1981.

*   *   *

STOLTZFUS, Ben Franklin 1927-

PERSONAL: Born September 15, 1927, in Sofia, Bulgaria; American citizen born abroad; son of B. Frank (a teacher) and Esther (a teacher; maiden name, Johnson) Stoltzfus; married Elizabeth Burton, August 20, 1955 (divorced, 1975); married Judith Palmer (an artist), November 8, 1975; children: Jan, Celia, Andrew. *Education:* Amherst College, B.A., 1949; Middlebury College, M.A., 1954; University of Wisconsin (now University of Wisconsin—Madison), Ph.D., 1959. *Politics:* Democrat. *Home:* 2040 Arroyo Dr., Riverside, Calif. 92506. *Office:* Department of Literatures and Languages, University of California, Riverside, Calif. 92521.

CAREER: Smith College, Northampton, Mass., instructor in French, 1958-60; University of California, Riverside, assistant professor, 1960-65, associate professor, 1965-66, professor of French, comparative literature, and creative writing, 1967—, vice-chairman of Division of Humanities, 1962, chairman of humanities interdisciplinary program, 1973-76, chairman of education abroad program, 1976-78. *Member:* American Association of Teachers of French, Modern Language Association of America, Association des Amis d'Andre Gide. *Awards, honors:* Fulbright scholarship for France, 1955-56, 1963-64; awards from University of California Creative Arts Institute, 1968 and 1975; awards from University of California Humanities Institute, 1969 and 1972; H.D.L. from Amherst College, 1974.

WRITINGS: Alain Robbe-Grillet and the New French Novel, Southern Illinois University Press, 1964; *Georges Chenneviere et l'unanimisme,* Minard, 1965; *The Eye of the Needle* (fiction), Viking, 1967; *Gide's Eagles,* Southern Illinois University Press, 1969; *Black Lazarus* (fiction), Winter House, 1972; *Gide and Hemingway,* Kennikat, 1978. Contributor to literature and language journals and literary magazines, including *Chelsea, Kayak,* and *Mosaic.*

WORK IN PROGRESS: IRS: A Presidential Memoir, a novel; *Cat O'Nine Tails,* nine stories; *Alain Robbe-Grillet: Structures and Themes.*

SIDELIGHTS: Stoltzfus wrote: "Men frequently walk a thin line between passion and intellect. In situations of conflict, often out of ignorance, passion dictates responses that are sometimes violent. Intellect's role, out of respect for life and stable, long-term goals, is to soothe the passions, nudging and coaxing them onward toward non-violent solutions.

"There need not be a difference, though there all too frequently is, between life and art. They can be one and the same, and the artist's responsibility is to both, constantly transforming one into the other. The work of art is not only a reflexive voice dealing with love and death and violence, and the meaning of art itself; it is also a place of mirrors and distortions. The artist must be like a thorn in the side of the establishment, reminding it that all forms of 'ideology' are oppressive, demonstrating by his life and his art that in spite of television, advertising, slogans, and coercions of all kinds, it is possible to resist the 'tyranny' of the system by playing with, hence exposing, the terrible seriousness of the cliché and the ready-made. To create is to play with contemporary myths, assembling fragments of reality into an artistic whole that challenges every callous, monolithic, and inhumane aspect of establishment 'ideology.' Art is also a theatre of play which mimes the great cosmic game. The work of art is thus always a personal signature attesting to man's passion, his rebellion, and his freedom."

AVOCATIONAL INTERESTS: The cinema, music, painting, travel, tennis, skiing, scuba diving.

*   *   *

STOODLEY, Bartlett Hicks 1907-1978

OBITUARY NOTICE—See index for *CA* sketch: Born July 15, 1907, in Somerville, Mass.; died December 8, 1978. Educator, attorney, and author. In addition to his position as a professor of sociology and later as professor emeritus at Wellesley College, Stoodley was a Fulbright professor at the University of the Philippines. He was also a visiting professor at Chung Chi College in Hong Kong, Queen's University in Ontario, St. Mary's University in Nova Scotia, and the University of Western Ontario. In 1962, he was awarded grants from the American Philosophical Society and from the United Board of Christian Education. His books include *The Concepts of Sigmund Freud* and *Society and Self.* (Date of death provided by Wellesley College.)

*   *   *

STOVER, W(illiam) H(arrison) M(owbray) 1898-1980

PERSONAL: Born in 1898 in Phoenix, Md.; died March 21, 1980; married Ruby Rives; children: William M. *Education:* Attended business college in Baltimore, Md. and Vanderbilt University.

CAREER: Remington Rand, Inc., member of staff in St. Louis, Mo., Houston, Tex., and New Orleans, La., from the 1920's to 1936; specialist in accounting machines for federal agencies in Washington, D.C., designing and installing systems, beginning in 1936; Leadership Training Institute of the District of Columbia, Washington, D.C., founder and president, 1945-62. Operated National Hospitalization, Inc. (insurance company); executive of W.H.M. Stover, Inc. (in hotel management and real estate). Associated with writer and lecturer, Dale Carnegie, and sponsor of Dale Carnegie programs in Washington, D.C., Maryland, Virginia, and West Virginia. Organized "Help Your Police Fight Crime" in the 1970's.

WRITINGS: Don't Just Deplore Discrimination, Do Something!, Vantage, 1964; *How to Find Inner Peace and Learn to Relax,* Hawthorn, 1973. Also author of *Don't Let Cancer Throw You.*

BIOGRAPHICAL/CRITICAL SOURCES: Washington Post, March 23, 1980.*

*   *   *

STRALEY, John A(lonzo)   1894-1966

OBITUARY NOTICE—See index for *CA* sketch: Born July 21, 1894, in Brooklyn, N.Y.; died December, 1966. Editor and author, Straley served as the mutual funds editor of *Investment Dealers' Digest* from 1949 until his death. Though he edited the *Bawl Street Journal,* a satire of the *Wall Street Journal,* for thirty-two years, in his later years Straley concentrated on writing fiction for Christian magazines. His other works include *What About Mutual Funds?* and *What About Common Stocks?* (Date of death provided by *Investment Dealers' Digest.*)

*   *   *

STRAYER, Joseph Reese   1904-

PERSONAL: Born August 20, 1904, in Baltimore, Md.; son of George Drayton and Cora (Bell) Strayer; married Lois Curry, September 12, 1929; children: Charles Drayton, Elizabeth Anne (Mrs. G. C. Corson). *Education:* Princeton University, A.B., 1925; Harvard University, M.A., 1926, Ph.D., 1930; also attended University of Paris, 1928-29. *Home:* 57 Balsam Lane, Princeton, N.J. 08540.

CAREER: Stevens Institute of Technology, Hoboken, N.J., instructor in history, 1929-30; Princeton University, Princeton, N.J., instructor, 1930-35, Shreve fellow, 1935-36, assistant professor, 1936-40, associate professor, 1940-42, Henry Charles Lea Professor of History, 1942-49, Dayton-Stockton Professor of History, 1949-73, professor emeritus, 1973—, chairman of department, 1941-61. Member of council of Borough of Princeton, 1964-67.

MEMBER: American Academy of Arts and Sciences (fellow), Mediaeval Academy of America (fellow; member of council, 1945-48; vice-president, 1949-51; president, 1966-69), American Philosophical Society, American Historical Association (president, 1971), American Council of Learned Societies (member of board of directors, 1948-51), British Academy (fellow), Phi Beta Kappa, Cosmos Club. *Awards, honors:* LL.D. from University of Caen, 1957; L.H.D. from Lehigh University, 1976, and Princeton University, 1980.

WRITINGS: The Administration of Normandy Under Saint Louis (monograph), Mediaeval Academy of America, 1932, reprinted, Kraus Reprint, 1970; (editor) *The Royal Domain in the Bailliage of Rouen,* Princeton University Press, 1936, reprinted, Variorum Reprints, 1976; (with Charles Holt Taylor) *Studies in Early French Taxation* (monograph), Harvard University Press, 1939, reprinted, Greenwood Press, 1972; (editor) John Lansing, *The Delegate From New York; or, Proceedings of the Federal Convention of 1787,* Princeton University Press, 1939, reprinted, Kennikat, 1967; (with Dana Carleton Munro) *The Middle Ages, 395-1500,* Appleton, 1942, 5th edition, 1970; (editor and author of introduction) *The Interpretation of History,* Princeton University Press, 1943; (editor with W. A. Morris) *English Government at*

Work, 1327-1336, Volume II: *Fiscal Administration,* Mediaeval Academy of America, 1947.

(With Hans W. Gatzke and E. Harris Harbison) *The Course of Civilization,* two volumes, Harcourt, 1961; *Feudalism,* Van Nostrand, 1965; *The Mainstream of Civilization,* Harcourt, 1969, 2nd edition (with Hans W. Gatzke and E. Harrison Harbison), 1973, 3rd edition, 1979, published in two volumes, Volume I: *To 1715,* Volume II: *Since 1660,* 1974, 3rd edition, 1979, published in three volumes, Volume I: *To 1500,* Volume II: *1350-1815,* Volume III: *Since 1879,* 1974; *Western Europe in the Middle Ages: A Short History,* Appleton, 1955, 2nd edition, Prentice-Hall, 1974.

Les Gens de justice du Languedoc sous Philippe le Bel (title means "Lawyers and Judges in Languedoc Under Philip the Fair"), Association Marc Bloch, 1970; *On the Medieval Origins of the Modern State,* Princeton University Press, 1970; *The Albigensian Crusades,* Dial, 1971; *Medieval Statecraft and the Perspectives of History: Essays,* Princeton University Press, 1971; (editor with Donald E. Queller) *Post Scripta: Essays on Medieval Law and the Emergence of the European State in Honor of Gaines Post,* Libreria Ateneo Salesiano, 1972; *The Reign of Philip the Fair,* Princeton University Press, 1980. Contributor to journals. Editor-in-chief of *Dictionary of the Middle Ages,* Scribner.

BIOGRAPHICAL/CRITICAL SOURCES: Times Literary Supplement, April 24, 1981.

*   *   *

STREAN, Herbert S(amuel)   1931-

PERSONAL: Born March 2, 1931, in Montreal, Quebec, Canada; came to the United States in 1944, naturalized citizen, 1954; son of Lyon Peter (a bacteriologist) and Lillian (a teacher; maiden name, Henken) Strean; married Marcia Ruth Silverman (in marine education), March 21, 1953; children: Richard, William. *Education:* New York University, B.A. (cum laude), 1951; Boston University, M.S.W., 1953; National Psychological Association for Psychoanalysis, Certificate in Psychoanalysis, 1962; Columbia University, D.S.W., 1968. *Politics:* Democrat. *Religion:* Jewish. *Home:* 1011 Sheffield Rd., Teaneck, N.J. 07666. *Office:* 7 West 96th St., New York, N.Y. 10025.

CAREER: New York University, New York City, part-time lecturer in social work, 1953-56; Jewish Board of Guardians, Child Guidance Institute, New York City, caseworker, 1955-61; Theodor Reik Clinic, New York City, chief social worker and assistant director of Child Therapy Division, 1958-59; Community Guidance Service, New York City, supervisor, 1962-66; Rutgers University, New Brunswick, N.J., assistant professor, 1966-67, associate professor, 1967-70, professor of social work, 1970—, distinguished professor, 1976. Private practice of social work and psychotherapy, 1959—. Instructor at State University of New York at Stony Brook, 1961-64. Caseworker, intake worker, supervisor, chief caseworker, and assistant director of Jewish Board of Guardians treatment center, Camp Ramapo, 1956-61; fellow in advanced training program in child therapy at Child Development Center, New York City, 1957-59, senior caseworker, group therapist, and research associate, 1959-61; director of training at Training Institute of National Psychological Association for Psychoanalysis, 1965-66; vice-president and training psychoanalyst at New York Center for Psychoanalytic Training, 1976—. *Military service:* U.S. Army, Mental Hygiene Consultation Service, 1953-55; became first lieutenant.

MEMBER: National Association of Social Workers, Academy of Certified Social Workers, Council of Social Work

Education, American Association of University Professors, American Orthopsychiatric Association, National Psychological Association for Psychoanalysis, Society for Psychoanalytic Training, Society for Clinical Social Workers, Clinical Social Workers of New York. *Awards, honors:* Robert Lindner Award from National Psychological Association for Psychoanalysis, 1959, for outstanding scholarship; Van Ophuisen Award from Jewish Board of Guardians, 1960, for paper; named social worker of the year by New Jersey branch of National Association of Social Workers, 1972.

WRITINGS: The Casework Digest, Scarecrow, 1968; *Roles and Paradigms in Psychotherapy,* Grune, 1969; *New Approaches in Child Guidance,* Scarecrow, 1970; *Social Casework: Theories in Action,* Scarecrow, 1971; *The Experience of Psychotherapy,* Scarecrow, 1973; *The Social Worker as Psychotherapist,* Scarecrow, 1974; *Personality Theory and Social Work Practice,* Scarecrow, 1975; *Crucial Issues in Psychotherapy,* Scarecrow, 1976; *Conjoint Therapy,* Human Services Press, 1978; *Clinical Social Work,* Free Press, 1978; *Psychoanalysis and Social Work,* Free Press, 1979; *The Extramarital Affair,* Free Press, 1980; *Controversial Issues in Psychotherapy,* Scarecrow, in press; *Freud and Women,* Ungar, in press.

Contributor: Francis Turner, editor, *Social Work Treatment,* Free Press, 1974; Joel Fisher, editor, *The Effectiveness of Casework,* C. C Thomas, 1976. Also contributor to *Sources of Conflict in Group Psychotherapy,* edited by Asya Kaydis, 1963. Contributor of about fifty articles to journals in the behavioral sciences. Member of editorial committee of *Psychoanalytic Review,* 1966-80, and *Clinical Social Work,* 1973—.

SIDELIGHTS: Strean wrote: "I still subscribe to Freud's notion that the goal of psychotherapy should be to help the patient enjoy working and loving. I believe the way to achieve this is to help the patient make his unconscious conscious. To help people discover how they write their own self-destructive scripts, they need love and understanding. I decry the manipulative therapies, such as behavior modification which negates the patient's wishes, feelings, hates, loves, etc. and focuses exclusively on behavior.

"In my recent book *The Extramarital Affair* I have demonstrated how the affair is symptomatic always of a neurotic marriage composed of two unhappy people and that to have two part-time marriages is a means of escape from intrapsychic conflict. In my book *Freud and Women* I demonstrate how Freud's ambivalent relationship toward his mother influenced many of his notions about people and in ways accounts for some of his male chauvinism."

*   *   *

STREITHORST, Tom   1932(?)-1981

OBITUARY NOTICE: Born c. 1932; died of heart failure, February 19, 1981, in Palo Alto, Calif. Journalist. Streithorst covered turbulent situations in Latin America and the Middle East for NBC News, *Washington Post,* and *Newsweek* before succumbing to a degenerative heart disease. In 1978 he underwent a heart transplant that was recorded by television cameras. Obituaries and other sources: *Newsweek,* March 2, 1981.

*   *   *

STROUD, Joe H(inton)   1936-

PERSONAL: Born June 18, 1936, in McGehee, Ark.; son of Joseph Hilliard (a banker) and Marion Rebecca (a teacher;

maiden name, McKinney) Stroud; married Janis Mizell, August 21, 1957; children: Rebecca McKinney, Joseph Scott, Alexandra Jane. *Education:* Hendrix College, B.A., 1957; Tulane University, M.A., 1959. *Home:* 1614 Keller Lane, Bloomfield Hills, Mich. 48013. *Office:* Detroit Free Press, 321 West Lafayette Blvd., Detroit, Mich. 48231.

CAREER/WRITINGS: Pine Bluff Commercial, Pine Bluff, Ark., 1959-60, began as reporter, became editor of editorial page; *Arkansas Gazette,* Little Rock, editorial writer, 1960-64; *Winston-Salem Journal and Sentinel,* Winston-Salem, N.C., 1964-68, began as editorial writer, became editor of editorial page; *Detroit Free Press,* Detroit, Mich., associate editor, 1968-73, editor, 1973—, senior vice-president, 1978—, author of weekly column. Member of general board of publications of United Methodist Church, 1975-76; member of advisory board of *Michigan Christian Advocate,* 1975-79; program chairman of National Conference of Editorial Writers, 1978. Corporate member of Merrill Palmer Institute, 1975—; member of board of governors of Cranbrook Institute of Science and member of board of directors of Detroit Symphony Orchestra, both 1978—. Member of board of directors of Southeast Michigan Chapter of American Red Cross, 1972—; chairman of advisory committee on service to military families, 1974-77, chairman of program evaluation committee, 1978-80; member of Detroit Committee on Foreign Relations.

MEMBER: American Society of Newspaper Editors, National Press Club, Detroit Economics Club, Detroit Club, Renaissance Club, Sigma Delta Chi, Pine Lake Country Club. *Awards, honors:* North Carolina School Board award, 1967; Michigan School Bell Award, 1973; William Allen White Award from Inland Daily Press Association, 1973, 1976, 1977; Overseas Press Club citation, 1974; Paul Tobenkin Award from Columbia University, 1976.

*   *   *

STROUSE, Jean   1945-

PERSONAL: Born September 10, 1945; daughter of Carl David (a physician) and Louise (Friedberg) Strouse. *Education:* Radcliffe College, B.A. (honors), 1967. *Residence:* New York, N.Y. *Agent:* Georges Borchardt, Inc., 136 East 57th St., New York, N.Y. 10022. *Office:* Newsweek, 444 Madison Ave., New York, N.Y. 10022.

CAREER: New York Review of Books, New York City, editorial assistant, 1967-69; Pantheon Books, New York City, associate editor, 1972-75; *Newsweek,* New York City, general editor, 1979—. *Member:* P.E.N. *Awards, honors:* National Endowment for the Humanities fellowship, 1976; Radcliffe Institute fellowship, 1976-77; Guggenheim fellowship, 1977-78; National Endowment for the Arts fellowship, 1979; National Book Critics Circle Award nomination for general nonfiction, 1980, and Bancroft Prize in American History and Diplomacy, 1981, both for *Alice James: A Biography.*

WRITINGS: Up Against the Law: The Legal Rights of People Under Twenty-One, New American Library, 1970; (editor) *Women and Analysis: Dialogues on Psychoanalytic Views of Femininity,* Viking, 1974; *Alice James: A Biography,* Houghton, 1980.

SIDELIGHTS: Strouse's first book, *Up Against the Law,* was described by Walter Clemons of the *New York Times* as "a cool, clear handbook for middle-class youths under 21," which, he added, reveals "some jarring things about justice in this country as it is administered to the young." Pointing out that many constitutional safeguards do not apply to minors, Strouse offers advice to young people on their rights in dealing with parents, schools, courts, and police. The book takes a critical view of juvenile courts, calling them "arbitrary, impersonal and punitive," and a cautionary view of legal self-help: "Only a lawyer familiar with the laws and practices in your area can fully advise you of your rights and legal options."

In subsequent books Strouse has concentrated, in varying ways, on the problems of women. In *Women and Analysis* she juxtaposes ten classic essays on the psychology of women with ten new essays in which the classic theories are re-evaluated. In her biography of Alice James, Strouse examines the life of an intelligent woman who was emotionally crippled by the conventions of nineteenth-century society.

Women and Analysis contains essays by Freud, Karen Horney, Helene Deutsch, Erik Erikson, and other psychoanalytic thinkers, along with "responses" written by Elizabeth Janeway, Margaret Mead, Juliet Mitchell, Robert Coles, Erikson himself, and other writers. Christopher Lasch, writing in the *New York Review of Books,* criticized Strouse's selection of essayists, saying that she gives "more weight to those who claim to have improved and updated Freud than to Freud himself." He attacked the "neofeminist" psychological theories represented in the anthology and noted that "the reader is likely to come away from this collection with the impression that most of Freud's ideas have been superseded or overthrown."

But Elizabeth Long of the *New York Times Book Review* saw *Women and Analysis* as a nonpolemical "introduction to the many facets of psychoanalytic thinking about women . . . [and] an opportunity to enter into conversation with a group of thinkers who are trying to understand the far-reaching effects of the differences between men and women within ourselves and society." Though she found some of the essays "less satisfying" than others, Long generally praised the book, saying that it "marks a new stage in the controversy by and about women: a time when . . . exhausted rhetoric must give way to reflection."

In her biography, *Alice James,* Strouse describes the life of the sister of Henry James, the novelist, and William, the psychologist. Alice was a potentially brilliant woman who, denied the opportunities for achievement granted to her brothers, "made a career of emotional collapse" and spent much of her life as an invalid. Strouse drew on Alice's letters and those written by her brothers, as well as Alice's diary, to reveal Alice's intelligence, her perception, and her often prickly personality. Henry wrote of her "vigour of mind, decision of character. . . . Her conversation is brilliant and trenchant." She suffered from an illness that was diagnosed variously as "neurasthenia," "melancholia," and "hysteria"—all names for the psychosomatic prostration that afflicted many Victorian women.

Alice James was widely praised for its perceptive portrayal of Alice's delicate and complex emotional sensibility as well as for its restraint: "No argument is ever forced by hindsight; there is no sentimentality, no bitterness, no easy diagnosis, no covering up," wrote Michael Ratcliffe in the *London Times.* "[The story is told] with such breadth, sympathy and wit, we are persuaded that the life of Henry and William's sister was not a tragedy and not a waste, but an end, ingeniously devised and fiercely suffered, in itself."

John Leonard of the *New York Times* observed that Strouse "weaves instead of hammering home her delicate points" and called the book "a Jamesian novel, subtle, evasive, embroidered, splendid." Vivian Gornick of the *Detroit News,* however, found this same restraint to be a major flaw:

"Analysis is subordinated to a thoroughgoing recapitulation of that prodigious collective entity called *The James Family.* . . . To write a conventional biography of Alice James with the James family at its center is to confirm the judgement of the very world from which this 'lesser life' is meant to be rescued. . . . Its power is diffused, and the purpose of the tale seems uncertain." Gornick would have preferred a more complete consideration of the "Victorian repressiveness" that caused Alice's breakdown and suggested that "a single long essay would perhaps have done better; then the idea of Alice's life would have been compacted and the purpose of telling it made certain."

Another critic, Diane Johnson of the *New York Times Book Review,* called Alice "too exasperating" to be either a heroine or a victim and observed that the book is "more than a biography, a complicated work of social history. Alice James lived at a time when widespread consciousness of women's problems first assumed its modern aspect. Miss Strouse renders these complexities with great skill."

BIOGRAPHICAL/CRITICAL SOURCES: New York Times, January 2, 1971, November 10, 1980; *New York Times Book Review,* August 18, 1974, December 14, 1980, May 5, 1981; *New York Review of Books,* October 3, 1974; *Hudson Review,* autumn, 1975; *Washington Post Book World,* November 30, 1980; *Detroit News,* January 11, 1981; *London Times,* February 26, 1981.

—*Sketch by Tim Connor*

*   *   *

STUART, Aimee   1886(?)-1981

OBITUARY NOTICE: Born c. 1886 in Glasgow, Scotland; died April 17, 1981, in Brighton, England. Playwright best known for her domestic comedies, including "Jeannie" and "Lace on Her Petticoat." Stuart also wrote plays with her husband, Philip Stuart, including "Nine Till Six" and "Sixteen." Obituaries and other sources: *Who Was Who Among English and European Authors, 1931-1949,* Gale, 1978; *Who Was Who in the Theatre, 1912-1976,* Gale, 1978; *International Motion Picture Almanac,* Quigley, 1980; *London Times,* April 24, 1981.

*   *   *

SUARES, Guy   1932-

PERSONAL: Born August 25, 1932, in Paris, France; son of Isaac (an editor) and Regina (Russo) Suares; married Claudel Violane, January 31, 1958 (divorced, 1970); children: Marie-Catherine, Annabelle, Dominique-Myriam. *Education:* Attended French-speaking public schools in Buenos Aires, Argentina; studied under Roger Blin, Tania Balachora, and Michel Vitold. *Religion:* Jewish. *Home:* 37 rue des Blancs Manteaux, Paris, France 75004. *Agent:* Editions Stock, 14 rue de l'Ancienne Comedie, Paris, France 75016. *Office:* Radio France Culture, 116 President Kennedy, Paris, France 75005.

CAREER: Grand Prix Productions, Paris, France, producer, beginning 1955. Director of La Comedie de la Loire, Tours, France, 1962-71. Playwright. *Awards, honors:* Chevalier of French Legion of Honor.

WRITINGS: Malraux, celui qui vient, Stock, 1973, translation by Derek Coltman published as *Malraux: Past, Present, Future; Conversations with Guy Suares,* Little, Brown, 1974; *Haim,* Stock, 1974; *La Memoire oubliee* (title means "The Forgotten Memory"), Stock, 1979. Also translator of works of Pablo Neruda for Editions Gallimard. Contributor to *Le Quotidien de Paris, Le Monde,* and *Le Figaro.*

SIDELIGHTS: Of all Suares's works, *Malraux* has commanded the most attention. The book is a photo album that records the life of Andre Malraux (1901—), novelist and former French President Charles de Gaulle's minister of cultural affairs. Included are well over three hundred photographs that trace Malraux's life, beginning with his boyhood. Generally, the pictures resemble each other stylistically. "The routine, when photographing Malraux," remarked a *Listener* reviewer, "is to offer two huge, black eyes and a wrinkled, handsome face wrapped round a cigarette." Many of the photographs are from Malraux's private file. Others are pictures taken during Suares's two interviews with the novelist.

The dialogue of these interviews plus a conversation between Malraux and Jose Bergamin, the Spanish poet and intellectual, comprise the text of *Malraux.* Suares, Malraux, and Bergamin discuss, among other things, history, culture, aesthetics, civilization, and faith. The conversation between Bergamin, a believer, and Malraux, an agnostic, presents an interesting juxtaposition of ideas.

A noticeable aspect of Suares's book is his personal esteem for Malraux. "There is a sort of hero-worship going on here," wrote the *Listener* reviewer, "and it feels dangerous." In *Choice,* a critic noted that Suares's "effusive admiration" may, at first, be disconcerting to a reader. And, in *Economist,* the reviewer felt that Suares's fascination for Malraux was "way the other side of idolatry." "Malraux," the critic commented, "is not merely a hero" for Suares "but a saint."

BIOGRAPHICAL/CRITICAL SOURCES: Atlantic Monthly, February, 1975; *Listener,* February 13, 1975; *Economist,* March 1, 1975; *Books and Bookmen,* May, 1975; *Choice,* June, 1975.

* * *

SULLIVAN, Denis G(artland) 1929-

PERSONAL: Born October 15, 1929, in Cleveland, Ohio; son of Frank J. (in business) and Helen M. (Hogan) Sullivan; married Margaret A. Henderson (an art historian), November 28, 1953; children: Kevin, Marc, David. *Education:* Attended Brown University, 1947-50; Oberlin College, B.A., 1955; Northwestern University, M.A., 1962, Ph.D., 1962. *Home:* Goodrich Four Corners, Norwich, Vt. 05055. *Office:* Department of Government, Dartmouth College, Hanover, N.H. 03755.

CAREER: University of Illinois, Champaign-Urbana, assistant professor, 1959-64, associate professor of political science, 1965-68; Dartmouth College, Hanover, N.H., professor of government, 1968—. *Military service:* U.S. Army, 1951-53; became second lieutenant. *Member:* American Political Science Association. *Awards, honors:* Grants from National Science Foundation, 1968, Ford Foundation, 1972, 1976, National Endowment for the Humanities, 1976, Sumitomo Fund, 1978, Toyota Twentieth Century and Anniversary Fund, 1979.

WRITINGS: (With Jeffrey L. Pressman, John J. Lyons, and Benjamin Page) *The Politics of Representation: The Democratic Convention, 1972,* St. Martin's, 1974; (with Pressman and C. F. Arterton) *Explorations in Convention Decision Making,* W. H. Freeman, 1976; (with R. T. Nakamura and R. F. Winters) *How America Is Ruled,* Wiley, 1980.

WORK IN PROGRESS: A book on the Japanese-American relationship and its political implications, with Joseph A. Massey, publication expected in 1982.

SULTANA, Donald Edward 1924-

PERSONAL: Born October 20, 1924, in Sliema, Malta; son of Carmel (a managing director of a shipping firm) and Carmelina (Pace) Sultana; married Myriam Vella, October 30, 1964. *Education:* Royal University of Malta, B.Sc., 1942, M.D., 1946; St. John's College, Oxford, B.A. (with honors), 1951, D.Phil., 1964. *Home:* 5 Howe St., Edinburgh EH3 6TE, Scotland. *Office:* Department of Rhetoric and English Literature, University of Edinburgh, David Hume Tower, George Sq., Edinburgh 8, Scotland.

CAREER: Royal University of Malta, Msida, lecturer in English, 1951-64; University of Edinburgh, Edinburgh, Scotland, lecturer, 1965-72, senior lecturer, 1973-78, reader in English literature, 1979—. *Member:* International P.E.N., Royal Commonwealth Society, Edinburgh University Staff Club, Oxford Union Club, Casino Maltese. *Awards, honors:* Rhodes scholar at Oxford University, 1946-50; Carnegie Foundation visiting lecturer in the United States, 1957.

WRITINGS: Samuel Taylor Coleridge in Malta and Italy, 1804-1806, Blackwell, 1969; *Benjamin Disraeli in Spain, Malta, and Albania, 1830-32* (monograph), Famesis, 1975; *"The Siege of Malta" Rediscovered: An Account of Sir Walter Scott's Mediterranean Journey and His Last Novel,* Scottish Academic Press, 1977; (editor and contributor) *New Approaches to Coleridge,* Barnes & Noble, 1981. Contributor to *British Book News.*

WORK IN PROGRESS: Benjamin Disraeli's Mediterranean Journey: A Literary Biography of All the Journey; an annotated edition of Samuel Taylor Coleridge's post-1800 poems, for Longman.

SIDELIGHTS: Sultana commented: "I am principally interested in the travels of English literary figures in the Mediterranean, mainly in the early nineteenth century and with particular reference to Malta and Italy, which, together with Britain, I know best. In my biographies I try to combine literature with history, aiming strictly at accuracy in the interpretation and presentation of facts, and at lucidity and correctness in style. My search for objective truth has probably been determined by choice of subject, for which I have tried to research in comparatively virgin fields, which have made the disciplined establishment of facts absolutely necessary."

BIOGRAPHICAL/CRITICAL SOURCES: Times Literary Supplement, March 27, 1981.

* * *

SUMMERS, Lionel M(organ) 1905-1975

OBITUARY NOTICE—See index for *CA* sketch: Born November 20, 1905, in Madrid, Spain; died March 29, 1975. Government official, attorney, educator, and author. Summers studied and practiced international arbitration. His works include *The International Law of Peace.* Obituaries and other sources: *Who Was Who in America,* 6th edition, Marquis, 1976.

* * *

SUMNER, Lloyd Quinton 1943-

PERSONAL: Born November 4, 1943, in Hillsville, Va.; son of William Henry and Naomi (Burcham) Sumner. *Education:* University of Virginia, B.Eng. Sci., 1967. *Home and office address:* Route 6, P.O. Box 68, Riner, Va. 24149.

CAREER: Computer Creations (computer art business), Charlottesville, Va., owner, 1966-76; worked as expedition leader, architect, homesteader, beekeeper, and builder, 1976-80; free-lance writer, 1980—. Owner of Lloyd Sumner Films, 1967-69. Photographer. *Member:* American Adventurers Association.

WRITINGS: Computer Art and Human Response, Victorious, 1968; *International Bicycle Touring,* World Publications, 1976; *The Long Ride,* Stackpole, 1978. Contributor to magazines, including *Adventure Travel, Bike World, Backpacker, Scope, Personality,* and *Lloyd's Trail-o-Gram.*

WORK IN PROGRESS: Around the World in Eighty Ways, completion expected in 1982.

SIDELIGHTS: Sumner commented: "I was the last of thirteen children, born on a small farm near Fancy Gap, Va. I developed computer art, sold it, and lectured about it around the world. I rode a bicycle for nearly thirty thousand miles around the world in four years (the subject of *The Long Ride*). I built a house and established a homestead where I live in luxury on one thousand dollars a year, and I am studying ways of living even more happily with less money.

"I am currently traveling around the world by as many different means as possible and selling my stories to magazines in the countries I visit. Recently I visited Antarctica and while there sold a piece of my computer art, thereby becoming the only artist in the world to sell his work on all seven continents."

* * *

SUNDERLAND, Eric 1930-

PERSONAL: Born March 18, 1930, in Ammanford, England; son of Leonard (a local government official) and Mary Agnes (Davies) Sunderland; married Jean Patricia Watson, October 19, 1957; children: Helen Rowena, Frances Anne. *Education:* University of Wales, B.A., 1950, M.A., 1951; University of London, Ph.D., 1954. *Religion:* Christian. *Home:* Pelaw Rise, Leazes Rd., Durham DH1 1QP, England. *Office:* Department of Anthropology, University of Durham, South End House, South Rd., Durham DH1 3TG, England.

CAREER: Worked as research scientist for National Coal Board, 1958-66; University of Durham, Durham, England, lecturer, 1958-66, senior lecturer, 1966-71, professor of anthropology, 1971—, pro-vice-chancellor, 1979—, director of Centre for Middle East and Islamic Studies, 1980—. *Military service:* British Army, Royal Artillery, 1954-56; became lieutenant. *Member:* International Association of Human Biologists, International Union of Anthropological and Ethnological Sciences (secretary-general, 1978—), Royal Anthropological Institute, Institute of Biology, Society for the Study of Human Biology, Eugenics Society (vice-president).

WRITINGS: Elements of Human and Social Geography: Some Anthropological Perspectives, Pergamon, 1973; *Some Bio-Social Aspects of Anthropology,* University of Durham Press, 1973; (editor with D. F. Robert) *Genetic Variation in Britain,* Taylor & Francis, 1973; (editor with M. T. Smith) *The Operation of Intelligence: Biosocial Pre-Conditions for the Operation of Intelligence,* Garland STPM Press, 1980. Contributor to scientific journals.

WORK IN PROGRESS: Research on human genetics and human biological variability.

SIDELIGHTS: Sunderland has traveled in Europe, North America, Asia, and Africa. His languages include Welsh and some Farsi.

SWAN, Christopher C(ushing) 1946-

PERSONAL: Born December 14, 1946, in Berkeley, Calif.; son of Robert (in sales) and Martha (an accountant; maiden name, McGlaughlin) Swan; married Sandra Dasmann (a poet and painter), May 10, 1980; children: Torrey Dasmann. *Education:* Attended high school in Corona del Mar, Calif. *Home:* 852 Allegheny Star Route, Nevada City, Calif. 95959. *Agent:* Frederick Hill, 2237 Union St., San Francisco, Calif. 94123.

CAREER: John Carl Warnecke & Associates (architects), San Francisco, Calif., draftsman, 1966-67; Benjamin Thompson & Associates (architects), Cambridge, Mass., draftsman, 1968-69; Robert Hawley & Associates (architects), San Francisco, draftsman, 1970-71; free-lance graphic designer, 1971—.

WRITINGS: (With Jeremy Hewes and Eileen Douse) *Cable Car,* Ten Speed Press, 1973, 2nd edition, 1977; (illustrator) Lenny Lipton, *The Super 8 Book,* Straight Arrow, 1975; (with Chet Roaman) *YU 88,* Sierra Club Books, 1977.

WORK IN PROGRESS: Window Music, on transportation; *The Vanishing Machine,* on technology; research on technology of transportation and on ecological restoration.

SIDELIGHTS: Swan wrote: "I am most concerned with the relationship between people, technology, and the environment. Unless there are drastic changes in these areas, I fear civilization is doomed."

* * *

SWANSEA, Charleen (Whisnant) 1932-

PERSONAL: Born May 27, 1932, in Greensboro, N.C.; daughter of Henry and Elvilee Swansea; married Jim Thompson; children: Ena Whisnant, Thomas Whisnant. *Education:* Meredith College, B.A., 1955; University of North Carolina, M.A., 1956. *Home:* 1710 I'on Ave., Sullivans Island, S.C. 29482. *Agent:* Wendy Weil, Julian Bach Literary Agency, Inc., 747 Third Ave., New York, N.Y. 10017. *Office:* 6366 Sharon Hills Rd., Charlotte, N.C. 28210.

CAREER: University of North Carolina, Raleigh, professor of English, 1956-57; Queens College, Charlotte, N.C., professor of English, 1958-64; *Southern Review,* Charlotte, N.C., executive director, 1963-81; writer. Gives concerts with flute, guitar, and poetry; writer-in-residence at Stanford University, 1977, Columbia University, Bryn Mawr College, Wesleyan University, University of North Carolina, Wofford College, Barber-Scotia College, Johnson Smith University, St. Andrews College, Lenoir-Rhyne College, Appalachian University, and Richmond Institute; director of poetry at Charlotte-Mecklenburg Public Schools, 1972—. Founder and senior editor of Red Clay Books, 1970—. Regional vice-president of International Poetry Therapy; consultant to National Endowment for the Humanities and North Carolina Arts Council. *Member:* International Guild of Women in Writing (member of board of directors).

WRITINGS: Poetry Power, Red Clay Books, 1970; *Word Magic,* Doubleday, 1973; (editor) *Smiles You Can Hear,* Red Clay Books, 1978; (editor) *Love Stories by New Women,* Avon, 1980; (editor) *Sense of Human,* Red Clay Books, 1981. Also editor of *American Women Poets: New writing From the South,* 1976. Also author of "Poetry Power" and "Something to Think About," two series of short films for television.

Contributor to magazines, including *Prairie Schooner, New Athenaeum,* and *Appalachian Review.* Editor of *Acorn* and *Carolina Quarterly;* founder and senior editor of *Red Clay*

Reader, 1964-70; poetry editor and member of board of directors of *Southern Voices,* 1973-75.

WORK IN PROGRESS: A novel about Ezra Pound, publication expected in 1982; short stories about women, completion expected in 1983.

SIDELIGHTS: Charleen Swansea told *CA:* "I grew up in the South, eldest child of a false-teeth manufacturer and a peripatetic clubwoman. I spent my teen summers on the road, selling Carolina's dentists on the superiority of my father's false teeth. My father gave me a '49 Ford and a .22 pistol, with which I was able to judiciously attract or repel other Southern hotbloods.

"I attended a small Baptist school for girls and University of North Carolina, where I completed a master's degree in modern poetry during the same year that I discovered Ezra Pound. He had been committed to a Washington mental hospital for making fascist radio speeches in Italy during World War II. After passing myself off as Pound's daughter to get into his ward, I studied with the first of my several mentors, including Conrad Aiken, e.e. cummings, and Buckminster Fuller.

"Pound taught me Chinese and gave me writing assignments. He encouraged and challenged me intellectually, broadened my outlook from southern to ecumenical. From Pound I learned to 'take what you got and make something of it.'

"I took my abilities and began a magazine, *Red Clay Reader.* I brought to it an obsession with good writing and flamboyance. The first issue, featuring both big-name writers and unknowns, came out in 1964. At three dollars a copy ('dirt cheap,' noted the cover) it sold as many as fifteen thousand copies an issue, making it the biggest 'little magazine' in the country.

"The seventh and last issue, devoted to women writers, appeared in 1970. Despite the magazine's surprising financial vitality, I was ready by then to move on to something new— a small press for books by new writers. Since 1970, Red Clay Books has published some thirty-two titles and has won many literary and graphic art awards.

"In 1981 I moved to the beach of South Carolina, where I intend to write novels and plan my next publishing projects."

Swansea was the subject of a film, "Charleen," in 1977.

BIOGRAPHICAL/CRITICAL SOURCES: Winston Salem Journal, November 5, 1971; *Ms.,* December, 1977; *Charlotte,* Volume X, number 3, 1976; *Charlotte Observer,* July, 1977; *Town and Country,* January, 1979; *National Geographic,* March, 1980.

SWIGG, Richard 1938-

PERSONAL: Born September 5, 1938, in London, England; son of Richard and Lilian Swigg; married Eileen Osborne (a teacher), April 4, 1964; children: Virginia Elaine, Alexander Richard John. *Education:* University of Liverpool, B.A. (with first class honors), 1963; University of Bristol, Ph.D., 1967. *Home:* 21 Keele Rd., Newcastle-under-Lyme, Staffordshire ST5 2JT, England. *Office:* Department of English, University of Keele, Keele, Staffordshire ST5 5BG, England.

CAREER: University of Keele, Keele, England, assistant lecturer, 1966-69, lecturer, 1969-80, senior lecturer in English, 1980—.

WRITINGS: Lawrence, Hardy, and American Literature, Oxford University Press, 1972; *Shakespeare's Great Confines,* Carcanet Press, 1981. Contributor of articles and reviews to magazines, including *Agenda, Poetry Nation Review,* and *Modern Language Review.*

WORK IN PROGRESS: In the Fullness of Time (tentative title), essays on contemporary culture, drama, poetry, and novels, completion expected in 1983.

SIDELIGHTS: Swigg commented: "Having grown up in diffuse and dulling South London, I find that the theme which constantly attracts me is that of focus struggled for amidst blurring, a sense of working limits defined amidst swamping hopelessness. My sympathies lie, therefore, with those who have a robust (but not conservatively brash) suspicion of nihilistic complacency, which is the surrender to fate and 'complexity' (when complexity is used as an excuse for evaded response). The non-tragic is, therefore, a theme: that which need not be tragic, yet, in becoming so, shows what the full extent of tragedy is, not its underestimated size."

*   *   *

SWISHER, Carl Brent 1897-1968

OBITUARY NOTICE—See index for *CA* sketch: Born April 28, 1897, in Weston, W.Va.; died June 14, 1968, in Baltimore, Md. Educator and author best known for his books on the Supreme Court and the Constitution. Swisher began his career in 1930 as an instructor in government at Columbia University and later became a Thomas P. Stran Professor of Economics at Johns Hopkins University. His teaching technique was marked by student involvement, and he specialized in relating Supreme Court decisions to economic and social conditions. Swisher's works include *American Constitutional Development, The Growth of Constitutional Power in the United States, Roger B. Taney,* and *The Taney Period: 1836-1864.* Obituaries and other sources: *New York Times,* June 16, 1968.

T

TAMES, Richard (Lawrence) 1946-

PERSONAL: Born January 30, 1946, in Ilford, England; son of Albert Edward (a company director) and Phyllis (Amos) Tames; married Elizabeth Elliston, April 15, 1968. *Education:* Pembroke College, Cambridge, B.A., 1967; Birkbeck College, London, M.Sc., 1974. *Home:* 76 Regent Sq., Bruce Rd., London E3 3HW, England.

CAREER: Haberdashers' Aske's School, Elstree, England, master, 1967-70; Chiswick Polytechnic, London, England, lecturer, 1970-71; researcher for Granada Television, 1972; secretary to the council of the Hansard Society for parliamentary government, 1973-74; University of London, School of Oriental and African Studies, London, assistant organizer of extramural studies, 1975-78, deputy organizer, 1978—. History teacher on adjunct faculty of Syracuse University, London campus, c. 1974—. *Member:* British Association of Japanese Studies.

WRITINGS: Japan Today, Kaye & Ward, 1976; *Modern France: State and Society,* Harrap, 1977; *The World of Islam: A Teacher's Handbook,* School of Oriental and African Studies, University of London, 1977; *China Today,* Kaye & Ward, 1978; *People, Power, and Politics,* Thomas Nelson, 1978; *The Japan Handbook: A Guide for Teachers,* Paul Norbury Publications, 1978; *The Arab World Today,* Kaye & Ward, 1980; *Japan in the Twentieth Century,* Batsford, 1981; *India and Pakistan in the Twentieth Century,* Batsford, 1981; *Emergent Nations: Strategies for Development,* Blackie & Son, 1981; *Makers of Modern Britain,* Batsford, 1982. Author of television scripts for BBC-Schools Television and Inner London Education Authority Schools Television.

SIDELIGHTS: Tames told *CA:* "For the past seven years I have served as a member of the adjunct faculty of Syracuse University's London campus, teaching British history. It's a stimulating experience in inter-cultural communication. Most of my working time, however, is spent in trying to assist British teachers in coming to terms with the curricular challenge of our multicultural society in an increasingly interdependent world. Recent years have surely shown the importance of understanding the achievements of the Japanese and the aspirations of the Muslims, whose cultures represent two of my major areas of interest."

TANN, Jennifer 1939-
(Geoffrey Booth)

PERSONAL: Born in 1939 in Bedford, England; daughter of John (a solicitor) and Frances (a music teacher; maiden name, Ruddle) Booth; married Roger Tann (a teacher and writer); children: Edmund, Oliver. *Education:* Victoria University of Manchester, B.A., 1960; University of Leicester, Ph.D., 1964. *Home:* 24 Amesbury Rd., Moseley, Birmingham 13, England. *Office:* Department of Management, University of Aston, Birmingham, England.

CAREER: Research associate for Historic Towns Project, 1964-66; University of Hull, Hull, England, tutor in industrial archaeology, 1960-69; University of Aston, Birmingham, England, lecturer in business history and economic history, 1969-73, reader in modern economic history, 1973—. Member of executive committee of Business Archives Council. *Member:* Post-Medieval Archaeological Society (member of council, 1975), Economic History Society, Economic History Association, Society of Architectural Historians of Great Britain, Newcomen Society.

WRITINGS: Gloucestershire Woollen Mills, Augustus M. Kelley, 1967; (with M. D. Lobel) *Historic Towns: Gloucester,* Lovell Johns, 1967; *The Development of the Factory,* Cornmarket Press, 1971; (contributor) Brian Bracegirdle, *Archaeology of the Industrial Revolution,* Heinemann, 1973; (under pseudonym Geoffrey Booth) *Industrial Archaeology,* Wayland, 1973; *Children at Work,* Batsford, 1981; *The Selected Papers of Boulton and Watt,* M.I.T. Press, Volume I, 1981.

Screenplays; all released by University of Aston Communications Media Unit: "From Back-to-Back to Bournville," 1972; "Five Percent and Philanthropy," 1976; "Aston's Villas," 1977; "Joseph's Dream," 1978; "Potbank," 1980; "Royal Glassmakers," 1980.

WORK IN PROGRESS: A biography of James Watt, publication by Faber expected in 1982; *International Diffusion of the Watt Engine,* publication expected in 1983.

SIDELIGHTS: Jennifer Tann commented: "I consider it important to investigate a project from many different viewpoints, not just a single discipline base."

TANNER, John (Ian) 1927-

PERSONAL: Born in 1927 in Chelsea, England; son of Robert Arthur (an academic) and I.D.M. (Manners) Tanner; married April Rothery, June 4, 1953; children: Sarah Jane. *Education:* Attended University of Nottingham, 1946-51; Pembroke College, Oxford, M.A., 1949, Ph.D., 1951. *Religion:* Anglican. *Home:* 57 Drayton Gardens, London S.W.10, England. *Agent:* Hope Leresche & Sayle, 11 Jubilee Pl., Chelsea, London SW3 3TE, England. *Office:* Royal Air Force Museum, Hendon, London NW9 5LL, England.

CAREER: Leighton House Art Gallery and Museum, Kensington, 1951-53; Royal Air Force College, Cranwell, England, curator, librarian, and tutor, 1953-63; University of Nottingham, Nottingham, England, extra-mural lecturer in history of art, 1959-63; Royal Air Force Museum, London, England, founding director, 1963—. Associated with Battle of Britain Museum, 1979, and Cosford Aero-Space museum, 1980. Member of local parish council.

MEMBER: Anglo-American Ecumenical Association (president), Royal Aeronautical Society (fellow), Society of Antiquaries, Royal Historical Society, Library Association, Museum Association, Athenaeum Club, Beefsteak Club, Buck's Club, Marylebone Cricket Club, Royal Air Force Club, Reform Club. *Awards, honors:* Cross of Merit of Malta, 1976; member of Papal Order of St. Gregory, 1977; knight of Venerable Order of St. John, 1977; commander of Order of the British Empire, 1978; Tissander Award, F.A.1, 1978; grand officer of merit, Vatican Order of the Holy Sepulchre, 1979.

WRITINGS: (With Julian Franklyn) *An Encyclopaedic Dictionary of Heraldry,* illustrated by Violetta Keeble, Pergamon, 1970; *How to Trace Your Ancestors; or, Find Your Greatest Grandfather,* Corgi, 1971; *The Royal Air Force Museum, Hedon: One Hundred Years of Aviation History,* Pitkin, 1973; (with W. E. May and W. Y. Carman) *Badges and Insignia of the British Armed Services,* St. Martin's, 1974; *Who's Famous in Your Family?,* Reader's Digest Association Ltd., 1975. Also author of *History of Man in Flight,* 1973. Contributor of numerous articles to journals.

WORK IN PROGRESS: Historical works, including catalogues of British air museums and studies of seventeenth-century theology.

AVOCATIONAL INTERESTS: Travel (United States, France, and Italy).

*   *   *

TARKENTON, Fran(cis Asbury) 1940-

PERSONAL: Born February 3, 1940, in Richmond, Va.; son of Dallas (a Methodist minister) and Frances Tarkenton; married Elaine Merrell; children: Angela, Matthew, Melissa. *Education:* University of Georgia, B.B.A., 1961. *Religion:* Methodist. *Residence:* Atlanta, Ga. *Office:* Tarkenton & Co., 3340 Peachtree Rd., N.E., Suite 444, Atlanta, Ga. 30326.

CAREER: Minnesota Vikings (National Football League team), Edina, quarterback, 1961-67; New York Giants (National Football League team), New York City, quarterback, 1967-72; Minnesota Vikings, quarterback, 1972-79; American Broadcasting Co. (ABC-TV), New York City, commentator on television program "Monday Night Football," 1979—, Los Angeles, Calif., co-host of television series "That's Incredible!," 1979—. Founder and chairman of the board of Tarkenton & Co. (formerly Behaviorial Systems, Inc.), 1972—; management consultant for such companies as Exxon, American Express, 3M, U.S. Steel, Pan American

World Airways, Inc., Hilton Hotels, Milliken, Levi Strauss, Fireman's Fund Insurance Companies, United Technologies, and Honeywell. Executive trainee with Coca Cola Co.; associated with advertising agency Batten, Barton, Durstine & Osborn; endorser of various products; engaged in diversified business enterprises; host of talk show in New York City. Affiliated with Diabetes Foundation and Viking Children's Fund. Major gift campaign chairman for Henrietta Egleston Children's Hospital; member of board of directors of Gannett Foundation; member of national board of advisors of Fiscal Policy Council, Inc.; chairman of national steering committee for the University of Georgia Bicentennial Fund Capital Campaign. *Member:* Fellowship of Christian Athletes. *Awards, honors:* Named outstanding man of the year in Georgia, 1968 and 1980; Jim Thorpe Trophy, 1975, for most valuable player in National Football League.

WRITINGS: No Time for Losing, Revell, 1967; (with Jack Olsen) *Better Scramble Than Lose* (autobiographical), Four Winds Press, 1969; (with Brock Yates) *Broken Patterns: The Education of a Quarterback* (autobiographical), Simon & Schuster, 1971; (with Jim Klobuchak) *Tarkenton* (autobiography), Harper, 1976. Also contributor of monthly management articles to *Sky* magazine.

SIDELIGHTS: "Of course it bothers me not to have played for a Super Bowl champion," Fran Tarkenton told *Time.* "But a failure? Lord no. I have played with and against the best players in football since 1961 and I have to believe I belong with the best quarterbacks ever." The record books agree.

By the time Tarkenton ended his football career in 1979, the scrambling quarterback held two all-time pro football records and led the National Football Conference (NFC) in passing for one season. After eighteen years as a quarterback in the National Football League (NFL), Tarkenton completed fifty-seven percent of his passes for more than forty-seven thousand yards. He holds the NFL record for the most touchdown passes, 342. And, in 1975, Tarkenton was the NFC's leader in passing. That same year, Tarkenton was awarded the prestigious Jim Thorpe Trophy as the NFL's most valuable player.

The one football honor which eluded him, as Tarkenton admits, was a Super Bowl victory. On three occasions, the quarterback led the Minnesota Vikings to the Super Bowl. In 1973, he guided the Vikings to a victory over the Dallas Cowboys in the NFC championship game and then to the Super Bowl where they were defeated by the Miami Dolphins. The following season, Tarkenton and the Vikings defended their title as the number one team in the NFC by defeating the Los Angeles Rams in the conference's championship game, but the Minnesota team lost the 1975 Super Bowl to the Pittsburgh Steelers. In the 1976 NFC championship game, Tarkenton and the Vikings defeated the Rams again before losing to the Oakland Raiders in the 1977 Super Bowl. These losses have made Tarkenton feel "empty," but, as he said, "Football is not the end of creation for me."

As the scrambler suggests in his autobiography, *Tarkenton,* an athlete should be capable of functioning in a world in which professional sports are only a part. Tarkenton believes that football players often possess a false sense of security; he knows that they lose their sense of perspective from the pampering they receive.

So Tarkenton followed his own advice. While he was a professional athlete, he was also a successful businessman. For instance, the various business enterprises in which Tarkenton was engaged in 1969, such as an executive training position with Coca Cola and the ownership of an apartment house in Georgia, yielded a greater income than the quarterback's football salary. In 1971, *Newsweek*'s Pete Axthelm reported that Tarkenton "had amassed a considerable fortune." The scrambler "is a millionaire several times over," observed a *Time* reporter, "a self-made corporate presence." And Gerald Eskenazi of the *New York Times* noted that "he is a wealthy man, with one of his companies consisting of more than 100 learning centers for the disadvantaged." Tarkenton's financial success prompted Roger Kahn of *Time* to write: "Our old preoccupation with what Clark Gable was paid at Metro has been replaced by speculation on Francis Tarkenton's net worth."

Tarkenton's books have also been successful. *Tarkenton, Broken Patterns,* and *Better Scramble Than Lose* are accounts of his quarterback career as well as an insider's view of pro football. Geared for football enthusiasts, the books present typical football playing tips, anecdotes, and stories.

AVOCATIONAL INTERESTS: Tennis, racquetball, golf, fishing, television, reading historical novels.

BIOGRAPHICAL/CRITICAL SOURCES: New York Times, July 23, 1971; *Newsweek,* August 23, 1971; *Time,* January 10, 1977; *Best Sellers,* April, 1977.

*   *   *

TARRANT, John
 See EGLETON, Clive (Frederick)

*   *   *

TATARKIEWICZ, Wladyslaw   1886-1980

PERSONAL: Born April 3, 1886, in Warsaw, Poland; died April 4, 1980, in Warsaw; son of Ksawery and Maria (Brzezinska) Tatarkiewicz; married Teresa Potworowska, 1919 (deceased); children: one son. *Education:* Attended University of Warsaw, University of Zurich, University of Paris, University of Berlin, and University of Marburg; earned Ph.D.

CAREER: University of Warsaw, Warsaw, Poland, professor of philosophy, 1915-62, professor emeritus, 1962-80. Professor at University of Lvov and University of Vilno. Past member of Polish Academy of Learning; honorary member of International Committee of History of Art. *Awards, honors:* French Legion of Honor; commander cross of Order of Polonia Restituta, 1938, with star, 1958; Polish State Prize, 1966; D.H.C. from Catholic University of Lublin, 1976.

WRITINGS: Historia filozofii, two volumes, 2nd edition, Wydawnictwo Zakladu narodowego imienia Ossolinskich, 1933, 6th edition published as *Historia filozofii,* Volume I: *Filozofia starozytra i sredniowieczna,* Volume II: *Filozofia nowozytna do roku 1830,* Volume III: *Filozofia XIX wieku i wspoiczesna,* Panstwowe Wydawnictwo Naukowe, 1968, 7th edition, 1970, translation of Volume III by Chester A. Kisiel published as *Nineteenth-Century Philosophy,* Wadsworth, 1973; *Zarys dziejow filozofii w Polsce,* translation by Christopher Kasparek published as *Outline of the History of Philosophy in Poland to World War II,* Polish Arts and Culture Foundation, c.1945; *Historia estetyki,* Zaklad Narodowy im. Ossolinskich, 1960, 2nd edition, 1962, translation by Cyril Barrett published as *History of Aesthetics,* Mouton, Volume I: *Ancient Aesthetics,* 1970, Volume II: *Medieval Aesthetics,* 1970, Volume III: *Modern Aesthetics,* 1974; *O szczesciu,* 3rd edition, Panstwowe Wydawnictwo Naukowe, 1962, 5th edition, 1962, translation by Edward Rothert and Danuta Zielinska published as *Analysis of Happiness,* Polish

Scientific Publishers, 1976; *Twentieth-Century Philosophy, 1900-1950,* translated by Kisiel, Wadsworth, 1973.

Other writings: *Die disposition der aristotelischen prinzipien,* A. Toepelmann, 1910; *Skupienie i marzenie* (title means "Concentration and Dreaming"), [Poland], 1935; *Dominik Merlini,* Budownictwo i Architektura, 1955; *Lazienki warszowskie* (summary in English, French, and Russian), Arkady, 1957, 3rd edition, 1972; (editor with Tadeusz Dobrowolski) *Historia sztuki polskiej w zarysie,* Wydawnictwo Literackie, 1962; *Estetyka starozytna,* 2nd edition, Zaklad Narodowy im. Ossolinskich, 1962; *O sztuce polskiej XVII i XVIII wieku: Architektura, rzezba,* Panstwowe Wydawnictwo Naukowe, 1966; *Estetyka nowozytna,* Zaklad Narodowy im. Ossolinskich, 1967; *Lazienki krolewskie i ich osobliwosci* (summary in English, German, and Russian), Arkady, 1967.

(Editor) *Jakiej filozofii polacy potrzebuja,* Panstwowe Wydawnictwo Naukowe, 1970; *Droga do filozofii i inne rozprawy filozoficzne* (title means "The Way to Philosophy and Other Philosophical Papers"), Panstwowe Wydawnictwo Naukowe, 1971; *Pisma zebrane,* Panstwowe Wydawnictwo Naukowe, 1971; *Droga przez estetyke,* Panstwowe Wydawnictwo Naukowe, 1972; *Dzieje szesciu pojec: Sztuka, piekno, forma, tworczose, edtworczosc, przezycie estetyczne,* Panstwowe Wydawnictwo Naukowe, 1975, 2nd edition, 1976; *Zapiski do autobiografii* (title means "Notes to Autobiography"), 1976; *O doskonalosci* (title means "On Perfection"), Panstwowe Wydawnictwo Naukowe, 1976; *Parerga,* Panstwowe Wydawnictwo Naukowe, 1978. Contributor to *Cambridge History of Poland.*

OBITUARIES: New York Times, April 4, 1980; *London Times,* April 25, 1980; *AB Bookman's Weekly,* May 5, 1980.*

*   *   *

TAUBERT, William H(owland)   1934-

PERSONAL: Born October 18, 1934, in Corning, N.Y.; son of William H. (in sales) and Marian (Lipps) Taubert; married Patricia Gordon, July 1, 1960; children: Jennifer, Nancy, Linda. *Education:* Rensselaer Polytechnic Institute, B.E.E., 1955, M.E.E., 1960; Harvard University, M.B.A., 1959; University of California, Los Angeles, Ph.D. (with distinction), 1968. *Home:* 120 Monarch Bay, South Laguna, Calif. 92677. *Office:* Hunt-Wesson Foods, Inc., 1645 West Valencia Dr., Fullerton, Calif. 92634.

CAREER: Hughes Aircraft Co., Culver City, Calif., manager, 1960-70; Hunt-Wesson Foods, Inc., Fullerton, Calif., vice-president, 1970—. Member of board of directors of Universal Product Code Council and South Coast Community Hospital. *Military service:* U.S. Navy, 1955-57; became lieutenant commander. U.S. Naval Reserve, 1957-65. *Member:* National Council of Physical Distribution Management, Grocery Manufacturers Association (chairman).

WRITINGS: (Contributor) M.J.C. Martin and R. A. Denison, editors, *Case Exercises in Operations Research, Wiley-Interscience,* 1971; (with E. S. Buffa) *Production-Inventory Systems: Planning and Control,* Irwin, 1972. Contributor of articles to *Management Science* and *Industrial Management Review.*

SIDELIGHTS: Taubert told *CA:* "Writing is one of the most demanding, frustrating, exhilarating, and rewarding experiences imaginable!"

*   *   *

TAYLOR, Arthur Samuel   1894-1963

OBITUARY NOTICE—See index for *CA* sketch: Born March

7, 1894, in Aledo, Ill.; died August, 1963. Educator and author. Taylor was Emeritus Professor of Social Science and a past chairman of the Social Science Division of Southern Oregon State College. He was also a speaker on subjects relating to southern Oregon regional history. A building on the Southern Oregon State College campus, Taylor Hall, bears the educator's name. Taylor's works include *A Guide to the Study and Reading of the Pacific Northwest, Our Great Northwest,* and *Logging.* (Date of death provided by Vaughn D. Bornet, professor of history and social science, Southern Oregon State College.)

* * *

TAYLOR, Jesse
See AMIDON, Bill (Vincent)

* * *

TELLER, Neville 1931-
(Edmund Owen)

PERSONAL: Born June 10, 1931, in London, England; son of Hyman (a company director) and Sarah (Ephron) Teller; married Sheila Brown (a teacher), October 20, 1958; children: Richard Henry Marshall, Adam James Grenville, Matthew David Alexander. *Education:* St. Edmund Hall, Oxford, B.A. (with honors), 1955, M.A., 1963. *Home:* 15 Ewhurst Close, Cheam, Surrey, England. *Agent:* Lorna Vestey, 33 Dryburgh Rd., London S.W.15, England. *Office:* Department of Health and Social Security, Alexander Fleming House, Elephant & Castle, London S.E.1, England.

CAREER: Butterworth & Co. Ltd. (publisher), Sevenoaks, England, marketing manager, 1966-68; Granada Publishing Ltd., St. Albans, England, marketing director, 1968-69; *London Times,* London, England, marketing coordinator, 1969-70; Department of Health and Social Security, London, civil servant, 1970—. *Member:* Society of Authors.

WRITINGS: Bluff Your Way in Marketing, Wolfe, 1966, 2nd revised edition, 1969; (editor) *Whodunit: Ten Tales of Crime and Detection,* Edward Arnold, 1970; (editor with Jane Cicely Sounders and D. H. Summers) *Hospice: The Living Idea,* Edward Arnold, 1981. Radio writer, sometimes under pseudonym Edmund Owen.

WORK IN PROGRESS: A radio dramatization of "The Sword in the Stone" by T. H. White.

SIDELIGHTS: Teller wrote: "I have been a radio writer since 1956, mainly though not exclusively for the British Broadcasting Corp. I specialize in abridgement, adaptation, dramatization, and serialization for reading on the air. The number of programs I have scripted runs into the thousands. A recent major work was a ninety-minute dramatization of *Party Going* by Henry Green. I have also researched and scripted such literary and historical features as 'The Horror at Bly,' an investigation of Henry James's *The Turn of the Screw;* 'The Queen and the Kaiser,' a study of the relationship between Queen Victoria and her grandson; a fifteen-part abridgement of *The Franchise Affair* by Josephine Tey; and 'Dizzy and the Faery Queen,' a feature on Queen Victoria and Disraeli.

"I have been fascinated by radio since boyhood—television and film have never held the same appeal. At university, as a committee member of the Oxford University Dramatic Society and secretary of the Experimental Theatre Club, I specialized in radio productions, and later moved very quickly into writing free-lance for radio, while pursuing a career in marketing and general management.

"In 1970 I moved out of the business world into civil service, but continued and gradually extended the scope of my radio work. The range of artistic and technical possibilities inherent in the sound medium for interesting moving and communicating with people, as individuals and en masse at one and the same time, is a never-ending source of wonder and delight. The radio writer's intense satisfaction stems from blending the words, sounds, music, and technical devices on his palette to produce in the mind's eye of his listening audience and on their emotions a precisely calculated effect.

"I pity those benighted parts of the civilized world where radio has degenerated into a form of aural wallpaper, and where artistry and craftsmanship by writer, producers, and actors for radio has atrophied. *Floreat* the BBC!"

* * *

TENNANT, Veronica 1947-

PERSONAL: Born January 15, 1947, in London, England; son of Harry and Doris (Bassous) Tennant; married John Robert Wright (a physician), June 11, 1969; children: Jessica Robin. *Education:* National Ballet School, Toronto, Ontario, graduated, 1964. *Office:* National Ballet of Canada, 157 King St. E., Toronto, Ontario, Canada M5C 1G9.

CAREER: National Ballet of Canada, Toronto, Ontario, principal dancer, 1965—, dancers' representative to board of directors of National Ballet Company, 1970-73. Guest artist at International Dance Festival 1971, Expo 70, Newport Musical Festival, 1973, Dance Detroit, 1975, and Stratford Shakespearean Festival, 1978; also appeared in major U.S. cities, including Metropolitan Opera House, New York, N.Y.; dancer on CBC-TV, including performances in "Cinderella," "Sleeping Beauty," and "Romeo and Juliet"; actress in "Hans Christian Andersen," 1979. Guest on television programs. Lecturer at University of Waterloo and York University. Member of Ontario Arts Council and Canadian Conference on the Arts. *Awards, honors:* Officer of Order of Canada, 1975.

WRITINGS: On Stage, Please (juvenile novel), Holt, 1979.

SIDELIGHTS: Tennant has danced the leading roles of many major ballets, including "The Nutcracker," "The Dream," "Swan Lake," "La Sylphide," "Coppelia," and "Giselle." A dancer of international stature, she was Mikhail Baryshnikov's first partner after his defection to the West. Among the other partners with whom she has performed are Rudolf Nureyev, Erik Bruhn, Ivan Nagy, Anthony Dowell, Edward Villella, and Peter Schaufuss. Penelope Doob of the National Ballet of Canada described Tennant as "a dramatic ballerina of formidable intensity." She added: "Tennant wins praise as much for her superb technique and sensitive phrasing as for the compelling conviction of her interpretations of the great roles—Giselle, Juliet, Aurora, Cinderella, the Sylphide. Her technical brilliance comes in part from her training at the National Ballet School, with its emphasis on precise virtuosity in the use of feet and legs and on an elegant, lyrical line with expressive and beautifully fluid arms, all virtues noticeable in Tennant's own style. Other graces—an inspired and intelligent use of the head, face, and eyes, extraordinary musicality, the ability to create instantly believable and yet highly individual interpretations of any role—come partly from the observation of other great dancers but mostly from the dancer herself. Tennant has learned from others—from Ulanova, her teacher for a few classes, an 'enormous breadth of movement that never seemed to stop'; from guest artists Marcia Haydee and Lynn Seymour a sense of how to approach dramatic roles, from Lois Smith 'her superb stage-craft.'''

BIOGRAPHICAL/CRITICAL SOURCES: Dance in Canada, fall, 1976; *Dance,* March, 1977; *Eccentric* (Birmingham/Bloomfield, Mich.), March 19,1981.

*   *   *

THACKRAY, Derek V(incent) 1926-

PERSONAL: Born June 8, 1926, in Leeds, England; son of Verneis James and Alice May (Walker) Thackray; married Lucy Elizabeth Inmam, December 31, 1957; children: Frances Elizabeth, Teresa Carmel. *Education:* University of Leeds, Teacher's Certificate, 1945; University of London, B.Sc. (with honors), 1956, Academic Diploma in Education, 1960, M.A., 1964, Ph.D., 1969. *Home:* Lilbourne Furze, Clifton-on-Dunsmore, Rugby, Warwickshire, England. *Office:* Northampton University Centre, University of Leicester, Barrack Rd., Northampton, England.

CAREER: Teacher at primary school in Leeds, England, 1948-53, and Church of England school in Leeds, 1953-56; teacher of geography and department head at boys' secondary modern school in Leeds, 1956-58, and grammar school in Morley, England, 1958-60; St. Paul's College of Education, Rugby, England, lecturer, 1960-62, senior lecturer in education, 1962-78, head of department, 1966-78; University of Leicester, Northampton University Centre, Northampton, England, lecturer in education, 1978—. Member of summer faculty at University of Victoria, 1971; part-time lecturer at Leeds College of Commerce, 1956-60; part-time tutor at Open University, 1973-75. *Military service:* British Army, Royal Educational Corps, 1945-48. *Member:* International Reading Association, Society of Authors and Artists, United Kingdom Reading Association (secretary).

WRITINGS—Elementary school textbooks: *Stories the Rhymes Tell,* Basil Blackwell, 1968, *Tarzan the Tortoise,* Longmans, Green, 1969; *Other Children,* Geoffrey Chapman, 1970; *This Is How We Live,* Geoffrey Chapman, 1971; *This Is How We Work,* Geoffrey Chapman, 1971; *This Is My Colour,* Tom Stacey, 1973; *This Is My Shape,* Tom Stacey, 1973; *Steps to Reading,* Tom Stacey, 1973; *Reading Readiness Profiles,* University of London Press, 1974; *This Is My Sound,* George Philip Alexander, 1975; *Reading Readiness Inventory,* University of London Press, 1976; *Reading Readiness Training Programme for Language Master,* Drake Associates, 1978; *Reading Readiness Workbooks,* two volumes, Hodder & Stoughton, 1980.

Books for adults: *Readiness to Read,* Geoffrey Chapman, 1971; (with J. A. Downing) *Reading Readiness,* University of London Press, 1971, 2nd edition, 1975; *Ready for School,* Hodder & Stoughton, 1978; (editor and contributor) *Growth in Reading,* Ward, Lock, 1979. Contributor to *Reading and the Curriculum,* Ward, Lock, 1971; *The Reading Curriculum,* University of London Press, 1973; *The Road to Effective Reading,* Ward, Lock, 1974; *Reading: What of the Future?,* Ward, Lock, 1975; *The Reading Connection,* Ward, Lock, 1980.

Contributor to educational psychology journals.

WORK IN PROGRESS: Research on reading readiness, reading, test construction and standardization, comparison of reading methods, and reading schemes; *Major Reading Schemes,* with wife, Lucy Elizabeth Thackray, publication by Thomas Nelson expected in 1983.

THAYER, Charles Wheeler 1910-1969

OBITUARY NOTICE—See index for *CA* sketch: Born February 9, 1910, in Villanova, Pa.; died of a heart attack, August 27, 1969, in Salzberg, Austria; buried in Byrn Mawr, Pa. Diplomat and author. Active in the Foreign Service since 1933, Thayer held various positions in such countries as Russia, Germany, Afghanistan, and England. His most notable position was chief of the U.S. Military Mission to Marshal Tito. His diplomatic career ended when Senator Joseph R. McCarthy threatened to publicize an alleged incident from Thayer's past. At the time, the *Washington Post* defended Thayer saying that his ''principle offense . . . is that he is a brother-in-law of Charles E. Bohler—at whom Senator McCarthy has chosen to direct the full force of his malevolence.'' Thayer's works include *Bears in the Caviar, Unquiet Germans, Natasha,* and *Muzzy.* Obituaries and other sources: *Washington Post,* August 29, 1969; *Who Was Who in America,* 5th edition, Marquis, 1973.

*   *   *

THAYER, Theodore 1904-1981

OBITUARY NOTICE: Born October 17, 1904, in Akron, N.Y.; died February 17, 1981, in Alpine, Calif. Educator, historian, and author. Thayer taught American history for more than twenty years at Rutgers University. Among his writings are *Colonial and Revolutionary Morris County* and *Washington and Lee: From Valley Forge to Monmouth.* Obituaries and other sources: *Directory of American Scholars:* Volume I, *History,* 6th edition, Bowker, 1974; *New York Times,* February 25, 1981; *AB Bookman's Weekly,* May 25, 1981.

*   *   *

THISBY
See TURNER, Dona M.

*   *   *

THOMAS, Alexander 1914-

PERSONAL: Born January 11, 1914, in New York, N.Y.; son of Herman and Rose Thomas; married Stella Chess (a physician), June 28, 1938; children: Joan, Richard, Leonard, Kenneth. *Education:* City College (now of City University of New York), B.S. (magna cum laude), 1932; New York University, M.D., 1936. *Home:* 2500 Johnson Ave., New York, N.Y. 10463. *Office:* 333 East 49th St., New York, N.Y. 10017.

CAREER: Mount Sinai Hospital, New York City, intern, 1936-39; Bellevue Hospital, New York City, assistant visiting clinical psychiatrist/neurologist, 1938-40, resident in psychiatry, 1946-48, assistant visiting psychiatrist/neurologist, 1951-57, associate visiting psychiatrist/neurologist, 1958-68, director of Division of Psychiatry, 1968-78. Diplomate of American Board of Psychiatry and Neurology, 1948; private practice in psychiatry. Assistant clinical psychiatrist/neurologist at University Hospital, 1948-53, assistant attending psychiatrist, 1954-59, associate attending psychiatrist, 1960-65, attending psychiatrist, 1966—; clinical instructor at New York University, 1949-53, assistant professor, 1953-59, associate professor, 1959-66, professor, 1966—. Member of task forces and commissions on mental health services in New York State and New York City. *Military service:* U.S. Army Air Forces, Medical Corps, 1942-46; became captain. *Member:* American Psychiatric Association (fellow; president of New York branch, 1973-74), American Orthopsychiatric Society, Society for Research in Child Development, American Association for the Advancement of Science, Phi Beta Kappa, Sigma Xi, Alpha Omega Alpha.

WRITINGS: (With others) *Behavioral Individuality in Early Childhood,* New York University Press, 1963; (with wife, Stella Chess, and Herbert G. Birch) *Your Child Is a Person: A Psychological Approach to Parenthood Without Guilt,* Viking, 1965; (with Chess and Birch) *Temperament and Behavior Disorders in Children,* New York University Press, 1968; (editor with Chess) *Annual Progress in Child Psychiatry and Child Development,* Brunner, Volume I, 1968, Volume II, 1969, Volume III, 1970, Volume IV, 1971, Volume V, 1972, Volume VI, 1973, Volume VII, 1974, Volume VIII, 1975, Volume IX, 1976, Volume X, 1977, Volume XI, 1978, Volume XII, 1979, Volume XIII, 1980.

(With Samuel Sillen) *Racism and Psychiatry,* Brunner, 1972; (with Ernst F. Mueller) *Einfuehrung in die Sozialpsychologie,* Verlag fuer Psychologie Hogrefe, 1974; *Psychologie der Handlung und Bewegung,* Hain, 1976; (with Chess) *Temperament and Development,* Brunner, 1977; (with Chess) *The Dynamics of Psychological Development,* Brunner, 1980. Contributor to psychiatry journals.

WORK IN PROGRESS: A book, tentatively titled *A General Theory of Psychological Development;* papers and a volume based on the author's work as the principal investigator of the New York Longitudinal Study and on data analyses of normal and deviant psychological development from infancy to early adult life; long-term studies of psychological development.

SIDELIGHTS: Thomas told *CA:* "My research with Dr. Chess has emphasized the role of the child's own characteristics, especially his temperament, in his development. Studies in temperament, based largely on our work, have developed at many research centers throughout the world. We are always very critical of those theories which put all the responsibility and blame for the child's development on what the mother does. This leaves out all the influences of the child's temperament and of the social environment."

BIOGRAPHICAL/CRITICAL SOURCES: American Journal of Orthopsychiatry, July, 1980.

* * *

THOMAS, David   1931-

PERSONAL: Born February 16, 1931, in Bridgend, Wales; son of William and Florence (Jones) Thomas; married Daphne Elizabeth Berry (a teacher), August 16, 1955; children: Sian Elizabeth, Huw David. *Education:* University College of Wales, Aberystwyth, University of Wales, B.A., 1954, M.A., 1957. *Home:* 6 Plymouth Dr., Barnt Green, Birmingham B45 8JB, England. *Office:* Department of Geography, University of Birmingham, P.O. Box 363, Birmingham B15 2TT, England.

CAREER: University of London, London, England, lecturer, 1957-68, reader in geography, 1968-70; University of Wales, St. David's University College Lampeter, Dyfed, professor of geography, 1970-78; University of Birmingham, Birmingham, England, professor of geography, 1978—.

WRITINGS: Agriculture in Wales During the Napoleonic Wars, University of Wales Press, 1963; *London's Green Belt,* Faber, 1970; (editor and contributor) *An Advanced Geography of the British Isles,* Hutton, 1974; *Wales: A New Study,* David & Charles, 1978.

THOMAS, Gwyn   1913-1981

OBITUARY NOTICE—See index for *CA* sketch: Born July 6, 1913, in Cymmer, South Wales; died c. April 14, 1981, in Cardiff, Wales. Novelist, playwright, broadcaster, educator, and author best known for his stories about coal miners in South Wales. Early in his career, Thomas was associated with the Workers' Educational Association and with the National Council of Social Service. During World War II, he taught Spanish at Cardigan Grammar School and at Barry Grammar School. He wrote primarily about the inhabitants of the Rhondda coal mining valleys who tried to find happiness despite strikes, poverty, and unemployment. Although his novels and short story collections, such as *All Things Betray Thee* and *The Alone to the Alone,* have commanded the most attention, Thomas's autobiography, *A Few Selected Exits,* his twelve radio plays, his five teleplays, and his West End success "The Keep" reflected his facility in other genres. In 1976 the author, whose literary influences were Robert Benchley, S. J. Perelman, and the Marx Brothers, received the Welsh Arts Council's principal prize. His works include *The World Cannot Hear You, The Love Man, The Dark Philosophers, Where Did I Put My Pity?,* and *A Welsh Eye.* Obituaries and other sources: *London Times,* April 18, 1981; *New York Times,* April 19, 1981; *Detroit Free Press,* April 19, 1981; *Washington Post,* April 20, 1981; *AB Bookman's Weekly,* May 4, 1981; *Publishers Weekly,* May 8, 1981.

* * *

THOMAS, Helen Shirley   1931-1968

OBITUARY NOTICE—See index for *CA* sketch: Born September 24, 1931, in Baltimore, Md.; died December 10, 1968. Educator and author. Thomas began her career as an instructor at Johns Hopkins College in 1931. She was an assistant professor at Goucher College. Thomas wrote *Felix Frankfurter: Scholar on the Bench.* (Date of death provided by Joan King, alumnae secretary, Goucher College.)

* * *

THOMPSON, Gene   1924-

PERSONAL: Born June 28, 1924, in San Francisco, Calif.; son of Andrew A. (a naval officer) and Rose (Greenblat) Thompson; married Sylvia Vaughn Sheekman (a writer), June 15, 1955; children: David Oxley, Benjamin Stuart, Dinah Vaughn, Amanda Greenleaf. *Education:* University of California, Berkeley, B.A., 1949; studied music and German in Heidelberg, Germany, 1950-54. *Politics:* Democrat. *Religion:* Jewish. *Home address:* P.O. Box 145, Idyllwild, Calif., 92349. *Agent:* Robert Lescher, 155 East 71st St., New York, N.Y. 10021.

CAREER: Writer, 1941—. *Member:* Writers Guild of America (West).

WRITINGS: Lupe (novel), Random House, 1977; *Murder Mystery,* (novel), Random House, 1980. Writer for television shows, including "Baretta," "Columbo," "Cannon," "Harry-O," "Marcus Welby, M.D.," "Lucille Ball," "Love American Style," "My Three Sons," "The Beverly Hillbillies," and "Bob Newhart."

WORK IN PROGRESS: A sequel to *Murder Mystery,* publication expected in 1981.

SIDELIGHTS: Thompson wrote: "I was brought to Hollywood by Groucho Marx when I was sixteen and employed by him as a comedy writer. When I was twenty-one, I left Hollywood for the university, returning some years later. I have worked on a broad spectrum of television shows, ranging from 'Lucille Ball' to 'Baretta' and 'Columbo.' Much of my training in comedy involved writing material performed before an audience in the studio, and this greatly influenced my prose style." Thompson's work has been published in England, France, Spain, South America, Italy, Germany and the Netherlands.

*   *   *

THOMPSON, Robert Farris   1932-

PERSONAL: Born December 30, 1932, in El Paso, Tex.; married Nancy Gaylord (a teacher); children: Alicia, Clark. *Education:* Yale University, B.A., 1955, M.A., 1961, Ph.D., 1965. *Home:* 63 Wall St., New Haven, Conn. 06510. *Office:* Department of the History of Art, Yale University, New Haven, Conn. 06520.

CAREER: Yale University, New Haven, Conn., acting instructor, 1964-65, instructor, 1965-66, assistant professor, 1966-69, associate professor, 1969-75, professor of art history, 1975—, chairman of Council of African Studies, 1974-75. Visiting curator at Museum of Ethnic Arts, University of California, Los Angeles, 1970. Member of U.S. delegation to First World Festival of Black Art, Dakar, Senegal, 1966; founding member of Social Science Research Council-American Council of Learned Societies Joint Committee on Afro-American Cultures and Societies, 1968—; consultant to governor of Puerto Rico and Library and Museum of the Performing Arts. *Member:* African Studies Association (chairman of arts and humanities committee, 1966-70). *Awards, honors:* Grants from Concilium on International and Area Studies for Nigeria, 1965, 1968.

WRITINGS: (Translator from Portuguese) F. da Costa, *The Antiquity of the Art of Painting*, Yale University Press, 1967; (contributor) Armstead L. Robinson, C. Foster, and D. Ogilvie, editors, *Black Studies in the University*, Yale University Press, 1969; (contributor) D. P. Biebuyck, editor, *Tradition and Creativity in Tribal Art*, University of California Press, 1969; *Black Gods and Kings: Yoruba Art at U.C.L.A.* (monograph), Museum and Laboratories of Ethnic Arts and Technology, University of California, Los Angeles, 1971; (contributor) Douglas Fraser and H. M. Cole, editors, *African Art and Leadership*, University of Wisconsin Press, 1972; (contributor) Warren L. d'Azevedo, editor, *The Traditional Artist in African Societies*, Indiana University Press, 1973; *African Art in Motion: Icon and Act in the Collection of Katerine Coryton White*, University of California Press, 1974. Contributor to art and African studies journals, popular newspapers, and magazines, including *Saturday Review*.

*   *   *

THOMSON, Daisy H(icks)   1918-
(Jonathan H. Thomson)

PERSONAL: Born in 1918, in Rothesay, Scotland; daughter of Jonathan (a civil engineer) and Margaret (Hicks) Roe; married William Hugh Thomson, March 1, 1945 (deceased); children: Angus Jonathan, Marguerita Hicks Thomson McGilchrist. *Education:* University of Edinburgh, M.A., 1938; attended Kerr Sanders Secretarial College, 1938-39. *Religion:* Protestant. *Home:* 20 Batts Hill, Redhill, Surrey RH1 2DH, England.

CAREER: Bute County Council, Rothesay, Scotland, assistant welfare officer, 1939-45; assistant registrar of births in Rothesay, 1939-45; writer, 1947—. *Member:* International P.E.N., Society of Authors, Romantic Novelists Association, Edinburgh University Graduate Society.

WRITINGS—Novels; first published by R. Hale, except as noted: *Prelude to Love*, 1963, Pyramid Publications, 1974; *To Love and Honour*, 1964, published as *To Love and Honor*, Pyramid Publications, 1974; *Portrait of My Love*, 1966, Pyramid Publications, 1974; *Jealous Love*, 1966, Pyramid Publications, 1974; *Love for a Stranger*, 1966, Pyramid Publications, 1974; *A Truce for Love*, 1967, Pyramid Publications, 1974; *By Love Betrayed*, 1967, Pyramid Publications, 1974; *Journey to Love*, 1967, Pyramid Publications, 1974; *Be My Love*, 1968, Pyramid Publications, 1974; *My Only Love*, 1969, Pyramid Publications, 1974; *Five Days to Love*, 1969, Pyramid Publications, 1974; *The Italian for Love*, 1970.

Summons to Love, 1971, Pyramid Publications, 1974; *Hello My Love*, 1972, Pyramid Publications, 1974; *Woman in Love*, 1973, Pyramid Publications, 1974; *The Beginning of Love*, 1975, Pyramid Publications, 1976; *The Summer of Love*, Pyramid Publications, 1976; *My One and Only Love*, Pyramid Publications, 1976; *From Solitude With Love*, Pyramid Publications, 1976; *Myrtle for My Love*, Pyramid Publications, 1977; *The Voice of Love*, Pyramid Publications, 1977; *In Love, in Vienna*, Harcourt, 1977; *Suddenly It Was Love*, Harcourt, 1977; *Love at Leisure*, Harcourt, 1978; *A Nightingale for Love*, Harcourt, 1978; *A Time for Love*, Harcourt, 1978; *The Face of Love*, Doubleday, 1979; *The Web of Love*, 1979; *To Love and Be Wise*, 1980; *The Island of Love*, 1980; *I Love You Julie*, 1980; *The Eve of Love*, 1980.

Author of short stories under pseudonym, Jonathan H. Thomson. Contributor to magazines, including *Good Housewife*, *She*, and *Country Fair*, and newspapers.

WORK IN PROGRESS: Research on Paris for a novel.

SIDELIGHTS: Daisy Thomson commented: "Writing has always been an interest, and seeing new places, meeting new people intrigue me and fire my imagination." *Avocational interests:* Reading, gardening, oil painting, travel.

*   *   *

THOMSON, Jonathan H.
See THOMSON, Daisy H(icks)

*   *   *

THOMSON, William A(rchibald) R(obson)   1906-

PERSONAL: Born November 6, 1906, in Kinghorn, Fife, Scotland; son of W. A. (a minister) and Alison (Robson) Thomson; married Marion Lucy Nannette Hill, 1934; children: two sons. *Education:* University of Edinburgh, M.B. Ch.B., 1929, M.D. (with honors), 1933. *Home:* 4 Rutland Court, Queen's Dr., London W3 0HL, England.

CAREER: Clinical assistant and clinical tutor at Royal Infirmary, Edinburgh, Scotland; assistant in medicine and Davidson research fellow in applied bacteriology at University of Edinburgh, Edinburgh; Paterson research scholar and chief assistant in cardiac department at London Hospital, London, England; first assistant in medical unit at St. Thomas Hospital; chairman of Leprosy Study Center, 1951-80. Bengue Memorial Award Lecturer at Royal Institute of Public Health and Hygiene; Cavendish lecturer of West London Medico-Chirurgical Society, 1975. Foundation member of British Institute for the Study of the Arts in Therapy. *Military service:* Served with Royal Navy; became surgeon lieutenant. *Member:* Royal Society of Medicine (fellow), Royal College of Physicians (Edinburgh; fellow), Royal Institute of Public Health and Hygiene (fellow), British Acadmey of Forensic Sciences (founding member; deputy chairman of executive council, 1972-77 and 1980-81), Athenaeum Club. *Awards, honors:* Abercrombie Award from Royal College of General Practitioners, 1973.

WRITINGS: The Searching Mind in Medicine, Burns & MacEachern, 1960; (editor) *The Practitioner's Handbook,* Cassell, 1960; (editor) *Sex and Its Problems,* Williams & Wilkins, 1968; *Thomson's Concise Medical Dictionary,* Churchill Livingstone, 1973; *Herbs That Heal,* A. & C. Black, 1976, Scribner, 1977; *A Dictionary of Medical Ethics and Practice,* John Wright, 1977; *Spas That Heal,* A. & C. Black, 1978; *Healing Plants,* Macmillan, 1978; (with Elizabeth Smith) *Healing Herbs,* BBC Publications, 1978; (editor) *Medicines From the Earth,* McGraw, 1978; *A Change of Air,* A. & C. Black, 1979; *Faiths That Heal,* A. & C. Black. Also editor of *Practical Dietetics,* 1960, *The Doctor's Surgery,* 1964, and *Calling the Lab,* 1971.

Editor of *Practitioner,* 1944-73, and *Black's Medical Dictionary,* 1948—. Medical correspondent for *London Times,* 1956-71. Medical consultant to *Daily Telegraph* and *Fishbein's Illustrated Medical and Health Encyclopaedia.* Contributor to *Gradwhol's Legal Medicine* and *Encyclopaedia Britannica.* Contributor to British medical journals.

*   *   *

THURMAN, Howard   1900-1981

OBITUARY NOTICE—See index for *CA* sketch: Born November 18, 1900, in Daytona Beach, Fla.; died after a long illness, April 10, 1981, in San Francisco, Calif. Clergyman, educator, and author. A Baptist minister who was brought up by his grandmother, a former slave, Thurman co-founded the Church for Fellowship of All Peoples, an interracial, nondenominational church in San Francisco. Influenced by the philosophy of nonviolence espoused by Mohondas K. Gandhi, the minister provided a foundation on which the leaders of the civil rights movement of the fifties and sixties could build. He taught at Howard University, Spellman College for Women, Morehouse College, and Boston University, where he was the first black to hold a full-time faculty position. In the 1960's Thurman established an educational trust bearing his name to help needy students. Besides his autobiography, *With Hand and Heart,* Thurman wrote twenty-one books on religion and race, including *Deep River: An Interpretation of Negro Spirituals, The Creative Encounter,* and *Apostles of Sensitiveness.* Obituaries and other sources: *New York Times,* April 14, 1981; *Washington Post,* April 16, 1981; *Time,* April 27, 1981; *Newsweek,* April 27, 1981.

*   *   *

TIERNEY, Brian   1922-

PERSONAL: Born May 7, 1922, in Scunthorpe, England; came to the United States in 1951, naturalized citizen, 1966; son of John Patrick and Helena (McGuire) Tierney; married Theresa O'Dowd, August 24, 1949; children: John, Helen, Christopher, Ann Jane. *Education:* Pembroke College, Cambridge, B.A., 1948, M.A. and Ph.D., both 1951. *Home:* 201 Willard Way, Ithaca, N.Y. 14850. *Office:* Department of History, Cornell University, Ithaca, N.Y. 14853.

CAREER: Catholic University of America, Washington, D.C., instructor, 1951-53, assistant professor, 1953-57, associate professor of history, 1957-59; Cornell University, Ithaca, N.Y., professor of medieval history, 1959—, Goldwin Smith Professor of Medieval History, 1966-77, Bryce and Edith M. Bowmar Professor of Humanistic Studies, 1977—. Visiting lecturer at University of California, Los Angeles, 1956; fellow of Institute for Advanced Study, Princeton, N.J.,

1961-62. *Military service:* Royal Air Force, 1941-46; received Distinguished Flying Cross and bar.

MEMBER: American Academy of Arts and Sciences (fellow), Mediaeval Academy of America (fellow), American Historial Association, American Catholic Historical Association (president, 1965). *Awards, honors:* Guggenheim fellowship, 1955-57; American Council of Learned Societies fellowships, 1961-62 and 1966-67; D.Th. from University of Uppsala, 1964; Society for Religion in Higher Education fellowship, 1966-67; National Endowment for the Humanities fellowship, 1977.

WRITINGS: Foundations of the Conciliar Theory: The Contribution of the Medieval Canonists From Gratian to the Great Schism, Cambridge University Press, 1955; *Medieval Poor Law: A Sketch of Canonical Theory and Its Application in England,* University of California Press, 1959; *The Crisis of Church and State, 1050-1300, With Selected Documents,* Prentice-Hall, 1964; (editor with Donald Kagan and L. Pearce Williams) *Great Issues in Western Civilization,* Volume I: *From Periclean Athens Through Louis XIV,* Volume II: *From the Scientific Revolution Through the Cold War,* Random House, 1967, 2nd edition published as Volume I: *From Periclean Athens Through Louis XIV,* Volume II: *From the English Civil War Through the Cold War,* 1972, 3rd edition, 1976; (editor) *The Middle Ages,* Volume I: *Sources of Medieval History,* Volume II: *Readings in Medieval History,* Knopf, 1970, 3rd edition, 1978; (with Sidney Painter) *Western Europe in the Middle Ages, 300-1475,* revised edition published as *A History of the Middle Ages, 284-1500),* Knopf, 1970, 3rd edition, 1978; *Origins of Papal Infallibility, 1150-1350: A Study on the Concepts of Infallibility, Sovereignty, and Tradition in the Middle Ages,* E. J. Brill, 1972; *Church Law and Constitutional Thought in the Middle Ages,* Variorum Reprints, 1971; (editor with Peter Linehan) *Authority and Power: Studies on Medieval Law and Government Presented to Walter Ulmann on His Seventieth Birthday,* Cambridge University Press, 1981. General editor of "Historical Issues Series," Random House, 1967.

WORK IN PROGRESS: Religion and Constitutional Thought, 1150-1650.

BIOGRAPHICAL/CRITICAL SOURCES: Times Literary Supplement, March 13, 1981.

*   *   *

TIFFANY, E. A.   1911-
(E. A. Samuels)

PERSONAL: Born March 23, 1911, in Duisburg, Germany (now West Germany); came to the United States in 1912, naturalized citizen; daughter of Fritz (a chemical engineer) and Ella (Fetz) Abegg; married Ely Edward Samuels, September 8, 1935 (deceased); married Robert P. Tiffany (an electrical engineer), November 6, 1976; children: (first marriage) Diane Irene. *Education:* University of Iowa, B.A., 1933; graduate study at Hofstra University. *Religion:* Episcopalian. *Home:* 210-7 Schuyler St., Jamestown, N.Y. 14701.

CAREER: University of Iowa, Iowa City, instructor in German, 1934; Hofstra University, Hempstead, N.Y., instructor in elementary education, 1966-73; reading teacher at public schools in Jamestown, N.Y., 1974-77. *Member:* American Association of University Women, Phi Delta Kappa.

WRITINGS: (Under name E. A. Samuels; editor with Miriam Hoffman) *Authors and Illustrators of Children's Books,* Bowker, 1972.

SIDELIGHTS: Tiffany told *CA:* "Children today are fortunate in having such a wealth of reading material from which to choose. Every category offers a tremendous selection to meet every level of need and reading ability. *Authors and Illustrators of Children's Books* was conceived with the desire to acquaint readers with the personalities behind the printed page." *Avocational interests:* Painting in oils and drawing in pastels (portraits, still lifes, nature subjects), knitting, macrame, sewing, reading.

*   *   *

TILLY, Charles 1929-

PERSONAL: Born May 27, 1929, in Lombard, Ill.; son of Otto Charles and Naneth Rowena (Stott) Tilly; married Louise Audino (a historian, professor, and university program director), August 15, 1953; children: Christopher, Kathryn, Laura, Sarah. *Education:* Harvard University, B.A. (magna cum laude), 1950, Ph.D., 1958; attended Balliol College, Oxford, 1950-51, and Facultes Catholiques de l'Ouest, 1955-56. *Politics:* Democratic socialist. *Home:* 1819 Hill St., Ann Arbor, Mich. 48104. *Office:* 214F Perry Building, University of Michigan, 330 Packard St., Ann Arbor, Mich. 48109.

CAREER: University of Delaware, Newark, instructor, 1956-58, assistant professor of history, 1958-62; Princeton University, Princeton, N.J., research associate, 1962-63; Harvard University, Cambridge, Mass., lecturer, 1963-65, visiting professor of sociology, 1965-66; University of Toronto, Toronto, Ontario, professor of sociology, 1965-69; University of Michigan, Ann Arbor, Hudson Research Professor of History, 1964-65, professor of sociology and history, 1969—, director of Center for Research on Social Organization, 1974—, co-director of Center for Western European Studies, member of executive committees of Center for Research on Conflict Resolution and Institute for Social Research. Fellow of Center for Advanced Study in the Behavioral Sciences, Palo Alto, Calif., 1968-69; member of Institute for Advanced Study, Princeton, 1970-71 and 1972; study director at Ecole des Hautes Etudes en Sciences Sociales, 1974-78 and 1980. Co-chairman of history panel of behavioral and social sciences survey of Social Science Research Council and National Academy of Sciences; member of council of Inter-University Consortium for Political and Social Research, 1970-73, member of Mathematical Social Science Board, 1970-76, chairman, 1977; chairman of Social Science Research Council committee on mathematics in the social sciences, 1978-79; member of executive committee of National Science Foundation advisory committee for social and economic sciences; consultant to National Endowment for the Humanities, Marketing Science Institute, and Canada Council. *Military service:* U.S. Navy, 1952-54; became lieutenant junior grade. *Member:* American Academy of Arts and Sciences (fellow), American Association for the Advancement of Science (fellow; member of council), Sociological Research Association.

WRITINGS: Recent Changes in Delaware's Population, Delaware Agricultural Experiment Station, 1962; *The Vendee,* Harvard University Press, 1964; *Migration to an American City,* Division of Urban Affairs and School of Agriculture, University of Delaware, 1965; (with Wagner Jackson and Barry Kay) *Race and Residence in Wilmington,* Teachers College Press, 1965; (with James Rule) *Measuring Political Upheaval,* Center for International Studies, Princeton University, 1965.

(Editor with David Landes, and contributor) *History as Social Science,* Prentice-Hall, 1971; (with Joe Feagin and Constance Williams) *Subsidizing the Poor: Boston's Experiment With Rent Subsidies,* Heath, 1972; *An Urban World,* Little, Brown, 1974; (with Edward Shorter) *Strikes in France, 1830-1968,* Cambridge University Press, 1974; (with wife, Louise Tilly, and brother, Richard Tilly) *The Rebellious Century,* Harvard University Press, 1975; (editor and contributor) *The Formation of National States in Western Europe,* Princeton University Press, 1975; (editor and contributor) *Historical Studies of Changing Fertility,* Princeton University Press, 1978; *From Mobilization to Revolution,* Addison-Wesley, 1978; *As Sociology Meets History,* Academic Press, 1981; (editor with L. Tilly, and contributor) *Class Conflict and Collective Action,* Sage Publications, 1981.

Contributor: Richard Bolan, editor, *Social Structure and Human Problems in the Boston Metropolitan Area,* Joint Center for Studies for Urban Problems (Cambridge, Mass.), 1965; James Q. Wilson, editor, *The Metropolitan Enigma,* Harvard University Press, 1968; Ralph W. Conant and Molly Apple Levin, editors, *Problems in Research on Community Violence,* Praeger, 1969; Talcott Parsons, editor, *American Sociology,* Basic Books, 1969; Hugh D. Graham and Ted R. Gurr, editors, *Violence in America,* Volume I, U.S. Government Printing Office, 1969, revised edition, Sage Publications, 1979.

D. P. Moynihan, editor, *Toward a National Urban Policy,* Harper, 1970; John C. McKinney and Edward A. Tiryakian, editors, *Theoretical Sociology: Perspectives and Developments,* Appleton, 1970; Melvin Richter, editor, *Essays in Theory and History,* Harvard University Press, 1970; Jacob M. Price and Val Lorwin, editors, *The Dimensions of the Past,* Yale University Press, 1972; William Aydelotte, Alan Bogue, and Robert Fogel, editors, *The Dimensions of Quantitative Research in History,* Princeton University Press, 1972; Edward B. Harvey, editor, *Perspectives on Modernization: Essays in Memory of Ian Weinberg,* University of Toronto Press, 1972; Herbert Hirsch and David Perry, editors, *Violence as Politics,* Harper, 1973; John W. Lewis, editor, *Peasant Rebellion and Communist Revolution in Asia,* Stanford University Press, 1974; Fred I. Greenstein and Nelson Polsby, editors, *Handbook of Political Science,* Addison-Wesley, 1975; Roger D. Price, editor, *Revolution and Reaction: 1848 and the Second Republic,* Croom Helm, 1975; Joseph Merriman, editor, *1830 in France,* New Viewpoints, 1975; Joseph Spielberg and Scott Whiteford, editors, *Forging Nations,* Michigan State University Press, 1976; Richard Maxwell Brown and Don Fehrenbacher, editors, *Tradition, Conflict, and Modernization: Perspectives on the American Revolution,* Academic Press, 1977; William McNeill, editor, *Human Migration: Patterns, Implications, Policies,* Indiana University Press, 1978; Mayer N. Zald and John D. McCarthy, editors, *The Dynamics of Social Movements,* Winthrop, 1979; Merriman, editor, *Consciousness and Class Experience in Nineteenth-Century Europe,* Holmes & Meier, 1979.

Co-editor of series "Studies in Urban History," for Harvard University Press, and "Studies in Social Discontinuity," for Academic Press. Contributor of about one hundred fifty articles and reviews to academic journals. Member of editorial board of *Journal of Interdisciplinary History, Journal of Family History, Journal of Urban History, Comparative Studies in Society and History, Social Science Research, Social Science History, Review of Social and Working Class History, Social Networks,* and *Historical Methods;* past member of editorial board of *Journal of American Institute of Planners, French Historical Studies, American Journal of Sociology, American Historical Review,* and *Journal of Conflict Resolution.*

WORK IN PROGRESS: The Contentious French, publication expected in 1982; *Europe Changes, 1500-1900;* research on European proletarianization and social change and collective action in France, 1600-1975, Great Britain, 1828-34, and London, England, 1750-1840.

SIDELIGHTS: Tilly commented: "I find the combination of teaching, researching, writing, and running a research center tough but—when things are going right—satisfying and productive. In the long run I hope to contribute to our understanding of four interwoven problems: first, how the development of capitalism and the growth of powerful national states shaped the world we live in today; second, how those changes affected the ways that ordinary people could and did act together on their shared interests, grievances, and aspirations; third, why, and with what effects, the people who run states make war; fourth, what implications the answers to these questions have to the choices and mistakes we are making today. Taking these problems seriously means doing sociology, history, and political analysis at the same time. My efforts to harmonize all three have always failed in one way or another—but the failures, happily, are usually of the kind from which one learns something worth learning."

*   *   *

TILMAN, Harold William 1898-1978

PERSONAL: Born February 14, 1898, in Wallasey, England; died, 1978; son of John Hinkes Tilman. *Education:* Attended Royal Military Academy, Woolwich. *Home address:* Bodowen, near Barmouth, Gwynedd, Wales.

CAREER: Writer. Farmer in Kenya, 1919-33; mountaineer and explorer, 1933-76. *Military service:* British Army, Royal Artillery, 1915-19 and 1939-45; served in Europe and the Middle East, worked with Albanian and Italian partisans during World War II; received Military Cross and Bar, Distinguished Service Order, mentioned in dispatches.

MEMBER: Royal Geographical Society (fellow), Alpine Club, Naval and Military Club, Ocean Cruising Club, Royal Cruising Club. *Awards, honors:* Founders' medal from Royal Geographical Society; LL.D. from University of St. Andrews, 1954; named freeman of city of Belluno, Italy; Blue Water Medal from Cruising Club of America, 1956; commander of Order of the British Empire, 1973.

WRITINGS: The Ascent of Nanda Devi, Macmillan, 1937; *Snow on the Equator,* G. Bell, 1937, Macmillan, 1938; *Mount Everest, 1938,* Cambridge University Press, 1938; *When Men and Mountains Meet,* Cambridge University Press, 1946; *Two Mountains and a River,* Cambridge University Press, 1949; *China to Chitral,* Cambridge University Press, 1951; *Nepal Himalaya,* Cambridge University Press, 1952; *Mischief in Patagonia,* Travel Book Club, 1956; *Mischief Among the Penguins,* Hart-Davis, 1957; *Mischief in Greenland,* Hollis & Carter, 1964; *Mostly "Mischief": Voyages to the Arctic and to the Antarctic,* Hollis & Carter, 1966; *Mischief Goes South,* Hollis & Carter, 1968; *In Mischief's Wake,* Hollis & Carter, 1971; *Ice With Everything,* Nautical Publishing, 1974; *Triumph and Tribulation,* Nautical Publishing, 1977, Ziff-Davis, 1978.

SIDELIGHTS: Tilman's mountaineering experiences include expeditions to Mount Kenya, Mount Kilimanjaro, and Mount Ruwenzari. He participated in the Mount Everest reconnaissance of 1935 and led an expedition there in 1938, then traveled to Sinkiang and Nepal. He also made annual trips to the Arctic and Antarctica from 1955 to 1976.

BIOGRAPHICAL/CRITICAL SOURCES: J.R.L. Anderson, *High Mountains and Cold Seas: A Biography of H. W. Tilman,* Mountaineers, 1980.

*   *   *

TOD, Ian J. 1945-

PERSONAL: Born August 1, 1945, in Coventry, England. *Education:* Cambridge University, B.A., 1967; University of London, Diploma in Architecture, 1969; University of Durham, M.A., 1970. *Home:* 9 Midland Rd., Leeds 6, England. *Office:* Tod Petherick, Architects, 4 Corn Exchange, Leeds LS1 7BP, England.

CAREER: Architect with Tod Petherick in Leeds, England. Associated with Hull School of Architecture. Visiting lecturer at University of Delft, University of London, Canterbury School of Architecture, Oslo School of Architecture, and Bradford University. Member of Architects Registration Council of the United Kingdom, 1976-80. *Member:* New Architecture Movement, Society for the Protection of Ancient Buildings, William Morris Society.

WRITINGS: William Morris: Father of the Modern Movement, Forum voor Architectuur, 1974; (with Michael Wheeler) *Utopia,* Harmony Books, 1975.

WORK IN PROGRESS: More Utopias; a celebration of William Morris, artist, designer, poet, writer, and socialist, 1834-96.

*   *   *

TOFT, (Eric) John 1933-

PERSONAL: Born October 29, 1933, in the Staffordshire Potteries, England; son of Eric (a steelworker) and Olive (an underglaze painter; maiden name, Smith) Toft. *Education:* Magdalen College, Oxford, M.A., 1958. *Politics:* "Romantic Socialist/Green Peace." *Religion:* "Anglican Catholic." *Home:* 1 Clarendon Ter., Brighton, Sussex, England. *Agent:* Olwyn Hughes, 48 Lensfield Rd., Cambridge, England. *Office:* Department of Humanities, Brighton Polytechnic, Falmer, Brighton, Sussex, England.

CAREER: English master at grammar school in Huntingdon, England, 1958-59; adult education lecturer in Oxford, England, 1959-61; lecturer in English at Malayan Teachers College, 1961-64; Brighton Polytechnic, Brighton, England, lecturer in English, 1965—. *Military service:* Royal Air Force, 1952-54.

WRITINGS—Novels: *The Bargees,* Dent, 1969; *The Wedge,* W. H. Allen, 1971; *The House of the Arousing,* W. H. Allen, 1973; *The Underground Tree,* W. H. Allen, 1978; *The Dew,* W. H. Allen, 1981. Contributor to *Powys Review.*

WORK IN PROGRESS: Research on Indian writing.

SIDELIGHTS: Toft told *CA:* "So far my novels form a sequence exploring the changes in working-class life since World War I. They are not, however, sociological studies, but are concerned with the growth of self-consciousness that is bringing an end to the first industrial proletariat in history. I am attempting to draw together childhood memories and the memories of my parents and other relatives to form a living record of the way in which ordinary people perceive the momentous changes that have occurred in their lifetimes.

"My favorite literature includes seventeenth-century poetry and prose, English Romantic poetry, and the nineteenth-century European novel, but I am also interested in Oriental thought and Christian mysticism. I visited Southeast Asia in 1970 and wrote a sequence of stories, which were first published in magazines, including *Encounter, Atlantic Quarterly,* and *London Magazine,* and then collected in the volume called *The House of the Arousing.*

"What particularly haunts me about my friendships with Malaysians (many of whom I taught between 1961 and 1964) is the way our different beliefs—Christian, Muslim, Hindu, Buddhist—are really so closely related to one another. I have recently visited India and hope to write a new novel about that experience. Again I regard the experience as essentially a religious one. It is *not* that I regard all religions as the same, nor should I like to see world peace brought about by a reduction of variety, but rather I believe that we should recognize our different religions as equal, beautiful works of the imagination and of spiritual aspiration. That sounds perhaps pretentious, but as far as expressing it in fiction goes, I like to show it through comedy, or rather, I suppose, tragicomedy. My stories start with misunderstanding and a slight panic-stricken paranoia and isolation, and move, I hope, to a new sense of connection and communion. That sex inevitably plays a part in this movement is an indication that I think it is an indivisible form of spirituality. Indeed, sex and religion seem to me to be awesomely alike in their power to divide as well as to unite people."

*   *   *

TOFTE, Arthur   1902-1980

OBITUARY NOTICE—See index for *CA* sketch: Born June 8, 1902, in Chicago, Ill.; died of cancer, May 21, 1980, in Wauwatosa, Wis. Advertising manager and author. Early in his career, Tofte served as advertising manager of Tom Thumb Miniature Golf Company. Later, from 1938 to 1969, he held various advertising and managerial positions with Allis-Chalmers Corporation. Though he began his career as a science-fiction writer in 1938, he wrote for only two years before taking a thirty-year hiatus. He resumed writing in the early seventies as part of the Roger Elwood stable. During the 1930's, Tofte was a member of the Milwaukee Fictioneers, a group of science-fiction writers made up of Stanley G. Weinbaum, Ralph Milne Farley, Lawrence Keating, and Robert Bloch. His writings include *Crash Landing on Iduna, Walls Within Walls,* and *The Ghost Hunters.* Obituaries and other sources: *Locus,* June, 1980.

*   *   *

TOLBY, Arthur
See INFIELD, Glenn (Berton)

*   *   *

TOLLES, Frederick B(arnes)   1915-1975

OBITUARY NOTICE—See index for *CA* sketch: Born April 18, 1915, in Nashua, N.H.; died April 18, 1975; buried in Nashua, N.H. Educator and author. A Howard M. and Charles F. Jenkins Professor of Quaker History and Research at Swarthmore College, Tolles was a member of the Historical Society of Pennsylvania's council from 1955 to 1970. He also edited *Quaker History* for sixteen years beginning in 1949. His works include *Meeting House and Country House, The Witness of William Penn,* and *The Journal of John Woolman.* Obituaries and other sources: *Who Was Who in America,* 6th edition, Marquis, 1976.

TORS, Ivan (Lawrence)   1916-

PERSONAL: Born June 12, 1916, in Budapest, Hungary; came to United States, 1939, naturalized citizen, 1943; son of Anthony (a dairy chemist) and Margaret (Bohm) Tors; married Constance Dowling (an actress), February 23, 1953 (died October, 1969); children: Steven, Peter, David, Alfred Ndegwa (foster son). *Education:* Attended University of Budapest, 1934-36, and Fordham University, 1939-40; Goddard University, M.A., 1977. *Office:* Universal Studios, Los Angeles, Calif. 91608.

CAREER: Royal Theatre, Budapest, Hungary, playwright, 1935; *Esti Korir* (newspaper), Budapest, journalist, 1937; Columbia Pictures, Hollywood, Calif., screenwriter, 1941-42; Metro-Goldwyn-Mayer (MGM), Hollywood, writer, 1945-52; United Artists, Hollywood, producer, 1952-54; Ivan Tors Films, Inc., Los Angeles, Calif., founder, 1953, president, 1953-73; Ziv-United Artists, Hollywood, producer, 1954-61; Metro-Goldwyn-Mayer, producer, 1962-66; Paramount Pictures, Hollywood, executive producer, 1966-67; associated with Universal Studios, Los Angeles, 1969-70. Director and producer of motion pictures, including "Rhino!," MGM, 1963; "Zebra in the Kitchen," MGM, 1965; "The Galyon File," Key Films, 1980; "March of the Desert," American National, 1981. Producer of motion pictures, including "Gog," United Artists, 1954; "Riders to the Stars," United Artists, 1954; "Underwater Warrior," MGM, 1957; "Flipper," MGM, 1962; "Flipper's New Adventure," MGM, 1964; "Clarence, the Cross-Eyed Lion," MGM, 1965; "Around the World Under the Sea," MGM, 1966; "Birds Do It," Columbia, 1966; "Namu, the Killer Whale," United Artists, 1966; "Africa, Texas Style," Paramount, 1967; "Gentle Giant," Paramount, 1967; "Daring Game," Paramount, 1968; "Hello Down There," Paramount, 1969; "The Aquarians," Universal, 1970; "Escape From Angola," American National, 1981. Producer of television programs, including "Sea Hunt," Columbia Broadcasting System (CBS), 1956-60; "Ziv Science Fiction Theatre," 1957-61; "Man and the Challenge," National Broadcasting Co. (NBC); "The Aquanauts," CBS, 1960-61; "Ripcord," 1961-62; "Flipper," NBC, 1963-66; "Daktari," CBS, 1965-68; "Island of the Lost," American Broadcasting Co (ABC), 1967; "Gentle Ben," CBS, 1967-69; "Cowboy in Africa," ABC, 1967-68; "Story"; "Jambo," NBC, 1969; "The Forty-ninth Man"; "Elephant Country," NBC, 1971; "Orientation and Navigation"; "Primus," Syndicated Television, 1971-72; "Encyclopedia of Wildlife," CBS, 1974-80; "Danny and the Mermaid," CBS, 1977; "Pain in Nature"; "Battle Taxi"; "Labyrinth of Odor"; "The Last of the Wild"; "Where the Lions Rule."

Owner of Ivan Tors Studios, North Miami, Fla., and underwater studios in the Bahamas; co-owner of Africa, U.S.A., an animal ranch in Soledad Canyon, Calif., until 1969. Lecturer at University of California, Irvine. Participant in scientific expedition to Tsavo National Park in Kenya. Founder of Michael Tors Foundation for Scientific Research; member of board of directors of Vista Hill Foundation. *Military service:* U.S. Army Air Forces, 1942-45; radio writer in Technical Training Command Branch; later served in Office of Strategic Services. *Member:* World Wildlife Fund (member of board of directors), Academy of Motion Picture Arts and Sciences, Directors Guild of America, Writers Guild of America (West), Explorers Club. *Awards, honors:* Writers Guild nomination for screenplay "In the Good Old Summertime," 1949; Humane Award of the Year from International Pet and Animal Show, 1966; award from California branch of Humane Society of the United States, 1967.

WRITINGS: My Life in the Wild, Houghton, 1979.

Plays: "Mimi" (three-act), first produced in Budapest, Hungary, at Royal Theatre, 1935; "Keep Your Distance" (three-act comedy), first produced in Carmel, Calif., 1942; "Wind Without Rain," first produced in Los Angeles, Calif., at Circle Theatre, 1951.

Screenplays: "Below the Deadline," Monogram, 1946; (with Irmgard Von Cube, Allen Vincent, and Robert Ardrey) "Song of Love," MGM, 1947; (with Albert Hackett and Frances Goodrich) "In the Good Old Summertime," MGM, 1949; (with Jan Lustig and James B. Williams) "That Forsyte Woman," MGM, 1950; (with Devery Freeman and Harry Ruskin) "Watch the Birdie," MGM, 1951; (with Sam Meyer) "Storm Over Tibet," Columbia, 1952; (with Curt Siodmak) "The Magnetic Monster," United Artists, 1953; (with Maxwell Shane) "The Glass Wall," Columbia, 1953.

Writer for television series, including "Sea Hunt." Contributor to magazines, including *Screen Actor.*

SIDELIGHTS: Although now well known for his love of animals, Tors did not become interested in them until he worked on the set of his television series "Sea Hunt." While using sharks and barracudas in the filming of the show, Tors realized these fish were not as dangerous as he had thought. Soon he developed a method for training wild animals, which he called "affection training." Tors utilizes this form of positive reinforcement to train such diverse animals as bears, monkeys, whales, lions, elephants, dolphins, snakes, and trantulas. At one point, Tors supplied 90 percent of all the animals used by Hollywood in television and motion pictures.

Always opposed to violence in films, Tors produces wholesome, family entertainment in which animals and their stunts often outshine their human co-stars. His television programs and motion pictures often promote wildlife conservation and better treatment for animals. His film "Namu, the Killer Whale" was inspired by a real-life incident involving a killer whale found in Canada. Tors read that the animal was to be transported to a cove in Seattle, Washington, so he flew to the area and sat on a dock near the whale while the creature acclimated itself to its new surroundings. Other animal "stars" of Tors's productions are Judy, the mischievous chimp of "Daktari," Flipper, the dolphin seen in two motion pictures and a television series, and Ben, the bear of "Gentle Ben."

BIOGRAPHICAL/CRITICAL SOURCES: Newsweek, February 21, 1966; *Los Angeles Times,* March 22, 1966; *Christian Science Monitor,* Feburary 4, 1967; *New York Daily News,* May 23, 1967; *Time,* June 16, 1967; *New York Times,* August 2, 1967; *Life,* September 29, 1967.

*   *   *

TOWNSEND, Doris McFerran 1914-
   (Catherine Clelland, Ann McFerran, Doris
   McFerran)

PERSONAL: Born April 1, 1914, in Minneapolis, Minn.; daughter of Robert Bayard (in construction) and Edith Elisabeth (Hoar) McFerran; married Floyd Raymond Cogswell, March 20, 1936 (divorced November, 1937); married William Porter Turner Townsend (a graphics designer), May 21, 1945; children: (stepdaughters) Lynn Mary Townsend Turley, Karen Ann Townsend McLaughlin. *Education:* University of Minnesota, B.A., 1934; University of Kansas, M.S., 1938. *Politics:* Democrat. *Religion:* Episcopalian. *Home and office:* 4540 Limerick Way, San Diego, Calif. 92117.

CAREER: WTCN-Radio, Minneapolis, Minn., copywriter and actress, 1933-34; WDGY-Radio, Minneapolis, copywriter and talk show host, 1935-36; McFadden Publishers, New York City, editor of *Radio-TV Mirror* (fan magazine), 1939-47; free-lance writer, 1952-60; Rutledge Books, New York City, editor-in-chief, 1961-73; writer, 1961-73. Counselor of disturbed high school boys, 1942-60. *Member:* Authors Guild, Alpha Delta Pi, Delta Phi Lambda.

WRITINGS: Dinny and Dreamdust (juvenile), Doubleday, 1962; *The One Thousand Fabulous Sandwiches Cookbook,* Thomas Nelson, 1965; *Fabulous Sandwiches Cookbook,* Benjamin Co., 1965; *Creative Living With Aluminum Foil,* Grosset, 1968; *The Complete Money-Saving Chicken Cookbook,* Rutledge Books, 1970; (editor) *The Smirnoff Brunch Book,* Rutledge Books, 1971; (with Charlotte Adams) *The Family Cookbook: Dessert,* Holt, 1972; *Culinary Crafting: The Art of Garnishing and Decorating Food,* Rutledge, 1976; (with Barbara Bloch) *Cook's Choice,* Rutledge, 1977; *Diet Without Hunger,* Larousse, 1978; *The Cook's Companion* (food encyclopedia), Crown, 1978; *Cheese Cookery,* H. P. Books, 1980.

Under name Ann McFerran; juveniles: (Editor) *Poems to Be Read Aloud to Children and By Children,* Thomas Nelson, 1965; *Elizabeth Blackwell: First Woman Doctor,* Grosset, 1966; *The Big and Little Book of ABC's,* Gibson, 1969; *Ten Thousand Bears,* Gibson, 1969. Also author of *The Joy of Family,* 1969.

Under name Doris McFerran: *Your Career in Civil Service,* Dutton, 1942; *Careers in Retailing for Young Women,* Dutton, 1943.

Contributor of articles and stories to magazines, under pseudonym Catherine Clelland.

WORK IN PROGRESS: A cookbook on herbs, spices, sweet and savory seasonings; a novel.

SIDELIGHTS: Doris Townsend told *CA:* "Supposedly my husband and I are retired. As it turns out, we are the busiest retirees on record. But we make time to enjoy San Diego and the rest of California and the West. We share our home with a yellow labrador and six cats. I vary my writing routine with styling and cooking for color food photography."

AVOCATIONAL INTERSTS: Travel (especially Mexico).

*   *   *

TRAVERS, Virginia
   See COIGNEY, Virginia

*   *   *

TRAVIS, Gretchen A.

PERSONAL: Born in Omaha, Neb.; daughter of Robert Earl and Grace (Newbranch) Travis; married Frank Chinnock (executive editor of *Golf*), July, 1979; children: (previous marriage) Linda Mockler, Andy Mockler. *Education:* Attended University of Omaha and University of Nebraska. *Politics:* Democratic.*Residence:* 20-3 Manville Lane, Pleasantville, N.Y. 10570. *Agent:* Paul R. Reynolds, Inc., 12 East 41st St., New York, N.Y. 10017.

CAREER: Omaha World-Herald, Omaha, Neb., in editorial department, 1942-46; worked with United Nations' displaced persons program in Germany, 1947-49; writer, 1950-68; Vernon Pope Public Relations, New York, N.Y., publicist, 1969-71; *Patent Trader,* Mt. Kisco, N.Y., reporter, 1971-72; *Reader's Digest,* Pleasantville, N.Y., staff reader for non-fiction condensed books and writer, 1973-79; full-time writer,

1979—. Administrative assistant at Hudson Institute, Croton, N.Y., 1970-71. Volunteer worker with Westchester Children's Association and League of North Westchester; guest speaker at Bedford Hills Correctional Facility.

WRITINGS—Suspense novels: *She Fell Among Thieves,* Doubleday, 1963; *Too Old to Die,* Putnam, 1965; *Roanleigh,* New American Library, 1966; *Holiday of Fear,* New American Library, 1967; *The Cottage,* Putnam, 1973; *Two Spruce Lane,* Putnam, 1975.

Contributor to *Ellery Queen's Mystery Magazine* and *Saint.*

WORK IN PROGRESS: Another suspense novel; a book about mastectomy survivors.

SIDELIGHTS: Gretchen Travis commented: "I wrote *The Cottage* while living in Malta, and most of *Two Spruce Lane* as a resident of St. Jean, Cap Ferrat, France. I have also lived in Sicily and Germany, and want to live in Greece someday. My books have been published in England, France, Italy, Scandinavia, South America, and Australia."

* * *

TRAVIS, Neal 1939(?)-

PERSONAL: Born in New Zealand; married wife, Maggi. *Education:* Attended high school. *Residence:* Manhattan, N.Y. *Agent:* c/o Crown Publishers Inc., One Park Ave., New York, N.Y. 10016.

CAREER: Writer. Journalist in New Zealand, Australia, and New Guinea, c. 1956-66; U.S. news correspondent for newspapers in Australia and London, England, beginning in 1966; editor of newspaper chain in Australia; author of "Page Six" column for *New York Post* in New York City; author of "Intelligencer" section of *New York* in New York City.

WRITINGS: Manhattan (novel), Crown, 1979.

WORK IN PROGRESS: Summer People.

SIDELIGHTS: Travis's first novel concerns the takeover of *Manhattan,* a fictional magazine similar in many ways to Travis's former employer *New York.* After seeing firsthand for twelve years how the city operates, Travis set out, without the security of a publisher's contract or an advance, to expose New York life in terms of its people and the power they wield. His account reveals the jealousies, political and sexual ambitions, and the hatreds of those who possess power and of those who would like to have it.

BIOGRAPHICAL/CRITICAL SOURCES: New York Times Book Review, April 29, 1979.*

* * *

TRESSLER, Donald K(iteley) 1894-1981

OBITUARY NOTICE—See index for *CA* sketch: Born November 7, 1894, in Cincinnati, Ohio; died February 28, 1981, in Norwalk, Conn. Educator, researcher, publisher, and author. A frozen-food specialist, Tressler had been associated with Clarence Birdseye and Birdseye Laboratories in the 1930's and with General Electric Company in the 1940's. Later, he taught at the New York State Agricultural Experiment Station of Cornell University where he developed the Tressler process, a method of making sherry from Concord grape wine. He held twenty patents that were related to food processing, and he was the co-founder of the Institute of Food Technology as well as editor of that organization's journal. Tressler was also chairman of AVI Publishing Company, a publisher that specializes in food-science books. His works include *Fruit and Vegetable Juice Processing Technology* and a three-volume set titled *Food Products For-*

mulary. Obituaries and other sources: *New York Times,* March 3, 1981; *Publishers Weekly,* April 3, 1981.

* * *

TRETICK, Stanley 1921-

PERSONAL: Born July 21, 1921, in Baltimore, Md.; son of William and Sophia (Rosenberg) Tretick; married Maureen Hesselroth, March 30, 1963. *Education:* Attended high school. *Home:* 2953 Arizona Ave. N.W., Washington, D.C. 20016.

CAREER: Washington Post, Washington, D.C., member of editorial department, 1940-42; United Press International, photographer for "News Features," 1945-61; *Look,* Washington, D.C., staff photographer, 1961-71; official photographer for presidential campaign of George McGovern, 1972; official photographer for presidential campaign of Jimmy Carter, 1976-77. Photography exhibited at Museum of Modern Art, 1951. *Military service:* U.S. Marine Corps Reserve, active duty, 1942-45; served in Pacific theater.

MEMBER: White House Photographers Association, U.S. Senate Photographers Gallery. *Awards, honors:* National Headliners Award, 1951, for Korean war photographs; Graflex Achievement Award, 1955; grand award from White House News Photographers Association, 1956; first prizes in color class, 1962, 1963, both for portraits of John F. Kennedy; first prize for picture story, first prize in color class, and grand award from White House Photographers Competition, 1966.

WRITINGS—Photographer: Laura Bergquist, *A Very Special President,* McGraw, 1965; William V. Shannon, *They Could Not Trust the King: Nixon, Watergate, and the American People* (foreword by Barbara W. Tuchman), Macmillan, 1974; Jack Hirshberg, *A Portrait of All the President's Men,* Warner Books, 1976.*

* * *

TRIFONOV, Yuri Valentinovich 1925-1981

OBITUARY NOTICE: Born August 28, 1925, in Moscow, U.S.S.R.; died after surgery, March 28, 1981, in Moscow, U.S.S.R. Author best known for his novellas on the moral dilemmas facing Soviet intellectuals in the post-Stalinist era. Unlike his dissident peers, Trifonov adhered to the Soviet system of censorship. He therefore reached many more Russian readers than his unpublishable colleagues. Trifonov's writings include *The Exchange, The House on the Embankment,* and *Place and Time.* In 1951 he was awarded the Stalin Prize for literature. Obituaries and other sources: *Who's Who in the Socialist Countries,* K. G. Sauer, 1978; *New York Times,* March 29, 1981; *Chicago Tribune,* March 29, 1981; *Time,* April 13, 1981; *AB Bookman's Weekly,* May 4, 1981.

* * *

TROISE, Joe 1942-

PERSONAL: Surname rhymes with "noise"; born August 28, 1942, in New York, N.Y.; son of Louis C. and Ann (Bivona) Troise. *Education:* City University of New York, B.A., 1964. *Office:* 3364 22nd St., Suite 7, San Francisco, Calif. 94110.

CAREER: Harcourt Brace Jovanovich, Inc., New York City, assistant editor, 1966-68; Columbia University, New York City, assistant director of admissions and financial aid, 1968-69; Mercedes-Benz of North America, Fort Lee, N.J., special representative, 1969-70; writer, researcher, and automotive consultant, 1970—. Guest on radio and television programs. *Member:* Society of Automotive Historians.

WRITINGS: Cherries and Lemons, Warner Books, 1980; *Drive It 'Til It Drops,* And Books, 1980.

WORK IN PROGRESS: The Automotive Almanac, publication expected in 1981; research on the ancient utopia of Uranopolis; a play, "The Man Who Talked to Cars."

SIDELIGHTS: Troise commented: "I think the history of the automobile should be taught in every public school in America. The types of cars we have created through the years are not only a response to events; often they have initiated them. I would like my books to reflect the importance of the automobile's effect upon our lives. My point of view is not only that of a technician, but also that of a historian and social scientist."

BIOGRAPHICAL/CRITICAL SOURCES: Wall Street Journal, August 14, 1980; *Us,* October 14, 1980.

* * *

TROY, George F(rancis), Jr. 1909-1969

OBITUARY NOTICE—See index for *CA* sketch: Born May 8, 1909, in Providence, R.I.; died of an apparent heart attack, June 21, 1969, in East Providence, R.I. Editor and author. Troy began his career as a reporter for the *Providence Journal* in 1933. In 1956, he became the literary editor of the *Journal*'s book review page, a position he held for thirteen years. Troy's works include *Headland* and *Native to the Grain.* Obituaries and other sources: *Publishers Weekly,* October 20, 1969.

* * *

TRUEBLOOD, Alan Stubbs 1917-

PERSONAL: Born May 3, 1917, in Haverford, Pa.; son of Howard M. (an engineer) and Louise (Nyitray) Trueblood. *Education:* Harvard University, B.A., 1938, M.A., 1941, Ph.D., 1951. *Home:* Willow Ave., Little Compton, R.I. 02837. *Office address:* Box E., Brown University, Providence, R.I. 02912.

CAREER: Chile-U.S. Cultural Institute, Santiago, Chile, educational director, 1942-43; Brown University, Providence, R.I., instructor, 1947-51, assistant professor, 1951-55, associate professor, 1955-63, professor of Spanish, 1963—, chairman of department of Hispanic and Italian studies, 1967-72, professor of Hispanic studies and comparative literature, 1972—, chairman of department of comparative literature, 1973-77, chairman of Renaissance studies program, 1977-79. Harvard University, visiting associate professor, 1959-60, visiting lecturer, 1963; Fulbright lecturer in American studies in Colombia, 1972; resident scholar at Merton College, Oxford, 1973. *Military service:* U.S. Naval Reserve, 1943-46; became lieutenant. *Member:* Renaissance Society of America, Dante Society of America, Cervantes Society of America, Academy of Literary Studies. *Awards, honors:* Fulbright research scholar, Chile, 1958; Guggenheim fellow, 1965-66; Wilson Prize from Harvard University Press, 1974, for *Experience and Artistic Expression in Lope de Vega;* translation grant from National Endowment for the Humanities, 1977-80.

WRITINGS: Experience and Artistic Expression in Lope de Vega, Harvard University Press, 1974.

WORK IN PROGRESS: A bilingual edition, with critical study, of selected poems by Antonio Machado (1875-1939) in verse translation; an introductory study and annotated translation of Lope de Vega's *La Dorotea,* with Edwin Honig.

SIDELIGHTS: Trueblood's book, *Experience and Artistic Expression in Lope de Vega,* is an analysis of *La Dorotea,* a little known seventeenth-century drama in prose by Spanish playwright Lope de Vega. Elias L. Rivers wrote in *Comparative Literature* that the integration of biographical and creative material in the early chapters of the book is both "systematic and thorough." He noted Trueblood's skill in translating the subtleties of Lope de Vega's language and his understanding of the creative process. Rivers said: "The subtlety of [Trueblood's] guidance is masterful; we are never bullied, but always convinced. Lope de Vega's prose action has at last encountered a reading at its own level of maturity."

Trueblood told *CA:* "My fundamental interest is in the creative process, particularly in literature. The concern that has motivated both my shorter pieces and my major work has been to discover the transmutations vital experience undergoes as a way of reaching an understanding of the artistic form that results. Hence my interest in literary translation as a form of re-creation. There is some correlation between my avocations—country living, gardening, and ocean swimming—and certain subjects of my writings: the pastoral, the symbolic sea."

BIOGRAPHICAL/CRITICAL SOURCES: Comparative Literature, spring, 1975; *Modern Language Review,* July, 1975; *Times Literary Supplement,* September 5, 1975.

* * *

TURNELL, (George) Martin 1908-1979

OBITUARY NOTICE—See index for *CA* sketch: Born March 23, 1908, in Birmingham, England; died July, 1979. Critic, translator, and author. Turnell was a literary critic for the *Times Literary Supplement, Southern Review,* and *Sunday Telegraph.* He translated many books, including Sartre's *Baudelaire,* Pascal's *Pensees,* and Revel's *On Proust.* His writings include *Poetry and Crisis, The Art of French Fiction, Modern Literature and Christian Faith,* and *The Rise of the French Novel.* (Date of death provided by wife, Helen Julia Turnell.)

* * *

TURNER, Dona M. 1951-
(Thisby, a joint pseudonym)

PERSONAL: Born July 16, 1951, in Washington D.C.; daughter of Arthur Eugene (an auto technician) and Claire (an administrator; maiden name, Nealon) Turner; married Robert C. Mozingo (an architect), August 18, 1979. *Education:* University of Maryland, B.F.A., 1973; San Francisco State University, teaching certificate, 1979. *Home:* 133 Dolores St., No. 3, San Francisco, Calif. 94103.

CAREER: Clerical worker in a photo lab and for a crafts importer, both in San Francisco, Calif., 1973-78; graphics and kit designer for Hohug Corp. (craft kit manufacturer), in Burlingame, Calif.; free-lance graphic designer; publisher and seller of black and white photo postcards with Vince Genovese under joint pseudonym Thisby. *Member:* Authors Guild.

WRITINGS: My Cat Pearl (juvenile), Crowell, 1980.

WORK IN PROGRESS: Pearl Camps Out; two children's books, about a cat, Puffins, and the tooth fairy, completion expected in 1981; a photo essay of San Francisco building facades.

SIDELIGHTS: My Cat Pearl describes the day in the life of a cat. Michele Slung of the *Washington Post Book World* wrote, "Using her own black cat, Pearl, as inspiration, Dona Turner has created a slight but highly affectionate tribute to feline domestic habits."

Turner told *CA:* "I consider *My Cat Pearl* completely autobiographical. The book was so easy to write because it was just exactly the routine around our house at the time. It was obvious, which is probably the book's greatest charm. It took maybe three minutes to write; I just looked at the cat sitting on my paper, and the whole story just came to me. I believe in inspiration. I don't like to rework my text—it loses so much vitality—and, of course, the text of *My Cat Pearl* is very brief. Also, since I have been a painter for many years I really enjoyed working on the illustrations for the book and at some point would like to illustrate other people's work as well."

BIOGRAPHICAL/CRITICAL SOURCES: Washington Post Book World, May 1, 1980.

* * *

TURNER, George (Reginald) 1916-

PERSONAL: Born October 8, 1916, in Melbourne, Australia. *Education:* Attended high school in Melbourne, Australia. *Home:* 4 Robertson Ave., St. Kilda, Victoria 3182, Australia.

CAREER: Commonwealth Employment Office, Melbourne, Australia, employment officer, 1945-49; Commonwealth Employment Office, Wangaratta, Australia, employment officer, 1949-50; Buck Mills, Wangaratta, textile technician, 1951-64; Volkswagen Ltd., Melbourne, senior employment officer, 1964-67; Carlton and United Breweries, Melbourne, beer transferrer, 1970—. *Military service:* Australian Imperial Forces, 1939-45. *Awards, honors:* Miles Franklin Award, 1962, for *The Cupboard Under the Stairs;* award from Commonwealth Literary Fund, 1968, for *The Lame Dog Man.*

WRITINGS: Scobie (novel), Simon & Schuster, 1959 (published in England as *Young Man of Talent,* Cassell, 1959); *A Stranger and Afraid* (novel), Cassell, 1961; *The Cupboard Under the Stairs* (novel), Cassell, 1962; *A Waste of Shame* (novel), Cassell, 1965; *The Lame Dog Man* (novel), Cassell, 1967; (with Orville Goldner) *The Making of "King Kong,"* Tantivy Press, 1975, Ballantine, 1976; *Transit of Cassidy,* Thomas Nelson, 1978; *Beloved Son* (science-fiction novel), Faber, 1978, Pocket Books, 1979. Editor of *The View From Earth,* a collection of science-fiction stories, 1977. Contributor to *Science Fiction Commentary.* *

* * *

TURNER, Lloyd 1924-

PERSONAL: Born August 14, 1924, in Winnemucca, Nev.; son of Lloyd L. (a bank president) and Theodora (Gardner) Turner; married Darlene Soper (a photographer), April 26, 1976. *Education:* Attended Morgan Art Institute and Berkeley College of Arts and Crafts, 1942-43. *Residence:* Marina Del Rey, Calif. *Agent:* Irv Schechter, 404 North Roxbury, Beverly Hills, Calif. 90210.

CAREER: Television writer, 1944—. Warner Bros., Hollywood, Calif., writer and illustrator of cartoons, 1944-50; KTLA-TV, Hollywood, Calif., writer for syndicated puppet show "Time for Beany," 1949-55; Dell Publishing Co., Inc., New York, N.Y., writer of comic books featuring Walt Disney and Warner Bros. characters, including Bugs Bunny and Daffy Duck, 1955-59; Jay Ward Productions, Hollywood, Calif., writer of commercials, features, and cartoons, including "Bullwinkle,' 1959-68; writer and story consultant for "Get Smart" and writer for "The Doris Day Show,"

1968; staff writer for "The Bob Hope Show," and writer for "The Mary Tyler Moore Show," "Barefoot in the Park," "Love American Style," "The Partridge Family," and "The Odd Couple," 1970; story consultant and writer for "The Good Life," 1971; writer for "Temperatures Rising," "Honeymoon Suite," and "Bridget Loves Bernie," 1972; writer of pilots "The Lovers" and "Three Way Street," and of shows "Girl With Something Extra," "Maude," "Love Thy Neighbor," "The Brian Keith Show," "All in the Family," "Thicker Than Water," and "Honeymoon Suite," 1973; writer of "Love Nest," for Ilson/Chambers Productions and writer and story editor of "All in the Family," 1974; TAT-Tandem, Hollywood, Calif., story editor of "The Jeffersons," 1974-76, executive story editor, 1976-77, producer of "Good Times," 1977-78; Paramount, Hollywood, Calif., executive creative consultant for "Mork and Mindy," 1978-79; writer for "House Calls," 1980. *Member:* Writers Guild of America, Dramatists Guild. *Awards, honors:* Nomination for best-written comedy episode from Writers Guild of America, 1970, for "The Apes of Rath," and "Get Smart."

WRITINGS: (With Gordon Mitchell and Don Nicholl) *Archie and the Computer* (one-act comedy), Samuel French, 1975.

WORK IN PROGRESS: A novel; television pilots.

AVOCATIONAL INTERESTS: Boating, fishing.

CA INTERVIEW

CA interviewed Lloyd Turner by phone on August 5, 1980, while he was working aboard his boat in Marina Del Rey, California.

CA: You studied at Morgan Art Institute. Did you intend then to be strictly an artist, or was writing part of your plan?

TURNER: I was quite a gifted artist as a young person and naturally drifted into commercial art. I was fascinated with Walt Disney and had it in the back of my mind that I'd like to become an animator at the Disney studios in Hollywood.

CA: But you landed at Warner Brothers cartoons instead of Disney. Is that where you started writing?

TURNER: Yes. I began as an "in–betweener" hoping to work toward being an animator. It seemed as though the in–betweeners did all the work—while across the hall the writers seemed to be having all the fun. They were always laughing, coming in late, and were privileged to park on the lot instead of in the street. I thought, "What am I doing in–betweening? I could be coming in late, laughing, and parking on the lot!" One day I walked up to Warren Foster, one of the veteran writers, and said, "What does a guy have to do to become a writer around here?" He looked at me and said, "What have you written?" I said, "Nothing." He said, "Go home and write something." It never occurred to me that I'd have to write something before they'd hire me as a writer. The thing was, I did. I went home, wrote a story, came back, and presented it to the producer. To my surprise, he got all the directors and writers together and held what was called a jam session on my story. I told the story with illustrated sketches and it was a terrifying experience. The story sounded so weak as I stumbled my way through it. It met with only mild approval—but what it did was serve as a foot in the door. When there was an opening they tried me out. And that was the beginning of my writing career. I was nineteen.

CA: Did writing come easily or was it difficult for you?

TURNER: For me, difficult. I find it unnatural to sit and think that hard. There are compulsive writers, like Sidney Sheldon or Mel Shavelson, who are not comfortable unless they're writing—they write around the clock and thrive. After six hours, I'm exhausted. I find that the best part of writing is not writing but having written.

CA: What about your early cartoon–writing days? Was that helpful in your later television writing?

TURNER: Cartoons were a lot of fun to write—the plots were so simple. They always seemed to have something to do with an appetite, catching the chicken, getting rid of the dog, getting the duck out of the house, or shooting the rabbit. The Tweety Bird character was irresistibly charming—Sylvester the cat would practically kill himself trying to make a Tweety Bird sandwich—but Tweety always thought the cat was playing with him. We never quite understood why Sylvester would go to such painful lengths to eat that little bird when it was all too obvious that there was nothing really succulent to eat. Tweety was nothing but head and feet.

Once you had a cat-and-mouse plot, it was a matter of seeing how many ways you could have the mouse escape and the cat get "hoist by his own petard." The best writers who consistently turned out the most ingenious cartoons at Warner Brothers were Warren Foster, Mike Maltese, and Ted Pierce. I got a good basic background for comedy writing working with these guys. A cartoon has a simpler structure, but it's not too far removed from, say, "Mork and Mindy." Although more sophisticated in many other ways, television situation comedies are usually based on a frustration or a shortcoming that can be examined with humor. For example, Maxwell Smart's ("Get Smart") inability to ever completely understand the situation in which he was placed is comparable to the coyote's inability to catch the Roadrunner.

CA: You've been writing for television since its early days. Would you comment on the changes that have taken place in programming?

TURNER: For one thing, it's more expensive now. I started writing for television in 1949 with a syndicated puppet show at KTLA called "Time for Beany." It probably didn't cost more than $1.98 to produce . . . well, maybe two bucks. "Beany" became a cult show during the early days of television—Dorothy Lamour had it written into her contract that between 6:30 and 7:00 p.m. she had to be free to watch it. Cecil B. DeMille came onto the set one day "just to see what it was all about" (and he was parting the Red Sea for Charlton Heston at the time!). Martin and Lewis, Lionel Barrymore, a lot of big stars were fans and stopped by the set to visit. A show with the simplicity and charm of "Beany" would be impossible in television today.

CA: You worked on "The Bob Hope Show" in 1970 as a staff writer. Does Hope employ a large staff of writers?

TURNER: At that time there were ten of us, and Mort Lachman was the producer. Our assignments and memos would come from Mort directed to "Group Ten." We worked independently for the most part—you never saw the other guys except on tape night. There was no working in rooms together; everybody was spread out. At eleven every morning, Mort would call and give you your assignment, which was to be delivered in one of two ways: "Into the office by seven" or "Over the wall at Hope's by six." Hope lived in a house with a huge wall around it. You'd drive up, push a button on a post in the driveway, a guy would come out and snatch the material out of your hand and disappear into the house.

CA: Did you see much of Bob Hope on the job?

TURNER: No. I was only with Hope for one season. Other writers—like Charlie Lee, Bill Larkin, Gig Henry, and Les White—were with him for fifteen years or more. He would speak to them from time to time, but the rest of us found him to be aloof.

CA: Are there censorship problems on programs that deal with adult subjects? Programs like "The Mary Tyler Moore Show," "All in the Family," or "Maude"?

TURNER: The network shows are watched over by network "program practice representatives" that go through every script. They literally count the *damns* and *hells,* and point out to you with great glee that they found three *hells* on one page and they "aren't going to stand for it." Sometimes a *damn* or a *hell* is the only thing that will convey the character's feeling at the moment. Norman Lear used to say, "Use 'em, but make *damn* sure they count."

CA: If a show offends a great many people, who has to deal with the reaction?

TURNER: It rarely comes back to the writer—it usually comes back to the company that produced it. When I was on "The Jeffersons" we used to get a lot of hate mail, particularly about Tom and Helen Willis, an interracial couple. A lot of people thought we were going to hell in a handbasket for having anything to do with that subject, but we ignored all the threats.

CA: You've done a number of television pilots. How does a pilot take shape—is it one perons's idea or a joint effort?

TURNER: It can be both. Out of one hundred pilots that come up, maybe one gets through. The mortality rate on pilot ideas is incredible. Sometimes writers work in teams. I get the concept and work up a presentation, then go to a network, sit down with the powers that be and pitch the idea. If it gets a response like "Boy, that *is* different," or "that looks like a good area," they will give you a development deal to go ahead. The next step is to write a treatment, then a script. When a pilot is made from the script and is well received, thirteen episodes are ordered. Then it depends on the ratings the first four or five weeks. If it looks like it might do something, the network continues it. Otherwise it's canceled.

CA: Isn't it difficult to predict whether a series idea will be well received?

TURNER: It's impossible! Last year, for example, I had an idea which dealt with a young girl growing up in the country. I pitched it to a network and they were very interested. Then there was a change in the executive staff—people were shuffled around and the project was put on the shelf. When they got back to it, I had to deal with a new regime who thought "country themes stunk." A year later there were at least five highly rated shows on the air with a country theme: "Dukes of Hazzard," "Flo," "Sheriff Lobo," etc. The important thing is interesting characters. If you have well-drawn, good characters that people care about, you can put them in any familiar surroundings and it can work.

CA: What are you working on now?

TURNER: I just finished a script for a television show called "House Calls"—a good, intelligent show. I know the producer Jerry Davis very well—he's one of the good guys. I agreed to write one script and see how it feels. If everything works out for all concerned, I may go on staff.

CA: Will that take you away from your fishing?

TURNER: No. Part of the deal is that I continue to work here on the boat most of the time. Right now I'm working on my next pilot project, but I'm sitting here looking over the stern of my boat into the harbor and it's a gorgeous day. It's very nice here.

CA: Do you have any other plans for the future?

TURNER: I have a number of ideas for screenplays and novels. I hope to start a novel the first of next year.

CA: So you really intend to keep combining your pleasure with your work?

TURNER: Yes. For many years I was under contract and put in very long days. With Norman Lear it was a great learning experience writing and producing various shows. But Lear wanted a lot of you—seven days a week, usually twelve to fifteen hours a day. It was your whole life. I'm through with that now. I love working on my boat. I can pay attention to that inner voice that is always saying, "You shouldn't be sitting here writing, you should be out fishing." And I can answer, "You're right. Start the engines!"

—Interview by Jean W. Ross

*   *   *

TUWHARE, Hone   1922-

PERSONAL: Born October 21, 1922, in Kaikohe, Northland, New Zealand; married wife, Jean, 1949. *Education:* Attended Seddon Memorial Technical College, 1939-41, and Otahuhu Technical College, 1941. *Agent:* Longman Paul Ltd., Milford, Auckland, New Zealand.

CAREER: Poet. Worked as a welder and boilermaker; president of Birkdale Maori Cultural Committee, Auckland, New Zealand, 1966-68; councillor of Borough of Birkenhead,

Auckland, 1968-70; organizer of Maori Artists and Writers Conference, Te Kahar, New Zealand, 1973. *Military service:* New Zealand Army, Maori Battalion and Second Division Cavalry, 1945-47. *Member:* Auckland Boilermakers Union. *Awards, honors:* Grant from New Zealand Internal Affairs Department, 1956; Robert Burns centennial fellowship, University of Otago, 1969.

WRITINGS—Poems: *No Ordinary Sun,* International Publications Service, 1964; *Come Rain Hail,* Bibliography Room, University of Otago, 1970; *Sapwood and Milk,* Caveman Press, 1972; *Something Nothing,* Caveman Press, 1973, International Publications Service, 1975.

SIDELIGHTS: Hone Tuwhare's poetry is considered unique because it unites elements of traditional Maori verse with modern European forms. His themes concern the changes of the old Maori way of life, man's relationship with nature, and the consoling effects of the New Zealand environment.

BIOGRAPHICAL/CRITICAL SOURCES: Landfall 74, June, 1965.*

*   *   *

TWIGGY
See HORNBY, Leslie

*   *   *

TYLER, (John) Poyntz   1907-1971

OBITUARY NOTICE—See index for *CA* sketch: Born in 1907 in Ashland, Va.; died March 23, 1971. Editor and author. In 1967, Tyler's novel, *A Garden of Cucumbers,* was adapted as the United Artists motion picture "Fitzwilly," starring Dick Van Dyke and Barbara Feldon. His other works include *Social Welfare in the United States, Airways of America,* and *Television and Radio.* (Date of death provided by agent, A. Watkins, Inc.)

U

ULENE, Art(hur Lawrence) 1936-

PERSONAL: Born July 13, 1936, in Los Angeles, Calif.; son of John and Fay Ulene; married Priscilla Kalkstein (a television producer), December 18, 1960; children: Douglas, Valerie, Steven. *Education:* University of California, Los Angeles, B.A., 1957, M.D., 1962. *Office:* 2401 West Olive St., Burbank, Calif. 91506.

CAREER: University of California, Los Angeles, Center for Health Science, intern in internal medicine, 1962-63, resident in obstetrics and gynecology, 1963-67; University of Southern California, Los Angeles, assistant clinical professor of obstetrics and gynecology, 1970—. Created "Feeling Fine," on KNBC-TV, 1975—; health commentator for "Today," on NBC-TV, 1976—, and for ABC-TV, 1978. Member of health advisory council of Clearing House for Corporate Social Responsibility; member of interpersonal skills subcommittee of National Board of Medical Examiners. *Military service:* U.S. Army, assistant chief of obstetrics and gynecology at Walter Reed Army Medical Center, 1967-70; became major. *Member:* American College of Obstetricians and Gynecologists. *Awards, honors:* National Media Awards from Kidney Foundation, 1977, and Epilepsy Foundation, 1977, Golden Mike Awards from Southern California Radio and Television News Association, 1977 and 1978, and Blakeslee Award from American Heart Association, 1978, all for program "Feeling Fine."

WRITINGS: Feeling Fine, J. P. Tarcher, 1977; *Help Yourself to Better Health,* Perogee, 1980.

WORK IN PROGRESS: Developing a comprehensive health library for distribution in health care settings.

SIDELIGHTS: Ulene's special interest has been the application of modern technology to health education. It was this interest that led him to conceive the idea for "Feeling Fine," the television feature that promotes better health through viewer participation. His work at the University of Southern California has resulted in the development of self-instructional materials that are in use in medical schools and nursing homes all over the United States. *Feeling Fine* is a best-selling guide to common-sense health care.

*　　*　　*

ULLMAN, Michael (Alan) 1945-

PERSONAL: Born November 22, 1945, in Boston, Mass.; son of Albert Daniel (a professor) and Althea (Hayes) Ullman; married Harriet Bowdish (an editor); children: Catherine Victoria. *Education:* Harvard University, A.B., 1967; University of Chicago, M.A., 1968; University of Michigan, Ph.D., 1976. *Home:* 136 Woodward St., Newton Highlands, Mass. 02161. *Office:* Department of English, Tufts University, Medford, Mass. 02155.

CAREER: Teacher at private high school in Cambridge, Mass., 1973-74; Boston College, Chestnut Hill, Mass., part-time lecturer, 1974-75, lecturer in English, 1975-79; Tufts University, Medford, Mass., part-time lecturer, 1979-80, visiting assistant professor of English, 1980—. Guest on television and radio programs. *Member:* Northeast Victorian Studies Association (member of board of directors, 1977-78).

WRITINGS: (And photographer) *Jazz Lives: Portraits in Words and Pictures,* New Republic Books, 1980. Author of "Michael Ullman on Jazz," a column in *New Republic.* Contributor of about twenty-five articles, photographs, and reviews to magazines, including *Real Paper, Boston, Ariel: A Journal of International English Literature, The New Boston Review,* and *Mother Jones,* and to newspapers. Reviewer for *Boston Phoenix.*

WORK IN PROGRESS: A collection of articles on jazz musicians, publication expected in 1982.

SIDELIGHTS: Ullman commented: "I am interested in writing about literature and music. While my field was originally Victorian literature, I have been moving toward American studies. I hope to introduce valuable musicians to the public. I often proceed by interviewing these musicians—my articles thus add in a small way to an important body of oral history. At the same time my articles represent my critical judgements, which I offer in language that, I hope, is readily comprehensible to the lay person.

"Writing what is essentially music journalism offers peculiar challenges. The writer must convey a sense of the music as well as a feeling for the person making it and often within space limitations that seem devastating. Ideally, the critic should have a musician's ear and a novelist's eye. He or she should make frank judgements without being unfairly dismissive. When working with a music that changes as rapidly as jazz, this is particularly difficult. One has to remain open to new sounds without being taken in by what is false or insincere. I listen to all kinds of jazz. My writing tends to be about "new music," the avant-garde, because the people playing these forms are rarely given the exposure they deserve."

*   *   *

ULMAN, William A. 1908(?)-1979

PERSONAL: Born c. 1908, in New York, N.Y.; died of congestive heart failure, August 21, 1979, in Chevy Chase, Md.; married wife, Averil; children: Timothy, Valerie Ann. *Education:* Attended Magdalen College, Oxford, and Yale University; received degree in journalism from Columbia University.

CAREER/WRITINGS: U.S. Army, Signal Corps, served in Europe during World War II, retiring in 1954 as colonel; Housing and Home Finance Agency (now Department of Housing and Urban Development), Washington, D.C., assistant administrator, 1954-57; free-lance writer, 1957-73; U.S. Department of Health, Education and Welfare (HEW; now Department of Health and Human Services), Washington, D.C., congressional liaison officer, 1973-76; free-lance writer, 1976-79. Correspondent for *Los Angeles Times* and *New York Herald Tribune.* Contributor to magazines, including *Saturday Evening Post, Collier's, Esquire,* and *New Yorker.* Co-author of books on politics. *Awards, honors*— Military: Bronze Star with two oak leaf clusters; Legion of Merit; commander of Order of the British Empire.

BIOGRAPHICAL/CRITICAL SOURCES: Washington Post, August 24, 1979.*

*   *   *

ULMER, (Roland) Curtis 1923-

PERSONAL: Born March 30, 1923, in Rose Hill, Miss.; married Irene Simmons (a career placement officer), October 15, 1965. *Education:* Florida State University, B.S., 1957, M.S., 1960, Ed.D., 1965. *Home:* 436 Milledge Circle, Athens, Ga. 30606. *Office:* Department of Adult Education, University of Georgia, 426 Tucker Hall, Athens, Ga. 30602.

CAREER: Writer. Meridian Municipal Junior College, Meridian, Miss., founder of evening adult education program, 1949; Mississippi State College for Women (now Mississippi University for Women), Columbus, registrar and director of adult education, 1964-65; Florida Board of Public Instruction, state coordinator of adult basic education program, 1965-67; University of Georgia, Athens, professor of adult education and chairman of department, 1967—. Guest professor at Red River Community College, summer, 1973, and University of Maine, summers, 1974-75; speaker at workshops. Member of National Talent Pool, 1969-71, and International Associates in Education, 1978-79. Member of Georgia governor's advisory committee for vocational education, 1971-74; chairman of Georgia Advisory Committee for Adult Education, 1975—; consultant to U.S. Marine Corps.

MEMBER: National Association for Public Continuing and Adult Education (past member of board of directors; president, 1977-78), National Association of State Directors of Adult Education (chairman, 1966-67), Georgia Association for Public School Adult Education (president, 1970-71), Mississippi Adult Education Association (president, 1958-59). *Awards, honors:* Grants from Southern Regional Education Board for In-Service Programs, 1971, U.S. Department of Labor, and U.S. Office of Education.

WRITINGS: (With Malcolm Knowles and Doris Statker) *An Approach to Consumer Education for Adults,* Office of Consumer Affairs, 1973; *Teaching the Culturally Disadvantaged Adult,* Prentice-Hall, 1973. Contributor to *A Handbook for*

Adult Basic Education, 1972. Editor of "Adult Education" series, Prentice-Hall, 1971-72. Contributor to education journals, including *Adult Leadership, Journal of Research and Development in Education,* and *Illinois Journal of Education.*

*   *   *

UNDERHILL, Alice Mertie (Waterman) 1900-1971

OBITUARY NOTICE—See index for *CA* sketch: Born September 14, 1900, in Watertown, S.D.; died September 6, 1971. Educator, nurse, and author. Underhill's writings include *Adventures of Kado* and *Sharna of Rocky Bay.* She also wrote more than one hundred fifty songs. Obituaries and other sources: *Something About the Author,* Volume 10, Gale, 1976.

*   *   *

UNGARO, Susan Kelliher 1953-

PERSONAL: Born June 7, 1953, in New York, N.Y.; daughter of Thomas G. and Mary C. Kelliher; married Colin Ungaro (a news editor). *Education:* William Paterson College, B.A., 1975, M.A., 1976. *Office: Family Circle,* 488 Madison Ave., New York, N.Y. 10022.

CAREER: Family Circle, New York, N.Y., editorial assistant, 1976-77, editor and reporter, 1977-79, senior editor, 1979—. *Member:* Women in Communications. *Awards, honors:* Awards from Consumer Information Center and President's Office of Consumer Affairs, both 1980, for outstanding contributions to increasing consumer awareness.

WRITINGS: The H & R Block Family Financial Planning Workbook, Macmillan, 1980.

SIDELIGHTS: Ungaro told *CA:* "As a senior editor at *Family Circle,* it's easy to feel enthusiastic about the work I do. I'm a woman writing and editing articles that help other women live better, spend their money better, and make the most of the opportunities available to them. I see 'consumerism' journalism as the up and coming area of interest to the public; it seems to be an excellent area for new writers to develop and work on their writing skills. Anytime you can help people get more for their hard-earned money, they're going to be interested in what you have to say."

*   *   *

URCH, Elizabeth 1921-
(Elise Brogan)

PERSONAL: Born September 10, 1921, in Larne, Northern Ireland; daughter of John Tullis (a railway supervisor) and Elizabeth (McNeilly) Blair; married Walter Henry Urch, April 24, 1943 (died February 5, 1959); children: Michael John, Maureen Elizabeth, Rosalind Patricia Urch Sadler. *Education:* Stran Millis College of Education, diploma in Education, 1941. *Religion:* Protestant. *Office:* Logierait School, Ballinluig, Perthshire, Scotland.

CAREER: Ministry of Aircraft Production, Bristol, England, Glasgow, Scotland, and Belfast, Northern Ireland, aeronautical inspector, 1941-43; assistant teacher at grammar schools in Larne, Northern Ireland, 1959-69; head teacher at Newbigging School in Perthshire, Scotland, 1969-72; Logierait School, Ballinluig, Scotland, head teacher, 1972—. Marriage counselor, 1953-59. Guest on television and radio programs, including "Thought for the Day," "Silver Lining," "Women's Hour," and "Matter of Concern."

WRITINGS: Be Still My Soul (nonfiction), Arthur James, 1964; *For God's Sake Watch Your Language,* St. Andrews

Press, 1978; (editor) *Ladders up to Heaven,* Arthur James, Part I: *Christmas,* 1980, Part II: *Friendship,* 1980, Part III: *Sorrow,* 1981, Part IV: *Worship,* 1981, Part V: *Odds and Ends,* 1982.

Under pseudonym Elise Brogan: *Queen of the Manse: The Musing of a Parson's Wife,* Victory Press, 1957.

Television and radio scripts; all for BBC-Radio, except as noted: "Silver Lining," 1959—; "Lift up Your Hearts," 1960—; "Thought for the Day," 1960—; "Prayer for the Day," 1961—; "Ere I Sleep," 1961—; "Week of Prayer," British Broadcasting Corp., 1969, "Matter of Concern," ITV, 1976.

WORK IN PROGRESS: Completing remaining parts of *Ladders up to Heaven.*

SIDELIGHTS: Elizabeth Urch wrote: "My first book, *Queen of the Manse,* was written just for the joy of writing. *Be Still My Soul* developed out of broadcasts on bereavement and was compiled in answer to many inquiries for help after a death in the family. The next book came out of a conviction that something needed to be said about trying to cover up an uncaring attitude with modern trendy caring language.

"My interests are in the unspoiled outdoors—hill-walking and the conservation of beautiful areas. Only there can I seem to unwind and divest myself of the frenetic bureaucratic nonsense which invades our 'civilized' society. In God's creation I find the peace needed to be able to return to the necessary turmoil of daily life."

Ladders up to Heaven contains writing which Elizabeth Urch began collecting as a young girl and which she wants to preserve.

*   *   *

URRY, W(illiam) G(eorge)   1913-1981

OBITUARY NOTICE: Born December 17, 1913, in Canterbury, England; died February 18, 1981, in Canterbury, England. Historian, archivist, educator, and author. Urry worked as an archivist at the Cathedral Library in Canterbury during the late 1940's. In 1969 he became a reader in medieval western palaeography at Oxford University. Urry wrote *Canterbury Under the Angevin Kings* and the unpublished "The Marlowes of Canterbury." Obituaries and other sources: *London Times,* February 27, 1981.

V

V., Nina
 See VICKERS, Antoinette L.

*   *   *

VAILLAND, Roger (Francois)   1907-1965

PERSONAL: Born October 15, 1907, in Acy-en-Multien, France; died May 11, 1965; son of an architect; married second wife, Elisabeth Naldi, 1954. *Education:* Attended lyceum in Paris, France. *Politics:* Communist.

CAREER: Co-founder of review, *Le Grand Jeu* (title means "The Great Game"); *Paris-Soir*, Paris, France, foreign correspondent in the Balkans, the Near East, and Ethiopia, 1930-40; full-time writer, 1945-65. *Military service:* Served with French resistance movement derailing troop transport trains during World War II. *Awards, honors:* Prix-Interallie, 1945, for *Drole de jeu;* Prix Goncourt, for *La Loi.*

WRITINGS—In English translation; novels, except as noted: *Drole de jeu,* [Paris], 1946, translation by Gerald Hopkins published as *Playing for Keeps,* Houghton, 1948 (published in England as *Playing With Fire,* Chatto & Windus, 1948); *La Loi,* Gallimard, 1957, translation by Peter Wiles published as *The Law,* Knopf, 1958; *Les Mauvais Coups,* Sagittaire, 1959, translation by Wiles published as *Turn of the Wheel,* Knopf, 1962; *La Fete,* Gallimard, 1960, translation by Wiles published as *The Sovereigns,* J. Cape, 1960, also published as *Fete,* Knopf, 1961; (author of adaptation with Roger Vadim and Claude Brule) *Les Liaisons dangereuses 1960* (screenplay), Julliard, 1960, translation by Bernard Shir-Cliff published as *Roger Vadim's "Les Liaisons dangereuses,"* Ballantine, 1962; *La Truite,* Gallimard, 1964, translation by Wiles published as *The Trout,* Dutton, 1965 (published in England as *The Young Trout,* Collins, 1965).

In French: *Heloise et Abelard* (three-act play), [Paris], 1947; *Bon Pied, bon oeil* (title means "Good Foot, Good Eye"), Correa, 1950; *Le Colonel Foster plaidera coupable* (five-act play), Les Editeurs Francais Reunis, 1951; *Un Jeune Homme seul* (title means "A Young Man Alone"), Correa, 1951; *Beau Masque,* Gallimard, 1954; *Trois cent vingt-cinq mille francs,* Correa, 1956; *Monsieur Jean* (three-act play), Gallimard, 1959.

Nonfiction: *La Bataille d'Alsace: Novembre-decembre 1944,* J. Haumont, 1945; *Quelques Reflexions sur la singularite d'etre francais* (title means "Some Reflections on the Singularity of Being French"), J. Haumont, 1946; (with Ray-

mond Manevy) *Un Homme du peuple sous la revolution,* Correa, 1947; *Le Surrealisme contre la revolution,* Editions sociales, 1948; *Boroboudour: Voyage a Bali, Java et autres iles* (travel book), Correa, 1951; *Experience du drame,* Correa, 1953; (editor) *Laclos par lui-meme: Images et textes* (title means "Laclos by Himself"), Editions du Seuil, 1953; *Eloge du cardinal de Bernis* (title means "Eulogy of Cardinal de Bernis"), Fasquelle, 1956; (editor) C. Suetonius Tranquillus, *Les Douze Cesars: Choises et commentees,* Editions Buchet-Chastel, 1962; *Le Regard froid: Reflexions, equisses, libelles, 1945-1962,* B. Grasset, 1963; *La Reunion,* Editions Rencontre, 1964; *Erits intimes,* Gallimard, 1968; *Lettres a sa famille,* Gallimard, 1972; *Le Saint Empire,* Editions de la Difference, 1979.

Omnibus volumes: *Ouevres completes,* Editions Rencontre, 1967, Volume I: *Drole de jeu,* Volume II: *Les Mauvais Coups; Bon Pied, bon oeil,* Volume III: *Un Jeune Homme seul; Trois cent vingt-cinq mille francs,* Volume IV: *Heloise et Abelard; Le Colonel Foster plaidera coupable,* Volume V: *Monsieur Jean; Experience du drame; Batailles pour l'humanite; Les Liaisons dangereuses 1960,* Volume VI: *Boroboudour; Choses vues en Egypte; La Reunion,* Volume VII: *Beau Masque,* Volume VIII: *Le Regard froid; Le Surrealisme contre la revolution,* IX: *Laclos par lui-meme; Suetone: Les Douze Cesars; Sur "Manon Lescant,"* Volume X: *Un Homme du peuple sous la revolution; Recits et reportages; Erits politiques,* Volume XI: *La Loi.*

Film scenarios include "Les Mauvais Coups" and a television adaptation, "Trois cent vingt-cinq mille francs." Author of essays. Contributor to journals, including *Les Oeuvres libres.*

BIOGRAPHICAL/CRITICAL SOURCES: National Review, December, 1946; *New Republic,* May 7, 1951; *Reporter,* November 13, 1958, November 12, 1959; *New York Times,* September 28, 1958; *Times Literary Supplement,* September 28, 1967; Rene Ballet, Elisabeth Vailland, and Henri Bourbon, *Roger Vailland,* P. Seghers, 1973; John Ernest Flower, *Roger Vailland: The Man and His Masks,* Hodder & Stoughton, 1975.

OBITUARIES: New York Times, May 13, 1965; *Newsweek,* May 24, 1965; *Publishers Weekly,* May 31, 1965.*

VAKAR, N(icholas) P(latonovich) 1897-1970

OBITUARY NOTICE—See index for *CA* sketch: Born June 26, 1897, in Kiev, Russia (now U.S.S.R.); died July 18, 1970. Journalist, educator, and author. After emigrating from Russia and settling in Paris in 1920, Vakar worked as a journalist and served as the managing editor of *La Revue du Bridge.* He was a professor at Wheaton College and a visiting professor at Middlebury Russian Summer School and at Ohio State University. His works include *Belorussia: The Making of a Nation* and *Word Count of Spoken Russian: The Soviet Usage.* (Death date provided by Wheaton College.)

* * *

VALDMAN, Albert 1931-

PERSONAL: Born February 15, 1931, in Paris, France; came to the United States in 1944, naturalized citizen, 1953; son of Jacques and Rose (Standman) Valdman; married Hilde Wieners, August 19, 1960; children: Bertrand Andre. *Education:* University of Pennsylvania, A.B., 1953; Cornell University, A.M., 1955, Ph.D., 1960. *Office:* Committee for Research and Development in Language Instruction, Indiana University, Ballantine 602, Bloomington, Ind. 47401.

CAREER: Linguistic scientist at Foreign Service Institute, 1957-59; Pennsylvania State University, University Park, assistant professor of Romance languages, 1959-60; Indiana University, Bloomington, member of faculty, 1960-66, professor of French, Italian, and linguistics, 1966—, chairman of department of linguistics, 1963-68. Visiting professor at Harvard University, summer, 1965; visiting lecturer at University of the West Indies, 1965-66; Fulbright lecturer at University of Nice, 1971-72 and 1975-76. *Member:* Phi Beta Kappa. *Awards, honors:* Guggenheim fellowship, 1968.

WRITINGS: Applied Linguistics: French, A Guide for Teachers, 2nd edition, Heath, 1961; (editor) *Structural Drill and the Language Laboratory,* Indiana University Press, 1963; (with Robert J. Salazar and Marie Antoinette Charbonneaux) *A Drillbook of French Pronunciation,* Harper, 1964, 2nd edition, 1970; (with Simon Belasco) *College French in the New Key,* Heath, 1965; (editor) *Trends in Language Teaching,* McGraw, 1966; (with Belasco) *Applied Linguistics and the Teaching of French,* Nittany Press, 1968; *Saint-Lucian Creole Basic Course,* Indiana University, Creole Institute, 1969; *Basic Course in Haitian Creole,* Indiana University Press, 1970; (editor) *Papers in Linguistics and Phonetics to the Memory of Pierre Delattre,* Mouton, 1972; *Introduction to French Phonology and Morphology,* Newbury House, 1976; (editor) *Pidgin and Creole Linguistics,* Indiana University Press, 1977; (editor with Arnold R. Highfield) *Theoretical Orientation in Creole Studies,* Academic Press, 1980; (editor with Highfield) *Historicity and Variation in Creole Studies,* Karoma, 1981.

In French: (With Belasco and Florence Steiner) *Son et sens* (title means "Sound and Meaning"), Scott, Foresman, 1972; (with Belasco and Steiner) *Scenes et sejours* (title means "Scenes and Stays"), Scott, Foresman, 1972; (editor with Hand R. Runte) *Identite culturelle et francophonie dans les Ameriques* (title means "Cultural Identity and Francophony in the Americas"), Indiana University Press, 1976; *Le Creole: Structure, statut et origine* (title means "Creole: Structure, Status, and Origin"), Klincksieck, 1978; (editor) *Creole et enseignement primaire en Haiti* (title means "Creole and Primary Education in Haiti"), Indiana University, Creole Institute, 1979. Also author of *Langue et culture* (title means "Language and Culture"), 1975, and *Le Francais hors de France* (title means "French Outside of France"), 1978.

WORK IN PROGRESS: Creole Dictionary, publication expected in 1981.

* * *

VALENTIN, Thomas 1922-1981

OBITUARY NOTICE: Born January 13, 1922, in Weilburg, Germany; died in 1981 in Lippstadt, West Germany. Educator and author of novels, short stories, plays, children's books, and television scripts. After teaching school for fifteen years, Valentin devoted his full attention to writing. His first novel, *Hoelle fuer Kinder,* appeared in 1961 and was followed in 1963 by a highly successful play, *Die Unberatenen.* This play was made into a film in 1966 and was produced as *The Ill-Advised* at London's Aldwych Theatre in 1976. Beginning in 1966 Valentin wrote extensively for television, with much popular success. Most of his work combines psychological insight with social criticism. Obituaries and other sources: *London Times,* February 23, 1981.

* * *

VAMPLEW, Wray 1943-

PERSONAL: Born December 23, 1943, in South Hiendley, England; son of Allen (a miner and railway worker) and Doris (a teacher; maiden name, Watson) Vamplew; married Janice Cameron (a research assistant), July 1, 1967; children: Peter Wray, Ailsa Kathryn. *Education:* University of Southampton, B.Sc., 1965; University of Edinburgh, Ph.D., 1969. *Home:* 32 Shamrock Rd., Hallett Cove, South Australia 5158. *Office:* Department of Economic History, Flinders University of South Australia, Bedford Park, South Australia.

CAREER: University of Edinburgh, Edinburgh, Scotland, lecturer in economic history, 1967-75; Flinders University of South Australia, Bedford Park, senior lecturer in economic history, 1975—. Member of Public Examinations Board of South Australia, 1980—; South Australian representative collecting sport statistics for Australian Bicentennial history reference section, 1981—. *Member:* Economic History Society, Economic History Association, Economic History Society of Australia and New Zealand, North American Society for Sports History. *Awards, honors:* Named coach of the year by Hallett Cove Junior Soccer Club, 1980.

WRITINGS: Salvesen of Leith, Scottish Academic Press, 1975; *The Turf: A Social and Economic History of Horse Racing,* Allen Lane, 1976.

Contributor: M. C. Reed, editor, *Railways in the Victorian Economy,* David & Charles, 1969; Donald McCloskey, editor, *Essays on a Mature Economy,* Methuen, 1971; I.R.C. Hirst and W. D. Reekie, editors, *The Consumer Society,* Tavistock, 1977; R. Campbell, editor, *Scottish Industrial History,* Scottish History Society, 1978; R. Cashman and M. McKernan, editors, *Sport in History,* Queensland University Press, 1979; T. C. Smout, editor, *The Search for Wealth and Stability,* Macmillan, 1979; R. Crawford, editor, *Proceedings of Symposium on History of Sport,* A.C.H.P.E.R., 1980. Also contributor to *Sport: Money, Morality, and the Media,* Cashman and McKernan, editors, 1981.

Editor of *Australian Historical Statistics, Australian Historical Statistics Bulletin,* and *Australian Historical Statistics Monograph.* Contributor to economic and history journals.

WORK IN PROGRESS: An economic history of sport in England, with special reference to commercialization and professionalism, publication expected in 1983; an economic history of sport in South Australia.

SIDELIGHTS: Vamplew wrote: "My current aim is to help make the study of sport more academically acceptable. To this end I organized the session on the economic history of leisure and recreation at the Seventh International Economic History Congress in Edinburgh in 1978, and have been invited to do the same at the next congress in Budapest.

"My work has concentrated on establishing the chronology of commercialization in major crowd-drawing sports in order to test the hypothesis that the rise of mass-spectator sport correlates with changes in working-class incomes and hours of labor. Sports-club accounts and balance sheets have been examined to assess whether or not clubs were profit-maximisers as this has implications for their market behavior and any assessment of entrepreneurial performance. An analysis of the operations of markets for sport and sportsmen has revealed that in some sports such markets were subject to enforced restrictions on dividends, wages, and the mobility of labor. Examination has also been made of occupational aspects of sports professionalism, looking at such things as recruitment, career structures, job security, earnings, and unionism."

* * *

VanBIBBER, Max A(rnold) 1913(?)-1981

OBITUARY NOTICE: Born c. 1913 in Dalhart, Tex.; died after a long illness, March 15, 1981, in Middletown, Conn. Cartoonist. VanBibber was associated throughout his career with the comic strip "Winnie Winkle," beginning as assistant to the strip's creator, Martin M. Branner. When Branner retired in 1962, VanBibber took over the strip until his own retirement in January, 1981. The comic strip featured the romantic and professional troubles of its heroine, Winnie Winkle. Obituaries and other sources: *The World Encyclopedia of Comics,* Chelsea House, 1976; *Washington Post,* March 17, 1981.

* * *

Van BUITENEN, J(ohannes) A(drian) B(ernard) 1928(?)-1979

PERSONAL: Born c. 1928, in the Netherlands; came to the United States in 1959; died after a short illness, September 21, 1979, in Champaign, Ill.; married Georgette van Buitenen; children: Hans, Jeannette. *Education:* University of Utrecht, Ph.D., 1953.

CAREER: Deccan College, Poona, India, sub-editor of Sanskrit dictionary, 1956-59; University of Chicago, Chicago, Ill., associate professor, 1959-64, professor of linguistics, 1964-79, George K. Bobrinsky Distinguished Service Professor, chairman of department of South Asian languages and civilizations, 1966-76.

WRITINGS: The Maitrayaniya Upanishad: A Critical Essay With Text, Translation, and Commentary, Mouton, 1962; *Ramanuja on the Bhagavadgita,* reprinted, Oriental Book Distributors, 1974; (editor and translator) *The Mahabharata: The Book of the Beginning,* three volumes, University of Chicago Press, 1980; (editor) *The Bhagavadgita in the Mahabharata: A Bilingual Edition,* University of Chicago Press, 1980. Also author of *Ramanuja's Vedarthasamgraha* and *Tales of Ancient India.*

OBITUARIES: New York Times, September 22, 1979.*

* * *

VAN BUREN, Raeburn 1891-

PERSONAL: Born January 12, 1891, in Pueblo, Colo.; son of George Lincoln (an inventor) and Luella (la Mar) Van Buren; married Fern Rita Ringo, December 8, 1920; children: Richard. *Education:* Attended Arts Students League, 1913. *Home:* 21 Clover Dr., Great Neck, N.Y. 11021.

CAREER/WRITINGS: Kansas City Star, Kansas City, Mo., sketch artist, 1909-12; free-lance illustrator, 1913—. Creator of comic strip "Abbie and Slats." Contributor of illustrations to periodicals, including *Saturday Evening Post, Collier's, Redbook, New Yorker, Esquire,* and *McCall's. Military service:* National Guard, 1917-19. *Awards, honors:* Named cartoonist of the year by B'Nai B'rith, 1958; nominated for best story strip cartoonist award by National Cartoonist Society, 1976; named to Cartoonist Hall of Fame, 1978.

* * *

VANDERVEEN, Bareld Harmannus 1932- (Bart H. Vanderveen)

PERSONAL: Born May 5, 1932, in Assen, Netherlands; son of Nicolaas (in business) and Aagje (Feitsma) Vanderveen; married Johanna Margaretha Boers, October 26, 1959; children: Margaret, Jacqueline. *Education:* Attended secondary schools in Assen and Groningen, Netherlands. *Religion:* Protestant Reformed. *Home:* Lavastraat 13, 8084 CL 't Harde, Netherlands. *Office:* Eperweg 111, 8084 HD 't Harde, Netherlands.

CAREER: Royal Dutch Touring Club, The Hague, Netherlands, assistant automotive engineer, 1949-51; worked at General Motors dealership, Assen, Netherlands, 1953-56; Olyslager Organization, writer, Soest, Netherlands, 1956-60, and Dorking, England, 1960-75; Sindorf Group, 't Harde, Netherlands, export manager and technical consultant, 1975—. Guest on television and radio programs. *Military service:* Royal Netherlands Army, 1951-53; became sergeant. *Member:* Nederlands Algemene Miniatuur Auto Club (NAMAC), Dutch Society of Military Vehicles, Pre-Fifty American Automobile Club (honorary member), Historic Commercial Vehicle Club, Military Vehicle Conservation Group, All-Wheel Drive Club (president), Land-Rover Register.

WRITINGS—All under name Bart H. Vanderveen; published by F. Warne: *The Observer's Fighting Vehicles Directory: World War II,* 1969, revised edition, 1972; *The Jeep,* 1970, revised edition, 1981; *Half-Tracks,* 1970; *The Observer's Book of Automobiles,* 1970; *Scammel Vehicles,* 1971; *American Cars of the 1930's,* 1971; *The Observer's Military Vehicles Directory: From 1945,* 1972; *American Cars of the 1940's,* 1972; *American Cars of the 1950's,* 1973; *British Cars of the Early 1930's,* 1973; *British Cars of the Late 1930's,* 1973; *The Observer's Army Vehicles Directory: To 1945,* 1974; *Tanks and Transport Vehicles of World War II,* 1974; *American Trucks of the Early 1930's,* 1974; *British Cars of the Late 1940's,* 1974; *Buses and Coaches: From 1940,* 1974; *Cross-Country Cars: From 1945,* 1975; *American Trucks of the 1930's,* 1975; *Motorcycles: To 1945,* 1975; *Armour on Wheels,* 1976; *Motorcycles and Scooters: From 1945,* 1976, revised edition, 1979; *Fire and Crash Vehicles: From 1950,* 1976.

Published by Ward, Lock, except as noted: *Source Book of Military Wheeled Vehicles,* 1972, revised edition, 1975; *Source Book of Military Tracked Vehicles,* 1973, revised edition, 1978; *Source Book of Passenger Vehicles,* 1973; *Source Book of Military Support Vehicles,* 1980; *Source Book of Armoured Fighting Vehicles,* 1981; *Bedford and Vauxhall Military Vehicles,* Marshall, Harris & Baldwin, 1981.

Editor; published by F. Warne, except as noted: *Wreckers and Recovery Vehicles*, 1972, revised edition, 1979; *Fire-Fighting Vehicles, 1840-1950*, 1972; *Earthmoving Vehicles*, 1972; (and contributor) *Source Book of Commercial Vehicles*, Ward, Lock, 1972, revised edition 1976; *Fairground and Circus Transport*, 1973; *Passenger Vehicles, 1893-1940*, 1973; *British Cars of the Early 1950's*, 1975; *British Cars of the Late 1950's*, 1975.

Contributor to automotive magazines in Japan, England, and the Netherlands.

SIDELIGHTS: Vanderveen wrote: "Ever since 1945, I have been very active in collecting literature on the history of military motor vehicles. My library contains about three thousand books on this subject and numerous photographs, scale models, and other items. I am not a full-time writer, however much I'd like to be, but it is my intention to publish more in the future."

*   *   *

VANDERVEEN, Bart H.
See VANDERVEEN, Bareld Harmannus

*   *   *

VANE, Michael
See HUMPHRIES, Sydney Vernon

*   *   *

VANEK, Jaroslav   1930-

PERSONAL: Born April 20, 1930, in Prague, Czechoslovakia; came to the United States in 1955, naturalized citizen, 1960; son of Josef and Jaroslava (Tucek) Vanek; married Wilda M. Marraffino, December 26, 1959; children: Joseph, Francis, Rosemarie, Steven, Teresa. *Education:* Sorbonne, University of Paris, degree in statistics, 1951; University of Geneva, lic.econ., 1954; Massachusetts Institute of Technology, Ph.D., 1957. *Religion:* Roman Catholic. *Home:* 414 Triphammer Rd., Ithaca, N.Y. 14850. *Office:* Department of Economics, Cornell University, Ithaca, N.Y. 14850.

CAREER: Harvard University, Cambridge, Mass., 1957-63, began as instructor, became assistant professor of economics; Cornell University, Ithaca, N.Y., member of faculty, 1964-66, professor of economics, 1966—, Carl Marks Professor of International Studies, 1969—, director of program in comparative economic development, 1968—, director of program participation and labor-managed systems, 1969—. Adviser to Agency for International Development, 1964; member of national economic advisory board of National Science Foundation, 1970. *Member:* American Economic Association, Federation for Economic Democracy (co-founder). *Awards, honors:* Guggenheim fellowship, 1961-62; Ford Foundation faculty fellowship, 1967-68.

WRITINGS: International Trade: Theory and Economic Policy, Irwin, 1962; *The Balance of Payments, Level of Economic Activity, and the Value of Currency*, Libraire E. Droz, 1962; *Natural Resource Content of U.S. Foreign Trade, 1870-1955* (monograph), M.I.T. Press, 1963; *General Equilibrium of International Discrimination: The Case of Customs Unions*, Harvard University Press, 1965; *Estimating Foreign Resource Needs for Economic Development*, McGraw, 1967; *Estimating Foreign Resource Needs for Economic Development*, McGraw, 1966; *Maximal Economic Growth: A Geometric Approach to Von Neumann's Growth Theory and the Turnpike Theorem*, Cornell University Press, 1968; *General Theory of Labor-Managed Market Economies*, Cornell Uni-

versity Press, 1970; *The Participatory Economy: An Evolutionary Hypothesis and a Strategy for Development*, Cornell University Press, 1971; (editor with J. Bhagwati, R. W. Jones, and R. A. Mundell) *Trade, Balance of Payments, and Growth: Papers in International Economics in Honor of Charles P. Kindleberger*, North Holland Publishing, 1971; (contributor) *Economic Structure and Development: Essays in Honour of Jan Tinbergen*, North Holland Publishing, 1973; *International Trade and Finance: Essays in Honour of Jan Tinbergen*, Macmillan, 1974; (editor) *Self-Management: Economic Liberation of Man*, Penguin, 1975; *The Labor-Managed Economy: Essays*, Cornell University Press, 1977. Contributor of articles to journals, including *Quarterly Journal of Economics, American Economic Review, Review of Economics and Statistics, Review of Economic Studies*, and *Journal of Political Economy*.

*   *   *

Van NOPPEN, Ina (Faye) W(oestemeyer)   1906-1980
(Ina Faye Woestemeyer)

OBITUARY NOTICE—See index for *CA* sketch: Born April 14, 1906, in Bethel, Kan.; died April 7, 1980. Educator and author. Van Noppen retired from her position as professor of history at Appalachian State University in 1972. Her works include *The Westward Movement: A Book of Readings on Our Chaging Frontiers* and *Western North Carolina Since the Civil War*. (Date of death provided by Curtis Williams.)

*   *   *

VAN TASSEL, David Dirck   1928-

PERSONAL: Born March 29, 1928, in Binghamton, N.Y.; son of Walter Raymond (a physician) and Etta May (a poet and editor; maiden name, Strathie) Van Tassel; married Helen Hamilton Liddell, July 29, 1950; children: David Dirck, Jr., Emily Field, Katharine Anne, Jonathan Judson, Jeanie Strathie. *Education:* Dartmouth College, A.B., 1950; University of Wisconsin (now University of Wisconsin—Madison), M.S., 1951, Ph.D., 1955. *Home:* 2940 Euclid Heights Blvd., Cleveland Heights, Ohio 44118. *Office:* Department of History, Case Western Reserve University, Cleveland, Ohio 44106.

CAREER: University of Texas, Austin, instructor, 1954-57, assistant professor, 1957-61, associate professor, 1961-65, professor of history, 1965-69, associate of Center for the History of Education, 1967; Case Western Reserve University, Cleveland, Ohio, visiting professor, 1968-69, professor of American history, 1969—, head of department of history, 1976-80. Visiting lecturer at University of Wisconsin, Madison, 1961. Founder, president, and chairman of board of directors of National History Days, 1979—; member of national advisory board of National Action Forum for Older Women, 1978—; member of national committee for Bicentennial Conference on American Genealogy and Family History. *Military service:* U.S. Army, Signal Corps, 1946-47.

MEMBER: American Association for the Advancement of Science, American Association for the Advancement of the Humanities, American Historical Association, American Association of University Professors (vice-president, 1978-79; president, 1979-80), American Civil Liberties Union, Academy of Independent Scholars (founding member), Organization of American Historians (chairman of nominating committee for Merle Curti Award in Intellectual History, 1976), Immigration History Society (member of executive board, 1973-79), American Studies Association (vice-president and chairman of program committee, 1964), Gerontological Society (chairman of history and archives committee, 1978-79; member of council, 1977-79), Ohio Academy of History, Cleveland Philosophical Club. *Awards, honors:* American Philosophical Society grants, 1957 and 1958; Guggenheim fellowship, 1963-64; grants from Huntington Library, 1972, National Endowment for the Humanities, 1974 and 1980, George Gund Foundation, and Cleveland Foundation.

WRITINGS: Recording America's Past: An Interpretation of the Development of Historical Studies in America, 1607-1884, University of Chicago Press, 1960; (editor) *American Thought in the Twentieth Century,* Crowell, 1967; (editor and contributor) *Science and Society in the United States,* Dorsey, 1966; (co-author) *A Guide to Computer-Assisted Historical Research in American Education,* Center for the History of Education, University of Texas, 1969; (editor with R. W. McAhren) *European Origins of American Thought,* Rand McNally, 1969; (editor with Stuart Spicker and Kathleen Woodward) *Aging and the Elderly: Humanistic Perspectives in Gerontology,* Humanities, 1978; (editor) *Aging, Death, and the Completion of Being,* University of Pennsylvania Press, 1979.

Contributor: William B. Hesseltine and Donald R. McNeil, editors, *In Support of Clio: Essays in Memory of Herbert A. Kellar,* State Historical Society of Wisconsin, 1958; Clifford L. Lord, editor, *Keepers of the Past,* University of North Carolina Press, 1965; J. Walton, editor, *Toward Better Teaching of History in Secondary Schools,* St. Stephen's Episcopal School, 1966.

General editor of "Series on the History of American Thought and Culture," Rand McNally, 1967-76. Contributor to *Dictionary of American History.* Contributor of more than twenty-five articles and reviews to academic journals and popular magazines, including *Gerontologist, American Quarterly,* and *American Heritage.* Editor of *Human Values and Aging Newsletter,* 1975—.

WORK IN PROGRESS: Encyclopedia of Cleveland History, an interpretive history of the city, publication by Kent State University Press expected in 1984.

*   *   *

Van VALKENBURG, Samuel 1891-1976

OBITUARY NOTICE—See index for *CA* sketch: Born September 14, 1891, in Leeuwarden, Holland; died in 1976. Educator and author. Van Valkenburg, a professor emeritus at Clark University since 1962, specialized in geography. His works include *Economic and Social Geography, Elements of Political Geography, Pacific Asia: A Political Atlas,* and *Mediterranean Lands.* (Date of death provided by Jane Kjems, secretary of Graduate School of Geography, Clark University.)

*   *   *

VARE, Robert 1945-

PERSONAL: Born May 8, 1945, in New York, N.Y.; son of Arthur (a stockbroker) and Minnie (a doctor; maiden name, Gallay) Vare. *Education:* University of Chicago, B.A., 1967, M.A., 1968. *Home:* 25 Sutton Pl. S., New York, N.Y. 10022. *Agent:* Robert Lescher, 155 East 71st St., New York, N.Y. 10021.

CAREER: Bergen Record, Hackensack, N.J., staff writer, 1968-69; *New York Post,* New York City, staff writer, 1969-72; free-lance writer, 1972-79; New School for Social Re-

search, New York City, member of faculty, 1979—. *Member:* Authors Guild, American Society of Magazine Editors.

WRITINGS: Buckeye: A Study of Coach Woody Hayes and the Ohio State Football Machine (Book-of-the-Month Club alternate), Harper, 1974.

Co-author of "El Grande de Coca Cola," a screenplay, 1978. Author of "Food for Thought," a column in *National Observer.* Contributor to magazines and newspapers, including *Esquire, New Republic, New York, New Times, Sports Illustrated, Village Voice, New York Times Magazine,* and *Cosmopolitan.* Senior editor of *Look,* 1978-79; editor of *Home Video,* 1980—.

WORK IN PROGRESS: A book of humorous essays.

SIDELIGHTS: Vare told *CA:* "*Buckeye* was a national bestseller and was cited by James Michener in his book, *Sports in America,* as being 'indispensible to understanding what sports are about in this country.' George Plimpton said of the book: '*Buckeye* is not only an unforgettable portrait of one of the sport world's most controversial figures, but also a remarkable document on the state of big-time college sports.'"

*   *   *

VAUGHAN, Robert (Richard) 1937-

PERSONAL: Born November 22, 1937, in Morley, Mo.; son of Robert Richard (a truck owner and operator) and Florence Aline (Prouty) Vaughan; married Virginia Grace Goff, May 5, 1957 (divorced February 5, 1964); married Ruthellen Spengeman (a teacher and writer), May 30, 1975; children: Robert Richard III, Thomas Goff. *Education:* Attended College of William and Mary. *Politics:* "Ticket splitter, more conservative than Democrats, more liberal than Republicans." *Religion:* Episcopal. *Home and office:* 205 North Kingshighway, Sikeston, Mo. 63801. *Agent:* Jay Garon, Jay Garon-Brooke Associates, Inc., 415 Central Park W., No. 17-D, New York, N.Y. 10025.

CAREER: U.S. Army, 1955-73, served as helicopter pilot in the United States, Korea, Germany, and Vietnam, leaving service as chief warrant officer; television talk show and cooking show host in Phoenix, Ariz., 1973-75; publisher and editor of newspaper in Sikeston, Mo., 1975-77; free-lance writer, 1977—. Member of Sikeston Library Board; member of Scott County Republican Committee; Scott County director of George Bush for President campaign, 1979-80. *Awards, honors*—Military: Distinguished Flying Cross, Purple Heart, Bronze Star, Air Medal with thirty-four Oak Leaf clusters. Other: Named best military aviation writer of the year by *Army Aviation Digest,* 1968, 1969, 1970, and 1971; Porgie Award from West Coast Books, 1977, for *The Power and the Pride.*

WRITINGS: Brandywine's War, Bartholomew House, 1971; *The Valkyrie Mandate,* Simon & Schuster, 1974; *The Power and the Pride,* Manor, 1977; *The Sin,* Zebra Books, 1979.

WORK IN PROGRESS: Historical romances and contemporary novels.

SIDELIGHTS: Vaughan wrote: "As a storekeeper must keep an inventory of goods, a writer must keep an inventory of experiences. Therefore my main interest is in developing new experiences, primarily through travel. I have visited all fifty states and more than thirty countries."

VAUGHN, Jesse Wendell 1903-1968

OBITUARY NOTICE—See index for *CA* sketch: Born March 4, 1903, in Dadevill, Mo.; died September 29, 1968. Attorney and author. Vaughn began his career as an attorney in 1930 in Windsor, Colorado. His writings include *With Crook at the Rosebud, The Reynolds Campaign on Power River,* and *Indian Fights: New Facts on Seven Encounters.* (Date of death provided by the city hall of Windsor, Colo.)

* * *

VENTURA, Piero Luigi 1937-

PERSONAL: Born December 3, 1937, in Milan, Italy; son of Piero (a butcher) and Angela (Bernasconi) Ventura; married Marisa Murgo (a writer), May 21, 1962; children: Marco Jacopo, Paolo and Andrea (twins). *Education:* Attended Art School of Castello Sforzesco, 1956-57, and Architecture University, 1958. *Religion:* Roman Catholic. *Home and office:* Via Domenichino 27, Milan 20149, Italy.

CAREER: Associated with Lambert (an advertising agency), 1959-65; P & T of Milan, Milan, Italy, art director, 1965-78; free-lance illustrator, 1978—. *Military service:* Italian Army, Artillery, 1958-59; became sergeant. *Member:* Illustrators Society of Italy, Society of Illustrators (United States). *Awards, honors:* Award of excellence from Society of Illustrators, 1976, for *Piero Ventura's Book of Cities; Piero Ventura's Book of Cities* was named book of the year by American Institute of Graphic Arts and Brooklyn Museum, both 1977; Prix de Treize from Office Chretienne du Livre, 1979, and award from Ministero Spagnolo della Cultura, 1980, both for *Il viaggio di Colombo;* art citation from Fiera of Bologna, 1980, for *I viaggi al Polo Nord.*

WRITINGS—Self-illustrated children's books: *Piero Ventura's Book of Cities,* Random House, 1975; *The Magic Well,* Random House, 1976; (with wife, Marisa Ventura) *The Painter's Trick,* Random House, 1977; *Il Viaggio di Colombo,* Mondadori, 1977, translation (based on book by Gian Paolo Ceserani) published as *Christopher Columbus,* Random House, 1978.

In Italian: *Il viaggio di Marco Polo* (title means "The Voyage of Marco Polo"), Mondadori, 1977; *Il viaggio di Cook* (title means "The Voyage of Cook"), Mondadori, 1978; *Il viaggio di Livingstone* (title means "The Voyage of Livingstone"), Mondadori, 1978; *I viaggi al Polo Nord* (title means "The Voyages to the Northern Pole"), Mondadori, 1979; *Atlante vivo del mare* (title means "Great Book of the Sea"), Mondadori, 1979; *L'uomo a cavallo* (title means "The Men and the Horse"), Mondadori, 1980; *Un anno nel bosco* (title means "A Year of the Wood"), Mondadori, 1980.

Illustrator: Guido Sperandio, *Vanuk, Vanuk,* translation by Jane Murgo, Doubleday, 1973; Gladys Yessayan Cretan, *Ten Brothers With Camels,* Golden Press, 1975.

WORK IN PROGRESS: A book on architecture for Mondadori.

* * *

VICKERS, Antoinette L. 1942-
(Eda Franchi, Nina V.)

PERSONAL: Born February 26, 1942, in Rochester, N.Y.; daughter of L. Louis (a physician) and Edith (Harman) Lapi; married Russell T. Vickers (a nuclear engineering manager), July 2, 1966. *Education:* University of Wisconsin, J.D., 1966. *Home and office:* 28 Bedford Rd., Summit, N.J. 07901.

CAREER: Veterans Administration, Newark, N.J., senior adjudicator, 1969-73; Ruth Russell Gray, Plainfield, N.J., associate attorney, 1973-74; private practice of law, 1974—; writer. Member of New Jersey governor's committee on insurance rating; speaker at women's political caucus. *Member:* New Jersey State Bar Association. *Awards, honors:* Il Solco Scholarship for Middlebury College, 1959.

WRITINGS: (Under pseudonym Eda Franchi) *The Long Road Back* (novel), New American Library, 1975. Contributor to magazines and newspapers.

WORK IN PROGRESS: Another novel, under pseudonym Nina V.

SIDELIGHTS: In her work as a lawyer, Antoinette Vickers represents Spanish- and Portuguese-speaking clients. While working for the Veterans Administration she presented two television programs in Spanish that were aimed at improving the image of the U.S. Government.

She wrote: "My writing today is my most creative means of communicating the joy, as well as the pain and grunt involved in everyday living. My most vital subject is living, which I no longer put off until things get better.

"My unfinished novel deals with conflict in female role integration. Each case that my heroine, Anita Fischer, Esq., deals with in her law practice represents a larger struggle. The Jameson appeal shows Anita in conflict with her partner. She fights to argue the firm's most important case, and conceals a two hundred thousand dollar offer of settlement from her partner and the client. Then her spouse is transferred to Chicago. Anita stays in New Jersey to gain full partnership and argue the Jameson appeal. She loses. The White case shows her in conflict with her spouse and the Internal Revenue Service, his employer. The Kiddeck case shows Anita in conflict with herself and her destiny. On the outside she succeeds; on the inside she disintegrates. Ultimately, she can no longer deny the fear and pain of being alone and maintaining a cross-country marriage."

AVOCATIONAL INTERESTS: "My husband and I have traveled to South America and enjoyed a trip up the Amazon River as far as the natives would take us. I sail extensively in the Caribbean and plan to go to Belize, where my husband and I have become involved in boat exchanges in bareboat charter. At age thirty-six, I put on ice skates for the first time since childhood and have become an avid figure skater and ice dancer."

* * *

VILJOEN, Helen Gill 1899-1974

OBITUARY NOTICE—See index for *CA* sketch: Born July 26, 1899, in Passaic, N.J.; died after a long illness, March 4, 1974, in Flushing, N.Y. Educator and author. Viljoen was one of the original faculty members of Queens College when it was founded in 1937 and retired as professor emeritus of English from that college in 1965. Her writings include *Ruskin's Scottish Heritage, The Froude-Ruskin Friendship,* and *The Brantwood Diary of John Ruskin, With Related Letters.* Obituaries and other sources: *New York Times,* March 6, 1974.

* * *

VINEY, Wayne 1932-

PERSONAL: Born March 4, 1932, in Wichita, Kan.; son of Glenn R. and Grace Wayne (Brown) Viney; married Wynona Rose Wentworth (a teacher), February 23, 1953; children: Donald Wayne, Michael David. *Education:* Oklahoma Baptist University, B.A., 1956; University of Oklahoma, M.S., 1960, Ph.D., 1964. *Religion:* Methodist. *Home:* 1421 Miramont, Fort Collins, Colo. 80524. *Office:* Department of Psychology, Colorado State University, Fort Collins, Colo. 80523.

CAREER: Oklahoma City University, Oklahoma City, Okla., head of department of psychology, 1960-66; Colorado State University, Fort Collins, professor of psychology, 1976—, head of department, 1967-73, associate dean of College of Natural Sciences, 1973-76. *Member:* American Psychological Association, American Association for the Advancement of Science, Cheiron, Rocky Mountain Psychological Association, Sigma Xi.

WRITINGS: (Editor with Michael Wertheimer and Marilyn Wertheimer) *History of Psychology: A Guide to Information Sources,* Gale, 1979.

WORK IN PROGRESS: Research on the work of Dorothea Dix.

* * *

VITZTHUM, Richard Carleton 1936-

PERSONAL: Born June 11, 1936, in Minneapolis, Minn.; son of Hans Christoph and Virginia (Corse) Vitzthum; married Marcella Ann McKenzie, April 16, 1960; children: Virginia, Thomas. *Education:* Amherst College, B.A., 1957; Harvard University, M.A.T., 1958; Stanford University, Ph.D., 1963. *Home:* Eight Ridge Rd., Severna Park, Md. 21146. *Office:* Department of English, University of Maryland, College Park, Md. 20742.

CAREER: University of Rochester, Rochester, N.Y., instructor in English, 1962-64; U.S. Naval Academy, Annapolis, Md., assistant professor of English, 1964-66; University of Maryland, College Park, assistant professor, 1966-69, associate professor, 1969-79, professor of English, 1979—.

WRITINGS: The American Compromise: Theme and Method in the Histories of Bancroft, Parkman, and Adams, University of Oklahoma Press, 1974; *Land and Sea: The Lyric Poetry of Philip Freneau,* University of Minnesota Press, 1978.

* * *

VIZZINI, Salvatore 1926-

PERSONAL: Born November 29, 1926, in Pittsburgh, Pa.; son of Samuel Anthony and Lillian Antonette (Wolfe) Vizzini; married Marginell DeLoach, March 5, 1949; children: Samuel J. *Education:* Received A.A. (with honors) from Miami-Dade Community College, B.A. (with honors) from Shaw University, and M.A. from University of Miami, Coral Gables; also attended U.S. Treasury Law Enforcement Academy, Brevard Junior College, and Biscayne College. *Home:* 308 Fountain Circle, Hunstville, Ala. 35801. *Office:* Huntsville Police Department, Hunstville, Ala.

CAREER: U.S. Treasury Department, Federal Bureau of Narcotics, Washington, D.C., special agent in Italy, France, Greece, Syria, Lebanon, Thailand, Cuba, and Puerto Rico, and organizer and administrative head of Narcotics Bureau in Istanbul, Turkey, 1953-66; South Miami Police Department, South Miami, Fla., chief of police, 1967-79; Huntsville Police Department, Huntsville, Ala., chief of police, 1980—. Guest lecturer at University of Miami, Coral Gables, Biscayne College, Florida International University, and Miami-Dade Community College; adjunct professor at University of Alabama, Huntsville. Consultant to U.S. Senate Select Committee to Investigate Organized Crime and Law Enforcement, 1968-69. *Military service:* U.S. Marine Corps,

1944-50; served in the South Pacific, China, and Japan. U.S. Air Force, special agent, 1951-53. *Member:* International Association of Chiefs of Police, Alabama Police Chiefs Association, Alabama Police Officers Association, Legion of Honor (member of advisory board). *Awards, honors:* Outstanding service awards from U.S. Treasury Department, 1956, 1961, 1962, and 1964; Italian Caribinieri Award, 1960; Turkish Ataturke Award, 1960; medal from governor of Florida, 1968; Legion of Honor, 1973; award from American Bicentennial Research Institute, 1973; award from American Justinian Society of Jurists, 1975.

WRITINGS: (With Oscar Fraley and Marshall Smith) *Vizzini,* Arbor House, 1972.

* * *

VOADEN, Herman Arthur 1903-

PERSONAL: Born January 19, 1903, in London, Ontario, Canada; son of Arthur and Louisa (Bale) Voaden; married Violet Kilpatrick, June 21, 1935. *Education:* Queen's University, Kingston, Ontario, B.A., 1923, M.A., 1926; also attended Yale University, 1930-31. *Home:* 8 Bracondale Hill Rd., Toronto, Ontario, Canada M6G 3P4.

CAREER: Teacher at collegiate school in Ottawa, Ontario, 1924-26; English teacher and department head at technical school, 1926-27; English teacher and department head at technical school and collegiate institute in Sarnia, Ontario, 1927-28; Central High School Commission, Toronto, Ontario, director of department of English, 1928-64; writer, 1964—. Director of Toronto Play Workshop, 1932-55; director of summer course in drama and play production at Queen's University, Kingston, Ontario, 1934-36, and director at university theatre; member of Canadian delegation to General Assembly of United Nations Educational, Scientific, and Cultural Organization (UNESCO), 1946; associate director and executive director of Canadian Conference of Arts, 1966-68.

MEMBER: Canadian Arts Council (president, 1945-48), Canadian Guild of Crafts (president, 1968-70), Royal Society of Arts (fellow), Arts and Letters Club. *Awards, honors:* Canadian Drama Award, 1937; member of Order of Canada, 1974; Medal of Courage, 1974.

WRITINGS: Earth Song (symphonic play), Playwrights, 1976. Also author of plays "Murder Pattern," 1975, "Wilderness," 1978, "Rocks," "Hill-Land," "Ascend as the Sun," "Maria Chapdelaine," "Dance Chorale," "Romeo and Juliet" (adaptation), "Emily Carr," "The Prodigal Son" (libretto), and "Esther" (libretto).

Editor: *Six Canadian Plays,* C. Clark, 1930; *Four Good Plays to Read and Act,* Longmans, Green, 1945; *On Stage,* 1945, revised edition published as *Nobody Waved Goodbye and Other Plays,* Macmillan, 1966; T. S. Eliot, *Murder in the Cathedral,* Kingswood, 1959; *Four Plays of Our Time,* Macmillan, 1960; *Drama Four,* Macmillan, 1966; *Julius Caesar,* St. Martin's, 1966; *Human Values in Drama,* Macmillan, 1966; *Look Both Ways: Theatre Experiences,* Macmillan, 1975. Also editor of *A Book of Plays,* 1935.

AVOCATIONAL INTERESTS: Theatre, travel.*

* * *

von ENDE, Richard Chaffey 1907-

PERSONAL: Born August 4, 1907, in Pittsburgh, Pa.; son of Hermann and Florence M. (Chaffey) von Ende; married Genevra Brady, July 1, 1939; children: Richard L., Frederick A.C., William L., Eleanor T. *Education:* Carnegie-Mellon

University, B.A., 1931, M.A., 1939; University of Pittsburgh, Ph.D., 1941. *Religion:* Episcopal. *Home:* 1242 South Willis, Abilene, Tex. 79605.

CAREER: Minister of music at Methodist church in Grove City, Pa., 1931-33; music teacher at public schools in Chicora, Pa., 1933-34, Butler, Pa., 1934-36, and Pittsburgh, Pa., 1936-45; Bethany College, Bethany, W.Va., head of music department, 1945-48; Texas Women's University, Denton, professor of music, 1948-50; McMurry College, Abilene, Tex., professor of music, head of department, and chairman of Division of Fine Arts, 1950-73; writer, 1941—. Member of board of directors of Abilene Symphony Orchestra, Abilene Metropolitan Ballet, and Abilene Fine Arts Museum. Church choir director. *Member:* National Association of Teachers of Singing (national judge, 1961), Texas Music Educators Association, Texas Association of Music Schools (president, 1965), Pennsylvania Music Educators Association, Pittsburgh Music Educators Association (president, 1944-45), Abilene Kiwanis Club.

WRITINGS: Administration of Music Education in Public Schools of Large Cities, privately printed, 1941; (editor) *Church Music: An International Bibliography,* Scarecrow, 1980.

AVOCATIONAL INTERESTS: Oil painting, travel (including Europe, Canada, and Mexico).

* * *

von SCHUSCHNIGG, Kurt   1897-1977

PERSONAL: Born December 14, 1897, in Riva, Austria (now Italy); naturalized U.S. citizen, 1956; died November 18, 1977, in Mutters, Austria; son of Artur (a military general) and Anna (Wopfner) von Schuschnigg; married Hermione Masera, 1924 (died, 1935); married Vera Czernin, June 1, 1938; children: (first marriage) one son; (second marriage) Cissy. *Education:* University of Innsbruck, J.U.D., 1922. *Religion:* Roman Catholic.

CAREER: Attorney, 1922-27; Austrian Parliament, Vienna, Christian Socialist member of Parliament from Tyrolean constituency, 1927-32; Government of Austria, minister of justice, 1932-34, minister of education, 1933-34, chancellor of Austria, 1934-38, minister of defense and foreign affairs, 1936-38, minister of public security, 1937; political prisoner of the Nazi government in Germany, under name Dr. Auster, 1938-45; St. Louis University, St. Louis, Mo., professor of government, 1948-68, professor emeritus, 1968-77. Deputy of

Austrian National Council, 1927; founder and chief of patriotic organization, Ostmaerkische Sturmscharen. *Military service:* Austrian Army, 1915-18, prisoner of war in Italy, 1918-19. *Awards, honors:* Grand Cordon of Order of Pius, Order of St. Gregory, Legion of Honor, Cross of the South of Brazil, and Order of Malta; LL.D. from Rockford College, 1948, Mount Mary College, 1952, and John Carroll University, 1962.

WRITINGS: Oesterreichs erneuerung: Die reden des bundeskanzlers, Druck und verlag "Carinthia," 1935; *Dreimal Oesterreich,* J. Hegner, 1937, translation by John Segrue, P. Eckstein, and others published as *My Austria,* Knopf, 1938, reprinted, AMS Press, 1979 (published in England as *Farewell Austria,* Cassell, 1938); (contributor) Hans Bayer, editor, *Oesterreichisches arbeitsrecht, mit erlaueterungen und entscheidungen der gerichte und einigungsaemter,* Manz, 1938; *Ein Requiem im rot-weiss-rot,* 1946, reprinted, Amalthea, 1978, translation by Franz von Hildebrand published as *Austrian Requiem,* Putnam, 1946; *The Law of Peace,* 1959; *Im Kampf gegen Hitler: Die Ueberwindung der Anschlussidee,* Molden, 1969, translation by Richard Barry published as *The Brutal Takeover: The Austrian Ex-Chancellor's Account of the Anschluss of Austria by Hitler,* Atheneum, 1971. Contributor to Austrian and American journals, including *Social Order.*

BIOGRAPHICAL/CRITICAL SOURCES: John A. Lukacs, *The Great Powers and Eastern Europe,* 1953; Dieter Wagner and Gerhard Tompowitz, *Anschluss: The Week That Hitler Seized Vienna,* 1972; *New York Times,* November 19, 1977.*

* * *

von WANGENHEIM, Chris   1942-1981

OBITUARY NOTICE: Born in 1942 in Breslau, Germany: died in an automobile accident on the Caribbean island of St. Martin, March 9, 1981. Fashion photographer. When he became a photographer at the age of twelve, von Wangenheim was considered a child prodigy, and by the time he came to the United States, in 1965, he was already beginning to build an international reputation. The *New York Times* called his photographs "daring, provocative and brilliantly inventive," and the editorial director of Conde Nast Publications observed that von Wangenheim's work showed "a European sophistication. . . . He combined an admirable love of women, a sensuous feeling, with a modern image." A book of von Wangenheim's work entitled *Women Alone* was in progress at the time of his death. Obituaries and other sources: *New York Times,* March 12, 1981; *Newsweek,* March 23, 1981.

W

WADE, David 1929-

PERSONAL: Born December 2, 1929, in Edinburgh, Scotland; son of John Roland (a civil servant) and Penelope Haig (Ferguson) Wade; married Penelope Ann Northen (a company director), May 21, 1953; children: Sarah, Stephen Peter. *Education:* Queen's College, Cambridge, B.A. (with honors), 1952. *Home and office:* 4-a Queen Anne's Gardens, London W.4, England.

CAREER: Associated with Simpkin Marshall Ltd. (wholesale booksellers), 1952-54, and Dexion Ltd. (industrial equipment manufacturers), 1954-63; writer, 1963—. Director of Procaudio Ltd. *Military service:* British Army, Intelligence Corps, 1948-49. *Member:* Society of Authors, National Union of Journalists, Broadcasting Press Guild.

WRITINGS—Radio plays; all first broadcast by British Broadcasting Corp. (BBC-Radio): "Trying to Connect You," 1968; "The Cooker," 1970; "The Guthrie Process," 1971; "The Goldspinners," 1971; "Three Blows in Anger," 1973, published in *Winter's Tales,* edited by A. D. Maclean, Macmillan, 1973; "The Ogden File," 1975; "The Nightingale" (adaptation of work by Hans Christian Andersen), 1975; "The King Who Made a Magic Carpet," 1976; "Summer of '39," 1977; "The Facts of Life," 1980.

Television plays for children: "The Magician's Heart" (adaptation of work by E. Nesbit), first broadcast by BBC-TV, 1973; "The King Who Became a Carpenter," first broadcast by BBC-TV, 1976.

Radio critic for *Listener,* 1965-67, and *Times,* 1967—.

WORK IN PROGRESS: Radio plays and documentaries.

*　　*　　*

WADE, Wyn Craig 1944-

PERSONAL: Born July 3, 1944, in South Bend, Ind.; son of Wyndel Calvin and Ruth M. (a clerk; maiden name, Dishon) Wade; married Barbara Barnett (in public relations), April 30, 1966; children: Derek Wyndel. *Education:* University of Michigan, B.A., 1966; University of Wisconsin—Madison, M.A., 1971; further graduate study at Michigan State University, 1976-78. *Politics:* "Civil libertarian." *Religion:* "Western mysticism." *Residence:* Mishawaka, Ind. *Agent:* Paul R. Reynolds, Inc., 12 East 41st St., New York, N.Y. 10017. *Office address:* P.O. Box 6071, South Bend, Ind. 46660.

CAREER: Wisconsin Division of Corrections, Madison, psychologist, 1968-71; Washington County Mental Health, Montpelier, Vt., clinical psychologist, 1971-76; Michigan State University, East Lansing, instructor in psychology, 1976-78; Indiana University, South Bend, instructor in non-fiction writing, 1980-81. Writer, 1977—. *Member:* American Association of University Professors, Titanic Historical Society (honorary member), Authors Guild.

WRITINGS: The Titanic: End of a Dream (Literary Guild selection), Rawson, Wade, 1979; *America's Shadow: A History of the Ku Klux Klan,* Simon & Schuster, 1982. Contributor to *Michigan History* and *Newsday.*

WORK IN PROGRESS: The Annotated Mikado, with wife, Barbara Wade; "contemplating a book on George A. Custer, a biography that would argue that he has become a scapegoat for our inequitable Indian policy."

SIDELIGHTS: Wade wrote: "A recurrent theme in my work is catastrophe and violence—how they intrude unexpectedly into one's organized and complacent life. My first book was prompted by a severe auto accident to my only child, which likewise prompted my career change from psychology to full-time writing. *America's Shadow* is the first complete history of the Ku Klux Klan, arguing that the Klan is a uniquely American institution and represents a dark and nefarious side of the American character.

"Presently, I seem to be amalgamating my ten years' experience as a psychotherapist and my interests in western mysticism, philosophy, and civil liberties into reflective non-fiction on American history, culture, and values. Reviewers of my first book found it startling in its straight-forwardness and surprising in its overthrow of traditional interpretations of the subject; this quite surprised me, since I have no investment or interest in being controversial or iconoclastic. I am nevertheless grappling with a new form of psychological history, as opposed to standard history (which bores me) and psycho-history (which I detest).

"I am an intensely reflective and solitary man, extremely devoted to my home and family."

AVOCATIONAL INTERESTS: Building, repairing, and playing pipe organs.

WALDEN, Howard T(albot) II   1897-1981

OBITUARY NOTICE—See index for *CA* sketch: Born January 3, 1897, in Hackensack, N.J.; died March 22, 1981, in Hackensack, N.J. Author best known for his books on fish and fishing. Among his works are *Upstream and Down, Angler's Choice: An Anthology of American Trout-Fishing, Deep Pool*, short stories, and a novel left incomplete at the time of his death. Obituaries and other sources: *New York Times*, March 26, 1981.

*   *   *

WALDMAN, Max   1920(?)-1981

OBITUARY NOTICE: Born c. 1920; died March 1, 1981, in New York, N.Y. Photographer, lecturer, and author. Leaving a career in advertising photography in the mid-1960's, Waldman became known for his photographic portraits of ballet and theatre celebrities. His dramatic photographs, themselves stylistically theatrical, have been exhibited at New York museums, including the New York Cultural Center. Some of his work is also represented in books of theatre and dance portraits such as *Waldman on Dance* and *Waldman on Theater*. Waldman's other books discuss various aspects of photography, a subject on which he also lectured. Obituaries and other sources: *New York Times*, March 3, 1981.

*   *   *

WALDRON, Martin O.   1925-1981

OBITUARY NOTICE: Born February 2, 1925, in Calcasieu Parish, La.; died of heart disease, May 27, 1981, in Hightstown, N.J. Journalist. Waldron began his career as a newsman in the southern United States. While a correspondent for the *St. Petersburg Times*, he wrote a series of articles reporting major spending abuses in the building of Florida's Sunshine State Parkway. These articles, which effected several changes in the Parkway building program and resulted in new laws, brought the *St. Petersburg Times* a Pulitzer Prize for public service. Waldron also received Florida's Outstanding Newsman Award, a Sigma Delta Chi Award, and three Associated Press awards. He joined the *New York Times* in 1965 as bureau chief in Houston. At the time of his death, Waldron was bureau chief in Trenton, N.J. Obituaries and other sources: *New York Times*, May 28, 1981.

*   *   *

WALFORD, Christian
See DILCOCK, Noreen

*   *   *

WALKER, George F.   1947-

PERSONAL: Born August 23, 1947, in Toronto, Ontario, Canada; son of Malcolm and Florence (Braybrook) Walker; married Susan Purdy; children: Renata. *Agent:* Great North Artists Management, Inc., 345 Adelaide St. W., Toronto, Ontario, Canada M5V 1R5.

CAREER: Factory Theatre Lab, Toronto, Ontario, dramaturge, 1972-73, resident playwright, 1972-76. *Awards, honors:* Five Canada Council Grants.

WRITINGS—Plays: Prince of Naples (first produced in Toronto at Factory Theatre Lab, 1971; produced as radio play by Canadian Broadcasting Corp. [CBC-Radio], 1973), Playwrights Canada, 1973; *Ambush at Tether's End* (first produced in Toronto at Factory Theatre Lab, 1971; produced as radio play by CBC-Radio, 1974), Playwrights Canada,

1974; *Sacktown Rag* (first produced in Toronto at Factory Theatre Lab, 1972), Playwrights Canada, 1972; *Bagdad Saloon* (first produced in London, England, at Bush Theatre, 1973; produced in Toronto at Factory Theatre Lab, 1973), Playwrights Canada, 1973 (also see below); "Demerit," first produced in Toronto at Factory Theatre Lab, 1974; (and director) *Beyond Mozambique* (first produced in Toronto at Factory Theatre Lab, 1974), Playwrights Canada, 1975 (also see below).

(And director) "Ramona and the White Slaves," first produced in Toronto at Factory Theatre Lab, 1976 (also see below); "Gossip," first produced in Toronto at Toronto Free Theatre, 1977; *Three Plays* (contains "Bagdad Saloon," "Beyond Mozambique," and "Ramona and the White Slaves"), Coach House Press, 1978; *Zastrozzi: The Master of Discipline* (first produced in Toronto at Toronto Free Theatre, 1977), Playwrights Canada, 1979; *Filthy Rich* (first produced in Toronto at Toronto Free Theatre, 1979), Playwrights Canada, 1979.

Other: "The Private Man" (radio play), first produced by CBC-Radio, 1973; "Microdrama" (teleplay), first produced by CBC-TV, 1976; "Strike" (teleplay), first produced by CBC-TV, 1976; "Sam, Grace, Doug, and the Dog" (teleplay), first produced by CBC-TV, 1976; "Overlap" (teleplay), first produced by CBC-TV, 1977; "Capital Punishment" (teleplay), first produced by CBC-TV, 1977.

WORK IN PROGRESS: The Beast of Corsica, "an epic about a contemporary of Napoleon who has discovered longevity through masochism. The play follows him through various low points in history until he disappears into the Manhattan Project and is mutated into another form."

BIOGRAPHICAL/CRITICAL SOURCES: Factory Lab Anthology, Talonbooks, 1974; *University of Toronto Quarterly,* summer, 1975; *Scene Changes,* October, 1975; *Village Voice,* April 2, 1979; *Books in Canada,* April, 1980.

*   *   *

WALLACE, DeWitt   1889-1981

OBITUARY NOTICE: Born November 12, 1889, in St. Paul, Minn.; died of pneumonia, March 30, 1981, in Mount Kisco, N.Y. Businessman, editor, publisher, and founder of *Reader's Digest.* Wallace conceived the idea for *Reader's Digest* in 1917 while recovering from wounds received in World War I. It was his wife, however, who encouraged and facilitated the project, and the first edition of the monthly magazine was published in February, 1922. By the 1980's the magazine's readership had grown to more than one hundred million in 163 countries. The magazine, which presents condensed versions of previously published articles, favors a mixture of self-help, humor, optimism, and patriotism. In 1950 the company began to publish *Reader's Digest Condensed Books,* a five-volume-per-year series containing four or five condensed books in each volume. Wallace and his wife, co-chairmen of the *Reader's Digest* until 1973, used much of their huge fortune for charitable, social, and cultural causes. Obituaries and other sources: John Bainbridge, *Little Wonder: The Reader's Digest and How It Grew,* Reynal, 1946; *Current Biography,* Wilson, 1956; *Who's Who in the World,* 2nd edition, Marquis, 1973; *The International Who's Who,* Europa, 1978; *New York Times,* April 1, 1981; *Washington Post,* April 1, 1981; *Newsweek,* April 13, 1981; *Time,* April 13, 1981; *AB Bookman's Weekly,* May 4, 1981.

WALLACE, Lillian Parker 1890-1971

OBITUARY NOTICE—See index for *CA* sketch: Born in 1890 in Pine City, Minn.; died May 30, 1971. Educator and author. Wallace was a professor emeritus of history at Meredith College from 1962 to 1971. She was also an accomplished pianist and organist. Her works include *The Papacy and European Diplomacy, 1869-78* and *A Free Church in a Free State*. (Date of death provided by son, Wesley H. Wallace.)

* * *

WALLACH, Sidney 1905-1979

PERSONAL: Born July 4, 1905, in Horochow, Poland; came to the United States in 1912, naturalized citizen; died June 24, 1979, in New York, N.Y.; son of Don Zevi and Bertha (Steinberg) Wallach; married Idalee Burrows, August 17, 1929 (deceased); married Pauline Rudnick (a professor of psychiatry), February 5, 1967; children: (first marriage) Roseanne (Mrs. Barry Stein), Don H. *Education:* City College (now of City University of New York), A.B., 1925; graduate study at Columbia University, 1925-26. *Religion:* Jewish.

CAREER: Journalist, editor, and foreign correspondent, 1923-33; American Jewish Committee, New York, N.Y., began as educational director, became executive director, 1933-42; Sidney Wallach Associates (consultants), president, beginning in 1942. Lecturer on civil rights, public relations, and minority problems. Managing editor of *Jewish Tribune*, 1931, and *Young Judean*, 1932; founder of *Current Jewish Record* (now *Commentary*), 1938; publisher of *Modern Mexico*, 1945-51; editor of *City College Alumnus*, 1948-50. Counsel to National Jewish Welfare Board, 1942-43, National Conference of Christians and Jews, 1942-44, and American Council for Judaism, 1943-50. Executive vice-president of American Institute for Tropics, 1952-59; executive secretary of American Committee for the Study of War Documents; assistant director of Theodore Roosevelt Centennial Commission, 1954-60; member of American Chess Foundation; vice-president of American Friends of Tel Aviv Museum; director of Jewish Conciliation Board of America.

WRITINGS: (Editor of abridgement) Matthew Calbraith Perry, *Narrative of the Expedition of an American Squadron to the China Seas and Japan, Under the Command of Commodore M. C. Perry*, Coward, 1952; (editor) *A Theodore Roosevelt Round-up: A Biographical Sketch*, Theodore Roosevelt Association, 1958; (editor with Ronald B. Sobel) *Justice, Justice Shalt Thou Pursue: Papers Assembled on the Occasion of the Seventy-Fifth Birthday of the Reverend Julius Mark, as an Expression of Gratitude of the Jewish Conciliation Board With Whose Services and Leadership Dr. Mark Has Long Been Identified*, Ktav, 1975. European correspondent for Seven Arts Feature Syndicate, 1928-29. Contributor to magazines.

OBITUARIES: New York Times, June 29, 1979.*

* * *

WALLING, William (Herbert) 1926-

PERSONAL: Born November 25, 1926, in Denver, Colo.; son of Herbert E. (an electrician) and Sophia Helen (a secretary; maiden name, Keinath) Walling; married Judith Ruth Malone, September 6, 1952; children: Elizabeth Anne, Julia Susan, Jill Kathleen. *Education:* University of California, Los Angeles, B.E., 1951. *Agent:* c/o St. Martin's Press, Inc., 175 Fifth Ave., New York, N.Y. 10010.

CAREER: Writer. Design specialist for Lockheed Missiles & Space Co., 1960—. *Military service:* U.S. Army Air Forces, aviation cadet, 1944-45. *Member:* Science Fiction Writers of America, Authors Guild.

WRITINGS: No One Goes There Now (science fiction novel), Doubleday, 1971; *The World I Left Behind Me*, St. Martin's, 1979.*

* * *

WALLS, Ronald 1920-

PERSONAL: Born June 23, 1920, in Edinburgh, Scotland; son of Thomas John (an optician) and Jane (Kemp) Walls; married Helen MacLeod, July 17, 1941 (deceased); children: Nicolas (deceased), David, Christopher. *Education:* University of Edinburgh, M.A. (with honors), 1941, license to preach, 1945, diploma in education, 1949; attended Collegio Beda, Rome, 1975-77. *Politics:* Socialist. *Home:* Corsee Cottage, High St., Banchory, Kincardineshire AB3 3RP, Scotland.

CAREER: Ordained minister of Church of Scotland, 1946, ordained Roman Catholic priest, 1977; minister of Church of Scotland in Logie-Easter, 1946-48; teacher at St. Ninian's Primary School in Edinburgh, Scotland, 1948-51, and at St. David's Secondary School in Dalkeith, Scotland, 1951-53; Converts' Aid Society, Edinburgh, Scottish organizer, 1953-75; St. Columba's Church, Banchory, Scotland, parish priest, 1977—. *Member:* International P.E.N.

WRITINGS: The One True Kirk, Burns & Oates, 1960; *The Glory of Israel*, Our Sunday Visitor, 1972; *Christ Who Lives in Me*, Our Sunday Visitor, 1977.

Translator: Josef A. Jungmann, *Pastoral Liturgy*, Challoner, 1962; Clemens Kopp, *The Holy Places of the Gospels*, Herder & Herder, 1963; Franz Michel Willam, *Our Way to God*, Bruce, 1964; Erik Peterson, *The Angels and the Liturgy*, Darton, Longman & Todor, 1964; Theodore Filthaut, *Learning to Worship*, Burns & Oates, 1965; Gerhard Podhradsky, *New Dictionary of the Liturgy*, Geoffrey Chapman, 1967; Jungmann, *Announcing the Word of God*, Burns & Oates, 1967; Josef Lortz, *The Reformation in Germany*, Darton, Longman & Todor, 1968; Karl Rahner, *Hearers of the Word*, Sheed, 1969; David Flusser, *Jesus*, Herder & Herder, 1969; Lorenz Stucki, *The Secret Empire: The Success Story of Switzerland*, Herder & Herder, 1971.

Contributor to *Herder Commentary on Documents of Vatican II*. Contributor to journals, including *Furrow, The Tablet*, and *Doctrine and Life*.

SIDELIGHTS: Walls wrote: "I would like to reissue my first book, *The One True Kirk*, adding a prologue and epilogue. This book is my autobiography up to the date I was received into the Catholic church. The story continues in May, 1974, when, going about my business for the church as a layman, I had a serious road accident which resulted in my wife's death. This event was the cause of my turning to the priesthood.

"I would also like to find time to write a short book about *The Second Book of Discipline*, mainly the work of Andrew Melville, who was the real force and brains behind the Protestant Reformation in Scotland. I think this sort of book would be important in the ecumenical dialogue, for Melville expounds the essence of the Reformed church. His teaching is largely unknown and ignored by most people today."

WALSCHAP, Gerard   1898-

PERSONAL: Born July 9, 1898, in Londerzeel, Belgium; son of Florent Jozef (a shopkeeper) and Maria (Peeters) Walschap; married M.A. Theunissen, 1979; children: Hugo, Guido, Lieven, Carla, Bruno. *Education:* Educated in Belgium. *Politics:* Socialist. *Religion:* Atheist. *Home:* 243 Chausee de Malines, 2000 Antwerp, Belgium. *Agent:* Ed. Manteau, Beeldhouwerstraat 12, 2000 Antwerp, Belgium.

CAREER: Writer. Worked as inspector of national libraries, 1940. *Member:* Royal Academy of Letters. *Awards, honors:* Commander of Order of the Crown, 1950; grand officer of Order of Leopold, 1955; Belgian State Prize, 1965; Netherlands State Prize, 1968; created baron, 1977.

WRITINGS—In English translation: *Trouwen,* 1933, translation by A. Brotherton published as *Marriage,* British Book Centre, 1963; *Celibaat,* 1934, translation by Brotherton published as *Ordeal,* Heinemann, 1963; *Een mens van goede wil,* 1936, translation by Adrienne Dixon published as *The Man Who Went Well,* Panther, 1975.

Other writings: all published by Manteau: *Adelaide,* 1929; *Eric,* 1931; *Carla,* 1933; *Sibylle,* 1938; *Het kind* (title means "The Child"), 1939; *Houtekiet,* 1939; *De wereld van Soo Moerman* (title means "The World of Soo Moerman"), 1941; *Denise,* 1942; *De consul,* 1943; *Genezing door aspirine* (title means "Cure by Aspirin"), 1943; *Ons geluk* (title means "Our Fortune"), 1946; *Zwart en wit* (title means "Black and White"), 1948; *Moeder* (title means "Mother"), *Zuster Virgelia* (title means "Sister Virgilia"), 1951; *Het kleine meisje en ik* (title means "The Little Girl and I"), 1953; *De francaise* (title means "The French Woman"), 1957; *De verloren zoon* (title means "The Lost Son"), 1958; *Tilman Armenaas,* 1960; *Nieuw deps,* 1961; *Het gastmaal* (title means "The Banquet"), 1966; *Het avondmaal* (title means "The Evening Meal"), 1968; *Het Oramporject* (title means "The Oram Project"), 1975; *De Heilige Jan Mus* (title means "The Saint Jan Mus"), 1979.

Contributor of short stories to *Delta I* and *Literary Review.*

* * *

WALTER, William Grey   1910-1977

PERSONAL: Born February 19, 1910, in Kansas City, Mo.; died May 6, 1977; son of Karl (an editor and banker) and Margaret (a journalist; maiden name, Hardy) Walter; married Katherine Monica Ratcliffe, 1933 (divorced, 1947); married Vivian Joan Dovey, 1947 (divorced, 1950); married Lorraine Josephine Donn Aldridge, June 20, 1950 (divorced, 1973); children: (first marriage) Nicolas Hardy, Jeremy Karl; (second marriage) Timothy Carol Grey. *Education:* King's College, Cambridge, B.A. (with first class honors), 1931, M.A., 1934, Sc.D., 1947.

CAREER: Borden Neurological Institute, Bristol, England, physiologist, 1932-39, scientific consultant, 1939-77, scientific director, 1950; Maudsley Hospital, London, England, Rockefeller Foundation fellow, 1935-39. Past president of Electrophysiological Technologists. Maudsley Lecturer of Royal Medico-Psychological Association, 1949; professor at University of Aix-Marseilles, 1949; Adolf Meyer Lecturer of American Psychiatric Association, 1959. Member of World Health Organization study group on psychobiological development of the child, 1953-55, and United Nations Educational, Scientific and Cultural Organization (UNESCO) study group for the establishment of International Brain Research Organization, 1959-60; consultant of British Aircraft Corp. *Awards, honors:* Ambrose Fleming Prize from Institute

of Electrical Engineers, 1942; Ph.D. from University of Aix-Marseilles, 1949; John Snow Medal, 1950; honorary degree from University of Liege, 1967.

WRITINGS: (Contributor) D. Hill and G. Parr, editors, *Electro-Encephalography,* Macdonald, 1950; *The Living Brain,* Norton, 1953; *The Curve of the Snowflake* (science-fiction novel), Norton, 1956 (published in England as *Further Outlook,* Duckworth, 1956); *Observations on Man, His Frame, His Duty, and His Expectations,* Cambridge University Press, 1969; *Introduction to Microbiology,* Van Nostrand, 1973. Also author of *Discussions on Child Development* and *Brain Mechanisms and Consciousness.* Contributor to scientific journals and popular magazines, including *Scientific American* and *Nature.* Co-founder and co-editor of *Electroencephalography and Clinical Neurophysiology,* 1947.*

* * *

WAND, (John) William (Charles)   1885-?

PERSONAL: Born January 25, 1885, in Grantham, England; deceased; son of Arthur James Henry and Elizabeth Ann Ovelin (Turner) Wand; married Amy Agnes Wiggins, 1911 (died, 1966); children: one son (deceased), one daughter. *Education:* St. Edmund Hall, Oxford, B.A. (with first class honors), 1907, M.A., 1911; also studied at Bishop Jacob Hostel.

CAREER: Ordained Anglican minister; curate of Anglican churches in Benwell, England, 1908-11, and Lancaster, England, 1911-14; vicar-choral of Anglican church in Sarum, England, 1914-19, vicar, 1919-25; Oxford University, Oxford, England, fellow, dean, and tutor at Oriel College, 1925-34, lecturer in theology at St. Edmund Hall, 1928-31, select preacher, 1930-32, lecturer in church history, 1931-34; archbishop of Brisbane, Australia, 1934-43; bishop of Bath and Wells, England, 1943-45, and London, England, 1945-55; St. Paul's, London, canon-residentiary and treasurer, 1956-69. Lecturer at Sarum Theological College, 1914-20, tutor, 1920-24; Warburton Lecturer at Lincoln's Inn, 1956-58. Fellow of St. Edmund Hall, Oxford, 1938, Oriel College, Oxford, 1941, and King's College, London, 1956. Dean of Chapels Royal, 1945-55. *Military service:* British Army, chaplain, 1915-19, honorary chaplain, 1919-22. Royal Air Force, chaplain, 1922-25. Australian Army, senior chaplain, 1935-43. Royal Naval Volunteer Reserve, honorary chaplain, beginning in 1947.

AWARDS, HONORS: Member of Privy Council; chaplain and sub-prelate of Order of St. John of Jerusalem, 1936; prelate of Order of the British Empire, 1946-57, named prelate emeritus, 1957; S.T.D. from University of Toronto, 1947; S.T.P. from Columbia University, 1947; D.Litt. from Ripon College, 1949; knight commander of Royal Victorian Order, 1955; D.D. from Oxford University, University of London, and University of Western Ontario, 1957.

WRITINGS: The Golden String: A Short Introduction to Christian Practice, Mowbray, 1926, revised edition, 1950; *The Development of Sacramentalism,* Methuen, 1928; *A History of the Modern Church From 1500 to the Present Day,* Methuen, 1930, 7th edition, 1952; *The Old Faith and the New Age,* Skeffington & Son, 1933; (with Edward Eyre) *Non-Papal Christianity From 1648 to the Present Day,* 1934; (editor) *The General Epistles of St. Peter and St. Jude,* Methuen, 1934; *A History of the Early Church to A.D. 500,* Methuen, 1937, 4th edition, 1963; *First Century Christianity,* Oxford University Press, 1937; (editor and author of preface) *The New Testament Letters,* [Australia], 1944, reprinted, Oxford University Press, 1947; *God and Goodness,* Eyre & Spottiswoode, 1947; *The Spirit of Church History,* Mowbray, 1947, 2nd edition, Morehouse-Gorham, 1948; (editor) *The Anglican Communion: A Survey,* Oxford University Press, 1948; *The Church: Its Nature, Structure, and Function,* Morehouse-Gorham, 1948; *The Latin Doctors,* Morehouse-Gorham, 1948; *Our Day of Opportunity,* S.P.C.K., 1948; *White of Carpentaria* (biography of Bishop Gilbert White), Skeffington & Sons, 1949; (editor) *Recovery Starts Within: The Book of the Mission to London, 1949* (Religious Book Club selection), Oxford University Press, 1949; *The Authority of the Scriptures,* Mowbray, 1949.

The Greek Doctors, Faith Press, 1950; *The Four Councils,* Faith Press, 1951; *The High Church Schism: Four Lectures on the Non-Jurors,* Faith Press, 1951; *What the Church of England Stands For: A Guide to Its Authority in the Twentieth Century,* Morehouse-Gorham, 1951, reprinted, Greenwood Press, 1972; *What St. Paul Said; or, the Teaching of St. Paul,* Oxford University Press, 1952; (contributor) *Christian Belief Today,* Morehouse-Gorham, 1952; *The Mystery of the Kingdom,* Faith Press, 1953; *The Second Reform,* Morehouse-Gorham, 1953; *The Kingdom of Heaven in Its Relation to Social and Cultural Life,* Industrial Christian Fellowship, 1954; *The Four Great Heresies,* Morehouse-Gorham, 1955, reprinted, AMS Press, 1979; *The Life of Jesus Christ,* Morehouse-Gorham, 1955, 2nd edition, Methuen, 1961; *Seven Steps to Heaven,* Longmans, Green, 1956; *The Road to Happiness,* Muller, 1957; *True Lights: Talks on Saints and Leaders of the Christian Church,* Morehouse-Gorham, 1958.

The Church Today, Penguin, 1960; *Anglicanism in History and Today,* Weidenfeld & Nicolson, 1961, Thomas Nelson, 1962; *Doctors and Councils,* Faith Press, 1962; *The Atonement,* S.P.C.K., 1963; (translator and editor of abridgement) *St. Augustine's City of God,* Oxford University Press, 1963; *Seven Words, Seven Virtues: Meditations for the Three Hours,* Mowbray, 1963; *Reflections on the Collects,* Mowbray, 1964; *Changeful Page: The Autobiography of William Wand,* Hodder & Stoughton, 1965; (editor of abridgement) *Daily Readings From William Temple,* Hodder & Stoughton, 1965; *Reflections on the Epistles,* Mowbray, 1966; *Transfiguration,* Faith Press, 1967; *What St. Paul Really Said,* Macdonald & Co., 1968, Schocken, 1969; (co-author) *Promise of Greatness,* 1968; *Reflections on the Gospels,* Mowbray, 1969; *Christianity: A Historical Religion?,* Hodder & Stoughton, 1971, Judson, 1972; *Letters on Preaching,* Hodder & Stoughton, 1975. Also author of *Oxford and the Groups,* 1934, *Westminster Commentary,* 1934, *European Civilisation,* 1937, *Union of Christendom,* 1938, and *The Temptation of Jesus,* 1965. Contributor to *Praying for Daylight,* edited by John Christopher Neil Smith, 1964; contributor to magazines and newspapers, including *Spectator.* Editor of *Church Quarterly Review,* 1956-68.

SIDELIGHTS: Wand's comprehensive work *A History of the Modern Church From 1500 to the Present Day* outlines church history from the Reformation onward. A *Spectator* critic maintained that the book is "as compact and lucid an account of an immense and complicated area of events as could be devised." A *Times Literary Supplement* reviewer was also complimentary: "Wand has attained a remarkable degree of success in the synoptic view which his study affords of the development of the various Christian bodies and of their proportionate contribution to the evangelization of non-Christian lands. No book of equal compass has marshalled so great and varied a mass of detail, bringing together in a comparative manner relevant information from all continents."

In a later volume, *New Testament Letters,* Wand noted in the introduction of the book that he was endeavoring "to encourage a different kind of Bible-reading, which will lead, not perhaps to close familiarity with favourite passages, but to knowledge of whole books." He continued, "we need to grasp complete arguments, doctrines, schemes of salvation, not merely choice aphorisms of comforting texts." A writer for the *Manchester Guardian* asserted that Wand was successful in his effort: "It is a fresh and stimulating presentation of the contents of these documents [letters of the New Testament] and one that will certainly make the reader think about the meaning of the text."

BIOGRAPHICAL/CRITICAL SOURCES: Times Literary Supplement, March 6, 1930, August 30, 1947; *Spectator,* August 23, 1930; *Manchester Guardian,* November 7, 1946; *Changeful Page: The Autobiography of William Wand,* Hodder & Stoughton, 1965.*

*   *   *

WANGENHEIM, Chris von
    See von WANGENHEIM, Chris

*   *   *

WANGENSTEEN, Owen Harding   1898-1981

PERSONAL: Born September 21, 1898, in Lake Park, Minn.; died of a heart attack, January 14, 1981, in Minneapolis, Minn.; son of Owen and Hannah (Hanson) Wangensteen; married Helen C. Griffin, January 6, 1923 (marriage ended); married Sarah Anne Davidson (a medical historian and writer), September 16, 1954; children: (first marriage) Mary Helen Wangensteen Brink, Owen Griffin, Stephen Lightner. *Education:* University of Minnesota, B.A., 1919, M.B., 1921, M.D., 1922, Ph.D., 1925. *Home:* 2832 West River Rd., Minneapolis, Minn. 55406.

CAREER: University of Minnesota Hospital, Minneapolis, intern, 1922, fellow in medicine, 1923; Mayo Clinic, Rochester, Minn., fellow in surgery, 1924; University of Minnesota Hospital, resident surgeon, 1925, instructor in surgery, 1926-27; Surgical Clinic and Physiological Institute, Berne, Switzerland, assistant professor of surgery, 1927-28; University of Minnesota, associate professor, 1928-31, professor of surgery, 1931-66, distinguished service professor, 1961, regents' professor, 1966-67, professor emeritus, 1967—, director of department, 1930-67. President of Minnesota Medical Foundation, 1948-54, U.S. Public Health Service Heart Council, 1954-57, and Research Facilities Council, 1959; chairman of National Institutes of Health surgery study section, 1952-53. Founder of Wangensteen Historical Library of Biology and Medicine, 1972.

MEMBER: International Surgical Society (American president, 1969-70; international vice-president, 1971-73), American College of Surgeons (president, 1959), National Academy of Sciences, American Surgical Association (president, 1968-69), American Medical Association, American Association of Thoracic Surgery, American Association for the Advancement of Science, American Physiological Society, Society for Experimental Biology and Medicine, Society for Experimental Pathology, Hellenic Surgical Society (honorary member), Norwegian Academy of Science (honorary member), Argentine Surgical Society (honorary member), German Surgical Congress (corresponding member), Royal College of Surgeons (fellow), French Academy of Surgery, Royal College of Surgeons of Edinburgh (honorary member), Royal College of Surgeons (fellow), French Academy of Surgery, Royal College of Surgeons of Edinburgh (honorary member),

Royal College of Surgeons of Ireland (honorary member), Minnesota Pathological Society (past president), Minnesota Academy of Medicine (president, 1953), Minnesota Surgical Society, Halsted Surgical Society (past president), Minneapolis Surgical Society, Sigma Xi, Alpha Omega Alpha. *Awards, honors:* Samuel D. Gross Prize from Philadelphia Academy of Surgery, 1935; John Scott Award from Philadelphia College of Physicians, 1941; LL.D. from State University of New York at Buffalo, 1946; Alvarenga Prize from Philadelphia College of Medicine, 1949; American Cancer Society award, 1949, and special citation, 1962; D.Sc. from University of Chicago, 1956, St. Olaf College, 1958, Temple University, 1961, Hamline University, 1963, Marquette University, 1970, and University of Athens, 1978; award from Pittsburgh Surgical Society, 1958; medallion from French National Academy of Medicine, 1959; distinguished service award from University of Minnesota, 1960; Passano Award, 1961; D.H.C. from Sorbonne, University of Paris, 1962; Quinquennial Lannelongue Prize from French Academy of Surgery, 1967; distinguished service awards from American Medical Association, 1968, and American Surgical Association, 1976; named outstanding Minnesotan by committee of the governor, 1969; Pemhina Trail Award from Red River Valley Historical Society, 1973.

WRITINGS: The Therapeutic Problem in Bowel Construction: A Physiological and Clinical Consideration, C. C Thomas, 1937, 2nd edition published as *Intestinal Obstructions: A Physiological and Clinical Consideration With Emphasis on Therapy; Including Description of Operative Procedures,* 1942, 3rd edition, 1955; *Cancer of the Esophagus and the Stomach,* American Cancer Society, 1951, 2nd edition, 1956; (with wife, Sara D. Wangensteen) *The Rise of Surgery: From Empiric Craft to Scientific Discipline,* University of Minnesota Press, 1978. Also author of *Experimental and Clinical Journal.* Contributor to medical journals. Co-editor of *Surgery,* 1937-70.

WORK IN PROGRESS: A book, unfinished at time of death.

SIDELIGHTS: While chief of surgery at the University of Minnesota for more than thirty years, Wangensteen became internationally known for his surgical innovations. Stressing experimentation and research in his department, the doctor developed a tube for removing often fatal intestinal blockages that sometimes occur in patients following surgery. He trained many well-known medical men, including Christiaan N. Barnard and Norman E. Shumway, the pioneers of heart transplants in humans. The surgical techniques employed by Barnard are often traced to Wangensteen's teachings and medical practices. In 1972 Wangensteen helped found the Wangensteen Historical Library of Biology and Medicine at the university. The library contains more than twenty-five thousand volumes, some of which date to the fifteenth century.

BIOGRAPHICAL/CRITICAL SOURCES: Scientific American, October, 1979.

OBITUARIES: New York Times, January 15, 1981; *Publishers Weekly,* February 6, 1981.*

* * *

WANGERMANN, Ernst 1925-

PERSONAL: Born January 22, 1925, in Vienna, Austria; son of Herbert (a barrister) and Margarete (Dostal) Wangermann; married Maria Josefa Fernandez (a teacher), September 7, 1966; children: John Paul, Michael Alexander. *Education:* Balliol College, Oxford, B.A., 1949, M.A. and D.Phil., 1953. *Religion:* "Non-practicing Roman Catholic." *Home:* 1 Hollin

Dr., Leeds LS16 5NE, England. *Office:* School of History, University of Leeds, Leeds LS2 9JT, England.

CAREER: Assistant master at grammar school in Essex, England, 1955-62; University of Leeds, Leeds, England, lecturer, 1962-69, senior lecturer, 1969-77, reader in modern history, 1977—. Visiting professor at University of Wisconsin—Madison, 1968. *Member:* Royal Historical Society, Association of University Teachers. *Awards, honors:* Theodor-Koerner-Preis from Koerner Stiftung, 1974, for work in Austrian social history.

WRITINGS: From Joseph II to the Jacobin Trials, Oxford University Press, 1959, 2nd edition, 1969; *The Austrian Achievement, 1700-1800,* Harcourt, 1973; *Aufklaerung und staatsbuergerliche erziehung* (title means "Enlightenment and Civic Education: Gottfried van Swieten as Reformer of Austrain Education, 1781-1791"), Oldenbourg, 1978.

WORK IN PROGRESS: The Austrian Enlightenment and Its Pamphlet Literature.

SIDELIGHTS: Wangermann wrote: "My main interests are the history of ideas and great ideological movements like the Enlightenment and Marxism. My research, chiefly in Austria, has been on the Austrian aspects of these movements. I believe in the importance of men and movements aspiring to reform society, despite the difficulties and risks entailed, which seem to me dwarfed by the disastrous consequences of resisting social change and worshiping the past. I have a strong attachment to my native land, its history, music, and countryside."

* * *

WARD, Barbara
See JACKSON, Barbara (Ward)

* * *

WARD, Russel (Braddock) 1914-

PERSONAL: Born November 9, 1914, in Adelaide, Australia; son of John Frederick (a school headmaster) and Winifred Florence (Braddock) Ward; married Margaret Alice Ind, September 10, 1939 (divorced May 1, 1968); married Barbara Susan Wood Holloway (a children's writer), January 10, 1970; children: (first marriage) Elizabeth Russel, Mark Russel; (second marriage) Charles Russel, Oliver Braddock, Sally Caroline. *Education:* University of Adelaide, B.A. (with honors), 1936, M.A. (with honors), 1951; University of Melbourne, diploma in education, 1938; Australian National University, Ph.D., 1955. *Politics:* "Radical." *Religion:* Agnostic. *Home:* 275 Beardy St., Armidale, New South Wales 2350, Australia.

CAREER: Teacher at Geelong Grammar School in Victoria, Australia, 1937-39, and at Sydney Grammar School in Sydney, Australia, 1939-41; teacher of history, English, French, and geography at secondary schools in Sydney, 1946-52 and 1956; University of New England, Armidale, Australia, lecturer, 1957-60, senior lecturer, 1960-63, associate professor, 1963-67, professor of history, 1967-79, professor emeritus, 1980—, member of university council, 1960—. *Military service:* Australian Army, Imperial Force, 1942–46. *Member:* Fellowship of Australian Writers (president, 1956), New Theatre League (president, 1941-42), University of New England Teachers Association (president, 1958 and 1959), University of New England Union (president, 1965 and 1966). *Awards, honors:* Ernest Scott Prize from University of Melbourne, 1958, for *The Australian Legend.*

WRITINGS: Man Makes History, Shakespeare Head Press, 1952; *Britons Make an Empire*, William Brooks & Co., 1953; (editor) *Poems Grave and Gay*, William Brooks & Co., 1954; *Three Street Ballads*, Ram's Skull Press, 1957; *The Australian Legend*, Oxford University Press, 1958.

(Editor) *The Penguin Book of Australian Ballads*, Ringwood, 1964; *Australia: The Modern Nation in Historical Perspective*, Prentice-Hall, 1965 (published in Australia as *Australia: A Short History*, Ure Smith, 1967, published as *Black and White*, Landsdowne, 1981); (with Peter O'Shaughnessy and Graeme Inson) *The Restless Years*, Jacaranda Press, 1968; (editor) *Such Was Life: Select Documents in Australian Social History*, Volume I (with John Robertson): *1788-1850*, Ure Smith, 1969, Volume II: *1851-1913*, Alternative Publishing Cooperative, 1980, Volume III: *1914-1980*, Alternative Publishing Cooperative, 1981.

(With Inson) *The Glorious Years*, Jacaranda Press, 1970; (editor and translator) E. Marin La Meslee, *The New Australia*, Heinemann, 1973; (editor and translator) La Meslee, *Socialism Without Doctrine*, Alternative Publishing Cooperative, 1977; *The History of Australia: The Twentieth Century*, Harper, 1977 (published in Australia as *A Nation for a Continent: The History of Australia, 1901-1975*, Heinemann, 1977; published in England as *The History of Australia, 1901-1975*, Heinemann, 1977).

Contributor: T.A.G. Hungerford, editor, *Australian Signpost*, F. W. Cheshire, 1956; A. L. McLeod, editor, *The Pattern of Australian Culture*, Cornell University Press, 1963; C. D. Narasimhaiah, editor, *An Introduction to Australian Literature*, Jacaranda Press, 1965; Cyril Pearl, editor, *Australia*, Angus & Robertson, 1965; I. V. Hansen, editor, *The Tiger and the Rose*, Oxford University Press, 1966; Nancy Keesing, editor, *Transition*, Oxford University Press, 1970; V. G. Venturini, editor, *Australia: A Survey*, Otto Harrassowitz, 1970; *Australia: This Land, These People*, Reader's Digest Association, 1971. Contributor to Australian history journals and *Meanjin Quarterly*. Co-editor of *Australian Dictionary of Biography*, 1969-77.

WORK IN PROGRESS: "I am writing two companion volumes to *A Nation for a Continent* (1977), one from prehistoric times to 1821 and one from 1821-1900. Both will be published by Heinemann and, I expect, by Harper in the U.S.A."

SIDELIGHTS: Ward commented: "I have always been passionately interested in the relationship between literature and history; that is, in the light thrown on each other by the literature of a period and by its social history. Most of what I have written is on this subject in Australia.

"I have always been a radical in politics. For the last decade or two I have been considered by conservatives as a dangerous communist and by younger radicals as a pillar of the 'establishment.'"

BIOGRAPHICAL/CRITICAL SOURCES: J. B. Hirst, editor, *The Australian Legend Revisited*, University of Melbourne, 1978; Rob Pascoe, *The Manufacture of Australian History*, Oxford University Press, 1979.

*   *   *

WARE, Ciji   1942-

PERSONAL: Born May 22, 1942, in Pasadena, Calif.; daughter of Harlan (a writer) and Ruth (an education administrator) Ware; married Stewart C. Billett, 1966 (marriage ended, 1974); married Anthony Cook (a journalist), December 27, 1976; children: (first marriage) James Ware. *Education:* Harvard University, B.A., 1964. *Home and office:* 1305 North Beverly Dr., Beverly Hills, Calif. 90210. *Agent:* Don Congdon, Harold Matson Co., Inc., 22 East 40th St., New York, N.Y. 10016.

CAREER: Worked as associate producer for National Educational Television for "Your Dollar's Worth," 1965-67, and "New Jersey Speaks for Itself," 1967-69; WNAC-TV, Boston, Mass., associate director and writer for "Dave Garroway," 1969; KNBC-TV, Los Angeles, Calif., reporter, c. 1969; writer for NBC-TV for "Dinah's Place," 1969-71; KCET-TV, Los Angeles, producer and host of "Community Issues Forum," 1972-74; consumer reporter for KNXT-TV, Los Angeles, 1974-76; commentator for KABC-Radio, Los Angeles, 1977—. Program host for KCET-TV. Lecturer at University of Southern California. Member of advisory committee to implement California's joint custody law and advisory board of Center for Legal Psychiatry, Santa Monica, Calif. *Member:* Harvard-Radcliffe Club of Los Angeles. *Awards, honors:* Local Emmy Award from Los Angeles Academy of Television Arts and Sciences, 1977, for writing, producing, and hosting "Childstealing"; Silver Gavel Award from American Bar Association, 1980, for article, "Joint Custody: One Way to End the War."

WRITINGS: (With Taylor Hackford) *Joint Custody: One Way to End the War*, Viking, 1981. Author of "Consumer Aware," a column in *New West*. Contributor to magazines and newspapers, including *New West*, *Travel and Leisure*, and *Los Angeles*.

WORK IN PROGRESS: Duchess of Gordon, a novel, publication expected in 1983; "Windmill," a film, with Anthony Cook; "The Duke of Beverly Hills," a film based on the magazine article of the same title, with Cook.

SIDELIGHTS: Ciji Ware told *CA:* "As the daughter of a writer I learned that the only way to survive as a scribe was to be able to work in several media, and never to depend on one employer. So I work as a journalist, writer, and television and radio broadcaster. It means keeping a lot of balls in the air, but then one is never without a ball to *throw* into the air!

"The joint-custody book has been a three-year project which entailed traveling all over the country talking to scores of successful joint custody parents who are the *genuine* experts in how to be parents together—separately—after divorce. *Joint Custody* is a practical, not theoretical, book which, hopefully, will show other parents how to *stay* parents—sharing the joys and the burdens—even though the marriage ends."

AVOCATIONAL INTERESTS: Genealogy, "trashy historical novels," travel (especially England), cooking.

*   *   *

WARREN, Thomas (Bratton)   1920-

PERSONAL: Born August 1, 1920, in Carrizo Springs, Tex.; son of Thomas Clayton (in real estate) and Emma (Russell) Warren; married Faye Brauer (a secretary), October 3, 1941; children: Karen Warren Waters, Jan Warren Coleman, Lindsay Davis. *Education:* Abilene Christian University, B.A. (magna cum laude), 1947; University of Houston, M.A., 1960; Vanderbilt University, M.A., 1967, Ph.D., 1969; also attended Texas Christian University, Southwestern Baptist Theological Seminary, and Harding University. *Politics:* Republican. *Home and office address:* Tennessee Bible College, P.O. Box 865, Cookesville, Tenn. 38501. *Agent:* Jon R. Coleman, Citizens Bank Building, Jonesboro, Ark. 72401.

CAREER: Ordained minister of Church of Christ, 1945; pastor of Churches of Christ in Liberty, Tex., 1947-50, Houston, Tex., 1951-53, and Fort Worth, Tex., 1950-51 and 1953-64; Freed-Hardeman College, Henderson, Tenn., professor of Bible and chairman of department, 1964-71; Harding University, Graduate School, Memphis, Tenn., professor of philosophy of religion, 1971-79; Tennessee Bible College, Cookeville, professor of philosophy of religion, dean of Graduate School, and executive vice-president of college, 1979—. Director of Institute for the Advancement of Christian Theism. *Military service:* U.S. Army Air Forces, aerial navigator, 1942-45; served in the South Pacific; became second lieutenant. *Member:* American Philosophical Association, Philosophy of Science Association, American Academy of Religion, Society of Christian Philosophers, Evangelical Theological Society, Southwestern Philosophical Society, Tennessee Philosophical Association.

WRITINGS: (With L. S. Ballard) *The Warren-Ballard Debate: On Salvation From Sin,* Telegram Book Co., 1952; *Lectures on Church Cooperation,* National Christian Press, Inc., 1958; *Marriage Is for Those Who Love God—And Each Other,* National Christian Press, Inc., 1962; *Our God: A Sun and Shield for Troubled Hearts,* National Christian Press, Inc., 1963; *Do Men Have the Right to Be Wrong?,* National Christian Press, Inc., 1968.

(Editor) *The Church,* Freed-Hardeman College Press, 1970; (editor with Flatt and West) *The Inspiration of the Bible,* National Christian Press, Inc., 1971; *Have Atheists Proved There Is No God?,* Gospel Advocate, 1974; *Biblical Hermeneutics: When Is an "Example" Binding?,* National Christian Press, Inc., 1975; (editor with Garland Elkins) *The Living Messages of the Books of the New Testament,* National Christian Press, Inc., 1976; (editor with Elkins) *The Living Messages of the Books of the Old Testament,* National Christian Press, Inc., 1977; (with A.G.N. Flew) *The Warren-Flew Debate: On the Existence of God,* National Christian Press, Inc., 1977; (editor and contributor) *Your Marriage Can Be Great,* National Christian Press, Inc., 1978; (editor with Elkin) *God Demands Doctrinal Preaching,* National Christian Press, Inc., 1978; (with W. I. Matson) *The Warren-Matson Debate: On the Existence of God,* National Christian Press, Inc., 1979; (editor with Elkins) *The Home as God Would Have It,* National Christian Press, Inc., 1979.

(Editor with Elkins) *The Church: The Beautiful Bride of Christ,* National Christian Press, Inc., 1980; *Sin, Suffering, and God,* National Christian Press, Inc., 1980; *Keeping the Lock in Wedlock,* National Christian Press, Inc., 1980; (editor with Elkins) *Some Modern Sects, Movements, and World Religions,* National Christian Press, Inc., 1981; (with J. E. Barnhart) *The Warren-Barnhart Debate: On Utilitarian Ethics Versus Christian Ethics,* National Christian Press, Inc., 1981; *The Psychological Hedonism of Jeremy Bentham,* National Christian Press, Inc., in press; *The All-Sufficiency of the Bible,* National Christian Press, Inc., in press; *Can Science Prove the Theory of Evolution?,* National Christian Press, Inc., in press; *God's Word Is Truth,* National Christian Press, Inc., in press. Editor of *Spiritual Sword,* 1969—.

WORK IN PROGRESS—All for National Christian Press, Inc.: *The Role of Logic in Religion,* 1983; *The Inspiration of the Bible,* 1983; *A Critique of Atheism,* 1983; *A Critique of Agnosticism,* 1984; *A Critique of Romanticism,* 1984; *The Bible Can Help You to Attain Peace of Mind,* 1984; *Christian Ethics,* 1985; *Christian Ethics—And Biomedical Ethics,* 1985; *Biblical Epistemology,* 1985.

SIDELIGHTS: Warren wrote: "While in the South Pacific I decided to switch my studies from advertising to philosophy and religion. I came to the view that *truth* is what really matters in human life. At present I am especially interested in working on (and presenting) the case for the existence of God; that human beings owe their ultimate origin to the creative work of God, the inspiration of the Bible, logic and its crucial role, and epistemology.

"As affirmed both in the debate with Dr. A.G.N. Flew (professor of philosophy at the University of California, Berkeley), I claim to know that the existence of the God of Judeo-Christian theism can be proved, that human beings owe their ultimate to the miraculous creative activity of God, *not* from non-living, non-purposive, non-intelligent matter. Each individual human being constitutes *proof* (properly reasoned about) that God does exist and that the first human pair was created, not evolved."

AVOCATIONAL INTERESTS: Sports, painting, cartooning.

*   *   *

WASSMER, Arthur C(harles) 1947-

PERSONAL: Born August 8, 1947, in Newark, N.J. *Education:* Barrington College, B.A., 1968; Princeton University, M.A., 1971; University of Washington, Seattle, Ph.D., 1974. *Agent:* Dominick Abel Literary Agency, 498 West End Ave., New York, N.Y. 10024.

CAREER: Clinical psychologist with Arthur C. Wassmer & Associates, Inc. Member of faculty at University of Washington, Seattle; director of Corporate Psychological Services. *Member:* American Psychological Association, Chamber of Commerce.

WRITINGS: Making Contact, Dial, 1978.

*   *   *

WATERMAN, Cary (Martha) 1942-

PERSONAL: Born February 3, 1942, in Bridgeport, Conn.; daughter of James M. (a photographer) and Emily (Siebert) Brown; married Charles K. Waterman (a writer), December 10, 1964; children: Amy, Bridgit, Devin. *Education:* University of Denver, B.A., 1964; Mankato State University, B.S., 1971, M.S., 1981. *Home:* 225 Shaubut St., Mankato, Minn. 56001.

CAREER: Mankato State University, Mankato, Minn., academic coordinator of Upward Bound program, 1979—. Poet-in-residence of Minnesota Poets in the Schools program, 1975-79. *Awards, honors:* Fellow of Minnesota State Arts Board, 1975; grant from Bush Foundation, 1977-78.

WRITINGS: First Thaw (poems), Minnesota Writers Publishing House, 1975; *The Salamander Migration* (poems), University of Pittsburgh Press, 1980. Contributor to *South Dakota Review* and *Moons & Lion Tailes.*

WORKS IN PROGRESS: Calamity Jane Poems; co-writing *Dark Lights the Tiger's Tail,* poems.

SIDELIGHTS: Cary Waterman commented: "I wrote the first poem I remember when I was in the fourth grade. It was about the snowfall. After that I did not let the misunderstanding of parents, teachers, or friends deter me from what I feel is my life effort, although I was about thirty before I actually thought of myself seriously as a writer. There is not much money in poetry, which actually has nothing to do with poetry. I teach in order to survive, but there are many times that I wish I did not have to."

WATKIN, Edward Ingram 1888-1981

OBITUARY NOTICE: Born in 1888 near Manchester, England; died c. March, 1981. Philosopher, essayist, and author. Watkin became a convert to the Roman Catholic faith at the age of twenty and began a long career of studying and writing in the area of Catholic philosophy. His 1935 book, *The Philosophy of Form,* was described in the *London Times* as "a new and independent approach" to problems in Catholic thought. In this book Watkin discusses intuition as the basis for thought. He wrote *The Catholic Centre* to encourage a more vital worship based on liturgical understanding and contemplative prayer. In 1942 he published *An Essay on Catholic Art and Culture,* a book on the culture known as Christendom. In many of his other books and essays Watkin promoted the idea of Catholic humanism. Among his other works are *The Philosophy of Mysticism, The Bow in the Clouds, Theism, Agnosticism and Atheism,* and *Poets and Mystics.* Obituaries and other sources: *Catholic Authors: Contemporary Biographical Sketches,* Volume I: *1930-47,* St. Mary's Abbey, 1948; *London Times,* March 12, 1981.

* * *

WAXMAN, Chaim I(saac) 1941-

PERSONAL: Born February 26, 1941, in New York, N.Y.; son of Nissan and Sara R. Waxman; married Chaya Lifshitz, June 12, 1962; children: Ari, Shani, Dani. *Education:* Yeshiva University, B.A., 1963, M.H.L., 1966; New School for Social Research, M.A., 1965, Ph.D., 1974. *Home:* 2526 Bayswater Ave., Far Rockaway, N.Y. 11691. *Office:* Department of Sociology, Rutgers University, New Brunswick, N.J. 08903.

CAREER: Yonkers Community Action Program, Yonkers, N.Y., community planner, 1965-66; Central Connecticut State College, New Britain, assistant professor of sociology, 1965-72; Brooklyn College of the City University of New York, Brooklyn, N.Y., assistant professor of sociology, 1972-75; Rutgers University, New Brunswick, N.J., assistant professor, 1975-78, associate professor of sociology and chairman of department, 1978—. Chairman of American Jewish Committee task force on Jewish family policy, 1978-79; consultant to Anti-Defamation League of B'nai B'rith and World Zionist Organization.

MEMBER: American Sociological Association, Association for the Sociological Study of Jewry (president, 1979-81), Association for Jewish Studies, American Professors for Peace in the Middle East, Eastern Sociological Society. *Awards, honors:* American scholarship from American Zionist Foundation, 1974.

WRITINGS: (Editor) *Poverty: Power and Politics,* Grosset, 1968; *The End of Ideology Debate,* Funk, 1968; (editor with Michael Curtis, Joseph Neyer, and Allen Pollack) *The Palestinians: People, History, Politics,* Transaction Books, 1975; *The Stigma of Poverty: A Critique of Poverty Theories and Policies,* Pergamon, 1977. Contributor of articles and reviews to sociology and Jewish studies journals. Book review editor of *Transaction/Society;* member of editorial board of *Middle East Review.*

WORK IN PROGRESS: A book on the sociology of American Jewry; a book on American family policy; editing a book on social history and ethnicity, with Joseph B. Maier, for Transaction Books; editing a book on social welfare.

SIDELIGHTS: Waxman told *CA:* "I view my writing as an extension of my teaching; that is, I focus upon an area that is of interest and concern to me and try to provide greater clarity to the issues involved. As an American Jew, I find that American society, Jews, and Judaism are of great importance to me, and I have attempted to add to their understanding and well-being.

"Until relatively recently, most sociologists of ethnic groups in American society were either outsiders of the groups which they studied or they were insiders but ones who viewed their ethnic groups from explicit or implicit assimilationist perspectives. Today, the situation has changed, and I see myself as part of a new breed of sociologists who are survivalist in perspective; that is, we are committed to the survival of the ethnic group, and our professional training enables us to provide richer analysis and understanding. In my work on the sociology of American Jewry, my objective is to explain the historical backgrounds and social and cultural processes which have made that group what it is today in comparison with other ethno-religious groups in American society.

"Because I have deep personal commitments and am fortunate to be healthy and energetic, I am involved in many public and communal activities. In addition to these and my family, I enjoy reading detective and suspense novels, doing crossword puzzles, collecting campaign and other buttons, and I am an amateur numismatist."

* * *

WEBB, Barbara (Helen) 1929-

PERSONAL: Born January 1, 1929, in Darjeeling, India; daughter of Harry Walter (in Indian army) and Helen Acton (Farquharson) Tobin; married John Herbert Webb (a company director), March 17, 1956; children: Sarah Helen, Mary Harriet. *Education:* Educated in Wantage, England. *Politics:* "Fluctuating!" *Religion:* Church of England. *Home:* Arbourtree House, Wombourne, Wolverhampton, West Midlands WV5 9DP, England.

CAREER: Secretary for shipping company and travel agency in Southampton, England, 1948-55; free-lance translator, 1955—, writer, 1958—. Joing organizer of Wombourne Volunteer Bureau, 1972-80; center organizer of British Red Cross Society, 1975-77. Vice-chairman of Standing Conference of Voluntary Social Work Organisations in Staffordshire, 1975-80. *Member:* Royal Cruising Club, Royal Lymington Yacht Club.

WRITINGS: (Editor) *The Yachtsman's Eight-Language Dictionary,* Adlard Coles, 1965, 2nd edition, 1978; *The Beginner's Book of Navigation,* Ward, Lock, 1975; (with Peter Cook) *The Complete Book of Sailing,* Ward, Lock, 1977.

Translator: (From German) Joachim Schult, *Yacht Racing Tactics,* Harrap, 1964; (from German) F. H. Af Chapman, *Architectura Navalis Mercatoria* (title means "Naval Architecture Merchant"), Adlard Coles, 1968; (from German) Otman Schaeuffelen, *Great Sailing Ships,* Adlard Coles, 1969; (from German) Kurt Schubert and Uwe Mares, *Handling the Racing Dinghy,* Nautical Publishing, 1972; (from German) Gunther Grell, *The Beginner's Book of Sailing,* Ward, Lock, 1972; (from German) Hans Fock, *Fast Fighting Boats,* Nautical Publishing, 1973; (from German) *Windsurfing,* Nautical Publishing, 1976; (from German) Hans Donat, *Practical Points on Boat Engines,* Nautical Publishing, 1977; (from French) Daniel Gilles and Michel Malinovsky, *Go Cruising,* Adlard Coles, 1977; (from German) Peter Brockhaus, *Sailboarding,* Adlard Coles, 1978; (from German) Winkler, *This Is Surfboard Sailing,* Nautical Publishing, 1979; (from Dutch) Gerard Dijkstra, *Self-Steering for Yachts,* Nautical Publishing, 1979; (and editor) Ramon Gliewe, *Come on Board,* Frederick Muller, 1981; Rainer Gutjahr, *Sailboard*

Racing, Nautical Publishing, 1981; (and editor) Schult, *The Sailing Dictionary,* Adlard Coles, 1981.

SIDELIGHTS: Barbara Webb wrote: "I have always been interested in languages, so I became involved in translating—mainly from German (relatively few British sailors speak German), but occasionally from French and Dutch. I have been interested in sailing since childhood. I am also deeply involved in local social work activities, especially with the elderly and housebound, in counseling, and in church work."

AVOCATIONAL INTERESTS: Skiing, windsurfing (sailboarding), music, prehistoric monuments, nature.

*　　*　　*

WEBB, James (C. N.)   1946-1980

PERSONAL: Born in 1946 in Edinburgh, Scotland; died May 9, 1980, in Dumfriesshire, Scotland; married Mary Webb. *Education:* Attended Trinity College, Cambridge.

CAREER: Worked as television producer and schoolmaster; full-time writer, 1969—.

WRITINGS: The Flight From Reason, Macdonald, 1971, published as *The Occult Underground,* Library Press, 1974; *The Occult Establishment,* Library Press, 1976; *The Harmonious Circle,* Putnam, 1980. Editor of "The Occult" series, Arno, 1976—. Contributor to *Man, Myth and Magic,* Marshall Cavendish, 1970; and *Encyclopedia of the Unexplained,* McGraw, 1974.

SIDELIGHTS: Webb has made a special study of the complex historical and cultural background of Western occultism, and has documented its relationship to extremist political movements. His in-depth surveys of the ideas and personalities preceding a renewed interest in the occult present an overall view of the problem of the twentieth century as a battleground between reason and unreason.*

*　　*　　*

WEBER, Burton Jasper   1934-

PERSONAL: Born January 30, 1934, in St. Louis, Mo.; son of Sol (a medical doctor) and Mamie Weber; married Helen Shian, September 14, 1959 (divorced, 1978); children: Samuel, Malachi. *Education:* Washington University, St. Louis, Mo., A.B., 1955; University of Minnesota, M.A., 1958, Ph.D., 1965. *Home:* 2030 McTavish, Regina, Saskatchewan, Canada S4S 0A2. *Office:* Department of English, University of Regina, Regina, Saskatchewan, Canada.

CAREER: University of Regina, Regina, Saskatchewan, assistant professor, 1965-70, associate professor, 1970-78, professor of English, 1978—.

WRITINGS: The Construction of Paradise Lost, Southern Illinois University Press, 1971; *Wedges and Wings: The Patterning of Paradise Regained,* Southern Illinois University Press, 1974. Contributor to literature journals.

SIDELIGHTS: Weber told *CA:* "I do not consider critics authors, and do not see why anyone should be interested in them. Unlike the structuralists, I think my subjects infinitely more interesting than myself."

*　　*　　*

WECHSLER, David   1896-1981

OBITUARY NOTICE: Born January 12, 1896, in Lespedi, Romania; died c. May, 1981, in New York, N.Y. Psychologist, educator, and author. For thirty-five years Wechsler was chief psychologist at New York City's Bellevue Hospital,

and he served as a clinical psychologist at New York University's College of Medicine for nearly thirty years before becoming professor there in 1970. As alternatives to conventional IQ tests, he developed a series of intelligence tests that have become standard diagnostic tools, including the Wechsler-Bellevue Intelligence Scale and the Wechsler-Adult Intelligence Scale. His publications include *The Selected Papers of David Wechsler,* which appeared in 1974. Obituaries and other sources: *American Men and Women of Science: The Social and Behavioral Sciences,* 12th edition, Bowker, 1973; *Who's Who in America,* 39th edition, Marquis, 1976; *Time,* May 18, 1981.

*　　*　　*

WEIL, Ann Yezner   1908-1969

OBITUARY NOTICE—See index for *CA* sketch: Born August 31, 1908, in Harrisburg, Ill.; died July 31, 1969. Educator and author. In the twenties, Weil was an elementary school teacher in Illinois and Indiana. She wrote children's books, including *The Silver Fawn, Pussycat's Breakfast, Red Sails to Capri,* and *Eleanor Roosevelt: Courageous Girl.* Obituaries and other sources: *Who Was Who in America,* 5th edition, Marquis, 1973; *Something About the Author,* Volume 9, Gale, 1976.

*　　*　　*

WEISER, Marjorie P(hillis) K(atz)   1934-
(Marjorie P. Katz)

PERSONAL: Born February 6, 1934, in New York, N.Y.; daughter of Joseph (a certified public accountant and attorney) and Cecelia (Klein) Pearle; married Herbert M. Katz, January 5, 1957 (divorced, 1973); married Norman Weiser (a radio producer and public relations manager), November 26, 1976; children: (first marriage) Daniel Seth, Nina Judith. *Education:* Hunter College (now of the City University of New York), B.A., 1955; attended Columbia University, 1955-56. *Politics:* "Generally liberal." *Religion:* Jewish. *Residence:* New York, N.Y. *Agent:* Charlotte Sheedy Literary Agency, 145 West 86th St., New York, N.Y. 10024. *Office:* Prentice-Hall, Inc., 521 Fifth Ave., New York, N.Y. 10175.

CAREER: Rockefeller Foundation, Office of Publications, New York City, editorial trainee, 1956-57; Funk and Wagnalls, New York City, associate editor in trade book department, 1957-60; free-lance writer, 1960-78; Prentice-Hall, Inc., New York City, development editor of college textbooks, 1978—. *Member:* Phi Beta Kappa.

WRITINGS: Ethnic America, H. W. Wilson, 1978; (with Jean S. Arbeiter) *Womanlist: A Book of Lists by, About, of Interest to, and Celebrating Women,* Atheneum, 1981.

Under name Marjorie P. Katz: (with Herbert M. Katz) *Museums, U.S.A.: A History and Guide,* Doubleday, 1965; (with Vivienne Colle) *Vivienne Colle's Make-It-Yourself Boutique,* M.Evans, 1967; (with H. M. Katz) *Museum Adventures* (juvenile), Coward, 1969; *Grace Kelly,* Coward, 1970; *Instant-Effect Decorating,* M. Evans, 1972; *Fingerprint Owls and Other Fantasies,* M. Evans, 1972; (with J. S. Arbeiter) *Pegs to Hang Ideas On* (juvenile), M. Evans, 1973; *Boxes, String, Shells, and Things: Gifts to Make* (juvenile), Macmillan, 1975; *Shaped by Hands: Indian Art of North America* (juvenile), Macmillan, 1975; (contributor) James Beard, Milton Glasser, and Bert Wolf, editors, *The Cook's Catalogue,* Harper, 1975. Contributor to *World Book Encyclopedia.* Contributor to *Woman's Day* and *House Beautiful.*

SIDELIGHTS: Marjorie Weiser wrote: "For me, the challenge of being an editor and writer lies in the opportunity to explore a variety of subject areas, and to present information to specific audiences. The joy of working both with ideas and people can be found in few other occupations—and here it produces a useful lasting product."

BIOGRAPHICAL/CRITICAL SOURCES: New York Times Book Review, March 22, 1981.

* * *

WEISSBERGER, L. Arnold 1907-1981

OBITUARY NOTICE: Born January 16, 1907, in New York, N.Y.; died of an embolism in the lungs, February 27, 1981, in New York, N.Y. Attorney, photographer, and author. Admitted to the bar in 1930, Weissberger became the attorney for such arts and entertainment celebrities as Igor Stravinsky, Laurence Olivier, and Orson Welles. Weissberger also served as chairman of the New Dramatists Inc., president of the Martha Graham Center of Contemporary Dance, and trustee of the Museum of the City of New York. An accomplished photographer as well, Weissberger produced two well-received volumes of portraits, *Close-Up* and *Famous Faces: A Photograph Album of Personal Reminiscences.* He was working on his memoirs, *Double Exposure,* at the time of his death. Obituaries and other sources: *New Yorker,* December 10, 1973; *Who's Who in the World,* 4th edition, Marquis, 1978; *New York Times,* March 1, 1981; *Newsweek,* March 16, 1981.

* * *

WELCH, Stuart Cary 1928-

PERSONAL: Born April 2, 1928, in Buffalo, N.Y.; married Edith Iselin Gilbert, June 14, 1954; children: Adrienne Edith, Thomas Cary, Samuel Manning, Lucia Cary. *Education:* Harvard University, A.B., 1950. *Home:* 63 Sparks St., Cambridge, Mass. 02138; and R.F.D. 1, Contoocook, N.H. 03229. *Office:* Fogg Art Museum, Harvard University, 32 Quincy St., Cambridge, Mass. 02138.

CAREER: Harvard University, Cambridge, Mass., lecturer in Near Eastern and Indian art, curator of manuscripts at library, and curator of Indian and Islamic Art. Consultant to Metropolitan Museum of Art.

WRITINGS: The Art of Mughal India: Painting and Precious Objects, Abrams, 1963; *Painting in British India, 1757-1857,* Museum of Fine Arts, Bowdoin College, 1963; (with Milo Cleveland Beach) *Gods, Thrones, and Peacocks: Northern Indian Painting From Two Traditions, Fifteenth to Nineteenth Centuries,* Abrams, 1965; *A King's Book of Kings: The Shah-nameh of Shah Tahmasp,* Metropolitan Museum of Art, 1972; *A Flower From Every Meadow: Indian Paintings From American Collections,* Asia Society, 1973; *Indian Drawings and Painted Sketches: Sixteenth Through Nineteenth Centuries,* Asia Society, 1975; *Persian Painting: Five Royal Safavid Manuscripts of the Sixteenth Century,* Braziller, 1976; *Royal Persian Manuscripts,* Thames & Hudson, 1976; *Room for Wonder: Indian Painting During the British Period, 1760-1880,* American Federation of Arts, 1978; *Imperial Mughal Painting,* Braziller, 1978; (with Beach) *The Grand Mogul,* Sterling and Francine Clark Art Institute, 1978; (with Martin Bernard Dickson) *The Houghton Shahnameh,* Harvard University Press, 1980.

BIOGRAPHICAL/CRITICAL SOURCES: New York Review of Books, March 22, 1979.

WELLS, Ellen B(aker) 1934-

PERSONAL: Born July 23, 1934, in Berlin, Germany; came to the United States in 1934; daughter of John West (a paleontologist) and Elizabeth (Baker) Wells. *Education:* Oklahoma State University, A.B., 1957; University of California, Berkeley, M.L.S., 1963; McGill University, M.A., 1973. *Home:* 6038 Richmond Highway, No. 713, Alexandria, Va. 22303. *Office:* Dibner Library, NMAH 5016, Smithsonian Institution, Washington, D.C. 20560.

CAREER: U.S. National Library of Medicine, Bethesda, Md., cataloger and curator of prints, 1964-68; McGill University, Montreal, Quebec, acting librarian at Osler Library of the History of Medicine, 1968-72; Cornell University, Ithaca, N.Y., associate librarian for History of Science Collections, 1972-78; Smithsonian Institution, Washington, D.C., chief of special collections, 1979—.

WRITINGS: (Editor) *Horsemanship: A Guide to Information Sources,* Gale, 1979; (editor) *The Horse: A Bibliography,* Garland Publishing, in press. Contributor to *Encyclopedia of Library and Information Science.* Contributor of more than twenty-five articles and reviews to library science and horse journals.

WORK IN PROGRESS: Research on the 1656 Plague of Rome, on scientists' libraries, M. E. Bloch's publications on fishes in the late eighteenth century, bibliography of *Black Beauty,* and eighteenth-century Italian horse training.

SIDELIGHTS: Ellen Wells wrote: "As a librarian responsible for rare books in the history of science and technology, I have an opportunity to do some research into the nature of scientific inquiry and publishing. My avocational and professional interests mesh in my study of horse books.

"I have enjoyed writing about horses in history and on the bibliography of horses and horsemanship because so few others are in the field. Most people seem to repeat what has been written without any critical judgement of their own. The purpose in my bibliographical efforts is to reveal to reading riders the wealth of information and history available beyond the local bookstore or library on an animal of such interest to them. By reading more of the history of the horse I think I am a better rider, and that I can contribute a little bit to the history of technology."

* * *

WELSH, Stanley L. 1928-

PERSONAL: Born September 7, 1928, in Rockport, Utah; son of David Hartwell (a miner) and Amanda (a cook; maiden name, Larson) Welsh; married Stella Leimomi Tree (a city councillor), June 23, 1949; children: Julie Ann, Kent James, Ruth Ellen, Blaine Tree, Kathy Jo, Betty Jean, Martin Larson, Eric Richard. *Education:* Brigham Young University, B.S., 1951, M.S. 1957; Iowa State University, Ph.D., 1960. *Home:* 129 North 1000 E., Orem, Utah 84057. *Office:* Department of Botany, Brigham Young University, Provo, Utah 84601.

CAREER: Brigham Young University, Provo, Utah, professor of botany and range science, 1960—. *Military service:* U.S. Army, 1946-47. *Member:* International Society for Plant Taxonomy, American Society for Plant Taxonomy, Sigma Xi.

WRITINGS: (With Michael Treshow and Glen Moore) *Guide to the Woody Plants of Utah,* Brigham Young University Press, 1964, 2nd edition, Pruett, 1964; (with Bill Ratcliffe) *Flowers of the Canyon Country,* Brigham Young University

Press, 1971; (with Moore) *Utah Plants: Tracheophyta*, Brigham Young University Press, 1973; (with C. A. Toft) *Water Stone Sky: A Pictorial Essay of Lake Powell*, Brigham Young University Press, 1974; *Anderson's Flora of Alaska and Adjacent Parts of Canada*, Brigham Young University Press, 1974; (with Ratcliffe) *Fowers of the Mountain Country*, Brigham Young University Press, 1975; *Utah II*, Graphic Arts Center, 1981. Contributor of articles on various aspects of the plant life of western North America to scholarly journals.

WORK IN PROGRESS: Checklist of Utah Plants, publication expected in 1981; *Utah Flora*, publication expected in 1985.

SIDELIGHTS: Welsh told *CA:* "Writing becomes a part of the life of anyone engaged in teaching and research. I have attempted two different styles, scientific and popular. The scientific papers reach only a small audience; the popular books are more widely read. Words have an intrinsic value alone, and that value is magnified depending on the arrangement within phrases, clauses, and sentences. The affair of thought lies with words."

* * *

WEST, John Frederick 1929-

PERSONAL: Born February 6, 1929, in Ashford, England; son of Frederick (a headmaster) and Lydia Mary (a musical infant teacher; maiden name, Anstey) West; married Vera Eveline Mackenzie, December 21, 1957; children: Sarah Vivienne, Richard Alexander. *Education:* Queen's College, Cambridge, B.A., 1952, M.A., 1959; Ph.D. (awarded by Council for National Academic Awards), 1976. *Home:* 86 Walsingham Rd., Woodthorpe, Nottingham NG5 4NR, England. *Office:* Centre for Extension Studies, Trent Polytechnic, Burton St., Nottingham NG1 4BU, England.

CAREER: Worked as an assistant forest manager in North Borneo timber concession, 1952-53; commercial assistant in Nigeria, 1953-54; laborer in Norway, 1955; teacher at two comprehensive secondary schools in Coventry, England, 1955-62, and at bilateral secondary school in Nottingham, England, 1962-66; Trent Polytechnic, Nottingham, lecturer, 1967-69, senior lecturer in communication, 1969—. *Military service:* British Army, 1947-49. *Member:* Viking Society for Northern Research, Nordic History Group, Foeroya Frooskaparfelag.

WRITINGS: The Great Intellectual Revolution, J. Murray, 1965, Citadel, 1966; (editor) *The Journals of the Stanley Expedition to the Faroe Islands and Iceland in 1789*, Foeroya Frodskaparfelag, Volume I, 1970, Volume II, 1975, Volume III, 1976; (translator) Hedin Bru, *The Old Man and His Sons*, Paul Eriksson, 1970; *Faroe: The Emergence of a Nation*, Paul Eriksson, 1973; (translator and editor) *Faroese Folktales and Legends*, Shetland Publishing, 1980; (translator) William Heinesen, *The Good Hope*, Thule Press, 1981. Contributor to history journals.

WORK IN PROGRESS: Translating major works of Faroese literature; research on the history of the Faroe Islands in the eighteenth century.

SIDELIGHTS: West wrote : "A student interest in mountaineering in Norway led me to an interest in Scandinavian literature and subsequent dedication to the culture of the Faroe Islands (population fifteen thousand in 1900, forty-two thousand in 1980), where I found a creativity comparable during this century with Periclean Athens. Why? How can such creativity be transplanted, and mankind thereby enormously enriched? I would like to find out."

* * *

WHALLEY, Joyce Irene

PERSONAL: Born in Essex, England; daughter of Ernest A. (in government service) and Ellen Louise (Brown) Whalley. *Education:* University of Wales, B.A. (with honors), 1944; University of London, diploma, 1949; also attended Warburg Institute, London. *Religion:* Church of England. *Office:* Victoria and Albert Museum, London SW7 2RL, England.

CAREER: Victoria and Albert Museum, London, England, assistant keeper of library, 1950—. *Military service:* British Army, 1945-47. *Member:* Art Libraries Society, National Art Collections Fund, National Trust (life member), Victorian Society, Children's Books History Society, Beatrix Potter Society, Royal Society for the Protection of Birds, Inland Waterways Association.

WRITINGS: English Handwriting, 1540-1843, H.M.S.O., 1969; *Cobwebs to Catch Flies: Illustrated Books for the Nursery and Schoolroom, 1700-1900*, University of California Press, 1974; *Writing Implements and Accessories*, David & Charles, 1975; *The Pen's Excellencie: Calligraphy in Western Europe and America*, Pentelic, 1980; *Catalogue of Beatrix Potter Collections of the Victoria and Albert Museum*, East/West Publications, 1981. Contributor of articles and reviews to journals.

WORK IN PROGRESS: Editing a sketchbook by Beatrix Potter, publication by F. Warne expected in 1982; a catalogue of the Samuel Pepys collection of calligraphy, Magdalene College, Cambridge, 1983.

SIDELIGHTS: Joyce Whalley commented: "Handwriting and writing implements have for so long been accepted as everyday things that many people have been surprised to find that even handwriting has a history. It is, however, something that everyone does, even if only in signing his name. But because everyone can do it and because it needs little equipment, calligraphy, or the art of fine writing, has become very popular in recent years; some of my publications have intended to provide patterns for would-be exponents as well as indicating the long tradition of fine writing in western Europe and in America. Equally interesting, historically, has been the shared heritage of children's books, the memory of which often remains with people throughout their lives; some of my books have, therefore, dealt with the background to this aspect of early reading among western people.

"Most of my publications have been commissioned as a result of my work at the Victoria and Albert Museum, the national art library where I am in charge of manuscripts and illustrated books of all periods and countries. As an art historian, my travels are inevitably art oriented."

* * *

WHEELWRIGHT, Edward Lawrence 1921-

PERSONAL: Born August 10, 1921, in Sheffield, England; son of Lawrence (a steel worker) and Gladys Wheelwright; married Wendy McGregor, August 17, 1945; children: Helga McGregor Wheelwright Howdin, Sarah Jane Wheelwright Muston. *Education:* University of St. Andrews, M.A. (with first class honors), 1949; attended Harvard University, 1958, University of Toronto, National Institute of Economic and Planning Research (London, England), National Planning Commission (New Delhi, India), and University of Djakarta.

Politics: Socialist. *Religion:* Atheist. *Home:* 14 Somerset St., Mosman, Sydney, New South Wales 2088, Australia. *Office:* Department of Economics, University of Sydney, Sydney, New South Wales 2006, Australia.

CAREER: University of Bristol, Bristol, England, assistant lecturer in economics, 1949-52; University of Sydney, Sydney, Australia, lecturer, 1952-57, senior lecturer, 1957-65, associate professor of economics, 1965—, acting head of department, 1967-68, founder and director of Transnational Corporations Research Project, 1975—. Visiting fellow at Research School of Pacific Studies, Australian National University, 1962; lecturer at University of Malaya and University of Singapore; visiting professor at Di Tella Institute of Economic Research, 1965-66, Institute of Economics, Moscow, Soviet Union, 1966, Academy of Science, Peking, China, 1966-67, and Institute of International Research, University of Chile, 1970-71; lecturer at Catholic University of Buenos Aires. Member of Committee of Enquiry Into Government Procurement Policy, 1973-74; member of Committee of Enquiry Into Australian Manufacturing Industry, 1974-75; United Nations consultant to government of Malaysia. *Military service:* Royal Air Force, 1941-46; became squadron leader; received Distinguished Flying Cross. *Member:* Economic Society, Australian Consumer Association, Teachers Federation, Friends of the Earth.

WRITINGS: Ownership and Control of Australian Companies, Law Book Co. of Australia, 1957; *Industrialisation in Malaysia,* Melbourne University Press, 1965; (editor) *Higher Education in Australia,* F. W. Cheshire, 1965; (with Brian Fitzpatrick) *The Highest Bidder: A Citizen's Guide to Problems of Foreign Investment in Australia,* Lansdowne Press, 1965; (with Judith Miskelly) *Anatomy of Australian Manufacturing Industry,* Law Book Co. of Australia, 1967; (with Bruce McFarlane) *The Chinese Road to Socialism,* Monthly Review Press, 1971; *Radical Political Economy: Collected Essays,* Australia and New Zealand Book Co., 1974; (editor with Ken Buckley) *Essays in the Political Economy of Australian Capitalism,* Australia and New Zealand Book Co., Volume I, 1975, Volume II, 1978, Volume III, 1978, Volume IV, 1980, Volume V, 1982; (editor with Frank J. B. Stilwell) *Readings in Political Economy,* two volumes, Australia and New Zealand Book Co., 1978; *Capitalism, Socialism, or Barbarism?: The Australian Predicament,* Australia and New Zealand Book Co., 1978; (editor with Greg Crough and Ted Wilshire) *Australia and World Capitalism,* Penguin, 1980; (with Crough) *Australia: The Client State,* Allen & Unwin, 1982.

Contributor: *Education for International Understanding,* Australian National Advisory Committee for United Nations Educational, Scientific, and Cultural Organization, 1959; Alex Hunter, editor, *Economics of Australian Industry,* Melbourne University Press, 1963; E. K. Fisk and T. H. Silcock, editors, *The Political Economy of Independent Malaya,* Australian National University Press, 1963; John Andrews, editor, *Australia's Resources and Their Utilisation,* Department of Adult Education, University of Sydney, 1965; (author of introduction) Hylda A. Rolfe, *The Controllers: Interlocking Directorates in Large Australian Companies,* F. W. Cheshire, 1967; V. G. Venturini, editor, *Australia: A Survey,* Institute of Asian Affairs (Hamburg, West Germany), 1970; F. M. Katz and R. K. Browne, editors, *Sociology of Education,* Melbourne University Press, 1970; Keith Hancock, Barry Hughes, and Robert Wallace, editors, *Applied Economics: Readings for Australian Students,* McGraw, 1972; John Playford, editor, *Capitalism in Australia: A Socialist Critique,* Penguin, 1972; Allan Ashbolt, editor, *Her-*

esies, Australian Broadcasting Commission, 1974; (author of introduction) Bob Debus and John Merson, editors, *Transcripts on the Political Economy of Development,* Australian Broadcasting Commission, 1977; Gareth Evans and John Reeves, editors, *Labor Essays 1980,* Drummond Press, 1980; W. E. Willmott, editor, *Essays in Honour of W. Rosenberg,* University of New Zealand Press, 1980; (author of introduction) Len Fox, *Multi-Nationals Take Over Australia,* APCOL, 1981; R. Birrell, D. Hill, and J. Stanley, editors, *Quarry Australia: Who Cares?,* Oxford University Press, 1981. Contributor to journals and popular magazines.

WORK IN PROGRESS: Research on the effect of transnational corporations on the Australian economy and society.

SIDELIGHTS: Wheelwright told *CA:* "My major interest is what makes the world tick. I decided that the main answer is to be found in the study of political economy. The economics profession is dominated by conservative 'dessicated calculating machines' who have no answer to the world's problems. I firmly believe, with John Ruskin, that 'there is no wealth but life'—hence the importance of studying how the other half lives.

"I am now concentrating on the spread of international capitalism and on the reaction to it in various parts of the world by governments, trade unions, consumer organizations, churches, and environmentalists. I see this as a prime mover in shaping the future of the world economically, politically, socially, and culturally."

The Chinese Road to Socialism has been translated into six languages.

AVOCATIONAL INTERESTS: "Early morning swimming in the sea year-round."

*　　　*　　　*

WHELPTON, (George) Eric　1894-1981
(Richard Lyte, John Parry)

OBITUARY NOTICE—See index for *CA* sketch: Born March 21, 1894, in Le Havre, France; died February 13, 1981. Educator, journalist, broadcaster, and author best known for his travel books. Whelpton taught in France at the Ecole des Roches and was head of modern languages at King's College School in England. During World War II he acted as a broadcaster for the British Broadcasting Corp., and later he joined the Political Intelligence Department of the Foreign Office. While living in Italy in 1922, Whelpton founded a newspaper, *The Italian Mail.* He received awards from the Austrian Tourist Board and from the Italian government. He wrote *Summer at San Martino, The Making of a European, The Making of an Englishman,* and *A Happy European.* Obituaries and other sources: *London Times,* February 18, 1981.

*　　　*　　　*

WHITAKER, Rogers E(rnest) M(alcolm)　1899-1981
(E. M. Frimbo)

OBITUARY NOTICE: Born January 15, 1899, in Arlington, Mass.; died of cancer, May 11, 1981, in the Bronx, N.Y. Editor and author. Whitaker joined the staff of the *New Yorker* in 1926, one year after the magazine's inception. As an editor and columnist he influenced the magazine's style for more than fifty years. He wrote "Talk of the Town" pieces, covered Ivy League football games, and reviewed nightclub entertainers in his "Table for Two" column. Whitaker's editing "helped to shape the writing in the magazine during its formative years," a former colleague remarked. "He had an impeccable ear for style and grammar." Whitaker was a railroad buff, and logged nearly three million miles on railroads throughout the world, including every existing railroad in the United States. He wrote a popular *New Yorker* feature about his train adventures under the name E. M. Frimbo. His 1974 book, *All Aboard With E. M. Frimbo,* was co-authored with *New Yorker* colleague Anthony Hiss, and recounts Whitaker's unusual railroad experiences. A critic for the *New York Times Book Review* called the book "a delight" and "a vote for romance." Obituaries and other sources: *New York Times Book Review,* November 17, 1974; *New York Times,* May 12, 1981; *Newsweek,* May 25, 1981.

*   *   *

WHITE, Lionel 1905-

PERSONAL: Born July 9, 1905, in Buffalo, N.Y.; son of Harold and Lena (Ostrander) White; married Helaine Levy, 1947 (marriage ended); married Hedy Bergida, 1970; *children:* January. *Home and office:* 1275 North Hills Dr., Upland, Calif. 91786. *Agent:* Joel Gotler, 91 Sunset Blvd., Los Angeles, Calif. 90069; and John Farquharson Ltd., 8 Bell Yard, London WC2A 2JU, England.

CAREER: Police and general assignment reporter for newspapers in Ohio, including *Cleveland Press, Cleveland Times,* and *Canton Daily News,* 1923-25; reporter, rewrite man, sports editor, and copy editor for newspapers in New York, including *City News, Bronx Home Star, Women's Wear Daily, Poughkeepsie Star,* and *Schenectady Union Star,* 1925-33; secretary to Roy Howard (editorial director of Scripps-Howard newspapers), New York City, 1927; *American Detective,* New York City, editor, beginning 1933; *True* magazine, New York City, editor, 1935-36; Hillman Periodicals, New York City, executive editor, 1936-39; publisher of fact detective magazines, including *World, World Detective,* and *Homicide Detective,* 1940-1951; mystery novelist, 1951—. *Military service:* U.S. Army, served in World War II.

WRITINGS—Novels: *Seven Hungry Men,* Arthur Bernhard, 1952; *The Snatchers,* Fawcett, 1953; *To Find a Killer,* Dutton, 1954, published as *Before I Die,* Tower, 1964; *Love Trap,* New American Library, 1955; *The Big Caper,* Fawcett, 1955; *Clean Break,* Dutton, 1955, published as *The Killing,* Tower, 1964; *Flight Into Terror,* Dutton, 1955; *Operation—Murder,* Fawcett, 1956; *The House Next Door,* Dutton, 1956; *Right for Murder,* Boardman, 1957; *Death Takes the Bus,* Fawcett, 1957; *Hostage for a Hood,* Fawcett, 1958; *Too Young to Die,* Fawcett, 1958; *Coffin for a Hood,* Fawcett, 1958; *Invitation to Violence,* Dutton, 1958; *The Merriweather File,* Dutton, 1959; *Rafferty,* Dutton, 1959; *Run Killer, Run,* Avon, 1959.

Lament for a Virgin, Fawcett, 1960; *Steal Big,* Fawcett, 1960; *The Time of Terror,* Dutton, 1960; *Marilyn K.,* Monarch, 1960; *A Grave Undertaking,* Dutton, 1961; *A Death at Sea,* Dutton, 1961; *Obsession,* Dutton, 1962; *The Money Trap,* Dutton, 1963; *The Ransomed Madonna,* Dutton, 1964; *The House on K Street,* Dutton, 1965; *A Party to Murder,* Fawcett, 1966; *The Night of the Rape,* Dutton, 1967; *The Crimshaw Memorandum,* Dutton, 1967; *Hijack,* Macfadden, 1969.

Death of a City, Bobbs-Merrill, 1970; *The Mexican Run,* Fawcett, 1974; *A Rich and Dangerous Game,* McKay, 1974; *Jailbreak,* R. Hale, 1976.

Other: (Editor with Philip C. Blackburn) Lewis Carroll, *Logical Nonsense: Works, Now, for the First Time, Complete,* Putnam, 1934; *Protect Yourself, Your Family, and Your Property in an Unsafe World,* Books for Better Living, 1974. Contributor of articles to numerous magazines, including *Cosmopolitan, Red Book,* and *True Detective.*

WORK IN PROGRESS: "As little as possible."

SIDELIGHTS: White is considered an expert in the field of "caper" novels, a subgenre of mystery fiction that details the planning, execution, and follow-up of a crime. His novels have been translated into a dozen languages, are available in braille, and have been published in both hardcover and paperback. About twelve of his novels have been made into motion pictures. Movies based on his work include Stanley Kubrick's "The Killing," Jean-Luc Godard's "Pierrot Le Fou," and "Night of the Following Day," which starred Marlon Brando.

White told *CA:* "Fiction writers should stick to fiction, and I am afraid that anything I say may very well be fiction and certainly shouldn't be believed in any case. I do feel that writing is a nice profession if you are too lazy or incompetent to make a living any other way, but, personally, I would prefer sailing, fishing, playing poker, or in fact doing almost anything that would take a minimum of mental and physical effort.

"One piece of practical advice I might give to beginners probably would be to stick to writing bad checks or home for money—both have a high word rate."

*   *   *

WHITEHOUSE, Jeanne 1939-
(Jeanne Whitehouse Peterson)

PERSONAL: Born May 8, 1939, in Walla Walla, Wash.; daughter of Earl Austin (a pharmacist) and Lillian (an educator and counselor; maiden name, Von Pinnon) Whitehouse; married David J. Kammer; children: Frances Elizabeth, Ellen Louise, Catherine Dell. *Education:* Washington State University, B.A., 1961; Columbia University, M.A., 1965; doctoral study at University of New Mexico, 1976—. *Home:* 207 Aliso Dr. N.E., Albuquerque, N.M. 87108. *Office:* c/o Elementary Education, University of New Mexico, Albuquerque, N.M. 87131.

CAREER: Elementary school teacher in Pullman, Wash., 1961-62; U.S. Peace Corps, Washington, D.C., volunteer worker in Sabah, Malaysia, 1962-64; University of New Mexico, Albuquerque, educational director for teacher's aides in Career Opportunity Program, 1971-74; part-time lecturer in children's literature in Albuquerque, 1975—.

WRITINGS—Under name Jeanne Whitehouse Peterson; juveniles: *I Have a Sister, My Sister Is Deaf,* Harper, 1977; *That Is That,* Harper, 1979; *While the Moon Shines Bright,* Harper, 1981.

WORK IN PROGRESS: Several stories.

SIDELIGHTS: Jeanne Whitehouse told *CA* that her books are based on her own experiences: "I have a deaf sister and for many years I wondered how I could share the warm feelings I have for her. My father died when I was ten, and *That Is That* mulls over how it feels to be left behind."

*   *   *

WILBY, Basil Leslie 1930-
(Gareth Knight)

PERSONAL: Born in 1930 in Colchester, England; son of Leslie Bernard (a postal telegraphist) and Constance Mabel (a postal telegraphist; maiden name, Sutherland) Wilby; married Roma Buckley Berryman (a teacher), March 12, 1960; children: Richard Duncan, Rebecca Julia. *Education:* Attended grammar school in Colchester, England. *Politics:* "Romantic *laissez-faire* liberal." *Religion:* "Non-denominational Christian with mystical and ritualistic tendencies.'' *Home:* 8 Acorn Ave., Braintree, Essex, England.

CAREER: Free-lance writer, 1960-65; Longman Group Ltd., Harlow, England, educational representative, 1965-70, university sales manager, 1970-76, further education publisher, 1976—. Member of board of directors of Helios Book Service Ltd. and Helios Book Service Publications Ltd., 1963—; consultant to C. G. Jung Foundation. *Military service:* Royal Air Force, 1948-56; became sergeant. *Awards, honors:* D.Hum. from Sangreal Foundation, 1976.

WRITINGS: (Editor) *The New Dimensions Red Book,* Helios, 1969; *Meeting the Occult,* Lutterworth, 1974.

Under pseudonym Gareth Knight: *A Practical Guide to Qabalistic Symbolism,* Samuel Weiser, 1965; *The Practice of Ritual Magic,* Aquarian, 1969; *Occult Exercises and Practices,* Aquarian, 1969; *Experience of the Inner Worlds,* Helios, 1975; *The Occult: An Introduction,* Kahn & Averill, 1975; *A History of White Magic,* Samuel Weiser, 1979.

Author of "The Pigeon Fancier" (three-act play), first produced in Leicester, England, at Phoenix Theatre, August 29, 1969. Contributor to magazines, including *Light, Atlantean, Sangreal, Quest, Gnostica News,* and *Hermetic Journal.* Editor of *New Dimensions,* 1962-65, 1973-76, and *Quadriga,* 1977—.

WORK IN PROGRESS: A book, *The Secret Tradition in Arthurian Legend;* research on occult philosophy and practice, with public weekend seminars.

SIDELIGHTS: Wilby told *CA:* "My main aim in literary works is to rescue the word 'magic' from its sinister and sensational associations and to present it as a world-view of important practical applications that give great insights into modern religious and scientific thinking, which took a turn for the worse, particularly in the seventeenth century, landing us in the mess we are in today.

"Briefly, when science broke away from the domination of the authoritarian religious establishment that had hitherto prevailed, it received, because of its struggle for intellectual freedom, a considerable materialistic bias. This was compounded by the Cartesian assumption that there is a great divide between 'subjective consciousness' and the 'objective world' and that they are two discrete realities acting somehow in parallel.

"As a result we have misunderstood great scientific thinkers of the past such as Francis Bacon and Isaac Newton. Bacon, commonly regarded as being the father of the scientific method, was in fact more of a Platonist than is nowadays admitted. Similarly, Issac Newton was, besides being perhaps the greatest scientific and mathematical genius of all time, a profound theologian and researcher of alchemy. These facts are either conveniently forgotten nowadays or dismissed as quaint peccadillos.

"However, with the passage of time, a threatening chasm has developed in human thought and practice. The inadequacy of the Cartesian assumptions, which are now so ingrained in our thinking that they appear to be 'common sense,' is being revealed by scientific experiment in the realms of atomic physics, where it is now realized that the observer is an intrinsic part of the phenomena observed. At the same time the new science of ecology shows an awareness that the mechanistic view of the world, resulting in the rape of the world by technological parasites, cannot be much longer countenanced if we are to survive.

"The link between the two polarities of 'objective' and 'subjective' realities lies in a proper understanding of the function of the imagination as a means of perception and 'participative creation.' Most of this was foreseen by the poet and thinker Samuel Taylor Coleridge (1772-1834), whose thought has been admirably synthesized from a vast range of books, articles, lecture notes, notebooks, and marginalia by Owen Barfield in *What Coleridge Thought* (Wesleyan University Press). Before the mid–seventeenth century, which saw the great divide, the linking ground was in 'natural magic'—hence my interest in the subject. Properly understood, it is a 'technology of the imagination' which builds the bridge between spirit and matter. It illuminates, rather than contradicts, both science and religious beliefs.''

AVOCATIONAL INTERESTS: Walking with his dog, music (deputy bandmaster of Bocking Concert Brass, playing flugel horn and glockenspiel, playing the trumpet with Braintree College Big Band, playing jazz piano), numismatics (Indian native states, Ancient India, and Roman Britain), chess.

* * *

WILF, Alexander 1905(?)-1981

OBITUARY NOTICE: Born c. 1905; died c. April, 1981, in Philadelphia, Pa. Political activist, printer, and author. Wilf spent several years in the Middle East working for the establishment of a free Palestine and helping to repatriate European Jews in Palestine. He later operated a printing business in the newly-independent Israel. Wilf wrote *The Ascent of Man* and *The Origin and Destiny of the Moral Species.* Obituaries and other sources: *AB Bookman's Weekly,* April 27, 1981.

* * *

WILKENS, Emily 1917-

PERSONAL: Born May 6, 1917, in Hartford, Conn.; daughter of Morris and Rose (Drey) Wilkens; married Irving L. Levey (a justice), December 21, 1947 (deceased); children: Jane, Hugh. *Education:* Pratt Institute, graduated, 1938. *Home:* 200 East End Ave., New York, N.Y. 10028.

CAREER: King Features Syndicate, New York, N.Y. magazine fashion illustrator, 1938-40; fashion designer for theatre and film industry, beginning 1942. President of Emily Wilkens Young Originals, Young in Figure, Inc., and Emily Wilkens Mantles and Things, Inc. Lecturer; guest on radio and television programs; lecturer and member of boards of directors and trustees at New York Fashion Institute of Technology. *Member:* Costume Institute (founder), Metropolitan Museum of Art, Fashion Group. *Awards, honors:* Coty Fashion Critics Award, 1945; Neiman Marcus Award, 1946; Fashion Trades Award, 1947; award from *Mademoiselle;* Emily Wilkens Chair in External Impressions was established at New York Fashion Institute of Technology, 1965.

WRITINGS: Here's Looking at You!: The Modern Slant on Smartness for the Junior Miss! (edited by Dorothy Roe Lewis), Putnam, 1948; *A New You: The Art of Good Grooming,* Putnam, 1965; *Secrets From the Super Spas,* Grosset, 1976. Author of "A New You," a column syndicated to newspapers in the United States, Canada, and Europe.

BIOGRAPHICAL/CRITICAL SOURCES: America, April, 1946.*

* * *

WILLENSON, Kim Jeremy 1937-

PERSONAL: Born February 10, 1937, in Milwaukee, Wis.; son of Lawrence Alvin and Miriam (Hannah) Willenson;

married Keiko Okubo, December 15, 1965 (divorced); children: Kevin Nori. *Education:* University of Wisconsin, B.S.; Columbia University, M.S. *Politics:* Liberal. *Religion:* Jewish. *Home:* 1638 Cliff Dr., Edgewater, Md. 21037. *Office:* Suite 1220, 1750 Pennsylvania Ave., Washington, D.C. 20006.

CAREER/WRITINGS: Wisconsin State Journal, Madison, Wis., reporter, 1959-61; *Washington Post,* Washington, D.C., reporter, 1962-63; United Press International, New York City, correspondent in Tokyo, Bangkok, Saigon, and Washington, D.C., 1963-74; *Newsweek,* New York City, writer, 1974-78, correspondent in Washington, D.C., 1979—. *Military service:* U.S. Army, 1957-59. *Member:* U.S. Naval Institute. *Awards, honors:* Mary Hemingway Award from Overseas Press Club, 1977, for coverage of war between Somalia and Ethiopia.

WORK IN PROGRESS: The Church of Bombs, an "exposition of the domination of United States' air operations by 'bomber generals' and the resultant waste of military resources on 'strategic' targets."

SIDELIGHTS: Willenson told *CA:* "In some respects, much of my career was shaped by the Indochina War. Asia and its politics and economics remain a subject of considerable interest to me, as do military affairs. I spent about ten years in Asia, and have concentrated, until recently, on foreign and military affairs since returning to the United States in 1972. The fundamental thesis of *The Church of Bombs* is that air power is most effective when used in direct support of tactical surface operations by army, marine, and naval units."

*   *   *

WILLIAMS, Bert Nolan   1930-

PERSONAL: Born August 19, 1930, in Toronto, Ontario, Canada; son of Wesley Abraham (in sales) and Evelyn (Nolan) Williams; married Angela Babando (an executive secretary), December 6, 1953; children: Richard. *Education:* Attended George Williams College (Montreal). *Politics:* "Radical conservative!" *Religion:* None. *Home:* 10 Muirhead Rd., Apt. 504, Willowdale, Ontario, Canada M2J 4P9.

CAREER: Scarborough Board of Education, Scarborough, Ontario, teacher, 1953-67, librarian, 1968-75; teacher, 1976—.

WRITINGS: Food for the Eagle (juvenile), Thomas Nelson, 1970; *Master of Ravenspur* (juvenile), Thomas Nelson, 1970; *The Rocky Mountain Monster* (juvenile), Thomas Nelson, 1973; *Son of Egypt* (juvenile), Scholastic-Tab, 1977. Author of "Brumaire" (three-act play), 1978. Contributor of more than one hundred articles, stories, and poems to magazines.

WORK IN PROGRESS: A murder mystery dealing with Viking relics; a murder mystery about an art tour; a children's fantasy.

SIDELIGHTS: Williams wrote: "My mother loved show business, and wanted me to be another Sammy Davis, Jr., but my complexion was too light. I don't know why I became a writer, but one of my earliest memories was being dragged to movies by my mother and aunt to see whatever was playing. We had three theatres within a couple of blocks, and in those days (early thirties) they showed double bills which changed every second day. As a result, I knew the elements of a story long before I learned to read (at which I was very slow).

"When I became a writer, I read everything I could about how others worked. Katherine Anne Porter read two chapters of the Bible before beginning her daily writing, and Ernest Hemingway sharpened twenty pencils. A good writer knows these things, and then synthesizes. I get up and sharpen twenty Bibles.

"I've written seventeen books, mostly fiction, but including one on military history for children. After tiring of fighting with insensitive children's publishers who not only don't know what children want, but don't even know what *they* want, most of my work is now adult, so I'll have the experience of dealing with insensitive adult publishers. I've written about six hundred short stories, magazine articles on practically *everything,* and poems, of which a hundred or more have seen print. I like writing for magazines, but there's very little market any more.

"I'm deeply concerned about the incredible Soviet military buildup, both in conventional and nuclear armaments, and of the seeming indifference to this on the part of most western leaders. I also worry about the possible breakup of Canada, a land I love very much."

AVOCATIONAL INTERESTS: "I collect toy soldiers, of which I have several thousand, all beautifully displayed in my den, along with a wall covered with paintings of Napoleon's victories. I consider Napoleon to have been the greatest man who ever lived. I also play jazz piano, a hangover from the lessons in all aspects of show business my mother exposed me to."

*   *   *

WILLIAMS, C(hristopher) J(ohn) F(ardo)   1930-

PERSONAL: Born December 31, 1930, in Walsall, England; son of Harold Fardo (a bank manager) and Amy Cecilia (a corsetiere; maiden name, Bottrill) Williams. *Education:* Balliol College, Oxford, B.A., 1954, M.A., 1956, D.Phil., 1965. *Politics:* Labour. *Religion:* Roman Catholic. *Home:* 1 Fossefield Rd., Midsomer Norton, Bath BA3 4AS, England. *Office:* Department of Philosophy, University of Bristol, Bristol BS8 1RJ, England.

CAREER: Downside Abbey, near Bath, England, lecturer in history of philosophy, 1960-62; University of Hull, Hull, England, assistant lecturer, 1962-64, lecturer in philosophy, 1964-66; University of Bristol, Bristol, England, lecturer, 1966-72, reader in philosophy, 1972—. Visiting professor at University of Notre Dame, 1970, 1977, and 1978; member of council of Downside Centre for Religious Studies. *Member:* Downside Symposium Group (foundation member; chairman, 1966-68).

WRITINGS: (Translator) Francois Petit, *The Problem of Evil,* Burns & Oates, 1959; *What Is Truth?,* Cambridge University Press, 1976; *What Is Existence?,* Oxford University Press, 1981; (translator and author of notes) *Aristotle's De Generatione et Corruptione,* Oxford University Press, 1981; (translator and author of notes) Paul of Venice, *Logica Magna, Prima Pars, Tractatus XIV: "On the Necessity and Contingency of the Future,"* Oxford University Press, in press. Contributor to philosophy journals. Editor of *Analysis,* 1971-76.

WORK IN PROGRESS: "I am developing ideas about identity, and a book, *What Is Identity?,* could emerge as a result of this. A long-term ambition is to write a book on the concepts of nature and person as used in the theology of the Trinity and of the Incarnation."

SIDELIGHTS: Williams wrote: "After reading 'Greats' at Oxford I trained for three years for the Roman Catholic priesthood, finally in the novitiate at Downside Abbey. Polio made ordination impossible (friends have called me a monk *manque*). Philosophy was something to fall back on and, though boring at times, has provided a considerable amount of fun. I enjoy yearly visits to France, where I am spoiled by a community of nuns. I believe, with Wittgenstein, that most metaphysics comes from misunderstood syntax."

*   *   *

WILLIAMS, Eric Eustace   1911-1981

OBITUARY NOTICE: Born September 25, 1911, in Port of Spain, Trinidad; died of a heart attack, March 29, 1981, in St. Anne, Trinidad. Historian, educator, politician, Prime Minister of Trinidad and Tobago, and author of books on the Caribbean. Following the completion of his doctoral degree at Oxford University, Williams taught for fourteen years at Washington's Howard University as a professor of social and political science. He returned to his native Trinidad in the mid-1950's and soon organized the colony's first political party. In 1956, with his party in power, Williams was appointed Chief Minister of Trinidad and Tobago and immediately began working to raise the colony's standard of living and to improve social and economic conditions. He also worked toward winning independence from Great Britain for his two-island territory. In 1962 Williams became Prime Minister of the newly-independent Trinidad and Tobago, and continued to stress improvements for the new nation. The *New York Times* observed that Williams, as leader of Trinidad and Tobago, "moderately and almost totally moved peacefully toward a democratic socialist vision of reality." A respected scholar, Williams wrote several definitive texts on the Caribbean region and its history, including *The Negro in the Caribbean, Capitalism and Slavery, History of the People of Trinidad and Tobago,* and *British Historians and the West Indies.* His autobiography, *Inward Hunger,* appeared in 1969. Obituaries and other sources: *Current Biography,* Wilson, 1966; *The International Who's Who,* Europa, 1978; *Who's Who in the World,* 4th edition, Marquis, 1978; *New York Times,* March 31, 1981; *Time,* April 13, 1981; *Newsweek,* April 13, 1981.

*   *   *

WILLIAMS, F(rederick) Winston   1935-

PERSONAL: Born July 13, 1935, in New York, N.Y.; son of Donald Rowe and Elizabeth (Winston) Williams; married Maria Lana Reyes, April 7, 1962 (marriage ended, 1975); children: Elizabeth, Frederick Winston, Jr., Philip, Carolyn Anne. *Education:* Attended Trinity College, Hartford, Conn., 1954-56. *Politics:* Democrat. *Religion:* "Unity." *Home:* 69 South Main St., Centerville, Mass. 02632. *Office:* Chester A. Crosby, Bridge St., Osterville, Mass.

CAREER: Victoria School, Quezon City, Philippines, founder and member of board of trustees, 1964; associated with Chester A. Crosby Boat Yard, Osterville, Mass.

WRITINGS: Nantucket Then and Now, Dodd, 1976. Contributor to magazines in the Philippines and the United States, including *National Geographic* and *Connecticut.*

WORK IN PROGRESS: One Life Within a Lifetime, an autobiography covering his years as a sailor, and his experiences with alcoholism, reincarnation, and spirituality, publication expected in 1982; a collection of short stories, publication expected in 1983.

SIDELIGHTS: Williams wrote: "My autobiography is a manifestation of my beliefs and values as a writer and individual. Having lived a full and adventurous life, including sailing around the world on a windjammer and living in foreign countries for fifteen years, I feel I have important statements

to make. Using my life story as a frame of reference, I relate how I have come to believe internal success is more important than external success."

*   *   *

WILLIAMS, (David) Gwyn   1904-

PERSONAL: Born August 24, 1904, in Port Talbot, Wales; son of Evan (a builder and contractor) and Sarah Jane (Merchant) Williams; married, 1928 (marriage ended); married second wife, 1949. children: Edward David, Ijan Roderick John, Teleri (daughter), Lowri (daughter), Gwydion (son). *Education:* University College of Wales, Aberystwyth, B.A., 1925; Jesus College, Oxford, M.A., 1944. *Home:* Treweithan, Trefenter, Aberystwyth, Cardiganshire, Wales. *Agent:* Curtis Brown Ltd., 1 Craven Hill, London W2 3EP, England.

CAREER: Teacher of English at schools in Egypt, 1927-35; University of Cairo, Cairo, Egypt, lecturer in English literature, 1935-42; University of Alexandria, Alexandria, Egypt, assistant professor of English, 1942-51; free-lance writer, broadcaster, and lecturer, 1951-56; University of Libya, Benghazi, professor of English, 1956-61; University of Instanbul, Istanbul, Turkey, professor of English literature, 1961-69; free-lance writer, broadcaster, and lecturer, 1969—. *Member:* Yr Academi Gymreig. *Awards, honors:* Major literature award from Welsh Arts Council, 1977, for "distinguished contribution to the literature of Wales."

WRITINGS: An Introduction to Welsh Poetry From the Beginning to the Sixteenth Century, Dufour, 1953; *This Way to Lethe* (novel), Faber, 1962; *Green Mountain: An Informal Guide to Cyrenaica and Jebel Akhdra,* Faber, 1963; *Turkey: A Traveller's Guide and History,* Faber, 1967; *Inns of Love: Selected Poems,* Christopher Davis, 1970; *The Avocet* (novel), Christopher Davies, 1970; *Eastern Turkey,* Faber, 1972; *Foundation Stock* (poems), Gomer Press, 1974; *Turci a'i phobl* (title means "Turkey and Its People"), Gwasg y dref wen, 1975; *Two Sketches of Womanhood* (stories), Christopher Davies, 1975; *The Land Remembers: A View of Wales,* Faber, 1977; *An Introduction to Welsh Literature,* University of Wales Press, 1978; *Choose Your Stranger* (poems), Alun Books, 1979; *Y ddefod goll* (poems; title means "The Lost Rite"), Alun Books, 1981; *Person and Persona,* University of Wales Press, 1981; *ABC of (D)GW* (autobiography), Gwasg Gomer, 1981.

Editor: *Presenting Welsh Poetry: An Anthology of Welsh Verse in Translation and of English Verse by Welsh Poets,* Dufour, 1959; (also translator) *The Burning Tree: Poems From the First Thousand Years of Welsh Verse,* Faber, 1956, revised edition published as *Welsh Poems: Sixth Century to 1600,* 1973, University of California Press, 1974; *Troelus a Chresyd* (title means "Troilus and Cressida"), Gwasg Gomer, 1976; (also translator) *To Look for a Word: Collected Translations From Welsh Poetry,* Gomer Press, 1976.

Translator: *The Rent That's Due to Love* (selected Welsh poems), Editions Poetry London, 1950; (anonymous) *Against Women,* Golden Cockerel, 1953; William Cynwal, *In Defense of Woman: A Welsh Poem,* Golden Cockerel, 1958.

WORK IN PROGRESS: ABC(D)GW, a "Welsh revision of my autobiography"; *El Hadad,* a novel in Welsh; *With a Tongue in Each Cheek,* a bilingual selection of new poems.

SIDELIGHTS: Williams told *CA:* "A creative artist attempts to place himself in relation to what appears to be an absurd world. The more varied his interests and the more human relationships he enjoys, the more directions he will follow to achieve some integration. My lifelong interest in Shakespeare culminated in *Person and Persona.* A growing awareness of 'Welshness' has led me to more writing in my first language, Welsh.''

BIOGRAPHICAL/CRITICAL SOURCES: Times Literary Supplement, January 9, 1981.

*   *   *

WILLIAMS, Robert Deryck   1917-

PERSONAL: Born November 27, 1917, in Birmingham, England; son of Robert (a solicitor) and Eileen (Parkin) Williams; married Grace Mary Sheard, July 15, 1945 (died, 1979); children: Margaret Jane, Susan Mary Williams Martin, Elizabeth Caroline. *Education:* St. John's College, Cambridge, B.A. (with first class honors), 1939, M.A., 1945. *Office:* Department of Classics, University of Reading, Reading, Berkshire, England.

CAREER: University of Reading, Reading, England, lecturer, 1945-71 professor of classics, 1971—. Visiting professor at University of Chicago, 1964-5, Australian National University, 1966, Pennsylvania State University, 1968, 1971, Melbourne University, 1975, William and Mary College, 1978, University of Otago (New Zealand), 1980. *Military service:* Royal Air Force, flying officer, 1941-45. *Member:* Classical Association (president, 1980-81), Virgil Society (president, 1972-76).

WRITINGS: (Editor and author of commentary) Virgil, *Aeneid V,* Clarendon Press, 1960; (editor and author of commentary) Virgil, *Aeneid III,* Clarendon Press, 1962; (editor and author of introduction and notes) Virgil, *Aeneid I-VI,* Macmillan, 1972; (editor and author of commentary) Statius, *Thebaid X,* E. J. Brill, 1972; (editor and author of introduction and notes) Virgil, *Aeneid VII-XII,* Macmillan, 1973; *Aeneas and the Roman Hero,* Macmillan, 1973; (author of introduction) Virgil, *Aeneid,* Australian Broadcasting Commission, 1977; (editor and author of introduction and notes) Virgil, *Eclogues and Georgics,* Macmillan, 1980. Contributor to classical journals.

WORK IN PROGRESS: Continuing research in Virgil.

*   *   *

WILLIAMSON, David Keith   1942-

PERSONAL: Born February 24, 1942, in Melbourne, Australia; son of Keith (a bank official) and Elvie (Armstrong) Williamson; married Carol Ann Cranby, 1965 (divorced, 1972); married Kristin Ingrid Lofven (a journalist), May 29, 1974; children: Rebecca, Matthew, Rory. *Education:* Monash University, B.E., 1964. *Home:* 79 Louisa Rd., Birchgrove, New South Wales 2041, Australia. *Agent:* Curtis Brown Ltd., 86 William St., Sydney, New South Wales 2021, Australia.

CAREER: General Motors, Melbourne, Australia, design engineer, 1965; lecturer in mechanical engineering at Swinburne College of Technology, 1966-72; writer, 1972—. Chairman of Australian National Playwrights Conference, 1979-80. *Member:* Australian Writers Guild (president, 1979-80). *Awards, honors:* Two awards from Australian Writers Guild for "The Removalists," both 1972, one for "Don's Party," 1973, two for "The Club," both 1978, and one for "Travelling North," 1980; shared George Devine Award from Royal Court Theatre, 1972, for "The Removalists"; most promising playwright award from *London Evening Standard,* 1973, for "The Removalists"; Eric Award from Melbourne Critics, 1974, for "Jugglers Three"; award from Australian Film Institute, 1975.

WRITINGS—Plays: *The Removalists* (two-act; first produced in Melbourne, 1971; produced in London at Royal Court Theatre, 1973; produced Off-Broadway at Actors Playhouse, 1973), Currency Press, 1972; *Don's Party* (two-act; first produced in Melbourne, 1971; produced in London at Royal Court Theatre, 1975), Currency Methuen, 1973; *"The Coming of Stork"; "Jugglers Three"; "What If You Died Tomorrow?": Three Plays* (contains "The Coming of Stork," first produced in Melbourne, 1970; "Jugglers Three, " first produced in Melbourne, 1972; "What If You Died Tomorrow" [two-act], first produced in Melbourne, 1973, produced in London at Comedy Theatre, 1974), Eyre Methuen, 1974; *The Bad Life,* Queenston, 1975; *The Department* (two-act; first produced in Adelaide, Australia, at the Playhouse, 1974), Currency Press, 1975; *A Handful of Friends* (two-act; first produced in Adelaide at the Playhouse, 1976), Currency Press, 1976; *The Club* (two-act; first produced in Washington, D.C., at Kennedy Center, 1978, produced on Broadway at Lyceum Theatre, 1978), Currency Press, 1978; "Travelling North" (two-act), first produced in London at Lyric Hammersmith Theatre, 1980.

Screenplays: "Stork," released by Tim Burstall and Roadshow, 1971; "The Removalists," released by Margaret Fink Productions, 1974; "Petersen," released by Tim Burstall and Roadshow, 1974; "Don's Party," released by Phillip Adams and Jack Lee, 1976; "Eliza Frazer," released by Tim Burstall and Roadshow, 1976; "The Club," released by South Australian Film Corp., 1980; "Partners," released by Tim Burstall and Associates, 1981.

WORK IN PROGRESS: A screenplay tentatively entitled "Pharlap."

SIDELIGHTS: Williamson told *CA:* "I'm spending approximately equal amounts of time on stage and film writing— very different types of writing that don't really complement each other; they provide two distinct types of experience. By the time I've had a gutful of one I can thankfully turn to the other."

*   *   *

WILSON, (Archibald) Duncan   1911-

PERSONAL: Born August 12, 1911, in Winchester, England; son of Archibald Edward (a schoolmaster) and Ethel (Schuster) Wilson; married Elizabeth Ann Martin Fleming, July 17, 1937; children: Catherine Wilson Barlow, David Fleming (deceased), Elizabeth Wilson Lupu. *Education:* Balliol College, Oxford, B.A., 1934, M.A., 1971. *Home:* Cala na Ruadh, Port Charlotte, Islay, Argyll PA48 7TS, Scotland.

CAREER: Teacher of classics at private boys' school in London, England, 1936-37; British Museum, London, assistant keeper in department of manuscripts, 1937-39; associated with central secretariat of Ministry of Information, London, 1939, and with press section of Ministry of Economic Warfare, London, 1939-41; Foreign Office, London, 1941-45, began as deputy, became head of German section in department of political intelligence; Control Commission for Germany, Berlin, chief British controller of press and radio, 1945-46; Foreign Office, London, first secretary in German political department, 1946-47, first secretary in Political Division of Control Commission for Germany, 1947-49, head of German commercial department, 1949-51, counselor at British embassy in Belgrade, Yugoslavia, 1951-53, head of economic relations department, 1954-55, director of research and acting librarian, 1955-57, British charge d'affaires in Peking, China, 1957-59, assistant under-secretary, 1960-64; ambassador to Yugoslavia, 1964-68; ambassador to the Soviet

Union, 1968-71; Cambridge University, Cambridge, England, master of Corpus Christi College, 1971-80; writer, 1980—. Traveling fellow at Queen's College, Oxford, 1934-35, and visiting fellow at Harvard University, 1959-60. Chairman of United Kingdom Council on Overseas Student Affairs, 1972-75, and Committee on Public Records, 1978-80; member of Standing Commission on Museums and Galleries, 1973-78; member of board of governors of King's School, Canterbury, England, 1972-80. *Member:* American Academy of Political and Social Science (fellow). *Awards, honors:* Grand Cross of Order of St. Michael and St. George, 1971.

WRITINGS: (With wife, Elizabeth Wilson) *Federation and World Order,* Thomas Nelson, 1939; (editor) *Communist China: Policy Documents, 1955-59,* Harvard University Press, 1962; *Life and Times of Vuk Stefanovic Karadzic,* Oxford University Press, 1970; *Leonard Woolf: A Political Biography,* Hogarth, 1978; *Tito's Yugoslavia,* Cambridge University Press, 1980. Contributor to *International Affairs.*

WORK IN PROGRESS: The Life of Gilbert Murray, "Hellenist and League of Nations enthusiast," completion expected in 1983.

SIDELIGHTS: Wilson wrote: "My written work has resulted mainly from my working career as a diplomat. I have also been interested in attempts to set up international organizations to regulate the conduct of the nation-states. My first book was a very naive expression of concern about this subject. *Leonard Woolf* was commissioned largely as a result of chance connections with friends. I was induced to take it on partly because of my interest in him as one of the founders of the League of Nations; my work as under-secretary at the Foreign Office included United Nations affairs.

"I am writing now on Gilbert Murray, again on commission. This study will, I hope, show him as a pioneer in the field of 'intellectual cooperation' with the League of Nations framework, as someone who recognized pretty realistically the limits of the possibilities of this sort of work, as a great worker in the field of public education, and as a passionate believer in the need to 'open up' the very narrow curriculum of classical studies in which so many British public servants were brought up at the end of the nineteenth and beginning of the twentieth centuries.

"My other main interest has been in music. Our younger daughter studied in Moscow, and my wife and I have many friends among Russian musicians, both inside and outside Russia."

*   *   *

WILSON, Ellen (Janet Cameron)   ?-1976

OBITUARY NOTICE—See index for *CA* sketch: Born in Pittsburgh, Pa.; died December 17, 1976. Educator and author. Wilson began her career as a teacher of English in 1931. A writer of children's books, she specialized in fiction and biographies. Her works include *Annie Oakley: Little Sure Shot, American Painter in Paris: A Life of Mary Cassatt,* and the "Three Boys" series, which is comprised of such books as *Three Boys and the Remarkable Cow.* Obituaries and other sources: *Something About the Author,* Volume 9, Gale, 1976. (Date of death provided by husband, William E. Wilson.)

*   *   *

WILSON, Eugene Smith   1905-1981

OBITUARY NOTICE: Born in 1905 in St. Louis, Mo.; died February 24, 1981, in Amherst, Mass. Educator and author.

Wilson joined the Amherst College administration in 1939 and became dean of admissions there in 1946, a position he held until his retirement in 1972. His numerous books include *After College What?, College Ahead!,* and *The College Student's Handbook.* Obituaries and other sources: *New York Times,* February 25, 1981.

*   *   *

WILSON, Francesca Mary   1888-1981

OBITUARY NOTICE: Born in 1888 in Newcastle-on-Tyne, Northumberland, England; died c. April, 1981. Welfare officer, educator, and author. Wilson devoted her life to helping the victims of wars. She served as a relief worker in the Russian famine following World War I, worked with refugees from the Spanish Civil War, and, as chief welfare officer, helped survivors of World War II's Dachau concentration camp. Some of her books, such as *In the Margins of Chaos* and *Aftermath,* tell of her experiences as a relief worker. Among her other publications are *Strange Island: Britain Through Foreign Eyes, 1395-1940, They Came As Strangers: The Story of Refugees in the British Isles,* and *Rebel Daughter of a Country House.* Obituaries and other sources: *London Times,* April 22, 1981.

*   *   *

WINEARLS, Jane   1908-

PERSONAL: Born January 29, 1908, in London, England; daughter of Henry Percival and Mabel Ellen (Bune) Winearls; married George Willing, August 5, 1939 (deceased); children: Ronald Murray (stepson). *Education:* Attended high school in London, England. *Politics:* "None, vote Liberal in desperation." *Religion:* "None in orthodox form. I believe in creative vitality in disciplined form." *Home:* 109 Belgrave Rd., London S.W.1, England.

CAREER: Worked at Court Photographers, London, England, 1925-31; free-lance teacher of dance, 1932-65; Studio Dance Co., England, founder and performer, 1934-65; University of Birmingham, Birmingham, England, lecturer in dance, 1965-78.

WRITINGS: Modern Dance: The Jooss Leeder Method, A. & C. Black, 1958, 2nd edition, 1968; *Modern Dance Studies: Dance Notation,* Oxford University Press, 1975; *Choreography, the Art of the Body: An Anatomy of Express,* Dance Book Shop (London), in press. Contributor of articles and reviews to dance magazines and scholarly journals.

SIDELIGHTS: Jane Winearls commented: "I am motivated by an obsessive interest in the what, why, how, where, and when of human movement elevated to the sophisticated art of dance. I have worked in Germany, Switzerland, and South Africa, and have conducted research in France and Italy. I have been pushed unwillingly into pioneering, owing to my being a divine discontent, and from the points of view of many frineds I have ruined my life for dance. What I have really done is found it, through dance. One must create or die, and to do so, must serve one's art and utilize one's gift with total devotion."

AVOCATIONAL INTERESTS: Reading, playing piano, singing.

*   *   *

WINSLOW, Ron(ald A.)   1949-

PERSONAL: Born October 27, 1949, in Defiance, Ohio; son of Ronald A. (an assistant school superintendent) and Doris (a credit manager; maiden name, Long) Winslow; married Carol Chapman, October 5, 1974 (divorced, 1980). *Education:* University of New Hampshire, B.A., 1971. *Home address:* P.O. Box 853, Durham, N.H. 03824. *Agent:* Philippa Brophy, Sterling Lord Agency, 660 Madison Ave., New York, N.Y. 10021. *Office:* Department of English, University of New Hampshire, Durham, N.H. 03824.

CAREER: Providence Journal, Providence, R.I., staff writer, 1971-78; University of New Hampshire, Durham, assistant professor of English, 1978—. *Awards, honors:* News writing awards from regional unit of United Press International, 1975, for "A Couple Separates to Survive," and Associated Press, 1978, for "Tuesday, December 13, 2:57 A.M.: Fire at Providence College"; citation from Save the Bay, 1977, for environmental reporting.

WRITINGS: Hard Aground: The Story of the "Argo Merchant" Oil Spill, Norton, 1978; *Open and Shut* (nonfiction), Norton, 1981. Contributor to *Boston* and newspapers, including *New York Times.*

WORK IN PROGRESS: Research on the environment, medicine, and education.

SIDELIGHTS: Winslow wrote: "By selecting interesting people and exciting stories, I like to write about important subjects, both to inform and entertain an intelligent, but general audience. *Hard Aground* is an adventure story about an oil spill; *Open and Shut* is a bizarre crime story which answers the question, 'How can lawyers defend someone they know is guilty?' It's important not to write down to an audience, but to respect readers while recognizing that they are not experts about every subject. I also think it's important to write from an informed, but general, point of view. It gives me the opportunity to ask the obvious questions that often yield fresh insights the experts miss.

BIOGRAPHICAL/CRITICAL SOURCES: Vineyard Gazette, August, 1978.

*   *   *

WINTER, David Brian 1929-

PERSONAL: Born November 19, 1929, in London, England; son of Walter George (a civil servant) and Winifred (Oughton) Winter; married Christine Ellen Martin (an educational nurse), April 15, 1961; children: Philip, Rebecca, Adrian. *Education:* King's College, London, B.A. (with honors), 1953; Institute of Education, London, post-graduate certificate in Education, 1954. *Religion:* Church of England. *Home:* 47 Holdenhurst Ave., London N12 0JA., England. *Agent:* Edward England, 12 Highlands Close, Crowborough, Sussex, England. *Office:* BBC-Radio, Broadcasting House, London W1A 1AA, England.

CAREER: Teacher of English and religious education at Ware Church of England secondary school in Ware, England, 1954-58, and at Tottenham County mixed grammar school in London, England, 1958-59; *Crusade,* London, editor, 1959-71; British Broadcasting Corp. (BBC-Radio), London, senior producer, 1971—. *Military service:* Royal Air Force, Supreme Allied Command, 1948-50. *Member:* Arts Centre Group (executive chairman). *Awards, honors:* Sandford St. Martin Open Award for radio, 1980, for radio series "God in My Language."

WRITINGS—All nonfiction, except as noted: *The Christian's Guide to Church Membership,* Moody, 1963; *Ground of Truth,* Falcon Books, 1964; *Old Faith, Young World,* Hodder & Stoughton, 1966; *For All the People,* Hodder & Stoughton, 1966; *New Singer, New Song* (biography of Cliff

Richard), Word Books, 1967; (with Stella Linden) *Two a Penny* (novel), Tyndale House Publishers, 1969; *What Now?,* Scripture Union, 1969, published as *How to Walk With God,* Harold Shaw, 1978.

Closer Than a Brother, Harold Shaw, 1971 (published in England as *Laurie, the Happy Man,* Hodder & Stoughton, 1971); (with John Bryant) *Well, God, Here We Are Again,* Hodder & Stoughton, 1971; *Hereafter,* Harold Shaw, 1972; (editor) *Matthew Henry's Commentary,* two volumes, Clifford E. Barbour, 1975; *One Hundred Days in the Arena,* Harold Shaw, 1978 (published in England as *After the Gospels,* Mowbray, 1978); *But This I Can Believe,* Hodder & Stoughton, 1980.

WORK IN PROGRESS: The Case for Christ, publication expected by Hodder & Stoughton.

SIDELIGHTS: Winter wrote: "Apart from my one novel, all of my books have been concerned with communicating Christianity in the contemporary culture. *Hereafter* has been published in seven languages. It is a case for 'life beyond death.' Since it was written in 1972, the increase of interest in the subject has been spectacular. Perhaps we are replacing the exploration of outer space with an exploration of 'inner spaces' in our own lives—our deep and hidden inner secrets and fears."

*   *   *

WINTER, R. R.
See WINTERBOTHAM, R(ussell) R(obert)

*   *   *

WINTERBOTHAM, R(ussell) R(obert)   1904-1971
(Russ Winterbotham; Ted Addy, J. Harvey Bond, Franklin Hadley, R. R. Winter, pseudonyms)

OBITUARY NOTICE—See index for *CA* sketch: Born August 1, 1904, in Salina, Kan.; died June 9, 1971. Journalist, cartoonist, and author. Winterbotham wrote for newspapers in several states, including Kansas, Missouri, Illinois, Oklahoma, New Mexico, and South Dakota. He was the author of the comic strips "Captain Midnight," "Captain Easy," "Red Ryder," "Chris Welkin," "Vic Flint," and "The Good Guys." Winterbotham wrote the "Little Blue Book" series, which is comprised of such works as *Curious and Unusual Deaths.* His other books include *Bye-Bye Baby, If Wishes Were Hearses, Tom Beatty: Ace Detective Scores Again, Keep 'Em Flying,* and *Len Robbins and the Phantom Dirigible.* Obituaries and other sources: *Something About the Author,* Volume 10, Gale, 1976.

*   *   *

WINTERBOTHAM, Russ
See WINTERBOTHAM, R(ussell) R(obert)

*   *   *

WOESTEMEYER, Ina Faye
See Van NOPPEN, Ina (Faye) W(oestemeyer)

*   *   *

WOLF, William

PERSONAL: Born in Somerville, N.J.; married Irene Siotis, 1954 (marriage ended, 1971); married Lillian Kramer (an editor and researcher), September 18, 1971; children: Julie, Karen. *Education:* Rutgers University, B.A. *Home and office:* 155 West 68th St., New York, N.Y. 10023.

CAREER: Cue, New York City, film critic, 1964-80; New York University, New York City, lecturer in film, 1973—. Adjunct professor at St. John's University, 1972—. *Member:* National Society of Film Critics, New York Film Critics Circle (past chairman).

WRITINGS: The Marx Brothers, Pyramid Publications, 1976; (with wife, Lillian Kramer Wolf) *Landmark Films: The Cinema and Our Century,* Paddington, 1979. Author of "On Film," a column in *New York.* Contributor to *Encyclopedia Americana* and *Collier's Encyclopedia.* Contributing editor of *New York,* 1980—.

*   *   *

WOLFF, Robert Paul   1933-

PERSONAL: Born December 27, 1933, in New York, N.Y.; son of Walter Harold (a teacher) and Charlotte (a secretary; maiden name, Ornstein) Wolff; married Cynthia Griffin (a professor of literature), June 9, 1962; children: Patrick Gideon, Tobias Barrington. *Education:* Harvard University, A.B., 1953, A.M., 1954, Ph.D., 1957, postdoctoral study, 1958. *Politics:* Socialist. *Religion:* None. *Home:* 16 Garfield Rd., Belmont, Mass. 02178. *Office:* Department of Philosophy, Brandeis University, Waltham, Mass. 02254.

CAREER: Harvard University, Cambridge, Mass., instructor in philosophy and social science, 1958-61; University of Chicago, Chicago Ill., assistant professor of philosophy, 1961-63; Wellesley College, Wellesley, Mass., visiting lecturer in philosophy, 1963-64; Columbia University, New York, N.Y., associate professor, 1964-69, professor of philosophy, 1971-81; Brandeis University, Waltham, Mass., professor of philosophy, 1981—. Visitng professor at Rutgers University, 1967-68; Matchette Lecturer at University of Wisconsin—Madison, 1969; Raphael P. Demos Memorial Lecturer at Vanderbilt University, 1974; Kant Memorial Lecturer at Goethe Institute of Boston, 1974; Gilbert Ryle Memorial Lecturer at Trent University, 1980; lecturer at more than fifty colleges and universities in the United States and Canada; guest on David Susskind's television program. Organizer and director of International Conference on the Idea of Democracy in Transitional Societies, Frascati, Italy, 1965-66; member of organizing committee of First Annual Socialist Scholars' Conference, 1968-69; consultant to Battelle Seattle Research Foundation. *Military service:* U.S. Army National Guard, 1957-63, active duty, 1957.

MEMBER: American Philosophical Association, American Association of University Professors, American Civil Liberties Union, American Association for Legal Philosophy and Political Theory, Massachusetts Society of Professors, Phi Beta Kappa, Chicago-Sane (member of governing board). *Awards, honors:* Chancellor's medal from University of Massachusetts.

WRITINGS: Kant's Theory of Mental Activity, Harvard University Press, 1963; (with Barrington Moore, Jr., and Herbert Marcuse) *A Critique of Pure Tolerance,* Beacon Press, 1965; *The Poverty of Liberalism,* Beacon Press, 1968; *The Ideal of the University,* Beacon Press, 1969; *The Defense of Anarchism,* Harper, 1970, 2nd edition, 1976; *The Autonomy of Reason: A Commentary on Kant's Groundwork of the Metaphysic of Morals,* Harper, 1973; *About Philosophy,* Prentice-Hall, 1976, revised edition, 1980; *Understanding Rawls: A Reconstruction and Critique of John Rawls' "A Theory of Justice,"* Princeton University Press, 1977.

Editor and author of introduction: *Political Man and Social Man,* Random House, 1966; *Kant: A Collection of Critical Essays,* Anchor Books, 1967; *The Essential David Hume,*

Mentor Books, 1969; *Kant: Foundations of the Metaphysics of Morals: Text and Commentary,* Bobbs-Merrill, 1969; *Ten Great Works of Philosophy,* Mentor Books, 1970; *Philosophy: A Modern Encounter,* with teacher's manual, Prentice-Hall, 1971; (also contributor) *The Rule of Law,* Simon & Schuster, 1971; *Styles of Political Action in America,* Random House, 1972; *1984 Revisited: Prospects for American Politics,* Knopf, 1973; *Introductory Philosophy,* Prentice-Hall, 1979.

Contributor: V. C. Chappell, editor, *Hume: A Collection of Critical Essays,* Doubleday, 1966; Eugene V. D. Rostow, editor, *Is Law Dead?,* Simon & Schuster, 1970; Fred R. Kallmayr, editor, *From Contract to Community: Political Theory at the Crossroads,* Dekker, 1978. Contributor of articles and reviews to learned journals, popular magazines, and newspapers, including *Atlantic Monthly, Nation, New Republic, Change,* and *Dissent.*

Member of board of editors of *Bulletin of Atomic Scientists,* 1963-67, *Social Theory and Practice,* 1972—, *Philosophical Forum,* 1972—, and *Political Theory,* 1972—.

WORK IN PROGRESS: The Language of Marxian Economics, for Princeton University Press, completion expected in 1983.

SIDELIGHTS: Wolff wrote: "The connecting thread running through all my intellectual efforts during the past quarter century is the effort to expose and analyze mystifications, whether in religion, politics, education, or economics. To an extent that is only now becoming apparent to me. This effort represents a keeping faith with the intellectual and political tradition of my grandfather Barnet Wolff, long-time socialist leader in New York City. In recent years, my work has been profoundly influenced by my continuing contact with my wife, literary critic and scholar Cynthia Griffin Wolff, whose work on Wharton, Richardson, Chopin, and Dickinson has taught me a great deal about how to read a text.

"I am currently at work on a full-scale literary, philosophical, and mathematical reinterpretation of Volume I of *Das Capital* by Karl Marx. My aim, which is, I think, quite unique among Marx scholars, is to exhibit the complex relationship between the formal structure of Marx's economic theories, the literary structure of his writing, and the ontological structure of bourgeois capitalist society as he understood it.

"There are three public recognitions of which I am, somewhat perversely, particularly proud: a full-page attack on me in the Soviet propaganda journal *Literaturnaya Gazetta;* a full-column attack on me by the late Westbrook Pegler; and an attack on me, in a speech, by former vice-president Spiro Agnew."

BIOGRAPHICAL/CRITICAL SOURCES: Jeffrey Reiman, *In Defense of Political Philosophy,* Torchbooks, 1972.

*   *   *

WOLRIGE GORDON, Anne   1936-

PERSONAL: Born October 16, 1936, in London, England; daughter of Peter D. (a writer) and Doe (a tennis player; maiden name, Metaxa) Howard; married Patrick Wolrige Gordon (a farmer and politician), June 2, 1962; children: Patrick Adam, Caroline, Louisa. *Education:* Attended secondary school in Sussex, England. *Politics:* Conservative. *Religion:* Anglican. *Home:* Ythan Lodge, Newburgh, Aberdeenshire AB4 0AD, Scotland.

CAREER: Worked with Moral Re-Armament, 1957-62; writer, 1967—.

WRITINGS: Peter Howard: Life and Letters, Hodder & Stoughton, 1969; *Dame Flora* (biography), Hodder & Stoughton, 1974.

Author of "Blindsight" (three-act play), first produced in London, England, at Westminster Theatre, 1970.

WORK IN PROGRESS: A novel; a play; a biography.

SIDELIGHTS: Anne Wolrige Gordon told *CA:* "My father was a journalist for the *Daily Express;* from 1940 onward he was a writer whose books sold over four million copies, and from 1960 he was in charge of the world work of Moral Re-Armament. My mother was a French tennis player who won Wimbledon in 1932. Not surprisingly, our entire family is involved in communications.

"I live on a small farm in northeast Scotland. My interests at the moment are my children. I do not think a career and family can be satisfactorily combined, so for another four years my writing has to take second place. This does not distress me as I have always written for other people rather than myself and get little pleasure from seeing my name in print. I consider self-expression the most boring kind of literature and definitely prefer biography to all the types of work I have done because it involves painting a portrait of somebody other than myself."

AVOCATIONAL INTERESTS: Children, music, gardens, theatre, international affairs.

*　　*　　*

WOOD, Christopher 1941-

PERSONAL: Born October 31, 1941, in Newcastle upon Tyne, England; son of Christopher Russell (a businessman) and Muriel Wynne (Richardson) Wood; married Sarah Drummond (a journalist), March 31, 1967; children: Alexander, Laura, Henry. *Education:* St. John's College, Cambridge, M.A., 1963. *Agent:* Curtis Brown Ltd., 1 Craven Hill, London W2 3EP, England. *Office:* Christopher Wood Gallery, 15 Motcomb St. London SW1, England.

CAREER: Christie's (auctioneers), London, England, director, 1969-76; Christopher Wood Gallery, London, managing director, 1977—. Member of Committee of Victorian Society. *Military service:* British Army, Northumberland Hussars, 1961-66; became second lieutenant. *Member:* Brook's Club.

WRITINGS: Dictionary of Victorian Painters, Antique Collectors' Club, 1971, 2nd edition, 1979; *Victorian Panorama: Paintings of Victorian Life,* Faber, 1976. Contributor to art magazines, including *Connoisseur* and *Nineteenth Century.*

WORK IN PROGRESS: Victorian Parnassus, a book on the classical movement in Victorian painting; *The Pre-Raphaelites.*

SIDELIGHTS: The second edition of Wood's *Dictionary of Victorian Painters* contains entries on eleven thousand artists and features nearly five hundred illustrations. Wood told *CA:* "My career as an art dealer does not allow much time for writing, but I am concerned to see more and better research done into nineteenth-century art. I hope to devote more time to writing later on."

*　　*　　*

WOOD, Ramsay 1943-

PERSONAL: Born March 3, 1943, in San Antonio, Tex.; son of Chalmers B. (a diplomat) and Barbara Ann (a pilot; maiden name, Lindner) Wood; married Annabelle M. Bremner (a film animator), June 21, 1970. *Education:* Attended Harvard University, 1961-64. *Office:* Frame-Up Ltd., Unit 3.4, Wem-

bley Commercial Centre, East Lane, Wembley, Middlesex HA9 7XD, England.

CAREER: Speleogist, London, England, editor and publisher, 1969-71; Frame-Up Ltd. (picture framers), Wembley, England, marketing director, 1970—. Owner of photojournalism firm, 1964-71; partner of Flying Carpet (Oriental carpet dealers), 1969-72. Fellow of Institute for the Comparative Study of History, Philosophy, and the Sciences, 1964-69. *Member:* Society of Authors, Authors Guild, Institute for Cultural Research, Crail Golfing Society, College of Storytellers (secretary).

WRITINGS: Kalila and Dimna: Selected Fables From Bidpai, illustrations by Margaret Kilrenny, Knopf, 1980. Contributor of articles and poems to *Four Quarters, Life,* and *Descant.*

WORK IN PROGRESS: An investigation of belief systems and emotional response, including cults, religious beliefs, and consumer protection, completion expected in 1983.

SIDELIGHTS: The fables of Bidpai were first set down in Sanskrit more than two thousand years ago. Since then they have been translated into hundreds of languages and become a part of most world cultures. Ramsay Wood's *Kalila and Dimna* is the first English translation of some of these ancient tales in more than a century. According to Richard Dyer of the *Boston Globe,* "[Wood's] versions . . . are racy and idiomatic and contemporary—a fish speaks of 'ecological balance'; a spokesman for some endangered animals is identified as a 'spokesbeast.' . . . In short this is a beautiful book full of mirth and human interest and unsentimental wisdom and vigorous writing; handsomely designed; cleanly printed; with charming line illustrations by Margaret Kilrenny."

Carlos Fuentes, author of *The Death of Artemio Cruz* and *Terra Nostra,* said of Wood's book: "The Spanish-language version of the tales of *Kalila and Dimna* has long been one of my bedside favourites. It is at the source of Spanish literature: no picaresque novels, even no Quixote, without these wise and vigorous, sly and funny tales. They are contemporary: they are eternal. They revealed to me as a boy the enormous debt that we who speak and write and dream in Spanish have to the culture of Islam—as well as to the culture of Judaism. *Kalila and Dimna* is the greatest present of the Islamic heritage; it is a fountain, everrunning, of sensual joy against mortified stone, against the eventual solemnity of Christian office (power and incense); overrunning with the knowledge we dare not rediscover, for fear of its negating us in the tradition of Islam. Today when we need, more than ever, to understand the Muslim nations, Ramsay Wood's fresh recreation of these tales becomes indispensable reading for the West. Indispensable, more than for political, for human, artistic, *glad* reasons. Wood's supurb stories should be set alongside Italo Calvino's recent retelling of the folk tales of Italy. No higher praise is necessary."

BIOGRAPHICAL/CRITICAL SOURCES: Boston Globe, August 19, 1980.

*　　*　　*

WORLOCK, Derek John Harford 1920-

PERSONAL: Born February 4, 1920, in London, England; son of Harford (in politics) and Dora (a worker for women's suffrage; maiden name, Hoblyn) Worlock. *Education:* Studied at Allen Hall, Ware, England, 1938-44. *Home:* Archbishop's House, 87 Green Lane, Mossley Hill, Liverpool L18 2EP, England.

CAREER: Ordained Roman Catholic priest, 1944; private secretary to Archbishop of Westminster, 1945-64; expert at Second Vatican Council, 1962-65; dean of Stepney, 1964-65; bishop of Portsmouth, England, 1965-76; archbishop of Liverpool, England, 1976—. Broadcaster on radio and television. Vice-president of Bishops' Conference of England and Wales; member of Holy See's Laity Council and Committee for the Family.

WRITINGS: (Editor) *Take One at Bedtime,* Sheed, 1963; (editor) *English Bishops at the Council: The Third Session of Vatican II,* preface by John Heenan, Burns, 1965; (editor) *Turn and Turn Again,* Sheed, 1971; *Give Me Your Hand,* St. Paul Publications, 1977. Also editor of *Seek Ye First,* 1949. Contributor to journals.

SIDELIGHTS: Worlock told *CA:* "Because my writing is so integrated in my life and vocation as a priest and bishop, I seldom have much choice in the subjects about which I speak and write. These are dictated by the circumstances, theological, social, or political, in which I find myself engaged. This may also be true of a journalist, which I am not. But in so far as it means a narrowing in the gap between religion and real life, it is a constraint which should be welcomed."

* * *

WRIGHT, Grahame 1947-1977

PERSONAL: Born October 30, 1947, in Leicester, England; died April 10, 1977; son of Bernard (a compositor) and Georgina (Hurst) Wright; married Gillian Elizabeth Savage (a ceramist), September 16, 1972. *Education:* Attended secondary school in Leicester, England.

CAREER: Worked as an assistant stage manager, 1970, and as an insurance clerk, 1971; editor of *Laboratory News,* 1974. *Awards, honors:* Arts council grant, 1974-75.

WRITINGS: Jog Rummage (novel), Heinemann, 1974, Random House, 1975. Also author of three unpublished novels and a number of unpublished stories and plays.

BIOGRAPHICAL/CRITICAL SOURCES: Burt Britton, *Self-Portrait: Book People Picture Themselves,* Random House, 1976.

[Sketch verified by wife, Gillian Wright]

* * *

WRIGHT, J(oseph) Patrick (Jr.) 1941-

PERSONAL: Born June 16, 1941, in Detroit, Mich.; son of Joseph Patrick (a journalist) and Alice (Heaney) Wright; married Mary Ann Hastings (a fashion consultant), August 22, 1970; children: Joseph Patrick III, Mary Russell. *Education:* Marquette University, B.A., 1963; attended Wayne State University, mid-1960's. *Religion:* Roman Catholic. *Home:* 917 Fisher Rd., Grosse Pointe, Mich. 48230. *Agent:* Jane Jordan Browne, Multimedia, Room 828, 410 South Michigan Ave., Chicago, Ill. 60605. *Office:* J. Patrick Wright Enterprises, Inc., 20490 Harper Ave., Harper Woods, Mich. 48225.

CAREER: Appleton Post-Crescent, Appleton, Wis., reporter, 1963-64; Wisconsin Newspress, Inc., Plymouth, assistant editor, 1964-65; *Royal Oak Daily Tribune,* Royal Oak, Mich., reporter, 1965-66; *Business Week,* New York, N.Y., correspondent, Detroit bureau, 1966-69, Detroit bureau chief, 1969-78; J. Patrick Wright Enterprises, Inc., Harper Woods, Mich., president, 1979—. *Member:* Detroit Press Club. *Awards, honors:* Three Foundation Awards from the Detroit Press Club for excellence in business reporting and writing.

WRITINGS: (With John Z. De Lorean) *On a Clear Day You Can See General Motors,* Wright Enterprises, 1979. Contributor of articles to *Atlantic, Washington Post, Los Angeles Times,* and numerous business and trade publications.

WORK IN PROGRESS: Two book proposals: a work of fiction and a work of nonfiction, both with a business connection; research in business management techniques, economics, energy, and psychology.

SIDELIGHTS: The circumstances of the publication of *On a Clear Day You Can See General Motors* attracted nearly as much attention as the book's content. Four years earlier, Wright had collaborated with former GM executive John Z. De Lorean on the memoir of De Lorean's years with the auto manufacturer, but De Lorean had decided not to publish it. Finally, Wright mortgaged his home to raise money and published the book himself, without De Lorean's permission. *On a Clear Day* was printed and shipped in strict secrecy, for fear of legal action by GM or De Lorean to prevent its distribution.

The book was an instant bestseller. De Lorean declined to repudiate its harsh criticism of GM's management practices, though he said he would have preferred changes in "tone and emphasis." Its descriptions of the "adolescent cliquishness and senseless make-work" in the upper levels of GM management and of the decision to produce the Corvair, even though the car's safety was in doubt, were scathing, as was the charge that GM "has not had a significant technical innovation since the automatic transmission."

Some at GM, it was reported, welcomed the book—particularly those senior middle managers who had suffered under the company's dress code, social restrictions, and other annoyances. One executive was quoted in *Monthly Detroit* as saying with satisfaction, "Finally somebody had the guts to fight city hall."

De Lorean, who had spent seventeen years at GM and narrowly missed becoming the corporation's president, told Wright how executives were pressured to make contributions to political candidates supported by the company; how "excessive emphasis on cost cutting" rewarded managers for producing shoddy cars; how GM spied on competitors; and of the pettiness, intrigue, and sycophancy that permeated the corporation's upper echelons. Wright helped De Lorean shape his memories into a comprehensive indictment of GM and, in De Lorean's words, "a bible for corporate reform."

Wright told *CA:* "*On a Clear Day* is not just a commentary on General Motors management; it is a commentary on management of big, mature American business. What interested me from the beginning was that it was the first book of its kind: a key executive of a major American corporation was willing to talk candidly and personally about what he felt were the good and bad aspects of his company and the business world about him. While most business biographies have been candy-coated efforts, bereft of conflict and personality, we were able to offer a rare, critical, inside look at big business management.

"One of the shocking revelations that look provided was how giant corporations use their massive power to bully employees, competitors, and suppliers. Ironically, it was an apparent abuse of that type of power that forced John De Lorean to try to suppress the book after its completion. He backed out of the project and told me he was doing so because he feared that GM management would ruin his new small car company as a reprisal for the content of our book. To me, however, the fact that even John De Lorean was being forced to knuckle under to the odious use of corporate power was a compelling argument for pursuing the project, which is why I sought to publish it on my own.

"During twelve years with *Business Week,* I had the opportunity to observe American business closely. It seems to me that today America is at a critical crossroads in its economic development. Many of the big businesses that have a critical impact on the nation's economy are no longer responding to the needs and demands of that economy or its many constituencies. This is because these businesses are often run by bet-hedgers who are unwilling or unable to take well-informed, innovative risks. In addition, these businesses are often tied up internally by burdensome bureaucracy and corporate politics.

"The real risk takers and innovators, in whose visions the future of our economy could well rest, are the small businessmen. But these innovators are often hampered by excessive government regulation and prohibitive and complicated tax policies. This load has to be lessened to make more effective use of this valuable national resource.

"One thing appears clear, however, and that is the growing public awareness of the stranglehold big business has on the national economy. In the 1970's we witnessed increasing demands for more public information about the inner workings of these corporate monoliths. This was evident in the wave of small, modestly successful, grass roots attempts by shareholders to reform major corporations from within.

"In the 1980's we will probably see a demand for increased accountability of big business, as well as further public disclosure of the decision-making process that takes place inside these giant companies. Making public corporations truly public is a laudable goal for this decade. The danger is that a drive toward such a goal could be lost in the wave of anti-government and anti-tax sentiment sweeping across the country. If this push to cut back government involvement at all levels results simply in expanded big business influence, the economic results for America will be bad. But if such public pressure lessens excessive burdens on small businessmen, then the country stands to benefit substantially, because the energies of these entrepreneurs will be freed for creation, innovation, and invention."

AVOCATIONAL INTERESTS: "I am an active sports enthusiast, playing amateur ice hockey and slow-pitch softball, and coaching boys' and girls' soccer, floor hockey, basketball, and baseball. I have traveled extensively throughout the continental United States and the Canadian provinces of Ontario and Quebec. My family and I are avid summertime campers."

BIOGRAPHICAL/CRITICAL SOURCES: Wall Street Journal, November 7, 1979, November 9, 1979, November 15, 1979; *Detroit News,* November 7, 1979; *Washington Post,* November 8, 1979, November 15, 1979; *Time,* November 19, 1979; *Publishers Weekly,* November 26, 1979; *Denver Post,* December 23, 1979; *Monthly Detroit,* January, 1980; *Milwaukee Journal,* January 29, 1980; *Venture,* February, 1980; *Miami Herald,* February 10, 1980; *Newsweek,* February 25, 1980; *Saturday Review,* March 29, 1980; *Boston Globe,* March 29, 1980; *Marketing,* July 9, 1980; *London Daily Mail,* August 14, 1980; *Edinburgh Scotsman,* August 14, 1980; *Irish Times,* August 27, 1980.

*   *   *

WYATT, Woodrow Lyle 1918-

PERSONAL: Born July 4, 1918; son of Robert Harvey Lyle and Ethel (Morgan) Wyatt; married Moorea Hastings, 1957 (marriage ended, 1966); married Veronica Banszky, 1966; children: (first marriage) one son; (second marriage) one daughter. *Education:* Worcester College, Oxford, M.A. *Home:* 19 Cavendish Ave., London N.W.8, England; and Conock Old Manor, Devizes, Wiltshire, England.

CAREER: Parliament, London, England, Labour member of Parliament for Aston Division of Birmingham, 1945-55, member of Parliamentary delegation to India, 1946, Parliamentary under-secretary of state and financial secretary at War Office, 1951; British Broadcasting Corp. (BBC-TV), England, co-creator of "Panorama," 1955-59; Parliament, Labour member of Parliament for Bosworth Division of Leicester, 1959-70; Woodrow Wyatt Holdings Ltd., England, chairman, 1976—. Chairman of Horserace Totalisator Board, 1976—. *Military service:* British Army, 1939-45; became major; mentioned in dispatches. *Member:* Zoological Society of London (member of council, 1968-71, 1973-77).

WRITINGS—Nonfiction: *Southwards From China: A Survey of South East Asia Since 1945,* Hodder & Stoughton, 1952; *Into the Dangerous World,* Weidenfeld & Nicolson, 1952, Roy, 1953; *The Peril in Our Midst,* Phoenix House, 1956; *Distinguished for Talent: Some Men of Influence and Enterprise,* Hutchinson, 1958; *Turn Again, Westminster,* Deutsch, 1973; *What's Left of the Labour Party?,* Sidgwick & Jackson, 1977; *To the Point,* Weidenfeld & Nicolson, 1981. Also author of *The Jews at Home,* 1950.

For children: *The Exploits of Mr. Saucy Squirrel,* Allen & Unwin, 1976; *The Further Exploits of Mr. Saucy Squirrel,* Allen & Unwin, 1977.

Author of weekly columns in *Reynolds News,* 1949-61, *Daily Mirror,* 1965-73, and *Sunday Mirror,* 1973—. Founder and editor of *English Story,* 1940-50; member of editorial staff of *New Statesman and Nation,* 1947-48.

Y

YEN-PING, Shen 1896(?)-1981
(Mao Dun)

OBITUARY NOTICE: Born c. 1896 in China; died March 27, 1981, in China. Chinese Minister of Culture, editor, and author of novels under the pen name Mao Dun. In 1919 he was among the founders of a society promoting realistic literature, and in the thirties was one of China's foremost leftist writers. His most celebrated novel, *Midnight,* was published in 1933. From 1949 to 1965 he served as China's cultural minister. In the subsequent decade, during the Cultural Revolution, he came under criticism, but in the late seventies he again became active in the arts. One of his novels, written in the 1950's, was published for the first time in 1981. He believed that literature should awaken the masses, and wrote that it "performs a positive function of stimulating the human mind." Obituaries and other sources: *New York Times,* March 28, 1981; *Washington Post,* March 29, 1981.

*   *   *

YERGIN, Daniel H.

PERSONAL—Education: Cambridge University, Ph.D., 1974. *Agent:* Lynn Goldberg, Random House, Inc., 201 East 50th St., New York, N.Y. 10022.

CAREER: Harvard University, Cambridge, Mass., currently lecturer.

WRITINGS: Shattered Peace: The Origins of the Cold War and the National Security State, Houghton, 1977; (editor with Robert Stobaugh) *Energy Future: Report of the Energy Project at the Harvard Business School,* Random House, 1979. Editor-in-chief of *Yale Daily News,* c. 1967.

SIDELIGHTS: Shattered Peace, according to H. E. Salisbury of the *New Republic,* is "the most comprehensive examination of the *American* side of the US-Soviet schism yet attempted." Although there is a long list of books seeking to determine the origins of the Cold War, Yergin's book is separated "from most of its predecessors," said Norman Graebner of the *Virginia Quarterly Review,* not by "its fundamental assumptions or conclusions," but by "its fine detail, based on a Cambridge University doctoral dissertation, and its highly professional style. The volume presents much that is new." Graebner added: "It is replete with sparkling vignettes of men and events. Always balanced in its judgments, *Shattered Peace* is narrative history at its best."

In his book, Yergin traces Cold War ideology to two opposing theories of the Soviet Union. On the one hand were the Riga axioms, named after the Baltic port in Latvia from where the United States observed the Soviet Union until official diplomatic recognition was made in 1933. Proponents of the Riga theory, including George F. Kennan, Charles W. Henderson, Charles E. Bohlen, and Elbridge Durbow, believed, in Graebner's words, "that Soviet foreign policy flowed directly from Marxist-Leninist ideology. . . . The USSR, in short, was a revolutionary state, committed to unrelenting ideological warfare in its drive for world mastery." From this perspective, suggested Naomi Bliven of the *New Yorker,* the Soviet Union was seen as "a monstrous polity that could not be dealt with by normal diplomacy."

The opposing vision of the U.S.S.R., which Yergin refers to as the Yalta axioms, was subscribed to primarily by Franklin D. Roosevelt. After successful cooperation against the common Nazi enemy during World War II, Roosevelt maintained the possibility of fruitful negotiation with Stalin. From this position, Soviet foreign policy was seen, not as a plan to realize ideological imperatives, but as an effort to establish security and a defensive sphere of influence. With Roosevelt's death, however, American foreign policy returned to the Riga forces. Thomas L. Pangle of the *Yale Review* explained: "Mistakenly (though understandably) fearful of a new Soviet Hitlerism, and resolved not to allow traditional spheres of influence, the Anglo-American alliance under Truman consistently exaggerated the evil intentions as well as the coherence or cunning of Stalin's policy."

Prompted by Russia's postwar policies and its eventual domination of Eastern Europe, Riga theorists reasserted their fears of Soviet expansionism, effectively creating an anti-Soviet consensus within both the government and the general populace. Graebner remarked that "the Truman Doctrine Speech, which defined the enemy as communism everywhere, shifted the emphasis of American perceptions of danger from anti-Sovietism to anti-communism, with its far more pervading visions of subversion." The subsequent Cold War took on dimensions not only "increasingly hysterical," as Graebner put it, but increasingly distinct from international power politics.

Assessing Yergin's historical narrative as "a relatively dispassionate and moderate version of the currently fashionable revisionism," Pangle concluded: "Although the author assigns to the United States most of the responsibility for the

Cold War, he argues that America's role cannot be interpreted in terms of either a cultural history of expansionism or the imperialist imperatives of a capitalist economy. Far from laying moralistic blame, Yergin traces America's mistakes to tragic misconceptions growing directly out of her moral commitment to Wilson's vision of the world legal order defined by the democratic self-determination of nations."

Shattered Peace was commended by reviewers for portraying, among other things, "the men who affected American policy toward the Soviet Union until 1950 as earnest, fallible human beings attempting not to repeat the mistakes of the past," noted Bliven. Edward N. Luttwak observed in *Commentary* that Yergin's story brightly illuminated "the sentiments and bureaucratic concerns of American policy makers." Bliven further declared that "personality is very much a part of Mr. Yergin's story—a reason that his book is fascinating. He is at his most convincing in portraying the relationships among the people in our government."

Yergin's next undertaking was *Energy Future,* a collection of essays by six authors examining America's energy problem and options from political, economic, and ecological perspectives. Steven Ferrey found that "vigorous solar and conservation initiatives to effect a transition to renewable resources" are essential to U.S. economic stability. He continued, "The strength and power of this text is the ineluctable logic it brings to the increasingly acrimonious rift between the champions of various energy strategies." Peter Passell of the *New York Times Book Review* called the book "the best single examination of America's energy problem in print. What explains this excellence is the competent integration of geopolitics, economics and science." John Kenneth Galbraith, in the *New York Review of Books,* also considered *Energy Future* "by far the best text currently available."

BIOGRAPHICAL/CRITICAL SOURCES: Washington Post Book World, May 29, 1977, July 15, 1979; *New York Times,* May 31, 1977; *New York Times Book Review,* June 12, 1977, July 29, 1979; *New Republic,* July 2, 1977; *Nation,* July 9, 1977; *Commentary,* August, 1977; *Christian Science Monitor,* August 31, 1977; *Yale Review,* winter, 1977-78; *New Statesman,* January 13, 1978; *New Yorker,* February 27, 1978; *Virginia Quarterly Review,* spring, 1978; *Los Angeles Times Book Review,* July 29, 1979; *Saturday Review,* September 1, 1979; *New York Review of Books,* September 27, 1979, October 25, 1979.*

—*Sketch by Andrea Geffner*

*   *   *

YORK, Elizabeth
  See YORK, Margaret Elizabeth

*   *   *

YORK, Margaret Elizabeth   1927-
  (Margaret Abbey, Joanna Makepeace, Elizabeth York)

PERSONAL: Born August 2, 1927, in Leicester, England; daughter of John Edward (a bus driver) and Edith (Makepeace) York. *Education:* Earned teacher's diploma, 1947, L.G.S.M., 1954, and drama diploma. *Politics:* "Liberal/Labour." *Religion:* "Christian/Theosophist." *Home:* 294 Abbey Lane, Leicester LE4 2AA, England. *Agent:* Harold Ober Associates, Inc., 40 East 49th St., New York, N.Y. 10017; and David Higham Associates Ltd., 5-8 Lower John St., Golden Sq., London W1R 4HA, England.

CAREER: Teacher of history, drama, and English, 1956-81; head of English department at comprehensive school in Leicester, England, 1970-76; writer. *Member:* Richard III Society (chairman of Leicester branch), Leicester Writers Club.

WRITINGS—All novels; under pseudonym Margaret Abbey: *The Warwick Heiress,* Pinnacle Books, 1970; *Francesca,* Ballantine, 1970; *Son of York,* Pinnacle Books, 1970; *Flight of the Kestrel,* Ballantine, 1973; *Brothers in Arms,* Ballantine, 1973; *Amber Promise,* Ballantine, 1973.

Other novels: (Under pseudonym Joanna Makepeace) *Divine Son of Ra,* Hutchinson, 1969; (under name Elizabeth York) *The Medea Legend,* Simon & Schuster, 1975; *Rider on a Pale Horse,* Macdonald/Futura, 1981. Also author of *Daughter of Isis, Chosen of the Gods, Pawns of Power, Not in Our Stars,* and *Etain of the Red Hair,* all under pseudonym Joanna Makepeace.

WORK IN PROGRESS: The Burgundian, a historical novel set in the fifteenth-century; a sequel to *Rider on a Pale Horse.*

SIDELIGHTS: Margaret York told *CA:* "I live with my mother and my dog, Benjy, in a small house in an industrial East Midlands town. My particular interests are comparative religion, mythology, and the occult. My favorite historical period is the fifteenth century, and I have a passionate interest in the defense of King Richard III. I am also interested in Egyptology, ancient Rome, and Greece. I have campaigned for conservation of animals and have acted and sung in amateur theatricals.

"I find my particular type of historical novel writing a great challenge. The storyline must fit neatly into the political situation. No error or license must be allowed to creep in. If Richard III meets my heroine in London he must have been in London *on that day,* or, if not recorded directly, certainly (if by any research I can prove absolute dating and timing) he must not have been elsewhere. The political situation is a masterly craft. It would be simpler to write novelized biography. I enjoy wrestling with a creative plot and thereby hope to give my readers something extra to their historical knowledge which, for most, I believe, is already extensive."

AVOCATIONAL INTERESTS: Books, theatre, classical music, travel, caravaning.

*   *   *

YOST, Edna   1889-1971

OBITUARY NOTICE—See index for *CA* sketch: Born November 16, 1889, in Clearfield County, Pa.; died September 10, 1971, in New York, N.Y.; Educator and author. Yost was one of the first authors to write about the achievements of women. Her books include *American Women of Science, Straight Talk to Disabled Veterans,* and *Famous American Pioneering Women.* Obituaries and other sources: *AB Bookman's Weekly,* October 4, 1971.

*   *   *

YOUNG, Collier   1908(?)-1980

OBITUARY NOTICE: Born c. 1908 in Indianapolis, Ind.; died after an automobile accident, December 25, 1980, in Santa Monica, Calif. Producer and screenwriter. Young became a story editor for RKO studios in Hollywood in 1940, and during World War II, as a Navy lieutenant commander, he made documentary films of the fighting in the South Pacific. In the 1950's he formed an independent film production company with actress and director Ida Lupino, who was then his wife. The company made several low-budget films that explored socially controversial topics such as rape, unwed motherhood, and bigamy. Young later wrote for television, creating ''The Rogues'' in the 1960's, a series which won favorable critical attention. Young's best-known series, ''Ironside,'' was produced from 1967 through 1975. Obituaries and other sources: *New York Times*, December 27, 1980.

*   *   *

YOUNGDAHL, Reuben K(enneth Nathaniel)   1911-1968

OBITUARY NOTICE—See index for *CA* sketch: Born May 17, 1911, in Minneapolis, Minn.; died March 2, 1968; buried in Lakewood Cemetery, Minneapolis, Minn. Clergyman and author. Youngdahl was ordained a minister of the Lutheran Church in 1934. He served as pastor for churches in Iowa and Minnesota. Youngdahl's writings include *Going God's Way, The Pathway to Peace,* and *Trumpets in the Morning.* Obituaries and other sources: *Who Was Who in America*, 5th edition, Marquis, 1973.

Z

ZAMOYSKI, Adam (Stefan Jan Maria Sariusz) 1949-

PERSONAL: Born January 11, 1949, in New York, N.Y.; son of Count Stefan and Princess Elizabeth (Czartoryska) Zamoyski. *Education:* Queen's College, Oxford, B.A., 1971, M.A., 1974. *Religion:* Roman Catholic. *Home:* 33 Ennismore Gardens, London S.W.7, England. *Agent:* A. P. Watt Ltd., 26/28 Bedford Row, London WC1R 4HL, England.

CAREER: Writer. Worked as free-lance writer for British Broadcasting Corp. (BBC) World Service and *Financial Times.*

WRITINGS: Chopin: A Biography, Collins, 1979, Doubleday, 1980; *Paderewski,* Atheneum, 1981; *The Battle of the Marchlands,* Columbia University Press, 1981. Contributor to *Times Literary Supplement, History Today, Spectator, Tatler,* and *Polish Daily.*

SIDELIGHTS: Count Zamoyski wrote: "My books attempt in a minor way to breach the wall of ignorance and misinformation surrounding Polish history and culture. Relative to its size and importance, Poland is the most neglected country in the world from this point of view, and I feel that more information should be made available to the English-speaking reader in whatever way the book market allows."

* * *

ZAVIN, Benjamin B. 1920(?)-1981

OBITUARY NOTICE: Born c. 1920; died after a brief illness, February 23, 1981, in New York, N.Y. Librettist, playwright, and author of television plays. Zavin wrote extensively for television and won a Christopher Award for his television play "A Day in Town." He wrote for Broadway musicals and the stage, including a 1973 play based on the writings of Robert and Elizabeth Browning entitled "I Love Thee Freely." Obituaries and other sources: *New York Times,* February 26, 1981.

* * *

ZELK, Zoltan 1906-1981

OBITUARY NOTICE: Born December 18, 1906, in Ermihalyfalva, Hungary; died April 23, 1981, in Budapest, Hungary. Poet, essayist, and author of children's stories. Zelk was the recipient of many prestigious awards for his writing, including the Baumgarten Prize, two Kossuth Prizes, and the Graves Prize. As part of a group of writers protesting political repression, Zelk contributed to conditions leading to Hungary's 1956 uprising. When the revolt was stifled by Soviet tanks in 1957, Zelk was sentenced to three years in prison. He was released a year later and resumed writing, producing more than twenty volumes of poetry during his career. Among his publications are *Witness of Creation, Hoar-frost on the Rose-tree,* and *Gull.* Obituaries and other sources: *Who's Who in the Socialist Countries,* K. G. Saur, 1978; *Chicago Tribune,* April 26, 1981; *Washington Post,* April 27, 1981.

* * *

ZEYDEL, Edwin H(ermann) 1893-1973

OBITUARY NOTICE—See index for *CA* sketch: Born December 31, 1893, in Brooklyn, N.Y.; died April, 1973. Educator, translator, and author. Zeydel began his career as an instructor in German at the University of Minnesota in 1916. He served as a translator for the Carnegie Endowment for International Peace, and, at one time, he was attached to the U.S. State Department. In addition to his position as professor emeritus at the University of Cincinnati, Zeydel was a visiting professor at Rutgers, The State University, Cornell University, Columbia University, and the University of Colorado. His works include *The Holy Roman Empire in German Literature, Second German Reader,* and *Napoleon III and the Rhine.* Obituaries and other sources: *The Writers Directory, 1976-78,* St. Martin's, 1976.

* * *

ZOOK, David H(artzler), Jr. 1930-?

OBITUARY NOTICE—See index for *CA* sketch: Born January 22, 1930, in Bellefontaine, Ohio; declared missing in action during Viet Nam conflict, October 4, 1967, presumed finding of death declared, April 28, 1978. Military officer, educator, and author. Zook was a major in the U. S. Air Force and a professor of history. His writings include *The Conduct of the Chaco War* and *Jose de San Martin.* (Information provided by wife, Patricia S. Zook.)

* * *

ZWARENSTEYN, Hendrik 1913-1976

OBITUARY NOTICE—See index for *CA* sketch: Born February 16, 1913, in Tuban, Java, Indonesia; died August 6,

1976. Attorney, educator, and author. Zwarensteyn held positions in government and business, such as district employment head of the Ministry of Social Affairs in Zaandam, Netherlands, and personnel director of Royal Verkade Factories Ltd. He was a professor of business law at Michigan State University. His works include *College Business Law* and *Fundamentals of Hotel Law*. (Date of death provided by wife, Sarah Zwarensteyn.)